AF819602

POWER PACK

10.	Active-Passive Voice	**2024-21**	**453-475**	**1-312**	**312**
		SSC CGL	454-461	1-110	110
		SSC CPO	461-462	111-125	15
		SSC CHSL	462-469	126-223	98
		SSC MTS	-	-	-
		SSC GD	-	-	-
		SSC Selection Post	469-471	224-241	18
		SSC Steno	471-475	242-312	71
11.	Narration	**2024-21**	**476-497**	**1-279**	**279**
		SSC CGL	477-485	1-114	114
		SSC CPO	486-487	115-131	17
		SSC CHSL	487-490	132-174	43
		SSC MTS	-	-	-
		SSC GD	-	-	-
		SSC Selection Post	490-491	175-189	15
		SSC Steno	491-497	190-279	90
12.	Rearrangement of Words to Form Sentences	**2024-21**	**498-513**	**1-144**	**144**
		SSC CGL	498-508	1-94	94
		SSC CPO	-	-	-
		SSC CHSL	508-512	95-132	38
		SSC MTS	-	-	-
		SSC GD	-	-	-
		SSC Selection Post	-	-	-
		SSC Steno	512-513	133-144	12
13.	Para Jumble	**2024-21**	**514-547**	**1-205**	**205**
		SSC CGL	515-538	1-144	144
		SSC CPO	538-541	145-158	14
		SSC CHSL	541-544	159-182	24
		SSC MTS	-	-	-
		SSC GD	-	-	-
		SSC Selection Post	544-545	183-186	4
		SSC Steno	545-547	187-205	19
14.	Cloze Test	**2024-21**	**548-610**	**1-901**	**901**
		SSC CGL	548-566	1-273	273
		SSC CPO	566-575	274-403	130
		SSC CHSL	575-593	404-656	253

POWER PACK

		SSC MTS	593-603	657-806	150
		SSC GD	-	-	-
		SSC Selection Post	603-607	807-861	55
		SSC Steno	607-610	862-901	40
15.	Reading Comprehension	**2024-21**	**611-646**	**1-271**	**271**
		SSC CGL	611-625	1-95	95
		SSC CPO	625-632	96-160	65
		SSC CHSL	632-635	161-181	86
		SSC MTS	-	-	-
		SSC GD	-	-	-
		SSC Selection Post	635-640	182-221	40
		SSC Steno	640-646	222-271	150
16.	Miscellaneous	**2024-21**	**647-650**	**1-38**	**38**
		SSC CGL	647-649	1-20	20
		SSC CPO	-	-	-
		SSC CHSL	649-649	21-26	6
		SSC MTS	649-650	27-35	9
		SSC GD	-	-	-
		SSC Selection Post	-	-	-
		SSC Steno	650	36-38	3

SSC Cutoff 2023-24

Exam	Tier	Year	SC	ST	EWS	OBC	UR	ESM
SSC CGL	TIER I	2024	126.45554	111.8893	142.01963	146.26291	153.18981	69.92674
		2023	126.68201	118.16655	143.44441	145.93743	150.04936	100.29326
	TIER II	2024	-	-	-	-	-	-
		2023	252	241	265	271	287	223
SSC CHSL	TIER I	2024	139.68408	129.44568	150.51731	156.61665	157.36168	78.23008
		2023	136.41166	124.52592	151.09782	152.26953	153.91142	102.47651
	TIER I	2024	89.8581	82.6568	111.4352	113.50911	119.80335	40.07024
		2023	79.3189	78.13852	103.97465	102.9603	115.04762	40
SSC CPO	Grade C	2024	-	-	-	-	-	-
		2023	136.08122	128.04746	-	145.03097	147.45086	147.45086
SSC STENO	Grade D	2024	-	-	-	-	-	-
		2023	109.41004	88.71217	40.15035	125.02167	131.32184	126.29805
SSC GD	Tier I	2024	148.21914	143.65896	151.15627	152.28771	153.56851	94.65261
		2023	129.75	126.45	139.16	140.75	142.03	75.01

1st EDITION

POWER PACK

SSC ENGLISH

CHAPTERWISE 8000+ TCS MCQ

All SSC Exams PYQs Till Jan 2025

SSC CGL, CHSL, CPO, MTS, Steno, GD, Selection Post etc

Authors
Srishti Agarwal
Akansha Diwedi

arihant
SUCCESS AND NOTHING LESS

arihant
SUCCESS AND NOTHING LESS

ARIHANT PUBLICATIONS (INDIA) LIMITED

卐 **Administrative & Production Offices**

Regd. Office
'Ramchhaya' 4577/15, Agarwal Road, Darya Ganj, New Delhi -110002
Tele: 011- 47630600, 43518550

卐 **Head Office**
Kalindi, TP Nagar, Meerut (UP) - 250002
Tel: 0121-7156203, 7156204

卐 **Sales & Support Offices**
Agra, Ahmedabad, Bengaluru, Bareilly, Chennai, Delhi, Guwahati, Hyderabad, Jaipur, Jhansi, Kolkata, Lucknow, Nagpur & Pune.

卐 **PRICE** ₹675.00

卐 **PO No :** TXT-XX-XXXXXXX-X-XX

Published by Arihant Publications (India) Ltd.

For further information about the books published by Arihant, log on to www.arihantbooks.com or e-mail at info@arihantbooks.com

CHAPTER INDEX

POWER PACK

S.No.	Chapter	Exams	Page No.	Ques. No.	No. of Ques.
1.	Fill in the Blanks	**2024-21**	**1-45**	**1-668**	**668**
		SSC CGL	1-11	1-155	155
		SSC CPO	11-12	156-172	17
		SSC CHSL	12-25	173-373	201
		SSC MTS	25-40	374-595	222
		SSC GD	-	-	-
		SSC Selection Post	40-42	596-624	29
		SSC Steno	42-45	625-668	44
2.	Spotting Error	**2024-21**	**46-114**	**1-860**	**860**
		SSC CGL	47-66	1-251	251
		SSC CPO	66-73	252-346	95
		SSC CHSL	73-94	347-614	268
		SSC MTS	94-106	615-759	145
		SSC GD	-	-	-
		SSC Selection Post	106-107	760-772	13
		SSC Steno	107-114	773-860	88
3.	Sentence Improvement	**2024-21**	**115-182**	**1-921**	**921**
		SSC CGL	115-135	1-276	276
		SSC CPO	135-143	277-385	109
		SSC CHSL	144-168	386-733	348
		SSC MTS	168-177	734-856	123
		SSC GD	-	-	-
		SSC Selection Post	177-179	857-875	19
		SSC Steno	179-182	876-921	46
4.	Synonyms	**2024-21**	**183-244**	**1-937**	**937**
		SSC CGL	183-201	1-273	273
		SSC CPO	201-209	274-389	116
		SSC CHSL	209-226	390-655	266
		SSC MTS	226-236	656-795	140
		SSC GD	236-240	796-873	78
		SSC Selection Post	240-242	874-893	20
		SSC Steno	242-244	894-937	44
5.	Antonyms	**2024-21**	**245-305**	**1-910**	**910**
		SSC CGL	245-266	1-319	319
		SSC CPO	266-274	320-435	116

POWER PACK

		SSC CHSL	274-295	436-751	316
		SSC MTS	295-300	752-832	81
		SSC GD	-	-	-
		SSC Selection Post	300-302	833-857	25
		SSC Steno	302-305	858-910	53
6.	Homonyms	**2024-21**	**306-313**	**1-126**	**126**
		SSC CGL	306-309	1-57	57
		SSC CPO	-	-	-
		SSC CHSL	309-312	58-93	36
		SSC MTS	312-312	94-108	15
		SSC GD	312-313	109-126	18
		SSC Selection Post	-	-	-
		SSC Steno	-	-	-
7.	One Word Substitution	**2024-21**	**314-359**	**1-549**	**549**
		SSC CGL	314-337	1-281	281
		SSC CPO	337-346	282-382	101
		SSC CHSL	346-353	383-467	85
		SSC MTS	353-358	468-534	67
		SSC GD	-	-	-
		SSC Selection Post	358-359	535-545	11
		SSC Steno	359-359	546-549	4
8.	Idioms & Phrases	**2024-21**	**360-416**	**1-804**	**804**
		SSC CGL	360-377	1-241	241
		SSC CPO	378-390	242-412	171
		SSC CHSL	390-404	413-625	213
		SSC MTS	404-412	626-739	114
		SSC GD	-	-	-
		SSC Selection Post	412-414	740-770	31
		SSC Steno	414-416	771-804	34
9.	Spelling Test	**2024-21**	**417-452**	**1-683**	**683**
		SSC CGL	418-431	1-273	273
		SSC CPO	431-436	274-364	91
		SSC CHSL	436-446	365-556	192
		SSC MTS	446-451	557-654	98
		SSC GD	-	-	-
		SSC Selection Post	451-452	655-683	29
		SSC Steno	-	-	-

01

Fill in the Blanks

Fill in the blanks with the appropriate word to make the sentence grammatically correct and meaningful is an important language skill tested in SSC Examinations. Such questions involve filling the blank with the correct grammatical word or with the correct word/phrase.

Types of Questions Asked

In the SSC Examination, fill in the blanks can be based on singular filler or more than one fillers. Further, the fillers are based either on grammar or vocabulary.

Type 1

Choose the correct preposition to fill in the given blank.

They were .... 100 m from Harish's house when the door to his house opened.

(a) inside (b) within (c) near (d) close to **Ans.** (c)

Type 2

Choose the correct word to fill in the given blank.

She was .... when she heard the news of her promotion.

(a) ecstatic (b) crestfallen (c) apathetic (d) mascot **Ans.** (a)

Type 3

Choose the correct word to fill in the given blanks.

He is .... rich, yet he .... about high taxes.

(a) extremely; speaks (b) obscenely; whines

(c) modestly; cribs (d) unduly; praises **Ans.** (b)

How to Solve the Questions

To fill in the blank and complete the sentence successfully, you need to understand the sentence properly.

Here is a small step by step process that you should follow to solve the questions.

Step 1 Read the complete sentence properly and carefully to find out what can be used to fill in the blank.

Step 2 In some cases, the blank requires a grammatical word. If this is the case, follow these steps

- If the blank requires a pronoun or a verb, check the noun to ensure that the pronoun and verb is in agreement with it.
- Also check the tense of the sentence and make sure that the correct tense structure is followed.
- Is the blank requires an adjective or determiner, check if the noun is countable or uncountable before choosing your answer.
- In case of prepositions, make sure you check what relation between the words that preposition is connecting and then, choose your answer.
- For adverbs and conjunctions, make sure that they fit the sentence.

Step 3 If the filler is vocabulary based, follow these steps

- Read the sentence to understand what should come in the blank.
- Read the options carefully to understand their meanings.
- Choose the word that best fits the sentence.

Step 4 After making your choice, read the complete sentence to make sure that the sentences correct and meaningful.

SSC Exam Scanner

Directions (Q. Nos. 1-668) Select the most appropriate option to substitute the underlined segment in the given sentence.

SSC CGL 2024 (Tier 1 & 2)

1. No other book in the series captivated readers as.............. as the final installment. **SSC CGL Tier-2 18.01.2025**

(a) much (b) many (c) most (d) more

Ans. (a)

The word 'much' is used to compare the degree of captivation among the books in the series, indicating that the final installment captivated readers to a higher degree than any other book.

2. Luck does not always favour us, so we must always depend .... our own efforts for success. **SSC CGL Tier-2 18.01.2025**

(a) in (b) for (c) at (d) upon

Ans. (d)

'Upon' is the correct preposition to use in this context. It indicates reliance or dependence on something, which fits the meaning of the sentence perfectly.

3. The mango is the.........fruit. **SSC CGL Tier-2 18.01.2025**

(a) sweetly (b) sweet (c) sweeter (d) sweetest

Ans. (d)

'Sweetest' is the superlative form of the adjective 'sweet' to indicate that the mango is the most sweet compare other fruits.

4. Mr. Amit Kumar, Proprietor of Xyling Pens is known for ....honesty and decent behaviour in the business arena.
SSC CGL Tier-2 18.01.2025

(a) her (b) it
(c) his (d) they

Ans. (c)

'His' is the most appropriate pronoun to fill in the blank. As the sentence refers to Mr. Amit Kumar, a male, the correct pronoun is 'his' to indicate possession of honesty and decent behaviour.

5. Prescription safety glasses provide the .... tailored protection for individuals with vision correction needs. SSC CGL Tier-2 20.01.2025

(a) finest
(b) finer
(c) fine
(d) more finely

Ans. (a)

The superlative form 'finest' is most appropriate to indicate the highest quality or best tailored protection for individuals with vision correction needs

6. The blueberries in the basket are blue. The denotation of the word 'blue' is.......... SSC CGL Tier-2 20.01.2025

(a) gloominess
(b) sadness
(c) a colour
(d) negativity

Ans. (c)

The denotation of the word 'blue' refers to its literal meaning, which is 'a colour'. In this context, it describes the colour of the blueberries.

7. This is the...........book that I have read till now. SSC CGL Tier-2 20.01.2025

(a) better interest
(b) most interesting
(c) interesting
(d) more interesting

Ans. (b)

'Most interesting' is the correct option as it is the superlative form, indicating the highest level of interest in comparison to other books read till now.

8. Rabindranath Tagore,........... poet, was famous for his poetical work, Gitanjali. SSC CGL Tier-2 20.01.2025

(a) no article required
(b) an
(c) a
(d) the

Ans. (d)

The correct article to fill in the blank is 'the' since Rabindranath Tagore is a specific and well-known poet, making it: 'Rabindranath Tagore, the poet, was famous for his poetical work, Gitanjali.'

9. Vinod had a ...... escape in the car accident. SSC CGL Tier-1 09.09.2024 (Shift-I)

(a) comfortable (b) full
(c) narrow (d) wide

Ans. (c)

The phrase 'narrow escape' means escaping from a dangerous situation by a very small margin. 'Narrow' describes the close call in escaping the accident.

10. Two of the fugitives managed to remain free by adeptly avoiding the .... of the police.
SSC CGL Tier-1 11.09.2024 (Shift-II)

(a) following
(b) repression
(c) pursuit
(d) discovery

Ans. (c)

The given sentence indicates that the fugitives were not caught by the police who were following them. The correct word to fill in the blank is 'pursuit', which means the act of chasing or seeking something or someone. This fits the context perfectly as the police were actively trying to catch the fugitives.

11. We have postponed this movie outing too many times, so we are going tomorrow, come .... or shine. SSC CGL Tier-1 12.09.2024 (Shift-II)

(a) rain (b) mountain
(c) hail (d) thunder

Ans. (a)

The correct filler for the blank is 'rain.' The idiom 'come rain or shine' means that an event will happen no matter what the circumstances are. This implies determination to proceed regardless of any hindrance.

12. To .... the ticket, Amith had to visit the travel agency many times.
SSC CGL Tier-1 12.09.2024 (Shift-III)

(a) contract (b) confirm
(c) conform (d) convention

Ans. (b)

The correct word to fill in the blank is 'confirm.' This means to establish the certainty or validity of something. In the context, Amith had to visit the travel agency repeatedly to ensure his ticket was validated and confirmed.

13. They .... their house for the past two months and it's finally starting to look fantastic.
SSC CGL Tier-1 18.09.2024 (Shift-III)

(a) were renovating
(b) will renovate
(c) has renovated
(d) have been renovating

Ans. (d)

Since, the sentence describes an action that started in the past and is still ongoing, the present perfect continuous tense 'have been renovating' is appropriate. This tense highlights the duration of the ongoing activity.

14. The US .... building was built in the year 1800.
SSC CGL Tier-1 19.09.2024 (Shift-III)

(a) capital (b) cannibal
(c) captain (d) capitol

Ans. (d)

The correct word is 'capitol', which refers to a building where a legislative body meets. The US Capitol is an iconic structure and 'capitol' is the correct term in this context.

15. Sharat is always .... about showing up for work because he believes that tardiness gets us nowhere. SSC CGL Tier-1 24.09.2024 (Shift-II)

(a) selective (b) patient
(c) drowsy (d) punctual

Ans. (d)

The word 'punctual' means being on time. The sentence indicates that Sharat values timeliness, making 'punctual' the appropriate choice.

16. Raj is very interested in studying human psychology, so he decided to pursue his master's degree in ....
SSC CGL Tier-1 25.09.2024 (Shift-I)

(a) Archaeology (b) Philosophy
(c) Psychology (d) Anatomy

Ans. (c)

Given Raj's interest in human psychology, the appropriate field of study for his master's degree would be 'Psychology'. This directly relates to his interest and is the correct option.

17. Akshaya .... hard for the entrance exam and received a high score.
SSC CGL Tier-1 26.09.2024 (Shift-I)

(a) studies (b) has studied
(c) was studied (d) studied

Ans. (d)

As the sentence is in the simple past tense, the correct filler for the given blank is 'studied'.

Options like 'studies' (present tense), 'has studied' (present perfect) and 'was studied' (passive voice) do not fit the simple past tense context appropriately.

18. Just bite the ……… and tell him the truth. **SSC CGL Tier-1 26.09.2024 (Shift-II)**

(a) bullet (b) gun
(c) dust (d) shot

Ans. (a)

The correct filler for the given blank is 'bullet' to complete the idiom 'bite the bullet,' which means to decide to do something difficult or unpleasant that one has been putting off or hesitating over.

19. The team ……… the championship before their star player got injured. **SSC CGL Tier-1 26.09.2024 (Shift-II)**

(a) was won (b) had won
(c) has won (d) win

Ans. (b)

As the given sentence presents two actions of the past, the past perfect tense 'had won' should be used to fill in the blank.

SSC CGL 2023 (Tier 1 & 2)

20. She is …… a peacock in the blue satin saree. **SSC CGL Tier-1 14.07.2023 (Shift-I)**

(a) very beautiful as (b) so beautiful as
(c) as beautiful as (d) beautiful like

Ans. (c)

'As...as' is a comparative structure used to compare two things. The given sentence compares her beauty with a peacock.

21. She reminds me always that I .... to be a little more careful. **SSC CGL Tier-1 14.07.2023 (Shift-II)**

(a) had (b) have
(c) must (d) has

Ans. (b)

The verb 'reminds' indicates an action in the present tense. We generally use the semi-modal 'have to' with 'I/you/we/they' to express a general obligation.

22. The police were on high alert on account of the ……… convict who had killed many people. **SSC CGL Tier-1 17.07.2023 (Shift-II)**

(a) run after (b) walk away
(c) eloped (d) run away

Ans. (d)

The sentence states that the police were on high alert because of an escaped convict. 'Run away' refers to a person who had escaped the police.

23. As cattle are to herd so are birds to ….. . **SSC CGL Tier-1 18.07.2023 (Shift-II)**

(a) flock (b) litter (c) pack (d) streak

Ans. (a)

A 'flock' is a group of birds.

24. 'Habitual' may be replaced by '……. .' **SSC CGL Tier-1 19.07.2023 (Shift-I)**

(a) stagnant (b) continual
(c) temperate (d) holistic

Ans. (b)

'Habitual' means 'a continuous habit,' making 'continual' the suitable replacement.

25. The match schedule was disturbed due to .... rain. **SSC CGL Tier-1 19.07.2023 (Shift-I)**

(a) detestable (b) incessant
(c) venerable (d) soothing

Ans. (b)

The correct filler for the given blank is 'incessant,' meaning continuous or unending rain.

'Detestable' means deserving intense dislike, 'venerable' means accorded a great deal of respect, and 'soothing' means having a calming effect.

26. Mohan .... the charge of 'Centre for Life Skills' from Mustafa. **SSC CGL Tier-1 21.07.2023 (Shift-I)**

(a) took out (b) took through
(c) took off (d) took over

Ans. (d)

The given sentence states that Mohan took control of the Centre for Life Skills from Mustafa. 'Took over' means to take control. 'Took out' implies removal, 'took through' implies guiding someone, and 'took off' implies leaving or removing something.

27. Radium is a white powder that …… table salt. **SSC CGL Tier-1 19.07.2023 (Shift-II)**

(a) looks like (b) look like
(c) will look like (d) looking like

Ans. (a)

The given sentence is in the simple present tense and the subject is singular.

Thus, 'looks like' is the correct filler.

28. The details were .... from one person to the other within no time **SSC CGL Tier-1 24.07.2023 (Shift-IV)**

(a) passed away (b) passed in
(c) passed down (d) passed out

Ans. (c)

The sentence states that the details were shared from one person to another quickly. 'Passed down' means to share information.

29. Don't take the wind out of my………and tell me I'm going nowhere with my life. **SSC CGL Tier-1 19.07.2023 (Shift-III)**

(a) boat (b) wings
(c) sails (d) sales

Ans. (c)

The correct filler for the blank is 'sails.' The idiom 'take the wind out of my sails' means to cause someone to lose confidence.

30. The doctor .... two tablets per day. **SSC CGL Tier-1 19.07.2023 (Shift-IV)**

(a) prescribed (b) advised
(c) ordered (d) proposed

Ans. (a)

The correct filler is 'prescribed,' meaning recommended or authorised by a doctor for treatment.

31. Meenakshi sweeps the ball excellently when she………an off-spin delivery. **SSC CGL Tier-1 20.07.2023 (Shift-II)**

(a) will get (b) has got
(c) got (d) gets

Ans. (d)

The correct filler for the blank is 'gets' as the sentence is in the simple present tense.

32. 'Rapid' may be replaced by '........'. **SSC CGL Tier-1 20.07.2023 (Shift-II)**

(a) Gradual (b) Legitimate
(c) Artistic (d) Speedy

Ans. (d)

The correct word to replace 'rapid' is 'speedy' as it means quick or fast.

33. Ishwar Chandra Vidyasagar fought hard against .... practices which affected Indian Society of his time **SSC CGL Tier-1 20.07.2023 (Shift-IV)**

(a) many evil (b) all evil
(c) most evil (d) more evil

Ans. (a)

The correct filler for the blank is 'many evil'. We generally use 'many' before plural countable nouns ('practices' in the given sentence).

34. The young one of a lion is called a .... **SSC CGL Tier-1 20.07.2023 (Shift-IV)**

(a) colt (b) chick (c) calf (d) cub

Ans. (d)

The correct filler for the blank is 'cub', which refers to the young one of a lion. 'Colt' refers to a young male horse. 'Chick' refers to a baby bird, especially of a hen. 'Calf' refers to a youn or bull.

35. The sermon of the priest was very short and......... .
SSC CGL Tier-1 24.07.2023 (Shift-I)
(a) coned (b) conveyance
(c) concise (d) consisted

Ans. (c)
The given sentence states that the sermon of the priest was very short and concise. 'Concise' means brief and clear, without unnecessary details.

36. Tibet is our .... country. Its people are called 'Tibetans'.
SSC CGL Tier-1 24.07.2023 (Shift-II)
(a) neighbour (b) neighbouring
(c) neighour's (d) neighbourhood

Ans. (b)
The correct filler for the blank is 'neighbouring.' It is used as an adjective to modify the noun 'country', meaning someone or something that is very near or close to you.

37. Mosquitoes....if there is no water logging. SSC CGL Tier-1 24.07.2023 (Shift-III)
(a) breed
(b) will breed
(c) will not breed
(d) will have been breeding

Ans. (c)
The given sentence is an example of the first conditional sentence, and the correct grammatical structure is 'if + simple present ...... will + V1'. Hence, the correct filler for the blank is 'will not breed.'

38. Hundreds of firms went bankrupt during the ....
SSC CGL Tier-1 25.07.2023 (Shift-I)
(a) recission (b) revision
(c) remission (d) recession

Ans. (d)
The correct filler for the blank is 'recession'. It means a significant decline in economic activity that lasts longer.

39. I take my .... off to our freedom fighters for their service to our country. SSC CGL Tier-1 25.07.2023 (Shift-III)
(a) boots (b) hat
(c) gun (d) socks

Ans. (b)
The correct filler for the given blank is 'hat.'
The idiom 'take your hat off to someone' means to show admiration or respect for someone's achievement.

40. 'Stories of dolphins' saving human lives ....throughout history.
SSC CGL Tier-1 25.07.2023 (Shift-IV)
(a) have been said (b) told
(c) have been told (d) had been said

Ans. (c)
Action is in present tense which is in continuation of past so 'have been told' is correct.

41. Shakuntala Devi was born on 4th November, 1929. In her childhood she ....to school.
SSC CGL Tier-1 26.07.2023 (Shift-I)
(a) never gone
(b) went never
(c) had never been
(d) ever been

Ans. (c)
Sentence is in past perfect tense where an action is ended in past so, 'had never been' is correct.

42. The termites were just the tip of the ......but the house was near collapsing in reality.
SSC CGL Tier-1 26.07.2023 (Shift-IV)
(a) mountain (b) iceberg
(c) shoe (d) heel

Ans. (b)
The correct filler for the blank is 'iceberg'. The 'tip of the iceberg' is an idiom that refers to a small noticeable part of a much larger problem.

43. .... in population is a hindrance to a country's growth.
SSC CGL Tier-1 26.07.2023 (Shift-IV)
(a) Contract (b) Decrease
(c) Reduce (d) Increase

Ans. (d)
The correct filler for the blank is 'increase'. It means a rise in population, which can be a hindrance to a country's growth.

44. A .... is a female horse.
SSC CGL Tier-1 27.07.2023 (Shift-II)
(a) vixen (b) doe
(c) mare (d) rooster

Ans. (c)
The correct filler for the given blank is 'mare,' which refers to a female horse. 'Vixen' is a female fox, 'doe' is a female deer, and 'rooster' is a male chicken.

45. A good leader be ready to .... criticism. SSC CGL Tier-2 02.03.2023
(a) settle (b) meet
(c) face (d) carry

Ans. (c)
The correct filler for the given blank is 'face'. A good leader must be ready to 'face' criticism.

46. The friends decided to play cards to .... time while waiting for the cab. SSC CGL Tier-2 02.03.2023
(a) ignore (b) kill
(c) move (d) case

Ans. (b)
The correct filler for the given blank is 'kill.' The phrase 'kill time' means to pass the time while waiting.

47. The house they bought was ...... spacious than their previous house.
SSC CGL Tier-2 02.03.2023
(a) mostly (b) most
(c) as (d) more

Ans. (d)
The correct filler for the given blank is 'more.' The sentence compares the spaciousness of two houses, requiring the comparative form 'more'.

48. The management wants to ...... restrictions at the workplace.
SSC CGL Tier-2 03.03.2023
(a) break (b) impose
(c) settle (d) encourage

Ans. (b)
The correct filler for the given blank is 'impose'. The management wants to 'impose' restrictions at the workplace.

49. Many students do not ...... attention in botany class.
SSC CGL Tier-2 03.03.2023
(a) exhibit (b) drive
(c) pay (d) trace

Ans. (c)
The correct filler for the given blank is 'pay'. 'Pay attention' is the correct phrase commonly used.

50. Tia wants a dog that was ...... than Larry's dog. SSC CGL Tier-2 03.03.2023
(a) smarty and strong
(b) smartest and strongest
(c) smarter and stronger
(d) smart and strong

Ans. (c)
The correct filler for the given blank is 'smarter and stronger'. The sentence compares the qualities of two dogs, making 'smarter and stronger' the suitable comparative form.

51. The movie was released...... expected. SSC CGL Tier-2 06.03.2023
(a) later than
(b) most later than
(c) later then
(d) more later than

Ans. (a)
The correct filler for the given blank is 'later than'. The sentence compares the release time of the movie to expectations and 'later than' is the grammatically correct form.

52. Rahul is ...... Coding.
SSC CGL Tier-2 06.03.2023
(a) skilled on (b) strong of
(c) experienced of (d) exprienced in

Ans. (d)

The correct filler for the given blank is 'experienced in'.

53. Nowadays, online shopping is easier ...... shopping in a market.
SSC CGL Tier-2 07.03.2023
(a) like (b) than
(c) then (d) as

Ans. (b)

The correct filler for the given blank is 'than'. The sentence compares online shopping to shopping in a market, making 'than' the correct comparative conjunction.

54. The committee will .... a survey on the government schemes.
SSC CGL Tier-2 07.03.2023
(a) conduct (b) fight
(c) hold (d) originate

Ans. (a)

The correct filler for the given blank is 'conduct'. The committee will 'conduct' a survey, meaning to organise and carry out.

55. When the victim narrated his version of the incident, the jury was ....
SSC CGL Tier-2 07.03.2023
(a) honestly satisfied
(b) perfectly satisfied
(c) completely satisfied
(d) excruciatingly satisfied

Ans. (c)

The correct filler for the given blank is 'completely satisfied'. This phrase indicates that the jury was fully convinced by the victim's narration.

56. By this time tomorrow, I.......the work assigned to me.
SSC CGL Tier-2 26.10.2023
(a) will have did (b) will do
(c) will have done (d) will be done

Ans. (c)

The sentence is in future perfect tense, so, 'will have done' is the correct filler.

57. ...... the thought. It will be a great idea someday. SSC CGL Tier-2 26.10.2023
(a) Hold onto (b) Hold to
(c) Hold on (d) Hold against

Ans. (a)

The correct filler for the given blank is 'Hold onto'. The phrase 'hold onto the thought' means to keep an idea or plan in mind.

58. Robin watched as the smoke ....steadily from the chimney.
SSC CGL Tier-2 26.10.2023
(a) hung (b) rose
(c) left (d) went

Ans. (b)

The correct filler for the given blank is 'rose'.
The sentence describes the smoke rising steadily from the chimney.

59. The girl was .... as she was drenched in the rain.
SSC CGL Tier-2 26.10.2023
(a) bolt (b) gold
(c) cold (d) tight

Ans. (c)

The correct filler for the given blank is 'cold'.
'Bolt' means a sudden movement, 'gold' is a precious metal and 'tight' means firmly held.

SSC CGL 2022 (Tier 1 & 2)

60. The angles are equal, consequently the sides are ....
SSC CGL Tier-1 01.12.2022 (Shift-I)
(a) equal (b) unequal
(c) larger (d) smaller

Ans. (a)

The correct filler for the given blank is 'equal'.

Since the angles are equal, the sides are consequently equal.

61. Ram was praised for his .... leadership.
SSC CGL Tier-1 01.12.2022 (Shift-I)
(a) imaginary (b) visionary
(c) magical (d) broad

Ans. (b)

The correct filler for the given blank is 'visionary'.

It means having a clear idea of what the future should be like.

62. The doctor directed the nurse to administer an .... medicine to the patient. SSC CGL Tier-1 01.12.2022 (Shift-II)
(a) official
(b) eminent
(c) alternative
(d) insightful

Ans. (c)

The correct filler for the given blank is 'alternative'. The doctor directed the nurse to administer an alternative medicine.

63. If you try to do something every day you will .... progress.
SSC CGL Tier-1 01.12.2022 (Shift-II)
(a) hold (b) get
(c) make (d) catch

Ans. (c)

The correct filler for the given blank is 'make'. It means to move forward in one's work or activity.

64. It is very difficult for her to ....
SSC CGL Tier-1 1.12.2022 (Shift-III)
(a) keep a secret (b) touch a secret
(c) make a secret (d) cry a secret

Ans. (a)

The correct filler for the given blank is 'keep a secret'.

It means not to tell anyone a secret that you know.

65. The planets are .... around the Sun.
SSC CGL Tier-1 01.12.2022 (Shift-III)
(a) revolving (b) circling
(c) rotating (d) rounding

Ans. (a)

The correct filler for the given blank is 'revolving'. It means turning with a circular movement.

66. If you are the one who is planning to lose weight remember to keep your snacking ....
SSC CGL Tier-1 01.12.2022 (Shift-III)
(a) outgoing (b) prejudiced
(c) uncontrolled (d) moderate

Ans. (d)

The correct filler for the given blank is 'moderate'. It means keeping snacking in check to manage weight. 'Outgoing' means sociable, 'prejudiced' means biased and 'uncontrolled' means not restrained.

67. The monster trucks have very .... engines, they can probably pull a train coach without any problem.
SSC CGL Tier-1 01.12.2022 (Shift-IV)
(a) dominant (b) forceful
(c) impressive (d) powerful

Ans. (d)

The correct filler for the given blank is 'powerful'. It accurately describes the strength of the engines. 'Dominant' means having power over others, 'forceful' means strong and assertive and 'impressive' means making a strong impact.

68. The contingent managed to .... successfully.
SSC CGL Tier-1 01.12.2022 (Shift-IV)
(a) park the deal
(b) close the deal
(c) heal the deal
(d) catch the deal

Ans. (b)

The correct filler for the given blank is 'close the deal'. It means to finalise a business agreement successfully.

'Park the deal' implies putting it on hold, 'heal the deal' is incorrect usage and 'catch the deal' implies capturing it, which doesn't make sense here.

69. I was running late so I only had time for a .... shower.
SSC CGL Tier-1 01.12.2022 (Shift-I)
(a) quick (b) hasty
(c) fast (d) shot

Ans. (a)

The correct filler for the given blank is 'quick' to show that the shower took place in a short amount of time.

The words 'fast' and 'hasty' in the context of the shower would tell about the speed of the shower instead of the time.

70. When there are negative and toxic thoughts .... your mind, you can never think positively.
SSC CGL Tier-1 02.12.2022 (Shift-I)
(a) plotting (b) shouting
(c) clouding (d) persuading

Ans. (c)

Clouding is the correct filler because the sentence implies 'covering' of mind with some kind of thoughts.

71. Every time my boss comes up with some good idea, he gets into.................. .
SSC CGL Tier-1 02.12.2022 (Shift-II)
(a) trouble (b) fun
(c) sleep (d) shock

Ans. (a)

The correct filler for the given blank is 'trouble'. 'Get into trouble' means to fall into difficulty.

72. Although I have a good job, I wish to take the .... of starting my own business. SSC CGL Tier-1 02.12.2022 (Shift-II)
(a) back (b) seat (c) look (d) risk

Ans. (d)

The correct filler for the given blank is 'risk'.

73. Be it a *chaat* or a refreshing lemonade, lemon is the need of the hour in .... summers.
SSC CGL Tier-1 02.12.2022 (Shift-III)
(a) banging (b) freezing
(c) scorching (d) alleviating

Ans. (c)

The correct filler for the given blank is 'scorching' to describe hot summers.

74. One must learn to .... a line between one's private and professional life.
SSC CGL Tier-1 02.12.2022 (Shift-III)
(a) draw (b) catch (c) bring (d) get

Ans. (a)

The correct filler for the given blank is 'draw'. The phrase 'drawing a line' refers to putting a limit on what one will do or allow to happen.

75. After having understood the ill effects, he said he would .... drinking alcohol.
SSC CGL Tier-1 02.12.2022 (Shift-IV)
(a) quit (b) finish
(c) close (d) terminate

Ans. (a)

The correct filler for the given blank is 'quit'. The sentence indicates a decision to stop drinking alcohol.

76. The patient was .... from the hospital. SSC CGL Tier-1 02.12.2022 (Shift-IV)
(a) liberated (b) discharged
(c) let out (d) released

Ans. (b)

The correct filler for the given blank is 'discharged'. It means to be officially allowed to leave an institution such as a hospital, prison, or the army.

77. Motorists committing this infraction are .... fined.
SSC CGL Tier-1 03.12.2022 (Shift-I)
(a) wholly (b) hardly
(c) slowly (d) heavily

Ans. (d)

The correct word to fill in the blank is 'heavily' because it is the right adverb to use with 'fined'.

78. Anita is an employee who has unconditional .... for her company. SSC CGL Tier-1 03.12.2022 (Shift-II)
(a) support (b) dedication
(c) attachment (d) love

Ans. (d)

The correct filler for the given blank is 'love'. It means a deep affection or attachment to her company.

79. He has experienced .... abuse.
SSC CGL Tier-1 03.11.2022 (Shift-II)
(a) palpable (b) visible
(c) physical (d) intangible

Ans. (c)

The correct filler for the given blank is 'physical'.

'Palpable' means something that can be felt, 'visible' means something that can be seen and 'intangible' means something that cannot be touched or seen.

80. Every person should know their own..........., what their skillset is and how unique they are.
SSC CGL Tier-1 03.12.2022 (Shift-III)
(a) calamities (b) punctualities
(c) specialties (d) fecundities

Ans. (c)

The correct filler for the given blank is 'specialties'. It means a particular part of a wider subject that someone concentrates on or is an expert in. 'Calamities' means disasters, 'punctualities' means being on time and 'fecundities' means fertility or the ability to produce abundantly.

81. The country's rapid .... has led to a rise in many people's standard of living. SSC CGL Tier-1 03.12.2022 (Shift-III)
(a) idea (b) life
(c) confidence (d) growth

Ans. (d)

The correct filler for the given blank is 'growth'.

The country's rapid growth has led to a rise in many people's standard of living.

82. They supplied the required human resource ....
SSC CGL Tier-1 03.12.2022 (Shift-III)
(a) faultlessly (b) heavy
(c) clear (d) able

Ans. (a)

The correct filler for the given blank is 'faultlessly'.

It means in a way that is perfect or without mistakes.

83. The anchor gave us a .... welcome, a pleasant smile and a bouquet on reaching the hotel.
SSC CGL Tier-1 03.12.2022 (Shift-IV)
(a) warm (b) worth
(c) winning (d) wonderful

Ans. (a)

The correct filler for the given blank is 'warm'. It means kind and friendly in a way that makes other people feel comfortable.

84. I listened to him with .... attention. SSC CGL Tier-1 03.12.2022 (Shift-IV)
(a) hefty (b) massive
(c) rapt (d) vast

Ans. (c)

The correct filler for the given blank is 'rapt'. It means completely interested and involved in something. 'Hefty' means large and heavy, 'massive' means very large and heavy and 'vast' means very large in extent.

85. He booked the tickets for the show .... SSC CGL Tier-1 05.12.2022 (Shift-I)
(a) in advance (b) in common
(c) in depth (d) in demand

Ans. (a)

The correct filler for the given blank is 'in advance'. It means before something happens. 'In common' means shared by others, 'in depth' means thorough and 'in demand' means in great demand.

86. Although she didn't reveal her plans clearly, I had a .... idea. SSC CGL Tier-1 05.12.2022 (Shift-I)
(a) rough (b) clear
(c) concise (d) complete
Ans. (a)
The correct filler for the given blank is 'rough'. It means approximate or not exact.

87. This drama is extremely informative .... life in Roman times. SSC CGL Tier-1 05.12.2022 (Shift-I)
(a) on (b) of
(c) about (d) for
Ans. (c)
The correct filler for the given blank is 'about'.
This drama is extremely informative about life in Roman times.

88. Arun and his wife were .... a baby boy after 18 years of their marriage. SSC CGL Tier-1 05.12.2022 (Shift-I)
(a) delighted with
(b) prepared with
(c) provided with
(d) blessed with
Ans. (d)
The correct filler for the given blank is 'blessed with'. It means to have something good or lucky happen to you. 'Delighted with' means very pleased, 'prepared with' means made ready and 'provided with' means supplied with.

89. I looked at her face and found she was getting disturbed. I decided to drop that .... SSC CGL Tier-1 05.12.2022 (Shift-IV)
(a) product (b) chance
(c) subject (d) pride
Ans. (c)
The correct filler for the given blank is 'subject'. In the sentence, it refers to a person or thing that is being discussed, described or dealt with.

90. We ensure that you will get a .... chauffeur with the right car for your day. SSC CGL Tier-1 06.12.2022 (Shift-I)
(a) novice (b) uniformed
(c) dabbler (d) riotous
Ans. (b)
The correct filler for the given blank is 'uniformed'. It refers to wearing a specific kind of clothing worn by a particular group. 'Novice' means a beginner, 'dabbler' means someone who takes part in an activity casually and 'riotous' means wild or uncontrolled.

91. She rubbed her hands over her arms and then .... her purse, headed inside the convenience store. SSC CGL Tier-1 06.12.2022 (Shift-I)
(a) snapping (b) slaying
(c) pinching (d) grabbing
Ans. (d)
The correct filler for the given blank is 'grabbing'. 'Snapping' means to break suddenly, 'slaying' means to kill and 'pinching' means to squeeze tightly.

92. Great people are always ready to .... responsibilities. SSC CGL Tier-1 06.12.2022 (Shift-II)
(a) kindle (b) secure
(c) shoulder (d) burden
Ans. (c)
The correct filler for the given blank is 'shoulder'. The term 'shouldering responsibility' means to accept or take responsibility for something. 'Kindle' means to start a fire, 'secure' means to make safe and 'burden' means to load heavily.

93. The judge directed the advocate general to .... an enquiry on the case. SSC CGL Tier-1 06.12.2022 (Shift-III)
(a) make (b) produce
(c) hold (d) get
Ans. (c)
The correct filler for the given blank is 'hold' as it indicates that an enquiry needs to be held on the case.

94. Always be in .... with your near and dear ones as life is uncertain and fragile. SSC CGL Tier-1 06.12.2022 (Shift-IV)
(a) touch (b) relation
(c) communication (d) connection
Ans. (a)
The correct filler for the given blank is 'touch'.

95. Akshay always gives .... to Johana for his success. SSC CGL Tier-1 07.12.2022 (Shift-I)
(a) blame (b) chance
(c) opportunity (d) credit
Ans. (d)
The correct filler for the given blank is 'credit'. It means approval or praise that you give to someone for something they have done.

96. Holm, a Danish traveller, had made a/an .... replica of the tablet, which in 1908 was deposited in the Metropolitan Museum of Art, New York. SSC CGL Tier-1 07.12.2022 (Shift-I)
(a) wild (b) obscure
(c) corrupt (d) exact
Ans. (d)
The correct filler for the given blank is 'exact'.

97. Brady straightened the .... baton in hand. SSC CGL Tier-1 07.12.2022 (Shift-II)
(a) charge (b) wooden
(c) swing (d) open
Ans. (b)
'Wooden' is the correct filler which appropriately works as adjective of 'baton'.

98. A faint mist .... over the valley. SSC CGL Tier-1 07.12.2022 (Shift-II)
(a) hung (b) swung
(c) swayed (d) dangled
Ans. (a)
The correct filler for the given blank is 'hung'.
It means to stay in the air for a long time. 'Swung' means to move back and forth, 'swayed' means to move slowly from side to side and 'dangled' means to hang loosely.

99. I am .... after five years. SSC CGL Tier-1 07.12.2022 (Shift-III)
(a) making an exam
(b) taking an exam
(c) keeping an exam
(d) frying an exam
Ans. (b)
The word 'take' is used with 'exam'. Hence, the correct filler for the given blank is 'taking an exam'. 'Making' implies creating, 'keeping' implies holding on to and 'frying' is completely unrelated.

100. Happiness can be spread by being grateful or .... compliments to someone. SSC CGL Tier-1 07.12.2022 (Shift-III)
(a) giving (b) paying
(c) accepting (d) sharing
Ans. (b)
The correct filler for the given blank is 'paying'.

101. It is easier to make a promise than to .... a promise. SSC CGL Tier-1 07.12.2022 (Shift-IV)
(a) maintain (b) follow
(c) justify (d) keep
Ans. (d)
The word 'keep' is used with 'promise'. Hence, the correct filler for the given blank is 'keep', meaning to do what you said you would do.

102. In all her sorrow she must weep or she will .... SSC CGL Tier-1 07.12.2022 (Shift-IV)
(a) die (b) laugh
(c) suffer (d) cry

Ans. (c)

The correct filler for the given blank is 'suffer'. It means to experience physical or mental pain.

103. She frankly confessed that she couldn't .... to purchase a car then. SSC CGL Tier-1 08.12.2022 (Shift-I)

(a) spend (b) afford
(c) stand (d) tolerate

Ans. (b)

The given sentence indicates that she is not able to buy or do something because she does not have enough money or time.

104. She became frustrated with her poor health and began to lose .... of her recovery.
SSC CGL Tier-1 08.12.2022 (Shift-I)

(a) weight (b) idea
(c) money (d) hope

Ans. (d)

The correct filler for the given blank is 'hope'. 'Lose hope' means to stop believing that something you want to happen might be possible.

105. More than 200 eminent Indian Americans attended the reception at the East Room, a venue which has .... some of the landmark events related to the India-US relationship.
SSC CGL Tier-1 08.12.2022 (Shift-II)

(a) witnessed (b) surpassed
(c) rebuffed (d) grounded

Ans. (a)

The correct filler for the given blank is 'witnessed'. When a place or period witnesses a particular event, that event happens in that place or during that period.
'Surpassed' means to exceed, 'rebuffed' means to reject and 'grounded' means to base on.

106. The .... weapons which are easily available in the market are a big threat to the security of some nations.
SSC CGL Tier-1 08.12.2022 (Shift-III)

(a) heated (b) deadly
(c) casual (d) valuable

Ans. (b)

The correct filler for the given blank is 'deadly'. It means causing or likely to cause death.

107. There is .... traffic every morning.
SSC CGL Tier-1 08.12.2022 (Shift-IV)

(a) long (b) heavy
(c) big (d) lengthy

Ans. (b)

The word 'heavy' is used with 'traffic' to indicate that there is a lot of something.

108. He is diligent, therefore he will .... SSC CGL Tier-1 09.12.2022 (Shift-I)

(a) remain (b) succeed
(c) fail (d) fall

Ans. (b)

The correct filler for the given blank is 'succeed'.

109. The girl has ...... chances winning the match. SSC CGL Tier-1 09.12.2022 (Shift-I)

(a) bountiful (b) high
(c) light (d) hefty

Ans. (b)

'High' is used with 'chance' to say that something has a good chance of happening.
'Bountiful' implies abundant, 'light' implies not heavy and 'hefty' implies heavy.

110. The crowing witch released a .... cackle as she turned the boy into a beast. SSC CGL Tier-1 09.12.2022 (Shift-I)

(a) gentle (b) low
(c) loud (d) soft

Ans. (c)

The correct filler for the given blank is 'loud' as it qualifies the noun 'cackle', which is a loud, high laughter.

111. Nitha can assemble the students of her class...... .
SSC CGL Tier-1 09.12.2022 (Shift-III)

(a) perfect (b) distract
(c) slow (d) quickly

Ans. (d)

The correct filler for the given blank is 'quickly'.

112. Of course, we agree with that measure, it is .... sensible.
SSC CGL Tier-1 09.12.2022 (Shift-III)

(a) slightly (b) hardly
(c) partially (d) perfectly

Ans. (d)

The correct filler for the given blank is 'perfectly'.
'Slightly' implies a little, 'hardly' implies barely and 'partially' implies incompletely.

113. Sunil cannot .... a trip to the US now because he has already spent a lot for the completion of his house.
SSC CGL Tier-1 09.12.2022 (Shift-IV)

(a) visit (b) afford
(c) spend (d) earn

Ans. (b)

The given sentence states that the person would not be able to pay for the trip because of spending a lot on the house. 'Afford' means to not have enough money to pay.

114. Writing down instructions, steps and remembering them can make you look really efficient and ....
SSC CGL Tier-1 09.12.2022 (Shift-IV)

(a) diligent (b) dormant
(c) operable (d) sluggish

Ans. (a)

'Diligent' means careful and using a lot of effort.
'Dormant' implies inactive, 'operable' implies able to be used and 'sluggish' implies slow-moving.

115. She couldn't continue with a .... diet to reduce her blood sugar.
SSC CGL Tier-1 12.12.2022 (Shift-I)

(a) practiced (b) shortened
(c) balanced (d) maintained

Ans. (c)

With respect to diet, 'balanced' is the correct word to fill the given blank.

116. I had a nice......... on my birthday with all my friends and relatives.
SSC CGL Tier-1 12.12.2022 (Shift-II)

(a) opportunity (b) dey
(c) experience (d) time

Ans. (d)

The correct filler for the given blank is 'time'. The idiom 'had a nice time' is used for situations in which one has fun and enjoys oneself.

117. A gaggle of journalists sit in a/an .... foyer waiting impatiently.
SSC CGL Tier-1 12.12.2022 (Shift-II)

(a) attic (b) hotel
(c) ranch (d) croft

Ans. (b)

The correct filler for the given blank is 'hotel'. 'Attic' implies a space below the roof, 'ranch' implies a large farm and 'croft' implies a small farm.

118. The sergeant could not stand the weather because it was......... cold.
SSC CGL Tier-1 12.12.2022 (Shift-III)

(a) bitterly (b) carefully
(c) smoothly (d) cautiously

Ans. (a)

The adjective 'bitterly' is generally used to refer to extremely cold weather. Thus, the correct filler for the given blank is 'bitterly'.

119. Kajol is one age-defying beauty and her sari collection is worth. ....
SSC CGL Tier-1 12.12.2022 (Shift-III)

(a) bookmarking (b) repudiating
(c) flirting (d) renouncing

Ans. (a)

The correct filler for the given blank is 'bookmarking'. It means worth taking a note of. 'Repudiating' means rejecting, 'flirting' means showing a romantic interest and 'renouncing' means giving up.

120. Either he is mad, or he feigns ………… SSC CGL Tier-1 12.12.2022 (Shift-IV)

(a) happiness (b) madness
(c) calmness (d) sadness

Ans. (b)

The correct filler for the given blank is 'madness'.

121. I felt ……… elated at the news.
SSC CGL Tier-1 12.12.2022 (Shift-IV)

(a) commonly (b) strangely
(c) customarily (d) typically

Ans. (b)

The correct filler for the given blank is 'strangely'. It means in an unusual or surprising way.

122. This statement of the political leader has created ……… confusion.
SSC CGL Tier-1 13.12.2022 (Shift-I)

(a) weighty (b) utter
(c) vast (d) heavy

Ans. (b)

The correct filler for the given blank is 'utter'. It means complete or absolute.

123. When I got the job, I knew what ……… money really is
SSC CGL Tier-1 13.12.2022 (Shift-I)

(a) effort-earned (b) honest-earned
(c) hard-earned (d) soft-earned

Ans. (c)

The correct filler for the given blank is 'hard-earned'. It means earned or achieved after a lot of effort. 'Effort-earned' and 'honest- earned' are not common phrases and 'soft-earned' implies easily earned.

124. The party was a ……… hour for everyone, except Mukesh.
SSC CGL Tier-1 13.12.2022 (Shift-II)

(a) happy (b) dry
(c) welcome (d) stable

Ans. (a)

The correct filler for the given blank is 'happy'. Options like 'dry', 'welcome' and 'stable' do not fit this context.

125. There was a ……… accident last night and the inspector on duty was unable to raise help.
SSC CGL Tier-1 13.12.2022 (Shift-II)

(a) serious (b) harsh
(c) goofy (d) gloomy

Ans. (a)

The correct filler for the given blank is 'serious'. With respect to 'accident', 'serious' is the correct word for the given blank. 'Harsh' means severe, 'goofy' means silly and 'gloomy' means dark or depressed.

126. To make your own gargle, ……… half a teaspoon of salt in a glass of lukewarm or partly cooled boiled water. SSC CGL Tier-1 13.12.2022 (Shift-III)

(a) cease (b) cast
(c) consolidate (d) dissolve

Ans. (d)

The correct filler for the given blank is 'dissolve'. It means to mix a solid with a liquid until it forms a solution. 'Cease' means to stop, 'cast' means to throw and 'consolidate' means to combine.

127. His heart pounded as he checked his rearview mirror and saw only the dark ………… of highway.
SSC CGL Tier-1 13.12.2022 (Shift-IV)

(a) emancipation (b) trench
(c) stretch (d) vitality

Ans. (c)

The correct filler for the given blank is 'stretch'. 'Emancipation' means liberation, 'trench' means a long, narrow ditch and 'vitality' means energy.

128. In the absence of the principal, the vice-principal …. for him.
SSC CGL Tier-2 29.01.2022

(a) deputes (b) exchanges
(c) officiates (d) replaces

Ans. (c)

The correct filler for the given blank is 'officiates'. 'Deputes' means to delegate authority.

129. The workers …… against the new labour laws. SSC CGL Tier-2 29.01.2022

(a) remonstrated (b) dissented
(c) implicated (d) opposed

Ans. (a)

It is mentioned in the given sentence that the workers are protesting or complaining against the new labour laws. Hence, the correct filler for the given blank is 'remonstrated', which means to complain or protest. 'Dissented' means to disagree, 'implicated' means to show involvement and 'opposed' means to be against.

130. He was …….. at his brother's refusal to help him financially.
SSC CGL Tier-2 29.01.2022

(a) indignant (b) indicated
(c) enchanted (d) enamoured

Ans. (a)

The given sentence states that he was (angry) at his brother's refusal to help him financially. Hence, 'indignant' means angry.

'Indicated' means pointed out, 'enchanted' means charmed and 'enamoured' means in love with.

131. Have you …. with the difficulties you might have to face?
SSC CGL Tier-2 29.01.2022

(a) considered (b) reckoned
(c) discussed (d) pondered

Ans. (b)

The correct filler for the given blank is 'reckoned'.

'Considered' means thought about, 'discussed' means talked over and 'pondered' means thought deeply about.

132. All is calm now ... the heart of Paris due to the lock down
SSC CGL Tier-2 03.02.2022

(a) in (b) at (c) on (d) by

Ans. (a)

The correct filler for the given blank is 'in'. We use the preposition 'in' to show a place inside or to a position inside a particular area or object.

133. …… 5,40,000 square foot building now houses ……… enormous collection of artworks and historic archives. SSC CGL Tier-2 03.02.2022

(a) No word required, the
(b) The, no word required
(c) The, a
(d) A, an

Ans. (d)

The correct fillers for the given blanks are 'A' and 'an'.

The 'building' mentioned in the given sentence is non-specific and the indefinite article 'a' will be used with '5,40,000 square foot building'. Further, 'an' would be used before 'enormous'.

134. The annual meeting our club has been ………. till next month.
SSC CGL Tier-2 08.08.2022

(a) dragged (b) deferred
(c) disrupted (d) deranged

Ans. (b)

The given sentence states that the annual meeting of our club has been postponed till next month. Hence, the correct filler for the given blank is 'deferred', which means to postpone. 'Dragged' means pulled, 'disrupted' means interrupted and 'deranged' means insane.

135. The boy …. to take the money.
SSC CGL Tier-2 08.08.2022

(a) ordered (b) denied
(c) reminded (d) refused

Ans. (d)

The given sentence states that the boy did not take the money. Hence, the correct filler for the given blank is 'refused'.

SSC CGL 2021 (Tier 1 & 2)

136. India is formally moving ahead to ......21 MIG-29 and 12 Sukhoi-30MKI fighters from Russia along with upgrades of their existing fleets.
SSC CGL Tier-1 13.08.2021 (Shift-I)

(a) advance
(b) accomplish
(c) achieve
(d) procure

Ans. (d)

The given sentence presents that India is going ahead in getting the 21 MIG-29 and 12 Sukhoi-30MKI fighters from Russia. Hence, the correct filler for the given blank is 'procure', which means 'to get'.

137. Work and domestic .... made Kajal short-tempered.
SSC CGL Tier-1 13.08.2021 (Shift-I)

(a) weights (b) gravities
(c) pressures (d) forces

Ans. (c)

The correct filler for the given blank is 'pressures', which aligns with work and domestic forces that make Kajal short-tempered.

138. The door ...... in the strong wind.
SSC CGL Tier-1 13.08.2021 (Shift-III)

(a) slammed (b) hooted
(c) sizzled (d) slapped

Ans. (a)

The given sentence presents how the door shut with a loud sound. Hence, the correct filler for the given blank is 'slammed', which means to shut forcefully and loudly.
'Hooted' means to make a loud sound, 'sizzled' means to make a hissing sound.

139. The advanced nations face no population problem since they were already settling down to zero growth ...... in population.
SSC CGL Tier-1 13.08.2021 (Shift-III)

(a) scale (b) degree
(c) rate (d) frequency

Ans. (c)

The correct filler for the given blank is 'rate' as it makes the correct collocation with 'growth'.
'Scale' means a system of measurement, 'degree' means a level or extent and 'frequency' means the number of occurrences.

140. Advertisers often use rhyme and ....
SSC CGL Tier-1 13.08.2021 (Shift-III)

(a) alteration
(b) alliteration
(c) designation
(d) denunciation

Ans. (b)

'Alliteration' is the correct word according to the sentence which means using similar sounding words.
'Alteration' means a change, 'designation' means a name or title and 'denunciation' means public condemnation.

141. You need not .... so much fuss about wearing a mask when you go out.
SSC CGL Tier-1 16.08.2021 (Shift-I)

(a) generate (b) do
(c) cause (d) make

Ans. (d)

The correct filler for the given blank is 'make' as it makes the correct collocation with 'fuss'.

142. My New Year's .... is to think positive always.
SSC CGL Tier-1 16.08.2021 (Shift-III)

(a) repetition (b) resolution
(c) confession (d) celebration

Ans. (b)

The correct filler for the given blank is 'resolution' as the correct phrase is 'New Year's resolution'.

143. Some patches of the ...... garden have a rich cover of grass now.
SSC CGL Tier-1 17.08.2021 (Shift-II)

(a) stretching (b) slouching
(c) sprawling (d) stroking

Ans. (c)

The given sentence states that some patches of the large garden have a rich cover of grass now. Hence, 'sprawling', which means covering a large area of land.
'Stretching' means extending, 'slouching' means standing or sitting in a lazy way and 'stroking' means gently moving your hand over something.

144. .... yourself with the new perfume. SSC CGL Tier-1 17.08.2021 (Shift-II)

(a) Pamper (b) Purify
(c) Percolate (d) Prosper

Ans. (a)

The correct filler for the given blank is 'pamper'. It means to treat with care and attention.
'Purify' means to make clean, 'percolate' means to filter through and 'prosper' means to succeed or thrive.

145. Keats and Shelley were poets of the same period; they were ....
SSC CGL Tier-1 18.08.2021 (Shift-I)

(a) colleagues
(b) associates
(c) contemporaries
(d) acquaintances

Ans. (c)

The correct filler for the given blank is 'contemporaries'. It means people existing or occurring in the same period.
'Colleagues' means people you work with, 'associates' means partners or companions and 'acquaintances' means people you know but who are not close friends.

146. She knew that to apologise would .... to admitting she had failed.
SSC CGL Tier-1 18.08.2021 (Shift-III)

(a) tantamount (b) tandem
(c) tantalising (d) tangible

Ans. (a)

The given sentence presents how if she apologises, it would be equivalent to saying that she had failed.
Hence, the correct filler for the given sentence is 'tantamount', which means equivalent to.
'Tandem' implies a pair, 'tantalizing' means tempting and 'tangible' means something that can be touched.

147. Credit card .... has increased in recent years.
SSC CGL Tier-1 20.08.2021 (Shift-I)

(a) fraud (b) flake
(c) freed (d) fluke

Ans. (a)

The correct filler for the given blank is 'fraud'. 'Flake' means a small piece, 'freed' means released and 'fluke' means a stroke of luck.

148. My neighbour was admitted to the hospital when he developed an allergic .... to some medicine he took. SSC CGL Tier-1 20.08.2021 (Shift-I)

(a) reaction (b) result
(c) retort (d) rejoinder

Ans. (a)

The correct filler for the given blank is 'reaction' as the correct collocation is 'allergic reaction'. 'Retort' means a sharp reply and 'rejoinder' means a reply.

149. The cabinet has .... a proposal to change the way universities are funded and managed.
SSC CGL Tier-1 20.08.2021 (Shift-II)

(a) endorsed (b) endeared
(c) evaporated (d) endangered

Ans. (a)

'Endorsed' is the correct filler according to the context of the sentence which means to publicly make a statement of supporting a plan. 'Endeared' means to make beloved, 'evaporated' means turned into vapour and 'endangered' means at risk.

150. We are bewildered by the power which science has suddenly placed in our laps and we are .... by the realisation of our unpreparedness to deal with a crisis. SSC CGL Tier-1 23.08.2021 (Shift-I)

(a) proud (b) demeaned
(c) condemned (d) humbled

Ans. (d)

The given sentence presents how we are confused by the benefits science has brought to us and, at the same time, we are made to realise that we are unprepared for a crisis. Hence, the correct filler for the given blank is 'humbled'.

'Demeaned' means degraded and 'condemned' means declared wrong.

151. The government has hardened its .... against the agitators and imposed a curfew in the area. SSC CGL Tier-1 23.08.2021 (Shift-I)

(a) manner (b) orientation
(c) bearing (d) stance

Ans. (d)

The given sentence presents how the government has become strict in their position against the agitators of the curfew. Hence, the correct filler for the given blank is 'stance', which means position.

152. If you .... to newsgroups, you often get hundreds of messages. SSC CGL Tier-1 23.08.2021 (Shift-II)

(a) subscribe (b) describe
(c) practice (d) offend

Ans. (a)

The correct filler for the given blank is 'subscribe' as we subscribe to newsgroups, blogs or webpages.

153. His .... of the topic was so good that students had few doubts at the end of the class. SSC CGL Tier-1 24.08.2021 (Shift-I)

(a) qualification (b) exhibition
(c) picturisation (d) exposition

Ans. (d)

The correct filler for the given blank is 'exposition'.

154. The lack of regular academic sessions has meant that in 2020 the country has had the .... share of students who have attended educational institutions. SSC CGL Tier-1 24.08.2021 (Shift-I)

(a) lower (b) lowest (c) low (d) last

Ans. (b)

The given sentence presents a comparison of the presence of students in 2020 with other years. Hence, the correct filler for the given blank will be the superlative degree of adjective 'lowest'.

155. The people of Rajasthan strictly .... to the traditional customs. SSC CGL Tier-1 24.08.2021 (Shift-III)

(a) appeal (b) adhere
(c) apply (d) abide

Ans. (b)

'Adhere' is correct filler according to the context of the sentence which means 'to stick firmly to something'.

'Appeal' means to make a serious request, 'apply' means to put into action, and 'abide' means to accept or act in accordance with.

SSC CPO 2024 (Tier 1 & 2)

156. The small coffee shop at the end of the road is .... SSC CPO Tier-2 08.01.2024

(a) our (b) my
(c) mine (d) their

Ans. (c)

The correct filler for the given blank is 'mine'. 'Mine' indicates possession.

157. Gautam .... all the documents by the time his senior advocate reached the court. SSC CPO Tier-2 08.01.2024

(a) examines
(b) had examined
(c) is examining
(d) will be examining

Ans. (b)

'Had examined' is the correct filler as the sentence is in 'past perfect tense'.

158. She was so busy .... writing that when the maid came .... she didn't hear her. SSC CPO Tier-2 08.01.2024

(a) in, in (b) at, up
(c) with, by (d) to, in

Ans. (a)

The correct fillers for the given blanks are 'in, in'. In the first blank, 'in' is used after 'busy' to indicate the activity in which someone is engaged. In the second blank, 'in' has been used to show the presence of a maid inside a room or house.

159. 'Hurry up ! There's still ......work left to do. SSC CPO Tier-2 08.01.2024

(a) lot (b) much
(c) whole (d) many

Ans. (b)

The correct filler for the given blank is 'much'. 'Much work' is the correct phrase.

160. 'He gazed around the room ...... lay hidden a treasure chest. SSC CPO Tier-2 08.01.2024

(a) whereby (b) whereas
(c) wherein (d) whereof

Ans. (c)

The given sentence states that he gazed around the room in which a treasure chest was hidden. Hence, the correct filler for the given blank is 'wherein', which is used to indicate a location.

161. Each one of the participants in the annual function .... an applause. SSC CPO Tier-2 08.01.2024

(a) deserve (b) deserves
(c) is deserving (d) have deserved

Ans. (b)

The given sentence states that each one of the participants in the annual function is worthy of applause. Hence, the correct filler for the given blank is 'deserves'.

162. 'The air quality is so bad ...... it becomes difficult to breathe. SSC CPO Tier-2 08.01.2024

(a) when (b) as
(c) that (d) since

Ans. (c)

'So...that' is a fixed conjunction pair. Hence, the correct filler for the given blank is 'that'.

163. 'If I go to Bangalore, I .... with my nephew. SSC CPO Tier-2 08.01.2024

(a) stay (b) will stay
(c) have stayed (d) stayed

Ans. (b)

'Will stay' is the correct sentence as the sentence is in 'future tense' and contains a conditional action.

164. 'I trust him completely. His conduct is ...... suspicion. SSC CPO Tier-2 08.01.2024

(a) under (b) over
(c) above (d) below

Ans. (c)

The correct filler for the given blank is 'above'.

The phrase 'above/beyond suspicion' is used when there is no doubt about the honesty of a person. 'Under' implies beneath, 'over' implies on top and 'below' implies lower.

SSC CPO 2023 (Tier 1 & 2)

165. The company had some initial problems, but now it is...... SSC CPO Tier-1 04.10.2023 (Shift-I)

(a) flying like a rock (b) flying a kite
(c) flying the nest (d) flying high

Ans. (d)

The correct filler for the given blank is 'flying high'.

166. They knew that the stock of the food was getting reduced and the fund ...... for that was not enough for the next week. **SSC CPO Tier-1 05.10.2023 (Shift-I)**

(a) allotted (b) abandoned
(c) alerted (d) asserted

Ans. (a)

The given sentence states that they knew that the stock of the food was getting reduced and the fund was not enough for the next week. Hence, the correct filler for the given blank is 'allotted', which means to set aside.

167. Being courteous ...... costs you nothing **SSC CPO Tier-1 05.10.2023 (Shift-II)**

(a) No article required
(b) a (c) the (d) an

Ans. (a)

Options like 'a', 'the' and 'an' do not fit this context. 'Being courteous' is a general statement that does not require an article.

168. It took seven years for Harish to ......his migraine. **SSC CPO Tier-1 05.10.2023 (Shift-III)**

(a) shake off (b) shake out
(c) shake up (d) shake down

Ans. (a)

'Shake off' means to successfully deal with or recover from an illness, injury, or negative feeling. The given sentence states that it took seven years for Harish to recover from his migraine.

Hence, 'shake off' is the most appropriate answer. 'Shake out' means to shake something to make it fall out, 'shake up' means to mix vigorously and 'shake down' means to extort money.

169. This is not .... exhaustive list of words. **SSC CPO Tier-1 05.10.2023 (Shift-I)**

(a) many (b) an
(c) a (d) No word required

Ans. (b)

As the word followed by the blank starts with a vowel sound, the correct filler for the given blank is 'an'.

SSC CPO 2022 (Tier 1 & 2)

170. After a tiring day, the workers decided to ...... to restore their energy. **SSC CPO Tier-1 10.11.2022**

(a) have an axe to grind
(b) put a spoke in the wheel
(c) bring to book
(d) hit the sack

Ans. (d)

'Hit the sack' is an idiom that means to go to bed. The given sentence states that after a tiring day, the workers decided to go to bed to restore their energy.

171. James Bernard was undoubtedly one of the greatest elocutionists of the world. Everyone agreed that he possessed the .... **SSC CPO Tier-1 10.11.2022 (Shift-I)**

(a) yellow press
(b) fourth estate
(c) curtain lecture
(d) gift of the gab

Ans. (d)

'Gift of the gab' is an idiom that means the ability to speak with eloquence and fluency. Hence, 'gift of the gab' is the most appropriate answer.

'Yellow press' means sensational journalism, 'fourth estate' means the press and 'curtain lecture' means a private scolding.

172. It is never advisable to have an axe to .... **SSC CPO Tier-1 11.11.2022 (Shift-III)**

(a) kill (b) rotate
(c) replace (d) grind

Ans. (d)

The correct filler for the given blank is 'grind'. 'An axe to grind' is an idiom that means to have a private reason for doing or being involved in something.

SSC CHSL 2024 (Tier 1 & 2)

173. He has not.........returned the money. **SSC CHSL Tier-2 18.11.2024**

(a) still (b) only
(c) yet (d) too

Ans. (c)

'Yet' is used to indicate that something expected has not happened up to the present time. This makes the sentence grammatically correct and meaningful.

174. His family lives.........Mahu in Madhya Pradesh. **SSC CHSL Tier-2 18.11.2024**

(a) at (b) on
(c) of (d) by

Ans. (a)

The preposition 'at' is used to indicate specific locations and in this context, 'at' correctly specifies the exact place where the family resides.

175. I was in.........state of unconsciousness for about half ....hour. **SSC CHSL Tier-2 18.11.2024**

(a) the ; a (b) a ; No article
(c) a ; an (d) No article ; an

Ans. (c)

'A' is used before words that begin with a consonant sound and 'an' is used before words that begin with a vowel sound, such as 'hour' (which sounds like it starts with a vowel).

176. ...., I'm going to walk my dog. **SSC CHSL Tier-2 18.11.2024**

(a) Annually (b) Now
(c) Rarely (d) Already

Ans. (b)

The adverb 'Now' indicates that the action will happen immediately. It specifies the time frame for the action and makes the sentence clear.

177. The rising rate of inflation is making life very hard for......... poor. **SSC CHSL Tier-2 18.11.2024**

(a) the (b) some (c) all (d) its

Ans. (a)

'The' is used before adjectives to refer to a specific group of people, in this case, 'the poor'.

178. In both countries we have leaders of .... ability. **SSC CHSL Tier-1 01.07.2024 (Shift-I)**

(a) powerful (b) almighty
(c) compelling (d) exceptional

Ans. (d)

The given sentence points out that the leaders have great quality. Hence, the correct filler is 'exceptional' which means unusual; not typical.

179. Yesterday, I ate only a .... of apples for my dinner. **SSC CHSL Tier-1 01.07.2024 (Shift-I)**

(a) pair (b) pier (c) pare (d) pear

Ans. (a)

As the given sentence refers to the number of apples, the correct filler for the given blank is 'pair'.

180. It took 4 hours straight to .... the deal with the regional company. **SSC CHSL Tier-1 01.07.2024 (Shift-II)**

(a) stop (b) get
(c) perform (d) close

Ans. (d)

The correct filler for the given blank is 'close'. The phrase 'close the deal' means to complete or to get a deal successfully.

181. The CEO's decision to cut benefits was a .... move. **SSC CHSL Tier-1 01.07.2024 (Shift-IV)**

(a) harsh (b) humorous
(c) rigorous (d) laborious

Ans. (a)

The correct filler for the given blank is 'harsh'.

182. I always love the .... of my mother's cooking.
SSC CHSL Tier-1 02.07.2024 (Shift-I)
(a) aroma (b) stench
(c) perfume (d) scent
Ans. (a)
The correct filler for the given blank is 'aroma' which fits well with the smell of mother's cooking.

183. Both the criminals were cruel and .... SSC CHSL Tier-1 02.07.2024 (Shift-II)
(a) sympathetic (b) warm
(c) brutal (d) diligent
Ans. (c)
The correct filler for the given blank is 'brutal' which fits well with the words 'criminal' and 'cruel'.

184. I was in the .... of a meeting when somebody called me.
SSC CHSL Tier-1 02.07.2024 (Shift-II)
(a) centre (b) corner
(c) round (d) middle
Ans. (d)
The correct filler for the given blank is 'middle'.

185. The teacher asked the students to .... electricity by switching off lights when they left the room.
SSC CHSL Tier-1 02.07.2024 (Shift-III)
(a) save (b) deposit
(c) rescue (d) retain
Ans. (a)
The given sentence states the teacher's advice to save electricity. Hence, the correct filler for the given blank is 'save'.

186. The genie asked Aladdin to .... a wish. SSC CHSL Tier-1 02.07.2024 (Shift-IV)
(a) make (b) take
(c) ask (d) tell
Ans. (a)
The correct filler for the given blank is 'make' to make the phrase 'make a wish'.

187. She could easily eat the .... biryani by herself.
SSC CHSL Tier-1 02.07.2024 (Shift-IV)
(a) whole (b) haul (c) hall (d) hole
Ans. (a)
The correct filler for the given blank is 'whole'.

188. She .... gracefully and greeted the interview committee with respect.
SSC CHSL Tier-1 03.07.2024 (Shift-I)
(a) grinned (b) leered
(c) smiled (d) smirked
Ans. (c)
The correct filler for the given blank is 'smiled'.

189. My sister's paintings were .... at the national museum.
SSC CHSL Tier-1 03.07.2024 (Shift-II)
(a) in display (b) on display
(c) upon display (d) into display
Ans. (b)
The correct filler for the given blank is 'on display' as it indicates that the paintings were put for public viewing.

190. Many developing nations are having a .... economy these days.
SSC CHSL Tier-1 03.07.2024 (Shift-III)
(a) boosting (b) resounding
(c) ringing (d) booming
Ans. (d)
The given sentence presents that economies of many countries are growing. Hence, the correct filler for the given blank is 'booming'.

191. He ....a long distance.
SSC CHSL Tier-1 03.07.2024 (Shift-III)
(a) runned (b) running
(c) ran (d) run
Ans. (c)
The correct filler for the given blank is 'ran'.

192. The boxer was knocked out cold by a powerful .... punch to the jaw.
SSC CHSL Tier-1 03.07.2024 (Shift-III)
(a) write (b) wright
(c) rite (d) right
Ans. (d)
The correct filler for the given blank is 'right'.

193. The movie 'Desperate Ghosts' was watched by my younger brother and he was .... horror.
SSC CHSL Tier-1 03.07.2024 (Shift-III)
(a) filled with (b) filled of
(c) filled on (d) filled off
Ans. (a)
The correct filler for the given blank is 'filled with'.

194. The .... in my shoelace created a lot of trouble.
SSC CHSL Tier-1 04.07.2024 (Shift-I)
(a) not (b) naught
(c) nought (d) knot
Ans. (d)
The correct filler for the given blank is 'knot'.

195. A sailor was .... through the high tides. SSC CHSL Tier-1 04.07.2024 (Shift-I)
(a) ceiling (b) sailing
(c) swelling (d) selling
Ans. (b)
The correct filler for the given blank is 'sailing'.

196. The crowd gave them a .... of applause. SSC CHSL Tier-1 04.07.2024 (Shift-I)
(a) yell (b) load
(c) laugh (d) round
Ans. (d)
The correct filler for the given blank is 'round'.

197. We need to .... a decision on the housing project tomorrow morning.
SSC CHSL Tier-1 04.07.2024 (Shift-II)
(a) make (b) draw
(c) build (d) frame
Ans. (a)
The correct filler for the given blank is 'make'.

198. The new construction sites have .... attack by the environmentalists.
SSC CHSL Tier-1 04.07.2024 (Shift-IV)
(a) come off (b) come upon
(c) come under (d) come out
Ans. (c)
The correct filler for the given blank is 'come under'.
Come off means to appear or sound like something.
Come upon means to meet someone unexpectedly.
Come out means to become public.

199. She went on a shopping spree with her friend and made him .... the fat bill.
SSC CHSL Tier-1 05.07.2024 (Shift-I)
(a) paid (b) do (c) pay (d) give
Ans. (c)
The correct filler for the given blank is 'pay'.

200. The captain dropped the trophy while he .... the victory with his teammates.
SSC CHSL Tier-1 05.07.2024 (Shift-II)
(a) celebrated
(b) celebrates
(c) is celebrating
(d) was celebrating
Ans. (d)
The correct filler for the given sentence is 'was celebrating' as the sentence talks about two actions happening simultaneously.

201. Which .... do you usually take to reach your office?
SSC CHSL Tier-1 05.07.2024 (Shift-II)
(a) rude (b) route
(c) root (d) rout
Ans. (b)
The correct filler for the given blank is 'route'.

202. He made .... use of the opportunity to travel.
SSC CHSL Tier-1 05.07.2024 (Shift-II)
(a) full (b) total
(c) entire (d) whole
Ans. (a)
The correct filler for the given blank is 'full'.

203. The bride had a big villa in comparison to the bridegroom's .... house.
SSC CHSL Tier-1 05.07.2024 (Shift-III)
(a) large (b) small
(c) distinct (d) different
Ans. (b)
The correct filler for the given blank is 'small'.

204. Raju is such a .... always prying into other people's business!
SSC CHSL Tier-1 05.07.2024 (Shift-III)
(a) cheeky (b) stingy
(c) nosy (d) perky
Ans. (c)
The correct filler for the given blank is 'nosy'.

205. He .... the truth.
SSC CHSL Tier-1 05.07.2024 (Shift-IV)
(a) spoken (b) speaking
(c) spoke (d) speak
Ans. (c)
The correct filler for the given blank is 'spoke'.

206. The grass on my lawn is glistening with the morning ....
SSC CHSL Tier-1 05.07.2024 (Shift-IV)
(a) duo (b) due
(c) dew (d) do
Ans. (c)
The correct filler for the given blank is 'dew' which refers to tiny drops of water that form on cool surfaces at night, when atmospheric vapour condenses.

207. In boarding schools, students need to .... by themselves.
SSC CHSL Tier-1 05.07.2024 (Shift-IV)
(a) wash the bed (b) turn the bed
(c) make the bed (d) run the bed
Ans. (c)
The correct filler for the given blank is 'make the bed'.

208. The ...... today will be cloudy and humid. **SSC CHSL Tier-1 08.07.2024 (Shift-I)**
(a) wither (b) waiter
(c) weather (d) whether
Ans. (c)
The correct filler for the given blank is 'weather'.

209. After finishing all my pending assignments, I plan to .... in Goa. **SSC CHSL Tier-1 08.07.2024 (Shift-I)**
(a) land a meal (b) forgive a debt
(c) take a holiday (d) go bankrupt
Ans. (c)
The correct filler for the given blank is 'take a holiday'.

210. He comes here ....
SSC CHSL Tier-1 08.07.2024 (Shift-II)
(a) quickly (b) formerly
(c) daily (d) lately
Ans. (c)
The correct filler for the given blank is 'daily'.

211. He hasn't .... any attention to my miserable state.
SSC CHSL Tier-1 08.07.2024 (Shift-II)
(a) made (b) had
(c) gave (d) paid
Ans. (d)
The correct filler for the given blank is 'paid'.

212. The company's .... commitment to sustainability is admirable.
SSC CHSL Tier-1 08.07.2024 (Shift-III)
(a) shakeable (b) resolute
(c) wavering (d) strong
Ans. (d)
The correct filler for the given blank is 'strong'.

213. The perfume she uses has a strong .... **SSC CHSL Tier-1 08.07.2024 (Shift-III)**
(a) sent (b) scent (c) cent (d) send
Ans. (b)
The correct filler for the given blank is 'scent'.

214. Rosy and Nicky couldn't provide any evidence to support .... arguments.
SSC CHSL Tier-1 08.07.2024 (Shift-III)
(a) there (b) theirs
(c) their (d) they're
Ans. (c)
The correct filler for the given blank is 'their'.

215. The .... purpose of the coaching was to identify the talented players.
SSC CHSL Tier-1 08.07.2024 (Shift-IV)
(a) mane (b) mine (c) mean (d) main
Ans. (d)
The correct filler for the given blank is 'main'.

216. Shyam has reserved a .... in the train for his wife as she will be giving .... to his child soon.
SSC CHSL Tier-1 08.07.2024 (Shift-IV)
(a) birth; birth (b) berth; birth
(c) berth; berth (d) birth; berth
Ans. (b)
The correct fillers for the given blanks are 'berth' and 'birth'.
Berth means a fixed bunk on a ship, train, or other means of transport. Birth means to produce or create something.

217. He .... to the manager about the terrible food in the hostel.
SSC CHSL Tier-1 08.07.2024 (Shift-IV)
(a) made a complaint
(b) terribly complained
(c) said a complaint
(d) said a big complaint
Ans. (a)
The correct filler for the given blank is 'made a complaint'.

218. Serena .... from fever since the 5th of this month.
SSC CHSL Tier-1 09.07.2024 (Shift-I)
(a) is suffering (b) has been suffering
(c) suffers (d) suffered
Ans. (b)
The correct filler for the given blank is 'has been suffering'.

219. The teacher asked the students to .... attention towards the instructions given for the project.
SSC CHSL Tier-1 09.07.2024 (Shift-I)
(a) make (b) keen
(c) had (d) pay
Ans. (d)
The correct filler for the given blank is 'pay' as it is used with 'attention'.

220. I am scared of snakes; likewise, you are .... of lizards.
SSC CHSL Tier-1 09.07.2024 (Shift-II)
(a) passionate (b) critical
(c) fond (d) fearful
Ans. (d)
The correct word to fill in the blank is 'fearful'.

221. I have observed that there is proper natural .... even at 6 o'clock on summer mornings.
SSC CHSL Tier-1 09.07.2024 (Shift-II)
(a) light (b) sparkle
(c) lucent (d) gleam
Ans. (a)
The correct filler for the given blank is 'light'.

222. I would like to reach the .... of the Everest.
SSC CHSL Tier-1 09.07.2024 (Shift-III)
(a) peek (b) pick
(c) pike (d) peak

Ans. (d)

The correct filler for the given blank is 'peak' which indicates the top of the Everest.

223. The cat's entry into the store room was .... SSC CHSL Tier-1 09.07.2024 (Shift-IV)

(a) quite (b) quiet
(c) cute (d) quit

Ans. (b)

The correct filler for the given blank is 'quiet'.

224. The .... of the whale is 2 tonnes. SSC CHSL Tier-1 09.07.2024 (Shift-IV)

(a) wait (b) weight
(c) vet (d) wet

Ans. (b)

The correct filler for the given blank is 'weight'.

225. In spring the leaves are <u>bright</u> green, whereas they appear .... in autumn. SSC CHSL Tier-1 09.07.2024 (Shift-IV)

(a) gleaming (b) luminous
(c) dazzling (d) dull

Ans. (d)

The correct filler for the given blank is 'dull'.

226. It is the .... to reach Delhi. SSC CHSL Tier-1 09.07.2024 (Shift-IV)

(a) lowest route
(b) strongest route
(c) quickest route
(d) fastest route

Ans. (d)

The correct filler for the given blank is 'fastest route'.

227. I find that students nowadays are not interested in .... letters by hand. SSC CHSL Tier-1 10.07.2024 (Shift-I)

(a) rioting (b) rating
(c) writing (d) righting

Ans. (c)

The correct filler for the given blank is 'writing'.

228. Seema has a dominating nature, so she wants to .... of everything in her life. SSC CHSL Tier-1 10.07.2024 (Shift-II)

(a) keep touch
(b) keep calm
(c) keep record
(d) keep control

Ans. (d)

The correct filler for the given blank is 'keep control'.

229. I am doubtful about his story, though you seem to be .... SSC CHSL Tier-1 10.07.2024 (Shift-II)

(a) regretting (b) uncertain
(c) pleasant (d) convinced

Ans. (d)

The correct filler for the given blank is 'convinced'.

230. I don't like dirty cars, so you should keep it .... SSC CHSL Tier-1 10.07.2024 (Shift-III)

(a) shabby (b) similar
(c) new (d) spotless

Ans. (d)

The correct filler for the given blank is 'spotless'.

231. He has .... vision because of his illness. SSC CHSL Tier-1 10.07.2024 (Shift-III)

(a) blurred (b) unfocused
(c) obscured (d) faded

Ans. (a)

The correct filler for the given blank is 'blurred'.

232. Tom is trying to ....as soon as possible. SSC CHSL Tier-1 10.07.2024 (Shift-IV)

(a) receive a job
(b) experience a job
(c) get a job
(d) learn a job

Ans. (c)

The correct filler for the given blank is 'get a job'.

233. Ujjwal was imprisoned for .... a crime. SSC CHSL Tier-1 11.07.2024 (Shift-I)

(a) making (b) undertaking
(c) committing (d) involving

Ans. (c)

The correct filler for the given blank is 'committing'.

234. Yesterday, he .... pizza and .... burgers in one go. SSC CHSL Tier-1 11.07.2024 (Shift-I)

(a) eight; ate (b) ate; ate
(c) eight; eight (d) ate; eight

Ans. (d)

The correct filler for the given blanks are 'ate' and 'eight'.

235. She suppressed a .... urge to yawn. SSC CHSL Tier-1 11.07.2024 (Shift-II)

(a) tough (b) stout
(c) hard (d) strong

Ans. (d)

The correct filler for the given blank is 'strong'.

236. You just wait in the lobby. I will be back after .... SSC CHSL Tier-1 11.07.2024 (Shift-III)

(a) a fast meal
(b) a quick shower
(c) a fast shower
(d) a quick food

Ans. (b)

The correct filler for the given blank is 'a quick shower'.

237. The guard did not want anything bad to happen, so he ordered the group to step back to avoid anything .... SSC CHSL Tier-1 11.07.2024 (Shift-III)

(a) customary (b) terrible
(c) habitual (d) diplomatic

Ans. (b)

The correct filler for the given blank is 'terrible'.

238. The artist received a .... from the audience. SSC CHSL Tier-1 11.07.2024 (Shift-IV)

(a) handful of applause
(b) round of applause
(c) bunch of applause
(d) plenty of applause

Ans. (b)

The correct filler for the given blank is 'round of applause'.

239. Currently, Mittu and Bittu ...... hard to meet the project deadline. SSC CHSL Tier-2 10.01.2024

(a) worked (b) are working
(c) have worked (d) were working

Ans. (b)

The correct filler for the given blank is present continuous tense 'are working'.

240. Tania ...... to the canteen. SSC CHSL Tier-2 10.01.2024

(a) were gone (b) were going
(c) was going (d) had going

Ans. (c)

The correct filler for the given blank is 'was going' as the subject of the sentence is singular.

241. I did not ...... to university yesterday. SSC CHSL Tier-2 10.01.2024

(a) gone (b) go
(c) went (d) going

Ans. (b)

The correct filler for the given blank is 'go' as we use the first form of the verb with 'do/does/did'.

242. The war .... badly damaged the country's infrastructure. SSC CHSL Tier-2 10.08.2024

(a) has (b) have (c) was (d) is

Ans. (a)

The correct filler for the given blank is 'has' as the sentence points out that the effects of war are still relevant in the present time, indicating that the sentence is in present perfect tense.

SSC CHSL 2023 (Tier 1 & 2)

243. My feet don't .... the ground for the rest of the day.
SSC CHSL Tier-1 09.03.2023 (Shift-I)
(a) slab (b) touch
(c) deal (d) purify
Ans. (b)
The correct filler for the given blank is 'touch'.
'Slab' implies a large, thick piece, 'deal' means to handle and 'purify' means to make pure.

244. However, even after independence in 1947, British expatriate firms did not suddenly .... from India.
SSC CHSL Tier-1 09.03.2023 (Shift-I)
(a) divest (b) consecrate
(c) close (d) disallow
Ans. (a)
The given sentence presents how even after India's independence, the British leaders did not leave India. Hence, the correct filler for the given blank is 'divest', which means 'to completely go away'.

245. Remember that, little sister: wait for a man to .... your honour, and you'll wait forever.
SSC CHSL Tier-1 09.03.2023 (Shift-II)
(a) comfort (b) cheer
(c) repeal (d) avenge
Ans. (d)
The correct filler for the given blank is 'avenge'. It means to punish somebody for hurting you in some way.

246. One of his rules was to always . ... and await instruction to enter.
SSC CHSL Tier-1 09.03.2023 (Shift-II)
(a) knock (b) rub
(c) blin (d) resist
Ans. (a)
The correct filler for the given blank is 'knock'.

247. The makers of sports drinks spend tens to hundreds of millions of dollars ...... their products each years.
SSC CHSL Tier-1 09.03.2023 (Shift-III)
(a) snacking (b) lingering
(c) varying (d) advertising
Ans. (d)
The correct filler for the given blank is 'advertising'.

248. Illusions are usually related with ...... processes.
SSC CHSL Tier-1 09.03.2023 (Shift-III)
(a) visual (b) audio
(c) oratory (d) digital
Ans. (a)
The correct filler for the given blank is 'visual'. 'Visual' means related to seeing or sight.
The given sentence states that illusions are usually related to visual processes.

249. The US has military. ... in many Middle Eastern countries.
SSC CHSL Tier-1 09.03.2023 (Shift-IV)
(a) forces (b) denizens
(c) personal (d) townies
Ans. (a)
The correct filler for the given blank is 'forces'. It means the soldiers and weapons that an army, etc. 'Denizens' means inhabitants, 'personal' means individual, and 'townies' means townspeople.

250. He was a handsome man in his. ...... thirties. SSC CHSL Tier-1 10.03.2023 (Shift-II)
(a) least (b) latter (c) lest (d) late
Ans. (d)
The correct filler for the given blank is 'late' as it mentions the age between 35 and 40.

251. In humans, lack of sleep leads to ...... memory and reduced cognitive abilities. SSC CHSL Tier-1 10.03.2023 (Shift-III)
(a) attended (b) impaired
(c) thankless (d) witnessed
Ans. (b)
The correct filler for the given blank is 'impaired'. It means weakened or damaged.

252. In this engineering design project you will learn how to build an infinity mirror, with built-in lights that make the mirror look like a deep .... with no end.
SSC CHSL Tier-1 10.03.2023 (Shift-III)
(a) tunnel (b) lodge
(c) funeral (d) signal
Ans. (a)
The correct filler for the given blank is 'tunnel'. 'Lodge' means a small house, 'funeral' means a ceremony for the dead and 'signal' means a sign.

253. In some places, roads were still unfinished, as were several areas where football fans are expected to .... SSC CHSL Tier-1 10.03.2023 (Shift-IV)
(a) congregate (b) unravel
(c) dissolve (d) clump
Ans. (a)
The correct filler for the given blank is 'congregate'. It means to gather into a crowd.
'Unravel' means to untangle, 'dissolve' means to melt and 'clump' means to form a mass.

254. This has given rise to the view that the legal code is ...... against women and the poor.
SSC CHSL Tier-1 13.03.2023 (Shift-II)
(a) baked (b) frank
(c) duplicitous (d) biased
Ans. (d)
The correct filler for the given blank is 'biased'. It means showing prejudice. 'Baked' means cooked, 'frank' means honest and 'duplicitous' means deceitful.

255. How can seawater from the oceans be. ... .fresh water that is suitable for people to drink?
SSC CHSL Tier-1 13.03.2023 (Shift-III)
(a) change about (b) surrender in
(c) minced on (d) turned into
Ans. (d)
The correct filler for the given blank is 'turned into'. It means to change into. 'Change about' means to alter, 'surrender in' means to give up and 'minced on' is not relevant.

256. I don't know if such thoughts have ever ..... to Liz Truss, who is still, at the time of writing, Britain's Prime Minister. SSC CHSL Tier-1 13.03.2023 (Shift-IV)
(a) yielded (b) monitored
(c) occurred (d) desisted
Ans. (c)
The correct filler for the given blank is 'occurred'. 'Yielded' means to produce, 'monitored' means observed and 'desisted' means to cease.

257. In addition, it is believed they possess crude electronic devices capable of triggering ...... bombs.
SSC CHSL Tier-1 14.03.2023 (Shift-I)
(a) intelligible (b) incendiary
(c) insensible (d) insipid
Ans. (b)
The given sentence presents how a device comprises bombs that can cause damage and destruction. Hence, the correct filler for the given blank is 'incendiary', which means something that can cause a fire.
'Intelligible' means understandable, 'insensible' means unconscious, and 'insipid' means lacking flavour.

258. I try to retrieve the note from my pocket while ...... the tray steady on my palm. SSC CHSL Tier-1 14.03.2023 (Shift-I)
(a) holding (b) scolding
(c) noting (d) plotting

Ans. (a)

The correct filler for the given blank is 'holding'.

259. Still flaccid and .... from lack of blood. Ed ambled slowly in front of the doors.

SSC CHSL Tier-1 14.03.2023 (Shift-II)

(a) liberal (b) levity
(c) lethargic (d) levy

Ans. (c)

The correct filler for the given blank is 'lethargic'. It means having little energy, feeling unwilling and unable to do anything. 'Liberal' means open-minded, 'levity' means lightness of mind and 'levy' means to impose a tax.

260. At first the water .... blue, then grey. SSC CHSL Tier-1 14.03.2023 (Shift-III)

(a) glanced (b) seemed
(c) heeded (d) lest

Ans. (b)

The correct filler for the given blank is 'seemed'. 'Glanced' means looked quickly, 'heeded' means paid attention to and 'lest' means for fear that.

261. Ram placed her in one of the ...... leather chairs opposite his desk.

SSC CHSL Tier-1 14.03.2023 (Shift-III)

(a) marinated (b) brewed
(c) quilted (d) stewed

Ans. (c)

The correct filler for the given blank is 'quilted'. It means made of two layers of cloth filled with padding held in place by lines. 'Marinated' means soaked in a marinade, 'brewed' means prepared by boiling and 'stewed' means cooked slowly.

262. Sir, can you reflect on the usefulness or, ... of blocking all the highways?

SSC CHSL Tier-1 14.03.2023 (Shift-III)

(a) impotence (b) futility
(c) scorch (d) incompatibility

Ans. (b)

The given sentence talks about the usefulness or uselessness of blocking all the highways. Hence, the correct filler for the given blank is 'futility'. 'Impotence' means inability, 'scorch' means to burn and 'incompatibility' means not fitting together.

263. A haze of panic blurred my vision something terrible was close to .... SSC CHSL Tier-1 15.03.2023 (Shift-I)

(a) happened
(b) happening
(c) happens
(d) has happened

Ans. (b)

The correct filler for the given blank is 'happening'. In the sentence, it means an event that happens.

264. No matter how many times I try I, always end up in the same ....

SSC CHSL Tier-1 15.03.2023 (Shift-I)

(a) sauce (b) meal
(c) pickle (d) account

Ans. (c)

The correct filler for the given blank is 'pickle'. 'In a pickle' means to be stuck in a difficult situation.

265. Habitat loss received little attention from all Twitter ....

SSC CHSL Tier-1 15.03.2023 (Shift-IV)

(a) forces (b) users (c) pools (d) band

Ans. (b)

The correct filler for the given blank is 'users'. 'Forces' means military, 'pools' means a shared resource and 'band' means a group.

266. Have you ever had a ...... bath using a bath wash?

SSC CHSL Tier-1 15.03.2023 (Shift-IV)

(a) barbaric (b) extinguishing
(c) refreshing (d) killing

Ans. (c)

The correct filler for the given blank is 'refreshing'.

'Barbaric' means savage, 'extinguishing' means putting out and 'killing' means causing death.

267. My heart ...... hard, bumping the broken glass nicked by sharp edges.

SSC CHSL Tier-1 16.03.2023 (Shift-II)

(a) thundered (b) thumped
(c) inhibited (d) lifted

Ans. (b)

The correct filler for the given blank is 'thumped' as it is the correct collocation for 'heart' (heartbeat). 'Thundered' means made a loud noise, 'inhibited' means restrained and 'lifted' means raised.

268. The ...... of revenge demanded a life for a life.

SSC CHSL Tier-1 16.03.2023 (Shift-II)

(a) cheering (b) moaning
(c) crowning (d) obligations

Ans. (d)

'Obligations' means the state of having to do something because you have promised. The given sentence states that the obligations of revenge demanded a life for a life.

'Cheering' means shouting in support, 'moaning' means groaning and 'crowning' means making someone king or queen.

269. Choosing the right software for any purpose can be a/an .... task for any business.

SSC CHSL Tier-1 16.03.2023 (Shift-III)

(a) intimating (b) challenging
(c) flickering (d) attributing

Ans. (b)

The correct filler for the given blank is 'challenging'. 'Intimating' means suggesting, 'flickering' means wavering and 'attributing' means assigning.

270. I dump the tray on the side and start ...... up the dishwasher.

SSC CHSL Tier-1 17.03.2023 (Shift-I)

(a) tantalising (b) upbringing
(c) alienating (d) loading

Ans. (d)

The correct filler for the given blank is 'loading'.

'Tantalising' means tempting, 'upbringing' means the way a child is raised and 'alienating' means causing someone to feel isolated.

271. Lecanemab was recently reported to have a small but ..... effect in reducing cognitive decline.

SSC CHSL Tier-1 17.03.2023 (Shift-I)

(a) optional (b) marginal
(c) microscopic (d) significant

Ans. (d)

The given sentence states that lecanemab was recently reported to have a small but noticeable effect in reducing cognitive decline. Hence, the correct filler for the given blank is 'significant', which means important or large enough to be noticed.

'Optional' means not compulsory, 'marginal' means slight and 'microscopic' means very small.

272. Earwax is a helpful and ...... part for your body's defences.

SSC CHSL Tier-1 17.03.2023 (Shift-II)

(a) tedious (b) natural
(c) flowing (d) transparent

Ans. (b)

The correct filler for the given blank is 'natural'.

'Tedious' means boring, 'flowing' means moving smoothly and 'transparent' means see-through.

273. ...... on the silver tray like a white snake, the wedding garland was as thick as my forearm.

SSC CHSL Tier-1 17.03.2023 (Shift-II)

(a) Circulated (b) Bartered
(c) Repeated (d) Coiled

Ans. (d)

The correct filler for the blank is 'coiled' as it indicates the manner in which the wedding garland is kept on the tray.

274. He was rewarded for his meekness ...... and understanding heart.
SSC CHSL Tier-1 17.03.2023 (Shift-II)

(a) on a wisely (b) with a wise
(c) wisest (d) with wiser

Ans. (b)

The correct filler for the given blank is 'with a wise'.

275. David always kept his ...... open for anything that might put them at risk.
SSC CHSL Tier-1 17.03.2023 (Shift-III)

(a) black eye (b) starry eyes
(c) eagle eyes (d) sheep eyes

Ans. (c)

'Eagle eyes' means a careful or close watch.

The given sentence states that David always kept his eagle eyes open for anything that might put them at risk. Hence, 'eagle eyes' is the most appropriate answer.

'Black eye' means a bruised eye, 'starry eyes' means dreaming and 'sheep eyes' means shy glances.

276. Howard tried to speak but all that came out was an ...... squeaky gargle.
SSC CHSL Tier-1 17.03.2023 (Shift-IV)

(a) implausible (b) sincere
(c) easy (d) inarticulate

Ans. (d)

The correct filler for the given blank is 'inarticulate'. It means unable to express oneself clearly.

'Implausible' means not believable, 'sincere' means genuine and 'easy' means not difficult.

277. We can usefully distinguish four types of claims that have been traditionally made using the. .... 'human nature'.
SSC CHSL Tier-1 17.03.2023 (Shift-IV)

(a) collateral (b) application
(c) nuance (d) expression

Ans. (d)

The correct filler for the given blank is 'expression'. 'Collateral' means security for repayment, 'application' means a request and 'nuance' means a subtle difference.

278. In the early autumn fierce fighting took place, the .... Serbians bearing a prominent part.
SSC CHSL Tier-1 20.03.2023 (Shift-I)

(a) cowardly (b) unabashed
(c) gallant (d) bore

Ans. (c)

The given sentence states that in the early autumn fierce fighting took place, the brave Serbians bearing a prominent part.

Hence, the correct filler for the given blank is 'gallant', which means brave and courageous.

279. ...... threats to elephants requires public and political will to take action. SSC CHSL Tier-1 20.03.2023 (Shift-I)

(a) Dignifying (b) Addressing
(c) Perplexing (d) Stagnating

Ans. (b)

The correct filler for the given blank is 'Addressing'.

'Dignifying' means making worthy, 'perplexing' means confusing and 'stagnating' means becoming inactive.

280. It was past the mid-hour of the night, and was quiet ...... and dark.
SSC CHSL Tier-1 20.03.2023 (Shift-III)

(a) riding (b) moonless
(c) glimmer (d) flasher

Ans. (b)

The correct filler for the given blank is 'moonless'.

281. We are the creative force of our life, and through our own decisions rather than our conditions, if use carefully to learn to do certain things, we can ...... those goals.
SSC CHSL Tier-1 20.03.2023 (Shift-III)

(a) reverberate (b) accomplish
(c) torment (d) expel

Ans. (b)

The given sentence talks about how if we use all resources properly, we can reach our goals. In this context, the correct filler for the given blank is 'accomplish'.

'Reverberate' means to echo, 'torment' means to cause pain and 'expel' means to force out.

282. The scientists ...... that the chefs relied on a specific motion.
SSC CHSL Tier-1 20.03.2023 (Shift-III)

(a) invented (b) found
(c) innovated (d) planned

Ans. (b)

As the sentence is referring to a discovery or realisation, the correct filler for the given blank is 'found'.

283. Just one ...... of paper can lead to a whole lot of fun.
SSC CHSL Tier-1 20.03.2023 (Shift-III)

(a) group (b) sheet
(c) bunch (d) bulk

Ans. (b)

The correct filler for the given blank is 'sheet'.

284. The machine can be ...... to deliver a certain number of coins.
SSC CHSL Tier-1 20.03.2023 (Shift-IV)

(a) met (b) abet
(c) slashed (d) set

Ans. (d)

The correct filler for the given blank is 'set'. It means to put or bring into a specified state.

285. A group of Googlers get together regularly to .... and decide which event will be celebrated with a doodle. SSC CHSL Tier-1 20.03.2023 (Shift-IV)

(a) brainstorm (b) discredit
(c) relief (d) salute

Ans. (a)

The given sentence states that a group of Googlers get together regularly to brainstorm and decide which events will be celebrated with a doodle. Hence, the correct filler for the given blank is 'brainstorm'.

286. Taking a deep ...... breath, I start again successfully loading the filter and placing the cup underneath.
SSC CHSL Tier-1 21.03.2023 (Shift-II)

(a) jamming (b) penetrating
(c) surrogating (d) calming

Ans. (d)

The correct filler for the given blank is 'calming'.

'Jamming' means blocking, 'penetrating' means piercing and 'surrogating' means substituting.

287. In space it is possible to identify and ...... some unique characteristics of human physiology and biology.
SSC CHSL Tier-1 21.03.2023 (Shift-III)

(a) isolate (b) excess
(c) replete (d) partition

Ans. (a)

The given sentence states that in space it is possible to identify and isolate some unique characteristics of human physiology and biology. Hence, the correct filler for the given blank is 'isolate', which means to separate. 'Excess' means more than necessary, 'replete' means filled and 'partition' means division.

288. The ...... heard that the relationship was stormy and had broken up several times.
SSC CHSL Tier-1 21.03.2023 (Shift-IV)

(a) impugn (b) impute
(c) inquiry (d) inordinate

Ans. (c)

The correct filler for the given blank is 'inquiry'. 'Impugn' means to challenge, 'impute' means to attribute and 'inordinate' means excessive.

289. Your ear has three main ...... outer, middle and inner.
SSC CHSL Tier-1 21.03.2023 (Shift-IV)

(a) plugs (b) subjects
(c) parts (d) events

Ans. (c)

The correct filler for the given blank is 'parts'. 'Plugs' means to stop, 'subjects' means topics and 'events' means occurrences.

290. The humour of the Gods is cruel; or ...... they see more than we do.
SSC CHSL Tier-1 21.03.2023 (Shift-IV)

(a) unlikely (b) perhaps
(c) odds (d) however

Ans. (b)

The correct filler for the given blank is 'perhaps' as the sentence tries to reason why the Gods are cruel.

291. The chief guest is ...... to arrive at the venue within half an hour.
SSC CHSL Tier-1 03.10.2023 (Shift-I)

(a) accepted (b) expieted
(c) expected (d) espected

Ans. (c)

The given sentence states that the chief guest is likely to arrive at the venue within half an hour. Hence, the correct filler for the given blank is 'expected'.

292. The chef's culinary creations were infused with a distinctive ...... that set them apart from typical restaurant fare.
SSC CHSL Tier-1 04.08.2023 (Shift-I)

(a) flare (b) fair
(c) flere (d) flair

Ans. (d)

The given sentence states that the chef's dishes had a unique style that set them apart from typical restaurant food. Hence, the correct filler for the given blank is 'flair', which means style or characteristics.

'Flare' means to blaze, 'fair' means just or a public event and 'flere' is not a relevant term.

293. My cousin owns a shop of food ......
SSC CHSL Tier-1 10.10.2023 (Shift-II)

(a) additives (b) addetivis
(c) aditives (d) addetives

Ans. (a)

The correct filler for the given blank is 'additives'.

It refers to a substance added to something in small quantities to improve or preserve it.

294. The ...... of the crime scene made it difficult for investigators to gather evidence.
SSC CHSL Tier-1 10.10.2023 (Shift-III)

(a) set (b) cite
(c) sleight (d) site

Ans. (d)

The correct filler for the given blank is 'site'. It refers to the piece of land where something is located.

295. .... year ago, Arihant decided to join .... NCC.
SSC CHSL Tier-1 11.08.2023 (Shift-I)

(a) A; an
(b) The; No article
(c) The; a
(d) A; the

Ans. (d)

The correct fillers for the given blanks are 'A; the'. 'A year ago' indicates a general time frame and 'the NCC' specifies a particular organisation.

296. Fingernails and toenails helped our ...... to climb trees, peel fruits and use simple tools. While their colour and condition offer clues about your ...... health. Nail polish turns them into fashion accessories.
SSC CHSL Tier-2 26.06.2023

(a) ancestors ; overall
(b) predecessor ; universal
(c) forefather ; all in all
(d) general ; altogether

Ans. (a)

The correct fillers for the given blanks are 'ancestors' and 'overall'. 'Ancestors' refers to the people who came before us in our family or evolutionary history and 'overall' means considering or including everything.

'Predecessor' means one who came before, 'universal' means applicable everywhere, 'forefather' means an ancestor, 'all in all' means everything considered, 'general' means common and 'altogether' means entirely.

297. Reptiles ...... from amphibians. For a long period of 160 million years in earth's history, reptiles were the dominant form of life on the planet and ...... in an enormous variety of shapes and sizes.
SSC CHSL Tier-2 26.06.2023

(a) developed; continued
(b) came; exhausted
(c) evolved; existed
(d) involved; lived

Ans. (c)

The correct fillers for the given blanks are 'evolved' and 'existed'. 'Evolved' means to develop or undergo changes gradually over time and 'existed' means to be present or to have lived during a specific period in history.

298. Quarrels in result in .... confrontations and bring all conversations to a complete standstill.
SSC CHSL Tier-2 26.06.2023

(a) cold (b) hot
(c) heated (d) sisputed

Ans. (c)

The given sentence states that quarrels lead to intense confrontations, causing all conversations to come to a standstill. Hence, the correct filler for the given blank is 'heated', which means intense or angry.

299. Mohnish and Ravi .... to Canada next month.
SSC CHSL Tier-2 02.11.2023

(a) has move (b) is moving
(c) has moving (d) are moving

Ans. (d)

The given sentence presents a definite future action which can be represented by the present continuous tense. Hence, the correct filler for the given blank is 'are moving'.

300. Stanley .... to play the violin now, with an amateur instructor.
SSC CHSL Tier-2 02.11.2023

(a) is learning (b) had learnt
(c) will learn (d) was learning

Ans. (a)

The given sentence presents an action that is ongoing, which is represented by the present continuous tense. Hence, the correct filler for the given blank is 'is learning'.

301. Neither of the biscuits you gave me .... chocolate chips.
SSC CHSL Tier-2 02.11.2023

(a) are contained (b) contain
(c) contains (d) is contain

Ans. (c)

As the given sentence presents a general statement and has a plural subject, a singular verb in present tense would be used. Hence, the correct filler for the given blank is 'contains'.

SSC CHSL 2022 (Tier 1 & 2)

302. When we believe that our mind is thinking .... thoughts at the same time, what actually is happening is that .... thoughts are .... in such quick .... so as to seem simultaneous.
SSC CHSL Tier-1 24.05.2022 (Shift-III)

(a) homogenous, measurable unchanging, velocity
(b) challenging, limited, fixed, interruption
(c) multiple, myriad, alternating succession
(d) uniform, countable, altering ramification

Ans. (c)

The given sentence talks about the mind thinking multiple thoughts at the same time, but actually having myriad thoughts alternating in such quick succession as to seem simultaneous.

Hence, the correct fillers for the given blanks are 'multiple, myriad, alternating, succession'.

303. My grandfather was a farmer and he ...... three acres of land.
SSC CHSL Tier-1 24.05.2022 (Shift-III)

(a) cultivated (b) advanced
(c) grown (d) cultured

Ans. (a)

The correct filler for the given blank is 'cultivated'. It means to prepare and use the land for growing plants for food or to sell.

304. The ...... crowd gave their newly elected leader a magnificent welcome. **SSC CHSL Tier-1 25.05.2022 (Shift-I)**

(a) noisy (b) jubilant
(c) troublesome (d) melancholic

Ans. (b)

The given sentence states that the crowd gave their newly elected leader a magnificent welcome. Hence, the correct filler for the given blank is 'jubilant', which means extremely happy.

305. Manpower exporters and overseas recruiters commonly ...... in illegal business practices for short-term ...... gain. **SSC CHSL Tier-1 25.05.2022 (Shift-II)**

(a) honoured, professional
(b) indulged, monetary
(c) regulated personal
(d) thrived, devotional

Ans. (b)

The given sentence states that manpower exporters and overseas recruiters commonly allow themselves to engage in illegal business practices for short-term monetary gain.

Hence, the correct fillers for the given blanks are 'indulged' and 'monetary'. 'Indulged' means to allow and 'monetary' means relating to money.

306. One day, I was handed a few volumes of new literature unlike anything I had ever read before and so ...... as to make me utterly forget my hopeless states.
SSC CHSL Tier-1 25.05.2022 (Shift-III)

(a) repelling (b) captivating
(c) boring (d) unrealistic

Ans. (b)

The correct filler for the given blank is 'captivating'. It means to hold the attention of someone by being extremely interesting.

307. The roof .... the weight of the snow. **SSC CHSL Tier-1 25.05.2022 (Shift-III)**

(a) collapsed under
(b) collapsed to
(c) collapsed with
(d) collapsed for

Ans. (a)

The correct filler for the given blank is 'collapsed under'.

'Collapsed to' implies falling to a location, 'collapsed with' implies falling with something and 'collapsed for' is grammatically incorrect.

308. My success was complete and the delighted directors .... me the privilege of developing automatic regulators which were much desired.
SSC CHSL Tier-1 26.05.2022 (Shift-I)

(a) contrasted (b) accorded
(c) disagreed (d) removed

Ans. (b)

'Accorded' means to agree with something. The given sentence states that the narrator's success was complete and the delighted directors accorded him the privilege of developing automatic regulators which were much desired.
'Contrasted' means showed differences, 'disagreed' means had a different opinion and 'removed' means taken away.

309. As soon as she opened the cages, the birds........ **SSC CHSL Tier-1 26.05.2022 (Shift-I)**

(a) flown away (b) flew away
(c) fly away (d) flies away

Ans. (b)

The given sentence is in the simple past tense, so the verb must be used in its simple past form (V2). Hence, the correct filler for the given blank is 'flew away'.

310. The minute you start ...... and tolerating ......, it becomes the new norm and the slide begins and therefore, we must constantly .... to given our best and be recognised, not simply aim to do just enough to ......that we don't get found out.
SSC CHSL Tier-1 26.05.2022 (Shift-II)

(a) compelling, excellence, strike encourage
(b) compromising, mediocrity, strive ensure
(c) conjecturing transcendence, strum, envision
(d) contradicting distinction, stink, endeavour.

Ans. (b)

'Compromising' fits as it implies settling for less. 'Mediocrity' reflects the quality being tolerated.
'Strive' suggests continuous effort to do better. 'Ensure' means to make certain, fitting the context of being recognised for our efforts. The chosen words align perfectly with the intended meaning of the sentence.

311. If you had consulted me, I would have ...... you.
SSC CHSL Tier-1 30.05.2022 (Shift-I)

(a) advising (b) advises
(c) advised (d) advise

Ans. (c)

The correct filler for the given blank is 'advised'. V3 is used with 'would have'.

312. A note of ...... during the leaders' meeting at the UN.
SSC CHSL Tier-1 30.05.2022 (Shift-I)

(a) friction surfaced
(b) discord surfaced
(c) grievance surfaced
(d) strife surfaced

Ans. (b)

The given sentence states how an argument came up during the meeting at the UN. Hence, the correct filler for the given blank is 'discord surfaced', where 'discord' means argument or fight. 'Friction' means conflict, 'grievance' means complaint and 'strife' means conflict.

313. The death of her father had made her sullen and ....
SSC CHSL Tier-1 30.05.2022 (Shift-I)

(a) jovial (b) smug
(c) joyful (d) melancholic

Ans. (d)

The given sentence presents how the person became sad after the death of her father.

Hence, the correct filler for the given blank is 'melancholic', which means sad and despairing.

'Jovial' means cheerful and 'smug' means self-satisfied.

314. In a .... move, the robbers chose their next place of attack over 255 km away from the locations they had earlier .... in Dewas.

SSC CHSL Tier-1 30.05.2022 (Shift-II)

(a) righteous, incorporated
(b) noble, decided
(c) shrewd, targeted
(d) corrupt, vanished

Ans. (c)

The correct filler for the given blank is 'shrewd'; targeted'.

The given sentence states that the robbers were able to make good decisions while choosing their next place of attack, which was over 255 km away from the locations they had earlier targeted in Dewas.

'Righteous' means morally right, 'incorporated' means included, 'noble' means honourable, 'decided' means made a decision, 'corrupt' means dishonest and 'vanished' means disappeared.

315. I have been studying this course ...... two years now.

SSC CHSL Tier-1 31.05.2022 (Shift-I)

(a) through (b) since
(c) for (d) almost

Ans. (c)

The correct filler for the given blank is 'for'.

The preposition 'for' is used to express how long something or someone has been doing something.

316. I met my professor yesterday and we ...... a long conversation about books and work. SSC CHSL Tier-1 31.05.2022 (Shift-I)

(a) did (b) spoke
(c) had (d) talked

Ans. (c)

The correct filler for the given blank is 'had'.

317. Very carefully I ...... the tree I have referred to, and avoiding contact with the creepers the upper...... and leaves of which might have been visible from where the tiger was lying, I climbed to the fork, where I had a comfortable seat and perfect ....

SSC CHSL Tier-1 31.05.2022 (Shift-II)

(a) stalled, roots, visibility
(b) starved, stem disclosure
(c) stormed, fruits, revelation
(d) stalked, tendrils, concealment

Ans. (d)

The correct fillers for the given blanks are 'stalked, tendrils, concealment'. 'Stalked' means followed stealthily, 'tendrils' are slender curling parts of a plant and 'concealment' means hiding.

318. Many times ...... starts with the creative ...... and the enduring passion of a single individual.

SSC CHSL Tier-1 31.05.2022 (Shift-III)

(a) tradition, lethargy
(b) stagnation, determination
(c) renovation, dullness
(d) innovation, spark

Ans. (d)

The correct fillers for the given blank are 'innovation' and 'spark'. 'Innovation' means a new idea, method or device and 'spark' means an exciting quality that somebody/something has.

319. Towards the end of February the weather turned very...... .

SSC CHSL Tier-1 01.06.2022 (Shift-I)

(a) slight (b) insipid
(c) mild (d) thin

Ans. (c)

The correct filler for the given blank is 'mild', which means warm and gentle. 'Slight' means small and 'insipid' means lacking flavour.

320. A diary entry is a ...... account of one's day and is a very useful tool for celebrities.

SSC CHSL Tier-1 01.06.2022 (Shift-I)

(a) person (b) personnel
(c) persona (d) personal

Ans. (d)

The correct filler for the given blank is 'personal'. 'Person' means an individual, 'personnel' means staff and 'persona' means a social facade.

321. We would have loved to stay ...... like children all our lives.

SSC CHSL Tier-1 01.06.2022 (Shift-II)

(a) innocent
(b) shy
(c) fragile
(d) cunning

Ans. (a)

The correct filler for the given blank is 'innocent'. 'Shy' means timid, 'fragile' means delicate and 'cunning' means sly.

322. The Mahatma Gandhi National Rural Employment Guarantee Act 2005 (Mahatma Gandhi NREGA) aims at enhancing ...... security of households in rural areas of the country by providing at least one hundred days of guaranteed ways employment in a financial year to every household whose adult members volunteer to do unskilled manual work.

SSC CHSL Tier-1 01.06.2022 (Shift-II)

(a) balanced (b) total
(c) strict (d) livelihood

Ans. (d)

'Livelihood' security fits as it refers to means of securing the necessities of life.

323. Other countries of comparable size and exposure to Information and Communication Technologies (ICT) have adopted a decentralised organisational structure, liberal policies and a ...... dispute resolution mechanism, deployed state-of-the-art infrastructure and used the private-public partnership to market Domain Name Registration Services (DNS), resulting in phenomenal growth of their country code domain name.

SSC CHSL Tier-1 02.06.2022 (Shift-I)

(a) short (b) narrow
(c) restricted (d) comprehensive

Ans. (d)

The given sentence presents that a complete and effective dispute mechanism will be used to avoid internet related crimes. Hence, the correct filler for the given blank is 'comprehensive' which means 'including all aspects of something'.

324. Though he is stout, he runs ....

SSC CHSL Tier-1 02.06.2022 (Shift-I)

(a) faster (b) fastest
(c) fast (d) fastly

Ans. (c)

The given sentence requires an adverb to given more information about the verb 'runs'.

Hence, they correct filler for the given blank is 'fast'.

325. He is a...... in shining armour.

SSC CHSL Tier-1 02.06.2022 (Shift-II)

(a) knit (b) nite
(c) night (d) knight

Ans. (d)

'Knight' refers to a person given a title of honour by a king or queen, which fits the idiom 'knight in shining armour'.

326. We love to swing from the branches ......the pond.

SSC CHSL Tier-1 03.06.2022 (Shift-I)

(a) over (b) on
(c) in (d) under

Ans. (a)

The correct filler for the given blank is 'over'.

327. Two ...... control the judge's decision; justice and impartiality
SSC CHSL Tier-1 03.06.2022 (Shift-III)
(a) officials (b) members
(c) principles (d) advocates
Ans. (c)
The correct filler for the given blank is 'principles'. It means a rule for good behaviour, based on what a person believes is right.

328. The Young Global Leaders Community is an ...... for a dynamic community of exceptional people with the vision, courage and influence to drive positive change in the world.
SSC CHSL Tier-1 06.06.2022 (Shift-II)
(a) impediment (b) input
(c) effort (d) accelerator
Ans. (d)
The correct filler for the given blank is 'accelerator'.
In the sentence, it refers to a person or thing that accelerates or increases the speed of something.

329. Constructive thinking should be developed through ...... reading .
SSC CHSL Tier-1 06.06.2022 (Shift-II)
(a) avid (b) narrow
(c) extensive (d) brief
Ans. (c)
The correct filler for the given blank is 'extensive'. It means large in area or amount.

330. In the Second World War, the British ...... thousands of so-called interceptors- mostly women- whose job it was to tune in every day and night to the radio ...... of the various divisions of the German military.
SSC CHSL Tier-1 06.06.2022 (Shift-III)
(a) averted, broadbills
(b) assented, broadsides
(c) assembled, broadcasts
(d) adhered, broadlooms
Ans. (c)
The correct filler for the given blank is 'assembled, broadcasts'. 'Assembled' and 'broadcasts' fit the context of gathering people and the transmission of information via radio.

331. A major ...... of modern times is that we have come to assume that all creation is ...... to the material interests of us, the homo-sapiens inhabiting earth, which has cut the ...... relationship we otherwise enjoyed with other constituents of creation. SSC CHSL Tier-1 07.06.2022 (Shift-I)
(a) fallacy, subservient, symbiotic
(b) frankness, superior, disadvantageous
(c) accuracy, domineering, encumbering
(d) felicity, disobedient, hindering
Ans. (a)
The correct filler for the given blank is fallacy, subservient, symbiotic. 'Fallacy' means a mistaken belief, fitting the context of a misconception. 'Subservient' means submissive or subordinate, fitting the context of being secondary to human interests. 'Symbiotic' means mutually beneficial, fitting the context of a once mutually supportive relationship.

332. We have already said that inconsistency is not a matter of ……… education or lack of logical .... SSC CHSL Tier-1 07.06.2022 (Shift-I)
(a) indefinite, stupor
(b) institutional, shiver
(c) inadequate, rigour
(d) inadvertent, snigger
Ans. (c)
'Inadequate' means insufficient, fitting the context of insufficient education. 'Rigour' means strictness or severity, fitting the context of logical strictness.

333. The app gets Larry' parents involved in the learning and improvement process, sending them advice about Larry's behaviours and progress and recommending motivational …... they might undertake that are ..... to Larry's situation and the program's ...... about his attitudes and behaviours.
SSC CHSL Tier-1 07.06.2022 (Shift-III)
(a) intermissions, directed, injunctions
(b) interpolations, disrupted, inventions
(c) interpolations, targeted, inventions
(d) interruptions, disillusioned, invasions
Ans. (c)
'Interpolations' means insertions or additions, fitting the context of motivational activities. 'Targeted' means aimed at a specific goal, fitting the context of being specific to Larry's situation. 'Inventions' means creations or innovative approaches, fitting the context of the program's recommendations.

334. She swallowed ..... her breakfast in a hurry. SSC CHSL Tier-1 07.06.2022 (Shift-III)
(a) in (b) up
(c) into (d) down
Ans. (d)
'Down' fits the context of swallowing, indicating the direction the food moves.

335. Funny stories made me and my brother ..... .
SSC CHSL Tier-1 08.06.2022 (Shift-I)
(a) conscious (b) determined
(c) giggly (d) gritty
Ans. (c)
The correct filler for the given blank is 'giggly'. It means to laugh in an excited, nervous or silly way.

336. The world is constantly living in risk, uncertainty and fear of ....
SSC CHSL Tier-1 09.06.2022 (Shift-I)
(a) life (b) body
(c) nature (d) death
Ans. (d)
The correct filler for the given blank is 'death'. 'Death' fits the context of the ultimate fear and uncertainty.

337. She raced ...... towards the train.
SSC CHSL Tier-1 09.06.2022 (Shift-III)
(a) crazily (b) berserk
(c) hectically (d) frantically
Ans. (d)
The correct filler for the given blank is 'frantically' which means in a hurried, excited or disorganised manner fitting the context of racing towards a train.

338. The young king tried to speak, but his tongue seemed to ...... the roof of his mouth and his lips refused to move. SSC CHSL Tier-1 09.06.2022 (Shift-III)
(a) divide to
(b) cleave to
(c) link to
(d) leave to
Ans. (b)
'Cleave to' means to adhere closely, fitting the context of the tongue sticking to the roof of the mouth.

339. I never could quite get the idea ...... my mind that I should do some teaching, yet I felt a great deal of satisfaction with the pastorate.
SSC CHSL Tier-1 10.06.2022 (Shift-I)
(a) out of (b) out act
(c) out some (d) out cast
Ans. (a)
The correct filler for the given blank is 'out of'. 'Out of my mind' means to make yourself stop thinking about something.

340. Wise managers ...... opinions, get information, ask advice, act ...... and know the art of ...... responsibilities to the subordinates.
SSC CHSL Tier-1 10.06.2022 (Shift-II)
(a) condemn, transnationally, elevating
(b) solicit, transparently, delegating
(c) coerce, translucently, relegating
(d) entrust, transiently, accelerating

Ans. (b)

'Solicit' means to ask for something, which fits the context of gathering opinions. 'Transparently' means openly and honestly, which fits the context of acting with clarity and integrity. 'Delegating' means assigning tasks, which fits the context of distributing responsibilities.

SSC CHSL 2021 (Tier 1 & 2)

341. ...... of adulterated food stuff being sold in the market.
SSC CHSL Tier-1 12.04.2021 (Shift-I)

(a) Wary (b) Beware
(c) Aware (d) Cautious

Ans. (b)

The given sentence states to be careful of adulterated foodstuff being sold in the market. Hence, the correct filler for the given blank is 'beware' which means to be careful.

342. As far as he is .... he will love to attend the party.
SSC CHSL Tier-1 13.04.2021 (Shift-I)

(a) anxious (b) concerned
(c) interested (d) confined

Ans. (b)

In the given sentence, the narrator is giving his own opinion about somebody that he will love to attend the party. Hence, the correct filler for the given blank is 'concerned'.

343. She was greatly .... by the nightmare she had.
SSC CHSL Tier-1 12.04.2021 (Shift-II)

(a) feared (b) perturbed
(c) dreaded (d) trembled

Ans. (b)

The given sentence states that girl was worried due to her nightmare. Hence, the correct filler for the given blank is 'perturbed' which means 'worried and troubled'.

344. Shekhar Gupta is one of the ...... journalists of India.
SSC CHSL Tier-1 12.04.2021 (Shift-II)

(a) imminent (b) exponent
(c) eminent (d) pertinent

Ans. (c)

'Eminent' means popular or respected, fitting the context of being a well-known journalist.

345. He was not ready at first to come with us for the picnic but we ...... him. **SSC CHSL Tier-1 13.04.2021 (Shift-II)**

(a) controlled
(b) consulted
(c) isolated
(d) persuaded

Ans. (d)

The given sentence states that he was not ready at first to come with us for the picnic but we made him believe us.

Hence, the correct filler for the given blank is 'persuaded' which means to get someone to agree.

346. Courts help in the resolution of ...... issues. **SSC CHSL Tier-1 13.04.2021 (Shift-II)**

(a) contentious
(b) presumptuous
(c) contemptuous
(d) conscientious

Ans. (a)

'Contentious' means likely to cause arguments, fitting the context of issues that require court resolution.

347. Can you please...me in sorting out these files on my computer?
SSC CHSL Tier-1 13.04.2021 (Shift-III)

(a) connive (b) assist
(c) abet (d) hinder

Ans. (b)

In the given sentence, the narrator ask for please help me in sorting out these files on my computer.

Hence, the correct filler for the given blank is 'assist' which means to help.

348. Courts are ...... of the Constitution as they are expected to see that it is always respected.
SSC CHSL Tier-1 15.04.2021 (Shift-II)

(a) leaders (b) dictators
(c) sentinels (d) masters

Ans. (c)

'Sentinels' means guards or watchkeepers, fitting the context of courts protecting and upholding the Constitution.

349. According to Soli Sorabjee, listening to cases being argued in court can be ...... but there are lighter moments too. **SSC CHSL Tier-1 15.04.2021 (Shift-II)**

(a) tedious (b) entertaining
(c) lively (d) fun

Ans. (a)

The given sentence states that listening to cases being argued in court can be boring. Hence, the correct filler for the given blank is 'tedious' which means long and boring.

350. There is an ...... in the advertising company for a copywriter .
SSC CHSL Tier-1 16.04.2021 (Shift-II)

(a) opening
(b) occasion
(c) incidence
(d) instance

Ans. (a)

The given sentence states there is a job that is available in the advertising company for a copywriter. Hence, the correct filler for the given blank is 'opening'.

351. We had out time of peace and goodwill, a time I will ...... as long as I live. **SSC CHSL Tier-1 19.04.2021 (Shift-II)**

(a) esteem (b) cherish
(c) think (d) care

Ans. (b)

'Cherish' means to hold dear or value highly, fitting the context of remembering a special time.

352. During her vacation, Shanta ...... her mother when she went to work in the mall. **SSC CHSL Tier-1 19.04.2021 (Shift-III)**

(a) accompanied (b) isolated
(c) abandoned (d) associated

Ans. (a)

The correct filler for the given blank is 'accompanied as it indicates that Shanta went with her mother to the mall.

353. It is claimed that if you take a certain homeopathic medicine, it will .... you against the coronavirus.
SSC CHSL Tier-1 04.08.2021 (Shift-I)

(a) shelter (b) immune
(c) reinforce (d) fortify

Ans. (d)

The given sentence talks about how taking certain homeopathic medicine would boost or strengthen you against coronavirus.

Hence, the correct filler for the given blank is 'fortify' which means 'to strengthen'.

354. Debjyoti's short animation film ...... highlights the stark contrast between the rich and the poor in India.
SSC CHSL Tier-1 04.08.2021 (Shift-I)

(a) poignantly (b) strictly
(c) carelessly (d) sweetly

Ans. (a)

'Poignantly' means evoking a keen sense of sadness or regret, fitting the context of highlighting a stark contrast.

355. The passengers waited ...... for the local train to arrive.
SSC CHSL Tier-1 04.08.2021 (Shift-III)

(a) hastily (b) meekly
(c) patiently (d) considerably

Ans. (c)

The correct filler for the given blank is 'patiently'.

356. Today you may not ...... what you hear, but that is the truth and you have to accept it.
SSC CHSL Tier-1 05.08.2021 (Shift-I)

(a) answer (b) reply
(c) enjoy (d) like

Ans. (d)

The sentence talks about telling and accepting the truth of someone (that person) and that person may or may not like it. Hence, the correct filler for the given blank is 'like'.

357. His voice was ...... by the sound of the helicopter.
SSC CHSL Tier-1 05.08.2021 (Shift-I)

(a) driven (b) drawn
(c) dawned (d) drowned

Ans. (d)

The correct filler for the given blank is 'drowned'.
Drowned means overwhelmed by a louder sound, fitting the context of the helicopter noise.

358. Despite their ...... impersonal rules that apply to all are essential in large systems.
SSC CHSL Tier-1 05.08.2021 (Shift-III)

(a) support (b) advantages
(c) benefits (d) limitations

Ans. (d)

'Limitations' means restrictions or weaknesses, fitting the context of rules that have drawbacks but are necessary.

359. The migrant crisis led several states to ...... existing labour laws in order to improve their condition.
SSC CHSL Tier-1 06.08.2021 (Shift-II)

(a) introduce (b) amend
(c) initiate (d) abandon

Ans. (b)

'Amend' means to make changes to improve something, fitting the context of revising labour laws.

360. The headmaster .... on the stage and gave a short speech.
SSC CHSL Tier-1 09.08.2021 (Shift-I)

(a) prescribed (b) appeared
(c) delighted (d) remembered

Ans. (b)

The given sentence states that the headmaster is came on the stage and gave a short speech.

Hence, the correct filler for the given blank is 'appeared'.

361. The kite was stuck so high on the tree that it was ...... the reach of the boys.
SSC CHSL Tier-1 09.08.2021 (Shift-II)

(a) below (b) beneath
(c) beside (d) beyond

Ans. (d)

The correct filler for the given blank is 'beyond'.

Preposition 'beyond' is used to refer to the other side of something.

362. With a lot of difficulty, he could ...... only two tickets for the train from Mumbai to Ranchi.
SSC CHSL Tier-1 09.08.2021 (Shift-III)

(a) procure (b) gain
(c) incur (d) attain

Ans. (a)

The given sentence states that with a lot of difficulties, he could obtain only two tickets for the train. Hence, the correct filler for the given blank is 'procure' which means to obtain something with difficulty.

363. The air .... has gone up significantly.
SSC CHSL Tier-1 10.08.2021 (Shift-I)

(a) rent (b) charge
(c) cost (d) fare

Ans. (d)

'Fare' means the price paid for a journey, fitting the context of air travel costs.

364. In the past month, the price of oil has ...... several times.
SSC CHSL Tier-1 10.08.2021 (Shift-I)

(a) fumbled (b) fluctuated
(c) faltered (d) failed

Ans.(b)

'Fluctuated' means to rise and fall irregularly, fitting the context of changing oil prices.

365. The mother monkey picked up her baby and climbed up the tree to ......
SSC CHSL Tier-1 10.08.2021 (Shift-II)

(a) safety (b) ability
(c) cruelty (d) agility

Ans. (a)

'Safety' means the condition of being safe, fitting the context of protection.

366. Doctors and nurses who are treating Covid-19 patients are finding it difficult ...... long working hours.
SSC CHSL Tier-1 11.08.2021 (Shift-I)

(a) for manage with
(b) to cope with
(c) to service for
(d) to carry on

Ans. (b)

'Cope with' means to deal successfully with a difficult matter or situation. In this sentence doctors and nurses are finding it difficult to deal with patients for long hours.

367. When you speak there are gestures and body language that ...... your words. **SSC CHSL Tier-1 11.08.2021 (Shift-II)**

(a) achieve
(b) accomplish
(c) accompany
(d) construct

Ans. (c)

'Accompany' means to go along with, fitting the context of gestures and body language happening simultaneously with speech.

368. Schools will restart physical classes partially and states have .... their own conditions and procedures to ensure the safety of students.
SSC CHSL Tier-1 11.08.2021 (Shift-II)

(a) accepted (b) devised
(c) insisted (d) adopted

Ans. (b)

'Devised' means to plan or invent by careful thought, fitting the context of states creating safety protocols.

369. Unable to check her ...... Alice ran after the rabbit down the rabbit hole.
SSC CHSL Tier-1 12.08.2021 (Shift-I)

(a) nervousness (b) pleasure
(c) wisdom (d) curiosity

Ans. (d)

The sentence is implying that Alice followed the rabbit because she wanted to know more. The correct filler for the given blank is 'curiosity' because it means a strong desire to know or learn something, fitting the context of Alice's actions.

370. Thunder and lightning was ...... with heavy rain.
SSC CHSL Tier-1 12.08.2021 (Shift-I)

(a) accrued (b) accorded
(c) accompanied (d) accustomed

Ans. (c)

The sentence is implying that thunder and lightning occurred at the same time as heavy rain.
The correct filler for the given blank is 'accompanied' because it means to occur at the same time as something else, fitting the context of simultaneous events. 'Accrued' means accumulated, 'accorded' means granted and 'accustomed' means used to, none of which relate to simultaneous occurrence.

371. Delhi University's new institution called School of Public Health will offer a ...... of programmes.
SSC CHSL Tier-1 12.08.2021 (Shift-II)

(a) scale (b) plethora
(c) few (d) branch

Ans. (b)

The correct filler for the given blank is 'plethora' because it means a very large amount of something, fitting the context of offering many programmes.

372. The marking of answer papers is ...... out by the course teacher.
SSC CHSL Tier-1 12.08.2021 (Shift-III)
(a) done (b) carried
(c) checked (d) crossed

Ans. (b)

The sentence is implying that the course teacher is responsible for marking the answer papers.

The correct filler for the given blank is 'carried' because 'carried out' means to perform or conduct, fitting the context of marking papers.

373. Scientists all over the world are engaged in ...... how to find a vaccine for Covid-19.
SSC CHSL Tier-1 12.08.2021 (Shift-III)
(a) researching (b) scrutinising
(c) investigating (d) inspecting

Ans. (c)

The given sentence stats how scientists have been working to see how to find a vaccine for Covid-19 Hence, the correct filler for the given blank is 'investigating.

SSC MTS 2024 (Tier 1 & 2)

374. Only when the floods get......... will world governments begin to act.
SSC MTS Tier-1 14.11.2024 (Shift-III)
(a) lucky (b) gullible
(c) worse (d) frequently

Ans. (c)

'Worse' is the most appropriate option to fill in the blank. 'Worse' indicates a more severe condition.

Gullible means easily deceived.

375. A majority of Indians prefer to use the Internet for.........booking and other financial services.
SSC MTS Tier-1 14.11.2024 (Shift-III)
(a) attending (b) accessing
(c) dispersing (d) improving

Ans. (b)

'Accessing' is the most appropriate option to fill in the blank. 'Accessing' means obtaining or retrieving information.

376. Fish live in aquariums and pigs live in..........
SSC MTS Tier-1 14.11.2024 (Shift-III)
(a) stables (b) dens
(c) sties (d) kennels

Ans. (c)

'Sties' is the most appropriate option to fill in the blank. 'Sties' are enclosures for pigs.

Stable is used for horses.

Den is used for wild animals.

Kennel is used for dogs.

377. Her company's new product launch was a real.........squib.
SSC MTS Tier-1 14.11.2024 (Shift-III)
(a) dirty (b) dear
(c) damp (d) deaf

Ans. (c)

'Damp' is the most appropriate option to complete the idiom 'damp squib'. 'Damp squib' means a complete failure.

378. Please pass.........the salt.
SSC MTS Tier-1 14.11.2024 (Shift-III)
(a) my (b) mine (c) me (d) I

Ans. (c)

'Me' is the most appropriate option to fill in the blank. 'Me' is the first-person singular pronoun in the objective case, used here as the object of the verb 'pass'.

379. With the increasing reliance on digital systems, ensuring robust cybersecurity measures is......... to protect against online threats.
SSC MTS Tier-1 13.11.2024 (Shift-III)
(a) extraneous (b) superfluous
(c) paramount (d) impartial

Ans. (c)

'Paramount' is the most appropriate option to fill in the blank. 'Paramount' means more important than anything else.

Extraneous means irrelevant or unrelated.

Superfluous means unnecessary.

380. The professor delivered a......... lecture on quantum physics. (simplified)
SSC MTS Tier-1 13.11.2024 (Shift-III)
(a) plain (b) refined
(c) lengthy (d) complex

Ans. (d)

'Complex' is the most appropriate antonym for 'simplified'. 'Complex' means consisting of many different parts.

Refined means elegant and cultured.

381. You need to rest the.........before baking the bread.
SSC MTS Tier-1 12.11.2024 (Shift-III)
(a) paste (b) lard
(c) doe (d) dough

Ans. (d)

'Dough' is the most appropriate option to fill in the blank. The correct sentence is: 'You need to rest the dough before baking the bread'. 'Dough' is a mixture of flour and liquid used for baking.

382. The teacher asked the students to remain........., but the noise continued to.......... She finally had to raise her voice to gain control.
SSC MTS Tier-1 12.11.2024 (Shift-III)
(a) calm; escalate
(b) quit; rise
(c) silent; ascend
(d) still; elevate

Ans. (a)

'Calm; escalate' is the most appropriate option to fill in the blanks.

383. Martin Luther King Jr. started a crusade for discrimination......... African Americans. He relied on peaceful demonstrations and demonstrators. His most famous march was a powerful rally of about 250,000 people in Washington in 1963, where he ....one of the most famous speeches in history.
SSC MTS Tier-1 11.11.2024 (Shift-III)
(a) against; delivered
(b) opposed; dropped
(c) versus; brought
(d) counter; dispatched

Ans. (a)

'Against; delivered' is the most appropriate option.

384. The company's decision to relocate had a negative......... on its employees.
SSC MTS Tier-1 11.11.2024 (Shift-III)
(a) conclusion
(b) effect
(c) establish
(d) accommodation

Ans. (b)

'Effect' is the most appropriate option to fill in the blank.

385. When we .... ourselves, we activate a variety of psychological processes that help us achieve our objectives and improve our overall well-being.
SSC MTS Tier-1 11.11.2024 (Shift-III)
(a) doubt (b) believe in
(c) demolish (d) linger

Ans. (b)

'Believe in' is the most appropriate option to fill in the blank. 'Believe in' means to have confidence in.

386. Doctors should never be .... than others when patients come for their treatment.
SSC MTS Tier-1 05.11.2024 (Shift-III)
(a) least caring (b) more caring
(c) most caring (d) less caring
Ans. (b)
'More Caring' is the most appropriate degree to fill in the blank.

387. I have never ....this kind of pain before surgery.
SSC MTS Tier-1 05.11.2024 (Shift-III)
(a) experienced (b) practised
(c) trained (d) dedicated
Ans. (a)
'Experienced' is the most appropriate option to fill in the blank.

388. What's.........book you've ever read?
SSC MTS Tier-1 04.11.2024 (Shift-III)
(a) interesting
(b) the most interesting
(c) more interesting
(d) the interesting
Ans. (b)
'The most interesting' is the most appropriate superlative adjective form to fill in the blank.

389. ....they like sweets?
SSC MTS Tier-1 04.11.2024 (Shift-III)
(a) Do (b) Had (c) Has (d) Does
Ans. (a)
'Do' is the most appropriate present tense form of the verb to fill in the blank.

390. Despite his initial........., he eventually agreed to join the team.
SSC MTS Tier-1 04.11.2024 (Shift-III)
(a) enthusiasm (b) reluctance
(c) determination (d) compassion
Ans. (b)
'Reluctance' is the most appropriate option to fill in the blank.

391. Industrialisation gives even the least talented person a chance to ....his livelihood.
SSC MTS Tier-1 04.11.2024 (Shift-III)
(a) live (b) give
(c) earn (d) break
Ans. (c)
'Earn' is the most appropriate option to fill in the blank. 'Earn' means to receive money for work.

392. The investigating team smelled a ....in the suspect's defence.
SSC MTS Tier-1 04.11.2024 (Shift-III)
(a) cat (b) bat
(c) dog (d) rat
Ans. (d)
'Rat' is the most appropriate option to fill in the blank. 'Smell a rat' means to suspect something is wrong.

393. After coming from a long journey he said, 'It feels so .... to be home.'
SSC MTS Tier-1 30.10.2024 (Shift-III)
(a) better (b) good
(c) much good (d) best
Ans. (b)
'Good' is the most appropriate adjective to fill in the blank. The correct sentence is: 'It feels so good to be home'. 'Good' is used to express a positive feeling or state.

394. The arrangements of the little boy's birthday party were .... nice. We could not help but appreciate it.
SSC MTS Tier-1 29.10.2024 (Shift-III)
(a) little (b) many
(c) extremely (d) few
Ans. (c)
'Extremely' is the correct option. It is an adverb that intensifies 'nice'. Adverbs like 'extremely' modify adjectives to intensify their meaning.

395. I will not be able to.............. my assignment in time.
SSC MTS Tier-1 28.10.2024 (Shift-II)
(a) completing (b) completed
(c) completes (d) complete
Ans. (d)
'Complete' is the most appropriate option. The sentence refers to the ability to finish an assignment.

396. The play was shortened by the ....of two scenes.
SSC MTS Tier-1 28.10.2024 (Shift-II)
(a) insirtion (b) addition
(c) ommision (d) omission
Ans. (d)
'Omission' is the correct spelling to fill in the blank. It means something that has been left out or excluded.

397. As 'brutal' is synonymous to 'harsh', 'naive' is synonymous to ....
SSC MTS Tier-1 28.10.2024 (Shift-II)
(a) worldly (b) hospitable
(c) simple (d) wise
Ans. (c)
'Simple' is the most appropriate synonym of 'naive' which means showing a lack of experience, wisdom or judgement.

398. The croissant was........, as was the coffee. **SSC MTS Tier-1 23.10.2024 (Shift-II)**
(a) ambitious (b) excellent
(c) inferior (d) eloquent
Ans. (b)
'Excellent' is the most appropriate option. It means extremely good or outstanding.

399. The writer's.........prose resonated with readers, evoking powerful emotions. **SSC MTS Tier-1 23.10.2024 (Shift-II)**
(a) sporadic (b) banal
(c) mundane (d) eloquent
Ans. (d)
'Eloquent' is the most appropriate option. It means fluent or persuasive in speaking or writing.
Sporadic means occurring at irregular intervals.
Banal means lacking in originality.
Mundane means lacking interest or excitement.

400. The orator declared that the women are.........than the men.
SSC MTS Tier-1 23.10.2024 (Shift-II)
(a) intelligent
(b) intelligenter
(c) most intelligent
(d) more intelligent
Ans. (d)
'More intelligent' is the most appropriate adjective and the correct comparative form.

401. The teacher emphasised the importance of.........correct grammar and punctuation in our writing.
SSC MTS Tier-1 23.10.2024 (Shift-II)
(a) using (b) used
(c) use (d) uses
Ans. (a)
'Using' is the most appropriate option. It is a gerund, correctly fitting the context.

402. Jack always looks handsome, even if he is a.........out of style.
SSC MTS Tier-1 23.10.2024 (Shift-II)
(a) less (b) more little
(c) little (d) least
Ans. (c)
'Little' is the most appropriate adjective to fill in the blank. It is used to mean 'to some extent'.

403. She treats her juniors......... contempt. **SSC MTS Tier-1 22.10.2024 (Shift-II)**
(a) with (b) for
(c) by (d) in
Ans. (a)
'With' is the most appropriate option. 'With' indicates the manner in which she treats them.

404. I always prefer a small, cosy cottage.........a high-rise apartment.
SSC MTS Tier-1 21.10.2024 (Shift-II)

(a) from (b) to
(d) than (d) for

Ans. (b)

'To' is the most appropriate option. 'To' is used to indicate a preference.

405. Woodcutting involves the removal of useless trees first, ...by medium and finest quality timber trees.
SSC MTS Tier-1 21.10.2024 (Shift-II)

(a) enacted
(b) followed
(c) compared
(d) adjusted

Ans. (b)

'Followed' is the most appropriate option. 'Followed' means to come after in sequence.

406. Due to ....'eve teasing', parents conclude that it is not worth the danger of sending their daughters to school.
SSC MTS Tier-1 18.10.2024 (Shift-II)

(a) rectified (b) narrow
(c) widespread (d) localized

Ans. (c)

'Widespread' is the most appropriate option to fill in the blank.
'Widespread' means widely prevalent or occurring over a wide area.

407. During the interview, the candidate was challenged to provide chapter and .... on his proposed plan.
SSC MTS Tier-1 18.10.2024 (Shift-II)

(a) lines (b) page
(c) verse (d) cover

Ans. (c)

'Verse' is the most appropriate option to complete the idiom. 'Chapter and verse' means to give precise and detailed information.

408. The Chinese Government has accepted slower economic development as the 'new normal', recognising the need for China to adopt a new growth model that depends less on fixed investment and exports and more on private consumption, services and innovation to .... economic growth.
SSC MTS Tier-1 18.10.2024 (Shift-II)

(a) drive (b) exhale
(c) success (d) bridle

Ans. (a)

'Drive' is the most appropriate option. It means to propel or push forward.

409. The explorers trekked........... through the dense jungle.
SSC MTS Tier-1 17.10.2024 (Shift-II)

(a) before (b) rarely
(c) bravely (d) ever

Ans. (c)

'Bravely' is the most appropriate adverb, which means in a courageous manner.

410. The inclusion of Durga Puja in the UNESCO's list of Intangible Cultural Heritage was only possible due to the arduous ....of all stakeholders.
SSC MTS Tier-1 17.10.2024 (Shift-II)

(a) efforts (b) ignorance
(c) affects (d) passivity

Ans. (a)

'Efforts' is the most appropriate option. 'Efforts' refers to the exertion of physical or mental energy.

411. In order to maintain good governance, every government servant must be held.........for his/her decisions.
SSC MTS Tier-1 17.10.2024 (Shift-II)

(a) accountable (b) irresponsible
(c) unaccountable (d) flexible

Ans. (a)

'Accountable' is the most appropriate option. It means responsible.

412. I have a .... for reading and want to become a writer when I grow up. **SSC MTS Tier-1 16.10.2024 (Shift-II)**

(a) tallow (b) dream
(c) unity (d) passion

Ans. (d)

'Passion' is the most appropriate option. 'Passion' denotes a strong feeling or enthusiasm.

Tallow means a hard fatty substance made from rendered animal fat.

413. The coaches decided to .... the regulations more strictly because the candidates were not paying attention during their training sessions.
SSC MTS Tier-1 16.10.2024 (Shift-II)

(a) provide (b) supply
(c) enforce (d) enjoy

Ans. (c)

'Enforce' is the most appropriate option. 'Enforce' means to compel observance of or compliance with (a law, rule or obligation).

414. .... we gave them was some homemade ice cream.
SSC MTS Tier-1 15.10.2024 (Shift-II)

(a) What (b) When
(c) Which (d) While

Ans. (a)

'What' is the most appropriate option. The sentence should read 'What we gave them was some homemade ice cream.'

415. The rising interest in and concern about animal welfare resulted in legislative laws and the formation of The Animal ....Committee in many nations. **SSC MTS Tier-1 15.10.2024 (Shift-II)**

(a) Customs (b) Considers
(c) Resistant (d) Ethics

Ans. (d)

'Ethics' is the most appropriate option. It refers to moral principles that govern a person's behaviour or the conducting of an activity, which fits the context of animal welfare.

416. Leisure activities are activities that people.........in during their free time while, they are not working.
SSC MTS Tier-1 14.10.2024 (Shift-I)

(a) encourage (b) engage
(c) evaluate (d) exempt

Ans. (b)

'Engage' is the most appropriate option. It means to participate in activities.
Exempt means to free from an obligation.

417. Prem is an excellent chess player. He is the.........student of the class too.
SSC MTS Tier-1 14.10.2024 (Shift-I)

(a) most intelligent (b) intelligently
(c) intelligent (d) more intelligent

Ans. (a)

'Most intelligent' is the most appropriate option. It indicates the superlative degree.

418. Kiara was born in India but she went to.........university in ....United Kingdom. **SSC MTS Tier-1 09.10.2024 (Shift-I)**

(a) a; the
(b) No article required; the
(c) the; No article required
(d) a; No article required

Ans. (a)

'A university in the United Kingdom' is the correct option. 'A' is used before a noun that starts with a consonant sound and 'the' is used before a specific place like 'United Kingdom'.

419. As technology evolves, consumers increasingly......... products with enhanced features and greater efficiency. **SSC MTS Tier-1 09.10.2024 (Shift-I)**

(a) demand
(b) might demand
(c) were demanding
(d) has demanded

Ans. (a)

'Demand' is the most appropriate option. It fits the context of a present continuous trend.

420. Personally, Ramesh was.........to his villagers than his elder brother.
SSC MTS Tier-1 09.10.2024 (Shift-I)

(a) more helpful
(b) helped
(c) most helpful
(d) helpfuller

Ans. (a)

'More helpful' is the most appropriate option. It forms the comparative degree.

421. Living within our environmental limits is one of the central .... of sustainable development.
SSC MTS Tier-1 08.10.2024 (Shift-II)

(a) demonstrates (b) principles
(c) illuminates (d) agencies

Ans. (b)

The most appropriate option is 'principles.' This indicates fundamental truths or propositions serving as the foundation for a belief or behaviour.

Demonstrates means shows or illustrates.

Illuminates means lights up or makes clear.

Agencies means organisations or establishments.

422. Never .... ever seen a more disgusting sight.
SSC MTS Tier-1 08.10.2024 (Shift-II)

(a) has I (b) did I
(c) have I (d) I have

Ans. (c)

'Have I' fits the sentence structure. It forms an inverted sentence for emphasis.

423. She was barking up the wrong .... when she filed a complaint against ragging with the tudents' union instead of the university administration.
SSC MTS Tier-1 08.10.2024 (Shift-II)

(a) dog (b) pillar
(c) disc (d) tree

Ans. (d)

'Tree' is the appropriate word for the idiom 'barking up the wrong tree,' meaning to pursue a mistaken or misguided line of thought.

424. Select the most appropriate idiom to fill in the blank. My car .... on the way to college yesterday.
SSC MTS Tier-1 08.10.2024 (Shift-II)

(a) broke out (b) broke in
(c) broke up (d) broke down

Ans. (d)

'Broke down' is the correct idiom. It means the car stopped working.

Broke out means to start suddenly.

Broke in means to enter forcibly.

Broke up means to end a relationship.

425. School classrooms have ....very little over the last century.
SSC MTS Tier-1 07.10.2024 (Shift-I)

(a) freed
(b) changed
(c) startled
(d) unconcerned

Ans. (b)

'Changed' is the appropriate verb as it indicates the modification or alteration of something.

Startled means to surprise suddenly.

426. Many ornithologists believe that the Northern mocking birds are .... wild birds in the jungle.
SSC MTS Tier-1 07.10.2024 (Shift-I)

(a) the noisy (b) noisier
(c) the noisiest (d) noisy

Ans. (c)

'The noisiest' is the superlative form of 'noisy,' indicating that they are the loudest among the wild birds.

427. Leisure activities can improve an individual's physical and mental health by............. stress and offering a pleasurable experience.
SSC MTS Tier-1 07.10.2024 (Shift-I)

(a) relieving (b) reconstructing
(c) upsetting (d) irritating

Ans. (a)

'Relieving' means reducing or easing stress, fitting the context of health benefits.

428. The ....of the scientific experiment raised questions about the validity of the results.
SSC MTS Tier-1 01.10.2024 (Shift-I)

(a) verbosity (b) ambiguity
(c) Transparency (d) meticulousness

Ans. (b)

'Ambiguity' fits the context of questioning the validity of the results. Ambiguity means something that is unclear or uncertain, which can raise doubts about the experiment's findings.

Verbosity means excessive wordiness. Transparency means clarity or openness. Meticulousness means great attention to detail.

429. Alex ....(study) two programming languages.
SSC MTS Tier-1 01.10.2024 (Shift-I)

(a) have study
(b) has been studying
(c) had studied
(d) has studied

Ans. (d)

'Has studied' is the present perfect tense of 'study'. This tense indicates an action that was completed at some point in the past but is relevant to the present.

430. Please put the dishes in the .... after you finish eating.
SSC MTS Tier-1 01.10.2024 (Shift-I)

(a) sync (b) sink
(c) shrink (d) cinque

Ans. (b)

'Sink' is the most appropriate option to fill in the blank.

'Sink' is the place where dishes are typically washed. Hence, the correct option is sink .

Sync word for the context.

Shrink means to reduce in size.

Cinque as it is an outdated term for five.

431. The student leader has.......politics recently. **SSC MTS Tier-1 01.10.2024 (Shift-I)**

(a) approached (b) jumped
(c) entered (d) gathered

Ans. (c)

'Entered' is the most appropriate option to fill in the blank. 'Entered politics' indicates starting a career or becoming involved in politics.

432. Cultural heritage is the lifeblood of any............and serves as a link between generations.
SSC MTS Tier-1 30.09.2024 (Shift-I)

(a) believe (b) civilisation
(c) birthright (d) lethargy

Ans. (b)

The word 'civilisation' appropriately fills the blank, referring to the culture, traditions and achievements of a society.

433. He is..............tired to finish his homework.
SSC MTS Tier-1 30.09.2024 (Shift-I)

(a) to (b) too
(c) most (d) more

Ans. (b)

The word 'too' indicates an excessive degree of tiredness, making it impossible for him to complete his homework.

434. Accepting how wonderful you truly are and incorporating this ....into your attitude and personality is perhaps one of the most difficult things to do in life.
SSC MTS Tier-1 30.09.2024 (Shift-I)

(a) insight (b) glitch
(c) folly (d) craziness

Ans. (a)

The word 'insight' fits correctly in the context of understanding and appreciating one's worth.

435. Please listen to all announcements .... SSC MTS Tier-1 30.09.2024 (Shift-I)

(a) attentively (b) hungrily
(c) easily (d) generally

Ans. (a)

'Attentively' is the most appropriate option to fill in the blank. It means paying close attention to something, which is suitable for listening to announcements.

436. Arun............his bicycle to school every day. SSC MTS Tier-1 30.09.2024 (Shift-I)

(a) rode (b) riding
(c) rides (d) ride

Ans. (c)

'Rides' is the most appropriate verb form to fill in the blank. The sentence requires the present simple tense to indicate a habitual action.

SSC MTS 2023 Tier-1

437. Police used .... evidence to convict a victim who was innocent
SSC MTS Tier-1 02.05.2023 (Shift-I)

(a) stunted (b) fabricated
(c) hateful (d) authentic

Ans. (b)

The sentence implies that the evidence used was false or manufactured. The correct filler for the given blank is 'fabricated' because it means made up or forged, fitting the context of false evidence. 'Stunted' means hindered growth and 'authentic' means genuine.

438. Wheat is widely .... but the output is not large.
SSC MTS Tier-1 02.05.2023 (Shift-I)

(a) gross (b) grilled
(c) grown (d) groan

Ans. (c)

The sentence implies that wheat is cultivated on a large scale. The correct filler for the given blank is 'grown' because it means cultivated or produced, fitting the context of farming. 'Gross' means total, 'grilled' means cooked on a grill and 'groan' means a sound of pain or displeasure.

439. The person driving the car ...., control over the wheels and knocked her down. SSC MTS Tier-1 02.05.2023 (Shift-I)

(a) lose (b) lost
(c) losing (d) loose

Ans. (b)

The correct filler for the given blank is 'lost' because it means failed to maintain control, fitting the context of the past tense in the sentence.

440. His intent was to become sole lord and to .... his tiny principality.
SSC MTS Tier-1 02.05.2023 (Shift-I)

(a) subsidise
(b) aggrandise
(c) jeopardise
(d) methodise

Ans. (b)

'Aggrandise' means to increase the power status or wealth. The given sentence states that his intent was to become the sole lord and to aggrandise his-tiny principality. Hence, the correct filler for the given blank is 'aggrandise'.

'Subsidise' means to support financially, 'jeopardise' means to put in danger and 'methodise' means to arrange systematically.

441. I strained .... to catch his options. SSC MTS Tier-1 02.05.2023 (Shift-II)

(a) hardly (b) hard
(c) hardest (d) hardness

Ans. (b)

The correct filler for the given blank is 'hard' to qualify the verb 'strained'.

442. Rohan was now standing on tiptoe to .... over at the inhabitants of the two beds.
SSC MTS Tier-1 02.05.2023 (Shift-II)

(a) look (b) view
(c) stare (d) peep

Ans. (a)

The correct filler for the given blank is 'look'. 'To look over' means to quickly examine something.

443. Plastic inhabits the oceans, ... up in the guts of seagulls and great white sharks.
SSC MTS Tier-1 02.05.2023 (Shift-II)

(a) building
(b) burning
(c) provoking
(d) sailing

Ans. (a)

The correct filler for the given blank is 'building'. 'Building up' means to accumulate something by putting parts or material together.

444. The last man standing was ...., a fully paid vacation to Las Vegas.
SSC MTS Tier-1 02.05.2023 (Shift-III)

(a) appreciated (b) discarded
(c) rewarded (d) allotted

Ans. (c)

The correct filler for the given blank is 'rewarded'. It means to give something to someone in recognition of their services, efforts or achievements.

445. It's .... for someone to buy a product that contains no sugar,
SSC MTS Tier-1 02.05.2023 (Shift-III)

(a) easier (b) easiest
(c) easily (d) ease

Ans. (a)

The sentence implies comparing the ease of buying such a product. The correct filler for the given blank is 'easier' because it is the comparative form, fitting the context of comparison.

446. She reduced the volume because the, ... music was becoming too much for her. SSC MTS Tier-1 02.05.2023 (Shift-III)

(a) concede (b) content
(c) constant (d) competent

Ans. (c)

The correct filler for the given blank is 'constant'.

It means occurring continuously over a period of time.

'Concede' means to admit, 'content' means satisfied and 'competent' means capable.

447. An excellent career .... has now arisen with a leading recruitment agency.
SSC MTS Tier-1 03.05.2023 (Shift-I)

(a) preferability
(b) opportunity
(c) division
(d) severance

Ans. (b)

The correct filler for the given blank is 'opportunity'.
'Opportunity' means a set of circumstances that makes it possible to do something, fitting the context of a career chance.

448. A pair of Eurasian jays .... over the forest yesterday.
SSC MTS Tier-1 03.05.2023 (Shift-I)

(a) did flew (b) flew
(c) fly (d) flown

Ans. (b)

We use past indefinite (V_2) to describe completed actions or events that occurred in the past.
Hence, the correct filler for the given blank is 'flew'.

449. Mr. Sharma opened the door of the store to ....
SSC MTS Tier-1 03.05.2023 (Shift-I)
(a) peek (b) pike
(c) piece (d) peak
Ans. (a)
The correct filler for the given blank is 'peek'. It means to look quickly or furtively.

450. We didn't mean to .... all of you waiting. SSC MTS Tier-1 03.05.2023 (Shift-II)
(a) creep
(b) make
(c) seep
(d) keep
Ans. (d)
The correct sentence structure using Infinitive is 'To + Base Verb' (to eat, to go, to study).
Hence, the correct filler for the given blank is 'keep'.

451. Everyone who studies forests knows trees have been dying in large and .... numbers.
SSC MTS Tier-1 03.05.2023 (Shift-II)
(a) peculiar (b) minority
(c) massive (d) scanty
Ans. (c)
The given sentence states that everyone who studies forests knows trees have been dying in large numbers. Hence, the correct filler for the given blank is 'massive'.
'Peculiar' means strange, 'minority' means a smaller number and 'scanty' means insufficient.

452. His father was killed in a ...., when the boy was nine years old.
SSC MTS Tier-1 03.05.2023 (Shift-III)
(a) dwell (b) drool
(c) dual (d) duel
Ans. (d)
The correct filler for the given blank is 'duel'. 'Dwell', 'drool' and 'dual' do not fit this context.
'Duel' means a contest with deadly weapons arranged between two people, fitting the context of his father's death. 'Dwell' means to live or reside, 'drool' means saliva flowing from the mouth and 'dual' means having two parts.

453. Each band is known across a wide area because all residents of a given region are typically tied to one another through a large .... of kinship and reciprocity.
SSC MTS Tier-1 03.05.2023 (Shift-III)
(a) variation (b) mesh
(c) network (d) clash
Ans. (c)
The correct filler for the given blank is 'network'. It means a group or system of interconnected people or things.
'Variation' means a change or difference, 'mesh' means to fit together and 'clash' means a conflict.

454. Potato milk is .... another option for those wanting an alternative to cow's milk.
SSC MTS Tier-1 03.05.2023 (Shift-III)
(a) though (b) yet
(c) so (d) but
Ans. (b)
The correct filler for the given blank is 'yet'. We generally use conjunction 'yet' to connect two contrasting ideas or adding information.

455. Join our networks to .... better Governance.
SSC MTS Tier-1 04.05.2023 (Shift-I)
(a) drain (b) disintegrate
(c) promote (d) sedate
Ans. (c)
The correct filler for the given blank is 'promote'.
It means to support or actively encourage (a cause, venture, etc.); further the progress of.
'Drain' means to remove liquid, 'disintegrate' means to break into parts and 'sedate' means to calm or tranquilise.

456. Eventually, the water will .... through the surrounding concrete.
SSC MTS Tier-1 04.05.2023 (Shift-I)
(a) statolith (b) aerate
(c) permeate (d) delegate
Ans. (c)
The correct filler for the given blank is 'permeate'. 'Permeate' means to spread throughout, fitting the context of water moving through concrete. 'Statolith' refers to a type of stone, 'aerate' means to introduce air into a material and 'delegate' means to assign responsibility.

457. Snow ...... lightly as everyone was leaving church.
SSC MTS Tier-1 04.05.2023 (Shift-II)
(a) falling
(b) is falling
(c) was falling
(d) fallen
Ans. (c)
The correct filler for the given blank is 'was falling'. 'Was falling' indicates a continuous past action, fitting the context of snow falling as people were leaving.

458. She was moving slowly and .... yesterday when she fell.
SSC MTS Tier-1 04.05.2023 (Shift-II)
(a) shakily (b) firmly
(c) vaguely (d) strongly
Ans. (a)
The correct filler for the given blank is 'shakily'. It means in a manner characterised by trembling or shaking.

459. His place was .... in the team after he displayed his explosive batting style.
SSC MTS Tier-1 04.05.2023 (Shift-III)
(a) fermented (b) affected
(c) belittled (d) cemented
Ans. (d)
The correct filler for the given blank is 'cemented'. It means firmly established.
'Fermented' means to undergo fermentation, 'affected' means influenced and 'belittled' means made to seem less important.

460. Don't you be clever with me, boy! I want to know what you're really .... SSC MTS Tier-1 04.05.2023 (Shift-III)
(a) on to (b) up to
(c) in to (d) up about
Ans. (b)
The correct filler for the given blank is 'up to'. It means involved in or doing something.

461. The first time that nuclear radiation has been washed off with a .... SSC MTS Tier-1 04.05.2023 (Shift-III)
(a) fast shower
(b) quick shower
(c) speedy shower
(d) energetic shower
Ans. (b)
The correct filler for the given blank is 'quick shower' which means it rains for a very short period of time.

462. The necessity of resisting the .... demands of the prophets led to the introduction of new rules for distinguishing true and false prophets. SSC MTS Tier-1 04.05.2023 (Shift-III)
(a) unimpeachable
(b) relentless
(c) irreparable
(d) imperturbable
Ans. (b)
The correct filler for the given blank is 'relentless'. It means continuous or persistent.
'Unimpeachable' means beyond doubt, 'irreparable' means not fixable and 'imperturbable' means calm.

463. Very special care should be taken to proportion the sand so as to make a .... perfectly mixture.
SSC MTS Tier-1 08.05.2023 (Shift-I)
(a) envious (b) obvious
(c) devious (d) impervious
Ans. (d)
The correct filler for the given blank is 'impervious'. It means not allowing fluid to pass through.
'Envious' means jealous, 'obvious' means clear and 'devious' means dishonest.

464. Towel off and ...... your moisturiser immediately
SSC MTS Tier-1 08.05.2023 (Shift-I)
(a) refer (b) touch
(c) surrender (d) apply
Ans. (d)
The correct filler for the given blank is 'apply' which means to put to use especially for some practical purpose.

465. That remark .... a stir.
SSC MTS Tier-1 08.05.2023 (Shift-II)
(a) built (b) constructed
(c) produced (d) created
Ans. (d)
The correct filler for the given blank is 'created'. It means to cause, fitting the context of causing a stir.

466. To .... your self-worth, write down some things that are positive about yourself. SSC MTS Tier-1 08.05.2023 (Shift-II)
(a) sanctify (b) overlook
(c) affirm (d) repudiate
Ans. (c)
The correct filler for the given blank is 'affirm'. It means the act of affirming one's own worthiness and value as an individual for beneficial effect.
'Sanctify' means to make holy, 'overlook' means to fail to notice and 'repudiate' means to reject.

467. I enjoy finding ways to make the most of my budget by being ....,
SSC MTS Tier-1 08.05.2023 (Shift-III)
(a) miser (b) lethargic
(c) frugal (d) gloomy
Ans. (c)
The correct filler for the given blank is 'frugal'. It means economical, fitting the context of budgeting. 'Miser' means a person who hoards wealth, 'lethargic' means sluggish and 'gloomy' means sad.

468. Today is cloudy, but yesterday the Sun .... SSC MTS Tier-1 09.05.2023 (Shift-I)
(a) flamed (b) shown
(c) shone (d) burned
Ans. (c)
The correct filler for the given blank is 'shone'. It means emitted light, fitting the context of sunlight. 'Flamed' means burned with a flame.

469. The story of human evolution .... a moving target in recent years. SSC MTS Tier-1 09.05.2023 (Shift-I)
(a) had being (b) has been
(c) have been (d) did has
Ans. (b)
The given sentence in present perfect continuous tense as the sentence talks about actions and states that began in the past and are still continuing at the time of speaking. Hence, the correct filler for the given blank is 'has been'.

470. I am sorry that I was unable to see .... of you over the summer.
SSC MTS Tier-1 09.05.2023 (Shift-I)
(a) more (b) many
(c) much (d) many more
Ans. (a)
The correct filler for the given blank is 'more' which is used to indicate a greater quantity or number.

471. John rushed to the spot and saw his wife and kid .... on the road.
SSC MTS Tier-1 09.05.2023 (Shift-II)
(a) lain (b) lying
(c) lie (d) laying
Ans. (b)
The correct filler for the given blank is 'lying'. It means being in a horizontal position, fitting the context of people on the ground.

472. Today I received a letter. Finally, I .... back from him.
SSC MTS Tier-1 09.05.2023 (Shift-II)
(a) herd (b) hard (c) heard (d) horde
Ans. (c)
The correct filler for the given blank is 'heard'. It means received news, fitting the context of communication.

473. Women ....their male relatives to the battlefield for the purpose of tending the wounded and carrying away the dead.
SSC MTS Tier-1 09.05.2023 (Shift-II)
(a) signify (b) forsake
(c) justify (d) accompany
Ans. (d)
The correct filler for the given blank is 'accompany'. It means to go with, fitting the context of joining someone.

474. The most common sports injury is a .... SSC MTS Tier-1 09.05.2023 (Shift-III)
(a) brush (b) bruise
(c) brews (d) breve
Ans. (b)
The correct filler for the given blank is 'bruise'. It means an injury causing discoloration of the skin, fitting the context of injuries. 'Brews' means to make beer and 'breve' is a musical note.

475. Since the temperatures can soar in summer, choose clothing that is lightweight and ....
SSC MTS Tier-1 09.05.2023 (Shift-III)
(a) breathable (b) airtight
(c) bulky (d) hefty
Ans. (a)
The correct filler for the given blank is 'breathable'. It means allowing air to pass through, fitting the context of clothing. 'Airtight' means not allowing air to escape, 'bulky' means large and difficult to handle and 'hefty' means heavy.

476. I am not sure ...... wearing this black dress. SSC MTS Tier-1 09.05.2023 (Shift-III)
(a) with (b) in
(c) about (d) off
Ans. (c)
The correct filler for the given blank is 'about'. It means having uncertainty regarding something, fitting the context of uncertainty about wearing a dress.

477. This .... piece of mischief by his brother brought a quiet laugh from David. SSC MTS Tier-1 10.05.2023 (Shift-I)
(a) nonsensical
(b) classical
(c) whimsical
(d) vesical
Ans. (c)
The correct filler for the given blank is 'whimsical'. It means unusual and strange in a way that might be funny or annoying, fitting the context of a mischievous act.
'Vesical' refers to the bladder.

478. This change is responsible for a recent ...... the number of cases of cancer in this age group.
SSC MTS Tier-1 10.05.2023 (Shift-I)
(a) rise to (b) rise at
(c) rise in (d) rise of
Ans. (c)
The phrase 'rise in' means to increase or grow larger.
The given sentence states that this change is responsible for a recent rise in the number of cases of cancer in this age group.
Hence, 'rise in', is the most appropriate answer.

479. For months, Drupad could not taste anything he ate as regret layered .... mud.
SSC MTS Tier-1 10.05.2023 (Shift-I)
(a) his mouth like
(b) his mouth as though
(c) his mouth comparable to
(d) his mouth allied to

Ans. (a)

The correct filler for the given blank is 'his mouth like'.

It means comparing the feeling to mud, fitting the context of an analogy.

480. During treatment, patients lay .... on the treatment couch for around 3 hrs.
SSC MTS Tier-1 10.05.2023 (Shift-I)
(a) arsine (b) alpine
(c) repine (d) supine

Ans. (d)

The correct filler for the given blank is 'supine'. It means lying face upwards, fitting the context of a treatment position.

'Arsine' is a toxic gas, 'alpine' means relating to high mountains and 'repine' means to complain.

481. If the anesthesia is not .... properly, he might wake up in the.............. of the surgery.
SSC MTS Tier-1 10.05.2023 (Shift-II)
(a) perpetuated/start
(b) administer/during
(c) perpetuated/middle
(d) administered/middle

Ans. (d)

The correct filler for the given blanks are 'administered' and 'middle'. 'Administered' means given or applied, fitting the context of anesthesia. 'Middle' means the central part, fitting the context of the timing during surgery.

482. Societies need to develop highly........ behavioural rules for survival.
SSC MTS Tier-1 10.05.2023 (Shift-III)
(a) readjusted (b) adopted
(c) adaptive (d) matched

Ans. (c)

The correct filler for the given blank is 'adaptive'.

It means having an ability to change to suit changing conditions.

483. The man who is supposed to be protecting them is somehow their fiercest and most .... enemy.
SSC MTS Tier-1 10.05.2023 (Shift-III)
(a) implacable (b) pedestrian
(c) ostentatious (d) quotidian

Ans. (a)

The correct filler for the given blank is 'implacable'. It means unable to be appeased, fitting the context of an unyielding enemy.

'Pedestrian' means ordinary, 'ostentatious' means showy and 'quotidian' means everyday.

484. Before about 1830, ... sermons, tracts and addresses routinely broached female intemperance.
SSC MTS Tier-1 10.05.2023 (Shift-III)
(a) confluence
(b) temperance
(c) congruence
(d) affluence

Ans. (b)

The correct filler for the given blank is 'temperance'. It means moderation, fitting the context of addressing female intemperance. 'Confluence' means the coming together of streams, 'congruence' means agreement and 'affluence' means wealth.

485. Vulgar language to........... votes is not something he will endorse.
SSC MTS Tier-1 11.05.2023 (Shift-I)
(a) segregate (b) divulge
(c) lump (d) garner

Ans. (d)

The correct filler for the given blank is 'garner'. It means to gather or collect, fitting the context of garnering votes. 'Segregate' means to separate, 'divulge' means to reveal and 'lump' means to group together.

486. I was really hoping to .... a decent movie this time, and I came up with an undisputed classic.
SSC MTS Tier-1 11.05.2023 (Shift-I)
(a) tirade (b) subside
(c) unearth (d) strut

Ans. (c)

The correct filler for the given blank is 'unearth'. It means to discover, fitting the context of finding a classic movie. 'Tirade' means a long, angry speech, 'subside' means to lessen and 'strut' means to walk with confidence.

487. The pudding fell .... floor with a heart-stopping crash.
SSC MTS Tier-1 11.05.2023 (Shift-I)
(a) upon the (b) up to the
(c) in to the (d) to the

Ans. (d)

The correct filler for the given blank is 'to the'. It indicates direction, fitting the context of falling. 'Upon' means on top of, 'up to' means reaching a point and 'into' means entering something.

488. The sedative effect of the drugs impairs people's ability to pay attention SSC MTS Tier-1 11.05.2023 (Shift-II)
(a) concentrate (b) segregate
(c) reverberate (d) dilate

Ans. (a)

The correct filler for the given blank is 'concentrate'. It means to focus, fitting the context of paying attention. 'Segregate' means to separate, 'reverberate' means to echo and 'dilate' means to expand.

489. She kept pictures of her parents all........ the house.
SSC MTS Tier-1 11.05.2023 (Shift-II)
(a) about (b) over
(c) through (d) out

Ans. (b)

The correct filler for the given blank is 'over'. It means throughout, fitting the context of placement.

490. At Gurukul they spend many years together, growing into the best of friends and........ was time for each to return to his home, they wept.
SSC MTS Tier-1 11.05.2023 (Shift-III)
(a) instantly it (b) soon it
(c) when it (d) after it

Ans. (c)

The correct filler for the given blank is 'when it'. As a subordinating conjunction, 'when' introduces a dependent clause that provides additional information about the timing or condition of the main clause.

491. The television is big, has an excellent picture and last but not........... it's cheap. SSC MTS Tier-1 11.05.2023 (Shift-III)
(a) close (b) final (c) end (d) least

Ans. (d)

The correct filler for the given blank is 'least'. The phrase 'last but not least' is a commonly used expression indicating that something is mentioned as the final item on a list, but it is not less important than the previous ones.

492. The frequency of large wildfires .... dramatically in recent decades. SSC MTS Tier-1 11.05.2023 (Shift-III)
(a) did increase (b) has increased
(c) increase (d) have increased

Ans. (b)

The phrase 'in recent decades' suggests an ongoing timeframe that continues into the present. To express this idea, we need to use the 'present perfect tense' (has + V_2). Hence, the correct filler for the given blank is 'has increased'.

493. Obesity is also a progressive condition, unlike anorexia nervosa, which tends to .... with age.
SSC MTS Tier-1 12.05.2023 (Shift-I)

(a) inebriate (b) ameliorate
(c) struggle (d) negate

Ans. (b)

The correct filler for the given blank is 'ameliorate'. It means to improve, fitting the context of a condition improving with age.

'Inebriate' means to intoxicate, 'struggle' means to strive and 'negate' means to nullify.

494. Sitting at the computer, I saw something large and dark fall past my .... vision followed by a dull thwack.
SSC MTS Tier-1 12.05.2023 (Shift-I)

(a) central (b) external
(c) peripheral (d) incidental

Ans. (c)

The correct filler for the given blank is 'peripheral'. It refers to something that is situated at the edge or boundary of something.

495. In my view, this falls within the exception permitting warranteless seizure in .... circumstances.
SSC MTS Tier-1 12.05.2023 (Shift-I)

(a) reverent (b) sparse
(c) recondite (d) exigent

Ans. (d)

The correct filler for the given blank is 'exigent'. It means urgent or requiring immediate action, fitting the context of warrantless seizure.

'Reverent' means respectful, 'sparse' means thinly dispersed and 'recondite' means obscure.

496. The question is why an .... Hollywood film should provoke such a hostile reaction.
SSC MTS Tier-1 12.05.2023 (Shift-II)

(a) elicit (b) innocuous
(c) obstinate (d) erroneous

Ans. (b)

The correct filler for the given blank is 'innocuous'. It means not harmful or offensive, fitting the context of an unexpected hostile reaction.

'Elicit' means to draw out, 'obstinate' means stubborn and 'erroneous' means wrong.

497. The respondents were very agile and .... in subduing the situation.
SSC MTS Tier-1 12.05.2023 (Shift-II)

(a) hassled (b) quick
(c) tedious (d) tasty

Ans. (b)

The correct filler for the given blank is 'quick'. It means fast or prompt, fitting the context of subduing a situation.

'Hassled' means bothered, 'tedious' means boring and 'tasty' means delicious.

498. Fetal .... screening uses ultrasound scanning to find certain abnormalities in the baby.
SSC MTS Tier-1 12.05.2023 (Shift-II)

(a) enfevering (b) anomaly
(c) abeyance (d) snuggle

Ans. (b)

The correct filler for the given blank is 'anomaly'. It means something that deviates from the norm, fitting the context of abnormalities. 'Enfevering' means causing fever, 'abeyance' means temporary suspension and 'snuggle' means to cuddle.

499. For years, people afflicted with the itchy skin condition used stinky coal tar derivatives to .... their symptoms.
SSC MTS Tier-1 12.05.2023 (Shift-II)

(a) obviate (b) refer
(c) deviate (d) alleviate

Ans. (d)

The correct filler for the given blank is 'alleviate'. It means to make symptoms less severe, fitting the context of treating a condition. 'Obviate' means to remove a need or difficulty, 'refer' means to mention and 'deviate' means to depart from an established course.

500. This initiative has been sharply criticised as grossly inefficient and .... **SSC MTS Tier-1 12.05.2023 (Shift-III)**

(a) Capricious
(b) Counterproductive
(c) Calumny
(d) Canonical

Ans. (b)

The correct filler for the given blank is 'counterproductive'. It means having the opposite of the desired effect, fitting the context of criticism. 'Capricious' means unpredictable, 'calumny' means false statements and 'canonical' means conforming to a general rule.

501. We cannot .... a religion or a political party that ignores the rights of half the human race.
SSC MTS Tier-1 12.05.2023 (Shift-III)

(a) disseminate (b) desiccate
(c) condemn (d) forgive

Ans. (d)

The correct filler for the given blank is 'forgive'. It means to stop feeling angry or resentful, fitting the context of ignoring rights. 'Disseminate' means to spread widely, 'desiccate' means to dry out and 'condemn' means to express strong disapproval.

502. The duke had capacity, but his life was so .... that what influence he had upon the king was for evil.
SSC MTS Tier-1 12.05.2023 (Shift-III)

(a) seditious (b) scrumptious
(c) lewd (d) ambitious

Ans. (c)

The correct filler for the given blank is 'lewd'. It means crude and offensive in a sexual way, fitting the context of negative influence. 'Seditious' means inciting rebellion, 'scrumptious' means delicious and 'ambitious' means having a strong desire for success.

503. Disturbing emotions begin to build into fear and then .... .
SSC MTS Tier-1 15.05.2023 (Shift-I)

(a) boldness (b) terror
(c) server (d) assurance

Ans. (b)

The correct filler for the given blank is 'terror'. It means the feeling of strong fear.

504. I bowed to him, but he .... not to see me. **SSC MTS Tier-1 15.05.2023 (Shift-I)**

(a) seems
(b) seeming
(c) seemingly
(d) seemed

Ans. (d)

The main clause (having the verb 'bowed') is already given in past tense and is connected to the second clause using the conjunction 'but'. So, the second clause will also be written in past tense.

Hence, the correct filler for the given blank is 'seemed'.

505. The researcher team took air .... from the room every five minutes to rule out the possibility of a virus.
SSC MTS Tier-1 15.05.2023 (Shift-I)

(a) instance (b) slices
(c) samples (d) droops

Ans. (c)

The correct filler for the given blank is 'samples'. It means small parts taken for testing, fitting the context of research.

506. The priest puts some .... water on the child's head.
SSC MTS Tier-1 15.05.2023 (Shift-II)

(a) hairy (b) holy
(c) haughty (d) wholly

Ans. (b)

The correct filler for the given blank is 'holy'.

It means sacred or associated with divinity or religious significance.

507. All the companies make an .... to be seen and heard within communities.
SSC MTS Tier-1 15.05.2023 (Shift-III)

(a) establishment (b) effort
(c) excuse (d) aisle

Ans. (b)

The correct filler for the given blank is 'effort'.

It means an attempt, fitting the context of being visible in communities.

508. Jacqueline represents retirement as the final result of a long course of dissatisfaction with .... life.
SSC MTS Tier-1 15.05.2023 (Shift-III)

(a) joyful (b) mundane
(c) barbaric (d) divine

Ans. (b)

The correct filler for the given blank is 'mundane'. It means ordinary or everyday, fitting the context of dissatisfaction.

509. She has a large............. sympathy and absolute fairness of temper.
SSC MTS Tier-1 13.06.2023 (Shift-I)

(a) mean (b) sparing
(c) generous (d) thrifty

Ans. (c)

The correct filler for the given blank is 'generous'.

It means showing a readiness to give more of something than is strictly necessary or expected, fitting the context of sympathy and fairness. 'Mean' means unkind, 'sparing' means moderate, and 'thrifty' means economical.

510. Sulochana, whose, ... I had so admired during the festival, seemed a different person.
SSC MTS Tier-1 13.06.2023 (Shift-I)

(a) polish (b) crudeness
(c) grace (d) shadow

Ans. (c)

The correct filler for the given blank is 'grace'.

It means the charming quality of being polite and pleasant.

511. After the first defeats he had to ....from France with the empress. **SSC MTS Tier-1 13.06.2023 (Shift-II)**

(a) fleet (b) fling
(c) flee (d) flea

Ans. (c)

The correct filler for the given blank is 'flee'. It means to run away from a place or situation of danger, fitting the context of escaping after defeats. 'Fleet' means a group of ships, 'fling' means to throw and 'flea' is a small insect.

512. Someone thinks Charles should .... the British throne and come out here instead.
SSC MTS Tier-1 13.06.2023 (Shift-II)

(a) reciprocate
(b) abdicate
(c) decorticate
(d) authenticate

Ans. (b)

The correct filler for the given blank is 'abdicate'. It means to renounce one's throne, fitting the context of leaving the British throne. 'Reciprocate' means to return a favor, 'decorticate' means to peel and 'authenticate' means to verify.

513. Slightly .... bitter oranges to remove the red colour which covers their skins.
SSC MTS Tier-1 13.06.2023 (Shift-III)

(a) grate (b) great
(c) grace (d) grade

Ans. (a)

The correct filler for the given blank is 'grate'. It means to reduce to small shreds by rubbing on a grater, fitting the context of removing the color from oranges.

514. Pay attention to what's happening and make .... adjustments based on your personal experience.
SSC MTS Tier-1 14.06.2023 (Shift-I)

(a) impartial (b) honest
(c) placid (d) reasonable

Ans. (d)

The correct filler for the given blank is 'reasonable'. It means fair and sensible, fitting the context of making adjustments.

'Impartial' means unbiased, 'honest' means truthful and 'placid' means calm.

515. Lumber has many .... beyond home building.
SSC MTS Tier-1 14.06.2023 (Shift-I)

(a) trunks (b) loses
(c) pluses (d) uses

Ans. (d)

The correct filler for the given blank is 'uses'. It means purposes or applications, fitting the context of the versatility of lumber.

516. Many people may not find the rewards .... with the time and effort required.
SSC MTS Tier-1 14.06.2023 (Shift-I)

(a) collude
(b) coffer
(c) commensurate
(d) capable

Ans. (c)

The given sentence states that many people may not find the rewards suitable compared to the time and effort invested.

Hence, the correct filler for the given blank is 'commensurate' which means suitable according to something.

'Collude' means to conspire, 'coffer' means a strongbox and 'capable' means having the ability.

517. Those unfamiliar with the saga are bound to be mystified by the more .... plot twists.
SSC MTS Tier-1 14.06.2023 (Shift-II)

(a) arcane (b) arbitrary
(c) aesthetic (d) anoint

Ans. (a)

The correct filler for the given blank is 'arcane'.

It means understood by few; mysterious or secret, fitting the context of plot twists that are difficult to understand.

'Arbitrary' means based on random choice, 'aesthetic' means concerned with beauty and 'anoint' means to smear with oil as part of a religious ceremony.

518. Our breathing rate can change almost instantaneously in response to stress or **SSC MTS Tier-1 14.06.2023 (Shift-II)**

(a) arousal (b) fund
(c) difference (d) attention

Ans. (a)

The correct filler for the given blank is 'arousal'. It means the feeling of being excited.

519. The issue of fairness, which remained, was for consideration at the hearing to .... the scheme.
SSC MTS Tier-1 14.06.2023 (Shift-II)

(a) acclamation (b) sanction
(c) altercation (d) stratification

Ans. (b)

The correct filler for the given blank is 'sanction'. 'Acclamation' means loud and enthusiastic approval, 'altercation' means a noisy argument and 'stratification' means the arrangement into different layers.

520. Ancient Indians were never this .... minded.
SSC MTS Tier-1 14.06.2023 (Shift-III)
(a) cramp (b) slim
(c) narrow (d) tiny
Ans. (c)
The correct filler for the given blank is 'narrow'.
The phrase 'narrow minded' means someone who is not willing to accept opinions or beliefs that are different from his own.

521. And to think after all these years you still have the .... to say such things to me!. SSC MTS Tier-1 14.06.2023 (Shift-III)
(a) tangential (b) brightness
(c) arrogance (d) fitness
Ans. (c)
The correct filler for the given blank is 'arrogance'. It means excessive pride or self-importance.

522. The show played to full houses for a five-night run and ended to .... applause on Saturday night.
SSC MTS Tier-1 14.06.2023 (Shift-III)
(a) semantic (b) redress
(c) tumultuous (d) barren
Ans. (c)
The correct filler for the given blank is 'tumultuous'. It means loud, excited and emotional, fitting the context of applause at the end of a successful show.
'Semantic' means relating to meaning in language, 'redress' means to set right and 'barren' means empty or lacking.

523. Her ribs were .... but no longer painful. SSC MTS Tier-1 15.06.2023 (Shift-I)
(a) soar (b) sore
(c) sour (d) sure
Ans. (b)
The word 'sore' means experiencing pain, discomfort, or tenderness. In this sentence, it suggests that her ribs were previously painful but are now no longer causing her pain. Hence, 'sore' is the most appropriate answer.

524. The .... term 'wasteland' is proposed to be replaced by the term 'urban commons'.
SSC MTS Tier-1 15.06.2023 (Shift-I)
(a) derogatory (b) lucrative
(c) imperative (d) indicative
Ans. (a)
The correct filler for the given blank is 'derogatory'. It means expressing a low or negative opinion, critical in nature.
'Lucrative' means profitable, 'imperative' means crucial and 'indicative' means suggestive.

525. Some were very shaky and unstable, others were ...., and a few were both! SSC MTS Tier-1 15.06.2023 (Shift-I)
(a) voluted (b) diluted
(c) convoluted (d) involuted
Ans. (c)
The correct filler for the given blank is 'convoluted'. It means complex and difficult to follow, fitting the context of describing unstable things. 'Voluted' refers to a spiral shape, 'diluted' means weakened and 'involuted' means intricate.

526. A loud thud woke up everybody and nobody knew what all the .... was about.
SSC MTS Tier-1 15.06.2023 (Shift-I)
(a) exoneration (b) commotion
(c) abomination (d) culmination
Ans. (b)
The correct filler for the given blank is 'commotion'.
It means a state of noisy and chaotic behavior, fitting the context of confusion or disturbance.
'Exoneration' means clearing of blame, 'abomination' means something detestable and 'culmination' means the highest point.

527. The greatest source of income in India is from agriculture and related industries.
SSC MTS Tier-1 15.06.2023 (Shift-II)
(a) derived (b) expressed
(c) assumed (d) voiced
Ans. (a)
The correct filler for the given blank is 'derived'. It means received from a source.

528. It's a challenge, as you yourself and men find it hard to turn ...... challenges.
SSC MTS Tier-1 15.06.2023 (Shift-II)
(a) up (b) below
(c) down (d) aside
Ans. (c)
The correct filler for the given blank is 'down'.
The phrasal verb 'turn down' means to reject something, fitting the context of rejecting challenges.

529. I think she's right to warn you not to .... your temper.
SSC MTS Tier-1 15.06.2023 (Shift-III)
(a) drop (b) last
(c) lose (d) forget
Ans. (c)
The correct filler for the given blank is 'lose'.
The phrase 'lose your temper' means to become angry or lose control of your emotions.

530. As he walked past the chambers, Samir asked everyone to quiet.
SSC MTS Tier-1 15.06.2023 (Shift-III)
(a) please (b) rise (c) up (d) down
Ans. (d)
The correct filler for the given blank is 'down'. 'Quiet down' means to become quiet or to reduce noise.

531. The life of the Church seems, indeed, to have been in a more stagnant and .... condition in this age than at any other and period of English history. SSC MTS Tier-1 15.06.2023 (Shift-III)
(a) tangential (b) torpid
(c) expedite (d) truculent
Ans. (b)
The correct filler for the given blank is 'torpid'. It means sluggish or inactive, fitting the context of a stagnant condition.
'Tangential' means hardly touching a matter, 'expedite' means to speed up and 'truculent' means eager to argue.

532. My friends, being incredibly nerdy linguists, ... to make fun of the syntax. SSC MTS Tier-1 16.06.2023 (Shift-I)
(a) braided (b) decided
(c) stalked (d) traded
Ans. (b)
The correct filler for the given blank is 'decided'. It means made a choice, fitting the context of an action taken.
'Braided' means intertwined, 'stalked' means followed stealthily and 'traded' means exchanged.

533. Indonesian police fired warning shots, tear gas and water cannon to try and ..... the crowd.
SSC MTS Tier-1 16.06.2023 (Shift-I)
(a) discrete (b) delimit
(c) deleterious (d) disperse
Ans. (d)
The correct filler for the given blank is 'disperse'. It means to scatter or spread over a wide area.
'Discrete' means separate, 'delimit' means set limits and 'deleterious' means harmful.

534. Aunt Petunia was .... a box of after-dinner mints.
SSC MTS Tier-1 16.06.2023 (Shift-II)
(a) passing round (b) passed around
(c) passing around(d) passed away

Ans. (c)

The given sentence is an example of past continuous tense and the subject is plural.
So, the correct grammatical structure is 'singular subject + was + V_4(ing)'. Hence, 'passing around' is the most appropriate answer.

535. In more civilised times even the most ……… enemies were treated with dignity. **SSC MTS Tier-1 16.06.2023 (Shift-II)**

(a) explicable (b) vindicable
(c) implacable (d) ineducable

Ans. (c)

The correct filler for the given blank is 'implacable'. It means unable to be placated or appeased, fitting the context of strong enemies.

Options like 'explicable', 'vindicable' and 'ineducable' do not fit this context. 'Explicable' means able to be explained, 'vindicable' means able to be justified and 'ineducable' means unable to be educated.

536. She was trying to help that little boy in the grocery. ………… **SSC MTS Tier-1 16.06.2023 (Shift-III)**

(a) road (b) asylum
(c) store (d) park

Ans. (c)

The correct filler for the given blank is 'store'. It means a place where goods are sold, fitting the context of a grocery.

537. Many Americans appear to be ………. those warnings seriously. **SSC MTS Tier-1 16.06.2023 (Shift-III)**

(a) understanding (b) sacking
(c) making (d) taking

Ans. (d)

The correct filler for the given blank is 'taking'. It means considering or acknowledging, fitting the context of warnings.

538. The event acts as a trigger or........ which catapults them into an awareness of this phenomena. **SSC MTS Tier-1 16.06.2023 (Shift-III)**

(a) dogma (b) catalyst
(c) elegy (d) harangue

Ans. (b)

The correct filler for the given blank is 'catalyst'.

It means something that speeds up a process, fitting the context of an awareness trigger. 'Dogma' means a set of beliefs, 'elegy' means a mournful poem and 'harangue' means a lengthy speech.

539. Still, this is a Frank Black album, with its ………… references and abstruse lyrics. **SSC MTS Tier-1 19.06.2023 (Shift-I)**

(a) obscure (b) intelligent
(c) informal (d) apparent

Ans. (a)

The correct filler for the given blank is 'obscure'. It means difficult to understand, fitting the context of abstruse lyrics.

540. The event promised to be a grand show will see a display of grit, …… and mettle. **SSC MTS Tier-1 19.06.2023 (Shift-I)**

(a) tyro (b) zeal
(c) umbrage (d) zenith

Ans. (b)

The correct filler for the given blank is 'zeal' which means great energy or excitement.

'Tyro' means a beginner, 'umbrage' means offense and 'zenith' means the highest point.

541. His students from his time at Manchester University remember his lectures as extraordinarily …………. **SSC MTS Tier-1 19.06.2023 (Shift-I)**

(a) rancid (b) ballistic
(c) flaccid (d) lucid

Ans. (d)

The given sentence states that his students remember his lectures as easy and clear to understand. Hence, the correct filler for the given blank is 'lucid' which means clear and easy to understand.

'Rancid' means spoiled, 'ballistic' means related to projectiles and 'flaccid' means weak.

542. He is quite …….and narrow. **SSC MTS Tier-1 19.06.2023 (Shift-II)**

(a) tall (b) elongated
(c) long (d) stretched

Ans. (a)

The correct filler for the given blank is 'tall'. It means having a greater than average height, fitting the context of describing a person.

543. The ……… mistake these couples made was not spending enough time seriously planning for a lifetime together in marriage. **SSC MTS Tier-1 19.06.2023 (Shift-II)**

(a) sporadic (b) credulous
(c) enigmatic (d) egregious

Ans. (d)

The correct filler for the given blank is 'egregious'. It means shocking or outstandingly bad, fitting the context of a serious mistake.

'Sporadic' means occurring irregularly, 'credulous' means gullible and 'enigmatic' means mysterious.

544. Different cells express different proteins depending on which promoters are either active or ……….. . **SSC MTS Tier-1 19.06.2023 (Shift-III)**

(a) dormant (b) effectual
(c) productive (d) lazy

Ans. (a)

The correct filler for the given blank is 'dormant'. It means inactive, fitting the context of promoters that are not active.

545. I think he is a worthy …….of the policy and a worthy adversary for the press. **SSC MTS Tier-1 19.06.2023 (Shift-III)**

(a) reciprocate (b) placate
(c) educate (d) advocate

Ans. (d)

The correct filler for the given blank is 'an advocate'.

An advocate is someone who supports or speaks in favour of a particular policy.

546. At times he acted as viceroy in William's absence; at times he led the royal forces to ……… rebellions. **SSC MTS Tier-1 19.06.2023 (Shift-III)**

(a) scrutinise (b) chastise
(c) compromise (d) baptise

Ans. (a)

The correct filler for the given blank is 'scrutinise'. It means to examine closely, fitting the context of leading forces to closely examine or deal with rebellions.

'Chastise' means to scold, 'compromise' means to settle differences and 'baptise' means to administer a religious sacrament.

547. I was ………… and was suddenly woken up by the loud noise of crackers bursting. **SSC MTS Tier-1 20.06.2023 (Shift-I)**

(a) fast asleep (b) quiet asleep
(c) quite asleep (d) long asleep

Ans. (a)

The correct filler for the given blank is 'fast asleep'.

The phrase 'fast asleep' means in a state of deep sleep.

548. Harry stepped in, his head almost ……… the sloping ceiling and blinked. **SSC MTS Tier-1 20.06.2023 (Shift-II)**

(a) embracing (b) touching
(c) grasping (d) cuddling

Ans. (b)

The correct filler for the given blank is 'touching'. It means coming into contact with, fitting the context of Harry's head almost reaching the ceiling.

549. There was a general hesitation and .... to ignore the problem.

SSC MTS Tier-1 20.06.2023 (Shift-II)

(a) disposition (b) deride
(c) demur (d) denigrate

Ans. (c)

The correct filler for the given blank is 'demur'. It means to raise doubts or show reluctance, fitting the context of hesitation.
'Disposition' means temperament, 'deride' means to mock and 'denigrate' means to criticise unfairly.

550. Hardik Pandya hit four .... fours and scored 72 runs in the match.

SSC MTS Tier-1 01.09.2023 (Shift-I)

(a) continuous (b) consecutive
(c) ongoing (d) constant

Ans. (b)

The given sentence indicates that Hardik Pandya scored 4 fours one after another.

Hence, the correct filler for the given blank is 'consecutive' which means happening one after the other wotjpit interruption.

551. Oberon doesn't like the way Demetrius .... to Helena. (Credit; A Midsummer Night's Dream)

SSC MTS Tier-1 01.09.2023 (Shift-I)

(a) talked (b) talks
(c) talking (d) to talk

Ans. (b)

The given sentence is an example of Simple Present Tense and the subject 'Demetrius' is singular. Hence, the correct filler for the given blank is 'talks'.

552. The hiring manager has already offered you the job; now ...... to accept or decline the offer.

SSC MTS Tier-1 01.09.2023 (Shift-I)

(a) a penny for your thoughts
(b) the ball is in your court
(c) pull your leg
(d) get your act together

Ans. (b)

The correct filler for the given blank is 'the ball is in your court', meaning it is now your responsibility to make a decision.
'A penny for your thoughts' means asking someone's thoughts, 'pull your leg' means joking and 'get your act together' means becoming organised.

553. Ours is .... house of all the houses in our area.

SSC MTS Tier-1 01.09.2023 (Shift-II)

(a) the more bigger
(b) the biggest
(c) the most biggest
(d) the bigger

Ans. (b)

The correct filler for the given blank is 'the biggest'. We use superlative degree with the definite article 'the'.

554. Early childhood experiences have a .... impact on brain development affecting learning, health, behaviour and ultimately, productivity and income.

SSC MTS Tier-1 01.09.2023 (Shift-II)

(a) perfect (b) profound
(c) basic (d) superficial

Ans. (b)

The given sentence states that the experiences that children have in their early years can have a deep impact on the way their brains develop. Hence, the correct filler for the given blank is 'profound'.

555. The tigress that was killed by the villagers was not only a man-eater, ... a mother.

SSC MTS Tier-1 01.09.2023 (Shift-III)

(a) but (b) but also
(c) and (d) but often

Ans. (b)

The correct filler for the given blank is 'but also' because we always use not only .... but also together.

556. He generally avoids arguments as he is ....by nature.

SSC MTS Tier-1 04.09.2023 (Shift-I)

(a) questionable
(b) reliable
(c) quick-minded
(d) peaceful

Ans. (d)

The given sentence states that he generally avoid arguments because of his calm nature. Hence, the correct filler for the given blank is 'peaceful'.

557. The students of class 7 gave their teacher a gift, which was .... to her.

SSC MTS Tier-1 04.09.2023 (Shift-II)

(a) revealing (b) shocking
(c) confusing (d) surprising

Ans. (d)

The correct filler for the given blank is 'surprising' as it indicates a positive reaction of the teacher.

558. He is .... of many chain snatching cases in Dariyaganj.

SSC MTS Tier-1 04.09.2023 (Shift-II)

(a) ackused (b) acxused
(c) akused (d) accused

Ans. (d)

The correct filler for the given blank is 'accused'.

559. Her stories paid ...... to her mother, whom she regarded as the goddess of bravery.

SSC MTS Tier-1 04.09.2023 (Shift-III)

(a) frustration
(b) sainthood
(c) absoluteness
(d) homage

Ans. (d)

The given sentence states that her stories showed deep respect and praise to her mother whom she considered a symbol of bravery and excellence. Hence, the correct filler for the given blank is 'homage' which means deep respect and praise shown for a person or god.

560. Suresh has been learning Tamil ...... two months.

SSC MTS Tier-1 05.09.2023 (Shift-I)

(a) from (b) since
(c) before (d) for

Ans. (d)

The correct filler for the given blank is 'for'. It indicates a duration of time.

561. Can you quote any in your favour?

SSC MTS Tier-1 05.09.2023 (Shift-I)

(a) answer
(b) summary
(c) lines
(d) precedent

Ans. (d)

The correct filler for the given blank is 'precedent'.
It means a legal decision that supports a position or argument.

562. Bhanu, the security guard, asks everyone entering my building to show their........... card.

SSC MTS Tier-1 05.09.2023 (Shift-II)

(a) identity (b) place
(c) self (d) name

Ans. (a)

With respect to security measure, 'identity' is the correct word to fill the blank.

563. The tone of his voice seemed to .... that he knew more than he was letting on.
SSC MTS Tier-1 06.09.2023 (Shift-I)
(a) incise (b) intent
(c) inculcate (d) imply

Ans. (d)
The given sentence presents what the tone of his voice indicates. Hence, the correct filler for the given blank is 'imply' which means 'to indicate or point out'.

564. The rusty door made a .... screeching noise.
SSC MTS Tier-1 06.09.2023 (Shift-I)
(a) low (b) soft
(c) harsh (d) smooth

Ans. (c)
A screeching noise is always harsh. Hence, the correct filler for the given blank is 'harsh'.

565. COVID-19 .... structural weaknesses in health systems worldwide and negatively impacted individuals, societies and economies.
SSC MTS Tier-1 06.09.2023 (Shift-I)
(a) concealed (b) laid
(c) hit (d) revealed

Ans. (d)
The correct filler for the given sentence is 'revealed' as it indicates that the COVID-19 pandemic showed something.

566. Varun has to .... his studies for the sake of his ill father.
SSC MTS Tier-1 06.09.2023 (Shift-I)
(a) sacrifice (b) imitate
(c) reverse (d) applaud

Ans. (a)
'The correct filler for the given blank is 'sacrifice'. 'Imitate' means to copy, 'reverse' means to turn around and 'applaud' means to praise.

567. Some things are meant to be, and death is .... for humans.
SSC MTS Tier-1 06.09.2023 (Shift-III)
(a) edible (b) spiral
(c) natural (d) viral

Ans. (c)
The correct filler for the given blank is 'natural'. 'Edible' means fit to eat, 'spiral' means winding and 'viral' means relating to a virus.

568. Most times, he is sitting alone, immersed in his own ....
SSC MTS Tier-1 06.09.2023 (Shift-III)
(a) synagogue (b) monologue
(c) mystagogue (d) prologue

Ans. (b)
The given sentence states that he is sitting alone and is lost in his own thoughts. Hence, the correct filler for the given blank is 'monologue' which means a long conversation by one person, typically one's thoughts.

569. They are going to give me a lovely present, but I cannot .... what it will be. SSC MTS Tier-1 08.09.2023 (Shift-I)
(a) give (b) gist (c) guess
(d) guest

Ans. (c)
The correct filler for the given blank is 'guess'. It means to estimate or think about something without having its proper information.

570. .... doctor suggested doing some eye exercises and wearing .... pair of powered glasses.
(∅ = No article)
SSC MTS Tier-1 08.09.2023 (Shift-II)
(a) A; a (b) ∅; a
(c) A; ∅ (d) The; a

Ans. (d)
The correct article for the first blank is 'The' as we are referring to a specific eye doctor. The correct article for a second blank is 'a'.

571. Many soldiers marched in .... at the international border.
SSC MTS Tier-1 08.09.2023 (Shift-II)
(a) dress (b) uniform
(c) fabric (d) clothes

Ans. (b)
The sentence refers to soldiers in their standard attire. 'Uniform' means standardised clothing worn by members of an organisation.

572. She was known for her .... attention to detail, always making sure everything was perfectly organised and in its proper place.
SSC MTS Tier-1 08.09.2023 (Shift-II)
(a) fastidious (b) scornful
(c) tedious (d) exact

Ans. (a)
The given sentence states that the girl is a perfectionist as she given full attention to detail.
Hence, the correct filler for the given blank is 'fastidious' which means perfectionist.

573. The mother ...... the chips because they were soggy.
SSC MTS Tier-1 08.09.2023 (Shift-III)
(a) saved (b) wasted
(c) discarded (d) recovered

Ans. (c)
The correct filler for the given blank is 'discarded'. It means to get rid of something or throw it away.

574. During the meeting, he went on a long and angry ...... about how the project was being mismanaged.
SSC MTS Tier-1 08.09.2023 (Shift-III)
(a) shout (b) whisper
(c) rant (d) mutter

Ans. (c)
The correct filler for the given blank is 'rant'. It means when someone speaks at length in an angry way.

575. Chaitnya was .... from the school due to his misappropriate behaviour.
SSC MTS Tier-1 08.09.2023 (Shift-III)
(a) expelled (b) xpelled
(c) expeled (d) xpeled

Ans. (a)
The correct filler for the given blank is 'expelled'. The context is that Chaitnya faced a serious consequence for his behavior. 'Expelled' means officially removed from an institution.

576. Ministry of education has announced that students can .... the board examinations twice.
SSC MTS Tier-1 11.09.2023 (Shift-I)
(a) take (b) participate
(c) give (d) get

Ans. (a)
The correct filler for the given blank is 'take' as it correctly collocates with 'examination'.

577. All praised him when he soared in the business world, but the same people .... him when he failed in business. SSC MTS Tier-1 11.09.2023 (Shift-I)
(a) nourished
(b) criticised
(c) supported
(d) dramatised

Ans. (b)
The given sentence presents how the man was respected when his business was successful but when his business failed, he received negative comments. Hence, the correct filler for the given blank 'criticised' which means 'to express disapproval or make negative comments'.

578. Augmented Reality (AR) continues to develop and become more .... among a wide range of applications.
SSC MTS Tier-1 11.09.2023 (Shift-I)
(a) rare (b) amicable
(c) idealistic (d) pervasive

Ans. (d)

The given sentence presents how AI is being developed and becoming popular. Hence, the correct filler for the given blank 'pervasive' which means spread throughout in all areas and popular.

579. A/An .... fellow cannot become an ideal teacher.
SSC MTS Tier-1 11.09.2023 (Shift-I)

(a) idle (b) bright
(b) intelligent (d) honest

Ans. (a)

The correct filler for the given blank is 'idle' which is used to refer to a person who is lazy and has nothing to do.

580. Virtual worlds are recently new phenomena in that they...... people to meet and socially interact with others in a variety of online environments.
SSC MTS Tier-1 11.09.2023 (Shift-II)

(a) forbid (b) bring
(c) choose (d) enable

Ans. (d)

The given sentence presents what the virtual worlds allow people to do. Hence, the correct filler for the given blank is 'enable' which means 'to allow or give the facility of'.

581. The Nile is the .... river of the world. SSC MTS Tier-1 11.09.2023 (Shift-III)

(a) long (b) longer
(c) more longer (d) longest

Ans. (d)

The correct filler for the given blank is 'longest'. Article 'the' is used before a superlative degree adjective.

582. I .... to many countries to find the source of true happiness.
SSC MTS Tier-1 11.09.2023 (Shift-III)

(a) triveled (b) travelled
(c) traveled (d) travalled

Ans. (b)

The correct filler for the given blank is 'travelled'.

The sentence talks about visiting many countries, and the word 'travelled' means journeyed or moved from one place to another.

583. He is a smug and very .... person who thinks only about himself.
SSC MTS Tier-1 11.09.2023 (Shift-III)

(a) noble (b) diffident
(c) egoistic (d) humble

Ans. (c)

The correct filler for the given blank is 'egoistic'.

The sentence describes someone who is self-centered and 'egoistic' means having an inflated sense of self-importance.

584. I know that I can count on my best friend to be by my side through ...... and thin. SSC MTS Tier-1 11.09.2023 (Shift-III)

(a) tough (b) heavy
(c) thick (d) fat

Ans. (c)

The correct filler for the given blank is 'thick'. The idiom 'through' thick and thin' means to persevere through good times as well as bad.

585. Make-up was .... she hardly wore. SSC MTS Tier-1 12.09.2023 (Shift-I)

(a) anything (b) something
(c) anybody (d) someone

Ans. (b)

The correct filler for the given blank is 'something' is used when the specific thing (in this sentence, make-up) being referred to is not known in detail.

586. Ravi has little in .... with his friend, Senthil.
SSC MTS Tier-1 12.09.2023 (Shift-I)

(a) common (b) contention
(c) formal (d) normal

Ans. (a)

The correct filler for the given blank is 'common'. The phrase 'in common' is used indicate similarity or shared interests.

587. Her dedication to her work was .... what anyone had expected.
SSC MTS Tier-1 12.09.2023 (Shift-III)

(a) over (b) beyond
(c) beside (d) through

Ans. (b)

The correct filler for the given blank is 'beyond'. It means surpassing or exceeding expectations. 'Over' means above, 'beside' means next to and 'through' means passing from one side to the other.

588. The old man distributed his property .... his ten grandchildren equally.
SSC MTS Tier-1 12.09.2023 (Shift-III)

(a) within (b) among
(c) towards (d) between

Ans. (b)

The correct filler for the given blank is 'among'. It is used for distribution involving more than two entities.

589. The toddler decided to make a mess because he wanted to .... the attention of its parents.
SSC MTS Tier-1 13.09.2023 (Shift-I)

(a) seek (b) elicit (c) please (d) extract

Ans. (a)

The correct filler for the given blank is 'seek' indicating that the toddler to wanting to gain his father's attention.

590. The teacher assured- 'You have completed your homework, ... ?'
SS MTS Tier-1 13.09.2023 (Shift-I)

(a) had you
(b) hadn't you
(c) haven't you
(d) have you

Ans. (c)

According to the rules of the question tag, we use the pronoun of the sentence and the opposite of the auxiliary verb used. Hence, the correct filler for the given blank is 'haven't you'.

591. A strong .... for mathematics and problem-solving can be very useful.
SSC MTS Tier-1 13.09.2023 (Shift-II)

(a) strength (b) aptitude
(c) functioning (d) perception

Ans. (b)

The correct filler for the given blank is 'aptitude'. It means a natural ability to do something.

592. Dr. APJ Abdul Kalam was a great man with a high level of ....
SSC MTS Tier-1 14.09.2023 (Shift-I)

(a) intelligent humour
(b) wise boredom
(c) intellect
(d) clever fatigue

Ans. (c)

The correct filler for the given blank is 'intellect' which means 'wisdom and knowledge'.

593. The commander, "Honourable Emperor, all the troops have lined up for the battle and are awaiting your orders." Emperor Chandragupta Maurya, "......... ".
SSC MTS Tier-1 14.09.2023 (Shift-I)

(a) We will march at dawn
(b) You should learn how to talk to an emperor
(c) We will be playing cards
(d) We are ready for the pilgrimage

Ans. (a)

The given dialogue presents the commander telling emperor Chandragupta Maurya that the army is ready.

The appropriate reply of the Emperor would indicate the time to take the army to war. Hence, the correct filler for the given blank is 'We will march at dawn'.

594. I wish we had .... come here.
SSC MTS Tier-1 14.09.2023 (Shift-II)
(a) right (b) clear
(c) never (d) agreed
Ans. (c)
The given sentence needs an adverb here to modify the verb 'come'.
Hence, the correct filler for the given blank is 'never'.

595. Winning the championship was a dream come true for the team, but being awarded the MVP trophy was ....
SSC MTS Tier-1 14.09.2023 (Shift-III)
(a) the silver lining
(b) the bird in the bush
(c) a cold turkey
(d) the icing on the cake
Ans. (d)
'The icing on the cake' something that makes a good situation even better.

SSC Selection Post 2024

596. We must try and incorporate positive thinking in our lives to .... countless benefits it has to offer.
SSC SP 20.06.2024 (Shift-II)
(a) ignore (b) release
(c) contain (d) derive
Ans. (d)
The given sentence presents that we should think positively to get its benefits.
Hence, the correct filler for the given blank is 'derive' which means 'to get'.

597. Many societies throughout history have understood the .... for harmony between the environment, society and economy.
SSC SP 20.06.2024 (Shift-IV)
(a) superfluity (b) caninity
(c) necessity (d) amenity
Ans. (c)
The given sentence states that societies throughout our history have understood the need for harmony. Hence, the correct filler for the given blank is 'necessity' which emphasises the need.

SSC Selection Post 2023

598. Conditions such as stress, depression and anxiety can all affect mental health and .... a person's routine.
SSC SP 27.06.2023 (Shift-I)
(a) fragment (b) crush
(c) dishevel (d) disrupt
Ans. (d)
The given sentence presents how mental conditions affect and destroy a person's routine.
Hence, the correct filler for the given blank is 'disrupt' which indicates the destruction or hampering of routine.

599. Plastic pollution is ...... the oceans' ecosystem, but humanity doesn't take serious action against it.
SSC SP 27.06.2023 (Shift-III)
(a) deciding (b) aiming
(c) making (d) affecting
Ans. (d)
The correct filler for the given blank is 'affecting' which fits well with the sentence about how plastic pollution impacts the oceans.

600. Every cloud has a .... lining.
SSC SP 27.06.2023 (Shift-III)
(a) diffused (b) silver
(c) blue (d) grey
Ans. (b)
The correct filler for the given blank is 'silver'.
The proverb 'every cloud has a silver lining' means every difficult or sad situation has a comforting or more hopeful aspect, even though this may not be immediately apparent.

601. We as human beings usually tend to forget that life itself is an accumulated process of ....
SSC SP 27.06.2023 (Shift-I)
(a) learning (b) recalling
(c) remembering (d) testing
Ans. (a)
The correct filler for the given blank is 'learning' as the sentence talks about how we learn throughout our lives.

602. You must .... what you cannot cure.
SSC SP 27.06.2023 (Shift-I)
(a) embracing (b) endure
(c) state (d) take
Ans. (b)
The given sentence presents how we must suffer from problems that have no cure. Hence, the correct filler for the given blank is 'endure' which means to suffer from.

603. One is sure ....what one sees.
SSC SP 28.06.2023 (Shift-II)
(a) about (b) with
(c) around (d) without
Ans. (a)
'Sure about' is a phrasal verb that means to be sure or certain about something

604. That night the dinner was special, I and the .... himself came out to I read out the menu list.
SSC SP 28.06.2023 (Shift-II)
(a) servant (b) public
(c) guest (d) chef
Ans. (d)
'Chef' is a professional cook who is highly' skilled in preparing and cooking food.
The given sentence states that the chef himself came out to read out the menu list during the special dinner that night. Hence, 'chef' is the most appropriate answer.

605. A fire ...... out in the basement of the house.
SSC SP 26.06.2023 (Shift-IV)
(a) broke (b) breaking
(b) burned (d) burnt
Ans. (a)
The phrasal verb 'broke out' means to start suddenly and violently. The given sentence states that a fire suddenly started in the basement of the house. Hence, 'broke' is the most appropriate answer.

606. The weather report shows the .... of rainfall.
SSC SP 28.06.2023 (Shift-IV)
(a) tranquillity (b) mobility
(c) validity (d) probability
Ans. (d)
'Probability' means the possibility of something happening. The given sentence states that there is a possibility of rainfall as per the weather report. Hence, 'probability' is the most appropriate answer.

607. Rome grew from a small town on the Tiber River in Italy into a .... empire that ultimately embraced England.
SSC SP 28 .06.2023 (Shift-IV)
(a) vast (b) voluminous
(c) bountiful (d) lofty
Ans. (a)
The word 'vast' means very large or widespread.
The given sentence states that Rome grew from a small town into a large empire. Hence, 'vast' is the most appropriate answer.

608. Their conviction and determination helped Kimirica overcome .... odds and become India's largest manufacturer of luxury hotel toiletries and guest room amenities.
SSC SP 30.06.2023 (Shift-I)
(a) undefeated (b) inviolable
(c) insurmountable (d) unstoppable

Ans. (c)

'Insurmountable' means something that is impossible to overcome due to its great difficulty.

The given sentence states that despite facing significant challenges or difficulties, Kimirica's conviction and determination helped them achieve their goal. Hence, 'insurmountable' is the most appropriate answer.

609. .... for an hour made me lose my breath. SSC SP 30.06.2023 (Shift-I)

(a) Sitting (b) Sleeping
(c) Walking (d) Eating

Ans. (c)

The given sentence states that the act of walking for an hour caused the speaker to lose their breath. Hence, 'walking' is the most appropriate answer.

610. It is only a rope, she .... herself, though it looked very much like a snake. SSC SP 30.06.2023 (Shift-II)

(a) retained
(b) replied
(c) remembered
(d) reassured

Ans. (d)

'Reassured' means to say or do something to remove doubts or fears.

The given sentence states that the girl removed her fear by saying to herself that it is only a rope. Hence, 'reassured' is the most appropriate answer.

611. When you apply the medicine, the wound .... SSC SP 30.06.2023 (Shift-III)

(a) Feels (b) kills
(c) heals (d) deals

Ans. (c)

'Heals' means to restore health. The given sentence states that when you apply the medicine, the wound heals. Hence, 'heals' is the most appropriate answer.

612. The Thar desert is .... in the state of Rajasthan. SSC SP 30.06.2023 (Shift-IV)

(a) bounded (b) seen
(c) situated (d) placed

Ans. (c)

'Situated' means located at a particular place. The given sentence states that the mar desert is located in the state of Rajasthan. Hence, 'situated' is the most : appropriate answer.

613. The propaganda was made to invade .... neighbouring countries. SSC SP 30.06.2023 (Shift-I)

(a) smaller (b) largest
(c) stranger (d) strongest

Ans. (a)

Smaller generally use comparative degree (smaller) to compare things. Hence, 'smaller' is the most appropriate answer.

SSC Selection Post 2022

614. His wife is expecting a child and we expect some .... news soon. SSC SP 01.08.2022 (Shift-I)

(a) pretty (b) beautiful
(c) happy (d) good

Ans. (d)

The word 'expecting' in the sentence indicates the birth of a child which is a good news. Hence, the correct filler for the given blank is 'good'.

615. A gentleman .... as to what success meant to me. SSC SP 01.08.2022 (Shift-I)

(a) featured (b) impaired
(c) inquired (d) tailored

Ans. (c)

As the given sentence presents a question asked by a gentlemen, the correct filler for the given blank is 'inquired'.

616. The blue embroidered saree is no doubt an .... piece of handwork, but because of its .... price no one was ready to buy it. SSC SP 01.08.2022 (Shift-I)

(a) exquisite; exorbitant
(b) embellished; errant
(c) extinct; ecstatic
(d) erudite; enormous

Ans. (a)

The correct filler for the given blanks are 'exquisite' and 'exorbitant'.

'Exquisite' indicates the beauty and the gracefulness of the saree and the word 'exorbitant' indicates its very high price.

617. Burkin once had a client who had a breast tumour that was not spotted until it had .... and she wanted to sue her internist for the delayed .... and was also aware it was her............ who was potentially at fault. SSC SP 01.08.2022 (Shift-I)

(a) metastasised, diagnosis, radiologist
(b) metamorphosed, autopsy, dermatologist
(c) metaphorised, necropsy, cardiologist
(d) metabolised, biopsy, nephrologist

Ans. (a)

The correct fillers for the given blanks are 'metastasised', 'diagnosis' and 'radiologist'.

The word 'metastasised' indicates that the tumour had spread to other body parts. 'Diagnosis' indicates the identification and radiologist is a medical doctor that specialise in diagnosing and treating injuries and diseases using medical imaging (radiology) procedures (exams/tests) such as X-rays.

618. Easter eggs used to be painted chicken eggs, but a modern is to substitute them with chocolate eggs or plastic eggs filled with confectionery such as jelly beans. SSC SP 02.08.2022 (Shift-III)

(a) legacy (b) ethic
(c) lore (d) custom

Ans. (d)

'Custom' means a traditional and widely accepted way of behaving or doing something that is specific to a particular society, place or time.

The given sentence states that Easter eggs used to be painted chicken eggs, but a modern custom is to substitute them with chocolate eggs or plastic eggs filled with confectionery such as jelly beans. Hence, 'custom' is the most appropriate answer.

619. Countries like China and the United States invest .... in wind, hydro, solar and biofuels. SSC SP 02.08.2022 (Shift-III)

(a) profoundly (b) achingly
(c) absolutely (d) heavily

Ans. (d)

'Heavily' means to a great degree or in a heavy manner.

Hence, 'heavily' is the most appropriate answer.

620. Freud's work with free association, dream analysis and the unconscious was of .... importance to the Surrealists in developing methods to liberate imagination. SSC SP 03.08.2022 (Shift-III)

(a) farthest (b) hugest
(c) remotest (d) utmost

Ans. (d)

'Utmost' means the most extreme greatest.

The given sentence states that Freud's work with free association, dream analysis and the unconscious was of utmost importance. Hence, 'utmost' is the most appropriate answer.

621. New York .... its roots back to 1624, when it was founded as a trading post by colonists of the Dutch Republic. SSC SP 04.08.2022 (Shift-II)

(a) traces (b) dates
(c) sketches (d) recalls

Ans. (a)

'Traces' means a sign or evidence of some past thing.

The given sentence states that New York traces its roots back to 1624, when it was founded as a trading post by colonists of the Dutch Republic. Hence, 'traces' is the most appropriate answer.

622. His .... violation of the moral code of conduct was too .... to be forgiven. **SSC SP 04.08.2022 (Shift-III)**

(a) flagrant; outrageous
(b) fragrant; outgoing
(c) obscure; outstanding
(d) magnificent; outlandish

Ans. (a)

Flagrant means conspicuously offensive and 'outrageous' means exceeding the limits of what is usual. The given sentence states that his 'flagrant' violation of the moral code of conduct was too outrageous to be forgiven' Hence, 'flagrant and 'outrageous' is the most appropriate answer.

623. According to the traditions, Easter Sunday is celebrated by .... part in an Easter vigil, lighting a new fire outside the church early on Sunday morning. **SSC SP 04.08.2022 (Shift-IV)**

(a) taking (b) being
(c) bearing (d) making

Ans. (a)

The phrase 'take part' means to join in an activity or be involved. The given sentence states that Easter Sunday is celebrated by taking part in an Easter vigil. Hence, 'taking' is the most appropriate answer.

624. Stereotypes may be used to justify ill-founded .... or ignorance and prevent people of stereotyped groups from entering or succeeding in various activities or fields. **SSC SP 05.08.2022 (Shift-III)**

(a) conclusions (b) thoughts
(c) prejudices (d) problems

Ans. (c)

'Prejudices' means a preconceived opinion that is not based on reason or actual experience.

The given sentence states that stereotypes may be used to justify ill-founded prejudices or ignorance, and prevent people of stereotyped groups.

SSC Steno 2024

625. His friends disagreed............ him on that point. **SSC Steno 11.12.2024 (Shift-I)**

(a) for (b) on
(c) to (d) with

Ans. (d)

The correct preposition is 'with'. The phrase 'disagreed with' is used to indicate opposition or differing opinions.

626. Technology hasn't left anything behind, it has...........almost everything. From the phones we use to the medicines we consume; it is all a product of technology. **SSC Steno 11.12.2024 (Shift-I)**

(a) affected (b) effected
(c) dislodged (d) evicted

Ans. (a)

The most appropriate option is 'affected' because it means to have an impact on, fitting the context of technology impacting almost everything.

627. At the sight of the police, the thief ran away in the...........of an eye. **SSC Steno 11.12.2024 (Shift-I)**

(a) back (b) sparkling
(c) core (d) blink

Ans. (d)

The correct phrase is 'in the blink of an eye' because it means very quickly or suddenly, fitting the context of the thief running away quickly.

628. The tiger looked at me with a serious .... **SSC Steno 11.12.2024 (Shift-I)**

(a) smile (b) nap
(c) stare (d) wink

Ans. (c)

The correct word is 'stare'. The sentence 'The tiger looked at me with a serious stare' fits the context as 'stare' means to look fixedly or intently.

629. Good books should be read again and............ **SSC Steno 11.12.2024 (Shift-I)**

(a) ever (b) never
(c) after (d) again

Ans. (d)

The correct adverb is 'again'. The sentence 'Good books should be read again and again' implies that good books are worth reading repeatedly.

630. Their plan of acquisition was ....flawed from the very beginning; it was bound to fail. **SSC Steno 11.12.2024 (Shift-I)**

(a) biblically (b) cheerfully
(c) fatally (d) amicably

Ans. (c)

The correct word is 'fatally'. The sentence 'Their plan of acquisition was fatally flawed from the very beginning' implies that the flaw was serious and led to inevitable failure.

631. It may seem...........that the hours of women's chores at home have not declined inspite of the availability of many appliances (gas, electric ranges, washing machines, etc). **SSC Steno 11.12.2024 (Shift-II)**

(a) perceiving (b) promising
(c) perplexing (d) persisting

Ans. (c)

The most appropriate word to fill in the blank is 'perplexing.' 'Perplexing' means confusing or puzzling, fitting the context of the unexpected situation described.

632. The seven............for accreditation were presented in a seminar organised by the university. **SSC Steno 11.12.2024 (Shift-II)**

(a) criteria (b) criterias
(c) criterions (d) criterion

Ans. (a)

The correct word is 'criteria'. 'Criteria' is the plural form of 'criterion', meaning a standard or principle by which something is judged or decided. The sentence refers to 'seven' standards, thus requiring the plural form 'criteria'.

633. Adult Education is a great step that must be taken by all the countries as it will...........a lot of issues. The third world countries must especially work to make this happen so they can prosper. **SSC Steno 11.12.2024 (Shift-II)**

(a) permeate (b) resolve
(c) stagnate (d) contradict

Ans. (b)

'Resolve' means to find a solution, which fits the context of addressing and solving issues.

634. There...........been too many incidents of thefts lately. **SSC Steno 11.12.2024 (Shift-II)**

(a) has not (b) was
(c) have (d) has

Ans. (d)

'Has' is the correct option. The phrase 'There has been' is used to indicate the existence of something in the present perfect tense, which is appropriate for describing incidents that have occurred recently.

635. The business operates .... the same way as the other businesses did.
SSC Steno 11.12.2024 (Shift-II)

(a) such (b) very
(c) much (d) had

Ans. (c)

'Much' is used to indicate a great degree or extent and fits well with the sentence structure, making it clear that the business operates in a similar manner to other businesses.

636. The Warrens are............their house by the end of this month.
SSC Steno 11.12.2024 (Shift-III)

(a) shifted (b) will shift
(c) going to shift (d) been shifting

Ans. (c)

The phrase 'going to shift' indicates a future intention or plan.

637. We are blessed with a prudent house keeper, but cursed with an ....house master.
SSC Steno 11.12.2024 (Shift-III)

(a) potential (b) prominent
(c) indiscreet (d) wise

Ans. (c)

'Prudent' means showing good judgement, being careful and sensible. The antonym 'indiscreet' means lacking discretion, being careless or unwise in speech or actions.

638. Siraj threw a stone to destroy the ....built by the bird in a tree.
SSC Steno 11.12.2024 (Shift-III)

(a) nest (b) house
(c) home (d) roof

Ans. (a)

The most appropriate word to fill in the blank is 'nest'.

A nest is what a bird builds in a tree to live in. The other options, 'house', 'home' and 'roof' are not specific to birds.

639. A city on a hill...............be hidden.
SSC Steno 11.12.2024 (Shift-III)

(a) ought (b) need
(c) yet (d) cannot

Ans. (d)

The most appropriate option is 'cannot'. A city on a hill cannot be hidden.

This phrase indicates that something prominently positioned cannot be concealed.

The context implies the impossibility of hiding a city that is on a hill, so 'cannot' is the most suitable choice.

640. The tree lost many of its......... in the heavy rain and storm.
SSC Steno 11.12.2024 (Shift-III)

(a) creepers (b) branches
(c) bark (d) root

Ans. (b)

The most appropriate word to fill in the blank is 'branches'. Branches are the parts of a tree that can be lost in heavy rain and storms, making 'branches' the most contextually accurate choice.

641. If only we............(has) started earlier, we would be there now.
SSC Steno 11.12.2024 (Shift-III)

(a) had (b) have
(c) has been (d) have been

Ans. (a)

The correct form of the verb is 'had'. The past perfect tense 'had started' indicates a past action that did not happen and contrasts it with the present result of that inaction ('we would be there now').

642. Our environment is facing a severe crisis like never before. Any recklessness in this regard could prove............to life on Earth.
SSC Steno 11.12.2024 (Shift-III)

(a) bland (b) innocuous
(c) fatal (d) harmless

Ans. (c)

The most appropriate word to fill in the blank is 'fatal'. 'Fatal' is an adjective meaning causing death or leading to disaster, fitting the context of a severe environmental crisis that could have dire consequences.

643. Our crops depend on the rainy season. Before the monsoon begins, farmers in communities begin their work in the fields. They irrigate their grounds and grow a variety of crops............ for this season using the natural water supply.
SSC Steno 11.12.2024 (Shift-III)

(a) appropriate
(b) incompatible
(c) inadequate
(d) manipulating

Ans. (a)

The most appropriate word to fill in the blank is 'appropriate'.

The sentence describes farmers growing crops suitable for the rainy season using the natural water supply.

644. Spending quality time with friends and family is also......... to have a healthy daily routine. These happy moments release happy hormones in the body. SSC Steno 11.12.2024 (Shift-III)

(a) obligatory
(b) sceptical
(c) unseasonable
(d) derogatory

Ans. (a)

The most appropriate word to fill in the blank is 'obligatory'. The sentence implies that spending quality time with loved ones is essential for a healthy daily routine.

645. Technology has made it possible for us to reach out to more students, and it has also made it possible for us to deliver the same lessons in a much more .... manner.
SSC Steno 10.12.2024 (Shift-I)

(a) lumbering (b) resourceful
(c) incompetent (d) encumbering

Ans. (b)

The appropriate option to fill in the blank is 'resourceful'. The sentence describes how technology has improved the delivery of lessons and 'resourceful' means being able to effectively use resources, making it the best fit.

646. Online shopping refers to purchasing goods available on the world wide web. You have different websites which have a huge .... of products that you can choose from.
SSC Steno 10.12.2024 (Shift-I)

(a) assessment
(b) assortment
(c) appraisal
(d) assignment

Ans. (b)

The appropriate option to fill in the blank is 'assortment'.

The sentence describes websites with a wide range of products, and 'assortment' accurately captures this variety.

647. It is terrible that education systems all over the world are being held in captivity due to poverty, both at the governmental and family levels, despite the fact that education is claimed to be so important for human progress and the ....of global economies. SSC Steno 10.12.2024 (Shift-I)

(a) revitalisation (b) dismantling
(c) abrogation (d) devastation

Ans. (a)

The most appropriate option to fill in the blank is 'revitalisation'. The sentence discusses the importance of education for human progress and improving global economies and 'revitalisation' means bringing new life or energy, making it the best fit.

648. I am...........busy.
SSC Steno 10.12.2024 (Shift-I)

(a) few (b) quite
(c) tidily (d) quiet

Ans. (b)

The appropriate option to fill in the blank is 'quite'. The sentence 'I am quite busy' means that you are very busy or occupied.

649. They could not reach the railway station before the train..........
SSC Steno 10.12.2024 (Shift-I)

(a) has been leaving (b) leave
(c) has leave (d) left

Ans. (d)

The most appropriate option to fill in the blank is 'left'. The sentence 'They could not reach the railway station before the train left' indicates that the train had already departed before they arrived.

650. Over and ....being hardworking, he is thoroughly honest.
SSC Steno 10.12.2024 (Shift-I)

(a) above (b) over
(c) again (d) ever

Ans. (a)

The appropriate adverb to fill in the blank is 'above'. The sentence 'Over and above being hardworking, he is thoroughly honest' indicates that in addition to being hardworking, he is also honest.

651. Although one's body language is a very powerful medium of expression, we express our thoughts, verbally or .... through language, which is our main way of communication.
SSC Steno 10.12.2024 (Shift-II)

(a) hyperbolically
(b) banefully
(c) anemically
(d) textually

Ans. (d)

The correct option is 'textually', which means expressing thoughts through written or printed language.

It fits the context of primary communication methods, complementing 'verbally' as another main way of expressing thoughts.

652. Venus didn't have any moons or satellites or even a............field, but it did have an atmosphere sort of similar to Earth's, except it was super-hot. **SSC Steno 10.12.2024 (Shift-II)**

(a) magnetic
(b) musicological
(c) pedagogic
(d) graphological

Ans. (a)

The correct option is 'magnetic'. Venus having a 'magnetic field' is the accurate scientific term to complete the sentence contextually.

Other options

Musicological is related to the scholarly study of music.

Pedagogic is related to teaching or education.

Graphological is related to handwriting analysis.

653. He is good..............for the job.
SSC Steno 10.12.2024 (Shift-II)

(a) partly (b) enough
(c) rather (d) altogether

Ans. (b)

The most appropriate adverb to fill in the blank is 'enough'. 'Enough' is used to indicate that the subject meets the required degree or standard for the job.

654. You can tell yourself that you would be willing to lose everything you have in order to get something you want: all of those things you're willing to lose are what make you .... **SSC Steno 10.12.2024 (Shift-II)**

(a) recognisable (b) unfortunately
(c) pessimist (d) distract

Ans. (a)

The most appropriate option is 'recognisable'.

The sentence implies that the things you're willing to lose are integral to your identity, making you recognisable. Other options do not fit the context.

655. I'm busy today. I'd rather we ....(has) the meeting tomorrow.
SSC Steno 10.12.2024 (Shift-II)

(a) had (b) has been
(c) had been (d) has

Ans. (a)

The correct form is 'had'. The sentence should read: 'I'd rather we had the meeting tomorrow.' 'Had' is the past subjunctive form used to express a preference for a different action or time.

656. One should keep......... surroundings neat and tidy. **SSC Steno 10.12.2024 (Shift-II)**

(a) ones (b) one's
(c) there (d) there's

Ans. (b)

The possessive pronoun 'one's' is used to indicate that the surroundings belong to the person referred to by 'one'. This matches the subject 'One' and is the appropriate possessive form.

657. The difference between a male and a female still ....in our society. In this era where women have such great achievements in every field, still in some sections of our community, a man is always termed as superior to women.
SSC Steno 10.12.2024 (Shift-II)

(a) insists (b) requires
(c) defects (d) persists

Ans. (d)

The word 'persists' means continues to exist, which accurately fits the context of the ongoing issue of gender difference in society. This word conveys the idea that the issue still exists despite progress in other areas.

Defects means flaws or imperfections.

658. If you are going to keep eating those cookies, you are going to ....your dinner.
SSC Steno 10.12.2024 (Shift-II)

(a) miss (b) cheer
(c) allow (d) mute

Ans. (a)

'Miss' is the most appropriate option. The phrase 'miss your dinner' implies that eating cookies will spoil your appetite, causing you to not eat your dinner.

659. Survival of mankind...........is in danger due to pollution.
SSC Steno 10.12.2024 (Shift-III)

(a) himself (b) itself
(c) herself (d) yourself

Ans. (b)

'Itself' is the appropriate pronoun to refer to the survival of mankind, maintaining the correct reflexive form.

660. ....the teacher entered the classroom, all the students stood up to greet him. **SSC Steno 10.12.2024 (Shift-III)**

(a) Yet
(b) Whereas
(c) Rather
(d) As soon as

Ans. (d)

'As soon as' is the correct option because it indicates an immediate action that occurred when the teacher entered the classroom.

661. Our chemistry teacher taught us how, through a chemical reaction, milk...........into curd.
SSC Steno 10.12.2024 (Shift-III)

(a) diverts (b) progresses
(c) happens (d) converts

Ans. (d)

'Converts' is the correct option because it means to change in form, substance, or function, fitting the context of milk turning into curd. The verb 'converts' accurately describes the chemical reaction process.

662. I always believe that ....is the best policy. **SSC Steno 10.12.2024 (Shift-III)**

(a) immorality
(b) honesty
(c) complexity
(d) sanctity

Ans. (b)

'Honesty' is the best policy. The phrase means that being truthful is the most effective way in the long run.

663. In the following passage, some words have been deleted. Read the passage carefully and select the most appropriate option to fill in each blank. Mount Vesuvius is ....(1).......... near Pompeii. It began to erupt and covered everything with stones and hot ash which fell like ....(2).......... from the sky. It ....(3).......... the city almost under 2 metres of volcanic molten material.
SSC Steno 10.12.2024 (Shift-III)

(a) (1) placed; (2) volcano; (3) hid
(b) (1) situated; (2) tornado; (3) treasured
(c) (1) located; (2) a blizzard; (3) buried
(d) (1) found; (2) hail; (3) ignored

Ans. (c)

'Located' fits the context of being placed near Pompeii, 'a blizzard' of hot ash is likened to the falling material, and 'buried' means to cover completely under molten material.

SSC Steno 2023

664. On 25th August, 1925, the Royal Commission on Indian Currency and Finance .... the establishment of the Central Bank of India.
SSC Steno 12.10.2023 (Shift-I)

(a) defined (b) figured
(c) censored (d) proposed

Ans.(d)

The given sentence presents that on 25th August, 1925, the Royal Commission on Indian Currency and Finance did something, Hence, the correct filler for the given blank is 'proposed'.

665. As the company's client base grew at an unexpected rate, management was forced tosome work until they could hire new staff. **SSC Steno 13.10.2023 (Shift-I)**

(a) man up
(b) dish out
(c) rat out
(d) farm out

Ans. (d)

The given sentence indicates that the company grew so quickly that they had to get help from other people who were no their full time employees.

Hence, the correct filler for the given blank is 'farm out'.

666. Select the most appropriate preposition to fill in the blank.
The boy jumped .... the sofa.
SSC Steno 13.10.2023 (Shift-I)

(a) on (b) of
(c) below (d) in

Ans. (a)

The correct filler for the given blank is 'on'.

667. My friend borrowed a large sum from me for investment in stocks but so far he hasn't had any considerable .... **SSC Steno 13.10.2023 (Shift-I)**

(a) profit (b) fund
(c) money (d) sum

Ans. (a)

The given sentence presents how a man borrowed money to earn profits but has failed to do so. Hence, the correct filler for the given blank is 'profit'.

668. Knowing that building the new park in the city centre would be a controversial issue, the mayor's office decided to let the public .... with their concerns.
SSC Steno 13.10.2023 (Shift-I)

(a) size up (b) fill up
(c) weigh in (d) beat to

Ans. (c)

The given sentence presents that after getting to know the reaction of people about building the new park in the city centre, the mayor's office decided something. Hence, the correct filler for the blank is 'weigh in' which means tried to understand.

02

Spotting the Error

Spotting the error or Error detection is a very important type of question asked in the SSC examination with generally 2-3 questions being asked from the topic.

Spotting the error questions are asked to test a candidate's knowledge of basic rules of grammar.

Types of Questions Asked

In SSC examination, a variety of questions are asked from spotting the error. These types are

Type 1

A sentence is given divided into three or four parts and the candidates are required to identify and select the option that is erroneous. If the given sentence is grammatically correct, they are required to mark 'No error' as their answer.

The museum's revolving doors (a)/ stopped the crooks (b)/ as they jam half way round. (c)/ No error (d) ***Ans.*** (c)

Type 2

A sentence is given with some parts underlined. There may be an error in the underlined segment of the sentence. Choose the part that contains the error.

He <u>could</u> not have <u>saw</u> the green of the shore <u>now but only</u> the tops of the blue hills.

(a) could (b) saw

(c) now (d) but only ***Ans.*** (b)

TYPE 3

Choose the grammatically correct sentence from the following.

(a) The Soul Company has greatly enhanced it's advertising expense.
(b) The Soul Company has greatly increased its advertising expense.
(c) The Soul Company has greatly enhanced its advertising expense.
(d) The Soul Company has greatly increased their advertising expense.

Ans. (b)

TYPE 4

Identify the option that rectifies the error in the given sentence.

My friend house is big, white but expensive.

(a) My friend house is big, white or expensive.
(b) My friend's house is big white so expensive.
(c) My friend's house is big, white and expensive.
(d) My friend house is big, white, nor expensive. ***Ans.*** (c)

How to Solve the Questions

To spot the errors in the sentence or to choose the grammatically correct sentence successfully, the very first thing that you need to do is to read the rules of grammar carefully (Refer to Chapter- Grammar at a Glance). Once you know all the rules, it becomes easy for you to find the error.

Here is a small step by step process that you should follow to solve the questions

- **Step 1** Read the complete sentence properly and carefully.
- **Step 2** Ensure that the sentence is meaningful and no word is incorrectly used.
- **Step 3** Make sure that the nouns, pronouns, verb forms, adverbs, prepositions and conjunctions used are correct. Pay attention to the placement of adverbs and adjectives.
- **Step 4** Give special focus to time expression such as during, for, since, last night, etc. These expression will help you identify the tense of the sentence. Also make sure that the correct tense structure is followed.
- **Step 5** Make sure that subject and the verb agrees and the pronouns used are according to the noun of the sentence.

While following these steps, you will find your answer.

SSC Exam Scanner

Directions (Q. Nos. 1-860) The following sentence has been divided into four segments. Identify the segment that contains an error.

or

Parts of the following sentence have been underlined and given as options. Select the option that contains an error.

or

Select the sentence that has a grammatical error.

SSC CGL 2024 (Tier 1 & 2)

1. It takes me an hour to get to work at the moment, but when the new road is finished it be much quicker.
SSC CGL Tier-2 18.01.2025
(a) It takes me an hour to get to work
(b) but when the new road is finished
(c) at the moment
(d) it be much quicker

Ans. (d)
The option containing an error is 'it be much quicker'. The correct form should be 'it will be much quicker'. The error is due to the missing auxiliary verb 'will' needed to form the future tense.

2. When I returned to the office, / no work was left / as my friend Rahul / has done everything.
SSC CGL Tier-2 20.01.2025
(a) When I returned to the office
(b) has done everything
(c) no work was left
(d) as my friend Rahul

Ans. (b)
The segment 'has done everything' contains a grammatical error. The correct phrase should be in the past perfect tense 'had done everything'.

3. I, you and she/have been working happily/in the same company and in the same branch/for the last nine years. **SSC CGL Tier-2 20.01.2025**
(a) I, you and she
(b) for the last nine years
(c) have been working happily
(d) in the same company and in the same branch

Ans. (a)
The segment 'I, you and she' contains a grammatical error.
The correct order should be 'you, she and I' to follow the appropriate pronoun order in English.

4. Mr. Abhilash and his family / have received / no informations / about the incident.
SSC CGL Tier-1 09.09.2024 (Shift-I)
(a) have received
(b) no informations
(c) about the incident
(d) Mr. Abhilash and his family

Ans. (b)
Part 'no informations' contains an error. The word 'information' is an uncountable nouns and thus, does not have a plural form.

5. My brother performed / extremely good / in the class test / held yesterday. **SSC CGL Tier-1 09.09.2024 (Shift-I)**
(a) held yesterday
(b) in the class test
(c) My brother performed
(d) extremely good

Ans. (d)
Part 'extremely good' contains an error. The expression is used to modify the verb 'performed' and hence, is an adverb phrase.
However, the word 'good' is used as an adjective. Hence, 'well' should be used to correct the sentence.

6. Every students in the hostel decided to travel to Delhi to witness the Republic Day Parade.
SSC CGL Tier-1 09.09.2024 (Shift-II)
(a) Republic Day Parade
(b) to witness the
(c) decided to travel to Delhi
(d) Every students in the hostel

Ans. (d)
Part 'Every students in the hostel' contains an error. The use of the plural 'students' with 'every' is incorrect. Because every is a singular subject in this sentence. Hence, replace it with 'student' to correct the sentence.

7. By this time next year / I will had graduated from college / and starting my first job / in the field of marketing.
SSC CGL Tier-1 09.09.2024 (Shift-II)
(a) in the field of marketing
(b) and starting my first job
(c) By this time next year
(d) I will had graduated from college

Ans. (d)
Part 'I will had graduated from college' contains an error. We do not use 'had' with 'will' the sentence is in future tense. Hence, replace it with 'have' to correct the sentence.

8. I are dancing with my husband at my sister's wedding.
SSC CGL Tier-1 09.09.2024 (Shift-III)
(a) husband at my (b) sister's wedding
(c) with my (d) I are dancing

Ans. (d)
Part 'I are dancing' contains an error. The pronoun 'I' takes the verb 'am.'

9. The tea at this cafe is best than at the Costa Cafe in our office.
SSC CGL Tier-1 09.09.2024 (Shift-III)
(a) at the Costa Cafe
(b) The tea at this cafe
(c) is best than
(d) in our office

Ans (c)
Part 'is best than' contains an error. As the sentence makes a comparison, 'better' should be used to correct the sentence.

10. After the concert was over, / they go to a restaurant, / had dinner together / and talked until midnight. **SSC CGL Tier-1 10.09.2024 (Shift-I)**
(a) had dinner together
(b) they go to a restaurant
(c) After the concert was over
(d) and talked until midnight

Ans. (b)
Part 'they go to a restaurant,' contains an error. As the sentence is in past tense, use 'went' in place of 'go' to correct the sentence.

11. Renewable energy / sources like solar and wind power / will replaced traditional fossil fuels / and help reduce carbon emissions.
SSC CGL Tier-1 10.09.2024 (Shift-I)
(a) and help reduce carbon emissions
(b) Renewable energy
(c) will replaced traditional fossil fuels
(d) sources like solar and wind power

Ans. (c)
Part 'will replaced traditional fossil fuels' contains an error. Add 'be' after 'will' to correct the sentence.

12. No other place in this country is so better as Gulmarg, Kashmir.
SSC CGL Tier-1 10.09.2024 (Shift-II)
(a) No other place
(b) in this country is
(c) so better as
(d) Gulmarg, Kashmir

Ans. (c)

Part 'so better as' contains an error. As the sentence presents a comparison, we should use the as.....as structure with the positive degree of adjective.

13. Our family is planning / a trip to Europe next summer / where we should visit several famous / landmarks and enjoy local cuisine. **SSC CGL Tier-1 10.09.2024 (Shift-II)**

(a) where we should visit several famous
(b) Our family is planning
(c) landmarks and enjoy local cuisine
(d) a trip to Europe next summer

Ans. (a)

Part 'where we should visit several famous' contains an error. The use of modal verb 'should' is incorrect in the sentence presenting future action. Hence, use of modal verb 'would' be correct.

14. My sister, Juliet, / got married / as her/was 23. **SSC CGL Tier-1 10.09.2024 (Shift-III)**

(a) was 23 (b) as her
(c) My sister, Juliet (d) got married

Ans. (b)

Part 'as her' contains an error. The use of objective pronoun 'her' is incorrect in the sentence. Hence, replace it with subjective case 'she' to correct the sentence.

15. The supermarket is open from 10 am still 10 pm. **SSC CGL Tier-1 10.09.2024 (Shift-III)**

(a) open
(b) from 10 am
(c) The supermarket
(d) still 10 pm

Ans. (d)

Part 'still 10 pm' contains an error. To mention a time duration using 'from', we use the preposition 'to' not 'still.'

16. It is he who work for the company for more than a decade. **SSC CGL Tier-1 11.09.2024 (Shift-I)**

(a) for more than a decade
(b) who work
(c) for the company
(d) It is he

Ans. (b)

Part 'who work' contains an error of tense.

The sentence should use the present perfect tense as the sentence states an action that has an effect on the present too. Hence, 'has worked' should be used to correct the sentence.

17. The windows / violent banged / during the / storm yesterday. **SSC CGL Tier-1 11.09.2024 (Shift-I)**

(a) during the
(b) The windows
(c) storm yesterday
(d) violent banged

Ans. (d)

Part 'violent banged' contains an error. The use of adjective 'violent' is incorrect as the sentence requires an adverb to modify the verb 'banged.' Hence, use 'violently' to correct the sentence.

18. Neither my brother nor my brothers-in-law / attended the meeting / as his health is not more good. **SSC CGL Tier-1 11.09.2024 (Shift-II)**

(a) Neither my brother nor my brothers-in-law
(b) attended the meeting
(c) No error
(d) as his health is not more good

Ans. (d)

Part 'as his health is not more good' contains an error. The use of 'his' for plural subject and the use of 'more' is incorrect. Hence, replace it with 'as their health is not much good' to correct the sentence.

19. Rahul thinks he is as smarter as his friends in the class. **SSC CGL Tier-1 11.09.2024 (Shift-II)**

(a) his friends
(b) he is as smarter as
(c) Rahul thinks
(d) in the class

Ans. (b)

Part 'he is as smarter as' contains an error. The structure 'as....as' takes the positive degree of adjective to make the comparison.

20. Solutions to the country's interior problems are still a long way away. **SSC CGL Tier-1 11.09.2024 (Shift-III)**

(a) problems are still
(b) a long way away
(c) Solutions to
(d) the country's interior

Ans. (d)

Part 'the country's interior' contains an error. The use of the word 'interior' is incorrect in the context of the sentence. Use the word 'internal' to correct the sentence.

21. They secret / decided / to leave / the town. **SSC CGL Tier-1 11.09.2024 (Shift-III)**

(a) They secret (b) decided
(c) the town (d) to leave

Ans. (a)

Part 'they secret' contains an error. The use of 'secret' is incorrect in the sentence. It should be as an adverb i.e., 'secretly.'

22. He ran quick to catch the bus. **SSC CGL Tier-1 12.09.2024 (Shift-I)**

(a) quiet (b) rapid
(c) insipid (d) quickly

Ans. (d)

The sentence contains an error. The use of 'quick' is erroneous as the sentence requires an adverb. Hence, replace it with 'quickly' to correct the sentence.

23. Mrs. Sreelakshmi's / musical intelligence / is superior than / Mrs. Suma's. **SSC CGL Tier-1 12.09.2024 (Shift-I)**

(a) Mrs. Suma's
(b) musical intelligence
(c) is superior than
(d) Mrs. Sreelakshmi's

Ans. (c)

Part 'is superior than' contains an error. When we make a comparison using the word 'superior', we do not use 'than' but use 'to.'

24. The employees were comfortable / with me and they talked about / their problems since / I has worked there as a manager. **SSC CGL Tier-1 12.09.2024 (Shift-II)**

(a) I has worked there as a manager
(b) with me and they talked about
(c) their problems since
(d)The employees were comfortable

Ans. (a)

Part 'I has worked there as a manager' contains an error. The correct tense for this part of the sentence will be present perfect continuous tense i.e., 'I have been working.'

25. Mr. Arun / will pay dear / for his / financial mistake. **SSC CGL Tier-1 12.09.2024 (Shift-II)**

(a) will pay dear (b) Mr. Arun
(c) for his (d) financial mistake

Ans. (a)

Part 'will pay dear' contains an error. The use of the word 'dear' is incorrect in the sentence. Replace it with adverb 'dearly' to correct the sentence.

26. My brother received / his MBA degree into / the university last year. **SSC CGL Tier-1 12.09.2024 (Shift-III)**

(a) the university last year
(b) his MBA degree into
(c) No error
(d) My brother received

Ans. (b)

Part 'his MBA degree into' contains an error.

The use of preposition 'into' is incorrect in the sentence. Hence, use 'from' to correct the sentence.

27. He replied / in a dry tone, / "Ouch! I will not work / for you anymore."

SSC CGL Tier-1 12.09.2024 (Shift-III)

(a) in a dry tone,
(b) He replied
(c) for you anymore."
(d) "Ouch! I will not work

Ans. (d)

Part 'Ouch! I will not work' contains an error. The use of the interjection 'ouch' is incorrect in the sentence.

28. Mr. Surya / have no interior / motive in offering / you support.

(a) Mr. Surya

SSC CGL Tier-1 13.09.2024 (Shift-I)

(b) you support.
(c) motive in offering
(d) have no interior

Ans. (d)

Part 'have no interior' contains an error of Subject-Verb agreement. As the subject of the sentence, Mr. Surya, is singular, singular verb 'has' should be used to correct the sentence.

29. By the end of / this month, he / will been working / for five years.

SSC CGL Tier-1 13.09.2024 (Shift-I)

(a) for five years
(b) will been working
(c) By the end of
(d) this month, he

Ans. (b)

Part 'will been working' contains an error. As the sentence talks of an action that started in the past, is continuing and will continue in the future, future perfect continuous tense 'will have been working' should be used.

30. I have the hundred reasons to not attend the meeting tomorrow.

SSC CGL Tier-1 13.09.2024 (Shift-II)

(a) I have the hundred reasons
(b) the meeting
(c) tomorrow
(d) to not attend

Ans. (a)

Part 'I have the hundred reasons' contains an error. The use of definite article 'the' is incorrect in the sentence. Use 'a' or no article to correct the sentence.

31. After I retire, I started a second career / as a writer and published several books / which allowed me to share my stories / and insights with a wider audience.

SSC CGL Tier-1 13.09.2024 (Shift-II)

(a) and insights with a wider audience
(b) After I retire, I started a second career
(c) as a writer and published several books
(d) which allowed me to share my stories

Ans. (b)

Part 'After I retire, I started a second career' contains an error of tense. The sentence is in past tense. Hence, 'retire' will be changed to 'retired.'

32. Although the team had trained diligently for months, they had still overwhelmed by the opponent's unexpected tactics.

SSC CGL Tier-1 13.09.2024 (Shift-III)

(a) No error
(b) had still overwhelmed
(c) trained diligently
(d) for months

Ans. (b)

Part 'had still overwhelmed' contains an error. The use of 'had' is incorrect in the given sentence. Replace it with 'was' to correct the sentence.

33. Due to the pandemic, / the prices of / medicines increased / everyday since / last December.

SSC CGL Tier-1 13.09.2024 (Shift-III)

(a) everyday since
(b) medicines increased
(c) last December.
(d) the prices of

Ans. (b)

Part 'medicines increased' contains an error. As the sentence presents an action started in the past and still continuing in the present, present perfect continuous tense 'medicines has been increasing' should be used.

34. UNESCO works to / strengthen an intellectual / and moral solidarity / of humankind.

SSC CGL Tier-1 17.09.2024 (Shift-I)

(a) strengthen an intellectual
(b) of humankind.
(c) UNESCO works to
(d) and moral solidarity

Ans. (a)

Part 'strengthen an intellectual' contains an error. Remove 'an' as it is not needed with adjectives.

35. Dr. Sinha has / brought about a new / book on social / impact of child labour.

SSC CGL Tier-1 17.09.2024 (Shift-I)

(a) impact of child labour
(b) book on social
(c) brought about a new
(d) Dr. Sinha has

Ans. (c)

Part 'brought about a new' contains an error. The use of preposition 'about' is not needed in the sentence. Hence, remove 'about' to correct the sentence.

36. (a) It is said that Joseph was not ready to go to war.
(b) Karl Marx was a renowned social scientist.
(c) Indian force are known for their loyalty and integrity.
(d) It is impossible to wake Christine up in the morning.

SSC CGL Tier-1 17.09.2024 (Shift-II)

Ans (c)

The grammatically correct sentence is- Indian force are known for their loyalty and integrity. As the subject of the sentence is singular- Indian Force. Hence, singular verb 'is' should be used in place of 'are.'

37. The principal gave up / the prizes to / the winners on / Republic Day.

SSC CGL Tier-1 17.09.2024 (Shift-II)

(a) The principal gave up
(b) the winners on
(c) the prizes to
(d) Republic Day

Ans. (a)

Part 'The principal gave up' contains an error. The phrasal verb 'gave up' means to refuse ownership. Hence, it should be replaced with 'gave out' which means to distribute.

38. Brr, the city view from the Eiffel Tower is amazing!

SSC CGL Tier-1 17.09.2024 (Shift-III)

(a) amazing (b) from (c) view (d) Brr

Ans (d)

Part 'Brr' is erroneous for the emotion of amazement presented by the sentence. Hence, use 'wow' to correct the sentence.

39. Having known that / the train was already on the platform, / they ran fastly / to catch it.

SSC CGL Tier-1 17.09.2024 (Shift-III)

(a) they ran fastly
(b) Having known that
(c) the train was already on the platform
(d) to catch it.

Ans (a)

Part 'they ran fastly' contains an error. The use of 'fastly' is incorrect and must be replaced with 'fast' to correct the sentence.

40. Deepa and Seema are both good with running, but Deepa is also good at catching the ball and throwing it to the right corner in time. **SSC CGL Tier-1 18.09.2024 (Shift-I)**

(a) to the right corner
(b) at catching the ball
(c) good with running
(d) in time

Ans. (c)

Part 'good with running' contains an error. The use of preposition 'with' is incorrect in the context of the sentence. Use 'at' to correct the sentence.

41. People admired him, for / he lived by the same principals / that he preached. **SSC CGL Tier-1 18.09.2024 (Shift-II)**

(a) that he preached
(b) No error
(c) he lived by the same principals
(d) People admired him, for

Ans. (c)

Part 'he lived by the same principals' contains an error. The use of 'principals' is incorrect in the sentence. It should be 'principles.'

42. We were on the way/ to the party;/ suddenly, there/ will a heavy downpour.
SSC CGL Tier-1 18.09.2024 (Shift-II)

(a) to the party;
(b) We were on the way
(c) will a heavy downpour
(d) suddenly, there

Ans. (c)

Part 'will a heavy downpour' contains an error. As the sentence is in past tense, use of 'was' is appropriate in place of 'will.'

43. He never talks / for anybody. / He is alone / all day.
SSC CGL Tier-1 18.09.2024 (Shift-III)

(a) He is alone
(b) for anybody
(c) He never talks
(d) all day

Ans (b)

Part 'for anybody' contains an error and should be replaced it with 'to somebody' to correct the sentence.

44. The police told the agitators to back in, else they would lathi-charge.
SSC CGL Tier-1 19.09.2024 (Shift-I)

(a) lathi-charge
(b) else they would
(c) the agitators to back in
(d) The police told

Ans (c)

Part 'the agitators to back in' contains an error.

The use of preposition 'in' is incorrect in the sentence. Use 'off' to correct the sentence.

45. We took dinner in a Chinese restaurant and were amazed to see the interior of a restaurant.
SSC CGL Tier-1 19.09.2024 (Shift-I)

(a) and were amazed to see
(b) the interior of a restaurant
(c) We took dinner
(d) in a Chinese restaurant

Ans (b)

Part 'the interior of a restaurant' contains an error. The use of article 'a' is incorrect. Hence, use 'the' as the restaurant is already being referred to.

46. Mr. Ali's shop / is further to / the hospital. **SSC CGL Tier-1 19.09.2024 (Shift-II)**

(a) is further to (b) No error
(c) Mr. Ali's shop (d) the hospital

Ans (a)

Part 'is further to' contains an error. The use of preposition 'to' is incorrect in the sentence. The correct preposition will be 'away.'

47. It rain a lot in this part of the country. **SSC CGL Tier-1 19.09.2024 (Shift-II)**

(a) of the country (b) It rain
(c) a lot (d) in this part

Ans (b)

Part 'it rain' contains an error of subject verb agreement. The word 'it' is singular. Hence, singular verb 'rains' should be used to correct the sentence.

48. She sings good.
SSC CGL Tier-1 19.09.2024 (Shift-III)

(a) better (b) best
(c) goodly (d) well

Ans (d)

The sentence contains an error. The use of adjective 'good' is incorrect to modify the verb 'sings.' Hence, it should be replaced with adverb 'well.'

49. In some countries, you are not able to drink until you are 21.
SSC CGL Tier-1 19.09.2024 (Shift-III)

(a) In some countries
(b) able to drink
(c) until you are 21
(d) you are not

Ans (b)

Part 'able to drink' contains an error. The use of 'able' is incorrect in the context of the sentence. The correct word to be used in the sentence is 'allowed.'

50. Two of the world's / best forwards / has played alongside / David Beckham. **SSC CGL Tier-1 23.09.2024 (Shift-I)**

(a) Two of the world's
(b) David Beckham.
(c) best forwards
(d) has played alongside

Ans (d)

Part 'has played alongside' contains an error of subject-verb agreement. As the subject of the sentence, two of the world's best forwards', the verb will be plural. Hence, 'have' should be used in place of 'has' to correct the sentence.

51. Ourselves should not boast of one's knowledge.
SSC CGL Tier-1 23.09.2024 (Shift-I)

(a) one's (b) boast
(c) Ourselves (d) knowledge

Ans (c)

Part 'ourselves' contains an error. 'Ourselves' can never form the subject of the sentence. Hence, it should be replaced with pronoun 'We' to correct the sentence.

52. He always wants to be in the company of those who are intellectually superior than him.
SSC CGL Tier-1 23.09.2024 (Shift-II)

(a) superior than him.
(b) be in the company of
(c) He always wants to
(d) those who are intellectually

Ans (a)

Part 'superior than him' contains an error. The word 'superior' takes 'to' to make the comparison and not 'than.'

53. I have sing 'Let It Go' before a crowd of thousands of people.
SSC CGL Tier-1 23.09.2024 (Shift-II)

(a) a crowd of (b) thousands of people
(c) I have sing (d) 'Let It Go' before

Ans (c)

Part 'I have sing' contains an error. The verb 'has/have' takes past participle form of the verb. Hence, use 'sung' to correct the sentence.

54. Mr. Suman / asked me / to pack / my luggages.
SSC CGL Tier-1 23.09.2024 (Shift-III)

(a) asked me (b) my luggages.
(c) to pack (d) Mr. Suman

Ans (b)

Part 'my luggages' contains an error. The word 'luggage' is an uncountable noun and thus, does not have any plural form. It is used as luggage in both singular and plural cases.

55. Camels tend to move slowly than other domestic animals in the plains. **SSC CGL Tier-1 24.09.2024 (Shift-I)**

(a) domestic animals in the plains.
(b) than other
(c) move slowly
(d) Camels tend to

Ans (c)

Part 'move slowly' contains an error. As the sentence makes a comparison, use 'move slower' to correct the sentence.

56. Deepak is studying B.tech. at IIT Delhi to become the engineer. **SSC CGL Tier-1 24.09.2024 (Shift-II)**

(a) B.tech. at IIT Delhi
(b) the engineer.
(c) to become
(d) Deepak is studying

Ans (b)

Part 'the engineer' contains an error. The use of 'the' is incorrect with 'engineer' and should be replaced by 'an' to correct the sentence.

57. Master Sam / is a heaviest / boy in / grade twelve. **SSC CGL Tier-1 24.09.2024 (Shift-II)**

(a) boy in (b) Master Sam
(c) grade twelve (d) is a heaviest

Ans (d)

Part 'is a heaviest' contains an error. Superlative degree of adjective take definite article 'the.'

58. Jerry driving / home late / when the incident / took place. **SSC CGL Tier-1 24.09.2024 (Shift-III)**

(a) took place.
(b) when the incident
(c) Jerry driving
(d) home late

Ans (c)

Part 'Jerry driving' contains an error. As the sentence is in past continuous tense, 'was' will be added before 'driving' to correct the sentence.

59. The lions became violently / when the visitors / started throwing / stones at them. **SSC CGL Tier-1 24.09.2024 (Shift-III)**

(a) stones at them.
(b) The lions became violently
(c) started throwing
(d) when the visitors

Ans (b)

Part 'The lions became violently' contains an error. The use of 'violently' is incorrect in the sentence and it should be replaced with 'violent.'

60. My dog / barks / very louder / at night. **SSC CGL Tier-1 25.09.2024 (Shift-I)**

(a) My dog (b) very louder
(c) barks (d) at night

Ans (b)

Part 'very louder' contains an error. The use of 'louder' is incorrect in the sentence and adverb 'loudly' should be used to correct the sentence.

61. The company specialises at / designing, crafting and manufacturing / exquisite, high-quality furniture / of exceptional craftsmanship. **SSC CGL Tier-1 25.09.2024 (Shift-I)**

(a) exquisite, high-quality furniture
(b) designing, crafting and manufacturing
(c) The company specialises at
(d) of exceptional craftsmanship

Ans (c)

Part 'The company specialises at' contains an error. The uses of preposition 'at' is incorrect. Use 'in' to correct the sentence.

62. He and his friends / does not / want to / attend the meeting. **SSC CGL Tier-1 25.09.2024 (Shift-II)**

(a) does not
(b) want to
(c) attend the meeting
(d) He and his friends

Ans (a)

Part 'does not' contains an error. The subject of the sentence is plural, so the verb should also be plural. Hence, replace 'does' with 'do' to correct the sentence.

63. In the recent past, the IT industry has emerged / as a major contributor to an industry revenue / as well as employment / opportunity provider in the country. **SSC CGL Tier-1 25.09.2024 (Shift-II)**

(a) opportunity provider in the country.
(b) In the recent past, the IT industry has emerged
(c) as a major contributor to an industry revenue
(d) as well as employment

Ans (c)

Part 'as a major contributor to an industry revenue' contains an error. The use of 'an' is incorrect in the sentence. Use 'the' in place of 'an' to correct the sentence.

64. While I was walking to the store, my friend calls me and ask for a favour. **SSC CGL Tier-1 25.09.2024 (Shift-III)**

(a) While I was walking
(b) my friend calls me and ask
(c) to the store
(d) for a favour.

Ans (b)

Part 'my friend calls me and ask' contains an error. As the sentence is in past tense, 'called and asked' should be used to correct the sentence.

65. Please go and meet the chairperson. / She will be / away for the/ few next days. **SSC CGL Tier-1 25.09.2024 (Shift-III)**

(a) She will be
(b) away for the
(c) few next days.
(d) Please go and meet the chairperson.

Ans (c)

Part 'few next days' contains an error. To correct it, the words would change order to 'next few days.'

66. The teacher asked him not to keep disturbing the class, but it had no affect. **SSC CGL Tier-1 26.09.2024 (Shift-I)**

(a) but it had no affect.
(b) him not to keep
(c) disturbing the class,
(d) The teacher asked

Ans (a)

Part 'but it had no affect' contains an error. The use of noun 'affect' is incorrect in the sentence. It should be 'effect' to correct the sentence.

67. My colleague always works latest than me. **SSC CGL Tier-1 26.09.2024 (Shift-II)**

(a) My colleague (b) latest
(c) always works (d) than me

Ans (b)

Part 'latest' contains an error. As the sentence makes a comparison, the comparative degree of adjective 'later' should be used to correct the sentence.

68. He was / bad injured / in the / last match. **SSC CGL Tier-1 26.09.2024 (Shift-III)**

(a) last match (b) in the
(c) bad injured (d) He was

Ans (c)

Part 'bad injured' contains an error. The use of adjective to modify the verb 'injured' is incorrect. Hence, use 'badly' to correct the sentence.

69. My sister and I / work very hard / nevertheless my brother does not do / any task assigned to him.
SSC CGL Tier-1 26.09.2024 (Shift-III)
(a) nevertheless my brother does not do
(b) work very hard
(c) any task assigned to him.
(d) My sister and I

Ans (a)

Part 'nevertheless my brother does not do' contains an error. The use of conjunction 'nevertheless' is incorrect. Hence, replace it with 'but.'

SSC CGL 2023 (Tier 1 & 2)

70. Neetu have been / waiting for me / since 10 o'clock / in the morning.
SSC CGL Tier-1 14.07.2023 (Shift-I)
(a) Neetu have been (b) in the morning
(c) since 10 o'clock (d) waiting for me

Ans. (a)

The part 'Neetu have been' contains an error of verb form. As the subject is singular, verb should also be singular. Hence, to correct the sentence, replace 'have' with 'has.'

71. (a) The participants of the competition are waiting for their turn curiously.
(b) The participants of the competition has been waiting for their turn curiously.
(c) A participants of the competition is waiting for their turn curiously.
(d) The participants of the competition is waiting for their turn curiously.
SSC CGL Tier-1 14.07.2023 (Shift-I)

Ans. (a)

Participants is a plural noun, so it requires the plural verb are waiting.

Options (b) and (d) incorrectly use has and is with a plural subject, which is grammatically incorrect. Option (c) incorrectly uses a participants, which mixes singular a with plural participants.

Hence, the correct sentence is given by option (a).

72. After knowing truth, / the jury took the right decision / in the case.
SSC CGL Tier-1 14.07.2023 (Shift-II)
(a) the jury took the right decision
(b) in the case
(c) after knowing truth
(d) No error

Ans. (c)

The part (c) 'after knowing truth' contains the error of article. Definite article 'the' is used before referring to something specific. To correct the sentence, add 'the' before 'truth.'

73. Darshan wished he hadn't / went to the theme park / in the first place.
SSC CGL Tier-1 14.07.2023 (Shift-III)
(a) Darshan wished he hadn't
(b) in the first place
(c) went to the theme park
(d) No error

Ans. (c)

The phrase 'went to the theme park' is incorrect. It should be 'gone to the theme park' because 'hadn't' requires the past participle form of the verb.

74. The availability of funds will be / ensured if they all tried to / submit the proposals on time.
SSC CGL Tier-1 14.07.2023 (Shift-IV)
(a) The availability of funds will be
(b) No error
(c) submit the proposals on time
(d) ensured if they all tried to

Ans. (d)

The part (d) 'ensured if they all tried to' contains an error.

The use of the verb form 'tried' is incorrect, because the sentence is in future tense. To correct the sentence, replace it with 'try.'

75. A. It is a nice party. I am enjoying the party.
B. It is a party. I am enjoying an party.
C. It is party. I am enjoying a party.
D. It is the party. I am enjoying an party. SSC CGL Tier-1 14.07.2023 (Shift-IV)
(a) D (b) C (c) B (d) A

Ans. (d)

The grammatically correct sentence is 'It is a nice party. I am enjoying the party.' The use of articles in sentences B, C, and D is incorrect. 'An party' should be 'a party' because 'party' starts with a consonant sound. 'It is party' should be 'It is a party' for correct article usage. 'It is the party' is contextually incorrect because 'the' specifies something already known, which isn't set up in the sentence.

76. He promised them / that he would sure repay / the loan urgently.
SSC CGL Tier-1 17.07.2023 (Shift-I)
(a) No error
(b) He promised them
(c) the loan urgently
(d) that he would sure repay

Ans. (d)

Part (d) 'that he would sure repay' contains an error. The use of 'sure' is incorrect and must be replaced by 'surely' to make the sentence correct.

77. Karan call the restaurant / to ask if he could / reserve a table for tomorrow SSC CGL Tier-1 17.07.2023 (Shift-I)
(a) Karan call the restaurant
(b) reserve a table for tomorrow
(c) to ask if he could
(d) No error

Ans. (a)

Part (a) 'Karan call the restaurant' contains an error. The sentence is in past tense.
Therefore 'call' should be replaced by 'called' to make the sentence error free.

78. (a) She is a Indian artist married to an European engineer.
SSC CGL Tier-1 17.07.2023 (Shift-II)
(b) She is an Indian artist married to an European engineer.
(c) She is an Indian artist married to a European engineer.
(d) She is a Indian artist married to a European engineer.

Ans. (c)

The sentence which uses the indefinite article correctly is 'She is an Indian artist married to a European engineer.' The article 'an' is used before 'Indian' as it begins with a vowel sound while article 'a' is used before 'European' as it begins with a non-vowel sound.

79. She always / invite me / to / dinner.
SSC CGL Tier-1 17.07.2023 (Shift-II)
(a) She always (b) to
(c) dinner (d) invite me

Ans. (d)

Part (d) 'invite me' contains the error of subject-verb agreement. Singular subject 'she' will take singular verb 'invites.' To correct it, replace 'invite' with 'invites.'

80. A. The Supriya is the best girl in the class.
B. Supriya is the best girl in the class.
C. Supriya is best girl in the class.
D. The Supriya is a best girl in the class. SSC CGL Tier-1 17.07.2023 (Shift-III)
(a) C (b) A (c) D (d) B

Ans. (d)

The grammatically correct sentence is 'Supriya is the best girl in the class.' Definite article 'the' is used before superlative degree of adjective.

81. I think Jeremy will not/have save enough money/by the time/the year ends. SSC CGL Tier-1 17.07.2023 (Shift-III)
(a) the year ends
(b) have save enough money
(c) by the time
(d) I think Jeremy will not

Ans. (b)

Part (b) 'have save enough money' contains an error. To correct it, replace 'save' with 'saved.' The part 'have save enough money' contains an error. To correct it, replace 'save' with 'saved' because has/have takes the past participle form of the verb. So, it should be 'have saved enough money.'

82. A. It is a old uniform but a memorable thing for me.
B. It is old uniform but a memorable thing for me.
C. It is the old uniform but memorable thing for me.
D. It is an old uniform but a memorable thing for me.
SSC CGL Tier-1 17.07.2023 (Shift-IV)

(a) D (b) C (c) B (d) A

Ans. (a)

The grammatically correct sentence is 'It is an old uniform but a memorable thing for me.' The indefinite article 'an' is used before a word starting with a vowel sound.

83. (a) She purchased a apple in the market with me.
(b) She purchased an apple in the market with me.
(c) She purchased apple in the market with me.
(d) She purchase a apple in the market with me. SSC CGL Tier-1 18.07.2023 (Shift-I)

Ans. (b)

The sentence with the correct use of indefinite article is 'She purchased an apple in the market with me.' The article 'an' is used before a word starting with a vowel sound.

84. Sajni had / interfere in / this matter.
SSC CGL Tier-1 18.07.2023 (Shift-I)

(a) interfere in (b) No error
(c) this mater (d) Sajni had

Ans. (a)

Part (a) 'interfere in' contains an error. As the sentence is in past tense, 'interfere in' should be replaced by 'interfered in' to make the sentence correct.

85. I fell / asleep while / I read / the book. SSC CGL Tier-1 18.07.2023 (Shift-II)

(a) the book (b) I read
(c) asleep while (d) I fell

Ans. (b)

Part (b) 'I read' contains an error of tense. To correct the sentence, replace it with 'I was reading' as the use of 'while' indicates that the action was ongoing or continuous.

86. I can't talk right now. / I am being really busy. / I'll call you later.
SSC CGL Tier-1 18.07.2023 (Shift-II)

(a) I can't talk right now
(b) I am being really busy
(c) No error
(d) I'll call you later

Ans. (b)

Part (b) 'I am being really busy' contains an error.

The given sentence is in simple present tense. Hence, the use of 'being' is incorrect and it must be removed to correct the sentence.

87. Aniket lives (A) / in the small apartment (B) / in the suburbs (C).
SSC CGL Tier-1 18.07.2023 (Shift-III)

(a) C (b) No error
(c) B (d) A

Ans. (c)

Part (B) of the given sentence contains an error. The use of article 'the' is incorrect in the context of the sentence because definite article 'the' is only used when referring to something specific. Hence, to correct the sentence, replace 'the' with 'a.'

88. The present-century threats to our environment, / which include interfering species, ailments, pollution and / a boiling temperature, were putting wildlife populations at peril.
SSC CGL Tier-1 18.07.2023 (Shift-III)

(a) which include interfering species, ailments, pollution and
(b) The present-century threats to our environment
(c) a boiling temperature, were putting wildlife populations at peril
(d) No error

Ans. (c)

Part (c) 'a boiling temperature, were putting wildlife populations at peril' is incorrect.

To correct it, replace 'populations' with 'population.' 'Population' is a collective noun, so the correct phrase should be 'a boiling temperature, were putting wildlife population at peril.'

89. My mother said / that Ben will done / the assignment / today.
SSC CGL Tier-1 18.07.2023 (Shift-IV)

(a) today
(b) My mother said
(c) that Ben will done
(d) the assignment

Ans. (c)

Part (c) 'that Ben will done' contains the error of verb form. The use of 'done' is incorrect and must be replaced with 'do' to make the sentence correct.

90. Mr. Ram Kumar, the cashier are / on temporary withdrawal / from service. SSC CGL Tier-1 18.07.2023 (Shift-IV)

(a) on temporary withdrawal
(b) Mr. Ram Kumar, the cashier are
(c) from service
(d) No error

Ans. (b)

Part (b) 'Mr. Ram Kumar, the cashier are' contains the error of subject-verb agreement. According to the subject-verb agreement, if the subject is singular, the verb will also be singular. Hence, 'is' should be used in place of 'are.'

91. (a) The rider who met with a accident was not wearing a helmet, the police said. SSC CGL Tier-1 19.07.2023 (Shift-I)
(b) The rider who met with an accident was not wearing an helmet, the police said.
(c) A rider who met with the accident was not wearing the helmet, an police said.
(d) The rider who met with the accident was not wearing a helmet, the police said.

Ans. (d)

The grammatically correct sentence is 'The rider who met with the accident was not wearing a helmet, the police said.' Options A, B and C have incorrect article usage: 'a accident' should be 'an accident' due to the vowel sound and 'an helmet' should be 'a helmet' because 'h' in 'helmet' is pronounced.

92. "Do you want to join us for lunch?" / "I'm sorry / my Physics class will start at 1 pm / and doesn't finish till 3 pm". SSC CGL Tier-1 19.07.2023 (Shift-I)

(a) my Physics class will start at 1 pm
(b) I'm sorry
(c) and doesn't finish till 3 pm
(d) Do you want to join us for lunch?

Ans. (a)

Part (a) 'my Physics class will start at 1 pm' contains the error of tense. As the sentence is in simple present tense, 'will start' must be replaced by 'starts' to make the sentence correct.

93. Sky appears blue / as it absorbs / all colours and / reflects only blue.
SSC CGL Tier-1 19.07.2023 (Shift-II)

(a) reflects only blue
(b) all colours and
(c) Sky appears blue
(d) as it absorbs

Ans. (c)

Part (c) 'Sky appears blue' contains an error of article. Add article 'The' before 'sky' to correct the sentence.

94. A celestial body or astronomical object is / a naturally occurring physical thing, association / or configuration that happens in the visible universe.

SSC CGL Tier-1 19.07.2023 (Shift-II)

(a) No error
(b) A celestial body or astronomical object is
(c) or configuration that happens in the visible universe
(d) a naturally occurring physical thing, association

Ans. (a)

The given sentence is grammatically correct and contextually meaningful.

95. Pritha will been cooking / the meal of your choice / before you / reach home. **SSC CGL Tier-1 19.07.2023 (Shift-III)**

(a) reach home
(b) Pritha will been cooking
(c) the meal of your choice
(d) before you

Ans. (b)

Part (b) 'Pritha will been cooking' contains the error of verb. We do not use 'been' with 'will.' Hence, 'been' must be replaced with 'be.'

96. She rarely approached nobody / to talk about the problems / that she was facing.

SSC CGL Tier-1 19.07.2023 (Shift-III)

(a) No error
(b) that she was facing
(c) She rarely approached nobody
(d) to talk about the problems

Ans. (c)

Part (c) 'She rarely approached nobody' contains the error of pronoun. To correct it, replace 'nobody' with 'anybody.'

97. The Dutta company <u>has not</u> <u>being</u> making new school bags <u>since</u> the lockdown <u>commenced</u>.

SSC CGL Tier-1 19.07.2023 (Shift-IV)

(a) since (b) has not
(c) being (d) commenced

Ans. (c)

The word 'being' is incorrect in the context of the sentence because the given sentence is in present perfect tense. Hence, 'being' must be removed and replaced with 'been' to correct the sentence.

98. It was (A) / by a chance (B) / he saw a movie in a theatre (C).

SSC CGL Tier-1 19.07.2023 (Shift-IV)

(a) A (b) C
(c) B (d) No error

Ans. (c)

Part (B) of the given sentence contains the error.

The article 'a' is not used in the phrase 'by chance.' Remove 'a' to correct the sentence.

99. My students / had expect / guidance from my end.

SSC CGL Tier-1 20.07.2023 (Shift-I)

(a) had expect
(b) guidance from my end
(c) My students
(d) No error

Ans. (a)

Part (a) 'had expect' has an error. As the sentence is in past perfect tense, 'expect' must be replaced by 'expected' to correct the sentence.

100. One of these / boxes have / the portrait / of the heiress.

SSC CGL Tier-1 20.07.2023 (Shift-I)

(a) boxes have (b) of the heiress
(c) the portrait (d) One of these

Ans. (a)

Part (a) 'boxes have' has an error of subject-verb agreement. As the subject is a singular and is referring to 'one' of the books, the verb must also be singular.

Hence, 'have' must be replaced with 'has' to correct the sentence.

101. You can fool some of the people all the time/and all the people some of the time/but you cannot fool all the people all the time.

SSC CGL Tier-1 20.07.2023 (Shift-II)

(a) No error
(b) You can fool some of the people all the time
(c) and all the people some of the time
(d) but you cannot fool all the people all the time.

Ans. (a)

The given sentence is grammatically correct and contextually meaningful.

102. Hardik's horoscope says / that the stars / will be exercised / a benign influence on his life.

SSC CGL Tier-1 20.07.2023 (Shift-III)

(a) will be exercised
(b) Hardik's horoscope says
(c) that the stars
(d) a benign influence on his life

Ans. (a)

Part (a) 'will be exercised' contains an error of tense. The given sentence is referring to a situation in simple future tense. To correct it, replace it with 'will exercise.'

103. A. Today is sixth day of our workshop. All the participants are highly enthusiastic.
B. Today is a sixth day of our workshop. All the participants are highly enthusiastic.
C. Today is the sixth day of our workshop. All the participants are highly enthusiastic.
D. Today is sixth day of our workshop. All participants are highly enthusiastic.

SSC CGL Tier-1 20.07.2023 (Shift-III)

(a) D (b) C
(c) B (d) A

Ans. (b)

The grammatically correct sentence is 'Today is the sixth day of our workshop. All the participants are highly enthusiastic.' Sentences (A), (B) and (D) do not have the correct use of the articles.

104. I <u>had gone</u> to Siliguri <u>before</u> I <u>go</u> to Raiganj. **SSC CGL Tier-1 20.07.2023 (Shift-IV)**

(a) go (b) before
(c) had (d) gone

Ans. (*)

The part of the sentence which contains an error is 'had gone.' It is not correct as the sentence is in past perfect tense. To correct the sentence, replace 'had gone' with 'will go.'

105. Identify the sentence that correctly uses the indefinite article.

SSC CGL Tier-1 20.07.2023 (Shift-IV)

(a) I have never seen an UFO in an English movie.
(b) I have never seen a UFO in a English movie.
(c) I have never seen a UFO in an English movie.
(d) I have never seen an UFO in a English movie.

Ans. (c)

The sentence with correct use of indefinite article is 'I have never seen a UFO in an English movie.'

The indefinite article 'a' will be used before 'UFO' because the beginning sound is not a vowel while 'an' would come before 'English' as the word begins with a vowel sound.

106. He will/return/in a/hour.
SSC CGL Tier-1 21.07.2023 (Shift-I)
(a) return (b) He will
(c) hour (d) in a

Ans. (d)

Part (d) 'in a' contains the error of article.

Article 'an' is used with words that start with a vowel sound. Hence, 'a' should be replaced by 'an' to correct the sentence.

107. Binay said that / he is coming / from / his village, Jaygarh.
SSC CGL Tier-1 21.07.2023 (Shift-II)
(a) from
(b) he is coming
(c) his village, Jaygarh
(d) Binay said that

Ans. (b)

Part (b) 'he is coming' contains the error of verb form. As the given sentence is in indirect speech, past form of the verb should be used. Hence, to correct the sentence, replace 'is coming' with 'was coming.'

108. She was waiting/for a opportunity/to start her/own business. SSC CGL Tier-1 21.07.2023 (Shift-II)
(a) own business
(b) to start her
(c) for a opportunity
(d) she was waiting

Ans. (c)

Part (c) 'for a opportunity' contains the error of article. Article 'an' is used with words starting with a vowel sound. Hence, to correct the sentence, replace 'a' with 'an.'

109. If things were not going to be normal / after the pandemic, mankind will / have to accept the new normal.
SSC CGL Tier-1 21.07.2023 (Shift-III)
(a) after the pandemic, mankind will
(b) have to accept the new normal
(c) If things were not going to be normal
(d) No error

Ans. (c)

Part (c) 'If things were not going to be normal' contains an error. The use of 'were' is incorrect in the context of the sentence.

Hence, it must be replaced with 'are' to make the sentence correct.

110. This will be most difficult of/ the adjustments we have to make/ because we have been used to/ spending a lot on guests.
SSC CGL Tier-1 21.07.2023 (Shift-III)
(a) spending a lot on guests
(b) the adjustments we have to make
(c) This will be most difficult of
(d) because we have been used to

Ans. (c)

Part (c) 'This will be most difficult of' contains an error. Add 'the' before the word 'most' corrects the sentence.

111. I am sure that / the postman would be / coming shortly / to deliver the letter. SSC CGL Tier-1 24.07.2023 (Shift-I)
(a) I am sure that
(b) coming shortly
(c) to deliver the letter
(d) the postman would be

Ans. (d)

Part (d) 'the postman would be' contains an error. The use of 'would' is incorrect as the sentence is referring to a near future event, while 'would' is used only in past contexts. Hence, 'would' should be replaced with 'will' to correct the sentence.

112. Maruti likes / adventure / stories, especially / an adventures of Tarzan. SSC CGL Tier-1 24.07.2023 (Shift-I)
(a) stories, especially
(b) an adventures of Tarzan
(c) Maruti likes
(d) adventure

Ans. (b)

Part (b) 'an adventures of Tarzan' is incorrect as the name of the book / story is 'The adventures of Tarzan.'

113. A honourable person (A) / deserves respect (B) / from everybody (C).
SSC CGL Tier-1 24.07.2023 (Shift-II)
(a) B (b) C
(c) No error (d) A

Ans. (d)

Part (A) of the given sentence contains an error of articles. Article 'an' should be used in place of 'a' as the initial sound of the word 'honourable' is a vowel.

114. The receptionist asked if Diya / will take a seat and / wait for the boss to call her in.
SSC CGL Tier-1 24.07.2023 (Shift-II)
(a) The receptionist asked if Diya
(b) No error
(c) will take a seat and
(d) wait for the boss to call her in

Ans. (c)

Part (c) 'will take a seat and' contains an error of modal. The use of 'will' is incorrect for the sentence in indirect speech. Hence, it must be replaced by 'would.'

115. I play / cricket in / my childhood / with my sister.
SSC CGL Tier-1 24.07.2023 (Shift-III)
(a) my childhood
(b) with my sister
(c) I play
(d) cricket in

Ans. (c)

Part (c) 'I play' of the given sentence contains an error of tense. The verb form 'played' should be used in place of 'play' as the sentence is in past tense.

116. The historians/are a great/asset to the/ field of academia.
SSC CGL Tier-1 24.07.2023 (Shift-III)
(a) field of academia
(b) are a great
(c) asset to the
(d) The historians

Ans. (d)

Part (d) 'the historians' contains an error of articles. The word 'the' must be removed to correct the sentence.'

The definite article 'the' is only used before nouns to indicate something specific or something that is known to the reader.

Hence, it can't be used with 'historians' in the context of the sentence.

117. (a) The warrior was waiting for an right time to attack the lion hiding in a cave. SSC CGL Tier-1 24.07.2023 (Shift-IV)
(b) The warrior was waiting for the right time to attack the lion hiding in the cave.
(c) An warrior was waiting for a right time to attack the lion hiding in the cave.
(d) The warrior was waiting for a right time to attack an lion hiding in the cave.

Ans. (b)

The grammatically correct sentence is 'The warrior was waiting for the right time to attack the lion hiding in the cave. Option (a), (c) and (d) have incorrect use of article.

Since, definite article 'the' is used before referring to something specific, it will be used before 'right time' and 'lion' as per the context of the sentence.

118. We hardly knew nothing/about the manager/who had recently joined.
SSC CGL Tier-1 25.07.2023 (Shift-I)
(a) We hardly knew nothing
(b) No error
(c) about the manager
(d) who had recently joined

Ans. (a)

Part (a) 'We hardly knew nothing' contains an error in the use of the word 'nothing.' 'Nothing' refers to the absence or lack of something specific. Hence, 'nothing' must be replaced with 'anything' to correct the sentence.

119. Here/ come/ the bus/ for Lucknow. **SSC CGL Tier-1 25.07.2023 (Shift-I)**

(a) for Lucknow (b) the bus
(c) come (d) Here

Ans. (c)

Part (c) 'come' contains an error of subject-verb agreement. The singular subject 'bus' would take a singular verb. Hence, 'come' must be replaced with 'comes' to correct the sentence.

120. Anti-party activities / improved my relations/with an opposition. **SSC CGL Tier-1 25.07.2023 (Shift-II)**

(a) Anti-party activities
(b) No error
(c) improved my relations
(d) with an opposition

Ans. (d)

Part (d) 'with an opposition' contains an error in the use of the article 'an.' Definite article the is used when referring to something specific. Hence, 'an' must be replaced with 'the' to correct the sentence.

121. All the horses, except one, always / behaved in a rough manner when / Robert come to clean the stable. **SSC CGL Tier-1 25.07.2023 (Shift-II)**

(a) behaved in a rough manner when
(b) Robert come to clean the stable
(c) No error
(d) All the horses, except one, always

Ans. (b)

Part (b) 'Robert come to clean the stable' contains an error of tense. The use of 'come' is incorrect as the sentence is in past tense. Hence, it must be replaced with 'came' to correct the sentence.

122. You wash / the dishes / and / I dry the same. **SSC CGL Tier-1 25.07.2023 (Shift-III)**

(a) and (b) You wash
(c) I dry the same (d) the dishes

Ans. (c)

Part (c) 'I dry the same' contains an error. The phrase 'the same' is not appropriate in the context of the sentence. The pronoun 'them' is used as the object of a verb that have already been mentioned. Replace 'the same' with 'them' to correct the sentence.

123. A. As a nation, India is a united country and shall always remain so.
B. As nation, India is a united country and shall always remain so.
C. As the nation, India is a united country and shall always remain so.
D. As a nation, India is an united country and shall always remain so. **SSC CGL Tier-1 25.07.2023 (Shift-III)**

(a) A (b) B
(c) D (d) C

Ans. (a)

The grammatically correct sentence is 'As a nation, India is a united country and shall always remain so.'
Indefinite article 'a' would be used before 'nation' because as per the context, the sentence isn't referring to anything specific. Article 'a' should also be used before 'united' because it begins with a consonant sound. All the other sentences except option (a) contain incorrect articles.

124. (a) It was a hectic day for Susan with a lot of purchases and a couple of meetings.
(b) It was a hectic day for Susan with the lot of purchase and a couple of meetings.
(c) It was a hectic day for Susan with the lot of purchase and an couple of meetings.
(d) It was the hectic day for Susan with a lot of purchase and the couple of meetings.
SSC CGL Tier-1 25.07.2023 (Shift-IV)

Ans. (a)

The grammatically correct sentence is 'It was a hectic day for Susan with a lot of purchases and a couple of meetings' because it uses the correct article 'a' before 'lot of purchases and couple of meetings.' Sentences (b), (c) and (d) use article incorrectly.

125. The doctor came / after the patient/ had/pass away. **SSC CGL Tier-1 25.07.2023 (Shift-IV)**

(a) The doctor came
(b) pass away
(c) after the patient
(d) had

Ans. (b)

Part (b) 'pass away' contains an error of tense.
The use of 'pass' is incorrect as the sentence is in past perfect tense. Hence, it must be replaced with 'passed' to correct the sentence.

126. When Mrs. Sinha came to see Varanasi in 2019, Nupur has already been teaching there for five years. **SSC CGL Tier-1 26.07.2023 (Shift-I)**

(a) When Mrs. Sinha came to see Varanasi <u>in 2019</u>, Nupur has already been teaching there for five years.
(b) <u>When Mrs. Sinha came to see Varanasi</u> in 2019, Nupur has already been teaching there for five years.
(c) When Mrs. Sinha came to see Varanasi in 2019, Nupur has already been teaching <u>there for five years.</u>
(d) When Mrs. Sinha came to see Varanasi in 2019, <u>Nupur has already been teaching</u> there for five years.

Ans. (d)

The underlined part of the sentence in given option (d) has the error of tense. The sentence should use the past perfect tense 'had been teaching' instead of 'has already been teaching' because the action of teaching started in the past and continued upto another point in the past, which is Mrs. Sinha's visit to Varanasi in 2019.

127. She is in an hurry to meet her brother. **SSC CGL Tier-1 26.07.2023 (Shift-I)**

(a) to meet (b) She is in
(c) her brother (d) an hurry

Ans. (d)

Part (d) 'an hurry' contains an error of article. Article 'a' will be used in place of 'an' as the word succeeding it starts with a consonant sound.

128. You should / see a oculist; / your eyes look / worse today. **SSC CGL Tier-1 26.07.2023 (Shift-II)**

(a) your eyes look
(b) You should
(c) worse today
(d) see a oculist

Ans. (d)

Part (d), 'see a oculist' contains an error of article. Article 'an' will be used in place of 'a' as the word succeeding it starts with a vowel sound.

129. My mother is a honest and well-known woman in the society. **SSC CGL Tier-1 26.07.2023 (Shift-III)**

(a) in the society
(b) My mother
(c) is a honest
(d) and well-known woman

Ans. (c)

Part (c) 'is a honest' contains an error of article. Article 'an' will be used in place of 'a' as the word succeeding it starts with a vowel sound.

130. He was always been a grumpy man, so I never liked him and avoided his company.
SSC CGL Tier-1 26.07.2023 (Shift-III)
(a) He was always been a grumpy man, so I never liked him and avoided his company.
(b) He was always been a grumpy man, so I never liked him and avoided his company.
(c) He was always been a grumpy man, so I never liked him and avoided his company.
(d) He was always been a grumpy man, so I never liked him and avoided his company.

Ans. (b)

The part underlined in option (b) contains an error. The given sentence is referring to an action that is still continuing in the present while past tense is used here.

Further, the continuous form 'been' does not work with the simple past tense 'was' so it should be eliminated from the sentence. To make the sentence correct, replace 'was' with 'has.'

131. In 2023, she will has been working in the company for three years.
SSC CGL Tier-1 26.07.2023 (Shift-IV)
(a) By 2023
(b) in company
(c) she will has been
(d) since three years

Ans. (c)

Part (c) 'she will has been' contains the error of verb form. The use of 'has' is incorrect as the sentence is the future perfect continuous tense. 'Has' must be replaced by 'have' to correct the sentence.

132. My younger brother were attending a short-term computer course these days. SSC CGL (Tier-I) 27.07.2023 (Shift-I)
(a) were attending
(b) My younger brother
(c) a shot-term computer course
(d) these days

Ans. (a)

Part (a) 'were attending' contains an error of subject-verb agreement as well as tense.

As the subject is singular and the sentence is referring to 'these days', implying present tense.

The use of 'were' is not appropriate in the given context. So, 'were' must be replaced by 'is' to correct the sentence.

133. They usually allege that there is / a delay in procuring stationery / due to the faulty purchase orders.
SSC CGL Tier-1 27.07.2023 (Shift-II)
(a) due to the faulty purchase orders
(b) a delay in procuring stationery
(c) They usually allege that there is
(d) No error

Ans. (d)

The given sentence is grammatically correct and contextually meaningful.

134. He is not rich (A) / so he cannot afford (B) / to buy a expensive car (C). SSC CGL Tier-1 27.07.2023 (Shift-II)
(a) C (b) A
(c) No error (d) B

Ans. (a)

Part (C) of the sentence contains an error of articles.

Article 'an' should be used in place of 'a' as the succeeding word starts with a vowel sound.

135. It can/get extreme cold/during/the winters. SSC CGL Tier-1 27.07.2023 (Shift-III)
(a) the winters (b) during
(c) It can (d) get extreme cold

Ans. (d)

Part (d) 'get extreme cold' contains an error in the use of the word 'extreme.' Its adverb form 'extremely' should be used to correct the sentence.

136. (a) The decision to change a hospital saved an life of the daughter of the doctor.SSC CGL Tier-1 27.07.2023 (Shift-IV)
(b) The decision to change the hospital saved the life of the daughter of the doctor.
(c) The decision to change an hospital saved the life of the daughter of the doctor.
(d) A decision to change a hospital saved the life of the daughter of the doctor.

Ans. (b)

The grammatically correct sentence is 'The decision to change the hospital saved the life of the daughter of the doctor.'

137. If / it will rain, / we will have / a tough time.
SSC CGL Tier-1 27.07.2023 (Shift-IV)
(a) If (b) a tough time
(c) we will have (d) it will rain

Ans. (d)

Part (d) 'it will rain' contains the error of tense. The use of 'will rain' is incorrect in the future conditional sentence. It must be replaced with 'rains' to correct the sentence.

138. He lived close to / the train station, / yet travelled by bus.
SSC CGL Tier-2 02.03.2023
(a) yet travelled by bus
(b) No error
(c) He lived close to
(d) the train station

Ans. (b)

The given sentence is grammatically correct and contextually meaningful.

139. My father give up / smoking when / I was twelve / years old.
SSC CGL Tier-2 02.03.2023
(a) My father give up
(b) smoking when
(c) I was twelve
(d) years old

Ans. (a)

Part (a) 'My father give up' contains the error of tense. As the given sentence is in past tense. The correct phrase would be 'My father gave up.'

140. We should sorted out/the problem ourselves/rather than depending/on the third party. SSC CGL Tier-2 03.03.2023
(a) rather than depending
(b) the problem ourselves
(c) We should sorted out
(d) on the third party

Ans. (c)

The part 'We should sorted out' contains an error. The correct phrase is 'sort out' because 'should' is followed by the base form of the verb. 'Sort out' means to solve or organise.

141. Dan needed help/to get/tight coat of him. SSC CGL Tier-2 03.03.2023
(a) No error
(b) Dan needed help
(c) to get
(d) tight coat of him

Ans. (d)

The part 'tight coat of him' contains an error. The correct phrase should be 'his tight coat off him.' This construction correctly uses possessive pronoun 'his' and the phrasal verb 'get off' to indicate removal.

142. The postman / delivers the letters / through hand, / door to door.
SSC CGL Tier-2 06.03.2023
(a) door to door (b) delivers the letters
(c) The postman (d) through hand

Ans. (d)

The part 'through hand' contains an error. The use of 'through' is incorrect here. The correct preposition is 'by,' so it should be 'by hand.' This means the postman delivers letters personally.

143. She watched / the thief who / steal the purse / in the bus.
SSC CGL Tier-2 06.03.2023
(a) the thief who (b) in the bus
(c) steal the purse (d) She watched
Ans. (c)
Part (c) 'steal the purse' contains an error. As the sentence is in past tense, use 'stole' to correct the sentence.

144. Everybody stared / when me / entered the / drawing room.
SSC CGL Tier-2 07.03.2023
(a) when me (b) Everybody stared
(c) drawing room (d) entered the
Ans. (a)
Part (a) 'when me' contains an error. To correct it, use 'when I' instead of 'when me.'

145. Daniel sat on / his new bike / and went afar / a ride.
SSC CGL Tier-2 07.03.2023
(a) a ride (b) his new bike
(c) and went afar (d) Daniel sat on
Ans. (c)
Part (c) 'and went afar' contains an error. Use 'went for' to correct the sentence.

146. This is/the book/whom I/wanted to buy. SSC CGL Tier-2 26.10.2023
(a) the book (b) wanted to buy
(c) whom I (d) This is
Ans. (c)
Part (c) 'whom I' contains an error. 'Whom' is used to refer to people in objective case. Hence, replace it with 'which' which is used to refer to objects.

147. Everyone should/respect those/parents, teachers/and elders.
SSC CGL Tier-2 26.10.2023
(a) and elders (b) parents, teachers
(c) respect those (d) Everyone should
Ans. (c)
Part (c) 'respect those' contains an error. Use 'their' in place of 'those.'

148. (A) They were /(B) married happily/ (C) before she/ (D) quit her job. SSC CGL Tier-2 26.10.2023
(a) B (b) D
(c) C (d) A
Ans. (a)
Part (B) 'married happily' contains an error. Adverb of manner is generally placed before the verb. Hence, 'happily married' should be used.

149. They want to/live in first floor/of this building. SSC CGL Tier-2 26.10.2023
(a) They want to
(b) of this building
(c) No error
(d) live in first floor
Ans. (d)
Part (d) 'live in first floor' contains an error. Use 'live on the first floor' to correct the sentence.

150. We/ has seen/ that movie/ before.
SSC CGL Tier-2 26.10.2023
(a) has seen (b) before
(c) that movie (d) We
Ans. (a)
Part (a) 'has seen' contains an error. As the subject is plural, verb should also be plural. Hence, replace 'has' with 'have.'

151. Throw a rounder stone to create ripples in the water.
SSC CGL Tier-2 26.10.2023
(a) Throw the roundest stone to create ripples in the water.
(b) Throw a more round stone to create ripples in the water.
(c) Throw a more rounder stone to create ripples in the water.
(d) Throw a round stone to create ripples in the water.
Ans. (d)
The correct phrase is 'Throw a round stone to create ripples in the water.' Options (a), (b) and (c) are incorrect because 'rounder' and 'more round' are not appropriate comparative forms here.
'Round' is already an adjective indicating shape and adding 'more' or 'rounder' is redundant and incorrect.

SSC CGL 2022 (Tier 1 & 2)

152. It was/ the very well-directed film/ and we enjoyed it.
SSC CGL Tier-1 11.04.2022 (Shift-I)
(a) the very well-directed film
(b) No error
(c) and we enjoyed it
(d) It was
Ans. (a)
Part 'the very well-directed film' contains an error.
The correct phrase should be 'a very well-directed film.' 'a' is used as an indefinite article before singular nouns when the noun is mentioned for the first time and isn't specific.

153. If the economy fails / this year it reflect badly / on the government.
SSC CGL Tier-1 11.04.2022 (Shift-I)
(a) this year it reflect badly
(b) No error
(c) on the government
(d) If the economy fails
Ans. (a)
Part 'this year it reflect badly' contains a subject-verb agreement error.
The correct verb form should be 'reflects' to match the singular subject 'it.'

154. We stayed / in Jim's flat / during he was / on holiday.
SSC CGL Tier-1 11.04.2022 (Shift-II)
(a) on holiday (b) during he was
(c) in Jim's flat (d) We stayed
Ans. (b)
Part 'during he was' contains a pronoun error. The correct phrase should be 'while he was' to make the sentence grammatically correct.

155. Do you /recall to meet/ her at the party / last night?
SSC CGL Tier-1 11.04.2022 (Shift-II)
(a) last night (b) her at the party
(c) Do you (d) recall to meet
Ans. (d)
Part 'recall to meet' contains a verb form error. The correct phrase should be 'recall meeting' because 'recall' is followed by the gerund (verb+ing) form.

156. It is not worth/ having the trouble/ to write to him/ as he never replies.
SSC CGL Tier-1 11.04.2022 (Shift-III)
(a) as he never replies
(b) to write to him
(c) It is not worth
(d) having the trouble
Ans. (d)
Part 'having the trouble' contains an idiomatic error.
The correct phrase should be 'worth the trouble' to make the sentence grammatically correct.

157. How many/ eggs were put/ into the basket? SSC CGL Tier-1 12.04.2022 (Shift-III)
(a) How many
(b) No error
(c) eggs were put
(d) into the basket
Ans. (b)
The given sentence is grammatically correct and contextually meaningful.

158. We have/ not met/ some of our friends/ since six months.
SSC CGL Tier-1 12.04.2022 (Shift-III)
(a) since six months
(b) not met
(c) some of our friends
(d) We have
Ans. (a)
Part 'since six months' contains a preposition error. The correct phrase should be 'for six months' because 'for' is used to indicate a period of time.

159. The policeman asked / many people but / no one was knowing / how the accident happened.
SSC CGL Tier-1 12.04.2022 (Shift-III)
(a) how the accident happened
(b) the policeman asked
(c) no one was knowing
(d) many people but
Ans. (c)
Phrase 'no one was knowing' is incorrect. The correct phrase should be 'no one knew' because it uses the simple past tense.

160. This question / is quite too / simple for me / to answer.
SSC CGL Tier-1 13.04.2022 (Shift-I)
(a) to answer (b) is quite too
(c) This question (d) simple for me
Ans. (b)
Phrase 'is quite too' is incorrect. The correct phrase should be 'is too' because 'quite' and 'too' are not used together.

161. You should/ have respond / to me query / sooner.
SSC CGL Tier-1 13.04.2022 (Shift-II)
(a) to my query (b) You should
(c) have respond (d) sooner
Ans. (c)
The phrase 'have respond' is incorrect. The correct phrase should be 'have responded' because 'should have' is followed by the past participle form of the verb.

162. There have been /three breaks-in fin our society/ this month.
SSC CGL Tier-1 18.04.2022 (Shift-II)
(a) three breaks-in
(b) this month
(c) in our society
(d) There have been
Ans. (a)
The phrase 'three breaks-in' is incorrect. The correct phrase should be 'three break-ins' because 'break-ins' is the correct plural form of the compound noun.

163. He/ can have been/ more polite/ to her. SSC CGL Tier-1 18.04.2022 (Shift-II)
(a) more polite (b) He
(c) to her (d) can have been
Ans. (d)
The phrase 'can have been' is incorrect. The correct phrase should be 'could have been' to indicate a hypothetical or past possibility.

164. You and I / have submitted / your work / on time.
SSC CGL Tier-1 21.04.2022 (Shift-I)
(a) on time (b) your work
(c) have submitted (d) You and I
Ans. (b)
The phrase 'your work' is incorrect. The correct phrase should be 'our work' to match the subject 'You and I.'

165. I find that / I get myself tired / very easily / these days.
SSC CGL Tier-1 21.04.2022 Shift-III
(a) these days (b) I find that
(c) I get myself tired (d) very easily
Ans. (c)
The phrase 'I get myself tired' misuses the reflexive pronoun 'myself.' The correct phrase is 'I get tired' because it appropriately reflects the speaker's state without unnecessary emphasis.

166. During an earthquake / it is advised to take / cover above a table / to save your life. SSC CGL Tier-1 01.12.2022 (Shift-I)
(a) cover above a table
(b) During an earthquake
(c) it is advised to take
(d) to save your life
Ans. (a)
The phrase 'cover above a table' is incorrect because the preposition 'above' suggests being on top of the table, which is not protective during an earthquake. The correct preposition is 'under,' indicating that one should be beneath the table for safety.

167. He used to reply / that the only place / for which he went / was the town library.
SSC CGL Tier-1 01.12.2022 (Shift-II)
(a) was the town library
(b) for which he went
(c) He used to reply
(d) that the only place
Ans. (b)
The phrase 'for which he went' is incorrect. The correct phrase should be 'to which he went' because 'to' is the appropriate preposition indicating direction towards a place.

168. <u>Has</u> Gita <u>any</u> previous knowledge of <u>work</u> <u>with</u> junior colleagues?
SSC CGL Tier-1 01.12.2022 (Shift-IV)
(a) with (b) Has (c) any (d) work
Ans. (d)
The word 'work' should be 'working' to match the context of previous experience with junior colleagues.

169. One can never imagine / how hot it gets in Delhi/ unless one doesn't go / there in person.
SSC CGL Tier-1 02.12.2022 (Shift-I)
(a) One can never imagine
(b) unless one doesn't go
(c) how hot it gets in Delhi
(d) there in person
Ans. (b)
The phrase 'unless one doesn't go' is incorrect. The correct phrase should be 'unless one goes' because 'unless' already implies a negative condition. Double negatives are incorrect in standard English.

170. Neither the doctors nor / the nurse were present / when the patient / reached the hospital.
SSC CGL Tier-1 02.12.2022 (Shift-II)
(a) Neither the doctors nor
(b) the nurse were present
(c) when the patient
(d) reached the hospital
Ans. (b)
The phrase 'the nurse were present' contains a subject-verb agreement error. The correct verb should be 'was' to match the singular subject 'the nurse.'

171. She often / accuses him for / a lack of morality.
SSC CGL Tier-1 02.12.2022 (Shift-IV)
(a) She often (b) a lack of morality
(c) No error (d) accuses him for
Ans. (d)
The phrase 'accuses him for' is incorrect. The correct phrase should be 'accuses him of' because 'accuse' is followed by the preposition 'of' when indicating the reason for accusation.

172. I have never played any game of side this track during the season.
SSC CGL Tier-1 03.12.2022 (Shift-I)
(a) I have never played any game off side this track <u>during the season</u>.
(b) I have never played any game <u>of side this track</u> during the season.
(c) <u>I have never played</u> any game off side this track during the season.
(d) I have never played <u>any game</u> off side this track during the season.

Ans. (b)

The phrase 'of side this track' is incorrect. The correct phrase should be 'offside this track' which is a term used in sports to indicate a position.

173. There is a whole world / out there that / is invisible from / the naked eye. **SSC CGL Tier-1 03.12.2022 (Shift-I)**

(a) the naked eye
(b) is invisible from
(c) There is a whole world
(d) out there that

Ans. (b)

The phrase 'is invisible from' is incorrect. The correct phrase should be 'is invisible to' because 'invisible to' is the correct idiomatic expression.

174. The manager told her that /she should be a bit more / careful while executed the/orders of the company. **SSC CGL Tier-1 03.12.2022 (Shift-III)**

(a) The manager told her that
(b) she should be a bit more
(c) orders of the company
(d) careful while executed the

Ans. (d)

The phrase 'careful while executed the' contains a verb tense error. The correct phrase should be 'careful while executing the' because 'executing' is the correct gerund form of the verb.

175. The newspaper reported / that it was a mystery / how the thieves enter / into the house. **SSC CGL Tier-1 03.12.2022 (Shift-IV)**

(a) into the house
(b) how the thieves enter
(c) that it was a mystery
(d) The newspaper reported

Ans. (b)

The phrase 'how the thieves enter' contains a verb tense error. The correct phrase should be 'how the thieves entered' because the sentence is in the past tense.

176. I had walked / for most of the day / to Kanpur and then / get on the train by Mumbai. **SSC CGL Tier-1 05.12.2022 (Shift-I)**

(a) for most of the day
(b) to Kanpur and then
(c) get on the train by Mumbai
(d) I had walked

Ans. (c)

The phrase 'get on the train by Mumbai' is incorrect. The correct phrase should be 'got on the train to Mumbai' to match the past tense and the correct preposition indicating destination.

177. He will make mistakes, but he will learn / by making mistakes. So, dear parents, / once you put the money in your / children's little pockets, forget all on it. **SSC CGL Tier-1 05.12.2022 (Shift-I)**

(a) children's little pockets, forget all on it
(b) once you put the money in your
(c) by making mistakes. So, dear parents
(d) He will make mistakes, but he will learn

Ans. (a)

The phrase 'forget all on it' is incorrect. The correct phrase should be 'forget all about it.' This follows the rule of correct idiomatic expression usage, where the appropriate phrase is 'forget all about it.'

178. There are no tables at the classroom. **SSC CGL Tier-1 05.12.2022 (Shift-IV)**

(a) There are no tables at the <u>classroom</u>.
(b) <u>There are</u> no tables at the classroom.
(c) There are <u>no tables</u> at the classroom.
(d) There are no tables <u>at the</u> classroom.

Ans. (d)

Part 'There are no tables at the classroom' contains an error. The preposition 'at' is incorrect. The correct preposition should be 'in.' This follows the rule of correct preposition usage, where 'in' is used to indicate something inside a place.

179. The prisoner was / accused for stealing / from his landlord. **SSC CGL Tier-1 06.12.2022 (Shift-I)**

(a) accused for stealing
(b) The prisoner was
(c) from his landlord
(d) No error

Ans. (a)

The phrase 'accused for' is incorrect. The correct phrase should be 'accused of.' This follows the rule of correct preposition usage, where 'accused' is followed by 'of' when indicating the reason for accusation.

180. When the train pulled in / at the station, it take / Joseph some time / to get off. **SSC CGL Tier-1 06.12.2022 (Shift-III)**

(a) When the train pulled in
(b) at the station, it take
(c) Joseph some time
(d) to get off

Ans. (b)

The verb 'take' is incorrect because it does not match the past tense context provided by 'pulled in.' The correct verb should be 'took' to align with the past tense. This adheres to the rule of verb tense consistency, which states that verbs in a sentence should consistently reflect the time frame being described.

181. You must / be hurry / otherwise you will / miss the train. **SSC CGL Tier-1 07.12.2022 (Shift-I)**

(a) miss the train
(b) be hurry
(c) You must
(d) otherwise you will

Ans. (b)

The phrase 'be hurry' is incorrect. The correct phrase should be 'be in a hurry.' This uses the correct idiomatic expression 'be in a hurry.'

182. The boy had run away / because he couldn't stand / his father beat him / for one more day. **SSC CGL Tier-1 07.12.2022 (Shift-I)**

(a) his father beat him
(b) because he couldn't stand
(c) The boy had run away
(d) for one more day

Ans. (a)

The verb 'beat' is incorrect in this context. The correct verb should be 'beating' to match the continuous action implied. This follows the rule of gerund usage, where certain verbs (like 'stand') are followed by the gerund form (verb+ing) to describe an ongoing action.

183. They all, except Shirin, were very sad / during the farewell party given / to the teacher retiring, and her / indifference were well noticed. **SSC CGL Tier-1 07.12.2022 (Shift-III)**

(a) They all, except Shirin, were very sad
(b) during the farewell party given
(c) indifference were well noticed
(d) to the teacher retiring and her

Ans. (c)

The verb 'were' is incorrect because it does not match the singular subject 'indifference.' The correct verb should be 'was.' This adheres to the rule of subject-verb agreement, which states that singular subjects require singular verbs.

184. He was / paid handsomely for / his ability to handle / the crowd skillful. **SSC CGL Tier-1 07.12.2022 (Shift-IV)**

(a) paid handsomely for
(b) his ability to handle
(c) the crowd skillful
(d) He was

Ans. (c)

The phrase 'the crowd skillful' is incorrect. The correct phrase should be 'the crowd skillfully' because 'skillfully' is the correct adverb form of 'skillful.' This ensures the sentence is grammatically correct.

185. He knows that / he has no other option / but to work hard.
SSC CGL Tier-1 08.12.2022 (Shift-I)

(a) He knows that
(b) but to work hard
(c) he has no other option
(d) No error

Ans. (b)

The phrase 'but to work hard' is incorrect. The correct phrase should be 'but work hard' because 'but' is used as a conjunction here and 'to' is redundant.

186. The article that she wrote / for the last week's Sunday Supplement / fairly criticises / the abuses of mobile phones.
SSC CGL Tier-1 08.12.2022 (Shift-II)

(a) The article that she wrote
(b) for the last week's Sunday Supplement
(c) the abuses of mobile phones
(d) fairly criticises

Ans. (c)

The phrase 'the abuses of mobile phones' is incorrect. The correct phrase should be 'the abuse of mobile phones' because 'abuse' is an uncountable noun in this context and does not need to be pluralised.

187. She has / not written / a single novel / by three years.
SSC CGL Tier-1 08.12.2022 (Shift-III)

(a) not written (b) She has
(c) by three years (d) a single novel

Ans. (c)

The phrase 'by three years' is incorrect.
The correct phrase should be 'in three years' because 'in' correctly denotes the duration of time.

188. The scooter that / I am using / these days is belonging / to my brother.
SSC CGL Tier-1 08.12.2022 (Shift-IV)

(a) to my brother
(b) I am using
(c) The scooter that
(d) these days is belonging

Ans. (d)

The phrase 'these days is belonging' is incorrect. The correct phrase should be 'these days belongs' because 'belonging' is not used in the present continuous tense. The verb 'belongs' correctly aligns with the subject 'the scooter.'

189. Children listens to people / speaking around them / for a long time before / they begin to speak.
SSC CGL Tier-1 09.12.2022 (Shift-I)

(a) Children listens to people
(b) speaking around them
(c) they begin to speak
(d) for a long time before

Ans. (a)

The phrase 'Children listens to people' is incorrect. The correct phrase should be 'Children listen to people' because the plural subject 'Children' requires the plural verb 'listen.'

190. The wedding gown / looked decently / despite being / studded with jewels.
SSC CGL Tier-1 09.12.2022 (Shift-III)

(a) The wedding gown
(b) despite being with
(c) looked decently
(d) studded with jewels

Ans. (c)

The phrase 'looked decently' is incorrect. The correct phrase should be 'looked decent' because 'decent' is the correct adjective to describe the gown's appearance.

191. I <u>told</u> Rahul <u>on</u> wait <u>for</u> two hours <u>at</u> the bus stop.
SSC CGL Tier-1 09.12.2022 (Shift-IV)

(a) at (b) for (c) told (d) on

Ans. (d)

The phrase 'on wait' is incorrect. The correct phrase should be 'to wait' because 'to' is the appropriate preposition used with the infinitive form of the verb 'wait.'

192. The meeting was held upon / for an hour / due to non-availability / of the committee members.
SSC CGL Tier-1 12.12.2022 (Shift-I)

(a) The meeting was held upon
(b) for an hour
(c) of the committee members
(d) due to non-availability

Ans. (a)

The phrase 'was held upon' is incorrect. The correct phrase should be 'was held for' because 'for' is the appropriate preposition to indicate a duration of time.

193. The audience has being / angry as the magician / is not performing / as expected. SSC CGL Tier-1 12.12.2022 (Shift-I)

(a) as expected
(b) angry as the magician
(c) The audience has being
(d) is not performing

Ans. (c)

The phrase 'has being' is incorrect. The correct phrase should be 'has been' because 'been' is the correct past participle form of 'be' used in the present perfect continuous tense.

194. No talking / on the dinner table / is an absolute rule.
SSC CGL Tier-1 12.12.2022 (Shift-III)

(a) No talking
(b) No error
(c) on the dinner table
(d) is an absolute rule

Ans. (b)

The sentence is grammatically correct and contextually meaningful.

195. The students usually asks / for a bonus time of / thirty minutes for / completing their projects.
SSC CGL Tier-1 12.12.2022 (Shift-IV)

(a) The students usually asks
(b) completing their projects
(c) for a bonus time of
(d) thirty minutes for

Ans. (a)

The segment 'the students usually asks' of the given sentence contains an error. As 'students' is a plural noun, a plural verb will be used with it. So, 'ask' should be used in place of 'asks' in the segment to make the sentence grammatically correct.

196. One of the students is always / late to the class; he has been warn / by the teacher many times; / but still, he keeps on being late.
SSC CGL Tier-1 13.12.2022 (Shift-I)

(a) One of the students is always
(b) by the teacher many times
(c) but still, he keeps on being late
(d) late to the class, he has been warn

Ans. (d)

There is an error in part (d). 'He has been warned' should be used in place of 'he has been warn' because the sentence belongs to present perfect tense.

197. Usually Rathessh hasn't take part in these types of events because of his hectic schedule.
SSC CGL Tier-1 13.12.2022 (Shift-II)

(a) Usually Rathessh hasn't
(b) take part in these types
(c) his hectic schedule
(d) of events because of

Ans. (a)

There is an error in part (a). Use 'doesn't' in place of 'hasn't' to make the sentence grammatically correct.

198. There can be precious / diamonds and metals / in the surface / just below you.
SSC CGL Tier-1 13.12.2022 (Shift-III)
(a) diamonds and metals
(b) just below you
(c) in the surface
(d) There can be precious

Ans. (b)

Segment (b) of the given sentence contains a grammatical error in it. 'Beneath' should be used in place of 'below' in segment (b) to make the sentence grammatically correct.

199. He describes the place vivid / that inspired in us / a wish to visit / the same. **SSC CGL Tier-1 13.12.2022 (Shift-IV)**
(a) He describes the place vivid
(b) the same
(c) that inspired in us
(d) a wish to visit

Ans. (a)

There is an error in part (a).

The part should be replaced by 'He described the place so vividly' to make the sentence grammatically correct and error free.

200. The boy, as well as / his friends, were / absent from the class / when the teacher came.
SSC CGL Tier-1 13.12.2022 (Shift-IV)
(a) his friends, were
(b) The boy, as well as
(c) when the teacher came
(d) absent from the class

Ans. (a)

There is an error in part (a) 'His friends, was' should be used in place of 'his friends, were' because when two subjects are joined with 'as well as' the verb should be used according to the first subject.

201. If you have / remained calm / you could have / saved the situation.
SSC CGL Tier-2 29.01.2022
(a) saved the situation
(b) you could have
(c) remained calm
(d) If you have

Ans. (d)

If you have 'If + had + V_3 .... could have + V_3 (third form of the verb)' is the correct grammatical structure for the given sentence.

Hence, 'If you had' is the most appropriate answer.

202. I will spend / my rest of remaining / life in my / native village.
SSC CGL Tier-2 29.01.2022
(a) my rest of remaining
(b) life in my
(c) native village
(d) I will spend

Ans. (a)

We cannot use 'rest' and 'remaining' together in a sentence as it becomes the case of superfluousness (not necessary). Hence, 'remaining' will be removed from the sentence and 'the rest of my life' the most appropriate answer.

203. We yet / have time / to catch / the bus. **SSC CGL Tier-2 29.01.2022**
(a) have time (b) to catch
(c) the bus (d) We yet

Ans. (d)

'Still' means starting in the past and continuing until now. However, 'still' generally comes before a verb in the present perfect form (has / have) and 'yet' usually comes at the end of the sentence. Similarly in the given sentence, the time for catching the bus has started in the past and continued till now. Hence, 'We still' is the most appropriate answer.

204. This dog seems / to be very ferocious, / otherwise, / it is harmless. **SSC CGL Tier-2 29.01.2022**
(a) otherwise
(b) to be very ferocious
(c) it is harmless
(d) This dog seems

Ans. (a)

'Otherwise' is a conjunction that means apart from that. However, 'But' is also a conjunction that is used for introducing an idea that contrasts with or is different from what has just been said. Similarly in the given sentence, the statement that the dog is harmless contrasts with its characteristic of being ferocious (violent). Hence, 'But' is the most appropriate answer.

205. The girl lay down / on the bed / besides her mother / and went to sleep. **SSC CGL Tier-2 29.01.2022**
(a) on the bed
(b) besides her mother
(c) The girl lay down
(d) and went to sleep

Ans. (b)

'Besides' means 'in addition to something' and 'Beside' means 'at the side of or next to somebody / something.' However, the given sentence states that the girl lay down on the bed next to her mother and went to sleep. Hence, 'beside her mother' is the most appropriate answer.

206. He went / to the bed/ with a / slight fever. **SSC CGL Tier-2 29.01.2022**
(a) slight fever (b) to the bed
(c) with a (d) He went

Ans. (b)

We generally use the phrases 'go to bed', 'gone to bed' or 'went to bed.' Hence, we will remove the definite article 'the' from the given sentence and 'went to bed' becomes the most appropriate answer.

207. The city turned out / to be very / different to what / he had expected.
SSC CGL Tier-2 29.01.2022
(a) to be very
(b) The city turned out
(c) he had expected
(d) different to what

Ans. (d)

There is a prepositional error in the given sentence. The preposition 'to' after 'different' must be replaced with 'from' because 'different' generally takes the preposition 'from' with it. Hence 'different from what' is the most appropriate answer.

208. Your name / precedes before / mine / in the list. **SSC CGL Tier-2 29.01.2022**
(a) mine
(b) Your name
(c) precedes before
(d) in the list

Ans. (c)

We do not use 'precedes' and 'before' together in a sentence as they have similar meanings and that will become a case of superfluousness (not necessary). Hence, 'before' must be removed from the sentence to make it grammatically correct.

209. You should / avail this opportunity / to demonstrate / your skills.
SSC CGL Tier-2 29.01.2022
(a) You should
(b) your skills
(c) avail this opportunity
(d) to demonstrate

Ans. (c)

'Avail' always takes the preposition of and a reflexive pronoun (myself, yourself, ourselves, etc.), in accordance with the given subject (You). Hence, 'avail yourself of this opportunity' is the most appropriate answer.

210. He was unable/ to help me because / he had been failed / to arrange the money. **SSC CGL Tier-2 29.01.2022**

(a) to help me because
(b) to arrange the money
(c) he had been failed
(d) He was unable

Ans. (c)

The given sentence is in the simple past tense so, the verb must be used in its simple past form (failed) and not in the past perfect form (had been failed). Hence, 'he failed' is the most appropriate answer.

211. He often / persists to ask / awkward questions / at the board meetings. **SSC CGL Tier-2 29.01.2022**

(a) He often
(b) persists to ask
(c) awkward questions
(d) at the board meetings

Ans. (b)

'Persist + in + V-ing' is the correct grammatical structure for the given sentence. Hence, the preposition 'to' must be replaced with the preposition 'in' and 'persists in asking (V-ing)' becomes the most appropriate answer.

212. His son-in-laws / have enhanced / his business / within a short period. **SSC CGL Tier-2 29.01.2022**

(a) have enhanced
(b) his business
(c) his son-in-laws
(d) within a short period

Ans. (c)

We do not use 'in-laws' because it is incorrect to add 's' in the suffix of law). However, we generally write son-in-law for a single male and sons-in-law for more than one male. Similarly, the given sentence talks about two males. Hence, 'His sons-in-law' is the most appropriate answer.

213. A businessman / at our colony / was found / COVID positive. **SSC CGL Tier-2 03.02.2022**

(a) at our colony (b) A businessman
(c) was found (d) COVID positive

Ans. (a)

The preposition 'at' is used when you are at a specific address, at a general location and at a point. However, the preposition 'in' is used in a space, neighbourhood, city and country. Similarly, the given sentence talks about a businessman in the neighbourhood (colony). Hence, 'in our colony' is the most appropriate answer.

214. Either of these / two roads / lead to / the post office. **SSC CGL Tier-2 03.02.2022**

(a) Either of these (b) the post office
(c) lead to (d) two roads

Ans. (c)

According to the 'Subject-Verb Agreement Rule', 'Either of / Neither of + Plural Subject + Singular Verb' is grammatically the correct structure. The given sentence has 'Roads' as a plural subject and 'leads' as a singular verb. Hence, 'leads to' is the most appropriate answer.

215. His father / prevented him / to go abroad / for higher studies. **SSC CGL Tier-2 03.02.2022**

(a) for higher studies
(b) His father
(c) to go abroad
(d) prevented him

Ans. (c)

We generally use the preposition 'from' with prevent not 'to.' Hence, we will replace 'to' with 'from' and 'from going abroad' becomes the most appropriate answer.

216. What is the name / of the Swami / whom autobiography /impressed you so much? **SSC CGL Tier-2 03.02.2022**

(a) What is the name
(b) whom autobiography
(c) impressed you so much
(d) of the Swami

Ans. (b)

'Whom' is an object pronoun that refers to the person who was the recipient of an action. However, 'Whose' is a possessive pronoun that refers to the person to whom something belongs.

Similarly, the given sentence refers to a Swami to whom the autobiography belongs. Hence, 'whose autobiography' is the most appropriate answer.

217. The crowd/of the migrant worker/ at the station/for the Shramik Special/is unforgettable. **SSC CGL Tier-2 03.02.2022**

(a) at the station
(b) of the migrant worker
(c) The crowd
(d) is unforgettable

Ans. (b)

'Crowd' means a large number of people in one placed and these people are migrant workers (not a single worker) in the given sentence. However, it is irrelevant to use the definite article 'the' as the workers are not specific. Hence, 'of migrant workers' is the most appropriate answer.

218. These experiments / had been going on / since several months. **SSC CGL Tier-2 08.08.2022**

(a) These experiments
(c) No error
(b) had been going on
(d) since several months

Ans. (d)

The given sentence is in 'past perfect continuous tense (Sub +had been + V_1-ing + obj. + since/for + time).' We generally use 'since' to denote a point of time and 'for' to denote a period of time. Hence, 'for several months' is the most appropriate answer.

219. Every Saturday, your mother prepares a pudding, isn't she? **SSC CGL Tier-2 08.08.2022**

(a) isn't she
(c) prepares a pudding
(b) Every Saturday, your mother
(d) No error

Ans. (a)

According to the 'Question Tag rule', if the statement is positive, the question tag will be negative and *vice-versa*.

Further, the sentence and the question tag must be in the same tense. The given sentence is in simple present tense. So, the same tense will be used for the question tag. The given sentence is positive so the question tag will be negative (doesn't). Hence, 'doesn't she' is the most appropriate answer.

220. The people / living in coastal areas / were evacuated / by time. **SSC CGL Tier-2 08.08.2022**

(a) were evacuated
(b) living in coastal areas
(c) by time
(d) The people

Ans. (c)

Phrase 'by time' will be replaced by 'on time' as both the phrases look similar but have different meanings. 'On time' means at a specific time and 'By time' means at the time. Hence, 'on time' is the most appropriate answer.

221. During the 17th century / there were great developments / at the sphere of knowledge. **SSC CGL Tier-2 08.08.2022**

(a) During the 17th century
(b) there were great developments

(c) No error
(d at the sphere of knowledge

Ans. (d)

There is a prepositional error in the given sentence.

The preposition 'At' must be replaced with 'In.' Hence, 'In the sphere of knowledge' is the most appropriate answer.

222. The gentleman had / a suitcase full with / wigs, ornaments and dresses.
SSC CGL Tier-2 08.08.2022

(a) a suitcase full with
(b) The gentleman had
(c) wigs, ornaments and dresses
(d) No error

Ans. (a)

'Full with' will be replaced with 'Full of' as the phrase 'Full of' means completely, including the whole of something.

Hence, 'A suitcase full of' is the most appropriate answer.

223. You should tell / these children to complete / their projects himself.
SSC CGL Tier-2 08.08.2022

(a) You should tell
(b) No error
(c) these children to complete
(d) their projects himself

Ans. (d)

There is an error of pronoun in the given sentence.

The reflexive pronoun 'himself' must be replaced with 'themselves' as there is a plural subject 'children' in the sentence. Hence, 'their projects themselves' is the most appropriate answer.

224. Open your / books at / page tenth.

(a) No error **SSC CGL Tier-2 08.08.2022**
(b) Open your
(c) page tenth
(d) books at

Ans. (c)

'Tenth' must be replaced with 'ten' as the word 'tenth' is used to denote the position of something and the word 'ten' is used to denote the number. Hence, 'page ten' is the most appropriate answer.

225. A misunderstanding / has crept / between he / and his sister.
SSC CGL Tier-2 08.08.2022

(a) and his sister
(b) between he
(c) has crept
(d) A misunderstanding

Ans. (b)

There is an error of pronoun in the given sentence. 'He' must be replaced with 'him' as we need to use the objective case of the third person pronoun 'he.'

Hence, 'between him' is the most appropriate answer.

226. Scarcely had he / took the medicine / when his headache was gone.
SSC CGL Tier-2 08.08.2022

(a) when his headache was gone
(b) No error
(c) took the medicine
(d) Scarcely had he

Ans. (c)

We generally use (V_3) with the helping verb 'has / have / had.' Hence, 'taken the medicine' is the most appropriate answer.

227. Contented people / seldom complaint / against / their fate.

(a) their fate **SSC CGL Tier-2 08.08.2022**
(b) against
(c) Contented people
(d) seldom complaint

Ans. (d)

'Complaint' will be replaced with 'complain' as we need a verb to make the sentence grammatically correct. Hence, 'seldom complain' is the most appropriate answer.

228. If you study hard, / you surely got selected / for the scholarship.
SSC CGL Tier-2 08.08.2022

(a) for the scholarship
(b) you surely got selected
(c) No error
(d) If you study hard

Ans. (b)

The given sentence is the first conditional sentence and the correct grammatical structure is (If + simple present tense, simple future tense). Hence, 'you surely will get selected' is the most appropriate answer.

229. He said that / he had forgot / to lock the door / before leaving.
SSC CGL Tier-2 08.08.2022

(a) to lock the door (b) He said that
(c) he had forgot (d) before leaving

Ans. (c)

We generally use (V_3) with the helping verbs 'has/have/had' and the 3rd form of 'forget' is 'forgotten.'

Hence, 'he had forgotten' is the most appropriate answer.

230. It turned out to be / the noisy park party / anybody had ever attended.
SSC CGL Tier-2 08.08.2022

(a) No error
(b) the noisy park party
(c) anybody had ever attended
(d) It turned out to be

Ans. (b)

'Superlative degree' denotes the form of an adjective or adverb that expresses the highest or a very high degree of quality of a thing, person, etc.

For example, most, best, worst, greatest, etc. However, we always place the definite article 'the' before any superlative adjective. Similarly, in the given sentence, we need to use superlative degree. Hence, 'The most noisy park party' is the most appropriate answer.

231. This story is quite interesting / but I have read / much interesting stories than this. **SSC CGL Tier-2 08.08.2022**

(a) much interesting stories than this
(b) but I have read
(c) No error
(d) This story is quite interesting

Ans. (a)

Use 'more' in place of 'much.' For comparison we use the word 'more' and not 'much.' Hence, 'More interesting stories than this' is the most appropriate answer.

SSC CGL 2021 (Tier 1 & 2)

232. Had you / not reached in time, / we will have / lost our lives.
SSC CGL Tier-1 13.08.2021 (Shift-I)

(a) not reached in time
(b) Had you
(c) lost our lives
(d) we will have

Ans. (d)

Part (d) 'we will have' contains an error. The correct phrase would be 'we would have' to make the sentence grammatically correct.

233. You must avoid riding in a crowded bus / or travelling in a metro / during rush hour / as both are quiet unpleasant experiences.
SSC CGL Tier-1 13.08.2021 (Shift-I)

(a) during rush hour
(b) or travelling in a metro
(c) You must avoid riding in a crowded bus
(d) as both are quiet unpleasant experiences

Ans. (d)

Part (d) 'as both are quiet unpleasant experiences' contains an error.

The adverb 'quite' should substitute the adverb 'quiet' (meaning, 'silent') to rectify the sentence.

234. Lack of required / vitamins and minerals / lead against / several complications / in the human body.

SSC CGL Tier-1 13.08.2021 (Shift-III)

(a) lead against
(b) Lack of required
(c) in the human body
(d) several complications

Ans. (a)

Part (a) 'lead against' contains an error. The correct preposition to be used with 'lead' is 'to.'

235. The Dussehra celebrations/in Mysore/this year/are grandest than/in any other part/of the state.

SSC CGL Tier-1 13.08.2021 (Shift-III)

(a) in any other part
(b) are grandest than
(c) The Dussehra celebrations
(d) in Mysore

Ans. (b)

Part (b) 'are grandest than' contains an error. The correct phrase would be 'are grander than' as a comparison is made between Mysore and other states.

236. It have been only/through writing/that men have been able/to spread their ideas to mankind.

SSC CGL Tier-1 16.08.2021 (Shift-I)

(a) to spread their ideas to mankind
(b) It have been only
(c) that men have been able
(d) through writing

Ans. (b)

Part (b) 'It have been only' contains an error. The correct phrase would be 'It is only.'

237. Won't you/please come/to help me/along this heavy box?

SSC CGL Tier-1 16.08.2021 (Shift-I)

(a) to help me (b) Won't you
(c) please come (d) along this heavy box

Ans. (d)

Part (d) 'along this heavy box' contains an error. The preposition 'with' should be used instead of 'along.'

238. The recruiters/were pleased/ to John's/ domain knowledge and personality.

SSC CGL Tier-1 16.08.2021 (Shift-III)

(a) to John's
(b) were pleased
(c) domain knowledge and personality
(d) The recruiters

Ans. (a)

Part (a) 'to John's contains an error. The preposition 'to' should be replaced with the preposition 'with' as 'with' is used with 'pleased.'

239. The sea has become / an cheap dumping ground / for all kinds / of waste products.

SSC CGL Tier-1 17.08.2021 (Shift-I)

(a) of waste products
(b) an cheap dumping ground
(c) for all kinds
(d) The sea has become

Ans. (b)

Part (b) 'an cheap dumping ground' contains an error. The correct phrase would be 'a cheap dumping ground.'

Article 'a' is used before a word beginning with a consonant sound.

240. He win/several accolades/for his/ music compositions.

SSC CGL Tier-1 17.08.2021 (Shift-III)

(a) several accolades
(b) for his
(c) He win
(d) music compositions

Ans. (c)

Part (c) 'He win' contains an error. The correct phrase would be 'He has won' as the sentence talks about an action whose effects are visible in the present indicating present perfect tense.

241. Lalitha will go/to sister's house/in Mumbai/this summer.

SSC CGL Tier-1 18.08.2021 (Shift-I)

(a) to sister's house
(b) this summer
(c) in Mumbai
(d) Lalitha will go

Ans. (a)

Part (a) 'to sister's house' contains an error.

The correct phrase can be 'to her sister's house' to make the sentence error free.

242. The weather / is much / more warmer/than it was a few days before. SSC CGL Tier-1 18.08.2021 (Shift-III)

(a) than it was a few days before
(b) is much
(c) The weather
(d) more warmer

Ans. (d)

Part (d) 'more warmer' contains an error.

The use of 'more' is redundant in the sentence, as warmer already indicates the comparative degree.

243. Ranbir could not went / to the award ceremony / as he was busy / shooting / for a film / in Maldives.

SSC CGL Tier-1 20.08.2021 (Shift-I)

(a) for a film
(b) as he was busy
(c) Ranbir could not went
(d) to the award ceremony

Ans. (c)

Part (c) 'Ranbir could not went' contains an error. The correct phrase would be 'Ranbir could not go.'

244. My brother/ who live in Pune / is arriving tomorrow.

SSC CGL Tier-1 20.08.2021 (Shift-II)

(a) No error
(b) is arriving tomorrow
(c) who live in Pune
(d) My brother

Ans. (c)

Part (c) 'who live in Pune' contains an error. 'Lives' should be used in place of 'live' to rectify the segment.

245. The Committee agreed/that small businesses/ has been adversely affected /by COVID-19.

SSC CGL Tier-1 20.08.2021 (Shift-II)

(a) The Committee agreed
(b) that small businesses
(c) has been adversely affected
(d) by COVID-19

Ans. (c)

Part (c) 'has been adversely affected' contains an error. The correct phrase would be, 'have been adversely affected' as the plural noun 'small businesses' should take plural verb 'have.'

246. The army/marched fearless / towards / the enemy cantonment.

SSC CGL Tier-1 23.08.2021 (Shift-I)

(a) marched fearless
(b) towards
(c) The army
(d) the enemy cantonment

Ans. (a)

Part (a) 'marched fearless' contains an error. The adverb 'fearlessly' should be used to modify the verb 'marched' and make the sentence grammatically correct.

247. The concept became / too much clear to me / after my tutor / showed me the diagram.

SSC CGL Tier-1 23.08.2021 (Shift-II)

(a) showed me the diagram
(b) The concept became
(c) after my tutor
(d) too much clear to me

Ans. (d)

Part (d) 'too much clear to me' contains an error. The correct phrase would be 'very clear to me.'

248. The food/in the new eatery/ is much best than/the one in RK Puram. **SSC CGL Tier-1 24.08.2021 (Shift-I)**

(a) The food
(b) is much best than
(c) the one in RK Puram
(d) in the new eatery

Ans. (b)

Part (b) 'is much best than' contains an error. With 'much', the comparative degree 'better' should be used. So, to make the sentence grammatically correct, 'is much better than' shall be used.

249. All those students/who are participating / in the play / have been notify/ to stay back for rehearsal / after 3:00 pm. **SSC CGL Tier-1 24.08.2021 (Shift-II)**

(a) after 3:00 pm
(b) to stay back for rehearsal
(c) have been notify
(d) who are participating

Ans. (c)

Part (c) 'have been notify' contains an error. Here, the sentence belongs to present perfect continuous.

So, 'have been notifying' should be used in place of 'have been notify' to make the sentence grammatically correct.

250. After entering the town, / go straight and then/ take a sharpest turn/towards your left /to reach the mall. **SSC CGL Tier-1 24.08.2021 (Shift-II)**

(a) take a sharpest turn
(b) After entering the town
(c) towards your left
(d) to reach the mall

Ans. (a)

Part (a) 'take a sharpest turn' contains an error. The correct phrase will be 'take the sharp turn' to make the sentence grammatically correct.

251. Mithila art tradition is passed on/ from one generation through a next /by children watching and helping /their mothers and grandmothers. **SSC CGL Tier-1 24.08.2021 (Shift-III)**

(a) their mothers and grandmothers
(b) Mithila art tradition is passed on
(c) from one generation through a next
(d) by children watching and helping

Ans. (c)

Part (c) 'from one generation through a next' contains an error. The correct phrase would be 'from one generation to the next.'

SSC CPO 2024 (Tier 1 & 2)

252. Specialists say that / this method speeds up / language learning tremendously. **SSC CPO Tier-2 08.01.2024**

(a) Specialists say that
(b) language learning tremendously
(c) No error
(d) this method speeds up

Ans. (c)

The given sentence is grammatically correct and contextually meaningful.

253. Two elderly gentlemen / told the rather improbable / story to mislead / the police personnel. **SSC CPO Tier-2 08.01.2024**

(a) story to mislead
(b) told the rather improbable
(c) the police personnel
(d) Two elderly gentlemen

Ans. (b)

'The' must be replaced with 'a.' Article 'the' is used for specific or particular nouns but the 'story' mentioned in the sentence is not specific. Hence, 'told a rather improbable' is the most appropriate answer.

254. We cannot postpone / discussion on this issue / although it is urgent. **SSC CPO Tier-2 08.01.2024**

(a) although it is urgent
(b) No error
(c) We cannot postpone
(d) discussion on this issue

Ans. (a)

Part (a) 'Although' must be replaced with 'as/ because.' The issue is urgent, that is why discussion on it cannot be postponed.

Here, we need a connector to show the cause or reason. Hence, 'because it is urgent' is the most appropriate answer.

255. Are you yet / afraid of going out / in the dark? **SSC CPO Tier-2 08.01.2024**

(a) in the dark
(b) Are you yet
(c) No error
(d) afraid of going out

Ans. (b)

Part (b) 'Yet' must be replaced with 'still.'

'Yet' is used to show contrast between two events. 'Still' is used to show that an action was happening in the past and continuing in the present. Hence, 'Are you still' is the most appropriate answer.

256. Rohit Sharma's century / was very acclaimed / in the media. **SSC CPO Tier-2 08.01.2024**

(a) was very acclaimed
(b) No error
(c) Rohit Sharma's century
(d) in the media

Ans. (a)

Part (a) 'Very' must be replaced with 'much.' 'Very' is used with present participles (V_{ing}) not with past participles (V_3). Hence, 'much acclaimed' is the most appropriate answer.

257. You can take a horse / to the water / but you cannot / make it to drink. **SSC CPO Tier-2 08.01.2024**

(a) You can take a horse
(b) make it to drink
(c) but you cannot
(d) to the water

Ans. (b)

Part (b) 'To' must be removed. There are some verbs that take a bare infinitive (without 'to') after them. These are 'make, let, bid, see, watch, observe.' Hence, 'make it drink' is the most appropriate answer.

258. One must do his/his duty proparly. **SSC CPO Tier-2 08.01.2024**

(a) One must do ones duty properly.
(b) One must do one's duty properly.
(c) One must do once duty proparly.
(d) One must do one's duty proprly.

Ans. (b)

Each pronoun has its own possessive adjective. For example- (I/my), (he/his), (she/her), (one/one's). Hence, option (b) is the correct sentence.

259. It is time someone takes / concrete steps to alleviate / the problem of unemployment / in the country. **SSC CPO Tier-2 08.01.2024**

(a) the problem of unemployment
(b) It is time someone takes
(c) in the country
(d) concrete steps to alleviate

Ans. (b)

Part (b) Simple past tense (Subject + V_2) is used after phrases such as 'It is time / It is about time / It is high time.' Therefore, 'takes' will be replaced with 'took (V_2).' Hence, 'It is time someone took' is the most appropriate answer.

260. None than you / deserve credit / for the success / of this project. **SSC CPO Tier-2 08.01.2024**

(a) deserve credit (b) for the success
(c) None than you (d) of this project

Ans. (c)

Part (c) 'Than' must be replaced with 'but.' The correct phrase is 'none but' or 'none other than', which means 'only.' Hence, 'none but you' is the most appropriate answer.

261. Hold my hand / you should not / get lost in the huge / crowd at the fair. **SSC CPO Tier-2 08.01.2024**

(a) lest you should not
(b) Hold my hand
(c) crowd at the fair
(d) get lost in the huge

Ans. (a)

Part (a) 'Lest' is used without 'not.' Hence, 'lest you should' is the most appropriate answer.

262. I will definitely accept / the responsibility / while the time comes. **SSC CPO Tier-2 08.01.2024**

(a) the responsibility
(b) No error
(c) I will definitely accept
(d) while the time comes

Ans. (d)

Part (d) 'While' must be replaced with 'when.' The phrase 'when the time comes' is used to state an action that will be done in the suitable circumstances. Hence, 'when the time comes' is the most appropriate answer.

263. Let us work out / the details of / our endeavour / shouldn't we? **SSC CPO Tier-2 08.01.2024**

(a) the details of (b) shouldn't we
(c) our endeavour (d) Let us work out

Ans. (b)

Part (b) 'Shall we' is the correct question tag for an imperative sentence starting with 'let us.' Hence, 'shall we' is the most appropriate answer.

264. I am understanding;/ you like her/ because she has /a generous nature. **SSC CPO Tier-1 27.06.2024 (Shift-I)**

(a) you like her
(b) I am understanding
(c) a generous nature
(d) because she has

Ans. (b)

Part (b) 'I am understanding' contains an error. Use 'I understand' to correct the sentence.

265. When he resigned, / the company offered him / a huge sum of money but / he refused to agree to it. **SSC CPO Tier-1 27.06.2024 (Shift-I)**

(a) a huge sum of money but
(b) When he resigned,
(c) he refused to agree to it.
(d) the company offered him

Ans. (c)

Part (c) 'he refused to agree to it' contains an error.

The use of 'agree to' is incorrect in the context of the sentence. It should be 'accept.'

266. Since his son has not yet completed the age of eighteen, <u>he was reluctant to fulfill his son's demand of getting a motorbike</u>. **SSC CPO Tier-1 27.06.2024 (Shift-I)**

(a) of getting a motorbike
(b) No error
(c) to fulfil his son's demand
(d) he was reluctant

Ans. (d)

Part (d) 'he was reluctant' contains an error. As the given sentence is in present tense, 'is' should be used in place of 'was.'

267. Can we go / visit a Statue of Liberty / on our trip to / the United States? **SSC CPO Tier-1 27.06.2024 (Shift-I)**

(a) on our trip to
(b) Can we go
(c) the United States?
(d) visit a Statue of Liberty

Ans. (d)

Part 'Visit a Statue of Liberty' contains an error. As 'Statue of Liberty' is a unique monument, article 'the' will be used with it.

268. We were/grateful for / a book / they gave us. **SSC CPO Tier-1 27.06.2024 (Shift-I)**

(a) they gave us (b) We were
(c) grateful for (d) a book

Ans. (d)

Part 'A book' contains an error. As we are referring to a specific book, article 'the' will be used with it.

269. We were driving / home / when suddenly / a deer runs across the road. **SSC CPO Tier-1 27.06.2024 (Shift-II)**

(a) home
(b) We were driving
(c) a deer runs across the road
(d) when suddenly

Ans. (c)

Part 'A deer runs across the road' contains an error. As the sentence is in past tense, 'ran' should be used.

270. His energetic attitude / showed that he had / soundly slept / the previous night. **SSC CPO Tier-1 27.06.2024 (Shift-II)**

(a) His energetic attitude
(b) showed that he had
(c) the previous night.
(d) soundly slept

Ans. (d)

Part 'Soundly slept' contains an error. The correct phrase should be 'slept soundly' to maintain proper adverb placement as adverb of manner is placed after the verb.

271. I will be arrange all the necessary materials for the programme. **SSC CPO Tier-1 27.06.2024 (Shift-II)**

(a) I was arrange all the necessary materials for the programme.
(b) I would arranging all the necessary materials for the programme.
(c) I is arrange all the necessary materials for the programme.
(d) I will be arranging all the necessary materials for the programme.

Ans. (d)

The error in the original sentence is in the tense used. 'I will be arrange' is incorrect because it combines 'will be' (future continuous tense) with 'arrange' (which should be in the present participle form 'arranging' for future continuous tense).

The correct sentence from the options provided is 'I will be arranging all the necessary materials for the programme.' This option correctly uses the future continuous tense ('will be arranging') to indicate an action that will be ongoing in the future.

272. Mrs. Gomathi was / that tired and weak / that she could / scarcely walk. **SSC CPO Tier-1 27.06.2024 (Shift-II)**

(a) Mrs. Gomathi was
(b) that she could
(c) scarcely walk.
(d) that tired and weak

Ans. (d)

Part 'that tired and weak' contains an adverbial usage error.

The correct adverbial usage should be 'so tired and weak that she could scarcely walk.'

273. It is a cheap reasonably / restaurant in this part of the town / where you can eat / delicious food. **SSC CPO Tier-1 27.06.2024 (Shift-II)**

(a) delicious food
(b) restaurant in this part of the town
(c) It is a cheap reasonably
(d) where you can eat

Ans. (c)

Part 'It is a cheap reasonably' contains the error. The correct phrase should be 'reasonably priced' instead of 'cheap reasonably.'

274. Ms. Malathi is living lonely in an apartment.
SSC CPO Tier-1 27.06.2024 (Shift-III)
(a) is living (b) lonely in
(c) Ms. Malathi (d) an apartment

Ans. (b)

Part 'lonely in' contains an error. The use of the word 'lonely' is incorrect. Remove it or place it after the word 'apartment' to correct the sentence.

275. The art historian argued that the painting's value has been greatly underestimated and that its unique style and technique deserved recognition from the art community and the public alike.
SSC CPO Tier-1 27.06.2024 (Shift-III)
(a) its unique style and technique
(b) has been greatly underestimated
(c) recognition from the art community
(d) and the public alike

Ans. (b)

Part 'Has been greatly underestimated' contains an error. As the sentence is in past perfect tense, the verb would be 'had been.'

276. Mr. Vinu / has never / slept in / a igloo. SSC CPO Tier-1 27.06.2024 (Shift-III)
(a) slept in
(b) a igloo
(c) Mr. Vinu
(d) has never

Ans. (b)

Part 'A igloo' contains an error. The use of article 'a' before 'igloo' is incorrect. As the word 'igloo' starts with a vowel, 'an' should be used.

277. My neighbours were / serious injured / in / the car accident.
SSC CPO Tier-1 27.06.2024 (Shift-III)
(a) serious injured
(b) My neighbours were
(c) the car accident
(d) in

Ans. (a)

Part 'Serious injured' contains an error.

The sentence requires an adverb to qualify the noun. Hence, 'seriously' must be used.

278. I am working with him since 2002, / but even today / I am unable / to understand his motives.
SSC CPO Tier-1 27.06.2024 (Shift-III)
(a) I am unable
(b) I am working with him since 2002,
(c) to understand his motives.
(d) but even today

Ans. (b)

Part 'I am working with him since 2002' contains an error. The sentence talks of an action that started in the past and is still in continuation. Hence, present perfect continuous tense 'have been working' should be used.

279. Mr. Thomas / is going / to buy / horse. SSC CPO Tier-1 28.06.2024 (Shift-I)
(a) is going (b) Mr. Thomas
(c) to buy (d) horse

Ans. (d)

Part 'Horse' contains the error. The error lies in the omission of the article 'a' before the word 'horse.' Therefore, option (d) is the correct answer.

280. By the time I reaching / the metro station, / the train had departed.
SSC CPO Tier-1 28.06.2024 (Shift-I)
(a) No error
(b) the metro station
(c) the train had departed
(d) By the time I reaching

Ans. (d)

Part 'By the time I reaching' contains the error.

The error lies in the incorrect verb form 'reaching.' It should be changed to 'reached' to match the past tense structure of the sentence.

281. Last night I dreamed that / I am looking for the/ abominable snowman high / up in the Himalayas.
SSC CPO Tier-1 28.06.2024 (Shift-I)
(a) abominable snowman high
(b) up in the Himalayas
(c) I am looking for the
(d) Last night I dreamed that

Ans. (c)

Part 'I am looking for the' contains the error. In reported speech or narrative past tense, the verb form 'am looking' should be changed to 'was looking' to maintain consistency with the past tense structure of the sentence.

282. My father / is / comparatively better / today. SSC CPO Tier-1 28.06.2024 (Shift-I)
(a) comparatively better
(b) is
(c) My father
(d) today.

Ans. (a)

Part 'Comparatively better' contains an error.

The word 'comparatively' is redundant here because the word 'better' already implies a comparison.

283. If I have recovered from fever, / I will start going / for swimming classes / from tomorrow.
SSC CPO Tier-1 28.06.2024 (Shift-I)
(a) I will start going
(b) for swimming classes
(c) from tomorrow
(d) If I have recovered from fever

Ans. (d)

Part 'If I have recovered from fever' contains an error.

The use of 'have recovered' is incorrect here because the sentence is in the future tense, indicating a condition that will happen in the future ('will start going'). Therefore, it should use the simple present tense ('If I recover from fever').

284. When my father will come, I will make sure that I discuss the possibilities of a new business venture with him.
SSC CPO Tier-1 28.06.2024 (Shift-II)
(a) No error
(b) I discuss the possibilities
(c) When my father will come
(d) I will make sure

Ans. (c)

Part 'When my father will come' contains an error. We do not use the future tense ('will come') after subordinate conjunctions like 'when', 'if', 'after', etc. Instead, we use the simple present tense to indicate future actions. Therefore, it should be 'When my father comes, I will make sure that I discuss the possibilities of a new business venture with him.'

285. Soldiers in / the Indian Armed Forces are / trained never to / fight cowardly SSC CPO Tier-1 28.06.2024 (Shift-II)
(a) fight cowardly
(b) Soldiers in
(c) the Indian Armed Forces are
(d) trained never to

Ans. (d)

Part 'Trained never to' contains an error. The word 'never' would be place before the verb 'trained.'

286. The committee work diligently to ensure fair and unbiased decision.
SSC CPO Tier-1 28.06.2024 (Shift-II)
(a) The committee is work diligently to ensure fair and unbiased decision.
(b) The committee works diligently to ensure fair and unbiased decision.
(c) The committee has work diligently to ensure fair and unbiased decision.
(d) The committee worked diligently to ensure fair and unbiased decision.

Ans. (b)

The grammatically correct sentence is- The committee works diligently to ensure fair and unbiased decision. This option corrects the verb form to 'works,' which agrees with the singular subject 'committee' in the present tense.

287. Ramesh licked (A) / honey and (B) / said that (C) / it tasted sweetly. (D)
SSC CPO Tier-1 28.06.2024 (Shift-III)

(a) D (b) A (c) B (d) C

Ans. (a)

The segment that contains the error is answer (D). The correct adverbial form should be 'sweet', not 'sweetly.' Therefore, the corrected segment should be 'it tasted sweet.'

288. Mr. Sukesh and / his family / ate the / food greedy.
SSC CPO Tier-1 28.06.2024 (Shift-III)

(a) ate the (b) Mr. Sukesh and
(c) his family (d) food greedy

Ans. (d)

Part 'Food greedy' contains an error. The correct adverbial form should be 'greedily.' Therefore, the corrected segment should be 'ate the food greedily.'

289. The people of / Jammu and Kashmir / has emphasised and / appreciated transparency.
SSC CPO Tier-1 28.06.2024 (Shift-III)

(a) appreciated transparency
(b) The people of
(c) has emphasised and
(d) Jammu and Kashmir

Ans. (c)

Part 'has emphasised and' contains an error. The correct verb form should agree with the plural subject 'people,' so it should be 'have emphasised and.' Therefore, the corrected sentence would be 'The people of Jammu and Kashmir have emphasised and appreciated transparency'.

290. Himalayas include the / highest mountains in / the world and feed / almost 20% of the Earths population.
SSC CPO Tier-1 28.06.2024 (Shift-III)

(a) almost 20% of the Earths population.
(b) highest mountains in
(c) the world and feed
(d) Himalayas include the

Ans. (d)

Part 'himalayas include the' contains an error. The correct form should be 'The Himalayas include,' as 'Himalayas' is a plural noun and requires a plural verb form. Therefore, the corrected sentence would be 'The Himalayas include the highest mountains in the world and feed almost 20% of the earths population.'

291. When Ramu was working / as a clerk, / he asked me money.
SSC CPO Tier-1 29.06.2024 (Shift-I)

(a) When Ramu was working
(b) as a clerk
(c) No error
(d) he asked me money

Ans. (d)

Part 'he asked me money' contains an error. The correct phrase should be 'he asked me for money.'

292. Mrs. Rani / works for / a international / school.
SSC CPO Tier-1 29.06.2024 (Shift-I)

(a) works for (b) school
(c) a international (d) Mrs. Rani

Ans. (c)

Part 'a international' contains an error. The correct phrase should be 'an international' as 'an' is used with words starting from a vowel sound.

293. (a) I will be drive into town later on.
(b) I will be driving into town later on.
(c) I might drive into town later on.
(d) I could be driving into town later on.
SSC CPO Tier-1 29.06.2024 (Shift-I)

Ans. (a)

The sentence with a grammatical error is 'I will be drive into town later on.' In option (a), 'drive' should be changed to 'driving' to form a grammatically correct sentence. The corrected version should be 'I will be driving into town later on.'

294. Mohan insisted to go there.
SSC CPO Tier-1 29.06.2024 (Shift-I)

(a) Error is with the tense. The correct sentence should read like this answer. Mohan insisting to go there.
(b) Error is in the sentence formation. Preposition and gerund are required. The correct sentence should read like this answer. Mohan insisted on going there.
(c) Error is with the verb. The correct sentence should read like this answer. Mohan insist to going there.
(d) Error is with the preposition. The correct sentence should read like this answer. Mohan insisted go there.

Ans. (b)

The sentence 'Mohan insisted to go there' contains an error is in the sentence formation. Preposition and gerund are required. The correct sentence should read like this Mohan insisted on going there. In this sentence, 'insisted on going' is the correct usage because 'insist on' is followed by a gerund (the '-ing' form of a verb) to indicate what Mohan insisted upon doing.

295. Most of the committee / are here to / decide the fate of / this ancient building. SSC CPO Tier-1 29.06.2024 (Shift-I)

(a) are here to
(b) Most of the committee
(c) decide the fate of
(d) this ancient building.

Ans. (a)

Part 'are here to' contains an error. As the word 'committee' is a collective noun, singular verb 'is' should be used.

296. The sons of the old farmer / fell off after their father / breathed his last / in the village.
SSC CPO Tier-1 29.06.2024 (Shift-II)

(a) in the village.
(b) breathed his last
(c) The sons of the old farmer
(d) fell off after their father

Ans. (d)

Part 'fell off after their father' contains an error. The use of 'fell off' is incorrect in the sentence. We need to use 'fell apart' which mean destroyed.

297. I had done / my cooking when / Vishnu came to see me.
SSC CPO Tier-1 29.06.2024 (Shift-II)

(a) No error
(b) I had done
(c) Vishnu came to see me
(d) my cooking when

Ans. (a)

The given sentence is grammatically correct and contextually meaningful.

298. There are four tributaries / of Ganga and it / is ranked as the fifth / most polluted river of the world.
SSC CPO Tier-1 29.06.2024 (Shift-II)

(a) is ranked as the fifth
(b) of Ganga and it
(c) There are four tributaries
(d) most polluted river of the world

Ans. (b)

Part 'of Ganga and it' contains an error. The use of 'it' is incorrect in the sentence as plural pronoun is used. Hence, use 'they are' in place of 'it is.'

299. Had you been / working regularly, / you had completed / the project yesterdaySSC CPO Tier-1 29.06.2024 (Shift-II)

(a) Had you been
(b) the project yesterday
(c) you had completed
(d) working regularly

Ans. (c)

Part 'you had completed' contains an error. The correct form should be 'you would have completed' instead of 'you had completed' to indicate the conditional past perfect tense correctly.

300. For the past / three years, / my uncle is /away from home.
SSC CPO Tier-1 29.06.2024 (Shift-III)

(a) three years
(b) For the past
(c) my uncle is
(d) away from home

Ans. (c)

Part 'my uncle is' contains an error. The correct form should be 'my uncle has been' instead of 'my uncle is' to indicate the continuous action over a period of time.

301. Although there is no proven data / the Centre for Policy Research estimate / that India has the largest stock / of iron ore in the world.
SSC CPO Tier-1 29.06.2024 (Shift-III)

(a) Although there is no proven data
(b) Centre for Policy Research estimate
(c) No error
(d) India has the largest stock

Ans. (b)

Part 'centre for Policy Research estimate' contains an error. The correct form should be 'Centre for Policy Research estimates' because it refers to a singular entity (Centre for Policy Research) and hence requires a singular verb form.

302. Mr. Prabhakar / was first man / to arrive / at the venue.
SSC CPO Tier-1 29.06.2024 (Shift-III)

(a) was first man
(b) Mr. Prabhakar
(c) to arrive
(d) at the venue

Ans. (a)

Part 'was first man' contains an error. The correct phrase should be 'was the first man' instead of 'was first man.' The definite article 'the' is necessary before 'first.'

303. Mr. Raghav / brushes his / teeth four / times the day.
SSC CPO Tier-1 29.06.2024 (Shift-III)

(a) brushes his (b) times the day
(c) Mr. Raghav (d) teeth four

Ans. (b)

Part 'times the day' contains the error. The correct phrase should be 'times a day' instead of 'times the day.'

304. Raveena has made / up her mind to / carried minimum / luggage with her. **SSC CPO Tier-1 29.06.2024 (Shift-III)**

(a) Raveena has made
(b) up her mind to
(c) carried minimum
(d) luggage with her.

Ans. (c)

Part 'carried minimum' contains an error. The correct form should be 'carry minimum,' not 'carried minimum.'

SSC CPO 2023

305. The dancers / swayed dainty / on the stage / last night.
SSC CPO Tier-1 03.10.2023 (Shift-I)

(a) last night (b) on the stage
(c) The dancers (d) swayed dainty

Ans. (d)

Part 'swayed dainty' contains the error. The verb should be followed by an adverb. Hence, we need to replace it by 'swayed gracefully' to correct the sentence.

306. We feed the horse oats / for a week because / it had eaten all the hay.
SSC CPO Tier-1 03.10.2023 (Shift-I)

(a) No error
(b) it had eaten all the hay
(c) We feed the horse oats
(d) for a week because

Ans. (c)

Part 'we feed the horse oats' contains an error. We need to replace 'feed' with 'fed' as the sentence is in the past tense.

307. He wrote his dairy / in code / so, that nobody / could understand it.
SSC CPO Tier-1 03.10.2023 (Shift-I)

(a) so, that nobody
(b) could understand it
(c) in code
(d) He wrote his dairy

Ans. (d)

Part 'he wrote his dairy' contains the error of tense. As the sentence presents a general statement, simple present tense, 'writes', should be used.

308. They will not attend / the event / as they're going / away at end of April. **SSC CPO Tier-1 03.10.2023 (Shift-I)**

(a) away at end of April
(b) as they're going
(c) the event
(d) They will not attend

Ans. (a)

Part 'at end of April' contains an error. Add 'the' before 'end' to correct the sentence.

309. I wanted to buy a candle holder/ but the store didn't have none/ so, I got a cake. **SSC CPO Tier-1 03.10.2023 (Shift-II)**

(a) No error
(b) I wanted to buy a candle holder
(c) but the store didn't have one
(d) so, I got a cake

Ans. (a)

The given sentence is grammatically correct and contextually meaningful.

310. You arrived two days ago / By the time you leave / you will have spent nine days here.
SSC CPO Tier-1 03.10.2023 (Shift-II)

(a) You arrived two days ago
(b) you will have spent nine days here
(c) By the time you leave
(d) No error

Ans. (d)

The given sentence is grammatically correct and contextually meaningful.

311. (a) The simple mistake which was committed by the boy haunted her for years.
(b) An simple mistake which was committed by the boy haunted her for years.
(c) The simple mistake which was committed by an boy haunted her for years.
(d) A simple mistake which was committed by an boy haunted her for years. **SSC CPO Tier-1 03.10.2023 (Shift-III)**

Ans. (a)

The simple mistake which was committed by the boy haunted her for years.(Correct Article).
(b) **An simple** mistake which was committed by the boy haunted her for years.(Incorrect Article)
(c) The simple mistake which was committed by haunted **an boy** her for years.(Incorrect Article)
(d) A simple mistake which was committed by **an boy** haunted her for years.(Incorrect Article)

312. There is a spectrum / of seas around that / land which attracts / tourists of all aging.
SSC CPO Tier-1 03.10.2023 (Shift-III)

(a) There is a spectrum
(b) land which attracts
(c) of seas around that
(d) tourists of all aging

Ans. (d)

'Aging' must be replaced with 'ages.' 'of all ages' is a phrase which means people belonging to all age groups. Hence, 'tourists of all ages' is the most appropriate answer.

313. Neem tastes / a little bitterly, / but is very useful. SSC CPO Tier-1 04.10.2023 (Shift-I)

(a) a little bitterly
(b) Neem tastes
(c) but is very useful
(d) No error

Ans. (a)

'Bitterly' must be replaced with the adjective 'bitter.' 'Taste' is a stative verb and stative verbs require an adjective after them, not adverb. Hence, 'a little bitter' is the most appropriate answer.

314. Rani was / extreme upset / with her results / this year. SSC CPO Tier-1 04.10.2023 (Shift-I)

(a) Rani was (b) this year
(c) with her results (d) extreme upset

Ans. (d)

'Extreme' must be replaced with 'extremely.' The given sentence requires an adverb to modify the meaning of the adjective 'upset'. Hence, 'extremely upset' is the most appropriate answer.

315. The postman / delivers the letters / through hand, / door to door. SSC CPO Tier-1 04.10.2023 (Shift-I)

(a) delivers the letters (b) The postman
(c) through hand (d) door to door

Ans. (c)

'By' is used to show the means or method used to do something whereas 'through' is used to talk about the process by which something happens. Similarly, the given sentence shows that the postman delivers the letters using his hands. Hence, 'by hand' is the most appropriate answer.

316. Luckily, I managed to get a room / in the college hostel / and I move in there. SSC CPO Tier-1 04.10.2023 (Shift-I)

(a) in the college hostel
(b) No error
(c) and I move in there
(d) Luckily, I managed to get a room

Ans. (c)

'Move' must be replaced with 'moved.' The given sentence is in past tense, so the verb must be used in the past form (moved). Hence, 'and I moved there' is the most appropriate answer.

317. Mr. Khanna and family / have visit / Manali during / the summer vacation. SSC CPO (Tier-I) 04.10.2023 (Shift-II)

(a) have visit
(b) Mr. Khanna and family
(c) the summer vacation
(d) Manali during

Ans. (a)

Use 'have visited' instead of 'have visit' as we use third form of verb with 'has/have.'

318. There was no other book / in the English language / which is as interesting as this one. SSC CPO Tier-1 04.10.2023 (Shift-II)

(a) There was no other book
(b) in the English language
(c) No error
(d) which is as interesting as this one

Ans. (a)

'There was no other book' is incorrect as the presence of the word 'other' is unnecessary. Remove 'other' to correct the sentence.

319. I have never / come to / such a kind person / like my friend. SSC CPO Tier-1 04.10.2023 (Shift-II)

(a) such a kind person
(b) like my friend
(c) come to
(d) I have never

Ans. (c)

The use of preposition 'to' is incorrect in the sentence. Use preposition 'across' is correct in the context of the sentence.

320. The university has putting off / the semester examination / for the second time now / due to technical issues. SSC CPO Tier-1 04.10.2023 (Shift-II)

(a) the semester examination
(b) due to technical issues
(c) for the second time now
(d) The university has putting off

Ans. (d)

'The university has putting off' is incorrect as the structure of present perfect continuous tense is has/have+ been + '-ing' form of verb. Hence, add 'been' after 'has.'

321. Anant was telling a story / about his most recent exploits / when a tree branch break the living room window. SSC CPO Tier-1 04.10.2023 (Shift-II)

(a) about his most recent exploits
(b) when a tree branch break the living room window
(c) Anant was telling a story
(d) No error

Ans. (b)

Part 'when a tree branch break the living room window' contains an error. As the given sentence is in past tense, use 'broke' in place of 'break.'

322. We should / not make an noise / in the class. SSC CPO Tier-1 04.10.2023 (Shift-III)

(a) not make an noise
(b) in the class
(c) We should
(d) No error

Ans. (a)

'An noise' must be replaced with 'a noise.' Article 'A' is used before the words starting from a consonant sound - (a conversation, a story). Hence, 'not make a noise' is the most appropriate answer.

323. I was wish / to meet her / on her birthday. SSC CPO Tier-1 04.10.2023 (Shift-III)

(a) to meet her (b) No error
(c) I was wish (d) on her birthday

Ans. (c)

'I was wish' must be replaced with 'I wish' as we generally use the expression 'I wish' to express wishes or desires. Hence, 'I wish' is most appropriate answer.

324. We have being / arranged the stay / for the guests at / a hillside resort. SSC CPO Tier-1 04.10.2023 (Shift-III)

(a) a hillside resort (b) We have being
(c) for the guests at (d) arranged the stay

Ans. (b)

'We have being' must be replaced with 'We have.' The given sentence is in present perfect tense and 'Plural Sub. + have + V_3(arranged)' is the correct grammatical structure for it. Hence, 'We have' is the most appropriate answer.

325. The students / are expected / to come/ in the right time. SSC CPO Tier-1 05.10.2023 (Shift-I)

(a) are expected (b) The students
(c) in the right time (d) to come

Ans. (c)

'In' must be replaced with 'at.' 'At' is used to indicate the specific time of an action. Hence, 'at the right time' is the most appropriate answer.

326. I am sure Helena / would passes / with flying colours. SSC CPO Tier-1 05.10.2023 (Shift-II)

(a) would passes
(b) I am sure Helena
(c) with flying colours
(d) No error

Ans. (a)

After a modal verb, we generally use the first form of the verb (V_1). Hence, 'would pass (V_1)' is the most appropriate answer.

327. One of their freighters, / a Neptune / will be leaving / in two weeks.
SSC CPO Tier-1 05.10.2023 (Shift-II)

(a) One of their freighters
(b) will be leaving
(c) a Neptune
(d) in two weeks

Ans. (c)

Article 'a' must be replaced with article 'the.' 'Neptune' mentioned in the given sentence is a specific ship and we generally use the definite article 'the' before any specific or particular noun. Hence, 'the Neptune' is the most appropriate answer.

328. (1) He could / (2) be pass his exams / (3) if he studied harder. / (4) No error **SSC CPO Tier-1 05.10.2023 (Shift-III)**

(a) 2 (b) 1 (c) 3 (d) 4

Ans. (a)

The use of 'be' is incorrect in 'be pass his exams.' Remove it to correct the sentence.

329. <u>Have</u> they <u>been work</u> in that particular shop <u>for</u> several years?
SSC CPO Tier-1 05.10.2023 (Shift-III)

(a) work (b) been
(c) for (d) Have

Ans. (a)

'Work' is incorrect in the context of the sentence. As the given sentence is in present perfect continuous tense, the correct form should be 'working' instead of 'work'.

SSC CPO 2022 (Tier 1 & 2)

330. The investors were / put off by the dirty / visage of the workshop.
SSC CPO Tier-1 09.11.2022 (Shift-I)

(a) visage of the workshop
(b) put off by the dirty
(c) No error
(d) The investors were

Ans. (c)

The given sentence is grammatically correct and contextually meaningful.

331. Psychology has been / defined the scientific study of / human psyche and behaviour.
SSC CPO Tier-1 09.11.2022 (Shift-I)

(a) defined the scientific study of
(b) Psychology has been
(c) human psyche and behaviour
(d) No error

Ans. (a)

'Defined' will be replaced by 'defined as' because it means to determine or identify the essential qualities or meaning of something. Hence, 'defined as the scientific study of' is the most appropriate answer.

332. Everyone was surprised / at his indefatigable courage and determination / to achieve what he desired. **SSC CPO Tier-1 09.11.2022 (Shift-II)**

(a) Everyone was surprised
(b) To achieve what he desired
(c) No error
(d) At his indefatigable courage and determination

Ans. (c)

The given sentence is grammatically correct and contextually meaningful.

333. He took a hurried glance / on the newspaper / and swiftly left for work. **SSC CPO Tier-1 09.11.2022 (Shift-III)**

(a) and swiftly left for work
(b) He took a hurried glance
(c) on the newspaper
(d) No error

Ans. (c)

Preposition 'at' will be used instead of 'on' as 'Glance at something' is the correct phrase which means to take a quick look at something. Hence, 'at the newspaper' is the most appropriate answer.

334. My granny says that / it is quite all right / to get married young, / though I do not absolute agree with her a bit on this.
SSC CPO Tier-1 09.11.2022 (Shift-III)

(a) My granny says that
(b) though I do not absolute agree with her a bit on this
(c) it is quite all right
(d) to get married young

Ans. (b)

The given sentence needs an adverb to modify the verb (agree) and not an adjective (absolute). Hence, 'though I do not absolutely agree with her a bit on this is the most appropriate answer.

335. As is usual with stories of this genre, / in spite of their varying socio political realities, / the youngsters have fallen in love / with each other madly.
SSC CPO Tier-1 10.11.2022 (Shift-II)

(a) he youngsters have fallen in love
(b) with each other madly
(c) in spite of their varying socio political realities
(d) As is usual with stories of this genre

Ans. (d)

The verb 'is' is incorrect in the given sentence as 'as usual' is the correct phrase that means in a way that often happens and is expected. The given sentence talks about something that often happens with the stories of this genre. Hence, 'As usual with stories of this genre' is the most appropriate answer.

336. He was enough tall / to be admitted / into the armed forces.
SSC CPO Tier-1 10.11.2022 (Shift-III)

(a) into the armed forces
(b) to be admitted
(c) No error
(d) He was enough tall

Ans. (d)

We will place the adjective 'tall' before the word 'enough' to correct the given sentence.
Hence, 'He was tall enough' is the most appropriate answer.

337. His cellphone is / different and costlier / than mine.
SSC CPO Tier-1 10.11.2022 (Shift-III)

(a) No error
(b) than mine
(c) His cellphone is
(d) different and costlier

Ans. (d)

'Different from and costlier' should be used in place of 'different and costlier' to make the sentence grammatically correct.

338. The knight was received/ compliments from the king / for his bravery. **SSC CPO Tier-1 11.11.2022 (Shift-II)**

(a) No error
(b) for his bravery
(c) complements from talking
(d) The knight was received

Ans. (d)

The word 'was' should be removed to make the sentence grammatically correct.

339. The helicopter of the enemies/ hovered exact/over their bunker.
SSC CPO Tier-1 11.11.2022 (Shift-I)

(a) No error
(b) hovered exact
(c) The helicopter of the enemies
(d) over their bunker

Ans. (b)

'Hovered exactly' should be used in place of 'hovered exact' to make the sentence error free.

340. Fortunately, he passed the exams/ with dint of/sheer hard work and diligence. **SSC CPO Tier-1 11.11.2022 (Shift-I)**
(a) sheer hard work and diligence
(b) with dint of
(c) No error
(d) Fortunately, he passed the exams

Ans. (b)

'By dint of' should be used in place of 'with dint of' to make the sentence error free. 'By dint of' means by 'means of.'

SSC CPO 2021 (Tier 2)

341. You need to sign / these important documents / by ink. **SSC CPO Tier-2 26.07.2021**
(a) these important documents
(b) to sign
(c) by ink
(d) You need

Ans. (c)

There is a prepositional error in the given sentence. The preposition 'by' must be replaced with 'in' because we generally write 'in ink' for example fill the form in blue ink, sign the cheque in ink, etc.

Similarly, in the given sentence, the documents need to be signed in ink. Hence, 'in ink' is the most appropriate structure.

342. Parul is / ten years / elder than / her sibling. **SSC CPO Tier-2 26.07.2021**
(a) elder than (b) Parul is
(c) her sibling (d) ten years

Ans. (a)

The comparative degree 'elder' will not be used with 'than' because it will become a case of superfluousness (not necessary). Hence, 'than' will be replaced with 'to' and 'elder to' is the most appropriate structure.

343. He is / afraid from / all insects / that crawl. **SSC CPO Tier-2 26.07.2021**
(a) He is (b) that crawl
(c) all insects (d) afraid from

Ans. (d)

Afraid generally takes the preposition 'of and not 'from', Hence, 'afraid of' is the most appropriate structure.

344. My neighbour is / an young businessman / who is very friendly / with everyone. **SSC CPO Tier-2 26.07.2021**
(a) who is very friendly
(b) an young businessman
(c) My neighbour is
(d) with everyone

Ans. (b)

We use the article 'a' before the words starting with a consonant (a, d, f, n, etc.), for example, a dirty shirt, a neglected department, etc. However, the article 'an' is used before words starting with a vowel (a, e, i, o, u) for example, an educated person, an imminent danger, etc. Hence, 'a young (consonant 'y') businessman' is the most appropriate structure.

345. He wanted to know / the reason / why his low score/ in Mathematics. **SSC CPO Tier-2 26.07.2021**
(a) why his low score
(b) He wanted to know
(c) the reason
(d) in Mathematics

Ans. (a)

If an interrogative sentence (in which a question is asked) is written in the indirect form (speech), then 'Wh-word (why, when, where) + Subject + Verb' is grammatically the correct structure for it.

Hence, 'why his (subject) score was (verb) low' is the most appropriate structure.

346. This is / only mistake / he has made / in the dictation. **SSC CPO Tier-2 26.07.2021**
(a) only mistake (b) in the dictation
(c) he has made (d) This is

Ans. (a)

The article 'the' is used to refer to specific or particular nouns and articles 'a/an' are used to modify non-specific or non-particular nouns. For example, if someone says, 'Let's buy the book'; it means a specific book but if someone says, 'Let's buy a book'; it means any book rather than a specific book.

Similarly, the given sentence talks about a specific mistake. Hence, 'the only mistake' is the most appropriate structure.

SSC CHSL 2024 (Tier 1 & 2)

347. The Supreme Court set away / the verdict of the High Court / and agreed to hear the plea / of the complainant. **SSC CHSL Tier-2 18.11.2024**
(a) the verdict of the High Court
(b) The Supreme Court set away
(c) of the complainant
(d) and agreed to hear the plea

Ans. (b)

The correct phrase is 'set aside,' which means to annul or reject a previous decision.

348. Passengers started behaving / violent when / they were asked / to leave the bus station. **SSC CHSL Tier-1 01.07.2024 (Shift-I)**
(a) to leave the bus station
(b) Passengers started behaving
(c) violent when
(d) they were asked

Ans. (c)

Part (c) 'violent when' contains an error. The use of 'violent' is incorrect. The adverb 'violently' should be used to modify the meaning of the verb 'behaving' to correct the sentence.

349. The couple / preferred to walk / until the last house / of the town. **SSC CHSL Tier-1 01.07.2024 (Shift-I)**
(a) The couple
(b) preferred to walk
(c) of the town
(d) until the last house

Ans. (d)

Part (d) 'until the last house' contains an error. Use 'to' in place of 'until' to correct the sentence.

350. She always/likes to/show on/her wealth. **SSC CHSL Tier-1 01.07.2024 (Shift-II)**
(a) show on (b) she always
(c) likes to (d) her wealth

Ans. (a)

Part (a) 'show on' contains an error. The phrasal verb 'show on' is incorrect for the sentence. The correct phrasal verb is 'show off' which means display someone or something that is a source of pride.'

351. <u>If it</u> <u>will rain</u> tomorrow, <u>I will</u> stay <u>at home</u>. **SSC CHSL Tier-1 01.07.2024 (Shift-II)**
(a) I will (b) at home
(c) will rain (d) If it

Ans. (c)

Part (c) 'will rain' contains an error. The sentence is a future hypothetical conditional wherein the 'if' clause is in present tense.

Hence, 'rains' should be used to correct the sentence.

352. Hard had she / thrown the basketball / when it fell / on the ground. **SSC CHSL Tier-1 01.07.2024 (Shift-II)**
(a) when it fell
(b) on the ground
(c) thrown the basketball
(d) Hard had she

Ans. (d)

Part (d) 'Hard had she' contains an error. Use 'Hardly' in place of 'Hard' to correct the sentence.

353. 'Ramayana' is an ancient Sanskrit epic; it is believed to be written around 500 BC to 100 BC.
SSC CHSL Tier-1 01.07.2024 (Shift-II)
(a) 'Ramayana' is an ancient
(b) Sanskrit epic; it is
(c) believed to be written
(d) around 500 BC to 100 BC

Ans. (a)

Part (a) 'Ramayana is an ancient' contains an error. Definite article 'the' is used with the name of holy books. Hence, add 'The' before 'Ramayana' to correct the sentence.

354. When it / come to football, / my brother is / an addict.
SSC CHSL Tier-1 01.07.2024 (Shift-IV)
(a) come to football (b) an addict
(c) my brother is (d) When it

Ans. (a)

Part (a) 'come to football' contains an error. As the subject of the sentence is singular, singular verb 'comes' should be used to correct the sentence.

355. Throw of / the old shoes; / nobody will wear / them now.
SSC CHSL Tier-1 01.07.2024 (Shift-IV)
(a) them now (b) nobody will wear
(c) the old shoes (d) Throw of

Ans. (d)

Part (d) 'throw of' contains an error. Use 'dispose of' or throw off to correct the sentence.

356. They have decided / to wind out / their business / without delay.
SSC CHSL Tier-1 07.07.2024 (Shift-I)
(a) They have decided
(b) their business
(c) to wind out
(d) without delay

Ans. (c)

Part (c) 'to wind out' contains an error. Use 'to wind up' which means to shut down to correct the sentence.

357. He organises / a children's fair every year / and his friends comes / to attend it.
SSC CHSL Tier-1 02.07.2024 (Shift-I)
(a) He organises
(b) a children's fair every year
(c) to attend it
(d) and his friends comes

Ans. (d)

Part (d) 'and his friends comes' contains an error.

As the subject 'friends' is singular, the singular verb should be used. Hence, 'come' should be used to correct the sentence.

358. I goes to / attend dance classes at / the National Dance Academy.
SSC CHSL Tier-1 02.07.2024 (Shift-II)
(a) No error
(b) attend dance classes at
(c) the National Dance Academy
(d) I goes to

Ans. (d)

Part (d) 'I goes to' contains an error. The pronoun 'I' takes the plural form of verb. Hence, use 'go' to correct the sentence.

359. I noticed that they/did not went to / the museum but entered / a shopping complex.
SSC CHSL Tier-1 02.07.2024 (Shift-II)
(a) the museum but entered
(b) did not went to
(c) a shopping complex
(d) I noticed that they

Ans. (b)

Part (b) 'did not went to' contains an error. The verb 'do/does/did' takes the base form of verb. Hence, use 'go' to correct the sentence.

360. The meeting was called off / due to a medical emergency of / the manager of the company.
SSC CHSL Tier-1 02.07.2024 (Shift-II)
(a) No error
(b) the manager of the company
(c) The meeting was called off
(d) due to a medical emergency of

Ans. (a)

The given sentence is grammatically correct and contextually meaningful.

361. We took / an ice / and applied it on / the wound.
SSC CHSL Tier-1 02.07.2024 (Shift-III)
(a) an ice
(b) We took
(c) and applied it on
(d) the wound

Ans. (a)

Part (a) 'an ice' contains an error. Remove 'an' to correct the sentence as ice is an uncountable noun.

362. Since the little girl answers / a few simple questions, / her parents say that / she is too intelligent.
SSC CHSL Tier-1 02.07.2024 (Shift-III)
(a) Since the little girl answers
(b) her parents say that
(c) she is too intelligent
(d) a few simple questions

Ans. (c)

Part (c) 'she is too intelligent' contains an error. The use of 'too' is incorrect. Use 'very' to correct the sentence.

363. It is difficult to live in (A) / the societal expectations (B) / when one has (C) / fewer resources (D).
SSC CHSL Tier-1 02.07.2024 (Shift-III)
(a) B (b) A
(c) D (d) C

Ans. (b)

Part (A) 'It is difficult to live in' contains an error. Use 'under' in place of 'in' to correct the sentence.

364. The teacher was / taken back by/ the audacity of (c)/ the new student.
A B C D
SSC CHSL Tier-1 02.07.2024 (Shift-IV)
(a) D (b) C
(c) A (d) B

Ans. (d)

Part (B) 'taken back by' contains an error. Use 'taken aback by' which means 'surprised by' to correct the sentence.

365. Ramya is working / hardly / to get good marks.
SSC CHSL Tier-1 03.07.2024 (Shift-I)
(a) hardly
(b) Ramya is working
(c) No error
(d) to get good marks

Ans. (a)

Part (a) 'hardly' contains an error. The correct adverb form for the sentence is 'hard.'

366. Petrified wood is type of fossilised wood that exhibits the original details of the wood.
SSC CHSL Tier-1 03.07.2024 (Shift-I)
(a) Petrified wood is the type of fossilised wood that exhibits a original details of the wood.
(b) A petrified wood is type of fossilised wood that exhibits an original details of the wood.
(c) The petrified wood is the type of fossilised wood that exhibits a original details of the wood.
(d) Petrified wood is a type of fossilised wood that exhibits the original details of the wood.

Ans. (d)

The given sentence is missing an article. Hence, the correct sentence is- Petrified wood is a type of fossilised wood that exhibits the original details of the wood.

367. The meeting / will taking / place next / Wednesday.
SSC CHSL Tier-1 03.07.2024 (Shift-II)
(a) place next (b) will taking
(c) The meeting (d) Wednesday

Ans. (b)

Part (b) 'will taking' contains an error. Use 'take' in place of 'taking' to correct the sentence.

368. Urgent activities are those things / that you must do immediately, / as they require quick action / and cannot be put on.
SSC CHSL Tier-1 03.07.2024 (Shift-II)

(a) and cannot be put on
(b) that you must do immediately
(c) Urgent activities are those things
(d) as they require quick action

Ans. (a)

Part (a) 'and cannot be put on' contains an error. Add 'hold' after 'on' to complete the meaning of the sentence.

369. (A) When Christy (B) grew out, (C) he turned out (D) to be a gentleman.
SSC CHSL Tier-1 03.07.2024 (Shift-II)

(a) D (b) C
(c) B (d) A

Ans. (c)

Part (B) 'grew out', contains an error. Use 'up' in place of 'out' to correct the sentence.

370. Rashmi was / quite amusing when / she heard about / what had happened.
SSC CHSL Tier-1 03.07.2024 (Shift-II)

(a) Rashmi was
(b) quite amusing when
(c) she heard about
(d) what had happened

Ans. (b)

Part (b) 'quite amusing when' contains an error.

The use of present participle adjective is incorrect in the sentence. Use past participle 'amused' to correct the sentence.

371. Today she said to her friend, 'You're the sweetest person I have met ever'.
SSC CHSL Tier-1 03.07.2024 (Shift-III)

(a) I have met ever'.
(b) her friend, 'You're
(c) Today she said to
(d) the sweetest person

Ans. (a)

Part (a) 'I have met ever' contains an error.

Place 'ever' before 'met' to correct the sentence.

372. Please remember to take / your notice to the reception area / if you want it to be displayed / upon the bulletin board.
SSC CHSL Tier-1 03.07.2024 (Shift-III)

(a) Please remember to take
(b) upon the bulletin board
(c) if you want it to be displayed
(d) your notice to the reception area

Ans. (b)

Part (b) 'upon the bulletin board' contains an error. Use 'on' in place of 'upon' to correct the sentence.

373. The class / teacher was / wounded in / a leg.
SSC CHSL Tier-1 03.07.2024 (Shift-III)

(a) a leg
(b) teacher was
(c) wounded in
(d) The class

Ans. (a)

Part (a) 'a leg' contains an error. Use article 'the' to correct the sentence.

374. Don't go / outside / because it is / raining heavy.
SSC CHSL Tier-1 03.07.2024 (Shift-III)

(a) Don't go (b) outside
(c) raining heavy (d) because it is

Ans. (c)

Part (c) 'raining heavy' contains an error. The verb requires an adverb and not an adjective.

Hence, use 'heavily' to correct the sentence.

375. I had seen / her with her mother / in the cinema hall / yesterday.
SSC CHSL Tier-1 03.07.2024 (Shift-III)

(a) in the cinema hall
(b) her with her mother
(c) yesterday
(d) I had seen

Ans. (d)

Part (d) 'I had seen' contains an error. As the sentence is in past tense, use 'saw' to correct the sentence.

376. I am sure / that he will praying / for a good crop / this year.
SSC CHSL Tier-1 04.07.2024 (Shift-I)

(a) that he will praying
(b) I am sure
(c) this year
(d) for a good crop

Ans. (a)

Part (a) 'that he will praying' contains an error. Add 'be' before 'praying' to correct the sentence.

377. My students are / waiting for / their flights / at the gate no. 6.
SSC CHSL Tier-1 04.07.2024 (Shift-I)

(a) at the gate no. 6
(b) waiting for
(c) their flights
(d) My students are

Ans. (a)

Part (a) 'at the gate no. 6' contains an error. Remove 'the' to correct the sentence.

378. I am very much / obliged of my friend / for the help / he rendered to me. **SSC CHSL Tier-1 04.07.2024 (Shift-I)**

(a) I am very much
(b) he rendered to me
(c) for the help
(d) obliged of my friend

Ans. (d)

Part (d) 'obliged of my friend' contains an error. Use 'obliged to' to correct the sentence.

379. She <u>will being studying</u> for her <u>exams tomorrow</u>.
SSC CHSL Tier-1 04.07.2024 (Shift-I)

(a) studying (b) tomorrow
(c) will being (d) exams

Ans. (c)

Part (c) 'will being' contains an error. Use 'be' in place of 'being' to correct the sentence.

380. I am writing to invite you / to give a presentation / for our Jobs and Careers Conference / for engineering graduates.
SSC CHSL Tier-1 04.07.2024 (Shift-II)

(a) for engineering graduates
(b) I am writing to invite you
(c) for our Jobs and Careers Conference
(d) to give a presentation

Ans. (c)

Part (c) 'for our Jobs and Careers Conference' contains an error.

Use 'in' in place of 'for' to correct the sentence.

381. (A) I am hearing / (B) that the heat wave / (C) is going to be / (D) worse this year**SSC CHSL Tier-1 04.07.2024 (Shift-II)**

(a) B (b) D
(c) C (d) A

Ans. (d)

Part (A) 'I am hearing' contains an error. Use 'hear' to correct the sentence as the verbs of sense do not take the -ing form of the verb.

382. This artwork / are a wonderful example / of the period's vogue / for realistic style.
SSC CHSL Tier-1 04.07.2024 (Shift-III)
(a) This artwork
(b) of the period's vogue
(c) for realistic style
(d) are a wonderful example

Ans. (d)

Part (d) 'are a wonderful example' contains an error. Use 'is' in place of 'are' to correct the sentence. As the subject of the sentence is singular, singular verb should be used.

383. Prateek was planning to ask Shreya for a favour. But he could not muster up the courage. So, he blacked out.
SSC CHSL Tier-1 04.07.2024 (Shift-III)
(a) Prateek was planning to ask Shreya for a favour. But he could not muster up the courage. So, he broke in.
(b) Prateek was planning to ask Shreya for a favour. But he could not muster up the courage. So, he chickened out.
(c) Prateek was planning to ask Shreya for a favour. But he could not muster up the courage. So, he checked out.
(d) Prateek was planning to ask Shreya for a favour. But he could not muster up the courage. So, he turned down.

Ans. (b)

The phrasal verb 'blacked out' in the given sentence is incorrect as it means to get unconscious.

The correct phrasal verb for the sentence would be 'chickened out' which means to get scared.

384. The companies were / giving in the prizes / to attract customers / during the festive season.
SSC CHSL Tier-1 04.07.2024 (Shift-III)
(a) The companies were
(b) giving in the prizes
(c) during the festive season
(d) to attract customers

Ans. (b)

Part (b) 'giving in the prizes' contains an error. Use 'out' to make the phrasal verb 'giving out' which means to distribute.

385. She was singing / beautifully in / the concert hall / last night.
SSC CHSL Tier-1 04.07.2024 (Shift-IV)
(a) the concert hall
(b) last night
(c) She was singing
(d) beautifully in

Ans. (c)

Part (c) 'She was singing' contains an error. As the sentence presents a time expression of the past, simple past tense should be used. Hence, use 'sang' in place of 'was singing' to correct the sentence.

386. I will be study around 7 o'clock.
SSC CHSL Tier-1 04.07.2024 (Shift-IV)
(a) around 7 o'clock
(b) be study
(c) will
(d) I

Ans. (b)

Part (b) 'be study' contains an error. Use 'studying' to correct the sentence.

387. My daughter participate / in the dance competition / that is organised every year/ by the Lion's Club.
SSC CHSL Tier-1 04.07.2024 (Shift-IV)
(a) in the dance competition
(b) that is organised every year
(c) My daughter participate
(d) by the Lion's Club

Ans. (c)

Part (c) 'My daughter participate' contains an error. Use 'participates' to correct the sentence. As the subject of the sentence is singular, singular verb should be used.

388. This is / a doll / and there is / a umbrella.
SSC CHSL Tier-1 05.07.2024 (Shift-I)
(a) This is
(b) a doll
(c) and there is
(d) a umbrella

Ans. (d)

Part (d) 'a umbrella' contains an error. Use 'an' as the word 'umbrella' starts with a vowel sound.

389. The aeroplane took down / without the passengers after / making a sudden announcement.
SSC CHSL Tier-1 05.07.2024 (Shift-I)
(a) making a sudden announcement
(b) No error
(c) without the passengers after
(d) The aeroplane took down

Ans. (d)

Part (d) 'The aeroplane took down' contains an error. The use of 'took down' meaning to defeat is incorrect in the sentence. Use 'off' making 'took off' to correct the sentence.

390. She shall being / travelling / by this time / tomorrow.
SSC CHSL Tier-1 05.07.2024 (Shift-I)
(a) travelling
(b) She shall being
(c) by this time
(d) tomorrow

Ans. (b)

Part (b) 'She shall being' contains an error. Use 'will be' to correct the sentence.

391. Emily is a American living in Paris for her work.
SSC CHSL Tier-1 05.07.2024 (Shift-I)
(a) a American
(b) living in Paris
(c) Emily is
(d) for her work

Ans. (a)

Part (a) 'a American' contains an error. Use 'an', as the word 'American' starts with a vowel sound, to correct the sentence.

392. The soldiers / were selected / on the section / of 'gallantry of spirits.'
SSC CHSL Tier-1 05.07.2024 (Shift-II)
(a) were selected
(b) The soldiers
(c) on the section
(d) of 'gallantry of spirits'

Ans. (c)

Part (c) 'on the section' contains an error. Use 'on the basis' to correct the sentence.

393. We has travelled / to many states / of India to get / an essence of its diversity.
SSC CHSL Tier-1 05.07.2024 (Shift-II)
(a) to many states
(b) of India to get
(c) an essence of its diversity
(d) We has travelled

Ans. (d)

Part (d) 'We has travelled' contains an error. Use 'have' to correct the sentence. As the subject of the subject is plural, plural verbs should be used.

394. With hard work, commitment / and proper guidance, / Sivaram has become / a IPS officer.
SSC CHSL Tier-1 05.07.2024 (Shift-III)
(a) With hard work, commitment
(b) and proper guidance
(c) a IPS officer
(d) Sivaram has become

Ans. (c)

Part 'a IPS officer' contains an error. Use 'an' before the abbreviation to correct the sentence.

395. A owl is a bird which has wide eyes, asymmetrical ears and is found mostly in forests.
SSC CHSL Tier-1 05.07.2024 (Shift-III)
(a) and is found mostly in forests
(b) asymmetrical ears
(c) A owl is a bird
(d) which has wide eyes

Ans. (c)

Part (c) 'A owl is a bird' contains an error. Use 'an' to correct the sentence.

396. The teacher will never / give you punishment / if you will / come on time. SSC CHSL Tier-1 05.07.2024 (Shift-III)

(a) give you punishment
(b) if you will
(c) come on time
(d) The teacher will never

Ans. (b)

Part (b) 'if you will' contains an error. Remove 'will' to correct the sentence. The given sentence is future conditional, the 'if' clause should be in present tense.

397. If she exercises daily, / she would / remain energetic / and fit forever. SSC CHSL Tier-1 05.07.2024 (Shift-III)

(a) remain energetic
(b) If she exercises daily
(c) and fit forever
(d) she would

Ans. (d)

Part (d) 'she would' contains an error. Use 'will' to correct the sentence.

398. Ms. Rose is a / sweetest of / all the girls / in the class. SSC CHSL Tier-1 05.07.2024 (Shift-IV)

(a) sweetest of
(b) all the girls
(c) in the class
(d) Ms. Rose is a

Ans. (d)

Part (d) 'Ms. Rose is a' contains an error. Use 'the' to correct the sentence as definite article is used before superlative degree of adjective.

399. The shop / usually opened / ten minutes / late. SSC CHSL Tier-1 05.07.2024 (Shift-IV)

(a) usually opened
(b) late
(c) The shop
(d) ten minutes

Ans. (a)

Part (a) 'usually opened' contains an error. Use 'opens' to correct the sentence. The given sentence presents a habitual action, so simple present tense should be used.

400. I am going / to buy a red car / with a leather seats / and a sunroof. SSC CHSL Tier-1 05.07.2024 (Shift-IV)

(a) I am going
(b) and a sunroof
(c) to buy a red car
(d) with a leather seats

Ans. (d)

Part (d) 'with a leather seats' contains an error. Remove 'a' to correct the sentence.

401. Mrs. Arunima / speaks / Telugu well. SSC CHSL Tier-1 08.07.2024 (Shift-I)

(a) speaks (b) Mrs. Arunima
(c) Telugu well (d) No error

Ans. (d)

The given sentence is grammatically correct and contextually meaningful.

402. According to the encyclopaedia, a oasis is an area which is made fertile by a source of freshwater. SSC CHSL Tier-1 08.07.2024 (Shift-I)

(a) a source of freshwater
(b) a oasis is an area
(c) According to the encyclopaedia,
(d) which is made fertile by

Ans. (b)

Part (b) 'a oasis is an area' contains an error. Use 'an' to correct the sentence.

403. He have / workers from / Ireland and France / in his factory. SSC CHSL Tier-1 08.07.2024 (Shift-I)

(a) in his factory
(b) workers from
(c) Ireland and France
(d) He have

Ans. (d)

Part (d) 'He have' contains an error. Use 'has' to correct the sentence. The subject of the given sentence is singular, the singular verb should be used.

404. During winters, most of the trains are not running on time in North India. SSC CHSL Tier-1 08.07.2024 (Shift-II)

(a) During winters
(b) on time in North India
(c) are not running
(d) most of the trains

Ans. (c)

Part (c) 'are not running' contains an error. Use 'do not run' to correct the sentence. As the sentence presents a general statement, Simple Present tense should be used.

405. That day we reached late for the competition and even though the competition went on smooth, I felt bad about Shivani losing it. SSC CHSL Tier-1 08.07.2024 (Shift-II)

(a) I felt bad
(b) losing it
(c) the competition went on smooth
(d) we reached late

Ans. (c)

Part (c) 'the competition went on smooth' contains an error. Use 'smoothly' to correct the sentence.

406. Are today / a working day / or a / holiday? SSC CHSL Tier-1 08.07.2024 (Shift-II)

(a) Are today
(b) holiday
(c) a working day
(d) or a

Ans. (a)

Part (a) 'Are today' contains an error. Use 'is today' to correct the sentence.

407. In this cold weather, / there's nothing / like good / cup of coffee. SSC CHSL Tier-1 08.07.2024 (Shift-III)

(a) In this cold weather
(b) like good
(c) cup of coffee
(d) there's nothing

Ans. (b)

Part (b) 'like good' contains an error. Add 'a' after 'like' to correct the sentence.

408. The general's address / was applauds / by all sections / of society. SSC CHSL Tier-1 08.07.2024 (Shift-III)

(a) by all sections
(b) was applauds
(c) of society
(d) the general's address

Ans. (b)

Part (b) 'was applauds' contains an error. Use 'applauded' to correct the sentence.

409. There's an quiet street down the left that you can use for your dance practice. SSC CHSL Tier-1 08.07.2024 (Shift-III)

(a) down the left
(b) that you can use
(c) There's an quiet street
(d) for your dance practice

Ans. (c)

Part (c) 'There's an quiet street' contains an error.

Use 'a' in the place of 'an' to correct the sentence.

410. A part / of an / apple is / rotten. SSC CHSL Tier-1 08.07.2024 (Shift-III)

(a) apple is (b) of an
(c) A part (d) rotten

Ans. (b)

Part (b) 'of an' contains an error. Use 'the' to correct the sentence.

411. To submit a report / on the recent fire accident, / a high level commitee / has been formed.
SSC CHSL Tier-1 08.07.2024 (Shift-III)
(a) To submit a report
(b) has been formed
(c) on the recent fire accident
(d) a high level commitee

Ans. (d)
Part (d) 'a high level commitee' contains an error. The correct spelling is 'committee.'

412. The Sun rises / in an East / and sets / in the West.
SSC CHSL Tier-1 08.07.2024 (Shift-IV)
(a) in the West
(b) and sets
(c) the Sun rises
(d) in an East

Ans. (d)
Part (d) 'in an East' contains an error. Use 'the' to correct the sentence.

413. The judges eliminated the / classical singer, as she dropped of / in the middle of the competition.
SSC CHSL Tier-1 08.07.2024 (Shift-IV)
(a) in the middle of the competition
(b) The judges eliminated the
(c) classical singer, as she dropped of
(d) No error

Ans. (c)
Part (c) 'classical singer, as she dropped of' contains an error. Use 'off' to correct the sentence.

414. How long are you working / for your current employer / and why don't you / look for better opportunities?
SSC CHSL Tier-1 08.07.2024 (Shift-IV)
(a) look for better opportunities
(b) and why don't you
(c) How long are you working
(d) for your current employer

Ans. (c)
Part (c) 'How long are you working' contains an error. Use 'have you been working' to correct the sentence.

415. In geography class, / the teacher told the students, / 'Switzerland lies / inside Germany, France, Austria and Italy.'
SSC CHSL Tier-1 09.07.2024 (Shift-I)
(a) inside Germany, France, Austria, and Italy
(b) In geography class
(c) Switzerland lies
(d) the teacher told the students

Ans. (a)
Part (a) 'inside Germany, France, Austria, and Italy' contains an error. Use 'surrounded by' in place of 'inside' to correct the sentence.

416. There are eight planets in our solar system and a Earth is the third planet from the Sun.
SSC CHSL Tier-1 09.07.2024 (Shift-I)
(a) planet from the Sun
(b) in our solar system
(c) and a Earth is the third
(d) There are eight planets

Ans. (c)
Part (c) 'and a Earth is the third' contains an error. Use 'the' in place of 'a' to correct the sentence.

417. You expressed your opinion/ very clearly /but I am sorry/ I cannot agree to you.
SSC CHSL Tier-1 09.07.2024 (Shift-I)
(a) You expressed your opinion
(b) very clearly
(c) I cannot agree to you
(d) but I am sorry

Ans. (c)
Part (c) 'I cannot agree to you' contains an error. Use 'with' in place of 'to' to correct the sentence.

418. This is the story of eight round planets, the few rocks in between, and some comets.
SSC CHSL Tier-1 09.07.2024 (Shift-II)
(a) This is story of eight round planets, few rocks in between and some comets.
(b) This is a story of eight round planets, few rocks in between, and some comets.
(c) This is the story of eight round planets, few rocks in between, and some comets.
(d) This is the story of eight round planets, a few rocks in between, and some comets.

Ans. (d)
The given sentence contains an error of articles. The correct sentence is- This is the story of eight round planets, a few rocks in between, and some comets.

419. Everyone have/ to join health orientation/ classes before/ going for trekking.
SSC CHSL Tier-1 09.07.2024 (Shift-II)
(a) to join health orientation
(b) Everyone have
(c) going for trekking
(d) classes before

Ans. (b)
Part (b) 'Everyone have' contains an error. Use 'has' to correct the sentence. The word 'everyone' is a singular subject which will take a singular verb.

420. Our plane / arrived at / the Mumbai airport / at the right time.
SSC CHSL Tier-1 09.07.2024 (Shift-II)
(a) arrived at
(b) Our plane
(c) at the right time
(d) the Mumbai airport

Ans. (d)
Part (d) 'the Mumbai airport' contains an error. Remove 'the' to correct the sentence.

421. The workers called out / the strike because / the management acceded to / all their demands.
SSC CHSL Tier-1 09.07.2024 (Shift-III)
(a) the strike because
(b) all their demands
(c) the management acceded to
(d) The workers called out

Ans. (d)
Part (d) 'the workers called out' contains an error.

The use of 'called out' which means 'to rebuke or humiliate' is incorrect in the sentence.

Use 'called off' which means 'to end' to correct the sentence.

422. She / did not watched / Frankenstein / last night.
SSC CHSL Tier-1 09.07.2024 (Shift-III)
(a) did not watched (b) Frankenstein
(c) She (d) last night

Ans. (a)
Part (a) 'did not watched' contains an error. Use 'watch' to correct the sentence. The verb 'did/do/does' takes the base form of the verb.

423. A company can / make money by / obtain resources / more affordably.
SSC CHSL Tier-1 09.07.2024 (Shift-III)
(a) A company can (b) make money by
(c) obtain resources (d) more affordably

Ans. (c)
Part (c) 'obtain resources' contains an error. Use 'obtaining' to correct the sentence.

424. When the famous businessman / faced a huge loss / in his business, / no one expressed sympathy.
SSC CHSL Tier-1 09.07.2024 (Shift-III)
(a) in his business
(b) When the famous businessman
(c) no one expressed simpathy
(d) faced a huge loss

Ans. (c)

Part (c) 'no one expressed simpathy' contains the spelling error. The correct spelling is 'sympathy.'

425. A great / culture of hospitality of / the Spanish / is well-known.
SSC CHSL Tier-1 09.07.2024 (Shift-IV)

(a) the Spanish
(b) culture of hospitality of
(c) A great
(d) is well-known

Ans. (c)

Part (c) 'A great' contains an error. Use 'the' correct the sentence.

426. After a while, / she look up / and saw that / it was getting dark.
SSC CHSL Tier-1 09.07.2024 (Shift-IV)

(a) and saw that
(b) it was getting dark
(c) she look up
(d) After a while

Ans. (c)

Part (c) 'she look up' contains an error. Use 'looked' to correct the sentence as the sentence is in past tense.

427. There was an gang of thieves spotted at our local bank, make sure to be careful.
SSC CHSL Tier-1 09.07.2024 (Shift-IV)

(a) at our local bank
(b) make sure to be careful
(c) There was an gang
(d) of thieves spotted

Ans. (c)

Part (c) 'There was an gang' contains an error. Use 'a' to correct the sentence.

428. The volunteer gave on to / the food packets to the / children of the orphanage.
SSC CHSL Tier-1 10.07.2024 (Shift-I)

(a) The volunteer gave on to
(b) the food packets to the
(c) No error
(d) children of the orphanage

Ans. (a)

Part (a) 'The volunteer gave on to' contains an error. Use 'out' in place of 'on to' correct the sentence. Gave out means to distribute.

429. It was my niece / who was leaving college / last year, and / not my son.
SSC CHSL Tier-1 10.07.2024 (Shift-I)

(a) last year, and
(b) not my son
(c) It was my niece
(d) who was leaving college

Ans. (d)

Part (d) 'who was leaving college' contains an error. Use 'left' to correct the sentence as the sentence is in simple past tense.

430. <u>Raveena's daughter</u> Kavya is <u>most intelligent</u> student and <u>she consistently</u> achieves <u>top grades</u>.
SSC CHSL Tier-1 10.07.2024 (Shift-I)

(a) Raveenas' daughter
(b) she has consistently
(c) most intelligent
(d) topper grades

Ans. (c)

Part (c) 'most intelligent' contains an error. Use 'an intelligent' to correct the sentence.

431. (A) It is sad / (B) that you / (C) are believing / (D) in superstitious rituals. SSC CHSL Tier-1 10.07.2024 (Shift-II)

(a) A (b) C (c) B (d) D

Ans. (b)

Part (C) 'are believing' contains an error. Use 'believe' to correct the sentence.

432. Since childhood, Monty / ate his food / fast and he / will not change.
SSC CHSL Tier-1 10.07.2024 (Shift-II)

(a) fast and he
(b) ate his food
(c) Since childhood, Monty
(d) will not change

Ans. (b)

Part (b) 'ate his food' contains an error. Use 'eats' in place of 'ate' to correct the sentence. The sentence presents a habit and would take simple present tense.

433. After your insistence, / my sister / checked / a mailbox again.
SSC CHSL Tier-1 10.07.2024 (Shift-II)

(a) a mailbox again
(b) After your insistence,
(c) my sister
(d) checked

Ans. (a)

Part (a) 'a mailbox again' contains an error. Use 'the' in place of 'a' to correct the sentence.

434. In order to connect / these themes to a wider / historical context, Rahul go / beyond aesthetic analysis. SSC CHSL Tier-1 10.07.2024 (Shift-II)

(a) In order to connect
(b) beyond aesthetic analysis
(c) these themes to a wider
(d) historical context, Rahul go

Ans. (d)

Part (d) 'historical context, Rahul go' contains an error. Use 'went' in place of 'go' to correct the sentence.

435. I used to eat into / in the evening / when my parents / were on night shifts. SSC CHSL Tier-1 10.07.2024 (Shift-III)

(a) I used to eat into
(b) when my parents
(c) in the evening
(d) were on night shifts

Ans. (a)

Part (a) 'I used to eat into' contains an error. Use 'out' in place of 'into' to correct the sentence.

436. (A) Ganga was / (B) out shopping at the mall / (C) and ran over / (D) her schoolmate.
SSC CHSL Tier-1 10.07.2024 (Shift-III)

(a) D (b) A
(c) B (d) C

Ans. (d)

Part (C) 'and ran over' contains an error.

The use of 'ran over', which means to kill by car, is incorrect in the sentence. Use 'ran into', which means to meet suddenly, to correct the sentence.

437. Shall have / you bring / your note-book / tomorrow?
SSC CHSL Tier-1 10.07.2024 (Shift-III)

(a) Shall have
(b) you bring
(c) tomorrow
(d) your note-book

Ans. (a)

Part (a) 'Shall have' contains an error. Use 'will' in place of 'shall' to correct the sentence.

438. Select the option with the correct use of article(s).
SSC CHSL Tier-1 10.07.2024 (Shift-IV)

(a) William Wordsworth was a romantic poet. He did things in an unusual manner.
(b) William Wordsworth was romantic poet. He did things in an unusual manner.
(c) William Wordsworth was the romantic poet. He did things in a unusual manner.
(d) William Wordsworth was a romantic poet. He did things in a unusual manner.

Ans. (a)

The given sentence which correctly uses articles is-

William Wordsworth was a romantic poet. He did things in an unusual manner.

439. The manager noticed / that Pragya / was first to reach / the office on Saturday.
SSC CHSL Tier-1 10.07.2024 (Shift-IV)
(a) that Pragya
(b) The manager noticed
(c) was first to reach
(d) the office on Saturday
Ans. (c)
Part (c) 'was first to reach' contains an error. Add 'the' before 'first' to correct the sentence.

440. The chief guest/gave out prizes/to the meritorious students/of the school. **SSC CHSL Tier-1 10.07.2024 (Shift-IV)**
(a) of the school
(b) gave out prizes
(c) to the meritorious students
(d) The chief guest
Ans. (b)
Part (b) 'gave out prizes' is incorrect. Gave out 'the' prizes will be used or 'gave away' the prizes can also be used.

441. Mathematics help / in developing / the logical mindset / of students.
SSC CHSL Tier-1 10.07.2024 (Shift-IV)
(a) in developing
(b) the logical mindset
(c) Mathematics help
(d) of students
Ans. (c)
Part (c) 'Mathematics help' contains an error.
Use 'helps' to correct the sentence. The names of subject form singular nouns and thus, would take singular verbs.

442. She was fond of walking along the path besides the lake.
SSC CHSL Tier-1 11.07.2024 (Shift-I)
(a) besides the lake (b) along the path
(c) She was (d) fond of walking
Ans. (a)
Part (a) 'besides the lake' contains error. Change 'besides' to 'beside' as besides means in addition to and beside means at the side or adjacent.

443. <u>Policeman</u> came to <u>my village</u> and asked about <u>a person</u> who burgled <u>a house</u> last night.
SSC CHSL Tier-1 11.07.2024 (Shift-I)
(a) Policeman (b) a house
(c) my village (d) a person
Ans. (a)
Part (a) 'Policeman' contains an error. Add 'The' before 'policeman' to correct the sentence.

444. Father took the newspaper / in his hand to / go through it once again.
SSC CHSL Tier-1 11.07.2024 (Shift-I)
(a) in his hand to
(b) Father took the newspaper
(c) go through it once again
(d) No error
Ans. (d)
The given sentence is grammatically correct and contextually meaningful.

445. When Serena / will arrive, / she will / call you.
SSC CHSL Tier-1 11.07.2024 (Shift-I)
(a) call you
(b) will arrive
(c) she will
(d) When Serena
Ans. (b)
Part (b) 'will arrive' contains an error. Use 'arrives' to correct the sentence. The given sentence is a future conditional in which one clause is in simple future and the other is in simple present.

446. It is his job / to chase out / clients with / outstanding debts.
SSC CHSL Tier-1 11.07.2024 (Shift-II)
(a) clients with
(b) to chase out
(c) outstanding debts
(d) It is his job
Ans. (b)
Part (b) 'to chase out' contains an error.
The use of 'chase out' is incorrect in the sentence. Use 'look for' to correct the sentence.

447. Mumbai is the / city of dreams / but it is / a expensive city too.
SSC CHSL Tier-1 11.07.2024 (Shift-II)
(a) a expensive city too
(b) but it is
(c) Mumbai is the
(d) city of dreams
Ans. (a)
Part (a) 'a expensive city too' contains an error. Use 'an' in place of 'a' to correct the sentence.

448. .... road to Taj Mahal passes through ...... forest. (ϕ = No article)
SSC CHSL Tier-1 11.07.2024 (Shift-II)
(a) A; the (b) ϕ; ϕ
(c) The; a (d) A; a
Ans. (c)
The correct filler for the given blanks are 'the' and 'a.'

449. He do not / fear the / repercussions of / this decision.
SSC CHSL Tier-1 11.07.2024 (Shift-II)
(a) repercussions of (b) this decision
(c) He do not (d) fear the
Ans. (c)
Part (c) 'He do not' contains an error. Use 'does' in place of 'do not' to correct the sentence. As the subject of the sentence is singular, singular verb should be used.

450. Between two evils, I always picks the one I have never tried before.
SSC CHSL Tier-1 11.07.2024 (Shift-III)
(a) Between two evils, I always pick the one I have never tried before.
(b) Between two evils, I always is picking the one I have never tried before.
(c) Between two evils, I always picked the one I have never tried before.
(d) Between two evils, I always picking the one I have never tried before.
Ans. (a)
The given sentence contains an error. The correct sentence is– Between two evils, I always pick the one I have never tried before.

451. The teacher will / certainly help you / if you will / ask her.
SSC CHSL Tier-1 11.07.2024 (Shift-III)
(a) certainly help you
(b) The teacher will
(c) if you will
(d) ask her
Ans. (c)
Part (c) 'if you will' contains an error. Remove 'will' to correct the sentence. The given sentence is a future conditional in which one clause is in simple future and the other is in simple present.

452. It was possible to achieve anything, / if one has the grit and determination / to keep going.
SSC CHSL Tier-1 11.07.2024 (Shift-III)
(a) No error
(b) It was possible to achieve anything,
(c) if one has the grit and determination
(d) to keep going
Ans. (b)
Part (b) 'It was possible to achieve anything,' contains an error. Use 'is' to correct the sentence.

453. My Vice-Chancellor works / eighteen hours / a day, / seven days week. **SSC CHSL Tier-1 11.07.2024 (Shift-III)**
(a) seven days week
(b) My Vice-Chancellor works
(c) eighteen hours
(d) a day

Ans. (a)

Part (a) 'seven days week' contains an error. Use 'seven days a week' to correct the sentence.

454. Geeta was working now / but she can be seen / swimming in the / river every evening.
SSC CHSL Tier-1 11.07.2024 (Shift-IV)

(a) swimming in the
(b) river every evening
(c) but she can be seen
(d) Geeta was working now

Ans. (d)

Part (d) 'Geeta was working now' contains an error. As the given sentence is in present tense, use 'is' to correct the sentence.

455. The manager asked / the cooking team, 'Who / among you is to baked the / Christmas cake this year?' SSC CHSL Tier-1 11.07.2024 (Shift-IV)

(a) Christmas cake this year?'
(b) The manager asked
(c) among you is to baked the
(d) the cooking team, 'Who

Ans. (c)

Part (c) 'among you is to baked the' contains an error.
Use 'among you will bake the' to correct the sentence. The given sentence is a future conditional in which one clause is in simple future and the other is in simple present.

456. Select the grammatically incorrect sentence. SSC CHSL Tier-1 11.07.2024 (Shift-IV)

(a) They often meet each other.
(b) They always meet each other.
(c) They quite meet each other.
(d) They hardly meet each other.

Ans. (c)

The grammatically incorrect sentence is- They quite meet each other. The correct sentence is- 'They frequently meet each other'.

457. The new / secretary / does not likes / me. SSC CHSL Tier-1 11.07.2024 (Shift-IV)

(a) me (b) secretary
(c) The new (d) does not likes

Ans. (d)

Part (d) 'does not likes' contains an error. Use 'does not like' to correct the sentence.

458. A man who has been accused of fraud / in an earlier job, he will never be / welcome in any other organisation. SSC CHSL Tier-2 10.01.2024

(a) No error
(b) welcome in any other organisation.
(c) A man who has been accused of fraud
(d) in an earlier job, he will never be

Ans. (d)

Part (d) 'in an earlier job, he will never be' contains an error. The use of 'he' is redundant in the sentence, remove it to correct the sentence.

459. I have three sisters; / Meera is the elder / and Charu is the youngest.

(a) No error SSC CHSL Tier-2 10.01.2024
(b) and Charu is the youngest
(c) I have three sisters
(d) Meera is the elder

Ans. (d)

Part (d) 'Meera is the elder' contains an error.

Use 'the eldest' as comparison is made between three sisters.

460. While astrology has / a long history / it is generally / considered pseudoscience. SSC CHSL Tier-2 10.01.2024

(a) it is generally
(b) a long history
(c) While astrology has
(d) considered pseudoscience

Ans. (d)

Part (d) 'considered pseudoscience' contains an error.

SSC CHSL 2023 (Tier 1 & 2)

461. The recent discoveries / have risen hopes / about possible applications.
SSC CHSL Tier-1 04.03.2023 (Shift-I)

(a) have risen hopes
(b) No error
(c) about possible applications
(d) The recent discoveries

Ans. (a)

Part (a) 'have risen hopes' should be replaced with 'raised' to make the sentence grammatically correct.

462. And it just recently awarded / a million-dollar contract / that reeks of corruption.
SSC CHSL Tier-1 09.03.2023 (Shift-I)

(a) a million-dollar contract
(b) that reeks of corruption
(c) No error
(d) And it just recently awarded

Ans. (c)

The given sentence is grammatically correct and contextually meaningful.

463. The recent discoveries / have risen hopes / about possible applications.
SSC CHSL Tier-1 09.03.2023 (Shift-I)

(a) have risen hopes
(b) No error
(c) The recent discoveries
(d) about possible application

Ans. (a)

Part (a) 'have + V_3' is the correct grammatical structure for the given sentence which is in the present perfect tense.

Hence, 'risen' will be replaced with 'raised' and 'have raised (V_3) hopes' is the most appropriate answer.

464. Today, in fit of frenzied rage and / jealousy, you would have / killed me, your brother.
SSC CHSL Tier-1 09.03.2023 (Shift-II)

(a) killed me, your brother
(b) No error
(c) jealousy, you would have
(d) Today, in fit of frenzied rage and

Ans. (d)

We will not write 'frenzied' with 'rage' as they both nearly have the same meanings which leads to a case of superfluousness (exceeding more than necessary).
Hence, 'frenzied' will be removed from the sentence and 'Today, in a fit of rage' is the most appropriate answer.

465. A study finds that the average staff cost at / a public sector bank is high than that at / its private sector counterpart.
SSC CHSL Tier-1 09.03.2023 (Shift-III)

(a) No error
(b) its private sector counterpart.
(c) a public sector bank is high than that at
(d) A study finds that the average staff cost at

Ans. (c)

We always use a comparative degree adjective like better, worse, greater, etc., when we do a comparison between two things.
Similarly, 'cost' at public and private banks is being compared in the given sentence.
Hence, 'cost at a public sector bank is higher than that at its private sector counterpart' is the most appropriate answer.

466. Atmospheric rivers are long, narrow bands / of moisture in the atmosphere that extends from the / tropics to higher latitudes.
SSC CHSL Tier-1 10.03.2023 (Shift-I)

(a) Atmospheric rivers are long, narrow bands
(b) of moisture in the atmosphere that extends from the
(c) tropics to higher latitudes
(d) No error

Ans. (b)

In the given sentence, 'narrow bands' is a plural subject that will take 'extend' as a plural verb. Hence, 'narrow bands of moisture in the atmosphere that extend' is the most appropriate answer.

467. It turns out / that my father / isn't alone. SSC CHSL Tier-1 10.03.2023 (Shift-I)

(a) No error
(b) that my father
(c) It turns out
(d) isn't alone.

Ans. (a)

The given sentence is grammatically correct and contextually meaningful.

468. This was no strange sight / to the boy by that time, / for he had neither gun or spear.
SSC CHSL Tier-1 10.03.2023 (Shift-II)

(a) to the boy by that time,
(b) for he had neither gun or spear
(c) No error
(d) This was no strange sight

Ans. (b)

Part (b) 'for he had neither gun or spear' contains an error.

'Neither .... nor' is a correlative conjunction; hence, 'nor' should be used in place of 'or' to make the sentence error free.

469. When we cook garlic, the sulphide / molecules raise into the air / and fill the room with their pleasing aroma.
SSC CHSL Tier-1 10.03.2023 (Shift-II)

(a) No error
(b) molecules raise into the air
(c) and fill the room with their pleasing aroma
(d) When we cook garlic, the sulphide

Ans. (b)

'Molecules raise into the air' contains an error.
'Rise' should be used in place of 'raise' to make the sentence grammatically correct.

470. He has been / told many a times to / mind his manners.
SSC CHSL Tier-1 10.03.2023 (Shift-III)

(a) No error
(b) He has been
(c) told many a times to
(d) mind his manners.

Ans. (c)

We will not use the indefinite article 'a' before 'times.'
Hence, 'told many times to' is the most appropriate answer.

471. I will never / judge you for / yours impromptu performance.
SSC CHSL Tier-1 13.03.2023 (Shift-I)

(a) I will never
(b) yours impromptu performance
(c) judge you for
(d) No error

Ans. (b)

We will not use another pronoun (yours) with the given pronoun (you). Instead, we will use an adjective 'your' that means relating to or belonging to you. Hence, 'judge you for your impromptu performance' is the most appropriate answer.

472. If conventional arrangements and / patterns are made more scarcer, other / arrangements and patterns will spring up.
SSC CHSL Tier-1 13.03.2023 (Shift-I)

(a) arrangements and patterns will spring up
(b) No error
(c) If conventional arrangements and
(d) patterns are made more scarcer, other

Ans. (d)

Whenever we do a comparison between two things or people we don't use 'more or very' with the comparative degree adjective ('scarcer' in the given sentence) because it becomes a case of superfluousness (not necessary). Hence, 'more' will be removed from the given sentence and 'patterns are made scarcer,' other becomes the most appropriate answer.

473. You care for him / even more than for myself / he cried bitterly.
SSC CHSL Tier-1 13.03.2023 (Shift-III)

(a) even more than for myself
(b) No error
(c) he cried bitterly
(d) You care for him

Ans. (a)

Part (a) 'even more than for myself contains an error. Replace 'even more than for myself' with 'even more than me' to make the sentence grammatically correct.

474. Once, I run in / the Sonoran Desert in Arizona / after a huge rain event.
SSC CHSL Tier-1 13.03.2023 (Shift-III)

(a) after a huge rain event
(b) No error
(c) Once, I run in
(d) The Sonoran Desert in Arizona

Ans. (c)

As the sentence is in past tense, replace 'run' with 'ran' to make the sentence grammatically correct.

475. As per the study, mosquito-borne / dengue fever infects little / 400 million people annually.
SSC CHSL Tier-1 13.03.2023 (Shift-IV)

(a) As per the study, mosquito-borne
(b) No error
(c) dengue fever infects little
(d) 400 million people annually

Ans. (c)

'Little' is used for uncountable nouns and 'people' in the given sentence are countable. Therefore, 'little' will be removed from the sentence.

Hence, 'dengue fever infects 400 million people annually' is the most appropriate answer.

476. It's 4 pm local time and quite a /large crowd has gathered from yesterday / evening around the giant stage.
SSC CHSL Tier-1 13.03.2023 (Shift-IV)

(a) evening around the giant stage
(b) large crowd has gathered from yesterday
(c) No error
(d) It's 4 pm local time quite a

Ans. (b)

'Since' is used to denote a point of time and 'yesterday evening' is that point of time in the given sentence. Hence, 'from' will be replaced with 'since' and 'large crowd has gathered since yesterday evening' becomes the most appropriate answer.

477. Smart phone age has lead / to substantial deterioration in / both duration and quality of sleep.
SSC CHSL Tier-1 14.03.2023 (Shift-I)

(a) No error
(b) to substantial deterioration in
(c) both duration and quality of sleep
(d) Smart phone age has lead

Ans. (d)

'Smart phone age has lead' contains an error in it. 'Led' (past participle of 'lead') should be used in place of 'lead' to make the sentence grammatically correct.

478. The five first girls / will get the discount / on our merchandise.
SSC CHSL Tier-1 14.03.2023 (Shift-I)

(a) The five first girls
(b) No error
(c) will get the discount
(d) on our merchandise

Ans. (a)

'The five first girls' contains an error. 'The first five girl' should be used in place of 'The five first girls' to make the sentence grammatically correct.

479. Scientists have a few tricks up / their sleeves for dealing with / the universe other objects.
SSC CHSL Tier-1 14.03.2023 (Shift-II)
(a) their sleeves for dealing with
(b) Scientists have a few tricks up
(c) No error
(d) the universe other objects

Ans. (d)
We will use the conjunction 'and' to connect two different words 'universe' and 'objects.' Hence, 'the universe and other objects' is the most appropriate answer.

480. You never know when / you are going to stumble to a / jewel in the most unexpected corner.
SSC CHSL Tier-1 14.03.2023 (Shift-III)
(a) You never know when
(b) you are going to stumble to a
(c) jewel in the most unexpected corner
(d) No error

Ans. (b)
There is a prepositional error in the given sentence.
The preposition 'to' will be replaced with 'upon' because we generally use the preposition 'upon' with 'stumble.' Hence, 'you are going to stumble upon a' is the most appropriate answer.

481. Around 30 percent of the / Indian population are estimated / to have latent TB.
SSC CHSL Tier-1 14.03.2023 (Shift-IV)
(a) Indian population are estimated
(b) No error
(c) to have latent TB
(d) Around 30 percent of the

Ans. (a)
'30 percent of + Subject + Singular verb' is the correct grammatical structure of the given sentence.
Hence, 'Indian' population is (singular verb) estimated' is the most appropriate answer.

482. A key institution is the judiciary, / especially the Supreme Court, with / a widely remit and a wise legacy.
SSC CHSL Tier-1 15.03.2023 (Shift-I)
(a) a widely remit and a wise legacy
(b) especially the Supreme Court, with
(c) A key institution is the judiciary
(d) No error

Ans. (a)
The given sentence needs an adjective 'wide' to tell a quality about the subject and not an adverb 'widely.' Hence, 'a wide remit and a wise legacy' is the most appropriate answer.

483. The Presidential election / turned out to be one of / the biggest landslide in history.
SSC CHSL Tier-1 15.03.2023 (Shift-I)
(a) turned out to be one of
(b) The Presidential election
(c) No error
(d) the biggest landslide in history.

Ans. (d)
'One of the + superlative degree of the adjective (best worst, etc. + Plural Subject' is grammatically correct structure.
Thus, 'landslides' will be used in the given sentence and 'biggest' will be the superlative degree adjective.
Hence, 'one of the biggest landslides in history' is the most appropriate answer.

484. Although people had been on watch and / the watchkeepers were very tired, / everyone were up and buzzing. SSC CHSL Tier-1 15.03.2023 (Shift-III)
(a) No error
(b) the watchkeepers were very tired
(c) everyone were up and buzzing
(d) Although people had been on watch and

Ans. (c)
According to the 'Subject-Verb Agreement Rule', a singular subject always takes a singular verb and a plural subject always takes a plural verb.
In the given sentence, 'everyone' is a singular subject that will take 'was' as a singular verb. Hence, 'everyone was up and buzzing' is the most appropriate answer.

485. Give yourself a / chance to be distracted / of bad news.
SSC CHSL Tier-1 15.03.2023 (Shift-IV)
(a) of bad news
(b) chance to be distracted
(c) Give yourself a
(d) No error

Ans. (a)
Part 'of bad news', contains an error. The preposition 'by' is used with 'distracted.' So, 'by' should replace 'of' to make the sentence error free.

486. The inflow of foreign portfolio funds / into Indian equities have pushed / up price-earning multiples and valuation.
SSC CHSL Tier-1 15.03.2023 (Shift-IV)
(a) The inflow of foreign portfolio funds
(b) into Indian equities have pushed
(c) No error
(d) up price-earning multiples and valuation

Ans. (b)
Part 'into Indian equities have pushed' contains an error.
'Has' should be used in place of 'have' to make the sentence grammatically correct.

487. People that are lonely / have higher levels of / the hormone cortisol.
SSC CHSL Tier-1 16.03.2023 (Shift-I)
(a) the hormone cortisol
(b) have higher levels of
(c) No error
(d) People that are lonely

Ans. (d)
Part 'people that are lonely' contains an error. The word 'that' is not used in the context of people. Hence, 'that' must be replaced by 'who' to make the sentence grammatically correct.

488. We talked about writing a will, but it / was one of those thing you never / get around to doing.
SSC CHSL Tier-1 16.03.2023 (Shift-I)
(a) get around to doing
(b) No error
(c) We talked about writing a will, but it
(d) was one of those thing you never

Ans. (d)
Part 'was one of those thing you never' contains an error. The word 'thing' can't be used in a plural context of the sentence which refers to a single item out of many. Hence, 'thing' must be replaced by 'things' to make the sentence grammatically correct.

489. If someone you are talking / to is open of learning more / encourage that continued curiosity.
SSC CHSL Tier-1 16.03.2023 (Shift-II)
(a) encourage that continued curiosity
(b) If someone you are talking
(c) to is open of learning more
(d) No error

Ans. (c)
Part 'to is open of learning more' contains an error. The preposition 'to' is used with 'open.'
So, 'to is open to learn more' should replace 'to is open to learning more' to make the sentence grammatically correct.

490. Vijay and Ajay is here / to celebrate 7 years / of their friendship.
SSC CHSL Tier-1 16.03.2023 (Shift-II)
(a) Vijay and Ajay is here
(b) No error
(c) of their friendship
(d) to celebrate 7 years

Ans. (a)

Part 'Vijay and Ajay is here' contains an error. As the subject of the sentence i.e., 'Vijay and Ajay' is plural, the plural verb 'are' should be used. Hence, 'are' should be used in place of 'is' to make the sentence grammatically correct.

491. The event Horizon Telescope can/help scientists analyse the shapes/ and behaviours of event horizons.
SSC CHSL Tier-1 16.03.2023 (Shift-III)

(a) and behaviours of event horizons
(b) No error
(c) The event Horizon Telescope can
(d) help scientists analyse the shapes

Ans. (b)

The given sentence is grammatically correct and contextually meaningful.

492. The London-based Brodsky/ Quartet, meanwhile, is one of/ the world's leading string quartet.
SSC CHSL Tier-1 16.03.2023 (Shift-IV)

(a) The London-based Brodsky
(b) the world's leading string quartet
(c) Quartet, meanwhile, is one of
(d) No error

Ans. (b)

'One of the + Plural Subject' is grammatically the correct structure. Similarly, 'quartets' will be the plural subject in the given sentence. Hence, 'one of the world's leading string quartets' is the most appropriate answer.

493. Ashwathama, Drona's / only son, has had developed/ a fondness for lavish living.
SSC CHSL Tier-1 17.03.2023 (Shift-I)

(a) No error
(b) a fondness for lavish living
(c) only son, has had developed
(d) Ashwathama, Drona's

Ans. (c)

The given sentence is in the present perfect tense, so the verb must be used in the present perfect form (has + V_3) and not it the past tense (had). Hence, 'Drona's only son, has developed (V_3) is the most appropriate answer.

494. Democrats are often more receptive / and accommodating of / foreign people and cultures.
SSC CHSL Tier-1 17.03.2023 (Shift-I)

(a) No error
(b) Democrats are often more receptive
(c) foreign people and cultures
(d) and accommodating of

Ans. (d)

We generally use the same form of the verb before and after that conjunction 'and.' Therefore, 'accommodating' must be replaced with 'accommodative.' Hence, 'receptive and accommodative of' is the most appropriate answer.

495. Balloons filled with helium / travel hundreds or / even thousands of mile. **SSC CHSL Tier-1 17.03.2023 (Shift-II)**

(a) even thousands of mile
(b) Balloons filled with helium
(c) No error
(d) travel hundreds or

Ans. (a)

Part 'even thousands of mile' contain an error. 'Miles' should be used in place of 'mile' to make the sentence grammatically correct.

496. More than 40 percent of the world's population / lives in regions where water / has becoming increasingly scarce. **SSC CHSL Tier-1 17.03.2023 (Shift-II)**

(a) More than 40 percent of the world's population
(b) No error
(c) has becoming increasingly scarce.
(d) lives in regions where water

Ans. (c)

Part 'has becoming increasingly scarce, contains an error in it.

'Become' should be used in place of 'becoming' to make the sentence grammatically correct.

497. Bushfire have created havoc / and exacerbated the conditions / of animals in the forest.
SSC CHSL Tier-1 17.03.2023 (Shift-IV)

(a) Bushfire have created havoc
(b) and exacerbated the conditions
(c) No error
(d) of animals in the forest

Ans. (a)

According to the 'Subject-Verb Agreement Rule', a singular subject always takes a singular verb and a plural subject always takes a plural verb.

In the given sentence, 'Bushfire' is a singular subject that will take 'has' as a singular verb.

Hence, 'Bushfire has created havoc' is the most appropriate answer.

498. You will never / regret this wonderful / experience with your life. **SSC CHSL Tier-1 17.03.2023 (Shift-IV)**

(a) regret this wonderful
(b) experience with your life.
(c) You will never
(d) No error

Ans. (b)

There is a prepositional error in the given sentence.

The preposition 'with' must be replaced with 'in.' Hence, 'experience in your life' is the most appropriate answer.

499. Shyam, so good with weapons, 'fail to find the words /to tell him that everything he'd done / so far, all the compromises he'd made, had been for love.
SSC CHSL Tier-1 20.03.2023 (Shift-I)

(a) to tell him that everything he'd done
(b) Shyam, so good with weapons, fail to find the words
(c) so far, all the compromises he'd made, had been for love
(d) No error

Ans. (b)

According to the 'Subject-Verb Agreement Rule', a singular subject always takes a singular verb and a plural subject always takes a plural verb.

In the given sentence, 'Shyam' is a singular subject that will take 'fails' as a singular verb. Hence, 'Shyam, so good with weapons, fails to find the words' is the most appropriate answer.

500. Her failure in life / is too much / painful for me.
SSC CHSL Tier-1 20.03.2023 (Shift-II)

(a) No error
(b) painful for me
(c) is too much
(d) Her failure in life

Ans. (c)

We will not use the adverb 'much' with the adjective 'painful' is the given sentence.

Therefore, 'much' will be removed. Hence 'too painful for me' is the most appropriate answer.

501. Bacteria are single-celled / organisms that can / reproduce on its own. **SSC CHSL Tier-1 20.03.2023 (Shift-II)**

(a) organisms that can
(c) Bacteria are single-celled
(b) No error
(d) reproduce on its own

Ans. (d)

We will use a plural pronoun 'their' for the plural subject 'organisms' in the given sentence, not a singular pronoun 'its.' Hence, 'reproduce on their own' is the most appropriate answer.

502. I felt that/I was be groomed/for success in the world.
SSC CHSL Tier-1 20.03.2023 (Shift-III)

(a) No error
(b) I felt that
(c) I was be groomed
(d) for success in the world

Ans. (c)

'I was be groomed' contains an error. 'Being' should be used in place of 'be' to make the sentence grammatically correct.

503. A guru is someone who does not / charge you a fee because someone / who is tied in greed couldn't release you.
SSC CHSL Tier-1 20.03.2023 (Shift-III)

(a) No error
(b) who is tied in greed couldn't release you
(c) charge you a fee because someone
(d) A guru is someone who does not

Ans. (b)

'Who is tied in greed couldn't release you' contains an error. 'Cannot' should be used in place of 'couldn't' to make the sentence grammatically correct.

504. Such was the education/ of the spartans with regard to/ one of the greatest of there kings.
SSC CHSL Tier-1 21.03.2023 (Shift-I)

(a) No error
(b) one of the greatest of there kings
(c) Such was the education
(d) of the spartans with regard to

Ans. (b)

The pronoun 'there' must be replaced with the number 'three' to grammatically correct the given sentence. Hence, 'one of the greatest of three kings' is the most appropriate answer.

505. Workers and companies in all / sectors can contribute their skills / to meet society new needs.
SSC CHSL Tier-1 21.03.2023 (Shift-II)

(a) to meet society new needs.
(b) Workers and companies in all
(c) sectors can contribute their skills
(d) No error

Ans. (a)

Part 'to meet society new needs' contains an error.

'Society's' should be used in place of 'society' to make the sentence grammatically correct.

506. We have more / then 6 years of / experience in field hockey.
SSC CHSL Tier-1 21.03.2023 (Shift-II)

(a) No error
(b) then 6 years of
(c) experience in field hockey
(d) We have more

Ans. (b)

Part 'then 6 years of' contains an error. The word 'then' does not fit in the context of the sentence.

It should be replaced with 'than' to make the sentence grammatically correct.

507. Near 800 million/ people worldwide lack/ updated sanitation.
SSC CHSL Tier-1 21.03.2023 (Shift-III)

(a) updated sanitation
(b) people worldwide lack
(c) No error
(d) Near 800 million

Ans. (d)

The given sentence needs an adverb (nearly) and not an adjective (near). Hence, 'nearly 800 million people' is the most appropriate answer.

508. That was a good/ conversation, look forward/ to meet you.
SSC CHSL Tier-1 21.03.2023 (Shift-III)

(a) That was a good
(b) to meet you
(c) conversation, look forward
(d) No error

Ans. (b)

'Look forward + to + V-ing' is the correct grammatical structure for the given sentence.
Hence, 'look forward to meeting (V-ing) you' is the most appropriate answer.

509. Babbal is / a oldest member / in our / Black Ice Club
SSC CHSL Tier-1 02.08.2023 (Shift-I)

(a) in our
(b) Black Ice Club
(c) Babbal is
(d) a oldest member

Ans. (d)

Part 'a oldest member' contains an error. Superlative degree is along preceded by the definite article 'the.' 'The' should replace 'a' make it grammatically correct.

510. He finally / recalled that / the thieves have leave / from front door.
SSC CHSL Tier-1 02.08.2023 (Shift-III)

(a) the thieves have leave
(b) recalled that
(c) He finally
(d) from front door

Ans. (a)

Part 'the thieves have leave' must be replaced with 'the thieves had left.' If two actions took place in the past then the 1st action must be in the past perfect tense (Had + V_3) and the 2nd action must be in the simple past tense (V_2). However, the V_3 form of 'leave' is 'left.' Hence, 'the thieves had left (V_3)' is the most appropriate answer.

511. He / lives / in 45 Church Street / with his family.
SSC CHSL Tier-1 02.08.2023 (Shift-IV)

(a) in 45 Church Street
(b) with his family
(c) lives
(d) He

Ans. (a)

'In' must be replaced with 'at' as we generally use the preposition 'at' for smaller or specific locations. Hence, 'at 45 Church Street' is the appropriate answer.

512. He sang / beautifully but / the judges were / unimpress at the end.
SSC CHSL Tier-1 02.08.2023 (Shift-IV)

(a) the judges were
(b) unimpress at the end
(c) He sang
(d) beautifully but

Ans. (b)

'Unimpress' must be replaced with the adjective 'unimpressed' as we generally use adjectives after stative verbs ('were' in the given sentence). Hence, 'unimpressed at the end' is the most appropriate answer.

513. Radhika is not capable on participating in a national level competition.
SSC CHSL Tier-1 03.08.2023 (Shift-I)

(a) about
(b) of
(c) on
(d) at

Ans. (b)

The word 'capable' is followed by the preposition 'of.'

Hence, 'on' should be replaced with 'of' to make it grammatically correct.

514. The Sun/revolves/around/a Earth.
SSC CHSL Tier-1 03.08.2023 (Shift-I)

(a) The Sun
(b) revolves
(c) a Earth
(d) around

Ans. (c)

'A Earth' contains an error. As Earth is a heavenly body.

The article 'the' should precede it. Hence, 'the Earth' should be used in place of 'a Earth.'

515. In course by time,/ he was wise enough to realise/mistakes of his past life. SSC CHSL Tier-1 03.08.2023 (Shift-III)

(a) In course by time
(b) he was wise enough to realise
(c) the mistakes of his past life
(d) No error

Ans. (a)

'By' must be replaced with 'of' as 'in course of time' is the correct phrase. This phrase is used when something happens over a period of time.

516. I like my puppies, Mac and Matt, but I like Matt best.
SSC CHSL Tier-1 03.08.2023 (Shift-IV)

(a) I like my puppies, Mac and Matt, but I like Matt better.
(b) I like my puppies, Mac and Matt, but I like Matt the best.
(c) I like my puppies, Mac and Matt, but I like Matt much.
(d) I like my puppies, Mac and Matt, but I like Matt most.

Ans. (a)

I like my puppies, Mac and Matt, but I like Matt better. (Correct Degree)

517. The company was sued/ for breach of contract/ but still deny/ any wrongdoing.
SSC CHSL Tier-1 04.08.2023 (Shift-I)

(a) The company was sued
(b) for breach of contract
(c) any wrongdoing
(d) but it still deny

Ans. (d)

'Deny' must be replaced with 'denied' as the given sentence is in the past tense.

Hence, 'but it still denied' is the most appropriate answer.

518. Honesty / is / a best / policy.
SSC CHSL Tier-1 04.08.2023 (Shift-III)

(a) policy (b) is
(c) a best (d) Honesty

Ans. (c)

'Superlative degree' denotes the form of an adjective or adverb that expresses the highest or a very high degree of quality of a thing, person, etc. For example, most, best, worst, greatest, etc.

However, we always place the definite article 'the' before any superlative adjective.

Similarly, in the given sentence, 'best' is the superlative degree adjective. Hence, 'the best' is the most appropriate answer.

519. The current state of the literature / on the efficacy under cognitive-behavioural therapy / for individuals with generalised anxiety disorder / suggests that it is a promising treatment option.
SSC CHSL Tier-1 04.08.2023 (Shift-III)

(a) The current state of the literature
(b) suggests that it is a promising treatment option
(c) on the efficacy under cognitive-behavioural therapy
(d) for individuals with generalised anxiety disorder

Ans. (c)

'Under' must be replaced with 'of.' 'Under' is used to denote the position of something/somebody at a lower level. 'of' is used to mention the parts or characteristics of something. Hence, 'on the efficacy of cognitive-behavioural therapy' is the most appropriate answer.

520. The rich / should / help / poor.
SSC CHSL Tier-1 04.08.2023 (Shift-IV)

(a) help (b) should (c) poor (d) The rich

Ans. (c)

Article 'the' is used when we use an adjective to represent the whole class. Similarly, in the given sentence, we are referring to the whole class of poor people. Hence, 'the poor' is the most appropriate answer.

521. He was / that angry / that he slammed the book / on the table.
SSC CHSL Tier-1 07.08.2023 (Shift-I)

(a) that he slammed the book
(b) that angry
(c) He was
(d) on the table

Ans. (b)

'That angry' must be replaced with 'so angry' as 'so...that' is a fixed conjunction pair.
Hence, 'so angry' is the most appropriate answer.

522. After working so much / in the fields yesterday / did you took a break? SSC CHSL Tier-1 07.08.2023 (Shift-III)

(a) did you took a break
(b) No error
(c) After working so much
(d) in the fields yesterday

Ans. (a)

'Took' must be replaced with 'take' as we generally use the first form of the verb (V_1) after 'did.' Hence, 'did you take a break' is the most appropriate answer.

523. Do you want / to visit a zoo / when you / go to Ahmedabad?
SSC CHSL Tier-1 07.08.2023 (Shift-III)

(a) Do you want
(b) go to Ahmedabad
(c) when you
(d) to visit a zoo

Ans. (d)

Article 'a' must be replaced with 'the' to specify a particular zoo. Hence,'to visit the zoo' is the most appropriate answer.

524. A lot of adulterants / are chemicals that can lead / to an range of health problems / in both children and adults. SSC CHSL Tier-1 07.08.2023 (Shift-IV)

(a) A lot of adulterants
(b) are chemicals that can lead
(c) in both children and adults
(d) to an range of health problems

Ans. (d)

'To an range of health problems' contains an error.

Hence, 'range' should be used in place of to 'an range.'

525. Suman has bought / a black and a white shawl / to wear with / her new dress.
SSC CHSL Tier-1 07.08.2023 (Shift-IV)

(a) to wear with
(b) her new dress
(c) a black and a white shawl
(d) Suman has bought

Ans. (c)

Part 'a black and a white shawl' contains an error.

Here, 'a black and white shawl' should be used because it is the same shawl. So, article 'a' is used only before first subject (black).

526. Were this boy / washing his clothes / yesterday when the matron / came for a regular round?
SSC CHSL Tier-1 08.08.2023 (Shift-I)

(a) washing his clothes
(b) yesterday when the matron
(c) Were this boy
(d) came for a regular round

Ans. (c)

According to the 'Subject-Verb Agreement Rule', a singular subject always takes a singular verb and a plural subject always takes a plural verb.

'This boy' is a singular subject that will take 'was' as a singular verb. Hence, 'was this boy' is the most appropriate answer.

527. Nobody from the gathering / of odd people could guess / the accident occurring blast.
SSC CHSL Tier-1 08.08.2023 (Shift-II)

(a) the accident occurring blast
(b) Nobody from the gathering
(c) No error
(d) of odd people could guess

Ans. (a)

Part 'the accident occurring blast', contains an error. The word 'causing' should be used in place of 'occurring' to correct the sentence.

528. I have read that/a Leaning Tower of Pisa is a/popular tourist attraction/in the world.
SSC CHSL Tier-1 08.08.2023 (Shift-II)

(a) I have read that
(b) a Leaning Tower of Pisa is a
(c) popular tourist attraction
(d) in the world

Ans. (b)

Part 'a Leaning Tower Pisa is a' contains an error. 'The Leaning Tower of Pisa is a' should be used in place of 'a Leaning Tower of Pisa' because, 'the' is used before the name of a famous building, monument, etc.

529. Sita spotted golden / deer and / requested Rama / to capture it.
SSC CHSL Tier-1 08.08.2023 (Shift-III)

(a) to capture it. (b) Sita spotted golden
(c) deer and (d) requested Rama

Ans. (b)

Article 'a' is used before the words starting from a consonant sound - (a conversation, a story).

Therefore, article 'a' must be used before the word 'golden.' Hence, 'Sita spotted a golden' is the most appropriate answer.

530. The committee was divided on the issue / and neither side were willing to / compromise on the compensation / amount to be given.
SSC CHSL Tier-1 08.08.2023 (Shift-III)

(a) and neither side were willing to
(b) amount to be given
(c) compromise on the compensation
(d) The committee was divided on the issue

Ans. (a)

'Were' must be replaced with 'was' as 'everyone/ each / every/ nothing/ everything/ anything/ either/ neither' represents a singular noun. Therefore, singular verbs will be used with them. Hence, 'and neither side was willing to' is the most appropriate answer.

531. The investigation conducting by the research team /yielded statistically significant results / providing substantial evidence /to support the hypothesis.
SSC CHSL Tier-1 08.08.2023 (Shift-IV)

(a) to support the hypothesis.
(b) yielded statistically significant results
(c) providing substantial evidence
(d) The investigation conducting by the research team

Ans. (d)

A participle phrase is a group of words which includes a past participle form (V_3) and functions as an adjective, providing additional information about the subject. Similarly, in the given sentence, the participle phrase 'conducted (V_3) by the team' provides additional information about the subject 'the investigation.' Hence, 'The investigation conducted by the research team' is the most appropriate answer.

532. It was Ravi, not his friends, / who were shouting / at late hours last night. SSC CHSL (Tier-I) 08.08.2023 (Shift-IV)

(a) It was Ravi, not his friends
(b) No error
(c) who were shouting
(d) at late hours last night

Ans. (c)

'Were' must be replaced with 'was' According to the 'Subject-Verb Agreement Rule', a singular subject always takes a singular verb and a plural subject always takes a plural verb.

'Ravi' is a singular subject that will take 'was' as a singular verb. Hence, 'who was shouting' is the most appropriate answer.

533. Washington Irving's writing career started at/ the tender age of nineteen when he joined/his brother Peter's newspaper. The Morning Chronical/as journalist.
SSC CHSL Tier-1 09.08.2023 (Shift-I)

(a) his brother Peter's newspaper. The Morning Chronical
(b) Washington Irving's written career started at
(c) as journalist
(d) the tender age of nineteen when he joined

Ans. (c)

Part 'as journalist' contains an error in it. 'As a journalist' should replace 'as journalist' to make the sentence grammatically correct.

534. Can you make / sure you have / a correct address / before you start driving? SSC CHSL Tier-1 09.08.2023 (Shift-II)

(a) Can you make
(b) sure you have
(c) a correct address
(d) before you start driving

Ans. (c)

Part 'a correct address' must be replaced with 'the correct address' as we generally use article 'the' before definite or particular nouns. Similarly, the given sentence is talking about a particular address. Hence, 'the correct address' is the most appropriate answer.

535. The food container / is not enough big to meet / the demands of the affected people.
SSC CHSL Tier-1 09.08.2023 (Shift-III)

(a) No error
(b) is not enough big to meet
(c) The food container
(d) the demands of the affected people

Ans. (b)

'Enough big' must be replaced with 'big enough' as 'enough' is a special adverb and always used after the adjective ('big' in the given sentence). Hence, 'is not big enough to meet' is the most appropriate answer.

536. By virtue off / the power given to the leader / the followers accepted his decision.
SSC CHSL Tier-1 09.08.2023 (Shift-IV)

(a) No error
(b) By virtue off
(c) the power given to the leader
(d) the followers accepted his decision .

Ans. (b)

'By virtue of' is the correct preposition and it is used to provide reason. Hence, 'by virtue of' is the most appropriate answer.

537. The team of scientists / were conducting / experiments to test / their hypothesis.
SSC CHSL Tier-1 09.08.2023 (Shift-IV)

(a) experiments to test
(b) The team of scientists
(c) their hypothesis
(d) were conducting

Ans. (d)

According to the 'Subject-Verb Agreement Rule', a singular subject always takes a singular verb and a plural subject always takes a plural verb. 'Team' is a singular subject that will take 'was' as a singular verb. Hence, 'was conducting' is the most appropriate answer.

538. This region / was struck by unusual/wave of violence /last year.
SSC CHSL Tier-1 10.08.2023 (Shift-I)
(a) was struck by unusual
(b) wave of violence
(c) This region
(d) last year

Ans. (a)

Article 'an' is used before the words starting from a vowel sound (an imminent danger, an apple). Therefore, article 'an' must be used before the word 'unusual.' Hence, 'was struck by an unusual' is the most appropriate answer.

539. With reference of your letter, / the organisation wishes to hire you / for the security services.
SSC CHSL Tier-1 10.08.2023 (Shift-I)
(a) With reference of your letter
(b) for the security services
(c) the organisation wishes to hire you
(d) No error

Ans. (a)

'Of' must be replaced with 'to' as 'with reference to' is the correct phrase which means about or concerning (something). Hence, 'with reference to your letter' is the most appropriate answer.

540. The English / often / fought / French. **SSC CHSL Tier-1 10.08.2023 (Shift-III)**
(a) French (b) often
(c) fought (d) The English

Ans. (a)

'French' contains an error.

'The French' should be used in place of 'French' in order to denote the French people.

541. It is imperative in understanding / the rising importance of artificial intelligence / in the public sector to increase the efficacy / and impact of the work done for public welfare.
SSC CHSL Tier-1 10.08.2023 (Shift-IV)
(a) the rising importance of artificial intelligence
(b) It is imperative in understanding
(c) and impact of the work done for public welfare
(d) in the public sector to increase the efficacy

Ans. (b)

'In understanding' must be replaced with 'to understand.' We generally use the phrase 'it is imperative / important + to + V_1' when the infinitive (to + V_1) tells us what is important. Hence, it is imperative to understand (V_1)' is the most appropriate answer.

542. The soldier met / a fearless death / fighting on behalf at his country.
SSC CHSL Tier-1 10.08.2023 (Shift-IV)
(a) The soldier met
(b) a fearless death
(c) No error
(d) fighting on behalf at his country

Ans. (d)

'On behalf at his country' must be replaced with 'on behalf of his country.' The phrase 'on behalf of' is used to indicate that someone is acting or speaking for another person, group or organisation.

Hence, 'fighting on behalf of his country' is the most appropriate answer.

543. (a) I need to buy an new iPhone.
(b) The cat sat on the windowsill
(c) She is the best singer in the choir.
(d) He is an artist who paints landscapes.
SSC CHSL Tier-1 11.08.2023 (Shift-I)

Ans. (a)

The sentence 'I need to buy an new iPhone' contains an error of article. The correct sentence is 'I need to buy a new iPhone.'

544. The man / is a / social animal.
SSC CHSL Tier-1 11.08.2023 (Shift-II)
(a) social animal (b) The man
(c) No error (d) is a

Ans. (b)

No article is used when a noun is used in the general sense.

Therefore, article 'the' must be removed before 'man.' Hence, 'man' is the most appropriate answer.

545. The poor undergoes / several problems in life / that could be / solved with money.
SSC CHSL Tier-1 11.08.2023 (Shift-III)
(a) that could be
(b) several problems in life
(c) The poor undergoes
(d) solved with money

Ans. (c)

An adjective represents the whole class of people when article 'the' is used before it. Similarly, 'the poor' represents all the poor people. We always use a plural verb after such adjectives. Hence, 'The poor undergo' is the most appropriate answer.

546. (a) He ate the sweets greedy
(b) I could not find it anywhere
(c) I haven't got none.
(d) He is much weak.
SSC CHSL Tier-1 11.08.2023 (Shift-III)

Ans. (b)

I could not find it anywhere. (Correct)
(a) He ate the sweets **greedy**. ('Greedily' will be used)
(c) I **haven't** got none. ('Have' will be used)
(d) He is much **weak**. (Weaker' will be used)

547. He speaks pleasantly / with her yesterday / evening but not today.
SSC CHSL Tier-1 11.08.2023 (Shift-IV)
(a) He speaks pleasantly
(b) with her yesterday
(c) No error
(d) evening but not today

Ans. (a)

'Speaks' must be replaced with 'spoke' as we generally use 'simple past tense (V_2)' to describe actions, events or states that occurred and were completed in the past.

Similarly, in the sentence, the action was completed yesterday. Hence, 'he spoke (V_2) pleasantly' is the most appropriate answer.

548. Hurray! Here is the toy / what I was looking for / as my birthday gift.
SSC CHSL Tier-1 14.08.2023 (Shift-I)
(a) Hurray! Here is the toy
(b) No error
(c) what I was looking for
(d) as my birthday gift

Ans. (c)

'What' must be replaced with 'that' as when we introduce a relative clause that provides more information about a noun, we typically use 'that' or 'which' instead of 'what.' Hence, 'that I was looking for' is the most appropriate answer.

549. The politician was accused / of accepting bribes / and lied about it / to the public.
SSC CHSL Tier-1 14.08.2023 (Shift-I)
(a) of accepting bribes
(b) The politician was accused
(c) and lied about it
(d) to the public

Ans. (c)

According to the 'Rule of Parallelism', two or more verbs must be in the same form if they are connected with one another.

Similarly, in the given sentence 'and' connects two verbs 'accepting (V_{ing})' and 'lied.'

Therefore, 'lying (V_{ing})' must be used in place of 'lied.' Hence, 'and lying about it' is the most appropriate answer.

550. The news / is / very good / to be true. SSC CHSL Tier-1 14.08.2023 (Shift-II)

(a) to be true (b) very good
(c) The news (d) is

Ans. (b)

'Very' must be replaced with 'too' as 'too good to be true' is an idiom that means something is so positive or favourable. Hence, 'to good' is the most appropriate answer.

551. This boy / is cleverest/of all / in the class. SSC CHSL Tier-1 14.08.2023 (Shift-III)

(a) in the class (b) This boy
(c) is cleverest (d) of all

Ans. (c)

We generally use article 'the' with a superlative degree i.e., cleverest. Hence, 'is the cleverest' is the most appropriate answer.

552. Identify the error in the use of preposition in the given sentence and select the correct option.
Her family lost their way on Daman. SSC CHSL Tier-1 14.08.2023 (Shift-III)

(a) over (b) in (c) upon (d) of

Ans. (b)

The preposition 'on' must be replaced with 'in' as 'in' is used to indicate location or position within a place or area. Similarly, in the sentence, 'Daman' is a location and we need to use the preposition 'in' before it. Hence, 'in' is the most appropriate answer.

553. Select the sentence that has a grammatical error. SSC CHSL Tier-1 14.08.2023 (Shift-IV)

(a) Rama can bowl fastly
(b) Go back to your room
(c) Don't talk so loudly
(d) Run quickly

Ans. (a)

The sentence with the grammatical error is 'Rama can bowl fastly.' The grammatically correct sentence is 'Rama can bowl very fast.'

554. I brought / an apple from / a place you recommended / me earlier. SSC CHSL Tier-1 14.08.2023 (Shift-IV)

(a) I brought
(b) me earlier
(c) a place you recommended
(d) an apple from

Ans. (c)

The part 'a place you recommended' contains an error of article. Use article 'the' as we one referring to a specific place.

555. He was youngest than his brother. SSC CHSL Tier-1 17.08.2023 (Shift-II)

(a) He was younger than his brother.
(b) He was youngest to his brother.
(c) He was too young than his brother.
(d) He was young to his brother.

Ans. (a)

Comparative degree of an adjective is used while making comparison between two people or things.

Hence, 'He was younger than his brother,' is the grammatically correct sentence.

556. When I was in 5th grade, / I use to / ride on my / red bicycle. SSC CHSL Tier-1 17.08.2023 (Shift-II)

(a) red bicycle
(b) I use to
(c) When I was in 5th grade,
(d) ride on my

Ans. (b)

'I use to' contains an error. 'I used to' should replace 'I use to' to make segment grammatically correct.

557. A owl was/hooting throughout/ the night. SSC CHSL Tier-1 17.08.2023 (Shift-IV)

(a) A owl was
(b) the night
(c) No error
(d) hooting throughout

Ans. (a)

Article 'A' must be replaced with article 'An.'

Article 'a' is used before the words starting from a consonant sound -(a conversation, a story). Whereas, the article 'an' is used before the words starting from a vowel sound (an imminent danger, an apple). Hence, 'An owl was' is the most appropriate answer.

558. They were laid / in the Sun/ the entire morning/ till Sudharshan came. SSC CHSL Tier-1 17.08.2023 (Shift-IV)

(a) till Sudharshan came
(b) They were laid
(c) the entire morning
(d) in the Sun

Ans. (b)

The given sentence is an example of passive voice of past continuous tense and the subject 'they' is plural. 'Plural Sub + were + V_{ing}' is the correct grammatical structure for his sentence. 'Laid' must be replaced with 'lying' as 'lying' means resting in a horizontal position. Hence, 'they were lying' is the most appropriate answer.

559. The police could not/ hold on the people/ for long as they/ gathered in large numbers. SSC CHSL Tier-2 26.06.2023

(a) for long as they
(b) hold on the people
(c) The police could not
(d) gathered in large numbers

Ans. (b)

'On' must be replaced with 'back' as the 'hold back' is a phrasal verb that means to stop or prevent someone or something. Hence, 'hold back the people' is the most appropriate answer.

560. The students were / able to get better from / college early so they/ went to the movies. SSC CHSL Tier-2 26.06.2023

(a) able to get better from
(b) went to the movies
(c) The students were
(d) college early so they

Ans. (a)

'Better' must be replaced with 'back' as the phrase 'get back' means to return. Hence, 'get back' is the most appropriate answer.

561. Those players who chose not to <u>play in the league</u> were banned from playing in <u>an World Cup</u>. SSC CHSL Tier-2 02.11.2023

(a) the World Cup
(b) play in a league
(c) play in league
(d) No error

Ans. (a)

Part 'an World Cup' contains an error. Use 'the' in place of 'an' as we use definite article 'the' before names of awards.

562. It was <u>the Home Minister</u> of the country who took the decision to change <u>a laws pertaining</u> to <u>migration</u> of people from one state to another. SSC CHSL Tier-2 02.11.2023

(a) No error
(b) a laws pertaining
(c) the Home Minister
(d) the migration

Ans. (b)

Part 'a laws pertaining' contains an error.

Use 'the' in the place of 'an' as we are referring to specific laws.

563. This lesser known heritage building is so beautiful as the Red Fort.
SSC CHSL Tier-2 02.11.2023
(a) This heritage building is as beautiful as the Red Fort.
(b) This lesser known heritage building is as much beautiful as the Red Fort.
(c) This lesser known heritage building is very much beautiful as the Red Fort.
(d) This less known heritage building is much beautiful than the Red Fort.

Ans. (b)
The correct sentence is 'This lesser known heritage building is as much beautiful as the Red Fort.'

564. Sincere students / like you and he should study / regularly to pass the examination. **SSC CHSL Tier-2 02.11.2023**
(a) like you and he should study
(b) No error
(c) regularly to pass the examination
(d) Sincere students

Ans. (a)
Part 'like you and he should study' contains an error. Use object pronoun 'him' to correct the sentence.

565. The committee requested / the Chief Investigator / to personally / look after the matter.
SSC CHSL Tier-2 02.11.2023
(a) look after the matter
(b) the Chief Investigator
(c) to personally
(d) The committee requested

Ans. (a)
Part 'look after the matter' contains an error. We need to use 'into' in the place of 'after.' Look into' means to investigate.

566. The film received critical acclaim for being a more innovative movie of the year. **SSC CHSL Tier-2 02.11.2023**
(a) film receives
(b) a most innovative
(c) acclaim at
(d) in the year

Ans. (b)
Part 'a more innovative' contains an error. Use the most innovative' to correct the sentence.

SSC CHSL 2022 (Tier 1 & 2)

567. Rahul sings / very sweet / when he is / in a good mood.
SSC CHSL Tier-1 24.05.2022 (Shift-III)
(a) very sweet
(b) when he is
(c) in a good mood
(d) Rahul sings

Ans. (a)
The given sentence needs an adverb to modify the verb(sings) and not an adjective(sweet). Hence, 'Rahul sings very sweetly' is the most appropriate answer.

568. After / a long and fun-filled day, / the children / slept themselves peacefully.
SSC CHSL Tier-1 24.05.2022 (Shift-III)
(a) a long and fun-filled day
(b) slept themselves peacefully
(c) the children
(d) After

Ans. (b)
The use of the reflexive pronoun 'themselves' is incorrect according to the grammatical context of the given sentence so it must be removed. Hence, 'slept peacefully' is the most appropriate answer.

569. The river / flowed besides / the hillock / in our village.
SSC CHSL Tier-1 25.05.2022 (Shift-I)
(a) in our village
(b) the hillock
(c) flowed besides
(d) The river

Ans. (c)
'Besides' means in addition to something and 'beside' means next something. Similarly, the given sentence states that the river flowed next to the hillock in our village. Hence, 'flowed beside' is the most appropriate answer.

570. He has been / excused by the teacher / by the time a formal complaint / for bullying was made.
SSC CHSL Tier-1 25.05.2022 (Shift-III)
(a) excused by the teacher
(b) for bullying was made
(c) by the time a formal complaint
(d) He has been

Ans. (d)
'By the time + V_2 (second form of the verb) , Had + V_3 (third form of the verb)' is grammatically correct structure for the given sentence. Hence, 'He had been excused (V_3)' is the most appropriate answer.

571. I goes / to the school / everyday / irrespective of the weather.
SSC CHSL Tier-1 27.05.2022 (Shift-I)
(a) everyday
(b) I goes
(c) irrespective of the weather
(d) to the school

Ans. (b)
Part 'I goes' contains an error. 'I go' should be used in place of 'I goes' to make the sentence grammatically correct. Simple present tense should be used in the given sentence as it talks about a habit.

572. Fatima and Sana has both taken the vaccine. **SSC CHSL Tier-1 27.05.2022 (Shift-I)**
(a) Fatima and Sana was both taken the vaccine.
(b) Fatima and Sana have both taken the vaccine.
(c) Fatima and Sana were both taken the vaccine
(d) Fatima and Sana are both taken the vaccine.

Ans. (b)
When two nouns are joined by 'and', we take a plural verb. Hence, 'Fatima and Sana have both taken the vaccine' is the correct sentence from the given options.

573. I am not sure / if the red car / in the parking slot / is your.
SSC CHSL Tier-1 27.05.2022 (Shift-I)
(a) in the parking slot
(b) I am not sure
(c) if the red car
(d) is your

Ans. (d)
Part (d) 'is your' contains an error. Possessive pronoun is needed in the sentence. Hence, 'is yours' should be used in place of 'is your' to make the sentence error free.

574. My boss keeps telling me / all the time / that money / doesn't grows on trees. **SSC CHSL Tier-1 27.05.2022 (Shift-I)**
(a) My boss keeps telling me
(b) all the time
(c) that money
(d) doesn't grows on trees

Ans. (d)
Part (d) 'doesn't grows on trees' contains an error. As 'money' is an uncountable noun, a plural verb will be used with it. Hence, 'doesn't grow on trees' should be used in place 'doesn't grows on trees' to make the sentence grammatically correct.

575. Ronaldo is / a famous / player of / the football.
SSC CHSL Tier-1 25.05.2022 (Shift-III)
(a) a famous (b) the football
(c) Ronaldo is (d) player of

Ans. (b)
'The' is not used before some words like football, cricket, jail, school, etc., because these nouns are non-specific in the general sense.

576. Whenever he is / on a holiday, / he travels by foot / to the temple nearby. SSC CHSL Tier-1 30.05.2022 (Shift-I)
(a) to the temple nearby
(b) Whenever he is
(c) he travels by foot
(d) on a holiday

Ans. (c)

Part (c) 'he travels by foot' contains an error.
'On' should be used in place of 'by' to make it grammatically correct, 'on foot' means walking.

577. He continued / staring at the elephant, / as if he had not see / one before. SSC CHSL Tier-1 31.05.2022 (Shift-I)
(a) as if he had not see
(b) staring at the elephant
(c) one before
(d) He continued

Ans. (a)

Part (a) 'as if he had not see' contains an error. 'As if he had not seen' should be used in place of 'as if he had not see' to make the sentence grammatically correct.
Spot the error in the given sentence and select the correct sentence from the options given. Fatima and Sana has both taken the vaccine.

578. Is Savita is joining us for lunch today? SSC CHSL Tier-1 31.05.2022 (Shift-I)
(a) Is Savita joining us for lunch today?
(b) Savita is joined us for lunch today?
(c) Savita joining us for lunch today?
(d) Are Savita joining us for lunch today?

Ans. (a)

The use of 'is' after 'Savita' is redundant. Hence, Option (a) correctly rectifies the error in the given sentence.

579. In its August 1992 issue, the highly respected British Journal of Addiction describe three unusual cases of carrot dependence.
SSC CHSL Tier-1 31.05.2022 (Shift-III)
(a) In its August 1992 issue, the highly respected British Journal of Addiction was describing three unusual cases of carrot dependence.
(b) In its August 1992 issue, the highly respected British Journal of Addiction describing three unusual cases of carrot dependence.
(c) In its August 1992 issue, the highly respected British Journal of Addiction described three unusual cases of carrot dependence.
(d) In its August 1992 issue, the highly respected British Journal of Addiction has been described three British Journal of Addiction has been described three.

Ans. (c)

In its August 1992 issue, the highly respected British Journal of Addiction described three unusual cases of carrot dependence. (Correct).

580. There was an interesting article / in the newspaper / about the dangers / to an environment.
SSC CHSL Tier-1 01.06.2022 (Shift-I)
(a) to an environment
(b) Three was an interesting article
(c) about the dangers
(d) in the newspaper

Ans. (a)

Part (a) 'to an environment' contains an error.
'Dangers to the environment' should be used in place of 'dangers to an environment' to make the sentence grammatically correct.

581. He sees us coming and unaware that we had learned of his treachery, greeted us with a smile.
SSC CHSL Tier-1 01.06.2022 (Shift-I)
(a) He saw us coming and unaware that we learned of his treachery, greeted us with a smile.
(b) He saw us coming and unaware that we had learned of his treachery, greeted us with a smile.
(c) He saw us coming and unaware that we were learning of his treachery, greeted us with a smile.
(d) He saw us come and unaware that we had learned of his treachery, greets us with a smile.

Ans. (b)

The given sentence is in past perfect tense wherein simple past and past perfect form is used. Hence, option (b) correctly rectifies the error in the given sentence.

582. When Sanathan asked Mr. Jignesh / for a fresh evaluation of his performance / in the last financial year, / little did him know that the results will come out worse than expected.
SSC CHSL Tier-1 01.06.2022 (Shift-III)
(a) When Sanathan asked Mr. Jignesh
(b) for a fresh evaluation of his performance
(c) in the last financial year
(d) little did him know that the results will come out worse than expected

Ans. (d)

We will replace the pronoun 'him' with the correct pronoun 'he' after the verb 'did' in the given sentence. Hence, 'little did he know that the results will come out worse than expected' is the most appropriate answer.

583. The Minister announced / that the bridge would constructed / within a week. SSC CHSL Tier-1 02.06.2022 (Shift-I)
(a) No error
(b) that the bridge would constructed
(c) The Minister announced
(d) within a week

Ans. (b)

Part 'that the bridge would constructed contains an error. 'That the bridge would be constructed' should be used in place of 'that the bridge would constructed' to make the sentence error free.

584. As a rule, single sentences should not be write or printed as paragraphs.
SSC CHSL Tier-1 03.06.2022 (Shift-III)
(a) As a rule, single sentences should not be wrote or printed as paragraphs.
(b) As a rule, single sentences should not write or print as paragraphs.
(c) As a rule, single sentences shall not have written or printed as paragraphs.
(d) As a rule, single sentences should not be written or printed as paragraphs.

Ans. (d)

As a rule, single sentences should not be written or printed as paragraphs. (Correct)
(a) As a rule, single sentences should not be wrote or printed as paragraphs. (Incorrect verb)
(b) As a rule, single sentences should not write or print as paragraphs. (Incorrect verb)
(c) As a rule, single sentences shall not have written or printed as paragraphs. (Incorrect verb)

585. Me and my friends / often go / to the cinema / together.
SSC CHSL Tier-1 06.06.2022 (Shift-II)
(a) together
(b) often go
(c) to the cinema
(d) Me and my friends

Ans. (d)

We always put the second person before the first person in positive sentence according to the order of pronouns.

Similarly in the given sentence, narrator is the first person and his 'friends' is the second person. Hence, 'My friends and I' is the most appropriate answer.

586. He wished he has more resources to support the poor.
SSC CHSL Tier-1 06.06.2022 (Shift-III)

(a) He wished his having more resources to support the poor.
(b) He wished he have more resources to support the poor.
(c) He wishing he has more resources to support the poor.
(d) He wished he had more resources to support the poor.

Ans. (d)

He wished he had more resources to support the poor. The given sentence is in the simple past tense so the verb must be used in the past form (V_2). However, the past form of 'has' is 'had.' Hence, 'he wished he had' is the most appropriate answer.

587. The students stopped / their chatter / as soon as them noticed / the teacher enter the classroom.
SSC CHSL Tier-1 07.06.2022 (Shift-I)

(a) their chatter
(b) The students stopped
(c) The teacher enter the classroom
(d) as soon as them noticed

Ans. (d)

'As soon as them noticed' will be replaced by 'as soon as they noticed.' Use of objective pronoun is incorrect here and a nominative pronoun will be used.

588. The mob/is believing / every word / the leader says.
SSC CHSL Tier-1 07.06.2022 (Shift-II)

(a) is believing (b) the leader says
(c) every word (d) The mob

Ans. (a)

The sentence is in the present indefinite tense. The word 'says' has been used at the end. So 'believes' will be used. The correct sentence will be 'The mob believes every word the leader says.' Hence, 'believes' is the most appropriate answer.

589. Investing on real estate / can earn you quick profit / but it comes with / a certain amount of risk attached to it.
SSC CHSL Tier-1 07.06.2022 (Shift-II)

(a) a certain amount of risk attached to it
(b) can earn you quick profit
(c) Investing on real estate
(d) but it comes with

Ans. (c)

The preposition 'on' will be replaced by 'in.' Invest in is a phrasal verb which means to put money, effort, time, etc., into something to make a profit or get an advantage. Hence, 'investing in real estate' is the most appropriate answer.

590. When the villagers put up a firm resistance to the fearsome bandit with all their might, he ultimately fleed the spot.
SSC CHSL Tier-I 07.06.2022 (Shift-III)

(a) When the villagers put up a firm resistance to the fearsome bandit with all their might, he ultimately flew the spot.
(b) When the villagers putted up a firm resistance to the fearsome bandit with all their might, he ultimately fleed the spot.
(c) When the villagers put up a firm resistance to the fearsome bandit with all their might, he ultimately flown the spot.
(d) When the villagers put up a firm resistance to the fearsome bandit with all their might, he ultimately fled the spot.

Ans. (d)

When the villagers put up a firm resistance to the fearsome bandit with all their might, he ultimately fled the spot. (Correct)

591. The General have ordered / that the troops should move / immediately .
SSC CHSL Tier-1 08.06.2022 (Shift-II)

(a) immediately
(b) No error
(c) that the troops should move
(d) The General have ordered

Ans. (d)

The 'General' is singular so singular verb 'has' will be used. 'Have' is incorrect. The correct sentence will be 'The General has ordered that the troops should move immediately.'

592. As she kept walking to me, my heart skipped a beat.
SSC CGL Tier-1 09.06.2022 (Shift-I)

(a) As she kept walking within me, my heart skipped a beat.
(b) As she kept walking from me, my heart skipped a beat.
(c) As she kept into me, my heart skipped a beat.
(d) As she kept walking towards me, my heart skipped a beat.

Ans. (d)

As she kept walking towards me, my heart skipped a beat. (Correct)

(a) As she kept walking within me, my heart skipped a beat. (Incorrect preposition)
(b) As she kept walking from me, my heart skipped a beat. (Incorrect preposition)
(c) As she kept into me, my heart skipped a beat. (Incorrect preposition)

593. There were more than thirty delegates who attend the training programme last summer.
SSC CHSL Tier-1 09.06.2022 (Shift-III)

(a) There are more than thirty delegates who attend the training programme last summer.
(b) There were more than thirty delegates who attends the training programme last summer.
(c) There was more than thirty delegates who attend the training programme last summer.
(d) There were more than thirty delegates who attended the training programme last summer.

Ans. (d)

There were more than thirty delegates who attended the training programme last summer. (Correct)

(a) There are more than thirty delegates who attend the training programme last summer. (Incorrect tense)
(b) There were more than thirty delegates who attends the training programme last summer. (Incorrect tense)
(c) There was more than thirty delegates who attend the training programme last summer. (Incorrect verb)

594. As soon as we went for an afternoon siesta, my pet rabbit Tia digged a huge hole right in the middle of the lawn.
SSC CHSL Tier-1 10.06.2022 (Shift-I)

(a) As soon as we were going for an afternoon siesta, my pet rabbit Tia digged a huge hole right in the middle of the lawn.
(b) As soon as we went for an afternoon siesta, my pet rabbit Tia dug a huge hole right in the middle of the lawn.
(c) As soon as we gone for an afternoon siesta, my pet rabbit Tia digged a huge hole right in the middle of the lawn.
(d) As soon as we gone for an afternoon siesta, my pet rabbit Tia dug a huge hole right in the middle of the lawn.

Ans. (b)

As soon as we went for an afternoon siesta, my pet rabbit Tia dug a huge hole right in the middle of the lawn. (Correct)

SSC CHSL 2021

595. Electric heaters / were providing / to all the officers / at the guest house. SSC CHSL Tier-1 12.04.2021 (Shift-I)
(a) at the guest house
(b) were providing
(c) to all the officers
(d) Electric heaters

Ans. (b)

The given sentence is in the passive voice, so the verb must be used in its past form(provided) and not in the continuous form(providing). Hence, 'were provided' is the most appropriate structure.

596. Einstein's school teachers / thought he would / never success / in life.
SSC CHSL Tier-1 12.04.2021 (Shift-II)
(a) thought he would
(b) never success
(c) in life
(d) Einstein's school teachers

Ans. (b)

Succeed is a verb that means to manage to achieve what you want. But, success is a noun. However, the given sentence needs a verb. Hence, 'never succeed' is the most appropriate structure.

597. That man would have / attacked you / if you went / that way.
SSC CHSL Tier-1 13.04.2021 (Shift-I)
(a) That man would have
(b) attacked you
(c) that way
(d) if you went

Ans. (d)

'If + sub + Had + V_3...would have + V_3' is grammatically the correct structure for the given sentence. Hence, 'If you had gone' is the most appropriate structure.

598. Employees were / given incentives / based at / their performance.
SSC CHSL Tier-1 13.04.2021 (Shift-I)
(a) given incentives
(b) based at
(c) Employees were
(d) their performance

Ans. (b)

The phrase 'based at' is used to refer to the main place where you live or work and the phrase 'based on' means to use particular ideas or facts to make a decision. However, the given sentence states that employees were given incentives based on their performance. Hence, 'based on' is the most appropriate structure.

599. Economists have declared that 2020 graduates / will face the worse job depression / since the Great Depression / because of the COVID-19 pandemic.
SSC CHSL Tier-1 15.04.2021 (Shift-II)
(a) Economists have declared that 2020 graduates
(b) will face the worse job depression
(c) because of the COVID-19 pandemic
(d) since the Great Depression

Ans. (b)

'Worse' is used as a comparative degree like your project is worse than Rahul's project.

But, 'worst' is used as a superlative degree which is used to show the highest degree of anything like most beautiful, best, fastest, etc. However, the given sentence states that 2020 graduates will face job depression of the highest degree since the Great Depression. Hence, 'will face the worst job depression' is the most appropriate structure.

600. Until I was / still a little weak, / I decided to walk home / from the metro station.
SSC CHSL Tier-1 16.04.2021 (Shift-I)
(a) from the metro station
(b) I decided to walk home
(c) still a little weak
(d) Until I was

Ans. (d)

'Until' is used to describe an effect that will take place and still is used to denote the continuity of the action. In the given sentence, the narrator described the continuity of the action of walking.

So, we will remove the word 'until.' Hence, 'I was still a little weak' is the most appropriate answer.

601. The government has announced / a gradual / reboot of air travel / who was halted / two months ago / due to lockdown.
SSC CHSL Tier-1 16.04.2021 (Shift-I)
(a) reboot of air travel
(b) due to lockdown
(c) The government has announced
(d) who was halted

Ans. (d)

Replace 'who' with 'which.' In the given sentence, the halting of air travel due to lockdown was specific. Hence, 'which was halted' is the most appropriate structure.

602. Keep looking and/ you are sure to find the meaning /of the word on that page.
SSC CHSL Tier-1 16.04.2021 (Shift-II)
(a) of the word on that page
(b) you are sure to find the meaning
(c) No error
(d) Keep looking and

Ans. (c)

The sentence is grammatically correct and contextually meaningful.

603. Most hotels/ offer for their guests/ complimentary breakfast/ during their stay there.
SSC CHSL Tier-1 16.04.2021 (Shift-II)
(a) complimentary breakfast
(b) during their stay there
(c) offer for their guests
(d) Most hotels

Ans. (c)

There is a prepositional error in the given sentence. The use of 'for' after 'offer' is irrelevant so it should be removed.

Hence, 'most hotels offer their guests complimentary breakfast' is the most appropriate structure.

604. After a long gap, / we went shopping / last Sunday and bought / that we wanted.
SSC CHSL Tier-1 19.04.2021 (Shift-I)
(a) we went shopping
(b) After a long gap
(c) that we wanted
(d) last Sunday and bought

Ans. (c)

'What' is used to refer to the thing or things that have been mentioned or said like shopping mentioned in the given sentence. Hence, 'what' is the most appropriate structure.

605. I'm sorry, sir. / How many is / the fine for / returning the books late?
SSC CHSL Tier-1 19.04.2021 (Shift-III)
(a) I'm sorry, sir
(b) returning the books late
(c) How many is
(d) the fine for

Ans. (c)

'Many' is used for countable nouns, for example how many apples. However, 'much' is used for uncountable nouns for example how much money, how much rice, etc. Similarly in the given sentence, fine is uncountable. Hence, 'how much is the fine for' is the most appropriate structure.

606. At the workshop, / they were taught how to nail / the pieces of wood together to create toys.
SSC CHSL Tier-1 04.08.2021 (Shift-III)
(a) No error
(b) they were taught how to nail
(c) the pieces of wood together to create toys
(d) At the workshop

Ans. (a)

Th given sentence is grammatically correct and contextually meaningful.

607. A probe has been ordered / by the incident / that occurred at the celebrations.
SSC CHSL Tier-1 05.08.2021 (Shift-I)
(a) A probe has been ordered
(b) that occurred at the celebrations
(c) by the incident
(d) No error

Ans. (c)

'Probe into' a correct phrase meaning (To begin inquiring into or investigating something). The correct sentence will be as follows 'A probe has been ordered into the incident that occurred at the celebrations.'

608. If you rent a house / near your office / it will save you time / as well as also money.
SSC CHSL Tier-1 06.08.2021 (Shift-I)
(a) If you rent a house
(b) as well as also money
(c) near your office
(d) it will save you time

Ans. (b)

'As well as' is a conjunction that means in addition. It connects two nouns, pronouns, etc., to each other. So, use only 'money' in place of 'also money.' The conjunction 'as well as' is not immediately followed by , 'also.' Hence, the correct sentence will be as 'If you rent a house near your office, it will save you time as well as money'.

609. Notwithstanding we were / all busy that weekend / we had to / cancel the outing.
SSC CHSL Tier-1 06.08.2021 (Shift-I)
(a) cancel the outing
(b) we had to
(c) Notwithstanding we were
(d) all busy that weekend

Ans. (c)

'Notwithstanding' means 'despite or in spite of something.'
It is used to indicate an aspect of contrast. So, 'Notwithstanding' will be replaced by 'as' to make the sentence grammatically correct.

610. Every participant gave / so outstanding performance / that it became difficult / to choose the winner. SSC CHSL Tier-1 06.08.2021 (Shift-III)
(a) Every participant gave
(b) so outstanding performance
(c) to choose the winner
(d) that it became difficult

Ans. (b)

'Such' is used for emphasising the degree of something. The given sentence tells about a performance of outstanding degree.
Hence, 'so outstanding performance' will be replaced by 'such an outstanding performance' to grammatically correct the given sentence.

611. The need today is for both sides / to introspect and re-examine the issue carefully / and resolve it amicably.
SSC CHSL Tier-1 09.08.2021 (Shift-I)
(a) to introspect and re-examine the issue carefully
(b) and resolve it amicably
(c) No error
(d) The need today is for both sides

Ans. (c)

The sentence is grammatically correct and contextually meaningful.

612. We are / yet living / in the / same house. SSC CHSL Tier-1 10.08.2021 (Shift-I)
(a) We are (b) same house
(c) in the (d) yet living

Ans. (d)

'Yet living' contains an error. Remove 'yet' to correct the sentence.

613. The Prime Minister chair a high-level meeting / with senior officials / to review the COVID situation.
SSC CHSL Tier-1 10.08.2021 (Shift-I)
(a) with senior officials
(b) The Prime Minister chair a high-level meeting
(c) to review the COVID situation
(d) No error

Ans. (b)

'The Prime Minister chair a high-level meeting' contains an error. The word 'conducted' should be used in place of 'chair' to make the sentence error free.

614. Your advices were timely / and guided me / to take the right decisions.
SSC CHSL Tier-1 10.08.2021 (Shift-III)
(a) to take the right decisions
(c) and guided me
(b) No error
(d) Your advices were timely

Ans. (d)

'Advice' does not have any plural form. Use 'pieces of advice / bits of advice' in place of 'advices' to make the sentence grammatically correct.

SSC MTS 2024 (Tier 1 & 2)

615. My cousin thinks that/English is difficult/than other subjects.
SSC MTS Tier-1 14.11.2024 (Shift-III)
(a) English is difficult
(b) My cousin thinks that
(c) than other subjects
(d) No error

Ans. (a)

'English is difficult' contains an error. The correct phrase should be 'English is more difficult'.

616. Meenu looks/ much better/ today.
SSC MTS Tier-1 14.11.2024 (Shift-III)
(a) Meenu looks (b) today.
(c) No error (d) much better

Ans. (c)

'No error' is the correct option. The sentence 'Meenu looks much better today' is grammatically correct.

617. It was an insight / and determination of the lady doctor / that people were / able to lead a normal life.
SSC MTS Tier-1 14.11.2024 (Shift-III)
(a) It was an insight
(b) and determination of the lady doctor
(c) able to lead a normal life
(d) that people were

Ans. (a)

'It was an insight' contains a grammatical error. The correct phrase should be 'It was the insight'.

618. I thought of this idea / just when you called / me yesterday.
SSC MTS Tier-1 14.11.2024 (Shift-III)
(a) I thought of this idea
(b) No error
(c) me yesterday
(d) just when you called

Ans. (d)

'Just when you called' contains the error. The correct phrase should be 'just as you called'. The conjunction 'as' is used to indicate that two events occur simultaneously.

619. Please hang with for two minutes while I finish cleaning the utensils.
SSC MTS Tier-1 13.11.2024 (Shift-III)
(a) Please hang with
(b) while I finish cleaning
(c) the utensils
(d) for two minutes

Ans. (a)

'Please hang with' contains an error. 'Hang on' means to wait for a short time.

620. The car which I bought last year was cheap than my bike.
SSC MTS Tier-1 13.11.2024 (Shift-III)

(a) The car
(b) last year
(c) which I bought
(d) was cheap than my bike

Ans. (d)

'Was cheap than my bike' contains an error.

The phrase should be 'was cheaper than my bike'. 'Cheaper' is the comparative form of 'cheap'.

621. My aunt came from Switzerland by the flight which was landing at 5:00 am yesterday.
SSC MTS Tier-1 13.11.2024 (Shift-III)

(a) Switzerland by the
(b) My aunt came from
(c) flight which was landing
(d) at 5:00 a.m yesterday.

Ans. (c)

'Flight which was landing' contains an error.

The phrase should be 'flight which landed'. 'Was landing' should be in past simple tense as the action was completed.

622. (a) She was not allow to enter the hotel as her clothes were dirty.
(b) She was not allowed to enter the hotel as her clothes were dirtier.
(c) She was not allowed to enter the hotel as her clothes was dirtier.
(d) She was not allowed to enter the hotel as her clothes were dirty
SSC MTS Tier-1 12.11.2024 (Shift-III)

Ans. (d)

'She was not allowed to enter the hotel as her clothes were dirty' is the grammatically correct sentence.

623. (a) A secondary section of the school is located at an end of the street.
(b) The secondary section of the school is located at the end of the street.
(c) The secondary section of a school is located at the end of a street.
(d) The secondary section of a school is located at an end of the street
SSC MTS Tier-1 12.11.2024 (Shift-III)

Ans. (b)

'The secondary section of the school is located at the end of the street' is the grammatically correct sentence.

624. I still / do not understand / why he did not / reply my email.
SSC MTS Tier-1 12.11.2024 (Shift-III)

(a) I still (b) why he did not
(c) reply my email
(d) do not understand

Ans. (c)

'Reply my email' contains a grammatical error. The correct phrase is 'reply to my email'.

625. If I wrote an email / to my boss now, / he will react / by yelling at me tomorrow in the morning.
SSC MTS Tier-1 11.11.2024 (Shift-III)

(a) he will react
(b) to my boss now,
(c) by yelling at me tomorrow in the morning.
(d) If I wrote an email

Ans. (d)

'If I wrote an email' contains a grammatical error. The correct phrase should be 'If I write an email.' The sentence should use the present tense to match 'he will react.'

626. If the players don't wear sunscreen, / their faces will / get reddest.
SSC MTS Tier-1 11.11.2024 (Shift-III)

(a) get reddest
(b) their faces will
(c) If the players don't wear sunscreen,
(d) No error

Ans. (a)

'Get reddest' contains an error. The correct phrase should be 'get red.' 'Red' is the correct adjective form here.

627. (a) She is an artist at a local gallery.
(b) The cat is sleeping on a mat.
(c) They have an information about the event.
(d) Can you bring me the keys to the car? **SSC MTS Tier-1 11.11.2024 (Shift-III)**

Ans. (c)

'They have an information about the event' contains a grammatical error. 'Information' is an uncountable noun and should not be preceded by 'an.'

628. She oftenly goes/shopping with/her friends / on Saturdays.
SSC MTS Tier-1 05.11.2024 (Shift-III)

(a) her friends (b) on Saturdays
(c) She oftenly goes (d) shopping with

Ans. (c)

Part 'she oftenly goes' contains a grammatical error. The correct phrase is 'She often goes'. The word 'oftenly' is incorrect.

629. The zoo is under the street from the temple. **SSC MTS Tier-1 05.11.2024 (Shift-III)**

(a) zoo (b) temple
(c) from (d) under

Ans. (d)

Part 'under' contains an error. The correct preposition is 'across.'

630. A good lawyer / always looks in the / case before he / attends court.
SSC MTS Tier-1 04.11.2024 (Shift-III)

(a) attends court (b) always looks in the
(c) case before he (d) A good lawyer

Ans. (b)

Part 'always looks in the' contains a grammatical error. The correct phrase should be 'always looks into the.'

631. Before the internet was available on mobile, I read often books for entertainment and information.
SSC MTS Tier-1 04.11.2024 (Shift-III)

(a) for entertainment and information
(b) was available on mobile
(c) Before the internet
(d) I read often books

Ans. (d)

Part 'I read often books' contains an error. The correct phrase should be 'I often read books.'

632. We have invited / our friends / for a / dinner. **SSC MTS Tier-1 30.10.2024 (Shift-III)**

(a) dinner (b) We have invited
(c) our friends (d) for a

Ans. (d)

Part 'for a' contains an error in the usage of indefinite articles. The correct phrase is 'for dinner' without the indefinite article 'a'.

633. Mohan is still confused about his higher studies.
SSC MTS Tier-1 30.10.2024 (Shift-III)

(a) No error
(b) Mohan is still
(c) his higher studies
(d) confused about

Ans. (a)

The sentence 'Mohan is still confused about his higher studies' is grammatically correct.

634. The manager had / thrown up the / drunk people sitting / inside his office premises.
SSC MTS Tier-1 30.10.2024 (Shift-III)

(a) drunk people sitting
(b) inside his office premises
(c) thrown up the
(d) The manager had

Ans. (c)

Part 'thrown up the' contains a grammatical error.

The correct phrase should be 'thrown out the'. 'Thrown up' is incorrect usage in this context.

635. You have spoilt / the little chance you / had at succeeding.
SSC MTS Tier-1 28.10.2024 (Shift-II)

(a) You have spoilt
(b) No error
(c) the little chance you
(d) had at succeeding

Ans. (c)

Part 'the little chance you' contains the error. The sentence should use 'your little chance' to be grammatically correct.

636. That question is / much difficult / but this one is / very easy.
SSC MTS Tier-1 28.10.2024 (Shift-II)

(a) much difficult
(b) very easy
(c) That question is
(d) but this one is

Ans. (a)

Part 'much difficult' contains the error. 'Much' should be replaced with 'very' to be grammatically correct.

637. (a) A famous poet wrote that poem.
(b) I went to watch a play with one of my friends.
(c) He resides near an university.
(d) A dog likes sunlight.
SSC MTS Tier-1 28.10.2024 (Shift-II)

Ans. (c)

Part 'he resides near an university' contains a grammatical error. The correct article is 'a university'.

638. The robbers stabbed him by a sharp knife and he started bleeding profusely on the spot.
SSC MTS Tier-1 28.10.2024 (Shift-II)

(a) profusely from the spot
(b) The robbers stabbed her
(c) but he started bleeding
(d) with a sharp knife

Ans. (d)

Part 'with a sharp knife' is the correct option to rectify the error.

639. (a) A lot of books and notes place in order look most fascinating.
(b) A lot of book and notes placed in order looks most fascinating.
(c) A lot of books and notes placed in order look fascinating.
(d) A lot of books and notes placed on order looks most fascinating.
SSC MTS Tier-1 23.10.2024 (Shift-II)

Ans. (c)

'A lot of books and notes placed in order look fascinating' is the grammatically correct sentence. This sentence uses the correct plural forms and subject-verb agreement.

640. If I was a king, I would have tried my best to remove poverty from my country.
SSC MTS Tier-1 22.10.2024 (Shift-II)

(a) I would has tried
(b) If I were a king
(c) my best by remove poverty
(d) on my country

Ans. (b)

'If I were a king', is the correct option to rectify the error.

The sentence should read 'If I were a king,
I would have tried my best to remove poverty from my country'. The use of 'were' is correct in this subjunctive mood, which is used for hypothetical situations.

641. Bindu asked Arya to fill out for / her so that she could / take care of / her sick father.
SSC MTS Tier-1 21.10.2024 (Shift-II)

(a) take care of
(b) her sick father
(c) her so that he could
(d) Bindu asked Arya to fill out for

Ans. (d)

Part 'bindu asked Arya to fill out for' contains an error in the phrasal verb. The correct form is 'fill in for.'

The sentence should read 'Bindu asked Arya to fill in for her so that she could take care of her sick father.'

642. (a) If you want to have an sound working knowledge of Japanese, you must read this book.
(b) If you want to have a sound working knowledge of Japanese, you must read this book.
(c) If you want to have a sound working knowledge of the Japanese, you must read this book.
(d) If you want to have sound working knowledge of the Japanese, you must read this book.
SSC MTS Tier-1 21.10.2024 (Shift-II)

Ans. (b)

'If you want to have a sound working knowledge of Japanese, you must read this book' is the grammatically correct sentence.

This sentence correctly uses the indefinite article 'a'.

643. My sister Mona / never drinks coffee; / she prefer tea / in the morning. SSC MTS Tier-1 17.10.2024 (Shift-II)

(a) in the morning
(b) My sister Mona
(c) never drinks coffee;
(d) she prefer tea

Ans. (d)

Part 'she prefer tea' contains a grammatical error. The correct form is 'She prefers tea'. This verb agreement is necessary because 'she' (third person singular) requires the verb to be in its singular form.

644. He was constantly / gazing on the / crime scene to / find some clues.
SSC MTS Tier-1 16.10.2024 (Shift-II)

(a) He was constantly
(b) crime scene to
(c) gazing on the
(d) find some clues

Ans. (c)

Part 'gazing on the' contains a grammatical error. The correct phrase is 'gazing at the'.

'Gazing' typically uses the preposition 'at' when referring to looking steadily and intently.

645. Shivani go to school tomorrow for prize distribution.
SSC MTS Tier-1 16.10.2024 (Shift-II)

(a) Shivani has gone to school tomorrow for prize distribution.
(b) Shivani goes to school tomorrow for prize distribution.
(c) Shivani had gone to school tomorrow for prize distribution.
(d) Shivani will go to school tomorrow for prize distribution.

Ans. (d)

'Shivani will go to school tomorrow for prize distribution' rectifies the error in the usage of the future tense. The sentence correctly uses the future tense to indicate a planned future event.

646. (a) Yesterday, we was painting the door when a neighbour stopping by to say hello.
(b) Yesterday, we are painting the door when a neighbour stop by to say hello.
(c) Yesterday, we were painting the door when a neighbour stopped by to say hello.
(d) Yesterday, we will be painting the door when a neighbour stops by to say hello.
SSC MTS Tier-1 16.10.2024 (Shift-II)

Ans. (c)

'Yesterday, we were painting the door when a neighbour stopped by to say hello' uses the correct tense.

The past continuous tense 'were painting' is correctly used to indicate an ongoing action in the past that was interrupted by another action 'stopped by.'

647. This is the best novel / I have read, / in a very long time.
SSC MTS Tier-1 15.10.2024 (Shift-I)

(a) No error
(b) in a very long time
(c) This is the best novel
(d) have read

Ans. (a)

'No error' is the correct option. The sentence is grammatically correct.

648. Sam and Teena / had wondering / what to do this weekend.
SSC MTS Tier-1 15.10.2024 (Shift-I)

(a) what to do this weekend
(b) had wondering
(c) No error
(d) Sam and Teena

Ans. (b)

Part 'had wondering' contains an error. The correct form is 'were wondering.'

649. The sky is covering / with dark clouds and / I hope soon it / will begin to rain.
SSC MTS Tier-1 15.10.2024 (Shift-I)

(a) with dark clouds and
(b) The sky is covering
(c) will begin to rain
(d) I hope soon it

Ans. (b)

Part 'the sky is covering' contains a grammatical error. The correct form is 'The sky is covered.'

650. (a) By the time we arrive at the party, they had been waiting for over an hour.
(b) By the time we arrived at the party, they had been waiting for over an hour.
(c) By the time we arrives at the party, they had been waiting for over an hour.
(d) By the time we arriving at the party, they had been waiting for over an hour. SSC MTS Tier-1 14.10.2024 (Shift-I)

Ans. (b)

'By the time we arrived at the party, they had been waiting for over an hour' uses the correct tense. The past perfect continuous tense is appropriate here.

651. Sushil, who recently joined our school/was awarded the Gold Cup/as he worked hardly / throughout the year.
SSC MTS Tier-1 14.10.2024 (Shift-I)

(a) throughout the year.
(b) Sushil, who recently joined our school
(c) was awarded the Gold Cup
(d) as he worked hardly

Ans. (d)

Part 'as he worked hardly' contains a grammatical error.

It should be 'as he worked hard.'

652. I have never seen so beautiful a landscape than this one.
SSC MTS Tier-1 14.10.2024 (Shift-I)

(a) I have never seen
(b) so beautiful
(c) a landscape
(d) than this one

Ans. (d)

Part 'than this one' contains an error. It should be 'as this one' to correctly form a comparison using 'so' or 'as.'

653. My son, who is a cricketer too, is a MA from Delhi University.
SSC MTS Tier-1 09.10.2024 (Shift-I)

(a) from Delhi University
(b) is a MA
(c) My son, who is
(d) a cricketer too

Ans. (b)

Part 'is a MA' contains an error. 'An' should be used before 'MA' because 'MA' is pronounced with a vowel sound at the beginning.

654. She forbade / him not / to enter that / room. SSC MTS Tier-1 09.10.2024 (Shift-I)

(a) she forbade (b) him not
(c) to enter that (d) room

Ans. (b)

Part 'him not' contains a grammatical error use of 'not' is superfluous as 'forbade' itself means 'to not allow'.

655. Tara was late for the meeting/but somehow managed/to catch out with/everything she had missed.
SSC MTS Tier-1 08.10.2024 (Shift-II)

(a) to catch out with
(b) everything she had missed
(c) Tara was late for the meeting
(d) but somehow managed

Ans. (a)

The segment 'to catch out with' contains an error in the phrasal verb; it should be 'to catch up with.'

656. He cheated in the (A) / examination, making his (B) / already-falling academic (C) / credentials worst. (D)
SSC MTS Tier-1 07.10.2024 (Shift-I)

(a) C (b) B
(c) D (d) A

Ans. (c)

The segment 'credentials worst' contains a grammatical error; it should be 'credentials worse.' 'Worse' is the comparative form of 'bad,' fitting the context of deteriorating academic credentials.

657. Tina dropped behind of / college and/went straight/into a good job.
SSC MTS Tier-1 07.10.2024 (Shift-I)

(a) college and
(b) into a good job
(c) Tina dropped behind of
(d) went straight

Ans. (c)

The segment 'Tina dropped behind of' contains an error in the phrasal verb; it should be 'Tina dropped out of.' 'Dropped out' means to withdraw or leave a programme or institution.

SSC MTS 2023 (Tier 1 & 2)

658. Restoring soil health would / help at mitigate the /effects of climate change. SSC MTS Tier-1 02.05.2023 (Shift-I)

(a) help at mitigate the
(b) effects of climate change.
(c) Restoring soil health would
(d) No error

Ans. (a)

Preposition 'at' will be removed as we directly use the bare infinitive after the verb bid, let, watch, see, make, help and hear.

Hence 'help mitigate the' is the most appropriate answer.

659. The front part is used for carving / the lines and the back end / for scratching of whole areas.
SSC MTS Tier-1 02.05.2023 (Shift-II)

(a) the lines and the back end
(b) No error
(c) The front part is used for carving
(d) for scratching of whole areas

Ans. (d)

Preposition 'of' will be removed as scratch is a transitive verb and it will not use any preposition with it. 'The' will be used before 'whole', Hence, 'for scratching the whole areas' is the most appropriate answer.

660. Companies will go / after one other in / their marketing campaigns.
SSC MTS Tier-1 02.05.2023 (Shift-III)
(a) their marketing campaigns
(b) after one other in
(c) Companies will go
(d) No error

Ans. (b)

'Other' will be replaced by 'another' as we generally use the reciprocal pronoun 'one another' to indicate a mutual relationship between two or more people or things. Hence,'after one another in' is the most appropriate answer.

661. Now its referring to the same / big lug who met his fate/ thanks to David's slingshot.
SSC MTS Tier-1 03.05.2023 (Shift-I)
(a) No error
(b) thanks to David's slingshot
(c) big lug who met his fate
(d) Now its referring to the same

Ans. (d)

It's a contraction and should be used where a sentence would read 'it is.' Its with no apostrophe is the possessive pronoun, like 'his' and 'her', for nouns without gender. Hence, 'Now it's referring to the same' is the most appropriate answer.

662. The police released a statement saying, / 'This was one of the most vicious / attack we have ever seen'.
SSC MTS Tier-1 03.05.2023 (Shift-III)
(a) No error
(b) The police released a statement saying
(c) 'This was one of the most vicious
(d) attack we have ever seen'

Ans. (d)

'One of the + Superlative degree of the adjective (best, worst, etc.) + Plural Subject' is grammatically the correct structure.
For example, one of the best men, one of the greatest kings, one of the worst phones, etc. Hence, 'attacks we have ever seen' is the most appropriate structure.

663. Participants in our / studies reviewed these / online dating profiles. SSC MTS Tier-1 04.05.2023 (Shift-I)
(a) online dating profiles
(b) Participants in our
(c) studies reviewed these
(d) No error

Ans. (d)

The sentence is grammatically correct and contextually meaningful.

664. While persimmons can be / use in pies and tarts, you / can also enjoy them plain.
SSC MTS Tier-1 04.05.2023 (Shift-III)
(a) While persimmons can be
(b) use in pies and tarts, you
(c) No error
(d) can also enjoy them plain

Ans. (b)

'Use' must be replaced with 'used' as the first clause of the sentence is in passive voice and the verb will always be in the 3rd form in the passive voice.
Hence, 'used in pies and tarts, you' is the most appropriate answer.

665. Your ears are itching / because you are having an / allergic reaction.
SSC MTS Tier-1 08.05.2023 (Shift-I)
(a) because you are having an
(b) Your ears are itching
(c) allergic reaction
(d) No error

Ans. (d)

The sentence is grammatically correct and contextually meaningful.

666. 'Don't you get / involve!' Sandhya / whispered urgently to him.
SSC MTS Tier-1 08.05.2023 (Shift-I)
(a) whispered urgently to him.
(b) involve! Sandhya
(c) Don't you get
(d) No error

Ans. (b)

'Involve' must be replaced with 'involved' in the given sentence. As we generally use past participles with the verb 'get.'
Hence, 'involved! Sandhya will' be the most appropriate answer.

667. India is already the third-largest / aviation market in / terms of domestic travel.
SSC MTS Tier-1 08.05.2023 (Shift-III)
(a) aviation market in
(b) India is already the third-largest
(c) No error
(d) terms of domestic travel

Ans. (c)

The sentence is grammatically correct and contexually meaningful.

668. The Gryffindors trooped back up / to the castle, none of them talking; / it have been another long day.
SSC MTS Tier-1 09.05.2023 (Shift-I)
(a) No error
(b) The Gryffindors trooped back up
(c) it have been another long day
(d) to the castle, none of them talking

Ans. (c)

'Have' must be replaced with 'has' in the given sentence.

According to the subject-verb agreement, a singular subject takes a singular verb and a plural subject always takes a plural verb.

Here, in the sentence 'it' is a singular subject. Hence,'it has been another long day' is the most appropriate answer.

669. Professor Murli's eyebrows/rose a little higher and his/gaze became distinctly coldest.
SSC MTS Tier-1 09.05.2023 (Shift-III)
(a) gaze became distinctly coldest
(b) No error
(c) Professor Murli's eyebrows
(d) rose a little higher and his

Ans. (a)

'Coldest' must be replaced by 'colder' as to maintain consistency, the correct usage would be to use the comparative degree throughout the sentence. In this correction, both 'higher' and 'colder' are in the comparative degree, indicating a comparison between two states or levels.

Hence, 'gaze became distinctly colder' is the most appropriate answer.

670. Early, during December 2021, / Lal was appointed as /the Secretary to the Lokpal.
SSC MTS Tier-1 10.05.2023 (Shift-I)
(a) the Secretary to the Lokpal
(b) Early, during December 2021
(c) Lal was appointed as
(d) No error

Ans. (b)

The error in the sentence is the use of the word 'during.' Since the sentence specifies December 2021, it implies that Lal was appointed as the Secretary to the Lokpal at some point within that month.

However, the word 'during' suggests a continuous action or a period of time, which is not appropriate in this context. Hence, 'Early in December 2021' is the most appropriate answer.

671. In 79 AD, the Mount Vesuvius blew / its top, burying the ancient / cities of Pompeii and Herculaneum.
SSC MTS Tier-1 10.05.2023 (Shift-I)
(a) In 79 AD, the Mount Vesuvius blew
(b) its top, burying the ancient
(c) cities of Pompeii and Herculaneum
(d) No error

Ans. (a)

Article 'the' must be removed as we generally use article 'the' with the names of mountains but we do not use 'the' if the name includes Mount or Mountain (Mount Olympus, Brokeback Mountain).

672. I hope that /we will arrive at / the ideal trade-off soon.
SSC MTS Tier-1 10.05.2023 (Shift-III)
(a) the ideal trade-off soon
(b) we will arrive at
(c) No error
(d) I hope that
Ans. (c)
The sentence is grammatically correct and contexually meaningfull.

673. If I was a clown, / I would have made / everyone smile.
SSC MTS Tier-1 11.05.2023 (Shift-I)
(a) everyone smile
(b) I would have made
(c) If I was a clown
(d) No error
Ans. (c)
'Was' must be replaced with 'were.' When expressing unreal or hypothetical situations in the present or future, the subjunctive mood is used, which requires the use of 'were' instead of 'was' after 'if.'
Hence, 'If I were a clown' is the most appropriate answer.

674. Many female mammals, / including rabbits and cats, ovulate / only when they mate.
SSC MTS Tier-1 11.05.2023 (Shift-II)
(a) No error
(b) Many female mammals
(c) only when they mate
(d) including rabbits and cats, ovulate
Ans. (a)
The sentence is grammatically correct and contextually meaningful.

675. One-to-one interaction / with parents is know / to be important.
SSC MTS Tier-1 11.05.2023 (Shift-II)
(a) with parents is know
(b) to be important
(c) No error
(d) One-to-one interaction
Ans. (a)
'Know' must be replaced with 'known' as the given sentences is in passive voice (is + V_3).
The 3rd form of the verb 'know' is 'known.' Hence, 'with parents is known' is the most appropriate answer.

676. Even if a evidence was/ relevant to the case, it couldn't/ is used to determine the reprobate.
SSC MTS Tier-1 12.05.2023 (Shift-I)
(a) relevant to the case, it couldn't
(b) even if a evidence was
(c) No error
(d) is used to determine the reprobate
Ans. (b)
'A evidence' must be replaced with 'the evidence.' 'Evidence' is an uncountable noun, so we cannot use article 'a / an.'
Here, the person talking about the evidence is familiar with it and we use article 'the' for things that are familiar or known to us. Hence, 'Even if the evidence was' is the most appropriate answer.

677. The kids there was so notorious, the /more I asked them to quiet down,/ the more loud they would scream. SSC MTS Tier-1 12.05.2023 (Shift-II)
(a) No error
(b) the more loud they would scream
(c) more I asked them to quiet down
(d) The kids were so notorious, the
Ans. (b)
The phrase 'the more loud' will be replaced with the correct comparative degree 'the louder.' Hence, 'the louder they would scream' is the most appropriate answer.

678. The Federalists wished to / make the Central Government / as strong possible. SSC MTS Tier-1 12.05.2023 (Shift-III)
(a) as strong possible
(b) The Federalists wished to
(c) No error
(d) make the Central Government
Ans. (a)
'As strong possible' will be replace with 'as strong as possible.' This is because 'As...as' is a comparative structure that shows similarity or equality between two elements.
It is used to compare two things or actions and indicates that they are of the same degree or level. Hence, 'as strong as possible' is the most appropriate answer.

679. Can you please / help me to / this project? SSC MTS Tier-1 12.05.2023 (Shift-III)
(a) this project
(b) Can you please
(c) No error
(d) help me to
Ans. (d)
'Help me to' will be replaced with 'help me with' as the verb 'help' is typically followed by the preposition 'with' when indicating assistance or support in accomplishing a task or project.
Hence, 'help me with' will be the most appropriate answer.

680. Her evaluation will give /me a best indication of /where I stand in the class. SSC MTS Tier-1 15.05.2023 (Shift-I)
(a) where I stand in the class
(b) Her evaluation will give
(c) No error
(d) me a best indication of
Ans. (d)
Article 'a' will be replaced with article 'the' as we use 'the' before superlative degree of adjectives.
Hence, 'the best indication' is the most appropriate answer.

681. No matter how mountains are / formed, they eventually becomes / too heavy and succumb to gravity.
SSC MTS Tier-1 15.05.2023 (Shift-II)
(a) formed, they eventually becomes
(b) No matter how mountains are
(c) too heavy and succumb to gravity
(d) No error
Ans. (a)
'Becomes' will be replaced with 'become' as according to the subject-verb agreement, Singular subject always takes singular verb and plural subject takes plural verb. Here in the sentence 'they' is a plural subject, so we need the plural verb 'become.' Hence, 'formed, they eventually become' is the most appropriate answer.

682. In humans, consumption of alcohol, / stimulate brain cells to / release mood-altering dopamine.
SSC MTS Tier-1 15.05.2023 (Shift-III)
(a) release mood-altering dopamine
(b) In humans, consumption of alcohol
(c) stimulate brain cells to
(d) No error
Ans. (c)
'Stimulate' will be replaced with 'stimulates' as it agrees with the subject 'consumption of alcohol' which is singular.
According to the subject verb-agreement, singular subject takes singular verb and plural subject takes plural verb.Hence, 'stimulates brain cells to' will be the most appropriate answer.

683. When he buckled down to his / work he became, the slyer / and cleverest of diplomats.
SSC MTS Tier-1 16.05.2023 (Shift-II)
(a) When he buckled down to his
(b) work he became, the slyer
(c) and cleverest of diplomats
(d) No error

Ans. (b)

'The slyer' will be replaced with 'the slyest' as 'slyer' is a comparative form and we need a superlative form of the adjective 'sly' i.e., 'slyest' to match the later part of the sentence. Hence, 'Work he became, the slyest' will be the most appropriate answer.

684. Humans have rapidly / changing the balance of / gases in the atmosphere.
SSC MTS Tier-1 16.05.2023 (Shift-III)
(a) Humans have rapidly
(b) changing the balance of
(c) gases in the atmosphere
(d) No error

Ans. (b)

The verb 'changing' is incorrect because we can not use 'V_4 (ing form) with the helping verb of present perfect tense (has/have).

The third form (V_3) 'changed' will be used in place of changing. Hence, 'changed the balance of' is the most appropriate answer.

685. Largest farmers usually / have more money, social power /and local influence.
SSC MTS Tier-1 17.05.2023 (Shift-I)
(a) Largest farmers usually
(b) No error
(c) have more money, social power
(d) and local influence

Ans. (a)

'Largest farmers' will be replaced with 'the largest farmers' as when referring to a specific group of farmers, the definite article 'the' is required before the superlative adjective 'largest.'

Hence, 'the largest farmers usually' will be the most appropriate answer.

686. You can find these / books into the extreme / corner of this shelf.
SSC MTS Tier-1 17.05.2023 (Shift-II)
(a) books into the extreme
(b) corner of this shelf
(c) You can find these
(d) No error

Ans. (a)

'Into' will be replaced with 'in' as the preposition 'in' indicates the location of the books. Hence, 'books in the extreme' will be the most appropriate answer.

687. Mothers can pass the HIV virus to / their newborns during delivery / as well, who says?
SSC MTS Tier-1 17.05.2023 (Shift-II)
(a) as well, who says?
(b) Mothers can pass the HIV virus to
(c) No error
(d) their newborns during delivery

Ans. (b)

Article 'the' must be removed as we don't use article 'the' before names. 'HIV' is the name of a virus. Hence, 'Mothers can pass HIV virus to' is the most appropriate answer.

688. Tax dispute settlement / might not work out in / the desired scale.
SSC MTS Tier-1 18.05.2023 (Shift-I)
(a) might not work out in
(b) the desired scale
(c) Tax dispute settlement
(d) No error

Ans. (a)

Preposition 'in' must be replaced with 'on' as we generally use 'on' to discuss the success on outcome of a particular activity or process. Hence, 'might not work out on' is the most appropriate answer.

689. The government have a rudimentary plan for / an ecosystem for defence startups / to fast-forward innovation.
SSC MTS Tier-1 18.05.2023 (Shift-II)
(a) to fast-forward innovation
(b) an ecosystem for defence startups
(c) The government have a rudimentary plan for
(d) No error

Ans. (c)

According to the 'Subject-Verb Agreement Rule', a singular subject always takes a singular verb and a plural subject always takes a plural verb. In the given sentence, 'government' is a singular subject that will take 'has' as a singular form. Hence, 'The government has a rudimentary plan for' is the most appropriate structure.

690. Do not be put of by the / mathematical equation, because / this is really not very complicated.
SSC MTS Tier-1 18.05.2023 (Shift-III)
(a) Do not be put of by the
(b) this is really not very complicated
(c) mathematical equation, because
(d) No error

Ans. (a)

'put off' is the correct phrasal verb to be used in place of 'put of.' Put of means to lose interest or enthusiasm in something. In the given sentence, it implies that you don't have to be discouraged by the mathematical equation.

Hence, 'do not be put off by the' is the most appropriate answer.

691. He consolidated control over all the / provinces of the Great Britain and some / of Northern Gaul while Maximian dealt with other uprisings. **SSC MTS Tier-1 19.05.2023 (Shift-I)**
(a) of Northern Gaul while Maximian dealt with other uprisings
(b) No Error
(c) He consolidated control over all the
(d) provinces of the Great Britain and some

Ans. (d)

The definite article 'the' should not be used before 'Great Britain' in this passage.

'Great Britain' is a proper noun and it does not require the definite article 'the' before it. Hence, 'provinces of Great Britain and some' is the most appropriate answer.

692. Here, in truth, lies / the crux of the / great problem of all.
SSC MTS Tier-1 19.05.2023 (Shift-II)
(a) great problem of all
(b) No error
(c) Here, in truth, lies
(d) the crux of the

Ans. (a)

'Great problem of all' will be replaced with 'greatest problem of all' as article 'the' is used before superlative degree adjectives.

Hence, 'greatest problem of all' is the most appropriate answer.

693. An appeasements policies / were all but a sham to misdirect / the local groups. **SSC MTS Tier-1 19.05.2023 (Shift-III)**
(a) the local groups
(b) were all but a sham to misdirect
(c) An appeasements policies
(d) No error

Ans. (c)

Article 'an' must be removed as we don't use an article before plural noun (appeasement policies) also appeasements must be replaced with appeasement as it is used as an adjective to modify the noun 'policies.' Hence, 'Appeasement policies' is the most appropriate answer.

694. Humans are drawn to / foods that is fatty, / sweet, rich and complex.
SSC MTS Tier-1 13.06.2023 (Shift-II)
(a) No error
(b) sweet, rich and complex
(c) Humans are drawn to
(d) foods that is fatty

Ans. (d)

The phrase 'that is' will be replaced with 'that are' because the antecedent (foods) of the relative pronoun 'that' is plural.
Plural verbs should be used for plural antecedent. Hence, 'that are' will the most appropriate answer.

695. It would be neat and / cleanest, a home worthy of /spending our lives together. SSC MTS Tier-1 13.06.2023 (Shift-III)
(a) cleanest, a home worthy of
(b) spending our lives together
(c) It would be heat and
(d) No error

Ans. (a)

'Cleanest' must be replaced with 'clean' as 'cleanest' is a superlative form of the adjective 'clean.' Superlatives are used to compare three or more items or qualities. However, in the sentence there is no comparison being made between multiple homes or qualities. So, we can use the adjective 'clean' alone. Hence, 'clean, a home worthy of' is the most appropriate answer.

696. Eddie just panics / when it gets close / nearer the end.
SSC MTS Tier-1 14.06.2023 (Shift-I)
(a) nearer the end
(b) No error
(c) when it gets close
(d) Eddie just panics

Ans. (a)

'Nearer' must be removed as the phrase 'close' and 'nearer' convey the same meaning of proximity or nearness. Hence, 'close to the end' is the most appropriate answer.

697. Susan had recently run on to / Catherine at the supermarket, they / were seeing each other after many years. SSC MTS Tier-1 14.06.2023 (Shift-III)
(a) were seeing each other after many years
(b) Catherine at the supermarket, they
(c) No error
(d) Susan had recently run on to

Ans. (d)

The correct phrasal verb is 'run into.' 'Run into' means to accidentally meet someone. Hence, 'Susan had recently run into' is the most appropriate answer.

698. Harry's eyes watered in / the chill as they soar upwards; he / could see nothing below now.
SSC MTS Tier-1 15.06.2023 (Shift-I)
(a) could see nothing below now
(b) the chill as they soar upwards; he
(c) Harry's eyes watered in
(d) No error

Ans. (b)

'Soar' must be replaced with 'soared' as the given sentence is in simple past tense and we need to use the pronoun 'he' for the singular noun (Harry). Hence, 'the chill as he soared upwards; he' is the most appropriate answer.

699. Neither Ram nor / his sisters are ready / to play the game.
SSC MTS Tier-1 15.06.2023 (Shift-II)
(a) to play the game
(b) No error
(c) his sisters are ready
(d) Neither Ram nor

Ans. (b)

The given sentence is grammatically correct and contextually meaningful.

700. Leaders are self-direct, / but learning and understanding / are the keys to self-direction.
SSC MTS Tier-1 15.06.2023 (Shift-III)
(a) No error
(b) but learning and understanding
(c) Leaders are self-direct
(d) are the keys to self-direction

Ans. (c)

'Self-direct' must be replaced with 'self-directed' as it is a past participle adjective.
These adjectives are commonly used to describe emotions, physical states or the condition of objects or people. Hence, 'Leaders are self-directed' is the most appropriate answer.

701. For example the parent mountain / of Mont Blanc, the / high peak in the Alps, is the Mount Everest.
SSC MTS Tier-1 16.06.2023 (Shift-I)
(a) No error
(b) high peak in the Alps, is the Mount Everest
(c) of Mont Blanc, the
(d) For example the parent mountain

Ans. (b)

'High' must be replaced with 'highest' as we generally use article 'the' with a superlative degree (highest). Hence, 'highest peak in the Alps, is the Mount Everest' is the most appropriate answer.

702. He best understand that / because of the fight it is no / longer his decision to make.
SSC MTS Tier-1 16.06.2023 (Shift-II)
(a) He best understand that
(b) longer his decision to make
(c) because of the fight it is no
(d) No error

Ans. (a)

Use of the superlative degree adverb 'best' is incorrect here.
The adverb 'better' is the comparative degree of 'well' and is used to give advice or suggestions on what is considered a more suitable action. 'Better + V_1' is the correct grammatical structure. Hence, 'He better understand that' is the most appropriate answer.

703. Even the most wise don't / know what's hidden in / the depths of their being.
SSC MTS Tier-1 16.06.2023 (Shift-III)
(a) No error
(b) know what's hidden in
(c) the depths of their being.
(d) Even the most wise don't

Ans. (d)

'The most wise' must be replaced with 'the wisest' as the correct superlative degree of the adjective 'wise' is 'wisest.'
Hence, 'Even the wisest don't' is the most appropriate answer.

704. The baby's faces are expressionless and / their pupils aren't visible which gives / the appearance of lifelessness and dreadfulness.
SSC MTS Tier-1 19.06.2023 (Shift-II)
(a) No error
(b) the appearance of lifelessness and dreadfulness
(c) their pupils aren't visible which gives
(d) The baby's faces are expressionless and

Ans. (d)

'Baby's' must be replaced with (babies) as we are referring to the faces of multiple babies. Hence, 'the babies faces are expressionless and' is the most appropriate answer.

705. In practice rounds, my caddie, Greg / and me works on my short / game with a baseball glove.
SSC MTS Tier-1 19.06.2023 (Shift-III)
(a) and me works on my short
(b) No error
(c) game with a baseball glove
(d) In practice rounds, my caddie, Greg

Ans. (a)

The pronoun 'me' must be replaced with 'I' we need to use to the subjective case of the pronoun. Also, the verb 'work' must be used to agree with the plural subject 'my caddie, Greg and I.' Hence, 'and I works on my short' is the most appropriate answer.

706. Disease-carrying parasites / is not picky / about hosts.
SSC MTS Tier-1 19.06.2023 (Shift-III)

(a) about hosts
(b) Disease-carrying parasites
(c) No error
(d) is not picky

Ans. (d)

The verb 'is' must be replaced with 'are' to agree with the plural subject parasites. Hence, 'are not picky' is the most appropriate answer.

707. 'I'm going to get / start on some / homework', said the professor angrily. SSC MTS Tier-1 20.06.2023 (Shift-I)

(a) No error
(b) I'm going to get
(c) homework', said the professor angrily
(d) start on some

Ans. (d)

'Start' must be replaced with 'started' as we generally as we the past participle form of the verb after 'get.' Hence, 'started on some' is the most appropriate answer.

708. Raising temperatures in the / springtime signal plants and / animals to come alive.
SSC MTS Tier-1 20.06.2023 (Shift-II)

(a) Raising temperatures in the
(b) springtime signal plants and
(c) animals to come alive
(d) No error

Ans. (a)

'Raising' must be replaced with 'Rising' as rise means to increase in value and raise means to lift or elevate something. Hence, 'Rising temperature in the' is the most appropriate answer.

709. Most impressive / was record breaking / 75.6 FPS one crysis.
SSC MTS Tier-1 20.06.2023 (Shift-III)

(a) 75.6 FPS on crysis
(b) Most impressive
(c) was record breaking
(d) No error

Ans. (c)

We generally use article 'a' with a singular countable noun (record breaking 75.6 FPS). Hence, 'was a record breaking' is the most appropriate answer.

710. I began with writing / one a week and / now I do so everyday.
SSC MTS Tier-1 20.06.2023 (Shift-III)

(a) one a week and
(b) I began with writing
(c) now I do so everyday
(d) No error

Ans. (a)

The phrase 'one a week' must replaced with 'once a week' as we need to use an adverb of frequency 'once' instead of 'one.'

Hence 'once a week' is the most appropriate answer.

711. The boy told his mother that he saw the most tall giraffe at the zoo.
SSC MTS Tier-1 01.09.2023 (Shift-I)

(a) The boy told his mother that he saw the tallest giraffe at the zoo.
(b) The boy told his mother that he saw the most taller giraffe at the zoo.
(c) The boy told his mother that he saw the most tallest giraffe at the zoo.
(d) The boy told his mother that he saw the more taller giraffe at the zoo.

Ans. (a)

The given sentence contains an error of degree of adjective. The superlative degree of 'tall' is 'tallest', not 'most tall.' Hence, the correct sentence is given by option (a).

712. Harish told me / in the morning / that Gaurav will / come tomorrow.
SSC MTS Tier-1 01.09.2023 (Shift-II)

(a) come tomorrow (b) Harish told me
(c) that Gaurav will (d) in the morning

Ans. (c)

The verb 'will' must be replaced with 'would' as the given sentence in the past tense, so we need to use the verb in past form. Hence, 'Gaurav would' is the most appropriate answer.

713. She performed / the dance routine / perfect, / impressing everyone.
SSC MTS Tier-1 01.09.2023 (Shift-II)

(a) She performed
(b) perfect
(c) impressing everyone
(d) the dance routine

Ans. (b)

'Perfect' must be replaced with 'perfectly' as we generally use adverbs to modify the meaning of the verb(performed). Hence, 'perfectly' is the most appropriate answer.

714. In America, / most of the people / can speak / the English well.
SSC MTS Tier-1 01.09.2023 (Shift-II)

(a) the English well
(b) most of the people
(c) can speak
(d) In America

Ans. (a)

The definite article 'the' is not used before the name of language.

Hence, 'English well' is the most appropriate answer.

715. It is commonly believed / that Democracy is / the best form / of the government.
SSC MTS Tier-1 01.09.2023 (Shift-III)

(a) of the government
(b) It is commonly believed
(c) that Democracy is
(d) the best form

Ans. (a)

Article 'the' must be removed as the word 'government' in the general sense refers to any form of government. It does not point towards any particular nation. Hence, 'of government' is the most appropriate answer.

716. He told me / that he goes / to the market / to buy a laptop.
SSC MTS Tier-1 01.09.2023 (Shift-III)

(a) He told me
(b) to buy a laptop
(c) to the market
(d) that he goes

Ans. (d)

Part (d) 'that he goes' contains an error. As the sentence is in indirect speech, 'went' should be used in place of 'goes' to correct the sentence.

717. A fiction is a constantly / evolving genre that gives us an peek / into the potential upsides and downsides / of intelligent machines. SSC MTS Tier-1 04.09.2023 (Shift-I)

(a) A fiction is an constantly
(b) into the potential upsides and downsides
(c) evolving genre that gives us an peek
(d) of intelligent machine

Ans. (c)

Article 'a' is used before the words starting from a consonant sound - (a conversation, a story, a peek). Whereas,the article 'an' is used before the words starting from a vowel sound(an imminent danger, an apple). Hence, 'evolving genre that gives us a peek' is the most appropriate answer.

718. If he / will come early, / we will leave / on time.
SSC MTS Tier-1 04.09.2023 (Shift-I)
(a) will come early (b) If he
(c) on time (d) we will leave

Ans. (a)
'Will come' must be replaced 'with' 'comes.' The given sentence is an example of the first conditional sentence and the correct grammatical structure is 'if + simple present .... will + V_1'. Hence, 'comes' is the most appropriate answer.

719. A lot of adulterants / are chemicals that can lead / to an range of health problems / in both children and adults. SSC MTS Tier-1 04.09.2023 (Shift-II)
(a) to an range of health problems
(b) are chemicals that can lead
(c) A lot of adulterants
(d) in both children and adults

Ans. (a)
Part (a) 'to an range of health problems' contains an error of article. Replace 'an' with 'a' to correct the sentence.

720. The ball/ I kicked / went highly / in the sky. SSC MTS Tier-1 04.09.2023 (Shift-II)
(a) The ball (b) went highly
(c) in the sky (d) I kicked

Ans. (b)
Part (b) 'went highly' contains an error. Replace 'highly' with 'high' to correct the sentence.

721. (a) The Mona Lisa is a famous painting by Leonardo da Vinci.
(b) She is the only person who can speak five languages fluently.
(c) He is a doctor who specialises in the treating rare diseases.
(d) I saw the movie that won the Academy Award for Best Picture.
SSC MTS Tier-1 04.09.2023 (Shift-III)

Ans. (c)
He is a doctor who specialises in the treating rare diseases. (Incorrect)
He is a doctor who specialises in treating rare diseases. (Correct)
The definite article 'the' is not used before gerunds.

722. After I complete my training programme / I will have been joining a team of astronauts / and preparing to / embark on a mission to Mars. SSC MTS Tier-1 04.09.2023 (Shift-III)
(a) I will have been joining a team of astronauts
(b) embark on a mission to Mars
(c) and preparing to
(d) After I complete my training programme

Ans. (a)
'Will have been' must be replaced with 'will be' as the given sentence is in the future continuous tense and the correct grammatical structure is 'Subject + will + be + V-ing.'
Hence, 'I will be joining a team of astronauts' is the most appropriate answer.

723. Earlier, he was feeling better, but things took a turn for the bad.
SSC MTS Tier-1 04.09.2023 (Shift-III)
(a) Earlier, he was feeling better, but things took a turn for the worst.
(b) Earlier, he was feeling good, but things took a turn for the bad.
(c) Earlier, he was feeling well, but things took a turn for the ill.
(d) Earlier, he was feeling better, but things took a turn for the ill.

Ans. (a)
Earlier, he was feeling better, but things took a turn for the worst. (Correct)
(b) Earlier, he was feeling good, but things took a turn for the bad. (Incorrect word)
(c) Earlier, he was feeling well, but things took a turn for the ill. (Incorrect degree)
(d) Earlier, he was feeling better, but things took a turn for the ill. (Incorrect word)

724. A night alone/ in a hotel/can be lonely prospect.
SSC MTS Tier-1 05.09.2023 (Shift-I)
(a) can be lonely prospect
(b) A night alone
(c) No error
(d) in a hotel

Ans. (a)
Article 'a' must be used before 'lonely prospect' as the adjective 'lonely' describes a noun and we need to use an article before the adjective to indicate that it's a singular, countable noun. Hence, 'can be a lonely prospect' is the most appropriate answer.

725. The new restaurant on Main Street is cheap than the old one.
SSC MTS Tier-1 05.09.2023 (Shift-I)
(a) the older one
(b) in Main Street
(c) newer restaurant
(d) is cheaper than

Ans. (d)
We generally use a comparative degree before 'than' and the correct comparative degree of 'cheap' is 'cheaper.' Hence, 'is cheaper than' is the most appropriate answer.

726. My relatives shall have reached Amritsar by now.
SSC MTS Tier-1 05.09.2023 (Shift-I)
(a) My (b) by now
(c) shall (d) reached

Ans. (c)
'Shall' must be replaced with 'will' as we generally use 'will' with 'He/She/It/You/they' or a noun and 'shall' with 'I' and 'we' only. Hence, 'will' is the most appropriate answer.

727. Several days later, / he received a written / commeunication from the magistrate/ that the case has been dropped. SSC MTS Tier-1 05.09.2023 (Shift-II)
(a) Several days later
(b) he received a written
(c) commeunication from the magistrate
(d) that the case has been dropped

Ans. (c)
Part (c) 'commeunication from the magistrate' contains the spelling error. The incorrectly spelt word is 'commeunication.' The correct spelling is 'communication.'

728. Did/her friend/went to/school yesterday?
SSC MTS Tier-1 05.09.2023 (Shift-II)
(a) went to (b) school yesterday
(c) her friend (d) did

Ans. (a)
Part 'went to' contains an error of tense. Replace 'went to' with 'go to' to correct the sentence as the verbs 'do/did/does' take base form of the verb.

729. They had been dancing / for an hour / when our dance teacher / had arrived.
SSC MTS Tier-1 05.09.2023 (Shift-II)
(a) when our dance teacher
(b) They had been dancing
(c) for an hour
(d) had arrived

Ans. (d)
Part (d) 'had arrived' contains an error of tense.
Replace 'had arrived' with 'arrived' to correct the sentence.

730. Shelley and Keats / are great writers / but I prefer / the last.
SSC MTS Tier-1 05.09.2023 (Shift-III)
(a) the last
(b) are great writers
(c) but I prefer
(d) Shelley and Keats

Ans. (a)

'the last' must be replaced with 'the latter' as the word 'latter' is used to refer to the second of two things or people. Hence, 'the latter' is the most appropriate answer.

731. This is the first time/I ate such/ a tasty cake **SSC MTS Tier-1 06.09.2023 (Shift-I)**

(a) I ate such
(b) This is the first time
(c) No error
(d) a tasty cake

Ans. (a)

Part (a) 'I ate such' contains an error of tense. Replace 'ate' with present perfect tense 'have eaten' as the sentence presents an act whose effect is visible in the present.

732. A old woman / suddenly laughed / sounding just / like an amused hen. **SSC MTS Tier-1 06.09.2023 (Shift-I)**

(a) like an amused hen
(b) sounding just
(c) A old woman
(d) suddenly laughed

Ans. (c)

Part (c) 'A old woman' contains an error of articles. The word 'an' should be used in place of 'a' to correct the sentence.

733. Existentialism has a reputation / for being angst-ridden and gloomy / mostly because of its emphasis / on pondering the meaningless of existence. **SSC MTS Tier-1 06.09.2023 (Shift-II)**

(a) on pondering the meaningless of existence
(b) mostly because of its emphasis
(c) Existentialism has a reputation
(d) for being angst-ridden and gloomy

Ans. (a)

Adjective 'meaningless' must be replaced with the noun 'meaning' as we need to use a noun to refer to the concept or state of existence. Hence, 'on pondering the meaning of existence' is the most appropriate answer.

734. (A) The mother exclaimed / (B) when she saw her son / (C) stumble on the race track, / (D) 'Look, he fells!' **SSC MTS Tier-1 06.09.2023 (Shift-II)**

(a) B (b) D
(c) C (d) A

Ans. (b)

'Fells' must be replaced with 'fell' as the correct past form of the verb 'fall' is 'fell.' Hence, 'Look, he fell!' is the most appropriate answer.

735. As soon as / I shall win / the lottery, I hope / to buy a Ferrari. **SSC MTS Tier-1 06.09.2023 (Shift-III)**

(a) the lottery, I hope
(b) As soon as
(c) I shall win
(d) to buy a Ferrari

Ans. (c)

If a clause begins with the words 'as long as, as soon as, when, until, unless, till', it is not written in future tense.

Simple present tense will be used as the second clause is given in present tense.

Hence, 'win' is the most appropriate answer.

736. (a) I saw a movie that was directed by Steven Spielberg.
(b) She is the only person who can solve this difficult math problem.
(c) He is an lawyer who works for a prestigious law firm.
(d) The Great Wall of China is a popular tourist attraction.
SSC MTS Tier-1 08.09.2023 (Shift-I)

Ans. (c)

'He is an lawyer who works for a prestigious law firm.' Article 'an' must be replaced with 'a' as we generally use article 'a' before the words starting with a consonant sound. Similarly, in the given sentence, the noun 'lawyer' starts with a consonant sound. Hence, 'a lawyer' is the most appropriate answer.

737. She was writing / a letter to her grandmother /when the power / gone out. **SSC MTS Tier-1 08.09.2023 (Shift-II)**

(a) gone out
(b) a letter to her grandmother
(c) She was writing
(d) when the power

Ans. (a)

Part 'gone out' contains an error of tense. Replace 'gone' with 'went' to correct the sentence.

738. The viable of life / depends on a pair / of conflicting realities. **SSC MTS Tier-1 08.09.2023 (Shift-III)**

(a) depends on a pair
(b) No error
(c) The viable of life
(d) of conflicting realities

Ans. (c)

'The viable of life' adjective 'viable' must be replaced with the noun 'viability' as we need to use a specific noun after the article 'the.' Hence, 'the viability of life' is the most appropriate answer.

739. I / shall be playing / for / four hours. **SSC MTS Tier-1 08.09.2023 (Shift-III)**

(a) four hours (b) I
(c) shall be playing (d) for

Ans. (c)

'Shall be playing' must be replaced with 'shall have been playing' as the given sentence mentions a period of time 'for four hours', so we need to use future perfect continuous tense (will/shall +have + been + V_1-ing). Hence, 'shall have been playing' is the most appropriate answer.

740. (A) Taylor, Richard and / (B) Francis plays for / (C) the state / (D) basketball team. **SSC MTS Tier-1 11.09.2023 (Shift-I)**

(a) D (b) A
(c) C (d) B

Ans. (d)

Part (B) 'Francis plays for' has an error. To correct the sentence, replace the verb 'plays' with 'play.' When we refer to more than one person, together, plural verb is used. Hence, as the subject (Taylor, Richa and Francis) is plural, the verb should also be in plural form.

741. As they driven through the dark, twisting lane / down which they had walked earlier, Lucius heard / the whistling of the night air in his ears. **SSC MTS Tier-1 11.09.2023 (Shift-I)**

(a) down which they had walked earlier, Lucius heard
(b) No error
(c) the whistling of the night air in his ears
(d) As they driven through the dark, twisting lane

Ans. (d)

Part (d) 'As they driven through the dark, twisting lane' has an error. To correct the sentence and maintain tense consistency, replace past participle form 'driven' with simple past form 'drove.'

742. This is the eldest standing structure of Chola architecture in India. **SSC MTS Tier-1 11.09.2023 (Shift-II)**

(a) This is the more older standing structure of Chola architecture in India.
(b) This is the most old standing structure of Chola architecture in India.
(c) This is the more elder standing structure of Chola architecture in India.
(d) This the oldest standing structure of Chola architecture in India.

Ans. (d)

The given sentence contains an error. We use the adjective 'oldest' for non-living things. Hence, the correct sentence is 'This the oldest standing structure of Chola architecture in India.'

743. A music / is a great way / to express / your emotions.
SSC MTS Tier-1 11.09.2023 (Shift-II)

(a) to express (b) is a great way
(c) A music (d) your emotions

Ans. (c)

Part (c) 'A music' contains an error. Remove 'a' to correct the sentence as music is an uncountable noun.

744. The SNAP-10 A / was launched on 3rd April, 1965 / on a Atlas-Agena D rocket / from Vandenberg Air Force Base.
SSC MTS Tier-1 12.09.2023 (Shift-I)

(a) at Vandenberg Air Force Base
(b) The SNAP-10 A
(c) was launched on 3rd April, 1965
(d) on an Atlas-Agena D rocket

Ans. (d)

Article 'a' must be replaced with article 'an' as we generally use article 'an' with the nouns starting with a vowel sound.

Similarly, in the given sentence, 'Atlas-Agena D' starts with a vowel sound. Hence, 'an' is the most appropriate answer.

745. This car is lesser expensive than the one I had come to buy.
SSC MTS Tier-1 12.09.2023 (Shift-I)

(a) for (b) came
(c) ones (d) less

Ans. (d)

'Lesser' is used to indicate something of lower importance or significance and 'less' used to indicate a lower amount or degree. Hence, 'less' is the most appropriate answer.

746. (A) It is said / (B) that fortune / (C) favour the / (D) brave.
SSC MTS Tier-1 12.09.2023 (Shift-I)

(a) B (b) C
(c) A (d) D

Ans. (b)

'Favour' must be replaced with 'favours.' According to the 'Subject-Verb Agreement Rule', a singular subject always takes a singular verb. Similarly, 'fortune' is a singular subject that will take 'favours' as a singular verb. Hence, 'favours the' is the most appropriate answer.

747. (a) I love the taste of fresh strawberries in the summer.
SSC MTS Tier-1 12.09.2023 (Shift-II)
(b) She is the winner of the Nobel Peace Prize.
(c) He is chef who specialises in Italian cuisine.
(d) The Earth revolves around the Sun.

Ans. (c)

He is chef who specialises in Italian cuisine is incorrect sentence. The article 'the' is used to refer to specific or particular nouns. Similarly, in the given sentence, 'chef' is a specific person. Hence, 'He is the chef who specialises in Italian cuisine' is the most appropriate answer.

748. When I bought the book, I thought it will be interesting.
SSC MTS Tier-1 12.09.2023 (Shift-II)

(a) When (b) bought
(c) will (d) thought

Ans. (c)

The verb 'will' must be replaced with 'would' as the given sentence in the past tense. Hence, 'would' is the most appropriate answer.

749. (A) It is a / (B) state of chaos / (C) since the / (D) chairman resigned.
SSC MTS Tier-1 12.09.2023 (Shift-III)

(a) D (b) A (c) B (d) C

Ans. (b)

'is' must be replaced with 'has been' as we generally use present perfect tense (has/have + V_3) to discuss a situation that began in the past and continues into the present.

Similarly in the given sentence, a state of chaos began in the past and still exists in the present. Hence, 'it has been a' is the most appropriate answer.

750. With cloud streaming, people can play games from a/ internet connected device, avoiding the need for pricey /dedicated hardware such as a game console.
SSC MTS Tier-1 13.09.2023 (Shift-I)

(a) No error
(b) dedicated hardware such as a game console
(c) With cloud streaming people can play games from a
(d) internet connected device, avoiding the need for pricey

Ans. (c)

Part (c) 'With cloud streaming people can play games from a' contains an error. The use of article 'a' is incorrect. We need to replace 'a' with 'any' to correct the sentence.

751. The team played / really well, but / they lose the game / in the final minutes.
SSC MTS Tier-1 13.09.2023 (Shift-I)

(a) really well, but
(b) in the final minutes
(c) they lose the game
(d) The team played

Ans. (c)

Part (c) 'they lose the game' contains an error of tense. As the given sentence is in past, 'lost' should be used in place of 'lose' to correct the sentence.

752. To much seriousness hardens the world, pinning it down with rules.
SSC MTS Tier-1 13.09.2023 (Shift-II)

(a) with rules
(b) hardens the
(c) to much
(d) world, pinning

Ans. (c)

'to' must be replaced with 'too' as 'too' is used to indicate an excessive or more than necessary amount. Hence,'too much' is the most appropriate answer.

753. The space agency wanted / to test with a chimp / before orbiting a astronaut / in a Mercury capsule.
SSC MTS Tier-1 13.09.2023 (Shift-III)

(a) The space agency want
(b) in an Mercury capsule
(c) before orbiting a astronaut
(d) to test with a chimp

Ans. (c)

Article 'A' is used before the words starting from a consonant sound (a conversation, a story). Whereas, the article 'An' is used before the words starting with a vowel sound(an imminent danger, an apple). Similarly, in the given sentence, 'astronaut' is a noun starting with a vowel sound. Hence, 'an astronaut' is the most appropriate answer.

754. If he had paid / attention to the announcement, / he had not / missed the train.
SSC MTS Tier-1 13.09.2023 (Shift-III)

(a) If he had paid
(b) he had not
(c) attention to the announcement
(d) missed the train

Ans. (b)

The given sentence is an example of a third conditional sentence and the correct grammatical structure is 'If + past perfect (had + V_3) ...... Would have + V_3' Hence, 'he would not have' is the most appropriate answer.

755. When Nisha will / have / finished / her task? SSC MTS Tier-1 14.09.2023 (Shift-I)
(a) have (b) When Nisha will
(c) finished (d) her task

Ans. (b)

Part (b) 'When Nisha will' contains an error. To correct the sentence, 'When Nisha will' should be replaced by 'When will Nisha', because, to form questions, wh-words should be followed by a verb/auxiliary verb.

756. My daughter was / invited to lunch / hosted by the Governor / at his residence. SSC MTS Tier-1 14.09.2023 (Shift-II)
(a) at his residence
(b) invited to lunch
(c) hosted by the Governor
(d) My daughter was

Ans. (b)

When we talk about a meal (lunch/dinner/breakfast) as a special event, we use the article 'the' before the meal. For example the lunch with the President of India. Hence, 'invited to the lunch' is the most appropriate answer.

757. When I was in high school/I participated in several extracurricular activities / such as the debate team and the school newspaper/ which help me developed my communication and writing skills. SSC MTS Tier-1 14.09.2023 (Shift-III)
(a) When I was in high school
(b) which help me developed my communication and writing skills
(c) such as the debate team and the school newspaper
(d) I participated in several extracurricular activities

Ans. (b)

The phrase 'which help me developed' must be replaced with 'which helped me develop.'

The given sentence is in the past tense so it must have the verb in the past form (V_2-helped) and not in the present form (help). We generally use the first form of the verb (V_1) after certain verbs such as help, let, bid, make, etc. Hence, 'which helped me develop' is the most appropriate answer.

758. The cholera / is / a / frightful disease. SSC MTS Tier-1 14.09.2023 (Shift-III)
(a) is (b) The cholera
(c) frightful disease (d) a

Ans. (b)

Article 'the' must be removed before 'cholera' as we generally don't use the definite article 'the' before the names of illnesses or diseases. Hence, 'cholera' is the most appropriate answer.

759. The twins are / (B) often told that /(C) they are resembling / (D) each other. SSC MTS Tier-1 14.09.2023 (Shift-III)
(a) C (b) A (c) B (d) D

Ans. (a)

We generally use simple present tense (Plural Sub. V_1) for generally held beliefs or opinions. Similarly, the given sentence states an opinion about twins. Hence, 'they resemble (V_1)' is the most appropriate answer.

SSC Selection Post 2024

760. King Solomon of Israel / is said to be one / of a wisest man / who ruled the Earth. SSC SP 20.06.2024 (Shift-II)
(a) is said to be one
(b) King Solomon of Israel
(c) of a wisest man
(d) who ruled the Earth

Ans. (c)

'Of a wisest man' contains an error. The phrase 'one of' takes the superlative degree of adjective with article 'the' and plural noun. Hence, use 'of the wisest man' to correct the sentence.

761. He has been (A) / watered the plants (B) / for one hour. (C) / No error (D) SSC SP 20.06.2024 (Shift-II)
(a) D (b) C (c) B (d) A

Ans. (d)

'Watered the plants' contains an error. As the sentence talks of an action that started in the past but is still going on, present perfect continuous tense 'has been watering' should be used to correct the sentence.

762. The toast was / raised in honour / of the chairman / yesterday at hall. SSC SP 20.06.2024 (Shift-II)
(a) raised in honour
(b) yesterday at hall
(c) The toast was
(d) of the chairman

Ans. (b)

'Yesterday at hall' contains an error. It should be 'in the hall yesterday.'

SSC Selection Post 2023

763. We must / take care / of one other / in times of crisis. SSC SP 27.06.2023 (Shift-III)
(a) take care (b) in times of crisis
(c) We must (d) of one other

Ans. (d)

'Of one other' contains an error. The expression 'one another' or 'each other' should be used to correct the sentence.

764. I caught / a white cat / rustling / beneath my room. SSC SP 27.06.2023 (Shift-IV)
(a) a white cat (b) I caught
(c) rustling (d) beneath my room

Ans. (d)

'Beneath my room' contains an error. Preposition 'in' should be used to indicate the position of the cat as inside the room.

765. Kids learn / a lot by / their / school activities and homework.
(a) Kids learn SSC SP 28.06.2023 (Shift-III)
(b) school activities and homework
(c) their
(d) a lot by

Ans. (d)

There is a prepositional error in the given sentence. 'A lot by' must be replaced with 'a lot from' as the preposition 'by' is generally used to indicate the way something is done and the preposition 'from' is used to indicate the source of gaining knowledge. Hence, 'a lot from' is the most appropriate answer.

766. A. I would like to spend an evening near pool with a cup of coffee.
B. I would like to spend an evening near pool with cup of coffee.
C. I would like to spend a evening near a pool with a cup of coffee.
D. I would like to spend an evening near a pool with a cup of coffee.
SSC SP 28.06.2023 (Shift-III)
(a) C (b) D (c) B (d) A

Ans. (b)

I would like to spend an evening near a pool with a cup of coffee.
(a) I would like to spend a evening near a pool with a cup of coffee. (Incorrect article)
(c) I would like to spend an evening near pool with cup of coffee. (Article missing)
(d) I would like to spend an evening near pool with a cup of coffee. (Article missing)

767. He is as concerned as me/regarding / the renewed / examination schedule. SSC SP 28.06.2023 (Shift-II)
(a) the renewed
(b) examination schedule
(c) regarding
(d) He is as concerned as me

Ans. (d)

Pronoun 'me' must be replaced with 'I' as the conjunction pair 'as....as' is used to do comparison between the same 'cases of pronoun.' So, we need to use the subjective case of pronoun i.e., 'I.' Hence, 'He is as concerned as I' is the most appropriate answer.

768. If you live / in a foreign country, / you should/ try and learn language.

SSC SP 30.06.2023 (Shift-I)

(a) If you live
(b) you should
(c) try and learn language
(d) in a foreign country

Ans. (c)

'and' must be replaced with 'to' as we generally use an 'to + infinitive (V_1)' after certain verbs like try, bid, let, make, need, etc. Hence, 'try to learn language' is the most appropriate answer.

769. There are more than two million/job-seekers who are already / completed their fitness test /for the post since 2020.

SSC SP 30.06.2023 (Shift-I)

(a) There are more than two million
(b) job-seekers who are already
(c) completed their fitness test
(d) for the post since 2020

Ans. (b)

'Are' must be replaced with 'have' as we need to use present perfect tense (have + V_3) to indicate actions that started in the past and continue into the present. Hence, 'job-seekers who have already' is the most appropriate answer.

770. After that long afternoon, / when I quietly entered her room / to hand over the packet to her/she asked me to sit reluctant. SSC SP 30.06.2023 (Shift-II)

(a) she asked me to sit reluctant
(b) After that long afternoon
(c) to hand over the packet to her
(d) when I quietly entered her room

Ans. (a)

'Reluctant' must be replaced with 'reluctantly' as we generally use adverbs to modify or describe verbs (sit). Hence, 'she asked me to sit reluctantly' is the most appropriate answer.

SSC SP 2022

771. The mall just opened and the visitors arrived now.

SSC SP 03.08.2022 (Shift-III)

(a) The mall has just opened and the visitors have arrived.
(b) The mall has just been opening and the visitors arrived.
(c) The mall just opens and the visitors arrives.
(d) The mall is just opening and the visitors are arriving.

Ans. (a)

The given sentence must be in present tense as the adverb 'Now' refers to the present time. So,we will use 'present perfect tense (Have + V_3)' to make the sentence grammatically correct. Hence, option (a) is the most appropriate answer.

772. After the thieves / had left, / George crept slow / out of his room.

SSC SP 04.08.2022 (Shift-II)

(a) had left
(b) After the thieves
(c) out of his room
(d) George crept slow

Ans. (d)

'slow' must be replaced with 'slowly' as we need an adverb to describe the verb 'crept', not an adjective 'slow.' Hence, 'George crept slowly' is the most appropriate answer.

SSC Steno 2024

773. I visited mall yesterday. It had unique designer shop of accessories. SSC Steno 11.12.2024 (Shift-I)

(a) I visited a mall yesterday. It had an unique designer shop of accessories.
(b) I visited a mall yesterday. It had unique designer shop of accessories.
(c) I visited a mall yesterday. It had a unique designer shop of accessories.
(d) I visited mall yesterday. It had a unique designer shop of accessories.

Ans. (c)

The correct sentence is 'I visited a mall yesterday.
It had a unique designer shop of accessories.' Using 'a' before 'mall' and 'a' before 'unique designer shop' makes the sentence grammatically correct.

774. Bill was looking impatient / at the useless guest / who showed / no signs of leaving the room.

SSC Steno 11.12.2024 (Shift-I)

(a) who showed
(b) Bill was looking impatient
(c) at the useless guest
(d) no signs of leaving the room.

Ans. (c)

The error is in 'at the useless guest'. The correct phrase should be 'at the ungracious guest' as it provides a more appropriate descriptor in this context.

775. A. I have bought/ B. a house in Jalandhar./ C. House is in a rural area/ D. No error

SSC Steno 11.12.2024 (Shift-I)

(a) D (b) A (c) B (d) C

Ans. (d)

The error is in part (C). The correct form is 'The house is in a rural area.' The definite article 'The' should be used before 'house' to specify the house mentioned.

776. I want my son to be pharmacist and my husband wants him to be a engineer. He wishes to be architect.

SSC Steno 11.12.2024 (Shift-I)

(a) I want my son to be pharmacist and my husband wants him to be an engineer. He wishes to be an architect.
(b) I want my son to be a pharmacist and my husband wants him to be an engineer. He wishes to be an architect.
(c) I want my son to be a pharmacist and my husband wants him to be a engineer. He wishes to be an architect.
(d) I want my son to be a pharmacist and my husband wants him to be an engineer. He wishes to be a architect.

Ans. (b)

The sentence should be: 'I want my son to be a pharmacist and my husband wants him to be an engineer. He wishes to be an architect.' The correct use of articles 'a' and 'an' before consonant and vowel sounds respectively rectifies the errors.

777. This smartphone is / superior than / the model I had been /using previously. SSC Steno 11.12.2024 (Shift-I)

(a) This smartphone is
(b) using previously.
(c) the model I had been
(d) superior than

Ans. (d)

The error is in 'superior than'. It should be 'superior to' because the correct comparative form is 'superior to'.

778. Akash would be staying to his uncle's place during the holidays.

SSC Steno 11.12.2024 (Shift-I)

(a) during (b) would
(c) staying (d) to

Ans. (d)

The error is in 'to'.

It should be 'at' because the correct preposition is 'at' when referring to staying at a place.

779. They decided to/consult a lawyer/ as soon as they/reach their/home town. SSC Steno 11.12.2024 (Shift-I)
(a) consult a lawyer
(b) as soon as they
(c) reach their
(d) home town

Ans. (c)

The error is in 'reach their'. It should be 'reached their' because the correct tense to use after 'as soon as they' is past tense.

780. Sanchit has been read since early morning for his class test. SSC Steno 11.12.2024 (Shift-I)
(a) for his
(b) class test
(c) Sanchit has been read
(d) since early morning

Ans. (c)

The error is in 'Sanchit has been read.' It should be 'Sanchit has been reading' because the correct tense for continuous action since early morning is present perfect continuous.

781. She spotted the novel [A] / and shouted, "Here the book lies [B] / that we were searching for[C] / all around."[D] SSC Steno 11.12.2024 (Shift-I)
(a) A (b) D (c) C (d) B

Ans. (d)

The error is in 'Here the book lies'. The correct phrase should be 'Here lies the book' to maintain proper word order and make sense.

782. She is not rich / and that is why, she cannot afford to / buy a expensive bungalow / near the sea-side. SSC Steno 11.12.2024 (Shift-I)
(a) near the sea-side.
(b) She is not rich
(c) and that is why, she cannot afford to
(d) buy a expensive bungalow

Ans. (d)

The error is in 'buy a expensive bungalow'. The correct form is 'buy an expensive bungalow' because 'expensive' begins with a vowel sound, and 'an' should be used before vowel sounds.

783. Coimbatore is one of / the biggest cities in Tamil Nadu / and is considered / as a Manchester of South India. SSC Steno 11.12.2024 (Shift-I)
(a) as a Manchester of South India.
(b) the biggest cities in Tamil Nadu
(c) Coimbatore is one of
(d) and is considered

Ans. (a)

The error is in 'as a Manchester of South India'. The correct form is 'the Manchester of South India' because 'Manchester' is used as a title or nickname here.

784. Let us, at any rate, / give him / an outline out the case, / and hear what he has to say. SSC Steno 11.12.2024 (Shift-I)
(a) an outline out the case
(b) give him
(c) and hear what he has to say
(d) Let us, at any rate

Ans. (a)

The error is in 'an outline out the case'. The correct phrase should be 'an outline of the case' to make grammatical sense.

785. Though the / global financial crisis, / China's economy continues / to grow at an impressive rate. SSC Steno 11.12.2024 (Shift-II)
(a) to grow at an impressive rate.
(b) China's economy continues
(c) Though the
(d) global financial crisis,

Ans. (c)

The segment with a grammatical error is 'Though the'. The correct expression should be 'Despite the' or 'Due to the'. 'Though' is a conjunction and the sentence needs a preposition to indicate the cause or condition affecting China's economy. Therefore, 'Though the' is incorrect in this context.

786. He would be meet us next week. SSC Steno 11.12.2024 (Shift-II)
(a) He would be meets us next week.
(b) He would not bemet us next week.
(c) He will be meet us next week.
(d) He will be meeting us next week.

Ans. (d)

'He will be meeting us next week' is correct because it uses the future continuous tense, formed by 'will be' + present participle ('meeting'), indicating an action that will happen in the future.

787. I am sorry / to intrude by / you at / such a time. SSC Steno 11.12.2024 (Shift-II)
(a) such a time (b) you at
(c) to intrude by (d) I am sorry

Ans. (c)

The phrase 'to intrude by' is incorrect. The correct phrase should be 'to intrude on', meaning to disturb or interrupt someone. The error lies in using 'by' instead of 'on'.

788. A Himalayas stretch across / the North-East part / of India and pass / through many countries. SSC Steno 11.12.2024 (Shift-II)
(a) of India and pass
(b) through many countries.
(c) the North-East part
(d) A Himalayas stretch across

Ans. (d)

The segment 'A Himalayas stretch across' contains an error because 'A' is an incorrect article. The correct article to use with 'Himalayas' is 'The' because it refers to a specific mountain range.

789. Villagers / who approached the agriculture officer / are uneducated and poor. SSC Steno 11.12.2024 (Shift-II)
(a) are uneducated and poor.
(b) No error
(c) who approached the agriculture officer
(d) Villagers

Ans. (b)

No error

790. Doctor she spoke to at a exhibition was very knowledgeable. The medicines prescribed by him have proved excellent for my father. SSC Steno 11.12.2024 (Shift-II)
(a) The doctor she spoke to at the exhibition was very knowledgeable. The medicines prescribed by him have proved excellent for my father.
(b) Doctor she spoke to at the exhibition was very knowledgeable. The medicines prescribed by him have proved excellent for my father.
(c) The doctor she spoke to at exhibition was very knowledgeable. The medicines prescribed by him have proved excellent for my father.
(d) The doctor she spoke to at the exhibition was very knowledgeable. A medicines prescribed by him have proved excellent for my father.

Ans. (a)

The sentence 'Doctor she spoke to at a exhibition was very knowledgeable' contains errors.

The correct article 'the' should be used with 'doctor' and 'exhibition' and the sentence should start with 'The doctor'.

791. I always love to eat snacks at the evening. SSC Steno 11.12.2024 (Shift-II)
(a) to (b) snacks
(c) always (d) at

Ans. (d)

The error in the sentence is the use of 'at' before 'the evening'. The correct preposition is 'in' for time periods such as 'in the evening', so the sentence should be 'I always love to eat snacks in the evening.' This ensures the sentence follows proper prepositional usage for clarity.

792. I shall be cook my favourite dish tonight for the party.
(a) the party SSC Steno 11.12.2024 (Shift-II)
(b) tonight for
(c) I shall be cook
(d) my favourite dish

Ans. (c)

The error in the sentence is the phrase 'I shall be cook'. The correct phrase should be 'I shall cook' or 'I will be cooking'.

Using 'be cook' is grammatically incorrect because 'shall be' is not followed by the base form of the verb. Correcting this ensures proper grammatical structure and clarity in the sentence.

793. Gandhi ji considered it wrongly to use unfair means even for fair ends.
SSC Steno 11.12.2024 (Shift-II)
(a) Gandhi ji considered
(b) even for fair ends
(c) it wrongly
(d) to use unfair means

Ans. (c)

The error in the sentence is the phrase 'it wrongly'.

The correct phrase should be 'it wrong' or 'wrongly' to maintain proper grammatical structure. 'Wrongly' can be used as an adverb to modify a verb, but in this context, 'wrong' as an adjective is more appropriate. For example, 'Gandhi ji considered it wrong to use unfair means even for fair ends.'

794. Raghu did not get the job / because he did not have / experience enough for the post.
SSC Steno 11.12.2024 (Shift-II)
(a) because he did not have
(b) No error
(c) Raghu did not get the job
(d) experience enough for the post

Ans. (d)

The error in the sentence is 'experience enough for the post'. The correct phrase should be 'enough experience for the post'. In English, quantifiers like 'enough' typically come before the noun they modify. This ensures proper word order and clarity in the sentence.

795. They were sitting on the chairs in the class talking to each other when they entered in a heated argument.
SSC Steno 11.12.2024 (Shift-II)
(a) on (b) to
(c) in (d) when

Ans. (c)

The error in the sentence is the preposition 'in' in 'entered in a heated argument'. The correct phrase should be 'entered into a heated argument' or simply 'entered a heated argument'. 'Entered into' is the appropriate preposition pair used with 'argument' to convey entering a state of heated discussion.

796. Mr. Arun had / written the letter / before the manager arrived.
SSC Steno 11.12.2024 (Shift-III)
(a) written the letter
(b) Mr. Arun had
(c) before the manager arrived
(d) No error

Ans. (d)

The sentence 'Mr. Arun had written the letter before the manager arrived' is grammatically correct. The past perfect tense 'had written' is appropriately used to indicate that the action of writing the letter was completed before the manager's arrival. There are no errors in the sentence structure or verb tense usage.

797. I will have been studying English for three years by the end of this course. SSC Steno 11.12.2024 (Shift-III)
(a) I had been studying English for three years by the end of this course.
(b) I have been studying English for three years by the end of this course.
(c) I will have been studying English for three years by the end of this course.
(d) I was studying English for three years by the end of this course.

Ans. (c)

The original sentence 'I will have been studying English for three years by the end of this course' is correct. It uses the future perfect continuous tense to indicate an action that will continue up to a certain point in the future.

798. It began / to rain / as soon as / she steps out of / the movie theatre.
SSC Steno 11.12.2024 (Shift-III)
(a) she steps out of
(b) as soon as
(c) to rain
(d) the movie theatre

Ans. (a)

The segment 'she steps out of' contains the grammatical error. The correct phrase should be 'she stepped out of' to maintain the past tense consistency with the rest of the sentence. The rest of the sentence uses past tense ('began', 'rained'), so 'steps' should be changed to 'stepped' to match this tense.

799. The boy you met on an train last night was quite impressed by you. He has expressed his wish to work under you. SSC Steno 11.12.2024 (Shift-III)
(a) The boy you met on train last night was quite impressed by you. He has expressed his wish to work under you.
(b) The boy you met on the train last night was quite impressed by you. He has expressed his wish to work under you.
(c) Boy you met on the train last night was quite impressed by you. He has expressed his wish to work under you.
(d) An boy you met on the train last night was quite impressed by you. He has expressed his wish to work under you.

Ans. (b)

The corrected sentence is 'The boy you met on the train last night was quite impressed by you. He has expressed his wish to work under you.' The error 'an train' should be corrected to 'the train' for grammatical accuracy. Articles 'a' and 'an' are used before words that begin with a consonant or vowel sound, respectively. 'The' is used for specific references.

800. (A) This is book/ (B) you are/ (C) searching for./ (D) No error
SSC Steno 11.12.2024 (Shift-III)
(a) A (b) B
(c) D (d) C

Ans. (a)

The segment 'This is book' contains the grammatical error. The correct phrase should be 'This is the book'. The article 'the' is required before the noun 'book' to specify which book is being referred to.

801. When a beggar appeared, / I offered him / an one rupee coin / but he did not take it. SSC Steno 11.12.2024 (Shift-III)
(a) an one rupee coin
(b) I offered him
(c) but he did not take it
(d) When a beggar appeared

Ans. (a)

The segment 'an one rupee coin' contains the grammatical error. The correct phrase should be 'a one rupee coin'. The article 'a' is used before words that begin with a consonant sound and 'one' begins with a consonant sound 'w'.

802. The committee's decision / have been / a topic / of controversy. SSC Steno 11.12.2024 (Shift-III)
(a) a topic
(b) of controversy.
(c) have been
(d) The committee's decision

Ans. (c)

The segment 'have been' contains the grammatical error. The correct phrase should be 'has been' because 'The committee's decision' is a singular subject and should be followed by the singular verb 'has'.

803. Sachin and Sehwag are / great batsmen / but the former is greater / than latter. SSC Steno 11.12.2024 (Shift-III)
(a) than latter
(b) great batsmen
(c) Sachin and Sehwag are
(d) but the former is greater

Ans. (a)

The segment 'than latter' contains the grammatical error. The correct phrase should be 'than the latter'. The definite article 'the' is required before 'latter'.

804. The police are searching about the missing jewellery. SSC Steno 11.12.2024 (Shift-III)
(a) about (b) are
(c) the (d) missing

Ans. (a)

The segment 'about' contains the error. The correct phrase should be 'for' instead of 'about'. The correct sentence should be 'The police are searching for the missing jewellery.'

805. A courage gives / enormous strength to people / to fight for what they want. SSC Steno 11.12.2024 (Shift-III)
(a) A courage gives
(b) No error
(c) enormous strength to people
(d) to fight for what they want.

Ans. (a)

The segment 'A courage gives' contains the grammatical error. Courage' is an uncountable noun and does not require the article 'A'. The sentence should start with 'Courage gives'.

806. Shyamali is / very / careful for / her health. SSC Steno 11.12.2024 (Shift-III)
(a) very (b) her health.
(c) careful for (d) Shyamali is

Ans. (c)

The segment 'careful for' contains the grammatical error. The correct phrase should be 'careful about' or 'careful with', as these prepositions correctly follow the adjective 'careful' to indicate caution or attention.

807. Radha climbed the / ladder cautious, / but she fell off / despite being careful SSC Steno 11.12.2024 (Shift-III)
(a) ladder cautious
(b) Radha climbed the
(c) despite being careful
(d) but she fell off

Ans. (a)

The segment 'ladder cautious', contains the grammatical error. The correct phrase should be 'ladder cautiously' as 'cautiously' is the adverb form needed to modify the verb 'climbed'.

808. John is really / good in / playing / the piano. SSC Steno 11.12.2024 (Shift-III)
(a) playing (b) John is really
(c) the piano (d) good in

Ans. (d)

The segment 'good in' contains the error. The correct phrase should be 'good at'. The preposition 'at' is correctly used with 'good' to indicate proficiency in an activity.

809. He will / come when / he will be / ready. SSC Steno 10.12.2024 (Shift-I)
(a) he will be (b) come when
(c) He will (d) ready

Ans. (a)

The segment with the grammatical error is 'he will be'. In English, we use the present tense after 'when' in future time clauses. Therefore, the correct sentence should be 'He will come when he is ready.'

810. My idea can be key idea for cracking difficult conflicts of extremely high level. SSC Steno 10.12.2024 (Shift-I)
(a) My idea can be a key idea for cracking difficult conflicts of a extremely high level.
(b) My idea can be key idea for cracking difficult conflicts of an extremely high level.
(c) My idea can be an key idea for cracking difficult conflicts of an extremely high level.
(d) My idea can be a key idea for cracking difficult conflicts of an extremely high level.

Ans. (d)

The error in the sentence is the missing article 'a' and the use of 'an' before a vowel sound. The correct sentence is 'My idea can be a key idea for cracking difficult conflicts of an extremely high level'.

This ensures proper use of articles and adjective-noun agreement.

811. Vishnu and his friends / were listening to / the radio all morning. SSC Steno 10.12.2024 (Shift-I)
(a) No error
(b) Vishnu and his friends
(c) the radio all morning
(d) were listening to

Ans. (a)

There is no error in the given sentence. 'Vishnu and his friends were listening to the radio all morning' is grammatically correct.

812. PIEZO2 plays an critical role along with Piezo1 to regulate a important physiological process for brain to understand. SSC Steno 10.12.2024 (Shift-I)
(a) PIEZO2 plays an critical role along with Piezo1 to regulate the important physiological process for brain to understand.
(b) PIEZO2 plays critical role along with Piezo1 to regulate a important physiological process for brain to understand.
(c) PIEZO2 plays a critical role along with Piezo1 to regulate an important physiological process for the brain to understand.
(d) PIEZO2 plays the critical role along with Piezo1 to regulate the important physiological process for brain to understand.

Ans. (c)

The error in the sentence is the use of 'an' before a consonant sound and the missing article 'the' before 'brain'.

The correct sentence is 'PIEZO2 plays a critical role alongwith Piezo1 to regulate an important physiological process for the brain to understand.'

This ensures proper use of articles and adjective-noun agreement.

813. The earth has a exceptional structure which may have helped in life's arrival SSC Steno 10.12.2024 (Shift-I)
(a) An Earth has exceptional structure which may have helped in life's arrival.

(b) An Earth has an exceptional structure which may have helped in life's arrival.
(c) The Earth has an exceptional structure which may have helped in life's arrival.
(d) A Earth has exceptional structure which may have helped in life's arrival.

Ans. (c)

The error in the sentence is the use of 'a' before a vowel sound. The correct sentence is 'The Earth has an exceptional structure which may have helped in life's arrival'. This ensures proper use of the article 'an' before the vowel sound in 'exceptional'.

814. I have known her for many years. This time, she took unusual decision in unprejudiced way.
SSC Steno 10.12.2024 (Shift-I)

(a) I have known her for many years. This time, she took an unusual decision in unprejudiced way.
(b) I have known her for many years. This time, she took an unusual decision in an unprejudiced way.
(c) I have known her for many years. This time, she took a unusual decision in an unprejudiced way.
(d) I have known her for many years. This time, she took unusual decision in an unprejudiced way.

Ans. (b)

The error in the sentence is the missing articles 'an' and 'a'. The correct sentence is 'I have known her for many years. This time, she took an unusual decision in an unprejudiced way.'

This ensures proper use of articles and adjective-noun agreement.

815. He will has been helping me with tending to my plants.
SSC Steno 10.12.2024 (Shift-I)

(a) helping me
(b) to my plants
(c) He will has been
(d) with tending

Ans. (c)

The error in the sentence is 'He will has been'. The correct phrase should be 'He has been' or 'He will be'. The sentence should be 'He has been helping me with tending to my plants.'

816. Select the grammatically correct sentence from the options given.
SSC Steno 10.12.2024 (Shift-I)

(a) A troll, a boy shared in on social media created an big laughter.
(b) The troll, a boy shared on an social media created a big laughter.
(c) An troll, the boy shared on the social media created the big laughter.
(d) The troll, the boy shared on social media created a big laughter.

Ans. (d)

The correct sentence is 'The troll, the boy shared on social media created a big laughter'. This sentence maintains proper grammatical structure and clarity.

817. That accident happened [A] /a long time ago, but [B] / I have shivered at [C] / the thought of it ever for [D].
SSC Steno 10.12.2024 (Shift-I)

(a) D (b) C (c) A (d) B

Ans. (a)

The segment with the grammatical error is 'the thought of it ever for'. The correct phrase should be 'the thought of it ever since'. This ensures proper idiomatic expression.

818. You have said that, / as he took money from you many times, / he owes you / five thousand rupees all together.
SSC Steno 10.12.2024 (Shift-I)

(a) he owes you
(b) five thousand rupees all together
(c) You have said that
(d) as he took money from you many times

Ans. (b)

The segment with the grammatical error is 'five thousand rupees all together'.

The correct phrase should be 'five thousand rupees altogether'.

'Altogether' means completely or entirely, fitting the context of the sentence.

819. It became a known fact that they most played techno music at every party.
SSC Steno 10.12.2024 (Shift-I)

(a) every (b) at
(c) that (d) most

Ans. (d)

The segment with the error is 'they most played'. The correct phrase should be 'they mostly played', which correctly modifies the verb 'played' to indicate frequency.

820. One of the great rivers / of China, a Hwang Ho, / originates from the / Eastern face of Tibet.
SSC Steno 10.12.2024 (Shift-II)

(a) One of the great rivers
(b) Eastern face of Tibet.
(c) of China, a Hwang Ho,
(d) originates from the

Ans. (c)

The segment with the error is 'of China, a Hwang Ho'.

The correct article should be 'the' instead of 'a' to refer to the specific river Hwang Ho. The correct segment should be 'of China, the Hwang Ho'.

821. When I saw / her, she write / a poem / with full attention.
SSC Steno 10.12.2024 (Shift-II)

(a) her, she write
(b) a poem
(c) with full attention.
(d) When I saw

Ans. (a)

The segment with the grammatical error is 'her, she write.' The correct form should be 'her, she was writing' to maintain past continuous tense consistency.

The correct sentence should be: 'When I saw her, she was writing a poem with full attention.'

822. The rain will / not have stop / before the match / begins.
SSC Steno 10.12.2024 (Shift-II)

(a) The rain will
(b) before the match
(c) begins
(d) not have stop

Ans. (d)

The segment with the grammatical error is 'not have stop'. The correct form should be 'not have stopped'. The verb 'stop' should be in the past participle form to match the future perfect tense.

823. I stayed in my hometown with my parents on the pandemic.
SSC Steno 10.12.2024 (Shift-II)

(a) with (b) on
(c) in (d) I

Ans. (b)

The error is in the segment 'on the pandemic'. The correct preposition should be 'during' instead of 'on,' as 'during' is used to indicate a period of time.

824. The day is longer than year on Venus.
SSC Steno 10.12.2024 (Shift-II)

(a) A day is longer than the year on Venus.
(b) A day is longer than a year on Venus.
(c) All day is longer than a year on Venus.
(d) Day is longer than the year on Venus.

Ans. (b)

The correct rectification is 'A day is longer than a year on Venus.' Using 'A day' and 'a year' provides the correct indefinite articles to make the sentence grammatically correct.

825. If we / were meeting at 6 p.m., / we will / have plenty of time.
SSC Steno 10.12.2024 (Shift-II)

(a) If we
(b) were meeting at 6 p.m.,
(c) we will
(d) have plenty of time

Ans. (c)

The segment with the grammatical error is 'we will'. The correct form should be 'we would' to match the past continuous tense 'were meeting'.

The sentence should be: 'If we were meeting at 6 pm, we would have plenty of time.'

826. In August, she will be / enjoying / all the fruits her grandmother / will plant last January.
SSC Steno 10.12.2024 (Shift-II)

(a) will plant last January.
(b) In August, she will be
(c) all the fruits her grandmother
(d) enjoying

Ans. (a)

The segment with the grammatical error is 'will plant last January'. The correct form should be 'planted last January' to maintain the correct past tense for the action that occurred.

827. Once on a time, there was a brave king.
SSC Steno 10.12.2024 (Shift-II)

(a) brave (b) on
(c) was (d) once

Ans. (b)

The error in the sentence is 'on'. The correct phrase should be 'Once upon a time' to align with the traditional storytelling opening.

828. I have thought at / what you said / and I've decided / to take your advice.
SSC Steno 10.12.2024 (Shift-II)

(a) to take your advice
(b) and I've decided
(c) I have thought at
(d) what you said

Ans. (c)

The segment with the grammatical error is 'I have thought at'. The correct form should be 'I have thought about'. The preposition 'at' should be replaced with 'about' to correctly convey the action of considering something.

829. In the next few months, / they will / have teach / hundreds of children.
SSC Steno 10.12.2024 (Shift-II)

(a) have teach
(b) they will
(c) hundreds of children
(d) In the next few months

Ans. (a)

The segment with the grammatical error is 'have teach'.

The correct form should be 'have taught'. The verb 'teach' should be in the past participle form to match the future perfect tense.

830. A) The Gita / (B) is most sacred book / (C) of the Hindus. / (D) No error
SSC Steno 10.12.2024 (Shift-II)

(a) C (b) B
(c) A (d) D

Ans. (b)

The part that contains the error is 'is most sacred book'. The correct form should be 'is the most sacred book'. The definite article 'the' is necessary before 'most sacred book' to specify that it is the particular book being referred to as the most sacred.

831. The compensation that the [A] / Government agreed to provide to [B] / the dependents of the [C] / train accident is fairly less [D].
SSC Steno 10.12.2024 (Shift-II)

(a) A (b) B
(c) D (d) C

Ans. (c)

The segment with the grammatical error is 'is fairly less'. The correct form should be 'is fairly low' or 'is quite low'. 'Less' is incorrect in this context.

832. (A) Show me file/ (B) which has been given/ (C) to you by the lawyer . / (D) No error
SSC Steno 10.12.2024 (Shift-III)

(a) B (b) C
(c) A (d) D

Ans. (c)

The error is in part (A). The definite article 'the' is missing before 'file'. In English grammar, definite articles are used to specify particular nouns.

833. The swimmer jumped on the pool with the whistle.
SSC Steno 10.12.2024 (Shift-III)

(a) whistle (b) on
(c) with (d) jumped

Ans. (b)

The error is in the use of 'on'. The correct preposition should be 'in'. Preposition 'in' is appropriate for indicating the swimmer's location relative to the pool.

834. Tide pool is a isolated pocket of water that is formed when sea water becomes trapped as tide goes out.
SSC Steno 10.12.2024 (Shift-III)

(a) A tide pool is a isolated pocket of water that is formed when sea water becomes trapped as a tide goes out.
(b) A tide pool is an isolated pocket of water that is formed when sea water becomes trapped as the tide goes out.
(c) Tide pool is isolated pocket of water that is formed when sea water becomes trapped as a tide goes out.
(d) The tide pool is isolated pocket of water that is formed when sea water becomes trapped as tide goes out.

Ans. (b)

The article 'an' should be used before 'isolated' because it starts with a vowel sound, and 'the' before 'tide' specifies the particular tide.

835. (A) The more it rains,/ (B) worse/ (C) the roads become./ (D) No Error
SSC Steno 10.12.2024 (Shift-III)

(a) C (b) B (c) A (d) D

Ans. (b)

The error is in part (B). The comparative form 'worse' should be preceded by 'the' to form the correct structure 'the worse'. The correct comparative construction is 'the more it rains, the worse the roads become', showing a proportional relationship.

836. Since 1988, / the people of Rajasthan / have been searching / for 25-year-old man.
SSC Steno 10.12.2024 (Shift-III)

(a) for 25-year-old man.
(b) the people of Rajasthan
(c) have been searching
(d) Since 1988

Ans. (a)

The error is in the use of 'for 25-year-old man'. The correct form should be 'for a 25-year-old man' to include the article 'a'. The indefinite article 'a' is necessary before singular countable nouns.

837. Dr. Paramahamsa has been working / as a Assistant Professor/ of Mathematics / in IIT Madras for five years.
SSC Steno 10.12.2024 (Shift-III)

(a) of Mathematics
(b) as a Assistant Professor
(c) Dr. Paramahamsa has been working
(d) in IIT Madras for five years

Ans. (b)

The error is in the use of 'a Assistant Professor'. The correct form should be 'an Assistant Professor'. The article 'an' is used before words that start with a vowel sound.

838. A youth must respect the elderly, the rich must help the needy and a powerful must help the weak. If we keep up this trend, then the world can be a beautiful place.
SSC Steno 10.12.2024 (Shift-III)

(a) The youth must respect the elderly, the rich must help the needy and the powerful must help weak. If we keep up this trend, then the world can be a beautiful place.
(b) The youth must respect the elderly, the rich must help the needy and powerful must help the weak. If we keep up this trend, then the world can be a beautiful place.
(c) The youth must respect the elderly, the rich must help the needy and the powerful must help the weak. If we keep up this trend, then the world can be a beautiful place.
(d) The youth must respect the elderly, rich must help needy and the powerful must help the weak. If we keep up this trend, then the world can be a beautiful place

Ans. (c)

The errors are the use of 'a youth', 'a powerful' and the lack of an article before 'weak'.

The correct sentence uses 'the youth', 'the powerful' and 'the weak' to maintain consistency with the definite articles.

839. Mr. Unkerton glanced / to the inspector, / who merely snorted / and looked at the ceiling.
SSC Steno 10.12.2024 (Shift-III)

(a) and looked at the ceiling.
(b) who merely snorted
(c) Mr. Unkerton glanced
(d) to the inspector,

Ans. (d)

The error is in 'to the inspector'. The correct preposition should be 'at' to indicate the direction of the glance. 'Mr. Unkerton glanced at the inspector.'

840. In August next year, / she will been / studying / for four years.
SSC Steno 10.12.2024 (Shift-III)

(a) for four years
(b) she will been
(c) In August next year
(d) studying

Ans. (b)

The error is in the use of 'she will been'. The correct form is 'she will have been'. The future perfect tense requires the auxiliary verb 'have' before the past participle 'been'.

841. I looked / of the newspaper headlines / but I didn't read / carefully. SSC Steno 10.12.2024 (Shift-III)

(a) carefully
(b) but I didn't read
(c) I looked
(d) of the newspaper headlines

Ans. (d)

The error is in the use of 'of the newspaper headlines'. The correct preposition should be 'at' or 'over' to indicate the action of looking. 'I looked at the newspaper headlines.'

842. Ravi always / boasts at / his / achievements.
SSC Steno 10.12.2024 (Shift-III)

(a) achievements
(b) boasts at
(c) Ravi always
(d) his

Ans. (b)

The error is in 'boasts at'. The correct preposition should be 'boasts of' to indicate the action of talking with excessive pride about one's achievements.

843. A first / Indian who / went to space / was Rakesh Sharma.
SSC Steno 10.12.2024 (Shift-III)

(a) went to space
(b) A first
(c) Indian who
(d) was Rakesh Sharma

Ans. (b)

The error is in the use of 'A first.'

The correct form should be 'The first' to refer to a specific individual who achieved this.

SSC Steno 2023

844. It takes me an hour / to get to work at the moment, / but when the new road is finished,/ it be much quicker. SSC Steno 12.10.2023 (Shift-I)

(a) but when the new road is finished
(b) to get to work at the moment
(c) it be much quicker
(d) it takes me an hour

Ans. (c)

Part (c) 'it be much quicker' contains an error.
Add 'will' before 'be' to correct the sentence.

845. Salman finishes the work / within hours but he / delays it if not / accompanying by Rohit.
SSC Steno 12.10.2023 (Shift-I)

(a) Salman finishes the work
(b) delays it if not
(c) within hours but he
(d) accompanying by Rohit

Ans. (d)

Part (d) 'accompanying by Rohit' contains an error. As the sentence is in past tense, 'accompanied' should be used.

846. I'm sure that time / changes things, but it / didn't change anything / unlike my perception of you.
SSC Steno 12.10.2023 (Shift-I)

(a) didn't change anything
(b) changes things, but it
(c) unlike my perception of you
(d) I'm sure that time

Ans. (c)

Part (c) 'unlike my perception of you' contains an error. The use of conjunction 'unlike' is incorrect. Use 'except' to correct the sentence.

847. She has been speaking / four languages / very fluent / since childhood. SSC Steno 12.10.2023 (Shift-I)

(a) since childhood
(b) four languages
(c) very fluent
(d) She has been speaking

Ans. (c)

Part (c) 'very fluent' contains the error. Use of 'fluent' is incorrect in the sentence. It should be an adverb. Hence, use 'fluently' to correct the sentence.

848. By the way a lorry/crashed into the car but/the boys were lucky and/escaped with only minor injuries. SSC Steno 12.10.2023 (Shift-I)

(a) the boys were lucky and
(b) crashed into the car but
(c) By the way a lorry
(d) escaped with only minor injuries

Ans. (c)

Part (c) 'By the way a lorry' contains an error. Use 'on the way' to correct the sentence.

849. The team played / extremely / good / during the match.
SSC Steno 12.10.2023 (Shift-I)

(a) extremely
(b) good
(c) during the match
(d) The team played

Ans. (b)

Part (b) 'good' is erroneous. The use of 'good' is incorrect.
Use 'well' as an adverb is used to modify the verb to correct the sentence.

850. If you have / faith in God, / everything turn out / to be all right.

(a) If you have SSC Steno 12.10.2023 (Shift-I)
(b) to be all right
(c) everything turn out
(d) faith in God

Ans. (c)

Part (c) 'everything turn out' contains an error.

Present conditional sentence takes present tense; in the conditional clause and future tense in the second clause. Hence, add 'will' after 'everything' to correct the sentence.

851. Yesterday, / I went / to the store and / buy some groceries.

SSC Steno 12.10.2023 (Shift-I)

(a) Yesterday
(b) buy some groceries
(c) to the store and
(d) I went

Ans. (b)

Part (b) 'buy some groceries' contain an error of tense.
The sentence is in past tense where the two verbs are joined and hence, 'bought' should be used in place of 'buy' to correct the sentence.

852. You must meet / Suyash sometime. / I think you like him.

SSC Steno 13.10.2023 (Shift-I)

(a) You must meet
(b) Suyash sometime
(c) I think you like him
(d) No error

Ans. (c)

Part (c) 'I think you like him' contains an error. Add 'will' before 'like' to indicate possibility.

853. He bought a / pen; a / pen was silver / grey in colour.

SSC Steno 13.10.2023 (Shift-I)

(a) pen was silver (b) He bought a
(c) grey in colour (d) pen; a

Ans. (d)

Part (d) 'pen; a' contains an error. As the pen has already been introduced, 'the' should be used to correct the sentence.

854. The CEO announced that/the company's profits has/fallen significantly/in the last quarter.

SSC Steno 13.10.2023 (Shift-I)

(a) The CEO announced that
(b) the company's profits has
(c) fallen significantly
(d) in the last quarter

Ans. (b)

Part (b) 'the company's profits has' contains an error. As the subject 'the company's profits' is plural, plural verb 'have' should be used to correct the sentence.

855. She have been spending / all her money on her flat / to make it more decorative. SSC Steno 13.10.2023 (Shift-I)

(a) No error
(b) all her money on her flat
(c) to make it more decorative
(d) She have been spending

Ans. (d)

Part (d) 'She have been spending' is erroneous.

The subject 'she' is a singular noun, so singular verb should be used. Hence, 'has' should be used to correct the sentence.

856. As twilight settled / upon the bustling city, / its streets come alive with / a symphony of flickering lights. SSC Steno 13.10.2023 (Shift-I)

(a) its streets come alive with
(b) a symphony of flickering lights
(c) upon the bustling city
(d) As twilight settled

Ans. (a)

Part (a) 'its streets come alive with' contains an error.
As the sentence is in past tense, 'came' should be used to correct the sentence.

857. I don't think / I can go throughout / the process of raising / two children on my own. SSC Steno 13.10.2023 (Shift-I)

(a) two children on my own
(b) I can go throughout
(c) I don't think
(d) the process of raising

Ans. (b)

Part (b) 'I can go throughout' contains an error.

The preposition 'through' should be used to correct the sentence.

858. She sat amid a / rocking chair, listening to / some music and / reminiscing about the past.

SSC Steno 13.10.2023 (Shift-I)

(a) She sat amid a
(b) rocking chair, listening to
(c) reminiscing about the past
(d) some music and

Ans. (a)

Part (a) 'she sat amid a' contains an error. Add 'on' in place of 'amid' to correct the sentence.

859. Shops are not allowed / to remain open / after 8:00 pm / from the lockdown. SSC Steno 13.10.2023 (Shift-I)

(a) from the lockdown.
(b) after 8:00 pm
(c) Shops are not allowed
(d) to remain open

Ans. (a)

Part (a) 'from the lockdown' contains an error.

The use of preposition 'from' is incorrect.

Use 'since' as the action is continuing in the present to correct the sentence.

860. I didn't sleep well last night because the dog is barking.

SSC Steno 13.10.2023 (Shift-I)

(a) <u>I didn't</u> sleep well last night because the dog is barking.
(b) I didn't sleep well last night because <u>the dog is barking</u>.
(c) I didn't sleep well <u>last night</u> <u>because</u> the dog is barking.
(d) I didn't <u>sleep well</u> last night because the dog is barking.

Ans. (b)

The part 'the dog is barking' contains the error. As the sentence is in past tense, use 'was barking' to correct the sentence.

03

Sentence Improvement

Sentence Improvement is another category of questions related to English grammar which is very important for SSC examination. Generally 3-4 questions of this category are asked in the examination.

Types of Questions Asked

Sentence Improvement questions are generally formed with a sentence in which a word or group of words is either underlined or in brackets.

Type 1

Select the option that will improve the underlined part of the given sentence. In case no improvement is needed, select 'No improvement required'.

<u>This were back</u> in the early days when we were fighting the Italians in Libya.

(a) This was back
(b) These were back
(c) It were back
(d) No improvement needed **Ans.** (a)

Type 2

Select the option that will improve the bracketed part of the given sentence. In case no improvement is needed, select 'No improvement required'.

Peter and I made a chair (with my hands) and Rima lifted him up on to it.

(a) With our hands
(b) By my hands
(c) By our hands
(d) No improvement **Ans.** (a)

How to Solve the Questions

To spot the errors in the sentence or correct the underlined part sentence successfully, you need to read the rules of grammar carefully (Refer to Chapter- Grammar at a Glance). Once you know all the rules, it becomes easy for you to find the error and correct it.

Here is a small step by step process that you should follow to solve the questions.

Step 1 Read the complete sentence properly and carefully but pay special focus to the underlined segment.

Step 2 Ensure that the sentence is meaningful and no word is incorrectly used.

Step 3 Make sure that the nouns, pronouns, verb forms, adverbs, prepositions and conjunctions used in the underlined segment are correct.
Pay attention to the placement of adverbs and adjectives.
Make sure that subject and the verb agrees and the pronouns used are according to the noun of the sentence.
Ensure that the correct tense structure is followed.

Step 4 Give special focus to time expression such as during, for, since, last night, etc. If the underlined segment contains a verb.

Step 5 Once you identify the error in the segment, you need to choose the option that corrects it. In most cases, when you identify the error, you know the correct substitution.

Step 6 Read all the options carefully. Two options may look exactly the same with some minor differences. Choose the option that fits the sentence perfectly.

SSC Exam Scanner

SSC CGL 2024 (Tier 1 & 2)

Directions (Q. Nos. 1-921) Select the most appropriate option to substitute/replace the underlined/bracketed segment in the given sentence. If there is no need to substitute it, select 'No substitution'.

1. 'Spy Family' is a graphic novel that is a narrative work in which the story is conveyed to the reader using <u>uninterrupted art in a traditional</u> comics format.
SSC CGL Tier-1 09.09.2024 (Shift-I)

(a) sequential art in a traditional
(b) existential art in a traditional
(c) sedimental art in a traditional
(d) longitudinal art in a traditional

Ans. (a)

The underlined part of the given sentence contains an error. The use of the word 'uninterrupted' is incorrect in the context of the sentence. Hence, use 'sequential art in a traditional' to improve the sentence.

2. She has been <u>studying for 2 o'clock</u>.
SSC CGL Tier-1 09.09.2024 (Shift-I)

(a) study from 2 o'clock
(b) studying since 2 o'clock
(c) study for 2 o'clock
(d) studying 2 o'clock

Ans. (b)

The underlined part of the sentence contains an error. The use of preposition 'for' is correct. 'For' is used to refer to a period of time, while 'since' is used to refer to a point in time.

Hence, replace it with 'studying since 2 o'clock' to correct the sentence.

3. Spreading awareness about the rights of the consumers and the relief open to them in case they did not get their money's worth of goods and service has rightly been identified as the first priority. **SSC CGL Tier-1 09.09.2024 (Shift-II)**

(a) were unable to get their money's worth
(b) No substitution
(c) did not getting their money's worth
(d) will not get their money's worth

Ans. (a)

The underlined part of the sentence is correct. However, it can be better articulated by replacing it with 'were unable to get their money's worth'.

4. Pollution levels have increased so largely that they are almost killing us. **SSC CGL Tier-1 09.09.2024 (Shift-II)**

(a) highly (b) slowly
(c) primarily (d) chiefly

Ans. (a)

The underlined word is incorrect in the context of the sentence. It should be replaced by 'highly' to correct the sentence.

5. (Each participant have) performed well. **SSC CGL Tier-1 09.09.2024 (Shift-III)**

(a) Each participant was
(b) Each participant has
(c) Each participant have been
(d) Each participant were

Ans. (b)

The bracketed part of the sentence contains an error. The word 'each' takes a singular verb. Hence, use 'has' to correct the sentence.

6. The question papers are placed in the lockers of the school in a way that they can't be reached. **SSC CGL Tier-1 09.09.2024 (Shift-III)**

(a) are irrepressible
(b) are inaccessible
(c) are affordable
(d) are affable

Ans. (b)

The underlined part of the sentence seems awkward in the context of the sentence. Replace it with 'are inaccessible.'

7. I have been living in Hyderabad since I am born. **SSC CGL Tier-1 10.09.2024 (Shift-I)**

(a) since I have born
(b) since I will be born
(c) since I born
(d) since I was born

Ans. (d)

The underlined part of the sentence contains an error. As the first clause is in present perfect continuous tense, the since clause will be in past tense. Hence, replace 'since I was born' to correct the sentence.

8. Rare species of frogs were very quicker identified by Stella. **SSC CGL Tier-1 10.09.2024 (Shift-II)**

(a) to frogs were very quickly
(b) of frogs were very quickly
(c) in frogs were very quicker
(d) of frogs were very quicklier

Ans. (b)

The underlined part of the sentence contains an error.

The use of 'quicker' is incorrect as the word is in positions to be an adjective. Hence, use 'quickly' to correct the sentence.

9. He was an irresponsible person to the matter of taking up responsibilities. **SSC CGL Tier-1 10.09.2024 (Shift-II)**

(a) at the matter of taking up
(b) in the matter of taking up
(c) by the matter of taking up
(d) along the matter of taking up

Ans. (b)

The underlined part of the sentence contains an error. The use of preposition 'to' is incorrect. Hence, replace it with 'in' to correct the sentence.

10. They could (always) stay in, or go for a walk. **SSC CGL Tier-1 10.09.2024 (Shift-III)**

(a) had better (b) not only
(c) either (d) neither

Ans. (c)

The bracketed part of the sentence is erroneous. The use of 'always' with 'or' is incorrect. It should be 'either'.

11. Charles Darwin is renowned for his book on evolution, 'On the Origin of Species', which laid down a treasure of substantiation that evolution occurs and projected a mechanism, that is, natural selection, for how it does so. **SSC CGL Tier-1 11.09.2024 (Shift-I)**

(a) laid into a treasure of substantiation
(b) laid about a treasure of substantiation
(c) laid away a treasure of substantiation
(d) laid out a treasure of substantiation

Ans. (d)

The underlined part of the sentence contains an error. The use of phrasal verb 'laid down' is incorrect as it means to state something plainly, especially as an official rule. Hence, replace it with 'laid out' which means stated.

12. The programme on TV was now shown the blurred faces of the inmates of the rehabilitation centre. **SSC CGL Tier-1 11.09.2024 (Shift-II)**

(a) were now showing the blurred faces of the inmates of the rehabilitation centre.
(b) was now showing the blurred faces of the inmates of the rehabilitation centre.
(c) were now showing the blurring faces of the inmates from the rehabilitation centre.
(d) was now showing the blurred faces of the inmates upon the rehabilitation centre.

Ans. (b)

The underlined part of the sentence contains an error. As the sentence presents a continuous action, the use of 'shown' is incorrect.
Hence, replace it with 'showing' to correct the sentence.

13. When I saw him, I will ask him to return the book he borrowed. **SSC CGL Tier-1 11.09.2024 (Shift-III)**

(a) shall see him
(b) have seen him
(c) had seen him
(d) see him

Ans. (d)

The underlined part of the sentence contains an error. The given sentence is a present conditional clause wherein the if/when clause is in present tense and the second clause is in future tense. Hence, 'see him' should be used to correct the sentence.

14. Gourav was no good than a foolish person. **SSC CGL Tier-1 12.09.2024 (Shift-I)**

(a) no better (b) not good
(c) no best (d) not best

Ans. (a)

The underlined part of the sentence contains an error.

The use of 'good' is incorrect as the sentence makes a comparison. Hence, replace it with 'better' to correct the sentence.

15. If I was the queen, I would give a handsome sum towards education. **SSC CGL Tier-1 12.09.2024 (Shift-I)**

(a) will be the queen
(b) were the queen
(c) have been the queen
(d) would be the queen

Ans. (b)

The underlined part of the sentence contains an error. In hypothetical conditional sentence we use 'were'.

16. Five years later, I was eating this same dish at the same restaurant. **SSC CGL Tier-1 12.09.2024 (Shift-II)**

(a) will have be eating
(b) has been eating
(c) am eating
(d) had been eating

Ans. (c)

The underlined part of the sentence contains an error. The pronoun 'I' takes 'am' as the primary auxiliary.

17. Beyond skills, experience and training, companies search for applicants who display excitement — those they believe shall carry out allocated responsibilities cheerfully and cooperatively. **SSC CGL Tier-1 12.09.2024 (Shift-III)**

(a) shall take up any designated obligations
(b) will execute assigned duties
(c) will demonstrate non-biased work
(d) should pick up all skills and works

Ans. (b)

The underlined part of the sentence is grammatically correct. However, it can be improved with - will execute assigned duties.

18. The mother asked the child, 'Will you tell me who did accompany you to the airport?' **SSC CGL Tier-1 12.09.2024 (Shift-III)**

(a) who accompanies you
(b) who does accompany you
(c) who accompanied you
(d) who must be accompanied you

Ans. (c)

The underlined part of the sentence contains an error of tense. Use 'who accompanied you' to correct the sentence.

19. Satya is always great to his friends who helped him when he was in trouble. **SSC CGL Tier-1 13.09.2024 (Shift-I)**

(a) greatful (b) thanked
(c) No substitution (d) grateful

Ans. (d)

The underlined word is incorrect in the context of the given sentence. The correct word for the sentence will be 'grateful' as the sentence presents that Satya was helped by her friends.

20. The team always anticipate a bowling friendly pitch on their easy victory in the T20 matches. **SSC CGL Tier-1 13.09.2024 (Shift-I)**

(a) pitch over their easy victory
(b) pitch for their easy victory
(c) pitch to their easy victory
(d) pitch of their easy victory

Ans. (b)

The underlined part of the sentence contains an error. Use of preposition 'on' is incorrect. The correct preposition will be 'for'.

21. The wedding was put on until January. **SSC CGL Tier-1 13.09.2024 (Shift-II)**

(a) put in (b) put off
(c) put down (d) put up

Ans. (b)

The underlined word is incorrect in the context of the given sentence. The phrasal verb 'put on' means to wear, which is incorrect. The correct word for the sentence will be 'put off' which means to delay.

22. Carnatic music is usually performed by a small troupe of actors, consisting of a principal performer, a melodic accompaniment and a rhythm accompaniment. **SSC CGL Tier-1 13.09.2024 (Shift-III)**

(a) board of directors
(b) ensemble of musicians
(c) panel of judges
(d) band of singers

Ans. (b)

The underlined phrase in incorrect in the context of the given sentence. As the sentence talks about singing, a group of actors is incorrect for the sentence. Hence, replace it with 'ensemble of musicians' to correct the sentence.

23. It is very hard for her to provide the necessities of her family. **SSC CGL Tier-1 17.09.2024 (Shift-I)**

(a) the necessities to her family
(b) the necessities by her family
(c) the necessity of her family
(d) the necessities from her families

Ans. (a)

The underlined part of the sentence contains an error. Replace it with 'the necessities to her family' to make the sentence meaningful.

24. To the general public, William was best known as a crusader for peace and as an admired critic about social, political and ethical subjects. **SSC CGL Tier-1 17.09.2024 (Shift-I)**

(a) for peace and as an admired critic by
(b) for peace and as an admired critic on
(c) about peace and as an admired critic about
(d) in peace and as an admired critic about

Ans. (b)

The underlined part of the sentence contains an error. The use of preposition 'about' is incorrect in the sentence. Replace it with 'on' to correct the sentence.

25. No matter how hard work you, your boss will not recognise your efforts. **SSC CGL Tier-1 17.09.2024 (Shift-I)**

(a) hard you work
(b) work you do hard
(c) hardly you work
(d) No substitution

Ans. (a)

The underlined part of the sentence contains an error.
The word order is incorrect in the sentence. The correct word order will be- hard you work.

26. As the rulers of the planet, humans like to think that it is the largest creatures that will emerge victorious from the struggle for survival. **SSC CGL Tier-1 17.09.2024 (Shift-II)**

(a) No substitution
(b) it is the most large creatures
(c) they are a largest creature
(d) they are the largest creatures

Ans. (d)

The underlined part of the sentence contains an error.

The subject of the sentence is 'humans' so, plural pronoun 'they are' should be used.

27. If it had not rained, they would not postpone the programmes. **SSC CGL Tier-1 17.09.2024 (Shift-III)**

(a) would be postponed
(b) no substitution
(c) would not have postponed
(d) would not postponed

Ans. (c)

The underlined part of the sentence contains an error.
The sentence is a past hypothetical sentence wherein if clause is in past perfect tense, the second clause in the present perfect tense. Hence, use 'would not have postponed' to correct the sentence.

28. Sivamani is working as an electrician for the past 22 years. **SSC CGL Tier-1 18.09.2024 (Shift-I)**

(a) had been worked
(b) has been working
(c) have been working
(d) would work

Ans. (b)

The underlined part of the sentence contains an error.

As the sentence presents an action that started in the past and is still continuing, present perfect continuous tense should be used. Hence, 'has been working' should be used to correct the sentence.

29. Rohan exercised and ate a lot, lest he should not be weak.
SSC CGL Tier-1 18.09.2024 (Shift-II)
(a) lest he should not weak.
(b) lest he would be weak.
(c) lest he would not be weak.
(d) lest he should be weak.

Ans. (d)

The underlined part of the sentence contains an error. The word 'lest' does not take any other negative word. Hence, remove 'not' to correct the sentence.

30. He (seek) for the wallet in his pocket.
SSC CGL Tier-1 18.09.2024 (Shift-II)
(a) Sought
(b) Had seeking
(c) Are seeking
(d) Seeking

Ans. (a)

The bracketed part of the sentence is erroneous.

As the sentence is in past tense, 'sought' would be used to correct the sentence.

31. Do you know where does she reside?
SSC CGL Tier-1 18.09.2024 (Shift-III)
(a) where does she resides?
(b) where she reside?
(c) where she resides?
(d) where do she reside?

Ans. (c)

The underlined part of the sentence contains an error. Replace it with 'where she resides' to correct the sentence.

32. A computer can't function without it's motherboard.
SSC CGL Tier-1 18.09.2024 (Shift-III)
(a) its (b) his
(c) their (d) it is

Ans. (a)

The underlined part of the sentence contains an error.

The use of 'it's' is incorrect as it means it is. The correct replacement would be the possessive adjective 'its'.

33. Transnational linkages, for example, sever the nation-state's integrity and corrupt state-society relations.
SSC CGL Tier-1 19.09.2024 (Shift-I)
(a) cohesion and erode
(b) divergence and relativity
(c) severance and revolution
(d) controversy and diminution

Ans. (a)

The underlined part of the sentence is incorrect in the context. Hence, replace it with 'cohesion and erode' to correct the sentence.

34. His house is smaller than you.
SSC CGL Tier-1 19.09.2024 (Shift-I)
(a) is smaller than yours
(b) is small as you
(c) is small than you
(d) is smaller than your

Ans. (a)

The underlined part of the sentence is erroneous. The objective pronoun 'yours' should be used to correct the sentence.

35. She was foolish enough to think that she be completely safe now.
SSC CGL Tier-1 19.09.2024 (Shift-II)
(a) has being completely safe
(b) have been completely safe
(c) is completely safe
(d) were completely safe

Ans. (c)

The underlined part of the sentence contains an error.

The use of 'be' is incorrect in the sentence. Hence, use 'is' in its place to correct the sentence.

36. No sooner did Mr. Piyahri Mishra finish his chemistry lecture that the students began to leave.
SSC CGL Tier-1 19.09.2024 (Shift-III)
(a) so the students began to leave.
(b) then the students began to leave.
(c) and the students began to leave.
(d) than the students began to leave.

Ans. (d)

The underlined part of the given sentence contains an error. 'No sooner' takes 'than' and not 'that'.

37. Sanat has just arrived in Mysore on transfer; he requests his friend Raghu to help him find an appropriate location.
SSC CGL Tier-1 23.09.2024 (Shift-I)
(a) an allocation recommendation
(b) a rented accommodation
(c) a proper junction
(d) a suitable elevation

Ans. (b)

The underlined part of the sentence contains an error. Use 'a rented accommodation' to correct the sentence.

38. This book giving us much information about our freedom fighters who lost their lives while serving our motherland.
SSC CGL Tier-1 23.09.2024 (Shift-I)
(a) gives us many information
(b) give us many information
(c) give us much information
(d) gives us much information

Ans. (d)

The underlined part of the sentence is erroneous. The use of 'giving' is incorrect and must be replaced with simple present 'gives' to correct the sentence.

39. The food intolerance industry has grown dramatically in the previous decade, chiefly because of a boost in Coeliac and Crohn's disease cases, as well as increasing awareness among health-conscious clients.
SSC CGL Tier-1 23.09.2024 (Shift-I)
(a) contextually because of a spark
(b) pretty much entirely because of a boil-down
(c) casually due to a growth
(d) owing primarily to a rise

Ans. (d)

The underlined part of the sentence is grammatically correct but awkward. Hence, we can improve it by using 'owing primarily to a rise'.

40. Aesthetic value is specifically a way in which we can get positive conclude value from the world at large.
SSC CGL Tier-1 23.09.2024 (Shift-II)
(a) can get positive convalescent value
(b) can get positive convulsive value
(c) can get positive conclusive value
(d) can get positive contrastive value

Ans. (c)

The underlined part of the given sentence contains an error. The use of form 'conclude' is incorrect and adjective form 'conclusive' should be used to correct the sentence.

41. Ranjith failed in all his exams as he had been addicted of social media.
SSC CGL Tier-1 23.09.2024 (Shift-III)
(a) as he had been addicted at
(b) as he had been addicted on
(c) as he had been addicted in
(d) as he had been addicted to

Ans. (d)

The underlined part of the given sentence contains an error.
The use of preposition 'of' is incorrect in the context of the sentence. Hence, replace it with 'to' to correct the sentence.

42. The cynical investors believed in every word the analysts said.
SSC CGL Tier-1 23.09.2024 (Shift-III)
(a) credulous (b) distrustful
(c) persuasive (d) credible

Ans. (a)

The word 'cynical' means believing that people are motivated purely by self-interest; distrustful of human sincerity or integrity. Hence, it does not seem correct in the sentence. Use 'credulous' which means having or showing too great a readiness to believe things.

43. A herd of cattle consists of related females, cubs and a small number of adult males.
SSC CGL Tier-1 24.09.2024 (Shift-I)
(a) pride of lions (b) pack of wolves
(c) school of fish (d) flock of birds

Ans. (a)
The underlined part of the sentence contains an error. As the sentence mentions cubs or the young ones of a lion, the correct expression would be 'pride of lions'.

44. It is nothing else your pride which makes you say such a thing.
SSC CGL Tier-1 24.09.2024 (Shift-I)
(a) else your pride that makes
(b) else your pride which make
(c) else but your pride which make
(d) else but your pride which makes

Ans. (d)
The underlined part of the sentence seems to be missing a contrasting conjunction. Hence, replace it with 'else but your pride which makes' to correct the sentence.

45. Mr. Adhil called back but he wasn't able to find the scooter part he needed. SSC CGL Tier-1 24.09.2024 (Shift-I)
(a) called down but he wasn't able to
(b) called off but he wasn't able to
(c) called around but he wasn't able to
(d) called up to but he wasn't able to

Ans. (c)
The underlined part of the sentence contains an error. The use of phrasal verb 'called back' is incorrect in the sentence. Replace it with 'called around' to correct the sentence.

46. I had not only helped her by giving hints but also with providing her links. SSC CGL Tier-1 24.09.2024 (Shift-II)
(a) helped her not only by
(b) helped her not by
(c) helped her only by
(d) helped not only her by

Ans. (a)
The underlined part of the sentence contains an error. The place of the main verb will be before the conjunction 'not only'.

47. Positive self-talk have a great affect on one's self-worth.
SSC CGL Tier-1 24.09.2024 (Shift-II)
(a) has a great affect
(b) have a great effect
(c) having a great affect
(d) has a great effect

Ans. (d)
The underlined part of the sentence contains an error. As the subject of the sentence is singular, the verb should also be singular. Hence, use 'has' to correct the sentence.

48. Arushya purchased the most good of all the suits kept in the shop.
SSC CGL Tier-1 24.09.2024 (Shift-III)
(a) the goods (b) the best
(c) the more good (d) the good

Ans. (b)
The underlined part of the sentence is incorrect. Use 'the best' to correct the sentence.

49. Even if you've never heard his name, you've probably met someone with his words tattooed in their skin or heard them sung at a music concert.
SSC CGL Tier-1 24.09.2024 (Shift-III)
(a) tattooed through their skin
(b) tattooed until their skin
(c) tattooed overdoing their skin
(d) tattooed on their skin

Ans. (d)
The underlined part of the sentence contains an error. The use of preposition 'in' is incorrect. Use 'on' to correct the sentence.

50. If he runs, he (get) there in time.
SSC CGL Tier-1 25.09.2024 (Shift-I)
(a) will get
(b) is getting
(c) got there in time
(d) has to get

Ans. (a)
The bracketed part of the sentence is incorrect as the sentence is a present conditional sentence wherein the if clause is in present tense and the other clause is in future tense. Hence, 'will get' is the correct option.

51. Ashoka was the greatest than all the Mauryan Emperors.
SSC CGL Tier-1 25.09.2024 (Shift-II)
(a) all Mauryan Emperors
(b) of the Mauryan Emperors
(c) to all another Mauryan Emperors
(d) to other Mauryan Emperors

Ans. (b)
The underlined part of the sentence contains an error. Use 'of the Mauryan Emperors' to correct the sentence.

52. I said I (don't) understand.
SSC CGL Tier-1 25.09.2024 (Shift-II)
(a) doesn't (b) am doing
(c) didn't (d) done

Ans. (c)
The bracketed part of the sentence contains an error. As the sentence is in past tense, 'didn't' should be used.

53. I picked up my little clock and it began to dance gracefully.
SSC CGL Tier-1 25.09.2024 (Shift-III)
(a) move gradually (b) lift smoothly
(c) chime prettily (d) work agreeably

Ans. (c)
The underlined part of the sentence is incorrect in the context of the clock. Hence, use 'chime prettily' to correct the sentence.

54. The chair I have bought recently is costly than what I bought last year.
SSC CGL Tier-1 26.09.2024 (Shift-I)
(a) is the costliest (b) is costlier
(c) was costly (d) will be costly

Ans. (b)
The underlined part of the sentence contains an error. As the sentence makes a comparison, 'is costlier' should be used.

55. RN Right's literary works helped redefine discussions in race relations in America in the mid-20th century.
SSC CGL Tier-1 26.09.2024 (Shift-I)
(a) by race relations in America
(b) beside race relations in America
(c) to race relations in America
(d) of race relations in America

Ans. (d)
Part 'in race relations in America' contains an error. Preposition 'in' before 'race' is incorrect in the sentence. Use 'of' to correct the sentence.

56. The chief guest concluded his speech as he requested to stop by the organisers.
SSC CGL Tier-1 26.09.2024 (Shift-III)
(a) No substitution
(b) he was requested
(c) he is requested
(d) he will be requested

Ans. (b)
The underlined part of the sentence contains an error. As the sentence is in indirect speech, 'he was requested' should be used to correct the sentence.

57. We will have to (put the meeting away) as the Director is not well.
SSC CGL Tier-1 26.09.2024 (Shift-III)
(a) put the meeting off
(b) put the meeting up
(c) put the meeting on
(d) put the meeting again

Ans. (a)
The bracketed part of the sentence is incorrect. Use 'put the meeting off' to correct the sentence.

SSC CGL 2023 (Tier 1 & 2)

58. The boys and the teacher wants to win. SSC CGL Tier-1 14.07.2023 (Shift-II)
(a) wants to won (b) want to won
(c) want win (d) want to win

Ans. (d)

The underlined part 'wants to win' contains the error of verb form. As the subject is plural, verb should also be plural according to the rules of subject-verb agreement. Hence, to correct the sentence, replace 'wants' with 'want'.

59. The fact that God created man in his personal view by giving him an intellectual spirit elevates him above the beasts of the field. SSC CGL Tier-1 14.07.2023 (Shift-II)
(a) own glory (b) own capacity
(c) own image (d) own idea

Ans. (c)

The phrase 'personal view' can be substituted 'own image' as per the context of the sentence.

60. The frog adopts itself to live both in water and on land. SSC CGL Tier-1 14.07.2023 (Shift-III)
(a) frog adepts itself
(b) frog alters itself
(c) No substitution
(d) frog adapts itself

Ans. (d)

The underlined part of the sentence contains an error. The use of the word 'adopts' is incorrect in the context of the sentence. To correct the sentence, replace the underlined part with 'frog adapts itself'.

61. We all should help each other. SSC CGL Tier-1 14.07.2023 (Shift-III)
(a) help mutually
(b) help one another
(c) help each one
(d) No substitution

Ans. (b)

The underlined part of the sentence contains an error. To correct the sentence, replace the underlined part with 'help one another'. 'Each other' is used for two people while 'one another' is used for more than two people.

62. It is reported that she has win a prize money of ten lakhs at a reality show. SSC CGL Tier-1 17.07.2023 (Shift-I)
(a) she will won
(b) she had win
(c) No substitution required
(d) she has won

Ans. (d)

The underlined part of the sentence contains an error. After 'has', the main verb 'should be in' the third form, so 'has won' should be used to correct the sentence.

63. Natwar was a fraudster who always tried to fooling others. SSC CGL Tier-1 17.07.2023 (Shift-I)
(a) betraying (b) deceive
(c) cheating (d) revealing

Ans. (b)

'Deceive' is the correct improvement for the given underlined word.

64. The Indian Independence Movement sought to establish the conceptions of freedom and social welfare as the goals of an independent Indian state, resulting in Fundamental Rights and Directive Principles. SSC CGL Tier-1 17.07.2023 (Shift-II)
(a) procedures of free mind
(b) concept of liberty
(c) symbols of victory
(d) methods to sympathise

Ans. (b)

'Conception' refers to the way in which something is perceived or the ability to form or understand mental concepts. The underlined segment can be replaced by 'concept of liberty' to improve the sentence. 'Concept' refers to a general idea or understanding of something while 'liberty' is synonymous with 'freedom'.

65. He was so curious that he rose many questions in the meeting. SSC CGL Tier-1 17.07.2023 (Shift-III)
(a) that he raised many questions
(b) that he rose much questions
(c) that he aroused many questions
(d) No substitution

Ans. (a)

The underlined part of the sentence contains an error of verb. To correct it, the verb 'rose' must be replaced by 'raised'.

66. The river (flowing) under the bridge. SSC CGL Tier-1 17.07.2023 (Shift-IV)
(a) was flow (b) flows
(c) is flow (d) is flowed

Ans. (b)

The bracketed part of the sentence has incorrect verb form. The appropriate verb form for the given sentence is 'flows'.

67. They have disposed all the old books. SSC CGL Tier-1 17.07.2023 (Shift-IV)
(a) disposed of (b) disposed out
(c) disposed on (d) disposed by

Ans. (a)

The underlined part of the sentence is incorrect as it is not complete. We use the preposition 'of' with the verb 'disposed' to mean to throw out. Hence, add 'of' after 'disposed' to make the sentence correct.

68. National development is defined as an improvement in people's daily arrangements, the provision of fundamental necessities to citizens such as food, education, social services, medical help, and so on, as well as an increase in per capita income. SSC CGL Tier-1 18.07.2023 (Shift-I)
(a) dividing techniques
(b) dining categories
(c) existing calamities
(d) living conditions

Ans. (d)

The underlined part of the sentence does not fit the context of the sentence. The phrase 'living conditions' should be used.

69. I will not go out if is raining. SSC CGL Tier-1 18.07.2023 (Shift-II)
(a) raining (b) it rains
(c) will rain (d) rained

Ans. (b)

The underlined part contains an error of tense.

The sentence is in Simple Future Tense and 'is raining' is not correct in the context. Thus, replace 'is raining' with 'it rains' to make the sentence meaningful.

70. Please ask the dog to get of my couch. SSC CGL Tier-1 18.07.2023 (Shift-II)
(a) get of mine (b) get off my
(c) get off mine (d) No substitution

Ans. (b)

The underlined part of the sentence contains an error of preposition. The use of 'of' is incorrect in the sentence. Hence, it must be replaced by 'off'.

71. The mob drove on the rampage and looted several shops in the locality. SSC CGL Tier-1 18.07.2023 (Shift-II)
(a) played on the rampage
(b) went on the rampage
(c) ran on the rampage
(d) strolled on the rampage

Ans. (b)

The phase 'go/went on a rampage' means rushing around in a mild or violent way, causing damage or destruction.

Hence, 'went on the rampage' is appropriate to substitute the underlined segment.

72. I have not seen you for last year. SSC CGL Tier-1 18.07.2023 (Shift-III)
(a) you since last year
(b) me for last year
(c) you about last year
(d) you for last years

Ans. (a)
The underlined part contains an error of preposition. To correct it, replace 'for' with 'since'. 'Since' is used to denote a point of time in the past.

73. I don't wear the sunglasses at the moment. SSC CGL Tier-1 18.07.2023 (Shift-III)
(a) I didn't wear
(b) I wore
(c) I was wearing
(d) I'm not wearing

Ans. (d)
The underlined part of the given sentence is not correct in the context of the sentence.
The sentence is referring to an ongoing action and Present Continuous Tense is appropriate. Hence, the underlined part must be replaced by 'I'm not wearing'.

74. Her hopes for building her own house were beaten when she lost her jewellery box. SSC CGL Tier-1 18.07.2023 (Shift-III)
(a) house were defeated when
(b) house were frustrated when
(c) house were relieved when
(d) house were dashed when

Ans. (d)
In the underlined part of the sentence, the use of the word 'beaten' is incorrect in the context of the sentence. To correct it, the word 'beaten' should be replaced with 'dashed'.

75. Irene went to office every single day by walk. SSC CGL Tier-1 18.07.2023 (Shift-IV)
(a) every day single by walk
(b) every single day walk
(c) every single day on foot
(d) every single day on walk

Ans. (c)
The underlined part of the sentence contains an error.
It should be replaced with 'every single day on foot'.

76. The company decided to sell their stake in their subsidiary because it was under massive debts. SSC CGL Tier-1 18.07.2023 (Shift-IV)
(a) sell their stake in its subsidiary
(b) No substitution
(c) sell its stake in their subsidiary
(d) sell its stake in its subsidiary

Ans. (d)
The underlined part of the sentence contains an error. The use of 'their' for singular noun 'company' is incorrect and thus, it must be replaced with 'its' to make the sentence correct.

77. In times of difficulty, she preys for an oracle to guide her. SSC CGL Tier-1 18.07.2023 (Shift-IV)
(a) pray (b) praise (c) price (d) prays

Ans. (d)
The word 'prays' should replace the underlined word to make the sentence contextually meaningful.

78. In today's digital age, information is widely available to everyone by many means of media such as television, newspapers, films and social media. SSC CGL Tier-1 19.07.2023 (Shift-I)
(a) with quite enough of mechanisms
(b) through any strategies
(c) *via* various forms
(d) among many techniques

Ans. (c)
The phrase '*via* various forms' means 'by many means'.

79. They are the people which are looking to expand their horizons in the fast growing tourism industry. SSC CGL Tier-1 19.07.2023 (Shift-II)
(a) which looked to expand
(b) who is looking to expand
(c) who are looking to expand
(d) that are looked to expand

Ans. (c)
The underlined part of the sentence contains an error of relative pronoun. The use of 'which' is incorrect for people and it must be replaced with 'who' to correct the sentence.

80. Either you and he will have to pay for this damage. SSC CGL Tier-1 19.07.2023 (Shift-III)
(a) or he (b) with he
(c) but he (d) nor he

Ans. (a)
The underlined part of the given sentence contains an error. We use 'or' with 'either'. Hence, 'or' should be used in place of 'and' to make the sentence correct.

81. Govind is improving his communication skills with a view to become a journalist. SSC CGL Tier-1 19.07.2023 (Shift-IV)
(a) form into (b) achieving
(c) making (d) becoming

Ans. (d)
The underlined word must be replaced with 'becoming' to correct the sentence. The idiom, 'with a view to doing something', means 'with the aim of doing something'.

82. Disability was viewed as God's retribution for wickedness in the past. SSC CGL Tier-1 20.07.2023 (Shift-I)
(a) revenge for legal works
(b) punishment for wrongdoing
(c) payback for doing help
(d) fine for misbehaviour

Ans. (b)
The underlined phrase 'retribution for wickedness' means 'punishment for wrongdoing'.

83. Many noticeable people were present at the function. SSC CGL Tier-1 20.07.2023 (Shift-II)
(a) No substitution (b) noteworthy
(c) celebrity (d) notable

Ans. (d)
The underlined word is incorrect in the context of the sentence. The word 'noticeable' means easily seen, clear or apparent. Hence, it must be replaced by 'notable', which means worthy of attention, important or famous.

84. The man was convicted for murder by the jury but he is not committed it. SSC CGL Tier-1 20.07.2023 (Shift-III)
(a) have not committed it
(b) has not committed it
(c) had not committed it
(d) am not committed it

Ans. (c)
The underlined part of the given sentence contains an error of tense. As the given sentence is in past perfect tense, the use of 'is' is incorrect. It must be replaced with 'had' to correct the sentence.

85. Neither John nor Simon are coming to the meeting. SSC CGL Tier-1 20.07.2023 (Shift-III)
(a) were coming to the meeting
(b) No substitution
(c) are coming to meeting
(d) is coming to the meeting

Ans. (d)
The underlined part of the given sentence contains the error of subject verb agreement. 'Neither .... nor' takes a singular verb and hence, 'are' must be replaced by 'is' to correct the sentence.

86. The family is neither interested in selling the house or rebuilding it. SSC CGL Tier-1 20.07.2023 (Shift-III)
(a) yet rebuilding
(b) not only rebuilding
(c) nor rebuilding
(d) but also rebuilding

Ans. (c)

The underlined part of the sentence contains an error of conjunction. 'Neither' takes 'nor'. Hence, 'or' must be replaced by 'nor'.

87. Brian remained silent during the board meeting, though Rahul was unaware that he had an ace up his sheath the entire time.
SSC CGL Tier-1 20.07.2023 (Shift-IV)
(a) an ace up his sleeve
(b) an ace up his fortune
(c) an ace up his teeth
(d) an ace up his head

Ans. (a)

The underline part of the sentence contains an error. The use of 'sheath' is incorrect in the sentence. Replace it with 'sleeve' to correct the sentence.

The idiom 'an ace up one's sleeve' means secret knowledge or skill that gives someone an advantage.

88. My friend is owing an expensive cell phone. **SSC CGL Tier-1 21.07.2023 (Shift-II)**
(a) own an expensive cell phone
(b) owns an expensive cell phone
(c) No substitution
(d) is own an expensive cell phone

Ans. (b)

The underlined part of the sentence contains an error. The use of verb form 'is owing' is incorrect in the context of the sentence as the sentence is in simple present tense and not continuous. Hence, it must be replaced by 'owns'.

89. The players distributed the reward between themselves.
SSC CGL Tier-1 21.07.2023 (Shift-II)
(a) between them
(b) among themselves
(c) between their selves
(d) amongst their self

Ans. (b)

The underlined part of the sentence contains an error. The use of preposition 'between' is incorrect in the context of the sentence. Hence, it must be replaced by 'among' as more than two people are mentioned. 'Between' is used in the context of two people or things.

90. Hardly we had boarded the train when it started to move.
SSC CGL Tier-1 21.07.2023 (Shift-II)
(a) will we boarded
(b) we are boarded
(c) is we boarded
(d) had we boarded

Ans. (d)

The underlined part of the sentence contains an error. Hence, it must be replaced by 'had we boarded' to correct it.

'Hardly' adverb is generally used when emphasising that one event quickly followed another. The verb describing the earlier event is usually in the past perfect tense. Also, helping verb 'had' comes before the subject 'we' in such situation. When 'Hardly' is in the initial position, 'Hardly' is followed by 'when' is such situations.

91. Greenhouse gas trapped beside Earth's atmosphere cause global warming.
SSC CGL Tier-1 21.07.2023 (Shift-III)
(a) trapped inside (b) No substitution
(c) trapped outside (d) trapped beyond

Ans. (a)

The underlined part of the sentence contains the error of preposition. The use of 'beside' is incorrect in the context of the sentence. Hence, it must be replaced by 'inside' to correct the sentence.

92. While he saw the bear, he ran to the nearest trees, dropped his gun and climbed to a safe place.
SSC CGL Tier-1 21.07.2023 (Shift-III)
(a) When he saw the bear
(b) No substitution
(c) No sooner did the bear
(d) Hardly he saw the bear

Ans. (a)

The underlined part of the sentence contains an error. The use of 'While' is incorrect as the sentence does not contrast. Hence, it must be replaced with 'When' to make the sentence correct.

93. The family has visit many parts of Europe when the man was working with an international educational agency. **SSC CGL Tier-1 21.07.2023 (Shift-III)**
(a) had visited (b) are visited
(c) have visit (d) has visiting

Ans. (a)

The underlined part of the given sentence contains an error of tense. As the given sentence is in past perfect tense, 'had visited' should be used in place of the underlined part.

94. The Moon is Earth's only natural satellite and the nearby large celestial body. **SSC CGL Tier-1 21.07.2023 (Shift-IV)**
(a) the near largest
(b) the nearest large
(c) No substitution
(d) the nearly large

Ans. (b)

The underlined part of the given sentence contains an error. The use of 'nearby' is incorrect in the context of the sentence. Hence, it must be replaced with 'nearest' to correct the sentence.

95. Parents should tell their children to exercise great care when crossed busy roads. **SSC CGL Tier-1 21.07.2023 (Shift-IV)**
(a) has crossed (b) crossing
(c) cross (d) has been crossing

Ans. (b)

The underlined verb form is incorrect and must be replaced by 'crossing' to correct the sentence.

Continuous form 'crossing' is appropriate because the sentence refers to an ongoing action.

96. This compartment is reserved for military person.
SSC CGL Tier-1 21.07.2023 (Shift-IV)
(a) military personal
(b) military personality
(c) military members
(d) military personnel

Ans. (d)

The underlined part of the sentence contains an error. The use of 'person' is incorrect in the context of the sentence.

Hence, it must be replaced by 'personnel' to correct the sentence. 'Personnel' refers to a body of person employed in an organisation.

97. If only I was young again.
SSC CGL Tier-1 24.07.2023 (Shift-I)
(a) I were young again.
(b) I be young again.
(c) I will be young again.
(d) I am young again.

Ans. (a)

The underlined part of the sentence contains the error of tense. 'Were' instead of 'was' is used with expressions that are hypothetical, wishful, imagined, desired, doubtful and otherwise contrary to fact -not real. Hence, 'were' should be used in place of 'was' to correct the sentence.

98. The girl in the water whistled with full might and waved my arms to draw attention to her plight.
SSC CGL Tier-1 24.07.2023 (Shift-II)
(a) her arms (b) our arms
(c) his arms (d) their arms

Ans. (a)

The underlined part of the given sentence contains an error of possessive adjective. The use of 'my' is incorrect as the sentence is referring to the girl as third person. Hence, it must be replaced by 'her'.

99. The government has finally agreed to wave the entertainment tax on the movie. SSC CGL Tier-1 24.07.2023 (Shift-II)

(a) waive (b) wager
(c) waiver (d) web

Ans. (a)

The underlined word is incorrect in the context of the sentence. Hence, it must be replaced with 'waive' meaning 'to give up'.

100. Abraham Lincoln has been the sixteenth President of the United States and save the Union at the American civil war.
SSC CGL Tier-1 24.07.2023 (Shift-II)

(a) No substitution
(b) save the Union alongside
(c) saved the Union during
(d) saved the Union on

Ans. (c)

The underlined part of the sentence contains an error of tense and preposition. The sentence is referring to the past tense and 'have' is not appropriate in this context. Also, preposition 'at' not suitable in the given context.

Hence, the underlined part must be replaced by 'saved the Union during' to correct the sentence.

101. Delegates of the conflicting countries formally meet at a conference to ironing out their differences.
SSC CGL Tier-1 24.07.2023 (Shift-III)

(a) No substitution (b) No ironed
(c) for iron in (d) to iron out

Ans. (d)

The underlined part of the sentence contains an error of tense. The use of verb form 'ironing' is incorrect in the context of the sentence. Here, infinite form of 'iron' is used with 'to' as per the context of the sentence. Hence, 'ironing' must be replaced by 'iron'.

102. You can always dependent on me.
SSC CGL Tier-1 24.07.2023 (Shift-IV)

(a) depend over me (b) depend for me
(c) depend at me (d) depend on me

Ans. (d)

The underlined part of the given sentence contains an error in the use of the word 'dependent'. Since the sentence is implying a verb in this context, instead of the adjective 'dependent'.

The phrase 'depend on' means to rely on or trust someone or something. Hence, it must be replaced with 'depend' to correct the sentence.

103. My friend Meera and her mother is visiting me this weekend.
SSC CGL Tier-1 25.07.2023 (Shift-II)

(a) have visiting (b) am visiting
(c) was visiting (d) are visiting

Ans. (d)

The underlined part of the sentence contains an error of Subject verb agreement. As the subject is plural, 'are' should be used in place of 'is'.

104. I've got a lot of homeworks this weekend. SSC CGL Tier-1 25.07.2023 (Shift-II)

(a) a lot of homework
(b) No substitution
(c) a lots of homework
(d) much homework

Ans. (a)

The underlined part of the sentence contains an error as the word 'homeworks' is incorrect. The word 'homework' does not have any plural form.

105. The young boy displayed an aptitude on scientific research.
SSC CGL Tier-1 25.07.2023 (Shift-III)

(a) aptitude for (b) aptitude at
(c) aptitude by (d) aptitude in

Ans. (a)

The underlined part of the sentence contains the error as the phrasal verb used is incorrect.

The correct phrasal verb is 'aptitude for' which means a natural ability or skill in a particular area.

106. He had given me that book in 1999.
SSC CGL Tier-1 25.07.2023 (Shift-III)

(a) did given me (b) was given me
(c) gives me (d) gave me

Ans. (d)

The underlined part of the sentence contains the error as the given sentence is in simple past tense not in past perfect tense.

Thus, 'gave me' should be used in place of 'had given me' to correct the sentences.

107. There is a charm on the midnight air which all cannot experience.
SSC CGL Tier-1 26.07.2023 (Shift-I)

(a) over the midnight air
(b) around the midnight air
(c) in the midnight air
(d) under the midnight air

Ans. (c)

The phrase 'on the midnight air' is not idiomatically correct. 'In the midnight air' suggests that the charm is in intrinsic quality of the midnight air itself, which is the meaning of the sentence is most likely try to convey.

108. After finishing this assignment, the employees make it a day.
SSC CGL Tier-1 26.07.2023 (Shift-I)

(a) call it a day
(b) consider it a day
(c) stop it a day
(d) ring it a day

Ans. (a)

The underlined part of the given sentence contains the error of idiom. The correct idiom is 'call it a day' meaning 'to end the day and stop the work'.

109. Honesty as well as discipline are required to succeed in life.
SSC CGL Tier-1 26.07.2023 (Shift-I)

(a) are requirement to succeed in life
(b) is required to succeed in life
(c) has required to succeed in life
(d) No substitution

Ans. (b)

The underlined part of the given sentence contains the error of subject verb agreement. When two subjects are joined with 'as well as' the verb agrees with the first subject. The verb 'is' should be used in place of 'are' because honesty is the singular subject.

110. I love to read certain stories from a Mahabharata.
SSC CGL Tier-1 26.07.2023 (Shift-IV)

(a) certain (b) to (c) love (d) the

Ans. (d)

The underlined word 'a' is erroneous because article 'the' is used before the names of works of famous literature or epics. Hence, 'a' should be replaced by 'the' to correct the sentence.

111. He described about the scenery yesterday. SSC CGL Tier-1 27.07.2023 (Shift-I)

(a) described about the scenary
(b) described the scenery
(c) describing about the scenery
(d) describe the scenery

Ans. (b)

The underlined part of the sentence contains an error of preposition. The use of preposition 'about' is unnecessary with 'described' and hence must be removed to correct the sentence.

112. I worked hard so that I might success.
SSC CGL Tier-1 27.07.2023 (Shift-I)

(a) that I may success
(b) that I might successful
(c) that I might succeed
(d) that I might successor

Ans. (c)

The underlined part of the sentence contains an error.

The use of the noun 'success' is incorrect in the context of the sentence. It must be replaced by the verb 'succeed' to correct the sentence.

113. The stranger stood quietly for few moments. SSC CGL Tier-1 27.07.2023 (Shift-I)

(a) for the few moments
(b) No improvement required
(c) for moments
(d) for a few moments

Ans. (d)

The underlined part of the sentence contains an error. Add 'a' before 'few' to correct the sentence.

114. Polyethylene terephthalate, one of the most often recycled plastics and the material used in the majority of water and soda bottles, can be transformed into everything from polyester fabric to automotive parts.
SSC CGL Tier-1 27.07.2023 (Shift-III)

(a) might be placed
(b) might be evolved
(c) may be converted
(d) may be devaluated

Ans. (c)

The phrase 'may be converted' means the same as 'can be transformed'.

115. The secretary to my boss is very efficient as he not only gives him the required information and also handles correspondence independently.
SSC CGL Tier-1 27.07.2023 (Shift-III)

(a) yet also handles
(b) but also handles
(c) along with also handles
(d) not also handles

Ans. (b)

The underlined part of the sentence contains an error of conjunction. The use of 'and' is incorrect as 'not only' takes 'but also'.

Hence, 'and' should be replaced by 'but' to correct the sentence.

116. Edward II is tragic than some other plays by the dramatist.
SSC CGL Tier-2 02.03.2023

(a) as least tragic as
(b) No substitution required
(c) the most tragic
(d) less tragic than

Ans. (d)

The adjective in the sentence is tragic. The adjective will be used in the comparative form. To make the comparative of tragic we will add 'less' before it. Hence, 'less tragic than' is the most appropriate answer.

117. Bloomberg Businessweek is not more popular than some other business magazines in the US.
SSC CGL Tier-2 07.03.2023

(a) No substitution required
(b) the most popular than
(c) as more popular than
(d) so popular than

Ans. (a)

The given sentence is grammatically correct.

118. This is the challenge task I have ever encountered. SSC CGL Tier-2 26.10.2023

(a) more challenging
(b) most challenging
(c) challenging
(d) much challenging

Ans. (b)

Definite article 'the' is used for a specific or particular thing and before a superlative degree adjective. 'Most challenging' is the correct superlative degree of 'challenging'. Hence, 'most challenging' is the most appropriate answer.

119. Ashoka was not only a great warrior but also a very wiser ruler.

(a) more wise SSC CGL Tier-2 26.10.2023
(b) No correction required
(c) wisest
(d) wise

Ans. (d)

'Very' is a positive adverb and takes a positive degree adjective after it. Hence, 'wise' is the most appropriate answer.

120. Cinema provides the most universal entertainment. SSC CGL Tier-2 26.10.2023

(a) No correction required
(b) a universal
(c) an universal
(d) more universal

Ans. (b)

There are some adjectives that can not be written in comparative or superlative degree. These adjectives are called absolute or non-gradable' adjectives. Some examples are universal, absolute, complete, perfect, empty, full, etc. Hence, 'a universal' is the most appropriate answer.

121. He is taller and most handsome than his friend. SSC CGL Tier-2 26.10.2023

(a) very more (b) more
(c) the more (d) the most

Ans. (b)

If two or more adjectives are joined with a conjunction, these adjectives are written in the same degree. In the given sentence, 'and' joins two adjectives, out of which one is comparative degree all. Therefore, the second adjective will also be written in comparative degree. 'More handsome' is the correct comparative degree of 'handsome.' Hence, 'more' is the most appropriate answer.

SSC CGL 2022 (Tier 1 & 2)

122. The student apologised the teacher for the delay in submitting the assignment.
SSC CGL Tier-1 11.04.2022 (Shift-III)

(a) No substitution required
(b) is apologising the teacher
(c) apologised to the teacher
(d) has apologised the teacher

Ans. (c)

The preposition 'to' is missing in the given sentence. Hence, 'apologised to the teacher' is the most appropriate answer.

123. I have been wondering at taking skating as a hobby.
SSC CGL Tier-1 11.04.2022 (Shift-II)

(a) on taking to (b) about taking up
(c) to take up
(d) No improvement required

Ans. (b)

There is a prepositional error in the given sentence. The preposition 'at' must be replaced with 'about' as we generally use the preposition 'about' with 'wonder'. Hence, 'about taking up' is the most appropriate answer.

124. He's not so friendly like she is
SSC CGL Tier-1 12.04.2022 (Shift-III)

(a) so friendly as
(b) as friendly like
(c) so friendly that
(d) No improvement required

Ans. (a)

'As' is used for comparing people or things and 'like' is used for giving examples. However, in the given sentence, two persons are being compared on the basis of friendliness. Hence, 'so friendly as' is the most appropriate answer.

125. We might as well watch a film on TV as there's nothing much to do.
SSC CGL Tier-1 12.04.2022 (Shift-III)

(a) No improvement required
(b) may as such
(c) may as well as
(d) might well

Ans. (a)

The sentence is grammatically correct.

126. The old lady needed love and care beyond money.
SSC CGL Tier-1 13.04.2022 (Shift-I)
(a) besides
(b) No substitution required
(c) beside
(d) beneath

Ans. (a)
'Besides' means in addition to or as well as somebody/something. The given sentence states that the old lady needed love and care as well as money. Hence, 'besides' is the most appropriate answer.

127. I imagine you have learnt a valuable lesson from this experience, didn't you? **SSC CGL Tier-1 13.04.2022 (Shift-I)**
(a) did you?
(b) haven't you?
(c) have you?
(d) No substitution required

Ans. (b)
According to the 'Question Tag rule', if the statement is positive, the question tag will be negative but in the contracted form (t) and *vice-versa*. However, the sentence and the question tag must be in the same tense.
Similarly, the given sentence is positive, so the question tag will be negative (haven't). Hence, 'haven't you?' is the most appropriate answer.

128. My father was always ordering about my sister. **SSC CGL Tier-1 13.04.2022 (Shift-II)**
(a) ordering on my sister
(b) ordering my sister about
(c) No improvement required
(d) giving order for my sister

Ans. (b)
The position of the preposition 'about' is incorrect in the given sentence, it must be placed after the noun sister. Hence, 'ordering my sister about' is the most appropriate answer.

129. None of the boys was willing to admit that he was in the wrong.
SSC CGL Tier-1 13.04.2022 (Shift-III)
(a) No substitution required
(b) willing to admitting
(c) ready to admitting
(d) admit

Ans. (a)
The sentence is grammatically correct.

130. You are welcome to partake this light refreshment.
SSC CGL Tier-1 13.04.2022 (Shift-III)
(a) No improvement required
(b) to partake of
(c) for partaking
(d) in partaken

Ans. (b)
The phrase 'partake of' means to experience something along with others or to have a portion.
The given sentence states that you are welcome to have a portion of this light refreshment. Hence, 'to partake of' is the most appropriate answer.

131. This TV channel has a larger viewership from another channel.
SSC CGL Tier-1 18.04.2022 (Shift-I)
(a) from the other channel
(b) than any other channel
(c) No substitution required
(d) from-any other channel

Ans. (b)
We always use 'than' when we compare two things, people, etc. Similarly in the given sentence, the viewership of a TV channel is being compared with all the other channels. Hence, 'than any other channel' is the most appropriate answer.

132. In spite of my niece's dog Casper is very mischievous, he is lovable.
SSC CGL Tier-1 18.04.2022 (Shift-I)
(a) Nevertheless my niece
(b) No substitution required
(c) Although my niece's
(d) However my nieces

Ans. (c)
The phrase 'in spite of' will be replaced with 'although' which means 'and yet'.
However, the given sentence states that the narrator's niece's dog Casper is very mischievous and yet he is lovable. Hence, 'although my niece's' is the most appropriate answer.

133. They each listened carefully to what each other said.
SSC CGL Tier-1 18.04.2022 (Shift-III)
(a) each another
(b) No improvement required
(c) the other
(d) one another

Ans. (c)
We will remove 'each' to grammatically correct the given sentence. Hence, 'the other' is the most appropriate answer.

134. While the online class was going on, they had to keep their cameras on.
SSC CGL Tier-1 18.04.2022 (Shift-II)
(a) No substitution required
(b) have their cameras on
(c) are keeping their cameras on
(d) had keep the camera on

Ans. (a)
The sentence is grammatically correct.

135. The dress may pleasantly be delivered to us at the earliest.
SSC CGL Tier-1 19.04.2022 (Shift-II)
(a) No substitution required
(b) may kindly
(c) might kindly
(d) must pleasantly

Ans. (b)
We will replace 'pleasantly' with 'kindly' to grammatically correct the given sentence. Hence, 'may kindly' is the most appropriate answer.

136. Since setting up, the charity has raised a million dollars.
SSC CGL Tier-1 19.04.2022 (Shift-II)
(a) Since being set up
(b) From setting up f
(c) Since setting
(d) No improvement required

Ans. (a)
The initial part of the given sentence is incomplete as it requires a gerund (being). Hence, 'since being set up' is the most appropriate answer.

137. I can't make out my mind about taking a vacation in winter.
SSC CGL Tier-1 19.04.2022 (Shift-III)
(a) make up
(b) made out
(c) No substitution required
(d) make on

Ans. (a)
'Make up one's mind' is a phrase that means to make a decision. Similarly in the given sentence, the narrator is unable to decide about taking a vacation.
Hence, 'make up' is the most appropriate answer.

138. There are a bit nice shops in the town centre. **SSC CGL Tier-1 20.04.2022 (Shift-II)**
(a) a bit nicer
(b) far more nicer
(c) No improvement required
(d) far nicer

Ans. (d)
We cannot use the article 'a' before shops (plural) and we cannot write 'more' with a comparative degree 'nicer'. Hence, 'far nicer' is the most appropriate answer.

139. Would you have been so kind as to close the window?
SSC CGL Tier-1 20.04.2022 (Shift-II)
(a) No substitution required
(b) Would you be
(c) Would you being
(d) Will you been

Ans. (b)

We generally use the modal verb 'would' when we want to politely request someone for something. Similarly in the given sentence, someone is asking politely to close the window. Hence, 'would you be' is the most appropriate answer.

140. Often it makes one wonder at the sights you see. SSC CGL Tier-1 20.04.2022 (Shift-III)
(a) one sees
(b) one see
(c) you saw
(d) No substitution required

Ans. (a)

'One' means any person, but not any particular person. However, when we use 'one' in a sentence we always use 'one' as a pronoun not pronouns like you, him, he, etc.

Moreover, 'one' is a singular subject, so it will take 'sees' as a singular verb. Hence, 'one sees' is the most appropriate answer.

141. It is quite difficult to make on what this doctor writes. SSC CGL Tier-1 20.04.2022 (Shift-III)
(a) make out
(b) make in
(c) No substitution required
(d) made on

Ans. (a)

'Make out' is a phrasal verb which means to see, hear or understand something with difficulty. The given sentence states that it is difficult to understand what this doctor writes. Hence, 'make out' is the most appropriate answer.

142. Whom was the person that you wanted me to contact there? SSC CGL Tier-1 21.04.2022 (Shift-I)
(a) No substitution required
(b) Who is the person
(c) Whom is the person
(d) Whom were the persons

Ans. (b)

If the relative pronoun is followed by a 'verb', then the relative pronoun must be 'who' and if it is followed by a 'noun or pronoun', then the relative pronoun must be 'whom'. Similarly, in the given sentence, the relative pronoun is followed by a 'verb (was)'. Hence, 'who is the person' is the most appropriate answer.

143. We had to undergo a great many difficulties. SSC CGL Tier-1 21.04.2022 (Shift-II)
(a) No improvement
(b) a great many difficulty
(c) great many difficulties
(d) much great difficulties

Ans. (a)

The sentence is grammatically correct.

144. I don't fancy to go out this evening. SSC CGL Tier-1 21.04.2022 (Shift-II)
(a) to going outside
(b) No improvement required
(c) to be going out
(d) going out

Ans. (d)

The sentence will take a bare infinitive (without the preposition 'to'). Hence, 'going out' is the most appropriate answer.

145. After finishing high school, I plan to pursuing law. SSC CGL Tier-1 01.12.2022 (Shift-I)
(a) No substitution
(b) plan to pursue
(c) plan in pursue
(d) plan to pursuing

Ans. (b)

V1 is used after 'to'. So, 'plan to pursue' is most appropriate to substitute 'plan to pursuing' in the given sentence.

146. Our guests arrived; they are sitting in the garden. SSC CGL Tier-1 01.12.2022 (Shift-I)
(a) shall arrive (b) have arrived
(c) are arriving (d) might arrive

Ans. (b)

'Have arrived' is most appropriate to substitute the underlined segment i.e., 'arrived' is the given sentence. Present Perfect Tense will be used in the sentence as per the context.

147. He was looking into his book for the last two hours but couldn't find it. SSC CGL Tier-1 01.12.2022 (Shift-I)
(a) looking down on his book
(b) looking above his book
(c) looking for his book
(d) looking after his book

Ans. (c)

'Looking for his book' should substitute the underlined segment in the given sentence. 'Look for somebody/something' is a phrasal verb which means to try to find something that has been lost.

148. Rajan is having three brothers and three sisters. SSC CGL Tier-1 01.12.2022 (Shift-II)
(a) Rajan has been having
(b) Rajan has
(c) Rajan was having
(d) Rajan having

Ans. (b)

'Rajan has' is appropriate to substitute the underlined segment in the given sentence. In the stative sense, we cannot use a continuous tense.

149. The new shop that opened last week are hardly sufficient stock of the products that it advertised about. SSC CGL Tier-1 01.12.2022 (Shift-IV)
(a) hardly hand't (b) hardly had
(c) hardly is having (d) is had

Ans. (b)

Based on the context of the sentence, 'hardly had' can substitute 'are hardly' as the sentence is in past tense.

150. Abu said that he saw the picture. SSC CGL Tier-1 02.12.2022 (Shift-I)
(a) he has seen the picture
(b) he will have seen the picture
(c) he would have seen the picture
(d) he had seen the picture

Ans. (d)

The most appropriate substitute for the underlined segment to make the sentence grammatically correct is 'he had seen the picture'.

151. Solomon always refers in the dictionary for clearing doubts about words. SSC CGL Tier-1 02.12.2022 (Shift-II)
(a) on the dictionary
(b) No substitution
(c) to the dictionary
(d) with the dictionary

Ans. (c)

The underlined segment is not grammatically correct because 'in' is not generally used with 'refer'. The word 'to' is generally used with the verb 'refer' as one always 'refers to' something. Thus, the correct answer is 'to the dictionary'.

152. Mr. Raghav racked his brain, but couldn't think where he had left the book. SSC CGL Tier-1 02.12.2022 (Shift-II)
(a) thought very hard
(b) had a series of consecutive thoughts
(c) knew it, but couldn't quite remember it
(d) thought he had heard something before

Ans. (a)

The phrase 'rack one's brain' means making a great effort to think of or remember something. Thus, the correct answer is 'thought very hard'.

153. One of my friends is gone to Goa for a holiday. SSC CGL Tier-1 02.12.2022 (Shift-II)
(a) has gone (b) are gone
(c) gone (d) were gone

Ans. (a)

The most appropriate option in order to make the sentence grammatically correct is 'has gone' because 'has' (instead of 'is') is used when the sentence is in present perfect tense.

154. Finally, here are a few examples of passages and their precis.
SSC CGL Tier-1 02.12.2022 (Shift-II)

(a) by passages and their precis
(b) of passages and there precis
(c) of passages and there precises
(d) No substitution

Ans. (d)

The given sentence is correct and does not need any substitution.

155. Our office is in the 2nd floor of the skyscraper.
SSC CGL Tier-1 02.12.2022 (Shift-III)

(a) is for the 2nd floor
(b) is on the 2nd floor
(c) is with the 2nd floor
(d) is at the 2nd floor

Ans. (b)

The correct answer is 'is on the 2nd floor' because the preposition 'on' is the right one in the context of the sentence.

156. Rajesh was angry at himself for making a silly mistake during the examination.
SSC CGL Tier-1 02.12.2022 (Shift-IV)

(a) for (b) on (c) above (d) with

Ans. (d)

The correct answer is 'with' because preposition 'with' is used with the word 'angry'.

157. We live in a populated country of 120 million people.
SSC CGL Tier-1 02.12.2022 (Shift-IV)

(a) congested (b) dense
(c) populous (d) No substitute

Ans. (c)

The appropriate option to substitute the word 'populated' is 'populous', which means having a large population.

158. I used to swim across the river when I was young.
SSC CGL Tier-1 03.12.2022 (Shift-I)

(a) will swim across
(b) was swimming across
(c) could swim across
(d) can swim across

Ans. (c)

The correct option to substitute the underlined segment, based on the context of the sentence, is 'could swim across'. 'Could' is used to describe an activity in the past.

159. Last before year, Shirley got very good grades.
SSC CGL Tier-1 03.12.2022 (Shift-I)

(a) The last year before
(b) Before last year
(c) The year before last
(d) Before year last

Ans. (c)

The most appropriate option to substitute the underlined segment is 'the year before last' because it has the correct order of the words to refer to the year before the previous year.

160. I am been working here for the past ten years. **SSC CGL Tier-1 03.12.2022 (Shift-I)**

(a) have been working here
(b) is been working here
(c) was been working here
(d) had been working here

Ans. (a)

The correct answer is 'have been working here' because the sentence needs to be in present perfect continuous tense as the action started in the past and continues till the present.

161. Oscar is the most prestigious award which is introduced to good actors in that year. **SSC CGL Tier-1 03.12.2022 (Shift-II)**

(a) rewarded to good
(b) nominated to fine
(c) awarded to the best
(d) attached to fine

Ans. (c)

The most appropriate option to substitute the underlined segment is 'awarded to the best' as 'awarded' is the right word to use in the context of an award and fits the sentence.

162. When I reached home late, I found my children waiting on me.
SSC CGL Tier-1 03.12.2022 (Shift-II)

(a) waiting with me
(b) waiting by me
(c) waiting about me
(d) waiting for me

Ans. (d)

The correct answer is 'waiting for me' because 'for' is more suitable in the context of awaiting someone.

163. Not only is my brother intelligent though hard working too.
SSC CGL Tier-1 03.12.2022 (Shift-II)

(a) or hard working
(b) but hard working
(c) so hard working
(d) yet hard working

Ans. (b)

The most appropriate option to substitute the underlined segment is 'but hard working' because 'but' is used as a linking word to connect ideas that contrast like in the given sentence where the person is intelligent but also hardworking.

164. During my Goa tour, I had visited beaches in Vasco, Baga and Vagator.
SSC CGL Tier-1 03.12.2022 (Shift-III)

(a) visited (b) have visited
(c) was visited (d) has visited

Ans. (a)

As the sentence describes an event that happened in the past, simple present tense will be used in it. So, 'visited' should substitute 'had visited' in the given sentence.

165. Have you want me to come with you to the dentist?
SSC CGL Tier-1 15.12.2022 (Shift-I)

(a) Had you want me
(b) Do you want me
(c) Has you wanted me
(d) No substitution required

Ans. (b)

'Do you want me' should be used in place of 'Have you want me' to make the sentence grammatically correct.

Do/Does is used in yes/no interrogative questions.

166. Don't disturb the boy, he prepares for his examination.
SSC CGL Tier-1 15.12.2022 (Shift-I)

(a) prepared (b) will be preparing
(c) was preparing (d) is preparing

Ans. (d)

The given sentence is referring to an action which is in progress. Hence, 'is preparing' should be used in place of 'prepares' to make the sentence grammatically correct.

167. Rita will never have changed her job if she would have been promoted.
SSC CGL Tier-1 15.12.2022 (Shift-I)

(a) No substitution
(b) should never have
(c) would never have
(d) shall never have

Ans. (c)

'Would never have' is most appropriate to substitute the underlined segment in the given sentence as per the context.

168. The art history teacher was sacked after she were thought taking school supplies. **SSC CGL Tier-1 05.12.2022 (Shift-I)**

(a) she was wondered
(b) she was dumped
(c) she was caught
(d) she was enlightened

Ans. (c)

'She was caught' makes sense with the given sentence. So, it should replace the understand segment in the given sentence.

169. I know she really wants the promotion, but she really hit me below the hand by telling the boss about my personal problems. **SSC CGL Tier-1 05.12.2022 (Shift-I)**

(a) hit me the bricks
(b) hit me below the books
(c) hit me below the bottle
(d) hit me below the belt

Ans. (d)

'Hit me below the belt' can correctly replace the underlined part of the given sentence. 'Hit below the belt' means to say something that is often too personal, usually irrelevant, and always unfair.

170. The banker warned me not to be careless from my ATM card. **SSC CGL Tier-1 05.12.2022 (Shift-III)**

(a) careless beside (b) careless with
(c) careless across (d) careless on

Ans. (b)

The preposition 'with' should be used with 'careless'.

So, the most appropriate preposition to substitute the underlined collocation is given in option (b) i.e. 'careless with'.

171. Every nook and corner of the house were unclean. **SSC CGL Tier-1 05.12.2022 (Shift-III)**

(a) of a house was unclean
(b) by the house were unclean
(c) to the house were unclean
(d) of the house was unclean

Ans. (d)

The pronoun 'every' agrees with a singular verb, So, the underlined segment in the given sentences can be substituted with 'of the house was unclean'.

172. Rearing of silk worms is called horticulture. **SSC CGL Tier-1 05.12.2022 (Shift-III)**

(a) Pisciculture (b) Agriculture
(c) Sericulture (d) Apiculture

Ans. (c)

The word 'sericulture' means the production of silk and the rearing of silkworms for the purpose. Hence; 'sericulture' is most appropriate to substitute 'horticulture' in the given sentence. 'Horticulture' refers to the study or activity of cultivating garden plants.

173. Santa Claus stays at the North Pole when he isn't out deliver gifts for Christmas. **SSC CGL Tier-1 05.12.2022 (Shift-III)**

(a) out to delivering
(b) out delivering
(c) No substitution
(d) out of deliver

Ans. (b)

'out delivering' from the given options is most appropriate to substitute 'out deliver' in the sentence.

174. Mother ordered John to switch on the light as it was time to sleep. **SSC CGL Tier-1 05.12.2022 (Shift-IV)**

(a) to switch of the light
(b) to switch in the light
(c) to switch off the light
(d) to switch out the light

Ans. (c)

The most appropriate option that can substitute the underlined segment is 'to switch off the light' because in the context of the sentence it is time to sleep and lights are switched off during this time.

175. The intern should take a right choice in choosing the right job for her. **SSC CGL Tier-1 05.12.2022 (Shift-IV)**

(a) rake a right choice
(b) make a right choice
(c) fix a right choice
(d) take the right choice

Ans. (b)

The most appropriate collocation to substitute the underlined word in the given sentence is 'make a right choice' because this term means to make the right decision or do the right thing which fits the context of the sentence.

176. Biden write a letter to the Russian President to restrain from war. **SSC CGL Tier-1 05.12.2022 (Shift-IV)**

(a) writes a letter
(b) wrote a letter
(c) write a good letter
(d) writing a surprise letter

Ans. (b)

The most appropriate answer is 'wrote a letter' as the sentence is in simple past tense and 'write' should be replaced by 'wrote'.

177. I have reached the hotel, by the time you call me. **SSC CGL Tier-1 06.12.2022 (Shift-I)**

(a) will be reaching the hotel
(b) No substitution
(c) will have reached the hotel
(d) had reached the hotel

Ans. (c)

The most appropriate option is 'will have reached the hotel' because the sentence is in the future perfect tense where an action would be completed at a time in the future.

178. Old people acquire experience through age. **SSC CGL Tier-1 06.12.2022 (Shift-I)**

(a) got experience
(b) developed experience
(c) experienced
(d) gain experience

Ans. (d)

The meaning of the word 'acquire' is to obtain, gain, learn or develop something. Thus, the correct option to replace the underlined segment 'acquire experience' is 'gain experience'.

179. He did not admit that his team played badly. **SSC CGL Tier-1 06.12.2022 (Shift-I)**

(a) never admitted
(b) yesterday admitted
(c) happily admitted
(d) willingly admitted

Ans. (a)

An adverb of frequency in a sentence tells us how often an action takes place and 'never' is an adverb of frequency as it tells us that something never happens. Thus, the correct answer is 'never admitted'.

180. The soldiers had no choice to 'report' the loss to their commander. **SSC CGL Tier-1 06.12.2022 (Shift-II)**

(a) no choice as to
(b) no choice how to
(c) No substitution required
(d) no choice but to

Ans. (d)

The phrase 'no choice but to do something' means that something can't be avoided and has to be done. Thus, the correct answer is 'no choice but to' as it fits the context of the sentence where there is no choice and the loss has to be reported to the commander.

181. She acted as if she is the one who was hurt. **SSC CGL Tier-1 06.12.2022 (Shift-III)**

(a) as if she has been
(b) as if she will be
(c) as if she would
(d) as if she was

Ans. (d)

The given sentence is in past tense. Thus, 'she is' is not right in the context of the sentence and 'is' should be replaced with 'was'. Hence, the correct answer is 'as if she was'.

182. I am working hard in order to earn a decent living.
SSC CGL Tier-1 06.12.2022 (Shift-IV)
(a) buying a decent living
(b) earning a better living
(c) purchase a reputed life
(d) No substitution
Ans. (d)
No substitution is required in the given sentence.

183. We congratulated him at his new job. He was delighted.
SSC CGL Tier-1 06.12.2022 (Shift-IV)
(a) congratulate him up
(b) congratulated him on
(c) congratulate him with
(d) congratulate him along
Ans. (b)
The preposition 'on' is used with 'congratulated'. So, 'congratulated him on' is the most appropriate collocation to substitute the underlined words in the given sentence.

184. She lived in well-resourced surroundings.
SSC CGL Tier-1 07.12.2022 (Shift-I)
(a) luxurious
(b) luxuriousness
(c) luxury
(d) No substitute
Ans. (a)
'Luxurious' is the most appropriate word to substitute the underlined segment in the given sentence as it means very expensive, beautiful and comfortable.

185. Unemployment has become a fiery question of the day.
SSC CGL Tier-1 07.12.2022 (Shift-III)
(a) become a burning question
(b) become a freezing question
(c) become a furious question
(d) become a flaming question
Ans. (a)
The underlined segment can be substituted with 'become a burning question'. The idiom 'burning issue/question' means something that people have strong opinions about and think is very important.

186. Estella had hardly heard the news (after) she began to weep.
SSC CGL Tier-1 07.12.2022 (Shift-III)
(a) while (b) well
(c) than (d) when
Ans. (d)
'Hardly......when' is the correct syntax. So, 'when' should substitute 'after' to make the sentence meaningful.

187. They spoke about the political turmoil in the state.
SSC CGL Tier-1 07.12.2022 (Shift-III)
(a) expressed (b) said
(c) talked (d) stated
Ans. (c)
'talked' should replace 'spoke' in the given sentence as per the context.

188. The yellow dress purchased by you is not much different than the one I have brought.
SSC CGL Tier-1 07.12.2022 (Shift-IV)
(a) different then the one
(b) different as the one
(c) different above the one
(d) different from the one
Ans. (d)
The preposition 'from' is used with 'different'. So, 'different from the one' can substitute the underlined segment in the given sentence.

189. There are many people in the world who believe that the earth is flat.
SSC CGL Tier-1 07.12.2022 (Shift-IV)
(a) who belief that
(b) who should believe that
(c) No substitution
(d) who believed
Ans. (c)
No substitution is required in the given sentence.

190. Give us some room for improvement.
SSC CGL Tier-1 07.12.2022 (Shift-IV)
(a) an opportunity for improvement
(b) room in a house for improvement
(c) advice for improvement
(d) a warning for improvement
Ans. (a)
The idiom 'Room for improvement' means a possibility or hope that someone or something will improve. So, 'an opportunity for improvement' from the given options is closest in meaning to it.

191. When I was your age, I was working two jobs to provide for my family.
SSC CGL Tier-1 08.12.2022 (Shift-I)
(a) to providing for (b) for provide to
(c) on providing (d) No substitution
Ans. (d)
No substitution is required in the given sentence.

192. They met yesterday, haven't they?
SSC CGL Tier-1 08.12.2022 (Shift-II)
(a) don't they? (b) isn't it?
(c) didn't they? (d) did they?
Ans. (c)
'didn't they?' is most appropriate to replace 'haven't they?' in the given sentence as per the context.

193. No sooner did this idea enter his head, than it carried conviction with it.
SSC CGL Tier-1 08.12.2022 (Shift-II)
(a) No sooner does this idea enter
(b) No substitution
(c) No sooner do his idea enter
(d) No sooner has his idea enter
Ans. (b)
No substitution is required in the given sentence.

194. Holi is a festival of revelry and camaraderie which is celebrated between the country.
SSC CGL Tier-1 08.12.2022 (Shift-II)
(a) No substitution
(b) celebrated upon the country
(c) celebrated at the country
(d) celebrated across the country
Ans. (d)
The word 'across' should be used in place of 'between' to make the sentence meaningful as it means in every part of a particular place or country. So, 'celebrated across the country' should substitute the underlined segment in the given sentence.

195. Many companies displaced paying income tax last year.
SSC CGL Tier-1 08.12.2022 (Shift-II)
(a) hedged to paying
(b) circumvent to paying
(c) hedged in paying
(d) evaded paying
Ans. (d)
'Evaded paying' can substitute the underlined segment in the given sentence. 'evaded' means to avoid paying money that you ought to pay, for example tax.

196. The rate of interest for the loan went out all our calculations.
SSC CGL Tier-1 08.12.2022 (Shift-III)
(a) under all our calculations
(b) No substitution
(c) beyond all our calculations
(d) besides all our calculations
Ans. (c)
'Beyond all our calculations' is most appropriate to substitute 'Out all our calculations' in the given sentence. 'Go beyond something' means to be more than or not limited to something.

197. Shyama does not laugh, nor she smiles.
SSC CGL Tier-1 08.12.2022 (Shift-III)
(a) nor she does smile
(b) she does smile
(c) nor does she smile
(d) nor she smile does
Ans. (c)

'Nor does she smile' is most appropriate to substitute the underlined segment in the given sentence.

198. It was an horrible day at the office for Roy, but he didn't allow it to spoil his evening plans.
SSC CGL Tier-1 08.12.2022 (Shift-IV)
(a) was a horrible day at the office
(b) were a horrible day at office
(c) No substitution
(d) horrible day at the office

Ans. (a)
'An' will not be used with 'horrible' as 'horrible' starts with a consonant. So, 'was a horrible day at the office' is most appropriate to substitute the underlined segment in the given sentence.

199. Computers and mobile phones have become a necessary and important part of our lives.
SSC CGL Tier-1 09.12.2022 (Shift-I)
(a) a requisite (b) an essential
(c) a required (d) a needed

Ans. (b)
'An essential' can substitute 'important' in the given sentence. 'Essential' means completely necessary.

200. He will talk about nothing but films.
SSC CGL Tier-1 09.12.2022 (Shift-I)
(a) was talking at (b) is talking in
(c) shall talking of (d) talks about

Ans. (d)
'Talks about' can substitute the underlined segment in the given sentence. The sentence describes a habit, so Simple Present Tense should be used in it.

201. After a prolonged discussion, Gayatri got a permission from her parents to study law.
SSC CGL Tier-1 09.12.2022 (Shift-I)
(a) got the permission
(b) got proper permission
(c) got permission
(d) got her permission

Ans. (c)
'A' will not be used before 'permission' as it is an uncountable noun. So, 'got permission' is the most appropriate option to substitute 'got a permission' in the given sentence.

202. We have only just enough money to live on now, and if my husband loses his job, we'll really be up again it.
SSC CGL Tier-1 09.12.2022 (Shift-III)
(a) be up gone it (b) be up across it
(c) be up cross it (d) be up against it

Ans. (d)
'Be up against it' should substitute the underlined phrase in the given sentence. 'Up against something' is a phrase which means in a very difficult situation, or with a serious problem to deal with.

203. Blind by a dust storm, they fell into disorder. **SSC CGL Tier-1 09.12.2022 (Shift-III)**
(a) Have been blind
(b) Blinded
(c) Blinding
(d) Being blind

Ans. (b)
'Blinded' is the most appropriate option to substitute, 'Blind' as the sentence talks about an event in the past tense. 'Blinded' means to make if difficult for someone to see for a short time.

204. He was not able to adopt himself to the new environment of the hostel.
SSC CGL Tier-1 09.12.2022 (Shift-IV)
(a) able to adept himself to
(b) able for adopt himself to
(c) able to adopt himself with
(d) able to adapt himself to

Ans. (d)
The appropriate option that can substitute the underlined segment in the given sentence is 'able to adapt himself to' because 'adapt' means to change your ideas or behaviour to make them suitable for a new situation.

205. Neither the teachers (or the principal likes the new budget) cuts.
SSC CGL Tier-1 09.12.2022 (Shift-IV)
(a) either the principal likes the new budget
(b) or the principal like the new budget
(c) nor the principal like the new budget
(d) nor the principal likes the new budget

Ans. (d)
Since 'neither' and 'nor' are used together in a sentence, the correct answer based on the context of the sentence is 'nor the principal likes the new budget.'
With 'neither…nor' the verb must agree with the second subject ('principal' in this case).

206. Scores given by the members are to be consolidated and sent in the head office immediately.
SSC CGL Tier-1 12.12.2022 (Shift-II)
(a) No substitution
(b) after the head office
(c) at the head office
(d) to the head office

Ans. (d)
The correct preposition is 'to' when referring to a destination. Thus, 'in' is not the correct preposition to be used in the given sentence and must be replaced with 'to'.

207. You must aware of friends who speak against you.
SSC CGL Tier-1 12.12.2022 (Shift-II)
(a) caution of (b) beware of
(c) scarce of (d) careful of

Ans. (b)
The meaning of 'beware of' is to be cautious and alert to risk or dangers. Thus, the most appropriate option that can substitute the underlined segment in the given sentence is 'beware of'.

208. The students were warned on coming late to school.
SSC CGL Tier-1 12.12.2022 (Shift-IV)
(a) warned against (b) warned at
(c) warned in (d) warned with

Ans. (a)
'Warned against' can substitute the underlined segment in the given sentences 'warn (somebody) against something' means to advise someone to not to do something because it may have dangerous or unpleasant results.

209. The students decided to surprise their teacher on her birthday.
SSC CGL Tier-1 13.12.2022 (Shift-I)
(a) her teacher on her birthday
(b) there teacher on her birthday
(c) No substitution
(d) their teacher at her birthday

Ans. (c)
No substitution is required in the given sentence as the sentence is grammatically correct and contextually meaningful.

210. The percentage of employees who called in sick and the number of employees who left their jobs within 2 years (were reflective of the level of job satisfaction).
SSC CGL Tier-1 13.12.2022 (Shift-I)
(a) are reflective of the level of job satisfaction.
(b) is reflective of the level of job satisfaction.
(c) were reflective on the level of job satisfaction.
(d) has reflected the level of job satisfaction.

Ans. (a)
Here, 'are reflective of the level of job satisfaction' replaces the given bracketed segment, to make the sentence grammatically correct.

211. He was sitting besides his best friend during the event. SSC CGL Tier-1 13.12.2022 (Shift-I)
(a) was sitting about his
(b) were sitting besides his
(c) was sitting beside his
(d) was sitting besides her

Ans. (c)

In the given sentence, 'beside' should be used as it means next to or very close to the side of someone or something. So, the most appropriate option that can substitute the underlined segment is 'was sitting beside his'.

212. Health club membership has grown by leaps and bounds after the pandemic. SSC CGL Tier-1 13.12.2022 (Shift-I)
(a) slowly and gradually
(b) hurriedly
(c) full of speed and excitement
(d) very quickly

Ans. (d)

The most appropriate option that can substitute the underlined segment in the given sentence is 'very quickly'. 'By leaps and bounds' means very quickly.

213. They decided to have a meeting to discuss about the project. SSC CGL Tier-1 13.12.2022 (Shift-II)
(a) to discuss over the project
(b) to discuss through the project
(c) to discuss the project
(d) to discuss beyond the project

Ans. (c)

'About' is not used with discuss. Hence, replace the underlined segment with 'to discuss the project' to make the sentence grammatically correct.

214. This package is ideal for infant teenager who are just getting started with babysitting. SSC CGL Tier-1 13.12.2022 (Shift-III)
(a) youngest teenagers
(b) younger teenagers
(c) young teenagers
(d) No substitution required

Ans. (c)

'Young teenagers' is most appropriate to substitute 'infant teenager' in the given sentence.

215. Kranthi loves to swim at the local swimming pool in order that relieve his work stress. SSC CGL Tier-1 13.12.2022 (Shift-IV)
(a) in order which
(b) No substitution required
(c) In order as to relieve
(d) in order to relieve

Ans. (d)

'In order to relieve' should substitute the underlined segment to make the sentence grammatically correct.

216. The bus is now full of passengers, it will leave soon. SSC CGL Tier-1 13.12.2022 (Shift-IV)
(a) is leaving (b) has to leave
(c) leaves (d) is going to leave

Ans. (d)

'Is going to leave' should substitute the underlined segment to make the sentence correct.

217. The man which was present at the meeting spoke against the chairperson. SSC CGL Tier-1 13.12.2022 (Shift-IV)
(a) The man which were present
(b) The men which was present
(c) The man who was present
(d) The man whom was present

Ans. (c)

For persons, 'who' is used. So, 'The man who was present' should substitute the underlined segment in the given sentence.

218. Do I need finish this work today itself? SSC CGL Tier-2 29.01.2022
(a) Must I to
(b) Need I
(c) No improvement required
(d) Do I must

Ans. (b)

'Modal + Subject + V_1 (first form of the verb)' is the correct grammatical structure for the given interrogative sentence. Hence, 'Need (modal) I (subject)' is the most appropriate answer.

219. The show flopped miserably to the utter disappointment of everybody. SSC CGL Tier-2 29.01.2022
(a) by the utterly
(b) for the utter
(c) No improvement required
(d) at an utter

Ans. (c)

The given sentence is grammatically correct.

220. The news about the surge in Covid-19 cases is broadcasted every morning. SSC CGL Tier-2 29.01.2022
(a) are broadcast
(b) is broadcast
(c) are broadcasted
(d) No improvement required

Ans. (b)

We can't make the past form of some verbs (forecast, cost, broadcast, etc) by simply adding 'ed' to them. It means the past form of these verbs remains the same as the present form like the past form of 'broadcast' is 'broadcast' and not broadcasted. However, we always use a singular verb after an uncountable noun(news). Hence, 'is broadcast' is the most appropriate answer.

221. Is this the same book like our teacher recommended? SSC CGL Tier-2 29.01.2022
(a) No improvement required
(b) same book who
(c) similar book that
(d) same book as

Ans. (d)

We generally use 'like' for giving examples of something.

However, the phrase 'same as' means someone or something that is exactly like another thing. Similarly, the given sentence talks about a book that is exactly the same book that the teacher recommended. Hence, 'same book as' is the most appropriate answer

222. Megha's habit of procrastination puts her colleagues on lot of trouble. SSC CGL Tier-2 29.01.2022
(a) to a lot of trouble
(b) in lot of troubles
(c) into lot troubles
(d) No improvement required

Ans. (a)

The phrase 'put someone to trouble' means make somebody work extra and cause problems. Similarly in the given sentence,

Megha's habit makes his colleagues do extra work and creates problems. Hence, 'to a lot of trouble' is the most appropriate answer.

223. It is the true fact that the second wave of Covid-19 that has gripped India is more deadly. SSC CGL Tier-2 29.01.2022
(a) the correct fact
(b) No improvement required
(c) a real fact
(d) a fact

Ans. (d)

The 'fact' mentioned in the given sentence is non-specific and we generally use the definite article 'a' before any non-specific or non-particular noun. Hence, 'a fact' is the most appropriate answer.

224. He felt dejected but the feeling passed out in a minute. SSC CGL Tier-2 29.01.2022
(a) No improvement required
(b) passed off
(c) passed on
(d) passed back

Ans. (b)

'Passed out' means to become unconscious for a short time. 'Passed off' means to evade or lightly dismiss an awkward remark.

However, the given sentence states that the feeling of dejection was evaded or dismissed in a minute. Hence, 'passed off' is the most appropriate answer.

225. The magistrate acquitted him of all charges and set him free. SSC CGL Tier-2 29.01.2022

(a) atoned him from
(b) No improvement required
(c) apprehended him in
(d) accused him for

Ans. (b)

The given sentence is grammatically correct.

226. These shoes are cheap as well durable. SSC CGL Tier-2 29.01.2022

(a) more cheaper than durable
(b) both cheap and durable
(c) improvement required
(d) neither cheaper nor durable

Ans. (b)

The phrase 'as well as' is incomplete in the given sentence and we are discussing two qualities (low price and durability) of the shoes.

Hence, 'both' which means 'the one as well as. the other' will be used for the two qualities and 'both cheap and durable' becomes the most appropriate answer.

227. He denied if he had caused the accident. SSC CGL Tier-2 29.01.2022

(a) not to had
(c) No improvement required
(b) of having
(d) that he had

Ans. (d)

We generally use 'if' in a conditional sentence but the given sentence is a general statement.

However, we generally use 'that' to introduce the next clause in a general statement. Hence, we will replace 'if' with 'that' and 'that he had' becomes the most appropriate answer.

228. Sal trees have been planted in relatively three-fourth of the forest area. SSC CGL Tier-2 29.01.2022

(a) No improvement required
(b) nearly three-fourths
(c) bout three-fourth
(d) around three-fourth

Ans. (b)

'Three-fourths + of + something' will be the correct grammatical structure for the given sentence. Hence, 'nearly three-fourths' is the most appropriate answer.

229. The shopkeeper was obliged to dispense to the service of his salesman. SSC CGL Tier-2 29.01.2022

(a) with the services
(b) by the services
(c) away services
(d) No improvement required

Ans. (a)

There is a prepositional error in the given sentence. The preposition 'to' must be replaced with 'with' because 'dispense' generally takes the preposition 'with'. Hence, 'with the services' is the most appropriate answer.

230. Why did you take this toy along the child? SSC CGL Tier-2 03.02.2022

(a) at
(b) No improvement required
(c) by
(d) from

Ans. (d)

The preposition 'along' that means from one end to or towards the other end of something must be replaced with 'from'. However, 'from' also means showing that somebody/ something is taken away, removed, or separated from somebody/something else. Similarly, the given sentence states that the toy is taken away from the child. Hence, 'from' is the most appropriate answer.

231. You must start your work without some farther delay. SSC CGL Tier-2 03.02.2022

(a) much far delay
(b) any further delay
(c) any farther delay
(d) No improvement required

Ans. (b)

'farther' means to a greater distance and 'Further' means to a greater degree.

However, the phrase 'without any further delay' means to immediately do something.

Hence, 'any further delay' is the most appropriate answer.

232. Often we ourselves are responsible for our ill health. SSC CGL Tier-2 03.02.2022

(a) themselves
(b) yourself
(c) ourself
(d) No improvement required

Ans. (d)

The given sentence is grammatically correct.

233. It was too an interesting movie.

(a) so SSC CGL Tier-2 03.02.2022
(b) such
(c) enough
(d) No improvement required

Ans. (b)

'Too' is used in the sentences with a negative sense. But, the given sentence has a positive sense as the movie was interesting.

However, 'such' is used for emphasising the degree of something like such a nice play, such a bad boy, etc. Hence, we will replace 'too' with 'such' to grammatically correct the sentence.

234. I found my bag to lie where I had left it. SSC CGL Tier-2 03.02.2022

(a) No improvement required
(b) to be lying
(c) lying
(d) to lay

Ans. (c)

'Lying' is derived from the word lie. It means to be in a specific state or, remain, or be kept in a specified state like the bag was kept in a specified position in the sentence. However, the given sentence will have bare infinitive means without the preposition 'to'. Hence, 'lying' is the most appropriate answer.

235. How many sums had you solve so far? SSC CGL Tier-2 03.02.2022

(a) No improvement required
(b) are you solving
(c) have you solved
(d) do you solve

Ans. (c)

According to the 'Subject-Verb Agreement Rule', a singular subject always takes a singular verb and a plural subject always takes a plural verb. In the given sentence, 'sums' is a plural subject that will take 'have' as a plural verb.

However, 'have + V_3 (the third form of the verb)' is the correct grammatical structure for the given sentence. Hence, 'have you solved is the most appropriate answer.

236. The report that markets are open is not true. SSC CGL Tier-2 03.02.2022

(a) was open
(b) have open
(c) No improvement required
(d) has opened

Ans. (c)

The given sentence is grammatically correct.

237. Keep the dog tied indoors; however it may bite some stranger.
SSC CGL Tier-2 08.08.2022

(a) No Improvement (b) else
(c) yet (d) still

Ans. (b)

'Else' means otherwise. The given sentence states that - Keep the dog tied indoors; else (otherwise), it may bite some stranger. Hence, 'else' is the most appropriate answer.

238. The apple tree was loaded of fruit.
SSC CGL Tier-2 08.08.2022

(a) No Improvement (b) loaded with
(c) loaded from (d) laden with

Ans. (d)

'Laden' means heavily loaded with something.

The given sentence states that the apple tree was laden (heavily loaded) with fruits. Hence, 'laden with' is the most appropriate answer.

239. The first step in making a kite is to fasten two sticks of bamboo together in the form of a cross.
SSC CGL Tier-2 08.08.2022

(a) in making a kite is to be fastened
(b) in making a kite is to fastening
(c) into making a kite is fasten
(d) No improvement required

Ans. (d)

The given sentence is grammatically correct.

240. Nobody was interested in the fish who Gopal had catch from the river.
SSC CGL Tier-2 08.08.2022

(a) which Gopal had catch
(b) No improvement required
(c) who Gopal had caught
(d) which Gopal had caught

Ans. (d)

'Who' must be replaced with 'which' as 'Which' is used for things and 'who' is used for people. Also, we generally use (V_3) with had/has/have. Hence, 'which Gopal had caught' is the most appropriate answer.

241. You can have a comfortable journey only then you are getting your seats reserved in advance.
SSC CGL Tier-2 08.08.2022

(a) only then you get
(b) No improvement required
(c) only when you are getting
(d) only if you get

Ans. (d)

We use the preposition 'If' in conditional sentences. The first conditional sentences are used to express situations in which the outcome is likely to happen in the future and is always used in simple present tense. Hence, 'only if you get' is the most appropriate answer.

242. Eighty girls sat there at four long tables, doing their homework by candlelight. **SSC CGL Tier-2 08.08.2022**

(a) to have done their homework with
(b) no improvement required
(c) to doing their homework by
(d) doing its homework by

Ans. (b)

The given sentence is grammatically correct.

243. I take pride to serve my country.
SSC CGL Tier-2 08.08.2022

(a) to be serving (b) No improvement
(c) to have served (d) in serving

Ans. (d)

'Take pride in someone or something' is the correct phrase. Hence, 'in serving' is the most appropriate answer.

244. Turn left outside the library door and walk down the corridor then you came to the main staircase.
SSC CGL Tier-2 08.08.2022

(a) No improvement required
(b) until you come to
(c) when you are come to
(d) until you came to

Ans. (b)

'Until' is used as a conjunction and Instead of a noun phrase, we use a subordinate clause after until which is in simple present tense. Hence, 'until you come to' is the most appropriate answer.

245. His tone was neither of anger nor sorrow. **SSC CGL Tier-2 08.08.2022**

(a) or sorrow
(b) No improvement required
(c) or of sorrow
(d) nor of sorrow

Ans. (d)

We will use the preposition 'of' with 'Nor' as the tone of the person is talked about. Hence, 'Nor of sorrow' is the most appropriate answer.

246. I reached at London only this morning. **SSC CGL Tier-2 08.08.2022**

(a) reach (b) reached
(c) No Improvement (d) am reaching

Ans. (b)

'Reach somewhere' is the correct phrase and 'Reach' will not have any preposition with it.

Hence, 'I reached London only this morning' is the most appropriate answer.

SSC CGL 2021 (Tier 1 & 2)

247. While washing your hands, rub them together for 20 seconds to remove the microbes on them.
SSC CGL Tier-1 13.08.2021 (Shift-I)

(a) the microbes on those
(b) the microbes on they
(c) the microbes on their
(d) No substitution

Ans. (d)

The underlined segment is grammatically and contextually correct.

248. The toy drummer plays the drum if you press the button at the back.
SSC CGL Tier-1 13.08.2021 (Shift-I)

(a) No substitution
(b) will play the drum if you will press
(c) playing the drum if you pressed
(d) played the drum if you are pressing

Ans. (a)

The underlined segment is grammatically and contextually correct.

249. Many of the apples was rotten.
SSC CGL Tier-1 13.08.2021 (Shift-III)

(a) No substitution
(b) was being rotten
(c) is rotten
(d) were rotten

Ans. (d)

The underlined segment contains an error. 'was rotten' should be substituted with 'were rotten'. With plural subject (apples) plural verb is used.

250. Although the children studied hard, but they could not understand the topic without the help of the teachers.
SSC CGL Tier-1 13.08.2021 (Shift-III)

(a) Although the children had study hard, but they
(b) No substitution
(c) Although the children studied hard, they
(d) Althrough the children have studied hard, but they

Ans. (c)

The underlined segment contains an error.

It should be substituted with 'Although the children studied hard, they' as two conjunctions never used together or in a single sentence.

251. The place is too much noisy.
SSC CGL Tier-1 16.08.2021 (Shift-I)
(a) too noisy
(b) much too much noisy
(c) No substitution
(d) much noisy

Ans. (a)

The underlined segment contains an error. The use of 'much' is redundant. So, 'too noisy' should be used in place of 'too much noisy'.

252. I wish I have come an hour sooner.
SSC CGL Tier-1 16.08.2021 (Shift-I)
(a) has
(b) had
(c) will
(d) No improvement required

Ans. (b)

The underlined segment contains an error, 'have' should be replaced with 'had' to rectify the sentence grammatically as past perfect tense is used to express wish.

253. I asked Rahul that how far was his office from his home.
SSC CGL Tier-1 16.08.2021 (Shift-III)
(a) how far his office was
(b) No substitution required
(c) that how far his office is
(d) then how far was his office

Ans. (a)

The underlined segment contains an error. 'That how far was his office' should be substituted with 'how far his office was', to make the sentence grammatically correct.

254. Among applied sciences, medicine is one which have given man some power over death.
SSC CGL Tier-1 16.08.2021 (Shift-III)
(a) is one which has given
(b) No substitution required
(c) are one which given
(d) is the one which gave

Ans. (a)

The underlined segment contains an error. 'Is one which have given' should be replaced with 'is one which has given' to improve the given sentence.

255. Hears to the news tonight at 9 pm, as there will be an important announcement about the budget.
SSC CGL Tier-1 17.08.2021 (Shift-I)
(a) Listened to
(b) Hear to
(c) No substitution required
(d) Listen to

Ans. (d)

The underlined segment contains an error. 'Hears to' should be replaced with 'Listen to' to improve the sentence.

256. Either the bears or the lion has escaped from the zoo.
SSC CGL Tier-1 17.08.2021 (Shift-I)
(a) is escaped from the zoo
(b) have escaped from the zoo
(c) No substitution required
(d) are escaped from the zoo

Ans. (c)

The underlined segment is grammatically and contextually correct.

257. No one are supposed to react to her prejudiced comments.
SSC CGL Tier-1 17.08.2021 (Shift-III)
(a) No one is supposed to react
(b) No substitution required
(c) No one has supposed to react
(d) No one had supposed to react

Ans. (a)

The underlined segment contains an error. 'No one are supposed to react' should be substituted with 'no one is supposed to react' to rectify the sentence.

258. The teacher asked the students for fill the form before entering the classroom.
SSC CGL Tier-1 17.08.2021 (Shift-III)
(a) the students to fill the form
(b) No substitution required
(c) the students for filled the form
(d) the students to filled the form

Ans. (a)

The underlined segment contains an error.

'The students for fill the form' should be substituted with 'the students to fill the form' to rectify the sentence grammatically.

259. When I met the couple yesterday I noticed that the wife was more taller than her husband.
SSC CGL Tier-1 18.08.2021 (Shift-I)
(a) much tall
(b) taller
(c) much tallest
(d) No substitution required

Ans. (b)

The underlined segment contains an error. 'More taller' should be substituted with 'taller' to improve the sentence. Two comparatives are not used single sentence.

260. The teacher advised the children to not went near the lake.
SSC CGL Tier-1 18.08.2021 (Shift-I)
(a) don't go
(b) No improvement
(c) not to go
(d) not to be going

Ans. (c)

The underlined segment contains an error. It should be 'to not went' replaced with 'not to go' to improve the sentence.

261. Fifty litres of milk are donated by the committee to the orphanage every week.
SSC CGL Tier-1 18.08.2021 (Shift-III)
(a) are donated by a committee
(b) are being donated by the committee
(c) No substitution
(d) is donated by the committee

Ans. (d)

The underlined segment contains an error. 'Are donated by the committee' should be substituted with 'is donated by the committee' to rectify the sentenc, as the subject of the sentence is singular.

262. He fell over in studies owing to his illness.
SSC CGL Tier-1 18.08.2021 (Shift-III)
(a) fell behind
(b) fell for
(c) No improvement required
(d) fell out

Ans. (a)

The underlined segment contains an error. 'Fell over' should be replaced with 'fell behind' to improve the sentence.

263. After the old building was pulled out, the building contractor surveyed the progress of the work.
SSC CGL Tier-1 20.08.2021 (Shift-I)
(a) was pulled over (b) No substitution
(c) was pulled up (d) was pulled down

Ans. (d)

The underlined segment contains an error 'was pulled out' should be substituted with 'was pulled down' to rectify the sentence.

264. The apple a day keeps the doctor away.
SSC CGL Tier-1 20.08.2021 (Shift-I)
(a) No substitution
(b) The apples a day
(c) An apple a day
(d) A apple a day

Ans. (c)

The underlined segment contains an error.

The correct proverb is 'An apple a day, keeps the doctor away'. Hence, option (c) is used to substitute the given underlined segment.

265. Sunil have been working as a personal assistant to the Director for two years.
SSC CGL Tier-1 20.08.2021 (Shift-II)
(a) is working (b) has been worked
(c) No substitution (d) has been working

Ans. (d)

The underlined segment contains an error. 'Have been working' should be replaced with 'has been working' to rectify the sentence, as the subject of the sentence is singular, so singular verb should be used.

266. The herd are grazing in the fields far away from the farmer's hut.
SSC CGL Tier-1 20.08.2021 (Shift-II)

(a) No substitution
(b) The herd has grazing
(c) The herd is grazing
(d) The herd is grazed

Ans. (c)

The underlined segment contains an error. 'The herd are grazing' should be replaced with 'the herd is grazing' to rectify the sentence. With the collective noun word 'herd' singular verb is used as per rules.

267. What were the examples that the writer gave to proved his point ?
SSC CGL Tier-1 23.08.2021 (Shift-I)

(a) given to prove his point
(b) gave to prove his point
(c) no substitution
(d) give for proving his point

Ans. (b)

The underlined segment contains an error. Replace it with 'gave to prove his point' to correct the sentence.

268. If you are not able to go out, did not worry. SSC CGL Tier-1 23.08.2021 (Shift-I)

(a) don't worried (b) do not worry
(c) worrying not (d) No substitution

Ans. (b)

The underlined segment contains an error. 'Did not worry' 'should be replaced with' 'do not worry' to make the sentence grammatically correct as the sentence is in simple present tense.

269. The warden punished the students who violates the rules of the hostel.
SSC CGL Tier-1 23.08.2021 (Shift-II)

(a) who is violating (b) who violated
(c) who are violate (d) No substitution

Ans. (b)

The underlined segment contains an error. 'Who violates' should be replaced with 'who violated' as the sentence is in past tense.

270. The minister, along with his team members, is expected to arrive shortly. SSC CGL Tier-1 23.08.2021 (Shift-II)

(a) No substitution
(b) are expected to arrive
(c) are expect to arrive
(d) are being expected to arrive

Ans. (a)

The underlined segment is grammatically and contextually correct.

271. Japan has made important and original contributions inside some fields like photography and electronics. SSC CGL Tier-1 24.08.2021 (Shift-I)

(a) No Substitution required
(b) for some field like
(c) in some fields like
(d) on some filed like

Ans. (c)

The underlined segment contains an error. 'Inside some fields like' should be replaced with 'in some fields like' to correct the sentence.

272. A need of an hour is to provide employment to the youth of the country. SSC CGL Tier-1 24.08.2021 (Shift-I)

(a) No improvement required
(b) The need in an
(c) The need of the
(d) The need of an

Ans. (c)

The underlined segment contains an error. 'A need of an hour' should be substituted with 'the need of the', to improve the sentence.

273. Bats huddle together to get warm of each other's body.
SSC CGL Tier-1 24.08.2021 (Shift-II)

(a) Warm off
(b) No improvement required
(c) Warmth from
(d) Warming from

Ans. (c)

The underlined segment contains an error. 'Warm of' should be replaced with 'warmth from' to correct the sentence.

274. The news are true.
SSC CGL Tier-1 24.08.2021 (Shift-II)

(a) are being true (b) No substitution
(c) is being true (d) is true

Ans. (d)

The underlined segment contains an error. 'Are true' should be replaced with 'is true'. A collective noun (news) takes a singular verb (is).

275. The prisoners are kept at constant surveillance.
SSC CGL Tier-1 24.08.2021 (Shift-III)

(a) kept with (b) No improvement
(c) kept under (d) kept by

Ans. (c)

The underlined segment contains an error. 'Kept at' should be replaced with 'kept under' as 'under' is the suitable preposition to be used after 'kept'.

276. The crowd have gathered around the area to watch the actors.
SSC CGL Tier-1 24.08.2021 (Shift-III)

(a) has gathered around the area
(b) have gathered in the area
(c) No substitution required
(d) have gather around the area

Ans. (a)

The underlined segment contains an error. 'Crowd have gathered around the area' should be replaced with 'crowd has gathered around the area'. Since, 'crowd' is a collective noun, singular verb 'has' should be used with it.

SSC CPO 2024

277. The referee declared that the participant who will score the highest points in the tally will take away the cash prize of 50 lakh.
SSC CPO 27.06.2024 (Shift-I)

(a) who can score the highest point
(b) who scores the highest point
(c) who could score the highest point
(d) who settles scores the highest point

Ans. (b)

The underlined part of the sentence contains error. The use of future tense is incorrect in the underlined part. It should be 'who scores the highest point'.

278. My friends are on a trip to the world.
SSC CPO 27.06.2024 (Shift-I)

(a) in the world
(b) by the world
(c) within the world
(d) around the world

Ans. (d)

The underlined part of the sentence contains error. Use 'around' in place of 'to'.

279. An awkward neither grammatically accurate sentence is the result of centre implanting.
SSC CPO 27.06.2024 (Shift-I)

(a) awkward but grammatically
(b) awkward either grammatically
(c) awkward beyond grammatically
(d) awkward unless grammatically

Ans. (a)

The underlined part of the sentence contains error. Use 'awkward but grammatically'.

280. Youth is the time when the seeds of character is sown.
SSC CPO 27.06.2024 (Shift-I)

(a) the seeds of character will have been sowing
(b) the seeds of character had been sown
(c) the seeds of character were sown
(d) the seeds of character are sown

Ans. (d)

The underlined part of the sentence contains error. As the subject 'seeds' is plural, plural verb 'are' should be used.

281. I prefer walking than riding.
SSC CPO 27.06.2024 (Shift-I)
(a) walking to riding
(b) walking above riding
(c) walking from riding
(d) walking with riding

Ans. (a)

The underlined part of the sentence contains error. We use preposition 'to' with the word 'prefer'.

282. Shakespeare is greater than any other English poet.
SSC CPO 27.06.2024 (Shift-I)
(a) was great than (b) was greater than
(c) is greater than (d) is greatest than

Ans. (b)

The underlined part of the sentence contains error. Use 'was greater than' as the sentence refers to a past comparison.

283. The culprit had been shot from the back by the police inspector.
SSC CPO 27.06.2024 (Shift-II)
(a) to (b) in
(c) by (d) off

Ans. (b)

The underlined part of the sentence contains an error. Use 'in' in place of 'from' to correct the sentence.

284. The authors writing style is characterised by its poetic language.
SSC CPO 27.06.2024 (Shift-II)
(a) lyrical language
(b) simple language
(c) lucid language
(d) prosaic language

Ans. (a)

The underlined part of the sentence contains an error.

This sentence maintains the sense that the authors writing style is characterised by using language that is poetic or expressive in nature.

'Lyrical' suggests a style that is melodious, expressive and artistic, similar to 'poetic.'

The most appropriate option that can substitute the underlined segment is 'lyrical language.'

285. After two hours of wandering in the desert, we realised we were on a wild horse race. SSC CPO 27.06.2024 (Shift-II)
(a) wild goose chase
(b) wild jackal hunt
(c) wild carpet rug
(d) wild shadow chase

Ans. (a)

The correct idiom to improve the underlined part of the given sentence is 'wild goose chase,' which means a futile or hopeless pursuit.

286. My friend vanished when the goons came to fight with me.
SSC CPO 27.06.2024 (Shift-III)
(a) mobilised when the thugs arrived
(b) disappeared when the thugs arrived
(c) condemned when the thugs arrived
(d) attacked when the thugs arrived

Ans. (b)

The underlined part of the sentence contains an error. Use 'disappeared when the thugs arrived' to correct the sentence.

287. After he leave, we discussed his suggestion. SSC CPO 27.06.2024 (Shift-III)
(a) he will be leaving (b) he has left
(c) he had left (d) he was leaving

Ans. (c)

The underlined part of the sentence contains an error. As the sentence talks of two actions that happened one after the other, past perfect tense 'had left' should be used.

288. Though very informative, Shweta's article was mercilessly rejected of the editor. SSC CPO 27.06.2024 (Shift-III)
(a) was mercilessly rejected of
(b) was mercilessly rejected on
(c) was mercilessly rejected each
(d) was mercilessly rejected by

Ans. (d)

The underlined part of the sentence contains an error. Use 'by' in place of 'of'.

289. No sooner had she finished her breakfast that she had received a phone call from her boss, informing her that she needed to come to work immediately. SSC CPO 27.06.2024 (Shift-III)
(a) that she received
(b) that she receives
(c) than she receives
(d) than she received

Ans. (a)

The underlined part of the sentence contains an error.

The correct structure is 'No sooner....than'. Further, as the sentence is in past tense, 'that she received' will be correct.

290. If I was very rich, I would spend all my time and money for the poor.
SSC CPO 27.06.2024 (Shift-III)
(a) No substitution
(b) If I were very rich
(c) If I have much riches
(d) If I am very rich

Ans. (b)

The underlined part of the sentence contains an error. Use 'if I were very rich' is correct as the sentence is presenting a future hypothetical situation.

291. My son will carry out my business in my absence. SSC CPO 28.06.2024 (Shift-I)
(a) carry at (b) carry on
(c) carry for (d) carry in

Ans. (b)

The underlined part of the sentence contains an error.

Use the phrasal verb 'carry on' which means to continue doing something. It fits the context as it implies that the son will continue to manage or operate the business while the speaker is absent.

292. The Centre of Excellence for Data Analytics (CEDA) provides quality data analytic services to various government departments on all levels as well as to public sector units at the Centre and in states.
SSC CPO 28.06.2024 (Shift-II)
(a) various government departments through all levels
(b) various government departments from all levels
(c) various government departments in all levels
(d) various government departments at all levels

Ans. (d)

The underlined part of the sentence contains an error. Use 'various government departments at all levels'.

293. This is the group of leaders in whom the ruling government has placed its trust. SSC CPO 28.06.2024 (Shift-II)
(a) No substitution
(b) in who the ruling government
(c) with who the ruling government
(d) on who the ruling government

Ans. (a)

The underlined part is grammatically and contextually correct.

294. You have tears, prepare to shed them now. SSC CPO 28.06.2024 (Shift-II)
(a) If you have tears,
(b) Yet you have tears,
(c) Until you have tears
(d) Unless you have tears,

Ans. (a)

The underlined part of the sentence contains an error.
Use 'If you have tears' as it retains the directness of the original statement

while suggesting a conditional scenario answer. If tears are present, then prepare to shed them.

295. In yesterday's fire accident, her feets are burnt badly.
SSC CPO 28.06.2024 (Shift-II)
(a) her feet was (b) her foots were
(c) her feet were (d) No substitution

Ans. (c)

The underlined part of the sentence contains an error.
Use 'her feet were'. 'Feet' is the plural form of 'foot.' The verb 'were' agrees with the plural subject 'feet.'

296. The minister promised to provide free laptops to the public if his (party came in power).
SSC CPO 28.06.2024 (Shift-II)
(a) party loses the election
(b) he loses the election
(c) party forms the government
(d) he comes to a party

Ans. (c)

The bracketed part of the sentence contains an error.

The sentence talks about a promise made by the minister regarding what will happen if his party gains power or forms the government. 'Party forms the government' accurately reflects the context of the ministers promise to provide free laptops once his political party assumes power.

297. A goose's eye view.
SSC CPO 28.06.2024 (Shift-II)
(a) dogs (b) hornets
(c) fools (d) birds

Ans. (d)

The underlined part of the sentence contains an error.

Use 'bird' 'A bird's eye view' is the idiom that refers to a view or perspective from high above.

298. The woman to who I sold my house was a criminal.
SSC CPO 28.06.2024 (Shift-III)
(a) No substitution (b) to whom I sold
(c) to whom I sell (d) to whom sold

Ans. (a)

The underlined part is grammatically and contextually correct.

299. Half of the property given to his sons by the businessman last year.
SSC CPO 28.06.2024 (Shift-III)
(a) No substitution
(b) Half of the property is given
(c) Half of the property was given
(d) Half of the property has been given

Ans. (c)

The underlined part of the sentence contains an error. As the sentence refers to past, the past tense form 'was given,' making the sentence grammatically correct and meaningful.

300. We should not underestimate the signification of female education.
SSC CPO 28.06.2024 (Shift-III)
(a) underestimate the significance
(b) underestimate at signification
(c) underestimate on signification
(d) underestimate signification

Ans. (a)

The underlined part of the sentence contains an error. The word 'signification' is not the correct word here. It should be 'significance,' which means importance or meaning.

301. A sharp fall in the price of jute have led the poor jute farmers to the brink of starvation.
SSC CPO 28.06.2024 (Shift-III)
(a) have lead the poor jute farmers
(b) have led the poor farmers
(c) has led the poor jute farmers
(d) No substitution

Ans. (c)

The underlined part of the sentence contains an error.

The subject 'a sharp fall' is singular, so the verb should agree with it in singular form. 'Has led' is the correct form of the verb to match with a singular subject.

302. His interpretation of the fact and understanding of reality was impressive. SSC CPO 29.06.2024 (Shift-I)
(a) understands of realities
(b) understand of realities
(c) understood of realities
(d) understanding of realities

Ans. (d)

The underlined part of the sentence contains an error. The sentence implies that he comprehended or perceived the facts in an impressive manner. The phrase 'understanding of realities' maintains the context of interpretation and correctly replaces 'interpretation of the facts' with 'understanding of realities.'

303. If his father will give money, he will buy a sports bike.
SSC CPO 29.06.2024 (Shift-I)
(a) No substitution
(b) If his father give money
(c) If his father gave money
(d) If his father gives money

Ans. (d)

The underlined part of the sentence contains an error.

When we use 'if' to introduce a conditional clause in the present tense, the main clause should use a future tense form.

304. He wanted to visiting the Golden Temple in Amritsar.
SSC CPO 29.06.2024 (Shift-I)
(a) wanted to be visit
(b) wanted to visited
(c) wanted to visitor
(d) wanted to visit

Ans. (d)

The underlined part of the sentence contains an error.

The original sentence 'He wanted to visiting...' is incorrect because after 'to,' the base form of the verb (infinitive without 'to') should be used.

305. What exactly have the teachers being doing wrong? SSC CPO 29.06.2024 (Shift-I)
(a) teachers been doing
(b) teachers being done
(c) teachers are doing
(d) teachers have been doing

Ans. (a)

The underlined part of the sentence contains an error. The correct form should be 'teachers been doing,' using the present perfect continuous tense to indicate actions that started in the past and continue into the present.

306. Had I known that you were planning to visit me, I should have done all the necessary arrangements.
SSC CPO 29.06.2024 (Shift-I)
(a) I would have made
(b) I should have made
(c) I would have do
(d) I must have made

Ans. (a)

The underlined part of the sentence contains an error.

The sentence structure 'I would have made' is correct and matches the conditional tense used in the sentence. It indicates a hypothetical past action that did not occur due to a condition (not knowing about the visit beforehand).

307. When our principal said she was leaving the company, I played out the opportunity to fill the job.
SSC CPO 29.06.2024 (Shift-II)
(a) glided at the opportunity
(b) jumped at the opportunity
(c) started at the opportunity
(d) ran to the opportunity

Ans. (b)

The phrase/idiom that will improve the underlined part of the sentence is 'jumped at the opportunity.' This idiom means to eagerly accept or seize an opportunity. It fits well in the context of being proactive in filling a job position after the principal's departure.

308. The core part in Artificial Intelligence (AI) is knowledge engineering, machine learning, machine perception and robotics.
SSC CPO 29.06.2024 (Shift-II)

(a) The core part on Artificial Intelligence
(b) The core part of Artificial Intelligence
(c) The core part from Artificial Intelligence
(d) The core part with Artificial Intelligence

Ans. (b)

The underlined part of the sentence contains an error. Use 'The core part of Artificial Intelligence'. Prepositions 'of' is commonly used to show possession or association.

309. Not a word didnt they speak to the others about the sad turn of events.
SSC CPO 29.06.2024 (Shift-II)

(a) did they speak
(b) No substitution
(c) do they speak
(d) had they speak

Ans. (a)

The underlined part of the sentence contains an error. To correct this, we should use the affirmative form of the sentence, which is 'did they speak.'

310. Mr. Patel is likely to win the elections in the sweeping majority.
SSC CPO 29.06.2024 (Shift-II)

(a) elections by a sweeping majority
(b) elections on a sweeping majority
(c) elections of a sweeping majority
(d) elections at a sweeping majority

Ans. (a)

The underlined part of the sentence contains an error. 'By a sweeping majority' correctly indicates the manner in which Mr. Patel is likely to win the elections, emphasising the magnitude or extent of the majority.

311. The veteran footballer was expected for reach here by 10 o clock, the notice said. SSC CPO 29.06.2024 (Shift-II)

(a) expected on reach here
(b) expected to reach here
(c) expected of reach here
(d) expected by reach here

Ans. (b)

The underlined part of the sentence contains an error. Use 'to' in place of 'for' to correct the sentence.

312. The Sumo wrestler seemed to be incapable in being tired.
SSC CPO 29.06.2024 (Shift-II)

(a) incapable of being tired
(b) incapable from being tired
(c) incapable to being tired
(d) incapable by being tired

Ans. (a)

The underlined part of the sentence contains an error. The phrase 'incapable of being tired' is the correct expression. It means that the Sumo wrestler does not seem to get tired.

313. The road is too busy for elderly people that they cannot cross safely.
SSC CPO 29.06.2024 (Shift-II)

(a) that it is difficult to cross.
(b) to cross safely.
(c) that it cannot be crossed properly.
(d) that it is impossible for them to cross.

Ans. (b)

The underlined part of the sentence contains an error. The most appropriate option to substitute the underlined words is answer. 'to cross safely' as the correct structure is 'too…to'.

314. Before she began, she asked the teacher whether she write with a pen or a pencil. SSC CPO 29.06.2024 (Shift-II)

(a) she can write (b) she wrote
(c) she should write (d) she did write.

Ans. (c)

The underlined part of the sentence contains an error.

Use 'she should write' to ask something.

315. He is feeding a male dog and female dog. SSC CPO 29.06.2024 (Shift-III)

(a) a dog and puppy
(b) a dog and a bitch
(c) a male dog and lady dog
(d) No substitution

Ans. (b)

The underlined part of the sentence contains an error. 'Bitch' is the correct term for a female dog.

316. The quality of students of an educational institute is of great importance and a crucial starting point. SSC CPO 29.06.2024 (Shift-III)

(a) The quality of students in an educational institute is in great importance and a crucial starting point.
(b) The quality of students in an educational institute is of great importance and a crucial starting point.
(c) No substitution
(d) The quality of students in an educational institute is of great importance and is a crucial start point.

Ans. (b)

The underlined part of the sentence contains an error. The correct sentence is- The quality of students in an educational institute is of great importance and a crucial starting point.

317. She asked me where my hometown is and where I worked.
SSC CPO 29.06.2024 (Shift-III)

(a) hometown has been
(b) hometown would be
(c) hometown were
(d) hometown was

Ans. (d)

The underlined part of the sentence contains an error.

The sentence is in reported speech, so the verb 'is' should be changed to 'was' to maintain consistency in past tense.

318. What flavour ice-cream do you want?
SSC CPO 29.06.2024 (Shift-III)

(a) No improvement required
(b) flavours ice-cream
(c) flavour of ice-cream
(d) ice cream flavoured

Ans. (c)

The underlined part of the sentence contains an error. The option that will improve the underlined part of the given sentence is 'flavour of ice-cream.'

319. Inspite mothers milk is vital to a childs health, a number of FMCG companies wrongly advertise artificially prepared infant formulas as being the best for the child.
SSC CPO 29.06.2024 (Shift-III)

(a) Mothers milk
(b) No substitution
(c) Though mothers milk
(d) Despite mothers milk

Ans. (c)

The underlined part of the sentence contains an error. The correct usage will be 'though' in place of 'in spite'.

320. Ice melts fastly, in the Sun.
SSC CPO 29.06.2024 (Shift-III)

(a) melts fastest (b) melt fastly
(c) melt fast (d) melts fast

Ans. (d)

The underlined part of the sentence contains an error. 'Fast' is the correct adverb to use here.
The adverb 'fastly' does not exist in standard English.

321. I will definitely return your notes at Saturday evening.
SSC CPO Tier-2 08.01.2024

(a) returned your notes on
(b) returning your notes at
(c) No improvement required
(d) return your notes by

Ans. (d)

Preposition 'by' is used to indicate a deadline or a specific time before which the action will be completed. The given sentence states that the notes will be returned by evening. Hence, 'return your notes by' is the most appropriate answer.

322. My sister resembles to my mother a lot in looks and in temperament.
SSC CPO Tier-2 08.01.2024

(a) is resembling to
(b) resembles
(c) has resemblance to
(d) No improvement

Ans. (b)

The verb 'resembles' does not take the preposition 'to' after it.
Hence, 'resembles' is the most appropriate answer.

323. Effective communication is a skill that can significant enhance your personal and professional life.
SSC CPO Tier-2 08.01.2024

(a) which can significant enhanced
(b) No improvement required
(c) which can significantly enhancing
(d) which can significantly enhance

Ans. (d)

The given sentence needs an adverb(significantly) to modify the verb (enhance) and not an adjective (significant). Hence, 'which can significantly enhance' is the most appropriate answer.

324. We have received no information so far to the main island.
SSC CPO Tier-2 08.01.2024

(a) No improvement required
(b) so farther from
(c) so far from
(d) such far from

Ans. (c)

'From' is used with 'receive' to indicate the source destination or sender. In the given sentence, 'the main island' is the source destination from which no information has been received so far. Hence 'so far from' is the most appropriate answer.

325. When he was falsely accused of embezzlement, he was beside himself in anger. **SSC CPO Tier-2 08.01.2024**

(a) No improvement
(b) he went beside himself
(c) he were beside himself
(d) he was besides himself

Ans. (a)

'Be beside oneself' is a phrase which means to be in an extremely emotional state. The given sentence states that the person was in an extreme state of anger. Hence, option (a) is the most appropriate answer.

326. She is married with a rich businessman and has enough money to splurge on luxuries.
SSC CPO Tier-2 08.01.2024

(a) has marriage with
(b) is married to
(c) has married with
(d) No improvement

Ans. (b)

'To' is used after the verb 'married' in the passive voice. Hence, 'is married to' is the most appropriate answer.

327. Sherpas have prospered and come along the way from being just porters to becoming mountaineers.
SSC CPO Tier-2 08.01.2024

(a) are coming along
(b) come all along
(c) No improvement
(d) come a long way

Ans. (d)

The phrase 'come a long way' means to make significant progress or improvement.
The given sentence states that Sherpas have prospered and made significant progress from being just porters to becoming mountaineers. Hence, 'come a long way' is the most appropriate answer.

328. You have a lot of coconut trees in your village, do you?
SSC CPO Tier-2 08.01.2024

(a) have you?
(b) don't you?
(c) don't they?
(d) No improvement required

Ans. (b)

According to the 'Question Tag rule', if the statement is positive, the question tag will be negative and Vice-versa. However, the sentence and the question tag must be in the same tense. Similarly, the given sentence is positive so the question tag will be negative(don't).
Hence, 'don't you?' is the most appropriate answer.

329. By next summer, I will have completed my internship and will have returned to school.
SSC CPO Tier-2 08.01.2024

(a) No improvement required
(b) have returned to school.
(c) will return to school.
(d) returned to school.

Ans. (d)

If two or more verbs are of the same tense then the helping verb is written only once before the first verb, In the given sentence, 'will have' is a helping verb of future perfect tense and has, been used for both verbs ('completed' and 'returned').
Hence, 'returned to school' is the most appropriate answer.

330. Tomorrow, they will be take a flight to their dream vacation destination.
SSC CPO Tier-2 08.01.2024

(a) will taking a flight
(b) be taking a flight
(c) No improvement required
(d) will be taking a flight

Ans. (d)

'Will be / shall be + ing form of verb' is the correct grammatical structure of Future continuous tense.
Hence, will be taking ing form of verb 'a flight' is the most appropriate answer.

331. As bombs keep falling on Gaza, hundreds of thousands of children have been order to flee their homes.
SSC CPO Tier-2 08.01.2024

(a) have been ordered to flee
(b) have been ordered fleeing
(c) No improvement required
(d) has been ordered to flee

Ans. (a)

'Subject + has / have + been + V_3' is the correct grammatical structure for passive voice of Present perfect tense, 'Ordered' is the correct third form of 'order'.
Hence, 'have been ordered to flee' is the most appropriate answer.

332. The pollution level ought to keep under control. **SSC CPO Tier-2 08.01.2024**

(a) No improvement required
(b) ought to be keeping
(c) ought to be kept
(d) ought to have kept

Ans. (c)

Passive voice is used when the action is performed upon the subject, not by the subject.

'Ought to + be + V_3' is the correct passive form. Hence, 'ought to be kept under' is the most appropriate answer.

SSC CPO 2023

333. Her paintings are way better <u>then</u> her sketches. **SSC CPO 03.10.2023 (Shift-I)**

(a) off
(b) than
(c) more
(d) No substitution required

Ans. (b)

The underlined segment contains an error. The word 'then' is contextually incorrect in the given sentence. Replace it with 'than' to correct the sentence.

334. Lots of kids (was visualised) crossing the road when the bus arrived. **SSC CPO 03.10.2023 (Shift-I)**

(a) were seen (b) have been seen
(c) are seen (d) was seen

Ans. (a)

The bracketed part of the sentence is contextually incorrect. Replace it with 'were seen' to correct the sentence.

335. <u>The use of chemicals, insecticides and pesticides</u> began after the Green Revolution. **SSC CPO 03.10.2023 (Shift-I)**

(a) A practice of chemicals, insecticides and pesticides
(b) The custom of chemicals, insecticides and pesticides
(c) Consumption of chemicals, insecticides and pesticides
(d) The usage of chemicals, insecticides and pesticides

Ans. (d)

'The usage of chemicals, insecticides and pesticides' is the correct option as 'us age' is used as noun (common practice).

336. He is <u>faster than smarter</u>. **SSC CPO 03.10.2023 (Shift-II)**

(a) more fast than smart
(b) faster than being smart
(c) fast than smart
(d) No substitution

Ans. (a)

When there is a comparison between two qualities of a single person or thing, we do not use normal comparative degree. E.g.- more smart than beautiful(not 'smarter than beautiful'). Similarly, the given sentence compares two qualities, 'fast' and 'smart'. Hence, 'more fast than smart' is the most appropriate answer.

337. The Taj Mahal is one of the <u>much</u> popular seven wonders of the world. **SSC CPO 03.10.2023 (Shift-II)**

(a) much more
(b) more
(c) most
(d) No substitution required

Ans. (c)

'One of the + Superlative degree adjective + Plural Subject' is grammatically the correct structure. For example, one of the best men, one of the greatest kings, one of the worst phones, etc. Hence, 'most' is the most appropriate answer.

338. She trusted her husband but he <u>stabbed her in the neck</u> when he usurped her inheritance. **SSC CPO 03.10.2023 (Shift-II)**

(a) snapped her in the neck
(b) stabbed her in the back
(c) stabbed her with a fork
(d) stabbed her prospects

Ans. (b)

'Stabbed her in the back' is the correct idiom that means to be unfaithful or disloyal to.

The given sentence states that she trusted her husband but he was unfaithful to her when he usurped her inheritance. Hence, 'stabbed her in the back' is the most appropriate answer.

339. I like to read books, but my brother prefers <u>to watching</u> movies. **SSC CPO 03.10.2023 (Shift-III)**

(a) No substitution (b) to watch
(c) in watching (d) on watching

Ans. (b)

We generally use an infinitive (V_1) with the preposition 'to'. Hence, 'to watch' is the most appropriate answer.

340. This case is serious. You need to <u>look into</u> this matter; otherwise, the situation will get out of control soon. **SSC CPO 03.10.2023 (Shift-III)**

(a) look after (b) No substitution
(c) look up (d) look at

Ans. (b)

The given sentence is grammatically correct.

341. The village Seoni is located 113 km <u>away from the capital city of MP, Bhopal</u>. **SSC CPO 04.10.2023 (Shift-I)**

(a) adjacent from city capital of MP, Bhopal
(b) proximate from capital of MP, Bhopal
(c) near from the city capital of MP, Bhopal
(d) far from the capital city of MP, Bhopal

Ans. (d)

'Far' means situated at a distance or away from a place. Hence, 'far from the capital city of MP, Bhopal' is the most appropriate answer.

342. Kiran's teacher was <u>doubtful on</u> her success. **SSC CPO 04.10.2023 (Shift-II)**

(a) doubtful beyond
(b) doubtful of
(c) doubtful in
(d) doubtful off

Ans. (b)

'Of' is a fixed preposition used after the word 'doubtful'. Hence 'doubtful of' is the most appropriate answer.

343. Harry is the one sitting <u>on</u> the corner. **SSC CPO 04.10.2023 (Shift-II)**

(a) in
(b) No substitution required
(c) onto
(d) upon

Ans. (a)

'In' is used to indicate the location or position of an object or a person. Similarly, in the given sentence, 'corner' is the position of Harry. Hence, 'in' is the most appropriate answer.

344. Naina is leaving and I am <u>think to apply</u> for her job. **SSC CPO 04.10.2023 (Shift-III)**

(a) thinking about apply
(b) thinking on applying
(c) thinking about applying
(d) thinking in applying

Ans. (c)

'Am' is a helping verb of Present Continuous Tense and 'is/am/are + V_{ing}' is the correct grammatical structure. 'About' is used to introduce the topic or subject of discussion or consideration. Also, we always use a gerund after a preposition. Hence, 'thinking about applying' is the most appropriate answer.

345. Malati has a difficult job, but she does it <u>good</u>. **SSC CPO 04.10.2023 (Shift-III)**

(a) nice (b) best (c) better (d) well

Ans. (d)

The given sentence needs an adverb (well) to modify the meaning of the verb 'does', not an adjective (good). Hence, 'well' is the most appropriate answer.

346. He travelled the whole world, but found <u>piece</u> at home. **SSC CPO 04.10.2023 (Shift-III)**

(a) No substitution required
(b) prize
(c) peach
(d) Peace

Ans. (d)

'Piece' means a portion of an object or a material while 'peace' means a state of being calm and free from any kind of worry or disturbance.

The word 'peace' makes the sentence meaningful. Hence 'peace' is the most appropriate answer.

347. Farmers have harvested wheat by using whatever labour that was available to them.
SSC CPO 04.10.2023 (Shift-III)
(a) by using dispersed labour
(b) by using amalgamated labour
(c) by using united labour
(d) by using limited labour

Ans. (d)

'Limited' means a small quantity or number of something.

The given sentence states that farmers have harvested their wheat by using a small number of labourers. Hence, 'by using limited labour' is the most appropriate answer.

348. You can become confident to speak English within one year.
SSC CPO 05.10.2023 (Shift-I)
(a) convinced to speaking
(b) confident in speaking
(c) reassured of speaking
(d) assured of speaking

Ans. (b)

'In' is used after the word 'confident' to show the specific area or subject in which someone is confident. Hence, 'confident in speaking' is the most appropriate answer.

349. The unexpected turn beside the project put the company in a big financial crisis. SSC CPO 05.10.2023 (Shift-I)
(a) No substitution required
(b) between the project
(c) until the project
(d) in the project

Ans. (d)

'In' is used to indicate involvement while 'beside' is used to show that two things are close to each other.

The given passage talks about the impact of unexpected change in the project. Hence, 'in the project' is the most appropriate answer.

350. The cat climbed a tree and perched itself on a branch.
SSC CPO 05.10.2023 (Shift-II)
(a) perked
(b) perished
(c) No substitution required
(d) parched

Ans. (c)

The given sentence is grammatically correct.

351. Fifty rupees feels too much for such a pen. SSC CPO 05.10.2023 (Shift-II)
(a) seems (b) looks
(c) price (d) minds

Ans. (a)

'Feels' is used for the sense of touch or emotion and 'seems' is used to show what something appears to be. The word 'seems' makes the sentence meaningful. Hence, 'seems' is the most appropriate answer.

352. Despite of an injury, he won the match. SSC CPO 05.10.2023 (Shift-II)
(a) In spite off
(b) Despite
(c) In despite of
(d) No substitution required

Ans. (b)

'Despite' means in spite of and it doesn't take any preposition with it. Hence, 'Despite' is the most appropriate answer.

353. Lily has dedicate her life towards becoming a doctor.
SSC CPO 05.10.2023 (Shift-II)
(a) No improvement required
(b) has dedicated
(c) is dedicate
(d) had dedicate

Ans. (b)

"Has/Have/Had + V_3 (third form of the verb)" is the correct grammatical structure. However, the third form of 'dedicate' is 'dedicated'. Hence, 'has dedicated' is the most appropriate answer.

354. It was a quite afternoon so, Dan decided to take a nap.
SSC CPO 05.10.2023 (Shift-III)
(a) an quiet
(b) an quite
(c) No substitution required
(d) a quiet

Ans. (d)

The underlined segment contains an error. The word 'quite' is incorrect in the context of the sentence. It should be replaced with 'Quiet' which is an adjective that means making little or no noise.

355. Unless you (do will not prepare) well you will not perform well.
SSC CPO 05.10.2023 (Shift-III)
(a) would not prepare
(b) prepare
(c) will do not prepare
(d) will prepare

Ans. (b)

The phrase 'do will not prepare' is incorrect. The correct construction should be 'prepare' to make the sentence grammatically correct and meaningful.

356. People say different things at different times SSC CPO 05.10.2023 (Shift-III)
(a) should say fanciful things at different times.
(b) says delectable things at different times.
(c) says whimsical things at different times.
(d) say diverse things at different times.

Ans. (d)

The given sentence is already clear and grammatically correct. However, to enhance the sentence, the word 'diverse' can be used instead of 'different' to add a bit more sophistication and specificity to the statement.

357. Health insurance are important today since, anyone can face a medical emergency without warning.
SSC CPO 05.10.2023 (Shift-III)
(a) will be important
(b) has been important
(c) was important
(d) is important

Ans. (d)

The underlined segment contains an error. In the given sentence, the verb should agree with the subject 'health insurance', which is singular. Therefore, the correct form of the verb is 'is'. Additionally, the sentence is discussing the present importance of health insurance so, the present tense 'is important' is the most appropriate option.

358. I like all games instead of cricket.
SSC CPO 05.10.2023 (Shift-III)
(a) rather (b) exclude
(c) object (d) except

Ans. (d)

The underlined segment contains an error. The most appropriate option to substitute the underlined segment in the given sentence is 'except' to make the sentence contextually meaningful and correct.

SSC CPO 2022

359. As Simon had already been to the park, he lead the way for the other children. SSC CPO 09.11.2022 (Shift-I)
(a) leading the way
(b) lead away
(c) led the way
(d) No substitution required

Ans. (c)

If two actions took place in the past then the 1st action must be in the Past perfect tense (Had + V_3) and the 2nd action must be in the Simple Past tense (V_2). Therefore, 'led the way' is the most appropriate answer.

360. Between Raima and Saima, the former is intelligent, while the latter is beautiful. SSC CPO 09.11.2022 (Shift-II)

(a) later is
(b) letter is
(c) No substitution required
(d) later was

Ans. (c)

The given sentence is grammatically correct.

361. They are cautious about their car as it's door is broken. SSC CPO 09.11.2022 (Shift-III)

(a) as it is
(b) as its
(c) No substitution required
(d) because it's

Ans. (b)

(It's) is a contraction of the words it and is/has and 'Its' is the possessive form of the pronoun 'It' which is used to refer to the noun 'Car'. Hence, 'as its' is the most appropriate answer.

362. He is a weak student and somehow pulled over the exams. SSC CPO 10.11.2022 (Shift-I)

(a) pulled through
(b) pulled down
(c) pulled up
(d) pulled together

Ans. (a)

The underlined segment contains an error. Here, 'pulled through' should replace 'pulled over' in the given sentence. Pulled through means to survive a difficult or dangerous situation.

363. Manthan and Pranav (sang together in a concert). SSC CPO 10.11.2022 (Shift-I)

(a) chanted together in a show
(b) enunciated together in a show
(c) enjoined together in a show
(d) articulated together in a show

Ans. (a)

'Chant' means to sing or intene. Hence, 'chanted together in a show' should replace the underlined part.

364. The story did not go by well enough. SSC CPO 10.11.2022 (Shift-I)

(a) go through (b) go down
(c) go off (d) go into

Ans. (b)

Go down is a phrasal verb which means (keep) from someone. Hence 'go down' is the most appropriate to substitute 'go by' in the given sentence.

Go down is a phrasal verb that means to not accept or believe.

365. The ship sank because the engineer has not called for help. SSC CPO 10.11.2022 (Shift-I)

(a) was not call for help
(b) did not call for help
(c) will not call for help
(d) did not called for help

Ans. (b)

The given sentence is in the past tense so the verb must be used in the past form (V_2) and not in the present perfect form(has not called). Hence, 'did not call for help' is the most appropriate answer.

366. How did you come about his purse? SSC CPO 10.11.2022 (Shift-III)

(a) come into (b) come off
(c) come out (d) come by

Ans. (d)

'Come by' is a phrase that means to manage to acquire or obtain something. The given sentence talks about acquiring a purse.

Hence, 'come by' is the most appropriate answer.

367. She paid a high price for the clothes she brought at the boutique. SSC CPO 10.11.2022 (Shift-III)

(a) bring at
(b) bought at
(c) No substitution required
(d) brought to

Ans. (b)

'Bring/Brought' means to carry or take somebody/something to a place with you & 'Buy/Bought' means to get something by paying money for it. However, the given sentence states that she paid a high price for the clothes she brought at the boutique. Hence, 'bought at' is the most appropriate answer.

368. His last trip around the world taking a toll on his health. SSC CPO 11.11.2022 (Shift-I)

(a) took a toll
(b) taken a toll
(c) No Substitution required
(d) take a toll

Ans. (a)

The underlined segment contains an error. As the given sentence talks about an event in the past, past tense should be used in the underlined segment of the given sentence. Hence, 'took a toll' is most appropriate to substitute 'taking a toll'.

369. Football fans are feeling proud of their teams when they win. SSC CPO 11.11.2022 (Shift-I)

(a) felt proud to their teams
(b) feel proud of their teams
(c) are feel to proud of their teams
(d) feeling proud of their teams

Ans. (b)

The underlined segment contains an error. 'Feel proud of their teams' is the most appropriate option to substitute the underlined segment in. Simple Present Tense will be used in the sentence as it talks about a fact.

370. He is waiting upon you in the compound. SSC CPO 11.11.2022 (Shift-I)

(a) waiting on (b) waiting at
(c) waiting for (d) waiting up

Ans. (c)

The underlined segment contains an error. 'waiting for' is most appropriate to substitute the underlined segment in the given sentence.

371. The child felt down from a great height. SSC CPO 11.11.2022 (Shift-I)

(a) child fallen down
(b) child fall down
(c) child fell down
(d) child falling down

Ans. (c)

The underlined segment contains an error. 'Child fell down' should substitute 'child felt down' in the given sentence. 'Felt' does not make sense in the given sentence. 'Fell' is correct because the sentence is in simple past tense.

372. It was delightful to heard the baby's voice. SSC CPO 11.11.2022 (Shift-I)

(a) was delightful to be heard
(b) was delightful to hear
(c) was delightful to heard
(d) was delightful to hearing

Ans. (b)

The underlined segment contains an error. 'It was delightful to hear' is most appropriate to substitute the underlined segment in the given sentence. As infinitive takes base form of verb (here, hear).

373. The application of the medicine seemed to lesson his pain. SSC CPO 11.11.2022 (Shift-II)

(a) No substitution required
(b) lesion
(c) lessen
(d) lessoned

Ans. (c)

'Lesson', means a period of time when you learn or teach something and 'Lessen' means to make something smaller or less in amount or degree. However, the given sentence states that the application of the medicine seemed to make his pain less.

Hence, 'lessen' is the most appropriate answer.

374. The flames of the fire leap into the air. **SSC CPO 11.11.2022 (Shift-II)**

(a) No substitution required
(b) leapt into
(c) leap in
(d) leaping into

Ans. (b)

We will use the past form(V2) of the verb 'leap' as the event had occurred in the past. Hence 'leapt into' is the most appropriate answer.

375. With tear, eyes, she said goodbye to he dear friend. **SSC CPO 11.11.2022 (Shift-II)**

(a) teary eyes
(b) tear up eyes
(c) No substitution required
(d) tearing eyes

Ans. (a)

'Teary eyes' is a phrase that means having eyes that are wet with tears. The given sentence states that she said goodbye to her dear friend with eyes that are wet with tears.

376. She has checked everything she needs before started work. **SSC CPO 11.11.2022 (Shift-II)**

(a) before starts work
(b) before start to working
(c) before start working
(d) before starting work

Ans. (d)

We will use the V-ing form of the verb 'start' to grammatically correct the given sentence.

Hence, before starting work' is the most appropriate answer.

377. Covid-19 pandemic has resulted in an slow change in flowing of capital generated by workers. **SSC CPO 11.11.2022 (Shift-III)**

(a) an deliberate change to flow of capital
(b) a sluggish change in the flow of capital
(c) an abrupt change in the flow of capital
(d) an sudden change to flow of capital

Ans. (b)

'Sluggish' in option (b) starts, with a consonant sound and we always use the indefinite article 'a' before words starting with a consonant sound. Hence, 'a sluggish change in the flow of capital' is the most appropriate answer.

SSC CPO 2021 (Tier 1 & 2)

378. He lost his heart because he could not cope with the difficult situation. **SSC CPO Tier-2 26.07.2021**

(a) No substitution (b) loss the heart
(c) lost heart (d) lose his heart

Ans. (c)

'Lost heart' is an idiom that mean, to begin to feel that one cannot do something that one has been trying to do.

Similarly, in the given sentence, he could not cope with the difficult situation so he lost heart. Hence, 'lost heart' is the most appropriate answer.

379. He replied mine letter after a month. **SSC CPO Tier-2 26.07.2021**

(a) replied to mine letter
(b) No substitution
(c) reply my letter
(d) replied to my letter

Ans. (d)

We use 'my' before a noun and 'mine' after a noun.

Similarly, in the given sentence, 'letter' is a noun so we will use 'my' before it. Hence, 'replied to my letter' is the most appropriate answer.

380. His fine voice has never heard in this hall again. **SSC CPO Tier-2 26.07.2021**

(a) No substitution
(b) never be heard
(c) will never be heard
(d) will never hear

Ans. (c)

We generally use 'again in a sentence to indicate that something happens a second time so obviously, it will happen in the future and for it, we will use a verb of the future tense(will).

Hence, 'will never be heard' is the most appropriate answer.

381. I am much taller than I was a year ago. **SSC CPO Tier-2 26.07.2021**

(a) that I were a year ago
(b) as I was the year before
(c) No substitution
(d) than a year before

Ans. (c)

The given sentence is grammatically correct.

382. He went to foreign for higher education. **SSC CPO Tier-2 26.07.2021**

(a) went to abroad
(b) has gone to foreign
(c) No substitution
(d) went abroad

Ans. (d)

'Abroad' means in/to a foreign country and we generally use abroad as an adverb in phrases like go/went abroad. So, the phrase 'went to foreign' is contextually incorrect.

Similarly, the given sentence states that he went abroad for higher education. Hence, 'went abroad' is the most appropriate answer.

383. It is time for the children to go to bed. **SSC CPO Tier-2 26.07.2021**

(a) to being in bed (b) should be in bed
(c) No substitution (d) for going in bed

Ans. (c)

The given sentence is grammatically correct.

384. What kind of the book do you want? **SSC CPO Tier-2 26.07.2021**

(a) kinds of a book
(b) No substitution
(c) Kind of the books
(d) kind of book

Ans. (d)

The article 'the' is used to refer to specific or particular nouns. However, in the given sentence, 'book' is not particularly specified so it can be any book.

So, We will remove the article 'the' before 'book'. Hence, 'kind of book' is the most appropriate answer.

385. The porter denied to take the money. **SSC CPO Tier-2 26.07.2021**

(a) denied taking
(c) denied for taking
(b) denied from taking
(d) No substitution

Ans. (a)

'Deny' is always followed by a gerund(V-ing) and never by an infinitive(with the preposition 'to') for example he denied seeing me, he denied giving me, etc. Similarly,the given sentence states that Porter denied taking the money. Hence, 'denied taking' is the most appropriate answer.

SSC CHSL 2024 (Tier 1 & 2)

386. Harish is clever than wise.
SSC CHSL Tier-2 18.11.2024
(a) cleverest than
(b) more clever than
(c) clever as
(d) more cleverer than

Ans. (b)

When comparing two qualities, we use 'more' + adjective + 'than' to make the sentence grammatically correct.
The structure 'more clever than' properly compares the two attributes, cleverness and wisdom, highlighting that cleverness is more pronounced.

387. Research in Social Sciences is plagued nowadays on gloomy definitions and measurements. SSC CHSL Tier-2 18.11.2024
(a) nowadays amid gloomy definitions
(b) nowadays by gloomy definitions
(c) nowadays during gloomy definitions
(d) nowadays onto gloomy definitions

Ans. (b)

'By' is the appropriate preposition to indicate the cause of the plague.
Hence, the correct option is: nowadays by gloomy definitions.

388. I am down with her complaints.
SSC CHSL Tier-1 01.07.2024 (Shift-I)
(a) passed out with
(b) fed up with
(c) held down with
(d) looked down with

Ans. (b)

The underlined part of the given sentence contains an error. The phrasal verb 'down with' means suffering from which does not fit the context of the sentence. Hence, replace it with 'fed up with' to correct the sentence.

389. This is best book for children to read.
SSC CHSL Tier-1 01.07.2024 (Shift-I)
(a) This is the best book
(b) This is good book
(c) This is very good book
(d) This is very best book

Ans. (a)

The underlined part of the given sentence contains an error. The superlative degree of adjective takes article 'the'. Hence, add 'the' before 'best'.

390. Rahul had strong pain in his stomach.
SSC CHSL Tier-1 01.07.2024 (Shift-I)
(a) severe (b) high
(c) deep (d) strict

Ans. (a)

From the given options, 'severe' can be replaced by 'strong'.

391. It is a general belief that the female ostrich guard the nest at night.
SSC CHSL Tier-1 01.07.2024 (Shift-I)
(a) guarded the nest at night
(b) guards the nest at night
(c) does guard the nest in night
(d) is guarding the nest at night

Ans. (b)

The underlined part of the sentence contains an error. As the subject of the sentence 'It is a general belief that the female ostrich' is singular, singular verb 'guards' should be used to correct the sentence.

392. The little boy cried with pain when he burnt his fingers.
SSC CHSL Tier-1 01.07.2024 (Shift-I)
(a) No substitution required
(b) when he burns his fingers
(c) while he burn his fingers
(d) as he burning his fingers

Ans. (a)

The underlined segment is grammatically and contextually correct.

393. As I have no time to discuss the points, so I wrote a email to her.
SSC CHSL Tier-1 01.07.2024 (Shift-II)
(a) so I wrote an e-mail for her
(b) so I wrote a e-mail to her
(c) I write an email to her
(d) I wrote an email to her

Ans. (d)

The underlined part of the sentence contains an error.
The conjunction 'as' does not take 'so'. Hence, remove 'so' to correct the sentence.

394. Children should avoid giving out personal details online (which will) identify them or their location.
SSC CHSL Tier-1 01.07.2024 (Shift-II)
(a) what will
(b) that could
(c) whichever can
(d) which might lead

Ans. (b)

The bracketed part of the sentence contains an error. Use 'that could' to correct the sentence.

395. The road which connecting the two states is overcrowded.
SSC CHSL Tier-1 01.07.2024 (Shift-II)
(a) connected (b) connects
(c) has connecting (d) have connected

Ans. (b)

The underlined part of the sentence contains an error. Use 'connects' to correct the sentence.

396. If you had apprised me about your problem earlier, I would have allow you to go.
SSC CHSL Tier-1 01.07.2024 (Shift-III)
(a) If you had apprised me about your problem earlier, I would have allowed you to go.
(b) If you apprised me about your problem earlier, I would have allowed you to go.
(c) If you had apprised me about your problem earlier, I would allow you to go.
(d) If you can apprise me about your problem earlier, I would have allowed you to go.

Ans. (a)

The given sentence contains an error. The verb 'has/have' takes the second form of the verb. Hence, the correct sentence is- If you had apprised me about your problem earlier, I would have allowed you to go.

397. Select the option with the correct use of article(s).
SSC CHSL Tier-1 01.07.2024 (Shift-III)
(a) She kept lot of rules in her life due to which she is flourishing today
(b) She kept an lot of rules in her life due to which she is flourishing today
(c) She kept a lot of rules in her life due to which she is flourishing today.
(d) She kept the lot of rules in her life due to which she is flourishing today.

Ans. (c)

The sentence that correctly uses the articles is- She kept a lot of rules in her life due to which she is flourishing today.

398. Harmit is not innocent such as Uday.
SSC CHSL Tier-1 01.07.2024 (Shift-III)
(a) Harmit is not as innocent more than Uday.
(b) Harmit is not as much as innocent as Uday.
(c) Harmit is not as innocent as Uday.
(d) Harmit is not innocent than Uday.

Ans. (c)

The given sentence contains an error. As there is a comparison between Harmit and Uday, 'as ... as' will be used. Hence, the correct sentence is- Harmit is not as innocent as Uday.

399. He was not happy until he gave up his job and live as a fakir in the forests. SSC CHSL Tier-1 01.07.2024 (Shift-III)
(a) unless he gave up his job and lives
(b) until he gave up his job and lived
(c) until he gave up his job and lives
(d) until he gives up his job and lived

Ans. (b)

The underlined part of the given sentence contains an error. As the given sentence is in past tense, 'lived' should be used to correct the sentence.

400. Dhruv's anger blazed of uncontrollably.
SSC CHSL Tier-1 01.07.2024 (Shift-III)
(a) anger blazed onwards
(b) anger blazed after
(c) anger blazed up
(d) anger blazed into
Ans. (c)
The underlined part of the given sentence contains an error. Use 'anger blazed up' to correct the sentence.

401. The company do not broke the law at any time.
SSC CHSL Tier-1 01.07.2024 (Shift-III)
(a) do not brakes
(b) did not breaking
(c) did not broken
(d) does not break
Ans. (d)
The underlined part of the given sentence contains an error. The use of 'do' is incorrect as the subject is singular, so singular verb is used. Use 'does' to correct the sentence.

402. I am so glad that I ran into you on the way. SSC CHSL Tier-1 01.07.2024 (Shift-IV)
(a) ran over
(b) No improvement required
(c) ran away
(d) ran out of
Ans. (b)
The underlined part is grammatically and contextually correct.

403. This win could enhance to be a historic turning point in the fortunes of the team.
SSC CHSL Tier-1 01.07.2024 (Shift-IV)
(a) prove (b) demonstrate
(c) accomplish (d) confirm
Ans. (a)
The underlined part of the sentence contains an error. Use 'prove' to correct the sentence.

404. Mothers have great animosity for their children.
SSC CHSL Tier-1 01.07.2024 (Shift-IV)
(a) affection (b) absurdity
(c) affectation (d) abasement
Ans. (a)
The underlined part of the sentence contains an error.
The use of word 'animosity' is incorrect in the context of the sentence. Use 'affection' to correct the sentence.

405. Sonam's cat used to chase the mouse into the kitchen and knock through a tower of pots and pans.
SSC CHSL Tier-1 01.07.2024 (Shift-IV)
(a) knock inside a tower of pots
(b) knock over a tower of pots
(c) knock away a tower of pots
(d) knock out a tower of pots
Ans. (b)
The underlined part of the sentence contains an error. Use 'over' in place of 'through' to correct the sentence.

406. Samita asked out a favour of going early today.
SSC CHSL Tier-1 02.07.2024 (Shift-I)
(a) asked for (b) asked over
(c) asked around (d) asked after
Ans. (a)
The underlined part of the sentence contains an error. The phrasal verb 'asked out' is incorrect. Use 'asked for' which means 'to request' to correct the sentence.

407. The plum tree in our garden is cover in blossoms, as are the trees outside my office window.
SSC CHSL Tier-1 02.07.2024 (Shift-I)
(a) is covering at
(b) are cover at
(c) is covered in
(d) No substitution required
Ans. (c)
The underlined part of the sentence contains an error. Use 'is covered in' to correct the sentence.

408. A soldier of the tenth legion leaped into the water as soon as the ship touches the shore.
SSC CHSL Tier-1 02.07.2024 (Shift-I)
(a) No substitution required
(b) the ship touched the shore
(c) the ship was touch the shore
(d) the ship touch the shore
Ans. (b)
The underlined part of the sentence contains an error.
As the sentence is in past tense, 'the ship touched the shore' should be used to correct the sentence.

409. We feel warm on the subject.
SSC CHSL Tier-1 02.07.2024 (Shift-I)
(a) warmly about (b) warming about
(c) warmer on (d) warmed on
Ans. (a)
The underlined part of the sentence contains an error.
Use 'warmly about' to correct the sentence.

410. The dictator ordered the traitor were jailed. SSC CHSL Tier-1 02.07.2024 (Shift-I)
(a) is (b) to be
(c) might (d) was
Ans. (b)
The underlined part of the sentence contains an error. Use 'to be' to correct the sentence.

411. He has broken his leg yesterday.
SSC CHSL Tier-1 02.07.2024 (Shift-II)
(a) He broke his leg yesterday.
(b) He had broke his leg yesterday.
(c) He have broken his leg yesterday.
(d) He has broke his leg yesterday.
Ans. (a)
The given sentence contains an error. As the sentence is in past tense, use 'broke' in place of 'has broken' to correct the sentence.

412. Please take many as you want.
SSC CHSL Tier-1 02.07.2024 (Shift-II)
(a) so much
(b) as much
(c) too much
(d) much of
Ans. (b)
The underlined part of the sentence contains an error. Use 'as much' to correct the sentence.

413. Rimjhim received a children's very illustrated colourful atlas on her 10th birthday. SSC CHSL Tier-1 02.07.2024 (Shift-II)
(a) a very illustrated colourful atlas children
(b) a very colourful illustrated children's atlas
(c) an very illustrated colourful children's atlas
(d) a colourful very illustrated children's atlas
Ans. (b)
The underlined part of the sentence contains an error.
Use 'a very colourful illustrated children's atlas' to correct the sentence.

414. I hope you have enjoying yourselves at the party tonight!
SSC CHSL Tier-1 02.07.2024 (Shift-II)
(a) enjoys yourselves
(b) will be enjoy himself
(c) are enjoying themselves
(d) enjoy yourselves
Ans. (d)
The underlined part of the sentence contains an error.
Use 'enjoy yourselves' to correct the sentence.

415. Their was a large snake found in the garden last evening.
SSC CHSL Tier-1 02.07.2024 (Shift-II)
(a) There was a large snake
(b) There was the larger snake
(c) There was not a large snake
(d) Their was the larger snake
Ans. (a)
The underlined part of the sentence contains an error. Use 'There was a large snake' to correct the sentence.

416. What are you looking around?
SSC CHSL Tier-1 02.07.2024 (Shift-III)
(a) What are you looking among?
(b) What are you looking for?
(c) What are you looking across?
(d) What are you looking through?
Ans. (b)
The given sentence contains an error. The use of phrasal verb 'looking around' is incorrect. The correct phrasal verb is 'looking for' which means 'to search for' to correct the sentence.

417. Then I unfurled the Indian tri-colour and keep it aloft at the roof of the world. SSC CHSL Tier-1 02.07.2024 (Shift-III)
(a) keeping
(b) held
(c) No substitution required
(d) hold
Ans. (b)
The underlined part of the sentence contains an error. The use of the word 'keep' is incorrect in the context as well as the past tense of the sentence. Use 'held' to correct the sentence.

418. Ramita has decided to forsake her participation in college activities until she improved her scores.
SSC CHSL Tier-1 02.07.2024 (Shift-III)
(a) Forsake (b) Improved
(c) Decided (d) Participation
Ans. (b)
'Improved' is incorrect in this sentence as the sentence is emphasising future course of action. Hence 'improves' should be used to make the sentence correct.

419. This book provides an unrestrained account of the natural resources in India. SSC CHSL Tier-1 02.07.2024 (Shift-III)
(a) exhausting (b) limlited
(c) exhaustive (d) excessive
Ans. (c)
The underlined part of the sentence contains an error. The word 'unrestrained', which means 'not controlled', is not correct in the sentence. Use 'exhaustive' meaning that which can finish, to correct the sentence.

420. The Privacy Shield establishes a process to allow companies to transfer consumer data from European Union countries to the United States in compliance in EU law. SSC CHSL Tier-1 02.07.2024 (Shift-III)
(a) No improvement
(b) in compliance for the
(c) in compliance under the
(d) in compliance with
Ans. (d)
The underlined part of the sentence contains an error. Use 'in compliance with' to correct the sentence.

421. I have met my friend yesterday.
SSC CHSL Tier-1 02.07.2024 (Shift-IV)
(a) had been meeting
(b) was meeting
(c) met my friend
(d) have been meeting
Ans. (c)
The given sentence contains an error of tense. The sentence is in simple past tense. So, use 'met my friend' to correct the sentence.

422. It will take two hours to walk across the forest.
SSC CHSL Tier-1 02.07.2024 (Shift-IV)
(a) through (b) over
(c) away (d) between
Ans. (a)
The underlined part of the given sentence contains an error. Use 'through' to correct the sentence.

423. The wizard, while performing an item, accidentally set his own hat on fire and prompted the fire alarm to go on. SSC CHSL Tier-1 02.07.2024 (Shift-IV)
(a) the fire alarm to go away
(b) the fire alarm to go under
(c) the fire alarm to go off
(d) the fire alarm to go above
Ans. (c)
The underlined part of the given sentence contains an error. Use 'off' in place of 'on' to correct the sentence.

424. You can be sentenced for trespassing on someone else's property.
SSC CHSL Tier-1 02.07.2024 (Shift-IV)
(a) conspiring against others
(b) entering without permission
(c) leaving without permission
(d) showing unselfish devotion
Ans. (b)
Trespassing means to enter any area without permission.

425. We set up on the journey early in the morning.
SSC CHSL Tier-1 02.07.2024 (Shift-IV)
(a) set off
(b) set in
(c) No improvement required
(d) set about
Ans. (a)
The underlined part of the given sentence contains an error. Use 'off' in place of 'up' to correct the sentence.

426. His mother's transfer from a small town to Delhi brought up a huge change in his schooling.
SSC CHSL Tier-1 03.07.2024 (Shift-I)
(a) from a small town to Delhi
(b) His mother's transfer
(c) in his schooling
(d) brought up a huge change
Ans. (d)
Part 'brought up a huge change' contains an error. The phrasal verb 'brought up' means to nurture which is incorrect for the sentence. The correct phrasal verb would be 'brought about'.

427. Mrs. Meera and family / received his letter / a week ago.
SSC CHSL Tier-1 03.07.2024 (Shift-I)
(a) No error
(b) Mrs. Meera and family
(c) received his letter
(d) a week ago
Ans. (a)
The given sentence is grammatically correct and contextually meaningful.

428. The woman lost much to her body weight due to diabetes.
SSC CHSL Tier-1 03.07.2024 (Shift-I)
(a) from her body weight due to
(b) for her body weight due to
(c) off her body weight due to
(d) of her body weight due to
Ans. (d)
The underlined part of the given sentence contains an error. Use 'of' in place of 'to' to correct the sentence.

429. In every country of the world, primary caregivers are the women of children and elders.
SSC CHSL Tier-1 03.07.2024 (Shift-I)
(a) women are the caregivers primary of
(b) the women primary caregivers are of
(c) primary caregivers women are of the
(d) women are the primary caregivers of
Ans. (d)
The underlined part of the given sentence contains an error. Use 'women are the primary caregivers of' to correct the sentence.

430. I will require a quiet room to work at.
SSC CHSL Tier-1 03.07.2024 (Shift-I)

(a) on (b) about
(c) with (d) in

Ans. (d)

The underlined part of the given sentence contains an error. Use 'in' to correct the sentence.

431. Gulliver hear his watch ticking in his pocket. SSC CHSL Tier-1 03.07.2024 (Shift-I)

(a) heard his watch tickling
(b) watch ticking
(c) could hear his watch ticking
(d) could hear his watch ticked

Ans. (c)

The underlined part of the given sentence contains an error. Add 'could' before 'hear' to correct the sentence.

432. An (imperfect positioning) of the Sun, Earth and Moon results in the Moon passing through only part of Earth's umbra, resulting in a partial lunar eclipse. SSC CHSL Tier-1 03.07.2024 (Shift-II)

(a) imperfect alliance
(b) imperfect revolution
(c) imperfect allegiance
(d) imperfect alignment

Ans. (d)

The phrase 'imperfect alignment' indicates 'imperfect positioning'.

433. The city of Hyderabad is located (on the heart from Telangana).
SSC CHSL Tier-1 03.07.2024 (Shift-II)

(a) with the heart in Telangana
(b) in the heart with Telangana
(c) of the heart in Telangana
(d) in the heart of Telangana

Ans. (d)

The bracketed part of the given sentence contains an error. Use 'in the heart of Telangana' to correct the sentence.

434. The new chief is gifted at the power of eloquence.
SSC CHSL Tier-1 03.07.2024 (Shift-II)

(a) gifted with (b) gifted for
(c) gifted among (d) gifted of

Ans. (a)

The underlined part of the given sentence contains an error.

Use 'gifted with' to correct the sentence.

435. I was looking for a barren seat in the bus but could not find one.
SSC CHSL Tier-1 03.07.2024 (Shift-II)

(a) hollow seat (b) deserted seat
(c) vacant seat (d) vacuous seat

Ans. (c)

The underlined part of the given sentence contains an error. Use 'vacant seat' to correct the sentence.

436. Little that I knew of the English language was not sufficient to make me an English teacher.
SSC CHSL Tier-1 03.07.2024 (Shift-III)

(a) So little (b) A little
(c) The little (d) Very little

Ans. (c)

The underlined part of the given sentence contains an error. Use 'The little' to correct the sentence.

437. The annual seed festival hosted in Auroville promote sharing of traditional knowledge and sustainable farming practices.
SSC CHSL Tier-1 03.07.2024 (Shift-III)

(a) promotes sharing of traditional
(b) promotes sharing of traditionally
(c) promotes sharing of tradition
(d) No improvement required

Ans. (a)

The underlined part of the given sentence contains an error. Use 'promotes sharing of traditional' to correct the sentence as the subject of the sentence is singular.

438. He was the fastest between all the contestants.
SSC CHSL Tier-1 03.07.2024 (Shift-III)

(a) No substitution (b) since
(c) amongst (d) from

Ans. (c)

The underlined part of the given sentence contains an error. Use 'amongst' to correct the sentence as we are referring to more than two contestants.

439. There is no place on the bench.
SSC CHSL Tier-1 03.07.2024 (Shift-III)

(a) more space (b) no life
(c) more place (d) no room

Ans. (d)

The underlined part of the given sentence contains an error. Use 'no room' to correct the sentence.

440. Chotu is a bright young child, who yearn to go to school but works in his uncle's dhaba.
SSC CHSL Tier-1 03.07.2024 (Shift-IV)

(a) worked (b) working
(c) yearns (d) yearned

Ans. (c)

The given sentence contains an error of subject verb agreement. Use 'yearns' as the subject is singular to correct the sentence.

441. If you behave well and exhibit good manners, then (people will be likely to remember you) in a positive way.
SSC CHSL Tier-1 03.07.2024 (Shift-IV)

(a) people likely you remember
(b) people are like remember you
(c) people will like in remember
(d) people are likely to remember you

Ans. (d)

The bracketed part of the given sentence contains an error. Use 'people are likely to remember you' to correct the sentence.

442. The sudden declaration of war between two countries led to a disarray. SSC CHSL Tier-1 03.07.2024 (Shift-IV)

(a) peaceful treaty
(b) disorderly situation
(c) refined argument
(d) elusive situation

Ans. (b)

The word 'disarray' means disorderly situation.

443. It was her who first saw the criminal.
SSC CHSL Tier-1 03.07.2024 (Shift-IV)

(a) she (b) them
(c) hers (d) him

Ans. (a)

The underlined part of the given sentence contains an error. Use 'she' to correct the sentence.

444. Greta Thunberg's tirade against environmental degeneration shocked the world leaders.
SSC CHSL Tier-1 03.07.2024 (Shift-IV)

(a) minute observation
(b) debatable account
(c) long and angry speech
(d) innate liberal opinion

Ans. (c)

A tirade is a long and angry speech.

445. If you are thinking about investing in share markets, isn't it make sense to find an expert?
SSC CHSL Tier-1 04.07.2024 (Shift-I)

(a) did it (b) is it
(c) doesn't it (d) do it

Ans. (c)

The underlined part of the given sentence contains an error. Use 'doesn't it' to correct the sentence.

446. He lived on the bank of a mighty river, broad and deep, that have always silently rolling on to a vast undiscovered ocean.
SSC CHSL Tier-1 04.07.2024 (Shift-I)

(a) which were always silently rolling
(b) which was always silently rolling
(c) that were always silently rolling
(d) what has always silently rolling

Ans. (b)

The underlined part of the given sentence contains an error. Use 'which was always silently rolling' to correct the sentence.

447. Applications are to be sent to the school's e-mail ID before 30th June.
SSC CHSL Tier-1 04.07.2024 (Shift-I)

(a) will be send to
(b) is sending
(c) No substitution required
(d) would be send to

Ans. (c)

The underlined part is grammatically correct and contextually meaningful.

448. The painting look good in this room.
SSC CHSL Tier-1 04.07.2024 (Shift-I)

(a) have looking (b) looking
(c) had look (d) looks

Ans. (d)

The underlined part of the given sentence contains an error. Use 'looks' to correct the sentence as the subject of the sentence is singular.

449. His flight departs in 5:00 pm.
SSC CHSL Tier-1 04.07.2024 (Shift-II)

(a) of (b) for
(c) at (d) from

Ans. (c)

The underlined part of the given sentence contains an error. Use 'at' to mention the exact time and to correct the sentence.

450. I gave my best dress to her on condition that she return it the very next day in a clean condition.
SSC CHSL Tier-1 04.07.2024 (Shift-II)

(a) on the condition that she would return
(b) on the condition that she return
(c) on condition that she returned
(d) on the conditions that she had return

Ans. (a)

The underlined part of the given sentence contains an error. Use 'on the condition that she would return' to correct the sentence.

451. The novel highlights the place of the endangered species in the rainforest.
SSC CHSL Tier-1 04.07.2024 (Shift-II)

(a) prowess
(b) position
(c) plight
(d) perspective

Ans. (c)

The underlined part of the given sentence contains an error. Use 'plight' to correct the sentence.

452. The boy watched a sci-fi movie in the lieu of playing in the game zone.
SSC CHSL Tier-1 04.07.2024 (Shift-II)

(a) in lieu of play
(b) in lieu off playing
(c) in lieu of playing
(d) on lieu of playing

Ans. (c)

The underlined part of the given sentence contains an error. Use 'in lieu of playing' to correct the sentence.

453. My entire family left me in the lurch when I went to them after I divorced my husband.
SSC CHSL Tier-1 04.07.2024 (Shift-II)

(a) refused to help me in my distress
(b) blamed only me for my failure
(c) scorned me for committing mistakes
(d) attempted to harass me

Ans. (a)

Left me in the lurch means to leave (someone) without help or protection when it is needed.

454. Pratigya arrived / to the / railway station / five hours early.
SSC CHSL Tier-1 04.07.2024 (Shift-III)

(a) railway station
(b) Pratigya arrived
(c) to the
(d) five hours early

Ans. (c)

Part (c) 'to the' contains an error. Use 'at' as preposition of in place of 'to' to correct the sentence.

455. The revolt of the labourers will be considered as an epoch in the world history.
SSC CHSL Tier-1 04.07.2024 (Shift-III)

(a) unpopular measure
(b) hostile event
(c) important period
(d) commendable act

Ans. (c)

The word 'epoch' means 'an important period'.

456. Many a women work for the betterment of their family.
SSC CHSL Tier-1 04.07.2024 (Shift-III)

(a) Many a woman worked for
(b) Many a women working for
(c) Many a woman works for
(d) Many a women works for

Ans. (c)

The underlined part of the given sentence contains an error. Use 'Many a woman works for' to correct the sentence.

The expression 'Many a' takes the singular form of noun.

457. He is almost quiet well.
SSC CHSL Tier-1 04.07.2024 (Shift-III)

(a) almost quietly (b) quiet
(c) very quite (d) quite

Ans. (d)

The underlined part of the given sentence contains an error. Use 'quite' to correct the sentence.

458. In the winter season, the poor woman needed a refuge where she could live freely and independently.
SSC CHSL Tier-1 04.07.2024 (Shift-III)

(a) school (b) shelter
(c) inn (d) tent

Ans. (b)

The word 'refuge' means a place or situation providing safety or shelter.

459. It is a high-pay job.
SSC CHSL Tier-1 04.07.2024 (Shift-III)

(a) high-paying
(b) low-paid
(c) high-paid
(d) low-pay

Ans. (a)

The underlined part of the given sentence contains an error.
Use 'high-paying' to correct the sentence.

460. He takes his always dog for a walk in the park.
SSC CHSL Tier-1 04.07.2024 (Shift-IV)

(a) takes his dog for always a walk
(b) takes his dog for an always walk
(c) always takes his dog for a walk
(d) his dog for a walk always takes

Ans. (c)

The underlined part of the given sentence contains an error.

Use 'always takes his dog for a walk' to correct the sentence.

461. She was thinking at the fun they had.
SSC CHSL Tier-1 04.07.2024 (Shift-IV)

(a) beside
(b) by
(c) No substitution required
(d) about

Ans. (d)

The underlined part of the given sentence contains an error. Use 'about' to correct the sentence.

462. A newer, more effective computer system was installed in place of the obsolete one.
SSC CHSL Tier-1 04.07.2024 (Shift-IV)

(a) out-dated (b) current
(c) modern (d) advanced

Ans. (a)

Obsolete means old and out-dated.

463. I had to write a letter of mistake to my father for the blunder I made.
SSC CHSL Tier-1 04.07.2024 (Shift-IV)
(a) apology
(b) No substitution required
(c) gratitude
(d) circumstance

Ans. (a)

The underlined part of the given sentence contains an error. Use 'apology' to correct the sentence.

464. They are leaving there coats there.
SSC CHSL Tier-1 05.07.2024 (Shift-I)
(a) their coats there
(b) they're coats there
(c) there coats their
(d) their coats their

Ans. (a)

The underlined part of the given sentence contains an error.

Use 'their coats there' to correct the sentence.

465. Even in cold weather, the reliable car always started on the first try.
SSC CHSL Tier-1 05.07.2024 (Shift-I)
(a) dependable
(b) inaccurate
(c) erratic
(d) flaky

Ans. (a)

'Reliable' means dependable.

'Erratic' means no ever or regular.

'Flaky' means unreliable.

466. Mrs. Lakshmi's purchases add around to ₹ 2,650.
SSC CHSL Tier-1 05.07.2024 (Shift-I)
(a) purchases add out to
(b) purchases add from to
(c) purchases add up to
(d) purchases add for to

Ans. (c)

The underlined part of the given sentence contains an error.

Use 'purchases add up to' to correct the sentence.

467. The girl which is wearing a blue shirt is my sister.
SSC CHSL Tier-1 05.07.2024 (Shift-II)
(a) which is wearing the blue shirt
(b) who is wearing a blue shirt
(c) which wear a blue shirt
(d) who wear a blue shirt

Ans. (b)

The underlined part of the given sentence contains an error.
Use 'who is wearing a blue shirt' to correct the sentence as relative pronoun 'who' is used for people.

468. The clamour distracted the priest and made him angry.
SSC CHSL Tier-1 05.07.2024 (Shift-II)
(a) loud and confused noise
(b) narrow-mindedness
(c) introduction of new things
(d) humorous deception

Ans. (a)

The word 'clamour' means a loud and confused noise, especially that of people shouting.

469. Employers in many developing countries report that a lack of skilled workers is a major and increasing bottleneck for their operations, affected their capacity to innovate.
SSC CHSL Tier-1 05.07.2024 (Shift-II)
(a) affect their capacity
(b) effecting their capacity
(c) effect their capacity
(d) affecting their capacity

Ans. (d)

The underlined part of the given sentence contains an error. Use 'affecting their capacity' to correct the sentence.

470. The dedicated teacher laboured assiduously to aid her pupils in achieving success.
SSC CHSL Tier-1 05.07.2024 (Shift-II)
(a) un-biased
(b) committed
(c) uninvolved
(d) apathetic

Ans. (b)

The word 'dedicated' means 'committed'. The other options are 'Un-biased' means fair or impartial. 'Apathetic' means not caring.

471. He asked his father when would come the next letter.
SSC CHSL Tier-1 05.07.2024 (Shift-III)
(a) No substitution required
(b) the next letter would come
(c) would the next letter come
(d) come the next letter

Ans. (b)

The underlined part of the given sentence contains an error. Use 'the next letter would come' to correct the sentence.

472. If you do hard work, you will have the expected results.
SSC CHSL Tier-1 05.07.2024 (Shift-III)
(a) good results
(b) required results
(c) desired results
(d) bad results

Ans. (c)

The underlined segment 'expected results' means 'desired results'.

473. Although I have a lot of work to do, I am determined to finish it all by the end of the day so that I can enjoy my weekend not having any imminent due dates.
SSC CHSL Tier-1 05.07.2024 (Shift-III)
(a) without any looming deadlines
(b) not with any pressure of due date
(c) with no pending reservations
(d) not leaving any work incomplete

Ans. (a)

The most appropriate substitution will be 'without any looming deadlines'. It means not having any imminent due dates.

474. Vihaan is clumsy at dancing.
SSC CHSL Tier-1 05.07.2024 (Shift-IV)
(a) all thumbs
(b) easy handed
(c) master skill
(d) heavy duty

Ans. (a)

The most appropriate substitution will be- all thumbs. It means not graceful and clumsy.

475. Play cards is not allowed here.
SSC CHSL Tier-1 05.07.2024 (Shift-IV)
(a) Play card
(b) Played cards
(c) Playing cards
(d) Playing card

Ans. (c)

The underlined part of the given sentence contains an error. Use 'playing cards' to correct the sentence.

476. There was a noise that was wake me up.
SSC CHSL Tier-1 05.07.2024 (Shift-IV)
(a) woken me up
(b) has woke me up
(c) woke me up
(d) wakes me up

Ans. (c)

The underlined part of the given sentence contains an error. Use 'woke me up' to correct the sentence.

477. Sarita speaks French best.
SSC CHSL Tier-1 08.07.2024 (Shift-I)
(a) worst
(b) better
(c) good
(d) well

Ans. (d)

The underlined part of the given sentence contains an error. Use 'well' to correct the sentence as the sentence needs an adverb and not an adjective.

478. We have carried out an successful raid on a fraudulent minister.
SSC CHSL Tier-1 08.07.2024 (Shift-I)
(a) the successful raid
(b) successful raid
(c) these successful raid
(d) a successful raid

Ans. (d)
'A successful raid' is the appropriate option as the word 'successful' starts with a consonant 's'.
Hence it will tape preposition (article) 'a' before it.

479. Yoga may manage pain and helping reduce stress.
SSC CHSL Tier-1 08.07.2024 (Shift-I)
(a) help reduction for
(b) helped reduce
(c) help reduced
(d) help in reducing

Ans. (d)
The underlined part of the given sentence contains an error. Use 'help in reducing' to correct the sentence.

480. I like played cricket after school.
SSC CHSL Tier-1 08.07.2024 (Shift-I)
(a) playing
(b) play
(c) played
(d) having to play

Ans. (a)
The underlined part of the given sentence contains an error. Use 'playing' to correct the sentence.

481. Since, my friend was not feeling well, she asked me to come over and take care of her.
SSC CHSL Tier-1 08.07.2024 (Shift-I)
(a) No improvement
(b) come across
(c) come into
(d) come through

Ans. (a)
The underlined part is grammatically and contextually correct.

482. They appointed him as the manager, as he was due for an promotion.
SSC CHSL Tier-1 08.07.2024 (Shift-II)
(a) next
(b) it's
(c) No substitution required
(d) a

Ans. (d)
The underlined part of the given sentence contains an error. Use 'a' to correct the sentence.

483. What is the time (in) your watch?
SSC CHSL Tier-1 08.07.2024 (Shift-II)
(a) by (b) with
(c) into (d) on

Ans. (a)
The bracketed part of the given sentence contains an error. Use 'by' to correct the sentence.

484. She developing a remarkable resistance to cold and altitude.
SSC CHSL Tier-1 08.07.2024 (Shift-II)
(a) developed
(b) has develop
(c) No substitution required
(d) has been developing

Ans. (a)
The underlined part of the given sentence contains an error.
Use 'developed' to correct the sentence.

485. He has grown into a beautiful youth.
SSC CHSL Tier-1 08.07.2024 (Shift-III)
(a) in a beautiful youth
(b) a beautiful youth
(c) in a handsome youth
(d) into a handsome youth

Ans. (d)
The underlined part of the given sentence contains an error. Use 'into a handsome youth' to correct the sentence.

486. The inspector smile after he was finished and patted Margie's head.
SSC CHSL Tier-1 08.07.2024 (Shift-III)
(a) No substitution required
(b) smiled
(c) was smiled
(d) has smiled

Ans. (b)
The underlined part of the given sentence contains an error.
Use 'smiled' to correct the sentence as the given sentence is in past tense.

487. Rohit is write to them three times.
SSC CHSL Tier-1 08.07.2024 (Shift-III)
(a) Rohit was beings written
(b) Rohit was write
(c) Rohit had write
(d) Rohit has written

Ans. (d)
The underlined part of the given sentence contains an error. Use 'Rohit has written' to correct the sentence.

488. We are decorate the living-room at the moment.
SSC CHSL Tier-1 08.07.2024 (Shift-III)
(a) We are being decorating
(b) We are being decorate
(c) We are decorates
(d) We are decorating

Ans. (d)
The underlined part of the given sentence contains an error. Use 'We are decorating' to correct the sentence.

489. Men (allowed) for Olympic artistic swimming for the first time at the 2024 Paris Games, the IOC confirmed on Thursday.
SSC CHSL Tier-1 08.07.2024 (Shift-IV)
(a) are likely (b) have permitted
(c) will approve (d) are eligible

Ans. (d)
The bracketed part of the given sentence contains an error. Use 'are eligible' to correct the sentence.

490. As there was no one to look thorough the orphan, he had to take refuge in the orphanage.
SSC CHSL Tier-1 08.07.2024 (Shift-IV)
(a) look down upon (b) look after
(c) look upon (d) look through

Ans. (b)
The underlined part of the given sentence contains an error. The use of 'look thorough' is incorrect. Use 'look after' to correct the sentence.

491. Loud noise effects our ability to concentrate.
SSC CHSL Tier-1 08.07.2024 (Shift-IV)
(a) affects (b) bestows
(c) results (d) intensifies

Ans. (a)
The underlined part of the given sentence contains an error. Use 'affects' to correct the sentence.

492. I cannot go out tonight because I will preparing of my interview tomorrow.
SSC CHSL Tier-1 08.07.2024 (Shift-IV)
(a) I have to prepare for
(b) I will have prepare for
(c) I have been prepare to
(d) I had to prepare to

Ans. (a)
The underlined part of the given sentence contains an error. Use 'I have to prepare for' to correct the sentence.

493. If it is sunny tomorrow, we go for a picnic. **SSC CHSL Tier-1 09.07.2024 (Shift-I)**
(a) will going (b) will went
(c) will go (d) goes

Ans. (c)
The underlined part of the given sentence contains an error. Use 'will go' to correct the sentence.

494. Even though she's a celebrity, she doesn't draw any attention towards herself. **SSC CHSL Tier-1 09.07.2024 (Shift-I)**
(a) is hard to come by
(b) keeps a low profile
(c) keeps hot under the collar
(d) keeps up with the Joneses

Ans. (b)

The most appropriate substitute for the given blank is 'keeps a low profile'. It means that it doesn't draw any attention towards herself.

'Is hard to come by' means hard to find or get.

'Keep hot under the collar' means to get annoyed or angry.

'Keep up with the Joneses' means to own the same things as other people.

495. There is an old rivalry between the three families for ages.

SSC CHSL Tier-1 09.07.2024 (Shift-I)

(a) of the three families
(b) No substitution required
(c) among the three families
(d) in the three families

Ans. (c)

The underlined part of the given sentence contains an error.

Use 'among' to correct the sentence as we are referring to more than two beings.

496. She finished her quickly breakfast and rushed to school.

SSC CHSL Tier-1 09.07.2024 (Shift-II)

(a) finished her breakfast quickly
(b) quickly her breakfast finished
(c) her breakfast finished quickly
(d) finished breakfast hers quickly

Ans. (a)

The underlined part of the given sentence contains an error. Use 'finished her breakfast quickly' to correct the sentence.

497. Writing can instil a number of emotions (as in a reader).

SSC CHSL Tier-1 09.07.2024 (Shift-II)

(a) until a reader
(b) among a reader
(c) within a reader
(d) instead a reader

Ans. (c)

The bracketed part of the given sentence contains an error. Use 'within a reader' to correct the sentence.

498. I consider that every matter must be considered in every point of view.

SSC CHSL Tier-1 09.07.2024 (Shift-II)

(a) of every point
(b) from every point
(c) at every point
(d) on every point

Ans. (b)

The underlined part of the given sentence contains an error. Use 'from every point' to correct the sentence.

499. Once bitten, thrice shy.

SSC CHSL Tier-1 09.07.2024 (Shift-II)

(a) always shy (b) never shy
(c) once shy (d) twice shy

Ans. (d)

The underlined part of the given sentence contains an error. Use 'twice shy' to correct the sentence.

500. Mahima is as smarter as Shilpi.

SSC CHSL Tier-1 09.07.2024 (Shift-III)

(a) as smart as
(b) more smart as
(c) most smart as
(d) smartest than

Ans. (a)

The underlined part of the given sentence contains an error. Use 'as smart as' to correct the sentence. The as….as expression takes the positive degree of adjective.

501. The small size of his store makes it impossible for him to stock all the items. **SSC CHSL Tier-1 09.07.2024 (Shift-III)**

(a) made them impossible
(b) making it impossible
(c) is made it impossible
(d) No substitution required

Ans. (d)

The underlined part is grammatically and contextually correct.

502. Bill Gates' fortune was bequeathed for the old age home.

SSC CHSL Tier-1 09.07.2024 (Shift-III)

(a) into the old age home
(b) to the old age home
(c) by the old age home
(d) with the old age home

Ans. (b)

The underlined part of the given sentence contains an error. Use 'to the old age home' to correct the sentence.

503. He never (talks) the truth.

SSC CHSL Tier-1 09.07.2024 (Shift-III)

(a) speaks (b) declares
(c) narrates (d) utters

Ans. (a)

The bracketed word of the given sentence contains an error. Use 'speaks' to correct the sentence.

504. Professor Singh is not in the office today. I ask you try call him tomorrow.

SSC CHSL Tier-1 09.07.2024 (Shift-III)

(a) suggest you try calling
(b) am suggesting you calling
(c) ask you to try called
(d) asked you to call

Ans. (a)

The underlined part of the given sentence contains an error. Use 'suggest you try calling' to correct the sentence.

505. Alexa have being working as a teacher for five years now.

SSC CHSL Tier-1 09.07.2024 (Shift-IV)

(a) Alexa has been working as a teacher for five years now.
(b) Alexa has being working as a teacher for five years now.
(c) Alexa is being working as a teacher for five years now.
(d) Alexa was been working as a teacher for five years now.

Ans. (a)

The given sentence has an error of subject verb agreement.

As singular subject takes a singular verb, the correct sentence would be- Alexa has been working as a teacher for five years now.

506. Grasslands should not be foraged and some places are to be closed for grazing. **SSC CHSL Tier-1 09.07.2024 (Shift-IV)**

(a) over-grazed and some areas should be
(b) cut and few areas
(c) grazed and some places is
(d) planted or

Ans. (a)

The underlined part of the given sentence contains an error.

Use 'over-grazed and some areas should be' to correct the sentence.

507. Things that do not come from the ground not safe to compost.

SSC CHSL Tier-1 09.07.2024 (Shift-IV)

(a) has not been safe
(b) are not safe
(c) is not safe
(d) be not safe

Ans. (b)

The underlined part of the given sentence contains an error.

Use 'are not safe'' to correct the sentence.

508. I quietly went out at the door into the veranda.

SSC CHSL Tier-1 09.07.2024 (Shift-IV)

(a) No substitution required
(b) by
(c) through
(d) from

Ans. (c)

The underlined part of the given sentence contains an error. Use 'through' to correct the sentence.

509. Modest stores and welcoming residents populated the charming tiny town.
SSC CHSL Tier-1 09.07.2024 (Shift-IV)
(a) delightful
(b) unpleasant
(c) hideous
(d) nasty
Ans. (a)
The word 'charming' means 'attractive, pleasant and delightful'.

510. UNICEF builds partnerships across the global community on accelerate gender equality.
SSC CHSL Tier-1 10.07.2024 (Shift-I)
(a) global community with accelerate
(b) global community till accelerate
(c) global community to accelerate
(d) global community in accelerate
Ans. (c)
The underlined part of the given sentence contains an error.
Use 'global community to accelerate' to correct the sentence.

511. Allusive handwriting creates a poor impression.
SSC CHSL Tier-1 10.07.2024 (Shift-I)
(a) Legal handwriting
(b) Eligible handwriting
(c) Descriptive handwriting
(d) Illegible handwriting
Ans. (d)
Allusive handwriting means illegible handwriting.

512. Mr. Sen is clever enough to handle his professional hazards.
SSC CHSL Tier-1 10.07.2024 (Shift-I)
(a) Foolish
(b) Callous
(c) Intelligent
(d) Bold
Ans. (c)
The underlined word denotes that Mr. Sen is intelligent.

513. Although uncountable files stack up on the tables of government officials, they prefer doing their work at a more leisure pace.
SSC CHSL Tier-1 10.07.2024 (Shift-I)
(a) at a more leisurely pace
(b) at a more leisure paced
(c) No improvement needed
(d) at a more leisurely paced
Ans. (a)
The underlined part of the given sentence contains an error. Use 'at a more leisurely pace' to correct the sentence.

514. Classical buildings in ancient Greek and Roman times were (characteristically built) from marble or some other attractive, durable stone. SSC CHSL Tier-1 10.07.2024 (Shift-I)
(a) typically built
(b) fascinating to build
(c) strange build
(d) mainly having been built
Ans. (a)
The bracketed word in the given sentence contains an error.
Use 'typically built' to correct the sentence.

515. The housing loan taken by Ramesh effected his daily expenses adversely.
SSC CHSL Tier-1 10.07.2024 (Shift-I)
(a) by Ramesh affected
(b) for Ramesh effected
(c) from Ramesh effected
(d) of Ramesh effected
Ans. (a)
The bracketed word of the given sentence contains an error. Use 'by Ramesh affected' to correct the sentence.

516. We shall rehearse thrice before the final performance at least we make errors in the dialogues.
SSC CHSL Tier-1 10.07.2024 (Shift-II)
(a) for we make errors
(b) but we make errors
(c) can we make errors
(d) lest we make errors
Ans. (d)
The underlined part of the given sentence contains an error. Use 'lest we make errors' to correct the sentence.

517. They studied during three hours.
SSC CHSL Tier-1 10.07.2024 (Shift-II)
(a) by (b) for
(c) at (d) from
Ans. (b)
The underlined part of the given sentence contains an error. Use 'for' to correct the sentence.

518. This newly arisen evidence could have proved to finally put the culprit behind bars.
SSC CHSL Tier-1 10.07.2024 (Shift-II)
(a) is proof
(b) can proof
(c) can be proven
(d) could have been proven
Ans. (a)
The underlined part of the given sentence contains an error. Use 'is proof' to correct the sentence.

519. The removal of petty restrictions has made life easier.
SSC CHSL Tier-1 10.07.2024 (Shift-II)
(a) big (b) consequential
(c) large (d) small
Ans. (d)
'Petty' will be replaced by 'small' to make the sentence contextually meaningful, as 'petty' means 'small' & 'unimportant'.

520. She's under the allusion that she'll get the job.
SSC CHSL Tier-1 10.07.2024 (Shift-III)
(a) illusion (b) hallucination
(c) vision (d) unreality
Ans. (a)
The underlined part of the given sentence contains an error. Use 'illusion' to correct the sentence.

521. The common masses have waited for three hours to meet the king in the royal court.
SSC CHSL Tier-1 10.07.2024 (Shift-III)
(a) has been waiting
(b) had waiting
(c) have been waiting
(d) will waiting
Ans. (c)
The underlined part of the given sentence contains an error. Use 'have been waiting' to correct the sentence.

522. Shelley was very happy (while) I accepted her invitation to her birthday party.
SSC CHSL Tier-1 10.07.2024 (Shift-III)
(a) when (b) as
(c) after (d) before
Ans. (a)
The bracketed part of the given sentence contains an error. Use 'when' to correct the sentence.

523. There was some drawing-pins in my desk. SSC CHSL Tier-1 10.07.2024 (Shift-III)
(a) There is some (b) There has some
(c) Theirs some (d) There are some
Ans. (d)
The underlined part of the given sentence contains an error.
Use 'There are some' to correct the sentence.

524. Mr. Sengupta's complaint to the higher authority was only a red herring. SSC CHSL Tier-1 10.07.2024 (Shift-III)
(a) candid confession
(b) fortunate evidence
(c) clever bluff
(d) discouraging act
Ans. (c)

A red herring means an idea or a subject which takes people's attention away from what is really important or a clever bluff.

525. Had you been to Dubai, I would also go with you.
SSC CHSL Tier-1 10.07.2024 (Shift-IV)
(a) I shall be gone
(b) I will have went
(c) I would has also gone
(d) I would have gone

Ans. (d)
The underlined part of the given sentence contains an error. Use 'I would have gone' to correct the sentence.

526. She argued against the unnecessary split in the committee.
SSC CHSL Tier-1 10.07.2024 (Shift-IV)
(a) division (b) blend
(c) combination (d) mix

Ans. (a)
The underlined part of the given sentence contains an error. Use 'division' to correct the sentence.

527. This serum contains ingredients enabling the hair to grow.
SSC CHSL Tier-1 10.07.2024 (Shift-IV)
(a) the enable grow hair
(b) for growth hair
(c) for growing many hair
(d) that enable the hair to grow

Ans. (d)
The underlined part of the given sentence contains an error. Use 'that enable the hair to grow' to correct the sentence.

528. Telangana artists (are know for the amazing bronze castings).
SSC CHSL Tier-1 10.07.2024 (Shift-IV)
(a) Are known for their amazing bronze castings
(b) Have been knew to the amazing bronze castings
(c) Is known to the amazing bronze castings
(d) Have to know the amazing bronze castings

Ans. (a)
The bracketed part of the given sentence contains an error. Use 'Are known for their amazing bronze castings' to correct the sentence.

529. It has been found that the trees are being destroyed by a moth.
SSC CHSL Tier-1 10.07.2024 (Shift-IV)
(a) have destroyed
(b) is being destroyed
(c) have been destroying
(d) No substitution required

Ans. (d)
The underlined part is grammatically and contextually correct.

530. Soorya walking to college every day.
SSC CHSL Tier-1 11.07.2024 (Shift-I)
(a) Soorya is walking to college every day.
(b) Soorya walked to college every day.
(c) Soorya walks to college every day.
(d) Soorya have walked to college every day.

Ans. (c)
The given sentence contains an error. As the sentence presents a habit, simple present tense should be used. Hence, the correct sentence is- Soorya walks to college every day.

531. The interdisciplinary approach utilised in this study facilitates comprehensive understanding of the complex phenomenon under investigation.
SSC CHSL Tier-1 11.07.2024 (Shift-I)
(a) facilitated a comprehensive understanding
(b) will have facilitated a comprehensive understanding
(c) utilises a comprehensive understanding
(d) is facilitates a comprehensive understanding

Ans. (a)
The underlined part of the given sentence contains an error.
Use 'facilitated a comprehensive understanding' to correct the sentence.

532. No sooner did we reach at the party that it began to rain.
SSC CHSL Tier-1 11.07.2024 (Shift-I)
(a) it began to rain
(b) before it began to rain
(c) than it began to rain
(d) as it began to rain

Ans. (c)
The underlined part of the given sentence contains an error. Use 'than it began to rain' to correct the sentence.

533. I cannot use my office at the moment because it being painted.
SSC CHSL Tier-1 11.07.2024 (Shift-I)
(a) it is being painted
(b) it had been paint
(c) it has being painted
(d) No substitution required

Ans. (a)
The underlined part of the given sentence contains an error.
Use 'it is being painted' to correct the sentence.

534. He passed away in the year 1950 at 10 a.m. on 13 July.
SSC CHSL Tier-1 11.07.2024 (Shift-II)
(a) in the year 1950 at 10 a.m. on 13 July
(b) at 10 a.m. on 13 July in the year 1950
(c) on 13 July at 10 a.m. in the year 1950
(d) in the year 1950 on 13 July at 10 a.m.

Ans. (b)
The underlined part of the given sentence contains an error. Use 'at 10 a.m. on 13 July in the year 1950' to correct the sentence.

535. I was in Oman around two months.
SSC CHSL Tier-1 11.07.2024 (Shift-II)
(a) from (b) for (c) into (d) since

Ans. (b)
The underlined part of the given sentence contains an error. Use 'for' to correct the sentence.

536. Neither Janki or I am to receive the award. SSC CHSL Tier-1 11.07.2024 (Shift-III)
(a) either (b) no (c) nor (d) not

Ans. (c)
The underlined part of the given sentence contains an error. Use 'nor' to correct the sentence. Neither is always followed by nor.

537. The film was made in Botswana, whose wildlife parks is larger to those in Kenya.
SSC CHSL Tier-1 11.07.2024 (Shift-III)
(a) are larger than
(b) are large than
(c) No substitution required
(d) as large than

Ans. (a)
The underlined part of the given sentence contains an error. Use 'are larger than' to correct the sentence. The comparative degree of sentence always takes 'than'.

538. He has recovered now and is feeling too strong to walk.
SSC CHSL Tier-1 11.07.2024 (Shift-III)
(a) too weak to walk
(b) weak enough to walk
(c) strong to walk
(d) strong enough to walk

Ans. (d)
The underlined part of the given sentence contains an error. Use 'strong enough to walk' to correct the sentence.

539. Peter was the last to know that she had been cheating of him.
SSC CHSL Tier-1 11.07.2024 (Shift-III)
(a) cheating up him
(b) cheating in him
(c) cheat of him
(d) cheating on him

Ans. (d)

The underlined part of the given sentence contains an error. Use 'cheating on him' to correct the sentence.

540. I opened the box beneath the table and took of a book, the 'Materia Medica'. SSC CHSL Tier-1 11.07.2024 (Shift-IV)

(a) took out
(b) take off
(c) took in
(d) No substitution required

Ans. (a)

The underlined part of the given sentence contains an error. Use 'took out' to correct the sentence.

541. Do not later about the street.
SSC CHSL Tier-1 11.07.2024 (Shift-IV)

(a) loiter around (b) litre about
(c) litter about (d) latter about

Ans. (a)

The underlined part of the given sentence contains an error. Use 'loiter around' to correct the sentence.

542. Well, I prefer eating at home from eating out.
SSC CHSL Tier-1 11.07.2024 (Shift-IV)

(a) and eating out (b) than eating out
(c) while eating out (d) to eating out

Ans. (d)

The underlined part of the given sentence contains an error. Use 'to eating out' to correct the sentence.

543. The experienced surgeon handled the delicate procedure with care and precision.
SSC CHSL Tier-1 11.07.2024 (Shift-IV)

(a) seasoned (b) amateur
(c) untrained (d) unskilled

Ans. (a)

The word 'seasoned' means 'experienced' which is appropriate to fill in the blank.

SSC CHSL 2023 (Tier 1 & 2)

544. A man may die, nations may rise and fall but an idea lived on.
SSC CHSL Tier-1 09.03.2023 (Shift-I)

(a) lives on
(b) lives in
(c) live on
(d) No improvement

Ans. (a)

The underlined part of the given sentence contains an error.

The simple present tense should be used in the given sentence as it describes a general truth. So, 'lives on' should be used in place of 'lived on' to improve the sentence.

545. Herbalism had become an all but extinct skill in the Western world.
SSC CHSL Tier-1 09.03.2023 (Shift-II)

(a) No improvement
(b) Herbalism has become but all an extinct skill
(c) Herbalism become an extinct skill
(d) Herbalism has become but an extinct skill

Ans. (a)

The given sentence is gramatically correct and contextually meaningful.

546. The Blue House is practising it's songs for the competition.
SSC CHSL Tier-1 09.03.2023 (Shift-IV)

(a) No improvement (b) practised it's
(c) practising its (d) practise its

Ans. (c)

'Practising its' will replace the underlined part of the sentence as 'its' is used to depict the possessiveness of the subject and 'it's' simply means 'it is'.

547. When you ride a horse, (you sat on it and control it's) movements.
SSC CHSL Tier-1 09.03.2023 (Shift-IV)

(a) you sit on it and afterwards control it's
(b) you seated on it and control it's
(c) you sit on it and control its
(d) No improvement

Ans. (c)

'you sit on it and control its' is the correct replacement as 'its' shows the required possessiveness though 'it's' is short form of 'it is'.

548. (Hardly had the news leak out that) my telephone started ringing.
SSC CHSL Tier-I 10.03.2023 (Shift-II)

(a) No sooner had the news leaked out than
(b) No sooner had the news leaked out that
(c) No improvement
(d) No sooner did the news leaked out than

Ans. (a)

'No sooner ...than' is a correlative conjunction. Further more the third form of a verb is used with 'had'.

Hence, 'No sooner had the news leaked out than' should replace the bracketed part.

549. This heap of rubbish has not been remove for 6 months.
SSC CHSL Tier-1 10.03.2023 (Shift-II)

(a) been removes since
(b) been removed for
(c) been removing from
(d) No improvement

Ans. (b)

The third form of verb is used with 'has'. So,'been removed for' should replace the underlined part to improve the given sentence.

550. Africa has glaciers on the Mount Kilimanjaro in Tanzania and on the Mount Kenya.
SSC CHSL Tier-1 10.03.2023 (Shift-II)

(a) No improvement
(b) Mount Kilimanjaro in Tanzania and the Mount Kenya
(c) the Mount Kilimanjaro in Tanzania and the Mount Kenya
(d) Mount Kilimanjaro in Tanzania and on Mount Kenya

Ans. (d)

No article is used before the name of individual mountains. So, 'Mount Kilimanjaro in Tanzania and on Mount Kenya' should replace the name of mountains in the underlined part to improve the sentence.

551. The councillor (said that, "We plan to make the statem as safer place for) everyone."
SSC CHSL Tier-1 10.03. 2023 (Shift-IV)

(a) said, "We plan to make the state a safest place for
(b) said, "We plan to make the state a safar place for
(c) No improvement
(d) said that, "We are planning to make the state a safe place for

Ans. (d)

The underlined segment can be improved by changing it to 'said that, 'We are planning to make the state a safe place for' to correct the sentence. This correction uses the continuous tense 'are planning' which aligns with the intended meaning and makes the sentence grammatically correct.

552. People who came into contact with the carrier are in danger of catching the disease.
SSC CHSL Tier-1 13.03.2023 (Shift-I)

(a) at dangerous of
(b) No improvement
(c) in danger off
(d) in dangers for

Ans. (b)

The sentence is correct as it is. The phrase 'in danger of catching the disease' is accurate and requires no substitution.

553. We (opened) on a new travel venture.
SSC CHSL Tier-1 13.03.2023 (Shift-I)

(a) No correction required
(b) Begun
(c) Initiated
(d) Embarked

Ans. (d)

The underlined segment 'opened' can be improved by changing it to 'embarked' because 'embarked' implies the start of a journey or venture, which is more precise in this context.

554. The play was (either as funny or as) disturbing as shivang told it was.
SSC CHSL Tier-1 13.03.2023 (Shift-II)

(a) No improvement
(b) either as funny nor as
(c) neither as funny nor as
(d) neither as funny or as

Ans. (c)

The correct phrase should be 'neither as funny nor as' because 'neither...nor' is the correct correlative conjunction pair to show a negative comparison between 'funny' and 'disturbing'.

555. Funny grow Chihuahua weight less than the average house cat.
SSC CHSL Tier-1 13.03.2023 (Shift-II)

(a) No improvement
(b) fully grow
(c) fullest grow
(d) funny growth

Ans. (b)

The underlined segment can be improved by changing it to 'fully grow' because 'fully grow' appropriately describes the state of a Chihuahua in comparison to an average house cat.

556. The guests (has just arrived).
SSC CHSL Tier-1 13.03.2023 (Shift-III)

(a) have just arrived
(b) arrives now
(c) just arrives
(d) No correction required

Ans. (a)

The given sentence contains a plural subject; hence, a plural verb should be used. Replace the bracketed part with 'have just arrived' to make the sentence grammatically correct. The subject 'guests' is plural, requiring the verb 'have'.

557. She hang up the clothes in the closet.
SSC CHSL Tier-1 13.03.2023 (Shift-III)

(a) have hung up (b) No improvement
(c) hung up (d) had hang up

Ans. (c)

'Hung up' should replace the underlined part to make the sentence grammatically correct.

558. He released the brake and the tractor slow moved forward.
SSC CHSL Tier-1 13.03.2023 (Shift-IV)

(a) No improvement (b) slow move
(c) slowly move (d) slowly moved

Ans. (d)

The underlined segment can be improved by changing it to 'slowly moved' to make the sentence grammatically correct. The adverb 'slowly' correctly modifies the verb 'moved'.

559. The dog will whine at the door when he wants to go out.
SSC CHSL Tier-1 13.03.2023 (Shift-IV)

(a) wants to gone
(b) want to go
(c) No improvement
(d) wants to going

Ans. (c)

The sentence is correct as it is. The phrase 'when he wants to go out' is accurate and does not require any improvement.

560. The Businessman also insited (that the police had issued him several summons).
SSC CHSL Tier-1 13.03.2023 (Shift-IV)

(a) that the police issued him with several summonses
(b) that the police issued him several summons
(c) No improvement
(d) that the police had issued him several summonses

Ans. (d)

The underlined segment can be improved by changing it to 'that the police had issued him several summonses' to make the sentence grammatically correct. 'Summonses' is the correct plural form of 'summons'.

561. The detention (arised two distinct) but closely linked questions.
SSC CHSL Tier-1 13.03.2023 (Shift-IV)

(a) raised two distinct
(b) rises two distinct
(c) No improvement
(d) increased two distinct

Ans. (a)

The correct phrase should be 'raised two distinct' to make the sentence grammatically correct. 'Raised' is the appropriate verb to indicate bringing up questions.

562. The weather on the weekend are supposed to be sunny.
SSC CHSL Tier-1 14.03.2023 (Shift-I)

(a) were supposed
(b) is supposed
(c) No improvement
(d) are supposing

Ans. (b)

The underlined part of the given sentence has an error. As 'weather' is an uncountable noun, the singular verb 'is' should be used with it. Hence, 'is supposed' improves the underlined part in the given sentence.

563. The thieves entered a house at night and decamp with valuable worth ₹ 50,000. **SSC CHSL Tier-1 14.03.2023 (Shift-II)**

(a) decamped with valuables
(b) No improvement
(c) decamps with valuable
(d) decamping with valuably

Ans. (a)

The correct phrase should be 'decamped with valuables' to make the sentence grammatically correct. 'Decamped' means to leave hurriedly and secretly, which fits the context.

564. They hired a maid to have cleaner the house. **SSC CHSL Tier-1 14.03.2023 (Shift-III)**

(a) to cleans (b) No improvement
(c) to clean (d) for cleaner

Ans. (c)

The underlined segment can be improved by changing it to 'to clean' to make the sentence grammatically correct. 'To clean' is the correct infinitive form to use after 'to have'.

565. Their appointment lasted for almost an hour. **SSC CHSL Tier-1 14.03.2023 (Shift-IV)**

(a) lastly for (b) lasting for
(c) No improvement (d) last for

Ans. (c)

The sentence is correct as it is. The phrase 'lasted for almost an hour' is accurate and does not require any improvement.

566. A young girl was kidnapped from the mainly street in 3 o'clock yesterday afternoon.
SSC CHSL Tier-1 14.03.2023 (Shift-IV)

(a) main street in
(b) main street on
(c) No improvement
(d) main street at

Ans. (b)

The correct phrase should be 'main street on' to make the sentence grammatically correct.

'On' is the correct preposition to use with 'street'.

567. I try to travelling lightly, packing only the bare essentials.
SSC CHSL Tier-1 15.03.2023 (Shift-I)

(a) No improvement
(b) travelled light
(c) travels lightly
(d) travel lightly

Ans. (d)

The underlined segment can be improved by changing it to 'travel lightly' to make the sentence grammatically correct. 'Travel lightly' is the correct phrase to use when referring to packing only the bare essentials.

568. There's even a (picture by which a witch is riding) a broomstick on the sides of the police cars. **SSC CHSL Tier-1 15.03.2023 (Shift-III)**

(a) No improvement
(b) picture that of a witch riding
(c) pictures of witch riding
(d) picture of a witch riding

Ans. (d)

The underlined segment can be improved by changing it to 'picture of a witch riding' to make the sentence grammatically correct. 'Of a witch riding' is the correct prepositional phrase to use.

569. The dog chased the ball into the neighbour's yard. **SSC CHSL Tier-1 15.03.2023 (Shift-III)**

(a) chase the ball
(b) No improvement
(c) chasing the ball
(d) has chasing the ball

Ans. (b)

The sentence is correct as it is verb 'chased' is in the past tense, which matches the context of the sentence.

570. Add more flour if the dough is too stickiest. **SSC CHSL Tier-1 15.03.2023 (Shift-III)**

(a) too stickier (b) too sticky
(c) No improvement (d) much stick

Ans. (b)

The underlined segment 'too stickiest' is incorrect.

The correct phrase is 'too sticky' because 'sticky' is the appropriate comparative form in this context.

571. 'Hello! How (is) you?'

(a) was **SSC CHSL Tier-1 15.03.2023 (Shift-IV)**
(b) am
(c) are
(d) No correction required

Ans. (c)

The brackted part of the give sentence has an error. 'Are' should be used in place of 'is' to make the sentence correct.

572. He always checks the weather in the morning before he leaves for working. **SSC CHSL Tier-1 15.03.2023 (Shift-IV)**

(a) leave for work (b) left for works
(c) leaves for work (d) No improvement

Ans. (c)

The underlined part of the sentence contains an error.

'Leaves for work' should be used to replace 'leaves for work' to improve the sentence.

573. There are a number of places of historical or religiously importance. **SSC CHSL Tier-1 15.03.2023 (Shift-IV)**

(a) No improvement
(b) religiosity important
(c) religious importance
(d) religious important

Ans. (c)

The underlined part of the sentence contains an error. The adjective 'religious' should be used in place of the adverb 'religiously' to improve the sentence.

574. She dedicated her entire life to the serviced of the poorest of the poor. **SSC CHSL Tier-1 16.03.2023 (Shift-I)**

(a) service of the poorest
(b) No improvement
(c) services off the poorest
(d) serviced of the poorer

Ans. (a)

'Service of the poorest' is most appropriate to improve the underlined part of the sentence because the noun 'service', which refers to the action of helping or doing work for someone fits the context of the sentence instead of the verb 'serviced'.

575. The efforts of the Government in providing health education and Primary Health Centres is borne fruits. **SSC CHSL Tier-1 16.03.2023 (Shift-I)**

(a) was bore
(b) have borne
(c) No improvement
(d) has borne

Ans. (b)

The part 'have borne' is appropriate to improve the underlined part of the sentence.

576. My new shoes gave me a blistered on my right heel. **SSC CHSL Tier-1 16.03.2023 (Shift-II)**

(a) No improvement
(b) me a blister
(c) me a blisters
(d) I a blister

Ans. (b)

The underlined part of the sentence contains an error.

'Blister' (Noun) should be used in place of 'blistered' (Verb) to improve the given sentence.

577. His word wield tremendous influence between his followers. **SSC CHSL Tier-1 16.03.2023 (Shift-II)**

(a) among his followers
(b) No improvement
(c) in his following
(d) within his followers

Ans. (a)

The underlined part of the sentence contains an error. 'Among' is used for more than two people while 'between' is used for two people. So, 'among his followers' should replace 'between his followers' to improve the sentence.

578. The shelf is too highest for me to reach. **SSC CHSL Tier-1 16.03.2023 (Shift-III)**

(a) too highly
(b) more higher
(c) No improvement
(d) too high

Ans. (d)

The underlined segment 'too highest' is incorrect. The correct phrase is 'too high' because 'high' is the appropriate form to use with 'too' to describe the shelf.

579. I can't concentrate on my work because I am thinking off that beautiful scene. **SSC CHSL Tier-1 16.03.2023 (Shift-IV)**

(a) was think of
(b) am thinking about
(c) is thinking about
(d) No improvement

Ans. (b)

The underlined segment 'thinking off' is incorrect.

The correct phrase is 'am thinking about' because 'about' is the correct preposition to use with 'thinking' in this context.

580. The actors is to shoot the scene three times. **SSC CHSL Tier-1 17.03.2023 (Shift-I)**

(a) No improvement
(b) had to shooting
(c) has to shoot
(d) had to shoot

Ans. (c)

The underlined segment 'is to shoot' is incorrect. The correct phrase is 'has to shoot' because it indicates a requirement or necessity in the present tense.

581. The crime scene were surround by yellow tape. **SSC CHSL Tier-1 17.03.2023 (Shift-II)**

(a) were surrounded
(b) was surrounded
(c) No improvement
(d) was surround

Ans. (b)

The underlined part of the sentence has an error.

As the subject of the sentence 'The crime scene' is singular, a singular verb 'was' should be used with it. So, 'was surrounded' improves the underlined part of the sentence.

582. I can hear the band which is playing patriotic tunes, in the playground.
SSC CHSL Tier-1 17.03.2023 (Shift-III)

(a) No improvement
(b) patriot tunes
(c) patriotic tuning
(d) patriotically tuned

Ans. (a)

The sentence is correct as it is.

The phrase 'patriotic tunes' is accurate and does not require any improvement.

583. I won't bore you with the details, but I finally finish my taxes.
SSC CHSL Tier-1 17.03.2023 (Shift-III)

(a) No improvement
(b) finally finished
(c) final finishing
(d) finally finishing

Ans. (b)

The underlined segment 'finally finish' is incorrect. The correct phrase is 'finally finished' because 'finished' is the past tense, which matches the context of the sentence.

584. Check all radiators for (meagre leaks, special) round pipework connections.
SSC CHSL Tier-1 17.03.2023 (Shift-III)

(a) small leaks, especially
(b) No improvement
(c) modest leaks, specially
(d) cramped leaks, specially

Ans. (a)

The bracketed segment 'meagre leaks, special' is incorrect. The correct phrase is 'small leaks, especially' because 'small' is the appropriate adjective, and 'especially' is the correct adverb to use in this context.

585. Remember to close the windows before you leave.
SSC CHSL Tier-1 17.03.2023 (Shift-IV)

(a) your leave
(b) No improvement
(c) you leaves
(d) you have leaving

Ans. (b)

The sentence is correct as it is. The phrase 'before you leave' is accurate and does not require any improvement.

586. None of the witnessed could identify the suspect.
SSC CHSL Tier-1 17.03.2023 (Shift-IV)

(a) No improvement
(b) witness and identify
(c) witnessed could identified
(d) witnesses could identify

Ans. (d)

The underlined segment 'witnessed' is incorrect. The correct phrase is 'witnesses could identify' because 'witnesses' is the correct plural form of the noun, and 'could identify' is the appropriate verb phrase.

587. The early morning flight is the lest expensive.
SSC CHSL Tier-1 20.03.2023 (Shift-II)

(a) least's expensive
(b) least expensive
(c) lastly expensive
(d) No improvement

Ans. (b)

The underlined segment 'lest expensive' is incorrect. The correct phrase is 'least expensive' because 'least' is the appropriate superlative form to use with 'expensive'.

588. Nonetheless, (many an old poets, such as Tennyson and Browning, has) kept their romance to the end.
SSC CHSL Tier-1 20.03.2023 (Shift-III)

(a) many a old poets, such Tennyson and Browning, has
(b) many old poets, such as Tennyson and Browning, have
(c) No improvement
(d) many old poets, such as Tennyson and Browning, has

Ans. (b)

The bracketed part of the sentence contains an error. The use of 'has' is incorrect. As 'many' indicates a plural noun, the plural verb 'have' will be used. Further, 'a' must be removed. So, 'many old poets, such as Tennyson and Browning, have' should replace the bracketed segment to improve the sentence.

589. His shoes were soacked from walk through the dew
SSC CHSL Tier-1 21.03.2023 (Shift-I)

(a) soaking from walking
(b) soak from walking
(c) No improvement
(d) soaks from walks

Ans. (a)

The underlined segment 'soacked from walk' is incorrect. The correct phrase is 'soaking from walking' because 'soaking' is the correct present participle and 'walking' is the correct gerund form to use in this context.

590. But what of the young people whom are part of the cricket crowds, some of who are presumably born in England?
SSC CHSL Tier-1 21.03.2023 (Shift-II)

(a) whom are part of the cricket crowds, some of whom are presumably born in England
(b) No improvement
(c) who are part of the cricket crowds, some of who are presumably born in England
(d) who are part of the cricket crowds, some of whom are presumably born in England

Ans. (d)

The underlined part of the sentence contains errors. The use of the words 'who' and 'whom' are incorrect. To correct the sentence, use 'whom' in place of 'who' and 'who' in place of 'whom'. Hence, 'who are part of the cricket crowds, some of whom are presumably born in England'.

591. We keeps a horse, two cows and six chickens.
SSC CHSL Tier-1 21.03.2023 (Shift-II)

(a) has keeps a
(b) keeping a
(c) keep a
(d) No improvement

Ans. (c)

As the subject of the sentence 'We' is plural, the plural verb 'keep' should be used with it. So, 'Keep a' will replace the underlined part in the given sentence.

592. If proper treat, the wound should heal within a few weeks.
SSC CHSL Tier-1 21.03.2023 (Shift-II)

(a) properly treatment
(b) No improvement
(c) properly treated
(d) proper treated

Ans. (c)

The underlined part of the sentence contains an error. The use of 'proper' is incorrect in the context of the sentence; the adverb 'properly' should be used in its place.

Hence, 'properly treated' will appropriately replaced the underlined part of the sentence.

593. There has been a noticeable fall in the number of children dying from malnutrition.
SSC CHSL Tier-1 21.03.2023 (Shift-III)

(a) noticeable falling
(b) No improvement
(c) noticeably falling
(d) noticeably falls

Ans. (b)

The sentence is correct as it is.

The phrase 'noticeable fall' is accurate and does not require any improvement.

594. Scientists have predicted that the cultivation of rice will be affected severe. **SSC CHSL Tier-1 21.03.2023 (Shift-III)**

(a) affect severe
(b) No improvement
(c) effecting severely
(d) affected severely

Ans. (d)

The underlined segment 'affected severe' is incorrect.

The correct phrase is 'affected severely' because 'severely' is the appropriate adverb to modify the verb 'affected'.

595. Dad said that, ''She would have been a great sister if she was just a bit more careful''.
SSC CHSL Tier-1 21.03.2023 (Shift-III)

(a) No improvement
(b) that, ''She would have been a great sister if she were just a bit more careful''
(c) ''She would have been a great sister if she were just a bit more careful''
(d) ''She would have been a greatest sister if she was just a bit more careful''

Ans. (b)

The underlined segment 'if she was' is incorrect. The correct phrase is 'if she were' because 'were' is the correct subjunctive form to use in this hypothetical situation.

596. I didn't have times to watch the whole movie.
SSC CHSL Tier-1 21.03.2023 (Shift-IV)

(a) time to watching
(b) time to watch
(c) No improvement
(d) timer to watched

Ans. (b)

The underlined part of the sentence has an error. 'Times to watch' does not make sense with the sentence and should be replaced with 'time to watch' to improve the sentence.

597. The number of women working outside homes has been steady increasing.
SSC CHSL Tier-1 21.03.2023 (Shift-IV)

(a) has been steadily
(b) have been steady
(c) had been steadier
(d) No improvement

Ans. (a)

The underlined part of the sentence has an error. 'Steady' does not fit in the context of the sentence. It should be replaced with 'Steadily' (adverb) to improve the sentence.

598. With the harsh words of the boss, Srujan felt sad but his colleague's words created insult to injury.
SSC CHSL Tier-1 02.08.2023 (Shift-I)

(a) attached insult to injury
(b) provoked insult to injury
(c) added injury to insult
(d) added insult to injury

Ans. (d)

'Added insult to injury' is the most appropriate option to substitute 'created insult to injury'. It is an idiom that means to act in a way that makes a bad situation worse.

599. Adyasha would have been looked gorgeous in ethnic apparel.
SSC CHSL Tier-1 02.08.2023 (Shift-I)

(a) was looked
(b) would have looked
(c) had looking
(d) would be looked

Ans. (b)

'Would have looked' will improve the underlined part in the given sentence. 'Would have' is followed by the V_3 form of the verb.

600. In today's would, technology must be used for feed the changing forces in society.
SSC CHSL Tier-1 02.08.2023 (Shift-II)

(a) must had been used to feed
(b) must have been used to feed
(c) must used to feed
(d) must be used to feed

Ans. (d)

The sentence is correct as it is. The phrase 'must be used to feed' is accurate and does not require any improvement.

601. She can draw very well and just as creative. **SSC CHSL Tier-1 02.08.2023 (Shift-II)**

(a) as creativer
(b) as creatively
(c) creative than
(d) creative

Ans. (b)

The underlined segment 'just as creative' is incorrect. The correct phrase is 'just as creatively' because 'creatively' is the appropriate adverb to use in this context.

602. The flames caught so quick that I had no time to think.
SSC CHSL Tier-1 02.08.2023 (Shift-III)

(a) quickly (b) quickest
(c) as quick as (d) quicker

Ans. (a)

The underlined segment 'so quick' is incorrect. The correct phrase is 'quickly' because 'quickly' is the appropriate adverb to modify the verb 'caught'.

603. I have been in Chennai since a week, but I am planning to return now. **SSC CHSL Tier-1 02.08.2023 (Shift-III)**

(a) for (b) from
(c) in (d) No substitution

Ans. (a)

The underlined segment 'since a week' is incorrect. The correct phrase is 'for a week' because 'for' is the correct preposition to use with a period of time.

604. Peter was brought in the penalty area. **SSC CHSL Tier-1 03.08.2023 (Shift-I)**

(a) was brought down of the
(b) was brought of the
(c) was brought on the
(d) was brought down in the

Ans. (d)

'Was brought down in the' can substitute the underlined segment in the given sentence 'brought down' means to cause someone to fall down by pushing or kicking the person when they are moving.

605. He will be looking as if he has not slept. **SSC CHSL Tier-1 03.08.2023 (Shift-I)**

(a) He looks (b) He has look
(c) He was looking (d) He will be look

Ans. (a)

As the sentence is in simple present tense, 'He looks' can substitute 'He will be looking'.

606. Mahesh's attitude annoyed me and I blew into.
SSC CHSL Tier-1 03.08.2023 (Shift-I)

(a) annoyed me and I blew over
(b) annoyed me and I blew off
(c) annoyed me and I blew down of
(d) annoyed me and I blew up

Ans. (d)

'Annoyed me and I blew up' is the most appropriate option that can substitute 'annoyed me and I blew into'. 'Blew up' means to suddenly become very angry.

607. No sooner did she shouted, than the thieves ran away leaving all the jewellery on the table.
SSC CHSL Tier-1 03.08.2023 (Shift-II)

(a) No sooner do she shouts
(b) No sooner does she shout
(c) No sooner had she shout
(d) No sooner did she shout

Ans. (d)

The underlined segment 'did she shouted' is incorrect. The correct phrase is 'did she shout' because 'did' is already in the past tense, so the main verb should be in the base form.

608. I don't think he can dance as wellest Elena. SSC CHSL Tier-1 03.08.2023 (Shift-II)

(a) weller than (b) wellest
(c) as well as (d) well than

Ans. (c)

The underlined segment 'as wellest Elena' is incorrect.

The correct phrase is 'as well as Elena' because 'as well as' is the correct comparative form.

609. Since the storm knocked in the power, we've been using

SSC CHSL Tier-1 03.08.2023 (Shift-III)

(a) No substitution required
(b) the storm knocked out the power
(c) the storm knocked over the power
(d) the storm knocked away the power

Ans. (b)

The underlined segment 'knocked in the power' is incorrect. The correct phrase is 'knocked out the power' because 'knocked out' is the correct phrasal verb to use in this context.

610. Could you please tell me which languages you are fluent in?

SSC CHSL Tier-1 03.08.2023 (Shift-III)

(a) you may be fluent in speaking
(b) you speak fluently
(c) you fluently speaking
(d) you have been fluent in speaking

Ans. (b)

The underlined segment 'you are fluent in' can be improved by changing it to 'you speak fluently' for better clarity and grammar.

611. I enjoy learn languages because I like them.

SSC CHSL Tier-1 03.08.2023 (Shift-IV)

(a) to learning
(b) lean
(c) learning
(d) No substitution required

Ans. (c)

The underlined segment 'learn' is incorrect. The correct form is 'learning' because the verb 'enjoy' is followed by a gerund.

612. Abraham narrated Reshma his last escapade in dramatic way.

SSC CHSL Tier-1 04.08.2023 (Shift-I)

(a) exertion (b) ordeal
(c) adventure (d) escape

Ans. (c)

The underlined segment 'escapade' can be improved by changing it to 'adventure' to better convey the meaning of an exciting or daring experience.

613. Mr. Arvind was accused of beating up before the students in the class.

SSC CHSL Tier-1 04.08.2023 (Shift-I)

(a) accused of beating up off the
(b) accused of beating up of the
(c) accused of beating up on the
(d) accused of beating up in the

Ans. (d)

The underlined segment 'accused of beating up before' is incorrect. The correct phrase is 'accused of beating up in the' because 'in' is the correct preposition to use in this context.

614. If we had moved to Italy when I was a child, I will had an Italian accent. SSC CHSL Tier-1 04.08.2023 (Shift-I)

(a) I will be have
(b) I would has
(c) I would have had
(d) I am having

Ans. (c)

The underlined segment 'will had' is incorrect.

The correct phrase is 'would have had' because it correctly follows the structure of a conditional sentence in the past perfect tense.

615. Lewis can handle many of the European languages with its dialectical varieties fluently.

SSC CHSL Tier-1 04.08.2023 (Shift-II)

(a) on its dialectical varieties
(b) with their dialectical varieties
(c) with a dialectical varieties
(d) with they dialectical varieties

Ans. (b)

The most appropriate substitute for the underlined segment is 'with their dialectical varieties' as the possessive adjective refers to plural European languages.

616. Despite having a broken leg, Sarah managed to finish the Marathon on record time.

SSC CHSL Tier-1 04.08.2023 (Shift-II)

(a) finish the marathon in record time
(b) finish a marathon on record time
(c) finish the marathon to record time
(d) finish the marathon at record time

Ans. (a)

The most appropriate substitute for the underlined segment is 'finish the marathon in record time'.

617. She is not as cleverest as John.

SSC CHSL Tier-1 04.08.2023 (Shift-II)

(a) as clever as (b) clever
(c) cleverest (d) cleverer by

Ans. (a)

The most appropriate substitute for the underlined segment is 'as clever as'.

618. Himanshu is braver than intelligent.

SSC CHSL Tier-1 04.08.2023 (Shift-II)

(a) more brave than intelligent
(b) most brave than intelligent
(c) braver than more intelligent
(d) most brave than more intelligent

Ans. (a)

The most appropriate substitute for the underlined segment is 'more brave than intelligent'. When we compare two adjective both adjective are in positive degree.

619. It is nothing but pride.

SSC CHSL Tier-1 04.08.2023 (Shift-IV)

(a) nothing ever (b) nothing else
(c) nothing seldom (d) nothing so

Ans. (b)

The underlined segment 'nothing but pride' can be improved by changing it to 'nothing else' to better convey the intended meaning.

620. Sujata has not and can never in the good books of her principal as she lacks honesty.

SSC CHSL Tier-1 07.08.2023 (Shift-I)

(a) has not been and can never be
(b) has not been and can never been
(c) has not be and can never be
(d) has not be and can never been

Ans. (a)

The underlined segment 'has not and can never' is incorrect.
The correct phrase is 'has not been and can never be' because it maintains parallel structure and correct tense usage.

621. The integration of cutting-edge technologies into the healthcare industry have the prospect of revolutionising the way medical professionals provide patient care.

SSC CHSL Tier-1 07.08.2023 (Shift-I)

(a) were the potential
(b) have the potential
(c) has the prospect
(d) will have potential

Ans. (c)

The underlined segment 'have the prospect' is incorrect.
The correct phrase is 'has the prospect' because the subject 'integration' is singular and requires a singular verb.

622. Our teachers has planned of going for a picnic to the Doon Valley.
SSC CHSL Tier-1 07.08.2023 (Shift-II)
(a) Our teachers has planned a picnic
(b) Our teachers has plan a picnic
(c) Our teachers is planned a picnic
(d) Our teachers have planned a picnic

Ans. (d)
The underlined segment 'has planned of going' is incorrect. The correct phrase is 'have planned a picnic' because the subject 'teachers' is plural and requires a plural verb.

623. The new employee was quickly promoted due to their hard work and dedication.
SSC CHSL Tier-1 07.08.2023 (Shift-II)
(a) due to his hard work and dedication
(b) due to the hard work and dedication of him
(c) due to hard work and dedication
(d) due to giving hard work and showing dedication.

Ans. (a)
The underlined segment 'due to their hard work and dedication' is incorrect. The correct phrase is 'due to his hard work and dedication of him' because 'employee' is singular and typically takes a singular pronoun.

624. I have been living in this country since last several years but have never experienced any discrimination.
SSC CHSL Tier-1 07.08.2023 (Shift-III)
(a) for the last several years
(b) in the last several years
(c) by the last several years
(d) from the last several years

Ans. (a)
The underlined segment 'since last several years' is incorrect. The correct phrase is 'for the last several years' because 'for' is the correct preposition to use with a period of time.

625. He got appreciation from every people in a country and abroad.
SSC CHSL Tier-1 07.08.2023 (Shift-III)
(a) from one and all in the country and abroad
(b) from one or all in a country and abroad
(c) from one and all form a country and aborad
(d) from one and all in country and abroad

Ans. (a)
The underlined segment 'from every people' is incorrect. The correct phrase is 'from one and all in the country and abroad' because it better conveys the meaning of receiving appreciation from everyone.

626. The invigilator did not know that the four friends were exchanging notes right at the front of him.
SSC CHSL Tier-1 07.08.2023 (Shift-IV)
(a) of front of him
(b) for front of him
(c) No substitution required
(d) in front of him

Ans. (d)
Here, 'in front of him' should be used in place of 'at the front of him' to improve the sentence.

627. The mermaid murmured that it had been very difficult for her to live far from human civilisation.
SSC CHSL Tier-1 07.08.2023 (Shift-IV)
(a) it had
(b) No correction required
(c) this have been
(d) this had been

Ans. (b)
The sentence is correct as it is. The phrase 'it had been very difficult' is accurate and does not require any improvement.

628. Although he was exhausted form working all day, John continues to study for his upcoming exam.
SSC CHSL Tier-1 08.08.2023 (Shift-I)
(a) will continue to study for his upcoming exam
(b) has been studying for his upcoming exam
(c) continued to study for his upcoming exam
(d) continues studying for his upcoming exam

Ans. (c)
The underlined segment 'continues to study' is incorrect. The correct phrase is 'continued to study' because it matches the past tense 'was exhausted'.

629. My parents had not call me yesterday.
SSC CHSL Tier-1 08.08.2023 (Shift-I)
(a) does not calliing (b) did not call
(c) do not call (d) have not call

Ans. (b)
The underlined segment 'had not call' is incorrect. The correct phrase is 'did not call' because it matches the past tense 'yesterday'.

630. One cannot exactly predict the way she behaves in public gatherings.
SSC CHSL Tier-1 08.08.2023 (Shift-I)
(a) deliberate (b) precipitate
(c) prefigure (d) proliferate

Ans. (c)
The underlined segment 'predict' can be improved by changing it to 'prefigure' because 'prefigure' means to suggest or indicate something beforehand.

631. The most important fruit in Kinnaur is apricot. It is possible to get it at everyplace in huge amount.
SSC CHSL Tier-1 08.08.2023 (Shift-I)
(a) found for a huge amount everywhere
(b) found everywhere in a huge amount
(c) found everywhere with a huge amount
(d) find everywhere in a huge amount

Ans. (b)
The underlined segment 'at everyplace in huge amount' is incorrect. The correct phrase is 'found everywhere in a huge amount' because it better conveys the intended meaning.

632. Can you please make sure that all the guests are gathered on the stage before the performance begins?
SSC CHSL Tier-1 08.08.2023 (Shift-II)
(a) guest is gathered on
(b) guests are gathered in
(c) guests are gathered by
(d) guests is gathered by

Ans. (c)
'Guests are gathered by' can substitute the underlined segment in the given sentence.

633. She makes sure that all the newly realised books are available in her personal library.
SSC CHSL Tier-1 08.08.2023 (Shift-IV)
(a) the newly released books
(b) the newly negated books
(c) the newly relieved books
(d) the newly reverberated books

Ans. (a)
The underlined segment 'realised books' is incorrect. The correct phrase is 'the newly released books' because 'released' is the appropriate term for books made available to the public.

634. The new restaurant is more better than the old one.
SSC CHSL Tier-1 09.08.2023 (Shift-I)
(a) most better
(b) better
(c) much more better
(d) the best

Ans. (b)
'Better' can substitute 'more better' in the given sentence as the comparative form of 'good' is 'better' and not 'more better'.

635. I have the bestest placement offer among all my classmates.
SSC CHSL Tier-1 09.08.2023 (Shift-II)
(a) the best
(b) the better
(c) more good
(d) good
Ans. (a)
The underlined segment 'bestest' is incorrect. The correct phrase is 'the best' because 'best' is the superlative form of 'good'.

636. The people who live here have had the same kind of lifestyle until hundreds of years.
SSC CHSL Tier-1 09.08.2023 (Shift-II)
(a) though hundreds of year
(b) for hundreds of years
(c) although hundreds of years
(d) since hundreds of year
Ans. (b)
The underlined segment 'until hundreds of years' is incorrect.
The correct phrase is 'for hundreds of years' because 'for' is the correct preposition to use with a period of time.

637. All colleagues of Rohit except Joseph have commemorated the elective courses they are planning to offer. **SSC CHSL Tier-1 09.08.2023 (Shift-II)**
(a) have considered the elective courses
(b) have castigated the elective courses
(c) have constipated the elective courses
(d) have commiserated the elective courses
Ans. (a)
The underlined segment 'commemorated the elective courses' is incorrect.
The correct phrase is 'have considered the elective courses' because 'considered' is the appropriate verb to use in this context.

638. The number of seats in the movie theatre were reduced to comply with the new social distancing guidelines.
SSC CHSL Tier-1 09.08.2023 (Shift-III)
(a) in the movie theater was reduced
(b) in the movie theater were being reduced
(c) of the movie theater were reduced
(d) in the movie theater are reduced
Ans. (a)
The underlined segment 'were reduced' is incorrect.
The correct phrase is 'was reduced' because the subject 'number' is singular and requires a singular verb.

639. Our former minister Mr. Sikhar is in the running from Shrinet Nagar for the post of Member of Legislative Assembly.
SSC CHSL Tier-1 09.08.2023 (Shift-III)
(a) contesting the elections
(b) making laws
(c) teaching students
(d) giving speeches
Ans. (a)
The underlined segment 'in the running' can be improved by changing it to 'contesting the elections' for better clarity and grammar.

640. She has gone to the stationery store to buy a scissor.
SSC CHSL Tier-1 09.08.2023 (Shift-III)
(a) buying a pair of scissors
(b) buy a scissors
(c) buy a pair of scissors
(d) buy a pair of scissor
Ans. (c)
The underlined segment 'a scissor' is incorrect.
The correct phrase is 'a pair of scissors' because 'scissors' is a plural noun and is typically used with 'pair of'.

641. As the orchestra began to play, the audience was transported to another world, enthralled by the psychological effects of the music and the skill of the musician, who performed each note with precision and passion.
SSC CHSL Tier-1 09.08.2023 (Shift-IV)
(a) influenced by the overall scenario
(b) impacted by feelings
(c) swept away by the emotive power
(d) taken in by the effect on emotions
Ans. (c)
The underlined segment 'psychological effects' can be improved by changing it to 'swept away by the emotive power' to better convey the intended meaning.

642. I need to put out my clothes before I leave for work this morning otherwise, I will be restless when I return. **SSC CHSL Tier-1 10.08.2023 (Shift-I)**
(a) need for put out
(b) need to put in
(c) need to put off
(d) need to put away
Ans. (d)
The underlined segment 'put out' is incorrect. The correct phrase is 'put away' because 'put away' means to place something in its proper place.

643. As the storm raged outside, the children huddled together under blankets, listening to the sound of the rain hitting the windows hard and hoping that the power wouldn't go out.
SSC CHSL Tier-1 10.08.2023 (Shift-I)
(a) climbing up to the windows
(b) setting off the windows
(c) pounding against the windows
(d) beating off the windows
Ans. (c)
The underlined segment 'hitting the windows hard' can be improved by changing it to 'pounding against the windows' for better clarity and imagery.

644. The newly admitted students has been give a pair of uniforms by the management.
SSC CHSL Tier-1 10.08.2023 (Shift-II)
(a) are been given pair
(b) has given pair
(c) have been given a pair
(d) have being given a pair
Ans. (c)
The underlined segment 'has been give' is incorrect.
The correct phrase is 'have been given a pair' because the subject 'students' is plural and requires a plural verb.

645. Pooja could feel the anger building off inside her.
SSC CHSL Tier-1 10.08.2023 (Shift-II)
(a) building upon inside her
(b) building of inside her
(c) building on inside her
(d) building up inside her
Ans. (d)
The underlined segment 'building off' is incorrect.
The correct phrase is 'building up' because 'building up' means to increase in intensity.

646. The healthcare system is in transition at those moment.
SSC CHSL Tier-1 10.08.2023 (Shift-II)
(a) at that moments (b) at the moment
(c) at a moment (d) at these moment
Ans. (b)
The underlined segment 'at those moment' is incorrect. The correct phrase is 'at the moment' because 'moment' is singular and requires the singular article 'the'.

647. The doctor knew that Ravindra would recover from dengue soon and do the kind of work he was doing before.
SSC CHSL Tier-1 10.08.2023 (Shift-III)

(a) would do
(b) had been done
(c) would have been doing
(d) had been doing

Ans. (d)

'Had been doing' is most appropriate to substitute 'was doing' in the sentence.

As per the context of the sentence past perfect continuous tense should be used in it.

648. The fields are full of crops existing in large quantities.
SSC CHSL Tier-1 10.08.2023 (Shift-III)
(a) that are sufficient
(b) that are limited
(c) that are customised
(d) that are abundant

Ans. (d)

'That are abundant' can substitute 'existing in large quantities' in the sentence. 'Abundant' means existing in very large quantities.

649. As it is a rainy season, it is raining cats and mice.
SSC CHSL Tier-1 10.08.2023 (Shift-III)
(a) it is raining tigers and lions
(b) it is raining cats and dogs
(c) it is raining dogs and wolves
(d) it is raining birds and beats

Ans. (b)

'It is raining cats and dogs' is the most appropriate option that can substitute the underlined segment in the given sentence. 'Raining cats and dogs' means to rain very heavily.

650. I have think tomorrow I will take my belongings to the new apartment.
SSC CHSL Tier-1 10.08.2023 (Shift-III)
(a) I think (b) I will think
(c) I had think (d) I am think

Ans. (a)

'I think' is the most appropriate option that can substitute 'I have think' in the given sentence.

651. She will accept his love proposal if he will express impressively.
SSC CHSL Tier-1 10.08.2023 (Shift-IV)
(a) if he has been pressed
(b) if he had express
(c) if he expresses
(d) if he expressed

Ans. (c)

The underlined segment 'will express' is incorrect.

The correct phrase is 'if he expresses' because the present simple tense is used in the conditional clause.

652. Could you please tell me which movie you would like to watch tonight? **SSC CHSL Tier-1 10.08.2023 (Shift-IV)**
(a) you may wish to scroll
(b) you have desire to see
(c) you are wishing to watch
(d) are you interested in watching

Ans. (d)

The underlined segment 'would like to watch' can be improved by changing it to 'are you interested in watching' for better clarity and grammar.

653. She was not allowed for going outside by her mother.
SSC CHSL Tier-1 11.08.2023 (Shift-I)
(a) not allowed to go
(b) not allowed to going
(c) not allowed by going
(d) not allowing to go

Ans. (a)

The most appropriate substitute for the underlined segment is 'not allowed to go'.

654. Her determination impressed all of the other colleagues and inspires them to continue pursuing their dreams.
SSC CHSL Tier-1 11.08.2023 (Shift-I)
(a) inspires them in continuing pursuing their
(b) inspired them to continue pursuing their
(c) inspires them to continue pursuing her
(d) inspires them to continue pursuing there

Ans. (b)

The most appropriate substitute for the underlined segment is 'inspired them to continue pursuing their'.

655. In according to his advise I look this medicine.
SSC CHSL Tier-1 11.08.2023 (Shift-II)
(a) accordance with
(b) accordingly
(c) accordance to
(d) accord with

Ans. (a)

The underlined segment 'In according to' is incorrect. The correct phrase is 'in accordance with' because 'in accordance with' is the correct idiomatic expression.

656. I am typing to study, if it is impossible with all this noise.
SSC CHSL Tier-1 11.08.2023 (Shift-II)
(a) that it is impossible
(b) but it is impossible
(c) while it is impossible
(d) unless it is impossible

Ans. (b)

The underlined segment 'if it is impossible' is incorrect. The correct phrase is 'but it is impossible' because 'but' is the correct conjunction to use in this context.

657. Everyone sincerely and positively were ready to find the solution for the serious issue of sewage system.
SSC CHSL Tier-1 11.08.2023 (Shift-II)
(a) Everyone were sincerely and positively
(b) Everyone was sincerely and positively
(c) No correction required
(d) Everyone had sincerely and positively

Ans. (b)

The underlined segment ' Everyone was sincerely and positively were ready' is incorrect.

The correct phrase is 'Everyone was sincerely and positively' because the subject 'Everyone' is singular and requires a singular verb.

658. Can you please tell me where is the city park?
SSC CHSL Tier-1 11.08.2023 (Shift-III)
(a) where the city park is
(b) where are city's park
(c) city park where
(d) where was the city park

Ans. (a)

The underlined segment 'where is the city park' is incorrect. The correct phrase is 'where the city park is' because the correct word order for an indirect question is used.

659. This hill is a nice place to meditate because one can enjoy solitude?
SSC CHSL Tier-1 11.08.2023 (Shift-III)
(a) is a nice place to be meditation
(b) is an excellent place to meditates
(c) No correction required
(d) is a nasty place to meditate

Ans. (c)

The sentence is correct as it is. The phrase 'is a nice place to meditate' is accurate and does not require any improvement.

660. No less than eight pedestrians were killed in the accident.
SSC CHSL Tier-1 11.08.2023 (Shift-IV)
(a) No few than
(b) None less than
(c) No fewer than
(d) No lesser than

Ans. (c)

The underlined segment 'No less than' is incorrect. The correct phrase is 'No fewer than' because 'fewer' is used for countable nouns like 'pedestrians'.

661. How do you think the internet has influenced how we utilise news and media? SSC CHSL Tier-1 11.08.2023 (Shift-IV)

(a) has managed the pattern we ingest
(b) has revoked the way we interact
(c) has maintained how we receive
(d) has impacted the way we consume

Ans. (d)

The underlined segment 'influenced how we utilise' can be improved by changing it to 'has impacted the way we consume' for better clarity and grammar.

662. Meenakshi called out for the neighbourhood to get support for her campaign.
SSC CHSL Tier-1 11.08.2023 (Shift-IV)

(a) called by the neighbourhood
(b) called of the neighbourhood
(c) called in the neighbourhood
(d) called around the neighbourhood.

Ans. (d)

The underlined segment 'called out for' is incorrect.

The correct phrase is 'called around the neighbourhood' because 'called around' means to visit or contact multiple people or places.

663. One of them who were hidings at the back of a rock fired at the villagers. SSC CHSL Tier-1 14.08.2023 (Shift-II)

(a) one of them who were hiding behind a rock
(b) one of them who was hide behind a rock
(c) one of them who hiding behind a rock
(d) one of them who was hiding behind a rock

Ans. (d)

The underlined segment 'were hidings' is incorrect. The correct phrase is 'was hiding behind a rock' because 'was hiding' is the correct past continuous form.

664. Despite facing numerous obstacles and setbacks, the determined entrepreneur refused to give up on her dream of creating a successful startup that would transform the sector. SSC CHSL Tier-1 14.08.2023 (Shift-III)

(a) that will improvise the sector
(b) that shall redesign the industry
(c) that could socialise the sector
(d) that would revolutionise the industry

Ans. (d)

The underlined segment 'transform the sector' can be improved by changing it to 'would revolutionise the industry' for better clarity and impact.

665. Amal brightened of when they said he could go with them.
SSC CHSL Tier-1 14.08.2023 (Shift-III)

(a) brightened in when they
(b) brightened on when they
(c) brightened upon when they
(d) brightened up when they

Ans. (d)

The underlined segment 'brightened of' is incorrect. The correct phrase is 'brightened up' because 'brightened up' means to become happier or more cheerful.

666. Amar is very good in mathematics.
SSC CHSL Tier-1 14.08.2023 (Shift-IV)

(a) good at
(b) good about
(c) good on
(d) good with

Ans. (a)

'Good at' should be used to correct the sentence.

667. The company is planning to cut back few employees.
SSC CHSL Tier-1 14.08.2023 (Shift-IV)

(a) reduce some
(b) lay off some
(c) refuse some
(d) lay down some

Ans. (b)

'Lay off some' should be used to correct the sentence. 'Lay off' means to fire which fits the context of the sentence.

668. No sooner did we arrived at the airport than we got onto our flight to Atlanta.
SSC CHSL Tier-1 14.08.2023 (Shift-IV)

(a) did we arrive at
(b) can we arrive by
(c) have we arrived at
(d) had we arrive at

Ans. (a)

'Did we arrive' should be used to correct the sentence.

We use the first form of verb with 'do/does/did'.

669. From a recent research, evident is it that a lot more women have been opting for professional courses.
SSC CHSL Tier-1 17.08.2023 (Shift-I)

(a) it is evident that more a lot women
(b) it is evidently that a lot more women
(c) it is evident that a lot more women
(d) it is evidence that a lot more women

Ans. (c)

'It is evident that a lot more women' is most appropriate to substitute the underlined segment in the given sentence.

670. The performance of the musicians was rather worst than expected by the audience.
SSC CHSL Tier-1 17.08.2023 (Shift-I)

(a) worst than expectation
(b) worse was expected
(c) worse than expected
(d) bad as expected

Ans. (c)

The underlined segment 'rather worst' is incorrect. The correct phrase is 'rather worse than expected' because 'worse' is the comparative form of 'bad'.

671. She is the least reliablest person of all. SSC CHSL Tier-1 17.08.2023 (Shift III)

(a) leastest reliable
(b) less reliable
(c) least reliable
(d) lesser reliable

Ans. (c)

The underlined segment 'least reliablest' is incorrect. The correct phrase is 'least reliable' because 'least reliable' is the correct superlative form.

672. The young artist spent countless hours perfecting her craft, trying with various methods and mediums and honing her creative vision until she had produced a stunning collection of works that showcased her unique talent and perspective.
SSC CHSL Tier-1 17.08.2023 (Shift-III)

(a) exploring with different factors
(b) experimenting with different techniques
(c) merging with different variations
(d) researching with different type

Ans. (b)

The underlined segment 'trying with various methods' can be improved by changing it to 'experimenting with different techniques' for better clarity and precision.

673. The students were restored to complete the assignment by Friday.
SSC CHSL Tier-1 17.08.2023 (Shift-III)

(a) declared
(b) expected
(c) designed
(d) No substitution required

Ans. (b)

The underlined segment 'restored to complete' is incorrect.

The correct phrase is 'expected to complete' because 'expected' is the appropriate verb to use in this context

674. The GDP of th counrty has growth rapidly since independence.
SSC CHSL Tier-1 17.08.2023 (Shift-III)
(a) had been grow rapidly
(b) has grown rapidly
(c) have grown been rapidly
(d) had grow rapidly

Ans. (b)

The underlined segment 'has growth rapidly' is incorrect.

The correct phrase is 'has grown rapidly' because 'has grown' is the correct present perfect form.

675. An ultralight airplane is very different from a conventional airplane. It is looking like a lawn chair with wings.
SSC CHSL Tier-2 26.06.2023
(a) No substitution required
(b) look like
(c) looked like
(d) looks like

Ans. (d)

'Simple present tense (Singular. Sub + V_1-s/es+obj)' will be used in the given sentence as it is used to describe a fact. Hence, 'looks like' is the most appropriate answer.

676. Raju did very well in the exam, he must study well.
SSC CHSL Tier-2 26.06.2023
(a) he may study well
(b) he should have studied well
(c) he must have studied well
(d) No substitution required

Ans. (c)

The underlined segment 'he must study well' is incorrect.

The correct phrase is 'he must have studied well' because the present perfect tense (have+V3) is used to indicate that the studying happened before the exam.

677. I decided to call out to various bookstores in the area to see if any of them had the book I needed.
SSC CHSL Tier-2 02.11.2023
(a) call around
(b) No substitution required
(c) call off
(d) call on

Ans. (a)

In the given sentence 'call around' would be the most appropriate phrase. It implies reaching out to multiple locations or sources in search of something.

678. Select the option that will improve the given sentence by using the most appropriate pronoun.
Pradeep, whom is a teacher, also works as a content writer.
SSC CHSL Tier-2 02.11.2023
(a) Pradeep, who is a teacher, also works as a content writer.
(b) Pradeep, whose is a teacher, also works as a content writer.
(c) Pradeep, which is a teacher, also works as a content writer.
(d) Pradeep, that is a teacher, also works as a content writer.

Ans. (a)

The use of 'whom' is incorrect in the sentence. It should be replaced by subject pronoun 'who' Hence, option (a) improves the sentence.

679. This lesser known heritage building is so beautiful as the Red Fort.
SSC CHSL Tier-2 02.11.2023
(a) This less known heritage building is much beautiful than the Red Fort.
(b) This heritage building is as beautiful as the Red Fort.
(c) This lesser known heritage building is very much beautiful as the Red Fort.
(d) This lesser known heritage building is as much beautiful as the Red Fort.

Ans. (b)

The underlined segment 'is so beautiful as' is incorrect. The correct phrase is 'This heritage building is as beautiful as the Red Fort' because 'as beautiful as' is the correct comparative form.

680. It was the home minister of the country who took the decision to change a laws pertaining to migration of people from one state to another. SSC CHSL Tier-2 02.11.2023
(a) No error
(b) an home minister
(c) the migration
(d) the laws pertaining

Ans. (d)

The underlined segment 'change a laws pertaining' is incorrect. The correct phrase is 'change the laws pertaining' because 'laws' is plural and requires 'the' as the definite article.

681. The film received critical acclaim for being a more innovative movie of the year. SSC CHSL Tier-2 02.11.2023
(a) Film receives
(b) Acclaim at
(c) In the year
(d) An innovative

Ans. (d)

The underlined segment 'a more innovative' is incorrect. The correct phrase is 'an innovative' because 'innovative' is a vowel sound and requires 'an' as the indefinite article.

682. The river Ganga has some of the purer water on earth.
SSC CHSL Tier-2 10.01.2023
(a) The river Ganga has some of the most purest water on earth.
(b) The river Ganga has some of the very purest water on earth.
(c) The river Ganga has some of the more purest water on earth.
(d) The river Ganga has some of the purest water on earth.

Ans. (d)

The given sentence contains an error of degree of adjective.

The sentence the correctly gives it in superlative degree is ''The river Ganga has some of the purest water on earth''.

SSC CHSL 2022 (Tier 1)

683. If we do nothing to curb this pollution, I guarantee we will face the wall in the future.
SSC CHSL Tier-1 21.05.2022 (Shift-I)
(a) face the wind (b) face the music
(c) face the dark (d) face the stick

Ans. (b)

The underlined segment 'face the wall' is incorrect. The correct phrase is 'face the music' because 'face the music' is an idiom meaning to accept the unpleasant consequences of one's actions.

684. Do you mind me to being here while you are working?
SSC CHSL Tier-1 24.05.2022 (Shift-I)
(a) you can mind me to be
(b) you minds me to be
(c) you mind me being
(d) you will mind me to being

Ans. (c)

The underlined segment 'you mind me to being' is incorrect.

The correct phrase is 'you mind me being' because 'being' is the correct gerund to use in this context.

685. One's family plays a very major role to continue the trends and age old traditions.
SSC CHSL Tier-1 24.05.2022 (Shift-II)
(a) passive role in making the trends
(b) futile part in making trends
(c) significant role in enduring the trends
(d) docile part in enduring trends

Ans. (c)

The underlined segment 'major role to continue the trends' is incorrect. The correct phrase is 'significant role in enduring the trends' because 'enduring' better conveys the idea of maintaining traditions over time.

686. All his bones could be counted because his body was totally shrivelled and wrinkled with age.
SSC CHSL Tier-1 25.05.2022 (Shift-I)

(a) wizened (b) shrunken
(c) dried (d) bony

Ans. (b)

The underlined segment 'shrivelled and wrinkled' can be improved by changing it to 'shrunken' to better describe a body that has become smaller and wrinkled with age.

687. My sincerity and patience drove me through all odds and problems of life. **SSC CHSL Tier-1 25.05.2022 (Shift-II)**

(a) carried me (b) flew me
(c) ran me (d) lifted me

Ans. (a)

The underlined segment 'drove me' is incorrect. The correct phrase is 'carried me' because 'carried' better conveys the idea of helping someone through difficulties.

688. I was look forward to helping you complete the project.
SSC CHSL Tier-1 25.05.2022 (Shift-III)

(a) look forward helping
(b) look forward to helping
(c) look forwarding to helps
(d) look forwarding to helping

Ans. (b)

The underlined segment 'look forward to helping' is correct as it is. The phrase 'look forward to' is followed by a gerund.

689. The teacher said, "The Sun raises in the East every day".
SSC CHSL Tier-1 26.05.2022 (Shift-II)

(a) the Sun will rise in the East
(b) the Sun rises in the East
(c) the Sun rises at the East
(d) No Substitution required

Ans. (b)

The underlined segment 'The Sun raises in the East' is incorrect.

The correct phrase is 'The Sun rises in the East' because 'rises' is the correct present tense form for habitual actions.

690. I was carried by her rapturous song. **SSC CHSL Tier-1 26.05.2022 (Shift-II)**

(a) carried off (b) carried away
(c) carried of (d) carried to

Ans. (b)

The underlined segment 'carried by' can be improved by changing it to 'carried away' to better convey the idea of being completely absorbed or captivated by something.

691. The Ukranian soldiers passed in several weeks.
SSC CHSL Tier-1 26.05.2022 (Shift-III)

(a) hanged to (b) get off
(c) held out (d) hanged in

Ans. (c)

The underlined segment 'passed in' is incorrect.

The correct phrase is 'held out' because 'held out' means to continue to survive or endure.

692. I told Pooja that she could have use my car to get around while she is in my hometown.
SSC CHSL Tier-1 26.05.2022 (Shift-III)

(a) that she could have use my car to get around with
(b) that she can use my car to get around
(c) that she could have use my car to get away
(d) that she can use my car to get away with

Ans. (b)

The underlined segment 'could have use' is incorrect. The correct phrase is 'can use' because 'can use' correctly indicates permission in the present tense.

693. In this scene, a close-up shot was taken by the cameraman for display the emotions.
SSC CHSL Tier-1 27.05.2022 (Shift-I)

(a) to show emotions
(b) for show of emotions
(c) in order of emotions
(d) in order to display the emotions

Ans. (d)

The underlined segment contains an error. 'in order to display the emotions' should be used to improve the underlined part of the sentence.

694. I called of an explanation for his rude behaviour.
SSC CHSL Tier-1 27.05.2022 (Shift-I)

(a) called out (b) called in
(c) called into (d) called

Ans. (a)

The underlined segment contains an error.
Here, 'called out' can be used to substitute the underlined segment in the given sentence. 'Called out' means to criticise or ask someone to explain their actions.

695. I would like to thank you for your coming out tonight.
SSC CHSL Tier-1 27.05.2022 (Shift-I)

(a) for comes out
(b) for you came out
(c) for coming out
(d) for you will come out

Ans. (c)

The underlined segment contains an error. 'for coming out' will improve the underlined part in the given sentence.

696. People was empty out of the malls and roads.
SSC CHSL Tier-1 27.05.2022 (Shift-I)

(a) was emptying out of
(b) were emptying of
(c) was emptying of
(d) were emptying out of

Ans. (d)

The underlined segment contains an error. 'were emptying out of' can substitute the underlined segment in the given sentence. As 'people' is a plural noun, a plural verb i'were' will used with it.

697. Life is hard, unpredictable, but though manageable.
SSC CHSL Tier-1 27.05.2022 (Shift-II)

(a) still controllable
(b) despite practicable
(c) although bearable
(d) though achievable

Ans. (c)

The underlined segment 'but though manageable' is incorrect. The correct phrase is 'although bearable' because 'although' correctly introduces a contrast and 'bearable' means manageable.

698. Reema and Aasha were frolicking in the park
SSC CHSL Tier-1 27.05.2022 (Shift-III)

(a) were enjoying in the garden
(b) were participating in the garden
(c) were playing in the garden
(d) were performing in the garden

Ans. (c)

The underlined segment 'were frolicking in the park' can be improved by changing it to 'were playing in the garden' to better convey the idea of light-hearted fun.

699. We love to play with our neighboar's children.
SSC CHSL Tier-1 30.05.2022 (Shift-I)

(a) neighbours
(b) naighbour's
(c) neighboars
(d) neighbour's

Ans. (d)

The underlined segment contains an error. The correct spelling of the underlined word is given in option (d). Hence, 'neighbour's' can substitute the underlined word in the given sentence.

700. The sweet and bitter memories of her past make her weak and sad.
SSC CHSL Tier-1 30.05.2022 (Shift-II)
(a) ought to make her pallid and unhappy
(b) had to make her pale and unhappy
(c) must make her pastel and unhappy
(d) made her feeble and unhappy

Ans. (d)

The underlined segment 'make her weak and sad' can be improved by changing it to 'made her feeble and unhappy' to better convey the impact of past memories.

701. My mom told me to have cleaning up the kitchen before I go outside.
SSC CHSL Tier-1 30.05.2022 (Shift-III)
(a) to have clean out
(b) to clean up
(c) to clean over
(d) to clean out

Ans. (b)

The underlined segment 'to have cleaning up' is incorrect. The correct phrase is 'to clean up' because 'clean up' is the correct phrasal verb to use in this context.

702. A visit in Ladakh is a must these days. SSC CHSL Tier-1 31.05.2022 (Shift-I)
(a) from (b) to (c) for (d) at

Ans. (b)

The underlined segment contains an error. 'to' should be used to substitute 'in' in the given sentence. The preposition 'to' is used with 'visit'.

703. The NCERT was set up ahead by the government to assist and advise the Central and State Governments on policies and programmes for qualitative improvement in school education.
SSC CHSL Tier-1 31.05.2022 (Shift-I)
(a) was set off
(b) was set forward
(c) was set over
(d) was set up

Ans. (d)

The underlined segment contains an error. 'was set up' should substitute the underlined segment in the given sentence. 'Set up' means to start a business, organisation or institution.

704. We will leave towards 6.00 a.m.
SSC CHSL Tier-1 01.06.2022 (Shift-I)
(a) at (b) on (c) for (d) from

Ans. (a)

The underlined segment contains an error. 'at' is most appropriate to substitute 'towards' in the given sentence as time is mentioned after the underlined segment.

705. Nowadays, many doctors advise to live in the countryside.
SSC CHSL Tier-1 01.06.2022 (Shift-I)
(a) to have live in the countryside
(b) lived in the countryside
(c) to lived in the countryside
(d) living in the countryside

Ans. (d)

The underlined segment contains an error. 'Living in the countryside' will improve the underlined part of the given sentence.

706. It is a bad habit to talk in while someone is speaking.
SSC CHSL Tier-1 01.06.2022 (Shift-I)
(a) cut in (b) intrude over
(c) burst in (d) walk over

Ans. (a)

The underlined segment contains an error. Here, 'cut in' is most appropriate to substitute the underlined segment in the given sentence. 'Cut in' means to interrupt someone who is talking.

707. It is possible to prevent oneself with respiratory diseases by maintaining a disciplined lifestyle.
SSC CHSL Tier-1 02.06.2022 (Shift-I)
(a) of prevent oneself
(b) to a disciplined lifestyle
(c) on maintaining
(d) from respiratory diseases

Ans. (d)

The underlined segment 'with respiratory diseases' is incorrect. The correct phrase is 'from respiratory diseases' because 'prevent from' is the correct idiomatic expression.

708. They had eaten an apple every day for breakfast.
SSC CHSL Tier-1 02.06.2022 (Shift-I)
(a) eaten (b) eat
(c) has eaten (d) eating

Ans. (b)

The underlined segment contains an error. Hence, 'eat' can be used in place of 'had eaten' in the given sentence. As the sentence expresses a habit, simple present tense will be used in the sentence.

709. It was apparent that the girl was heading into a serious disaster.
SSC CHSL Tier-1 02.06.2022 (Shift-II)
(a) heading along (b) heading for
(c) heading down (d) heading out

Ans. (b)

The underlined segment 'heading into' is incorrect. The correct phrase is 'heading for' because 'heading for' means moving towards something.

710. One must care as for family members as possible.
SSC CHSL Tier-1 02.06.2022 (Shift-III)
(a) most for family members
(b) as most for family members
(c) more for family members
(d) as much for family members

Ans. (d)

The underlined segment 'as for family members' is incorrect. The correct phrase is 'as much for family members' because 'as much for' is the correct comparative form.

711. The delegates talked of the matter for an hour but without any result.
SSC CHSL Tier-1 03.06.2022 (Shift-II)
(a) talked to (b) talked above
(c) talked from (d) talked over

Ans. (d)

The underlined segment 'talked of' is incorrect. The correct phrase is 'talked over' because 'talked over' means to discuss something thoroughly.

712. Reena got embarrassed and started crying. SSC CHSL Tier-1 03.06.2022 (Shift-II)
(a) frightened and started shouting
(b) humiliated and started weeping
(c) frustrated and started yelling
(d) conscious and started admiring

Ans. (b)

The underlined segment 'embarrassed and started crying' can be improved by changing it to 'humiliated and started weeping' to better convey the emotions involved.

713. Some politicians turn up their face at the hard life of downtrodden people. SSC CHSL Tier-1 03.06.2022 (Shift-III)
(a) turn up their eyes
(b) turn up their nose
(c) turn up their mouth
(d) turn up their ears

Ans. (b)

The underlined segment 'turn up their face' is incorrect. The correct phrase is 'turn up their nose' because 'turn up one's nose' is an idiom meaning to show disdain or contempt.

714. When we reached the hill station, it was raining the heaviest.
SSC CHSL Tier-1 06.06.2022 (Shift-I)
(a) heavily
(b) more heavy
(c) heavy
(d) most heavily
Ans. (d)
The underlined segment 'the heaviest' is incorrect.
The correct phrase is 'most heavily' as it is the correct superlative form for adverbs.

715. He was bereft of hope after the tragedy struck.
SSC CHSL Tier-1 06.06.2022 (Shift-II)
(a) filled (b) devoid
(c) roused (d) strained
Ans. (b)
The underlined segment 'bereft of hope' can be improved by changing it to 'devoid of hope' because 'devoid' means completely lacking in something.

716. The organisation had set up for a Free Mandela Committee and launched a lively campaign with the slogan 'Free Mandela'.
SSC CHSL Tier-1 06.06.2022 (Shift-III)
(a) had set up (b) had set to
(c) had set over (d) had set upon
Ans. (a)
The sentence is correct as it is. The phrase 'had set up' is accurate and does not require any improvement.

717. The minor project put forward by the government is now moving around into its third year.
SSC CHSL Tier-1 07.06.2022 (Shift-II)
(a) is now moving into
(b) is now moving along into
(c) is now moving at
(d) are now moving into
Ans. (a)
The underlined segment 'is now moving around into' is incorrect. The correct phrase is 'is now moving into' because 'moving into' means to advance to the next stage.

718. I cannot sit up with this sort of insult in office.
SSC CHSL Tier-1 07.06.2022 (Shift-III)
(a) go up with (b) put up with
(c) get up with (d) do up with
Ans. (b)
The underlined segment 'sit up with' is incorrect. The correct phrase is 'put up with' because 'put up with' means to tolerate or endure something.

719. Don't provoke Harsha, otherwise, she will give you a slap.
SSC CHSL Tier-1 08.06.2022 (Shift-II)
(a) Do not vacillate
(b) Do not exasperate
(c) Do not hesitate
(d) Do not equivocate
Ans. (b)
The underlined segment 'Do not provoke' can be improved by changing it to 'Do not exasperate' to better convey the idea of irritating or annoying someone.

720. She should run the fast to win the race.
SSC CHSL Tier-1 10.06.2022 (Shift-I)
(a) the fastest
(b) more fast
(c) a fastest
(d) the faster
Ans. (a)
The underlined segment 'the fast' is incorrect. The correct phrase is 'the fastest' because 'fastest' is the correct superlative form.

721. After wearing the complete sports gear, he looked lean, tough and sinewy.
SSC CHSL Tier-1 10.06.2022 (Shift-I)
(a) a toughie (b) wirey
(c) wiry (d) dewy
Ans. (c)
The underlined segment 'sinewy' can be improved by changing it to 'wiry' to better describe someone who is lean, tough, and strong.

722. Though Mr. Swami ran it debt, he did not stop wasting money.
SSC CHSL Tier-1 10.06.2022 (Shift-II)
(a) ran along (b) ran into
(c) ran to (d) ran over
Ans. (b)
The underlined segment 'ran it debt' is incorrect. The correct phrase is 'ran into debt' because 'ran into' is the correct phrasal verb to use in this context.

723. Shanti heard the children who were shouting outside.
SSC CHSL Tier-1 10.06.2022 (Shift-II)
(a) who were screaming outdoors
(b) who were playing outdoor
(c) who were thrashing in the open air
(d) who were flaying in the open air
Ans. (a)
The underlined segment 'who were shouting outside' can be improved by changing it to 'who were screaming outdoors' to better convey the idea of children making loud noises outside.

SSC CHSL 2021 (Tier 1 & 2)

724. My hands were eager for tore up that awful letter.
SSC CHSL Tier-2 12.04.2021 (Shift-II)
(a) for tearing upon (b) of tearing up
(c) No substitution (d) to tear up
Ans. (d)
The underlined segment contains an error. Hence, 'to tear up' is the most appropriate option to substitute the underlined segment in the given sentence.

725. Make a list of most the things you would like to do once this lockdown is over.
SSC CHSL Tier-2 12.04.2021 (Shift-II)
(a) each (b) No improvement
(c) many (d) all
Ans. (d)
The underlined segment contains an error. Hence, 'all' is more appropriate here to improve the given sentence.

726. My daughter could not find the words to say why she has been crying on a day when she should have been happy.
SSC CHSL Tier-2 19.04.2021 (Shift-III)
(a) can be crying (b) is been crying
(c) No substitution (d) was crying
Ans. (d)
The underlined segment contains an error. Hence, 'was crying' is the most appropriate option to substitute the underlined segment in the given sentence.

727. The green shirt is too lose for me to wear.
SSC CHSL Tier-2 19.04.2021 (Shift-III)
(a) lost for me
(b) loose for me
(c) No substitution required
(d) loss for me
Ans. (b)
The underlined segment contains an error. Loose means not fitting tightly or closely (of a garment) and lose means forget, leave or become unable to find.
Hence, 'loose for me' is the most appropriate option to substitute the underlined segment in the given sentence.

728. If he doesn't reach the station in time, he would sure miss the train.
SSC CHSL Tier-1 04.08.2021 (Shift-I)
(a) would surely miss
(b) will surely miss
(c) will sure missing
(d) No substitution

Ans. (b)

The underlined segment contains an error. Hence, 'will surely miss' should be used to substitute the underlined segment in the given sentence. The given sentence is conditional so will + V_1 should be used.

729. What a palace home!
SSC CHSL Tier-1 04.08.2021 (Shift-I)
(a) pushy (b) palatial
(c) palatable (d) No improvement

Ans. (b)

The underlined segment contains an error. To improve the given sentence 'palatial' should be used in place of 'palace'. Palatial means luxurious, deluxe and magnificent.

730. Unless someone makes a complaint, they will not clear the garbage from the street.
SSC CHSL Tier-1 10.08.2021 (Shift-I)
(a) Without someone makes a complaint
(b) No substitution required
(c) Despite someone makes a complaint
(d) Except someone makes a complaint

Ans. (b)

The sentence is correct as it is. The phrase 'Unless someone makes a complaint' is accurate and does not require any improvement.

731. Select the most appropriate option to substitute the underlined segment in the given sentence. If there is no need to substitute it, select 'No substitution'.
How long have you being seating on this bench?
SSC CHSL Tier-1 10.08.2021 (Shift-I)
(a) being sat
(b) been seating
(c) been sitting
(d) No substitution required

Ans. (c)

The underlined segment contains an error. Hence, 'been sitting' will substitute the underlined segment in the given sentence.

732. Mr. Sharma is kind as his father.
SSC CHSL Tier-1 12.08.2021 (Shift-III)
(a) as kind as
(b) No substitution required
(c) the kindest as
(d) kinder as

Ans. (a)

The underlined segment contains an error. To show similarity with someone as .... as is used. So, 'as kind as' is the most appropriate option to substitute the underlined segment in the given sentence.

733. He won't come to the party unless you will invite him personally.
SSC CHSL Tier-1 12.08.2021 (Shift-III)
(a) would invite
(b) invite
(c) No substitution required
(d) invited

Ans. (b)

The underlined segment contains an error. Hence, 'invite' should be used in place of 'will invite' to make the sentence grammatically correct.

SSC MTS 2024 (Tier 1 & 2)

734. Ramesh is fond at playing guitar in his free time.
SSC MTS Tier-1 14.11.2024 (Shift-III)
(a) for (b) in
(c) on (d) of

Ans. (d)

'Of' is the most appropriate option to substitute the underlined segment. 'Fond of' means having an affection or liking for something.

735. Whoever got the few answers has to leave the room.
SSC MTS Tier-1 13.11.2024 (Shift-III)
(a) most few (b) fewer
(c) more fewer (d) fewest

Ans. (d)

'Fewest' is the most appropriate option to substitute the underlined segment. 'Fewest' is the superlative form of 'few'.

736. Pankaj is a better cook.
SSC MTS Tier-1 12.11.2024 (Shift-III)
(a) goodest (b) best
(c) good (d) more good

Ans. (b)

'Best' is the correct alternative. The sentence should read: 'Pankaj is the best cook'. 'Best' is the superlative form of 'good'.

737. Shirin came off with a brilliant idea to solve the problem.
SSC MTS Tier-1 12.11.2024 (Shift-III)
(a) came off on a brilliant idea
(b) came up in a brilliant idea
(c) came up with a brilliant idea
(d) came off to a brilliant idea

Ans. (c)

'Came up with a brilliant idea' is the most appropriate option to substitute the underlined segment.

738. I have never had and never will be dependent on him.
SSC MTS Tier-1 11.11.2024 (Shift-III)
(a) never been (b) was never being
(c) never has (d) has never been

Ans. (a)

'Never been' is the most appropriate option.

The correct sentence is "I have never been and never will be dependent on him." It ensures the sentence structure is parallel.

739. Rahul was angry of his brother as he broke his pen.
SSC MTS Tier-1 11.11.2024 (Shift-III)
(a) at (b) on
(c) of (d) from

Ans. (a)

'At' is the most appropriate option to substitute the underlined segment.

740. Effective responses of climate change are imperative to protect the world's children and fulfil their rights. SSC MTS Tier-1 11.11.2024 (Shift-III)
(a) responses to climate change
(b) responses at climate change
(c) responses from climate change
(d) responses with climate change

Ans. (a)

'Responses to climate change' is the most appropriate substitution.

741. No sooner had she enter her apartment than she found a bouquet of flowers on her table.
SSC MTS Tier-1 05.11.2024 (Shift-III)
(a) No substitution
(b) No sooner did she entered her apartment than
(c) No sooner did she enter her apartment than
(d) No sooner has she enter her apartment than

Ans. (c)

'No sooner did she enter her apartment than' is the correct substitution.

742. According to Greek mythology, Sipylus is holier city of Lydia.
SSC MTS Tier-1 04.11.2024 (Shift-III)
(a) the holiest (b) most holiest
(c) the holier (d) most holy

Ans. (a)

'The holiest' will improve the underlined part of the given sentence. 'Holiest' is the superlative form of 'holy'.

743. The sports teacher saw across the game and punished the students who were cheating in the game.
SSC MTS Tier-1 30.10.2024 (Shift-III)
(a) underneath (b) through
(c) beside (d) beneath

Ans. (b)

'Through' will improve the underlined part of the sentence. 'Saw through' means to see the true nature of something.

744. Ramya would gladly help Manya if you had asked her.
SSC MTS Tier-1 30.10.2024 (Shift-III)

(a) is to gladly help
(b) will gladly help
(c) was to have gladly helped
(d) would have gladly helped

Ans. (d)

'Would have gladly helped' is the correct substitution. This is a correct use of the third conditional, which expresses a hypothetical situation in the past.

745. The house seemed much far than she expected.
SSC MTS Tier-1 29.10.2024 (Shift-III)

(a) farthest (b) more far
(c) farer (d) farther

Ans. (d)

'Farther' is the correct alternative.

It is used to compare physical distances. 'Much' is used as an intensifier before the comparative adjective 'farther'.

746. This novel is more interesting of all in the library.
SSC MTS Tier-1 29.10.2024 (Shift-III)

(a) the more interesting
(b) interesting
(c) most interesting
(d) the most interesting

Ans. (d)

'The most interesting' is the correct substitution. It is the superlative form, appropriate for comparing within a group.

- Superlatives indicate the highest degree among three or more items.

747. This is the old tree in the colony.
SSC MTS Tier-1 29.10.2024 (Shift-III)

(a) elder (b) older
(c) most old (d) oldest

Ans. (d)

'Oldest' is the correct substitution. 'Oldest' is the superlative form of 'old'.

748. While I was teaching the elder one, the younger one take an opportunity and ran away.
SSC MTS Tier-1 29.10.2024 (Shift-III)

(a) the younger one has taken an opportunity and ran away
(b) the younger one will take an opportunity and ran away
(c) No substitution
(d) the younger one took an opportunity and ran away

Ans. (d)

'The younger one took an opportunity and ran away' is the correct option that can substitute the underlined segment. 'Took' is the past tense of 'take', which is appropriate in this context.

749. The intersection of nature conservation and social justice is evident in efforts to ensure that marginalised communities and other backward classes should have equal access to natural reserves.
SSC MTS Tier-1 28.10.2024 (Shift-II)

(a) Unclear in initiatives to safeguard
(b) Manifest in actions to redesign
(c) obvious in attempts to recollect
(d) apparent in endeavours to guarantee

Ans. (d)

'Apparent in endeavours to guarantee' is the most appropriate substitution. It means clear in efforts to ensure.

750. Gold is **much** costly than any other metal. SSC MTS Tier-1 23.10.2024 (Shift-II)

(a) many (b) most
(c) more (d) most costlier

Ans. (c)

'More' is the most appropriate option. It is used for the comparative form.

751. Each of the participants **were given** a certificate.
SSC MTS Tier-1 22.10.2024 (Shift-II)

(a) have been given
(b) was given
(c) have given
(d) are given

Ans. (b)

'Was given' is the correct segment. 'Each' is singular, so the verb should be singular.

752. The branches of the tree is very long. SSC MTS Tier-1 18.10.2024 (Shift-II)

(a) has (b) was
(c) had (d) are

Ans. (d)

'Are' is the most appropriate option to substitute the underlined segment. 'Branches' is a plural noun, so, the verb 'are' is required to maintain subject-verb agreement.

753. He received the best employee award because he was the **more hardworking**.
SSC MTS Tier-1 18.10.2024 (Shift-II)

(a) No improvement required
(b) hardworking
(c) the hardworking
(d) most hardworking

Ans. (d)

'Most hardworking' is the correct improvement. This uses the superlative form to indicate that he was the hardest working compared to others.

754. He possesses one of the slimmer handsets in the world.
SSC MTS Tier-1 18.10.2024 (Shift-II)

(a) slimmest
(b) most slimmest
(c) slim
(d) most slim

Ans. (a)

'Slimmest' is the most appropriate option. 'Slimmest' is the superlative form of 'slim', indicating that it is the most slim compared to others.

755. Reduced price of cooking gas brought **happy** to the face of every citizen. SSC MTS Tier-1 17.10.2024 (Shift-II)

(a) happily (b) happiest
(c) happier (d) happiness

Ans. (d)

'Happiness' is the most appropriate option. It is a noun that conveys a state of well-being and joy, which fits the context of the sentence where the reduced prices have a positive impact on people.

756. Rishi Sunak, the Prime Minister of the United Kingdom and Leader of the Conservative Party, **was born into** Southampton to parents of Indian descent who immigrated to Britain from East Africa in the 1960s. SSC MTS Tier-1 17.10.2024 (Shift-II)

(a) No substitution required
(b) was born with
(c) was born on
(d) was born in

Ans. (d)

'Was born in' is the correct replacement. This indicates the place of birth.

757. No sooner had they left their home that it started raining heavily.
SSC MTS Tier-1 16.10.2024 (Shift-II)

(a) their home than it started
(b) there home than it started
(c) their home than it starts
(d) their home that it start

Ans. (a)

'Their home than it started' is the correct replacement.

This follows the correct structure of the correlative conjunction 'no sooner... than'.

758. Heba dropped of the club unexpectedly to say hello and catch up. SSC MTS Tier-1 15.10.2024 (Shift-I)
(a) dropped by the club unexpectedly
(b) dropped besides the club unexpectedly
(c) dropped between the club unexpectedly
(d) dropped for the club unexpectedly

Ans. (a)

'Dropped by the club unexpectedly' is the correct alternative.

The phrase 'dropped by' means to visit briefly or casually, which fits the context of Heba's unexpected visit.

759. Good nutrition is the bedrock at child survival, health and development. SSC MTS Tier-1 08.10.2024 (Shift-II)
(a) bedrock off child survival
(b) bedrock of child survival
(c) bedrock through child survival
(d) bedrock from child survival

Ans. (b)

The most appropriate option is 'bedrock of child survival.' This correctly uses the preposition 'of' to indicate the fundamental basis of child survival.

760. Arun asks Smita to copy the contents of the document word by word. SSC MTS Tier-1 07.10.2024 (Shift-I)
(a) word par word
(b) word with word
(c) word for word
(d) word to word

Ans. (c)

'Word for word' means to copy exactly and literally.

The other options are incorrect because they don't convey the idea of exact copying.

761. Raghav, who studies tourism at present, is planning to go abroad after his graduation. SSC MTS Tier-1 01.10.2024 (Shift-I)
(a) is studying
(b) studied
(c) study
(d) will study

Ans. (a)

'Is studying' can substitute 'who studies' in the given sentence. The present continuous tense 'is studying' better indicates an ongoing action at the present time.

SSC MTS 2023

762. No, they are normal people, (although they perceive the world different). SSC MTS Tier-1 02.05.2023 (Shift-II)
(a) but they perceive the world differently
(b) No substitution required
(c) from they perceive the world differently
(d) while they perceive the world different

Ans. (a)

Conjunction 'but' will be used instead of 'although' as we generally use 'but' to connect ideas that contrast and adverb 'differently' will be used to describe the verb 'perceive' Hence, 'but they perceive the world differently'·is the most appropriate answer.

763. You'll have to brakes hard when you go down the hill. SSC MTS Tier-1 02.05.2023 (Shift-III)
(a) brake hardly
(b) braked hard
(c) No improvement
(d) brake hard

Ans. (d)

The correct sentence structure using Infinitive is 'To + Base Verb' (to eat, to go,to study).

Hence, 'brake hard' is the most appropriate-answer.

764. The rodeo is (great way to unite soldier's skills and build) esprit de corps. SSC MTS Tier-1 03.05.2023 (Shift-I)
(a) a great way to unite soldiers skills and build
(b) No substitution required
(c) great way to unite soldier's skills and building
(d) a great way to unite an soldier's skill and build

Ans. (a)

We generally use article 'a' to refer to a non-specific or general noun.

Hence,'a great way to unite soldiers' skills and build' is the most appropriate answer.

765. The water leaked in with a hole in the roof. SSC MTS Tier-1 03.05.2023 (Shift-II)
(a) No improvement
(b) by a holed
(c) through a holes
(d) through a hole

Ans. (d)

'With' must be replaced with 'through' as we generally use the preposition (through) indicating movement or passage from one side or location to another. Hence, 'through a hole' is the most appropriate answer.

766. She ran 12 kms at a stretch, (which are a greater) distance for a rookie. SSC MTS Tier-1 04.05.2023 (Shift-I)
(a) No correction required
(b) which is quite some
(c) which are greatest
(d) what is great

Ans. (b)

'Which are a greater' must be replaced with 'which is quite some' in the given sentence. The word 'which' refers to the distance of 12 kms, and the word 'are' is plural because it agrees with the noun 'distances'.

However, in this case, we are only talking about one distance, so the verb 'is' will be used. The adverb 'quite' is used to emphasise the distance, and the word 'some' is used to indicate that the distance is significant. Hence, 'which is quite some' is the most appropriate answer.

767. MLA is a representative electing by the voters of a constituency to the legislature. SSC MTS Tier-1 04.05.2023 (Shift-II)
(a) elects by a
(b) elected by a
(c) No improvement
(d) elected by the

Ans. (d)

'Electing by the' must be replaced with 'elected by the' in the given sentence. As we generally use past participles (elected) to denote the current state of a person or thing. Hence, 'elected by the' will be the most appropriate answer

768. The rabbit was remain stationary to avoid being seen. SSC MTS Tier-1 04.05.2023 (Shift-III)
(a) No improvement
(b) remain stationary
(c) remained stationary
(d) were remained stationary

Ans. (c)

'Was remain' must be replaced by 'remained' as the given sentence is in the simple past tense, so the verb must be used in the simple past form (V_2). However, the past form of 'remain' is 'remained'. Hence, 'remained stationary' is the most appropriate structure.

769. Watch your step-the third stair have a broken tread.
SSC MTS Tier-1 08.05.2023 (Shift-I)

(a) has a break (b) No improvement
(c) has a broken (d) has a broke

Ans. (c)

'Have a broken' must be replaced with 'has a broken' in the given sentence. According to the subject, verb agreement singular subject always takes singular verb and plural subject always takes plural verb. Here, the subject 'third stair' is a singular subject. Hence, 'has a broken' is the most appropriate answer.

770. When my calculations are wrong, I have to pore over the spreadsheet to find the error,
SSC MTS Tier-1 08.05.2023 (Shift-II)

(a) No improvement
(b) to poring over
(c) to pored over
(d) to pore by

Ans. (a)

The sentence is grammatically correct. To pore over means to read a document very carefully.

771. The most worrying aspect of climate change is the effect it has on the world's food supply.
SSC MTS Tier-1 08.05.2023 (Shift-III)

(a) A most worry aspect
(b) A worried aspects
(c) The most worrying aspects
(d) No improvement

Ans. (d)

The sentence is grammatically correct.

772. The government appears (to be at war with it's own people.)
SSC MTS Tier-1 09.05.2023 (Shift-I)

(a) to be on war with it's own people
(b) to be at war against it's own people
(c) No substitution required
(d) to be at war with its own people

Ans. (d)

'It's' must be replaced with 'its' in the given sentence. The words 'its' is the possessive pronoun for the singular noun 'government'. Hence, 'to be at war with its own people' is the most appropriate answer.

773. The idea was to delivered governmental services at the citizen's doorstep.
SSC MTS Tier-1 09.05.2023 (Shift-II)

(a) delivering government serviced
(b) delivers governmental servicing
(c) No improvement.
(d) deliver government services

Ans. (d)

'Delivered' must be replaced with 'deliver' as the correct sentence structure using Infinitive is 'To + Base Verb' (to eat, to go, to study). Hence, 'deliver government services' is the most appropriate answer

774. Raccoons have being more active at night. SSC MTS Tier-1 09.05.2023 (Shift-III)

(a) are more (b) are few
(c) No improvement (d) are much

Ans. (a)

'Have being' must be replaced with 'are' as we generally use simple present tense (Sub + are + obj) to describe actions that are facts or generalisations. Hence, 'are more' is the most appropriate answer.

775. The film's director decide to reshoot the scene. SSC MTS Tier-1 10.05.2023 (Shift-II)

(a) deciding to reshoot
(b) decide to reshot
(c) decided to reshoot
(d) No improvement

Ans. (c)

The given sentence is in the simple past tense, so the verb must be used in the simple past form (V_2). However, the past form of 'decide' is 'decided'. Hence, 'decided to reshoot' is the most appropriate answer.

776. One of the main climbing routes, approaches the summit from the South-East (in the Nepal).
SSC MTS Tier-1 10.05.2023 (Shift-III)

(a) at the Nepal
(b) in Nepal
(c) No correction required
(d) from the Nepal

Ans. (b)

Article 'the' must be removed as we only use article 'the' with the name of the countries which have plural or singular nouns, are composed of multiple words or include words like 'republic', 'kingdom' or 'states'.

For example 'The United States of America', 'The Philippines', 'The Maldives' etc. Hence, 'in Nepal' is the most appropriate answer.

777. In the logo, the blue contrast wells with its complementary colour, yellow. SSC MTS Tier-1 11.05.2023 (Shift-I)

(a) No improvement (b) contrast well
(c) contrast we'll (d) contrasts well

Ans. (d)

'Wells' must be replaced with 'well' as 'well' is an adverb and we never make plurals of adverbs. Hence, 'contrasts well' is the most appropriate answer.

778. My history assignment is due on Wednesday.
SSC MTS Tier-1 11.05.2023 (Shift-II)

(a) are due at (b) No improvement
(c) were due on (d) is dues in

Ans. (b)

The sentence is grammatically correct.

779. Bonaparte, unlike Hoche, was not (eagerly to embark in) a serious Irish expedition.
SSC MTS Tier-1 11.05.2023 (Shift-III)

(a) eager to embark on
(b) No substitution required
(c) eagerest to embarked on
(d) eager into embark in

Ans. (a)

Adverb 'eagerly' must be replaced with the adjective 'eager' as adjectives are words that describe or modify nouns (Bonaparte). We generally use prepositions (on/upon) with the verb 'embark'. Hence, 'eager to embark on' is the most appropriate answer..

780. In the summer, the weathering can be very hot around here.
SSC MTS Tier-1 12.05.2023 (Shift-I)

(a) weathers could being
(b) No improvement
(c) weather is be
(d) weather can be

Ans. (d)

'Weathering can be' must be replaced with 'weather can be' as the. correct phrase to use is 'weather can be,' which conveys the intended meaning that the weather can be very hot in the summer. Hence, 'weather can be' is the most appropriate answer.

781. Training your dog have required a lot of patience.
SSC MTS Tier-1 12.05.2023 (Shift-II)

(a) require the lot (b) requires a lot
(c) required lot (d) No improvement

Ans. (b)

The phrase 'have-required a lot' will be replaced with 'requires a lot' because we use simple present tense to state general truths. The given sentence states a general truth about training dogs. Hence,'requires a lot' is the most appropriate answer.

782. The query isn't (whether he will admit it, but when).
SSC MTS Tier-1 12.05.2023 (Shift-III)

(a) No substitution required
(b) whether he will be admitting it or not, but when?
(c) whether or nor he will admit it, but when?
(d) where he will admit it or not, but when

Ans. (a)

The sentence is grammatically correct.

783. The (roof collapsing) in a roar of rock and rubble.
SSC MTS Tier-1 12.05.2023 (Shift-III)

(a) roof have collapsed
(b) No correction required
(c) roof was collapse
(d) roof collapsed

Ans. (d)

'Roof collapsing' will be replaced with 'roof collapsed' as it indicates that the action of the roof falling down has already happened in the past.

So we need simple past tense and verb form (V_2) that is 'collapsed'. Hence, 'roof collapsed' is the most appropriate answer.

784. The Tagore House is rehearsing a skit for the school's Annual Day Function. SSC MTS Tier-1 15.05.2023 (Shift I)

(a) has been rehearsing a skits
(c) is rehearsed an skit
(b) was rehearse a skit
(d) No improvement

Ans. (d)

The given sentence is grammatically correct.

785. The tourists (rendered to the) museum on time.
SSC MTS Tier-1 15.05.2023 (Shift-II)

(a) appeared at the
(b) occurred to the
(c) No correction required
(d) arrived at the

Ans. (d)

'Rendered to the' must be replaced with 'arrived at the' as 'Arrived at' is a commonly used phrase to indicate reaching a specific location. Hence, 'arrived at the' is the most 'appropriate answer.

786. The number of homes with running watered has been rising sharply since 1985. SSC MTS Tier-1 15.05.2023 (Shift-II)

(a) with run water
(b) with running water
(c) of ran watered
(d) No improvement

Ans. (b)

The phrase 'with running watered' must be replaced with 'with running water' as a noun is required after the preposition 'with'.

Also, the participle 'running' is acting as an adjective and requires a noun. Hence, 'with running water' is the most appropriate answer

787. She was fined of driving over the speed limit
SSC MTS Tier-1 15.05.2023 (Shift-III)

(a) fine of driving
(b) fined for drive
(c) fined for driving
(d) No improvement

Ans. (c)

The underlined segment 'fined of driving' is incorrect. The correct phrase is 'fined for driving' because 'for' is the correct preposition to indicate the reason for the fine.

788. The cat sits in the window and staring at the squirrel.
SSC MTS Tier-1 16.05.2023 (Shift-III)

(a) No improvement (b) stares at
(c) stares on (d) stared at

Ans. (b)

'Staring at' will be replaced with 'stares at' as the given sentence is in present tense. 'Sits' is the present form of the verb.

'At' is a fixed preposition used after the verb 'stare'. Hence, 'stares at' is the most appropriate answer.

789. He has 33 years of professional experience (on the field of) Public Administration.
SSC MTS Tier-1 16.05.2023 (Shift II)

(a) over field of
(b) in the field of
(c) No substitution required
(d) in the field off

Ans. (b)

'On the field of' must be replaced with 'in the field of' as the preposition 'in' is commonly used to indicate involvement or specialisation in a particular field. Hence, 'in the field' is the most appropriate answer.

790. The transit of the Planet of Love happen in pairs, eight years apart every century.
SSC MTS Tier-1 16.05.2023 (Shift-III)

(a) The transits of the Planet of Love happen in pairs
(b) No substitution required
(c) The transits of the Planet of Love happens at pairs
(d) The transit of Planet of Love happen in pairs

Ans. (a)

The phrase 'in pairs' indicates that two transits happen. So, plural noun 'transits' will be used in place of 'transit'. Hence, 'the transits of the Planet of Love happen in pairs' is the most appropriate answer.

791. The only course of action to (fend of the loud clamour off conspiracy theories) is to keep everyone fully informed. SSC MTS Tier-1 17.05.2023 (Shift-II)

(a) fend off the loud clamour of conspiracy theories
(b) No substitution required
(c) fend off the loud clamour off conspiracy theories
(d) fend of the loud clamour of conspiracy theories

Ans. (a)

The phrase 'fend off' means to defend against or repel something. The phrase should be followed by the preposition 'of' to indicate the object, which is 'the loud clamour of conspiracy theories'. Hence, 'fend off the loud clamour of conspiracy theories' is the most appropriate answer.

792. Some of them were nearly (as hard as ligament, and many an inch in length). SSC MTS Tier-1 17.05.2023 (Shift-I)

(a) as hard as ligaments, and many were an inch long
(b) No substitution required
(c) hard as ligament, and many an inch at length
(d) as hard as a ligament, and many an inches in length

Ans. (a)

'Ligament' must be replaced with 'ligaments' as it specifies the plural form of 'ligaments' to match the plural subject 'them' and provides the correct verb form 'were' and adjective 'long' for agreement.

Hence, 'as hard as ligaments and many were an inch long' is the most appropriate answer.

793. We were asked by (Jane's aunt where she was last night.
SSC MTS Tier-1 17.05.2023 (Shift-III)

(a) No substitution required
(b) Jane aunt's where she was last night?
(c) Jane's aunt where was she last night.
(d) Jane's aunt where was she was last night?

Ans. (a)

The given sentence is grammatically correct.

794. Cell phones keeps loved ones and those nearly them well connected.
SSC MTS Tier-1 18.05.2023 (Shift-I)

(a) No improvement
(b) keeping loved and nearly
(c) kept love and near
(d) keep loved ones and those near

Ans. (d)

According to the 'subject-Verb Agreement Rule', a plural subject (call phones) always takes a plural verb (keep).
And the preposition 'near' is used to denote the relationship with the noun/pronoun (than).
Hence, 'keep loved ones and those near' is the most appropriate answer.

795. You can't bought anything with one cent anymore.
SSC MTS Tier-1 18.05.2023 (Shift-II)

(a) should not bought anything
(b) No improvement
(c) could not buying anything
(d) can't buy anything

Ans. (d)

'Bought' must be replaced with 'buy' as we generally use bare infinitive after modal auxiliary verbs (can and could, may and might, will and shall, must, would, etc.).
Hence, 'can't buy anything' is the most appropriate answer.

796. There has been a spate of some unfortunately events in Madurai.
SSC MTS Tier-1 18.05.2023 (Shift-III)

(a) unfortunate events
(b) unfortunately event
(c) No improvement
(d) unfortunate some events

Ans. (a)

The phrase 'unfortunately events' will be replaced with 'unfortunate events' as we need an adjective before the noun 'events' to qualify its meaning, not an adverb.
Hence, 'unfortunate events' is the most appropriate answer.

797. I received word that you (were attempting) to contact me.
SSC MTS Tier-1 19.05.2023 (Shift-I)

(a) No correction required
(b) were strike
(c) has attempting
(d) was attempting

Ans. (a)

The sentence is grammatically correct.

798. Plots to dispose him came to nothing. **SSC MTS Tier-1 19.05.2023 (Shift-I)**

(a) No substitution required
(b) Plots to dispose off him comes
(c) Plots to dispose of him came
(d) Plots which dispose him came

Ans. (c)

The phrase 'dispose of ' means to get rid of or eliminate someone or something.
In this sentence, the sentence suggests that there were plots or plans to eliminate or get rid of him, but those plans ultimately failed or had no result.
Hence, 'plots to dispose of him came' is the most appropriate answer.

799. The Bank of New York has increased (interest rates four times from last January.)
SSC MTS Tier-1 19.05.2023 (Shift-II)

(a) interest rates four times since last January.
(b) the interest rates four time from last January.
(c) No substitution required
(d) interest rates from last January four times.

Ans. (a)

'From' will be replaced with 'since' because the preposition 'since' is used to denote point of time. Hence, 'interest rates four times since last January' is the most appropriate answer.

800. Drive two blocks and turn right at the traffic lights.
SSC MTS Tier-1 19.05.2023 (Shift-III)

(a) turn right in (b) No improvement
(c) turns right at (d) turn rightly at

Ans. (b)

The sentence is grammatically correct.

801. He lost his temper (by a driver) flashed her headlights as he overtook. **SSC MTS Tier-1 13.06.2023 (Shift-I)**

(a) afterwards a driver
(b) No correction required
(c) considering a driver
(d) after a driver

Ans. (d)

The phrase 'by a driver' will be replaced with 'after the driver' as we use the preposition 'after' to show that something happens at a later time than the other thing.
The action of flashing happened first and then the action of losing temper. It is to be noted that 'after' is used at the beginning of the first action. Hence, 'after a driver' is the most appropriate answer.

802. Christian turned round and (strided off into) the blackness and I got into my car. **SSC MTS Tier-1 13.06.2023 (Shift-II)**

(a) strode off
(b) strode of
(c) strided of
(d) No correction required

Ans. (a)

The phrase 'strided off into' will be replaced with 'strode off' as the given sentence is in the past and the correct past form of 'stride' is strode'. Hence, 'storde off' is the most appropriate answer.

803. How (can a book such as) be written before I'd lived the incidents it described?
SSC MTS Tier-1 13.06.2023 (Shift-III)

(a) No correction required
(b) could such a book
(c) must so a book
(d) such a book

Ans. (b)

The phrase 'could such a book' functions as a conditional statement expressing doubt or disbelief.
The modal verb 'could' suggests the possibility or ability of something happening, in this case, a book being written.
The word 'such' emphasises the particular type or nature of the book being referred to.
Together, this choice conveys the skepticism or questioning about the book's existence prior to the person's own experiences. Hence, 'could such a book' is the most appropriate answer .

804. I try to eat less meat and more vegetables.
SSC MTS Tier-1 14.06.2023 (Shift-I)

(a) to eats less
(b) to eat lesser
(c) to ate less
(d) No improvement

Ans. (d)

The sentence is grammatically correct.

805. (This bridge neither crossed the Thames and neither gave) access to a now-lost island in the river.
SSC MTS Tier-1 14.06.2023 (Shift-II)

(a) This bridge either crossed the Thames, and or gave
(b) This bridge neither crossed the Thames, nor gave
(c) This bridge either crossed the Thames, nor gave
(d) No substitution required

Ans. (b)

The phrase 'this bridge neither crossed the Thames, and neither gave' will be replaced with this bridge neither crossed the Thames, nor gave' because the conjunction 'neither' is paired with 'nor'. Hence, 'this bridge neither crossed the Thames, nor gave' is the most appropriate answer.

806. He lights his pipe, (and on many an evenings he helps me with) dishes.
SSC MTS Tier-1 14.06.2023 (Shift-III)
(a) and on many evenings he helped me with the
(b) and on many evenings he helps me with the
(c) and many an evenings he helps me With the
(d) No substitution required

Ans. (b)

'Many + plural noun' 'is the correct grammatical structure. Also article 'the' is generally used before known or familiar things. Since 'the dishes' are used by the person regularly, the person is familiar 'with the dishes'. Hence 'and on many evenings he helps me with the' is the most appropriate answer.

807. He gritted his teeth and tried to act as though he (either noticed nor cared). SSC MTS Tier-1 15.06.2023 (Shift-I)
(a) neither noticed nor cared
(b) No correction required
(c) either noticed or cared
(d) neither noticed cared

Ans. (a)

The word 'either' must be replaced with 'neither' as 'neither ...... nor' is a fixed conjunctional pair. Hence, 'neither noticed nor cared' is the most appropriate answer.

808. His temperament (disposed him to) argue readily with people.
SSC MTS Tier-1 15.06.2023 (Shift-II)
(a) disposed him of to
(b) dispose him to
(c) disposed him off to
(d) No correction required

Ans. (d)

The given sentence is grammatically correct.

809. He <u>had thrown the</u> wrapper into the garbage.
SSC MTS Tier-1 15.06.2023 (Shift-III)
(a) throw the
(b) thrown the
(c) No Improvement
(d) has throwing the

Ans. (c)

The given sentence is grammatically correct.

810. We saw him (the more) during Hogsmeade weekend.
SSC MTS Tier-1 16.06.2023 (Shift-I)
(a) the many
(b) the most
(c) the bigger
(d) No correction required

Ans. (b)

We generally use superlative degree 'most' with definite article 'the'. Hence, 'the most' is the most appropriate answer.

811. The relationship between two people is (by the way in what) they feel and behave to wards each other. SSC MTS Tier-1 16.06.2023 (Shift-II)
(a) the way by which
(b) by which ways
(c) the way in which
(d) No correction required

Ans. (c)

The phrase 'by the way in what' must be replaced with 'the way in which' as we generally use the phrase 'the way in which' to show the manner in which something is being done.

This phrase gives the same meaning as the relative adverb 'how'. Hence, 'the way in which' is the most appropriate answer.

812. We've made extraordinary (flowering as a) society in that regard. SSC MTS Tier-1 16.06.2023 (Shift-III)
(a) progress as a
(b) advance as a
(d) No correction required
(c) improvement by a

Ans. (a)

'Progress as a' functions as a prepositional phrase modifying the noun 'society'.

It indicates that the society has made extraordinary progress or advancement in a certain regard. Hence, 'progress as a' is the most appropriate answer.

813. If you want to have two cats, a male and a female <u>will usually gotten</u> along. SSC MTS Tier-1 19.06.2023 (Shift-I)
(a) will usual get
(b) No improvement
(c) will usually get
(d) will usually got

Ans. (c)

The phrase 'will usually gotten' will be replaced with 'will usually get' as we generally use the first form of the verb after modals. Hence, 'will usually get (V_1)' is the most appropriate answer.

814. Both of us felt the relationship (wasn't really gone somewhere.)
SSC MTS Tier-1 19.06.2023 (Shift-II)
(a) No correction required
(b) wasn't really going anywhere
(c) was going that direction
(d) won't really gone that path

Ans. (b)

We generally use the Gerund (going) as these are actually verb forms used as nouns to show activities.

Hence, 'wasn't really going anywhere' is the most appropriate answer.

815. I like to hang my laundry outside in the <u>Suns to dry</u>.
SSC MTS Tier-1 19.06.2023 (Shift-III)
(a) No improvement
(b) Sun to dried
(c) Sun to dries
(d) Sun to dry

Ans. (d)

The word 'Suns' must be replaced with 'Sun' as we don't make plurals of the proper noun 'Sun'.

Hence, 'Sun to dry' is the most. appropriate answer

816. She (had a reputation) brilliance.
SSC MTS Tier-1 20.06.2023 (Shift-I)
(a) No correction required
(b) have a reputation for
(c) has a reputation for
(d) has a reputation of

Ans. (c)

The phrase 'had a reputation' must be replaced with 'has a reputation for'. According to subject-verb agreement, a singular verb should be used for a singular subject.

Generally use the preposition 'for' to express reason. Hence, 'has a reputation for' is the most appropriate answer.

817. Though they allow celebrities and famous people to take pictures (inside the museum, but they does not allow the general public) to do the same. SSC MTS Tier-1 20.06.2023 (Shift-II)
(a) inside the museum, they do not allow the general public
(b) No substitution required
(c) inside the museum, but do not allowing the general public
(d) inside the museum, they does not allow general public

Ans. (a)

Inside the museum, they do not allow the general public

According to the 'Subject-Verb Agreement Rule', a singular subject always takes a singular verb and a plural subject (they) always takes a plural verb (do).

Hence, 'they do not allow the general public' is the most appropriate answer.

818. The people of Philippines has voted to elect a new president.
SSC MTS Tier-1 20.06.2023 (Shift-III)
(a) No substitution required
(b) The people of Philippines have voted
(c) The people of the Philippines have voted
(d) The people of the Philippines has voted

Ans. (c)

According to the 'Subject-Verb Agreement Rule', a plural subject (people) always takes a plural verb (have).

Hence, 'the people of the Philippines have voted' is the most appropriate answer.

819. Andrew will playing basketball at the college tournament.
SSC MTS Tier-1 01.09.2023 (Shift-I)
(a) are play the
(b) are play
(c) is playing
(d) is played

Ans. (c)

The underlined part of the given sentence contains an error of tense. Replace 'will' with 'is' to correct the sentence.

820. The energetic kitten is playful after having his breakfast.
SSC MTS Tier-1 01.09.2023 (Shift-III)
(a) its (b) it's
(c) it (d) it is

Ans. (a)

The underlined part of the given sentence contains an error.

Replace 'his' with 'its' to correct the sentence.

821. They would find someone drive the wagon back across the desert.
SSC MTS Tier-1 04.09.2023 (Shift-II)
(a) in drive in the
(b) to drive
(c) to drive the
(d) in driving

Ans. (c)

The underlined part of the given sentence contains an error. Add 'to' to correct the sentence.

822. No sooner did he finished his examination than he left for his cricket training centre.
SSC MTS Tier-1 05.09.2023 (Shift-II)
(a) No sooner did he finish
(b) No sooner than he finished
(c) No sooner than he did finished
(d) No sooner had he finish

Ans. (a)

The underlined part of the given sentence contains an error. The word 'finish' should be used in place of 'finished' to correct the sentence as we use first form of verb with 'do/does/did.

823. She will handling the baby as tenderly as possible.
SSC MTS Tier-1 06.09.2023 (Shift-I)
(a) wills handle
(b) shall handles
(c) will handle
(d) will handled

Ans. (c)

The underlined part of the given sentence contains an error.

The word 'handle' should be used in place of 'handling' to correct the sentence as it makes a comparison.

824. To preparing the vine for plant, it should be cut back to 2 ft.
SSC MTS Tier-1 06.09.2023 (Shift-II)
(a) prepares in vine in plant
(b) prepare a vine in planting
(c) prepared the vine of plant
(d) prepare the vine for planting

Ans. (d)

The underlined segment 'To preparing the vine for plant' is incorrect. The correct phrase is 'prepare the vine for planting' because 'prepare' is the correct infinitive form and 'planting' is the correct gerund form.

825. Virtual reality is the creation of a virtual environment presented to our senses in such a way that we experience it as if we were really there.
SSC MTS Tier-1 06.09.2023 (Shift-III)
(a) presenting to our senses
(b) presenting in our senses
(c) presents to our senses
(d) No substitution required

Ans. (d)

The sentence is correct as it is.

826. You are the beautiful woman I have ever seen. SSC MTS Tier-1 08.09.2023 (Shift-I)
(a) no rectification needed
(b) more beautiful
(c) beauty
(d) most beautiful

Ans. (d)

The underlined segment 'the beautiful woman' is incorrect. The correct phrase is 'the most beautiful woman' because 'most beautiful' is the correct superlative form.

827. France is a largest country.
SSC MTS Tier-1 08.09.2023 (Shift-III)
(a) smaller (b) larger
(c) smallest (d) large

Ans. (d)

The underlined segment 'a largest country' is incorrect.
The correct phrase is 'a large country' because 'large' is the correct adjective to use here.

828. I considered Geography as an easier subject.
SSC MTS Tier-1 11.09.2023 (Shift-I)
(a) the easy (b) the easier
(c) an easiest (d) an easy

Ans. (d)

The underlined segment 'an easier subject' is incorrect.
The correct phrase is 'an easy subject' because 'easy' is the correct adjective to use here.

829. Rashmi works at the hospital, don't she? SSC MTS Tier-1 11.09.2023 (Shift-II)
(a) does she? (b) has she?
(c) doesn't she? (d) do she?

Ans. (c)

Use 'doesn't she?' to correct the sentence.

830. I considered geography as an easier subject. SSC MTS Tier-1 11.09.2023 (Shift-I)
(a) the easy (b) the easier
(c) an easiest (d) an easy

Ans. (d)

'An easy' is the most appropriate option to replace the underlined words in the given sentence. As no comparison is made in the sentence, positive degree of adjective must be used.

831. I (am here) since 1981.
SSC MTS Tier-1 11.09.2023 (Shift-III)
(a) have been here
(b) had been here
(c) was here
(d) has have here

Ans. (a)

The bracketed segment 'am here' is incorrect. The correct phrase is 'have been here' because 'have been' indicates that the action started in the past and continues to the present.

832. Teenage is that phase of life when you are proposed to the world outside. SSC MTS Tier-1 12.09.2023 (Shift-I)
(a) you are exposed to
(b) you are excited with
(c) one are proposed to
(d) you are interrupted to

Ans. (a)

The underlined segment 'proposed to the world' is incorrect.

The correct phrase is 'exposed to the world' because 'exposed' means being introduced or made known.

833. Very early in the morning, at the beginning of January, Opu was lying in bed waiting for the Sun having rose.
SSC MTS Tier-1 12.09.2023 (Shift-II)

(a) waited for the Sun rising
(b) waited for the Sun having rose
(c) No improvement required
(d) waiting for the Sun to rise

Ans. (d)

The underlined segment 'having rose' is incorrect.

The correct phrase is 'waiting for the Sun to rise' because 'to rise' is the correct infinitive form.

834. Many a things are used for the show. SSC MTS Tier-1 13.09.2023 (Shift-I)

(a) a things is
(b) a things were
(c) a thing is
(d) a thing were

Ans. (c)

The underlined part of the given sentence contains an error of subject verb agreement. 'Many a' takes a singular verb.

Hence, 'are' should be replaced by 'is' to correct the sentence.

835. This film is a non-stop riot that many cite as one of the funny films of all time. SSC MTS Tier-1 13.09.2023 (Shift-I)

(a) No rectification needed
(b) funniest
(c) more funny
(d) funnier

Ans. (b)

The degree of the adjective is incorrect in the sentence. As the article 'the' precedes the adjective, the superlative degree of adjective 'funniest' should be used in the sentence.

836. If I hand her a flower and say, 'Given it to mamma,' she take it to her mother.
SSC MTS Tier-1 13.09.2023 (Shift-II)

(a) was taking it (b) takes it
(c) had took it (d) had taken it

Ans. (b)

The underlined segment 'she take it' is incorrect. The correct phrase is 'she takes it' because 'takes' is the correct present tense form.

837. They said that he is not going to call them.
SSC MTS Tier-1 13.09.2023 (Shift-III)

(a) he shall not call them
(b) he has not gone to call then
(c) they are not going to call them
(d) he was not going to call them

Ans. (d)

The underlined segment 'is not going to call' is incorrect. The correct phrase is 'he was not going to call' because it correctly matches the past tense.

838. Ramesh is owning a beautiful house in Noida. SSC MTS Tier-1 14.09.2023 (Shift-I)

(a) did owned (b) owns
(c) has owning (d) was owned

Ans. (b)

As the given sentence states a fact simple present tense 'owns' should be used.

839. His claim to be the smartly kid in the school was a bit hyperbole!
SSC MTS Tier-1 14.09.2023 (Shift-II)

(a) no rectification needed
(b) smartest
(c) smarter
(d) smart

Ans. (b)

The underlined segment 'smartly' is incorrect.

The correct phrase is 'smartest' because 'smartest' is the superlative form of 'smart.'

840. The rise in temperature is playing havoc with India's rainfall which is pertinent for India's agriculture sector. SSC MTS Tier-1 14.09.2023 (Shift-III)

(a) rainfall who is pertinent
(b) rainfall which is significant
(c) rainfall which is decant
(d) rainfall which was mendicant

Ans. (b)

The underlined segment 'pertinent' can be improved by changing it to 'significant' to better convey the importance of rainfall for India's agriculture sector.

SSC MTS 2022

841. The water at her place was cool and had a metallic taste.
SSC MTS Tier-1 05.07.2022 (Shift-I)

(a) was cooling and have
(b) No improvement required
(c) were cool and have
(d) was coolest and has

Ans. (b)

The sentence is correct as it is.

842. Many families are so poor to bear the cost of educating all their children. SSC MTS Tier-1 05.07.2022 (Shift-I)

(a) No improvement
(b) too poor
(c) to poor
(d) such poor

Ans. (b)

The underlined segment 'so poor' is incorrect.

The correct phrase is 'too poor' to convey the idea of an excessive degree of poverty.

843. I don't know why he is such secretly. SSC MTS Tier-1 05.07.2022 (Shift-II)

(a) are so secretly
(b) No improvement required
(c) is many secretive
(d) is so secretive

Ans. (d)

The underlined segment 'such secretly' is incorrect.

The correct phrase is 'so secretive' because 'so secretive' correctly describes the degree of being secretive.

844. I knew very little Spanish when I came here, but I have been learning and can now make myself understood.
SSC MTS Tier-1 05.07.2022 (Shift-III)

(a) when I come here,however
(b) upon arriving here,since
(c) No improvement required
(d) as soon as I came here, but

Ans. (c)

The sentence is correct as it is.

845. His mouth left open as he realise the truth. SSC MTS Tier-1 06.07.2022 (Shift-I)

(a) fell open as he perceived
(b) felt opened as he perceive
(c) was felt opened as he realise
(d) No improvement required

Ans. (a)

The underlined segment 'left open' can be improved by changing it to 'fell open' to better describe the action of his mouth opening due to surprise or realisation.

846. I noticed some strawberries grown in which of the gardens.
SSC MTS Tier-1 06.07.2022 (Shift-I)

(a) growing in which of
(b) grows upon one of
(c) No improvement required
(d) growing in one of

Ans. (d)

The underlined segment 'grown in which of the gardens' is incorrect. The correct phrase is 'growing in one of the gardens' to accurately describe the action.

847. He stood up from their chair to signal the end of the meeting. SSC MTS Tier-1 06.07.2022 (Shift-I)

(a) up from his
(b) upon of his
(c) No improvement
(d) below in their

Ans. (a)

The underlined segment 'their chair' is incorrect.

The correct phrase is 'his chair' to match the subject 'He.'

848. Although the waters may have receded, the aftermath of one of the world's biggest natural disaster had only just begun. SSC MTS Tier-1 06.07.2022 (Shift-I)

(a) the aftermath of one of the world's biggest natural disaster
(b) No improvement required
(c) the aftermath of one of the world's biggest natural disasters has
(d) the aftermath of one of the world's biggest natural disasters

Ans. (c)

The underlined segment 'disaster had' is incorrect. The correct phrase is 'disasters has' to correctly match the subject-verb agreement.

849. Abraham also had one sister, of who not much has been recorded. SSC MTS Tier-1 06.07.2022 (Shift-II)

(a) of what
(b) of whose
(c) of whom
(d) No substitution

Ans. (c)

The underlined segment 'of who' is incorrect.

The correct phrase is 'of whom' to correctly refer to the sister.

850. I am sorry of which my mother said. SSC MTS Tier-1 06.07.2022 (Shift-III)

(a) for what
(b) for which
(c) off that
(d) No improvement

Ans. (a)

The underlined segment 'of which' is incorrect.

The correct phrase is 'for what' to correctly refer to the reason for the apology.

851. He became the first Indian to be invited to perform at the advantageous Maple Theatre in Canada. SSC MTS Tier-1 07.07.2022 (Shift-I)

(a) prestigious
(b) inauspicious
(c) heterogeneous
(d) multifarious

Ans. (a)

The underlined segment 'advantageous' is incorrect. The correct phrase is 'prestigious' to better describe a well-known and respected theater.

852. Shall you pass me that pasta bowl? SSC MTS Tier-1 07.07.2022 (Shift-I)

(a) Shall pass you
(b) Can you pass
(c) Could passing you
(d) No improvement

Ans. (b)

The underlined segment 'Shall you pass' is incorrect. The correct phrase is 'Can you pass' to correctly form a polite request.

853. It has been my great misfortune to follow a speech more notable for its volume than for any sense. SSC MTS Tier-1 07.07.2022 (Shift-I)

(a) following a speech most notable
(b) No improvement required
(c) to follow a speech much notable
(d) to have being following a speech more notable

Ans. (b)

The sentence is correct as it is.

854. While the symptoms are troubling, they typically resolve within two weeks. SSC MTS Tier-1 07.07.2022 (Shift-III)

(a)No improvement (b) was troubling
(c) is troubling
(d) are troubled

Ans. (a)

The sentence is correct as it is.

855. My mother looked at Sana and me with her mouth slight openly. SSC MTS Tier-1 07.07.2022 (Shift-III)

(a) an openly slight
(b) No improvement
(c) open slight
(d) slightly open

Ans. (d)

The underlined segment 'slight openly' is incorrect.

The correct phrase is 'slightly open' to accurately describe the position of her mouth.

856. The scientists have so far focused on improve cropped yields. SSC MTS Tier-1 08.07.2022 (Shift-I)

(a) improving crop
(b) improvement crop
(c) No improvement required
(d) improve cropping

Ans. (a)

The underlined segment 'improve cropped yields' is incorrect. The correct phrase is 'improving crop' to accurately describe the action.

SSC Selection Post 2024, 2023

857. I have been yet to go to the flower exhibition at Delhi University. SSC SP 20.06.2024

(a) have yet been (b) have yet being
(c) had been yet (d) have yet

Ans. (d)

The underlined part of the given sentence contains an error. Remove 'been' to correct the sentence.

858. The rebels laid up their arms. SSC SP 27.06.2023 (Shift-IV)

(a) laid down (b) laid out
(c) laid on (d) laid by

Ans. (a)

The underlined part of the given sentence contains an error. Use 'laid down' which means to surrender to correct the sentence.

859. He was advised for walking alone in the neighbourhood. SSC SP 27.06.2023 (Shift-IV)

(a) No substitution
(b) advised about
(c) advised against
(d) advised on

Ans. (c)

The underlined part of the given sentence contains an error. Use 'advised against' which means to not do something to correct the sentence.

SSC Selection Post 2022

860. It is wrong to make accusations without will have any proof. SSC SP Level 27.06.2022

(a) without has any proof
(b) without being have any proof
(c) without to be have any proof
(d) without having any proof

Ans. (d)

The underlined part of the given sentence contains an error. Use 'without having any proof' to correct the sentence.

861. The volunteers of the organisation refused point of do what was requested. SSC SP 30.06.2022
(a) refused point blank to do
(b) redused point blank doing
(c) refused point blankedly to do
(d) refused in point blank of doing

Ans. (a)
The underlined segment 'refused point of do' is incorrect.
The correct phrase is 'refused point blank to do' because 'point blank' means directly and without hesitation.

862. Student were asked to write the historical events in the order of their occurence SSC SP 01.08.2022
(a) aesthetic order
(b) historic order
(c) chronological order
(d) dia clrovic order

Ans. (c)
The underlined segment 'the order of their occurrence' can be improved by changing it to 'chronological order' to accurately describe the arrangement of events by the order in which they occurred.

863. They made us to wait while they were checking our documents. SSC SP 01.08.2022
(a) made us wait
(b) made us to waits
(c) make us wait
(d) make us to waiting

Ans. (a)
The underlined part of the given sentence contains an error. Remove 'to' before 'wait' to correct the sentence.

864. Anyone reading these lines will thought that the writer is very sad. SSC SP 01.08.2022
(a) will have think that the writer is
(b) are think that the writer has
(c) have thinking that the writer is
(d) will think that the writer is

Ans. (d)
The underlined part of the given sentence contains an error. The modal 'will' takes the first form of verb. Hence, use 'think' to correct the sentence.

865. Reading has the capacity to make a man wise, but reading of only textbooks is like living in room of our same height. SSC SP 01.08.2022
(a) Reading makes a man wise
(b) Reading make a man wise
(c) Reading should make a man wise
(d) Reading shall make a man wise

Ans. (a)
The underlined part of the given sentence contains an error. However, it can be better written as 'reading makes a man wise'.

866. This statue of Lord Buddha is carved in jade. SSC SP 01.08.2022
(a) besides (b) by of
(c) out of (d) as of

Ans. (c)
The underlined part of the given sentence contains an error. Use 'out of' to correct the sentence.

867. The heading of the newspaper shout at the readers to stay inside their homes. SSC SP 03.08.2022 (Shift-III)
(a) had shouted at the leader
(b) No improvement required
(c) will shout at the reader
(d) shouted at the readers

Ans. (d)
The underlined segment 'shout' is incorrect. The correct phrase is 'shouted at the readers' because 'shouted' is the correct past tense form to match the context of the sentence.

868. Extreme sadness and pitiful cries of people filled the whole atmosphere. SSC SP 03.08.2022 (Shift-III)
(a) The effecting cries
(b) The continuous cries
(c) The heart-rending cries
(d) The loud cries

Ans. (c)
The underlined segment 'Extreme sadness and pitiful cries' can be improved by changing it to 'The heart-rending cries' to better convey the intense emotion involved.

869. The report claimed that a consensus was growing against the absolute authority in the country. SSC SP 04.08.2022 (Shift-II)
(a) Systematically collected laws
(b) Difference of opinion
(c) Centre of attraction
(d) Generally accepted agreement

Ans. (d)
The underlined segment 'consensus' is correctly defined as a 'generally accepted agreement,' making this the best substitution.

870. India went forward all odds and won the match against West Indies. SSC SP 04.08.2022 (Shift-IV)
(a) against (b) at
(c) among (d) in

Ans. (a)
The underlined segment 'went forward all odds' is incorrect. The correct phrase is 'went against all odds' because 'against all odds' is the correct idiomatic expression.

871. Anyone reading these lines will thought that the writer is very sad. SSC SP 1.08.2022 (Shift-III)
(a) will have think that the writer is
(b) have thinking that the writer is
(c) are think that the writer has
(d) will think that the writer is

Ans. (d)
The underlined segment 'will thought' is incorrect.
The correct phrase is 'will think' because 'think' is the correct present tense form to follow 'will.'

872. He brought these sweets for you and I. SSC SP 02.08.2022 (Shift-II)
(a) for I and you
(b) for you and I both
(c) for you and me
(d) No substitution required

Ans. (c)
The underlined segment 'for you and I' is incorrect.
The correct phrase is 'for you and me' because 'me' is the correct object pronoun.

873. The money arrived when I (little) expected it. SSC SP 02.08.2022 (Shift-II)
(a) The money arrived when I expected it.
(b) The money arrived when I least expected it.
(c) The money arrived when I less expected it.
(d) The money arrived when I little expected it.

Ans. (b)
The bracketed segment 'little expected it' is incorrect.
The correct phrase is 'least expected it' because 'least' is the correct superlative form.

874. In the introductory session, the teacher asked me to what district I came from. SSC SP 02.08 2022 (Shift-II)
(a) to which district
(b) which district
(c) No substitution required
(d) what district

Ans. (b)
The underlined segment 'to what district' is incorrect.
The correct phrase is 'which district' to correctly form the question.

875. I asked two people the way to Diana's house but no one of them knew it. **SSC SP 03.08. 2022 (Shift-IV)**

(a) whether either if them knew it
(b) if none of them knew it
(c) that no one of them knew it
(d) but neither of them knew it

Ans. (d)

The underlined segment 'no one of them' is incorrect.

The correct phrase is 'neither of them' because 'neither' correctly indicates that none of the two people knew the way.

SSC Steno 2024

876. After flip through half dozen profiles with the same name, he chance upon Elina's profile, he succeed in zeroing in on her now recognisable face. **SSC Steno 11.12.2024 (Shift-I)**

(a) flip through half dozen profile with the same name, he chance upon Elina's profile, he succeeded
(b) flipping through half a dozen profiles with the same name, he chanced upon Elina's profile, he succeeded
(c) flipping through half dozen profiles with the same name, he chanced upon Elina's profile, he succeed
(d) flipping through half dozen profile with the same name, he chance upon Elina's profile, he succeeded

Ans. (b)

'Flipping' is the correct gerund form, 'half a dozen' specifies the quantity correctly, and 'chanced' and 'succeeded' are correct past tense verbs.
Hence, 'flipping through half a dozen profiles with the same name, he chanced upon Elina's profile, he succeeded.'

877. What do you like to do on your free days other than to watching movies? **SSC Steno 11.12.2024 (Shift-I)**

(a) watch movie
(b) watching movies
(c) watches movies
(d) having watched movies

Ans. (b)

The correct substitution is 'watching movies' because the gerund form 'watching' is needed after the preposition 'than'.

878. I don't trust my friend because he has not and can never be trusted because of his deeds. **SSC Steno 11.12.2024 (Shift-I)**

(a) has not and can't be
(b) has not be and can never be
(c) has not been and can never be
(d) has been not and can never be

Ans. (c)

The phrase 'has not been and can never be' makes the sentence grammatically correct. The correct form maintains parallelism in the verb phrases.

879. I do not pay heed to walking excuses of the students. **SSC Steno 11.12.2024 (Shift-II)**

(a) sleeping excuses
(b) blind excuses
(c) deaf excuses
(d) lame excuses

Ans. (d)

The correct idiom is 'lame excuses'. The sentence 'I do not pay heed to lame excuses of the students' means that the speaker does not pay attention to weak or unconvincing excuses.

880. The bridge that connect the two sides of the city broke today. **SSC Steno 11.12.2024 (Shift-II)**

(a) that have been connecting
(b) that connects
(c) that have connect
(d) that has connect

Ans. (b)

The correct substitution is 'that connects.' The verb 'connects' is in the present tense and agrees with the singular subject 'bridge'.

881. Take a lot of care in writing official letters because they leave a trail behind. **SSC Steno 11.12.2024 (Shift-II)**

(a) a sound effect
(b) a lasting impression
(c) a longing desire
(d) a temporary exposure

Ans. (b)

The correct substitution is 'a lasting impression'.

Official letters often leave a significant and enduring effect, which aligns with the context.

882. (Everyone carefully were trying to) reason with the CEO regarding the need for work-life balance during the upcoming festivals. **SSC Steno 11.12.2024 (Shift-II)**

(a) Everyone was carefully trying to
(b) Everyone had carefully trying to
(c) Everyone were carefully trying to
(d) Everyone did carefully tried to

Ans. (a)

The correct word segment is 'Everyone was carefully trying to', which ensures subject-verb agreement and proper sentence structure. 'Everyone' is a singular subject, so it requires the singular verb 'was'. The original segment 'Everyone carefully were trying to' is incorrect because 'were' does not agree with the singular subject 'Everyone'.

883. While I was waiting for Asha for shopping, I spilled lemonade on my new trousers. **SSC Steno 11.12.2024 (Shift-II)**

(a) to hold shop
(b) to shop
(c) to shopper
(d) to see shopping

Ans. (b)

The underlined segment 'for shopping' is correctly substituted with 'to shop' to convey the intended meaning. 'To shop' is an infinitive that clearly indicates the purpose of waiting. The correct sentence is 'While I was waiting for Asha to shop, I spilled lemonade on my new trousers.'

884. Whether she wishes to relocate to Mumbai or continues to live here are her personal decisions. **SSC Steno 11.12.2024 (Shift-III)**

(a) is her personal decision
(b) were her personal decisions
(c) No substitution required
(d) have her personal decision

Ans. (a)

The correct substitution is 'is her personal decision'. The sentence should have singular verb 'is' to match the singular subject 'Whether she wishes to relocate to Mumbai or continues to live here.'

885. Radha and Sheela have been knowing each other since they were children. **SSC Steno 11.12.2024 (Shift-III)**

(a) had knowing themselves
(b) have been know each other
(c) have known each other
(d) had been known themselves

Ans. (c)

The correct substitution is 'have known each other'. The present perfect tense 'have known' indicates a continuous state from the past to the present. The phrase 'have been knowing' is incorrect because 'know' is a stative verb and does not use the continuous form.

886. Anya was a empath and had accurate intuitions regarding other people's feelings. **SSC Steno 11.12.2024 (Shift-III)**

(a) being a empath
(b) is an empath
(c) was an empath
(d) had an empathy

Ans. (c)

The correct substitution is 'was an empath'. This corrects the article usage error in the original sentence, as 'an' should be used before 'empath' because it starts with a vowel sound.

887. I look forward (see) you soon. **SSC Steno 11.12.2024 (Shift-III)**

(a) into see (b) to seeing
(c) to see (d) on seeing

Ans. (b)

The correct substitution is 'to seeing'. The gerund 'seeing' follows the preposition 'to' in the phrasal verb 'look forward to', which expresses anticipation or expectation.

888. Elegance and intelligence had the two most important traits of young ladies. **SSC Steno 10.12.2024 (Shift-I)**

(a) been the
(b) has been the
(c) are the
(d) am being the

Ans. (c)

The correct phrase to substitute the underlined segment is 'are the'. The sentence 'Elegance and intelligence are the two most important traits of young ladies' uses the present tense 'are' to agree with the plural subject 'Elegance and intelligence'.

889. The patient couldn't survive the injuries and succumbed with death **SSC Steno 10.12.2024 (Shift-I)**

(a) succumbed to death
(b) succumbed by death
(c) succumbed into death
(d) succumbed in death

Ans. (a)

The correct phrase to substitute the underlined segment is 'succumbed to death'.

The sentence 'The patient couldn't survive the injuries and succumbed to death' accurately conveys the intended meaning.

890. He was the most cleverest man I ever knew. **SSC Steno 10.12.2024 (Shift-I)**

(a) cleverest
(b) most cleverer
(c) more clever
(d) cleverer

Ans. (a)

The underlined part 'the most cleverest' is incorrect because 'cleverest' is already in the superlative form and does not require 'most'. The correct sentence is 'He was the cleverest man I ever knew'.

891. I know a person who parents live in Milan. **SSC Steno 10.12.2024 (Shift-II)**

(a) whom parents
(b) whose parents
(c) what parents
(d) which parents

Ans. (b)

The correct improvement is 'whose parents'.

The sentence should read: 'I know a person whose parents live in Milan.' This correctly indicates possession.

892. My mom made her muffins, but she didn't eat none. **SSC Steno 10.12.2024 (Shift-II)**

(a) she did eat none
(b) she did ate many
(c) she didn't eat any
(d) she didn't ate any

Ans. (c)

The correct substitution is 'she didn't eat any.' Double negatives ('didn't' and 'none') are grammatically incorrect. 'Any' is the appropriate word to use here.

893. Our defence minister has shown his silver will by introducing this scheme. **SSC Steno 10.12.2024 (Shift-II)**

(a) iron will (b) stony will
(c) diamond will (d) golden will

Ans. (a)

The phrase 'iron will' is the correct idiom to use. It means strong determination, which fits the context of the defence minister introducing a new scheme.

894. There are being several psychological theories that aid the diagnosis of a mental disorder or illness. **SSC Steno 10.12.2024 (Shift-III)**

(a) are severally
(b) are several
(c) is several
(d) have being several

Ans. (b)

The phrase 'are being several' is incorrect here. Remove 'being' to correct it.

895. Doctor wants Tony to cut back down junk foods. **SSC Steno 10.12.2024 (Shift-III)**

(a) to cut back off
(b) to cut back over
(c) to cut back out
(d) to cut back on

Ans. (d)

The phrase 'to cut back on' means to reduce the amount of something, which fits the context of reducing junk food consumption.

896. He behaves if he were a king. **SSC Steno 10.12.2024 (Shift-III)**

(a) will be behaving as
(b) could be behaving as
(c) behaves as if
(d) has been behaving as

Ans. (c)

The correct phrase is 'behaves as if'. The expression 'as if' is used to describe how someone behaves in a way that is not true or hypothetical, making it appropriate for the given context.

897. The resort manager planned to welcome the guests with open arms when they arrived. **SSC Steno 10.12.2024 (Shift-III)**

(a) without any delay
(b) in a secretive way
(c) in a cordial manner
(d) in a melancholy spirit

Ans. (c)

'in a cordial manner' is the appropriate substitution.

Welcoming guests 'with open arms' means doing so warmly and in a friendly manner.

In a melancholy spirit feeling sad or sorrowful.

898. What are there reason s for refusing the offer? **SSC Steno 10.12.2024 (Shift-III)**

(a) are there reason
(b) are their reasons
(c) is their reasons
(d) is there reasons

Ans. (b)

The correct form is 'are their reasons'. 'Their' is the possessive pronoun correctly referring to reasons belonging to them.

- There refers to a place.
- Their indicates possession.

SSC Steno 2023

899. My brother <u>is resembling</u> my mother. SSC Steno 12.10.2023 (Shift-I)
(a) resembles
(b) had resembled
(c) was resembling
(d) had been resembling

Ans. (a)

The underlined part of the given sentence contains an error.

As the sentence states a fact, simple present tense 'resembles' should be used' as it doesn't take any preposition.

900. No sooner had I reached the station <u>when the train started moving</u>. SSC Steno 12.10.2023 (Shift-I)
(a) than the train started moving
(b) when the train had started moving
(c) when the train start moving
(d) then the train had started moving

Ans. (a)

The underlined part of the given sentence contains an error. No sooner takes than.

Hence, use 'than' to correct the sentence.

901. <u>Suitable to</u> the instructions from the higher officials, the government land was allotted to the poor. SSC Steno 12.10.2023 (Shift-I)
(a) Despite of
(b) No substitution
(c) As of
(d) In accordance with

Ans. (d)

The underlined part of the sentence needs substitution.

The conjunction is unsuitable in the context of the sentence. Hence, use 'in accordance with' to improve the sentence.

902. They <u>wondered about in</u> sheepskins and goatskins in those days. SSC Steno 12.10.2023 (Shift-I)
(a) wander about in
(b) wondered in
(c) wandered about in
(d) wandered in

Ans. (c)

The underlined part of the sentence contains an error.

The use of the word 'wondered' is incorrect in the context of the sentence. Hence, use 'wandered' to correct the sentence.

903. Select the correct option to substitute the underlined segment in the given sentence. If no substitution is required, select 'No substitution'.
'Speak slow lest you <u>will</u> wake up mommy', said Emily to Tess. SSC Steno 12.10.2023 (Shift-I)
(a) should
(b) would
(c) No substitution
(d) could

Ans. (a)

The underlined part of the sentence need substitution. 'Lest' takes 'should'. Hence, use 'should' to correct the sentence.

904. Physical activity has been <u>projected to be helpful on avoidance</u> of depression, by the experts. SSC Steno 12.10.2023 (Shift-I)
(a) projected to be helpful in the avoidance
(b) projected to be helpful for avoidance
(c) projected to be helpful of avoidance
(d) projected to be helpful about avoidance

Ans. (a)

The underlined part of the sentence contains an error. Use 'projected to be helpful in the avoidance' to correct the sentence.

905. <u>Unless you don't answer my question</u>, I will not leave. SSC Steno 12.10.2023 (Shift-I)
(a) I don't answer my question
(b) you don't answer this question
(c) you answer my question
(d) you don't question my answer

Ans. (c)

The underlined part of the sentence contains an error. Unless does not take a negative word. Hence, use 'you answer my question' to correct the sentence.

906. The scientist says that while the complete core meltdown at Chernobyl was a major disaster, <u>it had fall far short of catastrophe</u> many nuclear power critics had feared, the so-called 'China Syndrome'. SSC Steno 12.10.2023 (Shift-I)
(a) it fell far short of the catastrophe
(b) it fell far away of the catastrophe
(c) it fell much short of the catastrophe
(d) it fell far shorter of the catastrophe

Ans. (a)

The underlined part of the sentence contains an error.

As the sentence is in past tense, use 'it fell far short of the catastrophe' to correct the sentence.

907. A few boys were <u>kept up</u> because of disobedience. SSC Steno 12.10.2023 (Shift-I)
(a) kept in
(b) kept back
(c) kept on
(d) kept off

Ans. (b)

The underlined part of the sentence contains an error. The use of phrasal verb 'kept up' means to continue without stopping or changing is incorrect.

Hence, 'kept back' which means 'to not go near something' correct the sentence.

908. He <u>was fatiguing because</u> he spent seven break-less hours on the computer. SSC Steno 12.10.2023 (Shift-I)
(a) was fatigueness because
(b) was fatigueless because
(c) was fatigued because
(d) has been fatiguing because

Ans. (c)

The underlined part of the sentence contains an error. Use 'was fatigued' to correct the sentence.

909. The excessive <u>using of pocket calculators</u> can stultify your capacity to do mental calculations. SSC Steno 12.10.2023 (Shift-I)
(a) used of pocket calculators
(b) use of pocket calculators
(c) aversion of pocket calculators
(d) utility of pocket calculators

Ans. (b)

The underlined part of the sentence contains an error. Use 'use of pocket calculators' to correct the sentence.

910. <u>Me and Samridhi</u> live here. SSC Steno 12.10.2023 (Shift-I)
(a) Samridhi with I
(b) Samridhi and I
(c) Samridhi and me
(d) I and Samridhi

Ans. (b)

The underlined part of the sentence contains an error. If two or more than two Subjective Case Singular Pronouns are present in a sentence, then we follow the 231 rule. Hence, the correct part would be 'Samridhi and I'.

911. They didn't catch you, are they?
SSC Steno 13.10.2023 (Shift-I)

(a) had they (b) wasn't it
(c) did they (d) didn't they

Ans. (c)

The underlined part of the sentence contains an error.

A question tag is constructed using the auxiliary verb present in the sentence and the pronoun which agrees with the subject. Hence, 'did they' should be used to correct the sentence.

912. The knowledge and abilities that students are expected to master as they progress through the four years of high school are referred to as the high school curriculum.
SSC Steno 13.10.2023 (Shift-I)

(a) deteriorate over
(b) grow with
(c) advance through
(d) regress along

Ans. (c)

The phrase 'advance' through means 'progress through'. Hence, it can replace the underlined segment.

913. Ravina was very sick today and we will take her to the hospital as she gets worse. SSC Steno 13.10.2023 (Shift-I)

(a) we took her to the hospital now before she gets worse
(b) we will take her to the hospital now before she gets worse
(c) No substitution
(d) we can take her to the hospital now before she get worse

Ans. (b)

The underlined part of the sentence contains an error. Use 'we will take her to the hospital now before she gets worse' to correct the sentence.

914. The manager of the hotel requested the boarder to mention his whereabouts in the register.
SSC Steno 13.10.2023 (Shift-I)

(a) motif of the heinous crime
(b) reason of moral degradation
(c) aftermath of the offence
(d) place of residence

Ans. (d)

The word 'whereabouts' refers to the place of residence.

915. It is easier to learn English than to learn German. SSC Steno 13.10.2023 (Shift-I)

(a) not to learn German
(b) No substitution required
(c) than learn German
(d) learning than German

Ans. (b)

The underlined part of the sentence is grammatically and contextually correct.

916. He ordered for four cups of tea and some snacks. SSC Steno 13.10.2023 (Shift-I)

(a) order for four cups of tea
(b) gave ordered for four cups of tea
(c) ordered four cups of tea
(d) ordered four for cups of tea

Ans. (c)

The underlined part of the sentence contains an error. The word 'ordered' does not take any preposition. Hence remove 'for' to correct the sentence.

917. Police termed it as of riot on which two of their colleagues were killed and many spectators got injured.
SSC Steno 13.10.2023 (Shift-I)

(a) as a riot in which two of their
(b) as a riot though which two of their
(c) as if riot about which two of their
(d) as a riot for which two of their

Ans. (a)

The underlined part of the sentence contains an error. Use 'as a riot in which two of their' to correct the sentence.

918. Either my sisters or my brother are coming to the meeting.
SSC Steno 13.10.2023 (Shift-I)

(a) my brother come
(b) my brothers is coming
(c) my brother is coming
(d) my brother do not come

Ans. (c)

The underlined part of the sentence contains an error.

Use 'my brother is coming' to correct the sentence as the subject 'my brother' is singular.

919. When the thief sees the sentry at the main gate, he managed to escape from the side gate.
SSC Steno 13.10.2023 (Shift-I)

(a) seeing the sentry
(b) has seen the sentry
(c) saw the sentry
(d) see the sentry

Ans. (c)

The underlined part of the given sentence contains an error. As the sentence is in past tense, 'saw the sentry' will be used to correct the sentence.

920. The road has been rough, they abandoned their journey further.
SSC Steno 13.10.2023 (Shift-I)

(a) be rough
(b) being rough
(c) was rough
(d) had been rough

Ans. (b)

The underlined part of the sentence contains an error. Use 'being rough' to correct the sentence.

921. She is the eldest member of our town. SSC Steno 13.10.2023 (Shift-I)

(a) No substitution
(b) is the old
(c) is the elder
(d) is the oldest

Ans. (d)

The underlined part of the sentence contains an error. 'Oldest' is used in terms of age.

Hence, 'oldest' should be used in place of 'eldest'.

04

Synonyms

A synonym is a word that has a similar meaning to another word.
For example,

Word	Synonyms
Adhere	Comply, Observe
Ferocious	Cruel, Fierce

Types of Questions Asked

Type 1

Select the most appropriate synonym of the given word.

Gregarious

(a) Anti-social (b) Introvert (c) Sociable (d) Excited *Ans.* (c)

Type 2

Select the most appropriate synonym of the underlined words in the following sentence.

The detective uncovered a clandestine operation.

(a) Secretive (b) Obvious
(c) Public (d) Revealed *Ans.* (a)

Type 3

Select the most appropriate synonym of the given word to fill in the blank in the sentence.

Inception

Since the .... of the year, you have been doing nothing.

(a) Initiative (b) Beginning (c) Initial (d) Origin *Ans.* (b)

How to Solve the Questions

To find the correct synonym, it is very important to develop a good vocabulary. Read newspapers, articles, journals, blogs, etc. to find new words and understand their meanings.

You can also solve sentence based questions on synonyms with these easy steps.

Step 1 Read the sentence with the underlined word or the word whose synonym you need.

Step 2 Understand the meaning of the word within the sentence. This will help you know the meaning of the word and help you find the synonym.

Step 3 Now, read the words in the options. You would easily find the synonym of the given word.

SSC Exam Scanner

Directions (Q. Nos. 1-937) Select the most appropriate synonym of the given word. *Or*

Select the most appropriate option to substitute the underlined/highlighted segment in the given sentence. *Or*

Select the most appropriate synonym of the word given in bracket to fill in the blank.

SSC CGL 2024 (Tier 1 & 2)

1. He walked leisurely towards the entrance. **SSC CGL Tier-2 18.01.2025**

(a) reassuringly (b) hastily
(c) without haste (d) with a kickstart

Ans. (c)

The most appropriate meaning of the underlined word 'leisurely' is 'without haste'. It means taking one's time in a relaxed manner.

2. Charisma **SSC CGL Tier-2 20.01.2025**

(a) Charm (b) Influence
(c) Atmosphere (d) Reputation

Ans. (a)

The synonym of 'charisma', which means a compelling attractiveness or charm that can inspire devotion in others, is 'charm'.

3. Innuendo **SSC CGL Tier-1 09.09.2024 (Shift-I)**

(a) Prose (b) Crude
(c) Ragged (d) Insinuation

Ans. (d)

Innuendo means a remark or remarks that suggest something unpleasant indirectly. Hence, its synonym is 'insinuation' which means an unpleasant hint or suggestion of something bad.

Prose means written or spoken language in its ordinary form, without metrical structure.

Crude means raw.

Ragged means torn and dirty.

4. Fatal **SSC CGL Tier-1 09.09.2024 (Shift-I)**

(a) Deadly (b) Additional
(c) Jovial (d) Easy

Ans. (a)

Fatal means something that can cause death or deadly.

Jovial means happy.

5. We'd better watch our step and not give him any excuse to **harass** us further. **SSC CGL Tier-1 09.09.2024 (Shift-I)**

(a) betray (b) relish
(c) soothe (d) intimidate

Ans. (d)

Harass means subject to aggressive pressure or intimidation or to make repeated small-scale attacks on someone.

Betray means to deceive someone.

Relish means to appreciate.

Soothe means to comfort.

6. Toxic **SSC CGL Tier-1 09.09.2024 (Shift-I)**

(a) Laudatory (b) Lanky
(c) Lethal (d) Licit

Ans. (c)

Toxic means poisonous containing or contaminated with a substance capable of injuring or killing a living thing. Hence, its nearest synonym is 'lethal' which means deadly.

Laudatory means praiseworthy.

Lancy means 'enclosure' or 'church'.

Licit means not forbidden; lawful.

7. No altruistic act is truly sincere. **SSC CGL Tier-1 09.09.2024 (Shift-I)**

(a) philanthropic
(b) phantasmal
(c) phenomenal
(d) phonotypical

Ans. (a)

Altruistic means having or showing a concern for the well-being of others, even if it results in disadvantage for yourself. Hence, its synonym is 'philanthropist' which means a person who seeks to promote the welfare of others, especially by the generous donation of money to good causes.

Phantasmal means something is unreal or only exists in the imagination.

Phenomenal means remarkable or exceptional, especially exceptionally good.

Phonotypical means relating to a phonetic symbol or text printed in phonetic symbols.

8. Abundant
SSC CGL Tier-1 09.09.2024 (Shift-II)
SSC CGL Tier-1 09.12.2022 (Shift-I)

(a) Ample (b) Scarce
(c) Barren (d) Difficult

Ans. (a)

Abundant means excess or in large quantity. Hence, its synonym is 'ample' which means the same.

Scarce means not enough.

Barren means not productive.

9. I would love to organise the farewell party at my house. **SSC CGL Tier-1 09.09.2024 (Shift-II)**

(a) Derange (b) Disorder
(c) Arrange (d) Confuse

Ans. (c)

Organise means to arrange properly.

Derange means make (someone) insane.

10. Berserk **SSC CGL Tier-1 09.09.2024 (Shift-II)**

(a) Demented (b) Absurd
(c) Stubborn (d) Lazy

Ans. (a)

Berserk means to become very angry and often violent or to be out of control due to intense anger or excitement. Hence, its synonym is 'demented' which means unable to think or act clearly because you are extremely worried, angry or excited by something.

Absurd means strange.

Stubborn means someone who doesn't change opinions.

11. Taut **SSC CGL Tier-1 09.09.2024 (Shift-III)**

(a) Slack (b) Tight
(c) Torn (d) Flaccid

Ans. (b)

Taut means stretched or pulled tight; not slack.

Slack means not taut or held tightly in position; loose.

Flaccid means (of part of the body) soft and hanging loosely or limply, especially so as to look or feel unpleasant.

12. Confiscate **SSC CGL Tier-1 09.09.2024 (Shift-III)**

(a) Restock (b) Destroy
(c) Seize (d) Titivate

Ans. (c)

Confiscate means take or seize (someone's property) with authority.

Titivate means arouse (someone) to interest or mild excitement, especially through sexually suggestive images or words.

13. Edible **SSC CGL Tier-1 09.09.2024 (Shift-III)**

(a) noisome
(b) mortal
(c) noxious
(d) nutritive

Ans. (d)

Edible means something that can be eaten. The word nearest in meaning to it is 'nutritive'.

Noisome means having an extremely offensive smell.

Noxious means harmful, poisonous or very unpleasant.

14. There are many factories in the operative area of the city. **SSC CGL Tier-1 09.09.2024 (Shift-III)**

(a) industrial (b) serviceable
(c) industrious (d) mechanical

Ans. (a)

Operative means functioning or having effect. Hence, its nearest means is 'industrial'.

15. The elaborate syllabi had to be .... (summarised) to make a presentation in the UGC assessment meeting. **SSC CGL Tier-1 09.09.2024 (Shift-III)**

(a) expanded (b) recapitulated
(c) prolonged (d) lengthened

Ans. (b)

Summarised means to give a brief statement of the main points of (something). Hence, its synonym is 'recapitulated' which means summarise and state again the main points of.

Expanded means to grow in size.

Prolonged means to increase in time.

Lengthened means to increase in length.

16. He was trembling with fear. **SSC CGL Tier-1 09.09.2024 (Shift-III)**

(a) Shivering (b) Weeping
(c) Running (d) Intrepid

Ans. (a)

Trembling means shaking or quivering, typically as a result of anxiety, excitement, or frailty. Hence, its synonym is 'shivering'.

Intrepid means fearless; adventurous (often used for rhetorical or humorous effect).

17. He tried to **alleviate** the sufferings of his neighbours. **SSC CGL Tier-1 09.09.2024 (Shift-III)**

(a) Swell (b) Add
(c) Intensify (d) Relieve

Ans. (d)

Alleviate means make (suffering, deficiency or a problem) less severe. Hence, its synonym is 'relieve'.

18. The Morbi bridge mishap has left Gujarat in a deplorable state. **SSC CGL Tier-1 10.09.2024 (Shift-I)**

(a) Jubilation
(b) Despicable
(c) Complaining
(d) Rejoicing

Ans. (b)

Deplorable means deserving strong condemnation; completely unacceptable. Hence, its synonym is 'despicable' which means deserving hatred and contempt.

Jubilation and **Rejoicing** means being happy.

19. Equivocal **SSC CGL Tier-1 10.09.2024 (Shift-I)**

(a) Clear (b) Ambiguous
(c) Representative (d) Balanced

Ans. (b)

Equivocal means open to more than one interpretation; ambiguous.

20. Stationary
SSC CGL Tier-1 10.09.2024 (Shift-II)

(a) Motile (b) Portable
(c) Swindle (d) Still

Ans. (d)

Stationary means not moving or not intended to be moved. Hence, its synonym is 'still'.

Motile means to be able to move independently.

Portable means capable of being carried or moved about.

Swindle means use deception to deprive (someone) of money or possessions.

21. Pugnacious
SSC CGL Tier-1 10.09.2024 (Shift-II)
SSC CGL Tier-1 10.06.2022 (Shift-II)
SSC CGL Tier-1 18.09.2024 (Shift-II)

(a) Ally (b) Belligerent
(c) Sly (d) Dogmatic

Ans. (b)

Pugnacious means eager or quick to argue, quarrel or fight. Hence, its synonym is 'belligerent' which means hostile and aggressive.

Ally means friend.

Sly means clever.

Dogmatic means inclined to lay down principles as undeniably true.

22. Solomon's reputation as an accountant is taintless.
SSC CGL Tier-1 10.09.2024 (Shift-III)

(a) flawed (b) faultless
(c) dubious (d) inconsistent

Ans. (b)

Taintless means perfect and faultless.

Dubious means doubtful, unsettled in opinion or lacking confidence.

Inconsistent means not staying the same throughout.

23. Mayra has the ability for mathematics.
SSC CGL Tier-1 10.09.2024 (Shift-III)

(a) astute (b) altitude
(c) aptitude (d) attitude

Ans. (c)

The synonym of 'ability' is **aptitude**.

Astute means having or showing an ability to accurately assess situations or people and turn this to one's advantage.

Altitude means height.

24. The media, these days, constructs .... (misleading) narratives on politics and celebrities to increase the viewership.
SSC CGL Tier-1 10.09.2024 (Shift-III)

(a) sincere (b) true
(c) candid (d) mendacious

Ans. (d)

Mendacious means not telling the truth; lying, misleading.
Hence, it is the correct filler for the given blank.

Candid means honest.

25. Evaluate **SSC CGL Tier-1 10.09.2024 (Shift-III)**

(a) Misjudge (b) Assess
(c) Unity (d) Misquote

Ans. (b)

Evaluate means to test or assess something.

26. Adversity **SSC CGL Tier-1 11.09.2024 (Shift-I)**

(a) Success
(b) Misfortune
(c) Pleasure
(d) Advantage

Ans. (b)

Adversity means hardship, suffering and misfortune.

27. Our legal system must frame proper legal rules for juvenile criminals.
SSC CGL Tier-1 11.09.2024 (Shift-I)

(a) senile (b) dotage
(c) old (d) young

Ans. (d)

Juvenile means a young person, a characteristic of children or a sign of immaturity.

Senile means (of a person) having or showing the weaknesses or diseases of old age, especially a loss of mental faculties.

Dotage means the period of life in which a person is old and weak.

28. FATIGUE **SSC CGL Tier-1 11.09.2024 (Shift-I)**
SSC CGL Tier-1 06.12.2022 (Shift-IV)
SSC CGL Tier-1 29.02.2024 (Shift-IV)

(a) Mission (b) Tiredness
(c) Vigour (d) Obese

Ans. (b)

Fatigue means tiredness.
Mission means goal.
Vigour means energy.
Obese means fat.

29. She was overstrung before her dance performance.
SSC CGL Tier-1 11.09.2024 (Shift-I)

(a) Cheerful (b) Calm
(c) Placid (d) Nervous

Ans. (d)

Overstrung means extremely nervous or tense.

Placid means not easily upset or excited.

30. Merit **SSC CGL Tier-1 11.09.2024 (Shift-II)**

(a) Fatigue (b) Oblique
(c) Virtue (d) Residue

Ans. (c)

Merit means morals and virtue.

Oblique means not expressed or done in a direct way.

Residue means a small amount of something that remains after the main part has gone or been taken or used.

31. Jovial **SSC CGL Tier-1 11.09.2024 (Shift-II)**

(a) Miserable (b) Solemnity
(c) Cheerful (d) Profane

Ans. (c)

Jovial means cheerful and happy.

Miserable means sad and unhappy.

Solemnity means the state or quality of being serious and dignified.

Profane means not relating to that which is sacred or religious; secular.

32. Layla is the Sultan's consort.
SSC CGL Tier-1 11.09.2024 (Shift-II)

(a) Foe (b) Alcoholic
(c) Enemy (d) Partner

Ans. (d)

Consort means friend or partner.

33. Paramount
SSC CGL Tier-1 11.09.2024 (Shift-III)

(a) inferior (b) collateral
(c) supreme (d) trivial

Ans. (c)

Paramount means superior or supreme.

Collateral means property (such as securities) pledged by a borrower to protect the interests of the lender.

34. Expertise **SSC CGL Tier-1 11.09.2024 (Shift-III)**

(a) Proficiency (b) Ignorance
(c) Clumsiness (d) Lack

Ans. (a)

Expertise means expert skill or knowledge in a particular field. Hence, its synonym is 'proficiency' which means the same.

Ignorance means not knowledgable.

Clumsiness means the quality of being awkward or careless in one's movements.

35. His **eloquent** speech always persuades people to work for their betterment.
SSC CGL Tier-1 11.09.2024 (Shift-III)
(a) Vague (b) Inarticulate
(c) Articulate (d) Short
Ans. (c)
Eloquent means fluent or persuasive in speaking or writing. Hence, its synonym is 'articulate' which means the same.
Vague means not clear.
Inarticulate means not spoken in a elegant way.

36. The .... (crux) of his argument was that education should continue throughout life.
SSC CGL Tier-1 11.09.2024 (Shift-III)
(a) essence (b) proposal
(c) etiquette (d) draft
Ans. (a)
Crux means summary or essence. Hence, essence is the correct filler for the blank.
Proposal means a plan, scheme or offer that can be accepted or rejected.
Etiquette means socially acceptable behaviour.
Draft means a preliminary version of a piece of writing.

37. Acquiesce SSC CGL Tier-1 12.09.2024 (Shift-I)
(a) Desist (b) Cease
(c) Thwart (d) Concur
Ans. (d)
Acquiesce means accept something reluctantly but without protest. Hence, its synonym is 'concur' which means the same.
Desist and **Cease** means to stop.
Thwart means to prevent (someone) from accomplishing something

38. His ambition in life is to become a happy and satisfied man.
SSC CGL Tier-1 12.09.2024 (Shift-I)
(a) Apathy (b) Satisfaction
(c) Eagerness (d) Amend
Ans. (c)
Ambition means a strong desire to do or achieve something. Hence, its nearest synonym is 'eagerness'.
Amend means to correct.

39. During Covid times, many organisations made .... (sentimental) appeals to raise funds for migrant workers.
SSC CGL Tier-1 12.09.2024 (Shift-I)
(a) mawkish
(b) sincere
(c) cynical
(d) practical
Ans. (a)
Mawkish means emotional and sentimental. Hence, it is the correct filler for the given blank.
Cynical means believing that people are motivated purely by self-interest; distrustful of human sincerity or integrity.

40. Many people love to visit enchanting hills. SSC CGL Tier-1 12.09.2024 (Shift-II)
(a) alluring (b) cool
(c) risky (d) echoing
Ans. (a)
Enchanting means attractive.
Hence, its synonym is **alluring** which means the same.

41. Repulse SSC CGL Tier-1 12.09.2024 (Shift-II)
(a) Repel (b) Substitute
(c) Recover (d) Reprove
Ans. (a)
Repulse means to cause dislike. Hence, its synonym is **repel** which means the same.
Reprove means reprimand (someone).

42. Listening to the same lecture everyday appeared very .... to him. (boring)
SSC CGL Tier-1 12.09.2024 (Shift-II)
(a) monotonous (b) furious
(c) nervous (d) monolithic
Ans. (a)
The synonym of boring is **monotonous** which is the correct filler for the given blank.
Monolithic means formed of a single large block of stone.

43. How did we end up in this rapturous situation?
SSC CGL Tier-1 12.09.2024 (Shift-III)
(a) ecstatic (b) terrifying
(c) misleading (d) disastrous
Ans. (a)
Rapturous means characterised by, feeling or expressing great pleasure or enthusiasm.
Hence, its synonym is **ecstatic** which means happy.

44. Rectify SSC CGL Tier-1 12.09.2024 (Shift-III)
SSC CGL Tier-1 05.12.2022 (Shift-II)
SSC CHSL Tier-1 09.07.2024 (Shift-IV)
(a) Mar (b) Amend
(c) Corrupt (d) Upset
Ans. (b)
Rectify means to correct or amend.
Mar means to impair the quality or appearance of spoil.
Corrupt means morally degenerate, dishonest or immoral.

45. Celebrate SSC CGL Tier-1 13.09.2024 (Shift-II)
(a) Daunt (b) Rejoice
(c) Bitch (d) Assure
Ans. (b)
Celebrate means to acknowledge (a significant or happy day or event) with a social gathering or enjoyable activity. Hence, its synonym is 'rejoice'.
Daunt means make (someone) feel intimidated or apprehensive.
Bitch is a female dog.
Assure means to tell someone something positively to dispel any doubts.

46. One of Ram's leisure activities is tennis. SSC CGL Tier-1 13.09.2024 (Shift-II)
(a) Main (b) Lead
(c) Languish (d) Recreation
Ans. (d)
Leisure refers to a time of relaxation of refreshment.
Hence, its synonym is **recreation** which means the same.
Languish means (of a person, animal or plant) lose or lack vitality; grow weak.

47. His approach was filled with such perseverance that it was difficult to overlook his merit.
SSC CGL Tier-1 13.09.2024 (Shift-III)
SSC CGL Tier-1 05.12.2022 (Shift-I)
(a) Ignorance (b) Doggedness
(c) Reluctance (d) Monotonous
Ans. (b)
Perseverance means persistence in doing something despite difficulty or delay in achieving success.
Hence, its synonym is 'Doggedness' which means the same.
Ignorance means not knowledgeable.
Reluctance means doubt or hesitance.

48. Bully SSC CGL Tier-1 17.09.2024 (Shift-I)
(a) Plough (b) Oxen
(c) Coddle (d) Oppressor
Ans. (d)
A **bully** is a person who habitually seeks to harm or intimidate those whom they perceive as vulnerable. Hence, its synonym is 'oppressor'.
Plough means a large farming implement with one or more blades fixed in a frame, drawn over soil to turn it over and cut furrows in preparation for the planting of seeds.
Oxen is a bull.
Coddle means to treat (someone) in an indulgent or overprotective way.

49. Thankful SSC CGL Tier-1 17.09.2024 (Shift-I)
(a) Ungrateful (b) Affirmation
(c) Obliged (d) Obscure

Ans. (c)

The word 'obliged' is a synonym of **thankful.**

Ungrateful means not thankful.

Affirmation means agreement.

Obscure means not clear.

50. Labour **SSC CGL Tier-1 17.09.2024 (Shift-I)**

(a) Mesh (b) Toil
(c) Dalliance (d) Relaxation

Ans. (b)

Labour means hardwork or toil.

Mesh means material made of a network of wire or thread.

Dalliance means a casual romantic or sexual relationship.

51. Experts acknowledged that some counterfeiting of document techniques are virtually impossible to detect. **SSC CGL Tier-1 17.09.2024 (Shift-II)**

(a) fiasco (b) forgery
(c) impromptu (d) frenzy

Ans. (b)

Forgery is the counterfeiting of document.

Fiasco means a complete failure, especially a ludicrous or humiliating one.

Impromptu means done without being planned, organised or rehearsed.

Frenzy means a state or period of uncontrolled excitement or wild behaviour.

52. I was completely mesmerised by the performance.
SSC CGL Tier-1 17.09.2024 (Shift-III)

(a) Irritated (b) Annoyed
(c) Bored (d) Fascinated

Ans. (d)

Mesmerised means capture the complete attention of (someone). Hence, its synonym is **fascinated.**

53. Exceptional
SSC CGL Tier-1 18.09.2024 (Shift-I)

(a) Trivial
(b) Emotional
(c) Total
(d) Outstanding

Ans. (d)

Exceptional means outstanding.
Trivial means insignificant.

54. Forsake **SSC CGL Tier-1 18.09.2024 (Shift-I)**
SSC CHSL Tier-1 10.08.2021 (Shift-I)

(a) Accelerate (b) Reveal
(c) Abandon (d) Clutch

Ans. (c)

To **forsake** means to abandon.

Accelerate means to quicken.

Clutch means to hold tightly.

55. An intense wish to learn something keeps the nerves active.
SSC CGL Tier-1 18.09.2024 (Shift-I)

(a) powerful (b) fixed
(c) lazy (d) half-hearted

Ans. (a)

Intense means powerful.

56. Condone **SSC CGL Tier-1 18.09.2024 (Shift-II)**

(a) Solicitude (b) Penalty
(c) Pardon (d) Solace

Ans. (c)

Condone means accept (behaviour that is considered morally wrong or offensive); pardon.

Solicitude means care or concern for someone or something.

Penalty means a fine.

Solace means peace.

57. Tendency **SSC CGL Tier-1 18.09.2024 (Shift-II)**

(a) Distaste (b) Decoy
(c) Proneness (d) Aversion

Ans. (c)

Tendency means an inclination towards a particular characteristic or type of behaviour.
Given words 'proneness' seems similar to it.

58. Bankrupts are those who are incapable to pay their debts.
SSC CGL Tier-1 18.09.2024 (Shift-II)

(a) capable (b) powerful
(c) incompetent (d) meagre

Ans. (c)

Incompetent means incapable.

59. Mellifluous
SSC CGL Tier-1 18.09.2024 (Shift-III)

(a) Distinct (b) Musical
(c) Loud (d) Cacophonous

Ans. (b)

Mellifluous means (of a sound) pleasingly smooth and musical to hear.
Distinct means different.

Cacophonous means harsh and unpleasant.

60. A period of free outdoor play can provide a very necessary respite from the hustle and bustle of the day.
SSC CGL Tier-1 18.09.2024 (Shift-III)

(a) progression
(b) commencement
(c) break
(d) continuation

Ans. (c)

Respite means break.
Commencement means beginning.

61. Garnish **SSC CGL Tier-1 19.09.2024 (Shift-I)**

(a) Dwindle (b) Tarnish
(c) Blemish (d) Decorate

Ans. (d)

Garnish means to decorate.

Dwindle means to cheat.

Tarnish means to spoil something.

Blemish means a flaw.

62. Determined
SSC CGL Tier-1 19.09.2024 (Shift-I)
SSC MTS 08.09.2023 (Shift-I)

(a) Hesitant (b) Loathe
(c) Faltering (d) Resolute

Ans. (d)

Resolute means determined or decisive, **Hesitant** means doubtful.

Loathe means hate.

Faltering means wavering or unstable.

63. Fallacy **SSC CGL Tier-1 19.09.2024 (Shift-I)**

(a) Error
(b) Veracity
(c) Evidence
(d) Verify

Ans. (a)

Fallacy means a mistaken belief, especially one based on unsound arguments. Hence, its synonym is an **error.**

Veracity means truth.

64. She is a very creative artist and one can see that in her paintings.
SSC CGL Tier-1 19.09.2024 (Shift-II)

(a) innovative (b) likeable
(c) pedantic (d) good

Ans. (a)

Creative means innovative.

Pedantic means excessively concerned with minor details or rules.

65. Morbid **SSC CGL Tier-1 19.09.2024 (Shift-II)**

(a) Blithe (b) Gloomy
(c) Grand (d) Bet

Ans. (b)

Morbid means characterised by an unusual interest in disturbing and unpleasant subjects, especially death and disease. Hence, its synonym is 'gloomy'.

Blithe means showing a casual and cheerful indifference considered to be callous or improper.

66. It takes time to adapt to a new environment.
SSC CGL Tier-1 19.09.2024 (Shift-II)

(a) apply (b) adjust
(c) understand (d) control

Ans. (b)

Adapt means to adjust to something.

67. Beseech **SSC CGL Tier-1 19.09.2024 (Shift-III)**

(a) Pamper (b) Implore
(c) Impart (d) Bequeath

Ans. (b)

Beseech means ask (someone) urgently and fervently to do something; implore. Entreat means to indulge with every attention, comfort and kindness, spoil.

Bequeath means to honour with a title.

68. Miraculous
SSC CGL Tier-1 19.09.2024 (Shift-III)

(a) Draining (b) Average
(c) Expected (d) Incredible

Ans. (d)

Miraculous means of the nature of a miracle or having the power to work miracles. Hence, its nearest synonym is **incredible.**

69. Magnificent
SSC CGL Tier-1 19.09.2024 (Shift-III)
SSC CHSL Tier-1 11.07.2024 (Shift-I)
SSC MTS 14.09.2023 (Shift-III)

(a) Slow (b) Sacred
(c) Scared (d) Splendid

Ans. (d)

Magnificent means extremely beautiful, elaborate or impressive. Hence, its synonym is **splendid.**

70. Adequate SSC CGL Tier-1 23.09.2024 (Shift-I)
SSC Steno Grade C&D 13.10.2023

(a) Evaluate (b) Hidden
(c) Sufficient (d) Reconcile

Ans. (c)

Adequate means sufficient or enough.

71. Brittle SSC CGL Tier-1 23.09.2024 (Shift-I)

(a) Furtive (b) Fickle
(c) Fragile (d) Fatal

Ans. (c)

Brittle means hard but liable to break easily; fragile.

Furtive means attempting to avoid notice or attention, typically because of guilt or a belief that discovery would lead to trouble; secretive.

Fickle means changing frequently, especially as regards one's loyalties or affections.

72. Cherish SSC CGL Tier-1 23.09.2024 (Shift-I)
SSC GD 02.02.2023 (Shift-I)

(a) Neglect (b) Breach
(c) Nurture (d) Afflict

Ans. (c)

Cherish means protect and care for (someone) lovingly.

Hence, its nearest synonym is 'nurture' which means care for and protect (someone or something) while they are growing.

Breach means a failure to do what is required by a law, an agreement or a duty.

Afflict means (of a problem or illness) cause pain or trouble to; affect adversely.

73. The city has **immense** coal piers.
SSC CGL Tier-1 23.09.2024 (Shift-I)

(a) diminutive (b) trifling
(c) set (d) huge

Ans. (d)

Immense means huge.

Diminutive means extremely or unusually small.

Trifling means insignificant.

74. Obstinate SSC CGL Tier-1 23.09.2024 (Shift-II)

(a) Obedient (b) Adaptive
(c) Stubborn (d) Submissive

Ans. (c)

Obstinate means stubbornly refusing to change one's opinion or chosen course of action, despite attempts to persuade.

Adaptive means adjustable.

Submissive means obedient.

75. The mothers, who suffer from postpartum depression, feel .... by their children. (vexed)
SSC CGL Tier-1 23.09.2024 (Shift-II)

(a) delighted (b) recovered
(c) pacific (d) annoyed

Ans. (d)

Vexed means annoyed. Hence, 'annoyed' is the correct filler for the given blank.

76. Dissipate
SSC CGL Tier-1 23.09.2024 (Shift-III)

(a) Glorious (b) Malicious
(c) Haste (d) Spend

Ans. (d)

Dissipate means (with reference to a feeling or emotion) disappear or cause to disappear. Hence, its nearest synonym is 'spend'.

Glorious means worthy of praise and honour.

Malicious means evil and wicked.

Haste means quick.

77. Dodge SSC CGL Tier-1 23.09.2024 (Shift-III)

(a) Avoid (b) Force
(c) Boarding (d) Amount

Ans. (a)

Dodge means to avoid.

78. I saw a shabby looking man living in the <u>cavity</u> of a mountain.
SSC CGL Tier-1 24.09.2024 (Shift-I)

(a) elevation (b) height
(c) mound (d) hole

Ans. (d)

A **cavity** is a hole.

79. This is a clear example of <u>conflict</u> of egos. SSC CGL Tier-1 24.09.2024 (Shift-I)

(a) clash (b) mingling
(c) infliction (d) crash

Ans. (a)

A conflict is a **clash** or quarrel.

Mingling means mix or cause to mix together.

Infliction means to cause pain.

80. This building is <u>colossal</u> and it can hold a village's population in it.
SSC CGL Tier-1 24.09.2024 (Shift-I)
SSC CHSL Tier-1 02.08.2023 (Shift-III)
SSC GD 01.02.2023 (Shift-I)

(a) very huge (b) temporary
(c) very beautiful (d) puny

Ans. (a)

Colossal means extremely large or great. Hence is synonym is 'very huge'.

81. Maverick SSC CGL Tier-1 24.09.2024 (Shift-I)

(a) Conformist (b) Orthodox
(c) Bohemian (d) Follower

Ans. (c)

Maverick means an unorthodox or independent-minded person. Hence, its synonym is **bohemian**. It means a social and cultural movement that promotes a way of life that rejects mainstream society's expectations and norms.

Conformist and **Orthodox** refer to a person who conforms to accepted behaviour or established practices.

82. At times, David behaves in a very <u>obdurate</u> manner to kids.
SSC CGL Tier-1 24.09.2024 (Shift-II)

(a) trusting (b) amiable
(c) obstinate (d) envious

Ans. (c)

Obdurate means stubbornly refusing to change one's opinion or course of action. Hence, its synonym is **obstinate** which means the same.

83. Sachin Tendulkar was an <u>indispensable</u> member of the Indian cricket team in his days.
SSC CGL Tier-1 24.09.2024 (Shift-II)
SSC CHSL Tier-1 09.08.2023 (Shift-II)

(a) Motivational
(b) Essential
(c) Optional
(d) Functional

Ans. (b)

Indispensable means absolutely necessary. Hence, its synonym is 'essential' or 'compulsory'.

84. Cascade SSC CGL Tier-1 24.09.2024 (Shift-II)

(a) Garden (b) Waterfall
(c) Criticise (d) Arcade

Ans. (b)

Cascade means a small, steep waterfall or a series of small waterfalls.

Arcade refers to a place where there are many electronic or other coin-operated games for the public.

85. Evoke SSC CGL Tier-1 24.09.2024 (Shift-III)

(a) Induce (b) Abandon
(c) Divert (d) Reduce

Ans. (a)

Evoke means to bring to mind or recollection or to make someone feel an emotion. Hence, its synonym is **induce** which means initiate or enhance a biochemical process.

Divert means to go away from something.

86. The soldiers spent long period .... (convalescing). SSC CGL Tier-1 24.09.2024 (Shift-III)

(a) attacking (b) travelling
(c) recovering (d) ailing

Ans. (c)

Convalescing means recovering.

87. Grotesque SSC CGL Tier-1 24.09.2024 (Shift-III)

(a) Shameful (b) Comely
(c) Ugly (d) Spontaneous

Ans. (c)

Grotesque means comically or repulsively ugly or distorted.

Spontaneous means without preparation.

88. Loving SSC CGL Tier-1 24.09.2024 (Shift-III)

(a) Subordinate (b) Affectionate
(c) Rejuvenate (d) Offish

Ans. (b)

Loving means affectionate.

Subordinate means inferior in position.

Rejuvenate means give new energy or vigour to; revitalise.

Offish means aloof or distant in manner; not friendly.

89. Necessary SSC CGL Tier-1 24.09.2024 (Shift-III)

(a) Potential (b) Essential
(c) Existential (d) Spatial

Ans. (b)

Necessary means essential.

Existential means of, relating to or affirming existence.

Spatial means relating to or occupying space.

90. Our university is <u>affiliated</u> with various institutes all over the world. SSC CGL Tier-1 25.09.2024 (Shift-I)

(a) disparate (b) diverse
(c) unalike (d) allied

Ans. (d)

Affiliated means (of a subsidiary group or a person) officially attached or connected to an organisation.

Hence, its antonym is 'allied' which means united and joined.

Disparate means essentially different in kind; not able to be compared.

91. We went to a <u>legitimate</u> Mexican restaurant for my birthday, where they served cuisine like you would find in Mexico. SSC CGL Tier-1 25.09.2024 (Shift-I)

(a) genuine (b) fictitious
(c) falsified (d) productive

Ans. (a)

Legitimate means genuine and true.

Fictitious means not real.

92. Derogatory SSC CGL Tier-1 25.09.2024 (Shift-I)

(a) Insulting
(b) Derivative
(c) Delegation
(d) Salutary

Ans. (a)

Derogatory means insulting.

Derivative means imitative of the work of another artist, writer, etc. and usually disapproved of for that reason.

Delegation is the act of assigning work, responsibility or decision-making to another person

Salutary means (especially with reference to something unwelcome or unpleasant) producing good effects; beneficial.

93. He said that he lacks the .... to stand in a queue. (patience) SSC CGL Tier-1 25.09.2024 (Shift-II)

(a) relevance (b) elegance
(c) endurance (d) acceptance

Ans. (c)

Endurance means the ability to keep doing something difficult, unpleasant, or painful for a long time.

Hence, it is the nearest synonym of **patience** that can fill in the blank.

94. The choice was **judicious** as further events proved. SSC CGL Tier-1 25.09.2024 (Shift-III) SSC GD 08.02.2023 (Shift-I) SSC CPO 29.069.2024 (Shift-II)

(a) prudent (b) silly
(c) hasty (d) ridiculous

Ans. (a)

Judicious means having, showing or done with good judgement or sense. Hence, its synonym is **prudent** which means the same.

95. It was his <u>decency</u> that he employed him. SSC CGL Tier-1 25.09.2024 (Shift-III)

(a) Rudeness (b) Deception
(c) Courtesy (d) Perversion

Ans. (c)

Decency means behaviour that conforms to accepted standards of morality or respectability. Hence, its synonym is **courtesy** which means the same.

Deception means dishonesty or lie.

Perversion means distortion or corruption of the original course, meaning, or state of something.

96. He was the most <u>honest</u> and good-hearted man that she had ever met. SSC CGL Tier-1 26.09.2024 (Shift-I)

(a) deceptive (b) sincere
(c) biased (d) fake

Ans. (b)

Honest is truthful and sincere.

Deceptive means dishonest and lying.

Biased means unfairly prejudiced for or against someone or something.

97. Even when he was left with plenty of fortune, he lived a <u>frugal</u> life. SSC CGL Tier-1 26.09.2024 (Shift-I)

(a) thrifty (b) purposeless
(c) extraordinary (d) hardworking

Ans. (a)

Frugal means thrifty and not wanting to spend money.

98. <u>Verity</u> is a good virtue for human life. SSC CGL Tier-1 26.09.2024 (Shift-II)

(a) Knowledge (b) Truth
(c) Information (d) Cooperation

Ans. (b)

Verity means a true principle or belief, especially one of fundamental importance.

99. Munificent SSC CGL Tier-1 26.09.2024 (Shift-II)

(a) Magnanimous (b) Malicious
(c) Miserly (d) Underappreciated

Ans. (a)

Munificent means characterised by or displaying great generosity. Hence, its synonym is 'magnanimous' which means the same.

Malicious means evil and wicked.

Miserly means not wanting to spend money.

100. Carcass SSC CGL Tier-1 26.09.2024 (Shift-II)

(a) Gale (b) Scrap
(c) Prison (d) Corpse

Ans. (d)

Carcass means a corpse or a dead body.

Gale means a very strong wind.

Scrap means waste.

101. She .... requested him to pay the bills. (persistently)
SSC CGL Tier-1 26.09.2024 (Shift-III)
(a) impetuously (b) obliviously
(c) tremendously (d) continuously
Ans. (d)
Persistently means continuously.
Impetuously means to do something quickly.
Obliviously means unaware.

SSC CGL 2023 (Tier 1 & 2)

102. Zealous SSC CGL Tier-1 14.07.2023 (Shift-I)
(a) Enthusiastic (b) Detached
(c) Apathetic (d) Indifferent
Ans. (a)
The word 'zealous' means showing great energy or enthusiasm in pursuit of a cause or objective.
Apathetic means detached or indifferent.

103. Read the given sentence and select the most appropriate synonym of the word 'ready' from the following options.
She was preparing dinner in an organised manner using well-equipped tools while listening to the radio. SSC CGL Tier-1 14.07.2023 (Shift-II)
(a) Preparing (b) Listening
(c) Organised (d) Equipped
Ans. (a)
The word 'preparing' in the sentence means the same as 'ready'.

104. Abound SSC CGL Tier-1 14.07.2023 (Shift-III)
(a) Increase (b) Flourish
(c) Succeed (d) Adequate
Ans. (b)
The word 'abound' means 'flourish'.

105. Matching SSC CGL Tier-1 14.07.2023 (Shift-IV)
(a) Appointing (b) Distinguishing
(c) Adoring (d) Resembling
Ans. (d)
The word **matching** is synonymous to 'resembling'.

106. The salesman <u>yielded</u> to the demands of his corrupt boss.
SSC CGL Tier-1 14.07.2023 (Shift-IV)
(a) conceded (b) courted
(c) hounded (d) trended
Ans. (a)
The underlined word 'yielded' means 'to surrender or give way to arguments, demands or pressure'. Hence, from the given options, 'conceded' meaning 'to yield' is its synonym.

107. Consent SSC CGL Tier-1 17.07.2023 (Shift-I)
(a) Avert (b) Assent
(c) Disturb (d) Dissent
Ans. (b)
The word 'consent' means 'to agree or assent'.

108. Read the given sentence and select the most appropriate synonym of the word 'vigilant' from the following options.
The burglar was very cautious, so he avoided the security perfectly as they didn't find any proof.
SSC CGL Tier-1 17.07.2023 (Shift-IV)
(a) Cautious (b) Proof
(c) Burglar (d) Security
Ans. (a)
The word 'vigilant' means 'careful' or cautious'.

109. Intriguing SSC CGL Tier-1 18.07.2023 (Shift-I)
(a) Glorifying
(b) Ravishing
(c) Stunning
(d) Interesting
Ans. (d)
The word 'intriguing' means 'interesting'.

110. The government's **utilitarian** stance was appreciated by all.
SSC CGL Tier-1 18.07.2023 (Shift-III)
SSC CHSL Tier-1 06.06.2022 (Shift-III)
(a) thrust (b) fanciful
(c) useful (d) distasteful
Ans. (c)
The word 'utilitarian' means designed to be functional or practical rather than attractive. Hence, its synonym is 'useful'.

111. The Committee wanted us to <u>explain</u> this in detail.
SSC CGL Tier-1 18.07.2023 (Shift-III)
(a) elaborate (b) trouble
(c) collect (d) keen
Ans. (a)
The word 'explain' means 'to elaborate'.

112. Certain SSC CGL Tier-1 18.07.2023 (Shift-IV)
(a) Approval (b) Definite
(c) Doubtful (d) Caution
Ans. (b)
The word 'certain' means 'definite'.

113. Tedious SSC CGL Tier-1 19.07.2023 (Shift-I)
SSC CHSL Tier-1 05.07.2024 (Shift-IV)
SSC MTS 13.09.2023 (Shift-III)
(a) Tiresome (b) Wholesome
(c) Repetitive (d) Threescore
Ans. (a)
The word 'tedious' means 'tiresome'. It refers to something that is boring and monotonous, often because it lasts too long.
'Tiresome' is a direct synonym as it implies causing one to feel bored or annoyed.

114. The <u>benevolent</u> gesture of the rich merchant was appreciated by all.
SSC CGL Tier-1 19.07.2023 (Shift-I)
SSC CHSL Tier-1 10.08.2023 (Shift-I)
SSC CPO 03.10.2023 (Shift-III)
(a) generous (b) sombre
(c) numb (d) sober
Ans. (a)
The underlined word 'benevolent' means 'kind and generous'.

115. He is very .... (eager) to join the Air Force. SSC CGL Tier-1 19.07.2023 (Shift-I)
(a) irksome (b) keen
(c) dubious (d) unconcerned
Ans. (b)
The correct word for the given blank is 'keen'. 'Keen' means having a strong desire or enthusiasm to do something. Therefore, being 'keen' to join the Air Force aligns with the given context of being 'eager'.

116. Adamant
SSC CGL Tier-1 19.07.2023 (Shift-III)
SSC GD 31.01.2023 (Shift-III)
(a) Flexible (b) Soft
(c) Stubborn (d) Adaptable
Ans. (c)
The word 'Adamant' means unshakable or insistent especially in maintaining a position or opinion. Hence, its synonym is 'Stubborn' which means refusing to change.

117. Abhijeet feels <u>extremely tired</u> after working all day long.
SSC CGL Tier-1 19.07.2023 (Shift-III)
(a) depressed (b) exhausted
(c) sleepy (d) bare
Ans. (b)
The word 'exhausted' means 'extremely tired'.

118. Authentic
SSC CGL Tier-1 19.07.2023 (Shift-III)
SSC CGL Tier-1 24.07.2023 (Shift-I)
(a) Genuine (b) False
(c) Doubtful (d) Corrupt
Ans. (a)
The word 'authentic' means 'true or genuine'.

119. One should <u>follow</u> the role models in life. SSC CGL Tier-1 19.07.2023 (Shift-IV)
(a) emulate (b) admire
(c) cherish (d) reward
Ans. (a)
The word 'emulate' meaning 'to copy or imitate' is nearest in meaning to the underlined word 'follow'.

120. The investment scheme had been a scam all along.
SSC CGL Tier-1 20.07.2023 (Shift-I)
(a) plain (b) swindle
(c) failure (d) successful
Ans. (b)
The underlined word 'scam' means 'doing something dishonest or fraud'. From the given options, 'swindle' means the same and is its synonym.

121. Hapless SSC CGL Tier-1 20.07.2023 (Shift-III)
(a) Happy
(b) Unfortunate
(c) Fortunate
(d) Distasteful
Ans. (b)
The word 'hapless' means 'unlucky and unfortunate'. Hence, 'unfortunate' is its synonym.

122. Immerse SSC CGL Tier-1 20.07.2023 (Shift-IV)
(a) Emerge (b) Distant
(c) Involve (d) Uncover
Ans. (c)
The word 'immerse' means 'to be involved'. Hence, 'involve' is the most appropriate synonym of 'immense'.

123. She looked .... (luminous) in the diamond necklace.
SSC CGL Tier-1 21.07.2023 (Shift-I)
(a) inpudent (b) strident
(c) transcendent (d) resplendent
Ans. (d)
The word 'resplendent', which means having a very bright or beautiful appearance, is a synonym of 'luminous'.

124. Genial SSC CGL Tier-1 21.07.2023 (Shift-II)
SSC CHSL Tier-1 14.03.2023 (Shift-IV)
(a) Optimistic
(b) Cheerful
(c) Despondent
(d) Positive
Ans. (b)
The word 'genial' means 'friendly and cheerful or convivial'.

125. Absorbed SSC CGL Tier-1 21.07.2023 (Shift-II)
(a) Preoccupied (b) Soaked
(c) Restored (d) Replaced
Ans. (b)
The word 'absorbed' means 'extremely wet or soaked'. Hence, 'soaked' is its closest synonym.

126. After my first visit to Boston, I spent almost every winter in the North. Once I went on a visit to a New England village with its frozen lakes and vast snow fields
SSC CGL Tier-1 21.07.2023 (Shift-III)
(a) minimal (b) shallow
(c) extensive (d) solid
Ans. (c)
The underlined word 'vast' means of very great extenet or quantity; immense or extensive.

127. Fierce SSC CGL Tier-1 21.07.2023 (Shift-III)
SSC CPO 04.10.2023 (Shift-III)
(a) Fanatic (b) Aggressive
(c) Fraud (d) Gentle
Ans. (b)
The word 'Fierce' means 'having or displaying an intense or ferocious aggressiveness'.
Hence, 'aggressive' is its closest synonym.

128. For many, a warming climatic system is expected to impact the availability of basic necessities like freshwater, food security and energy, while efforts to redress climate change, both through adaptation and mitigation, will similarly inform and shape the global development agenda. SSC CGL Tier-1 24.07.2023 (Shift-II)
(a) rise (b) cure
(c) balance (d) reduction
Ans. (d)
The underlined word 'mitigation' means 'reduction'.

129. Announced
SSC CGL Tier-1 24.07.2023 (Shift-III)
(a) Estrange (b) Declared
(c) Secret (d) Hid
Ans. (b)
The word 'announced' means 'declared'.
Estrange means to cause someone to no longer be friendly.

130. The hot Sun enervated the labourer to the extent that he collapsed.
SSC CGL Tier-1 24.07.2023 (Shift-IV)
(a) weaken (b) alleviate
(c) energise (d) elevate
Ans. (a)
The underlined word 'enervated' means feeling tired and weak. So, 'weaken' is its correct synonym.

131. Exuberance
SSC CGL Tier-1 24.07.2023 (Shift-IV)
(a) Vibrancy (b) Laziness
(c) Sympathy (d) Impartiality
Ans. (a)
Exuberance means overflowing energy and enthusiasm.
Vibrancy is a synonym of exuberance, meaning liveliness and energy.

132. Extol SSC CGL Tier-1 25.07.2023 (Shift-I)
(a) Reward (b) Punish
(c) Dismay (d) Praise
Ans. (d)
The word 'extol' means to 'praise'.

133. Gentle SSC CGL Tier-1 25.07.2023 (Shift-II)
(a) Fierce (b) Ferocious
(c) Cruel (d) Sympathetic
Ans. (d)
The word 'Gentle' means kind. From the given options, 'sympathetic' is its synonym.

134. Predicament
SSC CGL Tier-1 25.07.2023 (Shift-III)
(a) Ease (b) Quandary
(c) Blessing (d) Solution
Ans. (b)
The word 'predicament' means 'a difficult, unpleasant or embarrassing situation'.
From the given options, the word 'quandary' means a difficult situation or dilemma and hence, is its synonym.

135. Extinct SSC CGL Tier-1 25.07.2023 (Shift-IV)
(a) Vibrant (b) Vanished
(c) Active (d) Living
Ans. (b)
The word 'extinct' means 'vanished', as both means no longer existing.

136. A strong man is a mediator between divine and **mortal** fate.
SSC CGL Tier-1 26.07.2023 (Shift-I)
(a) delightful (b) sincere
(c) overjoyed (d) lethal
Ans. (d)
The word 'mortal' means 'someone who can die'. Hence, 'lethal' meaning 'deadly' is its nearest synonym.

137. His **modest** nature made all the difference.
SSC CGL Tier-1 26.07.2023 (Shift-II)
(a) courageous (b) horrific
(c) shy (d) dry
Ans. (c)
The word given in bold 'modest' means 'humble and shy'.

138. The internationally agreed declaration of the Small Island Developing States (SIDS) Accelerated Modalities of Action, the so-called S.A.M.O.A Pathway, recognises that SIDS remains a special case for sustainable development in view of their unique and particular vulnerabilities.
SSC CGL Tier-1 26.07.2023 (Shift-III)
SSC SP Higher Secondary 27.06.2023 (Shift-I)
(a) vast (b) unsuitable
(c) rare (d) imperishable
Ans. (d)
The word 'sustainable' means 'something that can exist in its form for a long time or imperishable'.

139. The heavy medications and strong drugs at the sanatorium will surely turn a patient completely lifeless and unresponsive.
SSC CGL Tier-1 26.07.2023 (Shift-IV)
(a) tombic (b) cadaverous
(c) zonic (d) wasted

Ans. (b)

The word **cadaverous** means 'very pale, thin or completely lifeless and unresponsive'.

Tombic means like or relating to atomb.

Zonic means a zone or beet 'wasted' means weak or emaciated.

140. This is credible information provided by the informer.
SSC CGL Tier-1 27.07.2023 (Shift-I)
(a) commendable
(b) dependable
(c) detachable
(d) digestible

Ans. (b)

The underlined word 'credible' means 'believable, authentic and dependable.'

141. Connote **SSC CGL Tier-1 27.07.2023 (Shift-II)**
(a) Comment (b) Criticise
(c) Care (d) Convey

Ans. (d)

The word 'Connote' means 'to convey the meaning of something'.

142. Select the synonym of the word *'Reproduce'* from the sentence.
Many scientific researches have proved that DNA replicates itself in the human body and is an enzyme based catalyst reaction.
SSC CGL Tier-1 27.07.2023 (Shift-II)
(a) Replicates (b) Reaction
(c) Proved (d) Researches

Ans. (a)

The word 'reproduce' means 'to produce a copy of something or replicate'.

Hence, the synonym of the word 'reproduce' from the sentence is 'replicates'.

143. I have thus far sketched the events of my life, but I have not shown how much I have depended on books not only for pleasure and for the wisdom they bring to all who read, but also for that knowledge which comes to others through their eyes and their ears. **SSC CGL Tier-1 27.07.2023 (Shift-III)**
(a) clarity (b) folly
(c) insight (d) emotion

Ans. (c)

The word 'wisdom' means 'intelligence and insight'.

144. The crowd cheered the cricketer.
SSC CGL Tier-1 27.07.2023 (Shift-IV)
(a) encouraged (b) distracted
(c) dropped (d) attracted

Ans. (a)

The underlined word 'cheered' means 'encouraged'.

145. Misanthropic
SSC CGL Tier-1 27.07.2023 (Shift-IV)
(a) Humanitarian (b) Sociable
(c) Antisocial (d) Philanthropic

Ans. (c)

The word 'misanthropic' means 'antisocial'.

146. It was a fairly foul day, as omens could be seen in abundance from the threshold of his border town ever since the dawn struck.
SSC CGL Tier-2 03.03.2023 (Shift-I)
(a) fairly, abundance
(b) foul, omens
(c) days, border
(d) threshold, dawn

Ans. (d)

The pair of synonyms is 'threshold and dawn'. The word 'threshold' means entrance and 'dawn' means 'the beginning or entry of the new day'.

147. The doctor has ...... (advised) medicine for the treatment of the disease. **SSC CGL Tier-2 03.03.2023 (Shift-I)**
(a) prevented (b) proscribed
(c) presented (d) prescribed

Ans. (d)

The correct word for the blank is 'prescribed'. 'Prescribed' means advised or recommended, especially by a doctor.

148. Bullying is a rather unacknowledged social evil. **SSC CGL Tier-2 03.03.2023 (Shift-I)**
(a) unidentified (b) notable
(c) infamous (d) named

Ans. (a)

The word **unacknowledged** means 'not recognised or identified'. 'Unidentified' is the closest synonym.

Notable means worthy of notice.

Infamous means well known for some bad quality or deed.

Named means having a specified name.

149. Even though James won the election, he has not brought any of his campaign promises ot fruition.
SSC CGL Tier-2 07.03.2023 (Shift-I)
(a) concealment
(b) nourishment
(c) disappointment
(d) accomplishment

Ans. (d)

The word **fruition** means 'accomplishment'. It refers to the realisation or fulfillment of a plan or project.

Concealment means the action of hiding something.

Nourishment means the food necessary for growth and health.

Disappointment means sadness or displeasure caused by the non-fulfillment of one's hopes or expectations.

150. The authority refused to pay any heed to the ...... demands made by the workers. (Trivial)
SSC CGL Tier-2 26.10.2023 (Shift-II)
SSC CHSL Tier-1 11.08.2023 (Shift-II)
(a) conceited (b) idiotic
(c) insignificant (d) majestic

Ans. (c)

The word **trivial** means 'insignificant'. It refers to something of little value or importance.

Conceited means excessively proud of oneself.

Idiotic means very stupid.

Majestic means having or showing impressive beauty or dignity.

SSC CGL 2022 (Tier 1 & 2)

151. Ostentatious
SSC CGL Tier-1 11.04.2022 (Shift-I)
(a) Showy (b) Tasteful
(c) Sudden (d) quick

Ans. (a)

The word **ostentatious** means 'showy'. It refers to something designed to impress or attract notice.

Tasteful means having or showing good taste.

Sudden means occurring or done quickly and unexpectedly.

Quick means moving fast or doing something in a short time.

152. Taciturn **SSC CGL Tier-1 11.04.2022 (Shift-II)**
(a) Verbose (b) Noisey
(c) Lively (d) Reserved

Ans. (d)

The word **taciturn** means 'reserved'. It refers to someone who is habitually silent or uncommunicative.

Noisy means making or given to making a lot of noise.
Lively means full of life and energy; active and outgoing.

153. Imminent
SSC CGL Tier-1 11.04.2022 (Shift-III)
(a) Unyielding (b) Ignorant
(c) Impending (d) Distant

Ans. (c)

The word **imminent** means 'impending'. It refers to something that is about to happen.

Unyielding means not giving way to pressure; hard or solid.

Ignorant means lacking knowledge or awareness in general.

Distant means far away in space or time.

154. Fluke **SSC CGL Tier-1 11.04.2022 (Shift-II)**

(a) Policy (b) Plan
(c) Chance (d) Contract

Ans. (c)

The word **fluke** means 'chance'. It refers to something that happens unexpectedly by luck.

Policy means a course or principle of action adopted or proposed by an organisation or individual.

Plan means a detailed proposal for doing or achieving something.

Contract means a written or spoken agreement, especially one concerning employment, sales, or tenancy, that is intended to be enforceable by law.

155. Urge **SSC CGL Tier-1 12.04.2022 (Shift-III)**

(a) Reply (b) Refuse
(c) Protest (d) Appeal

Ans. (d)

The word **urge** means 'appeal'. It refers to a strong desire or impulse to do something.

Reply means say or write something in response to what someone has said or written.

Refuse means indicate or show that one is not willing to do something.

Protest means express an objection to what someone has said or done.

156. Lacuna **SSC CGL Tier-1 13.04.2022 (Shift-I)**

(a) Misfortune
(b) Languor
(c) Apathy
(d) Hiatus

Ans. (d)

The word **lacuna** means 'hiatus'. It refers to a gap or missing part, especially in a document or series.

Misfortune means bad luck.

Languor means the state or feeling, often pleasant, of tiredness or inertia.

157. Solemn **SSC CGL Tier-1 13.04.2022 (Shift-I)**

(a) Dignified (b) Trivial
(c) Excited (d) Frivolous

Ans. (a)

The word **solemn** means 'dignified'. It refers to something that is serious and respectful.

Excited means very enthusiastic and eager.

Frivolous means not having any serious purpose or value.

158. Succulent **SSC CGL Tier-1 13.04.2022 (Shift-II)**

(a) Decent (b) Coarse
(c) Juicy (d) Foul

Ans. (c)

The word **succulent** means 'juicy'. It refers to something that is tender, moist, and tasty.

Decent means conforming with generally accepted standards of respectable or moral behaviour.

Coarse means rough or loose in texture or grain.

Foul means offensive to the senses, especially through having a disgusting smell or taste or being unpleasantly soiled.

159. Disrupt **SSC CGL Tier-1 13.04.2022 (Shift-II)**

(a) Breach (b) Injure
(c) Arrange (d) Organise

Ans. (a)

The word **disrupt** means 'breach'. It refers to interrupting or causing a disturbance.

Injure means do physical harm or damage to (someone).

Arrange means put (things) in a neat, attractive, or required order.

160. Trendy **SSC CGL Tier-1 13.04.2022 (Shift-III)**

(a) Common (b) Foreign
(c) Popular (d) Familiar

Ans. (c)

The word **trendy** means 'popular'. It refers to something that is currently fashionable or in style.

Common means occurring, found, or done often; prevalent.

Foreign means of, from, in, or characteristic of a country or language other than one's own.

Familiar means well known from long or close association.

161. Squawk **SSC CGL Tier-1 18.04.2022 (Shift-I)**

(a) Suggest
(b) Explore
(c) Scream
(d) Connote

Ans. (c)

The word **squawk** means 'scream'. It refers to making a loud, harsh noise.

Suggest means put forward for consideration.

Explore means travel through (an unfamiliar area) in order to learn about it.

162. Threshold **SSC CGL Tier-1 18.04.2022 (Shift-II)**

(a) Stairs (b) Exit
(c) Window (d) Doorway

Ans. (d)

The word **threshold** means 'doorway'. It refers to the entrance or beginning point of something.

Stairs means a set of steps leading from one floor of a building to another.

Exit means a way out of a building, room, or passenger vehicle.

Window means an opening in the wall or roof of a building or vehicle that is fitted with glass or other transparent material in a frame to admit light or air and allow people to see out.

163. Amass **SSC CGL Tier-1 18.04.2022 (Shift-III)**

(a) Gather (b) Spread
(c) Divide (d) ScatterArid

Ans. (a)

The word **amass** means 'gather'. It refers to collecting or accumulating a large amount of something.

Spread means open out (something) so as to extend its surface area, width, or length.

Divide means separate or be separated into parts.

Scatter means throw in various random directions.

164. Commute **SSC CGL Tier-1 19.04.2022 (Shift-I)**

(a) Consume (b) Convert
(c) Condense (d) Conserve

Ans. (b)

The word **commute** means 'convert'. It refers to changing something into a different form.

Consume means eat, drink, or ingest (food or drink).

Condense means make (something) denser or more concentrated.

Conserve means protect (something, especially an environmentally or culturally important place or thing) from harm or destruction.

165. Arid **SSC CGL Tier-1 19.04.2022 (Shift-III)**

(a) Dry (b) Lively
(c) Damp (d) Fertile

Ans. (a)

The word **arid** means 'dry'. It refers to a lack of moisture or water.

Lively means full of life and energy; active and outgoing.

Damp means slightly wet.

Fertile means (of soil or land) producing or capable of producing abundant vegetation or crops.

166. Saucy SSC CGL Tier-1 20.04.2022 (Shift-I)
(a) Tasty (b) Polite
(c) Smooth (d) Cheeky

Ans. (d)

The word **saucy** means 'cheeky'. It refers to someone who is boldly rude or disrespectful.

Tasty means (of food) having a pleasant, distinct flavor.

Polite means having or showing behavior that is respectful and considerate of other people.

Smooth means having an even and regular surface or consistency; free from perceptible projections, lumps, or indentations.

167. Lull SSC CGL Tier-1 20.04.2022 (Shift-III)
(a) Disturbances (b) Activity
(c) Noise (d) Calm

Ans. (d)

'Lull' means a temporary interval of quiet or lack of activity. Hence, its synonym is 'calm'.

168. Imbue SSC CGL Tier-1 21.04.2022 (Shift-I)
(a) Remove (b) Clear
(c) Instill (d) Deprive

Ans. (c)

Imbue means to inspire or permeate with a feeling or quality. Hence, its synonym is 'instill'.

Remove means to take something away.

Clear means easy to understand, free of obstacles.

Deprive means to deny someone the possession or use of something.

169. Livid SSC CGL Tier-1 21.04.2022 (Shift-II)
(a) Closed (b) Clear
(c) Pale (d) Furious

Ans. (d)

Livid means extremely angry. Hence, its synonym is 'furious'.

Pale means light in color or having less colour than usual.

170. Confusion SSC CGL Tier-1 1.12.2022 (Shift-I)
(a) Intrepidity (b) Stagnation
(c) Perusal (d) Commotion

Ans. (d)

Confusion means a situation when people do not understand what is happening, what they should do or who someone or something is.

Commotion from the given option is its most appropriate synonym as it means a sudden short period of noise, confusion or excited movement.

Intrepidity means fearless

Stagnation means stillness

Perusal menana quick glance.

171. Competent
SSC CGL Tier-1 1.12.2022 (Shift-II)
SSC CHSL Tier-1 02.07.2024 (Shift-I)
(a) Complex (b) Poor
(c) Capable (d) Beginner

Ans. (c)

'Competent' means having enough skill or knowledge to do something to a satisfactory standard. Hence, capable from the given options is the most appropriate synonym of 'Competent'.

172. The <u>sporadic</u> instructions of the invigilators distracted the examinee.
SSC CGL Tier-1 01.12.2022 (Shift-II)
(a) Continuous (b) Indirect
(c) Repetitive (d) Occasional

Ans. (d)

'Sporadic' means happening fairly often, but not regularly. So, 'occasional' from the given options is the most suitable synonym of 'sporadic'.

173. Moral SSC CGL Tier-1 02.12.2022 (Shift-IV)
(a) Ethical (b) Honourable
(c) Godliness (d) Symphony

Ans. (a)

The most appropriate synonym of the word **Moral** is 'ethical' as it means relating to beliefs about what is morally right and wrong. **Ethical means moral symphony refers to a long musical compositional.**

174. For Rahul, everything was a .... (modern) experience until he stepped onto the field.
SSC CGL Tier-1 01.12.2022 (Shift-IV)
(a) new (b) flashy
(c) global (d) Asiatic

Ans. (a)

The correct synonym of the word **modern** is 'new', Thus, the correct answer is 'new. Asiatic means belonging to Asia.

175. Even though Margaret had already eaten a large meal, she could not resist eating two slices of the <u>delectable</u> pie.
SSC CGL Tier-1 02.12.2022 (Shift-I)
(a) Stale (b) Delicious
(c) Nutritious (d) Rotten

Ans. (b)

'Delectable' means looking or tasting extremely good, and giving great pleasure. So, the most appropriate meaning of the word 'delectable' is 'delicious'.

176. Listening to the news of his father's <u>illness</u>, Soumen left for home with a heavy heart.
SSC CGL Tier-1 02.12.2022 (Shift-II)
(a) distrurbance (b) sickness
(c) disintegration (d) disorder

Ans. (b)

The word 'Illness' means a disease or period of being sick. The word 'Sickness' means the state of being ill. Thus, the correct synonym of the word 'Illness' is 'Sickness'.

177. If we want to progress, we must sometimes embrace .... (mutate).
SSC CGL Tier-1 02.12.2022 (Shift-II)
(a) replicate (b) imitate
(c) change (d) incise

Ans. (c)

The word 'Mutate' means change in form or nature.
Thus, the correct synonym is 'change'.
Replicate and **Imitate** mean to copy.
Incise means to decorate with cuts.

178. Visiting a book fair always fills my heart with a great <u>satisfaction</u>.
SSC CGL Tier-1 02.12.2022 (Shift-III)
(a) refreshment
(b) pride
(c) contentment
(d) bliss

Ans. (c)

Contentment means a state of happiness and satisfaction. Visiting a book fair always fills my heart with great satisfaction, so 'contentment' fits well in this context.

Refreshment means a light meal or drink.

Pride means a feeling of deep pleasure or satisfaction derived from one's own achievements.

Bliss means perfect happiness.

179. Deliberate
SSC CGL Tier-1 02.12.2022 (Shift-III)
(a) Casual (b) Hasty
(c) Planned (d) Rushed

Ans. (c)

The word **deliberate** means doing something consciously and intentionally.

Thus, the correct synonym of this word is 'planned'.

Hasty means quick and rushed.

180. Remorse SSC CGL Tier-1 02.12.2022 (Shift-IV)
SSC CPO Tier-1 09.11.2022 (Shift-III)
(a) Repentance (b) Slow
(c) Liberate (d) Affinity

Ans. (a)

Remorse means a strong female of being sorry that you have done something bad. So, the correct synonym of the word 'remorse' is 'repentance', which means regret or remorse.

Liberate means to free. Affinity means likeness.

181. Select the most appropriate synonym of the word *'stagnant'* from the following sentence.
Reeta was motionless after knowing that her brother had become mentally unstable after seeing the fatal accident on Tuesday night.
SSC CGL Tier-1 03.12.2022 (Shift-I)
(a) Motionless (b) Fatal
(c) Unstable (d) Accident
Ans. (a)
The correct synonym of the word 'stagnant' from the given sentence is 'motionless'.

182. There is a huge generation ...... (void) between Arun and his grandparents.
SSC CGL Tier-1 03.12.2022 (Shift-I)
(a) traditions (b) gap
(c) memory (d) experience
Ans. (b)
'Void' means a situation in which something important that is usually present is no longer there. So, the correct synonym of the word 'void' is 'gap'.

183. The perils of smoking tobacco can never be ignored.
SSC CGL Tier-1 03.12.2022 (Shift-I)
SSC CHSL Tier-1 08.08.2023 (Shift-II)
(a) Delights (b) Benefits
(c) Hazards (d) Humiliations
Ans. (c)
The word 'Peril' means serious and immediate danger. Thus, the correct synonym of 'peril' is 'hazards'.

184. Obligatory
SSC CGL Tier-1 03.12.2022 (Shift-II)
(a) Unnecessary (b) Compulsory
(c) Chosen (d) Optional
Ans. (b)
The meaning of the word 'obligatory' is mandatory or compulsory. Thus, the correct answer is 'compulsory'.

185. Rahul was sharing some of his childhood stories and they were hysterical.
SSC CGL Tier-1 03.12.2022 (Shift-II)
(a) Emotional (b) Dangerous
(c) Funny (d) Scary
Ans. (a)
The word 'hysterical' refers to something very emotional response in informal usage. Thus, the correct answer is 'emotional.'

186. The celebrity was inundated with birthday wishes from his admirers.
SSC CGL Tier-1 03.12.2022 (Shift-III)
(a) Annoyed (b) Preoccupied
(c) Rewarded (d) Overwhelmed
Ans. (d)
Inundated means to send or provide much more of something than someone can easily deal with. So, 'Overwhelmed' from the given options is its most appropriate synonym as it means to exist in such great amounts that someone cannot deal with them.
Annoyed means angry.
Preoccupied means busy.

187. Keen **SSC CGL Tier-1 03.12.2022 (Shift-IV)**
(a) Happy (b) Enthusiastic
(c) Wild (d) Imitate
Ans. (b)
Keen means wanting to do something. 'Enthusiastic' means feeling or showing a lot of interest and excitement about something. So, 'enthusiastic' is the most appropriate synonym of 'keen'.
Imitate means to copy.

188. Impede **SSC CGL Tier-1 05.12.2022 (Shift-I)**
(a) Intend (b) Prompt
(c) Respite (d) Hinder
Ans. (d)
Impede means to make it more difficult for someone to do something or more difficult for something to hopper. So, 'Hinder' from the given options is the most appropriate synonym of 'impede' as it means to stop someone or something from making progress or developing.
Intend means plan.
Prompt means immediate.
Respite means relief.

189. The audience was mesmerised by the speech delivered by the vivacious lady.
SSC CGL Tier-1 05.12.2022 (Shift-I)
SSC CHSL Tier-1 03.07.2024 (Shift-I)
(a) Energetic (b) Fearless
(c) Prosperous (d) Friendly
Ans. (a)
Vivacious means (of a woman) having a lot of energy and a happy attractive manner. So, 'Energetic' from the given options is the most appropriate synonym of 'vivacious'.
Prosperous means rich.

190. Mercy **SSC CGL Tier-1 05.12.2022 (Shift-I)**
(a) Legacy (b) Clarity
(c) Clemency (d) Plurality
Ans. (c)
Mercy means the act of forgiving someone or not treating them severely, especially someone who you have the authority to punish. 'Clemency' means forgiveness and less severe punishment for a crime. So, it is the most appropriate synonym of 'mercy'.
Legacy means heritage or ancestory.
Clarity means clear and easy to understand.
Plurality means many in number.

191. Tyranny **SSC CGL Tier-1 05.12.2022 (Shift-III)**
(a) Autocracy (b) Compassion
(c) Social (d) Discordance
Ans. (a)
The word 'tyranny' means a cruel, harsh and and unfair government in which a person or a small group of people have power over everyone else. So, 'Autocracy' is the most appropriate synonym.
Compassion means kindness.
Discordance means lack of harmony.

192. The president's concern for the homeless people was superficial and ended as soon as the media left the event. **SSC CGL Tier-1 05.12.2022 (Shift-III)**
(a) Shallow (b) Derogatory
(c) Regardless (d) Insubstantia
Ans. (a)
The underlined word **superficial** means appearing to be real or important when this is not true or correct. Hence, 'Shallow' from the given options is most similar in meaning to it.
Derogatory means insulting.
Insubstantial means useless.

193. No plausible explanation could be found for her disappearance.
SSC CGL Tier-1 05.12.2022 (Shift-IV)
(a) Just (b) Legal
(c) Credible (d) Useless
Ans. (c)
The word 'plausible' means seeming reasonable or probable. Thus, the correct answer is 'credible', which refers to something that can be believed.

194. Wrathful **SSC CGL Tier-1 05.12.2022 (Shift-IV)**
(a) Pleased (b) Amiable
(c) Furious (d) Cordial
Ans. (c)
The word **wrathful** means full of or characterised by extreme anger. Thus, the correct synonym is 'furious', which means extremely angry.
Amiable and **cordial** means friendly.

195. The promises made by the old minister were fulfilled.
SSC CGL Tier-1 06.12.2022 (Shift-I)
(a) Contemporary (b) Aged
(c) Recent (d) Vernal
Ans. (b)
The word 'old' means having lived for a long time. Thus, its correct synonym is 'Aged', which means very old.

Contemporary means belonging to the same time.

Vernal means occurring in spring.

196. Select the most appropriate synonym of the word *'Consensus'* from the following sentence.
The landowner and the tenant mutually came to an agreement for decisive acceptance of its clause.
SSC CGL Tier-1 06.12.2022 (Shift-I)
(a) Decisive (b) Acceptance
(c) Mutually (d) Agreement

Ans. (d)
The word 'Consensus' means a general agreement. Thus, its appropriate synonym from the given sentence is 'Agreement'.

197. The essayist's sole intention was to baffle his readers.
SSC CGL Tier-1 06.12.2022 (Shift-II)
SSC CHSL Tier-1 08.08.2023 (Shift-II)
SSC CPO 28.06.2024 (Shift-I)
(a) Puzzle (b) Influence
(c) Scold (d) Annoy

Ans. (a)
The word 'baffle' means to cause someone to be unable to understand or explain something. Thus, the correct synonym is 'puzzle', which means to cause someone to feel confused because they cannot understand something.

198. The students have decided to conspire to steal the test papers.
SSC CGL Tier-1 06.12.2022 (Shift-III)
(a) Enact (b) Moderate
(c) Plot (d) Assist

Ans. (c)
The meaning of the word **conspire** is to secretly plan with someone to do something bad or legal. Thus, its most appropriate meaning is 'plot', which means to make a secret plan with other people to do something bad.
Enact means to act.
Assist means to help.

199. Belief **SSC CGL Tier-1 06.12.2022 (Shift-IV)**
(a) Faith (b) Promise
(c) System (d) Religion

Ans. (a)
'Belief' means trust, faith or confidence in someone or something. Hence, 'Faith' from the given options is the most appropriate synonym of 'belief'.

200. Inherent **SSC CGL Tier-1 06.12.2022 (Shift-IV)**
(a) Increase (b) Superficial
(c) Inborn (d) Conclusion

Ans. (c)
The word **inherent** means existing as a natural or basic part of something. So, 'inborn' from the given options is its most appropriate synonym as it means natural or existing from birth.

201. The next move of the opponent was anticipated by the team.
SSC CGL Tier-1 07.12.2022 (Shift-I)
(a) Forgotten (b) Predicted
(c) Suspected (d) Dreaded

Ans. (b)
Anticipated means to expect that something will happen and be ready for it. The word 'Predicted' means to say or estimate that something will happen in the future.
Suspected means doubtful.
Dreaded means feared.

202. The way Sheetal imparts knowledge to her students is really praiseworthy.
SSC CGL Tier-1 07.12.2022 (Shift-I)
(a) discloses (b) transmits
(c) exposes (d) admits

Ans. (b)
'Transmits' is the most appropriate synonym of 'Imparts'. 'Impart' means to give information, knowledge, wisdom, etc to someone. The word 'Transmit' means to send or convey from one person or place to another.

203. The lights .... (lighting up) the artwork on the walls of the museum were looking beautiful.
SSC CGL Tier-1 17.12.2022 (Shift-I)
(a) enlightening (b) illuminating
(c) trafficking (d) mesmerising

Ans. (b)
Illuminating means to shine light on something and to make it more brighter and visible. So, it is the most appropriate word to fill the blank in the sentence.
Enlightening means providing information.
Trafficking refers to illegal transportation of goods and people.
Mesmerising is attractive.

204. He is in debt due to his judicious tastes and habits. **SSC CGL Tier-1 17.12.2022 (Shift-II)**
(a) affluent (b) frugal
(c) extravagant (d) moderate

Ans. (c)
Extravagant is most appropriate to substitute 'judicious' in the given sentence as it means spending too much of money, or using too much of something.
Affluent means rich.
Moderate means at medium level.

205. He gave a concise explanation of the company's retirement plan.
SSC CGL Tier-1 07.12.2022 (Shift-III)
(a) Clear (b) Verbose
(c) Terse (d) Sharp

Ans. (c)
Concise means expressed using only a few words, but in a way that is easy to understand.
So, 'terse' from the given options is most similar in meaning to 'concise' as it means (of a reply, message, etc.) using very few words.

206. Never teach your children to flout the rules and regulations of their, educational institution.
SSC CGL Tier-1 07.12.2022 (Shift-IV)
(a) Monitor (b) Revere
(c) Divulge (d) Mock

Ans. (d)
The underlined word **Flout** means to intentionally disobey a rule or law or to intentionally avoid behaviour that is usual. So, 'Mock' from the given options is the most appropriate synonym of 'Flout' as it means to defy or challenge.
Monitor means to overlook.
Revere means to respect.
Divulge means to get into.

207. Select the most appropriate synonym of the word 'Obscene' from the following sentence.
Vijay was suspended from duty because he gave dirty and prejudiced remarks to his female colleagues in the office. **SSC CGL Tier-1 07.12.2022 (Shift-IV)**
(a) Dirty (b) Suspended
(c) Prejudice (d) Colleagues

Ans. (a)
Dirty from the given sentence is the most appropriate synonym of 'obscene'.
'Obscene' means offensive, rude or disgusting according to accepted moral standards.
Suspended means removed from service temporarily.
Prejudiced means to dislike someone and prefer other.

208. My father took a moment to ponder before signing the deed of our ancestral home.
SSC CGL Tier-1 08.12.2022 (Shift-II)
(a) Hesitate (b) Contemplate
(c) Sigh (d) Brief

Ans. (b)
Ponder means to think carefully about something, especially for a noticeable length of time.
'Contemplate' from the given options is its most appropriate synonym as it means to spend time considering a possible future action, or to consider one particular thing for a long time in a serious and quiet way.

209. The wrestler retaliated the blow that he received.
SSC CGL Tier-1 08.12.2022 (Shift-III)
(a) Respected
(b) Welcomed
(c) Reciprocated
(d) Forgave

Ans. (c)

'Retaliated' means to return like for like, especially to get revenge. So, 'Reciprocated' from the given sentence is of the most appropriate synonym of 'Retaliated'.

210. The professor refused to comment on the erroneous description of the historical events in the journal.
SSC CGL Tier-1 08.12.2022 (Shift-III)
(a) Suitable (b) Lucid
(c) Inaccurate (d) Sensitive

Ans. (c)

The word **erroneous** means not correct; based on wrong information. So, 'inaccurate' from the given options is the most appropriate synonym of 'erroneous'. Lucid means clear and detailted.

Lucid means clear and detailed.

Inaccurate means not exact.

211. Iyadurai Solomon was a great teacher because he instilled in all the children a sense of their own worth.
SSC CGL Tier-1 08.12.2022 (Shift-III)
(a) stopped (b) took out
(c) inculcate (d) neglected

Ans. (c)

'Instilled' means to put a feeling, idea or principle gradually into someone's mind so that it has a strong influence on the way that person thinks or behaves. So, 'Inculcate' from the given options is the most appropriate synonym of 'instilled'.

The word 'instill' means to cause a quality to become part of someone's nature.

212. Empty **SSC CGL Tier-1 8.12.2022 (Shift-IV)**
(a) Priceless (b) Vacant
(c) packed (d) Filled

Ans. (b)

'Empty' means not containing any things or people.

So, 'Vacant' from the given options is the most appropriate synonym of 'Empty' as it means not filled or occupied; available to be used.

213. Wavering
SSC CGL Tier-1 08.12.2022 (Shift-IV)
(a) Sickly (b) Drenching
(c) Fluctuating (d) Unconvincing

Ans. (c)

Wavering means losing strength, determination or purpose, especially temporarily. So, 'fluctuating' from the given options is the most appropriate synonym of 'wavering'.

Drenching means something that is wet.

Unconvincing means failing to impress.

214. My uncle is a colonel who gets extremely angry over petty issues every now and then.
SSC CGL Tier-1 08.12.2022 (Shift-IV)
(a) furious (b) fierce
(c) heated (d) violent

Ans. (a)

'Furious' means extremely angry. So, 'furious' can substitute the underlined segment in the given sentence.

215. I could not sleep because I was too eager, so I got up early and dressed.
SSC CGL Tier-1 09.12.2022 (Shift-I)
(a) Apathetic (b) Tensed
(c) Satisfied (d) Exhilarated

Ans. (d)

Exhilarated means extremely happy, excited and full of energy. So, it is the most appropriate synonym of 'eager'.

Apathetic means indifferent.

216. Truth can never be concealed from anyone. **SSC CGL Tier-1 09.12.2022 (Shift-I)**
(a) Separated (b) Borrowed
(c) Disguised (d) Snatched

Ans. (c)

Concealed means to prevent something from being seen or known about. 'Disguised' is the most appropriate synonym of 'Concealed' as it means to hide an opinion, a feeling, etc.

217. Try to be frugal with your hard-earned money.
SSC CGL Tier-1 09.12.2022 (Shift-II)
(a) Imprudent (b) Economical
(c) Negligent (d) Honest

Ans. (b)

The word **frugal** means careful when using money or food. So, 'economical' from the given options is the most appropriate synonym of 'frugal'.

Imprudent means unwise.

Negligent means careless.

218. No one was prepared for the environmental calamity that hit the town in the middle of the night.
SSC CGL Tier-1 09.12.2022 (Shift-II)
SSC GD 07.02.2023 (Shift-I)
(a) Damage (b) Catastrophe
(c) Degradation (d) Stress

Ans. (b)

Calamity means a serious accident or bad event causing damage, destruction, disaster or suffering.

'Catastrophe' is its most appropriate synonym as it means a sudden event that causes very great trouble or destruction.

219. Demolish **SSC CGL Tier-1 09.12.2022 (Shift-II)**
(a) Create (b) Fabricate
(c) Ruin (d) Shape

Ans. (c)

Demolish means to completely destroy buildings or other structures. 'Ruin' from the given options is the most appropriate synonym of 'Demolish' as it means to spoil or destroy something completely.
Fabricate means to create.

220. The foreign company is chary of investing in Africa.
SSC CGL Tier-1 09.12.2022 (Shift-III)
(a) Keen (b) Fervent
(c) Confident (d) Cautious

Ans. (d)

The underlined word **chary** means unwilling to do something because you are afraid that something bad will happen. So, 'cautious' from the given options is the most appropriate synonym of 'chary'.

Fervent means to show strong feelings.

221. Select the most appropriate synonym of the word 'Encountered' from the following sentence.
Many people have been experiencing the starting of heat wave and some of them have avoided going outside their homes.
SSC CGL Tier-1 09.12.2022 (Shift-III)
(a) Outside
(b) Starting
(c) Avoided
(d) Experiencing

Ans. (d)

Experiencing from the given sentence is the most appropriate synonym of 'Encountered'.
Encountered means to experience, especially something unpleasant.

222. Anger **SSC CGL Tier-1 09.12.2022 (Shift-III)**
(a) Pleasure (b) Fury
(c) Comfort (d) Agony

Ans. (b)

Fury means a feeling of very strong anger that usually does not last very long.
Hence, it is the most appropriate synonym of 'anger'.

223. The director is at the <u>apex</u> of the managing committee.
SSC CGL Tier-1 9.12.2022 (Shift-IV)
(a) Core (b) Bottom
(c) Corner (d) Pinnacle
Ans. (d)
The meaning of the word **apex** is top or highest part of something. Thus, its correct synonym is 'pinnacle', which means the most successful, powerful, exciting, etc., part of something.
Core means basic and fundamental.

224. The fraudsters <u>hoodwinked</u> us and took away all our valuables.
SSC CGL Tier-1 09.12.2022 (Shift-IV)
(a) Coerced (b) Threatened
(c) Misguided (d) Deceived
Ans. (d)
The word **hoodwinked** means to deceive or trick someone. Thus, the correct synonym is 'deceived', which means to cause someone to believe something that is not true, especially for personal benefit.
Coerced means forced.
Misguided means going on the wrong path.

225. Permeate **SSC CGL Tier-1 12.12.2022 (Shift-I)**
(a) Remain (b) Diffuse
(c) Exude (d) Continue
Ans. (b)
Permeate means to spread through something and be present in every part of it. Among the given options, 'diffuse' is its correct synonym as it also means spread over a wide area.
Exude means to given out or come out of something.

226. Answer **SSC CGL Tier-1 12.12.2022 (Shift-I)**
(a) Recall (b) Remember
(c) Reply (d) Query
Ans. (c)
Answer means something you say when you reply to a question that someone has asked you. Hence, 'reply' is the most appropriate synonym of 'answer'.
Query means a question.

227. The good weather has been a <u>boon</u> for many businesses located near the beach. **SSC CGL Tier-1 12.12.2022 (Shift-II)**
(a) Luck (b) Signal
(c) Fortune (d) Beneficial
Ans. (d)
The word **boon** refers to something that is helpful and beneficial.
Thus, its most appropriate meaning is 'beneficial'.
Signal means sign or indignation.

228. Although Edward had noble blood, his <u>ignoble</u> qualities made him incapable of taking over the kingdom. **SSC CGL Tier-1 12.12.2022 (Shift-II)**
(a) Salient (b) Strange
(c) Ostentatious (d) Unworthy
Ans. (d)
The word **ignoble** means not honourable in character or purpose. Thus, its correct synonym is 'unworthy', which refers to not having adequate merit or character.
Salient means important.
Ostentatious means attracting envy.

229. Irrevocable
SSC CGL Tier-1 12.12.2022 (Shift-III)
(a) Unmediated (b) Congruent
(c) Irreversible (d) Irresponsive
Ans. (c)
The word **irrevocable** means something that is final and not able to changed, reversed or recovered. Thus, its correct synonym is 'irreversible', which refers to something that can't be undone, reversed or altered.
Unmeditated means direct.
Congruent means similar.
Irresponsive means not giving a reaction.

230. Your words seemed more like a demand rather than a .... (request).**SSC CGL Tier-1 12.12.2022 (Shift-IV)**
(a) plea (b) compromise
(c) contract (d) order
Ans. (a)
Plea is the most appropriate word to fill the blank in the given sentence. 'Plea' is a synonym of 'request' and means a request that is urgent or full of emotion.
Compromise means an argument with them in which you both get part of what was wanted.

231. The young fellow was innocent and without <u>guile</u>.
SSC CGL Tier-1 12.12.2022 (Shift-IV)
SSC CHSL Tier-1 24.05.2022 (Shift-II)
(a) Morality (b) Pride
(c) Greed (d) Deceit
Ans. (d)
The underlined word **Guile** means the use of clever but dishonest means to deceive someone.
So, 'Deceit' form the given options is the most appropriate synonym of 'Guile' as its means dishonest behaviour that is intended to make someone believe something that is not true.
Morality means values.

232. Marcella seemed <u>morose</u> and downcast when she refused to have dinner. **SSC CGL Tier-1 13.12.2022 (Shift-I)**
(a) Excited (b) Jocund
(c) Liberal (d) Gloomy
Ans. (d)
The underlined word **morose** means having sullen and gloomy disposition. Thus, 'gloomy' is the correct synonym.
Jocund means cheerful.
Liberal means open to accept new ideas.

233. The efforts of the doctors came to a <u>futile</u> end with the death of the patient. **SSC CGL Tier-1 13.12.2022 (Shift-I)**
(a) Terrifying (b) Starting
(c) Fruitless (d) Enriching
Ans. (c)
The underlined word **Futile** means incapable of producing any useful result. So, 'fruitless' would be its correct synonym. 'Fruitless' also means failing to achieve the desired results.
Terrifying means scaring.
Enriching mens to improve quality of something.

234. Roads in villages during rainy season become <u>muddy</u>.
SSC CGL Tier-1 13.12.2022 (Shift-I)
(a) fuzzy (b) filthy
(c) blurred (d) unsoiled
Ans. (b)
Muddy means covered with mud or containing mud. So, among the given words, 'filthy' is its correct synonym as it means very dirty.
Fuzzy means confusing.
Blurred means note clear.
Unsoiled means not dirty.

235. The poet managed to paint a <u>vivid</u> picture of the landscape by the river through words.
SSC CGL Tier-1 13.12.2022 (Shift-I)
(a) Evocative (b) Metaphoric
(c) Contemporary (d) Blurred
Ans. (a)
Vivid means producing very clear and detailed images in the mind. Thus, 'evocative' is its correct synonym as it also means bringing strong images, memories or feelings to mind.
Metaphoric means comparative.
Contemporary means belonging to the same time.
Blurred means not clear.

236. <u>Distant</u> **SSC CGL Tier-1 13.12.2022 (Shift-II)**
(a) Futuristic (b) Farsighted
(c) Forward (d) Faraway

Ans. (d)

Distant means far away in space or time. So, 'faraway' is its correct synonym.

Futuristic means belonging to the future.

Farsighted means wise.

Forward means direct.

237. You also worked with another eccentric genius.
SSC CGL Tier-1 13.12.2022 (Shift-III)

(a) Middle (b) Ecological
(c) Peculiar (d) Elusive

Ans. (c)

The underlined word **eccentric** means behaving in a way that is unusual and different from most people.

Hence, 'peculiar' from the given options is the most appropriate synonym of 'Eccentric' as it means behaving in a strange and slightly crazy way.

Ecological means relating to ecology.

Elusive refers to something that cannot be achieved.

238. He declined the offer to join the board of directors.
SSC CGL Tier-1 13.12.2022 (Shift-III)

(a) Delayed (b) Rejected
(c) Modified (d) Deferred

Ans. (b)

Declined means to refuse. Hence, 'rejected' from the given options is similar in meaning to 'declined' as it means to refuse to accept use or believe something or someone.

Modified means changed to improve.

Deferred means Delayed.

239. Chide SSC CGL Tier-1 13.12.2022 (Shift-IV)

(a) Scold (b) Rescue
(c) Follow (d) Prevent

Ans. (a)

Chide means to scold or rebuke. So, 'scold' is the most appropriate synonym of the given word.

240. Isn't knowledge supposed to make life sweeter and happier?
SSC CGL Tier-1 13.12.2022 (Shift-IV)

(a) Superiority (b) Profession
(c) Wisdom (d) Curriculum

Ans. (c)

Knowledge means facts, information and skills acquired through experience or education. So, 'wisdom' is its most appropriate synonym.

Wisdom means the body of knowledge and experience that develops within a specified society or period.

241. Abandon SSC CGL Tier-2 08.08.2022
SSC CPO 03.10.2023 (Shift-I)
SSC Steno 18.11.2022 (Shift-I)

(a) Leave (b) Start (c) Adopt (d) Allow

Ans. (a)

Abandon means to leave something or desert someone. Hence, its synonym is 'leave'.

242. Incumbent SSC CGL Tier-2 08.08.2022

(a) Occupant (b) Adventurer
(c) Contestant (d) Prophet

Ans. (a)

Incumbent means the current holder of an office or position. Hence, its synonym is 'occupant'.

Adventurer means a person who enjoys or seeks adventure.

Prophet means a person regarded as an inspired teacher or proclaimer.

243. Fictitious SSC CGL Tier-2 08.08.2022

(a) Factual (b) Imaginary
(c) Confirmed (d) Genuine

Ans. (b)

Fictitious means not real or true; imaginary or fabricated. Hence, its synonym is 'imaginary'.

Factual means based on or concerned with fact.

Confirmed means firmly established in a particular habit or way of life.

SSC CGL 2021 (Tier 1 & 2)

244. Regime SSC CGL Tier-1 13.08.2021 (Shift-I)

(a) Country (b) Space
(c) Territory (d) Rule

Ans. (d)

The word 'regime' means a system or ordered way of doing things. Hence, its correct synonym is 'rule'.

245. Generic SSC CGL Tier-1 13.08.2021 (Shift-I)

(a) Definite (b) Specific
(c) Precise (d) Universal

Ans. (d)

The word 'generic' means relating to or shared by a whole group of similar things; not specific to any particular thing.

Hence, its synonym is 'universal' which means applicable to all.

Precise, specific and **definite** indicate difference between things and people.

246. Yield SSC CGL Tier-1 13.08.2021 (Shift-III)
SSC Steno 18.11.2022 (Shift-I)

(a) Plantation (b) Garden
(c) Orchard (d) Harvest

Ans. (d)

Yield means the amount of a crop produced in a given area. Hence, its synonym is 'harvest'.

Plantation means a large agricultural property.

Garden means a piece of ground used for growing flowers, fruits, or vegetables.

Orchard means a piece of land planted with fruit trees.

247. Iota SSC CGL Tier-1 13.08.2021 (Shift-III)

(a) Lot (b) Bag (c) Bit (d) Box

Ans. (c)

Iota means an extremely small amount. Hence, its synonym is 'bit'.

Lot means a large number or amount.

Bag means a container made of flexible material.

Box means a container with a flat base and sides, typically square or rectangular.

248. Transmit SSC CGL Tier-1 16.08.2021 (Shift-I)

(a) Catch (b) Convey
(c) Receive (d) Accept

Ans. (b)

The word 'transmit' means to send or pass something from one person, place or thing to another.

Hence, its synonym is 'convey' which means to pass information.

249. Numerous SSC CGL Tier-1 16.08.2021 (Shift-I)

(a) Few (b) Several
(c) Numbered (d) Totalled

Ans. (b)

Numerous means many or several. Hence, its synonym is 'several'.

Few means a small number.

Numbered means included in a group.

Totalled means the complete number.

250. Adjust SSC CGL Tier-1 16.08.2021 (Shift-III)

(a) Adapt (b) Change
(c) Move (d) Shift

Ans. (a)

Adjust means to alter or move something slightly in order to achieve the desired fit, appearance or result. Hence, its synonym is 'adapt'.

251. Slack SSC CGL Tier-1 17.08.2021 (Shift-I)

(a) Lively (b) Careless
(c) Keen (d) Active

Ans. (b)

Slack means not taut or held tightly in position; loose. Hence, its synonym is 'careless'.

252. Munch SSC CGL Tier-1 17.08.2021 (Shift-I)

(a) Flew (b) Chew
(c) Drew (d) Burp

Ans. (b)

Munch means to chew food audibly or with enthusiasm. Hence, its synonym is 'chew'.

Drew means past tense of draw.

Burp means to expel gas noisily from the stomach through the mouth.

253. Termination SSC CGL Tier-1 17.08.2021 (Shift-I)

(a) Conduction (b) Conclusion
(c) Consolation (d) Conviction

Ans. (b)

Termination means the action of bringing something to an end. Hence, its synonym is 'conclusion'.

Conduction means the process by which heat or electricity is directly transmitted.

Consolation means comfort received by a person after a loss or disappointment.

Conviction means a formal declaration that someone is guilty of a criminal offense.

254. Grumble SSC CGL Tier-1 17.08.2021 (Shift-III)

(a) Call (b) Ring (c) Grin (d) Groan

Ans. (d)

Grumble means to complain about something in a bad-tempered way. Hence, its synonym is 'groan'.

Grin means to smile broadly.

255. Wander SSC CGL Tier-1 17.08.2021 (Shift-III)

(a) Run (b) Roam
(c) Think (d) Sing

Ans. (b)

Wander means to move slowly away from a fixed point or place. Hence, its synonym is 'Roam'.

256. Testify SSC CGL Tier-1 18.08.2021 (Shift-I)

(a) Oppose (b) Disprove
(c) Affirm (d) Invalidate

Ans. (c)

Testify means serve as evidence or proof that something exists or is the case. So, 'affirm' would be its correct synonym. Affirm means state emphatically or publicly.

257. Abolish SSC CGL Tier-1 18.08.2021 (Shift-I)

(a) Eliminate (b) Establish
(c) Introduce (d) Continue

Ans. (a)

Abolish means formally put an end to something. So, among the given, 'eliminate' would be its correct synonym.

Eliminate means completely remove or get rid of something.

258. Calm SSC CGL Tier-1 18.08.2021 (Shift-III)

(a) Cranky (b) Relaxed
(c) Joyful (d) Clean

Ans. (b)

The synonym of 'calm' is 'relaxed', as both means free from tension.

259. Poignant SSC CGL Tier-1 18.08.2021 (Shift-III)

(a) Quiet (b) Beautiful
(c) Touching (d) Happy

Ans. (c)

'Poignant' means evoking a keen sense of sadness or regret. Among the given options, 'touching' would be its correct synonym as it means arousing feeling of sympathy or gratitude.

260. Tag SSC CGL Tier-1 20.08.2021 (Shift-I)

(a) Label (b) Syphon
(c) Drain (d) Pump

Ans. (a)

The synonym of 'tag' is 'label'.

261. Detrimental SSC CGL Tier-1 20.08.2021 (Shift-I)

(a) Friendly (b) Smart
(c) Intellectual (d) Harmful

Ans. (d)

The synonym of 'detrimental' is 'harmful'. 'Detrimental' means tending to cause harm.

Intellectual means relating to the intellect.

262. Commence SSC CGL Tier-1 20.08.2021 (Shift-II)

(a) Start (b) Shoot
(c) Stand (d) Stop

Ans. (a)

Commence means to begin or start. Hence, its synonym is 'start'.

263. Principle SSC CGL Tier-1 20.08.2021 (Shift-II)

(a) Concrete (b) Headmaster
(c) Leader (d) Axiom

Ans. (d)

Principle means a fundamental truth or proposition that serves as the foundation for a system of belief or behaviour. Hence, its synonym is 'axiom'.

Concrete means existing in a material or physical form.

264. Banner SSC CGL Tier-1 23.08.2021 (Shift-I)

(a) March (b) Rally
(c) Poster (d) Protest

Ans. (c)

Banner means a long strip of cloth bearing a slogan or design. Hence, its synonym is 'poster'.

March means to walk in a military manner.

Rally means a mass meeting of people.

Protest means a statement or action expressing disapproval.

265. Absolve SSC CGL Tier-1 23.08.2021 (Shift-I)

(a) Accuse (b) Condemn
(c) Attack (d) Pardon

Ans. (d)

Absolve means to declare someone free from blame, guilt or responsibility. Hence, its synonym is 'pardon'.

Accuse means to charge someone with an offense.

266. Ponder SSC CGL Tier-1 23.08.2021 (Shift-II)

(a) Terminate (b) Celebrate
(c) Agitate (d) Meditate

Ans. (d)

Ponder means to think about something carefully, especially before making a decision. Hence, its synonym is 'meditate'.

Terminate means to bring to an end.

Agitate means to make someone troubled or nervous.

267. Bang SSC CGL Tier-1 23.08.2021 (Shift-II)

(a) Ride (b) Beat
(c) Rang (d) Sang

Ans. (b)

Bang means a sudden loud noise. Hence, its synonym is 'beat'.

268. Leverage SSC CGL Tier-1 24.08.2021 (Shift-I)

(a) Conclusion (b) Weakness
(c) Influence (d) Suggestion

Ans. (c)

Leverage means the exertion of force by means of a lever. Hence, its synonym is 'influence'.

Conclusion means the end or finish of an event or process. Weakness means the state of lacking strength.

Suggestion means an idea or plan put forward for consideration.

269. Integrate SSC CGL Tier-1 24.08.2021 (Shift-I)

(a) Distribute (b)Assimilate
(c) Disburse (d) Separate

Ans. (b)

Integrate means to combine one thing with another to make a whole. Hence, its synonym is 'assimilate'.

Distribute means to give shares of something.

Disburse means to pay out money.

Separate means to cause to move or be apart.

270. Abstain SSC CGL Tier-1 24.08.2021 (Shift-II)

(a) Refrain (b) Reduce
(c) Propose (d) Accept

Ans. (a)

Abstain means to restrain oneself from doing or enjoying something. Hence, its synonym is 'refrain'.

Reduce means to make smaller or less in amount.

Propose means to put forward an idea.

Accept means to consent to receive.

271. Cadence SSC CGL Tier-1 24.08.2021 (Shift-II)
(a) Pleasure (b) Freshness
(c) Habit (d) Rhythm

Ans. (d)

Cadence means a modulation or inflection of the voice. Hence, its synonym is 'rhythm'.

272. Drag SSC CGL Tier-1 24.08.2021 (Shift-III)
(a) Push (b) Pull (c) Tell (d) Call

Ans. (b)

Drag means to pull something along forcefully. Hence, its synonym is 'pull'.

273. Humdrum
SSC CGL Tier-1 24.08.2021 (Shift-III)
(a) Boring (b) Noisy
(c) Exciting (d) Lively

Ans. (a)

Humdrum means lacking excitement or variety; boring. Hence, its synonym is 'boring'.

SSC CPO 2024

274. He behaved ruthlessly with his junior, to say the least.
SSC CPO 27.06.2024 (Shift-I)
(a) Unexpectedly (b) Inhumanly
(c) Weirdly (d) Politely

Ans. (b)

The underlined word **ruthlessly** means 'rudely and harshly'. Hence, its synonym is 'inhumanly' which means lacking warmth and love.

Unexpectedly means suddenly.
Weirdly means strangely.
Politely means kindly.

275. A good critic should also be a person of great candour.
SSC CPO 27.06.2024 (Shift-I)
(a) will (b) resolution
(c) honesty (d) power

Ans. (c)

The underlined word **candour** means the quality of being open and honest.

Will means desire or determination.

Resolution means promise.

276. Reckon SSC CPO 27.06.2024 (Shift-I)
SSC GD 27.01.2023 (Shift-IV)
(a) Merit (b) Assess
(c) Count (d) Imagine

Ans. (d)

The word **reckon** means 'imagine consider or think about'.

Assess means to test.

277. The cacophony in the theatre was too much for us. SSC CPO 27.06.2024 (Shift-II)
(a) silence (b) smell
(c) noise (d) laughter

Ans. (c)

The word 'Cacophony' means a harsh, discordant mixture of sounds noise.

278. Mr. Satterthwaite was shrewd enough to penetrate her meaning.
SSC CPO 27.06.2024 (Shift-II)
(a) Aged (b) Funny
(c) Innocent (d) Smart

Ans. (d)

The word 'Shrewd' means having or showing sharp powers of judgement; smart.

279. Queen Gulnaar of Arabia mourned her...... beauty. (waning)
SSC CPO 27.06.2024 (Shift-II)
(a) false (b) frightening
(c) fading (d) futile

Ans. (c)

Waning means to decrease in size, extent or degree; to diminish gradually in power, intensity or importance. Hence, its synonym is 'Fading' which means to gradually becoming less bright, intense or clear; synonymous with 'waning.'

Frightening means causing fear or apprehension.

280. Ramya is an ardent follower of secularism. SSC CPO 27.06.2024 (Shift-II)
SSC MTS 18.07.2022 (Shift-I)
(a) committed (b) forced
(c) temporary (d) unhappy

Ans. (a)

The word 'Ardent' means passionate, enthusiastic or dedicated. Hence, its synonym is 'committed' which means devoted or dedicated to a cause, belief or activity.

281. Immune SSC CPO 27.06.2024 (Shift-II)
(a) Resistant (b) Asleep
(c) Variable (d) Safe

Ans. (a)

The word **Immune** refers to being resistant to or protected against a disease or condition.

Variable means likely to change or vary.

282. The environmental organisation issued a statement to condemn the deforestation happening in the protected area.
SSC CPO 27.06.2024 (Shift-II, III)
(a) Censure (b) Persuade
(c) Foster (d) Compel

Ans. (a)

The underlined word **condemn** means to criticise. Hence, its synonym is 'censure' which means to fault or reprimand.

Foster means to encourage.
Compel means to force.

283. Mourn SSC CPO 27.06.2024 (Shift-III)
(a) Dread (b) Amuse
(c) Grieve (d) Approve

Ans. (c)

The word **mourn** means 'to grieve or be sorrowful'.

Dread means to fear.

Amuse means to be laughable.

Approve mean to agree.

284. Pacify SSC CPO 28.06.2024 (Shift-I)
SSC CHSL Tier-I 11.08.2023 (Shift-I)
(a) Rebuke (b) Blame
(c) Strengthen (d) Soothe

Ans. (d)

The word **Pacify** means to calm or soothe someone who is angry, upset or agitated.

Rebuke means to criticise sharply.

Blame means to hold responsible for.

Strengthen means to make stronger or more powerful.

285. Dainty SSC CPO 28.06.2024 (Shift-I)
(a) Vulgar (b) Fine
(c) Elegant (d) Sable

Ans. (c)

The word **Dainty** is used for something delicate, elegant, fine and often small, especially in relation to food or objects.

Vulgar means lacking sophistication or good taste.

Fine means high quality or purity, but not necessarily delicate or dainty.

Sable refers to a type of animal or a dark colour.

286. Filthy SSC CPO 28.06.2024 (Shift-I)
(a) Tidy (b) Visual
(c) Shiny (d) Dirty

Ans. (d)

The word **Filthy** means covered or smeared with dirt; disgustingly dirty.

287. The regulation bans any direct or indirect promotion through radio or television of supernatural practices.
SSC CPO 28.06.2024 (Shift-I)
(a) Questionable (b) Obtuse
(c) Occult (d) Evident

Ans. (c)

The word **Occult** refers to supernatural practices, magic or mystical beliefs that are beyond ordinary understanding, often involving hidden or secret knowledge.

Questionable refers to something that raises doubts or uncertainty.

Obtuse means lacking sharpness or clarity; also used to describe someone who is insensitive or dull.

Evident means clearly visible or obvious.

288. Voracious SSC CPO 28.06.2024 (Shift-I) SSC MTS 22.07.2022 (Shift-II)

(a) Quenched (b) Appreciate
(c) Compensated (d) Greedy

Ans. (d)

The word **Voracious** describes someone who has a very eager approach to an activity, often in an insatiable or greedy manner, especially related to consuming food or knowledge.

Quenched means satisfied or relieved, often used in the context of thirst or desire.

Appreciate means to value or recognise the worth of something.

Compensated means to be paid for services rendered or to make up for something lost or lacking.

289. Rajans caused extremely painful headaches. SSC CPO 28.06.2024 (Shift-I)

(a) excruciating
(b) horrible
(c) extreme
(d) devastating

Ans. (a)

The word 'excruciating' means extremely painful.

290. The company plans to expand its business to the international market. SSC CPO 28.06.2024 (Shift-I)

(a) to reduce (b) to contract
(c) to increase (d) to limit

Ans. (c)

'To expand' means to increase.

291. Emotional stimulation provides the necessary ...... for creative imagination. (fecundity) SSC CPO 28.06.2024 (Shift-II)

(a) fertility (b) force
(c) fulcrum (d) freedom

Ans. (a)

The word **Fecundity** refers to the ability to produce offspring or the capacity for prolific production or reproduction.

Hence, its synonym is 'fertility' which means quality or state of being fertile; in the context of creativity, it implies the ability to produce ideas or creative works.

Fulcrum refers to the point on which a lever pivots or something that plays a central role or is crucial to an action or process.

292. Bind SSC CPO 28.06.2024 (Shift-II)

(a) Secure (b) Amuse
(c) Flourish (d) Disengage

Ans. (a)

The word **bind** means to tie or fasten something tightly; to hold or restrain. Its synonym is 'secure'.

Amuse means to entertain or make someone laugh.

Flourish means to thrive or grow well; to wave something in the air in a dramatic or impressive way.

Disengage means to detach or separate from something; to release or free

293. Eagerly SSC CPO 28.06.2024 (Shift-III)

(a) Stringently (b) Dubiously
(c) Keenly (d) Playfully

Ans. (c)

The word **Eagerly** means in a manner showing keen interest or enthusiasm; eagerly implies a strong desire or enthusiasm for something.

Stringently means strictly or rigorously.

Dubiously means with doubt or skepticism.

294. Entail SSC CPO 28.06.2024 (Shift-III)

(a) Assume (b) Necessitate
(c) Eliminate (d) Flaw

Ans. (b)

The word **Entail** means to involve something as a necessary part or consequence.

Assume means to take on or adopt (a role, responsibility, etc.) often without solid proof.

Eliminate means to remove or get rid of something completely.

Flaw refers to a defect or imperfection that detracts from the quality or completeness of something.

295. The hypothesis that the police believed in led to a lot of chaos. SSC CPO 28.06.2024 (Shift-III)

(a) speculation
(b) breakthrough
(c) trepidation
(d) encounter

Ans. (a)

The word **Hypothesis** refers to a supposition or proposed explanation made on the basis of limited evidence as a starting point for further investigation. Hence, its synonym is 'speculation' which refers to Ideas or guesses about something without firm evidence.

Breakthrough means an important discovery or development that solves a problem or opens up new possibilities.

Trepidation means a feeling of fear or agitation about something that may happen.

Encounter means a meeting, especially an unexpected or casual one.

296. Grisly SSC CPO 28.06.2024 (Shift-III)

(a) Pleasant (b) Atrocious
(c) Glorious (d) Dire

Ans. (b)

The word **grisly** means something that is grisly is extremely unpleasant or shocking, often involving death or injury. Hence, its synonym is 'atrocious' which means extremely wicked, brutal or cruel; appalling.

Pleasant means agreeable, enjoyable, or pleasing.

Glorious means having or deserving great fame, praise or honour.

Dire means extremely serious or urgent; causing great fear or suffering.

297. Concordant SSC CPO 28.06.2024 (Shift-III)

(a) Certain (b) Unanimous
(c) Abnormal (d) Harmonious

Ans. (d)

The word **Concordant** refers to something that is in agreement or harmony, especially in music or opinions.

Unanimous means fully in agreement; showing complete unity of opinion.

Abnormal means unusual, deviating from the normal or typical.

298. Fabulous SSC CPO 28.06.2024 (Shift-III)

(a) Remarkable (b) Resourceful
(c) Regrettable (d) Restful

Ans. (a)

The word **Fabulous** means something that is extremely good or impressive; often used to describe something wonderful or amazing. Hence, its synonym is 'remarkable.'

Resourceful means skilled at solving problems and finding ways around obstacles; inventive.

Regrettable means causing feelings of sorrow or disappointment; unfortunate.

Restful means providing relaxation or repose; peaceful and calming.

299. Looking after small children is a real conundrum for working parents. SSC CPO 29.06.2024 (Shift-I)

(a) peace (b) plan
(c) problem (d) pacification

Ans. (c)

The word **conundrum** means a confusing and difficult problem or question.

Pacification means the act of soothing or calming someone or a situation.

300. Habitual SSC CPO 29.06.2024 (Shift-I)
(a) Considerate (b) Continuous
(c) Diverse (d) Pertinent

Ans. (b)

The word **Habitual** means done or doing constantly or as a habit; usual; customary. Hence, its synonym is 'continuous'.

Considerate means a thoughtful of the rights and feelings of others.

Diverse means showing a great deal of variety; different from each other.

Pertinent means relevant or applicable to a particular matter.

301. Insipid SSC CPO 29.06.2024 (Shift-I)
SSC CPO 05.10.2023 (Shift-II)
(a) Dismal (b) Tasteless
(c) Obscure (d) Idle

Ans. (b)

The word **Insipid** means lacking flavour; lacking in qualities that interest, stimulate or challenge; dull; tasteless.

Dismal means depressing; dreary.

Obscure means not clear or plain; ambiguous or vague.

Idle means not active or in use; lazy.

302. Indigent SSC CPO 29.06.2024 (Shift-I)
(a) Bust (b) Low
(c) Impoverished (d) Affluent

Ans. (c)

The word **indigent** means needy; impoverished; lacking the basic necessities of life; poor.

Bust means to break or smash; to reduce to bankruptcy.

Affluent means wealthy; having an abundance of goods or riches.

303. Unhappiness SSC CPO 29.06.2024 (Shift-I)
(a) Woe (b) Wilful
(c) Willing (d) Wicked

Ans. (a)

The synonym of **unhappiness** is 'woe' which means deep distress or misery.

Wilful means deliberate; intentional.

Willing means eager; prepared.

Wicked means evil morally wrong.

304. His intriguing mastery of the English language allowed him to write **eloquently**.
SSC CPO 29.06.2024 (Shift-I)
(a) wellness known skill
(b) least known talent
(c) captivating expertise
(d) master

Ans. (c)

The word 'eloquently' means with 'expertise and knowledge.'

305. I will <u>strive</u> to win the race.
SSC CPO 29.06.2024 (Shift-II)
(a) trouble (b) Support
(c) Assume (d) Attempt

Ans. (d)

The word 'Strive' means to make great efforts or attempt; to struggle or work hard towards achieving something.

306. Efface SSC CPO 29.06.2024 (Shift-II)
SSC CHSL Tier-1 07.08.2023 (Shift-IV)
(a) Hidden (b) Makeup
(c) Daily (d) Destroy

Ans. (d)

The word 'Efface' means to erase or destroy completely; to make oneself inconspicuous.

307. I was <u>astonished</u> to know the truth.
SSC CPO 29.06.2024 (Shift-II)
(a) Stunned (b) Awesome
(c) Blindsided (d) Sickened

Ans. (a)

The word **Astonished** means feeling shocked or surprised. Hence, its synonym is 'stunned.'

Awesome means inspiring awe or admiration.

Blindsided means caught off guard or surprised by something unexpected.

Sickened means made ill or disgusted.

308. Her million-dollar wedding was a ...... display of wealth. (pompous)
SSC CPO 29.06.2024 (Shift-III)
SSC CHSL Tier-1 02.08.2023 (Shift-I)
(a) prestigious (b) outrageous
(c) mock (d) pretentious

Ans. (d)

The word **pompous** means characterised by a display of grandeur or self-importance. Hence, it synonym is 'pretentious' which means attempting to impress others by pretending to have greater importance, talent, or culture than is actually possessed; closely related to the idea of a display of wealth in a showy or ostentatious manner.

Prestigious means having high status or reputation.

Outrageous means shockingly bad or excessive.

Mock means not genuine or real; used to imitate or simulate something.

309. Destitute SSC CPO 29.06.2024 (Shift-III)
SSC CHSL Tier-1 09.08.2023 (Shift-II)
(a) Broken (b) Corrupt
(c) Broke (d) Firm

Ans. (c)

The word **Destitute** means extremely poor or broke; lacking the basic necessities of life.

Firm means strong or steady.

310. Chameleon usually <u>disguises</u> itself to avoid predators.
SSC CPO 29.06.2024 (Shift-III)
(a) changes (b) camouflages
(c) transposes (d) swaps

Ans. (b)

The word **Camouflages** means to disguise or blend into the surroundings for concealment or protection.

Transposes means to change the position or order of something.

Swaps means to exchange one thing for another.

311. Mundane SSC CPO Tier-2 8.01.2024
(a) exciting
(b) abnormal
(c) ordinary
(d) wonderful

Ans. (c)

Mundane means very ordinary and not at all interesting or unusual.

312. Vitiate SSC CPO Tier-2 8.01.2024
(a) annihilate (b) facilitate
(c) propagate (d) validate

Ans. (a)

Annihilate means to completely destroy something.

Vitiate means to damage or destroy something is its synonym.

Facilitate means to make a process or action easier.

Propagate means to spread, multiply, or promote the growth of something, such as an idea, belief, or organism.

Validate means to give official approval or acceptance.

313. Entice SSC CPO Tier-2 08.01.2024
(a) entreat (b) dissuade
(c) beguile (d) repulse

Ans. (c)

Beguile which means charm or enchant (someone), often in a deceptive way.

Entice means to attract or lure someone by offering something appealing or tempting is its synony.

Entreat means ask someone earnestly or anxiously to do something.

Dissuade means to discourage or persuade someone not to take a particular course of action.

SSC CPO 2023

314. Dreadful SSC CPO 03.10.2023 (Shift-I)
(a) Feeble (b) Terrible
(c) Auspicious (d) Propitious

Ans. (b)

The word 'dreadful' refers to something that is horrible and terrible.

315. Despite the **advancement** of technology in many Rural areas, in developing countries still lack access to basic necessities.
SSC CPO 03.10.2023 (Shift-I)
(a) Desist (b) Disguise
(c) Avenue (d) Apathy
Ans. (*)
None of the given options is synonymous to the word in the given sentence.

316. Justifiable SSC CPO 03.10.2023 (Shift-I)
(a) Indefensible (b) Neutral
(c) Maintainable (d) Reasonable
Ans. (d)
The word 'justifiable' means 'that which can be explained with reason or logic.'

317. Site SSC CPO 03.10.2023 (Shift-I)
(a) Lap (b) Location
(c) Globe (d) Pull
Ans. (b)
The word 'site' means 'location'.

318. Haphazard SSC CPO 03.10.2023 (Shift-I)
(a) Random
(b) Sociable
(c) Aggressive
(d) Confident
Ans. (a)
The word 'haphazard' means lacking any obvious principle of organisation. Its antonym is 'random' which means made, done, or happening without method or conscious decision.

319. Effective public transportation networks may greatly alleviate traffic **congestion** and enhance inhabitants quality of life general.
SSC CPO 03.10.2023 (Shift-II)
(a) Gridlock (b) Amplification
(c) Diversion (d) Laxity
Ans. (a)
Gridlock means a situation of severe traffic congestion. Effective public transportation networks may greatly alleviate traffic congestion and enhance inhabitants' quality of life in general. Hence, the correct synonym is 'gridlock'.
Amplification means the process of making something larger or more significant.
Diversion means turning something aside from its course.
Laxity means lack of strictness or care.

320. Select the most appropriate synonym of the word **'viable'** in the given sentence and choose the correct option.
The engineer's design was optimised for efficiency and scalability, with a focus sustainability.
SSC CPO 03.10.2023 (Shift-II)
(a) Scalability
(b) sustainability
(c) Efficiency
(d) Optimised
Ans. (b)
Viable means capable of working successfully; feasible. The sentence implies sustainability. Hence, the correct synonym is 'sustainability'.
Scalability means the capacity to be changed in size or scale.
Efficiency means the state or quality of being efficient.
Optimised means making the best or most effective use of a situation or resource.

321. Captivate SSC CPO 03.10.2023 (Shift-II)
(a) Study (b) Envelope
(c) Allure (d) Arrest
Ans. (c)
Captivate means to attract and hold the interest and attention of; charm. Hence, the correct synonym is 'allure'.
Study means to devote time and attention to gaining knowledge of an academic subject.
Envelope means a flat paper container with a sealable flap.
Arrest means to seize someone by legal authority.

322. Select the most appropriate synonym of the word 'disclosed' in the given sentence and choose the correct option.
The linguist's analysis of the language revealed patterns and structures that were previously unknown. SSC CPO 03.10.2023 (Shift-III)
(a) Linguist (b) Revealed
(c) Patterns (d) Unknown
Ans. (b)
Disclosed means to make known or public. Hence, the correct synonym is 'revealed'.
Linguist means a person skilled in foreign languages.

323. Unequivocal SSC CPO 03.10.2023 (Shift-III)
(a) Unambiguous
(b) Doubted
(c) Complete
(d) Articulate
Ans. (a)
Unequivocal means leaving no doubt; unambiguous. Hence, the correct synonym is 'unambiguous'.
Articulate means having or showing the ability to speak fluently and coherently.

324. O' Henry's short stories are read all over the world till now because they are pithy. SSC CPO 03.10.2023 (Shift-III)
(a) exaggerated yet short
(b) fascinating and lengthy
(c) concise and expressive
(d) elusive and unreal
Ans. (c)
Pithy means concise and expressive. Hence, the correct synonym is 'concise and expressive'.
Exaggerated yet short means overemphasised but brief.
Fascinating and lengthy means interesting and long.
Elusive and unreal means difficult to find or achieve and not real.

325. Vulnerable SSC CPO 03.10.2023 (Shift-III)
SSC Steno 12.11.2022 (Shift-I)
(a) Susceptible
(b) Amiable
(c) Guarded
(d) Delectable
Ans. (a)
Vulnerable means susceptible to physical or emotional attack or harm. Hence, the correct synonym is 'susceptible'.
Guarded means cautious and having possible reservations.

326. We shouldn't blame or envy anyone.
SSC CPO 03.10.2023 (Shift-III)
(a) Jealousy (b) Reap
(c) Love (d) Curse
Ans. (a)
Blame means to assign responsibility for a fault or wrong. Hence, the correct synonym is 'jealousy'.
Reap means to cut or gather.
Curse means an offensive word or phrase used to express anger or annoyance.

327. Saurabh imitates his boss perfectly.
SSC CPO 03.10.2023 (Shift-III)
SSC MTS 26.07.2022 (Shift-II)
(a) Admires (b) Worships
(c) Copies (d) Hates
Ans. (c)
Imitates means to take or follow as a model. Hence, the correct synonym is 'copies'.

328. The new professor is liked by his students for his amiable approach.
SSC CPO 04.10.2023 (Shift-I)
(a) academic (b) strict
(c) friendly (d) simple

Ans. (c)

Amiable means having or displaying a friendly and pleasant manner. Hence, the correct synonym is 'friendly'.

329. Spontaneous SSC CPO 04.10.2023 (Shift-I)
(a) Acquisitive (b) Attractive
(c) Instinctive (d) Exhaustive

Ans. (c)

Spontaneous means performed or occurring as a result of a sudden impulse or inclination. Hence, the correct synonym is 'instinctive'.

Acquisitive means excessively interested in acquiring money or material things.

Exhaustive means including or considering all elements or aspects.

330. The education system must **evolve** to keep pace with the rapid changes in the job market. SSC CPO 04.10.2023 (Shift-I)
(a) Censor (b) Emanate
(c) Demolish (d) Conceal

Ans. (b)

Evolve means to develop gradually. Hence, the correct synonym is 'emanate'.

Censor means to suppress unacceptable parts.

Conceal means to keep from sight; hide.

331. A gust of wind came abruptly and our sand castle toppled.
SSC CPO 04.10.2023 (Shift-I)
(a) blew out (b) tumbled down
(c) turned up (d) ran after

Ans. (b)

Toppled means overbalance or become unsteady and fall down. Hence, the correct synonym is 'tumbled down'.

Blew out means to be extinguished.

Turned up means to make an appearance.

Ran after means to chase or follow someone quickly.

332. Behold SSC CPO 04.10.2023 (Shift-I)
(a) Burden (b) Fortunate
(c) Predict (d) Look

Ans. (d)

Behold means to see or observe someone or something. Hence, the correct synonym is 'look'.

Burden means a load, typically a heavy one.

Fortunate means favored by or involving good luck.

Predict means to say or estimate that a specified thing will happen in the future.

333. Robe SSC CPO 04.10.2023 (Shift-II)
(a) Robbery (b) Mishap
(c) Success (d) Cloak

Ans. (d)

A 'robe' and a 'cloak' are both garments worn over other clothing, typically for warmth or ceremonial purposes.
Mishap is a sudden tragic events.

334. He is a person who holds old fashioned opinions.
SSC CPO 04.10.2023 (Shift-II)
(a) obsolete (b) ancient
(c) antique (d) senior citizen

Ans. (a)

The word 'obsolete' refers to something that is no longer in widespread use or that is considered outdated or old fashioned.

335. He uses one of the finest ingredients in his cooking.
SSC CPO 04.10.2023 (Shift-II)
(a) components (b) mixtures
(c) culinary (d) preparations

Ans. (a)

The most appropriate meaning of the underlined word 'ingredients' is 'components'.

336. Aggravate SSC CPO 04.10.2023 (Shift-II)
(a) annoy (b) mitigate
(c) enhance (d) satisfy

Ans. (a)

The word 'aggravate' means to irritate or annoy.

337. Extravagance SSC CPO 04.10.2023 (Shift-III)
(a) Self-indulgence
(b) Love
(c) Fortune
(d) Simplicity

Ans. (a)

Extravagance means lack of restraint in spending money or using resources. Hence, the correct synonym is 'self-indulgence'.

338. Cruise SSC CPO 04.10.2023 (Shift-III)
(a) Voyage (b) Bounce
(c) Fall (d) Distance

Ans. (a)

Cruise means to sail about in an area without a precise destination, especially for pleasure. Hence, the correct synonym is 'voyage'.

339. Sexual assault is a severe and **pervasive** issue that can have a significant Impact on a victim's life.
SSC CPO 04.10.2023 (Shift-III)
(a) Equatorial (b) Retrospective
(c) Widespread (d) Longitudinal

Ans. (c)

Pervasive means spreading widely throughout an area or a group of people. Hence, the correct synonym is 'widespread'.

Equatorial means of, at, or near the equator.

Retrospective means looking back on or dealing with past events or situations.

Longitudinal means running lengthwise rather than across.

340. Faithful SSC CPO 04.10.2023 (Shift-III)
(a) Cheerful (b) Unfaithful
(c) Daring (d) Loyal

Ans. (d)

Faithful means loyal, constant and steadfast. Hence, the correct synonym is 'loyal'.

341. She was yearning for a trip to the mountains SSC CPO 04.10.2023 (Shift-III)
(a) keenly desiring
(b) saving money for
(c) leaving for
(d) deeply repenting

Ans. (a)

Yearning means having an intense feeling of longing for something. Hence, the correct synonym is 'keenly desiring'.

342. Trousseau SSC CPO 04.10.2023 (Shift-III)
(a) Being true to oneself
(b) Single leg side of a trouser
(c) A large cabinet full of expensive clothes
(d) The clothes, linen and other belongings collected by a bride for her marriage

Ans. (d)

Trousseau means the clothes, linen and other belongings collected by a bride for her marriage.

343. The plane crash was a **harrowing** experience for everyone involved.
SSC CPO 05.10.2023 (Shift-I)
(a) Exterminate (b) Awesome
(c) Sad (d) Excruciating

Ans. (d)

Harrowing means extremely distressing. Hence, the correct synonym is 'excruciating'.

Exterminate means to kill or destroy completely.

344. Reminiscence SSC CPO 05.10.2023 (Shift-I)
(a) Harsh
(b) Oblivion
(c) Remembrance
(d) Benevolence

Ans. (c)

Reminiscence means the enjoyable recollection of past events. Hence, the correct synonym is 'remembrance'.

Harsh means unpleasantly rough or jarring to the senses.

Oblivion means the state of being unaware or unconscious.

Benevolence means the quality of being well-meaning.

345. Rehabilitate SSC CPO 05.10.2023 (Shift-I)
(a) Absolve (b) Develop
(c) Decline (d) Reinstall

Ans. (d)

Rehabilitate means to restore someone to health or normal life through training and therapy. Hence, its synonym is 'reinstall'.

346. The book narrated the athlete's prowess in a lucid manner. SSC CPO 05.10.2023 (Shift-I)
(a) difficult situation
(b) affluent days
(c) exceptional mastery
(d) refined arguments

Ans. (c)

Prowess means skill or expertise in a particular activity or field. Hence, its synonym is 'exceptional mastery'.

347. She has become a familiar figure in the world of politics. SSC CPO 05.10.2023 (Shift-I)
(a) Legend (b) Known
(c) Elevated (d) Fancy

Ans. (b)

Familiar means well-known from long or close association. Hence, its synonym is 'known'.

Legend means a famous person, often of historical or cultural importance.

Elevated means placed higher than the surrounding area.

Fancy means elaborate in structure or decoration.

348. Select the most appropriate synonym of the word 'factual' in the given sentence and choose the correct option.
The scientist's hypothesis was based on empirical evidence and rigorous experimentation. SSC CPO 05.10.2023 (Shift-I)
(a) Evidence (b) Hypothesis
(c) Empirical (d) Rigorous

Ans. (c)

Factual means concerned with what is actually the case. Hence, its synonym is 'empirical'.

Evidence means the available body of facts or information.

Hypothesis means a supposition or proposed explanation.

Rigorous means extremely thorough and careful.

349. Diabolical SSC CPO 05.10.2023 (Shift-II)
(a) Sophisticated
(b) Sycophant
(c) Celestial
(d) Malicious

Ans. (d)

Diabolical means characteristic of the Devil or so evil as to recall the Devil. Hence, its synonym is 'malicious'.

Sophisticated means having a refined knowledge of the world.

Sycophant means a person who acts obsequiously toward someone important.

Celestial means positioned in or relating to the sky, or outer space.

350. Major SSC CPO 05.10.2023 (Shift-II)
(a) Creviced (b) Considerable
(c) Diligent (d) Shallow

Ans. (b)

Major means important, serious or significant. Hence, its synonym is 'considerable'.

Creviced means having deep cracks or fissures.

Shallow means of little depth.

351. Vagrancy SSC CPO 05.10.2023 (Shift-II)
(a) Vagabond (b) Vagueness
(c) Fragrance (d) Exploration

Ans. (a)

Vagrancy means the state of living as a vagrant; homelessness. Hence, its synonym is 'vagabond'.

Vagueness means lack of certainty or distinctness.

Fragrance means a pleasant, sweet smell.

Exploration means the action of traveling in or through an unfamiliar area.

352. The manager noticed a discrepancy between the two audit reports. SSC CPO 05.10.2023 (Shift-II)
(a) deliberate mistake
(b) major difference
(c) selfish interest
(d) great similarity

Ans. (b)

Discrepancy means a lack of compatibility or similarity between two or more facts. Hence, its synonym is 'major difference'.

353. Improved rail transport is essential for business. SSC CPO 05.10.2023 (Shift-III)
(a) Recommended (b) Trivial
(c) Crucial (d) Technical

Ans. (c)

The underlined word 'essential' means absolutely necessary or extremely crucial and important.

Technical means relating to a particular subject.

354. Desolate SSC CPO 05.10.2023 (Shift-III)
(a) Fortunate (b) Sturdy
(c) Depressive (d) Hopeful

Ans. (c)

The word 'desolate' means barren, empty or bleak, often describing a place that is deserted or showing signs of abandonment. 'Depressive,' which conveys a sense of emptiness.

Sturdy means strongly built.

355. The concert was filled with rapt teenage listeners. SSC CPO 05.10.2023 (Shift-III)
(a) really fashionable
(b) boldly dressed
(c) truly energetic
(d) fully attentive

Ans. (d)

The underlined word 'rapt' means fully attentive or completely engrossed in something.

SSC CPO 2022 (Tier 1 & 2)

356. Radiant SSC CPO Tier-1 09.10.2022 (Shift-II)
(a) Dismal (b) Frowning
(c) Glowing (d) Depressing

Ans. (c)

Radiant means shining or glowing brightly. Hence, its synonym is 'glowing'.

Frowning means showing displeasure or disapproval.

Depressing means causing a feeling of severe despondency and dejection.

357. Glee SSC CPO Tier-1 09.11.2022 (Shift-II)
(a) Anxiety (b) Abhorrence
(c) Mirth (d) Distress

Ans. (c)

Glee means great delight or joy. Hence, its synonym is 'mirth'. Anxiety means a feeling of worry or unease.

Abhorrence means a feeling of repulsion; disgusted loathing.

Distress means extreme anxiety, sorrow, or pain.

358. Prodigal SSC CPO Tier-1 09.11.2022 (Shift-II)
(a) Economical (b) Scrimping
(c) Extravagant (d) Conserving

Ans. (c)

Prodigal means spending money or resources freely and recklessly; wastefully extravagant. Hence, its synonym is 'extravagant'.

Economical means giving good value or service in relation to the amount of money, time, or effort spent.

Scrimping means being thrifty or miserly.

Conserving means protecting from harm or destruction.

359. Populous SSC CPO Tier-1 09.11.2022 (Shift-II)

(a) Crowded (b) Inactive
(c) Sleepy (d) Lifeless

Ans. (a)

Populous means having a large population; densely populated. Hence, its synonym is 'crowded'.

360. We also must do something about mental and physical lethargy.
SSC CPO Tier-1 09.11.2022 (Shift-II)

(a) eagerness
(b) enthusiasm
(c) hebetude
(d) vigour

Ans. (c)

Lethargy means a lack of energy and enthusiasm. Hence, its synonym is 'hebetude'.

Eagerness means enthusiasm to do or to have something.

Enthusiasm means intense and eager enjoyment, interest, or approval.

Vigour means physical strength and good health.

361. Peril SSC CPO Tier-1 09.11.2022 (Shift-III)
SSC MTS 12.09.2023 (Shift-II)

(a) Doubt (b) Danger
(c) Benefit (d) Safety

Ans. (b)

Peril means serious and immediate danger. Hence, its synonym is 'danger'.

362. He **imputes** his ability to play great football to an inspirational coach.
SSC CPO Tier-1 10.11.2022 (Shift-I)

(a) Validates (b) Contributes
(c) Attributes (d) Amputates

Ans. (c)

Imputes means attributes or ascribes. Hence, its synonym is 'attributes'.

Validates means to confirm or support.

Contributes means to give something in order to help achieve or provide something.

Amputates means to cut off a part of the body.

363. Progress SSC CPO Tier-1 10.11.2022 (Shift-I)

(a) Development (b) Diminishment
(c) Halt (d) Stagnation

Ans. (a)

Progress means forward or onward movement towards a destination. Hence, its synonym is 'development'.

Diminishment means a reduction in the size, extent, or importance of something.

Halt means to stop.

Stagnation means a period of inactivity or lack of growth.

364. Their vision was very clear: if Indians were to play a meaningful role in the community of nations, they must be second to none in the application of advanced technologies to their real-life problems.
SSC CPO Tier-1 10.11.2022 (Shift-I)

(a) mistreatment (b) implementation
(c) corruption (d) misuse

Ans. (b)

Application in this context means the act of putting something to use. Hence, its synonym is 'implementation'.

365. Ideas are present in the consciousness, which when released and given scope to grow and take shape, can lead to successful events.
SSC CPO Tier-1 10.11.2022 (Shift-I)

(a) ignorance (b) thoughtlessness
(c) awareness (d) negligence

Ans. (c)

Consciousness means the state of being aware of and responsive to one's surroundings. Hence, its synonym is 'awareness'.

Ignorance means lack of knowledge or information.

Negligence means failure to take proper care over something.

366. Addicted SSC CPO Tier-1 10.11.2022 (Shift-I)

(a) Disinclined (b) Unaccustomed
(c) Inclined (d) Averse

Ans. (c)

Addicted means physically and mentally dependent on a particular substance. Hence, its synonym is 'inclined'.

Disinclined means unwilling.

Unaccustomed means not familiar with.

Averse means having a strong dislike of or opposition to something.

367. This discovery of of treasure under the bermuda triangle is probably a hoax. SSC CPO Tier-1 10.11.2022 (Shift-I)

(a) Analogy (b) Bonanza
(c) Delusion (d) Trick

Ans. (d)

Hoax means a humorous or malicious deception. Hence, its synonym is 'trick'.

Analogy means a comparison between two things.

Bonanza means a situation which creates a sudden increase in wealth.

Delusion means a false belief.

368. Penchant SSC CPO Tier-1 10.11.2022 (Shift-II)

(a) Bitterness (b) liking
(c) Sourness (d) Disliking

Ans. (b)

Penchant means a strong or habitual liking for something. Hence, its synonym is 'liking'.

369. Contrary SSC CPO Tier-1 10.11.2022 (Shift-II)

(a) Wobbly
(b) Crooked
(c) Straight
(d) Opposite

Ans. (d)

Contrary means opposite in nature, direction or meaning. Hence, its synonym is 'opposite'.

Wobbly means tending to move unsteadily from side to side.

370. Cogent SSC CPO Tier-1 10.11.2022 (Shift-II)

(a) Rational (b) Insane
(c) Tyrannical (d) Coward

Ans. (a)

Cogent means clear, logical and convincing. Hence, its synonym is 'rational'.

Insane means in a state of mind which prevents normal perception.

Tyrannical means exercising power in a cruel or arbitrary way.

Coward means a person who lacks courage.

371. Pester SSC CPO Tier-1 10.11.2022 (Shift-III)

(a) Abuse (b) Adore
(c) Annoy (d) Amuse

Ans. (c)

Pester means trouble or annoy (someone) with frequent or persistent requests. Hence, its synonym is 'annoy'.

372. Abridge SSC CPO Tier-1 10.11.2022 (Shift-III)
SSC SP 01.08.2022 (Matric Level)

(a) Expand (b) Earmark
(c) Shorten (d) Increase

Ans. (c)

Abridge means to shorten (a book, movie, speech or other text) without losing the sense.

Hence, its synonym is 'shorten'.

Earmark means to designate (something, typically funds or resources) for a particular purpose.

373. Dr. Brahm Prakash advised me to take care of the performance degraders and cautioned me against seeking optimal performance from the participating work centres.
SSC CPO Tier-1 10.11.2022 (Shift-III)
(a) Minimum (b) faulty
(c) Worst (d) best

Ans. (a)

Optimal means best or most effective. Hence, its synonym is 'minimum'.

374. The little girl had **obsequious** manners. SSC CPO Tier-1 10.11.2022 (Shift-III)
(a) mischievous (b) defiant
(c) headstrong (d) law-abiding

Ans. (a)

Obsequious means obedient or attentive to an excessive or servile degree. Hence, its synonym is 'mischievous'.

Defiant means showing defiance.

Headstrong means self-willed and obstinate.

Law-abiding means obedient to the laws of society.

375. He wanted to buy some books, but his purse did not permit that.
SSC CPO Tier-1 11.11.2022 (Shift-I)
(a) warrant (b) patent
(c) grant (d) tolerate

Ans. (c)

Permit means to give authorisation or consent to someone to do something. Hence, its synonym is 'grant'.

Warrant means to justify or necessitate.

Patent means a government authority or license.

Tolerate means to allow the existence, occurrence, or practice of something.

376. Revoke SSC CPO Tier-1 11.11.2022 (Shift-I)
(a) Sustain (b) Repeat
(c) Regret (d) Repeal

Ans. (d)

Revoke means to put an end to the validity or operation of (a decree, decision or promise). Hence, its synonym is 'repeal'.

Sustain means to strengthen or support physically or mentally.

377. Sneha opened the cupboards and glanced over her **meagre** supply of canned goods.
SSC CPO Tier-1 11.11.2022 (Shift-I)
(a) surplus (b) plenteous
(c) bountiful (d) scanty

Ans. (d)

Meagre means lacking in quantity or quality. Hence, its synonym is 'scanty'.

Surplus means an amount of something left over when requirements have been met.

Plenteous means existing in large amounts.

Bountiful means large in quantity; abundant.

378. Preposterous
SSC CPO Tier-1 11.11.2022 (Shift-I)
(a) Flashy (b) Outrageous
(c) Dreamy (d) Imaginative

Ans. (b)

Preposterous means contrary to reason or common sense; utterly absurd or ridiculous. Hence, its synonym is 'outrageous'.

Flashy means ostentatiously attractive or impressive.

Dreamy means having a magical or pleasantly unreal quality.

Imaginative means having or showing creativity or inventiveness.

379. Accredit SSC CPO Tier-1 11.11.2022 (Shift-I)
(a) Certify (b) Confide
(c) Rely (d) Trust

Ans. (a)

Accredit means to give credit or authority to. Hence, its synonym is 'certify'.

Confide means to tell someone about a secret or private matter while trusting them not to repeat it.

Rely means to depend on with full trust or confidence.

Trust means firm belief in the reliability, truth, or ability of someone.

380. Conjure SSC CPO Tier-1 11.11.2022 (Shift-II)
(a) Appeal (b) Quiet
(c) Appease (d) Content

Ans. (a)

Conjure means to call upon (a spirit or ghost) to appear, by means of a magic ritual. Hence, its synonym is 'appeal'.

Appease means to pacify or placate someone by acceding to their demands.

Content means in a state of peaceful happiness.

381. Rebellious
SSC CPO Tier-1 11.11.2022 (Shift-II)
(a) Manageable (b) Unruly
(c) Happy (d) Obedient

Ans. (b)

Rebellious means showing a desire to resist authority, control, or convention. Hence, its synonym is 'unruly'.

Manageable means able to be managed, controlled, or accomplished.

Obedient means complying or willing to comply with orders or requests.

382. Indignation
SSC CPO Tier-1 11.11.2022 (Shift-II)
(a) Offense (b) Designation
(c) Resignation (d) Defence

Ans. (a)

Indignation means anger or annoyance provoked by what is perceived as unfair treatment. Hence, its synonym is 'offense'.

Designation means the action of choosing a place for a special purpose.

Resignation means an act of retiring or giving up a position.

Defense means resistance against attack.

383. Bonhomie
SSC CPO Tier-1 11.11.2022 (Shift-III)
(a) Bad-natured (b) Enemy
(c) Friendship (d) Disagreeable

Ans. (c)

Bonhomie means cheerful friendliness; geniality. Hence, its synonym is 'friendship'.

384. The crowds gathered were **partisan** in nature. SSC CPO Tier-1 11.11.2022 (Shift-III)
(a) pitiful (b) Kind
(c) biased (d) Destructive

Ans. (c)

Partisan means strongly supporting a particular party, cause or person. Hence, its synonym is 'biased'.

Pitiful means deserving or arousing pity.

385. Gourmet SSC CPO Tier-1 11.11.2022 (Shift-III)
(a) Indifferent (b) Detached
(c) Epicure (d) Non-indulgent

Ans. (c)

Gourmet means a connoisseur of good food; a person with a discerning palate. Hence, its synonym is 'epicure'.

Indifferent means having no particular interest or sympathy.

Detached means separate or disconnected.

Non-indulgent means not allowing oneself to enjoy the pleasure of something.

386. She was a brave woman but she. felt daunted by the task ahead.
SSC CPO Tier-1 11.11.2022 (Shift-III)
(a) bold (b) intimidated
(c) appreciated (d) encouraged

Ans. (b)

Daunted means to feel intimidated or apprehensive. Hence, its synonym is 'intimidated'.

387. The scene of Ratan's friend's bike accident remains stamped in his memory. **SSC CPO Tier-1 11.11.2022 (Shift-III)**
(a) approved (b) scary
(c) shunned (d) imprinted
Ans. (d)
Stamped means to impress a pattern or mark. Hence, its synonym is 'imprinted'.

388. Cornucopia
SSC CPO Tier-1 11.11.2022 (Shift-III)
(a) Sink hole (b) Treasure trove
(c) Malaise (d) Avarice
Ans. (b)
Cornucopia means an abundant supply of good things. Hence, its synonym is 'treasure trove'.
Sink hole means a cavity in the ground, especially in limestone bedrock.
Malaise means a general feeling of discomfort, illness, or unease.
Avarice means extreme greed for wealth or material gain.

389. Obliterate
SSC CPO Tier-1 11.11.2022 (Shift-III)
(a) Patched (b) Healed
(c) Mended (d) Abolish
Ans. (d)
Obliterate means to destroy completely. Hence, its synonym is 'abolish'.
Patched means to repair something in a makeshift way.
Healed means to make or become healthy again.
Mended means to repair something that is broken or damaged.

SSC CHSL 2024 (Tier 1)

390. Abolish **SSC CHSL Tier-2 18.11.2024**
(a) Assist (b) Cancel
(c) Subside (d) Worship
Ans. (b)
'Abolish' means 'Cancel'. It refers to formally putting an end to a system, practice or institution. 'Cancel' is a suitable synonym as it captures the essence of completely stopping something from continuing.

391. Huxley was an exponent of Darwin's theory of evolution.
SSC CHSL Tier-2 18.11.2024
(a) Cease (b) Terminate
(c) Proponent (d) Conclude
Ans. (c)
'Proponent' is a synonym for 'exponent.' Both words mean someone who supports or advocates a particular idea or theory. 'Exponent' refers to a person who explains or supports an idea, just as 'proponent' does.

392. Dingy **SSC CHSL Tier-2 18.11.2024**
(a) Pure (b) Dreary
(c) Sterile (d) Bright
Ans. (b)
'Dreary' is a synonym for 'Dingy'. Both words describe something that is dull and gloomy. 'Dingy' implies being dirty or discoloured, often making a place feel unwelcoming.

393. The skunk had a conspicuous spinal stripe. **SSC CHSL Tier-1 01.07.2024 (Shift-I)**
SSC CHSL Tier-1 04.08.2023 (Shift-II)
SSC Steno 15.11.2021 (Shift-I)
(a) obscure (b) charming
(c) noticeable (d) faint
Ans. (c)
Conspicuous means attracting and noticeable.
Obscure means not discovered or known about; uncertain.
Faint means not visible.

394. The documentary explored the historical and cultural significance of the ....(antique) ruins in the region. **SSC CHSL Tier-1 01.07.2024 (Shift-I)**
SSC CPO 04.10.2023 (Shift-III)
(a) obsolete (b) contemporary
(c) modern (d) ancient
Ans. (d)
'Antique' means old and ancient. Hence, the correct filler is 'ancient'.

395. Respect **SSC CHSLTier-1 01.07.2024 (Shift-III)**
(a) Honour (b) Disrespect
(c) Attend (d) Invalidate
Ans. (a)
The synonym of 'respect' is 'honour'.
'Invalidate' means to state to be false.

396. Titanic **SSC CHSL Tier-1 01.07.2024 (Shift-IV)**
(a) Deep (b) Huge
(c) Attractive (d) Disastrous
Ans. (b)
'Titanic' means of exceptional strength, size or power; huge.

397. Fasten **SSC CHSL Tier-1 01.07.2024 (Shift-IV)**
(a) Loosen (b) Bolt
(c) Undo (d) Detach
Ans. (b)
The word 'Fasten' means close or do up securely.
Hence, its synonym is 'Bolt' which means a bar that slides into a socket to fasten a door or window.
Detach means disengage (something or part of something) and remove it.

398. Wonderful
SSC CHSL Tier-1 02.07.2024 (Shift-I)
(a) Upright (b) Synthetic
(c) Amazing (d) Awful
Ans. (c)
The synonym of 'Wonderful' is 'Amazing'.

399. The city's infrastructure was ill-equipped to handle the influx of .... (visitors) during the peak season. **SSC CHSL Tier-1 02.07.2024 (Shift-II)**
(a) tourists (b) citizens
(c) natives (d) residents
Ans. (a)
The word 'visitors' means 'tourists' which is appropriate to fill in the blank.

400. Implicate
SSC CHSL Tier-1 02.07.2024 (Shift-II)
(a) Complain (b) Confuse
(c) Accuse (d) Interrogate
Ans. (c)
The word 'implicate' means 'show (someone) to be involved in a crime/ accuse'.

401. Pliable **SSC CHSL Tier-1 02.07.2024 (Shift-II)**
(a) Severe (b) Probable
(c) Malleable (d) Rigid
Ans. (c)
'Pliable' means easily bent; flexible. Hence, its synonym is 'malleable' which means (of a metal or other material) able to be hammered or pressed into shape without breaking or cracking.
Rigid means stiff.

402. In a split second, her .... (intuitive) reaction kicked in as she swiftly reached out to catch the falling glass.
SSC CHSL Tier-1 02.07.2024 (Shift-III)
(a) shrewd (b) instinctive
(c) voluntary (d) insightful
Ans. (b)
The word 'intuitive' means using or based on what one feels to be true even without conscious reasoning; instinctive.
Shrewd means clever.
Voluntary means willing.
Insightful means to give information.

403. Select the most appropriate synonym of the word 'Abandon' from the given sentence.
SSC CHSL Tier-1 02.07.2024 (Shift-III)
(a) Forsake (b) Improved
(c) Decided (d) Participation
Ans. (a)
The word 'forsake' means to abandon or leave.

404. We should not discriminate against people who are different from us. **SSC CHSLTier-1 02.07.2024 (Shift-III)**
(a) differentiate (b) divide
(c) part (d) sever
Ans. (a)
The word 'discriminate' means to differentiate on the basis of race, gender, etc.

405. Remission **SSC CHSLTier-1 02.07.2024 (Shift-IV)**
(a) Pardon (b) Retribution
(c) Punishment (d) Overlook
Ans. (a)
The word 'remission' means the cancellation of a debt, charge or penalty; pardon.
Retribution means punishment.

406. Let us assume that we will do the job honestly. **SSC CHSLTier-1 02.07.2024 (Shift-IV)**
(a) allow (b) think (c) take (d) give
Ans. (b)
The word 'assume' indicates 'to think that something may be true or false'.

407. The Television show was hosted by a young and vivacious woman called Laura. **SSC CHSLTier-1 03.07.2024 (Shift-I)**
(a) legendary (b) atrocious
(c) liberal (d) energetic
Ans. (d)
The word 'vivacious' means attractively energetic and enthusiastic.
Legendary means very famous and admired or spoken about.
Atrocious means horrifying.
Liberal means free and open to new ideas.

408. Abscond **SSC CHSLTier-1 03.07.2024 (Shift-I)**
(a) Flee (b) Avoid
(c) Annoy (d) Stay
Ans. (a)
The word 'abscond' means to leave hurriedly and secretly, typically to escape from custody or avoid arrest. Hence, its synonym is 'flee' which means the same.

409. Confidential **SSC CHSLTier-1 03.07.2024 (Shift-I)**
(a) Public (b) Limited
(c) Secret (d) Open source
Ans. (c)
The word 'confidential' means a secret not to be discussed openly.

410. Interpret **SSC CHSLTier-1 03.07.2024 (Shift-I)**
(a) Clarify (b) Cleanse
(c) Celebrate (d) Complicate
Ans. (a)
'Interpret' means explain the meaning of (information or actions) for clarity.

411. Lead paint is an environmental .... (danger) and can harm children. **SSC CHSLTier-1 03.07.2024 (Shift-I)**
(a) conflict (b) empathy
(c) toil (d) hazard
Ans. (d)
The word 'hazard' means danger and thus, can be used to fill in the blank.

412. Frivolity **SSC CHSLTier-1 03.07.2024 (Shift-II)**
(a) Consequence (b) Substantial
(c) Meaningful (d) Insignificance
Ans. (d)
The word 'frivolity' means 'insignificance or non-importance'.

413. Ablaze **SSC CHSLTier-1 03.07.2024 (Shift-III)**
(a) Extinguished (b) Burning
(c) Brazen (d) Sharp
Ans. (b)
The word 'Ablaze' means 'to set on fire or burning.
Brazen means bold and unashamed.

414. Everyone revered my austere father who was the high priest of the famous Shiva temple. **SSC CHSLTier-1 03.07.2024 (Shift-III)** **SSC CHSLTier-1 02.06.2022 (Shift-I)**
(a) stern (b) composed
(c) morose (d) aged
Ans. (a)
The word 'austere' means severe or strict in manner or attitude.
Hence, the synonym of 'austere' is 'stern'.
'Morose' means sullen and ill-tempered.

415. Select the most appropriate synonym of the word 'echoed' to fill in the blank.
The thunderous applause .... through the stadium. **SSC CHSLTier-1 03.07.2024 (Shift-IV)**
(a) reverberated (b) recoiled
(c) bounced (d) pulsed
Ans. (a)
The correct filler for the given blank is 'reverberated' which means (of a loud noise) be repeated several times as an echo.

416. Chaste **SSC CHSLTier-1 03.07.2024 (Shift-IV)**
(a) Flashy (b) Corrupt
(c) Sullied (d) Pure
Ans. (d)
The word 'Chaste' means 'pure'.
Sullied means dirty or made impure.

417. They gave us the impression that Clara was a cold and calculating woman, who was only after power. **SSC CHSLTier-1 04.07.2024 (Shift-I)**
(a) callous (b) unscrupulous
(c) unsympathetic (d) manipulative
Ans. (d)
The word 'manipulative' means 'scheming and calculating'.

418. Lousy **SSC CHSLTier-1 04.07.2024 (Shift-II)**
(a) Praiseworthy (b) Moral
(c) Funny (d) Pitiful
Ans. (d)
The word 'Lousy' means very poor or bad. Hence, its synonym is 'pitiful' which means the same.

419. It did not take her very long to ascend to power. **SSC CHSLTier-1 04.07.2024 (Shift-II)**
(a) grab (b) climb
(c) reach (d) arise
Ans. (b)
The word 'ascend' means to rise and climb.

420. Peculiar **SSC CHSLTier-1 04.07.2024 (Shift-II)** **SSC MTS 04.09.2023 (Shift-I)**
(a) Revolutionary (b) Strange
(c) Frequent (d) Usual
Ans. (b)
The word 'Peculiar' means 'unusual and strange'.

421. Fertile **SSC CHSLTier-1 04.07.2024 (Shift-III)**
(a) Productive (b) Destructive
(c) Hectic (d) Amusing
Ans. (a)
The word 'Fertile' means able to produce something or productive.
Hectic means busy.

422. Desire **SSC CHSLTier-1 04.07.2024 (Shift-IV)**
(a) Loathing (b) Aversion
(c) Disgust (d) Longing
Ans. (d)
The word 'Desire' means 'a longing or want of something'.
Loathing and **Aversion** means dislike and disgust.

423. Select the most appropriate synonym of the word 'Swap' from the given sentence.
The original buyer attempted to resell the tickets online because there was no option to exchange them for a new date. **SSC CHSLTier-1 05.07.2024 (Shift-I)**
(a) Resell (b) Exchange
(c) Original (d) Option
Ans. (b)
The word 'swap' means 'to exchange'.

424. Appalled **SSC CHSLTier-1 05.07.2024 (Shift-I)**
(a) Applied (b) Clap
(c) Disgusted (d) Allied

Ans. (c)

'Appalled' means greatly dismayed, disgusted or horrified.

425. Permit SSC CHSLTier-1 05.07.2024 (Shift-II)

(a) Disgrace (b) Flout
(c) Approve (d) Abandon

Ans. (b)

The word 'permit' means to allow someone to do something.

Flout means to break a rule or law.

426. Accept SSC CHSLTier-1 05.07.2024 (Shift-IV)

(a) Agree (b) Refuse
(c) Present (d) Regret

Ans. (a)

The word 'accept' means 'to agree'.

427. Change SSC CHSLTier-1 05.07.2024 (Shift-IV)

(a) Resolute (b) Renew
(c) Adjust (d) Alter

Ans. (d)

Alter means to change.

Renew means to take a service again.

428. Erudite SSC CHSLTier-1 08.07.2024 (Shift-I)

(a) Humble (b) Honest
(c) Strong (d) Educated

Ans. (d)

The word 'erudite' means 'educated'.

429. Injustice SSC CHSLTier-1 08.07.2024 (Shift-I)

(a) Discrimination
(b) Equality
(c) Complacency
(d) Demand

Ans. (a)

The nearest synonym of 'injustice' is 'discrimination'.

Complacency means a feeling of quiet pleasure or security, often while unaware of some potential danger, defect, or the like.

430. The setting Sun turned the .... (calm) ocean into a sea of gold.
SSC CHSLTier-1 08.07.2024 (Shift-II)

(a) volatile (b) placid
(c) furtive (d) scattered

Ans. (b)

The word 'placid' means 'calm'.

Volatile means liable to change rapidly and unpredictably, especially for the worse.

Furtive means attempting to avoid notice or attention, typically because of guilt or a belief that discovery would lead to trouble; secretive.

431. He is just <u>jealous</u> that he didn't get picked for the job.
SSC CHSLTier-1 08.07.2024 (Shift-II)

(a) envious (b) spiteful
(c) greedy (d) suspicious

Ans. (a)

The word 'envious' means 'jealous'.
'Spiteful' means angry.

432. Venom SSC CHSLTier-1 08.07.2024 (Shift-III)

(a) Poison (b) Butter
(c) Fruit juice (d) Honey

Ans. (a)

The word 'venom' means 'poison'.

433. Callous SSC CHSLTier-1 08.07.2024 (Shift-III)
SSC CHSLTier-1 07.08.2023 (Shift-I)

(a) Cruel (b) Generous
(c) Affectionate (d) Exhausting

Ans. (a)

'Callous' means evil, cruel or brutal.

Exhausting means tiring.

434. Baffle SSC CHSLTier-1 08.07.2024 (Shift-III)
SSC CHSLTier-1 24.05.2022 (Shift-III)

(a) Explicate (b) Confuse
(c) Barbarous (d) Equalise

Ans. (b)

Baffle means to be confused.

Explicate means to analyse and develop (an idea or principle) in detail.

Barbarous means extremely brutal.

Equalise means to make things equal.

435. Sceptical SSC CHSLTier-1 09.07.2024 (Shift-I)

(a) Incredulous (b) Stoic
(c) Garrulous (d) Insensitive

Ans. (a)

'Sceptical' means doubtful. Hence, its synonym is 'incredulous' which means (of a person or their manner) unwilling or unable to believe something.

Stoic means a person who can endure pain or hardship without showing their feelings or complaining.

Garrulous means talkative.

436. Attire SSC CHSLTier-1 09.07.2024 (Shift-II)

(a) Park (b) Dress
(c) Theatre (d) Hote

Ans. (b)

The word 'attire' refers to the dress or clothes one wears.

437. The sun was shining bright and <u>intense</u> in the sky.
SSC CHSLTier-1 09.07.2024 (Shift-II)

(a) mild (b) strong
(c) subtle (d) weak

Ans. (b)

The word 'intense' means of extreme force, degree or strength. Hence, its synonym is 'strong'.

438. The girl tried to <u>alleviate</u> her brother's problem.
SSC CHSLTier-1 09.07.2024 (Shift-III)

(a) increase (b) soar
(c) reduce (d) worsen

Ans. (c)

The word 'alleviate' means 'to reduce'.

439. John is very <u>generous</u>; he regularly gives alms to the poor.
SSC CHSLTier-1 09.07.2024 (Shift-III)

(a) popular (b) great
(c) kind (d) shrewd

Ans. (c)

The word 'generous' means 'kind'.

440. The meeting was brought to a .... (rapid) conclusion.
SSC CHSLTier-1 09.07.2024 (Shift-III)

(a) stubborn (b) pervious
(c) grim (d) hasty

Ans. (d)

The word 'rapid' means quick. Hence, its synonym is 'hasty' which means the same and is the correct filler for the given blank.

441. Luminous
SSC CHSLTier-1 09.07.2024 (Shift-IV)

(a) Radiant (b) Laborious
(c) Luxurious (d) Amiable

Ans. (a)

The word **Luminous** means giving off light; bright or shining. Hence, its synonym is 'Radiant'.

'**Laborious** means requiring hard work.

Luxurious means rich and wealthy.

442. Retract SSC CHSLTier-1 10.07.2024 (Shift-I)

(a) Disturb (b) Please
(c) Implement (d) Revoke

Ans. (d)

The word 'retract' means 'to take back'. Hence, its synonym is 'revoke'.

443. Alert SSC CHSLTier-1 10.07.2024 (Shift-I)

(a) Inactive (b) Dull
(c) Smart (d) Vigilant

Ans. (d)

The word 'vigilant' means 'alert and careful'.

444. For Rana, unable to see a thing, the <u>parade</u> seemed to last forever.
SSC CHSLTier-1 10.07.2024 (Shift-I)

(a) hiding (b) darkness
(c) concealment (d) procession

Ans. (d)

'Parade' refers to a public procession, especially one celebrating a special day or event.

445. Estimate SSC CHSLTier-1 10.07.2024 (Shift-II)

(a) Evaluate (b) Appropriate
(c) Profit (d) Verify

Ans. (a)

The word 'estimate' means to check or evaluate an approximate value of something.

446. The removal of <u>petty</u> restrictions has made life easier.
SSC CHSLTier-1 10.07.2024 (Shift-II)
(a) big (b) consequential
(c) large (d) small
Ans. (d)
The word 'petty' means 'small'.

447. Absurd **SSC CHSLTier-1 10.07.2024 (Shift-III)**
(a) Sudden (b) Arbitrary
(c) Irrational (d) Abstruse
Ans. (c)
Absurd means strange and irrational.
Arbitrary means based on random choice or personal whim, rather than any reason or system.
Abstruse means difficult to understand; obscure.

448. Evasive **SSC CHSLTier-1 10.07.2024 (Shift-IV)**
(a) Cohesive (b) Ambiguous
(c) Accessible (d) Abrasive
Ans. (b)
'Evasive' means tending to avoid commitment or self-revelation, especially by responding only indirectly. Hence, its antonym is **Ambiguous** means confusing.

449. Indigenous
SSC CHSLTier-1 11.07.2024 (Shift-I)
(a) Aboriginal (b) Artificial
(c) Tangible (d) Literary
Ans. (a)
'Indigenous' means originating or occurring naturally in a particular place; native.
Hence, the synonym is 'Aboriginal' which means originating or occurring naturally in a particular place; native.

450. Select the most appropriate synonym of 'amazement' to fill in the blank.
Leena was filled with .... when she saw the diamond ring as her wedding gift.
SSC CHSLTier-1 11.07.2024 (Shift-I)
(a) happiness
(b) measurement
(c) haughtiness
(d) astonishment
Ans. (d)
The synonym of 'astonishment' is 'amazement' which is the correct filler for the given blank.

451. Perilous **SSC CHSLTier-1 11.07.2024 (Shift-II)**
SSC CHSLTier-1 08.11.2023 (Shift-II)
(a) Dangerous (b) Ugly
(c) Bad (d) Adverse
Ans. (a)
The underlined word 'Perilous' means 'Dangerous'.
'Adverse' means strict and severe.

452. Advanced
SSC CHSLTier-1 11.07.2024 (Shift-II)
(a) Foreign (b) Progressive
(c) Discarded (d) Elementary
Ans. (b)
'Advanced' means modern and recently developed.
Hence, its synonym is 'Progressive' which means moving forward or onward.

453. My grandmother is fond of giving <u>homilies</u> to all my friends who visit my place. **SSC CHSLTier-1 11.07.2024 (Shift-II)**
(a) suggestions (b) sermons
(c) alternatives (d) strictures
Ans. (b)
The word 'homilies' means a religious discourse which is intended primarily for spiritual edification rather than doctrinal instruction. Hence, its synonym is 'sermons' which means the same.

454. Anxiety **SSC CHSLTier-1 11.07.2024 (Shift-III)**
(a) Serenity (b) Distress
(c) Dilemma (d) Ease
Ans. (b)
The words 'Anxiety' and 'Distress' are synonymous.

455. Revolution
SSC CHSLTier-1 11.07.2024 (Shift-IV)
(a) Stagnation (b) Gyration
(c) Harmony (d) Order
Ans. (b)
The word 'revolution' means an instance of revolving. Hence, its synonym is 'gyration' which means a rapid movement in a circle or spiral; a whirling motion.
Stagnation means to be still.

456. Candid **SSC CHSLTier-1 11.07.2024 (Shift-IV)**
(a) Cruel (b) Bright
(c) Top (d) Honest
Ans. (d)
The word 'candid' means 'honest'.

SSC CHSL 2023 (Tier 1)

457. Apologetic
SSC CHSLTier-1 09.03.2023 (Shift-I)
(a) Contrite (b) Solid
(c) Stagnant (d) Derisive
Ans. (a)
The word **Apologetic** means showing or saying that you are sorry that something has happened, especially because you feel guilty or embarrassed about it. From the given options **Contrite** means the same and is synonym.
Contrite means regretful.

458. Magnanimity
SSC CHSLTier-1 09.03.2023 (Shift-I)
(a) Virulence
(b) Volatile
(c) Invidiousness
(d) Altruism
Ans. (d)
The word 'Magnanimity' means kindness and generosity, especially towards an enemy or someone you have defeated.
From the given options, 'Altruism' meaning willingness to do things that bring advantages to others, even if it results in disadvantage for yourself is its synonym.
Virulence means severity of a disease.
Volatile means easy to catch fire.
Invidiousness means unhappy .

459. Quandary **SSC CHSLTier-1 09.03.2023 (Shift-I)**
(a) Breeze (b) Impasse
(c) Clique (d) Clinch
Ans. (b)
The word **Quandary** means a difficult situation or problem, especially one in which you cannot decide what to do.
Impasse meaning a situation in which progress is impossible, especially because the people involved in it cannot agree is its synonym.
Clique means a small close kvit group.
Clinch means confirm.

460. Slick **SSC CHSL Tier-1 09.03.2023 (Shift-II)**
(a) Novice (b) Fractions
(c) Slippery (d) New
Ans. (c)
'Slick' means smooth and slippery. Hence, its synonym is 'slippery'.
Novice means a person new to or inexperienced in a field or situation.

461. Laggard **SSC CHSL Tier-1 09.03.2023 (Shift-II)**
(a) Prompt (b) Hustler
(c) Dawdling (d) Expeditious
Ans. (c)
Laggard means a person who makes slow progress and falls behind others. Hence, its synonym is 'dawdling'.
Prompt means done without delay; immediate.
Hustler means an aggressively enterprising person.
Expeditious means done with speed and efficiency.

462. Sacrilege **SSC CHSL Tier-1 09.03.2023 (Shift-II)**
(a) Blasphemy
(b) Modification
(c) consecration
(d) Reverence

Ans. (a)

Sacrilege means violation or misuse of what is regarded as sacred. Hence, its synonym is 'blasphemy'.

Modification means a change made.

Consecration means the action of making or declaring something sacred.

Reverence means deep respect for someone or something.

463. Ponderous SSC CHSL Tier-1 09.03.2023 (Shift-III)

(a) Unruly (b) Wondrous
(c) Buff (d) Heavy

Ans. (d)

Ponderous means slow and clumsy because of great weight. Hence, its synonym is 'heavy'.

Unruly means disorderly and disruptive.

Wondrous means inspiring a feeling of wonder.

Buff means a yellowish-beige colour.

464. Ridicule SSC CHSL Tier-1 09.03.2023 (Shift-IV)

(a) Pathology (b) Resolute
(c) Derision (d) Derivation

Ans. (c)

Ridicule means the subjection of someone or something to contemptuous and dismissive language or behaviour. Hence, its synonym is 'derision'.

Resolute means admirably purposeful, determined, and unwavering.

Derivation means the obtaining or developing of something from a source.

465. Anxious SSC CHSL Tier-1 10.03.2023 (Shift-II)

(a) Collected
(b) Flawless
(c) Apprehensive
(d) Accept

Ans. (c)

The word 'Anxious' means worried and nervous. 'Apprehensive' which means feeling worried about something that you are going to do or that is going to happen.

466. Gallivant SSC CHSL Tier-1 10.03.2023 (Shift-II)

(a) Gall (b) Meander
(c) Grave (d) Brave

Ans. (b)

The word **Gallivant** means to go from place looking for enjoyment. A 'Meander' which means the same as 'Gallivant'.

Gall means bold behaviour.

Grave means serious.

467. Glib SSC CHSL Tier-1 10.03.2023 (Shift-II)

(a) Sincere (b) Inarticulate
(c) Easy (d) Implausible

Ans. (c)

The word **Glib** means marked by ease and fluency in speaking or writing often to the point of being insincere or deceitful.

Inarticulate means unable to express clearly.

Implausible means not logical or reasonable

468. Whimsical SSC CHSL Tier-1 10.03.2023 (Shift-II)

(a) Weak (b) Respectful
(c) Humiliated (d) Funny

Ans. (d)

Whimsical means playfully quaint or fanciful, especially in an appealing and amusing way. Hence, its synonym is 'funny'.

Humiliated means made to feel ashamed and foolish.

469. Instigate SSC CHSL Tier-1 10.03.2023 (Shift-II)

(a) Deterrence (b) Settle
(c) Raise (d) Complacence

Ans. (c)

Instigate means to bring about or initiate an action or event. Hence, its synonym is 'raise'.

Deterrence means the action of discouraging an action or event through instilling doubt or fear of the consequences.

Settle means resolve or reach an agreement about an argument or problem.

Complacence means a feeling of smug or uncritical satisfaction with oneself or one's achievements.

470. Domicile SSC CHSL Tier-1 13.03.2023 (Shift-I)

(a) Wild (b) Dictator
(c) Home (d) Evict

Ans. (c)

Domicile means the country that a person treats as their permanent home, or lives in and has a substantial connection with. Hence, its synonym is 'home'.

Dictator means a ruler with total power over a country.

Evict means to expel someone from a property.

471. Jarred SSC CHSL Tier-1 13.03.2023 (Shift-II)

(a) Macho (b) Assented
(c) Altercated (d) Accorded

Ans. (c)

Jarred means to send a painful or damaging shock through something. Hence, its synonym is 'altercated'.

Macho means showing aggressive pride in one's masculinity.

Assented means to express approval or agreement.

Accorded means to give or grant someone power, status, or recognition.

472. Blasphemous SSC CHSL Tier-1 13.03.2023 (Shift-II)

(a) Authentic (b) Disrespectful
(c) Costly (d) Reality

Ans. (b)

Blasphemous means sacrilegious against God or sacred things; profane. Hence, its synonym is 'disrespectful'.

473. Simple SSC CHSL Tier-1 13.03.2023 (Shift-III)

(a) Decorated (b) Complex
(c) Elementary (d) Embellished

Ans. (c)

Elementary means easy, straightforward and simple. Hence, it is closest in meaning to 'simple'.

Embellished means decorated.

474. Conscientious SSC CHSL Tier-1 13.03.2023 (Shift-IV)

(a) Savage (b) Casual
(c) Carefree (d) Sedulous

Ans. (d)

Conscientious means wishing to do one's work or duty well and thoroughly. Hence, its synonym is 'sedulous'.

Savage means fierce, violent, and uncontrolled.

Casual means relaxed and unconcerned.

475. Edacious SSC CHSL Tier-1 13.03.2023 (Shift-IV)

(a) Solvent (b) Gluttonous
(c) Insolvent (d) Satiated

Ans. (b)

Edacious means relating to or given to eating. Hence, its synonym is 'gluttonous'.

Solvent means having assets in excess of liabilities.

Insolvent means unable to pay debts owed. Satiated means fully satisfied.

476. Hostility SSC CHSL Tier-1 14.03.2023 (Shift-I)

(a) Organise (b) Anchor
(c) Authorise (d) Enmity

Ans. (d)

The word 'hostility' means an occasion when someone is unfriendly or shows that they do not like something.

Hence, its synonym is 'enmity'.

Anchor means support.

Authorise means to gain official approval.

477. Oblivious SSC CHSL Tier-1 14.03.2023 (Shift-I)

(a) Aware (b) Careful
(c) Suspecting (d) Ignorant

Ans. (d)

The word Oblivious' means not knowing about or not noticing something that is happening around you. From the given options 'ignorant' means the same.

478. Saboteur SSC CHSL Tier-1 14.03.2023 (Shift-I)

(a) Sage (b) Mendicant
(c) Preservationist (d) Vandal

Ans. (d)

The word **Saboteur** means someone who deliberately damages or destroys the property of an enemy or opponent. From the given options 'Vandal' means the same and is its synonym.

Sage is a saint.

Mendicant refers to a beggar.

Preservationist refers to someone who support preservation of something.

479. Ferocious SSC CHSL Tier-1 14.03.2023 (Shift-II)

(a) Frightful (b) Mild
(c) conscientious (d) Tame

Ans. (a)

Ferocious means savagely fierce, cruel or violent. Hence, its synonym is 'frightful'.

Mild means gentle and not easily provoked.

Conscientious means wishing to do one's work or duty well and thoroughly.

Tame means not dangerous or frightened of people.

480. Wager SSC CHSL Tier-1 14.03.2023 (Shift-II)

(a) Gamble (b) scrutinise
(c) Crumble (d) Scrupulous

Ans. (a)

Wager means to risk money or something else on the outcome of a contest or uncertain event. Hence, its synonym is 'gamble'.

Scrutinise means to examine or inspect closely and thoroughly.

Crumble means to break or fall apart into small fragments.

Scrupulous means very concerned to avoid doing wrong.

481. Vault SSC CHSLTier-1 15.03.2023 (Shift-I)

(a) Ration (b) Crypt
(c) Raisins (d) Monarch

Ans. (b)

Vault means a large room or chamber used for storage, especially an underground one. Hence, its synonym is 'crypt'.

Ration means a fixed amount of a commodity officially allowed to each person.

Raisins mean dried grapes.

Monarch means a sovereign head of state.

482. Dandy SSC CHSLTier-1 15.03.2023 (Shift-I)

(a) Cartel (b) Disappointment
(c) Dud (d) Beautiful

Ans. (d)

Dandy means a man unduly devoted to style, neatness and fashion in dress and appearance. Hence, its synonym is 'beautiful'.

Cartel means an association of manufacturers or suppliers with the purpose of maintaining prices at a high level.

Disappointment means sadness or displeasure caused by the non-fulfillment of one's hopes or expectations.

Dud means a thing that fails to work properly.

483. Habitat SSC CHSL Tier-1 15.03.2023 (Shift-II)

(a) Motion (b) Clothed
(c) Bent (d) Niche

Ans. (d)

Habitat means the natural home or environment of an animal, plant or other organism. Hence, its synonym is 'niche'.

Motion means the action or process of moving or being moved.

484. Cajole SSC CHSL Tier-1 15.03.2023 (Shift-III)

(a) Dissuade (b) Persuade
(c) Bully (d) Disenchant

Ans. (b)

Cajole means to persuade someone to do something by sustained coaxing or flattery. Hence, its synonym is 'persuade'.

Dissuade means to persuade someone not to take a particular course of action.

Disenchant means to free from illusion.

485. Malign SSC CHSL Tier-1 15.03.2023 (Shift-III)

(a) Nihilistic (b) Insurgent
(c) Baleful (d) Radical

Ans. (c)

Malign means evil in nature or effect; malevolent. Hence, its synonym is 'baleful'.

Nihilistic means rejecting all religious and moral principles.

Insurgent means rising in active revolt.

Radical means relating to or affecting the fundamental nature of something.

486. Jape SSC CHSL Tier-1 15.03.2023 (Shift-IV)

(a) Quarrel (b) Quip
(c) Quit (d) Quick

Ans. (b)

The word 'Jape' refers to a trick that you play on someone to make them feel silly or look stupid. 'Quip' meaning humorous and clever remark.

Quarrel means to fight.

487. Caginess SSC CHSL Tier-1 15.03.2023 (Shift-IV)

(a) Ingenuous
(b) Guilefulness
(c) Desiccate
(d) Dopiness

Ans. (b)

The word **Caginess** means unwilling to give information. 'Guilefulness' which means using cleverness in order to deceive someone or get what you want.

Ingenous means innocent.

Desiccate means to dry something.

Dopiness means sleepiness.

488. Fortitude SSC CHSL Tier-1 15.03.2023 (Shift-IV)

(a) Plot (b) Vacillation
(c) Grim (d) Grit

Ans. (d)

The word **Fortitude** means courage shown when you are in great pain or experiencing a lot of trouble.

'Grit' meaning determination to succeed, even in very difficult situations is its synonym.

Plot means story.

Vacillation means in ability to decide.

Grim means serious.

489. Fabricate SSC CHSL Tier-1 16.03.2023 (Shift-I)

(a) Mimic (b) Flatten
(c) Detached (d) Concoct

Ans. (d)

The word **fabricate** means to invent or produce something false in order to deceive someone. 'Concoct' which means the same.

Mimic means to copy.

Flatten means to make something even.

Detached means to seperate.

490. Quail SSC CHSL Tier-1 16.03.2023 (Shift-I)

(a) Cringe (b) Approach
(c) Tyrant (d) Assail

Ans. (a)

The word 'quail' means to feel or show fear or apprehension, 'Cringe', which means to suddenly move away from someone or something because of being frightened.

Tyrant means cruel and oppressive ruler.

Assail means a violent attack.

491. Levitate SSC CHSL Tier-1 16.03.2023 (Shift-II)

(a) Float (b) Laydown
(c) Rusticate (d) Walk

Ans. (a)

Levitate means to rise or cause to rise and hover in the air. Hence, its synonym is 'float'.

Laydown means to place something down in a resting position.

Rusticate means to go to, live in, or spend time in the country.

492. Opaque SSC CHSL Tier-1 16.03.2023 (Shift-II)

(a) Clear (b) Unadulterated
(c) Translucent (d) Arcane

Ans. (d)

The word **Opaque** refers to something that is difficult to understand. From the given options 'Arcane', which refers to something that is mysterious, secret or understood by only a few people is its synonym.

Translucent means semi clear.

Unadulterated means pure.

493. Obliquity SSC CHSL Tier-1 16.03.2023 (Shift-II)

(a) Profundity (b) Incisiveness
(c) Surety (d) Opacity

Ans. (d)

Obliquity is a characteristic of being deliberately indirect or vague, especially to fool or deceive someone. From the given options 'Opacity', which refers to the quality of being obscure in meaning is its synonym.

Profundity means great knowledge.

Incisivenese means clear and direct.

494. Nark SSC CHSL Tier-1 16.03.2023 (Shift-III)

(a) Reassure (b) Irritate
(c) Solace (d) Obligation

Ans. (b)

Nark means to annoy or irritate someone. Hence, its synonym is 'irritate'.

Reassure means to say or do something to remove the doubts and fears of someone.

Solace means comfort or consolation in a time of distress or sadness.

Obligation means a duty or commitment.

495. Nascence SSC CHSL Tier-1 16.03.2023 (Shift-III)

(a) Cessation (b) Incipience
(c) Omega (d) Acrimonious.

Ans. (b)

Nascence means the process of coming into existence; beginning. Hence, its synonym is 'incipience'.

Cessation means the fact or process of ending or being brought to an end.

Omega means the last letter of the Greek alphabet, symbolising the end.

Acrimonious means angry and bitter.

496. Dreary SSC CHSL Tier-1 16.03.2023 (Shift-IV)

(a) Faith (b) Dull
(c) Superstitious (d) Active

Ans. (b)

Dreary means dull, bleak and lifeless; depressing. Hence, its synonym is 'dull'.

497. Ecclesial SSC CHSL Tier-1 16.03.2023 (Shift-IV)

(a) Profane (b) Secular
(c) Profuse (d) Churchly

Ans. (d)

Ecclesial means relating to the Christian Church or its clergy. Hence, its synonym is 'churchly'.

Profane means relating or devoted to that which is not sacred or biblical; secular.

Secular means denoting attitudes, activities, or other things that have no religious or spiritual basis.

498. Shapeless SSC CHSL Tier-1 17.03.2023 (Shift-II)

(a) Amoral (b) Amortisation
(c) Amorous (d) Amorphous

Ans. (d)

The word **Amorphous** means wigh no clear shape, design or structure or 'Shapeless'.

Amoral means locking morality.

Amorous means lustful.

Amortisation means paying off debts.

499. Attune SSC CHSL Tier-1 17.03.2023 (Shift-III)

(a) Assimilate (b) Skew
(c) Estrange (d) Disrupt

Ans. (a)

Attune means to bring into harmony; adjust. Hence, its synonym is 'assimilate'.

Skew means to suddenly change direction or position.

Estrange means to cause someone to be no longer close or affectionate to someone.

500. Obligation SSC CHSL Tier-1 17.03.2023 (Shift-IV)

(a) Imperative (b) Loophole
(c) Discharge (d) Quietus

Ans. (a)

Obligation means an act or course of action to which a person is morally or legally bound; a duty or commitment. Hence, its synonym is 'imperative'.

Loophole means an ambiguity or inadequacy in the law or a set of rules.

Discharge means tell (someone) officially that they can or must leave.

Quietus means death or something that causes death, regarded as a release from life.

501. Faddish SSC CHSL Tier-1 20.03.2023 (Shift-I)

(a) Unpopular (b) Phony
(c) Barge (d) Fashionable

Ans. (d)

Faddish means intensely fashionable or popular for a short time. Hence, its synonym is 'fashionable'.

Unpopular means not liked or popular.

Phony means not genuine; fraudulent.

Barge means move forcefully or roughly.

502. Thrifty SSC CHSL Tier-1 20.03.2023 (Shift-I)

(a) Prudent (b) wasteful
(c) Generous (d) Extravagant

Ans. (a)

Thrifty means using money and other resources carefully and not wastefully. Hence, its synonym is 'prudent'.

Wasteful means using or expending something of value carelessly.

Generous means showing a readiness to give more of something.

Extravagant means lacking restraint in spending money or using resources.

503. Elucidate SSC CHSL Tier-1 20.03.2023 (Shift-II)

(a) Exhaust (b) Examine
(c) Oracular (d) Explicate

Ans. (d)

Elucidate means to make (something) clear; explain. Hence, its synonym is 'explicate'.

Exhaust means to drain someone of their physical or mental resources.

Examine means inspect someone or something in detail to determine their nature or condition.

Oracular means relating to an oracle.

504. Jejune SSC CHSL Tier-1 20.03.2023 (Shift-III)

(a) Drab (b) Cosmopolitan
(c) Unchildlike (d) Poignant

Ans. (a)

The **Jejune** means dry, uninteresting and boring. From the given options, **Drab** means the same and is its synonym.

Cosmopolitan refers to a person who considers the world his home.

Poignant means deeply affecting.

505. Buddy SSC CHSL Tier-1 20.03.2023 (Shift-III)

(a) Foe (b) Enemy
(c) Associate (d) Stylist

Ans. (c)

The word 'buddy' means a friend. So, 'Associate' as it means someone who is closely connected to another person as a companion, friend or business partner.

506. Craven SSC CHSL Tier-1 20.03.2023 (Shift-III)
(a) Gallant (b) Unabashed
(c) Bold (d) Cowardly
Ans. (d)
The word 'craven' means very cowardly.
Gallant means bold
Unabashed means unashamed.

507. Wallow SSC CHSL Tier-1 20.03.2023 (Shift-IV)
(a) Straighten (b) Rise
(c) Flounder (d) Steady
Ans. (c)
Wallow means to roll about or lie relaxed in mud or water, especially to keep cool, avoid biting insects or spread scent. Hence, its synonym is 'flounder'.
Straighten means to make or become straight.
Steady means firmly fixed, supported, or balanced; not shaking or moving.

508. Famine SSC CHSL Tier-1 20.03.2023 (Shift-IV)
(a) Drought (b) Feast
(c) Abundance (d) Plenty
Ans. (a)
Famine means extreme scarcity of food. Hence, its synonym is 'drought'.
Feast means a large meal, typically a celebratory one.
Abundance and **Plenty** means a very large quantity of something.

509. Lair SSC CHSL Tier-1 20.03.2023 (Shift-IV)
(a) Concealment
(b) Arraign
(c) Apart
(d) Concurrent
Ans. (a)
Lair means a place where a wild animal, especially a fierce or dangerous one, lives. Hence, its synonym is 'concealment'.
Arraign means to call or bring someone before a court to answer a criminal charge.
Apart means to be separated by a distance.
Concurrent means existing, happening or done at the same time.

510. Bogus SSC CHSL Tier-1 21.03.2023 (Shift-I)
(a) Humane (b) Strong
(c) False (d) Criticise
Ans. (c)
Bogus means not genuine or true; fake. Hence, its synonym is 'false'.
Humane means having or showing compassion or benevolence.
Criticise means to indicate the faults of someone or something.

511. Nacreous
SSC CHSL Tier-1 21.03.2023 (Shift-III)
(a) Monochromatic (b) Pale
(c) Gloom (d) Iridescent
Ans. (d)
Nacreous means having an iridescent, lustrous and pearly appearance. Hence, its synonym is 'iridescent'.
Monochromatic means containing or using only one color.
Pale means light in colour or having less color than usual.
Gloom means partial or total darkness.

512. Oblate SSC CHSL Tier-1 21.03.2023 (Shift-IV)
(a) Heathen (b) Secular
(c) Mendicant (d) Layperson
Ans. (c)
The word **Oblate** refers to a person dedicated to a monastic or religious life. From the given options, 'Mendicant' meaning someone who belongs to a religious group that lives by asking the public for food, money, etc is its synonym.
Heathen means devil.
Secular means non religious.
Lay person is a common man.

513. Decimate
SSC CHSL Tier-1 21.03.2023 (Shift-IV)
(a) Establish (b) Harbour
(c) Mend (d) Wreck
Ans. (d)
The word **decimate** means to destroy or spoil something. From the given options, 'Wreck' means the same and is its synonym.
Harbour means to keep in one's mind.
Mend means to fix.

514. Enigmatic
SSC CHSL Tier-1 21.03.2023 (Shift-IV)
(a) Grumpy (b) Mysterious
(c) Literate (d) Illiterate
Ans. (b)
The word **enigmatic** means mysterious and impossible to understand completely.
Grumpy means angry and serious.

515. Soar SSC CHSL Tier-1 21.03.2023 (Shift-IV)
(a) Fly (b) Bitter
(c) Sour (d) Sweet
Ans. (a)
Soar means to fly or rise high in the air. Hence, its synonym is 'fly'.
Bitter means having a sharp, pungent taste or smell.
Sour means having an acid taste like lemon or vinegar.
Sweet means having the pleasant taste characteristic of sugar or honey.

516. Resentment
SSC CHSL Tier-1 02.08.2023 (Shift-I)
(a) Calmness (b) Happiness
(c) Anger (d) Relaxation
Ans. (c)
The word 'resentment' means a feeling of anger because you have been forced to accept something that you do not like.
So, 'Anger' from the given option is the most appropriate synonym of 'Resentment'.

517. Select the most appropriate synonym of the word **'Keen'** from the given sentence.
I am eager and happy to visit the beautiful city of Darjeeling next month with my family.
SSC CHSL Tier-1 02.08.2023 (Shift-II)
(a) beautiful (b) visit
(c) eager (d) happy
Ans. (c)
'Keen' means eager. Hence, its synonym is 'eager'.

518. The guest was heckled by the spectators.
SSC CHSLTier-1 02.08.2023 (Shift-II)
(a) Calmed (b) Aided
(c) Taunted (d) Helped
Ans. (c)
Heckled means to interrupt a speaker with derisive or aggressive comments or abuse. Hence, its synonym is 'taunted'.
Aided means **helped.**

519. Compel SSC CHSL Tier-1 02.08.2023 (Shift-III)
(a) Allow (b) Stop
(c) Give (d) Obligate
Ans. (d)
Compel means to force or oblige someone to do something. Hence, its synonym is 'obligate'.

520. Although the new fashion trend was quite popular, some critics were quick to deride it as a passing fad.
SSC CHSL Tier-1 02.08.2023 (Shift-III)
(a) Ridicule
(b) Hail
(c) Detest
(d) Applaud
Ans. (a)
Deride means to express contempt for; ridicule. Hence, its synonym is 'ridicule'.
Hail means to greet or acclaim enthusiastically.
Detest means to dislike intensely.
Applaud means to show approval or praise by clapping.

521. The security cameras can automatically ....(**rotate**) to monitor the entire hallway.
SSC CHSL Tier-1 02.08.2023 (Shift-IV)

(a) evolve (b) resolve
(c) revolve (d) devolve

Ans. (c)

Rotate means to move in a circle around an axis or center. Hence, its synonym is 'revolve'.

Resolve means to settle or find a solution to a problem.

Devolve means to delegate or transfer power to a lower level.

522. Select the most appropriate synonym of the word '**Scrutiny**' from the given sentence.
The company's strategic plan included a comprehensive analysis of market trends and consumer behaviour.
SSC CHSL Tier-1 02.08.2023 (Shift-IV)

(a) Behaviour (b) Comprehensive
(c) Trends (d) Analysis

Ans. (d)

Scrutiny means critical observation or examination. Hence, its synonym is 'analysis'.

523. Select the most appropriate synonym of the word '**Capable**' from the given sentence.
Jayesh was competent and the best candidate for the post of clerk in the interview, whereas others were inefficient and irritating.
SSC CHSL Tier-1 02.08.2023 (Shift-IV)

(a) best (b) irritating
(c) competent (d) inefficient

Ans. (c)

Capable means having the ability, fitness, or quality necessary to do or achieve a specified thing. Hence, its synonym is 'competent'.

524. Caves like Ajanta lie in perpetual darkness. **SSC CHSL Tier-1 03.08.2023 (Shift-I)**

(a) Permanent (b) Extreme
(c) Brief (d) Huge

Ans. (a)

The word 'perpetual' means continuing forever in the same way. Hence, it synonym is 'permanent'.
Brief means in a short span of time.

525. The event, in a cramped space, was totally bizarre in my view.
SSC CHSL Tier-1 03.08.2023 (Shift-III)

(a) Usual (b) Customary
(c) Odd (d) Normal

Ans. (c)

Bizarre means very strange or unusual. Hence, its synonym is 'odd'.

Customary means according to the customs or usual practices associated with a particular society, place, or set of circumstances.

526. Tranquil
SSC CHSL Tier-1 03.08.2023 (Shift-III)

(a) Anxious (b) Dilemma
(c) Fierce (d) Peaceful

Ans. (d)

Tranquil means free from disturbance; calm. Hence, its synonym is 'peaceful'.
Anxious means experiencing worry, unease, or nervousness.

Dilemma means a situation in which a difficult choice has to be made between two or more alternatives.

527. He was the discreet boy in our group but more hardworking than all of us.
SSC CHSL Tier-1 03.08.2023 (Shift-IV)

(a) loud (b) outspoken
(c) reserved (d) noisy

Ans. (c)

Discreet means careful and prudent in one's speech or actions. Hence, its synonym is 'reserved'.

Outspoken means frank in stating one's opinions.

528. The factory has been .... (**exhaling**) black smoke from its chimney.
SSC CHSL Tier-1 03.08.2023 (Shift-IV)

(a) emitting (b) preserving
(c) remitting (d) indicting

Ans. (a)

Exhaling means to breathe out.
'Emitting' means to produce and discharge something, especially gas or radiation. Hence, its synonym is 'emitting'.
Preserving means maintaining something in its original or existing state.
Remitting means canceling or refraining from exacting or inflicting a debt or punishment.
Indicting means formally accusing or charging someone with a serious crime.

529. Diminutive
SSC CHSL Tier-1 04.08.2023 (Shift-II)

(a) Miniature (b) Enormous
(c) Propaganda (d) Distinguish

Ans. (a)

Both **Diminutive** and 'Miniature' refer to something that is small in size.
Enormous means very big in size.
Propaganda means misleading information that promotes one point of view.
Distinguish means to differentiate.

530. The teacher was accused of brazen favouritism in assigning the grades.
SSC CHSL Tier-1 04.08.2023 (Shift-II)

(a) Modest (b) Shy
(c) Unashamed (d) Ashamed

Ans. (c)

The word 'Brazen' means 'Unashamed'.

531. The ruins of this building do tell us the story of a defunct organisation.
SSC CHSL Tier-1 04.08.2023 (Shift-II)

(a) obsolete (b) ancient
(c) contemporary (d) prominent

Ans. (a)

The words 'defunct' and 'obsolete' refer to something that is no longer in use.
Ancient means old.
Contemporary means belonging to the same time period.
Prominent means popular.

532. Camouflage
SSC CHSL Tier-1 04.08.2023 (Shift-II)
SSC Steno 17.11.2022 (Shift-I)

(a) Sabotage (b) Execute
(c) Gigantic (d) Disguise

Ans. (d)

The word **Camouflage** means 'Disguise'.
Sabotage means to destroy.
Execute means to carry out.
Gigantic means huge.

533. We cannot achieve success until these antiquated policies are not amended.
SSC CHSL Tier-1 04.08.2023 (Shift-IV)

(a) Outdated (b) Current
(c) New (d) Updated

Ans. (a)

Antiquated means old-fashioned or outdated. Hence, its synonym is 'outdated'.

534. The doctors say that majority of the people who attended the fest are ill due to eating of adulterated food.
SSC CHSL Tier-1 04.08.2023 (Shift-IV)

(a) Spicy (b) Lascivious
(c) Contaminated (d) Damp

Ans. (c)

Adulterated means having been made impure by adding inferior or unsuitable substances. Hence, its synonym is 'contaminated'.

Spicy means flavored with or fragrant with spice.

Lascivious means feeling or revealing an overt sexual interest or desire.
Damp means slightly wet.

535. Worn **SSC CHSL Tier-1 04.08.2023 (Shift-IV)**

(a) Dilemma (b) Energetic
(c) Dilapidated (d) Diminutive

Ans. (c)

Worn means damaged and shabby as a result of much use. Hence, its synonym is 'dilapidated'.

Dilemma means a situation in which a difficult choice has to be made.

Energetic means showing or involving great activity or vitality.

Diminutive means extremely or unusually small.

536. Select the synonym of word 'Magical' from the given sentence.

SSC CHSL Tier-1 04.08.2023 (Shift-IV)

The stories of The Arabian Nights are enchanting, interesting, vivacious and natural.

(a) enchanting (b) interesting
(c) natural (d) vivacious

Ans. (a)

Magical means enchanting or having the qualities of magic. Hence, its synonym is 'enchanting'.

537. The deteriorated building was declared unsafe for the inmates.

SSC CHSL Tier-1 07.08.2023 (Shift-IV)

(a) dilapidated (b) dissipated
(c) meliorated (d) reprobated

Ans. (a)

Deteriorated means to become progressively worse. Hence, its synonym is 'dilapidated'.

Meliorated means to make something bad or unsatisfactory better.

Reprobated means disapproved of or condemned.

538. Requirement

SSC CHSL Tier-1 07.08.2023 (Shift-I)

(a) Essential (b) Serious
(c) Vague (d) Importance

Ans. (a)

Requirement means a thing that is needed or wanted. Hence, its synonym is 'essential'.

539. Deterioration

SSC CHSL Tier-1 07.08.2023 (Shift-I)

(a) Retrogression (b) Demonstration
(c) Malfunction (d) Ramification

Ans. (a)

Deterioration means the process of becoming progressively worse. Hence, its synonym is 'retrogression'.

Demonstration means the action or process of showing the existence or truth of something.

Malfunction means to fail to function normally.

Ramification means a consequence of an action or event, especially when complex or unwelcome.

540. Objection SSC CHSL Tier-1 07.08.2023 (Shift-I)

(a) Moan (b) Disapproval
(c) Counter (d) Sanction

Ans. (b)

Objection means an expression or feeling of disapproval or opposition. Hence, its synonym is 'disapproval'.

Moan means to make a long, low sound expressing physical or mental suffering.

Counter means to speak or act in opposition to.

Sanction means to give official permission or approval for an action.

541. Sometimes, she passes sarcastic remarks on everyone.

SSC CHSL Tier-1 07.08.2023 (Shift-III)

(a) Quite (b) Hostile
(c) Complimentary (d) Exceptional

Ans. (b)

Sarcastic means marked by or given to using irony in order to mock or convey contempt. Hence, its synonym is 'hostile'.

Complimentary means expressing a compliment; praising or approving.

542. Despite having a lot of work to do, he spent the whole day engaging in frivolous activities like playing video games and watching TV.

SSC CHSL Tier-1 07.08.2023 (Shift-III)

(a) Worthless
(b) Detestable
(c) Secretive
(d) Mischievous

Ans. (a)

Frivolous means not having any serious purpose or value. Hence, its synonym is 'worthless'.

Detestable means deserving intense dislike.

Secretive means inclined to conceal feelings and intentions or not to disclose information.

Mischievous means causing or showing a fondness for causing trouble in a playful way.

543. Comprehend

SSC CHSL Tier-1 07.08.2023 (Shift-IV)

(a) Distort (b) Deter
(c) Assimilate (d) Complex

Ans. (c)

The word **Comprehend** means to understand something completely.

Hence, its synonym is 'Assimilate', which means to learn and understand something.

Distort means to damage.

Deter means to discourage.

544. Bewitching

SSC CHSL Tier-1 07.08.2023 (Shift-IV)

(a) Painful (b) Alluring
(c) Rude (d) Repulsive

Ans. (b)

The word 'Bewitching' means to attract and interest somebody very much.

Hence, its synonym is 'Alluring' which means attractive and exciting.

Repulsive means disgusting.

545. I ....(itemise) the work that will have to be done.

SSC CHSL Tier-1 08.08.2023 (Shift-I)

(a) impart (b) enumerate
(c) conceal (d) assess

Ans. (b)

Itemise means to list one by one. Hence, its synonym is 'enumerate'.

Impart means to make information known.

Conceal means to keep from sight.

Assess means to evaluate or estimate the nature, ability or quality of.

546. Assuagement

SSC CHSL Tier-1 08.08.2023 (Shift-I)

(a) Consignment (b) Stratification
(c) Ruthlessness (d) Mollification

Ans. (d)

Assuagement means the action of making an unpleasant feeling less intense. Hence, its synonym is 'mollification'.

Consignment means a batch of goods destined for or delivered to someone.

Stratification means the arrangement or classification of something into different groups.

Ruthlessness means a lack of compassion or pity.

547. Access to safe water, sanitation and hygiene is a human right-fundamental to everyone's health, dignity and prosperity.

SSC CHSL Tier-1 08.08.2023 (Shift-I)

(a) enthusiasm (b) immorality
(c) grace (d) wealth

Ans. (c)

Dignity means the state or quality of being worthy of honour or respect. Hence, its synonym is 'grace'.

Immorality means the state or quality of being immoral.

548. Colleague

SSC CHSL Tier-1 08.08.2023 (Shift-II)

(a) Co-worker (b) Consult
(c) Distend (d) Exempt

Ans. (a)

The word **Co-worker** is the most appropriate synonym of the word 'Colleague'.

Consult means to get advise.

Distent means to swell.

Exempt means free from obligation.

549. The decision of the committee may mitigate the growth of the organisation.
SSC CHSL Tier-1 08.08.2023 (Shift-III)

(a) Show (b) Accelerate
(c) Divert (d) Lessen

Ans. (d)

Mitigate means to make less severe, serious or painful. Hence, its synonym is 'lessen'.

Accelerate means to begin to move more quickly.

Divert means to cause someone or something to change course or turn from one direction to another.

550. The children did not like the abominable table manners of old aunt. SSC CHSL Tier-1 08.08.2023 (Shift-IV)

(a) Delectable (b) Stringent
(c) Obnoxious (d) Inflexible

Ans. (c)

Abominable means causing moral revulsion. Hence, its synonym is 'obnoxious'.

Stringent means strict, precise and exacting.

Inflexible means unwilling to change or compromise.

551. Makeshift
SSC CHSL Tier-1 09.08.2023 (Shift-I)

(a) Resourceful
(b) Provisional
(c) Perpetual
(d) Inconsiderate

Ans. (b)

The word 'makeshift' means temporary and of low quality but used because of a sudden need.

Hence, its synonym is 'Provisional' as it means for the present time but likely to change; temporary.

Perpetual means always continuting.

552. Select the synonym of 'Ambitious' from the given sentence.
He aspires to be a future diplomat but he will have to improve his decision-making skills.
SSC CHSL Tier-1 09.08.2023 (Shift-I)

(a) Aspires (b) Improve
(c) Decision (d) Skill

Ans. (a)

The word 'Ambitious' means to want or 'aspire' something very much or hope to achieve something or to be successful.

553. The fall of Ranjith for the petty material benefit was really ignominious.
SSC CHSL Tier-1 09.08.2023 (Shift-I)

(a) Unfaltering
(b) Amusing
(c) Reprehensible
(d) Ignorable

Ans. (c)

The word **Ignominious** means (especially of events or behaviour) embarrassing because of being a complete failure. Hence, its synonym is 'reprehensible' as it means (of summaries behaviour) extremely bad or unacceptable.

Unfaltering means steady and fixed.

Amusing means funny.

Ignorable means can be ignored.

554. The transient rains harm have cause to the crops in the North.
SSC CHSL Tier-1 09.08.2023 (Shift-III)

(a) Perpetual (b) Long
(c) Fleeting (d) Stable

Ans. (c)

Transient means lasting only for a short time. Hence, its synonym is 'fleeting'.

Perpetual means never ending or changing.

Long means measuring a great distance from end to end.

Stable means not likely to change or fail; firmly established.

555. Prolific SSC CHSL Tier-1 09.08.2023 (Shift-III)

(a) Productive (b) Lazy
(c) Unproductive (d) Unsuccessful

Ans. (a)

Prolific means producing much fruit or foliage or many offspring. Hence, its synonym is 'productive'.

556. His conceit prevented him from accepting any criticism, even if it was to be constructive.
SSC CHSL Tier-1 09.08.2023 (Shift-III)

(a) prejudice (b) modesty
(c) cowardice (d) egotism

Ans. (d)

Conceit means excessive pride in oneself. Hence, its synonym is 'egotism'.

Prejudice means preconceived opinion that is not based on reason or actual experience.

Modesty means the quality or state of being unassuming or moderate in the estimation of one's abilities.

Cowardice means lack of bravery.

557. Education gives people the ledge and skills they need to stay healthy get jobs and foster tolerance.
SSC CHSL Tier-1 09.08.2023 (Shift-IV)

(a) entrench
(b) distrust
(c) lethargy
(d) endurance

Ans. (d)

Foster means encourage or promote the development of something. Hence, its synonym is 'endurance'.

Entrench means to establish an attitude, habit, or belief so firmly that change is very difficult or unlikely.

Distrust means the feeling that someone or something cannot be relied on.

558. Precise SSC CHSL Tier-1 10.08.2023 (Shift-I)

(a) Vague (b) General
(c) Accurate (d) Ambiguous

Ans. (c)

Precise means marked by exactness and accuracy of expression or detail. Hence, its synonym is 'accurate'.

General means affecting or concerning all or most people, places, or things.

Ambiguous means open to more than one interpretation; not having one obvious meaning.

559. I am in a difficult predicament as I have two offers at a time.
SSC CHSL Tier-1 10.08.2023 (Shift-I)

(a) Dilemma (b) Success
(c) Offer (d) Advantage

Ans. (a)

Predicament means a difficult, unpleasant or embarrassing situation. Hence, its synonym is 'dilemma'.

Success means the accomplishment of an aim or purpose.

560. Demand for water is also rapidly rising due to population growth, urbantsation and increasing pressures from the agriculture and energy sector.
SSC CHSL Tier-1 10.08.2023 (Shift-I)

(a) promptly
(b) luxuriously
(c) leisurely
(d) hopefully

Ans. (a)

Rapidly means very quickly; at a great rate. Hence, its synonym is 'promptly'.

Luxuriously means in a comfortable and elegant way.

Leisurely means acting or done at leisure; unhurried or relaxed.

Hopefully means in a hopeful manner.

561. The Sustainable Development Goals are a call for action by all countries-poor, rich and middle-income-to promote prosperity while protecting the planet. SSC CHSL Tier-1 10.08.2023 (Shift-I)

(a) Conceal (b) Holistic
(c) Growl (d) Boost

Ans. (b)

Promote means support or actively encourage. Hence, its synonym is 'holistic'.

Conceal means to keep from sight; hide.

Growl means make a low guttural sound in the throat.

Boost means to increase or improve something.

562. Survey SSC CHSL Tier-1 10.08.2023 (Shift-II)

(a) Disregard (b) Slothful
(c) Scrutinise (d) Apathy

Ans. (c)

Survey means a general view, examination, or description of someone or something. Hence, its synonym is 'scrutinise'.

Disregard means to pay no attention to; ignore.

Slothful means lazy.

563. Select the most appropriate synonym of the word 'Flung' from the given sentence.
The entrepreneur's innovative strategies propelled his startup to success. SSC CHSL Tier-1 10.08.2023 (Shift-I)

(a) Strategies (b) Innovative
(c) Success (d) Propelled

Ans. (d)

Propelled means drive, push or cause to move in a particular direction. Hence, its synonym is 'flung'.

Strategies means plans of action designed to achieve a long-term or overall aim.

Innovative means introducing new ideas; original and creative in thinking.

564. Despite the professor's best efforts to explain the complex theory, it took me a while to decipher the meaning of the text.
SSC CHSL Tier-1 10.08.2023 (Shift-III)
SSC CHSL Tier-1 30.05.2022 (Shift-I)

(a) interpret (b) predict
(c) conceal (d) foresee

Ans. (a)

The word **Decipher** means to find the meaning of something that is difficult to understand. Hence, its synonym is 'Interpret'.

Conceal means to hide.
Foresee and **Predict** means to say something about the future.

565. Happiness is not something you .... (adjourn) for the future. It is something you design for the present.
SSC CHSL Tier-1 10.08.2023 (Shift-III)
SSC CHSL Tier-1 17.08.2023 (Shift-I)

(a) decimate (b) rejuvenate
(c) constitute (d) postpone

Ans. (d)

The word **Adjourn** means to stop a meeting, a trial, etc., for a short time and start it again later or postpone.
Constitute means to form.
Decimate means to destroy.
Rejuvenate means to gain energy or be fresh.

566. The COVID-19 outbreak has caused a global education crisis.
SSC CHSL Tier-1 10.08.2023 (Shift-III)

(a) legacy (b) catastrophe
(c) inhibition (d) hoard

Ans. (b)

The words **Crisis** and **catastrophe** means a terrible event in which there is a lot of destruction, suffering or death.
Legacy means heritage.
Inhibition means shyness.
Hoard means to collect.

567. Hesitate SSC CHSL Tier-1 10.08.2023 (Shift-III)

(a) Haste (b) Stumble
(c) Dither (d) Hassle

Ans. (c)

The words **Hesitate** and **dither** both means to keep being unable to make a final decision about something.
Haste mens fasts.
Stumble means to lose balance.
Hassle means problem.

568. Unique SSC CHSL Tier-1 10.08.2023 (Shift-III)

(a) General (b) Ordinary
(c) Exclusive (d) Usual

Ans. (c)

The word 'unique' means being the only one of its kind; unlike anything else. Hence, its synonym is 'exclusive'.

569. The chubby player was clearly told to bring his corpulent body into a good shape. SSC CHSL Tier-1 11.08.2023 (Shift-I)

(a) rotund (b) lanky
(c) deformed (d) plush

Ans. (a)

The underlined word **corpulent** refers to something or someone excessively large. Hence, its synonym is 'rotund' which refers to 'large and plump'.
Lanky means thin and tall.
Deformed means lacking proper shape.
Plush means rich and luxurious.

570. The old castle, with its towering walls, creaky gates and secret passages, was the perfect example of a medieval fortress.
SSC CHSL Tier-1 11.08.2023 (Shift-I)

(a) Epicentre (b) Crux
(c) Epitome (d) Antithesis

Ans. (c)

The world 'epitome' means a perfect example.

Epicentre means the point of seismic activity or earthquake.

Crux means main idea.

Antithesis means opposite.

571. She became frantic as she lost her purse on the busy streets of the markets. SSC CHSL Tier-1 11.08.2023 (Shift-IV)

(a) Hectic (b) Composed
(c) Audacious (d) Agitated

Ans. (d)

Frantic means wild or distraught with fear, anxiety or other emotion. Hence, its synonym is 'agitated'.

Hectic means full of incessant or frantic activity.

Composed means having one's feelings and expression under control; calm.

Audacious means showing a willingness to take surprisingly bold risks.

572. Fervour SSC CHSL Tier-1 11.08.2023 (Shift-IV)

(a) Apathy (b) Hatred
(c) Enthusiasm (d) Disgust

Ans. (c)

Fervour means intense and passionate feeling. Hence, its synonym is 'enthusiasm'.

573. Paragon SSC CHSL Tier-1 14.08.2023 (Shift-I)

(a) Transient (b) Epitome
(c) Associate (d) Grumpy

Ans. (b)

Paragon means a person or thing regarded as a perfect example of a particular quality. Hence, its synonym is 'epitome'.

Associate means to connect with something else in one's mind.

Grumpy means bad-tempered and irritable.

574. He lost the golden opportunity due to his habit of procrastination.
SSC CHSL Tier-1 14.08.2023 (Shift-I)

(a) indecisiveness (b) impulsiveness
(c) inquisitiveness (d) submissiveness

Ans. (a)

Procrastination means the action of delaying or postponing something. Hence, its synonym is 'indecisiveness'.

Impulsiveness means acting without thought or consideration.

Inquisitiveness means curiosity.

Submissiveness means the willingness to obey others unquestioningly.

575. The text ...... (implies) to several themes that need closer examination.
SSC CHSL Tier-1 14.08.2023 (Shift-I)
(a) alludes
(b) deceives
(c) embellishes
(d) apprehends

Ans. (a)

Imply means to strongly suggest the truth or existence of something not expressly stated. Hence, its synonym is 'alludes'.

Deceives means to mislead by a false appearance or statement.

Embellishes means to make something more attractive by adding decorative details.

Apprehends means to arrest someone for a crime.

576. Select the most appropriate synonym of '**potential**' in the given sentence.
I have seen Radhya growing in the last few years; she now has the capability to fight worse situations.
SSC CHSL Tier-1 14.08.2023 (Shift-II)
(a) Worse (b) Situations
(c) Growing (d) Capability

Ans. (d)

Potential means having or showing the capacity to develop into something in the future. Hence, its synonym is 'capability'.

577. Strength **SSC CHSL Tier-1 14.08.2023 (Shift-II)**
(a) Recluse (b) Weakness
(c) Power (d) Disability

Ans. (c)

Strength means the quality or state of being physically strong. Hence, its synonym is 'power'.

Recluse means a person who lives a solitary life and tends to avoid other people.

578. Feasibility
SSC CHSL Tier-1 14.08.2023 (Shift-II)
(a) Sustainability (b) Impropriety
(c) Heavy (d) Probability

Ans. (d)

Feasibility means the state or degree of being easily or conveniently done. Hence, its synonym is 'probability'.

Sustainability means the ability to be maintained at a certain rate or level.

Impropriety means failure to observe standards of honesty or modesty.

579. Elaborate
SSC CHSL Tier-1 14.08.2023 (Shift-II)
(a) Easy (b) Complex
(c) Simple (d) Plain

Ans. (b)

Elaborate means involving many carefully arranged parts or details. Hence, its synonym is 'complex'.

580. The <u>incorrigible</u> optimism displayed by Aishwarya in difficult situations turned out her to be a favourite among her friends.
SSC CHSL Tier-1 14.08.2023 (Shift-II)
(a) translucent (b) illustrious
(c) unchanged (d) barefooted

Ans. (b)

Illustrious means well-known, respected and admired for past achievements. Hence, synonym 'of incorrigible' is 'illustrious'.

Translucent means allowing light to pass through but not detailed shapes.

Barefooted means without shoes.

581. Fraudulent
SSC CHSL Tier-1 14.08.2023 (Shift-III)
(a) Genuine (b) Counterfeit
(c) Unimaginative (d) Dissimilar

Ans. (b)

Fraudulent means obtained, done by, or involving deception, especially criminal deception. Hence, its synonym is 'counterfeit'.

582. Quell **SSC CHSL Tier-1 17.08.2023 (Shift-I)**
(a) Invite (b) Beseech
(c) Encourage (d) Suppress

Ans. (d)

Quell means to put an end to a rebellion or other disorder, typically by the use of force. Hence, its synonym is 'suppress'.

Encourage means to give support, confidence, or hope to someone.

583. Select the synonym of 'Damage' from the given sentence.
SSC CHSL Tier-1 17.08.2023 (Shift-I)
Every war in the history originates because of the greed of the rulers which was satisfied after mass destruction.
(a) Satisfied (b) Destruction
(c) Greed (d) Originates

Ans. (b)

Damage means physical harm that impairs the value, usefulness or normal function of something. In the context of the sentence, 'destruction' is a synonym for 'damage'.

584. Repercussion
SSC CHSL Tier-1 17.08.2023 (Shift-I)
(a) Duplication (b) Consequence
(c) Recusation (d) Apprehension

Ans. (b)

Repercussion means an unintended consequence occurring after an event or action. Hence, its synonym is 'consequence'.

Duplication means the action or process of duplicating something.

Recusation means the act of refusing.

Apprehension means anxiety or fear that something bad will happen.

585. Select the most appropriate synonym of the word 'Bleak' from the given sentence.
He looked gloomy, frail, broken and slow after the sudden demise of his brother. **SSC CHSL Tier-1 17.08.2023 (Shift-II)**
(a) slow (b) gloomy
(c) frail (d) sudden

Ans. (b)

Bleak means lacking in warmth, life or kindliness; gloomy. Hence, its synonym is 'gloomy'.

Frail means weak and delicate.

586. Select the most appropriate synonym of the word 'Ravishing' from the given sentence.
The architect designed a stunning skyscraper with a sophisticated structural system.
SSC CHSL Tier-1 17.08.2023 (Shift-III)
(a) Sophisticated
(b) Skyscraper
(c) Stunning
(d) System

Ans. (c)

Ravishing means delightful; entrancing. Hence, its synonym is 'stunning'.

Sophisticated means having or showing a lot of experience and knowledge.

Skyscraper means a very tall building.

System means a set of things working together as parts of a mechanism.

587. She <u>detests</u> capsicum so much that she would prefer going empty stomach**SSC CHSL Tier-1 17.08.2023 (Shift-III)**
(a) prompts (b) marvels
(c) rebels (d) loathes

Ans. (d)

Detests means to dislike intensely. Hence, its synonym is 'loathes'.

Prompts means to cause or bring about.

Marvels means to be filled with wonder or astonishment.

Rebels means to rise in opposition.

588. Timid **SSC CHSL Tier-1 17.08.2023 (Shift-III)**
(a) Magical (b) Honest
(c) Fearless (d) Nervous

Ans. (d)

Timid means showing a lack of courage or confidence; easily frightened. Hence, its synonym is 'nervous'.

589. Dynamic SSC CHSL Tier-1 17.08.2023 (Shift-IV)
(a) Famous (b) Halt
(c) Innate (d) Energetic

Ans. (d)

Dynamic means characterised by constant change, activity or progress. Hence, its synonym is 'energetic'.

Halt means to bring or come to an abrupt stop.

Innate means inborn; natural.

590. Humble SSC CHSL Tier-1 02.11.2023 (Shift-I)
(a) Beautiful (b) Keen
(c) Modest (d) Amusing

Ans. (c)

The work 'Humble' and 'Modest' both means kind.

591. Decadence SSC CHSL Tier-2 10.01.2023
(a) Decline (b) Liberate
(c) Dispirited (d) Flowering

Ans. (a)

The words 'decline' and 'decadence' refer to a fall or deterioration.

Liberate means to be free.

Dispirited means hopeless.

Flowering means producing flowers.

592. Serene SSC CHSL Tier-2 10.01.2023
(a) Chaotic (b) Calm
(c) Agitated (d) Angry

Ans. (b)

Serene means calm, peaceful and untroubled, so 'calm' is its synonym.

Chaotic means confused.

Agitated means angry and irritated.

SSC CHSL 2022 (Tier 1)

593. Amble SSC CHSL Tier-1 24.05.2022 (Shift-I)
(a) Bustle (b) Stare
(c) Wander (d) Trot

Ans. (c)

Amble means to walk or move at a slow, relaxed pace. Hence, its synonym is 'wander'.

Bustle means to move in an energetic or noisy manner.

Stare means to look fixedly or vacantly at someone or something.

Trot means to proceed or cause to proceed at a pace faster than a walk.

594. The university team won the match in the end with a .... (cunning) move. SSC CHSL Tier-1 24.05.2022 (Shift-II)
(a) brilliant (b) Stick
(c) random (d) quick

Ans. (a)

Cunning means having or showing skill in achieving one's ends by deceit or evasion. Hence, its synonym is 'brilliant'.

595. Loathe SSC CHSL Tier-1 25.05.2022 (Shift-I)
(a) Entrench (b) Abhor
(c) Abjure (d) Meddle

Ans. (b)

Loathe means to feel intense dislike or disgust for. Hence, its synonym is 'abhor'.

Entrench means to establish something very firmly so that it is very difficult to change.

Abjure means to solemnly renounce a belief, cause, or claim.

Meddle means to interfere in something that is not one's concern

596. The archer doesn't get <u>perturbed</u> easily. SSC CHSL Tier-1 25.05.2022 (Shift-I)
(a) Initiated (b) Agitated
(c) Animated (d) Triumphed

Ans. (b)

Perturbed means feeling anxiety or concern; unsettled. Hence, its synonym is 'agitated'.

Initiated means to cause something to begin.

Animated means full of life or excitement.

Triumphed means to achieve a victory; be successful.

597. Serendipity SSC CHSL Tier-1 25.05.2022 (Shift-I)
(a) Sibilance (b) Godsend
(c) Catastrophe (d) Surreptitious

Ans. (b)

Serendipity means the occurrence and development of events by chance in a happy or beneficial way. Hence, its synonym is 'godsend'.

Sibilance means a hissing sound.

Catastrophe means an event causing great and usually sudden damage or suffering; a disaster.

Surreptitious means kept secret, especially because it would not be approved of.

598. The tie <u>complements</u> the shirt he is wearing. SSC CHSL Tier-1 25.05.2022 (Shift-III)
(a) diserrays (b) Relegates
(c) Matches (d) Drains

Ans. (c)

Complements means to add to something in a way that enhances or improves it; make perfect. Hence, its synonym is 'matches'.

Disarrays means to throw into a state of disorganisation or untidiness.

Relegates means to consign or dismiss to an inferior rank or position.

Drains means to cause the water or other liquid in something to run out, leaving it empty, dry, or drier.

599. His <u>finicky</u> attitude was the main cause of the conflict. SSC CHSL Tier-1 25.05.2022 (Shift-III)
(a) Fussy (b) Indolent
(c) Hasty (d) Nervous

Ans. (a)

Finicky means fussy about one's needs or requirements. Hence, its synonym is 'fussy'.

Indolent means wanting to avoid activity or exertion; lazy.

Hasty means done with excessive speed or urgency; hurried.

Nervous means easily agitated or alarmed.

600. He is <u>inclined</u> to stay with the present organisation. SSC CHSL Tier-1 26.05.2022 (Shift-II)
(a) struggled
(b) mystified
(c) motivated
(d) declined

Ans. (c)

Inclined means leaning or turning away from the vertical or horizontal; sloping. Hence, its synonym is 'motivated'.

Struggled means make forceful or violent efforts to get free of restraint or constriction.

Mystified means utterly bewildered or perplexed. Declined means politely refuse an invitation or offer.

601. Sanguinity SSC CHSL Tier-1 26.05.2022 (Shift-III)
(a) Acrimony
(b) Despondence
(c) timism
(d) Distrust

Ans. (b)

Sanguinity means optimism or positive thinking, especially in an apparently bad or difficult situation. Hence, its synonym is 'despondence'.

Acrimony means bitterness or ill feeling.

Timism means a belief in time management.

Distrust means the feeling that someone or something cannot be relied on.

602. Disseminate SSC CHSL Tier-1 27.05.2022 (Shift-I)
(a) Implement (b) Merge
(c) Circulate (d) Facilitate

Ans. (c)

Disseminate means to spread or disperse widely. Hence, its synonym is 'circulate'.

Implement means to put a decision, plan, agreement, etc., into effect.

Merge means to combine or join together.

Facilitate means to make an action or process easier.

603. Police fear that terrorists may, to assassinate the president during appearance at the summit. SSC CHSL Tier-1 27.05.2022 (Shift-II)

(a) Distress (b) Murder
(c) Rebuke (d) Deceive

Ans. (b)

Assassinate means to murder an important or famous person, especially for political reasons. Hence, its synonym is 'murder'.

Distress means extreme anxiety, sorrow, or pain.

Rebuke means to express sharp disapproval or criticism.

Deceive means to cause someone to believe something that is not true.

604. The Western side of the country has some ...... (vacant) islands to explore. SSC CHSL Tier-1 27.05.2022 (Shift-I)

(a) unexplored (b) uninhabited
(c) undesired (d) uninterested

Ans. (b)

The word in brackets 'vacant' means uninhabitated or having no people having unit. Hence, 'uninhabitated' is the correct filler.

605. Ecstasy SSC CHSL Tier-1 27.05.2022 (Shift-I)

(a) Mourning (b) Bliss
(c) Fantacy (d) Appreciation

Ans. (b)

The word 'ecstasy' means a feeling of extreme happiness. Hence, its synonym is 'Bliss' which ' means complete happines.

Mourning means sadness or sorrow at someone's death.

606. Startle SSC CHSL Tier-1 30.05.2022 (Shift-I)

(a) Scare (b) Humiliate
(c) Surprise (d) Shame

Ans. (c)

The word 'startle' means to make someone suddenly surprised or slight shocked.

Humiliate means to insult.

607. Overture SSC CHSL Tier-1 30.05.2022 (Shift-I)

(a) Slander (b) Conclusion
(c) Preamble (d) Plunk

Ans. (c)

The word 'overture' refers to a short piece of music written as an introduction to a long piece of music, especially on opera. Hence, its synonym is 'Preamble' which means an introduction.

Slander means to publicly insult.

Conclusion means end.

Plunk means to hit abruptly.

608. Reconnoitre SSC CHSL Tier-1 30.05.2022 (Shift-II)

(a) Glance (b) Disclaim
(c) Inspect (d) Overlook

Ans. (c)

Reconnoitre means to make a military observation of a region. Hence, its synonym is 'inspect'.

Glance means to take a brief or hurried look.

Disclaim means to refuse to acknowledge.

Overlook means to fail to notice something.

609. Rescind SSC CHSL Tier-1 30.05.2022 (Shift-II)

(a) Revoke (b) Sign
(c) Validate (d) Accredit

Ans. (a)

Rescind means to revoke, cancel or repeal a law, order or agreement. Hence, its synonym is 'revoke'.

Sign means to write one's name on a document.

Validate means to check or prove the validity or accuracy of something.

Accredit means to give credit to someone for something.

610. Opulence SSC CHSL Tier-1 30.05.2022 (Shift-III)

(a) View (b) Sagacity
(c) Recognition (d) Prosperity

Ans. (d)

Opulence means great wealth or luxuriousness. Hence, its synonym is 'prosperity'.

Sagacity means having or showing keen mental discernment and good judgement.

611. The new software provides a perfect solution to the complex issues pertaining to pick up and delivery. SSC CHSL Tier-1 30.05.2022 (Shift-III)

(a) Promoting (b) Denying
(c) Trusting (d) Referring

Ans. (d)

Pertaining means relating to or concerning. Hence, its synonym is 'referring'.

Promoting means to advance or raise to a higher position.

Denying means to state that something is not true.

612. Incite SSC CHSL Tier-1 31.05.2022 (Shift-I)

(a) Pacify (b) Tighten
(c) Inflame (d) Quote

Ans. (c)

The word **incite** means to encourage people to be violent or commit crimes by making them angry or excited. Hence, its synonym is 'Inflame' which means to make a situation worse by making people more angry or excited.

613. Fleck SSC CHSL Tier-1 31.05.2022 (Shift-I)

(a) Spot (b) Neglect
(c) View (d) Fault

Ans. (a)

The word 'Fleck' means a small mark or spot.

614. Arraign SSC CHSL Tier-1 30.05.2022 (Shift-I)

(a) Arrive (b) Prosecute
(c) Persecute (d) Arrange

Ans. (b)

Arraign means to call or bring someone before a court to answer a criminal charge. Hence, its synonym is 'prosecute'.

Persecute means to subject someone to hostility and ill-treatment.

615. Rampart SSC CHSL Tier-1 01.06.2022 (Shift-I)

(a) Denigration (b) Fortitude
(c) Bulwark (d) Portal

Ans. (c)

The word **rampart** means a high hill of earth or a stone wall, built around a city or castle to protect it against an enemy. Hence, its synonym is 'Bulwark' as it means a wall that is built for defence.

Denigration means to criticise someone.

Fortitude means courage.

Portal means a gate.

616. Vanity SSC CHSL Tier-1 01.06.2022 (Shift-II)

(a) Beauty (b) Empty
(c) Humility (d) Conceit

Ans. (d)

Vanity means excessive pride in or admiration of one's own appearance or achievements. Hence, its synonym is 'conceit'.

Humility means a modest view of one's own importance.

617. Allay SSC CHSL Tier-1 01.06.2022 (Shift-III)

(a) Relieve (b) Release
(c) Arrange (d) Allure

Ans. (a)

Allay means to diminish or put at rest fear, suspicion or worry. Hence, its synonym is 'relieve'.

Allure means to attract or charm.

618. Quaint SSC CHSL Tier-1 01.06.2022 (Shift-III)

(a) Quite (b) Queer
(c) Quack (d) Quiet

Ans. (b)

Quaint means attractively unusual or old-fashioned. Hence, its synonym is 'queer'.

Quack means a person who dishonestly claims to have special knowledge and skill in some field, typically medicine.

619. The headless monster winked at er from eyes embedded in **pudgy** shoulders.

SSC CHSL Tier-1 01.06.2022 (Shift-III)

(a) narrow (b) stubborn
(c) thick-bodied (d) bright

Ans. (c)

Pudgy means slightly fat. Hence, its synonym is 'thick-bodied'.

620. Banter SSC CHSL Tier-1 02.06.2022 (Shift-I)

(a) Repartee (b) Rebuke
(c) Reliance (d) Commendation

Ans. (a)

The word 'banter' means friendly conversation in which people make a lot of jokes with and amusing remarks about each other. Hence, its synonym is **Repartee** which means conversation that is full of clever and funny comments.

Rebuke means to scold.

Reliance means to depend on someone

Commendation means to qraise someone.

621. Salubrious

SSC CHSL Tier-1 02.06.2022 (Shift-II)

(a) Beneficial (b) Vicarious
(c) Insidious (d) Septic

Ans. (a)

Salubrious means health-giving; healthy. Hence, its synonym is 'beneficial'.

Vicarious means experienced in the imagination through the feelings or actions of another person.

Septic means infected with bacteria.

622. The **litigant** wished that justice would prevail.

SSC CHSL Tier-1 02.06.2022 (Shift-III)

(a) detective (b) culprit
(c) abuser (d) petitioner

Ans. (d)

Litigant means a person involved in a lawsuit. Hence, its synonym is 'petitioner'.

Detective means a person, especially a police officer, whose occupation is to investigate and solve crimes.

Culprit means a person who is responsible for a crime or other misdeed.

Abuser means a person who treats another person or animal with cruelty or violence.

623. Boldness

SSC CHSL Tier-1 02.06.2022 (Shift-III)

(a) Eagerness
(b) Hard-heartedness
(c) Wisdom
(d) Bravery

Ans. (d)

Boldness means the willingness to take risks and act innovatively. Hence, its synonym is 'bravery'.

Hard-heartedness means a lack of feeling or compassion.

624. It will be **illogical** to accept the demands of the protesters this time.

SSC CHSL Tier-1 03.06.2022 (Shift-I)

(a) unfavourable (b) absurd
(c) biased (d) factual

Ans. (b)

Illogical means lacking sense or clear, sound reasoning. Hence, its synonym is 'absurd'.

Unfavourable means not good and likely to cause problems or make something more difficult.

Biased means unfairly prejudiced for or against someone or something.

Factual means concerned with what is actually the case.

625. His strategy is to <u>protract</u> negotiations until the enemy are exhausted while assembling the forces necessary to crush them.

SSC CHSL Tier-1 03.06.2022 (Shift-I)

(a) Control (b) Prolong
(c) Accept (d) Cease

Ans. (b)

Protract means to prolong. Hence, its synonym is 'prolong'.

Control means to direct, influence, or have power over.

Cease means to bring or come to an end.

626. The <u>divisive</u> policy of this nation has led to its downfall.

SSC CHSL Tier-1 03.06.2022 (Shift-II)

(a) Spurring (b) Dethroning
(c) Alienating (d) Encouraging

Ans. (c)

Divisive means tending to cause disagreement or hostility between people. Hence, its synonym is 'alienating'.

Spurring means giving an incentive or encouragement to someone.

Dethroning means removing a ruler from power.

Encouraging means giving support, confidence or hope to someone.

627. Stymie SSC CHSL Tier-1 03.06.2022 (Shift-III)

(a) Tame (b) Amaze
(c) Hinder (d) Scare

Ans. (c)

Stymie means to prevent or hinder the progress of. Hence, its synonym is 'hinder'.

Tame means domesticated and not dangerous.

Amaze means to surprise someone greatly.

Scare means to cause great fear or nervousness.

628. The black marketers are <u>hoarding</u> large quantities of groceries.

SSC CHSL Tier-1 06.06.2022 (Shift-I)

(a) Doling Out (b) Designing
(c) Training Up (d) Piling Up

Ans. (d)

Hoarding means to accumulate for preservation, future use, etc., in a hidden or carefully guarded place. Hence, its synonym is 'piling up'.

Doling Out means to distribute shares of something.

Designing means to create something with a detailed plan.

Training Up means to teach someone the skills they need.

629. Laconic SSC CHSL Tier-1 06.06.2022 (Shift-I)
SSC MTS 12.09.2023 (Shift-I)

(a) Exaggerated
(b) Lengthy
(c) Talkative
(d) Concise

Ans. (d)

Laconic means using very few words. Hence, its synonym is 'concise'.

Exaggerated means represented as greater than is true or reasonable.

Lengthy means having considerable length.

Talkative means fond of talking.

630. Resplendent

SSC CHSL Tier-1 06.06.2022 (Shift-I)

(a) Magnificent (b) Astonished
(c) Enthusiastic (d) Exuberant

Ans. (a)

Resplendent means attractive and impressive through being richly colourful or sumptuous. Hence, its synonym is 'magnificent'.

Astonished means greatly surprised.

Enthusiastic means having or showing intense and eager enjoyment.

Exuberant means filled with or characterised by a lively energy and excitement.

631. Excruciating
SSC CHSL Tier-1 06.06.2022 (Shift-II)
(a) Facile (b) Enticing
(c) Alluring (d) Piercing

Ans. (d)

Excruciating means intensely painful. Hence, its synonym is 'piercing'.

Facile means appearing neat and comprehensive only by ignoring the true complexities.

Enticing means attractive or tempting.

Alluring means powerfully and mysteriously attractive or fascinating.

632. In his youth,Joyonto must have been <u>starlingly</u> handsome.
SSC CHSL Tier-1 06.06.2022 (Shift-III)
(a) enviously (b) lightly
(c) wrinkly (d) amazingly

Ans. (d)

Starlingly means surprisingly impressive. Hence, its synonym is 'amazingly'.

Enviously means feeling or showing envy.

Lightly means in a way that is gentle or delicate.

Wrinkly means having many lines or folds.

633. Abrogate
SSC CHSL Tier-1 06.06.2022 (Shift-III)
(a) Endure (b) Reveal
(c) Extend (d) Repeal

Ans. (d)

Abrogate means to repeal or do away with. Hence, its synonym is 'repeal'.

Endure means to suffer something painful or difficult patiently.

Reveal means to make known.

Extend means to cause to cover a larger area.

634. Slender SSC CHSL Tier-1 07.06.2022 (Shift-I)
(a) Lively (d) Energetic
(c) Defame (d) Frail

Ans. (d)

Slender means gracefully thin. Hence, its synonym is 'frail'.

Lively and **energetic** mean full of life and energy.

Defame means to damage the good reputation of someone.

635. Chastise SSC CHSL Tier-1 07.06.2022 (Shift-I)
(a) Discipline (b) Order
(c) Sever ties (d) Chase

Ans. (a)

Chastise means to rebuke or reprimand severely. Hence, its synonym is 'discipline'.

636. Bestial SSC CHSL Tier-1 07.06.2022 (Shift-I)
(a) Brutish (b) Greedy
(c) High-minded (d) Noble

Ans. (a)

Bestial means of or like an animal. Hence, its synonym is 'brutish'.

High-minded means having strong moral principles.

Noble means having or showing fine personal qualities.

637. Quintessential
SSC CHSL Tier-1 07.06.2022 (Shift-III)
(a) Fantastic (b)Typical
(c) Initial (d) Charming

Ans. (b)

Quintessential means representing the most perfect or typical example of a quality or class. Hence, its synonym is 'typical'.

638. The patient complained of <u>giddiness</u> after surgery.
SSC CHSL Tier-1 07.06.2022 (Shift-III)
(a) opponent (b) unsteadiness
(c) enthusiasm (d) pride

Ans. (b)

Giddiness means a sensation of whirling and a tendency to fall or stagger. Hence, its synonym is 'unsteadiness'.

Opponent means someone who competes against or fights another.

Enthusiasm means intense and eager enjoyment.

Pride means a feeling of deep pleasure derived from achievements.

639. His <u>perverse</u> thoughts were very disturbing so he decided to try seeing a therapist.
SSC CHSL Tier-1 08.06.2022 (Shift-I)
(a) Convergent (b) Deviant
(c) Cynical (d) Logical

Ans. (b)

Perverse means showing a deliberate and obstinate desire to behave in a way that is unreasonable or unacceptable. Hence, its synonym is 'deviant'.

Convergent means tending to move toward one point.

Cynical means believing that people are motivated by self-interest.

Logical means of or according to the rules of logic.

640. If you're feeling brave, try this ...... (savoury) dish made by me.
SSC CHSL Tier-1 08.06.2022 (Shift-III)
(a) salty (b) stale
(c) stinky (d) stenchy

Ans. (a)

Savoury means salty or spicy rather than sweet. Hence, its synonym is 'salty'.

Stale means no longer fresh and pleasant to eat.

Stinky means having a strong or unpleasant smell.

Stenchy means having a foul odor.

641. Stupendous
SSC CHSL Tier-1 08.06.2022 (Shift-III)
(a) Stunning (b) Magnifying
(c) Shining (d) Amplifying

Ans. (a)

Stupendous means extremely impressive. Hence, its synonym is 'stunning'.

Magnifying means making something appear larger.

Shining means giving out or reflecting bright light.

Amplifying means increasing the volume of sound.

642. Exorcise SSC CHSL Tier-1 09.06.2022 (Shift-II)
(a) Invent (b) Expel
(c) Introduce (d) Expect

Ans. (b)

Exorcise means to drive out an evil spirit. Hence, its synonym is 'expel'.

Invent means to create or design something that has not existed before.

Introduce means to bring something into use for the first time.

Expect means to regard something as likely to happen.

643. Affront SSC CHSL Tier-1 10.06.2022 (Shift-I)
(a) Depress (b) Fail
(c) Insult (d) Tolerate

Ans. (c)

Affront means an action or remark that causes outrage or offense. Hence, its synonym is 'insult'.

644. Ravenous
SSC CHSL Tier-1 10.06.2022 (Shift-I)
(a) Commodiolis (b) Iniquitous
(c) Scrumptious (d) Esurient

Ans. (d)

Ravenous means extremely hungry. Hence, its synonym is 'esurient'.

Commodious means roomy and comfortable.

Iniquitous means grossly unfair and morally wrong.

Scrumptious means extremely appetising or delicious.

645. Eccentric SSC CHSL Tier-1 10.06.2022 (Shift-III)
(a) Queer (b) Excellent
(c) Common (d) Charming

Ans. (a)

Eccentric means unconventional and slightly strange. Hence, its synonym is 'queer'.

646. Ludicrous SSC CHSL Tier-1 10.06.2022 (Shift-III)
(a) Intuitive (b) Crazy
(c) Astute (d) Intrinsic

Ans. (b)

Ludicrous means so foolish, unreasonable or out of place as to be amusing. Hence, its synonym is 'crazy'.

Intuitive means using or based on what one feels to be true.

Astute means having or showing an ability to accurately assess situations.

Intrinsic means belonging naturally.

SSC CHSL 2021 (Tier 1 & 2)

647. Severity SSC CHSL Tier-1 19.04.2021 (Shift-III)
(a) Anguish (b) Pain
(c) Seriousness (d) Support

Ans. (c)

The word 'severity' means the condition of being very bad, serious or unpleasant.

Anguish means pain.

648. Emerge SSC CHSL Tier-1 19.04. 2021 (Shift-III)
(a) Mingle (b) Withhold
(c) Appear (d) Leave

Ans. (c)

The word 'emerge' means come out or appear.

Mingle means mix together.

Withhold means to refuse to give.

649. Priority SSC CHSL Tier-1 12.04.2021 (Shift-II)
(a) Inference
(b) Deference
(c) Subservience
(d) Preference

Ans. (d)

The words 'Priority' and 'Preference' both means favour shown to one person or thing over another or others.

Inference means conclusion drawn from evidence.

Deference means respect.

Subservience means willingness to obey others.

650. Precision SSC CHSL Tier-1 12.04.2021 (Shift-II)
(a) Accuracy (b) Vagueness
(c) Estimation (d) Neglect

Ans. (a)

The word 'precision' means exact and accurate.

Vaguense means lack of clarity.

Estimation refers to a rough calculation.

Neglect means showing lack of care.

651. Wry SSC CHSL Tier-1 04.08.2021 (Shift-I)
(a) Straight (b) Frank
(c) Forthright (d) Crooked

Ans.(d)

The word 'Wry' means twisted into an expression of disgust, disappointment. Hence, its synonym is 'Crooked' which means twisted out of shape or out of place; illegal.

Frank means honest and true.

Forthright means direct.

652. Malignant SSC CHSL Tier-1 04.08.2021 (Shift-I)
(a) Vicious (b) Beneficial
(c) Loving (d) Healthy

Ans. (a)

The word 'Malignant' means evil in nature or effect; disposed to cause harm. Hence, its synonym is 'Vicious' which means deliberately cruel or violent.

653. Profuse SSC CHSL Tier-1 10.08.2021 (Shift-I)
(a) Meagre (b) Abundant
(c) Limited (d) Consistent

Ans. (b)

The word 'profuse' means very plentiful or abundant.

Limited means little.

Consistent means stable and continuous.

654. Ban SSC CHSL Tier-1 12.08.2021 (Shift-III)
(a) Ascertain (b) Prohibit
(c) Abandon (d) Band

Ans. (b)

The word 'ban' means officially or legally prohibit (something).

Ascertain means to make sure of.

655. Repulsive
SSC CHSL Tier-1 12.08.2021 (Shift-III)
SSC MTS 01.09.2023 (Shift-I)
(a) Respectable (b) Disgusting
(c) Attractive (d) Agreeable

Ans. (b)

The word 'repulsive' means arousing intense distaste or disgust.

SSC MTS 2024 (Tier 1)

656. Hamper SSC MTS Tier-1 13.11.2024 (Shift-III)
(a) Hinder (b) Gift
(c) Pamper (d) Irritate

Ans. (a)

'Hinder' is the most appropriate synonym of 'hamper'. 'Hamper' means to obstruct or impede.

657. Hire SSC MTS Tier-1 12.11.2024 (Shift-III)
(a) Endure (b) Engage
(c) Enhance (d) Engross

Ans. (b)

'Engage' is the most appropriate synonym of 'hire'. 'Hire' means to employ someone.

Endure means to suffer patiently.

Enhance means to improve.

Engross means to absorb all attention.

658. I did not like his <u>bossy</u> attitude.
SSC MTS Tier-1 11.11.2024 (Shift-III)
(a) benevolent
(b) idiosyncratic
(c) controlling
(d) sensible

Ans. (c)

'Controlling' is the most appropriate synonym of 'bossy.' 'Bossy' means fond of giving people orders.

Benevolent means well-meaning and kindly.

Idiosyncratic means peculiar or individual.

Sensible means practical and realistic.

659. <u>Disclaimer</u> on products in the markets saves manufacturer from unusual results on usage.
SSC MTS Tier-1 05.11.2024 (Shift-III)
(a) Guarantee (b) Approval
(c) Clause (d) Acceptance

Ans. (c)

'Clause' is the most appropriate meaning of 'disclaimer'. It is a statement that denies responsibility.

Guarantee means a formal assurance.

660. The doctor made a <u>tentative</u> diagnosis as he did not have the reports of her blood tests.
SSC MTS Tier-1 05.11.2024 (Shift-III)
(a) provisional (b) tedious
(c) hazardous (d) obsolete

Ans. (a)

'Provisional' is the word that has the same meaning as 'tentative.' It means not certain or fixed.

Tedious means too long, slow or dull.

Hazardous means dangerous.

Obsolete means no longer in use.

661. Gloomy SSC MTS Tier-1 04.11.2024 (Shift-III)
(a) Sticky (b) Vain
(c) Dismal (d) Buoyant

Ans. (c)

'Dismal' is the most appropriate synonym of 'gloomy'. 'Gloomy' means feeling down or sad.

Vain means having an excessively high opinion of one's appearance.

Buoyant means cheerful and optimistic.

662. Fabricate SSC MTS Tier-1 30.10.2024 (Shift-III)
(a) Construct (b) Garments
(c) Fascinate (d) Floral

Ans. (a)

'Construct' is the most appropriate synonym of 'Fabricate'. 'It means to make or build something.

Garments means items of clothing.

Fascinate means to attract or hold attention.

Floral means related to flowers.

663. Gregarious
SSC MTS Tier-1 30.10.2024 (Shift-III)
(a) Sociable
(b) Isolated
(c) Introverted
(d) Reserved

Ans. (a)

'Sociable' is the most appropriate synonym of 'Gregarious'. It means enjoying the company of others similar to sociable.

664. The town, where Haruki lived, stood in <u>imminent</u> danger of tidal waves.
SSC MTS Tier-1 29.10.2024 (Shift-III)
(a) eminent (b) immaculate
(c) impending (d) prominent

Ans. (c)

'Impending' has the same meaning as 'imminent'. Both words refer to something about to happen.

Eminent means famous and respected within a particular sphere.

Immaculate means perfectly clean.

Prominent means important or famous.

665. The vital role played by women at home and in the struggle for freedom, advanced the case for female <u>emancipation</u> soon after the war was over.
SSC MTS Tier-1 28.10.2024 (Shift-II)
(a) utility (b) objectivity
(c) freedom (d) bondage

Ans. (c)

'Freedom' has the same meaning (synonym) as 'emancipation'.

666. Urban people have a <u>bombastic</u> lifestyle, which is very different from those of rural folks.
SSC MTS Tier-1 22.10.2024 (Shift-II)
(a) common (b) delusive
(c) hollow (d) pretentious

Ans. (d)

'Pretentious' is the most appropriate meaning of 'bombastic'. 'Bombastic' means high-sounding but with little meaning; inflated.

Delusive means giving a false or misleading impression.

667. Shylock, the Jewish moneylender, and Antonio, the rich Merchant of Venice <u>loathed</u> each other.
SSC MTS Tier-1 21.10.2024 (Shift-II)
(a) lathered
(b) admired
(c) abhorred
(d) latte

Ans. (c)

'Abhorred' is the word that has the same meaning as 'loathed.' 'Loathed' means to feel intense dislike or disgust for.

Lathered means to form a frothy white mass of bubbles.

Admired means to regard with respect or warm approval.

Latte means a type of coffee drink.

668. The teacher made <u>judicious</u> use of technology to explain a sensitive topic. SSC MTS Tier-1 18.10.2024 (Shift-II)
(a) judgemental (b) difficult
(c) prominent (d) prudent

Ans. (d)

'Prudent' is the synonym of 'judicious.' 'Judicious' means having, showing or done with good judgement or sense.

669. Her <u>austere</u> lifestyle reflected her minimalist approach to living.
SSC MTS Tier-1 15.10.2024 (Shift-I)
(a) Sombre (b) Luxurious
(c) Giddy (d) Happy

Ans. (a)

'Sombre' is the most appropriate synonym of 'austere.' It means serious, grave or plain.

670. Corroborate
SSC MTS Tier-1 14.10.2024 (Shift-I)
(a) Suggest (b) Support
(c) Contend (d) Elaborate

Ans. (b)

'Support' is the most appropriate synonym of 'corroborate.' It means to confirm or give support to.

671. Select the most appropriate synonym of the word 'Plain' from the given sentence. Mr. Das believes and follows the principle of simple living and high thinking.
SSC MTS Tier-1 09.10.2024 (Shift-I)
(a) Simple (b) principle
(c) believes (d) High

Ans. (a)

'Simple' is the most appropriate synonym of 'Plain'. It means not elaborate or complicated.

672. The future looks **bleak** for the fishing industry.
SSC MTS Tier-1 08.10.2024 (Shift-II)
(a) Fearless (b) Expensive
(c) Ample (d) Depressing

Ans. (d)

'Depressing' is the most appropriate synonym for 'bleak.' It means causing a feeling of sadness or hopelessness.

Ample means more than enough.

673. The rivals in the institution .... (fabricated) evidence and manipulated the whole dataset.
SSC MTS Tier-1 07.10.2024 (Shift-I)
(a) forged (b) fluctuated
(c) destroyed (d) wrecked

Ans. (a)

'Forged' means fabricated or created falsely, fitting the context of tampering with evidence. The other options are incorrect because they don't match the context of falsifying evidence.

Fluctuated means to change irregularly.

Wrecked means to damage severely.

674. Select the most appropriate synonym of the word 'Scanty' from the given sentence.
India has varied regions which have excess, moderate and deficient rainfall all through the year.
SSC MTS Tier-1 01.10.2024 (Shift-I)
(a) Varied (b) Excess
(c) Moderate (d) Deficient

Ans. (d)

'Deficient' is the most appropriate synonym for 'scanty'. Both words describe something that is lacking or insufficient in quantity.

Varied means diverse.

Excess means too much.

Moderate means average or reasonable.

675. The disposal of <u>hazardous</u> waste in hospitals and factories is a serious problem and needs to be taken care of urgently. SSC MTS 01.10.2024 (Shift-I)
(a) hazy (b) benign
(c) belligerent (d) dangerous

Ans. (d)

'Dangerous' is the synonym for 'hazardous'. Both words mean something that poses a risk or is likely to cause harm.

Hazy means unclear.

Benign means harmless.

Belligerent means aggressive.

676. Inspire **SSC MTS Tier-1 01.10.2024 (Shift-I)**

(a) Stimulate (b) Reach
(c) Daunt (d) Aspire

Ans. (a)

'Stimulate' is the most appropriate synonym for 'inspire'. Both words means to encourage or motivate someone to take action or feel in a particular way.

Daunt means to discourage.

Aspire means to have a strong desire.

677. Energy **SSC MTS Tier-1 30.09.2024 (Shift-I)**

(a) Frailty (b) Power
(c) Speed (d) Strife

Ans. (b)

'Energy' refers to the capacity for vigorous activity or the ability to do work, which is closely related to 'power.' The other options (frailty, speed, strife) do not have the same meaning as 'energy.'

678. The project's tight deadline and complex requirements made it a gruelling task for the team.
SSC MTS Tier-1 30.09.2024 (Shift-I)

(a) accessible (b) challenging
(c) inclusive (d) empowering

Ans. (b)

'Challenging' is the most appropriate synonym for 'gruelling'. Both words indicate something that is extremely difficult and demanding.

Accessible means easy to approach.

Inclusive means comprehensive.

Empowering means giving power.

679. The detective's job was to discern the truth from the web of lies.
SSC MTS Tier-1 30.09.2024 (Shift-I)

(a) Confuse (b) Ignore
(c) Perceive (d) Fabricate

Ans. (c)

'Perceive' is the most appropriate synonym for 'discern.' Both words mean to recognise or understand something, especially after thinking about it carefully.

Fabricate means to invent falsely.

680. Ecstatic **SSC MTS Tier-1 30.09.2024 (Shift-I)**

(a) Happy (b) Angry
(c) Interested (d) Shocked

Ans. (a)

'Happy' is the most appropriate synonym for 'Ecstatic.' Both words indicate a state of great joy or excitement.

681. Select the most appropriate synonym of the word 'pursue' from the given sentence.
Dr. Kalam's success in the field of science has inspired young Indians to dream big and chase those dreams with immense hard work.
SSC MTS Tier-1 30.09.2024 (Shift-I)

(a) success (b) inspired
(c) chase (d) immense

Ans. (c)

'Chase' is the synonym for 'pursue.' Both words mean to go after or strive to achieve something. Success means achieving a goal. Inspired means to motivate. Immense means very large or great.

SSC MTS 2023

682. In the 20th century, many (radical) intellectuals embraced the mass media. **SSC MTS 02.05.2023 (Shift-I)**

(a) Sabbatical
(b) Egotistical
(c) Sceptical
(d) Fanatical

Ans. (d)

Radical means relating to or affecting the fundamental nature of something; far-reaching or thorough. Hence, its synonym is 'fanatical'.

Sabbatical means a period of paid leave granted to a university teacher or other worker for study or travel.

Egotistical means excessively conceited or absorbed in oneself.

Sceptical means not easily convinced; having doubts or reservations.

683. They wanted me to (expound) on this topic because I had some decent ideas on the subject.
SSC MTS 02.05.2023 (Shift-II)

(a) Paucity (b) Notoriety
(c) Partisan (d) Expatiate

Ans. (d)

Expound means to present and explain a theory or idea in detail. Hence, its synonym is 'expatiate'.

Paucity means the presence of something in only small or insufficient quantities.

Notoriety means the state of being famous or well known for some bad quality or deed.

Partisan means a strong supporter of a party, cause or person.

684. Ulterior **SSC MTS 02.05.2023 (Shift-III)**

(a) Anterior (b) Prior
(c) Ancient (d) Eventual

Ans. (d)

Ulterior means existing beyond what is obvious or admitted; intentionally hidden. Hence, its synonym is 'eventual'.

Anterior means near the front.

Prior means existing or coming before in time.

Ancient means belonging to the very distant past.

685. Valiance **SSC MTS 03.05.2023 (Shift-II)**

(a) Gallantry
(b) Cravenness
(c) Dastardliness
(d) Patience

Ans. (a)

Valiance means bravery or courage. Hence, its synonym is 'gallantry'.
Cravenness means cowardliness.
Dastardliness means wicked and cruel behaviour.

686. Gauge **SSC MTS 04.05.2023 (Shift-I)**

(a) Diagnose (b) Valve
(c) Attempt (d) Measure

Ans. (d)

Gauge means to measure or determine the quantity, capacity or dimensions of something. Hence, its synonym is 'measure'.
Diagnose means to identify the nature of an illness or other problem by examination.
Valve means a device for controlling the passage of fluid or air through a pipe.
Attempt means to make an effort to achieve or complete something.

687. In the absence of miraceles, my frustration spikes.
SSC MTS 04.05.2023 (Shift-II)

(a) Digs (b) Falls
(c) Losses (d) Increases

Ans. (d)

Spikes means to increase sharply. Hence, its synonym is 'increases'.

688. From start to finish, the treatment of the defendants was a travesty of legal due process. **SSC MTS 04.05.2023 (Shift-III)**

(a) magic (b) mockery
(c) tribute (d) slurry

Ans. (b)

Travesty means a false, absurd or distorted representation of something. Hence, its synonym is 'mockery'.

Tribute means an act, statement, or gift that is intended to show gratitude, respect, or admiration.

Slurry means a semi-liquid mixture, typically of fine particles of manure, cement, or coal suspended in water.

689. Jaded SSC MTS 08.05.2023 (Shift-II)

(a) Weariless (b) Unwearied
(c) Beguiled (d) Fatigued

Ans. (d)

Jaded means tired, bored or lacking enthusiasm. Hence, its synonym is 'fatigued'.

Weariless means not tired.

Unwearied means not weary or tired.

Beguiled means charmed or enchanted, sometimes in a deceptive way.

690. Valet SSC MTS 09.05.2023 (Shift-I)

(a) Carrier (b) Carrousel
(c) Kingpin (d) Butler

Ans. (d)

Valet means a man's personal male servant. Hence, its synonym is 'butler'.

Carrier means a person or thing that carries something.

Carrousel means a rotating machine or device.

Kingpin means a main or large bolt in a central position.

691. Calamity SSC MTS 09.05.2023 (Shift-II)

(a) Embark (b) Debauchery
(c) Debar (d) Debacle

Ans. (d)

Calamity means an event causing great and often sudden damage or distress. Hence, its synonym is 'debacle'.

Embark means to go on board a ship, aircraft, or other vehicle.

Debauchery means excessive indulgence in sensual pleasures.

Debar means to exclude or prohibit someone officially from doing something.

692. Abide SSC MTS 09.05.2023 (Shift-III)

(a) Repudiate (b) Decamp
(c) Dwell (d) Vamoose

Ans. (c)

Abide means to accept or act in accordance with. Hence, its synonym is 'dwell'.

Repudiate means to refuse to accept.

Decamp means to leave a place suddenly or secretly.

Vamoose means to leave hurriedly or quickly.

693. No need to read (voluminous) campaign literature or pore through printed recommendations.
SSC MTS 10.05.2023 (Shift-III)

(a) Commodious (b) Micro
(c) Sparkling (d) Reverberate

Ans. (a)

Voluminous means occupying or containing much space; large in volume. Hence, its synonym is 'commodious'.

Micro means extremely small.

Sparkling means shining brightly with flashes of light.

Reverberate means to be repeated several times as an echo.

694. Fetish SSC MTS 10.05.2023 (Shift-III)

(a) Awkward (b) Requirement
(c) Desire (d) Learning

Ans. (c)

Fetish means an excessive and irrational devotion or commitment to a particular thing. Hence, its synonym is 'desire'.

695. Paul Bunyan is considered <u>legend</u>.
SSC MTS 11.05.2023 (Shift-II)

(a) Spinster (b) Stoic
(c) Volunteer (d) Tradition

Ans. (d)

Legend means a traditional story sometimes popularly regarded as historical but unauthenticated. Hence, its synonym is 'tradition'.

Spinster means an unmarried woman, typically an older woman.

Stoic means a person who can endure pain or hardship without showing their feelings or complaining.

Volunteer means a person who freely offers to take part in an enterprise or undertake a task.

696. Inquisitive SSC MTS 11.05.2023 (Shift-II)

(a) Agile (b) Aloof
(c) Callous (d) Curious

Ans. (d)

Inquisitive means having or showing an interest in learning things; curious. Hence, its synonym is 'curious'.

Agile means able to move quickly and easily.

Aloof means not friendly or forthcoming.

Callous means showing or having an insensitive and cruel disregard for others.

697. Feat SSC MTS 11.05.2023 (Shift-III)

(a) Hallowed
(b) Handsy
(c) Accomplishment
(d) Obligation

Ans. (c)

Feat means an achievement that requires great courage, skill or strength. Hence, its synonym is 'accomplishment'.

Hallowed means greatly revered or respected.

Handsy means (informally) tending to touch people with one's hands, especially in an inappropriate way.

Obligation means a duty or commitment.

698. If you think atheists are all miserable, (nihilistic) amoralists, this book should put you straight.
SSC MTS 12.05.2023 (Shift-I)

(a) Canonical (b) Cynical
(c) Conical (d) Tyrannical

Ans. (b)

Nihilistic means rejecting all religious and moral principles in the belief that life is meaningless. Hence, its synonym is 'cynical'.

Canonical means according to or ordered by canon law.

Conical means having the shape of a cone.

Tyrannical means exercising power in a cruel or arbitrary way.

699. Virtuoso SSC MTS 12.05.2023 (Shift-I)

(a) Waive (b) Voluble
(c) Maestro (d) Novice

Ans. (c)

Virtuoso means a person highly skilled in music or another artistic pursuit. Hence, its synonym is 'maestro'.

Waive means to refrain from insisting on or using a right or claim.

Voluble means speaking or spoken incessantly and fluently.

Novice means a person new to or inexperienced in a field or situation.

700. He <u>has</u> been used as the (fall guy) for issues the housing and unemployment.
SSC MTS 12.05.2023 (Shift-II)

(a) Reticent (b) Confiscate
(c) Scapegoat (d) Weakling

Ans. (c)

Fall guy means a person who is falsely blamed for something, especially in order to protect the real culprit. Hence, its synonym is 'scapegoat'.

Reticent means not revealing one's thoughts or feelings readily.

Weakling means a person who is weak or lacking in strength.

701. Debased SSC MTS 12.05.2023 (Shift-III)

(a) Amenable (b) Unamenable
(c) Corrupted (d) Aggrandise

Ans. (c)

Debased means reduced in quality or value. Hence, its synonym is 'corrupted'.

Amenable means open and responsive to suggestion.

Unamenable means not responsive or submissive to control.

Aggrandise means to increase the power, status, or wealth of.

702. The story shows the importance of self-esteem. SSC MTS 15.05.2023 (Shift-I)

(a) Pride (b) Humility
(c) Disgrace (d) Shyness

Ans. (a)

Self-esteem means confidence in one's own worth or abilities; self-respect. Hence, its synonym is 'pride'.

Humility means a modest or low view of one's own importance.

Disgrace means loss of reputation or respect.

703. Aptitude SSC MTS 15.05.2023 (Shift-III)

(a) Attitude (b) Talent
(c) Stress (d) Faith

Ans. (b)

Aptitude means a natural ability to do something. Hence, its synonym is 'talent'.

Attitude means a settled way of thinking or feeling about something.

Stress means pressure or tension exerted on a material object.

Faith means complete trust or confidence in someone or something.

704. Immediate relocation is your best course of action. SSC MTS 15.05.2023 (Shift-III)

(a) Emergence (b) Ending
(c) Expiration (d) Migration

Ans. (d)

Relocation means the action of moving to a new place and establishing one's home or business there. Hence, its synonym is 'migration'.

Emergence means the process of coming into view or becoming exposed after being concealed.

Expiration means the end of the period for which something is valid.

705. Easiness SSC MTS 16.05.2023 (Shift-I)

(a) Gullibility
(b) Immunity
(c) Fraternity
(d) Indomitability

Ans. (b)

Easiness means the state or quality of being easy. Hence, its synonym is 'immunity'.

Gullibility means a tendency to be easily persuaded that something is real or true.

Fraternity means a group of people sharing a common profession or interests.

Indomitability means the quality of being impossible to subdue or defeat.

706. A sudden gust of wind hits the window SSC MTS 16.05.2023 (Shift-I)

(a) Below (b) Cramp
(c) Feel (d) Pump

Ans. (d)

Gust means a brief, strong rush of wind. Hence, its synonym is 'pump'.

Cramp means painful involuntary contraction of a muscle or muscles.

707. Little Red Riding hood is a fairy tale. SSC MTS 16.05.2023 (Shift-II)

(a) document (b) Fact
(c) Tail (d) Story

Ans. (d)

Fairy tale means a children's story about magical and imaginary beings and lands. Hence, its synonym is 'story'.

Document means a piece of written, printed, or electronic matter that provides information.

Fact means a thing that is known or proved to be true.

Tail means the hindmost part of an animal.

708. Subtle SSC MTS 16.05.2023 (Shift-III)

(a) Corrupt (b) Homely
(c) Exquisite (d) Wrong

Ans. (c)

Subtle means so delicate or precise as to be difficult to analyse or describe. Hence, its synonym is 'exquisite'.

Corrupt means having or showing a willingness to act dishonestly in return for money or personal gain.

Homely means (of a person) unattractive in appearance.

709. There are actually many different versions of Cinderella. SSC MTS 17.05.2023 (Shift-I)

(a) Problems (b) Features
(c) Variations (d) signals

Ans. (c)

Versions means a particular form of something differing in certain respects from an earlier form or other forms of the same type of thing. Hence, its synonym is 'variations'.

Problems means a matter or situation regarded as unwelcome or harmful and needing to be dealt with and overcome.

Features means a distinctive attribute or aspect of something.

Signals means gestures, actions, or sounds used to convey information or instructions.

710. Villainous SSC MTS 17.05.2023 (Shift-II)

(a) Wholesome (b) Lucid
(c) Nefarious (d) Famous

Ans. (c)

Villainous means relating to or guilty of wicked or criminal behaviour. Hence, its synonym is 'nefarious'.

Wholesome means conducive to or suggestive of good health and physical well-being.

Lucid means expressed clearly; easy to understand.

711. Confession had always rested on a clear distinction between moral and venial sins. SSC MTS 18.05.2023 (Shift-I)

(a) Genial (b) Pardonable
(c) Major (d) Intolerable

Ans. (b)

Venial means (of a fault or offense) slight and pardonable. Hence, its synonym is 'pardonable'.

Major means important, serious, or significant.

Intolerable means unable to be endured.

712. Upsetting SSC MTS 18.05.2023 (Shift-II)

(a) Dreamy (b) Aware
(c) Amusing (d) Perturbing

Ans. (d)

Upsetting means causing unhappiness, disappointment or worry. Hence, its synonym is 'perturbing'.

713. It broke Eleanora's heart to see her daughter become that (wraith) of her former self. SSC MTS 19.05.2023 (Shift-III)

(a) Spirit (b) Wail
(c) Being (d) Yore

Ans. (a)

Wraith means a ghost or ghostlike image of someone, especially one seen shortly before or after their death. Hence, its synonym is 'spirit'.

Wail means a prolonged high-pitched cry of pain, grief, or anger.

Yore means of long ago or former times.

714. Unfortunately he is merely the head of a rabble of warlords who are (firmly) rooted in the past. SSC MTS 13.06.2023 (Shift-II)

(a) Feebly (b) Languidly
(c) Stiffly (d) Impotently

Ans. (c)

Firmly means in a strong, steady way. Hence, its synonym is 'stiffly'.

Feebly means in a way that lacks strength or force.

Languidly means in a relaxed and unenergetic manner.

Impotently means in a powerless or helpless manner.

715. In the midst of the tumult of charges against him, a (welter) of conflicting poll numbers are being bandied about. SSC MTS 14.06.2023 (Shift-II)

(a) Turmoil (b) Dynamic
(c) Static (d) Peace

Ans. (a)

Welter means a large number of items in no order; a confused mass. Hence, its synonym is 'turmoil'.

Dynamic means characterised by constant change, activity, or progress.

Static means lacking in movement, action, or change.

Peace means freedom from disturbance; tranquility.

716. Liberty SSC MTS 15.06.2023 (Shift-I)

(a) Status (b) Freedom
(c) Dependence (d) Acclamation

Ans. (b)

Liberty means the state of being free within society from oppressive restrictions. Hence, its synonym is 'freedom'.

Status means the relative social, professional, or other standing of someone or something.

Dependence means the state of relying on or being controlled by someone or something else.

Acclamation means loud and enthusiastic approval.

717. I do not object to this (accolade) on the grounds that Edinburgh has little literary tradition.
SSC MTS 15.06.2023 (Shift-III)

(a) Stubborn (b) Criticism
(c) Praise (d) Indictment

Ans. (c)

Accolade means an award or privilege granted as a special honour or as an acknowledgement of merit. Hence, its synonym is 'praise'.

Stubborn means having or showing dogged determination not to change one's attitude or position.

Criticism means the expression of disapproval of someone or something.

Indictment means a formal charge or accusation of a serious crime.

718. Spreading from the ports, Formosan termites begna a (subterranean) colonisation of the country.
SSC MTS 16.06.2023 (Shift-I)

(a) Terrestrial (b) Underground
(c) Overt (d) Subcutaneous

Ans. (b)

Subterranean means existing, occurring, or done under the earth's surface. Hence, its synonym is 'underground'.

Terrestrial means of, on, or relating to the earth.

Overt means done or shown openly.

Subcutaneous means situated or applied under the skin.

719. Capricious SSC MTS 16.06.2023 (Shift-II)

(a) Arbitrary (b) Stable
(c) Steadfast (d) Cautious

Ans. (a)

Capricious means given to sudden and unaccountable changes of mood or behaviour. Hence, its synonym is 'arbitrary'.

Stable means not likely to change or fail.

Steadfast means resolutely or dutifully firm and unwavering.

Cautious means careful to avoid potential problems or dangers.

720. Gala SSC MTS 19.06.2023 (Shift-II)

(a) Carnival (b) Moist
(c) Mistakenly (d) Funeral

Ans. (a)

Gala means a social occasion with special entertainments or performances. Hence, its synonym is 'carnival'.

721. Disdain SSC MTS 19.06.2023 (Shift-III)

(a) Contempt (b) Acceptance
(c) Admiration (d) Withdraw

Ans. (a)

Disdain means the feeling that someone or something is unworthy of one's consideration or respect. Hence, its synonym is 'contempt'.

722. Enthuse SSC MTS 20.06.2023 (Shift-II)

(a) Unbothered (b) Carefree
(c) Fondle (d) Lazy

Ans. (c)

Enthuse means to express eager enjoyment, interest, or approval. Hence, its synonym is 'fondle'.

723. The athlete's perseverance and mental toughness .... (facilitate) her to overcome adversity and archieve her goals.
SSC MTS 01.09.2023 (Shift-I)

(a) restricted (b) enabled
(c) limited (d) hindered

Ans. (b)

Facilitate means to enable or help. Hence, 'enabled' will be the correct filler.

Restricted, limited and **hindered** means to stop someone from doing something.

724. Obsession SSC MTS 04.09.2023 (Shift-II)

(a) Discrimination
(b) Fascination
(c) Unconcern
(d) Sympathy

Ans. (b)

Obsession means 'extreme fascination'.

Discrimination means an unjust treatment on grounds of sex, religion, ethnicity, etc.

Sympathy means a feeling of sorrow for someone.

725. Amicable SSC MTS 04.09.2023 (Shift-II)

(a) Friendly (b) Proud
(c) Generous (d) Harsh

Ans. (a)

Amicable means having a spirit of friendliness; without serious disagreement. Hence, its synonym is 'friendly'.

726. Diminish SSC MTS 05.09.2023 (Shift-I)

(a) Demote (b) Relegate
(c) Prevent (d) Weaken

Ans. (d)

Diminish means to make or become less.

Hence, its synonym is 'weaken'.

Demote means to give someone a lower rank or less senior position.

Relegate means to consign or dismiss to an inferior rank or position.

Prevent means to stop something from happening.

727. Insist SSC MTS 05.09.2023 (Shift-I)

(a) Persist (b) Resist
(c) Heist (d) Assist

Ans. (a)

Insist means to demand something forcefully, not accepting refusal. Hence, its synonym is 'persist'.

Resist means to withstand the action or effect of.

Heist means a robbery or holdup.

Assist means to help.

728. Elegant SSC MTS 05.09.2023 (Shift-III)

(a) Mighty (b) Graceful
(c) Ugly (d) Tall

Ans. (b)

Elegant means pleasingly graceful and stylish in appearance or manner. Hence, its synonym is 'graceful'.

729. Design SSC MTS 05.09.2023 (Shift-III)
(a) Fabricate (b) Destroy
(c) Inspect (d) Copy
Ans. (a)
Design means to create, fashion, execute or construct according to plan. Hence, its synonym is 'fabricate'.

730. The athlete's injury was a....... (defeat) for the team's chances of winning the championship.
SSC MTS 06.09.2023 (Shift-II)
(a) progression (b) breakthrough
(c) stress (d) setback
Ans. (d)
Defeat means an instance of defeating or being defeated. Hence, its synonym is 'setback'.
Progression means the process of developing or moving gradually towards a more advanced state.
Breakthrough means a sudden, dramatic, and important discovery or development.

731. Distinguished SSC MTS 06.09.2023 (Shift-III)
(a) Mirrored (b) Dignified
(c) Dramatic (d) Mediocre
Ans. (b)
Distinguished means successful, authoritative and commanding great respect. Hence, its synonym is 'dignified'.
Mirrored means having a surface capable of reflecting.
Dramatic means relating to drama or the performance of drama.
Mediocre means of only moderate quality; not very good.

732. Obvious SSC MTS 08.09.2023 (Shift-I)
(a) Clear (b) Murky
(c) Ambiguous (d) Opaque
Ans. (a)
Obvious means easily perceived or understood; clear, self-evident or apparent. Hence, its synonym is 'clear'.
Murky means dark and gloomy.
Ambiguous means open to more than one interpretation; not having one obvious meaning.
Opaque means not able to be seen through; not transparent.

733. Ray was <u>cynical</u> about love.
SSC MTS 08.09.2023 (Shift-I)
(a) prolific (b) obese
(c) trusting (d) pessimistic
Ans. (d)
Cynical means believing that people are motivated by self-interest; distrustful of human sincerity or integrity. Hence, its synonym is 'pessimistic'.
Prolific means producing much fruit or foliage or many offspring.
Obese means grossly fat or overweight.
Trusting means showing or tending to have a belief in a person's honesty or sincerity; not suspicious.

734. The Sun was setting over the mountains, painting the sky with (energetic) shades of orange and pink. SSC MTS 08.09.2023 (Shift-II)
(a) vibrant (b) reactive
(c) faded (d) bright
Ans. (a)
The word 'vibrant' given the sense of energetic and thus, is appropriate to fill the blank.
Faded means losing colour.
Reactive means responding to a situation.

735. Grief SSC MTS 08.09.2023 (Shift-II)
(a) Pleasure (b) Jollity
(c) Pain (d) Content
Ans. (c)
The word 'Grief' means 'pain or sorrow.
Jollity means' lively and cheerful.
Content means satisfied.

736. Hope SSC MTS 08.09.2023 (Shift-III)
(a) Caution (b) Realism
(c) Cynicism (d) Wish
Ans. (d)
Hope means a feeling of expectation and desire for a certain thing to happen. Hence, its synonym is 'wish'.
Caution means care taken to avoid danger or mistakes.
Realism means the attitude or practice of accepting a situation as it is.
Cynicism means an inclination to believe that people are motivated purely by self-interest.

737. She's reading a....(secrecy) novel and can't wait to find out who the killer is. SSC MTS 08.09.2023 (Shift-III)
(a) crisis (b) complication
(c) difficulty (d) mystery
Ans. (d)
Secrecy means the action of keeping something secret or the state of being kept secret. Hence, its synonym is 'mystery'.
Crisis means a time of intense difficulty or danger.
Complication means a circumstance that complicates something; a difficulty.

738. Hazard SSC MTS 11.09.2023 (Shift-III)
(a) Marvel (b) Miracle
(c) Ardent (d) Accident
Ans. (d)
Hazard means a danger or risk. Hence, its synonym is 'accident'.
Marvel means to be filled with wonder or astonishment.
Miracle means an extraordinary and welcome event.
Ardent means enthusiastic or passionate.

739. The medical procedure was successful, but the patient experienced some minor...(troubles) during recovery.
SSC MTS 12.09.2023 (Shift-I)
(a) applications
(b) complications
(c) transformations
(d) obligations
Ans. (b)
Troubles means difficulties or problems. Hence, its synonym is 'complications'.
Applications means the action of putting something into operation.
Transformations means thorough or dramatic changes in form or appearance.
Obligations means an act or course of action to which a person is morally or legally bound.

740. Barbed SSC MTS 12.09.2023 (Shift-II)
(a) Passive (b) Kind
(c) Gentle (d) Spiteful
Ans. (d)
Barbed means having barbs or barbed wire. Hence, its synonym is 'spiteful'.

741. Enchanted SSC MTS 12.09.2023 (Shift-III)
(a) Disgusted (b) Cursed
(c) Appealing (d) Repelling
Ans. (c)
Enchanted means delighted or charmed. Hence, its synonym is 'appealing'.
Disgusted means feeling or expressing revulsion or strong disapproval.
Cursed means to wish harm upon someone.
Repelling means to drive or force back or away.

742. Glimpse SSC MTS 13.09.2023 (Shift-I)
(a) Examine (b) Glance
(c) Stare (d) Observe
Ans. (b)
Glimpse means a momentary or partial view. Hence, its synonym is 'glance'.

743. Mild SSC MTS 13.09.2023 (Shift-II)
(a) Scathing (b) Brittle
(c) Gentle (d) Severe
Ans. (c)
Mild means not severe, serious or harsh. Hence, its synonym is 'gentle'.
Scathing means severely critical.

744. Pretend SSC MTS 13.09.2023 (Shift-III)
(a) Feign (b) Benign
(c) Align (d) Reign
Ans. (a)
Pretend means to behave so as to make it appear that something is the case when in fact it is not. Hence, its synonym is 'feign'.
Benign means gentle and kind.
Align means to place or arrange things in a straight line.
Reign means to hold royal office; rule as king or queen.

745. The girl was manacled and locked in the room. SSC MTS 14.09.2023 (Shift-I)
(a) Unfastened
(b) Liberated
(c) Fettered
(d) Unbinded
Ans. (c)
The word 'manacled' means to chain or confine a person.
Hence, its correct synonym is 'fettered' which means 'to stop someone from progressing
Unfastened, **liberated** and **Unbinded** indicate freedom.

746. Plunge SSC MTS 14.09.2023 (Shift-I)
(a) Transgress (b) Dive
(c) Rush (d) Fly
Ans. (b)
The word 'Plunge' means a sudden jump, drop or fall. Hence, its correct synonym is 'Dive' which means to jump into water and go down quickly.
Transgress means to go beyond acceptable.

747. Shiya had more grit than her other siblings. SSC MTS 14.09.2023 (Shift-III)
(a) power (b) level
(c) gap (d) courage
Ans. (d)
Grit means courage and resolve; strength of character. Hence, its synonym is 'courage'.

SSC MTS 2022

748. Occlude SSC MTS 05.07.2022 (Shift-III)
(a) facilitate (b) promote
(c) Abstain (d) Obstruct
Ans. (d)
Occlude means to stop, close up or obstruct. Hence, its synonym is 'obstruct'.
Facilitate means to make an action or process easy or easier.

749. Segregate SSC MTS 06.07.2022 (Shift-II)
(a) Submerge (b) Isolate
(c) Nullify (d) Integrate
Ans. (b)
Segregate means to set apart from the rest or from each other. Hence, its synonym is 'isolate'.
Submerge means to cause to be under water.
Nullify means to make legally null and **void**.

750. Obtrusive SSC MTS 06.07.2022 (Shift-II)
(a) Pervasive (b) Exclusive
(c) Prominent (d) Modest
Ans. (c)
Obtrusive means noticeable or prominent in an unwelcome or intrusive way. Hence, its synonym is 'prominent'.
Exclusive means excluding or not admitting other things.

751. Caustic SSC MTS 08.07.2022 (Shift-I)
(a) Acidic (b) Photogenic
(c) Basic (d) Soothing
Ans. (a)
Caustic means able to burn or corrode organic tissue by chemical action. Hence, its synonym is 'acidic'.
Photogenic means looking attractive in photographs.
Soothing means having a gently calming effect.

752. Intervene SSC MTS 08.07.2022 (Shift-II)
(a) Embody (b) Combine
(c) Coalesce (d) Arbitrate
Ans. (d)
Intervene means to come between so as to prevent or alter a result or course of events. Hence, its synonym is 'arbitrate'.
Embody means to be an expression of or give a tangible or visible form to an idea.
Coalesce means to come together to form one mass or whole.

753. Concede SSC MTS 08.07.2022 (Shift-III)
(a) Reject (b) Permit
(c) Deny (d) Fascinate
Ans. (b)
Concede means to admit that something is true or valid after first denying or resisting it. Hence, its synonym is 'permit'.

754. We need to protest against this policy. SSC MTS 08.07.2022 (Shift-III)
(a) resist (b) assent
(c) validate (d) perk
Ans. (a)
Protest means a statement or action expressing disapproval of or objection to something. Hence, its synonym is 'resist'.
Assent means to express approval or agreement.
Validate means to check or prove the validity.
Perk means a benefit to which one is entitled.

755. Deficient SSC MTS 08.07.2022 (Shift-III)
(a) Sleek (b) Whole
(c) Incomplete (d) Integral
Ans. (b)
Deficient means not having enough of a specified quality or ingredient. Hence, its synonym is 'whole'.
Sleek means smooth and glossy.
Integral means necessary to make a whole complete.

756. Provoke SSC MTS 11.07.2022 (Shift-I)
(a) Inhibit (b) Slack
(c) Arouse (d) Constrain
Ans. (c)
The word 'provoke' means to cause a reaction, especially an angry one. Hence, its correct synonym is 'arouse' as it means to cause someone to have a particular feeling.
Inhibit means to stop.
Slack means slow.
Constrain means a restriction.

757. These figures have been greatly exaggerated. SSC MTS 11.07.2022 (Shift-I)
(a) understated (b) magnified
(c) belittled (d) ignore
Ans. (b)
The word 'exaggerate' means to make something seem better, larger, worse etc., than it really is. Hence, its correct synonym is 'magnified'.

758. Luxuriant SSC MTS 11.07.2022 (Shift-II)
(a) Meagre (b) Sparse
(c) Flourishing (d) Combative
Ans. (c)
Luxuriant means rich and profuse in growth. Hence, its synonym is 'flourishing'.
Sparse means thinly dispersed or scattered.
Combative means ready or eager to fight.

759. They saw fit to banish him from the party and exclude him from the election campaign. SSC MTS 11.07.2022 (Shift-III)
(a) persevere (b) revolt
(c) distress (d) exile
Ans. (d)
Banish means to send someone away from a country or place as an official punishment. Hence, its synonym is 'exile'.
Persevere means to continue in a course of action.
Revolt means to rise in rebellion.
Distress means extreme anxiety, sorrow, or pain.

760. The laws are strong but never enforced. SSC MTS 11.07.2022 (Shift-III)
(a) Diluted (b) Abandoned
(c) Imposed (d) Disregarded
Ans. (c)
Enforced means to compel observance of or compliance with a law. Hence, its synonym is 'imposed'.
Diluted means made thinner or weaker.
Disregarded means to pay no attention to.

761. Intricate SSC MTS 12.07.2022 (Shift-I)
(a) Basic (b) Complicated
(c) Painted (d) Developed
Ans. (b)
The word 'Intricate' means having a lot of small parts that are arranged in a complicated or delicate way.

762. All branded shoes are priced extravagantly. SSC MTS 12.07.2022 (Shift-I)
(a) modestly (b) economically
(c) expensively (d) meagerly
Ans. (c)
The word 'extravagantly' means in a way that causes you to spend too much money or use too much of something. Hence its correct synonym is 'expensively.'
Modestly, economically and **meagerly** mean spending less money.

763. Hurdle SSC MTS 12.07.2022 (Shift-II)
(a) Progress (b) Impediment
(c) Accessory (d) Aid
Ans. (b)
Hurdle means an obstacle or difficulty. Hence, its synonym is 'impediment'.

764. Laborious SSC MTS 12.07.2022 (Shift-II)
(a) Unsophisticated
(b) Profane
(c) Assiduous
(d) Pompous
Ans. (c)
Laborious means requiring considerable effort and time. Hence, its synonym is 'assiduous'.
Unsophisticated means lacking refined worldly knowledge or tastes.
Profane means relating or devoted to that which is not sacred.
Pompous means affectedly and irritatingly grand, solemn or self-important.

765. Probe SSC MTS 13.07.2022 (Shift-I)
(a) Search (b) Motivate
(c) Invite (d) Push
Ans. (a)
He word 'Probe' means to look for something or examine something, using a long thin object. Hence, its correct synonym is 'search'.

766. Clandestine SSC MTS 13.07.2022 (Shift-I)
(a) Blatant (b) Ornate
(c) Open (d) Undercover
Ans. (d)
The word 'Clandestine' means planned or done in secret, especially describing something that is not officially allowed. Hence, its correct synonym is 'undercover'.
Blatant means clear and open.
Ornate means to decorate.

767. Bulky SSC MTS 14.07.2022 (Shift-I)
(a) Airy
(b) Soft
(c) Massive
(d) Scanty
Ans. (c)
The word 'Bulky' means large and heavy and therefore, difficult to move and carry. Hence, its correct synonym is 'massive' as, it means very large, solid and heavy.
Scanty means insufficient.

768. Maestro SSC MTS 14.07.2022 (Shift-I)
(a) Genius (b) Senile
(c) Slender (d) Novice
Ans. (a)
The word 'Maestro' means someone who is very skilled and who people admire a lot. Hence its correct synonym is 'genius' as it means someone who has a very high level of intelligence, mental skill or ability, which only a few people have.
Senile means crazy.
Slender means thin.
Novice means an inexperienced person.

769. Aug SSC MTS 14.07.2022 (Shift-III)
(a) Imminent (b) Eminent
(c) Permanent (d) Illicity
Ans. (b)
Aug is short for 'August,' an honorific used to describe someone eminent, grand or venerable. Hence, its synonym is 'eminent'.
Permanent means lasting or intended to last or remain unchanged indefinitely.
Illicit means forbidden by law, rules, or custom.

770. Mandate SSC MTS 14.07.2022 (Shift-III)
(a) Question (b) Request
(c) Enquire (d) Command
Ans. (d)
Mandate means an official order or commission to do something. Hence, its synonym is 'command'.
Question means to ask a question.
Request means an act of asking politely or formally for something.
Enquire means to ask for information from someone.

771. Erring SSC MTS 15.07.2022 (Shift-I)
(a) Blundering
(b) Tidy
(c) Sloppy
(d) Flawless
Ans. (a)
The word 'Erring' means having failed to adhere to the proper or accepted standard, having done wrong. Hence its correct synonym is 'blundering' as it means often making serious mistakes, usually because of not taking care.
Sloppy means careless

772. Penniless SSC MTS 15.07.2022 (Shift-I)
(a) Broke (b) Reckless
(c) Cranky (d) Wealthy
Ans. (a)
The word 'Penniless' means having no money. Hence its correct synonym is 'Broke' which also means having no money.
Reckless means careless
Cranky means carinated

773. Tenderness SSC MTS 15.07.2022 (Shift-III)
(a) ruthlessness (b) severity
(c) kindness (d) spiteful
Ans. (c)
Tenderness means gentleness and kindness. Hence, its synonym is 'kindness'.
Spiteful means showing or caused by malice.

774. Acute SSC MTS 18.07.2022 (Shift-I)
(a) Obtuse (b) Faithful
(c) Chronic (d) Dire
Ans. (d)

Acute means having or showing a perceptive understanding or insight. Hence, its synonym is 'dire'.

Obtuse means annoyingly insensitive or slow to understand.

Chronic means persisting for a long time or constantly recurring.

775. Propitious SSC MTS 18.07.2022 (Shift-II)

(a) Conciliatory (b) Cogent
(c) Inimical (d) Auspicious

Ans. (d)

Propitious means giving or indicating a good chance of success. Hence, its synonym is 'auspicious'.

Conciliatory means intended or likely to placate or pacify.

Cogent means clear, logical and convincing.

Inimical means tending to obstruct or harm.

776. Bloom SSC MTS 19.07.2022 (Shift-II)

(a) Flower (b) Fade
(c) Drop (d) Wither

Ans. (a)

Bloom means a flower, especially one cultivated for its beauty. Hence, its synonym is 'flower'.

Fade means to gradually grow faint and disappear.

Wither means to become dry and shriveled.

777. Confiscated SSC MTS 19.07.2022 (Shift-III)

(a) Seized
(b) Marinated
(c) Acquitted
(d) Liberated

Ans. (a)

Confiscated means taken or seized with authority. Hence, its synonym is 'seized'.

Marinated means soaked in a marinade.

Acquitted means free someone from a criminal charge by a verdict of not guilty.

Liberated means set someone free from imprisonment, slavery, or oppression.

778. Satiate SSC MTS 19.07.2022 (Shift-III)

(a) Pamper (b) Culminate
(c) Satisfy (d) Agitate

Ans. (c)

Satiate means to satisfy a desire or appetite to the full. Hence, its synonym is 'satisfy'.

Pamper means to indulge with every attention, comfort and kindness.

Culminate means to reach a climax or point of highest development.

Agitate means to make someone troubled or nervous.

779. Flagrant SSC MTS 20.07.2022 (Shift-I)

(a) Favourable
(b) Wonderful
(c) Magnificent
(d) Atrocious

Ans. (d)

Flagrant means conspicuously or obviously offensive. Hence, its synonym is 'atrocious'.

780. Enthrall SSC MTS 20.07.2022 (Shift-III)

(a) Deceive (b) Repulse
(c) Forgive (d) Captivate

Ans. (d)

Enthrall means to capture the fascinated attention of. Hence, its synonym is 'captivate'.

781. This style is ideal for men of all ages who wish to convey a <u>dapper</u> look.
SSC MTS 21.07.2022 (Shift-I)

(a) Messy (b) Filthy
(c) Stylish (d) Healthy

Ans. (c)

Dapper means neat and trim in dress and appearance. Hence, its synonym is 'stylish'.

782. Culpable SSC MTS 21.07.2022 (Shift-II)

(a) Guilty (b) Irresponsible
(c) Immune (d) Innocent

Ans. (a)

Culpable means deserving blame. Hence, its synonym is 'guilty'.

Immune means resistant to a particular infection or toxin.

783. He was quick in his anger, but easily <u>appeased</u>. SSC MTS 21.07.2022 (Shift-II)

(a) unsatisfied (b) bugged
(c) dejected (d) pacified

Ans. (d)

Appeased means to pacify or placate someone by acceding to their demands. Hence, its synonym is 'pacified'.

Bugged means annoyed or bothered.

784. Revile SSC MTS 21.07.2022 (Shift-III)

(a) Silence (b) Incite
(c) Discourage (d) Abuse

Ans. (d)

Revile means to criticise in an abusive or angrily insulting manner. Hence, its synonym is 'abuse'.

Silence means complete absence of sound.

Incite means to encourage or stir up violent or unlawful behavior.

785. They are <u>perceptive</u> observers of social groups SSC MTS 22.07.2022 (Shift-I)

(a) Conflicted (b) Astute
(c) Imbecile (d) Witless

Ans. (b)

Perceptive means having or showing sensitive insight. Hence, its synonym is 'astute'.

Conflicted means having or showing confused and mutually inconsistent feelings.

Imbecile means a stupid person.

Witless means foolish; stupid.

786. Both songs have been reworked giving them fresh <u>impetus</u>.
SSC MTS 22.07.2022 (Shift-III)

(a) detachment (b) aversion
(c) disfavour (d) incitement

Ans. (d)

Impetus means the force or energy with which a body moves. Hence, its synonym is 'incitement'.

Detachment means the state of being objective or aloof.

Aversion means a strong dislike or disinclination.

Disfavour means disapproval or dislike.

787. Vanquish SSC MTS 25.07.2022 (Shift-I)

(a) Defeat (b) Acquit
(c) Surrender (d) Flee

Ans. (a)

Vanquish means to defeat thoroughly. Hence, its synonym is 'defeat'.

Acquit means to free someone from a criminal charge.

Surrender means to cease resistance to an enemy or opponent.

Flee means to run away from a place or situation of danger.

788. Bustle SSC MTS 25.07.2022 (Shift-II)

(a) Rush (b) Praise
(c) Force (d) Block

Ans. (a)

Bustle means to move in an energetic or noisy manner. Hence, its synonym is 'rush'.

789. Emphatic SSC MTS 25.07.2022 (Shift-III)

(a) Vigorous (b) Restrained
(c) Hesitant (d) Moderate

Ans. (a)

Emphatic means showing or giving emphasis. Hence, its synonym is 'vigorous'.

Restrained means characterised by reserve or moderation.

Hesitant means tentative, unsure, or slow in acting or speaking.

Moderate means average in amount, intensity, quality or degree.

790. Expository SSC MTS 26.07.2022 (Shift-II)
(a) Illustrative (b) temperamenta
(c) Obligatory (d) Dubious

Ans. (a)

Expository means intended to explain or describe something. Hence, its synonym is 'illustrative'.

Temperamental means liable to unreasonable changes of mood.

Obligatory means required by a legal, moral, or other rule.

Dubious means hesitating or doubting.

SSC MTS 2021

791. Indulgence SSC MTS 05.10.2021 (Shift-I)
(a) Accuracy (b) Leniency
(c) Diligence (d) Attentiveness

Ans. (b)

The word 'Indulgence' refers to the state of being tolerant. Hence, its correct synonym is 'leniency' which means tolerance.

Accuracy means exactness.

Diligence means devoted and hard working.

792. Fluorescent SSC MTS 06.10.2021 (Shift-III)
(a) elaborate (b) flowery
(c) perfumed (d) glowing

Ans. (d)

Fluorescent means glowing brightly.

Elaborate means in detail.

Flowery means decorated.

Perfumed means smelling good.

793. Graceful SSC MTS 06 Oct. 2021 (Shift-III)
(a) Elegant (b) Dangerous
(c) Pleasant (d) Friendly

Ans. (a)

The word 'graceful' means 'beautiful and elegant'.

794. Foment SSC MTS 02.11.2021 (Shift-I)
(a) Incite (b) Inspire
(c) Imply (d) Ignore

Ans. (a)

The word 'foment' means to instigate or stir up and undesirable course of action. Hence, its correct synonym is 'Incite' as it also means the same.

795. Wane SSC MTS 02.11.2021 (Shift-II)
(a) Increase (b) Rise
(c) Decline (d) Drown

Ans. (c)

The word 'wane' means to decline.

SSC GD 2024

796. Enervate SSC GD 20.02.2024 (Shift-I)
(a) Insecure (b) Desolation
(c) Secure (d) Devitalise

Ans. (d)

The word 'Enervate' means to weaken or drain of energy. Hence, its synonym is 'Devitalise' as it also means to weaken or make feeble.

Desolation means destruction.

797. Absolute SSC GD 20.02.2024 (Shift-II)
(a) Divine (b) Complete
(c) Final (d) Bounded

Ans. (b)

The word 'Absolute' and 'Complete' are synonyms both meaning total or full.

Divine means godly.

Bounded means restricted.

798. This query is no doubt a very correct and moral one, but it seems somewhat <u>cryptic</u>. SSC GD 20.02.2024 (Shift-III)
(a) common (b) clear
(c) obvious (d) mysterious

Ans. (d)

The underlined word 'cryptic' means 'mysterious' or 'puzzling' in this context.

799. Fantastically SSC GD 20.02.2024 (Shift-IV)
(a) Scarcely (b) Scantily
(c) Nominally (d) Fabulously

Ans. (d)

The word 'Fantastically' means in an extraordinarily good or impressive manner. Hence, its correct synonym is 'Fabulously'.

Scantily means in small quantity.

Nominally means in name only, not reality.

800. A successful outcome could ultimately lead to its use in (autonomous) planetary rovers and robot aircraft. SSC GD 20.02.2024 (Shift-IV)
(a) unanimous (b) occlude
(c) independent (d) obstruct

Ans. (c)

The bracketed word 'autonomous' means freedom or independence.

Unanimous means by the consent of all.

Occlude means to stop

Obstruct means to block.

801. That young woman has a <u>tendency</u> to date men who are similar to her father. SSC GD 21.02.2024 (Shift-I)
(a) Propensity (b) Apathy
(c) Inactivity (d) Indifference

Ans. (a)

The underlined word 'tendency' means a natural inclination or inclination towards something. Hence, its synonym is 'Propensity' as it also means to have a natural tendency to behave in a particular way.

802. Daring SSC GD 21.02.2024 (Shift-II)
(a) Patience (b) Fearless
(c) Coward (d) Trepid

Ans. (b)

The word 'Fearless' means the same as 'Daring'.

Trepid means fearful.

803. The mountaineers embarked on (an arduous) journey to conquer the formidable peak, facing treacherous terrain, extreme weather conditions and physical exhaustion along the way. SSC GD 21.02.2024 (Shift-IV)
(a) a severe
(b) an important
(c) a taxing
(d) a rewarding

Ans. (c)

The bracketed part 'an arduous' suggest that the journey was difficult and tiring. Hence, 'a taxing' can replace it as it also means difficult and exhausting.

804. Measure SSC GD 21.02.2024 (Shift-IV)
(a) Diagnose (b) Deviation
(c) Gauge (d) Propel

Ans. (c)

The word 'Measure' means to ascertain the size, amount or degree of something. Hence, its synonym is 'Gauge', which means to estimate or determine the magnitude, amount or volume of something.

Diagnose means to identify a medical condition.

Deviation means to go away from the natural path.

Propel means to push.

805. The trend of artwork among middle Eastern ladies is nothing new, yet nail paint is frequently <u>overlooked</u>. SSC GD 22.02.2024 (Shift-I)
(a) Appreciated (b) Pranked
(c) Sedated (d) Neglected

Ans. (d)

The underlined word 'Overlooked' means to fail, to notice or pay attention to something, which is synonymous with 'neglected.'

Pranked means joked.

Sedated means to be made unconscious.

806. Fill in the blank with the correct synonym of the word 'lavish'.
Her ………… donation to the cause greatly benefitted the community. SSC GD 22.02.2024 (Shift-I)
(a) stingy (b) contradictory
(c) generous (d) miserly

Ans. (c)

The word 'lavish' means characterised by or produced with great extravagance. Hence, its nearest synonym is 'generous'.

Stingy and **Miserly** refers to one who does not spend money.

Contradicting means opposite.

807. We cannot always follow instructions exactly, sometimes we need to incorporate our own ideas.

SSC GD 22.02.2024 (Shift-II)

(a) integrate (b) exclude
(c) part (d) separate

Ans. (a)

Both the words 'incorporate' and 'integrate' means 'to combine or merge into a unified whole'.

Exclude means to keep out.

Separate and **Part** means to cause to move away.

808. I have known you for a long time and possess the most circumstantial details about the plans you were devising. SSC GD 22.02.2024 (Shift-III)

(a) certain (b) credible
(c) coincidental (d) direct

Ans. (c)

The word 'circumstantial' and 'coincidental' are synonyms as they both means related to or coming together with circumstances.

809. Visitors board the train and wind their way through its corridors and lavish decor. SSC GD 22.02.2024 (Shift-IV)

(a) destitute (b) regular
(c) affluent (d) mundane

Ans. (c)

The word 'affluent' and 'lavish' are synonymous as both means having a lot of wealth or riches.

Destitute means poor.

Mundane means common and boring.

810. Cognitive SSC GD 23.02.2024 (Shift-I)

(a) Private (b) Obscure
(c) Latent (d) Perceivable

Ans. (d)

The word 'Cognitive' means the process of thinking, understanding and perception. Its synonym is 'Perceivable' which means able to be perceived or understood.

Latent means hidden.

Obscure means to block.

811. Lewis asked (tactlessly), as he did not know that the motive was

SSC GD 23.02.2024 (Shift-II)

(a) Blissfully (b) Ignorantly
(c) Civilly (d) Bluntly

Ans. (d)

The word 'Tactlessly' means lacking tact or consideration. Hence, its synonym is 'Bluntly', which means direct and without consideration for the feelings of others.

Blissfully means happily

Ignorantly means carelessly.

Civilly means politely.

812. In the age of technology, smartphones have become (ubiquitous), infiltrating every aspect of our lives, from communication and work to entertainment and even our daily routines. SSC GD 23.02.2024 (Shift-III)

(a) obsolete (b) candid
(c) omnipresent (d) irreplicable

Ans. (c)

The bracketed word 'ubiquitous' refers to something present, appearing or found everywhere. From the given options, the word 'omnipresent' which means 'being everywhere at once' is the closest in meaning to the given word. Hence, 'omnipresent' can replace 'ubiquitous' without changing the meaning of the sentence.

Obsolete means outdated.

Irreplicable means cannot be copied.

813. Curious SSC GD 23.02.2024 (Shift-III)

(a) Interested (b) Agile
(c) Benign (d) Callous

Ans. (a)

The word 'Curious' means 'interested to know or learn something'.

Agile means active.

Benign means harmless.

Callous means cruel.

814. Agreement SSC GD 23.02.2024 (Shift-IV)

(a) Census (b) Puny
(c) Consent (d) Celibate

Ans. (c)

The words 'Agreement' and 'Consent' are synonyms, both indicating an accord or concurrence.

Census means population count.

Puny means small.

Celibrate means an unmarried person.

815. Followed SSC GD 24.02.2024 (Shift-I)

(a) Transgressed
(b) Disobliged
(c) Obeyed
(d) Claimed

Ans. (c)

The word 'Followed' can means to comply with or obeyed.

Transgressed means to go away from the norm.

Disobliged means to offend.

816. To me this was both a perfect articulation of the problem and the suggestion of a solution.

SSC GD 24.02.2024 (Shift-II)

(a) Mispronounce (b) Damp
(c) Park (d) Enunciation

Ans. (d)

The underlined word 'articulation' is synonymous with 'enunciation' both of which mean expressing something clearly and precisely.

Damp means wet.

817. Attack SSC GD 24.02.2024 (Shift-III)

(a) Assault (b) Perform
(c) Bowl (d) Dwindle

Ans. (a)

The words 'Attack' and 'Assault' are synonyms, both referring to a violent or forceful attempt to cause harm or damage. **Dwindle** means to reduce.

SSC GD 2023

818. Forbore SSC GD 23.01.2023 (Shift-III)

(a) Refrain (b) Submit
(c) Yield (d) Surrender

Ans. (a)

The word 'forbore' means politely or patiently restrain an impulse to do something; refrain.

'**Submit**', '**Yield**' and '**Surrender**' are antonyms of forbore.

819. Select the most appropriate synonym of the capitalised word in the given sentence.

They tried to get official SANCTIONS for the scheme.

SSC GD 23.01.2023 (Shift-III)

(a) Committees (b) Unholiness
(c) Permissions (d) Substances

Ans. (c)

The word 'sanctions' means official permission or approval for an action.

Committees means a group of people appointed for a specific function by a larger group and typically consisting of members of that group.

Unholiness means wicked.

820. The teacher has ....(admitted) the student's sincere apologies.

SSC GD 23.01.2023 (Shift-III)

(a) acknowledged (b) executed
(c) neglected (d) denied

Ans. (a)

The word 'acknowledged' means 'admitted'.

Executed means killed as punishment for something.

Neglected means ignored.

Denied means refused.

821. The collision was witnessed by the pedestrians. **SSC GD 23.01.2023 (Shift-IV)**
(a) powerful blast
(b) funeral procession
(c) violent accident
(d) protest march

Ans. (c)
The word 'collision' means a violent impact of moving objects; crash.

822. Eligible **SSC GD 23.01.2023 (Shift-IV)**
(a) Efficient (b) Qualified
(c) Sufficient (d) Disinterested

Ans. (b)
The word 'eligible' means fit or proper to be chosen; worthy of choice; desirable; qualified'.

823. Ample **SSC GD 23.01.2023 (Shift-IV)**
(a) Entertain (b) Sample
(c) Temple (d) Sufficient

Ans. (d)
The word 'ample' means 'sufficient and enough in quantity or quality'.

824. The increasing population of a country can be a ...... (affliction) for the development of a country. **SSC GD 23.01.2023 (Shift-IV)**
(a) boom (b) bane
(c) boon (d) brittleness

Ans. (b)
The word 'affliction' means a cause of pain or harm. Hence, its synonym is 'bane' which means a source of harm or ruin.
Boom means a sudden and quick rise.
Brittleness means roughness.

825. Indebted **SSC GD 24.01.2023 (Shift-I)**
(a) Careless (b) Doubtful
(c) Envious (d) Thankful

Ans. (d)
The word 'indebted' means 'thankful for something'.
Envious means jealous.

826. Prashant is obstinate by nature. **SSC GD 24.01.2023 (Shift-I)**
(a) adamant (b) pliable
(c) generous (d) flexible

Ans. (a)
The word 'obstinate' means stubbornly refusing to change one's opinion or chosen course of action, despite attempts to persuade.
Hence, its synonym is 'adamant' which means the same.

827. He has a nasty habit of picking his nose. **SSC GD 24.01.2023 (Shift-I)**
(a) laudable (b) indolent
(c) cowardly (d) despicable

Ans. (d)
The word 'nasty' means 'bad and producing a dislike'.
Hence, its synonym is 'despicable' which means not likable.
Laudable means deserving praise.
Indolent means lazy.

828. Earned **SSC GD 24.01.2023 (Shift-IV)**
(a) Offered (b) Gave
(c) Gained (d) Accorded

Ans. (c)
The word 'Earned' means 'gained in return for labour or services'.
Accorded means give or grant someone (power, status or recognition).

829. Locating directions through the location of stars and constellations is a ....(handy) way at the sea. **SSC GD 24.01.2023 (Shift-IV)**
(a) near (b) simple
(c) useful (d) nice

Ans. (b)
The word 'handy' means 'simple and easy'. Hence, 'simple' can fill in the blank aptly.

830. Brave **SSC GD 24.01.2023 (Shift-IV)**
(a) Cautious (b) Timid
(c) Daring (d) Mild

Ans. (c)
The word 'Brave' means 'bold and daring'.
Cautious means careful.
Timid means fearful.
Mild means moderate.

831. He distracted him while his partner burgled his shop **SSC GD 25.01.2023 (Shift-I)**
(a) burnt (b) rooted
(c) arrived (d) looted

Ans. (d)
The word 'burgled' means 'looted'.

832. Select the most appropriate synonym of the word given below to fill in the blank in the following sentence.
Toying
My cat, Mili, loves .... with the toy mouse. **SSC GD 25.01.2023 (Shift-I)**
(a) licking (b) going
(c) dancing (d) playing

Ans. (d)
The word 'toying' means 'playing'.

833. Gloomy **SSC GD 25.01.2023 (Shift-III)**
(a) Unhappy (b) Blissful
(c) Hopeful (d) Light

Ans. (a)
The word 'gloomy' means 'sad and unhappy'. **Blissful** means happy.

834. Stratified **SSC GD 25.01.2023 (Shift-III)**
(a) Scattered (b) Consolidated
(c) Laminated (d) Ungraded

Ans. (a)
The word 'stratified' means arranged in separate layers. Hence, its nearest synonym is 'scattered'.
Consolidated means to combine.
Laminated means to cover with a plastic sheet for protection.
Ungraded means no classified in layers.

835. Annoyance **SSC GD 25.01.2023 (Shift-III)**
(a) Anger (b) Hatred
(c) Emotion (d) Agony

Ans. (a)
The word 'Annoyed' means 'angry and irritated'.
Agony means extreme pain.

836. The strict measures employed by the government ensured there was peace. **SSC GD 25.01.2023 (Shift-III)**
(a) liberal (b) austere
(c) orthodox (d) valiant

Ans. (b)
The word 'strict' means demanding that rules concerning behaviour are obeyed and observed. Hence, its synonym is 'austere' which means severe or strict in manner or attitude.
Liberal means willing respect or accept behaviour or opinions different from one's own; open to new ideas.
Orthodox means of the ordinary or usual type; normal/
Valiant means possessing or showing courage or determination.

837. Her debonair combined with quick wit added to her oratory skills. **SSC GD 27.01.2023 (Shift-II)**
(a) charming (b) corpulent
(c) amorous (d) churlish

Ans. (a)
The word 'debonair' means confident, stylish and charming (typically used of a man).
Corpulent means (of a person) fat.
Amorous means showing, feeling or relating to sexual desire.
Churlish means rude in a mean-spirited and surly way.

838. You have ...... (built up) a lot of muscles by going to the gym. **SSC GD 27.01.2023 (Shift-II)**
(a) enhanced (b) elevated
(c) boosted (d) gained

Ans. (d)
The correct filler the means 'built up' is 'gained'.

839. Noble SSC GD 27.01.2023 (Shift-IV)
(a) Agile (b) Regular
(c) Humble (d) Dignified

Ans. (d)

The word 'noble' means belonging by rank, title or birth to the aristocracy. Hence, its synonym is 'dignified' which means having or showing a composed or serious manner that is worthy of respect.

Agile means active.

Humble means kind and polite.

840. Nothing equalled the grief I felt at the death of my pet cat.
SSC GD 30.01.2023 (Shift-III)
(a) Freedom (b) Bondage
(c) Fear (d) Anguish

Ans. (d)

The word 'Anguish' means 'grief and sorrow'.

Bandage means slavery.

841. Alight SSC GD 30.01.2023 (Shift-III)
(a) Commence (b) Earn
(c) Enlighten (d) Descend

Ans. (d)

The word 'alight' means descend from a train, bus or other form of transport.

Enlighten means to gain knowledge.

842. Salty SSC GD 31.01.2023 (Shift-III)
(a) Feline (b) Prim
(c) Saline (d) Pricky

Ans. (c)

The word 'Saline' means 'Salty'.

Feline means related to a cat.

Prim means feeling or showing disapproval of anything regarded as improper; stiffly correct.

Pricky means unfriendly and easily offended or annoyed.

843. Early SSC GD 31.01.2023 (Shift-IV)
(a) Beforehand (b) Complex
(c) Late (d) Tardy

Ans. (a)

The word 'Beforehand' is a synonym of 'Early'.

Complex means difficult.

Tardy means late.

844. Obstruct SSC GD 31.01.2023 (Shift-IV)
(a) Separate (b) Block
(c) Magnify (d) Obey

Ans. (b)

The word 'Obstruct' means 'to stop or block'.

845. I was very much surprised to see mariam at the party.
SSC GD 31.01.2023 (Shift-IV)
(a) bowled (b) astonished
(c) stalked (d) aghast

Ans. (b)

The word 'astonished' means to be surprised and shocked.

Bowled means the act of throwing a ball.

Stalked means to follow secretly.

Aghast means filled with horror or shock.

846. Hesitation SSC GD 01.02.2023 (Shift-I)
(a) Readiness (b) Reluctance
(c) Prudence (d) Creativity

Ans. (b)

The word 'reluctance' means 'hesitation or doubt'.

Readiness means eagerness to do something.

Prudence means innocence.

847. I had the PRIVILEGE of meeting the magistrate. SSC GD 02.02.2023 (Shift-I)
(a) Recommendation
(b) Guidance
(c) Honour
(d) Atrocity

Ans. (c)

The word 'Privilege' means 'honour'.

Recommendation means suggestion or proposal as to the best course of action, especially one put forward by an authoritative body.

Atrocity means a very cruel, shocking action.

848. I was startled by his entry into the hall. SSC GD 02.02.2023 (Shift-I)
(a) glad (b) cherished
(c) frightened (d) miserable

Ans. (c)

The word 'startled' means 'shocked and frightened'.

Glad means happy.

Cherished means loved and cared.

Miserable means unhappy and angry.

849. We paid her a FLEETING visit before leaving the country.
SSC GD 06.02.2023 (Shift-I)
(a) Brief (b) Final (c) Hasty (d) Last

Ans. (a)

The word 'fleeting' means 'a small'. Hence, its synonym is 'brief' which means something small.

Hasty means quick.

850. The .... (glowing) fireflies lit up the field like city lights at night.
SSC GD 06.02.2023 (Shift-I)
(a) devious (b) dazzling
(c) furious (d) gracious

Ans. (b)

The word 'dazzling' means 'glowing'. Hence, it can fill the blank aptly.

Devious means evil.

Furious means angry.

Gracious means kind.

851. Antagonist SSC GD 06.02.2023 (Shift-I)
(a) Evil
(b) Adversary
(c) Nerd
(d) Amiable

Ans. (b)

The word 'Antagonist' means one that contends with or opposes another : adversary, opponent'.

Nerd is a person who is extremely enthusiastic and knowledgeable about a particular subject, especially one of specialist or niche interest.

852. Swindle SSC GD 07.02.2023 (Shift-I)
(a) Threat (b) Fraud
(c) Observation (d) Ride

Ans. (b)

The word 'Swindle' means a fraudulent scheme or a fraud action.

853. The treaty was signed by both the parties to retain the status-quo.
SSC GD 07.02.2023 (Shift-I)
(a) previous condition
(b) unnatural behaviour
(c) current situation
(d) class of societies

Ans. (c)

Status-quo is the current state of things.

854. Rohan .... (insufficient) the compassion required to be a doctor.
SSC GD 07.02.2023 (Shift-I)
(a) oversized (b) lacked
(c) was deprived (d) voided

Ans. (b)

The word 'insufficient' means a lack of something. Hence, 'lacked' can fill in the blank aptly.

855. Grandeur SSC GD 08.02.2023 (Shift-I)
(a) Magnificence
(b) Liable
(c) Commotion
(d) Power

Ans. (a)

The word 'grandeur' means 'grand splendour and impressiveness, especially of appearance or style.' Hence, its synonym is 'magnificence' which means the state of being very good, beautiful or deserving to be admired.

Liable means responsible.

Commotion means a disturbance.

856. He paused several times while delivering the speech.
SSC GD 08.02.2023 (Shift-I)
(a) persisted (b) stammered
(c) left (d) halted
Ans. (d)
The word 'paused' means 'stopped for some time'. Hence, its synonym is 'halted' which also means 'stopped'.
Persisted means to continue to do something.
Stammered means to say something with difficulty, repeating the initial letters of words and with sudden involuntary pauses.

857. The decision taken by the director is a/(an) judicious one.
SSC GD 08.02.2023 (Shift-I)
(a) honest (b) irrational
(c) thoughtful (d) foolish
Ans. (c)
The word 'Judicious' means 'Wise and thoughtful'.

858. Propel
Paddles are used to .... the boat.
SSC GD 08.02.2023 (Shift-I)
(a) rush (b) move
(c) carry (d) run
Ans. (b)
The word 'Propel' means drive or push something so that it moves forward.

859. Bliss **SSC GD 09.02.2023 (Shift-I)**
(a) Pain (b) Bane
(c) Joy (d) Educated
Ans. (c)
The word 'bliss' means extreme joy and happiness.
Bane means a cause of great distress or annoyance.

860. The manager's behaviour was the quintessence of professionalism.
SSC GD 09.02.2023 (Shift-I)
(a) insignificant appearance
(b) apparent display
(c) perfect example
(d) volatile aspect
Ans. (c)
The word 'quintessence' means the most perfect or typical example of a quality or class.

861. Scared **SSC GD 09.02.2023 (Shift-I)**
(a) Reassured (b) Calm
(c) Confident (d) Frightened
Ans. (d)
The word 'scared' means 'frightened and terrified'.
Reassured means to comfort.

862. Their relationship is quite .... (cordial). **SSC GD 09.02.2023 (Shift-I)**
(a) hostile (b) formal
(c) warm (d) artful
Ans. (c)
The word 'cordial' means 'warm and friendly'. **Artful** means creative.

863. Those unwilling to capitulate to new chancellor's demands will breathlessly fired.
SSC GD 09.02.2023 (Shift-II)
(a) believe (b) listen
(c) torture (d) surrender
Ans. (d)
The word 'capitulate' means cease to resist an opponent or an unwelcome demand; yield. Hence, its synonym is 'surrender' which means to stop resisting to an enemy or opponent and submit to their authority.

864. Frantic **SSC GD 09.02.2023 (Shift-II)**
(a) Violent (b) Gentle
(c) Lazy (d) Loyal
Ans. (a)
The word 'frantic' means distraught with fear, anxiety or other emotion. Hence, its nearest synonym is 'violent'.

865. A real warrior does not....(surrender) to his enemies.
SSC GD 09.02.2023 (Shift-II)
(a) expose (b) yield
(c) smile (d) cooperate
Ans. (b)
The word 'surrender' means to stop resisting to an enemy or opponent and submit to their authority.
Hence, its synonym is 'yield' which means to give way to someone or something that one can no longer resist.

866. Valid **SSC GD 13.02.2023 (Shift-II)**
(a) Illicit (b) Evil
(c) Logical (d) Fake
Ans. (c)
The word 'Valid' means 'correct and logical'.
Illicit means secret or hidden.

867. The most arrogant employee in his company was sacked by the boss. No one could tolerate his .... nature.
SSC GD 13.02.2023 (Shift-IV)
(a) pricey (b) plain
(c) dicey (d) haughty
Ans. (d)
The word 'haughty' means 'arrogant and egoist'. Hence, it can fill in the blank.
Dicey means doubtful.

868. Secure **SSC GD 13.02.2023 (Shift-IV)**
(a) Secret (b) Independent
(c) Safe (d) Comfortable
Ans. (c)
The word 'Secure' means 'certain to remain safe and unthreatened'.

869. Objective **SSC GD 13.02.2023 (Shift-IV)**
(a) Subjective
(b) Purpose
(c) Tyrannical
(d) Heartfelt
Ans. (b)
The word 'objective' means 'purpose or aim'.
Subjective means differing for people.
Tyrannical means exercising power in a cruel or arbitrary way.
Heartfelt means emotional.

SSC GD 2021

870. Visible **SSC GD 16.11.2021 (Shift-I)**
(a) Secret (b) Apparent
(c) Vague (d) Hidden
Ans. (b)
The word 'Apparent' means 'clearly visible'.
Vague means not clear and confusing.

871. Threat **SSC GD 16.11.2021 (Shift-I)**
(a) Suggestion (b) Proof
(c) Attention (d) Risk
Ans. (d)
The word 'Threat' means 'Risk'.

872. Ample **SSC GD 16.11.2021 (Shift-II)**
(a) Sparse (b) Sufficient
(c) Limited (d) Scarce
Ans. (b)
The word 'Ample' means 'sufficient or enough in quality and quantity'.
Sparse, Scarce and **Limited** means in less quantity.

873. Submissive **SSC GD 16.11.2021 (Shift-II)**
(a) Adamant (b) Obdurate
(c) Obedient (d) Obstinate
Ans. (c)
The word 'Submissive' means inclined or ready to submit or yield to the authority of another; unresistingly or humbly obedient.
Adamant, Obdurate and **Obstinate** mean stubbornly refusing to change one's opinion or chosen course of action, despite attempts to persuade one to do so.

SSC Selection Post 2024

874. Envoy **SSC SP 20.06.2024**
(a) Carrier (b) Chief
(c) Ambassador (d) Receiver

Ans. (c)

The word 'envoy' means a minister plenipotentiary, ranking below ambassador and above charge affairs.

Carrier means a person or thing that carries or delivers something.

Chief means a leader or ruler of a people or clan.

875. Warm SSC SP 20.06.2024 (Shift-IV)

(a) Unkind (b) Hostile
(c) Mean (d) Amicable

Ans. (d)

The word 'amicable' means 'warm and friendly'.

876. Concise SSC SP 20.06.2024 (Shift-IV)

(a) Brief (b) Grief
(c) Relief (d) Belief

Ans. (a)

The word 'concise' means 'short and brief'.

Grief means sorrow.

Relief means to reduce the pain.

SSC Selection Post 2023

877. Instant SSC SP 27.06.2023 (Shift-IV)

(a) Immediate (b) Precise
(c) Anticipated (d) Gradual

Ans. (a)

The word 'instant' means 'immediate'.

Precise means exact.

Anticipated means expected.

Gradual means slow.

878. The hapless incident was a result of sheer negligence by the authorities. SSC SP 27.06.2023 (Shift-IV)

(a) joyful (b) triumphant
(c) ill-fated (d) gratful

Ans. (c)

Hapless means unfortunate. Hence, its synonym is 'ill-fated'.

Joyful means feeling, expressing, or causing great pleasure and happiness.

Triumphant means having won a battle or contest.

Grateful means feeling or showing an appreciation of kindness.

879. There were a plethora of options available to the applicant SSC SP 28.06.2023 (Shift-III)

(a) destructive (b) recess
(c) excess (d) insufficient

Ans. (c)

Plethora means a large or excessive amount of something. Hence, its synonym is 'excess'.

Destructive means causing great and irreparable damage.

Recess means a small space created by building part of a wall further back from the rest.

Insufficient means not enough; inadequate.

880. The moral values in this nation were at their nadir during the autocrat's rule. SSC SP 30.06.2023 (Shift-I)

(a) highest point
(b) lowest point
(c) equatorial
(d) medial point

Ans. (b)

Nadir means the lowest point in the fortunes of a person or organisation. Hence, its synonym is 'lowest point'.

Highest point means the greatest or most significant point.

Equatorial means relating to, or near the equator. Medial point means situated in the middle.

881. Paranoia SSC SP 30.06.2023 (Shift-II)

(a) Assurance (b) Anxiety
(c) Belief (d) Faith

Ans. (b)

Paranoia means an irrational and persistent feeling that people are 'out to get you'. Hence, its synonym is 'anxiety'.

Assurance means a positive declaration intended to give confidence.

Faith means complete trust or confidence in someone or something.

882. As far as possible, solid waste should be managed at the household level so that minimum waste in delivered for management at the community level. SSC SP 30.06.2023 (Shift-III)

(a) Withdraw
(b) relocated
(c) replaced
(d) deposited

Ans. (d)

Delivered means brought or handed over to the proper recipient or address. Hence, its synonym is 'deposited'.

883. Awful SSC SP 30.06.2023 (Shift-IV)

(a) Inoffensive (b) Delightful
(c) Acceptable (d) Terrible

Ans. (d)

Awful means very bad or unpleasant. Hence, its synonym is 'terrible'.

Inoffensive means not causing harm or offense.

SSC Selection Post 2022

884. Gratification SSC SP 01.08.2022 (Shift-I)

(a) Pique
(b) Dejection
(c) Contentedness
(d) Dispiritedness

Ans. (c)

The word 'gratification' means pleasure, especially when gained from the satisfaction of a desire. Hence, its synonym is 'contentedness' which means satisfaction.

Pique means to raise interest.

Dejection and **Dispiritedness** means sadness and hopelessness

885. She evinced little enthusiasm for the outdoor games. SSC SP 01.08.2022 (Shift-I)

(a) showed (b) observed
(c) suppressed (d) pretended

Ans. (a)

The word 'evinced' means reveal the presence of (a quality or feeling); indicate; showed.

886. Blink SSC SP 01.08.2022 (Shift-IV)

(a) Attend (b) Ticker
(c) Blaze (d) Shine

Ans. (b)

Blink means shut and open the eyes quickly. Hence, its synonym is 'ticker'.

Attend means to be present at an event, meeting, or function.

Blaze means to burn fiercely or brightly.

Shine means to give out a bright light.

887. Alacrity SSC SP 03.08.2022 (Shift-III)

(a) Willingness
(b) Capriciousness
(c) Pleasure
(d) Mediocrity

Ans. (a)

Alacrity means brisk and cheerful readiness. Hence, its synonym is 'willingness'.

Capriciousness means given to sudden and unaccountable changes of mood or behaviour.

Mediocrity means the quality or state of being mediocre.

888. He appealed to the laws of th e land to vindicate from his assailants SSC SP 03.08.2022 (Shift-IV)

(a) prove (b) exonerate
(c) banish (d) assess

Ans. (b)

Vindicate means to clear someone of blame or suspicion. Hence, its synonym is 'exonerate'.

889. Compunction SSC SP 04.08.2022 (Shift-II)
(a) Punishment
(b) Scruples
(c) Scepticism
(d) Grief

Ans. (b)

Compunction means a feeling of guilt or moral scruple that prevents or follows the doing of something bad. Hence, its synonym is 'scruples'.

Scepticism means a skeptical attitude; doubt as to the truth of something.

Grief means deep sorrow, especially that caused by someone's death.

890. The eagle seized its prey in a <u>tenacious</u> grip. SSC SP 04.08.2022 (Shift-III)
(a) timorous (b) flexible
(c) persistent (d) passive

Ans. (c)

Tenacious means tending to keep a firm hold of something; clinging or adhering closely. Hence, its synonym is 'persistent'.

Timorous means showing or suffering from nervousness or a lack of confidence.

891. Abnegation SSC SP 04.08.2022 (Shift-IV)
(a) Abduction
(b) Sacrifice
(c) Renouncement
(d) Materialism

Ans. (c)

Abnegation means the act of renouncing or rejecting something. Hence, its synonym is 'renouncement'.

Abduction means the action of forcibly taking someone away against their will.

892. Embellish SSC SP 05.08.2022 (Shift-III)
(a) Decrease (b) Decorate
(c) Simplify (d) Reduce

Ans. (b)

Embellish means to make something more attractive by the addition of decorative details. Hence, its synonym is 'decorate'.

893. Sybarite SSC SP 05.08.2022 (Shift-II)
(a) debauchee (b) Gratuitous
(c) Ornery (d) Brusque

Ans. (a)

Sybarite means a person who is self-indulgent in their fondness for sensuous luxury. Hence, its synonym is 'debauchee'.

Gratuitous means uncalled for; lacking good reason; unwarranted.

Ornery means bad-tempered or difficult to deal with.

Brusque means abrupt or offhand in speech or manner.

SSC Steno 2024

894. Plentiful SSC Steno 11.12.2024 (Shift-I)
(a) Fondant
(b) Stingy
(c) Abundant
(d) Concordant

Ans. (c)

The most appropriate synonym of 'plentiful' is 'abundant' because both 'plentiful' and 'abundant' mean existing in large quantities or referring to something that is more than enough.

Fondant means a thick, creamy sugar mixture.

Stingy means unwilling to give or spend; ungenerous.

Concordant means in agreement; harmonious.

895. He was publicly scorned due to his <u>predilection</u> for luxurious items. SSC Steno 11.12.2024 (Shift-I)
(a) special liking
(b) dreamy meditation
(c) observant nature
(d) extreme indifference

Ans. (a)

The most appropriate meaning of 'predilection' is 'special liking'. Predilection means a preference or special fondness for something.

Observant nature means being attentive and noticing details.

Extreme indifference means lack of interest or concern.

896. Remote SSC Steno 11.12.2024 (Shift-I)
(a) Aloof (b) Remorse
(c) Sociable (d) Rash

Ans. (a)

The most appropriate synonym of 'remote' is 'aloof' because 'remote' means distant or far away, and 'aloof' means not friendly or forthcoming, detached.

Remorse means a feeling of deep regret.

Rash means acting without thinking.

897. Suman felt <u>ashamed and shy</u> about admitting his fault before his boss. SSC Steno 11.12.2024 (Shift-I)
(a) embarrassed
(b) brazen
(c) sad
(d) exalted

Ans. (a)

The correct substitution is 'embarrassed' because it means feeling self-conscious or ashamed, which fits the context of admitting a fault before a boss.

898. Why don't you come <u>visit</u> us sometime? SSC Steno 11.12.2024 (Shift-I)
(a) elude (b) see
(c) snub (d) ignore

Ans. (b)

The word 'visit' means to go to see and spend time with someone.

Elude means to escape from.

Snub means to ignore or reject.

Ignore means to pay no attention to.

899. Quandary SSC Steno 11.12.2024 (Shift-I)
(a) Dilemma (b) Harmony
(c) Solution (d) Certainty

Ans. (a)

The most appropriate synonym of 'quandary' is 'dilemma' because 'quandary' means a state of uncertainty or perplexity, especially as requiring a choice between equally unfavourable options and 'dilemma' has a similar meaning.

Harmony means a state of agreement or concord.

Solution means the act of solving a problem.

Certainty means a state of being sure or confident.

900. Procrastination SSC Steno 11.12.2024 (Shift-I)
(a) Limitation
(b) Suspension
(c) Resumption
(d) Action

Ans. (b)

The most appropriate synonym of 'procrastination' is 'suspension'. It refers to the act of delaying or postponing something.

901. Wholly SSC Steno 11.12.2024 (Shift-I)
(a) Lonely (b) Barely
(c) Entirely (d) Weekly

Ans. (c)

The synonym of 'wholly' is 'entirely'. 'Wholly' means completely or fully, and 'entirely' has the same meaning.

902. Sarika's husband had been undergoing <u>vicissitudes</u> in his fortune since 2002. SSC Steno 11.12.2024 (Shift-II)
(a) compilations (b) hibernations
(c) tribulations (d) consolations

Ans. (c)

The word 'vicissitudes' means 'tribulations'. 'Vicissitudes' refers to the changes or variations, particularly those that are challenging or difficult. In this context, it describes the hardships or fluctuations in Sarika's husband's fortune, making 'tribulations' an appropriate synonym.

903. His lecture was terse and interesting.
SSC Steno 11.12.2024 (Shift-II)
(a) overt (b) braggart
(c) inert (d) short
Ans. (d)
The synonym for 'terse' is 'short'. 'Terse' means brief and to the point, and in the context of the sentence, it describes the lecture as concise, which is synonymous with 'short.'

904. Abandon SSC Steno 11.12.2024 (Shift-II)
(a) Reclaim (b) Possess
(c) Desert (d) Commence
Ans. (c)
'Desert' is a synonym of 'abandon', which means to leave something or someone behind. It accurately captures the meaning of leaving or forsaking, which aligns with the meaning of 'abandon'.

905. Banish SSC Steno 11.12.2024 (Shift-III)
(a) Deport (b) Belligerent
(c) Recoil (d) Savage
Ans. (a)
'Banish' means to expel or send away. 'Deport' is a synonym because it also means to remove someone from a place, usually a country.

906. Enrage SSC Steno 11.12.2024 (Shift-III)
(a) Stimulate (b) Infuriate
(c) Eradicate (d) Expand
Ans. (b)
The synonym of 'enrage' is 'infuriate'. Both words mean to make someone extremely angry.

907. Divine SSC Steno 11.12.2024 (Shift-III)
(a) Artful (b) Modest
(c) Celestial (d) Perpetual
Ans. (c)
The synonym of 'divine' is 'celestial'. 'Divine' relates to something heavenly or god-like and 'celestial' means pertaining to the sky or heavens.

908. Your silly tricks will not impress me.
SSC Steno 11.12.2024 (Shift-III)
(a) expunge (b) bore
(c) neglect (d) impact
Ans. (d)
The synonym of 'impress' is 'impact'. Both words mean to have a strong effect on someone or something.

909. Hind SSC Steno 10.12.2024 (Shift-I)
(a) Fore (b) Anterior
(c) Ventral (d) Rear
Ans. (d)
The most appropriate synonym of the word 'hind' is 'rear'. Both 'Hind' and 'rear' refer to the back part of something.

910. Vanquish SSC Steno 10.12.2024 (Shift-I)
(a) Quantify (b) Conquer
(c) Describe (d) Verify
Ans. (b)
The most appropriate synonym of the word 'vanquish' is 'conquer'. 'Vanquish' means to defeat or overcome, and 'conquer' has a similar meaning, making it the best fit.

911. Ignoramus SSC Steno 10.12.2024 (Shift-I)
(a) Stupid (b) Cautious
(c) Playful (d) Deceitful
Ans. (a)
The most appropriate synonym of the word 'ignoramus' is 'stupid'. 'Ignoramus' refers to someone who is ignorant or lacks knowledge, and 'stupid' similarly implies a lack of intelligence or understanding.

912. Recumbent SSC Steno 10.12.2024 (Shift-II)
(a) Upstanding (b) Prostrate
(c) Upright (d) Review
Ans. (b)
The most appropriate synonym for 'recumbent' is 'prostrate'. Both 'Recumbent' and 'prostrate' means lying stretched out on the ground, especially face down.
Upstanding means honest and respectable.
Upright means standing or sitting straight.
Review means to examine or assess something.

913. Taciturnity SSC Steno 10.12.2024 (Shift-II)
(a) Eloquence (b) Talkative
(c) Silence (d) Tactic
Ans. (c)
The most appropriate synonym for 'taciturnity' is 'silence'. 'Taciturnity' means the state of being reserved or not speaking much.
Eloquence means fluent or persuasive speaking or writing.
Tactic means a planned action or strategy.

914. The lockdown during Covid-19 in certain places has imposed threatening constraints on market economy and it will take time to recover from this.
SSC Steno 10.12.2024 (Shift-II)
(a) Beliefs (b) Problems
(c) Restrictions (d) Faiths
Ans. (c)
'Restrictions' is the most appropriate synonym for 'constraints'. 'Constraints' means limitations or restrictions imposed on something.

915. Morality is contextual; therefore, it is foolish to believe that one's moral judgement would be perfect and immaculate. SSC Steno 10.12.2024 (Shift-III)
(a) indelicate (b) tarnished
(c) impeccable (d) grubby
Ans. (c)
'Impeccable' is the most appropriate synonym for 'immaculate', as both means perfect or without any flaws.

916. Prerogative SSC Steno 10.12.2024 (Shift-III)
(a) Satisfaction (b) Bias
(c) Privilege (d) Predisposition
Ans. (c)
'Privilege' is the most appropriate synonym of 'prerogative'. Prerogative means a right or privilege exclusive to a particular individual or class.

917. A slow, languid smile crossed her face, as if to voice the contentment of her heart. SSC Steno 10.12.2024 (Shift-III)
(a) sluggish (b) hurried
(c) lively (d) energetic
Ans. (a)
'Sluggish' is the most appropriate synonym for 'languid', as both mean slow-moving or inactive.

918. The women of this country never questioned anything.
Why are they so credulous?
SSC Steno 10.12.2024 (Shift-III)
(a) Suspicious of everything surrounding them
(b) Willing to believe promptly without adequate evidence
(c) Reluctant to face the difficulties of life with courage
(d) Indifferent to the basic necessities of life
Ans. (b)
'Willing to believe promptly without adequate evidence' is the most appropriate meaning of 'credulous'.
Credulous means having or showing too great a readiness to believe things.

919. She could sensen something ominous in the darkness of the night.
SSC Steno 10.12.2024 (Shift-III)
(a) inauspicious (b) propitious
(c) blissful (d) profane
Ans. (a)
'Inauspicious' is the synonym of 'ominous', as both means giving the impression that something bad or unpleasant is going to happen.
Propitious means giving or indicating a good chance of success.
Profane means not respectful of religious practice; irreverent.

920. Wanton SSC Steno 10.12.2024 (Shift-III)
(a) Abrogation (b) Obscene
(c) Prevent (d) Habit
Ans. (b)
'Obscene' is the most appropriate synonym of 'wanton,' both of which mean deliberate and unprovoked, often in a morally unacceptable way.

SSC Steno 2023

921. Apprehension SSC Steno 12.10.2023 (Shift-I)
(a) Courage (b) Fear
(c) Myth (d) Barbarous
Ans. (b)
The word 'Apprehension' means anxiety or fear that something bad or unpleasant will happen.

922. She was often oblivious to the potential consequences of her actions.
Steno Steno 13.10.2023 (Shift-I)
(a) barely (b) proficient
(c) obvious (d) unaware
Ans. (d)
The word 'oblivious' means 'not aware'.

923. Feeble SSC Steno 13.10.2023 (Shift-I)
(a) Rugged (b) Stout
(c) Wimpy (d) Stalwart
Ans. (c)
Feeble means weak. Hence, its synonym is 'Wimpy' which means 'thin and weak'.

SSC Steno 2022

924. Ritika was deprived of her father's property as she married a knave.
SSC Steno 17.11.2022 (Shift-I)
(a) Gallant (b) Novice
(c) Rogue (d) Chauffeur
Ans. (c)
The underlined word 'Knave' means a dishonest man.
Hence, its correct synonym is 'rogue'.
Galdant means brave.
Novice refers to a new and in experienced person.
Chauffeur is a person who drives a car.

925. The soldiers showed fortitude and resilience while facing the opponents.
SSC Steno 17.11.2022 (Shift-I)
(a) Ingenuity (b) Bravery
(c) Atrocity (d) Conscientiousness
Ans. (b)
The word 'Fortitude' means courage shown when you are in great pain or experiencing a lot of trouble. Hence, its correct synonym is 'Bravery'.
Ingenuity means honest
Atrocity means cruelty
Conscientiousness means responsible.

926. Lucky SSC Steno 17.11.2022 (Shift-I)
(a) Outrageous (b) Jealous
(c) Auspicious (d) Ominous
Ans. (c)
A 'Lucky' means having, bringing or resulting from good luck. Hence, its correct synonym is 'Auspicious' as it means suggesting a positive and successful future.
Outrageous means bad and shocking.
Ominous means threatening.

927. Our locality has a common space for observing various national days and for organising festivals.
SSC Steno 18.11.2022 (Shift-I)
(a) celebrating (b) forming
(c) witnessing (d) coordinating
Ans. (d)
'Coordinating' is a synonym of 'organising'.

928. He gave a large amount of donation for flood victims and everyone appreciated his magnanimous act.
SSC Steno 18.11.2022 (Shift-I)
(a) Vindictive (b) Chimerical
(c) Chivalrous (d) Cherubic
Ans. (c)
The word 'Magnanimous' means generous. Hence, its correct synonym is 'Chivalrous' which means to be considerate or benevolent.
Vindictive means revengeful.
Chimerical means impossible to achieve.
Cherukic means angelic.

929. Sycophant SSC Steno 18.11.2022 (Shift-I)
(a) Flatterer (b) Mammoth
(c) Killer (d) Psycho
Ans. (a)
The word 'Sycophant' refers to a person who tries to win favour from others by the means of flattery. Thus, the word 'Flatterer'' is the correct synonym for it.
Mammoth means great.
Psycho means crazy.

930. Gregarious SSC Steno 18.11.2022 (Shift-I)
(a) Anti-social (b) Introvert
(c) Sociable (d) Excited
Ans. (c)
The word 'Gregarious' means sociable. Thus, 'sociable' is the correct synonym for it.
Introvert means anti-social.

931. Solicit SSC Steno 18.11.2022 (Shift-I)
(a) Pretend (b) Degrade
(c) Request (d) Complicate
Ans. (c)
The word 'Solicit' means asking for something from someone. Hence, 'request' is its synonym.
Pretend means to act.
Degrade means to insult.
Complicate means to make difficult.

932. The visitors of the restaurant were enthralled by the dulcet tune that the pianist played.
SSC Steno 18.11.2022 (Shift-I)
(a) unpleasantly rough
(b) ear-piercing and loud
(c) sweet and soothing
(d) inaudible and indistinct
Ans. (c)
The underlined word 'Dulcet' means 'sweet and soothing'.

933. As the effect of anaesthesia dissipated, the patient regained consciousness. SSC Steno 18.11.2022 (Shift-I)
(a) Enhanced (b) Heightened
(c) Returned (d) Disappeared
Ans. (d)
The word 'dissipate' means to disappear gradually.

934. Carnage SSC Steno 11.11.2022 (Shift-I)
(a) Slaughter (b) Lust
(c) Plague (d) Revelry
Ans. (a)
The word 'Carnage' means the killing of a large number of people. Hence, its correct synonym is 'slaughter'.
Plague refers to a widespread fatal disease.
Revelry means festivities.

935. Emblem SSC Steno 11.11.2022 (Shift-I)
(a) Symbol (b) Expression
(c) Problem (d) Refinement
Ans. (a)
An 'emblem' is a symbolic object as a distinctive badge of a nation, organisation or family.
'Symbol' also means a thing that represents or stands for something else. Therefore, symbol and emblem are synonymous.

936. Batter SSC Steno 11.11.2022 (Shift-I)
(a) Clash (b) Struggle
(c) Beat (d) Fight
Ans. (c)
The word 'Batter' means to strike repeatedly with hard blows. 'Beat' also means the same.
'Clash' refers to a fight.

937. Austere SSC Steno 12.11.2022 (Shift-I)
(a) Unadorned (b) Luxurious
(c) Elaborate (d) Decorative
Ans. (a)
The word 'Austere' means having a plain appearance. So, 'Unadorned' is the correct synonym.

05

Antonyms

An antonym is a word that has the opposite meaning of another word.
For example
Unworthy, Infamous are antonyms of Meritorious
Subdues, Gentle are antonyms of Frantic

Types of Questions Asked

Various types of questions are asked on antonyms in the SSC Examination.

TYPE 1

Select the most appropriate antonym of the given word.
Placate
(a) Calm (b) Pacify (c) Incite (d) Tranquil ***Ans.*** (c)

TYPE 2

Select the most appropriate antonym of the underlined words in the following sentence.
The mountain path was treacherous, with steep cliffs and slippery rocks.
(a) Dangerous (b) Safe
(c) Unstable (d) Perilous ***Ans.*** (b)

TYPE 3

Select the most appropriate antonym of the given word to fill in the blank in the sentence.
Vivid
The artist's painting was intentionally ...., allowing viewers to interpret it in different ways.
(a) ambiguous (b) Undefined
(c) Labyrinth (d) Puzzle ***Ans.*** (a)

How to Solve the Questions

To find the correct antonyms, it is very important to develop a good vocabulary.

Read newspapers, articles, journals, blogs, etc., to find new words and understand their meanings.

You can also solve sentence based questions on synonyms with these easy steps.

- **Step 1** Read the sentence with the underlined word or the word whose antonym you need.
- **Step 2** Understand the meaning of the word within the sentence. This will help you know the meaning of the word and help you find the antonyms.
- **Step 3** Now, read the words in the options. Think of the meanings of the words given in the options.
- **Step 4** The word with the opposite meaning is your answer.

SSC Exam Scanner

Directions (Q. Nos. 1-910) Select the most appropriate antonym of the given word.

Or

Select the most appropriate option to substitute the underlined/highlighted segment in the given sentence.

Or

Select the most appropriate antonym of the word given in bracket or underline to fill in the blank.

SSC CGL 2024 (Tier 1 & 2)

1. Enhance **SSC CGL Tier-2 18.01.2025**
(a) Enrich (b) Impair (c) Miracle (d) Relevance
Ans. (b)
While 'enhance' means to improve or augment something, 'impair' means to weaken or damage it, which is the opposite of enhancement.

2. Generous **SSC CGL Tier-2 18.01.2025**
(a) Magnanimous (b) Altruistic
(c) Selfish (d) Benevolent
Ans. (c)
While 'generous' means showing kindness and willingness to give, 'selfish' means lacking consideration for others and being primarily concerned with one's own profit or pleasure.

3. Accumulated **SSC CGL Tier-2 18.01.2025**
(a) Bunched (b) Garnered
(c) Spared (d) Scattered
Ans. (d)
While 'accumulated' means to gather or collect, 'scattered' means to disperse or spread out, which is the opposite of accumulation.

4. Ameliorate SSC CGL Tier-2 20.01.2025
(a) Succour (b) Recondite
(c) Exacerbate (d) Motto

Ans. (c)

The antonym of 'ameliorate', which means to make better, is 'exacerbate', which means to make worse.

- **Recondite** Little known or obscure.
- **Motto** A short sentence or phrase that expresses a belief or purpose.
- **Succour** Assistance and support in times of hardship and distress.

5. Thrifty SSC CGL Tier-2 20.01.2025
(a) Indifferent (b) Thankful
(c) Extravagant (d) Intolerant

Ans. (c)

The word 'thrifty' means economical and careful with resources. Its antonym is 'extravagant', which means spending money or resources freely and wastefully.

6. Melancholy SSC CGL Tier-2 20.01.2025
(a) Mechanical (b) Profitable
(c) Miserable (d) Pleasant

Ans. (d)

The antonym of 'melancholy', which means a deep, pensive and long-lasting sadness, is 'pleasant', which means giving a sense of happy satisfaction or enjoyment.

- **Miserable** Extremely unhappy or uncomfortable.
- **Profitable** Yielding financial gain.
- **Mechanical** Related to machinery or lacking emotion and spontaneity.

7. The explosive used is of my own formulation and I can vouch for its efficiency. SSC CGL Tier-1 09.09.2024 (Shift-I)
(a) Maintain (b) Certify
(c) Invalidate (d) Witness

Ans. (c)

Vouch means to support or help. Hence, its antonym is 'invalidate' which means to prove as false.

Certify means to attest or confirm in a formal statement.

Witness is someone who is required to appear in court to answer questions about a case.

8. If you want to be a good detective, it helps to have an inquisitive nature. SSC CGL Tier-1 09.09.2024 (Shift-II) SSC CPO 04.10.2023 (Shift-II) CPO 05.10.2023 (Shift-I)
(a) Comprehensive
(b) Itemised
(c) Intrusive
(d) Disinterested

Ans. (d)

Inquisitive means curious and interested. Hence, its antonym is 'disinterested'.

Comprehensive means including or dealing with all or nearly all elements or aspects of something.

Itemised means present as a list of individual items.

Intrusive means causing disruption or annoyance through being unwelcome or uninvited.

9. Scary SSC CGL Tier-1 09.09.2024 (Shift-II)
(a) Bright
(b) Pristine
(c) Awful
(d) Comforting

Ans. (d)

The antonym of 'scary' is 'comforting'.

Pristine means perfectly clean.

10. Elisabeth stood at the piano, which did nothing to **allay** his anxiety. SSC CGL Tier-1 09.09.2024 (Shift-II)
(a) mitigate (b) simplify
(c) mollify (d) aggravate

Ans. (d)

Allay means to diminish or put at rest (fear, suspicion or worry).
Hence, its antonym is 'aggravate' which means make (a problem, injury, or offence) worse or more serious.

Mitigate means make (something bad) less severe, serious, or painful.

Mollify means reduce the severity of (something).

11. Miserable SSC CGL Tier-1 10.09.2024 (Shift-III) SSC SP 20.06.2024 (Shift-II), HSC Level
(a) Melodious (b) Settled
(c) Restrained (d) Cheerful

Ans. (d)

Miserable means sad and angry. Hence, its antonym is 'cheerful'.

Melodious means a sweet and pleasing voice.

Settled means resolve or reach an agreement about (an argument or problem).

Restrained means a limiting condition or measure, especially a legal one.

12. Timid SSC CGL Tier-1 10.09.2024 (Shift-I)
(a) Meek (b) Anxious
(c) Daring (d) Spooky

Ans. (c)

Timid means weak and showing a lack of courage or confidence. Hence, its antonym is 'daring'.
Meek means weak.
Spooky means scary.

13. She was elated about her promotion, but her colleague felt quite disheartened. SSC CGL Tier-1 10.09.2024 (Shift-I)
(a) cheerful (b) proud
(c) discouraged (d) delighted

Ans. (c)

Elated means happy.
Hence, its antonym is 'discouraged'.

14. Their sporting achievements at the highest level are being utterly ignored. SSC CGL Tier-1 10.09.2024 (Shift-II)
(a) extremely (b) correctly
(c) minimally (d) totally

Ans. (c)

Utterly means completely. Hence, its antonym is 'minimally'.

15. Most of the flowers bloom in the spring season but they start to .... during summer. SSC CGL Tier-1 10.09.2024 (Shift-II)
(a) flush (b) wither
(c) flourish (d) blossom

Ans. (b)

Bloom means to grow. Hence, its antonym is 'wither' which means to become dry and shrivelled.

Flush means (of a person's skin, face, etc.) become red and hot, typically as the result of illness or strong emotion.

Flourish means to grow.

Blossom means a flower or a mass of flowers, especially on a tree or bush.

16. Risible SSC CGL Tier-1 10.09.2024 (Shift-II)
(a) Serious (b) Curious
(c) Droll (d) Giddy

Ans. (a)

Risible means provoking laughter through being ludicrous. Hence, its nearest antonym is 'serious'.

Droll means curious or unusual in a way that provokes dry amusement.

Giddy means having a sensation of whirling and a tendency to fall or stagger; dizzy.

17. Most of the land near the town is barren, but the efforts of the farmers have turned it .... SSC CGL Tier-1 10.09.2024 (Shift-II) SSC CGL Tier-1 03.08.2023 (Shift-II)
(a) sterile (b) infertile
(c) fertile (d) unfruitful

Ans. (c)

Barren means too poor to produce much or any vegetation. Hence, its antonym is 'fertile'.

Sterile means unfruitful and infertile.

18. The ……… to the venue was decorated with beautiful lights. [exit] SSC CGL Tier-1 10.09.2024 (Shift-III)
(a) house (b) road
(c) entry (d) ceremony

Ans. (c)
The correct filler for the given blank is 'entry'. It is the opposite of 'exit'.

19. Mechanical SSC CGL Tier-1 10.09.2024 (Shift-III)
(a) Surrogate (b) Automatised
(c) Yielding (d) Manual

Ans. (d)
Mechanical means done by machine. Hence, its antonym is 'manual' which means done by hands.
Surrogate is a woman who carries and gives birth to a child for another person or couple.
Automatised means to make automatic.
Yielding means giving way under pressure; not hard or rigid.

20. Forbid SSC CGL Tier-1 11.09.2024 (Shift-I)
(a) Prohibit (b) Allow
(c) Call (d) Forsake

Ans. (b)
Forbid means refuse to allow (something). Hence, its antonym is 'allow'.
Prohibit means to stop someone to do something.
Forsake means to give up.

21. He was very <u>cruel</u> in dealing with the students. SSC CGL Tier-1 11.09.2024 (Shift-I)
(a) skittish (b) kind
(c) malevolent (d) kingly

Ans. (b)
The antonym of 'cruel' is 'kind'.
Skittish means (of an animal, especially a horse) nervous or excitable; easily scared.
Malevolent means evil.

22. Deficient SSC CGL Tier-1 11.09.2024 (Shift-II)
(a) Skimpy (b) Broken
(c) Ample (d) Terrible

Ans. (c)
Deficient means lacking.
Hence, its antonym is 'ample' which means more than enough.
Skimpy means (of clothes) short and revealing.

23. Meander SSC CGL Tier-1 11.09.2024 (Shift-II)
(a) Ramble (b) Deputise
(c) Confirm (d) Direct

Ans. (d)
Meander means curving or zigzag. Hence, its antonym is 'direct'.
Ramble means walk for pleasure in the countryside.
Deputise means temporarily act or speak on behalf of someone else.

24. In Shakespeare's 'The Merchant of Venice', Shylock's connivance aimed to <u>jeopardise</u> Antonio's life. SSC CGL Tier-1 11.09.2024 (Shift-II)
(a) Safeguard (b) Risk
(c) Peril (d) Jape

Ans. (a)
Jeopardise means put (someone or something) into a situation in which there is a danger of loss, harm, failure. Hence, its antonym is to 'safeguard'.
Peril means danger.
Jape means a practical joke.

25. Brittle SSC CGL Tier-1 11.09.2024 (Shift-III)
(a) Crunchy (b) Resilient
(c) Delicate (d) Aloof

Ans. (b)
Brittle means hard but liable to break easily. Hence, its antonym is 'resilient' which means strong.

26. <u>Success</u> is not a destination, it's a journey. SSC CGL Tier-1 12.09.2024 (Shift-III)
(a) Sensation (b) Opulence
(c) Victory (d) Failure

Ans. (d)
The antonym of 'success' is 'failure'.
Opulence means great wealth or luxuriousness.

27. Secure SSC CGL Tier-1 12.09.2024 (Shift-I)
(a) Succeed (b) Save
(c) Attack (d) Trundle

Ans. (c)
The antonym of 'secure' is 'attack'.
Trundle means (with reference to a wheeled vehicle or its occupants) move or cause to move slowly and heavily.

28. Receive SSC CGL Tier-1 12.09.2024 (Shift-I)
(a) Admit (b) Exile
(c) Reward (d) Fund

Ans. (b)
The nearest antonym of 'receive' is 'exile' which means to exit.

29. She has ……. (witty) remarks about everything. SSC CGL Tier-1 12.09.2024 (Shift-II)
(a) sorry (b) whimsical
(c) unamusing (d) woeful

Ans. (c)
Witty means wise but funny. Hence, its antonym is 'unamusing' which is the correct filler for the given blank.
Whimsical means fanciful.
Woeful means characterised by, expressive of or causing sorrow or misery.

30. Paralysed SSC CGL Tier-1 12.09.2024 (Shift-II)
(a) Demure (b) Stifled
(c) Sultry (d) Healthy

Ans. (d)
The antonym of 'paralysed' is 'healthy'.
Demure means reserved, modest and shy (typically used of a woman).
Stifled means make (someone) unable to breathe properly; suffocate.
Sultry means (of the air or weather) hot and humid.

31. Catastrophe SSC CGL Tier-1 12.09.2024 (Shift-III)
(a) Success (b) Nurture
(c) Immaculate (d) Disaster

Ans. (a)
Catastrophe means disaster.
Hence, its antonym is 'success'.
Nurture means care for and protect (someone or something) while they are growing.
Immaculate means perfectly clean, neat or tidy.

32. One must be very <u>strong</u> to lift this box of glass jars. SSC CGL Tier-1 12.09.2024 (Shift-III)
(a) Mighty (b) Weak
(c) Complicated (d) Rugged

Ans. (b)
The antonym of 'strong' is 'weak'.
Complicated means difficult. Rugged means a broken, rocky and uneven surface.

33. Monotonous SSC CGL Tier-1 12.09.2024 (Shift-III)
(a) Tiresome (b) Tedious
(c) Engrossing (d) Rational

Ans. (c)
Monotonous means repetitive and boring. Hence, its antonym is 'engrossing'.
Tiresome means tiring.
Tedious means difficult.
Rational means sensible.

34. Epitome SSC CGL Tier-1 13.09.2024 (Shift-I)
(a) Exhort (b) Expansion
(c) Lucid (d) Precise

Ans. (b)

Epitome means the highest order, place or position. Hence, its nearest antonym is 'expansion' as it indicates upwards movement.

Exhort means strongly encourage or urge (someone) to do something.

Lucid means expressed clearly, easy to understand.

Precise means correct and accurate.

35. An elephant is a large mammal.
SSC CGL Tier-1 13.09.2024 (Shift-I)

(a) Bumper (b) Gigantic
(c) Tiny (d) Heroic

Ans. (c)

The antonym of 'large' is 'tiny'.

Bumper means a device to absorb shock, a slang term and a break between a programme and commercial on radio or television.

Gigantic means huge.

36. The modern work is deliberately .... (ambiguous).
SSC CGL Tier-1 13.09.2024 (Shift-I)

(a) puzzling (b) certain
(c) dubious (d) vague

Ans. (b)

Ambiguous means confusing and not certain of anything. Hence, its antonym is 'certain' which is the correct filler for the given blank.

Puzzling means confusing.

Dubious means hesitating or doubting.

Vague means not clear.

37. Barbarity SSC CGL Tier-1 13.09.2024 (Shift-I)

(a) Callous (b) Compromise
(c) Compassion (d) Rivalry

Ans. (c)

'Barbarity' means cruelty.

Hence, its antonym is 'compassion' which means kindness.

Callous means cruel and evil.

Compromise means an agreement or settlement of a dispute that is reached by each side making concessions.

Rivalry means competition for the same objective or for superiority in the same field.

38. His mother never held a **grudge** against his father.
SSC CGL Tier-1 13.09.2024 (Shift-I)

(a) rancour (b) benevolence
(c) revulsion (d) malevolence

Ans. (b)

Grudge means a strong feeling of anger and dislike for a person who you feel has treated you badly, especially one that lasts for a long time.

Hence, its nearest antonym is 'Benevolence' which means kindness.

Rancour means bitterness or resentfulness, especially when long standing.

Revulsion means lack of attraction.

Malevolence means evilness.

39. Sheila .... (failed) all her classes.
SSC CGL Tier-1 13.09.2024 (Shift-II)

(a) passed (b) flunked
(c) fizzled (d) flopped

Ans. (a)

The antonym of 'failed' is 'passed' which is the correct filler for the given blank.

40. She .... the target by an inch and lost the gold medal. [hit]
SSC CGL Tier-1 13.09.2024 (Shift-II)

(a) touched
(b) bashed
(c) missed
(d) cleaned

Ans. (c)

The antonym of 'hit' is 'missed'.

41. I was happy to know that Sheila passed her final exams.
SSC CGL Tier-1 13.09.2024 (Shift-II)

(a) Sad (b) Joyful
(c) Upbeat (d) Excited

Ans. (a)

The antonym of 'happy' is 'sad'.

42. The war was followed by a long period of prosperity.
SSC CGL Tier-1 13.09.2024 (Shift-III)

(a) Security (b) Secure
(c) Affluence (d) Failure

Ans. (d)

Prosperity means success and wealth. Hence, its antonym is 'failure'. Affluence means wealth.

43. If someone babbles, it means that they talk in a confused or excited way. SSC CGL Tier-1 13.09.2024 (Shift-III)

(a) Gossips (b) Quiet
(c) Talkative (d) Rants

Ans. (b)

Babbles means continuously talking and making noise.

Hence, its antonym is 'quiet'.

44. Akash went to .... his school uniform. [sell]
SSC CGL Tier-1 13.09.2024 (Shift-III)

(a) loan (b) rent
(c) buy (d) make

Ans. (c)

The antonym of 'buy' is 'sell', which is the correct filler for the given blank.

45. Affirmative
SSC CGL Tier-1 13.09.2024 (Shift-III)

(a) Sanction (b) Negative
(c) Acquiescence (d) Accession

Ans. (b)

Affirmative means to agree or positive. Hence, its antonym is 'negative'.

Sanction means a threatened penalty for disobeying a law or rule.

Acquiescence means the reluctant acceptance of something without protest.

Accession means to take power or throne.

46. Entire SSC CGL Tier-1 17.09.2024 (Shift-I)

(a) Ingress (b) Thorough
(c) Incomplete (d) Undivided

Ans. (c)

Entire means complete.

Hence, its antonym is 'incomplete'.

Ingress means the action or fact of going in or entering; the capacity or right of entrance.

Thorough means complete.

47. Feeling discouraged, she finally finds the motivation for pursing her goal. SSC CGL Tier 1 17.09.2024 (Shift-I)

(a) inspired (b) energetic
(c) admired (d) disappointed

Ans. (a)

Discouraged means not inspired or motivated. Hence, its antonym is 'inspired'.

48. Attack SSC CGL Tier-1 17.09.2024 (Shift-II)

(a) Ambush (b) Defence
(c) Production (d) Engagement

Ans. (b)

The antonym of 'attack' is 'defence'.

Ambush is a surprise attack on a target that is either moving or temporarily stopped, carried out from a concealed position.

49. We should plan our actions judiciously before going to war.
SSC CGL Tier-1 17.09.2024 (Shift-II)

(a) irreverent (b) irrational
(c) irrelevant (d) irritatingly

Ans. (b)

Judiciously means rational. Hence, its antonym is 'irrational'.

Irreverent means disrespectful.

Irrelevant means not important.

50. The chef requires .... vegetables for the salad. [stale]
SSC CGL Tier-1 17.09.2024 (Shift-II)

(a) green (b) fresh (c) cut (d) leafy

Ans. (b)

The antonym of 'stale' is 'fresh'.

51. I refuse to let anything come in the way of my dreams.
SSC CGL Tier-1 17.09.2024 (Shift-II)
(a) repress (b) balk
(c) accord (d) permit

Ans. (d)

The antonym of 'refuse' is to permit or allow.

Repress means to subdue (someone or something) by force.

Balk means to hesitate or be unwilling to accept an idea or undertaking.

Accord means to give or grant someone (power, status or recognition).

52. Synthetic SSC CGL Tier-1 17.09.2024 (Shift-II)
(a) Artificial (b) Imitation
(c) Processed (d) Natural

Ans. (d)

Synthetic means artificial. Hence, its antonym is 'natural'. Imitation means a copy.

53. Candid SSC CGL Tier-1 17.09.2024 (Shift-III)
(a) Tender (b) Guileless
(c) Dishonest (d) Irrelevant

Ans. (c)

Candid means honest. Hence, its antonym is 'dishonest'.

Tender means soft.

Guileless means devoid of guile; innocent and without deception.

Irrelevant means not important.

54. Reluctant
SSC CGL Tier-1 17.09.2024 (Shift-III)
(a) Desperate (b) Obedient
(c) Enthusiastic (d) Beautiful

Ans. (c)

Reluctant means unwilling and hesitant; disinclined. Hence, its antonym is 'enthusiastic'.

55. The movie's plot was predictable, with cliched twists and turns.
SSC CGL Tier-1 17.09.2024 (Shift-III)
(a) undeviating
(b) evident
(c) unexpected
(d) infelicitous

Ans. (c)

Predictable means expected. Hence, its antonym is 'unexpected'.

Undeviating means showing no deviation; constant and steady.

Evident means clear.

Infelicitous means unfortunate; inappropriate.

56. The patient was suffering from a chronic disease.
SSC CGL Tier-1 17.09.2024 (Shift-III)
(a) common (b) universal
(c) usual (d) mild

Ans. (d)

Chronic means severe. Hence, its antonym is 'mild'.

57. Many people fought to **abolish** slavery during the Civil War.
SSC CGL Tier-1 17.09.2024 (Shift-III)
(a) kill (b) terminate
(c) establish (d) damage

Ans. (c)

Abolish means formally put an end to (a system, practice, or institution). Hence, its antonym is 'establish' which means to set up.

58. The appearance of most of the animals in jungle is deceptive in nature. SSC CGL Tier-1 18.09.2024 (Shift-I)
(a) honest (b) illusive
(c) ugly (d) beautiful

Ans. (a)

Deceptive means dishonest. Hence, its antonym is 'honest'.
Illusive means deceptive.

59. The long-standing feud between the two villages was settled due to the intervention of the two chiefs.
SSC CGL Tier-1 18.09.2024 (Shift-I)
SSC CGL Tier-1 12.12.2022 (Shift-II)
SSC MTS 01.09.2023 (Shift-I)
(a) Humility (b) Harmony
(c) Humble (d) Honesty

Ans. (b)

Feud means a prolonged and bitter quarrel or dispute. Hence, its antonym is 'harmony'.

Humility means Humble.

60. Autonomy
SSC CGL Tier-1 18.09.2024 (Shift-I)
(a) Dependence (b) Permanence
(c) Independence (d) Economical

Ans. (a)

Autonomy means independence.

Hence, its antonym is 'dependence'.

61. Despite his annoyance, Rahul knew that rushing the delicate process would only lead to mistakes.
SSC CGL Tier-1 18.09.2024 (Shift-II)
(a) Susceptibility (b) Absurdity
(c) Gnawer (d) Serenity

Ans. (d)

Annoyance means irritation.

Hence, its nearest antonym is 'serenity' which means peace.

Susceptibility means vulnerable or prone to attack.

Absurdity means strangeness.

Gnawer means small placental mammals having a single pair of constantly growing incisor teeth.

62. Dogmatic
SSC CGL Tier-1 18.09.2024 (Shift-II)
(a) Concerned (b) Liberal
(c) Conservative (d) Diplomatic

Ans. (b)

Dogmatic means inclined to lay down principles as undeniably true.

Hence, its antonym is 'liberal' which means willing to respect or accept behaviour or opinions different from one's own; open to new ideas.

Conservative means averse to change or innovation and holding traditional values.

Diplomatic means acting in a way that does not cause offence.

63. Envious SSC CGL Tier-1 18.09.2024 (Shift-III)
(a) Generous (b) Suspicious
(c) Malicious (d) Untrustworthy

Ans. (a)

Envious means a feeling of discontented or resentful longing aroused by someone else's possessions, qualities, or luck. Hence, its antonym is 'generous' which means kind.

Suspicious means doubtful.

Malicious means evil.

64. Dhara .... the way to Mumbai. [lost] SSC CGL Tier-1 18.09.2024 (Shift-III)
(a) paved (b) slept
(c) found (d) helped

Ans. (c)

The antonym of 'lost' is 'found' which is the correct filler for the given blank.

65. Coffee was too hot; it burnt my tongue. SSC CGL Tier-1 18.09.2024 (Shift-III)
(a) Scorching (b) Frigid
(c) Balmy (d) Subtle

Ans. (b)

The antonym of 'hot' is 'frigid' which means extremely cool.

Scorching means extremely hot.

Balmy means characterised by pleasantly warm weather.

Subtle means so delicate or precise as to be difficult to analyse or describe.

66. Triumphant
SSC CGL Tier-1 18.09.2024 (Shift-III)
(a) Flourishing (b) Unsuccessful
(c) Jubilant (d) Tender

Ans. (b)

Triumphant means successful. Hence, its antonym is 'unsuccessful'.
Flourishing means growing.
Jubilant means extremely happy.
Tender means soft.

67. Evenings get dark very early in this cold weather.
SSC CGL Tier-1 19.09.2024 (Shift-I)
(a) shadowy (b) dim
(c) bright (d) gloomy
Ans. (c)
The antonym of 'dark' is 'bright'.

68. Desolate **SSC CGL Tier-1 19.09.2024 (Shift-I)**
(a) Festive
(b) Allusive
(c) Frugal
(d) Melancholic
Ans. (a)
Desolate means feeling or showing great unhappiness or loneliness. Hence, its antonym is 'Festive'.
Allusive means using or containing suggestion rather than explicit mention.
Frugal means someone who does not want to spend money.
Melancholic means sad.

69. Capricious
Share market prices have remained .... for weeks.
SSC CGL Tier-1 19.09.2024 (Shift-I)
(a) fickle (b) stable
(c) mischievous (d) volatile
Ans. (b)
Capricious means given to sudden and unaccountable changes of mood or behaviour or unstable; fickle.
Hence, its antonym is 'stable'.
Mischievous means naughty.
Volatile means unstable.

70. I love the stunning view of the mountain.
SSC CGL Tier-1 19.09.2024 (Shift-II)
(a) toxic (b) superfluous
(c) smashing (d) mundane
Ans. (d)
Stunning means exceptionally beautiful. Hence, its antonym is 'mundane' which means common.
Superfluous means not necessary.

71. Hinder **SSC CGL Tier-1 19.09.2024 (Shift-II)**
SSC CGL Tier-1 20.07.2023 (Shift-IV)
(a) Praise (b) Facilitate
(c) Joy (d) Block
Ans. (b)
Hinder means to interfere and stop from continuation. Hence, its antonym is 'facilitate' which means to aid or help in continuation.

72. Inevitable
SSC CGL Tier-1 19.09.2024 (Shift-II)
(a) Inexorable (b) Clear
(c) Avoidable (d) Confident
Ans. (c)
Inevitable means unavoidable.
Hence, its antonym is 'avoidable'.
Inexorable means impossible to stop or prevent.

73. Absolve **SSC CGL Tier-1 19.09.2024 (Shift-III)**
(a) Commend (b) Accuse
(c) Excuse (d) Appeal
Ans. (b)
Absolve means to declare (someone) free from guilt, obligation or punishment. Hence, its antonym is 'accuse' which means 'to blame someone'.
Commend means to praise.
Appeal means to request.

74. Appreciate
SSC CGL Tier-1 23.09.2024 (Shift-III)
(a) Depict (b) Acknowledge
(c) Esteem (d) Depreciate
Ans. (d)
The antonym of 'appreciate' is to 'depreciate' which means to condemn or criticise.
Depict means to show.
Acknowledge means to accept.
Esteem means confidence.

75. Material **SSC CGL Tier-1 23.09.2024 (Shift-I)**
(a) Cheap (b) Abstract
(c) Concrete (d) Temporary
Ans. (b)
Material is something that can be touched. Hence, its antonym is 'abstract' which is something that can be felt.
Concrete means strong.

76. It was as if the newer hybrids had an insatiable appetite for chemicals.
SSC CGL Tier-1 23.09.2024 (Shift-II)
(a) satisfiable (b) urgent
(c) curbed (d) pressing
Ans. (a)
Insatiable means to be never satisfied. Hence, its antonym is 'satisfiable'.
Curbed means restricted.
Pressing means urgent.

77. Lady Stranleigh continued to smile at him brilliantly.
SSC CGL Tier-1 23.09.2024 (Shift-II)
(a) brightly (b) dimly
(c) cunningly (d) strangely
Ans. (b)
The antonym of 'brilliantly' is 'dimly'.

78. Purify **SSC CGL Tier-1 23.09.2024 (Shift-II)**
(a) Chant (b) Invite
(c) Pollute (d) Wash
Ans. (c)
The antonym of 'purify' is to 'pollute' or make dirty.

79. The teammates made several jibes at the opponent team members during the interview.
SSC CGL Tier-1 23.09.2024 (Shift-III)
(a) Consolation (b) Mockery
(c) Inspiration (d) Contradict
Ans. (d)
Jibes means be in accord; agree. Hence, its antonym is 'contradict'.
Consolation means the comfort received by a person after a loss or disappointment.
Mockery means joke to insult someone.

80. Her behaviour was so ostentatious that it attracted the attention of everyone in the room.
SSC CGL Tier-1 23.09.2024 (Shift-III)
(a) attractive (b) restrained
(c) gentle (d) repulsive
Ans. (b)
Ostentatious means characterised by pretentious or showy display; designed to impress. Hence, its nearest antonym is 'restrained' which means characterised by reserve or moderation; unemotional or dispassionate.
Repulsive means not attractive.

81. Her remarks were relevant to the discussion.
SSC CGL Tier-1 23.09.2024 (Shift-III)
(a) inappropriate (b) suitable
(c) introductory (d) conclusive
Ans. (a)
Relevant means appropriate.
Hence, its antonym is 'inappropriate'.

82. Lethargic
SSC CGL Tier-1 23.09.2024 (Shift-III)
SSC CHSL Tier-1 02.07.2024 (Shift-I)
(a) Active (b) Languid
(c) Moderate (d) Angry
Ans. (a)
Lethargic means lazy. Hence, its antonym is 'active'.
Languid means slow and lazy.

83. It was difficult to accommodate the avariciousness of the people.
SSC CGL Tier-1 24.09.2024 (Shift-I)
(a) Generosity (b) Criticism
(c) Hatred (d) Envy
Ans. (a)

Avariciousness means an intense, selfish desire for wealth or possessions. Hence, its antonym is 'generosity' which means kindness.

84. Barren SSC CGL Tier-1 24.09.2024 (Shift-I)

"Can you believe how much traffic there is today?", grumbled Tom, glancing at the congested road ahead.
SSC CGL Tier-1 24.09.2024 (Shift-II)

(a) Believe (b) Grumbled
(c) Glancing (d) Congested

Ans. (d)

Barren means (of land) too poor to produce much or any vegetation. Hence, its nearest antonym is 'congested' which means full.

85. Hostile SSC CGL Tier-1 24.09.2024 (Shift-II)

(a) Incoherent (b) Doubtful
(c) Eager (d) Friendly

Ans. (d)

Hostile means showing or feeling opposition or dislike; unfriendly. Hence, its antonym is 'friendly'. Incoherent means not understandable.

86. Foment SSC CGL Tier-1 24.09.2024 (Shift-II)

(a) Proximity (b) Remoteness
(c) Separation (d) Regulate

Ans. (d)

Foment means to cause trouble to develop. Hence, its antonym is 'regulate'.

Proximity means nearness.

Remoteness means aloofness.

87. Intelligible
SSC CGL Tier-1 24.09.2024 (Shift-III)

(a) Scriptable (b) Embezzle
(c) Incoherent (d) Deliberate

Ans. (c)

Intelligible means easily understood. Hence, its antonym is 'incoherent' which means not easily understood.

Scriptable means relating to data containers that store large amounts of data, independent of class instances.

Embezzle means steal or misappropriate (money placed in one's trust or belonging to the organisation for which one works).

Deliberate means done consciously and intentionally.

88. Ram failed initially but after a few years, he .... in every field.
SSC CGL Tier-1 25.09.2024 (Shift-I)

(a) elevated (b) succeeded
(c) enjoyed (d) reserved

Ans. (b)

The antonym of 'failed' is 'succeeded'.

89. Laudable SSC CGL Tier-1 25.09.2024 (Shift-I)

(a) Commendable (b) Severe
(c) Deplorable (d) Humorous

Ans. (c)

Laudable means praiseworthy. Hence, its antonym is 'deplorable' which means deserving strong condemnation; completely unacceptable.

Commendable means praiseworthy.

Severe means serious.

Humorous means funny.

90. Dissolve SSC CGL Tier-1 25.09.2024 (Shift-I)

(a) Vanish (b) Fade
(c) Solve (d) Appear

Ans. (d)

Dissolve means to disappear. Hence, its antonym is to 'appear'.

91. Nominal SSC CGL Tier-1 25.09.2024 (Shift-II)

(a) Nasty (b) Sound
(c) Constant (d) Significant

Ans. (d)

Nominal means existing in name only. Hence, its antonym is 'significant'.

92. Concede SSC CGL Tier-1 25.09.2024 (Shift-II)

(a) Surrender (b) Battle
(c) Avow (d) Deny

Ans. (d)

Concede means to agree. Hence, its antonym is to 'deny'.

Surrender means to give up.

Battle means war.

Avow means to promise.

93. Bombastic
SSC CGL Tier-1 25.09.2024 (Shift-II)

(a) Simple (b) Wicked
(c) Elevated (d) Pastoral

Ans. (a)

Bombastic means high-sounding but with little meaning; inflated. Hence, its antonym is 'simple'.

Elevated means to be set at a height.

Pastoral means related to agricultural.

94. Forgive SSC CGL Tier-1 25.09.2024 (Shift-II)

(a) Unburden (b) Requite
(c) Clear (d) Loathe

Ans. (d)

The antonym of 'forgive' is 'loathe' which means to hate.

95. The pool was too .... at this end for kids to play. [shallow]
SSC CGL Tier-1 25.09.2024 (Shift-II)

(a) green (b) blue
(c) deep (d) cold

Ans. (c)

The antonym of 'shallow' is 'deep', which is the correct filler for the given blank.

96. She left the party .... because of her parents' strict time restrictions. [late] SSC CGL Tier-1 25.09.2024 (Shift-III)

(a) exit (b) early
(c) small (d) suffer

Ans. (b)

The antonym of 'late' is 'early'.

97. I heard his suggestion, but I am quite unsure about the risks involved in it.
SSC CGL Tier-1 25.09.2024 (Shift-III)

(a) Thoughtful (b) Interested
(c) Certain (d) Doubtful

Ans. (c)

The antonym of 'unsure' is 'certain'.

98. The author's writing was so captivating that readers were [enthralled], while the other book left them completely uninterested.
SSC CGL Tier-1 26.09.2024 (Shift-I)

(a) interested (b) agreement
(c) bored (d) intrigued

Ans. (c)

Enthralled means interested. Hence, its antonym is 'bored'.

99. This library building is very high and has 25 floors.
SSC CGL Tier-1 26.09.2024 (Shift-I)

(a) Low (b) Sturdy
(c) Hale (d) Elevated

Ans. (a)

The antonym of 'high' is 'low'.

100. I do not have any access to the information in this matter.
SSC CGL Tier-1 26.09.2024 (Shift-I)

(a) Doubt (b) Reach
(c) Clue (d) Denial

Ans. (d)

Access means to allow. Hence, its antonym is 'denial' which means to refuse.

101. Profuse SSC CGL Tier-1 26.09.2024 (Shift-I)

(a) Scarce (b) Humble
(c) Prompt (d) Just

Ans. (a)

Profuse means (especially of something offered or discharged) very plentiful; abundant. Hence, its antonym is 'scarce' which means in low quantity.

Humble means kind and polite.

Prompt means quick.

102. Insert SSC CGL Tier-1 26.09.2024 (Shift-II)
(a) Remove (b) Inform
(c) Select (d) Inject
Ans. (a)
The antonym of 'insert' is to 'remove'.

103. He is always active in a party but ……… in the class.
SSC CGL Tier-1 26.09.2024 (Shift-II)
(a) inert (b) careless
(c) angry (d) naughty
Ans. (a)
The antonym of 'active' is 'inert' which means lazy.

104. In front of the big screen, this behaviour is generally considered taboo. SSC CGL Tier-1 26.09.2024 (Shift-II)
(a) Obedience (b) Acceptable
(c) Promotion (d) Prescription
Ans. (b)
A **taboo** is a a social or religious custom prohibiting or restricting a particular practice or forbidding association with a particular person, place or thing. Hence, its antonym is 'acceptable'.

105. Astute SSC CGL Tier-1 26.09.2024 (Shift-III)
(a) Stupid (b) Temporary
(c) Illegal (d) Dispute
Ans. (a)
Astute means sharp and clever. Hence, its antonym is 'stupid'.

106. Coy SSC CGL Tier-1 26.09.2024 (Shift-III)
(a) Shy (b) Uptight
(c) Recent (d) Extroverted
Ans. (d)
Coy means shy. Hence, its antonym is 'extroverted' which means outgoing and social.

107. 'Grisly' SSC CGL Tier-1 26.09.2024 (Shift-III)
The other day Jimmy behaved ……… with Jammy and that was quite ……… for me.
(a) rudely, attractive
(b) disgusting, atrocious
(c) ghastly, shameless
(d) pleasantly, comforting
Ans. (d)
Grisly means sadly.
Hence, its antonym is 'pleasantly' and 'comforting'.

108. Customary
SSC CGL Tier-1 26.09.2024 (Shift-III)
(a) Fashion (b) Protection
(c) Habitual (d) Unusual
Ans. (d)
Customary means usual or normal. Hence, its antonym is 'unusual'.

SSC CGL 2023 (Tier 1 & 2)

109. Her dog can climb under the fence.
SSC CGL Tier-1 14.07.2023 (Shift-I)
(a) over (b) sink
(c) behind (d) beneath
Ans. (a)
The antonym of 'under' is 'over'.

110. Henry is so servile that other people take advantage of him.
SSC CGL Tier-1 14.07.2023 (Shift-I)
(a) arrogant (b) sheepish
(c) bickering (d) cunning
Ans. (a)
The underlined word 'servile' means 'having or showing an excessive willingness to serve or please others'. Hence, from the given options, 'arrogant' meaning having or revealing an exaggerated sense of one's own importance or abilities, is its correct antonym.

111. Select the word most appropriate antonym of the word 'optimistic' from the given sentence.
Optimistic After the incident, Radha prepared herself to stay positive even in gloomy days.
SSC CGL Tier-1 14.07.2023 (Shift-II)
(a) Stay (b) Incident
(c) Positive (d) Gloomy
Ans. (d)
Among the words in the sentence, word 'gloomy' meaning 'sad and negative' is the antonym of the word 'optimistic'.

112. The thief was caught with a spurious Picasso painting.
SSC CGL Tier-1 14.07.2023 (Shift-II)
(a) fake (b) stolen
(c) splendid (d) authentic
Ans. (d)
The underlined word 'spurious' means 'false or fake'. Hence, its antonym is 'authentic'.

113. Israel has been a staunch ally of the United States.
SSC CGL Tier-1 14.07.2023 (Shift-III)
(a) Resolute
(b) Careless
(c) Confused
(d) Unsteady
Ans. (d)
The underlined word 'staunch' means 'very loyal and committed in attitude'. Hence, its antonym is 'unsteady' which means 'unstable'.

114. The emperor was considered as a wicked man.
SSC CGL Tier-1 14.07.2023 (Shift-IV)
(a) virtuous (b) savage
(c) fierce (d) vile
Ans. (a)
The underlined word 'wicked' means 'evil'. Hence, its antonym is 'virtuous' meaning 'moral and good'.

115. Derision SSC CGL Tier-1 14.07.2023 (Shift-IV)
(a) Disintegration
(b) Termination
(c) Admiration
(d) Estimation
Ans. (c)
The word 'derision' means 'ridicule or mock someone'. Hence, from the given options, 'admiration' is its nearest antonym.

116. Gullible SSC CGL Tier-1 17.07.2023 (Shift-I)
(a) Credulous (b) Pliant
(c) Cynical (d) Simple
Ans. (c)
The word 'gullible' means 'easily persuaded to believe something'. From the given options, 'cynical' meaning 'believing that people are motivated purely by self-interest; distrustful of human sincerity or integrity' is its antonym.

117. Is there any portal to redeem these coupons that I have collected from the store? SSC CGL Tier-1 17.07.2023 (Shift-I)
(a) Forsake (b) Deplore
(c) Forfeit (d) Embezzle
Ans. (c)
The underlined word 'redeem' means 'to compensate for the faults or bad aspects of'.
Hence, 'forfeit' meaning 'lose or be deprived of (property or a right or privilege) as a penalty for wrongdoing' is its antonym.
Forsake means to give up.
Deplore means to disapprove.
Forfeit means to lose as penalty.

118. Indolent SSC CGL Tier-1 17.07.2023 (Shift-II)
(a) Lazy (b) Unskilled
(c) Active (d) Sluggish
Ans. (c)
The word 'indolent' means 'lazy' and 'inactive'. Hence, 'active' is its antonym.

119. He regards himself as a patriot.
SSC CGL Tier-1 17.07.2023 (Shift-II)
(a) Nationalist (b) Dutiful
(c) Traitor (d) Loyal

Ans. (c)

The underlined word 'patriot' refers to a person who loves, supports and defends his country.

Hence, from the given options, 'traitor' meaning a person who betrays someone or something, such as a friend, cause or principle is its nearest antonym.

120. Lucy presented a lucid account of her achievements before the committee.

SSC CGL Tier-1 17.07.2023 (Shift-II)

(a) Orderly (b) Ambiguous
(c) Intelligible (d) Transparent

Ans. (b)

The underlined word 'lucid' means 'clear'.

Hence, from the given options, 'ambiguous' meaning 'not clear or decided' is its antonym.

121. Traitor SSC CGL Tier-1 17.07.2023 (Shift-II)

People should vote for honest and loyal leaders not for betrayer and defender.

(a) Honest (b) Defender
(c) Betrayer (d) Loyal

Ans. (d)

A traitor is a person who betrays someone or something, such as a friend, cause or principle. Hence, 'loyal' is its antonym.

122. Developed countries are at a disadvantage to have access to modern science and technologies.

SSC CGL Tier-1 17.07.2023 (Shift-II)

(a) Powered (b) Privileged
(c) Useless (d) Unhappy

Ans. (b)

The underlined phrase at a disadvantage means 'to be at a bad position'.

Hence, 'privileged' which means 'to be at a favourable position', is its antonym.

123. Triumph SSC CGL Tier-1 17.07.2023 (Shift-III)
SSC Steno 12.10.2023

(a) Defeat (b) Capture
(c) Attainment (d) Succeed

Ans. (a)

The word 'triumph' means 'victory'. Hence, from the given options, 'defeat' meaning 'loss' is its antonym.

124. Ranen feels that the notion of democracy is a farce.

SSC CGL Tier-1 17.07.2023 (Shift-III)

(a) Quotient (b) Law
(c) Reality (d) Portion

Ans. (c)

The underlined word 'notion' means 'a belief or conception'.

Thus, from the given options, 'reality' is its antonym.

125. Wax SSC CGL Tier-1 17.07.2023 (Shift-III)
SSC CHSL 02.06.2022 (Shift-II)

(a) Polish (b) Can
(c) Wail (d) Wane

Ans. (d)

The word 'wax' means (of the Moon between new and full) 'have a progressively larger part of its visible surface illuminated'. Hence, from the given options, 'wane' meaning (of the Moon) 'have a progressively smaller part of its visible surface illuminated, so that it appears to decrease in size' is its antonym.

126. She was upset seeing the scattered documents.

SSC CGL Tier-1 17.07.2023 (Shift-III)

(a) Perished (b) Dissipated
(c) Sprinkled (d) Gathered

Ans. (d)

The underlined word 'scattered' means 'throw in various random directions'. Hence, from the given options, 'gathered' meaning 'to be collected' is its antonym.

Perished means not seen or destroyed.

Dissipated means abandoned.

127. The patient found the doctor to be obtuse and distracted by constant calls on his phone.

SSC CGL Tier-1 17.07.2023 (Shift-III)

(a) Obese (b) Banal
(c) Astute (d) Obsolete

Ans. (c)

The word 'obtuse' means stupid and slow to understand. So, among the given words, 'astute' meaning 'very clever, good at judging or situations' is its antonym.

Obese means fat.

Banal means boring.

Obsolete means no longer useful.

128. His house was filthy with papers and eatables strewn everywhere.

SSC CGL Tier-1 17.07.2023 (Shift-IV)

(a) Dignified (b) Integral
(c) Barren (d) Clean

Ans. (d)

The underlined word 'filthy' means 'dirty'. Hence, 'clean' is its antonym.

129. He was uncomfortable at the sport event. SSC CGL Tier-1 17.07.2023 (Shift-IV)

(a) easeful (b) difficult
(c) awkward (d) troublesome

Ans. (a)

The word 'easeful' meaning 'comfortable', is an antonym of 'uncomfortable'.

130. Select the most appropriate antonym of the word 'sophisticated' from the given sentence.
The tribe had no access to modern technology or resources and had to rely on primitive tools and techniques for survival.

SSC CGL Tier-1 17.07.2023 (Shift-IV)

(a) Technology (b) Primitive
(c) Modern (d) Techniques

Ans. (b)

The word 'sophisticated' is often used for civilised man. Hence, the word 'primitive' is its antonym.

131. Choose the antonym of the word 'Effervescent' in the given sentence.
Sonali is bubbly and carefree in comparison to her sister Mitali's subdued nature.

SSC CGL Tier-1 17.07.2023 (Shift-IV)

(a) Bubbly (b) Comparison
(c) Carefree (d) Subdued

Ans. (d)

The word 'effervescent' means 'enthusiastic'. From the given sentence, 'subdued' meaning 'depressed' is its antonym.

132. Eloquent SSC CGL Tier-1 18.07.2023 (Shift-I)

(a) Modest (b) Crucial
(c) Impotent (d) Humble

Ans. (c)

The word 'eloquent' means 'fluent and strong'. Hence, from the given options, 'impotent' meaning 'weak' is its nearest antonym.

133. Identify the word in the given sentence that is the antonym of the word 'frugal'.

SSC CGL Tier-1 18.07.2023 (Shift-II)

At present, people are paying extravagant prices for houses because they have to have accommodation.

(a) Prices (b) Accommodation
(c) Present (d) Extravagant

Ans. (d)

The word 'frugal' means 'wanting to spend less money'.
Hence, the word 'extravagant', which means lacking restraint in spending money or resources, is its antonym.

134. Those streets are very lonely.

SSC CGL Tier-1 18.07.2023 (Shift-II)

(a) Crowded (b) Isolated
(c) Empty (d) Remote

Ans. (a)

The word 'crowded' is an antonym of 'lonely'.

135. <u>Seldom</u> had he been so joyous in other's happiness.
SSC CGL Tier-1 18.07.2023 (Shift-II)

(a) Hardly (b) Rarely
(c) Frequently (d) Occasionally

Ans. (c)

The underlined word 'Seldom' means 'rarely'. Hence, 'frequently' is its antonym.

136. He brought <u>disgrace</u> to his family by being involved in illegal activities. **SSC CGL Tier-1 18.07.2023 (Shift-II)**

(a) Suspicion (b) Shame
(c) Discord (d) Honour

Ans. (d)

The underlined word 'disgrace' means 'dishonour' or 'disrespect'. Hence, 'honour' is its antonym.

137. Divergence
SSC CGL Tier-1 18.07.2023 (Shift-II)

(a) Convergence (b) Existence
(c) Resilience (d) Transience

Ans. (a)

The word 'divergence' means 'a difference in opinions, interests, etc'. Hence, 'convergence' meaning 'the fact that two or more things, ideas, etc., become similar or come together' is its antonym.

138. The love between them is <u>blooming</u>.
SSC CGL Tier-1 18.07.2023 (Shift-IV)

(a) Flourishing (b) Sprouting
(c) Growing (d) Fading

Ans. (d)

The word 'blooming' means 'thriving or growing'. From the given options, 'fading' meaning 'to gradually faint' is its antonym.

139. The truck was carrying a <u>heavy</u> load. **SSC CGL Tier-1 18.07.2023 (Shift-IV)**

(a) Big (b) Massive
(c) Light (d) Large

Ans. (c)

The word 'light' is an antonym of 'heavy'.

140. I understand your <u>plight</u>.
SSC CGL Tier-1 18.07.2023 (Shift-IV)

(a) Predicament (b) Dilemma
(c) Quandary (d) Advantage

Ans. (d)

The underlined word 'plight' means 'a dangerous, difficult or otherwise unfortunate situation'. Hence, 'advantage' is its antonym.

141. He just needs to <u>calm down</u> a wee bit. **SSC CGL Tier-1 19.07.2023 (Shift-I)**

(a) Understand (b) Agitate
(c) Question (d) Dissipate

Ans. (b)

'Agitate' meaning 'irritated or angry' is an antonym of 'calm down'.

142. Managers who <u>delegate</u> reduce their work load.
SSC CGL Tier-1 19.07.2023 (Shift-II)

(a) Retain (b) Appoint
(c) Nominate (d) Depute

Ans. (a)

The word 'delegate' means 'to distribute or give responsibility or duty to others'.
From the given options, 'retain' meaning 'to keep to oneself' is its antonym.

143. Innate **SSC CGL Tier-1 19.07.2023 (Shift-II)**

(a) Learned (b) Aquatic
(c) Natural (d) Replete

Ans. (a)

The word 'innate' means 'natural'. Hence, 'learned' is its antonym.

144. Most of the things in life are <u>transient</u>. **SSC CGL Tier-1 19.07.2023 (Shift-II)**
SSC CHSL Tier-1 05.07.2024 (Shift-I)

(a) Boring (b) Permanent
(c) Toxic (d) Fleeting

Ans. (b)

The underlined word 'transient' means 'temporary'. Hence, 'permanent' is its antonym.

145. Theirs is <u>clandestine</u> affair.
SSC CGL Tier-1 19.07.2023 (Shift-III)

(a) Known (b) Private
(c) Sneaky (d) Illicit

Ans. (a)

The underlined word 'clandestine' means kept secret or done secretively, especially because illicit. Hence, 'known' is its antonym.

146. That is a picture worth seeing but this is an <u>absurd</u> piece of art.
SSC CGL Tier-1 19.07.2023 (Shift-III)

(a) Ordinary (b) Odd
(c) Eerie (d) Realistic

Ans. (d)

The underlined word 'absurd' means 'something that does not seem real'. Hence, 'realistic' is its antonym.

147. The panel picked the candidates <u>randomly</u> for the interview.
SSC CGL Tier-1 19.07.2023 (Shift-III)

(a) Casually (b) Unwillingly
(c) Systematically (d) Incidentally

Ans. (c)

The word 'randomly' means 'without method or conscious decision'. Hence, 'systematically' meaning 'in an organised manner' is its antonym.

148. Taking a <u>Brisk</u> walk can often induce a feeling of well-being.
SSC CGL Tier-1 19.07.2023 (Shift-IV)

(a) Slow (b) Late night
(c) Quick (d) Dusky

Ans. (a)

The underlined word 'brisk' means 'fast'.
Hence, 'slow' is its antonym.

149. Partial **SSC CGL Tier-1 19.07.2023 (Shift-IV)**

(a) Unjust (b) Prejudiced
(c) Doubtful (d) Unbiased

Ans. (d)

The word 'partial' means 'biased'. Hence, 'unbiased' is its antonym.

150. <u>Trivial</u> issues have always interested our boss.
SSC CGL Tier-1 19.07.2023 (Shift-IV)
SSC CGL Tier-1 27.07.2023 (Shift-I)

(a) Fierce (b) Hopeful
(c) Significant (d) Common

Ans. (c)

The underlined word 'Trivial' means 'small or insignificant'. Hence, 'Significant' is its antonym.

151. To <u>abate</u> her listlessness, she went for a long walk in the country.
SSC CGL Tier-1 19.07.2023 (Shift-IV)

(a) Lessen (b) Sustain
(c) Increase (d) Subside

Ans. (c)

The underlined word 'abate' means 'to reduce'. Hence, 'increase' is its antonym.

152. The teacher could judge that his intentions were ...., (nefarious) so he was not stopped from entering the hall. **SSC CGL Tier-1 20.07.2023 (Shift-I)**

(a) Pious
(b) Traitorous
(c) Envious
(d) Perfidious

Ans. (a)

The correct filler for the given blank is 'pious'.
The word 'pious' is the antonym of 'nefarious'.

Traitorous means relating to or characteristic of a traitor.

Envious means jealous.

Perfidious means deceitful and untrust worthy.

153. My teacher accepted my excuse for being late.
SSC CGL Tier-1 20.07.2023 (Shift-I)
(a) Trusted (b) Rejected
(c) Agreed (d) Believed
Ans. (b)
The word 'rejected' is the antonym of the underlined word 'accepted'.

154. The old port was abandoned a long ago. SSC CGL Tier-1 20.07.2023 (Shift-I)
(a) Quit (b) Shortened
(c) Kept (d) Rashed
Ans. (c)
The underlined word 'abandoned' means 'having been deserted or left'. Hence, 'kept' is its antonym.

155. Her mother always encouraged the idea of early marriage.
SSC CGL Tier-1 20.07.2023 (Shift-II)
(a) Motivated
(b) Supported
(c) Cheered
(d) Discouraged
Ans. (d)
The word 'discouraged' is an antonym of the underlined word 'encouraged'.

156. They live in the apartment above ours. SSC CGL Tier-1 20.07.2023 (Shift-II)
(a) over (b) after
(c) upward (d) below
Ans. (d)
The antonym of the underlined word 'above' is 'below'.

157. Aditi is meticulous by nature.
SSC CGL Tier-1 20.07.2023 (Shift-II, IV)
(a) Accurate (b) Precise
(c) Careless (d) Concise
Ans. (c)
The underlined word 'meticulous' means 'careful and perfect'. Hence, its antonym is 'careless'.

158. He was quite violent in his behaviour.
SSC CGL Tier-1 20.07.2023 (Shift-III)
(a) Crazy (b) Aggressive
(c) Gentle (d) Savage
Ans. (c)
The underlined word 'violent' means 'angry and rough'. Hence, 'gentle' is its antonym.

159. We usually had .... visitors dropping by, but now we have very less visitors.
SSC CGL Tier-1 20.07.2023 (Shift-III)
(a) Insufficient (b) A handful of
(c) Slighter (d) Umpteen
Ans. (d)
The correct filler for the given blank is 'umpteen'. The word 'umpteen' means 'a lot of ' and it is the appropriate antonym of 'less'.

160. Heavy outfits make the movement of trekkers sluggish.
SSC CGL Tier-1 20.07.2023 (Shift-III)
(a) Active (b) Distorted
(c) Eye catching (d) Comfortable
Ans. (a)
The underlined word 'sluggish' means 'lazy and slow'. Hence, 'active' is its antonym.

161. It was evident from his gestures that he was feeling guilty.
SSC CGL Tier-1 20.07.2023 (Shift-IV)
(a) Hidden (b) Profuse
(c) Correct (d) Visible
Ans. (a)
The underlined word 'evident' means 'clear and visible'. Hence, 'hidden' is its antonym.

162. Nervous SSC CGL Tier-1 20.07.2023 (Shift-IV)
(a) Hesitant (b) Shaky
(c) Courageous (d) Casual
Ans. (c)
The word 'nervous' means 'easily agitated and frightened'. Hence, 'courageous' is its antonym.

163. Perseverance
SSC CGL Tier-1 21.07.2023 (Shift-I)
(a) Irresolution (b) Obstinacy
(c) Readiness (d) Eloquence
Ans. (a)
The word 'Perseverance' means 'continued effort to do or achieve something despite difficulties, failure or opposition'.
Hence, from the given options 'Irresolution' meaning 'indecisiveness' is its antonym.

164. Her sudden arrival has disarranged my plans. SSC CGL Tier-1 21.07.2023 (Shift-I)
(a) Timing (b) Entrance
(c) Departure (d) Appearance
Ans. (c)
The word 'departure' is an antonym of the underlined word 'arrival'.

165. Select the most appropriate antonym of the word 'Unsure' from the given sentence.
SSC CGL Tier-1 21.07.2023 (Shift-I)
Himanshi is preparing customised gifts and handicrafts for suprising Mehul on his retirement, but the date is not certain yet.
(a) Date (b) Certain
(c) Customised (d) Handicrafts
Ans. (b)
The word 'Unsure' means 'uncertain'. Hence, 'certain' is its antonym.

166. He was acquitted of all the charges in the court today.
SSC CGL Tier-1 21.07.2023 (Shift-I)
(a) Conformed (b) Discharged
(c) Praised (d) Convicted
Ans. (d)
The underlined word 'acquitted' means 'free (someone) from a criminal charge by a verdict of not guilty'. Hence, from the given options, 'convicted' means 'having officially been found guilty of a crime' is its antonym.

167. Her modest behaviour was appreciated by everyone in the assembly. SSC CGL Tier-1 21.07.2023 (Shift-I)
(a) Distant (b) Unpresuming
(c) Conceited (d) Obvious
Ans. (c)
The underlined word 'modest' means 'humble'. From the given options, 'conceited' meaning 'egoistic' is its antonym.

168. There are .... (definite) weaknesses in their security arrangements.
SSC CGL Tier-1 21.07.2023 (Shift-III)
(a) monotonous (b) hazy
(c) subtle (d) vague
Ans. (d)
The correct filler for the given blank is 'vague'. Hence, antonym of 'definite' is 'vague'.

169. This is such a rowdy classroom.
SSC CGL Tier-1 21.07.2023 (Shift-III)
(a) Compliant (b) Chattering
(c) Disorderly (d) Noisy
Ans. (a)
The underlined word 'rowdy' means 'noisy and disorderly'. Hence, 'compliant' meaning 'calm and organised' is its antonym.

170. She will probably come tonight for a party. SSC CGL Tier-1 21.07.2023 (Shift-III)
(a) Definitely (b) Perhaps
(c) Apparently (d) Possibly
Ans. (a)
The antonym of 'probably' is 'definitely'.

171. One should not yell at children.
SSC CGL Tier-1 21.07.2023 (Shift-IV)
(a) Notify (b) Indemnity
(c) Whisper (d) Terrorise

Ans. (c)

The underlined word 'yell' means 'a loud, sharp cry of pain, surprise or delight'. Hence, 'whisper' is its antonym.

172. Clear SSC CGL Tier-1 24.07.2023 (Shift-I)

(a) Clean (b) Opaque
(c) Mess (d) Untidy

Ans. (b)

The word 'Opaque' meaning 'not able to be seen through; not transparent' is the antonym of 'Clear'.

173. My energy waned to see my college team performing poorly in the match. SSC CGL Tier-1 24.07.2023 (Shift-I)

(a) Declined (b) Dimmed
(c) Abated (d) Grew

Ans. (d)

The underlined word 'waned' means 'to reduce'. Hence, 'grew' is its antonym.

174. She is a veteran journalist known for her powerful writing style. SSC CGL Tier-1 24.07.2023 (Shift-I)

(a) Renowned (b) Creviced
(c) Conditioned (d) Novice

Ans. (d)

The underlined word 'veteran' means 'highly experience'. Hence, 'novice' meaning 'a person new to and inexperienced in a job or situation' is its antonym.

175. Fetish
Shilpi has a fixed indifference and obsession towards problems in life. SSC CGL Tier-1 24.07.2023 (Shift-I)

(a) Indifference (b) Fixed
(c) Problems (d) Obsession

Ans. (a)

The word 'Fetish' means 'Obsession'. Hence, 'Indifference' is its antonym.

176. The boy looked disheveled and lost. SSC CGL Tier-1 24.07.2023 (Shift-II)

(a) Tidy (b) Clumsy
(c) Infuriated (d) Excited

Ans. (a)

The underlined word 'disheveled' means 'dirty and rough'. Hence, 'tidy' is its antonym.

Clumsy means awkward in movement or in handling things.

Infuriated means to make someone extremely angry.

177. The apple tasted incredibly sweet. SSC CGL Tier-1 24.07.2023 (Shift-II)

(a) Delicious (b) Pleasant
(c) Bitter (d) Special

Ans. (c)

The word 'bitter' is the antonym of 'sweet'.

178. I must have a chance to rectify my error. SSC CGL Tier-1 24.07.2023 (Shift-II)

(a) worsen (b) alter
(c) reason (d) modify

Ans. (a)

The underlined word 'rectify' means 'to solve'. Hence, 'worsen' is its nearest antonym.

179. My complaint is that the gardener dozes off during work. SSC CGL Tier-1 24.07.2023 (Shift-IV)

(a) Challenge (b) Carp
(c) Praise (d) Demur

Ans. (c)

The word 'praise' is an antonym of the underlined word 'complaint'.

180. The lizard's light brown skin acts as camouflage in the desert sand. SSC CGL Tier-1 24.07.2023 (Shift-IV)

(a) Clothed (b) Mask
(c) Reveal (d) Vanishing

Ans. (c)

The underlined word 'camouflage' means 'hide or disguise the presence of (a person, animal, or object)'. Hence, 'reveal' it its antonym.

181. Incompetent SSC CGL Tier-1 25.07.2023 (Shift-IV)

(a) Forlorn (b) Desperate
(c) Hopeless (d) Dexterous

Ans. (d)

The word 'incompetent' means 'not having or showing the necessary skills to do something successfully.'

Hence, the word 'dexterous' meaning 'showing or having skill, especially with the hands' is its antonym.

182. The confectioner dusted a fine layer of sugar on the muffin. SSC CGL Tier-1 25.07.2023 (Shift-II)

(a) Scattered (b) Sprinkled
(c) Powdered (d) Cleaned

Ans. (d)

The underlined word 'dusted' in the given context means 'to let the dust collect'. Hence, 'cleaned' is its antonym.

183. He was riding his bike on a bumpy surface. SSC CGL Tier-1 25.07.2023 (Shift-II)

(a) Jerky (b) Uneven
(c) Choppy (d) Steady

Ans. (d)

The underlined word 'bumpy' means 'unsteady and unstable'. Hence, 'steady' is its antonym.

184. Jubilant SSC CGL Tier-1 25.07.2023 (Shift-III)

(a) Indifferent (b) Thoughtful
(c) Gay (d) Melancholic

Ans. (d)

The word 'jubilant' means happy and cheerful. Hence, 'melancholic' meaning 'sad and sorrowful' is its antonym.

185. Grow SSC CGL Tier-1 25.07.2023 (Shift-III)

(a) Shrink (b) Crimp
(c) Plant (d) Alter

Ans. (a)

The antonym of 'grow' is 'shrink' which means 'to reduce in size'.

186. Instead of becoming joyous to hear the breaking news, she became .... SSC CGL Tier-1 25.07.2023 (Shift-III)

(a) melancholic (b) vengeful
(c) ecstatic (d) exuberant

Ans. (a)

The word 'melancholic' meaning 'sad' is the antonym of 'joyous'. 'Vengeful' means seeking to harm someone in return for a perceived injury.

Ecstatic means state of sudden, intense overpowering emotion.

Exuberant means full of energy, excitement and cheerfulness.

187. His knowledge is superficial in nature. SSC CGL Tier-1 25.07.2023 (Shift-III)

(a) Deviant (b) Profound
(c) Artificial (d) Opposing

Ans. (b)

The underlined word 'superficial' means 'having no depth at all'. Hence, 'profound' meaning 'deep' is its antonym.

188. Her parents forbade her to marry her lover. SSC CGL Tier-1 25.07.2023 (Shift-IV)

(a) Prevented (b) Refused
(c) Declined (d) Allowed

Ans. (d)

The underlined word 'forbade' means 'to refuse'. Hence, 'allowed' is its antonym.

189. While most friends persuaded him to choose the career, there were a few who .... him from doing so. SSC CGL Tier-1 26.07.2023 (Shift-I)

(a) evaded (b) bombarded
(c) dissuaded (d) situated

Ans. (c)

The word 'persuaded' means 'to get to agree'.

Hence, 'dissuaded' means 'to get to disagree' is its antonym and the correct filler for the blank.

190. One may <u>accomplish</u> many things by a little effort.
SSC CGL Tier-1 26.07.2023 (Shift-I)
(a) Qualify (b) Retain
(c) Execute (d) Miss
Ans. (d)
The word 'accomplish' means 'to achieve something'. Hence, 'miss' is its nearest antonym.

191. The professor's lectures are very conventional and so <u>tedious</u>.
SSC CGL Tier-1 26.07.2023 (Shift-I)
(a) Interesting (b) Informative
(c) Idle (d) Boring
Ans. (a)
The underlined word 'tedious' means 'complex and boring'. Hence, 'interesting' is its antonym.

192. She <u>chided</u> her son for being impatient with the customers.
SSC CGL Tier-1 26.07.2023 (Shift-II)
(a) Reproved (b) Scolded
(c) Applauded (d) Rebuked
Ans. (c)
The underlined word 'chided' means 'scolded'. Hence, 'applauded' meaning 'praised' is its antonym.

193. Choose the antonym of the word 'disenfranchise' in the given sentence. SSC CGL Tier-1 26.07.2023 (Shift-II)
The Parliament of Tonoco authorised the king to take over the reins of the government and disable the power of the Council of Ministers.
(a) Authorised (b) Powers
(c) Disabled (d) Reins
Ans. (a)
Disenfranchise means to deprive someone of the right to vote of power, rights or privileges.
Authorised means to give legal or official approval to do something.

194. They <u>praised</u> her for her bravery.
SSC CGL Tier-1 26.07.2023 (Shift-III)
(a) Acclaimed (b) Rebuked
(c) Defended (d) Assaulted
Ans. (b)
The word 'rebuked' meaning 'scolded' is the antonym of the underlined word 'praised'.

195. Intentional
SSC CGL Tier-1 26.07.2023 (Shift-III)
(a) Cordial (b) Unplanned
(c) Amiable (d) Inanimate
Ans. (b)
The word 'intentional' means 'deliberate or planned'. Hence, 'unplanned' is its correct antonym.

196. I <u>confronted</u> the journalist with the evidence. SSC CGL Tier-1 26.07.2023 (Shift-III)
(a) Resisted (b) Avoided
(c) Challenged (d) Encountered
Ans. (b)
The word 'confronted' means 'come face to face with (someone) with hostile or argumentative intent'. Hence, 'avoided' would be its correct antonym.

197. Prohibition
SSC CGL Tier-1 26.07.2023 (Shift-III)
(a) Restriction (b) Inhibition
(c) Direction (d) Permission
Ans. (d)
The word 'prohibition' means 'to stop from doing something'. Hence, 'permission' meaning 'to allow to do something' is its antonym.

198. Selective SSC CGL Tier-1 26.07.2023 (Shift-IV)
(a) Stimulating (b) Careless
(c) Doubtful (d) Planned
Ans. (b)
The word 'selective' means tending to select carefully. Hence, 'careless' is its nearest antonym.

199. The crowd gave an <u>exultant</u> cheer to the football team when they were exiting the airport.
SSC CGL Tier-1 26.07.2023 (Shift-IV)
(a) Rejoicing (b) Disconsolate
(c) Jubilant (d) Elated
Ans. (b)
The underlined word 'exultant' means 'extremely happy'.
Hence, 'disconsolate' meaning 'sad' is its antonym.

200. The village fair was cancelled due to <u>incessant</u> rains.
SSC CGL Tier-1 27.07.2023 (Shift-I)
(a) Insistent (b) Daily
(c) Sporadic (d) Continual
Ans. (c)
The underlined word 'incessant' means 'continuous'. Hence, 'sporadic' meaning 'irregular' would be its correct antonym.

201. I <u>object</u> the false claims made against me.
SSC CGL Tier-1 27.07.2023 (Shift-I)
(a) Assent (b) Ease
(c) Restore (d) Ascertain
Ans. (a)
The underlined word 'object' means 'to stop because you have a problem with something'. Hence, 'assent' meaning 'to agree' would be its correct antonym.

202. Conceal SSC CGL Tier-1 27.07.2023 (Shift-I)
(a) Watch (b) See
(c) Reveal (d) Hide
Ans. (c)
The word 'conceal' means 'to hide'. Hence, the word 'reveal' which means 'to show' is its antonym.

203. Memory SSC CGL Tier-1 27.07.2023 (Shift-I)
(a) Suppress (b) Oblivion
(c) Retrospection (d) Impart
Ans. (b)
Memory means a person's ability to remember things. The antonym of 'memory' is 'oblivion'.
Olivion means a state in what in which you do not realise what is happening around you usually because you are unconscious or sleep.
Suppress means to forcibly put an end to something.
Retrospection refers to the action of looking back on or receiving past events or situations.
Impart means making information known.

204. I don't like to work with people who are not <u>flexible</u>.
SSC CGL Tier-1 27.07.2023 (Shift-II)
(a) Capable (b) Malleable
(c) Open-ended (d) Rigid
Ans. (d)
The underlined word 'flexible' means 'capable of bending easily without breaking.'
Hence, 'rigid' meaning 'unable to bend or be forced out of shape; not flexible' is its antonym.

205. My niece is an <u>amateur</u> artist. I hope she becomes famous one day.
SSC CGL Tier-1 27.07.2023 (Shift-III)
(a) Boring (b) Freelancing
(c) Expert (d) Decent
Ans. (c)
The underlined word 'amateur' means 'inexperienced or new at a job'.
Hence, 'expert' would be its suitable antonym.

206. Select the most appropriate antonym of the word 'Naive' from the given sentence.
SSC CGL Tier-1 27.07.2023 (Shift-III)
After years of working in politics, she had become cynical and jaded, convinced that all politicians were corrupt and that the system was rigged against the people.
(a) Jaded (b) Corrupt
(c) Cynical (d) Convinced

Ans. (c)

Naive means without enough experience of life and two ready to believe or trust other people. Hence, 'cynical' meaning 'believing that people are motivated purely by self-interest; distrustful of human sincerity or integrity', is its correct antonym.

207. She was wearing a ...... new outfit. (expensive)
SSC CGL Tier-1 27.07.2023 (Shift-IV)
(a) cheap (b) costly
(c) premium (d) precious

Ans. (a)

The correct filler for the given blank is 'cheap'. Hence, antonym of 'cheap' is 'expensive'.

208. Lament **SSC CGL Tier-1 21.07.2023 (Shift-IV)**
(a) Deplore (b) Decry
(c) Celebrate (d) Regret

Ans. (c)

The word 'lament' means 'to cry over a sorrow'. Hence, 'celebrate' is its antonym.

209. The <u>colossal</u> building stood amidst the ruins bearing sign of Victorian architecture. **SSC CGL Tier-2 02.03.2023**
(a) Enormous (b) Extraordinary
(c) Quaint (d) Tiny

Ans. (d)

Colossal means huge.
Tiny means very small is its antonym.
Enormous means huge.
Quaint means quiet and peaceful.

210. The new principal of the school is <u>stern</u> yet he understands the needs of his subordinates.
SSC CGL Tier-2 02.03.2023
(a) Flippant (b) Lenient
(c) Desolate (d) Noxious

Ans. (b)

Stern means strict and serious.
Lenient means merciful is its antonym.
Flippant means disrespectful.
Desolate means empty and isolated.
Noxious means harmful.

211. The reputed officer was removed from his past as he was having a <u>clandestine</u> affair.
SSC CGL Tier-2 03.03.2023
(a) Surreptitious (b) Overt
(c) Amorous (d) Casual

Ans. (b)

Clandestine means secret.
Overt which means openly is its antonym.
Surreptitious means secret.
Amorous means lustful.

212. The manager decided to resign from his post as the bank was declared to be <u>insolvent</u>.
SSC CGL Tier-2 06.03.2023
(a) Independent (b) Commercial
(c) Affluent (d) Bankrupt

Ans. (c)

Insolvent means 'bankrupt or poor'. Its antonym is 'affluent' which means 'rich'.

213. Select the most appropriate antonym for the word 'often' in the following sentence. **SSC CGL Tier-2 06.03.2023**
Usually at Christmas, uncle often brings lovely and cherished gifts for us.
(a) Seldom (b) Cherished
(c) Lovely (d) Usually

Ans. (a)

The antonym of 'often' is 'seldom'.

214. The audience <u>sneered</u> at the monologue uttered by the veteran actor. **SSC CGL Tier-2 07.03.2023**
(a) Waved (b) Lauded
(c) Unleashed (d) Ascribed

Ans. (b)

Sneered means 'to mock'.
Lauded which means praise is its antonym.
Waved is a movement of hands.
Unleashed means to release.
Ascribed means to regard something as cause.

215. Aunt May thought that Uncle Ken's job as a manager at Firpo's hotel in Shimla was a <u>stable</u> one.
SSC CGL Tier-2 07.03.2023
(a) Lucrative (b) Permanent
(c) Durable (d) Mutable

Ans. (d)

The antonym of word 'stable' is 'mutable' which means unstable or varied.
Lucrative means profitable.
Durable means long lasting.

SSC CGL 2022 (Tier 1 & 2)

216. Raze **SSC CGL Tier-1 11.04.2022 (Shift-I)**
(a) Build (b) Ease
(c) Comfort (d) Ruin

Ans. (a)

Raze means to completely destroy a building, town or other site. Hence, its antonym is 'build'.

217. Tenacious
SSC CGL Tier-1 11.04.2022 (Shift-II)
(a) Steadfast (b) Relentless
(c) Persistent (d) Yielding

Ans. (d)

Tenacious means tending to keep a firm hold of something; clinging or adhering closely. Hence, its antonym is 'yielding'.
Steadfast means resolutely or dutifully firm and unwavering.
Relentless means oppressively constant; incessant.
Persistent means continuing firmly or obstinately in an opinion or course of action despite difficulty or opposition.

218. Camaraderie
SSC CGL Tier-1 11.04.2022 (Shift-III)
(a) Dislike (b) Amity
(c) Companionship (d) Friendship

Ans. (a)

Camaraderie means mutual trust and friendship among people who spend a lot of time together. Hence, its antonym is 'dislike'.
Amity means a friendly relationship.

219. Criticise **SSC CGL Tier-1 11.04.2022 (Shift-III)**
(a) Disappoint (b) Forgive
(c) Prevent (d) Praise

Ans. (d)

Criticise means indicate the faults of (someone or something) in a disapproving way. Hence, its antonym is 'praise'.

220. Appal **SSC CGL Tier-1 12.04.2022 (Shift-I)**
(a) Alarm (b) Assure
(c) Amaze (d) Astound

Ans. (b)

Appal means greatly dismay or horrify. Hence, its antonym is 'assure'.
Alarm means an anxious awareness of danger.
Amaze means surprise (someone) greatly.
Astound means shock or greatly surprise.

221. Prey **SSC CGL Tier-1 12.04.2022 (Shift-II)**
(a) Predator (b) Sufferer
(c) Loot (d) Game

Ans. (a)

Prey means an animal that is hunted and killed by another for food. Hence, its antonym is 'predator'.

222. Linger **SSC CGL Tier-1 12.04.2022 (Shift-III)**
(a) Leave (b) Choose
(c) Entertain (d) Annoy

Ans. (a)

Linger means stay in a place longer than necessary because of a reluctance to leave. Hence, its antonym is 'leave'.

223. Clench SSC CGL Tier-1 13.04.2022 (Shift-I)
(a) Tighten (b) Clasp
(c) Hold (d) Relax

Ans. (d)

Clench means (with reference to the fingers or hand) close into a tight ball, especially as a manifestation of extreme anger. Hence, its antonym is 'relax'.

Tighten means make or become tight or tighter.

Clasp means grasp (something) tightly with one's hand.

Hold means grasp, carry, or support with one's arms or hands.

224. Ransack SSC CGL Tier-1 13.04.2022 (Shift-III)
(a) Seize (b) Raid
(c) Protect (d) Pilfer

Ans. (c)

Ransack means go through (a place) stealing things and causing damage. Hence, its antonym is 'protect'.

Seize means take hold of suddenly and forcibly.

Raid means a sudden attack on an enemy by troops, aircraft, or other armed forces in warfare.

Pilfer means steal (typically things of relatively little value).

225. Obscure SSC CGL Tier-1 18.04.2022 (Shift-I)
(a) Blurred
(b) Apparent
(c) Cloudy
(d) Veiled

Ans. (b)

Obscure means not discovered or known about; uncertain. Hence, its antonym is 'apparent'.

Blurred means unable to see or be seen clearly.

Cloudy means (of the sky or weather) covered with or characterised by clouds; overcast.

Veiled means partially conceal, disguise, or obscure.

226. Devious SSC CGL Tier-1 18.04.2022 (Shift-II)
(a) Dishonest (b) Crooked
(c) Crafty (d) Sincere

Ans. (d)

Devious means showing a skillful use of underhanded tactics to achieve goals. Hence, its antonym is 'sincere'.

Dishonest means behaving or prone to behave in an untrustworthy or fraudulent way.

Crooked means bent or twisted out of shape or out of place.

Crafty means clever at achieving one's aims by indirect or deceitful methods.

227. Sober SSC CGL Tier-1 18.04.2022 (Shift-III)
(a) Straight (b) Calm
(c) Drunk (d) Unwell

Ans. (c)

Sober means not affected by alcohol; not drunk. Hence, its antonym is 'drunk'.

228. Altercation SSC CGL Tier-1 19.04.2022 (Shift-I)
(a) Agreement (b) Argument
(c) Quarrel (d) Controversy

Ans. (a)

Altercation means a noisy argument or disagreement, especially in public. Hence, its antonym is 'agreement'.

Argument means an exchange of diverging or opposite views, typically a heated or angry one.

Quarrel means a heated argument or disagreement, typically about a trivial issue and between people who are usually on good term.

Controversy means prolonged public disagreement or heated discussion.

229. Taut SSC CGL Tier-1 19.04.2022 (Shift-II)
(a) Tight (b) Solid
(c) Strong (d) Slack

Ans. (d)

Taut means stretched or pulled tight; not slack. Hence, its antonym is 'slack'.

230. Obdurate SSC CGL Tier-1 20.04.2022 (Shift-III)
(a) Rigid (b) Callous
(c) Amenable (d) Secure

Ans. (c)

Obdurate means stubbornly refusing to change one's opinion or course of action. Hence, its antonym is 'amenable'.

Rigid means not able to be changed or adapted.

Callous means showing or having an insensitive and cruel disregard for others.

231. Proclaim SSC CGL Tier-1 21.04.2022 (Shift-II)
(a) Exhibit (b) Evince
(c) Conceal (d) Announce

Ans. (c)

Proclaim means to announce officially or publicly. Hence, its antonym is 'conceal'.

Exhibit means to show or display.

Evince means to reveal the presence of (a quality or feeling).

Announce means to make a formal public statement about a fact, occurrence, or intention.

232. Astound SSC CGL Tier-1 21.04.2022 (Shift-III)
(a) Confuse (b) Shock
(c) Clarify (d) Stun

Ans. (c)

Astound means to shock or greatly surprise. Hence, its antonym is 'clarify'.

233. Select the most appropriate antonym of the word 'Sinks' from the given sentence.
SSC CGL Tier-1 01.12.2022 (Shift-I)

Groups work together to create Christmas parade themes, which are then carried out in floats, musical groups and strolling figures.
(a) Floats (b) Create
(c) Parade (d) Strolling

Ans. (a)

Floats from the given options is the most appropriate antonym of 'Sinks'. 'Float' means to stay on the surface of a liquid without sinking whereas 'Sink' means to go down below the surface of a liquid. Hence, its antonym is 'Floats'.

Parade means walking in large numbers.

Strolling means walking in a relaxed way.

234. Rebellion SSC CGL Tier-1 01.12.2022 (Shift-I)
(a) Uprising
(b) Loyalty
(c) Sedition
(d) Allotment

Ans. (b)

Rebellion means action against authority, against the rules or against normal or accepted ways of behaving. Hence, its antonym is 'Loyalty'.

Uprising means starting a fight.

Sedition means acts of rebellion.

Allotment means to given a slot.

235. Hospitality SSC CGL Tier-1 01.12.2022 (Shift-I)
(a) Complaint (b) Cordiality
(c) Coldness (d) Wrathful

Ans. (c)

Hospitality means friendly behaviour towards visitors. 'Coldness' from the given option is its most appropriate antonym as it means a way of speaking or behaving that does not show kindness, love, or emotion and is not friendly. Hence, its antonym is 'coldness'.

Cordiality means friendshipness.

Wrathful means angry.

236. Failure to carry hall ticket to the exam is considered as a <u>trivial</u> issue. **SSC CGL Tier-1 01.12.2022 (Shift-II)**

(a) Underrated (b) Kind
(c) Problematic (d) Serious

Ans. (d)

'Trivial' means having little value or importance. Hence, its antonym is 'Serious'.

237. Casual **SSC CGL Tier-1 01.12.2022 (Shift-III)**

(a) Spiritual (b) Personal
(c) Formal (d) Traditional

Ans. (c)

'Casual' means not formal, relaxed in style or manner. Hence, its antonym is 'Formal' .

238. Conceit **SSC CGL Tier-1 01.12.2022 (Shift-III)**

(a) Concealment (b) Reveal
(c) Modesty (d) Hidden

Ans. (a)

'Conceit' means an attitude that shows you have too high an opinion of your own abilities or importance. A concealment means hiding. Hence, its antonym is 'Concealment'.

239. God has clearly <u>blessed</u> human beings for his glory. **SSC CGL Tier-1 01.12.2022 (Shift-IV)**

(a) Appointed (b) Produced
(c) Applied (d) Cursed

Ans. (d)

Blessed means to ask God to protect someone or something. Hence, its antonym is 'Cursed' as it means to ask God or a magical power to harm someone.

240. Select the most appropriate antonym of the word 'Mobile' from the given sentence. **SSC CGL Tier-1 02.12.2022 (Shift-I)**

The strange TV reporter standing over there covers all the funny and interesting things happening inside the town.

(a) Standing (b) Interesting
(c) Inside (d) Strange

Ans. (a)

The word 'Mobile' means being able to move. Thus, its most appropriate antonym is 'Standing'.

241. Oppose **SSC CGL Tier-1 02.12.2022 (Shift-I)**

(a) Embody (b) Resist
(c) Encourage (d) Elective

Ans. (c)

Oppose means to disagree or not approve of a plan or policy. So, its most appropriate antonym is 'Encourage' as it means to suggest that someone does something that you believe should be good.
Embody means example.
Resist means to bovid.
Elective means to optional.

242. Technology plays an <u>indispensable</u> role in the lives of human beings in the 21st century. **SSC CGL Tier-1 02.12.2022 (Shift-I)**

(a) Superfluous (b) Relentless
(c) Vigilant (d) Unprecedented

Ans. (a)

Indispensable means absolutely necessary. Thus, its correct antonym is 'Superfluous', which means unnecessary.
Relentless means continuous.
Vigilant means careful.
Unprecedented means never existed before.

243. The recent disaster of <u>unprecedented</u> floods in June 2013, in the state of Uttarakhand devastated many towns and villages on the banks of the rivers Bhagirathi, Pindar, Mandakini, Alaknanda and Sarju. **SSC CGL Tier-1 02.12.2022 (Shift-II)**

(a) Lacklustre (b) Tarnished
(c) Familiar (d) Deranged

Ans. (c)

Unprecedented means never done or known before. Thus, its correct antonym is 'Familiar', which means known for acquainted.
Lackluster means dull.
Tarnished means destroyed or damaged.
Deranged means crazy.

244. Regardless of their <u>diversity</u>, all flowers have a uniform function, the reproduction of the species through the production of seed. **SSC CGL Tier-1 02.12.2022 (Shift-III)**

(a) Melancholy (b) Equilibrium
(c) Affinity (d) Uniformity

Ans. (d)

Diversity means variety. Thus, its correct antonym is 'Uniformity'.
Melancholy means sadness.
Equilibrium means balance.
Affinity means closeness.

245. The number of tests conducted dropped further on Saturday with a total of 67,624 tests of which 20% were the less <u>precise</u> rapid antigen tests. **SSC CGL Tier-1 02.12.2022 (Shift-IV)**

(a) Complicated (b) Inevitable
(c) Rough (d) Adequate

Ans. (c)

Precise means exact and accurate. Thus, nearest antonym is 'Rough'.
Complicated means difficult.
Inevitable means unavoidable.

246. A few chocolates were <u>left</u> after the Halloween's trick or treat fair. **SSC CGL Tier-1 02.12.2022 (Shift-IV)**

(a) Stayed (b) Finished
(c) Right (d) Present

Ans. (b)

'Left' in the context of the sentence is used to show what had remained. Hence, its antonyms is 'Finished'.

247. Ambition **SSC CGL Tier-1 03.12.2022 (Shift-I)**

(a) Intent (b) Anxiety
(c) Object (d) Laziness

Ans. (d)

Ambition refers to a strong desire to do or achieve something. Thus, the correct antonym is 'Laziness'.
Intent means purpose.
Anxiety means stress.
Object means to oppose.

248. Built by King Narasimhadeva I of the Eastern Ganga dynasty from 1238-1250 CE, the 13th century late-style Kalingan temple forms part of the golden triangle of Odisha, along with Puri and Bhubaneswar and <u>attracts</u> tourists, pilgrims and history and art lovers. **SSC CGL Tier-1 03.12.2022 (Shift-II)**

(a) Embodies (b) Shrouds
(c) Elucidates (d) Deters

Ans. (d)

Attracts means to cause someone to have a liking for or interest in something. Thus, the correct antonym is 'Deters', which means to turn aside, discourage or prevent from acting.
Embodies means to represent.
Shrouds means hides.
Elucidates means explains.

249. The WHO issued a statement on Sunday morning that though the Omicron variant of Coronavirus may appear to be less <u>severe</u>, it should not be dismissed as 'mild'. **SSC CGL Tier-1 03.12.2022 (Shift-II)**

(a) Withered (b) Sick
(c) Gentle (d) Voracious

Ans. (c)

Severe means extremely bad or serious. Thus, its correct antonym is 'Gentle', which means not strong, violent or extreme.

Withered means damaged due to age or use.

Voracious means hungry or wanting large amounts of food.

250. Humble SSC CGL Tier-1 03.12.2022 (Shift-III)

(a) Dishonour
(b) Pleasantry
(c) Modest
(d) Arrogant

Ans. (d)

Humble means not rude or not believing that you are important. Hence, its antonym is 'Arrogant' which means unpleasantly rude and behaving as if you know more than people.

Peasantry refers to a class of people, specially poor farmers.

Modesty means kindness.

251. Although gardening is a laborious job, but it gives me boundless joy, strenuous happiness and immense satisfaction and I like this facile activity. SSC CGL Tier-1 03.12.2022 (Shift-III)

(a) Boundless (b) Facile
(c) Strenuous (d) Immense

Ans. (b)

Laborious means taking a lot of time and effort. 'Facile' from the given options, is its most appropriate antonym as it means easy or too easy, not needing effort.

Strenuous means difficult

Immense means two large.

252. DispatchSSC CGL Tier-1 03.12.2022 (Shift-III)

(a) Acquire (b) Transmit
(c) Deliver (d) Bulletin

Ans. (a)

'Dispatch' means to send someone or something somewhere. 'acquire' means to get something. Hence, 'acquire' is the most appropriate antonym of 'Dispatch'.

Transmit means to send.

Bulletin refers to news.

253. Exemplary
SSC CGL Tier-1 03.12.2022 (Shift-IV)

(a) Flattering
(b) Unsatisfactory
(c) Imitative
(d) Desirable

Ans. (b)

'Exemplary' means very good and suitable to be copied by other people. So, 'Unsatisfactory' from the given options, is its most appropriate antonym as it means not good enough.

Flattering means attractive.

Imitative means copied.

254. Select the most appropriate antonym of the word 'Polite' in the given sentence.
SSC CGL Tier-1 03.12.2022 (Shift-IV)

The rude and insensitive murderer pleaded for mercy in the court.

(a) Pleaded (b) Mercy
(c) Insensitive (d) Rude

Ans. (d)

'Polite' means behaving in a way that is socially correct and shows understanding of and care for other people's feelings. 'Rude' from the given sentence is the most appropriate antonym of 'Polite' as it means not polite, offensive or embarrassing.

Mercy means forgiveness.

255. Adversity
SSC CGL Tier-1 03.12.2022 (Shift-IV)

(a) Fortune (b) Affliction
(c) Brilliance (d) Penury

Ans. (a)

'Adversity' means a difficult period in your life in which you have many problems. So, 'Fortune' from the given options is the most appropriate antonym of 'Adversity'.

Affliction means sorrow.

Penury means poor.

256. The patient was happy that he was given ancient methods of treatment to cure his health condition.
SSC CGL Tier-1 05.12.2022 (Shift-I)

(a) Multiple (b) Modern
(c) Primitive (d) Slow

Ans. (b)

The most appropriate antonym of the word 'Ancient' is 'Modern'.

257. Native SSC CGL Tier-1 05.12.2022 (Shift-I)

(a) Vicinity (b) Foreign
(c) Aboriginal (d) Realm

Ans. (b)

'Native' means a local inhabitant or a person's place of birth. So, 'Foreign' is its most appropriate antonym.

258. Beowulf was praised for his valour displayed in the battlefield.
SSC CGL Tier-1 05.12.2022 (Shift-III)

(a) Forbearance (b) Erudition
(c) Cowardice (d) Idiosyncrasy

Ans. (c)

'Valour' means great courage and lack of fear, especially in war.

Hence, its antonym is 'Cowardice' which means a lack of courage.

Forbearance means patience.

Erudition means knowledge.

Idiosyncrasy means a way of behavious and thinking.

259. The Government ruthlessly decided to force its citizens to pay taxes even during famine.
SSC CGL Tier-1 05.12.2022 (Shift-IV)

(a) Leniently
(b) Indifferently
(c) Unscrupulously
(d) Tyrannically

Ans. (a)

'Ruthlessly' means having or showing no pity or compassion for others. Thus, the correct antonym is 'Leniently', which means mild or tolerant and not harsh, severe or strict.

Indifferently means carelessly.

Unscrupulously means dishonestly.

Tyrannically means authoritatively.

260. Cease SSC CGL Tier-1 05.12.2022 (Shift-IV)

(a) Origin (b) Halt
(c) Produce (d) Begin

Ans. (d)

The word 'Cease' means come or bring to an end.

Thus, the correct antonym is 'Begin', which means to start.

Halt means to stop.

261. Select the most appropriate antonym of the word 'Established' from the given sentence.
SSC CGL Tier-1 06.12.2022 (Shift-I)

Siben feels great satisfaction and gratified when he finds his pupils established successfully in the society when a lot have been displaced because of several failed attempts.

(a) Displaced (b) Fail
(c) Gratified (d) Pupils

Ans. (a)

'Established' means settled and having existed or done something for a long time. Thus, its correct antonym is 'Displaced', which refers to moving something from its proper or usual position.

Gratified means satisfied.

262. The game continued due to heavy rainfall after the pitch became completely wet.
SSC CGL Tier-1 06.12.2022 (Shift-II)

(a) Ongoing
(b) Played
(c) Stopped
(d) Disregarded

Ans. (c)

'Continued' refers to something happening or taking place without a break. Thus, the correct antonym is 'Stopped'.

263. Select the most appropriate antonym of the word 'Immoral' from the given sentence.
SSC CGL Tier-1 06.12.2022 (Shift-II)
The city of Hamburg and its surrounding region have generally decent health, with no pandemic illnesses having lately developed to any significant degree.
(a) Degree (b) Decent
(c) Illness (d) Region

Ans. (b)
The word 'Immoral' refers to something that goes against morality or the ideas regarding what is good. Thus, its correct antonym from the given sentence is 'Decent', which refers to conforming with generally accepted standards of respectable or moral behaviour.

264. On must aim to develop intrinsic motivation within learners for better retention of knowledge.
SSC CGL Tier-1 06.12.2022 (Shift-III)
(a) Elemental (b) Introjected
(c) Extrinsic (d) Inherent

Ans. (c)
'Intrinsic' refers to something that is essential and belongs naturally. Thus, its correct antonym is 'Extrinsic', which refers to something that is not part of the essential nature of something or someone.
Elemental means basic.
Introjected means without awareness.
Inherent means natural.

265. Select the most appropriate antonym of the word 'Identify' from the given sentence. My pet dog can classify and identify our family friends easily and doesn't overlook anonymous and unknown ones. SSC CGL Tier-1 06.12.2022 (Shift-III)
(a) Anonymous (b) Spot
(c) Classify (d) Overlook

Ans. (d)
'Identify' means to recognise or spot someone. Thus, its correct antonym is 'Overlook', which means to fail to notice something.
Anonymous means unknown.
Classify means to categorises.

266. The money she offered him was insufficient to persuade him to sell.
SSC CGL Tier-1 06.12.2022 (Shift-III)
(a) Clade
(b) Propagandise
(c) Discourage
(d) Influence

Ans. (c)
The meaning of the word 'Persuade' means to motivate or encourage someone. Thus, its correct antonym is 'Discourage', which means to persuade someone against an action.
Clade means species of the same descendent
Propagandise means to promote a particular view.

267. Select the most appropriate antonym of the word 'Leisure' from the given sentence.
After my working hours, I use my leisure time to take care of my flower garden, dig my restricted land, sow seeds and water the plants for proper growth and development.
SSC CGL Tier-1 06.12.2022 (Shift-IV)
(a) Growth (b) Working
(c) Restricted (d) Development

Ans. (b)
'Working' in the given sentence is the most appropriate antonym of 'Leisure'.
'Leisure' means time when you are not working or studying and can relax and do things you enjoy.

268. The managing director produced **cogent** reasons for the change in HR policies.
SSC CGL Tier-1 07.12.2022 (Shift-I)
(a) Compelling (b) Unconvincing
(c) Pertinent (d) Unexpected

Ans. (b)
'Cogent' means (of reason, argument) strong and convincing. So, 'Unconvincing' from the given options is its most appropriate antonym.
Compelling means forcing.
Pertinent means closely connected.

269. It is undesirable to invest a part of your earnings for future use.
SSC CGL Tier-1 07.12.2022 (Shift-II)
(a) Advisable (b) Foolish
(c) Unadvisable (d) Meek

Ans. (a)
'Advisable' means to be done in order to avoid problems or risks. Hence, it is the most appropriate antonym of 'Undesirable'.

270. The actor was ridiculed for her nonchalant attitude towards her work. SSC CGL Tier-1 07.12.2022 (Shift-II)
(a) Boisterous
(b) Unconcerned
(c) Considerate
(d) Retrospective

Ans. (c)
'Nonchalant' means not feeling or showing interest or excitement about anything. Hence, 'Considerate' from the given option is its most appropriate antonym as it means thinking about the feelings and need of other people.
Boisterous means energetic and noisy
Retrospective means thoughtful about the past.

271. Pacify SSC CGL Tier-1 07.12.2022 (Shift-II)
(a) Placate (b) Assuage
(c) Aggravate (d) Quell

Ans. (c)
'Pacify' means to cause someone who is angry or upset to be calm and satisfied.
'Aggravate' is the most appropriate antonym of 'Pacify' as it means to make someone angry or annoyed.
Placate, **Assuage** and **quell** means to provide comfort.

272. Select the most appropriate antonym of the word 'Penniless' from the given sentence.
SSC CGL Tier-1 07.12.2022 (Shift-III)
Living in a house with a spacious lawn, a proper parking space and a nice swimming pool is still a dream for many rich people in Mumbai.
(a) Rich (b) Space
(c) Spacious (d) Dream

Ans. (a)
'Penniless' means having no money. So, 'Rich' from the given sentence is the most appropriate antonym of 'Penniless'.

273. Accept SSC CGL Tier-1 07.12.2022 (Shift-III)
(a) Agree (b) Respond
(c) Deny (d) Confirm

Ans. (c)
'Accept' means to take something that someone gives you. 'Deny' from the given options is the most appropriate antonym of 'Accept' as it means to refuse to allow someone to have or do something.

274. Select the most appropriate antonym of the word 'Vivid' from the given sentence.
In my murky memory lane, I still could vividly apprehend and envision the pictures of Nischindipu while reading Bibhutibhushan Bandyopadhyay's 'Pather Panchali'.
SSC CGL Tier-1 07.12.2022 (Shift-III)
(a) Perceive (b) Apprehend
(c) Murky (d) Envision

Ans. (c)

'Vivid' means very brightly coloured. 'Murky' is the most appropriate antonym as it means dark or difficult to see through, especially because of bad light, thick cloud or dirt in the air or water.

Perceive means to identify.

Apprehend means to catch.

Envision means thought about the future.

275. An autoimmune disease is a condition in which your <u>immune</u> system mistakenly attacks your body. SSC CGL Tier-1 07.12.2022 (Shift-IV)

(a) Susceptible (b) Fragile
(c) Sick (d) Sedentary

Ans. (a)

'Immune' means protected or not vulnerable. 'Susceptible' from the given options is the most appropriate antonym of 'Immune' as it means easily influenced or harmed by something.

Fragile means weak and delicate.

Sedentary means lazy.

276. The <u>antonym</u> of a word is sometimes a prefix added to the actual word.

SSC CGL Tier-1 07.12.2022 (Shift-IV)

(a) Metaverse (b) Synonym
(c) Symphony (d) Metonymy

Ans. (b)

The word 'Antonym' means a word which is opposite in meaning to another word. Thus, its most appropriate antonym is 'Synonym', which refers to a word having a similar meaning to another word.

Metaverse refers to virtual world.

Symphony is a long piece of music.

Metonymy is a poetic device based on comparison.

277. Bulk SSC CGL Tier-1 08.12.2022 (Shift-I)

(a) Handful (b) Heavy
(c) Staple (d) Brunt

Ans. (a)

The word 'Bulk' means in large amounts. 'Handful' from the given options is the most appropriate antonym of 'Bulk' as it means very few.

Staple means common.

Brunt means effect.

278. The natural environment is in contrast with the 'built environment' which refers to areas that have been fundamentally transformed and <u>influenced</u> by human activity, such as cities, towns, substructures and so on.

SSC CGL Tier-1 08.12.2022 (Shift-I)

(a) Hackneyed
(b) Inimical
(c) Bipartisan
(d) Interested

Ans. (b)

'Inimical' is the most appropriate antonym of 'influenced' as it means harmful or limiting.

Hackneyed means boring.

Bipartisan means involving two parties.

279. Loyal SSC CGL Tier-1 08.12.2022 (Shift-I)

(a) Ardent (b) Fickle
(c) Stupid (d) Tragic

Ans. (b)

'Loyal' means firm and not changing your friendship with or support for a person or an organisation. 'Fickle' is its most appropriate antonym as it means likely to change your opinion or your feelings suddenly and without a good reason.

Ardent means loyal.

Tragic means sorrowful.

280. The dacoits <u>ravaged</u> the bungalow in the absence of its owner.

SSC CGL Tier-1 08.12.2022 (Shift-I)

(a) Exploded (b) Demolished
(c) Restored (d) Sealed

Ans. (c)

The underlined word 'ravaged' means to cause great damage to something. So, 'Restored' from the given options is the most appropriate antonym of 'Ravaged' as it means to return something to an earlier good condition or position.

Exploded means burst.

Demolished means destroyed.

Sealed means to close an envelope.

281. Vigilant SSC CGL Tier-1 08.12.2022 (Shift-II)

(a) Stagnant
(b) Dubious
(c) Robust
(d) Negligent

Ans. (d)

'Vigilant' means being careful to notice things, especially possible danger. So, 'Negligent' from the given options is the most appropriate antonym of 'Vigilant' as it means not being careful or giving enough attention to people or things that are your responsibility.

Stagnant means still.

Dubious means fake.

Robust means strong.

282. Evolutionary psychology is a recently <u>advanced</u> field of study, which has grown exponentially with interest since the 1980s.

SSC CGL Tier-1 08.12.2022 (Shift-II)

(a) Rudimentary
(b) Lackadaisical
(c) Operative
(d) Presumptuous

Ans. (a)

'Rudimentary' is the most appropriate antonym of 'Advanced' as it means basic.

Lackadaisical means uninterested operative means useful.

Presumptuous means confident.

283. Anxiety SSC CGL Tier-1 08.12.2022 (Shift-II)

(a) Discomfort (b) Relief
(c) Agitation (d) Stress

Ans. (b)

'Anxiety' means an uncomfortable feeling of nervousness or worry about something that is happening or might happen in the future.

Hence, 'Relief' from the given options is the most appropriate antonym of 'Anxiety' as it means a feeling of happiness that something unpleasant has not happened or has ended.

Agitation means irritation and discomfort.

284. Hazard SSC CGL Tier-1 08.12.2022 (Shift-III)

(a) Peril (b) Jeopardy
(c) Protection (d) Danger

Ans. (c)

'Hazard' means something that is dangerous and likely to ensure damage. So, 'Protection' from the given options is the most appropriate antonym of 'Hazard'.

Peril and **Jeopardy** refer to dangerous situations.

285. A balloon <u>contracts</u> when air is blown into it.

SSC CGL Tier-1 08.12.2022 (Shift-IV)

(a) Controls (b) Repulses
(c) Shrinks (d) Expands

Ans. (d)

The underlined word 'Contracts' means to make or become shorter or narrower or generally smaller in size. Hence, 'Expands' from the given options is the most appropriate antonym of 'Contracts' as it means to become larger in size and fill more space.

Repulses means causing dislike.

Shrinks means to reduce in size.

286. The soldiers were irresolute and so, they won the war for the infantry and the country.
SSC CGL Tier-1 09.12.2022 (Shift-III)
(a) Harsh (b) Variant
(c) Default (d) Decisive
Ans. (d)
'Irresolute' means unable to make decisions. So, 'Decisive' from the given options is the most appropriate antonym of 'Irresolute'.
Variant means a type.
Default means original.

287. Everlasting
SSC CGL Tier-1 09.12.2022 (Shift-IV)
(a) Eternal (b) Transient
(c) Fatuous (d) Misled
Ans. (b)
'Everlasting' means something that lasts forever or for a very long time. Thus, its correct antonym is 'Transient', which means lasting only for a short time; temporary.
Eternal means everlasting.
Fatuous means pointless.

288. Select the most appropriate antonym of the word 'Acquisition' from the given sentence.
SSC CGL Tier-1 09.12.2022 (Shift-IV)
The head coach got surprised with the level of enthusiasm shown by the players as they all were demoralised after the first loss.
(a) Enthusiasm
(b) Demoralised
(c) Surprised
(d) Loss
Ans. (d)
'Acquisition' refers to the act of obtaining or beginning to have something. Thus, its correct antonym is 'Loss', which means the fact or the process of losing something.
Enthusiasm means excitement.
Demoralised means loss of confidence.

289. Abominable
SSC CGL Tier-1 12.12.2022 (Shift-II)
(a) Worthy (b) Delectable
(c) Admirable (d) Detestable
Ans. (c)
'Abominable' means extremely bad, offensive or unpleasant. Thus, its correct antonym is 'Admirable', which means something excellent and deserving the highest esteem.
Delectable means tasty.
Detestable means disliked.

290. Select the most appropriate antonym of the word 'Strange' from the given sentence.
SSC CGL Tier-1 12.12.2022 (Shift-III)
The intriguing journal took a back place once more to the more mundane events at the Ouray inn.
(a) Events (b) Intriguing
(c) Mundane (d) Place
Ans. (c)
The meaning of the word 'Strange' refers to something that is unusual or surprising and not previously seen or encountered. Thus, its correct antonym is 'Mundane', which means something that is ordinary and not at all unusual
Intriguing means interesting.

291. Appropriate
SSC CGL Tier-1 12.12.2022 (Shift-III)
(a) Transparent (b) Improper
(c) Salient (d) Disturbing
Ans. (b)
The meaning of the word 'Appropriate' means suitable or proper in the circumstances. Thus, its correct antonym is 'Improper', which means inappropriate or not in accordance with the accepted standards.
Transparent means that light can pass through it.
Salient means important.

292. Social economics is a meta-discipline in which economics is entrenched in social, political and cultural behaviours.
SSC CGL Tier-1 12.12.2022 (Shift-IV)
(a) Averted (b) Startling
(c) Transient (d) Entrusted
Ans. (c)
'Entrenched' means strongly established and not likely to change. 'Transient' which means existing, happening or staying some were for a short period of time only.
Averted means avoided.
Startling means shocking.
Entrusted means given a responsibility.

293. The singer complained to the police that she was purportedly attacked back stage immediately after the concert. SSC CGL Tier-1 12.12.2022 (Shift-IV)
(a) Maliciously (b) Impossibly
(c) Dramatically (d) Severely
Ans. (b)
'Purportedly' means in a way that is stated to be true, although this may not be case. So, 'Impossibly' is the most appropriate antonym of 'Purportedly'.
Maliciously means evilly.
Dramatically means very suddenly.
Severely means heavily or too strongly.

294. Repulsive
SSC CGL Tier-1 13.12.2022 (Shift-II)
(a) Hopeless (b) Steadfast
(c) Pleasant (d) Superfluous
Ans. (c)
'Repulsive' means extremely unpleasant or unacceptable.
So, 'Pleasant' is its correct antonym.
Steadfast means determined.
Superfluous means present on the surface but not useful.

295. The concert sound was in cacophony with every instrument playing in synchronisation.
SSC CGL Tier-1 13.12.2022 (Shift-II)
(a) Euphony (b) Bedlam
(c) Harmony (d) Alimony
Ans. (c)
Cacophony means a harsh discordant mixture of sounds. So, 'Harmony' is its correct antonym as it refers to the combination of simultaneously sounded musical notes to produce a pleasing effect.
Euphony means pleasing to the ear.
Bedlam means noisy and confusing place.
Alimony refers to money given during divorce to support the less income partner.

296. Intense SSC CGL Tier-1 13.12.2022 (Shift-II)
SSC CPO 10.11.2022 (Shift-II)
(a) Moderate (b) Thrifty
(c) Stately (d) Lavish
Ans. (a)
The most appropriate antonym of the given word 'Intense' is 'Moderate'. Intense means existing in an extreme degree and moderate means not excessive.
Thrifty means cheap.
Stately means formal.
Lavish means luxurious.

297. You should donate your old clothes to the poor.
SSC CGL Tier-1 13.12.2022 (Shift-III)
(a) Young (b) New
(c) Modern (d) Fresh
Ans. (b)
'New' out of the given options is the most appropriate antonym of 'Old'.

298. Incoherent
SSC CGL Tier-1 13.12.2022 (Shift-III)
(a) Gloomy (b) Apparent
(c) Pensive (d) Rational

Ans. (d)

'Incoherent' means expressing yourself in a way that is not clear. 'Rational' is the most appropriate antonym of 'Incoherent' as it means based on clear thought and reason.

Gloomy and **Pensive** means sad.

Apparent means clear.

299. Select the most appropriate antonym of the word 'Dwindle' in the sentence given below.
SSC CGL Tier-1 13.12.2022 (Shift-IV)
Rahul advised Neerja to appreciate or motivate her younger brother and not to dwindle or neglect his ideas all the time.
(a) Motivate
(b) Deprecate
(c) Complement
(d) Neglect

Ans. (c)

'Dwindle' means to keep on becoming or making smaller or less; diminish. Thus, 'Complement', which means a thing that contributes extra features to something else in such a way as to improve or emphasise its quality, is its correct antonym.

Deprecate means to reduce.

Neglect means to ignore.

300. Inherent SSC CGL Tier-1 13.12.2022 (Shift-IV)
(a) Restricted (b) Extraneous
(c) Induce (d) Natural

Ans. (b)

'Inherent' means existing in something as a permanent, essential or characteristic attribute. So, among the given options 'Extraneous' is its correct antonym. 'Extraneous' means irrelevant or unrelated to the subject being dealt with.

Restricted means not free.

Induce means to forcefully begin.

SSC CGL 2021 (Tier 1 & 2)

301. Gradual SSC CGL Tier-1 13.08.2021 (Shift-I)
(a) Gentle (b) Abrupt
(c) Regular (d) Slow

Ans. (b)

'Gradual' means 'slowly and consistently'. Hence, its antonym is 'Abrupt' which means 'all of a sudden'.

302. Seize SSC CGL Tier-1 13.08.2021 (Shift-I)
(a) Grab (b) Lose
(c) Snatch (d) Catch

Ans. (b)

'Seize' means 'to capture'. Hence, its antonym is 'Lose'.

Snatch means to take forcefully.

303. Widespread
SSC CGL Tier-1 13.08.2021 (Shift-III)
(a) Limited (b) General
(c) Overall (d) Famous

Ans. (a)

The antonym of 'Widespread' would be 'Limited'. 'Widespread' means 'found' or distributed over a large area or number of people. Hence, its antonym is 'limited' which means 'restricted' in size, amount or extent; few, small or short.

304. Invade SSC CGL Tier-1 16.08.2021 (Shift-I)
(a) Seize (b) Assault
(c) Attack (d) Surrender

Ans. (d)

'Invade' means 'to enter a country, town, etc. using military force, in order to take control of it'. Its antonym is 'Surrender' as it means 'to stop fighting and admit defeat'.

Seize means to take something forcefully.

Assault means attack.

305. Toxic SSC CGL Tier-1 16.08.2021 (Shift-I)
(a) Healthy (b) Venomous
(c) Lethal (d) Harmful

Ans. (a)

'Toxic' means 'harmful'. Hence, its antonym is 'Healthy'.

306. Stalwart SSC CGL Tier-1 17.08.2021 (Shift-I)
(a) Firm (b) Robust
(c) Cowardly (d) Stout

Ans. (c)

A 'stalwart' is a loyal friend who is very hardworking. Hence, its nearest antonym is 'Cowardly'.

Stout means fat.

Robust and **Firm** means strong.

307. Slur SSC CGL Tier-1 17.08.2021 (Shift-I)
(a) Mixture (b) Assortment
(c) Compliment (d) Insult

Ans. (c)

'Slur' means 'to insult or abuse'. Hence, its antonym is 'Compliment' which means 'praise'.

Mixture refers to a combination of things.

Assortment means a collection of variety of things.

308. Dividing SSC CGL Tier-1 17.08.2021 (Shift-III)
(a) Detaching (b) Breaking
(c) Parting (d) Connecting

Ans. (d)

'Dividing' means 'separate or categorise'. So, its antonym is 'Connecting'.

Breaking, **Detaching** and **Parting** means to separate.

309. Segregate
SSC CGL Tier-1 17.08.2021 (Shift-III)
(a) Correlate (b) Allude
(c) Integrate (d) Implicate

Ans. (c)

'Segregate' means 'to keep one thing separate from another'. So, its antonym is 'integrate' as it means 'combine one thing with another to form a whole'.

Correlate means to have a mutual relationship.

Allude means to all to attention or suggest.

Implicate means to blame someone for a crime.

310. Hassled SSC CGL Tier-1 18.08.2021 (Shift-III)
(a) Annoyed (b) Worried
(c) Relaxed (d) Stressed

Ans. (c)

'Hassled' means 'to bother, annoy or harass'. So, its antonym is 'Relaxed'.

311. Fallacy SSC CGL Tier-1 18.08.2021 (Shift-III)
(a) Cheat (b) Flaw (c) Trick (d) Truth

Ans. (d)

'Fallacy' means 'a mistaken belief'. Its antonym is 'Truth'.

312. Revel SSC CGL Tier-1 18.08.2021 (Shift-I)
(a) Appreciate (b) Rejoice
(c) Mourn (d) Enjoy

Ans. (c)

'Revel' means 'to celebrate'. Hence, its antonym is 'Mourn' which means 'to feel or express deep sadness'.

313. Downcast
SSC CGL Tier-1 18.08.2021 (Shift-I)
(a) Successful (b) Cheerful
(c) Distressed (d) Disappointed

Ans. (b)

'Downcast' means 'disheartened' or 'discouraged'. Hence, its antonym is 'Cheerful'.

Distressed means anxious.

314. Blemish SSC CGL Tier-1 20.08.2021 (Shift-I)
(a) Damage
(b) Stain
(c) Discolouration
(d) Perfection

Ans. (d)

'Blemish' means 'imperfection, fault, flaw, etc'. Its antonym is 'Perfection'.

315. Censure SSC CGL Tier-1 20.08.2021 (Shift-II)

(a) Fault (b) Applause
(c) Blunder (d) Contempt

Ans. (b)

'Censure' means 'express severe disapproval of (someone or something), especially in a formal statement'. So, its antonym is 'Applause' which means 'approval or praise expressed by clapping'.

Blunder means mistake.

Contempt means hatred.

316. Fecund SSC CGL Tier-1 23.08.2021 (Shift-I)

(a) Barren (b) Polite
(c) Genial (d) Rude

Ans. (a)

'Fecund' means 'highly fertile'. Hence, its antonym is 'Barren'.

Genial means friendly and cheerful.

317. Sprightly SSC CGL Tier-1 24.08.2021 (Shift-I)

(a) Energetic (b) Active
(c) Lively (d) Lethargic

Ans. (d)

'Sprightly' means 'to be lively, active and full of energy'. Its antonym is 'Lethargic' which means 'to lazy or sleepy'.

318. Delight SSC CGL Tier-1 24.08.2021 (Shift-II)

(a) Sorrow (b) Pleasure
(c) Glee (d) Joy

Ans. (a)

The antonym of 'Delight' is 'Sorrow'.

Glee, Joy and **Pleasure** mean happy and delight.

319. Controlled SSC CGL Tier-1 24.08.2021 (Shift-III)

(a) Restrained (b) Excited
(c) Guarded (d) Calm

Ans. (b)

'Controlled' means 'calm and not showing emotion, even if you feel angry, afraid, etc. Its antonym is 'Excited' as it means 'very nervous and upset about something so, that you cannot relax'.

Restrained means controlled.

Guarded means careful.

SSC CPO 2024

320. Select the word from the sentence below, which is an antonym for the word 'Uniformity'.
SSC CPO 27.06.2024 (Shift-I)

A great variety of birds is found in the sanctuaries of India.

(a) Great (b) Variety
(c) Found (d) Sanctuaries

Ans. (b)

The word 'Uniformity' means 'similarity between all things'. Hence, its antonym is 'Variety' which means 'different'.

Sanctuaries mean refuge or safety from pursuit, persecution or other danger.

321. The repetitive and <u>monotonous</u> task of data entry made the work seem incredibly long and tedious.
SSC CPO 27.06.2024 (Shift-I)

(a) Pious
(b) Interesting
(c) Precarious
(d) Threatening

Ans. (b)

Monotonous means repetitive and boring. Hence, its antonym is 'Interesting'.

Pious means holy or related to God.

Precarious means not sure.

322. The speaker delivered a <u>profound</u> speech that left the audience deeply moved. SSC CPO 27.06.2024 (Shift-I)

(a) Deep (b) Inventive
(c) Shallow (d) Occult

Ans. (c)

Profound means deep and thoughtful. Hence, its antonym is 'Shallow' which means not deep.

Invective means insulting, abusive, or highly critical language.

Occult means mystical, supernatural, or magical powers, practices or phenomena.

323. The worker is known to **exert** himself a lot. SSC CPO 27.06.2024 (Shift-I)

(a) Crouch (b) Emerge
(c) Relax (d) Stress

Ans. (c)

Exert means to force or stress. Hence, its antonym is 'to relax'.

Crouch means a sitting posture.

Emerge means to come out.

324. Freezing SSC CPO 27.06.2024 (Shift-I)

(a) Summary (b) Brisk
(c) Gnawing (d) Tropical

Ans. (d)

The antonym of 'Freezing' is 'Tropical' which means characteristic of a region or climate that is frost-free with temperatures high enough to support year-round plant growth given sufficient moisture.

Gnawing means bite at or nibble (something) so as to wear it away.

325. Select the word from the sentence below, which is an antonym for the word 'Confusing'.
The stars twinkled in the dark sky, guiding travellers on their journey.
SSC CPO 27.06.2024 (Shift-I)

(a) Guiding (b) Twinkled
(c) Travellers (d) Journey

Ans. (a)

The antonym of 'Confusing' in the sentence is 'Guiding'.

326. "Well, what if it is? You are not afraid of anything, you know", returned the boy, looking <u>wicked</u>.
SSC CPO 27.06.2024 (Shift-II)

(a) Clean (b) Evil
(c) Righteous (d) Improper

Ans. (c)

'Wicked' means moral wrongdoing or mischievous behaviour. Hence, its antonym is 'Righteous' which means morally upright, virtuous and adhering to ethical principles.

327. Summary SSC CPO 27.06.2024 (Shift-II)

(a) Abrupt (b) Lengthy
(c) Elliptical (d) Significant

Ans. (b)

Summary is short description of a story. Hence, its antonym is 'Lengthy'.

Abrupt means sudden and unexpected.

Elliptical refers to something that is elliptical in shape or form.

Significant means important or meaningful.

328. Mighty SSC CPO 27.06.2024 (Shift-II)

(a) Weak (b) Forcible
(c) Forceful (d) Haughty

Ans. (a)

Mighty means possessing great power or strength. Hence, its antonym is 'Weak'.

Haughty means arrogantly superior or disdainful.

329. Select the word from the sentence below, which is an antonym for the word 'Resolve'.
My cousin Nisha's curiosity about life will never be satisfied because no one knows all the answers to all her questions. SSC CPO 27.06.2024 (Shift-III)

(a) About (b) Questions
(c) Knows (d) Satisfied

Ans. (b)

'Resolve' means to come to a solution. Hence, its antonym is 'Questions'.

330. Select the word from the sentence below, which is an antonym for the word 'Advance'.
SSC CPO 27.06.2024 (Shift-III)

Clive is a travel blogger who believes that with even an elementary or intermediate knowledge of the local language, you can enjoy your travel more.

(a) Destination (b) Believes
(c) Elementary (d) Knowledge

Ans. (c)

Advance means difficult and complex. Hence, its antonym would be 'Elementary'.

Destination means the end point of a journey.

331. What is the most appropriate antonym of the word 'Fluctuate'?
SSC CPO 27.06.2024 (Shift-III)

(a) Stabilise (b) Deflect
(c) Fickle (d) Vacillate

Ans. (a)

Fluctuate means rise and fall irregularly in number or amount. Hence, its antonym is 'Stabilise' which means to remain same.

Deflect means cause (something) to change direction; turn aside from a straight course.

Fickle means changing frequently, especially as regards one's loyalties or affections.

Vacillate means waver between different opinions or actions; be indecisive.

332. Confound SSC CPO 27.06.2024 (Shift-III)

(a) Expire (b) Discern
(c) Assure (d) Suppress

Ans. (c)

Confound means to confuse and very much surprise someone. Hence, its antonym is 'assure' which means 'to remove doubts'.

Expire means to come to the end of the period of validity.

Discern means to recognise or find out.

Suppress means to forcibly put an end to.

333. Oral SSC CPO 27.06.2024 (Shift-III)

(a) Verbal (b) Inscribed
(c) Obligatory (d) Dejected

Ans. (b)

Oral means verbal or spoken. Hence, its antonym is 'Inscribed' which means written somewhere.

Obligatory means required by a legal, moral, or other rule; compulsory.

Dejected means sad and depressed; dispirited.

334. Rapid SSC CPO 27.06.2024 (Shift-III)

(a) Active (b) Smart
(c) Lately (d) Slow

Ans. (d)

Rapid means quick and fast. Hence, its antonym is 'Slow'.

335. Convalesce SSC CPO 27.06.2024 (Shift-III)

(a) Collapse (b) Conceal
(c) Corrupt (d) Confront

Ans. (a)

'Convalesce' means to recover. Hence, its antonym is to 'Collapse'.

Conceal means to hide.

Confront means come face to face with.

336. The beauty of cherry blossoms is <u>ephemeral</u>, as the delicate pink petals bloom for only a short period. SSC CPO 28.06.2024 (Shift-I)

(a) Uniform
(b) Unwavering
(c) Permanent
(d) Transient

Ans. (c)

Ephemeral means lasting for a very short time, fleeting or transient. Hence, its antonym is 'Permanent'.

Uniform means consistent or unchanging in form, quality, or nature.

Unwavering means steady or constant, indicating something that does not change.

Transient means lasting for only a short time.

337. Indians tend to be quite <u>conservative</u> in most aspects of life, particularly in rural areas.
SSC CPO 28.06.2024 (Shift-I)

(a) Liberal (b) Fantastic
(c) Determined (d) Authentic

Ans. (a)

Conservative refers to a tendency to preserve existing traditions and resist change.

Hence, its antonym is 'Liberal' which means open to new behaviour or opinions and willing to discard traditional values.

Fantastic means imaginative or fanciful.

Determined means having made a firm decision and being resolved.

Authentic means genuine or real.

338. Which is the right set of antonyms from the options for 'Confidential'?
SSC CPO 28.06.2024 (Shift-I)

(a) Familiar, Revealed
(b) Offstage, Sneaking
(c) Public, Concealed
(d) Hushed, Common

Ans. (a)

'Confidential' means secretive. Hence, its antonyms are 'Familiar' which means well-known or easily recognised by someone and 'Revealed' which means made known or disclosed, especially after having been kept secret.

339. Aggravate SSC CPO 28.06.2024 (Shift-II)

(a) Exasperate (b) Alleviate
(c) Humiliate (d) Ignorant

Ans. (b)

Aggravate means to make (a problem, injury or offense) worse or more serious. Hence, its antonym is 'Alleviate' which means to make (suffering, deficiency, or a problem) less severe.

Exasperate means to irritate intensely or to infuriate.

Humiliate means to cause someone to feel ashamed or foolish by injuring their dignity or self-respect.

Ignorant means lacking knowledge or awareness.

340. The government is proposing to <u>incinerate</u> cattle carcasses at many sites, some of which are in populated areas.
SSC CPO 28.06.2024 (Shift-II)

(a) Oxidise (b) Blaze
(c) Extinguish (d) Combust

Ans. (c)

Incinerate means to burn something completely, typically in a self-sustaining fire at very high temperatures. Hence, its antonym is **Extinguish** which means to put out a fire or a flame, or to bring an end to something.

Oxidise and **Combust** are related to the process of burning or undergoing combustion.

Blaze refers to a large and dangerous fire.

341. The brave knight set out to <u>vanquish</u> the fearsome dragon and protect the kingdom from its menace. SSC CPO 28.06.2024 (Shift-II)

(a) Liberate (b) Measure
(c) Engage (d) Instill

Ans. (a)

Vanquish means to defeat thoroughly in a battle or contest. Hence, its antonym is 'Liberate' which means to set free from imprisonment, slavery or oppression.

Measure means to ascertain the size, amount or degree of something.

Engage means to occupy, attrac, or involve someone's interest or attention.

Instill means to gradually but firmly establish an idea or attitude, typically in a person's mind.

342. Upright SSC CPO 28.06.2024 (Shift-II)
(a) Stout (b) Immoral
(c) Brave (d) Ethical

Ans. (b)

Upright means honest, honourable, and morally correct. Hence, its antonym is 'Immoral' which means not conforming to accepted standards of morality; morally wrong or evil.
Stout means physically strong or heavily built; it does not relate to morality.
Ethical means relating to moral principles or the branch of knowledge dealing with these.

343. The arrival of spring brings an ebullient feeling as flowers bloom and the weather warms.
SSC CPO 28.06.2024 (Shift-II)
(a) Deciduous (b) Clamant
(c) Rude (d) Weary

Ans. (d)

Ebullient means cheerful and full of energy. Hence, its antonym is 'Weary', which means feeling or showing tiredness, especially as a result of excessive exertion or lack of sleep.
Deciduous relates to trees that shed their leaves annually.
Clamant means urgent or strongly expressed.

344. Tight SSC CPO 28.06.2024 (Shift-II)
(a) Cordial (b) Slack
(c) Comfortable (d) Resilient

Ans. (b)

Tight typically means firmly held together, restrictive or not loose. Hence, its antonym is 'Slack' which means loose, not taut or lacking tension.
Cordial means warm and friendly.
Comfortable means providing physical ease and relaxation.
Resilient means able to recoil or spring back into shape after bending, stretching, or being compressed.

345. Maria thinks the animals that live in freedom have a sad look in their eyes. SSC CPO 28.06.2024 (Shift-III)
(a) Carefree (b) Liberty
(c) Surrendered (d) Captivity

Ans. (d)

Captivity means the condition of being imprisoned or confined.
Hence, it is the correct antonym of 'Freedom'.

346. Accolade SSC CPO 28.06.2024 (Shift-III)
(a) Criticism (b) Tribute
(c) Promotion (d) Assurance

Ans. (a)

Accolade refers to an award or honour given as a mark of recognition or approval. Hence, its antonym is 'Criticism' which is the expression of disapproval of someone or something based on perceived faults or mistakes.
Tribute refers to an expression of praise or admiration.
Promotion refers to the advancement or elevation of someone to a higher position or rank.
Assurance means a positive declaration intended to give confidence.

347. The door was ajar and a faint wisp of smoke floated through it.
SSC CPO 28.06.2024 (Shift-III)
(a) Itchy (b) Lot
(c) Trickle (d) Wind

Ans. (b)

A wisp refers to a thin, delicate strand or fragment, often used to describe a faint trace of something, like smoke in this case. Hence, its antonym is 'Lot' which refers to a large quantity or amount.

348. Recession fettered the company from any further investments.
SSC CPO 29.06.2024 (Shift-I)
(a) Concealed (b) Valuable
(c) Depended (d) Liberated

Ans. (d)

Fettered means restricted or restrained. Hence, its antonym is 'Liberated' which means freed or released from restrictions.
Concealed means hidden or kept out of sight.

349. Her behaviour was consistent even in challenging situations.
SSC CPO 29.06.2024 (Shift-I)
(a) Appreciative (b) Standard
(c) Enthusiastic (d) Unpredictable

Ans. (d)

Consistent means behaving or acting in the same way over time, especially so as to be fair or accurate. Hence, its antonym is 'Unpredictable' which means not able to be predicted; changeable.
Appreciative means showing gratitude or pleasure.
Standard refers to a level of quality or attainment.
Enthusiastic means having or showing intense and eager enjoyment, interest, or approval.

350. The reports of the medical tests done are now accessible on phone.
SSC CPO 29.06.2024 (Shift-I)
(a) Useless (b) Free
(c) Restricted (d) Invisible

Ans. (c)

'Accessible' means able to be reached, used, or obtained easily. Hence, its antonym is 'Restricted' which means limited or controlled so that people cannot enter, use or obtain easily.

351. Cowardice SSC CPO 29.06.2024 (Shift-I)
(a) Boldness
(b) Abundance
(c) Hazard
(d) Vigour

Ans. (a)

Cowardice means the ability to face danger, difficulty, opposition, or pain; being easily frightened. Hence, its antonym is 'Boldness' which is the quality of having a strong, confident and courageous personality.
Abundance means a very large quantity of something.
Hazard means a danger or risk.
Vigour means physical strength and good health; energy and enthusiasm.

352. The teacher praised the student for his diligent work and consistent effort. SSC CPO 29.06.2024 (Shift-II)
(a) Frazzle (b) Persistent
(c) Lazy (d) Squander

Ans. (c)

Diligent means showing careful and persistent effort in doing something; hard-working. Hence, its antonym is 'Lazy'.
Frazzle means to exhaust physically or emotionally.
Persistent means continuing firmly or obstinately in a course of action despite difficulty or opposition.
Squander means to waste something, especially money or time, in a reckless and foolish manner.

353. Pitiable SSC CPO 29.06.2024 (Shift-II)
(a) Eradicate (b) Pleasant
(c) Grievous (d) Aggregate

Ans. (b)

Pitiable means deserving or arousing pity; pathetic. Hence, its antonym is 'Pleasant'.
Eradicate means to destroy completely; put an end to.
Grievous means causing grief or great sorrow; serious or severe.
Aggregate means formed by the combination of many separate units or items; total.

354. Quaint SSC CPO 29.06.2024 (Shift-II)
(a) Brisk (b) Ridiculous
(c) Ordinary (d) Distinct

Ans. (c)

Quaint refers to attractively unusual or old-fashioned. Hence, its nearest antonym is 'Ordinary'.
Ridiculous means deserving or inviting mockery; absurd.
Distinct means recognisably different in nature from something else of a similar type.

355. Languid SSC CPO 29.06.2024 (Shift-II)
(a) Exceptional (b) Lazy
(c) Loyal (d) Energetic

Ans. (d)

Languid displaying or having a disinclination for physical exertion or effort; slow and relaxed. Hence, its antonym is 'Energetic'.
Exceptional means unusually good; outstanding.

356. Suspend SSC CPO 29.06.2024 (Shift-II)
(a) Extend (b) Terminate
(c) Project (d) Resume

Ans. (d)

Suspend means to temporarily prevent from continuing or being in force or effect. Hence, its antonym is 'Resume'.

357. The artists abstract painting was enigmatic to the viewers. SSC CPO 29.06.2024 (Shift-II)
(a) Mysterious (b) Instigating
(c) Clear (d) Thrilling

Ans. (c)

Enigmatic means something that is mysterious, puzzling, or difficult to understand. Hence, its antonym is 'Clear'.
Mysterious means something that is difficult to understand.
Instigating means to incite or provoke.
Thrilling means something that is exciting or causing excitement.

358. We embraced each other overjoyed at our success, then I took photograph of Tenzing holding aloft the flags of Great Britain, Nepal, the United Nations and India. SSC CPO 29.06.2024 (Shift-III)
(a) Cradled (b) Junked
(c) Contained (d) Limited

Ans. (d)

'Embraced' means to hold or hug tightly, often in a gesture of celebration or affection. Hence, its antonym is 'Limited' which implies restrained or restricted.
Cradled means held in arms.
Junked means destroyed as waste.

359. The new government allowed all the corrupt ministers to feel the sufficiency of money by banning the specific currency. SSC CPO 29.06.2024 (Shift-III)
(a) Indeficiency (b) Plenty
(c) Enough (d) Dearth

Ans. (d)

'Sufficiency' means an adequate amount or enough.
Hence, its antonym is 'Dearth' which means a scarcity or lack of something, especially something essential.

360. The woman in the crowd broke down in hysterics. SSC CPO 29.06.2024 (Shift-III)
(a) Aghast (b) Cray
(c) Calm (d) Insanity

Ans. (c)

Hysterics refers to a state of uncontrollable and extreme emotion, often manifested as intense laughter or crying.
Hence, its antonym is 'Calm'.
Aghast means extremely shocked or horrified.
Cray (assuming a type of 'crazy') means insane or mentally deranged.
Insanity means extreme foolishness or irrationality; also can refer to a state of mental illness or madness.

361. Select the word from the sentence below, which is an antonym for the word 'Dishearten'. SSC CPO 29.06.2024 (Shift-III)
Many of the world's greatest art pieces are encouraged by kings and are inspired by nature and society.
(a) Greatest
(b) Pieces
(c) Inspired
(d) Encouraged

Ans. (d)

'Dishearten' means to cause someone to lose determination or confidence; to discourage. Hence, its antonym is 'Encouraged'.

362. Her sarcastic comment earned a few chuckles from the audience, who understood the irony in her words. SSC CPO 29.06.2024 (Shift-III)
(a) Unsavoury (b) Courteous
(c) Sardonic (d) Humorous

Ans. (b)

Sarcastic means characterised by sarcasm; using irony to mock or convey contempt. Hence, its antonym is 'Courteous' which means polite, respectful, showing good manners.
Unsavoury means unpleasant, disagreeable.
Sardonic means grimly mocking or cynical.
Humorous means funny, causing laughter.

SSC CPO 2023

363. Catastrophic SSC CPO 03.10.2023 (Shift-I)
(a) Calamity (c) Fortuitous
(c) Fiasco (d) Sabotage

Ans. (b)

Catastrophic means 'involving or causing sudden great damage or suffering'. Hence, its antonym is 'Fortuitous' which means 'happening by a lucky chance, fortunate'.
Calamity means a dangerous situation.
Fiasco means failure.
Sabotage means to destroy something deliberately.

364. Select the most appropriate antonym of the word 'Moving' in the given sentence and choose the correct option. SSC CPO 03.10.2023 (Shift-I)
The old grandfather clock chimed loudly, marking the passage of time with its steady tick-tock.
(a) Steady (c) Marking
(c) Chimed (d) Passage

Ans. (a)

The word 'Steady' means 'stable' is the antonym of 'Moving'.

365. Damp SSC CPO 03.10.2023 (Shift-I)
(a) Misty (b) Arid
(c) Tropical (d) Soaked

Ans. (b)

'Damp' means 'wet'. Hence, its antonym is 'Arid' which means 'dry'.
Misty and **Soaked** indicate different levels of dampness.
Tropical means supporting moisture.

366. The **negligent** attitude of the cops was criticised. SSC CPO 03.10.2023 (Shift-I)
(a) attentive (b) reluctant
(c) amplify (d) bored

Ans. (a)

'Negligent' means 'uncaring or ignoring'. Hence, its antonym is 'attentive'.
Amplify means to increase in continuity.

367. Select the most appropriate antonym of the word 'Discordant' in the given sentence and choose the correct option. **SSC CPO 03.10.2023 (Shift-II)**

The sweet melodious symphony of the piano filled the room, transporting the listeners to a world of beauty and emotion.

(a) Transporting (b) Melodious
(c) Emotion (d) Filled

Ans. (b)

Discordant means disagreeing or incongruous. Hence, its antonym is 'melodious'.

368. Rejoinder **SSC CPO 03.10.2023 (Shift-II)**

(a) Ordinary (b) Request
(c) Reply (d) Expedite

Ans. (c)

Rejoinder means a reply, especially a sharp or witty one. Hence, its antonym is 'reply'.

Expedite means make (an action or process) happen sooner or be accomplished more quickly.

369. Leniency **SSC CPO 03.10.2023 (Shift-II)**

(a) Penalty
(b) Discard
(c) Sternness
(d) Favour

Ans. (c)

Leniency means the fact or quality of being more merciful or tolerant than expected. Hence, its antonym is 'sternness'.

Penalty means a punishment imposed for breaking a law, rule, or contract.

Discard means get rid of (someone or something) as no longer useful or desirable.

Favour means approval, support or liking for someone or something.

370. Placid **SSC CPO 03.10.2023 (Shift-II)**

(a) Turbulent (b) Destined
(c) Pensive (d) Pristine

Ans. (a)

Placid means not easily upset or excited. Hence, its antonym is 'turbulent'.

Destined means certain to meet (a particular fate).

Pensive means engaged in, involving, or reflecting deep or serious thought.

Pristine means in its original condition; unspoiled.

371. Asset **SSC CPO 03.10.2023 (Shift-II)**

(a) Liability (b) Mole
(c) Wealth (d) Refuse

Ans. (a)

Asset means a useful or valuable thing, person, or quality. Hence, its antonym is 'liability'.

Mole means a small burrowing mammal.

372. Denounce **SSC CPO 03.10.2023 (Shift-II)**

(a) Criticise (b) Dainty
(c) Praise (d) Relieve

Ans. (c)

Denounce means publicly declare to be wrong or evil. Hence, its antonym is 'praise'.

Criticise means indicate the faults of (someone or something) in a disapproving way.

Dainty means delicately small and pretty.

373. Apathy **SSC CPO 03.10.2023 (Shift-II)**

(a) Sincerity (b) Interruption
(c) Interest (d) Ignorance

Ans. (c)

Apathy means lack of interest, enthusiasm, or concern. Hence, its antonym is 'interest'.

374. Specific **SSC CPO 03.10.2023 (Shift-III)**

(a) Topple (b) Lawful
(c) Stroll (d) Random

Ans. (d)

Specific means clearly defined or identified. Hence, its antonym is 'random'.

Topple means overbalance or cause to overbalance and fall.

375. Beneficent **SSC CPO 03.10.2023 (Shift-III)**

(a) Soft (b) Friendly
(c) Cruel (d) Lethargic

Ans. (c)

Beneficent means (of a person) generous or doing good. Hence, its antonym is 'cruel'.

376. Glad **SSC CPO 03.10.2023 (Shift-III)**

(a) Loyal (b) Sad (c) Keen (d) Pleased

Ans. (b)

Glad means feeling pleasure or happiness. Hence, its antonym is 'sad'.

377. Contempt **SSC CPO 03.10.2023 (Shift-III)**

(a) Regard (b) Mockery
(c) Deny (d) Immoral

Ans. (a)

Contempt means the feeling that a person or a thing is worthless or beneath consideration. Hence, its antonym is 'regard'.

Mockery means teasing and contemptuous language or behaviour directed at a particular person or thing.

Immoral means not conforming to accepted standards of morality.

378. Credit **SSC CPO 04.10.2023 (Shift-I)**

(a) Install (b) Impute
(c) Debit (d) Litigate

Ans. (c)

Credit means the ability of a customer to obtain goods or services before payment, based on the trust that payment will be made in the future. Hence, its antonym is 'debit'.

Install means place or fix (equipment or machinery) in position ready for use.

Impute means represent (something, especially something undesirable) as being done, caused, or possessed by someone; attribute.

Litigate means take (a dispute) to a court of law.

379. Select the most appropriate antonym of the word 'Hindrance' in the given sentence and choose the correct option. **SSC CPO 04.10.2023 (Shift-I)**

The refreshing breeze blew through the open window, bringing relief from the summer heat.

(a) Refreshing (b) Bringing
(c) Blew (d) Relief

Ans. (d)

Hindrance means a thing that provides resistance, delay or obstruction to something or someone. Hence, its antonym is 'relief'.

380. Vague **SSC CPO 04.10.2023 (Shift-I)**

(a) Dwarf (b) Regal
(c) Definite (d) Elegant

Ans. (c)

Vague means of uncertain, indefinite, or unclear character or meaning. Hence, its antonym is 'definite'.

Dwarf means (in folklore or fantasy literature) a member of a mythical race of short, stocky humanlike creatures who are generally skilled in mining and metalworking.

Regal means of, resembling, or fit for a monarch, especially in being magnificent or dignified.

Elegant means pleasingly graceful and stylish in appearance or manner.

381. Demolish **SSC CPO 04.10.2023 (Shift-I)**

(a) Inferior (b) Annihilate
(c) Fabricate (d) Unmethodical

Ans. (c)

Demolish means pull or knock down (a building). Hence, its antonym is 'fabricate'.

Inferior means lower in rank, status, or quality.

Annihilate means destroy utterly; obliterate.

Unmethodical means not done according to a systematic or established form of procedure.

382. Defunct SSC CPO 04.10.2023 (Shift-I)

(a) Convoluted (b) Redundant
(c) Extant (d) Stoicism

Ans. (c)

Defunct means no longer existing or functioning. Hence, its antonym is 'extant'.

Convoluted means (especially of an argument, story, or sentence) extremely complex and difficult to follow.

Redundant means not or no longer needed or useful; superfluous.

Stoicism means the endurance of pain or hardship without the display of feelings and without complaint.

383. Brave SSC CPO 04.10.2023 (Shift-I)

(a) Cowardly
(b) Cordial
(c) Courageous
(d) Elegant

Ans. (a)

Brave means ready to face and endure danger or pain; showing courage. Hence, its antonym is 'cowardly'.

Cordial means warm and friendly.

Elegant means pleasingly graceful and stylish in appearance or manner.

384. Transparent SSC CPO 04.10.2023 (Shift-II)

(a) Crossover (b) Linger
(c) Opaque (d) Oppress

Ans. (c)

Transparent means 'clear and penetrable by light'. Hence, its antonym is 'Opaque' which means 'not transparent or translucent, impenetrable to light'.

Crossover means the process of changing from one style to another.

Linger means to move slowly.

385. Abhor SSC CPO 04.10.2023 (Shift-II)

(a) Occupy (b) Despise
(c) Danger (d) Love

Ans. (d)

'Abhor' means to regard with disgust and hatred. Hence, its antonym is 'Love'.

386. Apex SSC CPO 04.10.2023 (Shift-II)

(a) Pinnacle (b) Bottom
(c) Farthest (d) Watchful

Ans. (b)

'Apex' refers to the highest point or peak of something. Hence, its antonym is 'Bottom'.

Pinnacle means highest point.

387. Bombastic SSC CPO 04.10.2023 (Shift-II)

(a) Essential (b) Sarcastic
(c) Plain (d) Rhythmic

Ans. (c)

'Bombastic' means high-sounding but with little meaning, inflated. Hence, its antonym is 'Plain'.

388. Redemption SSC CPO 05.10.2023 (Shift-III)

(a) Salvation (b) Blasphemy
(c) Corrugation (d) Conjunction

Ans. (b)

Redemption refers to the act of being saved or rescued from sin, error or evil. Its antonym is 'Blasphemy' which refers to the act of speaking disrespectfully or irreverently about sacred things.

Salvation means the state of being saved.

Corrugation means the process of wrinkling or folding.

Conjunction means joining.

389. Decline SSC CPO 05.10.2023 (Shift-III)

(a) Escape (b) Ascend
(c) Demonstrate (d) Traverse

Ans. (b)

Decline typically means to decrease or to move downward. Hence, its antonym is 'Ascend' that means to increase or to move upward.

Demonstrate means to show.

Traverse means to travel across or through.

390. Together SSC CPO 05.10.2023 (Shift-III)

(a) Apart (b) United
(c) Freight (d) Engulf

Ans. (a)

The antonym of 'Together' is 'Apart'.

Freight means to transport goods in bulk.

Engulf means to surround or cover.

391. Magnificent SSC CPO 05.10.2023 (Shift-III)

(a) Impressive (b) Peaceful
(c) Quiet (d) Modest

Ans. (d)

'Magnificent' means 'splendid or grand'. Hence, its antonym is 'Modest', which means humble or simple.

392. Resolute SSC CPO 05.10.2023 (Shift-III)

(a) Serious (b) Wavering
(c) Steadfast (d) Brave

Ans. (b)

'Resolute' means to be firmly determined or steadfast in purpose. Hence, its antonym is 'Wavering' as it conveys indecision or lack of determination.

393. All members of the association adhere to a strict code of practice. SSC CPO 05.10.2023 (Shift-III)

(a) Observe (b) Cling
(c) Flout (d) Comply

Ans. (c)

Adhere means 'to stick to or follow closely'.
Hence, its antonym is 'Flout' which means 'to disregard or disobey'.

Cling means to hold tightly.

Comply means to agree or obey.

394. She has a **penchant** for art and craft. SSC CPO 05.10.2023 (Shift-III)

(a) Anxiety (b) Hatred
(c) Fear (d) Joy

Ans. (b)

Penchant refers to a strong liking or preference for something. Hence, its antonym is 'Hatred'.

395. Superb SSC CPO 05.10.2023 (Shift-III)

(a) Infallible
(b) Incorrigible
(c) Inferior
(d) Splendid

Ans. (c)

Superb means 'excellent or outstanding'. Hence, its antonym is 'Inferior' which means 'to lower quality or standard'.

Infallible means that cannot fail.

Incorrigible means cannot be reformed.

Splendid means superb.

396. Malice SSC CPO 04.10.2023 (Shift-III)

(a) Tremor
(b) Haughtiness
(c) Torsion
(d) Kindness

Ans. (d)

Malice means the intention or desire to do evil; ill will. Hence, its antonym is 'kindness'.

Tremor means an involuntary quivering movement.

Haughtiness means the appearance or quality of being arrogantly superior and disdainful.

Torsion means the action of twisting or the state of being twisted, especially of one end of an object relative to the other.

397. Identify the antonym of 'Languid' in the given sentence. SSC CPO 04.10.2023 (Shift-III)
The animated infantry was marching forward for another rehearsal.
(a) Infantry (b) Forward
(c) Animated (d) Rehearsal
Ans. (c)
Languid means displaying or having a disinclination for physical exertion or effort; slow and relaxed. Hence, its antonym is 'animated'.
Infantry means soldiers marching or fighting on foot.
Forward means in the direction that one is facing or travelling.
Rehearsal means a practice or trial performance of a play or other work for later public performance.

398. The **malice** he developed for all caused a lot a damage. SSC CPO 04.10.2023 (Shift-III)
(a) Oppression (b) Sympathy
(c) Grace (d) Avarice
Ans. (b)
Malice means the intention or desire to do evil; ill will. Hence, its antonym is 'sympathy'.
Oppression means prolonged cruel or unjust treatment or control.
Grace means simple elegance or refinement of movement.
Avarice means extreme greed for wealth or material gain.

399. After losing his job and his home, he found himself **destitute** and living on the streets. SSC CPO 05.10.2023 (Shift-I)
(a) disturbed (b) affluent
(c) glorious (d) ridiculous
Ans. (b)
Destitute means without the basic necessities of life. Hence, its antonym is 'affluent'.

400. He is so **stingy** that I have never seen him spending money on basic necessities. SSC CPO 05.10.2023 (Shift-I)
(a) Obnoxious (b) Extravagant
(c) Indecent (d) Wicked
Ans. (b)
Stingy means unwilling to give or spend; ungenerous. Hence, its antonym is 'extravagant'.
Obnoxious means extremely unpleasant.
Indecent means not conforming with generally accepted standards of behaviour or propriety; obscene.
Wicked means evil or morally wrong.

401. Authentic SSC CPO 05.10.2023 (Shift-I)
(a) Fake (b) Different
(c) Basic (d) Genuine
Ans. (a)
Authentic means of undisputed origin and not a copy; genuine. Hence, its antonym is 'fake'.

402. The court **absolved** the defendant of all charges due to lack of evidence. SSC CPO 05.10.2023 (Shift-II)
(a) Condemned
(b) Criticised
(c) Attacked
(d) Accused
Ans. (a)
Absolved means declared (someone) free from blame, guilt, or responsibility. Hence, its antonym is 'condemned'.

403. Calm SSC CPO 05.10.2023 (Shift-II)
(a) Confused (b) Shocked
(c) Variable (d) Turbulent
Ans. (d)
Calm means not showing or feeling nervousness, anger, or other strong emotions. Hence, its antonym is 'turbulent'.

404. Ethical SSC CPO 05.10.2023 (Shift-II)
(a) Mourning (b) Discord
(c) Joyous (d) Immoral
Ans. (d)
Ethical means relating to moral principles or the branch of knowledge dealing with these. Hence, its antonym is 'immoral'.
Mourning means the expression of deep sorrow for someone who has died.
Discord means disagreement between people.
Joyous means full of happiness and joy.

405. Profane SSC CPO 05.10.2023 (Shift-II)
(a) Barnyard (b) Immaterial
(c) Perverse (d) Divine
Ans. (d)
Profane means relating or devoted to that which is not sacred or biblical; secular rather than religious. Hence, its antonym is 'divine'.
Barnyard means a yard adjacent to a barn.
Immaterial means unimportant under the circumstances; irrelevant.
Perverse means showing a deliberate and obstinate desire to behave in a way that is unreasonable or unacceptable.

406. Hideous SSC CPO 05.10.2023 (Shift-II)
(a) Attractive (b) Restorative
(c) Healthful (d) Lament
Ans. (a)
Hideous means ugly or disgusting to look at. Hence, its antonym is 'attractive'.
Restorative means having the ability to restore health, strength, or a feeling of well-being.
Lament means a passionate expression of grief or sorrow.

SSC CPO 2022

407. Emulate SSC CPO 09.11.2022 (Shift-I)
(a) Respect (b) Neglect
(c) Spoilt (d) Bash
Ans. (b)
Emulate means match or surpass (a person or achievement), typically by imitation. Hence, its antonym is 'neglect'.
Bash means strike hard and violently.

408. <u>Spurious</u> medicine can be fatal to the patient. SSC CPO 09.11.2022 (Shift-I)
(a) Genuine (b) Inferior
(c) Contemptuous (d) Virtuous
Ans. (a)
Spurious means not being what it purports to be; false or fake. Hence, its antonym is 'genuine'.
Inferior means lower in rank, status, or quality.
Contemptuous means showing contempt; scornful.
Virtuous means having or showing high moral standards.

409. Scanty SSC CPO 09.11.2022 (Shift-I)
(a) Expedient (b) Paltry
(c) Nasty (d) Abundant
Ans. (d)
Scanty means small or insufficient in quantity or amount. Hence, its antonym is 'abundant'.
Expedient means (of an action) convenient and practical although possibly improper or immoral.
Paltry means small or meager.
Nasty means highly unpleasant, especially to the senses; physically nauseating.

410. Asperity SSC CPO 09.11.2022 (Shift-I)
(a) Virility (b) Civility
(c) Acridity (d) Curiosity
Ans. (b)
Asperity means harshness of tone or manner. Hence, its antonym is 'civility'.
Virility means (in a man) the quality of having strength, energy, and a strong sex drive; manliness.

Acridity means having an irritatingly strong and unpleasant taste or smell.

Curiosity means a strong desire to know or learn something.

411. With her spry and athletic build, she won the race easily. SSC CPO 09.11.2022 (Shift-I)

(a) Agile (b) Lethargic
(c) Sleuth (d) Workaholic

Ans. (b)

Spry means (especially of an old person) active; lively. Hence, its antonym is 'lethargic'.

Agile means able to move quickly and easily.

Sleuth means a detective.

Workaholic means a person who compulsively works hard and long hours.

412. Read the given sentence and select the most appropriate antonym of the word 'Deplete' from the following options. SSC CPO 09.11.2022 (Shift-I)

Depletion of old things has become a fancy business as it brings back old memories but at a high cost.

(a) Restore (b) Old
(c) High (d) Fancy

Ans. (a)

Deplete means use up the supply or resources of. Hence, its antonym is 'restore'.

413. Stupendous SSC CPO 09.11.2022 (Shift-II)

(a) Terrible (b) Smart
(c) Perfect (d) Jealous

Ans. (a)

Stupendous means extremely impressive. Hence, its antonym is 'terrible'.

414. Colloquial SSC CPO 09.11.2022 (Shift-II)

(a) Informal (b) Slack
(c) Slang (d) Formal

Ans. (d)

Colloquial means (of language) used in ordinary or familiar conversation; not formal or literary. Hence, its antonym is 'formal'.

Informal means having a relaxed, friendly, or unofficial style, manner, or nature.

Slack means not taut or held tightly in position; loose.

Slang means a type of language consisting of words and phrases that are regarded as very informal.

415. Wily SSC CPO 09.11.2022 (Shift-II)

(a) Horrid (b) Honest
(c) Raunchy (d) Triumphant

Ans. (b)

Wily means skilled at gaining an advantage, especially deceitfully. Hence, its antonym is 'honest'.

Horrid means causing horror.

Raunchy means earthy, vulgar and often sexually explicit.

416. My teacher asked me to compress the file. SSC CPO 10.11.2022 (Shift-I)

(a) Search (b) Trace (c) Enlarge (d) Turn

Ans. (c)

'Compress' means 'to make something smaller'. Hence, its antonym is 'Enlarge' which means 'to make something bigger'.

Trace means to form carefully.

417. Novel SSC CPO 10.11.2022 (Shift-I)

(a) Formal (b) Ancient
(c) Traditional (d) Customary

Ans. (c)

'Novel' means 'interestingly new and unusual'. Hence, its antonym is 'Traditional'.

418. Rife SSC CPO 10.11.2022 (Shift-I)

(a) Scarce (b) Ripe
(c) Popular (d) Serene

Ans. (a)

'Rife' means 'full of something'. Hence, its antonym is 'Scarce' which means 'not easy to find or get'.

419. Jason was sent to school in England, where he excelled academically and developed an interest in theatre and writing. SSC CPO 10.11.2022 (Shift-I)

(a) Accomplished (b) Pursued
(c) Continued (d) Failed

Ans. (d)

'Excelled' means to 'do something very well or much better than most people'.
Hence, its antonym is 'Failed'.

Accomplished means to achieve a goal.

Pursued means followed.

420. Fascinating SSC CPO 10.11.2022 (Shift-I)

(a) Unforgettable (b) Tempting
(c) Seductive (d) Repulsive

Ans. (d)

'Fascinating' means 'extremely interesting'. Hence, its antonym is 'Repulsive' which means causing a feeling of strong dislike'.

421. He leaves behind an indelible contribution to the financial world. SSC CPO 10.11.2022 (Shift-II)

(a) Temporary (b) Futile
(c) Durable (d) Solitary

Ans. (a)

Indelible means making marks that cannot be removed. Hence, its antonym is 'temporary'.

Futile means incapable of producing any useful result; pointless.

Durable means able to withstand wear, pressure, or damage; hard-wearing.

Solitary means done or existing alone.

422. Pensive SSC CPO 10.11.2022 (Shift-II)

(a) Frivolous
(b) Unreflective
(c) Hollow
(d) Goofy

Ans. (a)

Pensive means engaged in, involving, or reflecting deep or serious thought. Hence, its antonym is 'frivolous'.

Unreflective means not engaging in reflection or contemplation.

Hollow means having a hole or empty space inside.

Goofy means foolish or harmlessly eccentric.

423. Vociferous SSC CPO 10.11.2022 (Shift-III)

(a) Silent (b) Sullen
(c) Gallant (d) Pugnacious

Ans. (a)

Vociferous means vehement or clamorous. Hence, its antonym is 'silent'.

Sullen means bad-tempered and sulky; gloomy.

Gallant means brave; heroic.

Pugnacious means eager or quick to argue, quarrel or fight.

424. Reprieve SSC CPO 10.11.2022 (Shift-III)

(a) Turn out
(b) Torrential
(c) Cease
(d) Continuation

Ans. (d)

Reprieve means cancel or postpone the punishment of (someone, especially someone condemned to death).
Hence, its antonym is 'continuation'.

Turn out means happen or develop in a particular way.

Torrential means (of rain) falling rapidly and in copious quantities.

Cease means bring or come to an end.

425. Sordid SSC CPO 10.11.2022 (Shift-III)
(a) Honourable (b) Censurable
(c) Shameful (d) Excellent

Ans. (a)

Sordid means involving ignoble actions and motives; arousing moral distaste and contempt. Hence, its antonym is 'honourable'.
Censurable means deserving or open to censure.

426. Sukhen always seeks to capitalise on opportunities. SSC CPO 10.11.2022 (Shift-III)
(a) Dismantle (b) Destroy
(c) Forfeit (d) Seize

Ans. (c)

Capitalise means to take advantage of something; make the most of. Hence, its antonym is 'forfeit'.

Dismantle means take (a machine or structure) to pieces.
Destroy means end the existence of (something) by damaging or attacking it.
Seize means take hold of suddenly and forcibly.

427. Utilitarian SSC CPO 10.11.2022 (Shift-I)
(a) Evident (b) Necessary
(c) Spacious (d) Unnecessary

Ans. (d)

Utilitarian means intended to be useful and practical rather than attractive or comfortable'. Hence, its antonym is 'Unnecessary'.

Spacious means having a large area.

428. The owner underestimated the damage caused to the walls of the apartment. SSC CPO 11.11.2022 (Shift-I)
(a) Calculated (b) Charged
(c) Misled (d) Exaggerated

Ans. (d)

'Exaggerated' means 'to make something seem better, larger, worse, etc'., than it really is underestimated. Hence, its antonym is 'Underestimated'.

429. The lunch menu includes some TEMPTING vegetarian offerings. SSC CPO 11.11.2022 (Shift-I)
(a) Repelling (b) Seductive
(c) Enticing (d) Tantalising

Ans. (a)

'Tempting' means 'attractive and making people want to have it, do it, etc'.
Hence, its antonym is 'Repelling' which means decking.
Seductive, **Enticing** and **Tantalising** indicate attractive and tempting.

430. Uncanny SSC CPO 11.11.2022 (Shift-I)
(a) Queer (b) Unduly
(c) Saintly (d) Ordinary

Ans. (d)

'Uncanny' means 'very strange and difficult to explain'. Hence, its antonym is 'Ordinary'.
Queer means strange.
Unduly means excessively.

431. The favouritism of the boss led to many DISGRUNTLED employees. SSC CPO 11.11.2022 (Shift-I)
(a) Disturbed (b) Determined
(c) Pleased (d) Miserable

Ans. (c)

'Disgruntled' means 'annoyed or disappointed, especially because things have not happened in the way that you wanted. Hence, its antonym is 'Pleased'.

432. Sting operations use subterfuge to obtain material for stories. SSC CPO 11.11.2022 (Shift-I)
(a) Society (b) Policy
(c) Suspicion (d) Honesty

Ans. (d)

'Subterfuge' means 'a secret trick or slightly dishonest way of doing something'. Hence, its antonym is 'Honesty'.

433. The subordinates will vituperate us when they are irritated. SSC CPO 11.11.2022 (Shift-II)
(a) Blame (b) Abuse
(c) Praise (d) Demean

Ans. (c)

Vituperate means blame or insult (someone) in strong or violent language. Hence, its antonym is 'praise'.
Demean means cause a severe loss in the dignity of and respect for (someone or something).

434. The penitent husband spends days at the wife's grave. SSC CPO 11.11.2022 (Shift-II)
(a) Unrepentant (b) Sorry
(c) Penniless (d) Pertinent

Ans. (a)

Penitent means feeling or showing sorrow and regret for having done wrong; repentant. Hence, its antonym is 'unrepentant'.
Penniless means having no money; very poor.
Pertinent means relevant or applicable to a particular matter; apposite.

435. Barbaric SSC CPO 11.11.2022 (Shift-III)
(a) Indifferent (b) Brutal
(c) Inquisitive (d) Civilised

Ans. (d)

Barbaric means savagely cruel; exceedingly brutal. Hence, its antonym is 'civilised'.

Indifferent means having noparticular interest or sympathy; unconcerned.

Brutal means savagely violent.

SSC CHSL 2024 (Tier 1 & 2)

436. **Allies** have always come to his rescue in spite of his attempts to defame him. SSC CHSL Tier-2 18.11.2024
(a) fellows'
(b) scholars'
(c) buddies'
(d) enemies'

Ans. (d)

'Enemies' is the antonym of 'allies'. While allies are supportive friends or partners, enemies are opposing forces.

437. Glory SSC CHSL Tier-1 01.07.2024 (Shift-I)
(a) Shame
(b) Honour
(c) Delight
(d) Gluttony

Ans. (a)

'Glory' means high renown or honour won by notable achievements. Hence, its antonym is 'shame'.

Delight means joy.

Gluttony means habitual greed or excess in eating.

438. Would you please support me for once in your life? SSC CHSL Tier-1 01.07.2024 (Shift-I)
(a) establish (b) refute
(c) document (d) disclaim

Ans. (b)

The antonym of 'Support' is to 'refute' which means prove that (someone) is wrong.
Disclaim means to refuse to acknowledge; deny.

439. Trivial SSC CHSL Tier-1 01.07.2024 (Shift-I)
(a) Vain (b) Essential
(c) Liable (d) Lavish

Ans. (b)

Trivial means insignificant and small. Hence, its antonym is 'essential'.

Vain means useless.

Liable means responsible.

Lavish means wealthy.

440. How can you be so joyless on hearing the news? SSC CHSL Tier-1 01.07.2024 (Shift-I)
(a) beaming (b) rapt
(c) blissful (d) dubious

Ans. (c)

The antonym of 'joyless' is 'blissful' which means 'happiness'.

Beaming means smiling broadly; grinning.

Rapt means completely fascinated or absorbed by what one is seeing or hearing.

Dubious means hesitating or doubting.

441. Resistance

SSC CHSL Tier-1 01.07.2024 (Shift-II)

(a) Awareness (b) Tolerance
(c) Tenderness (d) Reliance

Ans. (b)

Resistance means the refusal to accept or comply with something. Hence, its antonym is 'tolerance' which means the ability or willingness to tolerate the existence of opinions or behaviour that one dislikes or disagrees with.

Tenderness means with love and affection.

Reliance means to depend on.

442. The rocky terrain made the hike difficult and strenuous.

SSC CHSL Tier-1 01.07.2024 (Shift-II)

(a) demanding (b) lively
(c) intense (d) easy

Ans. (d)

'Strenuous' means complex and difficult. Hence, its antonym is 'easy'. 'Intense' means of extreme force, degree or strength.

443. Ria is liked by everyone as she is very amicable.

SSC CHSL Tier-1 01.07.2024 (Shift-II)

(a) hateful (b) unfriendly
(c) stupid (d) dangerous

Ans. (b)

'Amicable' means warm and friendly. Hence, its antonym is 'unfriendly'.

444. The committee deposed him from his office.

SSC CHSL Tier-1 01.07.2024 (Shift-II)

(a) interacted (b) demolished
(c) promoted (d) segregated

Ans. (c)

Deposed means remove from office suddenly and forcefully. Hence, its antonym is 'promoted' which means raise (someone) to a higher position or rank.

Demolished means to be destroyed.

Segregated means separated.

445. Language interacts with all aspects of human life and society.

SSC CHSL Tier-1 01.07.2024 (Shift-II)

(a) co-operates (b) interrelates
(c) disconnects (d) intermingles

Ans. (c)

'Interacts' means to communicate. Hence, its antonym is 'disconnects'.

Co-operates means assist someone or comply with their requests.

Interrelates means relate or connect to one another.

Intermingles means mix or mingle together.

446. Beautiful

SSC CHSL Tier-1 01.07.2024 (Shift-II)

(a) Pungent (b) Stingy
(c) Slimy (d) Ugly

Ans. (d)

The antonym of 'beautiful' is 'ugly'.

Pungent means having a sharply strong taste or smell.

Stingy means mean; ungenerous.

Slimy means slippery.

447. Select antonym of the word 'defeat' from the given sentence.
The first Battle of Panipat was fought on 21st April, 1526 where Babur introduced canon warfare and was able to gain victory on Delhi and subjugated sultanate ruler Ibrahim Lodi.

SSC CHSL Tier-1 01.07.2024 (Shift-II)

(a) Gain (b) Subjugated
(c) Warfare (d) Victory

Ans. (d)

Defeat means loss. Hence, its antonym is 'victory' which means 'to win'.

Subjugated means to bring under domination or control, especially by conquest.

448. It is no exaggeration to say the Hussain Sagar Lake is an integral element of Hyderabad and Hyderabad's history.

SSC CHSL Tier-1 01.07.2024 (Shift-III)

(a) essential (b) total
(c) extra (d) inherent

Ans. (c)

Integral means central and important. Hence, its antonym is 'extra'.

Inherent means natural or existing in something as a permanent, essential or characteristic attribute.

449. His opponents viewed him as stubborn, dogmatic and inflexible.

SSC CHSL Tier-1 01.07.2024 (Shift-III)

(a) Dishonest (b) Biased
(c) Careless (d) Amenable

Ans. (d)

Dogmatic means characterised by or given to the expression of opinions very strongly or positively as if they were facts.

Hence, its antonym is 'amenable' which means open and responsive to suggestion; easily persuaded or controlled.

Biased means showing an unreasonable like or dislike for someone or something based on personal opinions.

450. Bold
A person can be friendly, timid, clever or fearless based on the context of the situation.

SSC CHSL Tier-1 01.07.2024 (Shift-III)

(a) friendly (b) clever
(c) timid (d) fearless

Ans. (c)

The antonym of 'bold' is 'timid' which means 'showing a lack of courage or confidence; easily frightened'.

451. Shame SSC CHSL Tier-1 01.07.2024 (Shift-III)

(a) Disgrace
(b) Defamation
(c) Pride
(d) Fear

Ans. (c)

The antonym of 'shame' is 'pride'.

Disgrace means loss of reputation or respect as the result of a dishonourable action.

Defamation means the act of harming someone's reputation by saying or writing bad things about them.

452. A boisterous horse must have a rough bridle.

SSC CHSL Tier-1 01.07.2024 (Shift-IV)

(a) rowdy (b) loud
(c) bouncy (d) calm

Ans. (d)

Boisterous means noisy, energetic and cheerful. Hence, its antonym is 'calm'.

Rowdy means noisy and disorderly.

Bouncy means bouncing or causing things to bounce.

453. Stingy SSC CHSL Tier-1 01.07.2024 (Shift-IV)

(a) Generous (b) Humorous
(c) Lascivious (d) Deceitful

Ans. (a)

Stingy means not generous. Hence, its antonym is 'generous'.

Humorous means laughter worthy.

Lascivious means expressing a strong desire for sexual activity.

Deceitful means dishonest.

454. Prajakta is a very vain girl.

SSC CHSL Tier-1 01.07.2024 (Shift-IV)

(a) honourable (b) humble
(c) honest (d) hopeful

Ans. (b)

Vain means proud and arrogant. Hence, its antonym is 'humble' which means kind and polite.

455. Ralph's condition worsened in the hospital.
SSC CHSL Tier-1 01.07.2024 (Shift-IV)

(a) improved (b) scaled
(c) changed (d) traversed

Ans. (a)

The antonym of 'worsened' is 'improved'.

Scaled means covered with or made up of scales.

Traversed means travel across or through.

456. The organisation's furtive actions must be taken into notice and dealt with accordingly.
SSC CHSL Tier-1 01.07.2024 (Shift-IV)

(a) futuristic (b) truthful
(c) shady (d) foxy

Ans. (b)

'Furtive' means attempting to avoid notice or attention, typically because of guilt or a belief that discovery would lead to trouble; secretive. Hence, its antonym is 'truthful'.

Futuristic means relating to the future.

Shady means situated in or full of shade.

Foxy means resembling or likened to a fox.

457. My parents have a fertile land in the backyard. SSC CHSL Tier-1 02.07.2024 (Shift-I)

(a) barren (b) timid
(c) scanty (d) potent

Ans. (a)

The antonym of 'fertile' is 'barren' which means too poor to produce much or any vegetation.

Scanty means not enough.

Potent means having great power, influence or effect.

Timid means not courageous.

458. Enemy SSC CHSL Tier-1 02.07.2024 (Shift-I)

(a) Combatant (b) Colleague
(c) Friend (d) Attacker

Ans. (c)

The antonym of 'enemy' is 'friend'.

Combatant means a person or nation engaged in fighting during a war.

459. The equivocal tone of the Prime Minister in his speech caused uproar in the chamber.
SSC CHSL Tier-1 02.07.2024 (Shift-I)

(a) conflicting (b) iffy
(c) explicit (d) irresolute

Ans. (c)

Equivocal means open to more than one interpretation; ambiguous. Hence, its antonym is 'explicit' is fully revealed or expressed without vagueness, implication or ambiguity.

Conflicting means contradictory.

Iffy means full of uncertainty; doubtful.

Irresolute means showing or feeling hesitancy; uncertain.

460. He laboured very hard but could not yield anything from the barren piece of land.
SSC CHSL Tier-1 02.07.2024 (Shift-I)

(a) Fertile (b) Fruitless
(c) Vile (d) Sterile

Ans. (a)

The antonym of 'barren' meaning 'unproductive' its antonym is 'fertile'.

Vile means extremely unpleasant.

Sterile means not able to produce children or young.

461. The dearth of governmental policies on the basic rights and comforts of the impaired population leads to low standard of public life in a country.
SSC CHSL Tier-1 02.07.2024 (Shift-I)

(a) Brevity (b) Lacunae
(c) Abundance (d) Paucity

Ans. (c)

Dearth means lack of something. Hence, its antonym is 'Abundance' which means in large quantities.

Brevity means concise and exact use of words in writing or speech.

Lacunae means an unfilled space; a gap.

Paucity means lack

462. The firefighter summoned all her .... (cowardice) and rushed into the burning building.
SSC CHSL Tier-1 02.07.2024 (Shift-II)

(a) skills (b) erudition
(c) courage (d) expertise

Ans. (c)

The antonym of 'cowardice' is 'courage', which is the correct filler for the given blank.

463. She was known for her refined manners.
SSC CHSL Tier-1 02.07.2024 (Shift-III)

(a) crude (b) elegant
(c) shrewd (d) brood

Ans. (a)

'Refined' means made pure by removing unwanted material. Hence, its antonym is 'crude' which means simple and not skilfully done or made.

Elegant means beautiful and graceful.

Shrewd means evil.

Brood means a group.

464. The truth was revealed in the interrogation.
SSC CHSL Tier-1 02.07.2024 (Shift-III)

(a) evident
(b) found
(c) declared
(d) concealed

Ans. (d)

The antonym of 'revealed' is 'concealed', which means 'hidden'.

465. We should desecrate our national flag. SSC CHSL Tier-1 02.07.2024 (Shift-III)

(a) integrate (b) sanctify
(c) violate (d) damage

Ans. (b)

Desecrate means to treat (a sacred place or thing) with violent disrespect. Hence, its antonym is 'sanctify' which means the state or quality of being holy, sacred or saintly.

Integrate means 'to join'.

466. The upshot of the consultation with the doctor was an operation scheduled for the next week.
SSC CHSL Tier-1 02.07.2024 (Shift-IV)

(a) blame (b) cause
(c) result (d) estimate

Ans. (b)

Upshot means result. Hence, its antonym is 'cause'.

467. The plot of the novel is very dull.
SSC CHSL Tier-1 02.07.2024 (Shift-IV)

(a) diverting (b) riveting
(c) plodding (d) charming

Ans. (b)

The antonym of 'dull' is 'riveting' which means having the power to fix the attention.

Diverting means to shift attention to other things.

Plodding means to move slowly.

468. The State media houses present .... (vociferous) views compared to private media.
SSC CHSL Tier-1 02.07.2024 (Shift-IV)

(a) political (b) biased
(c) mild (d) assertive

Ans. (c)

Vociferous means expressing or characterised by strong opinions; loud and forceful. Hence, its antonym is 'mild'.

Biased means to show like or dislike towards something or someone due to personal opinion.

Assertive means confident and forceful.

469. Few people turned up to attend the tawdry promo of the new movie.
SSC CHSL Tier-1 02.07.2024 (Shift-IV)
(a) elegant (b) showy
(c) inferior (d) gawdy
Ans. (a)
Tawdry means showy but cheap and of poor quality. Hence, its antonym is 'elegant'.
Gawdy means showy.

470. Lenient SSC CHSL Tier-1 03.07.2024 (Shift-I)
(a) Strict (b) Rude
(c) Kind (d) Rowdy
Ans. (a)
Lenient means not harsh, severe or strict. Hence, its antonym is 'strict.
Rowdy means wild and uncontrolled.

471. Adverse SSC CHSL Tier-1 03.07.2024 (Shift-I)
(a) Listless (b) Striking
(c) Propitious (d) Critical
Ans. (c)
Adverse means unfavourable. Hence, its antonym is 'propitious' which means giving or indicating a good chance of success; favourable.
Listless means nervous and anxious.
Striking means gaining attention.
Critical means having negative views about something.

472. Anthony Trollope was an industrious and disciplined writer.
SSC CHSL Tier-1 03.07.2024 (Shift-II)
SSC CHSL Tier-1 07.07.2024 (Shift IV)
(a) exhausting (b) skittish
(c) dizzy (d) lazy
Ans. (d)
Industrious means hard working and dedicated. Hence, its antonym is 'lazy'.
Skittish means nervous or excitable; easily scared.
Dizzy means feeling faint, woozy, weak or unsteady.

473. Contaminate
She spent the entire night working non-stop to clean the blood stains from the rug.
SSC CHSL Tier-1 03.07.2024 (Shift-II)
(a) Rug (b) Spent
(c) Working (d) Clean
Ans. (d)
'Contaminate' means to make impure or dirty. Hence, its antonym is 'clean'.

474. Please don't touch that, it's flammable.
SSC CHSL Tier-1 03.07.2024 (Shift-II)
(a) non-combustible (b) non-explosive
(c) incendiary (d) fire-resistant
Ans. (a)
Flammable means easily set on fire. Hence, its antonym is 'non-combustible' which means not capable of igniting and burning.
Non-explosive means something that will not burst open.
Incendiary means designed to cause fires.

475. Fastidious
SSC CHSL Tier-1 03.07.2024 (Shift-II)
(a) Scrupulous (b) Lax
(c) Late (d) Speedy
Ans. (b)
Fastidious means very attentive to and concerned about accuracy and detail. Hence, its antonym is 'lax' which means not sufficiently strict, severe or careful.
Scrupulous means careful, thorough and extremely attentive to details.

476. Mr. Stein is a very cold and hard man. SSC CHSL Tier-1 03.07.2024 (Shift-III)
(a) clement (b) relaxed
(c) charitable (d) tolerant
Ans. (c)
The nearest antonym of 'hard' is 'charitable'.
Clement means inclined to be merciful.

477. My most vivid recollection of that summer is the ocean.
SSC CHSL Tier-1 03.07.2024 (Shift-III)
(a) vague (b) eloquent
(c) pictorial (d) lucid
Ans. (a)
Vivid means clear and descriptive. Hence, its antonym is 'vague' which means no clearly defined.
Eloquent means fluent or persuasive in speaking or writing.
Pictorial means of or expressed in pictures; illustrated.
Lucid means clear.

478. Sacred SSC CHSL Tier-1 03.07.2024 (Shift-III)
(a) Grave (b) Narrow
(c) Holy (d) Profane
Ans. (d)
Sacred means holy or related to God. Hence, its antonym is 'Profane' which means not relating to that which is sacred or religious; secular.

479. Alive SSC CHSL Tier-1 03.07.2024 (Shift-III)
(a) Wise (b) Animated
(c) Spry (d) Dead
Ans. (d)
The antonym of 'Alive' is 'Dead'.

480. You should never visit her without her consent.
SSC CHSL Tier-1 03.07.2024 (Shift-III)
(a) approval (b) permission
(c) knowledge (d) refusal
Ans. (d)
Consent means to agree to something. Hence, its antonym is 'Refusal'.

481. This makes readers contemplate the motives people have for performing acts of charity.
SSC CHSL Tier-1 03.07.2024 (Shift-IV)
(a) understate (b) follow up
(c) overlook (d) deviate
Ans. (c)
Contemplate means to think about something. Hence, its antonym is 'overlook'.

482. Cheerful
SSC CHSL Tier-1 03.07.2024 (Shift-IV)
(a) Sunny (b) Hilarious
(c) Gloomy (d) Joyful
Ans. (c)
The antonym of 'Cheerful' is 'gloomy'.

483. He tried to improve the working conditions in his office.
SSC CHSL Tier-1 03.07.2024 (Shift-IV)
(a) spatter (b) sprinkle
(c) specify (d) spoil
Ans. (d)
Here, 'improve' means to enhance the quality of something. Hence, 'spoil' (which means of make something bad) will be its antonym.

484. Important
SSC CHSL Tier-1 04.07.2024 (Shift-I)
(a) Recurring (b) Productive
(c) Trivial (d) Significant
Ans. (c)
The antonym of 'Important' is 'trivial' as it means insignificant.

485. Gentlemen always go for a lawful approach, but rouges choose .... ways to solve problems.
SSC CHSL Tier-1 04.07.2024 (Shift-I)
(a) legal (b) legitimate
(c) sophisticated (d) illicit
Ans. (d)
The antonym of 'lawful' is 'illicit' which means not legal.

486. Agile SSC CHSL Tier-1 04.07.2024 (Shift-II)
(a) Active (b) Apathetic
(c) Energetic (d) Sluggish

Ans. (d)

Agile means active and energetic. Hence, its antonym is 'sluggish' which means lazy and slow.

Apathetic means uncaring and indifferent.

487. There is also an increase in juvenile delinquency.
SSC CHSL Tier-1 04.07.2024 (Shift-II)
(a) Teenage (b) Adult
(c) Puerile (d) Minor

Ans. (b)

'Juvenile' means for or relating to young people. Hence, its antonym is 'adult'.

Puerile means childishly silly and immature.

488. Alluring SSC CHSL Tier-1 04.07.2024 (Shift-II)
(a) Enticing (b) Glamourous
(c) Repulsive (d) Fascinating

Ans. (c)

'Alluring' means attractive. Hence, its antonym is 'repulsive' which means to make someone dislike.

Enticing and **Glamourous** means attractive or appealing in an exotic or exciting way.

Fascinating means interesting.

489. Resourceful
SSC CHSL Tier-1 04.07.2024 (Shift-II)
(a) Incompetent (b) Ingenious
(c) Immaculate (d) Impeccable

Ans. (a)

The antonym of 'Resourceful' means 'Incompetent' which means not useful.

Ingenious means (of a person) clever, original and inventive.

Immaculate means clean and tidy.

Impeccable means flawless.

490. I have keen interest in reading the mind of those students who are boisterous at home but on their best behaviour at school.
SSC CHSL Tier-1 04.07.2024 (Shift-III)
(a) clamorous (b) frothing
(c) placid (d) raucous

Ans. (c)

'Boisterous' means noisy, energetic and cheerful. Hence, its antonym is 'placid' which means 'calm'.

Clamorous means making a loud and confused noise.

Frothing means bubbles formed in or on a liquid.

Raucous means making or constituting a disturbingly harsh and loud noise.

491. He purchased very cheap dresses.
SSC CHSL Tier-1 04.07.2024 (Shift-III)
(a) expensive (b) doltish
(c) lively (d) paltry

Ans. (a)

The antonym of 'cheap' is 'expensive'.

Doltish means (of a person) stupid; idiotic.

Paltry means very small or meagre.

492. The balloon started to deflate after being pricked with a needle. What is the antonym of 'deflate'?
SSC CHSL Tier-1 04.07.2024 (Shift-III)
(a) flatten (b) compress
(c) inflate (d) shrink

Ans. (c)

Deflate means let air or gas out of (a tyre, balloon, or similar object). Hence, its antonym is 'inflate' which means to swell with air or gas.

Flatten means to be made flat.

Compress and **Shrink** means to reduce in size.

493. Vehement
SSC CHSL Tier-1 04.07.2024 (Shift-IV)
(a) Reliable (b) Smashed
(c) Passionate (d) Mild

Ans. (d)

'Vehement' means showing strong feeling; forceful, passionate or intense. Hence, its antonym is 'mild'.

Reliable means dependable.

Smashed means broken.

Passionate means having, showing or caused by strong feelings or beliefs.

494. The growth of the cell wall is very rarely uniform.
SSC CHSL Tier-1 04.07.2024 (Shift-IV)
(a) paired (b) balanced
(c) fixed (d) variegated

Ans. (d)

'Uniform' means same for all. Hence, its antonym is 'Variegated' means various or different.

495. There is no transparency in the procedure followed by the company.
SSC CHSL Tier-1 04.07.2024 (Shift-IV)
(a) coherence (b) reliability
(c) clarity (d) opacity

Ans. (d)

'Transparency' means the quality of allowing light to pass through so that objects behind can be distinctly seen. Hence, its antonym is 'Opacity' which means the quality of being difficult to understand or know about, especially because things have been intentionally kept secret or made complicated.

Coherence means unity.

Reliability means dependable.

Clarity means the quality of being clear and easy to understand see or hear.

496. Noble SSC CHSL Tier-1 04.07.2024 (Shift-IV)
(a) Grand (b) Indescribable
(c) Common (d) Magical

Ans. (c)

'Noble' means someone with high or elevated character or who is impressive in appearance.
Hence, its antonym is 'common'.

497. The performance of the team in the lost match was dismal.
SSC CHSL Tier-1 04.07.2024 (Shift-IV)
(a) luminous (b) sadden
(c) cheap (d) dainty

Ans. (a)

'Dismal' means causing a mood of gloom or depression.
Hence, its antonym is 'luminous' which means well-lit.
Dainty means delicate.

498. Benevolent
SSC CHSL Tier-1 04.07.2024 (Shift-IV)
(a) Cruel (b) Happy
(c) Patient (d) Harmless

Ans. (a)

'Benevolent' means kind and noble.
Hence, its antonym is 'Cruel'.

499. He feels that wealthy people view him with contempt because he is poor. SSC CHSL Tier-1 05.07.2024 (Shift-I)
(a) derision (b) admiration
(c) scorn (d) obscurity

Ans. (b)

'Contempt' means dislike or hate.
Hence, its antonym is 'admiration'.
Derision means ridicule or mockery.

Scorn means a feeling and expression of contempt or disdain for someone or something.
Obscurity means the state of being unknown or unimportant.

500. Innocent SSC CHSL Tier-1 05.07.2024 (Shift-I)
(a) Guilty (b) Mischievous
(c) Unfair (d) Righteous

Ans. (a)

The antonym of 'innocent' is 'guilty'.

501. Cramped SSC CHSL Tier-1 05.07.2024 (Shift-I)
(a) Filthy (b) Spacious
(c) Tight (d) Crammed

Ans. (b)

'Cramped' means uncomfortably small or restricted. Hence, its antonym is 'spacious'.

Filthy means dirty.

Crammed means completely fill (a place or container) to the point of overflowing.

502. The news gave him inexpressible ecstasy. **SSC CHSL Tier-1 05.07.2024 (Shift-I)**

(a) delight (b) passion
(c) depression (d) disappointment

Ans. (c)

'Ecstasy' means happiness and joy. Hence, its antonym is 'depression'.

503. The vendor said that the apples were of superior quality. **SSC CHSL Tier-1 05.07.2024 (Shift-II)**

(a) Excellent (b) Distasteful
(c) Small (d) Inferior

Ans. (d)

The antonym of 'superior' is 'inferior'.

504. No one trusts her as her reasons are always explicit. **SSC CHSL Tier-1 05.07.2024 (Shift-II)**

(a) Precise (b) Ambiguous
(c) Exact (d) Distant

Ans. (b)

Explicit means clear and direct. Hence, its antonym is 'ambiguous' which means confusing.

Precise means exact.

505. Essays must be concise. **SSC CHSL Tier-1 05.07.2024 (Shift-II)**

(a) Excise (b) Lengthy
(c) Precise (d) Total

Ans. (b)

'Concise' means short and brief. Hence, its antonym is 'Lengthy'.

Excise means tax.

506. As a punishment for his betrayal to his country, the spy who sold secrets was sent to prison. **SSC CHSL Tier-1 05.07.2024 (Shift-III)**

(a) infidelity (b) loyalty
(c) perilous (d) nasty

Ans. (b)

'Betrayal' means an act of deliberate disloyalty. Hence, its antonym is 'loyalty'.

Infidelity means disloyalty.
Perilous means dangerous.

507. Skeptic **SSC CHSL Tier-1 05.07.2024 (Shift-III)**

(a) Believer (b) Atheist
(c) Careful (d) Infidel

Ans. (a)

'Skeptic' is a person inclined to question or doubt accepted opinions. Hence, its antonym is 'believer'.

Atheist means someone who does not believe in God.

Infidel means a person who has no religion or whose religion is not that of the majority.

508. Comical **SSC CHSL Tier-1 05.07.2024 (Shift-III)**

(a) Tragic (b) Remedial
(c) Farcical (d) Rebellious

Ans. (a)

'Comical' means 'Junny' or 'humorous'. Hence, its antonym is 'Tragic' which means 'serious' or 'sad'.

509. Her voice, soft and ...., (shrill) flowed effortlessly through the room. **SSC CHSL Tier-1 05.07.2024 (Shift-III)**

(a) mellow (b) nasal
(c) croaky (d) piercing

Ans. (a)

'Shrill' means (of a voice or sound) high-pitched and piercing. Hence, its antonym is 'mellow' which means (especially of a sound, flavour or colour) pleasantly smooth or soft; free from harshness.

The other options are

Nasal means relating to nose.

Croaky means (of a person's voice) deep and hoarse.

Piercing means having or showing shrewdness or keen intelligence.

510. Which of the following sentences contains the antonym of the word 'ignore'? **SSC CHSL Tier-1 05.07.2024 (Shift-III)**

(a) Avoid foods which make you sick.
(b) He did not succeed in gaining custody of his daughter.
(c) Ritika recognised Kavita in the gathering.
(d) To keep a tidy kitchen, do not neglect washing your dishes.

Ans. (c)

'Ignore' means refuse to take notice of or acknowledge; disregard intentionally. The antonym is 'recognised'. Its sentence with the antonym is- Ritika recognised Kavita in the gathering.

511. His jovial nature has won him many friends. **SSC CHSL Tier-1 05.07.2024 (Shift-IV)**

(a) Shrewd (b) Miserable
(c) Dumb (d) Cunning

Ans. (b)

'Jovial' means happy. Hence, its antonym is 'miserable' which means unhappy.

Shrewd means evil.

Cunning means clever.

512. Lazy **SSC CHSL Tier-1 05.07.2024 (Shift-IV)**

(a) Barren (b) Helpful
(c) Diligent (d) Genuine

Ans. (c)

The antonym of 'lazy' is 'diligent' which means hard-working.

513. Plausible
The trend of improvement is unlikely to continue for the foreseeable future. **SSC CHSL Tier-1 05.07.2024 (Shift-IV)**

(a) unlikely (b) trend
(c) foreseeable (d) future

Ans. (a)

'Plausible' means (of an argument or statement) seeming reasonable or probable. Hence, its antonym is 'unlikely'.

514. Absurd **SSC CHSL Tier-1 05.07.2024 (Shift-IV)**

(a) Reasonable (b) Foolish
(c) Nonsensical (d) Insane

Ans. (a)

'Absurd' means strange. Hence, its antonym is 'reasonable'.

515. Forbidden **SSC CHSL Tier-1 08.07.2024 (Shift-I)**

(a) Protected (b) Prevented
(c) Banned (d) Allowed

Ans. (d)

'Forbidden' means not allowed to do something. Hence, its antonym is 'allowed'.

516. He gave a haughty consent without honouring him with a single word. **SSC CHSL Tier-1 08.07.2024 (Shift-I)**

(a) proud (b) happy
(c) modest (d) indifferent

Ans. (c)

'Haughty' means arrogant. Hence, its antonym is 'modest' which means 'kind and polite'.

517. Generous **SSC CHSL Tier-1 08.07.2024 (Shift-I)**

(a) Needy (b) Mean
(c) Considerate (d) Clever

Ans. (b)

The antonym of 'generous' is 'mean'.

518. His grandfather was quite grumpy. **SSC CHSL Tier-1 08.07.2024 (Shift-II)**

(a) possible (b) tenable
(c) edible (d) amiable

Ans. (d)

'Grumpy' means irritated or angry. Hence, its antonym is 'Amiable' which means warm and friendly.

Tenable means capable of being held, maintained or defended.

Edible means something that can be eaten.

519. It's very cheap to display wealth by donning gaudy dresses.
SSC CHSL Tier-1 08.07.2024 (Shift-II)
(a) scanty (b) ornate
(c) cheap (d) sober
Ans. (d)
'Gaudy' means extravagantly bright or showy, typically so as to be tasteless. Hence, its antonym is 'Sober' which means graceful.
Scanty means in less quantity.
Ornate means decorated.

520. Morose SSC CHSL Tier-1 08.07.2024 (Shift-II)
(a) Jovial (b) Practical
(c) Dramatic (d) Hurried
Ans. (a)
'Morose' means sad and gloomy. Hence, its antonym is 'Jovial' which means happy.

521. Despondency
SSC CHSL Tier-1 08.07.2024 (Shift-II)
(a) Hopelessness (b) Satisfaction
(c) Cheerfulness (d) Dejection
Ans. (c)
'Despondency' means sad. Hence, its antonym is 'Cheerfulness'.

522. The humble pupil sat on the floor with respect.
SSC CHSL Tier-1 08.07.2024 (Shift-II)
(a) capitalist (b) corrupt
(c) sturdy (d) proud
Ans. (d)
'Humble' means polite. Hence, its antonym is 'proud'.
Capitalist means someone who uses their wealth to invest in trade and industry.
Corrupt means dishonest.
Sturdy means strong.

523. The CEO called for compulsory participation from each employee.
SSC CHSL Tier-1 08.07.2024 (Shift-III)
(a) voluntary (b) compliantly
(c) obligatory (d) overtly
Ans. (a)
'Compulsory' means necessary to do. Hence, its antonym is 'voluntary' which means willingly.
Compliantly means in a way that shows that you are willing to do what other people want you to do.
Obligatory means required by a legal, moral or other rule; compulsory.
Overtly means without concealment or secrecy; openly.

524. Logical SSC CHSL Tier-1 08.07.2024 (Shift-III)
(a) Subtle (b) Random
(c) Reasonable (d) Illogical
Ans. (d)
The antonym of 'Logical' is 'Illogical'.

525. Terminate
SSC CHSL Tier-1 08.07.2024 (Shift-IV)
(a) Mark (b) Die
(c) Conclude (d) Begin
Ans. (d)
'Terminate' means to end. Hence, its antonym is to 'Begin'.

526. Peace SSC CHSL Tier-1 08.07.2024 (Shift-IV)
(a) Harmony (b) Strange
(c) Turmoil (d) Refusal
Ans. (c)
The antonym of 'peace' is 'turmoil' which means chaos and confusion.

527. She was asked by the elders to wear a skirt covering her knees.
SSC CHSL Tier-1 09.07.2024 (Shift-I)
(a) exposing (b) expanding
(c) expecting (d) expounding
Ans. (a)
The antonym of 'covering' is 'exposing'.

528. The company has to be able to compete globally.
SSC CHSL Tier-1 09.07.2024 (Shift-I)
(a) support (b) attack
(c) pervert (d) impede
Ans. (a)
The antonym of 'compete' is 'support'.

529. The army advanced into enemy territory. SSC CHSL Tier-1 09.07.2024 (Shift-I)
(a) protruded (b) retreated
(c) arose (d) commuted
Ans. (b)
'Advanced' means to move forward. Hence, its antonym is 'retreated' means to go back.
Protruded means to stick out from or through something.
Commuted means to make the same journey regularly between work and home.

530. Which of the following sentences contains the antonym of the word 'important'?
SSC CHSL Tier-1 09.07.2024 (Shift-I)
(a) You always make me do all the trivial stuff.
(b) Choose the right colour to make your bike stand out!
(c) Namita also makes some very salient points in her newly revised preface.
(d) I have some urgent questions for you.
Ans. (a)
The antonym of 'important' is 'trivial' which means insignificant. Hence, the correct sentence is–You always make me do all the trivial stuff.

531. William Shakespeare is considered to be the most celebrated dramatist in the world of literature.
SSC CHSL Tier-1 09.07.2024 (Shift-I)
(a) laureate (b) acclaimed
(c) inglorious (d) illustrious
Ans. (c)
The antonym of 'celebrated' is 'inglorious' which means (of an action or situation) causing shame or a loss of honour.
Laureate means a person who is honoured with an award for outstanding creative or intellectual achievement.
Acclaimed means publicly praised; celebrated.
Illustrious means well-known, respected and admired for past achievements.

532. Abundance
SSC CHSL Tier-1 09.07.2024 (Shift-I)
(a) Fortune (b) Excitement
(c) Scarcity (d) Prosperity
Ans. (c)
'Abundance' means in large quantity. Hence, its antonym is 'scarcity' means 'in less quantity'.

533. Lewis was aggressive, ... (normal), moody and brilliantly clever. SSC CHSL Tier-1 09.07.2024 (Shift-II)
(a) feeble (b) eccentric
(c) dogmatic (d) selfish
Ans. (b)
The antonym of 'normal' is 'eccentric' which means strange.
Feeble means weak.

534. The dog was agitated and bit the child. SSC CHSL Tier-1 09.07.2024 (Shift-II)
(a) steady (b) nerveless
(c) quiescent (d) serene
Ans. (d)
'Agitated' means angry and irritated. Hence, its antonym is 'serene' which means peaceful.
Steady means firmly fixed, supported or balanced; not shaking or moving.
Nerveless means lacking vigour or feeling.
Quiescent means in a state or period of inactivity or dormancy.

535. The encounter made the audience squirm. SSC CHSL Tier-1 09.07.2024 (Shift-III)
(a) speak (b) relax
(c) chat (d) pray

Ans. (b)

'Squirm' means to be nervous. Hence, its antonym is 'relax'.

536. The coach was <u>optimistic</u> that Ronald will play the quarter final.
SSC CHSL Tier-1 09.07.2024 (Shift-III)

(a) tasteful (b) cheerful
(c) doubtful (d) helpful

Ans. (c)

The word 'optimistic' means positive and sure about something. Hence, its antonym is 'doubtful'.

537. The poet was lost in a <u>reverie</u>.
SSC CHSL Tier-1 09.07.2024 (Shift-III)

(a) reality (b) fantasy
(c) daydream (d) trance

Ans. (a)

The underlined word 'reverie' means a state of being pleasantly lost in one's thoughts; a daydream. Hence, its antonym is 'reality'.

538. Harry's behaviour was very <u>blunt</u> during his school days.
SSC CHSL Tier-1 09.07.2024 (Shift-IV)

(a) excited (b) polite
(c) dull (d) curious

Ans. (b)

'Blunt' means rude. Hence, its antonym is 'polite'.

539. Sluggish SSC CHSL Tier-1 10.07.2024 (Shift-I)

(a) Hassled (b) Lethargic
(c) Leisurely (d) Rapid

Ans. (d)

'Sluggish' means slow and lazy. Hence, its antonym is 'Rapid' which means fast.
Hassled means irritating inconvenience.
Lethargic means lazy.
Leisurely means in a slow manner.

540. Timid SSC CHSL Tier-1 10.07.2024 (Shift-I)

(a) Resolute (b) Blunt
(c) Audacious (d) Assertive

Ans. (c)

'Timid' means fearful. Hence, its antonym is 'Audacious' which means bold and brave.
Resolute means determined.
Blunt means rude.
Assertive means having or showing a confident and forceful personality.

541. Enormous
SSC CHSL Tier-1 10.07.2024 (Shift-I)

(a) Minute (b) Strong
(c) Monstrous (d) Tremendous

Ans. (a)

The word 'enormous' means huge. Hence, its antonym is 'minute' which means too small.

542. Powerful
SSC CHSL Tier-1 10.07.2024 (Shift-II)

(a) Strong (b) Impotent
(c) Manly (d) Wild

Ans. (b)

The antonym of 'powerful' is 'impotent' which means lacking power or strength.

543. The government is planning to <u>abolish</u> child care leave for female employees.
SSC CHSL Tier-1 10.07.2024 (Shift-II)

(a) Ensure (b) Eradicate
(c) Encourage (d) Establish

Ans. (d)

'Abolish' means to end a rule or law. Hence, its antonym is 'establish'.

544. Because the politician made a <u>candid</u> speech, he earned the respect of the voters.
SSC CHSL Tier-1 10.07.2024 (Shift-II)

(a) reticent (b) prudent
(c) deceitful (d) reckless

Ans. (c)

The word 'candid' means truthful and honest. Hence, its antonym is 'deceitful'.
Reticent means not revealing one's thoughts or feelings readily.
Prudent means innocent.
Reckless means careless.

545. Innovate
SSC CHSL Tier-1 10.07.2024 (Shift-II)

(a) Solve (b) Finance
(c) Invent (d) Copy

Ans. (d)

'Innovate' means to create something new. Hence, its antonym is to 'Copy'.

546. Stoic SSC CHSL Tier-1 10.07.2024 (Shift-III)

(a) Tolerant (b) Apathetic
(c) Fervent (d) Cooperative

Ans. (c)

'Stoic' means a person who can endure pain or hardship without showing their feelings or complaining. Hence, the antonym is 'Fervent' which means having or displaying a passionate intensity.
Apathetic means uncaring.

547. The stone was also said to have <u>occult</u> powers. SSC CHSL Tier-1 10.07.2024 (Shift-III)

(a) latent (b) intelligible
(c) ambiguous (d) unfathomable

Ans. (b)

'Occult' means mystical, supernatural or magical powers, practices or phenomena. Hence, its nearest antonym is 'intelligible'.
Latent means existing but not yet developed or manifest; hidden or concealed.
Unfathomable means unimaginable.

548. His father warned him not to use <u>vulgar</u> language at home.
SSC CHSL Tier-1 10.07.2024 (Shift-III)

(a) decorous (b) ribald
(c) impervious (d) licentious

Ans. (a)

'Vulgar' means lacking sophistication or good taste. Hence, its antonym is 'decorous' which means in keeping with good taste and propriety; polite and restrained.
Ribald means referring to sexual matters in an amusingly coarse or irreverent way.
Impervious means not allowing fluid to pass through.
Licentious means that they are very immoral in their behaviour.

549. Calm SSC CHSL Tier-1 10.07.2024 (Shift-III)

(a) Urban (b) Impressed
(c) Quiet (d) Upset

Ans. (d)

The antonym of 'Calm' is 'Upset'.

550. You can't stop the .... (outflow) of current.
SSC CHSL Tier-1 10.07.2024 (Shift-IV)

(a) deluge (b) influx
(c) torrent (d) income

Ans. (b)

'Outflow' means going outside. Hence, its antonym is 'influx' which means 'to come in'.
Deluge means a severe flood.
Torrent means a strong and fast-moving stream of water or other liquid.

551. Massive
SSC CHSL Tier-1 10.07.2024 (Shift-IV)

(a) Tiny (b) Tall
(c) Formidable (d) Heavy

Ans. (a)

Massive means 'huge'. Hence, its antonym is 'Tiny'.

552. His <u>feeble</u> opponent was no match to him and ultimately he won the challenge.
SSC CHSL Tier-1 10.07.2024 (Shift-IV)

(a) Strong (b) Mystic
(c) Major (d) Intelligent

Ans. (a)

'Feeble' means weak. Hence, its antonym is 'strong'.

553. Impulsive
SSC CHSL Tier-1 10.07.2024 (Shift-IV)

(a) Passive (b) Aggressive
(c) Hasty (d) Cautious

Ans. (d)

'Impulsive' means acting or done without forethought. Hence, the antonym is 'Cautious'.

Aggressive means angry.

Hasty means quick.

554. Commence
Let's put an end to this discussion about voodoo and instead talk about something amusing.
SSC CHSL Tier-1 10.07.2024 (Shift-IV)

(a) end (b) voodoo
(c) amusing (d) discussion

Ans. (a)

'Commence' means to begin. Hence, its antonym is to 'End'.

555. Abandon SSC CHSL Tier-1 11.07.2024 (Shift-I)

(a) Adopt (b) Randomise
(c) Destroy (d) Surrender

Ans. (a)

'Abandon' means to cease to support or look after (someone); desert. Hence, its antonym is to 'Adopt'.

Randomise means make (a set of items, people, etc.) unpredictable, unsystematic or random in order or arrangement.

556. He worked alone as he did not want anyone to <u>hamper</u> his project.
SSC CHSL Tier-1 11.07.2024 (Shift-I)

(b) care (b) help
(c) impede (d) finish

Ans. (b)

'Hamper' means to obstruct and impede. Hence, its antonym is 'Help'.

557. He is not <u>friendly</u> with him in the office. SSC CHSL Tier-1 11.07.2024 (Shift-I)

(a) revel (b) hostile
(c) gregarious (d) intelligent

Ans. (b)

The antonym of 'friendly' is 'hostile' which means 'not friendly'.

Revel means enjoy oneself in a lively and noisy way, especially with drinking and dancing.

Gregarious means (of a person) fond of company; sociable.

558. Precarious
SSC CHSL Tier-1 11.07.2024 (Shift-II)

(a) Luminous (b) Reliable
(c) Colossal (d) Doubtful

Ans. (b)

'Precarious' means not securely held or in position; dangerously likely to fall or collapse. Hence, its antonym is 'Reliable' which means dependable.

Luminous means giving off light; bright or shining.

Colossal means huge.

559. The vendor said that the apples were of <u>superior</u> quality.
SSC CHSL Tier-1 11.07.2024 (Shift-II)

(a) excellent (b) inferior
(c) small (d) distasteful

Ans. (b)

The antonym of 'superior' is 'inferior'.

560. Queer SSC CHSL Tier-1 11.07.2024 (Shift-III)

(a) Doubtful (b) Fantastic
(c) Eccentric (d) Ordinary

Ans. (d)

'Queer' means strange. Hence, its antonym is 'Ordinary'.

561. Contaminated
Crews were requested to purify the system since a brain-eating amoeba was discovered in the drinking water. SSC CHSL Tier-1 11.07.2024 (Shift-III)

(a) requested (b) discovered
(c) purify (d) system

Ans. (c)

'Contaminated' means to make dirty and unclean. Hence, its antonym is 'purify'.

562. I left the job because of a <u>hostile</u> working environment.
SSC CHSL Tier-1 11.07.2024 (Shift-III)

(a) morose (b) friendly
(c) rustic (d) violent

Ans. (b)

The underlined word 'hostile' means 'aggressive'. Hence, its antonym is 'friendy'.

563. The waters of Germany are <u>abundant</u> in fish, but there are few genera and species in them.
SSC CHSL Tier-1 11.07.2024 (Shift-IV)

(a) deficient (b) flourish
(c) allay (d) discord

Ans. (a)

'Abundant' means in large quantity. Hence, its antonym is 'deficient' which means in less quantity.

Flourish means to grow.

Discord means disagreement between people.

564. Ghastly SSC CHSL Tier-1 11.07.2024 (Shift-IV)

(a) Agitated (b) Bitter
(c) Relaxing (d) Pleasant

Ans. (d)

'Ghastly' means 'unpleasant' or 'bad'. Hence, 'pleasant' is its antonym.

565. Compulsory
SSC CHSL Tier-1 11.07.2024 (Shift-IV)

(a) Optional (b) Reliable
(c) Factional (d) Full-fledged

Ans. (a)

The antonym of 'compulsory' is 'optional'.

566. The athlete looked <u>unsettled</u> before the race.
SSC CHSL Tier-1 11.07.2024 (Shift-IV)

(a) confident (b) reticent
(c) triumphant (d) tangent

Ans. (a)

'Unsettled' means nervous and anxious. Hence, its antonym is 'confident'.

Reticent means not revealing one's thoughts or feelings readily.

Tangent means the straight line that just touches the curve at that point.

567. I have left it to his <u>discretion</u> to accept or decline my offer.
SSC CHSL Tier-1 11.07.2024 (Shift-IV)

(a) wisdom (b) calculation
(c) inattention (d) judgement

Ans. (c)

'Discretion' means saying something or taking decision precisely or attentively. Hence, 'inattention' is its nearest antonym.

SSC CHSL 2023 (Tier 1 & 2)

568. Frustrate SSC CHSL Tier-1 09.03.2023 (Shift-I)

(a) Foster (b) Fetter
(c) Circumvent (d) Irk

Ans. (a)

'Frustrate' means to make someone feel annoyed and impatient by presenting them from doing or getting something. 'Foster' meaning to help someone to develop over a period of time is its antonym.

Fetter means to chain.

Circumvent means to find a way around something.

Irk means to irritate.

569. Accessory
SSC CHSL Tier-1 09.03.2023 (Shift-II)

(a) Substitute (b) Surplus
(c) Essential (d) Option

Ans. (c)

Accessory means a thing which can be added to something else in order to make it more useful, versatile, or attractive. Hence, its antonym is 'essential'.

Surplus means an amount of something left over when requirements have been met; an excess of production or supply over demand.

570. Despondent
SSC CHSL Tier-1 09.03.2023 (Shift-III)
(a) Precise (b) Despaired
(c) Reproach (d) Hopeful

Ans. (d)

Despondent means in low spirits from loss of hope or courage. Hence, its antonym is 'hopeful'.

Precise means marked by exactness and accuracy of expression or detail.

Despaired means having lost all hope.

Reproach means address (someone) in such a way as to express disapproval or disappointment.

571. Knack SSC CHSL Tier-1 09.03.2023 (Shift-IV)
(a) Vile (b) Process
(c) Lesson (d) Inability

Ans. (d)

Knack means an acquired or natural skill at performing a task. Hence, its antonym is 'inability'.

Vile means extremely unpleasant.

572. Anomalous
SSC CHSL Tier-1 09.03.2023 (Shift-IV)
(a) Endemic (b) Outlandish
(c) Customary (d) Alien

Ans. (c)

Anomalous means deviating from what is standard, normal or expected. Hence, its antonym is 'customary'.

Endemic means (of a disease or condition) regularly found among particular people or in a certain area.

Outlandish means looking or sounding bizarre or unfamiliar.

Alien means belonging to a foreign country or nation.

573. Objurgation
SSC CHSL Tier-1 10.03.2023 Shift-I
(a) Hamper (b) Endorsement
(c) Reproof (d) Communication

Ans. (b)

Objurgation means a harsh reprimand or criticism. Hence, its antonym is 'endorsement'.

Hamper means hinder or impede the movement or progress of.

Reproof means an expression of blame or disapproval.

574. Fiend SSC CHSL Tier-1 10.03.2023 (Shift-II)
(a) Atrocious (b) Saint
(c) Junkie (d) Vile

Ans. (b)

Fiend means an evil spirit or demon. Hence, its antonym is 'saint'.

Atrocious means horrifyingly wicked.

Junkie means a person with a compulsive habit or dependency on a drug.

Vile means extremely unpleasant.

575. Inept SSC CHSL Tier-1 10.03.2023 (Shift-III)
(a) Wanting (b) Competent
(c) Barred (d) Callow

Ans. (b)

Inept means having or showing no skill; clumsy. Hence, its antonym is 'competent'.

Wanting means lacking in a certain required or necessary quality.

Barred means prevent or prohibit (someone) from doing something or going somewhere.

Callow means (of a young person) inexperienced and immature.

576. Wane SSC CHSL Tier-1 10.03.2023 (Shift-IV)
(a) Intensify (b) Evanesce
(c) Diminish (d) Contract

Ans. (a)

Wane means (especially of a condition or feeling) decrease in vigour, power, or extent; become weaker. Hence, its antonym is 'intensify'.

Evanesce means pass out of sight, memory, or existence.

Diminish means make or become less.

Contract means decrease in size, number or range.

577. Delinquency
SSC CHSL Tier-1 10.03.2023 (Shift-IV)
(a) Neglect (b) Fulfilment
(c) Tardiness (d) Default

Ans. (b)

Delinquency means minor crime, especially that committed by young people. Hence, its antonym is 'fulfilment'.

Neglect means fail to care for properly.

Tardiness means the quality or fact of being late; lateness.

Default means failure to fulfill an obligation, especially to repay a loan or appear in a court of law.

578. Relentless
SSC CHSL Tier-1 10.03.2023 (Shift-IV)
(a) Constant (b) Persistent
(c) Intermittent (d) Unabating

Ans. (c)

Relentless means oppressively constant; incessant. Hence, its antonym is 'intermittent'.

Constant means occurring continuously over a period of time.

Persistent means continuing firmly or obstinately in a course of action in spite of difficulty or opposition.

Unabating means without any reduction in intensity or strength.

579. Incredible
SSC CHSL Tier-1 13.03.2023 (Shift-I)
(a) Strained (b) Far-fetched
(c) Implausible (d) Believable

Ans. (d)

Incredible means difficult to believe; extraordinary. Hence, its antonym is 'believable'.

Strained means showing signs of tiredness or nervous tension.

Far-fetched means unlikely and unconvincing; implausible.

Implausible means (of an argument or statement) not seeming reasonable or probable; failing to convince.

580. Vain SSC CHSL Tier-1 13.03.2023 (Shift-I)
(a) Productive (b) Harmony
(c) Unpredictable (d) Calculable

Ans. (a)

Vain means producing no result; useless. Hence, its antonym is 'productive'.

Harmony means the combination of simultaneously sounded musical notes to produce chords and chord progressions having a pleasing effect.

Unpredictable means not able to be predicted.

Calculable means able to be measured or assessed.

581. Forthright
SSC CHSL Tier-1 13.03.2023 (Shift-I)
(a) Artless (b) Uninhibited
(c) Uncandid (d) Blunt

Ans. (c)

Forthright means (of a person or their manner or speech) direct and outspoken; straightforward and honest. Hence, its antonym is 'uncandid'.

Artless means without guile or deception.

Uninhibited means expressing one's feelings or thoughts unselfconsciously and without restraint.

Blunt means (of a knife, pencil, etc.) having a worn-down edge or point; not sharp.

582. Obfuscate
SSC CHSL Tier-1 13.03.2023 (Shift-III)
(a) Mend (b) Clarify
(c) Bid (d) Languish

Ans. (b)

'Obfuscate' means to make obscure, unclear or unintelligible. Hence, 'Clarify' is its antonym.

Mend means to fix.
Bid means to offer.
Languish means to weaken.

583. Opaque SSC CHSL Tier-1 13.03.2023 (Shift-III)
(a) Dark (b) Pellucid
(c) Glorify (d) Paragon

Ans. (b)

'Opaque' refers to something that cannot be seen through. A 'Pellucid' meaning translucent.
Glorify means to honour.
Paragon means a perfect example.

584. Brittle SSC CHSL Tier-1 13.03.2023 (Shift-III)
(a) Frail (b) Debilitated
(c) Robust (d) Decrepit

Ans. (c)

'Brittle' means weak or fragile. A 'Robust' meaning strong is its antonym.
Frail means weak and old.
Debilitated means weak.
Decrepit means worn down due to use or age.

585. Famish SSC CHSL Tier-1 14.03.2023 (Shift-I)
(a) Starve (b) Refrain
(c) Abstain (d) Eat

Ans. (d)

'Famish' means to suffer from extreme hunger. Hence, 'Eat' is its antonym.
Starve means to not eat.
Refrain means to stop from doing something.
Abstain means refrain.

586. Reprove
SSC CHSL Tier-1 14.03.2023 (Shift-III)
(a) Rap (b) Eulogise
(c) Pummel (d) Keelhaul

Ans. (b)

Reprove means reprimand or censure (someone). Hence, its antonym is 'eulogise'.
Rap means strike (a hard surface) with a series of rapid audible blows, especially in order to attract attention.
Pummel means strike repeatedly with the fists.
Keelhaul means punish (someone) severely.

587. Sinister SSC CHSL Tier-1 14.03.2023 (Shift-III)
(a) Propitious (b) Ominous
(c) Baleful (d) Foreboding

Ans. (a)

Sinister means giving the impression that something harmful or evil is happening or will happen. Hence, its antonym is 'propitious'.
Ominous means giving the impression that something bad or unpleasant is going to happen; threatening; inauspicious.
Baleful means threatening harm; menacing.
Foreboding means fearful apprehension; a feeling that something bad will happen.

588. Timorous
SSC CHSL Tier-1 15.03.2023 (Shift-I)
(a) Brazen (b) Scared
(c) Gutless (d) Reserved

Ans. (a)

Timorous means showing or suffering from nervousness, fear, or a lack of confidence. Hence, its antonym is 'brazen'.
Scared means fearful; frightened.
Gutless means lacking courage or determination.
Reserved means slow to reveal emotion or opinions.

589. Cupidity
SSC CHSL Tier-1 15.03.2023 (Shift-III)
(a) Largesse (b) Hatred
(c) Greed (d) Avarice

Ans. (a)

Cupidity means greed for money or possessions. Hence, its antonym is 'largesse'.
Avarice means extreme greed for wealth or material gain.

590. Contempt
SSC CHSL Tier-1 15.03.2023 (Shift-III)
(a) Approbation (b) Opprobrium
(c) Odium (d) Obloquy

Ans. (a)

Contempt means the feeling that a person or a thing is worthless or beneath consideration. Hence, its antonym is 'approbation'.
Opprobrium means harsh criticism or censure.
Odium means general or widespread hatred or disgust incurred by someone as a result of their actions.
Obloquy means strong public criticism or verbal abuse.

591. Sorcery SSC CHSL Tier-1 15.03.2023 (Shift-III)
(a) Spell (b) Reality
(c) Devilry (d) Dismiss

Ans. (b)

Sorcery means the use of magic, especially black magic. Hence, its antonym is 'reality'.
Spell means a form of words used as a magical charm or incantation.
Devilry means wicked activity.
Dismiss means order or allow to leave; send away.

592. Credible
SSC CHSL Tier-1 15.03.2023 (Shift-IV)
(a) Unlikely (b) Sheltered
(c) Unswerving (d) Conclusive

Ans. (a)

Credible means able to be believed or trusted. Hence, its antonym is 'Unlikely'.
Sheltered means protected.
Unswerving means not changing.

593. Bulwark SSC CHSL Tier-1 16.03.2023 (Shift-I)
(a) Fortification (b) Rampart
(c) Bastion (d) Assault

Ans. (d)

Bulwark means to drive danger or attack away from. 'Assault' meaning to attack someone violently is its antonym.
Fortification means the process of strengthening.
Rampart means a protective wall.
Bastion means wall.

594. Frighten SSC CHSL Tier-1 16.03.2023 (Shift-I)
(a) Startle (b) Reassure
(c) Petrify (d) Alarm

Ans. (b)

Frighten means make someone afraid or anxious. Hence, its antonym is 'Reassure' meaning to say or do something to remove the doubts or fears of someone.
Startle means to surprise.
Petrify means to frighten.
Alarm means to be aware of danger.

595. Amalgamate
SSC CHSL Tier-1 16.03.2023 (Shift-III)
(a) Integrate (b) Combine
(c) Dismantle (d) Coalesce

Ans. (c)

Amalgamate means combine or unite to form one organisation or structure. Hence, its antonym is 'dismantle'.
Integrate means combine (one thing) with another so that they become a whole.
Coalesce means come together to form one mass or whole.

596. Temerity SSC CHSL Tier-1 17.03.2023 (Shift-I)
(a) Diffidence (b) Audacity
(c) Assurance (d) Poison

Ans. (a)

Temerity means excessive confidence or boldness; audacity. Hence, its antonym is 'diffidence'.
Audacity means a willingness to take bold risks.
Assurance means confidence or certainty in one's own abilities.

597. Ideal SSC CHSL Tier-1 17.03.2023 (Shift-II)
(a) Optimal (b) Fitting
(c) Excellent (d) Flawed

Ans. (d)

Ideal means perfect or the best possible. Hence, its antonym is 'Flawed'.

Optimal means best.

Filling means perfect.

598. Antsy SSC CHSL Tier-1 17.03.2023 (Shift-II)
(a) Collected (b) Pure
(c) Perturbed (d) Adulation

Ans. (a)

Antsy means nervous and unable to keep still because you are waiting for something to happen.
Hence, its antonym is 'Collected' which means calm.

Perturbed means anxious

Adulation means praise.

599. Abstinence SSC CHSL Tier-1 17.03.2023 (Shift-II)
(a) Continence (b) Control
(c) Gluttony (d) Celibacy

Ans. (c)

'Abstinence' means the practice of not having something you enjoy, especially alcohol or sex, usually for reasons of religion or health.
'Gluttony' meaning the bad habit of eating or drinking too much is its antonym.

Continence means ability to control movements.

Celibacy means self-denial.

600. Inchoate SSC CHSL Tier-1 17.03.2023 (Shift-III)
(a) Artless (b) Refined
(c) Articulate (d) Formless

Ans. (b)

Inchoate means just begun and so not fully formed or developed; rudimentary. Hence, its antonym is 'refined'.

Articulate means having or showing the ability to speak fluently and coherently.

Formless means without a clear or definite shape or structure.

601. Babble SSC CHSL Tier-1 17.03.2023 (Shift-III)
(a) Drivel (b) Sense
(c) Jargon (d) Gibberish

Ans. (b)

Babble means talk rapidly and continuously in a foolish, excited, or incomprehensible way. Hence, its antonym is 'sense'.

Drivel means silly nonsense.

Jargon means special words or expressions used by a profession or group that are difficult for others to understand.

Gibberish means unintelligible or meaningless speech or writing.

602. Ignominy SSC CHSL Tier-1 17.03.2023 (Shift-IV)
(a) Esteem (b) Disrepute
(c) Stigma (d) Infamy

Ans. (a)

Ignominy means public shame or disgrace. Hence, its antonym is 'esteem'.

Disrepute means the state of being held in low esteem by the public.

Stigma means a mark of disgrace associated with a particular circumstance, quality, or person.

Infamy means the state of being well known for some bad quality or deed.

603. Vivacity SSC CHSL Tier-1 17.03.2023 (Shift-IV)
(a) Sap (b) Vim
(c) Lush (d) Apathy

Ans. (d)

Vivacity means the quality of being attractively lively and animated. Hence, its antonym is 'apathy'.

Sap means gradually weaken or destroy.

Vim means energy; enthusiasm.

Lush means (of vegetation) growing luxuriantly.

604. Legit SSC CHSL Tier-1 20.03.2023 (Shift-II)
(a) Bona fide (b) Endorsed
(c) Illegal (d) Canonical

Ans. (c)

Legit means conforming to the rules; legal. Hence, its antonym is 'illegal'.

Bona fide means genuine; real.

Endorsed means declare one's public approval or support of.

Canonical means according to or ordered by canon law.

605. Chastise SSC CHSL Tier-1 20.03.2023 (Shift-II)
(a) Mulct (b) Keelhaul
(c) Berate (d) Extol

Ans. (d)

Chastise means rebuke or reprimand severely. Hence, its antonym is 'extol'.

Mulct means extract money from (someone) by fine or taxation.

Keelhaul means punish severely.

Berate means scold or criticise (someone) angrily.

606. Coarse SSC CHSL Tier-1 20.03.2023 (Shift-III)
(a) Unrefined (b) Buttery
(c) Gruntted (d) Devoted

Ans. (b)

Coarse means having a rough surface that feels slightly hard.

Buttery meaning smooth is its antonym.

Unrefined means not purified.

Gruntted means a low and short guttural sound.

Devoted means dedicated.

607. Desiccate SSC CHSL Tier-1 21.03.2023 (Shift-I)
(a) Honour (b) Ascend
(c) Hydrate (d) Venerate

Ans. (c)

Desiccate means remove the moisture from (something); cause to become completely dry. Hence, its antonym is 'hydrate'.

Honour means regard with great respect.

Ascend means go up or climb.

Venerate means regard with great respect; revere.

608. Sane SSC CHSL Tier-1 21.03.2023 (Shift-I)
(a) Paranoid (b) Reposeful
(c) Stoical (d) Halcyon

Ans. (a)

Sane means of sound mind; not mad or mentally ill. Hence, its antonym is 'paranoid'.

Reposeful means having a calm and restful quality.

Stoical means enduring pain and hardship without showing one's feelings or complaining.

Halcyon means denoting a period of time in the past that was idyllically happy and peaceful.

609. Fanatic SSC CHSL Tier-1 21.03.2023 (Shift-II)
(a) Militant (b) Moderate
(c) Sectarian (d) Zealot

Ans. (b)

Fanatic means someone who has very strong religious or political beliefs that often make them behave in an unreasonable way. Hence, its antonym is 'Moderate'.

Militant means violent or related to military.

Sectarian means a member of sect.

Zealot means fanatic.

610. Algid SSC CHSL Tier-1 21.03.2023 (Shift-II)
(a) Igneous (b) Clean
(c) Algae (d) Gelid

Ans. (a)

Algid means chilly or cold.

Igneous meaning of or relating to fire ; fiery is its antonym.

Algae is another organism.

Gelid means icy cold.

611. Recondite
SSC CHSL Tier-1 21.03.2023 (Shift-II)
(a) Phlegm (b) Clear
(c) Abstract (d) Abstruse
Ans. (b)
Recondite means hard to understand; complicated. Hence, 'clear' is its correct antonym.
Phlegm means mucus lining our lungs and airways.
Abstract means not realistic.
Abstruse means difficult to understand.

612. Fret SSC CHSL Tier-1 21.03.2023 (Shift-IV)
(a) Anguish (b) Pine
(c) Relax (d) Anxious
Ans. (c)
Fret means to worry about something, especially when there is no need. Hence, its antonym is 'Relax'.
Anguish means pain or suffering.

613. Meagre SSC CHSL Tier-1 02.08.2023 (Shift-I)
(a) Regional (b) Racial
(c) Stupid (d) Generous
Ans. (d)
Mearge means too small in amount. Hence, its antonym is 'Generous, as it means larger than usual.

614. Wealthier countries are obligated to fulfil a <u>commitment</u> made in the Paris Agreement to provide $100 billion a year in International Climate Finance.
SSC CHSL Tier-1 02.08.2023 (Shift-I)
(a) Feeble (b) Drape
(c) Breach (d) Hale
Ans. (c)
Commitment means a promise or agreement to do something or a responsibility.
Hence, its antonym is 'Breach' as it means an act that breaks an agreement, a law, etc.
Feeble means weak.
Drape means to arrange loosely around something.
Hale means strong and healthy.

615. Fundamental
SSC CHSL Tier-1 02.08.2023 (Shift-I)
(a) Impact (b) Neutral (c) Least (d) Link
Ans. (c)
Fundamental means more important than anything else. Hence, its antonym is 'Least'.

616. Select the most appropriate antonym for 'Scarcity' in the given sentence SSC CHSL Tier-1 02.08.2023 (Shift-II)
In spite of having ice glaciers across the globe, people don't have excess of fresh drinking water.
(a) Excess (b) Water
(c) Glaciers (d) Fresh
Ans. (a)
Scarcity means the state of being scarce or in short supply; shortage. Hence, its antonym is 'excess'.

617. Penury SSC CHSL Tier-1 02.08.2023 (Shift-III)
(a) Emergency (b) Opulence
(c) Regression (d) Euphemism
Ans. (b)
Penury means extreme poverty; destitution. Hence, its antonym is 'opulence'.
Emergency means a serious, unexpected and often dangerous situation requiring immediate action.
Regression means a return to a former or less developed state.
Euphemism means a mild or indirect word or expression substituted for one considered to be too harsh or blunt when referring to something unpleasant or embarrassing.

618. Bhagat Singh was a young <u>firebrand</u>, whose militant activism and revolutionary fervour made him a symbol of resistance against the British Raj.
SSC CHSL Tier-1 02.08.2023 (Shift-IV)
(a) violent (b) radical
(c) moderate (d) ultra
Ans. (c)
Firebrand means a person who is passionate about a particular cause, typically inciting change and taking radical action. Hence, its antonym is 'moderate'.
Radical means relating to or affecting the fundamental nature of something; far-reaching or thorough.
Ultra means an extremist.

619. Sumptuous
SSC CHSL Tier-1 03.08.2023 (Shift-I)
(a) Unremitting (b) Lucrative
(c) Inexpensive (d) Delectable
Ans. (c)
Sumptuous means splendid and expensive looking. Hence, its antonym is 'Inexpensive'.
Unremitting means continuous.
Lucrative means profitable.
Delectable means delicious.

620. Amateur SSC CHSL Tier-1 03.08.2023 (Shift-I)
(a) Hobbyist (b) Devotee
(c) Layman (d) Professional
Ans. (d)
Amateur refers to someone who does not have much skill in what they do. Hence, its antonym is 'Professional'.
Hobbyist is one who does his hobby.
Layman is common man.

621. Comply SSC CHSL Tier-1 03.08.2023 (Shift-I)
(a) Deny (b) Engage
(c) Assist (d) Expect
Ans. (a)
'Comply' means to act according to an order, set of rules or request. Hence, its antonym is 'Deny'.

622. Awkward
SSC CHSL Tier-1 03.08.2023 (Shift-II)
(a) Graceful (b) Meaningful
(c) Innocent (d) Huge
Ans. (a)
Awkward means causing difficulty; hard to do or deal with. Hence, its antonym is 'graceful'.

623. On the day of independence a <u>jubilant</u> crowd from all over the country cheered and wept.
SSC CHSL Tier-1 03.08.2023 (Shift-II)
(a) triumphant (b) cryptic
(c) elated (d) gloomy
Ans. (d)
Jubilant means feeling or expressing great happiness and triumph. Hence, its antonym is 'gloomy'.
Cryptic means having a meaning that is mysterious or obscure.

624. Serendipity
SSC CHSL Tier-1 03.08.2023 (Shift-II)
(a) Tangibility (b) Misfortune
(c) Permanency (d) Tranquillity
Ans. (b)
Serendipity means the occurrence and development of events by chance in a happy or beneficial way. Hence, its antonym is 'misfortune'.
Tangibility means perceptible by touch.
Permanency means the state or quality of lasting or remaining unchanged indefinitely.
Tranquillity means the quality or state of being tranquil; calm.

625. Frugality
SSC CHSL Tier-1 03.08.2023 (Shift-III)
(a) Parsimony (b) Extravagance
(c) Providence (d) Economy
Ans. (b)
Frugality means the quality of being economical with money or food; thriftiness. Hence, its antonym is 'extravagance'.
Parsimony means extreme unwillingness to spend money or use resources.
Providence means the protective care of God or of nature as a spiritual power.

Economy means the state of a country or region in terms of the production and consumption of goods and services and the supply of money.

626. Acclimatise
SSC CHSL Tier-1 03.08.2023 (Shift-III)
(a) Disarrange (b) Prioritise
(c) Placate (d) Decriminalise
Ans. (a)
Acclimatise means become accustomed to a new climate or new conditions. Hence, its antonym is 'disarrange'.
Prioritise means designate or treat (something) as more important than other things.
Placate means make (someone) less angry or hostile.
Decriminalise means cease to treat (something) as illegal or as a criminal offense.

627. Gandhi's approach, while effective in mobilising large segments of Indian society, was criticised by some for being passive and overly accommodating.
SSC CHSL Tier-1 03.08.2023 (Shift-III)
(a) reconciling (b) strenuous
(c) disobliging (d) gratifying
Ans. (c)
Accommodating means fitting in with someone's wishes or demands in a helpful way. Hence, its antonym is 'disobliging'.
Reconciling means restore friendly relations between.
Strenuous means requiring or using great exertion.
Gratifying means giving pleasure or satisfaction.

628. He was a liberal who believed that men were inherently superior to women in every aspect of life.
SSC CHSL Tier-1 03.08.2023 (Shift-IV)
(a) conservative
(b) tolerant
(c) republican
(d) philanthropist
Ans. (a)
Liberal means open to new behaviour or opinions and willing to discard traditional values. Hence, its antonym is 'conservative'.
Tolerant means showing willingness to allow the existence of opinions or behaviour that one does not necessarily agree with.
Republican means a person advocating or supporting republican government.
Philanthropist means a person who seeks to promote the welfare of others, especially by the generous donation of money to good causes.

629. Hostile SSC CHSL Tier-1 03.08.2023 (Shift-IV)
(a) Hospitable (b) Bitter
(c) Nasty (d) Aggressive
Ans. (a)
Hostile means unfriendly; antagonistic. Hence, its antonym is 'hospitable'.
Bitter means having a sharp, pungent taste or smell; not sweet.
Nasty means highly unpleasant, especially to the senses; physically nauseating.
Aggressive means ready or likely to attack or confront; characterised by or resulting from aggression.

630. His deliberate activities brought him fame. SSC CHSL Tier-1 03.08.2023 (Shift-IV)
(a) dishonour (b) respect
(c) sorrow (d) strength
Ans. (a)
Fame means the state of being known or talked about by many people, especially on account of notable achievements. Hence, its antonym is 'dishonour'.

631. Imminent
SSC CHSL Tier-1 03.08.2023 (Shift-IV)
(a) Near (b) Unstoppable
(c) Distant (d) Impending
Ans. (c)
Imminent means about to happen. Hence, its antonym is 'distant'.
Impending means about to happen; imminent.

632. Copious SSC CHSL Tier-1 04.08.2023 (Shift-I)
(a) Galore (b) Enough
(c) Unsparing (d) Meagre
Ans. (d)
Copious means abundant in supply or quantity. Hence, its antonym is 'meagre'.
Galore means in abundance.
Unsparing means given freely and generously.

633. Select the most appropriate antonym for 'Apprehension' in the given sentence.
SSC CHSL Tier-1 04.08.2023 (Shift-I)
Shraddha was never in such a situation before; her excitement was understandable for her peers.
(a) Before (b) Excitement
(c) Peers (d) Situation
Ans. (b)
Apprehension means anxiety or fear that something bad or unpleasant will happen. Hence, its antonym is 'excitement'.
Before means during the period of time preceding (a particular event, date, or time).
Peers means look keenly or with difficulty at someone or something.
Situation means a set of circumstances in which one finds oneself; a state of affairs.

634. Abrogate
SSC CHSL Tier-1 04.08.2023 (Shift-I)
(a) Establish (b) Eradicate
(c) Demoralise (d) Sabotage
Ans. (a)
Abrogate means repeal or do away with (a law, right, or formal agreement). Hence, its antonym is 'establish'.
Eradicate means destroy completely; put an end to.
Demoralise means cause (someone) to lose confidence or hope.
Sabotage means deliberately destroy, damage, or obstruct (something), especially for political or military advantage.

635. Fierce SSC CHSL Tier-1 04.08.2023 (Shift-II)
(a) Sore (b) Gentle
(c) Vast (d) Noisy
Ans. (b)
The antonym of the given word 'Fierce' is 'Gentle'.
Sore means painful.
Vast means huge.

636. I wanted to ask if you have an/a .... bank account. Mine has been dormant for a year.
SSC CHSL Tier-1 04.08.2023 (Shift-III)
(a) quick (b) side (c) inert (d) active
Ans. (d)
Dormant means having normal physical functions suspended or slowed down for a period of time; in or as if in a deep sleep. Hence, its antonym is 'active'.
Inert means lacking the ability or strength to move.

637. Despicable
SSC CHSL Tier-1 04.08.2023 (Shift-III)
(a) Offensive (b) Rational
(c) Deplorable (d) Admirable
Ans. (d)
Despicable means deserving hatred and contempt. Hence, its antonym is 'admirable'.

Offensive means causing someone to feel resentful, upset, or annoyed.

Rational means based on or in accordance with reason or logic.

Deplorable means deserving strong condemnation.

638. Liable SSC CHSL Tier-1 04.08.2023 (Shift-III)

(a) Responsible (b) Tending
(c) Peaceful (d) Invulnerable

Ans. (d)

Liable means responsible by law; legally answerable. Hence, its antonym is 'invulnerable'.

639. They realised that the ghost was imperturbable.
SSC CHSL Tier-1 04.08.2023 (Shift-III)

(a) startling (b) contaminating
(c) exasperating (d) excitable

Ans. (d)

Imperturbable means unable to be upset or excited; calm. Hence, its antonym is 'excitable'.

Startling means very surprising, astonishing, or remarkable.

Contaminating means making something impure by exposure to or addition of a poisonous or polluting substance.

Exasperating means intensely irritating and frustrating.

640. She was in a state of ecstasy when she came to know that her son received a visa on his first attempt.
SSC CHSL Tier-1 04.08.2023 (Shift-III)

(a) agony (b) inspiration
(c) joyfulness (d) abash

Ans. (a)

Ecstasy means an overwhelming feeling of great happiness or joyful excitement. Hence, its antonym is 'agony'.

Abash means make (someone) feel embarrassed, disconcerted, or ashamed.

641. Select the most appropriate antonym of the word 'Regularity' from the given sentence.
SSC CHSL Tier-1 04.08.2023 (Shift-IV)

The doctor's examination revealed a significant abnormality in the patient's cardiovascular system.

(a) Examination (b) Abnormality
(c) Significant (d) Revealed

Ans. (b)

Regularity means the state or quality of being regular. Hence, its antonym is 'abnormality'.

642. Our economies and societies as a whole need to become resilient to climate impacts.
SSC CHSL Tier-1 07.08.2023 (Shift-I)

(a) Intricate (b) Lint
(c) Lapse (d) Weak

Ans. (d)

Resilient means able to withstand or recover quickly from difficult conditions. Hence, its antonym is 'weak'.

Intricate means very complicated or detailed.

Lint means short, fine fibers that separate from the surface of cloth or yarn, especially during processing.

Lapse means a temporary failure of concentration, memory, or judgment.

643. On the flight, I was in the company of an extremely **chivalrous** man.
SSC CHSL Tier-1 07.08.2023 (Shift-I)

(a) Noble
(b) Degraded
(c) Virtuous
(d) Courteous

Ans. (b)

Chivalrous means (of a man or his behaviour) courteous and gallant, especially towards women. Hence, its antonym is 'degraded'.

Noble means having or showing fine personal qualities or high moral principles and ideals.

Virtuous means having or showing high moral standards.

Courteous means polite, respectful, or considerate in manner.

644. Hamper
SSC CHSL Tier-1 07.08.2023 (Shift-II)

(a) Obscure (b) Reduce
(c) Hinder (d) Promote

Ans. (d)

Hamper means hinder or impede the movement or progress of. Hence, its antonym is 'promote'.

Obscure means not discovered or known about; uncertain.

Reduce means make smaller or less in amount, degree, or size.

Hinder means create difficulties for (someone or something), resulting in delay or obstruction.

645. Inept SSC CHSL Tier-1 07.08.2023 (Shift-II)

(a) Adorable (b) Kind
(c) Skilful (d) Elegant

Ans. (c)

Inept means having or showing no skill; clumsy. Hence, its antonym is 'skilful'.

646. The smell of .... (formerly) brewed coffee wafted through the air, beckoning him to start his day.
SSC CHSL Tier-1 07.08.2023 (Shift-II)

(a) hitherto (b) quickly
(c) preserved (d) subsequently

Ans. (d)

Formerly means before the point in time. Hence, its antonym is 'subsequently' which means after the point in time.

Hitherto means until now or until the point in time under discussion.

Quickly means at a fast speed; rapidly.

Preserved means maintain (something) in its original or existing state.

647. Although she was tired, she kept working on her project, ... (indefinite) to finish it before the deadline.
SSC CHSL Tier-1 07.08.2023 (Shift-III)

(a) bounded (b) believed
(c) contingently (d) incensed

Ans. (a)

Indefinite means lasting for an unknown or unstated length of time. Hence, its antonym is 'bounded'.

Contingently means subject to chance.

Incensed means very angry; enraged.

648. Intensive
SSC CHSL Tier-1 07.08.2023 (Shift-IV)

(a) Real (b) Dare
(c) Fierce (d) Superficial

Ans. (d)

Intensive means needing or using great energy or effort. Hence, its antonym is 'Superficial' which means don't want to think seriously about anything even important matters.

Dare means to be brave enough.

Fierce means strong and powerful.

649. The preparations for the picnic have been meticulously completed by the programme committee on time. SSC CHSL Tier-1 07.08.2023 (Shift-IV)

(a) mesmerisingly (b) prudently
(c) chaotically (d) serenely

Ans. (c)

Meticulously means very careful and with great attention to every detail. Hence, its antonym is 'Chaotically' which means in a completely confused way that lacks any order.

Mesmerisingly means attractively.

Prudently means carefully.

Serenely means calmly.

650. Extract SSC CHSL Tier-1 08.08.2023 (Shift-I)
(a) Insert (b) Fry
(c) Cut (d) Pull

Ans. (a)

Extract means remove or take out, especially by effort or force. Hence, its antonym is 'insert'.

651. One needs to be free of prejudices while dealing with judicial cases.
SSC CHSL Tier-1 08.08.2023 (Shift-I)
(a) favours (b) discriminations
(c) bigotries (d) equalities

Ans. (d)

Prejudices means preconceived opinion that is not based on reason or actual experience. Hence, its antonym is 'equalities'.

Favours means approval, support, or liking for someone or something.

Discriminations means the unjust or prejudicial treatment of different categories of people, especially on the grounds of race, age, or sex.

Bigotries means intolerance towards those who are different or hold different opinions from oneself.

652. It is a misconception that the more you learn, the more likely you are to succeed. SSC CHSL Tier-1 08.08.2023 (Shift-II)
(a) illusion (b) hallucination
(c) fallacy (d) certainty

Ans. (d)

Misconception means a wrong idea or conception of something. Hence, its antonym is 'Certainty' means something that is definitely true or that null definitely happen.

Illusion and **Hallucination** refer to a false appearance.

Fallacy is a false statement.

653. The doctor assured the patient that the tumour was benign and could be easily removed.
SSC CHSL Tier-1 08.08.2023 (Shift-II)
(a) favourable (b) malignant
(c) sterile (d) kind

Ans. (b)

Benign means not harmful in effect. Hence, its antonym is 'Malignant' means developing in an uncontrolled way and likely to cause someone's death.

Sterile means infertile.

654. He has harsh words for his opponents.
SSC CHSL Tier-1 08.08.2023 (Shift-III)
(a) sweet (b) penurious
(c) enliven (d) harsh

Ans. (a)

Harsh means unpleasantly rough or jarring to the senses. Hence, its antonym is 'sweet'.

Penurious means extremely poor; poverty-stricken.

Enliven means make (something) more entertaining, interesting, or appealing.

655. Pernicious
SSC CHSL Tier-1 08.08.2023 (Shift-III)
(a) Malicious (b) Wicked
(c) Injurious (d) Compassionate

Ans. (d)

Pernicious means having a harmful effect, especially in a gradual or subtle way. Hence, its antonym is 'compassionate'.

Malicious means characterised by malice; intending or intended to do harm.

Injurious means causing or likely to cause damage or harm.

656. Suspicious
Although the web server was, problematic, Sudha was certain that she will submit her form on the portal by evening.
SSC CHSL Tier-1 08.08.2023 (Shift-III)
(a) Certain (b) Problematic
(c) Submit (d) Portal

Ans. (a)

Suspicious means having or showing a cautious distrust of someone or something. Hence, its antonym is 'certain'.

657. The sound of rain tapping against the window was a .... (stimulating) melody, lulling him to sleep. SSC CHSL Tier-1 08.08.2023 (Shift-III)
(a) stressful (b) troubling
(c) subduing (d) harsh

Ans. (c)

Stimulating means encouraging or arousing interest or enthusiasm. Hence, its antonym is 'subduing'.

658. Witty SSC CHSL Tier-1 08.08.2023 (Shift-IV)
(a) Serious (b) Cynical
(c) Callous (d) Giddy

Ans. (a)

Witty means showing or characterised by quick and inventive verbal humour. Hence, its antonym is 'serious'.

Cynical means believing that people are motivated purely by self-interest.

Callous means showing or having an insensitive and cruel disregard for others.

Giddy means having a sensation of whirling and a tendency to fall or stagger; dizzy.

659. Darwin drew our attention to the gradual accumulation of unfavourable traits and its direct relationship with the survival of those presumed .... lucky species, which then serve as breeding grounds for more desirable traits.
SSC CHSL Tier-1 08.08.2023 (Shift-IV)
(a) advantageous (b) fulfilling
(c) steady (d) negative

Ans. (d)

Presumed means supposed to be true. Hence, its antonym is 'negative'.

Steady means firmly fixed, supported, or balanced; not shaking or moving.

660. Our administration uses .... techniques to get their work done. They do not rely on overt tactics.
SSC CHSL Tier-1 08.08.2023 (Shift-IV)
(a) covert (b) apparent
(c) clear (d) patent

Ans. (a)

Overt means done or shown openly; plainly apparent. Hence, its antonym is 'covert'.

Apparent means clearly visible or understood; obvious.

Patent means easily recognisable; obvious.

661. Conducting in-depth research and analysis of a startup as part of creating an investment memo is an important step for potential investors to evaluate the viability and potential of the startup.
SSC CHSL Tier-1 08.08.2023 (Shift-IV)
(a) liability (b) incredibility
(c) feasibility (d) extempore

Ans. (c)

Viability means ability to work successfully. Hence, its antonym is 'feasibility'.

Liability means the state of being responsible for something, especially by law.

Incredibility means the quality of being unbelievable or not convincing.

Extempore means spoken or done without preparation.

662. My friend believes in supernatural elements in the universe.
SSC CHSL Tier-1 08.08.2023 (Shift-IV)
(a) magical (b) usual
(c) unkind (c) unnatural

Ans. (b)

Supernatural means attributed to some force beyond scientific understanding or the laws of nature. Hence, its antonym is 'usual'.

663. After the rain stopped, the air smelled fresh and clean and the Sun .... (stared) out from behind the clouds.
SSC CHSL Tier-1 09.08.2023 (Shift-I)

(a) peeked (b) observed
(c) spied (d) surveyed

Ans. (a)

Stared means to see continuously. Hence, its antonym is 'Peeked' which means to see for some time or have a quick look.

Spied means to gather information secretly.

664. The newly selected secretary of the party has a/an impeccable image among the public.
SSC CHSL Tier-1 09.08.2023 (Shift-I)

(a) refurbished (b) blemished
(c) irresistible (d) arbitrary

Ans. (b)

Impeccable means perfect, with no problems or bad parts. Hence, its antonym is 'Blemished' means to have a flaw.

Refurbished means redecorated.

Irresistible means too attractive to be ignored.

Arbitrary means random.

665. Contemplate
SSC CHSL Tier-1 09.08.2023 (Shift-II)

(a) Ruminate (b) Disregard
(c) Meditate (d) Retract

Ans. (b)

Contemplate means look thoughtfully for a long time at. Hence, its antonym is 'disregard'.

Ruminate means think deeply about something.

Meditate means think deeply or focus one's mind for a period of time.

Retract means draw or be drawn back or back in.

666. Your views related to morality are outdated and puritanical.
SSC CHSL Tier-1 09.08.2023 (Shift-II)

(a) orthodox
(b) prudish
(c) permissive
(d) blasphemous

Ans. (c)

Puritanical means practicing or affecting strict religious or moral behaviour. Hence, its antonym is 'permissive'.

Orthodox means conforming to what is generally or traditionally accepted as right or true; established and approved.

Prudish means having or revealing a tendency to be easily shocked by matters relating to sex or nudity.

Blasphemous means sacrilegious against God or sacred things; profane.

667. Decent
My father taught me to be true and ethical in business as dishonesty leads to downfall.
SSC CHSL Tier-1 09.08.2023 (Shift-III)

(a) Dishonesty (b) Ethical
(c) Downfall (d) True

Ans. (a)

Decent means conforming with generally accepted standards of respectable or moral behaviour. Hence, its antonym is 'dishonesty'.

Ethical means relating to moral principles or the branch of knowledge dealing with these.

Downfall means a loss of power, prosperity, or status.

668. Many confessed after the physical torture by the cops.
SSC CHSL Tier-1 09.08.2023 (Shift-III)

(a) revealed (b) recognised
(c) acknowledged (d) denied

Ans. (d)

Confessed means admit or state that one has committed a crime or is at fault in some ways. Hence, its antonym is 'denied'.

Revealed means make (previously unknown or secret information) known to others.

Recognised means identify (someone or something) from having encountered them before.

Acknowledged means accept or admit the existence or truth of.

669. Affliction
SSC CHSL Tier-1 09.08.2023 (Shift-III)

(a) Predicament (b) Mortgage
(c) Jeopardy (d) Consolation

Ans. (d)

Affliction means something that causes pain or suffering. Hence, its antonym is 'consolation'.

Predicament means a difficult, unpleasant, or embarrassing situation.

Mortgage means a legal agreement by which a bank or other creditor lends money at interest in exchange for taking title of the debtor's property.

Jeopardy means danger of loss, harm, or failure.

670. Repel
Her bright blue eyes .... everyone in the party.
SSC CHSL Tier-1 09.08.2023 (Shift-IV)

(a) disgust (b) vacillate
(c) attract (d) amenable

Ans. (c)

Repel means to drive away or cause dislike or aversion. Hence, its antonym is 'attract'.

Vacillate means alternate or waver between different opinions or actions; be indecisive.

Amenable means open and responsive to suggestion; easily persuaded or controlled.

671. Ludicrous
SSC CHSL Tier-1 09.08.2023 (Shift-IV)

(a) Ridiculous
(b) Insane
(c) Wise
(d) Pathetic

Ans. (c)

Ludicrous means so foolish, unreasonable, or out of place as to be amusing; ridiculous. Hence, its antonym is 'wise'.

Ridiculous means deserving or inviting derision or mockery; absurd.

Insane means in a state of mind that prevents normal perception, behaviour, or social interaction; seriously mentally ill.

Pathetic means arousing pity, especially through vulnerability or sadness.

672. The .... (chill) of the Sun on his face was a welcome respite from the chilly morning air.
SSC CHSL Tier-1 09.08.2023 (Shift-IV)

(a) glow (b) blush
(c) warmth (d) brightness

Ans. (c)

Chill means an unpleasant feeling of coldness in the atmosphere, one's surroundings, or the body. Hence, its antonym is 'warmth'.

673. The doctor reassured Raman that the lump was benign which brought immense relief to both him and his family.
SSC CHSL Tier-1 09.08.2023 (Shift-IV)

(a) harsh (b) rugged
(c) malignant (d) healthy

Ans. (c)

Benign means gentle and kindly. Hence, its antonym is 'malignant'.

Rugged means having a broken, rocky and uneven surface.

674. Fixation
SSC CHSL Tier-1 09.08.2023 (Shift-IV)
(a) Formulation (b) Indifference
(c) Inclination (d) Reformation

Ans. (b)

Fixation means an obsessive interest in or feeling about someone or something. Hence, its antonym is 'indifference'.

Formulation means the action of devising or creating something.

Inclination means a person's natural tendency or urge to act or feel in a particular way.

Reformation means the action or process of reforming an institution or practice.

675. The Tokyo Games accelerated energy policies in Japan, demonstrating how they could make steps towards a low-carbon economy by powering the athletes' village with hydrogen from clean, green sources.
SSC CHSL Tier-1 10.08.2023 (Shift-II)
(a) inspiring (b) exploring
(c) collating (d) hiding

Ans. (a)

Accelerated means begin to move more quickly. Hence, its antonym is 'inspiring'.

Collating means collect and combine (texts, information, or data).

676. Hysterical
SSC CHSL Tier-1 10.08.2023 (Shift-II)
(a) Controlled (b) Resolute
(c) Manful (d) Shy

Ans. (a)

Hysterical means deriving from or affected by uncontrolled extreme emotion. Hence, its antonym is 'controlled'.

Resolute means admirably purposeful, determined and unwavering.

Manful means having or showing courage and resolution.

677. The flow of the river is very rapid now. Let's go in when it's a little .... SSC CHSL Tier-1 10.08.2023 (Shift-II)
(a) fast (b) quick
(c) delayed (d) slow

Ans. (d)

Rapid means happening in a short time or at a great rate. Hence, its antonym is 'slow'.

678. Profit SSC CHSL Tier-1 10.08.2023 (Shift-III)
(a) Earnings (b) Amount
(c) Sale (d) Expense

Ans. (d)

'Expense' is the antonym for 'Profit' as it means the amount of money that you spend on something.

679. I can't believe that you're .... (resolute) enough to not even decide what you want for dinner.
SSC CHSL Tier-1 11.08.2023 (Shift-I)
(a) reluctant (b) indecisive
(c) disinclined (d) gullible

Ans. (b)

Resolute means 'decisive'. Hence, its antonym is 'indecisive'.

Disinclined means unwilling.

Gullible means too trustful.

680. The singer's performance captivated the audience and left them mesmerised.
SSC CHSL Tier-1 11.08.2023 (Shift-I)
(a) enthralled
(b) disillusioned
(c) horrified
(d) resisted

Ans. (b)

Captivated means attracted. Hence, its antonyms is 'Disillusioned' means to realise that something is not as good as you realised.

681. Punctual SSC CHSL Tier-1 11.08.2023 (Shift-I)
(a) Dependable (b) Precise
(c) Late (d) Ready

Ans. (c)

Punctual means happening or doing something at the agreed or proper time. Hence, its antonym is 'late'.

682. Empowered
People feel liberated in modern democracies, yet it is believed they are enslaved in their minds.
SSC CHSL Tier-1 11.08.2023 (Shift-I)
(a) Liberated (b) Enslaved
(c) Minds (d) Modern

Ans. (b)

Empowered means 'to have authority or power'. Hence, its antonym is 'Enslaved' meaning 'to be held under bondage'.

Liberated means free.

Enthralled means charmed or captivated.

Resisted means to fight the effect of.

683. This novelist is known for his verbosity.
SSC CHSL Tier-1 14.08.2023 (Shift-IV)
(a) vengeance (b) succinctness
(c) humility (d) candour

Ans. (b)

Verbosity means using a lot of words. Hence, its antonyms is 'Succinctness' refers to brief usage of words.

Vengeance means revenge.

Humility is kindness.

Candour means honest.

684. 'Refuse' SSC CHSL Tier-1 14.08.2023 (Shift-IV)
Shama was allowed to visit the accommodation places for the devotees of the shrine.
(a) Allowed (b) Visit
(c) Accommodation (d) Shrine

Ans. (a)

The most appropriate antonym of the underlined word 'Refuse' is 'Allowed'.

Accommodation refers to a place where one can stay.

Shrine means temple.

685. Raciness
SSC CHSL Tier-1 14.08.2023 (Shift-IV)
(a) Filth (b) Perfection
(c) Lewdness (d) Obscenity

Ans. (b)

Raciness means indecency. Hence, 'Perfection' is its nearest antonym.

Filth means dirty.

Lewdness and **Obscenity** mean in decency.

686. The loyal nature of the princess was one of the reasons that the king trusted her very much.
SSC CHSL Tier-1 14.08.2023 (Shift-IV)
(a) infamous (b) treacherous
(c) livid (d) unyielding

Ans. (b)

The given word 'loyal' means being faithful to someone. Hence, its antonym is 'Treacherous' refers to 'betraying someone's 'trust'.

Livid means very angry.

Unyielding means not giving way to pressure.

687. Everyone feels that he is pompous, but I know the underlying truth that he is a man of great understanding and love.
SSC CHSL Tier-1 17.08.2023 (Shift-I)
(a) modest (b) lofty
(c) grandiose (d) haughty

Ans. (a)

'Pompous' means too serious and full of importance. Hence, its antonym is 'Modest' means not usually talking about or making obvious your own abilities and achievements.

Lofty means heavy.

Grandiose means grand.

Haughty means too proud.

688. We were very much enthusiastic about our tour to Agra.
SSC CHSL Tier-1 17.08.2023 (Shift-I)
(a) obsessed (b) anxious
(c) casual (d) inclined

Ans. (c)

Enthusiastic means having or showing intense and eager enjoyment, interest or approval. Hence, its antonym is 'casual'.

Obsessed means to show excessive concern.

Anxious means worried.

Inclined means to have a strong opinion on something.

689. Elusive SSC CHSL Tier-1 17.08.2023 (Shift-I)
(a) Explosive (b) Affordable
(c) Definite (d) Rigid

Ans. (c)

Elusive means difficult to describe, find, achieve or remember. Hence, its antonym is 'Definite'.

Explosive means to break violently.

Rigid means hard and firm

690. Repeal SSC CHSL Tier-1 17.08.2023 (Shift-I)
(a) Approval (b) Expense
(c) Separation (d) Adversity

Ans. (a)

Repeal means the act of removing the legal force of a law. Hence, its antonym is 'Approval'.

Expense means cost incurred.

Adversity means difficulty.

691. Sharp SSC CHSL Tier-1 02.11.2023 (Shift-I)
(a) Kindled (b) Handy
(c) Magnetic (d) Blunt

Ans. (d)

'Sharp' can refer to someone who is quick-witted intelligent. Hence, its antonym is 'Blunt' implies being straight-forward but lacking finesse or tact.

Kindled means to set on fire.
Handy means useful.

692. Denote SSC CHSL Tier-1 10.01.2023 (Shift-I)
(a) Convey
(b) Conclude
(c) Conceal
(d) Convince

Ans. (c)

Denote means to be a sign of indicate Hence, its antonyms is 'Conceal' means to keep from signt; hide.

Convey means to give information.

Conclude means to end.

Convince means to persuade.

SSC CHSL 2022

693. I felt terribly jaded after working all weekend.
SSC CHSL Tier-1 24.05.2022 (Shift-II)
(a) glutted (b) refreshed
(c) spent (d) vigorous

Ans. (b)

Jaded means tired, bored or lacking enthusiasm. Hence, its antonym is 'refreshed'.

694. The malice he developed for all caused a lot of damage.
SSC CHSL Tier-1 24.05.2022 (Shift-II)
(a) avarice (b) grace
(c) sympathy (d) oppression

Ans. (c)

Malice means the intention or desire to do evil; ill will. Hence, its antonym is 'sympathy'.

695. Detrimental
SSC CHSL Tier-1 24.05.2022 (Shift-III)
(a) Baseless (b) Harmless
(c) Senseless (d) Meaningless

Ans. (b)

Detrimental means tending to cause harm. Hence, its antonym is 'harmless'.

696. Eventually the patient succumbed to her illness.
SSC CHSL Tier-1 25.05.2022 (Shift-I)
(a) died (b) overcame
(c) surrendered (d) advanced

Ans. (b)

Succumbed means fail to resist pressure, temptation, or some other negative force. Hence, its antonym is 'overcame'.

697. His liberal policies were responsible for progress in the community.
SSC CHSL Tier-1 25.05.2022 (Shift-II)
(a) ineffectual (b) conservative
(c) central (d) hysterica

Ans. (b)

Liberal means open to new behaviour or opinions and willing to discard traditional values.

Hence, its antonym is 'conservative'.

698. They bestow upon him whatever he wishes. SSC CHSL Tier-1 25.05.2022 (Shift-III)
(a) intensify (b) gift
(c) deny (d) classify

Ans. (c)

Bestow means confer or present (an honour, right or gift). Hence, its antonym is 'deny'.

699. It was an impetuous decision to buy a car when he didn't have a job. SSC CHSL 26.05.2022 (Shift-I)
(a) dense (b) arguable
(c) tangible (d) sensible

Ans. (d)

Impetuous means acting or done quickly and without thought or care. Hence, its antonym is 'sensible'.

700. Former SSC CHSL Tier-1 26.05.2022 (Shift-I)
(a) External (b) Additional
(c) Featured (d) Latter

Ans. (d)

Former means having previously filled a particular role or been a particular thing. Hence, its antonym is 'latter'.

701. Savage SSC CHSL Tier-1 26.05.2022 (Shift-I)
(a) Brutal (b) Civilised
(c) Adequate (d) Impartial

Ans. (b)

Savage means fierce, violent and uncontrolled. Hence, its antonym is 'civilised'.

702. Variance
SSC CHSL Tier-1 26.05.2022 (Shift-II)
(a) Convention (b) Equal
(c) Harmony (d) Intellectual

Ans. (c)

Variance means the fact or quality of being different, divergent, or inconsistent. Hence, its antonym is 'harmony'.

703. She has a **penchant** for art and craft. SSC CHSL Tier-1 27.05.2022 (Shift-I)
(a) hatred (b) fear
(c) joy (d) anxiety

Ans. (a)

Penchant means a feeling of liking something very much or a tendency to do something a lot. Hence, its antonym is 'hatred'.

704. Hari's **intimate** nature has earned him many friends.
SSC CHSL Tier-1 27.05.2022 (Shift-I)
(a) unfriendly (b) affectionate
(c) timely (d) passionate

Ans. (a)

Intimate means private and friendly so that you feel comfortable. Hence, its antonym is 'unfriendly'.

705. Pseudo SSC CHSL Tier-1 27.05.2022 (Shift-II)
(a) Flawed (b) Genuine
(c) Artificial (d) Corrupt

Ans. (b)

Pseudo means not genuine; sham. Hence, its antonym is 'genuine'.

706. Ebb SSC CHSL Tier-1 27.05.2022 (Shift-III)
(a) Ripe (b) Moisture
(c) Flow (d) Stiff

Ans. (c)

Ebb means the movement of the tide out to sea. Hence, its antonym is 'flow'.

707. Sceptic SSC CHSL Tier-1 27.05.2022 (Shift-III)
(a) Doubter (b) Believer
(c) Disbeliever (d) Receiver
Ans. (b)
Sceptic means a person inclined to question or doubt all accepted opinions. Hence, its antonym is 'believer'.

708. The uneducated man was flummoxed by the legal document.
SSC CHSL Tier-1 27.05.2022 (Shift-II)
(a) happy (b) annoyed
(c) comfortable (d) scared
Ans. (c)
Flummoxed means bewildered or perplexed. Hence, its antonym is 'comfortable'.

709. Her **candid** remarks impressed the Board of members.
SSC CHSL Tier-1 30.05.2022 (Shift-I)
(a) blunt (b) sincere
(c) deceitful (d) unconventional
Ans. (c)
Candid means telling the truth, even when the truth may be unpleasant or embarrassing.
Hence, its antonym is 'deceitful' which means dishonest or hiding the truth.
Blunt means direct and honest, often rude.
Unconventional means not normal and unusual.

710. Vulgar SSC CHSL Tier-1 30.05.2022 (Shift-I)
(a) Senior (b) Decreased
(c) Ignorant (d) Refined
Ans. (d)
'Vulgar' means not behaving politely in social situations. Hence, its antonym is 'Refined', which means very polite and showing knowledge of social rules.

711. Let's ascertain whether his claims have any truth.
SSC CHSL Tier-1 30.05.2022 (Shift-II)
(a) detect (b) approve
(c) disprove (d) prove
Ans. (c)
Ascertain means find (something) out for certain; make sure of. Hence, its antonym is 'disprove'.

712. Suffice SSC CHSL Tier-1 30.05.2022 (Shift-III)
(a) Excessed (b) Immatured
(c) Satirise (d) Dissatisfy
Ans. (d)
Suffice means be enough or adequate. Hence, its antonym is 'dissatisfy'.

713. Pretence SSC CHSL Tier-1 31.05.2022 (Shift-I)
(a) Reality (b) Impotence
(c) Arrogance (d) Intolerance
Ans. (a)
'Pretence' means a way of behaving that is intended to make people believe something that is not true. Hence, its antonym is 'Reality'.
Impotence means helplessness.
Arrogance means pride.
Intolerance means unable to accept new views and beliefs.

714. Precocious
SSC CHSL Tier-1 31.05.2022 (Shift-I)
(a) Liberal (b) Gentle
(c) Backward (d) Lenient
Ans. (c)
'Precocious' means (especially of children) showing mental development or achievement much earlier than usual. Hence, its antonym is 'Backward'.
Liberal means open to new ideas
Lenient means not harsh and severe.

715. Sacred SSC CHSL Tier-1 01.06.2022 (Shift-I)
(a) Profane (b) Maniacal
(c) Inquisitive (d) Rational
Ans. (a)
'Sacred' means considered to be holy or connected with God in a special way. Its antonym is 'Profane' as it means showing a lack of respect for religious objects, places or beliefs.
Profane means secular or not religious.
Maniacal means crazy.

716. Uphold SSC CHSL Tier-1 01.06.2022 (Shift-I)
(a) Support (b) Maintain
(c) Endorse (d) Oppose
Ans. (d)
'Uphold' means to give support or to defend. Hence, its antonym is 'Oppose'.
Endorse means to support.

717. Treacherous
SSC CHSL Tier-1 01.06.2022 (Shift-I)
(a) Fantastic (b) Flexible
(c) Fluent (d) Faithful
Ans. (d)
'Treacherous' means guilty of involving betrayal or deception. Hence, its antonym is 'Faithful'.

718. There is .... (scarce) evidence that he is the thief.
SSC CHSL Tier-1 01.06.2022 (Shift-I)
(a) strong (b) mysterious
(c) scant (d) abundant
Ans. (d)
'Abundant' is the appropriate antonym of 'scarce' that can be used to fill the blank in the given sentence.
'Abundant' means existing or available in large quantities.
Scant means very small in quantity.

719. Broke away from their solicitous grip. SSC CHSL Tier-1 01.06.2022 (Shift-II)
(a) worried (b) heedless
(c) knowledgeable (d) interesting
Ans. (b)
Solicitous means characterised by or showing interest or concern. Hence, its antonym is 'heedless'.

720. Maverick
SSC CHSL Tier-1 01.06.2022 (Shift-III)
(a) Custodian (b) Versatility
(c) Conformist (d) Brilliance
Ans. (c)
Maverick means an unorthodox or independent-minded person. Hence, its antonym is 'conformist'.

721. Famous SSC CHSL Tier-1 02.06.2022 (Shift-I)
(a) Quiet (b) Concert
(c) Obscure (d) Affluent
Ans. (c)
'Famous' means known about many people in many places. Hence, its antonym is 'Obscure' which means not well known and usually not very important.
Concert means a musical performance given in public.
Affluent means rich.

722. Despair SSC CHSL Tier-1 02.06.2022 (Shift-II)
(a) Vile (b) Hope
(c) Annoy (d) Definite
Ans. (b)
Despair means the complete loss or absence of hope. Hence, its antonym is 'hope'.

723. The players seem to be suffering from exertion.
SSC CHSL Tier-1 02.06.2022 (Shift-III)
(a) inaction (b) suffocation
(c) traction (d) reaction
Ans. (a)
Exertion means physical or mental effort. Hence, its antonym is 'inaction'.

724. The cricketer is in sublime form.
SSC CHSL Tier-1 02.06.2022 (Shift-III)
(a) superior (b) interior
(c) inferior (d) exterior
Ans. (c)
Sublime means of such excellence, grandeur, or beauty as to inspire great admiration or awe. Hence, its antonym is 'inferior'.

725. Which word in the given sentence is the antonym of 'Nibble'?
SSC CHSL Tier-1 03.06.2022 (Shift-II)
They sprinted across the floor and leaped up to the elevated platforms, poking their soft

muzzles into the stanchions to gobble the grain.
(a) gobble (b) muzzles
(c) elevated (d) sprinted

Ans. (a)

Nibble means take small bites out of. Hence, its antonym is 'gobble'.

726. Marvellous
SSC CHSL Tier-1 03.06.2022 (Shift-III)
(a) Adverse (b) Terrible
(c) Tolerable (d) Mythical

Ans. (b)

Marvellous means causing great wonder; extraordinary. Hence, its antonym is 'terrible'.

727. Ardent SSC CHSL Tier-1 03.06.2022 (Shift-III)
(a) Admirable (b) Beautiful
(c) Sincere (d) Apathetic

Ans. (d)

Ardent means enthusiastic or passionate. Hence, its antonym is 'apathetic'.

728. Annoy SSC CHSL Tier-1 06.06.2022 (Shift-I)
(a) Comfort (b) Miff (c) Get (d) Ruffle

Ans. (a)

Annoy means irritate (someone); make (someone) a little angry. Hence, its antonym is 'comfort'.

729. Terse SSC CHSL Tier-1 06.06.2022 (Shift-II)
(a) Succinct (b) Verbose
(c) Loathe (d) Concise

Ans. (b)

Terse means sparing in the use of words; abrupt. Hence, its antonym is 'verbose'.

Succinct and **Concise** are synonyms of terse.

730. Select the most appropriate antonym of the word 'Exaggerate' from the given sentence.
SSC CHSL Tier-1 06.06.2022 (Shift-III)
Rajni did understate Sheila's embroider work as, according to her, it was worthless to decorate a piece of cloth with abstract ideas and than elaborate it to the audience on the stage.
(a) Elaborate (b) Embroidery
(c) Decorate (d) Understate

Ans. (d)

Exaggerate means represent (something) as being larger, better, or worse than it really is. Hence, its antonym is 'understate'.

Elaborate means involving many carefully arranged parts or details.

Embroidery means the art or pastime of embroidering cloth.

731. Delay SSC CHSL Tier-1 06.06.2022 (Shift-III)
(a) Scarce (b) Nice
(c) Haste (d) Weary

Ans. (c)

Delay means make (someone or something) late or slow. Hence, its antonym is 'haste'.

Scarce means insufficient for the demand.

Weary means feeling or showing tiredness.

732. Meagre SSC CHSL Tier-1 07.06.2022 (Shift-I)
(a) Civilised (b) Miserable
(c) Plentiful (d) Sparse

Ans. (c)

Meagre means lacking in quantity or quality. Hence, its antonym is 'plentiful'.

Civilised means at an advanced stage of social and cultural development.

Sparse means thinly dispersed or scattered.

733. Which word in the given sentence is the antonym of 'Doubtful'?
SSC CHSL Tier-1 07.06.2022 (Shift-I)
The poverty of his childhood played a decisive role in his adult life.
(a) decisive (b) played
(c) adult (d) poverty

Ans. (a)

Doubtful means feeling uncertain about something. Hence, its antonym is 'decisive'.

734. The negligent attitude of the cops was criticised
SSC CHSL Tier-1 07.06.2022 (Shift-II)
(a) sloppy (b) persistent
(c) attentive (d) bored

Ans. (c)

Negligent means failing to take proper care in doing something. Hence, its antonym is 'attentive'.

Sloppy means careless and unsystematic; excessively casual.

Persistent means continuing firmly or obstinately in an opinion or course of action.

735. Her father was quick to detect her concealed emotion.
SSC CHSL Tier-1 07.06.2022 (Shift-III)
(a) annoyed (b) disclosed
(c) arrogant (d) excited

Ans. (b)

Concealed means kept secret; hidden. Hence, its antonym is 'disclosed'.

736. Comic SSC CHSL Tier-1 08.06.2022 (Shift-I)
(a) Native (b) Costly
(c) Tragic (d) Empty

Ans. (c)

Comic means causing or meant to cause laughter. Hence, its antonym is 'tragic'.

737. My fascination with Tyler's items .... (approached) into distant memories.
SSC CHSL Tier-1 08.06.2022 (Shift-I)
(a) receded (b) escalated
(c) expanded (d) intensified

Ans. (a)

Approached means come near or nearer to (someone or something) in distance. Hence, its antonym is 'receded'.

Escalated means increase rapidly.

Expanded means become or make larger or more extensive.

Intensified means become or make more intense.

738. Frivolous
SSC CHSL Tier-1 08.06.2022 (Shift-II)
(a) Popular (b) Reputed
(c) Nervous (d) Serious

Ans. (d)

Frivolous means not having any serious purpose or value. Hence, its antonym is 'serious'.

739. The President claimed he was immune from prosecution.
SSC CHSL Tier-1 09.06.2022 (Shift-I)
(a) Claimed
(b) President
(c) Immune
(d) Prosecution

Ans. (d)

Immune means resistant to a particular infection or toxin owing to the presence of specific antibodies or sensitised white blood cells. Hence, its antonym is 'prosecution'.

Claimed means state or assert that something is the case, typically without providing evidence or proof.

President means the elected head of a republican state.

Immune means protected or exempt, especially from an obligation or the effects of something.

740. You have made only perfunctory attempts to understand me!
SSC CHSL Tier-1 09.06.2022 (Shift-II)
(a) adamant (b) careful
(c) basic (d) casual

Ans. (b)

Perfunctory means (of an action or gesture) carried out with a minimum of effort or reflection. Hence, its antonym is 'careful'.

741. Defile **SSC CHSL Tier-1 09.06.2022 (Shift-II)**

(a) Regularise (b) Labour
(c) Particularise (d) Purify

Ans. (d)

Defile means sully, mar or spoil. Hence, its antonym is 'purify'.

742. Siege **SSC CHSL Tier-1 10.06.2022 (Shift-I)**

(a) Deference (b) Trance
(c) Clearance (d) Inference

Ans. (c)

Siege means a military operation in which enemy forces surround a town or building, cutting off essential supplies, with the aim of compelling the surrender of those inside. Hence, its antonym is 'clearance'.

Deference means humble submission and respect.

Trance means a half-conscious state characterised by an absence of response to external stimuli.

Inference means a conclusion reached on the basis of evidence and reasoning.

743. Which word in the given sentence is the antonym of 'Jeopardy'?
SSC CHSL Tier-1 10.06.2022 (Shift-III)

We were reluctant to leave the relative safety of our hotel.

(a) Leave (b) Relative
(c) Safety (d) Reluctant

Ans. (c)

Jeopardy means danger of loss, harm, or failure. Hence, its antonym is 'safety'.

SSC CHSL 2021

744. Graceful
SSC CHSL Tier-1 19.04.2021 (Shift-III)

(a) Dangerous (b) Attractive
(c) Awkward (d) Pretty

Ans. (c)

The most appropriate antonym of 'Graceful' is 'Awkward'.

745. Vitiate **SSC CHSL Tier-1 12.04.2021 (Shift-II)**

(a) Violate (b) Affirm
(c) Annul (d) Cancel

Ans. (b)

'Vitiate' means to make faulty or defective. Hence, 'Affirm' would be its nearest antonym.

Annul means to cancel.

746. Augment **SSC CHSL Tier-1 12.04.2021 (Shift-II)**

(a) Multiply (b) Amplify
(c) Decrease (d) Increase

Ans. (c)

'Augment' means make something greater by adding or multiplying, increase. Hence, its antonym is 'Decrease'.

Amplify means to increase.

747. Sustenance
SSC CHSL Tier-1 04.08.2021 (Shift-I)

(a) Refreshment (b) Livelihood
(c) Starvation (d) Nourishment

Ans. (c)

'Sustenance' is food or drink that allows you to continue to be alive. Hence, its antonym is 'Starvation', which means suffering or death caused by lack of food.

748. Constant
SSC CHSL Tier-1 19.04.2021 (Shift-III)

(a) Unchanging (b) Competent
(c) Fluctuating (d) Static

Ans. (c)

'Constant' means a situation that does not change. Hence, its antonym is 'Fluctuating' which means rising and falling irregularly.

Competent means skilled.

Static means stable.

749. Expunge **SSC CHSL Tier-1 10.08.2021 (Shift-I)**

(a) Insert (b) Deplete
(c) Exhaust (d) Remove

Ans. (a)

'Expunge' means obliterate or remove completely. Hence, its antonym is 'Insert'.

Deplete means to reduce.

Exhaust means to use completely.

750. Buoyant **SSC CHSL Tier-1 12.08.2021 (Shift-I)**

(a) Enthusiastic (b) Lively
(c) Weighted (d) Bouncy

Ans. (c)

'Buoyant' means able to rise and float in the air or on the top of a liquid. Hence, its antonym is 'Weighted'.

751. Traditional
SSC CHSL Tier-1 12.08.2021 (Shift-III)

(a) Earthly (b) Customary
(c) Modern (d) Conventional

Ans. (c)

The most appropriate antonym of 'Traditional' is 'Modern'.

Customary and **conventional** mean traditional.

Earthly means of Earth.

SSC MTS 2024 (Tier 1 & 2)

752. Mountaineering requires a combination of physical strength, endurance, technical skill and mental <u>fortitude</u>.
SSC MTS Tier-1 14.11.2024 (Shift-III)

(a) enthusiasm (b) persistence
(c) timidity (d) excitement

Ans. (c)

'Timidity' is the most appropriate antonym that can substitute the underlined segment. 'Fortitude' means courage in pain or adversity, while 'timidity' means lack of courage or confidence.

Enthusiasm means eager enjoyment.

Persistence means continuing firmly.

Excitement means a state of enthusiasm or eagerness.

753. Radha stepped <u>backward</u> to avoid the incoming traffic.
SSC MTS Tier-1 14.11.2024 (Shift-III)

(a) beside (b) affront
(c) forward (d) behind

Ans. (c)

'Forward' is the most appropriate antonym of 'backward'. 'Backward' means in the direction of the back, while 'forward' means in the direction of the front.

754. The vegetation in this area of the forest is very <u>dense</u>.
SSC MTS Tier-1 13.11.2024 (Shift-III)

(a) Spatial (b) Sparse
(c) Spare (d) Spruce

Ans. (b)

'Sparse' is the most appropriate antonym of 'dense'. 'Dense' means closely packed together, while 'sparse' means thinly dispersed or scattered.

Spatial relates to space.

Spare means extra.

Spruce means neat in appearance.

755. Inferior **SSC MTS Tier-1 12.11.2024 (Shift-III)**

(a) Superior (b) Substandard
(c) Beautiful (d) Mediocre

Ans. (a)

'Superior' is the most appropriate antonym of 'Inferior'. It means lower in rank, status, or quality, while 'superior' means higher in rank, status or quality.

Substandard means below the usual or required standard.

Mediocre means of only moderate quality.

756. Compassionate
SSC MTS Tier-1 11.11.2024 (Shift-III)

(a) Hardworking (b) Disciplined
(c) Confident (d) Cruel

Ans. (d)

'Cruel' is the most appropriate antonym of 'compassionate.' 'Compassionate' means feeling or showing sympathy and concern for others.

757. The mother told the child to <u>erase</u> the extra dots from the given graph.
SSC MTS Tier-1 05.11.2024 (Shift-III)

(a) create (b) shatter
(c) delete (d) efface

Ans. (a)

'Create' is the most appropriate antonym of 'Erase.' It means to remove or delete, while 'create' means to bring into existence.

758. Predicament
SSC MTS Tier-1 04.11.2024 (Shift-III)

(a) Solution (b) Docile
(c) Mess (d) Redeem

Ans. (a)

'Solution' is the most appropriate antonym of 'predicament'. 'Predicament' means a difficult or unpleasant situation, while 'solution' means a way to solve a problem.

759. Obsequious
SSC MTS Tier-1 04.11.2024 (Shift-III)

(a) Ordained (b) Obliterate
(c) Ostracised (d) Obstinate

Ans. (d)

'Obstinate' is the most appropriate antonym of 'Obsequious'. 'Obsequious' means excessively submissive, while 'obstinate' means stubborn.

Ordained means to officially appoint.

Obliterate means to destroy completely.

Ostracised means excluded from a society or group.

760. Piquant SSC MTS Tier-1 30.10.2024 (Shift-III)

(a) Bitter (b) Bland
(c) Delicious (d) Delectable

Ans. (b)

'Bland' is the most appropriate antonym of 'Piquant'. 'It means having a pleasantly sharp taste or appetising flavour, while 'Bland' means lacking strong features or characteristics.

761. The athlete's (languid) performance disappointed the fans as well as coaches.
SSC MTS Tier-1 29.10.2024 (Shift-III)

(a) Vigorous (b) Listless
(c) Relaxed (d) Lethargic

Ans. (a)

'Vigorous' is the correct antonym of 'languid'. It means full of energy and effort.

762. The magician's performance was (captivating) and held the audience spellbound.
SSC MTS Tier-1 28.10.2024 (Shift-II)

(a) Boring (b) Enchanting
(c) Fascinating (d) Gripping

Ans. (a)

'Boring' is the most appropriate antonym of 'captivating'.

Enchanting means delightful.

Fascinating means extremely interesting.

Gripping means holding one's attention.

763. High-altitude climbing poses **significant** risks due to factors like altitude sickness, hypothermia and extreme weather conditions.
SSC MTS Tier-1 23.10.2024 (Shift-II)

(a) magnificent (b) tempestuous
(c) inconsequential (d) plentiful

Ans. (c)

'Inconsequential' is the most appropriate antonym that can substitute 'significant' in the given sentence. 'Inconsequential' means not important or significant.

Magnificent means extremely beautiful or impressive.

Tempestuous means characterised by strong and turbulent or conflicting emotion.

Plentiful means existing in large quantities.

764. Chaotic SSC MTS Tier-1 22.10.2024 (Shift-II)

(a) Obscure (b) Confused
(c) Systematic (d) Dressed

Ans. (c)

'Systematic' is the most appropriate antonym of 'Chaotic'. 'Chaotic' means in a state of complete confusion and disorder, while 'systematic' means done or acting according to a fixed plan or system; methodical.

Obscure means not discovered or known about.

765. The painting exhibited a .... blend of colours. (harmonious)
SSC MTS Tier-1 18.10.2024 (Shift-II)

(a) discordant (b) quavering
(c) polyphonic (d) thrilling

Ans. (a)

'Discordant' is the most appropriate antonym of 'harmonious'. It means disagreeing or incongruous.

Quavering means shaking or trembling.

Polyphonic means producing many sounds simultaneously.

Thrilling means causing excitement.

766. The team was gradually realising that the social gatherings were draining. SSC MTS Tier-1 17.10.2024 (Shift-II)

(a) flippant (b) absorbing
(c) unfruitful (d) frivolous

Ans. (b)

'Absorbing' is the most appropriate antonym that can substitute 'draining'. While 'draining' means exhausting and tiring, 'absorbing' means fully engaging one's interest or attention.

767. The name should also be **beneficial** to a strong, long-lasting marketing campaign.
SSC MTS Tier-1 16.10.2024 (Shift-II)

(a) Causal (b) Advantageous
(c) Detrimental (d) Desirable

Ans. (c)

'Detrimental' is the word that is opposite in meaning to 'beneficial'.

While 'beneficial' means advantageous or helpful, 'detrimental' means harmful or damaging.

768. Although our new boss knew he was wrong, he was too **obstinate** to accept that.
SSC MTS Tier-1 15.10.2024 (Shift-I)

(a) Competent (b) Fearless
(c) Adamant (d) Flexible

Ans. (d)

'Flexible' is the most appropriate antonym of 'obstinate.' While 'obstinate' means stubborn and unwilling to change, 'flexible' means adaptable and willing to change.

Competent means capable and efficient.

Adamant means unyielding or stubborn, which is a synonym.

769. Searing SSC MTS Tier-1 14.10.2024 (Shift-I)

(a) Mocking (b) Pressing
(c) Freezing (d) Thrilling

Ans. (c)

'Freezing' is the most appropriate antonym of 'searing.' It means extremely hot, 'freezing' means extremely cold.

Mocking means making fun of.

Pressing means urgent.

Thrilling means exciting.

770. Boisterous
SSC MTS Tier-1 14.10.2024 (Shift-I)

(a) Noisy (b) Benevolent
(c) Buoyant (d) Quiet

Ans. (d)

'Quiet' is the most appropriate antonym of 'boisterous.' While 'boisterous' means noisy and energetic, 'quiet' means calm and silent.

Benevolent means kind and well-meaning.

Buoyant means cheerful and optimistic.

771. Hollow SSC MTS Tier-1 09.10.2024 (Shift-I)

(a) Spurious (b) Worthwhile
(c) Crafty (d) Arched

Ans. (b)

'Worthwhile' is the most appropriate antonym of 'Hollow'. 'Hollow' means having a space inside, while 'worthwhile' suggests something is valuable or beneficial.

Spurious means false or fake.

Crafty means cunning or deceitful.

Arched means curved.

772. Bulging SSC MTS Tier-1 08.10.2024 (Shift-I)

(a) Contracting (b) Swelling

(c) Hanging (d) Weeping

Ans. (a)

'Contracting' is the most appropriate antonym for 'bulging.' While 'bulging' means swelling outward, 'contracting' means becoming smaller or tighter.

Swelling is a synonym for 'bulging.'

Hanging does not fit the context.

Weeping means shedding tears.

773. Entice SSC MTS Tier-1 07.10.2024 (Shift-I)

(a) Allure (b) Repulse

(c) Tangle (d) Invite

Ans. (b)

The most appropriate antonym for 'entice' is 'repulse'. While 'entice' means to attract or lure, 'repulse' means to repel or drive away.

Allure is a synonym for 'entice.'

Tangle means to twist together.

Invite means to request or ask.

SSC MTS 2023

774. Viscous SSC MTS 02.05.2023 (Shift-I)

(a) Grim (b) Brutal

(c) Watery (d) Thick

Ans. (c)

Viscous means having a thick, sticky consistency between solid and liquid. Hence, its antonym is 'watery'.

775. We should have warned you that they were coming.

SSC MTS 03.05.2023 (Shift-I)

(a) waked (b) imperiled

(c) predicted (d) prepared

Ans. (b)

Warned means inform someone in advance of an impending or possible danger, problem, or other unpleasant situation. Hence, its antonym is 'imperiled'.

776. A war has been unleashed on financial untouchability.

SSC MTS 03.05.2023 (Shift-II)

(a) confined (b) unchained

(c) regarded (d) free

Ans. (a)

Unleashed means release from a leash or restraint. Hence, its antonym is 'confined'.

777. Social justice has been one of the cherished goals of the makers of our Constitution. SSC MTS 03.05.2023 (Shift-III)

(a) relished (b) valued

(c) treasured (d) despised

Ans. (d)

Cherished means protect and care for (someone) lovingly. Hence, its antonym is 'despised'.

778. So it would appear that from now on I am going to have to be more (tactful) and diplomatic in my meanderings. SSC MTS 04.05.2023 (Shift-I)

(a) Sycophantic (b) Fawning

(c) Grovelling (d) Ungracious

Ans. (d)

Tactful means having or showing adroitness and sensitivity in dealing with others or with difficult issues. Hence, its antonym is 'ungracious'.

779. Any book on any subject risks irrelevance or smallness compared to this (behemoth).

SSC MTS 04.05.2023 (Shift-III)

(a) Monster (b) Colossus

(c) Dreadnought (d) Midget

Ans. (d)

Behemoth means a huge or monstrous creature. Hence, its antonym is 'midget'.

780. Abstract SSC MTS 08.05.2023 (Shift-II)

(a) Transcend (b) Romantic

(c) Utopian (d) Concrete

Ans. (d)

Abstract means existing in thought or as an idea but not having a physical or concrete existence. Hence, its antonym is 'concrete'.

781. Analogous SSC MTS 08.05.2023 (Shift-III)

(a) Matching (b) Puzzle

(c) Straight (d) Dissimilar

Ans. (d)

Analogous means comparable in certain respects, typically in a way that makes clearer the nature of the things compared. Hence, its antonym is 'dissimilar'.

782. Reverence SSC MTS 09.05.2023 (Shift-III)

(a) Venerate (b) Honour

(c) Scorn (d) Deference

Ans. (c)

Reverence means deep respect for someone or something. Hence, its antonym is 'scorn'.

Venerate means honour.

783. It was a very generous and jolly voice. SSC MTS 09.05.2023 (Shift-III)

(a) morose (b) tabular

(c) festive (d) witty

Ans. (a)

Jolly means happy and cheerful. Hence, its antonym is 'morose'.

Witty means intelligent.

784. Malign SSC MTS 10.05.2023 (Shift-I)

(a) Praise (b) Align

(c) Cheerful (d) Harangue

Ans. (a)

Malign means speak about (someone) in a spitefully critical manner. Hence, its antonym is 'praise'.

785. Apprentice SSC MTS 10.05.2023 (Shift-II)

(a) Crude (b) Neophyte

(c) Veteran (d) Essential

Ans. (c)

Apprentice means a person who is learning a trade from a skilled employer, having agreed to work for a fixed period at low wages. Hence, its antonym is 'veteran'.

Crude means rough or rude.

Neophyte means new person/beginner.

786. The lens in this collection is focused very carefully upon the (quotidian), with all of its utterly familiar vexations. SSC MTS 10.05.2023 (Shift-II)

(a) Mandatory (b) Normal

(c) Sporadic (d) Obligatory

Ans. (c)

Quotidian means of or occurring every day; daily. Hence, its antonym is 'sporadic'.

787. The company has responded (sluggishly) to these changes in technology. SSC MTS 10.05.2023 (Shift-III)

(a) Lethargically (b) Similarly

(c) Apathetically (d) Promptly

Ans. (d)

Sluggishly means in a slow-moving or inactive manner. Hence, its antonym is 'promptly'.

788. Rigid SSC MTS 10.05.2023 (Shift-III)

(a) Superior (b) Distaste

(c) Satiation (d) Flexible

Ans. (d)

Rigid means unable to bend or be forced out of shape; not flexible. Hence, its antonym is 'flexible'.

789. The new government's domestic policies could easily undermine the main foreign policy.

SSC MTS 11.05.2023 (Shift-I)

(a) Cripple (b) Weaken

(c) Spoil (d) Enhance

Ans. (d)

Undermine means erode the base or foundation of (a rock formation). Hence, its antonym is 'enhance'.

790. Anomaly SSC MTS 11.05.2023 (Shift-III)
(a) Omen (b) Tangible
(c) Regularity (d) Tangent

Ans. (c)

Anomaly means something that deviates from what is standard, normal, or expected. Hence, its antonym is 'regularity'.

791. Adhere SSC MTS 12.05.2023 (Shift-I)
(a) Establish (b) Approve
(c) Compel (d) Condemn

Ans. (d)

Adhere means stick fast to (a surface or substance). Hence, its antonym is 'condemn'.

792. For years he pursued a (vendetta) against the Morris family. SSC MTS 12.05.2023 (Shift-I)
(a) conflict (b) traduce
(c) tirade (d) harmony

Ans. (d)

Vendetta means a prolonged bitter quarrel with or campaign against someone. Hence, its antonym is 'harmony'.

793. An (unsullied) safety record swelled pride in concorde's technical achievement as the years passed. SSC MTS 12.05.2023 (Shift-II)
(a) undefiled (b) impeccable
(c) tarnished (d) perfect

Ans. (c)

Unsullied means not spoiled or made impure. Hence, its antonym is 'tarnished'.

Undefiled means not made corrupt, impure, or unclean.

Impeccable means in accordance with the highest standards; faultless.

794. Doze SSC MTS 12.05.2023 (Shift-III)
(a) Cold (b) Neglect
(c) Snooze (d) Wake

Ans. (d)

Doze means sleep lightly. Hence, its antonym is 'wake'.

Neglect means fail to care for properly.

Snooze means have a short, light sleep, especially during the day.

795. Our financial situation had become (precarious). SSC MTS 16.05.2023 (Shift-III)
(a) insecure (b) stable
(c) delicate (d) noisy

Ans. (b)

Precarious means not securely held or in position; dangerously likely to fall or collapse. Hence, its antonym is 'stable'.

796. Many children still do not have access to quality education that will harness their inherent abilities and talent. SSC MTS 17.05.2023 (Shift-I)
(a) direct (b) exploit
(c) handle (d) misapply

Ans. (d)

Harness means control and make use of (natural resources), especially to produce energy. Hence, its antonym is 'misapply'.

797. Suspicion SSC MTS 17.05.2023 (Shift-I)
(a) Niggle (b) Tremor
(c) Conviction (d) Uncertainty

Ans. (c)

Suspicion means a feeling or thought that something is possible, likely, or true. Hence, its antonym is 'conviction'.

Niggle means cause slight but persistent annoyance, discomfort, or anxiety.

Tremor means an involuntary quivering movement.

Uncertainty means the state of being uncertain.

798. Culpable SSC MTS 17.05.2023 (Shift-II)
(a) Rigorous (b) Reasonable
(c) Innocent (d) Edible

Ans. (c)

Culpable means deserving blame. Hence, its antonym is 'innocent'.

Rigorous means extremely thorough, exhaustive, or accurate.

799. We will brush out the damp hair. SSC MTS 17.05.2023 (Shift-III)
(a) droughty (b) saturated
(c) sticky (d) moist

Ans. (a)

Damp means slightly wet. Hence, its antonym is 'droughty'.

Saturated means holding as much water or moisture as can be absorbed; thoroughly soaked.

800. Discreet SSC MTS 18.05.2023 (Shift-I)
(a) Release (b) Zenith
(c) Open (d) Lose

Ans. (c)

Discreet means careful and circumspect in one's speech or actions, especially in order to avoid causing offense or to gain an advantage. Hence, its antonym is 'open'.

Zenith means the time at which something is most powerful or successful.

801. Maladroit SSC MTS 18.05.2023 (Shift-II)
(a) Skilful (b) Arrogant
(c) Inept (d) Awkward

Ans. (a)

Maladroit means ineffective or bungling; clumsy. Hence, its antonym is 'skilful'.

802. We frequently congratulate people on their accomplishment in becoming famous, but we seldom ever talk about the price of fame. SSC MTS 18.05.2023 (Shift-II)
(a) Execution (b) Feat
(c) Fiasco (d) Triumph

Ans. (c)

Accomplishment means something that has been achieved successfully. Hence, its antonym is 'fiasco'.

Execution means the carrying out of a plan, order, or course of action.

803. Administer SSC MTS 18.05.2023 (Shift-III)
(a) Steady (b) Forego
(c) Entertaining (d) Pictural

Ans. (b)

Administer means manage and be responsible for the running of (a business, organisation, etc.). Hence, its antonym is 'forego'.

Steady means firmly fixed, supported, or balanced; not shaking or moving.

Pictorial means relating to or consisting of pictures.

804. Tangle SSC MTS 19.05.2023 (Shift-I)
(a) Jam (b) Labyrinth
(c) Simple (d) Coil

Ans. (c)

Tangle means twist together into a confused mass. Hence, its antonym is 'simple'.

Jam means squeeze or pack tightly into a specified space.

Labyrinth means a complicated irregular network of passages or paths in which it is difficult to find one's way; a maze.

Coil means arrange or wind (something long and flexible) in a joined sequence of concentric circles or rings.

805. Hyped SSC MTS 19.05.2023 (Shift-II)
(a) Dilate (b) Upped
(c) Reduced (d) Parlayed

Ans. (c)

Hyped means promote or publicise (a product or idea) intensively, often exaggerating its importance or benefits. Hence, its antonym is 'reduced'.

Dilate means make or become wider, larger, or more open.

Upped means increased in level, amount, or intensity.

Parlayed means turned an initial stake or winnings from a previous bet into (a greater amount) by gambling.

806. She ventured to go back to the tree of the (tryst), the mulberry with the shining white fruit.
SSC MTS 19.05.2023 (Shift-III)
(a) Rendezvous (b) Engagement
(c) Date (d) Separation

Ans. (d)

Tryst means a private, romantic rendezvous between lovers. Hence, its antonym is 'separation'.

Rendezvous means a meeting at an agreed time and place, typically between two people.

807. Crude SSC MTS 13.06.2023 (Shift-I)
(a) Beastly (b) Ripe
(c) Stubble (d) Intense

Ans. (b)

Crude means in a natural or raw state; not yet processed or refined. Hence, its antonym is 'ripe'.

Beastly means very unpleasant.

Stubble means the cut stalks of grain plants left sticking out of the ground after the grain is harvested.

Intense means of extreme force, degree, or strength.

808. Mound SSC MTS 14.06.2023 (Shift-II)
(a) Victory (b) Valley
(c) Bell (d) Prominence

Ans. (b)

Mound means a rounded mass projecting above a surface. Hence, its antonym is 'valley'.

809. The Prime Minister is making no (rash) promises SSC MTS 15.06.2023 (Shift-II)
(a) considerate (b) immature
(c) audacious (d) bold

Ans. (a)

Rash means displaying or proceeding from a lack of careful consideration of the possible consequences of an action. Hence, its antonym is 'considerate'.

Immature means having or showing emotional or intellectual development appropriate to someone younger.

Audacious means showing a willingness to take surprisingly bold risks.

Bold means showing a willingness to take risks; confident and courageous.

810. Glamour SSC MTS 16.06.2023 (Shift-I)
(a) Charm (b) Magnanimous
(c) Appeal (d) Dullness

Ans. (d)

Glamour means the attractive or exciting quality that makes certain people or things seem appealing or special. Hence, its antonym is 'dullness'.

Magnanimous means very generous or forgiving, especially toward a rival or someone less powerful.

Appeal means the quality of being attractive or interesting.

811. Impertinent SSC MTS 16.06.2023 (Shift-II)
(a) Polite (b) Irrelevant
(c) Insolent (d) Personal

Ans. (a)

Impertinent means not showing proper respect; rude. Hence, its antonym is 'polite'.

Irrelevant means not connected with or relevant to something.

Insolent means showing a rude and arrogant lack of respect.

812. Our children need <u>vital</u> lessons in wealth management.
SSC MTS 19.06.2023 (Shift-I)
(a) clever (b) superfluous
(c) organic (d) healthy

Ans. (b)

Vital means absolutely necessary or important; essential. Hence, its antonym is 'superfluous'.

Organic means relating to or derived from living matter.

813. There is a point at which fear turn to <u>insanity</u>. SSC MTS 19.06.2023 (Shift-II)
(a) Wisdom (b) Lunacy
(c) Absurdity (d) Frenzy

Ans. (a)

Insanity means the state of being seriously mentally ill; madness. Hence, its antonym is 'wisdom'.

Lunacy means the state of being a lunatic; insanity.

Absurdity means the quality or state of being ridiculous or wildly unreasonable.

Frenzy means a state or period of uncontrolled excitement or wild behaviour.

814. Topple SSC MTS 19.06.2023 (Shift-II)
(a) Tumble (b) Steady
(c) Fumble (d) Plunge

Ans. (b)

Topple means overbalance or become unsteady and fall slowly. Hence, its antonym is 'steady'.

Tumble means fall suddenly, clumsily, or headlong.

Fumble means use the hands clumsily while doing or handling something.

Plunge means jump or dive quickly and energetically.

815. Misdemeanour
SSC MTS 19.06.2023 (Shift-III)
(a) Offense (b) Amalgamation
(c) Obedience (d) Gullible

Ans. (c)

Misdemeanour means a minor wrongdoing. Hence, its antonym is 'obedience'.

Offense means a breach of a law or rule; an illegal act.

Amalgamation means the action, process, or result of combining or uniting.

Gullible means easily persuaded to believe something; credulous.

816. There is an unhealthy tendency to (subjugate) films to the dictates raising public awareness.
SSC MTS 19.06.2023 (Shift-III)
(a) colonise (b) modest
(c) vanquish (d) liberate

Ans. (d)

Subjugate means bring under domination or control, especially by conquest. Hence, its antonym is 'liberate'.

Colonise means send settlers to (a place) and establish political control over it.

Modest means unassuming or moderate in the estimation of one's abilities or achievements.

Vanquish means defeat thoroughly.

817. Incompetence SSC MTS 20.06.2023 (Shift-I)
(a) Interfere (b) Attitude
(c) Efficient (d) Caustic

Ans. (c)

Incompetence means inability to do something successfully; ineptitude. Hence, its antonym is 'efficient'.

Interfere means prevent (a process or activity) from continuing or being carried out properly.

Caustic means able to burn or corrode organic tissue by chemical action.

818. Empathetic SSC MTS 01.09.2023 (Shift-III)
(a) Lonely (b) Merciless
(c) Charismatic (d) Frustrated

Ans. (b)

'Empathetic' means showing an ability to understand and share the feelings of another. Hence, 'merciless' is its antonym.

Charismatic means charming and fascinating.

Frustrated means irritated and angry.

819. Ecstasy SSC MTS 04.09.2023 (Shift-II)
(a) Euphoria (b) Coarse
(c) Natural (d) Despair

Ans. (d)

'Ecstasy' means 'happiness'. Hence, 'despair' means 'sorrow' is its antonym.
Euphoria means extreme excitement or pleasure.
Coarse means rough.

820. Humane SSC MTS 05.09.2023 (Shift-II)
(a) Proud (b) Kind
(c) Cruel (d) Imperfect

Ans. (c)

'Humane' means 'kind'. Hence, 'cruel' is its antonym.

821. The company is looking for some ....(idle) workers who can join the organisation immediately. SSC MTS 05.09.2023 (Shift-II)
(a) diligent (b) coy (c) callous (d) sober

Ans. (a)

The word in bracket 'idle' means lazy. Hence, its antonym is 'diligent' which means hardworking.
Callous means cruel.
Sober means serious and sensible.

822. Humility SSC MTS 05.09.2023 (Shift-II)
(a) Shyness (b) Timidity
(c) Arrogance (d) Obedience

Ans. (c)

Humility means 'kindness'. Hence, 'arrogance' is its antonym.
Timidity means cowardice.
Obedience means to follow orders willingly.

823. Enormous SSC MTS 06.09.2023 (Shift-I)
(a) Tiny (b) Inapposite
(c) Irrelevant (d) Gigantic

Ans. (a)

Enormous means 'large'. Hence, 'tiny' is its antonym.
Inapposite means inappropriate or wrong.
Irrelevant means useless.
Gigantic means huge.

824. Annoy SSC MTS 06.09.2023 (Shift-I)
(a) Gratify (b) Vex
(c) Irritate (d) Thrill

Ans. (a)

'Gratify' means to give someone joy, thrill, excitement or pleasure. Hence, it is the antonym of 'annoy'.
Vax means to irritate.

825. Authentic SSC MTS 11.09.2023 (Shift-I)
(a) Moderate (b) Actual
(c) False (d) Wise

Ans. (c)

'Authentic' means genuine or real. Hence, its antonym is 'false' which means artificial or fake.

826. Nonchalant SSC MTS 08.09.2023 (Shift-II)
(a) Flexible (b) Caring
(c) Marvelous (d) Covert

Ans. (b)

Nonchalant means 'uncaring and unconcerned'. Hence, 'caring' is its antonym.
Flexible means capable of bending without breaking.
Marvellous means beautiful and grand.
Covert means hidden.

827. Strengthen SSC MTS 11.09.2023 (Shift-II)
(a) Debilitate (b) Strain
(c) Fortify (d) Ascend

Ans. (a)

Strengthen means to make or become stronger. Hence, its antonym is 'debilitate' which means make (someone) very weak.
Strain means to put pressure on.
Fortify means to protect.
Ascend means to rise.

828. Fame SSC MTS 11.09.2023 (Shift-II)
(a) Name (b) Shame
(c) Scandal (d) Stingy

Ans. (b)

Fame means honour and popularity for something positive. Hence, its antonym is 'shame'.
Scandal means an unmoral act leading to public outrage.
Stingy means not willing to spend money.

829. Cheap SSC MTS 11.09.2023 (Shift-II)
(a) Expensive (b) Ignorant
(c) Old (d) Untangle

Ans. (a)

The antonym of 'cheap' is 'expensive'.
Ignorant means stupid and careless.
Untangle means to free from confusion.

830. A .... (distinct) sense of restlessness was bothering me when I left the cemetery. SSC MTS 13.09.2023 (Shift-I)
(a) terrible (b) critical (c) prior (d) vague

Ans. (d)

The word 'vague' meaning 'not clear or distinct' is an antonym of 'distinct' that will fill in the given blank.
Critical means important.
Prior means before.

831. They waited with anxiety for the final results. SSC MTS 13.09.2023 (Shift-I)
(a) Shrewdness (b) Wilderness
(c) Feebleness (d) Calmness

Ans. (d)

The word 'calmness' is an antonym of the underlined word 'anxiety'.
Shrewdness means cleverness.
Wilderness means forests.
Feebleness means weakness.

832. Addiction of drugs proved detrimental for his health. SSC MTS 14.09.2023 (Shift-I)
(a) Impartial (b) Potential
(c) Beneficial (d) Differential

Ans. (c)

The underlined word 'detrimental' means something damaging or having bad effects. Hence, its antonym is 'beneficial'.
Impartial means treating everyone equally.
Potential means ability.
Differential means showing differences.

SSC Selection Post 2024

833. The bowler signalled the wicket-keeper to catch the ball. SSC SP 20.06.2024 (Shift-I)
(a) Give (b) Change
(c) Throw (d) Drop

Ans. (d)

The antonym of 'catch' is 'to drop'.

834. The students were asked to assemble in the meeting hall. SSC SP 20.06.2024 (Shift-I)
(a) Pull together (b) Dispersed
(c) Collect (d) Gather

Ans. (b)

Assemble means to gather. Hence, its antonym is 'dispersed' which means to scatter.

835. It was certainly a cowardly act. SSC SP 20.06.2024 (Shift-IV)
(a) Believable (b) Brave
(c) Fearful (d) Comfortable

Ans. (b)

Cowardly means lacking courage. Hence, its antonym is 'brave'.

836. A frugal lifestyle doesn't necessarily reflect someone's personality. SSC SP 20.06.2024 (Shift-IV)
(a) Conventional (b) Cooperative
(c) Dynamic (d) Wasteful

Ans. (d)

Frugal means characterised by or reflecting economy in the use of resources or not wasting money. Hence, its antonym is 'wasteful'.

Conventional means traditional or usual.

Cooperative means marked by a willingness and ability to work with others.

Dynamic means marked by usually continuous and productive activity or change.

837. His **liberal** policies were responsible for progress in the community.
SSC SP 20.06.2024 (Shift-IV)
(a) Ccentral (b) Ineffectual
(c) Hysterical (d) Conservative

Ans. (d)

Liberal means not bound by authoritarianism, orthodoxy, or traditional forms. Hence, its antonym is 'conservative' which is marked by traditionalism.

Ineffectual means not producing the proper or intended effect.

Hysterical means feeling or showing extreme and unrestrained emotion.

SSC Selection Post 2023

838. Prudent SSC SP 27.06.2023 (Shift-IV)
(a) Wise (b) Atrocious
(c) Stupid (d) Crafty

Ans. (c)

Prudent means wise. Hence, its antonym is 'stupid'.

Atrocious means terrible.

Crafty means manipulative.

839. Hasten SSC SP 27.06.2023 (Shift-IV)
(a) Triumph (b) Spooky
(c) Present (d) Dawdle

Ans. (d)

Hasten means to walk quickly. Hence, its antonym is 'dawdle' which means to move slowly in a relaxed manner.

840. The old man was not only infirm but also blind and was unable to move around by himself.
SSC SP 27.06.2023 (Shift-III)
(a) Robust (b) Diffident
(c) Anaemic (d) Hospitable

Ans. (a)

Infirm means weak. Hence, its antonym is 'robust' which means strong and healthy.

Diffident means hesitant in acting or speaking through lack of self-confidence.

Anaemic means lacking blood.

Hospitable means friendly.

841. Keen SSC SP 27.06.2023 (Shift-III)
(a) Insensitive (b) Accurate
(c) Perceptive (d) Subtle

Ans. (d)

Keen means eager. Hence, its antonym is 'subtle' which means so delicate that it is not noticed.

Accurate means exact or precise.

Perceptive means thoughtful.

842. Artificial
My uncle, who is a native of Australia, is a logical thinker and says that natural and unnatural stones both look beautiful in gold jewellery. SSC SP 27.06.2023 (Shift-III)
(a) Unnatural (b) Native
(c) Natural (d) Logical

Ans. (c)

Artificial means made or produced by human beings rather than occurring naturally. Hence, its antonym is 'natural'.

843. Precious stones are expensive because they are not common.
SSC SP 27.06.2023 (Shift-I)
(a) Abundant (b) Rare
(c) Natural (d) Extinct

Ans. (b)

Common means occurring, found, or done often; prevalent. Hence, its antonym is 'rare'.

844. Suraj has always shown a willingness to accept and respect the differences in others' lives with impartiality and avoid prejudice
SSC SP 28.06.2023 (Shift-III)
(a) Willingness (b) Impartiality
(c) Avoid (d) Differences

Ans. (b)

Prejudice means preconceived opinion that is not based on reason or actual experience. Hence, its antonym is 'impartiality'.

845. Elegant
The table cloth on my brother's study table was classic and splendid, yet my mother found it very awkward and odd.
SSC SP 30.06.2023 (Shift-III)
(a) Classic (b) Odd
(c) Splendid (d) Awkward

Ans. (b)

Elegant means pleasingly graceful and stylish in appearance or manner. Hence, its antonym is 'odd'.

846. This is a/an *abundance* of fertile soil and magnificent grazing land.
SSC SP 27.06.2023 (Shift-II)
(a) dearth (b) plenitude
(c) adequacy (d) plethora

Ans. (a)

Abundance means a very large quantity of something. Hence, its antonym is 'dearth'.

Plenitude means an abundance.

Adequacy means the state or quality of being adequate.

Plethora means a large or excessive amount of something.

847. **Despair** SSC SP 28.06.2023 (Shift-I)
(a) Distant (b) Sorrow
(c) Optimism (d) Distinct

Ans. (c)

Despair means the complete loss or absence of hope. Hence, its antonym is 'optimism'.

848. The **melancholy** song brought tears to my eyes. SSC SP 28.06.2023 (Shift-IV)
(a) Seclusion (b) Ecstasy
(c) Tremendousness (d) Aesthetic

Ans. (b)

Melancholy means a feeling of pensive sadness, typically with no obvious cause. Hence, its antonym is 'ecstasy'.

Seclusion means the state of being private and away from other people.

Tremendousness means very great in amount, scale, or intensity.

Aesthetic means concerned with beauty or the appreciation of beauty.

849. Humane SSC SP 28.06.2023 (Shift-IV)
(a) Cordial (b) Merciless
(c) Forgiving (d) Generous

Ans. (b)

Humane means having or showing compassion or benevolence. Hence, its antonym is 'merciless'.

Cordial means warm and friendly.

Generous means showing a readiness to give more of something than is strictly necessary or expected.

850. Many sculptures of our history are like the unravelled path as we cannot garble and there is a lot of work that is yet to be interpreted or translated. SSC SP 30.06.2023 (Shift-III)
(a) Unravelled (b) Garble
(c) Interpreted (d) Translated

Ans. (a)

Garble means reproduce (a message, sound, or transmission) in a confused and distorted way. Hence, its antonym is 'unravelled'.

Unravelled means undo (twisted, knitted, or woven threads).

Interpreted means explain the meaning of (information, words, or actions).

SSC Selection Post 2022

851. Native SSC SP 01.08.2022 (Shift-I)
(a) Foreign (b) State
(c) Distant (d) Innate

Ans. (a)

Native refers to the original habitant of a place. Hence, its antonym is 'foreign'.

Innate means natural.

852. Majority SSC SP 01.08.2022 (Shift-I)
(a) Produce (b) Matrimony
(c) Adulthood (d) Minority

Ans. (d)

The antonym of 'majority' is 'minority'.

Matrimony means marriage.

853. Zeal SSC SP 01.08.2022
(a) Anger (b) Ardour (c) Allure (d) Apathy

Ans. (d)

Zeal means great energy or enthusiasm in pursuit of a cause or an objective. Hence, its antonym is 'apathy'.

Ardour means enthusiasm or passion.

Allure means the quality of being powerfully and mysteriously attractive or fascinating.

854. Delusion SSC SP 01.08.2022 (Shift-I)
(a) Reality (b) Fallacy
(c) Phantasm (d) Illusion

Ans. (a)

Delusion means something that is falsely or delusively believed. Hence, its antonym is 'reality'.

Fallacy means a false or mistaken idea.

Phantasm means a product of fantasy.

Illusion means a misleading image presented to the vision.

855. Despite the criticism, the government did not <u>rescind</u> the policy. SSC SP 02.08.2022 (Shift-II)
(a) Reinstate (b) Relegate
(c) Rewind (d) Revoke

Ans. (a)

Rescind means revoke, cancel, or repeal (a law, order, or agreement). Hence, its antonym is 'reinstate'.

Relegate means consign or dismiss to an inferior rank or position.

Rewind means wind (a tape or film) back to the beginning.

Revoke means put an end to the validity or operation of (a decree, decision or promise).

856. The orator gave his best <u>winsome</u> smile. SSC SP 04.08.2022 (Shift-III)
(a) Cunning (b) Satisfying
(c) Repelling (d) Winning

Ans. (c)

Winsome means attractive or appealing in appearance or character. Hence, its antonym is 'repelling'.

Cunning means having or showing skill in achieving one's ends by deceit or evasion.

857. The <u>penurious</u> little boy could not get the school lunch. SSC SP 05.08.2022 (Shift-II)
(a) Lazy (b) Naughty
(c) Unlawful (d) Munificent

Ans. (d)

Penurious means extremely poor; poverty-stricken. Hence, its antonym is 'munificent'.

SSC Steno 2024

858. Endless SSC Steno 11.12.2024 (Shift-I)
(a) Limited (b) Encompass
(c) Limitless (d) Associate

Ans. (a)

The most appropriate antonym of 'endless' is 'limited'.

Encompass means to include comprehensively.

859. Deplore SSC Steno 11.12.2024 (Shift-I)
(a) Ridicule (b) Prolong
(c) Decode (d) Relish

Ans. (d)

The most appropriate antonym of 'deplore' is 'relish' because 'deplore' means to feel or express strong disapproval, while 'relish' means to take great pleasure in something.

Prolong means to extend the duration of.

Decode means to convert into a readable form.

860. Identify the most appropriate antonym of the underlined word in the following sentence.
Dipesh loves to answer his boss' questions in <u>tactful ways</u>. SSC Steno 11.12.2024 (Shift-I)
(a) Affordable (b) Humble
(c) Ambiguous (d) Undiplomatic

Ans. (d)

The antonym of 'tactful' is 'undiplomatic'. Being tactful means handling situations with skill and sensitivity, while being undiplomatic means lacking these qualities and being blunt or insensitive.

861. Prefer SSC Steno 11.12.2024 (Shift-I)
(a) Disjoint (b) Choose
(c) Dislike (d) Regret

Ans. (c)

The antonym of 'prefer' is 'dislike'. Prefer means to favour something over another, while dislike means to have an aversion to something.

862. His <u>gloomy</u> demeanour is often criticised. SSC Steno 11.12.2024 (Shift-I)
(a) lively (b) slimy
(c) highly (d) poorly

Ans. (a)

The antonym of 'gloomy' is 'lively'. Gloomy means dark or pessimistic, while 'lively' means full of life and energy.

863. His request was <u>overlooked</u> by the management. SSC Steno 11.12.2024 (Shift-II)
(a) considered (b) ignored
(c) neglected (d) disdained

Ans. (a)

The antonym of 'overlooked' is 'considered'. The verb 'overlooked' means ignored or neglected, implying a lack of attention. The verb 'considered' means given thought or attention, making it the opposite of 'overlooked'.

864. Inquisitive SSC Steno 11.12.2024 (Shift-II)
(a) Curious (b) Dull
(c) Uninterested (d) Indolent

Ans. (c)

The antonym for 'inquisitive' is 'uninterested'.

'Inquisitive' means curious or eager for knowledge, while 'uninterested' means lacking interest or curiosity, making them opposites.

865. Mutely SSC Steno 11.12.2024 (Shift-II)
(a) Forcefully (b) Silently
(c) Loudly (d) Promptly

Ans. (c)

The word 'mutely' means to do something without speaking or silently. The most appropriate antonym from the given options would be 'Loudly', since it represents doing something with sound or noise.

866. She looked tired and <u>sallow</u> after the long day she'd had. SSC Steno 11.12.2024 (Shift-II)
(a) pallid (b) livid
(c) flushed (d) paled

Ans. (c)

'Flushed' is the opposite of 'sallow', which means a yellow or pale brown colour, typically associated with illness or fatigue. 'Flushed' indicates a healthy, reddish colour in the face, making it the most appropriate antonym.

867. Amrit felt a chill run down his spine as Mrityu gazed at him mid-conversation. SSC Steno 11.12.2024 (Shift-II)

(a) shot (b) glanced
(c) stared (d) shouted

Ans. (b)

'Glanced' is the opposite of 'gazed', which means to look steadily and intently.

'Glanced' indicates a brief or fleeting look, making it the most appropriate antonym.

868. The enemy, even if it is a child, is a challenge and needs to be removed from his path. SSC Steno 11.12.2024 (Shift-II)

(a) problem (b) solution
(c) nuisance (d) threat

Ans. (b)

'Solution' is the opposite of 'challenge', which means a difficult task or problem. 'Solution' indicates the resolution or answer to a problem, making it the most appropriate antonym.

869. I am astonished to see her *mercurial* demeanour in making any task a success. SSC Steno 11.12.2024 (Shift-II)

(a) capricious
(b) erratic
(c) fluctuant
(d) invariable

Ans. (d)

'Invariable' is the opposite of 'mercurial', which means subject to sudden or unpredictable changes in mood or behaviour. 'Invariable' means unchanging or constant, which accurately contrasts with the unpredictability of being mercurial.

870. Intent SSC Steno 11.12.2024 (Shift-II)

(a) Uncertain (b) Rigid
(c) Alert (d) Involved

Ans. (a)

'Uncertain' is the opposite of 'intent', which means having a firm purpose or determination. 'Uncertain' indicates a lack of clarity or decisiveness, suggesting that someone is unsure or wavering in their intentions.

871. This book is written by a famous author named GH Sullivan. SSC Steno 11.12.2024 (Shift-III)

(a) illegible (b) unknown
(c) uniform (d) illiterate

Ans. (b)

The word 'famous' means well-known and recognised by many people. The antonym of 'famous' is 'unknown', which describes someone or something that is not known or recognised.

872. Select the most appropriate antonym of the word 'Virtue' from the given sentence. Every person's actions have an innate power that determines the appropriate reward or punishment in addition to a moral value that produces merit or demerit. SSC Steno 11.12.2024 (Shift-III)

(a) merit (b) appropriate
(c) demerit (d) innate

Ans. (c)

The word 'virtue' refers to a moral excellence or a good quality. The antonym of 'virtue' is 'demerit', which means a fault or a bad quality.

873. The detective's astute observations led to the discovery of crucial evidence, unlike his oblivious partner. SSC Steno 11.12.2024 (Shift-III)

(a) idiotic (b) keen
(c) attentive (d) sharp

Ans. (a)

The word 'astute' means having or showing an ability to accurately assess situations and turn this to one's advantage. The antonym 'idiotic' means very stupid or foolish, which is the opposite of 'astute'.

874. Stretch SSC Steno 11.12.2024 (Shift-III)

(a) Lessen (b) Range
(c) Scope (d) Scale

Ans. (a)

The antonym of 'stretch' is 'lessen'. 'Stretch' means to extend, while 'lessen' means to reduce.

875. Accelerate SSC Steno 11.12.2024 (Shift-III)

(a) Heighten (b) Escalate
(c) Downsize (d) Augment

Ans. (c)

The antonym of 'accelerate' is 'downsize'. 'Accelerate' means to increase speed, while 'downsize' means to reduce in size or number.

876. Curiosity SSC Steno 11.12.2024 (Shift-III)

(a) Inquisitiveness (b) Indifference
(c) Restore (d) Lament

Ans. (b)

The antonym of 'curiosity' is 'indifference'. Curiosity implies a desire to know or learn, whereas indifference means a lack of interest or concern.

877. Reliable SSC Steno 10.12.2024 (Shift-I)

(a) Unknown (b) Untrustworthy
(c) Uncommon (d) Unfamiliar

Ans. (b)

The most appropriate antonym of the word 'reliable' is 'untrustworthy'. While 'reliable' means dependable and trustworthy, 'untrustworthy' means not reliable or dependable.

878. Admiration SSC Steno 10.12.2024 (Shift-I)

(a) Cognisance (b) Contempt
(c) Accomplish (d) Diminish

Ans. (b)

The most appropriate antonym of the word 'admiration' is 'contempt'. While 'admiration' means respect and warm approval, 'contempt' means a feeling that someone or something is worthless or beneath consideration, providing a clear contrast.

879. Rukhsana was left alone in the house again, but fear was now her constant companion. SSC Steno 10.12.2024 (Shift-I)

(a) boring (b) steady
(c) changing (d) friendly

Ans. (c)

The most appropriate antonym of the word 'constant' in this context is 'changing'. 'Constant' means unchanging or continuous, while 'changing' means variable or not staying the same, providing a clear contrast.

880. Select the most appropriate antonym of the word 'Concur' from the given sentence. SSC Steno 10.12.2024 (Shift-I)

Every time they met, he found it difficult to resist her odd magic.

(a) found (b) difficult
(c) resist (d) met

Ans. (c)

The most appropriate antonym of the word 'concur' is 'resist.'

While 'concur' means to agree or be in harmony, 'resist' means to oppose or withstand, providing a clear contrast.

881. Admonish SSC Steno 10.12.2024 (Shift-I)

(a) Abetment (b) Applaud
(c) Abide (d) Accede

Ans. (b)

The most appropriate antonym of the word 'admonish' is 'applaud'. While 'admonish' means to reprimand or scold, 'applaud' means to praise or commend, providing a clear contrast.

882. The development of the region also depended on the.............. (rapaciousness) of the corporate contribution via a social responsibility scheme. **SSC Steno 10.12.2024 (Shift-I)**

(a) generosity (b) voracity
(c) greed (d) violence

Ans. (a)

The most appropriate antonym of the word 'rapaciousness' is 'generosity'. While 'rapaciousness' means extreme greed, 'generosity' means the quality of being kind and giving, providing a clear contrast.

883. Amplify **SSC Steno 10.12.2024 (Shift-I)**

(a) Exaggerate (b) Lessen
(c) Dislike (d) Enrich

Ans. (b)

The most appropriate antonym of the word 'amplify' is 'lessen'. While 'amplify' means to increase or enlarge, 'lessen' means to decrease or reduce, providing a clear contrast.

884. The amateur proved them all wrong. **SSC Steno 10.12.2024 (Shift-I)**

(a) Assistant (b) Prefect
(c) Chef (d) Professional

Ans. (d)

The most appropriate antonym of the word 'amateur' is 'professional'. While 'amateur' refers to someone who engages in an activity as a hobby and lacks expertise, 'professional' refers to someone who is skilled and experienced in a particular field.

885. This narrow lane will take you to your destination. **SSC Steno 10.12.2024 (Shift-II)**

(a) mild (b) broad
(c) slender (d) straight

Ans. (b)

The most appropriate antonym for 'narrow' is 'broad'. 'Narrow' means limited in width; broad means wide in extent or range.

Mild means gentle or not severe.

Slender means slim or thin.

886. Exaggerate **SSC Steno 10.12.2024 (Shift-II)**

(a) Emphasise (b) Understate
(c) Embellish (d) Neglect

Ans. (b)

The most appropriate antonym for 'exaggerate' is 'understate'. 'Exaggerate' means to represent something as more significant than it is; understate means to represent something as less significant.

Emphasise means to give special importance.

Embellish means to make something more attractive by adding details.

Neglect means to fail to care for properly.

887. Fathomable **SSC Steno 10.12.2024 (Shift-II)**

(a) Inartistic
(b) Incoherent
(c) Inauspicious
(d) Incite

Ans. (b)

The most appropriate antonym for 'fathomable' is 'incoherent'. 'Fathomable' means understandable or comprehensible; inauspicious means not conducive to success or unpromising.

Other options

Inartistic means not artistic.

Incite means to encourage or stir up.

888. Inclusion **SSC Steno 10.12.2024 (Shift-II)**

(a) Gain (b) Boost
(c) Accrual (d) Omission

Ans. (d)

The most appropriate antonym for 'inclusion' is 'omission'. 'Inclusion' means the action or state of including or being included; omission means the action of excluding or leaving something out.

Boost means to increase or improve.

Accrual means the accumulation or increase of something over time.

889. The patient consumed mushrooms for hallucinatory experiences, but the doctor advised to consume only.........(hallucinogenic) drugs. **SSC Steno 10.12.2024 (Shift-II)**

(a) freaky (b) psychedelic
(c) regular (d) abnormal

Ans. (c)

The most appropriate antonym for 'hallucinogenic' is 'regular'. 'Hallucinogenic' means causing hallucinations; regular means normal or not causing hallucinations.

Freaky means strange or unusual.

Psychedelic means producing vivid visual or auditory experiences.

Abnormal means deviating from what is normal.

890. His was a stupendous performance in the competition. **SSC Steno 10.12.2024 (Shift-II)**

(a) Soothing (b) Unimpressive
(c) Mnemonic (d) Herculean

Ans. (b)

The most appropriate antonym for 'stupendous' is 'unimpressive'. 'Stupendous' means extremely impressive; unimpressive means not arousing admiration or interest.

Soothing means having a calming effect.

Mnemonic means aiding memory.

Herculean means requiring great strength or effort.

891. The team's performance was at its zenith in 2017. **SSC Steno 10.12.2024 (Shift-II)**

(a) Nadir (b) Peak
(c) Height (d) Sneak

Ans. (a)

'Nadir' is the most appropriate antonym for 'zenith'. Zenith means the highest point, while nadir means the lowest point.

Peak means the highest point.

Sneak means to move stealthily.

892. She made a courageous decision to quit her job. **SSC Steno 10.12.2024 (Shift-II)**

(a) coward (b) myopic
(c) calm (d) obstinate

Ans. (a)

'Coward' is the most appropriate antonym for 'courageous'. 'Courageous' means having bravery, while coward means lacking bravery.

Myopic means short-sighted.

Obstinate means stubborn.

893. My friend is not stubborn with regard to opinions; in fact, she is ....(intransigent). **SSC Steno 10.12.2024 (Shift-III)**

(a) pertinacious (b) obstinate
(c) subservient (d) tenacious

Ans. (c)

'Subservient' is the most appropriate antonym of 'intransigent', which means unwilling to change one's opinions or behaviour. Subservient means willing to obey others unquestioningly.

Pertinacious holding firmly to an opinion

Obstinate stubbornly refusing to change one's opinion

Tenacious tending to keep a firm hold on something

894. Latent SSC Steno 10.12.2024 (Shift-III)
(a) Early (b) Antique
(c) Manifest (d) Punctual
Ans. (c)
'Manifest' is the most appropriate antonym of 'latent', which means hidden or not yet developed.
Manifest means clear or obvious to the eye or mind.

895. A true friend always ………., but a selfish friend tries to mislead. SSC Steno 10.12.2024 (Shift-III)
(a) imbibes (b) deludes
(c) deplores (d) guides
Ans. (d)
'Guides' is the antonym of 'mislead'. Guiding means showing the way or directing, whereas misleading means causing someone to have the wrong idea or impression.
Imbibes means absorbs or assimilates.
Deludes means deceives or fools someone.
Deplores means to express strong disapproval of.

896. Only Mr. Sen's emotions were genuine, while others showed …………sadness at grandmother's death. SSC Steno 10.12.2024 (Shift-III)
(a) authentic (b) precise
(c) friendly (d) fake
Ans. (d)
'Fake' is the antonym of 'genuine'. Genuine means real or authentic, whereas fake means not real or counterfeit.
Precise means marked by exactness and accuracy of expression or detail.

897. Do not **linger** in the corridor. SSC Steno 10.12.2024 (Shift-III)
(a) delay (b) hasten
(c) idle (d) trifle
Ans. (b)
'Hasten' is the antonym of 'linger'. Hasten means to move or act quickly, which is the opposite of linger, meaning to stay in a place longer than necessary.

898. Languishing SSC Steno 10.12.2024 (Shift-III)
(a) Diminutive (b) Flourishing
(c) Mesmerising (d) Temporary
Ans. (b)
'Flourishing' is the antonym of 'languishing', which means to suffer or fail to make progress.
Flourishing means thriving or growing vigorously.

SSC Steno 2023

899. My favourite...... (deface) of his home is the large, farmhouse-style kitchen. SSC Steno 12.10.2023 (Shift-I)
(a) build (b) dimension
(c) regard (d) fact
Ans. (a)
'Deface' means to damage and spoil the appearance of something by writing or drawing on it. Hence, its antonym is 'build' which is the appropriate filler for the given blank.

900. Virtue SSC Steno 12.10.2023 (Shift-I)
(a) Acquire (b) Stout
(c) Precise (d) Vice
Ans. (d)
The word 'Virtue' means morals and values.
Hence, its antonym is 'Vice' which means bad habits.

901. Divulge
The culprit surprised everyone by opting to conceal the secret execution of his plans even after getting beaten by the police.
SSC Steno 12.10.2023 (Shift-I)
(a) Execution (b) Opting
(c) Conceal (d) Culprit
Ans. (c)
Divulge means make known (private or sensitive information); reveal. Hence, its antonym is 'Conceal' which means to hide.

902. Brave SSC Steno 12.10.2023 (Shift-I)
(a) Moving (b) Fearless
(c) Coward (d) Adulterous
Ans. (c)
Brave means ready to face and endure danger or pain; showing courage. Hence, its antonym is 'coward'.

903. It is a misconception that the more you learn, the more likely you are to succeed. SSC Steno 12.10.2023 (Shift-I)
(a) Hallucination (b) Fallacy
(c) Illusion (d) Certainty
Ans. (d)
'Misconception' means a view or opinion that is incorrect because it is based on faulty thinking or understanding.
Hence, its antonym is 'Certainty' which means absolutely true.

904. Humility
The little girl was humble enough to negate the ideology of her classmate whose arrogance was indomitable. SSC Steno 12.10.2023 (Shift-I)
(a) arrogance (b) indomitable
(c) negate (d) humble
Ans. (a)
'Humility' means kindness and politeness. Hence, its antonym is 'Arrogance' which means 'egoist and proud'.

905. Contentment SSC Steno 12.10.2023 (Shift-I)
(a) Sadness (b) Pleasure
(c) Greatness (d) Meanness
Ans. (a)
Contentment means happiness and satisfaction. Hence, its antonym is 'Sadness'.

906. Nominal SSC Steno 13.10.2023 (Shift-I)
(a) Identical (b) Liberal
(c) Adroit (d) Excessive
Ans. (d)
Nominal means very small; far below the real value or cost.
Hence, its antonym is 'Excessive' which means too much.

907. Decadent SSC Steno 13.10.2023 (Shift-I)
(a) Enflamed (b) Virtuous
(c) Muffled (d) Fluorescent
Ans. (b)
Decadent means characterised by or reflecting a state of moral or cultural decline. Hence, its antonym is 'Virtuous' means having or showing high moral standards.

908. Timorous SSC Steno 13.10.2023 (Shift-I)
(a) Muggy (b) Badgered
(c) Imbecilic (d) Brazen
Ans. (d)
'Timorous' means showing or suffering from nervousness or a lack of confidence. Hence, its antonym is 'Brazen' which means bold.

909. Frequent SSC Steno 13.10.2023 (Shift-I)
(a) Constant (b) Rare
(c) Persistent (d) Recurring
Ans. (b)
Frequent means regularly. Hence, its antonym is 'Rare' which means not often.

910. Frenzy SSC Steno 13.10.2023 (Shift-I)
(a) Copious (b) Harmony
(c) Obscurity (d) Haste
Ans. (b)
'Frenzy' means chaos and confusion. Hence, its antonym is 'Harmony' which means 'peace and order'.

06

Homonyms

Homonyms are words that may sound the same and whose spelling may be same, but they have different meanings.
For example, Assent and Ascent are homonyms. When you speak these words, they are pronounced the same. However,

- **Assent** means to agree with something.
- **Ascent** means to rise.

Types of Questions Asked

Generally, fill in the blanks are asked on homonyms.

Type 1

Select the most appropriate option to fill in the blanks.

Though he was already tired, the farmer had to .... the seeds.

(a) so (b) sew
(c) sow (d) chew **Ans.** (c)

Type 2

Choose the correct homonyms to fill in the given blanks.

.... of you must do the work comprising finding the .... of the given numbers.

(a) Sum, Some (b) Some, Some (c) Sum, Sum (d) Some, Sum

Ans. (d)

Type 3

Choose the correct word to fill in the given blanks.

You have got bigger piece of cake than me at the .... That's not ....

(a) fair (b) fare (c) fire (d) flair **Ans.** (a)

Type 4

Choose the correct homonym of the given word.

Course

(a) Curse (b) Coarse (c) Covers (d) Cars **Ans.** (b)

SSC Exam Scanner

Directions (Q. Nos. 1-126) Select the most appropriate option to fill in the blanks.

SSC CGL 2024 (Tier 1 & 2)

1. Rashid was not able to .... the pain after the accident.
SSC CGL Tier-2 18.01.2025
(a) beer (b) bare (c) buyer (d) bear
Ans. (d)
'Bear' means to endure or tolerate something difficult, making it the most appropriate choice in this context.

2. We should .... away all prejudices to live in harmony.
SSC CGL Tier-2 18.01.2025
(a) cast (b) caste (c) coast (d) cost
Ans. (a)
The most appropriate homophone to fill in the blank is 'cast'. In the context of the sentence, 'cast' means to throw away or get rid of, which fits the intended meaning of discarding prejudices to live in harmony.

3. The comedian's jokes were so funny that the entire audience erupted in ....
SSC CGL Tier-2 20.01.2025
(a) loiter (b) latter (c) laughter (d) later
Ans. (c)
'Laughter' is the most appropriate word to fill in the blank, as it conveys the idea of the audience erupting in joy and amusement due to the comedian's jokes

4. He has the .... to express his thoughts.
SSC CGL Tier-1 09.09.2024 (Shift-III)
(a) right (b) ride
(c) write (d) rite
Ans. (a)
The correct filler for the given blank is 'right'.
The word 'right' means having the ability or entitlement to express thoughts, which fits the context of the sentence.

5. The group of travellers were wonderstruck by the .... of the coin.
SSC CGL Tier-1 10.09.2024 (Shift-III)
(a) wait (b) white
(c) wide (d) weight
Ans. (d)
The correct filler for the given blank is 'weight'. The word 'weight' refers to the heaviness of the coin, which makes sense in the context of the travellers being wonderstruck.

6. He had .... the .... into smaller clips.
SSC CGL Tier-1 12.09.2024 (Shift-II)
(a) clipping, clips (b) clipping, clipped
(c) clips, clipping (d) clipped, clipping
Ans. (d)
The correct fillers for the given blanks are 'clipped' and 'clipping'. Clipped means to cut short and Clipping means small pages.

7. The homophone for the word 'there' is .... SSC CGL Tier-1 13.09.2024 (Shift-I)
(a) that (b) their
(c) those (d) clear
Ans. (b)
Homophones are words whose spellings or pronunciation may be the same but they have different meanings. Hence, the homophone of there is 'their'.

8. The .... was decorated with candles and chocolates everywhere.
SSC CGL Tier-1 13.09.2024 (Shift-II)
(a) flour (b) flower
(c) floor (d) flor
Ans. (c)
The correct filler for the given blank is 'floor'. The word 'floor' refers to the surface of a room, which makes sense in the context of being decorated with candles and chocolates.

9. Ram went to .... an ice cream.
SSC CGL Tier-1 17.09.2024 (Shift-I)
(a) buy (b) by (c) byre (d) bye
Ans. (a)
The correct filler for the given blank is 'buy'. The word 'buy' means to purchase something, which fits the context of Ram wanting to get an ice-cream.

10. The ointment will help to .... the wound. SSC CGL Tier-1 17.09.2024 (Shift-II)
(a) he'll (b) heel
(c) heal (d) kneel
Ans. (c)
The correct filler for the given blank is 'heal'. The word 'heal' means to make healthy or whole, which fits the context of the ointment helping the wound.

11. He .... his bike as fast as he could to reach home.
SSC CGL Tier-1 18.09.2024 (Shift-I)
(a) rode (b) road
(c) rowed (d) rote
Ans. (a)
The correct filler for the given blank is 'rode'. The word 'rode' is the past tense of 'ride,' which fits the context of him riding his bike to reach home.

12. The rowing instructor commanded them to .... in a ....
SSC CGL Tier-1 23.09.2024 (Shift-I)
A. row (verb)
B. roe
C. row (sequence)
(a) C, A (b) B, C (c) A, B (d) A, C
Ans. (d)
The correct fillers for the given blanks are A- row and C- row.
The first row is an act of moving the boat using oars and the second row refers to a queue.

13. The summer was .... hot this year. SSC CGL Tier-1 23.09.2024 (Shift-II)
(a) tow (b) two (c) to (d) too
Ans. (d)
The correct filler for the given blank is 'too'. The word 'too' means 'very' or 'excessively,' which fits the context of describing how hot the summer was.

14. Ruby gave her mother a hug and offered to knead the ....
SSC CGL Tier-1 25.09.2024 (Shift-III)
(a) flora (b) flavour
(c) floor (d) flour
Ans. (d)
The correct filler for the given blank is 'flour'.
The word 'flour' is a powder made from ground grains, which Ruby offered to knead.

15. The mother couldn't .... such an insult from her son in front of the others. SSC CGL Tier-1 25.09.2024 (Shift-III)
(a) bier (b) bare (c) beer (d) bear
Ans. (d)
The sentence indicates that she couldn't accept or tolerate the insults. Hence, the correct filler for the given blank is 'bear'.

16. I like bread made up of corn ....
SSC CGL Tier-1 26.09.2024 (Shift-II)
(a) flower (b) flour
(c) floor (d) failure
Ans. (b)
The correct filler for the given blank is 'flour'. The word 'flour' is made from ground corn, which is used to make bread.

17. The .... of the flowers spread everywhere when they bloom.
SSC CGL Tier-1 26.09.2024 (Shift-III)
(a) sent (b) saint (c) scent (d) cent
Ans. (c)
The correct filler for the given blank is 'scent'.
The word 'scent' refers to the smell of the flowers, which spreads everywhere when they bloom.

SSC CGL 2023 (Tier 1 & 2)

18. The hunter dogs followed the Hyena's ....
SSC CGL Tier-1 14.07.2023 (Shift-I)
(a) sense (b) scent
(c) cense (d) cents
Ans. (b)
The given sentence indicates how the dogs used their smelling abilities to follow the Hyena.
Hence, the correct filler for the given blank is 'scent' which means a distinctive smell.

19. Kiran had a short .... as a writer.
SSC CGL Tier-1 14.07.2023 (Shift-III)
(a) caress (b) career
(c) carer (d) carrier
Ans. (b)
The given sentence Kiran's profession as a writer.
Hence, the correct filler for the given blank is 'career' which indicates jobs or profession.

20. He was complimented for his appearance. His shirt .... his trousers perfectly.
SSC CGL Tier-1 17.07.2023 (Shift-I)
(a) competed (b) complement
(c) commented (d) complemented
Ans. (d)
The correct homonym of 'complimented' is 'complemented' which means to contribute extra features to (someone or something) in such a way as to improve or emphasise their qualities.

21. The patient looked ...... and tired.
SSC CGL Tier-1 17.07.2023 (Shift-I)
(a) pail (b) pale (c) pall (d) peel
Ans. (b)
The given sentence indicates that the patient lost the colour of his face and was tired.
Hence, the correct filler of the given blank is 'pale' which means of a whitish or colourless complexion.

22. Payments can be made by .... or in cash. SSC CGL Tier-1 17.07.2023 (Shift-II)
(a) chick (b) cheek
(c) cheque (d) cheeky
Ans. (c)
The given sentence presents the mode of payments. Hence, the correct filler for the given blank is 'cheque'.

23. You are the .... to the throne and should behave in such a manner.
SSC CGL Tier-1 17.07.2023 (Shift-III)
(a) hair (b) here
(c) hare (d) heir

Ans. (d)

The given sentence presents that 'you' will take the throne after his/her parents.

Hence, the correct filler for the given blank is 'heir' which means a person legally entitled to the property or rank of another on that person's death.

24. They are playing songs so .... that the entire neighbourhood is disturbed. **SSC CGL Tier-1 18.07.2023 (Shift-II)**

(a) lord (b) loved
(c) laud (d) loud

Ans. (d)

The given sentence states that the sound is so loud that it is disturbing the neighbourhood. Hence, the correct filler for the given blank is 'loud'.

25. There are rows of chairs on either side of the ....
SSC CGL Tier-1 18.07.2023 (Shift-III)

(a) ail (b) isle (c) I'll (d) aisle

Ans. (d)

The correct filler for the given blank is 'aisle'. Aisle means a narrow space between shelves.

26. I will just .... some figures for comparison.
SSC CGL Tier-1 19.07.2023 (Shift-I)

(a) cete (b) cite (c) site (d) sight

Ans. (b)

The given sentence states that the speaker would refer to some figures for comparison. Hence, the correct filler for the given blank is 'cite' which-means to refer or to quote.

27. The .... purpose of the coaching was to identify the talented players.
SSC CGL Tier-1 19.07.2023 (Shift-II)

(a) mean (b) mine
(c) mane (d) main

Ans. (d)

The given sentence indicates the central purpose of coaching. Hence, the correct filler for the given blank is 'main'.

28. The perfume she uses has a strong .... **SSC CGL Tier-1 19.07.2023 (Shift-III)**

(a) sent (b) scend
(c) scent (d) cent

Ans. (c)

The given sentence refers to the distinct smell of the perfume. Hence, the correct filler for the given blank is 'scent'.

29. The villagers kept the .... out, to collect the rain water.
SSC CGL Tier-1 20.07.2023 (Shift-I)

(a) crus (b) cruse
(c) crews (d) cruise

Ans. (b)

The given sentence presents that the villagers keep something out to collect the rain water.

Hence, the correct filler for the given blank is 'cruse' which is a small vessel.

30. I find that students nowadays are not interested in .... letters by hand.
SSC CGL Tier-1 20.07.2023 (Shift-III)

(a) righting (b) rioting
(c) rating (d) writing

Ans. (d)

The correct filler for the given blank is 'writing'.

31. Identify the option that defines the homonyms 'gate' and 'gait' most appropriately.
SSC CGL Tier-1 21.07.2023 (Shift-II)

(a) Gate means to achieve or receive and gait means a person's manner of walking.
(b) Gate means a hinged barrier used to close an opening in a wall, fence or hedge and gait means a person's manner of walking.
(c) Gate means general agreement on tariff and excise and gait means a person's manner of talking.
(d) Gate means a hinged barrier used to close an opening in a wall or fence, and gait means a cloth or leather leg covering reaching from the instep to above the ankle or to the mid-calf or knee.

Ans. (b)

Gate means to a hinged barrier used to close an opening in a wall, fence or hedge and gait means a person's manner of walking.

32. The princess firmly held the ...... in her hands.
SSC CGL Tier-1 24.07.2023 (Shift-III)

(a) rain (b) ran
(c) reign (d) rein

Ans. (d)

The given sentence indicates that the princess has the control of something. Hence, the correct filler for the given blank is 'rein' which means 'power or control over something'.

33. The room was very ....
SSC CGL Tier-1 24.07.2023 (Shift-IV)

(a) quit (b) quilt
(c) quiet (d) quite

Ans. (c)

The correct filler for the given blank is 'quiet'.

34. Raghav had a good .... for stage plays. **SSC CGL Tier-1 25.07.2023 (Shift-I)**

(a) trip (b) trope
(c) troop (d) troupe

Ans. (d)

The given sentence states that Raghav has something for stage plays. Hence, the correct filler for the given blank is 'troupe' which is a group of dancers, actors or entertainers.

35. Which .... do you usually take to reach your office?
SSC CGL Tier-1 25.07.2023 (Shift-I)

(a) route (b) root (c) rout (d) rude

Ans. (a)

The given sentence talks about the path taken for office. Hence, the correct filler for the given blank is 'route' which means way or path.

36. Yesterday, I ate only a .... of apples for my dinner.
SSC CGL Tier-1 25.07.2023 (Shift-II)

(a) pier (b) pear (c) pare (d) pair

Ans. (d)

The correct filler for the given blank is 'pair'. The word 'pair' means two of something, which fits the context of eating two apples for dinner.

37. .... droplets settled on top of leaves. **SSC CGL Tier-1 25.07.2023 (Shift-III)**

(a) Due (b) Doe
(c) Do (d) Dew

Ans. (d)

The correct filler for the given blank is 'Dew'. Dew refers to small water droplets that form on surfaces, especially during the night when the air is cooler.

38. Soon after the doctor gave her the next .... of the medicine, the patient began to ....
SSC CGL Tier-1 26.07.2023 (Shift-I)

(a) dose; dozed (b) dosed; doze
(c) dose; doze (d) doze; dose

Ans. (c)

The correct fillers for the given blanks are 'dose' and 'doze'. 'Dose' refers to a quantity of medicine taken or recommended while 'doze' means to sleep lightly.

39. The actress is very .... and takes pride in her appearance all the time.
SSC CGL Tier-1 26.07.2023 (Shift-I)

(a) vein (b) wane (c) vane (d) vain

Ans. (d)

The correct filler for the given blank is 'vain'. Vain means having or showing an excessively high opinion of one's appearance, abilities or worth.

40. Please .... more sugar to the juice so that it becomes sweeter.
SSC CGL Tier-1 26.07.2023 (Shift-II)

(a) aide (b) ad (c) aid (d) add

Ans. (d)

The correct filler for the given blank is 'add' with respect to sugar.

41. He confessed about his affairs as the .... made him speechless. SSC CGL Tier-1 26.07.2023 (Shift-III)

(a) gilled (b) gild (c) guild (d) guilt

Ans. (d)

The given sentence presents that 'he' confessed something due to shame. Hence, the correct filler for the given blank is 'guilt' which means a feeling of anxiety or unhappiness that you have done something immoral or wrong.

42. The group of travellers were wonderstruck by the .... of the coin. SSC CGL Tier-1 26.07.2023 (Shift-IV)

(a) wait (b) white
(c) weight (d) wide

Ans. (c)

The correct filler for the given blank is 'weight'.

43. What .... of a movie is this? SSC CGL Tier-1 26.07.2023 (Shift-IV)

(a) can (b) keen (c) con (d) kind

Ans. (d)

The correct filler for the given blank is 'kind'.

44. If you want .... the world. You should be the one to take the first step. SSC CGL Tier-1 26.07.2023 (Shift-IV)

(a) change (alter)
(b) change (loose money)
(c) change (transfer)
(d) change (switch)

Ans. (a)

The given sentence presents that if one wants to alter the world, one should be first to take steps. Hence, the correct filler for the given blank is 'change' whose meaning is 'alter'.

45. Select the nearest homonym of the given word.
Accept SSC CGL Tier-1 27.07.2023 (Shift-II)

(a) Accent (b) Expect
(c) Except (d) Expert

Ans. (c)

The correct homonym of 'Accept' is 'Except'. Accept means to agree to something while except means to deliberately leave something out.

46. The children enjoyed the .... very much. SSC CGL Tier-1 27.07.2023 (Shift-II)

(a) feer (b) fear (c) fere (d) fair

Ans. (d)

The correct filler for the given blank is 'fair'. A 'fair' in this context refers to an event with various attractions, games, rides and possibly food stalls.

47. I .... some essential items from the supermarket. SSC CGL Tier-1 27.07.2023 (Shift-II)

(a) bout (b) bought
(c) boat (d) bot

Ans. (b)

The correct filler for the given blank is 'bought'. The word 'bought' is the past tense of 'buy,' which means to purchase something from the supermarket.

48. She could easily eat the .... biryani by herself. SSC CGL Tier-1 27.07.2023 (Shift-III)

(a) haul (b) whole
(c) hall (d) hole

Ans. (b)

The given sentence indicates that she can eat the complete biryani by herself. Hence, the correct filler for the given blank is 'whole'.

49. We .... off old clothes and bought new ones for Diwali. SSC CGL Tier-1 27.07.2023 (Shift-IV)

(a) cost (b) coast (c) caste (d) cast

Ans. (d)

The correct filler for the given blank is 'cast' which makes 'cast off'. The phrasal verb cast off means to leave something.

50. Which .... does the minister take to reach the Assembly? SSC CGL Tier-2 02.03.2023

(a) root (b) rot (c) route (d) riot

Ans. (c)

The given questions asks about the path taken by the minister to reach the Assembly.
Hence, the correct filler for the given blank is 'route' which means 'way or path'.

51. Vishal is going to read the story .... SSC CGL Tier-2 02.03.2023

(a) load (b) allow
(c) aloud (d) allowed

Ans. (c)

The given sentence talks about how Vishal reads the story. Hence, the correct filler for the given blank is 'aloud'.

52. The wind ...... so powerfully that the door closed. SSC CGL Tier-2 03.03.2023

(a) blow (b) blew
(c) blues (d) blue

Ans. (b)

The given sentence refers to the movement of the wind. Hence, the correct filler for the given blank is 'blew'.

53. The farmers grow .... in their fields. SSC CGL Tier-2 06.03.2023

(a) maze (b) mays
(c) mase (d) maize

Ans. (d)

The given sentence indicates that the farmers grow a crop in the fields. Hence, the correct filler for the given blank is 'maize' which is a crop.

54. .... knowledge in this field is really profound. SSC CGL Tier-2 06.03.2023

(a) There (b) Their
(c) Dare (d) They're

Ans. (b)

The given sentence needs a possessive adjective. Hence, the correct filler for the given blank is 'Their'.

55. The athlete's .... was badly injured due to a fall on the track. SSC CGL Tier-2 07.03.2023

(a) toad (b) toe (c) tow (d) to

Ans. (b)

The given sentence presents how a particular part of the athlete's body was injured during an event. Hence, the correct filler for the given blank is 'toe'.

56. The security guard needs a .... of shoes. SSC CGL Tier-2 07.03.2023

(a) pare (b) pear
(c) payor (d) pair

Ans. (d)

The given sentence presents that the security guard needs shoes for his feet. We use the word 'pair' with 'shoes'. Hence, the correct filler for the given blank is 'pair'.

SSC CGL 2021 (Tier 1 & 2)

57. Some people were tired of the long .... in front of the mall and left without entering. SSC CGL Tier-1 18.08.2021 (Shift-I)

(a) waste (b) waist
(c) wait (d) weight

Ans. (c)

The given sentence talks about the people getting tired after standing in front of the mall and giving. Hence, the correct filler for the given blank is 'wait' which indicates patiently staying where one is.

SSC CHSL 2024 (Tier 1 & 2)

58. It's funny how every time he fails to apply the.........and......... the glass. SSC CHSL Tier-2 18.11.2024

(a) breaks; breaks
(b) brakes; breaks
(c) breaks; brakes
(d) brakes; brakes

Ans. (b)

The correct fillers for the given blanks are 'brakes' and 'breaks'.

'Brakes' refers to the stopping mechanism and 'breaks' means to cause damage to something.

59. He .... imitate the playful movement of the ....
SSC CHSL Tier-1 01.07.2024 (Shift-III)

Alternatives

A. does (female deer)
B. does
C. dose

(a) C, B (b) B, A (c) A, B (d) A, C

Ans. (b)

The correct fillers for the given blanks are 'does' and 'does'. The first 'does' is a verb and the second 'does' refers to female deer.

60. Sonu eats .... like a rabbit.
SSC CHSL Tier-1 01.07.2024 (Shift-III)

(a) karat (b) carrot
(c) carat (d) caret

Ans. (b)

The correct filler for the given blank is 'carrot'.

61. .... is a red-coloured root vegetable.
SSC CHSL Tier-1 02.07.2024 (Shift-II)

(a) beet (b) beat (c) bead (d) bit

Ans. (a)

The correct filler for the given blank is 'beet'.

62. Ravi is ....
SSC CHSL Tier-1 02.07.2024 (Shift-III)

(a) bawled (b) balled
(c) baled (d) bald

Ans. (d)

The correct filler for the given blank is 'bald', which means to not have any hair on the head.

63. Namita still cannot .... the pain of her cat's untimely demise.
SSC CHSL Tier-1 04.07.2024 (Shift-II)

(a) bier (b) bear
(c) beer (d) bare

Ans. (b)

The correct filler for the given blank is 'bear' which means 'to suffer from something'.

64. It is better to focus on your .... than to wander aimlessly.
SSC CHSL Tier-1 04.07.2024 (Shift-III)

(a) carrier (b) courier
(c) career (d) carreer

Ans. (c)

The correct filler for the given blank is 'career'.

65. The mechanics tried a lot to get that car .... from the accident spot.
SSC CHSL Tier-1 04.07.2024 (Shift-III)

(a) told (b) towed
(c) toed (d) toad

Ans. (b)

The correct filler for the given blank is 'towed' which means (of a motor vehicle or boat) pull (another vehicle or boat) along with a rope, chain, or tow bar.

66. Arun knows perfectly well how to mix the food items with ....
SSC CHSL Tier-1 05.07.2024 (Shift-III)

(a) sauce (b) saws
(c) sause (d) source

Ans. (a)

The correct filler for the given blank is 'sauce'.

67. The hospital is .... the river.
SSC CHSL Tier-1 08.07.2024 (Shift-I)

(a) buy (b) by (c) bye (d) bi

Ans. (b)

The correct filler for the given blank is 'by'.

68. The prince is the .... to the throne.
SSC CHSL Tier-1 08.07.2024 (Shift-IV)

(a) air (b) heir (c) err (d) ere

Ans. (b)

The correct filler for the given blank is 'heir'.

69. These people are artists. .... skills are extraordinary.
SSC CHSL Tier-1 08.07.2024 (Shift-IV)

(a) They or (b) There
(c) They're (d) Their

Ans. (d)

The correct filler for the given blank is 'Their'.

70. There was no one .... a few of my friends. SSC CHSL Tier-1 10.07.2024 (Shift-III)

(a) except (b) expect
(c) accept (d) excerpt

Ans. (a)

The correct filler for the given blank is 'except'.

71. Her father .... her to opt for a chemistry .... in her final year.
SSC CHSL Tier-1 11.07.2024 (Shift-II)

(a) aloud; course (b) aloud; coarse
(c) allowed; coarse (d) allowed; course

Ans. (d)

The correct fillers for the given blanks are 'allowed' and 'course'.

72. Please .... more sugar to the juice so that it becomes sweeter.
SSC CHSL Tier-1 11.07.2024 (Shift-II)

(a) ad (b) add (c) aide (d) aid

Ans. (b)

The correct filler for the given blank is 'add'.

73. It was against her .... to earn more .... than that decided by the Board of directors.
SSC CHSL Tier-1 11.07.2024 (Shift-III)

(a) principle, profit
(b) principal; profit
(c) principal; prophet
(d) principle; prophet

Ans. (a)

The correct fillers for the given blanks are 'principle' and 'profit'. Principle means a belief.

74. I .... that he has been promoted to the post of .... officer.
SSC CHSL Tier-1 11.07.2024 (Shift-III)

(a) herd; sealing (b) heard; sealing
(c) herd; ceiling (d) heard; ceiling

Ans. (b)

The correct fillers for the given blanks are 'heard' and 'sealing'.

SSC CHSL 2023 (Tier 1 & 2)

75. Even animals find it difficult to .... the loss of their loved ones.
SSC CHSL Tier-2 02.08.2023 (Shift-I)

(a) bear (b) wear
(c) where (d) bare

Ans. (a)

The given sentence talks about how the animals find it difficult to accept the loss of their loved ones.

Hence, the correct filler for the given blank is 'bear' which means to be able to accept and move on from the loss.

76. Kindly accept my ...... on my new haircut. It .... your personality.
SSC CHSL Tier-2 02.08.2023 (Shift-II)

(a) compliment; complaints
(b) compliment; complements
(c) compliment; compliments
(d) complement; complements

Ans. (b)

The correct fillers for the given blanks are 'compliment' and 'complements'. Compliment means praise and Complement refers to something that adds to the beauty of something.

77. My birthday will .... on a Friday this year.
SSC CHSL Tier-2 02.08.2023 (Shift-IV)

(a) fall: to go down onto the ground suddenly
(b) fall: to come at a particular time or happen in a particular place
(c) fall: to change to a particular condition
(d) fall: to be beaten or defeated

Ans. (b)

The correct filler for the given blank is 'fall' which, in the context of the sentence, would refer to a particular time or happen in a particular place.

78. The dog took a .... during his walk and lifted his .... to indicate that he was tired.
SSC CHSL Tier-2 03.08.2023 (Shift-I)
(a) pause; pours (b) pours; pores
(c) paws; pause (d) pause; paws

Ans. (d)

The correct fillers for the given blanks are 'pause' and 'paws'. Pause means to temporarily stop work. Paws refer to the feet of an animal.

79. He was convicted of assaulting a police officer, but he got off with a .... sentence.
SSC CHSL Tier-2 04.08.2023 (Shift-I)
(a) light : any device serving as a source of illumination
(b) light : not serious or profound
(c) light : the energy from the Sun
(d) light : lightly; with few burdens

Ans. (b)

The correct filler for the given blank is 'light' which, in the context of the sentence, would mean not serious or profound.

80. The doctors gave him more powerful drugs in the .... hope that he might recover.
SSC CHSL Tier-2 07.08.2023 (Shift-I)
(a) when (b) vein
(c) wane (d) vain

Ans. (d)

The given sentence presents how the doctor's action of giving the patient more powerful drugs was useless. Hence, the correct filler for the given blank is 'vain' which means 'of no use'.

81. The key was hanging on a ...... by the door. SSC CHSL Tier-2 07.08.2023 (Shift-I)
(a) nail : to catch someone, especially when they are doing something wrong or guilty.
(b) nail : a small metal spike, driven into wood to join things together or to serve as a hook.
(c) nail : a thin, hard area that covers the upper side of the end of each finger and each toe
(d) nail: to do something successfully.

Ans. (b)

The given sentence talks about the key which is hanging on a nail by the door.

Hence, the correct filler for the given blank is 'nail' which is a small metal spike used to join things together.

82. He was criticised for the .... leadership of his team. His casual body language seemed .... for a leader. SSC CHSL Tier-2 08.08.2023 (Shift-II)
(a) inapt; inapt (b) inapt; inept
(c) inept; inapt (d) inept; inept

Ans. (c)

The correct fillers for the given blanks are 'inept' and 'inapt'. Inept means having or showing no skill while inapt means not suitable or appropriate in the circumstances.

83. Developers .... the old buildings on the site to make way for new construction.
SSC CHSL Tier-2 09.08.2023 (Shift-I)
(a) raze (b) rays
(c) raise (d) rase

Ans. (a)

The given sentence talks about the destruction of a building.

Hence, the correct filler for the given blank is 'raze' which means to completely destroy a city, building, etc.

84. They do not say anything but stalk furiously out of the room.
'Stalk' here means ....
SSC CHSL Tier-2 10.08.2023 (Shift-II)
(a) the stem or main axis of a plant
(b) to walk in an angry or proud way
(c) to go through an area in search of prey
(d) recur constantly and spontaneously

Ans. (b)

Stalk in the given sentence means to walk in an angry or proud way.

85. I will ...... any job offer ...... for the one that requires me to work on weekends.
SSC CHSL Tier-1 10.08.2023 (Shift-IV)
(a) except, accept (b) expect, except
(c) expect, accept (d) accept, except

Ans. (d)

The correct fillers for the given blanks are 'accept' and 'except'. Accept means to agree to something while except means to deliberately leave something out.

86. The ..... of the new legislation has sparked a heated debate among lawmakers.
SSC CHSL Tier-1 11.08.2023 (Shift-I)
(a) affectation (b) effection
(c) effect (d) affect

Ans. (c)

The given sentence talks about the impact of the new legislation. Hence, the correct filler for the given blank is 'effect'.

87. The shareholders are planning to .... control of the company from the current directors.
SSC CHSL Tier-1 11.08.2023 (Shift-IV)
(a) roost (b) roast (c) wrest (d) rest

Ans. (c)

The given sentence talks about how shareholders are planning to forcefully take the control of the company from the current directors. Hence, the correct filler for the given blank is 'wrest' which means to forcefully grab or take something away.

88. I got .... while replacing the .... SSC CHSL Tier-1 17.08.2023 (Shift-IV)
(a) tyre, tire (b) tyred, tire
(c) tired, tier (d) tired, tyre

Ans. (d)

The correct fillers for the given blanks are 'tired' and 'tyre'. Tired means in need of sleep or rest; weary. Tyre refers-to a rubber ring placed over the rim of a wheel of a road vehicle.

89. Sarah just gave .... to a baby boy.
SSC CHSL Tier-1 17.08.2023 (Shift-I)
(a) birth (b) breath
(c) broth (d) berth

Ans. (a)

The given sentence talks about the birth of a child. Hence, the correct filler for the given blank is 'birth'.

90. Ants .... food during the summer and save it for winter.
SSC CHSL Tier-1 17.08.2023 (Shift-IV)
(a) horde (b) hoard
(c) heard (d) herd

Ans. (b)

The given sentence talk about how ants collect and save food during the summer for the winters.

Hence, the correct filler for the given blank is 'hoard' which means 'to collect' a lot of money or object.

91. A. I use a .... to weigh my ingredients while cooking.
B. The mountaineer is going to .... the rocky hills.
SSC CHSL Tier-2 02.11.2023 (Shift-I)
(a) horn (b) scale
(c) climb (d) crawl

Ans. (b)

The sentence A talks about an instrument used by someone to measure ingredients while cooking. Sentence B talks about climbing the mountains.

Hence, the correct filler for the given blank is 'scale'. The word refers to both an instrument for measurement and the act of climbing mountains.

SSC CHSL 2022 & 2021 (Tier 1 & 2)

92. The police returned to the ...... of the crime. **SSC CHSL Tier-1 27.05.2022 (Shift-I)**

(a) scene (b) zen
(c) seen (d) cene

Ans. (a)

The given sentence refers to the area where a crime had occurred. Hence, the correct filler for the given blank is 'scene' which means a place where something has happened.

93. For each question, four .... are given as options.
SSC CHSL Tier-1 19.04.2021 (Shift-III)

(a) alternates (b) alternative
(c) alterations (d) altercations

Ans. (b)

The given sentence talks about the choice given with questions.

Hence, the correct filler for the given blank is 'alternative' which means 'choices'.

SSC MTS 2024 (Tier 1 & 2)

94. I did not......that he would ...... the offer. **SSC MTS Tier-1 14.11.2024 (Shift-III)**

(a) except; accept (b) bate; bait
(c) bait; bate (d) expect; accept

Ans. (d)

'Expect; accept' is the most appropriate option to fill in the blanks. 'Expect' means to anticipate and 'accept' means to agree.

95. A buzzing......can......... dangerous.
SSC MTS Tier-1 13.11.2024 (Shift-III)

(a) bee; be (b) dear; deer
(c) deer; dear (d) be; bee

Ans. (a)

'bee; be' is the most appropriate option to fill in the blanks. The word 'bee' refers to the insect and 'be' is a verb meaning to exist or occur.

96. The citizens of Iraq wanted......... after years of war.
SSC MTS Tier-1 12.11.2024 (Shift-III)

(a) piece (b) pease (c) peice (d) peace

Ans. (d)

The correct filler for the given blank is 'peace'.

97. The team captain inquired of his teammates.........they preferred to choose batting as their initial option. s
SSC MTS Tier-1 12.11.2024 (Shift-III)

(a) whither (b) weather
(c) wither (d) whether

Ans. (d)

'Whether' is the most appropriate option to fill in the blank. 'Whether' is used to introduce alternatives.

98. I was trying to..............a pen to sign a form as my brother had been............ ₹ 500 for breaking the traffic rules.
SSC MTS Tier-1 29.10.2024 (Shift-III)

(a) find; find (b) fined; fined
(c) find; fined (d) fined; find

Ans. (c)

'Find; fined' is the most appropriate option to fill in the blanks.
'Find' means to discover and 'fined' means to impose a penalty.

99. Tom will...........the document to the office tomorrow.
SSC MTS Tier-1 28.10.2024 (Shift-II)

(a) male (b) mail (c) meal (d) mall

Ans. (b)

The correct filler for the given blank is 'mail' which means to sending a document.

100. Doves.........in the sky above me.
SSC MTS Tier-1 23.10.2024 (Shift-II)

(a) sour (b) shore
(c) soar (d) sore

Ans. (c)

The correct filler for the given blank is 'soar'. It means to fly or rise high in the air.

101. She.........the book to her friend.
SSC MTS Tier-1 23.10.2024 (Shift-II)

(a) lend (b) lent
(c) laned (d) leant

Ans. (b)

The correct filler for the given blank is 'lent'. 'Lent' is the past tense of 'lend' which means to give temporarily.

102. His.........is a brilliant student.
SSC MTS Tier-1 21.10.2024 (Shift-II)

(a) sune (b) sone (c) son (d) sun

Ans. (c)

The correct filler for the given blank is 'son'.

103. David decided to .... his old boat to get a new one.
SSC MTS Tier-1 18.10.2024 (Shift-II)

(a) sell (b) ceil (c) sale (d) cell

Ans. (a)

'Sell' is the most appropriate option to fill in the blank. It means to give something in exchange for money.

104. The teacher asked the students to stay .... during the exam.
SSC MTS Tier-1 18.10.2024 (Shift-II)

(a) quiet (b) quite
(c) quote (d) quit

Ans. (a)

'Quiet' is the most appropriate option to fill in the blank. It means making little or no noise.

105. Adithya ordered a juicy .... cooked to perfection at the highway restaurant.
SSC MTS Tier-1 16.10.2024 (Shift-II)

(a) stink (b) steak
(c) stoke (d) stake

Ans. (b)

'Steak' is the most appropriate word to fill in the blank.

'Steak' refers to a high-quality beef cut, typically served grilled or fried.

106. I checked the .... to see if it will rain or not. **SSC MTS Tier-1 16.10.2024 (Shift-II)**

(a) whether (b) wether
(c) weather (d) wither

Ans. (c)

'Weather' is the most appropriate option to fill in the blank. It refers to the atmospheric conditions.

107. Roger applied the .... in advance as he anticipated an accident.
SSC MTS Tier-1 08.10.2024 (Shift-II)

(a) break (b) brake
(c) broke (d) brig

Ans. (b)

'Brake' to fill in the blank. It refers to the device used to stop a vehicle.

108. Our .... conducted a .... to get everyone's opinion.
SSC MTS Tier-1 07.10.2024 (Shift-I)

(a) principle; pole (b) principal; pole
(c) principal; poll (d) principle; poll

Ans. (c)

The correct fillers for the given blanks are 'principal' and 'poll'. 'Principal' refers to the head of an educational institution and 'poll' refers to a survey.

SSC GD 2024 (Tier 1 & 2)

109. Her mother is a wonderful host, she prepared for us a seven .... meal all by herself. **SSC GD 20.02.2024 (Shift-I)**

(a) course (b) coarse
(c) coarser (d) courser

Ans. (a)

The given sentence talks about a set of dishes which was eaten by the speaker. Hence, the correct filler for the given blank is 'course'.

110. In the dense forest, a mother .... and her cubs roamed freely, enjoying the tranquility of their natural habitat. **SSC GD 20.02.2024 (Shift-III)**

(a) bare (b) beer (c) bear (d) ber

Ans. (c)

The given sentence refers to an animal named bear and her cubs enjoying their natural habitat. Hence, the correct filler for the given blank is 'bear'.

111. Of course it is. They just sit around .... maybe, when there's a war.
SSC GD 24.02.2024 (Shift-III)
(a) expect (b) except
(c) assent (d) accept

Ans. (b)

The given sentence presents a situation wherein people do something when they are not in war.

Hence, the correct filler for the given blank is 'except' which means to skip over.

SSC GD 2023 (Tier 1 & 2)

112. She liked .... flat.
SSC GD 23.01.2023 (Shift-III)
(a) they are (b) their
(c) there (d) they're

Ans. (b)

The correct filler for the given blank is 'their' which is a possessive adjective showing ownership of the flat.

113. We saw a .... in the city last year.
SSC GD 23.01.2023 (Shift-III)
(a) knew (b) no
(c) gnu (d) new

Ans. (c)

The correct filler for the given blank is 'gnu' which means a large African animal that has a long tail and horns that curve to the sides.

114. .... are the prime resource of a country and a tea is served in a ....
SSC GD 25.01.2023 (Shift-I)
(a) cattle; cattle (b) kettle; kettle
(c) kettle; cattle (d) cattle; kettle

Ans. (d)

The correct fillers for the given blanks are 'cattle' and 'kettle'. Cattle here indicates the domesticated animals which produce milk and other products and 'kettle' means a container or device in which water is boiled, having a lid, spout and handle.

115. The annual extraction of this .... costs around $10,000,000.
SSC GD 27.01.2023 (Shift-II)
(a) eor (b) arc
(c) ore (d) or

Ans. (c)

The correct filler for the given blank is 'ore' which means a naturally occurring solid material from which a metal or valuable mineral can be extracted profitably.

116. He planned a week long .... down the Nile. SSC GD 27.01.2023 (Shift-IV)
(a) crews (b) cruse
(c) crus (d) cruise

Ans. (d)

The given sentence presents that 'he' planned a journey on a water body. Hence, the correct filler for the given blank is 'cruise' which is a ship that takes someone on a journey through waterways.

117. The river .... provide a reserve .... for minerals that enrich the soil's fertility. SSC GD 30.01.2023 (Shift-III)
(a) right, right (b) banks, bank
(c) band, band (d) quail, quail

Ans. (b)

The correct fillers for the given blanks are 'banks' and 'bank'.

Banks here indicates the edges of the river where the water meets the land and 'bank' means a store house.

118. While teaching my son how to drive a car, I told him if he did'nt hit the...... in time he would .... the car's side mirror.
SSC GD 31.01.2023 (Shift-III)
(a) break; break (b) brake; break
(c) brake; brake (d) break; brake

Ans. (b)

The correct fillers for the given blanks are 'brake' and 'break'. Brake here indicates the act of stopping something and 'break' means to destroy and damage.

119. I taught my son the ...... way to tie a ....
SSC GD 31.01.2023 (Shift-IV)
(a) right; not (b) write; knot
(c) right; knot (d) write; not

Ans. (c)

The given sentence presents that the speaker taught his son the correct way to tie the knot.

Hence, the correct fillers for the given blanks are 'right' which means correct and 'knot'.

120. He received a .... during the ceremony. SSC GD 02.02.2023 (Shift-I)
(a) metal (b) medal
(c) meddle (d) mettle

Ans. (b)

The given sentence refers to an award that 'he' had won.

Hence, the correct filler for the given blank is 'medal' which a metal disc typically of the size of a large coin and bearing an inscription or design, made to commemorate an event or awarded as a distinction to someone such as a soldier or athlete.

121. He used to .... letters to his parents from Bangalore.
SSC GD 06.02.2023 (Shift-I)
(a) wright (b) rite
(c) write (d) right

Ans. (c)

The correct filler for the given blank is 'write'.

122. Select the most appropriate homonym of the given word.
Flea SSC GD 09.02.2023 (Shift-I)
(a) Flee (b) Fleece
(c) Flew (d) Fly

Ans. (a)

The homonym of the given word is 'flee'.

Flea refers to an insect.

Flee means to run away

123. I was looking forward to a .... evening at home. SSC GD 09.02.2023 (Shift-II)
(a) quit (b) quiet
(c) quite (d) quote

Ans. (b)

The given sentence presents that the speaker wanted a calm evening.

Hence, the correct filler for the given blank is 'quiet'.

124. I have made the basket for going to the picnic and I've packed some sandwiches ....
SSC GD 13.02.2023 (Shift-II)
(a) two (b) too
(c) to (d) toot

Ans. (b)

The given sentence presents that the speaker had also kept sandwiches in the basket.

Hence, the correct filler for the given blank is 'too' which means 'also'.

125. The authorities .... the unregistered companies.
SSC GD 13.02.2023 (Shift-II)
(a) sees (b) seize
(c) seas (d) cease

Ans. (b)

The given sentence presents that the authorities take over the unregistered companies.

Hence, the correct filler for the given blank is 'seize' which means 'to take hold of something'.

126. My uncle's legal ...... is his son.
SSC GD 13.02.2023 (Shift-II)
(a) heir (b) hair
(c) here (d) hare

Ans. (a)

The sentence refers to the legal successor of the uncle which is the uncle's son.

Hence, the correct filler for the given blank is 'heir'.

07

One Word Substitution

One Word Substitutions form an important part of Vocabulary. Thus, many questions are asked from this topic in the SSC examination. One Word Substitution, essentially, involves replacing a group of words or a lengthy phrase with a single word that conveys the same meaning.

For example

- A person who can use both hands with equal skill — **Ambidextrous**
- Something that lasts for a very short-time — **Ephemeral**
- To delay or postpone action — **Procrastinate**
- A person who is hired to drive a car — **Chauffeur**
- A list of all the sources consulted and cited in a written work — **Bibliography**
- The act of dropping rubbish on the ground in public places — **Littering**

Types of Questions Asked

Two types of questions are generally asked from one word substitutions.

Type 1

Select the option that can be used as a one-word substitute for the given group of words.

Code of diplomatic etiquette and precedence

(a) Hierarchy (b) Protocol (c) Diplomacy (d) Statesman ***Ans.*** (b)

Type 2

Select the option that can be used as a one word substitute for the underlined group of words.

He is hated by our group because he is <u>someone who criticises popular beliefs which he thinks is mistaken or unwise</u>

(a) Philistine (b) Iconoclast (c) Imposter (d) Cannibal ***Ans.*** (b)

SSC Exam Scanner

SSC CGL 2024 (Tier 1 & 2)

Directions (Q. Nos. 1-549) Select the option that can be used as a one word substitute for the given group of words.

Or

Select the most appropriate option that can substitute the bold/underlined/phrase/segment in the given sentence.

1. One who cannot make a mistake **SSC CGL Tier-2 18.01.2025**

(a) Inevitable (b) Infallible (c) Impregnable (d) Inimitable

Ans. (b)

'Infallible' refers to 'one who cannot make a mistake'. It means incapable of making mistakes or being wrong, which accurately matches the description given.

Inevitable means unavoidable.

Impregnable means unable to be overcome.

Inimitable means unique.

2. A sudden and violent change or upheaval **SSC CGL Tier-2 18.01.2025**

(a) Tranquility (b) Turbulence
(c) Serenity (d) Equanimity

Ans. (b)

'Turbulence' means 'a sudden and violent change or upheaval'.

Tranquility and **serenity** means calm.

Equanimity means composure and calmness.

3. Someone who walks on foot **SSC CGL Tier-2 20.01.2025**

(a) Stalker (b) Auditor (c) Decanter (d) Pedestrian

Ans. (d)

A 'pedestrian' is someone who walks on foot, fitting the description given in the question.

Stalker is a person who follows someone.

Auditor is a person who studies financial records.

Decanter is a decorated glass container.

4. Someone who loves and admires himself the most **SSC CGL Tier-2 20.01.2025**

(a) Recluse (b) Altruist (c) Narcissist (d) Omniscient

Ans. (c)

A 'narcissist' is someone who loves and admires himself the most, fitting the description given in the question.

Recluse is one who stays alone.

Altruist is one who helps others selflessly.

Omniscient is one who knows everything.

5. In the makeshift place of activity, debate or conflict, there were hundreds of people with the queen's team of advisors and servants sitting within the ring against the wall. SSC CGL Tier-2 20.01.2025

(a) casino (b) arena
(c) aviary (d) dormitory

Ans. (b)

The word 'arena' refers to 'makeshift place of activity, debate or conflict'.

Casino is a place where one plays gambling games.

Aviary is a place for keeping birds.

Dormitory is a place where a number of people live together.

6. The nation has chosen the government by the people over monarchy. SSC CGL Tier-2 20.01.2025

(a) oligarchy (b) autocracy
(c) democracy (d) theocracy

Ans. (c)

The term 'democracy', means a system of government where the citizens exercise power by voting.

Oligarchy is a government by a few.

Autocracy is a government by one person.

Theocracy is a government by a religious leader.

7. Speaking disrespectfully about sacred or religious things SSC CGL Tier-2 20.01.2025

(a) Blasphemy (b) Bigamy
(c) Belligerent (d) Biped

Ans. (a)

'Blasphemy' refers to speaking disrespectfully about sacred or religious things.

Bigamy is the offence of marrying two people.

Belligerent means hostile and aggressive.

Biped refers to an animal which uses two legs for walking.

8. A short interesting story about a real person or event SSC CGL Tier-1 09.09.2024 (Shift-I)

(a) Poem (b) Sketch
(c) Anecdote (d) Narrative

Ans. (c)

An **anecdote** is a short interesting story about a real person or event.

Poem is a composition in verse.

Sketch is a rough or unfinished drawing or painting, often made to assist in making a more finished picture.

Narrative is a spoken or written account of connected events; a story.

9. She is proficient in speaking many languages. SSC CGL Tier-1 09.09.2024 (Shift-I)

(a) Monolithic
(b) Multilingual
(c) Heterolinguistic
(d) Bilingual

Ans. (b)

Someone who is proficient in speaking many languages is called **multilingual**.

Monolithic means formed of a single large block of stone.

Heterolinguistic is a person who can speak more than one language.

Bilingual is someone who can speak two languages.

10. A person who likes to argue about anything SSC CGL Tier-1 09.09.2024 (Shift-I)

(a) Reticent (b) Coward
(c) Veracious (d) Contentious

Ans. (d)

A person who like to argue about everything is called **contentious**.

Veracious means speaking or representing the truth.

11. Unit of weight for precious stones SSC CGL Tier-1 09.09.2024 (Shift-I)

(a) Pure (b) Reliable
(c) Carat (d) Accurate

Ans. (c)

The unit of weight for precious stones is called a **carat**.

12. One who does not show response to good or bad SSC CGL Tier-1 09.09.2024 (Shift-II)

(a) Stoic (b) Sceptic
(c) Cynic (d) Phobic

Ans. (a)

A person who does not show response to good or bad is called a **stoic**.

Sceptic means someone who is doubtful.

Cynic is a person who believes that people are motivated purely by self-interest rather than acting for honourable or unselfish reasons.

Phobic means having or involving an extreme or irrational fear of or aversion to something.

13. Morbid compulsion to consume alcohol continuously SSC CGL Tier-1 09.09.2024 (Shift-III)

(a) Satyromania (b) Maniac
(c) Kleptomania (d) Dipsomania

Ans. (d)

Dipsomania means a morbid compulsion to consume alcohol continuously.

Satyromania means a man who has excessive and often uncontrollable sexual desire and behaviour.

Maniac means a crazy person.

Kleptomania is the excessive desire to steal.

14. An order of law requiring people to remain indoors SSC CGL Tier-1 09.09.2024 (Shift-III)

(a) Restriction (b) Curfew
(c) Limit (d) Check in

Ans. (b)

A **curfew** is an order of law requiring people to remain indoors.

Restriction and **Limit** means a limiting condition or measure, especially a legal one.

Check-in means to arrive and register at a hotel or airport.

15. A person who sells and arranges cut flowers. SSC CGL Tier-1 10.09.2024 (Shift-I)

(a) Horticulturist (b) Botanist
(c) Gardener (d) Florist

Ans. (d)

A **florist** is a person who sells and arranges cut flowers.

Horticulturist is an expert in garden cultivation and management.

Botanist is an expert in or student of the scientific study of plants.

16. A small group of people who spend their time together and do not welcome other people into that group SSC CGL Tier-1 10.09.2024 (Shift-I)

(a) Squad (b) Clique
(c) Employees (d) Lobby

Ans. (b)

A **clique** is a small group of people who spend their time together and do not welcome other people into that group.

Squad means a small organised group of military personnel.

Lobby means a room providing a space out of which one or more other rooms or corridors lead, typically one near the entrance of a public building.

17. A place where fruit trees are grown SSC CGL Tier-1 10.09.2024 (Shift-I)

(a) Orchard (b) Garden
(c) Quay (d) Museum

Ans. (a)

An **orchard** is a place where fruit trees are grown.

Quay means a stone or metal platform lying alongside or projecting into water for loading and unloading ships.

18. A government by the officials
SSC CGL Tier-1 10.09.2024 (Shift-I)
Or
A government that takes decisions based on the recommendations of state officials instead of elected representatives
SSC CPO 11.11.2022 (Shift-III)
(a) Autocracy (b) Bureaucracy
(c) Monarchy (d) Plutocracy

Ans. (b)

Bureaucracy is a government by the officials.

Autocracy means a system of government by one person with absolute power.

Monarchy means a form of government where a monarch, such as a king or queen, is the head of state and has supreme authority.

19. An often-imaginary place or state of utter perfection and happiness
SSC CGL Tier-1 10.09.2024 (Shift-II)
(a) Inferno (b) Dystopia
(c) Euphoria (d) Utopia

Ans. (d)

Utopia is a concept with defines an ideal and often imaginary place or state of utter perfection and happiness.

Inferno means a large fire that is dangerously out of control.

Dystopia means an imagined state or society in which there is great suffering or injustice, typically one that is post-apocalyptic.

Euphoria means extreme happiness.

20. Fear of closed spaces
SSC CGL Tier-1 10.09.2024 (Shift-III)
SSC MTS Tier-1 11.09.2023 (Shift-II)
(a) Photophobia
(b) Optophobia
(c) Agoraphobia
(d) Claustrophobia

Ans. (d)

Claustrophobia is the fear of closed spaces.

Photophobia is a fear of light.

Optophobia is an uncommon and debilitating phobia that causes people to fear opening their eyes.

Agoraphobia means an anxiety disorder that causes an intense fear of being in places where escape may be difficult or help may not be available.

21. A short section (as of a book) that leads to or explains the main part.
SSC CGL Tier-1 10.09.2024 (Shift-III)
(a) Foreword (b) Conclusion
(c) Postscript (d) Paraphrase

Ans. (a)

Foreword is a short section (as of a book) that leads to or explains the main part.

Postscript means is a note or series of notes added to the end of a letter, essay, book or article.

22. Choice between two unsatisfactory alternatives
SSC CGL Tier-1 10.09.2024 (Shift-III)
(a) Dilemma (b) Problem
(c) Confusion (d) Difficulty

Ans. (a)

Dilemma is a choice between two unsatisfactory alternatives.

23. Despite recent superficial moves toward political reconciliation, Libya remains in the grip of a bloodstained corrupt military <u>exclusive circle of people with a common purpose</u>.
SSC CGL Tier-1 11.09.2024 (Shift-I)
(a) oblique (b) pique
(c) clique (d) antique

Ans. (c)

A **clique** is an exclusive circle of people with a common purpose.

Oblique means not expressed or done in a direct way.

Antique means old and valuable things.

Pique means a feeling of irritation or resentment resulting from a slight, especially to one's pride.

24. An instrument for viewing distant objects in space.
SSC CGL Tier-1 11.09.2024 (Shift-I)
(a) Microscope (b) Spectrograph
(c) Telescope (d) Binoculars

Ans. (c)

A **telescope** is an instrument for viewing distant objects in space.

Spectrograph is a device that separates light from an object into its component wavelengths.

25. Awkward in movement or manner
SSC CGL Tier-1 11.09.2024 (Shift-I)
(a) Alert (b) Imbalanced
(c) Clumsy (d) Clownish

Ans. (c)

Clumsy means awkward in movement or manner.

26. A person who is trained to travel in a spacecraft.
SSC CGL Tier-1 11.09.2024 (Shift-II)
SSC CGL Tier-1 13.08.2021 (Shift-III)
SSC CPO 03.10.2023 (Shift-I)
(a) Astronaut (b) Anthropologist
(c) Alchemist (d) Curator

Ans. (a)

An **astronaut** is a person who is trained to travel in a spacecraft.

Anthropologist is a scientist who studies the origins, development and behaviours of humans.

Alchemist is someone who transforms things for the better.

A **curator** is a keeper of museum.

27. Failing to give proper care and attention **SSC CGL Tier-1 11.09.2024 (Shift-III)**
(a) Lax (b) Cautious
(c) Wild (d) Provident

Ans. (a)

Lax means failing to give proper care and attention.

Provident means frugal, saving.

28. Out of those group members, Rohan is the one <u>who opposes others</u>, no matter what they tell him.
SSC CGL Tier-1 11.09.2024 (Shift-III)
(a) antagonist (b) agonist
(c) anatomist (d) protagonist

Ans. (a)

An **antagonist** is someone who opposes others.

Agonist is a substance that mimics the actions of a neurotransmitter or hormone to produce a response when it binds to a specific receptor in the brain.

Anatomist is an expert in anatomy.

Protagonist is the main character of the story.

29. A false idea or belief
SSC CGL Tier-1 12.09.2024 (Shift-I)
(a) Reticence (b) Atrophy
(c) Fallacy (d) Entropy

Ans. (c)

Fallacy means a false idea or belief.

Reticence means an unwillingness to do something or talk about something.

Atrophy is the partial or complete wasting away of a part of the body.

Entropy is the measure of a system's thermal energy per unit temperature that is unavailable for doing useful work.

30. That which cannot be conquered
SSC CGL Tier-1 12.09.2024 (Shift-I)
(a) Invisible (b) Indelible
(c) Ineffable (d) Invincible

Ans. (d)

Invincible is used for something that cannot be conquered.

Indelible means (of ink or a pen) making marks that cannot be removed.

Ineffable means too great or extreme to be expressed or described in words.

31. In Indian mythology, most of the Asuras wish to be never able to die.
SSC CGL Tier-1 12.09.2024 (Shift-I)

(a) Invincible
(b) Impervious
(c) Invisible
(d) Immortal

Ans. (d)

Someone who can never die is called **immortal.**

Impervious means not allowing fluid to pass through.

32. He is an atheist, although he respects everyone's belief.
SSC CGL Tier-1 12.09.2024 (Shift-I)

(a) One who believes in God
(b) One who believes in nature
(c) One who is extremist
(d) One who does not believe in God

Ans. (d)

An atheist is someone who does not believe in God.

33. The list of subjects to be discussed at a meeting **SSC CGL Tier-1 12.09.2024 (Shift-II)**

(a) Minutes (b) Objectives
(c) Agenda (d) Menu

Ans. (c)

The list of subjects to be discussed at a meeting is called an agenda.

34. A place where birds are kept
SSC CGL Tier-1 12.09.2024 (Shift-III)

Or

A large cage, building or enclosure to keep birds
SSC CHSL Tier-1 10.08.2021 (Shift-I)
SSC CGL Tier-1 20.07.2023 (Shift-I)
SSC MTS Tier-1 01.09.2023 (Shift-I)

(a) Zoo (b) Aviary
(c) Sanctuary (d) Hive

Ans. (b)

An **Aviary** refers to a place where birds are kept.

Zoo is a facility in which animals are kept within enclosures for public exhibition and often bred for conservation purposes.

Sanctuary is a place where birds or animals can live and be protected, especially from being hunted or dangerous conditions.

Hive is a structure in which bees are kept, which is designed so that the beekeeper can collect the honey that they produce.

35. Incapable of being defeated
SSC CGL Tier-1 12.09.2024 (Shift-III)

(a) Invisible (b) Unavoidable
(c) Invincible (d) Ineluctable

Ans. (c)

Invincible means incapable of being defeated.

Ineluctable means unable to be resisted or avoided; inescapable.

36. Kamal is not willing to purchase a house on the 12th floor of a sea-side apartment, as she is fearful of heights. She is suffering from ....
SSC CGL Tier-1 13.09.2024 (Shift-I)

Or

Fear of heights.
SSC CHSL Tier-1 16.03.2023 (Shift-II)

(a) heliophobia (b) claustrophobia
(c) sociophobia (d) acrophobia

Ans. (d)

The fear of heights is called **acrophobia.**

Heliophobia is the fear of the Sun.

Sociophobia is a type of anxiety disorder.

Claustrophobia is a fear of closed spaces.

37. Cannot be corrected
SSC CGL Tier-1 13.09.2024 (Shift-I)
SSC CPO Tier-2 08.01.2024

Or

When her teacher calls her a person who cannot be corrected, she laughs at herself. **SSC CPO 10.11.2022 (Shift-II)**

(a) Illegible
(b) Incorrigible
(c) Incredible
(d) Ineligible

Ans. (b)

Incorrigible is something that cannot be correct.

Incredible means impossible to believe.

Ineligible means not eligible or qualified.

Illegible means not clear enough to be read.

38. A written statement made under oath
SSC CGL Tier-1 13.09.2024 (Shift-I)

(a) Testimony (b) Affirmation
(c) Affidavit (d) Statement

Ans. (c)

Affidavit is a written statement made under oath.

Testimony means a formal written or spoken statement, especially one given in a court of law.

Affirmation means agreement.

39. A large, flat area surrounded by seats used for sports or entertainment
SSC CGL Tier-1 13.09.2024 (Shift-II)

(a) Senate (b) Arena
(c) Department (d) Garden

Ans. (b)

An **Arena** is a large, flat area surrounded by seats used for sports or entertainment.

Senate is the group of politicians who have the most power to make laws in a government.

40. A period of ten years
SSC CGL Tier-1 13.09.2024 (Shift-II)

(a) Century (b) Decade
(c) Biennium (d) lustrum

Ans. (b)

A **decade** is a period of 10 years.

Century is a period of 100 years.

Biennium means a specified period of two years.

Lustrum means a purificatory sacrifice made after a census every five years.

41. One who eats a lot
SSC CGL Tier-1 13.09.2024 (Shift-II)

Or

A person who eats too much
SSC CPO 05.10.2023 (Shift-II)

(a) Chauffeur (b) Steward
(c) Glutton (d) Chef

Ans. (c)

A **glutton** is someone who eats a lot.

Chauffeur means someone who drives a car.

Steward means a person employed to look after the passengers on a ship, aircraft, or train.

Chef is someone who cooks.

42. An important person who represents his/her country in a foreign country
SSC CGL Tier-1 13.09.2024 (Shift-III)

(a) Amateur (b) Ambassador
(c) Altruist (d) Anonymous

Ans. (b)

An **ambassador** is an important person who represents his/her country in a foreign country.

Amateur is a person who participates in an activity for pleasure, not for pay.

Altruist is a person who cares about others and helps them despite not gaining anything by doing this.

Anonymous means not known.

43. A person who is unsure about God's existence
SSC CGL Tier-1 13.09.2024 (Shift-III)

(a) Ignorant (b) Atheist
(c) Agnostic (d) Theist

Ans. (c)

Agnostic is a person who is unsure about God's existence.

Ignorant is a person who does not have much knowledge.

Theist is a person who believes in God.

An **Atheist** is someone who does not believe in God.

44. One who speaks less in a forum.
SSC CGL Tier-1 13.09.2024 (Shift-III)

(a) Eccentric (b) Loquacious
(c) Gabby (d) Reticent

Ans. (d)

A **Reticent** is a person who speaks less in a forum.

Eccentric means strange.

Loquacious means talkative.

Gabby means excessively or annoyingly talkative.

45. Illiterate **SSC CGL Tier-1 13.09.2024 (Shift-III)**

(a) A person who cannot speak
(b) One who is well-educated
(c) A person who cannot read and write
(d) Highly rated thing

Ans. (c)

An Illiterate is a person who cannot read and write.

46. The study of coins
SSC CGL Tier-1 17.09.2024 (Shift-I)
SSC CPO 05.10.2023 (Shift-II)

(a) Numismatics (b) Choreography
(c) Informatics (d) Cartography

Ans. (a)

Numismatics is a study of coins.

Choreography is the act of making dance steps.

Informatics is the study of how information is represented, processed and communicated in systems, both natural and engineered

Cartography is the act of drawing maps.

47. A person who is inclined to see the worst aspect of things
SSC CGL Tier-1 17.09.2024 (Shift-I)

(a) Pessimist (b) Philanthropist
(c) Optimist (d) Altruist

Ans. (a)

A **Pessimist** is a person who is inclined to see the worst aspect of things.

Altruist is an unselfish person whose actions show concern for the welfare of others.

Philanthropist is one who donates money, time or other resources for welfare of others.

Optimist is a positive or hopeful person.

48. Almost immediately, they heard the high shrill piercing cry of tires on the side road. **SSC CGL Tier-1 17.09.2024 (Shift-II)**

(a) Beseech (b) Creche
(c) Screech (d) Bleach

Ans. (c)

A **Screech** is a high shrill piercing cry.

Beseech means to ask (someone) urgently and fervently to do something; implore; entreat.

Creche refers to a nursery where babies and young children are cared for during the working day.

49. A thing fit to eat.
SSC CGL Tier-1 17.09.2024 (Shift-II)
SSC CGL Tier-1 14.07.2023 (Shift-I)

(a) Edible (b) Unpalatable
(c) Uneatable (d) Toxic

Ans. (a)

The things that are fit to eat is **edible**.

Unpalatable means not pleasant to taste.

50. A person who deceives others by pretending to be someone else
SSC CGL Tier-1 17.09.2024 (Shift-II)

Or

Someone who dishonestly pretends to deceive under an assumed character **SSC CGL Tier-1 20.07.2023 (Shift-III)**

(a) Unrecognisable (b) Fraud
(c) Impostor (d) Inaccessible

Ans. (c)

An **impostor** is a person who deceives others by pretending to be someone else.

Fraud means someone who cheats others.

Inaccessible means unable to be reached or entered.

51. The workers received a sum for the services they <u>rendered</u>.
SSC CGL Tier-1 17.09.2024 (Shift-II)

(a) Recruitment (b) Remembrance
(c) Remuneration (d) Rejuvenation

Ans. (c)

Remuneration is a sum given for the services they rendered.

Rejuvenation means to renergise.

Recruitment means to hire someone.

52. Foul smell will come if the food is <u>not fresh</u>. **SSC CGL Tier-1 17.09.2024 (Shift-II)**

(a) brittle (b) crisp
(c) stale (d) odourless

Ans. (c)

Stale means not fresh.

Brittle means fragile or easily broken.

Crisp means new.

Odourless means without any smell.

53. <u>Capable of being done</u>
SSC CGL Tier-1 17.09.2024 (Shift-II)

(a) Suitable (b) Feasible
(c) Practical (d) Useful

Ans. (b)

Feasible means capable of being done.

54. One who eats the flesh of his own species **SSC CGL Tier-1 18.09.2024 (Shift-I)**

Or

One who eats human flesh.
SSC CGL Tier-1 25.09.2024 (Shift-II)

(a) Non-vegetarian (b) Vegan
(c) Cannibal (d) Mammal

Ans. (c)

A **Cannibal** is who eats the flesh of his own species or human flesh.

Mammal refers to a vertebrate animal whose young are nourished with milk from special mammary glands of the mother.

55. My father always tells amusing and true stories from his childhood at bedtime. **SSC CGL Tier-1 18.09.2024 (Shift-I)**

(a) anecdotes (b) sonnets
(c) fables (d) allegories

Ans. (a)

Anecdotes mean amusing and true stories.

Sonnets are 14 line poems.

Fables means a short story, typically with animals as characters, conveying a moral.

Allegories means a story, poem, or picture that can be interpreted to reveal a hidden meaning, typically a moral or political one.

56. Humour that describes the weaknesses of the other person is itself a crime among peer groups.
SSC CGL Tier-1 18.09.2024 (Shift-I)

(a) A joke (b) Attire
(c) Satire (d) A curse

Ans. (c)

A Satire refers to a humourous literature that describes the weaknesses of the other person is itself a crime among peer groups.

57. Most of the rivers dry up during the summer season, but the Ganga is full of water round the year because it is ....
SSC CGL Tier-1 18.09.2024 (Shift-II)

(a) biennial (b) biannual
(c) perennial (d) annual

Ans. (c)

Perennial means lasting or existing for a long or apparently infinite time; enduring or continually recurring. Hence, it can be used for round the year.

Biennial means lasting for two years or occurring every two years.

Biannual means occurring twice a year.

Annual means yearly.

58. Much more than usual or expected
SSC CGL Tier-1 18.09.2024 (Shift-III)
(a) Mordancy (b) Ordinate
(c) Subordinate (d) Exceeding

Ans. (d)

Exceeding means much more than usual or expected.

Mordancy means a biting or caustic quality of style or a sharply critical or bitter quality of thought or feeling.

Ordinate means the second number in a pair.

Subordinate means inferior in position.

59. A short stay that you make while on a longer journey
SSC CGL Tier-1 18.09.2024 (Shift-III)
(a) Saga (b) Stopover
(c) Refugee (d) Tent

Ans. (b)

Stopover is a short stay that you make while on a longer journey.

Refugee refers to people who move to another country to seek safety.

60. Having unlimited power
SSC CGL Tier-1 18.09.2024 (Shift-III)
Or
One who is all powerful.
SSC MTS Tier-1 14.09.2023 (Shift-I)
SSC CGL Tier-2 08.08.2022
(a) Omnipotent (b) Omnipresence
(c) Omniscient (d) Omnivorous

Ans. (a)

Omnipotent means to have unlimited power.

Omnipresence is one who is present everywhere.

Omniscient is one who knows everything.

Omnivorous are animals who eat plants as well as other animals.

61. A person who performs magic to entertain people
SSC CGL Tier-1 19.09.2024 (Shift-I)
(a) Alchemist (b) Angel
(c) Magician (d) Palmist

Ans. (c)

A **magician** is a person who performs magic to entertain people.

Alchemist is someone who transforms things for the better.

Palmist is a person who reads palms and suggested future.

62. A person who is kept captive for fulfilment of demands of money or conditions **SSC CGL Tier-1 19.09.2024 (Shift-I)**
(a) Hostage (b) Hermit
(c) Heretic (d) Introvert

Ans. (a)

A **hostage** is a person who is kept captive for fulfilment of demands of money or conditions.

Hermit is a person living in solitude as a religious discipline.

Heretic is a person believing in or practising religious heresy.

Introvert is a shy person.

63. The statistical study of human populations.
SSC CGL Tier-1 19.09.2024 (Shift-II)
Or
The study of population and its dynamics **SSC CHSL 25.05.2022 (Shift-III)**
(a) Photography (b) Palaeography
(c) Astronomy (d) Demography

Ans. (d)

Demography is the statistical study of human populations.

Palaeography is the study of historical writing systems, including handwriting, manuscripts and printed media.

64. In industries, it is very common to observe that people show undue favour to one's own relative during the hiring process.
SSC CGL Tier-1 19.09.2024 (Shift-II)
(a) nepotism (b) racism
(c) liberalism (d) communism

Ans. (a)

Nepotism refers to undue favour to one's own relative during the hiring process.

Liberalism is a political and moral philosophy based on the rights of the individual, liberty, consent of the governed, political equality, right to private property and equality before the law.

Communism is a political and economic system that aims to create a classless society where the state controls the means of production and wealth.

65. One who tends to look at the dark side of things
SSC CGL Tier-1 19.09.2024 (Shift-II)
SSC MTS 13.09.2023 (Shift-I)
Or
One who looks at the negative side of everything
SSC CGL Tier-1 20.07.2023 (Shift-III)
SSC CHSL Tier-1 14.03.2023 (Shift-I)
Or
One who always expects the worst possible outcome.
SSC CHSL Tier-1 04.08. 2023 (Shift-II)
(a) Dynamist (b) Polemist
(c) Optimist (d) Pessimist

Ans. (d)

A **pessimist** is one who tends to look at the dark side of things.

Dynamist is a person who supports a philosophical theory that explains phenomena in terms of a force or energy.

Polemist is a person who uses contentious rhetoric to support their position and undermine the opposing position.

66. An utter state of confusion
SSC CGL Tier-1 19.09.2024 (Shift-III)
(a) Pathos (b) Engross
(c) Innuendos (d) Chaos

Ans. (d)

Chaos is an utter state of confusion.

Pathos means a quality that evokes pity or sadness.

Engross means absorb all the attention or interest of. Innuendos means an allusive or oblique remark or hint, typically a suggestive or disparaging one.

Innuendo means a suggestive phrase.

67. Lack of interest, enthusiasm or concern **SSC CGL Tier-1 19.09.2024 (Shift-III)**
(a) Sympathy (b) Apathy
(c) Empathy (d) Antipathy

Ans. (b)

Apathy is a lack of interest, enthusiasm or concern.

Sympathy means feelings of pity and sorrow for someone else's misfortune.

Empathy means the ability to understand and share another person's feelings, experiences and perspective.

Antipathy means a deep-seated feeling of aversion.

68. The study of ancient things such as art, graves, ruins, etc.
SSC CGL Tier-1 19.09.2024 (Shift-III)
(a) Astrology (b) Archaeology
(c) Geology (d) Meteorology

Ans. (b)

Archaeology is the study of ancient things such as art, graves, ruins, etc.

Astrology is the study of the positions and movements of the planets, Sun, Moon and Stars and their supposed influence on human events and character.

Geology is the scientific study of the Earth, including its physical features, composition, structure and processes that have shaped it over time.

Meteorology means the scientific study of the atmosphere and its effects on weather, including weather forecasting.

69. A person who has supreme power or authority **SSC CGL Tier-1 19.09.2024 (Shift-III)**
(a) Secular (b) Sovereign
(c) Diversity (d) Foreign
Ans. (b)
Sovereign is the word used to refer to a person or institution which has supreme power or authority.

70. Speaking disrespectfully about sacred or religious things.
SSC CGL Tier-1 23.09.2024 (Shift-I)
Or
The action or offence of speaking sacrilegiously about God or sacred things; profane talk
SSC MTS Tier-1 19.05.2023 (Shift-I)
(a) Blasphemy (b) Mystic
(c) Atheist (d) Theist
Ans. (a)
Blasphemy is speaking disrespectfully about sacred or religious things.
Mystic is a person who seeks to obtain unity with or absorption into the Deity or the absolute.
Theist is a person who believes in God.

71. A thing that can be easily carried by hands **SSC CGL Tier-1 23.09.2024 (Shift-II)**
(a) Export (b) Import
(c) Potable (d) Portable
Ans. (d)
A thing that can be easily carried by hands is called **portable**.
Export means to send something to another land.
Import means to bring something from another land.
Potable is something that is safe to drink.

72. A place to park aeroplanes
SSC CGL Tier-1 23.09.2024 (Shift-III)
SSC MTS Tier-1 15.06.2023 (Shift-III)
Or
A huge building with a spacious area to house aircrafts
SSC CGL Tier-1 06.12.2022 (Shift-IV)
Or
A place where airplanes are kept for maintenance
SSC CGL Tier-2 27.07.2023 (Shift-III)
Or
A large building with an extensive floor area, typically for housing aircraft **SSC CGL Tier-1 16.08.2021 (Shift-I)**
(a) Hanger (b) Depot
(c) Shed (d) Hangar
Ans. (d)
Hangar is a place to park aeroplanes.
Hanger means a person who hangs something.
Depot means a place for the storage of large quantities of equipment, food, or goods.
Shed means a simple roofed structure used for garden storage, to shelter animals, or as a workshop.

73. Athens was suffering under the <u>rule of a powerful small group</u> that had no concern for the people's welfare.
SSC CGL Tier-1 23.09.2024 (Shift-III)
Or
The liberal leadership simply joined the ranks of the existing government by the few. **SSC CPO 29.06.2024 (Shift-I)**
(a) a democracy (b) an oligarchy
(c) a monarchy (d) a missionary
Ans. (b)
An **oligarchy** is a small but powerful group that takes an authoritative position.
A **democracy** is a government elected by the people.
A **monarchy** is a form of government where a monarch, such as a king or queen, is the head of state and has supreme authority.
A **missionary** is a member of a religious group who is sent to a specific area to promote their faith or provide services to the people there.

74. The evening time when the Sun has just set and it is almost dark.
SSC CGL Tier-1 23.09.2024 (Shift-III)
(a) Dusk (b) Night
(c) Dawn (d) Day break
Ans. (a)
Dusk is the evening time when the Sun has just set and it is almost dark.

75. A person who does not believe in God **SSC CGL Tier-1 24.09.2024 (Shift-I)**
SSC CGL Tier-1 20.08.2021 (Shift-I)
SSC CPO 27.06.2024 (Shift-II)
SSC CPO 28.06.2024 (Shift-II)
Or
A person who does not believe that God or Gods exist
SSC CGL Tier-1 14.07.2023 (Shift-IV)
SSC CPO 03.10.2023 (Shift-II)
(a) Amateur (b) Anarchy
(c) Autocrat (d) Atheist
Ans. (d)
An **Atheist** is a person who does not believe in God.
Amateur is a person who participates in an activity for pleasure, not for pay.
Anarchy is a state of disorder due to absence or non-recognition of authority or other controlling systems.
Autocrat is a ruler who has absolute power.

76. Dealing with things in a practical and sensible way
SSC CGL Tier-1 24.09.2024 (Shift-II)
(a) Pragmatic (b) Sceptic
(c) Stoic (d) Cynic
Ans. (a)
Pragmatic means practical and sensible.
Sceptic refers to a person who is doubtful of something.
Stoic refers to someone who does not show any emotion.
Cynic is a person who believes that people are selfish.

77. Anything pertaining to cats
SSC CGL Tier-1 24.09.2024 (Shift-II)
(a) Bovine (b) Canine
(c) Taurine (d) Feline
Ans. (d)
Feline is anything that pertains to cats.
Bovine means related to a cow.
Canine means related to a dog.
Taurine means related to a chemical that produces an amino acid that helps with bodily functions, including those of the digestive, cardiovascular, skeletal, muscular and nervous systems.

78. That which is no longer in existence
SSC CGL Tier-1 24.09.2024 (Shift-II)
(a) Extinct (b) Removed
(c) Vanished (d) Destroyed
Ans. (a)
Extinct means something that is no longer in existence.

79. Essence or main point of any passage, lecture or book
SSC CGL Tier-1 24.09.2024 (Shift-III)
(a) Gist (b) Significance
(c) Meaning (d) Heart
Ans. (a)
Gist is the essence of or main point of any passage, lecture or book.

80. We, as human beings, have a tendency of believing in the things that can be seen and touched.
SSC CGL Tier-1 24.09.2024 (Shift-III)
(a) impalpable (b) spiritual
(c) inexpressible (d) tangible
Ans. (d)
Things that can be seen and touched is called **tangible.**
Impalpable means unable to be felt by touch.

81. Fear of snakes
SSC CGL Tier-1 24.09.2024 (Shift-III)
(a) Claustrophobia
(b) Syngenesophobia
(c) Xenophobia
(d) Ophidiophobia

Ans. (d)

Ophidiophobia is the fear of snakes.

Syngenesophobia is an intense fear of relatives, including siblings.

Xenophobia means dislike of or prejudice against people from other countries.

82. A performer's first public appearance

SSC CGL Tier-1 25.09.2024 (Shift-I)

(a) Foundation (b) Debut
(c) Premise (d) Dawn

Ans. (b)

A performer's first public appearance means a **debut**.

Foundation and **Premise** refer to the base an argument, theory, or undertaking on.

Dawn refers to the first appearance of light in the sky before sunrise.

83. To go through an area making a lot of noise and causing damage

SSC CGL Tier-1 25.09.2024 (Shift-I)

(a) Brutality
(b) Cacophony
(c) Violence
(d) Rampage

Ans. (d)

Rampage means to go through an area making a lot of noise and causing damage.

Brutality means cruelty.

Cacophony means a harsh and unpleasant sound.

84. The ship launched out on a journey by water or sea of discovery.

SSC CGL Tier-1 25.09.2024 (Shift-II)

(a) voyage (b) rendezvous
(c) verso (d) vesper

Ans. (a)

A **voyage** is a journey by water or sea.

Rendezvous means a meeting at an agreed time and place.

Verso means a left-hand page of an open book, or the back of a loose document.

Vespers means a Christian evening prayer service that takes place in the late afternoon or evening.

85. The line, 'Round the rugged rocks the ragged rascal ran' uses the repetition of usually initial consonant sounds in two or more neighbouring words or syllables.

SSC CGL Tier-1 25.09.2024 (Shift-III)

Or

Words that begin with the same letter, syllable or sound

SSC CGL Tier-1 12.12.2022 (Shift-II

(a) alliteration (b) epithet
(c) simile (d) allegory

Ans. (a)

Alliteration is the repetition of usually initial consonant sounds in two or more neighbouring words or syllables.

Epithet is a descriptive word or phrase that is used to describe a person, place or thing and often appears in place of its name.

Simile is a literary device wherein we make a comparison

using words like and as.

Allegory is a literary device wherein a story, poem or picture that can be interpreted to reveal a hidden meaning, typically a moral or political one.

86. The soldier struck the enemy with the short sword fixed onto the end of the gun.

SSC CGL Tier-1 25.09.2024 (Shift-III)

(a) Baron (b) Bayonet
(c) Bigot (d) Baton

Ans. (b)

Bayonet refers to a short sword fixed onto the end of the gun.

Baron means a member of the lowest order of the British nobility.

Bigot means a person who has strong, unreasonable ideas, esp. about race or religion, and who thinks anyone who does not have the same beliefs is wrong.

Baton means a thick, heavy stick used as a weapon by police officers.

87. The <u>betrayer of the country</u> was at last unmasked.

SSC CGL Tier-1 25.09.2024 (Shift-III)

Or

Person who betrays his own country

SSC CGL Tier-1 19.07.2023 (Shift-I)

(a) traitor
(b) truant
(c) transgressor
(d) theist

Ans. (a)

Traitor means a betrayer of the country.

Truant means a pupil who stays away from school without leave or explanation.

Transgressor means a person who breaks a law or moral rule.

Theist means a person who believes in the existence of a god or gods, specifically of a creator who intervenes in the universe.

88. One who looks at the bright side of things/situations

SSC CGL Tier-1 26.09.2024 (Shift-I)

(a) Saint (b) Optimist
(c) Pessimist (d) Scientist

Ans. (b)

Optimist is the one who looks at the bright side of things/situations.

Saint is a person acknowledged as holy or virtuous and regarded in Christian faith as being in heaven after death.

89. His parents didn't allow him to enrol in the arts college because he is a dabbler in arts, science or literature.

SSC CGL Tier-1 26.09.2024 (Shift-I)

(a) Connoisseur (b) Taciturn
(c) Dilettante (d) Ignoramus

Ans. (c)

Dilettante is a dabbler in arts, science or literature.

Taciturn means (of a person) reserved or uncommunicative in speech; saying little.

Ignoramus means an ignorant or stupid person.

Connoisseur means a person who is an expert in the matter of taste.

90. Loud enough to be heard.

SSC CGL Tier-1 26.09.2024 (Shift-II)

(a) Audible (b) Audit
(c) Audacious (d) Audacity

Ans. (a)

Audible means something that is loud enough to hear.

Audit means an official inspection of an organisation's accounts, typically by an independent body.

Audacious and **Audacity** indicate boldness.

Audacity means courage.

91. Money collected from people for a cause.

SSC CGL Tier-1 26.09.2024 (Shift-II)

(a) Collection
(b) Deposit
(c) Fund
(d) Savings

Ans. (c)

Money collected from people for a cause is called a **fund**.

92. Study of flying airplanes

SSC CGL Tier-1 26.09.2024 (Shift-III)

(a) Aviation (b) Alchemy
(c) Astronomy (d) Acoustics

Ans. (a)

Aviation is the study of flying airplanes.

Alchemy is a process of transformation, creation, or combination.

Acoustics is the science that deals with the production, control, transmission, reception and effects of sound.

SSC CGL 2023 (Tier 1 & 2)

93. A person who believes that laws and governments are not necessary
SSC CGL Tier-1 14.07.2023 (Shift-II)

(a) Antagonist (b) Antichrist
(c) Anarchist (d) Adversary

Ans. (c)

An **anarchist** is a person who rebels against any authority, established order or ruling power believing that laws and government are not necessary.

Antichrist refers to a person or force opposing Christ or the Christian church.

Adversary refers to one's opponent in a contest, conflict or dispute.

94. A person who hates and avoids other people **SSC CGL Tier-1 14.07.2023 (Shift-III)**

(a) Masochist (b) Pervert
(c) Hermit (d) Misanthrope

Ans. (d)

A **misanthrope** is a person who hates and avoids all other people or hates mankind in general.

Masochist is a person who enjoys an activity that appears to be painful or tedious.

Pervert is a person with immoral behaviour.

Hermit is a person living in solitude as a religious discipline.

95. A place where coins, medals or tokens are made
SSC CGL Tier-1 14.07.2023 (Shift-III)
SSC CPO 04.10.2023 (Shift-I)

Or

A place where coins and medals are made. **SSC CGL Tier-1 05.12.2022 (Shift-III)**

(a) Hutch (b) Hangar
(c) Mint (d) Monastery

Ans. (c)

A **mint** is a place where coins or tokens are made.

Hutch is a chest or compartment for storage.

Monastery is a building or buildings occupied by a community of monks living under religious vows.

Hangar is a place for storing aircraft.

96. A person who abandons religion
SSC CGL Tier-1 14.07.2023 (Shift-III)

Or

A person who renounces a religious or political belief or principle.
SSC CHSL Tier-1 16.03.2023 (Shift-II)

(a) Egotist (b) Priest
(c) Apostate (d) Atheist

Ans. (c)

A person who abandons religion is an **apostate.**

Egotist is a person who considers himself or herself to be better or more important than other people.

Priest is someone who is authorised to perform the sacred rites of a religion.

97. A book or set of books giving information about all areas of knowledge
SSC CGL Tier-1 14.07.2023 (Shift-IV)

Or

A book or set of books giving information on many subjects or on many aspects of one subject and typically arranged alphabetically.
SSC CGL Tier-2 08.08.2022

Or

Book giving information about everything
SSC CHSL Tier-1 10.03.2023 (Shift-III)

(a) Encyclopedia
(b) Dictionary
(c) Volume
(d) Anthology

Ans. (a)

An **encyclopedia** is a book or a set of books giving information about all areas of knowledge.

Dictionary is a book or digital resource giving information on a particular subject or on a particular class of words, names or facts, usually arranged alphabetically.

Volume is a book forming part of a work or series.

Anthology is a collection of selected literary pieces or passages or works of art or music.

98. Irreverent behaviour towards anything held sacred or concerning God **SSC CGL Tier-1 17.07.2023 (Shift-I)**

(a) Agnosticism
(b) Pantheism
(c) Theism
(d) Blasphemy

Ans. (d)

Blasphemy is disrespectful behaviour towards anything scared or related to God.

Agnosticism is the view or belief that the existence of God, the divine or the supernatural is either unknowable in principle or currently unknown in fact.

Pantheism is the philosophical and religious belief that reality, the universe and nature are identical to divinity or a supreme entity.

Theism is belief in the existence of God as creator and ruler of the universe.

99. Huge fire for celebration
SSC CGL Tier-1 17.07.2023 (Shift-I)

(a) Firepower (b) Festivity
(c) Firefight (d) Bonfire

Ans. (d)

A bonfire is a huge fire that is made for a festival or celebration.

100. A place to play games and bet on them **SSC CGL Tier-1 17.07.2023 (Shift-I)**

(a) Motel (b) Hotel
(c) Casino (d) Pub

Ans. (c)

A **casino** is a place to play games or bet on them.

Motel is a hotel designed for motorists, usually having each room entered directly from the parking area for motor vehicles rather than through a central lobby.

Hotel is a commercial establishment offering lodging to travellers and sometimes to permanent residents.

Pub is an establishment where alcoholic beverages are sold and consumed.

101. Any female animal which feeds its young ones milk from her own body
SSC CGL Tier-1 17.07.2023 (Shift-II)

(a) Vertebrate (b) Parasite
(c) Mammal (d) Fauna

Ans. (c)

A **mammal** is an animal which feeds its young ones milk from her own body.

Vertebrate is an animal group distinguished by the possession of a backbone.

Parasite is an organism that lives in or on an organism of another species (its host) and benefits by deriving nutrients at the other's expense.

Fauna refers to the animals found in a region.

102. Certain to happen
SSC CGL Tier-1 17.07.2023 (Shift-II)

(a) Justifiable (b) Indispensable
(c) Convertible (d) Inevitable

Ans. (d)

Something that is certain to happen is called **inevitable.**

Justifiable means something that can be proven true with reason and logic.

Convertible means something that can be changed.

Indispensable means absolutely necessary.

103. Only the artists who make sculptures are allowed to take part in exhibitions.
SSC CGL Tier-1 17.07.2023 (Shift-II)

(a) Painter (b) Artisan
(c) Sculptor (d) Potter

Ans. (c)

A **sculptor** is an artist who makes sculptures out of clay or mud.

104. A similarity between like features of two things, on which a comparison may be based.

SSC CGL Tier-1 17.07.2023 (Shift-III)

(a) Analogy (b) Amalgamation
(c) Apathy (d) Ambiguity

Ans. (a)

Analogy refers to similarities between the features of two things.

Amalgamation means joining of two things.

Apathy means lack of any feeling.

Ambiguity means confusion.

105. The money paid to former wife, husband or partner when the marriage is ended.

SSC CGL Tier-1 17.07.2023 (Shift-III)

Or

Allowance given to a wife from her husband on separation

SSC CGL Tier-1 07.12.2022 (Shift-I)

(a) Alimony (b) Compensation
(c) Recompense (d) Maintenance

Ans. (a)

Alimony is the money paid to the former spouse when a marriage is ended.

Compensation means money that is paid to someone in exchange for something that has been lost or damaged.

Recompense means to make amends to (someone) for loss or harm suffered.

106. A group of people travelling together in a van SSC CGL Tier-1 17.07.2023 (Shift-III)

(a) Gypsies (b) Caravan
(c) Brood (d) Constellation

Ans. (b)

A **caravan** is a group of people travelling together in a van.

Gypsies refers to a member of a group of people who travel from place to place.

Brood is a group of birds.

Constellation is a group of stars.

107. A detailed description of a series of real or fictional events taking place over a long period of time.

SSC CGL Tier-1 17.07.2023 (Shift-IV)

(a) Witness (b) Journal
(c) Saga (d) Case study

Ans. (c)

A **saga** is a detailed description of a series of real or fictional events taking place over a long period of time.

Witness means a person who sees an event, typically a crime or accident, take place.

Journal means a newspaper or magazine that deals with a particular subject or professional activity.

Case Study means an intensive study about a person, a group of people or a unit, which is aimed to generalise over several units'.

108. A person who compiles a dictionary

SSC CGL Tier-1 17.07.2023 (Shift-IV)

(a) Plagiarist (b) Iconoclast
(c) Bibliophile (d) Lexicographer

Ans. (d)

A **lexicographer** is a person who compiles a dictionary.

Plagiarist is a person who copies the work of another and tries to submit it as his/her own.

Iconoclast is a person who attacks or criticises cherished beliefs or institutions.

Bibliophile is a lover and collector of books.

109. Harangue

SSC CGL Tier-1 17.07.2023 (Shift-IV)

(a) Strict disciplinarian
(b) Breaker of idols
(c) Airplane shed
(d) A lengthy and aggressive speech

Ans. (d)

A **harangue** is a lengthy and aggressive speech.

110. A sentimental memory of the past

SSC CGL Tier-1 18.07.2023 (Shift-I)

Or

An excessively intense desire for returning to past or lost conditions

SSC CGL Tier-1 05.12.2022 (Shift-IV)

(a) Hysteria (b) Nostalgia
(c) Mania (d) Euphoria

Ans. (b)

A sentimental memory of the past is called **nostalgia**.

Hysteria means exaggerated or uncontrollable emotion or excitement.

Mania means craziness.

Euphoria means the feelings of extreme satisfaction or happiness.

111. A large number of fish swimming together SSC CGL Tier-1 18.07.2023 (Shift-I)

(a) Shoal (b) Stream
(c) Sheaf (d) String

Ans. (a)

A **shoal** is a collective noun for a large number of fish swimming together.

Stream means a small, narrow river.

Sheaf is a bundle of grain stalks laid lengthways and tied together after reaping.

String is a material consisting of threads of cotton, hemp or other material twisted together to form a thin length.

112. A secret plan, made to do something (usually wrong)

SSC CGL Tier-1 18.07.2023 (Shift-II)

(a) Strategy
(b) Planning
(c) Conditioning
(d) Conspiracy

Ans. (d)

A **conspiracy** is a secret plan made to do something wrong.

Strategy means plans.

Conditioning means the process of training or accustoming a person or animal to behave in a certain way or to accept certain circumstances.

113. To put off doing something, especially out of habitual carelessness or laziness SSC CGL Tier-1 18.07.2023 (Shift-II)

SSC CGL Tier-1 08.12.2022 (Shift-IV)

(a) Accelerate (b) Lacerate
(c) Procrastinate (d) Recuperate

Ans. (c)

To **procrastinate** means to put off doing something especially out of habitual carelessness or laziness.

Accelerate means to increase in rate, amount or extent.

Lacerate means to tear or make cuts.

Recuperate means to recover from something.

114. A person who gives help and sympathy to people who need it

SSC CGL Tier-1 18.07.2023 (Shift-II)

(a) Preacher (b) Moralist
(c) Samaritan (d) Pardoner

Ans. (c)

A **Samaritan** is a person who gives help or sympathy to people who need it.

Preacher is a person who teaches religion.

Moralist refers to a person who promotes morality.

Pardoner refers to a person who forgives or excuses a fault.

115. A person who draws or produces maps SSC CGL Tier-1 18.07.2023 (Shift-III)

Or

While I was travelling in Europe, I met a <u>man who drew maps</u>.

SSC CGL Tier-1 12.12.2022 (Shift-II)

(a) Calligrapher (b) Choreographer
(c) Chauffeur (d) Cartographer

Ans. (d)

A **cartographer** is a person who draws or produces maps.

Calligrapher is a person who writes in beautiful handwriting.

Choreographer is a person who creates dance steps.

Chauffeur is a person who is hired to drive a car.

116. Something that is absolutely necessary, that you cannot do without **SSC CGL Tier-1 18.07.2023 (Shift-IV)**

Or

Something that is necessary or crucial **SSC MTS Tier-1 03.05.2023 (Shift-III)**

(a) Insular
(b) Indispensable
(c) Isolated
(d) Intolerant

Ans. (b)

Indispensable means something that is necessary and cannot be done away with.

Insular means ignorant of or uninterested in cultures, ideas or peoples outside one's own experience.

Isolated means far away from other places, buildings or people; remote.

Intolerant means failure or inability to tolerate.

117. Animal living both on land and water **SSC CGL Tier-1 18.07.2023 (Shift-IV)**

(a) Marine (b) Amphibian
(c) Arboreal (d) Terrestrial

Ans. (b)

An **amphibian** is an animal who can live both on land and water.

Marine means relating to or found in the sea.

Arboreal means relating to or resembling a tree.

Terrestrial means relating to the Earth.

118. The study of evolution of mankind **SSC CGL Tier-1 19.07.2023 (Shift-I)**

Or

The study of Man **SSC CPO 28.06.2024 (Shift-I)**

(a) Biology (b) Anthology
(c) Anthropology (d) Psychology

Ans. (c)

Anthropology is the study of evolution of mankind.

Biology is the scientific study of life and living organisms.

Anthology is a collection of selected literary pieces or passages or works of art or music.

Psychology is the scientific study of the human mind and its functions.

119. Child bereaved of one or both the parents **SSC CGL Tier-1 19.07.2023 (Shift-II)**

(a) Destitute (b) Orphan
(c) Lout (d) Desolate

Ans. (b)

An **orphan** is a child who has lost his/her parents and family.

Destitute mean poor and impoverished.

Lout means an aggressive man or boy.

Desolate means uninhabited and giving an impression of bleak emptiness.

120. Having a consistency that does not easily yield to pressure **SSC CGL Tier-1 19.07.2023 (Shift-II)**

(a) Substantial (b) Firm
(c) Ramrod (d) Close

Ans. (b)

Firm means having a consistency that does not easily give in to pressure.

Substantial means in large quantity.

Ramrod is a long, thin rod which can be used for pushing something into a narrow tube.

121. Government governed by wealth **SSC CGL Tier-1 19.07.2023 (Shift-III)**

Or

A government run by the wealthy people **SSC CHSL Tier-1 04.08.2021 (Shift-I)**

(a) Theocracy
(b) Autocracy
(c) Democracy
(d) Plutocracy

Ans. (d)

Plutocracy is the government governed by the wealth or wealthy.

Theocracy is a government in which the priests rule in the name of God.

Autocracy is a government where a single person or group rules.

Democracy is a government where people have the ultimate power.

122. Copying someone else's work and trying to submit as your own **SSC CGL Tier-1 19.07.2023 (Shift-III)** **SSC MTS 14.09.2023 (Shift-I)**

(a) Plagiarism (b) Hooliganism
(c) Altruism (d) Cynicism

Ans. (a)

Plagiarism refers to copying someone's work and submitting it as one's own.

Hooliganism means violent or rowdy behaviour by young troublemakers, typically in a gang.

Altruism means selfless concern for the well-being of others.

Cynicism refers to the belief that people are only interested in themselves and are not sincere.

123. A person who enjoys doing dangerous things, in a way that other people may think is stupid **SSC CGL Tier-1 19.07.2023 (Shift-IV)**

(a) Cavalier
(b) Lunatic
(c) Gallant
(d) Daredevil

Ans. (d)

A **daredevil** is a person who enjoys doing dangerous things in a way that other people may think is stupid.

Cavalier is a gallant or a gentleman of the royal court.

Lunatic refers to a crazy man.

124. Forsaken or neglected child who has no home and spends most of his/her time on the streets **SSC CGL Tier-1 19.07.2023 (Shift-IV)**

(a) Fugitive (b) Vulnerable
(c) Miscreant (d) Waif

Ans. (d)

A **waif** is a neglected child who has not home and spends his/her time on the streets.

Fugitive is a person, generally a criminal, who has run away from captivity.

Vulnerable means exposed to the possibility of being attacked or harmed, either physically or emotionally.

Miscreant means a person who has done something wrong or unlawful.

125. Gradual recovery of health and strength **SSC CGL Tier-1 20.07.2023 (Shift-I)**

(a) Convalescence
(b) Potency
(c) Benefaction
(d) Rejuvenation

Ans. (a)

Convalescence means gradual recovery of health and strength.

Potency means force or power.

Benefaction means donation or gift.

Rejuvenation refers to an action or process of giving new energy or vigour to something.

126. Capable of being bent or pulled into different shapes **SSC CGL Tier-1 20.07.2023 (Shift-I)**

(a) Lithe (b) Willowy
(c) Ductile (d) Lissome

Ans. (c)

Ductile means capable of being bent or pulled into a thin wire.

Lithe and **Lissome** means thin and graceful.

Willowy means tall and slim.

127. Manisha is a believer of fate
SSC CGL Tier-1 20.07.2023 (Shift-II)
Or
One who believes in fate.
SSC CGL Tier-1 24.07.2023 (Shift-II)
SSC CPO 10.11.2022 (Shift-III)
SSC CHSLTier-2 02.11. 2023 (Shift-I)
(a) Minimalist (b) Socialist
(c) Fatalist (d) Catalyst
Ans. (c)
A **fatalist** is someone who believes in fate.
Minimalist is a person who takes as little action or shows as little involvement in a situation as possible.
Socialist is someone who supports a political or economic philosophy that says society as a whole, rather than private companies, owns and regulates production, distribution and exchange of good.
Catalyst is a substance that increases the rate of a chemical reaction without itself undergoing any permanent chemical change.

128. Waver between different opinions or actions SSC CGL Tier-1 20.07.2023 (Shift-III)
(a) Sway (b) Viaduct
(c) Thrifty (d) Vacillate
Ans. (d)
Vacillate means to waver between different opinions or actions.
Sway means to move slowly from or side to side.
Viaduct is a specific type of bridge that consists of a series of arches, piers or columns supporting a long elevated railway or road.
Thrifty means using money and other resources carefully and not wastefully.

129. A person who kills somebody, especially for political reasons
SSC CGL Tier-1 20.07.2023 (Shift-IV)
(a) Monster (b) Criminal
(c) Hangman (d) Assassin
Ans. (d)
An **assassin** is a person who kills someone, especially for political reasons.
Monster is a large, ugly and frightening imaginary creature.
Hangman is one who hangs a condemned person.

130. By killing a large number of people, they thought they would get more benefits of the schemes.
SSC CGL Tier-1 20.07.2023 (Shift-IV)
Or
The murder of a large number of people from a particular nation or ethnic group
SSC CGL Tier-1 26.07.2023 (Shift-II)
(a) Homicide (b) Suicide
(c) Feticide (d) Genocide
Ans. (d)
Genocide means killing a number of people from a particular nation or ethnic group.
Suicide means killing of one's own self.
Feticide means killing a fetus.
Homicide means killing of another person.

131. A group of worshippers
SSC CGL Tier-1 21.07.2023 (Shift-I)
SSC CPO 10.11.2022 (Shift-I)
(a) Congregation (b) Crowd
(c) Caravan (d) Constellation
Ans. (a)
A **congregation** is a group of worshippers.
Crowd is a group of people.
Constellation is a group of stars.
Caravan is a group of pilgrims.

132. Bajrang is in extreme pain in his teeth. SSC CGL Tier-1 21.07.2023 (Shift-I)
Or
Extreme physical or mental sufferings
SSC MTS 04.05.2023 (Shift-II)
(a) ache (b) agony (c) hurt (d) sting
Ans. (b)
Agony means extreme pain.
Ache, Hurt and **Sting** refer to a continuous or prolonged dull pain in a part of one's body.

133. The place that a person treats as his permanent home or lives in and has a substantial connection with
SSC CGL Tier-1 21.07.2023 (Shift-II)
(a) Oasis (b) Domicile
(c) Embankment (d) Resort
Ans. (b)
Domicile is a place where one lives permanently.
Oasis is a spot in the desert where water is found.
Embankment is a wall or bank of Earth or stone built to prevent a river flooding an area.
Resort refers to a place that is frequented for holidays or recreation or for a particular purpose.

134. Capable of or adapted for turning easily from one to another of various tasks, fields of endeavour, etc., and is able to do many things
SSC CGL Tier-1 21.07.2023 (Shift-III)
Or
One who has the ability to do many different things
SSC CGL Tier-1 02.12.2022 (Shift-III)
(a) Versatile (b) Turncoat
(c) Talented (d) Flexible
Ans. (a)
Versatile refers to be able to adapt or be adapted to many different functions or activities.
Turncoat is a person who deserts one party or cause in order to join an opposing one.
Flexible means capable of bending easily without breaking.

135. Place where grains are stored
SSC CGL Tier-1 21.07.2023 (Shift-IV)
Or
There is a place for grains in the backyard of this house.
SSC CGL Tier-2 26.10.2023 (Shift-I)
(a) Tannery (b) Pantry
(c) Mint (d) Granary
Ans. (d)
A **granary** is a place where grains are stored.
Tannery is a place where animal skins are tanned and made into leather.
Pantry is a place for storing food items.
Mint is a place where coins are made.

136. A big clumsy often slow-witted person SSC CGL Tier-1 21.07.2023 (Shift-IV)
(a) Slouch (b) Chump
(c) Oaf (d) Ape
Ans. (c)
An **oaf** is a big and clumsy person.
Slouch means to stand, move or sit in a lazy, drooping way.
Chump is a person who is easily tricked.
Ape is an animal.

137. One who cannot hear
SSC CGL Tier-1 21.07.2023 (Shift-IV)
(a) Illegible (b) Inaudible
(c) Dumb (d) Deaf
Ans. (d)
Deaf is someone who cannot hear.
Inaudible is something that cannot be heard.
Dumb is someone who cannot speak.
Illegible means not clear enough to be read.

138. Termagant
SSC CGL Tier-1 21.07.2023 (Shift-IV)
(a) One who speaks many languages
(b) Overscrupulous about minute details
(c) A magnet with strong polarity
(d) A violent, overbearing, turbulent, brawling, quarrelsome woman
Ans. (d)
Termagant means a violent, overbearing, turbulent, brawling, quarrelsome woman.

139. Causing or wanting to cause harm or evil to someone
SSC CGL Tier-1 24.07.2023 (Shift-I)
(a) Chaotic (b) Malevolent
(c) Insipid (d) Rancour
Ans. (b)
Malevolent means 'causing and wanting to cause harm or evil to someone.'
Chaotic means in a state of complete confusion and disorder.
Insipid means lacking vigour or interest.
Rancour refers to bitterness or resentfulness, especially when long standing.

140. Causing or ending in death.
SSC CGL Tier-1 24.07.2023 (Shift-II)
(a) Gruesome (b) Foster
(c) Fatal (d) Grotesque
Ans. (c)
Fatal means 'causing or ending in death'.
Gruesome means causing repulsion or horror.
Foster means to encourage the development of something.
Grotesque means strange and unpleasant.

141. A person whose age is between 70 and 79 years old
SSC CGL Tier-1 24.07.2023 (Shift-III)
(a) Septuagenarian
(b) Aged
(c) Pensioner
(d) Oldie
Ans. (a)
A **septuagenarian** is a person whose age is between 70 and 79 years old.

142. A formal agreement between two or more nations or people
SSC CGL Tier-1 24.07.2023 (Shift-III)
(a) Pact (b) Concord
(c) Bond (d) Charter
Ans. (a)
A **pact** is a formal agreement between two or more people.
Concord means agreement or harmony between people or groups.
Bond means an official paper given by the government or a company to show that you have lent them money that they will pay back to you at a particular interest rate.
Charter means a written grant by the sovereign or legislative power of a country, by which a body such as a city, company or university is founded or its rights and privileges defined.

143. To move or travel back and forth frequently
SSC CGL Tier-1 24.07.2023 (Shift-IV)
(a) Grapple (b) Shuttle
(c) Rupture (d) Foster
Ans. (b)
The word **Shuttle** means 'to move or travel back and forth frequently'.
Grapple means to engage in a close fight or wrestle.
Rupture means to cause something to explode, break or tear.
Foster means to encourage the development of something.

144. Willing to take risks and try new ideas SSC CGL Tier-1 24.07.2023 (Shift-IV)
(a) Resolute (b) Desperate
(c) Adventurous (d) Mythical
Ans. (c)
Adventurous means willing to take risks and try new ideas.
Resolute means determined.
Desperate means feeling or showing hopelessness showing that a situation is so bad that it is impossible to deal with.
Mythical means occurring in or characteristic of myths or folk tales.

145. A speech by an actor at the end of a play SSC CGL Tier-1 25.07.2023 (Shift-I)
(a) Prologue (b) Monologue
(c) Epilogue (d) Duologue
Ans. (c)
An **epilogue** is a speech made at the end of a play or novel.
Prologue means a separate introductory section of a literary, dramatic or musical work.
Monologue means a long speech by one actor in a play or film or as part of a theatrical or broadcast programme.
Duologue means a play or part of a play with speaking roles for only two actors.

146. Someone who lives in solitude
SSC CGL Tier-1 25.07.2023 (Shift-I)
(a) Metropolitan (b) Cosmopolitan
(c) Recluse (d) Refugee
Ans. (c)
A **recluse** is someone who lives alone or in solitude.
Metropolitan is an inhabitant of a metropolis or large city.
Refugee is a person who has been forced to leave their country in order to escape war, persecution or natural disaster.
Cosmopolitan is a person who consider the world to be their home.

147. One who loves mankind
SSC CGL Tier-1 25.07.2023 (Shift-I)
SSC CGL Tier-2 07.03.2023 (Shift-I)
SSC CPO 27.06.2024 (Shift-III)
SSC CHSL Tier-1 16.03.2023 (Shift-II)
Or
One who makes an active effort to promote human welfare
SSC MTS Tier-1 08.09.2023 (Shift-II)
Or
One who loves humanity or believes in universal brotherhood.
SSC CGL Tier-1 09.12.2022 (Shift-IV)
(a) Atheist (b) Pessimist
(c) Optimist (d) Philanthropist
Ans. (d)
A **philanthropist** is a person who loves mankind.

148. Author's explanatory remarks at the beginning of a book.
SSC CGL Tier-1 25.07.2023 (Shift-I)
(a) Preface (b) Foreward
(c) Bibliography (d) Biography
Ans. (a)
A **preface** is an author's explanatory remarks at the beginning of a book.
Forward is a piece of writing at the beginning of a book, generally written by someone else.
Bibliography is a list of all the sources consulted and cited in a written work.
Biography is a story of a person's life.

149. Never changing and therefore boring.
SSC CGL Tier-1 25.07.2023 (Shift-II)
(a) Outdated (b) Impractical
(c) Idealistic (d) Monotonous
Ans. (d)
Monotonous means never changing and therefore, boring.
Outdated means old-fashioned and not modern.
Impractical means not adapted for use or action; not sensible or realistic.
Idealistic refers to something characterised by unrealistically aiming for perfection.

150. Changing secret and coded messages in a readable form
SSC CGL Tier-1 25.07.2023 (Shift-III)
(a) Decoupling (b) Encoding
(c) Decoding (d) Encrypting
Ans. (c)
Decoding means changing secret messages into readable form.
Decoupling means to separate something from something else.
Encoding means to convert into coded form.
Encrypting means to convert into a code for concealing data.

151. Enjoying or affording warm secure shelter or cover and opportunity for ease and contentment
SSC CGL Tier-1 25.07.2023 (Shift-III)

(a) Undisturbed (b) Easeful
(c) Untroubled (d) Snug

Ans. (d)

The word 'snug' means enjoying or affording a warm secure shelter or cover and opportunity for ease and contentment.

152. Kind, generous and forgiving.
SSC CGL Tier-1 25.07.2023 (Shift-III)

(a) Magnificent (b) Grandiloquent
(c) Portentous (d) Magnanimous

Ans. (d)

Magnanimous means kind, generous and forgiving.

Magnificent means very good or excellent.

Grandiloquent means pompous or extravagant in style, manner or quality especially in language.

Portentous means too serious and trying to be very important.

153. Too strong to be defeated or changed
SSC CGL Tier-1 25.07.2023 (Shift-IV)

(a) Invincible (b) Headstrong
(c) Vigorous (d) Sovereign

Ans. (a)

Invincible refers to the quality of being too strong to be defeated.

Headstrong means energetically wilful and determined.

Vigorous means strong and full of energy.

Sovereign refers to a supreme ruler, especially a monarch.

154. Which cannot be read
SSC CGL Tier-1 26.07.2023 (Shift-I)

Or

Incapable of being read
SSC CHSL Tier-1 14.03.2023 (Shift-I)

Or

That which is incapable of being read or understood **SSC CHSL 04.08.2021 (Shift-I)**
SSC MTS Tier-1 11.09.2023 (Shift-I)

(a) Illiterate (b) Inaudible
(c) Invisible (d) Illegible

Ans. (d)

Illegible means something that cannot be read.

Illiterate means uneducated.

Inaudible means something that cannot be heard.

Invisible means something that cannot be seen.

155. Life history written by oneself
SSC CGL Tier-1 26.07.2023 (Shift-II)

(a) Autography (b) Autobiography
(c) Autophagy (d) Autocracy

Ans. (b)

An **autobiography** is a life history written by oneself.

Autography refers to writing done with one's own hand.

Autophagy refers to a natural process in which body's cells clean our any damaged or unnecessary components.

Autocracy refers to a system of governance by one person with absolute power.

156. Being a practiced liar, it was totally normal for him to utter a <u>complete and blatant lie.</u>
SSC CGL Tier-1 26.07.2023 (Shift-III)

(a) blasphemy (b) whooper
(c) falsehood (d) perjury

Ans. (c)

Falsehood means a complete lie.

Whooper means something that is much bigger than the usual size.

Perjury is the crime of telling lies in court when you have promised to tell the truth.

Blasphemy is the act of speaking negatively about God.

157. Something belonging to or surviving from an earlier period.
SSC CGL Tier-1 26.07.2023 (Shift-III)

(a) Vestige (b) Dinosaur
(c) Ruin (d) Relic

Ans. (d)

A **relic** is something belonging to or surviving from an earlier period.

Vestige means a mark, trace or visible evidence of something that is no longer present or in existence.

158. A person who does not drink alcohol
SSC CGL Tier-1 26.07.2023 (Shift-III)

(a) Vegetarian (b) Celibate
(c) Teetotaller (d) Abstain

Ans. (c)

A **teetotaller** is a person who does not drink alcohol.

Vegetarian refers to a person who doesn't consume meat.

Celibate refers to a person who doesn't engage in sexual intercourse.

Abstain refers to restraining oneself from doing or enjoying something.

159. Someone who regards the world as his/her country
SSC CGL Tier-1 26.07.2023 (Shift-IV)
SSC MTS Tier-1 13.09.2023 (Shift-I)

Or

An outlook that is influenced by people from all over the world
SSC CHSL Tier-1 26.05.2022 (Shift-III)

(a) Atheist (b) Metropolitan
(c) Cosmopolitan (d) Philanthropist

Ans. (c)

A **cosmopolitan** is a person who regards the world as his/her own country.

Metropolitan refers to an inhabitant of a metropolis or large city.

Philanthropist is one who donates everything for the good of mankind.

160. Not informed about or aware of something
SSC CGL Tier-1 26.07.2023 (Shift-IV)

(a) Oblivious (b) Uneducated
(c) Absent (d) Inconscient

Ans. (a)

Oblivious means not informed about or aware of something.

161. Burial ground consisting of graves
SSC CGL Tier-1 26.07.2023 (Shift-IV)

(a) Courtyard
(b) Cemetery
(c) Sanctuary
(d) Auditorium

Ans. (b)

A **cemetery** is a burial ground for graves.

A **Courtyard** is an area that is surrounded by walls or building.

Sanctuary means a safe place.

An **Auditorium** is a place in a theatre where the audience sits.

162. Filled with fear or dread
SSC CGL Tier-1 26.07.2023 (Shift-IV)

(a) Prudent (b) Tremulous
(c) Corpulent (d) Hysterical

Ans. (d)

Hysterical means filled with extreme emotions.

Prudent means marked by wisdom or judiciousness.

Tremulous means shaking or quivering slightly.

Corpulent means fat.

163. The Prime Minister paid tributes to the martyrs by laying *circular arrangement of flowers*.
SSC CGL Tier-1 27.07.2023 (Shift-I)

(a) buds (b) ponies
(c) bouquets (d) wreaths

Ans. (d)

A **wreath** is a circular arrangement of flowers.

Buds means a small part of a plant, that develops into a flower or leaf.

Ponies means a horse of a small breed.

Bouquets refers to group of flowers.

164. The practice of writing dictionaries
SSC CGL Tier-1 27.07.2023 (Shift-I)
(a) Anthropology
(b) Lexicography
(c) Photography
(d) Philology

Ans. (b)

Lexicography is the practice of writing dictionaries.

Photography is the art or process of taking and processing photographs.

Philology refers to the study of language, especially its history and development.

Anthropology is the study of mankind.

165. He did not stop until it was remarked that he was <u>speaking at length about trivial things.</u>
SSC CGL Tier-1 27.07.2023 (Shift-II)
(a) twittering (b) writing
(c) rambling (d) littering

Ans. (c)

Rambling means to speak or write at length in a wandering or aimless manner, often without a clear structure of focus.

So, speaking at length about trivial things is called rambling.

Twittering means the act of talking quickly and nervously, saying things of very little importance or interest.

Littering means the act of dropping rubbish on the ground in public places.

166. Outer protective layer of a tree
SSC CGL Tier-2 27.07.2023 (Shift-II)
(a) Bark (b) Shrub
(c) Rind (d) Peel

Ans. (a)

A **bark** is an outer protective layer of the tree.

Shrub is a woody plant that is smaller than a tree, usually having several stems rather than a single trunk.

Rind is the tough outer skin of certain fruit, especially a citrus fruit.

Peel means to strip (something) of its skin, rind, bark, etc.

167. Willful destruction
SSC CGL Tier-2 02.03.2023
Or
The act of destroying or damaging something
SSC MTS Tier-1 09.05.2023 (Shift-I)
(a) Disaster (b) Combustion
(c) Calamity (d) Sabotage

Ans. (d)

Sabotage means wilful destruction.

Disaster and **Calamity** mean an event causing great and often sudden damage or distress.

Combustion means to burn.

168. A person who admires himself or herself too much, especially their appearance **SSC CGL Tier-2 02.03.2023**
Or
A person in love with himself
SSC CGL Tier-1 01.12.2022 (Shift-IV)
Or
A person who has excessive admiration of themselves
SSC CPO Tier-2 08.01.2024
SSC CHSL Tier-2 10.01.2024 (Shift-I)
(a) Narcissist (b) Egoist
(c) Selfish (d) Dictator

Ans. (a)

A **narcissist** is a person who admires himself/herself too much.

Egoist is a person who is preoccupied with his or her own interests; a selfish person.

Dictator is a person with unlimited governmental power.

169. Photographers who follow celebrities to get their pictures to sell them
SSC CGL Tier-2 03.03.2023
(a) Paparazzi (b) Reporter
(c) Editor (d) Interviewer

Ans. (a)

The **paparazzi** are photographers who follow famous people around, hoping to take interesting or shocking photographs of them that they can sell to a newspaper.

Reporter is a person who reports, especially one employed to report news or conduct interviews for the press or broadcasting media.

Editor is a person who is in charge of and determines the final content of a newspaper, magazine or multi-author book.

Interviewer is a person who takes an interview.

170. Someone who is reserved and shy
SSC CGL Tier-2 03.03.2023
(a) Introvert (b) Extrovert
(c) Chauffeur (d) Talkative

Ans. (a)

An **introvert** is a reserved and shy person.

Extrovert is a social and outgoing person.

Chauffur is a person who is hired to drive a car or vehicle.

Talkative is someone who talks a lot.

171. The science and art of growing vegetables, fruits and flowers
SSC CGL Tier-2 06.03.2023
(a) Herpetology (b) Horticulture
(c) Haplology (d) Herbing

Ans. (b)

The science and art of growing vegetables, fruits and flowers is called **Horticulture.**

Herpetology is the branch of zoology concerned with the study of amphibians and reptiles.

Haplology is a sound change involving the loss of a syllable when it is next to a phonetically identical (or similar) syllable.

172. One who is a boot licker and flatterer
SSC CGL Tier-2 06.03.2023
(a) Gold-digger (b) Gregarious
(c) Sycophant (d) Manipulative

Ans. (c)

A **sycophant** is a boot licker and a flatterer.

Gold-digger is a person who forms a relationship with another purely to extract money from them.

Gregarious means fond of company; sociable.

Manipulative means tending to influence or control someone or something to your advantage, often without anyone knowing it.

173. An arched structure in a garden having climbing plants.
SSC CGL Tier-2 07.03.2023
Or
A structure in the garden where climbing plants can grow and people can walk under
SSC CPO 04.10.2023 (Shift-III)
(a) Shelter (b) Pergola
(c) Path (d) Shed

Ans. (b)

An arched structure in the garden having climbing plants is called a **Pergola.**

Shelter means a place giving temporary protection from bad weather or danger.

Shed is typically a simple, single-story roofed structure, often used for storage, for hobbies or as a workshop.

174. She was known for her <u>ability to communicate effectively and express herself clearly in writing and speaking</u>. **SSC CGL Tier-2 26.10.2023**
(a) incoherence (b) articulation
(c) mumbling (d) rambling

Ans. (b)

Articulation is the ability to communicate effectively and clearly.

Incoherence means illogical, inconsistent or unclear.

Mumbling means speaking in a quiet and unclear manner.

Rambling means lengthy and confused manner of speaking.

SSC CGL 2022 (Tier 1 & 2)

175. To walk aimlessly

SSC CGL Tier-1 11.04.2022 (Shift-I)

(a) Amble (b) Crawl
(c) Sprint (d) Slither

Ans. (a)

Amble means to walk slowly or aimlessly.

Crawl means to move on hands and knees.

Sprint means to run at full speed over a short distance.

Slither means to move smoothly over a surface, like a snake.

176. Showing great attention to detail and correct behaviour

SSC CGL Tier-1 11.04.2022 (Shift-II)

(a) Punctual (b) Zealous
(c) Punctilious (d) Disciplined

Ans. (c)

Punctilious means showing great attention to detail and correct behaviour.

Punctual means being on time.

Zealous means showing great energy or enthusiasm.

Disciplined means showing controlled and orderly behaviour.

177. A medical condition in which somebody partly or completely loses their memory

SSC CGL Tier-1 12.04.2022 (Shift-III)

(a) Amnesia (b) Asphyxia
(c) Anaemia (d) Alopecia

Ans. (a)

Amnesia is the condition of losing memory.

Asphyxia means being deprived of oxygen.

Anaemia means a lack of red blood cells or hemoglobin.

Alopecia means hair loss.

178. The examination or observation of one's own mental and emotional processes

SSC CGL Tier-1 12.04.2022 (Shift-III)

(a) Assessment (b) Introspection
(c) Inspection (d) Valuation

Ans. (b)

Introspection means examining one's own thoughts and feelings.

Assessment means evaluation or estimation.

Inspection means careful examination.

Valuation means determining the value of something.

179. Sharpness and accuracy of judgement

SSC CGL Tier-1 13.04.2022 (Shift-II)

(a) Experience (b) Estimation
(c) Acumen (d) Knowledge

Ans. (c)

Acumen means sharpness and accuracy of judgement.

Experience means knowledge or skill from doing something.

Estimation means forming an opinion or judgement about something.

Knowledge means awareness or familiarity gained by experience or education.

180. Something that is strong and lasts a long time without breaking or becoming weaker.

SSC CGL Tier-1 13.04.2022 (Shift-II)

(a) Durable (b) Harsh
(c) Pliable (d) Secure

Ans. (a)

Durable means strong and lasting.

Harsh means unpleasantly rough or severe.

Pliable means easily bent or flexible.

Secure means safe and protected.

181. An image of a God used for workship

SSC CGL Tier-1 13.04.2022 (Shift-III)

(a) Model (b) Idol
(c) Icon (d) Temple

Ans. (b)

Idol means an image or representation of a god used for worship.

Model means a three-dimensional representation.

Icon means a person or thing regarded as a representative symbol.

Temple means a building devoted to worship.

182. Unfairly take something belonging to another for one's use

SSC CGL Tier-1 18.04.2022 (Shift-III)

(a) Misconstrue
(b) Misinterpret
(c) Misappropriate
(d) Misapprehend

Ans. (c)

Misappropriate means taking something unfairly for one's use.

Misconstrue means to misunderstand the meaning of something.

Misinterpret means to interpret something incorrectly.

Misapprehend means to understand something wrongly.

183. A problem that is so diffcult that it cannot be answered

SSC CGL Tier-1 18.04.2022 (Shift-III)

(a) Impossible
(b) Insoluble
(c) Terrible
(d) Solvable

Ans. (b)

Insoluble means a problem that cannot be solved.

Impossible means something that cannot be done or achieved.

Terrible means extremely bad or serious.

Solvable means capable of being solved.

184. An animal with a spinal cord

SSC CGL Tier-1 19.04.2022 (Shift-III)

(a) Amphibian (b) Mammal
(c) Invertebrate (d) Vertebrate

Ans. (d)

Vertebrate means an animal with a spinal cord.

Invertebrate means an animal lacking a backbone.

Mammal is a warm-blooded animal with hairs, backbone and mammary glands, which produce milk.

Amphibian are small vertebrates that require water to survive.

185. Able to be happy, successful, etc. again after something difficult or bad has happened

SSC CGL Tier-1 19.04.2022 (Shift-III)

(a) Reluctant (b) Remnant
(c) Resilient (d) Resistant

Ans. (c)

Resilient means able to recover quickly from difficult conditions.

Reluctant means unwilling and hesitant.

Remnant means a small remaining quantity of something.

Resistant means offering resistance to something.

186. A group of people

SSC CGL Tier-1 20.04.2022 (Shift-I)

(a) Crowd (b) Herd
(c) Flock (d) Brood

Ans. (a)

Crowd means a large group of people.

Herd means a large group of animals, especially hoofed mammals.

Flock means a number of birds of one kind feeding, resting, or travelling together.

Brood means a family of young animals, especially of a bird, produced at one hatching or birth.

187. A spear used for hunting large fish
SSC CGL Tier-1 20.04.2022 (Shift-II)

(a) Dagger (b) Lance
(c) Harpoon (d) Sword

Ans. (c)

Harpoon means a long spear-like instrument used for catching large fish.

Dagger means a short knife with a pointed and edged blade.

Lance means a long weapon for thrusting, having a wooden shaft and a pointed steel head, formerly used by a horseman in charging.

Sword means a weapon with a long metal blade and a hilt with a hand guard, used for thrusting or striking.

188. Lacking interest or excitement
SSC CGL Tier-1 20.04.2022 (Shift-III)

(a) Despot (b) Hostile
(c) Mundane (d) Miserly

Ans. (c)

Mundane means lacking interest or excitement.

Despot means a ruler with absolute power and authority.

Hostile means unfriendly or antagonistic.

Miserly means reluctant to spend money.

189. Policy of racial discrimination
SSC CGL Tier-1 21.04.2022 (Shift-II)

(a) Non-alignment (b) Diplomacy
(c) Commonwealth (d) Apartheid

Ans. (d)

Apartheid means a policy or system of segregation or discrimination on grounds of race.

Non-alignment means not allied with any other nation or bloc.

Diplomacy means the profession, activity, or skill of managing international relations.

Commonwealth means an international association consisting of the UK together with states that were previously part of the British Empire, and dependencies.

190. A four-footed animal
SSC CGL Tier-1 21.04.2022 (Shift-III)

(a) Mammal (b) Reptile
(c) Quadruped (d) Biped

Ans. (c)

Quadruped means an animal that has four feet.

Reptile means a class of animals that includes snakes, lizards, crocodiles, turtles and tortoises, and is characterised by a body covered with scales or hard plates and usually laying soft-shelled eggs on land.

Biped means an animal that uses two legs for walking.

191. A piece of a living tissue or plant that is transplanted surgically.
SSC CGL Tier-1 01.12.2022 (Shift-II)

(a) Gratis (b) Gourmet
(c) Gracious (d) Graft

Ans. (d)

A **Graft** is a piece of a tissue or plant that is transplanted

Gratis means without charge; free.

Gourmet means, relating to being high quality, expensive, or specialty food, typically requiring elaborate and expert preparation.

Gracious means marked by kindness and courtesy.

192. Feeling or showing extreme tiredness
SSC CGL Tier-1 01.12.2022 (Shift-III)

(a) Vitalised (b) Nervous
(c) Weary (d) Drowsy

Ans. (c)

Weary means feelings of extreme tiredness.

Vitalised means energised.

Nervous means fearful or stressed.

Drowsy means sleepy.

193. Navika is <u>a superb and impressive</u> child in her class.
SSC CGL Tier-1 01.12.2022 (Shift-III)

(a) Splendid (b) Brilliant
(c) Dazzling (d) Vivid

Ans. (b)

Brilliant means superb and impressive.

Splendid means magnificent; very impressive.

Dazzling means extremely bright, especially so as to blind the eyes temporarily.

Vivid means very clear and defined.

194. Giving the worrying impression that something bad is going to happen
SSC CGL Tier-1 01.12.2022 (Shift-IV)

(a) Desolate (b) Suspicious
(c) Ominous (d) Bleak

Ans. (c)

Ominous means giving a worrying impression that something bad is going to happen.

Desolate means feeling or showing great unhappiness or loneliness.

Suspicious means having or showing a cautious distrust of someone or something.

Bleak means cold and miserable.

195. Plants of a particular region
SSC CGL Tier-1 02.12.2022 (Shift-I)

(a) Flora (b) Flinch
(c) Fauna (d) Flotsam

Ans. (a)

Flora refers to the plants of a particular region.

Flinch means make a quick, nervous movement as an instinctive reaction to fear, pain or surprise.

Fauna refers to the animals belonging to a region.

Flotsam means the wreckage of a ship or its cargo found floating on or washed up by the sea.

196. A shortened version of a larger work
SSC CGL Tier-1 02.12.2022 (Shift-I)

(a) Summary (b) Precis
(c) Shorts (d) Abridgement

Ans. (d)

An **abridgement** is a smaller version of a larger piece of writing.

Summary means a brief statement or account of the main points of something.

Precis means a summary or abstract of a text or speech.

197. <u>The man supervising the exam</u> had a huge moustache.
SSC CGL Tier-1 02.12.2022 (Shift-II)

Or

One who supervises in an examination hall
SSC CGL Tier-1 20.08.2021 (Shift-II)
SSC SP Graduate Level 01.08.2022

(a) Examiner (b) Curator
(c) Controller (d) Invigilator

Ans. (d)

An **invigilator** is a man who supervises the exam.

Examiner is a person whose job is to inspect something; an inspector.

Controller is one who controls something.

Curator is a caretaker of a museum.

198. Adjust or make right; correct, amend
SSC CGL Tier-1 02.12.2022 (Shift-III)

(a) Recruit (b) Recreate
(c) Recourse (d) Rectify

Ans. (d)

Rectify means to adjust or make right.

Recruit means to enlist (someone) in the armed forces.

Recourse is a source of help in a difficult situation.

199. Having or showing an excessively high opinion of one's appearance, abilities or worth.
SSC CGL Tier-1 02.12.2022 (Shift-III)
(a) Superior (b) Vain
(c) Otiose (d) Domineering
Ans. (b)
Vain means having or showing an excessively high opinion of oneself.
Superior means higher in rank, status or quality.
Otiose means serving no practical purpose or result.
Domineering means inclined to exercise arbitrary and overbearing control over others.

200. The date when both, day and night are of approximately equal length.
SSC CGL Tier-1 02.12.2022 (Shift-III)
(a) Equilibrium (b) Equine
(c) Equator (d) Equinox
Ans. (d)
An **equinox** is the date when both day and night are of almost same length.
Equilibrium means balance.
Equine means relating to or affecting horses or other members of the horse family.
Equator is an imaginary line around the middle of a planet or other celestial body. It is halfway between the North Pole and the South Pole.

201. A speech made without preparation
SSC CGL Tier-1 02.12.2022 (Shift-II)
Or
Spoken or done without preparation
SSC CHSL Tier-1 11.08. 2023 (Shift-I)
SSC CPO 04.10.2023 (Shift-I)
SSC CHSL Tier-1 21.03.2023 (Shift-IV)
Or
Speech without prior preparation
SSC SP Matriculation 20.06.2024 (Shift-IV)
(a) Extempore (b) Rhetoric
(c) Deliberation (d) Spontaneous
Ans. (a)
An **extempore** is a speech made without any preparation or planning.
Rhetoric is the art of speaking or writing effectively.
Deliberation means long and careful consideration or discussion.
Spontaneous means (of a process or event) occurring without apparent external cause.

202. One who mediates in a deal or complex situation
SSC CGL Tier-1 03.12.2022 (Shift-I)
(a) Equaliser (b) Solicitor
(c) Pacifier (d) Negotiator
Ans. (d)
Negotiator is a person who mediates in a deal or a complex situation.
Equaliser means a person or thing that equalises.
A **solicitor** is a legal practitioner who traditionally deals with most of the legal matters in some jurisdictions.
Pacifier means something that makes people calm when they are angry or upset.

203. A loud appeal or demand
SSC CGL Tier-1 03.12.2022 (Shift-III)
(a) Protest (b) Entourage
(c) Clamour (d) Gambit
Ans. (c)
Clamour is a loud appeal or demand.
Protest means a statement or action expressing disapproval of or objection to something.
Entourage means a group of people attending or surrounding an important person.
Gambit means an act or remark that is calculated to gain an advantage, especially at the outset of a situation.

204. The study of languages
SSC CGL Tier-1 03.12.2022 (Shift-IV)
(a) Philology
(b) Anthropology
(c) Lexicography
(d) Philosophy
Ans. (a)
Philology is the study of history or development of languages.
Philosophy is a systematic study of general and fundamental questions concerning topics like existence, reason, knowledge, value, mind and language.
Anthropology is the study of mankind.
Lexicography is the act of compeling dictionaries.

205. Sharp and direct
SSC CGL Tier-1 03.12.2022 (Shift-IV)
(a) Acerbic (b) Zoonic
(c) Anodyne (d) Acidic
Ans. (a)
Acerbic means something that is sharp, cruel and direct.
Zoonic means an individual segment of an animal with a segmented body.
Anodyne means not likely to cause offence or disagreement and somewhat dull.
Acidic means being or containing an acid.

206. After my father passed away, I used to look at a <u>series of stars</u>, trying to find the unknown.
SSC CGL Tier-1 03.12.2022 (Shift-IV)
(a) Galaxy (b) Constellation
(c) Caravan (d) Horde
Ans. (b)
A **constellation** is a group or series of stars.
Galaxy is a group of planets.
Horde is a group of people.
Caravan is a group of pilgrims.

207. One who does something not professionally but for pleasure
SSC CGL Tier-1 03.12.2022 (Shift-IV)
(a) Professional (b) Mature
(c) Immature (d) Amateur
Ans. (d)
'Amateur' refers to someone who does something because they enjoy it instead of as a job.

208. A person having significant experience in an occupation
SSC CGL Tier-1 05.12.2022 (Shift-I)
(a) Fastidious (b) Veteran
(c) Novice (d) Agnostic
Ans. (b)
A **veteran** is a person having different experiences in an occupation.
Novice is a person new to and inexperienced in a job or situation.
Fastidious means very attentive about accuracy and detail.
Agnostic means a person who doesn't belive in the existence of God.

209. The act of washing oneself
SSC CGL Tier-1 05.12.2022 (Shift-I)
(a) Ablutions (b) Solutions
(c) Steaming (d) Bathing
Ans. (a)
Ablution means the process of washing yourself, cleaning your teeth, etc.

210. A very expensive and elaborately built tomb
SSC CGL Tier-1 05.12.2022 (Shift-III)
(a) Mausoleum (b) Cemetery
(c) Mosque (d) Masterpiece
Ans. (a)
Mausoleum refers to a large stately tomb or a building housing many tombs.
Mosque is a Muslim place of worship.

211. The act of killing one's mother
SSC CGL Tier-1 05.12.2022 (Shift-IV)
(a) Regicide (b) Homicide
(c) Uxoricide (d) Matricide

Ans. (d)

Matricide means killing of one's mother.

Regicide means killing of the king.

Homicide means the killing of one person by another.

Uxoricide means the killing of one's wife.

212. Today my dad will teach me how to make a small shelter for my dog.
SSC CGL Tier-1 06.12.2022 (Shift-II)
(a) kennel (b) canal
(c) burrow (d) shed

Ans. (a)

A **kennel** is a small home or shelter made for a dog.

Canal is artificial waterways.

Burrow is a hole or tunnel which acts as a home to small animals like a mouse.

Shed is typically a simple, single-story roofed structure, often used for storage, for hobbies or as a workshop.

213. Existing in a land from the earliest times or from before the arrival of colonists. SSC CGL Tier-1 06.12.2022 (Shift-II)
(a) Native (b) Ancient
(c) Aboriginal (d) Original

Ans. (c)

Aboriginal means existing is a land from the original times.

Native is a person born in a specified place or associated with a place by birth, whether subsequently resident there or not.

Ancient means old.

214. An eccentric manner of living
SSC CGL Tier-1 06.12.2022 (Shift-III)
(a) Bohemian (b) Numismatist
(c) Gourmet (d) Misanthrope

Ans. (a)

Bohemian means an eccentric manner of living wherein one does not accept the societal norms.

Numismatist is a specialist, researcher, or well-informed collector of coins.

Gourmet means of, relating to being high quality, expensive, or specialty food typically requiring elaborate and expert preparation.

Misanthrope is a person who hates mankind.

215. The property left to someone by a will. SSC CGL Tier-1 06.12.2022 (Shift-III)
(a) Ledger (b) Legacy
(c) Legend (d) Lexical

Ans. (b)

Legacy is the property left by someone in a will.

Ledger means a book or other collection of financial accounts.

Legend means a story from the past that is believed by many people but cannot be proved to be true.

Lexical means relating to the words or vocabulary of a language.

216. A small island
SSC CGL Tier-1 06.12.2022 (Shift-IV)
(a) Islet (b) Lagoon
(c) Closet (d) Isthmus

Ans. (a)

Islet is a small island.

Lagoon is a shallow body of water separated from a larger body of water by a narrow landform.

Closet is a tall cupboard or wardrobe with a door, used for storage.

Isthmus is a narrow strip of land with sea on either side, forming a link between two larger areas of land.

217. A group of stars having a particular shape. SSC CGL Tier-1 06.12.2022 (Shift-IV)
(a) Constellation
(b) Planet
(c) Orbit
(d) Galaxy

Ans. (a)

A **constellation** is a group of stars.

Orbit means the curved trajectory of an object such as the trajectory of a planet around a stars.

Galaxy is a group of planets.

218. Formal forgiveness of a person's sins
SSC CGL Tier-1 07.12.2022 (Shift-II)
(a) Ablutions (b) Absolution
(c) Absolutism (d) Forgiveness

Ans. (b)

Absolution is a formal forgiveness for a person's sins.

Ablutions is an act of washing oneself.

Absolutism means the holding of absolute principles in political, philosophical or theological matters.

219. Holding on to something or keeping an opinion with determination
SSC CGL Tier-1 07.12.2022 (Shift-III)
(a) Gracious (b) Tenacious
(c) Obnoxious (d) Loquacious

Ans. (b)

Tenacious means holding onto something or keeping an opinion with determination.

Gracious means courteous, kind and pleasant, especially towards someone of lower social status.

Obnoxious means arrogant and prideful.

Loquacious means talkative.

220. A perfectionist
SSC CGL Tier-1 07.12.2022 (Shift-IV)
(a) Meticulous
(b) Omniscient
(c) Optimist
(d) Ambidextrous

Ans. (a)

Meticulous means to perfection.

Omniscient means having complete knowledge.

Ambidextrous is a person who can write with both hands.

221. Fail to notice; ignore; condone (an offence etc.)
SSC CGL Tier-1 08.12.2022 (Shift-I)
(a) Overlong (b) Overlie
(c) Overly (d) Overlook

Ans. (d)

Overlook means to fail to notice or to ignore something.

Overlong means too long.

Overlie means to lie on top of.

Overly means excessively.

222. A room where dead bodies are kept until burial
SSC CGL Tier-1 08.12.2022 (Shift-I)
(a) Sanatorium (b) Museum
(c) Mortuary (d) Safari

Ans. (c)

Mortuary is a room where dead bodies are kept until burial.

Sanatorium is a room or building for sick children in a boarding school.

Museum is a building in which objects of historical, scientific, artistic or cultural interest are stored and exhibited.

Safari is an expedition for hunting or observing wild animals.

223. The action of damaging the good reputation of someone
SSC CGL Tier-1 08.12.2022 (Shift-I)
(a) Delegate
(b) Degeneration
(c) Defamation
(d) Defection

Ans. (c)

Defamation refers to the act of damaging the good reputation of someone.

Degeneration means the state or process of being or becoming degenerate; decline or deterioration.

Defection involves abandoning a person, cause or doctrine to which one is bound by some tie, as of allegiance or duty.

Delegate is a representative sent to an important event.

224. An exaggerated statement not to be taken seriously or literally.
SSC CGL Tier-1 08.12.2022 (Shift-III)
(a) Hypertext (b) Hyperbole
(c) Hypocrisy (d) Hippocrates
Ans. (b)
A **hyperbole** is an exaggerated statement not to be taken seriously or literally.
Hypertext means text which contains links to other texts.
Hypocrisy means the practice of claiming to have higher standards or more noble beliefs than is the case.
Hippocrates was a Greek physician and philosopher.

225. Cancel or do away with (a law or agreement)
SSC CGL Tier-1 08.12.2022 (Shift-III)
(a) Abrogate
(b) Cancellation
(c) Ultimation
(d) Prorogation
Ans. (a)
Abrogate means to cancel or do away with something (a law, agreement or custom officially).
Ultimation means the act or result of ultimating.
Prorogation means the action of discontinuing a session of a parliament or other legislative assembly without dissolving it.

226. A battle or anything involving or causing much bloodshed.
SSC CGL Tier-1 09.12.2022 (Shift-I)
(a) Autocracy (b) Sanguinary
(c) Ineffable (d) Redtapism
Ans. (b)
Sanguinary refers to an extremely violent battle involving a lot of bloodshed and injuries.
Autocracy means a system of government by one person with absolute power.
Ineffable means too great or extreme to be expressed or described in words.
Redtapism means excessive regulation or rigid conformity to formal rules that is considered redundant and bureaucratic and hinders action or decision-making.

227. Something which is worth believing
SSC CGL Tier-1 09.12.2022 (Shift-I)
(a) Spurious (b) Expedient
(c) Credible (d) Impending
Ans. (c)
Credible means something that can be believed.
Spurious means not being what it purports to be; false or fake.
Expedient means convenient and practical although possibly improper or immoral.
Impending means about to happen; forthcoming.

228. Strong hostility
SSC CGL Tier-1 09.12.2022 (Shift-III)
(a) Animalistic
(b) Anonymity
(c) Comity
(d) Animosity
Ans. (d)
Animosity means strong feelings of hatred or hostility.
Animalistic means behaving like an animal.
Anonymity means not known.
Comity means courtesy and considerate behaviour towards others.

229. My uncle is <u>someone who loves good food and knows a lot about it</u>.
SSC CGL Tier-1 12.12.2022 (Shift-I)
(a) Culinary (b) Connoisseur
(c) Chauffeur (d) Gourmet
Ans. (b)
A **connoisseur** is a person who loves good food and knows a lot about it.
Culinary means related to food or cooking.
Chauffeur is a person who is hired to drive a car or vehicle.
Gourmet means relating to being high quality, expensive, or specialty food, typically requiring elaborate and expert preparation.

230. To give up completely or agree to forgo, especially in favour of another
SSC CGL Tier-1 12.12.2022 (Shift-I)
(a) Surrender (b) Waive
(c) Forfeit (d) Cosign
Ans. (a)
To **surrender** means to give up something completely.
Waive means refrain from insisting on or using (a right or claim).
Forfeit means to give up.
Cosign means to sign (a loan or lease) jointly with another person in order to guarantee payment.

231. One who can speak two languages
SSC CGL Tier-1 12.12.2022 (Shift-I)
(a) Trilingual (b) Multilingual
(c) Monolingual (d) Bilingual
Ans. (d)
Bilingual is used for a person who speaks two languages.
Trilingual is a person who can speak three languages.
Multilingual is a person who can speak many languages.
Monolingual is a person who can speak one language.

232. One who runs away from law
SSC CGL Tier-1 12.12.2022 (Shift-II)
(a) Fatalist (b) Convict
(c) Fugitive (d) Lunatic
Ans. (c)
Fugitive is someone who runs away from law.
Convict is a criminal.
Lunatic is a crazy person.
Fatalist is someone who believes in fate.

233. Something that is capable of being accomplished
SSC CGL Tier-1 12.12.2022 (Shift-III)
(a) Feasible (b) Untenable
(c) Irrevocable (d) Eligible
Ans. (a)
Feasible means something that can be accomplished.
Untenable means (especially of a position or view) not able to be maintained or defended against attack or objection.
Irrevocable is not able to be changed, reversed or recovered.
Eligible means having the right to do or obtain something; satisfying the appropriate conditions.

234. The scientific study of plants and their structure.
SSC CGL Tier-1 12.12.2022 (Shift-III)
(a) Plantation (b) Environment
(c) Biology (d) Botany
Ans. (d)
Botany is the scientific study of plants and their structure.
Plantation means a large farm or estate in a tropical or semi-tropical zone, for the cultivation of cotton, tobacco, coffee, sugarcane, etc., typically by enslaved, unpaid or low-wage resident labourers.
Biology is the scientific study of life and of living organisms.
Environment means the surroundings or conditions in which a person, animal or plant lives or operates.

235. Sita seems <u>not to be affected by the pleasures and pains of life</u>.
SSC CGL Tier-1 12.12.2022 (Shift-IV)
(a) strict (b) active
(c) stoic (d) passive
Ans. (c)

The word 'Stoic' means someone who does not show their emotions and does not complain when bad things happen to them.

236. Having a feeling of guilt
SSC CGL Tier-1 12.12.2022 (Shift-IV)
(a) Refulgence
(b) Restitution
(c) Remorse
(d) Repugnance

Ans. (c)

Remorse means a feeling of guilt after someone has done something very bad.

Refulgence means a radiant or shining quality or state.

Restitution means the restoration of something lost or stolen to its proper owner.

Repugnance means intense disgust.

237. A person who criticises traditional beliefs and customs
SSC CGL Tier-1 12.12.2022 (Shift-IV)
(a) Heretic (b) Absconder
(c) Apostle (d) Iconoclast

Ans. (d)

A person who strongly opposes or criticises traditional beliefs and customs is called an **iconoclast**.

Heretic is a person who differs in opinion from established religious dogma.

Absconder is a fugitive who runs away and hides to avoid arrest or prosecution.

Apostle means belonging or relating to the early followers of Christ and to their teaching.

238. Something that is very small/ little
SSC CGL Tier-1 13.12.2022 (Shift-II)
(a) Thin (b) Tiny
(c) Few (d) Slender

Ans. (b)

Something that is very small or little is called tiny.

239. A poll taken of voters leaving the voting place that is usually used for predicting the winners.
SSC CGL Tier-1 13.12.2022 (Shift-II)
(a) Census (b) Consensus
(c) Exit poll (d) Results

Ans. (c)

An **exit poll** means a poll taken of voters leaving the voting place to predict the winner.

Census is a usually complete count of a population (as of a state).

Consensus is a general agreement.

240. A formal statement testifying to someone's character and qualifications
SSC CGL Tier-1 13.12.2022 (Shift-II)
(a) Testimonial (b) Manuscript
(c) Document (d) Affidavit

Ans. (a)

A **testimonial** is a formal agreement stating someone's character and achievements.

Manuscript means a book, document or piece of music written by hand rather than typed or printed.

241. Making of a false document with a false signature
SSC CGL Tier-1 13.12.2022 (Shift-III)
(a) Ruse (b) Forgery
(c) Insincerity (d) Deception

Ans. (b)

Forgery means an illegal copy of a document, painting, etc. or the crime of making such illegal documents.

Ruse means act.

Insincerity means dishonesty.

Deception means the act of causing someone to accept as true or valid what is false or invalid.

242. A list or collection of books or informative graphics
SSC CGL Tier-1 13.12.2022 (Shift-III)

Or

A list of books. SSC CPO 28.06.2024 (Shift-I)
(a) Bale (b) Hamlet
(c) Gallery (d) Catalogue

Ans. (d)

A **catalogue** is a list of something.

Bale refers to a bundle of cotton.

Hamlet means a small settlement, generally one smaller than a village, and strictly (in Britain) one without a church.

Gallery means a room or building for the display or sale of works of art.

243. An entertainer who performs difficult physical feats SSC CGL Tier-2 29.01.2022

Or

A person who entertains people by doing difficult feats
SSC CGL Tier-1 28.08.2021 (Shift-II)
(a) Archer (b) Acrobat
(c) Artist (d) Artisan

Ans. (b)

Acrobat means an entertainer who performs difficult physical feats.

Archer means a person who shoots with a bow and arrows.

Artist means a person who creates paintings or drawings.

Artisan means a worker in a skilled trade, especially one that involves making things by hand.

244. Made of artificial substance or material SSC CGL Tier-2 29.01.2022
(a) Synthetic (b) Offensive
(c) Expensive (d) Authentic

Ans. (a)

Synthetic means made of artificial substance or material.

Offensive means causing someone to feel resentful, upset, or annoyed.

Expensive means costing a lot of money.

Authentic means of undisputed origin and not a copy.

245. A decision on which one cannot go back SSC CGL Tier-2 29.01.2022
(a) Incorrigible (b) Irrevocable
(c) Improbable (d) Incredible

Ans. (b)

Irrevocable means a decision on which one cannot go back.

Improbable means not likely to be true or to happen.

Incredible means impossible to believe.

Incorrigible is someone who cannot be reformed.

246. Central character in a story or play
SSC CGL Tier-2 29.01.2022
(a) Emulator (b) Contender
(c) Protagonist (d) Adversary

Ans. (c)

Protagonist means the central character in a story or play.

Emulator means a person who tries to imitate someone or something.

Contender means a person or group competing with others to achieve something.

Adversary means one's opponent in a contest, conflict, or dispute.

247. A long wooden seat with a back for people to sit on in a church
SSC CGL Tier-2 29.01.2022
(a) Aisle (b) Pulpit
(c) Pew (d) Altar

Ans. (c)

Pew means a long wooden seat with a back for people to sit on in a church.

Aisle means a passage between rows of seats in a building such as a church or theater.

Pulpit means a raised platform in a church from which the preacher delivers a sermon.

Altar means a table in a Christian church at which the bread and wine are consecrated in communion services.

248. One who accompanies somebody to protect him SSC CGL Tier-2 29.01.2022

(a) Companion (b) Guide
(c) Defender (d) Escort

Ans. (d)

Escort means one who accompanies somebody to protect him.

Companion means a person or animal with whom one spends a lot of time.

Guide means a person who advises or shows the way to others.

Defender means a person who defends someone or something.

249. Too great to be expressed or described in words

SSC CGL Tier-2 03.02.2022

(a) Ineffable (b) Indelible
(c) Infallible (d) Indispensable

Ans. (a)

Ineffable means too great to be expressed or described in words.

Indelible means making marks that cannot be removed.

Infallible means incapable of making mistakes or being wrong.

250. A mass of snow, ice and rocks falling rapidly down a mountainside.

SSC CGL Tier-2 03.02.2022

(a) Blizzard (b) Glacier
(c) Avalanche (d) Typhoon

Ans. (c)

Avalanche means a mass of snow, ice, and rocks falling rapidly down a mountainside.

Blizzard means a severe snowstorm with high winds.

Glacier means a slowly moving mass of ice.

Typhoon means a tropical storm in the region of the Indian or Western Pacific oceans.

251. The original natives of a country

SSC CGL Tier-2 03.02.2022
SSC CPO 28.06.2024 (Shift-III)

(a) Savages (b) Aborigines
(c) Tribal (d) Cannibals

Ans. (b)

Aborigines means the original natives of a country.

Savages means people regarded as primitive and uncivilised.

Tribal means relating to a group of people who have the same language and customs.

Cannibals means people who eat the flesh of other human beings.

252. A set of rooms specially in a hotel for the use of one person or his family

SSC CGL Tier-2 03.02.2022

(a) Suite (b) Flat
(c) Apartment (d) Abode

Ans. (a)

Suite means a set of rooms specially in a hotel for the use of one person or his family.

Flat means a set of rooms forming an individual residence.

Apartment means a set of rooms forming an individual residence.

Abode means a place of residence.

253. A large single detached house with single or double story

SSC CGL Tier-2 08.08.2022

(a) Suite (b) Apartment
(c) Bungalow (d) Penthouse

Ans. (c)

Bungalow means a large single detached house with a single or double story.

Apartment means a set of rooms forming an individual residence.

Penthouse means an apartment on the top floor of a tall building.

254. Symbols of royalty

SSC CGL Tier-2 08.08.2022

(a) Sceptre (b) Relic
(c) Emblem (d) Regalia

Ans. (d)

Regalia means symbols of royalty.

Sceptre means an ornamental staff carried by rulers on ceremonial occasions.

Emblem means a symbolic object representing a quality or concept.

Relic means an object of historical interest.

255. One who speaks for others

(a) Spokesperson SSC CGL Tier-2 08.08.2022
(b) Orator
(c) Verbose
(d) Talkative

Ans. (a)

Spokesperson means one who speaks for others.

Orator means a public speaker, especially one who is eloquent or skilled.

Verbose means using more words than are needed.

Talkative means fond of talking.

256. A doctor who specialise in heart diseases SSC CGL Tier-2 02.08.2022 (Shift-I)

(a) Urologist (b) Cardiologist
(c) Nephorlogist (d) Dermatologist

Ans. (b)

Cardiologist means a doctor who specialises in heart diseases.

Urologist means a doctor who specialises in the urinary system.

Nephrologist means a doctor who specialises in kidney care.

Dermatologist means a doctor who specialises in skin diseases.

SSC CGL 2021 (Tier 1 & 2)

257. A herd or flock of animals being driven in a body

SSC CGL Tier-1 13.08.2021 (Shift-I)

(a) Drove
(b) Crowd
(c) Cluster
(d) Throng

Ans. (a)

A herd or flock of animals being driven by someone is called a **drove**.

Crowd and **Throng** are group of people.

Cluster is a group of similar things. or people positioned or occurring closely together.

258. A group of three novels or plays, each complete in itself

SSC CGL Tier-1 13.08.2021 (Shift-I)

(a) Triplet (b) Trivet
(c) Triumvir (d) Trilogy

Ans. (d)

The group of three complete novels or plays is called a **trilogy**.

Triplet is one of three children or animals born at the same birth.

Trivet is a three-legged stand.

Triumvir is (in ancient Rome) each of three public officers jointly responsible for overseeing any of the administrative departments.

259. One who does not take any alcoholic drink SSC CGL Tier-1 13.08.2021 (Shift-III)

(a) Perfectionist
(b) Teetotaller
(c) Vegetarian
(d) Astrologer

Ans. (b)

A person who does not take alcoholic drinks is called a **teetotaller**.

Perfectionist is someone who does everything without any flaws.

Vegetarian is a person who refrains from eating meat and lives on a diet made up of vegetables, fruits, grains, nuts and sometimes eggs or dairy products.

Astrologer is one who studies the stars and planets to make predictions about the future.

260. A person who listens to someone's private conversation without them knowing SSC CGL Tier-1 16.08.2021 (Shift-I)
(a) Spy
(b) Eavesdropper
(c) Secret agent
(d) Infiltrator
Ans. (b)
A person who listens to someone's private conversation without them knowing is called an **eavesdropper**.
Spy or **secret agent** is a person employed by a government or other organisation to secretly obtain information on an enemy or a competitor.
Infiltrator is a person who secretly becomes part of a group in order to get information or to influence the way the group thinks or behaves.

261. A place in a large institution, for the care of those who are ill
SSC CGL Tier-1 16.08.2021 (Shift-III)
(a) Hostel (b) Infirmary
(c) Hangar (d) Dormitory
Ans. (b)
A place in a large institution for the care of those who are ill is called an **infirmary**.
Hostel is an establishment which provides inexpensive food and lodging for a specific group of people such as students, workers or travellers.
Dormitory is a large bedroom for a number of people in a school or institution.

262. A group of stars
SSC CGL Tier-1 16.08.2021 (Shift-III)
(a) Astronomy (b) Constellation
(c) Congregation (d) Planets
Ans. (b)
A **constellation** is a group of stars.

263. One who studies the occult meanings of numbers and their supposed influence on human life
SSC CGL Tier-1 17.08.2021 (Shift-I)
(a) Astronomer (b) Numerologist
(c) Prophet (d) Astrologer
Ans. (b)
A person who studies the occult meanings of numbers and their supposed influence on human life is called a **numerologist**.
Astronomer refers to a person who is skilled in astronomy or who makes observations of celestial phenomena.
Prophet is one who declares publicly a message that one believes has come from God.
Astrologer is one who studies the stars and planets to make predictions about the future.

264. Having no boundaries or limits
SSC CGL Tier-1 17.08.2021 (Shift-I)
(a) Tremendous
(b) Infinite
(c) Enormous
(d) Colossal
Ans. (b)
Infinite means having no boundaries or limits.
Tremendous, **Enormous** and **Colossal** mean huge.

265. A news article that reports the recent death of a person
SSC CGL Tier-1 17.08.2021 (Shift-III)
(a) Mortuary (b) Review
(c) Editorial (d) Obituary
Ans. (d)
An **obituary** is a news article that reports the death of a person.
Mortuary is a room or building in which dead bodies are kept.
Review means to see carefully.
Editorial means relating to the commissioning or preparing of material for publication.

266. Soft, inner part of a nut or fruit-stone
SSC CGL Tier-1 17.08.2021 (Shift-III)
(a) Bean (b) Pulp
(c) Kernel (d) Caramel
Ans. (b)
Pulp is the small inner part of a nut or a fruit-stone.
Bean means an edible seed.
Kernel means a softer, usually edible part of a nut, seed or fruit stone contained within its shell.
Caramel is an orange-brown confectionery product made by heating a range of sugars.

267. To throw an event into confusion or disorder SSC CGL Tier-1 18.08.2021 (Shift-I)
(a) Explode (b) Detonate
(c) Disrupt (d) Erupt
Ans. (c)
The word **disrupt** means to throw an event into confusion or disorder.
Explode means to burst or shatter violently and noisily as a result of rapid combustion, excessive internal pressure or other process.
Detonate means explode or cause to explode.
Erupt means become active and eject lava, ash and gases.

268. Something that is to your advantage but happened by chance
SSC CGL Tier-1 18.08.2021 (Shift-I)
(a) Fortuitous (b) Purposeful
(c) Deliberate (d) Accidental
Ans. (a)
Something that is to one's advantage but happened by chance is called **fortuitous**.
Purposeful means useful.
Deliberate means planned.
Accidental means by accident and unplanned.

269. An imaginary ideal society free of poverty and suffering
SSC CGL Tier-1 18.08.2021 (Shift-III)
(a) Dreamland (b) Heaven
(c) Paradise (d) Utopia
Ans. (d)
An imaginary ideal society free of poverty and suffering is a 'Utopia'.

270. A dynamic campaign for political, social or religious change
SSC CGL Tier-1 18.08.2021 (Shift-III)
(a) Conflict (b) War
(c) Mutiny (d) Crusade
Ans. (d)
A dynamic campaign for political, social or religious change is called a **crusade**.
Conflict means a fight.
War means a state of armed conflict between different countries or different groups within a country.
Mutiny means an open rebellion against the proper authorities, especially by soldiers or sailors against their officers.

271. An arrangement of flowers that is usually given as a present.
SSC CGL Tier-1 20.08.2021 (Shift-I)
(a) Bracket (b) Basket
(c) Bouquet (d) Boutique
Ans. (c)
Bouquet means an arrangement of flowers that is usually given as a present.
Bracket means a right-angled support attached to and projecting from a wall for holding a shelf, lamp, or other object.
Basket means a container used to hold or carry things, typically made from interwoven strips of cane or wire.
Boutique means a small shop selling fashionable clothes or accessories.

272. A person preoccupied with an unrealistically optimistic approach to life SSC CGL Tier-1 20.08.2021 (Shift-II)
(a) Pragmatic (b) Practical
(c) Rational (d) Quixotic

Ans. (d)

A person preoccupied with an unrealistically optimistic approach to life is a **Quixotic** person.

273. The state of being subject to death
SSC CGL Tier-1 20.08.2021 (Shift-I)

(a) Mortality
(b) Morbidity
(c) Immortality
(d) Deadly

Ans. (a)

The state of being subject to death is called **mortality**.

Morbidity means the condition of suffering from a disease or medical condition.

Immortality means the something that will not die and live forever.

Deadly means something that can kill.

274. A musical composition made up of a series of songs or short pieces
SSC CGL Tier-1 23.08.2021 (Shift-I)

(a) Medley (b) Lyric
(c) Band (d) Orchestra

Ans. (a)

A musical composition made up of a series of songs or short pieces is called a **Medley**.

Lyric means (especially of poetry and songs) expressing personal thoughts and feelings.

Band is a group of people who have a common interest or purpose or who share a common feature.

Orchestra is a large instrumental ensemble typical of classical music, which combines instruments from different families.

275. A secret or disguised way of writing
SSC CGL Tier-1 23.08.2021 (Shift-II)

(a) Emblem (b) Symbol
(c) Cypher (d) Puzzle

Ans. (c)

A secret or disguised way of writing is called a **cypher**.

Emblem is a thing serving as a symbol of a particular quality or concept.

Puzzle is a game, toy or problem designed to test knowledge.

276. A short rest or sleep taken after lunch
SSC CGL Tier-1 24.08.2021 (Shift-I)

(a) Slumber (b) Leisure
(c) Doze (d) Siesta

Ans. (d)

A short rest or sleep taken after lunch is called **Siesta**.

Slumber and **Doze** means to sleep.

Leisure means entertainment and fun.

277. A corporation made up of a number of different companies that operate in diversified fields.
SSC CGL Tier-1 24.08.2021 (Shift-I)

(a) Correlation
(b) Conglomerate
(c) Agreement
(d) Association

Ans. (b)

A corporation made up of a number of different companies that operate in diversified fields is called a **conglomerate**.

Correlation and **association** indicates a relationship.

Agreement refers to a formal document.

278. An examination of a dead body to determine the cause of death
SSC CGL Tier-1 24.08.2021 (Shift-II)

(a) Suicide (b) Post-mortem
(c) Analysis (d) Homicide

Ans. (b)

An examination of a dead body to determine the cause of death is called **post-mortem**.

Suicide means killing of the self.

Analysis means detailed examination of the elements or structure of something.

Homicide means the killing of one person by another.

279. A person who presents a radio/television programme
SSC CGL Tier-1 24.08.2021 (Shift-II)

(a) Comedian (b) Choreographer
(c) Actor (d) Anchor

Ans. (d)

A person who presents a radio or television programme is called an **anchor**.

Comedian is an entertainer on stage or television whose act is designed to make the audience laugh.

Choreographer is a person who composes the sequence of steps and moves for a performance of dance.

Actor is a person whose profession is acting on the stage, in films or on television.

280. The art of effective or persuasive speaking or writing
SSC CGL Tier-1 24.08.2021 (Shift-III)

(a) Bombastic (b) Poetry
(c) Archaic (d) Rhetoric

Ans. (d)

The art of effective or persuasive speaking or writing is called **Rhetoric**.

Bombastic means showy in speech and given to using flowery or elaborate terms.

Poetry refers to rhythmic or musical language.

Archaic means old and outdated.

281. A person employed to drive a private or hired car
SSC CGL Tier-1 24.08.2021 (Shift-III)

(a) Escort (b) Chauffeur
(c) Captain (d) Pilot

Ans. (b)

A person employed to drive a private or hired car is a **chauffeur**.

Captain refers to a person who is in command.

Pilot refers to the person who operates the flying controls of an aircraft.

SSC CPO 2024

282. Attempting to impress by affecting greater importance or merit than is actually possessed.
SSC CPO 27.06.2024 (Shift-I)

(a) Pretentious (b) Imperious
(c) Airy (d) Glorious

Ans. (a)

Pretentious means attempting to impress by affecting greater importance or merit than is actually possessed.

Imperious means arrogant.

Airy means spacious, well lit and well ventilated.

Glorious means having, worthy of, or bringing fame or admiration.

283. A woman having more than one husband at the same time.
SSC CPO 27.06.2024 (Shift-I)

(a) Endogamy (b) Polymathy
(c) Polyandry (d) Monogamy

Ans. (c)

Polyandry refers to the phenomenon of a woman having more than one husband at the same time.

Endogamy means marriage within a specific group as required by custom or law.

Polymathy means learning in many fields; encyclopedic knowledge.

Monogamy means a relationship with only one partner at a time.

284. A professional rider in horse races.
SSC CPO 27.06.2024 (Shift-I)
SSC CPO Tier-2 26.07.2021
SSC CHSL Tier-1 10.03.2023 (Shift-I)

(a) Jockey (b) Stuntman
(c) Southpaw (d) Batsman

Ans. (a)

A **jockey** is a professional rider in horse races.

Stuntman refers to a person who performs stunts.

Southpaw refers to a left-handed person.

Batsman is a player, especially in cricket, who is batting or whose chief skill is in batting.

285. Rahul has done a study of statistics that contributed to the research.
SSC CPO 27.06.2024 (Shift-II)

(a) Demography
(b) Choreography
(c) Cartography
(d) Cinematography

Ans. (a)

Demography is the study of statistical changes in numbers of births, deaths, marriages and cases of disease in a community over a period of time.

Choreography refers to the sequence of steps and movements in dance.

Cartography refers to the science or practice of drawing maps.

Cinematography refers to the art of photography and camera work in film-making.

286. The doctor who deals with the female reproductive system.
SSC CPO 27.06.2024 (Shift-II)

(a) Ophthalmologist
(b) Orthodontist
(c) Cardiologist
(d) Gynaecologist

Ans. (d)

A **gynaecologist** is a specialist doctor who manages conditions that affect the female reproductive system.

An **ophthalmologist** is an eye care specialist.

An **orthodontist** is a type of dentist who specialises in straightening crooked teeth.

A **cardiologist** is a physician who's an expert in the care of your heart and blood vessels.

287. An open space usually rectangular and enclosed in a building.
SSC CPO 27.06.2024 (Shift-II)

(a) Quadruped (b) Quinton
(c) Quadrangle (d) Quintessential

Ans. (c)

A **quadrangle** is an open space usually rectangular and enclosed in a building.

Quadruped means an animal which has four feet.

Quinton means fifth in number.

Quintessential means essential.

288. A deal of agreement done in a company or firm.
SSC CPO 27.06.2024 (Shift-II)

(a) Concurrence (b) Acceptance
(c) Contract (d) Conformity

Ans. (c)

A **contract** is a deal of agreement done in a company or firm.

Concurrence means the fact of two or more events or circumstances happening or existing at the same time.

Conformity means behaviour in accordance with socially accepted conventions.

289. The act or process of going from the simple or basic to the complex or advanced. SSC CPO 27.06.2024 (Shift-II)

(a) Wither
(b) Ennoblement
(c) Evolution
(d) Flourishing

Ans. (c)

Evolution refers to the process of changing or going from the simple or basic to the complex or advanced.

Wither means to become dry and sapless.

Ennoblement means the conferring of nobility-the induction of an individual into the noble class.

Flourishing means developing rapidly and successfully; thriving.

290. An unpleasant mixture of loud sounds. SSC CPO 27.06.2024 (Shift-II)

(a) Harmony (b) Hegemony
(c) Irony (d) Cacophony

Ans. (d)

A **cacophony** is an unpleasant mixture of loud sounds.

Harmony means the combination of simultaneously sounded musical notes to produce a pleasing effect.

Hegemony means leadership or dominance, especially by one state or social group over others.

Irony refers to the use of words to express something other than and especially the opposite of the literal meaning.

291. A story intended to teach moral lessons. SSC CPO 27.06.2024 (Shift-II)

(a) Parboil (b) Parable
(c) Parole (d) Parasite

Ans. (b)

A **parable** is a simple story used to illustrate a moral or spiritual lesson.

Parboil means to boil food, usually vegetables, briefly and lightly.

Parole is the conditional release of prisoners before the full completion of their sentence.

Parasite means an organism that lives in or on an organism of another species (its host) and benefits by deriving nutrients at the other's expense.

292. Feeling of being in a place before having already experienced the present situation
SSC CPO 27.06.2024 (Shift-II)

(a) Deja-vu (b) Illusion
(c) Spirituality (d) Delusion

Ans. (a)

Deja-vu refers to the feeling of being in a place before having already experienced the present situation.

Illusion means a misleading image presented as a vision.

Spirituality means something that in ecclesiastical law belongs to the church.

Delusion means something that is believed to be true or real but that is actually false or unreal.

293. A lively, cheerful outgoing person.
SSC CPO 27.06.2024 (Shift-III)

(a) Orator (b) Ambivert
(c) Extrovert (d) Introvert

Ans. (c)

An **extrovert** is an outgoing, socially confident person.

Orator is a public speaker, especially one who is eloquent or skilled.

Introvert means a shy, reticent person.

Ambivert is a person who has features of both an introvert (= someone who prefers to spend time alone) and an extrovert (= someone who prefers to be with other people) in their personality.

294. Weak and cowardly
SSC CPO 27.06.2024 (Shift-III)

(a) Pusillanimous (b) Meek
(c) Timid (d) Anxious

Ans. (a)

Pusillanimous means showing a lack of courage or determination; meek and timid.

Timid and **Meek** indicate the lack of courage.

Anxious means worried.

295. He was promoted to a higher position in the first year due to his careful nature and hard- working efforts. SSC CPO 27.06.2024 (Shift-III)

(a) Business mindedness
(b) Extraordinary
(c) Elegance
(d) Diligence

Ans. (d)

Diligence means hardworking and careful.

296. The period of time in a person's life when they are developing into an adult. SSC CPO 28.06.2024 (Shift-I)

(a) Adolescence (b) Adultery
(c) Teenage (d) Childhood

Ans. (a)

Adolescence is the period of time in a person's life when they are developing into an adult.

Teenage is the period when an individual is in the age group of 13-19.

Adultery is the voluntary act of engaging in sexual relations by a married individual (man or woman) with someone other than their spouse.

297. Tin is *easy* to shape in any desired form **SSC CPO 28.06.2024 (Shift-I)**

(a) malleable (b) rigid
(c) immutable (d) gullible

Ans. (a)

Malleable means (of a metal or other material) able to be hammered or pressed into shape without breaking or cracking.

Rigid means not able to be changed or adapted.

Immutable means unchanging over time or unable to be changed.

Gullible means easily persuaded to believe something.

298. There was a huge fire for celebration on the occasion of Diwali. **SSC CPO 28.06.2024 (Shift-I)**

(a) Lohri (b) Flash
(c) Bonfire (d) Firecracker

Ans. (c)

A bonfire is a huge fire made during festivals or celebrations.

299. A film shown during the day, especially in the afternoon. **SSC CPO 28.06.2024 (Shift-I)**

(a) Dramatics (b) Matinee
(c) Cinema (d) Theatre

Ans. (b)

A **matinee** is a film shown during the day, especially in the afternoon.

Dramatics is the study or practice of theatrical arts (such as acting and stagecraft).

Cinema is a theatre where films are shown for public entertainment.

300. A doubtful look or examination of one's motives. **SSC CPO 28.06.2024 (Shift-II)**

(a) Introspect (b) Suspect
(c) Circumspect (d) Retrospect

Ans. (b)

Suspect is the doubtful look or examination of one's motives.

Introspect means to examine one's own thoughts or feelings.

Circumspect means careful to consider all circumstances and possible consequences.

Retrospect means the act of thinking now about something in the past.

301. Vivacious and enthusiastic **SSC CPO 28.06.2024 (Shift-II)**

(a) Introverted (b) Effervescent
(c) Rowdy (d) Brazen

Ans. (b)

Effervescent means vivacious and enthusiastic.

Introverted means shy.

Rowdy means noisy and disorderly.

Brazen means bold and without shame.

302. Consonance of sounds. **SSC CPO 28.06.2024 (Shift-II)**

(a) Troupe (b) Woodwinds
(c) Orchestration (d) Symphony

Ans. (d)

Symphony means a long piece of music usually in four parts and played by an orchestra. It is also called a consonance of sounds.

Troupe is a group of artists.

Woodwinds are a type of musical instrument that you play by blowing into its mouthpiece.

Orchestration means planning.

303. Dwarfed varieties of trees and shrubs in pots **SSC CPO 28.06.2024 (Shift-II)**

(a) Bonafide (b) Orchard
(c) Botanical (d) Bonsai

Ans. (d)

A **bonsai** is the Japanese art of growing and shaping miniature or miniature varieties of trees and shrubs in containers.

Bonafide means genuine; real.

Orchard refers to a piece of enclosed land planted with fruit trees.

Botanical means of or relating to plants or botany.

304. The patronage bestowed in consideration of family relationships and not of merit. **SSC CPO 28.06.2024 (Shift-II)**

(a) Egotism (b) Mannerism
(c) Neologism (d) Nepotism

Ans. (d)

Nepotism is the patronage bestowed in consideration of family relationships and not of merit.

Egotism is the fact of being excessively conceited or absorbed in oneself.

Neologism refers to a newly coined word or expression.

305. A place for storage of arms and ammunition **SSC CPO 28.06.2024 (Shift-II)**

(a) Mint (b) Arsenal
(c) Monastery (d) Scullery

Ans. (b)

An **arsenal** is a place where weapons (arms and ammunition) are stored.

Monastery is a building or buildings occupied by a community of monks living under religious vows.

Scullery is a small kitchen or room at the back of a house used for washing dishes and other dirty household work.

306. Referring to something from the past of high quality. **SSC CPO 28.06.2024 (Shift-III)**

(a) Epoch (b) Vintage
(c) Outdated (d) Culture

Ans. (b)

Vintage means belonging to the past but having very high quality and value.

307. The approach or style of teaching **SSC CPO 28.06.2024 (Shift-III)**

(a) Pedagogy (b) Media
(c) Philology (d) Platform

Ans. (a)

Pedagogy is to the method of how teachers teach, in theory and in practice.

Philology is the study of development of language.

308. A news article that reports the recent death of a person. **SSC CPO 28.06.2024 (Shift-III)**

(a) Culinary (b) Obituary
(c) Centenary (d) Mortuary

Ans. (b)

An **obituary** is a news article that reports the recent death of a person.

Culinary means having to do with cooking or the kitchen.

Centenary means of or relating to a period of 100 years.

Mortuary is a place in which the bodies of the dead are kept until burial.

309. Words inscribed on a tomb. **SSC CPO 28.06.2024 (Shift-III)**

(a) Epitaph (b) Prologue
(c) Epilogue (d) Post-script

Ans. (a)

An **epitaph** are the words that are inscribed on a tomb.

A **prologue** is an introductory section of a literary work that provides background information about the story or characters.

A **post-script** is something written at the end of a letter after you have signed your name.

Epilogue is a conclusion of a literary work.

310. Fertile watery place in a desert.
SSC CPO 28.06.2024 (Shift-III)
(a) Obsolete (b) Obscure
(c) Ode (d) Oasis
Ans. (d)
An **oasis** is a small area in a desert where water and plants are found.
Obsolete means outdated and no longer in use.
Obscure means not clear.
Ode refers to a lyric poem, typically one in the form of an address to a particular subject, written in varied or irregular metre.

311. Someone who speaks more than one language SSC CPO 28.06.2024 (Shift-III)
(a) Heretic (b) Fatalist
(c) Polyglot (d) Insolvent
Ans. (c)
A **polyglot** is someone who can speak more than one language.
Heretic is someone who has beliefs that are against the principles of a particular religion.
Insolvent means unable to pay debts owed.

312. During vacations, Geeta saw a saltwater lake separated from the sea by rocks and sand where she did kayak for the first time.
SSC CPO 29.06.2024 (Shift-I)
(a) Lagoon (b) River
(c) Ditch (d) Sea
Ans. (b)
River means a large natural stream of water flowing in a channel to the sea, a lake or another river.
Ditch means a narrow channel dug at the side of a road or field, to hold or carry away water.
Sea means the expanse of salt water that covers most of the earth's surface and surrounds its land masses.
Lagoon is a stretch of salt water separated from the sea by a sand bank or coral reef.

313. A soldier who fights for the sake of money. SSC CPO 29.06.2024 (Shift-I)
(a) Marine (b) Veteran
(c) Mercenary (d) Admiral
Ans. (c)
Mercenary refers to someone who is primarily concerned with making money at the expense of ethics.
Marine means relating to or found in the sea.
Veteran is a person who has had long experience in a particular field.
Admiral means the most senior commander of a fleet or navy.

314. A person who is filled with excessive enthusiasm SSC CPO 29.06.2024 (Shift-I)
(a) Horticulturist (b) Introvert
(c) Narcissist (d) Extrovert
Ans. (d)
An **extrovert** is an outgoing, socially confident person.
Horticulturist refers to a person who studies or grows garden plants.
Introvert refers to a shy, reticent person.

315. Madness or obsession with males
SSC CPO 29.06.2024 (Shift-II)
(a) Polygamy (b) Loquacious
(c) Misandrist (d) Andromania
Ans. (d)
Andromania is madness or obsession with males.
Polygamy is the practice of marrying multiple spouses.
Loquacious means talking or tending to talk much or freely.
Misandrist means a person who hates men.

316. A mythological animal with one horn on its forehead.
SSC CPO 29.06.2024 (Shift-II)
(a) Unicameral (b) Unipod
(c) Unific (d) Unicorn
Ans. (d)
A **unicorn** is a mythological animal with one horn on its forehead.
Unicameral means having or consisting of a single legislative chamber.
Unipod means a one-legged support (as for a camera).
Unific means tending to produce unity.

317. One who does not express himself freely. SSC CPO 29.06.2024 (Shift-II)
(a) Approachable (b) Immodest
(c) Introvert (d) Outgoing
Ans. (c)
Introvert means a shy, reticent person.
Approachable means friendly and easy to talk to.
Immodest means lacking humility or decency.
Outgoing means social.

318. A person who is a lover of women.
SSC CPO 29.06.2024 (Shift-III)
(a) Philologist (b) Monogamist
(c) Philogynist (d) Misogynist
Ans. (c)
Philogynist is a person who likes or admires women.
Philologist is a person who specialises in philology, the study of literary texts and written records.
Monogamist is a person with one relationship.
Misogynist is a person who hates women.

319. Modesty or shyness resulting from a lack of self-confidence.
SSC CPO 29.06.2024 (Shift-III)
(a) Assurance (b) Determination
(c) Conviction (d) Diffidence
Ans. (d)
Diffidence means modesty or shyness resulting from a lack of self-confidence.
Assurance means a positive declaration intended to give confidence; a promise.
Determination means the quality of being determined; firmness of purpose.
Conviction means a firmly held belief or opinion.

320. A person who is critical of the motives of others SSC CPO 29.06.2024 (Shift-III)
(a) Cynic (b) Interviewer
(c) Chauffeur (d) Curator
Ans. (a)
A **cynic** is a person who is critical of the motives of others,
Interviewer is a person who takes an interview.
Chauffeur is a person employed to drive a private or hired car.

321. The husks of corn or other grains separated by winnowing or threshing. SSC CPO Tier-2 08.01.2024
(a) Hay (b) Peel
(c) Fodder (d) Chaff
Ans. (d)
Chaff means the husks of corn or other grains separated by winnowing or threshing.
Hay means grass that has been mown and dried for use as fodder.
Peel means the outer covering or rind of a fruit or vegetable.
Fodder means food, especially dried hay or feed, for cattle and other livestock.

322. Irrational fear of water
SSC CPO Tier-2 08.01.2024
Or
Fear of water SSC CPO 03.10.2023 (Shift-I
(a) claustrophobia (b) acrophobia
(c) cacophobia (d) hydrophobia
Ans. (d)
Hydrophobia means an irrational fear of water.
Cacophobia means an irrational fear of ugliness.
Acrophobia is a fear of heights.

323. One who is skilled and eloquent in public speaking SSC CPO Tier-2 08.01.2024
(a) lecturer
(b) spokesperson
(c) orator
(d) actor
Ans. (c)
Orator means one who is skilled and eloquent in public speaking.
Lecturer means a person who gives lectures, especially as an occupation at a university or college of higher education.

324. A legal document authorising the police or another body to make an arrest or search premises
SSC CPO Tier-2 08.01.2024
(a) decree (b) warrant
(c) licence (d) permit
Ans. (b)
Warrant means a legal document authorising the police or another body to make an arrest or search premises.
Decree means an official order issued by a legal authority.
Licence means a permit from an authority to own or use something.
Permit means an official document giving someone authorisation to do something.

325. A statement open to more than one interpretation SSC CPO Tier-2 08.01.2024
(a) explicit (b) palpable
(c) tangible (d) ambiguous
Ans. (d)
Ambiguous means a statement open to more than one interpretation.
Explicit means stated clearly and in detail.
Palpable means able to be touched or felt.
Tangible means perceptible by touch.

326. To skip about playfully
SSC CPO Tier-2 08.01.2024
(a) trundle (b) scramble
(c) gamble (d) amble
Ans. (c)
Gamble means to skip about playfully.
Trundle means to move slowly and heavily, typically in a noisy or uneven way.
Scramble means to make one's way quickly or awkwardly up a steep gradient or over rough ground by using one's hands as well as one's feet.
Amble means to walk at a relaxed pace.

327. Natural talent for something
SSC CPO Tier-2 08.01.2024
(a) flavour (b) favour
(c) feeling (d) flair
Ans. (d)
Flair means a natural talent for something.
Flavour means the distinctive taste of a food or drink.
Favour means approval, support, or liking for someone or something.

328. A wooden frame for holding an artist's work while it is being painted or drawn SSC CPO Tier-2 08.01.2024
(a) lectern (b) platform
(c) easel (d) podium
Ans. (c)
Easel means a wooden frame for holding an artist's work while it is being painted or drawn.
Lectern means a tall stand with a sloping top to hold a book or notes, from which someone, typically a preacher or lecturer, can read while standing up.
Platform means a raised level surface on which people or things can stand.
Podium means a small platform on which a person may stand to be seen by an audience.

SSC CPO 2023

329. The pandemic deeply affected small business owners, as <u>they have no means of livelihood left</u>.
SSC CPO 03.10.2023 (Shift-I)
(a) Worker (b) Mason
(c) Pauper (d) Unemployed
Ans. (c)
Pauper means a person who is very poor and has no means of livelihood left.
Worker means a person who works, in particular.
Mason means a builder and worker in stone.
Unemployed means a person without a paid job but available to work.

330. Working or operating quickly and effectively in an organised way.
SSC CPO 03.10.2023 (Shift-I)
(a) Effusive (b) Extensive
(c) Excellent (d) Efficient
Ans. (d)
Efficient means working or operating quickly and effectively in an organised way.
Extensive means to vast and wide.
Effusive means showing or expressing gratitude, pleasure or approval in an unrestrained or heartfelt manner.

331. How did you become interested in learning <u>the art of producing beautiful handwriting</u>?
SSC CPO 03.10.2023 (Shift-I)
(a) Calligraphy (b) Lexicography
(c) Graphology (d) Demography
Ans. (a)
Calligraphy is the art of producing beautiful handwriting.
Graphology means inference of character from a person's handwriting.
Lexicography is the act of compiling dictionaries.
Demography is the study of human population.

332. A notice of the death of a person, often with a biographical sketch, as in a newspaper. SSC CPO 03.10.2023 (Shift-I)
(a) Obituary (b) Elegy
(c) Oblivion (d) Advertisement
Ans. (a)
An **obituary** is a notice of the death of a person printed in a newspaper.
Oblivion means the state of being unaware or unconscious of what is happening around one.
Elegy means a poem of seriousreflection, typically a lament for the dead.
Advertisement means a notice or announcement in a public medium promoting a product, service or event or publicising a job vacancy.

333. One who settles in another country.
SSC CPO 03.10.2023 (Shift-II)
(a) Traveller (b) Resident
(c) Refugee (d) Immigrant
Ans. (d)
Immigrant means one who settles in another country.
Traveller means a person who is travelling or who often travels.
Resident means a person who lives somewhere permanently or on a long-term basis.
Refugee means a person who has been forced to leave their country in order to escape war, persecution, or natural disaster.

334. Study of the science of insects.
SSC CPO 03.10.2023 (Shift-II)
(a) Microbiology (b) Anthropology
(c) Ecology (d) Entomology
Ans. (d)

Entomology means the study of the science of insects.

Microbiology means the study of microscopic organisms.

Ecology means the study of the relationships between living organisms and their environment.

335. Payal's father was seen desperately searching for the <u>medicine that can counteract the effect</u> of a venomous snakebite in Parul's left hand.

SSC CPO 03.10.2023 (Shift-II)

(a) Remedy (b) Antiseptic
(c) Antidote (d) Anti-serum

Ans. (c)

Antidote means a medicine that can counteract the effect of a venomous snakebite.

Remedy means a medicine or treatment for a disease or injury.

Antiseptic means a substance that prevents the growth of disease-causing microorganisms.

Anti-serum means a serum containing antibodies against specific antigens, used to treat or provide immunity to specific diseases.

336. The study of the human mind.

SSC CPO 03.10.2023 (Shift-II)

(a) Psychology
(b) Microbiology
(c) Epidemiology
(d) Anthropology

Ans. (a)

Psychology means the study of the human mind.

Epidemiology means the study of how diseases spread and can be controlled.

Microbiology is the study of microorganisms.

337. Happening repeatedly

SSC CPO 03.10.2023 (Shift-II)

(a) recurrent (b) rapport
(c) regression (d) recuperate

Ans. (a)

Recurrent means happening repeatedly.

Rapport means a close and harmonious relationship.

Regression means a return to a former or less developed state.

Recuperate means to recover from illness or exertion.

338. A keeper or custodian of a museum other collection.

SSC CPO 03.10.2023 (Shift-II)

(a) Cartographer (b) Chauffeur
(c) Curator (d) Calligrapher

Ans. (c)

Curator means a keeper or custodian of a museum or other collection.

Calligrapher means a person who writes in a decorative hand.

339. No longer used because something new has been invented.

SSC CPO 03.10.2023 (Shift-III)

(a) Ornamental (b) Obsolete
(c) Classic (d) Ancien

Ans. (b)

Obsolete means no longer used because something new has been invented.

Ornamental means serving or intended as an ornament.

Classic means judged over a period of time to be of the highest quality and outstanding of its kind.

Ancient means belonging to the very distant past and no longer in existence.

340. A pretence of having a virtuous and character, moral or religious beliefs or principles, etc., that one does not really possess. **SSC CPO 03.10.2023 (Shift-III)**

(a) Gullibility (b) Shrewdness
(c) Naivety (d) Hypocrisy

Ans. (d)

Hypocrisy means a pretence of having a virtuous and character, moral or religious beliefs or principles, etc., that one does not really possess.

Gullibility means easily persuaded to believe something.

Shrewdness means having or showing sharp powers of judgement.

Naivety means lack of experience, wisdom or judgement.

341. A state of intense happiness and self-confidence.

SSC CPO 03.10.2023 (Shift-III)

(a) Euphoria (b) Touche
(c) Intoxication (d) Oblivion

Ans. (a)

Euphoria means a state of intense happiness and self-confidence.

Touche means an acknowledgment during a discussion of a good or clever point made at one's expense by another person.

Intoxication means the state of being intoxicated, especially by alcohol.

Oblivion means the state of being unaware or unconscious of what is happening.

342. To criticise someone severely.

SSC CPO 03.10.2023 (Shift-III)

(a) Rate (b) Chastise
(c) Scoff (d) Remonstrate

Ans. (b)

Chastise means to criticise someone severely.

Rate means to assess the value of.

Scoff means to speak to someone or about something in a scornfully derisive or mocking way.

Remonstrate means to make a forcefully reproachful protest.

343. Huge fire for celebration.

SSC CPO 03.10.2023 (Shift-III)

(a) Agenda (b) Campaign
(c) Bonfire (d) Crossfire

Ans. (c)

Bonfire means a large fire built in the open air for celebration.

Agenda means a list of items to be discussed at a formal meeting.

Crossfire means gunfire from two or more directions passing through the same area.

344. To make a low continuous vibratory sound expressing contentment (of a cat).

SSC CPO 03.10.2023 (Shift-III)

(a) To meow (b) To buzz
(c) To roar (d) To purr

Ans. (d)

To purr means to make a low continuous vibratory sound expressing contentment (of a cat).

To meow means the sound a cat makes.

To buzz means a low, continuous humming or murmuring sound.

To roar means a full, deep, prolonged cry uttered by a lion or other large wild animal.

345. Minimum people needed for a meeting. **SSC CPO 03.10.2023 (Shift-III)**

(a) Forum (b) Quorum
(c) Addendum (d) Decorum

Ans. (b)

Quorum means the minimum number of people needed for a meeting.

Forum means a place, meeting, or medium where ideas and views on a particular issue can be exchanged.

Addendum means an item of additional material added at the end of a book or other publication.

Decorum means behaviour in keeping with good taste and propriety.

346. Something of monstrous size or power **SSC CPO 04.10.2023 (Shift-I)**

(a) Heavyweight (b) Bulk
(c) Amazon (d) Behemoth

Ans. (d)

Behemoth means something of monstrous size or power.

Heavyweight means a weight in boxing and other sports, typically the heaviest category.

Bulk means the mass or size of something large.

Amazon means a large, strong, and aggressive woman.

347. An ability to do several things at the same time. SSC CPO 04.10.2023 (Shift-I)
(a) Unitasking
(b) Indictment
(c) Blasphemy
(d) Multitasking

Ans. (d)

Multitasking means an ability to do several things at the same time.

Unitasking means doing one thing at a time.

Indictment means a formal charge or accusation of a serious crime.

Blasphemy is the act of talking negatively about god.

348. Someone who pretends to have certain moral standards while secretively that person practices those very moral lapses. SSC CPO 04.10.2023 (Shift-I)
(a) Actor (b) Hypocrite
(c) Sinner (d) Spy

Ans. (b)

Hypocrite means someone who pretends to have certain moral standards while secretly practicing those very moral lapses.

Sinner means a person who transgresses against divine law by committing an immoral act or acts.

Spy means a person who secretly collects and reports information on the activities, movements, and plans of an enemy or competitor.

349. The compulsion to tell lies SSC CPO 04.10.2023 (Shift-I)
(a) Mythomania
(b) Nymphomania
(c) Megalomania
(d) Pyromania

Ans. (a)

Mythomania means the compulsion to tell lies.

Nymphomania means excessive sexual desire in women.

Megalomania means obsession with the exercise of power, especially in the domination of others.

Pyromania means an obsessive desire to set fire to things.

350. A disease prevalent in a community or a specific region at a specific time, affecting a large area. SSC CPO 04.10.2023 (Shift-II)
(a) Eradicate (b) Epidemic
(c) Pandemic (d) Endemic

Ans. (b)

An **epidemic** is a disease prevalent in a community or a specific region at a time.

Pandemic is an epidemic of an infectious disease that has a sudden increase in cases and spreads across a large region.

Eradicate means destroy completely; put an end to.

Endemic means (of a disease) regularly occurring within an area or community.

351. He was <u>not willing</u> to attend the technical session of the conference. SSC CPO 04.10.2023 (Shift-II)
(a) Comprehensive (b) reluctant
(c) dejecting (d) curious

Ans. (b)

Reluctant means unwilling or hesitant to do something.

Dejecting means make sad or dispirited; depress.

Curious means eager to know or learn something.

Comprehensive means including or dealing with all or nearly all elements or aspects of something.

352. To have a strong emotional effect on. SSC CPO 04.10.2023 (Shift-II)
(a) To overwhelm (b) To yield
(c) To smother (d) To forfeit

Ans. (a)

To **overwhelm** means to have a strong emotional effect on.

To forfeit means to give up.

To smother means to make (someone) feel trapped and oppressed by acting in an overly protective or possessive manner towards them.

To yield means to give in or accept.

353. Very attractive and easy to feel love for SSC CPO 04.10.2023 (Shift-II)
(a) Adorable (b) Flamboyant
(c) Laudable (d) Mysterious

Ans. (a)

Adorable means very attractive.

Flamboyant means (of a person or their behaviour) tending to attract attention because of their exuberance, confidence, and stylishness.

Mysterious means difficult or impossible to understand explain or identify.

Laudable means (of an action, idea, or aim) deserving praise and commendation.

354. An animal or a person that eats all types of food, especially plants and meat SSC CPO 04.10.2023 (Shift-II)
(a) Vegetarian (b) Omnivore
(c) Herbivore (d) Carnivore

Ans. (b)

An **omnivore** is an organism that consumes both plants and animals.

Vegetarian and **Herbivore** refer to a person who refrains from eating meat and lives on a diet made up of vegetables, fruits, grains, nuts and sometimes eggs or dairy products.

Carnivore refers to an organism that mostly eats meat or the flesh of animals.

355. Extremely beautiful, elaborate or impressive SSC CPO 04.10.2023 (Shift-III)
(a) Transient (b) Magnificent
(c) Proficient (d) Deficient

Ans. (b)

Magnificent means extremely beautiful, elaborate or impressive.

Transient means lasting for only a short time; impermanent.

Proficient means competent or skilled in doing or using something.

Deficient means not having enough of a specified quality or ingredient.

356. A collection of historical documents or records providing information about a place, institution or group of people SSC CPO 04.10.2023 (Shift-III)
(a) Asylum (b) Museum
(c) Apostate (d) Archive

Ans. (d)

Archive means a collection of historical documents or records providing information about a place, institution or group of people.

Asylum means the protection granted by a nation to someone who has left their native country as a political refugee.

Museum means a building in which objects of historical, scientific, artistic, or cultural interest are stored and exhibited.

Apostate is a person who has renounced religious belief.

357. Since God is <u>an all-powerful</u> creator, he has absolute control over those whom he has created. SSC CPO 04.10.2023 (Shift-III)
(a) Omniscient (b) Voracious
(c) Omnipotent (d) Incorrigible

Ans. (c)

Omnipotent means having absolute control over those whom he has created.

Omniscient means knowing everything.

Voracious means wanting or devouring great quantities of food.

Incorrigible is someone who cannot change.

358. Centre of public attention
SSC CPO 05.10.2023 (Shift-I)
(a) Limelight (b) Ambiguity
(c) Fuzziness (d) Obscurity

Ans. (a)

Limelight means the centre of public attention.

Ambiguity means uncertainty or inexactness of meaning in language.

Fuzziness means lacking in clarity or definition.

Obscurity means the state of being unknown, inconspicuous, or unimportant.

359. One who goes from place to place, begging **SSC CPO 05.10.2023 (Shift-I)**
(a) Malleable (b) Mendicant
(c) Meticulous (d) Misogamist

Ans. (b)

Mendicant means one who goes from place to place begging.

Malleable means easily influenced or pliable.

Meticulous means showing great attention to detail.

Misogamist means a person who hates marriage.

360. To tell the nature of a disease by its symptoms. **SSC CPO 05.10.2023 (Shift-I)**
(a) Design (b) Diagnosis
(c) Decisive (d) Dosage

Ans. (b)

Diagnosis means to tell the nature of a disease by its symptoms.

Design means a plan or drawing produced to show the look and function or workings of a building, garment, or other object before it is made.

Decisive means settling an issue; producing a definite result.

Dosage means the size or frequency of a dose of a medicine or drug.

361. A book published after author's death. **SSC CPO 05.10.2023 (Shift-I)**
(a) Predecessor publication
(b) Posthumous publication
(c) Supernatural publication
(d) Posthuman publication

Ans. (b)

Posthumous publication means a book published after the author's death.

Predecessor publication means a book published before another one.

Supernatural publication means a book about supernatural phenomena.

Posthuman publication means a book about post-human topics.

362. Children and adolescents with <u>a morbid compulsion to steal</u> experience a growing sense of tension just before stealing, followed by pleasure, relief or gratification during or just after stealing.
SSC CPO 05.10.2023 (Shift-II)

Or

One who has persistent neurotic impulse to steal.
SSC CHSL Tier-1 09.03.2023 (Shift-I)
(a) Megalomania
(b) Kleptomania
(c) Dipsomania
(d) Pyromania

Ans. (b)

Kleptomania means a morbid compulsion to steal.

Megalomania means obsession with the exercise of power.

Dipsomania means an uncontrollable craving for alcohol.

Pyromania means an obsessive desire to set fire to things.

363. Requiring exceptional skill or caution in performance or handling
SSC CPO 05.10.2023 (Shift-III)
(a) Blunt (b) Abstract
(c) Sustainable (d) Tricky

Ans. (d)

A **tricky** thing requires exceptional skills or caution.

Blunt means not having a sharp edge or point.

Sustainable means able to be maintained at a certain rate or level.

Abstract means existing in thought or as an idea but not having a physical or concrete existence.

364. An act of exchanging information
SSC CPO 05.10.2023 (Shift-III)
(a) Touch (b) Hold
(c) Collaboration (d) Communication

Ans. (d)

Communication refers to the act of exchanging information.

Touch means to come into or be in contact with.

Hold means to grasp, carry, or support with one's arms or hands.

Collaboration means the action of working with someone to produce or create something.

SSC CPO 2022

365. Showing astute powers of judgement; clever and judicious
SSC CPO 09.11.2022 (Shift-I)
(a) Shriek (b) Shrift
(c) Shrewd (d) Shrike

Ans. (c)

Shrewd means showing astute powers of judgement; clever and judicious.

Shriek means a high-pitched piercing cry or sound.

Shrift means confession, especially to a priest.

Shrike means a songbird with a stout, hooked bill.

366. Profitable, yielding financial gain
SSC CPO 09.11.2022 (Shift-I)
(a) Ludicrous (b) Lucrative
(c) Luddite (d) Lugger

Ans. (b)

Lucrative means profitable, yielding financial gain.

Ludicrous means so foolish, unreasonable, or out of place as to be amusing.

Luddite means a person opposed to increased industrialisation or new technology.

Lugger means a small fishing or coasting boat with lug sails.

367. Cause to continue; keep up; preserve (a state of affairs, an activity, etc.
SSC CPO 09.11.2022 (Shift-II)
(a) Maintop (b) Mainly
(c) Maintain (d) Mainstay

Ans. (c)

Maintain means to cause to continue; keep up; preserve (a state of affairs, an activity, etc.).

Maintop means the platform at the top of the lower section of a mast.

Mainly means more than anything else.

Mainstay means a thing on which something else is based or depends.

368. Taking heed or care; being conscious
SSC CPO 09.11.2022 (Shift-II)
(a) Mindful (b) Mindless
(c) Mindset (d) Mind-read

Ans. (a)

Mindful means taking heed or care; being conscious.

Mindless means acting or done without justification or concern for the consequences.

Mindset means the established set of attitudes held by someone.

Mind-read means to perceive or know what another person is thinking.

369. The scientific study or worms and insects SSC CPO 09.11.2022 (Shift-II)

(a) Entomology
(b) Anatomy
(c) Zoology
(d) Anemology

Ans. (a)

Entomology means the scientific study of worms and insects.

Anatomy means the branch of science concerned with the bodily structure of humans, animals, and other living organisms.

Zoology means the scientific study of the behaviour, structure, physiology, classification, and distribution of animals.

Anemology means the study of wind.

370. Honour given for some achievement. SSC CPO 09.11.2022 (Shift-III)

(a) Placard (b) Laurel
(c) Party (d) Gift

Ans. (b)

Laurel means honour given for some achievement.

Placard means a poster or sign for public display.

371. Killing of a person by another SSC CPO 09.11.2022 (Shift-III)

(a) Homicide (b) Democide
(c) Genocide (d) Euthanasia

Ans. (a)

Homicide means killing of a person by another.

Democide means the murder of any person or people by their government.

Euthanasia means the painless killing of a patient suffering from an incurable and painful disease.

Genocide is killing of people of an ethnic group.

372. Treat with a vaccine, usually by injection to promote immunity against a disease SSC CPO 10.11.2022 (Shift-I)

(a) Innuendo (b) Inoculate
(c) Innumerate (d) Innovate

Ans. (b)

Inoculate means to treat with a vaccine, usually by injection, to promote immunity against a disease.

Innuendo means an allusive or oblique remark or hint, typically a suggestive or disparaging one.

Innumerate means without a basic knowledge of mathematics and arithmetic.

Innovate means to make changes in something established, especially by introducing new methods, ideas, or products.

373. None of the countries involved in war were ready to **broach** the issue of retreat. SSC CPO 10.11.2022 (Shift-II)

(a) turn down thoughtlessly
(b) bring up for discussion
(c) underestimate the worth of
(d) disregard contemptuously

Ans. (b)

Broach means to bring up for discussion.

Turn down thoughtlessly means to reject without consideration.

Underestimate the worth of means to undervalue.

Disregard contemptuously means to ignore in a scornful way.

374. Seeing the danger of <u>a group governed by old people</u>, Ratan planned to recruit young people for his project. SSC CPO 10.11.2022 (Shift-III)

(a) adhocracy (b) plutocracy
(c) gerontocracy (d) autocracy

Ans. (c)

Gerontocracy means a government or group governed by old people.

Adhocracy means a flexible, adaptable, and informal organisational structure without bureaucratic policies or procedures.

Autocracy means a system of government by one person with absolute power.

Plutocracy is the government by the wealthy.

375. Take hold of forcibly or suddenly SSC CPO 10.11.2022 (Shift-III)

(a) Seize (b) Liberate
(c) Release (d) Relinquish

Ans. (a)

Seize means to take hold of forcibly or suddenly.

Liberate means to set someone free from imprisonment, slavery, or oppression.

Release means to set free from confinement or bondage.

Relinquish means to voluntarily cease to keep or claim.

376. Try hard to do or achieve something SSC CPO 10.11.2022 (Shift-III)

(a) Endanger (b) Hardworking
(c) Endeavour (d) Indent

Ans. (c)

Endeavour means trying to achieve something.

Endanger means put (someone or something) at risk or in danger.

Indent means start (a line of text) or position (a block of text) further from the margin than the main part of the text.

377. The Bishop criticised the Government for its <u>having no sympathy</u> and an uncaring attitude to the homeless and the unemployed. SSC CPO 11.11.2022 (Shift-I)

(a) merciful (b) callous
(c) tender (d) compassionate

Ans. (b)

Callous means cruel and having no sympathy.

Merciful means forgiving.

Tender means soft.

Compassionate means kind.

378. One who is bad in spellings SSC CPO 11.11.2022 (Shift-II) SSC CHSL Tier-1 04.08. 2023 (Shift-II)

(a) Cacographer (b) Photographer
(c) Choreographer (d) Chauvinist

Ans. (a)

Cacographer means one who is bad at spellings.

Photographer means a person who takes photographs, especially as a job.

Choreographer means a person who composes the sequence of steps and moves for a performance of dance.

Chauvinist means a person displaying aggressive or exaggerated patriotism.

SSC CPO 2021 (Tier 2)

379. A person who shows people their seats SSC CPO Tier-2 26.07.2021

(a) usher (b) guard
(c) watchman (d) Cameraman

Ans. (a)

Usher means a person who shows people their seats.

Guard means a person who keeps watch, especially a soldier or other person formally assigned to protect a person or to control access to a place.

Watchman means a person employed to look after an empty building, especially at night.

Cameraman means a person who operates a camera for films or television.

380. To give one's authority to another
SSC CPO Tier-2 26.07.2021
Or
One appointed to act in place of another **SSC MTS Tier-1 11.05.2023 (Shift-III)**
(a) shirk (b) supervise
(c) usurp (d) delegate

Ans. (d)

Delegate means to give one's authority to another.

Shirk means to avoid or neglect a duty or responsibility.

Supervise means to observe and direct the execution of a task, project, or activity.

Usurp means to take a position of power or importance illegally or by force.

381. A fictitious name used by an uthor.
SSC CPO Tier-2 26.07.2021
(a) alibi (b) namesake
(c) homonym (d) pseudonym

Ans. (d)

Pseudonym means a fictitious name used by an author.

Alibi means a claim or piece of evidence that one was elsewhere when an act, typically a criminal one, is alleged to have taken place.

Namesake means a person or thing that has the same name as another.

Homonym means each of two or more words having the same spelling or pronunciation but different meanings and origins.

382. Someone taken a prisoner to fulfill demands **SSC CPO Tier-2 26.07.2021**
(a) dealer (b) hostage
(c) guest (d) host

Ans. (b)

Hostage means someone taken a prisoner to fulfill demands.

Dealer means a person who buys and sells goods.

Guest means a person who is invited to visit the home of or take part in a function organised by another.

Host means a person who receives or entertains other people as guests.

SSC CHSL 2024 (Tier 1 & 2)

383. Hospital for people with mental illnesses **SSC CHSL Tier-1 01.07.2024 (Shift-II)**
(a) Hangar (b) Druggist
(c) Asylum (d) Shelter

Ans. (c)

An **asylum** is a place where people with mental illness are kept and treated.

Hangar means a large building with an extensive floor area, typically for housing aircraft.

Druggist means a person who sells or dispenses drugs and medicines.

Shelter means a place where one is kept safe and secure.

384. A sudden violent event that brings about great loss or destruction.
SSC CHSL Tier-2 10.01.2024
(a) Blockbuster
(b) Farce
(c) Intrigue
(d) Catastrophe

Ans. (d)

A **catastrophe** is a sudden violent event that brings huge loss.

Blockbuster means hit and popular.

Farce is a comic dramatic work using buffoonery and horseplay, typically including crude characterisation and ludicrously improbable situations.

Intrigue means arouse the curiosity or interest of; fascinate.

385. A drug or other substance that induces sleep **SSC CHSL Tier-2 10.01.2024**
(a) Energetic (b) Reviver
(c) Stimulant (d) Sedative

Ans. (d)

A **sedative** is a drug or medicine that induces sleep.

Reviver means to make (someone or something) strong, active or healthy again.

Stimulant means a substance that raises levels of physiological or nervous activity in the body.

SSC CHSL 2023 (Tier 1)

386. Study of heavenly bodies
SSC CHSL Tier-1 09.03.2023 (Shift-I)
Or
The scientific study of the universe and planets
SSC CHSL Tier-1 19.04.2021 (Shift-III)
(a) Numerology (b) Astrology
(c) Stargazing (d) Astronomy

Ans. (d)

Astronomy refers to the scientific study of stars and planets.

Numerology means the study of numbers.

Astrology means the study that assumes and attempts to interpret the influence of the heavenly bodies on human affairs.

Stargazing means looking at the sky for stars.

387. One who hates institution of marriage **SSC CHSL Tier-1 09.03.2023 (Shift-I)**
(a) Pedantic (b) Polyglot
(c) Misogamist (d) Coquette

Ans. (c)

A **misogamist** hates the concept and institution of marriage.

Pedantic is an insulting word used to describe someone who annoys others by correcting small errors, caring too much about minor details, or emphasising their own expertise especially in some narrow or boring subject matter.

Polyglot is someone who speaks many languages.

Coquette is a woman who tries without sincere affection to gain the attention and admiration of men.

388. A specialist of kidney
SSC CHSL Tier-1 09.03.2023 (Shift-II)
(a) Obstetrician (b) Nephrologist
(c) Pathologist (d) Primatologist

Ans. (b)

Nephrologist means a specialist of kidney.

Obstetrician means a doctor who specialises in pregnancy and childbirth.

Pathologist means a scientist who studies the causes and effects of diseases.

Primatologist means a person who studies primates.

389. A person who is indifferent to pain and pleasure of life
SSC CHSL Tier-1 09.03.2023 (Shift-III)
(a) Vagabond (b) Amateur
(c) Stoic (d) Recluse

Ans. (c)

Stoic means a person who is indifferent to pain and pleasure of life.

Vagabond means a person who wanders from place to place without a home or job.

Amateur means a person who engages in a pursuit, especially a sport, on an unpaid basis.

Recluse is a person who chooses to live alone.

390. One who does not know reading or writing **SSC CHSL Tier-1 10.03.2023 (Shift-I)**
(a) Scholar (b) Illiterate
(c) Erudite (d) Fastidious

Ans. (b)

Illiterate means one who does not know reading or writing.

Scholar means a specialist in a particular branch of study, especially the humanities.

Erudite means having or showing great knowledge or learning.

Fastidious is someone who accepts perfection.

391. Recovering from an illness or medical treatment.

SSC CHSL Tier-1 10.03.2023 (Shift-II)

(a) Connoisseur (b) Bohemian
(c) Convalescent (d) Cosmopolitan

Ans. (c)

Convalescent means recovering from illness.

Bohemian is a socially unconventional person, especially one who is involved in the arts.

Connoisseur is an expert judge in matters of taste.

Cosmopolitan is a person who believes that he/she belongs to the world.

392. One who cures eye disease.

SSC CHSL Tier-1 13.03.2023 (Shift-II)

(a) Biologist
(b) Phonologist
(c) Prologist
(d) Ophthalmologist

Ans. (d)

Ophthalmologist means one who cures eye disease.

Biologist means a scientist who studies living organisms.

Phonologist means a person who studies phonology.

Prologist means an incorrect term; no such term exists.

393. A person who is never happy with what he has

SSC CHSL Tier-1 13.03.2023 (Shift-II)

(a) Miser (b) Heresy
(c) Malcontent (d) Malleable

Ans. (c)

Malcontent means a person who is never happy with what he has.

Miser means a person who hoards wealth and spends as little money as possible.

Heresy means belief or opinion contrary to orthodox religious doctrine.

Malleable means easily influenced or pliable.

394. The art of identifying a disease from its signs and symptoms

SSC CHSL Tier-1 13.03.2023 (Shift-III)

(a) Prognosis (b) Autopsy
(c) Diagnosis (d) Biopsy

Ans. (c)

Diagnosis refers to the art of identifying a disease from signs and symptoms.

Prognosis means the likely outcome or course of a disease; the chance of recovery or recurrence.

Autopsy means an examination of a body after death to determine the cause of death or the character and extent of changes produced by disease.

Biopsy is a procedure to remove a piece of tissue or a sample of cells from your body so that it can be tested in a laboratory.

395. Feeling or expressing overwhelming happiness or joyful excitement.

SSC CHSL Tier-1 13.03.2023 (Shift-III)

(a) Ecstatic (b) Escalate
(c) Scintillating (d) Intricate

Ans. (a)

Ecstatic means expressing overwhelming joy and happiness.

Escalate means to increase.

Scintillating means shining brightly and attractive

Intricate means delicate and complex.

396. A person who has escaped from captivity or is in hiding.

SSC CHSL Tier-1 14.03.2023 (Shift-I)

(a) Fanatic (b) Fugitive
(c) Fastidious (d) Farce

Ans. (b)

A **fugitive** is a person who has escaped from captivity.

Farce is a comic dramatic work using buffoonery and horseplay, typically including crude characterisation and ludicrously improbable situations.

Fanatic is a crazy person.

397. Killing one's father

SSC CHSL Tier-1 14.03.2023 (Shift-III)

(a) Insecticide (b) Suicide
(c) Tyrannicide (d) Patricide

Ans. (d)

Patricide means killing one's father.

Insecticide means a substance used for killing insects.

Suicide means the act of intentionally causing one's own death.

Tyrannicide means the act of killing a tyrant.

398. A publication containing astronomical or meteorological information

SSC CHSL Tier-1 14.03.2023 (Shift-IV)

(a) Allegory (b) Bane
(c) Conscription (d) Almanac

Ans. (d)

Almanac means a publication containing astronomical or meteorological information.

Allegory means a story, poem, or picture that can be interpreted to reveal a hidden meaning.

Bane means a cause of great distress or annoyance.

Conscription means compulsory enlistment for state service, typically into the armed forces.

399. A substance for killing algae

SSC CHSL Tier-1 14.03.2023 (Shift-IV)

(a) Algaecide (b) Prepuce
(c) Fungicide (d) Ruthenium

Ans. (a)

Algaecide means a substance for killing algae.

Prepuce means the foreskin of the penis.

Fungicide means a substance that destroys fungus.

Ruthenium means a chemical element with the symbol Ru and atomic number 44.

400. A person who is interested in material gains and is hostile to art/culture

SSC CHSL Tier-1 14.03.2023 (Shift-IV)

(a) Perfectionist (b) Sage
(c) Philistine (d) Egghead

Ans. (c)

Philistine means a person who is interested in material gains and is hostile to art/culture.

Perfectionist means a person who refuses to accept any standard short of perfection.

Sage means a profoundly wise person.

Egghead means an intellectual or very studious person.

401. Exclusive command possession

SSC CHSL Tier-1 15.03.2023 (Shift-II)

(a) Sanctum (b) Monopoly
(c) Hypergamy (d) Parvenu

Ans. (b)

Monopoly means exclusive command possession.

Sanctum means a sacred or holy place.

Hypergamy means the action of marrying a person of a superior caste or class.

Parvenu means a person of obscure origin who has gained wealth, influence, or celebrity.

402. One who is against religion.

SSC CHSL Tier-1 15.03.2023 (Shift-II)

(a) Poacher (b) Lunatic
(c) Bandit (d) Heretic

Ans. (d)

Heretic means one who is against religion.

Poacher means a person who hunts or catches game or fish illegally.

Lunatic means a mentally ill person.

Bandit means a robber or outlaw belonging to a gang and typically operating in an isolated or lawless area.

403. Give off gas bubbles
SSC CHSL Tier-1 15.03.2023 (Shift-II)

(a) Buoyant (b) Effervescent
(c) Flat (d) Effuse

Ans. (b)

Effervescent means to give off gas bubbles.

Buoyant means able or apt to stay afloat or rise to the top of a liquid or gas.

Flat means having a level surface; without raised areas or indentations.

Effuse means to pour out.

404. Rhythmic flow of sounds or words.
SSC CHSL Tier-1 15.03.2023 (Shift-IV)

(a) Cadence (b) Crescents
(c) Credence (d) Copious

Ans. (a)

Cadence refers to the rhythmic flow of sounds of words.

Crescents means a thing which has the shape of a single curve that is broad in the centre and tapers to a point at each end.

Credence means belief in or acceptance of something as true.

Copious means present in large quantity.

405. A person who attacks or criticises cherished belief or institutions.
SSC CHSL Tier-1 16.03.2023 (Shift-I)

(a) Impregnable (b) Insolvent
(c) Immoral (d) Iconoclast

Ans. (d)

Iconoclast is a person who criticises and attacks cherished traditional beliefs and customs.

Impregnable means unable to be captured or broken into.

Insolvent means unable to pay debts owed.

Immoral means not good or moral.

406. The origin or birth of a thing
SSC CHSL Tier-1 16.03.2023 (Shift-I)

(a) Coda (b) Quietus
(c) Genesis (d) Culmination

Ans. (c)

Genesis means the birth or origin of a thing.

Coda means a concluding part of a literary or dramatic work.

Quietus means death or something that causes death, regarded as a release from life.

Culmination means the end or conclusion of something.

407. Someone who avoids other people's company
SSC CHSL Tier-1 17.03.2023 (Shift-II)

(a) Gregarious (b) Amicable
(c) Amiable (d) Reclusive

Ans. (d)

Reclusive means living alone and avoiding other people.

Gregarious means fond of company; sociable.

Amicable and **Amiable** means friendly.

408. Lion like characteristics
SSC CHSL Tier-1 17.03.2023 (Shift-II)

(a) Feline (b) Porcine
(c) Leonine (d) Lionise

Ans. (c)

Leonine means having characteristics like that of a lion.

Porcine means having characteristics like that of a pig.

Lionise means to give a lot of public attention.

Feline means relating to cats.

409. A game that results neither in victory nor in defeat
SSC CHSL Tier-1 17.03.2023 (Shift-II)

(a) Draw (b) Void
(c) Fawn (d) Cynic

Ans. (a)

Draw is a game which ends with both teams having the same number of points.

Void means not valid.

Fawn means a young deer.

Cynic is a person who believes that mankind is selfish.

410. A lover of good food.
SSC CHSL Tier-1 20.03.2023 (Shift-III)

(a) Gourmand (b) Chauvinist
(c) Esoteric (d) Ergophile

Ans. (a)

Gourmand is a person who enjoys good food and wine.

Chauvinist is a person displaying excessive or prejudiced support for their own cause or group, in particular a man prejudiced against women.

Esoteric means intended for or likely to be understood by only a small number of people with a specialised knowledge or interest.

Ergophile is a person who enjoys working.

411. A fall of water from a great height
SSC CHSL Tier-1 21.03.2023 (Shift-II)

(a) Cascade (b) River
(c) Typhoon (d) Stream

Ans. (a)

Cascade means (of water) to fall downwards rapidly and in large quantities.

Typhoon is a storm.

Stream is a small river.

412. Exaggerated claims, not meant to be taken seriously.
SSC CHSL Tier-1 21.03.2023 (Shift-IV)

(a) Hypergamy (b) Hyperbole
(c) Hyperpyrexia (d) Hyperreal

Ans. (b)

A Hyperbole is a poetic device wherein we exaggerate claims so that it is not taken seriously.

Hypergamy means the act or practice of a person dating or marrying a spouse of higher social status or sexual capital than themselves.

Hyperpyrexia is condition which occurs when the body's temperature rises above 106.7 degrees Fahrenheit.

Hyperreal means very real.

413. When I was in class 5th, I won the first prize in <u>extempore</u> at my school.
SSC CHSL Tier-1 02.08. 2023 (Shift-I)

(a) A short piece of writing on a subject
(b) A sports event
(c) A speech delivered without prior preparation or rehearsal
(d) A dramatic performance on stage

Ans. (c)

'Extempore' is a speech delivered without prior preparation or rehearsal.

414. A person who loves and collects books.
SSC CHSL Tier-1 03.08. 2023 (Shift-I)
SSC CHSL Tier-1 08.06.2022 (Shift-II)

Or

A lover of books
SSC MTS Tier-1 06.09.2023 (Shift-I)

(a) Bibliophile
(b) Philanthropist
(c) Geologist
(d) Sommelier

Ans. (a)

A **bibliophile** is a person who loves and collects books.

Geologist is an expert in the field of geology, the study of what the Earth.

Sommelier is a wine waiter.

415. One's relatives or family related
SSC CHSL Tier-1 04.08.2023 (Shift-II)

(a) Kilt (b) Kindle
(c) Kin (d) Kine

Ans. (c)

Kin refers to one's relatives or family related.

Kilt means a knee-length pleated skirt usually of tartan worn by men in Scotland a knee-length pleated skirt usually of tartan worn by men in Scotland.

Kindle means arouse or inspire (an emotion or feeling).

Kine is plural of cow.

416. Affected by an undesirable condition or unpleasant feeling
SSC CHSL Tier-1 07.08.2023 (Shift-IV)

(a) Cancelled (b) Indifferent
(c) Modest (d) Stricken

Ans. (d)

Stricken means affected by an undesirable condition or unpleasant feeling.

Indifferent means having no feeling towards something.

Modest means polite and kind.

417. The theory or philosophy of law
SSC CHSL Tier-1 07.08.2023 (Shift-IV)

(a) Jurisprudence (b) Pacifism
(c) Cosmology (d) Philia

Ans. (a)

Jurisprudence means the theory or philosophy of law.

Pacifism is the opposition or resistance to war, militarism or violence.

Cosmology is a branch of astronomy that involves the origin and evolution of the universe, from the Big Bang to today and on into the future.

Philia is a positive feeling of liking.

418. Animals especially on a farm, regarded as an asset.
SSC CHSL Tier-1 07.08.2023 (Shift-IV)

(a) Livid (b) Livery stable
(c) Livelihood (d) Livestock

Ans. (d)

Livestock are animals that are regarded as assets.

Livid means angry.

Lively stable means happy.

Livelihood means money to fulfill the basic necessities of life.

419. The king's coronation ceremony was a grand affair, with all the nobles and dignitaries dressed in their finest insignia of royalty.
SSC CHSL Tier-1 08.08. 2023 (Shift-II)

(a) ornaments (b) regalia
(c) regals (d) specters

Ans. (b)

Regalia refers to the symbols of royalty.

Ornaments refers to objects used to make something more beautiful.

Regals means of relating to or suitable for a king.

Specters means something widely feared as a possible unpleasant or dangerous occurrence.

420. One who possesses outstanding technical ability in a particular art or field. SSC CHSL Tier-1 08.08. 2023 (Shift-II)

(a) Virtuous (b) Virtuoso
(c) Gourmand (d) Amateur

Ans. (b)

Virtuoso is used for someone who possess outstanding technical ability in a particular art or field.

Virtuous means moral.

Amateur refers to a person who engages in a pursuit, especially a sport, on an unpaid rather than a professional basis.

421. WHO is an organisation that raises money for a particular cause.
SSC CHSL Tier-1 09.08. 2023 (Shift-I)

(a) donation (b) volunteer
(c) charity (d) fundraiser

Ans. (d)

A **fundraiser** is an organisation that raises money for a particular cause.

Donation means a gift for charity, humanitarian aid or to benefit a cause.

Volunteer means to do something willingly.

422. A form of government in which power is held by the nobility.
SSC CHSL Tier-1 09.08.2023 (Shift-I)

(a) Democracy (b) Aristocracy
(c) Republic (d) Nobility

Ans. (b)

Aristocracy refers to the government of the people belonging to the high class or royalty.

Democracy is a system of government by the whole population or all the eligible members of a state, typically through elected representatives.

Republic is form of government in which a state is ruled by representatives of the citizen body.

Nobility means the quality or state of being noble in character, quality or rank.

423. The World Health Organisation has finally issued guidelines to prevent the spread of the Covid-19 <u>epidemic</u>.
SSC CHSL Tier-1 09.08.2023 (Shift-I)

(a) A large number of people or animals suffering from the same disease at the same time
(b) An infection which is caused by viruses
(c) An infection that spreads slowly
(d) A disease which lasts for more than fifty years

Ans. (a)

The word 'Epidemic' refers to the appearance of a particular disease in a large number of people at the same time.

424. A royal ceremony in which a crown is placed on the head of a new King or a Queen. SSC CHSL Tier-1 10.08.2023 (Shift-III)

(a) Corroboration
(b) Unseating
(c) Ousting
(d) Coronation

Ans. (d)

Coronation is a royal ceremony in which a crown is placed on the head of a new king or a queen.

Unseating means to cause (someone) to fall from a horse or bicycle.

Ousting means to throw out.

Corroboration means to verify.

425. Kidney beans were boiled quickly when Nisha added a substance that speeds up a chemical reaction without being consumed by the reaction itself.
SSC CHSL Tier-1 17.08.2023 (Shift-I)

(a) reactant (b) catalyst
(c) enzyme (d) solute

Ans. (b)

A **catalyst** is a substance that speeds up a chemical reaction without being consumed by the reaction itself.

Reactant means a substance that changes in a chemical reaction.

Enzyme means a biological catalyst and is almost always a protein.

Solute means the minor component in a solution, dissolved in the solvent.

426. As I walked through the old town, I couldn't help but feel a sentimental longing for the simpler times of my childhood.
SSC CHSL Tier-1 17.08.2023 (Shift-I)

(a) affection (b) homesickness
(c) inertia (d) nostalgia

Ans. (d)

Nostalgia means a sentimental longing.

Affection means love and care.

Homesickness means becoming ill due to being away from home.

Inertia means laziness.

427. Collection of written or spoken texts
SSC CHSL Tier-1 17.08.2023 (Shift-I)

(a) Data bank (b) Dictionary
(c) Corpus (d) Circa

Ans. (c)

Corpus refers to the collection of written or spoken texts.

Databank means a place where all data is stored.

Dictionary is a book or digital resource giving information on a particular subject or on a particular class of words, names or facts, usually arranged alphabetically.

Circa means the approximate date when something happened.

428. The inability to obtain adequate sleep
SSC CHSL Tier-2 02.11. 2023
(a) Insomnia
(b) Mythomania
(c) Andromania
(d) Pyromania

Ans. (a)

Insomnia is the inability to sleep properly.

Mythomania means an abnormal or pathological tendency to exaggerate or tell lies.

Andromania means an obsession with men.

Pyromania means an obsessive desire to set fire to things.

429. A phrase or words written in memory of a person who has died
SSC CHSL Tier-2 02.11. 2023
(a) Tombstone (b) Epitaph
(c) Calligraphy (d) Epigraph

Ans. (b)

An **epitaph** is a phrase written in the memory of a person who has died.

Tombstone means a large, flat inscribed stone standing or laid over a grave.

Calligraphy is the art of beautiful writing.

Epigraph means a quotation at the beginning of a book, chapter, etc., suggesting its theme.

SSC CHSL 2022 (Tier 1)

430. Unable to speak distinctly or express oneself clearly
SSC CHSL Tier-1 24.05.2022 (Shift-II)
(a) Inane (b) Inapt
(c) Inarch (d) Inarticulate

Ans. (d)

Inarticulate means unable to speak distinctly or express oneself clearly.

Inane means silly or stupid.

Inapt means not suitable or appropriate in the circumstances.

Inarch means to graft (a plant).

431. He is an excessively enthusiastic and strict follower of Judaism.
SSC CHSL Tier-1 25.05.2022 (Shift-II)
(a) a janissary (b) a zionist
(c) a zealot (d) a healer

Ans. (b)

Zionist means an excessively enthusiastic and strict follower of Judaism.

Janissary means a member of the Turkish infantry forming the Sultan's guard.

Zealot means a person who is fanatical and uncompromising in pursuit of their religious, political, or other ideals.

Healer means a person who cures others, especially someone who uses spiritual or traditional methods.

432. A short stay at a place that is not your own home
SSC CHSL Tier-1 25.05.2022 (Shift-III)
(a) Putrefy (b) Sojourn
(c) Perplex (d) Epitome

Ans. (b)

Sojourn means a short stay at a place that is not your own home.

Putrefy means to decay or rot and produce a fetid smell.

Perplex means to cause someone to feel completely baffled.

Epitome means a person or thing that is a perfect example of a particular quality or type.

433. Mohan <u>frequently wastes his money on luxurious objects</u> such as cars and digital devices.
SSC CHSL Tier-1 26.05.2022 (Shift-III)
(a) Extravagant (b) Businessman
(c) Consumer (d) Capitalist

Ans. (a)

Extravagant means frequently wasting money on luxurious objects such as cars and digital devices.

Businessman means a man who works in commerce.

Consumer means a person who purchases goods and services for personal use.

Capitalist means a wealthy person who uses money to invest in trade and industry for profit.

434. Several literary pieces of the Old English period are written by authors <u>whose names are not known</u>.
SSC CHSL Tier-1 27.05.2022 (Shift-I)
(a) Anomalies (b) Anonymous
(c) Renowned (d) Undercover

Ans. (b)

Anonymous means that the name of the person is not known.

Anomalies means something that deviates from what is standard, normal or expected.

Renowned means popular.

Undercover means taking a different identity for something.

435. The state of being full or complete
SSC CHSL Tier-1 25.05.2022 (Shift-II)
(a) Plunder (b) Plebiscite
(c) Plenitude (d) Pliability

Ans. (c)

Plenitude means the state of being full or complete.

Plunder means to steal goods using force, typically in a time of war or disorder.

Plebiscite means a direct vote by the electorate on an important public question.

Pliability means the quality of being easily bent or flexible.

436. The love of man or mankind
SSC CHSL Tier-1 27.05.2022 (Shift-III)
(a) Philology (b) Philanthropy
(c) Phylactery (d) Philosophy

Ans. (b)

Philanthropy means the love of man or mankind.

Philology means the study of language in written historical sources.

Phylactery means a small leather box containing Hebrew texts.

Philology is the study of development of languages.

437. Reject as invalid, especially by legal procedure
SSC CHSL Tier-1 30.05.2022 (Shift-I)
(a) Reiterate (b) Putrid
(c) Putrify (d) Quash

Ans. (d)

Quash means to reject something as it is invalid.

Reiterate means to repeat.

Putrid means very unpleasant; repulsive.

Putrify means to decay, producing a strong, unpleasant smell.

438. Merry, convivial, hearty and good humoured
SSC CHSL Tier-1 30.05.2022 (Shift-I)
(a) Jowl (b) Joyous
(c) Jovial (d) Jubilee

Ans. (c)

Jovial means happy, merry, hearty and good-humoured.

Jowl means the lower part of a person's or animal's cheek, especially when it is fleshy or drooping.

Jubilee is a special anniversary of an event, especially one celebrating twenty-five or fifty years of a reign or activity.

439. Allowing or assisting to discover
SSC CHSL Tier-1 31.05.2022 (Shift-I)
(a) Conceptual (b) Ineducative
(c) Unempirical (d) Heuristic
Ans. (d)
Heuristic means helping in the process of learning or discovery.
Conceptual means related to ideas and concepts formed in the mind.
Ineducative means lack of education.
Unempirical means not practical.

440. Direct and outspoken
SSC CHSL Tier-1 31.05.2022 (Shift-I)
(a) Forthright (b) Fortitude
(c) Formica (d) Fortify
Ans. (a)
Forthright means direct and honest.
Fortitude means strength of mind that enables a person to encounter danger or bear pain or adversity with courage.
Formica means a hard plastic that is used for covering surfaces such as kitchen tables or counters.
Fortify means to give up.

441. Something that is pertaining to controversy
SSC CHSL Tier-1 31.05.2022 (Shift-II)
(a) Poignancy (b) Laudatory
(c) Putative (d) Polemical
Ans. (d)
Polemical means something that is pertaining to controversy.
Poignancy means the quality of evoking a keen sense of sadness or regret.
Laudatory means expressing praise and commendation.
Putative means generally considered or reputed to be.

442. A person as a source of intellectual light or moral inspiration
SSC CHSL Tier-1 31.05.2022 (Shift-II)
(a) Lurch (b) Luminary
(c) Luminaire (d) Lunette
Ans. (b)
Luminary means a person as a source of intellectual light or moral inspiration.
Lurch means to make an abrupt, unsteady, uncontrolled movement or series of movements.
Luminaire means a complete electric light unit.
Lunette means something crescent-shaped, in particular.

443. To dispute angrily
SSC CHSL Tier-1 31.05.2022 (Shift-III)
(a) Wrench (b) Wreck
(c) Wrangle (d) Wrack
Ans. (c)
Wrangle means to dispute angrily.
Wrench means a sudden violent twist or pull.
Wreck means the destruction of a ship at sea.
Wrack means destruction or ruin.

444. The action of examining with care or reading carefully.
SSC CHSL Tier-1 01.06.2022 (Shift-I)
(a) Persuade (b) Perverse
(c) Perusal (d) Persiflage
Ans. (c)
Perusal means the action of examining with care or reading carefully.
Persuade means to cause someone to do something through reasoning or argument.
Perverse means showing a deliberate and obstinate desire to behave in a way that is unreasonable.
Persiflage means light and slightly contemptuous mockery or banter.

445. The manager behaves as if he <u>knows everything and has unlimited knowledge</u>.
SSC CHSL Tier-1 01.06.2022 (Shift-I)
(a) Omnipotent (b) Omniscient
(c) Omnipresent (d) Omnivorous
Ans. (b)
Omniscient is used for someone who knows everything and has unlimited knowledge.
Omnipresent means someone who is present everywhere.
Omnivorous means someone who can eat both plants and animals.
Omnipotent is someone with unlimited power.

446. At the party, Rohan was <u>pretending to be what he is not</u> to influence the investors for his company's shares.
SSC CHSL Tier-1 01.06.2022 (Shift-I)
(a) Canter (b) Autocrat
(c) Hypocrite (d) Goody
Ans. (c)
A **hypocrite** is someone who pretends to have certain beliefs or opinions that they do not really have.
Canter means a speed of movement on a horse that is quite fast but easy and comfortable.
Autocrat means a ruler with unlimited power, or someone who demands that people completely obey them.

447. One thing that can be divided
SSC CHSL Tier-1 02.06.2022 (Shift-I)
(a) Remainder (b) Quotient
(c) Dividend (d) Divisible
Ans. (d)
Divisible' means able to be divided, for example by a number.

448. Unselfish interest in the welfare of others SSC CHSL Tier-1 02.06.2022 (Shift-I)
(a) Celibacy (b) Misanthropy
(c) Egoism (d) Altruism
Ans. (d)
Altruism is when you care about or help other people, even though this brings no advantage to yourself.
Celibacy means the state of being unmarried.
Misanthropy means hatred of mankind.
Egoism refers to the means a philosophy concerned with the role of the self, or ego, as the motivation and goal of one's own action.

449. A person who leaves his/her own country to live in another country permanently
SSC CHSL Tier-1 02.06.2022 (Shift-III)
(a) Vagabond (b) Mercenary
(c) Emigrant (d) Immigrant
Ans. (c)
Emigrant means a person who leaves his/her own country to live in another country permanently.
Vagabond means a person who wanders from place to place without a home or job.
Mercenary means a professional soldier hired to serve in a foreign army.
Immigrant means a person who comes to live permanently in another country.

450. Lasting for a very short period of time SSC CHSL Tier-1 03.06.2022 (Shift-I)
(a) Permanent (b) Ceaseless
(c) Pungent (d) Ephemeral
Ans. (d)
Ephemeral means lasting for a very short period of time.
Permanent means lasting or intended to last or remain unchanged indefinitely.
Ceaseless means constant and unending.
Pungent means having a sharply strong taste or smell.

451. Strong taste or liking for something
SSC CHSL Tier-1 06.06.2022 (Shift-I)
(a) Insolvent (b) Parole
(c) Ebullient (d) Penchant
Ans. (d)

Penchant means a strong taste or liking for something.

Insolvent means unable to pay debts owed.

Parole means the release of a prisoner temporarily or permanently before the completion of a sentence.

Ebullient means cheerful and full of energy.

452. To renovate or improve

SSC CHSL Tier-1 06.06.2022 (Shift-II)

(a) Relocate (b) Revamp
(c) Resume (d) Revalue

Ans. (b)

Revamp means to renovate or improve.

Relocate means to move to a new place and establish one's home or business there.

Resume means to begin again or continue after a pause or interruption.

Revalue means to assess the value of something again.

453. Take and use the thoughts inventions, etc. of another person as one's own.

SSC CHSL Tier-1 07.06.2022 (Shift-I)

(a) Copyright (b) Compose
(c) Produce (d) Plagiarise

Ans. (d)

Plagiarise means to take and use the thoughts, inventions, etc. of another person as one's own.

Copyright means the exclusive legal right to print, publish, perform, film, or record literary, artistic, or musical material.

Compose means to write or create a work of art, especially music or poetry.

Produce means to make or manufacture from components or raw materials.

454. Easily provoked

SSC CHSL Tier-1 08.06.2022 (Shift-I)

(a) Invincible (b) Irascible
(c) Iridescent (d) Irrational

Ans. (b)

Irascible means easily provoked.

Invincible means too powerful to be defeated or overcome.

Iridescent means showing luminous colours that seem to change when seen from different angles.

Irrational means not logical or reasonable.

SSC CHSL 2021 (Tier 1)

455. Speed greater than that of sound

SSC CHSL Tier-1 12.04.2021 (Shift-I)

(a) Harmonic (b) Cacophonic
(c) Supersonic (d) Subsonic

Ans. (c)

Supersonic means speed greater than that of sound.

Harmonic means relating to or characterised by musical harmony.

Cacophonic means involving or producing a harsh, discordant mixture of sounds.

Subsonic means relating to or flying at a speed less than that of sound in air.

456. A large bundle bound for storage or transportation

SSC CHSL Tier-1 12.04.2021 (Shift-II)

(a) Bevy (b) Bouquet
(c) Bale (d) Brood

Ans. (c)

A **bale** is a large bundle of cotton bound for storage or transportation.

Bevy is a group of girls/ deer.

Bouquet is a group of flowers.

Brood is a group of young ones.

457. Doctor who deals with bone problems

SSC CHSL Tier-1 12.04.2021 (Shift-II)

(a) Orthodontist (b) Chiropodist
(c) Orthopaedist (d) Dermatologist

Ans. (c)

An **orthopaedist** is a doctor who deals with bones.

Orthodontist is a type of dentist who specialises in straightening crooked teeth.

Chiropodist is a person who treats the feet and their ailments.

Dermatologist is a doctor who specialises in the study of skin and the treatment of skin diseases.

458. Someone who studies elections and voting statistics

SSC CHSL Tier-1 12.04.2021 (Shift-III)

(a) Psychologist
(b) Psephologist
(c) Analyst
(d) Mathematician

Ans. (b)

Psephologist means someone who studies elections and voting statistics.

Psychologist means a person who studies the human mind and behaviour.

Analyst means a person who conducts analysis.

Mathematician means a person who specialises in mathematics.

459. Doing something awkwardly original a clumsy manner

SSC CHSL Tier-1 12.04.2021 (Shift-III)

(a) Fumbling (b) Faltering
(d) Hastening (d) Stumbling

Ans. (a)

Fumbling means doing something awkwardly, originally in a clumsy manner.

Faltering means losing strength or momentum.

Hastening means moving or acting quickly.

Stumbling means tripping or losing balance while walking.

460. Eat or drink food quickly and in large amounts

SSC CHSL Tier-1 19.04.2021 (Shift-III)

(a) Choke (b) Sip
(c) Gulp (d) Swish

Ans. (c)

Gulp means to eat or drink food quickly.

Choke means have severe difficulty in breathing because of a constricted or obstructed throat or a lack of air.

Sip means to drink water.

Swish means move with a hissing or rushing sound.

461. A period of two weeks

SSC CHSL Tier-1 06.08.2021 (Shift-I)

(a) Month (b) Century
(c) Decade (d) Fortnight

Ans. (d)

Fortnight means a period of two weeks.

Century means a period of one hundred years.

462. Something which cannot be taken by force

SSC CHSL Tier-1 06.08.2021 (Shift-II)

(a) Impregnable (b) Irresistible
(c) Imperative (d) Impromptu

Ans. (a)

Impregnable means something which cannot be taken by force.

Irresistible means too attractive or tempting to be resisted.

Imperative means of vital importance; crucial.

Impromptu means done without being planned or rehearsed.

463. A strong interest in something or someone

SSC CHSL Tier-1 06.08.2021 (Shift-III)

(a) Fixation (b) Empathy
(c) Apathy (d) Attachment

Ans. (a)

Fixation means a strong interest in something or someone.

Empathy means the ability to understand and share the feelings of another.

Apathy means lack of interest, enthusiasm, or concern.

Attachment means an emotional bond between people.

464. To come to an end
SSC CHSL Tier-1 06.08.2021 (Shift-III)
(a) Initiate (b) Exhale
(c) Inspire (d) Expire

Ans. (d)

Expire means to come to an end.

Initiate means to begin or start.

Exhale means to breathe out.

Inspire means to fill someone with the urge or ability to do or feel something.

465. Leather straps put around a horse's head to control it
SSC CHSL Tier-1 10.08.2021 (Shift-I)
(a) Bridle (b) Bridal
(c) Saddle (d) Stirrup

Ans. (a)

Bridle is a leather strap that is put around a horse's head to control it.

Bridal means relating to the bride.

Saddle means a seat on a bicycle, motorcycle, etc.

Stirrup means either of a pair of small light frames or rings for receiving the foot of a rider that are attached by a strap to a saddle and used to aid in mounting and as a support while riding.

466. A hunting weapon which comes back, used by Australian Aborigines
SSC CHSL Tier-1 12.08.2021 (Shift-III)
(a) Harpoon (b) Cutlass
(c) Slingshot (d) Boomerang

Ans. (d)

A hunting weapon which comes back to the thrower, traditionally used by Australian aboriginal people is called **boomerang**.

Harpoon means a long, heavy spear (a long, sharp weapon) attached to a rope, used for killing large fish.

Cutlass means a small knife.

Slingshot means a forked stick with an elastic band attached for shooting small stones.

467. Causing a strong dislike
SSC CHSL Tier-1 12.08.2021 (Shift-III)
(a) Redundant (b) Repulsive
(c) Hateful (d) Revealing

Ans. (b)

Repulsive means causing a strong dislike.

Redundant means repetitive.

Revealing means making interesting or significant information known, especially of a personal nature.

SSC MTS 2024 (Tier 1)

468. A serpent having many heads in Greek mythology.
SSC MTS Tier-1 14.11.2024 (Shift-III)
(a) Cobra (b) Python
(c) Hydra (d) Eopsin

Ans. (c)

In Greek mythology, **Hydra** is a serpent with many heads.

Cobra a type of snake.

Python a type of snake.

Eopsin a different mythical figure.

469. The Prime Minister will <u>address</u> the nation tomorrow.
SSC MTS Tier-1 12.11.2024 (Shift-III)
(a) To greet people
(b) A landmark
(c) A postal code for sending letters
(d) To deliver a speech

Ans. (d)

'Address' means to deliver a speech to an audience.

470. He devoted his entire life to the **study of the human mind**.
SSC MTS Tier-1 11.11.2024 (Shift-III)
(a) Philology (b) Psychology
(c) Physiology (d) Physics

Ans. (b)

Psychology is the study of the human mind.

Philology means the study of language.

Physiology means the study of the functions of living organisms.

Physics means the natural science studying matter, its motion and behaviour.

471. The rules of behaviour which guide one in a formal situation.
SSC MTS Tier-1 05.11.2024 (Shift-III)
(a) Affidavit (b) Protocol
(c) Bargain (d) Impropriety

Ans. (b)

Protocol refers to 'the rules of behaviour which guide one in a formal situation'.

Affidavit means a written statement confirmed by oath.

Bargain means an agreement between two parties.

Impropriety means improper conduct.

472. A grand function was organised to honour <u>the person who had died for a noble cause</u>.
SSC MTS Tier-1 04.11.2024 (Shift-III)
(a) martyr (b) volunteer
(c) prophet (d) philanthropist

Ans. (a)

Martyr is a person who has died for a noble cause.

Volunteer means a person who freely offers to take part in something.

Prophet means a person regarded as an inspired teacher or proclaimer of the will of God.

Philanthropist means a person who seeks to promote the welfare of others, especially by the generous donation of money to good causes.

473. A word, number, or other figure that looks the same when viewed (or rotated) upside down.
SSC MTS Tier-1 30.10.2024 (Shift-III)
(a) Anadiplosis (b) Alliteration
(c) Anagram (d) Ambigram

Ans. (d)

An **ambigram** is a word, number, or figure that looks the same when viewed upside down.

Anadiplosis means repetition of the last word of a preceding clause.

Alliteration means repetition of initial consonant sounds.

Anagram means a word formed by rearranging the letters of another.

474. A policy that separates people on the basis of race.
SSC MTS Tier-1 29.10.2024 (Shift-III)
(a) Apostle (b) Apartheid
(c) Apiary (d) Apostasy

Ans. (b)

Apartheid refers to a policy of racial segregation.

Apostle is a priest in christianity.

Apiary is a place for keeping bees.

Apostasy is the act of renouncing religion.

475. The method and practice of teaching.
SSC MTS Tier-1 29.10.2024 (Shift-III)
(a) Objective (b) Learning
(c) Pedagogy (d) Strategy

Ans. (c)

Pedagogy means the method and practice of teaching. Objective means a goal or aim.

Learning means acquiring knowledge. Strategy means a plane of action.

Objective means not influenced by feeling.

Strategy means a plan.

476. The scientific study of the structure and form of animals and plants
SSC MTS Tier-1 23.10.2024 (Shift-II)
(a) Biology (b) Morphology
(c) Zoology (d) Botany

Ans. (b)

Morphology is 'the scientific study of the structure and form of animals and plants'.

Biology means the study of living organisms.

Zoology means the study of animals.

Botany means the study of plants.

477. RK Laxman was well-known for his **drawings of people in such a highly exaggerated manner as to cause laughter.**
SSC MTS Tier-1 21.10.2024 (Shift-II)
(a) Portraits (b) Articles
(c) Caricatures (d) Sketches
Ans. (c)
Caricatures refers to 'drawings of people in such a highly exaggerated manner as to cause laughter'. A caricature is a depiction of a person in which certain striking characteristics are exaggerated to create a comic or grotesque effect.
Portraits means a painting, drawing, photograph or engraving of a person.
Articles means a piece of writing included with others in a newspaper, magazine or other publication.
Sketches means a rough or unfinished drawing or painting.

478. A person who travels from place to place, especially for work
SSC MTS Tier-1 21.10.2024 (Shift-II)
(a) Pilgrim (b) Vagrant
(c) Nomad (d) Itinerant
Ans. (d)
Itinerant is 'a person who travels from place to place, especially for work.'
Pilgrim means a person who journeys to a sacred place for religious reasons.
Vagrant means a person without a settled home or regular work who wanders from place to place and lives by begging.
Nomad means a number of people having no permanent abode and who travel from place to place to find fresh pasture for their livestock.

479. The place where soldiers live
SSC MTS Tier-1 18.10.2024 (Shift-II)
(a) Barracks (b) Unit
(c) Brigade (d) Regiment
Ans. (a)
Barracks refers to buildings used to house soldiers.
Unit a smaller military division.
Brigade a large military unit.
Regiment a military unit of ground troops.

480. Something that has the quality of being easily broken.
SSC MTS Tier-1 16.10.2024 (Shift-II)
(a) Broken (b) Damage
(c) Hard (d) Brittle
Ans. (d)
Brittle means hard but liable to break or shatter easily.
Broken means damaged and no longer in one piece.
Damage means harm or injury.
Hard means solid and firm.

481. The minister went to visit the **monuments set up for people who were buried in other countries.**
SSC MTS Tier-1 14.10.2024 (Shift-I)
(a) graves (b) cemetery
(c) cenotaphs (d) coffins
Ans. (c)
Cenotaphs refers to monuments set up for people who are buried elsewhere.
Graves refers to burial places.
Cemetery refers to a burial ground.
Coffins refers to the boxes used for burials.

482. A post without any remuneration
SSC MTS Tier-1 14.10.2024 (Shift-I)
(a) Illegible (b) Bigot
(c) Effeminate (d) Honorary
Ans. (d)
Honorary means a post without any remuneration.'
Illegible means unreadable.
Bigot means someone intolerant of different opinions.
Effeminate means showing characteristics regarded as typical of a woman.

483. Belonging or pertaining to an individual from birth
SSC MTS Tier-1 14.10.2024 (Shift-I)
(a) Congregational (b) Congenital
(c) Congruent (d) Congenial
Ans. (b)
Congenital means 'belonging or pertaining to an individual from birth.'
Congregational means relating to a congregation.
Congruent means in agreement or harmony.
Congenial means pleasant or agreeable.

484. A person who eats too much
SSC MTS Tier-1 09.10.2024 (Shift-I)
(a) Fatalist (b) Sycophant
(c) Glutton (d) Misogamist
Ans. (c)
Glutton is a person who eats too much. This term describes someone who has a great desire to consume food.
Fatalist means someone who believes in fate.
Sycophant means someone who flatters others for personal gain.
Misogamist means someone who hates marriage.

485. Because the politician's speech was <u>high-flown and pretentious,</u> it gained popularity.
SSC MTS Tier-1 09.10.2024 (Shift-I)
(a) schematising (b) austere
(c) mnemonic (d) bombastic
Ans. (d)
Bombastic is the one-word substitute for 'high-flown and pretentious'. It means using high- sounding but meaningless language.
Schematising means forming schemes.
Austere means strict or severe.
Mnemonic means relating to memory aids.

486. One who performs daring gymnastic feats SSC MTS Tier-1 09.10.2024 (Shift-I)
(a) Adonis (b) Acrobat
(c) Addict (d) Advocate
Ans. (b)
Acrobat 'one who performs daring gymnastic feats'.
Adonis means a very handsome young man.
Addict means someone dependent on a substance.
Advocate means someone who supports a cause.

SSC MTS 2023 (Tier 1)

487. The young of a frog
SSC MTS Tier-1 02.05.2023 (Shift-I)
(a) Kitten (b) Pup
(c) Tadpole (d) Antelope
Ans. (c)
Tadpole means the young of a frog.
Kitten means the young of a cat.
Pup means the young of a dog.
Antelope means a swift-running deer-like mammal.

488. The sound made by frogs
SSC MTS Tier-1 02.05.2023 (Shift-III)
(a) Trumpet (b) Moo
(c) Croak (d) Roar
Ans. (c)
Croak means the sound made by frogs.
Trumpet means the sound made by elephants.
Moo means the sound made by cows.
Roar means the sound made by lions.

489. That can be seen through
SSC MTS Tier-1 03.05.2023 (Shift-I)
(a) Defatigable (b) Transparent
(c) Opaque (d) Reverent
Ans. (b)
Transparent means that which can be seen through.
Defatigable means capable of being tired out.

Opaque means not able to be seen through; not transparent.

Reverent means feeling or showing deep and solemn respect.

490. A diagram showing the path of planets. SSC MTS Tier-1 03.05.2023 (Shift-II)

(a) Horoscope (b) Zodiac
(c) Planetarium (d) Platitude

Ans. (a)

Horoscope means a diagram showing the path of planets.

Zodiac means a belt of the heavens within about 8° either side of the ecliptic, including all apparent positions of the sun, moon and most familiar planets.

Planetarium means a building or room in which images of stars, planets, and constellations are projected on the inner surface of a dome.

Platitude is a moral remark.

491. Persons who are unfairly blamed for something that others have done SSC MTS Tier-1 04.05.2023 (Shift-I)

(a) Expedition
(b) Epitome
(c) Disdain
(d) Scapegoat

Ans. (d)

Scapegoat means persons who are unfairly blamed for something that others have done.

Expedition means a journey or voyage undertaken by a group of people with a particular purpose.

Disdain means the feeling that someone or something is unworthy of one's consideration or respect.

Epitome means perfect.

492. Difficult to interpret or understand SSC MTS Tier-1 04.05.2023 (Shift-III)

(a) Explicable (b) Emulate
(c) Enigmatic (d) Endemic

Ans. (c)

Enigmatic means difficult to interpret or understand.

Explicable means able to be explained or accounted for.

Emulate means to match or surpass, typically by imitation.

Endemic means regularly found among particular people or in a certain area.

493. Abundant garbage kept at one place SSC MTS Tier-1 08.05.2023 (Shift-I)

(a) Mound of garbage
(b) Hill of garbage
(c) Lot of garbage
(d) Heap of garbage

Ans. (d)

Heap of garbage means abundant garbage kept at one place.

Mound of garbage means a small hill or pile of garbage.

Hill of garbage means a large pile of garbage.

Lot of garbage means a large amount of garbage.

494. A person who easily believes without demanding proof SSC MTS Tier-1 08.05.2023 (Shift-II)

(a) Cosmopolitan (b) Credulous
(c) Streetwise (d) Wary

Ans. (b)

Credulous means a person who easily believes without demanding proof.

Streetwise means having the experience and knowledge necessary to deal with the potential difficulties or dangers of life in an urban environment.

Wary means feeling or showing caution about possible dangers or problems.

Cosmopolitan is a person belonging to the world.

495. A person appointed by two parties to solve a problem SSC MTS Tier-1 08.05.2023 (Shift-III)

(a) Advocate (b) Judge
(c) Arbitrator (d) Jury

Ans. (c)

Arbitrator means a person appointed by two parties to solve a problem.

Advocate means a person who publicly supports or recommends a particular cause or policy.

Judge means a public official appointed to decide cases in a court of law.

Jury means a group of people sworn to render a verdict in a legal case based on the evidence presented to them in court.

496. Experiences that are very unpleasant or difficult SSC MTS Tier-1 09.05.2023 (Shift-II)

(a) Pitfall (b) Ordeal
(c) Strident (d) Knack

Ans. (b)

Ordeal means experiences that are very unpleasant or difficult.

Pitfall means a hidden or unsuspected danger or difficulty.

Strident means loud and harsh; grating.

Knack means an acquired or natural skill at performing a task.

497. A local meeting of party members to select candidates, elect convention delegates; etc. SSC MTS Tier-1 10.05.2023 (Shift-I)

(a) Claque (b) Clique
(c) Caravan (d) Caucus

Ans. (d)

Caucus means a local meeting of party members to select candidates, elect convention delegates, etc.

Claque means a group of sycophantic followers.

Clique is a small close knit group of friends.

Caravan is a group of pilgrims.

498. Scientific tests or techniques used in connection with the detection of crime SSC MTS Tier-1 10.05.2023 (Shift-II)

(a) Post-mortem (b) Autopsy
(c) Forensics (d) Etymology

Ans. (c)

Forensics means scientific tests or techniques used in connection with the detection of crime.

Post-mortem means an examination of a dead body to determine the cause of death.

Autopsy means a post-mortem examination to discover the cause of death or the extent of disease.

Etymology means the study of the origin of words and the way in which their meanings have changed throughout history.

499. A portable case for holding papers, drawing, etc. SSC MTS Tier-1 11.05.2023 (Shift-II)

(a) Suitcase (b) Creche
(c) Portfolio (d) Cache

Ans. (c)

Portfolio means a portable case for holding papers, drawings, etc.

Creche means a nursery where babies and young children are cared for during the working day.

Cache means a collection of items of the same type stored in a hidden or inaccessible place.

500. Or Hard to please (very selective in his habits) SSC MTS Tier-1 11.05.2023 (Shift-II)

(a) Fastidious
(b) Squeamish
(c) Stubborn
(d) Impregnable

Ans. (a)

Fastidious means being careful that every detail is correct and perfect.

Squeamish means easily made to feel sick or disgusted.

Stubborn means determined to do what one wants and refuse to do anything else.

Impregnable means unable to be broken into or taken by force.

501. The sound of owls
SSC MTS Tier-1 12.05.2023 (Shift-I)

(a) Honk (b) Neigh
(c) Croak (d) Hoot

Ans. (d)

Hoot means the sound of owls.

Honk means the sound made by a goose.

Neigh means the sound made by a horse.

Croak means the sound made by a frog.

502. An adventurous or bold person
SSC MTS Tier-1 12.05.2023 (Shift-II)

(a) Judgemental (b) Foolhardy
(c) Debonair (d) Assaultive

Ans. (c)

Debonair means an adventurous or bold person.

Judgemental means having or displaying an overly critical point of view.

Foolhardy means recklessly bold or rash.

Assaultive means inclined to attack or acting aggressively.

503. Someone who knows a lot about the arts, food, drink or some other subject **SSC MTS Tier-1 15.05.2023 (Shift-I)**

(a) Pacifist (b) Gourmand
(c) Cynic (d) Connoisseur

Ans. (d)

Connoisseur means someone who knows a lot about the arts, food, drink or some other subject.

Pacifist means a person who believes that war and violence are unjustifiable.

Gourmand is a person who enjoys eating.

Cynic is a person who believes that mankind is selfish.

504. An exact copy of handwriting, printing **SSC MTS Tier-1 15.05.2023 (Shift-II)**

(a) Platitude (b) Maiden
(c) Potable (d) Facsimile

Ans. (d)

Facsimile means an exact copy of handwriting or printing.

Platitude means a remark or statement, especially one with a moral content, that has been used too often to be interesting or thoughtful.

Maiden means a girl or young woman, especially an unmarried one.

Potable means safe to drink; drinkable.

505. The sound of elephants
SSC MTS Tier-1 15.05.2023 (Shift-III)

(a) Trumpet (b) Quack
(c) Laurel (d) Screech

Ans. (a)

Trumpet means the sound of elephants.

Quack means the characteristic sound made by a duck.

Laurel means any of a number of shrubs and other plants with dark green glossy leaves.

Screech is a loud and harsh cry.

506. Government by two rulers or authorities
SSC MTS Tier-1 16.05.2023 (Shift-I)

(a) Monarchy (b) Bureaucracy
(c) Diarchy (d) Anarchy

Ans. (c)

Diarchy means government by two rulers or authorities.

Monarchy means a form of government with a monarch at the head.

Anarchy means a state of disorder due to the absence or non-recognition of authority.

Bureaucracy is a system of government wherein state officials take decisions.

507. A living organism that steals nourishment from other living beings
SSC MTS Tier-1 16.05.2023 (Shift-II)

(a) Vector (b) Parasite
(c) Insect (d) Co-Dependent

Ans. (b)

Parasite means a living organism that steals nourishment from other living beings.

Vector means an organism, typically a biting insect or tick, that transmits a disease or parasite from one animal or plant to another.

Insect means a small arthropod animal that has six legs and generally one or two pairs of wings.

Co-Dependent means a relationship where one person is physically or psychologically addicted and the other person is psychologically dependent on the first in an unhealthy way.

508. A long wandering or voyage usually marked by many changes of fortune
SSC MTS Tier-1 16.05.2023 (Shift-III)

(a) Odyssey (b) Ode
(c) Pilgrimage (d) Trip

Ans. (a)

Odyssey means a long wandering or voyage usually marked by many changes of fortune.

Pilgrimage means a journey to a place associated with someone or something well known or respected.

Trip means a journey or voyage.

Ode is a poem honouring someone.

509. One who is 100 years old or older
SSC MTS Tier-1 17.05.2023 (Shift-II)

(a) Centenarian (b) Immortal
(c) Mortal (d) Sententia

Ans. (a)

Centenarian means one who is 100 years old or older.

Immortal means living forever; never dying or decaying.

Mortal means subject to death.

Sententia means a brief expression of conventional wisdom.

510. A ground where the last funeral rites are performed
SSC MTS Tier-1 17.05.2023 (Shift-III)

(a) Tomb (b) Crematorium
(c) Barracks (d) Mortuary

Ans. (b)

Crematorium means a ground where the last funeral rites are performed.

Tomb means a large vault for burying the dead.

Barracks means a building or group of buildings used to house soldiers.

Mortuary means a place where dead bodies are kept before burial or cremation.

511. Destruction of a fetus
SSC MTS Tier-1 18.05.2023 (Shift-I)

(a) Fratricide (b) Ellipse
(c) Abhor (d) Feticide

Ans. (d)

Feticide means the destruction of a fetus.

Fratricide means the killing of one's brother or sister.

Ellipse means a regular oval shape.

Abhor means to regard with disgust and hatred.

512. To forbid something, especially by law **SSC MTS Tier-1 18.05.2023 (Shift-II)**

(a) Propound (b) Proscribe
(c) Quench (d) Quarantine

Ans. (b)

Proscribe means to forbid something, especially by law.

Propound means to put forward an idea or theory for consideration by others.

Quench means to satisfy one's thirst by drinking.

Quarantine means a state of enforced isolation designed to prevent the spread of disease.

513. A person holding conventional belief especially in matter of religion

SSC MTS Tier-1 19.05.2023 (Shift-III)

(a) Orthodox (b) Prudent
(c) Compere (d) Arsonist

Ans. (a)

Orthodox means a person holding conventional beliefs, especially in matters of religion.

Prudent means acting with or showing care and thought for the future.

Compere means a person who introduces the performers or contestants in a variety show.

Arsonist means a person who deliberately sets fire to property.

514. Information, especially of a biased or misleading nature, used to promote a political cause or point of view.

SSC MTS Tier-1 13.06.2023 (Shift-I)

(a) Welter (b) Propaganda
(c) Potable (d) Orchard

Ans. (b)

Propaganda means information, especially of a biased or misleading nature, used to promote a political cause or point of view.

Welter means a large number of items in no order; a confused mass.

Potable means safe to drink; drinkable.

Orchard means a piece of land planted with fruit trees.

515. Ethically good behaviour one has

SSC MTS Tier-1 13.06.2023 (Shift-II)

(a) Belief (b) Virtual
(c) Virtue (d) Values

Ans. (c)

Virtue means ethically good behaviour one has.

Belief means an acceptance that something exists or is true, especially one without proof.

Virtual means almost or nearly as described, but not completely or according to strict definition.

Values means the regard that something is held to deserve; the importance, worth, or usefulness of something.

516. A calculated move to gain an advantage

SSC MTS Tier-1 13.06.2023 (Shift-III)

(a) Grunt (b) Bonsai
(c) Gambit (d) Profit

Ans. (c)

Gambit means a calculated move to gain an advantage.

Grunt means a low, short guttural sound made by an animal or a person.

Bonsai means a tree or shrub that has been dwarfed, as by pruning and grown in a pot.

Profit means a financial gain, especially the difference between the amount earned and the amount spent.

517. A violent wind that has a circular movement

SSC MTS Tier-1 14.06.2023 (Shift-I)

(a) Drought (b) Deluge
(c) Tsunami (d) Hurricane

Ans. (d)

Hurricane means a violent wind that has a circular movement.

Drought means a prolonged period of abnormally low rainfall.

Deluge means a severe flood.

Tsunami means a long high sea wave caused by an earthquake or other disturbance.

518. A thing that is kept as a reminder of a person, place or event

SSC MTS Tier-1 14.06.2023 (Shift-II)

(a) Sinecure (b) Panacea
(c) Souvenir (d) Regalia

Ans. (c)

Souvenir means a thing that is kept as a reminder of a person, place or event.

Sinecure means a position requiring little or no work but giving the holder status or financial benefit.

Panacea means a solution or remedy for all difficulties or diseases.

Regalia means the emblems or insignia of royalty, especially the crown, scepter, and other ornaments used at a coronation.

519. Opposing or taking arms against a government or ruler.

SSC MTS Tier-1 14.06.2023 (Shift-III)

(a) Volunteer (b) Rebel
(c) Rubel (d) Participant

Ans. (b)

Rebel means opposing or taking arms against a government or ruler.

Volunteer means a person who freely offers to take part in an enterprise or undertake a task.

Rubel means a variant spelling of ruble, the currency of Russia.

Participant means a person who takes part in something.

520. License granted to an individual or group to market a company's goods or services in a particular territory

SSC MTS Tier-1 15.06.2023 (Shift-I)

(a) Branding (b) Marketing
(c) Monopoly (d) Franchise

Ans. (d)

Franchise means a license granted to an individual or group to market a company's goods or services in a particular territory.

Branding means the promotion of a particular product or company by means of advertising and distinctive design.

Marketing means the action or business of promoting and selling products or services.

Monopoly means the exclusive possession or control of the supply of or trade in a commodity or service.

521. A sacred place

SSC MTS Tier-1 15.06.2023 (Shift-II)

(a) Relic (b) Museum
(c) Sanctum (d) Retreat

Ans. (c)

Sanctum means a sacred place.

Retreat means a quiet or secluded place in which one can rest and relax.

522. The women stared at me with (great interest or concern).

SSC MTS Tier-1 16.06.2023 (Shift-II)

(a) Intellect (b) Control
(c) Curiosity (d) Possession

Ans. (c)

Curiosity means great interest or concern.

Intellect means the faculty of reasoning and understanding objectively.

Control means the power to influence or direct people's behaviour or the course of events.

Possession means the state of having, owning, or controlling something.

523. One who gives shape to stone

SSC MTS Tier-1 16.06.2023 (Shift-III)

(a) Curator (b) Sculptor
(c) Auditor (d) Vilify

Ans. (b)

Sculptor means one who gives shape to stone.

Auditor means a person who conducts an audit.

Vilify means to speak or write about in an abusively disparaging manner.

524. The branch of physics concerned with the properties of sound

SSC MTS Tier-1 20.06.2023 (Shift-II)

(a) Acoustics (b) Anchor
(c) Anarchist (d) Apiary

Ans. (a)

Acoustics means the branch of physics concerned with the properties of sound.

Anchor means a heavy object attached to a rope or chain and used to moor a vessel to the sea bottom.

Apiary means a place where bees are kept; a collection of beehives.

Anarchist refers to a person who stands against all forms of authority.

525. Disappointed and annoyed about something

SSC MTS Tier-1 20.06.2023 (Shift-III)

(a) Contented (b) Disgruntled
(c) Dissuade (d) Surreal

Ans. (b)

Disgruntled means disappointed and annoyed about something.

Contented means happy and at ease.

Dissuade means to persuade someone not to take a particular course of action.

Surreal means having the qualities of surrealism; bizarre.

526. Selling, purchasing and using an illegally copied product is a criminal offence. SSC MTS Tier-1 01.09.2023 (Shift-I)

(a) an obsolete
(b) a pirated
(c) an outlawed
(d) a crooked

Ans. (b)

The word **pirated** indicates an 'Illegally copied version of things'.

Obsolete means outdated and not used.

Outlawed means made illegal; banned.

Crooked means bent or not straight.

527. Study of sound and sound waves

SSC MTS Tier-1 04.09.2023 (Shift-II)

(a) Botany (b) Physics
(c) Demography (d) Acoustics

Ans. (d)

Acoustics is the study of sound and sound waves.

Botany is the study of plants, its structure and processes.

Physics is the study of matter and energy and the effect they have on each other.

528. A creature which depends on others

SSC MTS Tier-1 04.09.2023 (Shift-II)

(a) Microbes (b) Virus
(c) Parasite (d) Bacteria

Ans. (c)

Parasite is a creature that depends on others.

Microbes are organisms that are too small to be seen without using a microscope.

Virus is a submicroscopic infectious agent that replicates only inside the living cells of an organism.

Bacteria are microscopic living organisms that have only one cell.

529. A man whose wife is dead

SSC MTS Tier-1 05.09.2023 (Shift-II)

(a) Widower (b) Ascetic
(c) Widow (d) Bachelor

Ans. (a)

Widower is a man whose wife is dead.

Ascetic means characterised by severe self-discipline and abstention from all forms of indulgence, typically for religious reasons.

Widow is a female whose husband had died.

Bachelor is an unmarried man.

530. He simply continued to say something in order to convey information in a calm voice.

SSC MTS Tier-1 05.09.2023 (Shift-II)

(a) dictate (b) teach
(c) speak (d) spell

Ans. (c)

Speak means to say something to convey information.

531. The killing of a king

SSC MTS Tier-1 08.09.2023 (Shift-II)

(a) Regicide (b) Fratricide
(c) Sororicide (d) Patricide

Ans. (a)

Regicide means the killing of a king.

Fratricide means the killing of one's brother or sister.

Sororicide means the killing of one's sister.

Patricide means the killing of one's father.

532. Hundreds of people were removed from a place by the government recently due to a war-like situation.

SSC MTS Tier-1 08.09.2023 (Shift-II)

(a) assassinated (b) evacuated
(c) invaded (d) terminated

Ans. (b)

Evacuated means to be removed from a dangerous place to safety.

Assassinated means killed.

Invaded means (of an armed force) enter (a country or region) so as to subjugate or occupy it.

Terminated means ended abruptly.

533. One who lends money to others at a very high rate of interest.

SSC MTS Tier-1 11.09.2023 (Shift-I)

(a) Curator (b) Bankrupt
(c) Usurer (d) Numismatist

Ans. (c)

A **usurer** is a person who lends money at an unreasonably high rate.

Bankrupt means (of a person or organisation) declared in law as unable to pay their debts.

Numismatist is a specialist, researcher, or well-informed collector of coins.

534. I suppose dancing that well would require a lot of actual application.

SSC MTS Tier-1 11.09.2023 (Shift-II)

(a) prevention (b) perseverance
(c) practice (d) perception

Ans. (c)

Practice means the application of a thing.

Prevention means the action of stopping something from happening or arising.

Perseverance means continued effort to do or achieve something despite difficulties, failure or opposition.

Perception means the ability to see, hear or become aware of something through the senses.

SSC Selection Post 2024

535. A person who investigates, reports on and helps settle complaints

SSC SP 20.06.2024 (Shift-II)

(a) Spokesman (b) Bildungsroman
(c) Ombudsman (d) Superhuman

Ans. (c)

Ombudsman is one that investigates, reports on and helps settle complaints.

Spokesman is a person who represents another person or group.

Bildungsroman is a novel dealing with one person's formative years or spiritual education.

536. An absolute government by one man

SSC SP 20.06.2024 (Shift-II)

(a) Supremacy (b) Communism
(c) Aristocracy (d) Autocracy

Ans. (d)

Autocracy is a government where a single person or group rules.

Supremacy means at the highest point.

Communism is a political and economic system that seeks to create a classless society in which the major means of production.

537. A person in charge of the old people's home or a hostel

SSC SP 20.06.2024 (Shift-II)

(a) Watchman (b) Guard
(c) Warder (d) Warden

Ans. (d)

Warden is a person who is in charge of the old people's home or a hostel.

SSC Selection Post 2023

538. The war resulted in ruthless killing of many people. SSC SP 27.06.2023 (Shift-IV)
(a) sacrilege (b) fratricide
(c) carnage (d) murder
Ans. (c)
Carnage is the killing of many people.
Sacrilege means violation or misuse of what is regarded as sacred.
Fratricide means killing of a sibling.

539. Adversity always presents opportunities for the examination of one's own conscious thoughts and feelings. SSC SP 27.06.2023 (Shift-I)
(a) introspection
(b) judgement
(c) evaluation
(d) cognition
Ans. (a)
Introspection is the examination of one's own conscious thoughts and feelings.
Evaluation means to test.
Cognition means the process of acquiring knowledge and understanding through experience.

540. The wide variety of shared and different personal and group characteristics among human beings SSC SP 27.06.2023 (Shift-I)
(a) Diversity (b) Viscosity
(c) Community (d) Intensity
Ans. (a)
Diversity means the wide variety of shared and different personal and group characteristics among human beings.
Viscosity means resistance of a fluid (liquid or gas) to a change in shape, or movement of neighbouring portions relative to one another.
Community means group.
Intensity means the quality of being very serious.

541. Social organisation where males are heads of families SSC SP 27.06.2023 (Shift-III)
(a) Matriarchy (b) Patriarchy
(c) Polygamy (d) Hierarchy
Ans. (b)
Patriarchy is a social organisation where males are heads of families.
Matriarchy is a social organisation where males are heads of families.
Polygamy is the phenomenon of having many partners.
Hierarchy is a system in which members of an organisation or society are ranked according to relative status or authority.

SSC Selection Post 2022

542. The shells that were collected from the seashore are kept on the shelf as a reminder of the place. SSC SP 01.08.2022 (Shift-I)
(a) souvenir (b) solvent
(c) sling (d) gift
Ans. (a)
A **souvenir** means a reminder of the place.
Solvent is a substance that dissolves a solute, resulting in a solution.
Sling means a flexible strap or belt used in the form of a loop to support or raise a hanging weight.

543. A lot of people are seen gathering discussing and negotiating in front of our stall in the town. SSC SP 01.08.2022 (Shift-I)
(a) dealing (b) jostling
(c) bargaining (d) collecting
Ans. (c)
Bargaining means to discuss and negotiate the price of something.
Jostling means push, elbow, or bump against (someone) roughly, typically in a crowd.

544. Easy to understand SSC SP 01.08.2022 (Shift-I)
(a) Ambiguous (b) Ludicrous
(c) Lucid (d) Lackluster
Ans. (c)
Lucid means clear and easy to understand.
Ambiguous means confusing.
Ludicrous means stupid and unreasonable.
Lackluster means dull.

545. To the utmost or most absolute extent or degree SSC SP 01.08.2022 (Shift-I)
(a) Barely (b) Quite
(c) Merely (d) Primarily
Ans. (b)
Quite means to the utmost or most absolute extent or degree.
Barely means only just; almost not.
Merely means just; only.
Primarily means for the most part; mainly.

SSC Steno 2024

546. Jack was given the responsibility of driving, as he was the only **teetotaller.** SSC Steno 11.12.2024 (Shift-I)
(a) Person who habitually drinks to the point of losing control.
(b) Person who completely abstains from intoxicating drinks like alcohol.
(c) Person with imagination and creative potential.
(d) Responsible citizen of the country with high self-esteem.
Ans. (b)
A 'teetotaller' is a person who completely abstains from intoxicating drinks like alcohol. This term specifically refers to someone who chooses not to consume any alcoholic beverages, emphasising complete abstinence.

547. Even amidst the all-pervasive silence, the noise inside her head seemed **incessant.** SSC Steno 10.12.2024 (Shift-I)
(a) To occur at irregular intervals or occasionally
(b) To continue without any interruption
(c) To impact in a strikingly negative way
(d) To follow an unknown course
Ans. (b)
The most appropriate meaning of the word 'incessant' is 'to continue without any interruption'. It indicates something that persists unceasingly.

548. The patient **absconded** from the hospital at dawn. SSC Steno 10.12.2024 (Shift-I)
(a) Fled away hurriedly and secretly
(b) Collected acknowledgement of the payment
(c) Faced lack of cooperation from the nurse
(d) Learned to communicate with others
Ans. (a)
The most appropriate meaning of the word 'absconded' is 'fled away hurriedly and secretly'.
It indicates leaving or escaping in a sudden and secretive manner.

549. We should help each other to make a society that will be not concerned with any particular religious doctrines. SSC Steno 10.12.2024 (Shift-III)
(a) a secular society
(b) a humanist society
(c) a harmonious society
(d) a prejudiced society
Ans. (a)
The expression 'a secular society' is the correct substitution as it means not concerned with religious doctrines.
The term 'secular' refers to a society free from religious or spiritual basis.

08

Idioms and Phrases

In SSC examination, from Idioms and Phrases with 3-4 questions being asked.

An idiom is a special or figurative expression, word, or phrase with a meaning that differs from the literal meanings of its individual words.

Phrases or Phrasal verbs are combinations of a verb and one or more prepositions or adverbs.

Types of Questions Asked

Type 1

In this question, four alternatives are given for the Idioms/Phrases given in the bold/ underlined in the sentences.

Choose the alternative which best expresses the meaning of Idioms/Phrases.

I did not mind what he was saying, he was only **talking through his hat**.

(a) talking nonsense (b) talking irresponsibly
(c) talking ignorantly (d) talking insulting *Ans.* (a)

Type 2

Substitute the underlined word segment with most appropriate idiom.

The manager hesitated to assign the job to the newcomer as he was **young and inexperienced**.

(a) under a cloud (b) wet behind the ears
(c) in a pickle (d) as hard as nai *Ans.* (b)

Type 3

Choose the alternative which best expresses the meaning of Idioms/Phrases.

To stave off

(a) postpone (b) wait and see
(c) prevent (d) allow it to take its own course

Ans. (c)

Type 4

Fill in the blank with the most appropriate idiom.

This is strictly .... but some changes are going to happen in the near future.

(a) off the rails (b) off the key
(c) off the mark (d) off the record *Ans.* (c)

How to Solve the Questions

Solve questions based on Idioms and Phrases with these easy steps

Step 1 Read the sentence with the underlined idiom or the sentence which requires an idiom to understand its meaning.

Step 2 With step 1, you will find out what the idioms means in the sentence and then, select your answer.

Step 3 For fillers and substitutions, try to understand what the sentence want to convey. Now, read the idioms or phrases in the options. Think of their meanings.

Step 4 The idiom that fits the sentence the best, is your answer.

SSC Exam Scanner

Directions (Q. Nos. 1-804) Select the most appropriate meaning of the Bold/Underlined/Bracketed/Italisied Phrase.

Or

Fill in the blanks using the correct idiom. *Or*

Select the correct idiom that best fits the given sentence.

SSC CGL 2024 (Tier 1 & 2)

1. Complete the dialogue for Person B using the correct idiom.
Person A I am so nervous. I don't think I should make the speech tomorrow.
Person B No, You are just getting .... You have prepared for this. **SSC CGL Tier-2 18.01.2025**
(a) hot feet (b) cold feet
(c) cold hand (d) cold foot

Ans. (b)

The correct idiom to complete the dialogue is 'cold feet'. This idiom means experiencing nervousness or fear that prevents one from doing something planned, such as making a speech.

2. The team decided to pull out all the stops for their upcoming presentation. **SSC CGL Tier-2 18.01.2025**
(a) To do everything possible to make something successful
(b) Give up easily and without thinking much
(c) Keep things simple and straightforward
(d) Wait patiently for a more favourable time

Ans. (a)

The idiom 'pull out all the stops' means to do everything possible to make something successful.

3. A lot of people are still........... over the GDP issue. **SSC CGL Tier-2 20.01.2025**
(a) over the fence
(b) breaking a leg
(c) sitting on the fence
(d) by the fence

Ans. (c)

The idiom 'sitting on the fence' means to remain neutral or undecided in a situation. It is the most appropriate idiom for the given sentence.

4. Complete the dialogue for Person B using the correct idiom. Person A We are all going to the club this weekend. Do you want to come?
Person B Thank you for asking. But I don't like clubs. It's.........
SSC CGL Tier-2 20.01.2025
(a) not my cup, not my tea
(b) not my cup of coffee
(c) my cup of coffee
(d) not my cup of tea

Ans. (d)

The idiom 'not my cup of tea' is used to indicate that something is not to one's liking or preference. In this context, Person B is politely declining the invitation to the club by saying it's not their preference.

5. To have bigger fish to fry
SSC CGL Tier-1 09.09.2024 (Shift-I)
(a) To have an interest in cooking
(b) To know different kinds of fishing techniques
(c) To take calculated risks
(d) To have bigger things to take care of than the menial task at hand

Ans. (d)

'To have bigger fish to fry means' to have something more important to take care of than the menial task at hand.

6. Break a leg
SSC CGL Tier-1 09.09.2024 (Shift-II)
SSC CPO 05.10.2023 (Shift-I)
(a) Give advice on maintaining physical health.
(b) Encourage someone to engage in risky activities.
(c) Suggest taking a short break during work.
(d) Wish someone good luck before a performance.

Ans. (d)

'To break a leg' means to wish someone good luck before a performance.

7. Raju's job as a clerk seemed to be bad at first because of the low salary, but resulted in something good happening later because it saved him from being unemployed.
SSC CGL Tier-1 09.09.2024 (Shift-II)
(a) a boon in disguise
(b) a blessing in disguise
(c) a jolt in disguise
(d) a gift in disguise

Ans. (b)

'A blessing in disguise' means something that seems bad at first but resulted in something good.

8. Fatima was <u>at her wits' end</u> trying to decide on a serene place for spending the holidays in.
SSC CGL Tier-1 09.09.2024 (Shift-III)
(a) So worried, confused or annoyed that she does not know what to do next
(b) So worried, confused or annoyed that she became unconscious
(c) So calm and composed that she knows what to do next
(d) So worried, confused or annoyed that she insulted others for no reason

Ans. (a)

'At wits end' means worried, confused or annoyed such that one does not know what to do next.

9. To steal from a shop
SSC CGL Tier-1 09.09.2024 (Shift-III)
(a) Golden opportunity
(b) Green thumb
(c) Five-finger discount
(d) Black sheep

Ans. (c)

'Five-finger discount' means to steal from a shop.

'Golden opportunity' means a good opportunity.

'Green thumb' means natural talent for growing plants; green fingers.

'Black sheep' means a person who is different from the rest of a group, especially a family member who doesn't fit in.

10. On the ball
SSC CGL Tier-1 10.09.2024 (Shift-I)
SSC CGL Tier-1 20.07.2023 (Shift-I)
SSC CGL Tier-1 06.12.2022 (Shift-II
(a) Unaware of any changes or developments and lazy to react to them
(b) Aware of any changes or developments but slow to react to them
(c) Aware of any changes or developments and quick to react to them
(d) Aware of any changes or developments but doing nothing

Ans. (c)

'On the ball' means to be aware of any changes or developments and quick to react to them.

11. I'm .... about whether to accept the job offer or continue freelancing. Both options have their advantages.
SSC CGL Tier-1 10.09.2024 (Shift-I)
(a) on the fence
(b) cutting corners
(c) left out in cold
(d) up in arms

Ans. (a)

The correct idiom for the given blank is **'on the fence'** which means to be in a dilemma.

'Cutting corners' means to do something in the easiest, cheapest or fastest way, often at the expense of quality or standards.

'Left out in cold' means to be ignored.

'Up in arms' means protesting vigorously about something.

12. Your so-called friend has <u>cooked your goose</u>.
SSC CGL Tier-1 10.09.2024 (Shift-II)
(a) To complete a lot of work or a wide range of things
(b) When something develops completely and reaches maturity; when a child becomes an adult
(c) To spend a lot of time and energy but achieve nothing
(d) To interfere with, disrupt or ruin something for someone

Ans. (d)

'Cooked your goose' means to interfere with, disrupt or ruin something for someone.

13. 'Bite the bullet' means
SSC CGL Tier-1 10.09.2024 (Shift-II)
SSC CGL Tier-2 26.10.2023
SSC CPO 29.06.2024 (Shift-II)
SSC CPO 05.10.2023 (Shift-III)
(a) Enjoy a delicious meal
(b) Face a difficult situation with courage
(c) Avoid confrontation
(d) Give someone a piece of advice

Ans. (b)

'Bite the bullet' means to bravely endure a difficult or unpleasant situation, especially when there is no other choice.

14. Care a hang
SSC CGL Tier-1 10.09.2024 (Shift-III)
(a) Hanging clothes to dry
(b) Putting an outfit on a hanger
(c) Caring too much
(d) Showing no interest

Ans. (d)

'Care a hang' means to show no interest.

15. To tell others secret information only for enjoyment is not a good practice.
SSC CGL Tier-1 10.09.2024 (Shift-III)
(a) spill the words (b) spill the cat
(c) spill the onions (d) spill the beans

Ans. (d)

'To spill the beans' means to tell others secret information.

16. The doctors tried very hard to save his mother but they were unsuccessful.
SSC CGL Tier-1 11.09.2024 (Shift-I)
(a) faced the music
(b) drew the line
(c) moved heaven and earth
(d) ran like clockwork

Ans. (c)

'Moved heaven and earth' means tried very hard.

'Faced the music' means be confronted with the unpleasant consequences of one's actions.

'Drew the line' means to never do something because you think it is wrong.

'Ran like clockwork' means to happen exactly as planned, without any trouble.

17. Hit the nail on the head
SSC CGL Tier-1 11.09.2024 (Shift-I)
SSC CPO 05.10.2023 (Shift-I)
(a) They are experiencing a headache.
(b) They have accurately identified or explained something.
(c) They're uncertain about a decision.
(d) They hit a nail with a hammer.

Ans. (b)

'Hit the nail on the head' means to have accurately identified or explained something.

18. To read between the lines
SSC CGL Tier-1 11.09.2024 (Shift-II)
(a) To underline some words
(b) To read differently
(c) To read aloud to public
(d) To understand more than what the words suggest

Ans. (d)

'To read between the lines' means to understand more than what the words suggest.

19. Jump the gun
SSC CGL Tier-1 11.09.2024 (Shift-II)
SSC CHSL Tier-1 07.06.2022 (Shift-I)
(a) To start all over again
(b) Using a gun for sports
(c) To stop a process
(d) To do something too soon and too quickly

Ans. (d)

'Jump the gun' means to do something too soon and too quickly.

20. A dime a dozen
SSC CGL Tier-1 11.09.2024 (Shift-III)
SSC CGL Tier-1 17.07.2023 (Shift-II)
(a) Variety of amenities
(b) Something common and not special
(c) Very wealthy
(d) A fair trade

Ans. (b)

'A dime a dozen' means something common and not special.

21. She believed she had been blamed for the mistakes of others for what happened.
SSC CGL Tier-1 11.09.2024 (Shift-III)
(a) Made a sceptic
(b) Made a scapegoat
(c) Made a spinster
(d) Made a savage

Ans. (b)

'Made a scapegoat' means to blame someone for the mistakes of others.

22. Nobody's fool
SSC CGL Tier-1 11.09.2024 (Shift-III)
(a) Not easily deceived
(b) The wisest person
(c) A complete fool
(d) All are fools

Ans. (a)

'Nobody's fool' means not easily deceived.

23. The renowned publisher decided to withdraw a book from the market. No one was interested in the book as the arguments presented were ……… .
SSC CGL Tier-1 12.09.2024 (Shift-I)
(a) high and mighty
(b) out of the woods
(c) beside the mark
(d) under the rose

Ans. (c)

The correct filler for the given blank is **'beside the mark'** which means something is irrelevant or not to the point.

'High and mighty' means to behave with superiority.

'Out of the woods' means out of difficulty or problem.

'Under the rose' means secrecy or confidentiality

24. In my new office, all employees were different, so I felt like a fish out of water. **SSC CGL Tier-1 12.09.2024 (Shift-I)**
(a) Uncomfortable
(b) Homeless
(c) Frustrated
(d) Disappointed

Ans. (a)

'Fish out of water' means to be uncomfortable.

25. My sisters wished me good luck before I went on the stage to sing.
SSC CGL Tier-1 12.09.2024 (Shift-II)

Or

Roshan, it's time for you to give your speech to the whole school, wishing you luck to do well.
SSC CGL Tier-1 19.09.2024 (Shift-II)
(a) Told me to sit on the fence
(b) Told me to break a leg
(c) Told me to break the ice
(d) Told me to break an arm

Ans. (b)

'Told me to break a leg' means to wish good luck.

'Told me to sit on the fence' means to remain neutral, to refuse to take sides in a dispute.

'Told me to break the ice' means to remove the tension at a first meeting, at the opening of a party, etc.

'Told me to break an arm' means to crack or break one or more of the bones in the arm.

26. After years of fights with his neighbour Ram, Shekhar decided to hold out the……… and invited Ram for tea. **SSC CGL Tier-1 12.09.2024 (Shift-III)**
(a) poker face
(b) comparing apples to oranges
(c) chip on shoulder
(d) olive branch

Ans. (d)

The correct filler for the given blank is **'olive branch'** which means an offer of reconciliation.

'Poker face' means an impassive expression that hides one's true feelings.

'Comparing apples to oranges' means comparing two things that are very different and it's not sensible to do so.

'Chip on shoulder' means someone has an unpleasant or angry attitude or way of behaving.

27. Anand personally believes in the motto, "When life gives you lemons, make lemonade."
SSC CGL Tier-1 12.09.2024 (Shift-III)
(a) Earn the maximum out of business
(b) Nourish health
(c) Enjoy the most when the season is favourable
(d) Make the best out of difficult situations

Ans. (d)

'When life gives you lemons, make lemonade' is a proverb which means make the best out of difficult situations.

28. Turned a deaf ear to
SSC CGL Tier-1 13.09.2024 (Shift-I)
(a) Disregarded (b) At intervals
(c) By any means (d) Rebuked
Ans. (a)
'To turn a deaf ear' means to disregard or ignore.

29. A bad patch
SSC CGL Tier-1 13.09.2024 (Shift-I)
(a) A path that is untravelled
(b) A period of time when a person faces lots of troubles
(c) A person who takes a difficult path
(d) A dangerous road to walk on
Ans. (b)
'A bad patch' is a period of time when a person faces lots of troubles.

30. All his friends admired him because he was a straight shooter.
SSC CGL Tier-1 13.09.2024 (Shift-II)
(a) Excellent shooter
(b) Complicated and confusing person
(c) Miserly and pessimistic individual
(d) A thoroughly upright straightforward person
Ans. (d)
'A straight shooter' is a thoroughly upright straightforward person.

31. My uncle lives in New York, so I only see him once in a blue moon.
SSC CGL Tier-1 13.09.2024 (Shift-II)
SSC CGL Tier-1 21.07.2023 (Shift-II)
(a) Not very often (b) Monthly
(c) Weekly (d) Very often
Ans. (a)
'Once in a blue moon' means rarely or not very often.

32. Radhika stood by Monica's side through thick and thin.
SSC CGL Tier-1 13.09.2024 (Shift-III)
Or
Sanchit stands by his friends through thick and thin. SSC CPO 05.10.2023 (Shift-I)
(a) Under easy situations wherein she could ensure Monica's safety and security.
(b) In all the happy moments, personally spending most of her time.
(c) Under all conditions, no matter how challenging or difficult.
(d) In the moments when Monica couldn't complete some simple tasks.
Ans. (c)
'Through thick and thin' means under all conditions, no matter how challenging or difficult.

33. Everyone called the reporter a daredevil after he came back safely from the war zone.
SSC CGL Tier-1 13.09.2024 (Shift-III)
(a) a common man
(b) a fearless person
(c) an insignificant person
(d) a hypocrite
Ans. (b)
'A daredevil' is a fearless person.

34. In those days, we did not expect luxuries; we were thankful if we could keep the wolf from the door.
SSC CGL Tier-1 17.09.2024 (Shift-I)
(a) avoid starvation
(b) wallow in poverty
(c) relish food
(d) encourage starvation
Ans. (a)
'To keep the wolf from the door' means to avoid problems. In the context of the sentence, it means to avoid starvation.

35. My cousin works day and night to achieve success in life.
SSC CGL Tier-1 17.09.2024 (Shift-I)
(a) vale of tears
(b) around the clock
(c) great dealing
(d) a handful
Ans. (b)
'Day and night' means throughout the day and around the clock.

36. To bring to light
SSC CGL Tier-1 17.09.2024 (Shift-II)
(a) To engage in conversation
(b) To lighten
(c) To disclose
(d) To disengage
Ans. (c)
'To bring to light' means to disclose.

37. Rina pulled a long face since her husband had not bought her a diamond necklace on their anniversary.
SSC CGL Tier-1 17.09.2024 (Shift-II)
(a) to be euphoric (b) to be ecstatic
(c) to look saddened (d) to be electrified
Ans. (c)
'To pull a long face' means to look sad.

38. Easy does it
SSC CGL Tier-1 17.09.2024 (Shift-III)
(a) Used to tell someone to do something rarely
(b) Used to tell someone to do something violently
(c) Used to tell someone to do something slowly and carefully
(d) Used to tell someone to do something horridly
Ans. (c)
'Easy does it' is used to tell someone to do something slowly and carefully.

39. Cut corners
SSC CGL Tier-1 17.09.2024 (Shift-III)
SSC CGL Tier-1 21.07.2023 (Shift-IV)
(a) Complete a work
(b) Do something in an inexpensive and easy way
(c) Find a suitable place
(d) Clear a space
Ans. (b)
'Cut corners' means to do something in an inexpensive and easy way.

40. I thought Sadhna would always stick by me, but when I got into trouble, she turned out to be a/an ....
SSC CGL Tier-1 18.09.2024 (Shift-I)
(a) hard nut to crack
(b) open secret
(c) fair-weather friend
(d) white elephant
Ans. (c)
'Fair-weather friend' is used for a person whose friendship cannot be relied on in times of difficulty.
'Open secret' means a fact that should be a secret when in fact a lot of people know about it.
'White elephant' refers to something that is expensive or difficult to maintain, but has little or no value and is no longer wanted.
Hard nut to crack means difficult to solve.

41. Her thinning grey hair was hanging on her bony forehead.
SSC CGL Tier-1 18.09.2024 (Shift-I)
(a) falling about (b) urging ahead
(c) straggling over (d) sinking from
Ans. (c)
The underlined part of the sentence is incorrect in the context of the sentence. The correct usage will be 'straggling over' which means to spread or be spread in a scattered fashion or at irregular intervals.

42. His PhD degree seems to be (Penelope's web).
SSC CGL Tier-1 18.09.2024 (Shift-I)
(a) An important task
(b) A difficult task
(c) A secret task
(d) An endless task
Ans. (d)
'Penelope's web' means an endless task.

43. On cloud nine
SSC CGL Tier-1 18.09.2024 (Shift-II)
SSC CGL Tier-1 08.12.2022 (Shift-III)
SSC CGL Tier-1 23.08.2021 (Shift-I)
(a) Being angry with someone
(b) Being very delighted
(c) Flying in the sky
(d) Being very high

Ans. (b)

'On cloud nine' means being very happy or delighted.

44. A bitter pill

SSC CGL Tier-1 18.09.2024 (Shift-II)

(a) Facing a distressing situation
(b) Talking nonsense
(c) Arguing unnecessarily
(d) Getting furious easily

Ans. (a)

'A bitter pill' means facing a distressing situation.

45. Creature of habit

SSC CGL Tier-1 18.09.2024 (Shift-III)

(a) A mean person
(b) A bad habit
(c) A faithful dog
(d) One who does same thing in the same way

Ans. (d)

'Creature of habit' means one who does same thing in the same way.

46. Hit the roof

SSC CGL Tier-1 18.09.2024 (Shift-III)

(a) To destruct a building
(b) To become very angry
(c) To jump high
(d) To play joyfully

Ans. (b)

'Hit the roof' means to become very angry.

47. Start from scratch

SSC CGL Tier-1 19.09.2024 (Shift-I)
SSC CHSL Tier-1 06.06.2022 (Shift-I)

(a) To start or create something from the very beginning
(b) To address an issue
(c) To develop something out of waste material
(d) To point out something wrong

Ans. (a)

'To start from scratch' means to start or create something from the very beginning.

48. His illness became <u>a blessing in disguise</u> when he married his nurse.

SSC CGL Tier-1 19.09.2024 (Shift-I)

(a) an apparent misfortune that eventually has good results
(b) when someone finds it difficult to choose between two alternatives
(c) to present a counter-argument
(d) deal with a problem if and when it becomes necessary

Ans. (a)

'A blessing in disguise' refers to an apparent misfortune that eventually has good results.

49. I had heard of <u>henpecked husbands</u> and now, I felt that I saw one.

SSC CGL Tier-1 19.09.2024 (Shift-II)

(a) controlling husband
(b) bossy husbands
(c) oppressed husband
(d) dominating husbands

Ans. (c)

'Henpecked husbands' refers to men who are constantly controlled, oppressed and criticised by their wives.

50. After reflecting on the matter regarding his boss's selfish attitude, Raju decided to force himself to perform <u>an unpleasant action in a difficult situation in order to resolve the matter</u>.

SSC CGL Tier-1 19.09.2024 (Shift-III)

(a) bite the bullet
(b) dodge the bullet
(c) shoot the bullet
(d) ignore the bullet

Ans. (a)

'To bite the bullet' means to force himself to perform an unpleasant action in a difficult situation in order to resolve the matter.

51. A continuing unpleasant situation, created when one problem causes another problem that then makes the first problem worse

SSC CGL Tier-1 19.09.2024 (Shift-III)

(a) Vicious cycle
(b) Round cycle
(c) Repetitive cycle
(d) Enclosed cycle

Ans. (a)

'Vicious cycle' means a continuing unpleasant situation that is created when one problem causes another problem that then makes the first problem worse.

52. At a low ebb

SSC CGL Tier-1 23.09.2024 (Shift-I)

(a) In a depressed or weak state
(b) In a happy state
(c) In a critical moment
(d) In an unemployed mode

Ans. (a)

'At a low ebb' means in a depressed or weak state.

53. On and off

SSC CGL Tier-1 23.09.2024 (Shift-I)

(a) Now and then
(b) Know something thoroughly
(c) Remind
(d) Object to

Ans. (a)

'On and off' means now and then.

54. Left out in the cold

SSC CGL Tier-1 23.09.2024 (Shift-II)

(a) To go underground
(b) To be in hiding
(c) To be ignored
(d) To be extremely negative

Ans. (c)

'Left out in the cold' means to be ignored.

55. Break the ice

SSC CGL Tier-1 23.09.2024 (Shift-II)

(a) Nervousness before a performance
(b) Ill-feeling carried by a person over a period of time
(c) Respect for someone's achievements
(d) To say or do something that makes people feel more relaxed, especially at the beginning of a meeting, party

Ans. (d)

'Break the ice' means to say or do something that makes people feel more relaxed, especially at the beginning of a meeting, party.

56. Sejal visits the nearby temple <u>on and off</u>.

SSC CGL Tier-1 23.09.2024 (Shift-III)

(a) Periodically (b) Constantly
(c) Continuously (d) Regularly

Ans. (a)

'On and off' means now and then or periodically.

57. This year's budget is unlikely to pass as law since the President's proposed budgets typically face a <u>jaundiced eye</u> but this one has gotten even more scepticism.

SSC CGL Tier-1 23.09.2024 (Shift-III)

(a) Jealousy (b) Confidence
(c) Resentment (d) Good will

Ans. (c)

'Jaundiced eye' means to view something with prejudice, usually in a cynical or negative way. Hence, 'resentment' is the correct answer.

58. A time when money might unexpectedly be needed

SSC CGL Tier-1 24.09.2024 (Shift-I)

(a) A rainy day (b) A raw deal
(c) A rash of something
(d) A rap over the knuckles

Ans. (a)

'A rainy day' means a time when money might unexpectedly be needed.
'A raw deal' is a situation in which someone receives unfair or harsh treatment.
'A rash of something' means a large number of unpleasant events or undesirable things that have happened or appeared within a short period of time.
'A rap over the knuckles' means a punishment.

59. Instead of confusing others, let us call a spade a spade in front of the audience. SSC CGL Tier-1 24.09.2024 (Shift-I)
(a) Pretend superiority
(b) Remain silent
(c) Speak truthfully
(d) Be at strife

Ans. (c)

'Call a spade a spade' means to speak truthfully.

60. We need to .... a solution to this problem before it gets worse. SSC CGL Tier-1 24.09.2024 (Shift-I)
(a) cut down on (b) break down
(c) break up (d) come up with

Ans. (d)

The correct filler for the given blank is **'come up with'** which means produce something, especially when pressured or challenged.
'Cut down on' means to reduce the use of something.
'Break down' means to stop working.
'Break up' means to end.

61. Rahul won the extempore competition. He is lucky to be blessed with the gift of the gab.
SSC CGL Tier-1 24.09.2024 (Shift-II)
SSC CHSL Tier-1 11.07.2024 (Shift-I)
(a) an honest person
(b) a big surprise
(c) a lucky person
(d) a talent for speaking

Ans. (d)

'Gift of the gab' means a talent for speaking.

62. Nina has not yet learned how to straighten up and fly right. SSC CGL Tier-1 24.09.2024 (Shift-II)
(a) forget the wrongdoings of the others
(b) improve her absurd behaviour and act seriously
(c) be professional in flying the aircraft
(d) remember the past and prepare for the future

Ans. (b)

'Straighten up and fly right' means to improve her absurd behaviour and act seriously.

63. After months of dedication and effort, I finally completed the marathon. I can really .... for this accomplishment. SSC CGL Tier-1 24.09.2024 (Shift-III)
(a) eat like a horse
(b) up a creek without a paddle
(c) blow hot and cold
(d) pat myself on the back

Ans. (d)

The correct idiom for the given blank is **'pat myself on the back'** which means to praise oneself for doing something good.
'Eat like a horse' means to eat a lot of food.
'Up a creek without a paddle' means to be in a difficult or dangerous situation with no clear way out.
Blow hot and cold means to frequently change one's mind or attitude towards something, making it difficult to understand how someone truly feels.

64. The leader of the Legislative Assembly won the hearts of the members through his maiden speech during the session in state council. SSC CGL Tier-1 24.09.2024 (Shift-III)
(a) final speech (b) closure speech
(c) first speech (d) logical speech

Ans. (c)

'Maiden speech' is first speech.

65. The entire speech of the revivalist fell flat with the crowd that was present there. SSC CGL Tier-1 25.09.2024 (Shift-I)
(a) had a great impact on
(b) had moderate influence on
(c) had somewhat of a result on
(d) had no effect on

Ans. (d)

'Fell flat with' means to have no effect on.

66. Leela was in class when the big fight happened. So, if you want to know the details, you should ask her, you will get the truth given by somebody who is directly involved and therefore likely to be accurate. SSC CGL Tier-1 25.09.2024 (Shift-I)
(a) with kid gloves
(b) shooting off the cuff
(c) calling a spade a spade
(d) straight from the horse's mouth

Ans. (d)

'Straight from the horse's mouth' means given by somebody who is directly involved and therefore likely to be accurate.
'With kid gloves' means to do so with special consideration or in a tactful manner, often due to a perceived sensitivity.
'Shooting off the cuff' means to expose one's shirt cuffs beyond the coat sleeves.
'Calling a spade a spade' means to say the truth.

67. We all have to pull our socks up for the upcoming Board exam, if we want to get outstanding grades. SSC CGL Tier-1 25.09.2024 (Shift-II)
(a) act in a proper manner
(b) work harder than before
(c) calm down impudent contempt
(d) revive interest in old matters

Ans. (b)

'To pull our socks up' means to work harder than before.

68. Due to her impoverished state, most of her relatives treated her with contempt. SSC CGL Tier-1 25.09.2024 (Shift-III)
(a) Came in handy
(b) Turned up their nose at her
(c) Turned the corner at her
(d) Gave a wide space to her

Ans. (b)

'Turned up their nose at her' means treated her with contempt.
'Came in handy' means to be useful.
'Turned the corner' means to get past a difficult time, period, crisis and to start to improve.
'Gave a wide space' means to avoid or stay away from them.

69. Let the dust settle SSC CGL Tier-1 25.09.2024 (Shift-III)
(a) To make use of a situation
(b) Wait for the other person to make a move
(c) To make a space tidy
(d) To wait for a situation to become clear or certain

Ans. (d)

'Let the dust settle' means to wait for a situation to become clear or certain.

70. Ranveer never has the habit of making a beeline for his academic activities. SSC CGL Tier-1 26.09.2024 (Shift-I)
(a) behaving abnormally
(b) selecting inconsiderately
(c) going straight and quick
(d) immediately responding to things

Ans. (c)

'Making a beeline' means going straight and quick.

71. The company understood that these small protests of employees regarding low wages were just the tip of the iceberg. SSC CGL Tier-1 26.09.2024 (Shift-I)
(a) A small, noticeable part of a problem, the total size of which is non-existent
(b) A small, noticeable part of a problem, the total size of which is solvable
(c) A large part of a problem which is really noticeable
(d) A small, noticeable part of a problem, the total size of which is really much greater

Ans. (d)

'The tip of the iceberg' means a small, noticeable part of a problem, the total size of which is really much greater.

72. Bincy's mother kept her cards close to her chest. **SSC CGL Tier-1 26.09.2024 (Shift-II)**

(a) decided to show more affection
(b) informed that all the cards must be kept safe
(c) kept her purse and money by herself
(d) kept her plans and thoughts hidden

Ans. (d)

'Kept her cards close to her chest' means to keep her plans and thoughts hidden.

73. The playwright has faced many ups and downs in his literary career, which spanned for almost 30 years.
SSC CGL Tier-1 26.09.2024 (Shift-III)

(a) much truth and falsehood
(b) many agreements and disagreements
(c) much light and darkness
(d) many good and bad times

Ans. (d)

The phrase 'many ups and downs' means experiencing periods of success and failure, indicating both positive and negative times in a person's life.

74. Lucy's conceited conduct with her colleagues has left her high and dry.
SSC CGL Tier-1 26.09.2024 (Shift-III)

(a) helpless
(b) superseding
(c) impoverished
(d) surrounded by people

Ans. (a)

The phrase 'high and dry' means being in a difficult or hopeless situation without any help.

SSC CGL 2023 (Tier 1 & 2)

75. Lily-livered
SSC CGL Tier-1 14.07.2023 (Shift-I)

(a) Brave (b) Comical
(c) Not brave (d) Naughty

Ans. (c)

The idiom 'lily-livered' means weak and cowardly. Hence, 'not brave' is its correct answer.

76. Pooja tried to explain the problem, but soon she tied herself up in knots.
SSC CGL Tier-1 14.07.2023 (Shift-I)

(a) be forced to explain your actions and (probably) punished
(b) become very confused when you are trying to explain something
(c) make no progress in an argument or discussion
(d) won't modify an opinion or agree to even small changes that another person wants.

Ans. (b)

The underlined idiom 'tied herself up in knots' means 'to become confused while explaining something'.

77. To kick the bucket
SSC CGL Tier-1 14.07.2023 (Shift-II)

(a) To be ill (b) Be sad
(c) Be happy (d) To die

Ans. (d)

The idiom 'to kick the bucket' means 'to die'.

78. Miss the boat
SSC CGL Tier-1 14.07.2023 (Shift-II)

(a) Missing a good opportunity
(b) Missing your medium of travel
(c) Missing good moments of your life
(d) Being too late

Ans. (a)

The idiom 'miss the boat' means to be too slow to take advantage of an opportunity.

79. To bell the cat
SSC CGL Tier-1 14.07.2023 (Shift-III)

(a) To feed pets (b) To play with kids
(c) To love cats (d) To face risk

Ans. (d)

The idiom 'to bell the cat' means to face risk.

80. The police have not yet been able to solve the case; it seems to be ......
SSC CGL Tier-1 14.07.2023 (Shift-III)

(a) in a nutshell
(b) turning over a new leaf
(c) a hard nut to crack
(d) in a pink

Ans. (c)

The idiom 'a hard nut to crack' means a difficult problem or an opponent that is hard to beat.

81. Sharp practice
SSC CGL Tier-1 14.07.2023 (Shift-IV)

(a) Dishonesty (b) Frequently
(c) Briefly (d) Nearby

Ans. (a)

The idiom 'sharp practice' means a way of behaving, in business, that is dishonest but not illegal.

82. Vennela made a big fuss about a small problem.
SSC CGL Tier-1 14.07.2023 (Shift-IV)

(a) get a taste of your own medicine
(b) barking up the wrong tree
(c) add insult to injury
(d) a storm in a teacup

Ans. (d)

The idiom 'a storm in a teacup' means a disproportionate reaction of anger, concern or displeasure over some minor or trivial matter.

83. Today, the country's nationalists rule the roost and hand out the jobs.
SSC CGL Tier-1 17.07.2023 (Shift-I)

(a) to be in charge
(b) to be prejudiced
(c) to save a criminal
(d) to exploit someone

Ans. (a)

The underlined idiom 'to rule the roost' means to be in control or charge.

84. Keep someone at arm's length
SSC CGL Tier-1 17.07.2023 (Shift-I)

(a) Avoid becoming friendly with someone
(b) Avoid playing with someone
(c) Being someone's enemy
(d) Avoid becoming bitter with someone

Ans. (a)

The idiom 'to keep someone at arm's length' means to avoid becoming too friendly or involved with them.

85. Scrape the barrel
SSC CGL Tier-1 17.07.2023 (Shift-II)

(a) Trying to find something
(b) Hiding something
(c) Using all the ways to achieve the desired result
(d) To be forced to use one's last and weakest resource

Ans. (d)

The idiom 'to scrape the barrel' means to be forced to use one's last and weakest resource, often because all other resources have been exhausted. It suggests a situation where one has to resort to using whatever is left, even if it is not ideal.

86. Carolina opened a savings account to save money for later.
SSC CGL Tier-1 17.07.2023 (Shift-III)

(a) for a cold day (b) for a rainy day
(c) for a sunny day(d) for a hot day

Ans. (b)

The idiom 'for a rainy day' means to save resources for later use, particularly in times of need or emergency.

87. Do not beat about the bush when you have anything to say.
SSC CGL Tier-1 17.07.2023 (Shift-III)

Or

Beat around the bush
SSC CPO 28.06.2024 (Shift-I)
SSC CPO 29.06.2024 (Shift-II)

(a) to try to influence
(b) to shift blame on others
(c) to argue
(d) to avoid giving a definite answer or position

Ans. (d)

The idiom 'beat about the bush' means to avoid giving a definite answer or to not come to the point.

It suggests being indirect and not addressing the main issue directly.

88. Back against the wall
SSC CGL Tier-1 17.07.2023 (Shift-IV)

(a) Be in an easy situation from where escape is difficult
(b) Be in a difficult situation from where escape is difficult
(c) Be in a relationship which one wants to escape
(d) Be in a difficult situation from where escape is easy.

Ans. (b)

The idiom 'back against the wall' means to be in a difficult situation without many options of escape.

It indicates a position where one feels trapped and has limited choices.

89. To prime the pump
SSC CGL Tier-1 17.07.2023 (Shift-IV)

(a) Manipulate someone to achieve success
(b) Encourage the growth or action of something
(c) To use a pump efficiently
(d) Ask others to be ambitious

Ans. (b)

The idiom 'to prime the pump' means to encourage the growth or action of something.

90. Bad iron SSC CGL Tier-1 18.07.2023 (Shift-I)

(a) No steam (b) Not hot
(c) Bad luck (d) Bad behaviour

Ans. (c)

The idiom 'bad iron' means bad luck, referring to an unfortunate or unlucky situation.

91. Sweety has been .... since her painting won first prize.
SSC CGL Tier-1 18.07.2023 (Shift-I)

(a) walking on eggshells
(b) waiting in the wings
(c) walking into the lion's den
(d) walking on air

Ans. (d)

The idiom 'walking on air' means to feel extremely excited or happy, describing the elation Sweety feels after winning first prize.

92. By the skin of your teeth
SSC CGL Tier-1 18.07.2023 (Shift-II)

(a) Confident of victory
(b) Kind towards the weak
(c) Determined to strike
(d) Just barely

Ans. (d)

The idiom 'by the skin of your teeth' means by a narrow margin or just barely, indicating something that is achieved with very little room for error.

93. Through thick and thin
SSC CGL Tier-1 18.07.2023 (Shift-III)
SSC CPO 29.06.2024 (Shift-II)

(a) Only assist during good times
(b) Hope during trying times
(c) In good times and in bad times
(d) Weak and lonely

Ans. (c)

The idiom 'through thick and thin' means in good and bad times, describing unwavering support or loyalty regardless of circumstances.

94. Has he lost his mind? He is **falling foul** of everybody.
SSC CGL Tier-1 18.07.2023 (Shift-IV)

(a) quite puzzled with
(b) maintaining a sort of coldness
(c) having and amicable talk with
(d) quarrelling with

Ans. (d)

The phrase 'falling foul of' means quarrelling with, indicating that the person is in conflict or dispute with others.

95. To be in two minds
SSC CGL Tier-1 18.07.2023 (Shift-IV)

(a) To be dominated by someone else
(b) To work on somebody else's advice
(c) To be in a critical state
(d) To be uncertain

Ans. (d)

The idiom 'to be in two minds' means 'to be uncertain.' It describes a state of indecision where a person is torn between two options and unable to make a definitive choice.

96. Gift of the gab
SSC CGL Tier-1 19.07.2023 (Shift-I)
SSC CGL Tier-1 24.08.2021 (Shift-I)
SSC CPO 27.06.2024 (Shift-III)

(a) Fluency of speech
(b) Freedom of speech
(c) First speech
(d) Figures of speech

Ans. (a)

The idiom 'Gift of the gab' means fluency of speech. It refers to someone who is particularly good at speaking and can talk easily and persuasively.

97. Get into a scrape
SSC CGL Tier-1 19.07.2023 (Shift-I)

(a) Creating a problem
(b) Solving a problem
(c) Explaining a problem
(d) Involved in a problem

Ans. (d)

The idiom 'get into a scrape' means to be involved in a problem. It suggests finding oneself in a difficult or tricky situation, often due to one's actions or decisions.

98. Blow something out of (all) proportion.
SSC CGL Tier-1 19.07.2023 (Shift-II)

(a) Make things difficult for someone without reason
(b) Leave someone at a time when they need you to stay and help them
(c) Control the level of something in order to stop it increasing
(d) Behave as if something that has happened is much worse than it really is

Ans. (d)

The idiom 'blow something out of proportion' means behave as if something that has happened is much worse than it really is.
It describes an overreaction to a situation, where the importance or severity is exaggerated.

99. To go to the dogs
SSC CGL Tier-1 19.07.2023 (Shift-III)

(a) To win a race
(b) To become worse
(c) To stand on guard
(d) To win support

Ans. (b)

The idiom 'to go to the dogs' means to become worse.

100. Go back to the drawing board
SSC CGL Tier-1 19.07.2023 (Shift-IV)
SSC CHSL Tier-1 15.04.2021 (Shift-III)

(a) Mediate a task
(b) Accomplish a task
(c) Start over
(d) Leave a work unfinished

Ans. (c)

The idiom 'Go back to the drawing board' means to start over.

It is used when an original plan has failed and a new plan or approach is needed.

101. I'm going to be <u>in trouble</u> if I don't submit my homework to the teacher.
SSC CGL Tier-1 19.07.2023 (Shift-IV)

(a) a devil's advocate
(b) off base
(c) the lion's share
(d) up the creek

Ans. (d)

The idiom 'up the creek' means in trouble. It implies being in a difficult or problematic situation, often without an easy way out.

102. I was very excited about my new assignment. I sent the email without the required attachment. What have I done? **SSC CGL Tier-1 20.07.2023 (Shift-I)**

(a) Shook a leg
(b) As swift as an eagle
(c) Jumped the gun
(d) Tested the waters

Ans. (c)

The idiom **'jumped the gun'** meaning to act too soon or before the right time or without any care is appropriate for the given situation.

'Shook a leg' means make a start; rouse oneself.

'As swift as an eagle' means moving or able to move quickly.

'Tested the waters' means to check people's reaction to a plan before you decide to use it.

103. To face the music **SSC CGL Tier-1 20.07.2023 (Shift-II)**

(a) Not knowing the real chords in music
(b) Barring the entire audiences view at a concert
(c) Being challenged to a music competition
(d) To bear the negative consequences of wrongful actions

Ans. (d)

The idiom 'to face the music' means to bear the negative consequences of wrongful actions.

104. Stir up a hornet's nest **SSC CGL Tier-1 20.07.2023 (Shift-II)**

(a) Provoke trouble (b) Resist a fight
(c) Create doubts (d) Scare the birds

Ans. (a)

The idiom 'to stir up a hornet's nest' means to provoke trouble. It implies causing a disturbance or creating a situation that is likely to result in conflict or problems.

105. It is raining cats and dogs **SSC CGL Tier-1 20.07.2023 (Shift-III)**

(a) It is raining very heavily
(b) There are showers
(c) Something that does not upset you
(d) It is drizzling

Ans. (a)

The idiom 'raining cats and dogs' means raining very heavily.

106. Taking a bull by the horns **SSC CGL Tier-1 20.07.2023 (Shift-III)**

(a) Wearing a skull cap
(b) To decapitate a bull for beef
(c) To make a stupid decision thinking to be daring
(d) To deal with a difficult situation in a very direct or confident way

Ans. (d)

The idiom 'taking a bull by the horns' means to deal with a difficult situation in a very direct and confident way. It suggests facing a challenging issue head-on with courage and determination.

107. The peasants worked the whole day in the fields and stopped working in the evening and went to their homes. **SSC CGL Tier-1 20.07.2023 (Shift-IV)**

(a) gave it a whirl
(b) put ice on it
(c) ran around in circles
(d) called it a day

Ans. (d)

The idiom **'called it a day'** means to stop working.

'Gave it a whirl' means to give something a try or attempt.

'Put ice on it' means to calm down a situation or reduce tension.

'Ran around in circles' means to engage in activity without achieving anything meaningful, indicating inefficiency.

108. Mohan .... the charge of Centre for Life Skills from Mustafa. **SSC CGL Tier-1 21.07.2023 (Shift-I)**

(a) took out (b) took through
(c) took off (d) took over

Ans. (d)

The correct filler for the given blank is 'took over'.

Took over means assuming control of something and it fits the context of the sentence.

Took out means to remove or extract.

Took through means' to guide or lead someone through a process.

Took off means to leave the ground and begin to fly or to become successful quickly.

109. Under the cloud **SSC CGL Tier-1 21.07.2023 (Shift-I)**

(a) The classmates were dancing together under the rain.
(b) The driver was under suspicion after the police found blood on his car.
(c) The Red Fort looks beautiful amidst the cloudy weather and cold atmosphere.
(d) It was the best place to sit under the sky with hands full of food.

Ans. (b)

The idiom 'under the cloud' means under suspicion, in trouble or out of favour.

Hence, sentence (b) uses the idiom appropriately.

110. A perfect storm **SSC CGL Tier-1 21.07.2023 (Shift-II)**

(a) Pretty good judgement
(b) Healing from trauma
(c) The worst possible situation
(d) Appropriate for all occasions

Ans. (c)

The idiom 'a perfect storm' means an extremely bad situation in which many bad things happen at the same time.

111. Bad blood **SSC CGL Tier-1 21.07.2023 (Shift-II)** **SSC CPO Tier-2 08.01.2024**

(a) She is so scared of cockroaches that she fainted when she saw them crawling near her foot.
(b) The doctor dropped the bad news to Ravi as he was suffering from a serious disease.
(c) The gangster had some bitter relations with a local activist so he warned him to stay out of his business.
(d) Sushant always gets in trouble for telling lies but he never learns anything.

Ans. (c)

The idiom 'bad blood' means feelings of hate between people because of arguments in the past'.

Hence, from the given sentences, sentence (c) uses it appropriately.

112. Your cancer is now completely obsolete. **SSC CGL Tier-1 21.07.2023 (Shift-III)**

(a) moving like a worm
(b) as dead as a doornail
(c) dead even
(d) hanging by a thread

Ans. (b)

The idiom **'as dead as a doornail'** means totally or assuredly dead; also finished and obsolete.

Moving like a worm means to move slowly.

Dead even means a situation without any progress.

Hanging by a thread means to be close to failure.

113. Hit the jackpot **SSC CGL Tier-1 21.07.2023 (Shift-IV)**

(a) Found a piece of gold
(b) Harm the opportunity
(c) Receiving a reward
(d) Gaining a big success

Ans. (d)

The idiom 'hit the jackpot' means to gain a big success.

114. This incident occurred without a warning. **SSC CGL Tier-1 24.07.2023 (Shift-I)**

(a) on thin ice
(b) bolt from the blue
(c) ignorance is bliss
(d) play devil's advocate

Ans. (b)

The idiom **'bolt from the blue'** means occurred without a warning.

'On thin ice' means in a precarious or risky situation.

'Ignorance is bliss' means that sometimes it is better to not know all the facts about a situation.

'Play devil's' advocate' refers to someone who pretends to be against an idea that a lot of people support.

115. You showed me your true personality when you asked me to get out of the house at midnight. **SSC CGL Tier-1 24.07.2023 (Shift-I)**

(a) true colours (b) bed of roses
(c) hot potato (d) white elephant

Ans. (a)

The phrase **'true colours'** means true personality or behaviour.

'Bed of roses' refers to a comfortable or easy situation.

'Hot potato' refers to a controversial issue or situation which is awkward to deal with.

'White elephant' refers to a possession that is useless or troublesome, especially one that is expensive.

116. Ravish is ready to throw caution to the wind. **SSC CGL Tier-1 24.07.2023 (Shift-II)**

(a) fight with wind
(b) act foolishly
(c) spend lavishly
(d) take risk

Ans. (d)

The underlined idiom 'throw caution to the wind' means to take risk.

117. Mahesh has learnt not to take things seriously. **SSC CGL Tier-1 24.07.2023 (Shift-II)**

(a) your guess is as good as mine
(b) take it with a grain of salt
(c) that's the last straw
(d) pull someone's leg

Ans. (b)

The idiom **'to take it with a grain of salt'** means to not believe something completely or not take something seriously.

'Your guess is as good as mine' is used when someone doesn't know the answer to a question.

'That's the last straw' refers to the latest problem in a series of problems that makes a situation impossible to accept.

'Pull someone's leg' means to try to persuade someone to believe something that is not true as a joke.

118. Many analysts are tipping stable, blue-chip companies to weather the storm. **SSC CGL Tier-1 24.07.2023 (Shift-III)**

(a) to deal with a simple situation without being harmed
(b) to deal with a situation without thinking
(c) to deal with a difficult situation without being harmed
(d) to deal with a simple situation without harming anyone else

Ans. (c)

The underlined idiom 'to weather the storm' means to deal with a difficult situation without being harmed.

119. The details were .... from one person to the other within no time. **SSC CGL Tier-1 24.07.2023 (Shift-IV)**

(a) passed away (b) passed in
(c) passed down (d) passed out

Ans. (c)

The correct filler for the given blank is **'passed down'**. The phrasal verb 'passed down' means to hand over.

passed away means to die.

passed in means to move in a specific direction.

passed out means to faint.

120. Harry always speaks his eye but he is not always very diplomatic! **SSC CGL Tier-1 24.07.2023 (Shift-IV)**

(a) speaks his tongue
(b) reads his heart
(c) speaks his mind
(d) listens his ear

Ans. (c)

The underlined idiom is incorrect. The correct idiom is 'speaks his mind' which means to speak openly.

121. Pass the buck **SSC CGL Tier-1 24.07.2023 (Shift-IV)**

(a) Providing essential services
(b) Trying to calm down
(c) Blaming another person
(d) Saying something unpleasant

Ans. (c)

The idiom 'pass the buck' means to blame another person.

122. As soon as the principal came to know about the inspection in the school, he put everything in perfect order. **SSC CGL Tier-1 25.07.2023 (Shift-I)**

(a) apple pie order
(b) apple of discord
(c) alley apple
(d) apple of one's eye

Ans. (a)

The idiom **'apple pie order'** means in perfect order.

'Apple of discord' means a subject of contention and envy.

'Alley apple' refers to a loose brick or rock found in the street.

'Apple of one's eye' refers to something or someone very precious or dear to a person.

123. Shelley has been *contemplating* for a few days but still has not decided to quit the job. **SSC CGL Tier-1 25.07.2023 (Shift-I)**

(a) biting the dust
(b) chewing the cud
(c) cooling one's heels
(d) getting into hot waters

Ans. (b)

The idiom **'chewing the cud'** means think or talk reflectively or to contemplate.

'Biting the dust' means to end in failure or death.

'Cooling one's heels' means to be kept waiting.

'Getting into hot waters' means landing into difficulty, danger or trouble.

124. At cross purposes **SSC CGL Tier-1 25.07.2023 (Shift-II)**

(a) Developing and amplifying ideas given
(b) Finalising deals and plans
(c) Blindly following each other's ideas
(d) Disagreeing with each other's ideas

Ans. (d)

The idiom 'at cross purposes' means disagreeing with each other's ideas.

125. You must not participate in the marathon this year without any training. It is an *unreal hope* on your part! **SSC CGL Tier-1 25.07.2023 (Shift-II)**

(a) carrying coal to new castle
(b) a pipe dream
(c) a will-o-the-wisp
(d) to lose one's temper

Ans. (b)

The idiom **'a pipe dream'** means unreal hopes.

'Carrying coals to Newcastle' means doing something that is obviously superfluous.

'Will-o-the wisp' refers to a person or thing that is difficult or impossible to reach or catch.

To lose one's temper means to get angry.

126. The commanders entered by force into terrorists' camp. **SSC CGL Tier-1 25.07.2023 (Shift-II)**

(a) broke down (b) broke with
(c) broke into (d) broke off

Ans. (c)

The phrasal verb **'broke into'** means 'to enter forcefully'. Hence, it can substitute the underlined phrase.

'Broke down' means to divide into smaller parts or it refers to something that doesn't work or is in bad condition.

'Broke with' means to intentionally not continue doing something that is normal, excepted or traditional.

'Broke off' means to stop abruptly or to end a relationship.

127. I just went to Bali on a backpacking trip and did everything by the ear without any itinerary.
SSC CGL Tier-1 25.07.2023 (Shift-III)

(a) by spreading rumours
(b) by improvisation
(c) while criticising
(d) by asking

Ans. (b)

The idiom 'by the ear' means 'by improvisation' or doing something that is not planned beforehand.

128. You snooze, you lose
SSC CGL Tier-1 25.07.2023 (Shift-IV)

(a) If you oversleep you are likely to lose a job
(b) Laziness is not good
(c) You may lose your money if snoozing is not stopped
(d) If you are not alert, you are likely to miss opportunities

Ans. (d)

The idiom 'you snooze, you lose' means if you are not alert, you are likely to miss opportunities.

129. Out of the blue
SSC CGL Tier-1 25.07.2023 (Shift-IV)
SSC CGL Tier-1 24.08.2021 (Shift-II)

(a) Undoubtedly (b) Unexpectedly
(c) Unbelievably (d) Unconcerned

Ans. (b)

The idiom 'out of the blue' means 'suddenly and unexpectedly'.

130. Anita keeps on repeating that she is innocent but there is ....
SSC CGL Tier-1 26.07.2023 (Shift-I)

(a) no smoke without fire
(b) no pulling up of the socks
(c) no rubbing of the shoulders
(d) no love lost between

Ans. (a)

The correct idiom for the given blank is **'no smoke without fire'**. The expression is used to convey that there is usually some truth behind a rumour or that rumours generally orginate from factual basis.

Pulling up of socks means to try hard to improve your performance.

Rubbing of the shoulders means to meet and spend time with someone.

No love lost between means to have no love or respect between two people.

131. Though very rich, Alexander always saves for a rainy day.
SSC CGL Tier-1 26.07.2023 (Shift-II)

(a) saves money for later
(b) lives like a miser
(c) spends too much
(d) accumulates less wealth

Ans. (a)

The underlined idiom 'saves for a rainy day' means 'to save money or resources for later'.

132. His voice gets on my nerves.
SSC CGL Tier-1 26.07.2023 (Shift-II)

(a) makes me ill (b) pierces my eardrums
(c) irritates me (d) makes me sad

Ans. (c)

The underlined idiom 'gets on someone's nerves' means 'to irritate or to become extremely annoying to someone'.

133. In a soup
SSC CGL Tier-1 26.07.2023 (Shift-III)

(a) Extremely short of money
(b) To exhibit cowardice
(c) To get nothing
(d) In trouble

Ans. (d)

The idiom 'in a soup' means in trouble.

It is used to describe a situation where someone is facing difficulties or complications.

134. The better you know someone the less you like him.
SSC CGL Tier-1 26.07.2023 (Shift-III)

(a) Save for a rainy day
(b) Spill the beans
(c) The elephant in the room
(d) Familiarity breeds contempt

Ans. (d)

The idiom **'familiarity breeds contempt'** is a proverb that means that more you know about someone, the more likely you are to find faults and grow to dislike them, which aligns with the sentiment expressed in the original sentence.

'Save for a rainy day' means to save money for a time of need.

'Spill the beans' means to reveal secret information unintentionally.

'Elephant in the room' refers to a problem which is present but is avoided as a subject of discussion.

135. Pintu has been advised to reduce smoking by his family doctor.
SSC CGL Tier-1 26.07.2023 (Shift-III)

(a) lower down (b) up down
(c) less down (d) cut down

Ans. (d)

The phrasal verb 'cut down' means 'to reduce'.

136. I really don't want to pour cold water on your theory but it cannot be applied to real life situations.
SSC CGL Tier-1 26.07.2023 (Shift-IV)

(a) to destroy someone's written piece of work
(b) to take revenge on someone by destroying their lives' work under the pretext of bad quality
(c) to be critical or doubtful of a plan that someone is excited about
(d) to give goosebumps by showing a prospect

Ans. (c)

The underlined idiom 'to pour cold water on' means 'to be critical or doubtful of a plan that someone is excited about'.

137. Hard nut to crack
SSC CGL Tier-1 27.07.2023 (Shift-I)

(a) A problem difficult to solve
(b) To leave an effect
(c) A situation that can be altered
(d) To bid farewell

Ans. (a)

The idiom 'hard nut to crack' means a problem difficult to solve.'

It describes a situation or issue that is particularly challenging and requires significant effort to resolve.

138. Riya always considers sincerity, devotion and dedication as the highest priority of a good employee.
SSC CGL Tier-1 27.07.2023 (Shift-I)

(a) fair and square
(b) ever and among
(c) free and easy
(d) first and foremost

Ans. (d)

The idiom **'first and foremost'** means 'highest priority'.

'Fair and square' means honesty and straight for wordly.

'Ever and among' means occasionally.

'Free and easy' means informal and relaxed.

139. He is rich and famous and expects everyone to .... on him.
SSC CGL Tier-1 27.07.2023 (Shift-II)

(a) tap dance like mad
(b) dead duck
(c) give a song and dance
(d) dance attendance

Ans. (d)

The correct filler for the given blank is **'dance attendance'**. 'Dance attendance' is an idiomatic expression that means to be attentive, submissive or obedient to someone in a servile or obsequious manner.

140. The question was raised for discussion before the members during the assembly session.
SSC CGL Tier-1 27.07.2023 (Shift-II)

(a) came up (b) came off
(c) came round (d) came out

Ans. (a)

The phrasal verb **'came up'** means 'to be raised for discussion'.

Came off means 'to succeed' or 'to happen as planned.'

Came round means 'to regain consciousness' or 'to be persuaded to change one's opinion.'

Came out means 'to be revealed' or 'to be published.'

141. Treading on thin ice
SSC CGL Tier-1 27.07.2023 (Shift-II)

(a) Playing with a sharp cicile
(b) To be in a dangerous or risky position
(c) Skating on ice fallen in a hailstorm
(d) Making a thin ice sculpture

Ans. (b)

The idiom 'treading on thin ice' means to be in a dangerous or risky position. This phrase is used to describe a situation where one's actions could easily lead to trouble or danger.

142. Get up on the wrong side of the bed
SSC CGL Tier-1 27.07.2023 (Shift-III)

(a) Someone who is having a horrible day
(b) Destroy or ruin a plan
(c) Someone who is having a good day
(d) Go to bed or go to sleep

Ans. (a)

The idiom 'get up on the wrong side of the bed' means 'to have a horrible day.' It suggests that someone is in a bad mood or experiencing misfortune from the very start of the day, often without any specific reason.

143. My cousin sister Neetu had an aerial view of the trade fair from the top of the giant wheel.
SSC CGL Tier-1 27.07.2023 (Shift-III)

(a) a bird in the gilded cage
(b) bird's eye view
(c) birds of same feather
(d) bird brain

Ans. (b)

The underlined phrase 'aerial view' means the same as 'bird's eye view' which means the ability to see something from a very elevated position while viewing a large area below you.

'A bird in the gilded cage' means to live in luxury but without freedom.

'Birds of a feather' is used to refer to people who have the same interests.

Bird brain is used to describe a foolish person.

144. The driver very subtly .... the traffic violation he committed.
SSC CGL Tier-1 27.07.2023 (Shift-III)

(a) ironed through (b) ironed in
(c) ironed out (d) ironed aside

Ans. (c)

The correct filler for the given blank is 'ironed out'. **'Ironed out'** means to resolve or work out a solution to something.

145. The youth involved in the accident escaped by the skin of his teeth.
SSC CGL Tier-2 02.03.2023

(a) Barely managed to escape
(b) Very arrogant
(c) Always taking calculated decisions
(d) Deficiency of funds

Ans. (a)

The idiom 'by the skin of his teeth' means 'to be able to barely manage to escape'.

146. My father's office is at a close distance from home.
SSC CGL Tier-2 02.03.2023

(a) from hand to mouth
(b) a part and parcel
(c) at a stone's throw
(d) at sixes and sevens

Ans. (c)

The idiom **'at a stone's throw'** means 'at a close distance.'

From hand to mouth means living with just enough money for basic necessities.

A part and parcel means an essential or integral part.

At sixes and sevens means in a state of confusion or disorder.

147. The team members seem **to be running around in circles.**
SSC CGL Tier-2 02.03.2023

(a) to be extremely successful
(b) hardly any time to breathe
(c) to be very active but with few results
(d) very dynamic and hardworking

Ans. (c)

The idiom 'running around in circles' means 'to be very active but with few results.' It describes a situation where a lot of effort is expended without making meaningful progress, similar to how running in a circle gets you nowhere.

148. It was a catch 22 situation for the manager.
SSC CGL Tier-2 03.03.2023

(a) worthy successor to the throne
(b) a difficult situation in which the solution to a problem is impossible
(c) hailed as the ultimate champion
(d) a positive outcome in a tough situation.

Ans. (b)

The idiom 'a catch 22 situation' means 'a difficult situation in which the solution to a problem is impossible.' It describes a paradoxical situation where you can't solve a problem because the solution itself is part of the problem.

149. Mentally strong people do not .... to suicide over trivial issues.
SSC CGL Tier-2 06.03.2023

(a) make up
(b) give up
(c) conceive on
(d) fall in

Ans. (b)

The correct filler for the given blank is 'give up' in which means to accept.

Give up means to accept defeat.

Make up means to reconcile or invent something.

Conceive on means not a correct phrasal verb in this context.

Fall in means to collapse or become aligned.

150. Achilles' heel SSC CGL Tier-2 06.03.2023

(a) Irrelevant thing
(b) Vulnerable point
(c) Fast runner
(d) Costly item

Ans. (b)

Achilles' heel means a vulnerable point.

151. The actress' daughter is just a **chip off the old block.**
SSC CGL Tier-2 06.03.2023

Or

Amit is also a chip off the old block like his brother, Tandon.
SSC CPO 28.06.2024 (Shift-III)

(a) to get into the enemy's territory
(b) similar to one's parents in behaviour
(c) to console the dreary
(d) to chip off the edges

Ans. (b)

The idiom 'chip off the old block' means 'similar to one's parents in behaviour.'

It suggests that a child resembles his parent in terms of character or behaviour.

152. The employee took the manager's remark **with a pinch of salt.**
SSC CGL Tier-2 07.03.2023
(a) going for the truth
(b) distasteful and boring
(c) doubt the truth or value of something
(d) ever ready to condemn someone

Ans. (c)

The idiom 'take with a pinch of salt' means 'to doubt the truth or value of something.' It implies that one should view the statement with skepticism.

SSC CGL 2023 (Tier 1 & 2)

153. Water under the bridge
SSC CGL Tier-2 07.03.2023
SSC CHSL Tier-1 13.03.2023 (Shift-I)
(a) Past events that are not important anymore
(b) Difficult situations in one's life
(c) Promises that are made to someone and never fulfilled
(d) A seasoned crop with a heavy demand

Ans. (a)

The idiom 'water under the bridge' means 'past events that are not important anymore.'

It suggests that something has happened and is now in the past, and there is no point in worrying about it anymore.

154. Despite their differences, the two politicians decided to .... and work together for the greater good.
SSC CGL Tier-2 26.10.2023
(a) bury the hatchet
(b) burn the midnight oil
(c) bark up the wrong tree
(d) blow off steam

Ans. (a)

The idiom **'bury the hatchet'** means 'to end a conflict and make peace.'

Burn the midnight oil means to work late into the night.

Bark up the wrong tree means to pursue a mistaken or misguided course of action.

Blow off steam means to release pent-up energy or emotion.

SSC CGL 2022 (Tier 1 & 2)

155. Like a cakewalk
SSC CGL Tier-1 01.12.2022 (Shift-I)
(a) Smooth surface
(b) Pleasant experience
(c) Easy task
(d) Active

Ans. (c)

The idiom 'Like a cakewalk' means something that is very easy to achieve. Hence, 'Easy task' is the correct answer.

156. All eyes SSC CGL Tier-1 01.12.2022 (Shift-I)
(a) Watching with anger
(b) Watching eagerly
(c) Watching with no interest
(d) Not watching at all

Ans. (b)

The idiom 'All eyes' means to watch someone or something with a lot of interest.

So, 'watching eagerly' is the correct answer.

157. In weal and woe
SSC CGL Tier-1 01.12.2022 (Shift-II)
(a) In sad and gloomy days
(b) In happiness and good times
(c) In prosperity and adversity
(d) In despair and failure

Ans. (c)

The idiom 'in weal and woe' means 'in both prosperity and adversity.'
It refers to being there for someone or remaining committed through both good times and bad.

158. A greenhorn
SSC CGL Tier-1 01.12.2022 (Shift-II)
(a) Uneducated person
(b) Inexperienced person
(c) Clever person
(d) Skilled person

Ans. (b)

'A greenhorn' means a person who is not experienced.

159. He was murdered <u>in cold blood</u>.
SSC CGL Tier-1 01.12.2022 (Shift-III)
(a) in wild weather
(b) deliberately
(c) when blood was cold
(d) regretfully

Ans. (b)

The underlined idiom 'in cold blood' means in a cruel or deliberate way.

160. A skeleton in the cupboard
SSC CGL Tier-1 01.12.2022 (Shift-IV)
(a) A popular fact which is not hidden
(b) A popular fact to be kept secret
(c) An embarrassing fact not to be kept secret
(d) An embarrassing fact to be kept secret

Ans. (d)

The idiom 'a skeleton in the cupboard' means an embarrassing fact to be kept secret.

161. Fly into a passion
SSC CGL Tier-1 01.12.2022 (Shift-IV)
(a) To be aggressive at times
(b) To become aggressive often
(c) To become angry suddenly
(d) To be always angry

Ans. (c)

The idiom 'fly into a passion' means 'to become angry suddenly.'

162. The interviewees were slowly becoming impatient as they were left to .... in the waiting room for hours. SSC CGL Tier-1 02.12.2022 (Shift-I)
(a) draw the long bow
(b) cool their heels
(c) hold water
(d) flog a dead horse

Ans. (b)

The phrase **'to cool one's heels'** means to have to wait for something, especially when this is annoying and boring.

163. The little boy demanded colourful balloons, ribbons in the village fair. When the father didn't pay heed to his demands, the boy made a ....
SSC CGL Tier-1 02.12.2022 (Shift-II)
(a) cloven hoof (b) wry face
(c) a far cry (d) jaundiced eye

Ans. (b)

The correct answer is **wry face** because it refers to a disdainful grimace which is used to show disappointment.

164. By the end of the football match, feelings had <u>reached fever pitch</u>.
SSC CGL Tier-1 02.12.2022 (Shift-IV)
(a) in or to many places
(b) to get so strong that one cannot control them
(c) be extremely serious and worrying
(d) start well

Ans. (b)

'Fever pitch' refers to a very high level of excitement and activity. Thus, the correct answer is 'to get so strong that one cannot control them'.

165. To smell a rat
SSC CGL Tier-1 02.12.2022 (Shift-IV)
(a) To have reason to know the presence of a rat.
(b) To have reason to suspect.
(c) To know the smell of a rat.
(d) To learn the smell of a rat.

Ans. (b)

The idiom 'to smell a rat' means 'to begin to suspect trickery or deception.' It suggests sensing that something is wrong or that someone is being dishonest.

166. We decided to .... as we were missing him a lot.
SSC CGL Tier-1 03.12.2022 (Shift-I)
(a) give a visit (b) take a visit
(c) bring in a visit (d) pay him a visit

Ans. (d)

The correct option to fill in the blank is 'pay him a visit' as is 'pay someone a visit' is a phrase which means to go somewhere or spend time with someone.

167. Seeing my messy room, my mother taught me to keep everything in order. Now my room is ....
SSC CGL Tier-1 03.12.2022 (Shift-I)
(a) on demand
(b) of no avail
(c) spick and span
(d) high and dry

Ans. (c)

The correct option to fill the blank is **'spick and span'**, which means completely neat and clean.

168. Our school had decided to take us to the Himalayas for excursion. I .... to convince my mother to give consent.
SSC CGL Tier-1 03.12.2022 (Shift-II)
(a) fought fire with fire
(b) brought home the bacon
(c) made waves
(d) left no stone unturned

Ans. (d)

The correct idiom to fill in the blank is **'left no stone unturned'** means doing every possible thing to achieve something.

169. Cut a poor figure
SSC CGL Tier-1 03.12.2022 (Shift-III)
(a) In a poor state
(b) To put a good impression
(c) To put a bad impression
(d) Bad physical form

Ans. (c)

The idiom 'Cut a poor figure' means to appear or behave badly.

So, 'to put a bad impression' gives its most appropriate meaning.

170. Bear the palm
SSC CGL Tier-1 03.12.2022 (Shift-III)
(a) To bring joyful news
(b) To lose a game
(c) To advocate peace
(d) To be a winner

Ans. (d)

The idiom 'bear the palm' means 'to be the winner' or 'take the prize.' It signifies achieving victory or coming out on top.

171. They hired her to increase sales, but her strategies failed to ....
SSC CGL Tier-1 03.12.2022 (Shift-IV)
(a) move the needle (b) burn bridges
(c) spill the beans (d) get a second wind

Ans. (a)

The correct idiom to fill the given blank is **'move the needle'** means to make a significant difference.

172. "Just add a bit of cheese to your pasta and <u>Bob's your uncle!</u>" Reena suggested to me over dinner last night.
SSC CGL Tier-1 05.12.2022 (Shift-I)
(a) It ruins everything
(b) It becomes easily and quickly achievable
(c) It changes nothing
(d) It changes the appearance

Ans. (b)

The idiom 'Bob's your uncle' means 'it becomes easily and quickly achievable.'

It is used to indicate that a task is straightforward and simple to complete.

173. The trainee wanted to know the .... of the course to get a better understanding of the job prospects.
SSC CGL Tier-1 05.12.2022 (Shift-I)
(a) ins and outs (b) birds eye view
(c) crying need (d) tall talk

Ans. (a)

The correct idiom to fill in the blank is **'ins' and 'outs'** means all the facts and details about something.

174. He was sacked from his job because of a *grave error* on his part.
SSC CGL Tier-1 05.12.2022 (Shift-III)
(a) raining cats and dogs
(b) minding one's p's and q's
(c) picking holes in one's coat
(d) Himalayan blunder

Ans. (d)

The idiom 'Himalayan blunder' means very serious mistake or error.

175. I have been a vegetarian for a *very long time*. SSC CGL Tier-1 05.12.2022 (Shift-III)
(a) donkey's years
(b) duck in the thunderstorm
(c) die in harness
(d) Damocles' sword

Ans. (a)

The idiom **'donkey's years'** means for a very long time.

176. The company's profits were low and they were forced to .... staff.
SSC CGL Tier-1 05.12.2022 (Shift-III)
(a) lisp off (b) lay off
(c) lay on (d) lie on

Ans. (b)

The correct filler for the given blank is **'Lay off'**. It means to end someone's employment, especially temporarily.

177. The announcement of the new tourism policy of the government has <u>made some people excited or interested.</u>
SSC CGL Tier-1 05.12.2022 (Shift-IV)
(a) Pull out all the stops
(b) Run around in circles
(c) Quicken the pulse
(d) Reach for the moon

Ans. (c)

The idiom 'Quicken the pulse' means to fill one with excitement, interest or anticipation. Thus, it can replace the highlighted text.

178. The lecture by the French professor seemed <u>Latin and Greek</u> to the young students.
SSC CGL Tier-1 06.12.2022 (Shift-I)
(a) Interesting (b) Lucid
(c) Unbiased (d) Incomprehensible

Ans. (d)

The idiom 'Latin and Greek' refers to something incomprehensible or difficult to understand.

179. Some people still feel that they have very little *freedom* to be innovative in their work. SSC CGL Tier-1 06.12.2022 (Shift-I)
(a) elbow room (b) an old lady
(c) an old head on young shoulders
(d) to make a pile

Ans. (a)

The idiom **elbow room** refers to the freedom to do what one wants. Thus, it can substitute the word 'freedom'.

180. When the war breaks out, all the war mongering social media activists become <u>yellow-bellied</u>.
SSC CGL Tier-1 06.12.2022 (Shift-II)
(a) Zealots (b) Cowards
(c) Sceptics (d) Upset stomachs

Ans. (b)

The term 'yellow-bellied' refers to someone who is a coward and lacks courage.

181. A rolling stone gathers no moss
SSC CGL Tier-1 06.12.2022 (Shift-III)
(a) A person who settles for a short time and runs from place to place, enjoying his freedom.
(b) A person who does not settle anywhere for a short time and is always searching for gold.
(c) A person who settles for a long time and leads a boring and useless life.
(d) A person who does not settle in one place for a long time, does not gain wealth, name or fame.

Ans. (d)

The idiom 'a rolling stone gathers no moss' means 'a person who does not settle in one place for a long time, does not gain wealth, name or fame'.

182. The great director Satyajit Ray after receiving the Honorary Academy Award from Audrey Hepburn .... in his Kolkata home.

SSC CGL Tier-1 06.12.2022 (Shift-III)

(a) breathed his last
(b) nipped in the bud
(c) kept the ball rolling
(d) dug the grave

Ans. (a)

The correct idiom to fill in the blank is **'breath one's last'**. It means to die.

183. The world needs a global leader who can hold out a *gesture of peace*.

SSC CGL Tier-1 06.12.2022 (Shift-IV)

(a) mother wit (b) halcyon days
(c) a grass widow (d) an olive branch

Ans. (d)

The idiom **'An olive branch'** means a symbol, expression or gesture of peace. So, it can substitute the italicised words.

184. Nobody in the conference seemed to believe the cock and bull story about such a major movie star.

SSC CGL Tier-1 07.12.2022 (Shift-I)

(a) Factual story
(b) Wildly exaggerated or falsified story
(c) Interesting story
(d) Secretive story

Ans. (b)

The idiom 'Cock and bull story' means a story that is obviously not true, especially given as an excuse.

185. The game is now in full swing.

SSC CGL Tier-1 07.12.2022 (Shift-I)

(a) very passive (b) very uninteresting
(c) playing on the swings
(d) very active

Ans. (d)

The idiom 'in full swing' means at a stage when the level of activity is at its highest.

186. Take something at face value

SSC CGL Tier-1 07.12.2022 (Shift-II)

(a) Accept something as it looks without thinking about whether it might, in fact, not be quite what it appears
(b) According to the appearance of something
(c) Not laugh or change your expression even though you want to laugh
(d) Show that you do not like something by making an unpleasant expression

Ans. (a)

'Take something at face value' means to accept a situation or accept what someone says, without thinking there may be a hidden meaning.

187. Turn over a new leaf

SSC CGL Tier-1 07.12.2022 (Shift-III)

(a) To begin again (b) To stop finally
(c) To plant a tree (d) To take a break

Ans. (a)

The idiom 'Turn over a new leaf' means to change your life by starting to be a better person or stopping a bad habit. Hence, 'to begin again' gives its correct meaning.

188. The health personnel advised to .... of unhealthy food habits if we want to maintain our cardio-vascular health.

SSC CGL Tier-1 07.12.2022 (Shift-IV)

(a) pay lip service
(b) keep the pot boiling
(c) run short
(d) steer clear

Ans. (d)

The idiom 'steer clear' means 'to avoid someone or something that seems unpleasant, dangerous or likely to cause problems.' It advises maintaining distance from potential trouble.

189. Cudgel one's brain

SSC CGL Tier-1 08.12.2022 (Shift-I)

(a) Thinking about a debate
(b) To think hard
(c) Not to think
(d) To overthink

Ans. (b)

The idiom 'Cudgel one's brain' means to think very hard or try to remember something one has forgotten.

190. One has to be persistent in studies if he /she wants to get his/her dream job. Success will remain unattainable if one studies......... .

SSC CGL Tier-1 08.12.2022 (Shift-I)

(a) root and branch
(b) the three R's
(c) in ups and downs
(d) by fits and starts

Ans. (d)

The correct filler to fill the blank is **'By fits and starts'**. It means periods of activity mixed with periods when nothing happens.

191. I bought some extra copies from the stationery shop. These may come in handy during exams.

SSC CGL Tier-1 08.12.2022 (Shift-II)

(a) Be useful (b) Cause trouble
(c) Be sold (d) Bring luck

Ans. (a)

The idiom 'come in handy' means 'to be useful in a particular situation.' It implies that the extra copies bought from the stationery shop might be needed and prove to be useful during exams.

192. Play it by ear

SSC CGL Tier-1 08.12.2022 (Shift-II)
SSC CHSL Tier-1 02.08.2023 (Shift-IV)

(a) To do something without special preparation
(b) To plan
(c) To listen carefully
(d) To improve

Ans. (a)

The idiom 'Play it by ear' means to decide how to deal with a situation as it develops, rather than acting according to plans made earlier. So, 'to do something without special preparation' gives its correct meaning.

193. One has to .... the risks associated with global warming.

SSC CGL Tier-1 08.12.2022 (Shift-II)

(a) cook in mind
(b) bear in mind
(c) take in mind
(d) break in mind

Ans. (b)

The correct filler to fill the blank is 'Bear in mind'. 'Bear/keep something in mind' means to remember a piece of information when you are making a decision or thinking about a matter.

194. APJ Abdul Kalam's house, located on Mosque Street was within the reach of the famous temple of Rameswaram. It was just .... from it.

SSC CGL Tier-1 08.12.2022 (Shift-IV)

(a) a stone's throw away
(b) at one's fingertip
(c) at arm's length
(d) from pillar to post

Ans. (a)

The idiom **'a stone's throw away'** means 'a short distance.' This implies that APJ Abdul Kalam's house was very close to the famous temple of Rameswaram, just a brief walk away.

195. The news of his arrest spread rapidly in every ..... of the city.

SSC CGL Tier-1 09.12.2022 (Shift-I)

(a) rack and ruin
(b) ins and outs
(c) nook and corner
(d) life and soul

Ans. (c)

The correct filler to fill the blank is **'nook and corner'**. It means every place, everywhere.

196. The activist is working really hard and was determined to .... for this cause. **SSC CGL Tier-1 09.12.2022 (Shift-I)**

(a) have feet of clay
(b) blow his own trumpet
(c) move heaven and earth
(d) keep the wolf from the door

Ans. (c)

The correct idiom to fill the blank is 'Move heaven and Earth' means to do everything that is possible to do in order to make something happen.

197. I begged him to reconsider my application, but he put his foot down.
SSC CGL Tier-1 09.12.2022 (Shift-I)

(a) stamped his foot down
(b) agreed to reconsider
(c) refused to yield
(d) did not run

Ans. (c)

The idiom 'to put one's foot down' means to refuse very firmly to do or accept something. Hence, 'refused to yield' is the most appropriate meaning of the idiom.

198. To get cold feet
SSC CGL Tier-1 09.12.2022 (Shift-I)

(a) Ranita was not selected for the job as she got cold feet.
(b) Walking bare feet on grass gave him cold feet.
(c) After too much cycling Arun got cold feet.
(d) One can swim easily with cold feet.

Ans. (a)

The idiom 'To get cold feet' means to become nervous or frightened about something because you think you will fail.

199. Lose your marbles
SSC CGL Tier-1 09.12.2022 (Shift-IV)
SSC CPO Tier-2 08.01.2024

(a) To go insane
(b) To handle stress
(c) To lower down anger
(d) To be patient

Ans. (a)

The idiom 'Lose one's marbles' means to start behaving in a crazy way. Thus, the meaning of the given idiom is 'to go insane'.

200. She has .... her money and jewellery to help the poor.
SSC CGL Tier-1 12.12.2022 (Shift-I)

(a) given way (b) given away
(c) given in (d) given up

Ans. (b)

The correct filler for the given blank is **'given away'** which means to give something as a gift.

201. The anxious duke was found strolling in the garden to and fro.
SSC CGL Tier-1 12.12.2022 (Shift-III)1

(a) From North to South
(b) From West to East
(c) Forward and backward
(d) Upward and downward

Ans. (c)

The idiom 'to and fro' means a continuous or regular movement backward and forward.

202. Red tape **SSC CGL Tier-1 12.12.2022 (Shift-IV)**

(a) Catch someone at the moment they are doing something wrong.
(b) Official rules and bureaucracy that make it difficult to do something.
(c) Have a negative amount in your bank balance.
(d) Something unimportant that takes attention away from the main subject.

Ans. (b)

'Red tape' means official rules that seem unnecessary and prevent things from being done quickly and easily.

203. Hold water
SSC CGL Tier-1 13.12.2022 (Shift-II)

(a) Stop emphasising a point
(b) Appear to be of no value
(c) A diluted argument
(d) Appear to be valid or reasonable

Ans. (d)

The idiom 'hold water' means to appear to be valid or reasonable.

204. My mother said, "*Make consistent progress for success*."
SSC CGL Tier-1 13.12.2022 (Shift-III)

(a) slow and steady
(b) make a habit
(c) in and outs
(d) do's and don'ts

Ans. (a)

The phrase 'slow and steady' means 'making consistent progress over time.' It emphasises the importance of gradual but continuous improvement, often implying that this approach leads to success.

205. A village fair is a place that contains many interesting objects. People of all age groups eagerly wait for this.
SSC CGL Tier-1 13.12.2022 (Shift-IV)

(a) Aladdin's cave
(b) Ivory tower
(c) Road to Damascus
(d) Jewel in the crown

Ans. (a)

A place that contains many interesting objects is said to be **'Aladdin's cave'**. It is a place containing a vast collection of unusual objects.

206. I must tell you that it all went pear-shaped after you left the meeting in the middle.
SSC CGL Tier-1 13.12.2022 (Shift-IV)

(a) Became very entertaining
(b) Became tragic
(c) Turned out fine
(d) Went terribly wrong

Ans. (d)

The idiom 'went pear-shaped' means 'went terribly wrong' or 'failed miserably.' It describes a situation that has taken a turn for the worse, often unexpectedly.

207. They were not able to get the item from the store because it was ....
SSC CGL Tier-1 13.12.2022 (Shift-IV)

(a) out of stock
(b) in fashion
(c) in vain
(d) on leave

Ans. (a)

The correct filler for the blank is 'Out of stock'. It means unavailable for immediate sale in a shop.

208. To rise like a phoenix

(a) To be modest **SSC CGL Tier-2 29.01.2022**
(b) To set on fire
(c) To emerge with a new life
(d) To behave like a royal

Ans. (c)

The idiom 'to rise like a phoenix' means 'to emerge with a new life.' It refers to overcoming a difficult situation and being reborn stronger, just like the mythical phoenix bird that rises from its ashes.

209. Against one's grain
SSC CGL Tier-2 29.01.2022

(a) Against the law
(b) Against the society
(c) Against one's nature
(d) Against one's family

Ans. (c)

The idiom 'against one's grain' means 'against one's nature.' It describes doing something that is contrary to one's natural tendencies or inclinations.

210. Full of hot fair **SSC CGL Tier-2 03.02.2022**

(a) Talking nonsense
(b) Talking too much
(c) Being too proud
(d) Being hot tempered

Ans. (a)

The idiom 'full of hot air' means 'talking nonsense.'

It describes someone who talks a lot but says nothing of value or importance.

211. Not make head or tail
SSC CGL Tier-2 03.02.2022
(a) very boring and not at all fun
(b) not able to understand anything
(c) not find something interesting
(d) very unusual and strange
Ans. (b)
The idiom 'not make head or tail' means 'not able to understand anything.'
It signifies being completely confused or unable to make sense of something.

212. Not mince words
SSC CGL Tier-2 03.02.2022
(a) Not to be honest
(b) To speak in a garbled way
(c) Not to come directly to the point
(d) To speak in a direct way
Ans. (d)
The idiom 'not mince words' means 'to speak in a direct way.' It refers to expressing oneself plainly and directly, without sugar-coating or avoiding the truth.

213. To take stock of SSC CGL Tier-2 03.02.2022
(a) To assess (b) To discuss
(c) To assemble (d) To modify
Ans. (a)
The idiom 'to take stock of' means 'to assess.' It involves evaluating or reviewing a situation, often to make informed decisions.

214. On tenterhooks SSC CGL Tier-2 03.02.2022
SSC CHSL Tier-1 04.08.2021 (Shift-I)
(a) Anxious and tense
(b) Happy and joyous
(c) Alert and enthusiastic
(d) Neutral and undecided
Ans. (a)
The idiom 'on tenterhooks' means 'anxious and tense.' It describes a state of nervous anticipation or suspense.

215. Fight shy of SSC CGL Tier-2 08.08.2022
(a) To invite (b) To avoid
(c) To challenge (d) To perform
Ans. (b)
The idiom 'fight shy of' means 'to avoid.' It suggests keeping away from something or someone, often out of fear or dislike.

216. Clam up SSC CGL Tier-2 08.08.2022
(a) To be upset (b) To be frustrated
(c) To become silent (d) To lose temper
Ans. (c)
The idiom 'clam up' means 'to become silent.'
It refers to stopping talking suddenly, often because of fear, shyness, or reluctance to speak.

217. All in all SSC CGL Tier-2 08.08.2022
(a) Having all authority
(b) First in line
(c) Completely lost
(d) Every person
Ans. (a)
The idiom 'all in all' means 'having all authority.' It is used to describe someone who is in complete control or has the final say.

218. Cut a sorry figure
SSC CGL Tier-2 08.08.2022
(a) Render an apology
(b) Make a sculpture
(c) Create a poor impression
(d) Break a record
Ans. (c)
The idiom 'cut a sorry figure' means 'to create a poor impression.'
It describes someone who looks unsuccessful or unimpressive.

219. Bang for the buck
SSC CGL Tier-2 13.08.2022 (Shift-I)
(a) More value for money
(b) Less value for money
(c) A sorrowful heart
(d) Dash against something
Ans. (a)
The idiom 'bang for the buck' means 'more value for money.'
It implies getting the most out of one's expenditure, achieving the best possible return on investment.

SSC CGL 2021 (Tier 1 & 2)

220. Raise the bar
SSC CGL Tier-1 13.08.2021 (Shift-I)
(a) To grow taller
(b) To win a competition
(c) To raise the price
(d) To set higher goals
Ans. (d)
To 'raise the bar' means 'raise the standards or set higher goals' which need to be met in order to qualify for something.

221. Be at a loss for words
SSC CGL Tier-1 13.08.2021 (Shift-III)
(a) Not aware of the language
(b) Not know what to say
(c) Habituated to using difficult words
(d) Lost the urge to speak
Ans. (b)
The idiom 'be at a loss for words' means 'to not know what to say.'
It describes a situation where someone is so surprised, shocked, or overwhelmed that they are unable to articulate a response.

222. Want to curl up and die
SSC CGL Tier-1 13.08.2021 (Shift-III)
(a) Unable to sleep well
(b) Want to die comfortably
(c) Too tired from physical labour
(d) Feel terribly ashamed and sorry
Ans. (d)
The idiom 'want to curl up and die' means 'to feel terribly ashamed and sorry.'
It expresses a strong desire to escape from an embarrassing or humiliating situation.

223. To cut a long story short
SSC CGL Tier-1 16.08.2021 (Shift-I)
(a) Tell something briefly
(b) Like to tell long stories
(c) Tell something in a round about way
(d) Like to tell short stories
Ans. (a)
'To cut a long story short' means to tell something in brief, rather than giving a lengthy explanation for something.

224. Full of beans
SSC CGL Tier-1 16.08.2021 (Shift-I)
(a) A storeroom full of vegetables
(b) A dish made of French beans
(c) Full of energy
(d) Full of cowardice
Ans. (c)
The idiom 'full of beans' means 'full of energy and high spirit.'
It refers to someone who is very lively, enthusiastic and energetic.

225. A storm in a teacup
SSC CGL Tier-1 16.08.2021 (Shift-III)
(a) Disarranging the cutlery
(b) Unnecessary tension
(c) Lot of fuss that will soon be forgotten
(d) A sudden storm during tea time
Ans. (c)
'A storm in a teacup' means a situation in which people are very angry or upset about something that is not important.
So, a lot of fuss created that will soon be forgotten', gives its correct meaning.

226. At the eleventh hour
SSC CGL Tier-1 16.08.2021 (Shift-III)
(a) One hour before midnight
(b) At 11:00 PM
(c) At the very last minute
(d) At 11:00 AM
Ans. (c)
'At the eleventh hour' means 'at the very last minute' or almost too late.

227. Herculean task
SSC CGL Tier-1 17.08.2021 (Shift-I)

(a) A job that requires a lot of talking and information
(b) A job that makes everyone feel proud
(c) A job that requires a large amount of physical strength
(d) A job that only weak people are assigned

Ans. (c)

'Herculean task' means 'a task that requires a large amount of physical strength' or extremely difficult task.

228. Pipe dream
SSC CGL Tier-1 17.08.2021 (Shift-I)

(a) A dream or idea that keeps getting repeated
(b) A dream or idea that is loudly proclaimed
(c) A dream or idea that is unlikely to happen
(d) A dream or idea that is nearly accomplished

Ans. (c)

The idiom 'pipe dream' means an idea or plan that is impossible or very unlikely to happen.

229. Wild goose chase
SSC CGL Tier-1 17.08.2021 (Shift-III)

(a) A safari to spot rare animals
(b) A long search for hidden prey
(c) A worthless hunt or chase
(d) Going to watch uncommon birds

Ans. (c)

'Wild goose chase' means to waste resource working on something that does not exist.

Hence, a worthless hunt or chase would be its correct meaning.

230. Pat on the back
SSC CGL Tier-1 17.08.2021 (Shift-III)

(a) Mild form of disapproval or blame
(b) Praise or approval for doing something good
(c) Good massage for aches and pains
(d) Friendly tap to push someone

Ans. (b)

'To pat on the back' means 'to praise or approval for doing something good'.

231. A stumbling block
SSC CGL Tier-1 18.08.2021 (Shift-I)

(a) Removing stones on the way
(b) Putting stones along the way
(c) An obstacle to progress
(d) Skipping over a hurdle

Ans. (c)

The idiom 'a stumbling block' means 'an obstacle to progress.'

It signifies something that hinders or prevents advancement or success.

232. A kick in the teeth
SSC CGL Tier-1 18.08.2021 (Shift-I)

(a) A grave setback
(b) Severe toothache
(c) Removing tooth cavities
(d) Hitting someone hard

Ans. (a)

'A kick in the teeth' means something that is very shocking and disappointing.

So, 'to experience a grave setback', gives its correct meaning.

233. A bad egg SSC CGL Tier-1 20.08.2021 (Shift-I)

(a) Someone who doesn't like eggs
(b) Someone who is dishonest and unreliable
(c) Someone who likes to break eggs
(d) Someone who regularly makes mistakes

Ans. (b)

A bad egg is someone who is dishonest and unreliable; a good-for-nothing.

234. Tide someone over
SSC CGL Tier-1 20.08.2021 (Shift-I)

(a) Ask someone for financial assistance
(b) Give temporary help, usually financial
(c) Get a boat ready to cross a river or water body
(d) Complete a voyage successfully

Ans. (b)

The idiom 'tide someone over' means to help someone to work or operate normally through a difficult period, usually by lending then money.

235. To pay lip service
SSC CGL Tier-1 20.08.2021 (Shift-II)

(a) To be insincere
(b) To make loud statements
(c) To talk out of turn
(d) To ask for permission

Ans. (a)

'To pay lip service' means 'to make statements without following through, or to be insincere.

236. Draw the line at something
SSC CGL Tier-1 23.08.2021 (Shift-I)

(a) Accept something upto a particular point
(b) Agreeing to an idea
(c) Making pencil sketches
(d) Coming to a conclusion

Ans. (a)

'To draw a line at something' means to 'set a limit on what one is willing to do or accept'.

So, 'accept something upto a particular point' is the most appropriate meaning of the given idiom.

237. To be light years away
SSC CGL Tier-1 23.08.2021 (Shift-II)

(a) To be too distant for human beings to reach
(b) An extremely long time from now in the past or future
(c) When something seems like it is about to happen in the near future
(d) An unlikely event that happened suddenly

Ans. (a)

The idiom 'to be light years away' means 'to be too distant for human beings to reach.'

It describes something that is extremely far away, either in space or time.

238. Feel at sea SSC CGL Tier-1 24.08.2021 (Shift-I)

(a) Feel lost or confused
(b) Fell seasick
(c) Feel angry
(d) Feel comfortable while travelling by water

Ans. (a)

'To feel at sea' means 'to feel completely lost and deeply confused.'

239. Twiddling one's thumbs
SSC CGL Tier-1 24.08.2021 (Shift-II)

(a) Feeling angry
(b) Feeling sad
(c) Feeling hungry
(d) Feeling bored

Ans. (d)

'Twiddling one's thumbs' means be bored or idle because one has nothing to do.

240. To fight tooth and nail
SSC CGL Tier-1 24.08.2021 (Shift-III)

(a) To silently leave the scene of battle
(b) To fight or compete with great ferocity and intensity
(c) To use unusual weapons to fight
(d) To keep the enemy guessing about the weapons used

Ans. (b)

'To fight tooth and nail' means to try very hard to get something you want. So, 'to fight or compete with great ferocity and intensity' gives its correct meaning.

241. The fan the flames
SSC CGL Tier-1 24.08.2021 (Shift-III)

(a) To call for help to solve an issue
(b) To resolve the issue amicably
(c) To make a bad situation worse
(d) To cool the situation

Ans. (c)

The idiom 'the fan the flames' means to make a dangerous or unpleasant situation worse.

SSC CPO 2024

242. Hit the sack SSC CPO 27.06.2024 (Shift-I)
(a) Running on the beach
(b) Cracking the exams
(c) Going to sleep
(d) Making money quickly

Ans. (c)

The idiom 'hit the sack' means 'to go to sleep.' It implies going to bed and resting.

243. Sohan was very much perplexed to find that his younger brother Mohan had taken poison.
(a) At any rate SSC CPO 27.06.2024 (Shift-I)
(b) At his wit's end
(c) At logger heads
(d) At his disposal

Ans. (b)

The idiom 'at his wit's end' means 'to be completely puzzled and perplexed, not knowing what to do.

244. Planning to go for a movie just before the final-year examination is nothing but skating on thin ice.
SSC CPO 27.06.2024 (Shift-I)
(a) doing hard work
(b) being in a risky situation
(c) enjoying the moment
(d) going to hill stations

Ans. (b)

The idiom 'skating on thin ice' means to be doing something that is dangerous or involves risks.

245. Yeoman's service
SSC CPO 27.06.2024 (Shift-I)
(a) Excellent work done
(b) A thankless and tedious job
(c) Working under a cruel master
(d) Fraudulent service

Ans. (a)

The idiom 'yeoman's service' means very good, hard and valuable work that someone does especially to support a cause, to help a team, etc.

246. The Government must strive to provide an fair and square deal to the citizen of its country.
SSC CPO 27.06.2024 (Shift-I)
(a) exclusive and unreal
(b) honest and straightforward
(c) violent and immoral
(d) forward and backward

Ans. (b)

The idiom 'fair and square' means in an honest way and without any doubt.

247. By leaps and bounds
SSC CPO 27.06.2024 (Shift-I)
(a) Unknowingly (b) Normally
(c) Slowly (d) Rapidly

Ans. (d)

The idiom 'by leaps and bounds' means 'quickly and rapidly.' It describes a significant progress or increase made at a fast pace.

248. Be in seventh heaven
SSC CPO 27.06.2024 (Shift-I)
(a) To be ignored
(b) To start performing better
(c) To be in a state of extreme happiness
(d) To avoid talking about what's important

Ans. (c)

The idiom 'be in seventh heaven' means 'to be in a state of extreme happiness.' It expresses a feeling of great joy and bliss.

249. Bread and butter
SSC CPO 27.06.2024 (Shift-I)
SSC CPO 28.06.2024 (Shift-III)
SSC CHSL Tier 1 05.07.2024 (Shift-III)
(a) Comfortable living
(b) Means of livelihood
(c) The breakfast
(d) Money making

Ans. (d)

The idiom 'bread and butter' means the way of earning a livelihood or money.

250. Go down in flames
SSC CPO 27.06.2024 (Shift-II)
(a) To fail spectacularly
(b) To destroy completely
(c) To crash and burn
(d) To burn down completely

Ans. (a)

To go down in flames means to 'to fail spectacularly; to end suddenly and completely; be utterly ruined or wrecked'.

251. Only those having blue blood can dethrone the evil autocrat and restore equilibrium. SSC CPO 27.06.2024 (Shift-II)
(a) Political ideology
(b) Vigilant nature
(c) Aristocratic lineage
(d) Bitter relations

Ans. (c)

The idiom **'blue blood'** refers to someone of noble or aristocratic lineage.

252. Though Kalpana listened to Sheetal carefully, she knew that she should take it with a grain of salt.
SSC CPO 27.06.2024 (Shift-II)
(a) accept it as really useful and worthy
(b) move according to the trend
(c) regard it as exaggerated and not completely true
(d) be do it meticulously as taking salt

Ans. (c)

The idiom 'to take it with a grain of salt' means regard something as exaggerated; believe only part of something.

253. At the drop of a hat
SSC CPO 27.06.2024 (Shift-II)
(a) Consecutively (b) Eventually
(c) Certainly (d) Immediately

Ans. (d)

The idiom 'at the drop of a hat' means to do something immediately or without hesitation.

254. I will always stand by my friend.
SSC CPO 27.06.2024 (Shift-II)
(a) Be in a queue
(b) Stand next to
(c) Support in difficult situation
(d) Work together

Ans. (c)

The idiom 'stand by' in the context of the given situation means to support someone, especially in difficult times.

255. Read the books of APJ Abdul Kalam, who was a scholar.
SSC CPO 27.06.2024 (Shift-II)
(a) a queer fish (b) a man of letters
(c) a dare devil (d) a man of straw

Ans. (b)

The idiom **'a man of letters'** refers to 'someone who is a scholar or well-educated in literature and scholarly works.'

A queer fish is an unusual or eccentric person.

A dare devil is someone who enjoys taking dangerous risks.

A man of straw is a person of little substance or influence, often used as a front.

256. After the Pandemic, his business crumbled and he is in a difficult situation. SSC CPO 27.06.2024 (Shift-II)
(a) Bolt from the blue
(b) Give a cold shoulder
(c) Pull the last straw
(d) Be in a tight corner

Ans. (d)

The idiom **'be in a tight corner'** means 'to be in a difficult situation.' It describes a scenario where someone is facing problems or challenges that are hard to overcome.

Bolt from the blue means a sudden and unexpected event.

Give a cold shoulder means to ignore or show indifference.

Pull the last straw refers to the final problem or annoyance that leads to a tipping point.

257. Ignoring his father's warnings, he said, 'an elephant in the room' to his mother. SSC CPO 27.06.2024 (Shift-II)
(a) The elephant got stuck in the room
(b) There is an obvious problem
(c) Someone begins to suspect
(d) Someone hiding in the room

Ans. (b)

The idiom 'an elephant in the room' refers to an obvious problem or issue that everyone is aware of but chooses to ignore or avoid discussing.

258. I invited them to my anniversary dinner but they had other plans, so they decided to politely decline with the implication that they may come at a later date. SSC CPO 27.06.2024 (Shift-III)
(a) To spoil a moment
(b) To take a rain check
(c) Call it a day
(d) Took it with a grain of salt

Ans. (b)

The idiom **'to take a rain check'** means 'to politely decline with the implication that one may come at a later date.' It is a way of postponing an invitation or offer.

To spoil a moment means to ruin a special or enjoyable event.

Call it a day means to stop working or end an activity.

Took it with a grain of salt means to view something with skepticism or doubt.

259. He is very strict with his students but good-natured. SSC CPO 27.06.2024 (Shift-III)
(a) his eyes are bigger than his stomach
(b) his heart is in the right place
(c) he has a big mouth
(d) his heart misses a beat

Ans. (b)

The idiom **'his heart is in the right place'** means 'he has good intentions.' Despite being strict, his actions are motivated by a genuine desire to do good.

His eyes are bigger than his stomach means desiring more than one can manage or handle.

He has a big mouth means someone who talks too much or reveals secrets.

His heart misses a beat refers to a moment of surprise or excitement.

260. Popular cosmetics brands in India are very expensive. SSC CPO 27.06.2024 (Shift-III)
(a) up in arms
(b) flog a dead horse
(c) take it with a pinch of salt
(d) cost an arm and a leg

Ans. (d)

The idiom **'cost an arm and a leg'** means 'very expensive.' It implies that something costs a lot of money.

Up in arms means being very angry or upset about something.

Flog a dead horse means to waste effort on something that has no chance of succeeding.

Take it with a pinch of salt means to view something with skepticism or doubt.

261. To leave no stone unturned SSC CPO 27.06.2024 (Shift-III)
(a) To win everything that is available
(b) To control a person completely
(c) To do everything possible to achieve something
(d) To treat someone/something as if of no importance

Ans. (c)

The idiom 'to leave no stone unturned' means try every possible course of action in order to achieve something.

262. When I went to Egypt and lost my wallet and passport, I was .... SSC CPO 27.06.2024 (Shift-III)
(a) rolling up my sleeves
(b) putting my nose to the grindstone
(c) working my fingers to the bone
(d) up in a creek without a paddle

Ans. (d)

The correct idiom to fill in the blank is **'up in the creek without the paddle'**. The idiom means in trouble, in a serious predicament which fits the context perfectly.

263. John was always .... about becoming a millionaire without doing any hard work. SSC CPO 27.06.2024 (Shift-III)
(a) a storm in a tea cup
(b) eating like a horse
(c) building castles in the air
(d) having an ace up his sleeve

Ans. (c)

The correct idiom to fill in the blank is **'building castles in the air'**. The idiom refers to the habit of daydreaming which fits the context perfectly.

264. The players like the coach because he is honest, realistic and practical in dealing with them. SSC CPO 27.06.2024 (Shift-III)
(a) down to earth (b) by and large
(c) far and wide (d) sick and tired

Ans. (a)

The most appropriate idiom that can substitute the underlined words is 'down to earth'. This idiom means that practical and modest.

265. Despite multiple obstacles, she continued with her endeavour, demonstrating that she has nerves of steel. SSC CPO 28.06.2024 (Shift-I)
(a) Extraordinary beauty
(b) An absence of fear or anxiety
(c) Relentless determination
(d) The capacity to maintain composure when stressed

Ans. (b)

The idiom 'nerves of steel' is used for someone who can face situations without fear or anxiety, remaining calm and composed.

266. Its Christmas and everything looks so beautiful. It makes me believe that life is wonderful and pleasant. SSC CPO 28.06.2024 (Shift-I)
(a) I'm up in the air
(b) I'm facing the music
(c) I'm changing my tune
(d) life is a bowl of cherries

Ans. (d)

The idiom **life is a bowl of cherries** means 'life is wonderful and pleasant.' It suggests that life is full of enjoyable moments and is often used to express contentment and happiness.

I'm up in the air means to be uncertain or undecided.

I'm facing the music means to accept the consequences of one's actions.

I'm changing my tune means to change one's opinion or attitude.

267. Mathew decided to complete the marathon to prove that he is still fit as a fiddle in his eighties. SSC CPO 28.06.2024 (Shift-I) SSC CPO 05.10.2023 (Shift-I)
(a) an owner of a fit horse
(b) a man of great qualities
(c) proud and unreliable
(d) a fit and energetic person

Ans. (d)

The idiom 'fit as a fiddle' means a healthy, fit and energetic person. It describes someone who is healthy and in excellent physical condition.

268. The manager, decided at last to bring the stenographer to book for her illegal money transactions after trying to ignore it several times. SSC CPO 28.06.2024 (Shift-I)
(a) bring her for a detailed investigation
(b) take her into great confidence
(c) place her in a safe supportive position
(d) make her accountable for her conduct

Ans. (d)

The phrase 'bring to book' means to hold someone accountable for their actions.

269. We need to make sure that criminals like these get more from the authorities than a very mild punishment. **SSC CPO 28.06.2024 (Shift-I)**

(a) a slap on the wrist
(b) an axe to grind
(c) a blessing in disguise
(d) a taste of their own medicine

Ans. (a)

The idiom **'a slap on the wrist'** means 'a very mild punishment.' It suggests that the punishment is not severe enough for the offence committed.

An axe to grind means having a personal interest or grievance.

A blessing in disguise means something that seems bad at first but turns out to be good.

A taste of their own medicine means to experience the same unpleasant treatment that one has given to others.

270. In life, there will be many situations where you have to choose between the devil and the deep blue sea. **SSC CPO 28.06.2024 (Shift-I)**

(a) To be in dilemma to choose
(b) To be in the deep sea
(c) To be in a good condition
(d) To choose wisely

Ans. (a)

The idiom 'between the devil and the deep blue sea' means to be faced with two equally difficult choices or options, often in a dilemma where neither choice is desirable.

271. I don't know which career he will choose. He delays making strong decisions. **SSC CPO 28.06.2024 (Shift-I)**

(a) sits on the fence
(b) is as clean as a whistle
(c) turns a blind eye
(d) spills the beans

Ans. (a)

The idiom **'sits on the fence'** means 'delays making strong decisions.' It describes someone who is indecisive or avoids committing to a side.

Is as clean as a whistle means to be very clean or free of wrongdoing.

Turns a blind eye means to ignore something intentionally.

Spills the beans means to reveal a secret.

272. After his business failed, he had to reduce spending and adjust to a frugal lifestyle. **SSC CPO 28.06.2024 (Shift-II)**

(a) tighten his belt
(b) hit the nail on the head
(c) let the cat out of the bag
(d) kick the bucket

Ans. (a)

The idiom **'tighten his belt'** means 'to reduce spending and adjust to a frugal lifestyle.' It implies making financial cutbacks and living more economically.

Hit the nail on the head means to accurately identify or solve a problem.

Let the cat out of the bag means to reveal a secret.

Kick the bucket means to die.

273. Black sheep **SSC CPO 28.06.2024 (Shift-II)**

(a) Naive (b) Miscreant
(c) Disreputable (d) Intelligent

Ans. (c)

The idiom 'black sheep' typically refers to a person who is considered disgraceful or disreputable within a group or family, often behaving in a way that contrasts with the others who are more respectable or virtuous.

274. During the preparation for competitive exams, Meena avoided going to parties. **SSC CPO 28.06.2024 (Shift-II)**

(a) cracked a joke
(b) steered clear of
(c) fired a cracker
(d) whispered a secret

Ans. (b)

The idiom **'steered clear of'** means 'to avoid.' It suggests deliberately staying away from something or someone.

Cracked a joke means to tell a joke.

Fired a cracker means to set off a firecracker (literal meaning, not an idiom here).

Whispered a secret means to tell someone a secret in a quiet voice.

275. When pigs fly **SSC CPO 28.06.2024 (Shift-II)**

(a) Something that will never last long
(b) Something that will never deviate
(c) Something that will get completed
(d) Something that will never happen

Ans. (d)

The idiom 'when pigs fly' is used to describe something that will never happen or is highly unlikely to occur.

276. He always takes up difficult tasks – those which are beyond his capabilities. **SSC CPO 28.06.2024 (Shift-II)**

(a) Pull someone's leg
(b) Bite off more than you can chew
(c) No pain no gain
(d) Miss the boat

Ans. (b)

The idiom **'bite off more than you can chew'** means 'to take on more than one can handle.'

It describes someone who undertakes tasks or responsibilities that are beyond their ability to manage.

Pull someone's leg means to joke or tease someone.

No pain no gain refers to the the idea that effort and suffering are necessary to achieve success.

277. Have your head in the clouds **SSC CPO 28.06.2024 (Shift-II)**

(a) He had his head in the clouds during an important meeting.
(b) The pilot had his head in the clouds while flying a plane.
(c) They had their heads in the clouds by looking up at the sky during a meteor shower.
(d) She had her head in the clouds by wearing a cloud-shaped hat.

Ans. (a)

The idiom 'have your head in the clouds' means to be unaware of what is happening because you are thinking about something that is not practical or possible.

The sentence that correctly uses the idiom is -"He had his head in the clouds during an important meeting".

278. Sacred cow **SSC CPO 28.06.2024 (Shift-II)**

(a) Interrogate (b) Unquestionable
(c) Harmful (d) Hateful

Ans. (b)

The idiom 'sacred cow' refers to something that is regarded as immune from questioning or criticism, often due to its perceived sacredness or importance.

279. Amar was left in a difficult situation by his business partners. **SSC CPO 28.06.2024 (Shift-II)**

(a) High and dry
(b) Hard and fast
(c) Head and shoulders above
(d) Heart and soul

Ans. (a)

The idiom **'high and dry'** means 'left in a difficult situation.' It describes someone who has been abandoned and left to deal with problems alone.

Hard and fast means strict and unchanging.

Miss the boat means to miss an opportunity.

Head and shoulders above means far superior to others.

Heart and soul means fully committed or dedicated.

280. A team's captain always keeps a level head, even in the most challenging situations. SSC CPO 28.06.2024 (Shift-III)
(a) Prefers to keep his head covered with a cap
(b) Maintains an equal number of players on the field
(c) Remains calm and composed
(d) Keeps his head protected with a helmet

Ans. (c)

The idiom 'keeps a level head' means to remain calm and composed, especially during difficult or stressful situations.

281. Even after becoming bankrupt, Charlie is able to maintain an outward show SSC CPO 28.06.2024 (Shift-III)
(a) bring down the house
(b) keep up appearances
(c) bell the cat
(d) cut a sorry figure

Ans. (b)

The idiom **'keep up appearances'** means 'to maintain an outward show.' It refers to maintaining a facade of normalcy despite underlying difficulties.

Bring down the house means to receive an enthusiastic response from an audience.

Bell the cat means to take on a difficult or risky task.

Cut a sorry figure means to make a poor impression.

282. Get itchy feet SSC CPO 28.06.2024 (Shift-III)
(a) Judge something primarily on appearance
(b) Learn something by memorising it without a thought to what is being learnt
(c) To start to want to travel or do something different
(d) Join a popular trend or activity

Ans. (c)

The idiom 'get itchy feet' means to start to want to travel or do something different, often due to a desire for change or adventure.

283. He's still keeping his chin up despite all his health problems. SSC CPO 28.06.2024 (Shift-III)
(a) To keep ones chin clean and moist
(b) To stay safe during difficulty
(c) To stay cheerful during difficult times
(d) To save others during difficult times

Ans. (c)

The underlined phrase 'keeping his chin up' means to stay cheerful and optimistic during difficult times or adversity.

284. On thin ice SSC CPO 28.06.2024 (Shift-III)
(a) In a risky position
(b) Communicating with friends
(c) On a summer vacation
(d) On an investigating job

Ans. (a)

'On thin ice' describes being in a situation where one is at risk of causing trouble or facing consequences.

285. Keep your pants on SSC CPO 28.06.2024 (Shift-III)
(a) To wear the dress neatly
(b) To keep calm and quiet
(c) To make things proper
(d)To work like a tailor

Ans. (b)

The idiom 'keep your pants on' means to remain patient and composed.

286. Reena decided not to go to work today because she was feeling sick. SSC CPO 28.06.2024 (Shift-III)
(a) under the weather
(b) fit as a fiddle
(c) sitting on the fence
(d) going down in flames

Ans. (a)

The idiom **'under the weather'** means 'feeling sick.' It describes someone who is not feeling well.

Fit as a fiddle means in excellent health.

Going down in flames means failing spectacularly.

Sitting on the fence means to be in a dilemma.

287. Nip in the bud SSC CPO 29.06.2024 (Shift-I)
(a) To publicise a long-kept secret
(b) To stop something from growing beyond limit
(c) To complete a prolonged or unfinished work
(d) To suppress something at an early stage

Ans. (d)

The idiom 'nip in the bud' means to suppress something at an early stage, before it can develop into something larger or more serious.

288. Spill the beans SSC CPO 29.06.2024 (Shift-III) SSC CHSL Tier 1 05.07.2024 (Shift-IV)
(a) Reveal a secret
(b) Accomplish a lot
(c) Cornered by someone
(d) Tremble at possibilities

Ans. (a)

The idiom 'spill the beans' means to reveal a secret or disclose confidential information, often unintentionally or prematurely.

289. She now has more than a year as minister .... SSC CPO 29.06.2024 (Shift-I)
(a) under her belt
(b) on her thin ice
(c) in the fast lane
(d) down for the count

Ans. (a)

The idiom **'under her belt'** means 'to have achieved or acquired.' It indicates that she has gained experience or accomplishment.

On thin ice means in a risky or precarious situation.

In the fast lane means living a high-paced, sometimes risky life.

Down for the count means defeated or out of action.

290. From cradle to grave SSC CPO 29.06.2024 (Shift-I)
(a) Buying something very cheap or very expensive
(b) During the whole span of one's life
(c) Giving directions and telling someone to follow
(d) To achieve something you needed

Ans. (b)

The idiom 'from cradle to grave' means during the whole span of one's life, encompassing all stages from birth to death.

291. A piece of cake SSC CPO 29.06.2024 (Shift-I)
(a) A slice of sweet
(b) Something very easy
(c) A miserable person
(d) A difficult situation

Ans. (b)

The idiom 'a piece of cake' means something that is very easy to accomplish.

292. See eye to eye SSC CPO 29.06.2024 (Shift-I)
(a) To agree with someone
(b) To ignore someone
(c) To get upset with something
(d) To do something pointless

Ans. (a)

The idiom 'see eye to eye' means to agree with someone, especially in terms of opinions or viewpoints.

293. Chip on the shoulder SSC CPO 29.06.2024 (Shift-I)
(a) Happy (b) Offended
(c) Emotional (d) Elated

Ans. (b)

The idiom 'chip on the shoulder' refers to a persistent attitude of resentment or a grudge, often resulting from a feeling of inferiority or perceived injustice.

294. The meaning of which of the following options is good luck?
SSC CPO 29.06.2024 (Shift-I)

(a) Second banana (b) All wet
(c) Hang in there (d) Break a leg

Ans. (d)

The phrase 'Break a leg' is commonly used as a theatrical slang for wishing someone good luck.

Second banana means a supporter.

All wet means to be mistaken about something.

Hang in there means to continue trying despite failures.

295. She's feeling under the weather today. **SSC CPO 29.06.2024 (Shift-II)**

(a) She's feeling happy and energetic.
(b) She's feeling adventurous and ready for a challenge.
(c) She's feeling worried about something.
(d) She's not feeling well or is a bit sick.

Ans. (d)

The idiom 'under the weather' means that someone is not feeling well or is slightly sick.

296. A vicious cycle **SSC CPO 29.06.2024 (Shift-II)**

(a) a situation in which one problem causes another one, making the original problem impossible to solve.
(b) a situation in which one problem causes another one, making the first one easy to solve.
(c) a situation in which one problem creates another one, making the original problem easy to forget.
(d) a situation in which several problems merge and become one extremely complex problem.

Ans. (a)

The idiom 'a vicious cycle' refers to a situation where one problem or negative factor exacerbates another, leading to a worsening or self-perpetuating cycle.

297. The best of both worlds
SSC CPO 29.06.2024 (Shift-II)
SSC CPO 03.10.2023 (Shift-II)

(a) Everyone gets a chance
(b) Stay strong in a difficult situation
(c) Do a perfectly good job
(d) Good in every way

Ans. (d)

The idiom 'the best of both worlds' means to have the advantages or benefits of two different things at the same time, usually where one might expect to have to choose between them.

298. I have been living without a lot of money since I lost my job.
SSC CPO 29.06.2024 (Shift-II)

(a) receiving a kickback
(b) living hand to mouth
(c) keeping my chin up
(d) as genuine as a three-dollar bill

Ans. (b)

The most appropriate idiom that can substitute the underlined words is **'living hand to mouth.'**

This idiom means living with just enough money to cover basic needs, without any surplus. It accurately describes the situation of living without a lot of money.

299. At the last hour
SSC CPO 29.06.2024 (Shift-II)

(a) half (b) eleventh
(c) sixth (d) twelfth

Ans. (b)

The idiom 'at the eleventh hour' typically means doing something at the very last possible moment or just before a deadline.

300. Make waves **SSC CPO 29.06.2024 (Shift-III)**

(a) To cause difficulty
(b) To give up
(c) To take it easy
(d) To have patience

Ans. (a)

The idiom 'make waves' means to create trouble or disruption, especially by challenging the status quo or causing controversy.

301. Don't you think that the cats in the cradle? You never make time for me.
SSC CPO 29.06.2024 (Shift-III)

(a) Newly married life
(b) Busy in your work
(c) Complicated relationship
(d) Busy in minting money

Ans. (c)

The idiom 'cats in the cradle' suggests a complicated relationship. This interpretation sees the idiom extending beyond its typical meaning, where it often refers to neglect or absence rather than specifically complexity.

302. Up the ante **SSC CPO 29.06.2024 (Shift-III)**

(a) Increase demands
(b) Cost cutting
(c) Mediocre
(d) Expensive

Ans. (a)

The idiom 'up the ante' means to raise the stakes or increase the level of something, often referring to increasing demands or expectations.

303. All the kith and kin of my deceased landlady were present to attend her funeral. **SSC CPO 29.06.2024 (Shift-III)**

(a) office colleagues
(b) secret enemies
(c) special students
(d) blood relatives

Ans. (d)

The idiom 'kith and kin' collectively refers to one's family and relatives, encompassing both close family members (kin) and friends or acquaintances (kith) who are considered as part of one's social circle.

304. The team always .... to come up with unique advertisements for all its clients. **SSC CPO 29.06.2024 (Shift-III)**

(a) thinks outside the box
(b) throw caution to the winds
(c) take a back seat
(d) turn the tables

Ans. (a)

The correct filler for the given blank is **'thinks outside the box'**.

It implies thinking creatively or finding new solutions that are not limited by established norms or conventions.

305. I sometimes accept excess work to please my manager, so I take more responsibilities than one can manage.
SSC CPO 29.06.2024 (Shift-III)

(a) bite off more than I can chew
(b) get a taste of my own medicine
(c) burn my boats
(d) hear it straight from the horses mouth

Ans. (a)

The idiom **'bite off more than you I can chew'** means 'to take on more responsibilities than one can manage.'

Get a taste of your own medicine means to experience the same unpleasantness you have given to others.

Burn your boats means to commit irrevocably to a course of action.

Hear it straight from the horse's mouth means to get information directly from the source.

306. Rathna is known for .... tears.
SSC CPO 29.06.2024 (Shift-III)

(a) students
(b) babies
(c) animals
(d) crocodile

Ans. (d)

The correct filler is 'crocodile'. The phrase 'crocodile tears' refers to insincere or fake tears—tears that are not genuine but rather meant to manipulate or deceive.

307. Back to back **SSC CPO 29.06.2024 (Shift-III)**
(a) Present and discuss the details of something.
(b) Do something very fast or with great energy.
(c) Something follows immediately after something else.
(d) Try to get something.

Ans. (c)

The idiom 'back to back' refers to events or situations occurring consecutively without interruption.

308. Bring to book **SSC CPO Tier-2 08.01.2024**
(a) punish someone
(b) teach someone
(c) calm someone
(d) support someone

Ans. (a)

The idiom 'bring to book' means 'to punish someone.' It refers to holding someone accountable for their actions.

309. Split one's sides **SSC CPO Tier-2 08.01.2024**
(a) meet with an accident
(b) be extremely amused
(c) scream in pain
(d) undergo a surgery

Ans. (b)

The idiom 'split one's sides' means 'to be extremely amused.' It describes laughing very hard.

310. A mare's nest **SSC CPO Tier-2 08.01.2024**
SSC CPO Tier-1 09.11.2022 (Shift-II)
(a) a familiar situation
(b) a new situation
(c) a refreshing situation
(d) a confused situation

Ans. (d)

The idiom 'a mare's nest' means 'a confused situation.' It refers to a mess or muddle.

311. Rock the boat **SSC CPO Tier-2 08.01.2024**
(a) divert someone's attention
(b) overcome a difficult situation
(c) disturb a stable situation
(d) pester and irritate someone

Ans. (c)

The idiom 'rock the boat' means 'to disturb a stable situation.'

It implies causing trouble or disruption.

312. Have your heart in your mouth
SSC CPO Tier-2 08.01.2024
(a) to get worse and worse
(b) be extremely frightened
(c) to be extremely jealous
(d) to behave in a foolish manner

Ans. (b)

The idiom 'have your heart in your mouth' means 'to be extremely frightened.' It describes a state of intense fear or anxiety.

313. Forty winks **SSC CPO Tier-2 08.01.2024**
(a) a short sleep (b) a deep sleep
(c) a secret signal (d) a long leave

Ans. (a)

The idiom 'forty winks' means 'a short sleep.' It refers to a brief nap.

314. Cut from the same cloth
SSC CPO Tier-2 08.01.2024
(a) to be of a similar nature
(b) to come from the same source
(c) to share resources
(d) belong to the same family

Ans. (a)

The idiom 'cut from the same cloth' means 'to be of a similar nature.' It suggests that two people or things share similar characteristics.

SSC CPO 2023

315. An arm and a leg
SSC CPO 03.10.2023 (Shift-I)
(a) To ask for too much
(b) A large amount of money
(c) Everything is ready
(d) To be lost and bewildered

Ans. (b)

The idiom 'an arm and a leg' means 'a large amount of money.'
It suggests that something is very expensive.

316. A leopard can't change his spots.
SSC CPO 03.10.2023 (Shift-I)
(a) Someone who is cherished above all others
(b) A visual presentation is far more descriptive than words
(c) Something good that isn't recognised at first
(d) You cannot change who you are

Ans. (d)

'A leopard can't change his spots' means a person cannot change who he/she is.

317. Students often burn the midnight oil to qualify for competitive examinations. **SSC CPO 03.10.2023 (Shift-I)**
(a) put the things on fire at night
(b) want to be at a place full of light
(c) work until late at night
(d) sleep well

Ans. (c)

The idiom 'burn the midnight oil' means 'to work until late at night.' It is often used to describe the hard work and long hours students put in to prepare for exams.

318. Both Nitin and Uday are of the same interests. **SSC CPO 03.10.2023 (Shift-I)**
(a) under the weather
(b) birds of the same feather
(c) blowing smoke without fire
(d) different kettles of fish

Ans. (b)

The idiom **'birds of the same feather'** means 'people with similar interests.' It suggests that Nitin and Uday share common interests and get along well.

319. Bend over backwards
SSC CPO 03.10.2023 (Shift-I)
(a) Working hard to try to impress
(b) Working slowly and lazily
(c) Going backward
(d) Using wrongful means

Ans. (a)

'Bend over backwards' means to make every effort to achieve something, especially to be fair or helpful.

320. We dodged a bullet when we didn't fall for the agents' words.
SSC CPO 03.10.2023 (Shift-I)
(a) To give something a try
(b) To narrowly avoid situation
(c) To be out of your comfort zone
(d) To start performing better

Ans. (b)

The underlined idiom 'dodged a bullet' means 'to have escaped a bad situation'.

321. Arunima .... a lot during her vacation time. **SSC CPO 03.10.2023 (Shift-I)**
(a) gets on (b) gets after
(c) gets about (d) gets along

Ans. (c)

The correct filler for the given blank is **'gets about'**. It means to be socially active.

322. I hate to get off on the wrong foot.
SSC CPO 03.10.2023 (Shift-I)
(a) To start something with positive factors
(b) To start something with neutral factors
(c) To start a relationship or activity badly
(d) To start something with an injury on the wrong foot

Ans. (c)

'To get off on the wrong foot' means to make a bad start at something, especially a task or relationship.

323. More people in Turkey are on the breadline now than thirty years ago.
(a) Be very poor **SSC CPO 03.10.2023 (Shift-I)**
(b) Are well educated
(c) Be very expensive
(d) Earn a lot of money

Ans. (a)

The idiom 'on the breadline' means 'to be very poor.' It describes people who are living in poverty and struggling to make ends meet.

324. Left out in the cold **SSC CPO 03.10.2023 (Shift-I)**

(a) To serve stale and cold food
(b) To leave in hurry
(c) To bear extreme weather condition
(d) To be ignored

Ans. (d)

The idiom 'left out in the cold' means 'to be ignored or excluded.' It describes a situation where someone is not included in a group or activity.

325. I think we should...... before buying this car. **SSC CPO 03.10.2023 (Shift-II, III)**

(a) eat like a horse
(b) get off our high horse
(c) hold our horses
(d) stop to change horses

Ans. (c)

The idiom 'hold our horses' means 'to be patient.' It suggests that we should wait and think carefully before making a decision, such as buying a car.

326. All my efforts went in vain. The project on which I was working for the last two months has failed and we are .... **SSC CPO 03.10.2023 (Shift-II)**

(a) around the bend
(b) back to square one
(c) all in the seventh heaven
(d) on the fly

Ans. (b)

The idiom 'back to square one' means 'to start over from the beginning.' It suggests that after the project failed, all efforts have gone to waste and they have to start again.

327. Crack someone up **SSC CPO 03.10.2023 (Shift-II)**

(a) To criticise someone
(b) To make someone angry
(c) To make someone laugh
(d) To force someone to commit a mistake

Ans. (c)

The idiom 'crack someone up' means 'to make someone laugh.' It describes making someone laugh hard or finding something very funny.

328. What a small world! **SSC CPO 03.10.2023 (Shift-II)**

(a) What a coincidence!
(b) What a beautiful place!
(c) The world is a village.
(d) The world is great.

Ans. (a)

The idiom 'what a small world!' means 'what a coincidence!' It expresses surprise at meeting someone unexpectedly or discovering that you have mutual acquaintances.

329. Any sort of unfair conduct is not tolerated in international sports tournaments as it can completely ruin an athlete's career. **SSC CPO 03.10.2023 (Shift-II)**

(a) hand in the mud
(b) straw in the eye
(c) red handed
(d) foul play

Ans. (d)

The idiom 'foul play' means 'unfair conduct.' It refers to dishonest or deceitful actions that can ruin an athlete's career.

330. We should ask Emily to join our team. She is as keen as butter. **SSC CPO 03.10.2023 (Shift-II)**

(a) as keen as a bee
(b) as keen as salt
(c) as keen as mustard
(d) as keen as sugar

Ans. (c)

The idiom 'as keen as mustard' means 'very enthusiastic or eager.' It suggests that Emily is very enthusiastic and would be a good addition to the team.

331. He really *stinks and smells foul* after a hard session at the gym. **SSC CPO 03.10.2023 (Shift-II)**

(a) lame excuse (b) pen and ink
(c) an iron will (d) an old flame

Ans. (b)

The idiom **'pen and ink'** means 'to stinks or smells foul.' It refers to a strong, unpleasant odour.

Lame excuse means a poor or unconvincing justification.

An iron will means strong determination.

An old flame means a former romantic partner.

332. Ravi has a strong desire to be in college hockey team this year and he is working hard to gain such skills to fulfill his goal of life. He has clearly made up his mind to achieve his target. **SSC CPO 03.10.2023 (Shift-II)**

(a) Set sights on
(b) To move the goal posts
(c) To rise to the occasion
(d) To make the cut

Ans. (a)

The idiom **'set sights on'** means 'to have a strong desire to achieve a particular goal.' It indicates that Ravi is determined to join the college hockey team.

To move the goal posts means to change the rules or expectations in a way that makes success more difficult.

To rise to the occasion means to perform well in response to a challenge.

To make the cut means to meet the requirements or standards.

333. I was going to mention it, but it .... . **SSC CPO 03.10.2023 (Shift-III)**

(a) bore in mind
(b) slipped my mind
(c) changed my mind
(d) brought to mind

Ans. (b)

The idiom **'slipped my mind'** means 'to forget.' It indicates that the person intended to mention something but forgot.

Bore in mind means to remember or consider something.

Changed my mind means to alter one's decision or opinion.

Brought to mind means to remind someone of something.

334. I like her because she never likes to make .... **SSC CPO 03.10.2023 (Shift-III)**

(a) a drop in the bucket
(b) a quick buck
(c) a slap on the wrist
(d) a bed of roses

Ans. (b)

The idiom **'a quick buck'** means 'to make money easily.' It suggests that she does not try to make money quickly and perhaps unscrupulously.

A drop in the bucket means a very small amount compared to what is needed.

A slap on the wrist means a mild punishment.

A bed of roses means a situation that is comfortable and easy.

335. Keep count of **SSC CPO 03.10.2023 (Shift-III)**

(a) To act more politely
(b) To accept an invitation
(c) To remember a total
(d) To remind of a deadline

Ans. (c)

The idiom 'keep count of' means 'to remember a total.' It involves keeping track of numbers or amounts.

336. Grasping at straws **SSC CPO 03.10.2023 (Shift-III)**

(a) Trying to find the best way to compete with others when nothing you choose is likely to work
(b) Trying to find some way to succeed when nothing you choose is likely to work
(c) Trying to find some way to succeed when you see others are also doing the same
(d) Trying to find manipulative ways to succeed

Ans. (b)

The idiom 'grasping at straws' means 'trying to find some way to succeed when nothing you choose is likely to work.' It indicates desperation and futility in one's efforts.

337. You cannot throw dust into my eyes.

(a) hurt me **SSC CPO 03.10.2023 (Shift-III)**
(b) terrify me
(c) abuse me
(d) mislead or deceive me

Ans. (d)

The idiom **'throw dust into my eyes'** means 'to mislead or deceive me.' It refers to attempting to distract or confuse someone.

338. A plum job **SSC CPO 03.10.2023 (Shift-III)**

(a) A difficult job
(b) A rare job
(c) A job involving extensive travelling
(d) An easy and pleasant job

Ans. (d)

The idiom **'a plum job'** means 'an easy and pleasant job.' It refers to a job that is highly desirable and comes with good conditions.

339. He made a mess of that bookcase he was supposed to be repairing.
SSC CPO 03.10.2023 (Shift-III)

(a) brought a dog's breast
(b) made a clean breast
(c) made a pig's ear
(d) had a butcher hook

Ans. (c)

The idiom **'made a pig's ear'** means 'to make a mess of something.' It indicates that the repair job was done poorly.

340. Keep a straight face
SSC CPO 03.10.2023 (Shift-III)

(a) Get on extremely well with someone
(b) Not laugh or change your expression even though you want to laugh
(c) Become very confused
(d) Make more of an effort

Ans. (b)

The idiom 'keep a straight face' means 'not laugh or change your expression even though you want to laugh.' It describes maintaining composure.

341. Face the music
SSC CPO 03.10.2023 (Shift-III)

(a) To work every possible way to succeed
(b) To be cheated by someone you trust
(c) To have the problems with money
(d) To accept punishment for some mistakes which you have done

Ans. (d)

The idiom **'face the music'** means 'to accept punishment for some mistakes which you have done.' It suggests taking responsibility for one's actions.

342. Ram could not go to Delhi for vacation since he was banking on his arrears of pay which he did not get in time. **SSC CPO 03.10.2023 (Shift-III)**

(a) Calling on
(b) Sloping on
(c) Relying on
(d) Depending on his bank

Ans. (c)

The idiom **'relying on'** means 'depending on something or someone.' In this case, it means Ram was depending on his arrears of pay.

343. Our Director took a meeting and asked us to express our views on .... of the new HR policy.
SSC CPO 04.10.2023 (Shift-I)

(a) the pros and cons
(b) the ups and downs
(c) the bandwagon
(d) the hook

Ans. (a)

The idiom **'the pros and cons'** means 'the advantages and disadvantages.' It refers to considering both positive and negative aspects of the new HR policy.

The bandwagon means to follow a trend.

344. He got a burst of energy and started digging again. **SSC CPO 04.10.2023 (Shift-I)**

(a) took bull by the horns
(b) a fancy of someone
(c) heart on the sleeve
(d) second wind

Ans. (d)

The idiom **'second wind'** means 'a burst of energy after fatigue.' It indicates renewed energy to continue working.

A fancy of someone means not a known idiom.

345. Right now, my hands are full.
SSC CPO 04.10.2023 (Shift-I)

(a) My hands are swollen
(b) I'm very tired
(c) I'm very busy
(d) My hands are filled up

Ans. (c)

The idiom 'my hands are full' means 'I'm very busy.' It indicates having many tasks to do.

346. Boil the ocean **SSC CPO 04.10.2023 (Shift-I)**

(a) Try to do something impossible
(b) To make someone very angry
(c) Something which gets hot gradually
(d) Something very big

Ans. (a)

The idiom 'boil the ocean' means 'try to do something impossible.' It suggests attempting an unrealistic or impractical task.

347. We've sent a very strong protest letter. That should make them sit up and take notice. **SSC CPO 04.10.2023 (Shift-I)**

(a) Observe
(b) Attend
(c) Follow
(d) Consider

Ans. (d)

The idiom 'sit up and take notice' means 'to consider something seriously.'

It indicates paying close attention to something.

348. Burn one's bridges
SSC CPO 04.10.2023 (Shift-I)

(a) Impossible to return to an earlier state
(b) Having an overnight success
(c) Working very hard
(d) Attack on one's enemy

Ans. (a)

The idiom 'burn one's bridges' means 'impossible to return to an earlier state.' It suggests making a decision that cannot be undone.

349. I had to work late in the night for nearly three months to write my first book. **SSC CPO 04.10.2023 (Shift-I)**

(a) to take a back seat
(b) to blow a fuse
(c) to look through coloured glasses
(d) to burn the midnight oil

Ans. (d)

The idiom **'burn the midnight oil'** means 'to work late at night.' It describes working long hours, often late into the night.

To take a back seat means to play a less active role.

To blow a fuse means to become very angry.

To look through coloured glasses means to see things in a biased way.

350. You must lie in the bed you have made. **SSC CPO 04.10.2023 (Shift-I)**

(a) Sleep on the bed you made yourself
(b) Sleep in your own bed
(c) Be contended always
(d) Face the unpleasant consequences of your own acts

Ans. (d)

The idiom 'lie in the bed you have made' means 'to face the unpleasant consequences of your own acts.' It indicates accepting responsibility for one's actions.

351. Open your heart
SSC CPO 04.10.2023 (Shift-I)
(a) Immediately think of something
(b) Feel relieved because the stess is removed
(c) Could do something very easily
(d) Share your deepest feelings

Ans. (d)

The idiom 'open your heart' means 'to share your deepest feelings.' It involves being honest and expressive about your emotions.

352. The office management was in dire straits after the financial crash.
SSC CPO 04.10.2023 (Shift-II)
(a) To be extremely happy
(b) In a very bad situation
(c) Being direct or fair
(d) To walk on already trodden paths

Ans. (b)

'Dire straits' is an idiomatic expression that refers to a very difficult or desperate situation.

353. Do you believe that you have a possibility of getting that job?
SSC CPO 04.10.2023 (Shift-II)
(a) spill the beans (b) snow job
(c) stand a chance (d) shoot the breeze

Ans. (c)

'Stand a chance' means to have a possibility or likelihood of success in a particular situation.

354. Shelley ignored her father's wish of studying arts and instead took admission in commerce.
SSC CPO 04.10.2023 (Shift-II)
(a) Blew over
(b) Big fish
(c) Bid defiance to
(d) Beyond the pale

Ans. (c)

'Bid defiance to' means to openly resist or challenge someone's authority or wishes.

355. Get your act together
SSC CPO 04.10.2023 (Shift-II)
(a) To ruin one's plans
(b) To organise yourself so, that you can do something properly
(c) To get the conversation going
(d) To understand something complicated

Ans. (b)

'Get your act together' essentially means to gather oneself, become organised or prepare oneself to perform effectively.

356. There are others waiting to grab an opportunity, if you don't act fast, you are going to ....
SSC CPO 04.10.2023 (Shift-II)
(a) be in the same boat
(b) a full boat
(c) push the boat out
(d) miss the boat

Ans. (d)

The correct filler for the given blank is **'Miss the boat'**. It means to fail to take advantage of an opportunity because one did not act in time or was not prepared.

357. He started with an online company and became a millionaire. Then, he sold it and invested in the share market and earned more money. Now, he has invested in the transportation industry and is generating huge wealth. What does he have? SSC CPO 04.10.2023 (Shift-II)
(a) As genuine as a three-dollar bill
(b) Midas touch
(c) Rule of thumb
(d) Sticky fingers

Ans. (b)

The idiom **'Midas touch'** means 'the ability to generate wealth easily.' It refers to a person whose investments or ventures consistently turn out to be profitable, just like King Midas in the myth who turned everything he touched into gold.

As genuine as a three-dollar bill refers to something that is obviously fake or fraudulent.

Rule of thumb means a general principle derived from practice or experience.

Sticky fingers means a tendency to steal.

358. Part and parcel SSC CPO 04.10.2023 (Shift-II)
(a) Passing blame to someone else
(b) Agreement with someone
(c) A payment system for parcels
(d) Basic or essential element

Ans. (d)

'Part and parcel' refers to something that is an essential or integral component of a whole, something that cannot be separated from the whole. Therefore, it signifies a fundamental or indispensable element of something.

359. What we need is skilled and energetic planning and elbow grease.
SSC CPO 04.10.2023 (Shift-II)
(a) The grease that is earned through labour.
(b) Hard work that one puts into cleaning one's elbow.
(c) Hard work that one puts into removing grease.
(d) Hard work that one puts into doing something.

Ans. (d)

The idiom 'elbow grease' means 'hard work that one puts into doing something.'

It suggests that success requires significant effort and labour.

360. A snowball effect
SSC CPO 04.10.2023 (Shift-II)
(a) An accelerating growth of magnitude
(b) Trick someone completely
(c) Cold and uncomfortable
(d) Slow movement

Ans. (a)

'A snowball effect' refers to a situation in which something starts small and then grows or increases at an accelerating rate, similar to a snowball rolling down a hill and getting larger as it picks up more snow.

361. My final round of Spell Bee competition is coming up and to win this event, I need to study hard from today. SSC CPO 04.10.2023 (Shift-II)
(a) burn the books
(b) hit the books
(c) cut to the chase
(d) pour my heart Out

Ans. (b)

'Hit the books' means to study diligently or intensively.

362. The modern era statistics data provides useful advantage to the players at competent level.
SSC CPO 04.10.2023 (Shift-III)
(a) play it by ear
(b) put something on ice
(c) grist to the mill
(d) cost an arm and a leg

Ans. (c)

The idiom **'grist to the mill'** means 'something that provides useful advantage.'

It refers to any resource or information that can be put to good use.

Put something on ice means to delay or postpone something.

363. At some point in the past, there were rows of temporary shops that used to display various cooking utensils.
SSC CPO 04.10.2023 (Shift-III)
(a) In the past few years
(b) Long ago
(c) Before now
(d) Once upon a time

Ans. (d)

The idiom 'once upon a time' means 'at some point in the past.' It is often used to start stories, indicating that something happened long ago.

364. He ate the whole bunch of grapes <u>under the nose</u> of all of us.
SSC CPO 04.10.2023 (Shift-III)

(a) After much persuasion
(b) Sharing equally
(c) In full view of somebody
(d) Secretly

Ans. (c)

The idiom 'under the nose' means 'in full view of somebody.' It indicates doing something openly where others can see it.

365. Rahim had <u>to eat a humble pie</u> in starting a row with his neighbour over a trifle. **SSC CPO 04.10.2023 (Shift-III)**

(a) To feel sorry and apologise for a mistake.
(b) To be punished for doing something wrong
(c) To remain without food
(d) To take simple food

Ans. (a)

The idiom 'eat a humble pie' means 'to feel sorry and apologise for a mistake.' It implies acknowledging one's errors and showing humility.

366. Step up to the plate
SSC CPO 04.10.2023 (Shift-III)

(a) Take control of a situation
(b) Plan for better performance
(c) Implement a plan
(d) Think about a crisis

Ans. (a)

The idiom 'step up to the plate' means 'to take control of a situation.' It suggests taking responsibility or action, often in a challenging context.

367. Nancy held a grudge against her teacher for a long time, but she finally decided to <u>let bygones be bygones</u>.
SSC CPO 04.10.2023 (Shift-III)

(a) Ignore the past (b) Change the past
(c) Flatter someone (d) Take revenge

Ans. (a)

The idiom 'let bygones be bygones' means 'to ignore the past.' It suggests forgiving past offenses and moving on.

368. The boss wanted to <u>finish</u> the 'case' before the arrival of the Inspection team.

(a) be over one's head
(b) be over and done with
(c) be over and over
(d) be over a barrel

Ans. (b)

The idiom **'be over and done with'** means 'to finish something completely.' It indicates wanting to complete the 'case' before the Inspection team arrives.

369. Yamini is a great singer. She will <u>make it big</u> one day.
SSC CPO 04.10.2023 (Shift-III)

(a) Migrate and settle
(b) Educated and rich
(c) Succeed and become famous
(d) Become financially sound

Ans. (c)

The idiom 'make it big' means 'to succeed and become famous.' It indicates that Yamini will achieve significant success in her singing career.

370. Come what may
SSC CPO 05.10.2023 (Shift-I)

(a) No matter what happens
(b) To get frightened
(c) Meeting someone
(d) To be among the latest

Ans. (a)

The idiom 'come what may' means 'no matter what happens.' It expresses determination to proceed regardless of obstacles.

371. Christy should discuss her <u>face to face</u>. **SSC CPO 05.10.2023 (Shift-I)**

(a) Remained normal and realistic
(b) Almost always
(c) With another person in their presence rather than, say, by phone or letters
(d) Come to fully accept or understand something

Ans. (c)

The idiom 'face to face' means 'with another person in their presence rather than, say, by phone or letters.' It emphasises direct personal interaction.

372. Apple of discord
SSC CPO 05.10.2023 (Shift-I)

(a) Centre of attraction
(b) Distant love
(c) Practical
(d) Bone of contention break a leg

Ans. (d)

The idiom 'apple of discord' means 'bone of contention.' It refers to something that causes disagreement or conflict.

373. She can't <u>make up her mind</u> where to go for her summer vacation
SSC CPO 05.10.2023 (Shift-I)

(a) decide how to do her makeup
(b) decide on a suitable parlour
(c) decide between alternatives or come to a decision
(d) engage her mind in creative activities

Ans. (c)

The idiom 'make up her mind' means 'to decide between alternatives or come to a decision.' It indicates choosing where to go for summer vacation.

374. Hear someone out
SSC CPO 05.10.2023 (Shift-II)

(a) Dismiss someone from listening to you
(b) Keep someone out
(c) Hear from far away
(d) Let someone complete what they are saying

Ans. (d)

The idiom 'hear someone out' means 'to let someone complete what they are saying.'

It emphasises listening to someone fully without interruption.

375. Pull yourself together
SSC CPO 05.10.2023 (Shift-II)

(a) Feel agitated
(b) Discourage the orphans
(c) Calm down after an upsetting incident
(d) Encourage the rich

Ans. (c)

The idiom 'pull yourself together' means 'to calm down after an upsetting incident.' It suggests regaining composure and control of emotions.

376. Bite your tongue
SSC CPO 05.10.2023 (Shift-II)

(a) To avoid saying something
(a) To have something explored
(c) To scold someone verbally
(d) To drink very heavily

Ans. (a)

The idiom 'bite your tongue' means 'to avoid saying something.' It implies holding back from speaking out.

377. Doctors are <u>raising hue and cry</u> against the RTH bill.
SSC CPO 05.10.2023 (Shift-II)

(a) Abandon
(b) Enquire
(c) Postpone
(d) Protest

Ans. (d)

The idiom to 'raise hue and cry' means 'to protest.' It describes making a public outcry or loud protest.

378. To let the cat out of the bag
SSC CPO 05.10.2023 (Shift-II)

(a) To reveal a secret
(b) To hide the truth
(c) To be in a hurry
(d) To be careful

Ans. (a)

The idiom 'let the cat out of the bag' means 'to reveal a secret.' It suggests accidentally or intentionally disclosing information that was meant to be kept confidential.

379. I did not even listen to him; he was only talking through his hat.
SSC CPO 05.10.2023 (Shift-II)
(a) Talking ignorantly
(b) Talking non-stop
(c) Talking garrulously
(d) Talking nonsense
Ans. (d)
The idiom 'talking through his hat' means 'talking nonsense.' It describes someone speaking without knowledge or sense.

380. Most of the ministers are concerned with the .... of office than the service of man. **SSC CPO 05.10.2023 (Shift-II)**
(a) leaps and bounds
(b) wear and tear
(c) loaves and fishes
(d) Herculean task
Ans. (c)
The idiom **'loaves and fishes'** refers to 'seeking material benefits or rewards.' It suggests prioritising personal gain over service to others.
Leaps and bounds means significant progress or rapid advancement.
Wear and tear indicate damage resulting from normal use.
Herculean task means a difficult task.

381. I know every detail of his accident because I heard the facts directly from him. **SSC CPO 05.10.2023 (Shift-II)**
(a) Straight from horse's mouth
(b) Get something out of your system
(c) Pour one's heart out
(d) Speak of the devil
Ans. (a)
The idiom **'straight from the horse's mouth'** means 'to hear information directly from the source.' It indicates getting information from the most reliable source.
Get something out of your system means to express feelings to feel better.
Pour one's heart out means to share one's deepest feelings.
Speak of the devil means to mention someone who unexpectedly appears.

382. This is the critical point of the issue. One should always be focused on it.
SSC CPO 05.10.2023 (Shift-III)
(a) A black sheep
(b) The crux of the matter
(c) Chip off the old bock
(d) Don't cry over spilt milk
Ans. (b)
The idiom **'the crux of the matter'** means 'the critical point of the issue.' It indicates the most important or central aspect of a situation.
A black sheep refers to a person who is different from the rest of the family or group, often in a negative way.
Chip off the old block refers to someone who resembles their parent in character or appearance.
Don't cry over spilt milk means don't worry about things that cannot be undone.

383. She said she liked my hair but it turned out to be a left-handed compliment. **SSC CPO 05.10.2023 (Shift-III)**
(a) A joke (b) A flattery
(c) An insult (d) A praise
Ans. (c)
A 'left-handed compliment' is an idiom used to describe a statement that, despite being superficially complimentary, actually carries a hidden insult or criticism.

384. I have all the technical and communication skills necessary to crack any interview; it will be ....
SSC CPO 05.10.2023 (Shift-III)
(a) a storm in a tea cup
(b) a chip on my shoulder
(c) a hard nut to crack
(d) a piece of cake for me
Ans. (d)
'A piece of cake' means something that is very easy to do.

385. He seems to be undecided about whether to move to another city for better prospects.
SSC CPO 05.10.2023 (Shift-III)
(a) Bouncing off the walls
(b) Running out of steam
(c) Sitting on the fence
(d) Counting down the days
Ans. (c)
'Sitting on the fence' means to be undecided about moving to another city, hesitating to make a decision.

386. The team leader tried to remain positive or optimistic in the situation, even though they were facing tough competition and limited resources.
SSC CPO 05.10.2023 (Shift-III)
(a) to put a strong hand forward
(b) to put on a strong exterior
(c) to put a strong desire in front of
(d) to put a brave face on
Ans. (d)
The idiom 'to put a brave face on' means 'to remain positive or optimistic in a difficult situation.' It suggests maintaining an appearance of confidence and composure.

387. He was carried off his feet when he was declared to have won the prize.
SSC CPO 05.10.2023 (Shift-III)
(a) Was wild with excitement
(b) Was dizzy
(c) Became delirious
(d) Danced on his toes
Ans. (a)
'Carried off his feet' means to be over whelmed with excitement or emotion.

388. It took seven years for Harish to...... his migraine. **SSC CPO 05.10.2023 (Shift-III)**
(a) shake down (b) shake up
(c) shake out (d) shake off
Ans. (d)
In the given sentence, Harish is trying to get rid of his migraine so, the appropriate phrasal verb to fill in the blank would be **'shake off.'**

389. The new routine will suit you to a T.
SSC CPO 05.10.2023 (Shift-III)
(a) nicely (b) a little bit
(c) exactly (d) very poorly
Ans. (c)
'To a T' means exactly or precisely suited to someone or something.

SSC CPO 2022

390. They are rivals and cannot work together in harmony.
SSC CPO 09.11.2022 (Shift-I)
(a) Potter about (b) Make up
(c) Put down (d) Pull together
Ans. (d)
The idiom **'pull together'** means 'to work together in harmony.' It suggests cooperating and collaborating effectively.
Potter about means to spend time doing small or unimportant tasks.
Make up means to reconcile or forgive someone.
Put down means to criticise someone.

391. Crying wolf **SSC CPO 09.11.2022 (Shift-II)**
(a) To be in pain by getting hit by something
(b) To frighten someone in your comfort zone
(c) To ask for help when you don't need it
(d) To cry over little things that don't matter
Ans. (c)
The idiom 'crying wolf' means 'to ask for help when you don't need it.' It originates from the fable where a boy falsely cried wolf, leading people to ignore him when there was real danger.

392. Belly laugh SSC CPO 09.11.2022 (Shift-II)
(a) Mocking someone
(b) Laughing with inhibition
(c) A loud and unrestrained laugh
(d) To be subjected to mockery and ridicule

Ans. (c)

The idiom 'belly laugh' means 'a loud and unrestrained laugh.'

It describes a hearty and genuine laughter.

393. To give someone the cold shoulder
SSC CPO 09.11.2022 (Shift-II)
(a) To ignore someone
(b) To carry the burden of everyone
(c) To be carried on someone's back
(d) To listen to someone with empathy

Ans. (a)

The idiom 'to give someone the cold shoulder' means 'to ignore someone.' It suggests showing indifference or disregard to a person.

394. The mother-in-law deliberately <u>rained on the new bride's parade</u> when she asked her to change the dress of her choice.
SSC CPO 09.11.2022 (Shift-III)
(a) Force traditions upon someone
(b) Make someone tearful out of viciousness
(c) To spoil a moment
(d) Save one from embarrassment

Ans. (c)

The idiom 'rained on the new bride's parade' means 'to spoil a moment.' It describes ruining someone's enjoyable experience.

395. At the drop of a dime
SSC CPO 09.11.2022 (Shift-III)
(a) A way of saying that you are happy to see someone
(b) Something that is not popular
(c) Something that can happen very fast without hesitation
(d) Extremely easy to understand

Ans. (c)

The idiom 'at the drop of a dime' means 'something that can happen very fast without hesitation.' It indicates immediate action or response.

396. Snowed under
SSC CPO 09.11.2022 (Shift-III)
(a) Lazy (b) Silent
(c) Alm (d) Busy

Ans. (d)

The idiom 'snowed under' means 'busy.' It describes being overwhelmed with work or tasks.

397. He was <u>beaming from ear to ear</u>.
SSC CPO 10.11.2022
(a) Playing (b) Smiling broadly
(c) Criticising bitterly (d) Working

Ans. (b)

'Beaming from ear to ear' means showing that you are very happy or pleased by smiling a lot. Hence, 'smiling broadly' is its appropriate meaning.

398. At sea SSC CPO 10.11.2022
(a) To overcome
(b) Obsolete
(c) At a loss or perplexed
(d) To blunder

Ans. (c)

'At sea' means confused and not certain what to do. Hence, 'at a loss or perplexed' gives its most appropriate meaning.

399. You get a good and *comprehensive idea* of the town from the clock tower situated in the centre of the town.
SSC CPO 10.11.2022
(a) blind date
(b) body and soul
(c) bird's eye view
(d) blind alley

Ans. (c)

'Bird's eye view' means a good view of something from a higher position. Hence, it is the most appropriate idiom to substitute the italicised words in the given sentence.

Blind alley means a course of action that is useless.

400. Even when the child accused the relative of inappropriate behaviour, the parents continued to play perfect hosts at the party instead of addressing the <u>elephant in the room</u>.
SSC CPO 10.11.2022
(a) Ignoring someone who seeks attention through false stories
(b) Punishing someone for inappropriate behaviour
(c) Revealing the secrets
(d) A big problem everyone is ignoring or is afraid to talk about

Ans. (d)

The 'elephant in the room' refers to an obvious problem or a difficult situation that people do not want to talk about.

401. To stand one's ground
SSC CPO 10.11.2022
(a) To maintain one's position
(b) To fight for the same position
(c) To stand up
(d) To stand in one's own land

Ans. (a)

'Stand one's ground' means to stay where you are when someone threatens you, in order to show them that you are not afraid. Hence, 'to maintain one's position' is its correct meaning.

402. Get on like a house on fire
SSC CPO 11.11.2022
(a) Like someone immediately
(b) Get extremely well with someone
(c) Feel a lot of affection for one particular person, often without knowing why
(d) Do something good for someone you have done something bad to in the past

Ans. (b)

'Get on like a house on fire' means to become good friends and have a lot to talk to each other about.

403. Against the clock SSC CPO 11.11.2022
(a) Running faster with a clock in hand
(b) In a great hurry, as fast as possible
(c) Running faster without a clock
(d) Race with others to win

Ans. (b)

'Against the clock' means trying very hard to finish something before a particular time.

404. Get a second wind SSC CPO 11.11.2022
(a) To retell the same story
(b) To have renewed energy
(c) To commit the same mistake
(d) To get a second chance

Ans. (b)

'Get a second wind' means a return of strength or energy that makes it possible to continue in an activity that needs a lot of effort.

405. So far so good SSC CPO 11.11.2022
(a) Not impressed with how things are
(b) Things are going well so far
(c) No improvement in the work being done
(d) Good things can go far away

Ans. (b)

'So far so good' is used for saying that someone or something has been successful up to this point.

406. Hang in there SSC CPO 11.11.2022
(a) To remain unresolved
(b) To give up completely
(c) To spend time with people
(d) To persist in a difficult situation

Ans. (d)

'Hang in there' means to remain determined to succeed even when a situation is difficult.

407. Left, right and center SSC CPO 11.11.2022
(a) To have been happening for a long time and there is a lot of activity
(b) Happening in a lot of places or to a lot of people
(c) Start well
(d) The news went from one person to the next

Ans. (b)

'Left, right and center' means in all directions or to everyone.

408. Nine times out of ten, he tells lies. SSC CPO 11.11.2022
(a) All the time (b) Hardly
(c) In most cases (d) Sometimes

Ans. (c)

'Nine times out of ten' means almost every time.

409. To beat a retreat SSC CPO 11.11.2022
(a) To make a situation
(b) To leave a situation
(c) To solve a situation
(d) To face a situation

Ans. (b)

'To beat a retreat' means to run away from a dangerous or unpleasant situation.

SSC CPO 2021

410. I cannot take up any new assignment as I have my hands full. SSC CPO Tier-2 26.07.2021
(a) am very rich (b) need to seek help
(c) am very busy (d) am short of time

Ans (c)

The idiom 'have my hands full' means 'am very busy.' It indicates being occupied with a lot of tasks.

411. India's problem boils down to just one thing-lack of infrastructure for health services. SSC CPO Tier-2 26.07.2021
(a) fulfils something
(b) adapts to something
(c) heats up to (d) sums up to

Ans (d)

The idiom 'boils down to' means 'sums up to.' It describes reducing something to its essential point.

412. You must seize the opportunity to make amends for your earlier curtness. SSC CPO Tier-2 26.07.2021
(a) to correct a mistake
(b) to give a suggestion
(c) to make a proposal
(d) to offer a deal

Ans. (a)

The idiom 'make amends' means 'to correct a mistake.' It involves compensating for a previous wrongdoing.

SSC CHSL 2024 (Tier 1)

413. Call it a day SSC CHSL Tier-2 18.11.2024
(a) Stop working on something
(b) Begin with an assignment
(c) Name a particular day
(d) Involve many people for a simple job

Ans. (a)

'Call it a day' means 'stop working on something.' This idiom is used when someone decides to stop working for the day or to stop doing an activity. It implies wrapping up tasks and not doing any more work on them for that day. Hence, the correct option is: Stop working on something.

414. The fire fighters tried their best to extinguish the fire. SSC CHSL Tier-2 18.11.2024
(a) put in (b) put out
(c) put off (d) put on

Ans. (b)

The phrasal verb 'put out' means to extinguish. put in means to submit or install. put off it means to postpone. put on it means to dress or present.

415. The realtors of the new venture sold plots like hot cakes. SSC CHSL Tier-1 01.07.2024 (Shift-I)
(a) Sold innovatively
(b) Sold quickly and in large numbers
(c) Sold illegally
(d) Sold with great difficulty

Ans. (b)

'Sold plots like hot cakes' means to be sold very quickly and effortlessly.

416. Black and white SSC CHSL Tier-1 01.07.2024 (Shift-I)
(a) In dispute (b) A false invention
(c) In writing (d) Doubtful

Ans. (c)

'Black and white' means in writing.

417. At one's fingertips SSC CHSL Tier-1 01.07.2024 (Shift-II)
(a) To be unaware of something
(b) To take revenge
(c) Out of reach
(d) To have complete knowledge

Ans. (d)

'At one's fingertips' means to have complete knowledge.

418. Teja followed his friend's advice so now he is in deep water. SSC CHSL Tier-1 01.07.2024 (Shift-II)
(a) in deep thoughts
(b) in dilemma
(c) in trouble
(d) in good position

Ans. (c)

'In deep water' means to be in a difficult situation or trouble.

419. Blowing smoke SSC CHSL Tier-1 01.07.2024 (Shift-III)
(a) To tease someone relentlessly
(b) To hide something
(c) To burn something important
(d) To lie to perplex others

Ans. (d)

Blowing smoke means to lie to perplex others.

420. The arrival of Pragati in the house brought disharmony among the family members. SSC CHSL Tier-1 01.07.2024 (Shift-IV)
(a) tenterhooks
(b) a cry in the wilderness
(c) rift in the lute
(d) hair breadth

Ans. (c)

The most appropriate substitute for the underlined word is **'rift in the lute'**. It means sign of disharmony between persons, especially the first evidence of a quarrel that may become worse.

421. Dog eat dog SSC CHSL Tier-1 01207.2024 (Shift-I)
(a) Ruthlessly competitive
(b) Tit for tat
(c) Being calculative
(d) Like-minded people connect better

Ans. (a)

'Dog eat dog' means ruthlessly competitive.

422. Put in mind SSC CHSL Tier-1 01207.2024 (Shift-I)
(a) To calculate (b) To remind
(c) To forget (d) To understand

Ans. (b)

'Put in mind' means to remind.

423. Slip your mind SSC CHSL Tier-1 01207.2024 (Shift-II)
(a) Forget about something
(b) Think about something for a short time
(c) Immediately think of something
(d) Can't think of anything to say

Ans. (a)

Slip your mind means to forget about something.

424. Lose heart SSC CHSL Tier-1 02.07.2024 (Shift-II)
(a) To be suspicious of your success
(b) To get success by believing in yourself
(c) To stop believing that you can succeed
(d) To believe in your success

Ans. (c)

Lose heart means to stop believing that you can succeed.

425. After a day long trek, we were so tired that we were ready to ....

SSC CHSL Tier-1 02.07.2024 (Shift-III)

(a) face the music
(b) get into deep water
(c) go from rags to riches
(d) hit the sack

Ans. (d)

The correct idiom to fill in the blank is **'hit the sack'**, which means to go to sleep.

'To face the music' means to get punished for your action.

'To get into deep water' means to be in a difficult or awkward situation.

'To go from rags to riches' means to become rich suddenly.

426. The two brothers .... when their father died.

SSC CHSL Tier-1 02.07.2024 (Shift-III)

(a) fell down (b) fell out
(c) got the sack (d) look down upon

Ans. (b)

The correct phrasal verb for the given blank is **'fell out'**, which means to argue with someone and stop being friendly with them.

'Fell down' means to fall.

'Got the sack' means to be removed from a job.

'Look down upon' means to treat someone as unworthy.

427. On its last legs

SSC CHSL Tier-1 02.07.2024 (Shift-IV)

(a) Creeping on legs
(b) Last choice
(c) Slow movement
(d) In a bad condition

Ans. (d)

On its last legs means in a bad condition.

428. It feels like <u>I made a promise of more than my ability</u> when I promised to complete this worksheet in one day.

SSC CHSL Tier-1 02.07.2024 (Shift-IV)

(a) beat my brain out
(b) beat the drum
(c) bit off more than I could chew
(d) burnt a hole in my pocket

Ans. (c)

The most appropriate substitution for the underlined word is- **bit off more than I could chew**. It means to try to do something that is too difficult for you.

'Beat my brain out' means to hit someone repeatedly.

'Beat the drum' means to speak with enthusiasm.

'Burnt a hole in my pocket' means to cost a lot of money.

429. Last resort

SSC CHSL Tier-1 03.07.2024 (Shift-I)

(a) Last hotel on the way
(b) Last ride
(c) Last friend remaining
(d) Last course of action

Ans. (d)

Last resort means the only choice that remains after all others have been tried/ last course of action.

430. Ace in the hole

SSC CHSL Tier-1 03.07.2024 (Shift-I)

(a) A lot to do
(b) On the point of
(c) A second chance to do something
(d) A hidden advantage

Ans. (d)

Ace in the hole means a hidden advantage or resource kept in reserve until needed.

431. Stick to one's guns

SSC CHSL Tier-1 03.07.2024 (Shift-II)

(a) To become a rebel
(b) To shoot at
(c) To become unfaithful to
(d) To remain faithful to

Ans. (d)

Stick to one's guns means to refuse to compromise or change, despite criticism. It also means to remain faithful to something.

432. Have a bee in your bonnet

SSC CHSL Tier-1 03.07.2024 (Shift-II)

(a) Be preoccupied or obsessed with something
(b) Unable to stay at a place for long
(c) To keep worrying about yourself
(d) Having a cruel intention or grudge against someone

Ans. (a)

To have a bee in your bonnet means to be preoccupied or obsessed with something.

433. Around the clock

SSC CHSL Tier-1 03.07.2024 (Shift-III)

(a) Something that is done at night
(b) Something that is done within one hour
(c) Something that is time bound
(d) Something that goes on day and night

Ans. (d)

Around the clock means all day and all night.

434. Best thing since sliced bread

SSC CHSL Tier-1 03.07.2024 (Shift-III)

(a) Breaking news
(b) Something to be cautious about
(c) Extremely good, interesting
(d) Rated well amongst cooks

Ans. (c)

Best thing since sliced bread is used to emphasise one's enthusiasm about a new idea, person, or thing. It means extremely good, interesting.

435. Delivering that furniture to the tenth floor without the lift and an incline is <u>incredibly foolish and next to impossible</u> .

SSC CHSL Tier-1 03.07.2024 (Shift-IV)

(a) like a tree known by its fruits
(b) like nailing jelly to the tree
(c) as tight as the bark of the tree
(d) like going between the bark and the tree

Ans. (b)

The most appropriate substitute for the underlined words is **'like nailing jelly to the tree'**.

It means incredibly difficult or impossible.

436. This gun should be handled with care and ....

SSC CHSL Tier-1 03.07.2024 (Shift-IV)

(a) nip in the bud
(b) shot for safety
(c) mince the matters
(d) kept at arm's length

Ans. (d)

The correct idiom to fill in the blank is - **kept at arm's length**. It means to keep someone at distance.

437. Independence Day is considered as a <u>red-letter day</u> in the history of India.

SSC CHSL Tier-1 04.07.2024 (Shift-I)

(a) regular day
(b) uneventful day
(c) memorable day
(d) unimportant day

Ans. (c)

A red-letter day means a day that is pleasantly noteworthy or memorable.

438. Vishnu and Vignesh are always <u>like two peas in a pod</u>.

SSC CHSL Tier-1 04.07.2024 (Shift-I)

(a) Very similar to each other
(b) Smart and intelligent
(c) Happy and compassionate
(d) Good in every way

Ans. (a)

Two peas in a pod means very similar to each other.

439. Prakash could not make up his mind about what to do with the project.
SSC CHSL Tier-1 04.07.2024 (Shift-II)
(a) Abandon (b) Think
(c) Abide (d) Decide
Ans. (d)
Make up his mind to decide something.

440. You can best identify the fair-weather friends at the time of adversity.
SSC CHSL Tier-1 04.07.2024 (Shift-III)
(a) Friends who come in good weather conditions
(b) Best friends
(c) Friends who bring good rain
(d) Friend only at the time of prosperity
Ans. (d)
Fair-weather friends are people who become good friends when it is easy to be one and who stops being one when you are having problems.

441. I can't begin to talk on this situation right now; I am still wrapping my head around it.
SSC CHSL Tier-1 04.07.2024 (Shift-III)
(a) Ignoring something completely
(b) Understanding something complicated
(c) Comparing two things that can't be compared
(d) Revealing a secret nobody knows
Ans. (b)
'Wrapping my head around it' means to understand something, especially something strange or out of the ordinary.

442. A bolt from the blue
SSC CHSL Tier-1 04.07.2024 (Shift-IV)
(a) A sudden and unexpected event
(b) Thunder and rain in a strom
(c) Raining heavily
(d) A spontaneous but expected event
Ans. (a)
If a piece of news comes like a bolt from the blue, it is completely unexpected and very surprising.

443. Walk a tightrope
SSC CHSL Tier-1 04.07.2024 (Shift-IV)
(a) To walk on a narrow road
(b) To act carefully in a difficult situation
(c) To be tensed about something
(d) To try and balance yourself
Ans. (b)
Walk a tightrope means to act carefully in a difficult situation.

444. To be at daggers drawn
SSC CHSL Tier-1 05.07.2024 (Shift-I)
(a) To be about to collapse
(b) Ready to fight
(c) Under suspicion
(d) To be under control
Ans. (b)
'To be at daggers drawn' means to be ready to fight.

445. The United Nations is working to eliminate the vicious cycle of poverty.
SSC CHSL Tier-1 05.07.2024 (Shift-II)
(a) The barrier of poverty
(b) One problem causes other
(c) Loophole of something
(d) Strength of something
Ans. (b)
Vicious cycle refers to a sequence of reciprocal cause and effect in which two or more elements intensify and aggravate each other, leading inexorably to a worsening of the situation.

446. Bag and baggage
SSC CHSL Tier-1 05.07.2024 (Shift-II)
(a) At the service (b) By force
(c) With all goods (d) Fair and honest
Ans. (c)
Bag and baggage means with all goods.

447. Last year art critics praised Animesh as if he were a master, but he turned out to be a pleasure for a short time.
SSC CHSL Tier-1 05.07.2024 (Shift-III)
(a) a nine days' wonder
(b) a dish fit for Gods
(c) a house of cards
(d) a bull in a China shop
Ans. (a)
The most appropriate substitution will be **'a nine days' wonder'**. It means something that attracts great interest for a short while but is then forgotten.
'A dish fit for Gods' means a high quality meal.
'A house of cards' means a plan or system that is most likely to fail.
'A bull in a China shop' means careless.

448. When I got an opportunity to start a new business, Ravikanth queered my pitch. **SSC CHSL Tier-1 05.07.2024 (Shift-IV)**
(a) Supported me with money
(b) Helped me by standing beside me
(c) Ruined my plan
(d) Advised me
Ans. (c)
'Queered my pitch' means ruined my plan.

449. Fish out of water
SSC CHSL Tier-1 08.07.2024 (Shift-I)
(a) To be out of place
(b) No knowledge of marine life
(c) To die soon
(d) Not good at swimming
Ans. (a)
Fish out of water means to be out of place.

450. Bells and whistles
SSC CHSL Tier-1 08.07.2024 (Shift-I)
(a) To take on a difficult task
(b) An innovative development
(c) At a serious disadvantage
(d) Attractive but unnecessary features added to products
Ans. (d)
Bells and whistles means attractive but unnecessary features added to products.

451. Sell like hot cakes
SSC CHSL Tier-1 08.07.2024 (Shift-II)
(a) Extremely hot and humid
(b) Not bothering about money
(c) Selling out quickly
(d) Become very famous
Ans. (c)
'Sell like hot cakes' means selling very quickly.

452. Which of the following idioms means 'going to sleep'?
SSC CHSL Tier-1 08.07.2024 (Shift-II)
(a) Keep an ear to the ground
(b) Run around in circles
(c) Break new grounds
(d) Hit the sack
Ans. (d)
The idiom **'Hit the sack'** means to go to sleep.
'Keep an ear to the ground' means to be well informed.
'Run around in circles' means a purposeless action.
'Break new grounds' means to do something for the first time.

453. Where the shoe pinches
SSC CHSL Tier-1 08.07.2024 (Shift-III)
(a) Unknown paths
(b) Difficult roads
(c) Where the difficulty lies
(d) Where the shoe hurts
Ans. (c)
'Where the shoe pinches' refers to the place where difficulty lies.

454. Mala .... by cheating on the exam to win her bet with Priya.
SSC CHSL Tier-1 08.07.2024 (Shift-III)
(a) get the sack
(b) look down upon
(c) hit below the belt
(d) fell out
Ans. (c)
The correct idiom for the given blank is **'hit below the belt'**.
It means to say something that is often too personal, usually irrelevant and always unfair.

'Get the sack' means to be fired or removed from the job.

'Look down upon' means to think or treat someone or something as unimportant.

'Fell out' means to have a disagreement.

455. To read between the lines
SSC CHSL Tier-1 08.07.2024 (Shift-IV)
(a) To grasp the hidden meaning
(b) To read without concentration
(c) To read aloud
(d) To whisper

Ans. (a)

To read between the lines means to grasp the hidden meaning of something.

456. A piece of cake
SSC CHSL Tier-1 09.07.2024 (Shift-II)
(a) Despite the heavy rain, they managed to have a successful outdoor event.
(b) The restaurant was crowded, but they found a table without any difficulty.
(c) The puzzle was so challenging that it took hours for Sam to solve it.
(d) After months of practice, Emily performed her piano piece flawlessly during the concert.

Ans. (b)

A piece of cake means a very easy task to do. Hence, the sentence that uses the idiom correctly is- The restaurant was crowded, but they found a table without any difficulty.

457. Under the weather
SSC CHSL Tier-1 09.07.2024 (Shift-II)
(a) To feel secure
(b) To enjoy the weather
(c) To feel unwell
(d) To work against the weather

Ans. (c)

'Under the weather' means to be ill.

458. A wild goose chase
SSC CHSL Tier-1 09.07.2024 (Shift-III)
(a) Ideal seeking
(b) Fruitless search
(c) Fruitful search
(d) On a hunt

Ans. (b)

A wild goose chase is a fruitless activity or search.

459. An old head on young shoulders
SSC CHSL Tier-1 09.07.2024 (Shift-III)
(a) A young person who looks old
(b) A young person who is lazy
(c) A person who is slow at understanding things
(d) A young person who acts or speaks like an older person

Ans. (d)

'An old head on young shoulders' means being a young person who acts or speaks like an older person.

460. He got medals time after time by following the instructions of his mentor. SSC CHSL Tier-1 09.07.2024 (Shift-IV)
(a) Repeatedly (b) Twice
(c) Rarely (d) Once

Ans. (a)

The underlined part of the given sentence contains an error.

Use 'repeatedly' to correct the sentence.

461. Select the sentence that brings out the most appropriate meaning of the idiom 'Dog in the manger'.
SSC CHSL Tier-1 10.07.2024 (Shift-I)
(a) Mohit was so loyal and committed to his company that he rejected lucrative offers from different companies.
(b) To prove this is not a trap, I want to check the credibility of your plan.
(c) Rachit had some important work and so he cancelled the show tickets for everyone.
(d) You are here just because you have recognised your hidden potential.

Ans. (c)

Dog in the manger is used for a person who has no need of, or ability to use a possession that would be of use or value to others, but who prevents others from having it. The sentence that uses the idiom correctly is- Rachit had some important work and so he cancelled the show tickets for everyone.

462. The technicians who were repairing the broken elevator called it a day.
SSC CHSL Tier-1 10.07.2024 (Shift-I)
(a) Felt unhappy
(b) Shouted with anger
(c) Stopped to take a short break
(d) Stopped work for the day

Ans. (d)

The underlined idiom 'called it a day' means stopped work for the day.

463. Manish told Rounak time and again of the ill consequences of his habit of being late to the college.
SSC CHSL Tier-1 10.07.2024 (Shift-II)
(a) Repeatedly
(b) Hardly ever
(c) At intervals
(d) Not often

Ans. (a)

The underlined idiom 'time and again' means repeatedly.

464. They were waiting for their family members who were returning from a pilgrimage. Therefore, they were .... on the platform.
SSC CHSL Tier-1 10.07.2024 (Shift-II)
(a) running behind time
(b) playing a joke
(c) pacing up and down
(d) rolling up their sleeves

Ans. (c)

The correct idiom for the given blank is 'pacing up and down'. It means to be nervous and anxious.

465. With the increasing market prices and stagnant salaries, he is ....
SSC CHSL Tier-1 10.07.2024 (Shift-III)
(a) taking a break
(b) feeling the pinch
(c) beating the rap
(d) getting it off his chest

Ans. (b)

The correct idiom for the given blank is 'feeling the pinch' means to have problems with money because you are earning less than before.

466. Costing an arm and a leg
SSC CHSL Tier-1 10.07.2024 (Shift-IV)
(a) Very attractive and cheap
(b) Very rough and tough
(c) Very costly and luxurious
(d) Very entertaining and jovial

Ans. (c)

Costing an arm and a leg means to be very expensive.

467. Going through a sticky patch
SSC CHSL Tier-1 10.07.2024 (Shift-IV)
(a) To experience a bad period in life
(b) Try to paste something unsuccessfully
(c) To walk on a muddy road
(d) To feel sad

Ans. (a)

Going through a sticky patch means to experience a bad period in life.

468. A sting in the tail
SSC CHSL Tier-1 11.07.2024 (Shift-I)
(a) An unexpected, typically unpleasant or problematic end to something
(b) Something which seems bad at first but contains a pleasant part at the end
(c) To initiate a situation that is very complicated or problematic
(d) A situation in which a large group has to do something to satisfy a small group

Ans. (a)

A sting in the tail means an unexpected, typically unpleasant or problematic end to something.

469. I know Covid has made you terribly ill, but the good thing is that you have developed immunity against it for further infections.
SSC CHSL Tier-1 11.07.2024 (Shift-II)
(a) the silver spoon
(b) the silver lining in the cloud
(c) being in the quicksilver
(d) crossing palms with silver
Ans. (b)
The most appropriate substitute for the underlined words is- the silver lining in the cloud. It means every sad or unpleasant situation has a positive side to it.

470. Out of the frying pan and into the fire
SSC CHSL Tier-1 11.07.2024 (Shift-II)
(a) Things getting intense by the hour
(b) Being a horrible cook
(c) Being with someone through good times as well as bad times
(d) Things going from bad to worse
Ans. (d)
Out of the frying pan and into the fire means from a bad situation to one that is worse.

471. To throw dust in one's eyes
SSC CHSL Tier-1 11.07.2024 (Shift-III)
(a) To talk in an abusive language
(b) To mislead someone by tricks
(c) To make someone blind forever
(d) To hit someone with stone
Ans. (b)
To throw dust in one's eyes means to mislead someone by tricks.

472. Every piece of furniture in her house is in apple-pie order.
SSC CHSL Tier-1 11.07.2024 (Shift-III)
(a) Very neatly arranged
(b) Painted in light colours
(c) Very delicately arranged
(d) Kept in a disorganised way
Ans. (a)
The underlined idiom 'apple-pie order' means very neatly arranged.

473. After many years of rivalry, the two schools decided to .... and participate in a National Event together SSC CHSL Tier-1 11.07.2024 (Shift-IV)
(a) bell the cat
(b) bury the hatchet
(c) go cold turkey
(d) be in the doldrums
Ans. (b)
The correct idiom for the given blank is **'bury the hatchet'**. It means to end a quarrel or conflict and become friendly.

474. A jack of all trades cannot survive in the world of specialisation.
SSC CHSL Tier-1 11.07.2024 (Shift-IV)
(a) A good communicator
(b) A person who can do many things but is not an expert in any
(c) An expert of many jobs
(d) A businessman
Ans. (b)
A jack of all trades is someone who can do many things but is not an expert in any.

475. Shyama looks innocent but in reality, she is cunning.
SSC CHSL Tier-2 10.01.2024 (Shift-I)
(a) Fortune favours the brave.
(b) Beauty lies in the eyes of the beholder.
(c) Don't judge a book by its cover.
(d) Don't put all your eggs in one basket.
Ans. (c)
Don't judge a book by its cover is the idiom that best fits the sentence about Shyama. It means appearances can be deceptive.

476. The salesperson for the project offered a sneak peak of the project as we expressed our interest in the area and amenities.
SSC CHSL Tier-2 10.01.2024 (Shift-I)
(a) Getting a preview of something
(b) To try something new
(c) Sending a brief letter
(d) To be in a winning position
Ans. (a)
A 'sneak peak' refers to an opportunity to see something before it is officially available or released.

477. The teacher asked the students to .... their ideas during the class discussion.
SSC CHSL Tier-2 10.01.2024 (Shift-I)
(a) get on (b) put off
(c) bring up (d) bring about
Ans. (c)
The correct answer is 'bring up'. The phrasal verb 'bring up' means to introduce a topic for discussion.

478. The teacher asked the students to .... their essays before the deadline. SSC CHSL Tier-2 10.01.2024 (Shift-I)
(a) land in (b) put off
(c) hand in (d) hand up
Ans. (c)
The correct answer is 'hand in'. The phrasal verb 'hand in' means to submit work for consideration or judgement.

479. Keep your chin up.
SSC CHSL Tier-2 10.01.2024 (Shift-I)
(a) The students diligently completed their homework assignments before the deadline.
(b) Despite facing setbacks, she remained positive and determined to achieve her goals.
(c) The hiker enjoyed the breathtaking view from the mountaintop, taking in the natural beauty.
(d) The scientist conducted experiments and gathered data to support his research hypothesis.
Ans. (b)
The idiom 'Keep your chin up' means to remain cheerful in a difficult situation.
Hence, sentence in option (b) presents its meaning appropriately.

SSC CHSL 2023 (Tier 1)

480. Slap on the wrist
SSC CHSL Tier-1 09.03.2023 (Shift-I)
(a) A mild punishment
(b) Misunderstand each other
(c) Wild with excitement
(d) Criticise someone strongly and angrily
Ans. (a)
'A Slap on the wrist' means a punishment that is less severe than is expected or usual.

481. Body and soul
SSC CHSL Tier-1 09.03.2023 (Shift-I)
(a) Life and death
(b) To solve a difficulty
(c) Wholly and entirely
(d) Happiness and sorrow
Ans. (c)
'Body and soul' means completely.

482. A shot in the dark
SSC CHSL Tier-1 09.03.2023 (Shift-II)
(a) Shooting in the night
(b) Randomly doing something, the outcome of which is unknown
(c) Ablind man's cane
(d) Looking at the stars
Ans. (b)
The idiom 'a shot in the dark' means 'randomly doing something, the outcome of which is unknown.'
It suggests making a guess or attempt without having sufficient information.

483. A Bull market
SSC CHSL Tier-2 09.03.2023 (Shift-III)
(a) A fertile field
(b) A market where cattle is traded
(c) To boast
(d) Market where prices are rising
Ans. (d)
The idiom 'a bull market' means 'a market where prices are rising.'
It refers to a financial market in which the value of securities is expected to rise.

484. To shake in one's shoes
SSC CHSL Tier-1 09.03.2023 (Shift-IV)

(a) To be afraid
(b) To leave no remark
(c)An unpleasant scenario
(d) To fall to understand

Ans. (a)

The idiom 'to shake in one's shoes' means 'to be afraid.' It describes feeling scared or anxious.

485. Slack off SSC CHSL Tier-1 10.03.2023 (Shift-II)

(a) To ease pressure in something
(b) To make most effort
(c) To understand a hidden meaning
(d) To be very rude

Ans. (a)

'Slack off' means to make less effort than usual or to lazy in your work.

486. Pig in a poke
SSC CHSL Tier-1 10.03.2023 (Shift-II)

(a) To obstruct someone's work
(b) A brave man amongst all the cowards
(c) Somethings that is bought without examining properly
(d) To bring something to an end

Ans. (c)

'Pig in a poke' refers to something you bought without seeing it first and that is not as good of valuable as you expected.

487. Ace in the hole
SSC CHSL Tier-1 10.03.2023 (Shift-III)

(a) To create noisy disturbances so that competitors are unable to work.
(b) A major advantage that one keeps hidden until an ideal time.
(c) To attempt to do the impossible
(d) To suffer an injury on the lower body.

Ans. (b)

The idiom 'ace in the hole' means 'a major advantage that one keeps hidden until an ideal time.'

It refers to a secret strength or resource that can be used when needed.

488. For old time's sake
SSC CHSL Tier-1 10.03.2023 (Shift-IV)

(a) To consider the options
(b) Deliberately stop someone
(c) To be friends with an old person
(d) Because of sentimental memories of the past

Ans. (d)

The idiom 'for old time's sake' means 'because of sentimental memories of the past.' It refers to doing something to honour past relationships or experiences.

489. Sea change
SSC CHSL Tier-1 13.03.2023 (Shift-III)

(a) Major transformation
(b) Jealousy
(c) To pursue
(d) Hatred

Ans. (a)

'Sea change' means major change or transformation.

490. Wear your heart on your sleeve
SSC CHSL Tier-1 13.03.2023 (Shift-III)

(a) To go through a heart break
(b) To understand
(c) To suspect a trick
(d) To openly display one's emotions

Ans. (d)

'Wear your heart on your sleeve' means to openly display one's emotions and feelings.

491. How can seawater from the oceans be ...... fresh water that is suitable for people to drink?
SSC CHSL Tier-1 13.03.2023 (Shift-III)

(a) minced on (b) turned into
(c) surrender in (d) change about

Ans. (b)

The correct filler for the given blank is 'turned into'. It means 'to prove to be the case'.

492. To sleep like a dog
SSC CHSL Tier-1 14.03.2023 (Shift-I)

(a) To make noise while sleeping
(b) To sleep soundly
(c) To be less mindful
(d) To be insomniac

Ans. (b)

'To sleep like a dog' means to sleep soundly.

493. Armed to the teeth
SSC CHSL Tier-1 14.03.2023 (Shift-I)

(a) Different attacking techniques
(b) To have no weapon to fight
(c) Safeguard oneself in every possible way
(d) Fully armed, having many weapons

Ans. (d)

'Armed to teeth' means armed with a lot of weapons or with very effective weapons.

494. Apropos of nothing
SSC CHSL Tier-1 14.03.2023 (Shift-II)

(a) Any difficult situation or obstacle
(b) To be enraged
(c) Almost everything and anything has been included
(d) Having no relevance to any previous discussion or situation

Ans. (d)

The idiom 'apropos of nothing' means 'having no relevance to any previous discussion or situation.' It indicates something said or done that is unrelated to what has been discussed before.

495. Neck of the woods
SSC CHSL Tier-1 14.03.2023 (Shift-IV)

(a) Neighbourhood (b) Barren land
(c) Valley (d) Highways

Ans. (a)

The idiom 'neck of the woods' means 'neighbourhood.' It refers to a particular area or locality where someone lives or is familiar with.

496. Zero tolerance
SSC CHSL Tier-1 15.03.2023 (Shift-I)

(a) To detect someone in the group is betraying the others
(b) Riding in the front passenger seat of a car
(c) To escape and not have to pay
(d) A policy of not allowing any violations of a rule or law

Ans. (d)

The idiom 'zero tolerance' means 'a policy of not allowing any violations of a rule or law.' It refers to strict enforcement without exceptions.

497. To bridge the gap
SSC CHSL Tier-1 15.03.2023 (Shift-I)

(a) To reduce differences and reconcile
(b) To push people apart
(c) To mend a broken bridge
(d) To slander someone

Ans. (a)

The idiom 'to bridge the gap' means 'to reduce differences and reconcile.' It involves finding common ground and bringing people or ideas closer together.

498. High and dry
SSC CHSL Tier-1 15.03.2023 (Shift-IV)

(a) Occasionally (b) Abandoned
(c) Failed (d) Perplexed

Ans. (b)

'High and dry' means without any help or without the things that one needs or 'abandoned'.

499. The whole ball of wax
SSC CHSL Tier-1 15.03.2023 (Shift-IV)

(a) Everything (b) Sagacious
(c) Meagre (d) Complete disaster

Ans. (a)

'The whole ball of wax' means the everything.

500. Dead lock
SSC CHSL Tier-1 16.03.2023 (Shift-I)

(a) To attract
(b) To lose an important asset
(c) To be anxious
(d) A state in which progress is impossible

Ans. (d)

'Dead lock' refers to a situation, typically one involving opposing parties, in which no progress can be made.

501. Method to my madness
SSC CHSL Tier-1 16.03.2023 (Shift-II)

(a) Someone who is unpredictable and can cause damage if not kept in check.
(b) To get someone drunk.
(c) Strange or crazy actions that appear meaningless but in the end are done for a good reason.
(d) To state a fact so that there are no doubts or objections.

Ans. (c)

Method to my madness means that there is a purpose in doing something that is seemingly crazy.

502. To make one's mark
SSC CHSL Tier-1 16.03.2023 (Shift-II)

(a) To make no effort
(b) To prove a point
(c) To attain success
(d) To be indifferent

Ans. (c)

'To make one's work' means to become successful or famous.

503. To lay someone by the heels
SSC CHSL Tier-1 16.03.2023 (Shift-II)

(a) To confirm somebody in prison
(b) To praise someone
(c) To force someone for something
(d) To gain support

Ans. (a)

'To lay someone by the heels' means to arrest and imprison someone.

504. Have people rolling in the aisles
SSC CHSL Tier-1 16.03.2023 (Shift-III)

(a) To use false promise to pull people on one's side.
(b) Make an audience laugh uncontrollably
(c) To have a dispute with someone
(d) Willing to do something immediately

Ans. (b)

The idiom 'have people rolling in the aisles' means 'make an audience laugh uncontrollably.'

It describes making people laugh so hard that they are almost falling out of their seats.

505. To breast the tape
SSC CHSL Tier-1 16.03.2023 (Shift-IV)

(a) To shut someone's mouth
(b) To create problems
(c) To bring joy
(d) To win a race

Ans. (d)

The idiom 'to breast the tape' means 'to win a race.' It comes from the image of breaking the tape at the finish line of a race.

506. Good grief
SSC CHSL Tier-1 17.03.2023 (Shift-I)

(a) To dig a hole
(b) To be very systematic
(c) To try everything possible
(d) An expression of surprise or frustration

Ans. (d)

The phrase 'good grief' is an expression of surprise or frustration. It is often used to show disbelief or exasperation.

507. To jump out of one's skin
SSC CHSL Tier-1 17.03.2023 (Shift-I)

(a) To argue with someone
(b) To feel immense pain
(c) To show one's real side
(d) To be extremely surprised

Ans. (d)

The idiom 'to jump out of one's skin' means 'to be extremely surprised by something.' It describes a reaction to something startling or unexpected.

508. Penny wise and pound foolish
SSC CHSL Tier-1 17.03.2023 (Shift-II)

(a) Dissipating money without caring about consequences
(b) Careless with large amounts but not small
(c) To act like a fool
(d) An intelligent person who behaves foolishly

Ans. (b)

'Penny wise and pound foolish' means to be extremely careful about small amounts of money and not careful enough about larger amounts of money.

509. Get into hot water
SSC CHSL Tier-1 17.03.2023 (Shift-II)

(a) To get into trouble
(b) To reach nowhere
(c) A private end to serve
(d) To get a costly gift

Ans. (a)

'Get into hot water' means to get into trouble because of something you have done.

510. Appeal to Caesar
SSC CHSL Tier-1 17.03.2023 (Shift-III)

(a) An authority given to a foolish person
(b) To expect good from a wrong person
(c) To live in a false reality
(d) Appeal to the highest possible Authority

Ans. (d)

The idiom 'appeal to Caesar' means 'to appeal to the highest possible authority.'

It suggests taking a matter to the ultimate decision-maker.

511. A bite at the cherry
SSC CHSL Tier-1 17.03.2023 (Shift-IV)

(a) A wrong move
(b) An attempt or opportunity to do something
(c) To have a leverage over someone
(d) A dog bit

Ans. (b)

The idiom 'a bite at the cherry' means 'an attempt or opportunity to do something.' It implies getting a chance to try or achieve something.

512. Save your breath
SSC CHSL Tier-1 20.03.2023 (Shift-I)

(a) To make an effort that will be futile
(b) To hold one's anger
(c) To work hard
(d) To be resentful

Ans. (a)

The idiom 'save your breath' means 'to make an effort that will be futile.'

It suggests that speaking or trying to persuade someone would be pointless.

513. A beast of burden
SSC CHSL Tier-1 20.03.2023 (Shift-II)

(a) A liability
(b) An animal that carries luggage
(c) A person who works hardly
(d) A violent man

Ans. (b)

The idiom 'a beast of burden' means 'an animal that carries luggage.' It refers to animals like donkeys or mules that are used for carrying heavy loads.

514. New kid on the block.
SSC CHSL Tier-1 20.03.2023 (Shift-III)

(a) Don't hurt anyone that helps you
(b) Savings set aside for future use
(c) Nonsense or meaningless speech
(d) Someone new to the group or area

Ans. (d)

'New kid on the block' means someone who has just started a new activity.

515. Cast someone adrift.
SSC CHSL Tier-1 20.03.2023 (Shift-III)

(a) To blame someone for one's mistakes.
(b) To leave someone without any support or purpose
(c) Call someone repeatedly
(d) To change plane suddenly

Ans. (b)

'Cast someone adrift' means to stop supporting someone, or leave someone without any support or purpose.

516. To take the veil

SSC CHSL Tier-1 20.03.2023 (Shift-IV)

(a) To help someone
(b) To become nun
(c) To take a responsibility
(d) To show interest

Ans. (b)

The idiom 'to take the evil' means 'to become a nun.' It refers to the act of entering a religious life.

517. To the manner born

SSC CHSL Tier-1 20.03.2023 (Shift-IV)

(a) To have high manners
(b) To do something as though it is coming naturally
(c) To be sophisticated
(d) To give a ride to someone

Ans. (b)

The idiom 'to the manner born' means 'to do something as though it is coming naturally.' It describes someone who is naturally suited to a particular role or activity.

518. To miss the bus

SSC CHSL Tier-1 21.03.2023 (Shift-II)

(a) Escape by a thin margin
(b) Short lived glory
(c) To lose an opportunity
(d) A problem in a situation

Ans. (c)

The idiom 'to miss the bus' means 'to lose an opportunity.' It suggests failing to take advantage of a chance.

519. To have a nodding acquaintance

SSC CHSL Tier-1 21.03.2023 (Shift-II)

(a) To neglect all the parameters
(b) To have nothing in common
(c) To have a great experience
(d) Know somebody/something slightly

Ans. (d)

'To have a nodding acquaintance' means to know someone slightly or have a slight knowledge of a subject.

520. The whys and wherefores

SSC CHSL Tier-1 21.03.2023 (Shift-IV)

(a) Reasons (b) References
(c) Circumstances (d) Requirements

Ans. (a)

'The whys and wherefores' means the reasons or explanation for something.

521. As hard as nails

SSC CHSL Tier-1 21.03.2023 (Shift-IV)

(a) To feel no pain
(b) To be stubborn
(c) Hard working
(d) Physically or mentally tough

Ans. (d)

'As hard as nails' means not feeling or showing any emotions such as sympathy, fear or worry, very strong and good at fighting. Such a person is physically or mentally tough.

522. With the harsh words of the boss, Srujan felt sad, but his colleague's words <u>created insult to injury</u>.

SSC CHSL Tier-1 02.08.2023 (Shift-I)

(a) attached insult to injury
(b) provoked insult to injury
(c) added injury to insult
(d) added insult to injury

Ans. (d)

The idiom 'added insult to injury' means 'to make a bad situation worse by adding more discomfort or trouble.'

It describes making someone feel even worse about something that is already negative.

523. It's better to get less than what you want than get nothing.

SSC CHSL Tier-1 02.08.2023 (Shift-II)

(a) Half a loaf is better than none
(b) Waste not, want not
(c) Where there is smoke, there is fire
(d) A storm in a teacup

Ans. (a)

The idiom 'half a loaf is better than none' means 'it's better to get less than what you want than get nothing.' It emphasises the value of having something rather than nothing at all.

Waste not, want not is a proverb advising careful use of resources to avoid waste.

Where there is smoke, there is fire suggests that there is usually a basis for rumours or suspicion.

A storm in a teacup refers to a small event that has been exaggerated out of proportion.

524. The government arrested the opposition leader, making the situation worse.

SSC CHSL Tier-1 02.08.2023 (Shift-III)

(a) To cast pearls before swine
(b) To be on the last leg
(c) To add fuel to the fire
(d) To bite the dust

Ans. (c)

The idiom **'to add fuel to the fire'** means 'to make the situation worse.' It describes actions that exacerbate an already difficult or volatile situation.

To cast pearls before swine means to offer something valuable to someone who cannot appreciate it.

To be on the last leg means to be nearing the end of something, usually a journey or process.

To bite the dust means to fall to the ground, often in defeat or death.

525. Memory like sieve

SSC CHSL Tier-1 03.08.2023 (Shift-I)

(a) Being healthy
(b) Poor memory
(c) Feeling ill
(d) Remembering everything

Ans. (b)

'Memory like sieve' means to forget things easily.

Hence, 'poor memory' is its appropriate meaning.

526. The candidate blamed the persistent traffic jam as reason of his being late and the interviewer <u>believed him though he was not convinced</u>.

SSC CHSL Tier-1 03.08.2023 (Shift-I)

(a) Gave the benefit of doubt
(b) Changed his tune
(c) Though err is human and to forgive is divine
(d) Did not judge the book by its cover

Ans. (a)

'Give the benefit of doubt' means to decide that you will believe someone, even thought you are not sure that what is person saying is to true.

Hence, it can substitute the underlined expression.

527. Aurangzeb, the famous Mughal ruler found that he had caught someone more powerful than him in the form of the brave Maratha, Shivaji.

SSC CHSL Tier-1 03.08.2023 (Shift-II)

(a) Nipping in the bud
(b) Changing the hands
(c) Catching a tartar
(d) Blazing the trail

Ans. (c)

The idiom 'catching a tartar' means 'to encounter someone more powerful than oneself.'

It suggests unexpectedly facing a formidable opponent.

528. Geetika spoke a lot about her new movie. However, it came to nothing in the theatres.

SSC CHSL Tier-1 03.08.2023 (Shift-III)

(a) To give the devil his dues
(b) To get into hot water
(c) To dig the grave
(d) To end in smoke

Ans. (d)

The idiom 'to end in smoke' means 'to come to nothing.' It describes something that fails to produce the expected result.

529. Raima takes her classes very attentively.
SSC CHSL Tier-1 03.08.2023 (Shift-III)
(a) In accordance with
(b) By blazing a trail
(c) By losing in a cloud
(d) Be all ears
Ans. (d)
The idiom 'be all ears' means 'to listen very attentively.' It suggests being eager and attentive to hear something.

530. Make up one's mind
SSC CHSL Tier-1 03.08.2023 (Shift-IV)
(a) To disturb (b) To leave
(c) To decide (d) To cheat
Ans. (c)
The idiom 'make up one's mind' means 'to decide.' It indicates coming to a conclusion or making a choice.

531. After procrastinating for weeks, I finally had to bite the bullet and ask my boss for a raise.
SSC CHSL Tier-1 04.08.2023 (Shift-I)
(a) To give up easily
(b) To endure a painful or difficult situation with courage and determination
(c) To be indecisive
(d) To take the easy way out
Ans. (b)
The idiom 'bite the bullet' means 'to endure a painful or difficult situation with courage and determination.' It suggests facing something tough head-on.

532. Getting the long-awaited promotion is a milestone in her career.
SSC CHSL Tier-1 04.08.2023 (Shift-I)
(a) Burden
(b) Important event
(c) Wonder
(d) Mishap
Ans. (b)
The word 'milestone' in this context means 'an important event.' It signifies a significant achievement or stage in one's career.

533. Her son came from Europe to meet her ...... after 20 years.
SSC CHSL Tier-1 04.08.2023 (Shift-II)
(a) blowing off the steam
(b) like a cakewalk
(c) out of the blue
(d) stepping up his game
Ans. (c)
The correct idiom for the given blank is **'out of the blue'**. This idiom refers to something that is entirely unexpected.

534. When I was in Italy for a tour, the tourist guide provided by Azim was because of him, the whole tour was successful.
SSC CHSL Tier-1 04.08.2023 (Shift-III)
(a) Looking for a needle in a haystack
(b) Burning the midnight oil
(c) Worth his weight in gold
(d) Armed to the teeth
Ans. (c)
The idiom **'worth his weight in gold'** means 'extremely valuable or helpful.' It indicates that the tourist guide was very useful and contributed significantly to the success of the tour.
Looking for a needle in a haystack means searching for something very difficult to find.
Burning the midnight oil means working late into the night.
Armed to the teeth means fully equipped.

535. The new entrant in the class felt uncomfortable as all were unfamiliar to him.
SSC CHSL Tier-1 04.08.2023 (Shift-IV)
(a) Left out in cold
(b) Was not given a fig
(c) Was fish out of water
(d) Buried his head in the sand
Ans. (c)
The idiom **'a fish out of water'** means 'to feel uncomfortable in unfamiliar surroundings.' It describes the new entrant feeling uneasy because everyone was unfamiliar.
Left out in the cold means to be ignored or excluded.
Was not given a fig means to not care at all.
Buried his head in the sand means to ignore an obvious problem.

536. Like a cat on a hot tin roof
SSC CHSL Tier-1 07.08.2023 (Shift-IV)
(a) Studying very hard
(b) Being lazy
(c) Being in a state of agitation
(d) Urging somebody not to worry about something.
Ans. (c)
'Like a cat on a hot tin roof' means in an uneasy or agitated state.

537. Most of the people say that some people fight for the cause but most of them don't support it.
SSC CHSL Tier-1 07.08.2023 (Shift-IV)
(a) Are out of frying pan onto the fire
(b) Spare the rod and spoil the child
(c) Pay only lip service
(d) Mind their P's and Q's
Ans. (c)
The idiom 'pay only lip service' means that you support or agree with something without doing anything to prove it. Thus, it can substitute the underlined expression.

538. Devil's advocate
SSC CHSL Tier-1 08.08.2023 (Shift-II)
(a) One who takes an opposing position for the sake of an argument
(b) One who presents very logical arguments
(c) One who is very precise and accurate
(d) One who never argues
Ans. (a)
'Devil's advocate' refers to one who takes an opposing position for the sake of an argument.

539. The servants know the secrets of the family they are working for.
SSC CHSL Tier-1 09.08.2023 (Shift-I)
(a) ins and outs
(b) Latin and Greek
(c) Hornets nest
(d) Long and short
Ans. (a)
The idiom 'ins and outs' is the most appropriate for 'secrets' as it means the details or complicated facts about something.

540. Shruti is a strange person because of her attitude.
SSC CHSL Tier-1 09.08.2023 (Shift-I)
(a) A one man (b) A scarlet woman
(c) Queer fish (d) A straw man
Ans. (c)
'Queer fish' means a strange person.

541. The proud people forget the fact that the world is tangible.
SSC CHSL Tier-1 10.08.2023 (Shift-III)
(a) Hobson's choice
(b) Head and shoulders
(c) High and mighty
(d) Hard-nosed attitude
Ans. (c)
'High and mighty' is the most appropriate idiom for 'proud people'. It means behaving as if you are much more important than other people.

542. Richa was provoking her neighbours against her maid Shanta who spoke against her but none of them responded.
SSC CHSL Tier-1 11.08.2023 (Shift-I)
(a) Smelling a rat
(b) Egging on
(c) Carrying the conviction
(d) Rising like a phoenix

Ans. (b)

The idiom **'egging on'** means 'to provoke or encourage someone to do something.' Richa was trying to provoke her neighbours against her maid Shanta.

Smelling a rat means to suspect something is wrong.

Carrying the conviction means to have strong belief.

Rising like a phoenix means to emerge stronger from a difficult situation.

543. Tourists from all around the world visit Agra to see the Taj Mahal.

SSC CHSL Tier-1 11.08.2023 (Shift-I)

(a) Ever and anon (b) Cut and dried
(c) Few and far (d) Far and wide

Ans. (d)

The idiom 'far and wide' means all around the world and thus, it can substitute the underlined expression.

544. Teja is a successful businessman; he always makes hay when the Sun shines. **SSC CHSL Tier-1.08.2023 (Shift-II)**

(a) Makes hay while the Sun sets
(b) Makes hay while the Sun shines
(c) Makes hay while the Moon rises
(d) Makes hay while the stars twinkle

Ans. (b)

The idiom 'make hay while the Sun shines' means 'to take advantage of favourable circumstances.' It suggests that Teja takes advantage of opportunities to be successful.

545. Having a chip on one's shoulder

SSC CHSL Tier-1 11.08.2023 (Shift-II)

(a) Having an unnecessary feeling of guilt
(b) Having an irritated and unfriendly attitude
(c) Having a proud and self-centred arrogance
(d) Showing great resistance to any adversities

Ans. (b)

The idiom 'having a chip on one's shoulder' means 'having an irritated and unfriendly attitude.'

It describes someone who feels slighted and is looking for a confrontation.

546. I told Benny that the die was cast and there was no further escape.

SSC CHSL Tier-1 11.08.2023 (Shift-III)

(a) The course of action ended and it couldn't be restarted
(b) The course of action would never begin
(c) The course of action began and it could not be blocked
(d) The course of action yet to start and it could be postponed

Ans. (c)

The idiom 'the die was cast' means 'the course of action began and it could not be blocked.' It indicates that a decision was made and it is irreversible.

547. Turn his hand to

SSC CHSL Tier-1 11.08.2023 (Shift-III)

(a) To resolve
(b) To adapt or apply to
(c) To try new things
(d) To try hard

Ans. (b)

The idiom 'turn his hand to' means 'to adapt or apply to.' It refers to the ability to handle or engage in different types of activities or tasks successfully.

548. Throw cold water on

SSC CHSL Tier-1 14.08.2023 (Shift-I)

(a) To show indifference
(b) To rinse thorughly
(c) To encourage
(d) To talk nicely

Ans. (a)

The idiom 'throw cold water on' means 'to show indifference or discourage.' It implies dismissing or being negative about an idea or effort, thereby reducing enthusiasm or excitement.

549. Piyush is inexperienced in leather industry. **SSC CHSL Tier-1 14.08.2023 (Shift-I)**

(a) in great hands (b) a sore thumb
(c) hang fire (d) a greenhorn

Ans. (d)

The idiom 'a greenhorn' means 'inexperienced.' It describes someone who is new to a particular activity or field and lacks experience or expertise.

550. She's been beating around the bush all afternoon - I just wish she would come out and tell us what she really thinks. **SSC CHSL Tier-1 14.08.2023 (Shift-II)**

(a) Avoiding to talk directly about a topic or issue
(b) Trying to be overprotective
(c) Denying to have her head in the clouds
(d) There to give the cold shoulder

Ans. (a)

The idiom 'beating around the bush' means 'avoiding to talk directly about a topic or issue.' It describes not addressing the main point and instead talking about irrelevant things.

551. It's not polite to blow your own trumpet in front of others.

SSC CHSL Tier-1 14.08.2023 (Shift-II)

(a) Brag one's own accomplishment
(b) Criticise someone unfairly
(c) Play a musical instrument
(d) Give someone a compliment

Ans. (a)

The idiom 'blow your own trumpet' means 'to brag about one's own accomplishments.' It refers to boasting or speaking too proudly about oneself.

552. Cry for the Moon

SSC CHSL Tier-1 14.08.2023 (Shift-III)

(a) To start performing better
(b) To have patience
(c) To desire the unattainable
(d) To be extremely happy

Ans. (c)

The idiom 'cry for the Moon' means 'to desire the unattainable.' It describes wanting something that is impossible or very difficult to achieve.

553. Instead of taking the time to do the job properly, they decided to cut corners and save time by using cheap materials.

SSC CHST Tier-1 14.08.2023 (Shift-III)

(a) Avoid someone or something intentionally
(b) Physically cut a corner off of something
(c) Take a shortcut for easy way out in order to save efforts
(d) Break a promise or commitment

Ans. (c)

The idiom 'cut corners' means 'to take a shortcut or easy way out in order to save effort.' It implies doing something in the quickest or cheapest way, often sacrificing quality or thoroughness.

554. Have a narrow escape

SSC CHSL Tier-1 14.08.2023 (Shift-IV)

(a) Only just succeed in doing something
(b) Likely to fall in the near future
(c) Do something very risky
(d) Just manage to avoid danger of trouble

Ans. (d)

'Have a narrow escape' means to just be able to avoid danger or trouble.

555. The childhood days are peaceful days of our life.

SSC CHSL Tier-1 14.08.2023 (Shift-IV)

(a) halcyon days
(b) live wire days
(c) all years
(d) hard and fast days

Ans. (a)

The idiom 'halcyon days', means peaceful days and thus, it can substitute the underlined expression.

556. My mother asked my father to increase her personal use allowance.

SSC CHSL Tier-1 17.08.2023 (Shift-I)

(a) pell mell (b) rank and file
(c) pins and needles (d) pin money

Ans. (d)

'Pin money' refers to money given by a man to a woman in his family (such as his wife or daughter) for her own use. Hence, it can substitute the underlined expression.

557. The manager was punished for his negligence in work.
SSC CHSL Tier-1 17.08.2023 (Shift-I)

(a) Bid defiance
(b) Burn one's boats
(c) Bolt from the blue
(d) Bring to book

Ans. (d)

'Bring to book' is the most appropriate idiom for the given statement. It means to punish someone and make that person explain behaviour.

558. He was alone and knew the dangers ahead during his journey, but he <u>tried to keep up his confidence</u>.
SSC CHSL Tier-1 17.08.2023 (Shift-III)

(a) whistled in the dark
(b) made a sterner stuff
(c) stepped up his game
(d) wouldn't be caught dead

Ans. (a)

The idiom 'whistled in the dark' means 'to try to keep up one's confidence in a difficult situation.' It suggests maintaining a hopeful outlook or confidence despite knowing that the situation is challenging or dangerous.

559. Nitish's promotion is <u>due</u>.
SSC CHSL Tier-1 17.08.2023 (Shift-IV)

(a) On the cards
(b) Not worth his salt
(c) With due respect
(d) Done to death

Ans. (a)

The idiom 'on the cards' means 'likely to happen or due.' It indicates that an event or outcome is expected or anticipated.

560. In hot water SSC CHSL Tier-2 02.11.2023

(a) After accidentally breaking the valuable vase, Sarah found herself in trouble with her parents.
(b) The children enjoyed playing in the pool on a hot summer day.
(c) The company faced challenges due to the economic downturn but managed to overcome them.
(d) The chef added spices to the dish to enhance its flavour and make it more delicious.

Ans. (a)

The idiom 'in hot water' means 'to be in trouble.' The sentence about Sarah found herself in trouble with her parents after accidentally breaking the valuable fits this meaning.

561. I was unable to solve the geometry question myself. So, I have asked my teacher to help me out.
SSC CHSL Tier-2 02.11.2023

(a) You can't always get what you want.
(b) Two heads are better than one.
(c) Two wrongs don't make a right.
(d) When the going gets tough, the tough gets going.

Ans. (b)

The idiom 'two heads are better than one' means 'collaborating with someone else can yield better results.' It suggests that asking the teacher for help was a good idea because collaboration often leads to better outcomes.

562. Rajat irritated the street dog so much that it was about to bite him.
SSC CHSL Tier-2 02.11.2023

(a) If you play with fire, you'll get burned.
(b) If it ain't broke, don't fix it.
(c) If you can't beat 'em, join 'em.
(d) If you want something done right, you have to do it yourself.

Ans. (a)

The idiom 'if you play with fire, you'll get burned' means 'engaging in risky behaviour will lead to negative consequences.' Rajat irritating the street dog and risking a bite fits this meaning.

SSC CHSL 2022 (Tier 1)

563. A fly on the wall
SSC CHSL Tier-1 24.05.2022 (Shift-I)

(a) A vigilant security guard
(b) An unperceived observer
(c) Very intelligent person
(d) unwelcome guest

Ans. (b)

The idiom 'a fly on the wall' means 'an unperceived observer.' It describes someone who watches or listens to something without being noticed, often to gather information without interfering.

564. Gear up for
SSC CHSL Tier-1 24.05.2022 (Shift-II)

(a) Start off (b) Pass into
(c) Get ready (d) Put on

Ans. (c)

The idiom 'gear up for' means 'get ready.' It suggests preparing oneself for something.

565. Call upon
SSC CHSL Tier-1 24.05.2022 (Shift-II)

(a) To adjust (b) To stop
(c) To allow (d) To order

Ans. (d)

The idiom 'call upon' means 'to order.' It can also mean to ask someone to do something formally.

566. Lose your touch
SSC CHSL Tier-1 24.05.2022 (Shift-III)

(a) Doing someone a favour in hopes that the favour will be returned
(b) To be passed from one person to another
(c) Not being as successful as previously
(d) Something being very difficult to find

Ans. (c)

The idiom 'lose your touch' means 'not being as successful as previously.' It describes when someone is no longer as effective or skilled at something as they once were.

567. At one's elbow
SSC CHSL Tier-1 24.05.2022 (Shift-III)

(a) Next to someone
(b) Far away
(c) Strong grip
(d) Strong bond

Ans. (a)

The idiom 'at one's elbow' means 'next to someone.' It describes being very close to or nearby someone.

568. Blow up
SSC CHSL Tier-1 24.05.2022 (Shift-III)

(a) To suffice
(b) To live up greatly
(c) To destroy by an explosion
(d) To stand upright

Ans. (c)

The idiom 'blow up' means 'to destroy by an explosion.' It describes something being destroyed violently.

569. Tell upon
SSC CHSL Tier-1 25.05.2022 (Shift-III)

(a) To strike hard
(b) To advise someone
(c) To affect adversely
(d) To down

Ans. (c)

The idiom 'tell upon' means 'to affect adversely.' It describes having a negative effect on something or someone.

570. Win laurels
SSC CHSL Tier-1 26.05.2022 (Shift-II)

(a) To gain honour (b) To be decisive
(c) To change (d) To punish

Ans. (a)

The idiom 'win laurels' means 'to gain honour.' It signifies achieving recognition or acclaim for one's achievements.

571. Safe pair of hands
SSC CHSL Tier-1 26.05.2022 (Shift-III)

(a) Miss an opportunity
(b) Speak rashly without thinking carefully
(c) A secret or hidden advantage
(d) A person who can be trusted to do thing efficiently

Ans. (d)

The idiom 'safe pair of hands' means 'a person who can be trusted to do things efficiently.' It describes someone reliable and competent.

572. Let down
SSC CHSL Tier-1 26.05.2022 (Shift-III)

(a) To hire (b) To care about
(c) To fail (d) To nurse

Ans. (c)

The idiom 'let down' means 'to fail.' It describes disappointing someone by not meeting their expectations.

573. Donkey's years
SSC CHSL Tier-1 27.05.2022 (Shift-I)

(a) Leisure time (b) Bad time
(c) Long time (d) Good time

Ans. (c)

'Donkey's years' means an extremely long time.

574. Go to the wall
SSC CHSL Tier-1 27.05.2022 (Shift-I)

(a) To become strong
(b) To obtain protection
(c) To fail
(d) To start

Ans. (c)

'Go to the wall' means 'to fail', especially when this involves losing all your business and money.

575. Lion's share
SSC CHSL Tier-1 30.05.2022 (Shift-I)

(a) Largest share (b) Animal's share
(c) Limited share (d) Forceful share

Ans. (a)

'Lion's share' means the largest part of something.

576. Get the axe
SSC CHSL Tier-1 30.05.2022 (Shift-I)

(a) Burdened job (b) Lose the job
(c) Relaxed job (d) Get the job

Ans. (b)

'Get the axe' refers to a suitable in which a government, company or an organisation decides to end something or to get rid of a worker or their job.

577. Wipe the floor with someone
SSC CHSL Tier-1 30.05.2022 (Shift-I)

(a) To defeat someone
(b) To criticise someone
(c) To cheat someone
(d) To help someone

Ans. (a)

'Wipe the floor with someone' means to defeat someone very easily in a game or an argument.

578. Sum and substance
SSC CHSL Tier-1 31.05.2022 (Shift-I)

(a) Essence (b) Difficulty
(c) Deliberation (d) Assessment

Ans. (a)

'Sum and substance' means the general or basic meaning or essence of something said or written.

579. Under duress
SSC CHSL Tier-1 31.05.2022 (Shift-I)

(a) Under pressure (b) Under shelter
(c) Under confusions (d) Under support

Ans. (a)

'Under duress' means force, pressure or threats that make someone do something they do not want to.

580. Bed of roses
SSC CHSL Tier-1 01.06.2022 (Shift-I)

(a) Trying condition of life
(b) Lethargic condition of life
(c) Testing condition of life
(d) Pleasant condition of life

Ans. (d)

'Bed of roses' means a happy, comfortable or easy situation. Hence, 'pleasant condition of life' gives its appropriate meaning.

581. Pull a long face
SSC CHSL Tier-I 01.06.2022 (Shift-I)

(a) To look angry
(b) To look sad
(c) To flatter someone
(d) To chide someone

Ans. (b)

'Pull a long face' means a sad, disappointed or serious expression on someone's face.

582. White elephant
SSC CHSL Tier-1 02.06.2022 (Shift-I)

(a) Useful and expensive possession
(b) Memorable possession
(c) Costly but useless possession
(d) Motivational possession

Ans. (c)

'White elephant' means something that is completely useless, although it may have cost a lot of money.

583. To put someone's back up
SSC CHSL Tier-1 02.06.2022 (Shift-I)

(a) To flatter someone
(b) To irritate someone
(c) To help someone
(d) To deceive someone

Ans. (b)

'To put someone's back up' means to annoy someone.

584. Be at a loose end
SSC CHSL Tier-1 03.06.2022 (Shift-I)

(a) To have nothing to do
(b) On a turning point
(c) Defining moment
(d) In much trouble

Ans. (a)

The idiom 'be at a loose end' means 'to have nothing to do.' It describes a situation where someone is idle or has no particular activity to engage in.

585. The memory of all that blood was enough to <u>make my flesh crawl</u>.
SSC CHSL Tier-1 06.06.2022 (Shift-I)

(a) frightened me (b) worried me
(c) drew my attention (d) confused me

Ans. (a)

The idiom 'make my flesh crawl' means 'frightened me.' It describes a feeling of intense fear or disgust.

586. The attitude of the culprit made the judge <u>extremely angry</u>.
SSC CHSL Tier-1 06.06.2022 (Shift-II)

(a) Throw caution to the wind
(b) Make one's blood boil
(c) Play by the ear
(d) Back to the drawing board

Ans. (b)

The idiom 'make one's blood boil' means 'to make someone extremely angry.' It describes a situation where someone is infuriated.

587. The minister is <u>a little hard of hearing</u> SSC CHSL Tier-1 06.06.2022 (Shift-III)

(a) inaccessible (b) callous
(c) partially deaf (d) insensitive

Ans. (c)

The phrase 'hard of hearing' means 'partially deaf.' It refers to someone who has difficulty hearing.

588. Upset the apple-cart
SSC CHSL Tier-1 08.06.2022 (Shift-I)

(a) Withdraw
(b) Spoil careful plans
(c) Consider unsatisfactory
(d) To be offended

Ans. (b)

The idiom 'upset the apple-cart' means 'to spoil careful plans.' It describes causing disruption or failure in a well-organised plan.

589. Pocket an insult
SSC CHSL Tier-1 08.06.2022 (Shift-I)
(a) Insult someone strongly
(b) Endure insult and protest
(c) Tolerate insult without protest
(d) Rebel against insult

Ans. (c)

The idiom 'pocket an insult' means 'to tolerate insult without protest.' It describes enduring an insult without responding.

590. In your birthday suit
SSC CHSL Tier-1 08.06.2022 (Shift-II)
(a) Not wearing any clothes
(b) A suit which covers one's entire body
(c) Birthday celebrations
(d) A suit which is designed for only birthday functions

Ans. (a)

The idiom 'in your birthday suit' means 'not wearing any clothes.' It refers to being completely naked.

591. The coach was trying to twist the player's arm by asking him to practice throughout the day.
SSC CHSL Tier-1 08.06.2022 (Shift-II)
(a) To try to force someone to do something
(b) To refrain from resting
(c) To train someone in warfare
(d) To console the weak

Ans. (a)

The idiom 'twist the player's arm' means 'to try to force someone to do something.' It describes applying pressure on someone to get them to comply.

592. Cast aside
SSC CHSL Tier-1 08.06.2022 (Shift-II)
(a) To blow up (b) To bear with
(c) To display (d) To reject

Ans. (d)

The idiom 'cast aside' means 'to reject.' It describes discarding or dismissing something or someone.

593. Tick all the boxes
SSC CHSL Tier-1 08.06.2022 (Shift-II)
(a) To make a bad situation worse
(b) To fulfill the required norms
(c) To be extremely happy
(d) To make a decision

Ans. (b)

The idiom 'tick all the boxes' means 'to fulfill the required norms.' It refers to meeting all the criteria or expectations.

594. Get one's dander up
SSC CHSL Tier-1 09.06.2022 (Shift-I)
(a) Rush into someone
(b) Get into a difficult situation
(c) Lose one's temper
(d) To glare venomously

Ans. (c)

The idiom 'get one's dander up' means 'to lose one's temper.' It describes becoming angry or upset.

595. Hit the sack
SSC CHSL Tier-1 09.05.2022 (Shift-II)
(a) Miss the mark
(b) Confirm the target
(c) Complete the assignment
(d) Go to sleep

Ans. (d)

The idiom 'hit the sack' means 'to go to sleep.' It describes going to bed to rest.

596. In queer street
SSC CHSL Tier-1 09.05.2022 (Shift-II)
(a) Among scoundrels
(b) In prison
(c) Lost your way
(d) In debt

Ans. (d)

The idiom 'in queer street' means 'in debt.' It describes a situation of financial trouble.

597. The movers and shakers
SSC CHSL Tier-1 09.06.2022 (Shift-II)
(a) People who have lot of power and influence
(b) Transportation company
(c) Labourers
(d) Travelling agency

Ans. (a)

The idiom 'the movers and shakers' means 'people who have a lot of power and influence.' It describes influential and powerful individuals.

598. Face up to
SSC CHSL Tier-1 10.06.2022 (Shift-III)
(a) Look into face
(b) Personally
(c) Alter the face of
(d) To accept a difficult situation

Ans. (d)

The idiom 'face up to' means 'to accept a difficult situation.' It describes confronting and dealing with challenging circumstances.

SSC CHSL 2021 (Tier 1)

599. The eradication of Corona virus is still a far cry.
SSC CHSL Tier-1 12.04.2021 (Shift-I)
(a) very near
(b) very easy
(c) very fast
(d) very distant

Ans. (d)

The idiom 'a far cry' means 'very distant.' It indicates something that is very different from or far from being achieved.

600. Living in a fool's paradise
SSC CHSL Tier-1 12.04.2021 (Shift-I)
(a) To believe wrongly that your situation is good
(b) To be fooled by someone
(c) To live in luxuriously after fooling someone
(d) To live in a world of imagination

Ans. (a)

The idiom 'living in a fool's paradise' means 'to believe wrongly that your situation is good.' It describes a false sense of well-being.

601. To put one's foot in one's mouth
SSC CHSL Tier-1 12.04.2021 (Shift-II)
(a) To deliberately provoke someone
(b) To gather all of one's resources
(c) To be disorderly and stupid
(d) To accidentally embarrass or upset someone

Ans. (d)

The idiom 'to put one's foot in one's mouth' means 'to accidentally embarrass or upset someone.' It describes saying something that unintentionally causes embarrassment or offense.

602. She may be the principal but it is the school administrator who rules the roost.
SSC CHSL Tier-1 12.04.2021 (Shift-II)
(a) is proved right
(b) is in complete control
(c) is totally submissive
(d) is dependent upon her

Ans. (b)

If someone rules the roost in a particular place, it means that they have control and authority over people there.

603. To run around like a headless chicken
SSC CHSL Tier-1 13.04.2021 (Shift-II)
(a) To do things methodically one by one
(b) To be lazy and unwilling to work
(c) To do many things in a disorganised manner
(d) To be unable to catch escaping chicken.

Ans. (c)

The idiom 'to run around like a headless chicken' means 'to do many things in a disorganised manner.' It describes someone acting frantically and ineffectively without a clear plan or purpose.

604. Be glad to see the back of
SSC CHSL Tier-1 15.04.2021 (Shift-II)
(a) Be happy at another's success
(b) Be relieved at another's failure
(c) Be happy to see someone again
(d) Be happy when a person leaves

Ans. (d)

The idiom 'be glad to see the back of' means 'to be happy when a person leaves.' It suggests feeling relieved or pleased about someone's departure.

605. Provide a blueprint
SSC CHSL Tier-1 15.04.2021 (Shift-III)
(a) Propose a plan of a secret meeting
(b) Submit a printed application for a blue-collared job
(c) Give a detailed plan or scheme
(d) Have a building plan printed in blue

Ans. (c)

The idiom 'provide a blueprint' means 'to give a detailed plan or scheme.' It refers to presenting a comprehensive and well-structured plan.

606. To drag one's feet
SSC CHSL Tier-1 19.04.2021 (Shift-I)
(a) To walk unsteadily
(b) To walk with a limp
(c) To pull someone's legs
(d) To delay taking a decision

Ans. (d)

The idiom 'to drag one's feet' means 'to delay taking a decision.' It describes procrastinating or being reluctant to act promptly.

607. A grey area
SSC CHSL Tier-1 19.04.2021 (Shift-III)
(a) An unclear situation
(b) A special part of the brain
(c) An unspoken truth
(d) An unusual spot

Ans. (a)

The idiom 'a grey area' means 'an unclear situation.' It describes a situation that is not well defined or lacks clarity.

608. To be in the dark
SSC CHSL Tier-1 19.04.2021 (Shift-III)
(a) To always be in a bad mood about darkness
(b) To learn to face dark places without fear
(c) To be afraid of darkness and refuse to go out at night
(d) To not know something others are aware of

Ans. (d)

'To be in the dark' means keep someone unaware, not informed, keep somebody off from any act.

609. Under wraps
SSC CHSL Tier-1 04.08.2021 (Shift-I)
(a) Under estimate (b) Double layered
(c) Secretly (d) Underhand

Ans. (c)

'Under wraps' means known to only a few people. So, 'secretly' is appropriate meaning.

610. To go red in the face
SSC CHSL Tier-1 04.08.2021 (Shift-II)
(a) To shout at someone for doing something wrong
(b) To feel embarrassed
(c) To feel very happy and proud
(d) To feel extremely irritated

Ans. (b)

The idiom 'to go red in the face' means 'to feel embarrassed.' It describes the physical reaction of blushing due to embarrassment or shame.

611. Pull something off
SSC CHSL Tier-1 04.08.2021 (Shift-III)
(a) Drag something forcibly
(b) Take out the cover or lid
(c) Make something happen
(d) Make a lot of noise

Ans. (c)

The idiom 'pull something off' means 'to make something happen.'

It describes successfully achieving or accomplishing something difficult.

612. To have eggs on one's face
SSC CHSL Tier-1 05.08.2021 (Shift-I)
(a) To be embarrassed because of one's action
(b) To apply egg yolk on one's face for making it look beautiful
(c) To throw eggs on a speaker's face
(d) To buy eggs and break them

Ans. (a)

The idiom 'to have eggs on one's face' means 'to be embarrassed because of one's actions.'

It describes feeling foolish or humiliated due to a mistake.

613. Thick as thieves
SSC CHSL Tier-1 05.08.2021 (Shift-I)
(a) Having a close friendship
(b) Being very dishonest
(c) Never helping anyone
(d) Telling lies all the time

Ans. (a)

The idiom 'thick as thieves' means 'having a close friendship.' It describes a strong and inseparable bond between friends.

614. He is very impulsive and does things without rhyme or reason.
SSC CHSL Tier-1 06.08.2021 (Shift-I)
(a) without proper planning
(b) without a reasonable explanation
(c) without any resources
(d) Without anyone's help

Ans. (b)

The idiom 'without rhyme or reason' means 'without a reasonable explanation.' It describes actions that appear random or illogical.

615. Organic food seems to be in vogue these days.
SSC CHSL Tier-1 06.08.2021 (Shift-III)
(a) readily available (b) out of stock
(c) in fashion (d) very expensive

Ans. (c)

The idiom 'in vogue' means 'in fashion.'

It describes something that is currently popular or trendy.

616. A fire in someone's belly
SSC CHSL Tier-1 09.08.2021 (Shift-II)
(a) One who is energetic and enthusiastic about something
(b) One who is rich and powerful and exploits the poor
(c) one who comes from a middle class backcround
(d) one who continues to work without wanting a reward

Ans. (a)

The idiom 'a fire in someone's belly' means 'one who is energetic and enthusiastic about something.' It describes someone with strong passion and motivation.

617. Rank and file
SSC CHSL Tier-1 10.08.2021 (Shift-I)
(a) The manager of a personnel department
(b) Ordinary workers in a company
(c) Financial activities in a firm
(d) A very well-organised company

Ans. (b)

The idiom 'rank and file' means 'ordinary workers in a company.' It refers to the general workforce, excluding management.

618. My brother has decided to settle in London for good.
SSC CHSL Tier-1 10.08.2021 (Shift-I)
(a) forever
(b) briefly
(c) for a better income
(d) for a promotion

Ans. (a)

The idiom 'for good' means 'forever.' It indicates a permanent decision or action.

619. To come round
SSC CHSL Tier-1 10.08.2021 (Shift-II)
(a) To meet someone by chance
(b) To spend a lot of time with someone
(c) To go round and round
(d) To become conscious again

Ans. (d)

The idiom 'to come round' means 'to become conscious again.' It describes regaining consciousness after fainting or being unconscious.

620. A lean patch
SSC CHSL Tier-1 10.08.2021 (Shift-III)
(a) Cloth that is beginning to tear
(b) A part of hair that is thin
(c) Friendship that has ended
(d) A period of poor performance

Ans. (d)

The idiom 'a lean patch' means 'a period of poor performance.' It refers to a time when things are not going well, especially in terms of success or productivity.

621. Hand on every word
SSC CHSL Tier-1 11.08.2021 (Shift-I)

(a) Speak very slowly
(b) Listen very carefully
(c) Stop after hearing one word
(d) Stammer while speaking

Ans. (b)

The idiom 'hang on every word' means 'to listen very carefully.' It describes paying close attention to everything someone is saying.

622. Their marriage wasn't working but they kept up appearances.
SSC CHSL Tier-1 12.08.2021 (Shift-I)

(a) maintained an expression of well being
(b) maintained peace and harmony
(c) kept throwing parties
(d) revealed the truth

Ans. (a)

The idiom 'kept up appearances' means 'maintained an expression of well-being.'

It refers to pretending that everything is fine when it is not.

623. Method to one's madness
SSC CHSL Tier-1 12.08.2021 (Shift-II)

(a) Being very neat and particular about details
(b) Seeming disorderly yet having a structure
(c) Always behaving like a mad person
(d) Not following rules and conventions

Ans. (b)

The idiom 'method to one's madness' means 'seeming disorderly yet having a structure.' It describes actions that appear chaotic but have a purpose.

624. Not one's cup of tea
SSC CHSL Tier-1 12.08.2021 (Shift-III)

(a) Not absolutely true
(b) Not according to one's interest
(c) Beyond one's comprehension
(d) Of no concern for someone

Ans. (b)

The idiom 'not one's cup of tea' means 'not according to one's interest.' It describes something that someone does not particularly like or enjoy.

625. To cross one's mind
SSC CHSL Tier-1 12.08.2021 (Shift-III)

(a) To forget something
(b) To put a thought away from one's mind
(c) To move from one idea to another
(d) To think of something

Ans. (d)

The idiom 'to cross one's mind' means 'to think of something.' It describes having a thought or idea occur to someone.

SSC MTS 2024 (Tier 1)

626. Throw in the towel
SSC MTS Tier-1 13.11.2024 (Shift-III)

(a) To give up or surrender
(b) To prepare to fight
(c) To take responsibility for a situation while another person is temporarily absent
(d) To cause an activity or process to continue

Ans. (a)

'To give up or surrender' is the most appropriate meaning of the idiom 'throw in the towel'. It means to admit defeat.

627. The minister was in **partnership** with the queen in poisoning the King.
SSC MTS Tier-1 13.11.2024 (Shift-III)

(a) in cahoots (b) in the blues
(c) at one's beck and call
(d) run amok

Ans. (a)

'In cahoots' is the most appropriate idiom that can substitute the highlighted text. **'In cahoots'** means to be in partnership, typically for a dishonest purpose.

In the blues means feeling sad or depressed.

At one's beck and call means always ready to obey someone's orders.

Run amok means to behave uncontrollably.

628. To accept the gauntlet
SSC MTS Tier-1 12.11.2024 (Shift-III)

(a) To accept failure
(b) To accept a challenge
(c) To suffer financial loss
(d) To suffer a great insult

Ans. (b)

'To accept a challenge' is the most appropriate meaning of the idiom 'to accept the gauntlet'. It means to accept a challenge.

629. We often go camping, but I have never been to that particular part of town or country before.
SSC MTS Tier-1 11.11.2024 (Shift-III)

(a) neck of the woods
(b) get it in the neck
(c) knock on wood
(d) risk one's neck

Ans. (a)

'Neck of the woods' is the most appropriate idiom. It means a particular part of town or country.

Get it in the neck means to be punished or blamed.

Knock on wood means to wish for good luck.

Risk one's neck means to put oneself in danger.

630. Rajiv will understand some day that all his friends are fair weather friends. SSC MTS Tier-1 11.11.2024 (Shift-III)

(a) True friends help you when you need them.
(b) Friends generally have similar characteristics.
(c) A friend who stays only when times are convenient.
(d) A friend who meets you only during pleasant weather.

Ans. (c)

'A friend who stays only when times are convenient is the most appropriate meaning of the idiom 'fair weather friends.'

631. Despite the difficulties, Sarah started her business with great energy and hard work and performed remarkably well in the industry.
SSC MTS Tier-1 05.11.2024 (Shift-III)

(a) Hit the ground running
(b) Hit the hay
(c) Spilled the beans
(d) Let sleeping dogs lie

Ans. (a)

'Hit the ground running' is the most appropriate idiom to substitute the underlined segment. It means to start something energetically and successfully.

Hit the hay means to go to bed.

Spilled the beans means to reveal a secret.

Let sleeping dogs lie means to avoid interfering in a situation that could lead to trouble.

632. The negotiations reached a point where both parties had to (confront the consequences of their actions) and make tough decisions.
SSC MTS Tier-1 30.10.2024 (Shift-III)

(a) face the music
(b) break a leg
(c) cut corners
(d) get cold feet

Ans. (a)

'Face the music' can substitute the bracketed word segment correctly. 'Face the music' means to confront the consequences of one's actions.

Break a leg means good luck.

Cut corners means to do something the easiest or cheapest way.

Get cold feet means to become nervous or hesitant.

633. My old car was pressed into service as an emergency vehicle for my ailing grandmother.
SSC MTS Tier-1 30.10.2024 (Shift-III)
(a) Cared for by old people
(b) Asking for special maintenance
(c) To use for a particular purpose when a special need occurs.
(d) Used to take someone to the hospital.
Ans. (c)
'To use for a particular purpose when a special need occurs' is the most appropriate meaning of the idiom 'pressed into service'. It means to use something for a special purpose when a need arises.

634. A square peg in a round hole
SSC MTS Tier-1 29.10.2024 (Shift-III)
(a) a person who is criminal by nature.
(b) a person who is bankrupt.
(c) a person who does not fit the job.
(d) a person who fits the job.
Ans. (c)
'A person who does not fit the job' is the correct meaning of the idiom 'a square peg in a round hole'.

635. Hornet's nest
SSC MTS Tier-1 28.10.2024 (Shift-II)
(a) A bee's nest
(b) A troublesome or hazardous situation
(c) A difficult task
(d) A house built with great difficulty
Ans. (b)
A troublesome or hazardous situation' is the most appropriate meaning of the idiom 'hornet's nest.' It refers to a situation fraught with difficulties or danger, akin to disturbing a nest of hornets.

636. Out of spirits
SSC MTS Tier-1 22.10.2024 (Shift-II)
(a) Hurt (b) Obsolete
(c) Gloomy (d) Cheerful
Ans. (c)
'Gloomy' is the most appropriate meaning of 'out of spirits'. It means feeling low or depressed.
Obsolete means no longer in use.

637. The unexpected guest at the party was a bull in a China shop.
SSC MTS Tier-1 22.10.2024 (Shift-II)
(a) leisurely and relaxed
(b) careful and compassionate
(c) influential and meticulous
(d) careless and damaging
Ans. (d)
'Careless and damaging' is the most appropriate option. The sentence means that the unexpected guest behaved in a way that caused disruption or damage.

638. The new employee is really trying to fit in, but sometimes he feels out of place and uncomfortable.
SSC MTS Tier-1 22.10.2024 (Shift-II)
(a) a needle in a haystack
(b) a diamond in the rough
(c) a bird of a feather
(d) a fish out of water
Ans. (d)
'A fish out of water' is the most appropriate idiom that can substitute the underlined segment. 'A fish out of water' means feeling out of place or uncomfortable in a new environment.
A needle in a haystack means something hard to find.
A diamond in the rough means someone who has potential but needs refinement.
A bird of a feather means people who have similar interests.

639. Sarvana failed in the examination last week and is in extreme depression these days.
SSC MTS Tier-1 21.10.2024 (Shift-II)
(a) In the red (b) In the doldrums
(c) In the lurch (d) In cold blood
Ans. (b)
'In the doldrums' is the most appropriate idiom for 'in extreme depression.' It means a state of inactivity or stagnation, often associated with depression.
In the red means in debt or losing money.
In the lurch means to leave someone without help or in a difficult situation.
In cold blood means to act without emotion or pity, usually in a violent context.

640. I heard management is planning to transfer me to another department and demote me. I need to confirm if this is true by hearing it directly from the person involved and from my manager. SSC MTS Tier-1 16.10.2024 (Shift-II)
(a) straight from the horse's mouth
(b) in the seventh heaven
(c) bearing a grudge
(d) on pins and needles
Ans. (a)
'Straight from the horse's mouth' is the idiom that can substitute the underlined words. It means hearing it directly from the person involved, ensuring authenticity.
In the seventh heaven means extremely happy.
Bearing a grudge means holding resentment.
On pins and needles means being anxious or nervous.

641. Sean is notorious for revealing the secrets about the company.
SSC MTS Tier-1 16.10.2024 (Shift-II)
(a) Being in bad blood
(b) Biting the dust
(c) Spilling the beans
(d) Biting the bullet
Ans. (c)
'Spilling the beans' is the correct idiom. It means revealing secrets or confidential information.
Being in bad blood means having a hostile relationship.
Biting the dust means failing or dying. Not relevant to revealing secrets.
Biting the bullet means facing a painful situation bravely.

642. At the top of your lungs
SSC MTS Tier-1 15.10.2024 (Shift-I)
(a) Extremely loud (b) Extremely silly
(c) Exhausted
(d) Pretend superiority
Ans. (a)
'At the top of your lungs' means extremely loud. It implies shouting or speaking very loudly.

643. Like a bat out of hell
SSC MTS Tier-1 15.10.2024 (Shift-I)
(a) Defeated
(b) In a bad situation
(c) Very fast and wildly
(d) Impossible
Ans. (c)
'Like a bat out of hell' means very fast and wildly.

644. His sudden resignation left the company in a very difficult situation and to have to make a hard decision as they scrambled to find a replacement.
SSC MTS Tier-1 14.10.2024 (Shift-I)
(a) in the dark
(b) with a silver lining
(c) between a rock and a hard place
(d) on cloud nine
Ans. (c)
'Between a rock and a hard place' is the correct idiom. It means being in a difficult situation with no easy way out.
In the dark means uninformed.
With a silver lining means seeing the positive side.
On cloud nine means very happy.

645. An open book
SSC MTS Tier-1 14.10.2024 (Shift-I)
(a) Someone who gives advice based on theory not practice
(b) A helpful person
(c) A person of whom her mother is extremely proud
(d) A person or thing that is easy to learn about and understand

Ans. (d)

'An open book' means a person or thing that is easy to learn about and understand.

646. Knuckle down
SSC MTS Tier-1 09.10.2024 (Shift-I)

(a) To crush someone to the extent that they cannot get up
(b) To start working or studying hard
(c) To make others do their share of hardwork using power
(d) To engage in street fighting

Ans. (b)

'Knuckle down' means to start working or studying hard. This idiom implies putting in a serious effort to achieve something, often after a period of delay or procrastination.

647. The comedian's jokes were so funny that the audience was laughing uncontrollably.
SSC MTS Tier-1 09.10.2024 (Shift-I)

(a) in stitches (b) in bits and pieces
(c) on the ball (d) as easy as pie

Ans. (a)

'In stitches' is the correct idiom for laughing uncontrollably. This idiom describes a situation where someone is laughing so hard that they might metaphorically be 'stitched' together.

In bits and pieces means broken into small parts.

On the ball means being alert and quick to respond.

As easy as pie means something is very easy.

648. Run errands
SSC MTS Tier-1 07.10.2024 (Shift-I)

(a) To participate in a race through unfair me.
(b) To finish running before the end point.
(c) To do something incorrectly or erroneous in haste.
(d) To go out to buy or do something

Ans. (d)

The most appropriate meaning of the idiom 'run errands' is 'to go out to buy or do something.' This idiom refers to the act of completing small tasks or chores outside the home. The other options misinterpret the idiom.

649. He gnashed his teeth at his son's actions. SSC MTS Tier-1 07.10.2024 (Shift-I)

(a) expressed sadness
(b) expressed disappointment
(c) expressed joy
(d) expressed rage

Ans. (d)

The idiom 'gnashed his teeth' means to express rage, indicating a strong reaction of anger. The other options misinterpret the idiom.

650. Sonali is contemplating whether to accept the offer from Saanvi or not; she is still not in a position to be able to arrive at a decision.
SSC MTS Tier-1 01.10.2024 (Shift-I)

(a) blowing hot and cold
(b) getting her act together
(c) raising the eyebrows
(d) chewing the cud

Ans. (a)

'Blowing hot and cold' is the most appropriate expression. It means to be indecisive or to change one's opinion frequently.

Getting her act together means to become organised.

Raising the eyebrows means to cause surprise or disapproval.

Chewing the cud means to ponder or think deeply.

651. You overhear someone say, "He's always on cloud nine." What does this idiom mean in the given context?
SSC MTS Tier-1 01.10.2024 (Shift-I)

(a) Extremely happy
(b) Always busy
(c) Frequently daydreaming
(d) Often absent

Ans. (a)

'Extremely happy' is the meaning of the idiom 'on cloud nine.' This idiom is used to describe a state of great happiness or elation.

652. A piece of cake
SSC MTS Tier-1 30.09.2024 (Shift-I)

(a) Easy to do or achieve
(b) A cake that broke into pieces
(c) A slice of cake for eating
(d) A cake which is sold as a piece

Ans. (a)

'A piece of cake' means 'easy to do or achieve.' This idiom is used to describe tasks that are very simple or require little effort. The other options (a cake that broke into pieces, a slice of cake for eating, a cake which is sold as a piece) do not match the figurative meaning of the idiom.

653. What does it imply when people say to 'read between the lines'?
SSC MTS Tier-1 30.09.2024 (Shift-I)

(a) To avoid detailed information.
(b) To read something fast.
(c) To read with an ability to infer the meaning.
(d) To skip initial and final lines in a paragraph.

Ans. (c)

The phrase 'read between the lines' means to understand or find the hidden meaning in something, which requires the ability to infer.

SSC MTS 2023 (Tier 1)

654. A blind spot
SSC MTS Tier-1 02.05.2023 (Shift-I)

(a) A person who is blind
(b) A person with no emotional feelings
(c) A situation where no progress is made
(d) An area in your range of vision that you can not see properly

Ans. (d)

The idiom 'a blind spot' means 'an area in your range of vision that you cannot see properly.' It refers to a literal or metaphorical area where awareness is limited.

655. Get down to brass tacks
SSC MTS Tier-1 02.05.2023 (Shift-I)

(a) To become serious about something
(b) Get fired from the job
(c) Compromise, cooperation between people
(d) To be ready

Ans. (a)

The idiom 'get down to brass tacks' means 'to become serious about something.' It describes focusing on the essential details.

656. A bed of nails
SSC MTS Tier-1 02.05.2023 (Shift-III)

(a) A problematic or uncomfortable situation
(b) A quick and automatic response
(c) A person with no moral ethics
(d) A fiercely contested fight or dispute

Ans. (a)

The idiom 'a bed of nails' means 'a problematic or uncomfortable situation.' It refers to a difficult or painful circumstance.

657. To have an itching palm
SSC MTS Tier-1 03.05.2023 (Shift-I)

(a) To have no mercy
(b) To gain strength
(c) To have an urge to slap
(d) To be greedy for money

Ans. (d)

The idiom 'to have an itching palm' means 'to be greedy for money.' It describes someone who is eager to receive bribes or tips.

658. Out of the woods
SSC MTS Tier-1 03.05.2023 (Shift-II)

(a) Out of danger
(b) To lose contact
(c) To meet with disaster
(d) Not adhering to rules

Ans. (a)

The idiom 'out of the woods' means 'out of danger.'

It describes being safe from trouble or difficulty.

659. Buy a lemon
SSC MTS Tier-1 03.05.2023 (Shift-II)
(a) Wear fashionable clothing
(b) The ability to know what's happening
(c) To not complain
(d) To buy something that is worthless
Ans. (d)
The idiom 'buy a lemon' means 'to buy something that is worthless.' It refers to purchasing something, often a car, that turns out to be defective or unsatisfactory.

660. The first sample of ore from the trial boring is very promising, but we should remember that (one swallow does not make a summer.
SSC MTS Tier-1 04.05.2023 (Shift-I)
(a) The fact of failure or escape is not affected by the narrowness of the margin
(b) To come out of one trouble and get into a worse
(c) A single fortunate event does not mean that what follows will also be good.
(d) The whole of everything
Ans. (c)
The idiom 'one swallow does not make a summer' means 'a single fortunate event does not mean that what follows will also be good.' It suggests that one positive occurrence does not guarantee continued success.

661. To meet one's eyes
SSC MTS Tier-1 4.05.2023 (Shift-I)
(a) To look at someone directly while they are looking at you
(b) To confess something
(c) To make haste
(d) To meet someone regularly
Ans. (a)
The idiom 'to meet one's eyes' means 'to look at someone directly while they are looking at you.' It describes making direct eye contact.

662. A blast from the past
SSC MTS Tier-1 4.05.2023 (Shift-II)
(a) A competition where the outcome is difficult to judge or predict
(b) Punishment for the crime committed in the past
(c) Something powerfully nostalgic
(d) An unsolved argument
Ans. (c)
The idiom 'a blast from the past' means 'something powerfully nostalgic.' It refers to something that brings back strong memories from the past.

663. Against the clock
SSC MTS Tier-1 04.05.2023 (Shift-II)
(a) To take on a task that is a way to big
(b) On the point of achievement
(c) To avoid talking
(d) Rushed and short on time
Ans. (d)
The idiom 'against the clock' means 'rushed and short on time.' It describes working under time pressure.

664. In the groove
SSC MTS Tier-1 04.05.2023 (Shift-III)
(a) To muse on in an aimless manner
(b) Starting to perform very well
(c) Simplify the producers
(d) A widely debated issue
Ans. (b)
The idiom 'in the groove' means 'starting to perform very well.' It describes being in a rhythm or flow where things are going smoothly.

665. His mother and I (share the same opinion) about his decision to drop out of college.
SSC MTS Tier-1 08.05.2023 (Shift-I)
(a) see eye to eye
(b) feel blue
(c) leave no stone unturned
(d) paint the town red
Ans. (a)
The idiom 'see eye to eye' means 'to share the same opinion.' It describes agreeing with someone.

666. Walk on air
SSC MTS Tier-1 08.05.2023 (Shift-II)
(a) To work hard
(b) To describe an unusual situation
(c) To be extremely happy
(d) Feeling weakened or tired
Ans. (c)
The idiom 'walk on air' means 'to be extremely happy.' It describes feeling very joyful or elated.

667. Wet behind the ears
SSC MTS Tier-1 05.05.2023 (Shift-II)
(a) A sudden change in fortune due to a windfall
(b) To place a bad bet
(c) To be young and without experience
(d) To win a bet
Ans. (c)
The idiom 'wet behind the ears' means 'to be young and without experience.' It describes someone who is new to a situation and lacks experience.

668. That new budget bill was (totally useless) before it hit the Senate.
SSC MTS Tier-1 09.05.2023 (Shift-I)
(a) a cry wolf
(b) a dead duck
(c) cold feet
(d) a fuel to the fire
Ans. (b)
The idiom 'a dead duck' means 'totally useless.' It describes something that is ineffective or will not succeed.

669. To pull the trigger
SSC MTS Tier-1 09.05.2023 (Shift-III)
(a) To make an exaggerated statement
(b) To do unnecessary things
(c) To insult and disgrace the people
(d) To commit a course of action
Ans. (d)
The idiom 'to pull the trigger' means 'to commit a course of action.' It describes deciding to proceed with something.

670. On the job
SSC MTS Tier-1 09.05.2023 (Shift-III)
(a) In the war
(b) Avoiding the work
(c) Working at a particular job
(d) On the contrary
Ans. (c)
The idiom 'on the job' means 'working at a particular job.'
It refers to being engaged in work or duty.

671. The life and soul of the party
SSC MTS Tier-1 10.05.2023 (Shift-I)
(a) The only person who dances in the party
(b) Chief guest of the party
(c) A person who brings lots of gifts
(d) Person who brings lots of energy to the party
Ans. (d)
The idiom 'the life and soul of the party' means 'a person who brings lots of energy to the party.' It describes someone who makes an event lively and entertaining.

672. Later, Brooks' brother alleged that racism helped put the (pedal to the metal). **SSC MTS Tier-1 10.05.2023 (Shift-I)**
(a) Very excessive
(b) To go full speed, especially while driving a vehicle
(c) To enjoy yourself by going out
(d) Avoid responsibility by giving it to someone else
Ans. (b)
The idiom 'put the pedal to the metal' means 'to go full speed, especially while driving a vehicle.'
It describes accelerating to the maximum.

673. After repeated failures and disappointments he was tempted (to throw up the sponge), but continued perseverance finally brought success.
SSC MTS Tier-1 10.05.2023 (Shift-II)
(a) To catch somebody off guard
(b) To surrender or give up the contest
(c) To reveal secret information
(d) To be afraid

Ans. (b)

The idiom 'to throw up the sponge' means 'to surrender or give up the contest.' It describes quitting or admitting defeat.

674. Susie (has such strong resemblance to) Kate Winslet that sometimes people would ask her for her autograph.
SSC MTS Tier-1 10.05.2023 (Shift-III)

(a) dead ringer
(b) gone bananas
(c) jack of all trades
(d) pound the pavement

Ans. (a)

The idiom 'dead ringer' means 'has such a strong resemblance to.' It describes someone who looks very similar to another person.

675. In the long run
SSC MTS Tier-1 10.05.2023 (Shift-III)

(a) Lack of energy (b) Long walk
(c) In tough times (d) In the end

Ans. (d)

The idiom 'in the long run' means 'in the end.' It describes the final outcome or effect over a period of time.

676. To see the light
SSC MTS Tier-1 11.05.2023 (Shift-II)

(a) To gain conscious
(b) To misunderstand the situation
(c) To be optimistic
(d) Suddenly realise or understand something

Ans. (d)

The idiom 'to see the light' means 'to suddenly realise or understand something.' It describes gaining insight or clarity.

677. Go down like a lead balloon
SSC MTS Tier-1 11.05.2023 (Shift-III)

(a) To be received badly by an audience
(b) Put yourself in a tough position in order to support someone/something
(c) Surrender peacefully
(d) To gamble everything you have

Ans. (a)

The idiom 'go down like a lead balloon' means 'to be received badly by an audience.' It describes something that fails to impress or is poorly received.

678. I'm sorry I snapped at you earlier, I think I (am just in a bad mood today).
SSC MTS Tier-1 11.05.2023 (Shift-III)

(a) two wrongs don't make right
(b) clam up
(c) dressed to the nines
(d) got up on the wrong side of the bed

Ans. (d)

The idiom 'got up on the wrong side of the bed' means 'to be in a bad mood today.' It describes feeling irritable or cranky.

679. It takes two to tango
SSC MTS Tier-1 12.05.2023 (Shift-II)

(a) Two people are required for a couple dance
(b) To fight fiercely
(c) For an argument both parties are equally responsible
(d) An interesting idea

Ans. (c)

The idiom 'it takes two to tango' means 'for an argument, both parties are equally responsible.'

It suggests that two people are needed to create a situation.

680. To scratch one's head
SSC MTS Tier-1 15.05.2023 (Shift-I)

(a) To think hard in a puzzled way
(b) To think about good days
(c) To come up with an idea
(d) To lose all the wealth

Ans. (a)

The idiom 'to scratch one's head' means 'to think hard in a puzzled way.' It describes being confused and trying to understand something.

681. Dead men's shoes
SSC MTS Tier-1 15.05.2023 (Shift-II)

(a) Making oneself available for all the tasks being assigned
(b) A career where a lot of cheques are signed
(c) Job that one takes over from somebody who has left unexpectedly or died
(d) Acquiring the wealth of a dead man through malpractices

Ans. (c)

The idiom 'dead men's shoes' means 'a job that one takes over from somebody who has left unexpectedly or died.' It describes stepping into a role vacated by someone else.

682. To stretch one's legs
SSC MTS Tier-1 15.05.2023 (Shift-III)

(a) To leave a place without permission
(b) To go for a party
(c) To go for a walk after you have been sitting for a long time
(d) To measure one's worth

Ans. (c)

The idiom 'to stretch one's legs' means 'to go for a walk after you have been sitting for a long time.' It describes getting up and moving to relieve stiffness.

683. Drastic times call for drastic measures
SSC MTS Tier-1 15.05.2023 (Shift-III)

(a) When you are extremely desperate you need to take extremely desperate actions
(b) Don't rely on it until you sure of it
(c) Something that ends at the last minute or last few seconds
(d) Do not pull all your resources in one possibility

Ans. (a)

The idiom 'drastic times call for drastic measures' means 'when you are extremely desperate you need to take extremely desperate actions.' It describes taking bold actions in critical situations.

684. To sing a different tune
SSC MTS Tier-1 16.05.2023 (Shift-I)

(a) To change the way one talks about something
(b) To brag about something
(c) To be able to handle a jolt
(d) To buy or sell something

Ans. (a)

The idiom 'to sing a different tune' means 'to change the way one talks about something.'

It describes changing one's opinion or attitude.

685. Gut feeling
SSC MTS Tier-1 16.05.2023 (Shift-III)

(a) To have a dispute with someone
(b) A personal intuition you get, especially when feel something may not be right
(c) Very excited and/or joyful, especially when in love
(d) Doing things recklessly

Ans. (b)

The idiom 'gut feeling' means 'a personal intuition you get, especially when you feel something may not be right.' It describes a strong instinctive feeling.

686. Although Shagan was competently doing the project on her own, Pranav couldn't stop himself from (giving her unnecessary advice).
SSC MTS Tier-1 16.05.2023 (Shift-III)

(a) being a backseat driver
(b) devil's advocate
(c) a bitter pill to swallow
(d) cutting the mustard

Ans. (a)

The idiom 'being a backseat driver' means 'giving unnecessary advice.' It describes someone who offers unwanted suggestions or instructions.

687. To fly into a rage
SSC MTS Tier-1 17.05.2023 (Shift-I)
(a) To harm oneself
(b) To get very angry
(c) To make inappropriate gestures
(d) To be very excited
Ans. (b)
The idiom 'to fly into a rage' means 'to get very angry.' It describes suddenly becoming extremely angry.

688. Between a rock and a hard place
SSC MTS Tier-1 11.05.2023 (Shift-II)
(a) Stuck between two very bad options
(b) Willing to do anything
(c) On the point of achievement
(d) Avoiding the main topic, not speaking directly about the issue
Ans. (a)
The idiom 'between a rock and a hard place' means 'stuck between two very bad options.' It describes a difficult situation where both choices are undesirable.

689. To mind one's P's and Q's
SSC MTS Tier-1 17.05.2023 (Shift-III)
(a) To write English alphabets accurately
(b) To supervise something carefully
(c) To be polite and careful in one's behaviour and speech
(d) To make amends after a fight
Ans. (c)
The idiom 'to mind one's P's and Q's' means 'to be polite and careful in one's behaviour and speech.' It suggests being mindful of one's manners.

690. Rolling in cash
SSC MTS Tier-1 18.05.2023 (Shift-I)
(a) Have a large quantity of money
(b) A business magnate
(c) Buying things on interest
(d) To borrow a costly attire
Ans. (a)
The idiom 'rolling in cash' means 'to have a large quantity of money.' It describes being very wealthy.

691. Get the ball rolling
SSC MTS Tier-1 18.05.2023 (Shift-III)
(a) Get everyone's vote
(b) Behave in a crazy manner
(c) Collect one's belongings
(d) Set an activity in motion
Ans. (d)
The idiom 'get the ball rolling' means 'set an activity in motion.'
It describes initiating a process or project.

692. To go a long way
SSC MTS Tier-1 18.05.2023 (Shift-III)
(a) To become successful in life
(b) To join a foreign company
(c) To avoid short cuts
(d) To go on a long drive
Ans. (a)
The idiom 'to go a long way' means 'to become successful in life.' It suggests achieving significant success or progress.

693. Did you know David went to school wit my brother? It's (a small world), isn't it? SSC MTS Tier-1 19.05.2023 (Shift-I)
(a) Overwhelmed by what is happening in the moment
(b) Meeting someone not expected to be at a certain place
(c) A two-person conflict where both people are at fault
(d) An aggressive and bold confrontation
Ans. (b)
The idiom 'a small world' means 'meeting someone not expected to be at a certain place.'
It describes an unexpected encounter that highlights the interconnectedness of people.

694. In ones and twos
SSC MTS Tier-1 19.05.2023 (Shift-II)
(a) In small numbers
(b) By unfair means
(c) Large margin
(d) To count resources
Ans. (a)
The idiom 'in ones and twos' means 'in small numbers.' It describes people arriving or occurring in small, scattered groups.

695. The statement below has been given with bracketed text. Select the option with correct idiom for the bracketed text.
History certainly gives you (something to think about), doesn't it?
SSC MTS Tier-1 19.05.2023 (Shift-II)
(a) food for thought
(b) cup of Joe
(c) golden handshake
(d) forty winks
Ans. (a)
The idiom 'food for thought' means 'something to think about.' It describes information or ideas that provoke thoughtful consideration.

696. That were remarks made (in the heat of the moment).
SSC MTS Tier-1 19.05.2023 (Shift-III)
(a) At time when you cannot think carefully
(b) To exert all efforts
(c) To present a counter argument
(d) To be dismissed from your job
Ans. (a)
The idiom 'in the heat of the moment' means 'at a time when you cannot think carefully.' It describes acting impulsively due to strong emotions.

697. He (made an irreversible change, that will greatly impact his life) when he got that huge tattoo on his back.
SSC MTS Tier-1 13.06.2023 (Shift-I)
(a) beat the dead horse
(b) became the devil's advocate
(c) crossed the Rubicon
(d) put a rose on his nose
Ans. (c)
The idiom 'crossed the Rubicon' means 'made an irreversible change that will greatly impact his life.' It describes making a decision that commits one to a specific course of action with significant consequences.

698. Ethnic Cleansing
SSC MTS Tier-1 13.06.2023 (Shift-II)
(a) Worshipping of a certain ethnic or religious group on a massive scale
(b) Killing of a certain ethnic or religious group on a massive scale
(c) One who was previously unknown and is now prominent
(d) A large number of people either falling ill or dying
Ans. (b)
The idiom 'ethnic cleansing' means 'killing of a certain ethnic or religious group on a massive scale.' It describes the systematic extermination of a particular group.

699. The statement below has been given with bracketed text. Select the option with correct idiom for the bracketed text.
Don't start to think we've (won this game certainly), gentlemen.
SSC MTS Tier-1 14.06.2023 (Shift-I)
(a) swallowed the bitter truth
(b) held our horses
(c) have is/an in the game
(d) got this name in the bag
Ans. (d)
The idiom 'got this name in the bag' means 'won this game certainly.' It describes having secured a victory or success.

700. Fixed in one's ways
SSC MTS Tier-1 14.06.2023 (Shift-II)
(a) Something that shows potential or looks promising in the beginning but fails to deliver anything in the end
(b) To establish one's rule
(c) Not willing or wanting to change from your normal way of doing something
(d) An aggressive attack on someone by a group
Ans. (c)
The idiom 'fixed in one's ways' means 'not willing or wanting to change from your normal way of doing something.' It describes someone who is resistant to change.

701. Cold fish SSC MTS Tier-1 14.06.2023 (Shift-II)
(a) A person lacking in sympathy
(b) To make a log of money
(c) A dead body
(d) To retract one's statements
Ans. (a)
The idiom 'cold fish' means 'a person lacking in sympathy.' It describes someone who is unemotional or unfeeling.

702. Go bananas
SSC MTS Tier-1 14.06.2023 (Shift-III)
(a) To become excited or angry
(b) To win a match
(c) To finish household chores
(d) To feel low
Ans. (a)
The idiom 'go bananas' means 'to become excited or angry.'
It describes reacting with extreme emotion.

703. To pull your weight
SSC MTS Tier-1 15.06.2023 (Shift-I)
(a) To do your full share of work
(b) To help one's relatives
(c) To buy something
(d) To give something
Ans. (a)
The idiom 'to pull your weight' means 'to do your full share of work.' It describes contributing fairly to a task or responsibility.

704. They were really (selecting from the last or worst of the resources left) when they picked you.
SSC MTS Tier-1 15.06.2023 (Shift-I)
(a) scraping the bottom of the barrel
(b) rolling the stones
(c) pulling up snakes
(d) going haywire
Ans. (a)
The idiom 'scraping the bottom of the barrel' means 'selecting from the last or worst of the resources left.' It describes using whatever is left, even if it is of low quality.

705. Mom said these instructions are (not understood by her) and that we should show them to Dad.
SSC MTS Tier-1 15.06.2023 (Shift-II)
(a) Greek to her
(b) smart cookie to her
(c) pound the investment to her
(d) full of beans to her
Ans. (a)
The idiom 'Greek to her' means 'not understood by her.'
It describes something that is incomprehensible or difficult to understand.

706. Be at a crossroads
SSC MTS Tier-1 15.06.2023 (Shift-III)
(a) To have taken the wrong road
(b) To be confused
(c) To make a very important decision
(d) To have forgotten the way
Ans. (c)
The idiom 'be at a crossroads' means 'to make a very important decision.' It describes a critical point where a significant choice must be made.

707. To pick holes in someone's coat
SSC MTS Tier-1 16.06.2023 (Shift-I)
(a) To discharge one's duty well
(b) To deceive someone for personal gain
(c) To aspire for something difficult
(d) To find fault wight someone
Ans. (d)
The idiom 'to pick holes in someone's coat' means 'to find fault with someone.' It describes criticising or finding flaws in someone.

708. That's just like Julie - always (coming to conclusions too quickly) even before she knows the facts.
SSC MTS Tier-1 16.06.2023 (Shift-II)
(a) jumping in with both feet
(b) raring to go
(c) sailing in the same boat
(d) biting her own tongue
Ans. (a)
The idiom 'jumping in with both feet' means 'coming to conclusions too quickly.' It describes acting or deciding hastly without sufficient information..

709. Rust bucket
SSC MTS Tier-1 16.06.2023 (Shift-III)
(a) To be absent minded
(b) An old man
(c) A vehicle that is old or almost broken
(d) To be late for everything
Ans. (c)
The idiom 'rust bucket' means 'a vehicle that is old or almost broken.'
It refers to an old, dilapidated car or machine.

710. Hit the hay
SSC MTS Tier-1 19.06.2023 (Shift-I)
(a) To go to bed
(b) To buy or sell something
(c) To take revenge
(d) A sarcastic response
Ans. (a)
The idiom 'hit the hay' means 'to go to bed.' It describes going to sleep.

711. Let the bully have (a taste of his own medicine).
SSC MTS Tier-1 19.06.2023 (Shift-III)
(a) A dangerous person pretending harmless
(b) A result that is still unclear and can go either way
(c) When you are mistreated the same way you mistreat others
(d) A visual presentation is far more descriptive than words
Ans. (c)
The idiom 'a taste of his own medicine' means 'when you are mistreated the same way you mistreat others.' It describes experiencing the same negative treatment that one has given to others.

712. A broth of a boy
SSC MTS Tier-1 19.06.2023 (Shift-III)
(a) Not attached to someone
(b) To have specific food choices
(c) To behave foolishly
(d) A lively, energetic young person
Ans. (d)
The idiom 'a broth of a boy' means 'a lively, energetic young person.' It describes a young person who is full of life and energy.

713. To eat crow
SSC MTS Tier-1 20.06.2023 (Shift-I)
(a) To take great care
(b) To become non-vegetarian
(c) To take money back
(d) To admit that one is wrong
Ans. (d)
The idiom 'to eat crow' means 'to admit that one is wrong.' It describes having to acknowledge a mistake or defeat.

714. She started repaying the money she borrowed from me, but the amount she returned me is (insignificant compared) to what she still owes.
SSC MTS Tier-1 20.06.2023 (Shift-I)
(a) eat out of your hand
(b) jaw dropping
(c) an eye for an eye
(d) a drop in a bucket
Ans. (d)
The idiom 'a drop in a bucket' means 'insignificant compared to what she still owes.' It describes a small amount that has little impact in the larger context.

715. Long in the tooth
SSC MTS Tier-1 20.06.2023 (Shift-III)
(a) The show has come to an end
(b) Be optimistic, even difficult times will lead to better days
(c) To be old, often too old to do something
(d) Killing of a certain ethnic or religious group on a massive scale
Ans. (c)
The idiom 'long in the tooth' means 'to be old, often too old to do something.' It describes being advanced in age.

716. The hiring manager has already offered you the job; now, ... to accept or decline the offer.
SSC MTS Tier-1 01.09.2023 (Shift-I)
(a) a penny for your thoughts
(b) the ball is in your court
(c) pull your leg
(d) get your act together
Ans. (b)
The correct idiom to fill in the blanks is 'the ball is in your court' which means 'you have the power to take the decision'.

717. Let sleeping dogs lie
SSC MTS Tier-1 01.09.2023 (Shift-I)
(a) To let somebody sleep
(b) To fall sick intentionally
(c) Leave and existing situation as it is
(d) To care for the pet
Ans. (c)
The idiom 'let the sleeping dogs lie' means 'to leave the existing situation as it is.'

718. Call the shots
SSC MTS Tier-1 01.09.2023 (Shift-I)
(a) To be a follower that makes less important decision
(b) To be in a position to make decisions that influences a situation
(c) To be in a powerless position that follows orders
(d) To be in a neutral position
Ans. (b)
The idiom 'to call the shots' means 'to be the person who controls or organises a situation'. Such a person has the authority to take decisions that can influence a situation.

719. The exceutives were <u>running around in circles</u>, without any success.
SSC MTS Tier-1 01.09.2023 (Shift-III)
(a) Achieving maximum mileage
(b) Suffering huge profits and losses
(c) Successfully accomplishing the target
(d) Putting efforts into something that does not give a worthwhile result
Ans. (d)
The underlined idiom 'running around in circles' means 'putting efforts in something that does not give a worth while results.

720. Rajat is known for his notorious nature. He will be friendly to your face but likes ....
SSC MTS Tier-1 04.09.2023 (Shift-II)
(a) to blow his trumpet
(b) to stab you in the back
(c) to paint the whole town red
(d) to get all bent out of the shape
Ans. (b)
The correct idiom to fill in the blank is 'to stab you in the back' which means 'to cheat'.

721. Barking up the wrong tree
SSC MTS Tier-1 04.09.2023 (Shift-II)
(a) Provoke trouble
(b) To make a bad situation worse
(c) Getting a good start is important
(d) To be mistaken, to be looking for solutions in the wrong place
Ans. (d)
The idiom 'barking up the wrong tree' means to be mistaken or to be looking for solutions in the wrong place thought or course of action.'

722. The play I saw last night was a ....
SSC MTS Tier-1 04.09.2023 (Shift-II)
(a) hit the road (b) hit the hay
(c) smash hit (d) hit the roof
Ans. (c)
The correct idiom to fill in the blank is 'smash hit' which means 'popular'.

723. Shweta organises the sale of handmade pottery at a cheap rate.
SSC MTS Tier-1 04.09.2023 (Shift-II)
(a) Hush money
(b) Go for a song
(c) Having one's cake and eating it too
(d) Making a fuss out of something
Ans. (b)
The correct idiom for the situation is 'to go for the song' which means 'to be sold for an unexpectedly low price'.

724. Jane, please don't tell me fairy tales; I just want to know the real matter ..... .
SSC MTS Tier-1 05.09.2023 (Shift-II)
(a) in the cold (b) in a fort night
(c) in a long run (d) in a nutshell
Ans. (d)
The correct idiom to fill the blank is 'in a nutshell' which means 'summary'.

725. The shopkeeper was <u>sly as a fox</u> and tried to sell off the old stock.
SSC MTS Tier-1 05.09.2023 (Shift-II)
(a) smart and clever
(b) slow
(c) suspicious
(d) in confusion or disagreement
Ans. (a)
'As sly as a fox' means 'smart and clever'.

726. Bigger fish to fry
SSC MTS Tier-1 06.09.2023 (Shift-I)
(a) To barely get something done
(b) Having something more important to take care of
(c) Having work more than one's capacity
(d) To be similar to one's parents in some way
Ans. (b)
'Bigger fish to fry' means 'to have something more important to take care of'.

727. A storm in a tea cup
SSC MTS Tier-1 06.09.2023 (Shift-I)
(a) Much excitement over something trivial
(b) A signal for upcoming storm
(c) East money
(d) Suffering in silence
Ans. (a)
'A storm in a tea cup' means a situation in which people are very angry or upset about something that is not important.

728. From scratch
SSC MTS Tier-1 08.09.2023 (Shift-II)
(a) From a skin disease
(b) From the beginning
(c) From utter disorder
(d) From death
Ans. (b)
'From scratch' means 'from the very beginning'.

729. The detective went <u>the whole nine yards</u> in his investigation.
SSC MTS Tier-1 08.09.2023 (Shift-II)
(a) Measuring every step
(b) Everything, all the way
(c) Close affinity with the law
(d) Taking the distant call
Ans. (b)
'The whole nine yards' means everything, all the way.

730. After her husband passed away, Jane had to learn to <u>bite the bullet</u> and take care of the household on her own. SSC MTS Tier-1 11.09.2023 (Shift-I)
(a) Create a difficult situation
(b) Accept a difficult situation bravely
(c) Criticise someone harshly
(d) Run away from a difficult situation
Ans. (b)
'Bite the bullet' means to accept and face difficult situation.

731. Pay an arm and a leg for something.
SSC MTS Tier-1 11.09.2023 (Shift-I)
(a) Be devoted to unwanted things
(b) Pay a lot of money for something
(c) Give a lot of love and care to someone
(d) Pay a lot of attention to an incident
Ans. (b)
'Pay an arm and a leg' means to buy something extremely expensive.

732. A man of character, he <u>stuck to his guns</u> even in the most difficult situations. SSC MTS Tier-1 11.09.2023 (Shift-I)
(a) To do things that would please people
(b) To behave disrespectfully
(c) To find a treasure
(d) To stand firm against all difficulties and challenges

Ans. (d)

'Stuck to his guns' means to refuse to change one's decision or opinion about something, even though other people are against it.

733. To cross swords

SSC MTS Tier-1 11.09.2023 (Shift-II)

(a) To kill (b) To arrange
(c) To fight (d) To defend

Ans. (c)

'To cross swords' means 'to fight'.

734. Riddhi believes in <u>wearing her heart on her sleeve</u>. That is why she has no many friends.

SSC MTS Tier-1 11.09.2023 (Shift-II)

(a) To criticise everybody
(b) To wear a badge of honour
(c) To openly and freely express one's emotions
(d) To talk aloud

Ans. (c)

The underlined idiom 'Wearing her heart on her sleeve' means 'to openly and freely express one's emotions.'

735. You are an intellectual with a professional degree, you can do wonders as .... .

SSC MTS Tier-1 11.09.2023 (Shift-II)

(a) you are playing with fire
(b) you can say it again
(c) your mileage.05.vary
(d) the world is your oyster

Ans. (d)

The correct idiom to fill in the blank is 'the world is your oyster'. It means that you are in a position to take the opportunities that life has to offer.

736. The deal was .... for three months.

SSC MTS Tier-1 11.09.2023 (Shift-II)

(a) cut no ice
(b) broken the ice
(c) tipped of the iceberg
(d) put on ice

Ans. (d)

The correct idiom to fill in the blank is 'put on ice'. It means 'to postpone'.

737. I know it was wrong to distract his friends, but ....

SSC MTS Tier-1 13.09.2023 (Shift-I)

(a) all's fair in love and war
(b) all's unfair in the world
(c) all's unfair in love and war
(d) all's fair in the world

Ans. (a)

The idiom 'all's fair in love and war' means that anything goes when it comes to achieving love or victory in conflict. It suggests that usual rules and conventions do not apply in these situations.

738. Beauty of it

SSC MTS Tier-1 14.09.2023 (Shift-I)

(a) Make things worse
(b) Cause for dispute
(c) Quite ordinary
(d) Good points

Ans. (d)

'Beauty of it' means a quality that makes something special or good.

739. Today's question paper felt <u>like a cakewalk</u>. **SSC MTS Tier-1 14.09.2023 (Shift-I)**

(a) Very sweet (b) Very tasty
(c) Very easy (d) Very difficult

Ans. (c)

'Like a cakewalk' means something that is easily done.'

SSC Selection Post 2024

740. We should teach our wards not to <u>look down upon</u> anybody in human society. **SSC SP 20.06.2024**

(a) Talk leniently
(b) Kneel down
(c) Guess on something
(d) Despise somebody

Ans. (d)

'Look down upon' means to think of or treat (someone or something) as unimportant or not worthy of respect. Hence, 'to despise somebody' is its correct meaning.

741. Gift of the gab **SSC SP 20.06.2024 (Shift-II)**

(a) Someone's precious gift
(b) Very beautiful
(c) Attached to God
(d) Talent for speaking

Ans. (d)

If someone has the gift of the gab, they are able to speak easily and confidently and to persuade people.

742. Call it a day **SSC SP 20.06.2024 (Shift-II)**

(a) Stop working on something
(b) Start working on something
(c) The time at the end of the day
(d) Start a day badly

Ans. (a)

If you call it a day, you decide to stop what you are doing.

743. The imposition of lock down proved to be a ...... for many students who were not prepared for the examinations. **SSC SP 20.06.2024 (Shift-II)**

(a) feather in cap
(b) piece of cake
(c) blessing in disguise
(d) chip on their shoulder

Ans. (c)

The correct idiom to fill in the given blank is 'blessing in disguise' which means an apparent misfortune that eventually has good results.

744. A snake in the grass

SSC SP 20.06.2024 (Shift-IV)

(a) A worthless person
(b) A secret or hidden enemy
(c) A man of ability
(d) A man with a straightforward attitude

Ans. (b)

'A snake in the grass' refers to someone that you strongly dislike and disapprove of because, although they pretend to be. Hence, such a person is a secret or hidden enemy.

745. The construction of the office building of the company was taking place <u>in leaps and bounds.</u>

SSC SP 20.06.2024 (Shift-II)

(a) Progressing very quickly
(b) Stopped due to some legal issues
(c) Broken because of negligence
(d) Moving very slowly

Ans. (a)

'In leaps and bounds' means by very large degrees; rapidly or in quick progress.

SSC Selection Post 2023

746. He <u>brought his servant to book</u> for breaking the beautiful showpiece.

SSC SP 27.06.2023 (Shift-I)

(a) Scolded his servant
(b) Relieved his servant
(c) Rewarded his servant
(d) Sent his servant away

Ans. (a)

'Bring someone to book' means to scold or punish someone.

747. Easier said than done

SSC SP 27.06.2023 (Shift-I)

(a) Not as easy as it appears to be
(b) Not as moderate as it appears to be
(c) Not as restricted as it appears to be
(d) Not as difficult as it appears to be

Ans. (a)

If you say that something is easier said than done, you are emphasising that although it sounds like a good idea in theory, you think it would be difficult to actually do.

748. To show a clean pair of heels

SSC SP 27.06.2023 (Shift-I)

(a) To clean shoes fast
(b) Show clean shoes
(c) Show clean feet
(d) To run fast

Ans. (d)

'To show a clean pair of heels' means to run away quickly and without looking back.

749. His deep study of the case uncovered more problems. SSC SP 27.06.2023 (Shift-II)
(a) opened a Pandora's box
(b) opened the fire on
(c) opened conversation
(d) opened a season on

Ans. (a)

The idiom 'opened a Pandora's box' means 'uncovered more problems.' It describes a situation where a seemingly small action leads to unexpected and widespread problems.

750. My neigbour has decided to join the air force. SSC SP 27.06.2023 (Shift-III)
(a) Made up his mind
(b) Made a clean sweep
(c) Made a fuss
(d) Made his own way

Ans. (a)

The idiom 'made up his mind' means 'decided.' It describes coming to a firm decision.

751. I don't buy it SSC SP 27.06.2023 (Shift-III)
(a) Purchasing should be controlled
(b) Only good decisions can be agreed on
(c) I am not convinced
(d) I do not like to buy

Ans. (c)

'I'm not buying it' means 'I don't accept it as truthful' or I am not convinced.

752. On cloud nine SSC SP 27.06.2023 (Shift-IV)
(a) To be extremely cautious
(b) To be extremely happy
(c) To be extremely shaky
(d) To be extremely sad

Ans. (b)

'On cloud nine' means a condition of great joy or bliss.

753. She has gained a lot of fame but still she is very realistic and sensible. SSC SP 27.06.2023 (Shift-IV)
(a) down to earth (b) down to it
(c) down to bottom (d) down to drown

Ans. (a)

'Down to earth' means very realistic and sensible.

754. 'Honesty is the best policy' does not remain valid in the present times of corruption and greed. SSC SP 27.06.2023 (Shift-IV)
(a) Go through thick and thin
(b) Put up
(c) Keep pace with
(d) Hold good

Ans. (d)

The most appropriate substitute for the underlined segment is 'hold good' which means to remain valid.

755. Chanda always annoys everyone by praising herself all the time. SSC SP 28.06.2023 (Shift-I)
(a) Crying over the split milk
(b) Catching one's eyes
(c) Blowing her own trumpet
(d) Facing the music

Ans. (c)

The idiom 'blowing her own trumpet' means 'praising herself all the time.' It describes someone who is constantly boasting about their achievements.

756. Through the grapevine SSC SP 28.06.2023 (Shift-I)
(a) Through difficulties
(b) *Via* gossip
(c) Extremely ill
(d) Succeeded brilliantly

Ans. (b)

The idiom 'through the grapevine' means '*via* gossip.' It describes hearing information through informal or unofficial means.

757. Pull yourself together SSC SP 28.06.2023 (Shift-II)
(a) Fight violently
(b) Work overtime
(c) Help to needy
(d) Calm down

Ans. (d)

The idiom 'pull yourself together' means 'calm down.' It describes regaining composure after being upset or agitated.

758. Ruffle someone's feathers SSC SP 28.06.2023 (Shift-IV)
(a) Be relaxed and in control
(b) Do something very easily
(c) Make more of an effort
(d) Make someone annoyed

Ans. (d)

The idiom 'ruffle someone's feathers' means 'make someone annoyed.' It describes causing irritation or disturbance.

759. Julia has the habit of comparing apples to oranges. SSC SP 30.06.2023 (Shift-IV)
(a) Comparing two thing that cannot be compared
(b) Blaming other for her mistakes
(c) Choosing things after careful scrutiny
(d) Purchasing to different fruits for different purposes

Ans. (a)

The idiom 'comparing apples to oranges' means 'comparing two things that cannot be compared.' It describes trying to equate things that are fundamentally different.

760. Die a dog's death SSC SP 30.06.2023 (Shift-I)
(a) The old businessman died in peace after meeting his whole family on his deathbed.
(b) Yesterday, a poor vegetable seller died in an unfortunate accident.
(c) The doctor who udes illegal methods to conduct experiments on humans must die a shameful death.
(d) Wars compel people to starve to death and they are helpless.

Ans. (c)

The idiom 'die a dog's death' means 'to die a shameful death.'

It describes a disgraceful or dishonourable death.

761. Our secreatry is always in the mood for an argument. He must learn to keep quite. SSC SP 30.06.2023 (Shift-III)
(a) To go through
(b) To turn up
(c) To take off
(d) To hold his tongue

Ans. (d)

The idiom 'to hold his tongue' means 'to keep quiet.' It describes refraining from speaking, especially to avoid conflict.

762. Reghu's been trying to keep a lid on his emotions, but every now and then his anger erupts. SSC SP 30.06.2023 (Shift-III)
(a) make things difficult for someone
(b) either take less care of your appearance or relax completely and enjoy yourself
(c) leave someone at a time when they need you to stay and help them
(d) control the level of something in order to stop it increasing

Ans. (d)

The idiom 'keep a lid on' means 'control the level of something in order to stop it increasing.' It describes suppressing emotions or preventing a situation from escalating.

763. There are a number of things that the country needs to improve but the main part of the problem is corruption. SSC SP 30.06.2023 (Shift-III)
(a) Crux of the matter
(b) Last resort
(c) Grasping at straws
(d) Dodged a bullet.

Ans. (a)

The idiom 'crux of the matter' means 'the main part of the problem.' It describes the most important or central aspect of an issue.

764. A piece of information received by word of mouth has no authenticity.
SSC SP 30.06.2023 (Shift-IV)
(a) through an official order
(b) through rumours
(c) in written form
(d) in spoken form
Ans. (b)
The idiom 'through rumours' means 'received by word of mouth.' It describes information that is spread informally.

765. I finally understood how to operate the new smart television.
SSC SP 30.06.2023 (Shift-IV)
(a) Cast aside (b) hit the sack
(c) Don't know (d) Figured out
Ans. (d)
The idiom 'figured out' means 'understood.' It describes solving or comprehending something.

766. Athira would like to get him a special birthday present, but nothing springs to mind. SSC SP 30.06.2023 (Shift-IV)
(a) almost always
(b) forget about something
(c) dawns on
(d) from the beginning of time
Ans. (c)
The idiom 'dawns on' means 'comes to mind.' It describes realising or remembering something suddenly.

SSC Selection Post 2022

767. Hang in there SSC SP 01.08.2022
(a) There is no chance
(b) Let go off your stand
(c) Don't give up
(d) Put your ego aside
Ans. (c)
If you tell someone to hang in there or to hang on in there, you are encouraging them to keep trying to do something and not to give up.

768. Go the extra mile SSC SP 01.08.2022
(a) To show off physical strength
(b) To make an extra effort.
(c) To work for long hours
(d) To do rigorous exercise
Ans. (b)
'Go the extra mile' means to do more than one is required to do or to make an extra effort.

769. He got a job in the Railways through the back door. SSC SP 01.08.2022
(a) entered the office through the back entrance
(b) without appearing to others
(c) the main door is under repair
(d) in an indirect or unfair way
Ans. (d)
'Through the back door' means in a secret or indirect way.

770. I am of two minds about whether I should go to the convention.
SSC SP 01.08.2022
(a) holding a negative opinion
(b) holding a clear opinion
(c) holding a positive opinion
(d) holding conflicting opinions
Ans. (d)
'In two minds' means to not be decided or certain about something.

SSC Steno 2024

771. At the eleventh hour
SSC Steno 11.12.2024 (Shift-I)
(a) At the last possible moment
(b) At the distance
(c) At the break of the day
(d) At the present time
Ans. (a)
The meaning of the idiom 'at the eleventh hour' is 'at the last possible moment'. It refers to doing something just before the deadline.

772. All eyes and ears
SSC Steno 11.12.2024 (Shift-I)
(a) To be helpful
(b) To be restless
(c) To be attentive
(d) To be mistaken
Ans. (c)
The meaning of the idiom 'all eyes and ears' is 'to be attentive'.
It means to be fully focused and listening carefully.

773. The winner's performance was head and shoulders above all other participants' in the dance competition. SSC Steno 11.12.2024 (Shift-I)
(a) worse than others
(b) well informed of current trends
(c) caught between two alternatives
(d) much better than others
Ans. (d)
The meaning of the idiom 'head and shoulders above' is 'much better than others'. It means to be significantly superior or better in quality.

774. Turned a deaf ear
SSC Steno 11.12.2024 (Shift-I)
(a) To depend on (b) To defeat
(c) To disregard
(d) Trying to hear from the deafened ear
Ans. (c)
The meaning of the idiom 'turned a deaf ear' is 'to disregard'. This idiom means to ignore or pay no attention to something.

775. To have sticky fingers
SSC Steno 11.12.2024 (Shift-II)
(a) To be suspicious
(b) To have a tendency to steal
(c) To punish for a crime
(d) To remain joyful in a difficult situation
Ans. (b)
The idiom 'to have sticky fingers' means 'to have a tendency to steal'. This expression implies that someone habitually takes things that do not belong to them, as sticky substances pick up everything they touch.

776. Call it a day SSC Steno 11.12.2024 (Shift-II)
(a) To stop worrying over something
(b) To reach the destination
(c) To avoid meeting someone
(d) To decide to stop doing something
Ans. (d)
The idiom 'call it a day' means 'to decide to stop doing something'. This idiom indicates concluding an activity or work, often for the remainder of the day. The phrase originally stems.

777. Made his mark
SSC Steno 11.12.2024 (Shift-II)
(a) To make a colourful exit
(b) To distinguish himself
(c) To fail in the task
(d) To take a stand
Ans. (b)
The idiom 'Made his mark' means 'to distinguish himself'.
It indicates that someone has achieved something notable or left a significant impact.

778. On the ball SSC Steno 11.12.2024 (Shift-II)
(a) To be inattentive
(b) To be aware of any changes or developments and quick to react to them
(c) To be unaware of any changes happening around
(d) To not understand a situation well
Ans. (b)
The idiom 'On the ball' means to be aware of any changes or developments and quick to react them.
It indicates someone who is attentive and responsive to situations, making it the most appropriate meaning.

779. It was just an action **in the nick of time** that prepared all of us for further arrangements.
(a) just in time SSC Steno 11.12.2024 (Shift-II)
(b) forceful labour
(c) delayed as expected
(d) unnatural happenings

Ans. (a)

The idiom 'in the nick of time' means something done at the last possible moment, just in time to prevent something bad from happening. Therefore, 'just in time' is the most appropriate meaning.

780. Milk of human kindness
SSC Steno 11.12.2024 (Shift-II)

(a) Compassion (b) Bravery
(c) Luck (d) Victory

Ans. (a)

'Milk of human kindness' means 'compassion', which refers to showing kindness and understanding towards others. This idiom emphasises the natural human tendency to be caring and compassionate.

781. He gave his heart and soul to make the entire show a success.
SSC Steno 11.12.2024 (Shift-III)

(a) practical experience
(b) partially useful knowledge
(c) offer of peace and harmony
(d) entire energy and effort

Ans. (d)

The correct substitution is 'entire energy and effort'. The phrase 'heart and soul' means putting in all one's energy and effort. The other options, 'practical experience', 'partially useful knowledge' and 'offer of peace and harmony' do not convey the same intensity of effort and dedication.

782. Today's managers' meeting has given me a lot to think about as I decide whether or not to stay with this company. **SSC Steno 11.12.2024 (Shift-III)**

(a) belle of the ball
(b) bird's eye view
(c) roll with the punches
(d) food for thought

Ans. (d)

The most appropriate idiomatic expression that can substitute the underlined segment is 'food for thought'. This idiom means something that warrants serious consideration.

783. Ron always blows his own trumpet by mentioning his academic achievements. **SSC Steno 11.12.2024 (Shift-III)**

(a) To talk proudly about one's success
(b) To blow air into an instrument
(c) To save one's money with great effort using different means
(d) To ignore someone in the presence of others

Ans. (a)

The meaning of the idiom 'blows his own trumpet' is 'to talk proudly about one's success'.

This idiom is used to describe someone who boasts or brags about their achievements.

784. Meera wanted to prove to those around her that she was not a fair-weather friend.
SSC Steno 11.12.2024 (Shift-III)

(a) Helping and caring companion
(b) Reliable friend in tough times
(c) Unreliable friend in difficult times
(d) Friend for all situations

Ans. (b)

The meaning of the idiom 'fair-weather friend' is 'reliable friend in tough times'. A fair-weather friend is someone who is only supportive in good times, so the opposite is a friend who remains reliable during difficult times.

785. Lack of funds is the main obstacle for the company's growth.
SSC Steno 11.12.2024 (Shift-III)

(a) uphill battle
(b) odds and ends
(c) stumbling block
(d) storm in the teacup

Ans. (c)

The most appropriate idiom is 'stumbling block'. A stumbling block is an obstacle or hindrance, which fits the context of the company's growth being hindered by lack of funds.

786. Get your act together
SSC Steno 11.12.2024 (Shift-III)

(a) Get organised and work efficiently
(b) Write a letter
(c) Speak properly
(d) Behave in a rude way

Ans. (a)

The meaning of the idiom 'Get your act together' is 'get organised and work efficiently'. This idiom is used to tell someone to improve their behaviour or performance.

787. He goes hard with one and all.
SSC Steno 10.12.2024 (Shift-I)

(a) To be busy over trifles
(b) To remain neutral
(c) To be difficult
(d) To be unreliable

Ans. (c)

The idiom 'goes hard with one and all' means 'to be difficult'.

This indicates that the person is challenging or tough in their dealings with everyone.

788. Our neighbour told my brother to keep an eye on their pet dog in their absence. **SSC Steno 10.12.2024 (Shift-I)**

(a) To ignore something or someone
(b) To look after something or someone
(c) To wait for something that is disturbing
(d) To accomplish something too ambitious

Ans. (b)

The meaning of the idiom 'keep an eye on' is 'to look after something or someone'.

This idiom indicates watching or taking care of something or someone to ensure they are safe or well.

789. Extreme inflation in the country has led to a hike in the price of day-to-day commodity. It has made it difficult to............
SSC Steno 10.12.2024 (Shift-I)

(a) a blessing in disguise
(b) break a leg
(c) costs an arm and a leg
(d) keep body and soul together

Ans. (d)

The idiom that best fits the blank is 'keep body and soul together', which means to maintain oneself in a basic way, especially financially. The sentence refers to extreme inflation making it difficult to manage daily living expenses.

790. Unless sales improve next month, the company will be in a critical position in which failure seems imminent.
SSC Steno 10.12.2024 (Shift-I)

(a) a damp squib
(b) hitting the sack
(c) a mare's nest
(d) up against the wall

Ans. (d)

The idiom that best substitutes the underlined segment is 'up against the wall', which means in a critical or difficult situation where failure seems imminent.

791. I am feeling a bit under the weather.
SSC Steno 10.12.2024 (Shift-I)

(a) feeling angry
(b) feeling energetic
(c) feeling slightly ill
(d) feeling lazy and bored

Ans. (c)

The idiom 'feeling a bit under the weather' means 'feeling slightly ill'. It describes a state of minor illness or discomfort.

792. To get wind of **SSC Steno 10.12.2024 (Shift-I)**

(a) To get into difficulty
(b) To recover from something
(c) To escape so that you don't have to pay
(d) To hear a piece of information that someone was trying to keep secret

Ans. (d)

The idiom 'to get wind of' means 'to hear a piece of information that someone was trying to keep secret'.

793. Your guess is as good as mine

(a) To guess an incredible idea
(b) To have no idea of the answer
(c) To predict a disaster
(d) To be superstitious

Ans. (b)

The most appropriate meaning of the idiom 'your guess is as good as mine' is 'to have no idea of the answer.' It implies that the speaker is just as uncertain or uninformed as the listener.

794. Weal and woe **SSC Steno 10.12.2024 (Shift-II)**

(a) Joy and sorrow
(b) Early and late
(c) Hot and cold
(d) Simplicity and complexity

Ans. (a)

'Weal and woe' means 'joy and sorrow'.

The idiom represents the ups and downs or the good and bad times in life.

795. Loose cannon **SSC Steno 10.12.2024 (Shift-II)**

(a) Someone who is quiet and reserved in social situations.
(b) Someone who is unpredictable and liable to cause problems.
(c) Someone who is enthusiastic and very eager to take responsibilities.
(d) Someone who is well known and respected in society.

Ans. (b)

The most appropriate meaning of the idiom 'loose cannon' is 'someone who is unpredictable and liable to cause problems.' The idiom refers to a person whose actions are uncontrolled and potentially disruptive.

796. Diamond in the rough
SSC Steno 10.12.2024 (Shift-II)

(a) A top model
(b) Unpolished diamonds
(c) An industry of star-struck actors
(d) An unsophisticated person with Potential

Ans. (d)

'Diamond in the rough' means an unsophisticated person with potential. This idiom refers to someone who has intrinsic value or qualities that may not be immediately apparent but can shine with development and polishing.

797. A bird's eye view
SSC Steno 10.12.2024 (Shift-II)

(a) To move or rise into sight, especially from a distance
(b) A clear impression of what is happening
(c) To hold a negative or pessimistic opinion on something
(d) A limited understanding of something

Ans. (b)

'A bird's eye view' means a clear impression of what is happening.

This idiom is used to describe an overall view from a high position, giving a broad perspective.

798. Though the speaker used flowery expressions to convince the audience, they were intelligent enough to find out his ulterior intentions.
SSC Steno 10.12.2024 (Shift-III)

(a) to cast pearls before swine
(b) to be under somebody's thumb
(c) to not judge a book by its cover
(d) to read between the lines

Ans. (d)

'To read between the lines' means to understand the hidden meaning or implications of something, which fits the context of discovering the speaker's ulterior intentions.

SSC Steno 2023

799. The judge was **extremely angry** at the attitude of the culprit. **SSC Steno 13.10.2023**

(a) Throw caution to the wind
(b) Back to the drawing board
(c) Make one's blood boil
(d) Play by the ear

Ans. (c)

The highlighted part of the sentence can be replaced by 'to make one's blood boil' which means 'to be extremely angry.

800. They have been living from hand-to-mouth since they lost their property in that case. **SSC Steno 13.10.2023**

(a) Deal with a troublesome person
(b) Come to nothing
(c) Have just enough money to spend on basic needs
(d) Awkward situation

Ans. (c)

A hand-to-mouth existence is a way of life in which you have hardly enough food or money to live on.

801. The constant noise from the construction site next door is starting <u>to make me extremely angry</u>.
SSC Steno12.10.2023

(a) bringing me round
(b) drive me up the wall
(c) shove me under the table
(d) driving me blind

Ans. (b)

The most appropriate substitute is 'drive me up the wall' which means to make someone extremely angry.

802. Denim jackets are <u>in fashion</u> these days. **SSC Steno 12.10.2023**

(a) in lieu of
(b) in vogue
(c) in hand
(d) in a nut-shell

Ans. (b)

The most appropriate substitute of the given words is 'in vogue' which means 'popular or in fashion'.

803. Mr. Avinash is very nice and friendly, but his brother is very <u>toffee-nosed</u> **SSC Steno 12.10.2023**

(a) A person who is arrogant and cruel
(b) A person who thinks he is intelligent and perfect
(c) A person who thinks he is of a high social class and looks down on people of lower class
(d) A person who never trusts anyone

Ans. (c)

If you say that someone is toffee-nosed, you disapprove of them because they have a high opinion of themselves and a low opinion of other.

804. You shouldn't stress much. <u>This unpleasant situation could be hiding something positive in it</u>.
SSC Steno 13.10.2023

(a) hit the nail on the head
(b) over the moon
(c) on cloud nine
(d) every cloud has a silver lining

Ans. (d)

The most appropriate substitute is 'every cloud has a silver lining' which means every difficult or sad situation has a comforting or more hopeful aspect, even though this may not be immediately apparent.

09

Spelling Test

Spelling Test involves finding the incorrectly or correctly spelt words from the given options. It also includes selecting the correct spelling of the incorrectly spelt word or finding the sentence with the correct spelling.

Types of Questions Asked

In the SSC Examinations, spelling test is important topic as a variety of questions are asked from it.

Type 1

Select the incorrectly spelt word.

(a) Dispel (b) Dismiss (c) Disservice (d) Discribe ***Ans.*** (d)

Type 2

Select the correctly spelt word.

(a) Benidiction (b) Besmerch
(c) Beneficient (d) Benevolence ***Ans.*** (d)

Type 3

Select the correctly spelt word.

(a) Repitition (b) Repetition
(c) Repitetion (d) Repetetion ***Ans.*** (b)

Type 4

A part of the given sentence which has been underlined may contain a spelling error. Select the option that correctly rectifies the spelling error. If there is no error, select 'No error'.

They were forced to supplement their maegre earnings.

(a) Meagre (b) Meeger (c) Meager (d) No error ***Ans.*** (a)

Type 5

Parts of the given sentence have been given as options. One of them contains a spelling error. Select the option that rectifies the error.

Or

The sentence given below has one misspelt word. Spot the incorrectly spelt word and select its correct spelling.

The notarious and mercenary old man celebrated his centenarian at the aquarium.

(a) Aquarum (b) Notorious
(c) Centinarian (d) Mercenory ***Ans.*** (b)

Type 6

Parts of the given sentence have been given as options. One of them contains a spelling error. Select the option that contains the error.

The notarious and mercenary old man celebrated his centenarian at the aquarium.

(a) at the aquarium
(b) The notarious and
(c) celebrated his centenarian
(d) mercenary old man ***Ans.*** (b)

Type 7

From among the words given in bold, select the incorrectly spelt word in the sentence.

The popular **ridikule** of Puritanism in **burlesque** and **doggerel** is best **exemplified** in Butler's Hudibras.

(a) exemplified (b) ridikule
(c) burlesque (d) doggerel ***Ans.*** (b)

Type 8

Identify the correctly spelt sentence.

(a) Diabites is a chronic disease
(b) Diabetes is a chronic disease
(c) Daibetes is a chronic disease
(d) Diabeties is a chronic disease ***Ans.*** (b)

Type 9

Identify the sentence with a spelling error.

(a) The old man was afraid of the apparition of his wife.
(b) The adamant student refused to give up the arguement.
(c) The children watched the magician in fascination.
(d) Some people love to exaggerate during narrations. ***Ans.*** (b)

Type 10

Select the correct spelling of the word to fill in the blank.

Trouble and disease give us bad ....

(a) expereinces (b) xperiences
(c) xpreiences (d) experiences ***Ans.*** (d)

SSC Exam Scanner

Directions (Q. Nos. 1-683) In the following sentence, four words are underlined out of which one word is misspelt. Identify the incorrectly spelt word.

Or

Select the incorrectly/correctly spelt word.

Or

Identify the spelling error in the given sentence and select the option that rectifies the error.

Or

Identify the correctly spelt sentence/ sentence with the spelling error.

Or

Parts of a sentence has been given as options. One of them contains a spelling error. Select the part containing the error.

SSC CGL 2024 (Tier 1 & 2)

1. All criminal attitudes must be niped at the bud. **SSC CGL Tier-2 18.01.2025**
(a) Nipedd (b) Nipped
(c) Nipeed (d) Niiped

Ans. (b)

The correct spelling is 'nipped'.

2. The trainer tried to guage the learners' understanding of the subject by asking several new questions. **SSC CGL Tier-2 18.01.2025**
(a) Gaaug (b) Gaugg
(c) Gauge (d) Gaage

Ans. (c)

The correct spelling is 'gauge'. The word 'gauge' means to measure or assess something.

3. (a) Apparent (b) Practitionaire
(c) Recommend (d) Memento
SSC CGL Tier-2 20.01.2025

Ans. (b)

The correct spelling is 'practitioner', not 'practitionaire'.

4. Good characteristics are indispensible to succeed in life. **SSC CGL Tier-2 20.01.2025**
(a) Indispenscible (b) Indispensable
(c) Indespensible (d) Indespensable

Ans. (b)

The incorrectly spelt word is 'indispensible'.
The correct spelling is 'indispensable', which means absolutely necessary and essential.

5. (a) Embarrass (b) Connoisseur
(c) Relevent (d) Bureaucracy
SSC CGL Tier-1 09.09.2024 (Shift-I)

Ans. (c)

The incorrectly spelt word is 'relevent'. The correct spelling is 'relevant' which means correct.

6. After the recapture (A) of Tololing and the adjacent features, evacting (B) the enemy from this well-fortified (C) position became a priority.(D)
SSC CGL Tier-1 09.09.2024 (Shift-I)
(a) B (b) D (c) A (d) C

Ans. (a)

The incorrectly spelt word is 'evacting'. The correct spelling is 'evicting' which means to remove forcibly.

7. (a) I will definitely attend the conference.
(b) I will definitly attend the conference.
(c) I will definetely attend the conference.
(d) I will definately attend the conference.
SSC CGL Tier-1 09.09.2024 (Shift-II)

Ans. (a)

The correctly spelled sentence is- I will definitely attend the conference.

8. (a) Allocation (b) Abismal
(c) Allegation (d) Aversion
SSC CGL Tier-1 09.09.2024 (Shift-II)

Ans. (b)

The incorrectly spelt word is 'abismal'. The correct spelling is 'abysmal' which means extremely bad.

9. (a) Accommodate (b) Mischievious
(c) Millennium (d) Privilege
SSC CGL Tier-1 09.09.2024 (Shift-III)

Ans. (b)

The incorrectly spelt word is 'mischievious'. The correct spelling is 'mischievous'.

10. I receieved a parcel in the mail today. **SSC CGL Tier-1 09.09.2024 (Shift-III)**
(a) received (b) recived
(c) recieved (d) received

Ans. (a)

The correct spelling is 'received.'

11. He has to be conscious of his public manners as he is a decendent of a reputed family in this region.
SSC CGL Tier-1 10.09.2024 (Shift-I)
(a) Dicsendent (b) Descendent
(c) Discendent (d) Decendant

Ans. (b)

The incorrectly spelt word in the sentence is 'decendent'. The correct spelling is 'descendent'.

12. (a) Conscensus
(b) Entrepreneurship
(c) Collaegue
(d) Bizzaire
SSC CGL Tier-1 10.09.2024 (Shift-I)

Ans. (b)

The correctly spelt word is 'Entrepreneurship'. The correct spellings of the other words are- Consensus, Colleague and Bizarre.

13. Subir's long absence is likely to have ……… for employees in the office. **SSC CGL Tier-1 10.09.2024 (Shift-II)**
(a) repercusions (b) repercussions
(c) reperrcussions (d) rapercussions

Ans. (b)

The correctly spelt word to fill in the blank is 'repercussions' which means an unintended consequence of an event or action, especially an unwelcome one.

14. (a) Privelege (b) Priviledge
(c) Privilege (d) Privilej
SSC CGL Tier-1 10.09.2024 (Shift-II)

Ans. (c)

The correctly spelt word is 'Privilege'.

15. The transistors are used as the main ………, which are built into computer chips.
SSC CGL Tier-1 10.09.2024 (Shift-III)
(a) components (b) cumponents
(c) kamponents (d) kumponents

Ans. (a)

The correctly spelt word to fill in the blank is 'components'.

16. (a) Verminous (b) Vomitus
(c) Voluptuous (d) Verifibility
SSC CGL Tier-1 10.09.2024 (Shift-III)

Ans. (d)

The incorrectly spelt word is 'verifibility'. The correct spelling is 'verifiability'.

17. I was upstaires when somebody rang the doorbell.
SSC CGL Tier-1 11.09.2024 (Shift-I)
(a) Upstares (b) Upstaire
(c) Upsatires (d) Upstairs

Ans. (d)

The incorrectly spelt word in the sentence is 'upstaires'. The correct spelling is 'upstairs'.

18. His acquiantance with the author led to many fruitful collaborations.
SSC CGL Tier-1 11.09.2024 (Shift-I)
(a) acuiantance (b) acquaintance
(c) acquaintence (d) aquaintance
Ans. (b)
The incorrectly spelt word in the sentence is 'acquiantance'. The correct spelling is 'acquaintance'.

19. She recieved an award for her outstanding performance.
SSC CGL Tier-1 11.09.2024 (Shift-II)
(a) recieved (b) award
(c) performance (d) outstanding
Ans. (a)
The incorrectly spelt word is 'recieved'. The correct spelling is 'received.'

20. (a) Conscientous (b) Conscencious
(c) Conscientious (d) Conscietious
SSC CGL Tier-1 11.09.2024 (Shift-II)
Ans. (c)
The correctly spelt word is 'conscientious'.

21. All the chefs in the world are famous because of their .... skills. SSC CGL Tier-1 11.09.2024 (Shift-III)
(a) kulinary (b) kolinary
(c) culinary (d) colinary
Ans. (c)
The correct spelling to fill in the given blank is 'culinary'.

22. I took out a water tumbler (A) for a drink, but found the water in the metal container (B) had frozen so I couldn't quanch (C) my thirst. I ate some biscuits and offered (D) some to Hillary.
SSC CGL Tier-1 11.09.2024 (Shift-III)
(a) C (b) D
(c) B (d) A
Ans. (a)
The incorrectly spelt word is 'quanch'. The correct spelling is 'quench'.

23. (a) Embarrass (b) Occurrence
(c) Exhilerate (d) Accommodate
SSC CGL Tier-1 12.09.2024 (Shift-I)
Ans. (c)
The incorrectly spelt word is 'exhilerate'. The correct spelling word is 'exhilarate'.

24. (a) Exceed (b) Proceed
(c) Succeed (d) Preceed
SSC CGL Tier-1 12.09.2024 (Shift-I)
Ans. (d)
The incorrectly spelt word is 'preceed'. The correct spelling is 'proceed.'

25. (a) The paintings are structured chronologically, starting from cubism to surealism.
(b) The artist received recognition for her impressive etchings, buclic landscapes and recreation of natural scenes around her.
(c) The insouciance of the rock star considering the importance of the occasion, came as a shock to the audience who expected stressful moments.
(d) The focus of the exibition is to reinforce versatility and creative thinking.
SSC CGL Tier-1 12.09.2024 (Shift-II)
Ans. (c)
The sentence without any spelling error is- The insouciance of the rock star considering the importance of the occasion, came as a shock to the audience who expected stressful moments.
- In sentence 1, the incorrectly spelt word is 'surealism'. The correct spelling is 'surrealism'.
- In sentence 2, the incorrectly spelt word is 'buclic'. The correct spelling is 'bucolic'.
- In sentence 4, the incorrectly spelt word is 'exibition'. The correct spelling is 'exhibition'.

26. One must be confident of winning and gaining one's goals and must face situations, disasters, trials and setbecks of life with confidence.
SSC CGL Tier-1 12.09.2024 (Shift-II)
(a) Trials
(b) Disasters
(c) Confident
(d) Setbecks
Ans. (d)
The incorrectly spelt word in the given sentence is 'setbecks'. The correct spelling is setbacks.

27. (a) Centenary
(b) Consumerist
(c) Capitalist
(d) Countemptible
SSC CGL Tier-1 12.09.2024 (Shift-III)
Ans. (d)
The incorrectly spelt word is 'countemptible'. The correct spelling is 'contemptible'.

28. You need to be concious enough to listen to the question.
SSC CGL Tier-1 12.09.2024 (Shift-III)
(a) concious (b) enough
(c) question (d) listen
Ans. (a)
The incorrectly spelt word is 'concious'. The correct spelling is 'conscious'.

29. In spite of the dilemma that preveiled during the discussion sessions, the committee remained committed to finding an amicable solution to the issue.
SSC CGL Tier-1 13.09.2024 (Shift-I)
(a) amicable (b) committee
(c) preveiled (d) dilemma
Ans. (c)
The incorrectly spelt word in the sentence is 'preveiled'. The correct spelling is 'prevailed'.

30. (a) Reinforcement (b) Opportunity
(c) Atributes (d) Motivational
SSC CGL Tier-1 13.09.2024 (Shift-I)
Ans. (c)
The incorrectly spelt word is 'atributes'. The correct spelling is 'attributes'.

31. (a) Tangiable (b) Terracotta
(c) Tertial (d) Terracide
SSC CGL Tier-1 13.09.2024 (Shift-II)
Ans. (a)
The incorrectly spelt word is 'tangiable'. The correct spelling is 'tangible'.

32. (a) Occurence (b) Harassment
(c) Supersede (d) Exaggerate
SSC CGL Tier-1 13.09.2024 (Shift-I)
Ans. (a)
The incorrectly spelt word is 'occurence'. The correct spelling is 'occurrence'.

33. I felt absolutely (A) fit at the summit. My mind was absolutely clear. (B) I didn't feel tired, I felt exhelarated. (C) It was a very clear sensation.(D)
SSC CGL Tier-1 13.09.2024 (Shift-III)
(a) C (b) D (c) B (d) A
Ans. (a)
The incorrectly spelt word is C 'exhelarated'. The correct spelling is 'exhilarated'.

34. The government has ordered for the maintainance of the roads.
SSC CGL Tier-1 13.09.2024 (Shift-III)
(a) maintenance (b) maintainence
(c) maintainiance (d) maintennance
Ans. (a)
The incorrectly spelt word is 'maintainance'. The correct spelling is maintenance.

35. (a) Eficient (b) Contribution
(c) Miscalculation (d) Mediation
SSC CGL Tier-1 17.09.2024 (Shift-I)
Ans. (a)
The incorrectly spelt word is 'eficient'. The correct spelling is 'efficient'.

36. (a) The host institution must provide the delegates with accomodation at a subsidised rate.
(b) The occurrence of the lunar eclipse is often a mystery for children.
(c) The boss addressed the meeting.
(d) Rail lines go parallel.
SSC CGL Tier-1 17.09.2024 (Shift-I)

Ans. (a)

The sentence with the spelling error is- The host institution must provide the delegates with accomodation at a subsidised rate.

The spelling of 'accomodation' is incorrect. The correct spelling is 'accommodation'.

37. The thought of eating half-cooked food under compulsion fills me with …… . **SSC CGL Tier-1 17.09.2024 (Shift-II)**
(a) ripugnance (b) repegnance
(c) repugnance (d) repugnance

Ans. (b)

The correctly spelt word to fill in the blank is 'repugnance' which means intense disgust.

38. The resturant offers a wide variety of dishes. **SSC CGL Tier-1 17.09.2024 (Shift-II)**
(a) variety (b) resturant
(c) dishes (d) offers

Ans. (b)

The incorrectly spelt word in the sentence is 'resturant'. The correct spelling is 'restaurant'.

39. Educational technology has become a necesity if one desires excellent output. **SSC CGL Tier-1 17.09.2024 (Shift-III)**
(a) necesity (b) excellent
(c) Educational (d) technology

Ans. (a)

The incorrectly spelt word is 'necesity'. The correct spelling is 'necessity'.

40. (a) The new caches of materials reveal a secret pleascence that was hidden away from the rest of the world
(b) Statistical patterns and historical data cannot predict the futuristic problems that await a civilisation like ours.
(c) Many friends and memoirists have described the author in detail but there are no photos of the author available to the press.
(d) The author is famous for leading a life of subterfuge and contredictions which has led to challenges in understanding past works.
SSC CGL Tier-1 17.09.2024 (Shift-III)

Ans. (c)

The sentence with no spelling error is- Many friends and memoirists have described the author in detail but there are no photos of the author available to the press.

41. Helium is used with oxygen for asthma treatment because it ………… very easily.
SSC CGL Tier-1 18.09.2024 (Shift-I)
(a) difusez (b) difuses
(c) diffuses (d) diffuses

Ans. (c)

The correct spelling of the word to fill in the blank is 'diffuses.'

42. When numerous ideas are presented in a historical context, more than mere ……….. can be seen.
SSC CGL Tier-1 18.09.2024 (Shift-II)
(a) parallelism (b) paralialism
(c) paralelism (d) parallelism

Ans. (a)

The correctly spelt word to fill in the blank is 'parallelism.'

43. Calder Hall is a Nuclear Power Station in England which is known as the first Nuclear Power Station to generate electricity for ……….. purposes. **SSC CGL Tier-1 18.09.2024 (Shift-II)**
(a) comercial (b) comercail
(c) commerceil (d) commercial

Ans. (d)

The correctly spelt word to fill in the blank is 'commercial.'

44. Hiren loves to use ……… words while writing anything.
SSC CGL Tier-1 18.09.2024 (Shift-III)
(a) coloquial (b) colloquial
(c) colloquil (d) colloquiel

Ans. (b)

The correct filler for the given blank is 'colloquial'.

45. Economics began with growth and removel of poverty as its grand theme. **SSC CGL Tier-1 18.09.2024 (Shift-III)**
(a) Poverty (b) Grand
(c) Removel (d) Economics

Ans. (c)

The incorrectly spelt word in the sentence is 'removel'. The correct spelling is 'removal'.

46. Fundamentels of every subject need to be learnt on priority basis.
SSC CGL Tier-1 19.09.2024 (Shift-I)
(a) priority (b) basis
(c) Fundamentels (d) learnt

Ans. (c)

The incorrectly spelt word in the sentence is 'fundamentels'. The correct spelling is 'fundamentals'.

47. (a) What advice did he give to young entreprenuers?
(b) She tried to manoeuvre her trolley around people.
(c) The computer's software detected an anamoly caused by a virus.
(d) A clergyman read the liturgy from the prayer-book.
SSC CGL Tier-1 19.09.2024 (Shift-I)

Ans. (b)

The sentence with no spelling error is- She tried to manoeuvre her trolley around people.

48. Big Data has inandated / the education industry. / It has transformed it / by leaps and bounds. **SSC CGL Tier-1 19.09.2024 (Shift-II)**
(a) It has transformed it
(b) by leaps and bounds
(c) the education industry
(d) Big Data has inandated

Ans. (d)

Part 'Big Data has inandated' contains a spelling error.

The incorrectly spelt word is 'inandated'. The correct spelling is 'inundated' which means overwhelm (someone) with things or people to be dealt with.

49. (a) The athlete's achievements are impressive.
(b) The athlete's acheivements are impressive.
(c) The athlete's achievements are imprressive.
(d) The athletees achievements are impressive.
SSC CGL Tier-1 19.09.2024 (Shift-II)

Ans. (a)

The correctly spelled sentence is- The athlete's achievements are impressive.

50. The occurence of this phenomenon is quite rare.
SSC CGL Tier-1 19.09.2024 (Shift-III)
(a) occurrance
(b) occerence
(c) occurrence
(d) occurance

Ans. (c)

The incorrectly spelt word in the given sentence is 'occurence'. The correct spelling is 'occurrence'.

51. (a) Interrupt (b) Occurrence
(c) Beggining (d) Cemetery
SSC CGL Tier-1 19.09.2024 (Shift-III)

Ans. (c)

The incorrectly spelt word is 'beggining'. The correct spelling is 'beginning'.

52. 1. The new restraunt offers a wide variety of delicious dishes.
2. I can't beleive he made such a silly mistake in his presentation.
3. The teacher asked the students to complete the assigment by Friday.
4. She felt utterly embarassed by her colleague's comments.

SSC CGL Tier-1 23.09.2024 (Shift-I)

(a) delicious, beleive, assigment, utterly
(b) restraunt, silly, assigment, colleague
(c) delicious, silly, assigment, colleague
(d) restraunt, beleive, assigment, embarassed

Ans. (d)

In the first sentence, the misspelt word is 'restraunt'. The correct spelling is 'restaurant'.

In the second sentence, the misspelt word is 'beleive'. The correct spelling is 'believe'.

In the third sentence, the misspelt word is 'assigment'. The correct spelling is 'assignment'.

In the fourth sentence, the misspelt word is 'embarassed'. The correct spelling is 'embarrassed'.

53. My mother said that every relationship must have some amount of ....

SSC CGL Tier-1 19.09.2024 (Shift-I)

(a) phlexibility (b) flexebelity
(c) flexibility (d) flaxibilety

Ans.(c)

The correct spelling to fill in the given blank is 'flexibility'.

54. My grandmother .... the preparation of every festival celebration in my house.

SSC CGL Tier-1 23.09.2024 (Shift-II)

(a) initiates (b) inetiates
(c) enitiates (d) enetiates

Ans. (a)

The correct spelling of the word to fill in the blank is 'initiates'.

55. Can you please come back to reality from the fectitious world you live in? SSC CGL Tier-1 23.09.2024 (Shift-II)

(a) factitious (b) fractional
(c) factional (d) fictitious

Ans. (d)

The correct spelling is 'fictitious'.

56. I often fail to .... remember someone's name.

SSC CGL Tier-1 23.09.2024 (Shift-III)

(a) accuriately (b) accuratially
(c) acusatively (d) accurately

Ans. (d)

The correctly spelt word to fill in the blank is 'accurately'.

57. I doubt that these lifts can acommodate 100 people.

SSC CGL Tier-1 23.09.2024 (Shift-III)

(a) acomodate (b) accommodatte
(c) accomodate (d) accommodate

Ans. (d)

The incorrectly spelt word is 'acommodate'. The correct spelling is 'accommodate'.

58. (a) Measurement (b) Region
(c) Confidential (d) Strengths

SSC CGL Tier-1 24.09.2024 (Shift-I)

Ans. (a)

The incorrectly spelt word is 'measerement'. The correct spelling is 'measurement'.

59. (a) Connoisseur (b) Neccessary
(c) Privilege (d) Dilemma

SSC CGL Tier-1 24.09.2024 (Shift-I)

Ans. (b)

The incorrectly spelt word is 'neccessary'. The correct spelling is 'necessary'.

60. Definitions of .... are subjective to various interpretations.

SSC CGL Tier-1 24.09.2024 (Shift-II)

(a) sovereignty (b) suvereignty
(c) sovereinity (d) soverenty

Ans. (a)

The correct spelling to fill in the blank is 'sovereignty'.

61. (a) Guilty (b) Atempt
(c) Admit (d) Agree

SSC CGL Tier-1 24.09.2024 (Shift-II)

Ans. (b)

The incorrectly spelt word is 'Atempt'. The correct spelling is 'Attempt'.

62. (a) Possession (b) Unfourseen
(c) Referred (d) Weather

SSC CGL Tier-1 24.09.2024 (Shift-III)

Ans. (b)

The incorrectly splet word is 'unfourseen'. The correct spelling is 'unforeseen'.

63. (a) The restaurant serves delicious meals.
(b) The resturaunt serves delisious meals.
(c) The resturant serves deliscious meals.
(d) The resteraunt serves delicious meals.

SSC CGL Tier-1 24.09.2024 (Shift-III)

Ans. (a)

The sentence with the correct spelling is- The restaurant serves delicious meals.

64. (a) Exhilaration (b) Exilaration
(c) Exhillaration (d) Exhileration

SSC CGL Tier-1 25.09.2024 (Shift-I)

Ans. (a)

The correctly spelt word is 'exhilaration'.

65. Later on, he was truely apologetic for his misconduct in the meeting.

SSC CGL Tier-1 25.09.2024 (Shift-I)

(a) Trooly (b) Truily
(c) Truly (d) Treuly

Ans. (c)

The incorrectly spelt word in the given sentence is 'truly'. The correct spelling is 'truly'.

66. (a) There were no intermittent showers in the city, as was predicted during the whether forecast.
(b) She is very particular about pronounciation in her classes.
(c) The movie was very successful in the urban areas, but not among rural audiences.
(d) There wedding was during the summer, which is why we didn't attend it.

SSC CGL Tier-1 25.09.2024 (Shift-II)

Ans. (c)

The sentence with no spelling error is- The movie was very successful in the urban areas, but not among rural audiences.

67. Parul is known as a rigteous and honest lady.

SSC CGL Tier-1 25.09.2024 (Shift-II)

(a) rigteous (b) known
(c) lady (d) honest

Ans. (a)

The incorrectly spelt word is 'rigteous'. The correct spelling is 'righteous'.

68. In any time of crisis, there is always one mument that stands out from all the others.

SSC CGL Tier-1 25.09.2024 (Shift-III)

(a) mumunt (b) mumont
(c) momont (d) moment

Ans. (d)

The incorrectly spelt word in the given sentence is 'mument'. The correct spelling is 'moment'.

69. (a) Fermented apple juice is touted to have many health benefits though most are anecdotal and not supported by scientific facts.
(b) Intriguing as it is, the house was never sold because it was thought to be haunted.
(c) It is important for scientists to acknowledge their humanity and the implications of their inventions.
(d) There are many believes about ancient artefacts that some of them are patently not true.

SSC CGL Tier-1 25.09.2024 (Shift-III)

Ans. (d)

The sentence with a spelling error is- There are many believes about ancient artefacts that some of them are patently not true. The incorrectly spelt word is 'believes'. The correct spelling is 'beliefs'.

70. (a) Recieve (b) Necessary
(c) Possession (d) Accommodate
SSC CGL Tier-1 26.09.2024 (Shift-I)

Ans. (a)

The incorrectly spelt word is 'recieve'. The correct spelling is 'receive'.

71. (a) Researchers recommend that pesticides should not be used indiscriminately as they eliminate biodiversity for future generations.
(b) Journalism is often the work of painstaking rigour and perseverence that detail the socio-political experiences of our worlds.
(c) The venerated singer was also secretive, moody and very intense, famous for erratic and difficult behaviour
(d) Elephants are in trouble mainly because people desire ivory trinkets that are made of tusks, often gruesomely killing them to achieve their purpose.
SSC CGL Tier-1 26.09.2024 (Shift-I)

Ans. (b)

The sentence with spelling error is- Journalism is often the work of painstaking rigour and perseverence that detail the socio-political experiences of our worlds. The incorrect spelling is 'perseverence'. The correct spelling is 'perseverance'.

72. In our quest for power, we often fail to acknowlege the existence of other people.
SSC CGL Tier-1 26.09.2024 (Shift-II)
(a) acknowledje (b) accknowledge
(c) acknowledge (d) acknowlede

Ans. (c)

The incorrectly spelt word is 'acknowlege'. The correct spelling is 'acknowledge'.

73. (a) Accessibility (b) Aptitude
(c) Apparatus (d) Atrocios
SSC CGL Tier-1 26.09.2024 (Shift-II)

Ans. (d)

The incorrectly spelt word is 'atrocios'. The correct spelling is 'atrocious'.

74. Select the correct spelling of the word that means 'to replace'.
SSC CGL Tier-1 26.09.2024 (Shift-III)
(a) Superceed (b) Supersed
(c) Superseed (d) Supersede

Ans. (d)

The correct spelling is 'supersede' which means to replace.

75. (a) Convinient (b) Embarrass
(c) National (d) Discipline
SSC CGL Tier-1 26.09.2024 (Shift-III)

Ans. (a)

The incorrectly spelt word is 'convinient'. The correct spelling is 'convenient'.

SSC CGL 2023 (Tier 1 & 2)

76. The village beggars, no longer ill at ease in the gathering of gliterring dignitaries, sat in their assigned rows and joked with vegetarian Brahmin apprentices.
SSC CGL Tier-1 14.07.2023 (Shift-I)
(a) assigned
(b) apprentices
(c) beggars
(d) gliterring

Ans. (d)

The incorrectly spelt word is 'gliterring'. The correct spelling of the word is 'glittering'.

77. They denied having any associasion with the terrorists.
SSC CGL Tier-1 14.07.2023 (Shift-I)
(a) asociation (b) asocciation
(c) assosiation (d) association

Ans. (d)

The correct spelling of the given underlined word is 'association'.

78. The Collector paid floral tributes to the statue of Mahatma Gandhi after hosting. SSC CGL Tier-1 14.07.2023 (Shift-II)
(a) Floaral (b) Stateu
(c) Trebutes (d) Hoisting

Ans. (d)

In the given context, the word 'hosting' is not appropriate to be used with flag raising. The correct spelling of the word is 'hoisting'.

79. A lot of spontanity is required from the speaker in an extempore speech. The speaker is expected to brainstorm ideas and give speech instantaneously.
SSC CGL Tier-1 14.07.2023 (Shift-II)
(a) instantaneously
(b) extempore
(c) brainstorm
(d) spontanity

Ans. (d)

The incorrectly spelt word is 'spontanity'. The correct spelling of the word is 'spontaneity'.

80. The boys of our class have reported that considerable progress in the implimentation of their policies has been made.
SSC CGL Tier-1 14.07.2023 (Shift-III)
(a) implimentation
(b) implimantation
(c) implementation
(d) implemantation

Ans. (c)

The correct spelling of the underlined word is 'implementation'.

81. (a) Opportunity (b) Reliance
(c) Appraoch (d) Bureau
SSC CGL Tier-1 14.07.2023 (Shift-III)

Ans. (c)

The incorrectly spelt word is 'appraoch'. The correct spelling is 'approach'.

82. Seema was a timid girl. She did not talk to people who were not familiar to her. She was an introvert since adolosense.
SSC CGL Tier-1 14.07.2023 (Shift-IV)
(a) introvert (b) adolosense
(c) timid (d) familiar

Ans. (b)

The incorrectly spelt word is 'adolosense'. The correct spelling is 'adolescence'.

83. (a) Deceived (b) Reciept
(c) Resistance (d) Postponed
SSC CGL Tier-1 14.07.2023 (Shift-IV)

Ans. (b)

The incorrectly spelt word is 'reciept'. The correct spelling is 'receipt'.

84. Patrrol is very costly these days.
SSC CGL Tier-1 17.07.2023 (Shift-I)
(a) Petrole (b) Petrul
(c) Patrole (d) Petrol

Ans. (d)

The correct spelling of the underlined word is 'petrol'.

85. Select the incorrectly spelt word.
SSC CGL Tier-1 17.07.2023 (Shift-II)
(a) Nefew (b) Father
(c) Niece (d) Uncle

Ans. (a)

The incorrectly spelt word is 'nefew'. The correct spelling is 'nephew'.

86. (a) Fruitful (b) Unction
(c) Wilfull (d) Cradle
SSC CGL Tier-1 17.07.2023 (Shift-II)

Ans. (c)

The incorrectly spelt word is 'wilfull'. The correct spelling is 'wilful'. It means intentional or deliberate.

87. (a) Connotation (b) Pattron
(c) Dearth (d) Quarry
SSC CGL Tier-1 17.07.2023 (Shift-III)

Ans. (b)

The incorrectly spelt word is 'pattron'. The correct spelling is 'patron'. It refers to a person who gives finanical support to organisation or cause.

88. (a) Astute (b) Absolute
(c) Abrupt (d) Abendance
SSC CGL Tier-1 17.07.2023 (Shift-III)

Ans. (d)

The incorrectly spelt word is 'abendance'. The correct spelling is 'abundance'. It means in large quantity.

89. (a) Reasonable (b) Laughable
(c) Blessed (d) Prophane
SSC CGL Tier-1 17.07.2023 (Shift-IV)

Ans. (d)

The incorrectly spelt word is 'prophane'. The correct spelling is 'profane'.
It means non-religious.

90. Last-bench students are mysterous by nature.
SSC CGL Tier-1 17.07.2023 (Shift-IV)

(a) mystirious (b) misterous
(c) mysterious (d) misterious

Ans. (c)

The correct spelling is 'mysterious'.

91. (a) The mall road of our city is always teyming with street vendors.
(b) The mall road of our city is always tiiming with street vendors.
(c) The mall road of our city is always tyming with street vendors.
(d) The mall road of our city is always teeming with street vendors.
SSC CGL Tier-1 18.07.2023 (Shift-I)

Ans. (d)

The sentence that contains no spelling errors is 'The mall road of our city is always teeming with street vendors'.

92. (a) Horticulture (b) Ignision
(c) Copulate (d) Portion
SSC CGL Tier-1 18.07.2023 (Shift-II)

Ans. (b)

The incorrectly spelt word is 'ignision'. The correct spelling is 'ignition'. It means to start a fire.

93. (a) Concieve (b) Detect
(c) Predict (d) Stimulate
SSC CGL Tier-1 18.07.2023 (Shift-II)

Ans. (a)

The incorrectly spelt word is 'concieve'. The correct spelling is 'conceive'.

94. (a) Aristocrate (b) Advertise
(c) Occurrence (d) Preference
SSC CGL Tier-1 18.07.2023 (Shift-III)

Ans. (a)

The correct spelling is 'aristocrat'. An aristocrat is a member of the highest social class, often with a special title.

95. It is wierd to overreact on the consequences like this, it didn't even matter at the end of the day.
SSC CGL Tier-1 18.07.2023 (Shift-III)

(a) matter (b) overreact
(c) wierd (d) consequences

Ans. (c)

The incorrectly spelt word is 'wierd'. The correct spelling is 'weird'.

96. The agreement was termineted by mutal consent.
SSC CGL Tier-1 18.07.2023 (Shift-IV)

(a) The agreement was terminated by mutual consent.
(b) The agreement was tarminated by mutual consent.
(c) The agriment was terminated by mutual consent.
(d) The agreement was terminated by mutual concent.

Ans. (a)

The sentence with correct spellings is–The agreement was terminated by mutual consent.

97. (a) Avarise (b) Adverse
(c) Beige (d) Admonish
SSC CGL Tier-1 18.07.2023 (Shift-IV)

Ans. (a)

The incorrectly spelt word is 'avarise'. The correct spelling is 'avarice'. It means an extreme greed for wealth or material.

98. (a) Devide (b) Provide
(c) Subside (d) Confide
SSC CGL Tier-1 19.07.2023 (Shift-I)

Ans. (a)

The incorrectly spelt word is 'devide'. The correct spelling is 'divide'.

99. (a) Bonafide (b) Cultural
(c) Solusion (d) Trustworthy
SSC CGL Tier-1 19.07.2023 (Shift-I)

Ans. (c)

The incorrectly spelt word is 'solusion'. The correct spelling is 'solution'.

100. Science has made prrogress in leaps and bounds over the years.
SSC CGL Tier-1 19.07.2023 (Shift-II)

(a) leap (b) progress
(c) Sceince (d) bound

Ans. (b)

The correct spelling is 'progress'.

101. (a) Mischievous
(b) Miniature
(c) Metamorphic
(d) Mispell
SSC CGL Tier-1 19.07.2023 (Shift-III)

Ans. (d)

The incorrectly spelt word is 'mispell'. The correct spelling is 'misspell'.

102. (a) Achieve (b) Loyalty
(c) Trasury (d) Sprout
SSC CGL Tier-1 19.07.2023 (Shift-III)

Ans. (c)

The incorrectly spelt word is 'trasury'. The correct spelling is 'treasury'. It refers to the funds or revenue of a state, institution or a society.

103. (a) One needs to abide by certain instructions in every society.
(b) One needs to adide by certain instructions in every society.
(c) One needs to abide by certain instructiones in every society.
(d) One needs to abide by certain instructions in every socity.
SSC CGL Tier-1 19.07.2023 (Shift-IV)

Ans. (a)

The sentence with correct spelling and grammar is : 'One needs to abide by certain instructions in every society.'

104. (a) Arbitrary (b) Favourite
(c) Aggreement (d) Conviction
SSC CGL Tier-1 20.07.2023 (Shift-I)

Ans. (c)

The correct spelling is 'agreement'. It refers to a legal document.

105. (a) Rahul was ashamed of biheving so badly.
(b) Rahul was ashamed of bihaving so badly.
(c) Rahul was ashamed of beehaving so badly.
(d) Rahul was ashamed of behaving so badly. SSC CGL Tier-1 20.07.2023 (Shift-I)

Ans. (d)

The sentence with correct spelling is 'Rahul was ashamed of behaving so badly.'

106. The <u>sovenir</u> shops within the <u>amusement</u> parks do so well because the <u>visitors</u> are mostly children and the shops keep a good stock of objects that children find <u>fascinating</u>.
SSC CGL Tier-1 20.07.2023 (Shift-II)

(a) fascinating (b) visitors
(c) amusement (d) sovenir

Ans. (d)

Among the given underlined words, the incorrectly spelt word is 'sovenir'. The correct spelling is 'souvenir'. It is a thing that is kept as a reminder of a person, place or event.

107. (a) Erase (b) Dredge
(c) Sieze (d) North
SSC CGL Tier-1 20.07.2023 (Shift-II)

Ans. (c)

The correct spelling is 'seize'. It means to take control by force.

108. Being a milionaire, he is leading a luxurius life.
SSC CGL Tier-1 20.07.2023 (Shift-III)

(a) Being a millioneire, he is leading a luxrious life.
(b) Being a millionaire, he is leading a luxurious life.
(c) Being a millionaire, he is leeding a luxurous life.
(d) Being a millinaire, he is leading a luxurious life.

Ans. (b)

The sentence correct spelling is 'Being a millionaire, he is leading a luxurious life.'

109. (a) Consultancy (b) Constitution
(c) Conspirasy (d) Configuration
SSC CGL Tier-1 20.07.2023 (Shift-III)

Ans. (c)

The correct spelling is 'conspiracy'. It refers to a secret plan by a group to do something unlawful or harmful.

110. Labradors are gentle, docil dogs.
SSC CGL Tier-1 20.07.2023 (Shift-IV)

(a) Labradoors (b) Labradaurs
(c) gentil (d) docile

Ans. (d)

The correct spelling is 'docile'. It means obedient.

111. India needs to do better on rights and freedoms, welfare and justice, growth and development and in building a more egalitaerian society. SSC CGL Tier-1 20.07.2023 (Shift-IV)

(a) egalitarian (b) freedams
(c) developement (d) justise

Ans. (a)

The correct spelling is 'egalitarian'. It means to be equal.

112. (a) Nocturnal (b) Repulcive
(c) Scoreboard (d) Irrespective
SSC CGL Tier-1 21.07.2023 (Shift-I)

Ans. (b)

The correct spelling is 'repulsive'. It means to be disgusted.

113. Her duel attitude misguides everyone. SSC CGL Tier-1 21.07.2023 (Shift-I)

(a) daul (b) deul
(c) dual (d) dwell

Ans. (c)

The underlined word should be replaced by 'dual' to make the sentence contextually meaningful. 'Dual' denotes a reference to two.

114. (a) Treble (b) Nozzle
(c) Allmost (d) Moisture
SSC CGL Tier-1 21.07.2023 (Shift-II)

Ans. (c)

The correct spelling is 'almost'.

115. If more is desired than the instantanious impact on the mind, the advertising value of the poster falls sharply, within limits of outdoor publicity, however it is at present unchallenged.
SSC CGL Tier-1 21.07.2023 (Shift-II)

(a) unchallenged (b) instantanious
(c) desired (d) advertising

Ans. (b)

Among the given underlined words, the incorrectly spelt word is 'instantanious'. The correct spelling of the word is 'instantaneous'.

116. (a) Arrangement (b) Jeopardize
(c) Corruption (d) Remmission
SSC CGL Tier-1 21.07.2023 (Shift-III)

Ans. (d)

The correct spelling is 'remission'. It means the cancellation of debt, charge or penalty.

117. While driving his car, he applied breaks in time to save himself and his family from an accident.
SSC CGL Tier-1 21.07.2023 (Shift-III)

(a) brave (b) brakes
(c) bricks (d) braces

Ans. (b)

The underlined word is incorrect in the context of the sentence. It must be replaced with 'brakes' to make the sentence contextually meaningful.

118. (a) Adequate (b) Precaution
(c) Cowardise (d) Ridiculous
SSC CGL Tier-1 24.07.2023 (Shift-I)

Ans. (c)

The correct spelling is 'cowardice'.

119. (a) The psycologists who are a major part of the investigasion interviewed the witnesses.
(b) The psychologists who are a major part of the investigasion interviewed the witnesses.
(c) The psycologists who are a major part of the investigation interviewed the witnesses.
(d) The psychologists who are a major part of the investigation interviewed the witnesses.
SSC CGL Tier-1 24.07.2023 (Shift-I)

Ans. (d)

The sentence with correct spelling is 'The psychologists who are a major part of the investigation interviewed the witnesses.'

120. (a) Terrifying (b) Frosty
(c) Gauge (d) Effervescent
SSC CGL Tier-1 24.07.2023 (Shift-II)

Ans. (c)

The correct spelling is 'guage'. It means to estimate or determine.

121. (a) Dominate (b) Charishma
(c) Elegant (d) Cavalier
SSC CGL Tier-1 24.07.2023 (Shift-II)

Ans. (b)

The correct spelling is 'charisma'.

122. (a) Weave (b) Heave
(c) Obssess (d) Sieve
SSC CGL Tier-1 24.07.2023 (Shift-III)

Ans. (c)

The correct spelling is 'Obsess'.

123. (a) There was not enouf food in the beggar's house.
(b) There was not enough food in the beggar's house.
(c) There was not enauf food in the beggar's house.
(d) There was not enoufh food in the beggar's house.
SSC CGL Tier-1 24.07.2023 (Shift-III)

Ans. (b)

The correct spelling: 'There was not enough food in the beggar's house.'

124. (a) Hoarse (b) Imprint
(c) Precious (d) Visious
SSC CGL Tier-1 24.07.2023 (Shift-IV)

Ans. (d)

The correct spelling is 'vicious'. It means evil.

125. (a) Entrance (b) Brief
(c) Thunder (d) Statinary
SSC CGL Tier-1 24.07.2023 (Shift-IV)

Ans. (d)

The correct spelling is 'stationary'.

126. (a) Tour (b) Triumph
(c) Sandwitch (d) Process
SSC CGL Tier-1 25.07.2023 (Shift-I)

Ans. (c)

The correct spelling is 'sandwich'.

127. (a) Allimony (b) Structural
(c) Hallucinate (d) Halloween
SSC CGL Tier-1 25.07.2023 (Shift-I)

Ans. (a)

The correct spelling is 'alimony'. It is the money paid by a spouse to another after they have separated.

128. (a) Making healtcare more affordable is something I would do as President.
(b) Making healtcare more afordable is something I would do as President.
(c) Making healthcare more affordable is something I would do as President.
(d) Making healthcare more afordable is something I would do as Prescident
SSC CGL Tier-1 25.07.2023 (Shift-II)

Ans. (c)

The sentence with correct spelling is: 'Making healthcare more affordable is something I would do as President.'

129. (a) Receipt (b) Technically
(c) Harrasment (d) Vaccinate
SSC CGL Tier-1 25.07.2023 (Shift-II)

Ans. (c)

The correct spelling is 'harassment'. It means annoying or upsetting behaviour.

130. Successful people often have a role modal who inspired them to greatness.
SSC CGL Tier-1 25.07.2023 (Shift-III)
(a) gratenes (b) succesful
(c) inspaired (d) modal

Ans. (d)

The correct spelling is 'model'.

131. Mr. Singh is a phenomenally <u>sucsesful</u> salesperson.
SSC CGL Tier-1 25.07.2023 (Shift-III)
(a) sucessful (b) successful
(c) successfull (d) sucesfull

Ans. (b)

The correct spelling is 'successful'.

132. (a) Anxiety (b) Preparation
(c) Voluntary (d) Stetionery
SSC CGL Tier-1 25.07.2023 (Shift-IV)

Ans. (d)

The incorrect spelling is 'stetionery'.

133. (a) Felicitate (b) Cotarminous
(c) Ambient (d) Announce
SSC CGL Tier-1 25.07.2023 (Shift-IV)

Ans. (b)

The correct spelling is 'coterminous'. It means having the same borders or limit.

134. (a) Prefferance
(b) Preservation
(c) Preponderance
(d) Perseverance
SSC CGL Tier-1 26.07.2023 (Shift-I)

Ans. (a)

The correct spelling is 'preference'.

135. (a) The childrens playing in the kindergarden allmost broke the window of the principal's car.
(b) The children playing in the kindergarten almost broke the window of the principal's car.
(c) The childrens playing in the kindergarten almost broke the window of the principal's car.
(d) The children playing in the kindergarden allmost broke the window of the principle's car.
SSC CGL Tier-1 26.07.2023 (Shift-I)

Ans. (b)

The sentence with correct spelling is: 'The children playing in the kindergarten almost broke the window of the principal's car.'

136. (a) Hinterland (b) Haughty
(c) Drifter (d) Bellweather
SSC CGL Tier-1 26.07.2023 (Shift-II)

Ans. (d)

The correct spelling is 'bellwether'. It means the leading sheep of a flock with a bell on its neck.

137. To achieve somthing gigantic, you have to grind for a considerable amount of time.
SSC CGL Tier-1 26.07.2023 (Shift-II)
(a) somthing (b) considerable
(c) gigantic (d) achieve

Ans. (a)

The correct spelling is 'something'.

138. (a) Manisha got overwhelmed by the tremendus offer by a company to work in collaboration with internet personel.
(b) Manisha got overwhelmed by the tremendous offer by a company to work in collaboration with internet personnel.
(c) Manisha got overwellmed by the tremendous offer by a company to work in collaborasion with internet personnel.
(d) Manisha got overwhelmed by the tremendous offer by a company to work in collaborasion with internet personnal.
SSC CGL Tier-1 26.07.2023 (Shift-III)

Ans. (b)

The sentence with correct spelling is: 'Manisha got overwhelmed by the tremendous offer by a company to work in collaboration with internet personnel.'

139. (a) Believe (b) Audible
(c) Throat (d) Pronounciation
SSC CGL Tier-1 26.07.2023 (Shift-III)

Ans. (d)

The correct spelling is 'pronunciation'.

140. He is an <u>audacious</u> <u>entrepreneur</u> who started his own <u>business</u> with the <u>bear</u> minimum.
SSC CGL Tier-1 26.07.2023 (Shift-IV)
(a) business (b) audacious
(c) entrepreneur (d) bear

Ans. (d)

The word 'bear' is incorrectly spelt in the context of the sentence. It should be 'bare'.

141. (a) The body produces more saliva under fluorescent illumination which helps prevent cavities.
(b) The body produces more saliva under fluorescent illummination which helps prevent cavaties.
(c) The body produces more saliva under fluorescent illummination which helps prewent cavities.
(d) The body produces more saliva under fluorescent illumination which helps prewent cavaties.
SSC CGL Tier-1 26.07.2023 (Shift-IV)

Ans. (a)

The sentence with correct spelling is: 'The body produces more saliva under fluorescent illumination which helps prevent cavities.'

142. (a) Submisive (b) Validity
(c) Kaleidoscope (d) Animation
SSC CGL Tier-1 27.07.2023 (Shift-I)

Ans. (a)

The correct spelling is 'submissive'.

143. (a) Oligopoly (b) Xylophone
(c) Zenith (d) Robbust
SSC CGL Tier-1 27.07.2023 (Shift-I)

Ans. (d)

The correct spelling is 'robust'. It means strong and heathy.

144. Traditional people are used to using a calender for their routine activities in rural households.
SSC CGL Tier-1 27.07.2023 (Shift-II)
(a) traditional (b) households
(c) calender (d) activities

Ans. (c)

The correct spelling is 'calendar'.

145. Education plays a crucal role in breaking the cycle of poverty and child labour.
SSC CGL Tier-1 27.07.2023 (Shift-II)
(a) proverty (b) crucial
(c) braking (d) edukation

Ans. (b)

The correct spelling is 'crucial'. It means important.

146. (a) Dearth (b) Acceptible
(c) Corrupt (d) Barely
SSC CGL Tier-1 27.07.2023 (Shift-III)

Ans. (b)

The correct spelling is 'acceptable'.

147. (a) Sufficeint (b) Syrup
(c) Superior (d) Shrubbery
SSC CGL Tier-1 27.07.2023 (Shift-III)

Ans. (a)

The correct spelling is 'sufficient'. It means enough.

148. (a) Refusal (b) Wajes
(c) Stretch (d) Wearily
SSC CGL Tier-1 27.07.2023 (Shift-III)

Ans. (b)

The correct spelling is 'wages'.

149. (a) Greave (b) Groan
(c) Guarentee (d) Gravely
SSC CGL Tier-2 02.03.2023

Ans. (c)

The correct spelling is 'guarantee'.

150. (a) Descendant (b) Deceased
(c) Decimate (d) Desedent
SSC CGL Tier-2 02.03.2023

Ans. (a)

The correct spelling is 'descendent'.

151. One part of the philosophy of life's meaning consists of the systemetic attempt to identify what people have in mind when they think about the topic. SSC CGL Tier-2 02.03.2023
(a) attempt
(b) philosophy
(c) think
(d) systemetic

Ans. (d)

The correct spelling is 'systematic'.

152. (a) The granduor of the ancient Roman Empire is visible in many monuments in Italy and Greece.
(b) The grandour of the ancient Roman Empire is visible in many monuments in Italy and Greece.
(c) The grandeur of the ancient Roman Empire is visible in many monuments in Italy and Greece.
(d) The grandeur of the ancient Roman Empire is visible in many monuments in Italy and Greece.
SSC CGL Tier-2 03.03.2023

Ans. (c)

The sentence with correct spelling is: 'The grandeur of the ancient Roman Empire is visible in many monuments in Italy and Greece.'

153. The committee could not reach a <u>conscence</u> even after a six-hour long meeting yesterday.
SSC CGL Tier-2 06.03.2023
(a) consensus (b) conscius
(c) cautius (d) conscientios

Ans. (a)

The correct spelling is 'consensus'. It means a general agreement.

154. (a) Abhorrent (b) Abseil
(c) Acede (d) Abscess
SSC CGL Tier-2 06.03.2023

Ans. (c)

The correct spelling is 'Accede'. It means to agree to a demand, request or treaty.

155. If she had begun earlier, she might have suceeded in finishing the extremely intricate project before the deadline. SSC CGL Tier-2 07.03.2023
(a) deadline (b) intricate
(c) suceeded (d) earlier

Ans. (c)

The correct spelling is 'succeeded'.

156. The board reviewing the courses offered by the afiliated college found that the quality of academic programmes was usually good but somewhat irregular.
SSC CGL Tier-2 07.03.2023
(a) irregular (b) academic
(c) review (d) afiliated

Ans. (d)

The correct spelling is 'affiliated'.

157. She <u>vaccillates</u> a lot while making any decision. SSC CGL Tier-2 26.10.2023
(a) vasillates (b) vacillattes
(c) vacillates (d) vacilates

Ans. (c)

The correct spelling is 'vacillates'.

SSC CGL 2022 (Tier 1 & 2)

158. (a) Tution (b) Circuit
(c) Genuine (d) Manners
SSC CGL Tier-1 11.04.2022 (Shift-I)

Ans. (a)

The correct spelling is 'tuition'.

159. (a) Retort (b) Retrieve
(c) Revange (d) Return
SSC CGL Tier-1 11.04.2022 (Shift-II)

Ans. (c)

The correct spelling is 'revenge'.

160. (a) Statutory (b) Stratagy
(c) Stationary (d) Stationery
SSC CGL Tier-1 12.04.2022 (Shift-III)

Ans. (b)

The correct spelling is 'strategy'. It means a plan.

161. (a) Correspondence (b) Miscellaneous
(c) Exclaimation (d) Disciplinarian
SSC CGL Tier-1 13.04.2022 (Shift-II)

Ans. (c)

The correct spelling is 'exclamation'.

162. (a) Deceive (b) Leisure
(c) Believe (d) Wellfare
SSC CGL Tier-1 18.04.2022 (Shift-III)

Ans. (d)

The correct spelling is 'welfare'.

163. (a) Convert (b) Conect
(c) Concent (d) Convect
SSC CGL Tier-1 18.04.2022 (Shift-I)

Ans. (b)

The correct spelling is 'connect'.

164. (a) Ensure (b) Adjourn
(c) Purity (d) Exhast
SSC CGL Tier-1 19.04.2022 (Shift-I)

Ans. (d)

The correct spelling is 'exhaust'.

165. (a) Voluntary (b) Disparity
(c) Continuance (d) Convincing
SSC CGL Tier-1 21.04.2022 (Shift-I)

Ans. (c)

The correct spelling is 'continuanse'.

166. (a) Secratariat (b) Heartbeat
(c) Performance (d) Tongue
SSC CGL Tier-1 21.04.2022 (Shift-III)

Ans. (a)

The correct spelling is 'secretariat'.

167. (a) Giggle (b) Girdle
(c) Gingar (d) Giant
SSC CGL Tier-1 21.04.2022 (Shift-III)

Ans. (c)

The correct spelling is 'ginger'.

168. The erroneous information spread rapidly across the nation and created a stir.
SSC CGL Tier-1 01.12.2022 (Shift-I)
(a) erronous (b) No error
(c) eronneous (d) errauneous

Ans. (b)

The given sentence has no spelling error.

169. (a) Finery (b) Hiest
(c) Cringe (d) Defer
SSC CGL Tier-1 01.12.2022 (Shift-I)

Ans. (b)

The correct spelling is 'heist'. It refers to a crime in which valuable things are taken illegally and often violently from a place or person.

170. (a) Peircing (b) Sleek
(c) Pie (d) Itch
SSC CGL Tier-1 01.12.2022 (Shift-II)

Ans. (a)

The correct spelling is 'piercing'.

171. (a) Many communities in the world still feel that their voices and position has been dissenfranchised.
(b) Many communities in the world still feel that their voices and position has been dysenfranchised.
(c) Many communities in the world still feel that their voices and position has been dysenfrenchised.
(d) Many communities in the world still feel that their voices and position has been disenfranchised.

SSC CGL Tier-1 01.12.2022 (Shift-II)

Ans. (d)

The sentence with correct spelling is : Many communities in the world still feel that their voices and position has been disenfranchised.

172. (a) Slaughter (b) Cropping
(c) Traffickng (d) Tyrannical

SSC CGL Tier-1 01.12.2022 (Shift-III)

Ans. (c)

The correct spelling is 'trafficking' .

173. David was put off by the <u>glamming</u> eyes in the dark.

SSC CGL Tier-1 01.12.2022 (Shift-III)

(a) glamning (b) gleaning
(c) gleaming (d) glaming

Ans. (c)

The correct spelling is 'gleaming' means shining softly.

174. (a) Cemetery (b) Accommodate
(c) Intruder (d) Neccessary

SSC CGL Tier-1 01.12.2022 (Shift-IV)

Ans. (d)

The correct spelling is 'necessary'.

175. (a) Our government has launched a relatively extensive set of reforms for aborgines in the country.
(b) Our government has launched a relatively extensive set of reforms for aborigines in the country.
(c) Our government has launched a relatively extensive set of reforms for aboregynes in the country.
(d) Our government has launched a relatively extensive set of reforms for aborigynes in the country.

SSC CGL Tier-1 01.12.2022 (Shift-IV)

Ans. (b)

The sentence with correct spelling is : Our government has launched a relatively extensive set of reforms for aborigines in the country.

176. (a) Texture (b) Slege
(c) Savoury (d) Tamper

SSC CGL Tier-1 02.12.2022 (Shift-I)

Ans. (b)

The correct spelling is 'sledge'. It refers to a vehicle used for sliding over snow or ice.

177. (a) Benign (b) Mortifeid
(c) Insecurities (d) Dismay

SSC CGL Tier-1 02.12.2022 (Shift-I)

Ans. (b)

The correct spelling is 'mortified'. It refers to causing someone to feel very embarrassed or ashamed.

178. Siraj-ud-Daula <u>beseiged</u> Calcutta to take punitive actions against the East India Company.

SSC CGL Tier-1 02.12.2022 (Shift-II)

(a) besiezed (b) besiejed
(c) besieged (d) No error

Ans. (c)

The correct spelling is 'besieged'. It means a place surrounded by armed forces with the purpose of capturing it or forcing surrender.

179. The <u>adolocent</u> period of life, one of the most difficult stages of development, is known as the period of stress and storm.

SSC CGL Tier-1 02.12.2022 (Shift-II)

(a) adelescent
(b) adolescent
(c) adeloscent
(d) No error

Ans. (b)

The correct spelling is 'adolescent'. It refers to the process of developing from a child into an adult.

180. (a) Belief (b) Beneth
(c) Belly (d) Bellow

SSC CGL Tier-1 02.12.2022 (Shift-III)

Ans. (b)

The correct spelling is 'beneath'.

181. (a) Clemency (b) Avariciuos
(c) Hegemony (d) Nostalgic

SSC CGL Tier-1 02.12.2022 (Shift-III)

Ans. (b)

The correct spelling is 'avaricious'. It means having or showing extreme greed for wealth and material gain.

182. I would never <u>ascociate</u> with such a person. **SSC CGL Tier-1 02.12.2022 (Shift-IV)**

(a) associate (b) accosiate
(c) assosiate (d) asosiate

Ans. (a)

The correct spelling is 'associate'.

183. (a) Professional (b) Dubious
(c) Nefarious (d) Consumate

SSC CGL Tier-1 02.12.2022 (Shift-IV)

Ans. (d)

The correct spelling 'consummate'.

184. (a) I heard raucouos laughter from the next room.
(b) I heard raocous laughter from the next room.
(c) I heard raucus laughter from the next room.
(d) I heard raucous laughter from the next room.

SSC CGL Tier-1 03.12.2022 (Shift-I)

Ans. (d)

The sentence with correct spelling is : I heard raucous laughter from the next room.

185. Getting a compliment from her husband was a rare occurrance in Rashmila's life.

SSC CGL Tier-1 03.12.2022 (Shift-I)

(a) occurrence (b) ocurrance
(c) No error (d) ocurrancce

Ans. (a)

The correct spelling is 'occurrence'.

186. The rhime and rhythm of Papai's poems are highly symbolical and timely. **SSC CGL Tier-1 03.12.2022 (Shift-II)**

(a) rhyme (b) timely
(c) rhythm (d) symbolical

Ans. (a)

The correct spelling is 'rhyme'.

187. (a) Justice (b) Judege
(c) Attorney (d) Lawyer

SSC CGL Tier-1 03.12.2022 (Shift-II)

Ans. (b)

The correct spelling is 'judge'.

188. (a) He screeched hystericalli after seeing the accident.
(b) He screeched hystericaly after seeing the accident.
(c) He screeched hysteerically after seeing the accident
(d) He screeched hysterically after seeing the accident.

SSC CGL Tier-1 03.12.2022 (Shift-III)

Ans. (d)

The sentence with correct spelling is : He screeched hysterically after seeing the accident.

189. (a) Friwsk (b) Reply
(c) Rusk (d) Foliage

SSC CGL Tier-1 03.12.2022 (Shift-III)

Ans. (a)

The correct spelling is 'frisk'.
It means to search for a hidden weapon.

190. (a) Irritating (b) Pedestrian
(c) Enervating (d) Beguilling

SSC CGL Tier-1 03.12.2022 (Shift-IV)

Ans. (d)

The correct spelling is 'beguiling'. It means attractive and interesting.

191. (a) Adopt (b) Acces
(c) Abandon (d) Abase
SSC CGL Tier-1 03.12.2022 (Shift-IV)

Ans. (b)

The correct spelling is 'access'. It means the right to enter a place, use something, see someone, etc.

192. (a) Governance (b) Enforcement
(c) Insufficient (d) Innocense
SSC CGL Tier-1 05.12.2022 (Shift-I)

Ans. (d)

The correct spelling is 'innocence'. It means lack of guilt or corruption; purity.

193. (a) Striphe (b) Fright
(c) Delight (d) Knight
SSC CGL Tier-1 05.12.2022 (Shift-I)

Ans. (a)

The correct spelling is 'strife' means trouble or difficulty of any kind.

194. Sudhir's harrassment is not only perceivable and occasional but also has become a matter of humorous incident before his colleague.
SSC CGL Tier-1 05.12.2022 (Shift-I)

(a) colleague (b) harrassment
(c) humorous (d) perceivable

Ans. (b)

The correct spelling is 'harassment'. It means behaviour that annoys or upsets someone.

195. (a) Warden (b) Poliseman
(c) Engineer (d) Doctor
SSC CGL Tier-1 05.12.2022 (Shift-I)

Ans. (b)

The correct spelling is 'policeman'.

196. Tyrany must be dead to attain harmony, tranquillity and serenity.
SSC CGL Tier-1 05.12.2022 (Shift-III)

(a) tranquillity (b) tyrany
(c) serenity (d) harmony

Ans. (b)

The correct spelling is 'tyranny'. It refers to a cruel and oppresive government or rule.

197. (a) Movement (b) Kecthup
(c) Precise (d) Flashy
SSC CGL Tier-1 05.12.2022 (Shift-III)

Ans. (b)

The correct spelling is 'ketchup'.

198. (a) Dimolish (b) Conduct
(c) Biopic (d) Handful
SSC CGL Tier-1 05.12.2022 (Shift-IV)

Ans. (a)

The correct spelling is 'demolish'. It means to destroy.

199. Ratan is such an efficient sergeant that he doesn't need to imbibe any artillery craftmanship.
SSC CGL Tier-1 05.12.2022 (Shift-IV)

(a) artillery (b) efficient
(c) craftmanship (d) sergeant

Ans. (c)

The correct spelling is 'craftsmanship'.

200. (a) Compact (b) Compell
(c) Currently (d) Savage
SSC CGL Tier-1 06.12.2022 (Shift-I)

Ans. (b)

The correct spelling is 'Compel'. It means to force someone to do something.

201. (a) Assidous (b) Disapproval
(c) Devastation (d) Conjoined
SSC CGL Tier-1 06.12.2022 (Shift-I)

Ans. (a)

The correct spelling is 'assiduous'. It means showing great care and perseverance.

202. The Education Ministry believes that after the reopening of the schools, it will take some time to regain the equiliebrium.
SSC CGL Tier-1 06.12.2022 (Shift-II)

(a) equilibreum
(b) equelibrium
(c) No error
(d) equilibrium

Ans. (d)

The correct spelling of the underlined word is 'equilibrium'.

203. (a) Athlete (b) Practically
(c) Benefitted (d) Antartic
SSC CGL Tier-1 06.12.2022 (Shift-II)

Ans. (d)

The correct spelling is 'antarctic'.

204. (a) Thyriod (b) Disaster
(c) System (d) Distance
SSC CGL Tier-1 06.12.2022 (Shift-III)

Ans (a)

The correct spelling is 'thyroid'.

205. Apparently, he seems to be an amature person, but I know that he is a disciplined and committed person when it comes to doing something seriously.
SSC CGL Tier-1 06.12.2022 (Shift-III)

(a) amature (b) apparently
(c) committed (d) disciplined

Ans. (a)

The correct spelling is 'amateur'. It refers to a person who is not an expert at a particular activity.

206. Rather than being aggressive, you should be accomodative, magnanimous and benevolent in nature. SSC CGL Tier-1 06.12.2022 (Shift-IV)

(a) accomodative (b) magnanimous
(c) aggressive (d) benevolent

Ans. (a)

The correct spelling is 'accommodative'. It means willing to give someone what they want or need or to change in order to suit them.

207. (a) The art and science of designing buildings is called architecchure.
(b) The art and science of designing buildings is called architecture.
(c) The art and science of designing buildings is called archtiecture.
(d) The art and science of designing buildings is called architectrue.
SSC CGL Tier-1 06.12.2022 (Shift-IV)

Ans. (b)

The sentence with correct spelling is : The art and science of designing buildings is called architecture.

208. (a) My mother asked me to purchase two bread knives having serrated edges.
(b) My mother asked me to purchase two bread knives having seerated edges.
(c) My mother asked me to purchase two bread knives having serratted edges.
(d) My mother asked me to purchase two bread knives having serated edges. SSC CGL Tier-1 07.12.2022 (Shift-I)

Ans. (a)

The sentence with correct spelling is : My mother asked me to purchase two bread knives having serrated edges.

209. She is a nuisanse to her family.
SSC CGL Tier-1 07.12.2022 (Shift-I)

(a) nuisince (b) niusance
(c) newsance (d) nuisance

Ans. (d)

The correct spelling of the underlined word is 'nuisance'. It means a person, thing or situation that annoys you or causes problems.

210. (a) Languish (b) Altitude
(c) Discusion (d) Longitudinal
SSC CGL Tier-1 07.12.2022 (Shift-II)

Ans. (c)

The correct spelling is 'discussion'. It means the activity in which people talk about something and tell each other their ideas or opinions.

211. (a) Sabbatical (b) Confluence
(c) Sinhaleese (d) Conform
SSC CGL Tier-1 07.12.2022 (Shift-III)

Ans. (c)

The correct spelling is 'sinhalese'. It means the main group of people who live in Sri Lanka.

212. The nine-tailed fox is a mythicil creature from Japanese culture.
SSC CGL Tier-1 07.12.2022 (Shift-IV)
(a) mythycal (b) mitical
(c) mythical (d) mithical

Ans. (c)

The correct spelling is 'mythical'. It means existing only in stories.

213. (a) Ryan squaked about losing his job owing to a leg injury.
(b) Ryan squeked about losing his job owing to a leg injury.
(c) Ryan squawked about losing his job owing to a leg injury.
(d) Ryan skuawked about losing his job owing to a leg injury.
SSC CGL Tier-1 07.12.2022 (Shift-IV)

Ans. (c)

The sentence with no spelling error is : Ryan squawked about losing his job owing to a leg injury.

214. The outcome of the survey was a critical intervention to the questionaire prepared by Suraj and his committee.
SSC CGL Tier-1 08.12.2022 (Shift-I)
(a) questionaire (b) committee
(c) intervention (d) outcome

Ans. (a)

The correct spelling is 'questionnaire'. It refers to a list of questions that several people are asked so that information can be collected about something.

215. (a) The hippoputamus, also known as 'river horse', lives throughout sub-Saharan Africa.
(b) The hipopotamus, also known as 'river horse', lives throughout sub-Saharan Africa.
(c) The hippopotmaus, also known as 'river horse', lives throughout sub-Saharan Africa.
(d) The hippopotamus, also known as 'river horse', lives throughout sub-Saharan Africa.
SSC CGL Tier-1 08.12.2022 (Shift-I)

Ans. (d)

The sentence with no spelling error is : The hippopotamus, also known as 'river horse', lives throughout sub-Saharan Africa.

216. Kamal's repetative mistakes and slip of tongue often create embarrassing moments for him.
SSC CGL Tier-1 08.12.2022 (Shift-II)
(a) embarrassing (b) slip
(c) moments (d) repetative

Ans. (d)

The correct spelling is 'repetitive'. It means involving, doing or saying the same thing several times, especially in a way that is boring.

217. (a) Streamlining (b) Construction
(c) Barbaric (d) Evolutoin
SSC CGL Tier-1 08.12.2022 (Shift-II)

Ans. (d)

The correct spelling is 'evolution'. It means the way in which living things change and develop over the years.

218. (a) Contradiction (b) Abhorrent
(c) Condencing (d) Hereditary
SSC CGL Tier-1 08.12.2022 (Shift-III)

Ans. (c)

The correct spelling is 'condensing'. It means to change or make something change from gas to liquid.

219. (a) Bouquet (b) Hygene
(c) Mortgage (d) Champagne
SSC CGL Tier-1 08.12.2022 (Shift-III)

Ans. (b)

The correct spelling is 'hygiene'. It means the practice of keeping yourself and the things around you clean, in order to prevent illness or disease.

220. The staff members were attempting to manoeuvre the board of directors for the abolition of pay disparity.
SSC CGL Tier-1 08.12.2022 (Shift-IV)
(a) manouever (b) manoeuver
(c) manouvre (d) No error

Ans. (d)

The given sentence does not have any spelling errors in it.

221. In the coming millenium, some noticeable technological advancements will be accomplished. **SSC CGL Tier-1 08.12.2022 (Shift-IV)**
(a) noticeable (b) technological
(c) advancements (d) millenium

Ans. (d)

The correct spelling is 'millennium'. It means a period of 1,000 years or the time when a period of 1,000 years ends.

222. The ruthless story of Pankaj's assassination in the Carribean islands is thrilling to read.
SSC CGL Tier-1 09.12.2022 (Shift-I)
(a) Thrilling (b) Carribean
(c) Assassination (d) Ruthless

Ans. (b)

The correct spelling is 'caribbean'. It means relating to the islands of the Caribbean Sea and the countries that surround it, the people who live there or their culture.

223. Being a conscentious and single-minded person, Tubai has become inquisitive and perseverant in exploring young talents.
SSC CGL Tier-1 09.12.2022 (Shift-I)
(a) inquisitive
(b) perseverant
(c) conscentious
(d) exploring

Ans. (c)

The correct spelling is 'conscientious'. It means working hard and careful to do things well.

224. (a) Laproscopy (b) Generate
(c) Intermittent (d) Guise
SSC CGL Tier-1 09.12.2022 (Shift-I)

Ans. (a)

The correct spelling is 'Laparoscopy'. It refers to a surgical procedure used to examine the organs in the abdomen.

225. Handover that peace of paper to me so that I can evaluate the authenticity of his amorous claims.
SSC CGL Tier-1 09.12.2022 (Shift-I)
(a) peice (b) peices
(c) pieces (d) piece

Ans. (d)

The word 'peace' is incorrectly spelt in the context of the sentence. The correct spelling is 'piece'.

226. (a) Pollen (b) Mousy
(c) Quasi (d) Quever
SSC CGL Tier-1 09.12.2022 (Shift-III)

Ans. (d)

The correct spelling is 'quiver'. It means to shake with short quick movements.

227. (a) Flawless (b) Rudimentary
(c) Primitive (d) Impracticle
SSC CGL Tier-1 09.12.2022 (Shift-IV)

Ans. (d)

The correct spelling is 'impractical'.

228. The police came to the accident spot after receiving an annonymous phone call.
SSC CGL Tier-1 09.12.2022 (Shift-IV)
(a) anonnymous
(b) no error
(c) anonymous
(d) anonymaus

Ans. (c)

The correct spelling 'anonymous'. It means unknown.

229. He <u>deceaved</u> the fraternity by the news of his unparalleled accomplishment to accommodate himself in the academic field.
SSC CGL Tier-1 12.12.2022 (Shift-I)

(a) desieved (b) deseived
(c) decieved (d) deceived

Ans. (d)

The sentence with no spelling error is : The correct spelling is 'deceived'. It means 'to cheat'.

230. (a) Anxiety is one of the most insicdious conditions affecting the mental health of an individual.
(b) Anxiety is one of the most insidyous conditions affecting the mental health of an individual.
(c) Anxiety is one of the most insidious conditions aflecting the mental health of an individual.
(d) Anxiety is one of the most insidious conditions affecting the mental health of an individual.
SSC CGL Tier-1 12.12.2022 (Shift-I)

Ans. (d)

The sentence with no spelling error is: Anxiety is one of the most insidious conditions affecting the mental health of an individual.

231. It is a deeply regrettable fact that deforestation has had a substantial consequense on the environment.
SSC CGL Tier-1 12.12.2022 (Shift-II)

(a) deforestation (b) substantial
(c) regrettable (d) consequense

Ans. (d)

The correct spelling is 'consequence'.

232. (a) I saw the dress catalouge pieces of Asha's corchiture collection.
(b) I saw the dress catalougue pieces of Asha's couture collection.
(c) I saw the dress catalougue pieces of Asha's corchiture collection.
(d) I saw the dress catalogue pieces of Asha's couture collection.
SSC CGL Tier-1 12.12.2022 (Shift-II)

Ans. (d)

The sentence with no spelling error is : I saw the dress catalogue pieces of Asha's couture collection.

233. (a) People suffering from edzema have allergies with red and itchy skin.
(b) People suffering from ekzema have allergies with red and itchy skin.
(c) People suffering from eczema have allergies with red and itchy skin.
(d) People suffring from ekezema have allergies with red and itchy skin.
SSC CGL Tier-1 12.12.2022 (Shift-III)

Ans. (c)

The sentence with no spelling error is : People suffering from eczema have allergies with red and itchy skin.

234. The problematic and convoluted situation concerning Rakhtim's job is likely to exhilarate in the forseable future. SSC CGL Tier-1 12.12.2022 (Shift-III)

(a) convoluted
(b) forseable
(c) problematic
(d) exhilarate

Ans. (b)

The correct spelling is 'foreseeable'. It means to be predicted.

235. (a) Benchmark (b) Knight
(c) Aggravate (d) Subsistance
SSC CGL Tier-1 12.12.2022 (Shift-IV)

Ans. (d)

The correct spelling is 'subsistence'. It means the condition of only just having enough money or food to stay alive.

236. (a) Musk (b) Decide
(c) External (d) Angel
SSC CGL Tier-1 12.12.2022 (Shift-IV)

Ans. (c)

The correct spelling is 'external'. It means relating to the outside of something or of a person's body.

237. There lies no guarantee that the hierchical structural framework between the elite and downtrodden sections of the society is right.
SSC CGL Tier-1 13.12.2022 (Shift-I)

(a) downtrodden (b) hierchical
(c) guarantee (d) structural

Ans. (b)

The correct spelling is 'hierarchical'. It means arranged in order of rank.

238. (a) Diabites is a chronic disease.
(b) Diabetes is a chronic disease.
(c) Daibetes is a chronic disease.
(d) Diabeties is a chronic disease.
SSC CGL Tier-1 13.12.2022 (Shift-I)

Ans. (b)

The sentence with no spelling error is : Diabetes is a chronic disease.

239. Rajib's research aims to identify the strings that connect man and nature in order to provide a comprehensive examination and asesment of a variety of ecological issues. SSC CGL Tier-1 13.12.2022 (Shift-II)

(a) Strings
(b) Asesment
(c) Ecological
(d) Comprehensive

Ans. (b)

The correct spelling is 'assessment'. It means evaluation.

240. The poor woman is in excruciating mental anguish and her loved ones appear to have assisted in exarcerbating her traumatic experiences.
SSC CGL Tier-1 13.12.2022 (Shift-II)

(a) anguish (b) excruciating
(c) traumatic (d) exarcerbating

Ans. (d)

The correct spelling is 'exacerbating'. It means to make something worse, more violent or bitter.

241. (a) India has started the largest inocultaion drive in the world against Covid.
(b) India has started the largest inoculation drive in the world against Covid.
(c) India has started the largest inculation drive in the world against Covid.
(d) India has started the largest inokulation drive in the world against Covid.
SSC CGL Tier-1 13.12.2022 (Shift-III)

Ans. (b)

The sentence with no spelling error is : India has started the largest inoculation drive in the world against Covid.

242. Success is the continious journey towards the achievement of predetermined goals.
SSC CGL Tier-1 13.12.2022 (Shift-III)

(a) continuous (b) sucsess
(c) gaols (d) achivement

Ans. (a)

The correct spelling is 'continuous'.

243. Decades of enimity between Lomovs and Chubukovs came to an end with the marriage between the two families.
SSC CGL Tier-1 13.12.2022 (Shift-IV)

(a) No error (b) anaemity
(c) enemity (d) enmity

Ans. (d)

Among the given options, the correctly spelt word is 'enmity'.

244. (a) Furore from the protestors was heard outside the President's house.
(b) Furrow from the protestors was heard outside the President's house.
(c) Furorow from the protestors was heard outside the President's house.
(d) Furorow from the protestors was heard outside the President's house.
SSC CGL Tier-1 13.12.2022 (Shift-IV)

Ans. (a)

The sentence with no spelling error is : Furore from the protestors was heard outside the President's house.

SSC CGL 2021 (Tier 1 & 2)

245. (a) Creature (b) Specified
(c) Decrease (d) Pieceful
SSC CGL Tier-1 13.08.2021 (Shift-I)

Ans. (d)
The correct spelling is be 'peaceful'.

246. (a) Voilence (b) Exterminated
(c) Wildernesses (d) Unmanageable
SSC CGL Tier-1 13.08.2021 (Shift-I)

Ans. (a)
The correct spelling is 'violence'.

247. (a) Indolence (b) Inershia
(c) Idleness (d) Insolence
SSC CGL Tier-1 13.08.2021 (Shift-III)

Ans. (b)
The correct spelling is 'inertia'. It refers to a tendency to do nothing or to remain unchanged.

248. (a) Fiery (b) Scenic
(c) Friend (d) Neice
SSC CGL Tier-1 13.08.2021 (Shift-III)

Ans. (d)
The correct spelling is 'niece'.

249. (a) Vishious (b) Moisture
(c) Anxious (d) Mimic
SSC CGL Tier-1 16.08.2021 (Shift-I)

Ans. (a)
The correct spelling is 'vicious'. It means evil.

250. (a) Scrutinize (b) Cerebral
(c) Withdrawl (d) Arbitrary
SSC CGL Tier-1 16.08.2021 (Shift-I)

Ans. (c)
The correct spelling is 'withdrawal'.

251. (a) Professional (b) Electronics
(c) Dillemma (d) Perpetuate
SSC CGL Tier-1 16.08.2021 (Shift-III)

Ans. (c)
The correct spelling is 'Dilemma'. It refers to a situation in which a difficult choice has to be made between two or more alternatives.

252. (a) Processing (b) Boundary
(c) Photograp (d) Competency
SSC CGL Tier-1 16.08.2021 (Shift-III)

Ans. (c)
The correct spelling is 'photograph'.

253. (a) Cancellation (b) Incriminating
(c) Unpretensious (d) Embodiment
SSC CGL Tier-1 17.08.2021 (Shift-I)

Ans. (c)
The correct spelling is 'unpretentious'.

254. (a) Pledge (b) Acquarium
(c) Abridge (d) Bouquet
SSC CGL Tier-1 17.08.2021 (Shift-I)

Ans. (b)
The correct spelling is 'aquarium'.

255. (a) Comedian (b) Camoflage
(c) Custard (d) Caravan
SSC CGL Tier-1 17.08.2021 (Shift-III)

Ans. (b)
The correct spelling is 'camouflage'. It means to hide or disaguise.

256. (a) Astound (b) Amount
(c) Advice (d) Adress
SSC CGL Tier-1 17.08.2021 (Shift-III)

Ans. (d)
The correct spelling is 'address'.

257. (a) Seasonal (b) Celestial
(c) Hygeinic (d) Gymnastic
SSC CGL Tier-1 18.08.2021 (Shift-I)

Ans. (c)
The correct spelling is 'hygienic'.

258. (a) Scorpeon (b) Caterpillar
(c) Lizard (d) Chameleon
SSC CGL Tier-1 18.08.2021 (Shift-I)

Ans. (a)
The correct spelling is 'scorpion'.

259. (a) Sentimentally (b) Substantially
(c) Subseqently (d) Solicitation
SSC CGL Tier-1 18.08.2021 (Shift-III)

Ans. (c)
The correct spelling is 'subsequently'.

260. (a) Approval (b) Censure
(c) Criticism (d) Hellicopter
SSC CGL Tier-1 18.08.2021 (Shift-III)

Ans. (d)
The correct spelling is 'helicopter'.

261. (a) Cadre (b) Commit
(c) Carnivorous (d) Calender
SSC CGL Tier-1 20.08.2021 (Shift-I)

Ans. (d)
The correct spelling is 'calendar'.

262. (a) Drought (b) Doubt
(c) Dental (d) Dictonary
SSC CGL Tier-1 20.08.2021 (Shift-II)

Ans. (d)
The correct spelling is 'dictionary'.

263. (a) Adequate (b) Adamant
(c) Adviseable (d) Alternate
SSC CGL Tier-1 20.08.2021 (Shift-II)

Ans. (c)
The correct spelling is 'advisable'.

264. (a) Elite (b) Petete
(c) Concrete (d) Secrete
SSC CGL Tier-1 23.08.2021 (Shift-I)

Ans. (b)
The correct spelling is 'petite' which means 'small' or 'little'.

265. (a) Refurbish (b) Sanctity
(c) Esscalator (d) Automated
SSC CGL Tier-1 23.08.2021 (Shift-I)

Ans. (c)
The correct spelling is 'escalator'.

266. (a) Priority
(b) Detective
(c) Evidence
(d) Vacine
SSC CGL Tier-1 23.08.2021 (Shift-II)

Ans. (d)
The correct spelling is 'vaccine'.

267. (a) Innovation (b) Barricade
(c) Preshious (d) Infection
SSC CGL Tier-1 23.08.2021 (Shift-II)

Ans. (c)
The correct spelling is 'prescious'.

268. (a) Haphazard (b) Chandelier
(c) Aesthetic (d) Licenced
SSC CGL Tier-1 24.08.2021 (Shift-I)

Ans. (d)
The correct spelling is 'licensed'.

269. (a) Boasting (b) Evidence
(c) Overide (d) Ascetic
SSC CGL Tier-1 24.08.2021 (Shift-I)

Ans. (c)
The correct spelling is 'override'.

270. (a) Plough (b) Playful
(c) Plagiarise (d) Playright
SSC CGL Tier-1 24.08.2021 (Shift-II)

Ans. (d)
The correct spelling is 'playwright'.

271. (a) Nephew (b) Cousin
(c) Neice (d) Uncle
SSC CGL Tier-1 24.08.2021 (Shift-II)

Ans. (c)
The correct spelling is 'niece'.

272. (a) Anarchy (b) Monarchy
(c) Tyrany (d) Aristocracy
SSC CGL Tier-1 24.08.2021 (Shift-III)

Ans. (c)
The correct spelling is 'tyranny'. It means cruel or unfair control over people.

273. (a) Verbal (b) Melody
(c) Written (d) Speach
SSC CGL Tier-1 24.08.2021 (Shift-III)

Ans. (d)
The correct spelling is 'speech'.

SSC CPO 2024 (Tier 1 & 2)

274. (a) Disseminate (b) Enterprenuer
(c) Dilemma (d) Accommodate
SSC CPO Tier-1 27.06.2024 (Shift-II)

Ans. (b)
The correct spelt word is 'entrepreneur'.

275. Many promote bamboo planting for erosion prevention and to riverse the effects of global warming.
SSC CPO Tier-1 27.06.2024 (Shift-II)

(a) Reverse (b) Bambboo
(c) Efeccts (d) Prevension

Ans. (a)

The correct spelling is 'reverse'.

276. A <u>congragation</u> of monks reached Shimla for the convention.
SSC CPO Tier-1 27.06.2024 (Shift-II)

(a) congregetion (b) cangregation
(c) congretettion (d) congregation

Ans. (d)

The correct spelling is 'congregation'.

277. (a) Cheerfull (b) Tsunami
(c) Efficient (d) Responsibilities
SSC CPO Tier-1 27.06.2024 (Shift-II)

Ans. (a)

The correct spelt word is 'cheerful'.

278. The islands of Japan were connected to the Asian landmass about 12,000 years ago; the first Japanese travelled across the water in **serch** of animals to hunt.
SSC CPO Tier-1 27.06.2024 (Shift-II)

(a) landmass (b) serch
(c) connected (d) islands

Ans. (b)

The correct spelt word is 'search'.

279. (a) Directory (b) Dictionery
(c) Dispensery (d) Machinary
SSC CPO Tier-1 28.06.2024 (Shift-I)

Ans. (a)

The correctly spelled word is 'directory'. The correct spelling of other words are dictionary, dispensary and machinery.

280. The idea is to encourage tourism and allow visitors to enjoy the spectacular Rockies, but to ensure that it is done in **hermony** with the environment.
SSC CPO Tier-1 28.06.2024 (Shift-I)

(a) Enssure (b) Harmony
(c) Encaurage (d) Touresm

Ans. (b)

The correct spelling is 'harmony'.

281. (a) Granary (b) Dictionary
(c) Directory (d) Chancellary
SSC CPO Tier-1 28.06.2024 (Shift-I)

Ans. (d)

The correct spelling is 'chancellery'. It refers to the position, court or department of a chancellor.

282. (a) The skilled surgeon delicatly performed the intricate procedure, saving the patient's life with his stedy hands and unwavering focus.
(b) The skilled surgeon delicately performed the intrecate procedure, saving the patient's life with his steady hands and unwavering focus.
(c) The skiled surgeon delicatly performed the intricate procedure, saving the patient's life with his stedy hands and unwavering focus.
(d) The skilled surgeon delicately performed the intricate procedure, saving the patient's life with his steady hands and unwavering focus. **SSC CPO Tier-1 28.06.2024 (Shift-I)**

Ans. (d)

The sentence with correct spelling is: 'The skilled surgeon delicately performed the intricate procedure, saving the patient's life with his steady hands and unwavering focus.'

283. It may seem **pretintious** to say so but I cannot live without my essential articles.
SSC CPO Tier-1 28.06.2024 (Shift-I)

(a) essential (b) cannot
(c) articles (d) pretintious

Ans. (d)

The correct spelling is 'pretentious'.

284. (a) Programe (b) Unexpected
(c) Pilgrimage (d) Campaign
SSC CPO Tier-1 28.06.2024 (Shift-I)

Ans. (a)

The correct spelling is 'programme'.

285. Generousity is a godly feature among many individuals on the Earth. **SSC CPO Tier-1 28.06.2024 (Shift-II)**

(a) Generousity (b) feature
(c) godly (d) individuals

Ans. (a)

The correct spelling is 'generosity'.

286. (a) Refridgerator (b) Litrature
(c) Registration (d) Allegater
SSC CPO Tier-1 28.06.2024 (Shift-II)

Ans. (c)

The correctly spelt word is 'registration'. The correct spelling of other words are refrigerator, literature and alligator.

287. (a) The delicius aroma of freshely baked cookies wafted through the kitchen, making mouths water.
(b) The delicious arauma of freshely baked cookes wafted through the kitchen, making mouths water.
(c) The delicious aroma of freshly baked cookies wafted through the kitchen, making mouths water.
(d) The delicious arauma of freshly baked cookies waftad through the kitchen, making mouths water.
SSC CPO Tier-1 28.06.2024 (Shift-II)

Ans. (c)

The sentence with correct spelling is: 'The delicious aroma of freshly baked cookies wafted through the kitchen, making mouths water.'

288. (a) Passage (b) Reconsidered
(c) Prevention (d) Supremecy
SSC CPO Tier-1 28.06.2024 (Shift-II)

Ans. (d)

The correct spelling is 'supremacy'.

289. (a) Entrepreneur (b) Supersede
(c) Dissapear (d) Vicinity
SSC CPO Tier-1 28.06.2024 (Shift-II)

Ans. (c)

The correct spelling is 'disappear'.

290. (a) Irritate (b) Necessitate
(c) Reciept (d) Hindrance
SSC CPO Tier-1 28.06.2024 (Shift-III)

Ans. (c)

The correct spelling is 'receipt'.

291. (a) Dictionary (b) Reference
(c) Infurmary (d) Ordinary
SSC CPO Tier-1 28.06.2024 (Shift-III)

Ans. (c)

The correct spelling is 'infirmary'. It refers to a hospital.

292. (a) The scientiest meticulously analysed the complex data, uncovering ground-breaking insights that would revolutionice the field.
(b) The scientist meticulusly analysed the complex data, uncovering ground-breaking insights that would revaulutionise the field.
(c) The scientist meticulously anelysed the complex data, uncovering ground-breaking insights that would revolutionise the feild.
(d) The scientist meticulously analysed the complex data, uncovering ground-breaking insights that would revolutionise the field.
SSC CPO Tier-1 28.06.2024 (Shift-III)

Ans. (d)

The sentence with correct spelling is : 'The scientist meticulously analysed the complex data, uncovering ground-breaking insights that would revolutionise the field.' 'Revolutionise' is correctly spelled, meaning change something radically or fundamentally.

293. There are difficult times too, especially when the economy takes a dip and we have to lai people off.
SSC CPO Tier-1 28.06.2024 (Shift-III)

(a) economie (b) dificult
(c) lay (d) dipe

Ans. (c)

The correct spelling is 'lay'.

294. He was a benaevolent young man who would help his colleagues.
SSC CPO Tier-1 28.06.2024 (Shift-III)
(a) Benavolent (b) Benevolent
(c) Benevalant (d) Banevolent
Ans. (b)
The correct spelling of the given word is 'benevolent'. It means kind.

295. Large-scale hunting scenes and slaugter of wild animals is a heinous crime.
SSC CPO Tier-1 28.06.2024 (Shift-III)
(a) slaugter (b) heinous
(c) scenes (d) hunting
Ans. (a)
The correct spelling is 'slaughter'. It means to kill.

296. (a) Rhinoceros (b) Bueraucracy
(c) Acquaintance (d) Miscellaneous
SSC CPO Tier-1 29.06.2024 (Shift-I)
Ans. (b)
The correct spelling is 'bureaucracy'. It refers to a system of governance.

297. (a) Notation (b) Witharing
(c) Gallantry (d) Vagabond
SSC CPO Tier-1 29.06.2024 (Shift-I)
Ans. (b)
The correct spelling is 'withering'. It means to become dry or fail into decay.

298. The movie is just beggining.
SSC CPO Tier-1 29.06.2024 (Shift-I)
(a) Biginning (b) Beginning
(c) Beginnig (d) Begining
Ans. (b)
The correct spelling is 'beginning'.

299. They broght their dog to the park for a walk. SSC CPO Tier-1 29.06.2024 (Shift-I)
(a) brought (b) brahgt
(c) bruaght (d) braoght
Ans. (a)
The correct spelling is 'brought'.

300. (a) Ambigous (b) Luminous
(c) Gregarious (d) Nostalgia
SSC CPO Tier-1 29.06.2024 (Shift-I)
Ans. (a)
The correct spelling is 'ambiguous'. It means confusing.

301. (a) The profesional athlete pushed her body to the limit, surpassing all expectations and acheiving a new personal record.
(b) The profesional athlete pushed her body to the limit, surpasing all expectasions and achieving a new personal record.
(c) The professional athlete pushed her body to the limit, surpasing all expectations and acheving a new personal record.
(d) The professional athlete pushed her body to the limit, surpassing all expectations and achieving a new personal record.
SSC CPO Tier-1 29.06.2024 (Shift-II)
Ans. (d)
The sentence with correct spelling is : 'The professional athlete pushed her body to the limit, surpassing all expectations and achieving a new personal record.'

302. (a) Assimilation (b) Pluckiness
(c) Accumulation (d) Exestenalism
SSC CPO Tier-1 29.06.2024 (Shift-II)
Ans. (d)
The correct spelling is 'existentialism'.

303. Thousands of years ago, great masters of Ayurveda, notebly Sushrut and Charaka, discussed in detail the use of spices for culinary and medical purpose.
SSC CPO Tier-1 29.06.2024 (Shift-II)
(a) parpose (b) notably
(c) discused (d) cullinary
Ans. (b)
The correct spelling is 'notably'.

304. The boys seem irresponsibly insaucient about bullying the juniors. SSC CPO Tier-1 29.06.2024 (Shift-II)
(a) insoucient (b) insuociant
(c) insouciant (d) insouceant
Ans. (c)
The correct spelling is 'insouciant'. It means free from concern, worry or anxiety.

305. Mount Vesuvius is a volcano that erapts hot ashes which fall from the sky like a blizzard.
SSC CPO Tier-1 29.06.2024 (Shift-II)
(a) erapts (b) blizzard
(c) ashes (d) volcano
Ans. (a)
The correct spelling is 'erupts'.

306. The baby smiled and laughed at the pickaboo game.
SSC CPO Tier-1 29.06.2024 (Shift-II)
(a) peakaboo (b) pikaboo
(c) peekaboo (d) pekaboo
Ans. (c)
The correct spelling is 'peekaboo'. It is the name of a game.

307. (a) Matriculation (b) Prohibition
(c) Humorous (d) Addmission
SSC CPO Tier-1 29.06.2024 (Shift-III)
Ans. (d)
The correct spelling is 'admission'.

308. (a) Interogative (b) Auditions
(c) Interference (d) Greengrocers
SSC CPO Tier-1 29.06.2024 (Shift-III)
Ans. (a)
The correct spelling is 'interrogative'.

309. Everyone admired her because of her charesma, but she was a narcissist full of self-admiration and treachery.
SSC CPO Tier-1 29.06.2024 (Shift-III)
(a) treachery (b) self-admiration
(c) charesma (d) narcissist
Ans. (c)
The correct spelling is 'charisma'.

310. (a) Obscurity (b) Schedule
(c) Assasination (d) Buoyant
SSC CPO Tier-1 29.06.2024 (Shift-III)
Ans. (c)
The correct spelling is 'assassination'.

311. (a) Dilligence (b) Particularly
(c) Betrayal (d) Vacation
SSC CPO Tier-2 08.01.2024
Ans. (a)
'Diligence' is the correctly spelled word meaning careful and persistent work or effort.

312. (a) Insence (b) Enhance
(c) Immense (d) Elegance
SSC CPO Tier-2 08.01.2024
Ans. (a)
'Insence' is incorrectly spelled; the correct spelling is 'incense.'

313. (a) Exhiliarated (b) Officious
(c) Facetious (d) Conspicuous
SSC CPO Tier-2 08.01.2024
Ans. (a)
'Exhilarated' is the correctly spelled word meaning very happy, animated or elated.

314. (a) Temperament (b) Reticent
(c) Pertinent (d) Iminent
SSC CPO Tier-2 08.01.2024
Ans. (d)
'Iminent' is incorrectly spelled. The correct spelling is 'imminent.'

SSC CPO 2023

315. (a) Interrogate (b) Alienate
(c) Deserve (d) Asasinate
SSC CPO 03.10.2023 (Shift-I)
Ans. (d)
The correct spelling is 'assassinate'. It means to kill someone.

316. This was a blatent disregard to the advisory. By the host against it and in violation of norms of the meeting. SSC CPO 03.10.2023 (Shift-I)
(a) advisory (b) blatent
(c) disregard (d) violation

Ans. (b)

The correct spelling is 'blatant'. It means obvious.

317. (a) Adjacent (b) Accomplish (c) Agregate (d) Allure
SSC CPO 03.10.2023 (Shift-I)

Ans. (c)

The correct spelling is 'aggregate'. It means combined

318. (a) Serene (b) Triumph (c) Comparsion (d) Unveil
SSC CPO 03.10.2023 (Shift-I)

Ans. (c)

The correctly spelt word is 'comparison'.

319. A. The art of living is learnt easily by those who are positive and optimistic.
B. We can learn a lot about the art of living by having a peep into the lives of great men.
C. The daily routines of these great men dissiminate that they are different.
D. Their unique lifestyles help us learn certain habits and practices that they followed.
SSC CPO 03.10.2023 (Shift-II)
(a) The art of living is learnt easily by those who are positive and optimistic.
(b) We can learn a lot about the art of living by having a peep into the lives of great men.
(c) Their unique lifestyles help us learn certain habits and practices that they followed.
(d) The daily routines of these great men dissiminate that they are different.

Ans. (d)

'Dissiminate' is incorrectly spelled; the correct spelling is 'disseminate,' meaning spread or disperse something widely.

320. Gandhiji considared untouchability to be one of India's major social ills.
SSC CPO 03.10.2023 (Shift-II)
(a) untouchability
(b) major
(c) considared
(d) social

Ans. (c)

The correct spelling is 'considered'.

321. (a) Yearn (b) Merriment (c) Zenith (d) Miniture
SSC CPO 03.10.2023 (Shift-II)

Ans. (d)

'Miniture' is incorrectly spelled; the correct spelling is 'miniature,' meaning a small-scale replica or model.

322. He has won the medal for the twelth time. SSC CPO 03.10.2023 (Shift-II)
(a) Twwelfth (b) Twellth (c) Twelfth (d) Twelttth

Ans. (c)

The correct spelling is 'twelfth'.

323. (a) Pitza (b) Noodle (c) Pasta (d) Bread
SSC CPO 03.10.2023 (Shift-II)

Ans. (a)

The correct spelling is 'pizza'.

324. The ruins of many structures that still stand tall in their granduer are testimony to the fact that Mewar was not only the land of the courageous. SSC CPO 03.10.2023 (Shift-III)
(a) granduer
(b) courageous
(c) testimony
(d) ruins

Ans. (a)

'Granduer' is incorrectly spelled. The correct spelling is 'grandeur' meaning magnificence or splendor.

325. Traffic accidents are increasing steadily and large cities are plaged by traffic congestion. Worst of all is the air pollution caused by internal combustion engine, uninterruptedly.
SSC CPO 03.10.2023 (Shift-III)
(a) plaged (b) congestion (c) combustion (d) uninterruptedly

Ans. (a)

The correct spelling is 'plagued'.

326. A. A fisherman, enfeebled with age, could no longer go out to sea so he began fishing in the river.
B. Every morning he would go down to the river and sit there fishing the whole day long.
C. In the evening, he would sell whatever he had caught, buy food for himself and go home.
D. One hot afternoon, while he was bemoaning his fate, a large bird alited near him.
SSC CPO 03.10.2023 (Shift-III)
(a) A fisherman, enfeebled with age, could no longer go out to sea so he began fishing in the river.
(b) One hot afternoon, while he was bemoaning his fate, a large bird alited near him.
(c) Every morning he would go down to the river and sit there fishing the whole day long.
(d) In the evening, he would sell whatever he had caught, buy food for himself and go home.

Ans. (b)

'Alited' is incorrectly spelled; the correct spelling is 'alighted,' meaning landed or settled.

327. (a) Airplane (b) Helicopter (c) Gllidder (d) Ladybug
SSC CPO 03.10.2023 (Shift-III)

Ans. (c)

The correct spelling is 'glider'.

328. The disadvantages of listening to music at a loud volume include loss of heearing. SSC CPO 03.10.2023 (Shift-III)
(a) Lose
(b) Volume
(c) Lissening
(d) Hearing

Ans. (d)

The correct spelling is 'hearing'.

329. The Eustachian tube and vestubular complex in the middle and inner ear, respectively, have an important role to play. SSC CPO 04.10.2023 (Shift-II)
(a) vestibular (b) midle (c) respictevely (d) importent

Ans. (a)

The correct spelling is 'vestibular'.

330. Roshni does a fabulouous job at her company and has been offered a promotion. SSC CPO 04.10.2023 (Shift-II)
(a) fabulouous
(b) company
(c) promotion
(d) offered

Ans. (a)

The correct spelling is 'fabulous'.

331. (a) Ocassion (b) Agreeable (c) Formulae (d) Waitress
SSC CPO 04.10.2023 (Shift-II)

Ans. (a)

The correct spelling is 'occasion'.

332. Communities must build their resileince, including adopting appropriate technologies while making the most of traditional knowledge and diversifying their livelihoods to cope with current and future climate stress.
SSC CPO 04.10.2023 (Shift-II)
(a) livelihoods (b) diversifying (c) appropriate (d) resileince

Ans. (d)

The correct spelling is 'resilience'.

333. (a) Prefered (b) Reference (c) Revered (d) Answered
SSC CPO 04.10.2023 (Shift-III)

Ans. (a)

The correct spelling is 'preferred'.

334. As <u>affidevit</u> is a statement or declaration in writing an oath or <u>affirmation</u>, sworn before a person having <u>authority</u> to administer oath. SSC CPO 04.10.2023 (Shift-III)

(a) administer (b) authority
(c) affirmation (d) affidevit

Ans. (d)

The correct spelling is 'affidavit'.

335. The Egyptian Pharohs were the Kings of ancient Egypt and were considered as the literal embodiment of God himself.
SSC CPO 04.10.2023 (Shift-III)

(a) literal (b) embodiment
(c) pharohs (d) ancient

Ans. (c)

The correct spelling is 'pharaoh'.

336. Mrs. Lal taught me English <u>gramar</u>.
SSC CPO 05.10.2023 (Shift-I)

(a) gramerr (b) grammar
(c) grammarr (d) gramer

Ans. (b)

The correct spelling is 'grammar'.

337. Students should have a good vocabulary to write an essay efectively. SSC CPO 05.10.2023 (Shift-I)

(a) gud (b) voicabulary
(c) write (d) effectively

Ans. (d)

The correct spelling is 'effectively'. The other spellings are good, write and vocabulary.

338. It is beyond my cognative capacity to solve the mathematical problems. SSC CPO 05.10.2023 (Shift-I)

(a) problems (b) capacity
(c) cognative (d) mathematical

Ans. (c)

The correct spelling is 'cognitive'.

339. It is important to see school <u>holistically</u>, it is not a set of atomic items of rooms, library, assembly halls, canteen and playgrounds; it is all of these but in <u>symbiotic</u> relationship with each other, the <u>contors</u> of which are often far too obvious and often simply <u>mysterious</u>. SSC CPO 05.10.2023 (Shift-I)

(a) contors (b) mysterious
(c) holistically (d) symbiotic

Ans. (a)

The correct spelling is 'contour'.

340. (a) The country's GDP bloomed dispite the ongoing war situation.
(b) The country's GDP bloomed despete the ongoing war situation.
(c) The country's GDP bloomed dispete the ongoing war situation.
(d) The country's GDP bloomed despite the ongoing war situation.
SSC CPO 05.10.2023 (Shift-II)

Ans. (d)

The correct spelling is 'despite'.

341. But he waited with the <u>inconceivable</u> patience and <u>persistancy</u> of the race; besides, he was certain, the cat was a creature of absolute <u>convictions</u> and his faith in his <u>deductions</u> never wavered.
SSC CPO 05.10.2023 (Shift-II)

(a) convictions (b) deductions
(c) persistancy (d) inconceivable

Ans. (c)

The correct spelling is 'persistency'.

342. (a) Comuter (b) Committee
(c) Camouflage (d) Commission
SSC CPO 05.10.2023 (Shift-II)

Ans. (a)

The correct spelling is 'comutter'.

343. <u>Mountainering</u> is now looked upon as the king of sports.
SSC CPO 05.10.2023 (Shift-II)

(a) Mountainouring
(b) Mountaineering
(c) Mountainearing
(d) Mounteineering

Ans. (b)

The correct spelling is 'mountaineering'.

344. He had a round face made jovial by bright, almost boyish eyes and eyebrows ridiculusly small for a man his size. SSC CPO 05.10.2023 (Shift-III)

(a) ridicolusly (b) jouvial
(c) juvial (d) ridiculously

Ans. (d)

The correct spelling is 'ridiculously'.

345. Why is <u>everyone</u> so, dressed up? What's the <u>occaseon</u>? Is it a <u>wedding</u>? SSC CPO 05.10.2023 (Shift-III)

(a) wedding (b) occaseon
(c) everyone (d) dressed

Ans. (b)

The correct spelling is 'occasion'.

346. They were more often abnoxious than not, impatient with me because my services had been essentially imposed upon them.
SSC CPO 05.10.2023 (Shift-III)

(a) abnoxious (b) impatint
(c) servises (d) essentialy

Ans. (a)

The correct spelling is 'obnoxious'. It means extremely unpleasant.

347. They have begun to study in <u>sepparate</u> rooms.
SSC CPO 05.10.2023 (Shift-III)

(a) saperate (b) separate
(c) seprate (d) saparate

Ans. (b)

The correct spelling is 'separate'.

348. (a) Without basic intelligence, an individual is trapped within himself, manifesting conflicts and ignorance in the external world.
(b) An intellectual person.05.have all the knowledge of the world but won't know how to give it a shape.
(c) Knowledge will plague the individual if he does not have the intelligence to express it.
(d) One has to understand the rudimentery fact that intelligence and intellect are at two opposite poles. SSC CPO 05.10.2023 (Shift-III)

Ans. (d)

'Rudimentery' is incorrectly spelled. The correct spelling is 'rudimentary,' meaning basic or fundamental.

SSC CPO 2022

349. (a) Abcission (b) Abstruse
(c) Incision (d) Abyssal
SSC CPO 09.11.2022 (Shift-I)

Ans. (a)

'Abcission' is incorrectly spelled. The correct spelling is 'abscission,' meaning the natural detachment of parts of a plant, typically dead leaves and ripe fruit.

350. The pyramids that you see in Egypt were built by the Pharoh dynasties who ruled the ancient kingdom of Egypt for thousands of years.
SSC CPO 09.11.2022 (Shift-I)

(a) Egypt (b) Pharh
(c) dynasties (d) pyromids

Ans. (b)

The correct spelling is 'pharaoh'.

351. (a) Illicite (b) Illegal
(c) Impunity (d) Illegible
SSC CPO 09.11.2022 (Shift-II)

Ans. (a)

The correct spelling is 'illicit'.

352. (a) Perspicuiuos
(b) Purvey
(c) Peruse
(d) Pervade SSC CPO 09.11.2022 (Shift-III)

Ans. (a)

The correct spelling is 'perspicuious'.

353. (a) Membrane (b) Solvant
(c) Highlight (d) Exuberant
SSC CPO 09.11.2022 (Shift-III)

Ans. (b)

The correct spelling is 'solvent'.

354. (a) Pried (b) Prophet
(c) Prodigy (d) Proteg
SSC CPO 10.11.2022 (Shift-I)

Ans. (d)

The correct spelling is 'protege'. It means someone, especially a young person, who is taught and helped by someone who has influence, power or more experience.

355. (a) Impoverish (b) Ostacise
(c) Necessitate (d) Grandeur
SSC CPO 10.11.2022 (Shift-I)

Ans. (b)

The correct spelling is 'ostracise'. It means to stop accepting someone as a member of a group and refusing to talk or listen to them.

356. Rajib is not only an extremely reputed conoisseur of art but also a successful entrepreneur.
SSC CPO 10.11.2022 (Shift-II)
(a) conoisseur
(b) reputed
(c) entrepreneur
(d) successful

Ans. (a)

The incorrectly spelt word is 'conoisseur'. 'Connoisseur' is the correct spelling and it means someone who knows a lot about a particular thing and enjoys it a lot.

357. (a) Aquatic (b) Notorious
(c) Centinarian (d) Mercenary
SSC CPO 10.11.2022 (Shift-II)

Ans. (c)

The incorrectly spelt word is 'centinarian'. The correct spelling is 'centenarian' and it refers to someone who is 100 years old or more.

358. (a) Extacted (b) Expected
(c) Extracted (d) Acceptable
SSC CPO 10.11.2022 (Shift-III)

Ans. (a)

The correct spelling is 'exacted'.

359. Sharks often use their serated or smooth teeth for seizing prey, cutting or crushing.
SSC CPO 11.11.2022 (Shift-I)
(a) serated (b) prey
(c) seizing (d) crushing

Ans. (a)

The correct spelling is 'serrated'. It means having a row of sharp points along the edge.

360. (a) Assembly (b) Disipline
(c) Group (d) Leader
SSC CPO 11.11.2022 (Shift-I)

Ans. (b)

The correct spelling is 'discipline'. It means a way of training someone so that they learn to control their behaviour and obey rules.

361. (a) Intsrmenable (b) Intubate
(c) Incredible (d) Incredulous
SSC CPO 11.11.2022 (Shift-I)

Ans. (a)

The correct spelling is 'interminable'. It means continuing for a long time in a boring or annoying way.

362. (a) Flurorecence (b) Forebear
(c) Forgo (d) Flounder
SSC CPO 11.11.2022 (Shift-II)

Ans. (a)

The correct spelling is 'fluorescence'. It refers to the quality of a colour, material, etc. that appears very bright when light shines on it, so it can be seen in the dark.

363. (a) Quarrelsome (b) Ecclesiastical
(c) Bovine (d) Calamitious
SSC CPO 11.11.2022 (Shift-III)

Ans. (d)

'Calamitious' is incorrectly spelled. The correct spelling is 'calamitous,' meaning involving calamity or disastrous.

364. The most frequent medallion composition on a carpet consists of a more or less elaborate motif superimposed on the centre of a patterned field and often complemented with corner pieces, which are typically quadrants of the central medallion.
SSC CPO 11.11.2022 (Shift-III)
(a) medallion (b) elaborate
(c) complemented (d) quardant

Ans. (d)

'Quardant' is incorrectly spelled. The correct spelling is 'quadrant,' meaning each of four quarters of a circle.

SSC CHSL 2024 (Tier 1 & 2)

365. He is wimsical by natur. No one can seek an explanation from him for his absurd atitude towards others. **SSC CHSL Tier-2 18.11.2024**
(a) He is wimsical by nature. No one can seek an explanation from him for his absurd attitude towards others.
(b) He is whimsical by natur. No one can seek an explanation from him for his absurd atitude towards others.
(c) He is whimsical by nature. No one can seek an explanation from him for his abserd attitude towards others.
(d) He is whimsical by nature. No one can seek an explanation from him for his absurd attitude towards others.

Ans. (d)

'He is whimsical by nature.

No one can seek an explanation from him for his absurd attitude towards others.' This sentence contains all correctly spelled words: 'whimsical', 'nature', 'explanation', 'absurd' and 'attitude' are all spelled correctly.

366. (a) Intuition (b) Instinctual
(c) Implusive (d) Initiative
SSC CHSL Tier-2 18.11.2024

Ans. (c)

'Implusive' is incorrectly spelled. The correct spelling is 'Impulsive.' It means acting on a sudden urge or desire without thinking.

367. I have been morning the death of my pet dog. **SSC CHSL Tier-2 18.11.2024**
(a) merning (b) moruning
(c) mourning (d) murning

Ans. (c)

The correct spelling is 'mourning', which means to grieve.

368. (a) Encraoch (b) Delegate
(c) Illusion (d) Obtain
SSC CHSL Tier-1 01.07.2024 (Shift-I)

Ans. (a)

The incorrectly spelt word is 'encraoch'. The correct spelling is 'encroach'.

369. I begged him/to reconcider/the decision but / he refused to yield.
SSC CHSL Tier-1 01.07.2024 (Shift-I)
(a) the decision but
(b) I begged him
(c) he refused to yield
(d) to reconcider

Ans. (d)

Part (d) 'to reconcider' contains a spelling error. The correct spelling is 'reconsider'.

370. A distinguished academecian, Amartya Sen has taught in India, Britain and the United States.
SSC CHSL Tier-1 01.07.2024 (Shift-II)
(a) academecian (b) taught
(c) britain (d) distinguished

Ans. (a)

The incorrectly spelt word is 'academecian'. The correctly spelt word is 'academician'.

371. (a) Category (b) Hygiene
(c) Congratulate (d) Aquire
SSC CHSL Tier-1 01.07.2024 (Shift-II)

Ans. (d)

The incorrectly spelt word is 'aquire'. The correct spelling is 'acquire'.

372. (a) Foresee (b) Rebuke
(c) Seize (d) Dissappoint
SSC CHSL Tier-1 01.07.2024 (Shift-III)

Ans. (d)

The incorrectly spelt word is 'dissappoint'. The correct spelling is 'disappoint'.

373. 'Vande Mataram', a poignant poem, is obviously and indisputebly the premier national song of India.
SSC CHSL Tier-1 01.07.2024 (Shift-III)
(a) Obviously (b) Premier
(c) Indisputebly (d) Poignant

Ans. (c)

The incorrectly spelt word is 'indisputebly'. The correct spelling is 'indisputably'.

374. The precious bookshelf was carefully decorated with religiuos books. SSC CHSL Tier-1 01.07.2024 (Shift-IV)
(a) precious (b) decorated
(c) carefully (d) religiuos

Ans. (d)

The incorrectly spelt word is 'religiuos'. The correct spelling is 'religious'.

375. The committee heard that he had been negliegent in his duty.
SSC CHSL Tier-1 01.07.2024 (Shift-IV)
(a) negligent (b) dutie
(c) comitee (d) hurd

Ans. (a)

The incorrectly spelt word is 'negliegent'. The correct spelling is 'negligent'.

376. (a) Illuseon (b) Illusion
(c) Illuzion (d) Ilusion
SSC CHSL Tier-1 02.07.2024 (Shift-I)

Ans. (b)

The correctly spelt word is 'Illusion', which means a false idea or belief.

377. (a) Marijuena (b) Stationery
(c) Dictator (c) Lascivious
SSC CHSL Tier-1 02.07.2024 (Shift-I)

Ans. (a)

The incorrectly spelt word is 'marijuena'.
The correct spelling is 'marijuana' which is a drug that is smoked illegally in many countries.

378. Wether we want to admit it or not, we all wish everyone would like us.
SSC CHSL Tier-1 02.07.2024 (Shift-II)
(a) addmit (b) whether
(c) admitt (d) whither

Ans. (b)

The incorrectly spelt word is 'wether'. The correct spelling is 'whether'.

379. The prison is euphemistically called a 'rehabillitation centre'.
SSC CHSL Tier-1 02.07.2024 (Shift-II)
(a) rehabilition (b) rehabilitation
(c) rehbilitation (d) rehabilation

Ans. (b)

The correct spelling is 'rehabilitation'.

380. This will sound weired, but bear with me.
SSC CHSL Tier-1 02.07.2024 (Shift-III)
(a) wired (b) beer
(c) weird (d) bier

Ans. (c)

The incorrectly spelt word is 'weired'. The correct spelling is 'weird'.

381. (a) Betrey (b) Destroy
(c) Develop (d) Demolish
SSC CHSL Tier-1 02.07.2024 (Shift-III)

Ans. (a)

The incorrectly spelt word is 'betrey'. The correct spelling is 'betray'.

382. Maybe he wanted to make sure he didn't embarrese her.
SSC CHSL Tier-1 02.07.2024 (Shift-IV)
(a) sware (b) shure
(c) embarrass (d) emberess

Ans. (c)

The incorrectly spelt word is 'embarrese'. The correct spelling is 'embarrass'.

383. It has been a usual ocurrence for a few days now.
SSC CHSL Tier-1 02.07.2024 (Shift-IV)
(a) occerrence (b) occurrance
(c) occurence (d) occurrence

Ans. (d)

The correct spelling is 'occurrence'.

384. Nobody could move on after such a scandlous allegation is made on them. SSC CHSL Tier-1 03.07.2024 (Shift-I)
(a) skandelous (b) scandalous
(c) scandelous (d) scendolous

Ans. (b)

The correct spelling is 'scandalous'.

385. (a) Aspirant (b) License
(c) Autonomous (d) Ommision
SSC CHSL Tier-1 03.07.2024 (Shift-I)

Ans. (d)

The incorrectly spelt word is 'Ommision'. The correct spelling is 'Ommission'.

386. (a) Litrature (b) Reformation
(c) Schedule (d) Miserable
SSC CHSL Tier-1 03.07.2024 (Shift-II)

Ans. (a)

The incorrectly spelt word is 'litrature'. The correct spelling is 'literature'.

387. (a) Immigrete (b) Combat
(c) Relevant (d) Professional
SSC CHSL Tier-1 03.07.2024 (Shift-II)

Ans. (a)

The incorrectly spelt word is 'immigrete'. The correct spelling is 'immigrate'.

388. (a) Magnanimos
(b) Accompanied
(c) Fascination
(d) Psychology
SSC CHSL Tier-1 03.07.2024 (Shift-III)

Ans. (a)

The incorrectly spelt word is 'Magnanimos'. The correct spelling is 'Magnanimous'.

389. (a) Chief (b) Relevant
(c) Colleague (d) Judgment
SSC CHSL Tier-1 03.07.2024 (Shift-III)

Ans. (d)

The incorrectly spelt word is 'Judgment'. The correct spelling is 'Judgement'.

390. (a) Acknowledgment
(b) Apparent
(c) Fulfil
(d) Conscientous
SSC CHSL Tier-1 03.07.2024 (Shift-IV)

Ans. (d)

The incorrectly spelt word is 'Conscientous'. The correct spelling is 'Conscientious'.

391. I am contant with my day's work.
SSC CHSL Tier-1 04.07.2024 (Shift-I)
(a) contint (b) contante
(c) content (d) cuntent

Ans. (c)

The correct spelling is 'content'.

392. (a) Adulterous
(b) Amendment
(c) Advertisment
(d) Astounding
SSC CHSL Tier-1 04.07.2024 (Shift-I)

Ans. (c)

The incorrectly spelt word is 'Advertisment'. The correct spelling is 'Advertisement'.

393. The West Africans have a heritage of producing sculpture using wax and bronze.
SSC CHSL Tier-1 04.07.2024 (Shift-II)
(a) sculpture (b) bronze
(c) heritage (d) produsing

Ans. (d)

The incorrectly spelt word is 'produsing'. The correct spelling is 'producing'.

394. The boy found the project to be a peice of cake because it was incredibly easy.
SSC CHSL Tier-1 04.07.2024 (Shift-II)

(a) piece (b) incrediblly
(c) foaund (d) praject

Ans. (a)

The incorrectly spelt word is 'peice'. The correct spelling is 'piece'.

395. The mighty gaint brought a marigold for the princess.
SSC CHSL Tier-1 04.07.2024 (Shift-III)

(a) gaint (b) princess
(c) marigold (d) mighty

Ans. (a)

The incorrectly spelt word is 'gaint'. The correct spelling is 'giant'.

396. The calandar was reformed during the time of Julius Caesar.
SSC CHSL Tier-1 04.07.2024 (Shift-III)

(a) reeformed (b) celender
(c) riformed (d) calandar

Ans. (d)

The incorrectly spelt word is 'calandar'. The correct spelling is 'calendar'.

397. Shreya prefers wearing green coloured saree on marriage funcktions.
SSC CHSL Tier-1 04.07.2024 (Shift-IV)

(a) prefers (b) wearing
(c) funcktions (d) marriage

Ans. (c)

The incorrectly spelt word is 'funcktions'. The correct spelling is 'functions'.

398. (a) Physiologist
(b) Contagious
(c) Gracious
(d) Couragious
SSC CHSL Tier-1 04.07.2024 (Shift-IV)

Ans. (d)

The incorrectly spelt word is 'couragious'. The correct spelling is 'courageous'.

399. You shall recieve proper pay for your work.
SSC CHSL Tier-1 05.07.2024 (Shift-I)

(a) resieve (b) propper
(c) receive (d) propeer

Ans. (c)

The incorrectly spelt word is 'recieve'. The correct spelling is 'receive'.

400. He is one of the most <u>underated</u> players in the team.
SSC CHSL Tier-1 05.07.2024 (Shift-I)

(a) undereted (b) underatted
(c) underrated (d) underreted

Ans. (c)

The correct spelling is 'underrated'.

401. (a) Innoculate (b) Irreverent
(c) Immense (d) Immaculate
SSC CHSL Tier-1 05.07.2024 (Shift-II)

Ans. (a)

The incorrectly spelt word is 'innoculate'. The correct spelling is 'inoculate'.

402. The make-up room was filled / with incadescent lights / which added to the misery / of those subjected to make-up.
SSC CHSL Tier-1 05.07.2024 (Shift-II)

(a) which added to the misery
(b) with incadescent lights
(c) of those subjected to make-up
(d) The make-up room was filled

Ans. (b)

Part (b) 'with incadescent lights' contains a spelling error.
The correct spelling is 'incandescent' which means emitting light as a result of being heated.

403. (a) Aquarium (b) Mantain
(c) Accurate (d) Excellence
SSC CHSL Tier-1 05.07.2024 (Shift-III)

Ans. (b)

The incorrectly spelt word is 'Mantain'. The correct spelling is 'Maintain'.

404. It is his previlage to present all the candidates for ordination to the bishop of the diocese.
SSC CHSL Tier-1 05.07.2024 (Shift-III)

(a) deocease (b) privilege
(c) prevalage (d) odination

Ans. (b)

The incorrectly spelt word is 'previlage'. The correct spelling is 'privilege'.

405. (a) Scatered (b) Brazen
(c) Crowded (d) Imprudent
SSC CHSL Tier-1 05.07.2024 (Shift-IV)

Ans. (a)

The incorrectly spelt word is 'scatered'. The correct spelling is 'scattered'.

406. The police issued a <u>varant</u> to the criminals.
SSC CHSL Tier-1 05.07.2024 (Shift-IV)

(a) Warant (b) Varrant
(c) Warent (d) Warrant

Ans. (d)

The correct spelling is 'warrant'.

407. They were good-hearted girls, unclean, clothed in rags and profiundly ignorant.
SSC CHSL Tier-1 08.07.2024 (Shift-I)

(a) Hearted (b) Profiundly
(c) Unclean (d) Clothed

Ans. (b)

The incorrectly spelt word is 'profiundly'. The correct spelling is 'profoundly'.

408. (a) Comendation
(b) Reimbursement
(c) Competition
(d) Intertwined
SSC CHSL Tier-1 08.07.2024 (Shift-I)

Ans. (a)

The incorrectly spelt word is 'comendation'. The correct spelling is 'commendation'.

409. (a) Timorous (b) Amalgamate
(c) Unintended (d) Apropriate
SSC CHSL Tier-1 08.07.2024 (Shift-II)

Ans. (d)

The incorrectly spelt word is 'apropriate'. The correct spelling is 'appropriate'.

410. (a) Creator (b) Skewed
(c) Agressive (d) Apparent
SSC CHSL Tier-1 08.07.2024 (Shift-II)

Ans. (c)

The incorrectly spelt word is 'agressive'. The correct spelling is 'aggressive'.

411. Stomach sleepers were rated as being more gregairious and uncomfortable with criticism.
SSC CHSL Tier-1 08.07.2024 (Shift-III)

(a) gregarious (b) criticicm
(c) ratedd (d) stomac

Ans. (a)

The incorrectly spelt word is 'gregairious'. The correct spelling is 'gregarious'.

412. They adressed the special gathering perfectly.
SSC CHSL Tier-1 08.07.2024 (Shift-IV)

(a) addressed (b) special
(c) gathering (d) perfectly

Ans. (a)

The incorrectly spelt word is 'adressed'. The correct spelling is 'addressed'.

413. (a) Conscience (b) Consciencious
(c) Conspicuous (d) Conscious
SSC CHSL Tier-1 08.07.2024 (Shift-IV)

Ans. (b)

The incorrectly spelt word is 'consciencious'. The correct spelling is 'conscientious'.

414. (a) Dissociation
(b) Clandestine
(c) Pronounciation
(d) Denunciation
SSC CHSL Tier-1 09.07.2024 (Shift-I)

Ans. (c)

The incorrectly spelt word is 'Pronounciation'. The correct spelling is 'Pronunciation'.

415. I am in a hurry so I will see you tomorow.
SSC CHSL Tier-1 09.07.2024 (Shift-I)
(a) tomoorow (b) tomorrow
(c) toomorow (d) tomoorrow

Ans. (b)

The correct spelling is 'tomorrow'.

416. He was thrilled when he heard about there journey to wonderland.
SSC CHSL Tier-1 09.07.2024 (Shift-II)
(a) journey (b) thrilled
(c) there (d) heard

Ans. (c)

The incorrectly spelt word in the context of the sentence is 'there'.

The correct spelling is 'their'.

417. (a) Condimnation
(b) Intermingled
(c) Imprisonment
(d) Conglomerate
SSC CHSL Tier-1 09.07.2024 (Shift-II)

Ans. (a)

The incorrectly spelt word is 'Condimnation'. The correct spelling is 'Condemnation'.

418. The ministir ordered the engineers to build roads through high mountains and bridges across deep ravines in a week.
SSC CHSL Tier-1 09.07.2024 (Shift-III)
(a) ravines (b) engineers
(c) ministir (d) bridges

Ans. (c)

The incorrectly spelt word is 'ministir'. The correct spelling is 'minister'.

419. A natural clamity causing huge destruction and loss of life and property.
SSC CHSL Tier-1 09.07.2024 (Shift-IV)
(a) calamity (b) clamanity
(c) calamitey (d) climanity

Ans. (a)

The correct spelling is 'calamity'.

420. King Zheng is known to lead an army of a million armoured soldiers, a thousand chariots and ten thousand horses in his misssion to conquer the neighbouring kingdoms.
SSC CHSL Tier-1 09.07.2024 (Shift-IV)
(a) Misssion (b) Kingdoms
(c) Chariots (d) Thousand

Ans. (a)

The incorrectly spelt word is 'Misssion'. The correct spelling is 'Mission'.

421. It was a privvilege to receive the award from the President.
SSC CHSL Tier-1 10.07.2024 (Shift-I)
(a) privilegge (b) privileege
(c) privilege (d) privillege

Ans. (c)

The correct spelling is 'privilege'.

422. The Chinese are believed to have a longer history than that of any other civilisation in the wolrd.
SSC CHSL Tier-1 10.07.2024 (Shift-I)
(a) Wolrd (b) Civilisation
(c) Believed (d) Chinese

Ans. (a)

The incorrectly spelt word is 'wolrd'. The correct spelling is 'world'.

423. (a) Appraisal (b) Definate
(c) Stretch (d) Genuine
SSC CHSL Tier-1 10.07.2024 (Shift-II)

Ans. (b)

The incorrectly spelt word is 'Definate'. The correct spelling is 'Definite'.

424. She decided to file a complaint with HR after being harrasad by her supervisor for several weeks.
SSC CHSL Tier-1 10.07.2024 (Shift-II)
(a) harassed (b) harrassd
(c) harrased (d) harased

Ans. (a)

The correct spelling is 'harassed'.

425. (a) Connoisseur
(b) Circumlocution
(c) Haphazard
(d) Disintigrate
SSC CHSL Tier-1 10.07.2024 (Shift-III)

Ans. (d)

The incorrectly spelt word is 'Disintigrate'. The correct spelling is 'Disintegrate'.

426. The choice of buying a yahct was poor. SSC CHSL Tier-1 10.07.2024 (Shift-III)
(a) buying (b) yahct
(c) choice (d) poor

Ans. (b)

The incorrectly spelt word is 'yahct'. The correct spelling is 'yatch'.

427. (a) Dilemma (b) Committee
(c) Warranty (d) Neice
SSC CHSL Tier-1 10.07.2024 (Shift-IV)

Ans. (d)

The incorrectly spelt word is 'Neice'. The correct spelling is 'Niece'.

428. There are a number of artists currently creating unique, collectble teapots. SSC CHSL Tier-1 10.07.2024 (Shift-IV)
(a) currantly (b) collectable
(c) collectibile (d) currintly

Ans. (b)

The incorrectly spelt word is 'collectble'. The correct spelling is 'collectable'.

429. He lost all senisation in his legs through a cramp.
SSC CHSL Tier-1 11.07.2024 (Shift-I)
(a) syansation (b) sensition
(c) sansation (d) sensation

Ans. (d)

The incorrectly spelt word is 'senisation'. The correct spelling is 'sensation'.

430. To avoid indigetion, it is necessary to chew food properly.
SSC CHSL Tier-1 11.07.2024 (Shift-I)
(a) chew (b) necessary
(c) properly (d) indigetion

Ans. (d)

The incorrectly spelt word is 'indigetion'. The correct spelling is 'indigestion'.

431. (a) Psychometric
(b) Concentrate
(c) Vindication
(d) Conglomirate
SSC CHSL Tier-1 11.07.2024 (Shift-II)

Ans. (d)

The incorrectly spelt word is 'Conglomirate'. The correct spelling is 'Conglomerate'.

432. (a) Immediately (b) Immedeatly
(c) Imediately (d) Immidiately
SSC CHSL Tier-1 11.07.2024 (Shift-II)

Ans. (a)

The correct spelling is 'immediately'.

433. (a) Quintessential (b) Quintessintial
(c) Quintesential (d) Quientessential
SSC CHSL Tier-1 11.07.2024 (Shift-III)

Ans. (a)

The correct spelling is 'Quintessential'.

434. Psycology developed as a significant discipline of study in the twentieth century.
SSC CHSL Tier-1 11.07.2024 (Shift-III)
(a) Pscycology (b) Psychology
(c) Pcychology (d) Pscichology
Ans. (b)
The correct spelling is 'psychology'.

435. I was/alarmed lest/we should/be wreked. SSC CHSL Tier-1 11.07.2024 (Shift-IV)
(a) I was
(b) be wreked
(c) we should
(d) alarmed lest
Ans. (b)
Part (b) 'be wreked' contains an error. The correct spelling is 'wrecked'.

436. The advertisement of vacencies in education sector has received huge response.
SSC CHSL Tier-1 11.07.2024 (Shift-IV)
(a) vecencies (b) vacansies
(c) vecancies (d) vacancies
Ans. (d)
The incorrectly spelt word is 'vacencies'. The correct spelling is 'vacancies'.

437. The remoteness of the location made it difficult for the authoreties to reach out to the people.
SSC CHSL Tier-2 10.01.2024
(a) authorities (b) locasion
(c) remotness (d) deficult
Ans. (a)
The correct spelling is 'Authorities'.

438. He made a <u>sureptitiuos</u> phone call while his boss was out of the room.
SSC CHSL Tier-2 10.01.2024
(a) surreptitous (b) sureptitious
(c) surreptitious (d) sarreptitious
Ans. (c)
The correct spelling is 'Surreptitious'. It means done secretely.

439. (a) Maxim (b) Profligate
(c) Lisentious (d) Quandary
SSC CHSL Tier-2 10.01.2024
Ans. (c)
The correct spelling is 'licentious'. It means locking legal or moral values.

SSC CHSL 2023 (Tier 1 & 2)

440. (a) You remind me of someone I knew onse.
(b) You reminde me of someone I knew once.
(c) You remind me of someone I knew once.
(d) You remiend me of someone I knew once. SSC CHSL Tier-1 09.03.2023 (Shift-I)
Ans. (c)
The sentence with correct spelling is: You remind me of someone I knew once.

441. (a) Shuot (b) Broom
(c) Bloom (d) Gloomy
SSC CHSL Tier-1 09.03.2023 (Shift-I)
Ans. (a)
The correct spelling is 'shout'.

442. (a) Fine fthers do not make fine birds.
(b) Figne feathers do not make find brds.
(c) Fine fathears do not make fine birds.
(d) Fine feathers do not make fine birds. SSC CHSL Tier-1 09.03.2023 (Shift-I)
Ans. (d)
The sentence with no spelling error is Fine feathers do not make fine birds.

443. (a) Viscous (b) Boisterous
(c) Percieve (d) Benevolent
SSC CHSL Tier-1 10.03.2023 (Shift-II)
Ans. (c)
The correct spelling is 'perceive'. It means to become aware of or understand.

444. (a) Obsequios
(b) Maintainance
(c) Vacillate
(d) Stilletoes
Ans. (c)
The correctly spelt word is 'vacillate'. The correct spellings of other words 'obsequious', maintenance and 'stilettos'.

445. (a) Independant (b) Eminent
(c) Humorous (d) Splendid
SSC CHSL Tier-1 13.03.2023 (Shift-III)
Ans. (a)
The correct spelling is 'independent'.

446. (a) Greed (b) Circle
(c) Heap (d) Cateogry
SSC CHSL Tier-1 14.03.2023 (Shift-I)
Ans. (d)
The correct spelling is 'category'.

447. (a) Motivational quotes will not help you.
(b) Motivatinal quotes will not help you.
(c) Motivational qoutes will not help you.
(d) Motiviational quotes will not help you.
SSC CHSL Tier-1 14.03.2023 (Shift-I)
Ans. (a)
The sentence with no spelling error is 'Motivational quotes will not help you.'

448. (a) They give the impression that you are desperate.
(b) They give the impresion that you are desperate.
(c) They give the impression that you are desparate.
(d) They give the impressin that you are desperate.
SSC CHSL Tier-1 14.03.2023 (Shift-I)
Ans. (a)
The sentence with no spelling error is 'They give the impression that you are desperate.'

449. (a) A wel done introduction grabs the reader.
(b) A well done introduction grabbs the reader.
(c) A well done intrudoction grabs the reader.
(d) A well done introduction grabs the reader.
SSC CHSL Tier-1 15.03.2023 (Shift-IV)
Ans. (d)
The sentence with no spelling error is 'A well done introduction grabs the reader.'

450. (a) Majestic (b) Lovable
(c) Tokan (d) String
SSC CHSL Tier-1 15.03.2023 (Shift-IV)
Ans. (c)
The correct spelling is 'token'.

451. (a) Mouse (b) Brinjal
(c) Blink (d) Sliede
SSC CHSL Tier-1 16.03.2023 (Shift-II)
Ans. (d)
The correct spelling is 'slide'.

452. (a) A welcomng voice from the open doorway.
(b) A welcoming voice from the open dorway.
(c) A welcoming voice from the open doorway.
(d) A welcoming voise from the open doorway.
SSC CHSL Tier-1 16.03.2023 (Shift-II)
Ans. (c)
The sentence with no spelling error is 'A welcoming voice from the open doorway.'

453. (a) New seeds are made through polination.
(b) New seeds are made through pollination.
(c) New sieds are made through pollination.
(d) New seeds are made through pollination.
SSC CHSL Tier-1 16.03.2023 (Shift-III)
Ans. (b)

The sentence with no spelling error is 'New seeds are made through pollination.'

454. (a) Recruit (b) Remark
(c) Repeal (d) Revange
SSC CHSL Tier-1 16.03.2023 (Shift-III)

Ans. (d)

The correct spelling is 'revenge'.

455. (a) Treasure (b) Clouwn
(c) Mason (d) Poison
SSC CHSL Tier-1 17.03.2023 (Shift-II)

Ans. (b)

The correct spelling is 'clown'.

456. (a) Circumspect (b) Coffer
(c) Camor (d) Cloying
SSC CHSL Tier-1 20.03.2023 (Shift-III)

Ans. (c)

The correct spelling is 'clamour'. It refers to a loud and confusing noise.

457. (a) Besiege (b) Benign
(c) Bifurcate (d) Beneficiel
SSC CHSL Tier-1 20.03.2023 (Shift-III)

Ans. (d)

The correct spelling is 'beneficial'.

458. (a) He seemed to be taller than him.
(b) He seemed to bee taller then him.
(c) He semed to be taller than him.
(d) He seemed to be taler than him.
SSC CHSL Tier-1 21.03.2023 (Shift-II)

Ans. (a)

The sentence with no spelling error is : He seemed to be taller than him.

459. (a) Steam (b) Sleam
(c) Beam (d) Cream
SSC CHSL Tier-1 21.03.2023 (Shift-II)

Ans. (b)

The correct spelling is 'seam'.

460. (a) These components can wrok independently.
(b) These components can work independently.
(c) These components can work indepedently
(d) These componants can work independently.
SSC CHSL Tier-1 21.03.2023 (Shift-IV)

Ans. (b)

The sentence with no spelling error is : These components can work independently.

461. (a) Washing (b) Burnig
(c) Calling (d) Morning
SSC CHSL Tier-1 21.03.2023 (Shift-IV)

Ans. (b)

The correct spelling is 'burning'.

462. You need to acknowledge the itinary and accommodation details to your journey as per the given calendar. SSC CHSL Tier-1 02.08.2023 (Shift-I)
(a) calendar
(b) accommodation
(c) acknowledge
(d) itinary

Ans. (d)

The incorrectly spelt word is 'itinary'. The correctly spelling of the word is 'itinerary'. It means a plan of a journey, including the route and the places that you will visit.

463. Kasturi acts as a <u>liason</u> between patients and staff.
SSC CHSL Tier-1 02.08.2023 (Shift-I)
(a) liaision (b) laision
(c) liaison (d) liaisan

Ans. (c)

'Liaison' is the correct spelling. It means communication between two or more people or groups that work together.

464. (a) Business (b) Buisnesc
(c) Buisness (d) Busines
SSC CHSL Tier-1 02.08.2023 (Shift-II)

Ans. (a)

The correct spelling is 'Business'.

465. The <u>enchanteng scenary</u> of the beautiful lake was mesmerising.
SSC CHSL Tier-1 02.08.2023 (Shift-II)
(a) enchanting scenery
(b) encanting scenery
(c) enchenting seenary
(d) enchantine senery

Ans. (a)

The correct spelling is 'enchanting scenery'.

466. Jaysmita is one of the most .... persons I have ever met as she has many talents.
SSC CHSL Tier-1 02.08.2023 (Shift-III)
(a) versataile (b) versatele
(c) versateile (d) versatile

Ans. (d)

The correctly spelt word that can fill the blank is 'versatile'.

467. The civil engineers are trying to .... the bridge using the new technology.
SSC CHSL Tier-1 02.08.2023 (Shift-IV)
(a) elevate (b) illivate
(c) alivate (d) elivait

Ans. (a)

The correctly spelt word that can fill the blank is 'elevate'. It means to raise to a higher position.

468. Your lack of knowledge of recent advances in technology will be a sitback for your business.
SSC CHSL Tier-1 02.08.2023 (Shift-IV)
(a) advancess (b) knowleidge
(c) bussiness (d) setback

Ans. (d)

The correct spelling is 'setback'. It means a problem.

469. The chief guest is .... to arrive at the venue within half an hour.
SSC CHSL Tier-1 03.08.2023 (Shift-I)
(a) accepted (b) expieted
(c) expected (d) expceted

Ans. (c)

The correctly spelt word that will fill in the blank 'expected'.

470. Medical <u>termnalogy</u> is difficult to understand.
SSC CHSL Tier-1 03.08.2023 (Shift-I)
(a) tarmnalogy (b) tarminology
(c) terminology (d) terminiology

Ans. (c)

The correct spelling is 'terminology'. It means special words or expressions used in relation to a particular subject or activity.

471. (a) Grateful (b) Immigrate
(c) Ignorance (d) Hieararchy
SSC CHSL Tier-1 03.08.2023 (Shift-IV)

Ans. (d)

'Hieararchy' is incorrectly spelled. The correct spelling is 'hierarchy,' meaning a system in which members of an organisation or society are ranked according to relative status or authority.

472. (a) Ocasion (b) Occasion
(c) Occasien (d) Occassion
SSC CHSL Tier-1 03.08.2023 (Shift-IV)

Ans. (b)

'Occasion' is the correct spelling, meaning a particular event or time.

473. (a) Although the book was difficult to read, I persisted and eventualy understood the complex ideas.
(b) Although the book was difficult to read, I persisted and eventually understood the complex ideas.
(c) Although the book was difficult to read, I persisted and eventualy understood the complex ideas.
(d) Although the book was difficult to read, I persested and eventually understood the complex ideas.
SSC CHSL Tier-1 03.08.2023 (Shift-III)

Ans. (b)

The sentence with no spelling error is 'Although the book was difficult to read, I persisted and eventually understood the complex ideas.'

474. The preview version will give you a glimpse of the entaire book.
SSC CHSL Tier-1 04.08.2023 (Shift-II)
(a) glimse (b) preveiw
(c) varsion (d) entire
Ans. (d)
The correct spelling is 'entire'.

475. (a) Revolutionise (b) Professional
(c) Jewellry (d) Conscientiousness
SSC CHSL Tier-1 04.08.2023 (Shift-II)
Ans. (c)
The correct spelling is 'jewellery'.

476. After hours of persistent pursuit and percecution, the little prince was at last deserted by the rabble and left to himself.
SSC CHSL Tier-1 07.08.2023 (Shift-IV)
(a) persistent (b) rabble
(c) percecution (d) deserted
Ans. (c)
The correct spelling is 'persecution'. It means cruel and unfair retreatment of a person or group.

477. The Greeks are considered to be a courageous race valuing the knowledge, beauty and wisidiom.
SSC CHSL Tier-1 07.08.2023 (Shift-IV)
(a) wisidiom (b) knowledge
(c) valuing (d) courageous
Ans. (a)
The correct spelling is 'wisdom'.

478. (a) Obdurate (b) Cryptic
(c) Surrugocy (d) Drastic
SSC CHSL Tier-1 08.08.2023 (Shift-II)
Ans. (c)
The correct spelling is 'surrogacy'.

479. Drunkeness, riot and brawling were the order, there, every night.
SSC CHSL Tier-1 08.08.2023 (Shift-II)
(a) Riot (b) Drunkeness
(c) Order (d) Brawling
Ans. (b)
The correct spelling is 'drunkenness'.

480. Factories have to follow a proper procedure to dispose of the hazerdous material.
SSC CHSL Tier-1 08.08.2023 (Shift-III)
(a) disspose (b) proceedure
(c) hazardous (d) Factouries
Ans. (c)
'Hazardous' is the correct spelling, meaning dangerous or risky.

481. (a) Although he had never traveled abroad before, Jack felt confident navigating the unfamiliar castoms and language.
(b) Although he had never travelled abroad before, Jack felt confident navigating the unfamiliar customs and language.
(c) Although he had never traveled abroad before, Jack felt confidant navigating the unfamiliar customs and language.
(d) Although he had never traveled abroad before, Jack felt confident navigating the unfamilliar castoms and languages.
SSC CHSL Tier-1 08.08.2023 (Shift-III)
Ans. (b)
The sentence with no spelling error is : 'Although he had never travelled abroad before, Jack felt confident navigating the unfamiliar customs and language.'

482. (a) Interrogation (b) Magistrate
(c) Preliminary (d) Diciplinary
SSC CHSL Tier-1 08.08.2023 (Shift-IV)
Ans. (d)
'Diciplinary' is incorrectly spelled. The correct spelling is 'disciplinary,' meaning relating to discipline in behaviour or punishment.

483. Those friends meet <u>occassionaly</u>.
SSC CHSL Tier-1 08.08.2023 (Shift-IV)
(a) accationally (b) occasionally
(c) ocassionaly (d) occationally
Ans. (b)
The correct spelling is 'occasionally'.

484. (a) Suspicion (b) Susspicion
(c) Sussppicion (d) Suspicon
SSC CHSL Tier-1 09.08.2023 (Shift-I)
Ans. (a)
The correctly spelt word is 'suspicion'.

485. The Special Task Force will conduct a thorough probe in the land scam case which has Mr. Lakhan Lal as the prime akused.
SSC CHSL Tier-1 09.08.2023 (Shift-I)
(a) scam (b) prime
(c) thorough (d) akused
Ans. (d)
The correct spelling is 'accused' and it means the person who is on trial in a law court.

486. (a) Acquiesce (b) Artificial
(c) Conscientious (d) Mischievious
SSC CHSL Tier-1 09.08.2023 (Shift-II)
Ans. (d)
'Mischievious' is incorrectly spelled. The correct spelling is 'mischievous,' meaning causing or showing a fondness for causing trouble.

487. (a) Ambassador (b) Architecture
(c) Awful (d) Accomodate
SSC CHSL Tier-1 09.08.2023 (Shift-III)
Ans. (d)
The correct spelling is 'accommodate'.

488. The lack of mutual bonding was conspicuous form their shody body language in the marriage party.
SSC CHSL Tier-1 09.08.2023 (Shift-III)
(a) conspicuous (b) shody
(c) marriage (d) mutual
Ans. (b)
The correct answer is 'shoddy'. It means poor.

489. (a) Fulfilling (b) Fulfil
(c) Fulfilled (d) Fullfil
SSC CHSL Tier-1 10.08.2023 (Shift-III)
Ans. (b)
The correct spelling is 'fulfil'.

490. The colourful procession was the last item to be performed in the .... .SSC CHSL Tier-1 10.08.2023 (Shift-III)
(a) peasantry (b) pegentry
(c) pageantry (d) pegeantri
Ans. (c)
The correct spelling is 'pageantry'. It refers to impressive ceremonies or events, inviting many people wearing special clothes.

491. (a) Appreciate (b) Passenger
(c) Complaint (d) Personel
SSC CHSL Tier-1 11.08.2023 (Shift-I)
Ans. (d)
The correct spelling is 'personal'.

492. His <u>charesmatic</u> attitude is <u>admirble</u>.
SSC CHSL Tier-1 11.08.2023 (Shift-I)
(a) karismatic; admerable
(b) charismatic; admarable
(c) karismatic; admirable
(d) charismatic; admirable
Ans. (d)
The correct spellings of the underlined words in the given sentence is 'charismatic; admirable'.

493. (a) In spite of the challenges possed by the pandamic, the company adapted to remote work and successfully maintained productivity levels.
(b) In spite of the challenges posed by the pandamic, the company adapted to remote work and succeddfuly maintained productvity levels.
(c) In spite of the challenges posed by the pandemic, the company adapted to remote work and successfully maintained productivity levels.
(d) In spite of the challenges possed by the pandemic, the company adapted to remote work and

succesfully maintained productevity levels.
SSC CHSL Tier-1 11.08.2023 (Shift-II)

Ans. (c)

The sentence with no spelling error is 'In spite of the challenges posed by the pandemic, the company adapted to remote work and successfully maintained productivity levels.'

494. Whenever Susan received letters from the police, she .... ignored them. **SSC CHSL Tier-1 11.08.2023 (Shift-II)**

(a) intatienally (b) intoningly
(c) indentionally (d) intentionally

Ans. (d)

The correct spelling of the word to fill in the blank is 'Intentionally'. It means deliberately or on purpose.

495. (a) Laison (b) Lieutenant
(c) Entrepreneur (d) Fluorescents
SSC CHSL Tier-1 11.08.2023 (Shift-III)

Ans. (a)

'Laison' is incorrectly spelled. The correct spelling is 'liaison,' meaning communication or cooperation which facilitates a close working relationship between people or organisations.

496. The lower strata are mostly not benifitted by the reign of monarchy.
SSC CHSL Tier-1 11.08.2023 (Shift-III)

(a) monarchy (b) strata
(c) reign (d) benifitted

Ans. (d)

The correct spelling is 'benefited,' meaning received an advantage or profit from something.

497. The CEO's .... disregard for his employees' well-being led to high turnover and low morale in the company.
SSC CHSL Tier-1 14.08.2023 (Shift-IV)

(a) calous (b) callus
(c) callous (d) calus

Ans. (c)

The correct spelling of the word to fill in the blank is 'Callous'. It means showing or having an insensitive and cruel disregard for others.

498. You cannot/compensate for the/ wrongdoings you have/comitted in the past.
SSC CHSL Tier-1 14.08.2023 (Shift-IV)

(a) You cannot
(b) comitted in the past
(c) wrongdoings you have
(d) compensate for the

Ans. (b)

The part 'comitted in the past' contains an error of spelling. The correct spelling is 'committed'.

499. The city had a hundred thousand inhabitents—some think double as many. **SSC CHSL Tier-1 14.08.2023 (Shift-IV)**

(a) hundred (b) inhabitents
(c) double (d) thousand

Ans. (b)

The correctly spelt word is 'inhabitant'. It refers to a person or animal that lives in a place.

500. (a) Souvenir (b) Symbolise
(c) Suseptible (d) Sympathetic
SSC CHSL Tier-1 17.08.2023 (Shift-I)

Ans. (c)

The correct spelt is 'susceptible'. It means likely to be harmed.

501. Mihika was one of the .... in the Master Chef competition held in our society last year.
SSC CHSL Tier-1 17.08.2023 (Shift-I)

(a) contextants (b) contestents
(c) contestants (d) kontestants

Ans. (c)

The correct spelling of the word to fill in the blank is 'contestants'.

502. (a) Calendr (b) Conscientious
(c) Colleague (d) Conspicuous
SSC CHSL Tier-1 17.08.2023 (Shift-III)

Ans. (a)

The correct spelling is 'calendar'. It means a chart or series of pages showing the days weeks and months of a particular year.

503. There was a sudden esklation of violet acts which led to the starting of the second world war.
SSC CHSL Tier-1 17.08.2023 (Shift-III)

(a) esklation (b) starting
(c) violent (d) sudden

Ans. (a)

The correct spelling is 'escalation'. It means an increase in the intensity or seriousness of something.

504. (a) Subpoena (b) Noticeable
(c) Caucus (d) Milennium
SSC CHSL Tier-2 26.06.2023

Ans. (d)

The correct spelling is 'millennium'. It refers to a period of a thousand years.

505. (a) The novel, with its intrcate plot and multifaceted characters, captivated readers and left them pondering its deeper themes long after they finished reading.
(b) The novel, with its intricate plot and multifaceted characters, captivated readers and left them pondering its deeper themes long after they finished reading.
(c) The novel, with its intricate plot and multifacted characters, captivated readers and left them paundering its deeper themes long after they finished reading.
(d) The novel, with its intricete plot and multifacted characters, captivated readers and left them pondering its deeper themes long after they finished reading.
SSC CHSL Tier-2 02.11.2023

Ans. (b)

The sentence with correct spelling is: The novel, with its intricate plot and multifaceted characters, captivated readers and left them pondering its deeper themes long after they finished reading.'

'Pondering' is correctly spelled, meaning thinking about something carefully.

506. (a) Superindednt (b) Susceptibility
(c) Extemporise (d) Inconspicuous
SSC CHSL Tier-2 02.11.2023

Ans. (a)

The correct spelling is 'superintendent'. It refers to a person who manages or superintends an organisation or activity.

SSC CHSL 2022

507. (a) Nuptial (b) Decaffenated
(c) Supplementary (d) Noticeable
SSC CHSL Tier-1 24.05.2022 (Shift-I)

Ans. (b)

The correct spelling is 'decaffeinated,' meaning having had most or all of the caffeine removed.

508. (a) Xylophone (b) Oligopoly
(c) Robbust (d) Zenith
SSC CHSL Tier-1 24.05.2022 (Shift-I)

Ans. (c)

The correct spelling is 'robust,' meaning strong and healthy.

509. (a) Efficient (b) Layer
(c) Committee (d) Feeld
SSC CHSL Tier-1 24.05.2022 (Shift-II)

Ans. (d)

The correct spelling is 'field'.

510. Small drops **trickled** down the red and yellow **tassels** of **cannopies** and **dampened** the heads of little boys. **SSC CHSL Tier-1 24.05.2022 (Shift-III)**

(a) cannopies (b) tassels
(c) dampened (d) trickled

Ans. (a)

'Cannopies' is incorrectly spelled. The correct spelling is 'canopies,' meaning a covering or structure that provides shade or shelter.

511. The popular **ridikule** of Puritanism in **burlesque** and **doggerel** is best **exemplified** in Butler's Hudibras.
SSC CHSL Tier-1 25.05.2022 (Shift-I)
(a) exemplified (b) ridikule
(c) burlesque (d) doggerel
Ans. (b)
The correct spelling is 'ridicule'. It means the subjection of someone or something to mockery and derision.

512. (a) Informassional (b) Personnel
(c) Informal (d) Personal
SSC CHSL Tier-1 25.05.2022 (Shift-II)
Ans. (a)
The correct spelling is 'informational'. It means relating to or characterised by information.

513. (a) Occurrence (b) Accommodation
(c) Priviledge (d) Erroneous
SSC CHSL Tier-1 25.05.2022 (Shift-II)
Ans. (c)
The correct spelling is 'privilege,' meaning a special right, advantage or immunity granted or available only to a particular person or group.

514. (a) Ministry (b) Attention
(c) Attitude (d) Mimikry
SSC CHSL Tier-1 25.05.2022 (Shift-III)
Ans. (d)
The correct spelling is 'mimicry,' meaning the action or skill of imitating someone or something.

515. (a) Geet runs a pharmasutical chemist shop at New Delhi.
(b) My elder brother works in a pharmaceutical company.
(c) The pharmaetuical company develops and market drugs.
(d) Many phramaeutical companies supplied vaccines in pandemic.
SSC CHSL Tier-1 26.05.2022 (Shift-I)
Ans. (b)
The sentence with no spelling error is 'My elder brother works in a pharmaceutical company.'

516. (a) Cavalier (b) Elegant
(c) Charishma (d) Dominate
SSC CHSL Tier-1 26.05.2022 (Shift-III)
Ans. (c)
The correct spelling is 'charisma,' meaning compelling attractiveness or charm that can inspire devotion in others.

517. Almost all the governors of Bengal strongly **resented** the special **privileges** enjoyed by English company as it a huge loss to the **provinciel exchequer**.
SSC CHSL Tier-1 26.05.2022 (Shift-III)
(a) provinciel (b) resented
(c) exchequer (d) privileges
Ans. (a)
The correct spelling is 'provincial'. It means relating to a province.

518. (a) Fecilitation (b) Resplendent
(c) Jingoistic (d) Segregation
SSC CHSL Tier-1 27.05.2022 (Shift-I)
Ans. (a)
The correct spelling 'facilitation' and it means an expression of good wishes, congratulations.

519. And more than the muggings, the waiting to be mugged, fearing the dark that transformed **shoddy innocous** side streets into giant fangs **crouching**, springing to **demolish** this one last reminder.
SSC CHSL Tier-1 27.05.2022 (Shift-I)
(a) crouching (b) innocous
(c) demolish (d) shoddy
Ans. (b)
The correct spelling is 'innocuous'. It means not likely to upset or offend anyone.

520. (a) Supercede (b) Indefatigable
(c) Autopsy (d) Anonymous
SSC CHSL Tier-1 30.05.2022 (Shift-I)
Ans. (a)
The correct spelling is 'supersede'. It means to replace something, especially something older or more old-fashioned.

521. Now, I will not shoot a **sloth** bear **wantanly** but **unfortunately** for the poor **beast**.
SSC CHSL Tier-1 31.05.2022 (Shift-I)
(a) unfortunately (b) sloth
(c) beast (d) wantanly
Ans. (d)
The correct spelling is 'wantonly'. It means in a deliberate and unprovoked way.

522. (a) Repitetion (b) Portray
(c) Procedure (d) Separate
SSC CHSL Tier-1 31.05.2022 (Shift-I)
Ans. (a)
The correct spelling is 'repetition'. It means doing or saying the same thing many times.

523. Jane Austen was already writing in the early 1790s, as the **debates raged** on **radicalism**, women's rights and **premitivism**.
SSC CHSL Tier-1 01.06.2022 (Shift-I)
(a) radicalism (b) premitivism
(c) raged (d) debates
Ans. (b)
The correct spelling is 'primitivism'. It refers to the belief in the superiority of a simple way of life close to nature.

524. (a) Aquaintance (b) Treacherous
(c) Serendipity (d) Malicious
SSC CHSL Tier-1 01.06.2022 (Shift-I)
Ans. (a)
The correct spelling is 'acquaintance'. It means someone you know a little, who is not a close friend.

525. (a) Phiosophy (b) Geography
(c) Economics (d) Spychology
SSC CHSL Tier-1 01.06.2022 (Shift-II)
Ans. (a)
The correct spelling is 'philosophy'. It means the study of the fundamental nature of knowledge, reality and existence.

526. (a) Stingy (b) Culminate
(c) Picth (d) Hasty
SSC CHSL Tier-1 01.06.2022 (Shift-III)
Ans. (c)
The correct spelling is 'pitch'. It means the quality of a sound governed by the rate of vibrations producing it; the degree of highness or lowness of a tone.

527. (a) Movement (b) Career
(c) Carrier (d) Freadom
SSC CHSL Tier-1 02.06.2022 (Shift-I)
Ans. (d)
The correct spelling is 'freedom'.

528. He had to prepare for his <u>competation</u>.
SSC CHSL Tier-1 02.06.2022 (Shift-I)
(a) competetion (b) compitition
(c) competion (d) competition
Ans. (d)
The correct spelling is 'competition'.

529. (a) Summary (b) Emigrate
(c) Rivelry (d) Grandeur
SSC CHSL Tier-1 02.06.2022 (Shift-I)
Ans. (c)
The correct spelling is 'rivalry'. It means a situation in which people, teams, businesses, etc. compete with one another.

530. (a) Aries is the first sign of the zodiac.
(b) Many cities are named after zodaic signs.
(c) Water bearer is the symbol for zodiak Aquarius.
(d) The zodyac signs are split in twelve months.
SSC CHSL Tier-1 02.06.2022 (Shift-I)
Ans. (a)
The sentence with no spelling error is Aries is the first sign of the zodiac.

531. Tibet was ruled by a **theocracy** of **Buddhist** monks under **nominal suzeranity** of China.
SSC CHSL Tier-1 02.06.2022 (Shift-III)
(a) nominal (b) suzeranity
(c) Buddhist (d) theocracy
Ans. (b)
The correct spelling is 'suzerainty'. It means a situation in which a powerful region or people controls the foreign affairs of a tributary vassal state while allowing the vassal to govern itself.

532. Subsequent to the delegation's visit to the villages,/a new working commitee and a task force/have been formed to carry out/all the developmental works as promised to the people.
SSC CHSL Tier-1 03.06.2022 (Shift-II)
(a) Subsequent to the delegation's visit to the villages
(b) have been formed to carry out
(c) a new working commitee and a task force
(d) all the developmental works as promised to the people
Ans. (c)
Part 'a new working committee and a task force' contains a spelling error, correct spelling is 'committee,' meaning a group of people appointed for a specific function.

533. (a) Curiocity (b) Maturity
(c) Creativity (d) Generosity
SSC CHSL Tier-1 03.06.2022 (Shift-III)
Ans. (a)
The correct spelling is 'curiosity,' meaning a strong desire to know or learn something.

534. The action was unfortunately constructed not as the **necessity** of **conscience** but as deliberate **imprudance**, and the barrister was unofficially **reprimanded.**
SSC CHSL Tier-1 03.06.2022 (Shift-III)
(a) imprudance (b) conscience
(c) necessity (d) reprimanded
Ans. (a)
The correct spelling is 'imprudence,' meaning lack of care in a particular matter.

535. Kathmandu is vivid, **mercenery,** religious with small **shrines** to flower-adorned **deities** along the **narrowest** and busiest streets.
SSC CHSL Tier-1 06.06.2022 (Shift-I)
(a) shrines (b) deities
(c) mercenery (d) narrowest
Ans. (c)
The correct spelling is 'mercenary,' meaning primarily concerned with making money at the expense of ethics.

536. Evelyn Glennie has **brought percusion** to the front of the **orchestra** and **demonstrated** that it can be very moving.
SSC CHSL Tier-1 06.06.2022 (Shift-III)
(a) demonstrated
(b) percusion
(c) orchestra
(d) brought
Ans. (b)
The correct spelling is 'percussion,' which refers to musical instruments played by striking with the hand or with a stick.

537. (a) Certificate (b) Channel
(c) Champeon (d) Challenge
SSC CHSL Tier-1 08.06.2022 (Shift-I)
Ans. (c)
The correct spelling is 'champion,' which refers to a person who has defeated or surpassed all rivals in a competition.

538. (a) Copulate (b) Ignision
(c) Portion (d) Horticulture
SSC CHSL Tier-1 08.06.2022 (Shift-III)
Ans. (b)
The correct spelling is 'ignition,' which refers to the action of setting something on fire or starting the combustion in an engine.

539. It was really surprising/that the two bosom friends fought/over such a triviale matter/and stopped all communications with each other.
SSC CHSL Tier-1 08.06.2022 (Shift-III)
(a) It was really surprising
(b) over such a triviale matter
(c) and stopped all communications with each other
(d) that the two bosom friends fought
Ans. (b)
Part 'over such a triviale matter' contains a spelling error. 'Triviale' is incorrectly spelled. The correct spelling is 'trivial,' which means of little value or importance.

540. The Gadkaris were a **hereditary military** class which was **garisioned** in the Maratha **forts.**
SSC CHSL Tier-1 09.06.2022 (Shift-I)
(a) hereditary (b) forts
(c) garisioned (d) military
Ans. (c)
The correct spelling is 'garrisoned,' which means to station troops in a particular place.

541. (a) Immigration (b) Administrator
(c) Admission (d) Exploistation
SSC CHSL Tier-1 09.06.2022 (Shift-I)
Ans. (d)
The correct spelling is 'exploitation,' which refers to the action or fact of treating someone unfairly to benefit from their work.

542. The management is not perturbed about appointing/someone who is knowledgeable but is more inclined/towards filling the position with a person/who will be obsequous and will dance to their tunes.
SSC CHSL Tier-1 10.06.2022 (Shift-II)
(a) someone who is knowledgeable but is more inclined
(b) The management is not perturbed about appointing
(c) towards filling the position with a person
(d) who will be obsequous and will dance to their tunes
Ans. (d)
Part 'who will be obsequous and will dance to their tunes' contains a spelling error. 'Obsequous' is incorrectly spelled. The correct spelling is 'obsequious,' which means excessively obedient or attentive.

543. Reena, who **devoured** foreign **coloquialism** and **trivia, successfully** diverted the conversation.
SSC CHSL Tier-1 10.06.2022 (Shift-II)
(a) devoured (b) successfully
(c) coloquialism (d) trivia
Ans. (c)
'Coloquialism' is incorrectly spelled. The correct spelling is 'colloquialism,' which refers to a word or phrase that is not formal and is used in ordinary or familiar conversation.

544. (a) Interpretation (b) Tremendous
(c) Persistent (d) Pronounciation
SSC CHSL Tier-1 10.06.2022 (Shift-III)
Ans. (d)
The correct spelling is 'pronunciation', which refers to the way in which a word is pronounced.

545. Shanu's inquisitive mind could not/accept the seemingly ingenous reply/of the man and he resolved to solve the mystery/to mitigate the pain of the old couple.
SSC CHSL Tier-1 10.06.2022 (Shift-III)
(a) of the man and he resolved to solve the mystery
(b) accept the seemingly ingenous reply
(c) Shanu's inquisitive mind could not
(d) to mitigate the pain of the old couple
Ans. (b)

Part 'accept the seemingly ingenous reply' contains a spelling error. 'Ingenous' is incorrectly spelled. The correct spelling is 'ingenuous,' which means innocent and unsuspecting.

546. (a) Accessories (b) Dominate
(c) Pamplet (d) Politician
SSC CHSL Tier-1 10.06.2022 (Shift-III)

Ans. (c)
The correct spelling is 'pamphlet,' which refers to a small booklet or leaflet containing information or arguments about a single subject.

SSC CHSL 2021 (Tier 1 & 2)

547. (a) Exceed (b) Address
(c) Annax (d) Attempt
SSC CHSL Tier-1 12.04.2021 (Shift-II)

Ans. (c)
The correct spelling is 'annex'. It means to add something.

548. (a) Definately (b) Existence
(c) Mischievous (d) Violence
SSC CHSL Tier-1 12.04.2021 (Shift-II)

Ans. (a)
The correct spelling is 'definitely'.

549. (a) Science (b) Technology
(c) Seenary (d) Physics
SSC CHSL Tier-1 19.04.2021 (Shift-III)

Ans. (c)
The correct spelling is 'scenery'.

550. (a) Commitment (b) Development
(c) Failier (d) Approval
SSC CHSL Tier-1 19.04.2021 (Shift-III)

Ans. (c)
The correct spelling is 'failure'.

551. (a) Disappear (b) Until
(c) Twelth (d) Temperature
SSC CHSL Tier-1 04.08.2021 (Shift-I)

Ans. (c)
The correct spelling is 'twelfth'.

552. (a) Superior (b) Superstition
(c) Superflous (d) Supreme
SSC CHSL Tier-1 04.08.2021 (Shift-I)

Ans. (c)
The correct spelling is 'superfluous'. It means unceessary.

553. (a) Plump (b) Muscle
(c) Gnaw (d) Rinckle
SSC CHSL Tier-1 10.08.2021 (Shift-I)

Ans. (d)
The correct spelling is 'Wrinkle'.

554. (a) Mature (b) Mischief
(c) Misrable (d) Moisture
SSC CHSL Tier-1 10.08.2021 (Shift-I)

Ans. (c)
The correct spelling is 'miserable'. It means unhappy and uncomfortable.

555. (a) Terrible (b) Uprooted
(c) Haunted (d) Tendansy
SSC CHSL Tier-1 12.08.2021 (Shift-III)

Ans. (d)
The correct spelling is 'tendency'. It means habit.

556. (a) Rogue (b) Rocket
(c) Rockiry (d) Roaster
SSC CHSL Tier-1 12.08.2021 (Shift-III)

Ans. (c)
The correct spelling is 'rockery'. It refers to raised part of a garden which is built of rocks and soils.

SSC MTS 2024 (Tier 1 & 2)

557. (a) Comparison (b) Naviggetion
(c) Strengthen (d) Cleansing
SSC MTS Tier-1 14.11.2024 (Shift-III)

Ans. (b)
'Naviggetion' is incorrectly spelt. The correct spelling is 'navigation'.

558. (a) The scientist discovred a new planet in the galexy.
(b) The sceintist discovered a new palnet in the galaxy.
(c) The scientist discovered a new planet in the galaxy.
(d) The scienetist discovered a new planet in the galaxy.
SSC MTS Tier-1 13.11.2024 (Shift-III)

Ans. (c)
The sentence with no spelling error is : 'The scientist discovered a new planet in the galaxy'.

559. Is he ready to risk his <u>acredation</u> for the greater good?
SSC MTS Tier-1 12.11.2024 (Shift-III)
(a) accraditation (b) accredation
(c) acreditation (d) accreditation

Ans. (d)
'Accreditation' is the correct spelling of the underlined word.

560. The professor's.........lecture was filled with complex concepts.
SSC MTS Tier-1 12.11.2024 (Shift-III)
(a) lucyd (b) lucid
(c) lucide (d) lucied

Ans. (b)
'Lucid' is the correct spelling. It means clear and easy to understand.

561. If you try to conwince people that money is not very important, then you are barking up the wrong tree.
SSC MTS Tier-1 11.11.2024 (Shift-III)
(a) convince (b) convincee
(c) canvince (d) conveence

Ans. (a)
The correct spelling is 'convince'.

562. (a) Cautios (b) Anxious
(c) Curious (d) Bashful
SSC MTS Tier-1 05.11.2024 (Shift-III)

Ans. (a)
The correct spelling is 'cautious', which means careful to avoid potential problems or dangers.

563. The.........on the wall was beautifully painted.
SSC MTS Tier-1 04.11.2024 (Shift-III)
(a) pictur (b) picture
(c) picter (d) pickchure

Ans. (b)
'Picture' is the correctly spelt word to fill in the blank.

564. (a) Synchronous (b) Inadvertant
(c) Effeminate (d) Blatant
SSC MTS Tier-1 04.11.2024 (Shift-III)

Ans. (b)
The correct spelling is 'inadvertent', which means not resulting from or achieved through deliberate planning.

565. (a) Vigilante (b) Masquerade
(c) Squadroun (d) Caricature
SSC MTS Tier-1 30.10.2024 (Shift-III)

Ans. (c)
The correct spelling is 'squadron', which means a unit of the air force.

566. (a) Manoevre
(b) Consistent
(c) Embarrassment
(d) Occurrence
SSC MTS Tier-1 29.10.2024 (Shift-III)

Ans. (a)
The correct spelling is 'Maneuver', which means a movement or series of moves requiring skill and care.

567. Nylon was among the first synthitic fibre made by man and is known for its toughness, strength and resistance to oil and grease.
SSC MTS Tier-1 28.10.2024 (Shift-II)
(a) toughness (b) strength
(c) synthitic (d) resistance

Ans. (c)
The correct spelling is 'synthetic'.

568. (a) Machenical (b) Technical
(c) Annual (d) Regulator
SSC MTS Tier-1 23.10.2024 (Shift-II)

Ans. (a)
The correct spelling is 'Mechanical', which means relating to machines or machinery.

569. The police informed the statesman that the goons were up to something mischievious.
SSC MTS Tier-1 22.10.2024 (Shift-II)
(a) mischevious (b) mischevous
(c) mischievous (d) mischievous
Ans. (c)
'Mischievous' is the correct spelling of the underlined word.

570. (a) The audience applauded the musicians performance.
(b) The audience applauded the musician's performance.
(c) The audiance applauded the musicians performance.
(d) The audiance applauded the musician's perfomance.
SSC MTS Tier-1 21.10.2024 (Shift-II)
Ans. (b)
'The audience applauded the musician's performance' is the correctly spelled sentence.

571. (a) Excellent (b) Abandoned
(c) Celibrate (d) Dangerous
SSC MTS Tier-1 18.10.2024 (Shift-II)
Ans. (c)
The correct spelling is 'Celebrate,' which means to acknowledge a significant or happy event with a social gathering or enjoyable activity.

572. The neighbour came in disgoise and attacked her children.
SSC MTS Tier-1 17.10.2024 (Shift-II)
(a) disgoise (b) children
(c) attacked (d) neighbor
Ans. (a)
The correct spelling is 'disguise', which means to give a different appearance to conceal identity.

573. The scientist made an **appauling** discovery about the environmental impact of the drug.
SSC MTS Tier-1 16.10.2024 (Shift-II)
(a) appaulling (b) appalling
(c) apalling (c) appawling
Ans. (b)
The correct spelling is 'appalling'. It means causing shock or dismay; horrific.

574. In his persuit of excellence, he forgot to take care of his health.
SSC MTS Tier-1 15.10.2024 (Shift-I)
(a) persoot (b) pursuite
(c) pursuit (d) persuite
Ans. (c)
'Pursuit' is the correct spelling.

575. (a) Damaged (b) Fantastic
(c) Expensive (d) Forgetfull
SSC MTS Tier-1 14.10.2024 (Shift-I)
Ans. (d)
The correct spelling is 'forgetful.'

576. (a) Vacuum (b) Weired
(c) Separate (d) Until
SSC MTS Tier-1 09.10.2024 (Shift-I)
Ans. (b)
The correct spelling is 'Weird'. This word means something strange or unusual.

577. (a) Parallel (b) Miscellaneous
(c) Mediterranean (d) Peculliar
SSC MTS Tier-1 09.10.2024 (Shift-I)
Ans. (d)
The correct spelling is 'Peculiar', which means strange or unusual.

578. (a) Poignant (b) Relevant
(c) Eligible (d) Gourrmet
SSC MTS Tier-1 08.10.2024 (Shift-II)
Ans. (d)
The correct spelling is 'Gourmet.'

579. Uluru is the world's largest monolith and Australia's recognisable natural icon with an elliptical shape and a circumfarence of around 94 kilometres.
SSC MTS Tier-1 08.10.2024 (Shift-II)
(a) Monolith (b) Kilometers
(c) Elliptical (d) Circumfarence
Ans. (d)
The correct spelling is 'Circumference.'

580. (a) Spouse (b) Intransigence
(c) Unambiguous (d) Endengered
SSC MTS Tier-1 07.10.2024 (Shift-I)
Ans. (d)
The correct spelling is 'Endangered.'

581. The accideent on the highway caused a long traffic jam.
SSC MTS Tier-1 30.09.2024 (Shift I)
(a) acicdent (b) acident
(c) accidnt (d) accident
Ans. (d)
The word 'accident' is correctly spelled.

582. The rainbow only appears after a hurican. SSC MTS Tier-1 30.09.2024 (Shift I)
(a) hurrican (b) hurricane
(c) hurrecane (d) hurrecain
Ans. (b)
'Hurricane' is the correct spelling.

583. Select the incorrectly spelt word.
SSC MTS Tier-1 30.09.2024 (Shift I)
(a) consicstent (b) surrender
(c) disgust (d) trifle
Ans. (a)
The correct spelling is 'consistent.'

584. Select the option that rectifies the spelling error in the given sentence.
The student received an A+ for her exellent performance.
SSC MTS Tier-1 01.10.2024 (Shift I)
(a) Excellent
(b) perfarmence
(c) performence
(d) excelleant
Ans. (a)
'Excellent' rectifies the spelling error in 'exellent'.

585. Select the incorrectly spelt word.
SSC MTS Tier-1 01.10.2024 (Shift I)
(a) tentative (b) belated
(c) perepharal (d) stringent
Ans. (c)
The correct spelling is 'peripheral'.

586. The gardener's meticulous care ensured the vibrent colours of the flowers. SSC MTS Tier-1 01.10.2024 (Shift I)
(a) vibrent (b) care
(c) meticulous (d) gardener's
Ans. (a)
The correct spelling is 'vibrant', which describes something full of energy and bright colours.

SSC MTS 2023 (Tier 1)

587. (a) Tihgt (b) Locker
(c) Rift (d) Stock
SSC MTS Tier-1 02.05.2023 (Shift-I)
Ans. (a)
The correct spelling is 'tight.'

588. (a) Artiset (b) Banker
(c) Robber (d) Teacher
SSC MTS Tier-1 02.05.2023 (Shift-II)
Ans. (a)
The correct spelling is 'artist.'

589. (a) Declivity
(b) Decorous
(c) Cosmopolitan
(d) Copous
SSC MTS Tier-1 02.05.2023 (Shift-III)
Ans. (d)
The correct spelling is 'copious', which means abundant in supply or quantity.

590. (a) Discribe (b) Melting
(c) Advance (d) Start
SSC MTS Tier-1 03.05.2023 (Shift-II)
Ans. (a)
The correct spelling is 'describe.'

591. (a) Monitour (b) Slope
(c) Constant (d) Chemical
SSC MTS Tier-1 03.05.2023 (Shift-III)
Ans. (a)
The correct spelling is 'monitor.'

592. (a) Everything hurrt in a dull, constant way. SSC MTS Tier-1 04.05.2023 (Shift-I)
(b) Everything hurt in a dul, constant weigh.
(c) Everything hurt in a dull, constant way.
(d) Everything hurt in a dull, constent way.

Ans. (c)

The sentence with correct spelling is 'Everything hurt in a dull, constant way.'

593. (a) Drape (b) Neweset
(c) Vibe (d) Surround
SSC MTS Tier-1 04.05.2023 (Shift-II)

Ans. (b)

The correct spelling is 'newest.'

594. (a) Rhythm (b) Sieze
(c) Flowere (d) Recomend
SSC MTS Tier-1 08.05.2023 (Shift-I)

Ans. (a)

The correct spelling is 'rhythm.'

595. (a) Lattar (b) Critical
(c) Mastery (d) Loudly
SSC MTS Tier-1 09.05.2023 (Shift-II)

Ans. (a)

The correct spelling is 'letter.'

596. (a) Dominering (b) Domoneering
(c) Dominiering (d) Domineering
SSC MTS Tier-1 10.05.2023 (Shift-II)

Ans. (d)

The correct spelling is 'domineering', which means asserting one's will over another in an arrogant way.

597. (a) License (b) Neccesary
(c) Indispensable (d) Occasion
SSC MTS Tier-1 10.05.2023 (Shift-III)

Ans. (b)

The correct spelling is 'necessary.'

598. (a) Pernicious (b) Prefunctory
(c) Pariah (d) Peripheral
SSC MTS Tier-1 11.05.2023 (Shift-I)

Ans. (b)

The correct spelling is 'perfunctory', which means carried out with a minimum of effort or reflection.

599. (a) Plus (b) Dearest
(c) Worry (d) Moking
SSC MTS Tier-1 11.05.2023 (Shift-II)

Ans. (d)

The correct spelling is mocking, which means making fun of someone or something in a cruel way.

600. (a) Knowledge (b) Lightning
(c) Occassion (d) Millenium
SSC MTS Tier-1 11.05.2023 (Shift-III)

Ans. (c)

The correct spelling is 'occasion.'

601. (a) Deifinatn (b) Defination
(c) Definition (d) Definasion
SSC MTS Tier-1 12.05.2023 (Shift-II)

Ans. (c)

The correct spelling is 'definition', which means a statement that explains the meaning of a word or phrase.

602. (a) recind (b) rescind
(c) recsinf (d) resind
SSC MTS Tier-1 12.05.2023 (Shift-III)

Ans. (b)

The correct spelling is 'rescind', which means to revoke, cancel, or repeal a law, order, or agreement.

603. (a) Shout (b) Salute
(c) Belieif (d) Crops
SSC MTS Tier-1 15.05.2023 (Shift-III)

Ans. (c)

The correct spelling is 'belief', which refers to an acceptance that a statement is true or that something exists.

604. (a) Near death expereinces are still near death.
(b) Near death expriences are still near death.
(c) Near death experiences are still near deaath.
(d) Near death experiences are still near death.
SSC MTS Tier-1 16.05.2023 (Shift-I)

Ans. (d)

The sentence with correct spelling is 'Near death experiences are still near death.'

605. (a) Recently (b) Brush
(c) Structrure (d) Havoc
SSC MTS Tier-1 16.05.2023 (Shift-II)

Ans. (c)

The spelling with correct spelling is 'structure', which means the arrangement of and relations between the parts or elements of something complex.

606. (a) Indispensible (b) Liasion
(c) Privillige (d) Occurred
SSC MTS Tier-1 16.05.2023 (Shift-III)

Ans. (d)

The correct spelling is 'occurred', which means happened or took place.

607. (a) Loss (b) Losare
(c) Local (d) Loose
SSC MTS Tier-1 17.05.2023 (Shift-I)

Ans. (b)

The correct spelling is 'loser', which refers to a person or thing that loses or has lost something, especially a game or contest.

608. (a) Pleasurre (b) Slogan
(c) Heaven (d) Brinjal
SSC MTS Tier-1 17.05.2023 (Shift-II)

Ans. (a)

The correct spelling is 'pleasure', which means a feeling of happy satisfaction and enjoyment.

609. (a) Continue (b) Positon
(c) Source (d) Serious
SSC MTS Tier-1 17.05.2023 (Shift-III)

Ans. (b)

The correct spelling is 'position.'

610. (a) Sneha caught it and frouned.
(b) Sneha caught it and frownned.
(c) Sneha cuaght it and frowned.
(d) Sneha caught it and frowned.
SSC MTS Tier-1 18.05.2023 (Shift-II)

Ans. (d)

The sentence with correct spelling is 'Sneha caught it and frowned.'

611. (a) Contradictory (b) Disgsting
(c) Enclosed (d) Sizeable
SSC MTS Tier-1 18.05.2023 (Shift-III)

Ans. (b)

The correct spelling is 'disgusting', which means arousing revulsion or strong indignation.

612. (a) His performance exceeded all expectations SSC MTS 19.05.2023 (Shift-II)
(b) He was arrested for drunkeness on his way to the football ground.
(c) a dumbbell is a short bar with weigts on wither side.
(d) He was quite humorus, and I liked that about him.
SSC MTS Tier-1 19.05.2023 (Shift-II)

Ans. (a)

The sentence with no spelling error is 'His performance exceeded all expectations.'

613. (a) Apparent (b) Plege
(c) Aquire (d) Calender
SSC MTS Tier-1 19.05.2023 (Shift-II)

Ans. (b)

The correct spelling is 'pledge', which means a formal promise or agreement.

614. (a) What was the begining of the dispute?
(b) There is no comparision between the two books.
(c) She handlled the situation cooly.
(d) I got selected in D category.
SSC MTS Tier-1 13.06.2023 (Shift-I)

Ans. (d)

The sentence with no spelling error is 'I got selected in D category.'

615. (a) Pausity (b) Phlegmatic
(c) Phillistine (d) Philanthropy
SSC MTS Tier-1 13.06.2023 (Shift-III)

Ans. (a)

The correct spelling is 'paucity', which means the presence of something in only small or insufficient quantities or amounts; scarcity.

616. (a) Microsoft announced plans to make bids to accquire Byte Dance.
(b) The job of the artist is to make the revolution perceptible.
(c) Except that it'll be rooted in awkard, funny and compelling reality.
(d) She used the 14th Amendment to achelve equality.
SSC MTS Tier-1 14.06.2023 (Shift-I)

Ans. (b)

The sentence with no spelling error is The job of the artist is to make the revolution perceptible.

617. (a) Resistance (b) Acqiuant
(c) Persistent (d) Privilege
SSC MTS Tier-1 14.06.2023 (Shift-III)

Ans. (b)

The correct spelling is 'acquaint', which means to make someone aware of or familiar with.

618. (a) Referred (b) Recommend
(c) Separate (d) Publically
SSC MTS Tier-1 15.06.2023 (Shift-I)

Ans. (d)

The correct spelling is 'publicly', meaning in a manner that is open to or shared by the people.

619. (a) Inoculate (b) Memento
(c) Equiptment (d) Cemetery
SSC MTS Tier-1 15.06.2023 (Shift-II)

Ans. (c)

The correct spelling is 'equipment', referring to the necessary items for a particular purpose.

620. (a) Station (b) Magic
(c) Contaxte (d) Charity
SSC MTS Tier-1 15.06.2023 (Shift-III)

Ans. (c)

The correct spelling is 'contact', meaning the state or condition of physical touching or communication.

621. (a) The extended phenotype is noticeable when we look at parasites.
(b) The Secretary requested to be informed only as necesary to perform his job.
(c) They predicted a similarlly miniscule drop for September.
(d) Moving between floors, their journey seems both improbable and inevitible.
SSC MTS Tier-1 16.06.2023 (Shift-I)

Ans. (a)

The sentence with no spelling error is: 'The extended phenotype is noticeable when we look at parasites.'

622. (a) It turns out multiple groups have measured the concensus.
(b) The proposed cuts have caused considerable contraversy.
(c) The companies lose a lot of their overseas exposure.
(d) She was in a bouyant mood and was looking forward to her new life. **SSC MTS Tier-1 16.06.2023 (Shift-II)**

Ans. (c)

The companies lose a lot of their overseas exposure.

623. (a) Plageriasm
(b) Plagerism
(c) Plagiarism
(d) Plagiarsm
SSC MTS Tier-1 19.06.2023 (Shift-I)

Ans. (c)

The correct spelling is 'plagiarism', which refers to the practice of taking someone else's work or ideas and passing them off as one's own.

624. (a) It is demonstrably an unfair comparsion.
(b) The whole thing is foriegn to us.
(c) I'm the sole victim of Mother's tyrany.
(d) There is a room at the extreme end of the corridor.
SSC MTS Tier-1 19.06.2023 (Shift-II)

Ans. (d)

The sentence with no spelling error is : There is a room at the extreme end of the corridor.

625. (a) It was a letter that was shot throught with the writer's personality.
(b) There is plenty of student accomodation in Edinvurgh.
(c) He advised the government not to persue a gas deal with that company.
(d) Their skilled colleague soon satisfied them that they were wrong. **SSC MTS Tier-1 20.06.2023 (Shift-I)**

Ans. (d)

The sentence with no spelling error is : Their skilled colleague soon satisfied them that they were wrong.

626. (a) Stilettos (b) Bewilders
(c) Unforeseen (d) Viscious
SSC MTS Tier-1 20.06.2023 (Shift-II)

Ans. (d)

The correct spelling is 'vicious', meaning deliberately cruel or violent.

627. (a) Camoflague (b) Comparsion
(c) Guage (d) Presence
SSC MTS Tier-1 20.06.2023 (Shift-III)

Ans. (a)

The correct spelling is 'camouflage', which refers to the act of hiding or disguising something to blend in with the surroundings.

628. (a) Separate (b) Accommodate
(c) Definitely (d) Embarass
SSC MTS Tier-1 01.09.2023 (Shift-I)

Ans. (d)

The correct spelling is 'embarrass', which means to cause someone to feel self-conscious or ashamed.

629. (a) The doctor presribed some medicine to alleviate my parsistent cough, which has been boathering me for days.
(b) The doctor precribed some medicine to aleviate my persistent cough, which has been bothering me for days.
(c) The doctor prescribed some medicine to aleviate my parsistent cough, which has been boathering me for days.
(d) The doctor prescribed some medicine to alleviate my persistent cough, which has been bothering me for days.
SSC MTS Tier-1 01.09.2023 (Shift-I)

Ans. (d)

The sentence with no spelling error is : 'The doctor prescribed some medicine to alleviate my persistent cough, which has been bothering me for days.'

630. The <u>sergent</u> brought in a lot of changes as soon as he was given charge. **SSC MTS Tier-1 01.09.2023 (Shift-I)**
(a) seargeant (b) sergeannt
(c) sergant (d) sergeant

Ans. (d)

The correct spelling is 'sergeant', which refers to a non-commissioned officer in the armed forces.

631. Ozone is a <u>reactiev</u> gas that is not only important in protecting us from harmful ultraviolet <u>radiation</u> but is also a greenhouse gas and, at high smoke-level <u>concentrations</u>, harmful to human health and <u>vegetation</u>.
SSC MTS Tier-1 01.09.2023 (Shift-III)
(a) reactiev (b) radiation
(c) concentrations (d) vegetation

Ans. (a)

The correct spelling is 'reactive', which means showing a response to a stimulus.

632. We can also contribute to presaevation of water bodies by not dumping our garbage in them.
SSC MTS Tier-1 01.09.2023 (Shift-III)
(a) We can also contribute to presarvation of water bodies by not dumpeing our garbage in them.

(b) We can also contribute to preservation of water bodies by not dumping our garbage in them.
(c) We can also contribute to presarvation of water bodies by not dumping our garbage in them.
(d) We can also contribute to presarvation of water bodies by not dumping our garbag in them.

Ans. (b)

The sentence with no spelling error is 'We can also contribute to preservation of water bodies by not dumping our garbage in them.'

633. The questionaire used by the researcher was of top quality.
SSC MTS Tier-1 04.09.2023 (Shift-II)
(a) quesstionnaire (b) questionnaire
(c) questionnairre (d) questionnairee

Ans. (b)

The correct spelling is 'questionnaire', which refers to a set of printed or written questions used for gathering information.

634. The colours of the rainbow seemed to shine through the trianguler prism as the sun hit the object.
SSC MTS Tier-1 04.09.2023 (Shift-II)
(a) rainbouw (b) son
(c) triangular (d) objact

Ans. (c)

The incorrectly spelt word is the given sentence is 'trianguler'. The correct spelling is 'triangular'.

635. (a) Wholeness (b) Overwhelming
(c) Legandry (d) Inclusive
SSC MTS Tier-1 05.09.2023 (Shift-II)

Ans. (c)

The correct spelling is 'legendary'.

636. (a) Prevanseon (b) Prevention
(c) Previnsion (d) Prevension
SSC MTS Tier-1 05.09.2023 (Shift-II)

Ans. (b)

The correct spelling is 'prevention', which means the action of stopping something from happening or arising.

637. The hungery goblin scratched the grammar book with a feather.
SSC MTS Tier-1 06.09.2023 (Shift-I)
(a) hungery (b) scratched
(c) feather (d) grammar

Ans. (a)

The correct spelling is 'hungry'.

638. The questionnaire appeared to be misrably designed.
SSC MTS Tier-1 06.09.2023 (Shift-I)
(a) designed (b) questionnaire
(c) misrably (d) appeared

Ans. (c)

The correct spelling is 'miserably'.

639. All life depends on a healthy planet, but the interwoven system of atmosphere, oceans, watercourses, land, ice cover and biosphere, which form the natural environment, are threatned by human activities.
SSC MTS Tier-1 06.09.2023 (Shift-I)
(a) interwoven (b) threatned
(c) biosphere (d) watercourses

Ans. (b)

The correct spelling is 'threatened'.

640. The profesor's niece was planning a pleasant surprise for him.
SSC MTS Tier-1 08.09.2023 (Shift-II)
(a) profesor (b) planning
(c) pleasant (d) niece

Ans. (a)

The correct spelling is 'professor'.

641. He felt priviledged to have received the country's greatest honour.
SSC MTS Tier-1 08.09.2023 (Shift-II)
(a) previllaged (b) privileged
(c) privilegede (d) privilaged

Ans. (b)

The correct spelling is 'privileged'.

642. (a) The elderly woman was delighted to receive a boquet of fragrant flowers from her thougtful grandson, who had come to visit her at the nursing home.
(b) The elderly woman was delighted to receive a bouquet of fragrant flowers from her thoughtful grandson, who had come to visit her at the nursing home.
(c) The elderly woman was deligted to receive a bouque of fregrant flowers from her thoughtfull grandson, who had come to visit her at the nursing home.
(d) The elderly woman was delighed to recive a bouquet of fragrant flowers from her thoughtfull grandson, who had come to visit her at the nursing home.
SSC MTS Tier-1 08.09.2023 (Shift-II)

Ans. (b)

The sentence with no spelling error is 'The elderly woman was delighted to receive a bouquet of fragrant flowers from her thoughtful grandson, who had come to visit her at the nursing home.'

643. (a) Acknowlege (b) Territory
(c) Excellence (d) Business
SSC MTS Tier-1 11.09.2023 (Shift-I)

Ans. (a)

The correct spelling is 'acknowledge'. It means to accept or recognise.

644. The handloom shop at the ring road has many kinds of bags, such as paper, leather, cloth and cannvas. SSC MTS Tier-1 11.09.2023 (Shift-I)
(a) paper (b) cannvas
(c) leather (d) cloth

Ans. (b)

The correct spelling is 'canvas', which is a strong, coarse unbleached cloth used for bags, sails and tents.

645. (a) Grammar (b) Pleasant
(c) Familiar (d) Aweful
SSC MTS Tier-1 11.09.2023 (Shift-I)

Ans. (d)

The correct spelling is 'awful', which means very bad or unpleasant.

646. (a) My new phone has a high resolusion screen and powerful proccessor, which makes it pe rfect for streming videos and playing games.
(b) My new phone has a high resollution screen and powerfull proccessor, which makes it perfect for streaming videos ad playing games.
(c) My new phone has a high-resolution screen and powerful processor, which makes it perfect for streaming videos and playing games.
(d) My new phone has a high-resolustion screen and powerfull procesor, which makes it perfect for streming videos and playing games.
SSC MTS Tier-1 11.09.2023 (Shift-II)

Ans. (c)

The sentence with no spelling error is 'My new phone has a high-resolution screen and powerful processor, which makes it perfect for streaming videos and playing games.'

647. Being a doktor, my sister Meera is prepared for an emergency usually.
SSC MTS Tier-1 11.09.2023 (Shift-II)
(a) prepared (b) doktor
(c) usually (d) emergency

Ans. (b)

The correct spelling is 'doctor'.

648. (a) Curiousity (b) Vehemence
(c) Superficial (d) Synagogue
SSC MTS Tier-1 11.09.2023 (Shift-II)

Ans. (a)

The correct spelling is 'curiosity'.

649. (a) She acid the test desspite being sleep-deprived from studying for nearly 24 hours straight.
(b) She aced the test daspite being sleep-deprived from studying nor nearly 24 hours strait.

(c) She ased the test daspite being sleep-deprived from studying for nearly 24 hours strait.
(d) She aced the test despite being sleep-deprived from studying for nearly 24 hours straight.
SSC MTS Tier-1 13.09.2023 (Shift-I)

Ans. (d)
The sentence with no spelling error is 'She aced the test despite being sleep-deprived from studying for nearly 24 hours straight.'

650. (a) Essence
(b) Aggregate
(c) Transmisible
(d) Assembly
SSC MTS Tier-1 13.09.2023 (Shift-I)

Ans. (c)
The correct spelling is 'transmissible', which means able to be passed from one person or organism to another.

651. (a) Perceive (b) Recognition
(c) Vaccum (d) Shield
SSC MTS Tier-1 13.09.2023 (Shift-I)

Ans. (c)
The correct spelling is 'vacuum', which refers to a space entirely devoid of matter.

652. The forsec that generate conditions conducive to crime and riots are stronger in urban communities than in rurall areas.
SSC MTS Tier-1 14.09.2023 (Shift-I)
(a) The forsec that generate conditions conduciive to crime and riots are stronger in urban communities than in rurall areas.
(b) The forces that genereta conditions conducieve to crime and riotts are stronger in urban communities than in rural areas.
(c) The forces that generate conditions conducive to crime and riots are stronger in urban communities than in rural areas.
(d) The forces that genarete conditions conduciive to crime and riots are stronger in urban communities than in ruraal areas.

Ans. (c)
The sentence with no spelling error is : 'The forces that generate conditions conducive to crime and riots are stronger in urban communities than in rural areas.'

653. (a) Tomatos (b) Weather
(c) Vehicle (d) Professor
SSC MTS Tier-1 14.09.2023 (Shift-I)

Ans. (a)
The incorrectly spelt word is 'tomatos'. The correct spelling is 'tomatoes'.

654. All the members of my family are planning to visit Jammu and Kashmir this Nevember.
SSC MTS Tier-1 14.09.2023 (Shift-I)
(a) Nevember (b) Planning
(c) Visit (d) Members

Ans. (a)
The correct spelling is 'November'.

SSC Selection Post 2024

655. And so he was (A), for as she laughed (B) and talked, Jo had whiskd (C) things into place and given quite (D) a different air to the room. SSC SP 20.06.2024 (Shift-I)
(a) C (b) B
(c) D (d) A

Ans. (a)
The correct spelling is 'whisked'

656. (a) Experience (b) Noticeable
(c) Intterupt (d) Commodity
SSC SP 20.06.2024 (Shift-I)

Ans. (c)
The correct spelling is 'interrupt'.

657. (a) Occurence (b) Immediately
(c) Grateful (d) Parallel
SSC SP 20.06.2024 (Shift-II)

Ans. (a)
The correct spelling is 'occurrence'.

658. I like drinking lamonade.
SSC SP 20.06.2024 (Shift-II)
(a) Lemonaid (b) Lemenade
(c) Lemonade (d) Limonade

Ans. (c)
The correct spelling is 'lemonade', which is a drink made from lemon juice, water, and sugar.

659. These are the letters of administration that are useful for genaelogical studies and for investigations pertaining to state of society. SSC SP 20.06.2024 (Shift-IV)
(a) administration (b) genaelogical
(c) investigation (d) pertaining

Ans. (b)
The correct spelling is 'genealogical', which means the study of lines of family descent.

660. (a) Psychometric (b) Phisiology
(c) Psychiatry (d) Psychology
SSC SP 20.06.2024 (Shift-IV)

Ans. (b)
The correct spelling is 'physiology', which refers to the branch of biology that deals with the functions of living organisms.

661. The fencing was adoned with ornamental plants of various colours.
SSC SP 20.06.2024 (Shift-IV)
(a) Variouse (b) Fensing
(c) Adorned (d) Ornamenntal

Ans. (c)
The correct spelling is 'adorned', which means decorated.

662. (a) Publicly (b) Punctual
(c) Protien (d) Pursuit
SSC SP 27.06.2024 (Shift-IV)

Ans. (c)
The correct spelling is 'protein', which is a nutrient essential to the structure and function of all living cells.

SSC Selection Post 2023

663. How simple for the English businesman to word a cable that would be intelligible to Italian, Turkish and Chinese firms? If statesmen could discuss directly and accurately the problems.
SSC SP 27.06.2023 (Shift-III)
(a) statesmen (b) intelligible
(c) businesman (d) firms

Ans. (c)
The correct spelling is 'businessman', which refers to a man who works in commerce.

664. It remains for us to apply the tools of selection, rejection or compresion in order to understand.
SSC SP 27.06.2023 (Shift-III)
(a) compresion (b) rejection
(c) selection (d) understand

Ans. (a)
The correct spelling is 'compression', which means the action of compressing or being compressed.

665. She is the most underated cricketer in the country. SSC SP 27.06.2023 (Shift-I)
(a) underateed (b) underatted
(c) undderated (d) underrated

Ans. (d)
The correct spelling is 'underrated'.

666. In the unscientific age or community, there are official repositories of wisdom, such as Egyptian preists and Tibetan Lamas. SSC SP HSC Level 27.06.2023 (Shift-I)
(a) repositories (b) Egyptian
(c) unscientific (d) preists

Ans. (d)
The correct spelling is 'priests'.

667. We are going on a hiking expidition.
SSC SP 27.06.2023 (Shift-I)
(a) expedition (b) expedetion
(c) exhipidition (d) ixpedition

Ans. (a)

The correct spelling is 'expedition', which means a journey.

668. (a) Psychic (b) Though
(c) Truthfully (d) Suddeness
SSC SP 28.06.2023 (Shift-III)

Ans. (d)

The correct spelling is 'suddenness', which means the quality of being sudden or abrupt.

669. (a) Unconscious (b) Unnatural
(c) Vaccant (d) Vegeance
SSC SP 28.06.2023 (Shift-II)

Ans. (c)

The correct spelling is 'vacant', which means empty or unoccupied.

670. (a) Violence (b) Tyranny
(c) Valorous (d) Persuesive
SSC SP 30.06.2023 (Shift-II)

Ans. (d)

The correct spelling is 'persuasive', which means good at persuading someone to do or believe something.

671. (a) An Ethical Hacker identifies software vulnerabilities so that business owners can adress them before a baleful hacker uncovers them.
(b) An Ethickal Hacker identifies software vulnerabilities so that bussiness owners can address them before a baleful hacker uncovers them.
(c) An Ethical Hacker identifies software vulnerabilities so that business owners can address them before a baleful hacker uncovers them.
(d) An Ethickal Hacker identifies software vulnerabilities so that business owners can adress them before a baleful hacker uncovers them. SSC SP 27.06.2023 (Shift-II)

Ans. (c)

The sentence with no spelling error is is 'An Ethical Hacker identifies software vulnerabilities so that business owners can address them before a baleful hacker uncovers them.'

672. Women's **vulnarability** due to the denial of ownership of productive resources has been **focused** on in the **analysis** of how **progressive** laws shaped gender relations.
SSC SP 28.06.2023 (Shift-I)
(a) analysis (b) vulnarability
(c) progressive (d) focused

Ans. (b)

The correct spelling is 'vulnerability', which means the quality or state of being exposed to the possibility of being attacked or harmed.

673. The secret to tightrope walking is/ to graps the rope between the to/ and distribute one's weights evenly on the soles of one's feet.
SSC SP 28.06.2023 (Shift-I)
(a) to graps the rope between the toes
(b) evenly on the soul of one's feet
(c) and distribute ones weight
(d) The secrte of tightrope walk is

Ans. (a)

Part 'to graps the rope between the toes' contains a spelling error. The correct spelling is 'grasp'.

674. (a) Longevity (b) Leftinant
(c) Ludicrous (d) Location
SSC SP 28.06.2023 (Shift-IV)

Ans. (b)

The correct spelling is 'lieutenant', which is a rank in the army, navy or air force.

675. (a) Bourgeoisie (b) Burlesque
(c) Burgaler (d) Beggar
SSC SP 30.06.2023 (Shift-III)

Ans. (c)

The correct spelling is 'burglar', which refers to a person who illegally enters buildings to commit crimes, especially theft.

676. (a) Authority (b) Illegitimate
(c) Inaffectual (d) Authentic
SSC SP 30.06.2023 (Shift-IV)

Ans. (c)

The correct spelling is 'ineffectual', which means not producing any significant or desired effect.

677. (a) Games insteal in people the values of timliness, honesty and consistency in their routines.
(b) Games instil in people the values of timeliness, honesty and consistensy in their routeenes.
(c) Games instil in people the values of timeliness, honesty and consistency in their routines.
(d) Games insteal in people the values of timeliness, honesty and consistensy in their routines.
SSC SP 30.06.2023 (Shift-IV)

Ans. (c)

The sentence with no spelling error is 'Games instil in people the values of timeliness, honesty and consistency in their routines.'

SSC Selection Post 2022

678. (a) Kicked (b) Handicaped
(c) Twisted (d) Printed
SSC SP 01.08.2022 (Shift-I)

Ans. (b)

The correct spelling is 'handicapped', which refers to having a condition that markedly restricts one's ability to function physically, mentally, or socially.

679. (a) Tonsure (b) Ornate
(c) Mundane (d) Jwellery
SSC SP 01.08.2022 (Shift-I)

Ans. (d)

The correct spelling is 'jewellery', which refers to personal ornaments such as necklaces, rings, or bracelets.

680. I .... the idea of my latest project while visiting Goa on a vacation. SSC SP 01.08.2022 (Shift-I)
(a) kncieved (b) cuncieved
(c) qunciev ed (d) conceived

Ans. (d)

The correctly spelt word to fill in the blank is 'conceived', which means to create.

681. (a) Bailout (b) Blackbroad
(c) Citizen (d) Jailor
SSC SP 01.08.2022 (Shift-I)

Ans. (b)

The correct spelling is 'blackboard'.

682. She holered at her manager and told her that she does not need her service. SSC SP 01.08.2022 (Shift-I)
(a) manager (b) need
(c) holered (d) service

Ans. (c)

The incorrectly spelt word in the given sentence is 'holered'. The correct spelling is 'hollered' which means to shout someone's name to catch his/her attention.

683. Governments must translate their sustainable development goals into national legaslation.
SSC SP 01.08.2022 (Shift-I)
(a) legislation
(b) development
(c) translate
(d) sustainable

Ans. (a)

The correct spelling is 'legislation', which refers to laws, considered collectively.

10

Active-Passive Voice

Rules for Converting Active Voice into Passive Voice

Genera Rule The subject of a sentence in active voice becomes the object of a sentence in the passive voice. In the passive form, the subject is preceded with a 'by'.

e.g.,

- Kanika is cleaning the house. *(Active)*
- The house is being cleaned by Kanika. *(Passive)*

Rule 1 The main verb in the active voice is converted into its participles form (third form of verb) in the passive voice, preceded by the correct form of helping verb 'to be'. Accordingly, the changes in tenses, are made as follows,

Herein, S- Subject, O- Object

S.No.	Tense	Active Voice Structure	Passive voice Structure
(a)	Simple Present	S + V1 + O	O + am/is/are + V3 + by + S
(b)	Present Continuous	S + am/is/are/ + V1 + ing + O	O + am/is/are + being + V3 + by + S
(c)	Present Perfect	S + have/has + V3 + O	O + have/has + been + V3 + by + S
(d)	Simple Past	S + V2 + O	O + was/were + V3 + by + S
(e)	Past Continuous	S + was/were + V1 + ing + O	O + was/were + being + V3 + by + S
(f)	Past Perfect	S + had + V3 + O	O + had been + V3 + by + S
(g)	Simple Future	S + shall/will + V1 + O	O + shall/will + be + V3 + by + S
(h)	Future Perfect	S + shall/will + have + V3 + O	O + shall/will + have + been + V3 + by + S

Note Perfect Continuous tenses do not have passive voice.

Rule 2 Personal pronouns are changed while converting a sentence from active to passive voice in the following manner

S.No.	Active Voice	Passive Voice
(a)	I	Me
(b)	He	Him
(c)	She	Her
(d)	They	Them
(e)	We	Us
(f)	Who	Whom
(g)	It/You	Unchanged

Rule 3 If a sentence contains a preposition after the verb, it is maintained in its passive voice.

e.g.,

- Someone broke into the shop. *(Active)*
- The shop was broken into. *(Passive)*

Rule 4 When a sentence in active voice has a modal auxiliary (can, could, may, might, etc.), the modal verb does not change its form but 'be' is added to it.

e.g.,

- Shaurya can cook many international cuisines. *(Active)*
- Many international cuisines can be cooked by Shaurya. (Passive)

Rule 5 Questions Words (Wh) The question words such as 'what, why, when, where, which and how' do not change and remain at the starting position of the sentence.

Only "Who' is converted to 'By whom'

e.g.,

- **What** did you buy? (*Active*)
- **What** was bought by you? (*Passive*)
- **Who** told you about tomorrow's holiday? (*Active*)
- **By whom** were you told about tomorrow's holiday? (*Passive*)

Rule 6 'Yes/No' Questions: The questions that start with helping verbs do/ does/ did are changed into be verbs (is, am, are, was, were) in the passive voice.

e.g.,

- **Do** they perform fine arts? (*Active*)
- **Are** fine arts per formed by them? (*Passive*)

Rule 7 Subject is usually not mentioned in the imperative sentences. Thus, they can be changed into passive voice in the following manner

(i) Sentences with suggestion, advised or request etc.

e.g.,

- **Do not** harm the animals. (*Active*)
- The animals **should not be** harmed. (*Passive*)

Or

- **Let** the animals **not be** harmed. (*Passive*)

Or

- **You are advised** not to harm the animals. (*Passive*)

(ii) If the sentence starts with 'Let', change it into passive voice in the following manner

e.g.,

- **Let** him feed the dog. (*Active*)
- **Let** the dog **be** fed by him. (*Passive*)

SSC Exam Scanner

SSC CGL 2024 (Tier I & II)

1. Don't park your car here. *(Change in passive voice)*
   SSC CGL Tier-2 20.01.2025
   (a) Let your car not be parked here.
   (b) Let not your car be parked here.
   (c) Let your car be parked here.
   (d) Have not your car be parked here.

   Ans. (a) Refer to Rule 7 (ii)

2. Scientists have recently discovered a new species of marine life in the unexplored depths of the ocean. *(Change in passive voice)*
   SSC CGL Tier-2 20.01.2025
   (a) A new species of marine life was recently discovered in the unexplored depths of the ocean by scientists.
   (b) A new species of marine life had recently been discovered in the unexplored depths of the ocean by scientists.
   (c) A new species of marine life has recently been discovered in the unexplored depths of the ocean by scientists.
   (d) A new species of marine life was recently being discovered in the unexplored depths of the ocean by scientists.

   Ans. (c) Refer to Rule 1 (c)

3. After we come to power at the Centre, we will conduct a countrywide caste census. *(Change in passive voice)*
   SSC CGL Tier-2 20.01.2025
   (a) A countrywide caste census should be conducted by us when we come to power at the Centre.
   (b) A countrywide caste census will have been conducted by us after we come to power at the Centre.
   (c) A countrywide caste census will be conducted by us as and when we come to power at the Centre.
   (d) A countrywide caste census will be conducted by us after we come to power at the Centre.

   Ans. (c) Refer to Rule 1 (g)

4. Did you hear that noise? *(Change in passive voice)*
   SSC CGL Tier-2 18.01.2025
   (a) Has that noise been heard by you?
   (b) Wasn't that noise heard by you?
   (c) Is that noise heard by you?
   (d) Was that noise heard by you?

   Ans. (d) Refer to Rule 6

5. The explosion caused serious damage in Ukraine. *(Change in passive voice)*
   SSC CGL Tier-2 18.01.2025
   (a) Serious damage has been caused by the explosion in Ukraine.
   (b) Serious damage was caused by the explosion in Ukraine.
   (c) Serious damage in Ukraine has been caused by the explosion.
   (d) In Ukraine, serious damage had been caused by the explosion.

   Ans. (b) Refer to Rule 1 (d)

6. Everyone was surprised at his speech. *(Change in passive voice)*
   SSC CGL Tier-2 18.01.2025
   (a) His speech surprise everyone.
   (b) His speech surprised everyone.
   (c) His speech was surprising to everyone.
   (d) His speech is surprising everyone.

   Ans. (b) Refer to Rule 1 (d)

7. Ishika saw the tiger in the forest. *(Change in Passive voice)*
   SSC CGL Tier-1 09.09.2024 (Shift-I)
   (a) The tiger saw by Ishika in the forest.
   (b) The tiger was seen by the forest in Ishika.
   (c) The tiger was seen by Ishika in the forest.
   (d) The tiger sees Ishika in the forest.

   Ans. (c) Refer to Rule 1 (d)

8. Lovely tunes are composed by Domnica. *(Change in Active voice)*
   SSC CGL Tier-1 09.09.2024 (Shift-I)
   (a) Domnica composed lovely tunes.
   (b) Domnica composes tunes lovely.
   (c) Domnica will compose lovely tunes.
   (d) Domnica composes lovely tunes.

   Ans. (d) Refer to Rule 1 (a)

9. The meal was not prepared by us. *(Change in Active voice)*
   SSC CGL Tier-1 09.09.2024 (Shift-II)
   (a) We had not prepare the meal.
   (b) We did not prepare the meal.
   (c) We did not preparing the meal.
   (d) We did prepare the meal.

   Ans. (b) When such a sentence is transformed into active voice, the structure followed is Subject +did+ V1+ Object.

10. The homework must be done by you. *(Change in Active voice)*
    SSC CGL Tier-1 09.09.2024 (Shift-II)
    (a) You should have done the homework.
    (b) You do the homework.
    (c) You will do the homework.
    (d) You must do the homework.

    Ans. (d) Refer to Rule 4

11. The painting was admired by art enthusiasts from around the world. *(Change in Active voice)*
    SSC CGL Tier-1 09.09.2024 (Shift-III)
    (a) The painting was being admired by art enthusiasts from around the world.
    (b) Art enthusiasts from around the world admired the painting.
    (c) Art enthusiasts from around the world have admired the painting.
    (d) The painting has been admired by art enthusiasts from around the world.

    Ans. (b) Refer to Rule 1 (d)

12. He will be made President by the people. *(Change in Active voice)*
    SSC CGL Tier-1 09.09.2024 (Shift-III)
    (a) People will be making him the President.
    (b) The people will make him President.
    (c) By the people, he shall be made the President.
    (d) He will be made President by the people.

    Ans. (b) Refer to Rule 1 (g)

13. The contract was grabbed by the biggest telecom company in India. *(Change in Active voice)* **SSC CGL Tier-1 10.09.2024 (Shift-I)**
    (a) The biggest telecom company in India grabbed the contract.
    (b) The biggest telecom company in India grabs the contract.
    (c) The biggest telecom company in India will grab the contract.
    (d) The biggest telecom company in India has grabbed the contract.

    Ans. (a) Refer to Rule 1 (d)

14. By whom was grammar taught to you? *(Change in Active voice)* SSC CGL Tier-1 10.09.2024 (Shift-I)
(a) Did he teach you grammar?
(b) Who had taught you grammar?
(c) You were taught grammar by whom?
(d) Who taught you grammar?
Ans. (d) Refer to Rule 5.

15. The shareholders will elect him a director. *(Change in Active voice)* SSC CGL Tier-1 10.09.2024 (Shift-II)
(a) He will be elected as director by the shareholders.
(b) The shareholders have elected him a director.
(c) The shareholders elected him a director.
(d) He will be elected a director.
Ans. (a) Refer to Rule 1 (g)

16. The letter will be delivered by the postman tomorrow. *(Change in Active voice)* SSC CGL Tier-1 10.09.2024 (Shift-II)
(a) The postman delivered the letter tomorrow.
(b) The postman will have delivered the letter tomorrow.
(c) The postman will deliver the letter tomorrow.
(d) The postman will be delivering the letter tomorrow.
Ans. (c) Refer to Rule 1 (g)

17. Historians us how this country was divided into three. *(Change in Passive voice)* SSC CGL Tier-1 10.09.2024 (Shift-III)
(a) We are told by historians how this country has been divided into three.
(b) We are told by historians how this country divided into three.
(c) We are told by historians how this country was divided into three.
(d) We have been told by historians how this country was divided into three.
Ans. (c) Refer to Rule 1 (a)

18. The company will launch the new product next month and they are already promoting it through various marketing channels. *(Change in Passive voice)* SSC CGL Tier-1 10.09.2024 (Shift-III)
(a) The new product will be launched by the company next month, and it is already being promoted through various marketing channels.
(b) The new product were been launched by the company next month and it already was promoting through various marketing channels.
(c) The new product was launched by the company next month, and it is already promoted through various marketing channels.
(d) The new product will have been launched by the company next month, and it was already being promoted through various marketing channels
Ans. (a) Refer to Rule 1 (g)

19. The teachers of our school have already taken this training. *(Change in Passive voice)* SSC CGL Tier-1 11.09.2024 (Shift-I)
(a) This training has already been taken by the teachers of our school.
(b) This training has been taken by the teachers of our school.
(c) This training has already been taken by our school teachers.
(d) This training was already taken by the teachers of our school.
Ans. (a) Refer to Rule 1 (c)

20. Ravi will play the match. *(Change in Passive voice)* SSC CGL Tier-1 11.09.2024 (Shift-I)
(a) The match is played by Ravi.
(b) The match will have been played by Ravi.
(c) The match will be playing by Ravi.
(d) The match will be played by Ravi.
Ans. (d) Refer to Rule 1 (g)

21. Each candidate was making tall promises. *(Change in Passive voice)* SSC CGL Tier-1 11.09.2024 (Shift-II)
(a) Tall promises were being made by each candidate.
(b) Tall promises are made by each candidate.
(c) Tall promises will be made by each candidate.
(d) Tall promises are being made by each candidate.
Ans. (a) Refer to Rule 1 (e)

22. The car was repaired by the mechanic. *(Change in Active voice)* SSC CGL Tier-1 11.09.2024 (Shift-II)
(a) The mechanic repairs the car.
(b) The mechanic has repaired the car.
(c) The mechanic is repairing the car.
(d) The mechanic repaired the car.
Ans. (d) Refer to Rule 1 (d)

23. The letter was being typed by the secretary when the phone rang. *(Change in Active voice)* SSC CGL Tier-1 11.09.2024 (Shift-III)
(a) The secretary will type the letter when the phone rings.
(b) The secretary types the letter when the phone rings.
(c) The secretary was typing the letter when the phone rang.
(d) The secretary is typing the letter when the phone rings.
Ans. (c) Refer to Rule 1 (e)

24. He must deliver pizza. *(Change in Passive voice)* SSC CGL Tier-1 11.09.2024 (Shift-III)
(a) Pizza has to be delivered by him.
(b) Pizza have to be delivered by him.
(c) Pizza must be delivered by him.
(d) Pizza can be delivered by him.
Ans. (c) Refer to Rule 1 (a)

25. Sonam does not like bananas. *(Change in Passive voice)* SSC CGL Tier-1 12.09.2024 (Shift-I)
(a) Banana is not liked by Sonam.
(b) Bananas have not been liked by Sonam.
(c) Bananas are not liked by Sonam.
(d) Bananas had not been liked by Sonam
Ans. (c) Refer to Rule 1 (a)

26. Someone has taken my secret diary. *(Change in Passive voice)* SSC CGL Tier-1 12.09.2024 (Shift-I)
(a) My secret diary had been taken by someone.
(b) My secret diary has to be taken by someone.
(c) My secret diary has been taken by someone.
(d) My secret diary will have been taken by someone
Ans. (c) Refer to Rule 1 (c)

27. The drug pedlar was arrested by the narcotics team. *(Change in Active voice)* SSC CGL Tier-1 12.09.2024 (Shift-II)
(a) The narcotics team was arrested the drug pedlar.
(b) The narcotics team arrest the drug pedlar.
(c) The narcotics team arrested the drug pedlar.
(d) The narcotics team has arrested the drug pedlar.
Ans. (c) Refer to Rule 1 (d)

28. Scientists were conducting experiments on the newly discovered species. *(Change in Passive voice)* **SSC CGL Tier-1 12.09.2024 (Shift-II)**
(a) Experiments on the newly discovered species had been conducted by the scientists.
(b) The newly discovered species has been conducting experiments by scientists.
(c) The newly discovered species has been experimented on by scientists.
(d) Experiments were being conducted on the newly discovered species by scientists

Ans. (d) Refer to Rule 1 (e)

29. I will never overlook this creativity. *(Change in Passive voice)* **SSC CGL Tier-1 12.09.2024 (Shift-III)**
(a) This creativity will never be overlooked by me.
(b) This creativity will be overlooked by me.
(c) This creativity will being overlooked by me.
(d) This creativity will not never be overlooked by me.

Ans. (a) Refer to Rule 1 (g)

30. Who invited you to this party? *(Change in Passive voice)* **SSC CGL Tier-1 12.09.2024 (Shift-III)**
(a) By whom you are invited to this party?
(b) By whom are you invited to this party?
(c) By whom you were invited to this party?
(d) By whom were you invited to this party?

Ans. (d) Refer to Rule 5

31. The team will announce the winner tomorrow. *(Change in Passive voice)* **SSC CGL Tier-1 13.09.2024 (Shift-I)**
(a) The team will announce tomorrow the winner.
(b) The winner will announce tomorrow by the team.
(c) The winner will be announced by the team tomorrow.
(d) Tomorrow will be announced the winner by the team.

Ans. (c) Refer to Rule 1 (g)

32. Don't let Dylan fool you! *(Change in Passive voice)* **SSC CGL Tier-1 13.09.2024 (Shift-I)**
(a) Do not be fooled by Dylan.
(b) Do not ever be fooled by Dylan.
(c) Do not be fool by Dylan.
(d) Do not have been fooled by Dylan

Ans. (a) Refer to Rule 7 (i)

33. The children have made the box. *(Change in Passive voice)* **SSC CGL Tier-1 13.09.2024 (Shift-II)**
(a) The box is being made by the children.
(b) Children had made the box.
(c) The box had been made by the children.
(d) The box has been made by the children.

Ans. (d) Refer to Rule 1(c)

34. They are organising a concert for charity. *(Change in Passive voice)* **SSC CGL Tier-1 13.09.2024 (Shift-I)**
(a) A concert is being organised by them for charity.
(b) They are organising a charity concert.
(c) They are being organised a concert for charity.
(d) A concert for charity is organising by them.

Ans. (a) Refer to Rule 1(b)

35. Martha made pancakes yesterday. *(Change in Passive voice)* **SSC CGL Tier-1 13.09.2024 (Shift-III)**
(a) Pancakes had been made by Martha yesterday.
(b) Pancakes were being made by Martha yesterday.
(c) Pancakes were made by Martha yesterday.
(d) Pancakes was made by Martha yesterday.

Ans. (c) Refer to Rule 1 (d)

36. I will be gifted a fancy doll by them the next day. *(Change in Active voice)* **SSC CGL Tier-1 13.09.2024 (Shift-III)**
(a) They gifted me a fancy doll yesterday.
(b) They are gifting me a fancy doll the next day.
(c) They gift me a fancy doll the previous day.
(d) They will gift me a fancy doll tomorrow.

Ans. (d) Refer to Rule 1(g)

37. He will give a lecture on personality development. *(Change in Passive voice)* **SSC CGL Tier-1 17.09.2024 (Shift-I)**
(a) A lecture on personality development can be given by him.
(b) A lecture will be given on personality development.
(c) A lecture on personality development will be given by him.
(d) A lecture on personality development will be giving by him.

Ans. (c) Refer to Rule 1(g)

38. His behaviour vexes me sometimes. *(Change in Passive voice)* **SSC CGL Tier-1 17.09.2024 (Shift-I)**
(a) He is being vexing me with his behaviour
(b) Sometimes he vexes me with his behaviour.
(c) I am sometimes vexed by his behaviour.
(d) His behaviour is vexed.

Ans. (c) Refer to Rule 1(a)

39. They are building a new hospital in the city. *(Change in Passive voice)* **SSC CGL Tier-1 17.09.2024 (Shift-II)**
(a) A new hospital was built in the city by them.
(b) A new hospital has been built in the city by them.
(c) A new hospital will be built in the city by them.
(d) A new hospital is being built in the city by them.

Ans. (d) Refer to Rule 1(b)

40. They have built a new bridge across the river. *(Change in Passive voice)* **SSC CGL Tier-1 17.09.2024 (Shift-II)**
(a) A new bridge has been built across the river by them.
(b) A new bridge by them has been built across the river.
(c) A new bridge has built across the river by them.
(d) The river has been built a new bridge by them.

Ans. (a) Refer to Rule 1(c)

41. By whom were you injured? *(Change in Active voice)* **SSC CGL Tier-1 17.09.2024 (Shift-II)**
(a) Who has injured you?
(b) Who injured you?
(c) Who had injured you?
(d) Who had been injuring you?

Ans. (b) Refer to Rule 5

42. Were the plants being grafted by the gardener? *(Change in Active voice)* **SSC CGL Tier-1 17.09.2024 (Shift-II)**
(a) Was the gardener grafting the plants?
(b) Was the gardener grafted the plants?
(c) Were the plants grafting the gardener?
(d) Were the gardener grafting the plants?

Ans. (a) Refer to Rule 6

43. Dipesh will send Rakesh away to college for certain reasons. *(Change in Passive voice)* **SSC CGL Tier-1 18.09.2024 (Shift-I)**
(a) Rakesh will have to be sent away to college for certain reasons by Dipesh.
(b) Rakesh will be sent away to college for certain reasons by Dipesh.
(c) Rakesh would have been sent away to college for certain reasons by Dipesh.
(d) Rakesh would be sent away to college for certain reasons by Dipesh.

Ans. (b) Refer to Rule 1(g)

44. Why are you repeatedly called by her? *(Change in Active voice)* **SSC CGL Tier-1 18.09.2024 (Shift-I)**
(a) Why she calls you repeatedly?
(b) Why had she called you repeatedly?
(c) Why was she calling you repeatedly?
(d) Why does she call you repeatedly?
Ans. (d) Refer to Rule 5

45. Can you compose an inspiring poem? *(Change in Passive voice)* **SSC CGL Tier-1 18.09.2024 (Shift-II)**
(a) Can an inspiring poem be composed?
(b) An inspiring poem can be composed by you.
(c) Can an inspiring poem be composed by you?
(d) Can an inspiring poem by you composed?
Ans. (c) Refer to Rule 6

46. The tutor was not teaching the student. *(Change in Passive voice)* **SSC CGL Tier-1 18.09.2024 (Shift-II)**
(a) The student was teaching the tutor.
(b) The student was not taught by the tutor.
(c) The student was not being taught by the tutor.
(d) The student was not being teaching by the tutor.
Ans. (c) Refer to Rule 1(e)

47. People will respect his bravado. *(Change in Passive voice)* **SSC CGL Tier-1 18.09.2024 (Shift-III)**
(a) His bravado will being respected by people.
(b) His bravado will have to be respected by people.
(c) His bravado will be respected by people.
(d) His bravado will be respect by people.
Ans. (c) Refer to Rule 1(g)

48. People know Stellenbosch for its greenery and delicious street foods. *(Change in Passive voice)* **SSC CGL Tier-1 18.09.2024 (Shift-III)**
(a) Stellenbosch was known to people for its greenery and delicious street foods.
(b) Stellenbosch is known to people for its greenery and delicious street foods.
(c) Stellenbosch had been known to people for its greenery and delicious street foods.
(d) Stellenbosch have been known to people for its greenery and delicious street foods.
Ans. (b) Refer to Rule 1(a)

49. The cashier had finished the assigned task on time. *(Change in Passive voice)* **SSC CGL Tier-1 19.09.2024 (Shift-I)**
(a) The assigned task is finished by the cashier on time.
(b) The assigned task has been finished by the cashier on time.
(c) The assigned task had been finished by the cashier on time.
(d) The assigned task was finished by the cashier on time.
Ans. (c) Refer to Rule 1(f)

50. Data is being collected by the researcher. *(Change in Active voice)* **SSC CGL Tier-1 19.09.2024 (Shift-I)**
(a) The researcher has collected data.
(b) The researcher is collecting data.
(c) The researcher has been collecting data.
(d) The researcher will be collecting data.
Ans. (b) Refer to Rule 1(b)

51. The concert tickets were bought by my friend. *(Change in Active voice)* **SSC CGL Tier-1 19.09.2024 (Shift-II)**
(a) My friend has bought the concert tickets.
(b) My friend bought the concert tickets.
(c) My friend buys the concert tickets.
(d) My friend is buying the concert tickets.
Ans. (b) Refer to Rule 1(d)

52. Inayat did not greet her. *(Change in Passive voice)* **SSC CGL Tier-1 19.09.2024 (Shift-II)**
(a) She was not going to be greeted by Inayat.
(b) She was not at all greeted by Inayat.
(c) She was not greeted by Inayat.
(d) She was not being greeted by Inayat.
Ans. (c) Refer to Rule 1(d)

53. Meenakshi could have sent a reply. *(Change in Passive voice)* **SSC CGL Tier-1 19.09.2024 (Shift-III)**
(a) A reply could have be sent by Meenakshi.
(b) A reply could have been sent by Meenakshi.
(c) A reply could have sent by Meenakshi.
(d) A reply could have been send by Meenakshi
Ans. (b) Refer to Rule 4

54. The school will hire new teachers. *(Change in Passive voice)* **SSC CGL Tier-1 19.09.2024 (Shift-III)**
(a) New teachers will join the school.
(b) The school will be hiring new teachers.
(c) New teachers are hired by the school.
(d) New teachers will be hired by the school.
Ans. (d) Refer to Rule 1(g)

55. The teenager delivered the speech. *(Change in Passive voice)* **SSC CGL Tier-1 23.09.2024 (Shift-I)**
(a) The speech has been delivered by the teenager.
(b) The speech is delivered by the teenager.
(c) The speech was delivered by the teenager.
(d) The speech was being delivered by the teenager.
Ans. (c) Refer to Rule 1(d)

56. I have booked an apartment in the new residential colony. *(Change in Passive voice)* **SSC CGL Tier-1 23.09.2024 (Shift-I)**
(a) An apartment have been booked by me in the new residential colony.
(b) An apartment had been booked by me in the new residential colony.
(c) An apartment is been booked by me in the new residential colony.
(d) An apartment has been booked by me in the new residential colony.
Ans. (d) Refer to Rule 1(c)

57. Mr. Amar refused him admittance. *(Change in Passive voice)* **SSC CGL Tier-1 23.09.2024 (Shift-I)**
(a) Admittance will be refused to him by Mr. Amar.
(b) Admittance shall be refused to him by Mr. Amar.
(c) Admittance would be refused to him by Mr. Amar.
(d) Admittance was refused to him by Mr. Amar.
Ans. (d) Refer to Rule 1(d)

58. Trigonometry has been taught by him for donkey's years. *(Change in Active voice)* **SSC CGL Tier-1 23.09.2024 (Shift-I)**
(a) He had been teaching trigonometry for donkey's years.
(b) He has been trigonometry teaching for donkey's years.
(c) He is teaching trigonometry for donkey's years.
(d) He has been teaching trigonometry for donkey's years.
Ans. (d) Refer to Rule 1(c)

59. The baker baked the cake. *(Change in Passive voice)* **SSC CGL Tier-1 23.09.2024 (Shift-III)**
(a) The cake was baked by the baker
(b) The cake had been baked by the baker.
(c) The baker has been baking the cake.
(d) The cake has been baked by the baker.
Ans. (a) Refer to Rule 1(d)

60. Select the option that expresses the given sentence in passive voice.
(a) I prefer tea to coffee.
(b) Children are participating in sand-art competition.
(c) She sketches beautifully.
(d) The consignment was delivered yesterday.

Ans. (d) In passive voice, something is done on an object.

61. He has written a best-selling novel. *(Change in Passive voice)* **SSC CGL Tier-1 24.09.2024 (Shift-I)**
(a) A best-selling novel was being written by him
(b) A best-selling novel has been written by him.
(c) A best-selling novel was written by him.
(d) A best-selling novel would have been written by him.

Ans. (b) Refer to Rule 1(c)

62. He wrote an inspiring speech for the event. *(Change in Passive voice)* **SSC CGL Tier-1 24.09.2024 (Shift-I)**
(a) An inspiring speech was being written by him for the event.
(b) An inspiring speech was written by him for the event.
(c) An inspiring speech is written by him for the event.
(d) An inspiring speech has been written by him for the event.

Ans. (b) Refer to Rule 1(d)

63. He was given a reward for his contribution by the Governor. *(Change in Active voice)* **SSC CGL Tier-1 24.09.2024 (Shift-II)**
(a) For his contribution, he was rewarded by the governor.
(b) The governor rewarded him.
(c) The governor gave him a reward for his contribution.
(d) Rewarded by the governor, as he contributed along.

Ans. (c) Refer to Rule 1(d)

64. We have to say little in this matter. *(Change in Passive voice)* **SSC CGL Tier-1 24.09.2024 (Shift-I)**
(a) Little had to be said in this matter.
(b) In this matter, little is to be said.
(c) In this matter, little must be said.
(d) Little has to be said in this matter.

Ans. (d) Refer to Rule 1(c)

65. The chef prepares the meal with great care. *(Change in Passive voice)* **SSC CGL Tier-1 24.09.2024 (Shift-III)**
(a) The meal was prepared with great care by the chef.
(b) The meal will be prepared with great care by the chef.
(c) The meal is prepared with great care by the chef.
(d) The meal has been prepared with great care by the chef.

Ans. (c) Refer to Rule 1(a)

66. The novels of Dickens are being read by Mayank. *(Change in Passive voice)* **SSC CGL Tier-1 24.09.2024 (Shift-III)**
(a) Mayank is reading the novels of Dickens.
(b) Mayank has been reading the novels of Dickens.
(c) Mayank was reading the novels of Dickens.
(d) Mayank had been reading the novels of Dickens.

Ans. (a) Refer to Rule 1(b)

67. A comic play was performed by the comedian. *(Change in Active voice)* **SSC CGL Tier-1 25.09.2024 (Shift-I)**
(a) The comedian performs a comic play.
(b) The comedian performed a comic play.
(c) The comedian performance a comic play.
(d) The comedian do perform a comic play.

Ans. (b) Refer to Rule 1(d)

68. The research team is conducting experiments on a new drug that could revolutionise the treatment of the disease. *(Change in Passive voice)* **SSC CGL Tier-1 25.09.2024 (Shift-I)**
(a) Experiments have been conducted on a new drug that could have revolutionised the treatment of the disease through the research team.
(b) Experiments were being conducted on a new drug that could revolutionise the treatment of the disease by the research team.
(c) Experiments are conducted on a new drug that could revolutionise the treatment of the disease from the research team.
(d) Experiments are being conducted on a new drug that could revolutionise the treatment of the disease by the research team.

Ans. (d) Refer to Rule 1(b)

69. He had cleaned the bathroom. *(Change in Passive voice)* **SSC CGL Tier-1 25.09.2024 (Shift-II)**
(a) The bathroom has cleaned by him.
(b) The bathroom had cleaned by him.
(c) The bathroom had been cleaned by him.
(d) The bathroom has been cleaned by him.

Ans. (c) Refer to Rule 1(f)

70. Why didn't she bring her son to my house? *(Change in Passive voice)* **SSC CGL Tier-1 25.09.2024 (Shift-II)**
(a) Why wasn't her son brought by her to my house?
(b) Why isn't her son brought to my house?
(c) Why wasn't her son brought to my house?
(d) Why isn't her son brought by you to my house?

Ans. (a) Refer to Rule 5

71. We should clean the house regularly. *(Change in Passive voice)* **SSC CGL Tier-1 25.09.2024 (Shift-III)**
(a) The house should have been cleaned regularly by us.
(b) The house should be being cleaned regularly by us.
(c) The house should be cleaned regularly by us.
(d) The house should be clean regularly by us.

Ans. (c) Refer to Rule 5

72. His father's arm was bandaged by the kind nurse. *(Change in Active voice)* **SSC CGL Tier-1 25.09.2024 (Shift-III)**
(a) The kind nurse has bandaged his father's arm.
(b) The kind nurse had bandaged his father's arm.
(c) The kind nurse bandages his father's arm.
(d) The kind nurse bandaged his father's arm.

Ans. (d) Refer to Rule 1(d)

73. Rohit did not slap Kunal. *(Change in Passive voice)* **SSC CGL Tier-1 26.09.2024 (Shift-I)**
(a) Kunal was not being slapped by Rohit.
(b) Kunal had not been slapped by Rohit.
(c) Kunal was not slapped by Rohit.
(d) Kunal has not been slapped by Rohit

Ans. (c) Refer to Rule 1(d)

74. Will you give me an independent project? *(Change in Passive voice)* **SSC CGL Tier-1 26.09.2024 (Shift-I)**
(a) Will you be given an independent project by me?
(b) Would an independent project be given?
(c) Would I be given an independent project?
(d) Will I be given an independent project by you?

Ans. (d) Refer to Rule 5

75. The issue has been successfully resolved by the customer care team. *(Change in Active voice)*
SSC CGL Tier-1 26.09.2024 (Shift-II)
(a) The customer care team successfully resolves the issue.
(b) The customer care team successfully resolved the issue.
(c) The issue has successfully resolved the customer care team.
(d) The customer care team has successfully resolved the issue.

Ans. (d) Refer to Rule 1(c)

76. Gill scored 3 centuries in Tata IPL 2023. *(Change in Passive voice)*
SSC CGL Tier-1 26.09.2024 (Shift-II)
(a) 3 centuries has been scored by Gill in Tata IPL 2023.
(b) 3 centuries were scored by Gill in Tata IPL 2023.
(c) 3 centuries had been scored by Gill in Tata IPL 2023.
(d) 3 centuries were being scored by Gill in Tata IPL 2023.

Ans. (b) Refer to Rule 1(d)

77. A famous company conducted the workshop for its customers. *(Change in Passive voice)*
SSC CGL Tier-1 26.09.2024 (Shift-III)
(a) The workshop were conducted by a famous company for its customers.
(b) The workshop had been conducted by a famous company for its customers.
(c) The workshop was conducted by a famous company for its customers.
(d) The workshop is conducted by a famous company for its customers.

Ans. (c) Refer to Rule 1(d)

78. How have they been ordered by the minister? *(Change in Active voice)*
SSC CGL Tier-1 26.09.2024 (Shift-III)
(a) How have the minister ordered them?
(b) How had the minister ordered them?
(c) How did the minister order them?
(d) How has the minister ordered them?

Ans. (d) Refer to Rule 5

SSC CGL 2023 (Tier I & II)

79. The company's Board of Directors will announce the financial results at the annual meeting tomorrow. *(Change in Passive voice)*
SSC CGL Tier-1 14.07.2023 (Shift-I)
(a) The financial results will have been announced by the company's Board of Directors at the annual meeting tomorrow.
(b) The financial results are being announced by the company's Board of Directors at the annual meeting tomorrow.
(c) The company's Board of Directors announced the financial results at the annual meeting tomorrow.
(d) The financial results will be announced by the company's Board of Directors at the annual meeting tomorrow.

Ans. (d) Refer to Rule 1(g)

80. How you will ask everyone if the children were not reading the books?. *(Change in Passive voice)*
SSC CGL Tier-1 14.07.2023 (Shift-II)
(a) Were the books being read by the children?
(b) Were the books not being read by the children?
(c) Were the book not being read by the children?
(d) Were the children reading the books?

Ans. (b) Refer to Rule 5

81. He won't receive any better choice than this from anywhere. *(Change in Passive voice)*
SSC CGL Tier-1 14.07.2023 (Shift-I)
(a) Any better choice won't be received by him than this from anywhere.
(b) Any better choice wouldn't have received by him than this from anywhere.
(c) Any better choice shouldn't be received by him than this from anywhere.
(d) Any better choice won't have been be received by him than this from anywhere.

Ans. (a) Refer to Rule 1(g)

82. The little boy called up his best friend on his birthday. *(Change in Passive voice)*
SSC CGL Tier-1 14.07.2023 (Shift-III)
(a) His best friend has been called up by the little boy on his birthday.
(b) His best friend was called up by the little boy on his birthday.
(c) His best friend is called up by the little boy on his birthday.
(d) His best friend was being called up by the little boy on his birthday.

Ans. (b) Refer to Rule 1(d)

83. Who stole my tickets? *(Change in Passive voice)*
SSC CGL Tier-1 14.07.2023 (Shift-III)
(a) My tickets was stolen by whom?
(b) My tickets got stolen by who?
(c) By whom were my tickets stolen?
(d) My tickets were stolen by who?

Ans. (c) Refer to Rule 5

84. Did you not buy the return tickets to Dehradun? *(Change in Passive voice)*
SSC CGL Tier-1 14.07.2023 (Shift-IV)
(a) Was the return tickets to Dehradun not bought by you?
(b) Were the return tickets to Dehradun not being bought by you?
(c) Had the return tickets to Dehradun not bought by you?
(d) Were the return tickets to Dehradun not bought by you?

Ans. (d) Refer to Rule 6

85. How you will tell your parents that Mahesh and his team were helping the fire and rescue team? *(Change in Passive voice)*
SSC CGL Tier-1 14.07.2023 (Shift-IV)
(a) The fire and rescue team helped by Mahesh and his team.
(b) The fire and rescue team was being helped by Mahesh and his team.
(c) The fire and rescue team being help by Mahesh and his team.
(d) Mahesh and his team were been helping the fire and rescue team.

Ans. (b) Refer to Rule 5

86. Joseph opened the Bible. *(Change in Passive voice)*
SSC CGL Tier-1 17.07.2023 (Shift-I)
(a) The Bible is being opened by Joseph.
(b) Joseph is opening the Bible.
(c) The Bible was opened by Joseph.
(d) Joseph opens the Bible.

Ans. (c) Refer to Rule 1(d)

87. The ball of yarn was being nudged by the kitten. *(Change in Active voice)*
SSC CGL Tier-1 17.07.2023 (Shift-I)
(a) The kitten was nudged by the ball of yarn.
(b) The kitten is nudging the ball of yarn.
(c) The kitten was nudging the ball of yarn.
(d) The kitten has been nudging the ball of yarn.

Ans. (c) Refer to Rule 1(e)

88. She might have completed her research by that time. *(Change in Passive voice)* **SSC CGL Tier-1 17.07.2023 (Shift-II)**
(a) Her research might be completed by her by that time.
(b) Her research might had been completed by her by that time.
(c) Her research might have been completed by her by that time.
(d) Her research might have completed by her by that time.

Ans. (c) Refer to Rule 1(c)

89. By whom was the coffee made? *(Change in Active voice)* **SSC CGL Tier-1 17.07.2023 (Shift-II)**
(a) Who made the coffee?
(b) Who had made the coffee?
(c) Who has made the coffee?
(d) Who makes the coffee?

Ans. (a) Refer to Rule 5

90. Pudding had already been prepared by her. *(Change in Active voice)* **SSC CGL Tier-1 17.07.2023 (Shift-III)**
(a) She has already prepared pudding.
(b) She had already prepared pudding.
(c) She have already prepared pudding.
(d) She will prepare pudding.

Ans. (b) Refer to Rule 1(f)

91. How you will tell your parents that Darshana was laughed at by all her classmates? *(Change in Active voice)* **SSC CGL Tier-1 17.07.2023 (Shift-III)**
(a) All her classmates laughed at Darshana.
(b) All her classmates laughing at Darshana.
(c) Darshana is laughed at by all her classmates.
(d) All her classmates will been laugh at Darshana.

Ans. (a) Refer to Rule 5

92. She is laughing at me. *(Change in Passive voice)* **SSC CGL Tier-1 17.07.2023 (Shift-IV)**
(a) I am being laughed at by her.
(b) I have been laughed by her.
(c) I was being laughed at by her.
(d) I had been laughed by her.

Ans. (a) Refer to Rule 1(b)

93. The audience loved her performance. *(Change in Passive voice)* **SSC CGL Tier-1 17.07.2023 (Shift-IV)**
(a) The audience will love her performance.
(b) The performance is loved by the audience.
(c) Her performance was loved by the audience.
(d) The performance was loved by her.

Ans. (c) Refer to Rule 1(d)

94. He does not buy shirts. *(Change in Passive voice)* **SSC CGL Tier-1 18.07.2023 (Shift-I)**
(a) Shirts are not bought by him.
(b) Shirts are not brought by him.
(c) Shirts were not been bought by him.
(d) Shirts were not bought by him.

Ans. (a) Refer to Rule 1(a)

95. She is building a new house. *(Change in Passive voice)* **SSC CGL Tier-1 18.07.2023 (Shift-I)**
(a) A new house is being built by her.
(b) She had built a new house.
(c) She has built a new house.
(d) A new house has been built by her.

Ans. (a) Refer to Rule 1(b)

96. The award was presented to her by the director. *(Change in Active voice)* **SSC CGL Tier-2 26.12.2023 (Shift-I)**
(a) She presented the award to the director.
(b) The award presented to her by the director.
(c) The director presented the award to her.
(d) She was presenting the award to the director.

Ans. (c) Refer to Rule 1(d)

97. By whom were you taught English grammar and composition? *(Change in Active voice)* **SSC CGL Tier-2 26.12.2023 (Shift-I)**
(a) Who has taught you English grammar and composition?
(b) Whom taught you English grammar and composition?
(c) Who had taught you English grammar and composition?
(d) Who taught you English grammar and composition?

Ans. (d) Refer to Rule 5

98. Access denied. *(Change in Passive voice)* **SSC CGL Tier-2 26.12.2023 (Shift-I)**
(a) Let the access be denied.
(b) Let it be known that access will be denied.
(c) Access has been denied.
(d) Access is being denied.

Ans. (b) Refer to Rule 7 (ii)

SSC CGL 2022 (Tier I & II)

99. Give the child a nourishing diet. *(Change in Passive voice)* **SSC CGL Tier-1 11.04.2022 (Shift-II)**
(a) The child is given a nourishing diet.
(b) The child was given a nourishing diet.
(c) The child should be given a nourishing diet.
(d) The child must have given a nourishing diet.

Ans. (c) When such a sentence is transformed into passive voice, the structure followed is Object + should be + V3 + by + Subject.

100. The poems of great English poets are being translated into other languages. *(Change in Active voice)* **SSC CGL Tier-1 11.04.2022 (Shift-II)**
(a) They were translating the poems of great English poets into other languages.
(b) They are translating the poems of great English poets into other languages.
(c) They have translated the poems of great English poets into other languages.
(d) They translated the poems of great English poets into other languages.

Ans. (b) Refer to Rule 1(b)

101. They catch whale sharks commercially in some place around the world. *(Change in Passive voice)* **SSC CGL Tier-1 11.04.2022 (Shift-III)**
(a) Whale sharks were caught commercially in some places around the world.
(b) Whale sharks are being caught commercially in some places around the world.
(c) Whale sharks have been caught commercially in some places around the world.
(d) Whale sharks are caught commercially in some places

Ans. (d) Refer to Rule 1(a)

102. Who is creating this mess? *(Change in Passive voice)* **SSC CGL Tier-1 18.04.2022 (Shift-I)**
(a) By whom is this mess being created?
(b) Who has created this mess?
(c) By whom has this mess been created?
(d) By whom this mess being created?

Ans. (a) Refer to Rule 5.

103. Most lizards rely on camouflage to hide from their enemies. *(Change in Passive voice)* **SSC CGL Tier-1 18.04.2022 (Shift-III)**
(a) Camouflage has been relied on by most lizards to hide from their enemies.
(b) Camouflage is relied on by most lizards to hide from their enemies.
(c) Camouflage was relied on by most lizards to hide from their enemies.
(d) Most lizards are being relied on by camouflage to hide from their enemies.

Ans. (b) Refer to Rule 1(a)

104. My manager will be assigned a new project by me. *(Change in Active voice)* **SSC CGL Tier-1 19.04.2022 (Shift-II)**
(a) I will be assigning a new project to my manager.
(b) My manager is assigning me a new project.
(c) My manager has assigned me a new project.
(d) I am being assigned a new project by my manager.

Ans. (a) Refer to Rule 1(g)

105. Can you carry my bag upstairs? *(Change in Passive voice)* **SSC CGL Tier-1 19.04.2022 (Shift-II)**
(a) Was my bag carried upstairs by you?
(b) Could your bag be carried upstairs by me?
(c) Can my bag be carried upstairs by you?
(d) Can our bag be carried upstairs by me?

Ans. (c) Refer to Rule 6

106. Hold the rope firmly. *(Change in Passive voice)* **SSC CGL Tier-1 20.04.2022 (Shift-III)**
(a) Let the rope hold you firmly.
(b) Let the rope firmly hold you.
(c) Let the rope be hold firmly.
(d) Let the rope be held firmly.

Ans. (d) Refer to Rule 7 (ii)

107. Manu will tell her later. *(Change in Passive voice)* **SSC CGL Tier-1 01.12.2022 (Shift-I)**
(a) She will be tell later by Manu.
(b) She will tell later by Manu.
(c) She will be told later by Manu.
(d) She will be tell later.

Ans. (c) Refer to Rule 1(g)

108. Has the villa been occupied by them? *(Change in Active voice)* **SSC CGL Tier-1 01.12.2022 (Shift-I)**
(a) Did they occupied the villa?
(b) Had they occupied the villa?
(c) Have they occupied the villa?
(d) Do they occupied the villa?

Ans. (c) Refer to Rule 6

109. Priya washes her clothes in the evening. *(Change in Passive voice)* **SSC CGL Tier-1 01.12.2022 (Shift-I)**
(a) The clothes was washed by Priya in the evening.
(b) The clothes is washed by Priya in the evening.
(c) The clothes are washed by Priya in the evening.
(d) The clothes were washed by Priya in the evening.

Ans. (c) Refer to Rule 1(a)

110. The clothes will be delivered by the shop on Monday. *(Change in Active voice)* **SSC CGL Tier-1 01.12.2022 (Shift-I)**
(a) The shop will be delivering the clothes on Monday.
(b) The shop will deliver the clothes on Monday.
(c) The shop would be delivering the clothes on Monday.
(d) The shop would deliver the clothes on Monday.

Ans. (b) Refer to Rule 1(g)

SSC CPO 2024 (Tier-I & II)

111. The meal will have been made ready by the cook by the time you reach the guest house. *(Change in Passive voice)* **SSC CPO Tier-2 08.01.2024**
(a) The cook will make the meal ready by the time you reach the guest house.
(b) The cook have made the meal ready by the time you reach the guest house.
(c) The cook will have made the meal ready by the time you reach the guest house.
(d) The cook will be making the meal ready by the time you reach the guest house.

Ans. (c) Refer to Rule 1(h)

112. Grow more trees. *(Change in Passive voice)* **SSC CPO Tier-2 08.01.2024**
(a) Let more trees be grown.
(b) More trees should be growing.
(c) More trees should grow.
(d) You should grow more trees.

Ans. (a) Refer to Rule 7 (ii)

113. May you be blessed with good health. *(Change in Passive voice)* **SSC CPO Tier-2 08.01.2024**
(a) God bless you with good health.
(b) good health bless you.
(c) God should bless you with good health.
(d) You should be blessed with good health.

Ans. (a) The sentence is in imperative mood. When such a sentence is transformed into passive voice, the structure followed is Subject + bless + Object + with + Complement.

114. Bhavna saw him carrying your suitcase. *(Change in Passive voice)* **SSC CPO Tier-2 08.01.2024**
(a) He was seen by Bhavna carrying your suitcase.
(b) Your suitcase carried by him was seen by Bhavna.
(c) He had been seen by Bhavna carrying your suitcase.
(d) Your suitcase was seen by Bhavna carrying him.

Ans. (a) Refer to Rule 1 (e)

115. We had repaired the roads before the monsoon set in. *(Change in Passive voice)* **SSC CPO Tier-2 08.01.2024**
(a) The roads have been repaired before the monsoon set in by us.
(b) The roads were repaired before the monsoon set in by us.
(c) The roads had been repaired before the monsoon set in by us.
(d) The roads are repaired before the monsoon set in by us.

Ans. (c) Refer to Rule 1 (f)

116. The workers will not be satisfied with empty promises. *(Change in Passive voice)* **SSC CPO Tier-2 08.01.2024**
(a) Empty promises will not satisfy the workers.
(b) Empty promises would not satisfy the workers.
(c) Empty promises do not satisfy the workers.
(d) Empty promises cannot satisfy the workers.

Ans. (a) Refer to Rule 1 (g)

117. Take these two pills with warm water. *(Change in Passive voice)* **SSC CPO Tier-2 08.01.2024**
(a) Warm water should be taken with these two pills.
(b) You take these two pills with warm water.
(c) You are ordered to take these two pills with warm water.
(d) These two pills should be taken with warm water.

Ans. (d) The imperative sentence structure in passive voice is Object + should be + V3 + with + Complement.

118. Let the fire be kept burning at night. *(Change in Active voice)*
SSC CPO Tier-2 08.01.2024
(a) You must burn the fire at night.
(b) The fire should be burnt at night.
(c) Let the fire burning at night.
(d) Keep the fire burning at night.
Ans. (d) Refer to Rule 7 (ii)

119. One can achieve nothing without hard work. *(Change in Passive voice)*
SSC CPO Tier-2 08.01.2024
(a) Nothing is achieved without hard work.
(b) Nothing will be achieved without hard work.
(c) Nothing has been achieved without hard work.
(d) Nothing can be achieved without hard work.
Ans. (d) The sentence is in present tense. When such a sentence is transformed into passive voice, the structure followed is Object + can + be + V3.

120. Why didn't your father accompany you? *(Change in Passive voice)*
SSC CPO Tier-2 08.01.2024
(a) Why were you not accompanied by your father?
(b) Why have you not been accompanied by your father?
(c) Why didn't you be accompanied by your father?
(d) Why wasn't your father accompanied by you?
Ans. (a) Refer to Rule 5

121. Everybody wants others to respect them. *(Change in Passive voice)*
SSC CPO Tier-2 08.01.2024
(a) They want others to be respected by everybody.
(b) Everybody wants to respect others.
(c) Everybody wants to be respected by others.
(d) Everybody wanted to be respected by others.
Ans. (c) When such a sentence is transformed into passive voice, the structure followed is Subject + wants to + be + V3 + by + Object.

122. It is said that Einstein was a genius. *(Change in Active voice)*
SSC CPO Tier-2 08.01.2024
(a) People are saying that Einstein was a genius.
(b) People said that Einstein was a genius.
(c) People have said that Einstein was a genius.
(d) People say that Einstein was a genius.
Ans. (d) When such a sentence is transformed into active voice, the structure followed is Subject + say + that + Object + was/were + Complement.

123. It was decided by Salim Ali to devote his life to the preservation of Indian birds. *(Change in Active voice)*
SSC CPO Tier-2 08.01.2024
(a) Salim devoted his life to the preservation of Indian birds.
(b) Salim Ali decided to devote his life to the preservation of Indian birds.
(c) Salim Ali has decided to devote his life to the preservation of Indian birds.
(d) Salim Ali had decided to devote his life to the preservation of Indian birds.
Ans. (b) When such a sentence is transformed into active voice, the structure followed is Subject + V2 + to + V1 + Object + Complement.

124. Jack played hide and seek. *(Change in Passive voice)*
SSC CPO Tier-2 10.01.2022
(a) Hide and seek was played by Jack.
(b) Hide and seek had been played by Jack.
(c) Hide and seek will be played by Jack.
(d) Hide and seek is played by Jack.
Ans. (a) Refer to Rule 1 (d)

125. The villain of the play was hated by the audience. *(Change in Active voice)*
SSC CPO Tier-2 10.01.2022
(a) The audience hated the villain of the play.
(b) The villain hated the audience of the play.
(c) The audience had hated the villain of the play.
(d) The audience was hating the villain of the play.
Ans. (a) Refer to Rule 1 (d)

SSC CHSL 2024 (Tier 1 & 2)

126. Doctors saved many lives during the pandemic. *(Change in passive voice)*
SSC CHSL Tier-2 18.11.2024
(a) Many lives have been saved by doctors during the pandemic.
(b) Many lives were saved by doctors during the pandemic.
(c) Many lives were being saved by doctors during the pandemic.
(d) Many lives are saved by doctors during the pandemic.
Ans. (b) Refer to Rule 1 (d)

127. I remember my mother taking me to the stadium. *(Change in passive voice)*
SSC CHSL Tier-2 18.11.2024
(a) I remember being taken to the stadium by my mother.
(b) I was taken to the stadium by mother that I remembered.
(c) My mother remembered me taken to the stadium.
(d) I was remembered being taken to the stadium by my mother.
Ans. (a) Refer to Rule 1 (b)

128. The new sunshades have protected our windows during the rainy season. *(Change in passive voice)*
SSC CHSL Tier-2 18.11.2024
(a) Our windows are being protected by the new sunshades during the rainy season.
(b) Our windows have been protected by the new sunshades during the rainy season.
(c) Our windows are being protected by the new windows during the rainy season.
(d) Our sunshades have been protected by the new windows during the rainy season.
Ans. (b) Refer to Rule 1 (c)

129. Perumal has given a challenging assignment to the newly admitted students. *(Change in Passive voice)*
SSC CHSL Tier-2 10.01.2024
(a) A challenging assignment has been given by Perumal to the newly admitted students.
(b) A challenging assignment will have been given by Perumal to the newly admitted students.
(c) A challenging assignment was given by Perumal to the newly admitted students.
(d) A challenging assignment had been given by Perumal to the newly admitted students.
Ans. (a) Refer to Rule 1 (c)

130. They built a new house last year. *(Change in Passive voice)*
SSC CHSL Tier-2 10.01.2024
(a) A new house was being built by them last year.
(b) They had been building a new house last year.
(c) A new house was built by them last year.
(d) A new house is being built by them last year.
Ans. (c) Refer to Rule 1 (d)

131. The teacher will explain the lesson tomorrow. *(Change in Passive voice)* **SSC CHSL Tier-2 10.01.2024**

(a) The lesson is being explained by the teacher tomorrow.
(b) The lesson was explained by the teacher tomorrow.
(c) The lesson will be explained by the teacher tomorrow.
(d) The lesson will have been explained by the teacher tomorrow.

Ans. (c) Refer to Rule 1 (g)

132. Pranav painted his house. *(Change in Passive voice)* **SSC CHSL Tier-1 13.03.2023 (Shift-III)**

(a) The house was painted by Pranav.
(b) House painting was done by Pranav.
(c) Pranav's house was painted by him.
(d) Painting of the house was done by Pranav.

Ans. (c) Refer to Rule 1 (d)

133. Meghna has taken all the cash. *(Change in Passive voice)* **SSC CHSL Tier-1 10.03.2023 (Shift-II)**

(a) All the cash has been taken by Meghna.
(b) All the cash had been taking by Meghna.
(c) All the cash was taken by Meghna.
(d) All the cash had been taken by Meghna.

Ans. (a) Refer to Rule 1 (c)

134. Ravi gave you the information? *(Change in Passive voice)* **SSC CHSL Tier-1 09.03.2023 (Shift-I)**

(a) You have been given the information?
(b) Was the information given to you by Ravi?
(c) Have the information been given to you?
(d) Has the information given to you?

Ans. (b) Refer to Rule 1 (d)

135. Suresh speaks French here. *(Change in Passive voice)* **SSC CHSL Tier-1 16.03.2023 (Shift-I)**

(a) French is been spoken here by Suresh.
(b) French are spoken here by Suresh.
(c) French is spoken here by Suresh.
(d) French was spoken here by Suresh.

Ans. (c) Refer to Rule 1 (a)

136. The villagers have rebuilt the hospital. *(Change in Passive voice)* **SSC CHSL Tier-1 15.03.2023 (Shift-IV)**

(a) The hospital has rebuilt by the villagers.
(b) The hospital had been rebuilt by the villagers.
(c) The hospital has been rebuilt by the villagers.
(d) The hospital was rebuilt by the villagers.

Ans. (c) Refer to Rule 1 (c)

137. The President loved that lady. *(Change in Passive voice)* **SSC CHSL Tier-1 14.03.2023 (Shift-I)**

(a) That lady is love by the President.
(b) That lady was being loved by the President.
(c) That lady was loved by the President.
(d) That lady is loved by the President.

Ans. (c) Refer to Rule 1 (d)

138. The cat ate all the pastries. *(Change in Passive voice)* **SSC CHSL Tier-1 20.03.2023 (Shift-III)**

(a) All the pastries were eaten by the cat.
(b) All the pastries is eaten by the cat.
(c) All the pastries had been eaten by the cat.
(d) All the pastries are eaten by the cat.

Ans. (a) Refer to Rule 1 (d)

139. My father cooks breakfast everyday. *(Change in Passive voice)* **SSC CHSL Tier-1 17.03.2023 (Shift-II)**

(a) Breakfast was being cooked everyday by my father.
(b) Breakfast was cooked everyday by my father.
(c) Breakfast was cook everyday by my father.
(d) Breakfast is cooked everyday by my father.

Ans. (d) Refer to Rule 1 (a)

140. Daniel and Mary invited us to their wedding. *(Change in Passive voice)* **SSC CHSL Tier-1 16.03.2023 (Shift-II)**

(a) We were invited to Daniel and Mary's wedding.
(b) We are invited to Daniel and Mary's wedding.
(c) We had been invited to Daniel and Mary's wedding.
(d) We have been invited to Daniel and Mary's wedding.

Ans. (a) Refer to Rule 1 (d)

141. The child locked the shutters. **SSC CHSL Tier-1 21.03.2023 (Shift-IV)**

(a) The shutters had been locked by the child.
(b) The shutters were locked by the child.
(c) The shutters are locked by the child.
(d) The shutters would be locked by the child.

Ans. (b) Refer to Rule 1 (d)

142. Susan writes recipes for the cookbook. *(Change in Passive voice)* **SSC CHSL Tier-1 21.03.2023 (Shift-II)**

(a) Recipes were written by Susan for the cookbook.
(b) Recipes are written by Susan for the cookbook.
(c) Recipes are being written by Susan for the cookbook.
(d) Recipes are write by Susan for the cookbook.

Ans. (b) Refer to Rule 1 (a)

143. They cancelled the meeting due to bad weather. (Chance in Passive voice) **SSC CHSL Tier-1 03.08.2023 (Shift-I)**

(a) They meeting is cancelled by them because of bad weather.
(b) The meeting was cancelled due to bad weather.
(c) They cancelled the meeting and bad weather was the cause.
(d) The bad weather is the reason they cancelled the meeting.

Ans. (b) Refer to Rule 1 (d)

144. The work will be finished by the mason within a short time. (Chane in Active voice) **SSC CHSL Tier-1 03.08.2023 (Shift-I)**

(a) The mason will be finishing the work within a short time.
(b) The mason would have finish the work within a short time.
(c) The mason would finish the work within a short time.
(d) The mason will finish the work within a short time.

Ans. (d) Refer to Rule 1 (g)

145. The child will recite the poem. *(Change in Passive voice)* **SSC CHSL Tier-1 02.08.2023 (Shift-I)**

(a) By child poem will be recited.
(b) The poem will be recited by the child.
(c) The poem is recited by the child.
(d) The poem will recite by the child.

Ans. (b) Refer to Rule 1 (g)

146. French is taught to us by Miss Glenn. *(Change in Active voice)* **SSC CHSL Tier-1 02.08.2023 (Shift-I)**

(a) Miss Glenn taught us French.
(b) Miss Glenn teach us French.
(c) Miss Glenn teaches us French.
(d) Miss Glenn is teaching us French.

Ans. (c) Refer to Rule 1 (a)

147. The matches are being shown live on Sports TV. *(Change in Active voice)* **SSC CHSL Tier-1 02.08.2023 (Shift-II)**
(a) Sports TV is showing the matches live.
(b) Sports TV would be showing the matches live.
(c) Sports TV will be showing the matches live.
(d) Sports TV can be showing the matches live.

Ans. (a) Refer to Rule 1 (b)

148. The chef prepares the food in the kitchen. *(Change in Active voice)* **SSC CHSL Tier-1 02.08.2023 (Shift-III)**
(a) The food will be prepared by the chef in the kitchen.
(b) The food prepares by the chef in the kitchen.
(c) The food is preparing by the chef in the kitchen.
(d) The food is prepared by the chef in the kitchen.

Ans. (d) Refer to Rule 1 (a)

149. The Governor of the state inaugurated the exhibition in a grand way. *(Chance in Passive voice)* **SSC CHSL Tier-1 02.08.2023 (Shift-IV)**
(a) The exhibition had been inaugurated by the Governor of the state in a grand way.
(b) The exhibition inaugurated by the Governor of the state in a grand way.
(c) The exhibition has been inaugurated by the Governor of the state in a grand way.
(d) The exhibition was inaugurated by the Governor of the state in a grand way.

Ans. (d) Refer to Rule 1 (d)

150. A play is being staged by our group this evening. *(Change in Active voice)* **SSC CHSL Tier-1 03.08.2023 (Shift-II)**
(a) A play staged our group this evening.
(b) Our group stages a play this evening.
(c) Our group is staging a play this evening.
(d) Our group staged a play this evening.

Ans. (c) Refer to Rule 1 (b)

151. His brother needed some urgent help at that moment. *(Change in Passive voice)* **SSC CHSL Tier-1 03.08.2023 (Shift-III)**
(a) Some urgent help was needed by his brother at that moment.
(b) Urgent help was needed by his brother at that moment.
(c) Some urgent help is needed by his brother at that moment.
(d) Some urgent help was needed by his brother at this moment.

Ans. (a) Refer to Rule 1 (d)

152. I was kept waiting for more than an hour to get an appointment by the staff. *(Change in Active voice)* **SSC CHSL Tier-1 03.08.2023 (Shift-IV)**
(a) The staff had kept me waiting for more than an hour to get an appointment.
(b) The staff keep me waiting for more than an hour to get an appointment.
(c) The staff kept me waiting for more than an hour to get an appointment.
(d) The staff kept me wait for more than an hour to get an appointment.

Ans. (c) Refer to Rule 1 (d)

153. The book was written by the author over a period of two years. *(Change in Active voice)* **SSC CHSL Tier-1 04.08.2023 (Shift-I)**
(a) The author wrote the book over a period of two years.
(b) The book was written over a period of two years.
(c) The book was being written by the author over a period of two years.
(d) The period of two years was taken by the author to write the book.

Ans. (a) Refer to Rule 1 (d)

154. The test was passed by only a few students. *(Change in Active voice)* **SSC CHSL Tier-1 04.08.2023 (Shift-I)**
(a) Only a few students passed the test.
(b) The test was not passed by many students.
(c) Many students did not pass the test.
(d) Very few students passed the test.

Ans. (a) Refer to Rule 1 (d)

155. His wife was killed by him. *(Change in Active voice)* **SSC CHSL Tier-1 04.08.2023 (Shift-II)**
(a) Him kills his wife. (b) He has killed his wife.
(c) He killed his wife. (d) He kills his wife.

Ans. (c) Refer to Rule 1 (d)

156. The storm uprooted a large number of trees yesterday. *(Change in Passive voice)* **SSC CHSL Tier-1 04.08.2023 (Shift-II)**
(a) Large number of trees were uprooted by the storm yesterday.
(b) A large number of trees was uprooted by the storm yesterday.
(c) Trees was uprooted yesterday in a large number by the storm.
(d) A large number of trees were uprooted by the storm yesterday.

Ans. (d) Refer to Rule 1 (d)

157. You should apply for the job before the deadline. (Change in Passive voie) **SSC CHSL Tier-1 04.08.2023 (Shift-III)**
(a) You should be applying for the job before the deadline
(b) The job should be applied for before the deadline.
(c) The job could be applied for after the deadline.
(d) The deadline should not be crossed for the job application.

Ans. (b) When such a sentence is transformed into passive voice, the structure followed is Object + should be + V3 + by + Subject.

158. Was the painting stolen by the thief? *(Change in Active voice)* **SSC CHSL Tier-1 04.08.2023 (Shift-III)**
(a) Was the painting being stolen by the thief?
(b) Did not the thief steal the painting?
(c) Was the thief not stealing the painting?
(d) Did the thief steal the painting?

Ans. (d) Refer to Rule 6

159. The bell is rung by the peon. *(Change in Active voice)* **SSC CHSL Tier-1 04.08.2023 (Shift-IV)**
(a) The peon ranged the bell. (b) The peon rings the bell.
(c) The peon has rang the bell. (d) The peon rang the bell.

Ans. (b) Refer to Rule 1 (a)

160. The tiger was killed on an unfortunate day by a hostile hunter. *(Change in Active voice)* **SSC CHSL Tier-1 07.08.2023 (Shift-I)**
(a) A hostile hunter had killed the tiger on an unfortunate day.
(b) A hostile hunter kills the tiger on an unfortunate day.
(c) The tiger is killed by a hostile hunter on an unfortunate day.
(d) A hostile hunter killed the tiger on an unfortunate day.

Ans. (d) Refer to Rule 1 (d)

161. Austin kept the cake in the refrigerator. *(Change in Passive voice)* **SSC CHSL Tier-1 07.08.2023 (Shift-II)**
(a) The cake is kept in the refrigerator by Austin.
(b) The cake was kept in the refrigerator by Austin.
(c) The cake was being kept by Austin in the refrigerator.
(d) The cake was kept in the Austin by the refrigerator.

Ans. (b) Refer to Rule 1 (d)

162. The other details will be given by the concerned teacher. *(Change in Active voice)* **SSC CHSL Tier-1 07.08.2023 (Shift-III)**
(a) The teacher will give the other concerned details.
(b) The concerned teacher gave the other details.
(c) The concerned teacher will give other details.
(d) The concerned teacher will give the other details.
Ans. (d) Refer to Rule 1 (g)

163. The agency had been robbed by the masked intruders. *(Change in Active voice)* **SSC CHSL Tier-1 07.08.2023 (Shift-IV)**
(a) Two masked intruders had rob the agency.
(b) Two masked intruders had been robbed the agency.
(c) Two masked intruders had robbed the agency.
(d) Two masked intruders have been robbing the agency.
Ans. (c) Refer to Rule 1 (f)

164. Tall promises were being made by each candidate. *(Change in Active voice)* **SSC CHSL Tier-1 07.08.2023 (Shift-IV)**
(a) Each candidate made tall promises.
(b) Each candidate can make tall promises.
(c) Each candidate has made tall promises.
(d) Each candidate was making tall promises.
Ans. (d) Refer to Rule 1 (e)

165. The director hired the new employee after the interview. *(Change in Passive voice)* **SSC CHSL Tier-1 08.08.2023 (Shift-II)**
(a) The new employee will be hired by the director after the interview.
(b) The new employee was hired by the director after the interview.
(c) The new employee is being hired by the director after the interview.
(d) The new employee hired by the director after the interview.
Ans. (b) Refer to Rule 1 (d)

166. The speech of Dr. APJ Abdul Kalam influences young minds. *(Change in Passive voice)* **SSC CHSL Tier-1 08.08.2023 (Shift-II)**
(a) Young minds get influenced by Dr. APJ Abdul Kalam.
(b) Young minds were influenced by the speech of Dr. APJ Abdul Kalam.
(c) Young minds are influenced by the speech of Dr. APJ Abdul Kalam.
(d) The speech of Dr. APJ Abdul Kalam is very influencing.
Ans. (c) Refer to Rule 1 (a)

167. The teacher did not allow the students to leave the lecture. *(Change in Passive voice)* **SSC CHSL Tier-1 09.08.2023 (Shift-I)**
(a) The students are not allowed to leave the lecture.
(b) The students had not been allowed to leave the lecture by the teacher.
(c) The students had not allowed the teacher to leave the lecture.
(d) The students were not allowed to leave the lecture by the teacher.
Ans. (d) Refer to Rule 1 (d)

168. The professor assigns the homework every week. *(Change in Passive voice)* **SSC CHSL Tier-1 09.08.2023 (Shift-I)**
(a) The homework is assigning by the professor every week.
(b) The homework will be assigned by the professor every week.
(c) The homework assigns by the professor every week.
(d) The homework is assigned by the professor every week.
Ans. (d) Refer to Rule 1 (a)

169. The company will release the new product next month. *(Change in Passive voice)* **SSC CHSL Tier-1 09.08.2023 (Shift-II)**
(a) The new product will be released by the company next month.
(b) The new product will release by the company next month.
(c) The new product will be releasing by the company next month.
(d) The new product is released by the company next month.
Ans. (a) Refer to Rule 1 (g)

170. Let the book be read by me. *(Change in Active voice)* **SSC CHSL Tier-1 09.08.2023 (Shift-III)**
(a) Let me read the book.
(b) Let me had read the book.
(c) Let me have read the book.
(d) Let me please read the book.
Ans. (a) Refer to Rule 7 (ii)

171. The car was manufactured by the company in a factory overseas. *(Change in Active voice)* **SSC CHSL Tier-1 09.08.2023 (Shift-IV)**
(a) The factory overseas was used by the company to manufacture the car.
(b) The company manufactured the car in a factory overseas.
(c) The car was being manufactured by the company in a factory overseas.
(d) The car was manufactured in a factory overseas by the company.
Ans. (b) Refer to Rule 1 (d)

172. The garment business has made Archie rich. *(Change in Passive voice)* **SSC CHSL Tier-1 09.08.2023 (Shift-IV)**
(a) Archie has been made rich by the garment business.
(b) Archie have been made rich by the garment business.
(c) Archie had been made rich by the garment business.
(d) Archie is made rich by the garment business.
Ans. (a) Refer to Rule 1 (c)

173. The dog was run over by a truck. *(Change in Active voice)* **SSC CHSL Tier-1 10.08.2023 (Shift-I)**
(a) A truck had run over the dog.
(b) A truck runs over the dog.
(c) A truck has run over the dog.
(d) A truck ran over the dog.
Ans. (d) Refer to Rule 1 (d)

174. We hope that we shall win the match against Australia. *(Change in Passive voice)* **SSC CHSL Tier-1 10.08.2023 (Shift-II)**
(a) It is hoped that the match against Australia shall be won by us.
(b) It is expected that the match against Australia should be won by us.
(c) It is hoped that the match against Australia was won by us.
(d) It is sure that the match against Australia was won by us.
Ans. (a) Refer to Rule 1 (g)

175. Why is the rotten apple being eaten by you? *(Change in Passive voice)* **SSC CHSL Tier-1 10.08.2023 (Shift-III)**
(a) Why were you eating the rotten apple?
(b) Why you are eating the rotten apple?
(c) Why have you eaten the rotten apple?
(d) Why are you eating the rotten apple?
Ans. (d) Refer to Rule 5

176. The meeting was called off. *(Change in Active voice)*
SSC CHSL Tier-1 10.08.2023 (Shift-III)
(a) The meeting had been called off.
(b) They called off the meeting.
(c) Someone called off the meeting.
(d) They were calling off the meeting.
Ans. (c) Refer to Rule 1 (d)

177. When will the results of the dance competition be announced? *(Change in Active voice)*
SSC CHSL Tier-1 11.08.2023 (Shift-I)
(a) When will they are announcing the results of the dance competition?
(b) When will they announce the results of the dance competition?
(c) When will they announced the results of the dance competition?
(d) Will they announce the results of the dance competition?
Ans. (b) Refer to Rule 1 (g)

178. Do you obey your elders? *(Change in Passive voice)*
SSC CHSL Tier-1 11.08.2023 (Shift-I)
(a) Are your elders obeyed by you?
(b) Are you obeying by your elders?
(c) Have your elders obeyed by you?
(d) Do your elders obeyed by you?
Ans. (a) Refer to Rule 6

179. Suresh stole my book. *(Change in Passive voice)*
SSC CHSL Tier-1 11.08.2023 (Shift-II)
(a) My book is being stolen by Suresh.
(b) My book got stolen by Suresh.
(c) My book was stolen by Suresh.
(d) My book was being stolen by Suresh.
Ans. (c) Refer to Rule 1 (d)

180. Indian army airlifted thousands of people from Ukraine. *(Change in Passive voice)*
SSC CHSL Tier-1 11.08.2023 (Shift-III)
(a) Thousands of people had been airlifted from Ukraine by the Indian Army.
(b) Thousands of people have been airlifted from Ukraine by the Indian Army.
(c) Thousands of people are airlifted from Ukraine by the Indian Army.
(d) Thousands of people were airlifted from Ukraine by the Indian Army.
Ans. (d) Refer to Rule 1 (d)

181. By whom can the problem be solved? *(Change in Active voice)*
SSC CHSL Tier-1 11.08.2023 (Shift-III)
(a) Whom can solve the problem?
(b) Who can solved the problem?
(c) Whom can solved the problem?
(d) Who can solve the problem?
Ans. (d) Refer to Rule 5

182. The movie was directed by the famous filmmaker and produced by the studio. *(Change in Active voice)*
SSC CHSL Tier-1 11.08.2023 (Shift-IV)
(a) The famous filmmaker directed the movie and the studio produced it.
(b) The movie was being directed by the famous filmmaker and produced by the studio.
(c) The movie was directed and produced by the famous filmmaker and the studio.
(d) The famous filmmaker and the studio collaborated to make the move.
Ans. (a) Refer to Rule 1 (d)

183. The student asked the teacher a question during class. *(Change in Passive voice)*
SSC CHSL Tier-1 14.08.2023 (Shift-I)
(a) A question was asked by the student to the teacher during class.
(b) A question is being asked by the student to the teacher during class.
(c) A question asked by the student to the teacher during class.
(d) A question will be asked by the student to the teacher during class.
Ans. (a) Refer to Rule 1 (d)

184. Would pizza or burger rather be eaten by you? *(Change in Active voice)*
SSC CHSL Tier-1 14.08.2023 (Shift-II)
(a) Would you rather eat pizza or burger?
(b) Would you rather eaten pizza or burger?
(c) Would you rather ate pizza or burger?
(d) Would you eat pizza or burger?
Ans. (a) When such a sentence is transformed into active voice, the structure followed is Subject + V1 + Object.

185. The package was delivered by the courier to the recipient's doorstep. *(Change in Active voice)*
SSC CHSL Tier-1 14.08.2023 (Shift-II)
(a) The recipient received the package delivered by the courier.
(b) The package was being delivered by the courier to the recipient's doorstep.
(c) The courier delivered the package to the recipient's doorstep.
(d) The package was delivered to the recipient's doorstep by the courier.
Ans. (c) Refer to Rule 1 (d)

186. The victim was found innocent as well as honest by the police. *(Change in Active voice)* **SSC CHSL Tier-1 14.08.2023 (Shift-III)**
(a) The police find the victim innocent as well as honest.
(b) The police has found the victim innocent and honest.
(c) The police found the victim innocent as well as honest.
(d) The police finds the victim innocent and honest.
Ans. (c) Refer to Rule 1 (d)

187. The entrance of the museum was opened by the official. *(Change in Active voice)*
SSC CHSL Tier-1 14.08.2023 (Shift-III)
(a) The official opened the entrance of the museum.
(b) The official had opened the entrance of the museum.
(c) The official open the entrance of the museum.
(d) The officials opening the entrance of the museum.
Ans. (a) Refer to Rule 1 (d)

188. The snake was killed by Shyam. *(Change in Active voice)*
SSC CHSL Tier-1 14.08.2023 (Shift-IV)
(a) Shyam killed the snake.
(b) Shyam kills the snake.
(c) Shyam has killed the snake.
(d) Shyam had killed the snake.
Ans. (a) Refer to Rule 1 (d)

189. Let the door be shut. *(Change in Active voice)* SSC CHSL Tier-1 14.08.2023 (Shift-IV)

(a) You are requested to shut the door.
(b) The door should be shut.
(c) Let you shut the door.
(d) Shut the door.

Ans. (d) Refer to Rule 7 (ii)

190. This was talked about in the meeting by the officers. *(Change in Active voice)* SSC CHSL Tier-1 17.08.2023 (Shift-I)

(a) The officers were talking about in the meeting.
(b) The officers talked about this in the meeting.
(c) The officers in the meeting had talked about it.
(d) The officers talk about this in the meeting.

Ans. (b) Refer to Rule 1 (d)

191. The students must complete the assignment by Friday. *(Change in Passive voice)* SSC CHSL Tier-1 17.08.2023 (Shift-I)

(a) The assignment must be completed by the students by Friday.
(b) The assignment will be completed by the students by Friday.
(c) The students will have completed the assignment by Friday.
(d) The assignment must be complete by Friday by the students.

Ans. (a) The sentence is in future tense. When such a sentence is transformed into passive voice, the structure followed is Object + must be + V3 + by + Subject.

192. The letter was written by the author and mailed to the publisher. *(Change in Active voice)* SSC CHSL Tier-1 17.08.2023 (Shift-III)

(a) The letter was written and mailed to the publisher by the author.
(b) The author wrote the letter and mailed it to the publisher.
(c) The publisher received the letter written by the author.
(d) The letter was being written by the author and mailed to the publisher.

Ans. (b) Refer to Rule 1 (d)

193. I was never supported by my family. *(Change in Passive voice)* SSC CHSL Tier-1 17.08.2023 (Shift-IV)

(a) My family have never supported me.
(b) My family had never supported me.
(c) My family never supported me.
(d) My family never supports me.

Ans. (c) Refer to Rule 1 (d)

194. An agitated gathering of workers in the company disturbed the meeting. *(Change in Passive voice)* SSC CHSL Tier-1 17.08.2023 (Shift-IV)

(a) Meeting of the company was disturbed.
(b) An agitated meeting of workers in the company disturbed the gathering.
(c) The meeting was disturbed by an agitated gathering of workers in the company.
(d) The gathering agitated the meeting of the company.

Ans. (c) Refer to Rule 1 (d)

195. Simran was plucking the flowers. *(Change in Passive voice)* SSC CHSL Tier-2 26.06.2023

(a) The flowers are plucked by Simran.
(b) The flowers will be plucked by Simran.
(c) The flowers have been plucked by Simran.
(d) The flowers were being plucked by Simran.

Ans. (d) Refer to Rule 1 (e)

196. The seller shall dispatch the parcel soon to Chennai. *(Change in Passive voice)* SSC CHSL Tier-2 26.06.2023

(a) The parcel will be dispatched soon to Chennai by the seller
(b) The parcel must be dispatched by the seller to Chennai soon
(c) The parcel might be dispatched by the seller to Chennai soon.
(d) The parcel can be dispatched by the seller to Chennai soon.

Ans. (a) Refer to Rule 1 (g)

197. He is eating an apple. *(Change in Passive voice)* SSC CHSL Tier-2 02.11.2023 (Shift-I)

(a) He has been eating an apple.
(b) An apple was eaten by him.
(c) He was eating an apple.
(d) An apple is being eaten by him.

Ans. (d) Refer to Rule 1 (b)

198. The team won the tournament after weeks of hard work and commitment. *(Change in Passive voice)* SSC CHSL Tier-2 02.11.2023 (Shift-I)

(a) The tournament was won by the team after weeks of hard work and commitment.
(b) The tournament was being won by the team after weeks of hard work and commitment.
(c) The tournament was winning by the team after weeks of hard work and commitment.
(d) The tournament had been won by the team after weeks of hard work and commitment.

Ans. (a) Refer to Rule 1 (d)

199. The rescue team could have completed the task if there had been uninterrupted power supply. *(Change in Passive voice)* SSC CHSL Tier-2 02.11.2023 (Shift-I)

(a) The task can have completed by the rescue team if there was uninterrupted power supply.
(b) The task could be completed by the rescue team if there was uninterrupted power supply.
(c) The task could have to be completed by the rescue team if there was uninterrupted power supply.
(d) The task could have been completed by the rescue team if there had been uninterrupted power supply.

Ans. (d) Refer to Rule 1 (c)

200. The most recent studies on the human body are likely to alter the face of health sciences. *(Change in Passive voice)* SSC CHSL Tier-1 25.05.2022 (Shift-I)

(a) The most recent studies on the human body are likely to be altered by the face of health sciences.
(b) The face of health sciences will be altering the mot recent studies on the human body
(c) The face of health sciences is likely to be altered by the most recent studies on the human body.
(d) The most face of health sciences is likely to alter the recent studies on the human body.

Ans. (c) Refer to Rule 1 (a)

201. Has the assignment been uploaded by you? *(Change in Active voice)* SSC CHSL Tier-1 25.05.2022 (Shift-II)

(a) Have you been uploaded the assignment?
(b) Have you uploaded the assignment?
(c) Did you upload the assignment?
(d) Were you uploading the assignment?

Ans. (b) Refer to Rule 6

202. The incident was narrated by somebody to Naresh. *(Change in Active voice)* **SSC CHSL Tier-1 26.05.2022 (Shift-I)**
(a) Somebody was narrating the incident to Naresh.
(b) Somebody narrated the incident to Naresh.
(c) Somebody was about to narrate the incident to Naresh.
(d) Somebody will narrate the incident to Naresh.

Ans. (b) Refer to Rule 1 (d)

203. The new bride is going to be admired by everyone in the family. *(Change in Active voice)* **SSC CHSL Tier-1 26.05.2022 (Shift-III)**
(a) Everybody in the family is going to admire the new bride.
(b) Everybody in the family was admiring the new bride.
(c) Everybody in the family has been going to admire the new bride.
(d) Everybody in the family was going to admire the new bride.

Ans. (a) The sentence is in future continuous tense. When such a sentence is transformed into active voice, the structure followed is Subject + is/am/are going to + V1 + Object.

204. Admittance was refused to him by the airport security. *(Change in Active voice)* **SSC CHSL Tier-1 26.05.2022 (Shift-III)**
(a) The airport security is refusing him admittance.
(b) The airport security has refused him admittance.
(c) The airport security has refused him admittance.
(d) The airport security refused him admittance.

Ans. (d) Refer to Rule 1 (d)

205. Four grams of sodium chloride was added to the mixture by the research team. *(Change in Active voice)* **SSC CHSL Tier-1 27.05.2022 (Shift-III)**
(a) The research team added the mixture to four grams of sodium chloride.
(b) Four grams of sodium chloride added the mixture to the research team.
(c) The research team added four grams of sodium chloride to the mixture.
(d) The mixture added four grams of sodium chloride to the research team.

Ans. (c) Refer to Rule 1 (d)

206. All the electric poles in the suburbs were destroyed by the cyclone last year. *(Change in Active voice)* **SSC CHSL Tier-1 30.05.2022 (Shift-II)**
(a) The cyclone destroyed all the electric poles in the suburbs last year.
(b) The cyclone was being destroyed with all the electric poles in the suburbs last year.
(c) The cyclone was destroyed by all the electric poles in the suburbs last year.
(d) The cyclone destroyed all the suburbs by the electric poles last year.

Ans. (a) Refer to Rule 1 (d)

207. The car was being washed by me. *(Change in Active voice)* **SSC CHSL Tier-1 30.05.2022 (Shift-I)**
(a) I had been washing the car. (b) I was washing the car.
(c) I did the washing car. (d) I washed the car.

Ans. (b) Refer to Rule 1 (e)

208. The utensils have been cleaned. *(Change in Active voice)* **SSC CHSL Tier-1 30.05.2022 (Shift-I)**
(a) Someone is cleaning the utensils.
(b) Someone was cleaning the utensils.
(c) Someone cleaned the utensils.
(d) Someone has cleaned the utensils.

Ans. (d) Refer to Rule 1 (c)

209. This match is being watched today by more than thirty-three million people worldwide. *(Change in Active voice)* **SSC CHSL Tier-1 31.05.2022 (Shift-I)**
(a) This match is watching more than thirty-three million people worldwide today.
(b) More than thirty-three million people worldwide have been watching this match today.
(c) More than thirty-three million people worldwide are watching this match today.
(d) Today more than thirty-three million people worldwide have watched this match.

Ans. (c) Refer to Rule 1 (b)

210. The Finance Minister will announce the budget. *(Change in Passive voice)* **SSC CHSL Tier-1 31.05.2022 (Shift-I)**
(a) The budget will have announced by the Finance Minister.
(b) The budget were announced by the Finance Minister.
(c) The budget are announced by the Finance Minister.
(d) The budget will be announced by the Finance Minister.

Ans. (d) Refer to Rule 1 (g)

211. Our team has been defeated. *(Change in Active voice)* **SSC CHSL Tier-1 01.06.2022 (Shift-I)**
(a) Our team defeated the opposition.
(b) The opposition had been defeated by our team.
(c) The opposition defeated our team.
(d) The opposition has defeated our team.

Ans. (d) Refer to Rule 1 (c)

212. I laughed at the clown. *(Change in Passive voice)* **SSC CHSL Tier-1 01.06.2022 (Shift-I)**
(a) The clown was laughed at by me.
(b) The clown was being laughed by me.
(c) The clown is being laughed at by me.
(d) The clown is laughed by me.

Ans. (a) Refer to Rule 1 (d)

213. The door was opened by the children for their father. *(Change in Active voice)* **SSC CHSL Tier-1 02.06.2022 (Shift-I)**
(a) The children was opened the door for their father.
(b) The children are opens the door for their father.
(c) The children opened the door for their father.
(d) The children opens the door for their father.

Ans. (c) Refer to Rule 1 (d)

214. I am going to ask all employees about the incident that took place in the canteen yesterday. *(Change in Passive voice)* **SSC CHSL Tier-1 02.06.2022 (Shift-I)**
(a) All the employees are gone to be asked about the incident that took place in the canteen yesterday.
(b) All the employees are going to be asked about the incident that took place in the canteen yesterday.
(c) All the employees are asked by me about the incident that took place in the canteen yesterday.
(d) All the employees will go to be questioned by me about the incident that took place in the canteen yesterday.

Ans. (b) Refer to Rule 1 (b)

215. As was customary, the young prince was brought to the podium in a diamond studded carriage for the coronation ceremony. *(Change in Active voice)* **SSC CHSL Tier-1 03.06.2022 (Shift-II)**
(a) As was customary, the young prince brings himself to the podium in a diamond studded carriage for the coronation ceremony.

(b) As was customary, the young prince is bought to the podium in a diamond studded carriage for the coronation ceremony.
(c) As was customary, the young prince brought in a diamond studded carriage to the podium for the coronation ceremony.
(d) As was customary, the palace staff brought the young prince to the podium in a diamond studded carriage for the coronation ceremony.

Ans. (d) Refer to Rule 1 (d)

216. He ordered the police to pursue the robber and his gang. *(Change in Passive voice)* **SSC CHSL Tier-1 06.06.2022 (Shift-III)**
(a) Order the police to pursue the robber gang.
(b) Pursue the robber and gang were the orders by police.
(c) The robber and gang were pursued.
(d) The police were ordered to pursue the robber and his gang.

Ans. (d) Refer to Rule 1 (d)

217. The national anthem was being sung very enthusiastically by young students in the annual event. *(Change in Active voice)* **SSC CHSL Tier-1 06.06.2022 (Shift-III)**
(a) The young students in the annual event were singing the national anthem very enthusiastically.
(b) The national anthem was sung very enthusiastically for young students in the annual event.
(c) The young students in the annual event had been singing the national anthem very enthusiastically.
(d) The national anthem sang the young students very enthusiastically.

Ans. (a) Refer to Rule 1 (e)

218. They propose to build a dam for irrigation purposes. *(Change in Passive voice)* **SSC CHSL Tier-1 07.06.2022 (Shift-I)**
(a) Build a dam for irrigation purposes.
(b) For the irrigation purposes a dam has been built.
(c) Irrigation dam is built.
(d) It is proposed to build a dam for irrigation purposes.

Ans. (d) Refer to Rule 1 (a)

219. Usnis has not used the computer for weeks. *(Change in Passive voice)* **SSC CHSL Tier-1 09.06.2022 (Shift-I)**
(a) The computer did not used by Usnis for weeks.
(b) The computer has not been used by Usnis for weeks.
(c) The computer was not been used by Usnis for weeks.
(d) The computer has not being used by Usnis for weeks.

Ans. (b) Refer to Rule 1 (c)

220. A new policy for peace and tolerance was formulated by the member nations in the Universal Council meeting yesterday. *(Change in Passive voice)* **SSC CHSL Tier-1 09.06.2022 (Shift-I)**
(a) The member nations formulated a new policy for peace and tolerance in the Universal Council meeting yesterday.
(b) The member nations in the Universal Council meeting yesterday were formulated a new policy for peace and tolerance.
(c) The member nations in the Universal Council meeting yesterday were formulating a new policy for peace and tolerance.
(d) A new policy formulated the member nations in the Universal Council meeting yesterday for peace and tolerance.

Ans. (a) Refer to Rule 1 (d)

221. The disaster management team rescued the flood victims. *(Change in Passive voice)* **SSC CHSL Tier-1 12.04.2021 (Shift-II)**
(a) The flood victims are being rescued by the disaster management team.
(b) The flood victims have been rescued by the disaster management team.
(c) The flood victims were rescued by the disaster management team.
(d) The flood victims are rescued by the disaster management team.

Ans. (c) Refer to Rule 1 (d)

222. Teachers should cover all the topics in the syllabus. *(Change in Passive voice)* **SSC CHSL Tier-1 19.04.2021 (Shift-III)**
(a) All the topics in the syllabus should be covered by teachers.
(b) Teachers should be covered the syllabus in all the topics.
(c) Teachers should be covered all the topics in the syllabus.
(d) All the topics in the syllabus should cover teachers.

Ans. (a) When such a sentence is transformed into passive voice, the structure followed is Object + should be + V3 + by + Subject.

223. The Central Board to Secondary Education has launched a new helpline for students. *(Change in Passive voice)* **SSC CHSL Tier-1 04.08.2021 (Shift-I)**
(a) A new helpline for students is launched by the Central Board of Secondary Education.
(b) A new helpline for students will be launched by the Central Board of Secondary Education.
(c) A new helpline for students had been launched by the Central Board of Secondary Education.
(d) A new helpline for students has been launched by the Central Board of Secondary Education.

Ans. (d) Refer to Rule 1 (c)

SSC Selection Post 2024

224. The animals were frightened by the noise. *(Change in Active voice)* **SSC SP 20.06.2024**
(a) The noise had frightened the animals.
(b) The animals frightened the noise.
(c) The noise frightened the animal.
(d) The noise frightened the animals.

Ans. (d) Refer to Rule 1 (d)

225. English will be taught by Mr. Jha. *(Change in Active voice)* **SSC SP 20.06.2024**
(a) Mr. Jha would teach English.
(b) English would be taught by Mr. Jha.
(c) Mr. Jha will teach English.
(d) Mr. Jha teaches English.

Ans. (c) Refer to Rule 1 (g)

226. Jim will translate it. *(Change in Passive voice)* **SSC SP 20.06.2024 (Shift-II)**
(a) It will be translate by Jim.
(b) It will be translated by Jim.
(c) It would translate by Jim.
(d) It is translated by Jim.

Ans. (b) Refer to Rule 1 (g)

227. About 200 birds were driven out of their habitats by the City Council based on a Health Department recommendation. *(Change in Active voice)* **SSC SP 20.06.2024 (Shift-II)**
(a) A Health Department recommendation was the basis for the City Council to drive out 200 birds from their habitats.
(b) The City Council drove about 200 birds out of their habitats, based on a Health Department recommendation.
(c) About 200 birds is driven out of their habitats based on a Health Department recommendation.
(d) The City Council has driven about 200 birds out of their habitats based on a Health Department recommendation.
Ans. (b) Refer to Rule 1 (d)

228. The novel was being read by many people. *(Change in Active voice)* **SSC SP 20.06.2024 (Shift-II)**
(a) The novel was read by many people.
(b) Many people were reading the novel.
(c) The novel is being read by many people.
(d) Many people had read the novel
Ans. (b) Refer to Rule 1 (d)

229. The police is interrogating the peons of my school. *(Change in Passive voice)* **SSC SP 20.06.2024 (Shift-IV)**
(a) The peons of my school are being interrogated by the police.
(b) The peons of my school has been being interrogated by the police.
(c) The peons of my school have been being interrogated by the police.
(d) The peons of my school were being interrogated by the police.
Ans. (a) Refer to Rule 1 (b)

SSC Selection Post 2023

230. The storm destroyed the entire village. *(Change in Passive voice)* **SSC SP 27.06.2023 (Shift-IV)**
(a) The entire village was destroyed by the storm.
(b) The storm was destroying the entire village.
(c) The village was being destroyed entirely by the storm.
(d) The village was entirely destroyed by the storm.
Ans. (a) Refer to Rule 1 (d)

231. He ordered the police to pursue the robber and his gang. *(Change in Passive voice)* **SSC SP 27.06.2023 (Shift-IV)**
(a) The police were ordered to pursue the robber and his gang.
(b) Order the police to pursue the robber gang.
(c) Pursue the robber and gang were the orders by police.
(d) The robber and gang were pursued.
Ans. (a) Refer to Rule 1 (d)

232. The manager was being scolded by Rishikesh. *(Change in Active voice)* **SSC SP 27.06.2023 (Shift-I)**
(a) Rishikesh was scolding the manager.
(b) Rishikesh scolded the manager.
(c) Rishikesh has been scolding the manager.
(d) Rishikesh will be scolding the manager.
Ans. (a) Refer to Rule 1 (e)

SSC Selection Post 2022

233. My brother was being laughed at by them. *(Change in Active voice)* **SSC SP 01.08.2022**
(a) They were laughing at my brother.
(b) They had been laughing at my brother.
(c) They have been laughing at my brother.
(d) They laughed at my brother.
Ans. (a) Refer to Rule 1 (e)

234. People say that she is a kind lady. *(Change in Passive voice)* **SSC SP 01.08.2022**
(a) It is claimed people that she is a kind lady.
(b) It is said that she is a kind lady.
(c) It was said that she is a kind lady.
(d) It is said by people that she is a kind lady.
Ans. (b) When such a sentence is transformed into passive voice, the structure followed is It + is + V3 + that + Subject + V1 + Object

235. Are fossil fuels not impacting human heart? *(Change in Passive voice)* **SSC SP 01.08.2022**
(a) Did human health not being impacted by fossil fuel?
(b) Was human health not being impacted by fossil fuel?
(c) Is human health not impacted by fossil fuel?
(d) Is human health not being impacted by fossil fuel?
Ans. (d) Refer to Rule 6

236. You can take one casual leave per month. *(Change in Passive voice)* **SSC SP 01.08.2022**
(a) One casual leave per month will be taken.
(b) One casual leave per month could be taken.
(c) One casual leave per month is to be taken.
(d) One casual leave per month can be taken.
Ans. (d) When such a sentence is transformed into passive voice, the structure followed is Object + can be + V3 + by + Subject.

237. She will be wearing a pink dress to the wedding. *(Change in Passive voice)* **SSC SP 03.08.2022 (Shift-III)**
(a) A pink dress will be wear by her to the wedding.
(b) A pink dress will be worn by her at the wedding.
(c) A pink dress would be worn by her at the wedding.
(d) A pink dress would be worn by her to the wedding.
Ans. (b) Refer to Rule 1 (g)

238. Why would Celia burn the letter? *(Change in Passive voice)* **SSC SP 04.08.2022 (Shift-III)**
(a) Why is the letter burned by Celia?
(b) Why the letter burned by Celia?
(c) Why Celia would burn the letter?
(d) Why would the letter be burned by Celia?
Ans. (d) Refer to Rule 5

239. My father had to attend the meeting on Saturday. *(Change in Passive voice)* **SSC SP 05.08.2022 (Shift-III)**
(a) The meeting had been attended by my father on Saturday.
(b) The meeting has to be attended by my father on Saturday.
(c) The meeting had been to be attended by my father on Saturday.
(d) The meeting had to be attended by my father on Saturday.
Ans. (d) When such a sentence is transformed into passive voice, the structure followed is Object + had to be + V3 + by + Subject.

240. People say that she is a kind lady. *(Change in Passive voice)* **SSC SP 01.08.2022 (Shift-III)**
(a) It is said by people that she is a kind lady.
(b) It is said that she is a kind lady.
(c) It is claimed people that she is a kind lady.
(d) It was said that she is a kind lady.
Ans. (b) When such a sentence is transformed into passive voice, the structure followed is It + is + V3 + that + Subject + V1 + Object.

241. The author was writing the novel when the house caught fire. *(Change in Passive voice)* **SSC SP 05.08.2022 (Shift-I)**
(a) The novel has been written by the author when the house caught fire.
(b) The novel was being written by the author when the house caught fire.
(c) The novel was written by the author when the house caught fire.
(d) The novel had been written by the author when the house caught fire.
Ans. (b) Refer to Rule 1 (e)

SSC Steno 2024

242. These toys were made by my uncle. *(Change in Active voice)* **SSC Steno 11.12.2024 (Shift-I)**
(a) My uncle was making these toys.
(b) My uncle made these toys.
(c) My uncles have made these toys.
(d) My uncle had made these toys.
Ans. (b) Refer to Rule 1 (d)

243. Lee is humming a soothing tune for the masses. *(Change in Passive voice)* **SSC Steno 11.12.2024 (Shift-I)**
(a) A soothing tune has been hummed by Lee for the masses.
(b) A soothing tune had been hummed for the masses by Lee.
(c) A soothing tune was being humming by Lee for the masses.
(d) A soothing tune is being hummed for the masses by Lee.
Ans. (d) Refer to Rule 1 (b)

244. The job work had been learnt by me. *(Change in Active voice)* **SSC Steno 11.12.2024 (Shift-I)**
(a) I have learnt the job work. (b) I will learn the job work.
(c) I would learn the job work. (d) I had learnt the job work.
Ans. (d) Refer to Rule 1 (f)

245. I am upset because my cell phone has been stolen. *(Change in Active voice)* **SSC Steno 11.12.2024 (Shift-I)**
(a) I was upset because they have stolen my cell phone.
(b) I am upset because someone has stolen my cell phone.
(c) I am upset because someone has been stealing my cell phone.
(d) I have been upset because an unknown person has stolen my cell phone.
Ans. (b) 'I am upset because my cell phone has been stolen' in active voice becomes 'I am upset because someone has stolen my cell phone.' The active voice clarifies the subject (someone) performing the action (has stolen).

246. The door was opened by Samira when the fire was reported by Mithali. *(Change in Active voice)* **SSC Steno 11.12.2024 (Shift-I)**
(a) When Mithali reports the fire, Samira opened the door.
(b) Samira opened the door when the fire was being reported by Mithali.
(c) Samira opened the door and Mithali reported the fire.
(d) Samira opened the door when Mithali reported the fire.
Ans. (d) Refer to Rule 1 (d)

247. Jaundice is caused by drinking contaminated water. *(Change in Active voice)* **SSC Steno 11.12.2024 (Shift-I)**
(a) Drinking contaminated water caused jaundice.
(b) Drinking contaminated water can cause jaundice
(c) Drinking contaminated water has caused jaundice.
(d) Drinking contaminated water causes jaundice.
Ans. (d) Refer to Rule 1 (a)

248. Mrs. Leela opened the window. *(Change in Passive voice)* **SSC Steno 11.12.2024 (Shift-I)**
(a) The window was being opened by Mrs. Leela.
(b) The window is opened by Mrs. Leela.
(c) The window was opened by Mrs. Leela.
(d) The window is being opened by Mrs. Leela.
Ans. (c) Refer to Rule 1 (d)

249. You must send applications to the university before 30th December. *(Change in Passive voice)* **SSC Steno 11.12.2024 (Shift-I)**
(a) Applications has to be sent to the university before 30th December.
(b) Applications were to be sent to the university before 30th December.
(c) Applications must be sent to the university before 30th December.
(d) Applications are to be sent to the university before 30th December
Ans. (c) Refer to Rule 4

250. How was it written by Pragya? *(Change in Active voice)* **SSC Steno 11.12.2024 (Shift-I)**
(a) How has Pragya written it?
(b) How did Pragya write it?
(c) How does Pragya write it?
(d) How will Pragya write it?
Ans. (b) Refer to Rule 5

251. Mr. Thomas helps Mr. Anil. *(Change in Passive voice)* **SSC Steno 11.12.2024 (Shift-I)**
(a) Mr. Anil is helped by Mr. Thomas.
(b) Mr. Anil was helped by Mr. Thomas.
(c) Mr. Anil was being helped by Mr. Thomas.
(d) Mr. Anil is being helped by Mr. Thomas.
Ans. (a) Refer to Rule 1 (a)

252. The function hall has been decorated attractively by the boys. *(Change in Active voice)* **SSC Steno 11.12.2024 (Shift-I)**
(a) The boys attractively decorated the function hall.
(b) The boys will decorate the function hall attractively.
(c) The boys have decorated the function hall attractively.
(d) The boys had decorated the function hall attractively.
Ans. (c) Refer to Rule 1 (c)

253. He must be written to by us. *(Change in Active voice)* **SSC Steno 11.12.2024 (Shift-II)**
(a) We can write. (b) We must write to him.
(c) We are writing to him. (d) I have been writing to him.
Ans. (b) Refer to Rule 4

254. When is this car driven by you? *(Change in Active voice)* **SSC Steno 11.12.2024 (Shift-II)**
(a) When will you drive this car?
(b) When should you drive this car?
(c) When did you drive this car?
(d) When do you drive this car?
Ans. (d) Refer to Rule 5

255. The experiment is being completed by the whole class. *(Change in Active voice)* **SSC Steno 11.12.2024 (Shift-II)**
(a) The whole class has completed the experiment.
(b) The whole class completes the experiment.
(c) The whole class has been completing experiment.
(d) The whole class is completing the experiment.
Ans. (d) Refer to Rule 1 (b)

256. When will you play the musical instrument in the event? *(Change in Passive voice)* **SSC Steno 11.12.2024 (Shift-II)**
(a) When was the music instrument played by you in the event?
(b) When will the music instrument be played in the event?
(c) When will the music instrument be played by you in the event?
(d) When should the music instrument be played by you in the event?
Ans. (c) Refer to Rule 5

257. Mr. Suman opened the door. *(Change in Passive voice)* **SSC Steno 11.12.2024 (Shift-II)**
(a) The door was being opened by Mr. Suman.
(b) The door was opened by Mr. Suman.
(c) The door is opened by Mr. Suman.
(d) The door is being opened by Mr. Suman.
Ans. (b) Refer to Rule 1 (d)

258. People think the government will change the economic policies. *(Change in Passive voice)* **SSC Steno 11.12.2024 (Shift-II)**
(a) People thought that the government will change the economic policies.
(b) The government will think to change the economic policies.
(c) The government has been thinking to change the economic policies.
(d) It is thought that the economic policies will be changed by the government.
Ans. (d) Refer to Rule 1 (g)

259. The questions were framed by the content creators just to assess the skills of the test takers. *(Change in Active voice)* **SSC Steno 11.12.2024 (Shift-II)**
(a) The content creators framed the questions just to assess the skills of the test takers.
(b) The content creators had framed the questions just to assess the skills of the test takers.
(c) The content creators were framing the questions just to assess the skills of the test takers.
(d) The content creators could frame the questions just to assess the skills of the test takers.
Ans. (a) Refer to Rule 1 (d)

260. Somebody paid the workers 2000 rupees. *(Change in Passive voice)* **SSC Steno 11.12.2024 (Shift-II)**
(a) The workers were paid 2000 rupees.
(b) The workers were being paid 2000 rupees.
(c) 2000 rupees has been paid to the workers.
(d) 2000 rupees is paid to the worker
Ans. (b) Refer to Rule 1 (d)

261. The letter had been posted by me before I met him. *(Change in Active voice)* **SSC Steno 11.12.2024 (Shift-II)**
(a) I had posted the letter before I met him.
(b) I had posted the letter after meeting him.
(c) The letter has been posted by me before I had met him.
(d) I met him after posting the letter.
Ans. (a) Refer to Rule 1 (f)

262. I shared a clipping of myself dead-lifting and doing back squats. *(Change in Passive voice)* **SSC Steno 11.12.2024 (Shift-II)**
(a) A clipping of myself doing dead-lifting and back squats is shared by me.
(b) A clipping of myself doing dead-lifting and back squats are being shared by me.
(c) A clipping of myself doing dead-lifting and back squats was shared by me.
(d) Dead-lifting and back squats are being done by myself.
Ans. (a) Refer to Rule 1 (a)

263. Stones were thrown at the dog. *(Change in Active voice)* **SSC Steno 11.12.2024 (Shift-II)**
(a) They had been throwing stones at the dog.
(b) They throw stones at the dog.
(c) They were throwing stones at the dog.
(d) They threw stones at the dog.
Ans. (d) Refer to Rule 1 (d)

264. Leo Tolstoy wrote many stories for children. *(Change in Passive voice)* **SSC Steno 11.12.2024 (Shift-II)**
(a) Many stories were written by children for Leo Tolstoy.
(b) Many stories were written for children by Leo Tolstoy.
(c) Many stories have been written for children by Leo Tolstoy.
(d) Many children wrote stories for Leo Tolstoy.
Ans. (b) Refer to Rule 1 (d)

265. The couple was trolled by everyone. *(Change in Active voice)* **SSC Steno 11.12.2024 (Shift-III)**
(a) Everyone had trolled the couple.
(b) Everyone trolled the couple.
(c) Everyone trolls the couple.
(d) The social media trolled the couple.
Ans. (b) Refer to Rule 1 (d)

266. Srikar had been promised good support by Mahitha. *(Change in Active voice)* **SSC Steno 11.12.2024 (Shift-III)**
(a) Mahitha will have promised Srikar good support.
(b) Mahitha has promised Srikar good support.
(c) Mahitha had promised good support to Srikar.
(d) Mahitha promises good support to Srikar.
Ans. (c) Refer to Rule 1 (f)

267. How did you pay the bill? *(Change voice)* **SSC Steno 11.12.2024 (Shift-III)**
(a) How is the bill paid by you?
(b) How the bill is to be paid by you?
(c) How the bill has been paid by you?
(d) How was the bill paid by you?
Ans. (d) Refer to Rule 5

268. Do not mind Hari's insulting words. *(Change in Passive voice)* **SSC Steno 11.12.2024 (Shift-III)**
(a) Let Hari's insulted words be minded.
(b) Let not Hari's insulting words be minded.
(c) Let's don't mind Hari's insulting words.
(d) Let Hari not mind the insulting words.
Ans. (b) Refer to Rule 7 (ii)

269. These days most of the researchers conduct research with the help of internet. *(Change in Passive voice)* **SSC Steno 11.12.2024 (Shift-III)**
(a) These days the research is conducted with the help of internet by most of the researchers.
(b) These days most of the researchers are conducting their research with the help of internet.
(c) These days most of the research is being done with the help of internet.
(d) These days the research has been done with the help of internet by most of the researchers.
Ans. (a) Refer to Rule 1 (a)

270. The interviewers were asking difficult questions. *(Change in Passive voice)* **SSC Steno 11.12.2024 (Shift-III)**
(a) Difficult questions are being asked by the interviewers.
(b) Difficult questions are asked by the interviewers.
(c) Difficult questions were asked by the interviewers.
(d) Difficult questions were being asked by the interviewers.
Ans. (d) Refer to Rule 1 (e)

271. Are they watching the programmes? *(Change in Passive voice)* **SSC Steno 11.12.2024 (Shift-III)**
(a) Are the programmes being watched by them?
(b) Have the programmes been watched by them?
(c) Had the programmes been watched by them?
(d) Were the programmes being watched by them?
Ans. (a) Refer to Rule 6

272. The helper threw the trash in the dustbin. *(Change in Passive voice)* **SSC Steno 11.12.2024 (Shift-III)**
(a) The trash has been thrown in the dustbin by the helper.
(b) The trash is thrown in the dustbin by the helper.
(c) The trash had been thrown in the dustbin by the helper.
(d) The trash was thrown in the dustbin by the helper.
Ans. (d) Refer to Rule 1 (d)

273. Mrs. Sandhaya teaches us English. *(Change in Passive voice)* **SSC Steno 11.12.2024 (Shift-III)**
(a) English is taught to us by Mrs. Sandhaya.
(b) English has been taught to us by Mrs. Sandhaya.
(c) English was being taught to us by Mrs. Sandhaya.
(d) English is being taught to us by Mrs. Sandhaya.
Ans. (a) Refer to Rule 1 (a)

274. Mr. Varun had answered all the questions. *(Change in Passive voice)* **SSC Steno 11.12.2024 (Shift-III)**
(a) All the questions had been answered by Mr. Varun.
(b) All the questions have been answered by Mr. Varun.
(c) All the questions are answered by Mr. Varun.
(d) All the questions were answered by Mr. Varun.
Ans. (a) Refer to Rule 1 (f)

275. Who is making such a loud noise? *(Change in Passive voice)* **SSC Steno 11.12.2024 (Shift-III)**
(a) By whom is such a loud noise being made?
(b) By whom has such a loud noise been made?
(c) By whom is such loud noise made?
(d) By whom was such loud noise being made?
Ans. (a) Refer to Rule 5

276. The telephone was invented by Graham Bell in the second half of the 18th Century. *(Change in Active voice)* **SSC Steno 11.12.2024 (Shift-III)**
(a) Graham Bell has invented the telephone in the second half of the 18th Century.
(b) Graham Bell invents the telephone in the second half of the 18th Century.
(c) Graham Bell invented the telephone in the second half of the 18th Century.
(d) Graham Bell will have invented the telephone in the second half of the 18th Century.
Ans. (c) Refer to Rule 1 (d)

277. Who took Bruno for a walk? *(Change in Passive voice)* **SSC Steno 10.12.2024 (Shift-I)**
(a) With whom Bruno is taken for a walk?
(b) By whom was Bruno taken for a walk?
(c) By whom will Bruno be taken for a walk?
(d) By whom has Bruno been taken for a walk?
Ans. (b) Refer to Rule 5

278. The FIFA Cup 2022 will be won by France. *(Change in Active voice)* **SSC Steno 10.12.2024 (Shift-I)**
(a) France wins the FIFA Cup 2022
(b) France would win the FIFA Cup 2022
(c) France will win the FIFA Cup 2022
(d) France will be winning the FIFA Cup 2022
Ans. (c) Refer to Rule 1 (g)

279. She is doing the homework. *(Change in Passive voice)* **SSC Steno 10.12.2024 (Shift-I)**
(a) The homework was done by her.
(b) The homework was being done by her.
(c) The homework has been done by her.
(d) The homework is being done by her.
Ans. (d) Refer to Rule 1 (b)

280. Malathi loves Reena. *(Change in Passive voice)* **SSC Steno 10.12.2024 (Shift-I)**
(a) Reena was loved by Malathi.
(b) Reena is loved by Malathi.
(c) Reena was being loved by Malathi.
(d) Reena is being loved by Malathi.
Ans. (b) Refer to Rule 1 (a)

281. The wounded woman was being helped by some youngsters. *(Change in Active voice)* **SSC Steno 10.12.2024 (Shift-I)**
(a) Some youngsters have helped the wounded woman.
(b) Some youngsters helped the wounded woman.
(c) The woman found help by some youngsters.
(d) Some youngsters were helping the wounded woman.
Ans. (d) Refer to Rule 1 (e)

282. Devotional songs are sung superbly by Sastri. *(Change in active voice)* **SSC Steno 10.12.2024 (Shift-I)**
(a) Sastri sings devotional songs superbly.
(b) Sastri is singing devotional songs superbly.
(c) Sastri has been singing devotional songs superbly.
(d) Sastri has superbly sung devotional songs.
Ans. (a) Refer to Rule 1 (a)

283. A selected group of activists had been invited by the minister before the announcement of the strike. *(Change in Active voice)* **SSC Steno 10.12.2024 (Shift-I)**
(a) The minister had been inviting a selected group of activists before the announcement of the strike.
(b) The minister had invited a selected group of activists before the announcement of the strike.
(c) The minister invited a selected group of activists before the announcement of the strike.
(d) The minister was inviting a selected group of activists before the announcement of the strike.
Ans. (b) Refer to Rule 1 (f)

284. I am not forced to study hard by my parents. *(Change in Active voice)* **SSC Steno 10.12.2024 (Shift-I)**
(a) My parents did not force me to study hard.
(b) My parents will not force me to study hard.
(c) My parents do not force me to study hard.
(d) My parents are not forcing me to study hard.
Ans. (c) Refer to Rule 1 (a)

285. Some students are known to grow wise early. *(Change in Active voice)* **SSC Steno 10.12.2024 (Shift-I)**
(a) Some students have been knowing that they grow wise early.
(b) People know that some students grow wise early.
(c) Few of us know that students grow early.
(d) We all know that students grew wise early.
Ans. (b) Refer to Rule 1 (a)

286. It is time to have tea. *(Change in passive voice)*
SSC Steno 10.12.2024 (Shift-I)
(a) Tea is to be taken by it.
(b) Tea is to be had.
(c) Time must be taken to prepare tea.
(d) It is time for tea to be had.

Ans. (d) The sentence 'It is time to have tea' in passive voice is 'It is time for tea to be had'.

287. The cake was baked by the chef in the kitchen. *(Change in Active voice)*
SSC Steno 10.12.2024 (Shift-I)
(a) The chef baked the cake in the kitchen.
(b) The kitchen was baking the cake by the chef.
(c) The cake is being baked by the chef in the kitchen.
(d) The cake was being baked by the chef in the kitchen.

Ans. (a) Refer to Rule 1 (d)

288. Parents should be respected by their children. *(Change in Active voice)*
SSC Steno 10.12.2024 (Shift-I)
(a) Children are to respect their parents.
(b) Children shall be respecting their parents.
(c) Children should respect their parents.
(d) Children should be respecting their parents

Ans. (c) Refer to Rule 1 (d)

289. The shopkeeper lifted the shutter to open his shop. *(Change in Passive voice)*
SSC Steno 10.12.2024 (Shift-II)
(a) To open his shop, the shutter is lifted by the shopkeeper.
(b) The shutter is being lifted by the shopkeeper to open his shop.
(c) The shutter will be lifted by the shopkeeper to open his shop.
(d) The shutter was lifted by the shopkeeper to open his shop.

Ans. (d) Refer to Rule 1 (d)

290. Were you laughing at the poor masses? *(Change in Passive voice)*
SSC Steno 10.12.2024 (Shift-II)
(a) Are the poor masses being laughed at by you?
(b) Have the poor masses been laughed at by you?
(c) Were the poor masses being laughed at by you?
(d) Had the masses been laughed at by you?

Ans. (c) Refer to Rule 6

291. The interference of the police force would have controlled the situation. *(Change in Passive voice)*
SSC Steno 10.12.2024 (Shift-II)
(a) The situation would have been controlled by the interference of the police force.
(b) The situation could be controlled by the interference of the police force.
(c) The situation could have been controlled by the interference of the police force.
(d) The situation would be controlled by the interference of the police force.

Ans. (a) Refer to Rule 1 (h)

292. We have reorganised the department over the last year. *(Change in passive voice)*
SSC Steno 10.12.2024 (Shift-II)
(a) Last year, the department was reorganised.
(b) The department is being reorganised over the last year.
(c) The department is reorganised by me.
(d) The department has been reorganised over the last year

Ans. (d) Refer to Rule 1 (c)

293. They will have to pull down this building as they have not complied with the building regulations of the city. *(Change in passive voice)*
SSC Steno 10.12.2024 (Shift-II)
(a) This building is to be pulled down by them as the building regulations of the city have not been complied with by them.
(b) This building will have to be pulled down by them as the building regulations of the city have not been complied with.
(c) This building will be pulled down as the building regulations of the city have not been complied with by them.
(d) This building needs to be pulled down by them as the building regulations of the city have not been complied with.

Ans. (b) Refer to Rule 1 (g)

294. Suma is making tea. *(Change in Passive voice)*
SSC Steno 10.12.2024 (Shift-II)
(a) Tea is being made by Suma.
(b) Tea was made by Suma.
(c) Tea was being made by Suma.
(d) Tea has been made by Suma.

Ans. (a) Refer to Rule 1 (b)

295. Let the door be closed. *(Change in Active voice)*
SSC Steno 10.12.2024 (Shift-II)
(a) The door will be closed.
(b) The door is closed.
(c) Close the door.
(d) Please let him close the door

Ans. (c) Refer to Rule 7 (ii)

296. Who built this colossal architectural structure? *(Change in Passive voice)*
SSC Steno 10.12.2024 (Shift-II)
(a) Who had this colossal architectural structure built?
(b) By whom was this colossal architectural structure built?
(c) By whom has this colossal architectural structure been built?
(d) By whom is this colossal architectural structure built?

Ans. (b) Refer to Rule 5

297. This saree was bought by my son on the occasion of my birthday. *(Change in Active voice)* **SSC Steno 10.12.2024 (Shift-II)**
(a) My son has bought the saree on the occasion of my birthday.
(b) My son had bought this saree on the occasion of my birthday.
(c) My son has bought this saree on the occasion of my birthday.
(d) My son bought this saree on the occasion of my birthday

Ans. (d) Refer to Rule 1 (d)

298. The secretary has planted a lot of saplings to save the environment. *(Change in Passive voice)*
SSC Steno 10.12.2024 (Shift-II)
(a) A lot of saplings were planted by the secretary to save the environment.
(b) A lot of saplings are planted by the secretary to save the environment.
(c) A lot of saplings have been planted by the secretary to save the environment.
(d) A lot of saplings are being planted by the secretary to save the environment.

Ans. (c) Refer to Rule 1 (c)

299. Who has told you to buy trash from the market? *(Change in Passive voice)* **SSC Steno 10.12.2024 (Shift-II)**

(a) Who could tell you to buy trash?
(b) The buying of trash has been told by whom?
(c) By whom have you been told to buy trash?
(d) By whom had you been told to buy trash?

Ans. (c) Refer to Rule 5

300. Was your bicycle stolen by him? *(Change in Active voice)* **SSC Steno 10.12.2024 (Shift-II)**

(a) Did he steal your bicycle?
(b) Had he stolen your bicycle?
(c) Has he stolen your bicycle?
(d) Was he stealing your bicycle?

Ans. (a) Refer to Rule 6

301. He will visit the orphanage tomorrow. *(Change in Passive voice)* **SSC Steno 10.12.2024 (Shift-III)**

(a) The orphanage must be visited by him tomorrow.
(b) The orphanage will be visited by him tomorrow.
(c) The orphanage is visited by him tomorrow.
(d) The orphanage should be visited by him tomorrow.

Ans. (b) Refer to Rule 1 (g)

302. Mr. Prakash writes short stories. *(Change in Passive voice)* **SSC Steno 10.12.2024 (Shift-III)**

(a) Short stories are written by Mr. Prakash.
(b) Short stories were written by Mr. Prakash.
(c) Short stories have been written by Mr. Prakash.
(d) Short stories are being written by Mr. Prakash

Ans. (a) Refer to Rule 1 (a)

303. His finger had been cut by the sharp knife. *(Change in Active voice)* **SSC Steno 10.12.2024 (Shift-III)**

(a) The sharp knife had cut his finger.
(b) The sharp knife cuts his finger.
(c) The sharp knife has cut his finger.
(d) The sharp knife had been cutting his finger.

Ans. (a) Refer to Rule 1 (f)

304. Ms. Jyothi will finish the task in a week. *(Change in Passive voice)* **SSC Steno 10.12.2024 (Shift-III)**

(a) The task will have been finished by Ms. Jyothi in a week.
(b) The task will be finished by Ms. Jyothi in a week.
(c) The task was being finished by Ms. Jyothi in a week.
(d) The task is being finished by Ms. Jyothi in a week.

Ans. (b) Refer to Rule 1 (g)

305. Why did your manager refuse to give you the pay raise? *(Change in Passive voice)* **SSC Steno 10.12.2024 (Shift-III)**

(a) Why had your manager refused to give you the pay raise?
(b) Why has the pay raise been refused to be given to you by your manager?
(c) Why have you been refused the pay raise by your manager?
(d) Why was the pay raise refused to be given to you by your manager?

Ans. (d) Refer to Rule 5

306. Geography is taught to us by Mr. Anand. *(Change in Active voice)* **SSC Steno 10.12.2024 (Shift-III)**

(a) Mr. Anand will teach us Geography.
(b) Mr. Anand teaches us Geography.
(c) Mr. Anand shall teach us Geography.
(d) Mr. Anand will be teaching us Geography.

Ans. (b) Refer to Rule 1 (a)

307. They think that the Governor will resign. *(Change in Passive voice)* **SSC Steno 10.12.2024 (Shift-III)**

(a) They thought that the Governor would be resigning.
(b) It is thought that the Governor will resign.
(c) They think that the Governor is resigning.
(d) It is thought that the Governor will be resigning.

Ans. (b) 'It is thought that the Governor will resign, is the correct passive voice. Herein, the main clause is transformed into an impersonal construction, maintaining the future tense.

308. A lot of masks have been distributed by the social workers. *(Change in Active voice)* **SSC Steno 10.12.2024 (Shift-III)**

(a) The social workers had distributed a lot of masks.
(b) The social workers are distributing a lot of masks.
(c) The social workers have distributed a lot of masks.
(d) The social workers would distribute a lot of masks.

Ans. (c) Refer to Rule 1 (c)

309. The entire cake was eaten by Maria. *(Change in Active voice)* **SSC Steno 10.12.2024 (Shift-III)**

(a) Maria was eating the entire cake.
(b) Maria ate the entire cake.
(c) Maria had eaten the entire cake.
(d) Maria is eating the entire cake.

Ans. (b) Refer to Rule 1 (d)

310. Seema will have told you the truth. *(Change in Passive voice)* **SSC Steno 10.12.2024 (Shift-III)**

(a) You will have been told the truth by Seema.
(b) You are told the truth by Seema.
(c) Seema had told you the truth.
(d) You would have told the truth to Seema.

Ans. (a) Refer to Rule 1 (g)

311. A blog page has been created by the head of the department for the conference. *(Change in Active voice)* **SSC Steno 10.12.2024 (Shift-III)**

(a) The head of the department has created a blog page for the conference.
(b) The head of the department was creating a blog page for the conference.
(c) The head of the department has been creating a blog page for the conference.
(d) The head of the department created a blog page for the conference.

Ans. (a) Refer to Rule 1(c)

312. She was laughed at by all her friends. *(Change in Active voice)* **SSC Steno 10.12.2024 (Shift-III)**

(a) All her friends had laughed at her.
(b) All her friends laugh at her.
(c) All her friends had been laughing at her.
(d) All her friends laughed at her.

Ans. (d) Refer to Rule 1(d)

11

Narration

When we change the direct speech into indirect speech, the commas and the quotation marks are removed in indirect speech.

All the sentences are changes to simple statement in indirect speech.

The conjunction 'that' is generally to join the two parts of the introductory part and the exact words of the speaker.

General rules for direct-indirect speech conversion are as follows

Rule 1 When we convert a sentence from direct to indirect speech, the tense of the speech may or may not change depending on the reporting verb (the verb that is placed before the statement given in the inverted commas).

e.g., She **says**, "I am not going to the concert." (Herein 'says' is the reporting verb)

(a) If the reporting verb is in Present, the tense of the verbs in the introductory phrase and exact words of the speaker does not change. e.g.,

- My mother **says**, "You **are not going** to the mall." *(Direct Speech)*
- My mother **says** that **I am not going** to the mall. *(Indirect Speech)*

(b) The tense also does not change when we refer to a universal truth, a habitual fact, a historical fact, an imaginary sentence or when we are talking about two simultaneous actions.

(c) If the reporting verb is in Past Tense, the tense of the speech in double quotation marks undergoes a change as given in the table.

S.No.	Direct Speech	Indirect Speech
(i)	Simple Present	Simple Past
(ii)	Present Continuous	Past Continuous
(iii)	Present Perfect	Past Perfect
(iv)	Present Perfect Continuous	Past Perfect Continuous
(v)	Simple Past	Past Perfect
(vi)	Past Continuous	Past Perfect Continuous
(vii)	Past Perfect/ Past Perfect Continuous	No change
(viii)	Simple Future/ Future Continuous/ Future Perfect/ Future Perfect Continuous	Will/Shall changes to would

Rule 2 The pronouns are changed according to the speaker of the sentence.

1. The pronoun in the indirect speech remains unchanged if the speaker is in first person.
2. The pronoun in the indirect speech is changed to second person if the speaker is in second person.
3. The pronoun in the indirect speech is changed to third person in accordance with the gender of the speaker, if the speaker is in third person.

Note Refer to Pronouns Ch-1 Grammar at a Glance to understand the different persons of pronouns.

Rule 3 Modal verbs are changed in the following manner

- May - might
- Can - could
- Must - had to
- Ought to - ought to

Rule 4 Time indicators

Direct Speech	Indirect Speech
Now	Then
Ago	Before
Today	That day
Tonight	That night
Yesterday	The previous day/the day before
Tomorrow	The next day/ the following day
In an hour	An hour later

Rule 5 Place indicators – 'Here' will be converted to 'There', 'This' will be converted to 'That', 'These' will be converted to 'Those', etc.

Rule 6 Changes in Interrogative Sentences When we have to change a direct question into indirect speech, we make the following changes

1. The reporting verb 'said/ said to' is changed to 'asked/ enquired. 'The question form is converted to statement form.
2. If the question starts with helping verbs (is, were, have, does, etc.) or modal verbs (can, would, may, etc.), then they are replaced by conjunctions 'if' or 'whether'.
3. If the question starts with -wh words (why, when, what, which) or how, no conjunctions are used. Other changes are done according to rules mentioned above.

Rule 7 Changes in Imperative Sentences If the direct speech contains a request or a command, the reporting verb changes to told, requested, ordered, commanded, suggested, advised, etc., according to the intent of the spoken words. Other changes are done according to rules mentioned above. e.g.,

- He **said** to me, "Go to school now." *(Direct speech)*
- He **advised** me to go to school then. *(Indirect speech)*

Rule 8 Changes in Exclamatory Sentences While changing exclamatory sentences into indirect speech, we make the following changes

I. The reporting verb 'said/ said to' is changed to 'exclaimed'.

II. The exclamatory word (interjection) is replaced by 'exclaimed with joy/ sorrow/ regret/ surprise/ contempt, etc.' Other changes are done according to rules mentioned above. e.g.,

- The old man said, "**Alas!** Mr. Goel has lost his son." *(Direct speech)*
- The old man **exclaimed with sorrow** that Mr. Goel had lost his son. *(Indirect speech)*

SSC Exam Scanner

Directions (Q. Nos. 1-279) Select the option that expresses the given sentence in Direct/Indirect or Reported speech.

SSC CGL 2024 (Tier 1 & 2)

1. 'I am determined to publish my findings,' the scientist asserted confidently. **SSC CGL Tier-2 18.01.2025**
   (a) The scientist confidently asserted that she is determined to publish her findings.
   (b) The scientist confidently asserted that she would be determined to publish her findings.
   (c) The scientist confidently asserted that she was determined to publish her findings.
   (d) The scientist confidently asserted that she had determined to publish her findings.

   Ans. (c) Refer to Rule 1(c) (i)

2. The teacher informed that the exam had been postponed. **SSC CGL Tier-2 18.01.2025**
   (a) The teacher informed, 'The exam has been postponed.'
   (b) The teacher informs, 'The exam has been postponed.'
   (c) The teacher informed, 'The exam was being postponed.'
   (d) The teacher informs, 'The exam had been postponed.'

   Ans. (a) Refer to Rule 1(c) (iii)

3. The District Magistrate ordered the police to work all night and put an end to those riots. **SSC CGL Tier-2 18.01.2025**
   (a) The District Magistrate told the police, "Work all night and put an end to their riots."
   (b) The District Magistrate told the police, "Work all night and put to end these riots."
   (c) The District Magistrate told the police, "Work all night and put an end to these riots."
   (d) The District Magistrate told the police, "Work all night to put an end these riots."

   Ans. (b) Refer to Rule 7

4. Kanhaiya said to me, "Do you want to sing?" **SSC CGL Tier-2 20.01.2025**
   (a) Kanhaiya enquires if I want to sing.
   (b) Kanhaiya said that whether I would sing.
   (c) Kanhaiya said that I would sing or not.
   (d) Kanhaiya asked me if I wanted to sing.

   Ans. (d) Refer to Rule 6

5. The soldier said to his fellow soldiers, "I have buried our brave comrade here." **SSC CGL Tier-2 20.01.2025**
   (a) The soldier told us that I had buried their brave comrade here.
   (b) The soldier told his fellow soldiers that I had buried our brave comrade there.
   (c) The soldier told his fellow soldiers that he had buried their brave comrade there.
   (d) The soldier told us that he had buried our brave comrade there.

   Ans. (c) Refer to Rule 1(c) (iii)

6. He said, "I shall need a copy of the documents." **SSC CGL Tier-2 20.01.2025**
   (a) He said that he would need a copy of the documents.
   (b) He said that he is going to need a copy of the document.
   (c) He said that he will need a copy of the documents.
   (d) He said that he shall need a copy of the document.

   Ans. (a) Refer to Rule 1(c) (viii)

SSSC CGL 2023 (Tier 2)

7. Raghav said to Meera, 'Are you upset with me?' **SSC CGL Tier-2 02.03.2023**
   (a) Raghav asked Meera if she was upset with her.
   (b) Raghav asked Meera if she was upset with him.
   (c) Raghav asked Meera if she was upset with me.
   (d) Raghav asked Meera why she was upset with him.

   Ans. (b) Refer to Rule 6

8. Shikha said, "The heavy rain this week has spoiled all my travel plans". **SSC CGL Tier-2 02.03.2023**
   (a) Shikha said that the heavy rain that week had spoiled all her travel plans.
   (b) Shikha told me that the heavy rain that week had spoiled all her travel plans.
   (c) Shikha said that the heavy rain that week has spoiled all her travel plans.
   (d) Shikha said that the heavy rain this week had spoiled all her travel plans.

   Ans. (a) Refer to Rules 1(c) (iii) and 5

9. My brother said to me, "Don't play in the rain." **SSC CGL Tier-2 02.03.2023**
   (a) My brother said to me don't play in the rain.
   (b) My brother forbade me to play in the rain.
   (c) My brother assured me not to play in the rain.
   (d) My brother refused me to not play in the rain.

   Ans. (b) Refer to Rule 7

10. "So help me heaven!", the man cried, "I shall never lie again." **SSC CGL Tier-2 03.03.2023**
    (a) The man cries out to heaven to help him not to lie again ever.
    (b) The man called upon heaven to witness his resolve that he would never lie again.
    (c) The man requested heaven to help him and see that he lie again.
    (d) The man called heaven and ordered to help him and see to it that she never lies again.

    Ans. (b) The exclamation 'So help me heaven!' is transformed into an invocation and 'shall' changes to 'would' to reflect the future in the past.

11. Hira inquired how I was doing being all alone in my house. **SSC CGL Tier-2 03.03.2023**
    (a) Hira said to me, "Are you doing fine being all alone in your house".
    (b) Hira said to me, "How are you doing being all alone in my house."
    (c) Hira said to me, "How are you". doing being all alone in your house?"
    (d) Hira said to me, "How you are doing being all alone in your house?"

    Ans. (c) Refer to Rule 6

12. Joey said to the girl, "How are you doing?" **SSC CGL Tier-2 03.03.2023**
    (a) Joey asked the girl if she was doing fine.
    (b) Joey asked the girl how was she doing.
    (c) Joey asked the girl that how was she doing.
    (d) Joey asked the girl how she was doing.

    Ans. (d) Refer to Rule 6

13. I said to Mohan, "He has a green book".
SSC CGL Tier-2 06.03.2023

(a) I tell Mohan that he had a green book .
(b) I told Mohan that he have a green book.
(c) I told Mohan that he had a green book.
(d) I told Mohan that he has a green book.

Ans. (c) Refer to Rule 1(c) (iii)

14. She asked, "Are you meeting my partners next week?"
SSC CGL Tier-2 06.03.2023

(a) She asked about our meeting her partners next week.
(b) She asked if we meet her partners next week.
(c) She asked if we were meeting her partners the following week.
(d) She asked if we were meeting her partners next week.

Ans. (c) Refer to Rules 4 and 6

15. I warned Rita not to be late the next day.
SSC CGL Tier-2 06.03.2023

(a) I warned to Rita, 'Don't be late tommorrow'.
(b) I warning Rita, 'Not be late tomorrow'.
(c) I warned Rita, 'Not be late tomorrow'.
(d) I warned Rita, ''Don't be late tomorrow.''

Ans. (d) Refer to Rules 7 and 4

16. Harry said that he would not be in town on Friday.
SSC CGL Tier-2 07.03.2023

(a) Harry saying, "I will not be in town on Friday".
(b) Harry said, "I will not be in town on Friday".
(c) Harry said, "I can't be in town on Friday".
(d) Harry said, "I must not be in town on Friday."

Ans. (b) Refer to Rule 1(c) (viii)

17. She said impatiently, "I don't need any help".
SSC CGL Tier-2 07.03.2023

(a) She said impatiently that, I don't need any help.
(b) She said impatiently that, she didn't need any help.
(c) She said impatiently she don't need any help.
(d) She said impatiently that she doesn't need any help.

Ans. (b) Refer to Rule 1(c) (i)

18. The mother said that the kids were playing.
SSC CGL Tier-2 07.03.2023

(a) The mother said, "The kids have been playing".
(b) The mother has said "The kids were playing".
(c) The mother told, "The kids had been playing".
(d) The mother said, "The kids are playing".

Ans. (d) Refer to Rule 1(c) (ii)

19. He said, ''Two and two make four.'' **SSC CGL Tier-2 26.10.2023**

(a) He says that two and two made four.
(b) He said that two and two make four.
(c) He says that two and two make four.
(d) He said that two and two made four.

Ans. (b) Refer to Rule 1(b)

20. Select the most appropriate option in direct speech.
SSC CGL Tier-2 26.10.2023

(a) The principal said to me, ''You are incharge of the admission cell".
(b) The principal say me, ''You are incharge of the admission cell".
(c) The principal said to I, ''You are incharge of the admission cell".
(d) The principal said me, "You are incharge of the admission cell".

Ans. (a) The principal said to me, ''You are incharge of the admission cell." This sentence correctly uses the direct speech format with appropriate pronouns and punctuation.

21. He said, "I bought this book for my brother".
SSC CGL Tier-2 26.10.2023

(a) He said that he buy this book for his brother.
(b) He said that he had bought that book for his brother.
(c) He said that he has bought this book for his brother.
(d) He said that he bought this book for his brother.

Ans. (b) Refer to Rule 1(c) (v)

SSC CGL 2022 (Tier 1 & 2)

22. He asked me when I had booked the flight tickets.
SSC CGL Tier-1 11.04.2022 (Shift-I)

(a) He said to me, "When do you book the flight tickets?"
(b) He said to me, "When did you book the flight tickets?"
(c) He said to me, "When are you booking the flight tickets?"
(d) He said to me, "When you had book the flight tickets?"

Ans. (b) Refer to Rule 6

23. She said, "The stars are shining brightly tonight."
SSC CGL Tier-1 11.04.2022 (Shift-III)

(a) She said the stars are shining brightly tonight.
(b) She said that the stars were shining brightly that night.
(c) She said the stars were shining brightly tonight.
(d) She asked if the stars were shining brightly that night.

Ans. (b) Refer to Rules 1(c) (ii) and 4

24. The teacher said, "You must work hard for your exams".
SSC CGL Tier-1 13.04.2022 (Shift II)

(a) The teacher was advising her students to do work hard for their exams.
(b) The teacher told students for working hard for their exams.
(c) The teacher was telling her students to work hard for their exams.
(d) The teacher advised her students to work hard for their exams.

Ans. (d) Refer to Rule 7

25. They cried, ''Bravo! Well done.''
SSC CGL Tier-1 18.04.2022 (Shift-III)

(a) They shouted in joy that they had done well.
(b) They cried in joy for doing well.
(c) They cried loudly for doing well.
(d) They exclaimed with wonder that they had done well.

Ans. (a) Refer to Rule 8

26. The guard told the children to stay away from the flower beds. **SSC CGL Tier-1 19.04.2022 (Shift-III)**

(a) The guard says to the children, "Stay away from the flower beds".
(b) The guard told to the children, "Stay away from the flower beds".
(c) The guard said, "Children, should you stay away from the flower beds."
(d) The guard said, "Children, stay away from the flower beds".

Ans. (d) The guard said, "Children, stay away from the flower beds." This sentence correctly uses direct speech format with appropriate punctuation and verb tense.

27. She said to him, "May God shower his choicest blessing on you!" **SSC CGL Tier-1 20.04.2022 (Shift-I)**
(a) She wished that God may shower his choicest blessings on you.
(b) She wished that may God shower your choicest blessings on him.
(c) She wished that God might shower his choicest blessings on you.
(d) She wished that God might shower his choicest blessings on him.
Ans. (d) Refer to Rule 8

28. She exclaimed with sorrow that life had become miserable. **SSC CGL Tier-1 20.04.2022 (Shift-III)**
(a) She said, "Oh! What miserable life has become".
(b) She said, "Alas! How miserable life has become".
(c) She said, "How miserable had become life!"
(d) She said, "Life has become miserable".
Ans. (b) Refer to Rule 8

29. Mother said to her, "I expected a better result from you". **SSC CGL Tier-1 21.04.2022 (Shift-I)**
(a) Mother told her that she had expected a better result from her.
(b) Mother told her that she expected a better result from her.
(c) Mother told her that she was expecting a better result from you.
(d) Mother told her that she expected a better result from you.
Ans. (a) Refer to Rule 1(c) (ii)

30. She said, "I am in no mood to work now." **SSC CGL Tier-1 01.12.2022 (Shift-I)**
(a) She said that she has been in no mood to work then.
(b) She said that she was in no mood to work now.
(c) She said that she was in no mood to work then.
(d) She said that she has been in no mood to work now.
Ans. (c) Refer to Rule 1(c) (i)

31. He said that something might be missing in there. **SSC CGL Tier-1 01.12.2022 (Shift-II)**
(a) He said, "Something may be missing in here".
(b) He said, "Something had to be missing in there".
(c) He said, "Something is been missing in here".
(d) He said, "Something could be missing in here".
Ans. (a) Refer to Rule 3

32. She asked me why I had been smoking that day. **SSC CGL Tier-1 01.12.2022 (Shift-III)**
(a) She said to me, "Why were you smoking today?"
(b) She said to me, "Why are you smoking today?"
(c) She said to me, "Why you smoke today?"
(d) She says to me, "Why were you smoking this day?"
Ans. (a) Refer to Rule 6

33. Shyam asked me how I had persuaded his sister. **SSC CGL Tier-1 02.12.2022 (Shift-I)**
(a) "How are you persuading my sister?" Shyam asked me.
(b) "How did you persuaded my sister?" Shyam asked me.
(c) "How did you persuade my sister?" Shyam asked me.
(d) "How have you persuade my sister?" Shyam asks me.
Ans. (c) Refer to Rule 6

34. Mr. Sharma asked him if Maya had invited him for lunch. **SSC CGL Tier-1 02.12.2022 (Shift-II)**
(a) Mr. Sharma said to him, "Has Maya invited you for lunch?"
(b) Mr. Sharma said to me, "Has Maya invited you for lunch?"
(c) Mr. Sharma said to him, "Had Maya invited us for lunch?"
(d) Mr. Sharma said to him, "Did Maya invited us for lunch?
Ans. (a) Refer to Rule 6

35. She said, "She must leave all the bad habits". **SSC CGL Tier-1 02.12.2022 (Shift-III)**
(a) She said she has to leave all the bad habits.
(b) She said that she must have leave all the bad habits.
(c) She said that she had to leave all the bad habits.
(d) She said that she could leave all the bad habits.
Ans. (c) Refer to Rule 3

36. Priya said, "Yes, I am confounded". **SSC CGL Tier-1 02.12.2022 (Shift-IV)**
(a) Priya admitted that she was confound.
(b) Priya admit that she was confounded.
(c) Priya admitted that she was confounded.
(d) Priya admitted that she is confounded.
Ans. (c) 'Yes' is omitted and 'am' changes to 'was' in indirect speech.

37. Latika said to him, "I got a hefty discount on this television." **SSC CGL Tier-1 03.12.2022 (Shift-I)**
(a) Latika told him that she has got a hefty discount on that television.
(b) Latika told him that she is getting a hefty discount on that television.
(c) Latika told him that she had got a hefty discount on that television.
(d) Latika told him that she has got a hefty discount on this television.
Ans. (c) Refer to Rule 1(c) (v)

38. The surgeon says that I should get anaesthesia for the surgery. **SSC CGL Tier-1 03.12.2020 (Shift-II)**
(a) The surgeon says, "You should get anaesthesia for the surgery."
(b) The surgeon says, "I should get anaesthesia for the surgery."
(c) The surgeon said, "You should get anaesthesia for the surgery."
(d) The surgeon says, "You could get anaesthesia for the surgery."
Ans. (a) Refer to Rule 2

39. He said, "Let us wait for the award". **SSC CGL Tier-1 03.12.2022 (Shift-III)**
(a) He proposed that they should wait for the award.
(b) He said that he should wait for the award.
(c) He proposed that he should wait for the award.
(d) He said that they should waited for the award.
Ans. (a) Refer to Rule 7

40. Leena said that his relatives were landing the next day. **SSC CGL Tier-1 03.12.2022 (Shift-III)**
(a) Leena said, "My relatives land tomorrow".
(b) Leena said, "His relatives are landing today".
(c) Leena said, "His relatives were landing tomorrow".
(d) Leena said, "His relatives are landing tomorrow".
Ans. (d) Refer to Rules 1(c) (ii) and 4

41. Kavya said to her husband, "I don't mind being a busy woman". SSC CGL Tier-1 03.12.2022 (Shift-IV)
(a) Kavya told her husband that she had not mind being a busy woman.
(b) Kavya told her husband that she do not mind being a busy woman.
(c) Kavya said to her husband she did not mind being a busy woman.
(d) Kavya told her husband that she did not mind being a busy woman.

Ans. (d) Refer to Rule 1(c) (i)

42. Priya assured me, "I can stay in tonight". SSC CGL Tier-1 05.12.2022 (Shift-I)
(a) Priya told me that she could stay in that night.
(b) Priya told me that she could stay in tonight.
(c) Priya told me that she could stay in this night.
(d) Priya told me that she can stay in that night.

Ans. (a) Refer to Rules 3 and 4

43. Aryan told me that I knew where to find him. SSC CGL Tier-1 05.12.2022 (Shift-I)
(a) Aryan said to me, "You know where to find me".
(b) Aryan said to me, "You knowing where to find me".
(c) Aryan said to me, "You are known where to find me".
(d) Aryan says to me, "You know where to find me".

Ans. (a) Refer to Rules 1(c) (i)

44. John said that he was there to resolve that fight for them. SSC CGL Tier-1 05.12.2022 (Shift-III)
(a) John says, "I am here to resolve this fight for you".
(b) John said to me, "You are here to resolve this fight for you".
(c) John said, "I am here to resolve this fight for you".
(d) John said, "I was here to resolve this fight for you".

Ans. (c) Refer to Rules 1(c) (i)

45. Madhurima explained, "I am planning to quit my graduation". SSC CGL Tier-1 05.12.2022 (Shift-IV)
(a) Madhurima explained that she were planning to quit her graduation.
(b) Madhurima explained that she planned to quit her graduation.
(c) Madhurima explained that she was planning to quit her graduation.
(d) Madhurima explained that she had been planning to quit her graduation.

Ans. (c) Refer to Rule 1(c) (ii)

46. Raveena asked me if I had her maid's number. SSC CGL Tier-1 06.12.2022 (Shift-I)
(a) Raveena asked me, "Do you have my maid's number?"
(b) Raveena asked me, "Are you having my maid's number".
(c) Raveena said to me, "Does you have my maid's number".
(d) Raveena asked to me, "Have you have my maid's number".

Ans. (a) Refer to Rule 6

47. He said to him, "Is your name not Ahmed?" SSC CGL Tier-1 06.12.2022 (Shift-I)
(a) He enquired is your name not Ahmed.
(b) He enquired whether his name was not Ahmed.
(c) He said whether his name was not Ahmed.
(d) He said is your name not Ahmed.

Ans. (b) Refer to Rule 6

48. Radha said, "Why didn't he forward his petition to me?" SSC CGL Tier-1 06.12.2022 (Shift-II)
(a) Radha enquired why he had not forwarded his petition to her.
(b) Radha enquired why he has not forwarded his petition to her.
(c) Radha enquired why had he not forwarded his petition to her.
(d) Radha enquired why he had not forward his petition to her.

Ans. (a) Refer to Rule 6

49. "We had opened the lock". they told me. SSC CGL Tier-1 06.12.2022 (Shift-III)
(a) They said that we had opened the lock.
(b) They said to me that they have opened the lock.
(c) They told me that they had opened the lock.
(d) They says that we had opened the lock.

Ans. (c) Refer to Rule 2 for pronouns.

50. Professor told me that I could not rescue myself from that bait. SSC CGL Tier-1 06.12.2022 (Shift-IV)
(a) Professor says to me, "You cannot rescue yourself from this bait".
(b) Professor said to me, "You have not rescued yourself from this bait".
(c) Professor said to us, "You cannot rescue yourself from this bait".
(d) Professor said to me, "You cannot rescue yourself from this bait".

Ans. (d) Refer to Rule 3 for modals.

51. She said that she could not believe him. SSC CGL Tier-1 07.12.2022 (Shift-I)
(a) She said, "You cannot believe him".
(b) She said, "I may not believe him".
(c) She said, "I cannot believe him".
(d) She says, "I could not believed him".

Ans. (c) Refer to Rule 3 for modals.

52. The secretary assures the audience that he/she is going to help them. SSC CGL Tier-1 07.12.2022 (Shift-II)
(a) The secretary said to the audience, 'I am going to help you.'
(b) The secretary says to the audience, "I am going to help you."
(c) The secretary says to the audience, "I was going to help you."
(d) The secretary says to the audience, "I will be going to help you."

Ans. (b) Refer to Rule 2 for pronouns

53. She said to me, "You will speak at the conference tomorrow". SSC CGL Tier-1 07.12.2022 (Shift-II)
(a) She told me that I would speak at the conference that day.
(b) She told me that I might speak at the conference the next day.
(c) She told me that I will speak at the conference the today.
(d) She told me that I would speak at the conference the next day.

Ans. (d) Refer to Rule 1 (c)(viii)

54. We asked them who had called them. SSC CGL Tier-1 07.12.2022 (Shift-IV)
(a) We said to them, "Who are calling you?"
(b) We said to them, "Who calls you?"
(c) We said to them, "Who has called him?"
(d) We said to them, "Who has called you?"

Ans. (d) Refer to Rule 6

55. The blind man said to me, "Can you help me cross the road?" **SSC CGL Tier-1 08.12.2022 (Shift-I)**
(a) The blind man asked me if I could help him cross the road.
(b) The blind man asked me if I will help him cross the road.
(c) The blind man asked me if I could help him crossed the road.
(d) The blind man asked me if I can help him cross the road.
Ans. (a) Refer to Rule 6

56. The professor said, "I want you to pursue your dreams". **SSC CGL Tier-1 08.12.2022 (Shift-II)**
(a) The professor said that I want you to pursue your dreams.
(b) The professor said that he wanted me to pursue my dreams.
(c) The professor says that he wants me to pursue my dreams.
(d) The professor told me that I wanted you to pursue your dreams.
Ans. (b) Refer to Rule 1(c) (i)

57. Anita said to the mother, "Your child has been crying since morning." **SSC CGL Tier-1 08.12.2022 (Shift-III)**
(a) Anita told the mother that her child was crying since morning.
(b) Anita told the mother that her child had been crying since morning.
(c) Anita told the mother that her child had been cry since morning.
(d) Anita told the mother that your child had been crying since morning.
Ans. (b) Refer to Rule 1(c) (iii)

58. Rohan asked me if Rohit still cried. **SSC CGL Tier-1 08.12.2022 (Shift-IV)**
(a) Rohan said to me, "Did Rohit still cry?"
(b) Rohan says to me, "Does Rohit still cry?"
(c) Rohan said to me, "Does Rohit still cry?"
(d) Rohan said to me, "Has Rohit still cried?"
Ans. (a) Refer to Rule 6

59. He said that he was sorry for all that. **SSC CGL Tier-1 09.12.2022 (Shift-I)**
(a) "I am sorry for all then", he says.
(b) "I was sorry for all this", he said.
(c) "I am sorry for all that", he says.
(d) "I am sorry for all this", he said.
Ans. (d) Refer to Rules 1(c) (i) and 5

60. The doctor said that they had performed their bit. **SSC CGL Tier-1 09.12.2022 (Shift-I)**
(a) The doctor said, "We performed our bit".
(b) The doctor said, "We are performing our bit".
(c) The doctor said, "We have performed our bit".
(d) The doctor says, "We had performed our bit".
Ans. (c) Refer to Rule 1(c) (iii)

61. The old man asked the boy where the postman was. **SSC CGL Tier-1 09.12.2022 (Shift-III)**
(a) The old man says to the boy, "Where is the postman?"
(b) The old man said to the boy, "Where has been the postman?"
(c) The old man said to the boy, "Where is the postman?"
(d) The old man said to the boy. "Where was the postman?"
Ans. (c) Refer to Rule 6

62. "Meena, will you assist me to pack our belongings?", asked her mother. **SSC CGL Tier-1 09.12.2022 (Shift-IV)**
(a) Meena's mother asked her whether she will assist her to pack their belongings.
(b) Meena's mother asked her whether if she would assist her to pack their belongings.
(c) Meena's mother asked her whether she would assist her to pack their belongings.
(d) Meena's mother asked her whether she can assist her to pack their belongings.
Ans. (c) Refer to Rule 6

63. Renu said to her brother, "You were watching the show without me". **SSC CGL Tier-1 12.12.2022 (Shift-I)**
(a) Renu told her brother that he had watched the show without her.
(b) Renu told her brother that he were watching the show without her.
(c) Renu told her brother that he has been watching the show without her.
(d) Renu told her brother that he had been watching the show without her.
Ans. (d) Refer to Rule 1(c) (vi)

64. He says to Gayatri, "You are writing an apology to the warden". **SSC CGL Tier-1 12.12.2022 (Shift-II)**
(a) He told Gayatri that she is writing an apology to the warden.
(b) He tells Gayatri that she is writing an apology to the warden.
(c) He say to Gayatri that she was writing an apology to the warden.
(d) He tells Gayatri that she was writing an apology to the warden.
Ans. (b) Refer to Rule 1(c) (ii)

65. Ramita said, "I wish I didn't have to meet my step-mother". **SSC CGL Tier-1 12.12.2022 (Shift-III)**
(a) Ramita said she wished she hadn't have to meet her step-mother.
(b) Ramita said she wished she didn't meet her step-mother.
(c) Ramita said she wished she didn't have to meet her step-mother.
(d) Ramita said she wished hadn't met her step-mother
Ans. (c) Refer to Rule 2 for pronouns.

66. Meena said that her parents were getting divorced. **SSC CGL Tier-1 12.12.2022 (Shift-IV)**
(a) Meena said, "My parents get divorced".
(b) Meena said, "My parents are getting divorced".
(c) Meena said, "My parents will be getting divorced".
(d) Meena said, "My parents were getting divorced".
Ans. (b) Refer to Rule 1(c) (ii)

67. Shravan said that the prisoner had slept throughout the journey. **SSC CGL Tier-1 13.12.2022 (Shift-I)**
(a) Shravan said, "The prisoner sleeps throughout the journey".
(b) Shravan said, "The prisoner had slept throughout the journey".
(c) Shravan said, "The prisoner had been sleeping throughout the journey".
(d) Shravan says, "The prisoner has slept throughout the journey".
Ans. (b) Refer to Rule 1(c) (vii)

68. My teacher forbids to trust one's relatives. SSC CGL Tier-1 13.12.2022 (Shift-II)

(a) My teacher says, ''Never trusted your relatives''.
(b) My teacher says, ''Never trust my relatives''.
(c) My teacher says, ''Never trust your relatives''.
(d) My teacher said, ''Never trust your relatives''.

Ans. (c) Refer to Rule 7

69. Farah said to her aunt, "I am studying contemporary art". SSC CGL Tier-1 13.12.2022 (Shift-III)

(a) Farah told her aunt that she was study contemporary art.
(b) Farah told her aunt that she is studying contemporary art.
(c) Farah told her aunt that she had been studying contemporary art.
(d) Farah told her aunt that she was studying contemporary art.

Ans. (d) Refer to Rule 1(c) (ii)

70. She tells me that I am her lucky charm. SSC CGL Tier-1 13.12.2022 (Shift-IV)

(a) She says to me, "You was my lucky charm".
(b) She says to me, "I am your lucky charm".
(c) She says to me, "You are my lucky charm".
(d) She said to me, "You are my lucky charm".

Ans. (c) The present tense 'am' remains unchanged and the pronouns are adjusted appropriately.

71. The teacher ordered the students to go straight to their classrooms. SSC CGL Tier-2 29.01.2022

(a) "Go straight to their classrooms," the teacher said to the students.
(b) The teacher said to the students, "Please go straight to your classrooms."
(c) The teacher said, "Students, to go straight to their classrooms."
(d) ''Go straight to your classrooms'', the teacher said to the students.

Ans. (d) Refer to Rule 7

72. The investigator asked me, "Did you see or hear anything in the dead of night?". SSC CGL Tier-2 29.01.2022

(a) The investigator asked me if I saw or heard anything in the dead of night.
(b) The investigator asked me if I see or hear anything in the dead of night.
(c) The investigator asked me if I had seen or heard anything in the dead of night.
(d) The investigator asked me that if I had seen or heard anything in the dead of night.

Ans. (c) Refer to Rule 6

73. Her parents asked her if the match proposed by them would be acceptable to her. SSC CGL Tier-2 29.01.2022

(a) Her parents said her, "Would the match proposed by them be acceptable to her?"
(b) Her parents said to her,"Was the match proposed by them acceptable to her?"
(c) Her parents said her, ''Will be the match proposed by us be acceptable to you?''
(d) Her parents said to her, "Will the match proposed by us be acceptable to you?"

Ans. (d) Refer to Rule 6

74. The actor said that what he did in films was something he had never attempted in real life. SSC CGL Tier-2 29.01.2022

(a) The actor said, "What he did in films is something he has never attempted in real life."
(b) The actor said, "What I do in films is something I have never attempted in real life."
(c) The actor said, "What I am doing in films is something I have never attempted in real life".
(d) The actor said, "What he did in films was something he had never attempted in real life".

Ans. (b) The present tense 'do' and 'have' remain unchanged in direct speech.

75. The old man said to her, "Good luck to you! May you succeed in your venture" SSC CGL Tier-2 29.01.2022

(a) The old man exclaimed good luck to you and wished that she may succeed in her venture.
(b) The old man wished you good luck and prayed that you might succeed in your venture.
(c) The old man wished her good luck and prayed that she might succeed in her venture.
(d) The old man told her good luck and prayed that may she succeed in her venture.

Ans. (c) Refer to Rule 8

76. ''Please lend me some money, Raman. I need it urgently", said Sumesh. SSC CGL Tier-2 29.01.2022

(a) Sumesh requested Raman to lend him some money as he needed it urgently.
(b) Sumesh requested Raman please lend me some money as I need it urgently.
(c) Sumesh requested to Raman to please lend him some money as he needed it urgently.
(d) Sumesh requested Raman to lend me some money as I needed it urgently.

Ans. (a) Refer to Rule 7

77. Harsh said, "How happy I am to receive the best student award!" SSC CGL Tier-2 29.01.2022

(a) Harsh exclaimed happily that he was receiving the best student award.
(b) Harsh exclaimed with joy that he was very happy to receive the best student award.
(c) Harsh exclaimed with joy that how happy he was to receive the best student award.
(d) Harsh exclaimed happily that I am very happy to receive the best student award.

Ans. (b) Refer to Rule 7

78. Mother said that when we pluck a flower it dies so we should let it beautify the world as long as it lives. SSC CGL Tier-2 29.01.2022

(a) Mother says, "When we pluck a flower it dies so we should let it beautify the world as long as it lives".
(b) Mother said, "When we pluck a flower it dies so you should let it beautify the world as long as it lived".
(c) Mother said, "When we pluck a flower it dies so we should let it beautify the world as long as it lives".
(d) Mother said, "When we plucked a flower it died so we should let it beautify the world as long as it lived".

Ans. (c) The simple present tense 'pluck' and 'dies' remain unchanged in direct speech.

79. Father said, "On the news tonight they mentioned a possibility of a power strike". **SSC CGL Tier-2 03.02.2022**
(a) Father said that on the news that night they had mentioned a possibility of a power strike.
(b) Father wondered why on the news tonight they mentioned a possibility of a power strike.
(c) Father asked if on the news that night they had mentioned a possibility of a power strike.
(d) Father said that on the news tonight they mentioned a possibility of a power strike.

Ans. (a) Refer to Rules 1 (c)(v) and 4

80. "Good gracious! It's snowing!" he said. **SSC CGL Tier-2 03.02.2022**
(a) He remarked that it is snowing.
(b) He happily said that it is snowing.
(c) He said that good gracious it's snowing.
(d) He exclaimed with astonishment that it was snowing.

Ans. (d) Refer to Rule 8

81. She enquired if all those potatoes were to be peeled for dinner. **SSC CGL Tier-2 03.02.2022**
(a) She said, "Should I peel all these potatoes for dinner?"
(b) She said, "All those potatoes were to be peeled for dinner?"
(c) She said, "Are all these potatoes to be peeled for dinner?"
(d) She said, "Are all those potatoes peeling for dinner?"

Ans. (c) Refer to Rule 6

82. The captain told the crew that the ship had to reach London that night. **SSC CGL Tier-2 03.02.2022**
(a) The captain said to the crew, "The ship had to reach London that night".
(b) The captain said to the crew, "The ship has to reach London tonight".
(c) The captain said to the crew, "The ship had reached London tonight".
(d) The captain said to the crew, "The ship will have to reach London that night".

Ans. (b) Refer to Rules 1 (c)(iii) and 4

83. Anurag said, "The coming elections in Bihar will be the main topic of discussion for the next fortnight". **SSC CGL Tier-2 03.02.2022**
(a) Anurag predicted that the coming elections in Bihar would be the main topic of discussion for the following fortnight.
(b) Anurag informed that the coming elections in Bihar were the main topic of discussion for the following fortnight.
(c) Anurag commented that the coming elections in Bihar will be the main topic of discussion for the next fortnight.
(d) Anurag exclaimed that the coming elections in Bihar are the main topic of discussion for the coming fortnight.

Ans. (a) Refer to Rules 1(c)(viii) and 4

84. The fisherman asked his contractor if those salmons were to go on that morning's fish train?" **SSC CGL Tier-2 03.02.2022**
(a) The fisherman said to his contractor, "Are those salmons going on that morning's fish train?"
(b) The fisherman said to his contractor, "Are these salmons to go on this morning's fish train?"
(c) The fisherman said to his contractor, "Were these salmons to go on that morning's fish train?"
(d) The fisherman said to his contractor, "Is those salmons to go on that morning's fish train?"

Ans. (b) Refer to Rule 6

85. Anne said, "Next week I have my first skating lesson". **SSC CGL Tier-2 03.02.2022**
(a) Anne said that in the following week she had her first skating lesson.
(b) Anne said that in the next week she has her first skating lesson.
(c) Anne said that the following week had my first skating lesson.
(d) Anne said that the next week have my first skating lesson.

Ans. (a) Refer to Rules 1 (c)(iii) and 4

86. "I wish I had something to eat. I am so hungry" said Chippa. **SSC CGL Tier-2 03.02.2022**
(a) Chippa said he wishes he has something to eat as he is so hungry.
(b) Chippa said I wish I have something to eat as I am so hungry.
(c) Chippa said he wishes he had something to eat as he was so hungry.
(d) Chippa said he wished he had something to eat as he was so hungry.

Ans. (d) Refer to Rule 2 for pronouns.

87. The driver asked a passerby if he could tell him the way to the market. **SSC CGL Tier-2 03.08.2022**
(a) The driver said to a passerby, "Tell me the way to the market, will you?"
(b) The driver said to a passerby, "Please, will you tell me the way to the market?"
(c) The driver said to a passerby, "Can you tell me the way to the market?"
(d) The driver said to a passerby, "Could he tell him the way to the market?"

Ans. (c) Refer to Rule 6

88. "Oh, how could I ever thank you, Sir!" said the convict to the Bishop. **SSC CGL Tier-2 08.08.2022**
(a) The convict told the Bishop that it was difficult for him to thank him.
(b) Exclaiming gratefully, the convict said to the Bishop that he could never thank him enough.
(c) The convict said to the Bishop that he could never thank him enough.
(d) The convict exclaimed gratefully to the Bishop that how he could ever thank him.

Ans. (b) Refer to Rule 8

89. She said to herself, "Shall I have a happy married life?" **SSC CGL Tier-2 08.08.2022**
(a) She asked that if she should have a happy married life.
(b) She thought that she should have a happy married life.
(c) She wondered if she would have a happy married life.
(d) She wondered if she shall have a happy married life.

Ans. (c) Refer to Rule 7

90. She said, "Ruhi slipped when she was trying to board the bus". **SSC CGL Tier-2 08.08.2022**
(a) She said that Ruhi had slipped when she was trying to board the bus.
(b) She says that Ruhi slipped when she was trying to board the bus.
(c) She said that Ruhi has slipped when she was trying to board the bus.
(d) She said that Ruhi slipped when she was trying to board the bus.

Ans. (a) Refer to Rule 1(c)(v)

91. She said to me, "Can you look after my baby for a short while?" SSC CGL Tier-2 08.08.2022

(a) She asked me that if I could look after her baby for a short while.
(b) She asked me if you can look after my baby for a short while.
(c) She asked me if I can look after my baby for a short while.
(d) She asked me if I could look after her baby for a short while.

Ans. (d) Refer to Rule 6

92. Rahul said to Mohit, "I am taking my family to Kashmir for a vacation tomorrow". SSC CGL Tier-2 08.08.2022

(a) Rahul told Mohit that he was taking his family to Kashmir for a vacation the following day.
(b) Rahul told Mohit that he is taking his family to Kashmir for a vacation tomorrow.
(c) Rahul told Mohit that I was taking my family to Kashmir for a vacation the following day.
(d) Rahul told Mohit that I am taking my family to Kashmir for a vacation tomorrow.

Ans. (a) Refer to Rules 1 (c)(ii) and 4

93. He said, ''Oh, how I would have loved to visit Kashmir this year''. SSC CGL Tier-2 08.08.2022

(a) He exclaimed that he would have really loved to visit Kashmir that year.
(b) He exclaimed that how he would have loved to visit Kashmir that year'.
(c) He exclaimed how I would have loved to visit Kashmir this year.
(d) He said that he will have loved to visit Kashmir this year.

Ans. (a) Refer to Rule 8

94. I told you that I had bought a new book for you the day before. SSC CGL Tier-2 08.08.2022

(a) I told to you, "I have bought a new book for you yesterday".
(b) I said to you, "I have bought a new book for you the day".
(c) I said to you, "I bought a new book for you yesterday".
(d) I said to you, ''You have bought a new book for me the day before".

Ans. (c) Refer to Rules 1 (c)(v) and 4

95. The teacher asked me why I had reached the examination hall so late. SSC CGL Tier-2 08.08.2022

(a) The teacher said to me, "Why are you reaching the examination hall so late?"
(b) The teacher said to me, "Why had I reached the examination hall so late?"
(c) The teacher said to me, "Why did you reach the examination hall so late?"
(d) The teacher said to me, "Why you reached the examination hall so late?"

Ans. (c) Refer to Rule 6

96. I said to you, "He cannot be trusted completely". SSC CGL Tier-2 08.08.2022

(a) I told you that he could not be trusted completely.
(b) You told me that he could not be trusted completely.
(c) I said you that he cannot be trusted completely.
(d) You told me that he cannot be trusted completely.

Ans. (a) Refer to Rule 3

97. "Remove all the stains carefully and clean the windows", said the contractor to the worker. SSC CGL Tier-2 08.08.2022

(a) The contractor said to the worker that you should remove all the stains carefully and clean the windows.
(b) The contractor requested the worker to remove all the stains carefully and clean the windows.
(c) The contractor told the worker that by removing all the stains crefully, the windows will be cleaned.
(d) The contractor instructed the worker to remove all the stains carefully and clean the windows.

Ans. (d) Refer to Rule 7

98. Granny said to Nina, "I don't know why you think it is so wonderful". SSC CGL Tier-2 08.08.2022

(a) Granny said to Nina that she doesn't know why she thinks it was so wonderful.
(b) Granny said to Nina that she didn't know why she thought it was so wonderful.
(c) Granny said to Nina that she hadn't know why she was thinking it was so wonderful.
(d) Granny said to Nina that I don't know why you think it is so wonderful.

Ans. (b) Refer to Rule 1 (c)(i)

99. "What a hopeless fellow you are!" said the teacher to the student. SSC CGL Tier-2 08.08.2022

(a) The teacher told the student that you are a very hopeless fellow.
(b) The teacher told the student that he was a very hopeless fellow.
(c) The teacher said the student was what a hopeless fellow .
(d) The teacher told the student what are a hopeless fellow he was.

Ans. (b) The exclamation 'What a hopeless fellow' changes to 'that he was a very hopeless fellow' in indirect speech.

SSC CGL 2021 (Tier 1 & 2)

100. "Everything is going to be alright", said the doctor. SSC CGL Tier-1 13.08.2021 (Shift-I)

(a) The doctor said that everything is going to be alright.
(b) The doctor said that everything are going to be alright.
(c) The doctor said that everything was going to be alright.
(d) The doctor said that everything will be alright.

Ans. (c) Refer to Rule 1 (c)(ii)

101. "Read the instructions before you start making the dish," Deepa's mother said to her. SSC CGL Tier-1 13.08.2021 (Shift-III)

(a) Deepa's mother told to her to read the instructions before you start making the dish.
(b) Deepa's mother told her to read the instructions before you had made the dish.
(c) Deepa's mother said her to read the instructions before she start making the dish.
(d) Deepa's mother told her to read the instructions before she started making the dish.

Ans. (d) Refer to Rule 7

102. "Whom did you see at the shopping mall today?" I asked my daughter. SSC CGL Tier-1 16.08.2021 (Shift-I)
(a) I asked my daughter whom she had seen at the shopping mall that day.
(b) I asked my daughter who she has seen at the shopping mall today.
(c) I asked my daughter that whom she saw at the shopping mall on that day.
(d) I asked my daughter that whom did she saw at the shopping mall that day.

Ans. (a) Refer to Rule 6

103. 'Is the door closed?' Alka asked Tarun. SSC CGL Tier-1 16.08.2021 (Shift-III)
(a) Alka asked Tarun is the door close.
(b) Alka asked Tarun whether the door was closed.
(c) Alka asked Tarun if the door is closed.
(d) Alka asked Tarun whether she closed the door.

Ans. (b) Refer to Rule 6

104. 'How beautiful she is!' said Betty. SSC CGL Tier-1 17.08.2021 (Shift-I)
(a) Betty exclaimed with joy how beautiful she was.
(b) Betty exclaimed with joy that she was very beautiful.
(c) Betty exclaimed with joy how beautiful she is.
(d) Betty exclaimed with joy she is very beautiful.

Ans. (b) Refer to Rule 8

105. "I will work hard to get the first rank in class," said Rohan. SSC CGL Tier-1 17.08.2021 (Shift-III)
(a) Rohan said that he would work hard to get the first rank in class.
(b) Rohan said that he could work hard to get the first rank in class.
(c) Rohan said that he ought to work hard to get the first rank in class.
(d) Rohan said that he should work hard to get the first rank in class.

Ans. (a) Refer to Rule 1 (c)(viii)

106. Sneha said to me, "I was watching TV." SSC CGL Tier-1 18.08.2021 (Shift-I)
(a) Sneha told me that she had been watching TV.
(b) Sneha said to me that I was watching TV.
(c) Sneha told me that she was watching TV.
(d) Sneha told me that I was watching TV.

Ans. (a) Refer to Rule 1 (c)(vi)

107. Raj said to his friend, "Please help me in this task". SSC CGL Tier-1 18.08.2021 (Shift-III)
(a) Raj requested his friend to help him in that task.
(b) Raj ordered his friend to help him in this task.
(c) Raj threatened his friend to help him in this task.
(d) Raj said to his friend please help me in this task.

Ans. (a) Refer to Rule 7

108. The professor said to the media persons, "From our research we have come to the conclusion that there is life on that planet." SSC CGL Tier-1 20.08.2021 (Shift-I)
(a) The professor said to the media persons from our research you had come to the conclusion that there was life on that planet.
(b) The professor told to the media persons that from your research you have come to the conclusion that there is life on that planet.
(c) The professor said to the media persons that from their research they had come to the conclusion that there was life on that planet.
(d) The professor informed the media persons that from our research we have come to the conclusion that there had been life on that planet.

Ans. (c) Refer to Rule 1 (c)(iii)

109. Kamal said, "I have done my work". SSC CGL Tier-1 20.08.2021 (Shift-II)
(a) Kamal said that I have done my work.
(b) Kamal said I have done my work.
(c) Kamal said that he has done his work.
(d) Kamal said that he had done his work.

Ans. (d) Refer to Rule 1 (c)(iii)

110. The counter clerk asked the visitor, "What is your name?" SSC CGL Tier-1 23.08.2021 (Shift-I)
(a) The counter clerk asked the visitor his name.
(b) The counter clerk asks the visitor your name.
(c) The counter clerk is asking the visitor your name.
(d) The counter clerk has asked the visitor his name.

Ans. (a) Refer to Rule 6

111. "Alas, I have broken my brother's watch!" said he. SSC CGL Tier-1 23.08.2021 (Shift-II)
(a) He exclaimed with sorrow I have broken my brother's watch.
(b) He exclaimed with sorrow that he had broken his brother's watch.
(c) He exclaimed with sorrow that he may have broken his brother's watch.
(d) He exclaimed with sorrow that he has broken his brother's watch.

Ans. (b) Refer to Rule 8

112. "I live in Mumbai", she said. SSC CGL Tier-1 24.08.2021 (Shift-I)
(a) She said that she has been living in Mumbai.
(b) She said that she had been living in Mumbai.
(c) She said that she lived in Mumbai.
(d) She says that she was living in Mumbai.

Ans. (c) Refer to Rule 1 (c)(i)

113. He said to me, "It was raining all day". SSC CGL Tier-1 24.08.2021 (Shift-II)
(a) He told me that it had been raining all day.
(b) He told me it is raining all day.
(c) He told me it has been raining all day.
(d) He told me it was raining all day.

Ans. (a) Refer to Rule 1 (c)(ii)

114. Nelson said, "I was playing cricket". SSC CGL Tier-1 24.08.2021 (Shift-III)
(a) Nelson said that he was playing cricket.
(b) Nelson said I was playing cricket.
(c) Nelson said that he had been playing cricket.
(d) Nelson said that I was playing cricket.

Ans. (c) Refer to Rule 1 (c)(vi)

SSC CPO 2024 (Tier 1 & 2)

115. I suggested to my brother that we should go to the hills for a change. SSC CPO Tier-2 08.01.2024
(a) I requested to my brother, "We should go to the hills for a change".
(b) I said to my brother, "We shall go to the hills for a change".
(c) I said to my brother, "Shall we go to the hills for a change?"
(d) I said to my brother, "Let us go to the hills for a change".

Ans. (d) The suggestion 'we should go' changes to the proposal 'Let us go' in direct speech.

116. The old man prayed to God to help him in his hour of sorrow SSC CPO Tier-2 08.01.2024
(a) The old man said, "O God, help me in his hour of sorrow".
(b) The old man said, "O God must help him in his hour of sorrow".
(c) The old man said, "O God, help me in my hour of sorrow".
(d) The old man said, "O God, help him in my hour of sorrow".

Ans. (c) Refer to Rule 7

117. He said to his friend, "Let us leave for the trek tomorrow". SSC CPO Tier-2 08.01.2024
(a) He suggested to his friend that they should leave for the trek the next day.
(b) He told his friend to leave for the trek the next day.
(c) He suggested his friend that let us leave for the trek tomorrow.
(d) He suggested to his friend to leave for the trek the next day.

Ans. (a) The direct suggestion 'Let us leave' changes to 'they should leave' in indirect speech and 'tomorrow' changes to 'the next day'.

118. You said, "Priya kept watching television till her mother exploded at her". SSC CPO Tier-2 08.01.2024
(a) You said that Priya had kept watching television till her mother exploded at her.
(b) You said that Priya kept watching television till her mother had exploded at her.
(c) You said that Priya kept watching television till her mother exploded at her.
(d) You said that Priya had kept watching television till her mother had exploded at her.

Ans. (c) The past simple 'kept watching' remains unchanged in indirect speech.

119. I asked my friend how one could be merry when everything was so messed up. SSC CPO Tier-2 08.01.2024
(a) I said to my friend, "Could one be merry when everything is so messed up?"
(b) I asked to my friend, "How can one be merry when everything was so messed up?"
(c) I said to my friend, "How can one be merry when everything is so messed up?"
(d) I said to my friend, "How one could be merry when everything was so messed up?"

Ans. (c) Refer to Rule 6

120. He says that he will clear all his dues by the following month. SSC CPO Tier-2 08.01.2024
(a) He says, "I will clear all my dues by next month".
(b) He says, "I will clear all his dues by next month".
(c) He said, "I will clear all my dues by next month".
(d) He said, "I would clear all my dues by next month".

Ans. (a) Refer to Rule 4 for time phrase changes

121. Ankit said to Ashna, "Do you know that the annual meeting has been postponed?" SSC CPO Tier-2 08.01.2024
(a) Ankit asked Ashna that do you know that the annual meeting has been postponed.
(b) Ankit asked Ashna if she would be knowing that the annual meeting had been postponed.
(c) Ankit asked Ashna if she had known that the annual meeting was postponed.
(d) Ankit asked Ashna if she knew that the annual meeting had been postponed.

Ans. (d) Refer to Rule 6

122. I said to him, "Please stay here tonight". SSC CPO Tier-2 08.01.2024
(a) I asked him if he would stay there that night.
(b) I requested him to please stay there tonight.
(c) I requested him to stay there that night.
(d) I asked him to please stay here that night.

Ans. (c) Refer to Rule 7

123. Isha told Shivani that they didn't need to buy tickets for the match as she had been given free passes for two. SSC CPO Tier-2 08.01.2024
(a) Isha said to Shivani, "We didn't need to buy tickets for the match as I am given free passes for two".
(b) Isha said to Shivani, "We don't need to buy tickets for the match as I have been given free passes for two".
(c) Isha said to Shivani, "They didn't need to buy tickets for the match as she was given free passes for two".
(d) Isha said to Shivani, "They didn't need to buy tickets for the match as I am given free passes for two."

Ans. (b) The indirect speech 'didn't need' changes to 'don't need' in direct speech and 'had been given' changes to 'have been given'.

124. She exclaimed with regret that she had acted very foolishly. SSC CPO Tier-2 08.01.2024
(a) "Oh! I regret having acted foolishly," she said.
(b) "Alas! How foolishly I have acted," she said .
(c) "I have acted foolishly," she said.
(d) "Ah! Have I acted foolishly?" she said.

Ans. (b) Refer to Rule 8

125. She said, "If only I could relive my past!" SSC CPO Tier-2 08.01.2024
(a) She said that she could relive her past.
(b) She wished that she could relive her past.
(c) She wished if she could relive my past.
(d) She wished that if she could relive her past.

Ans. (b) Refer to Rule 8

SSC CPO 2021 (Tier 1 & 2)

126. The little girl said that those butterflies were very colourful. SSC CPO Tier-2 26.07.2021
(a) The little girl said, "Those butterflies were very colourful".
(b) The little girl said, "These butterflies are very colourful."
(c) The little girl says, "How colourful were these butterflies!'
(d) The little girl said, "Are those butterflies very colourful?"

Ans. (b) Refer to Rule 1 (c)(i) and 5

127. The manager lauded the salesman and said that his performance had been exceptional. **SSC CPO Tier-2 26.07.2021**
(a) The manager said to the salesman, "Oh! Your performance had been exceptional."
(b) The manager said to the salesman, "Well done! Your performance has been exceptional."
(c) The manager said to the salesman, "Well done! Your performance has being exceptional."
(d) The manager said to the salesman, "Bravo! How exceptional his performance is!"
Ans. (b) Refer to Rule 8

128. The young man exclaimed that it was a great feast. **SSC CPO Tier-2 26.07.2021**
(a) The young man said, "What a great feast it is!"
(b) The young man said, "It has being a great feast!"
(c) The young man says, "It is a great feast."
(d) The young man said, "Is it a great feast?"
Ans. (a) Refer to Rule 8

129. He told you that he had not known that it was your birthday that day. **SSC CPO Tier-2 26.07.2021**
(a) He said to you, "I do not know that it was your birthday that day."
(b) You said to him, "I do not know that it is your birthday today."
(c) He said to you, "You did not know that it was my birthday today."
(d) He said to you, "I did not know that it is your birthday today."
Ans. (d) Refer to Rules 1(c) (v) and 4

130. He said to me, "What a pity! You missed the party." **SSC CPO Tier-2 26.07.2021**
(a) He exclaimed that it was a pity I had missed the party.
(b) He exclaimed that it was a pity you missed the party.
(c) He exclaimed what a pity it was that you missed the party.
(d) He told to me that it was a pity I had missed the party.
Ans. (b) Refer to Rule 8

131. "Let us go to the hills for a vacation," Mother said to us. **SSC CPO Tier-2 26.07.2021**
(a) Mother ordered us to go to the hills for a vacation.
(b) Mother said that should we go to the hills for a vacation.
(c) Mother suggested that let us go to the hills for a vacation.
(d) Mother suggested that we should go to the hills for a vacation.
Ans. (d) Refer to Rule 7

SSC CHSL 2024 (Tier 1 & 2)

132. He will say that he is okay. **SSC CHSL Tier-2 18.11.2024**
(a) He would say, 'I am okay.'
(b) He will say, 'I am always okay.'
(c) He will say, 'I was okay.'
(d) He will say, 'I am okay.'
Ans. (d) Refer to Rule 2 for pronouns.

133. The patient says, 'I am fine.' **SSC CHSL Tier-2 18.11.2024**
(a) The patient says that he will be fine.
(b) The patient says that he is fine.
(c) The patient says that he would be fine.
(d) The patient says that he was fine.
Ans. (b) Refer to Rule 2 for pronouns.

134. He always says to me, 'I am perturbed.' **SSC CHSL Tier-2 18.11.2024**
(a) He always tells me that he is mostly perturbed.
(b) He always tells me that he is perturbed.
(c) He always tells me that he is perturbed by change.
(d) He always tells me that he is going to be perturbed.
Ans. (b) Refer to Rule 2 for pronouns.

135. He said to the mechanic, "Will you have the car ready by tomorrow morning?" **SSC CHSL Tier-2 10.01.2024**
(a) He asked the mechanic if he would have the car ready by the next morning.
(b) He told the mechanic if he will have the car ready for the next morning.
(c) He asked the mechanic if he will have the car ready by the previous morning.
(d) He said the mechanic whether he would has the car ready by the following morning.
Ans. (a) Refer to Rule 6

136. Anil said to Ria, "I know where everything is kept in the kitchen." **SSC CHSL Tier-2 10.01.2024**
(a) Anil told Ria that he knows where everything was kept in the kitchen.
(b) Anil told Ria that he knew where everything is kept in the kitchen.
(c) Anil asked Ria that he knows where everything was kept in the kitchen.
(d) Anil told Ria that he knew where everything was kept in the kitchen.
Ans. (d) Refer to Rule 1(c)(i)

SSC CHSL 2023 (Tier 1 & 2)

137. The sage said, ''Man proposes and God disposes''. **SSC CHSL Tier-1 09.03.2023 (Shift-I)**
(a) The sage said that man had proposed and God had disposed.
(b) The sage said that man proposed and God disposed.
(c) The sage said that man proposes and God dispose.
(d) The sage said that man proposes and God disposes.
Ans. (d) Refer to Rule 1(b)

138. The father said to his daughter, ''You mother will be waiting for me''. **SSC CHSL Tier-1 09.03.2023 (Shift-III)**
(a) The father told his daughter that her mother was waiting for me.
(b) The father told his daughter that her mother would be waiting for him.
(c) The father told his daughter that my mother would be waiting for him.
(d) The father told his daughter that her mother will be waiting for him.
Ans. (b) Refer to Rule 1(c)(viii)

139. The mayor said to the marshals, ''Dont't conduct any drill tomorrow''. **SSC CHSL Tier-1 10.03.2023 (Shift-I)**
(a) The mayor ordered the marshals not to conduct any drill the previous day.
(b) The mayor ordered the marshals not to conduct any drill tomorrow.
(c) The mayor ordered the marshals not to conducted any drill the next day.
(d) The mayor ordered the marshals not to conduct any drill the next day.
Ans. (d) Refer to Rule 7

140. My mother said, "I am meeting your father today."
SSC CHSL Tier-1 10.03.2023 (Shift-II)
(a) My mother said that she was meeting my father that day.
(b) My mother says that she was meeting my father today.
(c) The mother said that she has been meeting my father that day.
(d) My mother said that she were meeting my father that day.

Ans. (a) Refer to Rules 1(c)(ii) and 4

141. The surgeon says, "You should get anaesthesia for the surgery. SSC CHSL Tier-1 10.03.2023 (Shift-IV)
(a) The surgeon says you should get anaesthesia for the surgery.
(b) The surgeon said that I shall get anaesthesia for the surgery.
(c) The surgeon says that I should have got anaesthesia for the surgery.
(d) The surgeon says that I should get anaesthesia for the surgery.

Ans. (d) Refer to Rule 2 for pronouns.

142. The student said to her, "I don't remember your name."
SSC CHSL Tier-1 13.03.2023 (Shift-I)
(a) The student said to her that I did not remember her name.
(b) The student said to her that he/she cannot remember her name.
(c) The student told her that he/she did not remember her name.
(d) The student told her that he/she do not remember her name."

Ans. (c) Refer to Rule 1(c)(i)

143. She said to her,"Please pay attention to the detials".
SSC CHSL Tier-1 13.03.2023 (Shift-II)
(a) She requests her that pay attention to the details.
(b) She commanded her for paying attention to the details.
(c) She requested her to pay attention to the details.
(d) She requested her that to pay attention to the details.

Ans. (c) Refer to Rule 7

144. He said that he had taken French lessons on Duolingo.
SSC CHSL Tier-1 13.03.2023 (Shift-III)
(a) He says, "He has taken French lessons on Duolingo".
(b) He said, "I take French lessons on Duolingo".
(c) He said, "I have taken French lessons on Duolingo".
(d) He said, "You took French lessons on Duolingo".

Ans. (c) Refer to Rule 1(c)(iii)

145. She said that she would not be coming to the school that day. SSC CHSL Tier-1 13.03.2023 (Shift-IV)
(a) She had said, "She must not be coming to the school today".
(b) She said, "You will not be coming to the school today".
(c) She said, "I may not come to the school tomorrow".
(d) She said."I will not be coming to the school today".

Ans. (d) Refer to Rules 1(c)(viii) and 4

146. The professor said, "You must learn these words regularly." SSC CHSL Tier-1 14.03.2023 (Shift-I)
(a) The professor said that I had to learn those words regularly.
(b) The professor said that you had to learn these words regularly.
(c) The professor said that I must learn those words regularly.
(d) The professor said I should learn these words regularly.

Ans. (a) Refer to Rule 3 for modals.

147. Shubham said that his father was playing cricket with him. SSC CHSL Tier-1 15.03.2023 (Shift-I)
(a) Shubham said, "My father played cricket with me".
(b) Shubham said, "My father is playing cricket with me".
(c) Shubham said, "My father was playing cricket with me".
(d) Shubham said, "My father had played cricket with me".

Ans. (b) Refer to Rule 1(c)(ii)

148. He said that he would be taking a leave of absence for two weeks as there had been a death in his family.
SSC CHSL Tier-1 15.03.2023 (Shift-III)
(a) He said two "I am going to take a leave for two weeks as there had been a death in my family".
(b) He said, "I would be taking a leave of absence for two weeks as there been a death in my family".
(c) He said, "I will be taking a leave of absence for two weeks as there is a death in my family".
(d) He said, "I will be taking a leave of absence for two weeks as there has been a death in my family".

Ans. (d) Refer to Rules 1(c)(viii) and 1(c)(iii)

149. I explained, "I don't belong here".
SSC CHSL Tier-1 15.03.2023 (Shift-IV)
(a) I explained that I do not belong there.
(b) I explained that I did not belong here.
(c) I explained that I did not belong there.
(d) I said that I did not belonged here.

Ans. (c) Refer to Rules 1(c)(i) and 5

150. Tina said, "My parents are getting divorced".
SSC CHSL Tier-1 16.03.2023 (Shift-I)
(a) Tina said that her parents are getting divorced.
(b) Tina said that her parents were get divorced.
(c) Tina said that her parents were getting divorced.
(d) Tina said that her parents have been getting divorce.

Ans. (c) Refer to Rule 1(c)(ii)

151. "I have heard the podcast before", Nita says.
SSC CHSL Tier-1 16.03.2023 (Shift-II)
(a) Nita says that she has heard the podcast before.
(b) Nita says that she had heard the podcast ago.
(c) Nita says that she is hearing the podcast before.
(d) Nita says that she had heard the podcast before.

Ans. (a) Refer to Rule 1(c)(iii)

152. He said, "I will go to Indonesia tomorrow".
SSC CHSL Tier-1 16.03.2023 (Shift-III)
(a) He said that he would go to Indonesia tomorrow.
(b) He said that he would go to Indonesia the next day.
(c) He said that he would be going to Indonesia the next day.
(d) He said he would go to Indonesia by tomorrow.

Ans. (b) Refer to Rules 1(c)(viii) and 4

153. The teacher asked me if I had seen the match.
SSC CHSL Tier-1 16.03.2023 (Shift-IV)
(a) "Did you see the match?" the teacher said to me.
(b) "Did you had saw the match?" the teacher said to me.
(c) "Did you saw the match?" the teacher said to me.
(d) "Did you seen the match?" the teacher said to me.

Ans. (a) Refer to Rule 6

154. "Who is it?" Vikram asked, his euphoria fading.
SSC CHSL Tier-1 17.03.2023 (Shift-I)
(a) With a faded euphoria, Vikram asked who is it.
(b) As his euphoria faded, Vikram asks as to who was it.
(c) With his euphoria faded, Vikram asked who it is.
(d) With his euphoria fading, Vikram asked who it was.

Ans. (d) Refer to Rule 6

155. He said, "You were making excuses."
SSC CHSL Tier-1 17.03.2023 (Shift-II)
(a) He said that I was making excuses.
(b) He said that you were making excuses.
(c) He said that you had been making excuses.
(d) He said that I had been making excuses.

Ans. (d) Refer to Rule 1(c)(vi)

156. Rahul asked me, "Are we going to New York next year?"
SSC CHSL Tier-1 17.03.2023 (Shift-III)
(a) Rahul asked that are we going to New York next year.
(b) Rahul asked me that were we going to New York next year.
(c) Rahul asked me that would we go to New York next year?
(d) Rahul asked me if we were going to New York next year.

Ans. (d) Refer to Rule 6

157. Pritam said, "The prisoner had slept throughout the journey."
SSC CHSL Tier-1 17.03.2023 (Shift-IV)
(a) Pritam said that the prisoner had been sleeping throughout the journey.
(b) Pritam said that the prisoner had sleep throughout the journey.
(c) Pritam said that the prisoner had slept throughout the journey.
(d) Pritam said that the prisoner has slept throughout the journey.

And. (c) Refer to Rule 1(c)(vii)

158. She said to her maid, "Clean the utensils properly".
SSC CHSL Tier-1 20.03.2023 (Shift-II)
(a) She ordered her maid to clean the utensils properly.
(b) She commanded her maid that kindly clean the utensils properly.
(c) She orders her maid to clean the utensils properly.
(d) She commands her maid that clean the utensils properly.

Ans. (a) Refer to Rule 7

159. I said, "I'm not very happy at work".
SSC CHSL Tier-1 20.03.2023 (Shift-III)
(a) I told her that I was not very happy at work.
(b) I told her that I had not been very happy at work.
(c) I told her I would not be very happy at work.
(d) I told her that I am not very happy at work.

Ans. (a) Refer to Rule 1(c)(i)

160. Ravi said, "I may sell this tie".
SSC CHSL Tier-1 20.03.2023 (Shift-IV)
(a) Ravi said that he may sell that tie.
(b) Ravi said that he might sell that tie.
(c) Ravi said that I might sell that tie.
(d) Ravi said that he should sell this tie.

Ans. (b) Refer to Rule 3

161. Miranda said to her teacher, "I was sick for a day".
SSC CHSL Tier-1 21.03.2023 (Shift-II)
(a) Miranda told her teacher that she is sick for a day.
(b) Miranda told her teacher that she had been sick for a day.
(c) Miranda told her teacher that she was sick for a day.
(d) Miranda told her teacher that she has been sick for a day.

Ans. (b) Refer to Rule 1(c)(v)

162. Lee said to his wife, "I am very happy today".
SSC CHSL Tier-1 21.03.2023 (Shift-IV)
(a) Lee told his wife that he has been very happy that day.
(b) Lee told his wife that he was very happy that day.
(c) Lee told his wife he was very happy today.
(d) Lee told his wife that he was very happy today.

Ans. (b) Refer to Rules 1(c)(i) and 4

163. Madhav applauded her, saying that she had done well.
SSC CHSL Tier-2 26.06.2023
(a) Madhav say, "Bravo! You have done well".
(b) Madhav said, "Bravo! You have done well".
(c) Madhav said, "Bravo! You been done well".
(d) Madhav say, "Bravo! You have be done well".

Ans. (b) Refer to Rule 8

164. My son exclaimed with joy that it was an attractive site.
SSC CHSL Tier-2 26.06.2023
(a) My son said, "It is an attractive site".
(b) My son said, "What an attractive site it is!"
(c) My son said, "What an attractive site it was".
(d) My son said, "It was an attractive site".

Ans. (b) Refer to Rule 8

165. The captain said to the soldiers, "Follow the enemy".
SSC CHSL Tier-2 02.11.2023
(a) The captain commanded his soldiers to follow the enemy.
(b) The captain said his soldiers to follow the enemy.
(c) The captain requested his soldiers to follow the enemy.
(d) The captain charged his soldiers to followed the enemy.

Ans. (a) Refer to Rule 7

166. Rakesh said, "Wow! What a beautiful house".
SSC CHSL Tier-2 02.11.2023
(a) Rakesh exclaimed that it was a beautiful house.
(b) Rakesh exclaimed with surprise that it was must be beautiful house.
(c) Rakesh exclaimed with sorrow that it was a beautiful house.
(d) Rakesh told that it had been a beautiful house.

Ans. (a) Refer to Rule 8

SSC CHSL 2022 (Tier 1 & 2)

167. He said, "It's been raining since last night".
SSC CHSL Tier-1 25.05.2022 (Shift-III)
(a) He said that it had rained since last night.
(b) He said that it had been raining since the night before.
(c) He's said that it had been raining since yesterday.
(d) He said that it's raining since last night.

Ans. (b) Refer to Rules 1(c)(iv) and 4

168. Gogol offered me to go to the market in his car.
SSC CHSL Tier-1 06.06.2022 (Shift-II)
(a) "Let me take you to the market," Gogol offered.
(b) "Can I take to the market" Gogol asked me.

(c) "Let's go to the market in my car", Gogol told me.
(d) "Can you come with me to the market", Gogol asked me.

Ans. (c) The indirect offer 'offered me to go' changes to direct suggestion 'Let's go to the market in my car'.

169. Fiona enquired whether I had gone to school on Tuesday. **SSC CHSL Tier-1 10.06.2022 (Shift-III)**
(a) "Had you been going to school on Tuesday?" Fiona asked me.
(b) "Where are you going on Tuesday?" Fiona asked me.
(c) "Did you go to school on Tuesday?" Fiona asked me.
(d) "Are you gone to school on Tuesday? Fiona enquired.

Ans. (c) Refer to Rule 6

SSC CHSL 2021 (Tier 1 & 2)

170. "I like having South Indian breakfast", said Arun to the receptionist. **SSC CHSL Tier-1 12.04.2021 (Shift-II)**
(a) Arun tells the receptionist that he has liked South Indian breakfast.
(b) Arun is telling the receptionist that he likes South Indian breakfast.
(c) Arun told the receptionist that he will like South Indian breakfast.
(d) Arun told the receptionist that he liked having South Indian breakfast.

Ans. (d) Refer to Rule 1(c)(i)

171. Select the correct indirect form of the given sentence.
The yoga instructor said to us, "Doing yoga daily will help you to develop a healthy mind and body". **SSC CHSL Tier-1 19.04.2021 (Shift-III)**
(a) The yoga instructor said to us that daily yoga will help us to develop a healthy mind and body.
(b) The yoga instructor was told them that daily yoga would help them to develop a healthy mind and body.
(c) The yoga instructor said to us that doing daily yoga will be helping us to develop a healthy mind and body.
(d) The yoga instructor told us that doing yoga daily would help us to develop a healthy mind and body.

Ans. (d) Refer to Rule 1(c)(viii)

172. Anju said to Vijaya, "You can stay with us whenever you are in Delhi". **SSC CHSL Tier-1 04.08.2021 (Shift-I)**
(a) Anju told Vijaya that she could stay with them whenever she was in Delhi.
(b) Anju told Vijaya that she could stay with them whenever you were in Delhi.
(c) Anju told Vijaya that she can stay with us whenever she is in Delhi.
(d) Anju told Vijaya that you can stay with us whenever you are in Delhi.

Ans. (a) Refer to Rules 1(c)(i) and 3

173. Mother said, "All the guests will arrive tonight". **SSC CHSL Tier-1 10.08.2021 (Shift-I)**
(a) Mother said that all the guests would arrive that night.
(b) Mother said that all the guests will arrive tonight.
(c) Mother told that all the guests would arrive tonight.
(d) Mother said that all the guests will arrive that night.

Ans. (a) Refer to Rules 1(c)(viii) and 4

174. "Our teacher returned from Mumbai last month", she said. **SSC CHSL Tier-1 12.08.2021 (Shift-III)**
(a) She said that her teacher had returned from Mumbai the earlier month.
(b) Her teacher returned from Mumbai last month, she said.
(c) She said that their teacher had returned from Mumbai the previous month.
(d) She said that her teacher had returned from Mumbai the previous month.

Ans. (c) Refer to Rules 1(c)(v) and 4

SSC Selection Post 2024

175. The employee said "I somehow managed to submit the project last night." **SSC SP 20.06.2024 (Shift-I)**
(a) The employee said that I somehow managed to submit the project the previous night.
(b) The employee said that I have somehow managed to submit the project last night.
(c) The employee said that he had somehow managed to submit the project last night.
(d) The employee said that he had somehow managed to submit the project the previous night.

Ans. (d) Refer to Rules 1(c)(v) and 4

176. The teacher said that plants have life in them. **SSC SP 20.06.2024 (Shift-I)**
(a) The teacher said, "Plants have life in them."
(b) The teacher says, "A plant has life in them."
(c) The teacher said, "Plants too have life in them."
(d) The teacher said. "The plant had life in them."

Ans. (a) Refer to Rule 1(b)

177. I said to Amit, "I am not participating in the annual function." **SSC SP 20.06.2024 (Shift-II)**
(a) I said Amit that I was not participating in the annual function.
(b) I told Amit that he was not participating in the annual function.
(c) I told Amit that I was not participating in the annual function.
(d) I told to Amit that I was not participating in the annual function.

Ans. (c) Refer to Rule 1(c)(ii)

178. Select the option that expresses the given sentence in reported speech.
Sheena said, 'I am flying a kite.' **SSC SP 20.06.2024 (Shift-IV)**
(a) Sheena said that she had flown a kite.
(b) Sheena said that she has been flying a kite.
(c) Sheena said that she was flying a kite.
(d) Sheena says she was flying a kite.

Ans. (c) Refer to Rule 1(c)(ii)

SSC Selection Post 2023

179. Liam asked if we could proceed with the award ceremony. **SSC SP 27.06.2023 (Shift-I)**
(a) Liam said, "Can we proceed with the award ceremony?"
(b) Liam said, "Will we proceed with the award ceremony?"
(c) Liam said, "Should we proceed with the award ceremony?"
(d) Liam said, "Could we please proceed with the award ceremony?"

Ans. (a) Refer to Rule 6

180. Aravind said, "My teacher is correcting the answer sheets." **SSC SP 27.06.2023 (Shift-I)**

(a) Aravind said his teacher was be corrected the answer sheets.
(b) Aravind said that his teacher is being correcting the answer sheets.
(c) Aravind said that his teacher was correcting the answer sheets.
(d) Aravind said that teacher is corrected the answer sheets.

Ans. (c) Refer to Rule 1(c)(ii)

181. Bibiya asked the doctor if she could get the discharge in the morning. **SSC SP 27.06.2023 (Shift-III)**

(a) Bibiya asked the doctor, "Can I get the discharge in the morning?"
(b) Bibiya asked the doctor, "How can I get the discharge in the morning?"
(c) Bibiya asked the doctor, "Could I have got the discharge in the morning?"
(d) Bibiya asked the doctor, "If I can get the discharge in the morning?"

Ans. (a) Refer to Rule 6

182. "We will have a thorough search before opening the room," the inspector told his subordinates. **SSC SP 27.06.2023 (Shift-IV)**

(a)The inspector told his subordinates that they would be having a thorough search before opening the room.
(b) The inspector told his subordinates that they can have a thorough search before opening the room.
(c) The inspector told his subordinates that they will had a thorough search before opening the room.
(d) The inspector told his subordinates that they would have a thorough search before opening the room.

Ans. (d) Refer to Rule 1(c)(viii)

183. The teacher said, "She had started the fight". **SSC SP 27.06.2023 (Shift-IV)**

(a) The teacher complained that she has started the fight.
(b) The teacher said that she had started the fight.
(c) The teacher ordered that she had started the fight.
(d) The teacher said that she has started the fight.

Ans. (b) Refer to Rule 1(c)(vii)

SSC Selection Post 2022

184. "Where have you put the medical kit?" I asked my nephew. **SSC SP 01.08.2022 (Shift-I)**

(a) I asked my nephew where he had put the medical kit.
(b) I asked my nephew where he has put the medical kit.
(c) I asked my nephew that where he had put the medical kit.
(d) I asked my nephew where had he put the medical kit.

Ans. (a) Refer to Rules 6 and Rule 1(c)(iii)

185. "Has he come to office today?" You asked me. **SSC SP 01.08.2022 (Shift-I)**

(a) You asked me if he is coming to office today.
(b) You asked me whether he is in office today.
(c) You asked me if he has come to office today.
(d) You asked me whether he had come to office that day.

Ans. (d) Refer to Rule 6

186. The swallow asked the skylark, "Will we be able to shift the eggs from this tree by tomorrow?" **SSC SP 01.08.2022 (Shift-I)**

(a) The swallow asked the skylark whether they would be able to shift the eggs from that tree by the next day.
(b) The swallow asked the skylark whether they could be able to shift the eggs from this tree by tomorrow.
(c) The swallow asked the skylark whether they would have been able to shift the eggs from the tree by the next day.
(d) The swallow asked the skylark whether they will be able to shift the eggs from that tree by the next day.

Ans. (a) Refer to Rule 6

187. My mother said to my sister, "Did you receive a mail from your teacher?" **SSC SP 01.08.2022 (Shift-I)**

(a) My mother told my sister that did she receive a mail from her teacher.
(b) My mother said to my sister whether did she receive a mail from her teacher.
(c) My mother asked my sister if she had received a mail from her teacher.
(d) My mother advised my sister if did she received a mail from her teacher.

Ans. (c) Refer to Rule 6

188. My father asked how I had done that. **SSC SP 01.08.2022 (Shift-I)**

(a) My father asked, "How I had do that?"
(b) My father asked "How I did this".
(c) My father asked "How I had done that" .
(d) My father asked "How did you do this?"

Ans. (d) Refer to Rule 6

189. "Stop! Don't fight" said the mother to her children. **SSC SP 01.08.2022 (Shift-I)**

(a) The mother exclaimed to her children angrily to stop and don't fight.
(b) The mother exclaimed angrily to her children to stop and not fight.
(c) The mother exclaimed to her children to pause and not engage in a fight.
(d) The mother told her children to stop and not fight.

Ans. (b) Refer to Rule 7

SSC Steno 2024

190. She said, "Bravo! You have done well." **SSC Steno 11.12.2024 (Shift-I)**

(a) She applauded her saying that she had done well.
(b) She told her saying that she had done well.
(c) She applauded her saying that she did well.
(d) She applauded her saying that she has done well.

Ans. (a) Refer to Rule 8

191. Little Sam requested to let him rest there. **SSC Steno 11.12.2024 (Shift-I)**

(a) Little Sam said, "Do rest here."
(b) Little Sam said, "Let us rest here."
(c) Little Sam said, "Let me be resting here."
(d) Little Sam said, "Let me rest here."

Ans. (d) Refer to Rule 7

192. My father said, "Neha shall come back by 3:00 pm." **SSC Steno 11.12.2024 (Shift-I)**

(a) My father said that Neha should come back by 3:00 pm.
(b) My father told that Neha should come back by 3:00 pm.
(c) My father told that Neha shall come back by 3:00 pm.
(d) My father said that Neha will come back by 3:00 pm.

Ans. (d) The indirect speech changes 'shall' to 'will' to reflect a future action mentioned in the past.

193. Mother warned me not to make a mess of the living room again. SSC Steno 11.12.2024 (Shift-I)
(a) Mother warned, "Don't you dare to have made a mess of the living room again."
(b) Mother told me, "Do not make a mess from the living room again."
(c) Mother warned, "Don't make a mess of the living room again!"
(d) Mother instructed, "You may not be making a mess of the living room again."

Ans. (c) Refer to Rule 7

194. She said, "How beautiful is the rain!" SSC Steno 11.12.2024 (Shift-I)
(a) She exclaimed with joy that the rain had been beautiful.
(b) She exclaimed with joy that the rain has been beautiful.
(c) She exclaimed with joy that the rain is beautiful.
(d) She exclaimed with joy that the rain was beautiful.

Ans. (d) Refer to Rule 8

195. Mrs. Lisa suggested that we should purchase the property. SSC Steno 11.12.2024 (Shift-I)
(a) Mrs. Lisa said, "Let us purchase the property."
(b) Mrs. Lisa said, "Property must be purchased by us."
(c) Mrs. Lisa told, "You may purchase the property."
(d) Mrs. Lisa said, "Please purchase the property."

Ans. (a) Refer to Rule 7

196. "I will teach you," said the old man to his grandson. SSC Steno 11.12.2024 (Shift-I)
(a) The old man told his grandson that he taught him.
(b) The old man told his grandson to teach him.
(c) The old man said that he will teach you.
(d) The old man told his grandson that he would teach him.

Ans. (d) Refer to Rule 1 (c)(viii)

197. He said, "I can't attend the meeting tomorrow." SSC Steno 11.12.2024 (Shift-I)
(a) He said that he couldn't attend the meeting tomorrow.
(b) He said that he couldn't attend the meeting the next day.
(c) He said that he can't attend the meeting tomorrow.
(d) He said that he can't attend the meeting the next day.

Ans. (b) Refer to Rules 3 and 4

198. He exclaimed that he was a very stupid fellow. SSC Steno 11.12.2024 (Shift-I)
(a) "How a stupid fellow are you!" he remarked.
(b) "What a stupid fellow you are!" he remarked.
(c) "Are you a stupid fellow!" he remarked.
(d) "How a stupid fellow you are!" he remarked.

Ans. (b) Refer to Rule 8

199. The Minister explained that he was working for the benefit of the country. SSC Steno 11.12.2024 (Shift-I)
(a) The Minister explains, "I will work for the benefit of the country."
(b) The Minister explained, "I am working for the benefit of the country."
(c) The Minister explained, "He was working for the benefit of the country."
(d) The Minister explained, "I was working for the benefit of the country."

Ans. (b) Refer to Rule 1(c)(ii)

200. She asked, "Are you coming to the party?" SSC Steno 11.12.2024 (Shift-I)
(a) She asked are you going to the party.
(b) She asked if I was coming to the party.
(c) She asked if I am coming to the party.
(d) She asked if I can come to the party.

Ans. (b) Refer to Rule 6

201. He promised, "He will not do the mistake again." SSC Steno 11.12.2024 (Shift-I)
(a) He promised that he would not do the mistake next time.
(b) He promised that he would not did the mistake next time.
(c) He promised that he will not do the mistake again.
(d) He promises that he will not do the mistake again.

Ans. (a) Refer to Rule 1 (c)(viii)

202. Megha asked Reena where she was going that day. SSC Steno 11.12.2024 (Shift-I)
(a) Megha asked Reena, "Where were you going that day?"
(b) Megha asked Reena, "Where were you going today?"
(c) Megha asked Reena, "Where have you been going today?"
(d) Megha asked Reena, "Where are you going today?"

Ans. (d) Refer to Rule 4 and 6

203. He said, "Alas! I am a ruined man." SSC Steno 11.12.2024 (Shift-II)
(a) He applauded with sorrow that he was a ruined man.
(b) He confessed with sorrow that he was a ruined man.
(c) He cried out with sorrow that he was a ruined man.
(d) He wished that he was a ruined man.

Ans. (c) Refer to Rule 8

204. The manager said to the peon, "Why were you absent yesterday?" SSC Steno 11.12.2024 (Shift-II)
(a) The manager enquired why the peon was absent the previous day.
(b) The manager asked the peon why he was absent the previous day.
(c) The manager asked the peon why he had been absent the previous day.
(d) The manager asked the peon why had he been absent the previous day.

Ans. (c) Refer to Rule 4 and 6

205. She told her friend that she had been studying for her examination. SSC Steno 11.12.2024 (Shift-II)
(a) She told her friend, "I had studied for my examination."
(b) She told her friend, "I am studying for my examination."
(c) She told her friend, "I was studying for my examination."
(d) She tells her friend, "I have been studying for my examination."

Ans. (c) Refer to Rule 1(c)(vi)

206. Calling me a friend, Surjit Singh encouraged me and advised me not to lose heart. SSC Steno 11.12.2024 (Shift-II)
(a) Surjit Singh asked me, "Cheer up, friend. Do not lose heart."
(b) Surjit Singh demanded, "Cheer up, friend. Do not lose heart."
(c) Surjit Singh said, "Cheer up, friend. Do not lose heart."
(d) Surjit Singh ordered me, "Cheer up, friend. Do not lose heart."

Ans. (c) Refer to Rule 8

207. They said, "We were planning to visit you next week." SSC Steno 11.12.2024 (Shift-II)
(a) They said that they have been planning to visit him next week.
(b) They said that they had planned to visit him next week.
(c) They said that they are planning to visit him the coming week.
(d) They said that they had been planning to visit him the following week.

Ans. (d) Refer to Rules 1(c)(vi) and 4

208. The father said, "Ramu, try again." SSC Steno 11.12.2024 (Shift-II)
(a) The father advised Ramu to try again.
(b) The father requested Ramu to try again.
(c) The father told Ramu that he tried again.
(d) The father said that Ramu tries again.

Ans. (a) Refer to Rule 7

209. "I have not completed the assignment yet," the student admitted. SSC Steno 11.12.2024 (Shift-II)
(a) The student admitted that he/she hadn't been able to complete the assignment yet.
(b) The student admitted that he/she hasn't been able to complete the assignment yet.
(c) The student admitted that he/she hasn't completed the assignment yet.
(d) The student admitted that he/she hadn't completed the assignment yet.

Ans. (d) Refer to Rule 1(c)(iii)

210. She said, "Don't the children like the cake?" SSC Steno 11.12.2024 (Shift-II)
(a) She enquired about whether the children liked the cake.
(b) She asked me whether the children didn't like the cake.
(c) She asked whether the children liked the cake.
(d) She wondered why the children didn't like the cake.

Ans. (c) Refer to Rule 6

211. The boss said to the secretary, "Don't forget to order A3 size paper." SSC Steno 11.12.2024 (Shift-II)
(a) The boss instructed the secretary not to forget to order A3 size paper.
(b) The boss told the secretary that she didn't forget to order A3 size paper.
(c) The boss asked the secretary to order A3 size paper.
(d) The boss told the secretary that she should not forget to order A3 size paper.

Ans. (a) Refer to Rule 7

212. Tom said that he had a strange experience the day before. SSC Steno 11.12.2024 (Shift-II)
(a) Tom exclaimed, "What a strange experience it was!"
(b) Tom said, "I will have a strange experience the day before."
(c) Tom said, "I must have a strange experience the day before."
(d) Tom said, "I had a strange experience yesterday."

Ans. (d) Refer to Rule 2 and 4

213. He said, "My mother will be here tomorrow." SSC Steno 11.12.2024 (Shift-II)
(a) He said that his mother would be there the next day.
(b) He said that his mother would be here tomorrow.
(c) He said that my mother will be here the next day.
(d) He said that my mother will be here tomorrow.

Ans. (a) Refer to Rules 1(c)(viii) and 4

214. "Why is he crying?" he asked. SSC Steno 11.12.2024 (Shift-II)
(a) He asked why he was crying.
(b) She asked why he is crying.
(c) She asked why he was crying.
(d) He asked why she crying.

Ans. (a) Refer to Rule 6

215. Ram said, "I watched football." SSC Steno 11.12.2024 (Shift-III)
(a) Ram said that I shall watch football.
(b) Ram said that he had watched football.
(c) Ram said that they watched football.
(d) Ram said that he watches football

Ans. (b) Refer to Rule 1(c)(v)

216. He said, "I am going to the party tonight." SSC Steno 11.12.2024 (Shift-III)
(a) He said that he would go to the party that night.
(b) He said that he was going to the party tonight.
(c) He said that he was going to the party that night.
(d) He said that he is going to the party tonight.

Ans. (c) Refer to Rules 1(c)(ii) and 4

217. The tourist said, "Wow! what a wonderful view." SSC Steno 11.12.2024 (Shift-III)
(a) The tourist exclaimed with joy that it was a wonderful view.
(b) The tourist explained with joy that the view is wonderful.
(c) The tourist said that the view is wonderful.
(d) The tourist told what a wonderful view it is.

Ans. (a) Refer to Rule 8

218. She said, "I cannot call you at this time." SSC Steno 11.12.2024 (Shift-III)
(a) She said that she could not call me at that time.
(b) She said that she cannot call me at that time.
(c) She said that she would not call me at this time.
(d) She said that she could not call me this time.

Ans. (a) Refer to Rules 3 and 5

219. They said that they were practising for the next annual function. SSC Steno 11.12.2024 (Shift-III)
(a) They said, "They were practising for the next annual function."
(b) They said, "We are practising for the next annual function."
(c) They said, "We are practising for tomorrow's annual function."
(d) They said, "We have been practising for the next annual function."

Ans. (b) Refer to Rules 1(c)(ii) and 4

220. Rathan said, "I have written a poem." SSC Steno 11.12.2024 (Shift-III)
(a) Rathan said that he has written a poem.
(b) Rathan said that I had written a poem.
(c) Rathan said that he wrote a poem.
(d) Rathan said that he had written a poem.

Ans. (d) Refer to Rule 1(c)(iii)

221. The traffic police told me that I couldn't park my two-wheeler there. SSC Steno 11.12.2024 (Shift-III)
(a) The traffic police said to me, "I can't park my two-wheeler there."
(b) The traffic police told me, "I couldn't park my two-wheeler here."

(c) The traffic police said to me, "You can't park your two-wheeler here."
(d) The traffic police said, "Do not park the two-wheeler here."

Ans. (c) Refer to Rules 3 and 5

222. Mohan said, "I shall go as soon as it is possible." SSC Steno 11.12.2024 (Shift-III)
(a) Mohan said that he would go as soon as it is possible.
(b) Mohan said that he will go as soon as it is possible.
(c) Mohan said that he would go as soon as it was possible.
(d) Mohan said that he will go as soon as it was possible.

Ans. (c) Refer to Rules 1(c)(viii) and 1(c)(i)

223. The traveller asked the owner if he could stay in that tavern. The peasant replied that he could. SSC Steno 11.12.2024 (Shift-III)
(a) The traveller said, "Could I stay in this tavern?" The peasant replied, "He should."
(b) The traveller said, "May I stay in this tavern?" The peasant replies, "You can."
(c) The traveller said, "Can I stay in this tavern?" The peasant replied, "You can."
(d) The traveller said, "Can I stay in this tavern?" The peasant replied, "She could."

Ans. (c) Refer to Rules 3 and 6

224. He said that it would be fun if I could join. SSC Steno 11.12.2024 (Shift-III)
(a) He said, "It will be fun if you can join."
(b) He said, "It will have been fun if you had joined."
(c) He said, "It will have been fun if I could have joined."
(d) He said, "It will have been fun if I had joined."

Ans. (a) Refer to Rules 3 and 6

225. My aunt said that they had shifted to a new house. SSC Steno 11.12.2024 (Shift-III)
(a) "I am shifting to a new house," said my aunt.
(b) "We will be shifting to a new house," said my aunt.
(c) "We are shifting to a new house," said my aunt.
(d) "We have shifted to a new house," said my aunt.

Ans. (d) Refer to Rule 1(c)(v)

226. Ammu said, "How brilliant I am!" SSC Steno 11.12.2024 (Shift-III)
(a) Ammu exclaimed that she was being brilliant.
(b) Ammu exclaimed that she is brilliant.
(c) Ammu exclaimed that she was brilliant.
(d) Ammu exclaimed that she has been brilliant.

Ans. (c) Refer to Rule 8

227. The solicitor said, 'Let us solve the dispute over the land.' SSC Steno 10.12.2024 (Shift-I)
(a) The solicitor wished that they should solve the dispute over the land.
(b) The solicitor suggested that they might solve the dispute over the land.
(c) The solicitor suggested that they should solve the dispute over the land.
(d) The solicitor ordered that we should solve the dispute over the land.

Ans. (c) Refer to Rule 7

228. She said she was seeing her brother the following day. SSC Steno 10.12.2024 (Shift-I)
(a) She said, 'I am seeing my brother tomorrow.'
(b) She says, 'I will see my brother tomorrow.'
(c) She said, "I was seeing my brother tomorrow."
(d) She said, "I should see my brother tomorrow.

Ans. (a) Refer to Rules 1(c)(ii) and 4

229. The customer asked the tailor, 'Will you have the dress ready by Tuesday?' SSC Steno 10.12.2024 (Shift-I)
(a) The customer asked the tailor if he should have the dress ready by Tuesday.
(b) The customer asked the tailor if he would have the dress ready by Tuesday.
(c) The customer asked the tailor if he will have the dress ready by Tuesday.
(d) The customer asked the tailor if he would like to have the dress ready by Tuesday.

Ans. (b) Refer to Rules 6 and 1(c)(viii)

230. She asked me why I was not eating. SSC Steno 10.12.2024 (Shift-I)
(a) She said, "Why don't you eat?"
(b) She said, "Why am I not eating?"
(c) She said, "Why are you not eating?"
(d) She said, "Why is he not eating?"

Ans. (c) Refer to Rule 6

231. Raju said to Reghu, "Stay back." SSC Steno 10.12.2024 (Shift-I)
(a) Raju ordered Reghu to stay back.
(b) Raju had ordered Reghu to stay back.
(c) Raju orders Reghu to stay back.
(d) Raju has ordered Reghu to stay back.

Ans. (a) Refer to Rule 7

232. She said, "I have finished my work." SSC Steno 10.12.2024 (Shift-I)
(a) She said that she had finished her work.
(b) She said that she would finish her work.
(c) She said that she will finish her work.
(d) She said that she has finished her work.

Ans. (a) Refer to Rule 1(c)(iii)

233. My friend said to me, "Do you know the recipe of mango ice-cream?" SSC Steno 10.12.2024 (Shift-I)
(a) My friend asked me that I knew the recipe of mango ice-cream.
(b) My friend asked me if I know the recipe of mango ice-cream.
(c) My friend asked me if I knew the recipe of mango ice-cream.
(d) My friend asked me that I know the recipe of mango ice-cream.

Ans. (c) Refer to Rule 6

234. "I am playing the keyboard," she explained. SSC Steno 10.12.2024 (Shift-I)
(a) She explained that she is playing the keyboard.
(b) She said that she had been playing the keyboard.
(c) She said that she is playing the keyboard.
(d) She explained that she was playing the keyboard.

Ans. (d) Refer to Rule 1(c)(ii)

235. She said to me, "I shall come to meet you tomorrow." SSC Steno 10.12.2024 (Shift-I)
(a) She asked me that could she come to meet me the next day.
(b) She tells me that she could come to meet me tomorrow.
(c) She told me that she will come to meet me tomorrow.
(d) She told me that she would come to meet me the next day.

Ans. (d) Refer to Rules 1(c)(viii) and 4

236. She said that she could bake cookies. SSC Steno 10.12.2024 (Shift-I)

(a) She had said, "I can bake cookies."
(b) She said, "I can bake cookies."
(c) She says, "I can bake cookies."
(d) She said, "I may bake cookies."

Ans. (b) Refer to Rule 3

237. They said that they had been waiting for the bus for over an hour. SSC Steno 10.12.2024 (Shift-I)

(a) "We have been waiting for the bus for over an hour," they said.
(b) "We waited for the bus for over an hour," they said.
(c) "We had waited for the bus for over an hour," they said.
(d) "We are waiting for the bus for over an hour," they said.

Ans. (a) Refer to Rule 1(c)(iv)

238. He said, "I have finished my homework." SSC Steno 10.12.2024 (Shift-I)

(a) He said that he had to finish his homework.
(b) He said that he has finished his homework.
(c) He said that he would finish his homework.
(d) He said that he had finished his homework.

Ans. (d) Refer to Rule 1(c)(iii)

239. He told me that he would have finished the project by the following day. SSC Steno 10.12.2024 (Shift-II)

(a) "I have finished the project by tomorrow," he said to me.
(b) "I would finish the project," he said to me tomorrow.
(c) "I will finish the project by the next day," he said to me.
(d) "I will have finished the project by tomorrow," he said to me.

Ans. (d) Refer to Rule 1(c)(viii)

240. The Headmistress said, "What a performance!" SSC Steno 10.12.2024 (Shift-II)

(a) The Headmistress said that what a performance.
(b) The Headmistress exclaimed that it was a great performance.
(c) The Headmistress praised what a great performance.
(d) The Headmistress exclaimed what a great performance.

Ans. (b) Refer to Rule 8

241. He said, "Shall I ever reach my destination?" SSC Steno 10.12.2024 (Shift-II)

(a) He said he shall never reach his destination.
(b) He said I shall never reach his destination.
(c) He wondered if he would ever reach his destination.
(d) He said to me I shall never reach my destination

Ans. (c) Refer to Rule 7

242. The doctor advised me to take bed rest and eat nutritious food. SSC Steno 10.12.2024 (Shift-II)

(a) The doctor told me, "I should take bed rest and eat nutritious food."
(b) The doctor said to me, "You take bed rest and eat nutritious food."
(c) The doctor said to me, "I take bed rest and eat nutritious food."
(d) The doctor said to me, "Take bed rest and eat nutritious food."

Ans. (d) Refer to Rule 7

243. He ordered his soldiers to take that bird away. Its gilded cage reminded him of his father whom he had imprisoned. SSC Steno 10.12.2024 (Shift-II)

(a) He said to his soldiers, "May this bird be taken away. Its gilded cage reminds me of my father whom I imprisoned."
(b) He said to his soldiers, "Take the bird away. Its gilded cage reminded him of his father whom I imprison."
(c) He said to his soldiers, "Take this bird away. Its gilded cage reminded me of my father whom I imprison."
(d) He said to his soldiers, "Take this bird away. Its gilded cage reminds me of my father whom I imprisoned.

Ans. (d) Refer to Rule 7

244. "Dear daughter," she said caressing her cheeks, "have you come to comfort me in my time of need?" SSC Steno 10.12.2024 (Shift-II)

(a) Caressing her daughter's cheeks, she asked affectionately if she had come to comfort her in her time of need.
(b) Caressing her daughter's cheeks, she said affectionately if she had been coming to comfort her in her time of need.
(c) Caressing her daughter's cheeks, she asked affectionately if she did come to comfort her in her time of need.
(d) Caressing her daughter's cheeks, she said affectionately if she has come to comfort her in her time of need.

Ans. (a) Refer to Rule 7

245. Koushik said to Tarun, "You are a good cricketer." SSC Steno 10.12.2024 (Shift-II)

(a) Koushik told Tarun that he had been a good cricketer.
(b) Koushik told that Tarun is a good cricketer.
(c) Koushik told Tarun that he was a good cricketer.
(d) Koushik tells Tarun that he is a good cricketer.

Ans. (c) Refer to Rule 1(c)(i)

246. Ravi said that he might go to the mall. SSC Steno 10.12.2024 (Shift-II)

(a) Ravi said, "I will go to the mall."
(b) Ravi said, "I can go to the mall."
(c) Ravi said, "I could go to the mall."
(d) Ravi said, "I may go to the mall."

Ans. (d) Refer to Rule 3

247. Sakshi said that she would do it then or never. SSC Steno 10.12.2024 (Shift-II)

(a) Sakshi said, "I would do it then or never."
(b) Sakshi said, "I have to do it now or never."
(c) Sakshi said, "I will do it now or never."
(d) Sakshi said, "I will do it then or never."

Ans. (c) Refer to Rule 1(c)(viii)

248. He asked me affectionately what he could do for me. SSC Steno 10.12.2024 (Shift-II)

(a) He said to me, "What should be done for you?"
(b) He said to me, "What can be done for me?"
(c) He said to me, "What can I do for you, dear?"
(d) He said to me, "What could he do?"

Ans. (c) Refer to Rule 6

249. Jatin said, "I was at home yesterday." SSC Steno 10.12.2024 (Shift-II)

(a) Jatin said that he was at home yesterday.
(b) Jatin said that he had been at home the day before.
(c) Jatin said he was at home the day before.
(d) Jatin said he was at home.

Ans. (b) Refer to Rules 1(c)(v) and 4

250. My sister requested me to bring her a watch. SSC Steno 10.12.2024 (Shift-III)
(a) She said, "My sister, please bring me a watch."
(b) "Please bring me a watch," said my sister.
(c) My sister said, "Will you bring me a watch?"
(d) "Please bring my sister a watch," said she.

Ans. (b) Refer to Rule 7

251. He said to her, "Do you know French?" SSC Steno 10.12.2024 (Shift-III)
(a) He asked her that does she know French.
(b) He asked her whether she has known French.
(c) He asked her if she knew French.
(d) He asked her if she knows French.

Ans. (c) Refer to Rule 6

252. "I am not feeling well," said Mary. SSC Steno 10.12.2024 (Shift-III)
(a) Mary says that she is not feeling well.
(b) Mary said that she is not feeling well.
(c) Mary says that she wasn't feeling well.
(d) Mary said that she was not feeling well.

Ans. (d) Refer to Rule 1(c)(ii)

253. The student requested them to take him to the reception. SSC Steno 10.12.2024 (Shift-III)
(a) "Take me to the reception," said the student.
(b) "Please take me in the reception," said the student.
(c) "Please take me to the reception," said the student.
(d) "Take me to the reception now," said the student

Ans. (c) Refer to Rule 7

254. "You were warned by us three days ago," the manager shouted at him. SSC Steno 10.12.2024 (Shift-III)
(a) The manager shouted at him that he was warned by them three days ago.
(b) The manager shouted at him that he was warned by them three days earlier.
(c) The manager shouted at him that he had been warned by them three days before.
(d) The manager shouted at him that he was warned by them three days before.

Ans. (c) Refer to Rule 7

255. "I am going to play with my friends," the child says to his mother. SSC Steno 10.12.2024 (Shift-III)
(a) The child asked his mother that he is going to play with his friends.
(b) The child told his mother that I am going to play with my friends.
(c) The child said to his mother that he was going to play with his friends.
(d) The child tells his mother that he is going to play with his friends.

Ans. (d) Refer to Rule 1(c)(ii)

256. The reporter reported, "The US President is arriving to India this week." SSC Steno 10.12.2024 (Shift-III)
(a) The reporter reports that the US President is arriving to India that week.
(b) The reporter reported that the US President was arriving to India that week.
(c) The reporter reported that the US President was arriving to India this week.
(d) The reporter reported that the US President is arriving to India next week.

Ans. (b) Refer to Rules 1(c)(ii) and 4

257. He exclaimed with delight that he had won the first prize. SSC Steno 10.12.2024 (Shift-III)
(a) "Wow! I might win the first prize," said he.
(b) "Hurrah! I have won the first prize," said he.
(c) "Hurrah! I win the first prize," said he.
(d) "Hurrah! I will win the first prize," said he.

Ans. (b) Refer to Rule 7

258. Gita said, "I lost my umbrella." SSC Steno 10.12.2024 (Shift-III)
(a) Gita said that I lost my umbrella.
(b) Gita said that she had lost her umbrella.
(c) Gita expressed that she has lost her umbrella.
(d) Gita told me that he lost her umbrella.

Ans. (b) Refer to Rule 1(c)(v)

259. The principal said that he would hold a meeting the next day. SSC Steno 10.12.2024 (Shift-III)
(a) "I will be holding a meeting tomorrow," the principal said.
(b) "Tomorrow, I will hold a meeting," says the principal.
(c) "I will hold a meeting tomorrow," said the principal.
(d) "A meeting will be held by me," said the principal.

Ans. (c) Refer to Rules 1(c)(viii) and 4

260. My friend said to me, "Do you want to accompany us on this tour?" SSC Steno 10.12.2024 (Shift-III)
(a) My friend asked me if he wanted to accompany them on that tour.
(b) My friend asked me if I wanted to accompany us on that tour.
(c) My friend asked me if I wanted to accompany them on that tour?
(d) My friend asked me if I wanted to accompany them on that tour.

Ans. (d) Refer to Rule 6

261. Ritu said, "I am eating apples." SSC Steno 10.12.2024 (Shift-III)
(a) Ritu said that she was eating apples.
(b) Ritu told that she was eating apples.
(c) Ritu said that she has been eating apples.
(d) Ritu said that she had been eating apples.

Ans. (a) Refer to Rule 1(c)(ii)

SSC Steno 2023

262. The class teacher told, "Kneel down in the corridor." SSC Steno 12.10.2023 (Shift-I)
(a) The class teacher ordered to kneel down in the corridor.
(b) The class teacher ordered that they should kneel down in the corridor.
(c) The class teacher told that they kneel down in the corridor.
(d) The class teacher had ordered to kneel down in the corridor.

Ans. (a) Refer to Rule 7

263. He said, "I am living in Ludhiana." SSC Steno 12.10.2023 (Shift-I)
(a) He asked that he is living in Ludhiana.
(b) He said that he is living in Ludhiana.
(c) He said that he was living in Ludhiana.
(d) He said that he has been living in Ludhiana.

Ans. (c) Refer to Rule 1(c)(ii)

264. My mother asked me, "Who is the new Mathematics teacher?" SSC Steno 12.10.2023 (Shift-I)
(a) My mother asked me who the new Mathematics teacher is.
(b) My mother asked me who the new Mathematics teacher were.
(c) My mother asked me who the new Mathematics teacher was.
(d) My mother asked me who new the Mathematics teacher was.

Ans. (c) Refer to Rule 6

265. Neeraj said that he would go as soon as it was possible. SSC Steno 12.10.2023 (Shift-I)
(a) Neeraj say, "I should go as soon as it is possible".
(b) Neeraj says, "I may went as soon as it was possible".
(c) Neeraj said, "I shall go as soon as it is possible".
(d) Neerajsay, "I shall went as soon as it is possible".

Ans. (c) Refer to Rule 1(c)(viii)

266. She said to me, "I have often told you not to play with fire." SSC Steno 12.10.2023 (Shift-I)
(a) She told me that she has often told me not to play with fire.
(b) She asked me that she had often told me not to play with fire.
(c) She said to me that she has often told me not to play with fire.
(d) She told me that she had often told me not to play with fire.

Ans. (d) Refer to Rule 1(c)(iv)

267. Riya asked, "Are you feeling fine?" SSC Steno 12.10.2023 (Shift-I)
(a) Riya asked me if I was feeling fine?
(b) Riya asked me if I was feeling fine.
(c) Riya asked her if she was feeling fine.
(d) Riya told me if I was feeling fine.

Ans. (b) Refer to Rule 6

268. Mohan said to Hari, "I will study for the exam." SSC Steno 12.10.2023 (Shift-I)
(a) Mohan would say to Hari that he will study for the exam.
(b) Mohan said to Hari that he will study for the exam.
(c) Mohan told Hari that he would study for the exam.
(d) Mohan suggested Hari that he would study for the exam.

Ans. (c) Refer to Rule 1(c)(viii)

269. The security asked him who he was and which flat he wished to visit. SSC Steno 12.10.2023 (Shift-I)
(a) The security said, "Who are you? Which flat do you wish to visit?"
(b) The security said, "Who are you? Which flat are you wishing to visit?"
(c) The security said, "Who are you? Which flat you wish to be visited?"
(d) The security said, "Who are you? Which flat you wished to visit?"

Ans. (a) Refer to Rules 6

270. My sister asked me, "When will I be allowed to go to the church?" SSC Steno 12.10.2023 (Shift-I)
(a) My sister asked me that when she would be allowed to go to the church.
(b) My sister prayed when she will be allowed to go to the church.
(c) My sister asked me when she would be allowed to go to the church.
(d) My sister asked me when she will be allowed to go to the church.

Ans. (c) Refer to Rules 6 and 1(c)(viii)

271. She told me that she would come to the party.
(a) She said, "I will come to the party." SSC Steno 13.10.2023 (Shift-I)
(b) She said, "I have to come to the party."
(c) She said, "I was coming to the party."
(d) She said, "I am coming to the party."

Ans. (a) Refer to Rule 1(c)(viii)

272. The old man advised him to always speak the truth. SSC Steno 13.10.2023 (Shift-I)
(a) The old man advised, "Truth be told."
(b) "I advised you to always speak the truth," the old man said.
(c) The old man said to him, "Always speak the truth."
(d) "Truth shall always be spoken," advised the old man.

Ans. (c) Refer to Rule 7

273. Harish says that there is going to be a snowfall. SSC Steno 13.10.2023 (Shift-I)
(a) Harish says, "There was going to be a snowfall."
(b) Harish says, "There will be going to be a snowfall."
(c) Harish says, "There is going to be a snowfall."
(d) Harish says, "There may be a snowfall."

Ans. (c) Refer to Rule 1(b)

274. Sonia said, "I have finished my meal." SSC Steno 13.10.2023 (Shift-I)
(a) Sonia said that she has finished her meal.
(b) Sonia said that she had finished my meal.
(c) Sonia said that she has finished my meal.
(d) Sonia said that she had finished her meal.

Ans. (d) Refer to Rule 1(c)(iii)

275. She exclaimed delightfully, "What a beautiful sunset!" SSC Steno 13.10.2023 (Shift-I)
(a) She exclaimed with delight that it was a beautiful sunset.
(b) She exclaimed that it was a beautiful sunset.
(c) She exclaimed with delight on seeing the beautiful sunset!
(d) She exclaimed delightedly about the sunset.

Ans. (a) Refer to Rule 8

276. Louise said that it was getting late. SSC Steno 13.10.2023 (Shift-I)
(a) Louise said, "It was got late."
(b) Louise said, "It got late."
(c) Louise said, "It gets late."
(d) Louise said, "It is getting late."

Ans. (d) Refer to Rule 1(c)(i)

277. He said, "I will go and return quickly." SSC Steno 13.10.2023 (Shift-I)
(a) He said that he would go and I will return quickly.
(b) He said that I would go and return quickly.
(c) He said that he would go and return quickly.
(d) He said that he will gone and returned quickly.

Ans. (c) Refer to Rule 1(c)(viii)

278. Shalini exclaimed that the painting was enchanting. SSC Steno 13.10.2023 (Shift-I)
(a) Shalini exclaimed, "Ahha! Look at the paintings!"
(b) "Oh! What a painting!" thought Shalini.
(c) "The painting was enchanting," said Shalini.
(d) Shalini said, "Such an enchanting painting this is!"

Ans. (d) Refer to Rule 8

279. Teena said that the servant might come the next day. SSC Steno 13.10.2023 (Shift-I)
(a) Teena said, "The servant will come tomorrow."
(b) Teena said, "The servant will be coming tomorrow."
(c) Teena said, "The servant may come today."
(d) Teena said, "The servant may come tomorrow."

Ans. (d) Refer to Rule 3 and 4

12

Rearrangement of Words to Form Sentences

'Rearrangement of Words to Form Sentences' or 'Jumbled words' is a type of question that is sometimes asked in the SSC Examination.

Types of Questions Asked

In the SSC examinations, a few types of questions are asked from this topic.

Type 1

Parts of a sentence are given below in jumbled order. Arrange the parts in the correct order to form a meaningful sentence.

Next to the Punjabi

A. clad in beautiful sarees B. family was a group from Chennai in

C. which all the women were

(a) BAC (b) ACB (c) BCA (d) ABC **Ans.** (c)

Type 2

Select the correct option to form a meaningful sentence.

A. is credited with saying B. do not dry your feet

C. if you want to leave your footprint on the sand of time

D. Dr. APJ Abdul Kalam, former President of India

(a) DCAB (b) DACB (c) CABD (d) ABCD **Ans.** (b)

How to Solve the Questions

To re-jumble the words to form a correct and meaningful sentence requires you to know the various patterns in which a sentence is written. These patterns called the syntax these are

- **Pattern 1** Subject + Verb + Direct Object
- **Pattern 2** Subject + Verb + Subject complement (which gives more information about the subject)
- **Pattern 3** Subject + Verb + Indirect Object + Direct Object
- **Pattern 4** Subject + Verb + Object + Preposition + Object of the preposition
- **Pattern 5** Subject + Verb + Object + Adjectives denoting a situation (open, close, strong, deep, etc.)
- **Pattern 6** Subject + Verb + Preposition + Prepositional Object
- **Pattern 7** Subject + Verb + Infinitive

Note Remember the subject and the object can be a noun, pronoun, gerund, infinitive or participle phrase.

SSC Exam Scanner

Directions (Q. Nos. 1-144) Parts of a sentence are given below in jumbled order. Arrange the parts in the correct order to form a meaningful sentence.

Or

Select the correct option to form a meaningful sentence.

SSC CGL 2024 (Tier 1 & 2)

1. A. it requires constant sustenance
B. in order for life to be liveable,
C. that enable it to grow and develop
D. and favourable circumstances **SSC CGL Tier-2 18.01.2025**
(a) ABCD (b) DCBA
(c) BADC (d) BDAC

Ans. (c)

The correct logical sequence to form a meaningful sentence is B, A, D, C. This arrangement provides a clear and coherent structure, emphasising the necessity of constant sustenance and favourable circumstances for life to grow and develop.

2. 1. India has been a land
P. and the learned man has been held in higher esteem
Q. of learning through the ages
R. but in the sense that learning has always been very highly valued
S. not indeed in the sense that education has been universal
6. than the warrior or the administrator. **SSC CGL Tier-2 18.01.2025**
(a) SRQP (b) QSRP (c) PSQR (d) RQSP

Ans. (b)

The correct order for the segments is QSRP. This ensures a logical flow. It starts with the overall context of India as a land of learning, explaining the nuance that education was not universal and emphasising the high value placed on learned individuals. The final segment highlights the respect held for scholars over warriors or administrators.

3. a. beginning in the 19th century,
b. was long a mystery and
c. the origin of the Moon
d. three competing theories emerged to solve it **SSC CGL Tier-2 18.01.2025**

(a) dcab (b) bdca
(c) abdc (d) cbad

Ans. (d)

The correct order for the sentence parts is cbad.

This creates a logical and meaningful sentence by first mentioning the origin of the Moon, describing it as a mystery, specifying the time period (19th century) and finally indicating that three competing theories emerged.

4. Through the dense forest, / the hikers / trekked / for hours / before reaching / the mountain peak. **SSC CGL Tier-2 20.01.2025**

(a) The hikers for hours through the dense forest trekked before reaching the mountain peak.
(b) The hikers trekked for hours through the dense forest before reaching the mountain peak.
(c) Through the dense forest for hours trekked the hikers before reaching the mountain peak.
(d) Before reaching the mountain peak, the hikers through the dense forest trekked for hours.

Ans. (b)

The correct order is 'The hikers trekked for hours through the dense forest before reaching the mountain peak.'

This arrangement ensures a logical flow of the sentence.

5. 1. An outstanding feature of the 21st century has been
P. greater security and education which
Q. the improvement of the income and
R. living conditions of the
S. working man leading to
6. has meant greater political power. **SSC CGL Tier-2 20.01.2025**

(a) SRQP (b) QRSP
(c) SPQR (d) PRQS

Ans. (b)

The correct order is QRSP.

Segment Q introduces the improvement, followed by R specifying the living conditions, S leading to greater security and education and P elaborating on the implications.

6. O. as it was the last one of the evening
P. the city bus was overcrowded
Q. and this gave an opportunity
R. to the pickpockets
S. to try their skill **SSC CGL Tier-1 09.09.2024 (Shift-II)**

(a) SRPOQ (b) PSORQ
(c) POQRS (d) SROPQ

Ans. (c)

The correct order is POQRS.
The sentence starts with introducing the subject 'The city bus was overcrowded.'
The phrase 'as it was the last one of the evening' explains why the bus was overcrowded. This leads to the consequence 'and this gave an opportunity' to whom 'to the pickpockets' to do what 'to try their skill.'

7. A. the use of animal research
B. throughout the past century
C. and it continues to be used to understand many diseases
D. has been of considerable importance
E. in the field of scientific and medical advancements **SSC CGL Tier-1 09.09.2024 (Shift-II)**

(a) AECDB (b) ECDBA
(c) ADEBC (d) EDCBA

Ans. (c)

The correct order is ADEBC.
The sentence starts with 'The use of animal research,' followed by its importance 'has been of considerable importance.' This is specified further 'in the field of scientific and medical advancements.'

The time frame is given next 'throughout the past century,' and the sentence concludes with its continued relevance 'and it continues to be used to understand many diseases.'

8. P. having the opportunity of observing people's
Q. we respect and appreciate their point of views
R. the advantage of travelling different places and
S. culture, custom and lifestyle, is that **SSC CGL Tier-1 09.09.2024 (Shift-III)**

(a) RQPS (b) PSQR
(c) RPSQ (d) SQPR

Ans. (c)

The correct order is RPSQ.

The sentence starts with 'The advantage of travelling different places' followed by its opportunity to observe people's culture custom etc. which ultimately implants a feeling of respect and appreciation for their point of views.

9. O. delicious
R. she
Q. a
P. baked
S. chocolate cake **SSC CGL Tier-1 10.09.2024 (Shift-II)**

(a) RPQOS (b) QOSRP
(c) OPQRS (d) SRPQO

Ans. (a)

The correct order is RPQOS.

The sentence logically begins with the subject 'She,' followed by the action 'baked,' the article and adjective 'a delicious' and concluding with the object 'chocolate cake.'

10. O. its first constitution
P. and soon got himself elected
Q. the administration of the country
R. general Ayub Khan took over
S. after Pakistan framed **SSC CGL Tier-1 10.09.2024 (S.hift-II)**

(a) SORQP (b) SPORQ
(c) POSRQ (d) ROPQS

Ans. (a)

The correct order is SORQP.
The sentence starts with 'After Pakistan framed,' followed by 'its first Constitution,' introducing the main event. Then, it transitions to 'general Ayub Khan took over the administration of the country and soon got himself elected.'

11. P. technology has revolutionised
Q. and it has transformed the way
O. every aspect of our lives
R. we communicate and connect **SSC CGL Tier-1 10.09.2024 (Shift-III)**

(a) RPQO (b) RPOQ
(c) POQR (d) ORQP

Ans. (c)

The correct order is POQR.

The sentence logically starts with 'Technology has revolutionised,' which introduces the main subject. It is followed by 'every aspect of our lives,' then explains the effect 'and it has transformed the way we communicate and connect.'

12. A. while the employees
B. meeting on time
C. the boss arrived at the
D. despite the heavy traffic
E. were late **SSC CGL Tier-1 11.09.2024 (Shift-I)**

(a) DCBAE (b) DACEB
(c) BACED (d) ACEDB

Ans. (a)

The correct order is DCBAE.
The sentence begins with 'Despite the heavy traffic,' introducing the condition, followed by 'the boss arrived at the meeting on time' showing the main event and finally 'while the employees were late' to contrast the situation.

13. A. he had to take the bus
B. his friend, who used to give
C. to his office because he had
D. him a lift, was on vacation
E. never learned to drive and

SSC CGL Tier-1 11.09.2024 (Shift-I)

(a) DACEB (b) ACEBD
(c) EBADC (d) BADEC

Ans. (b)

The correct order is ACEBD.
The sentence logically starts with 'He had to take the bus to his office because.'
Then, explains the reason with 'he had never learned to drive and his friend, who used to give him a lift, was on vacation.'

14. P. kindness and empathy
Q. in a world that can be
O. bring light and positivity
R. harsh and challenging

SSC CGL Tier-1 11.09.2024 (Shift-II)

(a) PORQ (b) ROQP
(c) QRPO (d) QROP

Ans. (c)

The correct order is QRPO.

The sentence begins with 'In a world that can be harsh and challenging,' setting the scene, followed by 'kindness and empathy bring light and positivity,' explaining the effect.

15. O. population is expected to triple in
P. the next 50 years
Q. among the world's poorest countries
R. population shrinkage in that period
S. whereas many rich countries will see

SSC CGL Tier-1 11.09.2024 (Shift-II)

(a) POSQR (b) RSOPQ
(c) SPORQ (d) QOPSR

Ans. (d)

The correct order is QOPSR.
The sentence starts with 'Among the world's poorest countries,' introducing the subject, followed by 'population is expected to triple in the next 50 years,' and concludes with 'whereas many rich countries will see population shrinkage in that period.'

16. P. an open mind
Q. seek it with
O. for personal growth and development
R. knowledge is a powerful tool

SSC CGL Tier-1 11.09.2024 (Shift-III)

(a) PQRO (b) ORPQ
(c) QROP (d) ROQP

Ans. (d)

The correct order is ROQP.

The sentence starts with 'Knowledge is a powerful tool for personal growth and development,' introducing the main idea, followed by 'seek it with an open mind,' giving advice.

17. P. the sun
Q. to our planet, Earth
O. provides essential energy
R. sustaining life and warmth

SSC CGL Tier-1 12.09.2024 (Shift-II)

(a) POQR (b) QROP
(c) ROQP (d) ORPQ

Ans. (a)

The correct order is POQR.

The sentence logically starts with 'The sun provides essential energy,' followed by 'to our planet, Earth,' introducing the subject and concludes with 'sustaining life and warmth.'

18. I / that / the chef / to work / in /
(a) (b) (c) (d) (e)
the new / heard / restaurant /
(f) (g) (h)
is going / across the road.
(i) (j)

SSC CGL Tier-1 12.09.2024 (Shift-II)

(a) acgbhifedj (b) abdcefhgij
(c) abdcgefhij (d) agbcidefhj

Ans. (d)

The correct order is agbcidefhj.

The sentence formed will be: 'I heard that the chef is going to work in the new restaurant across the road.'

19. O. went
P. yesterday
Q. we
R. to the
S. park **SSC CGL Tier-1 12.09.2024 (Shift-II)**

(a) RQOSP (b) OPQRS
(c) PSROQ (d) QORSP

Ans. (d)

The correct order is QORSP.
The sentence starts with 'We went,' followed by 'to the park' and concludes with 'yesterday,' giving a complete timeline.

20. A. needs to be
B. the shelf in
C. a piece of wood
D. the kitchen
E. need to buy
F. replaced, so I will

SSC CGL Tier-1 12.09.2024 (Shift-II)

(a) BEFCAD (b) ACDBFE
(c) DEBACF (d) BDAFEC

Ans. (d)

The correct order is BDAFEC.

The sentence logically starts with 'The shelf in the kitchen needs to be replaced,' introducing the main problem, followed by 'so I will need to buy a piece of wood,' explaining the solution.

21. A. smoking in
B. your youth stunts
C. the body and
D. clouds the brain

SSC CGL Tier-1 13.09.2024 (Shift-I)

(a) ABCD (b) CABD
(c) DCBA (d) DBCA

Ans. (a)

The correct order is ABCD.
The sentence logically starts with 'Smoking in your youth stunts,' followed by 'the body and clouds the brain,' providing a complete statement about the effects of smoking.

22. A. the upper part of the river
B. continuous rain on
C. week, there had been
D. during the previous

SSC CGL Tier-1 13.09.2024 (Shift-II)

(a) DBAC (b) DCBA
(c) ADCB (d) ABCD

Ans. (b)

The correct order is DCBA.
The sentence logically starts with 'During the previous week,' introducing the time frame, followed by 'there had been continuous rain' and specifying the location 'on the upper part of the river.'

23. O. also benefit from knowing
P. there are several reasons
Q. why even parents would
R. more about how and why
S. children do the things that they do

SSC CGL Tier-1 13.09.2024 (Shift-III)

(a) RQOPS (b) OPQSR
(c) PQORS (d) PQROS

Ans. (c)

The correct order is PQORS.

The sentence begins with 'There are several reasons,' introducing the main idea, followed by 'why even parents would also benefit from knowing' and concludes with 'more about how and why children do the things that they do.'

24. In November, Lakshman fell (P) / with fever (Q) / seriously ill (R) and pneumonia (S).

SSC CGL Tier-1 13.09.2024 (Shift-III)

(a) PQSR (b) PRQS
(c) PQRS (d) RQSP

Ans. (b)

The correct order is PRQS.
The sentence starts with 'In November, Lakshman fell,' followed by 'seriously ill,' then 'with fever,' and ends with 'and pneumonia,' providing a logical sequence of the events.

25. A. false news websites
B. spreading propaganda about politics
C. thrive because the advertisements and politicians
D. and social networking sites
E. make a lot of money

SSC CGL Tier-1 17.09.2024 (Shift-II)

(a) AECBD (b) ADCBE
(c) ADECB (d) AEDCB

Ans. (b)

The correct order is ADCBE.
The sentence starts with 'False news websites and social networking sites,' introducing the subjects, followed by 'thrive because the advertisements and politicians,' and concludes with 'spreading propaganda about politics make a lot of money.'

26. P. willing to go
Q. is not
R. my son
S. camping

SSC CGL Tier-1 17.09.2024 (Shift-II)

(a) RQPS (b) SPRQ
(c) PQRS (d) QRSP

Ans. (a)

The correct order is RQPS.
The sentence logically starts with 'My son,' followed by 'is not willing to go camping,' providing a clear statement of his reluctance.

27. A. so I am not very sure
B. I have a driving license
C. of myself reaching home safely
D. but no real driving experience

SSC CGL Tier-1 18.09.2024 (Shift-II)

(a) BCAD (b) BDCA
(c) BDAC (d) CABD

Ans. (c)

The correct order is BDAC.

The sentence starts with 'I have a driving license but no real driving experience,' introducing the main idea, and concludes with 'so I am not very sure of myself reaching home safely,' providing the reason.

28. P. dreams provide an escape
Q. where reality is suspended
R. into a world
O. of endless possibilities

SSC CGL Tier-1 18.09.2024 (Shift-II)

(a) OPQR (b) PROQ
(c) QORP (d) RPOQ

Ans. (b)

The correct order is PROQ.

29. A. new facts and advanced
B. but my opinion is
C. he has discovered
D. unchanged
E. new arguments

SSC CGL Tier-1 18.09.2024 (Shift-III)

(a) DACBE (b) CAEBD
(c) BDAEC (d) EBDCA

Ans. (b)

The correct order is CAEBD.

The sentence starts with 'He has discovered new facts and advanced new arguments,' followed by 'but my opinion is unchanged,' creating a clear contrast.

30. Though Sheela loves watching horror movies, .../....../....../ ......she rented another romantic today.

SSC CGL Tier-1 19.09.2024 (Shift-I)

(a) she planned to try something different yesterday / so she rented the latest romantic / and to her surprise she enjoyed it very much / so much so that
(b) and to her surprise she enjoyed it very much /so much so that /so she rented the latest romantic /she planned to try something different yesterday
(c) so she rented the latest romantic / and to her surprise she enjoyed it very much / so much so that / she planned to try something different yesterday
(d) so much so that / and to her surprise she enjoyed it very much / she planned to try something different yesterday / so she rented the latest romantic

Ans. (a)

The correct filler for the given blank is: she planned to try something different yesterday / so she rented the latest romantic / and to her surprise she enjoyed it very much / so much so that.

This sequence logically narrates the events in the order they happened: She planned something, rented a movie, enjoyed it, and was surprised by how much she liked it.

31. A. a lot
B. my daily routine
C. i have missed
D. since my retirement
E. at the workplace

SSC CGL Tier-1 19.09.2024 (Shift-II)

(a) CBEAD (b) BACED
(c) BEADC (d) BADEC

Ans. (a)

The correct order is CBEAD.
The sentence starts with 'I have missed,' introducing the main idea, followed by 'my daily routine at the workplace,' and concludes with 'a lot since my retirement,' providing the time frame and extent of the feeling.

32. A. all the plants and animals of today
B. it is written that Brahma is the God of creation
C. and it is He who has made
D. in the book of Hindu mythology

SSC CGL Tier-1 19.09.2024 (Shift-II)

(a) DACB (b) DBCA
(c) DCBA (d) CABD

Ans. (b)

The correct order is DBCA.

33. P. society benefits from diversity
Q. enriching cultures and
O. by fostering understanding and empathy
R. perspectives from around the world **SSC CGL Tier-1 19.09.2024 (Shift-III)**

(a) QPRO (b) POQR
(c) RPOQ (d) ROQP

Ans. (b)

The correct order is POQR.

The sentence starts with 'Society benefits from diversity,' introducing the main idea, followed by 'by fostering understanding and empathy' and concludes with 'enriching cultures and perspectives from around the world,' describing the benefits in detail.

34. O. attitude is
P. or tendency in individuals
Q. a broad-based behaviour
R. which implies
S. a hypothetical postulate

SSC CGL Tier-1 23.09.2024 (Shift-I)

(a) SQPRO (b) OSRQP
(c) OPQRS (d) OPSRQ

Ans.(b)

The correct order is OSRQP.

The sentence starts with 'Attitude is a hypothetical postulate,' introducing the main subject, followed by 'which implies a broad-based behaviour,' and concludes with 'or tendency in individuals,' providing a comprehensive explanation.

35. P. and has also created a wide gap between them
Q. laid too much stress on
R. teachers and students
S. online mode of education has
SSC CGL Tier-1 23.09.2024 (Shift-II)
(a) SRPQ (b) RQPS
(c) SQRP (d) PSQR
Ans. (c)
The correct order is SQRP.
The sentence starts with 'Online mode of education has,' introducing the subject, followed by 'laid too much stress on teachers and students,' and concludes with 'and has also created a wide gap between them,' explaining the consequences.

36. O. want
P. movie tonight
Q. do you
R. to watch
S. the SSC CGL Tier-1 23.09.2024 (Shift-II)
(a) RSPQO (b) QORSP
(c) OSQPR (d) OSPQR
Ans. (b)
The correct order is QORSP.
The sentence logically starts with 'Do you want,' followed by 'to watch the movie' and concludes with 'tonight?' forming a complete question.

37. P. always favours
Q. only the
R. fortune
S. bold SSC CGL Tier-1 23.09.2024 (Shift-II)
(a) SQPR (b) RPQS
(c) SRQP (d) PQRS
Ans. (b)
The correct order is RPQS.

38. A. only for themselves
B. is full of
C. people who live
D. the world
SSC CGL Tier-1 23.09.2024 (Shift-II)
(a) BCAD (b) ABCD
(c) DBAC (d) DBCA
Ans. (d)
The correct order is DBCA.

39. A. at the same time giving happiness to the poor
B. by providing them with food, clothes, money or grain
C. festivals in India are celebrated to share happiness
D. by being in the presence of the members of the family and
SSC CGL Tier-1 24.09.2024 (Shift-III)
(a) ACBD (b) CBAD
(c) CABD (d) CDAB
Ans. (d)
The correct order is CDAB.

40. P. unlock their potential
Q. empowers individuals to
O. and shape their future
R. the power of education
SSC CGL Tier-1 23.09.2024 (Shift-III)
(a) QROP (b) OPRQ
(c) RQPO (d) RPOQ
Ans. (c)
The correct order is RQPO.

41. P. her face
Q. I have
R. for a year
S. not seen
SSC CGL Tier-1 24.09.2024 (Shift-I)
(a) PQRS (b) PSQR
(c) SPQR (d) QSPR
Ans. (d)
The correct order is QSPR.
The sentence starts with 'I have,' followed by 'not seen,' then the object 'her face,' and concludes with 'for a year.'

42. A. and was searching for them
B. the grandmother couldn't find
C. all around the house
D. placed them on her head
E. her spectacles because she had
SSC CGL Tier-1 25.09.2024 (Shift-I)
(a) BADEC (b) BEDAC
(c) CABED (d) ADBEC
Ans. (b)
The correct order is BEDAC.

43. P. achieve success
Q. when you
R. and polite
S. stay humble
SSC CGL Tier-1 25.09.2024 (Shift-I)
(a) PRQS (b) SRQP
(c) RQPS (d) PQRS
Ans. (b)
The correct order is SRQP.

44. P. for a
Q. exercise daily
R. one must
S. good body
SSC CGL Tier-1 25.09.2024 (Shift-II)
(a) PRQS (b) PRSQ
(c) RQPS (d) PQRS
Ans. (c)
The correct order is RQPS.

45. A. the Industrial Revolution denotes
B. and continued until the middle of the 19th century
C. a significant period of social, economic and technological revolution
D. that commenced in the latter part of the 18th century
SSC CGL Tier-1 25.09.2024 (Shift-II)
(a) DCBA (b) ACDB
(c) ABCD (d) CADB
Ans. (b)
The correct order is ACDB.

46. P. hard work and perseverance
Q. no matter how difficult
O. lead to success
R. the journey may seem
SSC CGL Tier-1 25.09.2024 (Shift-III)
(a) POQR (b) ORQP
(c) RPQO (d) RPOQ
Ans. (a)
The correct order is POQR.

47. O. that the Soviet army had liberated
P. from the fascist forces came under
Q. the East European countries
R. the control of the USSR
S. after the Second World War
SSC CGL Tier-1 26.09.2024 (Shift-I)
(a) SROPQ (b) POQSR
(c) POSQR (d) SQOPR
Ans. (d)
The correct order is SQOPR.
The sentence starts with 'After the Second World War,' providing the time frame, followed by 'the East European countries,' introducing the subject, then 'that the Soviet army had liberated from the fascist forces,' and concludes with 'came under the control of the USSR.'

48. Founding father / is / of / New Historicism / Greenblatt / considered / the. SSC CGL Tier-1 26.09.2024 (Shift-II)
(a) The founding father of New Historicism is considered Greenblatt.
(b) The founding father is considered Greenblatt of New Historicism.
(c) Greenblatt is considered the founding father of New Historicism.
(d) Greenblatt is the founding father of New Historicism considered.
Ans. (c)
This order places 'Greenblatt' as the subject, 'is considered' as the verb phrase, and 'the founding father of New Historicism' as the object.

49. P. once said
Q. a wise man
R. that action speaks

S. louder than words

SSC CGL Tier-1 26.09.2024 (Shift-II)

(a) QSRP (b) QPRS
(c) PQRS (d) SQPR

Ans. (b)

The correct order is QPRS.

50. A. to become severely seasick
B. a world tour, but he was
C. a nervous flyer and tended
D. he wanted to go on

SSC CGL Tier-1 26.09.2024 (Shift-III)

(a) BADC (b) ADBC
(c) CADB (d) DBCA

Ans. (d)

The correct order is DBCA.

The sentence starts with 'He wanted to go on a world tour,' followed by its contrast 'but he was a nervous flyer,' and concludes with it result of his nervousness 'and tended to become severely seasick.'

51. A. one of the primary obstacles encountered
B. is the risk of sample contamination
C. during the analysis of Controlled Dangerous Substance (CDS)
D. from improper handling and collecting methodologies
E. proof bloodstain patterns and DNA evidence

SSC CGL Tier-1 26.09.2024 (Shift-III)

(a) EACDB (b) ACEBD
(c) AECDB (d) ABCDE

Ans. (b)

The correct order is ACEBD.

SSC CGL 2023 (Tier 1 & 2)

52. S1. He sat in his seat
A. hardly showing any signs of hearing
B. beside the bed
C. gazing sternly
D. at the patient's face
S6. what they were saying to him.

SSC CGL Tier-1 25.07.2023 (Shift-I)

(a) DABC (b) BCDA
(c) DCAB (d) DBAC

Ans. (b)

The correct order is BCDA.

53. S1. A moment comes
A. long suppressed
B. and when the soul of a nation
C. which comes but rarely in history
D. when we step out from the old to the new, when an age ends
S6. finds utterance.

SSC CGL Tier-1 26.07.2023 (Shift-III)

(a) CBAD (b) CDBA
(c) ABCD (d) DCBA

Ans. (b)

The correct order is CDBA.

54. S1. In Dr. Babasaheb Ambedkar
A. but also an elder statesman, national leader and
B. we have not only a crusader against the caste system
C. a valiant fighter for the causes of the downtrodden in India
D. whose contribution in the form of the Constitution of India.
S6. will be cherished forever by posterity.

SSC CGL Tier-2 07.03.2023 (Shift-I)

(a) DABC (b) CABD
(c) BACD (d) ABCD

Ans. (c)

The correct order is BACD.

55. A. In Shakespeare's hands, English drama
B. that first shone forth in his early history plays
C. William Shakespeare is considered as the greatest dramatist and poet of English language
D. achieved a matchless brilliance

SSC CGL Tier-1 27.07.2023 (Shift-III)

(a) DBAC (b) ABCD
(c) CADB (d) BCAD

Ans. (c)

The correct order is CADB.

The sentence starts with 'William Shakespeare is considered as the greatest dramatist and poet of English language,' followed by 'In Shakespeare's hands, English drama achieved a matchless brilliance,' and concludes with relative clause 'that first shone forth in his early history plays.'

56. A. I love
B. so that
C. every morning
D. for a walk
E. to go
F. I can keep myself fit and healthy

SSC CGL Tier-2 06.03.2023 (Shift-I)

(a) BCDE (b) DEBC
(c) CBDE (d) EDCB

Ans. (d)

The correct order is EDCB.

The sentence starts with 'I love,' which is a clear subject and verb.

Following this, 'to go' introduces the infinitive form, and 'for a walk' specifies the activity.

'Every morning' provides the time context, and 'so that I can keep myself fit and healthy' concludes with the purpose.

57. A. then a nurse and a doctor came
B. after the terrible accident
C. a car took Raman to the hospital
D. the two men carried him to a bed and put him in it carefully

SSC CGL Tier-2 03.03.2023 (Shift-I)

(a) DCBA (b) ABCD
(c) BCDA (d) ACDB

Ans. (c)

The correct order is BCDA.

The sequence of events flows logically. It starts with 'After the terrible accident,' which sets the scene. Next, 'a car took Raman to the hospital' describes the immediate action following the accident.

'The two men carried him to a bed and put him in it carefully' continues the sequence, and finally, 'then a nurse and a doctor came' completes the scenario.

SSC CGL 2022 (Tier 1 & 2)

58. While physical movement
P. activities may not require physical
Q. is important for children, all learning
R. the part of teachers and students
S. movement and facial expressions on

SSC CGL Tier-1 01.12.2022 (Shift-II)

(a) PRQS (b) RSPQ
(c) QSRP (d) QPSR

Ans. (d)

The correct order is QPSR.

The sentence begins with 'While physical movement is important for children,' setting up the main topic. 'All learning activities may not require physical movement' contrasts the initial statement.

'And facial expressions' adds another element that may not be required, and 'on the part of teachers and students' specifies who it applies to.

59. Michael Holding, who
P. 20 years, has finally drawn curtains on
Q. commentary panel for more than
R. was a member of the Sky Sports
S. his stint behind the microphone

SSC CGL Tier-1 01.12.2022 (Shift-III)

(a) RQPS (b) QPRS
(c) SPQR (d) PSQR

Ans. (a)

The correct order is RQPS.

The sentence starts with 'Michael Holding, who was a member of the Sky Sports commentary panel for more than 20 years,' providing a background on Michael Holding.

'Has finally drawn curtains' indicates the action he has taken, and 'on his stint behind the microphone' specifies what he has ended.

60. We have been

P. able to identify certain patterns in
Q. the microbiome and immune response
R. that are clearly linked to the progression and
S. severity of brain injury

SSC CGL Tier-1 01.12.2022 (Shift-IV)

(a) PQSR (b) QPSR
(c) RSPQ (d) PQRS

Ans. (d)

The correct order is PQRS.

The sentence starts with 'We have been able to identify certain patterns,' introducing the subject. 'In the microbiome and immune response' specifies where the patterns were identified. 'That are clearly linked to the progression and severity of brain injury' explains the significance of the patterns.

61. The rattlesnake

P. it has specialised Jacobson's
Q. organs, which gives it a heightened
R. knows when to lie low because
S. sense of smell to detect prey

SSC CGL Tier-1 01.12.2022 (Shift-IV)

(a) RPQS (b) SPRQ
(c) QSPR (d) QPRS

Ans. (a)

The correct order is RPQS.

The sentence starts with 'The rattlesnake knows when to lie low,' introducing the subject and action. 'Because it has specialised Jacobson's organs' explains why the rattlesnake knows when to lie low.

'Which gives it a heightened sense of smell' further clarifies the function of these organs, and 'to detect prey' completes the purpose.

62. A single uranium

P. pencil eraser, contains the same energy
Q. pellet, slightly larger than a
R. as a ton of coal, 3 barrels of oil
S. or 17000 cubic feet of natural gas

SSC CGL Tier-1 02.12.2022 (Shift-II)

(a) PRSQ (b) RSPQ
(c) QPRS (d) RPQS

Ans. (c)

The correct order is QPRS.

The sentence starts with 'A single uranium pellet, slightly larger than a pencil eraser,' introducing the subject. 'Contains the same energy' describes what the pellet contains.

'As a ton of coal, 3 barrels of oil' provides a comparison, and 'or 17000 cubic feet of natural gas' adds another comparison to complete the sentence.

63. There are

P. reports that toy shops and other
Q. to prepare for the Christmas rush
R. non-food retailers are struggling to
S. get enough stock into their warehouses

SSC CGL Tier-1 02.12.2022 (Shift-III)

(a) RPSQ (b) PRSQ
(c) SQRP (d) QRPS

Ans. (b)

The correct order is PRSQ.

The sentence starts with 'There are reports that toy shops and other non-food retailers,' introducing the subject. 'Are struggling to get enough stock into their warehouses' describes the issue. 'To prepare for the Christmas rush' specifies the reason for the struggle.

64. According to the report,

P. the 2021 projections reflect growing
Q. recognition of climate change issues
R. and the importance of nuclear power in
S. reducing emissions from electricity generation

SSC CGL Tier-1 02.12.2022 (Shift-IV)

(a) QRSP (b) QPRS
(c) PSQR (d) PQRS

Ans. (d)

The correct order is PQRS.
The sentence starts with 'According to the report,' providing the source of information. 'The 2021 projections reflect growing recognition of climate change issues' introduces the main idea.
'And the importance of nuclear power in reducing emissions from electricity generation' concludes by explaining the significance of nuclear power in this context.

65. The spectacular

P. Indian economy, were largely based on coal
Q. expansion of electrification of the
R. the last 20 years and the considerable
S. Chinese economic growth of

SSC CGL Tier-1 03.12.2022 (Shift-II)

(a) QRPS (b) SQRP
(c) PRQS (d) SRQP

Ans. (d)

The correct order is SRQP.
The sentence starts with 'The spectacular Chinese economic growth of,' providing context. Followed by 'the last 20 years and the considerable expansion of electrification of the,' specifying the time and event.
'Indian economy, were largely based on coal,' provides the final detail.

66. A 2007-2009 study

P. explored forward thinking techniques
Q. to synchronise time on board deep
R. space probes for accurate navigation, in
S. particular looking into low-cost options

SSC CGL Tier-1 03.12.2022 (Shift-III)

(a) RSPQ (b) PSRQ
(c) SPRQ (d) PQRS

Ans. (d)

The correct order is PQRS.

The sentence starts with 'A 2007-2009 study explored forward thinking techniques,' introducing the study. It is followed by 'to synchronise time on board deep space probes for accurate navigation,' specifying the purpose, and 'in particular looking into low-cost options,' concludes the specific aspect explored.

67. The nanostructures on the

P. with added or 'doped', iron and phosphor
Q. surface made of nickel selenide
R. offers the high performance and stability
S. that are needed for industrial-scale electrolysis

SSC CGL Tier-1 03.12.2022 (Shift-IV)

(a) QPRS (b) QRSP
(c) RPQS (d) SPQR

Ans. (a)

The correct order is QPRS.
The sentence starts with 'The nanostructures on the surface made of nickel selenide,' introducing the subject.
Followed by 'with added, or doped, iron and phosphor,' specifying modifications. 'Offers the high performance and stability that are needed for industrial-scale electrolysis,' concludes the function and requirement.

68. Jobseekers are not

P. being unemployed are a test of faith
Q. self-purification, where the difficulties of
R. relentlessly to a pilgrimage of

S. fatalistic but reapply themselves
SSC CGL Tier-1 05.12.2022 (Shift-III)

(a) PQSR (b) SRQP
(c) SPQR (d) RPSQ

Ans. (b)

The correct order is SRQP.

The sentence starts with 'Jobseekers are not fatalistic but reapply themselves,' indicating their attitude. 'Relentlessly to a pilgrimage of self-purification,' describing their effort. 'Where the difficulties of being unemployed are a test of faith,' providing the challenge they face.

69. Lighting has

P. to become a disrupter and
Q. become human-centric as our
R. requirements change during the day and
S. lighting has to adapt to our change in needs
SSC CGL Tier-1 05.12.2022 (Shift-I)

(a) PSQR (b) RPQS
(c) QRSP (d) PQRS

Ans. (d)

The correct order is PQRS.

The sentence starts with 'Lighting has to become a disrupter,' indicating the necessity.

It is followed by 'and become human-centric as our requirements change during the day,' which specifies the need for adaptability.

'And lighting has to adapt to our change in needs,' completes the necessity for change.

70. We are encouraged

P. help accelerate their return to
Q. by how women are embracing online
R. work and promote economic mobility
S. learning to develop new skills that can SSC CGL Tier-1 05.12.2022 (Shift-IV)

(a) QSPR (b) PSQR
(c) PRQS (d) SPRQ

Ans. (a)

The correct order is QSPR.

71. Electrolytes like

P. important for balancing the water in your body
Q. are present in the body's fluids and are
R. are electrically charged minerals that
S. sodium, potassium, chloride and magnesium
SSC CGL Tier-1 06.12.2022 (Shift-II)

(a) PQSR (b) SPRQ
(c) SQRP (d) SRQP

Ans. (d)

The correct order is SRQP.

The sentence starts with 'Electrolytes like sodium, potassium, chloride and magnesium,' introducing the subject. It is followed by 'are electrically charged minerals that are present in the body's fluids,' which specifies the nature and presence.

'And are important for balancing the water in your body,' concludes the function.

72. One element that

P. is timing, in particular ensuring that
Q. is essential to navigating deep space
R. the time on board spacecraft is synchronised
S. with the time on the ground
SSC CGL Tier-1 06.12.2022 (Shift-III)

(a) PRQS
(b) PSQR
(c) RSPQ
(d) QPRS

Ans. (d)

The correct order is QPRS.

The sentence starts with 'One element that is essential to navigating deep space,' introducing the subject. Followed by 'is timing, in particular ensuring that the time on board spacecraft,' specifying the element. 'Is synchronised with the time on the ground,' concludes the requirement.

73. The decision not

P. to include any kind of wealth or
Q. crisis, has proven controversial
R. income tax, which would be the fairer option
S. for solving the social care funding
SSC CGL Tier-1 06.12.2022 (Shift-IV)

(a) SQPR (b) PRSQ
(c) RSPQ (d) QPRS

Ans. (b)

The correct order is PRSQ.

The sentence starts with 'The decision not to include any kind of wealth or income tax,' introducing the subject. Followed by 'which would be the fairer option,' specifying the alternative. 'For solving the social care funding crisis, has proven controversial,' concludes the context and consequence.

74. Thorium has

P. and is part of a nuclear programme in India
Q. of nuclear reactor in countries including
R. been tested as a fuel in other types
S. the United States, Germany and the United Kingdom,
SSC CGL Tier-1 07.12.2022 (Shift-I)

(a) RQSP (b) RPQS
(c) PSQR (d) SPQR

Ans. (a)

The correct order is RQSP.

The sentence starts with 'Thorium has been tested as a fuel in other types of nuclear reactor,' introducing the subject and action.

It is followed by 'in countries including the United States, Germany and the United Kingdom,' which specifies the locations. 'And is part of a nuclear programme in India,' concludes the additional context.

75. The Google Doodle

P. with a cup of green tea, beaker and
Q. Tsujimura working in her laboratory
R. some green tea leaves by the side
S. features a graphical representation of SSC CGL Tier-1 07.12.2022 (Shift-I)

(a) RSPQ (b) PQSR (c) RPQS (d) SQPR

Ans. (d)

The correct order is SQPR.

76. Kemp's ridleys are

P. usually found in nearshore and
Q. inshore waters of the Northern
R. Gulf of Mexico, especially in Louisiana waters,
S. which are their primary feeding grounds
SSC CGL Tier-1 07.12.2022 (Shift-II)

(a) SRQP (b) QPSR
(c) PQRS (d) PRSQ

Ans. (c)

The correct order is PQRS.

The sentence starts with 'Kemp's ridleys are usually found in nearshore and inshore waters of the Northern,' introducing the subject and location.

It is followed by 'Gulf of Mexico, especially in Louisiana waters,' specifying the exact location, and 'which are their primary feeding grounds,' concludes with the purpose of the location.

77. In December 2018,

P. caused a landslide that
Q. an eruption of the volcano Anak Krakatau
R. triggered a tsunami in the Sunda Strait (Indonesia)
S. and killed more than 400 people
SSC CGL Tier-1 08.12.2022 (Shift-I)

(a) SQPR (b) RPQS
(c) QPRS (d) PRQS

Ans. (c)

The correct order is QPRS.

The sentence starts with 'In December 2018, an eruption of the volcano Anak Krakatau,' introducing the subject and time frame.

It is followed by 'caused a landslide that triggered a tsunami in the Sunda Strait (Indonesia),' which specifies the event and location, and 'and killed more than 400 people,' concludes with the impact.

78. The ministry officials

P. recommend the shortlisted names to

Q. the awards selection committee

R. sieve through the applicants' credentials and

S. have been working overtime to

SSC CGL Tier-1 08.12.2022 (Shift-III)

(a) SRPQ (b) QRPS
(c) SPQR (d) PQRS

Ans. (a)

The correct order is SRPQ.

The sentence starts with 'The ministry officials have been working overtime to,' introducing the subject and action. It is followed by 'sieve through the applicants' credentials and recommend the shortlisted names,' which specifies the task. 'To the awards selection committee,' concludes with the recipient of the recommendation.

79. The researchers

P. decision centres called the orbitofrontal

Q. analysed the electrical activity recorded

R. cortex and dorsal anterior cingulate cortex

S. from neurons in two of the brain's

SSC CGL Tier-1 08.12.2022 (Shift-IV)

(a) QSPR (b) RSPQ
(c) RPQS (d) PQSR

Ans. (a)

The correct order is QSPR.

The sentence starts with 'The researchers analysed the electrical activity recorded,' introducing the subject and action.

It is followed by 'from neurons in two of the brain's decision centres,' which specifies the source. 'Called the orbitofrontal cortex and dorsal anterior cingulate cortex,' concludes with the specific brain regions.

80. In addition to

P. primary threat to the Kemp's ridley sea turtle

Q. capture in fishing gear like shrimp

R. threatened nesting habitat, accidental

S. trawls and gill nets continues to be the

SSC CGL Tier-1 09.12.2022 (Shift-I)

(a) SPQR (b) SQRP
(c) RQSP (d) PQSR

Ans. (c)

The correct order is RQSP.

The sentence starts with 'In addition to threatened nesting habitat,' introducing the primary issue.

It is followed by 'accidental capture in fishing gear like shrimp trawls and gill nets,' which specifies another threat. 'Continues to be the primary threat to the Kemp's ridley sea turtle,' concludes with the impact on the species.

81. The issue of

P. compulsory vaccination is difficult

Q. multiple interests all protected by human

R. because the governments need to consider

S. rights law and strike a fair balance between them

SSC CGL Tier-1 09.12.2022 (Shift-I)

(a) PRQS (b) PQRS
(c) RSPQ (d) QSPR

Ans. (a)

The correct order is PRQS.

The sentence starts with 'The issue of compulsory vaccination is difficult,' introducing the subject.

It is followed by 'because the governments need to consider multiple interests,' which specifies the challenge. 'All protected by human rights law,' providing the legal context, and 'and strike a fair balance between them,' concludes with the goal.

82. We looked for

P. strong relationships at locations in the

Q. genome that are not well studied in

R. apple and looked for which compounds we

S. could identify and which had nutritional value

SSC CGL Tier-1 09.12.2022 (Shift-I)

(a) QSRP (b) QRPS
(c) SPQR (d) PQRS

Ans. (d)

The correct order is PQRS.

The sentence starts with 'We looked for strong relationships at locations in the genome,' introducing the action and subject.

It is followed by 'that are not well studied in apple,' which specifies the focus. 'And looked for which compounds we could identify,' provides additional context, and 'and which had nutritional value,' concludes with the objective.

83. American alligators were

P. now this species is classified as least concern

Q. list in 1967, their population increased and

R. once threatened by extinction but

S. after being placed on the endangered species

SSC CGL Tier-1 09.12.2022 (Shift-III)

(a) SQPR (b) RPQS
(c) RSQP (d) PQSR

Ans. (c)

The correct order is RSQP.

The sentence starts with 'American alligators were once threatened by extinction,' introducing the subject and situation.

It is followed by 'but after being placed on the endangered species list in 1967,' which specifies the action taken.

'Their population increased,' provides the result, and 'and now this species is classified as least concern,' concludes with the current status.

84. NFTs are

P. digital collectables that exist on

Q. and are better known for recently

R. taking the art world by storm

S. online ledgers known as blockchains

SSC CGL Tier-1 09.12.2022 (Shift-IV)

(a) PSQR (b) RPQS
(c) RQPS (d) SPRQ

Ans. (a)

The correct order is PSQR.

The sentence starts with 'NFTs are digital collectables that exist on,' introducing the subject and nature.

It is followed by 'online ledgers known as blockchains,' which specifies the technology.

'And are better known for recently,' provides additional context, and 'taking the art world by storm,' concludes with the impact.

85. Medieval people undertook

P. purify themselves of sin, to transform

Q. pilgrimages individually, travelling to

R. themselves through a trial of faith

S. distant shrines as a penance to

SSC CGL Tier-1 12.12.2022 (Shift-I)

(a) QSPR (b) QPRS
(c) SPQR (d) PSRQ

Ans. (a)

The correct order is QSPR.

The sentence starts with 'Medieval people undertook pilgrimages individually, travelling to,' which introduces the subject and their actions.

It is followed by 'distant shrines as a penance to purify themselves of sin,' which specifies the purpose and destination.

'To transform themselves through a trial of faith,' concludes with the ultimate goal.

86. Peer pressure

P. when it comes to choosing the right

Q. course and therefore, career path

R. and lack of guidance are some of

S. the reasons for indecisiveness

SSC CGL Tier-1 12.12.2022 (Shift-III)

(a) SPQR (b) QSPR

(c) RSPQ (d) PQRS

Ans. (c)

The correct order is RSPQ.

The sentence starts with 'Peer pressure and lack of guidance are some of,' introducing the factors.

It is followed by 'the reasons for indecisiveness when it comes to choosing the right course and therefore, career path,' which specifies the outcome and context.

87. Birds heart, lungs and

P. uptake and intensive exertion compared

Q. to humans which enables them to function

R. efficiently at these very high altitudes

S. muscles are more efficient for oxygen

SSC CGL Tier-1 12.12.2022 (Shift-III)

(a) QRPS (b) PRQS

(c) SPQR (d) QSRP

Ans. (c)

The correct order is SPQR.

The sentence starts with 'Birds heart, lungs and muscles are more efficient for oxygen,' introducing the subject and their efficiency.

It is followed by 'uptake and intensive exertion compared to humans,' which specifies the comparison. 'Which enables them to function which specifies at these very high altitudes,' concludes with the result.

88. The absence of

P. data on the migrant workers was

Q. formulating effective policy decisions and

R. preventing the governments from

S. strategies for the welfare of migrant workers

SSC CGL Tier-1 12.12.2022 (Shift-IV)

(a) QPRS (b) RPQS

(c) PSRQ (d) PRQS

Ans. (d)

The correct order is PRQS.

The sentence starts with 'The absence of data on the migrant workers was,' introducing the problem.

It is followed by 'preventing the governments from formulating effective policy decisions,' which specifies the consequence.

'And strategies for the welfare of migrant workers,' concludes with the impact.

89. Russell Wilson, an NFL

P. about Naomi Osaka saying that her

Q. has been spectacular to watch

R. humility and dedication to others

S. player for the Seattle Seahawks, wrote

SSC CGL Tier-1 13.12.2022 (Shift-I)

(a) PRQS (b) QPRS

(c) SPRQ (d) RPQS

Ans. (c)

The correct order is SPRQ.

The sentence starts with 'Russell Wilson, an NFL player for the Seattle Seahawks, wrote,' introducing the subject and his action.

It is followed by 'about Naomi Osaka saying that her humility and dedication to others,' which specifies the content of his writing. 'Has been spectacular to watch,' concludes with his opinion.

90. Back in April

P. an afternoon walking around

Q. the Tillman Sand Ridge Heritage Preserve

R. I was visiting family in South Carolina

S. and my Brother and I spent

SSC CGL Tier-1 13.12.2022 (Shift-II)

(a) QPRS (b) PQRS

(c) RQPS (d) RSPQ

Ans. (d)

The correct order is RSPQ.

The sentence starts with 'Back in April, I was visiting family in South Carolina,' introducing the time and context.

It is followed by 'and my Brother and I spent an afternoon walking around,' which specifies the activity.

'The Tillman Sand Ridge Heritage Preserve,' concludes with the location.

91. Apart from generating

P. real income for players, play-to-earn

Q. games also create communities

R. where gamers and creators can meet, share

S. wisdom and do deals with one another

SSC CGL Tier-1 13.12.2022 (Shift-III)

(a) RSQP (b) PQRS

(c) PRQS (d) SPRQ

Ans. (b)

The correct order is PQRS.

The sentence starts with 'Apart from generating real income for players,' introducing the main idea.

It is followed by 'play-to-earn games also create communities,' which specifies an additional benefit.

'Where gamers and creators can meet, share wisdom and do deals with one another,' concludes with the details of the benefit.

92. Genome-wide

P. with metabolites that influence

Q. traits like flavour, disease resistance and texture

R. analysis of each apple enabled

S. identification of genetic markers associated

SSC CGL Tier-1 13.12.2022 (Shift-IV)

(a) PQRS (b) QRPS

(c) QRSP (d) RSPQ

Ans. (d)

The correct order is RSPQ.

The sentence starts with 'Genome-wide analysis of each apple enabled,' introducing the subject and the action.

It is followed by 'identification of genetic markers associated with metabolites,' which specifies the outcome. That influence traits like flavour, disease resistance and texture,' concludes with the impact.

93. A great transition/marked/ the 20th century/for mankind

(a) A great transition marked the 20th century for mankind.

(b) The 20th century marked a great transition for mankind.

(c) A great transition for mankind marked the 20th century.

(d) For mankind, a great transition marked the 20th century.

SSC CGL Tier-1 07.12.2022 (Shift-II)

Ans. (b)

The correct order is: The 20th century marked a great transition for mankind.

This order logically places 'The 20th century' as the subject, 'marked' as the verb, 'a great transition' as the object, and 'for mankind' providing the context.

SSC CGL 2021 (Tier 1)

94. The continued
P. the growing sales of sneakers
Q. dominance of the athleisure trend
R. along with the pursuit of comfort
S. has had a significant impact on
SSC CGL Tier-1 02.12.2021 (Shift-I)
(a) RPSQ (b) PSRQ
(c) QRPS (d) QSPR
Ans. (d)
The correct order is QSPR.
The sentence starts with 'The continued dominance of the athleisure trend,' introducing the main idea.
'Has had a significant impact on' describes the effect and 'the growing sales of sneakers' specifies what has been impacted.
'Along with the pursuit of comfort' adds an additional factor.

SSC CHSL 2023 (Tier 1 & 2)

95. Climate change is
P. climate caused by natural forces in combination
Q. a broad topic that includes periodic alterations in Earth's
R. with the effects of various human activities like burning of
S. fossil fuels and changes in land cover and biodiversity
SSC CHSL Tier-1 04.03.2023 (Shift-I)
(a) PSQR (b) QRPS
(c) RSQP (d) SRPQ
Ans. (b)
The correct order is QPRS.
The sentence starts with 'Climate change is a broad topic that includes periodic alterations in Earth's,' introducing the subject.
It is followed by 'climate caused by natural forces in combination with the effects of various human activities,' which specifies the causes and 'like burning of fossil fuels and changes in land cover and biodiversity,' provides specific examples.

96. P. versions of the European poor laws, charitable and
Q. in former colonies, such as Ghana, Jamaica, India
R. missionary activities and the introduction of Western juvenile justice procedures
S. and Philippines the basic welfare services grew out of modified
SSC CHSL Tier-1 09.03.2023
(a) PSQR (b) QPRS
(c) PRSQ (d) QSPR
Ans. (d)
The correct order is QSPR.
The sentence starts with 'In former colonies, such as Ghana, Jamaica, India,' introducing the context. It is followed by 'and Philippines the basic welfare services grew out of modified versions of the European poor laws,' which specifies the origin. 'Charitable and missionary activities and the introduction of Western juvenile justice procedures,' concludes with the specific activities.

97. The researchers
P. performed experiments and developed a model
Q. which explains how the worm's taste sensors
R. to direct its foraging behaviour
S. process information from the environment
SSC CHSL Tier-1 10.03.2023 (Shift-II)
(a) RPQS (b) PQSR
(c) PSQR (d) PRQS
Ans. (b)
The correct order is PQSR.
The sentence starts with 'The researchers performed experiments and developed a model,' introducing the subject and action.
It is followed by 'which explains how the worm's taste sensors process information from the environment to direct its foraging behaviour,' which specifies the function and outcome.

98. If a product placement
P. we are either less likely to notice the placement
Q. our attention is fixated on what will happen next,
R. or more likely to be annoyed by it if we do notice it
S. appears at the climax, the moment when **SSC CHSL Tier-1 10.03.2023 (Shift-II)**
(a) SPQR (b) PRSQ
(c) SQPR (d) RSQP
Ans. (c)
The correct order is SQPR.
The sentence starts with 'If a product placement appears at the climax, the moment when,' introducing the condition.
It is followed by 'our attention is fixated on what will happen next,' which specifies the context.
'We are either less likely to notice the placement,' indicates one possibility, and 'or more likely to be annoyed by it if we do notice it,' provides the alternative outcome.

99. There were two final
A. the story was the tale of Kunti
B. a story and a parchment
C. gifts the sorceress gave me
D. mother of Arjun. The parchment was a map of Bharat's many kingdoms
SSC CHSL Tier-1 10.03.2023 (Shift-II)
(a) CBAD (b) DCBA
(c) ABCD (d) ADCB
Ans. (a)
The correct order is CBAD.
The sentence starts with 'There were two final gifts the sorceress gave me,' introducing the subject and items.
It is followed by 'a story and a parchment,' which specifies the gifts. 'The story was the tale of Kunti, mother of Arjun,' further details the story, and 'the parchment was a map of Bharat's many kingdoms,' concludes with the details of the parchment.

100. They walked down the hall of
A. rocked them to sleep and played songs for them
B. had cost them seventy-five
C. thousand rupees. This house clothed and fed them
D. their soundproofed home, which
SSC CHSL Tier-1 13.03.2023 (Shift-III)
(a) DBCA (b) ACBD
(c) BADC (d) CBAD
Ans. (a)
The correct sequence is DBCA.
The sentence starts with 'They walked down the hall of their soundproofed home, which,' introducing the setting. It is followed by 'had cost them seventy-five thousand rupees,' which specifies the cost. 'This house clothed and fed them, rocked them to sleep and played songs for them,' provides the benefits and functions of the house.

101. Many psychological, neurological
P. and different thinking skills that make them leaders rather than followers
Q. studies generally indicate that leaders truly are born with different personality traits
R. to discover if leadership truly can be a learned trait and
S. and sociological tests have been conducted by scientists
SSC CHSL Tier-1 13.03.2023 (Shift-III)
(a) QPSR (b) SRQP
(c) PQSR (d) SQRP
Ans. (b)

The correct order is SRQP.

The sentence starts with 'Many psychological, neurological and sociological tests have been conducted by scientists,' introducing the subject and action.

It is followed by 'to discover if leadership truly can be a learned trait,' which specifies the goal. 'Studies generally indicate that leaders truly are born with different personality traits,' provides the general findings, and 'and different thinking skills that make them leaders rather than followers,' concludes with the specific traits.

102. The study led

P. collaborators from Bristol, Cambridge and Germany

Q. by scientists at the University of Bath and including

R. used fossils and analysed genetic difference between

S. modern snakes to reconstruct snake evolution

SSC CHSL Tier-1 13.03.2023 (Shift-III)

(a) QSRP (b) QPRS
(c) SPQR (d) PRQS

Ans. (b)

The correct order is QPRS.

The sentence starts with 'The study led by scientists at the University of Bath and including collaborators from Bristol, Cambridge and Germany,' introducing the subject and participants.

It is followed by 'used fossils and analysed genetic differences between modern snakes,' which specifies the method. 'To reconstruct snake evolution,' concludes with the goal.

103. P. contributed to the destruction of Sir Walter Raleigh's 'Lost Colony'

Q. a severe three-year drought in the late 16th century probably

R. at Roanoke Island in what is now North Carolina and a subsequent

S. seven-year drought led to high mortality at the Jamestown Colony in Virginia

SSC CHSL Tier-1 14.03.2023 (Shift-I)

(a) QRSP (b) PSQR
(c) QPRS (d) PRSQ

Ans. (c)

The correct order is QPRS.

The sentence starts with 'A severe three-year drought in the late 16th century probably contributed to the destruction of Sir Walter Raleigh's 'Lost Colony' at Roanoke Island,' introducing the event and location.

It is followed by 'in what is now North Carolina and a subsequent seven-year drought,' which specifies the location and subsequent event.

'Led to high mortality at the Jamestown Colony in Virginia,' concludes with the impact.

104. Forest planning rules

P. recognises the growing risks to national

Q. forests from climate change as well as expands

R. opportunities for public input and engagement

S. were updated in 2012 and the new rule explicitly

SSC CHSL Tier-1 14.03.2023 (Shift-I)

(a) PSQR (b) QRPS
(c) SPQR (d) PQRS

Ans. (c)

The correct order is SPQR.

The sentence starts with 'Forest planning rules were updated in 2012 and the new rule explicitly recognises the growing risks to national forests,' introducing the subject and action.

It is followed by 'from climate change as well as expands opportunities for public input and engagement,' which specifies the content and outcome.

105. A newly

P. reflected on why he chose to work for his

Q. appointed division manager, trained in accounting,

R. company despite better offers and realised that

S. it was the friendly, collaborative and ethical culture

SSC CHSL Tier-1 15.03.2023 (Shift-IV)

(a) SPRQ (b) SQRP
(c) QPRS (d) RQPS

Ans. (c)

The correct order is QPRS.

The sentence starts with 'A newly appointed division manager, trained in accounting, reflected on why he chose to work for his company,' introducing the subject and action.

It is followed by 'despite better offers and realised that it was the friendly, collaborative and ethical culture,' which specifies the reason.

106. P. useful for the Government to utilise the expertise and

Q. in the present international scenario, it is necessary and

R. and winning over the support of their counterparts in other countries

S. services of the Members of Parliament effectively for sensitising

SSC CHSL Tier-1 15.03.2023 (Shift-IV)

(a) SPRQ (b) PRSQ
(c) PSQR (d) QPSR

Ans. (d)

The correct order is QPSR.

The sentence starts with 'In the present international scenario, it is necessary and useful for the Government to utilise the expertise and services of the Members of Parliament,' introducing the context and necessity.

It is followed by 'effectively for sensitising and winning over the support of their counterparts in other countries,' which specifies the purpose.

107. It is not uncommon

SSC CHSL Tier-1 16.03.2023 (Shift-I)

P. for parents and others in a particular animal

Q. group to teach their young through example how to

R. of drought or other environmental change

S. find food or water when it becomes scarce because

(a) SPRQ (b) PQSR
(c) PQRS (d) QSPR

Ans. (b)

The correct order is PQSR.

The sentence starts with 'It is not uncommon for parents and others in a particular animal group,' introducing the subject.

It is followed by 'to teach their young through example how to find food or water,' which specifies the action. 'When it becomes scarce because of drought or other environmental change,' provides the context and reason.

108. P. elderly is on the increase and, although they constitute only

Q. a small minority of the retired population, their

R. in all advanced industrial societies, the proportion of infirm

S. claim on social services is disproportionately heavy

SSC CHSL Tier-1 16.03.2023 (Shift-I)

(a) RPQS (b) RSPQ
(c) PSRQ (d) QPSR

Ans. (a)

The correct order is RPQS.

The sentence starts with 'In all advanced industrial societies, the proportion of infirm,' introducing the subject.

It is followed by 'elderly is on the increase and, although they constitute only a small minority of the retired population,' which specifies the context and proportion. 'Their claim on social services is disproportionately heavy,' concludes with the impact.

109. Many people
P. learn better when they have something tangible
Q. hold in their hands and get their head
R. to work with, a physical object they can
S. round and low-cost 3D printers make that possible

SSC CHSL Tier-1 16.03.2023 (Shift-I)

(a) QPRS (b) PRQS
(c) QRSP (d) PRSQ

Ans. (b)

The correct order is PRQS.

The sentence starts with 'Many people learn better when they have something tangible,' introducing the main idea.

It is followed by 'to work with, a physical object they can hold in their hands,' which specifies the tangible item.

'And get their head round and low-cost 3D printers make that possible,' concludes with the benefit and means.

110. P. despite pandemic related travel complications, the
Q. Governments of India and France facilitated interactions
R. NPCIL a binding techno-commercial offer on 22nd April, 2021
S. between EDF and NPCIL which allowed EDF to submit to

SSC CHSL Tier-1 16.03.2023 (Shift-II)

(a) QRSP (b) PQSR
(c) RQSP (d) RPSQ

Ans. (b)

The correct order is PQSR.

The sentence starts with 'Despite pandemic related travel complications, the,' introducing the context.

It is followed by 'Governments of India and France facilitated interactions between EDF and NPCIL,' which specifies the action. 'Which allowed EDF to submit to NPCIL a binding techno-commercial offer on 22nd April, 2021,' concludes with the result and date.

111. P. won the right to host the 2020 Games, explicitly stated that
Q. Tokyo 2020 represented a key way to open up Japanese
R. culture and people to the watching and visiting world
S. Shinzo Abe, who was Prime Minister at the time Japan

SSC CHSL Tier-1 17.03.2023 (Shift-II)

(a) QRSP (b) RPQS
(c) SRPQ (d) SPQR

Ans. (d)

The correct order is SPQR.

The sentence starts with 'Shinzo Abe, who was Prime Minister at the time Japan won the right to host the 2020 Games,' introducing the subject and context.

It is followed by 'explicitly stated that Tokyo 2020 represented a key way to open up Japanese culture and people to the watching and visiting world,' which specifies the statement and its significance.

112. Many retailers have invested
P. time and money into understanding its
Q. make them healthier so they can continue to be marketed
R. promotions work and changing product ingredients to
S. complexity, refitting shops, trialling which

SSC CHSL Tier-1 20.03.2023 (Shift-III)

(a) SRPQ (b) PQRS
(c) QRPS (d) PSRQ

Ans. (d)

The correct order is PSRQ.

The sentence starts with 'Many retailers have invested time and money into understanding its complexity,' introducing the subject and action.

It is followed by 'refitting shops, trialling which promotions work,' which specifies the activities. 'And changing product ingredients to make them healthier,' provides the purpose. 'So they can continue to be marketed,' concludes with the goal.

113. P. undermining the strict application of comparative anthropology
Q. in the early 20th century, it was almost universally assumed
R. that traditional cultures would be completely assimilated
S. into colonial cultures within a few decades, thus

SSC CHSL Tier-1 21.03.2023 (Shift-II)

(a) PQRS (b) QRSP
(c) PSQR (d) QPRS

Ans. (b)

The correct order is QRSP.

The sentence starts with 'In the early 20th century, it was almost universally assumed,' introducing the context and assumption.

It is followed by 'that traditional cultures would be completely assimilated into colonial cultures within a few decades,' which specifies the belief. 'Thus undermining the strict application of comparative anthropology,' concludes with the consequence.

114. Some algal blooms
P. beneficial to aquatic life, since these tiny
Q. nutrient conditions are optimal and they can be
R. occur naturally when temperature, water and
S. organisms form the base of the food chain

SSC CHSL Tier-1 21.03.2023 (Shift-II)

(a) RQSP (b) QPRS
(c) PRSQ (d) RQPS

Ans. (d)

The correct order is RQPS.

The sentence starts with 'Some algal blooms occur naturally when temperature, water and nutrient conditions are optimal,' introducing the subject and conditions.

It is followed by 'and they can be beneficial to aquatic life,' which specifies the benefit.

'Since these tiny organisms form the base of the food chain,' concludes with the reason.

115. P. bendable electronics and sensing technologies research
Q. people using 'aerohaptics', creating feelings of touch with jets of air
R. my colleagues and I working in the University of Glasgow's
S. group have now developed a system of holograms of

SSC CHSL Tier-1 21.03.2023 (Shift-IV)

(a) SRQP (b) QPSR
(c) PQRS (d) RPSQ

Ans. (d)

The correct order is RPSQ.

The sentence starts with 'My colleagues and I working in the University of Glasgow's bendable electronics and sensing technologies research group,' introducing the subject and context.

It is followed by 'have now developed a system of holograms of people using 'aerohaptics',' which specifies the development. 'Creating feelings of touch with jets of air,' concludes with the mechanism.

116. A. fell before me
B. a carcass of an animal
C. when suddenly
D. my heart skipped a beat
SSC CHSL Tier-1 02.08.2023 (Shift-I)

(a) BACD (b) CDBA
(c) ABCD (d) DCBA

Ans. (b)

The correct order is CDBA.

117. A. in accordance with hierarchical status
B. of the services rendered
C. reward are given
D. and are not related to the economic value **SSC CHSL Tier-1 02.08.2023 (Shift-I)**

(a) ABDC (b) ADBC
(c) CADB (d) CBAD

Ans. (c)

The correct order is CADB.

The sentence starts with 'Reward are given,' introducing the subject.

It is followed by 'in accordance with hierarchical status,' which specifies the criteria.

'And are not related to the economic value of the services rendered,' concludes with the context and detail.

118. Such post-structuralist pronouncements ....
A. not only in the Anglo-American Academia
B. on the literature of the Third World War
C. however, are a common feature of the literary theory practiced
D. but also in the Third World War countries
SSC CHSL Tier-1 02.08.2023 (Shift-I)

(a) ABCD (b) ADCB
(c) BCAD (d) CABD

Ans. (c)

The correct order is BCAD.

The sentence starts with 'Such post-structuralist pronouncements on the literature of the Third World War,' introducing the subject.

It is followed by 'however, are a common feature of the literary theory practiced,' which specifies the context. 'Not only in the Anglo-American Academia,' provides the primary context, and 'but also in the Third World War countries,' concludes with the broader context.

119. A. between the two countries
B. will inevitably count
C. the recent political incident
D. against the peace process
SSC CHSL Tier-1 03.08.2023 (Shift-I)

(a) CDBA (b) CDAB
(c) CBAD (d) CBDA

Ans. (d)

The correct order is CBDA.

The sentence starts with 'The recent political incident,' introducing the subject.

It is followed by 'will inevitably count against the peace process,' which specifies the impact.

'Between the two countries,' concludes with the context.

120. A. or brave man to make
B. money the chief object of his thoughts
C. for a well-educated, intellectual
D. it is physically impossible
SSC CHSL Tier-1 03.08.2023 (Shift-I)

(a) ABCD (b) DCAB
(c) CDAB (d) CABD

Ans. (b)

The correct order is DCAB.

The sentence starts with 'It is physically impossible,' introducing the statement.

It is followed by 'for a well-educated, intellectual or brave man to make money the chief object of his thoughts,' which specifies the subject and context.

121. P. provided it is technologically accessible, economically feasible
Q. which can be used to satisfy our needs
R. and culturally acceptable can be termed as 'Resource'
S. everything is available in our environment
SSC CHSL Tier-1 04.08.2023 (Shift-II)

(a) SPRQ (b) SQPR
(c) QRSP (d) QSPR

Ans. (b)

The correct order is SQPR.

The sentence starts with 'Everything available in our environment,' introducing the subject.

It is followed by 'which can be used to satisfy our needs,' which specifies the potential use. 'Provided it is technologically accessible, economically feasible and culturally acceptable,' adds the conditions. 'Can be termed as 'Resource',' concludes with the definition.

122. P. an unparalleled popularity
Q. the Lotus temple has always enjoyed
R. as shown by its pre-dominance in literature and art
S. throughout the length and breadth of India from the earliest times down to the present day,
SSC CHSL Tier-1 07.08.2023 (Shift-IV)

(a) QPSR (b) PSQR
(c) QRSP (d) QPRS

Ans. (a)

The correct order is QPSR.

The sentence starts with 'The Lotus temple has always enjoyed,' introducing the subject and action.

It is followed by 'an unparalleled popularity,' which specifies the attribute. 'Throughout the length and breadth of India from the earliest times down to the present day,' provides the time and extent.

'As shown by its pre-dominance in literature and art,' concludes with the evidence.

123. P. and the impact of their
Q. the author's journey of self-discovery
R. the memoir explores
S. upbringing on their identity
SSC CHSL Tier-1 08.08.2023 (Shift-II)

(a) RQPS (b) RQSP
(c) QPSR (d) SPRQ

Ans. (a)

The correct order is RQPS.

The sentence starts with 'The memoir explores,' introducing the subject.

It is followed by 'the author's journey of self-discovery,' which specifies the focus. 'And the impact of their upbringing on their identity,' provides additional context.

124. A. that the only true individual
B. is the holy man
C. it has frequently been claimed
D. which the traditional society of India tolerates
SSC CHSL Tier-1 08.08.2023 (Shift-II)

(a) DCAB (b) CADB
(c) ABDC (d) CDAB

Ans. (b)

The correct order is CADB.

The sentence starts with 'It has frequently been claimed,' introducing the statement.

It is followed by 'that the only true individual which the traditional society of India tolerates,' which specifies the subject and context. 'Is the holy man,' concludes with the identification.

125. A. the importance
B. to be treated
C. of treating other people
D. now he knows
E. as he would like
SSC CHSL Tier-1 09.08.2023 (Shift-I)

(a) DACEB (b) BDCAE
(c) CDBAE (d) CEBAD

Ans. (a)

The correct order is DACEB.

The sentence starts with 'Now he knows,' introducing the subject.

It is followed by 'the importance of treating other people,' which specifies the realisation.

'As he would like to be treated,' concludes with the principle.

126. A. dictators may rise to power and inaugurate
B. a new regime with dramatic suddenness
C. and success under suitable conditions
D. democracy is always a slow growth
SSC CHSL Tier-1 10.08.2023 (Shift-III)

(a) DCAB (b) ACBD
(c) ABDC (d) ABCD

Ans. (d)

The correct order is ABCD.

The sentence starts with 'Dictators may rise to power and inaugurate,' introducing the subject and action.

It is followed by 'a new regime with dramatic suddenness,' which specifies the impact. 'And success under suitable conditions,' adds the condition. 'Democracy is always a slow growth,' concludes with the comparison.

127. A. agenda for sustainable development
B. as the world faces cascading and
C. interlinked global crises and conflicts
D. the aspirations set out in the 2030
E. are in jeopardy
SSC CHSL Tier-1 10.08.2023 (Shift-III)

(a) ABEDC (b) CBADE
(c) BCDAE (d) AEDCB

Ans. (c)

The correct order is BCDAE.

The sentence starts with 'As the world faces cascading and interlinked global crises and conflicts,' introducing the context.

It is followed by 'the aspirations set out in the 2030 agenda for sustainable development,' which specifies the aspirations. 'Are in jeopardy,' concludes with the impact.

128. A. We must not complain
B. thorns bear flowers
C. but rather be grateful that
D. that roses have thorns
SSC CHSL Tier-1 11.08.2023 (Shift-I)

(a) ADCB (b) ADBC
(c) ACDB (d) ABCD

Ans. (a)

The correct order is ADCB.

The sentence starts with 'We must not complain,' introducing the subject.

It is followed by 'that roses have thorns,' which specifies the reason. 'But rather be grateful that thorns bear flowers,' concludes with the positive perspective.

129. P. and allows them to come out of their imaginary world
Q. which helps in illuminating and enlightening the dark world
R. of the blind or visually impaired persons
S. eye donation is a very generous act towards society
SSC CHSL Tier-1 14.08.2023 (Shift-IV)

(a) SQPR (b) SRQP
(c) SPQR (d) SQRP

Ans. (d)

The correct order is SQRP.

The sentence starts with 'Eye donation is a very generous act towards society,' introducing the subject.

It is followed by 'which helps in illuminating and enlightening the dark world,' which specifies the impact. 'Of the blind or visually impaired persons' specifies the beneficiary (subject) of donation. 'And allows them to come out of their imaginary world,' concludes with the additional benefit.

130. P. the news of her husband's death
Q. to break to her as gently as possible
R. great care was taken
S. knowing that Mrs. Mallard was afflicted with a heart trouble
SSC CHSL Tier-1 14.08.2023 (Shift-IV)

(a) SPRQ (b) SPQR
(c) SQPR (d) SRQP

Ans. (d)

The correct order is SRQP.

The sentence starts with 'Knowing that Mrs. Mallard was afflicted with a heart trouble,' introducing the context.

It is followed by 'great care was taken,' which specifies the action. 'To break to her as gently as possible the news of her husband's death,' concludes with the objective and subject.

131. O. On a regular basis can improve
P. engaging in physical activity
Q. the risk of chronic diseases and boost mental health
R. cardiovascular health, reduce
SSC CHSL Tier-1 17.08.2023 (Shift-I)

(a) RPOQ (b) PROQ
(c) PORQ (d) OQRP

Ans. (c)

The correct order is PORQ.

The sentence starts with 'Engaging in physical activity on a regular basis,' introducing the subject.

It is followed by 'can improve cardiovascular health,' which specifies the benefit.

'Reduce the risk of chronic diseases and boost mental health,' concludes with additional benefits.

132. A. to his neighbours
B. first name is Adam
C. that no one even
D. he is so rude
E. knows that his
SSC CHSL Tier-1 17.08.2023 (Shift-I)

(a) DACEB (b) BDACE
(c) ACBDE (d) CEBAD

Ans. (a)

The correct order is DACEB.

The sentence starts with 'He is so rude to his neighbours,' introducing the subject and action.

It is followed by 'that no one even knows that his first name is Adam,' which specifies the consequence.

SSC Steno 2024

133. The first part 'Zombies are not real' is fixed. Zombies are not real / sound effects (P) / make it believable (Q) / but special (R) / and visuals (S)
SSC Steno 11.12.2024 (Shift-I)

(a) RPSQ (b) PRSQ
(c) PQRS (d) PQSR

Ans. (a)

The correct logical sequence is RPSQ.

The sentence begins with the fixed part 'Zombies are not real.' The next logical part is 'but special' (R), introducing a contrast. This is followed by 'sound effects' (P) and 'and visuals' (S) to explain what makes it believable. Finally, 'make it believable' (Q) concludes the sentence, explaining the impact of the special effects and visuals.

134. The initial days / are not (P) / of my high school (Q) / to remember (R) / very good (S). **SSC Steno 11.12.2024 (Shift-I)**

(a) P, R, S, Q (b) R, Q, P, S
(c) P, S, R, Q (d) Q, P, S, R

Ans. (d)

The correct order is Q, P, S, R. The sentence starts with 'The initial days of my high school' as the subject, followed by 'are not' as the verb, then 'very good' as the complement, and ends with 'to remember' as the infinitive phrase.

135. He wrapped himself / two sweatshirts (P) / with a blanket, (Q) / was wearing (R) / though he (S) **SSC Steno 11.12.2024 (Shift-II)**

(a) P, Q, S, R (b) S, P, Q, R
(c) Q, R, P, S (d) Q, S, R, P

Ans. (d)

The correct sequence is QSRP.

136. O. arid deserts
P. from lush forests to
Q. hikers encountered diverse ecosystems
R. trekking through the wilderness **SSC Steno 11.12.2024 (Shift-II)**

(a) OPQR (b) RQPO
(c) PRQO (d) QPOR

Ans. (b)

The correct order is RQPO.

The present participle 'trekking' (R) introduces the action and sets the context. The subject 'hikers' (Q) follows, along with the verb 'encountered', which describes what the hikers experienced. The phrase 'diverse ecosystems' is detailed by the range 'from lush forests to arid deserts' (P and O).

137. P. the paintings of Sayed Haider Raza blended
Q. considered as one of the
R. foremost pioneers of Indian modern art
S. parisian modernism with the colours of Indian Rajput art **SSC Steno 11.12.2024 (Shift-II)**

(a) P, Q, R, S (b) R, P, S, Q
(c) P, S, Q, R (d) Q, R, P, S

Ans. (d)

The correct order is QRPS.

138. P. some experienced teachers say that
Q. teaching about English is easy and
R. teaching English is difficult as
S. the latter needs dedication, resources and many more **SSC Steno 11.12.2024 (Shift-II)**

(a) PSQR (b) PSRQ
(c) PQRS (d) PRSQ

Ans. (c)

The correct order is PQRS.

139. A. by the doctor to drink
B. the lady was compelled
C. such a vile medicine that
D. but killed by him
E. she was all **SSC Steno 11.12.2024 (Shift-II)**

(a) CBDAE
(b) BACED
(c) ACDEB
(d) DACBE

Ans. (b)

The order BACED creates a coherent and meaningful sentence. It starts with the main subject and verb ('The lady was compelled'), followed by the reason ('by the doctor to drink such a vile medicine that'), and finally the result ('she was all but killed by him').

140. The first part 'R' is fixed.
R. Men usually make more decisions
A. and certainly the most important ones
B. earning a livelihood in most parts of the world
C. since men play a bigger role in
D. they have a major say in economic matters **SSC Steno 10.12.2024 (Shift-I)**

(a) ACDB (b) ACBD
(c) DCAB (d) BADC

Ans. (b)

The correct order is ACBD.

It links men making more decisions to their important role in economic matters, emphasising their influence due to earning a livelihood in most parts of the world. It logically connects each part to form a coherent and meaningful paragraph.

141. P. the South Pole of the Moon
Q. and where no man has ever been before
R. the Artemis mission will explore
S. where ice has been confirmed to exist within craters **SSC Steno 10.12.2024 (Shift-I)**

(a) S, R, Q, P (b) Q, P, S, R
(c) P, R, Q, S (d) R, P, S, Q

Ans. (d)

The correct order is RPSQ.

It begins with the subject and action (the Artemis mission will explore), then specifies the location (the South Pole of the Moon), followed by additional information about the location (where ice has been confirmed to exist within craters and where no man has ever been before).

142. A. lost all his teeth
B. cannot eat hard food
C. as he has
D. consequently, he **SSC Steno 10.12.2024 (Shift-I)**

(a) DACB (b) ADBC
(c) BDAC (d) CADB

Ans. (*)

The correct order is DBCA.

It begins with the cause (consequently), followed by the effect (he cannot eat hard food) and then explains the reason (as he has lost all his teeth).

143. P. and innovative solutions
Q. creativity is the driving force
O. behind new ideas
R. for progress and change **SSC Steno 10.12.2024 (Shift-III)**

(a) QROP (b) ROQP
(c) ORQP (d) PQRO

Ans. (a)

The correct order is QROP. The sentence should start with the main clause 'creativity is the driving force', followed by 'behind new ideas', which is a subordinate clause.

Then 'for progress and change' further explains the purpose and finally 'behind new ideas' and 'and innovative solutions' completes the thought, linking all parts cohesively.

144. A. They do taste kind of funny.
B. I've done so all my life.
C. But it keeps them on the knife.
D. I always eat peas with honey. **SSC Steno 10.12.2024 (Shift-III)**

(a) CBAD
(b) ABDC
(c) DBAC
(d) BACD

Ans. (c)

The correct order is DBAC.

The paragraph should start with the main action 'I always eat peas with honey', followed by 'I've done so all my life', then 'But it keeps them on the knife' and concluding with 'They do taste kind of funny'.

13

Para Jumble

Para Jumble, as the name suggests, is nothing but paragraphs whose sentences are jumbled up. In other words, they are questions of sentence arrangement or sentence sequencing. These questions assess the examinee's ability to comprehend the meaning of individual sentences and arrange them in a coherent and logical sequence.

Types of Questions Asked

In SSC Examinations, two types of questions are generally asked from this topic.

Type 1

Given below are four jumbled sentences. Select the option that gives their correct order forming a meaningful and coherent paragraph.

A. We have spent over 4000 hours guiding over the past 8 years.
B. The Pilanesberg National Park in South Africa is one of the best wildlife experiences in terms of the abundance.
C. We've witnessed the gore and bloodshed of a lion down an impala.
D. And yes, we have basically seen it all.

(a) BADC (b) BCDA (c) ACBD (d) CABD ***Ans.*** (b)

Type 2

The first and the last parts of the passage are numbered 1 and 6. The rest of the passage is split into four parts and named P, Q, R and S. These four parts are not given in their proper order. Read the passage and find out, which of the four combinations is correct.

1. The Cinema is a very valuable teaching aid.
P. The Cinema is entertaining also.
Q. Historical films help the teacher of History.
R. Science can also be taught very effectively through Cinema.
S. Large number of people like social films.
6. Thus, Cinema has a great impact on our society.

(a) RQSP (b) SQRP (c) PQRS (d) QRPS ***Ans.*** (d)

How to Solve the Questions

There is no set method of finding the correct order of sentences. However, there are certain basic steps that you have to follow to successfully attempt para jumbles.

1. Read each and every sentence very carefully. Do not look at the options if they are given in the question.
2. Find the opening line of the paragraph. Remember that the opening line
   - may start with 'a', 'an', 'the', 'nowadays', 'once', etc.
   - does not start or end with a transition word
   - gives a new information of the topic
   - does not start with a pronoun
3. Try to find the closing sentence. A closing sentence starts with words with words like 'thus', 'hence' 'therefore', 'eventually', 'finally', etc.
4. Look for transition words, pronouns and linking words.
5. While looking for a correct sequence, you must look for relationships between sentences. These relationships act as links between sentences and help us find a pair of sentences that come together. To find such links look for
   - **Nouns and Pronouns** Try to see if a noun is being replaced by a pronoun in any two sentences. This means they are to be written one after the other.
   - **Chronology** Often sentences refer to a time sequence. Look for sentences where one event comes after another as such sentences are always placed together.
6. Try to understand the flow of the sentences and re-order them to make a sequence.
7. Reread your sentence to make sure that your sequence is logical and meaningful.

In some cases, the first and the last sentence are given. In such questions, find the sentence that links to the first sentence and then follow step 4 and 5 to come to the correct sequence.

The Grammar Valley

Trasition words are some words that connect two sentences referring to the same theme. These words are above all, after all, after word, again, all in all, also, as a rule, as well as, aside from, at the same time, barring, besides, but, consequently, earlier, first of all, for example, for instance, for now, for one thing, for the time being, furthermore, generally, hence, however, in addition, in conclusion, in other words, in short, in time, instead, later, later one, likewise, meanwhile, moreover, nevertheless, next, on the other hand, otherwise, rather, similarly, simultaneously, soon, still, subsequently, then, therefore, thus, to begin with, while, with this in mind yet, etc.

SSC Exam Scanner

SSC CGL 2024 (Tier 1 & 2)

Directions (Q. Nos. 1-205) Sentences of a paragraph are given below in jumbled order. Arrange the sentences in the correct order to form a meaningful and coherent paragraph.

Or

Given below are six sentences of a paragraph. Sentence A is the beginning whereas sentence F is the last sentence. The middle four sentences are jumbled up. Select the option that gives their correct order forming a meaningful and coherent paragraph.

1. A. Psychotherapy is a voluntary relationship between the one seeking treatment or the client and the one who treats or the therapist.
   B. The relationship is conducive for building the trust of the client so that problems may be freely discussed.
   C. The purpose of the relationship is to help the client to solve the psychological problems being faced by her or him.
   D. Psychotherapies aim at changing the maladaptive behaviours, decreasing the sense of personal distress and helping the client to adapt better to her/his environment.
   E. Inadequate marital, occupational and social adjustment also require that major changes be made in an individual's personal environment.

   SSC CGL Tier-2 18.01.2025

   (a) DCABE (b) CDEBA
   (c) EDACB (d) ACBDE

   Ans. (d)

   The correct order for the sentences is A, C, B, D, E. This arrangement starts by introducing psychotherapy (A) and its purpose (C). It then elaborates on the relationship between the client and therapist (B), the aims of psychotherapy (D) and the necessity of major changes in an individual's environment for proper adjustment (E).

2. A. As cost of raw materials cannot be reduced, exporters try to cut labour costs.
   B. Large MNCs in the garment industry in Europe and America order their products from Indian exporters.
   C. These large MNCs with worldwide network look for the cheapest goods in order to maximise their profits.
   D. To get these large orders, Indian garment exporters try hard to cut their own costs.
   E. Where earlier a factory used to employ workers on a permanent basis, now they employ workers only on a temporary basis so that they do not have to pay workers for the whole year.

   SSC CGL Tier-2 18.01.2025

   (a) DCABE (b) BCDAE
   (c) CDAEB (d) ADECB

   Ans. (b)

   The correct order for the sentences is B, C, D, A, E. This order ensures a logical flow, starting with the introduction of large MNCs in the garment industry (B) and their search for the cheapest goods to maximise profits (C). It then describes how Indian garment exporters try to cut their own costs to secure these large orders (D), the methods they use to cut labour costs (A) and the shift to employing workers on a temporary basis to avoid year-round payments (E).

3. A. It consists of a terracotta army of approximately 8000 life-sized men and horses.
   B. Each of the horses and men is individually sculpted by a 3-inch-thick terracotta clay and looks unique.
   C. Shi Huangdi was the founder of Qin Dynasty and was the first ruler of unified China in 221 BC.
   D. His mausoleum was recently discovered in 1974 by Chinese peasants who were drilling a well.

   SSC CGL Tier-2 18.01.2025

   (a) CDAB (b) CABD
   (c) CADB (d) CBAD

   Ans. (a)

   The correct order for the sentences is C, D, A, B.

   This order ensures a logical flow, starting with the introduction of Shi Huangdi and the discovery of his mausoleum, followed by details about the terracotta army and its unique characteristics.

4. 1. There are some backward areas in Andhra Pradesh.
   A. Rayalaseema is one of them.
   B. Massive degradation of natural resources and extensive changes in land use have resulted in poor crop productivity in Rayalaseema.
   C. The National Soil Survey and Land Use Planning Organisation is doing its job by giving suggestions to the farmers of Rayalaseema.
   D. Soil Organic Carbon (SOC), which is crucial for maintaining soil quality, has decreased by 84% in the region. Poor soil fertility and soil degradation, like in Rayalaseema region, are the major causes of food shortage.
   5. The advice is about which crops are to be cultivated and which not.

   SSC CGL Tier-2 20.01.2025

   (a) CBAD (b) CDBA
   (c) DCBA (d) ABDC

   Ans. (d)

   The correct order is 'ABDC'.
   Sentence A introduces Rayalaseema as one of the backward areas. Sentence B discusses the degradation of natural resources and poor crop productivity. Sentence D gives more details about soil degradation. Sentence C mentions the actions taken by the National Soil Survey and Land Use Planning Organisation.

5. A. These can turn around to track stars with the rotation of Earth.
   B. Observatories are places to study place.
   C. They are mostly built on the mountain tops.
   D. Telescopes are placed in the dome-shaped roof of the building.

   SSC CGL Tier-1 09.09.2024 (Shift-II)

   (a) BCDA (b) DCBA
   (c) ACDB (d) CBDA

   Ans. (a)

   The first sentence will be Sentence B which introduces the main theme of 'observatories'. The second sentence is C as it uses the pronoun 'They'. The third sentence is D as it introduces 'telescopes'. Sentence D is followed by A which presents the purpose of telescopes. Hence, the correct order is BCDA.

6. A. More children go to school than at any time in the past. But more children today are out of school than any time in the past.
B. But it is not enough to blame the high birth rate for this state of affairs.
C. Indeed, it can be reasonably argued that continued mass illiteracy is not the result but the cause of the high birth rate.
D. There are more literate people in India today than ever before. But there are also more illiterates than ever before.
SSC CGL Tier-1 10.09.2024 (Shift-I)
(a) ABCD (b) CBAD
(c) DABC (d) BADC

Ans. (c)
The first sentence of the paragraph will be Sentence D as it introduces illiteracy. The second sentence will be sentence A which expands on the situation. The third sentence will be sentence B which presents a contrast. The last sentence will be sentence C which concludes the paragraph. Thus, the correct order is DABC.

7. A. It is also called a nuclear family.
B. It is good to be in a small family because there is better management of resources.
C. A small family is one with parents and a maximum of two children.
SSC CGL Tier-1 10.09.2024 (Shift-II)
D. The advantages of a small family are numerous.
(a) CADB (b) BACD
(c) CBDA (d) ACBD

Ans. (a)
The first sentence will be C as it introduces the small family and what it is constituted of. Next will be sentence A as it gives another name for the small family. The third sentence will be D as it states that a small family has advantages. The last sentence will be B as it expands on D. Hence, the correct order is CADB.

8. A. It contains high levels of Vitamin A and D.
B. Cod liver oil is thus used to treat arthritis.
C. This supplement is made from the liver of cod fish.
D. Cod liver oil is a nutritional supplement.
SSC CGL Tier-1 11.09.2024 (Shift-II)
(a) ABCD (b) CBAD
(c) DCAB (d) BACD

Ans. (c)
The first sentence will be sentence D as it presents the main topic- Cod Liver oil. The second sentence will be C as it present more information about it using 'this'. Sentence A comes third as it present more information. The last sentence is B as it contains 'thus'. Hence, the correct order is DCAB.

9. A. A big fancy dress ball was arranged to celebrate their homecoming.
B. It must have been a terrible shock for a young girl.
C. They had been married a month, just home from their honeymoon.
D. Just as the guests were starting to arrive, Charnley locked himself into his bedroom and shot himself.
SSC CGL Tier-1 11.09.2024 (Shift-III)
(a) BCDA (b) ABCD
(c) BCAD (d) DACB

Ans. (c)
The first sentence of the paragraph will be B as it introduces the story wherein the girl was shook. The next sentence will be C as it sets the background for the shock. It will be followed by sentence A presents how there was a party. The last sentence will be D as it reveals the reason for the shock. Hence, the correct order is BCAD.

10. A. The genuine beliefs, though not unconsciously acquired by most children; and even if they depart from these beliefs in later life.
B. Something of them remains deeply implanted, ready to emerge in a time of stress of crisis.
C. The importance of education in forming character and opinion is very great and well recognised by all.
D. Education is, as a rule, the strongest force on the side of what exists and again fundamental change **SSC CGL Tier-1 12.09.2024 (Shift-I)**
(a) DCAB (b) DABC
(c) CBAD (d) CABD

Ans. (c)
The first part of the sentence is 'C' which introduces the 'importance of education'. The next sentence is 'B' which tells about implanted beliefs in children. Next sentence will be 'A' which emphasises some remaining beliefs thought most of them being departed. The last sentence will be 'D' which concludes 'education' as the strongest force. Hence, the correct order is 'CBAD'.

11. A. This past summer, my dream finally came true.
B. Strange lands, exciting places and new cultures have always fascinated me.
C. Ever since I was a little girl, I dreamed about travelling overseas.
D. I got to travel to England, France, Switzerland and Germany.
SSC CGL Tier-1 12.09.2024 (Shift-III)
(a) DCBA (b) CBAD
(c) ABCD (d) BADC

Ans. (b)
The first sentence of the paragraph will be C as it introduces the main character 'I'. The second sentence will be B which expands on the dreams of I. The third sentence will be A which states that I's dream came true. The last sentence will be D which expands on it. Thus, the correct order is CBAD.

12. A. Mobile phones or smartphones are becoming popular all over the world.
B. But at the same time, it also harms us in many ways.
C. It is the most widely used medium of communication today.
D. Today, it is very affordable and available to everyone.
SSC CGL Tier-1 12.09.2024 (Shift-III)
(a) ABCD (b) DACB
(c) CABD (d) ACDB

Ans. (d)
The first sentence of the paragraph will be A as it introduces the main theme- Mobile phone. The second sentence will be C as refers to them with pronoun 'it'. The third sentence will be D which states the present day condition. The last sentence will be B which contrasts the statement in D. Thus, the correct order is ACDB.

13. A. When we connect this design with a wire, electricity flows.
B. These metal strips were put in a sulphuric acid solution.
C. He made two strips of different metals.
D. Alessandro Volta discovered electric battery.
SSC CGL Tier-1 13.09.2024 (Shift-II)
(a) CBDA (b) DCBA
(c) BCDA (d) ACDB

Ans. (b)
The first sentence of the paragraph will be D as it introduces Alessandro Volta and his discovery. The second sentence

will be C which starts describing how he made the discovery. The third sentence will be B which expands the description. The last sentence will be A which concludes on it. Thus, the correct order is DCBA.

14. A. That's why silky is deliciously different and exceptionally versatile, natural, thick and durable ice cream.
B. Beautifully firm, nice, silky rather than thin and watery, it stays in shape and stands on top of fruits or pastries without soaking in.
C. Silky thick double ice-cream has a unique, fresh taste and texture.

SSC CGL Tier-1 17.09.2024 (Shift-I)

(a) ABC (b) BAC
(c) CBA (d) BCA

Ans. (c)

The correct order is CBA.
The advertisement thus formed will be- Silky thick double ice-cream has a unique, fresh taste and texture. Beautifully firm, nice, silky rather than thin and watery, it stays in shape and stands on top of fruits or pastries without soaking in. That's why Silky is deliciously different and exceptionally versatile, natural, thick and durable ice-cream.

15. A. It was as simple as announcing what you have in your store or the services you offer in your premises.
B. Over the years, advertising has evolved into a major industry that goes beyond informing to persuading and influencing.
C. Advertising was initially meant to make people aware of the goods available in the market.
D. It is a form of brainwashing consumers.

SSC CGL Tier-1 17.09.2024 (Shift-II)

(a) BADC (b) ADBC
(c) DABC (d) CABD

Ans. (d)

The first sentence of the paragraph will be C as it introduces the main theme- Advertisement.
The second sentence will be A which expands the definition.
The third sentence will be B which states the idea of evolution of advertisement.
The last sentence will be D which concludes on it. Thus, the correct order is CABD.

16. A. However, their population is declining nowadays due to noise pollution.
B. It is one of the most common birds along with the other two species, the European starling and the rock pigeon.
C. Their constant presence outside our homes makes it easy to overlook them.
D. House sparrows can be found in most places with and without houses (or other structures).

SSC CGL Tier-1 19.09.2024 (Shift-I)

(a) DACB (b) BDCA
(c) DABC (d) DBCA

Ans. (d)

The first sentence of the paragraph will be D as it introduces the main theme- House sparrows. The second sentence will be B which expands on their species. The third sentence will be C which states the idea of it being a common bird. The last sentence will be A which concludes it with 'however'. Thus, the correct order is DBCA.

17. A. These are responsible for producing the major fuel used across the globe.
B. The country has 100 major oil and gas fields.
C. The economy of Saudi Arabia is based on petroleum.
D. The chief oil field is Ghawar Field having an estimated 70 billion reserve resource.

SSC CGL Tier-1 23.09.2024 (Shift-I)

(a) DCAB (b) ABCD
(c) CBAD (d) BACD

Ans. (c)

The first sentence of the paragraph will be C as it introduces the main theme- The economy of Saudi Arabia is based on Petroleum. The second sentence will be B which expands on it. The third sentence will be A which states how it is profitable. The last sentence will be D which concludes it with the chief oil field. Thus, the correct order is CBAD.

18. A. The door of the flat was ajar.
B. The taxi stopped.
C. Mr. Satterthwaite flung himself out and raced up the stone stairs to the second floor like a young athlete.
D. He pushed it open, and the great voice welcomed him.

SSC CGL Tier-1 24.09.2024 (Shift-I)

(a) BACD (b) ABCD
(c) BCAD (d) DCBA

Ans. (c)

The correct order is BCAD.
The paragraph formed will be- The taxi stopped. Mr. Satterthwaite flung himself out and raced up the stone stairs to the second floor like a young athlete.
The door of the flat was ajar.
He pushed it open and the great voice welcomed him which will depict a proper sequence.

19. A. It regulates the operation of all body organs protects the body and mind from becoming unbalanced as a result of negative circumstances and unhealthy lifestyles.
B. It only requires frequent practice of the proper body motions and breathing techniques.
C. The physical benefits of yoga can be enjoyed for a lifetime without risk or injury.
D. It regulates the relationship between the body, the intellect and the spirit.

SSC CGL Tier-1 24.09.2024 (Shift-II)

(a) DABC (b) CBDA
(c) BACD (d) ABCD

Ans. (b)

The first sentence of the paragraph will be C as it introduces the main theme- Physical benefits of yoga. The second sentence will be B which expands on it. The third sentence will be D which states its benefits. The last sentence will be A which further expands its benefits. Thus, the correct order is CBDA.

20. A. Summative assessment is the assignment of the student's performance at the end of the academic term.
B. This new pattern ensures that besides just textbook teaching and learning, effective child-teacher interaction is encouraged.
C. The CBSE envisages two types of examinations: formative and summative.
D. Formative assessment is a part of the teaching-learning process and is done through conversation, quizzes, interviews, projects, assignments, etc.

SSC CGL Tier-1 25.09.2024 (Shift-III)

(a) BCAD (b) DACB
(c) ABCD (d) CDAB

Ans. (d)

The first sentence of the paragraph will be C as it introduces the main theme- CBSE envisages two types of examinations, formative and summative.
The second sentence will be D which expands on formative assessment. The third sentence will be A which expands on summative assessment. The last sentence will be B which concludes it. Thus, the correct order is CDAB.

21. A. The world's biggest radio telescope is in Puerto Rico.
B. It is called Arecibo dish.
C. It was built 40 years ago.
D. It is also 300 metres across.
SSC CGL Tier-1 26.09.2024 (Shift-I)
(a) ABDC (b) CBDA
(c) DCAB (d) DCBA

Ans. (a)
The correct order is ABDC.
The paragraph formed will be- 'The world's biggest radio telescope is in Puerto Rico.
It is called Arecibo dish. It is also 300 metres across. It was built 40 years ago,' which will appropriately depict proper sequence.

22. A. He remembered her as she once was an eager, glowing girl.
B. He had not seen her for nearly thirteen years.
C. Mr. Satterthwaite went to meet her.
D. And now he saw – a Frozen Lady. **SSC CGL Tier-1 26.09.2024 (Shift-II)**
(a) DCBA (b) CBAD
(c) DBAC (d) ABCD

Ans. (b)
The correct order is CBAD.
The paragraph formed will be-
Mr. Satterthwaite went to meet her. He had not seen her for nearly thirteen years.
He remembered her as she once was – an eager, glowing girl. And now he saw – a Frozen Lady.

23. A. This figure is predicted to climb as the percentage of Americans residing in rural areas falls by an average of 1.6% annually.
B. The United Nations reports that India's urban population is growing at a rate of 1.1 % annually, while the country's rural population is shrinking at a rate of 0.37 percent annually.
C. While 82% of Americans live in urban settings, only 30% of Indians do so.
D. It's still a considerably smaller percentage of the Indian population than it is in the US that resides in urban areas.
SSC CGL Tier-1 26.09.2024 (Shift-III)
(a) DBAC (b) ACBD
(c) BDCA (d) BDAC

Ans. (c)
The first sentence of the paragraph will be B as it introduces the main theme- United Nations reports about Indian Urban population.
The second sentence will be D which expands on it. The third sentence will be C which makes a comparison between Indian and American population.
The last sentence will be A which concludes it. Thus, the correct order is BDCA.

SSC CGL 2023 (Tier 1 & 2)

24. A. In Bihar and Central India, in particular, every district had smelters that used local deposits of ore to produce iron which was widely used for the manufacture of implements and tools of daily use.
B. The smelting was done by men while women worked on the bellows, pumping air that kept the charcoal burning.
C. But iron smelting in India was extremely common till the end of the 19th century.
D. Production of Wootz steel required a highly specialised technique of refining iron.
SSC CGL Tier-1 14.07.2023 (Shift-I)
(a) ACDB (b) DCAB
(c) BCDA (d) CBDA

Ans. (b)
Sentence D will be the first sentence as it introduces the main theme- Iron smelting or refining iron. Sentence C comes second as it starts with 'but' and presents how iron smelting had been present in India. It is followed by sentence A which presents specific regions of India and how popular smelting was in these regions. The last sentence is B as it presents who did the smelting in India. Thus, the correct sequence is DCAB.

25. A. He repeated the experiment, increasing the amount until he had weighed up to a thousand pounds.
B. During the spring of 1717, the iron foundries in a remote district were often visited by a thin, middle-aged man with a notebook.
C. Three cauldrons were next prepared under his directions.
D. He would weigh out two pounds of iron, have them heated till they were red-hot and then weigh them again.
SSC CGL Tier-1 14.07.2023 (Shift-I)
(a) BDAC (b) ABDC
(c) BCAD (d) CABD

Ans. (a)
Sentence B will be the first sentence as it introduces the main theme- Who visited the iron foundries in spring 1717.
Sentence D comes second as it presents what the man would do. It is followed by sentence A which presents how the experiment continued till a certain point. The last sentence is C as it presents the end result. Thus, the correct sequence is BDAC.

26. A. The top band is made of saffron, which symbolises power and courage.
B. The Constituent Assembly adopted our National Flag, Tiranga, which means tricolour, on 22nd July, 1947.
C. As a symbol of nationalism and freedom, it is fashioned from khadi, which is domestically spun Indian cotton.
D. It features three horizontal stripes that are all the same width. **SSC CGL Tier-1 14.07.2023 (Shift-I)**
(a) CBAD (b) CBDA
(c) BCDA (d) BDCA

Ans. (c)
Sentence B will be the first sentence as it introduces the main theme- Adoption of the National Flag.
Sentence C comes second as it presents what it represents and the cloth used to make it.
It is followed by sentence D which presents how it looks. The last sentence is A as it presents new information about one of the stripes. Thus, the correct sequence is BCDA.

27. Sentences of a paragraph are given below while the first and the last sentences (S1 and S6) are in the correct order, the sentences in between are jumbled up and named P, Q, R, S. Arrange the sentences in the correct order to form a meaningful and coherent paragraph.

(S1) Newspapers, especially of the popular variety, aim to do two things to inform and to entertain.

(P) Entertainment may be principally found in the center pages of the newspaper in some of the feature articles and in some local news stories.

(Q) The principal aim of the short news report on the front pages is to inform.

(R) Most newspapers are published daily and the news reporters must make sure that they have up-to-the minute news.

(S) In their news reports they will aim to create a sense of immediacy, to convey the impression that they have 'rushed' the news to the reader and 'that the information contained is the very latest'.

(S6) Reporters also wish to create a sense of authenticity, that is, that their news is accurate and genuine.

SSC CGL Tier-1 14.07.2023 (Shift-II)

(a) QSRP (b) RPSQ
(c) SRPQ (d) PQRS

Ans. (d)

Sentence P will be the first sentence as it continues the main theme of S1- Newspapers and presents where the entertainment section can be found. Sentence Q comes second as it presents the purpose of shorts news on the front. It is followed by sentence R which states how newspapers are published daily and the reporters have to be up-to-date. The last sentence is S as it presents the effect of the latest news. Thus, the correct sequence is PQRS.

28. A. During the summer, I noticed that the leaves of the tree were beginning to wither.

B. I am especially proud of it, not only because it has survived several winters, but because it occasionally produces luscious peaches.

C. The tree had grown against a warm wall on a sheltered side of the house.

D. Last summer, I spent many days in the garden watching thousands of ants crawling up the trunk of my prize peach tree.

SSC CGL Tier-1 14.07.2023 (Shift-II)

(a) DCBA (b) ABCD
(c) CDBA (d) BDAC

Ans. (a)

Sentence D will be the first sentence as it introduces the main theme- What the writer had observed about ants and his peach tree. Sentence C comes second as it presents the location of the tree. It is followed by sentence B which states that the writer is proud of it. The last sentence is A as it presents the reason what the writer had notices in summer. Thus, the correct sequence is DCBA.

29. A. The outcome is much more likely to be favourable if there is substantial international aid than if there is not.

B. Many of the underdeveloped countries will promote the growth of their economies in one way or the other, no matter whether they receive substantial outside aid in the process or not.

C. By substantial aid I mean not only large amounts of technical assistance but also of capital.

D. The character of that development, however, is likely to be strongly influenced by the types of and amounts of aid available.

SSC CGL Tier-1 14.07.2023 (Shift-II)

(a) BDAC (b) ABDC
(c) DABC (d) DBCA

Ans. (a)

Sentence B will be the first sentence as it introduces the main theme- How underdeveloped economies will develop. Sentence D comes second as it presents how development will come. It is followed by sentence A which states the need of international aid. The last sentence is C as it elaborate what aid indicates. Thus, the correct sequence is BDAC.

30. A. Through a subtle analysis, Woolf raises certain concerns regarding discrimination against women in a male-dominated society.

B. It's also against the need for freedom of expression in women, and the right to human dignity and equality.

C. In 'Shakespeare's Sister', Virginia Woolf explores the plight of women in society in England during the 15th and 16th centuries.

D. It is against the denial of education to the girl-child and violence against women.

SSC CGL Tier-1 14.07.2023 (Shift-III)

(a) BACD (b) DCBA
(c) ADBC (d) CADB

Ans. (d)

Sentence C will be the first sentence as it introduces the main theme- The Shakespeare's Sister by Virginia Woolf.

Sentence A comes second as it states what Woolf does in the story. It is followed by sentence D which states its main theme. The last sentence is B as it elaborates the theme. Thus, the correct sequence is CADB.

31. A. But the question that perturbs Ruskin's mind is what social pressure can be exercised against a dishonest person.

B. The merchant, for instance, must supply perfect and pure things to the people.

C. Ruskin believes that in every civilised society there exist five intellectual professions, namely the soldier, the pastor, the physician, the lawyer and the merchant.

D. Persons belonging to these professions are expected to perform their duty honestly.

SSC CGL Tier-1 14.07.2023 (Shift-IV)

(a) BACD (b) DABC
(c) CDBA (d) ABDC

Ans. (c)

Sentence C will be the first sentence as it introduces the main theme- Ruskin's belief. Sentence D comes second as it elaborates on the belief. It is followed by sentence B which states an example. The last sentence is A as it states what Ruskin is filled with questions about something. Thus, the correct sequence is CDBA.

32. A. But she has no idea an aunt and uncle are waiting for her.

B. 'The Strange Child' is the story of a young girl who believes she is the only one on the planet.

C. Her parents simply vanished into thin air one day.

D. She travels the world in search of Nevada because she aspires to reside in the Mojave Desert.

SSC CGL Tier-1 14.07.2023 (Shift-IV)

(a) DABC (b) BDAC
(c) BACD (d) BCDA

Ans. (*)

Sentence B will be the first sentence as it introduces the main theme- The story of the 'Strange Child' who is an orphan. Sentence D comes second as it presents how she feels about her parents. It is followed by sentence C which presents how she travels. The last sentence is A. Thus, the correct sequence is BDCA.

33. A. We often make all things around us the way we want them.
B. Even during our pilgrimages, we have begun to look for whatever makes our heart happy, gives comfort to our body and peace to the mind.
C. Our mind is resourceful enough to find shortcuts in simple and easy ways.
D. It is as if external solutions will fulfil our needs and we do not want to make any special efforts even in our spiritual search.

SSC CGL Tier-1 14.07.2023 (Shift-IV)

(a) CABD (b) ADBC
(c) ABDC (d) DABC

Ans. (a)

Sentence C will be the first sentence as it introduces the main theme- The resourcefulness of our mind. Sentence A comes second as it presents how our mind works. It is followed by sentence B which presents how it works even during pilgrimages. The last sentence is D which states how we do not want to struggle. Thus, the correct sequence is CABD.

34. A. It's because the 'practical people' in society boast of having a practical approach to life.
B. It is very likely for youngsters to seek advice from their elders.
C. Emphasising upon the times that prevailed, the youth very much get their queries answered systematically.
D. In the similar context even the elders are, in most likelihood, expected to give their advice as a word of guidance.

SSC CGL Tier-1 14.07.2023 (Shift-IV)

(a) BDCA (b) CDAB
(c) ACDB (d) DCAB

Ans. (a)

Sentence B will be the first sentence as it introduces the main theme- Seeking advice from elders. Sentence D comes second as it presents how elders give advice. It is followed by sentence C which presents how youth gets answered. The last sentence is A. Thus, the correct sequence is BDCA.

35. A. Many countries throughout the world have achieved full digitalisation.
B. Initially, the entire world transitioned to digitalisation.
C. This type of internet is known as a Metaverse.
D. This existing kind of internet technology, which gives us access to various aspects, is about to change into a better and newer version.
E. The Metaverse is an intriguing technology that has been described as the 'newer version of the internet'.

SSC CGL Tier-1 17.07.2023 (Shift-I)

(a) BCEDA (b) DCEBA
(c) ABCDE (d) EADCB

Ans. (b)

Sentence D will be the first sentence as it introduces the main theme- The changing world of Internet. Sentence C comes second as it presents the name of the new internet- Metaverse. It is followed by sentence E which describes Metaverse. Sentence B comes next stating the beginning of Metaverse. The last sentence is A as it presents the current status of the world. Thus, the correct sequence is DCEBA.

36. A. According to Homer, Achilles was brought up by his mother at Phthia with his inseparable companion Patroclus.
B. Achilles was the bravest, handsomest and greatest warrior of the army of Agamemnon in the Trojan War.
C. Later non-Homeric tales suggest that Patroclus was Achilles' kinsman or lover.
D. Achilles, in Greek mythology, is the son of the mortal Peleus, king of the Myrmidons and the Nereid Thetis. SSC CGL Tier-1 17.07.2023 (Shift-II)

(a) ABCD (b) DBAC
(c) DABC (d) CABD

Ans. (b)

Sentence D will be the first sentence as it contains the main idea i.e., Achilles. Sentence B comes second as it describes Achilles. It will be followed by Sentence A which states how Homer describes Achilles. The last sentence is Sentence C which states how Achilles was seen by Non-Homeric representations. Thus, the correct sequence is DBAC.

37. A. "Well, you can't make me", she said, looking back at me.
B. She went on, "Well, you might try", I responded and she laughed.
C. She came in and we said hello, then she just looked at me and said, "What do you want?" McKechnie remembered.
D. "Well, I want you to grin and seem pleased", I added.

SSC CGL Tier-1 17.07.2023 (Shift-III)

(a) ACBD (b) DCBA
(c) BCDA (d) CDAB

Ans. (d)

Sentence C will be the first sentence as it introduces the starts of the conversation. Sentence D comes second as it presents how 'I' replies. It is followed by sentence A which presents the reaction of 'she'. The last sentence is B. Thus, the correct sequence is CDAB.

38. A. After examining these three approaches carefully I crossed the bridge and examined the Kedarnath pilgrim road for half a mile.
B. There were three approaches to the bridge, one from the North, one from the South and between these two a well-beaten footpath from the Rudraprayag bazaar.
C. Satisfied that the leopard had not crossed the river. I determined to put in operation my plan for closing the two bridges at night and thus confining the leopard to my side of the river.
D. Next, I examined the footpath on which three nights previously my goat had been killed.

SSC CGL Tier-1 17.07.2023 (Shift-III)

(a) CDAB (b) ABDC
(c) ABCD (d) DABC

Ans. (a)

Sentence C will be the first sentence as it introduces how the narrator has planned something. Sentence D comes second as it presents how he examined the footpath where his goat was killed. It is followed by sentence A which presents what he did next. The last sentence is B as it describes the path. Thus, the correct sequence is CDAB.

39. Sentences of a paragraph are given below. While the first and the last sentences (S1 and S6) are in the correct order, the sentences in between are jumbled up and named P, Q, R, S. Arrange the sentences in the correct order to form a meaningful and coherent paragraph.

(S1) Today, the world has become a much smaller place, thanks to the adventures and miracles of science.

P. We are slowly realising that the world is a single cooperative group.

Q. Other religions have become forces with which we have to reckon and we are seeking for ways and means by which we can live together in peace and harmony.

R. Mingling of population is bringing about interchange of thought.

S. Foreign nations have become our next-door neighbours.

(S6) We cannot have religious unity and peace so long as we assert that we are in possession of the light and all others are groping in the darkness.

SSC CGL Tier-1 18.07.2023 (Shift-I)

(a) SRPQ (b) PQRS
(c) SRQP (d) QRSP

Ans. (a)

Sentence S will be the first sentence as it states that foreign worlds have become our neighbours.
Sentence R comes second as it presents how intermingling of thought has impacted us. It is followed by sentence P which states that we are realising that the world is a single cooperative group. The last sentence is Q as it elaborate on the idea of sentence P. Thus, the correct sequence is SRPQ.

40. A. After a few months, the two countries engaged in the Kargil War.

B. Furthermore, a number of violent wars were fought between India and Pakistan.

C. In February 1999, during the winter invasion, India and Pakistan signed the Lahore Declaration, which was predicated on peace.

D. The engagements were extremely challenging for the Indian Army since they had to fight on rough rocky terrain.

SSC CGL Tier-1 18.07.2023 (Shift-II)

(a) DCAB (b) CABD
(c) CDBA (d) DABC

Ans. (b)

Sentence C will be the first sentence as it introduces the main theme- The Lahore Declaration. Sentence A comes second as it presents how after two months, India and Pakistan had a Kargil War.
It is followed by sentence B which presents that further wars were fought. The last sentence is D which states how it impacted the Indian Army. Thus, the correct sequence is CABD.

41. A. But, while the court's action solved one problem, it created another and because of the closure, many workers lost their jobs.

B. For instance, the courts directed industries in residential areas in Delhi to close down or shift out of the city.

C. In recent years, while the courts have come out with strong orders on environmental issues, these have sometimes affected people's livelihoods adversely.

D. Several of these industries were polluting the neighbourhood and discharge from these industries were polluting the River Yamuna because they hade been set up without following the rules.

SSC CGL Tier-1 18.07.2023 (Shift-III)

(a) CBDA (b) BDCA
(c) CDAB (d) BCAD

Ans. (a)

Sentence C will be the first sentence as it introduces the main theme- Orders on environmental issues and their impacts. Sentence B comes second as it presents an example. It is followed by sentence D which elaborates on the example. The last sentence is A as it presents how it created another problem. Thus, the correct sequence is CBDA.

42. A. The shopman was very interested in selling the creamy box to her as he would gain a big margin.

B. The man on the counter showed her 'an exquisite little enamel box' with a very fine glaze as if baked in cream.

C. As the box was too expensive, priced twenty-eight guineas, she asked the shopkeeper to keep it for her.

D. She went inside a little antique shop in Curzon Street. This was the usual shop where the shopkeeper was ridiculously fond of serving her.

SSC CGL Tier-1 18.07.2023 (Shift-IV)

(a) DCBA
(b) ADBC
(c) BDAC
(d) DBAC

Ans. (d)

Sentence D will be the first sentence as it contains the main idea i.e., the antique shop in Curzon Street.
Sentence B comes second as it states what the man at the counter showed. It will be followed by Sentence A which why the man wanted to sell the box. The last sentence is sentence C which states what the girl asked the man to do. Thus, the correct sequence is DBAC.

43. A. But at the same time, this is also true that when one reads a few works of the same genre, one naturally comes to know a rough structure of that genre.

B. The essence of suspense is whether the reader will be able to gauge the criminal before the detective tells who he is.

C. This leads to a different kind of approach to understanding literature in general and detective fiction in particular.

D. It is found that when one knows a genre and its structure and rules, it may often not make us enjoy a piece of literary work in the same manner as one usually does. **SSC CGL Tier-1 19.07.2023 (Shift-I)**

(a) DACB (b) BDCA
(c) CBAD (d) ADCB

Ans. (a)

Sentence D will be the first sentence as it introduces how the knowledge of genres impacts reading.
Sentence A comes second as it presents a fact about how one understand the structure of a genre.
It is followed by sentence C which states how this structure increase understanding of reading. The last sentence is B. Thus, the correct sequence is DACB.

44. A. It could possibly lead to serious injuries, hence a mate for N' Pongo became inevitable.
B. Within the span of one year, N' Pongo grew double the size and the need to obtain a mate for him arose, for it becomes unsafe for the humans around.
C. Every afternoon he was brought out onto the lawn to show off his skills in front of his admirers.
D. Owing to his attractive appearance and disposition, good manners and a well-developed sense of humour, N' Pongo soon became the darling of the zoo.

SSC CGL Tier-1 19.07.2023 (Shift-I)

(a) DCBA (b) DABC
(c) CDAB (d) BDAC

Ans. (a)

Sentence D will be the first sentence as it introduces N' Pongo. Sentence C comes second as it points out how he was shown off.

It is followed by sentence B which states the growth of N' Pongo. The last sentence is A as it points out the need for a mate for N' Pongo. Thus, the correct sequence is DCBA.

45. A. Graphology tells them about the candidates' temperaments, highlighting both, weaknesses and strengths.
B. Many companies use it for executive recruitment and analysis.
C. Despite public scepticism, graphology plays a covert role in British management.
D. Modern graphology began early in the 19th century when French churchman Jean Hippolyte Michon created the first graphological 'catalogue'.

SSC CGL Tier-1 19.07.2023 (Shift-II)

(a) DCBA (b) ABCD
(c) ABDC (d) CBDA

Ans. (a)

Sentence D will be the first sentence as it introduces modern graphology. Sentence C comes second as it points out the role of graphology in British management.

It is followed by sentence B which states how it is used.

The last sentence is A as it further elaborate the use. Thus, the correct sequence is DCBA.

46. A. Quipu, a type of knotted rope employed by the Incas of South America, served as a memory aid.
B. Different colours were used to dye the strings.
C. Yellow represented money while red stood for battle or warriors.
D. Do you realise that five yellow knots represented five gold coins?

SSC CGL Tier-1 19.07.2023 (Shift-II)

(a) BCAD (b) BDAC
(c) ADBC (d) ABCD

Ans. (d)

Sentence A will be the first sentence as it introduces Quipu. Sentence B comes second as it presents the string used in it. It is followed by sentence C which focuses on the symbolisation of different colours of the string. The last sentence is D. Thus, the correct sequence is ABCD.

47. A. Symptoms like nervousness, increased heart rate and feeling weak are some of the starting signs of anxiety.
B. Whereas anxiety attacks, sweating, trembling and having a feeling of impending danger might suggest advanced anxiety levels.
C. Most people don't even realise they have anxiety or take corrective measures until it amplifies and gets out of control.
D. Anxiety is a sad reality of today's time that has plagued a number of us in a variety of different ways.

SSC CGL Tier-1 19.07.2023 (Shift-III)

(a) CDAB (b) DCAB
(c) DACB (d) CDBA

Ans. (b)

Sentence D will be the first sentence as it introduces the main theme- Anxiety. Sentence C comes second as it presents how most people do not realise that they have anxiety. It is followed by sentence A which states its symptoms. The last sentence is B as it presents what happens in anxiety attacks. Thus, the correct sequence is DCAB.

48. A. Mendel's simple 'laws of heredity' came to be widely known and were uncritically assumed to apply to all human characteristics.
B. With Charles Darwin's popularisation of the concept of evolution, man became interested in his biological origins and affiliations.
C. Starting with the work on heredity of Gregor Mendel in the 1860s and the recognition of its significance in 1900, interest shifted to the problem of man's ontogenetic origins.
D. This interest was centred on man's phylogenetic origins.

SSC CGL Tier-1 19.07.2023 (Shift-III)

(a) ADCB (b) DCAB
(c) CDBA (d) BDCA

Ans. (d)

Sentence B will be the first sentence as it introduces the main theme- The impact of Charles Darwin's evolution on mankind. Sentence D comes second as it presents specific area of interests it included. It is followed by sentence C which presents how man's interest shifted. The last sentence is A as it refers to Mendel's thoery. Thus, the correct sequence is BDCA.

49. A. The olive tree grows slowly yet lives a long time.
B. The normal lifespan of an olive tree is 300-400 years but olive trees as ancient as 3000 years have been discovered.
C. The olive is a well-known Mediterranean-native evergreen tree whose fruit and oil are used in cuisine and cooking.
D. As a result, the olive tree is known as the 'immortal tree' in mythology and botany.

SSC CGL Tier-1 19.07.2023 (Shift IV)

(a) CDAB (b) CABD
(c) DBCA (d) ABCD

Ans. (b)

Sentence C will be the first sentence as it introduces the main theme- The olive. Sentence A comes second as it presents more information about the olive tree. It is followed by sentence B which presents the life span of an olive tree. The last sentence is D which states that it is called the immortal tree. Thus, the correct sequence is CABD.

50. A. So the problems of India should not be viewed as the failure of this great nation.
B. The uniqueness of this nation lies in its unity in diversity due to which there are problems here and there at times.
C. India, a very large country with many religions, many mini-cultures and many languages, has been achieving success in all fields.

D. But even small countries with monolithic societies have more problems than this second largest country.

SSC CGL Tier-1 19.07.2023 (Shift IV)

(a) DBAC (b) CADB
(c) CBDA (d) BDAC

Ans. (c)

Sentence C will be the first sentence as it introduces the main theme- How India is achieving success in all fields. Sentence B comes second as it presents that because of diversity there are problems. It is followed by sentence D which presents how all societies have such problems. The last sentence is A as it presents how the problems are not failures. Thus, the correct sequence is CBDA.

51. A. Both, Ratan and Moti were idlers and did not work.
B. Their wives had introduced order and industry in the house.
C. Ratan and Moti's wives would work hard and would earn the bread for their family.
D. This made them lazier.

SSC CGL Tier-1 20.07.2023 (Shift-I)

(a) CDAB (b) ABDC
(c) BADC (d) ACBD

Ans. (d)

Sentence A will be the first sentence as it introduces the main theme- Ratan and Moti. Sentence C comes second as it presents their contrast to their wives. It is followed by sentence B which presents how the wives impacted their house. The last sentence is D as it presents how Ratan and Moti become lazier. Thus, the correct sequence is ACBD.

52. A. The first is the herbalist, who generally enjoys the prestige and reputation of being the real traditional medical professional.
B. Over the years, I have come to distinguish three types of medical practitioners in African societies and to classify the extent to which each uses medicinal plants.
C. Thirdly, the witch doctor, the practitioner who is credited with the ability to intercept the evil deeds of a witch.
D. The second group represents the divine healers.

SSC CGL Tier-1 20.07.2023 (Shift-I)

(a) BDAC (b) BADC
(c) CBAD (d) ACDB

Ans. (b)

Sentence B will be the first line as it contains the main idea i.e., three types of medical practitioners in African societies. Sentence A comes second as it states the first type. Further, Sentence D states the second type and Sentence C states the third type. So, C will follow D. Thus, the correct sequence is BADC.

53. A. He used to commit one theft a year on average. The stolen money lasted for the year.
B. He chose the house at Shotover Grange to commit his next burglary. He studied the design of the house carefully for a fortnight.
C. He found that the family had gone to London and the servants to the movie. He broke into the house one afternoon.
D. He hoped to get fifteen thousand pounds worth of jewels from the safe. **SSC CGL Tier-1 20.07.2023 (Shift-II)**

(a) BCDA (b) DCBA
(c) BDAC (d) ABCD

Ans. (d)

Sentence A will be the first sentence as it introduces the main topic he and his act of theft. Sentence B comes second as it presents his target for theft. It is followed by sentence C which focuses on the fact that the target was easy for 'he'. The last sentence is D as it mentions what he hoped to get. Thus, the correct sequence is ABCD.

54. A. Chronic infections such as typhoid, chickenpox and others, for example, are no longer feared.
B. A factor contributing to the rapid rise of the population in recent years has been the drop in the death rate.
C. Because of medical breakthroughs, the death rate has decreased.
D. In 2001, the death rate in India was approximately 8.5 per thousand people.

SSC CGL Tier-1 20.07.2023 (Shift-II)

(a) BDCA (b) DBCA
(c) CDAB (d) ADBC

Ans. (a)

Sentence B will be the first sentence as it introduces the main theme- Population rise and drop in death rate. Sentence D comes second as it presents 2001 statistics. It is followed by sentence C which presents the reason for decrease in death rate. The last sentence is A as it presents evidence. Thus, the correct sequence is BDCA.

55. A. There are 1.52 billion Aadhaar cards given to the whole population as of February 2019.
B. A financial inclusion programme called the Prime Minister's Jan Dhan Yojana (PMJDY) makes services like banking, remittance and insurance accessible to every Indian at a reasonable price.
C. Under the acronym JAM-Jan Dhan Yojana for Financial Inclusion, Aadhaar Biometric Identification and Mobile Telecommunications- India is on the verge of a social revolution.
D. Beneficiaries may open an account with no balance.

SSC CGL Tier-1 20.07.2023 (Shift-II)

(a) ABCD (b) BCDA
(c) CABD (d) DCBA

Ans. (c)

Sentence C will be the first sentence as it introduces the main theme- JAM-Jan Dhan Yojana for financial inclusion. Sentence A comes second as it presents how Aadhaar was given to all in the policy.

It is followed by sentence B which presents what the policy includes. The last sentence is D. Thus, the correct sequence is CABD.

56. A. Swarms have wreaked havoc on crops and caused famines and mass migrations.
B. Since pre-historic times, locusts have caused plagues.
C. Traditional methods of control rely on the use of pesticides from the ground or the air, although biological control approaches are also making great strides.
D. Changes in agricultural practices and improved observation of areas where swarms tend to form have lately allowed control measures to be implemented at an earlier stage.

SSC CGL Tier-1 20.07.2023 (Shift-II)

(a) DCBA (b) BADC
(c) BDAC (d) ABDC

Ans. (b)

Sentence B will be the first line as it contains the main idea i.e., how locusts have impacted us. Sentence A comes second as it states the impact in form of damage.

Further, Sentence D states how locusts have been controlled and Sentence C mentions the methods of control. So, C will follow D. Thus, the correct sequence is BADC.

57. A. It centres on the sinking of the RMS Titanic.
B. The film proved immensely popular, holding the all time box-office gross record for more than a decade after its release.
C. Titanic is an American romantic adventure film released in 1997.
D. Most of the film's story is then told in flashbacks as the protagonist recounts the Titanic's fateful 1912 voyage.

SSC CGL Tier-1 20.07.2023 (Shift-IV)

(a) CDAB (b) BADC
(c) CADB (d) ABDC

Ans. (c)

Sentence C will be the first sentence as it introduces the main theme- The movie Titanic. Sentence A comes second as it states the central plot of the movie. It is followed by sentence D which states that picturisation of the movie. The last sentence is B as it presents the movie's popularity. Thus, the correct sequence is CADB.

58. A. Due to tight deadlines for delivery and increased focus on performance outcomes, many employees are unable to enjoy a proper work life.
B. Stress could emanate out of various situations such as lifestyle, health or relationship issues, lack of support system at home and competitive focus on acquiring material symbols of success and career advancement.
C. In today's fast-moving world, many young professionals are vulnerable to stress.
D. To add to this, the current economy has impacted many companies' revenues and profits which, in effect, have put many jobs at risk resulting in the frequency of counselling support and guidance going up significantly.

SSC CGL Tier-1 20.07.2023 (Shift-IV)

(a) DABC (b) ABCD
(c) DCBA (d) CBAD

Ans. (d)

Sentence C will be the first sentence as it introduces the main theme- Stress in the modern world. Sentence B comes second as it presents how stress is created.

It is followed by sentence A which presents the reason for stress in corporate world. The last sentence is D. Thus, the correct sequence is CBAD.

59. A. It superseded India's previous educational strategy, which was created in 1986.
B. The Indian Union Cabinet approved the country's National Education Strategy on 29th July, 2020.
C. And it provides a framework for education from the primary grades up to higher education, as well as for vocational training in both urban and rural settings.
D. This policy significantly improves India's educational system. Restructuring India's educational system is the primary goal of the National Education Policy, 2022.

SSC CGL Tier-1 21.07.2023 (Shift-I)

(a) DBCA (b) ABDC
(c) BCDA (d) BADC

Ans. (d)

Sentence B will be the first line as it contains the main idea i.e., National Education Strategy, 2020. Sentence A comes second as it states that it supersedes the earlier strategy. Furthers, Sentence D states what the new strategy does and Sentence C furthers it. So, C will follow D. Thus, the correct sequence is BADC.

60. A. Because of the region's scorching heat and aridity, a considerable amount of water evaporates.
B. As a result, the salt and other minerals become increasingly concentrated.
C. It is then unable to exit the lake and is forced to evaporate.
D. The Dead Sea is one of the saltiest bodies of water on the planet, with about ten times the salt content of typical saltwater.
E. This is because water flows into the Dead Sea from a single primary tributary, the Jordan river.

SSC CGL Tier-1 21.07.2023 (Shift-I)

(a) DECAB (b) DCBAE
(c) DEABC (d) DACEB

Ans. (a)

Sentence D will be the first sentence as it introduces the main theme- The Dead Sea. Sentence E comes second as it presents why it is Dead Sea. It is followed by sentence C which presents that it is not suitable for life. Sentence A comes next stating the weather condition of the region.

The last sentence is B as it presents that salt and other minerals are concentrated. Thus, the correct sequence is DECAB.

61. A. Bauxite is used as a main raw material for the production of aluminium.
B. Precipitation is a pre-final stage for actual production.
C. Sodium aluminate is acquired in the next step.
D. The smelting process actually extracts aluminium as a final product from its oxide.

SSC CGL Tier-1 21.07.2023 (Shift-I)

(a) ABCD (b) ACBD
(c) DCAB (d) ADCB

Ans. (b)

Sentence A will be the first sentence as it introduces the main theme- Production of aluminium and use of bauxite in it.

Sentence C comes second as it presents what is required in the next step. It is followed by sentence B which presents the pre-final stage.

The last sentence is D as it presents the smelting process. Thus, the correct sequence is ACBD.

62. A. She dashed from one side to the other, taking care not to destroy the lovely flowers in the garden.
B. Karen took a stroll in a lovely garden full of tulips and butterflies.
C. She discovered a swing constructed of tree branches behind a large bush.
D. Karen went onto the swing without hesitation and began swinging, causing the wind to dishevel her hair.
E. The small girl adored the outdoors and relished the breeze blowing through her hair.

SSC CGL Tier-1 21.07.2023 (Shift-I)

(a) BEACD (b) DBCAE
(c) BDECA (d) BDCAE

Ans. (a)

Sentence B will be the first sentence as it introduces the main theme- What Karen did.

Sentence E comes second as it states how she loved being outdoors. It is followed by sentence A which states how she enjoyed outdoors.

Sentence C comes next which states what she discovered. The last sentence is D as it presents how Karen enjoyed her discovery. Thus, the correct sequence is BEACD.

63. A. In 1944, he was honoured by King George VI with a Knighthood and became Sir Alexander Fleming.

B. On receiving this great honour, Fleming said in his usual modest way, "Wherever I go, people thank me for saving their lives. I didn't do anything; I just found a remedy that was there."

C. Fleming became famous overnight and was regarded as one of the most distinguished scientists of his time.

D. The next year, he and his fellow bacteriologists, whose combined efforts had led to the great discovery, were honoured with a joint Nobel Prize.

SSC CGL Tier-1 21.07.2023 (Shift-II)

(a) DBCA (b) ADBC
(c) CADB (d) BCDA

Ans. (c)

Sentence C will be the first sentence as it introduces the main theme- Fleming and how he became famous. Sentence A comes second as it states that he was honoured by a king. It is followed by sentence D which states that he won a Nobel Prize. The last sentence is B as it presents his reaction to his prize. Thus, the correct sequence is CADB.

64. A. It was the night before the day fixed for his coronation and the young king was sitting alone in his beautiful chamber.

B. And, indeed, it was the hunters who had found him, coming upon him almost by chance as, bare-limbed and pipe in hand, he was following the flock of the poor goat herd who had brought him up and whose son he had always fancied himself to be.

C. The lad–for he was only a lad, being but sixteen years of age–was not sorry at their departure and had flung himself back with a deep sigh of relief on the soft cushions of his embroidered couch, lying there, wild-eyed and open-mouthed, like a brown woodland Faun or some young animal of the forest newly snared by the hunters.

D. His courtiers had all taken their leave of him, bowing their heads to the ground, according to the ceremonious usage of the day and had retired to the Great Hall of the Palace, to receive a few last lessons from the Professor of Etiquette; there being some of them who had still quite natural manners, which in a courtier is, I need hardly say, a very grave offence.

SSC CGL Tier-1 21.07.2023 (Shift-II)

(a) ADCB (b) CBDA
(c) ACDB (d) CDBA

Ans. (a)

Sentence A will be the first sentence as it presents the young king and the setting of his coronation. Sentence D comes second as it presents his courtiers. It is followed by sentence C which describes the feelings of the young king. The last sentence is B as it presents what he wanted to be. Thus, the correct sequence is ADCB.

65. A. Water gives itself away for our agriculture and other uses.

B. Trees give flowers, fruits and wood.

C. Giving soothes an individual with the vibration of joy.

D. Unconditional giving is a natural principle and evident everywhere in nature which gives us solid, liquids and minerals.

SSC CGL Tier-1 21.07.2023 (Shift-III)

(a) ACDB (b) CDAB
(c) CBDA (d) BDCA

Ans. (b)

Sentence C will be the first sentence as it introduces how Giving affects us. Sentence D comes second as it presents how unconditional giving exists everywhere. It is followed by sentence A which presents how water gives. The last sentence is B as it presents how trees give. Thus, the correct sequence is CDAB.

66. A. The movement began in reaction to the ugliness of the industrial age.

B. This idea was amplified by JW von Goethe, JL Tieck and others in Germany.

C. Aestheticism was a European arts movement which centred on the doctrine that art exists for the sake of its beauty alone.

D. Its philosophical foundations were laid in the 18th century by Immanuel Kant.

SSC CGL Tier-1 24.07.2023 (Shift-I)

(a) BADC (b) CADB
(c) CBDA (d) ADBC

Ans. (b)

Sentence C will be the first sentence as it introduces the main theme- Aestheticism. Sentence A comes second as it states when the movement began. It is followed by sentence D which states the person who laid its foundation. The last sentence is B as it presents who supported the idea. Thus, the correct sequence is CADB.

67. A. Another boy tried his luck and won a comb, a fountain pen, wristwatch and a table lamp one after the other in many chances that he played.

B. An old man won a beautiful clock. The old man did not want the clock, so the shopkeeper took it back and paid ₹ 15 to the old man.

C. Bhaiya encouraged him, but Rasheed was not lucky when he tried his luck. He won only cheap items like pencils and an inkbottle and soon lost all his money.

D. He sold all the items to the shopkeeper and went away happily. Rasheed also wanted to play and try his luck.

SSC CGL Tier-1 24.07.2023 (Shift-I)

(a) BADC (b) DCAB
(c) BDCA (d) BCDA

Ans. (a)

Sentence B will be the first line as it contains the main idea i.e., an old man winning a clock and what happened next. Sentence A comes second as it states what another boy won. Further, Sentence D states what the boy did and Sentence C states what Rasheed won. So, C will follow D. Thus, the correct sequence is BADC.

68. A. "The most essential thing I learnt from 'Ready Now!' was the need of having a backup plan in case of an emergency", she stated.

B. The instruction, according to Nickola, was inspiring and confirmed her capacity to live effectively with a disability.

C. "I made sure I had a generator, wheelchair batteries and at least a week's worth of food, water and prescription medication."

D. "When I heard about the impending snowstorm, I emailed all of my caregivers to see who lived nearby and would be accessible."

SSC CGL Tier-1 24.07.2023 (Shift-I)

(a) ADCB (b) ACBD
(c) CDAB (d) BCDA

Ans. (a)

Sentence A will be the first sentence as it presents what the narrator learnt. Sentence D comes second as it presents what the narrator did in case of emergency.

It is followed by sentence C which presents another thing that the narrator ensured. The last sentence is B as it presents her inspiration. Thus, the correct sequence is ADCB.

69. A. Anime is a style of animation popular in Japanese films.

B. Modern anime began in 1956 and found lasting success in 1961 with the establishment of Mushi Productions.

C. At the turn of the 21st century, anime began to attain wide international popularity with the Pokemon television series.

D. Much of the genre is aimed at children but anime films are sometimes marked by adult themes and subject matter.

SSC CGL Tier-1 24.07.2023 (Shift-I)

(a) BADC (b) DBAC
(c) ADBC (d) ACBD

Ans. (c)

Sentence A will be the first sentence as it introduces the main theme- Anime. Sentence D comes second as it presents its audience.

It is followed by sentence B which states the beginning of modern anime. The last sentence is C as it presents its popularity. Thus, the correct sequence is ADBC.

70. A. The so-called harmless activities of a small number of people are increasingly becoming a serious problem for the internet.

B. You would have seen an increasing amount of 'junk mail' showing up in your email box.

C. It is basically electronic junk mail or junk newsgroup postings.

D. Spam is the flooding of the internet with many copies of the same message, in an attempt to force the message on people who would not otherwise choose to receive it.

SSC CGL Tier-1 24.07.2023 (Shift-II)

(a) CADB (b) BADC
(c) ACBD (d) DABC

Ans. (d)

Sentence D will be the first sentence as it introduces the main theme- Spam. Sentence A comes second as it presents how spam is becoming a problem. It is followed by sentence B which refers to junk mail.

The last sentence is C as it elaborates on junk mail. Thus, the correct sequence is DABC.

71. A. The Olympic Games have come to be regarded as the world's foremost sports competition.

B. Olympic Games is an athletic festival that originated in ancient Greece and was revived in the late 19th century.

C. Before the 1970s, the games were officially limited to competitors with amateur status but in the 1980s many events were opened to professional athletes.

D. Currently, the games are open to all, even the top professional athletes in basketball and football (soccer).

SSC CGL Tier-1 24.07.2023 (Shift-III)

(a) ABDC (b) BCDA
(c) CADB (d) BDCA

Ans. (b)

Sentence B will be the first sentence as it introduces Olympic Games. Sentence C comes second as it describes how the games have changed after 1980s. It is followed by sentence D which states the current status of Olympic Games. The last sentence is A which states its position in sports. Thus, the correct sequence is BCDA.

72. A. We recognise some aspects of an SF narrative with the realities of this world and some elements are estranged from the reality so as to take us to an unreal world.

B. Therefore, it is often suggested that 'cognitive estrangement' is a necessary means through which the SF is usually understood.

C. Science Fiction is a genre which manifests in itself the use of scientific premises often in a fantastical manner in a narrative.

D. It is highly seeped into the reality of this world.

SSC CGL Tier-1 24.07.2023 (Shift-III)

(a) CDBA (b) BCAD
(c) DACB (d) ADBC

Ans. (a)

Sentence C will be the first sentence as it introduces the main theme- Science Fiction. Sentence D comes second as it states how it has entered our world. It is followed by sentence B which states how science fiction is understood. The last sentence is A as it states how we understand science fiction. Thus, the correct sequence is CDBA.

73. A. I would attach as many as four of them to a crosspiece, notably arranged on a thin spindle and transmit the motion of the same to a large disc and so derive considerable 'power'.

B. In my next attempt I seem to have acted under the first instinctive impulse which later dominated me to harness the energies of nature to the service of man.

C. These creatures were remarkably efficient, for once they were started they had no sense to stop and continued whirling for hours and the hotter it was the harder they worked.

D. I did this through the medium of May-bugs or June-bugs as they are called in America which were a veritable pest in the country and sometimes broke the branches of trees by the sheer weight of their bodies.

SSC CGL Tier-1 24.07.2023 (Shift-IV)

(a) BACD (b) ACBD
(c) BDAC (d) DACB

Ans. (c)

Sentence B will be the first sentence as it introduces the main theme- The narrator's act and encouragement. Sentence D comes second as it presents what the narrator did.

It is followed by sentence A which furthers the narrator's experiment. The last sentence is C as it presents what he observed. Thus, the correct sequence is BDAC.

74. A. Those verses are collectively known as the Bhagavad Gita.
B. His hesitation before the battle against his family became the occasion for his friend and charioteer, Lord Krishna, to deliver a discourse on Dharma.
C. Arjuna was one of the five Pandava brothers, who are the heroes of the Indian epic, the 'Mahabharata'.
D. He was the son of the God Indra and was famous for his archery.
SSC CGL Tier-1 24.07.2023 (Shift-IV)
(a) DCBA (b) CDBA
(c) ABDC (d) BADC

Ans. (b)

Sentence C will be the first sentence as it introduces the main theme- Arjuna, the Pandava brother. Sentence D comes second as it describes his parentage. It is followed by sentence B which states how he got the lesson on Dharma. The last sentence is A as it states that these lessons form Bhagavad Gita. Thus, the correct sequence is CDBA.

75. A. There is a general belief that these medicines heal ailments safely.
B. The 'safe healing' is actually that which doesn't have any side effects.
C. Positive healing without any unwanted effect on the body drives the trend.
D. Herbal medicines are a new trend these days.
SSC CGL Tier-1 24.07.2023 (Shift-IV)
(a) ADCB (b) DACB
(c) DABC (d) ACDB

Ans. (c)

Sentence D will be the first sentence as it introduces the main theme- Herbal Medicines.

Sentence A comes second as it presents the general belief regarding herbal medicines. It is followed by sentence B which states that it is safe healing. The last sentence is C as it presents how positive healing drives the trend of herbal medicine. Thus, the correct sequence is DABC.

76. A. Lord Ganesha, the Destroyer of Obstacles, is worshipped for his wisdom and brilliance.
B. People adore the goddess Lakshmi and Lord Ganesha on Diwali.
C. This 'New Year' i.e., Diwali is marked by merchants establishing new account books.
D. Goddess Lakshmi is also worshipped on Diwali for wealth and success.
SSC CGL Tier-1 25.07.2023 (Shift-I)
(a) DABC (b) BADC
(c) ADBC (d) CDBA

Ans. (b)

Sentence B will be the first line as it contains the main idea i.e., Diwali. Sentence A comes second as it states why Lord Ganesha is worshipped. Further, Sentence D states why Lord Lakshmi is worshipped and Sentence C states that Diwali is marked as New Year by business people. So, C will follow D. Thus, the correct sequence is BADC.

77. A. Several times I have visited the narrow, dirty streets where the poor live and I grow hot and indignant to think that good people should be content to live in fine houses and become strong and beautiful, while others are condemned to live in hideous, sunless tenements and grow ugly, withered and cringing.
B. Dear little creatures, they crouch in my heart and haunt me with a constant sense of pain.
C. The children who crowd these grimy alleys, half-clad and underfed, shrink away from your outstretched hand as if from a blow.
D. In the country one sees only nature's fair works and one's soul is not saddened by the cruel struggle for mere existence that goes on in the crowded city.
SSC CGL Tier-1 25.07.2023 (Shift-II)
(a) BACD (b) ADBC
(c) CABD (d) DACB

Ans. (d)

Sentence D will be the first sentence as it introduces the narrator's philosophy about crowded cities. Sentence A comes second as it presents the narrators' experience and thoughts about hat experience. It is followed by sentence C which states what the narrator saw in his experience. The last sentence is B. Thus, the correct sequence is DACB.

78. A. Many species of bamboo flower once in several years and then die.
B. The stem itself is hollow and is connected to a network of rhizomes, which spreads out beneath the surface of the soil.
C. Roots grow out of this network of rhizomes and help the plants to absorb and distribute food and water from the soil.
D. The bamboo is a variety of grass, with a woody, many-jointed stem. SSC CGL Tier-1 25.07.2023 (Shift-II)
(a) ADCB (b) DBCA
(c) BCAD (d) CADC

Ans. (b)

Sentence D will be the first sentence as it introduces the main theme- The bamboo. Sentence B comes second as it presents the structure of a bamboo stem. It is followed by sentence C which states how its roots help the bamboo. The last sentence is A as it presents that bamboo's flowers many times. Thus, the correct sequence is DBCA.

79. A. And also, they contribute to the development of social and environmental solutions for the planet's future.
B. Companies do play an important role in modern society.
C. Because of their systematic relevance and their impact on policy-making, companies must use their influence in ways that benefit the public good.
D. Some corporations have become so large that their activities and strategic decisions have a direct impact on government policy and citizens' lives.
SSC CGL Tier-1 25.07.2023 (Shift-III)
(a) DCAB (b) DBCA
(c) ADCB (d) BDCA

Ans. (d)

Sentence B will be the first sentence as it introduces the main theme- The role of companies in modern society. Sentence D comes second as it presents how companies impact government policy. It is followed by sentence C which presents another impact. The last sentence is A as it presents the need for companies to create a positive influence. Thus, the correct sequence is BDCA.

80. A. Through the development of technologies, telecommunications, transportation and other areas, globalisation has developed very quickly in the last few decades, resulting in economic, social, political, and cultural integration on a global scale.
B. Although technology has had both positive and harmful effects

on human life, its negative repercussions must be addressed appropriately.

C. Globalisation has made significant positive contributions to economies all across the world.

D. For example– Science and Technology have made remarkable strides, providing businesses with a fantastic opportunity to expand quickly even outside of national borders.

SSC CGL Tier-1 25.07.2023 (Shift-IV)

(a) ACDB (b) BCDA
(c) ACBD (d) CDBA

Ans. (a)

Sentence A will be the first sentence as it introduces the main theme- The role of technology in globalisation.
Sentence C comes second as it presents how globalisation had impacted economies. It is followed by sentence D which presents an example for the statement given in Sentence C. The last sentence is B as it presents how we must address the negatives of technology. Thus, the correct sequence is ACDB.

81. A. Ashwagandha is an adaptogenic herb that has multiple benefits like improving thyroid functioning and reducing blood sugar levels.

B. But remember to consult a specialist while deciding the dosage and duration of continued intake.

C. It relaxes the nervous system and lowers cortisol (stress hormone) levels in the blood, thus, making you feel calm and relaxed overall.

D. You can consume Ashwagandha powder or Ashwagandha capsules.

SSC CGL Tier-1 25.07.2023 (Shift-IV)

(a) ADBC (b) DABC
(c) ACDB (d) ADCB

Ans. (c)

Sentence A will be the first sentence as it introduces the main theme- Ashwagandha.
Sentence C comes second as it presents uses. It is followed by sentence D which presents how it is consumed. The last sentence is B as it presents that we should take it after proper specialist advice. Thus, the correct sequence is ACDB.

82. A. Louis was enthralled by the concept of a raised dots system.

B. He made up his mind to use the technique to represent an alphabetic code.

C. Blind persons could read large-letter books that are bulky with the aid of this alphabet code.

D. Additionally, he developed the six-dot cell technology, which was at his fingertips.

SSC CGL Tier-1 25.07.2023 (Shift-IV)

(a) DCAB (b) BCDA
(c) ABCD (d) CDBA

Ans. (c)

Sentence A will be the first sentence as it introduces the main topic Louis and how he was attracted to the dots system. Sentence B comes second as it presents what he decided. It is followed by sentence C which focuses how his decision would impact blind people. The last sentence is D as it mentions what he developed. Thus, the correct sequence is ABCD.

83. A. In Catholic, Eastern Orthodox, Anglican, Oriental Orthodox and Lutheran teaching, all of their faithful departed in heaven are considered saints, although some are deemed deserving of more praise or emulation.

B. In religious belief, a saint is a person who is viewed as possessing an uncommon degree of holiness, similarity or proximity to God.

C. The term 'saint', however, is used differently depending on the setting and denomination.

D. Some saints receive official ecclesiastical recognition and, as a result, a public cult of veneration through the process of canonisation in the Catholic Church or glorification in the Eastern Orthodox Church.

SSC CGL Tier-1 26.07.2023 (Shift-I)

(a) BCAD (b) BCDA
(c) CBDA (d) BDAC

Ans. (a)

Sentence B will be the first sentence as it introduces the main theme- Who is a saint.
Sentence C comes second as it states that there are different meanings of saint. It is followed by sentence A which states the examples. The last sentence is D as it elaborates on sentence A. Thus, the correct sequence is BCAD.

84. A. Android began in 2003 as a project of the American technology company Android Inc., to develop an operating system for digital cameras.

B. In 2004, the project changed to become an operating system for smartphones.

C. Android is an operating system for cellular telephones and tablet computers.

D. In 2005, Android Inc. was bought by the American search engine company Google Inc. that transformed the OS into what it is today.

SSC CGL Tier-1 26.07.2023 (Shift-I)

(a) CABD (b) ABDC
(c) DCAB (d) BADC

Ans. (a)

Sentence C will be the first sentence as it introduces the main theme- Android. Sentence A comes second as it presents how Android was developed. It is followed by sentence B which presents how it became an operating system for phones. The last sentence is D as it presents that android was bought by Google. Thus, the correct sequence is CABD.

85. A. India has an upbeat vision of a liberal, non-violent, relatively pluralistic democracy with non-threatening global leadership.

B. Epics from mythologies like the 'Mahabharata' and 'Ramayana' are likened to classic Greek works like the Odyssey and Iliad and between 1 and 1000 AD. India was lauded as the 'Golden Bird' for its GDP, which was higher than China at the time.

C. Luminaries like Mahatma Gandhi and Rabindranath Tagore, as well as the arts of literature, music, dance, the software industry, Ayurveda, etc., generate a staggering array of soft power assets that highlight India's appeal to the world's population.

D. With Ashoka, Buddha and Gandhi serving as the primary leaders, Indians are known for their core values of respect, harmony and fraternity.

SSC CGL Tier-1 26.07.2023 (Shift-I)

(a) ACDB (b) CBAD
(c) ABDC (d) BCDA

Ans. (a)

Sentence A will be the first sentence as it introduces the main theme- India's vision of democracy. Sentence C comes second as it presents India's appeal. It is followed by sentence D which presents what India is known for. The last sentence is B as it presents India's glory. Thus, the correct sequence is ACDB.

86. A. According to him, ₹ 75 lakhs has been spent to make the gymnasium fully equipped with state-of-the-art fitness machines.
B. The Honourable Commissioner of Police inaugurated the gymnasium and swimming pool and appended the management for their efforts in providing such amenities to students.
C. A new indoor gymnasium and swimming pool was inaugurated at APJ International School, Goa.
D. Mr. Mercia, the Principal of the school familiarised the guests about the cost incurred and the various facilities available.

SSC CGL Tier-1 26.07.2023 (Shift-II)

(a) CBDA (b) BDCA
(c) ADBC (d) DABC

Ans. (a)

Sentence C will be the first sentence as it introduces the main theme- A new indoor gymnasium and swimming pool. Sentence B comes second as it presents who inaugurated it. It is followed by sentence D which presents how the principal of the school gave the information about the cost incurred. The last sentence is A as it presents the details. Thus, the correct sequence is CBDA.

87. A. Diwali, referred to as the 'festival of lights', ushers in the winter season with joy, shopping, presents and a slew of new occasions and celebrations, such as Dussehra, Dhanteras, Govardhan, Bhaidooj and Naraka Chaturdashi.
B. In the spiritual world, the event symbolises 'the triumph of light over darkness'.
C. The five-day festival of Diwali is observed during the Hindu month of Kartika as an event.
D. In India, Diwali is also known as Deepawali.

SSC CGL Tier-1 26.07.2023 (Shift-II)

(a) BACD (b) DBCA
(c) CDBA (d) ACBD

Ans. (d)

Sentence A will be the first sentence as it introduces the main theme- Diwali. Sentence C comes second as it presents when it is celebrated. It is followed by sentence B which presents what it symbolises. The last sentence is D as it presents more information. Thus, the correct sequence is ACBD.

88. A. This has an impact not just on global poverty, but also on Indians' awareness of the country's poverty for the first time in a decade.
B. And, for the first time in a decade, this update includes India's poverty data.
C. From 15th September, 2022, a new global poverty line has been established, with the World Bank revising its data in the Poverty and Inequality Platform on this basis.
D. According to Sunitha Sinha, Roy and Roy van der Weide of the World Bank's Policy Research Working Paper, "poverty in India had dropped over the recent decade, although not as much as previously thought."

SSC CGL Tier-1 26.07.2023 (Shift-II)

(a) DBAC (b) CBAD
(c) CADB (d) DBCA

Ans. (b)

Sentence C will be the first sentence as it introduces the main theme- The establishment of new poverty line. Sentence B comes second as it presents how it includes Indian poverty data. It is followed by sentence A which presents its impact. The last sentence is D. Thus, the correct sequence is CBAD.

89. A. The 1995 World Summit for Social Development had also emphasised the pivotal role of women in eradicating poverty and mending the social fabric.
B. Women are rational in approach, careful in handling situations and want to do things as best as possible.
C. The Fourth World Conference of Women held in Beijing in September 1995 had emphasised that no enduring solution of society's most threatening social, economic and political problems could be found without the participation and empowerment of the women.
D. Today's woman is a highly self-directed person, alive to the sense of her dignity and the importance of her functions in the private domestic domain and the public domain of the world of work.

SSC CGL Tier-1 26.07.2023 (Shift-III)

(a) ABDC (b) DBCA
(c) DBAC (d) BCAD

Ans. (b)

Sentence D will be the first sentence as it introduces the main theme- The woman of the present. Sentence B comes second as it presents how women are rational in approach. It is followed by sentence C which states that the Fourth World Conference of Women recognised the importance of women. The last sentence is A as it presents how the 1995 World Summit also recognised this. Thus, the correct sequence is DBCA.

90. A. Nostalgia helps us maintain a positive psychological status when counteracting the negative impact of difficult situations.
B. Nostalgia is a sentimental longing for one's past.
C. The adaptive functions of nostalgia are many, with one effect being pain relief.
D. It is a self-conscious, perhaps bittersweet but predominantly positive social emotion.

SSC CGL Tier-1 26.07.2023 (Shift-IV)

(a) CDBA (b) BDAC
(c) ABCD (d) CADB

Ans. (b)

Sentence B will be the first sentence as it introduces the main theme- Nostalgia.
Sentence D comes second as it describes it further. It is followed by sentence A which present how nostalgia helps us. The last sentence is C as it presents the pain relief quality of nostalgia. Thus, the correct sequence is BDAC.

91. A. It is not a walker's paradise. So walking is not a fashionable pastime here.
B. London is known for its hectic face, frensied movements, high decibels and dust kicked by the speeding vehicles.
C. On the contrary, life in the countryside is laid back and easy paced. Unless it is raining, people set out for walk.

D. For these reasons, Max never went out for a walk, nor did anyone ask him to accompany.

SSC CGL Tier-1 27.07.2023 (Shift-I)

(a) ADCB (b) BADC
(c) DCAB (d) CADB

Ans. (b)

Sentence B will be the first line as it contains the main idea i.e., London. Sentence A comes second as it states how it is not suitable for walking. Further, Sentence D states that it was the same for Max and Sentence C contrasts the city with the countryside. So, C will follow D. Thus, the correct sequence is BADC.

92. A. The government's recent efforts have concentrated on strengthening these ties.
B. The textile industry in India is one of the country's oldest, stretching back several centuries.
C. The textile business immensely diverse, with hand-spun and hand-woven textiles at one end of the spectrum and capital-intensive modern mills at the other.
D. Its tight ties to agriculture (for raw materials such as cotton) and the country's old history and traditions in terms of textiles set it apart from other sectors in the country.

SSC CGL Tier-1 27.07.2023 (Shift-I)

(a) DABC (b) ABCD
(c) BCDA (d) CBDA

Ans. (c)

Sentence B will be the first sentence as it introduces the textiles industry in India. Sentence C comes second as it describes the textiles industry. It is followed by sentence D which states that it is tied to agriculture. The last sentence is A as it presents how the efforts of the government strengthened the ties. Thus, the correct sequence is BCDA.

93. A. The other half had been sued at least twice and Levinson found that just on the basis of those conversations, she could find clear differences between the two groups.
B. Recently the medical researcher Wendy Levinson recorded hundreds of conversations between a group of physicians and their patients.
C. The surgeons who had never been sued spent more than three minutes longer with each patient than those who had been sued did.
D. Roughly half of the doctors had never been sued.

SSC CGL Tier-1 27.07.2023 (Shift-II)

(a) BDAC (b) CABD
(c) ABCD (d) BCAD

Ans. (a)

Sentence B will be the first sentence as it introduces the main theme- the recording of a medical researcher. Sentence D comes second as it presents how many doctors have never been sued. It is followed by sentence A which present how other have been sued. The last sentence is C as it presents the difference between the doctors who are sued and who are not sued. Thus, the correct sequence is BDAC.

94. A. In a study sponsored by World Health Organisation and carried out by Harvard School of Public Health, the global burden and injury indicated that stress diseases and accidents are going to be the killers in 2020.
B. Road traffic accidents are going to be the third largest killers.
C. These accidents are also an indicator of psycho-social stress in a fast-moving society.
D. The heart disease and depression-both stress diseases-are going to rank first and second in 2020.

SSC CGL Tier-1 27.07.2023 (Shift-II)

(a) BCDA (b) CBAD
(c) DACB (d) ADBC

Ans. (d)

Sentence A will be the first sentence as it introduces the main theme- The findings of the World Health Organisation regarding stress diseases. Sentence D comes second as it presents the first ranking of heart disease and depression related to stress. It is followed by sentence B which presents how road accident will become third killers. The last sentence is C as it presents what the road accident represents. Thus, the correct sequence is ADBC.

95. A. My grandmother always went to school with me because the school was attached to the temple.
B. When we both finished, we would be back together.
C. While the children sat in rows on either side of the verandah singing the alphabet or prayer in chorus, my grandmother sat inside reading the scriptures.
D. The priest taught us the alphabet and the morning prayer.

SSC CGL Tier-1 27.07.2023 (Shift-III)

(a) ACBD (b) ABDC
(c) ADCB (d) ADBC

Ans. (c)

Sentence A will be the first sentence as it presents how the grandmother went with the narrator. Sentence D comes second as it presents what the priest did at the school which was near the temple. It is followed by sentence C which presents what the narrator and the grandmother did. The last sentence is B as it presents how they would come back together. Thus, the correct sequence is ADCB.

96. A. He later tried to franchise his restaurant.
B. Colonel Harland Sanders' real-life story of being disappointed numerous times in his life and still making his ambition come true late in life is truly motivating.
C. He began selling chicken at the age of 40, but his dream of opening a restaurant was repeatedly denied owing to conflicts and wars.
D. He is a seventh-grade dropout who tried many things in life but found them bitter.

SSC CGL Tier-1 27.07.2023 (Shift-III)

(a) BCDA (b) BDCA
(c) BDAC (d) BACD

Ans. (b)

Sentence B will be the first sentence as it introduces the main theme- Colonel Harland Sanders. Sentence D comes second as it presents how he is a seventh-grade dropout. It is followed by sentence C which presents his work and his dream. The last sentence is A as it presents how he tried to franchise his restaurant. Thus, the correct sequence is BDCA.

97. A. Tigers are the largest members of the cat family. They are found in many parts of Asia.
B. They mostly live in dark forests and sleep during the day. They come out for hunting pigs and deer by night.

C. It is assumed that, probably, around 3000 tigers live in the wild. This species looks spectacular and grand and they are very graceful in their movements.

D. It is almost impossible for us to see them against a jungle background, especially when they are standing still, because of their striped coats. Unlike, most cats, the tiger likes bathing very much. **SSC CGL Tier-2 02.03.2023**

(a) ABCD (b) CDBA
(c) ACBD (d) ADBC

Ans. (c)

Sentence A will be the first sentence as it introduces the main theme- Tigers. Sentence C comes second as it presents more information about tigers. It is followed by sentence B which presents their appropriate habitat. The last sentence is D as it presents more information. Thus, the correct sequence is ACBD.

98. For the four-sentence (S1 to S4) paragraph below, sentences S1 and S4 are given. From the options P, Q, R and S select the appropriate sentences for S2 and S3, respectively.

S1 : The men and women took their places after the initial mingling and immediately a surge of conversation filled the room.

S2 :

S3 :

S4 : One or two of the women were actually bouncing up and down on the sofa cushions.

P. So, the two parties had to lean forward, their elbows on their knees.

Q. At the beginning they mingled awkwardly, clutching their drinks and walking here and there.

R. Several people made a last-minute dash to the bathroom before the conversation could start.

S. The men's chairs were far enough away from the women's couches. **SSC CGL Tier-1 02.03.2023 (Shift-I)**

(a) P, R (b) R, Q
(c) Q, S (d) S, P

Ans. (d)

The correct statement that would make the appropriate paragraph is S and P.

99. A. Many fitness trainers encourage their clients to include these foods in their diet to build muscle.

B. Power foods can be included in your everyday diet in a variety of ways.

C. The secret to getting the most out of power foods is, of course, knowing how to cook them properly, buying seasonal produce and recognising your preferred flavour profile.

D. Power foods are high in nutrients such as fibre, potassium and minerals. **SSC CGL Tier-2 02.03.2023**

(a) DBCA (b) DABC
(c) BCAD (d) ADBC

Ans. (b)

Sentence D will be the first sentence as it introduces the main theme- Power foods. Sentence A comes second as it presents that many trainers want these foods to be included in diet. It is followed by sentence B which states that we can include power foods in diets. The last sentence is C as it presents how to eat power foods. Thus, the correct sequence is DABC.

100. A. Healthy, strong trees act as carbon sinks, offsetting carbon and reducing the effects of climate change.

B. Trees help to clean the air we breathe. Through their leaves and bark, they absorb harmful pollutants and release clean oxygen for us to breathe.

C. Increasing levels of carbon dioxide caused by deforestation and fossil fuel combustion trap heat in the atmosphere.

D. In urban environments, trees absorb pollutant gases like nitrogen oxides, ozone and carbon monoxide and sweep up particles like dust and smoke. **SSC CGL Tier-2 02.03.2023**

(a) BDCA (b) DBAC
(c) CDAB (d) ABCD

Ans. (a)

Sentence B will be the first sentence as it introduces the main theme- How trees clean the air. Sentence D comes second as it presents how trees help in urban areas. It is followed by sentence C which presents effects of deforestation. The last sentence is A as it presents how trees maintain the weather. Thus, the correct sequence is BDCA.

101. A. They stand undefeated in the realms of Shakespeare and Homer.

B. India is a country where people are full of immense prolixity and exemplary storytelling.

C. Additionally, the philosophical discourse and discussions on various dilemmas of life associated with the Bhagavad Gita are highly appreciated by scholars from all over the world.

D. Mahabaharata and Ramayana are two great examples of colossal works that unquestionably enjoy the virtue of being peak sources for the cultural ethos of the country. **SSC CGL Tier-2 02.03.2023**

(a) DACB (b) BDAC
(c) ACBD (d) BACD

Ans. (b)

Sentence B will be the first sentence as it introduces the main theme- Storytelling in India. Sentence D comes second as it presents examples of Mahabharata and Ramayana. It is followed by sentence A which presents how these books are great. The last sentence is C as it presents the richness of philosophical discourse. Thus, the correct sequence is BDAC.

102. A. The principles that emerged from those trials, known as the Nuremberg Code, are broadly applicable to many types of health-related research involving human participants, including clinical trials.

B. The growing breadth and complexity of contemporary health challenges have produced a range of difficult questions that cannot always be adequately addressed by relying exclusively on existing policies, guidelines or codes of conduct.

C. Recent formal efforts to articulate international standards of ethics applicable to health and healthcare can be traced to the Nuremberg trials of 1947, during which the horrors of Nazi medical experiments came to light.

D. Ethical questions related to health, health care and public health cover topics as diverse as moral issues around reproduction, state obligations in the provision of healthcare services and appropriate measures to control infectious disease. SSC CGL Tier-2 02.03.2023

(a) DCAB (b) ACDB
(c) DACB (d) DABC

Ans. (a)

Sentence D will be the first sentence as it introduces the main theme- Ethical questions related to health.

Sentence C comes second as it presents how these questions led to Nuremberg trials. It is followed by sentence A which states that these trials lead to Nuremberg Code. The last sentence is B as it presents the need of more efficient solutions. Thus, the correct sequence is DCAB.

103. A. She shot the movie on the widest canvas possible using the same kind of equipment that captured Star Wars landscapes and applied a muted colour grading to every frame.

B. She said last year that she wanted the ensemble film to look like 'a faded postcard'.

C. Polley lends the central conversation a visual gravitas normally reserved for epics.

D. Women Talking, adapted by the writer-director Sarah Polley from Miriam Toews's 2018 novel, is vibrant cinema.

SSC CGL Tier-2 03.03.2023

(a) DABC (b) DBCA
(c) CABD (d) DCAB

Ans. (d)

Sentence D will be the first sentence as it introduces the main theme- Women Talking, a movie adapted from a novel. Sentence C comes second as it presents what the movie shows. It is followed by sentence A which presents the method of shooting the movie. The last sentence is B as it presents the reason why she directed the movie in that manner. Thus, the correct sequence is DCAB.

104. A. On the afternoon of that eventful day, I stood on the porch, dumb, expectant and guessed vaguely from my mother's signs and from the hurrying to and fro in the house that something unusual was about to happen, so I went to the door and waited on the steps.

B. I did not know what the future held of marvel or surprise for me and anger and bitterness had preyed upon me continually for weeks and a deep languor had succeeded this passionate struggle.

C. The most important day I remember in all my life is the one on which my teacher, Anne Mansfield Sullivan, came to me and I am filled with wonder when I consider the immeasurable contrasts between the two lives which it connects and it was the third of March, 1887, three months before I was seven years old.

D. The afternoon Sun penetrated the mass of honeysuckle that covered the porch and fell on my upturned face and my fingers lingered almost unconsciously on the familiar leaves and blossoms which had just come forth to greet the sweet Southern spring.

SSC CGL Tier-2 03.03.2023

(a) DABC (b) CBAD
(c) CADB (d) CDAB

Ans. (c)

Sentence C will be the first sentence as it introduces the main theme- The most important day in the narrator's life. Sentence A comes second as it states with the explanation of the event. It is followed by sentence D which further the description. The last sentence is B as it presents the narrators' emotions about it. Thus, the correct sequence is CADB.

105. A. When faced with uncertainty, humans look out for the action of others and become a victim of ineffective rational thinking during compelling, confusing situations.

B. According to him, in an emergency, we tend to forget that everybody else observing the event is also likely to be looking out for social evidence.

C. Robert B. Cialdini explains this reaction with a psychological phenomenon called 'pluralistic ignorance'.

D. Since, we all prefer to appear poised and unflustered among others, we are likely to search for answers placidly, with brief, camouflaged glances at those around us. SSC CGL Tier-2 03.03.2023

(a) ACBD (b) BCDA
(c) ABCD (d) ABDC

Ans. (a)

Sentence A will be the first sentence as it introduces the main theme- How humans react to difficulties. Sentence C comes second as it presents an observation by someone. It is followed by sentence B which presents the explanation.

The last sentence is D as it furthers the explanation. Thus, the correct sequence is ACBD.

106. A. The temperature of the world has increased, resulting in global warming.

B. The melting of the ice caps will increase the sea level, thereby drowning many islands and coastal regions.

C. The increased amount of carbon emission is considered as the reason behind global warming.

D. The increase in the global temperature is melting the polar ice caps. SSC CGL Tier-2 03.03.2023

(a) ABCD (b) ACBD
(c) ACDB (d) BADC

Ans. (c)

Sentence A will be the first sentence as it introduces the main theme- Global warming and rising temperatures. Sentence C comes second as it presents the reason behind global warming. It is followed by sentence D which presents that result of global warming. The last sentence is B as it presents the impact of the result. Thus, the correct sequence is ACDB.

107. A. Road accidents have become very common in India.

B. Condition of roads in India is pathetic.

C. Increasing number of vehicles leave little space on roads.

D. Roads are narrow and remain congested most of the time.

SSC CGL Tier-2 03.03.2023

(a) ACBD (b) BDCA
(c) BCDA (d) CDBA

Ans. (b)

Sentence B will be the first sentence as it introduces the main theme- The condition of roads.

Sentence D comes second as it presents the problem with roads in India.

It is followed by sentence C which presents that the increasing number of vehicles which effects the space on roads. The last sentence is A as it presents the effect in the form of road accidents. Thus, the correct sequence is BDCA.

108. P. Perhaps, no definition of democracy is more popular and universally acceptable than what is given by Abraham Lincoln.
Q. He defines democracy as "a government of the people, by the people and for the people".
R. Certainly, democracy is the most representative form of government.
S. To bind the people and take the nation ahead on the path of progress, democracy is the most suitable form of government for India. **SSC CGL Tier-2 06.03.2023**
(a) PSRQ (b) QRSP
(c) PQRS (d) SRQP

Ans. (c)

Sentence P will be the first sentence as it introduces the main theme- The definition of democracy given by Abraham Lincoln. Sentence Q comes second as it presents the definition. It is followed by sentence R which presents the author's view. The last sentence is S as it presents why democracy is the most suitable form of government. Thus, the correct sequence is PQRS.

109. A. Fort Hare was more than that: it was a beacon for African scholars from all over Southern, Central and Eastern Africa.
B. Until 1960, the University College of Fort Hare, in the municipality of Alice, about twenty miles due East from Healdtown, was the only residential center of higher education for blacks in South Africa.
C. For young black South Africans like myself, it was Oxford and Cambridge, Harvard and Yale, all rolled into one.
D. The regent was anxious for me to attend Fort Hare and I was gratified to be accepted there. I felt that I was being groomed for success in the world. **SSC CGL Tier-2 06.03.2023**
(a) BACD (b) BCAD
(c) CABD (d) BDAC

Ans. (a)

Sentence B will be the first sentence as it introduces the main theme- University College of Fort Hare and the fact that it was the home to black students. Sentence A comes second as it presents why Fort Hare was important for Africans. It is followed by sentence C which presents what it represented for the author. The last sentence is D as it presents that the author joined the university. Thus, the correct sequence is BACD.

110. A. We reached there at about 10 am.
B. The first ride we took was the Fury Wheel. It was really big, all of us were yelling and crying!
C. Yesterday, my friends and I went on a short picnic to an amusement park.
D. Even though we had reached on time, there was a serpentine queue for the tickets. I took the entrance ticket. **SSC CGL Tier-2 06.03.2023**
(a) CADB (b) ABCD
(c) CDBA (d) ADBC

Ans. (a)

Sentence C will be the first sentence as it introduces the main theme- The narrator and his friends going to picnic at an amusement park. Sentence A comes second as it presents the time of their arrival. It is followed by sentence D which presents that it took them some time to get the entry tickets. The last sentence is B as it presents the first ride they took. Thus, the correct sequence is CADB.

111. A. Helping parents become savvier at picking care options and tossing retention bonuses to caregivers are others.
B. These fixes, importantly, can make childcare more affordable for parents and offer life rafts to centres haemorrhaging workers.
C. The most proposed government solution for childcare involves building on top of this flawed system is offering more vouchers to purchase private childcare.
D. But they do little to address the structural needs: improved quality for kids, better wages and working conditions for workers and more choices in the low-income neighbourhoods. **SSC CGL Tier-2 06.03.2023**
(a) CDBA (b) CBDA
(c) CABD (d) BADC

Ans. (c)

Sentence C will be the first sentence as it introduces the main theme- Childcare solutions. Sentence A comes second as it presents some options for making childcare easy. It is followed by sentence B which presents that these measure make childcare affordable. The last sentence is D as it presents the flaws in childcare. Thus, the correct sequence is CABD.

112. A. In speed, in comfort, in beauty, in equipment she was a masterpiece.
B. It was the envy and admiration of the maritime nations of the world.
C. The Titanic was the Queen Alary of her day and the pride of the White Star Line.
D. Everything about her was attractive and fascinating. **SSC CGL Tier-2 06.03.2023**
(a) CBAD (b) ABCD
(c) CDAB (d) DCAB

Ans. (a)

Sentence C will be the first sentence as it introduces the main theme- The Titanic. Sentence B comes second as it presents how the ship made many jealous. It is followed by sentence A which presents its qualities. The last sentence is D as it presents that it was attractive. Thus, the correct sequence is CBAD.

113. A. The Sustainable Development Goals (SDGs) were adopted by all United Nations Member States in 2015 to end poverty, reduce inequality and build more peaceful, prosperous societies by 2030.
B. The SDGs cannot be achieved without the realisation of child rights.
C. Also known as the Global Goals, the SDGs are a call to action to create a world where no one is left behind.
D. As world leaders work to deliver on the 2030 promise, children around the globe are standing up to secure their right to good health, quality education, a clean planet and more. **SSC CGL Tier-1 07.03.2023 (Shift-I)**
(a) ABDC (b) ADCB
(c) ACBD (d) ADBC

Ans. (c)

Sentence A will be the first sentence as it introduces the main theme- Sustainable Development Goals. Sentence C comes second as it further defines SDGs. It is followed by sentence B which states the requirement of achieving the SDGs.

The last sentence is D as it presents the work done to achieve 2030 goals. Thus, the correct sequence is ACBD.

114. P. The prices of cooking gas, pulses and vegetables have registered a sharp rise.

Q. In recent years the prices of essential commodities have gone up sharply.

R. The low-income groups and the salaried classes are the worst sufferers.

S. Living has become quite a costly affair these days.

SSC CGL Tier-2 07.03.2023

(a) RPSQ (b) QSRP
(c) SRQP (d) PQRS

Ans. (c)

Sentence S will be the first sentence as it introduces the main theme of how living had become costly. Sentence R comes second as it presents who suffers the most. It is followed by sentence Q which presents the current scenario. The last sentence is P as it presents the examples of commodities whose price had risen. Thus, the correct sequence is SRQP.

115. A. I was almost drowned a dozen times; was nearly boiled alive and just missed being cremated.

B. Now, my well-being is simply the result of a careful and measured mode of living and perhaps the most astonishing thing is that three times in my youth. I was rendered by illness a hopeless physical wreck and given up by physicians.

C. More than this, through ignorance, and light-heartedness, I got into all sorts of difficulties, dangers and scrapes from which I extricated myself as by enchantment.

D. But as I recall these incidents to my mind I feel convinced that my preservation was not altogether accidental.

SSC CGL Tier-2 07.03.2023

(a) CADB (b) BADC
(c) BCAD (d) DCAB

Ans. (c)

Sentence B will be the first sentence as it introduces the main theme- What is the cause of the narrator's well-being. Sentence C comes second as it presents how he came out of difficulties. It is followed by sentence A which states the variety of problems he faced. The last sentence is D as it presents that he preserved. Thus, the correct sequence is BCAD.

116. A. Instead, they are constrictors, meaning they squeeze their prey to death before swallowing it whole.

B. Agile on water but awkward on land, the green anaconda is one of the largest snakes in the world.

C. Most people assume that anacondas are very poisonous, but they are actually non-venomous.

D. At 29 feet long and 550 pounds, these snakes are huge!

SSC CGL Tier-2 07.03.2023

(a) BACD (b) BDCA
(c) BCAD (d) DABC

Ans. (b)

Sentence B will be the first sentence as it introduces the main theme- The green anaconda. Sentence D comes second as it presents the size of these snakes. It is followed by sentence C which states that they are not poisonous. The last sentence is A as it presents how they kill their prey. Thus, the correct sequence is BDCA.

117. A. No country has yet achieved the combination of very high human development with a light ecological footprint and the impacts of climate change and biodiversity loss are growing.

B. Compounded by a climate emergency, political polarisation and challenged multilateralism, continued conflicts and forced displacement, the number of people living in poverty rose in 2020 for the first time since 1998 by an estimated 119-124 million and inequalities are growing, and the traditional social contract is no longer working for many.

C. The Challenge of Reaching Agenda 2030 was already significant, even before the COVID-19 pandemic hit.

D. Today's development challenges are dynamic, interconnected puzzles of multidimensional risk that require systemic solutions and multilateral cooperation is vital in addressing these shared challenges that cross boundaries of geography and time.

SSC CGL Tier-2 07.03.2023

(a) DBAC (b) ABDC
(c) BCDA (d) CBDA

Ans. (d)

Sentence C will be the first sentence as it introduces the main theme- Challenge of Reaching Agenda, 2030.

Sentence B comes second as it presents the different aspects of the challenge. It is followed by sentence D which presents the requirement to face the challenge. The last sentence is A as it presents that no country is ready to face the challenge. Thus, the correct sequence is CBDA.

SSC CGL 2022 (Tier 1 & 2)

118. A. Schools are closed for the Christmas and winter break at this time of the year.

B. Christmas and New Year are the time of the year to celebrate.

C. All over the city, winter carnivals and Christmas bazaars lend, fun and warmth in the cold.

D. For the second time in a row, we are likely to see restrained celebrations for fear of the pandemic raising its ugly head again. **SSC CGL Tier-1 12.04.2022 (Shift-III)**

(a) BADC (b) BACD
(c) ABCD (d) BCDA

Ans. (b)

Sentence B will be the first sentence as it introduces the main theme- Christmas and New year. Sentence A comes second as it states how schools are closed. It is followed by sentence C which describes the celebration. The last sentence is D as it presents how this year, the celebration will be restricted due to the pandemic. Thus, the correct sequence is BACD.

119. A. Finally, it can be termed as the channel for all trade, and what is more important, of all ideas.

B. It also provides a framework to all economic development.

C. It is the road which determines the site of many cities and the growth and nourishment of all.

D. The road is one of the great fundamental institutions of mankind.

SSC CGL Tier-1 13.04.2022 (Shift-III)

(a) CABD (b) DCBA
(c) BDAC (d) DBAC

Ans. (b)

Sentence D will be the first sentence as it introduces the importance of road. Sentence C comes second as it points out how roads are crucial to determine the site of cities. It is followed by sentence B which states how it is essential for economic development. The last sentence is A as it uses 'finally'. Thus, the correct sequence is DCBA.

120. A. The sectors included agriculture, public health and public utilities among others.
B. The GGI framework covered 10 sectors and 58 industries.
C. The Good Governance Index (GGI) 2022 scores have been declared.
D. The objective was to provide quantifiable data to compare the performance of different States and Union Territories in these sectors.

SSC CGL Tier-1 20.04.2022 (Shift-I)

(a) CADB (b) CBAD
(c) ABDC (d) BACD

Ans. (b)

Sentence C will be the first sentence as it contains the main idea i.e., the declaration of the Good Governance Index. Sentence B comes second as it states what it covers. Sentence A comes third as it states some sectors included in it. Sentence D is last as it indicates its objective. Thus, the correct sequence is CBAD.

121. A. Expert mechanics laboured over the plane for three hours.
B. A small nut had fallen into a channel which prevented the gear from moving.
C. A huge plane was forced to crash land when its landing gear got stuck.
D. They were amazed when they discovered what had caused the mechanical failure.

SSC CGL Tier-1 21.04.2022 (Shift-II)

(a) DBAC (b) BADC
(c) ACBD (d) CADB

Ans. (d)

Sentence C will be the first sentence as it introduces the plane landing. Sentence A comes second as it states how expert mechanics worked to correct it. It is followed by sentence D which states what they amazed. Sentence B will be the last sentence as it presents the reason for the landing. Thus, the correct sequence is CADB.

122. A. When this extra water vapour condenses into precipitation, it results in heavier rain or, if it's cold enough, heavier snow.
B. The atmosphere can store an additional 4% of water vapour for every additional °F of warming.
C. More water evaporates from soils, plants, lakes and seas as the atmosphere warms.
D. One of the most obvious indications of climate change is heavier rainfall.

SSC CGL Tier-1 01.12.2022 (Shift-I)

(a) CBDA (b) DCBA
(c) ACDB (d) BCAD

Ans. (b)

Sentence D will be the first sentence as it introduces indications of climate change. Sentence C comes second as it points out how more water evaporates from water bodies. It is followed by sentence B which states how much water can the atmosphere store. The last sentence is A. Thus, the correct sequence is DCBA.

123. A. They also wore felt caps to cover their ears.
B. They wore trousers tucked into leather boots.
C. This place was famous for its skilful archers and horsemen.
D. In the 5th and 4th centuries BC, today's South Ukraine was known as Scythia.

SSC CGL Tier-1 01.12.2022 (Shift-II)

(a) BCDA (b) CBDA
(c) ABCD (d) DCBA

Ans. (d)

Sentence D will be the first sentence as it introduces Scythia. Sentence C comes second as it points out that the place was famous for its archers and horsemen. It is followed by sentence B which states what they wore. The last sentence is A. Thus, the correct sequence is DCBA.

124. A. A panther is reported to have broken into a house yesterday in search of food and shelter.
B. The villagers heard his cries and ran to the house but the scared animal had run away through the window by then.
C. It secretly slouched into a room where a young man named Johnny was sleeping, who suddenly woke up and realised that the beast was roaming around his bed.
D. Just as the panther was about to leap on him, he swiftly shot out of bed and hid in a closet.

SSC CGL Tier-1 01.12.2022 (Shift-II)

(a) ABDC (b) BDCA
(c) ACDB (d) DCAB

Ans. (c)

Sentence A will be the first sentence as it introduces how a panther had broken into a house.

Sentence C comes second as it presents what happened. It is followed by sentence D which describes the young man's act of locking himself in a cupboard.

The last sentence is B as it presents how villagers acted and how the panther had run away. Thus, the correct sequence is ACDB.

125. P. We are naturally social creatures.
Q. A bit of solitude-as everyone from Thoreau to Proust have written about-is one of our most powerful tools for disconnecting and recharging.
R. This does not mean you need to lock yourself away in a room at the end of the day.
S. However, all that time with people takes its toll.

SSC CGL Tier-1 01.12.2022 (Shift-III)

(a) PQRS (b) QSRP
(c) SPQR (d) PSQR

Ans. (d)

Sentence P will be the first sentence as it states that we are social creatures. Sentence S comes second as it states how being social takes a toll.

It is followed by Sentence Q which states the importance of solitude. Sentence R will be the last sentence. Thus, the correct sequence is PSQR.

126. P. Main source of water for Wular Lake is River Jhelum.
Q. Wular Lake is also said to be a remnant of Satisar Lake that existed in ancient times.
R. This lake also has a small island in its centre called the 'Zaina Lank'.
S. This island was constructed by King Zainul-Abi-Din.

SSC CGL Tier-1 02.12.2022 (Shift-I)

(a) RPQS (b) PQRS
(c) QSRP (d) PRSQ

Ans. (d)

Sentence P will be the first sentence as it introduces the main source of water for Wular Lake. Sentence R comes second as it states that the lake has a small island in the centre. It is followed by Sentence S which states who constructed the island. Sentence Q will be the last sentence as it presents another fact about Wular Lake. Thus, the correct sequence is PRSQ.

127. A. This usually results from a conviction on the part of the worker that the boss is genuinely interested in his growth and development.
B. More attention should be paid to make this contact constructive and productive.
C. The most vital spot in management is the contact between the workers and the boss.
D. Constructive conditions prevail when mutual confidence and respect exists between the supervisor and the supervised.
SSC CGL Tier-2 29.01.2022
(a) CBDA (b) CADB
(c) DBCA (d) DABC

Ans. (a)

Sentence C will be the first sentence as it introduces the main topic of the paragraph contact between workers and boss.

Sentence B comes second as it presents how this contact should be constructive and productive. It is followed by sentence D which states that constructive conditions need mutual confidence and respect. The last sentence is A as it presents how constructive conditions can be achieved. Thus, the correct sequence is CBDA.

128. A. How do you manage to complete so much work? he asked the student.
B. Looking at the huge pile of books on a student's desk, a man said, "What a burden, my son! I pity you."
C. "I focus on only one lesson at a time," the student further added.
D. "I don't think of all the work I have to do." were the student.
SSC CGL Tier-2 29.01.2022
(a) ACDB (b) BADC
(c) ACBD (d) BDAC

Ans. (d)

Sentence B will be the first sentence as it contains the question asked by a man to a students. Sentence D states the student's reply.

Further, Sentence A states another question. The last sentence will be Sentence C which states the student's answer. Thus, the correct sequence is BDAC.

129. A. Most of these superpowers are not rich in natural resource and have faced political turmoil.
B. Human capital ultimately makes the difference, both, in an enterprise and a nation.
C. The new economic superpowers of today amply testify this thesis.
D. Yet, they have achieved economic affluence in a relatively short period.
SSC CGL Tier-1 29.01.2022 (Shift-I)
(a) BCDA (b) ADBC
(c) ACDB (d) BCAD

Ans. (d)

Sentence B will be the first sentence as it contains the main idea i.e., the importance of human capital. Sentence C comes second as it states the example of superpowers of the world. It is followed by Sentence A which states how these superpowers lack natural resources. The last sentence is Sentence D states the contrast. Thus, the correct sequence is BCAD.

130. A. He swore that the eight thousand roubles that he had were his own money.
B. He had not seen the merchant after they had had tea together.
C. Aksenov swore that he had not killed the merchant.
D. But his voice was broken and trembled with fear as though he were guilty. **SSC CGL Tier-2 03.02.2022**
(a) CBAD (b) ADBC
(c) ABDC (d) CADB

Ans. (a)

Sentence C will be the first sentence as it contains the main idea i.e., Aksenov and his statement that he did not kill the merchant.

Sentence B comes second as it states that he had not seen the merchant for some time. Sentence A comes third as it states the money was his. Sentence D is last as it indicates that Aksenov was guilty. Thus, the correct sequence is CBAD.

131. A. These thunderstorms were a huge relief after the heat wave conditions the region had experienced.
B. The Weather Department forecasts more storms in the coming days.
C. Thunderstorms and strong winds were reported in Northern India.
D. The Weather Department has also said monsoon is likely to hit South India soon.
SSC CGL Tier-2 03.02.2022
(a) CABD (b) DCAB
(c) CADB (d) BACD

Ans. (a)

Sentence C will be the first sentence as it defines thunderstorms. Sentence A comes second as it presents how thunderstorms present a relief. It is followed by sentence B which states the forecast. The last sentence is D as it presents when the monsoon will hit South India. Thus, the correct sequence is CABD.

132. A. Paper, pencil, whiteboard, textbook are the tools you need if you want to go to school.
B. But recently, you can add another one to the list: an iPad.
C. But today, it is also being used to make learning fun.
D. The tablet is useful for searching the internet and watching videos.
SSC CGL Tier-2 03.02.2022
(a) CDAB (b) ADBC
(c) CADB (d) ABDC

Ans. (d)

Sentence A will be the first sentence as it lists the things needed for school. Sentence B comes second as it presents how we cannot another thing called iPad. It is followed by sentence D which further states the use of iPad/tablet. The last sentence is C as presents how it is being used today. Thus, the correct sequence is ABDC.

133. A. He had agreed to feed him, pay him twelve rupees a month, and find him somewhere to stay.
B. A month's salary was paid in advance.
C. Fotik had learned to handle his job quite well in the last five days.
D. Upen Babu was a good man who had helped a lot.
SSC CGL Tier-2 08.08.2022
(a) ADBC (b) CDAB
(c) CBDA (d) DACB

Ans. (b)

Sentence C will be the first sentence as it introduces Fotik. Sentence D comes second as it states that Upen Babu had helped him. It is followed by sentence A which presents how Upen Babu helped him. The last sentence is B as it presents the salary status. Thus, the correct sequence is CDAB.

134. A. It was interesting to find out that the centre operates 24 hours a day all year round.
B. The recent trip to the recycling centre was a very useful experience.
C. However, it was surprising to learn that the centre only collects 50% of the waste as a lot of it is used as landfill.
D.The main aim of the visit was to find out about the systems put in place to recycle waste.
SSC CGL Tier-2 08.08.2022

(a) BCAD (b) ACDB
(c) BDAC (d) ABCD

Ans. (c)

Sentence B will be the first sentence as it contains the main idea i.e., a trip to a recycling plant. Sentence D states the main purpose of the trip. Further, Sentence A states an interesting fact about the recycling plant. The last sentence will be Sentence C which also states another surprising fact about the plant. Thus, the correct sequence is BDAC.

135. A. Miss Tredgold rapped on the door twice with her gloved knuckle.
B. A few moments passed before the door opened to reveal a man in grey sweater and blue jeans.
C. Florentyna stood by her side, silent for the first time since leaving school.
D. At last they came to a halt outside a newly painted red door which displayed the number 118.
SSC CGL Tier-2 08.08.2022

(a) DACB (b) ADBC
(c) CDAB (d) DBCA

Ans. (a)

Sentence D will be the first sentence as it introduces that some people came to a door. Sentence A comes second as it presents one of the people and how she knocks on the door. It is followed by sentence C which states who is with the person. The last sentence is B as it presents who was at the other end of the door. Thus, the correct sequence is DACB.

136. A. An allergy is a reaction of the immune system to a substance which is normally harmless.
B. These antibodies then attach themselves to cells, which contain histamine, which inflames the tissues.
C. One-third of us are affected by an allergy at some point in our lives.
D. The immune system in allergy sufferers makes antibodies against harmless substances because it believes them to be dangerous. **SSC CGL Tier-2 08.08.2022**

(a) DCAB (b) CBDA
(c) CADB (d) ACBD

Ans. (c)

Sentence C will be the first sentence as it introduces how all of us have suffered from allergies.

Sentence A comes second as it defines allergies. It is followed by Sentence D which states how the immune system produces some antibodies. Sentence B will be the last sentence as it presents how these antibodies affects our tissues. Thus the correct sequence is CADB.

137. A. Thus, Daphne cannot resist the opportunity to scold them about their behaviour.
B. The children have been annoying each other just before the meal starts.
C. Daphne's family mealtimes are usually tense because this is a time when conflicts in the family surface.
D. Also, they are rude about the food she has cooked, and Daphne gets upset by this.
SSC CGL Tier-2 08.08.2022

(a) CDAB (b) CBDA
(c) BCAD (d) BACD

Ans. (b)

Sentence C will be the first sentence as it introduces the main topic of the paragraph 'Daphne's family's mealtimes. Sentence B comes second as it presents the annoying behaviour of the children.

It is followed by sentence D which states how the family is rude. The last sentence is A as it presents how Daphne scolds them. Thus, the correct sequence is CBDA.

SSC CGL 2021 (Tier 1 & 2)

138. A. But the eagle, in wrath, gave the beetle a flap of his wing and straightaway seized upon the hare and devoured him.
B. The beetle therefore interceded with the eagle, begging of him not to kill the poor suppliant and pleaded with him not to kill so small an animal.
C. When the eagle flew away, the beetle flew after him, to learn where his nest was.
D. A hare, being pursued by an eagle, took himself for refuge to the nest of a beetle, whom he begged to save him.
SSC CGL Tier-1 13.08.2021 (Shift-I)

(a) CBAD (b) DBAC
(c) DCAB (d) ACDB

Ans. (b)

Sentence D will be the first sentence as it contains the main idea i.e., a hare, being pursued by an eagle. Sentence B comes second as it states that the beetle, therefore, interceded with the eagle.

It will be followed by Sentence A wherein the eagle, in wrath, gave the beetle a flap of his wing. The last sentence is Sentence C which states that when the eagle flew away, the beetle flew after him. Thus, the correct sequence is DBAC.

139. A. When we got near, we saw it was the steam rising from hot springs.
B. We saw in the distance a great column of smoke.
C. We wondered if it came from a chimney or a burning house.
D. We thought of taking a bath in the hot water.
SSC CGL Tier-1 13.08.2021 (Shift-I)

(a) ACDB (b) ABCD
(c) BCAD (d) BCDA

Ans. (c)

Sentence B will be the first sentence as it contains the main idea i.e., a great column of smoke.

Sentence C comes second as it states that they wondered where the smoke came from. It is followed by Sentence A which states that they found the steam to be rising from hot springs. The last sentence is Sentence D states that we thought of taking a bath in the hot water. Thus, the correct sequence is BCAD.

140. A. When he reached his town, he went to his house and knocked at the door.
B. A man went away from his home.
C. Disappointed, he decided to take it himself.
D. One day he wrote letter to his family, but could not find anyone to take the letter to his town.

SSC CGL Tier-1 13.08.2021 (Shift-III)

(a) DACB (b) BDCA
(c) ABCD (d) CBAD

Ans. (b)

Sentence B will be the first sentence as it contains the main idea i.e., the story of a man going away from his home. Sentence D comes second as it states that one day the man wrote a letter to his family, but could not find anyone to take the letter. Further, Sentence C states that the man got disappointed so he decided to take it himself making it the third sentence. The last sentence will be Sentence A which states that when he reached his town, he went to his house and knocked at the door. Thus, the correct sequence is BDCA.

141. A. At length the olive tree's branches broke with the snow's weight, at once despoiling it of its beauty and killing the tree.
B. A shower of snow fell upon them and finding the olive full of foliage, it settled upon its branches.
C. Finding the fig tree without leaves, the snow fell through the branches to the ground and did not injure it at all.
D. The olive tree ridiculed the fig tree because, while she was green all the year round, the fig tree changed its leaves with the seasons.

SSC CGL Tier-1 13.08.2021 (Shift-III)

(a) ACBD (b) ABCD
(c) DBAC (d) DACB

Ans. (c)

Sentence D will be the first sentence as it contains the main idea i.e., the olive tree ridiculing the fig tree. Sentence B comes second as it states that a shower of snow fell upon them, and finding the olive full of foliage, it settled upon its branches. It is followed by Sentence A which states that the olive tree's branches broke with the snow's weight. The last sentence will be Sentence C as it points out that the fig tree was without leaves so the snow fell through the branches to the ground and did not injure it at all. Thus, the correct sequence is DBAC.

142. A. This invention has helped us to heal wounds caused by bacteria.
B. Penicillin is one of the most useful drugs man has invented.
C. In the beginning however, very few people knew of this discovery and its use.
D. Its use has saved the lives of hundreds of thousands of soldiers.

SSC CGL Tier-1 16.08.2021 (Shift-I)

(a) DCBA (b) ABCD
(c) BADC (d) CABD

Ans. (c)

Sentence B will be the first line as it contains the main idea i.e., Penicillin. Sentence A comes second as it states that the invention of Penicillin has helped us to heal wounds caused by bacteria. Further, Sentence D states that its use has saved the lives of hundreds of thousands of soldiers and Sentence C states that very few people knew of this discovery and its use in the beginning. So, C will follow D. Thus, the correct sequence is BADC.

143. A. Then I took him by the hand and led him across the street.
B. I was going to the market when I saw a blind man trying to cross the street.
C. He expressed his gratitude with folded hands.
D. I walked across to the blind man.

SSC CGL Tier-1 16.08.2021 (Shift-I)

(a) DABC (b) BDAC
(c) ABCD (d) CBDA

Ans. (b)

Sentence B will be the first sentence as it contains the main idea i.e., a sight where a blind man was crossing the road. Sentence D states that the narrator walked across to the blind man. Further, Sentence A states that the narrator hold his hand and led him across the street which forms the third sentence. The last sentence will be Sentence C which states that the blind man expressed his gratitude to the narrator with folded hands. Thus, the correct sequence is BDAC.

144. A. "I have already spent it," the thief replied.
B. "What! I will take you to the police right now," Arun thundered.
C. "Give me back my money," Arun said to the thief.
D. "Sir, please have some mercy on me," the thief pleaded.

SSC CGL Tier-1 24.08.2021 (Shift-III)

(a) CBAD (b) BCAD
(c) ADBC (d) CABD

Ans. (d)

Sentence C will be the first sentence as it introduces Arun and the thief. Sentence A comes second as it given us the answer to the question asked in sentence C.

It is followed by Sentence B which shows Arun's reaction to the thief's answer. The last sentence would be sentence D as it presents the thief asking for mercy. Thus, the correct sequence is CABD.

SSC CPO 2024

145. A. The month was January.
B. On the first morning of the festival the mejhi would be set alight invoking the blessings of Agni, the god of fire.
C. There would be much feasting and merriment during the festival.
D. Each household would build a mejhi - a pile of firewood stacked neatly together in their backyard.
E. The Bihu festival was fast approaching.
F. "Let's build a champion mejhi this year," Ricky suggested a few days before the festival.

SSC CPO Tier-2 08.01.2024

(a) EDBC (b) CBED
(c) CBDE (d) ECDB

Ans. (d)

Sentence E will be the first sentence as it states that the Bihu festival is fast approaching.

Sentence C comes second as it presents how the festival is celebrated. It is followed by sentence D which presents the preparations.

The last sentence is B as it presents what happens on the first day of the festival. Thus, the correct sequence is ECDB.

146. A. When I studied Engineering thirty-five years back, I was the only girl in the course.
B. People often ask me how I managed.
C. I could only see boys and more boys everywhere.
D. But when I look back I feel it was not very difficult.
E. Having a girl in the class was unusual for the boys and initially I was the target for a lot of teasing.
F. But over a period of time they became my best friends.
SSC CPO Tier-2 08.01.2024
(a) CBDE (b) ECDB
(c) CBED (d) BDEC

Ans. (a)

Sentence C will be the first sentence as it states how the narrator saw only boys in her class. Sentence B comes second as it presents what people asked her. It is followed by sentence D which presents that the narrator found it not to be difficult. The last sentence is E as it presents how she was bullied by the boys. Thus, the correct sequence is CBDE.

147. A. My mother,Vimala Kulkarni, told me similar words when I got married.
B. They were usually like: 'You must adjust to your new house and in-laws, try to learn how they eat and cook their food, go out of your way to be friendly and helpful to everybody' etc.
C. When I was young, before a girl got married, her mother would give her some words of advice.
D. But along with this, she said something which helped me immensely in later life.
SSC CPO Tier-2 08.01.2024 (Shift-I)
(a) CBAD (b) CDBA
(c) ACBD (d) BDAC

Ans. (a)

Sentence C will be the first sentence as it introduces the main theme of the paragraph- what a girl is told by her mother when she is married. Sentence B comes second as it presents the words spoken by mothers. It is followed by sentence A which states that the speakers' mother also said the same. The last sentence is D as it points out that she said something else too. Thus, the correct sequence is CBAD.

148. A. I have seen a great many houses in my time, little and big, new and old, built of stone and of wood but of one house I have kept a very vivid memory.
B. It was, properly speaking, rather a cottage than a house - a tiny cottage of one story, with three windows, looking extraordinarily like a little old hunchback woman with a cap on.
C. The cottage was lost to sight among the mulberry-trees, acacias and poplars planted by the grandfathers and great grandfathers of its present occupants.
D. It had white stucco walls, tiled roof and a dilapidated chimney
SSC CPO Tier-2 08.01.2024
(a) ACBD (b) BDAC
(c) ABDC (d) CDBA

Ans. (c)

Sentence A will be the first sentence as it introduces the speaker's experience and vivid memory. Sentence B comes second as it presents how the narrator recognised the cottage. It is followed by sentence D which further describes the cottage. The last sentence is C as presents how The the cottage was hidden. Thus, the correct sequence is ABDC.

149. A. The Egyptians believed that the body and soul were important to human existence, in life and in death.
B. This ensured the soul's return to the body so that the deceased would live happily ever after.
C. Their funerary practices, such as mummification and burial in tombs, were designed to assist the deceased find their way in . the after world.
D. The tombs were thus, filled with food, tools, domestic wares, treasures - all the necessities of life.
SSC CPO Tier-2 08.01.2024
(a) ACDB (b) ABCD
(c) ADCB (d) ABDC

Ans. (c)

Sentence A will be the first sentence as it introduces the main theme of Egyptian belief about existence after death. Sentence D comes second as it presents how they build their tombs in regard to their belief. It is followed by sentence C which presents their funerary practices. The last sentence is B as it presents how this leads to the soul coming back to live a life after death. Thus, the correct sequence is ADCB.

150. A. The invention of the airplane was no exception.
B. However, the idea of flying an aircraft was quite repulsive to some people.
C. Many great inventions are initially greeted with ridicule and disbelief.
D. Most people who heard about the first powered flight on 17, December 1903 were excited and impressed.
SSC CPO Tier-2 08.01.2024 (Shift-I)
(a) DBCA (b) CADB
(c) CDAB (d) DABC

Ans. (b)

Sentence C will be the first sentence as it introduces the topic- great invention. Sentence A comes second as it presents the new invention of airplane. It is followed by sentence D which describes the positive reaction of people. The last sentence is B as presents the negative reaction. Thus, the correct sequence is CADB.

151. A. She was a busy person and had no time to visit her mother.
B. It was Mothers' Day.
C. She thought her mother would be pleased to receive the flowers.
D. A woman stopped at a flower shop to order some flowers to be sent to her mother. **SSC CPO Tier-2 08.01.2024**
(a) BDAC (b) BCDA
(c) DABC (d) CADB

Ans. (a)

Sentence B will be the first sentence as it states the importance of the Mother's day. Sentence D comes second as it presents an action by a woman. It is followed by sentence A which presents that she is a busy person and so, cannot visit her mother. The last sentence is C as it presents her decision to send flowers to her mother. Thus, the correct sequence is BDAC.

152. 1. A vacation is looked forward to as a time to relax.
A. But, destiny had other plans for me.
B. I was very excited to go on a vacation to Goa.

C. My bags were packed and I decided to retire early for the night.

D. It is a welcome break from the daily routine which is often monotonous.

6. I fell off the bed and fractured my foot! **SSC CPO Tier-2 08.01.2024**

(a) BCDA (b) ABDC
(c) CBAD (d) DBCA

Ans. (d)

Sentence D will be the first sentence as it elaborates on the main idea of vacations presented in 1.

Sentence B comes second as it describes how the narrator is excited. It will be followed by Sentence C which describes the narrator's preparation. The last sentence is Sentence A which contrasts his reality. Thus, the correct sequence is DBCA.

153. 1. During the Colonial Rule in India, Robert Bruce was the first who noticed tea plants growing near Rangpur 1823.

A. The species was found to be similar to that grown in Chinese tea gardens.

B. By 1862, the Assam tea industry comprised around 160 gardens.

C. The leaves of the plants were examined and the consequence was something fruitful.

D. Mr. Maniram Dewan was the first Indian tea planter who established the commercial plantation that we know today as the Assam tea.

6. Today the region has grown to become one of the world's largest tea-producing belts.

SSC CPO Tier-2 08.01.2024

(a) BDAC (b) DCBA
(c) CADB (d) ADCB

Ans. (c)

Sentence C will be the first sentence as it elaborates on 1 and states what was found after the leaves were examined. Sentence A comes second as it presents that the leaves were similar to those found in Chinese tea gardens. It is followed by sentence D which states the name of the person who commercialised Assam tea. The last sentence is B as presents the growth of the Assam tea industry. Thus, the correct sequence is CADB.

154. 1. Nicholas Chorier is not a usual photographer.

A. He uses a kite to hoist his camera into the skies and clicks photographs while the camera dangles mid-air.

B. He is a aerial kite photographer.

C. Fascinated, he literally tied his two hobbies, kite flying and photography, together for a living.

D. During a trip to India to make a photo report on kite making, he learnt about this unique style of photography.

6. Today he is one of the most well-known aerial kite photographers in the world.

SSC CPO Tier-2 08.01.2024

(a) DABC (b) BADC
(c) ACDB (d) BCDA

Ans. (b)

Sentence B will be the first sentence as it states why Nicholas Chorier is special- He is an aerial kite photographer. Sentence A will come second as it presents what is aerial kite photography. It will be followed by sentence D which elaborate on how he came across such photography. The last sentence will be sentence C as it points out his fascination and decision. Thus, the correct sequence is BADC.

155. Given below are six sentences of a paragraph. Sentence A is the beginning whereas sentence F is the last sentence of the para. The middle four sentences are jumbled up. Select the option that gives their correct order forming a meaningful and coherent paragraph.

A. It was midday.

B. Voldyrev, a tall country gentleman with a cropped head and prominent eyes, took off his overcoat, mopped his brow with his handkerchief, and went into the government office.

C. "Where can I make an inquiry here?" he said, addressing a porter who was bringing a trayful of glasses from the furthest recesses of the office.

D. Voldyrev coughed and went towards the window.

E. 'To that one sitting near the window!' said the porter, indicating with the tray the furthest window.

F. There, at a green table spotted like typhus, was sitting a young man with his hair standing up in four tufts on his head, with a long pimply nose and a long faded uniform. **SSC CPO Tier-2 08.01.2024**

(a) BDEC (b) CBED
(c) ECDB (d) BCED

Ans. (d)

Sentence B will be the first sentence as it introduces Voldyrev. Sentence C comes second as it presents his questions. It is followed by sentence E which states the answer. The last sentence is D as it presents that he went to the direction he was directed towards. Thus, the correct sequence is BCED.

SSC CPO 2021 (Tier 1 & 2)

156. A. A singer called Mukandan Misra and his wife lived in Behat near Gwalior.

B. Tired, the group settled down to rest in a shady grove.

C. Once Swami Haridas was travelling through the forest with his disciples.

D. Tansen, their only child was very naughty.

E. Often he would run away to the woods and soon learnt to imitate the calls of birds and animals.

F. Tansen thought it would be fun to frighten the resting men with the roar of a tiger.

SSC CPO Tier-2 26.07.2021

(a) ABDECF (b) ADECBF
(c) ACEBDF (d) AEBCDF

Ans. (b)

Sentence A comes first as it introduces Mukandan Misra and his family. Sentence D comes second as it introduces his son Tansen. Sentence E comes third as it states how Tansen imitated the sound of animals and birds. It is followed by sentence C which states what happened one day when Swami Haridas visited the forest with his group. Sentence B states that the group sat under a tree. Sentence F comes last as it states how Tansen scared the group. Hence, the correct order is ADECBF.

157. A. Suddenly I noticed smoke pouring in through the seams of the ceiling.

B. Groping our way to the front door we all ran out into the front yard.

C. The smoke began to fill the room so quickly that we could barely see.

D. I ran to the neighbours to call the fire department.

E. By the time we made our way outside, the whole roof was engulfed in flames.

F. I saw mother run back into the house and I screamed, "Mom! No!" **SSC CPO Tier-2 26.07.2021**

(a) ACBEDF (b) ABCDEF
(c) ADEBCF (d) AEDCBF

Ans. (a)

Sentence A comes first as it states that the narrator saw smoke. Sentence C comes second as it presents how the smoke filled the room. Sentence B comes third as it states how the speaker and his/her companions ran outside with difficulty. It is followed by sentence E which states how the fire had spread. Sentence D states that the narrator ran to call his neighbours. Sentence F comes last as it states the last action. Hence, the correct order is ACBEDF.

158. Sentences of a paragraph are given below in a jumbled order. Arrange these sentences to form a meaningful and coherent paragraph.

A. The Zip on the bag got jammed and wouldn't open no matter how hard I pulled at it.

B. We were flying to England for a week.

C. I also remembered that I had put the frequent flyer card in the carry bag hanging around my neck.

D. As we were checking in, I remembered that I was a member of the frequent flyer programme. **SSC CPO Tier-2 26.07.2021**

(a) DBAC (b) BACD
(c) ABDC (d) BDCA

Ans. (d)

Sentence B will be the first sentence as it introduces the main characters- A group comprising the narrator. Sentence D comes second as it what the narrator remembers. It is followed by sentence C which presents that other thing that the narrator remembered. The last sentence is A as it presents how the narrator got embarrassed. Thus, the correct sequence is BDCA.

SSC CHSL 2024 (Tier 1 & 2)

159. S1. CV Raman's story begins in a village near Tiruchirapalli (known in his days as Trichinopoly) in Southern India.

P. When he was four years old, Raman's family moved to Visakhapatnam.

Q. He was born on 8th November, 1888, the second child of R. Chandrashekhara Iyer and Parvati Ammal.

R. Chandrasekhara Iyer was an athletic man and he took active interest in sports.

S. His father took up a job there, as a lecturer in Mrs. AV Narasimha Rao College, where he taught Physics, Mathematics and Physical Geography.

S6. His young son Raman was not physically very strong, but was very intelligent and he preferred to read books and work at his studies. **SSC CHSL Tier-2 18.11.2024**

(a) QPSR (b) SRPQ
(c) PQSR (d) QPRS

Ans. (a)

The paragraph starts with Q, which introduces Raman's birth, followed by P detailing the family's move to Visakhapatnam, S elaborating on his father's job and R adding information about his father's interests. Thus, the correct sequence is QPSR.

SSC CHSL 2023 (Tier 1 & 2)

160. P. The average adult gets two to four colds a year, while the average child may get six to eight.

Q. It is the most frequent infectious disease in humans.

R. They occur more commonly during the winter.

S. The common cold, also known simply as the cold, is a viral infectious disease of the upper respiratory tract that primarily affects the nose. **SSC CHSL Tier-1 20.03.2023 (Shift-III)**

(a) QPSR (b) QSRP
(c) SQPR (d) PQRS

Ans. (c)

Sentence S will be the first sentence as it introduces the main theme- Common cold. Sentence Q comes second as it presents that is a the most frequent infectious disease. It is followed by sentence P which presents evidence for the previous statement. The last sentence is R as it presents when they occur. Thus, the correct sequence is SQPR.

161. P. In July 1977, Marley was found to have a type of malignant melanoma (cancer) under the nail of a toe.

Q. He died on 11th May, 1981 at Cedars of Lebanon Hospital in Miami (now University of Miami Hospital) at the age of 36.

R. Despite his illness, he continued touring until his health deteriorated as the cancer had spread throughout his body.

S. Marley turned down his doctors' advice to have his toe amputated, citing his religious beliefs. **SSC CHSL Tier-1 21.03.2023 (Shift-II)**

(a) PSQR (b) PSRQ
(c) RSQP (d) PQSR

Ans. (b)

Sentence P will be the first sentence as it introduces the main theme- Marley's diagnosis. Sentence S comes second as it presents how Marley reacted to the prospect of treatment. It is followed by sentence R which states how he continues touring despite his failing health. The last sentence is Q as it presents his death. Thus, the correct sequence is PSRQ.

162. A. So, then why are not Silican Valley entrepreneurs clamouring to decode the ancient wisdom?

B. The failure rate in finding a new drug is as high as 95%.

C. Because these once-thriving cultures are now reduced to an endangered tribe.

D. According to industry data it takes $2.6 Billion and on average, fourteen years to develop a new drug. **SSC CHSL Tier-1 02.08.2023 (Shift-I)**

(a) BADC (b) DCBA
(c) DBAC (d) ACDB

Ans. (c)

Sentence D will be the first sentence as it introduces the main theme- development of a new drug. Sentence B comes second as it presents the percentage probability of its failure. It is followed by sentence A which asks a question. The last sentence is C as it presents the answer to the question. Thus, the correct sequence is DBAC.

163. A. The Post-COVID period has caused many asymptomatic diseases.
B. Though it cannot be believed for sure; the change in social life may be a major cause.
C. These are people who suffered infection once or never at all.
D. Some propose that survival post infection has changed the mindset of people.
SSC CHSL Tier-1 08.08.2023 (Shift-IV)
(a) BDCA (b) BDAC
(c) ACDB (d) ACBD

Ans. (c)

Sentence A will be the first sentence as it introduces the main theme- Post COVID health issues. Sentence C comes second as it presents the people who faced those diseases. It is followed by sentence D which presents how people's mindset had changed after suffering from COVID. The last sentence is B as it presents that the doubt on such a belief. Thus, the correct sequence is ACDB.

164. A. Isabel saw a strange rabbit running through the bushes.
B. Following it, she found a door which she opened with the help of keys.
C. After that, she felt a strange sensation in her body.
D. She thought as if she was in a dream. SSC CHSL Tier-1 09.08.2023 (Shift-I)
(a) CDAB (b) DCAB
(c) BCDA (d) ABCD

Ans. (d)

Sentence A will be the first sentence as it introduces the main theme- Isabel seeing a strange rabbit. Sentence B comes second as it presents how she found a door which she opened with keys. It is followed by sentence C which presents how she felt after opening the door. The last sentence is D as it presents that she felt as if she was in a dream. Thus, the correct sequence is ABCD.

165. A. The new movie was highly anticipated by fans of the franchise.
B. As the lights dimmed, the audience grew quiet in anticipation.
C. The movie began with an exciting action sequence that had the audience on the edge of their seats.
D. The movie theatre was packed with people eager to see it.
SSC CHSL Tier-1 09.08.2023 (Shift-III)
(a) CBDA (b) BCDA
(c) ADBC (d) DBAC

Ans. (c)

Sentence A will be the first sentence as it introduces the main theme- A new movie. Sentence D comes second as it presents how the movie was popular among people. It is followed by sentence B which presents how people reacted in movie theatre when the movie started. The last sentence is C as it presents the start of the movie. Thus, the correct sequence is ADBC.

166. A. Human relationships are a matter of great concern for every one of us.
B. Nevertheless, social scientists have attached many other elements that actually help us for a good social life.
C. As it helps us all to have a coordinated, balanced and approachable life.
D. The present generation fails to take cognisance of all such elements and fall prey to a lonely life risking happiness.
SSC CHSL Tier-1 11.08.2023 (Shift-I)
(a) ADBC (b) DABC
(c) ABCD (d) ACBD

Ans. (d)

Sentence A will be the first sentence as it introduces the main theme- Human relationships. Sentence C comes second as it presents how human relationships help us. It is followed by sentence B which presents many other elements that help us. The last sentence is D as it presents how the present generation pays no value to these elements. Thus, the correct sequence is ACBD.

167. A. I once met a gentleman who told me about a game he plays with his grandchildren.
B. He shares a titbit or two and it starts off a conversation.
C. He then asks his teenage grandchildren if they know who those people are.
D. He picks some names of politicians, rock stars or even criminals from his generation.
SSC CHSL Tier-1 14.08.2023 (Shift-IV)
(a) ABCD (b) ACBD
(c) BACD (d) ADCB

Ans. (d)

Sentence A will be the first sentence as it uses the word 'once' and presents how the narrator got to know of a game. Sentence D comes second as it presents the description of the game. It is followed by sentence C which presents the questions asked in the game. The last sentence is B as it presents how this leads to the man telling more about the questions. Thus, the correct sequence is ADCB.

168. A. It is almost a definition of a gentleman to say he is one who never inflicts pain.
B. He is mainly occupied in merely removing the obstacles which hinder the free and unembarrassed action of those about him and he concurs with their movements rather than takes the initiative himself.
C. The true gentleman in like manner carefully avoids whatever may cause a jar or a jolt in the minds of those with whom he is cast; all clashing of opinion or collision of feeling, all restraint or suspicion or gloom or resentment; his great concern being to make everyone at their ease and at home.
D. His benefits may be considered as parallel to what are called comforts or conveniences in arrangements of a personal nature: like an easy chair or a good fire, which do their part in dispelling cold and fatigue, though nature provides both means of rest and animal heat without them. SSC CHSL Tier-2 26.06.2023
(a) BACD (b) ABCD
(c) DCBA (d) DBAC

Ans. (b)

Sentence A will be the first sentence as it provides a definition of a gentleman as someone who does not inflict pain. Sentence B comes second as it introduces the idea that the gentleman's main role is to remove obstacles and follow the lead of others. It is followed by Sentence C as it elaborates on the gentleman's avoidance of conflict and his focus on making everyone feel at ease. The last sentence is D as it compares the gentleman's actions to the comforts and conveniences that make life easier, but are not essential. Thus, the correct sequence is ABCD.

169. 1.Ranga is the accountant's son.
A. He returned to his village after his studies were over.
B. He is one rare breed of village folk who loved studies.
C. On his return the villagers milled around his house to see whether he has changed or not.
D. He had gone to Bangalore to pursue his studies.

2. His idea about marriage are now quite different.

SSC CHSL Tier-2 26.06.2023

(a) BDAC (b) BCAD
(c) BCDA (d) BDCA

Ans. (a)

Sentence B will be the first sentence as it elaborates of the main theme- Ranga and states how he loved to study. Sentence D comes second as it presents that he went to Bangalore to study. It is followed by sentence A which presents his return. The last sentence is C as it presents how villagers came to see him. Thus, the correct sequence is BDAC.

SSC CHSL 2022 (Tier 1 & 2)

170. A. These great leaders never escaped from their responsibilities and challenges because they knew greatness would come through great responsibilities.

B. Leadership is one of the crucial elements in the field of management because most of the time success or failure depends on the managerial skills of a leader.

C. There are not many leaders in the present world because, unlike ancient times, people are not ready to accept responsibilities.

D. Ancient India produced millions of people with leadership because it is an inner part of Indian culture to create leaders in every sphere of life. Chandragupta Maurya, Gandhi, Buddha, Bose, etc., were leaders on this soil.

SSC CHSL Tier-1 27.05.2022 (Shift-I)

(a) ADBC (b) BCAD
(c) ADCB (d) BCDA

Ans. (d)

Sentence B will be the first sentence as it introduces the main theme- Leadership. Sentence C comes second as it presents the cause of lack of leader in the world. It is followed by sentence D which presents the abundance of leaders in ancient India. The last sentence is sentence A gives the why there was an abundance. Thus, the correct sequence is BCDA.

171. A. The deeper you immerse it, the greater will be the difference in the water level.

B. This difference in the levels in the U-tube is a measure of the pressure applied by your palm.

C. If you immerse the funnel into a bucket of water, you will again see the difference in the water level in the U-tube.

D. When you gently apply pressure on the rubber film with your palm, you will find that a difference in the water level is created in the manometer.

SSC CHSL Tier-1 30.05.2022 (Shift-I)

(a) BACD (b) CBAD
(c) DBCA (d) ABCD

Ans. (c)

Sentence D will be the first sentence as it contains the main idea i.e., the difference in the water level is created in the manometer. Sentence B comes second as it describes the measures of the pressure of the water levels in the U - tube. It will be followed by Sentence C which describes you will again see the difference in the water level if you immerse the funnel into a bucket of water. The last sentence is Sentence A which it concludes the deeper you immerse it, the greater will be the difference. Thus, the correct sequence is DBCA.

172. A. The current concern is that it is rising day by day due to various resources of pollutants.

B. It has been there in different forms since a long time, even before human evolution, such as volcanic eruptions, wildfire which led to various photochemical reactions in the atmosphere.

C. Pollution has become a very common yet serious issue in today's world.

D. And, one of the main pollutants are humans and man-made machines.

SSC CHSL Tier-1 31.05.2022 (Shift-I)

(a) CBAD (b) ABCD
(c) CDBA (d) CADB

Ans. (a)

Sentence C will be the first sentence as it introduces the main theme of the paragraph- Pollution. Sentence B comes second as it presents the prevalence of pollution- the Hornbill festival. It is followed by sentence A which states the current situation of pollution.

The last sentence is D as it points out the main pollutants. Thus, the correct sequence is CBAD.

173. A. Two astronomers – Johannes Kepler from Germany and Galileo from Italy – supported the Copernicus theory after nearly a century passed by.

B. Copernicus' view was that the Sun was stationary and the Earth and the planets moved in orbits around the Sun.

C. Nicholas Copernicus, a Polish priest, proposed a model in 1514.

D. There are many popular theories about the solar system. Ancient people believed that the Sun moved around the Earth and the Earth was static.

SSC CHSL Tier-1 02.06.2022 (Shift-I)

(a) BCAD (b) ABCD
(c) DCBA (d) DACB

Ans. (c)

Sentence D will be the first sentence as it introduces the main theme- theories about the Solar System. Sentence C comes second as it points out the theory of Copernicus. It is followed by sentence B which states the theory given by Copernicus. The last sentence is A as it support received by the theory. Thus, the correct sequence is DCBA.

SSC CHSL 2021 (Tier 1 & 2)

174. A. We found both to be very quiet and subdued.

B. Later,when we became good friends, they told us about their tragic loss.

C. The Mehras were newcomers to the neighbourhood.

D. My wife and I called on them to ask if they needed any help.

SSC CHSL Tier-1 12.04.2021 (Shift-II)

(a) CDAB (b) BDAC
(c) DBAC (d) ACDB

Ans. (a)

Sentence C will be the first sentence as it introduces Mehras. Sentence D comes second as it presents how the narrators offers them help. It is followed by sentence A which presents that the narrator's view on the Mehras. The last sentence is B as it presents that they became friends. Thus, the correct sequence is CDAB.

175. A. Her face had the most extraordinary expression of horror and amusement.

B. My mother looked up in time to see me fall.

C. But I missed and went sprawling across the kitchen floor.

D. My hand reached out to grab the handle of the door that led into the kitchen.

SSC CHSL Tier-1 12.04.2021 (Shift-II)

(a) CBDA (b) DCBA
(c) BDAC (d) ABCD

Ans. (b)

Sentence D will be the first sentence as it introduces the narrator and his act.

Sentence C comes second as it points out how the narrator fell during his act. It is followed by sentence B which states that his mother looked at the narrator fall. The last sentence is A as it presents his mother's reaction. Thus, the correct sequence is DCBA.

176. A. I saw a middle-aged man sitting beneath the tree with his knees drawn up to his chest.
B. When I was a street away from my house, I saw a huge banyan tree to my right.
C. My heart went out to him as he was crying bitterly.
D. His head was bowed and his body was shivering continuously.
SSC CHSL Tier-1 19.04.2021 (Shift-III)
(a) ADBC (b) BADC
(c) ACDB (d) BDCA

Ans. (b)

Sentence B will be the first sentence as it introduces the narrator. Sentence A will come second as it presents what the narrator saw. It will be followed by sentence D wherein the narrator describes the man he saw. The last sentence will be sentence C as it points out what the narrator felt. Thus, the correct sequence is BADC.

177. A. He often spread rumours that his neighbours were thieves.
B. After being released, one of them sued him for wrongly accusing them.
C. One evening, some of them were arrested by the police.
D. After the investigation, they were proven innocent.
SSC CHSL Tier-1 19.04.2021 (Shift-III)
(a) ABCD (b) ADBC
(c) DCAB (d) ACDB

Ans. (d)

Sentence A will be the first sentence as it introduces 'he' and his rumours about his neighbours. Sentence C comes second as it presents how the neighbours were arrested. It is followed by sentence D which presents that the rumours were found false. The last sentence is B as it presents that he was sued. Thus, the correct sequence is ACDB.

178. A. He lived in a small house near the main road of a village.
B. As both, he and his wife, worked hard, they made a small fortune.
C. But one thing caused them great sorrow; they had no children.
D. After he got married, he started a tailor's shop.
SSC CHSL Tier-1 04.08.2021 (Shift-I)
(a) ABDC (b) BDAC
(c) ADBC (d) BACD

Ans. (c)

Sentence A will be the first sentence as it introduces the character 'he'. Sentence D comes second as it presents how he started the tailor's shop. It is followed by sentence B which presents how the man with his wife made a small fortune. The last sentence is C as it presents their sorrow. Thus, the correct sequence is ADBC.

179. A. We gently put the fledgling back into the nest.
B. One morning, we found one of the four fallen on the ground.
C. The robin couple built a nest in our verandah and laid four eggs.
D. Once they had hatched, they busily took turns feeding the four.
SSC CHSL Tier-1 04.08.2021 (Shift-I)
(a) CDBA (b) ACDB
(c) BADC (d) DABC

Ans. (a)

Sentence C will be the first sentence as it introduces the robin couple and their eggs. Sentence D comes second as it presents what happened after the eggs were hatched. It is followed by sentence B which states what happens in the morning. The last sentence is A as it presents how the narrator helped them. Thus, the correct sequence is CDBA.

180. A. The word 'Jama' means 'a robe or shawl' and 'War' means 'Yard (the measuring unit)'.
B. Jamawar (also spelled as Jamavar) is a fabric that has its roots in Kashmir.
C. People in the earlier times used to buy a yard of the shawl to protect themselves from the chilly winter.
D. The Jamawar is an adulterated form of Pashmina silk since it contains a blend of cotton and wool. **SSC CHSL Tier-1 10.08.2021 (Shift-I)**
(a) BACD (b) BCAD
(c) DCBA (d) DCAB

Ans. (a)

Sentence B will be the first sentence as it introduces the main theme-Jamawar. Sentence A comes second as it presents the history of the name of the fabric. It is followed by sentence C which states how people used the fabric. The last sentence is D as it presents more about Jamawar. Thus, the correct sequence is BACD.

181. A. His school was closed as it was the height of summer.
B. It was on one such day that Ranji discovered a pool in the forest.
C. As he had no friends yet, he wandered alone in the hills and forests.
D. Ranji had been less than a month in Rajpur.
SSC CHSL Tier-1 10.08.2021 (Shift-I)
(a) ACBD (b) CBDA
(c) BADC (d) DACB

Ans. (d)

Sentence D will be the first sentence as it introduces Ranji. Sentence A comes second as it presents why Ranji is in Rajpur. It is followed by sentence C how he spent time in Rajpur. The last sentence is B as it presents Ranji's discovery. Thus, the correct sequence is DACB.

182. A. The man who had caught me was a dreadful sight.
B. Suddenly I was picked up, whirled through the air and made to sit on a tombstone.
C. He was about forty years old, hard-faced and fierce.
D. I was only a child and small for my age. **SSC CHSL Tier-1 12.08.2021 (Shift-III)**
(a) CBAD (b) BACD
(c) DBAC (d) DCBA

Ans. (c)

Sentence D will be the first sentence as it introduces the narrator and an event which occurred during his childhood. Sentence B comes second as it starts explaining the event. It will be followed by Sentence A which presents a man who scared the narrator. The last sentence is Sentence C which presents the description of the man. Thus, the correct sequence is DBAC.

SSC Selection Post 2023

183. A. I was taking a stroll along the beach, when I came across a heap of plastic waste.
B. Realising the importance of removing the waste, joined them.
C. Some children came to clean the beach, seeing the dumped waste.
D.The adjacent industry had dumped the waste, which was floating, into the water, therefore polluting the sea water.
SSC SP 28.08.2023 (Shift-II)
(a) DCAB (b) BADC
(c) ADBC (d) ADCB

Ans. (d)

Sentence A will be the starting line as it contains the main idea of the para jumble i.e; heap of plastic waste. and Sentence D states that the nearby industry dumped the waste. So, D will follow A.

Further, Sentence C states that some children had come to clean the beach and Sentence B states that they understand the importance of removing waste. So, B will follow C. Thus, the correct sequence is ADCB.

SSC Selection Post 2022

184. A. Ram was sitting on a tree and was eating an apple.
B. The monkey had thrown an apple at him.
C. While eating the apple, something hit his head.
D. He looked up to find a monkey sitting on a branch of the tree.

SSC SP 01.08.2022

(a) ACBD (b) BCAD
(c) ACDB (d) CBOD

Ans. (c)

Sentence A will be the first sentence as it introduces Ram and what he is doing. Sentence C comes second which shows what happened while he was sitting beneath the tree. It is followed by Sentence D which shows his reaction. Sentence B comes last as it presents the culprit. Hence, the correct order is ACDB.

185. A. He had a tiny room in a basement, the one window of which looked out on to the street.
B. There was hardly a pair of boots in the neighbourhood that had not been once or twice through his hands.
C. In a certain town there lived a cobbler, Martin Avdeitch by name.
D. Through it one could see the feet of those who passed by, but Martin recognised the people by their boots. **SSC SP 4.08.2022 (Shift-III)**

(a) CADB (b) CBDA
(c) CDBA (d) CABD

Ans. (a)

Sentence C will be the first sentence as it introduces the topic- Martin Aveditch. Sentence A comes second as it presents where he lived and gives brief description of his house. It is followed by sentence D which further describes what could be seen from the window of his house and how he recognised people. The last sentence is B as presents that he was a shoemaker. Thus, the correct sequence is CADB.

186. A. In this style of essay, it is critical to incorporate precise details that allow the reader to experience the emotion.
B. When creating a narrative essay, you should have a cast of people, a setting, a compelling storyline and a satisfying ending.
C. Not only should they express their emotions or employ their senses, but they should also allow the tale to convey a point.
D. A narrative essay tells a tale from a certain point of view or can say a story of the personal experiences one had. **SSC SP 05.08.2022 (Shift-II)**

(a) DBAC (b) BCAD
(c) CDBA (d) DABC

Ans. (a)

Sentence D will be the first sentence as it contains the main theme- A narrative essay. Sentence B comes second as it points out the ideas needed to create a narrative essay. It will be followed by Sentence A which states the need of precise details. The last sentence is Sentence C which states the purpose of a narrative essay. Thus, the correct sequence is DBAC.

SSC Steno 2024

187. A. They think there are some bitter learning experiences
B. Which, over a period of time, guide them to take a good path
C. Many successful people believe that
D. There is no failure in anybody's life **SSC Steno 11.12.2024 (Shift-I)**

(a) CDAB (b) BDAC
(c) CBDA (d) CBAD

Ans. (a)

The correct order is C, D, A, B. This order maintains a logical flow, starting with the belief of successful people, explaining there is no failure, then mentioning learning experiences and concluding with how they guide over time.

188. A. Often one fails to grab that chance.
B. Life often gives us one single chance to flourish.
C. Getting a chance to do good is not easy.
D. If you get a chance, grab it and give your best.

SSC Steno 11.12.2024 (Shift-I)

(a) BCAD (b) ABCD
(c) DABC (d) DCAB

Ans. (a)

The paragraph starts with the idea that life gives us a chance to flourish (B), mentions that getting such a chance is not easy (C), often we miss the chance (A) and concludes with the advice to grab the chance and give our best (D). Hence, the correct order is BCAD.

189. A. The King Cobra is the world's largest venomous snake.
B. Even, the baby King Cobra is one-and-a-half foot long when born.
C. It is mostly found in parts of Africa.
D. The Cobra is the only snake that builds a nest.

SSC Steno 11.12.2024 (Shift-I)

(a) BDAC (b) ABCD
(c) BACD (d) CBAD

Ans. (b)

The correct logical sequence is: ABCD. It introduces the King Cobra, mentions its size at birth, specifies its habitat, and concludes with a unique characteristic.

190. Parts of a paragraph are given below in jumbled order. Arrange the parts in the correct order to form a meaningful paragraph. The first part 'R' is fixed.
R. The knowledge so far
A. Available about the endocrine gland is very limited.
B. Hormones are the body's chemical messengers.
C. These are the glands that make all the hormones.
D. They influence almost every cell, organ and function of our bodies.

SSC Steno 11.12.2024 (Shift-I)

(a) CABD (b) BCDA
(c) ACBD (d) ABCD

Ans. (c)

The correct order is A, C, B, D. The paragraph starts with the limited knowledge about endocrine glands (A), then explains that these glands make hormones (C), defines hormones (B), and concludes with their influence on the body (D).

191. A. People come from divergent families, nations, faiths, political structures and ethnicities.
B. Their beliefs constitute distinct moral frameworks.
C. Respect for these ideals or for human dignity will define society's functioning.
D. Respect and compromise are essential components of human dignity among the diverse members of any community.

SSC Steno 11.12.2024 (Shift-I)

(a) CBAD (b) BCDA
(c) BADC (d) DABC

Ans. (d)

The correct order is DABC. Sentence (D) sets the context by emphasising the need for respect and compromise. Sentence (A) describes the diversity of people.

Sentence (B) explains their distinct moral frameworks. Sentence (C) concludes by highlighting the impact of respect on society's functioning.

192. A. Positive thinking leads a man to success. One who thinks that he can achieve the things will put his best to achieve.

B. Self-confidence, determination, perseverance and hard work are the key factors of success.

C. He will not fetter by the problems in the path of success and one day he will win positively.

D. Every small or big, easy, or complex problem has its solution. There is a way out of every labyrinth, there is an answer to every enigma.

SSC Steno 11.12.2024 (Shift-II)

(a) BCAD (b) ACBD
(c) DCBA (d) CDBA

Ans. (b)

The correct sequence is ACBD. A introduces the idea of positive thinking leading to success. C follows by explaining how one will persist despite problems. B lists key factors of success, like self-confidence, determination and hard work. D concludes with the notion that every problem has a solution, reinforcing the message of persistence and positivity.

193. A. Ask your employer for information on the child care scheme.

B. If the employer does not contribute to the costs, the government will do so.

C. The employers of both parents are expected to contribute to child care.

D. The Government policy on child care was designed as a welfare scheme for citizens.

SSC Steno 11.12.2024 (Shift-II)

(a) BACD (b) CDBA
(c) BDAC (d) DCAB

Ans. (d)

The correct order is DCAB. The paragraph should start with the general statement about the government policy on child care (D), followed by the expectations from the employers (C), then the specific action that parents should take (A) and conclude with what happens if the employers do not contribute (B).

194. A. Nowadays, society has become corrupted by cunning, manipulative and toxic people.

B. The responsibility should be taken by mentally strong people.

C. There lies a responsibility for others to make society a better place to live in.

D. Being robust, they can devote their time or resources to change noxious individuals.

SSC Steno 11.12.2024 (Shift-III)

(a) CBAD (b) DCBA
(c) ACBD (d) ABCD

Ans. (c)

The correct order is ACBD.

This arrangement ensures that the ideas flow logically from identifying the problem, assigning the responsibility to strong individuals, acknowledging their role in improving society and finally describing their capability to change toxic individuals.

195. R. Mahatma Gandhi led a long struggle against untouchability

A. Dr. BR Ambedkar, the father of the Indian Constitution, belonged to the lower

B. Such as entry into temples and public places

C. And worked for the welfare of the so called lower castes

D. Caste and made many efforts to secure basic rights for them

SSC Steno 11.12.2024 (Shift-III)

(a) DBAC (b) CDBA
(c) BCAD (d) CADB

Ans. (d)

The correct order is 'CADB'. This arrangement ensures that the ideas flow logically from Gandhi's struggle against untouchability, Ambedkar's background, his efforts for securing basic rights, and examples of those rights.

196. A. However, the most consumed tea in the world is Indian tea.

B. Tea was originated in China by its ruler, Shennong.

C. India also has the credit of being the world's largest producer.

D. This is because of the tropical and sub-tropical climate present here.

SSC Steno 10.12.2024 (Shift-I)

(a) BACD (b) CBAD
(c) DCAB (d) ABCD

Ans. (a)

The correct logical sequence is BACD. This sequence presents a coherent narrative about the origin, popularity, and production of tea, linking it to India's climate.

197. P. Applied arts require an object to be functional, as well as beautiful.

Q. They recognised that their work belonged to the higher social classes who had the wealth to purchase art and the leisure time to enjoy it.

R. Fine art is categorised as something which only has an aesthetic or conceptual function.

S. There are a number of different categories of objects and processes under the umbrella term of art which need to be explored.

T. In the twentieth century, artists began to challenge the established notion of art.

U. Art is typically divided into two areas: fine art (such as painting, sculpture, music and poetry), and the applied arts (such as pottery, weaving, metal working, furniture making and calligraphy).

SSC Steno 10.12.2024 (Shift-I)

(a) RPSTUQ (b) SURPTQ
(c) SUPQRT (d) SRPUTQ

Ans. (b)

The correct order is SURPTQ. It introduces the concept of art and its categories, followed by the distinctions between fine and applied arts and concludes with a historical perspective on how these notions were challenged and perceived by different social classes.

198. A. Telugu movie industry is proud of many great producers, directors, artists and musicians.

B. Savithri was one such great artist who influenced Telegu movie industry single-handedly for many years.

C. Her initial interest was in dance so she learnt dance before entering movies.

D. She is still worshipped for her matchless expressions and dialogue delivery.

SSC Steno 10.12.2024 (Shift-II)

(a) BCDA (b) CDAB
(c) ABCD (d) ACDB

Ans. (c)

The correct order is ABCD. The paragraph starts by introducing the Telugu movie industry and its pride (A), followed by Savithri's significant influence (B), her initial interest in dance (C) and concluding with her being worshipped for her expressions and dialogue delivery (D). This order maintains coherence and logical flow.

199. A. Researchers from five medical centres around the country found that insomniacs were also significantly likely to have poor health, such as chest pain, arthritis, and depression, as well as difficulties doing daily duties.
B. Even temporary sleep loss can disrupt the body's capacity to break down carbohydrates, interfere with hormones and aggravate diabetes and high blood pressure.
C. So, make time for whatever helps you sleep, whether it's exercise, massages, yoga, meditation, or a fragrance bath.
D. Sleep deprivation has frightening consequences for many biological processes. **SSC Steno 10.12.2024 (Shift-II)**

(a) DACB (b) DABC
(c) DCAB (d) DCBA

Ans. (b)

The most logical sequence is D, A, B, C. The paragraph starts by explaining the consequences of sleep deprivation (D), followed by the findings of researchers (A), then detailing how sleep loss affects health (B) and concluding with advice on improving sleep (C).

200. A. The Booker is awarded on 17th October, which also happens to be Garner's 88th birthday, a coincidence that itself feels a little magical.
B. 'If the rocks, caves, lakes, fens, bogs and dens of the land of Britain had a voice, it would sound like Alan Garner telling a story.'
C. This year Alan Garner became the oldest author ever to be shortlisted for the Booker Prize for his small but mighty novel Treacle Walker.
D. Treacle Walker, a dreamlike fable of a convalescent boy named Joseph, a rag-and-bone man and a bog-dwelling spirit is at once a characteristically cryptic tale of a child threatened by dark forces, a meditation on time and mortality and a vivid example of folk horror. **SSC Steno 10.12.2024 (Shift-II)**

(a) BDAC (b) DACB
(c) ADBC (d) CADB

Ans. (d)

The most logical sequence is C, A, D, B. The paragraph starts with the current achievement of Alan Garner (C), followed by the award coinciding with his birthday (A), then describing the novel Treacle Walker (D) and concluding with a quote praising Garner's storytelling (B).

201. A. I must tell you that I am referring to the tax year which began on 1st April.
B. Let me be the first to wish you a very happy New Year.
C. In case none of your friends or family did so.
D. Now, before you ask whether the spring sunshine has gone to my head. **SSC Steno 10.12.2024 (Shift-II)**

(a) BACD (b) ADCB
(c) DBCA (d) CBDA

Ans. (c)

The correct order is DBCA.
The paragraph starts with a casual statement addressing a possible question (D), followed by a New Year's wish (B), a mention in case no one else has done so (C) and finally a clarification about the tax year (A).

202. A. Before we could react or comprehend, the waters had wiped out all the shanties on the beach.
B. The word 'tsunami' sends shivers down my spine.
C. Suddenly, on a bright afternoon I noticed a lot of waves grow bigger and splash quickly.
D. I still remember my vacation in Thailand the day the tsunami struck. **SSC Steno 10.12.2024 (Shift-II)**

(a) CDAB (b) BDCA
(c) ABCD (d) DABC

Ans. (b)

The correct order is B, D, C, A.
The paragraph starts with the word 'tsunami' creating a sense of fear (B), then recalling a specific event (D), followed by the description of the waves (C) and concluding with the impact of the tsunami (A).

203. A. Booming with private developers
B. And it is changing the landscape of the urban and semi-urban habitat
C. Making the Indian elevator industry the second highest market in the world
D. India's real estate business is **SSC Steno 10.12.2024 (Shift-II)**

(a) DBAC (b) DACB
(c) ABCD (d) BACD

Ans. (b)

The correct order is DACB. The sentence should start with the subject 'India's real estate business is' and logically follow with a description of its state ('booming with private developers'). Then, the effect of this booming business is mentioned ('making the Indian elevator industry the second highest market in the world'), and finally, it explains the consequence ('and it is changing the landscape of the urban and semi-urban habitat').

204. A. Freedom of thought and expression are fundamental human rights.
B. There are two important human rights.
C. Through good deeds, one can gain dignity.
D. Everyone has the inherent right to be treated with dignity and courtesy at all times. **SSC Steno 10.12.2024 (Shift-III)**

(a) BCAD (b) BCDA
(c) ACDB (d) DCBA

Ans. (b)

The correct order is BCDA. The paragraph starts with introducing the two important human rights. Next, it states everyone's inherent right to dignity and courtesy, followed by mentioning that dignity can be gained through good deeds and concludes with freedom of thought and expression as fundamental human rights.

205. A. Peace of mind is commonly correlated with happiness, contentment, tranquility, contemplation, exercise and relaxation.
B. Thus, we all need peace of mind in our lives.
C. Peace of mind, thus, give us all these attributes.
D. One of the most important aspects of the mind is getting peace. **SSC Steno 10.12.2024 (Shift-III)**

(a) BCDA (b) DACB
(c) BDCA (d) DCBA

Ans. (b)

The correct order is DACB. The paragraph should start with the importance of getting peace, followed by correlating peace of mind with various attributes. It then states that peace of mind gives us these attributes, and concludes with the need for peace of mind in our lives.

14

Cloze Test

A cloze test is an exercise where a passage is provided with certain words missing from it. Actually it is a combination of fill in the blanks and reading comprehension. It is important to understand the flow and context of a passage.

Tips to Handle Cloze Test

Read thoroughly Read the passage thoroughly to get an idea of the passage. Read slowly and gain an understanding of the text. Once the theme of the paragraph is clear, it becomes easy to fill in the blanks.

Link the sentences together Always remember, it is a passage, so the sentences are linked to one another. Never make a mistake of treating every sentence an individual one.

Type of word to fill in Look at the blanks carefully and try to assess which kind of word to put in the blank. Words can be based on grammar, prepositions, tenses, vocabulary etc.

Tone Passage may contain some specific tone like narrative, critical, sarcastic, humorous etc. So, always make a right choice of a word.

Negate options Sometimes, words are too close, eliminating wrong choices can help.

Key words Pay close attention to key words/ clues in the sentences before and after the given blank.

SSC Exam Scanner

SSC CGL 2024 (Tier 1 & 2)

Directions (Q. Nos. 1-901) In the following passage, some words have been deleted. Read the passage carefully and select the most appropriate option to fill in each blank.

PASSAGE-1

Climate change ....(1)......... an imminent threat to our planet, demanding urgent global action. The rise in greenhouse gas emissions, deforestation and unsustainable practices contribute to extreme weather events, rising sea levels and disruptions in ecosystems. To ....(2)......... these effects, a collaborative international effort is essential. Nations ....(3)......... commit to reducing carbon emissions, transitioning to renewable energy sources and implementing sustainable practices. Cooperation on technological advancements and sharing resources will foster a collective resilience against the impacts of climate change. The urgency of this issue calls for a united front, where governments, businesses and individuals work together to create a sustainable and resilient future for the ....(4)......... to come. **SSC CGL Tier-2 18.01.2025**

1. Select the most appropriate option to fill in blank number 1.
   (a) will pose (b) poses
   (c) posed (d) will be posing

   Ans. (b) 'Poses' is the correct option for blank number 1. It indicates a present and ongoing threat, fitting the context of climate change being an imminent danger to our planet.

2. Select the most appropriate option to fill in blank number 2.
   (a) widen (b) inflate
   (c) mitigate (d) maximise

   Ans. (c) 'Mitigate' is the correct option for blank number 2. It means to make less severe, serious, or painful, which aligns with the goal of reducing the harmful effects of climate change.

3. Select the most appropriate option to fill in blank number 3.
   (a) must (b) would
   (c) might (d) could

   Ans. (a) 'Must' is the correct option for blank number 3. It expresses a strong obligation or necessity, indicating that nations are required to take action against climate change.

4. Select the most appropriate option to fill in blank number 4.
   (a) generations
   (b) businessmen
   (c) poor people
   (d) backward nations

   Ans. (a) 'Generations' is the correct option for blank number 4. It refers to future generations who will benefit from a sustainable and resilient future created by current efforts to combat climate change.

PASSAGE-2

The greatest disease in the West today is not TB or leprosy; it is being unwanted, unloved and uncared for. We can cure ……(1)…… diseases with medicine, but the only cure for loneliness, despair and hopelessness is love. There are many in the world who are ……(2)…… or a piece of bread but there are many more dying for a little love.

The poverty in the West is a different kind of poverty – it is not only a poverty of ……(3)…… but also of ……(4)…… . There's a hunger for affection as there is a hunger for God.

SSC CGL Tier-2 20.01.2025

5. Select the most appropriate option to fill in blank number 1.
(a) masculine (b) stubborn
(c) physical (d) radical

Ans. (c) The correct option to fill in blank number 1 is 'physical', as it refers to diseases that can be treated with medicine.

6. Select the most appropriate option to fill in blank number 2.
(a) ignoring (b) dying
(c) neglecting (d) disregarding

Ans. (b) The correct option to fill in blank number 2 is 'dying', as it describes the desperate need for something, like a piece of bread.

7. Select the most appropriate option to fill in blank number 3.
(a) profusion (b) loneliness
(c) abundance (d) lavishness

Ans. (b) The correct option to fill in blank number 3 is 'loneliness', as it contrasts with material poverty and highlights the emotional and social aspects of poverty.

8. Select the most appropriate option to fill in blank number 4.
(a) covetous (b) spirituality
(c) educate (d) materialistic

Ans. (b) The correct option to fill in blank number 4 is 'spirituality', as it refers to the deeper, non-material aspects of life that people yearn for, alongside physical needs.

PASSAGE-3

There is a saying that coming events cast their shadows before. ………(1)………, it is not universally true. Something can happen within a second, and one may not ………(2)……… it. ………(3)………, some instances show that predictions based on certain signs have gone wrong. People generally say that natural calamities can be predicted by observing the animals. But what if animals are suffering from some disease and don't show any signs before the event appears? They may fail to make peculiar sounds or actions about the events which are going to take place. ………(4)………, some unnatural calamities that are likely to appear may forecast their shadows by some bad omens. ………(5)……… we should not completely cancel out the possibilities that animals can sense certain unnatural happenings. **SSC CGL Tier-1 09.09.2024 (Shift-I)**

9. Select the most appropriate option to fill in blank number 1.
(a) Moreover
(b) Therefore
(c) Furthermore
(d) However

Ans. (d) 'However' introduces a contrasting statement.

10. Select the most appropriate option to fill in blank number 2.
(a) legalise (b) foresee
(c) rescind (d) affect

Ans. (b) 'Foresee' means to predict something before it happens.

11. Select the most appropriate option to fill in blank number 3.
(a) Therefore (b) Moreover
(c) Nevertheless (d) However

Ans. (b) 'Moreover' adds additional information or evidence.

12. Select the most appropriate option to fill in blank number 4.
(a) Besides
(b) Secondly
(c) Therefore
(d) Despite

Ans. (a) 'Besides' introduces an additional point.

13. Select the most appropriate option to fill in blank number 5.
(a) However
(b) Nevertheless
(c) Moreover
(d) Therefore

Ans. (d) 'Therefore' concludes with a logical result.

PASSAGE-4

From the beginning ………(1)……………. the eighteenth century, the ladies of European cities covered ………(2)…………… faces in layers of paint and powder. This particular fashion was largely brought ………(3)…………… by the urgent need to disguise the ravages of smallpox, ………(4)…………… left their faces pitted and scarred. During this same period, the 'beauty spot' was introduced to cover ………(5)……… a facial defect. **SSC CGL Tier-1 09.09.2024 (Shift-II)**

14. Select the most appropriate option to fill in blank number 1.
(a) in (b) on
(c) of (d) about

Ans. (c) 'Of' indicates a relationship between the beginning and the eighteenth century.

15. Select the most appropriate option to fill in blank number 2.
(a) their (b) there
(c) them (d) they're

Ans. (a) 'Their' is a possessive pronoun showing ownership of the faces by the ladies.

16. Select the most appropriate option to fill in blank number 3.
(a) within (b) around
(c) to (d) about

Ans. (d) 'About' indicates the cause or reason for something happening.

17. Select the most appropriate option to fill in blank number 4.
(a) that (b) which
(c) when (d) who

Ans. (b) 'Which' is a relative pronoun used to provide additional information about 'ravages of smallpox.'

18. Select the most appropriate option to fill in blank number 5.
(a) on (b) to
(c) for (d) up

Ans. (d) 'Up' is used to indicate covering something to conceal it.

PASSAGE-5

Tea prices in the domestic .... (1)........... continue to rule high in the current year despite the expectation of a higher production as compared to the previous year. During the past three months, tea prices have been ....(2).......... with the prices of other companies. Unlike last year, tea prices have generally shown ....(3)............, when tea prices rose dramatically, this year, prices seem to have ....(4)........... at a rather high level. In the subsequent four months, the ....(5)............ average price showed a downtrend.

SSC CGL Tier-1 09.09.2024 (Shift-III)

19. Select the most appropriate option to fill in blank number 1.
(a) market (b) area
(c) zone (d) field

Ans. (a) 'Market' refers to the place where tea prices are regulated.

20. Select the most appropriate option to fill in blank number 2.
(a) aligning (b) favouring
(c) countering (d) encountering

Ans. (a) 'Aligning' means matching with the prices of other companies.

21. Select the most appropriate option to fill in blank number 3.
(a) an inflow (b) an innate
(c) a reduction (d) an uptrend

Ans. (d) 'An uptrend' indicates a general increase in tea prices.

22. Select the most appropriate option to fill in blank number 4.
(a) stabilised (b) moderated
(c) equated (d) abated

Ans. (a) 'Stabilised' means maintaining at a rather high level.

23. Select the most appropriate option to fill in blank number 5.
(a) monthly (b) half yearly
(c) weekly (d) yearly

Ans. (a) 'Monthly' refers to the average price over a month.

PASSAGE-6

The third National Wildlife Action Plan for 2017- 2031, underlying India's plan for wildlife conservation, was unveiled ....(1).......... the Global Wildlife Programme conference. The plan recognises ....(2).......... addresses concerns pertaining to climate changes and its impact on wildlife .

The plan details the importance of ecosystems for food production, health and other aspects of ....(3).......... survival and sustainable development. It also emphasises preservation of genetic ....(4).......... and sustainable utilisation of species and ecosystems which has direct bearing on our scientific advancements and support to millions of rural communities.

The plan underscores rehabilitation of threatened wildlife species ....(5).......... inland aquatic, coastal and marine ecosystems while conserving their habitats.

SSC CGL Tier-1 10.09.2024 (Shift-I)

24. Select the most appropriate option to fill in blank number 1.
(a) at (b) for
(c) in (d) to

Ans. (a) 'At' is used to indicate the location of the unveiling.

25. Select the most appropriate option to fill in blank number 2.
(a) to (b) and
(c) in (d) for

Ans. (b) 'And' connects two related ideas or addresses.

26. Select the most appropriate option to fill in blank number 3.
(a) group (b) human
(c) species (d) breed

Ans. (b) 'Human' pertains to the survival and sustainable development of humans.

27. Select the most appropriate option to fill in blank number 4.
(a) conflict (b) diversity
(c) focus (d) rejection

Ans. (b) 'Diversity' refers to the variety within genetic material.

28. Select the most appropriate option to fill in blank number 5.
(a) including (b) gathering
(c) counting (d) mixing

Ans. (a) 'Including' specifies the scope of the ecosystems mentioned.

PASSAGE-7

American have been arguing about pandemic ....(1).......... for two years, and the debate is particularly fraught among parents of small children, for good reasons. While ....(2).......... such as masking and isolation mean temporary discomfort or inconvenience for most people, their ....(3).......... for still-developing young children are more mysterious and possibly more significant and lasting.

Children with speech or language disorders offer perhaps the ....(4).......... example of these murky trade-offs. Pandemic restrictions vary by state, county and school district, but I spoke with parents in California, New York, Massachusetts, Washington, New Jersey, Iowa and Maryland, who said their children's speech therapy has been ....(5).......... : first by the loss of in-person therapy and then by masking requirements, in places that have them.

SSC CGL Tier-1 10.09.2024 (Shift-II)

29. Select the most appropriate option to fill in blank number 1.
(a) restrictions (b) intemperance
(c) advantages (d) handicap

Ans. (a) 'Restrictions' are the rules or limitations due to the pandemic.

30. Select the most appropriate option to fill in blank number 2.
(a) brandings (b) measures
(c) models (d) sluggishness

Ans. (b) 'Measures' are actions taken to control the situation.

31. Select the most appropriate option to fill in blank number 3.
(a) marginalisation
(b) foundations
(c) disapproval
(d) consequences

Ans. (d) 'Consequences' refer to the effects of the measures.

32. Select the most appropriate option to fill in blank number 4.
(a) clearest (b) vague
(c) indistinct (d) nebulous

Ans. (a) 'Clearest' example highlights the most evident case.

33. Select the most appropriate option to fill in blank number 5.
(a) disrupted (b) regulated
(c) measured (d) normalised

Ans. (a) 'Disrupted' means interrupted or affected negatively.

PASSAGE-8

As a result of Covid-19, the quick ....(1).......... to digital training has exposed the hazards of student disengagement and the resulting consequences of lower student performance across ....(2).......... courses. The latest ....(3).......... has altered the education of millions of people around the world. New approaches and improvements in the school system are urgently required. Considering the increasing digital divide, the strategy may exacerbate existing inequality disparities.

More than 500 million students, at various levels, around the world were forced to ....(4).......... their studies. These changes have caused and will continue to cause some inconvenience, but they will also foster innovation and future reforms inside this education system.

During a global Covid-19 pandemic, the 'pile-on effect' of the coronavirus can have long-term consequences for schooling, notably for the most vulnerable. Children, ...(5).......... basic, core learning (reading, math, languages, etc.) was weak to begin with, face a significant risk of regression.

During Covid-19, millions of children whose right to education has already been violated, particularly girls, are exposed to greater health and well-being hazards (both psychosocial and physical). **SSC CGL Tier-1 10.09.2024 (Shift-III)**

34. Select the most appropriate option to fill in blank number 1.
(a) end (b) transition
(c) set (d) stagnation

Ans. (b) 'Transition' refers to the shift to digital training.

35. Select the most appropriate option to fill in blank number 2.
(a) numerous (b) fewer
(c) particular (d) limit

Ans. (a) 'Numerous' means many, referring to various courses.

36. Select the most appropriate option to fill in blank number 3.
(a) local (b) endemic
(c) epidemic (d) pandemic

Ans. (d) 'Pandemic' is the global outbreak affecting education.

37. Select the most appropriate option to fill in blank number 4.
(a) suspend (b) resume
(c) reopened (d) carry on

Ans. (a) 'Suspend' means to temporarily stop their studies.

38. Select the most appropriate option to fill in blank number 5.
(a) which (b) whose
(c) whom (d) who

Ans. (b) 'Whose' indicates possession for the children mentioned.

PASSAGE-9

Azadi Ka Amrit Mahotsav is an ....(1).......... by the Government of India to celebrate and remember 75 years of independence and the beautiful history of its people, culture and achievements. This Mahotsav is ....(2).......... to the people of India, who have not only been instrumental in bringing India this far in its volutionary journey but also ....(3).......... the power and potential to realise Prime Minister, Narendra Modi's ....(4).......... of activating India 2.0, fuelled by the spirit of Aatmanirbhar Bharat. The formal journey of Azadi Ka Amrit Mahotsav began on 12th March, 2021, beginning a ....(5).......... to our 75th anniversary of independence and will finish a year later on 15th August, 2023. **SSC CGL Tier-1 11.09.2024 (Shift-I)**

39. Select the most appropriate answer for blank number 1.
(a) associate (b) initiative
(c) obligation (d) occult

Ans. (b) 'Initiative' is a new plan or programme started by the government.

40. Select the most appropriate answer for blank number 2.
(a) dedicated (b) alienated
(c) refused (d) withhold

Ans. (a) 'Dedicated' means devoted to the people of India.

41. Select the most appropriate answer for blank number 3.
(a) clarifies (b) possess
(c) concludes (d) obtains

Ans. (b) 'Possess' means having the power and potential.

42. Select the most appropriate answer for blank number 4.
(a) graphics (b) vision
(c) design (d) control

Ans. (b) 'Vision' refers to the Prime Minister's goal or dream.

43. Select the most appropriate answer for blank number 5.
(a) allocation (b) countdown
(c) custom (d) breakdown

Ans. (b) 'Countdown' refers to the time remaining until the anniversary.

PASSAGE-10

Appearances may not reveal the man. So, you shouldn't make ....(1).......... about a man's character based on how he ....(2).......... . People smile and smile, yet prove to be ....(3).......... . On the other hand, people with rough exteriors prove to be the ....(4).......... and most considerate people on earth. They are the people who are beautiful from ....(5).......... . **SSC CGL Tier-1 11.09.2024 (Shift-II)**

44. Select the most appropriate option to fill in blank number 1.
(a) ascend (b) derivations
(c) deficient (d) assumptions

Ans. (d) 'Assumptions' are beliefs about a man's character.

45. Select the most appropriate option to fill in blank number 2.
(a) admits (b) shows
(c) glitters (d) looks

Ans. (d) 'Looks' refers to a man's physical appearance.

46. Select the most appropriate option to fill in blank number 3.
(a) grumpy (b) ecstatic
(c) joyful (d) sparkling

Ans. (a) 'Grumpy' describes someone who seems unfriendly.

47. Select the most appropriate option to fill in blank number 4.
(a) bitterest (b) strangest
(c) gloomiest (d) kindest

Ans. (d) 'Kindest' refers to the most considerate people.

48. Select the most appropriate option to fill in blank number 5.
(a) within (b) personality
(c) style (d) exterior

Ans. (a) 'Within' means beautiful from the inside.

PASSAGE-11

Now, we have Mr. X as the President of India. It has come as a surprise ....(1).......... Scheduled Tribes who are ....(2).......... the most marginalised groups of the country. The Adivasis of India have been ....(3).......... socially, economically and culturally. Despite various efforts taken by the Government of India, they are still under ....(4).......... and suffering. Therefore, the ....(5).......... a leader from a marginalised community or group does not indicate that now the entire community will be uplifted. However, this kind of move may bring certain changes in the status of the Adivasis.

SSC CGL Tier-1 11.09.2024 (Shift-III)

49. Select the most appropriate option to fill in blank number 1.
(a) off (b) in (c) to (d) at

Ans. (c) 'To' is used to indicate surprise directed towards the Scheduled Tribes.

50. Select the most appropriate option to fill in blank number 2.
(a) through (b) therefore
(c) onto (d) among

Ans. (d) 'Among' is used to refer to being part of the most marginalised groups.

51. Select the most appropriate option to fill in blank number 3.
(a) censored (b) marginalised
(c) elevated (d) uplifted

Ans. (b) 'Marginalised' means treated as insignificant or peripheral.

52. Select the most appropriate option to fill in blank number 4.
(a) abundance (b) forest
(c) river (d) poverty

Ans. (d) 'Poverty' refers to the state of being extremely poor.

53. Select the most appropriate option to fill in blank number 5.
(a) rejection of (b) president of
(c) exclusion of (d) elevation of

Ans. (d) 'Elevation of' means the act of raising someone to a higher position.'Elevation of' means the act of raising someone to a higher position.

PASSAGE-12

The beginning of the story is ....(1).......... in its presentation but ....(2).......... the style eases out and becomes haunting in its simplicity. The author brings out the human elements in his story. This common element of sympathy and sacrifice is given a new ....(3).......... by the old artist who shows by his last desperate act that one can be a hero for one day if only one cares ....(4).......... . O Henry's treatment of his material is balanced and controlled, a fine ......(5)....... of humour and pathos. **SSC CGL Tier-1 12.09.2024 (Shift-I)**

54. Select the most appropriate option to fill in blank number 1.
(a) prone (b) delectable
(c) quaint (d) habitual

Ans. (c) 'Quaint' means attractively unusual or old-fashioned.

55. Select the most appropriate option to fill in blank number 2.
(a) hardly (b) recently
(c) initially (d) gradually

Ans. (d) 'Gradually' means slowly over a period of time.

56. Select the most appropriate option to fill in blank number 3.
(a) supervision (b) condition
(c) dimension (d) infection

Ans. (c) 'Dimension' refers to a new aspect or feature of something.

57. Select the most appropriate option to fill in blank number 4.
(a) through (b) though
(c) tough (d) enough

Ans. (d) 'Enough' means to the required degree or extent.

58. Select the most appropriate option to fill in blank number 5.
(a) legend (b) ascend
(c) blend (d) amend

Ans. (c) 'Blend' means a mix of homour and pathos.

PASSAGE-13

People often say that the stars govern their fate but they forget the fact that success or failure is the result of one's own ....(1).......... . If we sow chaff, we can't reap grain; and the result or consequence of an action depends on what one does and to the extent he ....(2).......... it. If we work hard, we succeed only to the extent that we work. People who think that the law of karma is ....(3).......... may feel that if one is destined to get something he will always get it whether he strives for it or not. But experience tells us that reward and punishments are the direct result of our action. Honesty and hard work never go unrewarded and ....(4).......... and evil deeds never go ....(5).......... . In fact even the law of karma, in its proper sense, means the fruit we get is decided by whatever actions we did in the past.

SSC CGL Tier-1 12.09.2024 (Shift-II)

59. Select the most appropriate option to fill in blank number 1.
(a) power (b) incidents
(c) case (d) actions

Ans. (d) 'Actions' refer to things one does.

60. Select the most appropriate option to fill in blank number 2.
(a) does (b) have
(c) create (d) put

Ans. (a) 'Does' is the verb that fits with the subject 'one.'

61. Select the most appropriate option to fill in blank number 3.
(a) supreme (b) greatest
(c) more (d) most

Ans. (a) 'Supreme' means highest in rank or authority.

62. Select the most appropriate option to fill in blank number 4.
(a) horribly (b) badly
(c) dishonesty (d) fairness

Ans. (c) 'Dishonesty' refers to deceitful or fraudulent behaviour.

63. Select the most appropriate option to fill in blank number 5.
(a) unpunished (b) vile
(c) punished (d) waste

Ans. (a) 'Unpunished' means not receiving punishment.

PASSAGE-14

Gandhi, ...(1).......... father of the Indian nation, practiced 'ahimsa' in his personal and political life. He firmly believed that nonviolence is not meant merely for monks, saints and priests; it is for commoners too. If violence is the law of the.........(2).......... beasts, non-violence is the law of the civilised human species. 'The spirit of the brute is inactive and so he knows no law; he knows only physical might. The dignity of man requires obedience to a higher law, to strength of the spirit,' Gandhi said. Ahimsa, to Gandhiji, meant that one should love all; even ......(3)...... enemies.

And the expression of love, ahimsa, should be in such a manner that it impresses itself indelibly upon the so-called enemy and then the enemy must return that love. It is a practically ....(4).......... philosophy. Gandhi was realistic; he believed that non-violence provides the fullest protection to one's self-respect and sense of humour. It won't work in the defence of ....(5).......... gains and immoral acts. He called his marches off when people indulged in violence during protests for India's freedom. His faith in 'ahimsa' played an influential role in enabling the creation of an independent India in 1947, with minimum bloodshed, breaking the shackles framed by the British. **SSC CGL Tier-1 12.09.2024 (Shift-III)**

64. Select the most appropriate option to fill in blank number 1.
(a) an (b) for (c) the (d) a
Ans. (c) 'The' is the definite article used before 'father of the Indian nation.'

65. Select the most appropriate option to fill in blank number 2.
(a) forest-living (b) life
(c) forest-lived (d) alive
Ans. (a) 'Forest-living' describes beasts that live in the forest.

66. Select the most appropriate option to fill in blank number 3.
(a) her (b) its (c) one's (d) one
Ans. (c) 'One's' is a possessive pronoun indicating ownership.

67. Select the most appropriate option to fill in blank number 4.
(a) prove (b) approved
(c) proven (d) proving
Ans. (c) 'Proven' means demonstrated to be true.

68. Select the most appropriate option to fill in blank number 5.
(a) relevant (b) ill-gotten
(c) ill-will (d) moral
Ans. (b) 'Ill-gotten' means obtained in an illegal or unfair manner.

PASSAGE-15

Sleeping, dreaming and waking are three important ....(1).......... for ordinary humans. But for those who have ....(2).......... transcendental knowledge, all three are almost same and there is not much difference among these three. 'The world and life is a myth and it keeps on changing' ....(3).......... Adi Shankaracharya, the greatest 'Advaita' preacher. Ramana Maharshi observed no difference between dreaming and waking states. What he said is that it is from one unreal world to another ....(4).......... world. There is no difference between the images one sees when waking up and the images he/she sees during dreams.

According to this great sage of the modern century, the first one is daydream and the second one is a night dream.

The usual philosophers say that mind and body are the two elements and mind is the source of all diverse thoughts. In the waking up state, the mind is active with all tensions and dissatisfactions, so happiness is missing: during sleep as the mind is absent and so is the physical world, the real happiness ....(5).......... . It is said that deep sleep, where there is no feeling of body, mind and the world, is the natural state of human beings. **SSC CGL Tier-1 13.09.2024 (Shift-I)**

69. Select the most appropriate option to fill in blank number 1.
(a) problems (b) aspects
(c) methods (d) angles
Ans. (b) 'Aspects' refer to different facets of sleeping, dreaming, and waking.

70. Select the most appropriate option to fill in blank number 2.
(a) large (b) deep
(c) superficial (d) depth
Ans. (b) 'Deep' suggests profound transcendental knowledge.

71. Select the most appropriate option to fill in blank number 3.
(a) tells by (b) was said
(c) saying (d) says
Ans. (d) 'Says' attributes the statement to Adi Shankaracharya.

72. Select the most appropriate option to fill in blank number 4.
(a) confused (b) reality
(c) unreal (d) unimaginary
Ans. (c) 'Unreal' contrasts with reality, fitting the context of dreams and waking states.

73. Select the most appropriate option to fill in blank number 5.
(a) is gained (b) gains
(c) gained (d) was gained
Ans. (a) 'Is gained' indicates the attainment of real happiness.

PASSAGE-16

Earthquake is the.........(1).......... breaking and displacement of substantial portions of the earth's outer rocky crust. During an earthquake, rock disturbances can cause rivers to change their flow. Landslides ....(2).......... by earthquakes can cause significant destruction and loss of life.

Tsunamis are a ....(3).......... of damaging waves caused by large earthquakes that occur under the ocean. Earthquakes rarely directly kill anyone. Many ....(4).......... and injuries are caused by falling debris and the fall of structures. The ....(5).......... of an earthquake relies on how much and how far rock cracks and shifts. **SSC CGL Tier-1 13.09.2024 (Shift-II)**

74. Select the most appropriate option to fill in blank number 1.
(a) innovative
(b) expansive
(c) deliberate
(d) abrupt
Ans. (d) 'Abrupt' describes sudden breaking and displacement.

75. Select the most appropriate option to fill in blank number 2.
(a) triggered (b) subdued
(c) blocked (d) prevented
Ans. (a) Triggered' means caused by earthquakes.

76. Select the most appropriate option to fill in blank number 3.
(a) interruption (b) arrest
(c) disorder (d) succession
Ans. (d) 'Succession' refers to a series of waves caused by undersea earthquakes.

77. Select the most appropriate option to fill in blank number 4.
(a) survival (b) fatalities
(c) durability (d) viability
Ans. (b) 'Fatalities' are deaths resulting from the earthquake's effects.

78. Select the most appropriate option to fill in blank number 5.
(a) depth (b) corpse
(c) discipline (d) magnitude
Ans. (d) 'Magnitude' measures the size and energy of an earthquake.

PASSAGE-17

………(1)……... a letter came to inform them that Raka's mother Tara had another breakdown and was in a nursing home in Geneva and that Raka's grandmother Asha, ………(2)……... seen another grandchild safely into the world, was flying to Switzerland to be with her, Nanda Kaul ………(3)……... her lips, ………(4)……... the blue sheets of paper with that distasteful sprawl ………(5)……... them and hid them in her desk. **SSC CGL Tier-1 13.09.2024 (Shift-III)**

79. Select the most appropriate option to fill in blank number 1.
(a) When (b) Sooner
(c) For (d) Unless
Ans. (a) 'When' introduces a clause indicating time.

80. Select the most appropriate option to fill in blank number 2.
(a) have (b) has (c) had (d) having
Ans. (d) 'Having' indicates the completion of an action before another.

81. Select the most appropriate option to fill in blank number 3.
(a) stuck (b) dirt (c) dusted (d) pursed
Ans. (d) 'Pursed' means to press lips together tightly.

82. Select the most appropriate option to fill in blank number 4.
(a) folded up (b) cleared up
(c) hid away (d) tucked away
Ans. (a) 'Folded up' indicates the action taken with the sheets of paper.

83. Select the most appropriate option to fill in blank number 5.
(a) across (b) at (c) in (d) by
Ans. (a) 'Across' indicates the direction of the sprawl on the paper.

PASSAGE-18

I have a recurring dream. Actually, I have a few: one is about dismembering a body, I'd rather not get into it, but the ………(1)……... pertinent one is about college. It's the end of the semester, and I suddenly ………(2)……... that there is a class I forgot to attend, ever, and now I have to sit for the final exam. I wake up panicked, my GPA in peril. How could I have done this? Why do I so ………(3)……... dissatisfy myself? Then I remember I haven't been in college in more than a decade. Someone with ………(4)……... knowledge of my academic career might point out that this nightmare scenario is not that far removed from my actual collegiate experience and that at certain times in my life, it did not take the magic of slumber to find me completely unprepared for a final. And, well, ………(5)……... of what may or may not be true of my personal scholastic rigour, I suspect the school stress dream is quite a common one. **SSC CGL Tier-1 17.09.2024 (Shift-I)**

84. Select the most appropriate option to fill in blank number 1.
(a) better (b) best
(c) strong (d) more
Ans. (d) 'More' emphasises greater pertinence.

85. Select the most appropriate option to fill in blank number 2.
(a) realise (b) praise
(c) offer (d) promise
Ans. (a) 'Realise' means to become aware of something.

86. Select the most appropriate option to fill in blank number 3.
(a) unpredictability (b) consistently
(c) conflictingly (d) clumsily
Ans. (b) 'Consistently' means always behaving the same way.

87. Select the most appropriate option to fill in blank number 4.
(a) instigate (b) distant
(c) remote (d) bleak
Ans. (c) 'Remote' means distant or unrelated.

88. Select the most appropriate option to fill in blank number 5.
(a) nevertheless (b) notwithstanding
(c) regardless (d) in as much
Ans. (c) 'Regardless' means without being affected by any other considerations.

PASSAGE-19

The adverse ………(1)……... of climate change and environmental degradation are increasingly driving human mobility the world over, particularly in countries with high exposure and low………(2)……... capacity. While most climate-related mobility currently occurs within countries, desperation and deteriorating environments can also compel people to seek a livelihood elsewhere through ………(3)……... migration. While climate change negatively impacts everyone, everywhere, those already in vulnerable situations due to geography, poverty, gender, age, disability, origin or other status, including migrant women who ………(4)……... climate-sensitive livelihoods and children who are less able to survive extreme weather events, are at the greatest risk of suffering harm. It is ………(5)……... to recognise this reality and take meaningful action to protect the human rights of those most affected by climate change, including migrants. **SSC CGL Tier-1 17.09.2024 (Shift-II)**

89. Select the most appropriate option to fill in blank number 1.
(a) renounce (b) affects
(c) effects (d) practice
Ans. (c) 'Effects' refer to the consequences of climate change.

90. Select the most appropriate option to fill in blank number 2.
(a) adaptive (b) adoptive
(c) minimum (d) affective
Ans. (a) 'Adaptive' means having the capacity to adjust to new conditions.

91. Select the most appropriate option to fill in blank number 3.
(a) regard (b) fast
(c) fixate (d) irregular

Ans. (d) 'Irregular' describes migration that is not regular or typical.

92. Select the most appropriate option to fill in blank number 4.
(a) depend from (b) depend at
(c) depend on (d) depend in

Ans. (c) 'Depend on' means to rely on something.

93. Select the most appropriate option to fill in blank number 5.
(a) optional (b) secondary
(c) resistant (d) imperative

Ans. (d) 'Imperative' means absolutely necessary or urgent.

PASSAGE-20

Rory Cooper was a top aide to former House Majority Leader Eric Cantor, the up-and-coming Virginia Republican who lost a 2014 House primary. He was also a prominent Never Trumper, openly ....(1).......... how awful he found the 45th president.

The cause Cooper has ....(2).......... himself to for the past year, though, is closer to home. He is, as he puts it in his Twitter bio, 'Apparently Mr. Open the Schools'.

A father of a fifth grader, a second grader and a kindergartner, Cooper is ....(3).......... because the public schools in Fairfax, Virginia, where he lives, have not reopened. Fairfax, in the Washington, DC, suburbs, is one of the school districts that has moved ....(4).......... toward in-person learning and it is still not close: only in the past few weeks have students started to return to classrooms and only about half of those eligible have opted to go back, for an ....(5).......... of two days a week. **SSC CGL Tier-1 17.09.2024 (Shift-III)**

94. Select the most appropriate option to fill in blank number 1.
(a) frisking (b) skipping
(c) detailing (d) ignoring

Ans. (c) 'Detailing' means describing something in detail.

95. Select the most appropriate option to fill in blank number 2.
(a) committed (b) pacified
(c) sorted (d) isolated

Ans. (a) 'Committed' means dedicated to a cause.

96. Select the most appropriate option to fill in blank number 3.
(a) indebted (b) provoked
(c) excited (d) frustrated

Ans. (d) 'Frustrated' means feeling upset or annoyed.

97. Select the most appropriate option to fill in blank number 4.
(a) plainest (b) slowest
(c) longest (d) strangest

Ans. (b) 'Slowest' indicates the pace of progress toward in-person learning.

98. Select the most appropriate option to fill in blank number 5.
(a) average (b) amount
(c) ideal (d) understanding

Ans. (a) 'Average' refers to the typical amount, in this case, days per week.

PASSAGE-21

The limbs of the flying squirrel are interlinked with a membrane. When the creature ....(1).......... into the air, the membrane opens and the squirrel seems to ....(2).......... swiftly downwards. This movement gives the ....(3).......... of flight. However, it is not flying really. It is a ....(4).......... in the air from a higher level. It is also noteworthy that a squirrel cannot ....(5).......... its direction while it is in flying mode. **SSC CGL Tier-1 18.09.2024 (Shift-I)**

99. Select the most appropriate option to fill in blank number 1.
(a) spring (b) cross
(c) hurdle (d) leaps

Ans. (d) 'Leaps' means to jump into the air.

100. Select the most appropriate option to fill in blank number 2.
(a) skate (b) skim (c) wheel (d) glide

Ans. (d) 'Glide' means to move smoothly and swiftly.

101. Select the most appropriate option to fill in blank number 3.
(a) affect (b) suspicion
(c) fancy (d) impression

Ans. (d) 'Impression' refers to the effect of appearing to fly.

102. Select the most appropriate option to fill in blank number 4.
(a) progress (b) motion
(c) sign (d) wave

Ans. (b) 'Motion' indicates movement in the air.

103. Select the most appropriate option to fill in blank number 5.
(a) adopt (b) replace (c) adept (d) swap

Ans. (d) 'Swap' means to change direction.

PASSAGE-22

This Diwali is more significant because we are going to celebrate it after three years, without the evil shadow of Covid-19 that ....(1).......... looming over all festivities. The lockdowns and endless bad news of death and ....(2).......... had turned our country into a zone of gloom. But, this season of Diwali ....(3)..........all the sorrows of people by lighting the candle of hope in their lives. We can see the lights, the candles, the lanterns and the busy people coming out of their houses and purchasing toys for their children. Let's ....(4).......... those people who have made such a huge contribution to ....(5).......... good thoughts and saving people's lives. **SSC CGL Tier-1 18.09.2024 (Shift-II)**

104. Select the most appropriate option to fill in blank number 1.
(a) is (b) were
(c) are (d) was

Ans. (d) 'Was' indicates the past continuous action of looming.

105. Select the most appropriate option to fill in blank number 2.
(a) economic boom (b) demonetisation
(c) disease (d) new birth

Ans. (c) 'Disease' refers to the health crisis caused by Covid-19.

106. Select the most appropriate option to fill in blank number 3.
(a) had recognised (b) has hovered
(c) has shed (d) has adopted

Ans. (c) 'Has shed' means to get rid of something.

107. Select the most appropriate option to fill in blank number 4.
(a) salute (b) berate
(c) terminate (d) onerous
Ans. (a) 'Salute' means to show respect.

108. Select the most appropriate option to fill in blank number 5.
(a) stagnating (b) impeding
(c) implicating (d) spreading
Ans. (d) 'Spreading' refers to the dissemination of good thoughts.

PASSAGE-23

According to a poll conducted in 2018–19 by an online internship and training platform, ...(1).......... number of businesses actively ....(2).......... intern profiles has increased over the previous five years. This study demonstrates that India received 80% more internship applications in 2018, with 2.2 million applications ....(3).......... 1.27 million in 2017.

The rise was influenced ....(4).......... part by an increase in the number of industries seeking fresh perspectives and innovativeideas to improve ....(5).......... on existing projects. Obtaining an internship prior to entering the job market, which was once viewed as a Western concept, is quickly gaining steam in Indian workplaces.

SSC CGL Tier-1 18.09.2024 (Shift-III)

109. Select the most appropriate option to fill in blank number 1.
(a) few (b) a (c) the (d) an
Ans. (c) 'The' specifies a particular number of businesses.

110. Select the most appropriate option to fill in blank number 2.
(a) seeking (b) neglecting
(c) declining (d) reducing
Ans. (a) 'Seeking' means looking for intern profiles.

111. Select the most appropriate option to fill in blank number 3.
(a) similar to (b) according to
(c) compared to (d) combine to
Ans. (c) 'Compared to' means to measure against another number.

112. Select the most appropriate option to fill in blank number 4.
(a) on (b) to (c) up (d) in
Ans. (d) 'In' indicates part of the influence.

113. Select the most appropriate option to fill in blank number 5.
(a) effecting (b) effortless
(c) efficiencies (d) efficient
Ans. (c) 'Efficiencies' refer to the improved effectiveness of projects.

PASSAGE-24

When Ojeya Cruz Banks moved to Ohio from New Zealand ....(1).......... years ago, she was overwhelmed by the logistics of uprooting her life. But Cruz Banks, a Denison University professor and a single mom, who is also my neighbour and friend, was ....(2).......... to find a house next to a public elementary school. She assumed that she would be able to walk to pick up her daughter, a needed convenience given that she didn't yet have a car. Unfortunately, when she went to register her daughter for kindergarten, she was met with an ....(3).......... surprise: The only ....(4).......... option was a half-day programme that would bus students to a day-care centre on the outskirts of the town for the afternoon. The district did offer a limited number of full-day slots, but those had all been claimed in a lottery earlier that spring and came with a tuition cost. "I was like, 'Cost me? What? Public school costs money here?'" she told me. Many parents across the United States, like Cruz Banks, may assume that free, full-day kindergarten is a ....(5).......... part of the country's public education system. I was one of them, until my youngest had to enter our district's lottery several months ago. When he was assigned to the half-day programme, I swung between alarm and frustration.

SSC CGL Tier-1 19.09.2024 (Shift-I)

114. Select the most appropriate option to fill in blank number 1.
(a) several (b) particular
(c) enormous (d) immense
Ans. (a) 'Several' refers to a number more than two.

115. Select the most appropriate option to fill in blank number 2.
(a) distraught (b) dispassionate
(c) relieved (d) worried
Ans. (c) 'Relieved' means feeling reassured.

116. Select the most appropriate option to fill in blank number 3.
(a) agreeable (b) unpleasant
(c) amusing (d) enjoyable
Ans. (b) 'Unpleasant' describes the surprise encountered.

117. Select the most appropriate option to fill in blank number 4.
(a) futile (b) available
(c) nonviable (d) inaccessible
Ans. (b) 'Available' refers to the option that exists.

118. Select the most appropriate option to fill in blank number 5.
(a) disapproved (b) ceaseless
(c) inessential (d) required
Ans. (d) 'Required' means necessary or essential.

PASSAGE-25

Recently, the ....(1).......... of heart-attacks in young Indians ....(2).......... increased tremendously. Doctors are surprised to note that young men and women with seemingly healthy lifestyle are suffering deadly heart attacks. ....(3).......... diet and exercise play a ....(4).......... role in a person's overall wellbeing, mental health is also a valuable factor. The ....(5).......... urban lifestyle is causing anxiety and depression in young Indians which may be a major factor behind the increased numbers.

SSC CGL Tier-1 19.09.2024 (Shift-III)

119. Select the most appropriate option to fill in blank number 1.
(a) amount (b) number
(c) percent (d) height
Ans. (b) 'Number' quantifies heart attacks.

120. Select the most appropriate option to fill in blank number 2.
(a) have been (b) had
(c) has (d) have
Ans. (c) 'Has' indicates an increase in heart attacks.

121. Select the most appropriate option to fill in blank number 3.
(a) Since (b) Although
(c) In spite of (d) However
Ans. (b) 'Although' introduces a contrasting idea.

122. Select the most appropriate option to fill in blank number 4.
(a) historic (b) epic
(c) monumental (d) increased
Ans. (c) 'Monumental' means very important or significant.

123. Select the most appropriate option to fill in blank number 5.
(a) fast-paced (b) cosmic
(c) rapidly (d) wilderness
Ans. (a) 'Fast-paced' describes the rapid urban lifestyle.

PASSAGE-26

Augmented reality and virtual reality are two types of reality technologies that either augment or replace a real-world environment with a ....(1).......... one. In augmented reality, a virtual environment coexists ....(2).......... the actual world, to be instructive and offer more data about the real world that a user can access without having to search. When a handset is pointed at a piece of malfunctioning ....(3).........., for example, industrial AR apps might provide rapid troubleshooting information. Virtual reality is a ....(4).......... environmental simulation that completely replaces the user's surroundings with a totally virtual world. For example, VR may provide a user with a box containing a cartoon ....(5).......... of Mike Tyson in a virtual boxing ring. SSC CGL Tier-1 23.09.2024 (Shift-I)

124. Select the most appropriate option to fill in blank number 1.
(a) simulated (b) catered
(c) revealed (d) suffocated
Ans. (a) 'Simulated' means created as a model.

125. Select the most appropriate option to fill in blank number 2.
(a) with (b) behind
(c) along (d) beyond
Ans. (a) 'With' indicates coexisting environments.

126. Select the most appropriate option to fill in blank number 3.
(a) equipment (b) arsenal
(c) outfit (d) baggage
Ans. (a) 'Equipment' refers to the machinery.

127. Select the most appropriate option to fill in blank number 4.
(a) comprehensive (b) conclusive
(c) transgressive (d) reprehensive
Ans. (a) 'Comprehensive' means complete and detailed.

128. Select the most appropriate option to fill in blank number 5.
(a) glossary (b) network
(c) rendition (d) resistance
Ans. (c) 'Rendition' refers to a performance or depiction.

PASSAGE-27

Culture is ....(1).........., understanding and protecting, like the cultivation of a garden, not the destruction or eradication of its roots. Understanding the roots and seeds, taking much care and providing instructed nourishment ....(2).......... important for good gardening. Culture also is similar; understanding its acquaintance ....(3).......... literature and art and careful protection are required. Culture is the way of life of a particular society in which a group of people live together in one place. The society's culture is visible in its literature, arts, social system, language and religion. It is a combination of traditions, customs, institutions, food habits, manners, morals, thoughts, tastes, views and beliefs. Usually, families ....(4).......... culture to the younger generations. As family system is becoming weak, schools, colleges and universities should take up this responsibility as education should promote potential values of its culture. The role of universities ....(5).......... only to issue course completed certificates. SSC CGL Tier-1 23.09.2024 (Shift-II)

129. Select the most appropriate option to fill in blank number 1.
(a) creation (b) to create
(c) create (d) creating
Ans. (d) 'Creating' refers to the act of nurturing and protecting culture.

130. Select the most appropriate option to fill in blank number 2.
(a) is (b) were (c) was (d) are
Ans. (d) 'Are' indicates a plural subject requiring careful nourishment.

131. Select the most appropriate option to fill in blank number 3.
(a) for (b) on (c) with (d) in
Ans. (c) 'With' refers to the acquaintance of culture with literature and art.

132. Select the most appropriate option to fill in blank number 4.
(a) transmitting (b) transmitted
(c) transmit (d) transmits
Ans. (c) 'Transmit' means passing culture to younger generations.

133. Select the most appropriate option to fill in blank number 5.
(a) should be restricted (b) restrict
(c) should restricted (d) should not be restricted
Ans. (d) 'Should not be restricted' suggests universities have broader roles.

PASSAGE-28

Music is perhaps the most popular and widely practiced ....(1).......... of fine arts, transcending all kinds of cultural and linguistic barriers. Any form of fine art is ....(2).......... to master and almost impossible to perfect, and music is no exception. Nature, it is learnt, has blessed almost two-thirds of the human race with musical ability of some sort. Music has the power to ....(3).......... out the deepest emotions. In fact, it is a magic medicine and many seek refuge in it when they are depressed or stressed. It is this intimacy that makes us listen to music ....(4).......... even hum or sing sometimes. This singing, or realistically speaking, expressing one's emotion musically sometimes takes a serious turn.

The desire to sing before an audience is innocent and beautiful, and indeed, it is perfectly alright to have such a genuine desire. But it is also important to understand that singing is an ....(5).......... art — a highly refined one at that, which requires systematic, prolonged and strict training to be acceptable. SSC CGL Tier-1 23.09.2024 (Shift-III)

134. Choose the most appropriate option to fill in blank number 1.
(a) format (b) substance (c) form (d) design
Ans. (c) 'Form' refers to the type of fine art that music is.

135. Choose the most appropriate option to fill in blank number 2.
(a) difficult (b) irksome (c) serious (d) easy
Ans. (a) 'Difficult' indicates the challenge in mastering music.

136. Choose the most appropriate option to fill in blank number 3.
(a) bring (b) catalyse
(c) yield (d) effect
Ans. (a) 'Bring' means to elicit or evoke emotions.

137. Choose the most appropriate option to fill in blank number 4.
(a) or (b) neither (c) nor (d) either
Ans. (a) 'Or' indicates an alternative action.

138. Choose the most appropriate option to fill in blank number 5.
(a) uncomplicated (b) uniform
(c) mixed (d) intricate
Ans. (d) 'Intricate' describes music as a complex and refined art.

PASSAGE-29

The Human Development Index (HDI) is a summary ....(1).......... of average accomplishment in important areas of human development, ...(2).......... living a long and healthy life, being informed and having a good quality of living. The HDI is the geometric mean of the normalized ....(3).......... for each dimension. The health component is ....(4).......... by life expectancy at birth, while the education dimension is measured by the average number of years of schooling for individuals aged 25 and above, as well as the ....(5).......... number of years of schooling for school-age children. **SSC CGL Tier-1 24.09.2024 (Shift-I)**

139. Select the most appropriate option to fill in blank number 1.
(a) regiment (b) assessment
(c) involvement (d) collect
Ans. (b) 'Assessment' refers to the evaluation of human development.

140. Select the most appropriate option to fill in blank number 2.
(a) segregating (b) exaggerating
(c) including (d) manifesting
Ans. (c) 'Including' means incorporating various aspects.

141. Select the most appropriate option to fill in blank number 3.
(a) features (b) contents
(c) indices (d) glimpses
Ans. (c) 'Indices' are measurements used in the HDI.

142. Select the most appropriate option to fill in blank number 4.
(a) levitated (b) escaped
(c) triggered (d) measured
Ans. (d) 'Measured' refers to how the health component is assessed.

143. Select the most appropriate option to fill in blank number 5.
(a) accompanied (b) hypnotised
(c) predicted (d) neglected
Ans. (c) 'Predicted' indicates anticipated years of schooling.

PASSAGE-30

The mathematician Federico Ardila-Mantilla grew up in Colombia, an ....(1).......... student but gifted in math. He was failing most of his classes at his high school in Bogota when someone ....(2).......... him to apply to MIT. He had not heard of the school. To his surprise, he got in, and he went on scholarship. Mathematically, he did well. One of his professors, an acid-tongued theoretician known to ....(3).......... his audience to a herd of cows, routinely tucked 'open' math problems into homework assignments, withouttelling the students.

These had never been solved by anyone. Ardila solved one. He went on to receive his bachelor's and Ph.D. in math from MIT.

But his academic experience was also one of isolation. Part of it had to do with his own ....(4).......... . Part of it was cultural. As a Latino, he was very much in the minority in the department, and he did not feel comfortable in American mathematical spaces.

No one had tried to explicitly ....(5).......... him, yet he felt alone. In math, collaborating with others opens up new kinds of learning and thinking. But in his nine years at MIT, Ardila worked with others only twice. **SSC CGL Tier-1 24.09.2024 (Shift-II)**

144. Select the most appropriate option to fill in blank number 1.
(a) apprehensive (b) apologetic
(c) indifferent (d) excellent
Ans. (c) 'Indifferent' means uninterested or unmotivated.

145. Select the most appropriate option to fill in blank number 2.
(a) dissuaded (b) suggested
(c) removed (d) dispirited
Ans. (b) 'Suggested' means advised to apply to MIT.

146. Select the most appropriate option to fill in blank number 3.
(a) compare (b) malign
(c) strangulate (d) differentiate
Ans. (a) 'Compare' refers to likening the audience to a herd of cows.

147. Select the most appropriate option to fill in blank number 4.
(a) introversion (b) molestation
(c) quantification (d) interrogation
Ans. (a) 'Introversion' means a tendency to be inwardly focused.

148. Select the most appropriate option to fill in blank number 5.
(a) exclude (b) fabricate
(c) incorporate (d) stratify
Ans. (a) 'Exclude' means to leave someone out.

PASSAGE-31

A dance which is created or choreographed and performed according ....(1).......... the tenets of the Natya Shastra is called a classical dance. The two broad ....(2).......... of classical dancing are the tandava and the lasya. Power and force are typical of the tandava; grace and delicacy of the lasya. Tandava is ....(3).......... with Shiva and lasya with Parvati.

Dance which is pure movement is called Nritta and dance which is ....(4).......... in nature is called nritya. A dancer, in the classical tradition, has to have years of training before he or she can begin to perform on the stage. The four main ....(5).......... of classical dancing in India are: Bharatanatyam, Kathakali, Manipuri, Kathak. Bharatanatyam is the oldest and most popular dance-form of India.

SSC CGL Tier-1 24.09.2024 (Shift-II)

149. Select the most appropriate option to fill in blank number 1.
(a) to (b) for
(c) of (d) with

Ans. (a) 'To' indicates following the tenets of the Natya Shastra.

150. Select the most appropriate option to fill in blank number 2.
(a) criteria (b) options
(c) display (d) aspects

Ans. (d) 'Aspects' refers to different elements of classical dancing.

151. Select the most appropriate option to fill in blank number 3.
(a) renovate (b) informed
(c) flourished (d) associated

Ans. (d) 'Associated' means connected with Shiva and Parvati.

152. Select the most appropriate option to fill in blank number 4.
(a) vegetative (b) commodious
(c) haphazard (d) interpretative

Ans. (d) 'Interpretative' refers to dance that conveys meaning.

153. Select the most appropriate option to fill in blank number 5.
(a) terminologies (b) schools
(c) characters (d) functions

Ans. (b) 'Schools' refers to different styles of classical dance.

PASSAGE-32

Listening starts with hearing but goes ....(1).......... . Hearing, in other words, is necessary, but is not a sufficient ....(2).......... for listening. Listening involves hearing with attention. Listening is a process that ....(3).......... concentration. While listening, one should also be observant. In other words, listening has to do with the ears ....(4).......... with the eyes and the mind. Listening is to be understood as the total process that involves hearing with attention, being observant and making interpretations. Good communication is essentially a/an ....(5)........ process.

SSC CGL Tier-1 24.09.2024 (Shift-III)

154. Select the most appropriate option to fill in blank number 1.
(a) towards (b) across
(c) beyond (d) throughout

Ans. (c) 'Beyond' means going further than just hearing.

155. Select the most appropriate option to fill in blank number 2.
(a) place (b) decorum
(c) condition (d) scenario

Ans. (c) 'Condition' refers to a necessary requirement for listening.

156. Select the most appropriate option to fill in blank number 3.
(a) calls for (b) disposes of
(c) takes for (d) brings up

Ans. (a) 'Calls for' means requires concentration.

157. Select the most appropriate option to fill in blank number 4.
(a) although (b) rather
(c) as well as (d) yet

Ans. (c) 'As well as' means in addition to the ears, using the eyes and mind.

158. Select the most appropriate option to fill in blank number 5.
(a) onerous (b) obnoxious
(c) interactive (d) pecuniary

Ans. (c) 'Interactive' means involving active participation in communication.

PASSAGE-33

The Kuno Palpur National Park, located in Madhya Pradesh's Chambal ....(1).......... , has an area of 750 square kilometres. It now has leopards, jackals, spotted deer, sambhar, neelgai, chinkara, wild boar, and four-horned antelope, making it a perfect ....(2).......... base for felids. Despite strong objections from Gujarat, which ....(3).......... that lions were part of the state's heritage, that MP had a poor ....(4).......... in wildlife management and that Kuno Palpur had other big cat species that would ....(5).......... lion relocation, the sanctuary was chosen for the lion reintroduction project in 2013.

SSC CGL Tier-1 25.09.2024 (Shift-I)

159. Select the most appropriate option to fill in blank number 1.
(a) reason (b) region (c) reign (d) river

Ans. (b)
'Region' refers to the area in Madhya Pradesh.

160. Select the most appropriate option to fill in blank number 2.
(a) guard (b) fun (c) aid (d) prey

Ans. (d)
'Prey' base means suitable for predators like felids.

161. Select the most appropriate option to fill in blank number 3.
(a) restricted (b) accused
(c) claimed (d) adjourned

Ans. (c)
'Claimed' means argued or asserted by Gujarat.

162. Select the most appropriate option to fill in blank number 4.
(a) summary (b) gaze (c) record (d) loss

Ans. (c)
'Record' refers to past performance in wildlife management.

163. Select the most appropriate option to fill in blank number 5.
(a) Innocuous (b) Jeopardise
(c) channelise (d) safeguard

Ans. (b) 'Jeopardise' means put at risk or endanger.

PASSAGE-34

We naturally seek the company of those whose ....(1).......... are the same as our own. Fools do not like the ....(2).......... of wise men and wise men avoid fools. Serious-minded people do not find much in common with ....(3).......... folk and vice versa. Sinners feel uncomfortable with ....(4).......... and do not seek their company. We can, therefore, as a rule, judge a man's ....(5).......... by the company he keeps.

SSC CGL Tier-1 25.09.2024 (Shift-II)

164. Select the most appropriate option to fill in blank number 1.
(a) organisations (b) institutes
(c) apathy (d) tastes
Ans. (d) 'Tastes' refers to preferences or likes.

165. Select the most appropriate option to fill in blank number 2.
(a) company (b) culture
(c) serious (d) antagonist
Ans. (a) 'Company' refers to the presence of others.

166. Select the most appropriate option to fill in blank number 3.
(a) solemn (b) thoughtful
(c) grave (d) frivolous
Ans. (d) 'Frivolous' means carefree or not serious.

167. Select the most appropriate option to fill in blank number 4.
(a) knave (b) rowdy
(c) saints (d) commoners
Ans. (c) 'Saints' refers to holy or virtuous people.

168. Select the most appropriate option to fill in blank number 5.
(a) futurities (b) character
(c) heirloom (d) legacy
Ans. (b) 'Character' means moral qualities or reputation.

PASSAGE-35

The rise in global temperature ....(1).......... already occurred is leading to extreme weather events that bring ....(2).......... heat waves and droughts, devastating floods and increasingly powerful hurricanes and tropical storms. The combination of these factors met the impact on human health is increasing and is ....(3).......... accelerate. But there is room for hope, particularly if governments take action now to ....(4).......... the pledges made at Glasgow in November 2021 and to go further in resolving the climate crisis.

Who is ....(5).......... governments to lead a just, equitable, and fast phase out of fossil fuels and transition to a clean energy future. **SSC CGL Tier-1 25.09.2024 (Shift-III)**

169. Select the most appropriate option to fill in blank number 1.
(a) which had (b) that is
(c) which have (d) that has
Ans. (d) 'That has' refers to the rise in global temperature.

170. Select the most appropriate option to fill in blank number 2.
(a) intense (b) mild (c) maximise (d) minor
Ans. (a) 'Intense' means extreme or severe.

171. Select the most appropriate option to fill in blank number 3.
(a) rarely to (b) likely to
(c) barely to (d) hardly to
Ans. (b) 'Likely to' means probable or expected.

172. Select the most appropriate option to fill in blank number 4.
(a) honour (b) take
(c) watch (d) keep
Ans. (a) 'Honour' means to fulfill or respect pledges.

173. Select the most appropriate option to fill in blank number 5.
(a) calling at (b) calling on
(c) calling for (d) calling from
Ans. (b) 'Calling on' means urging or appealing to governments.

PASSAGE-36

2022 sees us entering a third year of the pandemic and the harm ....(1).......... children is increasingly evident : A record rise in child poverty. Setbacks to progress on ....(2).......... vaccinations. Disruption to education for entire generation.

That harm ....(3).......... as an unintended side effect of the world's efforts to manage the crisis. COVID has been a uniquely dis-equalising crisis. Lopsided ....(4).......... vaccines aside, learning losses have been greatest among poorest children and job losses have been disproportionately borne by women and youth. What next for the world's children in the year ahead? As in the past two years, prospects for children will continue to hinge ....(5).......... on the pandemic and how it is managed. **SSC CGL Tier-1 26.09.2024 (Shift-II)**

174. Select the most appropriate option to fill in blank number 1.
(a) did to (b) done to
(c) does to (d) seems to
Ans. (b) 'Done to' refers to the impact on children.

175. Select the most appropriate option to fill in blank number 2.
(a) different (b) irregular
(c) routine (d) similar
Ans. (c) 'Routine' refers to regular or standard vaccinations.

176. Select the most appropriate option to fill in blank number 3.
(a) had emerged (b) has emerged
(c) have emerged (d) was emerged
Ans. (b) 'Has emerged' means has come into view or become apparent.

177. Select the most appropriate option to fill in blank number 4.
(a) keeps to (b) access to
(c) seems to (d) assess to
Ans. (b) 'Access to' means the ability to obtain or make use of vaccines.

178. Select the most appropriate option to fill in blank number 5.
(a) almost (b) minor (c) foremost (d) most
Ans. (c) 'Foremost' means most important or primary.

PASSAGE-37

Social media companies ....(1).......... claim that they promote democracy and are dedicated to the empowerment of ordinary individuals. The assertion ....(2).......... entirely unfounded. Recent history shows how ....(3).......... citizens have been mobilised against totalitarian regimes on social networking sites. Starting from MeToo to Black Lives Matter, digital networks ....(4).......... indispensable in bringing together critical voices against social and political (5)......... . **SSC CGL Tier-1 26.09.2024 (Shift-II)**

179. Select the most appropriate option to fill in blank number 1.
(a) frequently (b) seldom
(c) never (d) don't
Ans. (a) 'Frequently' means often or commonly.

180. Select the most appropriate option to fill in blank number 2.
(a) cannot (b) should
(c) shall (d) may not be
Ans. (d) 'May not be' means possibly not being.

181. Select the most appropriate option to fill in blank number 3.
(a) alien (b) common (c) neutral (d) foreign
Ans. (b) 'Common' means usual or widespread.

182. Select the most appropriate option to fill in blank number 4.
(a) can (b) were (c) that (d) have been
Ans. (d) 'Have been' means ongoing or continuous.

183. Select the most appropriate option to fill in blank number 5.
(a) election (b) democracy
(c) injustice (d) justice
Ans. (c) 'Injustice' refers to unfair treatment or wrongs.

SSC CGL 2023 (Tier 1 & 2)

PASSAGE-38

Human life is ....(1).......... a unique blessing, which in turn depends on the ....(2).......... of the self. He who is not aware of the self can neither have peace nor can he foster peaceful coexistence. We have to link our soul with God and body with the physical world for substance. ....(3).......... the formless God is invisible to the naked eye, our mind often wanders wherever it goes. ....(4).........., we are unable to develop any love for the divine. And religion like the white light of heavens ....(5).......... multi-coloured fragmentations by the prisms of men and loses its gravity. Instead of uniting, it becomes a major dividing force. French philosopher Teilhard de Chardin, thinking deeply on meaning of our existence and relationship with the divine, expounds, "we are not human beings having a spiritual experience".

SSC CGL Tier-1 14.07.2023 (Shift-I)

184. Select the most appropriate option to fill in blank number 1.
(a) considering (b) to consider
(c) considered (d) consider
Ans. (c) 'Considered' means regarded as.

185. Select the most appropriate option to fill in blank number 2.
(a) witness (b) known
(c) awareness (d) aware
Ans. (c) 'Awareness' refers to knowledge or perception.

186. Select the most appropriate option to fill in blank number 3.
(a) Since (b) From (c) As per (d) For
Ans. (a) 'Since' means because or due to.

187. Select the most appropriate option to fill in blank number 4.
(a) As a result (b) As a reaction
(c) Causing (d) As a reason
Ans. (a) 'As a result' means consequently.

188. Select the most appropriate option to fill in blank number 5.
(a) break into (b) breaks to
(c) break from (d) breaks into
Ans. (d) 'Breaks into' means divides into parts.

PASSAGE-39

Learning a new language can be challenging, but it's also ......(1) .... It can open up new opportunities for communication and cultural exchange. When learning a new language, Its important to be patient and ....(2).......... yourself time to progress. One way to make language learning easier is to .... (3)......... to it everyday, even if it's just for a few minutes. This helps in building consistency and reinforces what you're learning. Practising speaking and listening is also important, not just reading and writing. By immersing yourself in the language and culture, you can accelerate your .... (4) .... and gain a deeper understanding of the language. Learning a new language is not only practical, but it's also ...... (5) ...... and can be a fun experience.

SSC CGL Tier-1 14.07.2023 (Shift-IV)

189. Select the most appropriate option to fill in blank number 1.
(a) insignificant (b) rewarding
(c) pointless (d) customising
Ans. (b) 'Rewarding' means providing satisfaction.

190. Select the most appropriate option to fill in blank number 2.
(a) give (b) neglect
(c) rush (d) force
Ans. (a) 'Give' means to allow oneself time.

191. Select the most appropriate option to fill in blank number 3.
(a) hesitate (b) commit
(c) forget (d) procrastinate
Ans. (b) 'Commit' means to dedicate oneself to something.

192. Select the most appropriate option to fill in blank number 4.
(a) pitch (b) complacency
(c) progress (d) stamina
Ans. (c) 'Progress' means advancement in learning.

193. Select the most appropriate option to fill in blank number 5.
(a) daunting (b) arduous
(c) intimidating (d) enjoyable
Ans. (d) 'Enjoyable' means pleasant and fun.

PASSAGE-40

Ambition is a vital ingredient for success. Without ambition to push us, we will not be ....(1).......... of great achievements. We all need that special something ....(2)......... ourselves to give us the willpower to reach a higher goal ....(3)......... we imagine ourselves capable ......(4)....... Yet, ambition, ...(5).......... money and fire, is a good servant, but a bad master. **SSC CGL Tier-1 17.07.2023 (Shift-II)**

194. Select the most appropriate option to fill in blank number 1.
(a) able (b) capable
(c) durable (d) curable
Ans. (b) 'Capable' means having the ability to achieve.

195. Select the most appropriate option to fill in blank number 2.
(a) in (b) with
(c) without (d) within
Ans. (d) 'Within' means inside oneself.

196. Select the most appropriate option to fill in blank number 3.
(a) then (b) than
(c) that (d) what
Ans. (b) Than' is used to introduce a comparison.

197. Select the most appropriate option to fill in blank number 4.
(a) about (b) off (c) of (d) on
Ans. (c) 'Of' indicates possession or belonging.

198. Select the most appropriate option to fill in blank number 5.
(a) as (b) like
(c) such (d) similarly
Ans. (b) 'Like' is used to indicate similarity.

PASSAGE-41

All state universities and colleges in Uttar Pradesh, one of the ……(1)…… in India, will now ………(2)……… a 'save water' ritual named 'Jal Bharo' in place of 'lamp lighting' to inaugurate their annual convocation. The Governor of the state, who is also chancellor of state universities, instructed that every university and college in the state should install rainwater harvesting plants on its campus.

'Jal Bharo' signifies ………(3)……… the vision of 'Jal Shakti'. This ceremony symbolises the ………(4)……… importance of water conservation, whereas the lamp lighting ceremony symbolised removing darkness through education and spreading the light of learning. It is really a ………(5)……… initiative. Every educational institute in India should ensure to save and recharge groundwater by installing rainwater harvesting plants. These kinds of initiatives provide awareness of using and saving water, the elixir of life.

SSC CGL Tier-1 18.07.2023 (Shift-I)

199. Select the most appropriate option to fill in blank number 1.
(a) more big states (b) big state
(c) biggest states (d) bigger state
Ans. (c) 'Biggest states' refers to one of the largest states in India.

200. Select the most appropriate option to fill in blank number 2.
(a) organise (b) organising
(c) have managed (d) managing
Ans. (a) 'Organise' means to arrange or coordinate.

201. Select the most appropriate option to fill in blank number 3.
(a) holding (b) proceeding
(c) moving (d) strengthening
Ans. (d) 'Strengthening' means to make stronger or reinforce.

202. Select the most appropriate option to fill in blank number 4.
(a) sheer (b) complete (c) immense (d) total
Ans. (c) 'Immense' means vast or great in size.

203. Select the most appropriate option to fill in blank number 5.
(a) laudable (b) louder
(c) labelled (d) lower
Ans. (a) 'Laudable' means worthy of praise.

PASSAGE-42

We need the energy to move and we ……(1)….. on oil for it. Without it, our jobs, our free time and our mobility ………(2)…….. all be very different. Everyday we ……(3)……. 70 million barrels of oil. Every year we consume 2,200 million tonnes of coal and 2,500 billion cubic metres of gas. It's a long story! Total ……(4)…….. in 1924 and for many years it was a French state oil company.

In 1999, Total joined Petrofina, the Belgian oil and gas company and in 2000, Total ……(5)…… with its main French competitor, Elf Aquitaine and the name became Total Fina Elf. Now it's called Total again and it's France's biggest company.

SSC CGL Tier-1 19.07.2023 (Shift-III)

204. Select the most appropriate option to fill in blank number 1.
(a) hang (b) turn
(c) settle (d) depend
Ans. (d) 'Depend' means to rely on oil for energy.

205. Select the most appropriate option to fill in blank number 2.
(a) can (b) shall
(c) could (d) will
Ans. (b) 'Shall' indicates a strong possibility.

206. Select the most appropriate option to fill in blank number 3.
(a) consume (b) devour
(c) take (d) absorb
Ans. (a) 'Consume' means to use up or eat.

207. Select the most appropriate option to fill in blank number 4.
(a) had founded (b) was founded
(c) founded (d) were founded
Ans. (b) 'Was founded' refers to the establishment of total in the past.

208. Select the most appropriate option to fill in blank number 5.
(a) merged (b) combine
(c) join (d) incorporate
Ans. (a) 'Merged' means combined with another company.

PASSAGE-43

Fountains are used today to decorate city parks and squares; to honour individuals or events; for recreation ………(1)………. for entertainment. A splash pad or spray pool allows city residents to enter, get wet and cool off in summer. The musical fountain ………(2)………. moving jets of water coloured lights and recorded music, controlled by a computer, for dramatic effects. Fountains can ………(3)………. also be musical instruments played ………(4)………. obstruction of one or more of their water jets. Drinking fountains provide fresh ………(5)………. in public buildings, parks and public spaces.

SSC CGL Tier-1 20.07.2023 (Shift-IV)

209. Select the most appropriate option to fill in blank number 1.
(a) because (b) nor
(c) and (d) yet
Ans. (c) 'And' is used to add another item in the list.

210. Select the most appropriate option to fill in blank number 2.
(a) be combined (b) combine
(c) combines (d) combined
Ans. (c) 'Combines' is a singular verb that agrees with the subject 'musical fountain.'
As per the rules of subject-verb arrangement, single subject 'musical fountain' will take a singular verb 'combines'.

211. Select the most appropriate option to fill in blank number 3.
(a) itself (b) themselves
(c) herself (d) himself
Ans. (b) The word 'fountains' is plural and would take an appropriate plural pronoun (themselves).

212. Select the most appropriate option to fill in blank number 4.
(a) with (b) by
(c) off (d) on
Ans. (b) 'By' indicates the means by which something is done.

213. Select the most appropriate option to fill in blank number 5.
(a) flow of money (b) melodious music
(c) positive thought (d) drinking water
Ans. (d) 'Drinking water' refers to fresh water provided by drinking fountains.

PASSAGE-44

Social media can have ......(1)......... effects on mental health, with studies suggesting that excessive use can lead to feelings of anxiety, depression and loneliness.

To combat these negative effects, experts recommend setting ....(2)........ for social media use.

Other strategies include ......(3)........ with friends and family in person, engaging in hobbies or physical activity and seeking professional ......(4)......... if necessary. As such it's important to be ....(5)........ of its potential drawbacks and take steps to use it in a healthy and balanced way.

SSC CGL Tier-1 24.07.2023 (Shift-I)

214. Select the most appropriate option to fill in blank number 1.
(a) delirious (b) desirous
(c) detrimental (d) positive
Ans. (c) 'Detrimental' means harmful or damaging.

215. Select the most appropriate option to fill in blank number 2.
(a) principles (b) goals
(c) rules (d) standards
Ans. (c) 'Rules' means guidelines or principles.

216. Select the most appropriate option to fill in blank number 3.
(a) cooperating (b) involving
(c) entrusting (d) interacting
Ans. (d) 'Interacting' means engaging with others.

217. Select the most appropriate option to fill in blank number 4.
(a) concern (b) advise
(c) information (d) guidance
Ans. (d) 'Guidance' means advice or help.

218. Select the most appropriate option to fill in blank number 5.
(a) indifferent (b) cognizant
(c) sceptical (d) ignorant
Ans. (b) 'Cognizant' means aware or knowledgeable.

SSC CGL 2022 (Tier 1 & 2)

PASSAGE -45

How should one read a story to a child? usually a personality or character of the story ......(1)...... the child interest the most. ...(2)... use different voice ......(3)...... each character or act out various ......(4)...... from the story, to bring life to those characters. ......(5)...... out parts from the story will make story sessions fun and memorable for the kids.

SSC CGL Tier-1 11.04.2022 (Shift-III)

219. Select the most appropriate option to fill in the blank number 1.
(a) caught (b) catch
(c) catches (d) has caught
Ans. (c) 'Catches' means to attract or hold, fitting the context of what interests the child most in a story.

220. Select the most appropriate option to fill in the blank number 2.
(a) Either (b) So
(c) Also (d) However
Ans. (a) 'Either' introduces an alternative, fitting the context of using different voices or acting out characters.

221. Select the most appropriate option to fill in the blank number 3.
(a) for (b) by (c) with (d) from
Ans. (a) 'For' indicates the purpose, fitting the context of using different voices for each character.

222. Select the most appropriate option to fill in the blank number 4.
(a) pages (b) sheets (c) parts (d) words
Ans. (c) 'Parts' refers to different sections, fitting the context of acting out parts from the story.

223. Select the most appropriate option to fill in the blank number 5.
(a) saying (b) acting (c) telling (d) asking
Ans. (b) 'Acting' means to perform or play a role, fitting the context of making story sessions fun and memorable.

PASSAGE-46

An old man lived in the village. He was one of the ......(1)...... unfortunate people in the world. The whose village was tired ......(2)...... him; he was always gloomy, he ......(3)...... complained and was always in a bad mood. The ......(4)...... he lived, the more vile he was becoming and the more ......(5)...... were his words. SSC CGL Tier-1 12.04.2022 (Shift-I)

224. Select the most appropriate option to fill in the blank number 1.
(a) maximum (b) utmost
(c) most (d) main
Ans. (c) 'Most' indicates the highest degree, fitting the context of being the most unfortunate person.

225. Select the most appropriate option to fill in the blank number 2.
(a) from (b) of (c) by (d) at
Ans. (b) 'Of' indicates belonging, fitting the context of the village being tired of him.

226. Select the most appropriate option to fill in the blank number 3.
(a) mostly (b) commonly
(c) cyclically (d) constantly
Ans. (d) 'Constantly' means continuously, fitting the context of always complaining.

227. Select the most appropriate option to fill in the blank number 4.
(a) long (b) lengthy (c) longer (d) longest
Ans. (c) 'Longer' indicates more time, fitting the context of the longer he lived.

228. Select the most appropriate option to fill in the blank number 5.
(a) fatal (b) mortal (c) poisonous (d) toxic
Ans. (d) 'Toxic' means harmful, fitting the context of his words becoming more harmful.

PASSAGE-47

The modern-day student is extremely ……(1)........ with technology. They do read quite a bit because of social media. While their writing skills may not be top-notch, they do write, courtesy ……(2)........ affinity to various platforms on the internet. However, one skill that has been ……(3)........ affected is listening skills. They are extremely poor ……(4)........ listeners. If this issue is not addressed, what we may be heading to in the future is a huge chunk of people across the globe, with poor skills of listening, and a huge number of passive listeners. Researchers say that listening is the prime ingredient for empathy and the world will be in extreme poverty in terms of number of ……(5)........ on the planet. **SSC CGL Tier-1 01.12.2022 (Shift-II)**

229. Select the most appropriate option to fill in blank number 1.
(a) hindered (b) disconnected
(c) dreary (d) savvy

Ans. (d) 'Savvy' means knowledgeable or proficient, fitting the context of being extremely familiar with technology.

230. Select the most appropriate option to fill in blank number 2.
(a) their (b) they're (c) dare (d) there

Ans. (a) 'Their' is a possessive pronoun, fitting the context of their affinity to various platforms.

231. Select the most appropriate option to fill in blank number 3.
(a) thoroughly (b) through
(c) holistically (d) daily

Ans. (a) 'Thoroughly' means completely, fitting the context of listening skills being thoroughly affected.

232. Select the most appropriate option to fill in blank number 4.
(a) passive (b) active
(c) distinctive (d) demonstrative

Ans. (b) 'Active' means fully engaged, fitting the context of being poor active listeners.

233. Select the most appropriate option to fill in blank number 5.
(a) sympathisers (b) empathisers
(c) donors (d) characters

Ans. (b) 'Empathisers' means those who understand and share the feelings of others, fitting the context of a lack of empathy.

PASSAGE-48

In ancient times, Hieun Tsang, a Chinese traveller came to India during the .... ………(1)………. of King Harsha. He praised the India .... (2) ……… 'people with pure moral principles'. In 2014, India .... ………(3)………. 85th in the corruption perception index of the Transparency International. What .... (4)...... downfall! Isn't it ironical that we India .... (5) ……… by the ideals of honesty and integrity, self-denial and .... (6) ……… but in practice willingly resort to the .... (7) ……… forms of corruption to promote our interests? The .... (8) ……… of corruption is eating into the .... (9) ……… of our society and we have become helpless .... (10) ……… of our own degradation.

SSC CGL Tier-2 29.01.2022

234. Select the most appropriate option to fill in blank number 1.
(a) authority (b) reign
(c) command (d) vigour

Ans. (b)
'Reign' means the period during which a sovereign rules, fitting the context of Hieun Tsang coming to India during the reign of King Harsha.

235. Select the most appropriate option to fill in blank number 2.
(a) as (b) by (c) like (d) such

Ans. (a) 'As' means in the role of, fitting the context of India being ranked 85th as per the corruption perception index.

236. Select the most appropriate option to fill in blank number 3.
(a) ranked (b) piled
(c) graded (d) Stacked

Ans. (a) 'Ranked' means assigned a position in a hierarchy, fitting the context of India being ranked 85th in the corruption perception index.

237. Select the most appropriate option to fill in blank number 4.
(a) a (b) the (c) some (d) any

Ans. (a) 'A' is an indefinite article introducing the downfall, fitting the context of 'a downfall'.

238. Select the most appropriate option to fill in blank number 5.
(a) declare (b) affirm (c) swear (d) assert

Ans. (c) 'Swear' means to make a solemn statement, fitting the context of swearing by the ideals of honesty and integrity.

239. Select the most appropriate option to fill in blank number 6.
(a) prejudice (b) sacrifice
(c) omission (d) erosion

Ans. (b) 'Sacrifice' means giving up something valued, fitting the context of ideals of self-denial and sacrifice.

240. Select the most appropriate option to fill in blank number 7.
(a) viler (b) vile (c) more vile (d) Vilest

Ans. (b) 'Vile' means extremely unpleasant, fitting the context of resorting to vile forms of corruption.

241. Select the most appropriate option to fill in blank number 8.
(a) melancholy (b) malaise
(c) despair (d) deficiency

Ans. (b) 'Malaise' means a general feeling of discomfort or unease, fitting the context of the malaise of corruption.

242. Select the most appropriate option to fill in blank number 9.
(a) threats (b) vitals (c) necessity (d) imperative

Ans. (b) 'Vitals' means essential parts, fitting the context of corruption eating into the vitals of society.

243. Select the most appropriate option to fill in blank number 10.
(a) onlookers (b) visionaries
(c) sorcerers (d) performers

Ans. (a) 'Onlookers' means spectators or observers, fitting the context of people becoming helpless onlookers of degradation.

PASSAGE-49

A new swarm of locusts entered Rajasthan's Jaisalmer on Sunday. This is the fifth swarm to .... ………(1)………. the state in four days from .... (2) ……… western border with Pakistan. Since, the first locust swarm .... ………(3)………. the state's Sri Ganganagardistrict on April 11, as many as 25 swarms .... (4) ……… entered Rajasthan. Some swarms moved to Chhattisgarh and Madhya Pradesh, ... (5) ……… which agricultural departments issued advisories to farmers asking them to be on high alert. **SSC CGL Tier-2 03.02.2022**

244. Select the most appropriate option to fill in blank number 1.
(a) introduce (b) come
(c) enter (d) insert
Ans. (c) 'Enter' means to come or go into, fitting the context of a new swarm of locusts entering Rajasthan.

245. Select the most appropriate option to fill in blank number 2.
(a) its (b) it (c) his (d) their
Ans. (a) 'Its' is a possessive pronoun, fitting the context of the Western border of Pakistan.

246. Select the most appropriate option to fill in blank number 3.
(a) invaded (b) invade
(c) was invading (d) is invading
Ans. (a) 'Invaded' means entered by force, fitting the context of the first locust swarm invading the state's Sri Ganganagar district.

247. Select the most appropriate option to fill in blank number 4.
(a) having (b) have (c) to have (d) has
Ans. (b) 'Have' means to possess or hold, fitting the context of many swarms having entered Rajasthan.

248. Select the most appropriate option to fill in blank number 5.
(a) until (b) before
(c) since (d) after
Ans. (d) 'After' means following in time, fitting the context of swarms moving to other states after entering Rajasthan.

PASSAGE-50

The working of the stomach was .... (1). .... by a strange accident. In 1822. a man named Alexis St. Martin was .... (2). .... hit by a shot gun. The bullet had seriously ....(3).......... the chest wall and made a hole in .... (4). .... stomach. He was brought to an American army .... (5). By .... William Beaumont. The doctor saved the patient but he .... (6). .... not close the hole properly. Beaumont took it as a .... (7) .... opportunity to see the inside of the stomach .... (8). .... the hole. He made some wonderful observations. Beaumont .... (9) .... that the stomach was churning food. Its wall secreted a fluid .... (10). .... could digest the food. He also observed that the end of the stomach opens into the intestine only after the digestion of the food inside the stomach is completed.

SSC CGL Tier-2 08.08.2022

249. Select the most appropriate option to fill in blank number 1.
(a) discover (b) discovered
(c) discovering (d) to be discovered
Ans. (b) 'Discovered' means found out, fitting the context of the working of the stomach being discovered by accident.

250. Select the most appropriate option to fill in blank number 2.
(a) badly (b) nicely
(c) extremely (d) poorly
Ans. (a) 'Badly' means seriously or severely, fitting the context of Alexis St. Martin being badly hit by a shotgun.

251. Select the most appropriate option to fill in blank number 3.
(a) damaged (b) devastated
(c) decayed (d) decreased
Ans. (a) 'Damaged' means harmed or injured, fitting the context of the bullet damaging the chest wall.

252. Select the most appropriate option to fill in blank number 4.
(a) her (b) its (c) his (d) him
Ans. (c) 'His' is a possessive pronoun, fitting the context of a hole in his stomach.

253. Select the most appropriate option to fill in blank number 5.
(a) doctor (b) major
(c) colonel (d) registrar
Ans. (a) 'Doctor' means a medical practitioner, fitting the context of being brought to an American army doctor.

254. Select the most appropriate option to fill in blank number 6.
(a) should (b) could
(c) had (d) would
Ans. (b) 'Could' means was able to, fitting the context of the doctor not being able to close the hole properly.

255. Select the most appropriate option to fill in blank number 7.
(a) strong (b) fast
(c) countless (d) great
Ans. (d) 'Great' means significant, fitting the context of a great opportunity to observe the inside of the stomach.

256. Select the most appropriate option to fill in blank number 8.
(a) between (b) across
(c) imagined (d) obtained
Ans. (b) 'Across' means from one side to the other, fitting the context of seeing the inside of the stomach across the hole.

257. Select the most appropriate option to fill in blank number 9.
(a) acquired (b) found
(c) imagined (d) obtained
Ans. (b) 'Found' means discovered, fitting the context of finding that the stomach was churning food.

258. Select the most appropriate option to fill in blank number 10.
(a) Whom (b) What (c) Who (d) Which
Ans. (d) 'Which' introduces a clause specifying the fluid, fitting the context of a fluid which could digest the food.

SSC CGL 2021 (Tier 1 & 2)

PASSAGE-51

What every tourist must take back from Bhutan is pure honey, especially Putka, 'Antibiotic' honey produced ....(1).......... Melipona Bees (stingless bees) a breed found in protected areas ....(2).......... 700 to 1500 metres above sea level. Due ....(3).......... their small seize, they can get larger nutrients ....(4).......... regular honeybees. It has a tangy/sour taste and can ....(5).......... your sore throat in a matter of minutes.

SSC CGL Tier-1 13.08.2021 (Shift-I)

259. Select the most appropriate option to fill in blank number 1.
(a) through (b) with
(c) of (d) by
Ans. (d) 'By' means indicating the agent performing an action, fitting the context of honey produced by Melipona Bees.

260. Select the most appropriate option to fill in blank number 2.
(a) between (b) after
(c) midst (d) among
Ans. (a) 'Between' means in the space separating two points, fitting the context of bees found in protected areas between 700 to 1500 metres.

261. Select the most appropriate option to fill in blank number 3.
(a) to (b) for (c) of (d) at
Ans. (a) 'To' means indicating a relationship, fitting the context of the small size allowing bees to get larger nutrients.

262. Select the most appropriate option to fill in blank number 4.
(a) then (b) though (c) than (d) and
Ans. (c) 'Than' is used to introduce a comparison, fitting the context of bees getting larger nutrients than regular honeybees.

263. Select the most appropriate option to fill in blank number 5.
(a) soothe (b) pacify (c) appease (d) calm
Ans. (a) 'Soothe' means to relieve or ease, fitting the context of the honey soothing a sore throat.

PASSAGE-52

It is true that the more you study, the more you ....(1).......... your horizon and hence your point of view undergoes a ....(2).......... . A person with higher education certainly has a better ....(3).......... and ideas to help in community and societal ....(4).......... . Ideas that are gathered from such people provide a global ....(5).......... for the nation as a whole. SSC CGL Tier-1 16.08.2021 (Shift-I)

264. Select the most appropriate option to fill in blank number 1.
(a) expand (b) convert
(c) exchange (d) narrow
Ans. (a) 'Expand' means to increase, fitting the context of expanding one's horizon through study.

265. Select the most appropriate option to fill in blank number 2.
(a) succession (b) backwardness
(c) enlargement (d) transformation
Ans. (d) 'Transformation' means a thorough change, fitting the context of undergoing a transformation.

266. Select the most appropriate option to fill in blank number 3.
(a) routine (b) outlook (c) scope (d) luck
Ans. (b) 'Outlook' means perspective or point of view, fitting the context of having a better outlook and ideas.

267. Select the most appropriate option to fill in blank number 4.
(a) ripening (b) elaboration
(c) development (d) maturity
Ans. (c) 'Development' means progress or growth, fitting the context of contributing to community and societal development.

268. Select the most appropriate option to fill in blank number 5.
(a) proportion (b) posture
(c) perspective (d) prejudice
Ans. (c) 'Perspective' means a particular attitude or view, fitting the context of providing a global perspective for the nation.

PASSAGE-53

The Panchatantra is a legendary collection of short stories from India. ....(1).......... composed in the 2nd century BC, Panchatantra is ....(2).......... to be written by Vishnu Sharma ....(3).......... with many other scholars. The purpose behind the composition ....(4).......... to implant moral values and governing ....(5).......... in the young sons of the king. SSC CGL Tier-1 18.08.2021 (Shift-I)

269. Select the most appropriate option to fill in blank number 1.
(a) Originally (b) Eventually
(c) Firstly (d) Ultimately
Ans. (a) 'Originally' means at the beginning, fitting the context of Panchatantra being originally composed in the 2nd century BC.

270. Select the most appropriate option to fill in blank number 2.
(a) established (b) believed
(c) alleged (d) designed
Ans. (b) 'Believed' means thought to be, fitting the context of Panchatantra being believed to be written by Vishnu Sharma.

271. Select the most appropriate option to fill in blank number 3.
(a) along (b) beside
(c) next (d) near
Ans. (a) 'Along' means together with, fitting the context of Vishnu Sharma along with other scholars.

272. Select most appropriate option to fill in blank number 4.
(a) were (b) are (c) be (d) was
Ans. (d) 'Was' means past tense of is, fitting the context of the purpose behind the composition was to implant moral values.

273. Select the most appropriate option to fill in blank number 5.
(a) faculties (b) flairs
(c) skills (d) gifts
Ans. (c) 'Skills' means abilities, fitting the context of governing skills in the young sons of the king.

SSC CPO 2024

PASSAGE-54

Superheroes are fictional characters with ....(1).......... powers who use their powers to fight crime and protect the public. Some popular superheroes include Superman, Batman, Spiderman and Wonder Woman. Superheroes often have backstories that ....(2).......... how they have gained their powers, ...(3).......... being born with special powers, being bitten by a radioactive spider or being exposed to cosmic radiation. They usually have a specific outfit or clothing that they wear to hide their identity and protect ....(4).......... while fighting crime. Superheroes have been a staple of popular culture ....(5).......... decades, appearing in comics, movies, television shows and video games.
SSC CPO 27.06.2024 (Shift-I)

274. Select the most appropriate option to fill in blank number 1.
(a) extraordinary (b) pragmatic
(c) hereditary (d) familiar
Ans. (a) 'Extraordinary' means very special, fitting the context of superheroes having extraordinary powers.

275. Select the most appropriate option to fill in blank number 2.
(a) explaining (b) was explain
(c) explain (d) had explain
Ans. (c) 'Explain' means to make clear, fitting the context of backstories explaining how superheroes gained their powers.

276. Select the most appropriate option to fill in blank number 3.
(a) therefore (b) subsequently
(c) instead (d) such as
Ans. (d) 'Such as' means for example, fitting the context of examples of how superheroes gained their powers.

277. Select the most appropriate option to fill in blank number 4.
(a) themselves (b) ourselves
(c) herself (d) himself

Ans. (a) 'Themselves' means the persons referred to, fitting the context of superheroes protecting themselves while fighting crime.

278. Select the most appropriate option to fill in blank number 5.
(a) for (b) on (c) under (d) above

Ans. (a) 'For' indicates duration, fitting the context of superheroes being a staple of popular culture for decades.

PASSAGE-55

A series of ......(1)...... of shell or ivory or thin metal clothed her left upper arm all the way down to her fingers. A necklace ......(2)...... three pendants bunched together and a few bangles above the elbow and ......(3)...... on the right hands display an almost modern art. She speaks of the ......(4)......, ever hopeful human spirit. She reminds us that it is important to visit museums in our country to experience the ......(5)...... that a work of art leaves on our senses, to find among all the riches one particular vision of beauty that speaks to us alone.

SSC CPO 27.06.2024 (Shift-II)

279. Select the most appropriate option to fill in blank number 1.
(a) bangles (b) toe-rings
(c) anklets (d) ear-rings

Ans. (a) 'Bangles' means circular bracelets, fitting the context of bangles on her upper arm.

280. Select the most appropriate option to fill in blank number 2.
(a) by (b) with (c) upon (d) in

Ans. (b) 'With' means accompanied by, fitting the context of a necklace with three pendants.

281. Select the most appropriate option to fill in blank number 3.
(a) toe (b) wrist (c) waist (d) ankle

Ans. (b) 'Wrist' means the joint connecting the hand with the forearm, fitting the context of bangles on the wrist.

282. Select the most appropriate option to fill in blank number 4.
(a) unbelievable (b) ungrateful
(c) unsafe (d) undaunted

Ans. (d) 'Undaunted' means not intimidated, fitting the context of the ever hopeful human spirit.

283. Select the most appropriate option to fill in blank number 5.
(a) affect (b) result
(c) blow (d) impact

Ans. (d) 'Impact' means a strong effect, fitting the context of the impact a work of art leaves on our senses.

PASSAGE-56

Why do people yawn? No one seems to know the exact ......(1)...... . Some people believe that we yawn ......(2) ...... we do not have enough oxygen in our bodies. In ......(3) ......words, we yawn to breathe in ......(4) ...... oxygen. People also believe that yawning is associated ......(5) ...... boredom.

SSC CPO 27.06.2024 (Shift-III)

284. Select the most appropriate option to fill in blank number 1.
(a) explanation (b) basis
(c) reason (d) reality

Ans. (c) 'Reason' means a cause, fitting the context of the reason why people yawn.

285. Select the most appropriate option to fill in blank number 2.
(a) when (b) as
(c) why (d) while

Ans. (a) 'When' means at the time, fitting the context of yawning when there is not enough oxygen.

286. Select the most appropriate option to fill in blank number 3.
(a) some (b) new (c) rather (d) other

Ans. (d) 'Other' means different, fitting the context of explaining yawning in other words.

287. Select the most appropriate option to fill in blank number 4.
(a) less (b) little (c) much (d) more

Ans. (d) 'More' means a greater amount, fitting the context of yawning to breathe in more oxygen.

288. Select the most appropriate option to fill in blank number 5.
(a) on (b) in
(c) with (d) by

Ans. (c) 'With' means accompanied by, fitting the context of yawning being associated with boredom.

PASSAGE-57

"Can I come along with you on your fishing trip, please?" asked Millie. Her two elder brothers ....(1).......... at her scornfully. "Fishing is a mans ....(2).......... ," said her older brother, Derek. "Girls are not ....(3).......... at fishing." ....(4).......... a while, however, Millie managed to persuade her brothers to take her ....(5).......... . When they reached the fishing pond, the two brothers wandered off by themselves.

SSC CPO 28.06.2024 (Shift-I)

289. Select the most appropriate option to fill in blank number 1.
(a) looked (b) observed
(c) saw (d) watched

Ans. (a) 'Looked' means directed their eyes, fitting the context of her brothers looking at her scornfully.

290. Select the most appropriate option to fill in blank number 2.
(a) matches (b) gaming
(c) competition (d) sport

Ans. (d) 'Sport' means an activity involving physical exertion, fitting the context of fishing being a man's sport.

291. Select the most appropriate option to fill in blank number 3.
(a) good (b) sound
(c) likeable (d) acceptable

Ans. (a) 'Good' means skilled, fitting the context of girls not being good at fishing.

292. Select the most appropriate option to fill in blank number 4.
(a) Nearly (b) After
(c) Then (d) Before

Ans. (b) 'After' means following in time, fitting the context of Millie persuading her brothers after a while.

293. Select the most appropriate option to fill in blank number 5.
(a) among them (b) within
(c) along (d) with them

Ans. (c) 'Along' means together with, fitting the context of Millie going along with her brothers.

PASSAGE-58

Mowgli is a ......(1)...... character from Rudyard Kiplings classic The Jungle Book. Raised by wolves in the Indian jungle, Mowgli ......(2)...... thrilling adventures and forms friendships with various animals, like Bagheera the panther and Baloo the bear.

Throughout the story, he ......(3)..... the challenges of living among both humans and jungle creatures, all while learning essential life lessons. The Jungle Book continues to ......(4) ...... readers of all ages with its ......(5) ...... portrayal of Mowglis remarkable journey of self-discovery and the beauty of the natural world. **SSC CPO 28.06.2024 (Shift-II)**

294. Select the most appropriate option to fill in blank number 1.
(a) beloved (b) overlooked
(c) scorned (d) despised

Ans. (a) 'Beloved' means dearly loved, fitting the context of Mowgli being a loved character.

295. Select the most appropriate option to fill in blank number 2.
(a) exaggerates (b) enunciates
(c) excavates (d) experiences

Ans. (d) 'Experiences' means undergoes or encounters, fitting the context of Mowgli experiencing thrilling adventures.

296. Select the most appropriate option to fill in blank number 3.
(a) navigates (b) customises
(c) procures (d) coordinates

Ans. (a) 'Navigates' means to find a way through, fitting the context of Mowgli navigating challenges.

297. Select the most appropriate option to fill in blank number 4.
(a) register (b) captivate
(c) magnify (d) manipulate

Ans. (b) 'Captivate' means to attract and hold, fitting the context of The Jungle Book captivating readers.

298. Select the most appropriate option to fill in blank number 5.
(a) enchanting (b) surprising
(c) abnormal (d) ordinary

Ans. (a) 'Enchanting' means delightfully charming, fitting the context of the portrayal of Mowgli's journey being enchanting.

PASSAGE-59

It is important to ......(1)...... a healthy lifestyle to maintain good physical and mental well- being. Regular ......(2)...... helps improve cardiovascular health and boosts the immune system. Eating a balanced diet rich in ......(3)...... vitamins and minerals is crucial for overall health. Additionally, ...(4)...... stress through activities like yoga or meditation can enhance mental clarity. Getting an adequate amount of ......(5)...... each night is essential for restorative activity and optimum bodily functions. **SSC CPO 28.06.2024 (Shift-III)**

299. Select the most appropriate option to fill in blank number 1.
(a) adopt (b) adeptly (c) adapt (d) adept

Ans. (a) 'Adopt' means to take up or start, fitting the context of adopting a healthy lifestyle.

300. Select the most appropriate option to fill in blank number 2.
(a) exalt (b) exclaim
(c) exertion (d) exercise

Ans. (d) 'Exercise' means physical activity, fitting the context of improving cardiovascular health.

301. Select the most appropriate option to fill in blank number 3.
(a) necessarily
(b) necessity
(c) necessitate
(d) essential

Ans. (d) 'Essential' means necessary, fitting the context of a balanced diet rich in essential vitamins and minerals.

302. Select the most appropriate option to fill in blank number 4.
(a) managing (b) manages
(c) management (d) managed

Ans. (a) 'Managing' means to control or handle, fitting the context of managing stress through activities.

303. Select the most appropriate option to fill in blank number 5.
(a) resting (b) relax
(c) slumber (d) sleep

Ans. (d) 'Sleep' means rest, fitting the context of getting an adequate amount of sleep each night.

PASSAGE-60

It was an unusual dark night. In the ......(1)...... of an enjoyable dream, Jim thought he heard his dog ......(2)...... loudly. He groaned and glanced ......(3)...... his clock sleepily. 12 o' clock the green fluorescent ......(4)...... of his clock read. Suddenly, Jim ......(5)...... hushed voices outside his house.

He immediately became alert and jumped out of bed. As his parents had gone on a holiday, Jim was alone at home. He decided to look who was outside. **SSC CPO 29.06.2024 (Shift-I)**

304. Select the most appropriate option to fill in blank number 1.
(a) middle (b) side
(c) between (d) end

Ans. (a) 'Middle' means the center, fitting the context of being in the middle of a dream.

305. Select the most appropriate option to fill in blank number 2.
(a) jumping
(b) shouting
(c) barking
(d) dancing

Ans. (c) 'Barking' means making a loud noise, fitting the context of Jim hearing his dog barking.

306. Select the most appropriate option to fill in blank number 3.
(a) in (b) on
(c) at (d) upon

Ans. (c) 'At' means directing attention, fitting the context of glancing at the clock.

307. Select the most appropriate option to fill in blank number 4.
(a) hands (b) points
(c) dial (d) light

Ans. (a) 'Hands' means indicators on a clock, fitting the context of the clock hands reading 12 o'clock.

308. Select the most appropriate option to fill in blank number 5.
(a) thought (b) heard
(c) listened (d) saw

Ans. (b) 'Heard' means to perceive sound, fitting the context of Jim hearing hushed voices.

PASSAGE-61

Childhood is an important phase in a person's life. Children are free from worries, tensions and stresses so they lead a very ......(1)...... life. This is the only reason they create golden and beautiful memories during this period which are ......(2)...... in their adulthood. It is the responsibility of parents and guardians to shape the future of a child as he is very ......(3)...... and can drift in any direction. If they have made any mistakes, we should ......(4)...... them instead of misbehaving with them. How we have behaved with them will be ......(5)...... on their minds which will reflect in later stages. **SSC CPO 29.06.2024 (Shift-II)**

309. Select the most appropriate option to fill in blank number 1.
(a) carefree (b) careful
(c) stressful (d) cautious
Ans. (a) 'Carefree' means without worries, fitting the context of children leading a carefree life.

310. Select the most appropriate option to fill in blank number 2.
(a) cherished (b) blocked
(c) dumped (d) neglected
Ans. (a) 'Cherished' means valued or loved, fitting the context of cherishing memories in adulthood.

311. Select the most appropriate option to fill in blank number 3.
(a) mature (b) innocent (c) crafty (d) guilty
Ans. (b) 'Innocent' means without guilt, fitting the context of a child being innocent.

312. Select the most appropriate option to fill in blank number 4.
(a) damage (b) create
(c) design (d) rectify
Ans. (d) 'Rectify' means to correct, fitting the context of rectifying children's mistakes.

313. Select the most appropriate option to fill in blank number 5.
(a) published (b) bleached
(c) imprinted (d) coloured
Ans. (c) 'Imprinted' means fixed in the mind, fitting the context of behaviour being imprinted on children's minds.

PASSAGE-62

Literature is a reflection of society and often ......(1)...... insight into the human experience. Through various forms like novels, poems, and plays, literature allows us to ......(2)...... different emotions and perspectives. It can serve as a ......(3)...... for social issues, shedding light on topics that need attention. Reading literature not only enhances our language skills but also ......(4)...... empathy by helping us understand the feelings of characters. In a rapidly changing world, literature ......(5)...... a timeless portal to diverse worlds and cultures.
SSC CPO 29.06.2024 (Shift-III)

314. Select the most appropriate option to fill in blank number 1.
(a) denies (b) suggests
(c) offers (d) garners/provides
Ans. (c) 'Offers' means to provide, fitting the context of literature offering insight.

315. Select the most appropriate option to fill in blank number 2.
(a) explain (b) exploit
(c) explore (d) exclaim
Ans. (c) 'Explore' means to investigate or experience, fitting the context of exploring different emotions and perspectives.

316. Select the most appropriate option to fill in blank number 3.
(a) planking (b) plank (c) platform (d) planks
Ans. (c) 'Platform' means a stage for activities, fitting the context of literature serving as a platform for social issues.

317. Select the most appropriate option to fill in blank number 4.
(a) withers (b) avoids
(c) cultivates (d) provokes
Ans. (c) 'Cultivates' means to develop, fitting the context of literature cultivating empathy.

318. Select the most appropriate option to fill in blank number 5.
(a) became (b) becomes
(c) become (d) becoming
Ans. (b) 'Becomes' means to turn into, fitting the context of literature becoming a portal to diverse worlds and cultures.

PASSAGE-63

Days after Prime Minister Narendra Modi inaugurated the Ghaziabad priority ......(1)...... of the Delhi-Meerut Rapid Rail Transit System (RRTS),the ......(2) of high-rise societies in the National Capital Region called for direct ......(3) ...... to the public transport service points.

The residents in ......(4) ......areas of Noida and Ghaziabad said they would be forced to continue ......(5) ......on private vehicles without proper connectivity to the RRTS and ......(6) ...... public transport modes.

"The RRTS is a great development; we want ......(7)...... connectivity to key points like Metro stations, railway stations, Delhi and the RRTS.......(8)...... any proper public transport, many residents are forced to opt ......(9)...... a personal car," the president of the New Era Flat Owners Welfare Association, Abhishek Kumar, ...(10)...... . The 17 km priority section of the Delhi-Ghaziabad-Meerut RRTS corridor was inaugurated by PM Modi on 7th October and it started commercial operations on the next day. **SSC CPO Tier-2 08.01.2024**

319. Select the most appropriate option to fill in blank number 1.
(a) fragment (b) section
(c) system (d) piece
Ans. (b) 'Section' means a part of a whole, fitting the context of a priority section of the Delhi-Meerut RRTS.

320. Select the most appropriate option to fill in blank number 2.
(a) landlords (b) tenants
(c) people (d) residents
Ans. (d) 'Residents' means inhabitants, fitting the context of high-rise societies' residents.

321. Select the most appropriate option to fill in blank number 3.
(a) connected (b) connectivity
(c) connecting (d) connect
Ans. (d) 'Connect' means to establish a link, fitting the context of residents calling for direct connect to public transport.

322. Select the most appropriate option to fill in blank number 4.
(a) lot (b) very (c) many (d) much
Ans. (c) 'Many' means numerous, fitting the context of residents in many areas of Noida and Ghaziabad.

323. Select the most appropriate option to fill in blank number 5.
(a) depending (b) depended
(c) depends (d) depend

Ans. (a) 'Depending' means relying on, fitting the context of depending on private vehicles.

324. Select the most appropriate option to fill in blank number 6.
(a) other (b) further (c) extra (d) another

Ans. (a) 'Other' means additional, fitting the context of other public transport modes.

325. Select the most appropriate option to fill in blank number 7.
(a) consecutive (b) successive
(c) upright (d) direct

Ans. (d) 'Direct' means straightforward, fitting the context of wanting direct connectivity.

326. Select the most appropriate option to fill in blank number 8.
(a) In spite of (b) Despite
(c) Without (d) With

Ans. (c) 'Without' means in the absence of, fitting the context of without proper public transport.

327. Select the most appropriate option to fill in blank number 9.
(a) on (b) for (c) to (d) of

Ans. (b) 'For' means in place of, fitting the context of opting for a personal car.

328. Select the most appropriate option to fill in blank number 10.
(a) professed (b) assumed
(c) said (d) replied

Ans. (c) 'Said' means stated, fitting the context of Abhishek Kumar's statement.

PASSAGE-64

The door behind them was ....(1)......... There was no escape. A strange light was ....(2) .... from a corner, one that did not ....(3).......... the room but made darkness visible. ....(4) .... alien voice was heard which sounded like jargon, ...(5) .... to the hapless friends. They went down ....(6) .... their knees sobbing, pleading for their lives but the ....(7) .... sounds continued. Slowly, a form seemed to ....(8) .... right before their eyes which ....(9) .... their blood and chilled their ....(10) .... It was formless mass with no face!

SSC CPO Tier-2 08.01.2024

329. Select the most appropriate option to fill in blank number 1.
(a) vacant (b) sealed
(c) ajar (d) unbolted

Ans. (b) 'Sealed' means closed tightly, fitting the context of the door being sealed with no escape.

330. Select the most appropriate option to fill in blank number 2.
(a) preceding (b) commencing
(c) reclining (d) emanating

Ans. (d) 'Emanating' means coming out from a source, fitting the context of a strange light emanating from a corner.

331. Select the most appropriate option to fill in blank number 3.
(a) kindle (b) extinguish
(c) ignite (d) illuminate

Ans. (d) 'Illuminate' means to light up, fitting the context of the light making darkness visible.

332. Select the most appropriate option to fill in blank number 4.
(a) The (b) An
(c) A (d) Any

Ans. (b) 'An' is an indefinite article, fitting the context of an alien voice being heard.

333. Select the most appropriate option to fill in blank number 5.
(a) incomprehensible
(b) indelible
(c) invincibleq
(d) incorrigible

Ans. (a) 'Incomprehensible' means not understandable, fitting the context of the voice sounding like jargon and being incomprehensible to the friends.

334. Select the most appropriate option to fill in blank number 6.
(a) by (b) on
(c) at (d) in

Ans. (b) 'On' means in contact with the surface of, fitting the context of going down on their knees.

335. Select the most appropriate option to fill in blank number 7.
(a) bizarre (b) familiar
(c) regular (d) customary

Ans. (a) 'Bizarre' means very strange, fitting the context of the sounds being bizarre.

336. Select the most appropriate option to fill in blank number 8.
(a) assume (b) emerge
(c) extract (d) derive

Ans. (b) 'Emerge' means to become visible, fitting the context of a form seeming to emerge.

337. Select the most appropriate option to fill in blank number 9.
(a) flowed (b) spilled
(c) locked (d) curdled

Ans. (d) 'Curdled' means to cause to turn, fitting the context of curdling their blood.

338. Select the most appropriate option to fill in blank number 10.
(a) head (b) eyes
(c) skin (d) bones

Ans. (d) 'Bones' means the rigid structure inside the body, fitting the context of chilling their bones.

SSC CPO 2023

PASSAGE-65

The Amazon rainforest is an awe-inspiring natural wonder that ....(1).......... across several South American countries, including Brazil, Peru, Colombia and Ecuador. Covering an ....(2) .... area of 5.5 million square kilometres, it is the largest tropical rainforest on Earth. The Amazon jungle is ....(3)........... for its remarkable biodiversity, harbouring an astonishing array of plant and animal species that are still being discovered and studied. The dense vegetation of the jungle creates a .... (4) .... and complex ecosystem, supporting countless species and providing crucial ecosystem services such as carbon sequestration and climate regulation. It is also home to .... (5) .... communities that have thrived within its rich confines for centuries, preserving their traditions and deep connection to the land.

SSC CPO 03.08.2023 (Shift-I)

339. Select the most appropriate option to fill in blank number 1.
(a) reaches (b) lengths
(c) amounts (d) spans
Ans. (d) 'Spans' means to extend across, fitting the context of the Amazon rainforest spanning several countries.

340. Select the most appropriate option to fill in blank number 2.
(a) gauged (b) rated
(c) estimated (d) evaluated
Ans. (c) 'Estimated' means roughly calculated, fitting the context of an estimated area of 5.5 million square kilometers.

341. Select the most appropriate option to fill in blank number 3.
(a) great (b) acclaimed
(c) renowned (d) pre-eminent
Ans. (c) 'Renowned' means well-known, fitting the context of the Amazon jungle being renowned for its biodiversity.

342. Select the most appropriate option to fill in blank number 4.
(a) vigour (b) spirited
(c) vibrant (d) lavish
Ans. (c) 'Vibrant' means full of energy, fitting the context of the jungle creating a vibrant and complex ecosystem.

343. Select the most appropriate option to fill in blank number 5.
(a) late (b) ancient
(c) indigenous (d) organic
Ans. (c) 'Indigenous' means native to an area, fitting the context of communities that have thrived within the rainforest for centuries.

PASSAGE-66

South Korea is the most cosmetically ....(1).......... country on Earth. Beauty editors estimate that it is because of the government's heavy investment ....(2) .... industry. It is ahead of its competitors and its citizens ....(3).......... twice as much on skincare products as consumers in the United States, the UK and France. Korean shoppers are ....(4) .... the world's most discerning. Eight out of 10 Korean women in their 20s and 30s use an app that ....(5) .... like cosmetics-specific, to debate the merits of various common ingredients. **SSC CPO 03.10.2023 (Shift-II)**

344. Select the most appropriate option to fill in blank number 1.
(a) early (b) advanced
(c) ancient (d) primitive
Ans. (b) 'Advanced' means highly developed, fitting the context of South Korea being the most advanced in cosmetics.

345. Select the most appropriate option to fill in blank number 2.
(a) of the (b) in the
(c) by the (d) from the
Ans. (b) 'In the' means within, fitting the context of heavy investment in the industry.

346. Select the most appropriate option to fill in blank number 3.
(a) cherish (b) propagate
(c) comply (d) spend
Ans. (d) 'Spend' means to use money, fitting the context of citizens spending on skincare products.

347. Select the most appropriate option to fill in blank number 4.
(a) though (b) although
(c) maybe (d) perhaps
Ans. (d) 'Perhaps' means maybe, fitting the context of Korean shoppers being perhaps the world's most discerning.

348. Select the most appropriate option to fill in blank number 5.
(a) stops (b) functions
(c) dissolves (d) malfunctions
Ans. (b) 'Functions' means works or operates, fitting the context of an app that functions like a cosmetics-specific app.

PASSAGE-67

When another old cave is discovered in the South of France,it is not ....(1).......... in news. Rather, it is an ordinary event. Such discoveries are so .... (2) .... these days that hardly anybody pays heed to them. However, when the Lascaux cave complex was discovered in 1940 the world was ....(3).......... Painted directly on its walls were hundreds of scenes showing how people lived thousands of years ago. The scenes show people hunting animals, such as bison or wild cats. Other images .... (4) .... birds and most noticeably, horses, which appear in more than 300 wall images, by far .... (5) .... all other animals.
SSC CPO 03.10.2023 (Shift-III)

349. Select the most appropriate option to fill in blank number 1.
(a) usually (b) nearly
(c) merrily (d) suitably
Ans. (a) 'Usually' means commonly, fitting the context of old cave discoveries usually not making news.

350. Select the most appropriate option to fill in blank number 2.
(a) ghastly (b) frequent
(c) delusional (d) disorderly
Ans. (b) 'Frequent' means occurring often, fitting the context of discoveries being frequent.

351. Select the most appropriate option to fill in blank number 3.
(a) overthrown (b) crushed
(c) encouraged (d) baffled
Ans. (d) 'Baffled' means confused, fitting the context of the world being baffled by the Lascaux cave discovery.

352. Select the most appropriate option to fill in blank number 4.
(a) depict (b) determine
(c) imprint (d) require
Ans. (a) 'Depict' means to represent in images, fitting the context of images depicting people and animals.

353. Select the most appropriate option to fill in blank number 5.
(a) outlasting (b) outreaching
(c) outnumbering (d) outsourcing
Ans. (c) 'Outnumbering' means being more numerous, fitting the context of horses outnumbering other animals in the images.

PASSAGE-68

It is said that everyone lives ....(1).......... selling something. What you can ....(2).......... from this statement is that teachers live by selling knowledge, philosophers live by selling wisdom and priests earn their living by selling spiritual comfort. Though it may be possible to measure the value of material goods in terms of money, it is extremely difficult to ....(3).......... the true value of the services which people perform for us.

There are times when we would ....(4)......... give everything we possess to save our lives,yet we might grudge paying a surgeon a high fee for offering us precisely the same service. The ....(5)......... of society are such that skills have to be paid for in the same way that goods are paid for at a shop. **SSC CPO 04.10.2023 (Shift-I)**

354. Select the most appropriate option to fill in blank number 1.

(a) by (b) over (c) of (d) into

Ans. (a) 'By' means indicating the means, fitting the context of everyone living by selling something.

355. Select the most appropriate option to fill in blank number 2.

(a) revive (b) separate
(c) choose (d) derive

Ans. (d) 'Derive' means to obtain, fitting the context of deriving meaning from the statement.

356. Select the most appropriate option to fill in blank number 3.

(a) conceal (b) extort
(c) mock (d) estimate

Ans. (d) 'Estimate' means to calculate roughly, fitting the context of estimating the value of services.

357. Select the most appropriate option to fill in blank number 4.

(a) thoughtfully (b) perfectly
(c) thoroughly (d) willingly

Ans. (d) 'Willingly' means by choice, fitting the context of willingly giving everything to save lives.

358. Select the most appropriate option to fill in blank number 5.

(a) conditions (b) interferences
(c) obstacles (d) connections

Ans. (a)

'Conditions' means circumstances, fitting the context of conditions requiring skills to be paid for like goods.

PASSAGE-69

Among the largest species of cats in the world, tigers are powerful hunters with ....(1).......... teeth, strong jaws and agile bodies. They range across Asia from Russia all the way to Sumatra and mainland South-East Asia. Researchers still have much to learn ....(2).......... these beautiful, endangered ....(3).......... . There is currently one recognised species of tiger, Panthera tigris. Scientists have further ....(4).......... the tiger into nine sub-species: the extinct Bali, Caspian and Javan sub-species and the living Malayan, Sumatran, South China, Indochinese, Bengal and Amur (or Siberian) sub-species. Of these six sub-species AZA-accredited zoos currently manage three: Amur, Malayan and Sumatran. The Smithsonian's National Zoo and Conservation Biology Institute is home to Sumatran and Amur tigers, Sumatran tigers are ....(5).......... as Critically Endangered on the International Union for Conservation of Nature's Red List and Amur tigers have been classified as Endangered.
SSC CPO 04.10.2023 (Shift-II)

359. Select the most appropriate option to fill in blank number 1.

(a) long (b) small
(c) blunt (d) sharp

Ans. (d) 'Sharp' means having a thin edge that can cut or pierce, fitting the context of tigers having sharp teeth.

360. Select the most appropriate option to fill in blank number 2.

(a) with (b) into
(c) about (d) along

Ans. (c) 'About' means concerning, fitting the context of researchers learning about tigers.

361. Select the most appropriate option to fill in blank number 3.

(a) rabbits (b) cats
(c) elephants (d) dogs

Ans. (b) 'Cats' refers to the species, fitting the context of tigers being large species of cats.

362. Select the most appropriate option to fill in blank number 4.

(a) declared (b) restricted
(c) generalised (d) classified

Ans. (d) 'Classified' means arranged in categories, fitting the context of scientists classifying tigers into sub-species.

363. Select the most appropriate option to fill in blank number 5.

(a) numerated (b) detailed
(c) recorded (d) listed

Ans. (d) 'Listed' means included in a list, fitting the context of tigers being listed as Critically Endangered and Endangered.

PASSAGE-70

Discrimination refers to the inequitable or ....(1).......... treatment of individuals or collectives on the basis of attributes such as ethnicity, sex, age and sexual orientation. Studies have indicated that the perception of discrimination can .... (2) .... a series of stress-induced alterations in an individual's mental, physiological and behavioural responses. The experience of stress is known to elicit unfavourable emotional reactions, including but not limited to ....(3).......... despair and resentment. Furthermore, anxiety has been linked to a rise in health-compromising behaviours such as smoking, drinking and ....(4).......... drug use, while simultaneously causing a .... (5) .... in health-promoting activities such as quality sleep and vigorous exercise. **SSC CPO 04.10.2023 (Shift-III)**

364. Select the most appropriate option to fill in blank number 1.

(a) tragic (b) biased
(c) systematic (d) pathetic

Ans. (b) 'Biased' means unfairly prejudiced, fitting the context of discrimination being biased treatment.

365. Select the most appropriate option to fill in blank number 2.

(a) motivate (b) inspire
(c) support (d) trigger

Ans. (d) 'Trigger' means to cause to begin, fitting the context of discrimination triggering stress-induced alterations.

366. Select the most appropriate option to fill in blank number 3.

(a) deafness (b) impairment
(c) death (d) anxiety

Ans. (d) 'Anxiety' means a feeling of worry, fitting the context of emotional reactions including anxiety.

367. Select the most appropriate option to fill in blank number 4.

(a) prescribed (b) mandatory
(c) legitimate (d) illicit

Ans. (d) 'Illicit' means forbidden by law or rules, fitting the context of drug use being illicit.

368. Select the most appropriate option to fill in blank number 5.
(a) unfruitful (b) upheaval
(c) decline (d) rise

Ans. (c) 'Decline' means a decrease, fitting the context of a decline in health-promoting activities.

PASSAGE-71

Swans are large water birds that ....(1)......... to the family Anatidae, which also includes ducks and geese. They .... (2) .... for their beauty and grace and are often used as symbols of love, fidelity and elegance. They are also famous for their ....(3)......... features, such as their long necks, large wingspans and striking white feathers. .... (4) .... not all swan species are white; the black Swan .... (5) .... has black feathers with a red bill. Swans are found on every continent and are known for their strong pair bonds. They mate for life and can live up to 20 years.

SSC CPO 05.10.2023 (Shift-I)

369. Select the most appropriate option to fill in blank number 1.
(a) belonging (b) belong (c) belonged (d) belongs

Ans. (b) 'Belong' means to be a member of, fitting the context of swans belonging to the family Anatidae.

370. Select the most appropriate option to fill in blank number 2.
(a) are known (b) have knowing
(c) had know (d) were known

Ans. (a) 'Are known' means recognised or identified, fitting the context of swans being known for their beauty.

371. Select the most appropriate option to fill in blank number 3.
(a) popular (b) distinctive (c) similar (d) finite

Ans. (b) 'Distinctive' means characteristic, fitting the context of swans' distinctive features.

372. Select the most appropriate option to fill in blank number 4.
(a) Consequently (b) Formerly
(c) Because (d) However

Ans. (d) 'However' means despite this, fitting the context of not all swan species being white.

373. Select the most appropriate option to fill in blank number 5.
(a) for example (b) in addition
(c) after all (d) of course

Ans. (a) 'For example' means as an illustration, fitting the context of the black swan having black feathers.

PASSAGE-72

The concept of motivation focuses on explaining what moves behaviour. In fact, the term ....(1)......... is derived from the Latin word 'movere, referring to movement of activity. Most of our everyday explanation of .... (2) .... is given in terms of motives. Motives also help in making ....(3)......... about behaviour. A person will work hard in school, in sports, in business, in music and in many other situations, if he/she has a very strong need for .... (4) .... Hence, motives are the general states that enable us to make predictions about behaviour in many different situations. In other words, motivation is one of the .... (5) .... of behaviour. Instincts, drives, needs, goals and incentives come under the broad cluster of motivation.

SSC CPO 05.10.2023 (Shift-II)

374. Select the most appropriate option to fill in blank number 1.
(a) human behaviour (b) instinct
(c) motivation (d) psychology

Ans. (c) 'Motivation' means the reason for people's actions, fitting the context of motivation explaining what moves behaviour.

375. Select the most appropriate option to fill in blank number 2.
(a) behaviour (b) motivation
(c) goal (d) incentive

Ans. (a) 'Behaviour' means the way in which one acts, fitting the context of explaining behaviour in terms of motives.

376. Select the most appropriate option to fill in blank number 3.
(a) directions (b) predictions
(c) decisions (d) clarifications

Ans. (b) 'Predictions' means forecasts of future behaviour, fitting the context of making predictions about behaviour.

377. Select the most appropriate option to fill in blank number 4.
(a) motivation (b) desire
(c) grow (d) achievements

Ans. (d) 'Achievements' means accomplishments, fitting the context of a strong need for achievements.

378. Select the most appropriate option to fill in blank number 5.
(a) meaning (b) ways
(c) determinants (d) causes

Ans. (c) 'Determinants' means factors that decisively affect behaviour, fitting the context of determinants of behaviour.

PASSAGE-73

Rabindranath Tagore founded a small school at Santiniketan in 1901 and Kala Bhavan, an art school, in 1919 which .... (1) .... became a part of the Visvabharati University founded in 1921. It is located in an .... (2) .... village some distance from the city of Calcutta, Kala Bhavan presented an alternative methodology of art training, in which studio based practice was .... (3) .... in favour of learning through observation and living as a part of nature. The natural surroundings with the .... (4) .... of bare red earth dotted with trees, the colours of the changing seasons, the animals and birds .... (5) .... inspiration to students.

SSC CPO 05.10. 2023 (Shift-III)

379. Select the most appropriate option to fill in blank number 1.
(a) better (b) later
(c) faster (d) slower

Ans. (b) 'Later' means at a time in the future, fitting the context of Kala Bhavan becoming part of the Visvabharati University later.

380. Select the most appropriate option to fill in blank number 2.
(a) normal (b) magical
(c) reliable (d) idyllic

Ans. (d) 'Idyllic' means extremely happy, fitting the context of Santiniketan being an idyllic village.

381. Select the most appropriate option to fill in blank number 3.
(a) accepted (b) rejected
(c) investigated (d) aspired

Ans. (b) 'Rejected' means dismissed, fitting the context of rejecting studio-based practice.

382. Select the most appropriate option to fill in blank number 4.
(a) vistas (b) murk
(c) haze (d) band

Ans. (a) 'Vistas' means pleasing views, fitting the context of vistas of bare red earth dotted with trees.

383. Select the most appropriate option to fill in blank number 5.
(a) groomed (b) refused
(c) provided (d) agreed

Ans. (c) 'Provided' means supplied, fitting the context of providing inspiration to students.

SSC CPO 2022

PASSAGE-74

The soft layer of the Earth's ......(1)....... on which plants grow is referred to as soil. Soil includes a huge amount of both organic and inorganic ......(2)....... In the soil, the organic components known as humus are formed from ......(3)....... plant and animal remnants.

These' are combined with weathered particles of various rocks to form soil. Weathering occurs as a result of different chemical and physical ...... (4) ...... that occur on the Earth's surface. Soil formation is a ......(5)....... process in general. For example, the creation of a 2.5 cm thick soil layer might take more than 1000 years. **SSC CPO 02.08.2022 (Shift-III)**

384. Select the most appropriate option to fill in blank number 1.
(a) surface (b) boundary
(c) location (d) atmosphere

Ans. (a) 'Surface' means the outermost layer, fitting the context of the Earth's surface where plants grow.

385. Select the most appropriate option to fill in blank number 2.
(a) components (b) solvent
(c) pesticides (d) plants

Ans. (a) 'Components' means parts or elements, fitting the context of soil including organic and inorganic components.

386. Select the most appropriate option to fill in blank number 3.
(a) deformed
(b) deoxidised
(c) desterilised
(d) decomposed

Ans. (d) 'Decomposed' means broken down, fitting the context of humus formed from decomposed plant and animal remnants.

387. Select the most appropriate option to fill in blank number 4.
(a) compositions (b) fluctuations
(c) interactions (d) connections

Ans. (c) 'Interactions' means actions between elements, fitting the context of chemical and physical interactions.

388. Select the most appropriate option to fill in blank number 5.
(a) gradual (b) chemical
(c) steep (d) abrupt

Ans. (a) 'Gradual' means occurring slowly, fitting the context of soil formation being a gradual process.

PASSAGE-75

All elephants ....(1).......... several distinctive features, the most notable of which is a long trunk or proboscis, used for many .... (2) ...., particularly breathing, lifting water and grasping objects. Their incisors grow ....(3).......... tusks, which can serve as weapons and as tools for moving objects and digging.

Elephants' large ear flaps help to control their body temperature. Their pillar-like legs .... (4) .... carry their great weight. African elephants have larger ears and concave backs while Asian elephants have smaller ears and convex or level backs. One of the biggest threats to elephant populations is the ivory trade, as the animals are poached for their ivory tusks. Other threats to .... (5)..... elephants include habitat destruction and conflicts with local people. Elephants are used as working animals in Asia. In the past they were used in war; today, they are often put on display in zoos and circuses. **SSC CPO 10.11.2022**

389. Select the most appropriate option to fill in blank number 1.
(a) have (b) will have (c) had (d) has

Ans. (a) 'Have' means to possess, fitting the context of elephants having several distinctive features.

390. Select the most appropriate option to fill in blank number 2.
(a) schemes (b) means
(c) capacities (d) purposes

Ans. (d) 'Purposes' means intended uses, fitting the context of the trunk being used for many purposes.

391. Select the most appropriate option to fill in blank number 3.
(a) for (b) too (c) into (d) towards

Ans. (c) 'Into' means transforming, fitting the context of incisors growing into tusks.

392. Select the most appropriate option to fill in blank number 4.
(a) can (b) should (c) would (d) could

Ans. (a) 'Can' means able to, fitting the context of legs being able to carry their weight.

393. Select the most appropriate option to fill in blank number 5.
(a) wild (b) tame
(c) dangerous (d) elegant

Ans. (a) 'Wild' means untamed, fitting the context of threats to wild elephants.

SSC CPO 2021, 2020

PASSAGE-76

The rise and .... (1) .... of singers, music videos with lavish production budgets that amass hundreds of millions of views on YouTube, new sensations born virtually .... (2) ...., the overhang of drugs, guns and violence and the thrill of taste-making can all get .... (3) .... These are heady days in Punjab's .... (4) .... industry and Mohali is where the action is. It is a veritable music factory, some 20 songs are written, composed, recorded and released (5).... every day, by some reckoning. **SSC CPO 11.11.2021**

394. Select the most appropriate word to fill in blank number 1.
(a) failure (b) uprise
(c) down (d) fall

Ans. (d) 'Fall' means decline, fitting the context of the rise and fall of singers.

395. Select the most appropriate word to fill in blank number 2.
(a) tonight (b) overnight
(c) every night (d) at night

Ans. (b) 'Overnight' means suddenly, fitting the context of new sensations born overnight.

396. Select the most appropriate word to fill in blank number 3.
(a) overwhelming (b) easy
(c) boring (d) monotonous

Ans. (a) 'Overwhelming' means intense, fitting the context of the thrill of taste-making getting overwhelming.

397. Select the most appropriate word to fill in blank number 4.
(a) fashion (b) music
(c) film (d) food

Ans. (b) 'Music' means a related industry, fitting the context of Punjab's music industry.

398. Select the most appropriate word to fill in blank number 5.
(a) everywhere (b) there
(c) nowhere (d) here

Ans. (d) 'Here' means in this place, fitting the context of songs being written, composed, and released here.

PASSAGE-77

Necessity, they say, is the mother of invention. Dr. Burjor P. Banaji, pioneer of Lasik surgery in India has ....(1)......... over a dozen surgical instruments. When ....(2)......... senior eye surgeon at Max Eye Care started Lasik, there were ....(3)......... surgeons doing it worldwide and no ....(4)......... instruments were available either. "As I want things ....(5)........., I designed a whole slew of instruments that made my surgery more efficient," says Banaji. **SSC CPO 24.11.2020 (Shift-I)**

399. Select the most appropriate option to fill in the blank number 1.
(a) discovered (b) invented
(c) recovered (d) founded

Ans. (b) 'Invented' means created, fitting the context of Dr. Banaji inventing over a dozen surgical instruments.

400. Select the most appropriate option to fill in blank number 2.
(a) they (b) these (c) those (d) the

Ans. (d) 'The' means indicating a specific person, fitting the context of referring to the senior eye surgeon.

401. Select the most appropriate option to fill in the blank number 3.
(a) any (b) little (c) few (d) more

Ans. (c) 'Few' means not many, fitting the context of few surgeons doing it worldwide.

402. Select the most appropriate option to fill in the blank number 4.
(a) limited (b) correct
(c) exact (d) specific

Ans. (d) 'Specific' means clearly defined, fitting the context of no specific instruments being available.

403. Select the most appropriate option to fill in the blank number 5.
(a) popular (b) punitive
(c) perfect (d) prolific

Ans. (c) 'Perfect' means ideal, fitting the context of wanting things perfect.

SSC CHSL 2024 (Tier 1 & 2)

PASSAGE-78

During active sleep, the body is still, ...(1)... the brain is active. The eyes dart back and forth behind closed lids, blood pressure ...(2)... and the breathing pattern speeds up. An EEG of someone during rapid eye movement sleep looks almost the same as the EEG of a person in the waking state, although one is still asleep and the body is still immobile. Rapid eye movement sleep plays a vital role in harmonising the experiences we have in the world outside. An EEG of someone during rapid eye movement sleep looks almost the same as the EEG of a person in the ...(3)... state, although one is still asleep and the body is still ...(4)... . Rapid eye movement during sleep plays a vital role in harmonising the experiences we have in the world outside. **SSC CHSL Tier-2 18.11.2024**

404. Select the most appropriate option to fill in blank number 1.
(a) neither (b) therefore
(c) so (d) but

Ans. (d) 'But' is used to show contrast between the still body and the active brain.

405. Select the most appropriate option to fill in blank number 2.
(a) relaxes (b) beeps
(c) stables (d) increases

Ans. (d) 'Increases' is the correct verb to describe a rise in blood pressure.

406. Select the most appropriate option to fill in blank number 3.
(a) sleeping (b) standing
(c) waking (d) eating

Ans. (c) 'Waking' describes the state when someone is awake and active.

407. Select the most appropriate option to fill in blank number 4.
(a) conscious (b) immobile
(c) performing (d) active

Ans. (b) 'Immobile' means not moving, which accurately describes the body's state during this sleep phase.

PASSAGE-79

As Paul was (1) .... his supper, Aunt Jenny (2) .... him questions that have been full of deceit , and had a very deep meaning, for she wanted to trap him. It seemed as if she was endowed with a (3) .... which could hunt for dark and mysterious tact.

She asked, 'Did you now not want to swim, Paul?'

Paul felt an uncomfortable (4) ....

He (5) .... Aunt Jenny's face; however it informed him nothing. So, he said, 'No, ma'am.' **SSC CHSL Tier-1 01.07.2024 (Shift-I)**

408. Select the most appropriate option to fill in blank number 1.
(a) eating (b) churning
(c) feeding (d) grazing

Ans. (a) 'Eating' is the verb that accurately describes the action of consuming food, fitting the context of Paul having his supper.

409. Select the most appropriate option to fill in blank number 2.
(a) demanded (b) allowed
(c) submitted (d) asked

Ans. (d) 'Asked' is the verb that fits best in the context of Aunt Jenny posing questions to Paul. The verb 'asked' indicates a request for information, which aligns with the sentence's meaning.

410. Select the most appropriate option to fill in blank number 3.
(a) technique (b) purpose
(c) talent (d) weakness

Ans. (c) 'Talent' is a noun implying a special natural ability relevant to the context of Aunt Jenny's skill in detecting deceit.

411. Select the most appropriate option to fill in blank number 4.
(a) drop (b) suspicion
(c) view (d) guess

Ans. (b) 'Suspicion' is a noun that conveys Paul's feeling of doubt or distrust towards Aunt Jenny's questions.

412. Select the most appropriate option to fill in blank number 5.
(a) chased (b) ruffled
(c) searched (d) pursued

Ans. (c) 'Searched' is the verb that indicates Paul examining Aunt Jenny's face for clues about her intentions.

PASSAGE-80

The period from 1858-1905 was the seed time of Indian nationalism; and the early nationalists (1) .... the seeds well and deep. Instead of basing their nationalism or appeals to (2) .... sentiments and passing emotions, or abstract rights of freedom and liberty, or on obscurantist appeals to the past, they (3) .... it in a hard-headed and penetrating analysis of the complex mechanism of modern imperialism and the chief contradiction between the interests of the Indian people and British rule. The result was that they (4) .... a common political and economic programme which (5) .... rather than divided the different sections of the people. Later on, the Indian people could gather around this programme and wage powerful struggles.

SSC CHSL Tier-1 01.07.2024 (Shift-II)

413. Select the most appropriate option to fill in blank number 1.
(a) buried (b) scattered
(c) threw (d) sowed

Ans. (d) 'Sowed' means planted seeds, fitting the context of the early nationalists planting the seeds of Indian nationalism.

414. Select the most appropriate option to fill in blank number 2.
(a) shallow (b) grounded
(c) profound (d) deep

Ans. (c) 'Profound' means deep and serious, fitting the context of the sentiments appealed to by the nationalists.

415. Select the most appropriate option to fill in blank number 3.
(a) controlled (b) rooted
(c) drove (d) minded

Ans. (b) 'Rooted' means established firmly, fitting the context of basing nationalism on a well-thought-out analysis.

416. Select the most appropriate option to fill in blank number 4.
(a) evolved (b) banished
(c) uprooted (d) collapsed

Ans. (a) 'Evolved' means developed over time, fitting the context of creating a common political and economic programme.

417. Select the most appropriate option to fill in blank number 5.
(a) united (b) dissolved
(c) classified (d) complicated

Ans. (a) 'United' means brought together, fitting the context of the programme uniting different sections of the people.

PASSAGE-81

Many parents think of overweight children as 'cute' and cuddly. However, obesity must not be (1) .... as a healthy sign. (2) .... obese children grow up, they will be more prone (3) .... health problems like high blood pressure (4) .... diabetes. Today, overweight children are becoming a common (5) .... in many countries.

SSC CHSL Tier-1 01.07.2024 (Shift-III)

418. Select the most appropriate option to fill in blank number 1.
(a) saw (b) seen
(c) see (d) seeing

Ans. (b) 'Seen' is the past participle of 'see,'fitting the context of how obesity should not be viewed as a healthy sign.

419. Select the most appropriate option to fill in blank number 2.
(a) When (b) Who
(c) What (d) Where

Ans. (a) 'When' indicates the time at which something happens, fitting the context of obese children growing up.

420. Select the most appropriate option to fill in blank number 3.
(a) to (b) in
(c) at (d) on

Ans. (a) 'To' is a preposition used to indicate direction or result, fitting the context of children being prone to health problems.

421. Select the most appropriate option to fill in blank number 4.
(a) neither (b) or
(c) nor (d) never

Ans. (b) 'Or' is a conjunction used to link alternatives, fitting the context of health problems like high blood pressure or diabetes.

422. Select the most appropriate option to fill in blank number 5.
(a) sight (b) might
(c) light (d) tight

Ans. (a) 'Sight' means something that is seen, fitting the context of overweight children becoming a common occurrence.

PASSAGE-82

During the days of slavery, there lived (1) .... very hard-working slave. One day, (2) .... freedom, he ran away from his masters house. As he passed a forest, he saw a lion (3) .... with pain, for a huge thorn had pierced its paw. The slave felt sorry for the lion and took out the thorn gently. The grateful lion licked the slaves hand. But just then, both of (4) .... were captured by the soldiers.

The king ordered, 'Let the runaway slave (5) ……… thrown in front of a hungry lion.'But, when the slave was thrown in front of the lion, the lion licked him and quietly sat beside him. The amazed king asked the reason. The slave told the king everything. The king pardoned the slave. The lion was also freed and sent to the forest. **SSC CHSL Tier-1 01.07.2024 (Shift-IV)**

423. Select the most appropriate option to fill in blank number 1.

(a) the (b) a
(c) an (d) two

Ans. (b) 'A' is an indefinite article fitting the context of introducing 'a very hard-working slave'for the first time.

424. Select the most appropriate option to fill in blank number 2.

(a) gain (b) gains
(c) to gain (d) gained

Ans. (c) 'To gain' is an infinitive verb phrase indicating the purpose of the slave's action of running away.

425. Select the most appropriate option to fill in blank number 3.

(a) roars (b) roared
(c) roar (d) roaring

Ans. (d) 'Roaring' is a present participle describing the lion's continuous action of expressing pain.

426. Select the most appropriate option to fill in blank number 4.

(a) her (b) him
(c) us (d) them

Ans. (d) 'Them' is a pronoun referring to both the slave and the lion, fitting the context of their capture by the soldiers.

427. Select the most appropriate option to fill in blank number 5.

(a) been (b) being
(c) be (d) is

Ans. (c) 'Be' is a base form verb used after the modal 'let' to indicate the action of throwing the slave in front of a lion.

PASSAGE-83

(1) ……… health benefits, including protection from cardiovascular disease and cancer, have been (2) ……… to antioxidants; however, according to dietitian Vinson, these benefits depend on how well antioxidants are absorbed and (3) ……… by the body.

According to the study, coffee has more antioxidant power than other well-known foods and drinks, like tea, milk, chocolate, and cranberries. Dates had the highest antioxidants per serving out of all the foods and drinks (4) ………, but because dates are not consumed to the same extent as coffee, the latter comes out on (5) ………, according to Vinson.

SSC CHSL Tier-1 02.07.2024 (Shift-I)

428. Select the most appropriate option to fill in blank number 1.

(a) numerous (b) countable
(c) limited (d) few

Ans. (a) 'Numerous' means many, fitting the context of describing a large number of health benefits.

429. Select the most appropriate option to fill in blank number 2.

(a) attributed (b) negative
(c) similar (d) parallel

Ans. (a) 'Attributed' means credited to, fitting the context of assigning health benefits to antioxidants.

430. Select the most appropriate option to fill in blank number 3.

(a) utilised (b) impede
(c) rejected (d) hinder

Ans. (a) 'Utilised' means used, fitting the context of how antioxidants are absorbed and used by the body.

431. Select the most appropriate option to fill in blank number 4.

(a) assimilated (b) analysed
(c) synthesised (d) consumed

Ans. (d) 'Consumed' means eaten or used up, fitting the context of comparing foods and drinks based on consumption.

432. Select the most appropriate option to fill in blank number 5.

(a) bottom (b) lowest
(c) below (d) top

Ans. (d) 'Top' means the highest position, fitting the context of coffee being ranked the highest in antioxidant power.

PASSAGE-84

If we look at the global population, out of every six persons living in this world, one is an Indian and (1) .... a Chinese. The population of Pakistan is very (2).......... and accounts for roughly about one-tenth of China or India. Though China is the largest nation and geographically (3).......... the largest area among the three nations, its density is the lowest. Scholars point out the one child (4).......... in China in the late 1970s as the major reason for low population growth. They also state that this measure led to a (5).......... in the sex ratio, the proportion of females per 1000 males.

SSC CHSL Tier-1 02.07.2024 (Shift-II)

433. Select the most appropriate option to fill in blank number 1.

(a) many (b) another
(c) either (d) second

Ans. (d) 'Second' means another person, fitting the context of one being an Indian and another being a Chinese.

434. Select the most appropriate option to fill in blank number 2.

(a) small (b) obscure
(c) much (d) a little

Ans. (a) 'Small' means not large, fitting the context of describing Pakistan's population size.

435. Select the most appropriate option to fill in blank number 3.

(a) grasps (b) occupies
(c) rents (d) lodges

Ans. (b) 'Occupies' means takes up space, fitting the context of China having the largest geographical area.

436. Select the most appropriate option to fill in blank number 4.

(a) average (b) statute
(c) ordeal (d) standard

Ans. (b) 'Statute' means a law, fitting the context of the one-child policy being a significant measure in China.

437. Select the most appropriate option to fill in blank number 5.

(a) decline
(b) suspension
(c) diminish
(d) failure

Ans. (a) 'Decline' means a decrease, fitting the context of the sex ratio being affected by the one-child policy.

PASSAGE-85

Cities are the great havens for knowledge, culture and social life. Vibrant cultures are found in cities because it takes a (1).............. population to support museums, concert halls, sports teams, and night-life districts. Cities also offer rich social opportunities. People in rural areas enjoy only limited social opportunities because (2)........... the small local population. City dwellers can choose their friends and mates from among a large number of people of (3)........... interests and inclinations. We are not likely to abandon the city as a (4)........... institution, but we need to make sure that our transport arrangements do not (5)........... the city's other functions. **SSC CHSL Tier-1 02.07.2024 (Shift-III)**

438. Select the most appropriate option to fill in blank number 1.
(a) large (b) small
(c) lazy (d) dumb

Ans. (a) 'Large' means big, fitting the context of a population size needed to support cultural and social institutions.

439. Select the most appropriate option to fill in blank number 2.
(a) off (b) with (c) of (d) for

Ans. (c) 'Of' indicates a cause or reason, fitting the context of limited social opportunities due to the small local population.

440. Select the most appropriate option to fill in blank number 3.
(a) wasteful (b) declining
(c) similar (d) feigning

Ans. (c) 'Similar' means alike, fitting the context of people choosing friends and mates with similar interests and inclinations.

441. Select the most appropriate option to fill in blank number 4.
(a) psychological (b) educational
(c) cultural (d) religious

Ans. (c) 'Cultural' means related to culture, fitting the context of not abandoning the city as a cultural institution.

442. Select the most appropriate option to fill in blank number 5.
(a) boost (b) help
(c) damage (d) support

Ans. (c) 'Damage' means harm, fitting the context of ensuring transport arrangements do not harm the city's other functions.

PASSAGE-86

It is generally (1) .... that the methodology of teaching-learning is the concern of teachers only. Learners have (2) .... or nothing to do with it. But this is not true. The teaching-learning (3) .... are concerns of learners as well. Knowing and understanding that how different subjects are taught are important for the learners of all subjects, but it has more (4) .... for the learners of physical education. When we talk about you as learners of physical education, we mean that you have actually participated in the subject area, rather than (5) ...... studied it. **SSC CHSL Tier-1 02.07.2024 (Shift-IV)**

443. Select the most appropriate option to fill in blank number 1.
(a) hoped (b) wished
(c) planned (d) believed

Ans. (d) 'Believed' means considered to be true, fitting the context of the common assumption about teaching-learning methodology.

444. Select the most appropriate option to fill in blank number 2.
(a) light (b) minute
(c) little (d) sparse

Ans. (c) 'Little' means almost none, fitting the context of learners having minimal involvement.

445. Select the most appropriate option to fill in blank number 3.
(a) forms (b) breaks
(c) customs (d) methods

Ans. (d) 'Methods' means ways or processes, fitting the context of teaching-learning processes.

446. Select the most appropriate option to fill in blank number 4.
(a) reference (b) recurrence
(c) relevance (d) consistency

Ans. (c) 'Relevance' means importance or significance, fitting the context of its importance to learners of physical education.

447. Select the most appropriate option to fill in blank number 5.
(a) merely (b) hardly
(c) purely (d) entirely

Ans. (a) 'Merely' means just or simply, fitting the context of learners actually participating rather than just studying.

PASSAGE-87

On the afternoon of 30th March, 1981, many Americans experienced a
(1) .... of déjà-vu. Déjà-vu is a name given to the feeling that a person has seen or experienced an event before. Many Americans could not help having that feeling on this day.

The (2) .... hit TVs and radios immediately. President Ronald Raegan had been shot. He was leaving a hotel in Washington DC, turned to wave at some of the people gathered to see him, and fell towards the ground. Before he could hit the ground, his Secret Service Agents (3) .... him into the car and rushed to the nearest hospital. This same story had been heard before. On 22nd November, 1963, President John F. Kennedy was riding in a motorcade through Dallas, Texas. He smiled and waved to the crowd that had gathered to see him. (4) .... rang out from a nearby building. The President collapsed into the backseat of the car and was immediately taken to the nearest hospital. He was (5) .... dead at the hospital. Now, just seventeen years later, the news sounded eerily the same. **SSC CHSL Tier-1 03.07.2024 (Shift-I)**

448. Select the most appropriate option to fill in blank number 1.
(a) feeling (b) dealing
(c) blinking (d) recalling

Ans. (a) 'Feeling' is a noun that fits the context of déjà-vu, which is the sensation of having experienced something before.

449. Select the most appropriate option to fill in blank number 2.
(a) arrow (b) sceptre
(c) news (d) ball

Ans. (c) 'News' is a noun that fits the context of information being broadcasted on TVs and radios.

450. Select the most appropriate option to fill in blank number 3.
(a) whisked (b) pulled
(c) called (d) pushed

Ans. (a) 'Whisked is a verb that means quickly moved, fitting the context of the agents swiftly taking the President to the car.

451. Select the most appropriate option to fill in blank number 4.
(a) Shots (b) Alarm
(c) Music (d) Prayers

Ans. (a) 'Shots' is a noun that fits the context of the sounds that caused the President to collapse.

452. Select the most appropriate option to fill in blank number 5.
(a) acting (b) shot
(c) pronounced (d) almost

Ans. (c) 'Pronounced' is a verb that fits the context of the doctors officially declaring the President dead at the hospital.

PASSAGE-88

There is nothing more (1) .... than when you sit down at your table to study with the most sincere of intentions and instead of being able to finish the task at hand you find your thoughts (2) .... However, there are certain techniques that you can use to (3) .... your concentration. To begin with, one should (4) .... to create the physical environment that is conducive to (5) .... thought. **SSC CHSL Tier-1 03.07.2024 (Shift-II)**

453. Select the most appropriate option to fill in blank number 1.
(a) exciting (b) frustrating
(c) surprising (d) interesting

Ans. (b) 'Frustrating' means causing irritation or annoyance, fitting the context of being unable to finish the task at hand.

454. Select the most appropriate option to fill in blank number 2.
(a) worrying (b) tiring
(c) interesting (d) wandering

Ans. (d) 'Wandering' means moving aimlessly, fitting the context of thoughts drifting away while trying to study.

455. Select the most appropriate option to fill in blank number 3.
(a) enhance (b) convince
(c) commit (d) discover

Ans. (a) 'Enhance' means to improve or increase, fitting the context of techniques used to improve concentration.

456. Select the most appropriate option to fill in blank number 4.
(a) attempt (b) announce
(c) imagine (d) lead

Ans. (a) 'Attempt' means to try or make an effort, fitting the context of creating a conducive physical environment.

457. Select the most appropriate option to fill in blank number 5.
(a) dazzling (b) focussed
(c) cautious (d) joyful

Ans. (b) 'Focussed' means concentrated or directed, fitting the context of an environment conducive to concentrated thought.

PASSAGE-89

The tuatara, which lives on New Zealand's islands, is affectionately known as Living fossil. It is called that because it is the only (1)......... reptile in a group of reptiles that dates back about 220 million years to the time of the dinosaurs. The colour of the tuatara is grey or olive green. It (2)......... to a length of around 60 cm. The fact that this lizard has three eyes is its most (3)......... feature.

The pineal eye is the name given to the cone-shaped third eye. This eye is in a space between the brain and head. It has an eyelid over the third eye, which closes on a horizontal level. The tuatara has teeth that are (4)......... from those of other reptiles. The lower jaw has only one row of teeth, while the upper jaw has two rows.

The tuatara is most active at night. It eats the eggs of birds, frogs, rats and insects. A tuatara's average lifespan is less than 77 years, but some species can live up to 100 years. In the spring, the female tuatara lays 8 to 15 eggs. These eggs are (5)......... during summer. **SSC CHSL Tier-1 03.07.2024 (Shift-III)**

458. Select the most appropriate option to fill in blank number 1.
(a) living (b) being
(c) entity (d) life

Ans. (a) 'Living' means alive, fitting the context of describing the tuatara as the only living reptile from its ancient group.

459. Select the most appropriate option to fill in blank number 2.
(a) creates (b) develops
(c) links (d) nourishes

Ans. (b) 'Develops' means grows, fitting the context of the tuatara growing to a length of around 60 cm.

460. Select the most appropriate option to fill in blank number 3.
(a) intriguing (b) absorbing
(c) diverting (d) escalating

Ans. (a) 'Intriguing' means interesting, fitting the context of describing the most fascinating feature of the tuatara.

461. Select the most appropriate option to fill in blank number 4.
(a) separate (b) distinct
(c) discrete (d) sharp

Ans. (b) 'Distinct' means different, fitting the context of describing how the tuatara's teeth differ from those of other reptiles.

462. Select the most appropriate option to fill in blank number 5.
(a) pollinated (b) fertilised
(c) germinated (d) fructified

Ans. (b) 'Fertilised' means having undergone fertilisation, fitting the context of eggs being fertilised during summer.

PASSAGE-90

Trees are (1)......... best gift of nature for us. They make the environment beautiful and clean. Water and sunlight are very important to helping trees grow. Human beings get food from trees. Trees also give us wood and shade. Houses, chairs and toys (2) .... from wood we receive from trees. Trees can be called the best friends of mankind. Many animals get their food from leaves, vegetables and fruits grown (3) .... trees. They also live in the shadows of trees. We (4) .... cutting trees to save nature. Children and adults need to plant more trees and teach each other to stop causing harm to (5) .... One tree can save many lives. **SSC CHSL Tier-1 03.07.2024 (Shift-IV)**

463. Select the most appropriate option to fill in blank number 1.
(a) the (b) a (c) an (d) No article

Ans. (a) 'The' is a definite article, fitting the context of describing 'the best gift of nature'as something specific and well-known.

464. Select the most appropriate option to fill in blank number 2.
(a) are made (b) had make
(c) was make (d) will made

Ans. (a) 'Are made' is a present passive verb form, fitting the context of describing what houses, chairs, and toys are made from.

465. Select the most appropriate option to fill in blank number 3.
(a) on (b) out
(c) of (d) for

Ans. (c) 'Of' is a preposition indicating relationship, fitting the context of food grown from trees.

466. Select the most appropriate option to fill in blank number 4.
(a) can stopped (b) may stopped
(c) should stop (d) have stop

Ans. (c) 'Should stop' is a modal verb phrase, fitting the context of advising people to take action to save nature.

467. Select the most appropriate option to fill in blank number 5.
(a) nurturing (b) nature
(c) nurture (d) natural

Ans. (b) 'Nature' is a noun, fitting the context of stopping harm to the natural environment.

PASSAGE-91

Oil is almost certainly one of the ocean's greatest resources. 33% of the world's oil comes from seaward fields in seas. Oils are liquids that easily burn and do not (1)......... in water. Most of the time, they are made of chains of carbon and hydrogen atoms. There are three (2)......... types of oils: mineral, essential and fixed oils. From plants, essential oils are thin, scented oils. Because they frequently have an odour, essential oils are (3)......... in perfumery and food flavouring. Aromatic extraction processes like cold pressing, distillation and extraction are typically used to prepare essential oils. Fatty acids are used by animals and plants to make fixed oils. They are especially non-volatile oils that are found in the seeds of cotton, corn, flax, sunflowers, peanuts, coconuts and olives, as well as in fatty animal tissues. Mineral oils are (4)......... from petroleum which has been underground for millions of years from sea organism skeletons. Mineral oils are one of the petroleum by-products with the lowest prices. Mineral oils are colourless and transparent. They are made up of a (5)......... of hydrocarbons. **SSC CHSL Tier-1 04.07.2024 (Shift-I)**

468. Select the most appropriate option to fill in blank number 1.
(a) dissolve (b) diffuse
(c) melt (d) evaporate

Ans. (a) 'Dissolve' means to mix into a liquid, fitting the context of oils not mixing in water.

469. Select the most appropriate option to fill in blank number 2.
(a) initial (b) original
(c) early (d) primary

Ans. (d) 'Primary' means main or chief, fitting the context of describing the three main types of oils.

470. Select the most appropriate option to fill in blank number 3.
(a) applied (b) utilised
(c) operated (d) employed

Ans. (b) 'Utilised' means used, fitting the context of essential oils being used in perfumery and food flavouring.

471. Select the most appropriate option to fill in blank number 4.
(a) produced (b) invented
(c) renewed (d) fabricated

Ans. (a) 'Produced' means made or generated, fitting the context of mineral oils being extracted from petroleum.

472. Select the most appropriate option to fill in blank number 5.
(a) collaboration (b) cooperation
(c) combination (d) association

Ans. (c) 'Combination' means a mixture or blend, fitting the context of mineral oils being made up of various hydrocarbons.

PASSAGE-92

Once upon a time, there was a man (1) .... used to tell the fortunes of people. One day, he was telling the fortune as usual when a man came to him and said, 'Somebody (2) .... broken the door of your house and has stolen many valuables. Go home at once!"

The fortune teller was (3) .... shocked to hear the news. He could not utter a word out of shock. He just ran to his house as fast as he could. He was in such a hurry that he left all his things behind. Now, one of his customers saw him rushing and (4) .... 'Every day he (5) .... the fortunes of so many people but today he could not see his own future!'The fortune teller felt very embarrassed. **SSC CHSL Tier-1 04.07.2024 (Shift-II)**

473. Select the most appropriate option to fill in blank number 1.
(a) whose (b) whom
(c) by whom (d) who

Ans. (d) 'Who' is a relative pronoun, fitting the context of describing the man who tells fortunes.

474. Select the most appropriate option to fill in blank number 2.
(a) shall have (b) had
(c) have (d) has

Ans. (b) "Had" is the past perfect tense, fitting the context of an action that was completed before the current moment.

475. Select the most appropriate option to fill in blank number 3.
(a) so less (b) so more
(c) many (d) quite

Ans. (d) 'Quite' means very, fitting the context of describing the extent of the fortune teller's shock.

476. Select the most appropriate option to fill in blank number 4.
(a) comments (b) commented
(c) commenting (d) comment

Ans. (b) 'Commented' is the past tense, fitting the context of describing the customer's reaction.

477. Select the most appropriate option to fill in blank number 5.
(a) tell (b) tells (c) telling (d) told

Ans. (b) 'Tells' is the present tense, fitting the context of the fortune teller's regular activity.

PASSAGE-93

Famines were (1) .... during the period of British rule due to many reasons (2) .... unemployment following import of machine-made goods from Britain, overexploitation of farmers and (3) .... access to food. India suffered two very severe droughts in 1965 and 1966. India achieved (4) .... in food grains by the year 1976 through the implementation of the seedwater- fertiliser-led (5) .... The country is no longer exposed to real famines. However, lack of purchasing power continues to haunt people in some parts of the country. **SSC CHSL Tier-1 04.07.2024 (Shift-III)**

478. Select the most appropriate option to fill in blank number 1.
(a) caused (b) excruciated
(c) paused (d) discouraged
Ans. (a) 'Caused' means brought about, fitting the context of famines occurring due to several reasons.

479. Select the most appropriate option to fill in blank number 2.
(a) excluding large-scale (b) excluding small-scale
(c) including small-scale (d) including large-scale
Ans. (d) 'Including large-scale' fits the context of listing reasons such as large-scale unemployment.

480. Select the most appropriate option to fill in blank number 3.
(a) basic (b) restricted
(c) unlimited (d) inflated
Ans. (b) 'Restricted' means limited, fitting the context of limited access to food during famines.

481. Select the most appropriate option to fill in blank number 4.
(a) goal (b) incompetency
(c) success (d) self-sufficiency
Ans. (d) 'Self-sufficiency' means being able to sustain oneself without external aid, fitting the context of achieving independence in food grains.

482. Select the most appropriate option to fill in blank number 5.
(a) Blue Revolution (b) Pink Revolution
(c) Green Revolution (d) White Revolution
Ans. (c) 'Green Revolution' refers to the agricultural revolution involving seed-water-fertiliser, fitting the context of increased food grain production.

PASSAGE-94

Nutrition experts have researched the bad effects of junk food and have come to the (1)......... that junk food manufacturing companies are fooling the people by (2)......... deceptive advertisements that show junk food as healthy. We must substitute junk food with (3)......... food like fruits and vegetables.

So, the next time you think of (4)......... that burger, hotdog, pizza, samosa, kachori or even ice cream in a restaurant, eating joint or a party, stop your instincts and look for some healthier food (5)......... instead. **SSC CHSL Tier-1 04.07.2024 (Shift-IV)**

483. Select the most appropriate option to fill in blank number 1.
(a) conclusion (b) derivation
(c) solution (d) assumption
Ans. (a) 'Conclusion' means a judgment or decision reached after consideration, fitting the context of what nutrition experts have determined about junk food.

484. Select the most appropriate option to fill in blank number 2.
(a) observing (b) showing
(c) blowing (d) assuming
Ans. (b) 'Showing' means displaying or indicating, fitting the context of deceptive advertisements that portray junk food as healthy.

485. Select the most appropriate option to fill in blank number 3.
(a) powerful (b) expensive
(c) healthier (d) cleaner
Ans. (c) 'Healthier' means more conducive to good health, fitting the context of substituting junk food with nutritious options like fruits and vegetables.

486. Select the most appropriate option to fill in blank number 4.
(a) skipping (b) grabbing
(c) building (d) turning
Ans. (b) 'Grabbing' means quickly taking, fitting the context of the instinct to quickly grab junk food.

487. Select the most appropriate option to fill in blank number 5.
(a) comparisons (b) chances
(c) additions (d) options
Ans. (d) 'Options' means choices, fitting the context of looking for healthier food alternatives instead of junk food.

PASSAGE-95

The Sun is about 1.4 million kilometres (1) .... diameter, while the Earth is about 13,000 kilometres wide. This indicates that the Sun's width would need to be filled by more than one hundred Earths. Sunspots are dreary (2) .... on the Sun's surface that are two thousand degrees celsius cooler than the rest of the surface. The coolest piece of the sunspot is the dim focus called the umbra.

The penumbra surrounds it. On the Sun's surface, some sunspots are just specks. Additionally, they appear in groups up to ten times larger than Earth. They can sometimes reach 2,00,000 miles in length. As the Sun rotates, these groups (3) .... to travel across the Sun over two weeks. Every 11 years, the number of sunspots reaches its maximum. The solar or sunspot cycle (4) .... to this. The Earth's weather may become more extreme and warm during the peak of sunspot activity. According to the (5) .... made by satellites like Nimbus 7, when sunspots are at their largest, less heat reaches Earth. **SSC CHSL Tier-1 05.07.2024 (Shift-I)**

488. Select the most appropriate option to fill in blank number 1.
(a) in (b) of
(c) on (d) at
Ans. (b) 'Of' indicates measurement, fitting the context of describing the Sun's diameter.

489. Select the most appropriate option to fill in blank number 2.
(a) regions (b) section
(c) belt (d) province
Ans. (a) 'Regions' means areas, fitting the context of parts of the Sun's surface.

490. Select the most appropriate option to fill in blank number 3.
(a) act (b) show
(c) shape (d) appear
Ans. (d) 'Appear' means come into view, fitting the context of sunspot groups moving across the Sun.

491. Select the most appropriate option to fill in blank number 4.
(a) refers (b) pass
(c) cite (d) entrust
Ans. (a) 'Refers' means mentions or relates to, fitting the context of the sunspot cycle.

492. Select the most appropriate option to fill in blank number 5.
(a) perceptions (b) inspections
(c) observations (d) invalidations
Ans. (c) 'Observations' means findings, fitting the context of what satellites have recorded.

PASSAGE-96

For decades, humans have tried to theorise the origin and evolution of the universe. Many theories have been proposed and rejected. However, the Big Bang theory has been the most (1) .... accepted. According to this theory, the universe began as a single point, or singularity, around 13.8 billion years ago. This singularity contained all the matter and energy that would eventually (2)......... the stars, galaxies and other structures that make up our universe today. The Big Bang theory is supported by a (3)......... of observational evidence, including the cosmic microwave background radiation, the (4)......... of light elements in the universe and the large-scale structure of the cosmos. Despite its success, the Big Bang theory is still an active area of research, with scientists seeking to better understand the earliest moments of the universe and the (5).........of dark matter and energy.

SSC CHSL Tier-1 05.07.2024 (Shift-II)

493. Select the most appropriate option to fill in blank number 1.

(a) widely (b) vastly
(c) largely (d) loosely

Ans. (a) 'Widely' means to a great extent, fitting the context of being the most commonly accepted theory.

494. Select the most appropriate option to fill in blank number 2.

(a) form (b) design
(c) prepare (d) destroy

Ans. (a) 'Form' means to take shape, fitting the context of matter and energy forming stars and galaxies.

495. Select the most appropriate option to fill in blank number 3.

(a) rich (b) wealth
(c) debt (d) store

Ans. (b) 'Wealth' means a large amount, fitting the context of abundant observational evidence.

496. Select the most appropriate option to fill in blank number 4.

(a) abundance (b) plenty
(c) fortune (d) success

Ans. (a) 'Abundance' means a large quantity, fitting the context of the presence of light elements.

497. Select the most appropriate option to fill in blank number 5.

(a) nature (b) environment
(c) capture (d) brand

Ans. (a) 'Nature' means the fundamental qualities, fitting the context of understanding dark matter and energy.

PASSAGE-97

Romantic poetry is a literary movement that emerged in the late 18th century and continued through the mid-19th century. It is (1)......... by an emphasis on emotion, imagination and individualism. Romantic poets sought to express their innermost thoughts and feelings through their poetry, often exploring (2)......... such as love, beauty and mortality. One of the defining features of Romantic poetry is its use of language and imagery to evoke powerful emotions in the reader. Many Romantic poets, such as William Wordsworth and Samuel Taylor Coleridge (3)......... that poetry should be written in the language of common people, rather than in the lofty, formal language of the past. They also incorporated vivid descriptions of nature and the natural world into their poetry, using it as a source of inspiration and spiritual renewal. (4)......... important aspect of Romantic poetry is its focus on the individual and the subjective experience. Romantic poets believed that each persons experience of the world was unique and valuable, and sought to capture this individuality in their writing. This led to a greater emphasis on personal expression and introspection in poetry, (5)......... a rejection of the traditional poetic forms and structures of the past.

SSC CHSL Tier-1 05.07.2024 (Shift-III)

498. Select the most appropriate option to fill in blank number 1.

(a) characterises (b) characteristic
(c) characterised (d) characterising

Ans. (c) 'Characterised' means described by, fitting the context of Romantic poetry being described by an emphasis on emotion, imagination and individualism.

499. Select the most appropriate option to fill in blank number 2.

(a) concerns (b) arguments
(c) problems (d) themes

Ans. (d) 'Themes' means topics or subjects, fitting the context of Romantic poets exploring subjects like love, beauty, and mortality.

500. Select the most appropriate option to fill in blank number 3.

(a) could believe (b) will believe
(c) believes (d) believed

Ans. (d) 'Believed' means held a particular opinion, fitting the context of Romantic poets' belief about how poetry should be written.

501. Select the most appropriate option to fill in blank number 4.

(a) Mostly (b) Additional
(c) Another (d) Farther

Ans. (c) 'Another' means an additional one, fitting the context of describing another important aspect of Romantic poetry.

502. Select the most appropriate option to fill in blank number 5.

(a) whereas (b) therefore
(c) as well as (d) but

Ans. (b) 'Therefore' means for that reason, fitting the context of explaining the result of a greater emphasis on personal expression and introspection in poetry.

PASSAGE-98

Today, lets explore the significant role of human beings in shaping the world as we know it. Can you (1)......... a world without human beings? Who would have (2)......... the resources and created social and cultural environment? The people are (3)......... to develop the economy and the society. The people make and use resources and are themselves resources with (4)......... quality. Coal is but a piece of rock, until people were able to (5).......... technology to obtain it and make it a 'resource'.

SSC CHSL Tier-1 05.07.2024 (Shift-IV)

503. Select the most appropriate option to fill in blank number 1.

(a) ignore (b) fabricate
(c) neglect (d) imagine

Ans. (d) 'Imagine' means to form a mental picture, fitting the context of considering a world without human beings.

504. Select the most appropriate option to fill in blank number 2.

(a) broken (b) destroyed
(c) crippled (d) utilised

Ans. (d) 'Utilised' means made use of, fitting the context of using resources and creating a social and cultural environment.

505. Select the most appropriate option to fill in blank number 3.
(a) crucial (b) frantic
(c) hopeful (d) hasty

Ans. (a) 'Crucial' means extremely important, fitting the context of the significant role people play in developing the economy and society.

506. Select the most appropriate option to fill in blank number 4.
(a) deviating (b) alternating
(c) inconstant (d) varying

Ans. (d) 'Varying' means differing, fitting the context of people being resources with different qualities.

507. Select the most appropriate option to fill in blank number 5.
(a) fashion (b) mint
(c) invent (d) open

Ans. (c) 'Invent' means to create or design, fitting the context of developing technology to obtain and use coal as a resource.

PASSAGE-99

Family plays a vital role in our lives, serving as a source of love, support and stability. It is (1)......... the family unit that we develop lasting bonds, learn essential values, and find comfort during (2) .... times. Families provide a nurturing environment for personal growth and emotional well-being. They (3) .... guidance, share experiences, and create cherished memories. The strength and (4) .... of a family contribute to individual happiness, societal harmony, and the (5) .... of a strong community. **SSC CHSL Tier-1 08.07.2024 (Shift-I)**

508. Select the most appropriate option to fill in blank number 1.
(a) within (b) among
(c) beyond (d) between

Ans. (a) 'Within' indicates inside, fitting the context of developing bonds and values within the family unit.

509. Select the most appropriate option to fill in blank number 2.
(a) joyful (b) challenging
(c) initial (d) wasteful

Ans. (b) 'Challenging' means difficult, fitting the context of finding comfort during difficult times.

510. Select the most appropriate option to fill in blank number 3.
(a) deliver (b) offer
(c) contribute (d) propose

Ans. (b) 'Offer' means to provide, fitting the context of families providing guidance and sharing experiences.

511. Select the most appropriate option to fill in blank number 4.
(a) intrusion (b) cohesion
(c) disruption (d) commotion

Ans. (b) 'Cohesion' means unity or togetherness, fitting the context of family strength and unity contributing to happiness and harmony.

512. Select the most appropriate option to fill in blank number 5.
(a) foundation (b) undermining
(c) collision (d) erosion

Ans. (a) 'Foundation' means the basis or groundwork, fitting the context of a strong community being built on the foundation of strong families.

PASSAGE-100

Hierarchy is key in ensuring normal functioning of our increasingly (1)......... society. In the US, there is an enormous variety of industries, professional branches, specialisations, as well as a great (2)......... of other domains of human activity or interests. So, competence here is valued and opinion influencers have an important role to play. In fact, leadership evolves as a necessity almost in any realm of human activity/ thinking, (3)......... where more people are involved.

Thus, it isn't hard (4)......... why even in academic institutions throughout the US and worldwide, students are given leadership essay assignments. Most students will take on leadership roles with various degrees of responsibility and impact in their lives, hence, becoming (5)......... with typical challenges, solutions, or skills required is essential.

SSC CHSL Tier-1 08.07.2024 (Shift-II)

513. Select the most appropriate option to fill in blank number 1.
(a) systematic (b) complex
(c) easy (d) fine

Ans. (b) 'Complex' means complicated or intricate, fitting the context of describing society's increasing complexity.

514. Select the most appropriate option to fill in blank number 2.
(a) worry (b) difficulty
(c) uniformity (d) diversity

Ans. (d) 'Diversity' means a range of different things, fitting the context of various domains of human activity or interests.

515. Select the most appropriate option to fill in blank number 3.
(a) especially (b) only
(c) easily (d) tactfully

Ans. (a) 'Especially' means particularly, fitting the context of emphasizing realms with more people involved.

516. Select the most appropriate option to fill in blank number 4.
(a) focusing (b) rejecting
(c) polishing (d) accepting

Ans. (d) 'Accepting' means recognising as valid, fitting the context of understanding why students are given leadership assignments.

517. Select the most appropriate option to fill in blank number 5.
(a) familiar (b) unusual
(c) unequal (d) strange

Ans. (a) 'Familiar' means well-known, fitting the context of becoming acquainted with challenges, solutions or skills required.

PASSAGE-101

Trees provide so many benefits (1)......... our everyday lives. They filter clean air, provide fresh drinking water, help (2)............. climate change and create homes for thousands of species of plants and animals. (3).......... a billion trees can help save the Earth from climate change and biodiversity loss. When we restore and (4)........... critical forests, we remove carbon and support biodiversity. A billion is a big number, but we know we can do it together. (5).......... the planet by planting your tree today. This can protect and restore forests for future. **SSC CHSL Tier-1 08.07.2024 (Shift-III)**

518. Select the most appropriate option to fill in blank number 1.
(a) in (b) to
(c) for (d) with
Ans. (b) 'To' means indicating relationship, fitting the context of describing the benefits provided to our everyday lives.

519. Select the most appropriate option to fill in blank number 2.
(a) crib (b) cut
(c) curb (d) crust
Ans. (c) 'Curb' means to control or limit, fitting the context of helping to control climate change.

520. Select the most appropriate option to fill in blank number 3.
(a) In planting (b) With planting
(c) By planting (d) Planting
Ans. (c) 'By planting' means through the action of planting, fitting the context of how planting a billion trees can help save the Earth.

521. Select the most appropriate option to fill in blank number 4.
(a) sabotage (b) conserve
(c) observe (d) curtail
Ans. (b) 'Conserve' means to protect and preserve, fitting the context of restoring and preserving critical forests.

522. Select the most appropriate option to fill in blank number 5.
(a) Denigrate (b) Complement
(c) Sustain (d) Supplement
Ans. (c) 'Sustain' means to maintain or support, fitting the context of maintaining the planet by planting trees.

PASSAGE-102

A few months after Conrads death, the nobles met at Aix-la-Chapelle and elected Henry to be their king. At this time, it was the (1)................ in Europe to hunt various birds, such as the wild duck and partridge, with falcons. The falcons were long-winged birds of prey, (2)................ hawks. They were trained to (3)................ on their masters wrist and wait patiently until they were told to fly. Then they would swiftly (4) .... at their prey and bear it to the ground. Henry was very fond of falconry and hence was known as Henry the Fowler, or Falconer. As soon as the other dukes had elected him king, a messenger was sent to Saxony to (5)................ him of the honour done for him. After a search of some days, he was at last found, far up in the Hartz Mountains, hunting with his falcons.

SSC CHSL Tier-1 08.07.2024 (Shift-IV)

523. Select the most appropriate option to fill in blank number 1.
(a) custom (b) ritualistic
(c) motive (d) conventions
Ans. (a) 'Custom' means a traditional practice, fitting the context of describing the practice of hunting birds with falcons.

524. Select the most appropriate option to fill in blank number 2.
(a) subjugating (b) echoing
(c) favouring (d) resembling
Ans. (d) 'Resembling' means looking similar to, fitting the context of falcons being similar to hawks.

525. Select the most appropriate option to fill in blank number 3.
(a) lurch (b) chirp
(c) sitting (d) perch
Ans. (d) 'Perch' means to sit or rest on a high place, fitting the context of falcons sitting on their master's wrist.

526. Select the most appropriate option to fill in blank number 4.
(a) leapt (b) flight
(c) dart (d) dashed
Ans. (c) 'Dart' means to move swiftly, fitting the context of falcons quickly attacking their prey.

527. Select the most appropriate option to fill in blank number 5.
(a) inform (b) nullify
(c) communicate (d) convey
Ans. (a) 'Inform' means to tell, fitting the context of a messenger informing Henry of his election as king.

PASSAGE-103

The disclaimer read that no animals were harmed (1)............ the filming of that scene. However, they forgot that the brand of lipstick that was applied (2)............ the heroines lips for that scene was manufactured from crushed cochineal bugs, which release a pigment commonly used in red lipstick. The other items in the film studio (3)............ used animal fats during their manufacturing. The actors who (4)............ that they are vegan in past interviews are unaware of their indirect involvement in such acts of cruelty against animals. The indirect cruelty against animals does not stop here. For example, the extensive disposal of plastic waste in oceans has made plastic a part of the animal food chain, which is detrimental (5) .... our entire ecosystem.

SSC CHSL Tier-1 09.07.2024 (Shift-I)

528. Select the most appropriate option to fill in blank number 1.
(a) during (b) around
(c) from (d) for
Ans. (a) 'During' means throughout the duration of an event, fitting the context of the period when filming occurred.

529. Select the most appropriate option to fill in blank number 2.
(a) on (b) to
(c) over (d) upon
Ans. (a) 'On' means placed upon, fitting the context of lipstick being applied on the heroine's lips.

530. Select the most appropriate option to fill in blank number 3.
(a) long (b) also
(c) least (d) too
Ans. (b) 'Also' means in addition to, fitting the context of additional items using animal fats in their manufacturing.

531. Select the most appropriate option to fill in blank number 4.
(a) were confessing (b) had confessed
(c) confessed (d) are confessing
Ans. (b) 'Had confessed' means previously admitted, fitting the context of actors admitting their veganism in past interviews.

532. Select the most appropriate option to fill in blank number 5.
(a) to (b) on
(c) in (d) for
Ans. (a) 'To' means indicating effect, fitting the context of something being detrimental to the entire ecosystem.

PASSAGE-104

Our country, India, is one of the 12 mega bio-diversity countries of the world. With about 47,000 plant species, India (1)......... tenth place in the world and fourth in Asia in plant diversity. There are (2)......... 15,000 flowering plants in India, which account for 6 per cent of the world's (3)......... number of flowering plants. The country has many non-flowering plants, (4)......... as ferns, algae and fungi. India also has approximately 90,000 (5)......... of animals, as well as a rich variety of fish in its fresh and marine waters. **SSC CHSL Tier-1 09.07.2024 (Shift-II)**

533. Select the most appropriate option to fill in blank number 1.
(a) have (b) occupies
(c) had (d) occupy

Ans. (b) 'Occupies' means takes up space, fitting the context of India's ranking in plant diversity.

534. Select the most appropriate option to fill in blank number 2.
(a) a (b) many
(c) of (d) about

Ans. (d) 'About' means approximately, fitting the context of describing the number of flowering plants in India.

535. Select the most appropriate option to fill in blank number 3.
(a) exact (b) nearly
(c) exactly (d) total

Ans. (d) 'Total' means the sum, fitting the context of the world's total number of flowering plants.

536. Select the most appropriate option to fill in blank number 4.
(a) as (b) such
(c) in (d) for

Ans. (b) 'Such' means of this kind, fitting the context of giving examples of non-flowering plants.

537. Select the most appropriate option to fill in blank number 5.
(a) specie (b) species
(c) kind (d) type

Ans. (b) 'Species' means different kinds, fitting the context of describing the variety of animals in India.

PASSAGE-105

Conversation is indeed the (1)......... teachable of all arts. All you need to do in order to become a good conversationalist is to find a (2) .... that interests you and your listeners. But the important thing is that you must talk about the other (3)......... hobby rather than your own. Therein lies the secret of your (4)......... . Talk to your friends about the things that interest them, and you will get a reputation for good fellowship, charming wit, and a brilliant mind. There is nothing that (5) .... people so much as your interest in their interest. **SSC CHSL Tier-1 09.07.2024 (Shift-III)**

538. Select the most appropriate option to fill in blank number 1.
(a) more easily (b) more likely
(c) most easily (d) most occasionally

Ans. (c) 'Most easily' means the easiest to teach, fitting the context of describing conversation as an art that can be taught with ease.

539. Select the most appropriate option to fill in blank number 2.
(a) credit (b) subject
(c) luxury (d) result

Ans. (b) 'Subject' means a topic, fitting the context of finding a topic that interests both you and your listeners.

540. Select the most appropriate option to fill in blank number 3.
(a) worker's (b) self's
(c) victim's (d) fellow's

Ans. (d) 'Fellow's' means belonging to another person, fitting the context of talking about the other person's hobby.

541. Select the most appropriate option to fill in blank number 4.
(a) popularity (b) audacity
(c) irrationality (d) capacity

Ans. (a) 'Popularity' means the state of being liked or admired, fitting the context of gaining a reputation for good fellowship.

542. Select the most appropriate option to fill in blank number 5.
(a) accompanies (b) admits
(c) pleases (d) advances

Ans. (c) 'Pleases' means brings satisfaction, fitting the context of making people happy by showing interest in their interests.

PASSAGE-106

How does a camel survive in the desert? Many people think that the camel stores water in its hump, but the hump is really made up of fats.

When a camel (1) .... find water, it passes less urine to conserve (2) .... small amount of water it has in its body. Furthermore, the camel has a higher body temperature than (3) .... of most mammals. This means that it starts to sweat (4) .... a higher temperature than that which human beings, for example, (5) .... to perspire. This also helps it to keep water loss through sweating to a minimal.
SSC CHSL Tier-1 09.07.2024 (Shift-IV)

543. Select the most appropriate option to fill in blank number 1.
(a) do not (b) cannot
(c) hasn't (d) can

Ans. (b) 'Cannot' means is unable to, fitting the context of a camel being unable to find water.

544. Select the most appropriate option to fill in blank number 2.
(a) the (b) which
(c) a (d) very

Ans. (a) 'The' is a definite article, fitting the context of referring to the specific small amount of water in the camel's body.

545. Select the most appropriate option to fill in blank number 3.
(a) some (b) the
(c) that (d) all

Ans. (c) 'That' is a relative pronoun, fitting the context of comparing the camel's body temperature to that of most mammals.

546. Select the most appropriate option to fill in blank number 4.
(a) in (b) with
(c) at (d) for

Ans. (c) 'At' indicates a specific point, fitting the context of the temperature at which the camel starts to sweat.

547. Select the most appropriate option to fill in blank number 5.
(a) started (b) start
(c) starting (d) starts

Ans. (b) 'Start' is the base form of the verb, fitting the context of humans beginning to perspire.

PASSAGE-107

I was reading a book two days back. It was titled Charlie and the Chocolate Factory by Roland Dahl. It was fantastic. It has now become my favourite (1) .... It is about a boy named Charlie who is (2) .... poor. He wins a golden ticket that (3) .... him to enter the most famous chocolate factory in the world. He (4) .... it with his grandfather. But the other kids who accompany him are nasty. They are all spoilt. But you have to read the book to (5) .... out more about them. The amazing part of the book is that it is like a dream come true. **SSC CHSL Tier-1 10.07.2024 (Shift-I)**

548. Select the most appropriate option to fill in blank number 1.
(a) text (b) guide (c) book (d) manual

Ans. (c) 'Book' is a common noun fitting the context of describing the item as a favourite.

549. Select the most appropriate option to fill in blank number 2.
(a) very (b) nicely
(c) properly (d) finally

Ans. (a) 'Very' is an adverb fitting the context of describing Charlie as extremely poor.

550. Select the most appropriate option to fill in blank number 3.
(a) bears (b) gets
(c) suffers (d) allows

Ans. (d) 'Allows' means permits, fitting the context of the golden ticket permitting Charlie to enter the factory.

551. Select the most appropriate option to fill in blank number 4.
(a) examines (b) explores
(c) visits (d) inspects

Ans. (c) 'Visits' means goes to see, fitting the context of Charlie going to the factory with his grandfather.

552. Select the most appropriate option to fill in blank number 5.
(a) find (b) unlearn
(c) spot (d) locate

Ans. (a) 'Find' means to discover, fitting the context of encouraging the reader to discover more about the other characters.

PASSAGE-108

There is nothing more (1) .... than when you sit down at your table to study with the most sincere of intentions and instead of being able to finish the task at hand you find your thoughts (2) .... However, there are certain techniques that you can use to (3) .... your concentration. To begin with, one should (4) .... to create the physical environment that is conducive to (5) .... thought.
SSC CHSL Tier-1 10.07.2024 (Shift-II)

553. Select the most appropriate option to fill in blank number 1.
(a) frustrating (b) exciting
(c) interesting (d) surprising

Ans. (a) 'Frustrating' means causing irritation or annoyance, fitting the context of being unable to finish the task at hand.

554. Select the most appropriate option to fill in blank number 2.
(a) wandering (b) interesting
(c) tiring (d) worrying

Ans. (a) 'Wandering' means moving aimlessly, fitting the context of thoughts drifting away while trying to study.

555. Select the most appropriate option to fill in blank number 3.
(a) enhance (b) commit
(c) discover (d) convince

Ans. (a) 'Enhance' means to improve or increase, fitting the context of techniques used to improve concentration.

556. Select the most appropriate option to fill in blank number 4.
(a) attempt (b) imagine
(c) announce (d) lead

Ans. (a) 'Attempt' means to try or make an effort, fitting the context of creating a conducive physical environment.

557. Select the most appropriate option to fill in blank number 5.
(a) focussed (b) joyful
(c) cautious (d) dazzling

Ans. (a) 'Focussed' means concentrated or directed, fitting the context of an environment conducive to concentrated thought.

PASSAGE-109

In todays fast-paced and technology-driven world, (1) .... is crucial to disconnect occasionally for the sake of our health. (2) .... exposure to screens and the demands of the digital era can lead to stress, anxiety and reduced well-being. Taking time to unplug and engage (3) .... activities that promote relaxation, such as spending time in nature, (4) .... hobbies or simply enjoying quality time with loved ones allows us to recharge, find balance and (5) .... our mental and physical health. **SSC CHSL Tier-1 10.07.2024 (Shift-III)**

558. Select the most appropriate option to fill in blank number 1.
(a) that (b) this
(c) these (d) it

Ans. (d) 'It' is a pronoun that fits the context of emphasising the importance of disconnecting occasionally for health.

559. Select the most appropriate option to fill in blank number 2.
(a) Interrupted (b) Sporadic
(c) Constant (d) Redundant

Ans. (c) 'Constant' means continuous, fitting the context of continuous exposure to screens and digital demands causing stress.

560. Select the most appropriate option to fill in blank number 3.
(a) in (b) into
(c) to (d) for

Ans. (a) 'In' is a preposition fitting the context of engaging in activities that promote relaxation.

561. Select the most appropriate option to fill in blank number 4.
(a) constructing (b) pursuing
(c) chasing (d) trailing

Ans. (b) Pursuing' means following or engaging in activities, fitting the context of engaging in hobbies.

562. Select the most appropriate option to fill in blank number 5.
(a) precede (b) focus
(c) prioritise (d) underscore

Ans. (c) 'Prioritise' means to give priority to, fitting the context of prioritising mental and physical health.

PASSAGE-110

Water is (1) .... for life and for good health. Not only is it necessary for us to be able to meet our daily needs but safe drinking water can (2) .... many water-related diseases. India has one of the largest number of cases of (3) .... such as diarrhoea, dysentery, and cholera. Over 1,600 Indians, most of them children below the age of five,
(4) .... die every day because of waterrelated diseases. These deaths can be prevented if people have (5) .... to safe drinking water. **SSC CHSL Tier-1 10.07.2024 (Shift-IV)**

563. Select the most appropriate option to fill in blank number 1.
(a) primary (b) essential
(c) intrinsic (d) insistent

Ans. (b) 'Essential' means absolutely necessary, fitting the context of water being crucial for life and health.

564. Select the most appropriate option to fill in blank number 2.
(a) forbid (b) prevent
(c) restrain (d) hamper

Ans. (b) 'Prevent' means to stop from happening, fitting the context of safe drinking water stopping many water-related diseases.

565. Select the most appropriate option to fill in blank number 3.
(a) diseases (b) distress
(c) laments (d) sufferings

Ans. (a) 'Diseases' means illnesses, fitting the context of health issues like diarrhoea, dysentery and cholera.

566. Select the most appropriate option to fill in blank number 4.
(a) distinctly (b) assuredly
(c) reportedly (d) ostensibly

Ans. (c) 'Reportedly' means according to reports, fitting the context of the reported number of deaths due to water-related diseases.

567. Select the most appropriate option to fill in blank number 5.
(a) entrance (b) access
(c) providence (d) accession

Ans. (b) 'Access' means the ability to obtain, fitting the context of people needing access to safe drinking water.

PASSAGE-111

What is literacy? It is the golden key that (1)........... the gates to a whole new world. It heralds the dawn of a new (2)............ . But the media hype seems to give the impression that literacy simply means the ability to sign one's name, instead of putting thumb impression. Isn't that a very (3)..........., simplistic interpretation of the word?
Taking up this narrow meaning of the word, politicians proclaim that their states have achieved 80 or 90 per cent literacy or even (4)............ . But quite often, what happens is, once the training course is over, to produce (5)..........., the neo-literates soon lapse into illiteracy.
SSC CHSL Tier-1 11.07.2024 (Shift-I)

568. Select the most appropriate option to fill in blank number 1.
(a) opens (b) closes
(c) controls (d) leads

Ans. (a) 'Opens' means to unlock or make accessible, fitting the context of literacy being a golden key that opens new opportunities.

569. Select the most appropriate option to fill in blank number 2.
(a) year (b) day
(c) month (d) season

Ans. (b) 'Day' means a new period or era, fitting the context of a new beginning heralded by literacy.

570. Select the most appropriate option to fill in blank number 3.
(a) limited (b) daunted
(c) wide (d) small

Ans. (a) 'Limited' means restricted or narrow, fitting the context of describing a simplistic interpretation of literacy.

571. Select the most appropriate option to fill in blank number 4.
(a) better (b) higher
(c) lower (d) moderate

Ans. (b) 'Higher' means greater or more, fitting the context of politicians proclaiming high literacy rates.

572. Select the most appropriate option to fill in blank number 5.
(a) education (b) literates
(c) beginners (d) pupils

Ans. (b) 'Literates' means people who can read and write, fitting the context of neo-literates lapsing into illiteracy.

PASSAGE-112

When Prime Minister Narendra Modi announced that rupees with the denominations of 500/- and 1000/- would (1)........... to be the legal tender from the 9th of November, the whole country was stunned. This decision caused a sensation in the whole country. Social media was flooded with messages and information. People started counting the cash they had (2)........... for years legally or illegally. The main objective of this move was to curb black money, corruption and fake money menace. All the people but those who indulged in (3)........... welcomed the move. The whole opposition shook hands against this move under one pretence or the other.
They called this decision a (4)........... law and wanted the government to roll it back. Severe criticisms were made to target the decision. The government also carried out (5)............ attacks. **SSC CHSL Tier-1 11.07.2024 (Shift-II)**

573. Select the most appropriate option to fill in blank number 1.
(a) collaborate (b) seize
(c) cease (d) unify

Ans. (c) 'Cease' means to stop or discontinue, fitting the context of the denominations no longer being legal tender.

574. Select the most appropriate option to fill in blank number 2.
(a) dispersed (b) distributed
(c) accumulated (d) withdrawn

Ans. (c) 'Accumulated' means gathered or collected, fitting the context of people counting cash they had stored for years.

575. Select the most appropriate option to fill in blank number 3.
(a) amalgamation (b) indecision
(c) malpractices (d) announcement

Ans. (c) 'Malpractices' means unethical practices, fitting the context of people involved in black money and corruption.

576. Select the most appropriate option to fill in blank number 4.
(a) like (b) draconian
(c) comprehensive (d) fragile

Ans. (b) 'Draconian' means excessively harsh, fitting the context of severe criticisms against the decision.

577. Select the most appropriate option to fill in blank number 5.
(a) ineffectual (b) revengeful
(c) case (d) example

Ans. (a) 'Ineffectual' means not producing the desired effect, fitting the context of the government's retaliatory actions.

PASSAGE-113

Organic agriculture offers a means to substitute costlier agricultural inputs such as HYV seeds, chemical fertilisers and pesticides with locally produced organic inputs that are cheaper and thereby generate good returns on (1) .... Organic agriculture also generates income through exports as the demand for organically grown crops is on a (2) .... Studies across countries have shown that organically grown food has more nutritional value than chemical farming, thus providing us with healthy foods. Since organic farming requires more labour input than (3) .... farming, India will find organic farming an attractive (4) .... Finally, the produce is pesticide-free and produced in an environmentally (5) .... way. **SSC CHSL Tier-1 11.07.2024 (Shift-III)**

578. Select the most appropriate option to fill in blank number 1.
(a) loss (b) profit
(c) expenditure (d) investment

Ans. (d) 'Investment' means the action of investing money for profit, fitting the context of organic agriculture generating good returns.

579. Select the most appropriate option to fill in blank number 2.
(a) decline (b) rise
(c) growth (d) stagnation

Ans. (b) 'Rise' means an increase, fitting the context of the growing demand for organically grown crops.

580. Select the most appropriate option to fill in blank number 3.
(a) insipid (b) mechanical
(c) rigorous (d) conventional

Ans. (d) 'Conventional' means traditional, fitting the context of contrasting organic farming with traditional farming methods.

581. Select the most appropriate option to fill in blank number 4.
(a) obstacle (b) proposition
(c) burden (d) challenge

Ans. (b) 'Proposition' means a suggestion or plan, fitting the context of organic farming being seen as an attractive option.

582. Select the most appropriate option to fill in blank number 5.
(a) sustainable (b) innovative
(c) destructive (d) harmful

Ans. (a) 'Sustainable' means capable of being maintained over the long term, fitting the context of organic produce being environmentally friendly.

SSC CHSL 2023 (Tier 1)

PASSAGE-114

Many fruits and vegetables change ......(1)...... as they ripen. For example, tomatoes, strawberries and red bell peppers all change from green to red. Colour is just one way along with size, texture and smell that you can tell if a fruit or vegetable is ......(2)...... to be havested or eaten. Imagine a factory that ......(3)...... strawberries into plastic containers to be ......(4)...... to grocery stores across the country. It might be useful to have a machine that automatically ......(5)...... any green strawberries that were picked before they were ripe. Or, you might want a machine on the farm that automatically recognises strawberries by colour and only picks the red ones to begin with. **SSC CHSL Tier-1 09.03.2023 (Shift-I)**

583. Select the most appropriate option to fill in blank number 1.
(a) clothes (b) shape
(c) colour (d) size

Ans. (c) 'Colour' means the visual appearance, fitting the context of fruits and vegetables changing colour as they ripen.

584. Select the most appropriate option to fill in blank number 2.
(a) sober (b) ready
(c) trepid (d) steady

Ans. (b) 'Ready' means prepared or fit, fitting the context of being ready to be harvested or eaten.

585. Select the most appropriate option to fill in blank number 3.
(a) breaks (b) packs
(c) tapes (d) halts

Ans. (b) 'Packs' means to put into containers, fitting the context of packing strawberries into plastic containers.

586. Select the most appropriate option to fill in blank number 4.
(a) shipped off (b) suited to
(c) managed of (d) accounted to

Ans. (a) 'Shipped off' means sent, fitting the context of shipping strawberries to grocery stores.

587. Select the most appropriate option to fill in blank number 5.
(a) sustains (b) rejects
(c) proceeds (d) detains

Ans. (b) 'Rejects' means to refuse to accept, fitting the context of a machine rejecting green strawberries.

PASSAGE-115

Through the ......(1)....... , lonely years of my childhood when my father's palace ......(2)...... to tighten its grip ......(3)...... me until I couldn't ......(4)...... , I would go to my nurse and ask for a story. And though she knew many wondrous and edifying tales, the one I made her tell me over was the ......(5)...... of my birth. **SSC CHSL Tier-1 10.03.2023 (Shift-II)**

588. Select the most appropriate option to fill in the blank number 1.
(a) beautiful (b) timid
(c) menial (d) long

Ans. (d) 'Long' means extended, fitting the context of the long, lonely years of childhood.

589. Select the most appropriate option to fill in the blank number 2.
(a) seemed (b) thought
(c) perhaps (d) besides

Ans. (a) 'Seemed' means appeared, fitting the context of the palace seeming to tighten its grip.

590. Select the most appropriate option to fill in the blank number 3.
(a) surround (b) around
(c) revolving (d) encompassing

Ans. (b) 'Around' means surrounding, fitting the context of the grip tightening around.

591. Select the most appropriate option to fill in the blank number 4.
(a) breathing (b) breath (c) breathe (d) breathed
Ans. (c) 'Breathe' means to take air into the lungs, fitting the context of not being able to breathe.

592. Select the most appropriate option to fill in the blank number 5.
(a) story (b) ode (c) poem (d) news
Ans. (a) 'Story' means a tale or narrative, fitting the context of asking for the story of birth.

PASSAGE-116

On an unfortunate accident, first aid experts stress that ...(1)... what to do for an ...(2)... victim until a doctor or other trained person gets to the accident scene can ...(3)... a life, especially in cases of stoppage of breathing, severe bleeding and shock. People with special problems such as diabetes, epilepsy or allergy are ...(4)... to wear some sort of emblem identifying the problem, as a safeguard against administration of medication that might be injurious or even ...(5)....

SSC CHSL Tier-1 10.08.2023 (Shift-III)

593. Select the most appropriate option to fill in blank number 1.
(a) knowing (b) regarding
(c) attempting (d) before
Ans. (a) 'Knowing' means having knowledge of, fitting the context of knowing what to do for an injured victim.

594. Select the most appropriate option to fill in blank number 2.
(a) injured (b) efficient (c) inquiring (d) accidental
Ans. (a) 'Injured' means hurt, fitting the context of an injured victim until a trained person arrives.

595. Select the most appropriate option to fill in blank number 3.
(a) soothe (b) save (c) harm (d) take
Ans. (b) 'Save' means to rescue from harm, fitting the context of saving a life.

596. Select the most appropriate option to fill in blank number 4.
(a) benefitted (b) urged
(c) invited (d) allowed
Ans. (b) 'Urged' means strongly advised, fitting the context of people being urged to wear an emblem.

597. Select the most appropriate option to fill in blank number 5.
(a) appropriate (b) beneficial
(c) fatal (d) remedial
Ans. (c) 'Fatal' means causing death, fitting the context of medication being injurious or even fatal.

PASSAGE-117

Communication is very important for us humans in our daily lives. It means talking to others, ...(1)...... our thoughts and feelings and listening to what others have to say. When we communicate well, we can understand each other better and work together more ......(2)...... . Communication is especially important at work, where we need to work as a team and achieve common goals. Good communication helps us to avoid misunderstandings and ......(3)......, and makes us more productive. In our personal relationships, communication helps us to express our feelings and needs to our friends, family and partners. When we communicate well, we can build stronger relationships and understand each other better. Communication is also important for society as a whole. It helps us to share information, ideas and knowledge and to understand different cultures and ......(4)....... . Communication can also help us to make positive changes in our communities and ......(5)...... for important causes. Overall, communication is a very important skill that we all need to learn and practice. It can help us in many different ways and make our lives more fulfilling and successful.

SSC CHSL Tier-1 11.08.2023 (Shift-I)

598. Select the most appropriate option to fill in blank number 1.
(a) sharing (b) modifying (c) classifying (d) converging
Ans. (a) 'Sharing' means to communicate thoughts, fitting the context of sharing thoughts and feelings.

599. Select the most appropriate option to fill in blank number 2.
(a) economically (b) effectively
(c) sufficiently (d) vibrantly
Ans. (b) 'Effectively' means in an efficient manner, fitting the context of working together more effectively.

600. Select the most appropriate option to fill in blank number 3.
(a) distractions (b) justifications
(c) mistakes (d) quizzes
Ans. (c) 'Mistakes' means errors, fitting the context of avoiding misunderstandings and mistakes.

601. Select the most appropriate option to fill in blank number 4.
(a) fears (b) assumptions
(c) perspectives (d) biases
Ans. (c) 'Perspectives' means views or angles, fitting the context of understanding different cultures and perspectives.

602. Select the most appropriate option to fill in blank number 5.
(a) propagate (b) advocate
(c) inoculate (d) recommend
Ans. (b) 'Advocate' means to support a cause, fitting the context of advocating for important causes.

PASSAGE-118

India will host an international summit on Buddhism here on 20th and 21st April. Delegates from 30 countries will participate, a notable exception .... (1) .... China. Tibetan spiritual leader, the Dalai Lama, is also unlikely to attend the two-day conclave. The maiden conference being organised by the Union Culture Ministry and the International Buddhist Confederation will discuss .... (2) .... global issues through a Buddhist perspective. Over 170 delegates from countries such as Mexico, Cambodia, Laos, Thailand and Japan and 150 from India will participate in the summit to be held in the national capital. The delegates .... (3) .... prominent scholars, monks, diplomats and members of Buddhist organisations across the globe. The largest number of delegates are from Sri Lanka (20) and Vietnam (30). Abhijit Haldar, Director General of International Buddhist Confederation, said that while no delegate had been confirmed from China, there would be two participants from Taiwan. "The invitations .... (4) .... sent to various Buddhist institutions and not to governments" Mr. Haldar added. He also mentioned that the Dalai Lama .... (5) .... not attend the event due to health issues.

SSC CHSL Tier-1 17.07.2023 (Shift-III)

603. Select the most appropriate option to fill in blank number 1.
(a) been (b) being
(c) be (d) are
Ans. (b) 'Being' means existing, fitting the context of China being a notable exception.

604. Select the most appropriate option to fill in blank number 2.
(a) classical (b) contemporary
(c) old (d) ancient
Ans. (b) 'Contemporary' means modern or current, fitting the context of discussing contemporary global issues.

605. Select the most appropriate option to fill in blank number 3.
(a) included (b) include
(c) including (d) includes
Ans. (c) 'Including' means containing as part, fitting the context of delegates including prominent scholars.

606. Select the most appropriate option to fill in blank number 4.
(a) had (b) were (c) has (d) was
Ans. (b) 'Were' means past tense of are, fitting the context of invitations being sent to institutions.

607. Select the most appropriate option to fill in blank number 5.
(a) ought to (b) might
(c) used to (d) dare
Ans. (b) 'Might' means indicating possibility, fitting the context of the Dalai Lama possibly not attending.

SSC CHSL 2022 (Tier 1)

PASSAGE-119

Personification gives ...... (1) ...... qualities to non-living things or ideas. Imagery is a language used by poets, novelists and other writers to create images in the mind of the ...... (2) .... Rhyme scheme is the ...... (3) ...... that is created at the end of the lines of poetry. Irony is defined as when ...... (4) ...... meaning is completely ...... (5)...... from the literal meaning. **SSC CHSL Tier-1 27.05.2022 (Shift-I)**

608. Select the most appropriate option to fill in blank number 1.
(a) supernatural (b) divine
(c) animal (d) human
Ans. (d) 'Human' means relating to people, fitting the context of personification giving human qualities to non-living things.

609. Select the most appropriate option to fill in blank number 2.
(a) actors (b) speakers
(c) readers (d) humans
Ans. (c) 'Readers' means those who read, fitting the context of creating images in the mind of the readers.

610. Select the most appropriate option to fill in blank number 3.
(a) pattern (b) visual
(c) word (d) idea
Ans. (a) 'Pattern' means an arrangement, fitting the context of the rhyme scheme being a pattern created at the end of the lines.

611. Select the most appropriate option to fill in blank number 4.
(a) actual (b) common
(c) superficial (d) unintentional
Ans. (a) 'Actual' means real, fitting the context of the actual meaning being different from the literal meaning.

612. Select the most appropriate option to fill in blank number 5.
(a) different (b) similar
(c) parallel (d) against
Ans. (a) 'Different' means not the same, fitting the context of the actual meaning being different from the literal meaning.

PASSAGE-120

Most of the valley had been ...... (1) ...... over the ages by the river waters, ... (2) ...... rainfall and fierce winds. All except for one giant monolith, a ...... (3) ...... tower-like mountain of a single rock. It stood at a proud ...... (4)......... of eight hundred and fifty metres from the valley floor, towering well above the ......(5)...... shoulders. **SSC CHSL Tier-1 30.05.2022 (Shift-I)**

613. Select the most appropriate option to fill in blank number 1.
(a) dried (b) decoded
(c) eroded (d) wiped
Ans. (c) 'Eroded' means worn away, fitting the context of the valley being eroded by river waters, rainfall, and winds.

614. Select the most appropriate option to fill in blank number 2.
(a) empty (b) heavy
(c) less (d) scanty
Ans. (b) 'Heavy' means intense, fitting the context of heavy rainfall.

615. Select the most appropriate option to fill in blank number 3.
(a) humongous (b) small
(c) neat (d) tiny
Ans. (a) 'Humongous' means very large, fitting the context of a humongous tower-like mountain.

616. Select the most appropriate option to fill in blank number 4.
(a) weight (b) height
(c) length (d) width
Ans. (b) 'Height' means the measurement from base to top, fitting the context of the mountain standing at a height of 850 meters.

617. Select the most appropriate option to fill in blank number 5.
(a) shelf's (b) mountain
(c) valley (d) valley's
Ans. (d) 'Valley's' means belonging to the valley, fitting the context of the mountain towering above the valley's shoulders.

PASSAGE-121

The most urgent areas of attention and immediate action are nutrition, health and education of children, whose well-being ...... (1)...... the health of the society and caring outlook of the polity. Since, the causes of malnutrition of children are many, like exploding population, ... (2) .... against the female child, weak and suffering mothers, the remedy calls for 'care of the mother and care by mother',...... (3)...... an effective control over population explosion. Ignorance on what food should be taken is another ...... (4)...... factor that results in malnutrition among women and children.

The implementation of various schemes to fight the ...... (5)...... of malnutrition and undernourishment of children requires planning, co-ordination and monitoring by high-powered bodies right down to the village level.
SSC CHSL Tier-1 31.05.2022 (Shift-I)

618. Select the most appropriate option to fill in blank number 1.
(a) reflects (b) thinks (c) groups (d) efforts

Ans. (a) 'Reflects' means shows, fitting the context of children's well-being reflecting the health of society.

619. Select the most appropriate option to fill in blank number 2.
(a) bias (b) advanced (c) neutral (d) law

Ans. (a) 'Bias' means prejudice, fitting the context of bias against the female child.

620. Select the most appropriate option to fill in blank number 3.
(a) regardless(b) against (c) instead (d) besides

Ans. (d) 'Besides' means in addition to, fitting the context of care of the mother being besides effective control over population.

621. Select the most appropriate option to fill in blank number 4.
(a) advisory (b) explanatory
(c) contradictory (d) contributory

Ans. (d) 'Contributory' means helping to cause, fitting the context of contributory factors resulting in malnutrition.

622. Select the most appropriate option to fill in blank number 5.
(a) menace (b) solace
(c) balance (d) embrace

Ans. (a) 'Menace' means a threat, fitting the context of the menace of malnutrition and undernourishment.

PASSAGE-122

Although everyone wants to be successful in life, there are .... (1) .... people who know the elements of success, the factors that go to build up success. Today, success is being .... (2) .... with making money, with amassing millions and billions. Some people equate it with power and position. Many of us tend to equate success with visible material acquisitions. Outer things and external achievements are not a .... (3)........... of success. Power, prestige, position, social influence and higher degrees awarded by universities — all these are outer things. They only touch the fringe of life; they do not enter the depths within. A man may have all these and yet maybe intellectually barren; he may be emotionally barren and spiritually sterile. Would you call such a man .... (4).........? What then is success all about? What is true success? Success can be defined as the ability to be happy and make others happy; the ability to love and be loved; the ability to remain in peaceful .... (5)......... with oneself; with those around you and with God's cosmic laws.

SSC CHSL Tier-1 01.06.2022 (Shift-I)

623. Select the most appropriate option to fill in blank number 1.
(a) a few (b) most of
(c) lot of (d) a majority

Ans. (a) 'A few' means a small number, fitting the context of a few people knowing the elements of success.

624. Select the most appropriate option to fill in blank number 2.
(a) challenged (b) confused
(c) decreased (d) amazed

Ans. (b) 'Confused' means mistaken for, fitting the context of success being confused with making money.

625. Select the most appropriate option to fill in blank number 3.
(a) reason (b) measure
(c) thought (d) gift

Ans. (b) 'Measure' means a standard of comparison, fitting the context of outer things not being a measure of success.

626. Select the most appropriate option to fill in blank number 4.
(a) sober (b) successful
(c) sensible (d) thoughtful

Ans. (b) 'Successful' means achieving desired results, fitting the context of calling such a man successful.

627. Select the most appropriate option to fill in blank number 5.
(a) harmony (b) inner beauty
(c) pride (d) praise

Ans. (a) 'Harmony' means peace, fitting the context of being in peaceful harmony with oneself and others.

PASSAGE-123

Salander sat for a while ...... (1) ...... the telephone after Armansky hung up. She went to her work corner in the living room ...... (2) ...... looked at the notes she had pinned up on the wall and the papers she had ...... (3) ...... on the desk. What she had managed to collect was mostly press cuttings and articles ...... (4) .... from the internet. She took the papers and dropped ...... (5) ...... in a desk drawer.

SSC CHSL Tier-1 02.06.2022 (Shift-I)

628. Select the most appropriate option to fill in blank number 1.
(a) to be holding (b) holds
(c) holding (d) hold

Ans. (c) 'Holding' means to keep in one's possession, fitting the context of sitting while holding the telephone.

629. Select the most appropriate option to fill in blank number 2.
(a) and (b) so (c) but (d) although

Ans. (a) 'And' means connecting words, fitting the context of going to the work corner and looking at the notes.

630. Select the most appropriate option to fill in blank number 3.
(a) tacked (b) slacked
(c) mounded (d) stacked

Ans. (d) 'Stacked' means to pile, fitting the context of papers stacked on the desk.

631. Select the most appropriate option to fill in blank number 4.
(a) cropped (b) uploaded (c) cut (d) downloaded

Ans. (d) 'Downloaded' means obtained from the internet, fitting the context of articles downloaded from the internet.

632. Select the most appropriate option to fill in blank number 5.
(a) it (b) them (c) they (d) that

Ans. (b) 'Them' means referring to objects, fitting the context of dropping the papers in a drawer.

PASSAGE-124

Everything .... (1) .... us makes our environment. Living and non-living things form the .... (2) .... of our surroundings. Plants, animals! find microbes are parts of our environment. Plants, animals and microbes have affected the environment in multiple .... (3) .... like clearing of forests, building houses and farms; making roads, etc. This is the root .... (4) .... of air, water and land pollution on the planet. Ecologists across the globe are making efforts to educate mankind about the. .... (5) .... of nature, the crisis we face and the methods of managing these crises.

SSC CHSL Tier-1 10.06.2022 (Shift-III)

633. Select the most appropriate option to fill in blank number 1.
(a) over (b) beyond
(c) across (d) around

Ans. (d) 'Around' means on all sides, fitting the context of everything around us making up our environment.

634. Select the most appropriate option to fill in blank number 2.
(a) fractions (b) ingredients
(c) components (d) fragments

Ans. (c) 'Components' means parts or elements, fitting the context of living and non-living things forming components of our surroundings.

635. Select the most appropriate option to fill in blank number 3.
(a) plans (b) courses
(c) means (d) ways

Ans. (d) 'Ways' means methods or means, fitting the context of plants, animals, and microbes affecting the environment in multiple ways.

636. Select the most appropriate option to fill in blank number 4.
(a) cause (b) source
(c) origin (d) motive

Ans. (a) 'Cause' means the reason for something, fitting the context of pollution being the cause of air, water, and land pollution.

637. Select the most appropriate option to fill in blank number 5.
(a) surprise (b) wonders
(c) compassion (d) sensation

Ans. (b) 'Wonders' means marvels or amazing things, fitting the context of educating mankind about the wonders of nature.

SSC CHSL 2021 (Tier 1)

PASSAGE-125

The doctor left some medicine with the instructions for giving them. One was to .... (1) .... down the fever and another to overcome the acid condition. "The germs .... (2)......... influenza can exist only in acid condition," he explained. He said there was .... (3)......... to worry if the fever did not go up above 103°. This was as .... (4)......... of flu and there was no danger if pneumonia could be .... (5).......... .

SSC CHSL Tier-1 12.04.2021 (Shift-II)

638. Select the most appropriate option to fill in blank number 1.
(a) bring (b) shrink
(c) reduce (d) decrease

Ans. (c) 'Reduce' means to make smaller, fitting the context of the medicine reducing the fever.

639. Select the most appropriate option to fill in blank number 2.
(a) on (b) at
(c) to (d) of

Ans. (d) 'Of' means belonging to, fitting the context of germs of influenza existing in acidic conditions.

640. Select the most appropriate option to fill in blank number 3.
(a) nothing (b) anything
(c) nobody (d) everything

Ans. (a) 'Nothing' means not anything, fitting the context of there being nothing to worry about if the fever doesn't exceed 103°.

641. Select the most appropriate option to fill in blank number 4.
(a) explosion (b) erosion
(c) epidemic (d) epidermis

Ans. (c) 'Epidemic' means a widespread occurrence of an infectious disease, fitting the context of flu being an epidemic.

PASSAGE-126

These are the various symbols used on garbage bins. The wheeled-bin ...(1)... which is crossed out indicates that the item ...(2)... be disposed of separately from household waste. The item should be handed in for recycling ...(3)... to local environmental regulations for waste disposal. By ...(4)... a marked item from household waste, you will help reduce the volume of waste sent to landfills. It will also ...(5) ...any potential negative impact on human health and the environment. For more information, please contact your nearest civic official.

SSC CHSL Tier-1 19.04.2021 (Shift-III)

642. Select the most appropriate option to fill in blank number 1.
(a) symbol (b) photo (c) item (d) disposal

Ans. (a) 'Symbol' means a mark or sign, fitting the context of the wheeled-bin symbol indicating separate disposal from household waste.

643. Select the most appropriate option to fill in blank number 2.
(a) shouldn't (b) can't
(c) have (d) won't

Ans. (a) 'Shouldn't' means ought not to, fitting the context of items that shouldn't be disposed of with household waste.

644. Select the most appropriate option to fill in blank number 3.
(a) proposed (b) according
(c) subject (d) accordance

Ans. (b) 'According' means in agreement with, fitting the context of handing in items for recycling according to local environmental regulations.

645. Select the most appropriate option to fill in blank number 4.
(a) discarding (b) separating
(c) throwing (d) spoiling

Ans. (b) 'Separating' means to divide or keep apart, fitting the context of separating marked items from household waste.

646. Select the most appropriate option to fill in blank number 5.
(a) increase (b) encourage
(c) minimise (d) maximise

Ans. (c) 'Minimise' means to make as small as possible, fitting the context of minimising the negative impact on health and the environment.

PASSAGE-127

A year is hardly sufficient time for a Master to ...(1)... about a new school, leave alone absorb a distinct tradition like ...(2)... . Most of the new appointees had not served in a residential school and ...(3)... time to learn. But the short tenure did not allow ...(4)... . They could not develop understanding of the student and his ...(5)... .

SSC CHSL Tier-1 04.08.2021 (Shift-I)

647. Select the most appropriate option for blank number 1.
(a) learnt (b) learn (c) learns (d) learning

Ans. (b) 'Learn' means to acquire knowledge, fitting the context of a Master learning about a new school.

648. Select the most appropriate option for blank number 2.
(a) ourselves (b) himself
(c) mine (d) ours
Ans. (d) 'Ours' means belonging to us, fitting the context of absorbing a distinct tradition like ours.

649. Select the most appropriate option for blank number 3.
(a) needing (b) need
(c) needed (d) needs
Ans. (b) 'Need' means to require, fitting the context of new appointees needing time to learn.

650. Select the most appropriate option for blank number 4.
(a) them (b) those (c) these (d) that
Ans. (d) 'That' means indicating something specific, fitting the context of the short tenure not allowing that time.

651. Select the most appropriate option for blank number 5.
(a) environmentalist (b) environmental
(c) environment (d) environmentally
Ans. (c) 'Environment' means the surroundings, fitting the context of developing an understanding of the student's environment.

PASSAGE-128

Kashmiri carpets have been appreciated since a long time for their intricate work. Their uniqueness ...(1)... in their manufacturing. These carpets are ...(2)... handmade and are knotted, not tufted. You can ...(3)... different carpets from a variety of silk or woolen ones. These are ...(4)... in colourful themes. The main art of carpet manufacturing is ...(5)... with the knotting. These knots determine the durability and value of the carpet. **SSC CHSL Tier-1 10.08.2021 (Shift-I)**

652. Select the most appropriate option to fill in blank number 1.
(a) is lying (b) lying
(c) lies (d) lie
Ans. (d) 'Lie' means to be situated, fitting the context of the uniqueness of Kashmiri carpets lying in their manufacturing.

653. Select the most appropriate option to fill in blank number. 2.
(a) absolutely (b) merely
(c) simply (d) purely
Ans. (d) 'Purely' means entirely, fitting the context of the carpets being purely handmade.

654. Select the most appropriate option to fill in blank number 3.
(a) indicate (b) elect
(c) choose (d) decide
Ans. (c) 'Choose' means to select, fitting the context of choosing different carpets from a variety.

655. Select the most appropriate option to fill in blank number 4.
(a) devised (b) designed
(c) defined (d) described
Ans. (b) 'Designed' means created according to a plan, fitting the context of carpets being designed in colourful themes.

656. Select the most appropriate option to fill in blank number 5.
(a) assisted (b) abetted
(c) attended (d) associated
Ans. (d) 'Associated' means connected with, fitting the context of the main art of carpet manufacturing being associated with knotting.

SSC MTS 2024 (Tier 1)

PASSAGE-129

Until that moment, every director in Hollywood had accepted as gospel ...(1)... that the audience should not be taxed too much. Welles struck a ...(2) ... at these beliefs, without displaying the slightest of qualms. Visually, 'Citizen Kane' was shot with a harsh sharpness which ...(3)... every scene. Traditionally, every make-up man and cameraman in Hollywood had to keep a careful ...(4) ... on the appearance of the heroine. Welles refused to follow this ...(5) ... in the case of his own heroine. For the first time, dialogue was presented in its realistic form. **SSC MTS Tier-1 13.11.2024 (Shift III)**

657. Select the most appropriate option to fill in blank number 1.
(a) followers (b) blasphemy
(c) truth (d) Bible
Ans. (c) 'Truth' is the most appropriate option to fill in blank number 1. The phrase 'gospel truth' means an unquestionable truth.

658. Select the most appropriate option to fill in blank number 2.
(a) blue (b) blow
(c) bellow (d) blew
Ans. (b) 'Blow' is the most appropriate option to fill in blank number 2. The phrase 'struck a blow' means to challenge or undermine something.

659. Select the most appropriate option to fill in blank number 3.
(a) permeated (b) promoted
(c) prevented (d) permitted
Ans. (a) 'Permeated' is the most appropriate option to fill in blank number 3. 'Permeated' means to spread throughout something.

660. Select the most appropriate option to fill in blank number 4.
(a) ear (b) nose
(c) leg (d) eye
Ans. (d) 'Eye' is the most appropriate option to fill in blank number 4. The phrase 'keep a careful eye on' means to watch closely.

661. Select the most appropriate option to fill in blank number 5.
(a) practicals (b) prose
(c) practice (d) practice
Ans. (c) 'Practice' is the most appropriate option to fill in blank number 5. 'Practice' refers to the regular use of an activity or procedure.

PASSAGE-130

Indian villages showcase the country's rich culture and customs. Most Indians live in villages, ...(1).......... agriculture, modest living and close-knit communities are the norms. Villagers wake up to roosters crowing and farm ....(2).......... day. Farming is the main employment, and generations labour ....(3).......... the same land. Traditions, communal events and a slower pace ....(4)..........village life from metropolitan life.

Villagers' togetherness and shared duty make it part of India's identity, ...(5).......... the lack of contemporary conveniences. **SSC MTS Tier-1 05.11.2024 (Shift-III)**

662. Select the most appropriate option to fill in blank number 1.
(a) where (b) what (c) which (d) when

Ans. (a) 'Where' is the most appropriate option to fill in blank number 1.

663. Select the most appropriate option to fill in blank number 2.
(a) all (b) towards (c) before (d) after

Ans. (a) 'All' is the most appropriate option to fill in blank number 2.

664. Select the most appropriate option to fill in blank number 3.
(a) on (b) with (c) at (d) in

Ans. (d) 'In' is the most appropriate option to fill in blank number 3.

665. Select the most appropriate option to fill in blank number 4.
(a) compare (b) balance
(c) distinguish (d) equate

Ans. (c) 'Distinguish' is the most appropriate option to fill in blank number 4.

666. Select the most appropriate option to fill in blank number 5.
(a) in spite (b) beside (c) instead of (d) despite

Ans. (d) 'Despite' is the most appropriate option to fill in blank number 5.

PASSAGE-131

Man, it would seem, has (1)............. from arboreal apes. They lived a happy life in tropical forests, eating coconuts when they were hungry, and throwing them at each other when they were not. They were (2)............. occupied in gymnastics and acquired an (3)............. which to us is truly (4)............. . But after some millions of years of this arboreal paradise, their numbers increased to the point where the supply of coconuts was no longer (5)............. . **SSC MTS Tier-1 30.10.2024 (Shift-III)**

667. Select the most appropriate option to fill in blank number 1.
(a) descended (b) ascended
(c) recommended (d) extended

Ans. (a) 'Descended' is the most appropriate option to fill in blank number 1.

668. Select the most appropriate option to fill in blank number 2.
(a) perpetually (b) professionally
(c) bisectionally (d) conspiratorially

Ans. (a) 'Perpetually' is the most appropriate option to fill in blank number 2. 'Perpetually' means continuously.

669. Select the most appropriate option to fill in blank number 3.
(a) civility (b) density (c) agility (d) variability

Ans. (c) 'Agility' is the most appropriate option to fill in blank number 3.

670. Select the most appropriate option to fill in blank number 4.
(a) disappointing (b) boring
(c) astonishing (d) frightening

Ans. (c) 'Astonishing' is the most appropriate option to fill in blank number 4.

671. Select the most appropriate option to fill in blank number 5.
(a) deficient (b) delicate
(c) adequate (d) consecrate

Ans. (c) 'Adequate' is the most appropriate option to fill in blank number 5.

PASSAGE-132

It is true that strangers meeting for the first time seem to feel ......(1)...... if they do not engage ......(2)...... small talk. Usually, this is ......(3)...... and even necessary if strangers are to size each other up. But, this small talk aside, what are some ......(4)...... rules for general conversation? In the first place, certain ......(5)...... should be taboo. Kitchen topics, bus time-tables and other dull or specialised things should be barred from general discussion. **SSC MTS Tier-1 23.10.2024 (Shift-II)**

672. Select the most appropriate option to fill in blank number 1.
(a) discomforts (b) comforting
(c) uncomfortable (d) comforts

Ans. (c) 'Uncomfortable' is the most appropriate option. It means feeling uneasy.

673. Select the most appropriate option to fill in blank number 2.
(a) by (b) from
(c) on (d) in

Ans. (d) 'In' is the most appropriate option. 'Engage in' means to take part in.

674. Select the most appropriate option to fill in blank number 3.
(a) remedy (b) harmless
(c) comedy (d) happy

Ans. (b) 'Harmless' is the most appropriate option. It means not causing harm. Remedy means a treatment or cure.

675. Select the most appropriate option to fill in blank number 4.
(a) eliminating (b) illuminative
(c) elementary (d) alimentary

Ans. (c) 'Elementary' is the most appropriate option. It means basic and fundamental.
Alimentary means relating to nourishment or sustenance.

676. Select the most appropriate option to fill in blank number 5.
(a) books (b) subjects
(c) objects (d) essays

Ans. (b) 'Subjects' is the most appropriate option. It means topics or themes.

PASSAGE-133

We are familiar with the quote, 'If winter comes, can spring be far ......(1)......?' Winters are depressing, but we bear because we know that it will not ......(2)...... till perpetuity. Spring ......(3)...... a new life in us. As the spring begins to set itself, the nights become shorter and the days get longer. Gardens and lawns become colourful, buds ......(4)...... as flowers, birds chirp and butterflies fly from one flower to another to ......(5)...... on the sweet nectar. The dullness is taken over by brightness. **SSC MTS Tier-1 21.10.2024 (Shift-II)**

677. Select the most appropriate option to fill in blank number 1.
(a) behind and far (b) behind and below
(c) behind (d) far behind

Ans. (d) 'Far behind' is the most appropriate option. 'Far behind' means at a considerable distance away.

678. Select the most appropriate option to fill in blank number 2.
(a) last (b) rest
(c) hold (d) hold on

Ans. (a) 'Last' is the most appropriate option. 'Last' means to continue for a specified period of time.

679. Select the most appropriate option to fill in blank number 3.
(a) infuses (b) immerse
(c) inculcate (d) imbue

Ans. (a) 'Infuses' is the most appropriate option. 'Infuses' means to fill or pervade with a particular quality.
Inculcate means to instill an attitude, idea, or habit by persistent instruction.
Imbue means to inspire or permeate with a feeling or quality.

680. Select the most appropriate option to fill in blank number 4.
(a) come out (b) fall over
(c) pull out (d) take out

Ans. (a) 'Come out' is the most appropriate option. 'Come out' means to appear or become visible.
Fall over means to tumble or trip.
Pull out means to withdraw or remove.
Take out means to remove from a place.

681. Select the most appropriate option to fill in blank number 5.
(a) gulp (b) food (c) gobble (d) suck

Ans. (d) 'Suck' is the most appropriate option. 'Suck' means to draw into the mouth by creating a partial vacuum.

PASSAGE-134

Language is a powerful device that (1)............ communication and interaction between individuals. It serves as a crucial tool for expressing thoughts, emotions and ideas. (2) .... richness of language can be observed in various forms, including spoken and written interaction. People employ language to convey their intentions, share knowledge and build relationships. It is a fundamental aspect of human interaction and plays a vital role in shaping societies and cultures. Without language, cooperation would be (3)............., as it serves as the foundation for collaboration and understanding among diverse communities. Furthermore, language is dynamic and stationary, evolving over time to adapt to changing environments. New words are (4)............ into the vocabulary, reflecting advancements in technology, science and culture. The ability to modify and adapt language is a key aspect of linguistic competence. (5)............, the importance of language cannot be underestimated. It is a fundamental tool for human expression and interaction, facilitating the exchange of ideas and the formation of connections among people. **SSC MTS Tier-1 15.10.2024 (Shift-1)**

682. Select the most appropriate option to fill in blank number 1.
(a) facilitates
(b) qualifies
(c) delays
(d) experiences

Ans. (a) 'Facilitates' is the most appropriate option. It means to make an action or process easier, which fits the context of language aiding communication and interaction.

683. Select the most appropriate option to fill in blank number 2.
(a) An (b) A
(c) No article (d) The

Ans. (d) 'The' is the correct article. The sentence should read 'The richness of language,' using the definite article to specify the richness being discussed.

684. Select the most appropriate option to fill in blank number 3.
(a) challenges (b) challenging
(c) challenger (d) challenge

Ans. (b) 'Challenging' is the correct form.

685. Select the most appropriate option to fill in blank number 4.
(a) integral (b) integrated
(c) integration (d) integrity

Ans. (b) 'Integrated' is the most appropriate option.

686. Select the most appropriate option to fill in blank number 5.
(a) In spite of (b) In order to
(c) In conclusive (d) In any case

Ans. (d) 'In any case' is the most appropriate option. It means regardless of the circumstances and fits the concluding statement about the importance of language.

PASSAGE-135

The standard of living of any country means the average ....(1)......... share of the goods and services which the country produces. A country's standard of living, therefore, ...(2)......... first and foremost on its capacity to produce wealth. 'Wealth', in this sense, is not money, for we do not live ....(3).........money but on things that money ....(4)......... buy; 'goods' such as food and clothing and 'services' such as transport and entertainment. A country's capacity to produce wealth depends upon many factors, most of which have an effect on one another. Wealth depends to a great extent ....(5)......... a country's natural resources, such as coal, gold and other minerals, water supply and so on.
SSC MTS Tier-1 09.10.2024 (Shift-1)

687. Select the most appropriate option to fill in blank number 1.
(a) person's (b) per son
(c) persons' (d) person

Ans. (a) 'Person's' is the correct option. It denotes the average share belonging to a person.

688. Select the most appropriate option to fill in blank number 2.
(a) depended (b) dependent
(c) depending (d) depends

Ans. (d) 'Depends' is the correct form to use. It indicates present tense, showing current dependence.

689. Select the most appropriate option to fill in blank number 3.
(a) in (b) on
(c) by (d) into

Ans. (b) 'On' is the correct preposition. We do not live on money but on the things it can buy.

690. Select the most appropriate option to fill in blank number 4.
(a) should (b) ought
(c) can (d) must

Ans. (c) 'Can' is the correct option. It indicates the ability of money to buy things.

691. Select the most appropriate option to fill in blank number 5.
(a) over (b) in
(c) upon (d) with

Ans. (c) Upon' is the correct preposition. Wealth depends to a great extent upon a country's natural resources.

PASSAGE-136

Dolphins ....(1).......... regarded as the friendliest creatures in the sea and stories of them helping drowning sailors have been common since Roman times. The more we ....(2)...........about dolphins, the more we realise that their society is more complex ....(3)......... people previously imagined. They look ....(4)........other dolphins when they are ill, care for pregnant ....(5)........... and protect the weakest in the community, as we do. **SSC MTS Tier-1 07.10.2024 (Shift-1)**

692. Select the most appropriate option to fill in blank number 1.
(a) is (b) are
(c) was (d) has
Ans. (b) 'Are' is the correct form to use with the plural subject 'Dolphins' in this context.

693. Select the most appropriate option to fill in blank number 2.
(a) learns (b) learned
(c) learning (d) learn
Ans. (d) 'Learn' fits the present continuous passive form, indicating ongoing learning about dolphins.

694. Select the most appropriate option to fill in blank number 3.
(a) for (b) than
(c) to (d) the
Ans. (b) 'Than' is used for making comparisons, fitting the context of complexity.

695. Select the most appropriate option to fill in blank number 4.
(a) into (b) after
(c) on (d) up
Ans. (b) 'After' means to take care of, fitting the context of looking after ill dolphins.

696. Select the most appropriate option to fill in blank number 5.
(a) mothers (b) fathers
(c) brothers (d) uncles
Ans. (a) 'Mothers' fits the context of caring for pregnant individuals.

PASSAGE-137

My next pet, Ari, was a pigeon. He became convinced that he was not a bird at all and refused to .... (1) .... If he wanted to get on a table or a chair, he stood below it, cooing until someone picked him up. He would even try to come ...... (2)......... walks with us. This, however, we had to stop for, ... (3)......... you carried him on your shoulder or else you let him walk behind. If you let him walk, you had to slow down your own .... (4)......... to suit his, for should you get too far ahead, you would find him running after you, cooing frantically, his chest pouted out with ....(5).......... **SSC MTS Tier-1 30.09.2024 (Shift-1)**

697. Select the most appropriate option to fill in blank number 1.
(a) fly (b) file
(c) flea (d) read
Ans. (a) The context suggests that Ari, the pigeon, refused to use his natural ability to fly. Hence, the correct option is 'fly'.

698. Select the most appropriate option to fill in blank number 2.
(a) by (b) on (c) at (d) in
Ans. (b) The correct preposition is 'on' as in 'come on walks with us', which means to join someone for a walk.

699. Select the most appropriate option to fill in blank number 3.
(a) either (b) never
(c) neither (d) ever
Ans. (a) The context requires a word that introduces alternatives, making 'either' the best fit. It aligns with the structure 'either you carried him on your shoulder or let him walk behind.'

700. Select the most appropriate option to fill in blank number 4.
(a) piece (b) peace
(c) space (d) pace
Ans. (d) The correct word is 'pace' because it refers to the speed at which someone walks.

701. Select the most appropriate option to fill in blank number 5.
(a) inclination (b) indignation
(c) intimation (d) ignition
Ans. (b) The correct word is 'indignation', which means a feeling of anger or annoyance provoked by what is perceived as unfair treatment.

PASSAGE-138

It was one January morning, very early - a pinching, frosty morning - the cove all grey ....(1)......... hoar-frost and the ripple lapping softly on the stones. The captain had ....(2)....... earlier than usual and set out down the beach. Mother was upstairs with father and I was ....(3)....... the breakfast table against the captain's return when the parlour door opened and a man stepped in on whom I had never set my eyes before. He was a pale, tallowy creature, wanting two fingers of the left hand and ....(4)....... he wore a cutlass, he did not look much like a fighter. I had always my eye open for seafaring .....(5)...... with one leg or two and I remember this one puzzled me. **SSC MTS Tier-1 01.10.2024 (Shift-I)**

702. Select the most appropriate option to fill in blank number 1.
(a) with (b) about
(c) among (d) amongst
Ans. (a) The context suggests that the cove was all grey with hoar-frost. 'With' correctly indicates the presence of hoar-frost.

703. Select the most appropriate option to fill in blank number 2.
(a) waltzed (b) risen
(c) written (d) danced
Ans. (b) 'Risen' is the past participle of 'rise' and correctly fits the past perfect tense used if here.

704. Select the most appropriate option to fill in blank number 3.
(a) throwing (b) lying
(c) playing (d) laying
Ans. (d) 'Laying' is used for setting or placing something down, which fits the context.

705. Select the most appropriate option to fill in blank number 4.
(a) threw (b) throw
(c) though (d) through
Ans. (c) 'Though he' wore a cutlass ,he did not look much like a fighter. 'Though' is a conjunction used to introduce a contrast, which is suitable here.

706. Select the most appropriate option to fill in blank number 5.
(a) flowers (b) birds
(c) plants (d) men
Ans. (d) 'Men' is the plural noun that fits the context of seafaring individuals.

SSC MTS 2023

PASSAGE-139

When Jane died .... (1) .... 1850, she was called "one of the most distinguished novelists .... (2) .... England has produced" and "the first who .... (3) .... that beautiful kind of fiction, the historical romance". The Porter sisters' careers ended .... (4) .... as the Bronte sisters were getting started in the early Victorian .... (5) ....

SSC MTS Tier-1 03.05.2023 (Shift-II)

707. Select the most appropriate option to fill in blank number 1.
(a) on (b) in (c) at (d) into
Ans. (b) 'In' means during, fitting the context of Jane dying in 1850.

708. Select the most appropriate option to fill in blank number 2.
(a) who (b) what
(c) whose (d) which
Ans. (d) 'Which' means referring to something, fitting the context of being one of the novelists which England has produced.

709. Select the most appropriate option to fill in blank number 3.
(a) introduced (b) dismissed
(c) casted (d) energised
Ans. (a) 'Introduced' means brought into use, fitting the context of introducing the historical romance.

710. Select the most appropriate option to fill in blank number 4.
(a) lest (b) just
(c) that (d) must
Ans. (b) 'Just' means exactly, fitting the context of careers ending just as the Bronte sisters were starting.

711. Select the most appropriate option to fill in blank number 5.
(a) terms (b) period
(c) session (d) spell
Ans. (b) 'Period' means a length of time, fitting the context of the early Victorian period.

PASSAGE-140

"I am proud to .... (1) .... to a religion which has taught the world both tolerance .... (2) .... universal acceptance", he declared .... (3) .... 11th September, 1893. "We believe not only in universal toleration, ... (4) .... we accept all religions as true. I am proud to belong to a nation which has sheltered the persecuted and the .... (5) .... of all religions and all nations of the Earth."

SSC MTS Tier-1 04.05.2023 (Shift-II)

712. Select the most appropriate option to fill in blank number 1.
(a) belong (b) live
(c) behest (d) gain
Ans. (a) 'Belong' means to be a member of, fitting the context of belonging to a religion.

713. Select the most appropriate option to fill in blank number 2.
(a) and (b) as well as
(c) or (d) also
Ans. (a) 'And' means in addition to, fitting the context of tolerance and universal acceptance.

714. Select the most appropriate option to fill in blank number 3.
(a) upon (b) in
(c) on (d) at
Ans. (c) 'On' means at a specific date, fitting the context of declaring on 11th September, 1893.

715. Select the most appropriate option to fill in blank number 4.
(a) yet (b) though
(c) and (d) but
Ans. (d) 'But' means introducing a contrast, fitting the context of believing in universal toleration but accepting all religions.

716. Select the most appropriate option to fill in blank number 5.
(a) toilers (b) refugees
(c) workers (d) peons
Ans. (b) 'Refugees' means people seeking refuge, fitting the context of sheltering the persecuted and refugees.

PASSAGE-141

.... (1) .... people think that we can learn a lot about the culture of foreign country .... (2) .... by living in that country. However, this is not necessarily true. Often, the longer we stay in a .... (3) .... country, the more we realise how little we actually know about the culture of that country. Books and talks about other people's .... (4) .... can even be dangerous because they concentrate on cultural differences and .... (5) .... national character and sometimes a lot of information they contain is untrue.

SSC MTS Tier-1 09.05.2023 (Shift-III)

717. Select the most appropriate option to fill in blank number 1.
(a) Many (b) Few
(c) Every (d) Each
Ans. (a) 'Many' means a large number, fitting the context of many people thinking they can learn about a foreign culture by living there.

718. Select the most appropriate option to fill in blank number 2.
(a) precisely (b) directly
(c) formally (d) simply
Ans. (d) 'Simply' means easily or plainly, fitting the context of simply living in that country.

719. Select the most appropriate option to fill in blank number 3.
(a) benign (b) foreign
(c) sovereign (d) reign
Ans. (b) 'Foreign' means from another country, fitting the context of a foreign country.

720. Select the most appropriate option to fill in blank number 4.
(a) conjecture (b) caricature
(c) stature (d) culture
Ans. (d) 'Culture' means the customs and social behaviour of a society, fitting the context of other people's culture.

721. Select the most appropriate option to fill in blank number 5.
(a) considerate (b) exaggerate
(c) proliferate (d) concentrate
Ans. (b) 'Exaggerate' means to represent something as larger or more intense than it really is, fitting the context of exaggerating national character.

PASSAGE-142

Gaming in the banking sector seems virtually .... (1) .... to eliminate. The only effective measure to end it would be to .... (2) .... bankers personally liable for losses, to remove the sense that their actions - their games - have .... (3) .... personal financial or legal consequences. It is this, rather .... (4) .... removing the cap on bankers' bonuses, that has the best chance of preventing the financial system blowing .... (5) .... again. **SSC MTS Tier-1 10.05.2023 (Shift-II)**

722. Select the most appropriate option to fill in blank number 1.
(a) feasible (b) impossible
(c) penetrable (d) liable

Ans. (b) 'Impossible' means not able to occur, fitting the context of gaming in the banking sector being virtually impossible to eliminate.

723. Select the most appropriate option to fill in blank number 2.
(a) gave (b) bake
(c) take (d) make

Ans. (d) 'Make' means to cause, fitting the context of making bankers personally liable for losses.

724. Select the most appropriate option to fill in blank number 3.
(a) never (b) none
(c) not (d) no

Ans. (d) 'No' means not any, fitting the context of actions having no personal financial or legal consequences.

725. Select the most appropriate option to fill in blank number 4.
(a) then (b) but
(c) so (d) than

Ans. (d) 'Than' means used to introduce the second element in a comparison, fitting the context of this having a better chance than removing the cap on bonuses.

726. Select the most appropriate option to fill in blank number 5.
(a) on (b) into (c) up (d) off

Ans. (c) 'Up' means to increase or intensify, fitting the context of preventing the financial system from blowing up again.

PASSAGE-143

If you enjoy .... (1) .... crime shows on TV, you know that fingerprints play a large role in .... (2) .... people. But, you might be .... (3) .... to find out that using fingerprints for identification is not a new science. In fact, it is very old .... (4) .... back at least as far as 1885-1913 BCE. In Babylon, when people agreed to a business contract, they pressed their fingerprints into the clay in which the contract was written. .... (5) .... have also been found on clay seals from ancient China. **SSC MTS Tier-1 10.05.2023 (Shift-III)**

727. Select the most appropriate option to fill in blank number 1.
(a) marking (b) watching
(c) calling out (d) writing

Ans. (b) 'Watching' means to look at something for a period of time, fitting the context of enjoying watching crime shows.

728. Select the most appropriate option to fill in blank number 2.
(a) identifying (b) pertaining
(c) chortling (d) masking

Ans. (a) 'Identifying' means to recognise, fitting the context of fingerprints playing a role in identifying people.

729. Select the most appropriate option to fill in blank number 3.
(a) certain (b) calculable
(c) blocked (d) surprised

Ans. (d) 'Surprised' means feeling or showing surprise, fitting the context of being surprised to find out the history of fingerprint use.

730. Select the most appropriate option to fill in blank number 4.
(a) portraying (b) dating
(c) stating (d) going

Ans. (b) 'Dating' means to establish the date of something, fitting the context of dating back to ancient times.

731. Select the most appropriate option to fill in blank number 5.
(a) Thumbprints (b) Sculptures
(c) Footprints (d) Paintings

Ans. (a) 'Thumbprints' means impressions made by thumbs, fitting the context of thumbprints found on clay seals.

PASSAGE-144

As an industrial solvent, pyridine is used in a .... (1) .... range of manufacturing processes. It is also a by-product of coking coal, a crucial .... (2) .... for steel production. The Tees area was home to both steel and chemical .... (3) .... and the discharge of contaminated effluent .... (4) .... the river and surrounding wetlands has been .... (5) .... practice, often with minimal or no treatment. **SSC MTS Tier-1 12.05.2023 (Shift-I)**

732. Select the most appropriate option to fill in blank number 1.
(a) wide (b) wider
(c) widest (d) widely

Ans. (a) 'Wide' means extending over a large area, fitting the context of a wide range of manufacturing processes.

733. Select the most appropriate option to fill in blank number 2.
(a) code (b) desire
(c) load (d) input

Ans. (d) 'Input' means something put into a system, fitting the context of coking coal being crucial for steel production.

734. Select the most appropriate option to fill in blank number 3.
(a) fabrication
(b) industries
(c) monopoly
(d) salutation

Ans. (b) 'Industries' means economic activity concerned with the processing of raw materials, fitting the context of steel and chemical industries.

735. Select the most appropriate option to fill in blank number 4.
(a) into (b) on
(c) to (d) in

Ans. (a) 'Into' means moving to a location, fitting the context of discharge of effluent into the river.

736. Select the most appropriate option to fill in blank number 5.
(a) maniac (b) common
(c) bogus (d) ruckus

Ans. (b) 'Common' means occurring frequently, fitting the context of the discharge practice being common.

PASSAGE-145

In a gallery at the Metropolitan Muse of At .... (1) .... New York, paintings of a father and daughter .... (2) .... face to face. Larger than life, the monumental portraits .... (3) .... competing conceptions of royal power. The father, Henry VIII, ... (4) .... directly at the viewer, conveying aggression through his wide stance, bulging leg muscles and .... (5) .... padded clothing.

SSC MTS Tier-1 15.05.2023 (Shift-II)

737. Select the most appropriate option to fill in blank number 1.
(a) to (b) in (c) on (d) at
Ans. (b) 'In' means located inside, fitting the context of a gallery in the Metropolitan Museum of Art.

738. Select the most appropriate option to fill in blank number 2.
(a) rest (b) hang (c) poised (d) hanged
Ans. (b) 'Hang' means to be suspended, fitting the context of paintings hanging face to face.

739. Select the most appropriate option to fill in blank number 3.
(a) believe (b) sell
(c) present (d) settle
Ans. (c) 'Present' means to show or display, fitting the context of the portraits presenting conceptions of royal power.

740. Select the most appropriate option to fill in blank number 4.
(a) books (b) shocks
(c) looks (d) hooks
Ans. (c) 'Looks' means to direct one's gaze, fitting the context of Henry VIII looking directly at the viewer.

741. Select the most appropriate option to fill in blank number 5.
(a) totally (b) excessively
(c) commonly (d) acutely
Ans. (b) 'Excessively' means to a greater degree, fitting the context of excessively padded clothing.

PASSAGE-146

By contrast, depression is a .... (1) .... long-term downturn in economic activity in one or more .... (2) .... Depression is a more .... (3) .... downturn than a recession, which is seen by some economists as part of the modern business cycle. The latter refers to .... (4) .... that occur around a long-term growth trend and typically involve shifts over time between .... (5) .... of relatively rapid economic growth (an expansion or boom) and periods of relative stagnation or decline (a contraction or recession).

SSC MTS Tier-1 16.05.2023 (Shift-I)

742. Select the most appropriate option to fill in blank number 1.
(a) curtained (b) abstained
(c) stained (d) sustained
Ans. (d) 'Sustained' means continuing for a long time, fitting the context of a sustained long-term downturn in economic activity.

743. Select the most appropriate option to fill in blank number 2.
(a) services (b) autonomies
(c) economies (d) astronomies
Ans. (c) 'Economies' means economic systems, fitting the context of one or more economies.

744. Select the most appropriate option to fill in blank number 3.
(a) severe (b) tamed (c) feral (d) simple
Ans. (a) 'Severe' means very great, fitting the context of depression being a more severe downturn.

745. Select the most appropriate option to fill in blank number 4.
(a) firmness (b) stability
(c) fluctuations (d) sustainability
Ans. (c) 'Fluctuations' means variations, fitting the context of shifts that occur around a growth trend.

746. Select the most appropriate option to fill in blank number 5.
(a) perpetually (b) periods
(c) perpetuity (d) prods
Ans. (b) 'Periods' means lengths of time, fitting the context of periods of economic growth and decline.

PASSAGE-147

After a rejection, we tend to beat ourselves up over the things that might have .... (1) .... us to be rejected and might even end up dwelling on these negative .... (2) .... a process called rumination. This habit, however, inevitably causes us to .... (3) .... worse. "The first thing a lot of people do when they get rejected is to be unkind to .... (4) .... and they start coming up with all kinds of ideas about what's .... (5) .... with them", Gottlieb notes.

SSC MTS Tier-1 16.05.2023 (Shift-II)

747. Select the most appropriate option to fill in blank number 1.
(a) lead (b) led (c) leading (d) let
Ans. (b) 'Led' means caused, fitting the context of things that might have led to being rejected.

748. Select the most appropriate option to fill in blank number 2.
(a) endurance (b) formalities
(c) emotions (d) stoppages
Ans. (c) 'Emotions' means feelings, fitting the context of dwelling on negative emotions.

749. Select the most appropriate option to fill in blank number 3.
(a) feel (b) swirl
(c) share (d) recognise
Ans. (a) 'Feel' means to experience, fitting the context of causing us to feel worse.

750. Select the most appropriate option to fill in blank number 4.
(a) himself (b) yourself
(c) themselves (d) itself
Ans. (c) 'Themselves' means referring to people in general, fitting the context of people being unkind to themselves.

751. Select the most appropriate option to fill in blank number 5.
(a) strong (b) taming (c) syncing (d) wrong
Ans. (d) 'Wrong' means incorrect, fitting the context of coming up with ideas about what's wrong with them.

PASSAGE-148

It was this .... (1) .... that made John so particularly unusual, even for a wizard. This scar was .... (2) .... hint of John's very mysterious past, of the reason .... (3) .... the Samuel's doorstep eleven years .... (4) .... At the age of one, John .... (5) .... a curse from the greatest Dark sorcerer of all time.

SSC MTS Tier-1 18.05.2023 (Shift-III)

752. Select the most appropriate option to fill in blank number 1.
(a) blister (b) scar
(c) scab (d) defect
Ans. (b) 'Scar' means a mark left on the skin, fitting the context of John having a scar.

753. Select the most appropriate option to fill in blank number 2.
(a) the only (b) that only
(c) the alone (d) that individual
Ans. (a) 'The only' means the single one, fitting the context of the scar being the only hint.

754. Select the most appropriate option to fill in blank number 3.
(a) he had been left on (b) he had been left up
(c) he have been left on (d) he was been left in
Ans. (a) 'He had been left on' means placed on, fitting the context of being left on the doorstep.

755. Select the most appropriate option to fill in blank number 4.
(a) ago (b) prior (c) before (d) sooner
Ans. (a) 'Ago' means before now, fitting the context of eleven years ago.

756. Select the most appropriate option to fill in blank number 5.
(a) has had someway survived
(b) had somehow existed through
(c) have somehow survived
(d) had somehow survived
Ans. (d) 'Had somehow survived' means managed to live through, fitting the context of John surviving a curse.

PASSAGE-149

Workers' compensation benefits in Pennsylvania should pay for your medical .... (1) .... and a portion of your lost wages. However, you cannot be .... (2) .... for pain and suffering or other non-financial damage that your illness or injury may .... (3) .... you. A personal injury or wrongful death lawsuit, on the other hand, ... (4) .... compensation for the ill worker or surviving family members. If someone .... (5) .... your employer or a co-worker was to blame for your illness, you could pursue such a claim.

SSC MTS Tier-1 19.05.2023 (Shift-II)

757. Select the most appropriate option to fill in blank number 1.
(a) states (b) regulations
(c) bills (d) rules
Ans. (c) 'Bills' means invoices for services, fitting the context of paying medical bills.

758. Select the most appropriate option to fill in blank number 2.
(a) repudiated (b) paid
(c) stiffed (d) signed
Ans. (b) 'Paid' means compensated, fitting the context of not being paid for pain and suffering.

759. Select the most appropriate option to fill in blank number 3.
(a) cause (b) has caused
(c) have caused (d) causing
Ans. (c) 'Have caused' means resulted in, fitting the context of injury causing damage.

760. Select the most appropriate option to fill in blank number 4.
(a) hosts (b) allows
(c) hovers (d) boasts
Ans. (b) 'Allows' means permits, fitting the context of a lawsuit allowing compensation.

761. Select the most appropriate option to fill in blank number 5.
(a) beyond (b) along
(c) besides (d) beside
Ans. (d) 'Beside' means next to, fitting the context of blaming someone beside the employer or a co-worker.

PASSAGE-150

You may wonder if anyone would .... (1) .... to be diagnosed before they are even aware they have Alzheimer's .... (2) .... A recent survey shows that, indeed, they would. .... (3) .... three-quarters of the respondents said they would want .... (4) .... if they had Alzheimer's disease, even if they were not yet experiencing .... (5) ....

SSC MTS Tier-1 19.05.2023 (Shift-III)

762. Select the most appropriate option to fill in blank number 1.
(a) drop (b) surrender
(c) want (d) got
Ans. (c) 'Want' means to desire, fitting the context of wanting to be diagnosed before awareness.

763. Select the most appropriate option to fill in blank number 2.
(a) health (b) disease
(c) contamination (d) bug
Ans. (b) 'Disease' means an illness, fitting the context of Alzheimer's disease.

764. Select the most appropriate option to fill in blank number 3.
(a) Totally (b) Casually
(c) Firmly (d) Nearly
Ans. (d) 'Nearly' means almost, fitting the context of nearly three-quarters of the respondents.

765. Select the most appropriate option to fill in blank number 4.
(a) knowing (b) to know
(c) knows (d) known
Ans. (b) 'To know' means to learn or be aware, fitting the context of wanting to know if they had the disease.

766. Select the most appropriate option to fill in blank number 5.
(a) indexes (b) symptoms
(c) evidences (d) marks
Ans. (b) 'Symptoms' means signs of illness, fitting the context of experiencing symptoms.

PASSAGE-151

At the core of the .... (1) .... lies the fierce .... (2) .... between two branches of the Kuru dynasty, the Pandavas and the Kauravas. The lifelong struggle .... (3) .... the cousins for the throne of Hastinapur culminates .... (4) .... bloody battle of Kurukshetra, in which .... (5) .... kings of that period participated and perished.

SSC MTS Tier-1 13.06.2023 (Shift-III)

767. Select the most appropriate option to fill in blank number 1.
(a) dull (b) exercise
(c) bright (d) epic
Ans. (d) 'Epic' means a long narrative poem, fitting the context of the core of the epic.

768. Select the most appropriate option to fill in blank number 2.

(a) rivalry (b) commute
(c) hostile (d) friendship

Ans. (a) 'Rivalry' means competition, fitting the context of fierce rivalry between the Pandavas and the Kauravas.

769. Select the most appropriate option to fill in blank number 3.

(a) amongst (b) inside
(c) between (d) along

Ans. (c) 'Between' means in the middle of, fitting the context of the struggle between the cousins.

770. Select the most appropriate option to fill in blank number 4.

(a) in that (b) inside
(c) in the (d) in to

Ans. (d) 'Into' means indicating direction, fitting the context of culminating into a bloody battle.

771. Select the most appropriate option to fill in blank number 5.

(a) total (b) almost
(c) most (d) each

Ans. (c) 'Most' means the majority, fitting the context of most kings participating and perishing.

PASSAGE-152

Alkaline hydrolysis is rare today as a funeral .... (1) .... for humans. Offered to the public for the first time just over a .... (2) .... ago, it is now permitted and regulated in 26 US states and practiced .... (3) .... In North America, where It remains unfamiliar to most people who .... (4) .... a loved one or who are thinking about what could .... (5) .... to their own bodies when they die.

SSC MTS Tier-1 19.06.2023 (Shift-II)

772. Select the most appropriate option to fill in blank number 1.

(a) judgement (b) proceeding
(c) activity (d) practice

Ans. (d) 'Practice' means a customary way of operation, fitting the context of a funeral practice.

773. Select the most appropriate option to fill in blank number 2.

(a) date (b) vintage
(c) decade (d) period

Ans. (c) 'Decade' means ten years, fitting the context of being offered to the public a decade ago.

774. Select the most appropriate option to fill in blank number 3.

(a) primarily (b) manly
(c) approximately (d) lastly

Ans. (a) 'Primarily' means mainly, fitting the context of being practiced primarily in North America.

775. Select the most appropriate option to fill in blank number 4.

(a) has lost (b) lose
(c) have lost (d) loose

Ans. (c) 'Have lost' means no longer have, fitting the context of people who have lost a loved one.

776. Select the most appropriate option to fill in blank number 5.

(a) curtail (b) happen
(c) syndicate (d) gravitate

Ans. (b) 'Happen' means to occur, fitting the context of what could happen to their own bodies.

PASSAGE-153

That evening we sat in the courtyard of the hotel once more,....... (1) .... the Sun sink below the Western isles. I told alexi what had happened that day. I ..... (2) .... I could glimpse the grey stone wall of Lismore House...... (3) .... its island hilltop, the red light of the setting Sun glinting from the windows and from there the wasted frame of Jonathan Blake gazing out across the sea, on nothing, his boy waiting for him to die. But it was my...... (4) ...... simply the image on my mind, like the image burned on to your eyes when you have...... (5) .... too long at the Sun, the passing footprint of a creature long gone.

SSC MTS Tier-1 01.09.2023 (Shift-I)

777. Select the most appropriate option to fill in blank number 1.

(a) watching (b) wallowing
(c) risking (d) practising

Ans. (a) 'Watching' means to observe, fitting the context of watching the sun sink.

778. Select the most appropriate option to fill in blank number 2.

(a) fancied (b) groped
(c) imbibed (d) translated

Ans. (a) 'Fancied' means imagined, fitting the context of imagining seeing the grey stone wall.

779. Select the most appropriate option to fill in blank number 3.

(a) off (b) on
(c) aside (d) for

Ans. (b) 'On' means supported by, fitting the context of the wall being on its island hilltop.

780. Select the most appropriate option to fill in blank number 4.

(a) dribble (b) straw
(c) fantasy (d) habitat

Ans. (c) 'Fantasy' means imagination, fitting the context of it being a fantasy image in the mind.

781. Select the most appropriate option to fill in blank number 5.

(a) resumed (b) rusted
(c) blocked (d) stared

Ans. (d) 'Stared' means to look fixedly, fitting the context of staring too long at the sun.

PASSAGE-154

Photosynthesis is the ......(1)...... used by plants, algae and some bacteria to turn sunlight into energy. The process chemically ......(2)...... carbon dioxide and water into food and oxygen. The chemical reaction often ......(3)...... on a pigment called chlorophyll, which gives plants their green colour, Photosynthesis is also the ......(4)...... our planet is blanketed in an oxygen-rich atmosphere plants absorb carbon dioxide from the ......(5)...... air and release water and oxygen *via* microscopic pores on their leaves called stomata.

SSC MTS Tier-1 01.09.2023 (Shift-III)

782. Select the most appropriate option to fill in blank number 1.

(a) process (b) guess
(c) chaos (d) area

Ans. (a) 'Process' means a series of actions, fitting the context of photosynthesis being a process.

783. Select the most appropriate option to fill in blank number 2.
(a) converts (b) exceeds
(c) crates (d) bows

Ans. (a) 'Converts' means changes, fitting the context of converting carbon dioxide and water into food and oxygen.

784. Select the most appropriate option to fill in blank number 3.
(a) relies (b) creates
(c) hopes (d) wants

Ans. (a) 'Relies' means depends on, fitting the context of relying on chlorophyll.

785. Select the most appropriate option to fill in blank number 4.
(a) goal (b) sense
(c) reason (d) occasion

Ans. (c) 'Reason' means cause, fitting the context of photosynthesis being the reason for an oxygen-rich atmosphere.

786. Select the most appropriate option to fill in blank number 5.
(a) a far (b) distant
(c) surrounding (d) close

Ans. (c) 'Surrounding' means all around, fitting the context of absorbing carbon dioxide from the surrounding air.

PASSAGE-155

As a boy, I was always exploring lonely places-neglected gardens and orchards, unoccupied houses, patches of scrub or wasteland, the fields outside the town, the fringes of the forest. On one of my rambles .....(1)........ the bungalow, I pushed my way through a thicket of lantana bushes and stumbled over a thick stone slab, twisting my ankle slightly as I fell. For sometime, I sat on the grass massaging my foot. When the pain eased, I looked more ....(2).... at the stone slab and was surprised to find that it was a gravestone. It was almost entirely covered by ivy; obviously no one had been near it for years. I tugged at the ivy and some of it came away in my hands. There was some .....(3)...... lettering on the grave, half-obscured by grass and moss. I could make out a name Rose, but little more. I sat there for some time, ...(4)...... over my discovery. I was wondering why 'Rose' should have been buried at so lonely a spot when there was a .....(5)....... not far away.

SSC MTS Tier-1 04.09.2023 (Shift-II)

787. Select the most appropriate option to fill in blank number 1.
(a) before (b) behind
(c) by dint of (d) below

Ans. (b) 'Behind' means at the back of, fitting the context of rambling behind the bungalow.

788. Select the most appropriate option to fill in blank number 2.
(a) closely (b) emptily
(c) frankly (d) lawfully

Ans. (a) 'Closely' means in a detailed manner, fitting the context of looking closely at the stone slab.

789. Select the most appropriate option to fill in blank number 3.
(a) idiotic (b) sturdy
(c) blurred (d) nomadic

Ans. (c) 'Blurred' means not clear, fitting the context of the lettering on the grave being blurred.

790. Select the most appropriate option to fill in blank number 4.
(a) sleeping (b) pondering
(c) being (d) pulling

Ans. (b) 'Pondering' means thinking deeply, fitting the context of pondering over the discovery.

791. Select the most appropriate option to fill in blank number 5.
(a) dormitory (b) kennel
(c) sanctuary (d) cemetery

Ans. (d) 'Cemetery' means a burial ground, fitting the context of wondering why 'Rose' was buried at a lonely spot instead of a cemetery.

PASSAGE-156

The most common hazard in forests is forest fire. Forest fires are as old as the forests themselves. They pose a ......(1)...... not only to the forest wealth but also to the entire regime to fauna and flora seriously disturbing the biodiversity and the ecology and environment of a region. During summer, when there is no rain for months, the forests ......(2)...... littered with dry senescent leaves and twinges, which could burst into flames ignited by the slightest spark.

The Himalayan forests, particularly, Garhwal Himalayas have been burning ......(3)...... during the last few summers, with colossal loss of vegetation cover of that region. The youngest mountain ranges of the Himalayas are the most ......(4)...... stretches of the world susceptible to forest fires. The forests of the Western are more ......(5)...... vulnerable to forest fires as compared to those in the Eastern Himalayas. This is because forests of the Eastern Himalayas grow in high rain density.

SSC MTS Tier-1 11.09.2023 (Shift-I)

792. Select the most appropriate option to fill in blank number1.
(a) mercy (b) trend
(c) failure (d) threat

Ans. (d) 'Threat' means a danger, fitting the context of forest fires posing a threat.

793. Select the most appropriate option to fill in blank number 2.
(a) keep (b) build
(c) become (d) drive

Ans. (c) 'Become' means to come into being, fitting the context of forests becoming littered with dry leaves.

794. Select the most appropriate option to fill in blank number 3.
(a) rarely (b) regularly
(c) badly (d) enough

Ans. (b) 'Regularly' means occurring frequently, fitting the context of forests regularly burning during summers.

795. Select the most appropriate option to fill in blank number 4.
(a) outrageous (b) vulnerable
(c) greasy (d) mysterious

Ans. (b) 'Vulnerable' means susceptible to harm, fitting the context of the Himalayas being vulnerable to fires.

796. Select the most appropriate option to fill in blank number 5.
(a) closely (b) frequently
(c) deeply (d) barely

Ans. (b) 'Frequently' means happening often, fitting the context of Western Himalayas being more frequently vulnerable.

PASSAGE-157

A cashless India is the first step towards making the dream of digital India a reality. Government is trying to ....(1)........ a cashless environment in the country. Demonetisation appears to be a stepping ....(2)........ in that direction. To help facilitate this, government even ....(3)........ its own app 'BHIM' built for the same purpose. The ....(4)........ of conducting online financial transactions is probably the biggest motivator to go digital. You will no longer need to carry wads of cash, plastic cards or even queue up for ATM withdrawals. It's also safer and easier spending option when you are travelling. Making transactions digitally makes it easy to keep track of your finances. The ....(5)........ enormous for everyone if you leave out the low-income group, which will face a huge challenge. For the rest of the country, it is constructive and simple. However, the convenience of net-banking, m-banking, card or mobile wallet transactions can make you spend more thanyour budget.

SSC MTS Tier-1 11.09.2023 (Shift-II)

797. Select the most appropriate option to fill in blank number 1.
(a) preach (b) determine
(c) precede (d) create

Ans. (d) 'Create' means to bring into existence, fitting the context of creating a cashless environment.

798. Select the most appropriate option to fill in blank number 2.
(a) method (b) matter
(c) stairs (d) stone

Ans. (d) 'Stone' means a step in progress, fitting the context of demonetisation being a stepping stone.

799. Select the most appropriate option to fill in blank number 3.
(a) followed (b) sensed
(c) launched (d) submitted

Ans. (c) 'Launched' means to start or introduce, fitting the context of launching the 'BHIM' app.

800. Select the most appropriate option to fill in blank number 4.
(a) hassle (b) ease
(c) agony (d) delay

Ans. (b) 'Ease' means the absence of difficulty, fitting the context of the ease of conducting online transactions.

801. Select the most appropriate option to fill in blank number 5.
(a) attempts (b) scenarios
(c) benefits (d) severity

Ans. (c) 'Benefits' means advantages, fitting the context of the benefits of a cashless society.

PASSAGE-158

Modern football ...(1) ... in Britain in the 19th century. Since before medieval times, 'folk football' games had been played in towns and villages according to local customs and with a ...(2)... of rules. Industrialisation and ...(3) ..., which reduced the amount of leisure time and space available to the working class, combined with a history of legal prohibitions against particularly ...(4)... and destructive forms of folk football to undermine the game's status from the early 19th century onward. However, football was taken up as a winter game between residence houses at public (independent) school such as Winchester, Charterhouse and Eton. Each school had its own rules; some allowed limited handling of the ball and others did not. The ...(5)... in rules made it difficult for public schoolboys entering university to continue playing except with former schoolmates.

SSC MTS Tier-1 14.09.2023 (Shift-I)

802. Select the most appropriate option to fill in blank number 1.
(a) terminated (b) culminated
(c) originated (d) fragmented

Ans. (c) 'Originated' means began, fitting the context of modern football originating in Britain.

803. Select the most appropriate option to fill in blank number 2.
(a) optimum (b) variance
(c) minimum (d) maximum

Ans. (b) 'Variance' means variation, fitting the context of a variance of rules.

804. Select the most appropriate option to fill in blank number 3.
(a) normalisation (b) urbanisation
(c) standardisation (d) implementation

Ans. (b) 'Urbanisation' means the process of making an area more urban, fitting the context of reduced leisure time due to urbanisation.

805. Select the most appropriate option to fill in blank number 4.
(a) traces (b) undercurrents
(c) calm (d) violent

Ans. (d) 'Violent' means involving physical force, fitting the context of prohibitions against violent forms of folk football.

806. Select the most appropriate option to fill in blank number 5.
(a) grouse (b) grunt
(c) variance (d) control

Ans. (c) 'Variance' means variation, fitting the context of variance in rules making it difficult for schoolboys to continue playing.

SSC Selection Post 2024

PASSAGE-159

The roots of some plants get swollen with the .... (1) .... If storage food which can be used as vegetables. The plants which have such roots are called root crops. These are .... (2) .... staple foods with .... (3) .... giving carbohydrates. These also have large water .... (4) .... Some .... (5) .... are carrot, beetroot, radish, turnip, sweet potato, etc.

SSC SP 20.06.2024

807. Select the most appropriate option to fill in blank number 1.
(a) occupancy (b) residence
(c) presence (d) existence

Ans. (c) 'Presence' means existence, fitting the context of swollen roots with the presence of storage food.

808. Select the most appropriate option to fill in blank number 2.
(a) peptic (b) unhealthy
(c) nutritious (d) fattening

Ans. (c) 'Nutritious' means nourishing, fitting the context of root crops being nutritious.

809. Select the most appropriate option to fill in blank number 3.
(a) power (b) energy
(c) strength (d) capacity

Ans. (b) 'Energy' means the capacity to do work, fitting the context of giving carbohydrates for energy.

810. Select the most appropriate option to fill in blank number 4.

(a) gain (b) utility
(c) content (c) worth

Ans. (c) 'Content' means the amount contained, fitting the context of having large water content.

811. Select the most appropriate option to fill in blank number 5.

(a) examples (b) illustration
(c) case (d) samples

Ans. (a) 'Examples' means instances, fitting the context of examples of root crops.

PASSAGE-160

Tim Wright knows all about making companies more efficient. His firm, check-up, sends' secret shoppers' into retail and leisure companies in order to make sure that customers are receiving good service.

After ....(1).... visit, the secret shoppers prepare a report for the company to let them know how the service was. "Companies like to know", says Mr. Wright, "that ....(2)...... customers go into a store just a few minutes before closing time, they will still get good service." Check-up ....(3)..... set-up in the west of England and after two years moved to London so it could offer a nationwide service. ....(4)..... the last three years, Check-up's profits have increased dramatically as companies have come to realise the great importance of good customer service. Last week, an important new contract was ....(5)..... with a major supermarket chain. **SSC SP 20.06.2024 (Shift-II)**

812. Select the most appropriate option to fill in blank number 1.

(a) our (b) their
(c) there (d) his

Ans. (b) 'Their' means belonging to them, fitting the context of secret shoppers preparing their visit reports.

813. Select the most appropriate option to fill in blank number 2.

(a) while (b) when
(c) as (d) then

Ans. (b) 'When' means at the time, fitting the context of knowing that customers get good service when they visit.

814. Select the most appropriate option to fill in blank number 3.

(a) is (b) was
(c) are (d) has

Ans. (a) 'Is' means exists, fitting the context of Check-up being set up in the west of England.

815. Select the most appropriate option to fill in blank number 4.

(a) For (b) During
(c) Until (d) From

Ans. (a) 'For' means during, fitting the context of profits increasing for the last three years.

816. Select the most appropriate option to fill in blank number 5.

(a) signing (b) sign
(c) signed (d) have signed

Ans. (c) 'Signed' means completed a contract, fitting the context of a new contract being signed.

PASSAGE-161

Sustainability is .....(1)..... longer just a buzzword. It .....(2)..... a necessity and the primary agenda of the world today. Like many other countries, India too is witnessing a growth of .....(3)..... green economy. It .....(4)..... estimated that India's renewable energy target will create more than 3.4 million new job opportunities .....(5)..... 2030. In fact, a recent survey stated that a Sustainability Manager is going to be one of the top 10 jobs this decade. **SSC SP 20.06.2024 (Shift-IV)**

817. Select the most appropriate option to fill in blank number 1.

(a) any (b) never
(c) no (d) not

Ans. (c) 'No' means not any, fitting the context of sustainability being no longer just a buzzword.

818. Select the most appropriate option to fill in blank number 2.

(a) will be (b) is
(c) might be (d) was

Ans. (b) 'Is' means exists, fitting the context of sustainability being a necessity.

819. Select the most appropriate option to fill in blank number 3.

(a) his (b) hers (c) its (d) their

Ans. (c) 'Its' means belonging to it, fitting the context of the growth of its green economy.

820. Select the most appropriate option to fill in blank number 4.

(a) will be (b) were (c) had been (d) is

Ans. (d) 'Is' means exists, fitting the context of it being estimated that renewable energy targets will create jobs.

821. Select the most appropriate option to fill in blank number 5.

(a) with (b) since (c) by (d) for

Ans. (c) 'By' means no later than, fitting the context of job opportunities being created by 2030.

SSC Selection Post 2023

PASSAGE-162

Power foods are foods that provide .....(1)..... levels of nutrients like fibre, potassium and minerals. With people becoming increasingly health conscious today, a lot of fitness trainers encourage their clients to include these foods in their daily diet to .....(2)..... muscle development. There are various ways of incorporating power foods in your daily diet. Of course, the key to enjoying power foods is proper preparation of these foods, the .....(3)..... of season-fresh foods and identifying your choice of flavour among power foods. Some of the recommended power food combinations are those that are prepared in our kitchens on a regular basis. Take for instance, the combination of chickpeas and onions. This combination is a powerful source of iron which is required by the body to transport oxygen to its various parts. Iron .....(4)..... can lead to anaemia, fatigue, brain fog and tiredness. A study by the journal of agricultural and food chemistry says that sulphur compounds in onion and garlic help in the absorption of iron and zinc from chickpeas. The combination is a hit with teenagers who need to be .....(5)..... about getting iron in their diet. A quick way to prepare this power food is to make a chickpea salad with chopped onions, chaat masala and cilantro. **SSC SP 27.06.2023 (Shift-I)**

822. Select the most appropriate option to fill in blank number 1.
(a) thriving (b) rich
(c) flourishing (d) prosperous

Ans. (b) 'Rich' means containing a lot, fitting the context of foods providing rich levels of nutrients.

823. Select the most appropriate option to fill in blank number 2.
(a) spike (b) magnify
(c) intensify (d) increase

Ans. (d) 'Increase' means to make larger, fitting the context of increasing muscle development.

824. Select the most appropriate option to fill in blank number 3.
(a) wield (b) apply (c) handle (d) use

Ans. (d) 'Use' means to employ, fitting the context of the use of season-fresh foods.

825. Select the most appropriate option to fill in blank number 4.
(a) deficiency (b) inadequacy
(c) lack (d) drought

Ans. (a) 'Deficiency' means lack of something, fitting the context of iron deficiency leading to health issues.

826. Select the most appropriate option to fill in blank number 5.
(a) vibrant (b) diligent
(c) swamped (d) immersed

Ans. (b) 'Diligent' means showing care, fitting the context of teenagers being diligent about getting iron in their diet.

PASSAGE-163

Bottled water demonstrates how much humans .....(1)..... nature, reflecting the tremendous value they place on it. On the other hand, bottled water indicates .....(2)..... for nature's complexities, displaying the irony that may lead to the mutual annihilation of humanity and the .....(3)..... . The finest example is the .....(4)..... of bottled water, which is the commercialisation of natural resources. Holding bottled water, it is clear to see a gorgeous image of a lake and a small .....(5)..... of blue and green plastic around its neck. **SSC SP 27.06.2023 (Shift-III)**

827. Select the most appropriate option to fill in blank number 1.
(a) commodify (b) satisfy
(c) glorify (d) beautify

Ans. (a) 'Commodify' means to treat something as a mere commodity, fitting the context of humans commodifying nature.

828. Select the most appropriate option to fill in blank number 2.
(a) admiration (b) contempt
(c) acceptance (d) affectation

Ans. (c) 'Acceptance' means the act of accepting, fitting the context of acceptance for nature's complexities.

829. Select the most appropriate option to fill in blank number 3.
(a) collections (b) humans
(c) trash (d) environment

Ans. (d) 'Environment' means the natural world, fitting the context of mutual annihilation of humanity and the environment.

830. Select the most appropriate option to fill in the blank number 4.
(a) corruption (b) recycling
(c) recollection (d) sale

Ans. (d) 'Sale' means the exchange of a commodity for money, fitting the context of the sale of bottled water.

831. Select the most appropriate option to fill in blank number 5.
(a) beam (b) bunch
(c) group (d) piece

Ans. (d) 'Piece' means a part or portion, fitting the context of a small piece of plastic around its neck.

PASSAGE-164

The Publications Division (PD), one of the leading publishing houses in the country and the largest in the public sector, functions .....(1)..... the Ministry of Information and Broadcasting. It attempts to promote National Integration by .....(2)..... information and creating awareness about the various activities, regions, people and the .....(3)..... cultures and beliefs of the Nation. The Division publishes and sells books at affordable prices through its outlets in important cities and also .....(4)..... agents.

It also participates in exhibitions and books fairs to promote the sale of books and journals. Till date, 7,600 titles .....(5)..... published, of which 1,500 are live today. Besides books, the Publication Division has also brought out 21 journals about various issues of national and social significance.

SSC SP 27.06.2023 (Shift-IV)

832. Select the most appropriate option to fill in blank number 1.
(a) of (b) in (c) under (d) on

Ans. (c) 'Under' means managed by, fitting the context of functioning under the Ministry.

833. Select the most appropriate option to fill in blank number 2.
(a) concealing (b) disseminating
(c) pouring (d) assembling

Ans. (b) 'Disseminating' means spreading information, fitting the context of promoting national integration by disseminating information.

834. Select the most appropriate option to fill in blank number 3.
(a) same (b) myriad (c) clear (d) absolute

Ans. (b) 'Myriad' means countless or innumerable, fitting the context of various cultures and beliefs.

835. Select the most appropriate option to fill in blank number 4.
(a) through (b) as (c) about (d) in

Ans. (a) 'Through' means by means of, fitting the context of selling books through agents.

836. Select the most appropriate option to fill in blank number 5.
(a) have being (b) have been
(c) have be (d) had being

Ans. (b) 'Have been' means something has occurred, fitting the context of 7,600 titles having been published.

PASSAGE-165

Shark Tank has struck a chord with the aspiring, hardworking people who have a .....(1)..... and a stake in India's future in a very short period since its .....(2)..... What is particularly exciting to observe are the stories from across India .....(3)..... centre stage to carve out their individuality via entrepreneurial .....(4)..... . The sharks have made incredible .....(5)..... with new ventures ranging from gadget start-ups to food firms.

SSC SP 28.06.2023 (Shift-IV)

837. Select the most appropriate option to fill in blank number 1.
(a) vision (b) priority (c) perception (d) consistency
Ans. (a) 'Vision' means an aspirational view, fitting the context of people who have a vision and stake in India's future.

838. Select the most appropriate option to fill in blank number 2.
(a) birth (b) debut (c) departure (d) formation
Ans. (b) 'Debut' means first appearance, fitting the context of Shark Tank's debut.

839. Select the most appropriate option to fill in blank number 3.
(a) gratifying (b) measuring
(c) taking (d) reinventing
Ans. (c) 'Taking' means assuming a particular position, fitting the context of stories taking centre stage.

840. Select the most appropriate option to fill in blank number 4.
(a) intergrity (b) enthusiasm
(c) collaboration (d) limitation
Ans. (b) 'Enthusiasm' means intense eagerness, fitting the context of carving individuality via entrepreneurial enthusiasm.

841. Select the most appropriate option to fill in blank number 5.
(a) agreements (b) promises
(c) accounts (d) association
Ans. (a) 'Agreements' means mutual arrangements, fitting the context of incredible agreements with new ventures.

PASSAGE-166

Palaeontologists are like detectives who .... (1) ...... the evidence that .... (2) ...... animals left behind. Those clues to what dinosaurs were like are found in fossils— the ancient ...... (3) .... of an organism, such as teeth, bone or shell-or .... (4) .... of animal activity, such as .... (5)......... and trackways. **SSC SP 30.06.2023 (Shift-III)**

842. Select the most appropriate option to fill in blank number 1.
(a) examine (b) dominate (c) control (d) conduct
Ans. (a) 'Examine' means to inspect or scrutinise, fitting the context of palaeontologists examining evidence.

843. Select the most appropriate option to fill in blank number 2.
(a) surviving (b) vanished
(c) extinct (d) inactive
Ans. (c) 'Extinct' means no longer in existence, fitting the context of extinct animals.

844. Select the most appropriate option to fill in blank number 3.
(a) memories (b) fragments
(c) remains (d) leftovers
Ans. (c) 'Remains' means parts left after other parts have been removed or destroyed, fitting the context of remains of an organism.

845. Select the most appropriate option to fill in blank number 4.
(a) proposal (b) submission
(c) evidence (d) compliance
Ans. (c) 'Evidence' means an indication, fitting the context of evidence of animal activity.

846. Select the most appropriate option to fill in blank number 5.
(a) routes (b) pathways (c) canals (d) footprints
Ans. (d) 'Footprints' means tracks left by a foot, fitting the context of footprints and trackways.

SSC Selection Post 2022

PASSAGE-167

Whales and dolphins are .... (1) .... to be very unusual creatures. Do you know they breathe air and are warm-blooded? The .... (2) .... for them being warm-blooded is because of their belonging to the mammal group. They mostly eat other animals as their .... (3) .... Most of these animals live in the sea. There are very rare and few dolphins in the world which .... (4) .... in fresh water, rivers and lakes. These animals or marine mammals have many records to their .... (5) .... , the biggest animal in the world and the largest hunter. These mammals are some of the fastest, deepest, diving and cleverest creatures. **SSC SP 01.08.2022**

847. Select the most appropriate option to fill in blank number 1.
(a) contemplated (b) considered
(c) imagined (d) maintained
Ans. (b) 'Considered' means thought to be, fitting the context of whales and dolphins being considered unusual.

848. Select the most appropriate option to fill in blank number 2.
(a) reason (b) thought
(c) motive (d) ground
Ans. (a) 'Reason' means a cause, fitting the context of the reason for being warm-blooded.

849. Select the most appropriate option to fill in blank number 3.
(a) kill (b) catch
(c) eat (d) prey
Ans. (d) 'Prey' means an animal hunted by another, fitting the context of animals being their prey.

850. Select the most appropriate option to fill in blank number 4.
(a) exits (b) settle
(c) life (d) live
Ans. (d) 'Live' means to reside, fitting the context of dolphins living in fresh water.

851. Select the most appropriate option to fill in blank number 5.
(a) debit (b) praise
(c) approval (d) credit
Ans. (d) 'Credit' means acknowledgment, fitting the context of records to their credit.

PASSAGE-168

.... (1) .... a bear encased in fat is a very messy job and as I .... (2) .... back to the rest house for a hot bath and a late breakfast, I met a very .... (3) .... forest Guard, whose headquarters were at Dabidhura. Being in urgent need of bear's fat for his father, who was .... (4) .... with rheumatism, he was hurrying to try to get a share of the fat when he ran into a herd of .... (5) .... cattle, followed by a boy who informed him that a tiger had killed one of his cows. **SSC SP 01.08.2022**

852. Select the most appropriate option to fill in blank number 1.
(a) Skimming (b) Steaming
(c) Skinning (d) Stirring
Ans. (c) 'Skinning' means to remove the skin from, fitting the context of skinning a bear.

853. Select the most appropriate option to fill in blank number 2.
(a) floated (b) plodded
(c) fluttered (d) pranced

Ans. (b) 'Plodded' means to walk heavily, fitting the context of plodding back to the rest house.

854. Select the most appropriate option to fill in blank number 3.
(a) contented (b) ecstatic
(c) abominable (d) agitated

Ans. (d) 'Agitated' means feeling troubled or nervous, fitting the context of meeting an agitated forest guard.

855. Select the most appropriate option to fill in blank number 4.
(a) endowed (b) inclined
(c) crippled (d) equipped

Ans. (c) 'Crippled' means severely damaged, fitting the context of being crippled with rheumatism.

856. Select the most appropriate option to fill in blank number 5.
(a) stationary (b) stagnant
(c) listless (d) stampeding

Ans. (d) 'Stampeding' means rushing wildly, fitting the context of a herd of stampeding cattle.

PASSAGE-169

Darrah Wildlife Sanctuary is another name for Mukundra Hills National Park. Rajasthan is .... (1) .... to the Darrah Wildlife Sanctuary. The sanctuary is situated on the Southern outskirts of the town of Kota. Darrah was designated a (protected area) Wildlife Sanctuary in 1955 and visitors must now .... (2) .... consent from a local forest .... (3) .... before visiting the park. The Sanctuary's overall size is around 250 sq. km. Previously, the Darrah Sanctuary served as the Maharaja of Kota's royal .... (4) .... grounds. This location is around 50 kilometres from Kota. It is located on the Chambal River's Eastern bank and is drained by its .... (5) ....

SSC SP 01.08.2022

857. Select the most appropriate option to fill in blank number 1.
(a) destination (b) neighbour
(c) far (d) home

Ans. (d) 'Home' means a place where something is located, fitting the context of Rajasthan being home to the sanctuary.

858. Select the most appropriate option to fill in blank number 2.
(a) restrain (b) relinquish
(c) donate (d) obtain

Ans. (d) 'Obtain' means to acquire, fitting the context of obtaining consent before visiting.

859. Select the most appropriate option to fill in blank number 3.
(a) deployer (b) invader
(c) ranger (d) hunter

Ans. (c) 'Ranger' means a keeper of a park, fitting the context of obtaining consent from a local forest ranger.

860. Select the most appropriate option to fill in blank number 4.
(a) evading (b) playing
(c) hunting (d) dancing

Ans. (c) 'Hunting' means chasing and killing animals for sport, fitting the context of royal hunting grounds.

861. Select.the most appropriate option to fill in blank number 5.
(a) effluent (b) tributaries
(c) distributaries (d) outflow

Ans. (b) 'Tributaries' means smaller rivers that flow into a larger one, fitting the context of being drained by tributaries.

SSC Steno 2024

PASSAGE-170

It's ......(1)...... to have a conversation about health and wellness without talking about mental health. In the United States, nearly one in five adults has a mental illness or mental health condition. That's nearly 52 million people. However, mental health isn't just about having or not having a mental illness. Our well-being is ....(2).........by all aspects of our lives and that, in turn, affects how we experience life, work and time with our loved ones.

Now, the conversation is more ....(3)......... than ever. In 2021, the prevalent feeling of the year was languishing. Research found that more than 55% of workers weren't mentally ill, but they weren't thriving either. As the pandemic has brought physical health at the centre stage in an unprecedented way, it's time ....(4)......... look at the other major components of well-being. The conversation around mental health awareness has never been as public, as prevalent, or as important. After all, building ....(5)......... is a critical ingredient to learning how to care for your mental health.

SSC Steno 11.12.2024 (Shift-I)

862. Select the most appropriate option to fill in blank number 1.
(a) advisable (b) impossible
(c) easy (d) beneficial

Ans. (b) 'Impossible' fits the context as it highlights the necessity of including mental health in conversations about health and wellness.

863. Select the most appropriate option to fill in blank number 2.
(a) effected (b) affected
(c) different (d) indifferent

Ans. (b) 'Affected' is the correct choice as it means influenced or impacted, fitting the context of how various aspects of our lives influence our well-being.

864. Select the most appropriate option to fill in blank number 3.
(a) unnecessary (b) critical
(c) difficult (d) irrelevant

Ans. (b) 'Critical' is appropriate because it emphasises the importance of the ongoing conversation about mental health.

865. Select the most appropriate option to fill in blank number 4.
(a) for (b) about
(c) of (d) to

Ans. (d) 'To' is the correct preposition, making the phrase 'it's time to look' grammatically correct.

866. Select the most appropriate option to fill in blank number 5.
(a) dreams (b) awareness
(c) hospitals (d) family

Ans. (b) 'Awareness' is the right choice as building awareness is essential to understanding and caring for mental health.

PASSAGE-171

Child prodigies are a miraculous category of children that ....(1)......... bestowed with undying attention because of their exceptional skills in every domain of their curricula. When we speak of ....(2)......... changes in society, we grant its responsibility to child prodigies. ....(3)......... these are children who thrive everywhere, their parents are overjoyed when they win the lottery, and their peers are envious of them, research shows that young prodigies rarely go on to change the course of history. According to psychologists, many of history's most ....(4)......... and important figures weren't particularly talented as kids. To paraphrase TS Eliot, their careers tend to end not with a bang, but ....(5)......... . Although child prodigies frequently possess a wealth of intelligence and ambition, their inability to develop unique thoughts prevents them from advancing society.

SSC Steno 11.12.2024 (Shift-II)

867. Select the most appropriate option to fill in blank number 1.
(a) are (b) were (c) is (d) was

Ans. (a) The appropriate option to fill in blank number 1 is 'are'. The sentence refers to child prodigies, a plural noun, which requires the plural verb 'are' to maintain subject-verb agreement.

868. Select the most appropriate option to fill in blank number 2.
(a) forgotten (b) ordinary
(c) remarkable (d) professional

Ans. (c) The appropriate option to fill in blank number 2 is 'remarkable'. The sentence discusses changes in society attributed to child prodigies and 'remarkable' emphasises the notable and extraordinary nature of these changes.

869. Select the most appropriate option to fill in blank number 3.
(a) Nonetheless (b) So that
(c) Which (d) Neither

Ans. (a) The appropriate option to fill in blank number 3 is 'Nonetheless'. This word indicates a contrast, emphasising that despite the accomplishments and admiration, research shows young prodigies rarely change the course of history.

870. Select the most appropriate option to fill in blank number 4.
(a) notable (b) lame
(c) researcher (d) dumb

Ans. (a) The appropriate option to fill in blank number 4 is 'notable'. This word highlights that the figures being referred to are significant and important, fitting the context of influential historical figures.

871. Select the most appropriate option to fill in blank number 5.
(a) a reconcile (b) an impalpable
(c) an indomitable (d) a whimper

Ans. (d) The appropriate option to fill in blank number 5 is 'a whimper'. The phrase 'not with a bang, but a whimper' is a paraphrase of TS Eliot's line, indicating an anticlimactic end to the careers of child prodigies.

PASSAGE-172

Presently, a soprano voice of richness and depth floated from the open windows of the parlour, resonating ....(1)......... the darkening greenery. All at once it was as if the entire scene before them was ....(2)......... by that voice, infused with unexpected life: the Western sky, streaked with bands of pale gold and purple; the two houses, standing grey and disconsolate against that sky; the ....(3)......... of trees casting deep black shadows here and there across the ground. The same voice that ....(4)......... everything suddenly to life also drew them into another, much deeper world: a world that was normally hidden, a world that ....(5)......... into eternity.

SSC Steno 11.12.2024 (Shift-III)

872. Select the most appropriate option to fill in blank number 1.
(a) over (b) but
(c) aside (d) besides

Ans. (a) The most appropriate option to fill in blank number 1 is 'over'. The preposition 'over' indicates that the sound of the voice spreads or carries above the darkening greenery.

873. Select the most appropriate option to fill in blank number 2.
(a) belated (b) lapsed
(c) untried (d) awakened

Ans. (d) The most appropriate option to fill in blank number 2 is 'awakened'. The past participle 'awakened' suggests that the scene was brought to life by the voice, infusing it with unexpected vitality.

874. Select the most appropriate option to fill in blank number 3.
(a) transition (b) branches
(c) pack (d) material

Ans. (b) The most appropriate option to fill in blank number 3 is 'branches'. The noun 'branches' fits the context, as branches are part of trees and can cast deep black shadows.

875. Select the most appropriate option to fill in blank number 4.
(a) chiselled (b) lightened
(c) brought (d) transacted

Ans. (c) The most appropriate option to fill in blank number 4 is 'brought'. The verb 'brought' suggests that the voice animated or enlivened everything, fitting the context of the passage.

876. Select the most appropriate option to fill in blank number 5.
(a) pleaded for (b) asked for
(c) handed over (d) stretched out

Ans. (d) The most appropriate option to fill in blank number 5 is 'stretched out'. The phrase 'stretched out' implies an expansive, limitless quality, fitting the context of a world that extends into eternity.

PASSAGE-173

Earthquakes represent a highly consequential and perilous category of ....(1)......... disasters. These phenomena arise as a result of several variables and result in subsequent consequences. An earthquake refers to the abrupt release of accumulated strain ....(2)......... within the Earth's crust, leading to seismic shaking that propagates outward from the ....(3)......... . In essence, seismic activity refers to the abrupt displacement of the Earth's surface, commonly referred to as an earthquake, tremor or temblor. Earthquakes exhibit a range of magnitudes, encompassing both imperceptible tremors and catastrophic events capable of causing ....(4)......... urban devastation. Seismicity refers to the occurrence, magnitude and classification of earthquakes. Earthquakes can also arise as a ....(5)...... of volcanic activity. Moreover, these phenomena have diverse impacts that disrupt both individuals livelihoods and physical assets.

SSC Steno 10.12.2024 (Shift-I)

877. Select the most appropriate option to fill in blank number 1.
(a) unrealistic (b) artificial
(c) natural (d) unnatural

Ans. (c) The appropriate option to fill in blank number 1 is 'natural'. The sentence refers to earthquakes as a type of disaster and 'natural' fits the context, indicating that they are naturally occurring events.

878. Select the most appropriate option to fill in blank number 2.
(a) light (b) energy
(c) mineral (d) metal

Ans. (b) The appropriate option to fill in blank number 2 is 'energy'. The sentence describes the release of strain within the Earth's crust and 'energy' fits the context, indicating the force or power released during an earthquake.

879. Select the most appropriate option to fill in blank number 3.
(a) middleman (b) paradoxical
(c) opened (d) epicentre

Ans. (d) The appropriate option to fill in blank number 3 is 'epicentre'. The sentence describes seismic shaking propagating outward from a central point and 'epicentre' fits the context as the point on the Earth's surface directly above the focus of an earthquake.

880. Select the most appropriate option to fill in blank number 4.
(a) limited (b) small
(c) extensive (d) minimal

Ans. (c) The appropriate option to fill in blank number 4 is 'extensive'. The sentence describes the potential impact of catastrophic earthquakes, and 'extensive' fits the context, indicating widespread or significant urban devastation.

881. Select the most appropriate option to fill in blank number 5.
(a) consequence (b) classification
(c) name (d) direction

Ans. (a) The appropriate option to fill in blank number 5 is 'consequence'. The sentence describes the possibility of earthquakes arising as a result of volcanic activity, and 'consequence' fits the context, indicating a result or effect of volcanic activity.

PASSAGE-174

The Kodagu district administration ....(1)......... planned a Honey Festival in the gardens of Raja Seat in Madikeri on 24th and 25th December. The festival, which has been planned in association with Kodagu Zilla Panchayat and Horticulture Department, ...(2)......... aimed at encouraging ....(3)......... in Kodagu in view of the worldwide demand for Coorg honey. The festival is ....(4)......... to bring together not only people engaged in apiculture, but also scientists, societies and companies ....(5)......... in producing honey. **SSC Steno 10.12.2024 (Shift-II)**

882. Select the most appropriate option to fill in blank number 1.
(a) have (b) has
(c) had (d) has been

Ans. (b) 'Has' is the correct form to indicate the present perfect tense, showing that the planning has been completed recently and still has relevance now.

883. Select the most appropriate option to fill in blank number 2.
(a) have (b) was
(c) is (d) had

Ans. (c) 'Is' is used here to indicate the present tense, emphasising that the festival is currently aimed at encouraging specific activities.

884. Select the most appropriate option to fill in blank number 3.
(a) horticulture (b) apiculture
(c) agriculture (d) sericulture

Ans. (b) 'Apiculture' refers to beekeeping, which is the relevant activity in the context of producing Coorg honey.
Other options
Horticulture is the art or practice of garden cultivation.
Agriculture is the practice of farming.
Sericulture is the production of silk and the rearing of silkworms.

885. Select the most appropriate option to fill in blank number 4.
(a) excepted (b) accepted
(c) sophisticated (d) expected

Ans. (d) 'Expected' is used to indicate anticipation or what is planned to happen.

886. Select the most appropriate option to fill in blank number 5.
(a) captivated (b) engrossed
(c) engaged (d) related

Ans. (c) 'Engaged' means involved in a particular activity or area.

PASSAGE-175

Food brings people together and cooking at home is a great way to unite your family over the ....(1)......... table. Everyone loves a home-cooked meal– even moody teenagers or picky eaters. And, if you live alone, that doesn't mean you have to cook or eat ....(2)......... . If you live alone, invite a friend, co-worker or neighbour over. Sharing meals with others is a great way to ....(3)......... your social network. Getting appreciative feedback on a ....(4)......... you've prepared for someone can bring a real boost to your self-esteem too.

The simple act of talking to a friend or loved-one over food can play a big role in relieving stress and ....(5)......... mood.

Gather the family together and stay up to date with each other's daily lives. **SSC Steno 10.12.2024 (Shift-III)**

887. Select the most appropriate option to fill in blank number 1.
(a) console (b) vanity (c) dining (d) study

Ans. (c) 'Dining' is the most appropriate option because it refers to the table where people gather to eat, fitting the context of family meals.

888. Select the most appropriate option to fill in blank number 2.
(a) every day (b) healthy
(c) alone (d) together

Ans. (c) 'Alone' is the most appropriate option because it contrasts with the suggestion of inviting someone over to share a meal, fitting the context of cooking or eating by oneself.

889. Select the most appropriate option to fill in blank number 3.
(a) harm (b) expand
(c) reduce (d) break

Ans. (b) 'Expand' is the most appropriate option because it means to increase in size or scope, fitting the context of increasing one's social network.

890. Select the most appropriate option to fill in blank number 4.
(a) card (b) biscuits (c) tea (d) meal

Ans. (d) 'Meal' is the most appropriate option because it refers to the food prepared and shared, fitting the context of a home-cooked meal.

891. Select the most appropriate option to fill in blank number 5.
(a) falling (b) boosting
(c) depreciating (d) lowering

Ans. (b) 'Boosting' is the most appropriate option because it means to increase or improve, fitting the context of improving one's mood.

SSC Steno 2023

PASSAGE-176

Global warming is a significant .... (1) .... issue that requires immediate attention. The .... (2) .... of greenhouse gases in the atmosphere has led to a .... (3) .... increase in average temperatures worldwide. This phenomenon .... (4) .... various adverse effects on the environment, including .... (5) .... weather patterns and rising sea levels. **SSC Steno 12.10.2023**

892. Select the most appropriate option to fill in blank number 1.
(a) environmental (b) controversial
(c) detrimental (d) beneficial

Ans. (a) 'Environmental' means relating to the natural world, fitting the context of global warming being an environmental issue.

893. Select the most appropriate option to fill in blank number 2.
(a) extraction (b) production
(c) reduction (d) emission

Ans. (d) 'Emission' means the act of releasing something, fitting the context of the emission of greenhouse gases.

894. Select the most appropriate option to fill in blank number 3.
(a) ineffective (b) gradual
(c) large (d) temporary

Ans. (b) 'Gradual' means happening slowly over time, fitting the context of a gradual increase in average temperatures.

895. Select the most appropriate option to fill in blank number 4.
(a) causes (b) results
(c) contributes (d) prevents

Ans. (a) 'Causes' means brings about, fitting the context of global warming causing various adverse effects.

896. Select the most appropriate option to fill in blank number 5.
(a) predictable (b) stable
(c) constant (d) erratic

Ans. (d) 'Erratic' means unpredictable, fitting the context of global warming causing erratic weather patterns.

PASSAGE-177

Necessity is an .... (1) .... force that compels a man to do things. It stirs the mind so .... (2) .... that it causes great unrest that continues until the necessity is .... (3) .... As order comes out of .... (4) .... chaos so does an invention out of some .... (5) .... **SSC Steno 12.10.2023**

897. Select the most appropriate option to fill in blank number 1.
(a) inconceivable (b) irresistible
(c) essential (d) unpredictable

Ans. (b) 'Irresistible' means impossible to resist, fitting the context of necessity being an irresistible force.

898. Select the most appropriate option to fill in blank number 2.
(a) gracefully (b) slowly
(c) massively (d) violently

Ans. (d) 'Violently' means with great force, fitting the context of the mind being stirred violently.

899. Select the most appropriate option to fill in blank number 3.
(a) concerned (b) committed
(c) fulfilled (d) perturbed

Ans. (c) 'Fulfilled' means satisfied or completed, fitting the context of the necessity being fulfilled.

900. Select the most appropriate option to fill in blank number 4.
(a) perfect (b) analytical
(c) utter (d) least

Ans. (c) 'Utter' means complete, fitting the context of order coming out of utter chaos.

901. Select the most appropriate option to fill in blank number 5.
(a) necessity (b) abstrusity
(c) amity (d) ability

Ans. (a) 'Necessity' means something essential, fitting the context of inventions coming out of necessity.

15

Reading Comprehension

Reading Comprehension is a crucial language activity that assesses an individual's ability to understand and analyse a given passage. It involves various aspects, evaluating the reader's comprehension, analytical skills and critical thinking.

In some of the SSC Examinations, 5 questions are generally asked from one comprehension.

How to Solve the Comprehension

To answer the questions based on reading comprehension accurately, use the following steps

1. Read the passage quickly to get the basic idea of the theme and structure of the passage. It will help you find the summary and title of the passage.
2. Now, read only the questions carefully to understand what is asked as an answer.
3. Now, read the passage again. This reading should be thorough as you want to find out the probable answers to the question you have read.
4. Herein, it is suggested that you note down the paragraph in which you can find the answer.
5. Now, go back to the question and examine all answer choices thoroughly.
6. Go back to the paragraph that you may have identified to be containing the answer.
7. Compare the options and eliminate the incorrect choices based on the information that you see in the paragraph.
8. Select the answer that aligns best with the question based on the passage.
9. If two options are very close, mark the one that maintains the focus.
10. Choose the answer that best aligns with the passage, is factually accurate and directly answers the question.
11. For **Tone/ Description of the paragraph questions**, remember
    If a passage just gives factual information, it is **informative**.
    If it gives practical solutions to a problem, it is **practical.**
    If it presents information regarding only aspect of things generally negative or positive, it is **biased/prejudiced**.
    If it presents both side of a theme, it is **balanced/analytical/ evaluative**.
    If it points out the flaws in things, it is **critical**.
12. For **Vocabulary based questions** Underline unfamiliar words while reading the passage. Now understand their meaning in the sentence and then choose your answer.

SSC Exam Scanner

Directions (Q. Nos. 1-271) Read the following passages and answer the questions that follow.

SSC CGL 2024 (Tier 2)

PASSAGE - 1

The extraction of indigo dye involves harvesting the small, green leaves of the Indigofera plant before its flowers bloom. These leaves undergo a process of soaking in water and churning until a navy blue froth is released. The upper portion of the resulting mixture is drained for irrigation, while the leaves are repurposed as fertiliser. After allowing the water and fine sediment to settle for a day, the liquid is separated from the sediment. The obtained deep blue paste is then subjected to filtration to remove dirt and impurities, followed by compression into cakes and drying for several days. Once dried, the indigo is ready for use as a dye. Lime ($Ca(OH)2$) can be added to the initial water and leaves mixture, and various natural sugars can be dissolved into the paste to enhance the extraction process. **SSC CGL Tier-2 20.01.2025**

1. What is the overall tone of the passage?
(a) Humorous and light-hearted
(b) Critical and analytical
(c) Informative and instructional
(d) Emotional and sentimental

Ans. (c)

The overall tone of the passage is informative and instructional, as it provides detailed instructions and information about the indigo dye extraction process.

2. What is the central theme of the passage describing the extraction process of indigo dye from the Indigofera plant?
(a) The impact of lime and natural sugars on the indigo extraction process.
(b) The various uses of indigo dye in different industries.
(c) The intricate process of harvesting and processing indigo leaves.
(d) The cultivation and growth cycle of the Indigofera plant.

Ans. (c)

The central theme of the passage is the intricate process of harvesting and processing indigo leaves, explaining the steps involved in extracting indigo dye from the Indigofera plant.

3. Select the most appropriate synonym of the word 'impurities' from the options given below.
(a) Purity (b) Scum (c) Pureness (d) Cleanliness

Ans. (b)

The synonym of 'impurities' is 'scum', which refers to unwanted substances or contaminants.

4. In the extraction process described, what is the purpose of allowing the water and fine sediment at the bottom of the tank to settle for a day?
(a) To enhance the aroma of the indigo dye.
(b) To facilitate the separation of liquid from sediment.
(c) To create a unique texture in the final indigo paste.
(d) To promote the growth of additional indigo leaves.

Ans. (b)

The purpose of allowing the water and fine sediment to settle for a day is to facilitate the separation of liquid from sediment.

PASSAGE - 2

Reading is an important communication skill that has many benefits and it has great impact on a person's life. We should develop a reading habit as it allows us to learn new information and gives us access to a wide range of opportunities and ideas. So, reading regularly not only broadens our aspect and knowledge but also improves our intelligence, perspective, judgement and understanding of the world. It helps to stimulate creativity and imagination, to relieve the stress and pressure, and to provide a source of entertainment.

The major benefit of reading is to develop the analytical and critical skills of a reader. The former involves gathering information and breaking it down into parts for better understanding, while the latter involves evaluating the same information and making judgements based on evidence. Reading a book or any content improves our language and vocabulary, so we can easily comprehend the words and their use in the context. It also helps in cognitive development in young children so at the primary level, children are more involved in reading rather than writing. **SSC CGL Tier-2 20.01.2025**

5. Which skill is used by a reader when he evaluates the same information and makes judgements based on evidence?
(a) Critical skill (b) Technical skill
(c) Analytical skill (d) Drawing skill

Ans. (a)

The skill used by a reader when he evaluates the same information and makes judgements based on evidence is critical skill. This involves evaluating information and making judgements based on evidence.

6. Cognitive development in a child is related to
(a) technical development (b) mental development
(c) social development (d) environmental development

Ans. (b)

Cognitive development in a child is related to mental development, as it involves the growth of a child's ability to think and reason.

7. According to the passage, what is the role of reading?
(a) To give strength to the body.
(b) To learn new information to avail opportunity.
(c) To not to share information.
(d) To make environment healthy.

Ans. (b)

According to the passage, the role of reading is to learn new information. This helps in accessing a wide range of ideas and enhancing knowledge which helps in availing more opportunities

8. Which skill is used by a reader when he gathers information and breaks it down in a logical pattern to solve a problem?
(a) Speaking skill (b) Critical skill
(c) Analytical skill (d) Reasoning skill

Ans. (c)

The skill used by a reader when he gathers information and breaks it down in a logical pattern to solve a problem is analytical skill.

This involves breaking down information into parts for better understanding.

PASSAGE - 3

Engaging in regular physical activity is not only beneficial for physical well-being but also has a profound impact on mental health. Studies have shown that exercise releases endorphins, chemicals in the brain that act as natural painkillers and mood elevators.

Additionally, consistent exercise has been linked to reduced symptoms of anxiety and depression. Contrary to common misconceptions, it doesn't require intense workouts; even moderate activities like walking or yoga can contribute to improved mental well-being. Making exercise a regular part of one's routine not only supports physical fitness but also nurtures a positive and resilient mindset. **SSC CGL Tier-2 20.01.2025**

9. Select the most appropriate title for the given passage.
(a) The Impact of Technology on Health
(b) The Importance of a Balanced Diet
(c) Importance of Regular Physical Activities
(d) The Benefits of Mindfulness Meditation

Ans. (c)

The most appropriate title for the passage is 'Importance of Regular Physical Activities', as the passage focuses on the benefits of physical activities.

10. Select the option that provides an accurate summary of the main points discussed in the passage.
(a) The passage discusses the negative effects of technology on health.
(b) Exercise only impacts physical well-being, not mental health.
(c) Engaging in regular physical activity positively impacts mental health by releasing endorphins and reducing symptoms of anxiety and depression.
(d) Exercise requires intense workouts for mental health benefits.

Ans. (c)

The passage states that engaging in regular physical activity positively impacts mental health by releasing endorphins and reducing symptoms of anxiety and depression.

11. Determine the tone of the passage by choosing the option that reflects the overall emotional quality of the writing.
(a) Informative (b) Critical
(c) Dramatic (d) Humorous

Ans. (a)

The tone of the passage is informative, as it provides detailed information about the benefits of physical activity on mental health.

12. Which of the following is a fact mentioned in the passage?
(a) Exercise releases endorphins, contributing to improved mental well-being.
(b) Exercise requires intense workouts for mental health benefits.
(c) Regular exercise has no impact on mental health.
(d) Only intense physical activities are linked to reduced anxiety and depression.

Ans. (a)

Exercise releases endorphins, contributing to improved mental well-being. This fact is mentioned in the passage as a benefit of engaging in regular physical activity.

PASSAGE - 4

The French Revolution is a revolutionary movement that occurred in France between 1787 and 1799 and reached to its ....(1)......... in 1789. This revolution had many causes but the most important of all was ....(2)......... of bourgeoisie, who were merchants, manufacturers and professionals. The peasants, many of them landowners, wanted to get rid of the practices of absolute monarchy and feudalism. Another factor was an increase in population due to decreased mortality rates. It was followed by economic predicament and minor revolts were common. This led to a clarion call for social reforms. Intellectuals like Rene Descartes wrote about new things about political, social and economic matters. A fundamental political and societal change was to occur. The French Revolution played a critical role in shaping modern nations by showing the world the power inherent in the will of the people. **SSC CGL Tier-2 18.01.2025**

13. Select the most appropriate option to fill in blank number 1.
(a) foundation (b) middle
(c) pinnacle (d) fall

Ans. (c)

'Pinnacle' is the most appropriate option to fill in blank number 1. It signifies the highest point or peak of something, indicating that the French Revolution reached its peak in 1789.

14. Select the most appropriate option to fill in blank number 2.
(a) sorrow (b) joy
(c) killing (d) hankering

Ans. (d)

'Hankering' is the most appropriate option to fill in blank number 2. 'Hankering' means a strong desire or longing for something. In this context, it refers to the strong desire of the bourgeoisie for change.

15. What is the meaning of the phrase 'a clarion call' in the passage?
(a) A strongly expressed demand
(b) A call for forces
(c) Declaration of war
(d) Beginning of a new phase

Ans. (a)

The phrase 'a clarion call' means a strongly expressed demand. In the context of the passage, it refers to the urgent and clear demand for social reforms.

16. Select the most appropriate synonym of the word 'Inherent'.
(a) Artificial (b) Incited
(c) Natural (d) Borrowed

Ans. (c)

'Inherent' means existing as a natural or essential part of something.

PASSAGE - 5

Algae are photosynthetic creatures that have pigments that aid in photosynthesis, such as chlorophyll. They do not, however, have the actual stems, roots or leaves found in vascular plants.
While some of them have many cells, others are unicellular. They might establish colonies as well.
The majority of algae are aquatic. Some are terrestrial, and they can be found on rocks, trees and moist soil. Certain algae species co-exist well with other living things. For instance, lichens are a symbiotic relationship between green (and often blue-green) algae and fungi. Algae are members of a multiphyletic group.
This indicates that there is no common ancestor and that the species in this category are not necessarily closely related. They do not have other morphoanatomical characteristics typical of vascular plants, but they do have one thing in common: they are eukaryotes with the principal pigment being chlorophyll, which allows them to perform photosynthesis. Phycology is the scientific name for the study of algae. The blue-green algae is one example of a reference. But some sources do not classify them as algae because they are prokaryotes. **SSC CGL Tier-2 18.01.2025**

17. According to the passage, which is the main pigment in algae for photosynthesis?
(a) Chlorophyll (b) Xanthophyll
(c) Carotenoid (d) Melanin

Ans. (a)

Chlorophyll is the main pigment in algae for photosynthesis. This pigment allows algae to capture light energy and convert it into chemical energy during photosynthesis.

18. What is the central theme of the passage?
(a) The Anatomy of Vascular Plants
(b) The Diversity and Characteristics of Algae
(c) The Prokaryotic Nature of Blue-Green Algae
(d) The Symbiotic Relationship Between Algae and Fungi

Ans. (b)

The central theme of the passage is 'The Diversity and Characteristics of Algae.' The passage discusses various aspects of algae, including their photosynthetic abilities, habitat, relationships with other organisms and classification.

19. Which statement accurately describes vascular plants based on the information in the passage?
(a) Vascular plants have true stems, roots and leaves, unlike algae.
(b) Vascular plants are unicellular in structure.
(c) Algae and vascular plants share the same morphoanatomical characteristics.
(d) Vascular plants lack stems, roots and leaves.

Ans. (a)

Vascular plants have true stems, roots and leaves, unlike algae. This statement accurately distinguishes vascular plants from algae.

20. What does the term 'multiphyletic group' mean in the context of algae?
(a) Being closely related species.
(b) No common ancestor, not closely related.
(c) Having diverse morphoanatomical characteristics.
(d) Having a common ancestor.

Ans. (b)

In the context of algae, 'multiphyletic group' means no common ancestor and not closely related. This indicates that the species within this group do not share a single common ancestor and are not necessarily closely related to each other.

PASSAGE - 6

Subhas Chandra Bose, a prominent Indian nationalist leader, was convinced that India could not achieve independence without the use of force and he believed that a military campaign was necessary to achieve this goal. In 1942, Bose formed the Indian National Army (INA) with the help of the Japanese. Bose travelled to Japan in 1941 to seek their support in the struggle against British rule in India. The Japanese were interested in having Bose's help in their own efforts to expand their influence in South-East Asia. Bose's vision was to create a military force to fight against the British in India with the help of Japanese weapons and training. The INA was formed in Singapore in September 1942 with the slogan 'Jai Hind' (Victory to India). The INA consisted of soldiers who were primarily from the Indian community in South-East Asia. They were trained by Japanese officers and were equipped with Japanese weapons. The INA fought alongside Japanese forces in Burma and other parts of South-East Asia during World War II. Bose's leadership of the INA and his military campaigns against the British in India made him a popular figure among many Indians. The consequences of the formation of the INA were significant. The INA's campaigns against the British in India and the Indian soldiers' role in the Burma campaign had a psychological impact on the British forces. The British were shocked that Indian soldiers had turned against them, undermining their confidence in maintaining control over India. The INA also had a significant impact on the Indian independence movement. Bose's vision of a socialist India with equal rights for all citizens inspired many Indians. The INA became a symbol of the struggle against British colonialism and Bose's slogan of 'Jai Hind' became a rallying cry for the independence movement.

However, the INA's military campaigns were not successful in achieving their goal of freeing India from British rule. The INA suffered significant losses in battles and their efforts were undermined by the Japanese surrender in 1945.

SSC CGL Tier-2 18.01.2025

21. What ultimately undermined the INA's efforts to free India from British rule?
(a) The Japanese surrender in 1945
(b) The lack of support from the Indian and British people
(c) Gandhi's death
(d) The inferior military tactics of the British forces

Ans. (a)

The ultimate factor that undermined the INA's efforts to free India from British rule was the Japanese surrender in 1945. This event led to significant setbacks for the INA, including loss of support and resources.

22. How did Subhas Chandra Bose view India's fight for independence?
(a) Through political negotiations
(b) Through economic sanctions
(c) Through military campaigns
(d) Through non-violent means

Ans. (c)

Subhas Chandra Bose viewed India's fight for independence through military campaigns. He believed that armed struggle was necessary to achieve India's liberation from British rule.

23. What was the primary reason for the Japanese to support Subhas Chandra Bose and the formation of the INA?
(a) They believed in Bose's vision of a communist India.
(b) They wanted to expand their influence in South-East Asia.
(c) They were looking for allies in their fight against the British empire.
(d) They believed in India's right to self-determination.

Ans. (b)

The primary reason for the Japanese to support Subhas Chandra Bose and the formation of the INA was that they wanted to expand their influence in South-East Asia. This strategic alliance was in line with their broader goals during World War II.

24. What was the significance of Bose's slogan 'Jai Hind'?
(a) It symbolised the struggle against British colonialism.
(b) It was a call to arms for the Indian and British Army.
(c) It represented Bose's vision of a capitalist India.
(d) It manifests the vision of selected communities.

Ans. (a)

The significance of Bose's slogan 'Jai Hind' was that it symbolised the struggle against British colonialism. It became a rallying cry for the Indian Independence Movement, inspiring many to join the fight for freedom.

SSC CGL 2023 (Tier 2)

PASSAGE -7

The number of Indian students going abroad for higher studies has increased by 68.79% in the past year, according to data provided by the Minister of State in the Ministry of Education, Subhas Sarkar. As per the data provided by him in the Lok Sabha, the number of Indian enrolled in foreign varieties increased from 4.44 lakh in 2021 to 7.5 lakh in 2022.

He clarified that while the Bureau of Immigration and Ministry of Home Affairs maintain departure and arrival data of Indians, there is no index for capturing the category of Indians going abroad for higher education.

"Purpose of Indians going abroad for higher education is captured manually based either on their verbal disclosure or the type of visa of the destination country produced by them at the time of immigration clearance." Sarkar said.

According to the data provided by the ministry, the number of Indian nationals increased from 4.54 lakh in 2017 to 5.17 lakh in 2018. There was a significant increase in 2019 as well, with 5.86 lakh students flying out of the country. However, during the Covid pandemic, the number of Indian nationals in foreign varsities saw a drastic dip as only 2.59 lakh students were registered.

While the number continued to remain low, it saw a slight increase in 2021 with 4.4 lakh registrations. However, the number has significantly jumped to 7.5 lakh in 2022. The reports from some of the popular study-abroad destinations such as the US, UK and Australia.

For the UK, the Immigration Statistics Report states that 1,27,731 visas were granted to Indian students in September 2022, an increase of 93,470 (+273%) against 34,261 in 2019. Similarly, in the US, the number of Indian students has more than doubled and the Open Doors Report 2022 has predicted that the number of Indian students heading to America is likely to surpass those from China in 2022-23. **SSC CGL Tier-2 02.03.2023 (Shift-I)**

25. In 2019, how many Indian students went abroad?
(a) 5.17 lakh (b) 4.54 lakh (c) 5.86 lakh (d) 4.44 lakh

Ans. (c)

According to the passage, 5.86 lakh students flew out of the country.

26. Which of the following countries is not very popular with Indian students for studies?
(a) Australia (b) USA (c) UK (d) China

Ans. (d)

China is not very popular with Indian students for studies.

27. How do we know the number of students getting visas for studies in UK?
(a) From the records of Ministry of Home Affairs
(b) From the Immigration Statistics Report
(c) From the records of the Bureau of Immigration
(d) From the Ministry of Education

Ans. (b)

We know the number of students getting visas for studies in UK from the Immigration Statistics Report.

28. The passage is mainly about
(a) Immigration of Indians to UK, US and Australia
(b) Indians enrolled in foreign universities
(c) Indians going to America for higher studies
(d) Indians going abroad for higher studies

Ans. (d)

The given passage presents statistical data of Indians going abroad for higher studies.

PASSAGE - 8

We sit in the last row, bumped about but free of stares. The bus rolls out of the dull crossroads of the city and we are soon in the open countryside, with fields of sunflowers as far as the eye can see, their heads all facing us. Where there is no water, the land reverts to the desert. While still on level ground, we see in the distance the tall range of the Mount Bogda, abrupt like a shining prism laid horizontally on the desert surface. It is over 5,000 metres high and the peaks are under permanent snow, in powerful contrast to the flat desert all around. Heaven Lake lies part of the way up this range, about 2,000 metres above sea level, at the foot of one of the highest snow-peaks.

As the bus climbs, the sky, brilliant before, grows overcast. I have brought nothing warm to wear. It is all down at the hotel in Urumqi. Rain begins to fall. The man behind me is eating overpoweringly smelly goat's cheese. The bus window leaks inhospitably but reveals a beautiful view. We have passed quickly from the desert through arable land to pasture and the ground is now green with grass, the slopes dark with pine. A few cattle drink at a clear stream flowing past moss-covered stones; it is a constable landscape. The stream changes into a white torrent and as we climb higher, I wish more and more that I had brought with me something warmer than the pair of shorts that have served me so well in the desert. The stream (which, we are told, rises in Heaven Lake) disappears and we continue our slow ascent. About noon, we arrive at Heaven Lake and look for a place to stay at the foot, which is the resort area. We get a room in a small cottage and I am happy to note that there are thick quilts on the bed.

Standing outside the cottage, we survey our surroundings. Heaven Lake is long, sardine-shaped and fed by snowmelt from a stream at its head. The lake is an intense blue, surrounded on all sides by green mountain walls, dotted with distant sheep. At the head of the lake, beyond the delta of the inflowing stream, is a massive snow-capped peak which dominates the vista; it is part of a series of peaks that culminate, a little out of view, in Mount Bogda itself.

For those who live in the resort, there is a small mess-hall by the shore. We eat here sometimes and sometimes buy food from the vendors outside, who sell kabab and naan until the last buses leave. The kababs, cooked on skewers over charcoal braziers, are particularly good; highly spiced and well-done. Horse's milk is available too from the local Kazakh herdsmen, but I decline this. I am so affected by the cold that Mr. Cao, the relaxed young man who runs the mess, lends me a spare pair of trousers, several sizes too large but more than comfortable. Once I am warm again, I feel a pre-dinner spurt of energy – dinner will be long in coming – and I ask him whether the lake is good for swimming in.

SSC CGL Tier-2 02.03.2023 (Shift-I)

29. Select the most appropriate antonym of the word 'Accept' from the passage.
(a) Reject (b) Refuse
(c) Decline (d) Turn down

Ans. (c)

The correct antonym of the word 'Accept' is 'Decline'.

30. Select an appropriate title for the passage.
(a) Shorts to Trousers (b) Lake Heaven
(c) Peasant Life (d) Journey to Mount Bogda

Ans. (b)

The given passage presents the author's journey and the description of Heaven Lake. Hence, its appropriate title will be 'Lack Heaven'.

31. What is the tone of the passage?
(a) Romantic (b) Angry
(c) Serene (d) Agitated

Ans. (c)

The author of the passage calmly and peacefully describes his journey to Lake Heaven. Hence, the tone of the passage can be said to be serene.

32. What is the protagonist wearing in the bus?
(a) A dhoti (b) Trousers
(c) A pair of shorts (d) Long sleeved shirt

Ans. (c)

The protagonist is wearing a pair of shorts in the bus.

PASSAGE - 9

From 28th January to 4th February, 2023, a Chinese-operated, large white high-altitude balloon was seen in North American airspace, including Alaska, Western Canada and the contiguous United States. The American and Canadian militaries asserted that the balloon was for surveillance, while the Chinese

Government maintained it was a civilian meteorological research airship that had been blown off course. Analysts said that the balloon's flight path and structural characteristics made it dissimilar from those which have typically been used for meteorological research. The US Department of State said that the balloon was capable of locating electronic communication devices, including mobile phones and radios and that American U-2 reconnaissance aircraft deployed to track the balloon in the air revealed that the balloon carried antennas and other equipment "clearly for intelligence surveillance and inconsistent with the equipment on board weather balloon". The State Department said that the spy balloon was part of a global Chinese military-directed surveillance effort in which Chinese spy balloons have flown over more than 40 nations in five continents.

On 4th February, the US Air Force shot down the balloon over US territorial waters off the coast of South Carolina, on the order of US President Joe Biden. Debris from the wreckage was recovered and sent to the FBI Laboratory in Quantico, Virginia, for analysis.

The incident increased US-China tensions. The incident prompted US Secretary of State Antony Blinken to delay a diplomatic visit to Beijing, which was set to be his first since 2018. It also further strained Canada-China relations, as Canada summoned the Chinese ambassador because of the violation of Canadian airspace. On 3rd February, the US Department of Defence announced that a second Chinese balloon was passing over Latin America, which China also said belonged to it. On 10th February, the Air Force shot down another aerial object over US territory at the order of President Biden. **SSC CGL Tier-2 02.03.2023 (Shift-I)**

33. The passage is mainly about
(a) the strained relations between US and China
(b) a Chinese spy balloon flying over US and Canadian territories
(c) China's global military-directed surveillance
(d) Chinese balloons flying all over the world

Ans. (b)

The passage is mainly about how the US shot down a Chinese spy balloon flying over the US and Canada territories.

34. Read the statements given below.
A. The US Air Force shot down the Chinese balloon over US territorial waters.
B. Tensions between China and US have increased and the visit of the US Secretary of State to Beijing has been postponed.

Codes
(a) Both A and B are true, but B is not the correct reason for A.
(b) Both A and B are true and B is the correct reason for A.
(c) A is false and B is true.
(d) A is true and B is false.

Ans. (b)

The given passage clearly states that the US shot down the Chinese spy balloon keeping in mind tensions between the US and China.

35. How did US make sure that the balloon flying over its territory was a 'spy' balloon?
(a) The FBI lab confirmed that it was a spy balloon.
(b) The analysts studied its flight path and said so.
(c) It's reconnaissance aircraft saw the antennas and equipment of the balloon.
(d) It got the samples of the balloon checked in a lab.

Ans. (c)

The US made sure that the balloon flying over its territory was a 'spy' balloon with the help of its reconnaissance aircraft. It saw the antennas and equipment of the balloon.

36. The word 'contiguous' means
(a) adjoining (b) far off
(c) spreading (d) separated

Ans. (a)

The word 'contiguous' means adjoining or sharing a common border.

PASSAGE -10

Amidst a maze of rocks tucked in the Aravalli mountain ranges of Haryana, a team of archaeologists discovered cave paintings they believe belong to the Upper Palaeolithic age. The cave paintings have been discovered just outside the national capital and a stone's throw away from a holy grove called Mangar Bani- the region's only surviving patch of primary forest.

While the residents of the villages have been familiar with the paintings for ages, the Haryana Government's Museum and Archaeology Department took note of them just recently. A fact-finding team was sent to the area in the last week of June. The team came across cave paintings comprising images of human figurines, animals, foliage and geometric drawings. While some have paled over time, others are still very visible. They also discovered rock art and open-air ceremonial sites.

Banani Bhattacharya, Deputy Director of the Department of Archaeology and Museums informed, "So far, cave paintings in Delhi-NCR have only been found here. The paintings are yet to be dated but at least some of them belong to the Upper Palaeolithic period in all likelihood. We are viewing the paintings in continuation with the Soanian culture which has been found in Shivalik hills, Narmada and Aravallis."

Most of the cave paintings found were in ochre colour but some were in white. As per experts, cave paintings in white are usually from a later stage (early contemporary era), while Stone Age paintings are more often than not in ochre. "Stone Age paintings generally use red and ochre colours. Stones of these colour used to be available locally and inhabitants crushed the stones for preparing the colour for paintings" added Bhattacharya. The Upper Palaeolithic age began around 40,000 years ago and lasted till around 10,000 years ago. While yet to be established through archaeological dating, Bhattacharya says the Mangar cave art is 20,000-40,000 years old.

Bhattacharya claimed that the discovery is extremely significant. "Starting from the Lower Palaeolithic to Middle Palaeolithic then Upper Palaeolithic, we see the evolution here. We have found significant remains from Lower Palaeolithic till Middle and Upper Palaeolithic period too", she explained. "Though tools from the Palaeolithic age have been identified earlier in parts of the Aravallis, it is for the first time that cave paintings and rock art of a large magnitude have been found in Haryana, she added. **SSC CGL Tier-2 03.03.2023 (Shift-I)**

37. The cave paintings found in Aravalli hills are significant mainly because
(a) they are the only prehistoric cave paintings found in Aravalli hills
(b) they are found in such a large magnitude for the first time
(c) they have been discovered just outside the national capital, Delhi
(d) they depict the evolution from Lower to Upper Palaeolithic period

Ans. (d)

The cave paintings of Aravalli hills are significant mainly because they depict the evolution from Lower to Upper Palaeolithic period.

38. Most of the cave paintings found in Mangar Forest area in Haryana are in which colour?
(a) Black (b) White (c) Red (d) Ochre

Ans. (d)

Most of the cave paintings found in Mangar Forest area in Haryana are in ochre colour.

39. Which of the following statements is not correct according to the passage?
(a) The cave men crushed the locally available stones for preparing the colour for paintings.
(b) The paintings comprise images of human figurines, animals, foliage and geometric drawings.
(c) The Mangar cave art is 20,000-40,000 years old.
(d) The paintings in red belong to early contemporary era.

Ans. (d)

According to the passage, the statement that 'the paintings in red belong to the early contemporary era' is not correct. These paintings belong to the 'stone age era' as per the passage.

40. The archaeological findings in the Mangar Forest consist of all the following except
(a) tools (b) ceremonial sites
(c) cave paintings (d) rock art

Ans. (a)

The archaeological findings in the Mangar Forest consist of cave paintings of humans, animals, shapes, ceremonial sites and rock art.

PASSAGE - 11

Total area sown under Rabi crops has increased by 3.25% from 697.98 lakh hectares in 2021-22 to 720.68 lakh hectares in 2022-23. This is 22.71 lakh hectares more this year compared to corresponding period of 2021-22. Comparing with normal sown area (average of the last five years), the increase is to the tune of 13.71% from 633.80 to 720.68 lakh hectares. The increase in area is across all crops, highest being in rice. Out of 22.71 lakh hectares increase in all Rabi crops, increase in rice area is 11.20 lakh hectares from 35.05 lakh hectares in 2021-22 to 46.25 lakh hectares in 2022-23. However, this is lower than normal sown area of 47.71 lakh hectares. Maximum increase in area under rice is in states of Telangana and West Bengal.

Area under oilseeds increased by 7.31% from 102.36 lakh hectares during 2021-22 to 109.84 lakh hectares this year. The increase in area under oilseeds at the rate of 7.31% is more than double the rate of increase of 3.25% in all crops together. Rajasthan, Madhya Pradesh and Chhattisgarh accounted for major expansion in area of oilseeds. Rapeseed and Mustard contributed maximum in increasing oilseeds area during this Rabi season. Mustard area increased by 6.77 lakh hectares from 91.25 lakh hectares in 2021-22 to 98.02 lakh hectares in 2022-23.

Thus, out of 7.49 lakh hectares increase in area under oilseeds, rapeseed and mustard alone accounted for 6.44 lakh hectares. Pulse production is being focused to make country self-sufficient in these commodities. Area under pulses increased by 0.56 lakh hectares from 167.31 to 167.86 lakh hectares. Mung bean and lentil accounted for increase in area under pulses.

The United Nations General Assembly has declared the year 2023 as the International Year of Millets and India is at the forefront in celebrating the event in a big way. In order to create awareness about the benefits of millets as superfood and to meet its growing demand around the world, the government is promoting millet production through the NFSM-Nutri Cereals component of National Food Security Mission programme in 212 districts of 14 states. Coarse cum Nutri-cereals saw an increase of 2.08 lakh hectares in area under cultivation from 51.42 lakh hectares in 2021-22 to 53.49 lakh hectares in 2022-23.

SSC CGL Tier-2 03.03.2023 (Shift-I)

41. Match the following crops with their areas.

Crop		Areas in 2022-23
A. Millets	1.	98.02 lakh hectares
B. Pulses	2.	53.49 lakh hectares
C. Mustard	3.	167.86 lakh hectares

Codes

	A	B	C		A	B	C
(a)	1	3	2	(b)	3	1	2
(c)	2	1	3	(d)	2	3	1

Ans. (d)

The correct matching is A-2, B-3, C-1.
According to the passage, the crop and the area covered by them in 2022-2023 is
Millets– 53.49 lakh hectares
Pulses– 167.86 lakh hectares
Mustard– 98.02 lakh hectares

42. On which of the following crops is the Indian Government specially focusing this year?
(a) Rice (b) Oilseeds
(c) Pulses (d) Millets

Ans. (d)

The Indian Government is specially focusing on millets in this year.

43. The main theme of the passage is
(a) increase in the area of Rabi crops in 2022-23
(b) area under Rabi crop in last five years
(c) increase in the production of pulses
(d) increase in the area of oilseeds like mustard

Ans. (a)

'Increase in the area of Rabi crops in 2022-2023' is the main theme of the passage.

44. Which state recorded the maximum increase in sown area of the rice crop?
(a) Chhattisgarh (b) Telangana
(c) Rajasthan (d) Madhya Pradesh

Ans. (b)

Telangana recorded the maximum increase in sown area of the rice crop.

PASSAGE - 12

My grandmother like everybody's grandmother, was an old woman. She had been old and wrinkled for the twenty years that I had known her. People said that she once had been young and pretty and had even had husband, but that was hard to believe. My grandmother's portrait hung above the mantelpiece in the drawing room. He wore a big turban and loose fitting clothes. His long, white beard covered the best part of his chest and he looked at least a hundred years old. He did not look the sort of person who would have a wife or children. He looked as if he could only have lots and lots of grandchildren. As my grandmother being young and pretty, the thought was almost revelling. She often told us of the games she used to play as a child. That seemed quite absurd and undignified on her part and we treated it like the fables of the prophets she used to tell us.

SSC CGL Tier-2 03.03.2023 (Shift-I)

45. Select the most appropriate fact from the given options.
(a) The author and grandma lived for twenty years.
(b) Grandma was twenty years old.
(c) The author was twenty when grandma died.
(d) The author was twenty years old when he wrote the story.

Ans. (c)

The fact that the author had known his grandmother for twenty years indicates that he was 20 years old when his grandmother died.

46. Select an appropriate title for the given passage.
(a) The Grandchildren (b) My Grandfather
(c) Grandmothers (d) My Grandmother

Ans. (d)

The given passage presents the author's description of his grandmother.

47. Select the most appropriate antonym of the given word.
Revolting
(a) Attractive (b) Unpleasant
(c) Rebel (d) Peace

Ans. (a)

'Revolting' means arousing dislike. Hence, its antonym is 'attractive' which means to produce liking for someone.

48. Select the most appropriate inference drawn from the passage.
(a) The author looked upon his grandmother, as an old woman like every grandmother.
(b) People said that the grandmother was pretty.
(c) Grandmother had a husband.
(d) Grandmother loved to talk of her childhood.

Ans. (a)

The most important inference that can be drawn is that the author looked upon his grandmother as an old woman like every grandmother.

PASSAGE - 13

The sage of science, Einstein, was sitting in a depressive and pensive mood one evening. His eyes were brimming with tears. The pain was evident on his face. He peeped out of the window of his room. The Sun had set a few minutes back. The sky was filled with a reddish glow. At this sunset, he felt that it was humanity that had sunk into devilish darkness and the reddish glow in the sky was the blood of humanity spilling all over the sky from Earth. With tired steps, he walked back to his chair and settled down. It was the 9th of August, 1945.

Three days back, he had felt the same agony as if someone had torn him apart. He was deeply hurt and depressed when he heard on the radio that America had dropped an atom bomb on the Japanese city, Hiroshima. Today, within three days another bomb was dropped on another city, Nagasaki and lakhs of people had been killed.

He had heard that the blast released so much energy that it had paled all past destructions in comparison and death had played out a pitiable dance of destruction. The flames that broke out of the bomb were burning, melting and exploding buildings. Scared of the heat of the bomb, people had jumped into lakes and rivers, but the water was boiling and the people too were burnt and killed. The animals in the water were already boiled to death. Animals, trees, herbs, fragrant flowering plants were all turned into ashes. The atomic energy destruction had just not stopped there. It had entered the atmosphere there and had spread radiation that would affect people for generations to come and would also bring about destructive irreversible biological change in animals and plants.

As the news of the atomic attack reached Einstein and he became aware of the glaring horror of the abuse of atomic energy, his distress and restlessness knew no bounds. He could not control himself and picked up his violin to turn his mind on to other things. While playing the violin, he tried to dissolve his distress in its sad notes, but couldn't.

He was burning on the embers of destruction; his heart was filled with an ocean of agony and tears just continued streaming uncontrollably out of his eyes. Night had fallen. His daughter came up and asked him to eat something as he had not taken anything for the last four days. His voice was restrained and he said, "I don't feel like eating."

He could not sleep that night. Lying down, he was thinking how he had drawn the attention of the then American President Roosevelt towards the destructive powers of an atomic bomb. He had thought that this would be used to scare Hitler and put an end to the barbarism that Hitler was up to. However, Roosevelt kept him in the dark and made false promises.

Eventually, he had abused Einstein's equation of that resulted in the destructive experiments. His actions had made science and scientists as murderers. Einstein kept on thinking for a long time. Eventually, he slipped into sleep. When he woke up at dawn, there was a new dawn in him too. The atomic threat had transformed his heart.

SSC CGL Tier-2 06.03.2023 (Shift-I)

49. Why did Einstein refuse to eat?
(a) As he felt happy (b) As he felt worried
(c) As he felt guilty (d) As he felt sick

Ans. (c)

Einstein refused to eat because he felt guilty of bringing about huge damage and destruction to Japan's Hiroshima and Nagasaki by introducing the power of an atomic bomb to the American President, Roosevelt.

50. Select an appropriate title for the passage.
(a) War and Destruction (b) Death in Hiroshima
(c) Einstein and His Violin (d) Atom Bombs

Ans. (a)

The appropriate title of the passage can be 'War and Destruction.'

51. What is the central theme of the passage?
(a) Einstein and his life
(b) Atomic war and its consequences
(c) Einstein and his love for music
(d) Science and its bad side

Ans. (b)

The central theme of the passage is 'Atomic war and its consequences'.

The passage presents the war and destruction caused by the atomic bomb attack by America on Japan's Hiroshima and Nagasaki.

52. Select the most appropriate antonym of 'Set' from the passage.
(a) Stand (b) Get up
(c) Rise (d) Level
Ans. (c)
The antonym of the word 'Set' is 'Rise'.

PASSAGE - 14

The Indian Space Research Organisation (ISRO) announced another successful mission. ISRO Chairman S. Somanath said that three small satellites successfully separated and were injected into orbit.

ISRO had launched three small satellites powered by its SSLV-D2 launch vehicle from Satish Dhawan Space Centre at Sriharikota on 10th February, 2023 at 09:18 AM IST. The launch vehicle was carrying EOS-07, Janus-1 and AzaadiSAT-2 satellites and aimed to inject them into a 450 km circular orbit. The launch took place at the first launch pad at SDSC SHAR, Sriharikota.

The SSLV-D2 had to take a 15 minutes flight to inject EOS-07, Janus-1 and AzaadiSAT-2 satellites into 450 km circular lower orbit. "It is configured with three solid propulsion stages and a velocity terminal module.

It is a 34 m tall, 2 m diameter vehicle having a lift-off mass of 120 t", said ISRO. The EOS-07 satellite weighs 156.3 kg and is made by ISRO. About 13 minutes into its flight, the SSLV rocket ejected EOS-07 and soon after that the other two satellites Janus-1 and AzaadiSAT-2 were ejected — all at an altitude of 450 km, said ISRO.

With the new rocket in its portfolio, ISRO will have three rockets — Polar Satellite Launch Vehicle (PSLV) and its variants (cost about 200 crore), Geosynchronous Satellite Launch Vehicle (GSLV-MkII cost about ₹ 272 crore and LVM3 ₹ 434 crore) and SSLV (Development cost of three rockets about 56 crore each) and production cost may go down later.

"New experiments include mm-Wave Humidity Sounder and Spectrum Monitoring Payload. Janus-1, a 10.2 kg satellite belongs to ANTARIS, USA. A 8.7 kg satellite AzaadiSAT-2 is a combined effort of about 750 girl students across India guided by Space Kidz India, Chennai", it added.

SSLV caters to the launch of up to 500 kg satellites to Low Earth Orbits on 'launch-on- demand' basis. "It provides low-cost access to space, offers low turn-around time and flexibility in accommodating multiple satellites and demands minimal launch infrastructure", as per a statement by ISRO.

SSC CGL Tier-2 06.03.2023 (Shift-I)

53. Which satellite was injected into the orbit first?
(a) EOS-07 (b) Janus-1
(c) AzaadiSAT-2 (d) Antaris
Ans. (a)
The satellite to be injected in the orbit first was EOS-07.

54. Match the satellites with their weight.

	Satellites		Weight
a.	EOS-07	1.	10.2 kg
b.	AzaadiSAT-2	2.	156.3 kg
c.	Janus-1	3.	8.7 kg

Codes

	A	B	C		A	B	C
(a)	2	1	3	(b)	1	3	2
(c)	2	3	1	(d)	3	1	2

Ans. (c)
The correct matching is A-2, B-3, C-1.

55. What is the passage mainly about?
(a) New experiments on satellites by ISRO
(b) Launch of three small satellites in orbit by ISRO
(c) Development of SSLV rocket by ISRO
(d) Efforts to cut costs of satellites by ISRO
Ans. (b)
The passage is mainly about the launch of three small satellites in orbit by ISRO.

56. After reading the passage it can be inferred that it is
(a) a government release (b) a news item
(c) a magazine article (d) an editorial
Ans. (b)
It can be inferred that the passage is a news item.

PASSAGE - 15

Wetlands are amongst the most productive ecosystems on the Earth and provide many important services to human society. They exhibit enormous diversity according to their genesis, geographical location, water regime and chemistry, dominant species and soil and sediment characteristics.

Globally, the areal extent of wetland ecosystems ranges from 917 million hectares (m ha) to more than 1,275 m ha. One of the first widely used wetland classifications systems, devised by Cowardin et al., 1979, categorised wetlands into marine (coastal wetlands), estuarine (including deltas, tidal marshes, and mangrove swamps), lacustrine (lakes), riverine (along rivers and streams) and palustrine (marshes, swamps and bogs) based on their hydrological, ecological and geological characteristics.

Ramsar Convention on Wetlands was an international treaty signed in 1971. Overall, 1052 sites in Europe; 289 sites in Asia; 359 sites in Africa; 175 sites in South America; 211 sites in North America and 79 sites in Oceania region have been identified as Ramsar sites or wetlands of international importance.

As per the Ramsar Convention definition most of the natural water bodies (such as rivers, lakes, coastal lagoons, mangroves, peat land, coral reefs) and man- made wetlands (such as ponds, farm ponds, irrigated fields, sacred groves, salt pans, reservoirs, gravel pits, sewage farms and canals) in India constitute the wetland ecosystem distributed in different geographical regions ranging from Himalayas to Deccan plateau. As of February, 2022, India has 49 Ramsar sites covering an area of 10,93,636 hectares, the highest in South Asia.

As per the estimates, India has about 757.06 thousand wetlands with a total wetland area of 15.3 m ha, accounting for nearly 4.7% of the total geographical area of the country. Out of this, areas under inland wetlands accounts for 69%, coastal wetlands 27% and other wetlands (smaller than 2.25 ha) 4%.

Gujarat has the highest proportion (17.5%) and Mizoram has the lowest proportion (0.66%) of the area under wetlands. Among Union Territories, Lakshadweep has the highest proportion (around 96%) and Chandigarh has the least proportion (3%) of geographical area under wetlands. **SSC CGL Tier-2 06.03.2023 (Shift-I)**

57. Which of the following questions cannot be answered after reading the above passage?
(a) How many Ramsar sites are there in the world?
(b) What is the classification of wetlands?
(c) Why are wetlands important for human societies?
(d) How much area is covered by wetlands in India?

Ans. (c)

The question 'Why are wetlands important for human societies?' cannot be answered after reading the passage.

58. Match the continents with the number of Ramsar sites.

Continents	No. of Ramsar sites
A. North America	1. 1052 sites
B. Europe	2. 211 sites
C. Africa	3. 289 sites
D. Asia	4. 359 sites

Codes

	A	B	C	D		A	B	C	D
(a)	2	1	4	3	(b)	2	3	4	1
(c)	4	1	2	3	(d)	3	4	1	2

Ans. (a)

The correct matching is A-2, B-1, C-4, D-3.

59. In India, what kind of wetlands occupy the largest area?
(a) Coastal wetlands (b) Mangrove swamps
(c) Inland wetlands (d) Small wetlands

Ans. (c)

Inland wetlands occupy the largest area in India with 69% of the total wetland area in the country.

60. Under which category of wetlands, are delta and mangrove swamps included?
(a) Marine (b) Estuarine
(c) Lacustrine (d) Palustrine

Ans. (b)

Estuarine category of wetlands includes delta and mangrove swamps.

PASSAGE - 16

Notwithstanding logistical challenges posed by COVID-19 pandemic, India continues to expand its rice exports footprint in the African, Asian and European Union markets, thus having the largest share in global rice trade.

The robust global demand also helped India's growth in rice exports. In 2020-21, India's rice exports (Basmati and Non-Basmati) rose by a huge 87 per cent to 17.72 Million Tonne (MT) from 9.49 MT achieved in 2019-20.

In terms of value realisation, India's rice exports rose by 38 per cent to USD 8815 million in 2020-21 from USD 6397 million reported in 2019-20. In terms of Rupees, India's rice export grew by 44 per cent to ` 65298 crore in 2020-21 from ` 45379 crore in the previous year. In the first seven months of the current financial year (2021-22), India's rice exports rose by more than 33 per cent to 11.79 MT from 8.91 MT achieved during April-October, 2020-22. It is anticipated that India's rice exports in 2021-22 would likely surpass the record feet of 17.72 MT achieved in 2020-21.

In 2020-21, India shipped non-basmati rice to nine countries - Timor-Leste, Puerto Rico, Brazil, Papua New Guinea, Zimbabwe, Burundi, Eswatini, Myanmar and Nicaragua, where exports were carried out for the first time or earlier the shipment was smaller in volume. India's Non-Basmati rice exports was valued at USD 4796 million (₹ 35448 crore) in 2020-21, with Basmati Rice exports a close second at USD 4018 million (₹ 29,849 crore). In terms of volume of Basmati rice exports in 2020-21, top ten countries-Saudi Arabia, Iran, Iraq, Yemen, United Arab Emirates, United States of America, Kuwait, United Kingdom, Qatar and Oman have a share of close to 80 per cent in total shipments of aromatic long grained rice from India.

Top ten countries – Nepal, Benin, Bangladesh, Senegal, Togo, Cote D Ivoire, Guinea, Malaysia, Iraq, United Arab Emirates have a share of 57 per cent in India's total exports of Non-Basmati rice in 2020-21 in terms of volume. **SSC CGL Tier-2 07.03.2023 (Shift-I)**

61. What is the estimate of rice export in the year 2021-22?
(a) It will remain the same as the 17.72 MT rice export achieved in 2020-22.
(b) It may fall below the 17.72 MT rice export achieved in 2020-21.
(c) It will exceed the 17.72 MT rice export achieved in 2020-21.
(d) It will not pass beyond the 17.72 MT rice export achieved in 2020-21.

Ans. (c)

The estimate of rice export in the year 2021-22 will exceed the 17.72 MT rice export achieved in 2020-21.

62. Which of the following questions cannot be answered on the basis of the above passage?
(a) How much Basmati rice was exported by India in 2020-21?
(b) How much rice (Basmati and Non-Basmati) was exported by India in 2020-21?
(c) Which top 10 countries buy Non-Basmati rice from India?
(d) What was the value of Basmati rice export from India?

Ans. (a)

The given passage presents rice (Basmati and non-Basmati) exports of India in 2020-2021.

It also names the countries that buys Basmati and non-Basmati rice from India. Further, it states the value of Basmati rice exported from India. The passage does not answer the quantity of Basmati rice that was exported by India in 2020-2021.

63. Which of the following countries imported rice from India for the first time?
(a) Iraq (b) Bangladesh
(c) Brazil (d) United Arab Emirates

Ans. (c)

Brazil is the country that imported rice from India for the first time.

64. Which of the following countries imports Basmati rice from India?
(a) Malaysia (b) Nepal
(c) Bangladesh (d) Kuwait

Ans. (d)

Kuwait imports Basmati rice from India.

PASSAGE - 17

As the Sun inches closer to its peak activity in its solar cycle, an explosion has been picked up behind the North- Eastern limb of the star in our solar system. Solar observatories saw bits and pieces of the explosion, which remain obscured in view from Earth's orbit.

The explosion was spotted on 31st July at around 2309 UT and Earth-orbiting satellites registered a long-lasting C9.3-class solar flare. "The intensity is probably an underestimate because it was partially eclipsed by the edge of the Sun. Nasa's Solar Dynamics Observatory (SDO) saw hot debris flying away from the blast site," space weather, which tracks the solar activity, reported.

While the explosion was powerful, experts have predicted that Earth is not in the line of fire from the Sun. Scientists are expected to get a view of the active region later this week as it comes to sight. Earth is not in the line of fire.

The explosion is significant because it may herald an active region set to emerge over the Sun's North-Eastern limb later this week. A new sunspot group could bring an end to weeks of relative quiet," space weather said in its report.

SSC CGL Tier-2 07.03.2023 (Shift-I)

65. Select the most appropriate synonym of the given word from the passage.
Partially
(a) Supportively (b) Partly
(c) Frankly (d) Completely

Ans. (b)

The words 'Partially' and 'Partly' mean 'to a limited extend.'

66. Select the most appropriate synonym of the given word from the passage.
Debris
(a) Detritus (b) Rays (c) Specks (d) Liquid

Ans. (a)

The word 'detritus' means waste or debris of any kind.

67. Select the most appropriate synonym of the given word from the passage.
Spotted
(a) Witnessed (b) Speckled
(c) Splotchy (d) Placed

Ans. (a)

The synonym of 'Spotted' is 'Witnessed.

68. Select the most appropriate synonym of the given word from the passage.
Peak
(a) Glance (b) Point (c) Bottom (d) Zenith

Ans. (d)

The words 'Peak' and 'Zenith' mean the highest point.

PASSAGE - 18

Tens of thousands of people who lost their homes in a catastrophic earthquake huddled around campfires in the bitter cold and clamoured for food and water on Thursday, three days after the temblor hit Turkey and Syria and killed more than 19,300 on Monday, 6th February, 2023. Emergency crews used pick axes, shovels and jackhammers to dig through twisted metal and concrete - and occasionally still pulled out survivors.

In the Turkish city of Antakya, dozens scrambled for aid in front of a truck distributing children's coats and other supplies. Many of those who lost their homes found shelter in tents, stadiums and other temporary accommodation, but others slept outdoors. In Antakya, over 100 bodies were awaiting identification in a makeshift morgue outside a hospital.

Authorities called off search-and- rescue operations in the cities of Kilis and Sanliurfa, where destruction was not as severe as in other impacted regions.

The UN is authorised to deliver aid through only one border crossing, and road damage has prevented that thus far. UN Officials pleaded for humanitarian concerns to take precedence over wartime politics.

The scale of loss and suffering remained massive. Turkish authorities said on Thursday that the death toll had risen to more than 16,100 in the country, with more than 64,000 injured. In Syria, which includes government- held and rebel-held areas, more than 3,100 have been reported dead and more than 5,000 injured. Rescue teams urged quiet in the hope of hearing stifled pleas for help and the Syrian paramedic group known as the White Helmets noted that every second could mean saving a life. But more and more often, the teams pulled out dead bodies.

It was not clear how many people were still unaccounted for in both countries. Turkey's disaster-management agency said more than 110,000 rescue personnel were now taking part in the effort and more than 5,500 vehicles, including tractors, cranes, bulldozers and excavators had been shipped.

The Foreign Ministry said 95 countries have offered help. More than half of that number have sent a total of nearly 6,500 rescuers. Another 2,400 more are still expected to arrive. International aid for Syria was far more sparse.

Efforts there have been hampered by the civil war and the isolation of the rebel-held region along the border that is surrounded by Russia-backed government forces.

SSC CGL Tier-2 07.03.2023 (Shift-I)

69. How many foreign rescue workers are engaged in the rescue work?
(a) 2400 rescue workers (b) 1,10,000 rescue workers
(c) 5000 rescue workers (d) 6500 rescue workers

Ans. (d)

6500 foreign rescue workers are engaged in the rescue work.

70. Match the words with their meaning.

Words	Meanings
A. Clamoured	1. Checked
B. Scrambled	2. Screamed
C. Hampered	3. Jostled

Codes

	A	B	C		A	B	C
(a)	2	3	1	(b)	2	1	3
(c)	3	1	2	(d)	1	3	2

Ans. (a)

The correct matching is A-2, B-3, C-1.

The word 'clamoured' means 'screamed', 'scrambled' means 'jostled' or 'confused' and 'hampered' means 'checked'.

71. The passage highlights all the following except
(a) Syria's rebel-held areas and the Civil War going on there
(b) the foreign aid being offered to Turkey and Syria
(c) the suffering of people in the earthquake hit areas of Turkey and Syria
(d) the rescue work being carried out in Turkey and Syria

Ans. (a)

The given passage present how an earthquake affected Turkey and Syria.

It presents the rescue work and the foreign aid offered to the nation. The passage does not mention Syria's rebel-held areas and the civil war going on there.

72. Why is the International aid much lesser in Syria than in Turkey?
(a) Because Syria is a war-torn country and there are areas under rebels.
(b) Because the destruction was not as severe in Syria as in Turkey.
(c) Because the UN is allowed only one border crossing and Syria is not allowing that.
(d) Because the roads have been damaged there.

Ans. (a)

International aid was much lesser in Syria than in Turkey because Syria is a war-torn country and there are areas under rebels.

PASSAGE - 19

The discovery of a new bird species has sparked excitement among ornithologists and bird enthusiasts worldwide.

The bird named the Sapphire-winged Warbler, discovered in a remote tropical island's rainforests, is a unique bird with vibrant blue feathers and a distinctive melodic song. Birdwatchers and nature enthusiasts have been flocking to the island in hopes of catching a glimpse of this elusive and captivating creature. The discovery of the Sapphire-winged Warbler highlights the importance of preserving and protecting habitats. Amidst the excitement surrounding the discovery of the Sapphire-winged Warbler, researchers have embarked on a mission to uncover the bird's migratory patterns.

Equipped with satellite tracking devices, they aim to trace the remarkeable journey of this species across vast distances. By unravelling its migratory routes and stopover locations, scientists hope to gain insight into the challenges the Sapphire-winged Warbler faces during its arduous travels. The local community on the tropical island had embraced the newfound avian resident with great enthusiasm. Efforts are underway to raise awareness about the importance of conservation and to create protected areas that ensure the continued existance of this esquisite species.

SSC CGL Tier-2 26.10.2023

73. Select the most appropriate title for the given passage.
(a) The Migratory Journey of the Sapphire-winged Warbler
(b) Conservation Efforts in Tropical Rainforests
(c) The Unique Features of the Sapphire-winged Warbler
(d) The Curious Behaviour of Birds in Remote Island

Ans. (a)

The appropriate title for the passage is 'The Migratory Journey of the Sapphire-winged Warbler'.

74. Which statement best reflects a fact mentioned in the given passage?
(a) The Sapphire-winged Warbler is the largest bird species in the avian kingdom.
(b) Schools on the island organise annual bird-watching.
(c) The Sapphire-winged Warbler is the only species on the tropical island.
(d) Researchers are using satellite tracking devices to study the bird's migratory patterns.

Ans. (d)

The given passage mentions that researchers have embarked on a mission to uncover the Sapphire- winged Warblers migratory patterns with satellite tracking devices with the aim to trace the remarkable journey of this species across vast distances.

75. Identify the most appropriate synonym of the word 'Stare' from the passage.
(a) Arduousness (b) Vibrancy
(c) Excitement (d) Glimpse

Ans. (d)

The words 'stare' and 'glimpse' mean to see something.

76. Based on the given passage, which of the following inferences can be made ?
(a) The discovery of the Sapphire-winged Warbler has sparked global interest in bird watching.
(b) The Sapphire-winged Warbler is an aggressive and territorial bird species.
(c) Conservation efforts are solely focused on protecting the Sapphire-winged Warbler.
(d) The scientific community has lost interest in studying avian species.

Ans. (a)

According to the passage, people worldwide, including ornithologists and bird enthusiasts, are excited about the discovery of the Sapphire-winged Warbler. They are travelling to the remote tropical island to see this unique bird. This indicates a global interest in bird watching.

PASSAGE - 20

On woody plants known as vines, luscious, smooth-skinned berries called grapes grow in dense clusters. In particular, grapes are grown in France, Italy, Spain, Australia Chile, Romania, Georgia, South Africa and California, all of which have warm summers and moderate winters. Table grapes are larger and sweeter grapes that are intended for fresh consumption.

To create wine, 80% of the grapes are crushed. The fermentation process turns grapes into wine. To make raising, grapes must also be dried.

Grapes ripen in the area of California in August. They are cut from the vines and left on raisins, they are further cooked and steeped in particular treatments.

According to studies, one acre of grapes can make roughly 15,000 glasses of wine on average. Grapes of Thompson, Flame, Ruby, Perlette and Tokay varieties are popular. **SSC CGL Tier-2 26.10.2023**

77. What does the fermentation process do ?
(a) Turns grapes into raisins (b) Makes grapes larger
(c) Crushes the grapes (d) Turns grapes into wine

Ans. (d)

As per the passage, fermentation turns grapes into wine.

78. Based on your reading of the passage, select the most appropriate word which best describes 'Luscious'.
(a) Smooth (b) Soft
(c) Juicy (d) Large

Ans. (c)

The word 'Luscious' means juicy and sweet in taste.

79. In which region do grapes ripen in August ?
(a) Chile (b) California
(c) France (d) Australia

Ans. (b)

It is mentioned in the passage that grapes ripen in the area of California in August.

80. Select the most appropriate title for the passage.
(a) Grapes and its Uses (b) Grapes and World
(c) Wine Making (d) Varieties of Grapes

Ans. (a)

The most appropriate title for the passage is 'Grapes and its Uses'.

SSC CGL 2022 (Tier 2)

PASSAGE - 21

A piano teacher described an interesting encounter she had with a young lady who came to inquire about music lessons. The young lady asked her, "How long will this course take? My father tells me that it is in fashion now to be able to play musical instruments and that I should learn one quickly. I want something that will be quick, fast and easy like, like ... " When the amused teacher explained that it would take a lifetime of meticulous practice to learn music, her face fell and needless to say, she never came back.

The single most important factor that distinguishes those of us who succeed in any venture and those of us who don't is this instant coffee attitude. Most of us went results quickly. We want to reach the top immediately and get worked up when things go wrong. Perseverance and patience are forgotten words.

We get upset, frustrated and angry when a skill or activity requires us to put in a lot of effort and time. We get dejected and want to give it up.

But such thinking serves no good. For, it doesn't solve the problem. Life is tough for those with an 'instant coffee' attitude. Success, real success and happiness come to those who have a 'bread-making' attitude those who are willing to knead the dough, wait for hours for it to rise, only to punch it down and knead some more, wait for another couple of hours for it to rise again and then bake it before it is ready to be eaten. Nothing is instantaneous. For every endeavour - whether in the area of career, academics, music, sports, relationships, physical fitness or even in spirituality - it is a long, arduous journey.

Only if we are willing to put in the time, painstaking effort and have faith, can we get results. If we don't accept this difficult-but-true fact of life, our lives will be far from being happy and fulfilling. For we may not make that extra effort which can change the course of life dramatically, for the good.

The major problems with these 'instant coffee' solutions are that they are invariably short lived. If we stubbornly refuse to give up this search for quick solutions, all we do is end up on the wrong track.

SSC CGL Tier-2 29.01.2022

81. What do you understand by the term 'instant coffee attitude'?
(a) Passion to learn something
(b) Short-lived pleasure
(c) Expecting quick results
(d) Keeping up with the latest trends

Ans. (c)

According to the passage, instant coffee attitude is expecting easy and fast results without making any effort.

82. When an activity requires too much effort we feel
(a) frustrated (b) happy
(c) inspired (d) fulfilled

Ans. (a)

The given passage states that when an activity requires a lot of effort, we feel angry, dejected and frustrated.

83. Why did the young lady approach the piano teacher for music lessons?
(a) The piano teacher was highly accomplished.
(b) She was willing to practise hard to become a successful piano player.
(c) It was considered fashionable to be able to play musical instruments.
(d) She was a music lover and was keen to take lessons.

Ans. (c)

The first paragraph of the passage states that the lady came to the piano teacher because her father had told her that it was fashionable to be able to play musical instruments.

84. What kind of attitude does the writer advocate for a life of fulfilment?
(a) One of perseverance and patience
(b) One of instant gratification
(c) One of anger and dejection dismissed
(d) One of stubbornness and refusal

Ans. (a)

According to the author of the given passage, we should make effort with perseverance and patience to get success in life.

85. What does 'bread making' attitude consist of ?
(a) Instantaneous results (b) Painstaking efforts
(c) Futile labour (d) Talent and skill

Ans. (b)

The 'bread making' attitude includes taking painstaking efforts with perseverance and patience to get success in life.

PASSAGE - 22

Although pollution of land, sea and air has been well documented, the latest and the least recognised version is the swelling tide of noise which is engulfing urban as well as rural areas. This has long-term implications on the ecology, health and productivity of a fast developing country like India. Unlike other pollutants, noise lacks visibility, seldom registering on the consciousness, except as a trifling irritant to be dismissed at will and therefore less likely to be perceived as a threat. Available data indicates that noise does pose a threat to health and is known to have caused a number of complications. Declining productivity among workers in certain industries has been directly correlated with noise levels, particularly those under constant exposure to the menace.

The first-ever survey of the impact of noise on health, conducted by All India Institute of Medical Science (AIIMS), has established that noise not only impairs the physical and psychological functioning of the human organism but also causes nausea, vomiting, pain, hypertension and a lot of other complications, including cardio-vascular complaints.

A study by Post Graduate School of Basic Medical Sciences, Chennai confirms such conclusions. In 50 per cent of industries, it was found that workmen exposed to higher intensities of noise in occupational capacities were often irritated, short-tempered and impatient and more likely to resort to agitation and disrupt production. This was true of units in heavy industrial pockets in and around the four metropolitan centres.

Recreational noise, another ugly facet, is becoming more widespread in cities and towns. Loudspeakers are turned at full volume during marriages, festivals, jagr, musical programmes particularly at night, without the least consideration for others. Even at 50 dB, sound can awaken a person from a deep slumber.

As experiments have shown, loudspeakers with output from 60 to 80 dB cause the pupils of a slumbering person to dilate, with increasing intake of oxygen, resulting in palpitation. The effect is more pronounced in narrow lanes.

TV sets are played at full volume at prime time, invariably disturbing neighbours. Noise making seems to have become the latest status symbol, be it an election campaign or slogan shouting or advertising ownership" of a TV set.

SSC CGL Tier-2 29.01.2022

86. In what way does noise become a status symbol?
(a) Exposing workmen to high intensity sounds
(b) Showing off the loud volume of one's TV
(c) Awakening people from deep sleep
(d) Conducting late night musical shows

Ans. (b)

The last paragraph of the passage indicates that noise becomes a status symbol as people keep their TV on loud volume to show off their TV set.

87. According to a survey conducted by AIIMS, noise do not cause
(a) heart related complaints
(b) eye infections
(c) hypertension
(d) nausea and vomiting

Ans. (b)

As per the passage, the study conducted by AIIMS shows that noise can leads to nausea, hypertension, vomiting, pain, cardiovascular diseases, etc., not eye infections.

88. Noise can be differentiated from other pollutants because
(a) it does not impact the productivity of the workers in industries
(b) it is regarded as a small irritant which may be easily dismissed
(c) it is not detrimental to our health in any way
(d) it is prevalent only in the urban areas of the country

Ans. (b)

According to the passage, noise is not visible and so, is considered as a small irritant without any major impact. Hence, it is often dismissed.

89. Recreational noise is created during
(a) discord between agitated workers
(b) running of the heavy machinery
(c) weddings and festivals
(d) shouting of slog

Ans. (c)

As per the passage, recreational noise is the noise created by loudspeakers during marriages, festivals, jagrans, musical programmes, etc.

90. Which of the following statements is false?
(a) Loudspeakers with low decibel sound can cause palpitations.
(b) Several studies have been conducted on air, water and land pollution.
(c) There is a direct correlation between productivity of works and noise.
(d) Noise pollution is not visible to the eyes.

Ans. (a)

Except (a) all of the given sentences are mentioned in the passage.

PASSAGE - 23

The severe cyclonic storm, Nisarga, which made a landfall South of Alibag in Maharashtra's Raigad district on Wednesday 11:30 a.m. is an indication of an increasing frequency of severe cyclones developing in the Arabian Sea in the past trend that studies have linked to climate change.

In the past two years, there have been seven cyclones in the Arabian sea, though, according to India Meteorological Department (IMD), ratio of cyclones in the Arabian Sea and the Bay of Bengal which just witnessed the destructive cyclone Amphan on 21st May. The Inter-governmental Panel on Climate Change (IPCC) last year came out with a special report, Ocean and Cryosphere in a Changing Climate, in which it said that extreme rainfall and extreme sea level events associated with some tropical cyclones are being seen to have a cascading impact on coastal areas.

"There is emerging evidence for an increase in annual global proportion of Category 4 or 5 tropical cyclones in recent decades", the IPCC report had said. A Category 4 cyclone has a speed of 209-251 kmph and is referred to as an extremely severe cyclonic storm, while a Category 5 cyclone has a wind speed of more than 252 kmph and is referred to as a super cyclone. The IPCC report refers to a 2017 study led by Atmospheric and Oceanic Sciences Programme, Princeton University, USA, which found that in 2014 and 2015, post-monsoon Extremely Severe Cyclonic Storms (ESCS) were first observed over the Arabian Sea causing widespread damage. The study had concluded that climate change had led to an increase in the occurrence of ESCSs in the Arabian Sea.

"Our research suggests that cyclones would be more frequent during the post monsoon season (October-December) by a series climate model simulations. However, we didn't find any significant changes in cyclone activity during the pre-monsoon season through the climate simulations. It is very difficult to identify if a cyclone (like Nisarga) is generated in line with climate change", said Hiroyuki Murakami, the lead author of the study.

"Coastal hazards will be exacerbated by an increase in the average intensity, magnitude of storm surge, rising mean sea levels and precipitation rates of tropical cyclones", the IPCC report further stated.

SSC CGL Tier-2 03.02.2022

91. According to the research on cyclones, the frequency of cyclones is expected to be more during
(a) January-March
(b) October-December
(c) July- September
(d) April-June

Ans. (b)

As per the passage, cyclones are more frequent during the post monsoon season in October- December.

92. Match the word with their meaning

A. Cascading	(1) Intensify
B. Precipitation	(2) Drop-down
C. Exacerbate	(3) Rainfall

Codes

	A	B	C		A	B	C
(a)	3	2	1	(b)	2	1	3
(c)	1	3	2	(d)	2	3	1

Ans. (d)

The correct matching is A-2, B-3, C-1.
Cascading means the drop-down of the water, precipitation means rainfall and exacerbate means to intensify.

93. The passage is mainly focused on
(a) the research on super cyclones
(b) the effect of climate change on cyclone Nisarga
(c) the frequency of cyclones in the Arabian Sea and Bay of Bengal
(d) link of frequent cyclones with climate change

Ans. (c)

The given passage focuses on the increasing frequency of cyclones in the Arabian Sea and the Bay of Bengal.

94. The hazards in coastal areas worsen due to the increase which of the following?
1. Precipitation rate of the cyclone
2. Magnitude of storm
3. The rise of sea level

Codes
(a) (1) and (3) are true
(b) (2) and (3) are true
(c) (1) and (2) are true
(d) (1), (2) and (3) all are true

Ans. (d)

Statements 1, 2 and 3 all are true.

As per the last paragraph of the passage, coastal hazards worsen due to magnitude of the storm, rising sea levels and precipitation rates.

95. Which of the following is a Category 4 cyclone?
(a) One with a wind speed of 209-251 kmph
(b) One with a wind speed of less than 150 kmph
(c) One with a wind speed of more than 252 kmph
(d) One with a wind speed of 150-208 kmph

Ans. (a)

According to the passage, a category 4 cyclone has a speed of 209-251 kmph and is referred to as an extremely severe cyclonic storm.

SSC CPO 2024 (Tier 1 & 2)

PASSAGE - 24

A fact that draws our attention is that, according to his position in life, an extravagant man is either admired or loathed. A successful business man does nothing to increase his popularity by being prudent with his money. A person who is wealthy is expected to lead a luxurious life and to be lavish with his hospitality. If he is not so, he is considered mean and his reputation in business may even suffer in consequence. The paradox remains that he had not been careful with his money in the first place; he would never have achieved his present wealth.

Among the low income group, a different set of values exists. The young clerk, who makes his wife a present of a new dress when he has not paid his house rent, is condemned as extravagant. Carefulness with money to the point of meanness is applauded as a virtue.

Nothing in his life is considered more worthy than paying his bills. The ideal wife for such a man separates her housekeeping money into joyless little piles- so much for rent, for food, for the children's shoes, she is able to face the milkman with equanimity every month, satisfied with her economising ways and never knows the guilt of buying something she can't really afford. As for myself, I fall into neither of these categories.

If I have money to spare I can be extravagant, but when, as is usually the case, I am hard up and then I am the meanest man imaginable.

SSC CPO Tier-2 08.01.2024

96. Which of these is not true?
(a) A low-income person is considered worthy if he pays bills on time.
(b) The rich amass wealth by spending money economically.
(c) The author is at liberty to be extravagant at all times.
(d) People who lead a luxurious life are expected to entertain lavishly.

Ans. (c)

According to the last paragraph of the passage, the author is not extravagant at all time. In fact, he is the meanest man imaginable as he does not have much money on him.

97. Which of these can be inferred from the passage?
(a) Wealthy people are stingy as far as philanthropy is concerned.
(b) Extravagance is applauded in some and condemned in others.
(c) For the wealthy, prudence with money is considered a virtue.
(d) People who have a meagre income are expected to be spendthrifts.

Ans. (b)

The given passage posits that extravagance is applauded in some and condemned in others.

98. If a successful businessman is judicious with his money
(a) his prestige improves
(b) his reputation suffers
(c) his business flourishes
(d) his popularity rises

Ans. (c)

According to the given passage, a businessman has to be economical to make sure that his business flourishes.

99. Select the antonym of 'loathed' as used in the passage.
(a) Despised
(b) Shunned
(c) Adored
(d) Cursed

Ans. (c)

The word 'loathed' means 'disliked and hated'.

Hence, its antonym is 'adored' which means 'liked'.

100. The word 'equanimity' in the passage means
(a) tranquillity
(b) agitation
(c) anxiety
(d) frustration

Ans. (a)

The word 'equanimity' means calmness and composure, especially in a difficult situation. Hence, its synonym is 'tranquillity' which means the same.

PASSAGE - 25

Academics has always been an essential part of human development. It prepares us to survive in the outside world and establish an identity of our own. In India, from an early age we have been taught that education is limited to the boundaries of academics only; the idea of getting out into the field, for gaining practical experience is always considered a hoax. This has hindered students' development.

In the 21st century, the pure academic type of education is slowly paving way for a whole new type. The shift in the whole education system is evident. People have now come to understand that education should focus on students' overall development, rather than restricting him/her to the classroom.

Co-curricular activities that take place outside the classroom help in the growth of the child, in more than one way. Participating in such activities helps youngsters grow mentally, socially and individually. Intellectual development of a student takes place in the classroom, but for the aesthetic development such as team-building, character-building and physical growth, students must step out into the outside world.

Similarly, in colleges and institutions, there is a need for practical exposure so that the students can experience the actual working of an industry. Most professional colleges including B-schools, have started providing practical exposure to students through regular guest lectures, industrial visits, conferences and so on. Guest lectures are very important for all- round development of students as guest speakers talk about their real- life experiences and not what is there in the text books.

Through such events students are made to participate and coordinate different events wherein, they get to know how exactly things are managed. Classroom teaching provides the foundation and co-curricular or extra-curricular activities provide practical exposure and opportunities to implement what students learn in the classroom. This helps in developing the overall personality of the students, inculcating various soft-skills in them, which otherwise are difficult to teach. **SSC CPO Tier-1 08.01.2024 (Shift-I)**

101. Which of these does not provide industry exposure to students of business schools?

(a) Text books (b) Conferences
(c) Industrial visits (d) Guest lectures

Ans. (a)

Text books do not provide industry exposure to students of business schools. According to the given passage, students gain industry exposure with industrial visits, guest lectures and conferences.

102. The new education system has shifted focus on

(a) social and aesthetic development
(b) intellectual development
(c) academic development
(d) spiritual development

Ans. (a)

The given passage presents that the news education system focused on overall development, especially on social and aesthetic development, team-building, character- building and physical growth.

103. Select the correct meaning of 'implement' as used in the passage

(a) commerce (b) enforce
(c) inculcate (d) coordinate

Ans. (b)

The word 'implement' means 'to put into effect or enforce'.

104. What is the passage mainly about?

(a) Importance of teaching soft skills to students
(b) Preparing students for survival in the real world
(c) The need to change the education system in 21st century
(d) Participation of students in extra-curricular activities

Ans. (a)

The passage focuses on the need of developing the overall personality of the students while inculcating various soft skills in them.

105. What has hindered the development of students?

(a) Expanding academics to the outside world
(b) Indulging in co-curricular activities
(c) Getting out into the field
(d) Not gaining practical experience

Ans. (d)

According to the passage, students in India do not gain practical experience which hinders their development.

PASSAGE - 26

There are no ancient nations anywhere in the world. All nations are modern. Ancient Greece, ancient Egypt, ancient India - all of them may have had great civilisations whose architecture, art and literature are objects of admiration. But they are not nations.

To realise this truth, you will have to forget for the time being the history you were taught at school. Because it is that history, drilled into your heads from the time you were children and constantly renewed by national festivals and ceremonies, the speeches of your leaders and novels, films, and television serials, that make it seem obvious to you that your nation is ancient. In actual fact, it is not true. Your nation is not - indeed no nation on earth is - ancient.

Only modern people can imagine that way.

SSC CPO Tier-1 27.06.2024 (Shift-I)

106. Find out the correct antonym of the following word.

Realise

(a) Misunderstand (b) Understand
(c) Comprehend (d) Grasp

Ans. (a)

The word 'realise' means to understand. Hence, its antonym is 'misunderstand'.

107. Which of the following statements is correct?

(a) Only modern people can imagine the existence of ancient nations.
(b) History books should be read again and again because they celebrate ancient nations.
(c) Ancient India is an ancient civilisation but not an ancient nation.
(d) Novels, films and speeches of leaders celebrate the modernity of nations.

Ans. (a)

The given passage indicates that no nation can be called ancient. It is only the thinking of the modern people which can think of any nation as ancient.

108. Find out the correct synonym of the following word.

Obvious

(a) Dubious (b) Clear (c) Ambiguous (d) Doubtful

Ans. (b)

The word 'obvious' means clear and direct.

109. Why does the author of the passage ask us to forget the history that we were taught at school?

(a) Because the history book taught us that our nation is ancient.
(b) Because only the modern people imagine that way.
(c) Because the history book taught us that there are no ancient nations in the world.
(d) Because the history book asks us to celebrate festivals which make us believe that our nation is modern.

Ans. (a)

The author of the given passage wants us to forget what we have read in history in schools because these books teach us that our nation can be ancient.

110. What does the expression 'drill into your heads' mean?

(a) Make someone learn or understand something by repeating it
(b) Threaten someone repeatedly drill machine
(c) Force someone to move his/her head in a particular direction
(d) Repeatedly question someone regarding a certain issue

Ans. (a)

The phrase 'drill into your heads' indicates to make someone learn or understand something by repeating it.

PASSAGE - 27

Every minute, the equivalent of one garbage trucks worth of plastic is dumped into our ocean. Plastic pollution is a global problem.

Approximately 7 billion of the 9.2 billion metric tonnes of plastic produced from 1950-2017 became plastic waste, ending up in landfills or being dumped. Plastic pollution can alter habitats and natural processes, reducing ecosystems ability to adapt to climate change, directly affecting millions of livelihoods, food production capabilities and social well-being.

UNEPs body of work demonstrates that the problem of plastic pollution doesn't exist in a vacuum. The environmental, social, economic and health risks of plastics need to be assessed alongside other environmental stressors, like climate change, ecosystem degradation and resource use.

SSC CPO Tier-1 27.06.2024 (Shift-II)

111. Which of the following is the best description of the tone of the passage?

(a) Populist (b) Laudatory
(c) Informative (d) Patronising

Ans. (c)

The passage provides factual information about plastic pollution, its impact on ecosystems and human well-being and the need for assessment alongside other environmental stressors.

It aims to inform the reader about the severity and implications of plastic pollution rather than adopting a populist, laudatory or patronising tone.

112. Which of the following represents the structure of the passage?

(a) Definition (b) Sequence
(c) Cause-effect (d) Time order

Ans. (c)

The passage discusses the causes (plastic pollution) and its effects (altering habitats, affecting livelihoods, etc.). It explains how plastic pollution directly impacts various aspects of the environment and human society, making it a cause-effect structure.

113. Select the most appropriate antonym of the given word.

Exist

(a) Prevail (b) Cease (c) Imprint (d) Resent

Ans. (b)

The word 'exist' means to have actual being. Hence, its opposite is 'cease' which means to come to an end or to stop existing.

114. Which of the following most accurately states the main idea of the passage?

(a) Plastic pollution (b) Climate change
(c) Plastic waste (d) UNEP

Ans. (a)

The passage primarily discusses the issue of plastic pollution, including its scale, impact on ecosystems and human life and the need for comprehensive assessment alongside other environment issues.

115. Select the most appropriate antonym of the given word.

Alter

(a) Alight (b) Change
(c) Preserve (d) Absorb

Ans. (c)

The word 'alter' means to change or modify something. Hence, its antonym is 'preserve' which means to maintain or keep something unchanged.

PASSAGE- 28

New media is a catch-all term used for various kinds of electronic communications that are conceivable due to innovation in computer technology. In contrast to old media, which includes newspapers, magazines, books, television and other such non-interactive media, new media comprises websites, online video/audio streams, emails, online social platforms, online communities, online forums, blogs, internet telephony, web advertisements, online education and much more. It is not very easy to draw a line between the new and old media because the so-called old media has found new ways of representation in digital forms, leaving behind its conventional methods of representation.

New media is considered to be the multimedia and digital form of communication happening *via* desktop and laptop computers as well as phones, tablets and other devices. New media has introduced user interaction, rather than simply consuming media. New media can be customised to user's preferences and it can be selectively linked from one form of content to another.

SSC CPO Tier-1 28.06.2024 (Shift-I)

116. Select the most appropriate synonym of the word 'Customise'.

(a) Personalise (b) Realise
(c) Generalise (d) Ritualised

Ans. (a)

The word 'customise' means to modify or tailor something to meet individual preferences.
Hence, its synonym is 'personalise' as it also refers to making something specific to an individual's needs or preferences.

117. Why is it not easy to draw a line between old media and new media?

(a) Because new media can be customised to user's preferences.
(b) Because new media is considered to be the multimedia and digital form of communication.
(c) Because both include various kinds of medium.
(d) Because old media has found new ways of representation in digital forms.

Ans. (d)

The passage states that old media has adapted and found new ways of representation in digital forms, blurring the distinction between old and new media. This makes the differentiation between the two categories challenging.

118. How does the passage distinguish new media from old media?

(a) New media includes user interaction, whereas, through old media, we only consume information.
(b) New media increases screen time and could be addictive and unhealthy, unlike old media.
(c) New media is fast and digitally based, whereas old media has never been beyond the conventional methods of representation.
(d) New media caters to a larger audience and is more popular than old media.

Ans. (a)

The passage highlights that new media involves user interaction, such as customisation and linking of content, whereas old media is characterised as non-interactive, where consumers primarily receive information without active participation.

119. Which of the following is not a type/kind of new media?
(a) Web advertisements (b) Television
(c) Emails (d) Online video streams

Ans. (b)

The passage categorises television under old media, contrasting it with new media that includes websites, online streams, emails and various digital platforms.

120. What does the term Catch-all mean?
(a) A category which includes all the types of media
(b) A category that includes all the sources of information
(c) A category that includes all the sources of entertainment
(d) A category which includes many different things

Ans. (d)

In a broader sense, 'Catch-all' can refer to a category that includes a wide variety of different things or items. This interpretation aligns with the idea that new media encompasses diverse forms of electronic communications, covering everything from websites and social platforms to online video/audio streams and more.

PASSAGE - 29

Facial recognition is based on AI technology that recognises human faces. In fact, the technology considers a number of factors for face recognition: jawline length, the form of the cheekbones, eye sockets depth, and so on. A majority of these factors assist the technology 'recall' who's the proprietor of the face. Other than unlocking your phone, facial identification brings different advantages to the agencies.

The primary component to start with is surveillance. With the assistance of face recognition technology, it will likely be less complicated to catch any burglars, thieves or different trespassers. On the governmental level, facial recognition can help us to find out terrorists or other criminals. Face recognition is the most effective means in today's world.

The procedure of recognising a face takes a second or much less. Considering that facial recognition is almost instant, it offers a quick and successful verification of a person.

SSC CPO Tier-1 28.06.2024 (Shift-III)

121. Based on your reading of the passage, select the most appropriate antonym of 'excessive.'
(a) Accurate (b) Lavish (c) Extreme (d) Moderate

Ans. (d)

The word 'excessive' implies something beyond what is necessary or normal.

Hence, its antonym is 'moderate' which means within reasonable limits or not extreme.

122. Read the following line from the passage and select the most appropriate option that describes it. Considering that facial recognition is almost instant, it offers a quick and successful verification of a person.
(a) Face recognition is uneasy and verifies a person successfully.
(b) Face recognition is easy and verifies a person unsuccessfully.
(c) Face recognition is not on spot and verifies a person partly.
(d) Face recognition is fast and verifies a person successfully.

Ans. (d)

The passage states that facial recognition is almost instant and provides quick and successful verification of a person's identity.

123. As per the passage which facial factors are not recognised with face recognition?
(a) Jawline length (b) Face shape
(c) Cheekbones structure (d) Eye sockets

Ans. (b)

The passage mentions factors like jawline length, the form of cheekbones and eye sockets depth as considerations for facial recognition. However, it does not explicitly mention 'face shape' as a factor that the technology considers.

124. Select the most appropriate title for the given passage.
(a) Hacking and Safety (b) AI interface
(c) Face Recognition (d) Human Face

Ans. (c)

The passage primarily discusses facial recognition technology, its workings, and its benefits.

125. What is the primary component of face recognition?
(a) Surveillance (b) Verification
(c) Identification (d) Locking

Ans. (a)

According to the passage, the primary component of facial recognition is surveillance. Facial recognition technology aids in surveillance by helping to identify individuals for various purposes, including catching criminals and enhancing security measures.

PASSAGE - 30

Have you ever taken the time to stop and consider the dirt under your feet? Leonardo da Vinci said, "We know more about the movement of celestial bodies than about the soil underfoot." Yet, our very survival as humans - and life on this planet - is intimately linked with the health of a thin layer of soil enveloping the Earth.

Soil provides society with essential food, feed, fibre and raw materials, as well as being home to a quarter of the earths biodiversity. Soils are also the largest organic carbon reservoir on Earth and although highly dynamic, are very fragile. Chop a forest down and it might grow back in 50 years, but lose 10 cm of soil and get ready to wait 1,000 years to get it back. Without soil, our planet would be unrecognisable to us, and more like the barren and inhospitable surface of the Moon or Mars.

Until recently, we did not even know how deep the soil is below our feet. Like the best mysteries, a bit of digging is required for soils to be fully understood and for their history to be laid bare.

When they are visible, a range of questions arise. What does the variation in colour with depth mean? How much carbon is stored? Is the soil dense or light, damaged or healthy? Answering these questions is important, but presents a significant challenge and may require years of training. **SSC CPO Tier-1 29.06.2024 (Shift-II)**

126. Select the most suitable word from the passage which means difficult to stay or live in.
(a) Inhospitable (b) Dense
(c) Barren (d) Essential

Ans. (a)

The word 'Inhospitable' refers to a place or environment that is difficult or unpleasant to live in.

127. How many years are required to renew the loss of 10 cm of soil?
(a) 1,00,000 (b) 1,000 (c) 100 (d) 10,000

Ans. (b)

The passage states that if 10 cm of soil is lost, it can take up to 1,000 years to regenerate that amount of soil naturally.

128. What is the tone of the speaker?
(a) Derisive (b) Dogmatic
(c) Sarcastic (d) Alarming

Ans. (d)

The speakers tone is alarming as they emphasise the critical importance of soil for human survival and the fragile nature of soil resources.

129. Identify the most suitable title for the given passage.
(a) Moon and Mars Expedition
(b) Necessity of Mining
(c) The Uninhabitable Universe
(d) Mysteries Under Man's Feet

Ans. (d)

The most suitable title for the passage is 'Mysteries Under Man's Feet.'

This title reflects the theme of exploring and understanding the soil beneath our feet, which the passage discusses as an essential yet often overlooked aspect of our environment.

130. Mankind's survival, according to the passage, solely depends on
(a) inventions (b) celestial bodies
(c) soil (d) reproduction

Ans. (c)

The passage explicitly states that our survival as humans and life on this planet are intimately linked with the health and preservation of soil. Soil provides essential resources for human existence, including food, fiber and raw materials and supports biodiversity.

SSC CPO 2023 (Tier 1 & 2)

PASSAGE - 31

We started our research into organisational and personal excellence by studying a slightly different topic. We figured that if we could learn why certain people were more effective than others, then we could learn exactly what they did, clone it and pass it on to others. We asked people to identify who they thought were their most effective colleagues.

In fact, over the past twenty-five years, we have asked over twenty thousand people to identify the individuals in their organisations who could really get things done. We wanted to find those who were not just influential but who were far more influential than the rest. **SSC CPO Tier-1 03.10.2023 (Shift-I)**

131. Which real life situation can be the most appropriate to be inferred from the passage?
(a) Inflation has direct influence on the morals and ethics of an individual.
(b) If we do something wrong to decent people, the same comes to haunt us even after many years.
(c) People nowadays do not have patience and want quick success and does not matter what path they choose to obtain their targets.
(d) Jassie is an efficient employee whose work ethics can be a case study to learn more about organisational and personal excellence.

Ans. (d)

The author of the passage states that they want people who work efficiently. Hence, Jassie can be their case study because she is an efficient employee with a great work ethics.

132. Select the most suitable structure for the above passage.
(a) Chronological (b) Cause and effect
(c) Pragmatic (d) Compare and contrast

Ans. (c)

The author of the given passage is practical and pragmatic.

133. Select the most appropriate antonym of the given word.
Effective
(a) Deniable (b) Harmonious
(c) Fruitless (d) Courteous

Ans. (c)

The word 'effective' means 'fruitful'. Hence, its antonym is 'fruitless'.

134. Select the most appropriate title to the given passage.
(a) Research Grants in Organisations
(b) Learn, Clone and Pass
(c) Most Effective Colleagues
(d) Different Topics

Ans. (c)

The given passage talks about a case study conducted by the organisation to find the most effective employee.

135. Select the statement that most appropriately sums up the passage given.
(a) Some people cannot be identified due to their most effective ways in 25 years.
(b) Research grants in an organisation should be increased for personal excellence.
(c) It takes 25 years of research to make people more effective and influential.
(d) Some people are more effective and more influential than others to get things done.

Ans. (d)

The given passage states that some people are more effective than the others while getting things done.

PASSAGE - 32

Throughout history, the intricacies of the human mind have been the subject of fascination and inquiry. From ancient philosophers to modern-day neuroscientists, the workings of the brain have been studied and analysed in an attempt to unravel its mysteries. However, despite centuries of research, much remains unknown about the complexities of human cognition and consciousness. One of the most fascinating aspects of the human mind is its ability to create and imagine. The human mind has the capacity to conceptualise and bring into being ideas that were previously unknown or unimaginable, from artistic expression to scientific discovery. The process of creativity has captured the attention of scholars and laypeople alike and is both enigmatic and awe-inspiring.

There have been many theories proposed to explain the process of creativity. Some suggest that it is a purely subconscious process, while others argue that creativity is a result of conscious effort and intentional problem-solving. Still others suggest that creativity arises from a combination of conscious and subconscious processes. Despite the ongoing debate over the nature of creativity, one thing is clear: it is a multifaceted and complex phenomenon. Creativity can manifest in a wide range of human activities, from the creation of art and literature to the development of scientific theories and inventions. It can occur in both individual and collective contexts and can be driven by a variety of factors such as curiosity, passion or the desire for recognition.

Creativity also has the potential to bring about positive change in the world. Throughout history, creative individuals and groups have used their talents to address social, political and environmental challenges, often inspiring others to take action and make a difference. From the abolitionist movement to the civil rights movement to the environmental movement, creativity has played a crucial role in promoting social justice and positive change.

Despite the many benefits of creativity, it is not without its challenges. The process of creative expression can be fraught with obstacles, from self-doubt and insecurity to external pressures and constraints. Moreover, not all creative ideas are successful or well-received and many artists and innovators face rejection and criticism as they seek to bring their ideas to fruition. Despite these challenges, however, the human drive to create and imagine persists. Individuals and groups continue to harness the power of creativity to make a difference in the world. From the humblest amateur artist to the most celebrated innovator, the human capacity for creativity remains one of our greatest strengths and sources of inspiration. **SSC CPO Tier-1 03.10.2023 (Shift-II)**

136. Select the most appropriate antonym for the word 'Fraught'.

(a) Beset (b) Devoid (c) Calm (d) Tranquil

Ans. (b)

The word 'fraught' means 'to be full of something'. Hence, its antonym is 'devoid' which means a lack of something.

137. What is the main focus of the passage?

(a) The complexities and challenges of cognitive processes.
(b) The nature of creativity, its benefits and challenges.
(c) The nature of fancy and imagination.
(d) The mysteries of the human mind.

Ans. (b)

The given passage presents what creativity is all about, how it benefits us and the world and the various challenges it faces.

138. Which of the following factors can drive creativity?

(a) Fancy and imagination
(b) Self-doubt and insecurity
(c) Curiosity and passion
(d) External pressures and constraints

Ans. (c)

According to the given passage, creativity is driven by curiosity, passion or a desire for recognition.

139. According to the passage, what is one of the challenges of creative expression?

(a) The limited capacity of the human mind.
(b) The lack of appreciation for creative ideas.
(c) The absence of external pressures and constraints.
(d) The overemphasis on conscious problem-solving.

Ans. (b)

The challenges faced by creativity include self-doubt, insecurity to external pressures, lack of appreciation and criticism.

140. Select an appropriate title for the passage.

(a) The Power of Creativity
(b) The Complexities of Human Cognition
(c) The History of the Human Mind
(d) The Role of the Human Mind in Promoting Positive Change

Ans. (a)

The given passage presents how creativity holds the power to change the world. Hence, an appropriate title for the passage is 'The Power of Creativity.'

PASSAGE - 33

As a society, we have come a long way in terms of progress and development. We have eradicated diseases, explored space and created technological wonders that were once thought impossible. Yet, there is still one issue that continues to plague us: stupidity. Yes, stupidity. The thing that seems to be contagious and has been spreading faster than the common cold. It's everywhere you look - on social media, in politics, in the workplace. You can't escape it. It's as if we've all collectively decided that intelligence and common sense are no longer important. Why bother using your brain when you can just rely on your gut feelings and conspiracy theories?

Take politics, for example. It used to be that politicians were expected to be knowledgeable and well-informed about the issues they were dealing with. Now, it seems that all you need is a catchy slogan and some empty promises to win an election. And don't even get me started on social media. It's a breeding ground for stupidity. People will believe anything they read as long as it confirms their preconceived biases. And don't even think about trying to present them with actual facts and evidence. That's just a waste of time.

But it's not just individuals who are to blame for this epidemic of stupidity. Our education system is failing us as well. We're teaching our kids how to pass tests instead of how to think critically and solve problems. It's no wonder we have a generation of adults who can't even find their way around a basic math problem Of course, there are some who would argue that stupidity is just a different way of thinking. That it's a valid perspective that deserves to be respected. To those people, I say this: if you want to be stupid, go ahead. Just don't expect the rest of us to respect your opinions when they're based on nothing but ignorance and misinformation.

It's time for us to take a stand against stupidity. We need to start valuing intelligence and critical thinking again. We need to hold our leaders accountable for their actions and demand that they be knowledgeable and well-informed. We need to teach our children how to think, not just how to memorise.

It won't be easy, but it's a fight worth fighting.

Because if we '- don't, we'll be stuck in a world where stupidity reigns supreme and there's no telling what kind of damage that could do. Solet's all do our part and start using our brains again. It's time to put an end to the epidemic of stupidity once and for all. **SSC CPO Tier-1 04.10.2023 (Shift-I)**

141. According to the author of the passage, who among the following is not responsible for the spread of stupidity?

(a) Individuals (b) Children
(c) Education system (d) Politicians

Ans. (b)

According to the given passage, children are not responsible for the spread of stupidity.

142. What could be a suitable title for the passage?
(a) The Joy of Living in a World of Ignorance
(b) The Importance of Critical Thinking
(c) The Evils of Social Media
(d) The Benefits of Stupidity

Ans. (b)

The given passage focuses on the spread of stupidity and the need to start valuing critical thinking and power solving methods. Hence, a suitable title for the passage is 'The Importance of Critical Thinking'.

143. What is the tone of the passage?
(a) Serious (b) Joyful
(c) Melancholic (d) Sarcastic

Ans. (d)

The given passage sarcastically points out the widespread idea of stupidity to point out the need of critical thinking.

144. Which of the following techniques has been used by the other of the passage to convey the message?
(a) Factual and chronological account
(b) Examples and anecdotes
(c) Parody and mimicry
(d) Humour and exaggeration

Ans. (d)

The author uses humour and exaggeration to point out how we all spread stupidity to point out the need of critical thinking.

145. According to the passage, what is the solution to the issue stupidity in society?
(a) Electing politicians with catchy slogans
(b) Teaching students how to pass tests
(c) Encouraging critical thinking and problem-solving skills
(d) Embracing ignorance and misinformation

Ans. (c)

According to the author of the passage, stupidity can be avoided by encouraging critical thinking and problem solving methods.

PASSAGE - 34

What if globally designed products could radically change how we work, produce and consume? Several examples across continents show the way we are producing and consuming goods could be improved by relying on globally shared digital resources, such as design, knowledge and software.

Imagine a prosthetic hand designed by geographically dispersed communities of scientists, designers and enthusiasts in a collaborative manner *via* the web.

All knowledge and software related to the hand is shared globally as digital commons. People from all over the world who are connected online and have access to local manufacturing machines (from 3D printing and CNC machines to low-tech crafts and tools) can, ideally with the help of an expert, manufacture a customised hand.

This is the case of the open bionics project, which produces designs for robotic and bionic devices.

There are no patent costs to pay for. Less transportation of materials is needed, since a considerable part of the manufacturing takes place locally, maintenance is easier, products are designed to last as long as possible and costs are thus, much lower.

SSC CPO Tier-1 04.10.2023 (Shift-II)

146. Identify the most suitable title for the given passage.
(a) Knowledge Explosion (b) Customised Hand
(c) Shared Information (d) Digital Globalisation

Ans. (d)

The passage discusses how globally shared digital resources, such as design, knowledge and software, can impact how goods are produced and consumed worldwide. It highlights the collaborative nature of design projects and the benefits of relying on shared digital resources for manufacturing processes.

147. What is the term used in the passage for globally shared digital things?
(a) Digital commons (b) Digital information
(c) Digital resources (d) Digital world

Ans. (c)

The passage refers to globally shared digital resources, such as design, knowledge and software, as digital commons. This term emphasises the idea of shared ownership and accessibility of digital assets across geographical boundaries.

148. What is the tone of the author?
(a) Speculative (b) Caustic
(c) Acerbic (d) Belligerent

Ans. (a)

The author discusses the potential impact of globally shared digital resources on how goods are produced and consumed, presenting examples and highlighting the benefits of such a model. The tone is forward-looking and exploratory indicating a speculative approach to the topic.

149. Which of the following is not a globally shared digital resource?
(a) Knowledge (b) Design
(c) Automobile (d) Software

Ans. (c)

In the passage, the author discusses globally shared digital resources such as knowledge, design and software. However, automobiles are physical objects and not digital resources.

150. Select the most suitable word from the passage which means 'Scattered'.
(a) Collaborative (b) Shared
(c) Customised (d) Dispersed

Ans. (d)

The word 'scattered' means 'spread out'. Hence 'dispersed' is its correct synonym.

SSC CPO 2022 (Tier 1 & 2)

PASSAGE - 35

Migaloo is by far one of the world's most recognisable whales, because he is completely white. Thanks to genetic sampling of Migaloo's skin, scientists have identified that he's male and his albino appearance is a result of a variation in the gene responsible for the colour of his skin.

Simply by looking different, Migaloo has become an icon within Australia's east coast humpback whale population. Indeed, Migaloo has his own Twitter account with over 10,000 followers and website where fans can lodge sightings and learn more about humpback whales. He was first discovered in 1991 off Byron Bay, Australia and has since played hide and seek for many years, with many not knowing where or when he'll show up next. He's even surprised Kiwi fans by showing up in New Zealand waters.

With the last official sighting two years ago, the time has once again come for us to ask: where is Migaloo?

Already this year there have been false sightings, such as a near all white whale spotted off New South Wales. To make things more confusing, regular-looking humpbacks can trick whale watchers when they flip upside down, due to their white bellies.

SSC CPO Tier-1 09.11.2022 (Shift-II)

151. What is the theme of the passage?
(a) Protection of Whales
(b) The Extinction of Migaloo
(c) The Sighting of Migaloo
(d) Whale Hunting and its Aftermath

Ans. (c)

The given passage focuses on the first sighting of the Migaloo and the how it is not seen in the present day Australia. Hence, the theme is 'The Sighting of Migaloo'.

152. How can regular-looking humpbacks trick whale watchers?
(a) By posting tweets on Twitter
(b) By appearing secretly and unexpectedly
(c) By showing their white coloured bellies
(d) By displaying their huge size

Ans. (c)

The given passage points out that humpbacks can easily trick people by showing their white coloured bellies which are similar to Migaloos.

153. Where was Migaloo first discovered?
(a) South Wales (b) Australia
(c) Jamaica (d) New Zealand

Ans. (b)

According to the passage, a Migaloo was first discovered in 1991 off Byron Bay, Australia.

154. Select the suitable word given in the passage which means 'turn over with a sudden quick movement'.
(a) Albino (b) Flip
(c) Humpback (d) Lodge

Ans. (b)

'Flip' means a sudden quick movement to turn.

155. What is the tone of the speaker?
(a) Pessimistic (b) Descriptive
(c) Cynical (d) Melancholic

Ans. (b)

The tone of the speaker is descriptive.

PASSAGE - 36

It is not an exaggeration to say that the question of where and when the Black Death, the deadliest pandemic ever, originated is one of the biggest mysteries in human history. After all, the Black Death was the first wave of the second plague pandemic of the 14th to early 19th centuries. It killed some 50-60% of the population in Europe, the Middle East and North Africa and an unaccountable number of people in Central Asia.

Different proposals, based on competing theories, have been put forward. But in 2017, I came across some records describing an intriguing medieval cemetery in Kara-Djigach, Chuy Valley, Northern Kyrgyzstan, which I suspected may hold the key.

As part of a multi-disciplinary team co-led by Maria Spyrou at University of Tubingen, we have now investigated several specimens from individuals buried at that site—and come up with an answer.

The idea that the Black Death originated in the east—territories overlapping, roughly speaking, Central Asia, Mongolia and China—dates back to the contemporaries of the pandemic in Europe and the Islamic world.

The modern, academic Chinese origin theory dates back to at least to in 1756-8 and a publication about the history of Central Asia by French scholar Joseph de Guignes. **SSC CPO Tier-1 10.11.2022 (Shift-I)**

156. What is the tone of the speaker?
(a) Humorous (b) Explanatory
(c) Pessimistic (d) Informal

Ans. (b)

The tone of the speaker is explanatory.

The passage explains how different researches have tried to solve the mystery behind the Black Death.

157. What is the theme of the passage?
(a) Pitfall of Black Death (b) Impact of Black Death
(c) Origin of Black Death (d) History of Black Death

Ans. (c)

The passage focuses on the 'Origin of Black Death'.

158. How does the passage describe Black Death?
(a) The first wave of the second plague pandemic.
(b) The worst specimen of human created tragedy.
(c) The specimen of human evolution and its evidence.
(d) The initiator of all the future pandemics.

Ans. (a)

In the passage, Black death is described as the first wave of the second plague pandemic.

159. Select the suitable word given in the passage which means 'areas of land under the jurisdiction of a ruler or state'.
(a) Territories (b) Contemporaries
(c) Population (d) Mysteries

Ans. (a)

'Territories' refer to areas of land under the jurisdiction of a ruler or state.

160. Which of the following may be the probable origin of Black Death, according to the passage?
(a) Kyrgyzstan (b) India
(c) Mongolia (d) China

Ans. (a)

Kyrgyzstan may be the probable origin of Black Death, according to the passage.

SSC CHSL 2024 (Tier 1 & 2)

PASSAGE - 37

Lena was an avid explorer. She had a deep fascination for the mysteries hidden within the dense forests. One day, while wandering through a secluded forest, she stumbled upon an ancient-looking map half-buried in the undergrowth. The map depicted a trail that led to a legendary waterfall rumoured to possess magical properties. Driven by her curiosity, Lena decided to follow the trail. As she walked deeper into the forest, the atmosphere grew more enchanting. Sunlight filtered through the thick canopy, casting dappled patterns on the ground.

The sound of rustling leaves and distant bird calls created a symphony of nature around her. Guided by the map's markings, Lena navigated through challenging terrains and crossed a narrow rope bridge suspended over a crystal-clear stream. Finally, after hours of journeying, Lena arrived at the foot of the legendary waterfall. Its cascading waters sparkled like diamonds in the sunlight and a gentle mist enveloped the surroundings. Lena felt a sense of wonder and tranquillity as she dipped her hand in the cool waters, as if the legends were coming alive. She sat by the waterfall, captivated by its beauty, pondering the ancient stories that had led her here. **SSC CHSL Tier-2 18.11.2024**

161. What intrigued Lena's curiosity in the forest?

(a) She heard whispers in the wind.
(b) She found a hidden cave.
(c) She stumbled upon an ancient map.
(d) She discovered an old book.

Ans. (c)

Lena's curiosity was sparked when she discovered the ancient-looking map in the forest, which led her to follow the trail.

162. Select the most appropriate Antonym of the underlined word in the given sentence.

What surrounded Lena as she journeyed through the forest?

(a) Freed (b) Created (c) Girded (d) Bolt

Ans. (a)

While 'surrounded' means to be enclosed or encompassed on all sides, 'freed' means to be released from confinement or enclosure.

163. Select the correct spelling of the underlined word in the given sentence.

What was Lena's reason for following the trial on the map?

(a) Triall (b) Trail (c) Treil (d) Trale

Ans. (b)

'Trail' is the correct spelling.

164. Where did Lena find the map?

(a) Buried in the sand
(b) In a bookstore in town
(c) Underneath a bridge
(d) Half-buried in the undergrowth

Ans. (d)

Lena found the map partially buried in the vegetation or undergrowth of the secluded forest.

PASSAGE - 38

As a result of increasing population and expansion of residential areas, forest lands are being encroached. This is not all; even the wildlife is under extreme threat. As our fauna is facing a dearth of adequate shelter in forests, they are heading towards towns and hence, get killed by hunters. Consequently, many animal species have either become extinct or are on the verge of extinction. The Black Buck is almost endangered and found only in two countries, Nepal and India. In India, this antelope is found in many national parks like Guindy National Park, Point Calimere and Vellandu sanctuaries of Tamil Nadu, Rollapadu of Andhra Pradesh, few parts of Rajasthan and Haryana. As far as their habitat is concerned, they live in open grasslands, dry areas or thinly populated areas and near water resources. They live in the desert areas of Rajasthan and coastal areas because they cannot sustain cold climate. They are the fastest running animals on this planet. Further, this animal is active during the day, but slows down in its activities after mid-day. They are social beings.

Hence, they move with their herds, which can vary from 3 to 23 mates. They cohabit twice in a year and give birth twice in a year. Prior to independence, this antelope was extensively hunted which affected their population so much that this species has reached the stage of extinction in many parts of the country. Poachers kill them mainly for material gain. Its skin has an enormous value in the market. In order to protect this species, the IUCN has declared this species nearly threatened.

Hence, under Schedule I of the Wildlife Protection Act of 1972, numerous stern measures have been taken. To specify a few, Kaimur Wildlife Sanctuary (Bihar), Gir Forest National Park, Velavadar Wildlife Sanctuary (Gujarat), National Chambal Sanctuary, etc.

Despite these acts, hunting is adversely affecting our wildlife. There are some solutions to this problem but the best one is to boycott the products made from endangered species at an international level. This seems to be effective but will it prevent animal hunting? That's a question. **SSC CHSL Tier-2 18.11.2024**

165. What is the theme of this passage?

(a) Endangered species (b) Over-population
(c) Land encroachment (d) Forests and their uses

Ans. (a)

The passage primarily discusses the threat to wildlife, particularly endangered species like the Black Buck, due to habitat encroachment and hunting, emphasising their endangered status.

166. Choose the word which closely means 'adversely'.

(a) Digressing (b) Detrimentally
(c) Scarcely (d) Distressing

Ans. (b)

'Detrimentally' closely means 'adversely'.

Both words imply something harmful or damaging.

167. What is the author's tone in this passage?

(a) Concerned (b) Revengeful
(c) Impressed (d) Agitated

Ans. (a)

The author's tone reflects worry and urgency about the declining wildlife populations and the threats they face, indicating concern.

168. The Black Buck is killed because of hunters'......... .

(a) material gain (b) need
(c) fun (d) personal gratification

Ans. (a)

The passage states that hunters kill Black Bucks mainly for their valuable skin, which indicates the hunters' motivation is material gain.

PASSAGE - 39

Leadership does not exist without followership. A leader has to be accepted by the group which the former is supposed to lead. To gain acceptability, the leader should cause an emotive impact on the group members.

The strength of character exhibited by leaders makes them dear to their followers.

A leader is one who effectively inspires followers to achieve worthwhile things. What character of the leader motivates the followers? It is not pomp and show, neither flattery nor sanctioning more incentives.

Pomp and show creates a sense of awe and the leader is deified rather as emulated. Flattery is unrealistic and cannot serve as a long-term motivational tool. A leader's style should be one that can be emulated by all irrespective of cadre, class and calibre.

Simplicity in one's day-to-day conduct is the only thing that can be adopted by all. **SSC CHSL Tier-2 10.01.2024**

169. Which of the following desired qualities of a leader is mentioned in the passage?

(a) Simplicity (b) Deified
(c) Pomp and show (d) Flattery

Ans. (a)

The passage mentions that a leader's style should be one that can be emulated by all irrespective of cadre, class and calibre.

Simplicity in one's day-to-day conduct is the only thing that can be adopted by all.

170. Select the most appropriate synonym of the given word.

Emulate

(a) Relax (b) Imitate
(c) Suppose (d) Exhibit

Ans. (b)

The word 'emulate' means to match or surpass, typically by imitation.

171. According to the passage, why should the leader generate an emotive impact?

(a) To exhibit the character of his followers.
(b) To mould the character of a leader.
(c) To gain acceptance by the members of the group.
(d) To acquire social knowledge.

Ans. (c)

The passage suggests that the leader should generate an emotive impact to gain acceptance by the members of the group.

This is because emotions can influence the behaviour and decisions of the group members. Therefore, by generating an emotive impact, the leader can guide the group members towards the desired goals.

172. Select the best summary of the passage?

(a) A leader effectively inspires and guides his followers to achieve desired goals.
(b) A leader's style cannot serve as a long-term motivation among the group.
(c) Motivation is the innate quality that enables an individual to be intellectually strong.
(d) Administrative knowledge is essential for the followers to get success.

Ans. (a)

The passage discusses the qualities of a leader and how a leader can inspire followers to achieve worthwhile things.

PASSAGE - 40

In 1888, an Atlantic contributor made the case for a 'science of names.'

"Parents are strangely careless and unscientific in giving names to children", the contributor complained. "They forget that not only from the social point of view it is very advantageous to have one's name remembered but that from the business point of view notoriety is capital and must be obtained by persistent and ingenious advertising." Indeed, the contributor argued, a good name will give a child 'a start in life equivalent to a cash capital of at least fifteen thousand dollars.' One way to ensure this head start? 'Be guided by euphonic quality only.' Although not all of this contributor's guidance can or should still apply today, the importance of a name to a child's identity has stayed front of mind for many parents. A name can determine whether a child fits in or stands out and many parents differ on which of those outcomes is preferable. **SSC CHSL Tier-2 10.01.2024**

173. According to the contributor, the parents are strangely careless and unscientific in giving names to children because ....

(a) they do it without considering the business point of view
(b) they do it without discussing it with their relatives and friends
(c) they do it without considering the actual meaning of the name
(d) they do it without considering the latter's interest in it

Ans. (a)

The passage mentions that parents are unscientific in giving names to children because they forget that from the business point of view, notoriety is capital and must be obtained by persistent and ingenious advertising.

174. Select the most appropriate word in the passage which means 'pleasing and sweet sound'.

(a) Identity (b) Advantageous
(c) Outcomes (d) Euphonic

Ans. (d)

The word 'euphonic' means having a pleasant, harmonious sound.

175. What will be given to a child if he gets a good name?

(a) A good bank balance
(b) A perfect address
(c) A professional attitude
(d) A headstart in life

Ans. (d)

According to the author of the given passage, a good name will give a child 'a start in life equivalent to a cash capital of at least fifteen thousand dollars'.

176. What is the tone of the speaker in the passage?

(a) Humorous (b) Sarcastic
(c) Persuasive (d) Melancholic

Ans. (c)

The tone of the speaker in the passage is persuasive as the speaker is trying to convince the reader about the importance of a good name and how it can give a child a headstart in life.

SSC CHSL 2023 (Tier 1 & 2)

PASSAGE - 41

Such examples of commercial success, of innovation, drive vision, determination, adaptability and adventure are anchored in the basic Indian openness to and talent for, acquiring material wealth. For every success story there are, of course, dozens of failures. Traditional India firms have their strengths, but also their weaknesses and of these perhaps the most debilitating are a lack of team work and a weakness for quick profit. These reflect ingrained ways of thinking and planning, as does the distrust of anyone outside the family, which inhibits the adoption of modern practices of management. But such weaknesses are more than compensated for by the desire to succeed, which is probably more intense in India, given the omnipresent fear of poverty, the cut-throat competition for each opportunity and the asphyxiating hold of hierarchy. **SSC CHSL Tier-1 03.08.2023 (Shift-II)**

177. What has the Indian talent for acquiring material wealth led to?
(a) Commercial success, stagnation, innovation
(b) Adaptability, quick profit, opportunity
(c) Commercial success, innovation, adaptability
(d) Determination, team work, adventure

Ans. (c)

The first line of the passage states that the Indian talent for acquiring wealth has led to commercial success, innovation, drive, vision, determination and adaptability.

178. What are the weaknesses of traditional Indian firms?
(a) Ingrained ways of thinking and adoption of modern practices, of management
(b) A weakness for quick profit and the openness to acquiring wealth.
(c) A lack of team work and cut-throat competition
(d) A lack of team work and a weakness for quick profit

Ans. (d)

According to the passage, the traditional Indian firms have a weakness which is a lack of team work and a weakness for quick profit.

179. Why is the desire to succeed more intense in India?
(a) Due to the hold of hierarchy, fear of poverty and lack of team work
(b) Due to fear of poverty, a lack of team work and distrust of the outsider
(c) Due to cut-throat competition, distrust of the outsider and fear of poverty
(d) Due to fear of poverty, cut-throat competition and the hold of hierarchy

Ans. (d)

The passage mentions that the desire to succeed is present due to the fear of poverty, the cut-throat competition for each opportunity and the hold of hierarchy.

180. Select the most appropriate antonym of the given word with reference to its usage in the passage.
Debilitating
(a) Enfeebling (b) Crippling
(c) Invigorating (d)Undermining

Ans. (c)

The word 'debilitating' means making someone very weak and infirm. Hence, its antonym is 'invigorating' which means to fill someone with energy.

181. Select the most appropriate synonym of the given word with reference to its usage in the passage.
Asphyxiating
(a) Emancipating (b) Liberating
(c) Smothering (d) Unfettering

Ans. (c)

The word 'Asphyxiating' means to kill (someone) by depriving them of air. Hence, its synonym is 'smothering' which means the same.

SSC Selection Post 2024

PASSAGE - 42

The advancement of science has brought about profound changing every aspect of our lives, from medical treatment to the way we communicate. The capacity of artificial intelligence, sometimes known as AI, to accomplish jobs that previously required human intellect has caused a revolution in a number of different sectors.

The altering of organisms for issues relating to food security and renewable energy. Technologies that utilise renewable energy sources, such as solar panels and wind turbines, help to lower the emissions of greenhouse gases. Manufacturing has been radically altered with the introduction of 3D printing and the Internet of Things (IoT) has enabled better resource management via the connection of previously disconnected ordinary products. Because of the tremendous effects these technologies have on society, their use must be carefully considered from an ethical standpoint. **SSC SP 20.06.2024**

182. Which of the following statements concerning the effects of scientific advancements may be derived from the passage?
(a) The development of renewable energy technologies has led to a complete elimination of greenhouse gas emissions.
(b) Scientific innovations have the potential to revolutionise various sectors and improve efficiency in society.
(c) There is no longer any need for human intelligence since AI has taken over energy field.
(d) The only way to solve problems with food security and renewable energy is through genetic engineering.

Ans. (b)

From the very first line, we can derive that scientific innovations have the potential to revolutionise various sectors and improve efficiency in society.

183. Which of the following best capture the underlying theme of the passage?
(a) The connection between renewable energy and greenhouse gas emissions
(b) The ethical considerations of Artificial Intelligence (AI) in society
(c) The impact of scientific advancements on medical treatment.
(d) The transformative power of technology in tourism sector

Ans. (b)

The last line of the passage points out that the passage focuses on the ethical consideration of artificial intelligence in our society.

184. According to the paragraph, which phrase describes computers capacity to undertake human intelligence-based tasks?
(a) Profound (b) Revolution
(c) Artificial Intelligence (d) Communication

Ans. (c)

Artificial Intelligence is the capacity of the computers or devices to undertake human intelligence-based tasks.

185. Which technologies are stated in the text as utilising renewable or green energy sources?
(a) Solar panels and wind turbines
(b) Medical treatment and communication
(c) Genetic engineering and 3D printing
(d) Artificial Intelligence (AI) and the Internet of Things (IoT)

Ans. (a)

As per the passage, solar panels and wind turbines are utilising renewables or green energy.

186. According to the passage, by linking which sort of products do the Internet of Things (IoT) provide improved resource management?

(a) 3D printing technologies
(b) Previously disconnected ordinary products
(c) Renewable energy technologies
(d) Artificial Intelligence (AI) technologies

Ans. (b)

As per the passage, by connecting previously disconnected ordinary things with Internet of Things, we can provide improved resource management.

PASSAGE - 43

Seeking to move towards a cashless economy, the government has proposed income tax benefits for people making payments through credit or debit cards, besides doing away with transaction charges on the purchase of petrol, gas and rail tickets with plastic money. This is the first serious effort to tackle the predominance of cash in India's economy. India is a hugely cash-dependent economy. The RBI and commercial banks annually spend around ₹ 21,000 crore in currency operations costs while the citizens of Delhi alone spend ₹ 9.1 crore and 60 lakh hours in collecting cash.

The scale of this burden is unique to India considering that it is among the most cash-intensive economies with a cash-to-GDP ratio of 12%, almost four times as much as other markets such as Brazil (3.93%), Mexico (5.3%) and South Africa (3.73%). Moreover, cash transactions and black money are directly linked, since a cash trail is nigh impossible to track. As such, electronic transactions and the ease of audit they afford should make the government's job much easier in terms of curbing illegal transactions.

What the switchover to payments by credit and debit cards means is that the payer must have money in the bank. This can be facilitated through a greater recourse to direct cash transfer of subsidies to banks. But, those who avail of this may not belong to the section that pays income tax. Given that less than three per cent of our population pays income tax, transactions by plastic cards may not amount to much. But, the scene is changing. For instance, payments by mobiles have grown from just 860 transactions in November 2010 to 4.4 million in August 2014. With the spread of Internet and expansion of e-commerce, online payments are fast catching on among the middle class. These are mostly cashless transactions.

It is also necessary to remember that a move towards a cashless economy will eliminate the cost of printing and distributing cash. If to these expenses are added the cost of storage and maintaining the currencies in the over 60,000 ATMs, the outlay becomes prohibitive. The answer is a buoyant economy that will reduce the numbers of those who still regard cash as the only reliable legal tender.

SSC SP 20.06.2024 (Shift-II)

187. According to the author of the passage, which of the following is directly linked?

(a) Credit transaction and black money
(b) Black and white money
(c) Cash and credit transactions
(d) Cash transactions and black money

Ans. (d)

According to the author of the passage, cash transactions and black money are directly linked.

188. How would e-transactions help the Government of India?

(a) Increasing the audit work at government level
(b) Curbing illegal transactions
(c) Increasing the paperwork of the government
(d) Increasing the cash transportation charges at government level

Ans. (b)

According to the passage, e-transactions will help the Government of India by curbing illegal transactions.

189. Which of the following statements is incorrect according to the passage?

(a) The RBI and commercial banks annually spend around ₹ 21,000 crore in currency operations costs.
(b) Citizens of Delhi alone spend ₹ 9.1 crore and 60 lakh hours in collecting cash.
(c) Less than 4% of our population pays income tax.
(d) Payments by mobiles have grown from 860 transactions in 2010 to 4.4 million in 2014.

Ans. (c)

As per the passage, less than 3% of our population pays income tax.

190. How does the spread of the internet and expansion of e-commerce help people?

(a) Online payments don't attract people at all.
(b) Online payments are fast catching.
(c) Online payments are expensive.
(d) Online payments are slow catching.

Ans. (b)

As per the passage, with the spread of internet and expansion of e-commerce, more and more people are using online payment methods.
Online payments are fast catching.

191. According to the author of the passage, what type of economy exists is India?

(a) Developed economy (b) Labour intensive economy
(c) Dependent economy (d) Cash-intensive economy

Ans. (d)

According to the author of the passage, India is a cash-intensive economy.

PASSAGE - 44

Dhamaal is a mix of Sufi and African (mostly East African) musical and dance traditions. It refers particularly to the spiritual practices of the Siddis of Gujarat.

The Siddis begin almost every Dhamaal song by blowing into a conch shell. This is often followed by the slow playing of East African percussion instruments like the musindo and the slow thumping of feet that marks the onset of the singing and dancing Dhamaals. The ritual of foot thumping is a crucial part of spiritual East African dance and musical traditions.

The Siddis are followers of Islam and arrived in India from Muslim communities in East and Central Africa. Dhamaals are performed in memory of their spiritual leaders, among them Bava Gor, Mai Misra, Baba Habash and Sidi Nabi Sultan. According to Siddi folklore they arrived from Ethiopia through the Nubian

Valley, Syria and the Indian Ocean to the coast of Kuda in the Bhavnagar district of Gujarat.

Usually, Dhamaal songs and dances are performed to celebrate the anniversary of the birth and death of spiritual leaders. They are performed in two ways – Dance Dhamaal and Baithaaki Dhamaal. The Baithaaki Dhamaal is performed in the sitting position and the Dance Dhamaal is performed in both sitting and dance positions.

During the performance of Baithaaki Dhamaal the focus is more on the lyrics and less on the musical instruments. During Dance Dhamaal the focus is more on the sounds of the instruments. These are often played in a frenzied manner and accompanied by frenzied dance movements. The spiritual songs that are sung during the Dhamaals are known as zikrs. **SSC SP 20.06.2024 (Shift-IV)**

192. What is played in a Dhamaal song after blowing into a conch shell?

(a) Baithaaki (b) Lyre (c) Table (d) Musindo

Ans. (d)

According to the passage, Musindo is played in a Dhamaal song after blowing into a conch shell.

193. Select the most suitable word from the passage which means 'excited'.

(a) Spiritual (b) Ritual (c) Frenzied (d) Percussion

Ans. (c)

The word 'frenzied' means 'excited'.

194. What is the tone of the speaker?

(a) Informative (b) Biased
(c) Aggressive (d) Sarcastic

Ans. (a)

As the given passage given us factual information about 'Dhammal', the tone of the speaker is 'informative'.

195. Who is not a spiritual leader of the Siddis?

(a) Baba Habash (b) Mai Misra
(c) Gulam Ali (d) Sidi Nabi Sultan

Ans. (c)

According to the passage, Gulam Ali is not a spiritual leader of the Siddis.

Dhamaals are performed in memory of their spiritual leaders, which include Bava Gor, Mai Misra, Baba Habash and Sidi Nabi Sultan.

196. Identify the most suitable title for the passage.

(a) What's Missing in Dhamaal?
(b) The Saga of the Siddis
(c) Wonders of Indian Dance
(d) The Bhavnagar Treat

Ans. (b)

The most suitable title for the passage is 'The Saga of the Siddis'.

SSC Selection Post 2023

PASSAGE - 45

When the dance had finished, Odysseus stood, his voice raised for all to hear. "We are truly honoured by your performance; not everyone can say that they have seen the dancers of Scyros. As tokens of our admiration we have brought gifts for you and your king." A murmur of excitement. Luxuries did not come often to Scyros; no one here had the money to buy them.

"You are too kind." Lycomedes' face was flushed with genuine pleasure; he had not expected this generosity. The servants brought trunks forth at Odysseus' signal and began unloading them on the long tables. I saw the glitter of silver, the shine of glass and gems. All of us, men and women both, leaned towards them, eager to see.

'Please, take what you like,' Odysseus said. The girls moved swiftly to the tables and I watched them fingering the bright trinkets: perfumes in delicate glass bottles stoppered with a bit of wax; mirrors with carved ivory for handles; bracelets of twisted gold; ribbons, dyed deep in purples and reds. Among these were a few things I assumed were meant for Lycomedes and his counsellors: leather-bound shields, carved spear hafts and silvered swords with supple kidskin sheathes. Lycomedes' eyes had caught on one of these, like a fish snagged by a line. Odysseus stood near, presiding benevolently.

Achilles kept to the back, drifting slowly along the table. He paused to dab some perfume on his slender wrists, stroke the smooth handle of a mirror. He lingered a moment over a pair of earrings, blue stones set in silver wire.

A movement at the far end of the hall caught my eye. Diomedes had crossed the chamber and was speaking with one of his servants, who nodded and left through the large double doors. Whatever it was could not be important; Diomedes seemed half-asleep, his eyes heavy-lidded and bored.

I looked back to Achilles. He was holding the earrings up to his ears now, turning them this way and that, pursing his lips, playing at girlishness. It amused him, and the corner of his mouth curved up. His eyes flicked around the hall, catching for a moment on my face. I could not help myself. I smiled.

SSC SP 27.06.2023 (Shift-IV)

197. Which word in the passage is opposite in meaning to 'advanced'?

(a) Flushed (b) Lingered
(c) Crossed (d) Snagged

Ans. (b)

The word 'advanced' means 'to move forward'. Hence, its opposite is 'lingered' as it means to stay in a place longer than necessary because of a reluctance to leave.

198. "He was holding the earrings up to his ears now, turning them this way and that, pursing his lips, playing at girlishness."

What do you infer as the most probable reason for Achilles' behaviour?

(a) Achilles was selecting an ideal gift for Lycomedes.
(b) Achilles was in charge of selecting the best accessories for war.
(c) Achilles was in a woman's disguise and was playing his part.
(d) Achilles was playing the part of an ideal host.

Ans. (c)

The given sentence indicates that Achilles was in a woman's disguise and was playing his part.

199. Why was Odysseus distributing the gifts?

(a) Because he was very generous and wanted to help the people of Scyros who could not afford such gifts.
(b) Because he knew Achilles' fascination for jewellery and wanted to gift him earrings and other ornaments.
(c) Because he was pleased after witnessing the performance of the dancers of Scyros.
(d) Because he wanted to take Lycomedes to war and had come to gift him swords and shields.

Ans. (c)

As per the passage, Odysseus was distributing the gifts because he was pleased after witnessing the performance of the dancers of Scyros.

200. "Lycomedes' eyes had caught on one of these, like a fish snagged by a line." What can be inferred from this statement?

(a) He was attracted to the unique looking sword which looked like a fishing line with a hook.

(b) Being a warrior, he was attracted to the sword and all the more since he could not afford one like that on his own.

(c) He was very cunning and wanted to take the shields and swords in order to fight Odysseus later on.

(d) He was a greedy man and wanted to take the best gifts for himself without sharing anything with others.

Ans. (b)

The given sentence shows that Lycomedes, as a warrior, was attracted to the sword and all the more since he could not afford one like that on his own.

201. What is the passage based upon?

(a) A palace scene where the king and his counsellors are deciding to give gifts to the poor people who had just completed their dance performance in front of everyone.

(b) A palace scene where the king is distributing gifts to the performers who are very poor and cannot afford to buy such gifts on their own.

(c) A palace scene where a dance performance is taking place and thereafter, gifts are distributed to the performers and their selecting the trinkets are described.

(d) A palace scene where gifts are being distributed after a dance performance and detailed descriptions of the gifts and the way that people are choosing them are presented.

Ans. (d)

The passage is based upon a palace scene where gifts are being distributed after a dance performance. It also gives a detailed descriptions of the gifts and the way that people are choosing them are presented.

PASSAGE - 46

"For me, trees have always been the most penetrating preachers. I revere them when they live in tribes and families, in forests and groves. And even more I revere them when they stand alone. They are like lonely persons.

Not like hermits who have stolen away out of some weakness, but like great, solitary men, like Beethoven and Nietzsche. In their highest boughs the world rustles, their roots rest in infinity; but they do not lose themselves there, they struggle with all the force of their lives for one thing only: to fulfil themselves according to their own laws, to build up their own form, to represent themselves.

Nothing is holier, nothing is more exemplary than a beautiful, strong tree. When a tree is cut down and reveals its naked death-wound to the sun, one can read its whole history in the luminous, inscribed disk of its trunk: in the rings of its years, its scors, all the struggle, all the suffering, all the sickness, all the happiness and prosperity stand truly written, the narrow years and the luxurious years, the attacks withstood, the storms endured. And every young farm-boy knows that the hardest and noblest wood has the narrowest rings, that high on the mountains and in continuing danger the most indestructible, the strongest, the ideal trees grow." **SSC SP 27.06.2023 (Shift-I)**

202. Where can one read the complete history of a tree?

(a) On its leaves in sunny days

(b) On its branches when it is full-grown

(c) On its skin when it is counted

(d) On its trunk when it is cut-down

Ans. (d)

According to passage, we can read the complete history of a tree on its trunk when it is cut-down.

203. Where does the world rustle, according to the given passage?

(a) Around the trunk of trees

(b) Over the forest in the sunny days

(c) In the highest boughs of trees

(d) In the deepest roots of trees

Ans. (c)

According to passage, the world rustles in the highest boughs of trees.

204. Select the most suitable word given in the passage that means 'very good and perfect'.

(a) Holier (b) Penetrating

(c) Luminous (d) Exemplary

Ans. (d)

The word 'exemplary' means 'very good and perfect'.

205. Which of the following labels is most appropriate for the author of the given passage?

(a) Arrogant theorist (b) Nostalgic dreamer

(c) Environment enthusiast (d) Social activist

Ans. (c)

The author of the given passage seems to be an environmental enthusiast as he/shows a deep love and respect for the environment.

206. What is the tone of the speaker?

(a) Emotional (b) Apathetic

(c) Vituperative (d) Sarcastic

Ans. (a)

The tone of the speaker is 'emotional'.

PASSAGE - 47

Virtual learning refers to an environment where students study a digital-based curriculum taught by instructors that lecture online via video or audio. This instruction can take place either in a self-paced (asynchronous) environment or in a real-time (synchronous) environment. There are many reason why people choose virtual learning over instruction in a traditional classroom. For example, the flexibility of virtual learning makes it an appropriate choice for full-time workers who would like to continue their education or cannot attend in person classes.

The virtual learning environment is also a good choice for people who enjoy self-learning. Some virtual learning options have classes to attend at scheduled times, while others allow you to learn at your own pace.

With this self-paced option, you have a lot of autonomy with the intensity and overall cadence of your learning while still enjoying the benefits of guided lessons.

Virtual learning gives students access to coursework from anywhere, at any time, making learning super convenient. Asynchronous classes also give an immense amount of flexibility for lectures and studying.

Even with the flexibility of the course, online courses are associated with higher retention rates and graduation rates. A study conducted by Arizona State University found that students taking virtual classes benefit from increased access and cost savings of as much as 50 percent. **SSC SP 27.06.2023 (Shift-III)**

207. What is the most appropriate antonym of the word 'autonomy' from the passage?
(a) Dependence (b) Preference
(b) Liberty (d) Availability

Ans. (a)

The word 'autonomy' means 'freedom'. Hence, its opposite is 'dependence'.

208. What is the most appropriate antonym of the word 'retention' from the passage?
(a) Perception (b) Preventive
(c) Retaining (d) Relinquishment

Ans. (d)

The word 'retention' means 'an ability to retain things in mind'.

Hence, its antonym is 'relinquishment' which means the act of giving up.

209. Which of the following options represent the structure of the passage?
(a) Compare and Contrast (b) Chronological
(c) Descriptive (d) Spatial

Ans. (c)

The given passage describes virtual learning and its various aspects. Hence, the structure of the passage is 'descriptive'.

210. Which of the following most accurately states the central idea of the passage?
(a) Self-paced learning
(b) Flexible learning environment
(c) Guided learning environment
(d) Virtual learning and its advantages

Ans. (d)

The given passage presents virtual leaning and the various advantages it has.

211. Which of the following is the best description of the tone of the passage?
(a) Biased (b) Technical
(c) Cynical (d) Dogmatic

Ans. (b)

The tone of the passage is 'technical'.

SSC Selection Post 2022

PASSAGE - 48

Sniffer dog Tucker uses his nose to help researchers find out why a killer whale population off the North-West coast of the United States is on the decline. He searches for whale faeces floating on the surface of the water, which are then collected for examination. He is one of the elite team of detection dogs used by scientists studying a number of species including right whales and killer whales.

Conservation canines are fast becoming indispensable tools for biologists according to Aimee Hurt, associate director and co-founder of Working Dogs for Conservation, based in Three Forks, Montana. Over the last few years, though, so many new conservation dog projects have sprung up that Hurt can no longer keep track of them all. Her organisation's dogs and their handlers are fully booked to assist field researchers.

"Dogs have such a phenomenal sense of smell, " explained Sam Wasser, director of the Centre for Conservation biology at the University of Washington in Seattle. He has worked with scat-detection dogs since 1999. Scientists have been using Conservation Canines in their research since 1999. These dogs have enabled them to non-invasively access vast amount of genetic and physiological information which is used to tackle conservation problems around the world. Such information has proved vital for determining the causes and consequences of human disturbances on wildlife as well as the actions needed to mitigate such impacts.

The ideal detection dog is extremely energetic with an excessive play drive. These dogs will happily work all day long, motivated by the expectation of a ball game as a reward for sample detection. The obsessive, high energy personalities of detection dogs also make them difficult to maintain as pets. As a result, they frequently find themselves abandoned to animal shelters, facing euthanasia. The programme rescues these dogs and offers them a satisfying career in conservation research. **SSC SP 01.08.2022**

212. What is the appropriate title for the passage?
(a) Importance of Conservation Canines
(b) Dog Euthanasia
(c) Role of Special Dogs
(d) Whale Detection

Ans. (a)

The given passage focuses on how Conservation canines are fast becoming indispensable tools for biologists. Hence, the correct title for the passage will be 'Importance of Conservation Canines'

213. What is the summary of the passage?
(a) Life of a retired conservation canine
(b) The playtime of a conservation canine
(c) The qualities of conservation canines
(d) Life of a Detection Dog

Ans. (c)

The passage presents the various qualities possessed by conservation canines.

214. What is the theme of the passage?
(a) The energy levels of conservation canines
(b) The life of conservation canines
(c) The job of conservation canines
(d) The death of conservation canines

Ans. (b)

The passage presents the various ways in which conservation canines work in their life.

215. What is the role of conservation canines?
(a) Play ball games (b) Find Whales
(c) Sample Detection (d) Hunt animals

Ans. (c)

The given passage shows that conservation canines detect samples with their heightened senses.

216. How does the dog detect the whale?
(a) Sniffs whale skin (b) Listens to whale voices
(c) Watches for whales (d) Sniffs whale faeces

Ans. (d)

As per the passage, a dog detects a whale by searching/ sniffing for whale faeces floating on the surface of the water.

PASSAGE - 49

From language to cultures-there are annals about India's diversity writ in bold. At the heart of everything we hold close is our love for food; the aroma from warm hearths wafts in the air, a heady mix of history and meals. So heady, that we often forget that food has a large carbon footprint and the menace of ever-growing fast-food businesses that contribute the lion's share to this problem. However, India's rich traditional and local edible biodiversity, with its focus on home cooked food, presents a ray of hope. Indian members of Relais and Chateaux, in partnership with Slow Food International, hope to bring back our forefathers' wisdom when it comes to eating, through the Slow Food movement, which started in the 1980s and aims to bring to the fore the connection of plate with people and the planet.

Calling for the protection and promotion of traditional techniques associated with regional food cultures is Jaisal Singh, owner of Sujan group of hotels. **SSC SP 01.08.2022**

217. What does the term 'lion's share' refer to in this context?
   (a) Relating to non-vegetarian diet
   (b) The share of the head of the institution
   (c) The largest part of something
   (d) Something that is negligible

Ans. (c)

A lion's share refers to the larger part of something.

218. Which of the following can be the most appropriate title of the passage?
   (a) Retracing Traditional and Local Wisdom of Eating
   (b) A Heady Mix of History and Meals
   (c) Aroma from Warm Hearths
   (d) The Menace of Large Carbon Footprint

Ans. (a)

The most appropriate title of the passage is 'Retracing Traditional and Local Wisdom of Eating' as the given passage focuses on the traditional food biodiversity and ways of cooking.

219. What, according to the passage, is a possible way to manage the large carbon footprint caused by the fast-food Industry?
   (a) By going back to traditional techniques of cooking and regional food cultures.
   (b) By not participating in fast-food businesses at all.
   (c) By consuming only home-cooked food.
   (d) By associating with Slow Food International.

Ans. (a)

According to the passage, by going back to traditional techniques of cooking and regional food cultures, one can manage the large carbon footprint caused by the fast food industry.

220. Which of the following sums up the central idea of the passage?
   (a) Jaisal Singh the owner Sujan group of hotels has also been an important member of this traditional techniques associated with regional food cultures.
   (b) Given the large carbon foot-print and menace of fast-food businesses an attempt has been made to bring back our forefathers' wisdom about eating to restore the connection of plate with people and planet.
   (c) Fast food businesses are at the root of large carbon foot-print. The possible solution lies only in eating home cooked food and stop eating out.
   (d) Annals about India's diversity have been writ on varied subjects from languages to cultures. However, the love for food and the ever-growing fast-food businesses has been the central subject of the interest.

Ans. (b)

The given passage presents how with the large carbon foot-print and menace of fast-food businesses, an attempt has been made to bring back the wisdom of our forefathers about eating to restore the connection of plate with people and planet.

221. Which event mentioned in the passage took place in the 1980s?
   (a) Beginning of slow food movement
   (b) Documents of the annals about India's diversity
   (c) Partnership of Indian members of Relais and Chateaux and Slow Food International
   (d) Leaving of large carbon footprint by food

Ans. (a)

The given passage mentions the beginning of the slow food movement.

SSC Steno 2024

PASSAGE - 50

A Fox, one day, fell into a deep well and could find no means of escape. Meanwhile, a Goat, overcome with thirst, came to the same well, and seeing the Fox, enquired the reason for which the fox was in the well.

Concealing his sad plight under a merry guise, the Fox indulged in a lavish praise of the water, saying it was excellent beyond measure, and told the goat that he deliberately jumped in the well to enjoy its benefits.

He kept encouraging the goat to jump in the well. The Goat, mindful only of his thirst, thoughtlessly jumped down, but just as he drank, the Fox informed him of the difficulty they were both in and suggested a scheme for their common escape. 'If' said he, "you will place your forefeet upon the wall and bend your head, I will run up your back and escape, and will help you out afterwards." The Goat readily assented and the Fox leaped upon his back.

Steadying himself with the Goat's horns, he safely reached the mouth of the well and made off as fast as he could. When the Goat upbraided him for breaking his promise, he turned around and cried out, "You foolish old fellow! If you had as many brains in your head as you have hairs in your beard, you would never have gone down before you had inspected the way up, nor have exposed yourself to dangers from which you had no means of escape." **SSC Steno 11.12.2024 (Shift-I)**

222. Select the most appropriate title for the passage.
   (a) The Fox and the Goat
   (b) The Kind Fox
   (c) The Fox and the Forest
   (d) The Cunning Goat

Ans. (a)

The passage is about an interaction between a fox and a goat in a well. Hence, an appropriate title is 'The Fox and the Goat.'

223. What moral lesson can be drawn from the passage?
(a) Look before you leap.
(b) Pride comes before a fall.
(c) Honesty is the best policy.
(d) One good turn deserves another.
Ans. (a)
The moral is 'Look before you leap', as the goat jumped into the well without considering the consequences.

224. How did the goat get into the well?
(a) He descended into the well by mistake.
(b) He fell into the well.
(c) He was thrown into the well by a passer-by.
(d) He was lured by the fox.
Ans. (d)
The fox lured the goat into the well by praising the water and encouraging him to jump in.

225. Identify the tone of the passage.
(a) Didactic (b) Assertive
(c) Informal (d) Cheerful
Ans. (a)
The tone is 'didactic', as the story teaches a moral lesson.

226. Why did the fox invite the goat into the well?
(a) Because they were friends.
(b) Because the fox wanted the goat to drink the water.
(c) Because the fox felt lonely in the well.
(d) Because the fox needed support to get out of the well.
Ans. (d)
The fox invited the goat into the well because he needed support to get out.

PASSAGE - 51

"It is not a lip or eye we beauty call/ But the joint force and full result of all," wrote Alexander Pope, the English intellectual poet and contemporary of John Dryden. The very idea of beauty is subjective because we never take it in totality.

Years ago, one saw a painting at an art museum in Warsaw, Poland. Some unknown Polish painter made it during World War I. It was about an undraped woman, who had a chiselled body but no face. There was a comment in the corner of that painting: Impose your idea of beauty on it and think of a face for her. Everyone will visualise according to his one idea of beauty. This is indeed intriguing. Beauty, especially feminine beauty, is always stereotyped and reduced to concrete and unaltered idioms. The core concept of beauty lies in being abstract. 'Koi soorat de do ke tarasta hoon main/ Meri taameer ki mitti abhi narm hai dekho'. Give me a face, an appearance; my clay's still wet. The moment we try to concretise and quantify beauty, it loses its aura and its appeal. There is a term in French. 'Jene sais quoi', I know not what. Beauty ought to have this quality that cannot be adequately described or expressed, yet that makes somebody or something more attractive and interesting. Beauty is always an open-ended idea. Neither can you bind it, nor can you define it. It is like love, indefinable, yet so desirable. And like love, it can only be felt and experienced. You can never appreciate it superficially. Then it becomes voyeuristic and too quotidian. **SSC Steno 11.12.2024 (Shift-II)**

227. The central theme of the passage is ....
(a) beauty is indefinable but can be felt and experienced
(b) one should enjoy beauty in youth
(c) beautiful women can inspire others
(d) physical health is more important than beauty
Ans. (a)
The passage discusses the abstract nature of beauty and how it cannot be fully defined or quantified, but rather felt and appreciated on a deeper level.

228. Select the most appropriate antonym of the given word.
Intriguing
(a) Gripping (b) Boring
(c) Historical (d) Interesting
Ans. (b)
While 'intriguing' means arousing interest or curiosity, 'boring' means dull and uninteresting, which is its opposite.

229. Select an appropriate title for the passage.
(a) Beauty is What Strikes the Soul
(b) Beauty of Women is Inspiring
(c) Alexander Pope and His Beauty
(d) Poets and Beauty
Ans. (a)
The most appropriate title for the passage is 'Beauty is What Strikes the Soul.' The passage emphasises the abstract and subjective nature of beauty, suggesting that true beauty resonates with the soul rather than just physical appearance.

230. What does the French term 'Je ne sais quoi' mean?
(a) I know not where is it (b) I know what
(c) I know not what (d) I know where is it
Ans. (c)
The French term 'Je ne sais quoi' means 'I know not what'. It refers to a quality that is difficult to describe but makes someone or something attractive or interesting.

231. Which of the following statements is not true according to the passage?
(a) Beauty is like love.
(b) Beauty is an open-ended idea.
(c) One visualises according to his idea of beauty.
(d) Physical beauty is more impressive than inner beauty.
Ans. (d)
The statement "Physical beauty is more impressive than inner beauty" is not true according to the passage. The passage argues that beauty is subjective and abstract, emphasising inner qualities and the indefinable nature of true beauty over mere physical appearance.

PASSAGE - 52

The use of plastic bags has been a contentious issue for many years. On one hand, they are convenient for carrying groceries and other items. On the other hand, they are a major contributor to pollution and can have devastating effects on the environment. One of the main causes of plastic bag pollution is their widespread use. They are given out for free at almost every store and are used for just a few minutes before being discarded. This means that there are billions of plastic bags in circulation at any given time, many of which end up as litter on streets, in parks and in waterways. Another cause of plastic bag pollution is their slow degradation. Plastic bags can take up to 1,000 years to decompose, which means that they will continue to pollute the environment for centuries to come. This is especially problematic in oceans where they can harm marine life and damage ecosystems. The effects of plastic bag pollution are wide-ranging and can be devastating. They can harm wildlife and marine life, damage ecosystems and even contribute to the spread of disease. Plastic bags that end up in oceans can be mistaken as food by marine animals, leading to starvation or suffocation. They can also entangle animals, making it difficult for them to move or escape predators. Plastic bags can also damage coral reefs, which are vital habitats for many species of marine life. In addition to harming wildlife, plastic bags can also affect human health. Plastic bags that end up in waterways can contaminate drinking water and food sources, leading to the spread of disease. They can also block drainage systems, causing flooding and other problems. To address the problem of plastic bag pollution, many cities and countries have implemented plastic bag bans or fees. These policies have been effective in reducing the use of plastic bags and in turn reducing pollution. Consumers can also take action by choosing to bring reusable bags when shopping, or by using paper bags instead of plastic bags. In conclusion, the use of plastic bags has severe consequences on the environment and human health.

The cause of the problem is the widespread use and slow degradation of plastic bags, while the effects are wide-ranging and can be devastating. To mitigate these effects, individuals and governments can take actions such as implementing plastic bag bans, choosing to use reusable bags or paper bags instead of plastic bags. **SSC Steno 11.12.2024 (Shift-II)**

232. According to the passage, which of the following is not an effect of plastic bag pollution on the environment?
(a) Contamination of drinking water and food sources
(b) Harm to wildlife and marine life
(c) Air pollution
(d) Damage to ecosystems

Ans. (c)
According to the passage, air pollution is not mentioned as an effect of plastic bag pollution. The passage primarily discusses contamination of drinking water and food sources, harm to wildlife and marine life, and damage to ecosystems.

233. What is the main cause of plastic bag pollution?
(a) Their easy decomposition
(b) Lots of proper disposal methods
(c) Their widespread use and slow degradation
(d) Careful recycling

Ans. (c)
The main cause of plastic bag pollution is their widespread use and slow degradation. The passage explains that plastic bags are used widely and take up to 1,000 years to decompose, leading to long-term pollution.

234. Select the most appropriate antonym of the given word. Contaminate
(a) Extract (b) Purify (c) Collect (d) Pollute

Ans. (b)
While 'contaminate' means to make something impure or polluted, 'purify' means to remove impurities and make clean making it an opposite.

235. Select the most appropriate title for the passage.
(a) The Causes and Effects of Plastic Bag Pollution
(b) The Future of Marine Life
(c) The Consequences of a Damaged Ecosystem
(d) The Convenience of Plastic Bags: Ignoring the Negative Impact

Ans. (a)
The most appropriate title for the passage is 'The Causes and Effects of Plastic Bag Pollution'. The passage discusses both the causes of plastic bag pollution and its wide-ranging effects on the environment and human health.

236. Identify the structure of the passage.
(a) Chronological (b) Descriptive
(c) Compare and Contrast (d) Classification

Ans. (b)
The passage provides detailed descriptions of the causes, effects and possible solutions to plastic bag pollution.

PASSAGE - 53

The crystal clear, blue water and the magnificent Sun make the Caribbean Island of Saint Maarten a favourite vacation spot, one that is popular with North Americans during their winter holidays from December through March, as well as with South Americans and Europeans from April through August. The French and Dutch settled on the island in the 1600s, and to this day, the island is divided between the two of them. The French capital is Marigot; the Dutch capital is Philipsburg. Tourists soon discover that St. Maarten has an intriguing history. Ancient artifacts found on the island date back to the Stone Age, 6,000 years ago! Tourists also learn that 1,200 years ago the Arawak Indians inhabited all the islands of the West Indies and were a peaceful people living under the guidance of their chiefs. Three hundred years after the Arawaks first arrived on St. Maarten, in the 1300s, they were defeated and forced to abandon the island by a hostile tribe of Indians originating in South America. This new tribe was called the Carib. The Caribbean Sea was named after them. Unlike the Arawaks, they had no permanent chiefs or leaders, except in times of strife. And they were extremely warlike. **SSC Steno 11.12.2024 (Shift-III)**

237. Which two groups of people settled in the island after 1600 AD?
(a) The French and the Dutch
(b) The French and the Caribs
(c) The Arawaks and the Caribs
(d) The Dutch and the Arawaks

Ans. (a)
The passage states that the French and Dutch settled on the island in the 1600s, dividing it between them, with Marigot as the French capital and Philipsburg as the Dutch capital.

238. Select the most appropriate antonym of the given word in the context of the passage. Intriguing
(a) Torrid (b) Stimulating
(c) Boring (d) Crunching

Ans. (c)
'Intriguing' means fascinating or captivating. Hence, the opposite would be something dull, boring or uninteresting.

239. Select the most appropriate synonym of the given word from the passage. Hostile
(a) Ancient (b) Warlike
(c) Permanent (d) Magnificent

Ans. (b)
The synonym of 'hostile' from the passage is 'warlike'.

240. The passage talks about two groups of people: one which was peaceful by nature and one which wasn't. List them in that order.
(a) Arawaks and Caribs (b) Arawaks and Dutch
(c) French and Caribs (d) Dutch and French

Ans. (a)
The passage describes the Arawaks as peaceful and the Caribs as warlike, listing them in that order. The Arawaks lived peacefully under the guidance of their chiefs, while the Caribs were described as having no permanent leaders except in times of strife and being extremely warlike.

241. Which of the following statements can be inferred from the passage?
(a) Both the Arawaks and Caribs had permanent chiefs.
(b) The Arawaks first arrived at Saint Maarten around 1300 AD.
(c) The Carib tribe defeated the French in 1600 AD.
(d) The Arawaks first arrived at Saint Maarten around 1000 AD.

Ans. (d)

The passage mentions that the Arawaks inhabited the islands of the West Indies 1,200 years ago, which is around 1000 AD. This timeline indicates that the Arawaks first arrived at Saint Maarten around 1000 AD.

PASSAGE - 54

Once upon a time, in a land far, far away, there lived a group of mischievous monkeys. These monkeys were known throughout the land for their love of mischief and pranks. They were always up to something, and the other animals in the forest never knew what to expect from them. One day, the monkeys decided to play a prank on the elephants. They climbed up to the top of a tall tree and began throwing ripe bananas at the unsuspecting elephants below. The elephants, not used to being pelted with fruit, were confused and startled. They trumpeted in alarm and ran around in circles, trying to figure out what was happening. The monkeys, meanwhile, were having the time of their lives. They laughed and chattered as they threw more and more bananas at the elephants. The elephants, however, were not amused. They decided to teach the monkeys a lesson and began to shake the tree with all their might. The monkeys, realising they had gone too far, quickly climbed down from the tree and ran away as fast as they could. They knew they had made a big mistake and felt guilty for causing so much trouble. From that day on, the monkeys decided to stick to less destructive pranks, like stealing the ranger's hat or putting honey in the bird feeder. They learned their lesson and lived happily ever after, never bothering the elephants again.

The moral of the story: monkeys will be monkeys, but sometimes even they need to learn when to stop monkeying around.

SSC Steno 11.12.2024 (Shift-III)

242. What can be inferred about the monkeys' behaviour after the incident with the elephants?
(a) They only play less harmful pranks.
(b) They stop playing pranks altogether.
(c) They continue to play pranks on the elephants.
(d) They only play pranks during certain times of the day.

Ans. (a)

After the incident with the elephants, the monkeys decided to stick to less harmful pranks, like stealing the ranger's hat or putting honey in the bird feeder.

243. Select the most appropriate antonym of the given word.
Unsuspecting
(a) Wary (b) Trusting
(c) Unguarded (d) Naïve

Ans. (a)

'Unsuspecting' means not aware of potential danger. Hence, its antonym is 'Wary' which means being cautious and alert to potential dangers.

244. Select the most appropriate title for the passage.
(a) The Banana Bandit's Misadventure
(b) The Great Elephant Uprising: A Cautionary Tale
(c) Monkeying Around: A Tale of Mischief and Pranks
(d) Trouble in the Trees: A Monkey's Mischief

Ans. (c)

The most appropriate title for the passage is 'Monkeying Around: A Tale of Mischief and Pranks'. This title reflects the mischievous behaviour of the monkeys and their pranks.

245. Identify the tone of the passage.
(a) Humorous (b) Worried
(c) Assertive (d) Encouraging

Ans. (a)

The tone of the passage is 'humorous'. The passage describes the monkeys' playful and mischievous antics in a light-hearted and amusing manner.

246. What did the elephants do to teach the monkeys a lesson?
(a) They started shaking the tree with all their might.
(b) They started chasing the monkeys.
(c) They threw bananas back at the monkeys.
(d) They called the ranger.

Ans. (a)

The passage describes how the elephants decided to shake the tree to make the monkeys realise they had gone too far with their prank.

PASSAGE - 55

The topic of renewable energy is becoming increasingly important as concerns about climate change and the depletion of non-renewable resources continue to grow. Renewable energy sources, such as solar and wind power, have the potential to provide a clean and sustainable source of power for the world's growing population. One of the major advantages of renewable energy is that it is not limited by the same supply constraints as fossil fuels. Unlike oil, coal, and natural gas, which are finite resources that will eventually run out, renewable energy sources like solar and wind power will never run out. Additionally, renewable energy sources do not produce the greenhouse gases that are responsible for climate change, making them a much more environmentally friendly option. Despite the clear benefits of renewable energy, there are still significant challenges that need to be overcome in order for it to become a viable alternative to fossil fuels. One of the main challenges is the cost of renewable energy, which is currently higher than traditional fossil fuels. However, as technology continues to improve and economies of scale are achieved, the cost of renewable energy is expected to decrease.

Another challenge is the need for reliable and efficient energy storage solutions, which are essential for the widespread adoption of renewable energy. Without effective energy storage solutions, renewable energy sources like solar and wind power can only be used when the sun is shining or the wind is blowing, which greatly limits their overall usefulness.

Overall, renewable energy has the potential to play a critical role in addressing the world's energy needs and reducing dependence on fossil fuels. While challenges remain, with continued research and development, renewable energy is likely to become increasingly viable and important in the coming years.

SSC Steno 10.12.2024 (Shift-II)

247. Select the most appropriate title for the passage.
(a) The Future of Nuclear Energy
(b) The Role of Technology in Energy Production
(c) The Environmental Impact of Non-Renewable Energy Sources
(d) The Advantages and Challenges of Renewable Energy

Ans. (d)

The most appropriate title is 'The Advantages and Challenges of Renewable Energy'. The passage discusses both the benefits and challenges of renewable energy in detail.

248. Select the most appropriate antonym of the given word.
Viable

(a) Irresolvable (b) Indignant
(c) Inaccurate (d) Impracticable

Ans. (d)

Viable means capable of working successfully. Hence, its antonym is 'impracticable' which means not feasible or workable.

Irresolvable means impossible to solve.
Indignant means feeling or showing anger or annoyance.
Inaccurate means not correct or precise

249. Identify the tone of the passage.

(a) Informative (b) Sarcastic
(c) Satirical (d) Subjective

Ans. (a)

The passage provides factual information about renewable energy, its benefits, and the challenges it faces without showing any personal bias or emotion.

250. What is the main challenge facing the adoption of renewable energy?

(a) Abundance of fossil fuels in the world
(b) Cost of renewable energy is currently higher than traditional fossil fuels
(c) Insufficient demand for renewable energy
(d) Lack of skilled labour for the production of renewable energy

Ans. (b)

The main challenge is that the cost of renewable energy is currently higher than traditional fossil fuels. The passage mentions this as one of the significant barriers to the adoption of renewable energy.

251. What is the main advantage of renewable energy over fossil fuels?

(a) The renewable energy sources will eventually run out.
(b) It is cheaper than traditional fossil fuels.
(c) It is not limited by the same supply constraints as fossil fuels.
(d) It produces the greenhouse gases that are responsible for climate change.

Ans. (c)

The main advantage of renewable energy over fossil fuels is that it is not limited by the same supply constraints. Renewable energy sources like solar and wind power are abundant and will never run out, unlike finite fossil fuels.

PASSAGE - 56

The process of photosynthesis is one of the most important biological processes on Earth. It is the way that plants, algae and some types of bacteria convert energy from the Sun into chemical energy in the form of organic compounds. These organic compounds, such as sugars, are then used by the organism as a source of energy and as building blocks for growth and reproduction.

The basic process of photosynthesis can be broken down into two main stages: the light dependent reactions and the light-independent reactions (also known as the Calvin cycle). In the light-dependent reactions, energy from sunlight is absorbed by pigments in the chloroplasts of plant cells, and is used to convert water into oxygen and high-energy electrons. These electrons are then used to power the synthesis of ATP and NADPH, which are energy-rich molecules that are used in the light-independent reactions.

In the light-independent reactions, the energy from ATP and NADPH is used to fix carbon dioxide into organic compounds, such as glucose. This process is known as carbon fixation and is mediated by a series of enzymes called the Calvin cycle. These reactions take place in the stroma of the chloroplasts, and the end result is the production of glucose and other sugars.

Photosynthesis is not only important for the survival of plants, but also for all other organisms that depend on plants as a source of food. In addition, the oxygen produced during photosynthesis is crucial for the survival of animals and other organisms that require oxygen for respiration.

Without the process of photosynthesis, the Earth's atmosphere would not contain the high levels of oxygen that are necessary for most forms of life to survive. Overall, photosynthesis is a vital process that plays a critical role in the Earth's ecosystem, providing the energy and organic compounds needed for the growth and survival of all forms of life. **SSC Steno 10.12.2024 (Shift-II)**

252. Identify the structure of the passage.

(a) Introduction, Main Body, Conclusion
(b) Cause and Effect
(c) Compare and Contrast
(d) Problem and Solution

Ans. (a)

The structure of the passage is 'Introduction, Main Body, Conclusion'. The passage begins with an introduction to photosynthesis, provides details in the main body and concludes with its importance.

253. Which of the following is not a correct statement about the light-dependent reactions of photosynthesis?

(a) They power the synthesis of ATP and NADPH.
(b) They convert water into oxygen and high-energy electrons.
(c) They use energy from sunlight to produce glucose.
(d) The energy from sunlight is absorbed by pigments in the chloroplasts of plant cell.

Ans. (c)

It is not correct that light-dependent reactions use energy from sunlight to produce glucose.

The light-dependent reactions produce ATP and NADPH, which are used in the light-independent reactions Calvin cycle) to produce glucose.

254. Identify the tone of the passage.

(a) Informal and personal (b) Informative and neutral
(c) Inquisitive and subjective (d) Assertive and passive

Ans. (b)

The tone of the passage is informative and neutral. The passage provides factual information about the process of photosynthesis without expressing personal opinions or emotions.

255. Which of the following is not a correct statement about the light-independent reactions of photosynthesis?

(a) They are also known as the Calvin cycle.
(b) They use energy from ATP and NADPH to produce glucose.
(c) They use energy from ATP and NADPH to produce oxygen.
(d) They take place in the stroma of the chloroplasts.

Ans. (c)

It is not correct that light-independent reactions use energy from ATP and NADPH to produce oxygen. The light-independent reactions (Calvin cycle) use ATP and NADPH to fix carbon dioxide and produce glucose.

256. Select the most appropriate title for the passage.
(a) The Calvin Cycle and Carbon Fixation
(b) Photosynthesis in Algae and Bacteria
(c) The Importance of Photosynthesis in the Earth's Ecosystem
(d) The Role of Pigments in Photosynthesis

Ans. (c)

'The Importance of Photosynthesis in the Earth's Ecosystem' is the most appropriate title. The passage discusses the process of photosynthesis and its crucial role in sustaining life on Earth.

PASSAGE - 57

As a graduate student, it is important for them to remember that the skills and knowledge they gain during their studies will be valuable not only in their chosen field, but also in their future career. In addition to mastering the subject matter of their programme, they should also strive to develop critical thinking, problem-solving and communication skills. These abilities are highly valued by employers and will serve them well in any career path they choose. Furthermore, as a graduate student, they will have the opportunity to conduct research and make original contributions to their field. This experience will not only help them gain a deeper understanding of the subject matter, but will also give them the opportunity to publish their findings and build their professional network. Additionally, it is important for them to take advantage of any opportunities to gain practical experience in their field. This can include internships, co-op programmes or volunteer work. These experiences will not only help them to develop valuable skills, but they will also help them to gain a better understanding of the real-world applications of their field, and they can also help them to make important connections in the industry.

Finally, it is important for them to remember that graduate school is a challenging and demanding experience, but it is also an incredibly rewarding one. With hard work, dedication, and a positive attitude, they will be well on their way to achieving their goals and making a meaningful impact in their field.

SSC Steno 10.12.2024 (Shift-II)

257. Which of the following is not an important aspect of a graduate student's experience to achieve academic and professional success?
(a) Gaining practical experience through internships, co-op programmes or volunteer work
(b) Conducting research and making original contributions to their field
(c) Building a professional network
(d) Forming support groups from different ethnic groups to stay connected

Ans. (d)

Forming support groups from different ethnic groups to stay connected is not mentioned as an important aspect for achieving academic and professional success in the passage.

258. Select the most appropriate title for the passage.
(a) The Role of Research in Graduate School
(b) Skills and Experience: The Key to Success as a Graduate Student
(c) Career Advancement Schemes for Graduate Students
(d) The Importance of Positive Attitude during Graduate Days

Ans. (b)

'Skills and Experience: The Key to Success as a Graduate Student' is the most appropriate title for the passage. The passage emphasises the importance of developing various skills and gaining practical experience for academic and professional success.

259. Identify the main theme of the passage.
(a) The ways in which graduate school can be utilised to create political opportunities
(b) Methods to include experiential learning in graduate school to inculcate discipline
(c) The importance of experience-based knowledge to increase the learning potential of graduate students
(d) The importance of developing various skills and gaining practical experience as a graduate student in order to achieve academic and professional success

Ans. (d)

The main theme of the passage is the importance of developing various skills and gaining practical experience as a graduate student in order to achieve academic and professional success.

260. Select the most appropriate antonym of the given word.
Rewarding
(a) Comforting (b) Inspiring
(c) Discouraging (d) Stimulating

Ans. (c)

Rewarding means providing satisfaction or benefit. Hence, its antonym is discouraging which means causing someone to lose confidence or enthusiasm.

261. Which of the following is not important for a graduate student to achieve academic and professional success?
(a) Having a corporate job
(b) Mastering a positive attitude
(c) Mastering the subject matter of their programme
(d) Developing critical thinking, problem-solving and communication skills

Ans. (a)

Having a corporate job is not mentioned as important for a graduate student to achieve academic and professional success in the passage. The passage focuses on skills, practical experience and a positive attitude.

SSC Steno 2023

PASSAGE - 58

Sustainable utensils are proving to be a crucial tool in our collective efforts towards building a greener and more environmentally conscious world. These utensils, often made from renewable resources such as bamboo or plant-based materials like cornstarch, offer a myriad of benefits. Firstly, sustainable utensils significantly reduce our reliance on single-use plastics. Plastic cutlery, traditionally used for convenience, contributes to the vast amounts of waste that end up in landfills and oceans, polluting ecosystems and harming marine life. By switching to sustainable alternatives, we can minimise this environmental damage.

Secondly, sustainable utensils are biodegradable or compostable, meaning they can break down naturally over time. This ensures that even if they do end up in landfills, they won't persist for centuries like plastic does. Instead, they return to the Earth without leaving a lasting negative impact. These utensils can be reused multiple times, further reducing waste.

Many sustainable options are durable and washable, making them a viable long-term solution.

SSC Steno 12.10.2023

262. What is the main focus of the passage?
(a) The benefits and harms of single-use plastic
(b) The economic benefits of sustainable utensils
(c) The importance of sustainable alternatives
(d) The environmental benefits of the sustainable utensils

Ans. (d)

The passage focuses on how sustainable utensils are proving to be a crucial tool in our efforts towards building a greener and more environmentally conscious world.

263. What distinguishes sustainable utensils from plastic cutlery?
(a) They have a lower environmental impact
(b) They are more expensive
(c) They have a shorter life span
(d) They are made from non-renewable resources

Ans. (a)

According to the passage, plastic cutlery contributes to the larger part of waste in the world which impacts the environment negatively.
In contrast sustainable utensils have lower environmental impact.

264. Based on the information provided in the passage, which among the following is not an example of sustainable utensil?
(a) Bioplastic cutlery (b) Edible cutlery
(c) Wooden cutlery (d) Plastic cutlery

Ans. (d)

As per the passage, plastic cutlery is not an example of sustainable utensil.

265. Which materials are commonly used to make sustainable utensils?
(a) Bamboo and cornstarch
(b) Ceramic and wood
(c) Plastic and aluminium
(d) Metal and glass

Ans. (a)

According to the passage, sustainable utensils are made from renewable resources such as bamboo or plant-based materials like cornstarch, which offer a myriad of benefits.

266. Which of the following is not a characteristic of sustainable utensils?
(a) Reusability (b) Non-recyclability
(c) Durability (d) Biodegradability

Ans. (b)

As per the passage, sustainable utensils are made from renewable and recyclable resources.

PASSAGE - 59

In a study, the University of Colorado in Denver observed a group of nurses who visited pregnant mothers. After the women gave birth, the nurses made approximately twenty visits before the children turned two years old.
When the benefits to the children were studied, there searchers found that the children were emotionally less vulnerable to fear. The children learned languages sooner. They also had higher mental development scores than the control group without the nurses' support. The benefits to the children because of this simple intervention of the nurses' support were observed even fifteen years later. **SSC Steno 12.10.2023**

267. What is the style of the passage?
(a) Narrative (b) Descriptive
(c) Expository (d) Classification

Ans. (c)

The given passage presents the findings of a study conducted by University of Colorado. Hence, the passage can be said to be 'expository' which is a style of writing wherein the author provides an effective explanation of a topic.

268. Which statement best summarises the passage?
(a) Study on nurses have impact even after fifteen years.
(b) Nurses should visit pregnant mothers regularly.
(c) Pregnant women are emotionally less vulnerable to fear.
(d) Community support is vital in the emotional development of a child.

Ans. (d)

The passage presents the impact of the presence of a community in the form of a group of nurses which affects the development of a child.
Hence, we can state that the passage is about how community support is vital in the emotional development of a child.

269. Select the most appropriate antonym of the given word.
Unsusceptible
(a) Vulnerable (b) Development
(c) Approximately (d) Intervention

Ans. (a)

'Unsusceptible' means not weak or prone to be harmed. Hence, its antonym is 'Vulnerable' which means exposed to the possibility of being attacked or harmed, either physically or emotionally.

270. What is the most suitable title of the passage?
(a) Pregnant Mothers and Nurses
(b) Social Support and Its Benefits
(c) Intervention of the Nurses
(d) Control Group and Nurses

Ans. (b)

The passage presents the impact of the presence of a community in the form of a group of nurses which affects the development of a child. Hence, the most appropriate title of the passage is 'Social Support and Its Benefits.'

271. What can one infer from the passage?
(a) The community plays an important role in offering social support to mothers.
(b) Some children learn languages quickly.
(c) Control group without nurses' support have relatively elevated mental development.
(d) Nurses' intervention reduce vulnerability to fear in pregnant mothers.

Ans. (a)

The passage presents the impact of the presence of a community in the form of a group of nurses affects the development of a child. Hence, we can infer that the community plays an important role in offering social support to mothers.

16

Miscellaneous

This chapter comprises questions based on English grammar which cannot be placed in any other category. However, remember these questions are as important as any other category of questions.

To solve questions, a good knowledge about the structure and use of adverbs, prepositions and tenses is required *(Refer to free booklet containing 151+ Grammar Rules).*

SSC Exam Scanner

SSC CGL 2024 (Tier 1)

1. Select the sentence in which the '-ing' form of verb expresses the continuity of an action/event.
SSC CGL Tier-1 18.09.2024 (Shift-I)
(a) Reading novels is my favourite pastime.
(b) I am fond of reading science fiction.
(c) Please do not disturb me. I am preparing for exams.
(d) The optician advised me to use reading glasses.

Ans. (c)
In the sentence "Please do not disturb me. I am preparing for exams", the verb 'preparing' is in the present continuous tense. This tense is used to express an action that is currently ongoing or happening at the moment of speaking. The other sentences use the '-ing' form of the verb as a noun (gerund) or adjective, rather than to indicate continuity of an action.

2. Select the option with the correct use of future tense.
SSC CGL Tier-1 23.09.2024 (Shift-III)
(a) By next December, I will have been completed six years in this home.
(b) By next December, I will be completed six years in this home.
(c) By next December, I will have complete six years in this home.
(d) By next December, I will have completed six years in this home.

Ans. (d)
This sentence correctly uses the future perfect tense, which is formed using 'will have' followed by the past participle of the verb (completed).
This tense is used to express an action that will be completed before a specific point in the future. The other options contain incorrect verb forms or tense structures.

SSC CGL 2023 (Tier 1)

3. Select the option that expresses the given sentence in past tense form.
SSC CGL Tier-1 17.07.2023 (Shift-IV)
The declarations which come out from that office are not dependable.
(a) The declarations which will come out from that office may not be dependable.
(b) The declarations which come out from that office were not dependable.
(c) The declarations which came out from that office are not dependable.
(d) The declarations which came out from that office were not dependable.

Ans. (d)
The sentence changes from present tense ('come out' and 'are not dependable') to past tense ('came out' and 'were not dependable').
This shift accurately reflects that the action and state described occurred in the past.

4. Select the option that expresses the given sentence in past tense form.
SSC CGL Tier-1 26.07.2023 (Shift-II)
The methods Arunima adopts for taming the dogs create awe and wonder among them.
(a) The methods Arunima adopted for taming the dogs created awe and wonder among them.
(b) The methods Arunima adopts for taming the dogs created awe and wonder among them.
(c) The methods Arunima adopted for taming the dogs create awe and wonder among them.
(d) The methods Arunima adopts for taming the dogs will create awe and wonder among them.

Ans. (b)
The sentence changes from present tense ('adopts' and 'create') to past tense ('adopted' and 'created').
This transformation follows the structure: Subject + V_2 + object, where 'V_2' indicates the past form of the verb.

SSC CGL 2022 (Tier 1)

5. Select the sentence with the appropriate use of adverb of manner. **SSC CGL Tier-1 01.12.2022 (Shift-I)**
(a) He done his work regularly.
(b) He has just done his work.
(c) He does his work carefully.
(d) He has done his work on my table.

Ans. (c)

'Carefully' is an adverb of manner, which describes how the action is done. The other sentences either lack an adverb of manner or use it incorrectly.

6. Select the appropriate option to replace the underlined word with the adverb of time.

I went to Paris <u>regularly</u>.

SSC CGL Tier-1 01.12.2022 (Shift-II)

(a) twice (b) often
(c) yesterday (d) happily

Ans. (c)

'Yesterday' is an adverb of time, indicating when the action happened. In the context of the sentence "I went to Paris regularly", the word 'yesterday' correctly replaces 'regularly' to show a specific time when the action took place.

7. Select the appropriate adverb for the underlined word in the sentence. **SSC CGL Tier-1 02.12.2022 (Shift-I)**

He led me to the room that had <u>obvious</u> been built later than the rest of the house.

(a) obliviously (b) obliviousness
(c) obviousness (d) obviously

Ans. (d)

The most appropriate adverb as per the context of the sentence is 'obviously'. 'Obviously' means in a way that is clear for almost anyone to see or understand.

8. Select the sentence with the appropriate use of preposition.

SSC CGL Tier-1 02.12.2022 (Shift-III)

(a) It has been raining till morning.
(b) It has been raining from morning.
(c) It has been raining by morning.
(d) It has been raining since morning.

Ans. (d)

The sentence with the correct use of the preposition is "It has been raining since morning". The preposition 'since' is correct in the context of the sentence as it indicates the duration of rainfall.

9. Select the sentence with the appropriate use of adverb of frequency.

SSC CGL Tier-1 03.12.2022 (Shift-II)

(a) Radha goes to Nagpur with great affection.
(b) Radha goes to Nagpur for her office work.
(c) Radha often goes to Nagpur.
(d) Radha goes to Nagpur to meet her uncle.

Ans. (c)

The word 'often' is an adverb of frequency because it shows how many times something was done. Thus, the correct answer is "Radha often goes to Nagpur".

10. Select the sentence with the appropriate use of preposition.

SSC CGL Tier-1 05.12.2022 (Shift-III)

(a) They rise with the morning lark and labour till almost dark.
(b) They rise with the morning lark and labour utmost almost dark.
(c) They rise with the morning lark and labour by almost dark.
(d) They rise with the morning lark and labour still almost dark.

Ans. (a)

The sentence given in option (a) i.e. "They rise with the morning lark and labour till almost dark" has the appropriate usage of preposition in it. Preposition 'till' denotes the time of action upto a particular point.

11. Select the sentence with the appropriate use of preposition.

SSC CGL Tier-1 05.12.2022 (Shift-IV)

(a) We have been playing for 4 O'clock.
(b) We have been playing from 4 O'clock.
(c) We have been playing to 4 O'clock.
(d) We have been playing since 4 O'clock.

Ans. (d)

The preposition 'since' is used to refer back to a previous point in time.

Thus, the sentence having the appropriate use of the preposition is "We have been playing since 4 O'clock".

12. Select the sentence with the appropriate use of preposition.

SSC CGL Tier-1 06.12.2022 (Shift-II)

(a) By means of rope ladders they scaled the wall.
(b) Along with means of rope ladders they scaled the wall.
(c) In means of rope ladders they scaled the wall.
(d) Of means of rope ladders they scaled the wall.

Ans. (a)

The sentence with the appropriate use of preposition is "By means of rope ladders they scaled the wall' . The phrase 'by means of something' means using a particular method or system as is given in the sentence where rope ladders are used to scale the wall.

13. Select the sentence with the appropriate use of preposition.

SSC CGL Tier-1 06.12.2022 (Shift-III)

(a) Children are fond to sweets.
(b) Children are fond off sweets.
(c) Children are fond with sweets.
(d) Children are fond of sweets.

Ans. (d)

The sentence with the correct use of the preposition is "Children are fond of sweets".

'Fond of' is a common collocation, meaning to have a liking for something.

14. Select the sentence with the appropriate use of preposition.

SSC CGL Tier-1 07.12.2022 (Shift-II)

(a) Ashok was in the bus stop.
(b) Ashok was to the bus stop.
(c) Ashok was on the bus stop.
(d) Ashok was at the bus stop.

Ans. (d)

The sentence "Ashok was at the bus stop" has the appropriate usage of the preposition 'at.' The preposition 'at' denotes a specific place, indicating Ashok's location in relation to the bus stop.

15. Select the most appropriate collocation to substitute the underlined words in the given sentence. **SSC CGL Tier-1 08.12.2022 (Shift-IV)**

The MNC is about to <u>be bankrupt</u>, according to reliable sources.

(a) take bankrupt (b) go bankrupt
(c) come bankrupt (d) give bankrupt

Ans. (b)

The verb 'go' is used with 'bankrupt'. So, 'go bankrupt' is the most appropriate collocation to substitute the underlined words in the given sentence. 'Go bankrupt' means to have no money.

16. Select the appropriate adverb for the underlined words in the sentence. **SSC CGL Tier-1 08.12.2022 (Shift-IV)**

We considered <u>in brief</u> the long term solution to the problem.

(a) briefly (b) briefless
(c) brief (d) briefness

Ans. (a)

'Briefly' is the most appropriate adverb for 'in brief' as it means for a short time.

17. Select the sentence with the appropriate use of preposition.

SSC CGL Tier-1 09.12.2022 (Shift-I)

(a) He arrived to Sunday morning.
(b) He arrived at Sunday morning.
(c) He arrived in Sunday morning.
(d) He arrived on Sunday morning.

Ans. (d)

The sentence "He arrived on Sunday morning" is correct because the preposition 'on' is used with days of the week and specific parts of those days (e.g., on Sunday morning).

18. Select the sentence with the appropriate use of a preposition. **SSC CGL Tier-1 12.12.2022 (Shift-II)**

(a) Are you interested along with modern art?
(b) Are you interested into modern art?
(c) Are you interested with modern art?
(d) Are you interested in modern art?

Ans. (d)
The preposition 'in' is used to show involvement in a particular thing and is generally used with the word 'interested'.

19. Select the appropriate adverb for the underlined word in the sentence. **SSC CGL Tier-1 13.12.2022 (Shift-II)**

I complete forgot her birthday and I don't know how to make it up to her.

(a) completeness (b) completed
(c) completely (d) completing

Ans. (c)
The appropriate adverb for the underlined word 'complete' is 'completely.'
The sentence "I completely forgot her birthday and I don't know how to make it up to her" uses 'completely' to modify the verb 'forgot.'

20. Select the sentence with the appropriate use of preposition. **SSC CGL Tier-1 13.12.2022 (Shift-III)**

(a) The lion and the unicorn fought between the crown.
(b) The lion and the unicorn fought for the crown.
(c) The lion and the unicorn fought by the crown.
(d) The lion and the unicorn fought up the crown.

Ans. (b)
The sentence 'The lion and the unicorn fought for the crown' is correct because the preposition 'for' indicates the reason or purpose of the fight. 'Fight for' means to try hard to do or get something.

SSC CHSL 2024, 2023 (Tier 1 & 2)

21. The youth.........nowadays. life / of / today / a / leading / are / miserable **SSC CHSL Tier-2 18.11.2024**

(a) today are leading of a miserable life
(b) of today are leading a miserable life
(c) are today leading of a miserable life
(d) today are leading a miserable life of

Ans. (b)
'The youth of today are leading a miserable life nowadays.'
This sequence correctly arranges the words to form a grammatically correct sentence, ensuring clarity and coherence.

22. The people of.........to survive. are / this / island / commodities / deprived / essential / needed / remote / of **SSC CHSL Tier-2 18.11.2024**

(a) remote island are deprived of essential commodities needed this
(b) this remote island are needed essential commodities deprived of
(c) this island are deprived of essential commodities needed remote
(d) this remote island are deprived of essential commodities needed

Ans. (d)
'The people of this remote island are deprived of essential commodities needed to survive.' This arrangement forms a coherent and grammatically correct sentence, conveying the intended meaning clearly.

23. I missed the.........for the next. usually / hour / which / for / board / had / wait / an / bus / I / and / to **SSC CHSL Tier-2 18.11.2024**

(a) bus which I board and had to wait for an usually hour
(b) bus which I usually board and had to wait for an hour
(c) hour and had to wait for an bus which I usually board
(d) bus I usually board which had to wait for an hour and

Ans. (b)
'I missed the bus which I usually board and had to wait for an hour for the next.'
This arrangement forms a coherent and grammatically correct sentence, detailing the sequence of events clearly.

24. Select the sentence in the future tense. **SSC CHSL Tier-1 01.07.2024 (Shift-I)**

(a) I will be twenty five next Sunday.
(b) I have been twenty five next Sunday.
(c) I should be twenty five next Sunday.
(d) I could be twenty five next Sunday.

Ans. (a)
Future tense form of verb uses the modal verb 'will/shall' in all forms. Hence, the sentence in future tense is– I will be twenty five next Sunday.

25. Select the option that expresses the given sentence in positive degree of comparison. **SSC CHSL Tier-1 02.08.2023 (Shift-I)**

She is the dullest child in the class.

(a) She is very duller in the class.
(b) Dullest child in the class is she.
(c) No other child in the class is as dull as she.
(d) In the class of all she is dull.

Ans. (c)
The positive degree is used to compare a single entity without comparing it to others. It uses the structure 'as + positive degree + as'.
Hence, the correct sentence is – No other child in the class is as dull as she.

26. Select the option that expresses the following sentence in positive degree of comparison. **SSC CHSL Tier-1 10.08.2023 (Shift-III)**

Istanbul is a beautiful city.

(a) The city of Istanbul is as beautiful as other cities.
(b) Istanbul is a very beautiful city.
(c) Beautiful city is the Istanbul.
(d) No other place I have seen is as beautiful as Istanbul.

Ans. (d)
The sentence 'No other place I have seen is as beautiful as Istanbul' expresses the given sentence in the positive degree of comparison.
The positive degree is used to compare Istanbul with other places without implying any superiority or inferiority.

SSC MTS 2024 (Tier 1)

27. Select the option that expresses the given sentence in future continuous tense form. I shall come again in the afternoon for lunch. **SSC MTS Tier-1 14.11.2024 (Shift-III)**

(a) I will be coming again in the afternoon for lunch.
(b) I shall have come again in the afternoon for lunch.
(c) I will come again in the afternoon for lunch.
(d) I shall be coming again in the afternoon for lunch

Ans. (d)
'I shall be coming again in the afternoon for lunch' expresses the sentence in future continuous tense. It indicates an ongoing action that will happen in the future.

28. Identify the error in the usage of the future tense in the given sentence and choose the sentence from the following options. Parvati finish the painting in one hour. **SSC MTS Tier-1 13.11.2024 (Shift-III)**

(a) Parvati had been finishing the painting in one hour.
(b) Parvati was finished the painting in one hour.
(c) Parvati will finish the painting in one hour.
(d) Parvati has been finishing the painting in one hour.

Ans. (c)

'Parvati will finish the painting in one hour' is the sentence in the future tense.

The future tense verb form indicates an action that will happen.

29. Read the following sentence and select its future tense form from the given below.
Rachel and Rahul joined forces on a project and successfully completed it within a month.
SSC MTS Tier-1 12.11.2024 (Shift-III)

(a) Rachel and Rahul will join forces on a project and successfully complete it within a month.
(b) Rachel and Rahul have joined forces on a project and successfully completed it within a month.
(c) Rachel and Rahul are joining forces on a project and successfully completing it within a month.
(d) Rachel and Rahul should join forces on a project and successfully complete it within a month.

Ans. (a)

'Rachel and Rahul will join forces on a project and successfully complete it within a month' is in future tense. The correct future tense sentence describes an action that will happen.

30. Select the option that expresses the given sentence in future continuous tense form.
Shall I meet you soon?
SSC MTS Tier-1 05.11.2024 (Shift-III)

(a) Shall I have met you soon?
(b) Shall I be meeting you soon?
(c) Will we be meeting soon?
(d) Will I be meeting you soon?

Ans. (b, d)

Both the sentences 'shall I be meeting you soon?' and 'Will I be meeting you soon?' express the given sentence in future continuous tense form.

31. Change the following sentence into positive degree.
Sushma is one of the smartest girls in the class. **SSC MTS Tier-1 21.10.2024 (Shift-II)**

(a) No other girl is as smart as Sushma.
(b) Few girls in the class are as smart as Sushma.
(c) Sushma is smarter than any other girls in the class.
(d) Sushma is the smart girl of the class

Ans. (b)

'Few girls in the class are as smart as Sushma' changes the sentence to positive degree. This rephrasing maintains the original meaning using a positive comparison.

32. Which of the following sentences contains an adverbial error?
SSC MTS Tier-1 18.10.2024 (Shift-II)

(a) She writes slowly and steadily.
(b) He sang beautifully at the talent show.
(c) They danced gracefully across the stage.
(d) The teacher spoke clear and concise.

Ans. (d)

'The teacher spoke clear and concise' contains an adverbial error. The correct form should be 'The teacher spoke clearly and concisely'. Adverbs should be used to modify the verb 'spoke'.

33. Read the following sentence and select its future tense form from the options given below. Ramya finished her dissertation early.
SSC MTS Tier-1 18.10.2024 (Shift-II)

(a) Ramya has finished her dissertation early.
(b) Ramya is finishing her dissertation early.
(c) Ramya had finished her dissertation early.
(d) Ramya will finish her dissertation early.

Ans. (d)

'Ramya will finish her dissertation early' is in future tense. This sentence uses the future simple tense to indicate an action that will take place in the future.

34. Read the following sentence and select its future tense form from the following options.
The food company promoted newly launched products at affordable prices. **SSC MTS Tier-1 17.10.2024 (Shift-II)**

(a) The food company promotes newly launched products at affordable prices.
(b) The food company will be promoting newly launched products at affordable prices.
(c) The food company had promoted newly launched products at affordable prices.
(d) The food company is promoting newly launched products at affordable prices.

Ans. (b)

'The food company will be promoting newly launched products at affordable prices' is in future tense.

This sentence uses the future continuous tense to indicate an ongoing future action.

35. Identify the odd word from the given options.
SSC MTS Tier-1 07.10.2024 (Shift-I)

(a) Billiards (b) Carom
(c) Golf (d) Table tennis

Ans. (c)

'Golf' is the odd word. Unlike billiards, carom and table tennis, which are indoor games played on tables, golf is an outdoor sport played on a large course.

SSC Steno 2024, 2023

36. Which of the following sentences is in the past continuous tense?
SSC Steno 10.12.2024 (Shift-I)

(a) They watched TV all evening.
(b) They would have watched TV all evening.
(c) They shall be watching TV all evening.
(d) They were watching TV all evening.

Ans. (d)

The sentence 'They were watching TV all evening' is in the past continuous tense. It describes an action that was ongoing in the past.

37. Select the correct interrogative sentence. **SSC Steno 10.12.2024 (Shift-III)**

(a) What is a name of the next station?
(b) What is a name of a next station?
(c) What is the name of the next station?
(d) What is the name of a next station?

Ans. (c)

'What is the name of the next station?' is the correct interrogative sentence. It uses the definite article 'the' to specify the next station.

38. Select the option that can be used as a substitute for the underlined group of words. **SSC Steno Grade 13.10.2023**
Istanbul is a beautiful city.

(a) The city of Istanbul is as beautiful as other cities.
(b) Istanbul is a very beautiful city.
(c) Beautiful city is the Istanbul.
(d) No other place I have seen is as beautiful as Istanbul.

Ans. (a)

The sentence 'The city of Istanbul is as beautiful as other city' represents the exact meaning of the sentence.

POWER PACK

arihant
SUCCESS AND NOTHING LESS

151+
Grammar Rules

HIGHLY USEFUL FOR ALL SSC EXAMS

Free Booklet with POWER PACK

SSC English

Chapterwise 8000+ TCS MCQs

Top 151+ Grammar Rules

The SSC Examination asks various types of questions based on Grammar to test the grammatical knowledge and language skills of candidates. These types of questions range from spotting the error, sentence improvement, fill in the blanks to cloze tests. Hence, it is crucial for us to remember the various rules of grammar.

Let us carefully examine each of these parts one by one.

Noun

Some Important Collective Nouns

Collection of People

- An army/ regiment/ corps of soldiers
- An assembly of listeners/ worshippers
- A band of musicians/ pilgrims
- A bevy of ladies/girls/women
- A class/ group/ delegation of students
- A board of directors/ trustees/ examiners
- A caravan of pilgrims/ merchants
- A choir of singers
- A company of boys
- A crew of sailors
- A crowd of people/spectators
- The council of ministers
- A flock of tourists
- A gang of robbers/thieves/coolies
- A jury/ panel of judges
- A pack of thieves
- A panel of experts
- A posse of policemen
- A staff of employees
- A senate of Councilors
- A team of players
- A troupe of dancers/actors/acrobats. children
- A troop of soldiers/policemen/actors
- A tribe of natives/ aborigines

Collection of Animals

- An army/ a nest/ a swarm/ a column/ a colony of ants
- A cloud of bats
- A flock of sheep/goat/birds
- A flock/ brood of chickens
- A flight/ flock of birds
- A flight of insects
- A herd of cows/deer/elephants/cattle
- A hive of bees
- A swarm of bees/flies/locust/insects
- A kennel of dogs
- A litter of puppies/kittens/cubs
- A gaggle of geese
- A pack of wolves
- A pride of lions/peacocks
- A parliament of owls
- A school of fish/dolphin
- A shoal/ school of fish
- A string of camels
- A stud of horses
- A troop of monkeys/ lions
- A train of donkeys
- A team of horses/ducks/oxen
- A murder of crows
- A band of gorillas
- A company of parrots
- A bale of turtles
- A leap (leep) of leopards

Collection of Things

- An album of photographs/ autographs/ stamps
- An anthology of poems
- A bale of cotton/ wood
- A batch of cookies
- A bouquet of flowers
- A bunch of keys/grapes/plantains/flowers
- A bundle of sticks/papers/clothes
- A blade of grass
- A cloud of dust
- A fleet of ships
- A forest of trees
- A galaxy/ constellation of stars
- A group of islands
- A hedge of bushes
- A heap of ruins/ashes/ sand
- A library of books
- A pack of cards
- Peals of laughter
- A pile of books/papers
- A quiver of arrows
- A range of mountains
- A stack of wood/hay/corn
- A stream of bananas
- A stock of goods/ coal
- A string of pearls
- A series of events
- A suit of rooms/ furniture/ armour
- A tuft of hair
- A wad of notes

Rules of Nouns

Rule 1 A Proper Noun can act as a common noun. When this happens, an article is placed before the Proper Noun.

e.g.,

- Vinayak is the **Newton** of our class.
- Let's take an **Uber**.

In these examples, *Newton* and *Uber* are used as common nouns. Newton as a common noun indicates any person with great scientific mind and *Uber* refers to a cab service.

Rule 2 We can easily confuse material nouns with some descriptive adjectives. Remember Material nouns are name of products from which other things are made.

e.g.,

- **Platinum** is the most precious metal.
- She was eating from a **golden** spoon.

In the first sentence, *Platinum* is a material noun. However, in the second sentence, *golden* is an adjective which is followed by a noun.

Look Out For These Uncountable Nouns!

Advice, information, hair, luggage, business, work, word (in the sense of promise, message, discussion), mischief, bread, cattle, scenery, abuse, vacation, money, knowledge, evidence, employment, alphabet, poetry, food, furniture, baggage, fuel, paper, equipment, machinery, material, sugar, etc.

Rule 3 Uncountable nouns act like singular nouns.

e.g.,

- I need advices. (✗)
- I need advice. (✓)

As such, these nouns do not take indefinite articles (a or an)

e.g.,

- He gave me an information. (✗)
- He gave me information. (✓)

Rule 4 We can show the singularity or plurality of uncountable nouns by using certain phrases.

(A) For singularity, use

(i) a piece/a word of advice
(ii) a word of abuse
(iii) an act of mischief
(iv) a loaf of bread
(v) an article of luggage, etc.

(B) For plurality, use

(i) some advice
(ii) a lot of knowledge
(iii) plenty of information
(iv) much fuel, etc.

Rule 5 The use of the nouns that have the same form in both singular and plural (Offspring, deer, fish, sheep, aircraft, species, etc.) show their singularity or plurality in the sentence through the verb.

e.g.,

- Sheep are economically useful.
- A sheep is grazing in the field.

Rule 6 Some nouns ending in 's' or 'es' are singular nouns. These include

(A) **Branches of learning** including Mathematics, Physics, Mechanics, Politics, Statistics, Statics and Economics.

(B) **Diseases** including Mumps, Measles, Rickets etc.

(C) **Games and sports** including Billiards, Aquatics, Gymnastics, Athletics etc.

(D) **Titles of books** including The Three Musketeers, Gulliver's Travels, Arabian Nights, War and Peace, Tales from Shakespeare, etc.

(E) **Descriptive names of countries** including United States, United Arab Emirates etc.

(F) **Some other nouns** such as Innings, Series, News, Summons, etc.

Do not Confuse!

Statistics as a subject is used with singular verb. However, when Statistics is taken as a collection of data is used with plural verb.
"She is majoring in **statistics** at the university."(Singular)
"These economic **statistics** reveal a decline in unemployment rates."(Plural)

Rule 7 Some of the nouns exist in plural form only. They are

(A) **Articles of dress** such as trousers, breeches, Jeans, etc.

(B) **Names of instruments** such as scissors, spectacles, shears, scales, tongs, etc.

(C) **Other nouns** such as alms, thanks, proceeds, riches, contents, credentials, orders, refreshments, requirements, customs, rations, archives, annals, ashes, arrears, assets, stairs, spirits, statistics (data), quarters, earnings, manners, outskirts, savings, auspices (support), surroundings, etc.

Rule 8 A compound noun comprising a numerical + noun does not take a plural form when it is used as an adjective.

e.g.,

- I gave him two hundreds rupees. (✗)
  I gave him two hundred rupees. (✓)
- I gave him five dozens pencils. (✗)
  I gave him five dozen pencils. (✓)

Rule 9 Noun after preposition is repeated in singular form.

e.g.,

(i) Word for word (ii) Hour after hour
(iii) Door to door

Rule 10 The phrase 'one of' always takes a plural noun.

e.g.,

- One of the boy went to see the match. (✗)
  One of the boys went to see the match. (✓)

Rule 9 Young children are considered to be of neuter gender.

e.g.,

- The infant is crying for his toy. (✗)
- The infant is crying for its toy. (✓)

Pronouns

Personal Pronouns

	Singular		Plural	
	Subjective	Objective	Subjective	Objective
Ist Person	I	Me	We	Us
IInd Person	You	You	You	You
IIIrd Person	He, She, It	Him, Her, It	They	Them

Possessive Pronouns

	Singular	Plural
First Person	Mine	Ours
Second Person	Yours	Yours
Third Person	His, Hers	Theirs

Rules of Pronouns

Rule 1 Personal Pronouns are used according to the number, gender and person as the Nouns for which they are used.

e.g.,

(i) Ram is a revered deity in India. **He** is called the Ideal man.

(ii) Rakesh and Bhima are going to the fair. **They** would return late at night.

Rule 2 When all the three persons of personal pronouns is present in the sentence, we follow a certain order of pronouns.

(A) If two or more than two Subjective Case Singular Pronouns are present in a sentence, then we follow the **231 Rule**. This means

2nd person, 3rd person and 1st person.

e.g.,

- **You** and **she** will be going to the party. (2nd person and 3rd person)
- **She** and **I** should finish this dress by today. (3rd person and 1st person)
- You, he and I will go to the India Gate tomorrow. (2nd person, 3rd person and 1st person)

(B) If two or more than two Subjective Case Singular Pronouns are present in a sentence and something wrong is talked about or a mistake is accepted, then we follow the **123 Rule**. This means

1st person, 2nd person and 3rd person.

e.g.,

- **I** and **she** have made the mistake. (1st person and 2nd person)
- **You** and **he** have committed the crime. (2nd person and 3rd person)
- **I**, you and **she** will accept our mischief. (1st person, 2nd person and 3rd person)

(C) If two or more than two Subjective Case Plural Pronouns are present in a sentence, then also we follow the **123 Rule**.

e.g.,

- **We** and **you** are going to hike. (1st person and 2nd person)
- **You** and **they** will work together on this project. (2nd person and 3rd person)
- **We**, **you** and **they** need to meet soon. (1st person, 2nd person and 3rd person)

Rule 3 Uses of pronoun 'It'

(A) To refer to non-living things, animals, infants and insects.

e.g.,

- The chair looks exquisite. **It** was bought from the local antique shop.
- A chameleon is a mysterious creature. **It** has the ability to camouflage.
- The baby was crying. **It** was hungry.
- The caterpillar was crawling slowly. **It** was going near that leaf.

(B) In statement containing time, weather, climate, temperature and distance.

e.g.,

- **It** is 8 o'clock now.
- **It** is sunny in the afternoon.
- **It** rains all year round here.
- **It** is 11 degree Celsius outside.
- **It** is 8km to the left.

(C) As a subject to empathize on the noun or pronoun.

e.g.,

- **It** is she who mistook him for her brother.

Rule 4 Different cases of pronouns are used in different situations in a sentence.

(A) When a sentence starts with 'it' which is followed by any form of verb 'be' (is am, are, was, were), the pronoun following the verb is in Subjective Case.

e.g.,

- It is **him** who is to be blamed. (✗)
- It is **he** who is to be blamed. (✓)

(B) Objective case comes after preposition and words including let, like, between... and, but and except.

e.g.,

(i) He smiled at **I**. (✗)
He smiled at **me**. (✓)

(ii) Let **she** do this chores. (✗)
Let **her** do this chores. (✓)

(C) If there is a comparison between two pronouns, pronouns of the same case are used.

e.g.,

- He writes faster than **her**. (✗)
- He writes faster than **she**. (✓)

Rule 5 Possessive pronouns can be used as a subject of the verb, as the object of the verb and the object of the preposition.

e.g.,

- **Hers** was bought from the Duty free store. (as a subject)
- He has kept my clothes as well as **theirs**. (as an object)
- I prefer your hotel to **his**. (as an object of the preposition)

Rule 6 We use reflexive pronouns after many words including acquit, absent, avail, reconcile, amuse, resign, avenge, revenge, enjoy, exert, apply, adapt, adjust, pride, overreach, etc.

e.g.,

- You should avail of every chance in life. (✗)
- You should avail **yourself** of every chance in life. (✓)

Special Case!

The verb 'enjoy' presents a special case vis-a-vis the use of reflexive pronouns. If the verb 'enjoy' is followed by an object, it does not take a reflexive pronoun. However, if the object is not present, reflexive pronoun is used.

e.g., They enjoyed the picture last evening.
In this sentence, we have an object- the picture. Hence, no reflexive pronoun is needed.
They enjoyed **themselves** during summer vacation.
In this sentence, there is no object. Thus, reflexive pronoun is needed.

Rule 7 Different interrogative pronouns are used for different nouns. The same is followed for some relative pronouns including who, whom, which/ that and whose.

- **Who** is used to refer to people in subjective case
- **Whom** is used to refer to people in objective case
- **Whose** is used to show ownership
- **Which** are used for non-living thing, animals and in some cases, people.
- **What** is used for things only

Rule 8 We do not use reflexive pronouns with these verbs- Keep, stop, turn, qualify, bathe, move, rest, hide, etc.

e.g.,

- You should keep yourself away from bad people. (✗)
- You should keep away from bad people. (✓)

Rule 9 Each other is used when referring to two person or things. One another is used while referring to more than two persons or things.

e.g.,

- Raman and Mayank know **each other** since their childhoods.
- Siblings often fight with **one another**.

Rule 10 Relative pronoun 'Which' is used in place of 'Who' when we are referring to a choice between two or more than two things or persons.

e.g.,

- Of the two sisters who is the more intelligent. (✗)
  Of the two sister which is more intelligent. (✓)
- Who is your father in the crowd? (✗)
  Which is your father in the crowd? (✓)

Rule 11 Uses of Relative Pronoun 'that'

(A) If two pronouns or nouns are joined by 'and'- one is a living being and the other is non-living being then, relative pronoun 'that' is used.

e.g., The man and his cat that she saw yesterday are our neighbours.

(B) If the pronoun 'all' is used for non-living things, 'that' is used after it.

e.g., All **that** glitters is not gold.

Rule 12 The word 'same' is not a pronoun. Hence, do not use it.

e.g.,

- He bought a house and is living in **the same**. (✗)
- He bought a house and is living **in it**. (✓)

Rule 13 When one is used as a pronoun, one's is used as possessive pronoun and oneself is used as reflexive pronoun.

e.g.,

- One should do his duty himself. (✗)
- One should do one's duty oneself. (✓)

Articles

Rule 1 'A' is used before a word beginning

(i) With a consonant.

e.g.,

- **a** boy
- **a** Kite
- **a** student

(ii) With a vowel starting with the sound of a consonant.

e.g.,

- **a** one eyed man
  (the word 'one' starts with the sound of 'w')
- **a** university student
  (the word 'university' starts with the sound of 'y')
- **a** European
  (the word 'European' starts with the sound of 'y')
- **a** unique book
  (the word 'unique' starts with the sound of 'y')

Rule 2 'An' is used before a word beginning

(i) With a vowel.

e.g.,

- **an** apple
- **an** elephant
- **an** igloo
- **an** orange
- **an** umbrella

(ii) With a silent 'h'. This means that while pronouncing the word, the sound of h is mute.

e.g.,

- **an** hour
- **an** heir
- **an** honourable person
- **an** honest man

Rule 3 With an abbreviation

(i) 'An' is used when the first consonant letter is pronounced with the sound of a vowel.

e.g.,

- **An** L.L.B student
- **An** M.P.
- **An** S.P.
- **An** X-ray
- **An** F.I.R.

(ii) 'A' is used when the first consonant letter is pronounced with the consonant sound.

e.g.,

- **A** B.A.
- **A** D.M.

Rule 4 Indefinite articles are used when a person or thing is singled out as a representative of a class of things, animals or persons. Here, 'a' or 'an' is used in the sense of 'any'.

e.g.,

- **A** lion is a ferocious animal.
- **A** river is a lifeline of many villages.

Rule 5 In place of the word 'per'.

e.g.,

- Twenty kilometers **a** liter
- Ten thousand **a** month
- 150 Rupee **a** day

Rule 6 Before the words that denote numbers to indicate one.

e.g.,

- **A** hundred
- **A** million

Rule 7 Before a person not known to the speaker or the listener. Herein, 'a' indicates 'someone named'.

e.g.,

- **A** Mr. Gupta
(Someone named Mr. Gupta)
- **A** Mrs. Sharma
(Some named Mrs. Sharma)

Rule 8 When singular nouns are used after words many, rather, quite and such.

e.g.,

- Many **a** man would welcome such change.
- It is rather **a** pity.
- It was quite **an** impossible project.
- It was such **an** intelligent decision.

Rule 9 Uses of 'The'

1. When we talk of a particular person or a thing as already mentioned, known or under discussion.

e.g.,

- **The** book is not available in the market. (The book is already known to the speaker and listener)
- Let us study **the** lesson carefully. (The lesson is already known to the speaker and listener)

2. Before proper nouns that refer to unique objects. These include

(A) **Historical Buildings** the Statue of Unity, the Taj Mahal, etc.

(B) **Mountain Ranges** the Himalayas, the Eastern Ghats, etc.

(C) **Names of Planets, Stars and Sun** the Earth, the Moon, the Sun etc.

(D) **Rivers, Oceans, Canals, Bays and Gulfs** the Ganges, the Indian Ocean, the Suez Canal, the Bay of Bengal, the Persian Gulf, etc.

(E) **Group of Islands and Deserts** the Andaman and Nicobar, the Sahara, etc.

(F) **Holy Books** the Ramayana, the Vedas, etc.

(G) **Musical Instruments** the Flute, the Harmonium, etc.

(H) **Descriptive Names of Countries and States** the UK, the USA, the Netherlands, etc.

(I) **Names of Newspapers and Magazines** the Times of India, the Frontline, etc.

(J) **Names of Trains, Ships, Flights and Hotels** the Rajdhani Express, the Titanic, the Boeing, the Maurya Sherton, etc.

(K) **Sports Cups and Trophies** the Ranji, the Singer Cup, the World Cup, etc.

(L) **Cardinal Points of Directions** the East, the North, the South and the West

(M) **Names of Castes and Communities** the Rajputs, the Marathas, etc.

(N) **Organs of Government** the Judiciary, the Legislative, etc.

(O) **Names of Political Parties** the Congress, the BJP, the Labour Party, etc.

(P) **Names of Armed Forces** the Army, the Police, the Airforce, etc.

(Q) **Names of Dynasties, Empires, Wars, Revolutions and Centuries** the Gupta dynasty, the British Empire, the Middle Ages, the Civil War, the Vedic Ages, the Sixth Century, etc.

3. Before ordinals like first, second, third, fourth, etc. and superlative degree of adjectives.

e.g.,

- **The** first man
- **The** best photo

4. To present a class of animals or things.

e.g.,

- **The** dog is the most faithful animal.
- **The** pineapple is a tropical fruit.

5. Before an adjective when it represents a class of persons.

e.g.,

- **The** rich should help the poor.
- **The** old are respected by the young.

6. To express double comparisons. (Double comparison)

e.g.,

- The sooner, the better.
- The higher you go, **the** colder it is.

7. Before comparative degree of adjective when we are making a choice between two nouns.

e.g.,

- She is the weaker of **the** two sisters.
- Who is **the** more beautiful of **the** two sisters?

8. Before physical positions.

e.g.,

- **The** top of the mountain.
- **The** back of the house.

9. Before the words 'same and whole' and after the words 'all and both' used with plural nouns.

e.g.,

- This is **the** same book that you gave me.
- **The** whole class was absent.
- All **the** boys were present there.
- Both **the** brothers were honest.

10. Before a common noun to give it the force of a superlative.

e.g.,

- He is **the** man for this job.

11. Before a common noun to give it the sense of an abstract noun.

e.g.,

- **The** judge in him. (sense of justice)
- **The** mother in her. (feelings of a mother)
- **The** beast in him. (cruelty of a beast)

12. Before the names of gadgets referred to in the context of inventions.

e.g.,

- **The** telephone was first used in 90's
- **The** wireless is a fast developing technology.

13. Before the name of professions used collectively.

e.g.,

- **The** Press
- **The** Bench

14. Before the case in apposition

e.g.,

- Netaji, the hero of Modern India, ought to be remembered.
- Who can underestimate Mr. Vajpayee, the former Prime Minister?

15. Before dates comprising preposition 'of'.

e.g.,

- **The** 10th of May
- **The** 5th of September

16. Before the names of language to signify a particular linguistic group or nationality.

e.g.,

- The Chinese are hard working.
- The Japanese are very efficient.

Adjectives

Rule 1 Position of Adjectives

(A) Generally adjective come before a noun. This position is called Attributive.

e.g.,

- She is an **honest** girl.
- Burj Khalifa is a **tall** building.

(B) Some adjectives can be used after the noun. This position is called Predicative.

e.g.,

- The girl is **honest**.
- The infant is very **tiny**.

(C) Adjectives are placed after noun when the noun is followed by preposition.

e.g.,

- The subject is a worthy matter of note. (✗)
  The subject is a matter worthy of note. (✓)

(D) The following adjectives cannot be used before nouns (attributively)- 'Afraid, asleep, due, ready, unable, alike, aware, glad, sorry, well, alone, ill, sure, worth'.

e.g.,

- Alone she is responsible for my problems. (✗)
  She alone is responsible for my problems. (✓)

Rule 2 Use of possessive adjectives

(A) When two subjects are joined by 'as well as, together with, along with, and not, in addition to, like, unlike, with, rather than, except, no less than, nothing but, more (noun) than one,' the possessive adjective is used in accordance with the first subject.

e.g.,

- My sister along with her friends is doing their job at Delhi. (✗)
  My sister along with her friends is doing her job at Delhi. (✓)

(B) When two subjects are joined by 'either-or, neither-nor, not only-but also, none-but', the possessive adjective is used according to the nearest subject.

e.g.,

- Neither the students nor the teacher were in their proper uniform. (✗)
  Neither the students nor the teacher were in his/her proper uniform. (✓)

(C) When the pronouns 'each, every, neither, either, anyone', are used as subject, the possessive adjective 'our or their' should be used. They may refer to two or more than two objects or persons.

e.g.,

- Each of the girls went to her houses. (✗)
  Each of the girls went to their houses. (✓)

(D) Possessive adjectives are not used with nouns such as 'separation, leave, excuse, mention, report, pardon, sight, favour.'

e.g.,

- Your separation is very painful to me. (✗)
  Separation from you is very painful to me. (✓)

Rule 3 The plural demonstrative adjective 'these' and 'those' should not be used with singular noun 'kind' 'type' and 'sort'.

e.g.,

- I will not do these kind/sort of acts. (✗)
  I will not do this kind/ sort of acts. (✓)

Rule 4 When multiple adjectives are used to qualify a noun, we follow a specific order of adjectives.

The order is

Order of Adjective	Examples
Ordinals	First, second, third
Cardinals	One, two, some, few
Opinion/ Quality	Beautiful, expensive, strong, big
Size	Small, long, thick, huge
Age	New, modern, antique
Shape	Circular, oval, rectangular, straight
Colour	Red, yellow, blue, green
Origin	Chinese, Italian, French, Indian
Material	Silk, Wooden, Golden, Bronze

e.g.,

- Twenty-year old black American Negro.
- A small Indian Stadium.
- A big round black Indian plastic table.
- A spacious dark cell.

Rule 5 Basic Rules of Degree of Comparison

(A) Generally we use 'than' after the comparative degree of adjective.

e.g.,

- Shaily is **more graceful** than Jaslin.

(B) Definite article 'the' is used with superlative degree of adjectives.

e.g.,

- Usian Bolt is **the fastest** runner in the world.

(C) We always compare similar things.

e.g.,

- The climate of Chennai is warmer than Delhi. (✗)
  The climate of Chennai is warmer than that of Delhi. (✓)

(D) We never use double comparatives or superlatives together.

e.g.,

- Jay is more better than Vihaan at Tennis. (✗)
  Jay is better than Vihaan at Tennis. (✓)

Rule 6 There are some adjectives which do not have any comparative and superlative degree. Such adjectives already denote the highest degree of something. These adjectives are 'Perfect, unique, ideal, chief, universal, extreme, complete, entire, excellent, absolute, impossible, eternal, supreme', etc.

e.g.,

- I have never seen a more complete book on General Studies. (✗)
  I have never seen a complete book on General Studies. (✓)

Rule 7 Some adjectives such as 'prior, junior, senior, superior, inferior, prefer (verb), preferable, elder', etc. are only used to make comparison and do not have any comparative or superlative forms. These adjectives are followed by 'to' instead of 'than'.

e.g.,

- He is senior than me in service. (✗)
  He is senior to me in service. (✓)

Rule 8 When two adjectives qualify the same noun, both the adjectives should be expressed in the same degree.

e.g.,

- He is the most active and energetic social worker in our club. (✗)
  He is the most active and the most energetic social worker in our club. (✓)

Rule 9 When two or more qualities of a noun or pronoun are compared, we use 'more + positive degree of adjective'.

e.g.,

- She is cleverer than honest. (✗)
  She is more clever than honest. (✓)

Rule 10 Both 'as' and 'than' are required to be used when a sentence contains adjectives in positive and comparative forms.

e.g.,

- She is as honest, if not more honest than her brother. (✗)
  She is as honest as, if not more honest than her brother. (✓)

Rule 11 Positive Degree of Adjectives is used for comparison, when the word 'times' is used for comparison.

e.g.,

- Your income is many times higher than Tushar's. (✗)
  Your income is many times as high as Tushar's. (✓)

But we use comparative degree when the sentence is without 'times'

e.g., This book is five rupees cheaper than yours.

Rule 12 When we have to compare two or more than things and make a choice, we use 'the' before and 'of ' after the adjective.

e.g., He is **the taller** of the two brothers.

Rule 13 When we use adjectives between 'as......as' and 'not so.....as' we use the adjective in positive degree.

e.g., Delhi is **as populous** as Shangai.

Rule 14 When definite article 'the' is used before an adjective, the adjective becomes a common noun representing a class of people.

e.g.,

- The rich (all rich people)
  The Greedy (all greedy people)

Rule 15 When two adjectives require different prepositions, appropriate prepositions should be used with both adjectives.

e.g.,

- He is senior and older than I. (✗)
  He is senior to and older than I. (✓)

Confusing Adjectives

- 'Far/ Farther/ Farthest' means more distant.
  'Far/ Further/ Furthest' means additional.

e.g.,

- Moradabad is **farther** from Delhi than Meerut.
- No **further** help from government is required.

- 'Other' means the second of the two.
  'Another' means additional one.

e.g.,

- The **other** boy is great at mathematics.
- I am still thirsty, please give me **another** glass of water.

- 'Old/Older/Oldest' is used for persons (not related by blood) and things. It refers to both age and time.
  'Old/ Elder/Eldest' is used for persons only in case of blood relations. It refers to age only.

e.g.,

- My sister is **elder** to me.
- My friend is **older** than I.

- 'Later' is the opposite of earlier in reference to time.
  'Latter' is the opposite of former in reference to position.

e.g.,

- He came **later** than I.
- Josh and Mayank are brothers but the latter is more intelligent than the former.

Verbs

Rule 1 Some words remain the same in all three forms. Such words include- cut, bet, burst, cost, hit, hurt, let, put, read, set, shut, split, spread, forecast, telecast, etc.

Rule 2 Linking verbs are intransitive verbs as they do not take an object. However, these verbs do need another word to make complete sense. So, these verbs are also called Verbs of Incomplete Prediction.

- **Verbs that show state of being** is, am, are, was, were, being, been, seem and become.
- **Verbs that describe the five senses** appear, look, smell, touch, feel, sound and taste.
- **Verbs that show change, growth and inactivity** grow, remain, prove, turn, stay, act and get.

Rule 3 Generally a sentence starts with a noun or a pronoun. However, when we express a wish or prayer, the verb is inverted (verb is placed before the subject).

e.g., **May** you succeed in life!

Rule 4 Use of some Verbs

(A) Some verb namely 'make, get and have' are called **causative verbs**. These verbs cause something to happen.

e.g.,

- I **made** my friend write a letter.
- He **got** his house painted by expert painters.
- He **had** a house demolished.

(B) Some verbs namely 'grow, become, go, turn, run', etc. show the beginning, development, change of condition or the final stage of something. These verbs are called **inchoative verbs**.

e.g.,

- My father is **getting** weaker.
- The leaves **become** red in autumn.
- It is **growing** dark.

Rule 5 Some verbs can never be used transitively as they are not done on something. These include come, go, fall, die, sleep, be, etc.

e.g.,

- He **went** to the market.
- He **fell** asleep.

Rule 6 Use of Primary Auxiliaries

(A) Helping Verbs to be (is, am, are, was and were) generally take '–ing' or past participle form of the verb.

e.g.,

- I am dance. (✗)
  I am dancing. (✓)
- His initials are tattoo. (✗)
  His initials are tattooed. (✓)

(B) Helping Verb to do (do, does and did) always take Base form of the verb.

e.g.,

- He does wanted to play. (✗)
  He does want to play. (✓)
- He did went to the market. (✗)
  He did go to the market. (✓)

(C) Helping Verbs to have (has, have and had) take Past participle form of the verb.

e.g.,

- Wuhan has present the project. (✗)
  Wuhan has presented the project. (✓)
- Shivam had go to the auditorium. (✗)
  Shivan had gone to the auditorium. (✓)

Rule 7 Gerunds are used with certain words including avoid, mind, detest, can't help, can't bear, resist, enjoy, resent, stop, start, postpone, defer, worth, prefer, consider, practise, finish, risk, pardon, excuse, forgive, it is no use/good, propose, miss, imagine, regret, means, anticipate, love, like, hate and dislike.

e.g.,

- We stopped **writing**.
- She enjoyed **riding** on the hills.
- You should avoid **spending** extra money.
- Suhani does not mind **helping** me.
- It is no use/good **waiting** for her.

Rule 8 Use of Complete Infinitives

(A) As a Noun, an Adjective or an Adverb

e.g.,

- **To err** is human. (as a Subjective case noun)
- This is the movie **to watch**. (Here, 'to watch' is an adjective that indicates that the movie is a must watch.)
- She ran **to catch** the bus in time. (as an adverb)

(B) With some verbs and adjectives namely- Agree, happy, desire, need, dare, hope, expect, decide, want, wish, refuse, eager, fail, glad, happy, heard, astonished, delighted, glad, horrified, easy, etc.

e.g.,

- She had agreed **to meet** me.
- I refused **to go** to the mall.

(C) To express manner using words such as know, learn, explain, teach, discover, wonder, show, ask, remember, forget, etc. In this case, the infinitives follows the word 'how'.

e.g.,

- He knows how **to write** English.
- We taught him how **to cook** food.

(D) Infinitives can be used to give positive or a negative meaning to the sentence.
The word 'enough' is used after and the word 'very' is used before adjective when infinitives express affirmative meaning.

e.g.,

- She is good enough **to help** me.
- She is very happy **to come** here.

Adjective 'too' is used before adjective when infinitives express negative meaning.

e.g., She is too ill **to go** out.

(E) If there are more than one infinitive in a sentence, we use the 'to' only once with the first infinitive.

e.g.,

- I went to the mall **to shop, eat and enjoy** my day.

Rule 9 Use of Direct/ Bare Infinitives

(A) After the verbs—let, bid, make, know, help, feel, hear, watch, behold, notice, observe and see.

e.g.,

- I made the student **write** an essay.
- The teacher let him **go** out.

(B) With but, than, and, except, as and or.

e.g.,

- He did nothing but cry.
- She did no more than sleep the whole day.

Rule 10 Sometimes, we insert another word (known as adverb) between 'to' and its verb in an infinitive. Such a construction is called **Split Infinitive**, which is a grammatically incorrect form and must not be used.

e.g.,

- You are requested to kindly stay for some time. (✗)
  You are kindly requested to stay for some time. (✓)

Rule 11 Use of Participle

(A) A participle form of verb can act as the main verb in the sentence.

e.g.,

- I **watched** a movie.
- I **was watching** a movie.

Note The use of Participle form of verb is important while understanding phrases and clauses.

(B) The participle as a Non-finite verb is used as an adjective in a sentence.

e.g.,

- The **burning** candle resulted in the fire.
- The **burnt** wood was black in colour.

(C) A participle must correctly be associated with the subject it is describing. When the participle is not correctly associated, it is called a misplaced or dangling participle.

e.g.,

- Being a fine day, we went for a picnic. (✗)
  It being a fine day, we went for a picnic. (✓)

Adverbs

Rule 1 Position of Adverbs

(A) Adverbs of manner/ Place/ time are generally placed after the verb.

e.g.,

- They performed **badly**. (Manner)
- They performed **here**. (Place)
- They performed **yesterday**. (Time)

If there is an object in the sentence, they are placed after the object or the verb.

e.g.,

- He performed the ballad **badly**. (Manner)
- He performed the ballad **here**. (Place)
- He performed the ballad **yesterday**. (Time)
  However, in some cases of transitive verbs, adverbs of manner can be placed before the verb.

e.g., He **briefly** narrated the incident to me.

(B) Adverbs of frequency such as always, often, already, just, never, ever, sometimes, frequently, generally, recently, usually, seldom, hardly', rarely, normally, etc. are generally placed before the verb they modify.

e.g.,

- My brother comes often every Sunday. (✗)
  My brother often comes every Sunday. (✓)
- He goes usually to the movie every Friday. (✗)
  He usually goes to the movie every Friday. (✓)

(C) If more than one adverb is present in the sentence, it takes the following order-

- Adverbs of manner
- Adverbs of place
- Adverbs of frequency
- Adverbs of time

e.g.,

Shreya walked **slowly** (manner) **down** the alley (place) **every** evening (frequency) **before sunset** (time) to walk her dog.

Rule 2 If the sentence is introduced by an adverb, the verb is placed before the subject (inverted form of verb) is used.

e.g.,

- **Seldom** he visits his parents. (✗)
  Seldom does he visit his parents. (✓)
  Or
  He **seldom** visits his parents. (✓)

Rule 3 Linking verbs 'be, become, seem, appear, taste, smell, sound, feel, turn, get, grow, keep, look, make, prove,' etc. are not modified by adverbs. They take adjectives.

e.g.,

- Her voice sounds harshly. (✗)
  Her voice sound harsh. (✓)

Rule 4 Use of some Adverbs

(A) Adverb 'else' is followed by the word 'but'.

e.g.,

- It is nothing else than sheer madness. (✗)
  It is nothing else but sheer madness. (✓)

(B) Adverbs 'other' and 'otherwise' are followed by 'than'.

e.g.,

- She had no other alternative but stay here. (✗)
  She had no other alternative than stay here. (✓)

(C) Adverb 'as' should be used to introduce predicative of the verbs regard, describe, define, treat, view, and know.

e.g.,

- I regard him my brother. (✗)
  I regard him as my brother. (✓)
- Science has been defined the study of nature. (✗)
  Science has been defined as the study of nature. (✓)

Case of Exception Adverb 'as' should be avoided to introduce predicative of the verbs name, elect, think, consider, call, appoint, make and choose.

e.g.,

- She is considered as the best dancer in the town. (✗)
  She is considered as the best dancer in the town. (✓)
- The teacher called him as stupid. (✗)
  The teacher called him as stupid. (✓)

(D) Adverbs 'too, as well and also' are used in the sense of besides and in addition to in affirmative sentences.
Adverb 'also' cannot be used at the end of the sentence.

e.g.,

- She found her bag and money **too/as** well.
- She found her bag and **also** her money.

(E) Adverb **'so/ neither'** is used after conjunctions in the structure **So/ Neither + Auxiliary Verb + Subject** in assertive sentences when an action is related to two people.

e.g.,

- She won the prize and **so** did her sister.
- She will not lend money but **neither** will he.

(F) Adverb 'so' and 'too' is generally used with Infinitives, when used with adjectives. 'So' also takes the word 'that'.

e.g.,

- He is **so** haughty **that** no one wants to talk to him.
- She is **too** poor **to** study further.

Note This rule does not indicate that we do not use 'so' and 'too' without infinitives and 'that'.

e.g., It is **too** bad and **so** sad.

(G) Adverb 'very' modifies Present Participle Adjective, Adverb and Positive degree of adjectives.

e.g.,

- It is a much interesting picture. (✗)
  It is a very interesting picture. (✓)

(H) Adverb 'much' is used with Past Participle Adjectives and Comparative degree of Adjectives.

e.g.,

- I was very exhausted in the evening. (✗)
  I was much exhausted in the evening. (✓)

(I) Adverb 'rather' is used in a negative before a noun. In contrast, adverb 'fairly' is used in a positive sense.

e.g.,

- It is **rather** a nuisance.
- He is **fairly** wise.

Adverb 'rather' is also used in case of preference with the phrase **would rather, had rather, rather than, etc.**

- e.g., I'd like to play inside **rather than** going out with my friends.

GRAMMAR BYTE!

We use **very** and **much** in superlative degree and the phrase 'very much' with comparative degree.

e.g.,

- She is the very best teacher in our school. (Here 'very' means 're ally')
- She is much the best teacher in our school. (Here 'much' means 'decidedly')
- He feels very much better now.

It is also important to remember that adverbs 'very' and 'much' may be used in the place of 'so' and 'too'.

e.g.,

- My brother is so healthy. (✗)
- My brother is very healthy. (✓)
- She is too healthy. (✗)
- She is very healthy. (✓)

(J) Adverb 'much too' is followed by an adjective.

e.g., He looks **much too** vindictive for the role.

The expression 'too much' is used with noun.

e.g., He is in too much pain.

(K) Adverb 'yet' means 'up to the time of speaking'. It is generally used with negative and interrogative sentences.

e.g., John has not **yet** submitted his application.

(L) Adverb 'still' emphasises that the action is still continuing. It is used with affirmative and interrogative sentences.

e.g., He is **still** not here.

(M) Adverb 'quite' has two meanings: 'very' and 'sufficient'.

e.g.,

- The movie is **quite** boring. (Here, 'quite' carries the meaning 'very')
- Sneha is **quite** capable of living by herself for a couple of days. (Here, 'quite' carries the meaning 'sufficient')

Rule 5 Use of Negative Adverbs

(A) Adverb 'never' is not used to replace adverb 'not'. We use 'do/ did/ does not' in place of never.

e.g.,

- I never went to Ooty last year. (✗)
  I did not go to Ooty last year. (✓)

(B) We avoid using two negative words in a sentence. Hence, Negative adverbs should not be used with the words negative in meaning.

e.g.,

- She hardly knows nothing about the family. (✗)
  She hardly knows anything about the family. (✓)

(C) The adverb phrases 'seldom or ever' and 'little or anything' are wrong in use. The correct phrases are 'seldom or never', 'seldom', if ever', 'little or nothing', 'little if anything'.

e.g.,

- We seldom or ever meet our relatives these days. (✗)
  We seldom or never meet our relatives these days. (✓)
  Or
  We seldom if ever meet our relatives these days. (✓)

(D) We do not use of adverb of negation, with 'deny', 'forbid' and 'both'.

e.g.,

- She denied that she had not given him books. (✗)
  She denied that she had she had given him books. (✓)

Confusing Adjectives and Adverbs

We can often confuse different adverbs, adjectives and nouns.

(A) 'Fast, straight, outright, direct, hard, hardly, late, light, high, safe, quiet', etc. are used both as an adjective and adverb.

e.g.,

- He was a **fast** runner. (Adjective)
- The darkness closed in even as she was returning home **fast**. (Adverb)
- This **straight** path lead us to the beach. (Adjective)
- Please go **straight** and then turn left. (Adverb)

(B) 'Late' is both an adjective and an adverb. 'Lately' is an adverb meaning recently.

e.g.,

- The **late** comer was punished. (Adjective)
- He came **late** to the class. (Adverb)
- Rohit is not coming to school **lately**. (Adverb)

(C) 'Hard' is both an adjective and adverb used in affirmative sense. 'Hardly' is an adverb used in negative meaning.

e.g.,

- Their story is **hard** to believe. (Adjective)
- She has thought very **hard** about her future plans. (Adverb)
- He could **hardly** complete the task on time. (Adverb)

(D) 'Enough' is both an adjective and adverb. As an 'adverb' it is always placed after the adjective it modifies. As an 'adjective' it is placed before a noun.

e.g.,

- He has **enough** money to spend. (Adjective)
- She is wise **enough** to allow her son to go. (Adverb)

(E) 'Good' is an adjective while 'well' is its equivalent adverb.

e.g.,

- You did a **good** job. (Adjective)
- He performed **well** in the exams. (Adverb)

Prepositions

Uses of Some Commonly used Prepositions

Before we understand the use of different prepositions, we must remember that a preposition can have many uses. The uses of some commonly used prepositions are given below.

Common Prepositions	Their Uses	Examples
On	To specify days and dates	I will come back from Japan **on** Friday.
	To refer to a position on a surface	My Laptop is lying **on** the desk.
	To refer to devices	I will watch the match **on** the TV.
At	To refer to exact time	We left on the evening of the sixth **at** 5:30 pm.
	To indicate a place	I am waiting for my brother **at** home.
In	To specify day, month, season, year	The Foot Festival will start **in** December.
	To show that something is located inside another thing	My little sister hid my phone **in** my bag.
	To show position	We went to the festival **in** a cab.
To	To refer to a period	I will be in Mumbai from Friday **to** Sunday
	To indicate direction/ destination	We are going **to** the Airport.
For	To indicate the duration or time	He has been ill **for** quite some time now.
	To indicate the receiver of something	I've brought a cup of coffee **for** you.
	To indicate purpose	The drowning man shouted **for** someone to help him.
	To refer to an exchange:	I got two burgers for 50 Rupees.

Of	To indicate relating to, belonging to	A friend **of** mine is coming today.
	To indicate being part of something	The lid **of** the tiffin is broken.
	To indicate measurement	2 kilograms **of** potatoes cost ₹ 30.
With	To indicate agent	I wrote the letter **with** a pen.
	To indicate being together	I ordered a sandwich **with** a drink.
By	To indicate the latest time by which the action would be over	The meeting should have finished **by** 4:30 pm.
	To indicate proximity	I live by the old building on the Main Street.
	To show means	Little children go to school **by** bus.
Into	To show a movement or direction	The mob broke **into** the building.
From	To show the time period of action	The doctor said, "I will see you **from** 12 to 1 pm tomorrow."
	To show how far apart two places are	His house is around a kilometre **from** my house.
	To indicate source	The river originates **from** the Himalayas.
Before	To show that something happened earlier than the time or event mentioned	I will go for my coaching classes **before** the exam.
	To refer to a place	Please drop me at the bus stop **before** the Police Station.
After	To refer to a 'later' time	He will meet me day **after** tomorrow.
	To show 'next to' a place	What do those letters **after** your name mean?
During	To denote the length of time in which something happens.	**During** summer vacations, we went to the beach.
Above	To show that something is on the top of another thing	The plane is flying **above** the clouds.
Below	To show that something is on the lower level than another thing	She lives on the floor **below** mine.
Over	To show that something is in direct contact with or is covering another	They made her comfortable and put a blanket **over** her.
	To indicate that something covers from one side of something to the other; across something	There is a bridge **over** the river.
	To indicate that someone or something is present in every part of the region	He has friends all **over** the world.
Under	To show that something is on the lower level	The cat is hiding **under** the table.
	To indicate junior position in ranks.	He is **under** me.
Between	To show the position of a thing in the middle of two things	The hotel is **between** the temple and the school.
Across	To show something on the other side	You can go on a ride **across** the country.
Along	To show that something is moving in a constant direction on a horizontal surface	The track is **along** the river.
Around	To show a movement taking place in a circular fashion	The girls danced **around** the bonfire.
Beside	To tell the location of something in relation. It means 'next to'.	The person sitting **beside** me is wearing a yellow hat.

Besides	In addition to	**Besides** these clothes, I don't own anything.
Since	To indicate that something started in the past and continues till now.	I have not slept **since** last night.
Until/till	To show when something will happen, begin, or end	I waited for them **until/till** 7:00 PM.
	To indicate 'upto' the time of'	They haven't completed the project **till** today.
Behind	To show the position of a thing at the back side of another thing.	Look **behind** you.
Ahead	Further forward in space or time than someone or something.	The car was **ahead** of us.
Toward	To show the direction	The man started walking **toward** the exit.
Away	To show movement from here to another place	She moved **away** from this place.
Down	To show movement to a lower level	We are going **down** a mountain.
Up	To show movement to a higher level	My sister lives **up** the road.
Against	In the opposite direction	He is going **against** the river's flow.
	To indicate position as in contact with something	There is a ladder **against** the wall.

Rules Concerning Prepositions

Rule 1 Position of Prepositions

(A) A preposition is usually placed before its object.

e.g., The book is **on** the table.

(B) A preposition is placed at the end when the object of the preposition is an interrogative pronoun.

e.g.,

- To whom are you talking? (✗)
  Who are you talking to? (✓)
  Or
- Whom are you talking to? (✓)

(C) When the object of the preposition is a relative pronoun 'that' or the relative pronoun is 'hidden', the preposition comes at the end.

e.g.,

- This is the book for that I have been looking. (✗)
  This is the book that I have been looking for. (✓)

(D) When an infinitive qualifies a noun, the preposition should be placed after the infinitive, if required.

e.g.,

- It is not a safe place to live. (✗)
  It is not a safe place to live in. (✓)

(E) In some interrogative sentence, the preposition is used at the beginning.

e.g.,

- **By** which car did you come?
- **For** whom did you buy these earrings?

Rule 2 Use of preposition in relation to its object

(A) Note the use of different prepositions with different objects (Direct or Indirect) for verbs such as 'provide, supply, furnish, entrust, present,' etc.

e.g.,

- I provided him **with** money.
- I provided money **to** him.

(B) Note the use of verbs 'rob, inform, explain, recommend, compensate,' etc., in relation to objects.

e.g.,

(a) Rob a person of something.
(b) Inform someone of something.
(c) Explain something to a person.
(d) Recommend/Suggest/Propose something/ some-body to others.
(e) Compensate someone for something.

Rule 3 Verbs like 'say, suggest, propose, speak, reply, explain, talk, listen, write' are followed by the preposition 'to' if there is a person as the object.

e.g.,

- She will write her friend. (✗)
  She will write to her friend. (✓)

Rule 4 When two adjectives require different prepositions, appropriate prepositions should be used with both adjectives.

e.g.,

(i) He is senior and older than I. (✗)
He is senior to and older than I. (✓)

Rule 5 Generally all prepositions except 'to' is followed by a gerund. 'To' takes the base form of a verb to make an infinitive.

e.g.,

- She insisted on see the manager. (✗)
  She insisted on seeing the manager. (✓)

Case of Exception!

There are certain cases where the use of gerund after a preposition is incorrect.

I went for seeing him. (✗)

It should be-

I went to see him. (✓)

Further, we also use 'to' + Gerund is also used with certain verbs and phrases like 'be used to, accustomed to, averse to, with a view to, addicted to, devoted to, in addition to, look forward to, object to, owing to, given to, taken to, prone to', etc.

e.g., She is used **to swimming** at dawn.

Rule 6 Omission of Prepositions

(A) Preposition are not used before adverbs of place here and there

e.g.,

- You should be at here. (✗)
  You should be here. (✓)

(B) Preposition 'on' is not used before today, tomorrow, yesterday, the day before yesterday, the day before tomorrow and Next/last + days of the week.

e.g.,

- I need you to submit the report on today. (✗)
  I need you to submit the report today. (✓)

(C) Preposition 'in' is not used in the structure-all/this + day/night/morning/afternoon/ month/ week/year/, etc.

e.g.,

- I will do this in all year. (✗)
  I will do this all year. (✓)

(D) Prepositions are not used after the verbs-Stress, emphasise, discuss (matter), investigate, comprise, accompany, consider, violate, demand, resemble, pervade, precede, succeed, reach (at), resign (post), attack, invade, resist, eschew, befall, order, direct, join, sign, affect, ensure, board, describe, await, lack, regret, ridicule, advise, fine, beg, command, request, inform, tell, urge, etc.

e.g.,

- The police are investigating into the case. (✗)
  The police are investigating the case. (✓)
- The teacher emphasised on the need of discipline in life. (✗)
  The teacher emphasised the need of discipline in life. (✓)
- I have ordered for his transfer. (✗)
  I have ordered his transfer. (✓)

(E) Weakened Case of Preposition

In some situations, prepositions are omitted as their use does not make much difference to the sentence.

e.g.,

- He earns fifty rupees a day.
- She visits me once a month.

Note In the given sentences, the presence of the preposition 'in' would not make any different. It would not make the sentence incorrect.

Confusing Prepositions

Some preposition seems to have a similar usage. These prepositions, however, are used in different situations.

(A) **In**, **On** and **At**

'In' refers to names of countries, states, cities, towns, and large islands in a wider sense.

e.g., He lives **in** Delhi.

'On' is used for names of streets, avenues, etc.

e.g., I live **on** Broadway.

'At' is used for speaking of comparatively smaller places or specific addresses.

e.g., He lives **at** Rohini in Delhi.

(B) **On** and **Upon**

- 'On' denotes position

e.g., The Vase is **on** the table.

- 'Upon' denotes movement.

e.g., He threw the book **upon** the table.

(C) **Within** and **In**

- 'Within' means before the end of time.

e.g., He will return **within** ten minutes.

- 'In' means at the end of time while denoting a period of time.

e.g., He will return **in** ten minutes.

(D) **Under**, **Below** and **Beneath**

- 'Under' is used to show position of one thing.

e.g., She kept money **under** the bed.

- 'Below' is used to show position of one thing in comparison to other thing.

e.g., The book is kept **below** the dictionary.

- 'Beneath' has the same meaning as under, but it is better to use it for abstract meanings.

e.g., He would think it **beneath** him to do such a small work. (Unworthy of him)

(E) **Over** and **Above**

- 'Over' is used to when there is direct contact between things.

e.g., We put a sheet **over** his body.

- 'Above' is used when there is no contact between things.

e.g., The flags waved **above** our heads.

(F) **Between** and **Among**

- 'Between' is used while referring to two persons/things.

e.g., The two brothers divided the property **between** themselves.

- 'Among' is used while referring to more than two persons/things.

e.g., The two brothers and their sisters divided the property **among** themselves.

(G) **From** and **Between**

- 'From' is used to show duration with 'to/till/until'.

e.g., He works in the office **from** Ten to Five.

- 'Between' is used to show duration with 'and'.

e.g., The Reception will be held **between** 5 pm. and 9 pm.

(H) **Since** and **For**

- 'Since' is used with a specific point in time.

e.g., I have been waiting **since** morning

- 'For' is used with a period of time.

e.g., I have been waiting **for** two hours.

Fixed Prepositions

"Fixed prepositions" denote prepositional phrases or expressions where specific prepositions consistently accompany particular words. This means that we cannot use other prepositions with them.

These prepositions are

- Abound in (V)
- Abound with (Adjective)
- Absolve from
- Absorb in
- Abstain from
- Access to
- Adhere to
- Approve of
- Assent to
- Acquaint with
- Addicted to
- Assured of
- Attain to
- Attraction for
- Attracted to
- Avail of
- Aloof from
- Advance for
- Advance by
- Abide by
- Accused of
- Acquit of
- Annoy with
- Aspire to
- Amuse at
- Answer to
- Answer for
- Account for
- Ask for
- Attend to

- Allowance for
- Aptitude for
- Act upon
- Adapt to
- Accustomed to
- Alien to
- Aware of
- Born of
- Believe in
- Benefit by
- Beware of
- Compensate for
- Compete with
- Compete for
- Comply with
- Congratulate on
- Certain of
- Confident of
- Count on
- Cope with
- Complaint against
- Complain of
- Commit to
- Confide in
- Confide to ·
- Commence of
- Disappoint of
- Despair of
- Disposed to
- Discriminate against
- Discriminate between
- Fly into
- Feed on
- Fondness for
- For lack of/For want of
- Grieve for
- For short of
- Grieve at Guard from Grieve over
- Hear by
- Infer from
- Insight into
- Impress upon
- Invest with
- Irritated at
- Judge of
- Jump to
- Known to
- Known by
- Known for
- Key to
- Lean on
- Likeness between
- Married to
- Married with
- Neglectful of
- Need for
- (in) need of
- Originate in
- Occupied with
- Operate on/upon
- Oblivious of
- Offend at
- Part with
- Part from
- Preface to
- Profit by ·
- Profit from
- Prone to
- Prompt in
- Replace by
- Revenge oneself on (verb)
- Revenge for (noun)
- Reason with
- Sure of
- Sequel to
- Slow at
- Substitute for
- Scare of
- Speak of
- Start on
- Suffer from ·
- Show off
- Tantamount to
- Treat of
- Triumph over
- Vexed at
- Wait upon
- Wait for
- Warn against
- Warn of
- Wish for
- Worthy of
- Wanting in
- Yearn for
- Zealous for/about

Conjunctions

Uses of Conjunctions

Conjunction	Uses	Example
Coordinating Conjunction		
For	Used when we have to express a reason or a cause	I could not attend the wedding **for** I had fever.
And	To join together two sentences or words that are related to each other	She called me **and** told me about her situation.
Nor	used to combine two words or ideas both of which are to be negated	The teacher did not smile, **nor** did she speak to the class.
But	To join words or sentences with contrasting or opposite ideas	I like to read poetry **but** sometimes I read gothic novels too.

Conjunction	Uses	Example
Or	To join words or sentences which offer a choice	Do the chores of the house **or** clean your room.
Yet	To express a contradictory or contrasting concept to an existing logical idea or point.	He's seventy-two, **yet** he still swims, runs and plays football regularly.
So	To express result, outcome or consequence of something	Everyone was busy in work **so** I brought all the items myself.
Subordinating Conjunction		
Although/ Though/ Even though	To join words or sentences those have opposite ideas	**Although** she lives far away, she always comes on time. I bought the book **though** it is very expensive. I was late to my work **even though** I woke up on time.
Because	To express a reason or a cause	Lata Mangeshkar is my favourite singer **because** I love her voice.
As	To express a reason or a cause	You should take an umbrella **as** it is going to rain today.
	To make a comparison	I danced **as** I was expected to do so.
If/whether	To make a comparison	You will win the prize **if** you work hard for it.
Unless	To show a condition	**Unless** it is raining outside, you have to go to school.
Till/ Until	To connect an action to a point in time.	He stayed in the classroom **till** he finished the work. I'll be here **until** 2 o'clock.
Than	To make a comparison	She is wiser **than** her brother.
Where	To indicate place or location	I will meet you **where** we always used to meet.
Before	To suggest that the second event happened soon after the first one.	I need to tell her the truth **before** anyone else does.
After	To express the sequence of happening of two things.	**After** you'd left, I got a phone call from Sona.
When	To introduce a clause expressing when an action takes place.	I was there **when** children were playing.
Since	To give reason for something	I have played in this park **since** I was a child.
While	To show that actions or events happen at the same time.	Can you clean the house **while** I take a bath?
Rather than	To show preferences or choice.	I would live in Delhi **rather than** London.
Whereas	To show contrast between the two clauses.	She is intelligent **whereas** her brother is not.
Correlative Conjunction		
Both....and	To combine two ideas	Kenneth scores well because he is **both** hardworking **and** intelligent.
Either....or	To express a choice	I want to travel to **either** Manali **or** Ladakh.
Neither...nor	To express that none of the choices can be taken	**Neither** Meenal **nor** Sheela wants to go into that room.

Conjunction	Uses	Example
Whether...or	To express doubt	Tell me **whether** you will do it **or** not.
Not only...but also	To includes another aspect of a thing	We are **not only** composing the music for the film **but also** directing the film.
No sooner...than	To show that one action immediately followed another action	**No sooner** had they completed the work, **than** they demanded the wages.
Such...that	To show a cause and effect relationship between two actions	The man spoke with **such** passion **that** all the listeners were moved to tears.
Scarcely/ Hardly... When	To indicate simultaneous actions	He had **hardly** finished the task **when** another file arrived.

Rules of Conjunctions

Rule 1 Two Conjunctions cannot be used in the sentence.

e.g.,

- **Although** he was tired, **still** he cooked. (✗)
- **Although** he was tired, he cooked. (✓)

Rule 2 'Both' should be followed by 'and' and not by 'as well as', Negative is avoided with 'Both'.

e.g.,

- **Both** Kamal **as well** as Arun prepared for the Viva. (✗)
- **Both** Kamal **and** Arun prepared for the Viva. (✓)

Rule 3 Correlative Conjunctions should be placed immediately before the words they emphasise. (qualify/ modify).

e.g.,

- She not only came to see me but also to take her old books. (✗)
  She came not only to see me but also to take her old books. (✓)
- Neither she is intelligent nor honest. (✗)
  She is neither intelligent nor honest. (✓)

Rule 4 'Either ... or', 'neither ... nor', 'both ... and', 'not only ... but also' should be followed by the same parts of speech.

e.g.,

- You can **either** sit **or** stand in the metro.
- **Neither** Meena **nor** KPranya passed the exam.
- She **not only** forgot her wallet **but also** left her keys.

Rule 5 We do not use negatives with clauses containing conjunctions – until/ till, unless, and lest.

e.g.,

- **Until** she does not her homework, she would not get the dessert. (✗)
  Until she does her homework, she would not get the dessert. (✓)
- **Unless** she does not go the bank, she will not go to the party. (✗)
  Unless she does not go the bank, she will not go to the party. (✓)

- I was afraid to open the door **lest** he should not follow me. (✗)
  I was afraid to open the door **lest** he should follow me. (✓)

Rule 6 We do not use the word 'then' with conjunction 'if'.

e.g.,

- **If** he performs well, **then** he will be selected by the team. (✗)
  If he performs well, he will be selected by the team. (✓)

Rule 8 The word 'doubtful' and 'doubt' are followed by conjunction 'if/whether' in affirmative sentences.

e.g.,

- I doubt **whether** she is going to the US.
  In negative and interrogative sentence, the words are followed by 'that'.

e.g.,

- I do not doubt **that** she will cross the level.

Rule 8 Correlative Conjunctions 'no sooner ...than' and 'scarcely/ hardly... when' take an inverted form of verb.

e.g.,

- No sooner had she finished her speech than the lights went out. (✗)
  No sooner she had finished her speech than the lights went out. (✓)
- Scarcely Lena had got through the door when the phone rang. (✗)
  Scarcely had Lena got through the door when the phone rang. (✓)

Modals

Functions of Modals

1. **May** and **Might**

(A) Possibility or Probability

e.g.,

- It **may** rain today.
- He **might** go to Delhi tomorrow.

(B) Ask or Give Permission

e.g.,

- **May** I come in?
  Yes, you **may** come in.
- **Might** I begin to reveal the truth?
  No, you **might** not!

(C) 'May' is also used for informal request.

e.g.,

- **May** I have the salt please?

(D) 'May' is also used to make a wish or prayer

e.g.,

- **May** you enjoy marital happiness!
- **May** you live long!

(E) Indicate a Purpose

e.g.,

- She works hard so that she **may** pass.
- She came so that she **might** see me.

(F) 'May' is not used in the interrogative when it occurs after a 'Wh-' word.

e.g.,

- When may we expect you? (✗)
  When are you likely to arrive? (✓)

(G) Use of 'may' and 'might' in perfect tense: 'May' is used when you are not certain about a past action. 'Might' is the past form of **May** and is used when the uncertainty no longer exists in the present (i.e. something did not happen but it was possible).

e.g.,

- He **may** have been wounded. (We do not know so far, but he is perhaps injured, possibility exists)
- He **might** have been wounded. (That was a possibility in the past but he was not wounded).

2. **Can** and **Could**

(A) To Show Ability

e.g.,

- She **can** write English well.
- Meetu **could** play cards.

(B) To Show Capability

e.g.,

- She **can** pass the MBA examination.
- They **could** eat an entire family meal box by themselves

Note 'Ability' and 'Capability' seem to have the same meaning. However, they have a very small difference. 'Ability' refers to the potential of the person in doing/achieving something, with a high chance that they might successfully do so. 'Capability' refers to the potential of the person to do something though they might not be able to do it successfully.

(C) Polite Request

'Can' is used in cases of making a friendly request while 'could' is used to make a formal request in a more polite/courteous manner.

e.g.,

- **Can** you please do it for me?
- **Could** you please lend me some money?

(D) Permission/Order

e.g.,

- **Can** I go now?
  Yes, you **can** go now.
- **Could** I take your book?
  You **could** take my book.

(E) Offer

e.g.,

- **Can** I get you some fruits?
- **Could** I carry the bag for you?

(F) Possibility

e.g.,

- She **can** fall on the road as it is slippery.
- She **could** be sixteen.

(G) Could + Have is used for past ability while indicating that the action did not take place.

e.g.,

- I **could have** revealed the secret. (but I did not)
- You **could have** borrowed some money. (but you did not)

3. **Will** and **Would**

(A) The use of 'will' in second and third persons denotes pure future actions. With first person, 'will' denotes threat or warning.

e.g.,

- He **will** go tomorrow.
- You **will** work here.
- I **will** see you. (threat, warning)

(B) To show promise

e.g.,

- I **will** give you a gift of your choice.
- I **would** buy the bag for you.

(C) To indicate a willingness/ intention to do something

e.g.,

- We **will** help you in the best possible way.
- He informed me that he **would** dance at my wedding.

(D) To show the determination to do something.

e.g.,

- I **will** change the system of our organisation.
- I **would** definitely learn how to speak German.

(E) To express formal request

e.g.,

- **Will** you please help me?
- **Would** you please give me your bike?

(F) To highlight a characteristic or habit

e.g.,

- The lion **will** kill the other animals. (Characteristics)
- He **would** drink a cup of coffee in the morning. (Habit)

(G) 'Would' is also used to express possibility or probability.

e.g.,

- Who is she? She **would** be his sister. (possibly she is)
- She **would** be sixteen. (possibly she is)

(H) 'Won't (will not) or Would you' in interrogative denotes 'invitation'.

e.g.,

- **Won't you** have a cup of tea? (invitation; I want you to have a cup of tea.)
- **Would you** like a cup of tea?

(I) 'Will' is also used for commands and instructions.

e.g.,

- All the cadets **will** attend the parade.

4. **Shall**

(A) To ask for suggestion, request, advice with the first person (I, We) in the interrogative sentence

e.g.,

- What **shall** we do now? (Advice)
- **Shall** I have a cup of coffee from your shop? (Request)
- **Shall** we open a new shop? (Suggestion)

(B) With the second person pronoun (You) and third person pronoun (He/she/it/ they) to indicate threat/ warning, command and promise.

e.g.,

- If you sit with bad boys, you **shall** be punished. (Threat/ warning)
- You **shall** go now. (Command)
- She **shall** get a bicycle. (Promise)

(C) It expresses certainty of an event.

e.g.,

- If you work hard, you **shall** pass the entrance test.

5. **Should**

(A) To express a 'duty/obligation, expectation and advice.'

e.g.,

- You should stand by your brother. (Duty)
- Promises **should** be kept. (Obligation)
- The rich **should** help the poor. (Expectation)
- You **should** work hard. (advice)

(B) To refer to a future event in the past

e.g.,

- I told him that I **should** go there.
- Did I not tell you that I **should** qualify?

(C) To express condition

e.g.,

- Walk carefully lest you **should** fall.
- **Should** you work hard, you will get success.

(D) Should + Have is used to express obligation in the past. It denotes an obligation that was not fulfilled.

e.g.,

- You **should** have stood by your brother. (but you did not)
- She **should** have left a message. (but she didn't)

6. **Must**

(A) To express a 'necessity or obligation' (in place of 'should')

e.g.,

- You **must** follow instructions.
- I **must** leave now.

(B) To indicate an order

e.g.,

- You **must** not leave now.
- They **must** not play here.

(C) To express 'strong possibility' (in place of 'may')

e.g.,

- It is ten. The teacher **must** be in the class.
- She **must** be working in the office now.

(D) To indicate Determination

e.g.,

- I **must** help him.

(E) To show a Deduction or Inference

e.g.,

- He has a big house. He **must** be rich.
- She reads a lot. She **must** be learned.

Uses of Semi Modals

1. Ought to

(A) To express strong sense of moral obligation or duty in place of 'should & must'

e.g.,

- You **ought** to respect your parents.
- You **ought** to take food before leaving.

> **'Ought to'** is normally used for 'should & must', when there is strong sense of moral duty, advice or indication of correct action.

(B) To give advice

e.g.,

- You **ought** to study hard to achieve success.

(C) 'Ought to + Have' is used in relation to past action of duty that was not fulfilled or an action that was neglected in the past.

e.g.,

- You **ought to** have taken care of your wife. (but he didn't)
- He **ought to** have been present at the wedding of his friend. (but he wasn't)

2. Dare

(i) As an auxiliary verb, it is generally used in negative or interrogative sense with bare infinitive.

e.g.,

- Rani **dare** cross me again.
- Rani **dare** not cross me again.
- Does he **dare** to oppose you?

(ii) It is used at places where we are to use courage.

e.g.,

- **Dare** I cross my dad?
- **Dare** you go outside now?

> As auxiliary verbs, **dare** and **need** do not change forms according to the number of person of the subject

3. Need and Need Not

(A) As an auxiliary verb, 'need' is used mainly in the negative and the interrogative forms with bare infinitives.

e.g.,

- **Need** I write to him?

(B) 'Need not' is used for an action which is not necessary.

e.g.,

- He **need not** go there again.
- Rohit **need not** phone her now.

(B) 'Need not + Have' is used for an action which was not necessary but was performed.

e.g.,

- You **need not** have gone there. (but you did)
- Rohit **need not** have phoned her yesterday. (but Rohan did)

4. Used to

(A) To express past habits that are usually discontinued. They are not used with present tense.

e.g.,

- Aadar **used to** be fond of the Beatles.
- I **used to** study with my cousin sister.

(B) 'Used to' is also used as an adjective (be used to). It is equal to 'accustomed to'.

e.g.,

- He is **used to** getting up early.
- I was **used to** driving through crowded streets.

Tenses

Simple Present Tense

Structure	Singular Subject + V^1 + s/es + Object I/Plural Subject + V^1 + Object
Example	She lives in Delhi. They live in Delhi.

Present Continuous Tense

Structure	Singular Subject + is/am + V^1 + -ing + Object Plural Subject + are + V^1 + -ing + Object
Example	She is living in Delhi. They are living in Delhi.

Present Perfect

Structure	Singular Subject + has + V^3 + Object I/ Plural Subject+ have + V^3 + Object
Example	She has lived in Delhi. They have lived in Delhi.

Present Perfect Continuous Tense

Structure	Singular Subject + has been + V^1 + -ing + Object I/ Plural Subject+ have been + V^1 + -ing + Object
Example	She has been living in Delhi. They have been living in Delhi.

Simple Past Tense

Structure	Singular/ Plural Subject + V^2 + Object
Example	She lived in Delhi.

Past Continuous Tense

Structure	Singular Subject + was + V^1 + -ing + Object Plural Subject+ were + V^1 + -ing + Object
Example	She was living in Delhi. They were living in Delhi.

Past Perfect Tense

Structure	Singular/ Plural Subject + had + V^3 + Object
Example	They had lived in Delhi.

Past Perfect Continuous Tense

Structure	Singular/ Plural Subject + had been + V^1 + -ing + Object
Example	She had been living in Delhi.

Simple Future Tense

Structure	Singular/ Plural Subject + will/ shall + V^1 + Object
Example	She will live in Delhi.

Future Continuous Tense

Structure	Singular/ Plural Subject + will/ shall be + V^1 + -ing + Object
Example	They will be living in Delhi.

Future Perfect Tense

Structure	Singular/ Plural Subject + will/ shall have + V^3 + Object
Example	She will have lived in Delhi for six years now.

Future Perfect Continuous Tense

Structure	Singular/ Plural Subject + will/ shall have been + V^1 + -ing + Object
Example	They will have been living in Delhi.

Conditional Sentence

1. **First Conditional** contains possible condition and its probable result.

   Structure 'If' clause in the Simple Present Tense + main clause in Simple Future Tense

   Function To talk about real and possible future situations and their probable results.

   Example If it rains tomorrow, I will bring an umbrella.

2. **Second Conditional** contains hypothetical condition and its probable result.

   Structure 'If' clause in Simple Past Tense + main clause containing would + base form of verb

   Function To talk about unreal or improbable present or future situations and their hypothetical results.

   Example If I won the lottery, I would buy a big house.

3. Third Conditional contains an unreal past condition and its probable result in the past

   Structure 'If' clause clause in Past Perfect Tense + main clause containing would/could/might + have + past participle form of verb

   Function To talk about unreal situations in the past and their hypothetical results.

   Example If she had studied harder, she would have passed the exam.

Subject Verb Agreement

Rules Involved in Subject-Verb Agreement

Rule 1 If the subject is singular, it takes a singular verb and if the subject is plural, it takes a plural verb.

e.g.,

- My mother **wakes** up early in the morning.
- These sculptors **are** magnificent.

Rule 2 When two or more nouns are joined by the conjunction 'and', a plural verb is used.

e.g.,

- The doctors and the nurse **are going** to attend the seminar.
- Rita and Gita **were** best friends in college.

Rule 3 When there are two subjects but they refer to one idea, a singular verb is used.

e.g.,

- Peanut butter and jelly **is** my favourite breakfast. (Peanut Butter and jelly refers to a single food item)
- Time and tide **waits** for none. (Time and tide refers to the passing of time)

Rule 4 When there is one subject in the sentence and more than one verb, all the verbs must agree with the subject.

e.g.,

- My brother **likes** video games and **thinks** he can set up and run a gaming centre.
- My cousin sister **likes** chocolate but **hates** mint chocolate ice-cream.

Rule 5 When two or more singular nouns are joined by 'or' or 'nor', a singular verb is used.

e.g.,

- A pen or a pencil **is** mandatory to be carried into the seminar.
- My aunt nor my uncle is **coming** for the event next month.

Rule 6 Two singular subjects connected by either/or and neither/nor require a singular verb.

e.g.,

- Either India or South Africa **is going** to qualify for the semi-finals.
- Neither Raashi nor Mona **is coming** for the party tonight.

Rule 7 When a singular and plural subject are connected by either/or or neither/nor, the plural subject should be placed last and a plural verb should be used.

e.g.,

- Neither the diary nor the pens **are** on the rack.
- Neither he nor his friends **are playing** tonight.

Rule 8 When the subject has two nouns or pronouns joined by connectors like **as well as, with, along with, in addition to, and together with**, etc. the verb agrees with the first one.

e.g.,

- Cow milk as well as soy milk **is** good for health.
- The Chief Minister together with the governor **is** arriving for the protest.

Rule 9 Uncountable nouns take a singular verb.

e.g.,

- The time for the unveiling of the magazine **has come**.
- Water **flows** from high to low.

Rule 10 Collective nouns take a singular verb.

e.g.,

- My team **has designed** the interior of this cafe.
- A flock of sheep **was cared** for by the shepherd.

However, when the units of the collective noun are separated into groups, a plural verb is used.

e.g.,

- The family members **are** in disagreement about where to go for the picnic.
- The jury members **have caused** delay in the verdict for his case.

Rule 11 We use plural verbs with quantifiers such as both, few and many. 'Much' takes a singular verb.

e.g.,

- A few people **are** already in the hall.
- Both she and I **are visiting** the cafe today.

Rule 12 A singular verb must be used with the singular indefinite pronouns– each, neither, either, anyone, everyone, no one, someone, anybody, everybody, nobody, somebody, anything, everything, nothing, and something.

e.g.,

- Nobody **has brought** their car.
- Each of the boys **has come** home.

Rule 13 When two subjects are joined by not only....but also, the verb agrees with the subject that is closest to it.

e.g.,

- Not only I but also my mother **was excited** for my admission.
- Not only my uncle but my cousins also **were overjoyed** at his selection.

Rule 14 Titles of books, magazines and films take singular verbs, even if they contain plural nouns.

e.g.,

- The Birds **is** a movie from 1963.
- Harry Potter **is** my favourite book.

Rule 15 Some subjects might appear plural (e.g., News, Gymnastics, Physics, Statistics etc.) but are actually singular in meaning and so take a singular verb.

e.g.,

- Measles **is** the only childhood disease I haven't had.
- Physics **was** always my favourite subject.

Rule 16 A singular verb is generally used after words denoting an amount (time, money, measurement, weight, volume).

e.g.,

- 100 kilograms **is** an unhealthy weight for anybody.
- Thirty miles **is** not a long distance.

Rule 17 Statements that have 'many/ a great many/ a good many/ a number of/a large of/ many of/both of/few of/a few of/ some/some of / plenty of/ lots of/ a lot of/ all/ all of/ most/ most of/ enough/ a great deal of' then the noun and verb both are plural.

e.g.,

- A great many farmers **are** working.
- Many boys **were** accused.
- A large number of candidates **have** appeared in the examination.

Rule 18 Expression having 'Half of/two third of / one fourth of ', etc., takes plural verb when the noun is countable, but if the noun is uncountable then verb is singular.

e.g.,

- Three fourth of the work **is** done.
- Half of the boys from the class **were** absent.

Uses of Quantifiers

1. Few, a few and the few

'Few', 'a few' and 'the few' have similar meanings as 'little', 'a little' and 'the little'. However, they are generally used with countable nouns.

e.g.,

- I have only **few** friends.
- A **few** suggestions wouldn't hurt you.
- There are refreshments for **the few** guests that stayed behind.

2. Little, a little and the little

(i) 'Little' means 'hardly any' or the lack of something.

e.g., We have **little** money right now.

(ii) 'A little' signifies that even though it is not much, there is enough of an item.

e.g., There's **a little** ice-cream left; who will eat it?

(iii) 'The little' means 'not much but all that is'.

e.g., The cat has knocked over **the little** milk in the jug.

Note Both 'Little' and 'A little' mean the same thing. However, they are used in different contexts. 'Little' has negative implications while 'A little' has positive implications.

3. Much and Many

We use 'much' with singular uncountable nouns and 'many' with plural nouns.

e.g.,

- I haven't got **much** change; I've only got a hundred rupee note.
- Are there **many** campsites near your place?

4. Some and Any

The words 'some' and 'any' are used with both countable and uncountable nouns when the exact number or amount of something is not known. The only different between them is that 'some' has a positive implication whereas 'any' has a negative implication.

e.g.,

- So you have **some** time for the meeting?
- She can come **any** minute now.

5. More, Less and Fewer

(i) We use 'more' or 'less' before singular uncountable nouns by adding 'than' after it to indicate an additional or lesser quantity of something.

e.g.,

- I do **more** work than Suresh.
- Satish does **less** work than me.

(ii) We use 'fewer' before plural countable nouns to refer to a group of things smaller than another.

e.g., **Fewer** students succeeded in passing than last year.

6. Most and Several

(i) We usually use 'most' with plural uncountable nouns to refer to a large quantity or number.

e.g., **Most** people here cannot be trusted.

(ii) We usually use 'several' with plural nouns to refer to a number which is not very large

e.g., **Several** people were crushed in the stampede.

7. Another and Other

We use 'another' only with singular countable nouns, whereas 'other' can be used with singular countable, plural countable or uncountable nouns.

e.g.,

- Bring me **another** knife, as this one is blunt.
- I would prefer the **other** house.

8. Each and Every

We use 'each' when the number in the group is limited or definite, and 'every' is used when the number is indefinite or unknown.

e.g.,

- **Each** student in my class was promoted.
- **Every** person in the world has a parent.

9. Either and Neither

(i) We use 'either' to refer to two things, people, situations, etc. It may mean one or the other of two or each of the two.
e.g. I don't agree with **either** Ram or Shyam.

(ii) We use 'neither' with only singular countable nouns and a singular verb. 'Neither' is the negative of either.
e.g. **Neither** of the two boys passed the exam.

Rules of Question Tag

Rule 1 We form the question tags by using the auxiliary verb and the pronoun relating to the subject of the sentence.

e.g., They **were** at the concert, **weren't** they?

Rule 2 If the sentence is negative, we usually add a positive question tag and vice versa.

e.g.,

- She **doesn't** like coffee, **does** she?
- She **did** her masters in psychology, **didn't** she?

Rule 3 If there is another main verb, we use do in the correct form.

e.g., We told you not to drive on the highway, **didn't we**?